FAMILIAR QUOTATIONS

FAMILIAR QUOTATIONS

A Collection of Passages, Phrases,
and Proverbs Traced to Their
Sources in Ancient and
Modern Literature

By

JOHN BARTLETT

ELEVENTH EDITION
Revised and Enlarged

CHRISTOPHER MORLEY, *Editor*

LOUELLA D. EVERETT, *Associate Editor*

BOSTON

LITTLE, BROWN AND COMPANY

1938

PREFACE TO THE ELEVENTH EDITION

What makes words memorable? It would be useful if we knew, but I doubt we ever shall. The subtle adhesions of adult memory are unintentional and unconscious; that is the true Learning by Heart we were told of in school, when they really meant Learning by Rote. Grown minds have an abated regard for the operations of conscious intelligence. We have found (in many a secret surprise) that the images which sink deepest are often those we scarcely knew, at the time, we were noticing at all. Like a skillful diver they went through the outer film of sense with very little splash.

The mind has a delicate property of surface tension, a retracting and tightening function, which creates a superficial envelope against too easy interruption or dispersion of the precious Me within. Whatever somehow punctures that protection is latent for memory. All we dare say about it is that it satisfies some inner necessity of our own, whether it be John Milton or Eddie Guest. It is most likely to be metrical, because we are so ourselves. Well did the word *incantation*, meaning "speech singable," come to assume the suggestion of witchcraft. One can melodize words for years without stopping to consider how silly they are. Who cares? The magic happens —

> It creeps into your mind, you find it there.
> You are my poem then, for in my heart
> Lovelier than a sonnet, you made rhyme
> And I had memorized you unaware.

The iniquity of oblivion — willfully translating Sir Thomas Browne's phrase to mean the unfairness of man's forgettings — weighs heavy on anthologists. In BARTLETT the problem is at least double: not only to preserve as many as possible of those Household Words which were the original editor's prime search, but to seize also some of the Mindhold Words (even of our own day) which the world hardly yet knows it has absorbed. This is in no sense a collection

[v]

of personal choices. It is foremost a salvage of those words which users of the English tongue have shown evidence not willingly to let die. This involves a debatable proportion of adipose sentiment and mediocre art — certainly not the least valuable part of the work for any student of intellectual coefficients. The Public must love bad verse, it reads so much of it. It is not often that one finds the

> jewel five words long
> That on the stretched forefinger of all Time
> Sparkles forever,

or

> All the charm of all the Muses
> Flowering in a lonely word.

One of the pleasures of this re-editing has been that one collaborator, by long experience with inquiries for the affable familiar ghosts of print, knows acutely what readers want; and the other believes himself to know what they ought to want. They have striven for a happy compromise; in the final decisions I must take full responsibility.

So we have here, within evident fallibilities, a viva voce of English confession from Caedmon bashful in the byre down to Nathalia Crane equally bashful at the paper-box factory in Brooklyn. Chronological arrangement sets the whole story in perspective. My own choice would be to read backward, beginning with moods familiar to-day and tracing upstream and uphill to the far woodlands where still tingles the voice of that first cuckoo-singer. When I was a boy in Baltimore I used to hear often of a place called Blue Ridge Summit. I never went there; it would probably disillusion; but what a picture of mystic beauty was in the name! To this day I think of the earliest masters of our tongue as not merely a beginning but also a goal. Chaucer is to me truly a Blue Ridge Summit. No poet was in the least astonished by Professor Einstein's pronouncements about the relativity of Time. We knew it always: here is Chaucer thinking the very thoughts that came to us, so hot and immediate and self-englamoured, to-day of days. It is not we who think, but life that thinks us, and Chaucer seems more modern to me than most radio announcers.

(In fact I'm not at all sure that the present era is "modern" at all.

We seem to be sliding rapidly into medievalism, the Thirty Years' War kind of thing. The poets are the most savage historians. There have been plenty who thought "The world falls asunder, being old," — and ends "Not with a bang but a whimper." — And in this preface, by the way, I'm going to quote whatever comes into my head without always grieving to identify. I've done enough identifying for a lifetime.)

You don't labor in a Pandect like this without perceiving that it's not just a scrapbook of belles-lettres, but also a sort of anthropology; a social history; a diary of the race. Here are the Now It's Got To Be Tolds of a good many generations. What is the quality of permanence that makes it worth while to pack in our scanty baggage, for one more trudging hike forward, the remarks of our predecessors? Man is a sententious animal, splendid in syllables and pompous in afterthought; nothing makes so bewildered an impression on him as the disparity between his words and his behavior. He shrewdly learns not to put too much of what he thinks into writing, lest he be held responsible. Therefore he is the more astonished, touched with delight and compunction, when he observes that what he himself had hidden someone else has uncovered. Having learned so much of the cunning of concealment he is fit to appreciate the joy of exposure. One of the most appealing phases of the entertainment called Literature is a psychological strip-tease.

It would be hard to aver which gives us more pleasure when we find it in print: what we wanted to say, or what we wanted not to say. The most familiar dictum of course is that of Pope —

> Nature to advantage dressed,
> What oft was thought, but ne'er so well expressed.

Our satisfaction lies in that delicate divergence between the words before us and the words we ourselves would have used for the same thought (if we had had the same thought). We must not *quite* have had it; but we must have been troubled by its approach. The happy man lives subconsciously to-day among thoughts that he will render articulate to-morrow. Nothing is more exciting (you can see hints and murmurs of it in all sorts of places) than to watch the world getting ready to think ideas quite different from those it is at the moment openly proclaiming.

[vii]

A book like this can be the bliss of solitude: but solitude is chiefly a bliss when it can be terminated at will. Probably the "quality of permanence" is most often found in those passages that strike through into the central loneliness of the heart, for which it scarcely expected any relief. Rilke, the brilliant young German, once said, "Love consists in this, that two solitudes protect and touch and greet each other." And literature is at its happiest in that function of companionship. It offers us the verification of our own secrets without any possible embarrassment. The same Rilke wrote a book, a very moving one for a few readers, called *The Journal of My Other Self*. I like to think that for some this BARTLETT can be the journal of another self, continuing over some six or seven hundred years. Not just a work of reference, but a work of conference; a nest egg for the mind. I have occasionally imagined the editors as Huck and Tom on the raft, floating down the big river and trying to pull aboard, from so much miscellaneous jetsam, what would be enduringly useful. The shock of accuracy is not the only quality that helps words to live; there is also the shock of surprise. And there is the haphazard contingent of mere chance. The great saying requires wit, occasion, and — good luck. Many such have undoubtedly gone into the record wrongly ascribed. Most of our hodiernal instinctive palavers were already old when Heywood collected them in 1546. As the title page of a famous eighteenth-century volume of erotica put it: *Prostant apud Neminem, sed tamen Ubique.*[1] This can hardly be duly translated; as every lover of language knows, nothing ever can. One can render, but there is always a shrinkage in carrying across. The more volatile the wine, the more ullage.

Still pursuing — just for the joy of speculation — this quiddity of endurance in written thought. The pleasure of self-identification; the delight of ideas shrewdly or beautifully put; and then how about a certain overtone of sincerity? Hard to define but recognizable to intuition. There has been much lamentation lately about the decline of poetry, the unintelligibility of modern verse, a general feeling that (as Roy Campbell said) the young poet is an angry man wearing his liver on his sleeve. Then one evening this spring I listened

---

[1] "For sale by no one, but available everywhere." *Nugae Venales sive Thesaurus Ridendi,* 1720. A good example of this kind of thing in our own time would be Mark Twain's disgraceful — and delightful — *1601.*

to the radio (I don't often) and heard (feeling that significant chilblain on the withers) voices saying something new in a new way. It was Archibald MacLeish's remarkable fable "The Fall of the City"; the first time (I think) that a play in verse, written designedly for that oral medium, had been broadcast. Here was a true poet using a fresh technique with beauty and power, saying things of meaning, adapting all the resources of an ancient skill to the opportunities of to-day. The ear is an unsophistered recipient. Among so vast a listening there must have been many who were not likely to observe the conscious efficacy of the poet's devices, or even his political wit, but they must have felt the thrill of that drama on the clairaudient nerve. I said to myself with delight, Here begins a whole new era for poetic drama. And I shall continue to disregard, as I always have, any grievances about the failure of the arts. True, they are painfully subject to imitative corruptions of mode, but (as the Chinaman said) in due season we are granted the artists we require; and they the emotions they need. The emotion comes first.

Sincerity — passion — the sense that the man has something to say — the old alarm "there's something burning" — these rise above, or make unnecessary, "pretty little tricks of style." How it pleases to hear Sir Walter Raleigh (the modern one, distinguished learner and teacher of letters) confess in a fine sonnet "I never cared for literature as such." He continues: —

> The spondee, dactyl, trochee, anapaest,
> Do not inflame my passions in the least;
> And cultured persons do not please me much. . . .

But there is one kind of writing, he exclaims, that surely blasts our indifference: —

> One book among the rest is dear to me;
> As when a man, having tired himself in deed
> Against the world, and falling back to write,
> Sated with love, or crazed by vanity,
> Or drunk with joy, or maimed by Fortune's spite,
> Sets down his Paternoster and his Creed.

Of these personal outcries, wrung from men and women in the strong twist of life, there are plenty in BARTLETT. There is also more laughter than you might suppose. The English-speaking peoples are considered sombre-minded, but they often have a way of making a joke when no one is listening. They even laugh at themselves, which makes it unanimous. — It often strikes me as odd, by the way, that some of the most amusing books in the world have no reputation for humor. I have seen a roomful of people in the purest mirth over Dr. Johnson's *Lives of the Poets,* which is not commonly thought of as a work of merriment. But, as Swift suggested in the "Voyage of Laputa," extracting sunshine from cucumbers is an unlikely project, and too many of the professionals of letters have the cucumber temperament. The sudden glory that maketh those grimaces called laughter (Hobbes) must always remain rare, though a man who retains any of the impressible gust of childhood can scarcely walk along a city street without at least a twitching cheek. But, taken in print, we are mostly a solemn crowd. As Dr. Johnson said of Pope's grotto, "An Englishman has more frequent need to solicit than exclude the sun." And I think that in this new edition BARTLETT is a little less gloomy than before. But old John Bartlett himself, as his letters show, had his lighter moments. His first edition appeared while he was a bookseller in Cambridge, Massachusetts; and only a creature of humor can survive the difficulties of that exacting trade. Let the others hanker, as Jeremy Taylor said, for "strange flesh and heaps of money and popular noises."

The arts, we were saying, are specially susceptible to changes of fashion. One of the prime values of chronological arrangement is that it's possible to trace the diverse tastes, the prevailing moods, of different epochs; and to see how zigzag are the frontiers between periods which textbooks mark off (for convenience only) so net and clear. Everything has to be said all over again, in its own tone of voice, for each succeeding generation. (And thank goodness: if people realized, for instance, that almost everything conceivably sayable had been said in Montaigne, why should they ever buy another book?) I suppose it is natural for the very young to resent, or reject, the thought that everything has already been said; at any rate a strong instinct bids them listen to it only from some of their own kidney. Take for instance the note of *lacrimae rerum.* About every thirty or forty years some singer is likely to pluck that string with just the touch the human ear craves. Toward 1790 it was Robert Burns. In the 1820's, Byron. About 1860 FitzGerald was adapting the tune

[x]

from Omar. In the late 90's it was A. E. Housman; in the 20's of our own century, Miss Millay. It will be due again presently, and will be (quite rightly) hailed by its contemporaries as thrillingly new, poignant, unique. In the condensation of BARTLETT the reader has the pleasure of tracing down his own paths of affiliation and literary genealogy; and the rather frequent cross references often show the same thought expressed in different ways, which is the supreme vintage-tasting luxury of the connoisseur. I have smiled a good many times at the remark made by a publisher on the wrapper of a recent book of verse by a young writer. " ——— ," they said, "scorns the devices of his poetic elders." As if that were conceivably so of anyone sensitive enough, or grateful enough to our inheritance, to be worth the name of poet. Certainly no one ever undertook the task of editing an anthology without saluting old footprints in joy and reverence, as Chaucer himself did in that exquisite passage at the close of his Troilus. Let me quote a word from the king of critics in our lifetime, the magnificent Saintsbury, who spoke of "the most degrading of intellectual slaveries — that of the exclusive Present." [1]

So much may be said as reassurance for those who might have feared that our good old BARTLETT had too violently Gone Modern. At the same time rather extensive clearances have been made. The job, I have said to myself many times, is really that of sweeping the hearth of literature. A menial service, in one sense, yet also in any civilized household an important one. We serve here, no matter how many the errors of judgment and oversight, as proxy for Posterity. It costs a pang to sweep out some worthy who "flourished" in his time and was a hearty favorite fifty years ago but is plainly no longer necessary. (Humanity can't go on carrying all its baggage forever.) Ancient footnotes that have come downstream through former editions have often been dropped when they seemed pointless: one remembers the man (I forget who) described by Dr. Johnson as having "a rage for saying something when there was nothing to be said." A good many shrill huzzas from the patriots of '76 (especially around Boston) have faded out, and perhaps some allusions to unfamiliar names such as Axel Oxenstiern and Von Münch Bellinghausen. Wordsworth's bleatings when he was fecund rather than facund; lozenges from the original Smith Brothers (of the *Rejected Ad-*

[1] "Trollope Revisited," in his *Collected Essays,* Vol. II.

dresses); lesser bits of Byron, once so fashionable; Robert Pollok, a meteor in his day and confidently consigned to immortality by his epitaph — how much of that sort of thing is still essential to this wallowing world? How about the mysterious "Miss Wrother," to whom Hope "told a flattering tale" but disappointment followed? Sometimes mere chance intervened to prolong someone's foundering clutch on futurity. I was about to throw Letitia Landon overboard when Governor Alfred Landon of Kansas was nominated to the Presidency (in 1936). So I pulled L. E. L. back onto the raft as a small kindness toward keeping the name going. (L. E. L. may yet live longer than that candidacy.) Sometimes an old tidbit was left in with perhaps a little touch of malice, to emphasize the ironies of time — for instance Nat Willis's "On the Death of Harrison," who

> ascended Fame's ladder so high:
> From the round at the top he has stepped to the sky.

But there are awkward questions to ask one's self. How much of "Aurora Leigh" is still desirable? Who was Thomas Kibble Hervey, and how did he get into BARTLETT X when his exact contemporary Nathaniel Hawthorne didn't? For there were some curious gaps in the Tenth Edition. No Herman Melville, no Emily Dickinson, no O. Henry — most astonishing of all, not a line of William Blake. Even De Quincey and Hazlitt appeared only in footnotes.

The questions we asked ourselves just above are ill to answer; however answered there is sure to be grievance somewhere. In such a job one resigns one's self to being the most reprobated editor in print. Perhaps even, to the observer twenty-three years hence, present oversights will seem as fantastic as those of 1914 do now. Previous editors adhered, almost with pedantry, to the touchstone of *familiarity*. Only phrases or quotations that had gained wide recognition, become hypodermic, were admitted. It becomes then a significant footnote in literary history to observe that in 1914 neither Melville nor Emily Dickinson had gained enough currency to catch the eye of our toastmaster. In the matter of new inclusions this edition is not so stringent: we have tried to make literary power the criterion rather than width and vulgarity of fame.

But the hearth must be swept; the new clean fire is not to be choked by too much debris of the past. Every fire builder knows that a bed of

[xii]

ashes and used coals helps the fresh blaze, catches the glow and ra-
diates warmth, gives depth and bottom to the flame — up to a point.
But there comes a time to open the chute and rake out old cinders. I
breathe a small secret sigh over some of the vanished authors, and
keep their names to myself. Unless some morbid scholiast compares
the indexes of the Eleventh and Tenth Editions they will never be
missed. And there continues to be joy in those who go bravely on
toward the unknown future by the glory of one great line alone —
for instance John William Burgon, with his "rose-red city, half as
old as Time." As for Axel Oxenstiern and Von Münch Bellinghausen, they deserve a footnoted or marginal immortality for their names
alone, and as far as I can help them toward it I shall. They fascinate
me as the pale anonymous curate (squelched by Dr. Johnson) fascinated Max Beerbohm. See Beerbohm's essay "A Clergyman" — indeed, see all his essays.

The tactful editor does not too intrusively nudge his guests. What
a genial impudence was that of the magazine that used to allot "Reading Time" — so many minutes and seconds — for its customers to
accomplish a given piece. Suppose, in the middle of an article or
story, one actually paused to meditate? If we had to specify any limited duration for this work, I suppose it would have to be twenty-
three years, since that seems to be the established elapse between editions of BARTLETT; 1891 — 1914 — 1937 — we should be ripe for
another about 1960. I observe that longevity has been vouchsafed to
BARTLETT editors. Old J. B. died at eighty-five, and Dr. Dole at
eighty-four. The present editors are hopeful. I like the letter J. B.
wrote to his publisher on June 4, 1891, when correcting proof for the
Ninth Edition. He then described his book as "a middle-aged gentleman of thirty-six years, with the tallow which age brings. . . .
There never was such a repertory before and it can never be super-
seded. You will be troubled at not finding some of your good things,
but what could I do. The sensation of fulness is agreeable, that of
repletion is painful."
We have eased the old gentleman of some spiritual tallow; but the
interesting thing is to see how well the senior matter persists. I have
not used a tape measure on the galley proofs, but with one portentous
exception the order of the leaders in space allotted runs pretty much

as it did. Shakespeare and the King James Bible are far in the lead. After them come Milton and Pope. The excitement is to see that Kipling now stands, in the matter of space conceded, just about abreast of Tennyson and Byron. Then come Dr. Johnson, Wordsworth, Browning, Emerson and Longfellow. This reckoning has not been precisely calculated, but I think no fair-minded observer will deny that it approximates the general human suffrage up to date. And more than our predecessors, we have paid willing homage to the Muse of our own day. How vast a world of doing and saying (and doubting) has come to view since Dr. Dole wrote the Tenth Edition preface in — mark the date — July, 1914. Of the modern short-buskined goddess we have at least been able (with Herrick)

to descrie
The happy dawning of her thigh.

Dr. Dole spoke of himself as Elisha inheriting the mantle of Elijah. The successor of Elisha, one remembers, was Jehu; of whom I only know that they broke a box of oil over his head and he drove (or was driven) furiously.[1]

One does not without a twinge of sentiment say good-by to so long a pastime. I can't help feeling like Old Kaspar in Southey's poem, who sits at his cottage door in the sunset while the grandchildren are playing with the skulls — the skulls of dead authors. The cottage is actual, too: I built myself a pine-wood cabin, as aloofly jungled as a Long Island suburb would permit, to consort with the shade of John Bartlett. And my mind goes back to a bitter wintry day when an unexpected visitor joined me. I went out to the cabin to work, and was startled to see sheets of MS. all over the floor, pictures fallen from the top of the shelves, and a certain 1855 Overholt bottle (long empty, but souvenir of an old literary pilgrimage) toppled over but fortunately undamaged. At first I supposed some human mischief, but picking up Miss Everett's folios of beautiful typescript I saw unmistakable proof that the intruder was a bird. Then, from a shadowy perch just under the roof, he swooped across and gave me a start. It was an owl, a handsome fellow with tall ears and speckled breast. He must have come down the chimney. Flattened warily in the triangle of the rafters he watched me steadily. I whistled at him, tried

[1] II Kings, 9.

to frighten him through the open door, but he only coasted from side to side — coming too near my head for comfort. I had no mind to sit there with him perched above me, so I gathered papers and left him in charge, with the door open for exit.

Was it, or was it not, the shade of J. B. himself, offering suggestions? There was a certain facial resemblance . . . and the 1855 bottle was a coincidence: that was the year of BARTLETT's first publication (also *Leaves of Grass*). And the book he had chosen for most frequent perching was the Webster's Unabridged. At any rate it was suggestive to be visited by the bird of wisdom in person. We have tried to adhere to the admirable motto long used on the publisher's colophon, *Non refert quam multos sed quam bonos habeas*. Though there have been times when the editors felt like the Elizabethans described by Virginia Woolf — "Thought plunged into a sea of words and came up dripping." And I have smiled too at a passage in Melville's preface to *Moby Dick* —

This mere painstaking burrower and grubworm of a poor devil appears to have gone through the long Vaticans and street-stalls of the earth, picking up whatever random allusions he could anyways find in any book whatsoever, sacred or profane.

I have left to the end what is the most urgent to be said. Looking wistfully, from time to time, into important books of consultation, I saw something apropos in Professor Clarke Ansley's preface to the *Columbia Encyclopedia* (1935). "The traditional rule for preparing a reference work is, Find the right woman and do what she says." I cannot sufficiently pay tribute to Miss Louella D. Everett, on whom fell the onerous preliminary spadework, and whose accuracy and patience are beyond the scope of creatures like myself. Miss Everett's ideal vision of an all-embracing treasury was, in some respects, beyond the bounds of physical and editorial possibility, and we had our mutual heartburns over problems of omission. But I used to tell her, and still urge it, that there is need of a companion and quite different kind of volume, which might be called *Not in Bartlett* — for which I suggest a pleasant early-Victorian kind of subtitle: *The Librarian's Godsend*. Miss Everett's devotion to this enterprise can never be fully estimated except by her collaborator. As Browning said of Justinian's Pandects, she

made precise
What simply sparkled in men's eyes before,
Twitched in their brow or quivered on their lip,
Waited the speech they called but would not come.

If this book is efficient in arrangement and cross-fertility it is due to her indexophile habits. She is Patience personified and this is her monument. One remembers the story current in the press a few years ago, about a vast new post-office building in Pittsburgh. It was magnificent in every circumstance of Federal grandeur, with classic façade, marble paving, pneumatic chutes, sorting and filing niceties, stamp-moistening tricks, apertures for "Letters in Bulk" and what not. The only thing that was forgotten was a quite ordinary slot where a citizen could mail an everyday letter. The most elaborate lavish of Letters in Bulk is futile if access is difficult for the individual emergency.

The section of Translations — which obviously cannot be exhaustive in a book chiefly devoted to the memorabilia of our own tongue — was first examined by Professor J. D. M. Ford, professor of the French and Spanish Languages at Harvard, who made important suggestions. It was subsequently edited in detail by Mr. Theodore McClintock, who has had large experience in educational publishing and whose knowledge of German has been of much value. Mr. McClintock also copy-edited the whole text from beginning to end. The Index, the most wearisome and certainly the most indispensable feature of BARTLETT, is the work of Miss Beatrice L. Miller.

Correspondents and friends who have helped with suggestions, whether available or not, are gratefully thanked, and necessarily without identification. But no editorial scruple can forgo mention of Mr. Roger L. Scaife, of Little, Brown and Company, who has been this edition's appointed overseer from the beginning. It was he who knew with unerring instinct both when to castigate and when to condole. To renew the image of Jehu, it was Mr. Scaife who, as requirement prompted, either broke the box of oil or drove furiously.
And so to press —

CHRISTOPHER MORLEY.

Roslyn Heights, L. I.
May 22, 1937

PREFACE.

THE object of this work is to show, to some extent, the obligations our language owes to various authors for numerous phrases and familiar quotations which have become " household words."

This Collection, originally made without any view of publication, has been considerably enlarged by additions from an English work on a similar plan, and is now sent forth with the hope that it may be found a convenient book of reference.

Though perhaps imperfect in some respects, it is believed to possess the merit of accuracy, as the quotations have been taken from the original sources.

Should this be favorably received, endeavors will be made to make it more worthy of the approbation of the public in a future edition.

CAMBRIDGE, May, 1855.

FACSIMILE OF PREFACE TO FIRST EDITION

PREFACE TO THE NINTH EDITION

"Out of the old fieldes cometh al this new corne fro yere to yere,"
And out of the fresh woodes cometh al these new flowres here.

The small thin volume, the first to bear the title of this collection, after passing through eight editions, each enlarged, now culminates in its ninth, — and with it, closes its tentative life.

This extract from the Preface of the fourth edition is applicable to the present one : —

"It is not easy to determine in all cases the degree of familiarity that may belong to phrases and sentences which present themselves for admission; for what is familiar to one class of readers may be quite new to another. Many maxims of the most famous writers of our language, and numberless curious and happy turns from orators and poets, have knocked at the door, and it was hard to deny them. But to admit these simply on their own merits, without assurance that the general reader would readily recognize them as old friends, was aside from the purpose of this collection. Still, it has been thought better to incur the risk of erring on the side of fulness."

With the many additions to the English writers, the present edition contains selections from the French, and from the wit and wisdom of the ancients. A few passages have been admitted without a claim to familiarity, but solely on the ground of coincidence of thought.

I am under great obligations to M. H. Morgan, Ph.D., of Harvard University, for the translation of Marcus Aurelius, and for the translation and selections from the Greek tragic writers. I am indebted to the kindness of Mr. Daniel W. Wilder, of Kansas, for the quotations from Pilpay, with contributions from Diogenes Laertius, Montaigne, Burton, and Pope's Homer; to Dr. William J. Rolfe for quotations from Robert Browning; to Mr. James W. McIntyre for quotations from Coleridge, Shelley, Keats, Mrs. Browning, Robert

[xix]

Browning, and Tennyson. And I have incurred other obligations to friends for here a little and there a little.

It gives me pleasure to acknowledge the great assistance I have received from Mr. A. W. Stevens, the accomplished reader of the University Press, as this work was passing through the press.

In withdrawing from this very agreeable pursuit, I beg to offer my sincere thanks to all who have assisted me either in the way of suggestions or by contributions; and especially to those lovers of this subsidiary literature for their kind appreciation of former editions.

Accepted by scholars as an authoritative book of reference, it has grown with its growth in public estimation with each reissue. Of the last two editions forty thousand copies were printed, apart from the English reprints. The present enlargement of text equals three hundred and fifty pages of the previous edition, and the index is increased with upwards of ten thousand lines.

JOHN BARTLETT

Cambridge, March, 1891

predecessors, and epigrammed quotations will not be found included
in its pages. The present editor hopes that a book which has given
so much pleasure and proved so useful in the past may still had
favor with those interested in the best things in literature

PREFACE TO THE TENTH EDITION

"BARTLETT'S FAMILIAR QUOTATIONS" has long since been accepted as indispensable to every scholar and to every writer; it is a book for every library and every household. Embodying years of labor and research on the part of its author, "Familiar Quotations" passed through nine editions, each enlarged, and attained a sale of three hundred thousand copies before Mr. Bartlett's death in 1905 at the age of eighty-five. Unrevised for twenty-three years, it has still remained the best book of the kind, though a considerable body of apothegms have been knocking for admittance to its classic hall of fame.

In this new edition the main body of John Bartlett's compilation, up to the beginning of the nineteenth century, has been left practically unchanged; the chief purpose of the revision has been to incorporate in the work quotations from those writers whose place in literature has been achieved since the issue of the Ninth Edition in 1891. The selections from Poe, Whittier, Longfellow, Lowell, and other "best writers of their day" have been filled out extensively, and many new authors are represented by passages which have met with the seal of popular approval and are distinctly worthy of perpetuation. In this way the book has been greatly enriched. The attempt has been made not to admit anything which John Bartlett's impeccable judgment would have rejected. It is not always easy for Elisha to wear the mantle of Elijah; but it is Elisha's business to carry on his predecessor's work in the same spirit.

A collection of all possible quotations which would satisfy that multitudinous race of folk who apply to the almost omniscient editors of "Notes and Queries" columns for aid in tracing the origin of some favorite quotation, half forgotten, would have to be as big as the Encyclopedia. In the Tenth Edition of "Familiar Quotations" the aim has been to maintain the high literary standard set by its predecessors, and ephemeral quotations will not be found included in its pages. The present editor hopes that a book which has given so much pleasure and proved so useful in the past may still find favor with those interested in the best things in literature.

NATHAN HASKELL DOLE

Boston, July, 1914

INDEX OF AUTHORS

Note: Names, not British or American, preceded by the prepositional forms *d'*, *de*, *du*, *de la*, and *von*, are listed in order of the names, not in order of the prepositional forms.

The asterisk (*) preceding a name indicates that quotations from that author included as Notes are so numerous that the editors consider it impracticable to give the numbers of all the pages where they occur.

ABBOT, WILLIS JOHN, *note* . . . 753
ABERCROMBIE, LASCELLES . . . 867
ABRANTES, DUC D' 1062
    DUC D', *note* . . . 1003
ABRANTES, DUCHESSE D', *note* . . 993
ADAMS, CHARLES FOLLEN . . . 661
ADAMS, CHARLES FRANCIS . . . 431
ADAMS, FRANKLIN PIERCE . . . 867
    F. P., *note* . . 270, 331, 714
ADAMS, HENRY BROOKS 635
ADAMS, JAMES BARTON, *note* . . 681
ADAMS, JOHN 268
    JOHN, *note* . . . 339, 340
ADAMS, JOHN QUINCY 291
    JOHN QUINCY, *note* . . 203
ADAMS, SAMUEL, *note* 240
ADAMS, SARAH FLOWER 423
ADDAMS, JANE 750
*ADDISON, JOSEPH 194
ADE, GEORGE 791
    GEORGE, *note* 359
ADELER, MAX 684
ADY, THOMAS, *note* 164
AE 801
AESCHYLUS 963
    note 145
AESOP 961
AGUECHEEK 570
AÏDÉ, CHARLES HAMILTON . . . 582
AIKEN, CONRAD 904
AIKIN, LUCY, *note* 136
AINGER, ALFRED 942
AINSWORTH, WILLIAM HARRISON . 423
AKENSIDE, MARK, *note* . . . 200
AKINS, ZOË 887
ALCAEUS 959
ALCOTT, AMOS BRONSON . . . 393
ALCOTT, LOUISA MAY 594
ALDINGTON, RICHARD . . . 913
ALDIS, DOROTHY KEELEY . . . 925
ALDRICH, HENRY 184
ALDRICH, JAMES 473
ALDRICH, THOMAS BAILEY . . . 620
    THOMAS BAILEY, *note* . . 509

ALDUS (MANUTIUS) 1022
ALEXANDER, CECIL FRANCES . . 516
    CECIL FRANCES, *note* . 372
ALEXANDER, JOSEPH ADDISON . . 395
ALFORD, HENRY 473
ALGER, HORATIO 605
ALGER, WILLIAM ROUNSEVILLE, *note* 389
    W. R., *note* . . 437, 474, 566
ALI BEN ABOU TALEB 1017
ALIGHIERI, DANTE 1020
ALLEN, ELIZABETH AKERS . . . 595
ALLEN, HERVEY 905
    HERVEY, *note* . . . 904
ALLEN, JAMES LANE 691
ALLEN, WILLIAM 427
ALLINGHAM, WILLIAM 573
    WILLIAM, *note* . . . 978
ALLISON, YOUNG EWING . . . 710
    YOUNG EWING, *note* . . 704
ALPHONSO THE LEARNED . . . 1020
ALTGELD, JOHN PETER . . . 684
AMELIA, PRINCESS 342
AMES, FISHER, *note* 581
AMIEL, HENRI-FRÉDÉRIC . . . 1073
ANACREON 960
ANDERSON, HAROLD MACDONALD . 840
ANDERSON, SHERWOOD 841
ANGELL, WALTER FOSTER, *note* . 752
ANSPACHER, LOUIS KAUFMAN . . 848
ANSTER, JOHN, *note* 1058
ANTIN, MARY 862
ANTONINUS, MARCUS AURELIUS . 1009
    MARCUS AURELIUS, *note* . 989
APULEIUS, LUCIUS, *note* . . . 116
ARBUTHNOT, DR. JOHN, *note* . . 628
ARIOSTO, LUDOVICO, *note* . 356, 1035
ARISTOPHANES 971
ARISTOTLE 975
    note 173
ARKWRIGHT, PELEG 664
ARNIM AND BRENTANO, *note* . . 433
ARNOLD, SIR EDWIN 596
    SIR EDWIN, *note* . . . 437
ARNOLD, GEORGE 605

[xxiii]

ARNOLD, MATTHEW 545
    MATTHEW, *note* . 337, 1065
ARNOLD, SAMUEL J. 320
ARRIANUS, FLAVIUS, *note* . . . 980
ASHBY-STERRY, JOSEPH 637
ATHENAEUS 1012
ATHERTON, GERTRUDE 725
ATWELL, ROY 860
AUBREY, JOHN 171
    JOHN, *note* . 118, 130, 167
AUDEN, WYSTAN HUGH 937
AUGUSTINE, SAINT 1016
    SAINT, *note* 112, 126, 1012
AUSLANDER, JOSEPH 925
AUSONIUS, DECIMUS MAGNUS, *note* 1013
AUSTEN, JANE 322
AUSTIN, ALFRED 612
    ALFRED, *note* . . . 1040
AUSTIN, HENRY WILLARD . . 731
AUSTIN, MARY HUNTER . . . 801
AVEBURY, LORD 605
AVONMORE, LORD, *note* . . . 340
AYTOUN, WILLIAM EDMONDSTOUNE 500

BABCOCK, MALTBIE DAVENPORT . 731
BACKUS, BERTHA ADAMS . . . 848
BACON, LADY ANN, *note* . . . 9
BACON, FRANCIS 109
    FRANCIS, *note* . 16, 183, 987
BACON, LEONARD 892
BACON, SIR NATHANIEL, *note* . . 9
BAILEY, PHILIP JAMES 506
    PHILIP J., *note* . 469, 714
BAILEY, URANIA LOCKE STOUGHTON 539
BAILLIE, JOANNA 288
BAIRNSFATHER, BRUCE 943
BAKER, KARLE WILSON . . . 848
    KARLE WILSON, *note* . . 628
BALFOUR, ARTHUR JAMES . . . 687
BALZAC, HONORÉ DE 1066
BANCROFT, GEORGE, *note* . . 394
BANGS, JOHN KENDRICK . . . 760
BANKS, GEORGE LINNAEUS . . 543
BANNING, KENDALL 855
BANVILLE, THÉODORE DE, *note* . . 743
BARBAULD, ANNA LETITIA AIKEN . 272
BARBER, MARGARET FAIRLESS . . 805
    MARGARET FAIRLESS, *note* . 705
BARÈRE, BERTRAND 1059
    BERTRAND, *note* . . . 240
BARHAM, RICHARD HARRIS . . 350
BARING, MAURICE 825
BARING-GOULD, SABINE . . . 605
BARKER, DAVID 507
BARLOW, JOEL 280
BARNARD, LADY ANNE LINDSAY . 277
BARNARD, CHARLOTTE ALINGTON . 582
BARNFIELD, RICHARD 120

BARNHART, HENRY A. 731
BARR, MATTHIAS 589
BARRETT, EATON STANNARD . . 349
BARRIE, SIR JAMES MATTHEW . . 750
    SIR JAMES MATTHEW, *note* 312
BARRINGTON, GEORGE . . . 280
    GEORGE, *note* . . . 201
BARROW, ISAAC, *note* . . . 195
BARRY, MICHAEL JOSEPH . . . 511
* BARTAS, GUILLAUME DE SALLUSTE
    DU 1031
BARTHÉLEMY, AUGUSTE MARSEILLE,
    note 342
BASHFORD, HENRY HOWARTH . . 861
BASSE, WILLIAM, *note* . . . 119
BASSUS, *note* 985
BATES, DAVID 473
BATES, KATHARINE LEE . . . 737
BAX, CLIFFORD 887
BAXTER, RICHARD 166
BAYARD, CHEVALIER, *note* . . 19
BAYLE, PIERRE, *note* 415
BAYLY, THOMAS HAYNES . . . 388
BEACONSFIELD, EARL OF 418
    EARL OF, *note* 275, 319, 379, 414
BEATTIE, JAMES 269
BEATTY, PAKENHAM 473
BEAUMARCHAIS, PIERRE DE . . 1055
    PIERRE DE, *note* . . 360
BEAUMONT, FRANCIS 129
* BEAUMONT AND FLETCHER . 130, 947
BECCARIA, CESARE BONENSANO, *note* 223
BECK, MICHAEL WENTWORTH . . 505
BEDDOES, THOMAS LOVELL . . 406
BEDE, SAINT, *note* . . . 354, 993
BEE, BERNARD ELLIOTT . . . 552
BEECHER, HENRY WARD . . . 500
BEERBOHM, MAX 818
BEERS, ETHEL LYNN 569
BEERS, HENRY AUGUSTIN . . . 684
BELL, HENRY GLASSFORD . . . 423
BELLAMY, EDWARD 697
BELLAMY, FRANCIS M. . . . 718
BELLAMY, G. W. 647
BELLINGHAUSEN, VON MÜNCH . 1070
    VON MÜNCH, *note* 219
BELLOC, HILAIRE 809
BENCHLEY, ROBERT CHARLES . . 905
BENEDICT, SAINT 1016
    SAINT, *note* . . . 499
BENÉT, LAURA 881
BENÉT, STEPHEN VINCENT . . 927
BENÉT, WILLIAM ROSE . . . 887
BENJAMIN, JUDAH P., *note* . . 797
BENJAMIN, PARK 448
BENNETT, HENRY HOLCOMB . . 767
BENNETT, JOHN 774
BENNETT, WILLIAM COX . . . 539

BENSERADE, ISAAC DE 1043
BENSON, ARTHUR CHRISTOPHER . 761
BENSON, STELLA 913
BENTHAM, JEREMY, *note* . . . 223
BENTLEY, RICHARD 187
    RICHARD, *note* . . . 218
BENTON, THOMAS HART . . . 338
BERGERAC, SAVINIEN CYRANO DE,
   note 1047
BERKELEY, GEORGE 203
    GEORGE, *note* . . 30, 265
BERNARD OF CLUNY 1017
BERNERS, JULIANA, *note* . . . 115
BERNHARDI, FRIEDRICH A. J. VON . 1083
BERTAUT, JEAN, *note* 74
BERTIN, MADEMOISELLE . . 1061
BETHELL, RICHARD 402
BETTELHEIM, A. S., *note* . . . 112
BEYLE, HENRI 1063
BIBESCO, ELIZABETH ASQUITH . . 913
BICKERSTAFF, ISAAC 269
    ISAAC, *note* . 18, 29, 136
BICKERSTETH, EDWARD HENRY . . 561
BIDPAI 976
   note 16, 17
BIERCE, AMBROSE 661
BILLINGS, JOSH 518
    JOSH, *note* . . 873, 920
BINYON, LAURENCE 804
BIRDSEYE, GEORGE 668
BIRRELL, AUGUSTINE 697
BISHOP, MORRIS 878
BISHOP, THOMAS BRIGHAM . . 612
BISSON, ALEXANDER 1090
BLACKER, COLONEL VALENTINE . 329
BLACKMORE, RICHARD DODDRIDGE . 561
BLACKSTONE, SIR WILLIAM . . 248
BLACKWOOD, FREDERICK TEMPLE
   HAMILTON 566
BLAINE, JAMES GILLESPIE . . . 583
BLAIR, ROBERT, *note* . 145, 179, 186
BLAKE, JAMES W. 761
BLAKE, WILLIAM 281
BLANCHAN, NELTJE, *note* . . . 435
BLANCHARD, LAMAN 406
BLANCHET, *note* 27, 1024
BLAND, EDITH NESBIT . . . 731
BLAND, ROBERT, *note* . . . 125
BLANDING, DON 920
BLIND, MATHILDE 655
BLISS, DANIEL 272
BLISS, M. LINDSAY, *note* . . . 388
BLUNT, WILFRID SCAWEN . . . 647
BOBART, JACOB, *note* . . . 202, 950
BODINUS, JEAN, *note* . . . 264
BOETHIUS, ANTICIUS MANLIUS SE-
   VERINUS, *note* . . . 231, 440
BOGART, JOHN B. 677

BOILEAU-DESPRÉAUX, NICHOLAS . 1049
   NICHOLAS, *note* 177, 216, 361, 472
BOKER, GEORGE HENRY . . . 552
BOLINGBROKE, VISCOUNT . . . 200
    VISCOUNT, *note* . 229, 400
BOLITHO, WILLIAM 907
* BONAPARTE, NAPOLEON . . . 1060
BONAR, HORATIUS 445
BOND, CARRIE JACOBS . . . 761
BONE, DAVID WILLIAM . . . 825
BONE, JAMES 819
BONER, JOHN HENRY 677
BOOTH, BARTON, *note* . . . 143
BORBONIUS, MATTHIAS, *note* . . 209
BORROW, GEORGE 407
BOSQUET, PIERRE FRANÇOIS JOSEPH 1070
BOSSIDY, JOHN COLLINS . . . 752
BOSSUET, JACQUES BÉNIGNE . . 1048
BOSWELL, JAMES 272
   J., *note* . 121, 233, 239, 254
BOTTOMLEY, GORDON 826
BOUCICAULT, DION 548
BOULTON, HAROLD EDWIN . . 752
BOURDILLON, FRANCIS WILLIAM . 707
BOUVÉ, PAULINE CARRINGTON RUST 752
BOWEN, EDWARD ERNEST . . . 621
BOYLE, ROGER, *note* 167
BRACTON, HENRY DE . . . 945
BRADFORD, GAMALIEL . . . 767
BRADFORD, JOHN 18
BRADLEY, KATHARINE . . . 683
BRADLEY, MARY EMILY . . . 612
BRADY, NICHOLAS 185
   NICHOLAS, *note* 141
BRAGG, EDWARD STUYVESANT . . 569
BRAILSFORD, HENRY NOEL . . 821
BRAINARD, JOHN GARDINER CAL-
   KINS 375
BRAINARD, MARY GARDINER . . 626
BRALEY, BERTON 872
   BERTON, *note* . 562, 636, 1073
BRANCH, ANNA HEMPSTEAD . . 841
   ANNA HEMPSTEAD, *note* . 712
BRANN, WILLIAM COWPER . . . 714
BRATHWAITE, RICHARD . . . 940
BRENNAN, GERALD 715
BRERETON, JANE 204
BRETON, NICHOLAS, *note* . . 23
BRIDGES, MADELINE 671
BRIDGES, ROBERT 668
BRIGHT, JOHN 478
BRILLAT-SAVARIN, ANTHELME . 1059
      note 1040
BRINE, MARY DOW 715
BROMLEY, ISAAC HILL . . . 601
BRONTË, CHARLOTTE . . . 507
BRONTË, EMILY 516
BROOKE, HENRY, *note* . . . 238

BROOKE, LORD 27
          LORD, note 9, 395
BROOKE, RUPERT 893
BROOKS, MARIA GOWEN 375
BROOKS, NOAH 583
BROOKS, PHILLIPS 612
BROOKS, VAN WYCK 889
BROUGH, ROBERT BARNABAS . . 573
BROUGHAM, LORD 331
          LORD, note 259
BROUN, HEYWOOD CAMPBELL . . 898
          HEYWOOD CAMPBELL, note 697
BROWN, ALICE 725
BROWN, FRANCES 507
BROWN, THOMAS (TOM) . . . 188
BROWN, THOMAS EDWARD . . . 583
BROWNE, CHARLES FARRAR . . . 606
          CHARLES FARRAR, note . 389
BROWNE, MATTHEW 553
* BROWNE, SIR THOMAS . . . 144
BROWNE, WILLIAM 133
          WILLIAM, note 112
BROWNELL, HENRY HOWARD . . 539
          HENRY HOWARD, note . 764
* BROWNING, ELIZABETH BARRETT . 427
* BROWNING, ROBERT 484
BRUYÈRE, JEAN DE LA 1050
BRYAN, GEORGE SANDS 855
BRYAN, WILLIAM JENNINGS . . 752
          WILLIAM JENNINGS, note . 621
BRYANT, WILLIAM CULLEN . . . 371
          WILLIAM C., note . . 26, 986
BRYCE, JAMES 637
          JAMES, note . . . 278, 532
BUCHAN, JOHN 837
BUCHANAN, ROBERT 655
BUCK, PEARL SYDENSTRICKER . . 913
BUCKE, RICHARD MAURICE . . . 627
BUCKHAM, JAMES 732
BUCKINGHAM, DUKE OF, note . . 116
BUCKINGHAMSHIRE, DUKE OF . . 185
          DUKE OF, note 164
BUFFON, COMTE DE, note . . 122, 379
BULLEIN, WILLIAM, note . . . 79
BUNGAY, GEORGE W. 566
BUNN, ALFRED 386
BUNNER, HENRY CUYLER . . . 715
          HENRY CUYLER, note . 478
BUNSEN, BARON CHRISTIAN KARL
          JOSIAS, note 1024
BUNTLINE, NED, note 713
BUNYAN, JOHN 171
          JOHN, note . 14, 16, 79, 142
BURCHARD, SAMUEL DICKINSON . 494
BURDETTE, ROBERT JONES . . . 669
          ROBERT JONES, note . 583
BURGESS, GELETT 791
BURGON, JOHN WILLIAM . . . 500

BURGON, JOHN WILLIAM, note . . 443
* BURKE, EDMUND 258
BURLEIGH, GEORGE SHEPARD . . 543
BURNAND, SIR FRANCIS COWLEY . 627
BURNET, GILBERT, note 421
* BURNS, ROBERT 284
BURROUGHS, JOHN 627
          JOHN, note 535
BURTON, HENRY 647
BURTON, RICHARD 756
BURTON, SIR RICHARD FRANCIS . 543
* BURTON, ROBERT 121
BUSCH, WILHELM 1077
          WILHELM, note 217
BUSSY-RABUTIN, COMTE DE, note . 188
BUTLER, BENJAMIN FRANKLIN . 516
BUTLER, NICHOLAS MURRAY . . 761
* BUTLER, SAMUEL 141
BUTLER, SAMUEL 613
BUTLER, WILLIAM, note 798
BUTLER, WILLIAM ALLEN . . . 561
BUTTERWORTH, HEZEKIAH . . . 643
BYNNER, WITTER 868
BYRD, WILLIAM, note 20
BYROM, JOHN 221
          JOHN, note 116, 170
* BYRON, GEORGE NOEL GORDON,
          LORD 351

CABELL, JAMES BRANCH . . . 855
CABLE, GEORGE WASHINGTON . . 670
CAECILIUS STATIUS 978
CAEDMON 3
CAINE, HALL 711
CALHOUN, JOHN C. 338
          JOHN C., note 188
CALVERLEY, CHARLES STUART . . 589
          C. S., note . . . 551, 965
CAMBRONNE, PIERRE JACQUES
          ÉTIENNE, COUNT 1061
CAMDEN, WILLIAM 21, 948
CAMPBELL, ANNE 899
CAMPBELL, BARTLEY 942
CAMPBELL, CALDER 395
CAMPBELL, LORD JOHN, note . . 331
CAMPBELL, JOSEPH 868
CAMPBELL, ROY 933
* CAMPBELL, THOMAS 327
CAMPION, THOMAS 121
          THOMAS, note 133
CANBY, HENRY SEIDEL 849
CANNING, GEORGE 293
CANNING, JOSIAH DEAN . . . 507
CARBERY, ETHNA 792
CAREW, THOMAS 140
          THOMAS, note 185
CAREY, HENRY 189
CARLETON, WILL 677

CARLETON, WILL, *note* . . . 180, 482
CARLIN, FRANCIS 869
CARLYLE, JANE WELSH 402
CARLYLE, THOMAS 375
   T., *note* 186, 472, 607, 1020
CARMAN, BLISS 757
CARNEY, JULIA A. FLETCHER . . 553
CAROVÉ, FREDERICK WILHELM, *note* 433
CARPENTER, EDWARD 670
CARPENTER, HENRY BERNARD . . 647
CARPENTER, JOSEPH EDWARDS . . 500
CARROLL, LEWIS 598
   LEWIS, *note* 320
CARRUTH, WILLIAM HERBERT . . 737
   WILLIAM HERBERT, *note* 491
CARRUTHERS, ROBERT, *note* . . 331
CARRYL, CHARLES EDWARD . . . 655
CARRYL, GUY WETMORE . . . 821
CARTER, WILLIAM LORENZO . . 501
CARTWRIGHT, WILLIAM . . . 164
CARY, ALICE 540
CARY, PHOEBE 557
CASE, LIZZIE YORK 648
CASE, PHILO HENRIETTA . . . 557
CASEMENT, SIR ROGER 771
CATHER, WILLA SIBERT . . . 841
CATINAT, MARSHAL, *note* . . . 1005
CATO THE CENSOR, *note* . . 998, 1001
CATULLUS, CAIUS VALERIUS, *note* . 992
CAUX, GILLES DE, *note* . . . 250
CAWEIN, MADISON JULIUS . . . 774
CAZALIS, HENRI 1078
CENTLIVRE, SUSANNAH 190
* CERVANTES, MIGUEL DE . 1033, 947
CHADWICK, JOHN WHITE . . . 648
   JOHN WHITE, *note* . 639
CHAFEE, ZECHARIAH, JR., *note* . 201
CHALMERS, PATRICK REGINALD . 842
CHALONER, JOHN ARMSTRONG . 762
CHAMBERLAIN, JOSEPH . . . 621
CHAMBERS, ROBERT WILLIAM . 774
CHAMFORT, SÉBASTIEN R. N. . 1056
CHANDLER, BESSIE, *note* . . 402
CHANNING, WILLIAM ELLERY . 333
CHANNING, WILLIAM ELLERY . 517
CHANNING, WILLIAM HENRY . 473
CHAPMAN, ARTHUR 821
* CHAPMAN, GEORGE . . . 28
CHAPMAN, JOHN JAY, *note* . . 1020
CHAPMAN, ROBERT WILLIAM . 869
CHARLES I OF ENGLAND, *note* . 251
CHARLES II OF ENGLAND . . 940
CHARLES, ELIZABETH RUNDLE . 573
CHARRON, PIERRE, *note* . . . 207
CHASE, SALMON PORTLAND . . 445
CHATHAM, EARL OF 230
   EARL OF, *note* . . . 152
* CHAUCER, GEOFFREY . . . 3

CHENEY, JOHN VANCE 687
   JOHN VANCE, *note* . . 53
CHERRY, ANDREW 288
CHESTER, ANSON GLEASON . . 569
CHESTERFIELD, EARL OF . . . 222
   EARL OF, *note* . . . 253
CHESTERTON, GILBERT KEITH . 826
   G. K., *note* . . . 758
CHILD, LYDIA MARIA 403
CHILDE, WILFRED ROWLAND, *note* . 858
CHILDS, GEORGE WILLIAM . . . 577
CHILO, *note* 965
CHIVERS, THOMAS HOLLEY . . 431
CHOATE, RUFUS 393
CHOLMONDELEY, HESTER H., *note* . 136
CHORLEY, HENRY FOTHERGILL . 446
CHRISTY, DAVID, *note* . . . 432
CHRYSOSTOM, DIO 994
CHRYSOSTOM, SAINT, *note* . . . 1023
CHURCH, EDWARD A. 671
CHURCH, FRANCIS PHARCELLUS . 643
CHURCHILL, CHARLES . . . 262
   C., *note* 15, 245, 472, 1030
CHURCHYARD, THOMAS, *note* . 74
CIBBER, COLLEY 193
   COLLEY, *note* 67, 72, 145, 977
CICERO, MARCUS TULLIUS . . 980
   note . . . 206, 259, 289, 318
CLARE, JOHN 369
CLARENDON, EDWARD HYDE, *note* . 270
CLARIBEL 582
CLARK, BADGER, JR. 878
CLARK, CHARLES HEBER . . . 684
CLARK, JOHN ABBOT, *note* . . 774
CLARKE, JAMES FREEMAN . . . 473
CLARKE, JOHN, *note* . . 227, 365
CLARKE, JOSEPH IGNATIUS CONSTAN-
  TINE 683
CLARKE, MACDONALD 389
   MACDONALD, *note* . . 320
CLAY, HENRY 328
   HENRY, *note* 319
CLEAVELAND, ELIZABETH HANNAH
  JOCELYN 557
CLEMENS, SAMUEL LANGHORNE . 615
   S. L., *note* 702
CLEVELAND, GROVER 627
   GROVER, *note* . . . 419
CLIFFORD, JOHN 622
CLOUGH, ARTHUR HUGH . . . 519
   ARTHUR HUGH, *note* 300, 468
COATES, FLORENCE EARLE . . 697
COATSWORTH, ELIZABETH J. . . 917
COBB, IRVIN SHREWSBURY, *note* . 599
COCKBURN, ALICIA RUTHERFORD . 240
CODRINGTON, CHRISTOPHER, *note* . 187
COFFIN, ROBERT BARRY . . . 566
COFFIN, ROBERT PETER TRISTRAM . 914

COHAN, GEORGE MICHAEL . . . 849
COKE, SIR EDWARD 21
    SIR EDWARD, note . . . 129
COLBY, FRANK MOORE 774
    FRANK MOORE, note . . 1061
COLE, SAMUEL VALENTINE . . . 706
COLERIDGE, HARTLEY 386
    HARTLEY, note 296
* COLERIDGE, SAMUEL TAYLOR . . 314
COLESWORTHY, DANIEL CLEMENT . 474
COLLIER, ROBERT 553
COLLINS, MORTIMER 569
COLLINS, WILLIAM 249
COLMAN, GEORGE, THE YOUNGER . 288
    GEORGE, note 1008
COLTON, CHARLES CALEB . . . 333
COLUM, MARY M., note . . . 878
COLUM, PADRAIC 869
CONANT, ISABEL FISKE . . . 828
CONANT, JAMES BRYANT . . . 917
CONE, HELEN GRAY 737
CONGREVE, WILLIAM 193
    WILLIAM, note 52, 223, 468
CONKLING, GRACE HAZARD . . 849
CONKLING, ROSCOE 578
CONNELLY, MARCUS COOK . . . 908
CONOVER, OBADIAH MILTON . . 562
CONRAD, JOSEPH 726
CONRIED, HEINRICH 716
CONSTABLE, HENRY, note . . . 304
CONSTANT, HENRI BENJAMIN . . 1060
CONWELL, RUSSELL HERMAN . . 665
COOGLER, J. GORDON 804
COOK, ALBERT JAY 861
COOK, ELIZA 511
COOKE, EDMUND VANCE . . . 792
COOKE, ROSE TERRY 570
    ROSE TERRY, note . . . 180
COOLBRITH, INA DONNA . . . 671
COOLIDGE, CALVIN 819
COOLIDGE, SUSAN 682
COOPER, SIR ANTHONY ASHLEY, note 421
COOPER, EDITH 683
COOPER, GEORGE 637
COOPER, JAMES FENIMORE, note . 387
COPELAND, CHARLES TOWNSEND . 753
    C. T., note 493
CORBET, RICHARD 128
CORBETT, ELIZABETH T., note . . 733
CORCORAN, PETER 941
CORNEILLE, PIERRE 1043
    PIERRE, note 169
CORNEILLE, THOMAS, note . . . 358
CORNFORD, FRANCES 890
CORNUEL, MADAME, note . . . 1005
CORNWALL, BARRY 350
CORY, WILLIAM JOHNSON . . . 553
CORYAT, THOMAS, note . . . 321

COTTON, NATHANIEL 226
COURTNEY, MARGARET 548
COWLEY, ABRAHAM 167
    ABRAHAM, note . . 111, 151
* COWPER, WILLIAM 262
COX, KENYON 719
COXE, ARTHUR CLEVELAND . . . 517
CRABBE, GEORGE 280
    GEORGE, note . 79, 249, 468
CRAIK, DINAH MARIA MULOCK . 567
    D. M. M., note 9
CRANCH, CHRISTOPHER PEARSE . 501
    C. P., note . . . 379, 594
CRANE, NATHALIA 938
CRANE, STEPHEN 813
CRANFIELD, LIONEL, note . . . 141
CRANSTOUN, HELEN D'ARCY . . 290
CRAPSEY, ADELAIDE 849
CRASHAW, RICHARD 165
CRASTER, MRS. EDWARD . . . 942
CRAWFORD, FRANCIS MARION . . 712
    F. M., note 751
CRAWFORD, JOHN WALLACE (CAP-
    TAIN JACK) 684
CRAWFORD, JULIA 396
CRITTENDEN, JOHN JORDAN, note . 472
CROCKETT, DAVID 349
CROKER, JOHN WILSON, note . . 187
CROMWELL, OLIVER 141
    OLIVER, note 329
CROSLAND, THOMAS WILLIAM HODG-
    SON 802
CROSS, MARIAN EVANS . . . 520
CROWELL, GRACE NOLL . . . 845
    GRACE NOLL, note 562, 1073
CUFFE, WILLIAM ULICK O'CONNOR 678
CULLEN, COUNTEE 935
    COUNTEE, note . . . 904
CUMBERLAND, RICHARD . . . 179
CUMMINGS, EDWARD ESTLIN . . 920
CUNNINGHAM, ALLAN 345
CURRAN, JOHN PHILPOT . . . 277
CURTIS, GEORGE WILLIAM . . . 558
CURTIUS, QUINTUS, note . . . 21
CUSHMAN, CHARLOTTE . . . 508
CUTLER, JULIAN STEARNS . . . 712
CUTTER, GEORGE WASHINGTON . . 402
CYRILLUS, note 995

DALLAS, MARY KYLE 628
DALY, THOMAS AUGUSTINE . . 813
DANA, MARY STANLEY BUNCE . 474
DANA, RICHARD HENRY . . . 349
DANA, RICHARD HENRY . . . 505
DANIEL, SAMUEL 30
    SAMUEL, note 27
DANTE, ALIGHIERI 1020
DANTON, GEORGES JACQUES . . 1059

DANTON, GEORGES JACQUES, *note* . 25
D'ARCY, HUGH ANTOINE . . . 665
DARIO, RUBÉN 858
DARLEY, GEORGE 382
DARLING, CHARLES HIAL, *note* . . 822
DARWIN, CHARLES ROBERT . . . 448
DARWIN, ERASMUS 267
    ERASMUS, *note* . . 215, 269
DAVENANT, SIR WILLIAM . . . 146
DAVEY, NORMAN 899
DAVIDSON, JOHN 728
    JOHN, *note* . . 710, 754
DAVIES, SIR JOHN 114
DAVIES, SCROPE 941
DAVIES, WILLIAM HENRY . . . 814
    WILLIAM HENRY, *note* . . 492
DA VINCI, LEONARDO 1022
DAVIS, CHARLES T. 811
    CHARLES T., *note* . . . 361
DAVIS, FLORENCE BOYCE, *note* . . 752
DAVIS, JEFFERSON, *note* . . . 539
DAVIS, MOLLIE E. MOORE . . . 707
DAVIS, ROBERT HOBART (BOB) . . 804
DAVIS, THOMAS OSBORNE . . . 502
    THOMAS OSBORNE, *note* . 738
DAY, BETH 716
DAY, CLARENCE 828
DAY, HOLMAN FRANCIS . . . 775
DE BARY, ANNA BUNSTON . . . 811
DECATUR, STEPHEN, *note* . . 262, 472
DEFFAND, MARIE DU 1053
DEFOE, DANIEL 187
    DANIEL, *note* . . 126, 655
DEKKER, THOMAS 115
    THOMAS, *note* 117
DE LA MARE, WALTER 822
DELAND, MARGARET WADE . . . 728
DELILLE, JACQUES 1056
DELTA 393
DE MAP, WALTER 940
DE MORGAN, AUGUSTUS, *note* . . 190
DEMOSTHENES 976
    note 277
DENHAM, SIR JOHN 166
DENMAN, LORD THOMAS . . . 331
DENNIS, JOHN 186
DE QUINCEY, THOMAS 347
DERZHAVIN, GABRIEL ROMANOVITCH 1057
DESART, LORD 678
DÉSAUGIERS, MARC ANTOINE . . 1062
DESCHAMPS, ÉMILE, *note* . . 1056
DESPREZ, FRANK 711
DE VERE, AUBREY THOMAS . . 503
DE VERE, MARY AINGE . . . 671
DE VOTO, BERNARD 925
DEWEY, GEORGE 638
DIBDIN, CHARLES 274
    CHARLES, *note* . . 511, 776

DIBDIN, THOMAS 305
* DICKENS, CHARLES 494
DICKINSON, CHARLES MONROE . . 662
DICKINSON, EMILY 583
DICKINSON, GOLDSWORTHY LOWES . 762
DICKINSON, JOHN, *note* . . . 404
DIDACUS STELLA, *note* . . . 122
DIGBY, SIR KENELM 144
DIGBY, KENELM HENRY . . . 396
DILLON, GEORGE 938
DILLON, WENTWORTH 180
DIO CHRYSOSTOM 994
DIODORUS SICULUS 1092
* DIOGENES LAERTIUS 1012
DIONYSIUS OF HALICARNASSUS, *note* 200
DIONYSIUS THE ELDER 973
DISRAELI, BENJAMIN 418
    B., *note* . 275, 319, 379, 414
DISRAELI, ISAAC 291
DIVINE, CHARLES 905
DIX, JOHN ADAMS 390
DIXON, RICHARD WATSON . . . 601
DOANE, WILLIAM CROSWELL . . 597
    W. C., *note* . . 330, 454, 586
DOBELL, SYDNEY THOMPSON . . 558
DOBSON, HENRY AUSTIN . . . 648
    H. A., *note* 113, 180, 434, 716
DODD, LEE WILSON 856
DODDRIDGE, PHILIP 225
DODGE, MARY ABIGAIL 638
DODGE, MARY MAPES 638
DODGE, SAMUEL 474
DODGSON, CHARLES LUTWIDGE . . 598
    CHARLES LUTWIDGE, *note* 320
DODSLEY, ROBERT 225
DOLBEN, DIGBY MACKWORTH . . 687
DOLE, CHARLES FLETCHER . . . 678
DOLE, NATHAN HASKELL . . . 707
DOLLARD, JAMES B. 819
DOMETT, ALFRED 478
DONNE, JOHN 117
    JOHN, *note* 9, 110
DONNELLY, IGNATIUS, *note* . . . 260
DOOLEY, MR. 796
DORO, EDWARD 938
DORR, JULIA CAROLINE RIPLEY . . 562
DOS PASSOS, JOHN RODERIGO . . 925
DOSTOYEVSKY, FYODOR 1074
DOTEN, LIZZIE 570
DOUDNEY, SARAH 665
    SARAH, *note* 137
DOUGLAS, LORD ALFRED . . . 811
DOUGLAS, GEORGE NORMAN . . 802
DOUGLAS, MARIAN 665
DOWDEN, EDWARD 666
DOWLING, BARTHOLOMEW . . . 554
DOWNING, MAJOR JACK . . . 369
DOWSON, ERNEST 795

Dowson, Ernest, *note* 1105
Doyle, Sir Arthur Conan . . 737
    Sir Arthur C., *note* . 18, 490
Doyle, Sir Francis Hastings . . 474
Drake, Joseph Rodman . . . 382
Drayton, Michael 30
    Michael, *note* . . . 6
Drennan, William 941
Drinkwater, John 873
Driscoll, Louise 837
Driver, William 407
Drummond, Captain Thomas, *note* 420
Drummond, William, *note* . 113, 126
Drummond, William Henry . . 712
* Dryden, John 173, 947
DuBois, William Edward Burg-
    hardt 802
Dubourg, George 394
Dufferin, Lady 432
Dufferin, Lord 566
Duganne, Augustine Joseph
    Hickey 554
Dumas, Alexandre, the Elder . 1067
    A., the Elder, *note* 106, 1062
Dumas, Alexandre, the Younger 1075
Du Maurier, George Louis Pal-
    mella Busson 606
    George, *note* . . 551
Dunbar, Paul Laurence . . . 820
Dunbar, William, *note* . 316, 1080
Duncombe, Lewis, *note* . . . 292
Dunne, Finley Peter 796
Dunsany, Lord 849
D'Urfey, Thomas 186
Dwight, John Sullivan . . . 501
Dyer, Edward 20
Dyer, John 223
Dyer, John 941

Eastwick, Edward Backhouse,
    note 275
Eaton, Arthur Wentworth Ham-
    ilton 738
Eddy, Mary Baker 548
Edgett, Edwin Francis . . . 797
Edmond, Amanda M. 558
Edward VIII of England . . . 921
Edwards, Amelia Blanford, *note* 341
Edwards, Jonathan 226
Edwards, Richard 19
Edwin, John 276
Eggleston, Edward, *note* . . . 323
Eldon, Lord, *note* 259
Eliot, Charles William . . . 608
Eliot, George 520
Eliot, Thomas Stearns . . . 899
Elizabeth, Queen of England . 19

Elizabeth, Queen, *note* . . . 12
Ellerton, John 402
Elliot, Jared, *note* 248
Elliott, Ebenezer 338
Elliott, Jane, *note* . . . 240, 936
Ellis, Havelock 738
    Havelock, *note* . . . 751
Ellis, Henry 329
    Henry, *note* 189
Elmslie, W. G. 687
* Emerson, Ralph Waldo . . . 408
Emmet, Daniel Decatur . . . 505
Emmet, Robert 329
Engels, Friedrich, *note* . . . 1072
England, George Allan . . . 845
English, Thomas Dunn . . . 521
Ennius, Quintus 978
Epictetus 1007
    note 989
Erasmus, Desiderius 1023
    note 4, 143, 994
Erskine, John 856
Esenwein, Joseph Berg, *note* . . 643
Estienne, Henri, *note* . . . 138, 242
Euclid 977
Eusden, Laurence 205
Euwer, Anthony 845
* Euripides 967
Evarts, William Maxwell . . 517
Everett, David 292
Everett, Edward 374
Eytinge, Margaret, *note* . . . 815

Fabens, Joseph Warren . . . 544
Faber, Frederick William . . 503
Fabricius, Georgius 1027
Fairbanks, Charles B. . . . 570
Fairless, Michael 805
    Michael, *note* . . . 705
Falkenbury, Francis E. . . . 914
Fanshawe, Catherine Maria . 290
Farningham, Marianne . . . 608
Farquhar, George 200
    George, *note* 12, 116, 171
Farragut, David Glasgow . . 402
Farrand, Margaret L. 924
Fawcett, Edgar 685
Fénelon, François de Salignac
    de la Mothe 1051
    François, *note* . . 222
Ferriar, John 288
Ficke, Arthur Davison . . . 878
    Arthur Davison, *note* . 80
* Field, Eugene 698
Field, Kate 638
Field, Michael 683
Field, Nathaniel 132
    Nathaniel, *note* . . . 1039

FIELD, RACHEL, *note* 323
* FIELDING, HENRY . . 228, 946, 947
FIELDS, JAMES THOMAS 508
FILICAJA, VINCENZO DA, *note* . . 354
FILLMORE, MILLARD 396
FINCH, FRANCIS MILES 571
FIRKINS, CHESTER, *note* . . . 571
FIRKINS, OSCAR W. 771
FISH, HOWARD 941
FISH, WILLISTON 732
FISKE, JOHN, *note* 472
FITZ-GEFFREY, CHARLES, *note* . 201, 986
FITZGERALD, EDWARD 449
FITZSIMMONS, ROBERT, *note* . . 969
FLECKER, JAMES ELROY 881
FLETCHER, ANDREW 186
FLETCHER, GILES 21
            GILES, *note* 79
FLETCHER, JOHN 126
            JOHN, *note* . 13, 16, 27, 170
FLETCHER, LOUISA 879
FLETCHER, PHINEAS, *note* . . . 213
FLINT, ANNIE JOHNSON . . . 763
FLORUS, *note* 1009
FOCH, MARSHAL FERDINAND . . 1083
FOLEY, JAMES WILLIAM 829
FOLLEN, ELIZA LEE CABOT . . . 350
FONTAINE, JEAN DE LA . . . 1045
            JEAN DE LA, *note* 170, 1034
FOOTE, SAMUEL 246, 947
FORD, FORD MADOX (HUEFFER) . 823
FORD, HENRY, *note* 337
FORD, JOHN 132, 947
            JOHN, *note* 116
FORD, LENA GUILBERT 824
FORSTER, EDWARD MORGAN . . 856
FORTESCUE, JOHN 9
FOSS, SAM WALTER 732
            SAM WALTER, *note* 218, 409, 708
FOSTER, STEPHEN COLLINS . . . 567
            STEPHEN COLLINS, *note* . 328
FOUCHÉ, JOSEPH 1060
FOULKE, WILLIAM DUDLEY . . . 688
FOUQUÉ, BARON DE LA MOTTE . . 1063
FOURNIER, ÉDOUARD, *note* 183, 941, 1061
FOWLER, ELLEN THORNEYCROFT . 837
FOX, CHARLES JAMES, *note* . . . 341
FOX, GEORGE 170
FOX-SMITH, CECILY 873
FOXE, JOHN, *note* . . . 17, 304
F. P. A. 867
            note . . . 270, 331, 714
FRANCE, ANATOLE 1078
            ANATOLE, *note* . . 528, 835
FRANCIS, JOSEPH GREEN . . . 691
FRANCIS I OF FRANCE 1024
FRANCK, RICHARD 171
* FRANKLIN, BENJAMIN . . . 226

FRAZER, SIR JAMES GEORGE . . . 713
            SIR JAMES GEORGE, *note* . 766
FREEMAN, JOHN 869
FREILIGRATH, FERDINAND . . . 1070
FRENCH, L. VIRGINIA 586
FRENEAU, PHILIP 279
FRERE, JOHN HOOKHAM . . . 292
FROHMAN, CHARLES, *note* . . . 534
FROISSART, JEAN 1022
FROST, ROBERT 837
FROTHINGHAM, RICHARD, *note* . . 227
FULLER, HENRY BLAKE . . . 729
FULLER, MARGARET 475
            MARGARET, *note* . . . 311
* FULLER, THOMAS 147
FYLEMAN, ROSE 846

GAGE, FRANCES DANA 446
GAGE, THOMAS, *note* 312
GALE, NORMAN 763
GALLAGHER, CHARLES THEODORE,
            note 752
GALSWORTHY, JOHN 797
            J., *note* 18, 311, 418, 497
GANNETT, WILLIAM CHANNING . 650
GARFIELD, JAMES ABRAM . . . 590
GARLAND, HAMLIN 753
GARNETT, RICHARD 617
GARRICK, DAVID 242
            DAVID, *note* . 19, 117, 121
GARRISON, THEODOSIA . . . 829
GARRISON, WILLIAM LLOYD . . 424
            WILLIAM LLOYD, *note* . 419
GARTH, SIR SAMUEL 187
GASCOIGNE, GEORGE, *note* 12, 15, 17, 18
            GEORGE, *note* . . . 29
GASKELL, ELIZABETH CLEGHORN . 475
GATH 660
GAULTIER, JULES DE, *note* . . . 858
GAUTIER, THÉOPHILE 1071
            THÉOPHILE, *note* . . . 593
* GAY, JOHN 205
GEORGE V OF ENGLAND . . . 942
GEORGE VI OF ENGLAND . . . 943
GETTY, THE REVEREND DR., *note* . 467
GIBBON, EDWARD 270
            EDWARD, *note* . 28, 229, 972
GIBBONS, JAMES SLOANE . . . 475
GIBBONS, THOMAS 246
GIBRAN, KAHLIL 879
GIBSON, WILFRID WILSON . . . 850
GIDE, ANDRÉ PAUL GUILLAUME . . 1086
GIFFORD, RICHARD 249
            RICHARD, *note* . . 111, 242
GILBERT, JAMES STANLEY . . . 811
GILBERT, WILLIAM SCHWENCK . . 622
            W. S., *note* . . . 95, 256
GILDER, RICHARD WATSON . . . 671

GILDER, RICHARD WATSON, *note* . 562
GILDERSLEEVE, BASIL LANNEAU, *note* 554
GILDERSLEEVE, MRS. C. 650
GILFILLAN, ROBERT 390
GILL, JULIA 539
GILLILAN, STRICKLAND . . . 805
GILMAN, CAROLINE HOWARD . . 374
GILMAN, CHARLOTTE PERKINS
    STETSON 753
GILMAN, SAMUEL 363
GISSING, GEORGE 729
GLADDEN, WASHINGTON . . 624
GLADSTONE, WILLIAM EWART . . 450
GLAENZER, RICHARD BUTLER . . 842
GLASGOW, ELLEN 829
GLENCONNER, LADY PAMELA WYND-
    HAM 814
GLOVER, RICHARD 240
* GOETHE, JOHANN WOLFGANG VON 1057
GOGARTY, OLIVER ST. JOHN . . . 850
GOLDBERG, ISAAC 894
* GOLDSMITH, OLIVER 249
GOODRICH, ORRIN 475
GOODRICH, SAMUEL GRISWOLD . . 369
GOODWIN, JOHN CHEEVER . . . 700
GOOGE, BARNABY, *note* 8, 9
GORDON, ADAM LINDSAY . . 601
    ADAM LINDSAY, *note* . . 577
GORDON, WILLIAM, *note* . . . 298
GORE-BOOTH, EVA 820
GORMAN, HERBERT, *note* . . . 874
GOSSE, EDMUND 691
    EDMUND, *note* 918, 1042, 1050
GOSSON, STEPHEN, *note* . . 14, 17, 976
GOUGH, JOHN BALLANTINE . . 512
    JOHN BALLANTINE, *note* . 605
GOULD, HANNAH FLAGG . . . 362
GOURMONT, REMY DE 1084
GOWER, JOHN, *note* 14
GRAFFLIN, MARGARET JOHNSTON . 692
GRAFTON, RICHARD 18
GRAHAM, HARRY 830
GRAHAM, JAMES 164
GRAHAM, ROBERT BONTINE CUN-
    NINGHAME 707
GRAHAME, KENNETH 742
GRANGE, JOHN, *note* 9
GRANT, ULYSSES S. 549
GRANVILLE-BARKER, HELEN . . 870
GRAVES, JOHN WOODCOCK . . 396
GRAVES, RICHARD, *note* . . . 249
GRAVES, ROBERT 924
GRAY, DAVID, *note* 386
* GRAY, THOMAS 243
GREELEY, HORACE 479
GREEN, JOHN RICHARD 628
    JOHN RICHARD, *note* . 371, 508
GREEN, MATTHEW 223

GREENE, ALBERT GORTON . . . 404
GREENE, ROBERT 940
    ROBERT, *note* . . . 69, 124
GREENE, SARAH PRATT McLEAN . 719
GREENWELL, DORA 544
GRELLET, ÉTIENNE DE 1062
    ÉTIENNE DE, *note* . . . 682
GRENFELL, JULIAN 900
GRENVILLE, GEORGE 240
GREVILLE, FULKE 27
    FULKE, *note* . . . 9, 395
GREVILLE, MRS. 248
GRIFFIN, GERALD 416
GRIMMELSHAUSEN, HANS JAKOB
    CHRISTOFFEL VON . . . 1045
GUALTIER, PHILIPPE, *note* . . . 46
GUEDALLA, PHILIP 906
GUEST, EDGAR ALBERT . . . 870
GUINEY, LOUISE IMOGEN . . . 758
GUITERMAN, ARTHUR 815
    ARTHUR, *note* 56, 822, 828
GUITRY, SACHA, *note* 745
GURNEY, DOROTHY FRANCES . . 918
GUYON, JEANNE 1051

HADRIAN, EMPEROR 1009
HAGEDORN, HERMANN . . . 874
HAGEMAN, SAMUEL MILLER . 688
HAKEWILL, GEORGE, *note* . . . 112
HALDANE, JOHN BURDON SANDER-
    SON 914
HALE, EDWARD EVERETT . . . 550
    EDWARD EVERETT, *note* . . 372
HALE, NATHAN, *note* 195
HALE, SARAH JOSEPHA . . . 362
HALEY, MOLLY ANDERSON . . . 901
HALIBURTON, THOMAS CHANDLER . 387
HALIFAX, MARQUIS OF 183
HALL, GRANVILLE STANLEY . . . 683
HALL, JAMES NORMAN 894
HALL, JOSEPH 120
HALL, ROBERT 290
HALLACK, CECILY W. 918
HALLECK, FITZ-GREENE 362
    FITZ-GREENE, *note* . . 289
HALLIWELL, JAMES ORCHARD . . 540
    JAMES ORCHARD, *note* 404
HALPINE, CHARLES GRAHAM . . 578
HAMILTON, ALEXANDER, *note* . . 341
HAMILTON, ANNA E. 666
HAMILTON, GAIL 638
HAMILTON, ROBERT BROWNING . 861
HAMILTON, WILLIAM GERARD . 261
HAMMERSTEIN, OSCAR, 2ND, *note* . 456
HAMMOND, JAMES HENRY . . 432
HAMMURABI, KING OF BABYLON . 958
HANNAH, JOHN, *note* . . . 20, 114
HARBAUGH, HENRY, *note* . . . 507

HARBAUGH, THOMAS CHALMERS . 692
HARDENBERG, FRIEDRICH VON, *note* 1048
HARDY, THOMAS 650
HARE, JULIUS CHARLES, *note* . . 174
HARGRAVE, FRANCIS, *note* . . . 264
HARIRI, ABU MOHAMMED KASIM
    BEN ALI 1017
HARRIGAN, EDWARD 679
HARRINGTON, SIR JOHN 29
HARRIS, JOEL CHANDLER . . . 688
    JOEL CHANDLER, *note* . . 712
HARRIS, LEE O., *note* 320
HARRISON, JANE ELLEN 700
HARRISON, WILLIAM, *note* . . . 18
HARRISON, WILLIAM HENRY . . 319
HARTE, FRANCIS BRET 643
    FRANCIS BRET, *note* . . 442
HASTINGS, LADY FLORA . . . 431
HAVERGAL, FRANCES RIDLEY . . 625
HAWKER, ROBERT 280
HAWKER, ROBERT STEPHEN . . 416
HAWKINS, ANTHONY HOPE, *note* . 622
HAWTHORNE, ALICE 573
HAWTHORNE, HILDEGARDE, *note* . 562
HAWTHORNE, NATHANIEL . . . 421
    NATHANIEL, *note* . . . 509
HAY, LORD CHARLES 941
HAY, JOHN 639
    JOHN, *note* 565, 605
HAYDEN, JOSEPH 767
HAYNE, PAUL HAMILTON . . . 586
    PAUL HAMILTON, *note* . . 509
*HAZLITT, WILLIAM 329
HAZZARD, JOHN EDWARD . . . 870
HEARN, MARY ANNE 608
HEATH, CLARA B. SAWYER . . . 628
HEATON, ROSE HENNIKER . . . 700
HEBER, REGINALD 342
    REGINALD, *note* 266
HEGEL, GEORG WILHELM FRIEDRICH 1062
HEGGE, ROBERT, *note* 127
HEINE, HEINRICH 1065
HELPS, SIR ARTHUR, *note* . . . 600
HEMANS, FELICIA DOROTHEA . . 370
    FELICIA DOROTHEA, *note* 364
HEMINGWAY, ERNEST 930
HEMMINGER, G. L. 943
HENDRICK, BURTON J. 943
HENDYNG, *note* 9, 15, 16
HENLEY, WILLIAM ERNEST . . 692
    WILLIAM E., *note* . 470, 579
HENRY V OF ENGLAND, *note* . . 12
HENRY VI OF ENGLAND . . . 9
*HENRY, MATHEW 187
HENRY, O. 800
HENRY, PATRICK 270
    PATRICK, *note* 261
HERBERT, ALAN PATRICK . . . 908

*HERBERT, GEORGE 135
HERFORD, OLIVER 767
HERODOTUS 969
    note . 136, 963, 966, 967
HERRICK, ROBERT 133
    ROBERT, *note* 96, 112, 163, 976
HERSCHELL, WILLIAM 824
HERVEY, THOMAS KIBBLE . . . 423
HESIOD 958
    note 206
*HEYWOOD, JOHN 11
*HEYWOOD, THOMAS 129
HIGGINSON, ELLA 763
HIGGINSON, THOMAS WENTWORTH 554
    T. W., *note* . . . 509
HILL, AARON 204
    AARON, *note* . . . 165, 1040
HILL, BENJAMIN H. 599
HILL, ROWLAND 274
HILLYER, ROBERT 924
HINKSON, KATHARINE TYNAN . . 758
    KATHARINE TYNAN, *note* 566
HIPPOCRATES 971
    note 3, 96
HITLER, ADOLF 1090
HOAR, GEORGE FRISBIE, *note* . . 517
HOBBES, THOMAS 132
    THOMAS, *note* 674
HOCH, EDWARD WALLIS, *note* . . 657
HODGSON, RALPH 816
HOFFENSTEIN, SAMUEL 909
    SAMUEL, *note* . . . 915
HOFFMAN, CHARLES FENNO . . 431
HOFFMAN, PHOEBE 926
HOFFMANN, AUGUST HEINRICH . 1066
HOGG, JAMES 294
HOLLAND, JOSIAH GILBERT . . 521
    JOSIAH GILBERT, *note* . 525
HOLLAND, NORAH MARY . . . 842
HOLLAND, SIR RICHARD 9
HOLLIDAY, ROBERT CORTES . . 861
HOLM, SAXE 591
HOLME, JAMIE SEXTON, *note* . 509
HOLMES, OLIVER WENDELL . . . 450
    O. W., *note* . 437, 482, 921
HOLMES, OLIVER WENDELL (JR.) . 655
HOLYOAKE, GEORGE JACOB, *note* . 562
HOME, JOHN 248
    JOHN, *note* 139
HOMER 958
    note 733, 983
HONEYWOOD, ST. JOHN, *note* . 345
HOOD, THOMAS 390
    THOMAS, *note* . 242, 310, 388
HOOK, JAMES 275
HOOKER, JOSEPH 502
HOOKER, RICHARD 22
    RICHARD, *note* . . . 4, 15

HOOPER, ELLEN STURGIS . . . 508
HOOVER, HERBERT CLARK . . . 830
HOPE, LAURENCE 775
HOPKINS, ALPHONSO ALVA . . . 666
HOPKINS, CHARLES, note . . . 388
HOPKINS, GERARD MANLEY . . . 672
HOPKINSON, JOSEPH 294
* HORACE 982
HORNE, RICHARD HENRY HENGIST . 417
HOUGHTON, LORD 458
　　　　LORD, note 386
HOUSMAN, ALFRED EDWARD . . 742
　　　　ALFRED EDWARD, note . 143
HOVEY, RICHARD 771
HOW, WILLIAM WALSHAM . . . 555
HOWARD, ROWLAND 591
HOWE, EDGAR WATSON 711
HOWE, JULIA WARD 522
HOWE, MARK ANTONY DE WOLFE . 771
HOWELL, JAMES, note 113, 125, 140, 388
HOWELLS, MILDRED 820
* HOWELLS, WILLIAM DEAN . . 628
HOWITT, MARY 394
HOWITT, WILLIAM 365
HOYLE, EDMOND 197
HOYT, DANIEL WEBSTER . . . 679
HUBBARD, ELBERT 745
HUDSON, WILLIAM HENRY . . . 655
HUENEFELD, EHRENFRIED GUN-
　　　THER VON 1091
HUGHES, LANGSTON 934
HUGHES, RICHARD 932
HUGHES, THOMAS 550
HUGO, VICTOR 1067
　　　　VICTOR, note 432
HUME, DAVID, note 400
HUMPHREY, ROBERT, note . . . 13
HUNT, GEORGE WARD 562
HUNT, LEIGH 346
HURDIS, JAMES, note 23
HUTCHESON, FRANCIS 222
HUTCHINSON, JESSE, JR. . . . 502
HUTCHISON, PERCY ADAMS . . . 851
HUXLEY, ALDOUS LEONARD . . . 921
　　　　ALDOUS LEONARD, note . 254
HUXLEY, HENRIETTA A. HEATHORN 562
HUXLEY, THOMAS HENRY . . . 563
HUYSMANS, JORIS KARL . . . 1083

IBSEN, HENRIK 1075
　　　　HENRIK, note 487
IBYCUS 963
IGNATIUS LOYOLA, SAINT . . . 1024
IGNATIUS THEOPHORUS, SAINT, note 708
INGALLS, JOHN JAMES 601
INGELOW, JEAN 540
INGERSOLL, ROBERT GREEN . . . 602
　　　　ROBERT GREEN, note . 583

INGRAM, JOHN KELLS 555
INSULIS, ALANUS DE, note . . . 8
IRON, RALPH 717
　　　　RALPH, note . . 751, 763, 797
IRONQUILL 660
* IRVING, WASHINGTON 343
IRWIN, WALLACE 843

JACKSON, ANDREW 292
JACKSON, HELEN HUNT 591
JAMES, GEORGE PAYNE RAINSFORD . 394
　　　　GEORGE P. R., note . . 279
JAMES, HENRY 666, 766
JAMES, WILLIAM 662
JANVIER, FRANCIS DE HAES . . 513
JANVIER, MARGARET THOMSON . . 679
JARRETT AND PALMER 942
JAY, W. M. L. 605
JEANS, SIR JAMES HOPWOOD . . 846
JEBB, SIR RICHARD CLAVERHOUSE . 656
JEFFERIES, RICHARD 689
JEFFERS, ROBINSON 894
JEFFERSON, JOSEPH 578
JEFFERSON, THOMAS 273
　　　　THOMAS, note . . 163, 188
JEFFERYS, CHARLES 432
JENNER, EDWARD 276
JENYNS, SOAME 226
JEROME, JEROME KLAPKA . . . 745
JEROME, SAINT 1016
　　　　SAINT, note 1118
JERROLD, DOUGLAS 417
　　　　DOUGLAS, note . . . 64
JEWETT, SARAH ORNE 693
JOHNS, ORRICK 895
JOHNSON, ANDREW 446
JOHNSON, CHARLES FREDERICK . 625
JOHNSON, E. PAULINE 763
JOHNSON, GEORGE WASHINGTON . 640
JOHNSON, HUGH S. 874
JOHNSON, JAMES WELDON . . . 816
JOHNSON, LIONEL 798
JOHNSON, ROBERT UNDERWOOD . 711
JOHNSON, ROSSITER 652
* JOHNSON, SAMUEL 230
JOHNSTONE, ERNEST FENWICK . . 798
JOHNSTONE, GORDON 843
JONAS, SAMUEL ALROY 652
JONES, ELIJAH 564
JONES, FREDERICK SCHEETZ, note . 752
JONES, JAMES K. 564
JONES, THOMAS SAMUEL, JR. . . 874
JONES, SIR WILLIAM 275
　　　　SIR WILLIAM, note . . 21, 335
* JONSON, BEN 118, 947
JORDAN, THOMAS 164
JOYCE, JAMES 874
JOYCE, JOHN ALEXANDER . . . 656

JUDSON, EDWARD Z. C., *note* . . 713
JUNIUS 225
JUNOT, ANDOCHE 1062
    ANDOCHE, *note* . . . 1003
JUNOT, LAURE, *note* 993
JUVENAL 1006
    note . . 131, 174, 230, 257

KAFKA, FRANZ 1090
KANTOR, MACKINLAY 936
KEATS, JOHN 382
    JOHN, *note* 29, 390
KEBLE, JOHN 365
KEITH, GEORGE 22
KELLER, HELEN 861
KELLOGG, ELIJAH 502
KEMBLE, FRANCES ANNE . . 454
KEMBLE, JOHN PHILIP . . . 283
KEMP, HARRY 880
KEMP, WILLIAM, *note* . . . 6
KEMPIS, THOMAS À 8
    THOMAS À, *note* . . . 4
KEN, THOMAS 183
KENKO 1026
KENNEDY, CHARLES RANN . . 817
KENRICK, WILLIAM, *note* . . 286
KENYON, BERNICE LESBIA . . 926
KENYON, JAMES BENJAMIN, *note* 470, 693
KEY, FRANCIS SCOTT . . . 332
KEY, THOMAS HEWITT, *note* . . 360
KILBY, QUINCY 713
KILMER, ALINE 901
KILMER, JOYCE 890
    JOYCE, *note* . . . 614, 651
KING, BENJAMIN FRANKLIN, JR. . 729
KING, HENRY 134
KING, STODDARD 907
    STODDARD, *note* . . . 798
KING, WILLIAM, *note* . 101, 113, 146
KINGLAKE, ALEXANDER WILLIAM,
    note 542
KINGSLEY, CHARLES 523
KINNEY, COATES 568
*KIPLING, RUDYARD 776
KITTREDGE, WALTER 608
KLEISER, GRENVILLE 802
KNIBBS, HENRY HERBERT . . 830
KNICKERBOCKER, HERMAN W. . . 803
KNIGHT, CHARLES, *note* . . 439
KNOLLES, RICHARD, *note* . . 173
KNOTT, JAMES PROCTOR . . 645
KNOWLES, FREDERIC LAWRENCE . 805
KNOWLES, JAMES SHERIDAN . . 347
KNOX, WILLIAM 362
KOTZEBUE, AUGUST FRIEDRICH FER-
    DINAND VON 1060
KROUT, MARY HANNAH . . . 729

LA BRUYÈRE, JEAN DE 1050
LA FONTAINE, JEAN DE 1045
    JEAN DE, *note* 170, 1034
LAHORS, JEAN 1078
LAMARTINE, ALPHONSE M. L. . . 1064
LAMB, CHARLES 323
    CHARLES, *note* . . . 177
LAMB, MARY 290
LAMB, WILLIAM 332
LAMBERT, SAMUEL C., *note* . . 630
LAMPTON, WILLIAM JAMES . . . 746
LANCASTER, ALBERT EDWARD . . 746
LANDON, LETITIA ELIZABETH . . 404
LANDOR, WALTER SAVAGE . . 325
    W. S., *note* . . 302, 415
LANE, GEORGE MARTIN . . . 555
*LANG, ANDREW 673
LANGBRIDGE, FREDERICK . . 694
LANGHORNE, JOHN 269
LANGLAND, WILLIAM, *note* . 4, 9, 66
LANGTON, BENNET, *note* . . 1015
LANIER, SIDNEY 663
LANIGAN, GEORGE THOMAS . . 679
    G. T., *note* . . . 499
LARCOM, LUCY 568
    LUCY, *note* . . . 725
LARDNER, RINGGOLD WILMER . . 884
LATHBURY, MARY ARTEMISIA . 656
LATIMER, FREDERICK PALMER . . 839
LATIMER, HUGH 10
LAVATER, JOHANN KASPAR . . 1056
LAWRENCE, DAVID HERBERT . . 883
LAWRENCE, EDWIN GORDON . . 746
LAWRENCE, JAMES, *note* . . 527
LAWRENCE, THOMAS EDWARD . . 901
LAWSON, HENRY 754
LAYARD, SIR AUSTEN HENRY . . 513
LAZARUS, EMMA 694
LEA, FANNY HEASLIP 882
LEACOCK, STEPHEN 805
    STEPHEN, *note* . . . 615
LEAR, EDWARD 498
LEARNED, WALTER 685
    WALTER, *note* . . . 387
LECKY, WILLIAM EDWARD HARTPOLE 640
LECLERC, GEORGES LOUIS, *note* . 122, 379
LEDWIDGE, FRANCIS 912
LEE, AGNES 817
LEE, CHARLES 267
LEE, HENRY 281
LEE, NATHANIEL 186
LEE, VERNON, *note* . . . 486
LEE-HAMILTON, EUGENE . . 679
LE GALLIENNE, RICHARD . . . 792
    RICHARD, *note* 534, 737
LEGARÉ, JAMES MATTHEWS . . 555
LEHMANN, RUDOLPH CHAMBERS . 862
LEIGH, HARRY SAMBROOKE . . 630

LEIGHTON, ROBERT 551
        ROBERT, note . . . 242
LEITH, W. COMPTON 799
LELAND, CHARLES GODFREY . . 559
LEMON, MARK 454
LENIN, NIKOLAI 1086
LENT, EMMA A. 640
LEO XIII, POPE 1071
LEONARD, WILLIAM ELLERY . . 843
LE SAGE, ALAIN RENÉ . . . 1052
        ALAIN RENÉ, note 527, 1026
LESSING, GOTTHOLD EPHRAIM, note 254
L'ESTRANGE, SIR ROGER . . . 167
LETTS, WINIFRED MARY . . . 875
LEUTSCH AND SCHNEIDEWIN, note 435
                        note 968
LEVERIDGE, RICHARD 193
LEVY, NEWMAN 902
        NEWMAN, note . . . 416
LEWIS, CECIL DAY 936
LEWIS, JUDD MORTIMER . . . 799
LEWIS, SINCLAIR 884
LEYBOURNE, GEORGE 640
LIGNE, CHARLES JOSEPH, PRINCE DE 1055
LINCOLN, ABRAHAM 455
        ABRAHAM, note 123, 291, 341
LINCOLN, JOSEPH CROSBY, note . 818
LINDBERGH, CHARLES AUGUSTUS . 934
LINDSAY, NICHOLAS VACHEL . . 856
        VACHEL, note . . . 596, 684
LINLEY, GEORGE 392
LINNAEUS, CARL 1054
LINTON, WILLIAM JAMES . . . 499
LIPPARD, GEORGE 551
LIPPMANN, WALTER, note . . . 772
LISLE, JOSEPH ROUGET DE . . . 1059
LITCHFIELD, GRACE DENIO . . . 694
LITTLE, MISS L. M. 754
LIVY, note 14, 570
LLOYD, DAVID, note 183
LOCKE, DAVID ROSS 603
LOCKE, JOHN 685
LOCKER-LAMPSON, FREDERICK . . 545
LOCKHART, JOHN GIBSON . . . 374
        JOHN GIBSON, note . 269, 308
LODGE, HENRY CABOT 700
LODGE, THOMAS 27
LOGAN, JOHN 276
LOGAN, MINGO CHIEF . . . 249
LOGAU, FRIEDRICH VON . . . 435
        FRIEDRICH VON, note . . 138
LOINES, RUSSELL HILLARD . . . 943
LOMBROSO, CESARE 1077
        CESARE, note . . . 1063
LONG, JOHN LUTHER 759
* LONGFELLOW, HENRY WADSWORTH 433
        HENRY W. . . . 947
LONGUS 1017

LOUIS XIV OF FRANCE, note . . 1060
LOUNSBURY, THOMAS RAYNESFORD,
    note 278
LOVELACE, RICHARD 168
        RICHARD, note . . 76, 145
LOVEMAN, ROBERT 772
LOVER, SAMUEL 389
        SAMUEL, note . . . 116, 307
LOWE, JOHN 277
LOWE, ROBERT 479
LOWELL, AMY 831
* LOWELL, JAMES RUSSELL . . . 524
LOWELL, ROBERT TRAILL SPENCE . 509
        R. T. S., note 443
LOWNDES, WILLIAM, note . . . 222
LOYOLA, SAINT IGNATIUS . . . 1024
LUBBOCK, SIR JOHN 605
LUCAN 994
LUCAS, EDWARD VERRALL . . . 803
LUCAS, ST. JOHN 858
LUCRETIUS 981
        note . . . 23, 132, 352
LUDLOW, FITZHUGH 625
LUMMIS, CHARLES FLETCHER . . 746
LUTHER, MARTIN 1023
        MARTIN, note 126
LYALL, SIR ALFRED COMYN . . 618
LYCURGUS, note 175
LYDGATE, JOHN, note 8
* LYLY, JOHN 23
LYNDSAY, SIR DAVID 11
LYON, GEORGE WASHINGTON . . 946
LYONS, JAMES GILBORNE . . . 397
LYTLE, WILLIAM HAINES . . . 568
LYTTELTON, LORD 239
LYTTON, EDWARD BULWER . 425, 947
        E. B., note . . 123, 437
LYTTON, EDWARD ROBERT BULWER 592
        E. R. B., note 425

MABIE, HAMILTON WRIGHT . . 683
* MACAULAY, THOMAS BABINGTON . 397
MACCALL, WILLIAM, note . . . 444
MACCARTHY, JOSEPH P. . . . 768
MACDONALD, GEORGE 559
MACDOWELL, EDWARD 759
MACHEN, ARTHUR 768
MACHIAVELLI, NICOLÒ . . . 1023
        NICOLÒ, note . . . 998
MACKAY, CHARLES 503
        CHARLES, note . . 269, 310
MACKAYE, PERCY 839
MACKINTOSH, SIR JAMES . . . 290
        SIR JAMES, note . 191
MACKLIN, CHARLES, note . . 171, 628
MACLAGAN, T. 664
MACLEISH, ARCHIBALD . . . 914
MACLEOD, FIONA 717

MACLEOD, NORMAN 499
MACMAHON, MARSHAL MAURICE DE 1070
MACMANUS, MRS. SEUMAS . . 792
MACY, ARTHUR 664
MADDEN, SAMUEL 204
    SAMUEL, note . . . 138
MADELEVA, SISTER MARY . . 896
MAETERLINCK, MAURICE . . 1084
MAHON, LORD 426
    LORD, note 230, 299
MAHONY, FRANCIS SYLVESTER . . 423
MAIMON, MOSES BEN (MAIMON-
    IDES) 1020
MALINS, JOSEPH 640
MALLOCH, DOUGLAS 846
MALONE, EDMUND, note . . . 195
MALONE, WALTER 793
MALTHUS, THOMAS ROBERT, note . 448
MANGAN, JAMES CLARENCE . . 417
MANN, HORACE 387
MANN, THOMAS 1088
MANNERS, JOHN JAMES ROBERT . 518
MANSFIELD, KATHERINE . . . 907
MANUTIUS (ALDUS) 1022
MAP, WALTER DE 940
MARCUS AURELIUS ANTONINUS . 1009
    note 989
MARCY, WILLIAM LEARNED . . 349
MARKHAM, ANNA CATHERINE, note 596
MARKHAM, EDWIN 708
    EDWIN, note . . 335, 688
MARKHAM, GERVASE, note . . . 123
* MARLOWE, CHRISTOPHER . . 31
MARMION, SHACKERLEY, note . . 113
MARQUIS, DONALD ROBERT PERRY 851
    DON, note . 122, 282, 724, 829
MARRIOTT, JOHN 333
MARSHALL, THOMAS RILEY . . 714
MARSTON, JOHN, note 9, 11, 12, 13, 14, 116
MARSTON, PHILIP BOURKE . . . 701
* MARTIAL 995
MARTIN, AIME, note 1043
MARTIN, EDWARD SANDFORD . . 719
MARTIN, HENRI, note 1024
MARVEL, IK 551
MARVELL, ANDREW 169
MARX, KARL 1071
    KARL, note 662
MASEFIELD, JOHN 831
    JOHN, note 604
MASON, CAROLINE ATHERTON BRIGGS 555
MASON, DANIEL GREGORY . . . 824
MASON, WALT 763
    WALT, note 439
MASON, WILLIAM 249
MASSEY, GERALD 574
* MASSINGER, PHILIP . 128, 946, 947
MASTERS, EDGAR LEE 806

MATTOCKS, BREWER 656
MAUGHAM, WILLIAM SOMERSET . 835
MAULE, SIR WILLIAM HENRY . . 361
MAXWELL, LADY 446
MAY, JULIA HARRIS 603
MAYNARD, THEODORE 910
McCALLUM, DANIEL CRAIG, note 137, 666
McCARTHY, DENIS ALOYSIUS . . 811
    DENIS ALOYSIUS, note . 512
McCARTHY, JUSTIN HUNTLY . . 759
McCORD, DAVID T. W. 926
McCRAE, JOHN 820
McCREERY, JOHN LUCKEY . . 618
    JOHN LUCKEY, note . 435
McFEE, WILLIAM 870
McKIM, JOHN, note 1024
McLEOD, IRENE RUTHERFORD . . 912
McMASTER, GUY HUMPHRIES . . 579
McMASTER, JOHN BACH, note . . 274
McNALLY, LEONARD 280
McNAUGHTON, JOHN HUGH . . 579
MEE, WILLIAM 362
MELBOURNE, VISCOUNT . . . 332
MELCHIOR, CARDINAL, note . . . 113
MELLEN, GRENVILLE, note . . . 684
MELVILLE, HERMAN 530
    HERMAN, note . . . 380
MENANDER 976
    note . . . 990, 1120
MENCKEN, HENRY LOUIS . . . 862
MENKEN, ADAH ISAACS . . . 618
MERCIER, LOUIS SÉBASTIEN . . 1056
MEREDITH, GEORGE 574
    GEORGE, note . . . 446
MEREDITH, OWEN 592
    OWEN, note 425
MEURIER, GABRIEL, note . . . 58
MEW, CHARLOTTE 812
MEYNELL, ALICE 701
MEYNELL, VIOLA 911
    VIOLA, note 530
MICHELANGELO 1023
MICKLE, WILLIAM JULIUS . . 269
MIDDLESEX, EARL OF, note . . . 141
MIDDLETON, RICHARD 875
* MIDDLETON, THOMAS 116
MIFFLIN, LLOYD 683
MILLAY, EDNA ST. VINCENT . 915
    EDNA ST. VINCENT, note . 428
MILLER, CINCINNATUS HEINE (JOA-
    QUIN) 657
    JOAQUIN, note . 435, 643, 705
MILLER, EMILY HUNTINGTON . . 604
MILLER, HERMAN 427
MILLER, THOMAS 446
MILLER, WILLIAM 475
MILMAN, HENRY HART 363
MILNE, ALAN ALEXANDER . . . 876

MILNES, RICHARD MONCKTON . . 458
    RICHARD MONCKTON, *note* 386
* MILTON, JOHN 148
MIMNERMUS 959
MINER, CHARLES 333
MINOT, JOHN CLAIR 821
MITCHELL, AGNES E. 618
MITCHELL, DONALD GRANT . . 551
MITCHELL, SILAS WEIR 579
MOIR, DAVID MACBETH 393
* MOLIÈRE, JEAN BAPTISTE . . . 1046
MONKHOUSE, COSMO 653
MONNOYE, BERNARD DE LA, *note* . 252
MONRO, HAROLD 858
MONROE, JAMES 283
MONSELL, JOHN SAMUEL BEWLEY,
    note 165
MONTAGU, JOHN, *note* . . . 223
MONTAGU, LADY MARY WORTLEY . 221
    LADY M. W., *note* . 128, 313
MONTAGUE, CHARLES EDWARD . 799
MONTAGUE, JAMES JACKSON . . 824
* MONTAIGNE, MIGUEL DE . . . 1027
MONTENAEKEN, LEON, *note* . . 607
MONTGOMERY, JAMES 305
    JAMES, *note* . . 430
MONTGOMERY, ROBERT . . . 440
    ROBERT, *note* . . 355
MONTGOMERY, ROSELLE MERCIER . 835
    R. M., *note* . . 528
MONTROSE, MARQUIS OF . . . 164
MOODY, WILLIAM VAUGHN . . . 806
MOORE, CLEMENT CLARKE . . 332
MOORE, EDWARD 240
    EDWARD, *note* . . 74, 237
MOORE, FRANK FRANKFORT . . 716, 946
MOORE, GEORGE 709
MOORE, JOHN TROTWOOD . . . 733
MOORE, JULIA A. 685
MOORE, MERRILL 936
* MOORE, THOMAS 333
MORAN, MICHAEL 375
MORE, HANNAH 275
MORE, HENRY, *note* 139
MORE, PAUL ELMER 772
MORE, SIR THOMAS 10
    SIR THOMAS, *note* . . 27, 74
MOREHEAD, JOHN MOTLEY, *note* . 786
MORGAN, MORRIS HICKEY, *note* . 427
MORLEY, CHRISTOPHER . . . 911
    C., *note* 213, 373, 701, 1065
MORLEY, JOHN, VISCOUNT . . . 641
MORRIS, GEORGE POPE 404
    GEORGE POPE, *note* . 328, 332
MORRIS, SIR LEWIS 604
MORRIS, ROBERT 586
MORRIS, WILLIAM 608
MORRISON, M. T. 653

MORROW, ELIZABETH CUTTER (MRS.
    DWIGHT WHITNEY) . . . 824
MORTON, DAVID 891
MORTON, THOMAS 290
MOTHERWELL, WILLIAM . . . 389
MOULTON, LOUISE CHANDLER . 619
    L. C., *note* . . . 406, 607
MOULTRIE, JOHN 395
MUHLENBERG, WILLIAM AUGUSTUS 387
MULLIGAN, JAMES HILARY . . . 675
MULLINS, HELENE 931
MUMFORD, LEWIS 924
MUNBY, ARTHUR JOSEPH . . . 576
MUNRO, HECTOR HUGH (SAKI) . 812
MÜNSTER, ERNST F. 1060
MURPHY, ARTHUR, *note* . . . 14
MURRAY, SIR GILBERT 794
    SIR GILBERT, *note* . . 893
MURRAY, WILLIAM HENRY HARRI-
    SON (ADIRONDACK) 653
MUSSET, ALFRED DE 1070
    ALFRED DE, *note* . . 51, 649
MUSSOLINI, BENITO 1090
MUTSUHITO, EMPEROR OF JAPAN . 1083
MYERS, FREDERIC WILLIAM HENRY 667

NADAUD, GUSTAVE 1073
    GUSTAVE, *note* . . . 562
NAIRNE, LADY 291
NANCY, LORD 942
NAPIER, SIR CHARLES JAMES . . 339
NAPIER, MARK, *note* 164
* NAPOLEON I 1060
NASBY, PETROLEUM V. 603
NASH, OGDEN 934
    OGDEN, *note* . . . 859, 865
NASH, THOMAS, *note* 61
NATHAN, GEORGE JEAN 863
NATHAN, ROBERT 922
NAYLOR, JAMES BALL 754
NEALE, JAMES MASON 518
NEAVES, LORD CHARLES, *note* . 448
NEHERAI, MEIR BEN ISAAC . . . 1017
NEIHARDT, JOHN GNEISENAU . . 871
NELSON, HORATIO 283
NEPOS, CORNELIUS 982
NERI, SAINT PHILIP, *note* . . . 18
NESBIT, EDITH 731
NESBIT, WILBUR DICK, *note* . . 713
NETTLESHIP, RICHARD LEWIS . . 683
NEUMAN, HERMAN 1070
NEVILL, RALPH, *note* 722
NEWBOLT, SIR HENRY 764
NEWMAN, JOHN HENRY, CARDINAL 403
    CARDINAL, *note* . . 484
NEWTON, A. EDWARD 772
    A. EDWARD, *note* . 418, 505
NEWTON, BYRON RUFUS . . . 759

NEWTON, EDDIE 817
NEWTON, SIR ISAAC 184
NICHOLS, ROBERT MALISE BOWYER 918
NICOLL, SIR WILLIAM ROBERTSON . 706
NICOLSON, ADELA FLORENCE CORY . 775
* NIETZSCHE, FRIEDRICH WILHELM 1079
NIZAMI, note 566
NOBLE, JAMES ASHCROFT, note . . 192
NOBLES, MILTON 686
NOEL, RODEN BERKELEY WRI-
    OTHESLEY 609
NOEL, THOMAS 395
NORRIS, FRANK 812
NORRIS, JOHN 186
NORTH, CHRISTOPHER, note . . 360
NORTHBROOKE, JOHN, note . . . 16
NORTON, CAROLINE ELIZABETH
    SHERIDAN 446
NORTON, CHARLES ELIOT . . . 571
NORTON, GRACE FALLOW . . . 843
NOVALIS, note 1048
NOYES, ALFRED 864

O'BRIEN, FITZ-JAMES 576
O'BRIEN, LUCIUS 401
OCCIDENTE, MARIA DEL 375
O'CONNELL, DANIEL, note . . . 419
OGILVIE, WILLIAM HENRY . . . 807
O'HARA, THEODORE 541
O'KEEFE, PATRICK F. 821
O'KEEFFE, JOHN 276
O'KELLY, DENNIS 246
OLDHAM, JOHN, note 231
OLDYS, WILLIAM 223
OLIPHANT, CAROLINA 291
OLSON, TED 843
O'MALLEY, FRANK WARD . . . 843
OMAR IBN AL-HALIF, note . . . 180
OMAR KHAYYÁM 1018
    KHAYYÁM, note 461, 462, 468, 471
ONASANDER 1006
O'NEILL, EUGENE 902
O'NEILL, MOIRA 840
O'REILLY, JOHN BOYLE . . . 675
    JOHN BOYLE, note . . 392
O'REILLY, MILES 578
ORRERY, EARL OF, note 167
ORTON, JOB, note 225
OSBORN, SELLECK 344
OSBORNE, LOUIS SHREVE . . . 706
OSGOOD, FRANCES SARGENT . . 499
OSGOOD, KATE PUTNAM . . . 658
O'SHAUGHNESSY, ARTHUR WILLIAM
    EDGAR 676
O'SHEEL, SHAEMAS 891
* OSLER, SIR WILLIAM 694
OSSOLI, MARGARET FULLER . . 475
    MARGARET FULLER, note . 311

OSTENSO, MARTHA 932
OTWAY, THOMAS 185
OUSLEY, CLARENCE 768
OVERBURY, SIR THOMAS . . . 128
OVID 986
    note 7, 65, 196
OWEN, ANITA, note 336
OWEN, MOSES 641
OWEN, ROBERT 306
OWEN, WILFRED 918
OWENS, VILDA SAUVAGE . . . 864
OXENHAM, JOHN 794
OXENSTIERN, AXEL, note . . . 130

PAGE, EMILY REBECCA 642
PAGE, WALTER HINES 716
PAGE, WILLIAM TYLER 803
PAGET, VIOLET, note 486
PAINE, ALBERT BIGELOW . . . 945
PAINE, THOMAS 271
    THOMAS, note 424
PALEY, WILLIAM 274
PALGRAVE, FRANCIS TURNER . . 564
PALMER, WILLIAM PITT . . . 427
PANAT, CHARLES LOUIS ÉTIENNE,
    CHEVALIER DE 1060
PARACELSUS, PHILIPPUS AUREOLUS,
    note 1033
PARKER, DOROTHY 918
PARKER, EDWARD HAZEN . . . 555
PARKER, JOHN L 630
PARKER, MARTYN 115
PARKER, THEODORE 476
PARLEY, PETER 369
PARR, SAMUEL 276
PARNELL, THOMAS 201
PARSONS, THOMAS WILLIAM . . 531
PARTON, JAMES note 868
PARTRIDGE, SIBYL F. 645
PASCAL, BLAISE 1047
    BLAISE, note . . . 112, 988
PASTNOR, PAUL 732
PATER, WALTER 645
PATMORE, COVENTRY KERSEY DIGH-
    TON 556
PATTEN, GEORGE WASHINGTON . . 447
PAUL, JOHN 610
PAULL, MINNA 653
PAYNE, JOHN HOWARD 365
PEABODY, JOSEPHINE PRESTON . . 835
PEACHTREE, SIR EUSTACE . . . 184
PEACOCK, THOMAS LOVE . . . 347
PEARSE, PADRAIC H. 859
PEARSON, EDMUND LESTER . . 865
PEARY, ROBERT EDWIN . . . 719
PEATTIE, DONALD CULROSS . . 930
PEELE, GEORGE 27, 947
    GEORGE, note 17, 27, 127, 340

PEGLER, WESTBROOK 922
PENN, WILLIAM 184
    WILLIAM, *note* 183
PEPYS, SAMUEL 180
    SAMUEL, *note* . . 56, 257
PERCIVAL, JAMES GATES . . . 386
* PERCY, THOMAS 255
PERCY, WILLIAM ALEXANDER . . 885
PERRY, BLISS 755
PERRY, CARLOTTA 689
    CARLOTTA, *note* . . . 327
PERRY, LILLA CABOT 689
    LILLA CABOT, *note* . . . 554
PERRY, NORA 600
PERRY, OLIVER HAZARD . : . 348
PERSIUS, *note* 171, 992
PETERSON, HENRY 518
PETRARCH, FRANCESCO, *note* . . 187
PETTEE, JOHN TYLER 551
PHAEDRUS 991
    note 433, 961
PHELPS, EDWARD JOHN . . . 551
PHELPS, WILLIAM LYON, *note* . 534, 628
PHILIPS, JOHN 200
    JOHN, *note* 258
PHILLIPS, CHARLES 362
PHILLIPS, HARRY IRVING (H. I.) . 896
PHILLIPS, STEPHEN 773
PHILLIPS, WENDELL 479
PHILLPOTTS, EDEN 765
PHILOSTRATUS, *note* 119
PIATT, SARAH MORGAN BRYANT . 625
PIERPONT, JOHN 348
    JOHN, *note* 226
PIKE, ALBERT 459
PILPAY 976
    note 16, 17
PINCKNEY, CHARLES COTESWORTH 276
PINDAR 964
PINDAR, PETER 272
    PETER, *note* . . . 119, 138
PINERO, SIR ARTHUR WING . . 716
    SIR ARTHUR WING, *note* . 254
PINKNEY, EDWARD COOTE . . . 405
PIOZZI, HESTER LYNCH THRALE . 272
    H. L. T., *note* 361
PITT, WILLIAM 230
    WILLIAM, *note* 152
PITT, WILLIAM 274
PITTER, RUTH 931
PLANCHÉ, JAMES ROBINSON . . 387
PLATO 973
    note 207, 960
PLAUTUS 978
    note 7, 206, 302
PLAYFORD, JOHN 170
* PLINY THE ELDER 992
PLINY THE YOUNGER 1008

PLINY THE YOUNGER, *note* . . 254, 380
PLOMER, WILLIAM 936
PLUNKETT, EDWARD JOHN MORE-
    TON DRAX 849
* PLUTARCH 995
POE, EDGAR ALLAN 459
    E. A., *note* . 418, 568, 658, 1112
POLLARD, JOSEPHINE 667
POLLOCK, EDWARD 557
POLLOK, ROBERT 393
POMFRET, JOHN 190
    JOHN, *note* . . 179, 189
POMPADOUR, JEANNE ANTOINETTE
    DE 1055
PONTING, HERBERT GEORGE . . 817
POORE, BENJAMIN PERLEY, *note* . 404
* POPE, ALEXANDER 206
POPE, WALTER 172
PORTER, ALAN 933
PORTER, MRS. DAVID 587
PORTER, HORACE, *note* . . . 601
PORTER, WILLIAM SYDNEY . . . 800
PORTEUS, BEILBY 268
POTTER, HENRY CODMAN . . . 619
POULSSON, EMILIE 711
POUND, EZRA 885
POWELL, SIR JOHN, *note* . . . 21
POWERS, HORATIO NELSON . . 568
PRAED, WINTHROP MACKWORTH . 405
    W. M., *note* . . . 135, 311
PRESCOTT, WILLIAM HICKLING . . 387
PRESTON, KEITH 882
PRESTON, MARGARET JUNKIN . 541
PRIMROSE, ARCHIBALD PHILIP . 686
PRIOR, JAMES, *note* 261
* PRIOR, MATTHEW 189
PROCLUS, *note* 1005
PROCTER, ADELAIDE ANNE . . . 564
PROCTER, BRYAN WALLER . . 350
PROCTOR, EDNA DEAN 642
PROPERTIUS 985
PROUDFIT, DAVID LAW . . . 664
PROUST, MARCEL 1086
PROUT, FATHER 423
PROWSE, WILLIAM JEFFREY . . . 625
PRYNNE, WILLIAM, *note* . . . 136
* PUBLILIUS (PUBLIUS) SYRUS . 986
PULTENEY, SIR WILLIAM . . . 203
PUNSHON, WILLIAM MORLEY . 560
PUTNAM, H. PHELPS 923

QUARLES, FRANCIS 134
    FRANCIS, *note* . . . 1023
QUILLER-COUCH, SIR ARTHUR
    THOMAS 768
QUINCY, JOSIAH 274
QUINCY, JOSIAH, JR. 319
QUINTILIAN 995

QUINTILIAN, *note* . . . 4, 215, 1027
QUINTUS ENNIUS 978
QUITARD, *note* 115

* RABELAIS, FRANÇOIS . . . 1024
RACINE, JEAN BAPTISTE . . . 1050
   JEAN BAPTISTE, *note* . 131, 980
RADCLIFFE, ANN 290
RALEIGH, SIR WALTER . . . 21
RALEIGH, SIR WALTER . . . 759
RALPH, W. S. 619
RAMSAY, ALLAN 204
RANDALL, HENRY S., *note* . 260, 946
RANDALL, JAMES RYDER . . . 646
   JAMES RYDER, *note* . . 586
RANDOLPH, INNES 630
RANDOLPH, JOHN 320
RANDS, WILLIAM BRIGHTY . . 553
RANKE, LEOPOLD VON, *note* . 1024
RANSOM, JOHN CROWE . . . 903
RASPE, RUDOLF ERICH . . . 1055
RAVENSCROFT, THOMAS . . . 135
RAY, JAMES, *note* 143
RAYMOND, ROSSITER WORTHINGTON 653
READ, HERBERT 919
   HERBERT, *note* . . . 672
READ, THOMAS BUCHANAN . . 551
REALF, RICHARD 609
REDMAN, BEN RAY 925
REEDY, WILLIAM MARION . . 765
REESE, LIZETTE WOODWORTH . 719
REID, DOROTHY E. 931
REYNOLDS, GEORGE NUGENT . 294
REYNOLDS, JOHN HAMILTON . 941
REXFORD, EBEN EUGENE . . 690
RHODES, CECIL JOHN . . . 711
RHODES, WILLIAM BARNES . . 319
RHYS, ERNEST 746
RICE, ALICE HEGAN 812
RICE, GRANTLAND 865
   GRANTLAND, *note* . . 770
RICE, RUTH MASON 882
RICE, SIR STEPHEN 945
RICE, WALLACE 746
   WALLACE, *note* . . . 310
RICHARD, PAUL 1088
RICHARDS, EDWARD HERSEY . . 836
RICHARDS, LAURA ELIZABETH . 701
   LAURA ELIZABETH, *note* 659
RICHARDSON, ROBERT . . . 702
RIDDELL, HENRY SCOTT . . . 393
RIESENBERG, FELIX 859
RILEY, JAMES WHITCOMB . . 696
   J. W., *note* . 408, 707, 710, 973
RILKE, RAINER MARIA . . . 1089
RIMBAUD, ARTHUR 1084
RIPLEY, ROBERT LEROY . . . 943
RITTENHOUSE, JESSIE BELLE . . 847

ROBBINS, LEONARD H. 847
ROBERTS, CHARLES GEORGE DOUG-
   LAS 755
ROBERTS, ELIZABETH MADOX . . 891
ROBERTS, THEODORE GOODRIDGE . 847
ROBINSON, AGNES MARY FRANCES . 730
ROBINSON, ANNIE DOUGLAS GREEN 665
ROBINSON, EDWIN ARLINGTON . . 807
   EDWIN ARLINGTON, *note* 984
ROBINSON, EDWIN MEADE . . . 854
ROBINSON, JAMES HARVEY . . . 768
ROBINSON, JOSHUA DAVENPORT . 580
ROCHE, JAMES JEFFREY . . . 686
* ROCHEFOUCAULD, FRANÇOIS, DUC
   DE LA 1043
ROCHESTER, EARL OF 184
ROELOFSON, EMILY BRUCE . . . 658
ROGERS, CAMERON, *note* . . . 431
ROGERS, ROBERT CAMERON . . . 765
ROGERS, SAMUEL 289
   S., *note* . 109, 146, 188, 271
ROGERS, WILL 859
ROLAND, MANON JEANNE . . . 1058
ROMAINE, HARRY 755
RONSARD, PIERRE DE 1027
ROONEY, JOHN JEROME . . . 794
ROOSEVELT, FRANKLIN DELANO . 876
   F. D., *note* 654
ROOSEVELT, THEODORE 734
   THEODORE, *note* . . 1112
ROOT, E. MERRILL 925
ROOT, GEORGE FREDERICK . . . 541
RORTY, JAMES 912
ROSCOMMON, EARL OF 180
ROSE, ALEXANDER MACGREGOR . 684
ROSEBERY, EARL OF 686
ROSENBACH, ABRAHAM S. WOLF . 844
ROSSETTI, CHRISTINA GEORGINA . 587
ROSSETTI, DANTE GABRIEL . . . 577
ROSTAND, EDMOND 1085
ROUGET DE LISLE, JOSEPH . . . 1059
ROUSSEAU, JEAN JACQUES . . . 1054
ROWE, NICHOLAS 198
RUMBOLD, RICHARD 169
   RICHARD, *note* . . . 409
RUSKIN, JOHN 531
   JOHN, *note* 98, 159, 570, 611
RUSSELL, BERTRAND ARTHUR WIL-
   LIAM 821
   BERTRAND, *note* . . 915
RUSSELL, GEORGE W. (AE) . . 801
RUSSELL, IRWIN 712
RUSSELL, LORD JOHN, *note* . 230, 1006
RUSSELL, THOMAS 1095
RUSSELL, SIR WILLIAM HOWARD . 541
RUTLAND, DUKE OF 518
RYAN, ABRAM JOSEPH 609
RYAN, RICHARD 388

SABATINI, RAFAEL 840
SAINT JOHN, HENRY 200
    HENRY, note . . 229, 400
SAINT-SIMON, LOUIS DE ROUVROY,
    note 123, 984
SAINTE-BEUVE, CHARLES-AUGUSTIN 1069
    C.-A., note . . . 858
SAINTSBURY, GEORGE 680
    GEORGE, note . . . 1046
SAKI 812
SALLUST 981
    note 111, 470, 693
SALVANDY, NARCISSE ACHILLE,
    COMTE DE 1065
SANDBURG, CARL 854
SANDWICH, LORD, note 223
SANDYS, SIR EDWIN, note . . . 205
SANGSTER, MARGARET ELIZABETH . 642
SANGSTER, MARGARET E. . . . 923
SANTAYANA, GEORGE 769
SAPPHO OF LESBOS 960
SARETT, LEW 904
SARGENT, EPES 502
SASSOON, SIEGFRIED 891
SAVAGE, MINOT JUDSON . . . 658
SAVAGE, RICHARD 223
SAVILE, SIR GEORGE 183
SAWYER, CHARLES CARROLL . . 604
SAXE, JOHN GODFREY 509
    JOHN GODFREY, note . . 346
SAYERS, DOROTHY L. 919
SCARRON, PAUL, note 143
SCHAUFFLER, ROBERT HAVEN . 860
SCHAUFFLER, WILLIAM G., note . 18
SCHELLING, FRIEDRICH VON, note . 1060
SCHERMERHORN, ELIZA LEWIS HEN-
    ING 427
SCHIDONI, BARTHOLOMEW . . . 1043
SCHILLER JOHANN CHRISTOPH
    FRIEDRICH VON 1059
SCHMOLKE, BENJAMIN . . . 1052
SCHNECKENBURGER, MAX . . . 1073
SCHOPENHAUER, ARTHUR . . . 1063
SCHREINER, OLIVE 717
    OLIVE, note 751, 763, 797
SCHURZ, CARL 580
SCOLLARD, CLINTON 755
SCOLLARD MRS CLINTON . . . 847
SCOTT, CLEMENT WILLIAM . . 658
    CLEMENT WILLIAM, note . 633
SCOTT, FRED NEWTON 755
SCOTT, JOHN 261
SCOTT, ROBERT FALCON . . . 803
* SCOTT, SIR WALTER . . . 306, 946
SCOTT, WILLIAM 275
SCOTT, WINFIELD 349
SCOVILLE, BENJAMIN 653
SEAMAN, SIR OWEN 760

SEARS, EDMUND HAMILTON . . . 477
SÉBASTIANI, FRANÇOIS HORACE BAS-
    TIEN 1062
SEDAINE, MICHEL JEAN 1055
SEDLEY, SIR CHARLES 183
SEEGER, ALAN 904
SEGUR, note 253, 254
SEIBERG, T LAURENCE . . . 817
SELDEN, JOHN 130
    JOHN, note 113
SELVAGGI, note 176
* SENECA 990
SERVICE, ROBERT WILLIAM . . . 844
SEWALL, JONATHAN M. 276
SEWARD, THOMAS, note 124
SHAFTESBURY, EARL OF, note . 377
* SHAKESPEARE, WILLIAM . . 32, 947
SHARMAN, JULIAN, note . . . 13
SHARP, WILLIAM 717
SHARPE, R. L. 680
SHARPE, R. S. 941
SHARSWOOD, GEORGE 477
SHAW, GEORGE BERNARD . 719, 902
    GEORGE BERNARD, note . . 482
SHAW, HENRY WHEELER . . . 518
    HENRY WHEELER, note . 873, 920
SHEEHAN, PATRICK AUGUSTINE,
    note 18
SHEERES, SIR HENRY, note . . . 13
SHEFFIELD, JOHN 185
    JOHN, note 164
SHELDON, ARTHUR FREDERICK . 804
SHELLEY, MARY WOLLSTONECRAFT . 389
* SHELLEY, PERCY BYSSHE . . . 365
SHENSTONE, WILLIAM 242
    WILLIAM, note . 236, 335
SHEPARD, ODELL 882
SHEPHERD, RICHARD HERNE, note . 29
SHERBROOKE, VISCOUNT . . . 479
SHERIDAN, HELEN SELINA . . . 432
SHERIDAN, PHILIP HENRY . . . 594
SHERIDAN, RICHARD BRINSLEY . . 277
    R. B., note . . 53, 79, 84
SHERMAN, FRANK DEMPSTER . . 756
SHERMAN, SIDNEY 427
SHERMAN, STUART PRATT . . . 871
SHERMAN, WILLIAM TECUMSEH . 542
SHERWOOD, KATE BROWNLEE . 659
SHIPMAN, HERBERT 809
SHIPTON, MARTHA (MOTHER) . . 940
SHIRAS, CHARLES P. 560
SHIRLEY, JAMES 141
SHORTER, MRS. CLEMENT . . . 794
SIDNEY, ALGERNON 169
    ALGERNON, note . . . 183
SIDNEY, SIR PHILIP 27
    SIR PHILIP, note . . 129, 137
SIEGEL, ELI 945

SIENKIEWICZ, HENRYK 1083
SIGERSON, DORA 794
SIGISMUND, HOLY ROMAN EMPEROR,
    note 1047
SIGOURNEY, LYDIA HUNTLY . . . 363
SILIUS ITALICUS, note 139
SILL, EDWARD ROWLAND . . . 659
    EDWARD ROWLAND, note . . 1100
SILVA, JOSÉ ASUNCIÓN 1085
SIMMONS, LAURA 847
SIMMS, WILLIAM GILMORE . . . 431
SIMONIDES OF CEOS 960
SIMPLICIUS 970
SIMPSON, JANE CROSS 480
SIMS, GEORGE ROBERT 687
SINCLAIR, JOHN 941
SIRMOND, JOHN, note 184
SISMONDI, JEAN CHARLES LÉONARD
    DE, note 1024
SITWELL, EDITH 896
SKELTON, JOHN 9
    JOHN, note 17
SLADE, MARY B. C. 569
SLICK, SAM 387
SMART, CHRISTOPHER 248
    CHRISTOPHER, note . . 229
SMILEY, JOSEPH BERT 773
SMITH, ADAM, note 240
SMITH, ALEXANDER 587
    A., note . . 10, 360, 437, 1024
SMITH, ARABELLA EUGENIA . . 680
SMITH, DEXTER 665
SMITH, EDGAR 730
SMITH, EDMUND, note 216
SMITH, HORACE 332
SMITH, CAPTAIN JOHN, note . . 312
SMITH, LANGDON 734
SMITH, MRS. LANTA WILSON, note 509
SMITH, LOGAN PEARSALL . . . 787
    LOGAN PEARSALL, note . . 683
SMITH, MARION COUTHOUY . . 712
SMITH, MAY RILEY 665
SMITH, NORA ARCHIBALD . . . 747
SMITH, SAMUEL FRANCIS . . . 447
SMITH, SEBA 369
SMITH, SYDNEY 312
    SYDNEY, note 177, 246, 259, 265
SMITH, WALTER CHALMERS . . 560
SMOLLETT, TOBIAS 248
SOCRATES 970
    note 45, 229
SOMERVILLE, WILLIAM . . . 199
    WILLIAM, note . . 31
SOPHOCLES 964
    note . . . 170, 175, 966
SORBIENNE. note 188
SOTHEBY, WILLIAM, note . . 986
SOULE, JOHN BABSON LANE . . 505

SOUTH, ROBERT 183
SOUTHERNE, THOMAS, note . . . 131
SOUTHEY, CAROLINE BOWLES . . 349
* SOUTHEY, ROBERT 320
SOUTHWELL, ROBERT 29
    ROBERT, note 12, 20, 997
SPALDING, SUSAN MARR, note . . 597
SPENCER, HERBERT 580
    HERBERT, note . . 448, 536
SPENCER, HIRAM LADD . . . 581
SPENCER, WILLIAM ROBERT . . 294
    WILLIAM ROBERT, note . 53
SPENDER, STEPHEN 938
* SPENSER, EDMUND 24
SPEYER, LEONORA 821
SPINOZA, BENEDICT (BARUCH) . . 1048
    BENEDICT (B.), note . 986, 990
SPOFFORD, HARRIET PRESCOTT . . 619
SPOONER, ALLEN CROCKER . . . 403
SPRAGUE, CHARLES 364
    CHARLES, note . 415, 512
SPRING-RICE, SIR CECIL ARTHUR . 747
SPROAT, NANCY DENNIS . . . 291
SQUIRE, SIR JOHN COLLINGS . . 882
STAËL, GERMAINE NECKER DE . . 1060
    GERMAINE NECKER DE, note 117
STAFFORD, WENDELL PHILLIPS . . 760
STANHOPE, PHILIP DORMER . . 222
    PHILIP DORMER, note . 253
STANHOPE, PHILIP HENRY . . 426
    PHILIP HENRY, note 230, 299
STANLEY, BESSIE ANDERSON . . 860
STANLEY, SIR HENRY M. . . . 653
STANLEY, THOMAS, note . . 201
STANTON, CHARLES E. . . . 747
STANTON, EDWIN M., note . . . 706
STANTON, FRANK LEBBY . . . 730
STANTON, HENRY THOMPSON . . 609
STARRETT, VINCENT 892
STATIUS, CAECILIUS 978
STEDMAN, EDMUND CLARENCE . . 604
    EDMUND CLARENCE, note 63
STEELE, SIR RICHARD 197
    SIR RICHARD, note . . . 126
STEIN, GERTRUDE 836
STENDHAL, HENRI BEYLE DE . . 1063
STEPHEN, JAMES KENNETH . . 747
    J. K., note . . 300, 304
STEPHEN, SIR LESLIE, note . . . 379
STEPHENS, JAMES 877
STERLING, GEORGE 809
STERN, G. B., note 496
* STERNE, LAURENCE 241
STESICHORUS 959
STEVENS, GEORGE A. 247
STEVENSON, ROBERT LOUIS . . 702
    R. L., note . 524, 681, 786
STIDGER, WILLIAM LEROY . . . 886

STILES, EZRA, *note* . . . 260, 946
STILL, JOHN 20
STOCKTON, FRANK RICHARD . . 609
STODDARD, CHARLES WARREN . . 667
STODDARD, RICHARD HENRY . . 565
      R. H., *note* . . . 390, 483
STOKES, ROSE PASTOR . . . 860
STOLBERG, BENJAMIN, *note* . . 761
STOLBERG, CHRISTIAN, *note* . . 317
STONE, SAMUEL JOHN . . . 647
STORY, JOSEPH 332
STORY, WILLIAM WETMORE . . 533
STOUGHTON, WILLIAM . . . 179
STOWE, HARRIET BEECHER . . 480
      HARRIET BEECHER, *note* . 375
STOWELL, LORD 275
STRACHEY, GILES LYTTON . . 865
STRAFFORD, EARL OF, *note* . . 46
STRINGER, ARTHUR 836
STRODE, WILLIAM 144
STRUNSKY, SIMEON 860
STUART, MARY 20
STUBBS, CHARLES WILLIAM . . 681
      CHARLES WILLIAM, *note* . 487
STUDDERT-KENNEDY, GEOFFREY AN-
    KETELL 880
STURM, JULIUS KARL REINHOLD . 1071
SUCKLING, SIR JOHN 163
      SIR J., *note* 29, 99, 134, 1038
SUETONIUS, *note* 202
SULLIVAN, MARIAN DIX . . . 406
SULLIVAN, TIMOTHY DANIEL, *note* 511
SUMNER, CHARLES 480
      CHARLES, *note* . . . 188
SUMNER, WILLIAM GRAHAM . . 654
      WILLIAM GRAHAM, *note* . 876
SUTTNER, BARONESS BERTHA VON . 1083
SWAIN, CHARLES 418
SWEENEY, JOSEPH 843
* SWIFT, JONATHAN 190
SWINBURNE, ALGERNON CHARLES . 630
      A. C., *note* . 489, 618
SYDENHAM, LORD, *note* . . . 379
SYMONDS, JOHN ADDINGTON . . 654
SYMONS, ARTHUR 789
      A., *note* . 485, 488, 492, 493
SYNGE, JOHN MILLINGTON . . 817
      JOHN MILLINGTON, *note* . 306
* SYRUS, PUBLILIUS 986

TABB, JOHN BANISTER . . . 681
      JOHN BANISTER, *note* . . 828
* TACITUS 1006
TAGGARD, GENEVIEVE . . . 923
TAGORE, RABINDRANATH . . 1084
TALEB, ALI BEN ABOU . . . 1017
TALFOURD, SIR THOMAS NOON . 386

TALLEYRAND-PÉRIGORD, CHARLES
    MAURICE DE 1059
TAPPAN, EVA MARCH . . . 714
TARKINGTON, NEWTON BOOTH . . 809
TARLTON, RICHARD, *note* . . 13, 189
TATE, NAHUM 185
      NAHUM, *note* 141
TAWNEY, RICHARD HENRY . . 866
TAYLOR, ANN 339
TAYLOR, BAYARD 565
TAYLOR, BERT LESTON . . . 794
TAYLOR, EDWARD T. (FATHER) . 371
TAYLOR, SIR HENRY 401
TAYLOR, JANE 344
TAYLOR, JEFFERYS 369
      JEFFERYS, *note* . . . 143
TAYLOR, JEREMY 165
      JEREMY, *note* . . 112, 126
TAYLOR, JOHN 127
      JOHN, *note* . . . 19, 976
TAYLOR, THOMAS 513
TEASDALE, SARA 882
TEKAHIONWAKE 763
TEMPLE, SIR WILLIAM . . . 172
* TENNYSON, ALFRED, LORD . 462, 946
TENNYSON-TURNER, CHARLES . . 447
TERENCE 979
      note . . . 12, 19, 121
TERTULLIAN 1012
      note 143
THACKERAY, WILLIAM MAKEPEACE 481
      W. M., *note* 61, 241, 337
      W. M., *note* . . . 1035
THALES OF MILETUS, *note* . . 26
THAXTER, CELIA LAIGHTON . . 619
THAYER, ERNEST LAWRENCE . . 770
THAYER, LOUIS EDWIN . . . 855
THEOBALD, LEWIS 221
THEOCRITUS 977
      note 206
THEODORIDAS 1092
THEOGNIS 960
THEOPHORUS, SAINT IGNATIUS, *note* 708
THOMAS AQUINAS, SAINT, *note* . 139
THOMAS OF ERCILDOUN . . . 3
THOMAS, EDITH MATILDA . . 714
      EDITH MATILDA, *note* . 1014
THOMAS, EDWARD 855
THOMAS, FREDERICK WILLIAM . . 448
THOMPSON, FRANCIS . . . 748
THOMPSON, JOHN R. . . . 557
THOMPSON, MAURICE . . . 676
THOMPSON, WILL HENRY . . 690
THOMSON, JAMES 223
      JAMES, *note* . . 136, 152
THOMSON, JAMES 610
THOREAU, HENRY DAVID . . 513
      HENRY DAVID, *note* . . 876

THORNBURY, GEORGE WALTER . . 577
THORPE, ROSA HARTWICK . . . 705
THRALE, HESTER LYNCH . . . 272
    HESTER LYNCH, note . . 361
THUCYDIDES 969
    note 999
TIBULLUS, ALBIUS, note 78
TICKELL, THOMAS 205
    THOMAS, note . . 151, 215
TILLOTSON, JOHN 172
TILTON, THEODORE 620
    THEODORE, note . . . 509
TIMROD, HENRY 581
TINNEY, FRANK ALOYSIUS ROBERT . 943
TOBIN, JOHN 295
TOCQUEVILLE, ALEXIS CHARLES
    HENRI CLÉREL DE . . . 1070
TOLSTOI, COUNT LYOF NIKOLAYE-
    VITCH 1076
    COUNT L. N., note . . 1047
TOMLINSON, H. M. 824
TOMPKINS, JULIET WILBOR . . . 818
TOPLADY, AUGUSTUS MONTAGUE . 272
TORRENCE, RIDGELY 840
TOWNE, CHARLES HANSON . . . 847
    CHARLES HANSON, note . 738
TOWNSEND, GEORGE ALFRED . . 660
TOWNSEND, MARY ASHLEY . . . 626
TRENCH, HERBERT 789
TRENCH, MRS. MELESINA, note . 178
TRENCH, RICHARD CHEVENIX . . 441
TRENCK, FREDERICK VON DER, note . 226
TREVELYAN, GEORGE OTTO, note 293, 458
TROLLOPE, ANTHONY 505
    ANTHONY, note . . 496
TROUBETZKOY, AMÉLIE RIVES . . 770
TROWBRIDGE, JOHN TOWNSEND . 572
TRUMBULL, JOHN 277
TUCKER, BLANCHE ROOSEVELT, note 440
TUCKER, JOSIAH 240
TUPPER, MARTIN FARQUHAR . . 477
TURGENIEV, IVAN SERGEYEVICH . 1072
TURGOT, ANNE ROBERT JACQUES,
    note 226
TURNER, NANCY BYRD 866
TURNER, WALTER JAMES . . . 907
* TUSSER, THOMAS 19
TWAIN, MARK 615
    MARK, note 702
TWEEDSMUIR, LORD 837
TYLER, ROYALL 283
TYNDALL, JOHN 542
    JOHN, note 1032

UHLAND, JOHANN LUDWIG . . . 1063
UNDERHILL, EVELYN 840
UNDERWOOD, ELLEN H. 682
UNTERMEYER, LOUIS 886

UNTERMEYER, LOUIS, note . . . 934
UPSON, ARTHUR 847
URMY, CLARENCE 734

VALERIUS MAXIMUS, note . . . 969
VALÉRY, PAUL 1088
VANBRUGH, SIR JOHN 190
VAN BUREN, MARTIN, note . . . 230
VANDEGRIFT, MARGARET . . . 679
VANDERBILT, WILLIAM H. . . . 946
VANDIVER, WILLARD DUNCAN . . 714
VAN DOREN, MARK 923
VAN DYKE, HENRY 709
    HENRY, note 508, 542, 1126
VAN RENSSELAER, MARIANA GRIS-
    WOLD 706
VARDHILL, ANNA JANE 338
VARRO, MARCUS TERENTIUS, note . 111
VAUGHAN, HENRY 170
VAUVENARGUES, MARQUIS DE, note . 27
VAUX, SIR THOMAS 19
VEBLEN, THORSTEIN 730
VEGETIUS, FLAVIUS, note . . . 268
VENABLE, WILLIAM HENRY . . 626
    WILLIAM HENRY, note . 596
VENNING, RALPH 169
    RALPH, note 9
VERY, JONES 502
VEST, GEORGE GRAHAM, note . . 352
VICTORIA, QUEEN OF ENGLAND . 534
VILLARS, DUC DE, note 293
VILLIERS, GEORGE, note . . . 116
VILLON, FRANÇOIS 1022
    FRANÇOIS, note . . . 434
VINCI, LEONARDO DA 1022
* VIRGIL 982
VOLNEY, CONSTANTIN DE, note . 399
* VOLTAIRE, FRANÇOIS MARIE AROUET 1052
VOSS, JOHANN HEINRICH . . . 1058

WADE, JOSEPH AUGUSTINE . . . 388
WALAEUS, JAN, note 379
WALKER, KATHARINE KENT CHILD 654
WALKER, WILLIAM 170
WALKER, WILLIAM SIDNEY . . . 386
WALLACE, EDGAR 845
WALLACE, HORACE BINNEY, note . 227
WALLACE, WILLIAM ROSS . . . 534
WALLER, EDMUND 145
    EDMUND, note 30
WALLER, JOHN FRANCIS 478
WALPOLE, HORACE 246
    HORACE, note 200, 248, 399
WALPOLE, SIR ROBERT 200
WALSH, THOMAS 840
WALSH, WILLIAM 189
WALTER, HOWARD ARNOLD . . . 880
WALTON, IZAAK 139

WALTON, IZAAK, *note* 114
WARBURTON, WILLIAM 223
WARD, ARTEMUS 606
    ARTEMUS, *note* 389
WARD, ELIZABETH STUART PHELPS 677
WARD, NATHANIEL, *note* . . . 136
WARD, THOMAS 126
WARE, EUGENE FITCH 660
WARFIELD, BENJAMIN BRECKINRIDGE 706
WARMAN, CY 717
WARNER, CHARLES DUDLEY . . 581
    CHARLES DUDLEY, *note* . 517
WARNER, SYLVIA TOWNSEND . . 919
WARTON, THOMAS 258
    THOMAS, *note* . . 3, 230
WASHBURN, HENRY STEVENSON . 502
    H. S., *note* . . . 435
WASHINGTON, BOOKER TALIAFERRO 734
WASHINGTON, GEORGE 268
    GEORGE, *note* . . 1041
WATERMAN, NIXON 750
WATSON, JOHN WHITTAKER . . 560
WATSON, WILLIAM, *note* . . 136
WATSON, SIR WILLIAM 735
    SIR WILLIAM, *note* 780, 1126
WATTERSON, HENRY 654
WATTS, ISAAC 198
    ISAAC, *note* . . . 135, 340
WATTS-DUNTON, THEODORE . . 600
WEATHERLY, FREDERIC EDWARD . 690
WEAVER, JOHN VAN ALSTYN . 919
WEAVER, RAYMOND M., *note* . . 530
WEBB, CHARLES HENRY . . . 610
    CHARLES HENRY, *note* . . 446
WEBB, MARY 872
WEBSTER, DANIEL 339
    DANIEL, *note* . . 310, 312
WEBSTER, HENRY DE LAFAYETTE . 560
* WEBSTER, JOHN 127
WEDGWOOD, JOSIAH 941
WEEMS, MASON LOCKE 941
WELCH, WILLIAM H., *note* . . 449
WELLES, WINIFRED 920
    WINIFRED, *note* . . 1092
WELLESLEY, ARTHUR . . . 292
WELLINGTON, DUKE OF . . . 292
WELLS, CAROLYN 812
WELLS, HERBERT GEORGE . . 795
WELLS, ROLLIN JOHN . . . 690
WELSH, ROBERT GILBERT . . 836
WENTWORTH, THOMAS, *note* . 46
WESLEY, JOHN 226
    JOHN, *note* . . . 112
WEST, REBECCA, *note* . . . 878
WESTBURY, LORD 402
WESTCOTT, EDWARD NOYES . . 687
WESTON, EDWARD PAYSON, *note* . 371
WESTWOOD, THOMAS . . . 505

WHARNCLIFFE, LORD, *note* . . . 313
WHARTON, EDITH 766
WHAURR, THE REVEREND CORNELIUS 942
    note 394
WHEELOCK, JOHN HALL . . . 892
WHETSTONE, GEORGE, *note* . . 14
WHEWELL, WILLIAM . . . 375
    WILLIAM, *note* . . . 112
WHICHER, GEORGE MEASON . . 756
WHISTLER, JAMES MCNEILL . . 611
WHITE, ELWYN BROOKS . . 931
WHITE, GILBERT 247
WHITE, HENRY KIRKE . . . 348
    HENRY KIRKE, *note* . . 399
WHITE, JAMES TERRY . . . 682
    JAMES TERRY, *note* . . 534
WHITE, JOSEPH BLANCO . . 326
WHITE, WILLIAM ALLEN . . 804
WHITEHEAD, WILLIAM . . . 242
WHITING, WILLIAM 566
WHITLOCK, BRAND, *note* . . 804
WHITMAN, SARAH HELEN POWER . 418
* WHITMAN, WALT 534
WHITNEY, ADELINE DUTTON TRAIN 560
WHITTAKER, FREDERICK . . . 643
* WHITTIER, JOHN GREENLEAF . 441
WHYTE-MELVILLE, GEORGE JOHN . 545
    G. J., *note* . . 1117
WICKHAM, ANNA 880
WIDDEMER, MARGARET . . . 866
    MARGARET, *note* . 407, 575
WIGGAM, ALBERT EDWARD . . 818
WIGGIN, KATE DOUGLAS . . 722
WILCOX, ELLA WHEELER . . 718
    E. W., *note* 509, 520, 525, 570
WILDE, OSCAR FINGAL O'FLAHERTIE
    WILLS 722
    OSCAR, *note* . . 129, 526, 751
WILDER, THORNTON NIVEN . . 927
WILEY, HERBERT V. 913
WILKES, JOHN, *note* . . . 222
WILLARD, EMMA 350
WILLIAM, PRINCE OF ORANGE . 940
WILLIAMS, MRS. BERTYE YOUNG . 904
WILLIAMS, H. J. 836
WILLIAMS, ROGER, *note* . . 140
WILLIAMS, SARAH 661
WILLIS, NATHANIEL PARKER . . 431
    NATHANIEL PARKER, *note* . 387
WILLSON, DIXIE 925
WILLSON, FORCEYTHE . . . 635
WILMOT, JOHN 184
WILSON, HARRY LEON . . . 801
WILSON, JOHN, *note* . . . 360
WILSON, JOHN 654
WILSON, MCLANDBURGH . . 848
WILSON, SUSAN, *note* . . . 511
WILSON, T. P. CAMERON . . 907

WILSON, WOODROW 724
   WOODROW, *note* . . . 608
WINDHAM, WILLIAM, *note* . . . 398
WINNER, SEPTIMUS 573
WINSLOW, BENJAMIN DAVIS, *note* . 509
WINSLOW, EDWARD, *note* . . . 188
WINTER, WILLIAM 626
WINTHROP, ROBERT CHARLES . . 472
WISEWELL, MARY E., *note* . . . 533
WISTER, OWEN 756
WITHER, GEORGE 132
   GEORGE, *note* 22, 40, 118, 1036
WOLCOT, JOHN 272
   JOHN, *note* . . . 119, 138
WOLFE, CHARLES 364
WOLFE, HUMBERT 887
WOLFE, THOMAS 932
WOODBERRY, GEORGE EDWARD . 718
WOODBINE WILLIE 880
WOODROW, JOHN E. 789
WOODRUFF, JULIA LOUISE MATILDA 605
WOODWARD, WILLIAM E. . . . 836
   WILLIAM E., *note* . . 592
WOODWORTH, SAMUEL . . . 348
WOOLF, VIRGINIA 877
WOOLLCOTT, ALEXANDER . . . 897
WOOLLCOTT, WILLIAM W. . . . 866
WOOLMAN, JOHN 247
WOOLSEY, JOHN M., *note* . . 874

WOOLSEY, SARAH CHAUNCEY . . 682
WORDSWORTH, ELIZABETH . . . 942
* WORDSWORTH, WILLIAM . . . 295
WORK, HENRY CLAY 600
WORSLEY, PHILIP STANHOPE, *note* . 986
WOTTON, SIR HENRY 114
WREN, SIR CHRISTOPHER . . . 179
WROTHER, MISS 395
WYATT, SIR THOMAS 18
WYCHERLY, WILLIAM, *note* . . 171
WYCLIFFE, JOHN 8
   JOHN, *note* . . . 14, 15
WYLIE, ELINOR HOYT 897

XAVIER, SISTER MARY 645

YBARRA, THOMAS R. 867
YEATS, WILLIAM BUTLER . . . 789
YELVERTON, BARRY, *note* . . . 340
YONGE, NICHOLAS, *note* . . . 989
YORK, EVA ROSE, *note* 682
* YOUNG, EDWARD 201
YOUNG, GEORGE W. 791
YOUNG, SIR JOHN, *note* . . . 118

ZAMOYSKI, JAN 1031
ZANGWILL, ISRAEL 774
ZEUXIS 975
ZOUCH, THOMAS, *note* . . . 140

ANONYMOUS AND COLLECTIVE WORKS AND GROUPS OF QUOTATIONS

APOCRYPHA, THE 1123
BIBLE, THE DOUAY 1126
BIBLE, THE KING JAMES . . . 1097
BOOK OF COMMON PRAYER, AMER-
ICAN 1127
BOOK OF COMMON PRAYER, ENGLISH 1128
EGYPT, ANCIENT 958
EPITAPHS 948
GESTA ROMANORUM 1075

JUNIUS, LETTERS OF 950
KORAN, THE 1126
MISCELLANEOUS 940
MISCELLANEOUS TRANSLATIONS . 1092
NEW ENGLAND PRIMER, THE . . 947
NEW TESTAMENT 1114
OLD TESTAMENT 1097
OXYRHYNCHUS LOGIA (AGRAPHA) . 1126
UNKNOWN AUTHORSHIP, OF . . 949

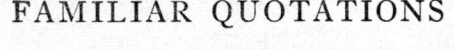

FAMILIAR QUOTATIONS

CAEDMON [1]
[*Floruit* 670]
From the text of Benjamin Thorpe [*1782–1870*]

Light was first
Through the Lord's word
Named day:
Beauteous, bright creation!
Creation. The First Day

The fiend with all his comrades
Fell then from heaven above,
Through as long as three nights and days,
The angels from heaven into hell;
And them all the Lord transformed to devils,
Because they his deed and word
Would not revere.
Ibid. The Fall of the Rebel Angels

THOMAS OF ERCILDOUN
[1220–1297]

Whate'er betide,
Haig shall be Haig of Bemersyde.
Quoted by SIR WALTER SCOTT:
Thomas the Rhymer, Part 2,
Minstrelsy of the Scottish
Border

ANONYMOUS
[*Circa* 1250]

Sumer is icumen in,
Lhude sing cuccu!
Groweth sed, and bloweth med,

<hr>

[1] It is pleasant to remember that the Muse of English Verse was born in a stable. The Venerable Bede in his *Ecclesiastical History* (*Book IV, Chapter 24*) tells the legend of Caedmon, the bashful hostler, who retired to the barn when his turn came to recite. There, in his sleep, he was visited by "a person" who said "Caedmon, sing me something." With those words begins the story of English poetry.

And springth the wude nu —
Sing cuccu!
Cuckoo Song.[1] Stanza 1

GEOFFREY CHAUCER
[1340–1400]
From the text of Walter William Skeat [*1835–1912*],[2] *and also the Globe Edition* [*Macmillan, 1907*]

Hard is his herte that loveth nought
In May.
The Romaunt of the Rose. Line 85

The tyme, that may not sojourne,
But goth, and never may retourne,
As water that doun renneth ay,
But never drope retourne may.
Ibid. Line 381

As round as appel was his face.
Ibid Line 819

The more she yaf awey,
The more, y-wis, she hadde alwey.
Ibid. Line 1159

A ful gret fool is he, y-wis,
That bothe riche and nigard is.
Ibid. Line 1171

To rede, and dryve the nyght away.
The Book of the Duchesse. Line 49
Morpheus,
Thou knowest him wel, the god of sleep.
Ibid. Line 136

I was waked
With smale foules a gret hepe,
That had affrayed me out of slepe.
Ibid. Line 294

The lyf so short, the craft so long to lerne,[3]
Th' assay so hard, so sharp the conquering.
The Parlement of Foules. Line 1

<hr>

[1] The most ancient English song that appears with the musical notes attached. — THOMAS WARTON [1728–1790]: *History of English Poetry*

[2] *The Complete Works of Geoffrey Chaucer.* Oxford University Press [1933].

[3] Ars longa, vita brevis (Art is long: life is brief). — HIPPOCRATES: *Aphorism I*

3

For out of olde feldes, as men seith,
Cometh al this newe corn fro yeer to
yere;
And out of olde bokes, in good feith,
Cometh al this newe science that men
lere.
          The Parlement of Foules. Line 22
The jalous swan, ayens his deth that
singeth.
                    Ibid. Line 342
Nature, the vicaire of th' almyghty
lorde.
                    Ibid. Line 379
A fool can noght be stille.
                    Ibid. Line 574
Now welcom somer, with thy sonne
soft,[1]
That hast this wintres weders over-
shake.
                    Ibid. Line 680
Flee fro the prees, and dwelle with soth-
fastnesse.
                    Truth. Line 1
Werk wel thy-self, that other folk canst
rede.
                    Ibid. Line 6
The wrastling for this worlde axeth a
fal.
                    Ibid. Line 16
A fool may eek a wys man ofte gyde.
          *Troilus and Criseyde.
                    Book I, Line 630*
Eek somtyme it is craft to seme flee
Fro thing which in effect men hunte
faste.
                    Ibid. Line 747
Of harmes two, the lesse is for to chese.[2]
          Ibid. Book II, Line 470
Lord, this is an huge rayn!
This were a weder for to slepen inne!
          Ibid. Book. III, Line 656
Right as an aspen leef she gan to quake.
                    Ibid. Line 1200

[1] In a somer sesun, when softe was the
sonne. — WILLIAM LANGLAND [1330–1400]:
The Vision of Piers Plowman, Prologue
[2] Of two evils the less is alway to be
chosen. — THOMAS À KEMPIS: *Imitation of
Christ, Book III, Chap. XII.* HOOKER: *Polity,
Book V, Chap. LXXXI*
  Of two evils I have chose the least. — PRIOR:
Imitation of Horace
  E duobus malis minimum eligendum (Of
two evils, the least should be chosen). —
ERASMUS: *Adages.* CICERO: *De Officiis, III, 1*

For of fortunes sharp adversitee
The worst kinde of infortune is this,
A man to have ben in prosperitee,
And it remembren, whan it passed is.
          *Troilus and Criseyde.
                    Book III, Line 1625*
Oon ere it herde, at the other out it
went.[1]
          Ibid. Book IV, Line 434
A wonder last but nyne night never in
toune.[2]
                    Ibid. Line 588
Thus maketh vertue of necessitee.[3]
                    Ibid. Line 1586
I am right sory for your hevinesse.
          Ibid. Book V, Line 140
He that nought n'assayeth, nought n'a-
cheveth.
                    Ibid. Line 1786
Go, litel book, go litel myn tragedie.
                    Ibid.
Farewel my boke, and my devocion!
          *The Legend of Good Women,
                    Prologue, Line 39*
Of alle the floures in the mede,
Than love I most these floures white
and rede,
Swiche as men callen daysies in our
toun.
                    Ibid. Line 41
Whan that Aprille with his shoures sote
The droghte of Marche hath perced to
the rote.
          *The Canterbury Tales, Prologue.
                    Line 1*

[1] Went in at the tone eare and out at the
tother. — HEYWOOD: *Proverbes, Part II,
Chap. IX*
[2] This wonder lasted nine daies. — HEY-
WOOD: *Proverbes, Part II, Chap. I*
  See Shakespeare, page 70.
[3] Also *The Knightes Tale, Line 3042;* and
The Squieres Tale, Line 593
  To make a virtue of necessity. — SHAKE-
SPEARE: *Two Gentlemen of Verona, Act IV.
Sc. 1, L. 62.* MATHEW HENRY: *Comm. on Ps.
XXXVII.* DRYDEN: *Palamon and Arcite*
  See Burton, page 125.
  In the additions of Hadrianus Julius to the
Adages of Erasmus, he remarks, under the
head of *Necessitatem edere,* that a very famil-
iar proverb was current among his country-
men — "Necessitatem in virtutem commutare"
(To make necessity a virtue).
  Laudem virtutis necessitati damus (We give
to necessity the praise of virtue). — QUINTIL-
IAN: *Inst. Orat., I, 8, 14*

And smale fowles maken melodye,
That slepen al the night with open yë,
(So priketh hem nature in hir corages):
Than longen folk to goon on pilgrim-
ages.

The Canterbury Tales, Prologue.
Line 9

And of his port as meke as is a mayde.
Ibid. Line 69

He was a verray parfit gentil knight.
Ibid. Line 72

He coude songes make and wel endyte.
Ibid. Line 95

Ful wel she song the service divyne,
Entuned in hir nose ful semely;
And Frensh she spak ful faire and
fetisly,
After the scole of Stratford atte Bowe,
For Frensh of Paris was to hir unknowe.
Ibid. Line 122

Amor vincit omnia.[1]
Ibid. Line 162

His palfrey was as broun as is a berye.
Ibid. Line 207

Therfore, in stede of weping and
preyeres,
Men moot yeve silver to the povre
freres.
Ibid. Line 231

A Clerk ther was of Oxenford also.
Ibid. Line 285

For him was lever have at his beddes
heed
Twenty bokes, clad in blak or reed,
Of Aristotle and his philosophye,
Than robes riche, or fithele, or gay
sautrye,
But al be that he was a philosophre,
Yet hadde he but litel gold in cofre.
Ibid. Line 293

And gladly wolde he lerne, and gladly
teche.
Ibid. Line 308

No-wher so bisy a man as he ther nas,
And yet he semed bisier than he was.
Ibid. Line 321

For he was Epicurus owne sone.
Ibid. Line 336

He was a good felawe.[1]
The Canterbury Tales, Prologue.
Line 395

His studie was but litel on the bible.
Ibid. Line 438

For gold in phisik is a cordial,
Therfore he lovede gold in special.
Ibid. Line 443

This noble ensample to his sheep he
yaf,
That first he wroghte, and afterward
he taughte.
Ibid. Line 496

If gold ruste, what shal iren do?
Ibid. Line 500

But Cristes lore, and his apostles
twelve,
He taughte, and first he folwed it himselve.
Ibid. Line 527

And yet he hadde a thombe of gold.[2]
Ibid. Line 563

And whan that he wel dronken hadde
the wyn,
Than wolde he speke no word but
Latyn.
Ibid. Line 637

Who-so shal telle a tale after a man,
He moot reherce, as ny as ever he can,
Everich a word, if it be in his charge,
Al speke he never so rudeliche and
large;
Or elles he moot telle his tale untrewe,
Or feyne thing, or finde wordes new.
Ibid. Line 731

For May wol have no slogardye a-night.
The sesoun priketh every gentil herte,
And maketh him out of his sleep to
sterte.
Ibid. The Knightes Tale. Line 1042

Ech man for himself.
Ibid. Line 1182

May, with alle thy floures and thy
grene,
Wel-come be thou, fair fresshe May.
Ibid. Line 1510

---

[1] Love overcomes all obstacles. — VIRGIL:
Eclogue 10, L. 69

[1] King of good fellows. — SHAKESPEARE:
King Henry V, Act V, Sc. 2, L. 260
[2] In allusion to the proverb, "Every honest
miller has a golden thumb."

That feeld hath eyen, and the wode
hath eres.[1]
> *The Canterbury Tales. The
> Knightes Tale. Line 1522*

Now up, now doun, as boket in a welle.
> *Ibid. Line 1533*

Cupido,
Up-on his shuldres winges hadde he
two;
And blind he was, as it is ofte sene;
A bowe he bar and arwes brighte and
kene.
> *Ibid. Line 1963*

Up roos the sonne, and up rose Emelye.
> *Ibid. Line 2273*

Myn be the travaille, and thyn be the
glorie!
> *Ibid. Line 2406*

She was al his chere.
> *Ibid. Line 2683*

What is this world? what asketh man
to have?
Now with his love, now in his colde
grave
Allone, with-outen any companye.
> *Ibid. Line 2777*

This world nis but a thurghfare full of
wo,
And we ben pilgrimes, passing to and
fro;
Deeth is an ende of every worldly sore.
> *Ibid. Line 2847*

Jesu Crist, and sëynt Benedight,
Blesse this hous from every wikked
wight.
> *Ibid. The Milleres Tale. Line 3483*

And broghte of mighty ale a large quart.
> *Ibid. Line 3497*

Yet in our asshen olde is fyr y-reke.[2]
> *Ibid. The Reeve's Prologue.
> Line 3882*

The gretteste clerkes been noght the
wysest men.
> *The Canterbury Tales. The Reves
> Tale. Line 4054*

Thurgh thikke and thurgh thenne.[1]
> *Ibid. Line 4066*

So was hir joly whistle wel y-wet.
> *Ibid. Line 4155*

At Cristemasse merie may ye daunce.
> *Ibid. The Man of Lawe, Prologue.
> Line 126*

For in the sterres, clerer than is glas,
Is writen, god wot, who-so coude it rede,
The deeth of every man.
> *Ibid. Line 194*

Sathan, that ever us waiteth to bigyle.
> *Ibid. Line 582*

Mordre wol out, certein, it wol nat
faille.[2]
> *Ibid. The Prioresses Tale. Line 1766*

This may wel be rym dogerel.
> *Ibid. Melibeus, Prologue. Line 2115*

Ful wys is he that can him-selven
knowe.[3]
> *Ibid. The Monkes Tale. Line 3329*

He was of knighthode and of fredom
flour.
> *Ibid. Line 3832*

For dronkenesse is verray sepulture
Of mannes wit and his discrecioun.
> *Ibid. The Pardoner's Tale.
> Line 448*

---

[1] Fieldes have eies and woodes have eares.
— HEYWOOD: *Proverbes, Part II, Chap. V*
Wode has erys, felde has sigt. — *King Edward and the Shepherd, MS.* [*circa* 1300]
Walls have ears. — HAZLITT: *English Proverbs, etc., P. 446* [*ed. 1869*]
> Woods have tongues
> As walls have ears.
TENNYSON: *Idylls of the King, Balin and Balan, L. 522*

[2] E'en in our ashes live their wonted fires.
— GRAY: *Elegy, St. 23*

[1] Through thicke and thin. — SPENSER: *The Faerie Queene, Book III, Canto I, St. 17.* DRAYTON: *Nymphidiæ.* MIDDLETON: *The Roaring Girl, Act IV, Sc. 2.* KEMP: *Nine Days' Wonder.* BUTLER: *Hudibras, Part I, Canto II, L. 370.* DRYDEN: *Absalom and Achitophel, Part II, L. 414.* POPE: *Dunciad, Book II.* STERNE: *Tristram Shandy, Book II, Chap. 9.* COWPER: *John Gilpin, St. 10*

[2] Also in *The Nonne Preestes Tale, Lines 4242 and 4247.*
Murder will out. — CERVANTES: *Don Quixote, Part I, Book III, Chap. 8*
Murder, though it have no tongue, will speak
With most miraculous organ.
SHAKESPEARE: *Hamlet, Act II, Sc. 2, L. 630*
See also Burton, page 122.

[3] Thales was asked what was very difficult; he said, "To know one's self." — DIOGENES LAERTIUS: *Thales, IX*
Know then thyself, presume not God to scan;
The proper study of mankind is man.
ALEXANDER POPE: *An Essay on Man, Epistle II, L. 1*

Gret swering is a thing abhominable,
And false swering is yet more reprev-
able.

> *The Canterbury Tales, Prologue.*
> *The Pardoner's Tale. Line 631*

Thus walke I, lyk a restelees caityf,
And on the ground, which is my modres
gate,
I knokke with my staf, bothe erly and
late,
And seye, "leve moder, leet me in!"

> *Ibid. Line 728*

In his owene grece I made him frye.[1]

> *Ibid. The Wife of Bath's Prologue.*
> *Line 487*

What thing we may nat lightly have,
Ther-after wol we crye al-day and
crave.

> *Ibid. Line 517*

Greet prees at market maketh dere
ware,
And to greet cheep is holde at litel prys.

> *Ibid. Line 522*

And for to see, and eek for to be seye.[2]

> *Ibid. Line 552*

I holde a mouses herte nat worth a
leek,[3]
That hath but oon hole for to sterte to,
And if that faille, thanne is al y-do.

> *Ibid. Line 572*

Loke who that is most vertuous alway,
Privee and apert, and most entendeth
ay
To do the gentil dedes that he can,

And tak him for the grettest gentil
man.

> *The Canterbury Tales. The Tale*
> *of the Wyf of Bathe. Line 1113*

That he is gentil that doth gentil dedis.[1]

> *Ibid. Line 1170*

The lady of the hous [2] ay stille sat.

> *Ibid. The Somnour's Tale. Line 2200*

For though we slepe or wake, or rome,
or ryde,
Ay fleeth the tyme, it nil no man abyde.

> *Ibid. The Clerkes Tale. Line 118*

Love is noght old as when that it is
newe.

> *Ibid. Line 857*

This flour of wyfly pacience.

> *Ibid. Line 919*

No wedded man so hardy be t'assaille
His wyves pacience, in hope to finde
Grisildes, for in certein he shall faille!

> *Ibid. Line 1180*

It is no childes pley
To take a wyf with-oute avysement.

> *Ibid. The Marchantes Tale.*
> *Line 1530*

Love is blind.

> *Ibid. Line 1598*

My wit is thinne.

> *Ibid. Line 1682*

Ther nis no werkman, what-so-ever he
be,
That may bothe werke wel and hastily; [3]
This wol be doon at leyser parfitly.[4]

> *Ibid. Line 1832*

The Pegasee,
The hors that hadde winges for to flee.

> *Ibid. The Squieres Tale. Line 207*

Therfor bihoveth him a ful long spoon
That shal ete with a feend.[5]

> *Ibid. Line 602*

---

[1] Frieth in her own grease. — HEYWOOD:
Proverbs, Part I, Chap. XI

Melted him in his own grease. — SHAKE-
SPEARE: *Merry Wives of Windsor, Act II,
Sc. 1, L. 69*

[2] To see and to be seen. — BEN JONSON:
Epithalamion, St. III, L. 4. GOLDSMITH: *Citizen of the World, letter 71*

Spectatum veniunt, veniunt spectentur ut
ipsæ (They come to see; they come that they
themselves may be seen). — OVID: *The Art of
Love, I, 99*

[3] Consider the little mouse, how sagacious
an animal it is which never entrusts his life
to one hole only. — PLAUTUS: *Truculentus,
Act IV, Sc. 4*

The mouse that hath but one hole is quickly
taken. — GEORGE HERBERT: *Jacula Prudentum*
The mouse that always trusts to one poor hole
Can never be a mouse of any soul.

POPE: *Paraphrase of the Prologue, L. 298*

[1] Handsome is that handsome does. — OLI-
VER GOLDSMITH: *The Vicar of Wakefield,
Chap. 1*

[2] Are you the lady of the house? — SHAKE-
SPEARE: *Twelfth-Night, Act I, Sc. 5, L. 198*

[3] Haste makes waste. — HEYWOOD: *Proverbes, Part I, Chap. II*

Nothing can be done at once hastily and
prudently. — PUBLIUS SYRUS: *Maxim 357*

[4] Ease and speed in doing a thing do not
give the work lasting solidity or exactness of
beauty. — PLUTARCH: *Life of Pericles*

[5] Hee must have a long spoon, shall eat

Men loven of propre kinde newfangelnesse.
> *The Canterbury Tales. The Squieres
> Tale. Line 610*

I am lorn with-outen remedye.
> *Ibid. Line 629*

Fy on possessioun
But-if a man be vertuous with-al.
> *Ibid. The Frankelin to the Squier.
> Line 686*

Pacience is an heigh vertu certeyn.
> *Ibid. The Frankeleyns Tale.
> Line 773*

Servant in love, and lord in mariage.
> *Ibid. Line 793*

Tak this for fynal answer as of me.
> *Ibid. Line 987*

It is agayns the proces of nature.
> *Ibid. Line 1345*

Trouthe is the hyeste thing that men
may kepe.
> *Ibid. Line 1479*

For whan a man hath over-greet a wit,
Ful oft him happeth to misusen it.
> *Ibid. The Canon Yeoman's Prologue.
> Line 648*

But al thing which that shyneth as the
gold
Nis nat gold, as that I have herd it
told.[1]
> *Ibid. The Chanouns Yemannes Tale.
> Line 962*

---

with the devill. — HEYWOOD: *Proverbes, Part
II, Chap. V*
  He must have a long spoon that must eat
with the devil. — SHAKESPEARE: *Comedy of
Errors, Act IV, Sc. 3, L. 64*
  [1] Hit is not al gold that glareth. *The Hous
of Fame, I, 272*
Tyrwhitt says this is taken from the *Para-
bolæ of* ALANUS DE INSULIS, who died in
1294, — Non teneas aurum totum quod splen-
det ut aurum (Do not hold everything as
gold which shines like gold).
  All is not golde that outward shewith
bright. — LYDGATE: *On the Mutability of
Human Affairs*
  Gold all is not that doth golden seem. —
SPENSER: *Faerie Queene, Book II, Canto VIII,
St. 14*
  All that glisters is not gold. — SHAKESPEARE:
Merchant of Venice, Act II, Sc. 7, L. 65.
GOOGE: *Eglogs, etc.* [1563]. HERBERT: *Jacula
Prudentum*
  All is not gold that glisteneth. — MIDDLE-
TON: *A Fair Quarrel, verse 1*

The firste vertu, sone, if thou wolt lere,
Is to restreyne and kepe wel thy tonge.
> *The Canterbury Tales. The
> Maunciples Tale. Line 332*

Thing that is seyd, is seyd; and forth
it gooth.
> *Ibid. Line 355*

For the proverbe seith: that manye
smale maken a greet.[1]
> *Ibid. The Persones Tale. Sect. 21*

Litel Lowys my sone, I aperceyve wel
by certeyne evydences thyn abilite to
lerne sciences touching nombres and
proporciouns. . . . Therefore have I
yeven the a suffisant Astrolabie as for
oure orizonte compowned after the latitude of Oxenforde.
> *A Treatise on the Astrolabe.*[2]

JOHN WYCLIFFE
[? –1384]

I believe that in the end the truth will
conquer.
> *To the Duke of Lancaster* [1381]
> (*Quoted by* J. R. GREEN: *A Short
> History of the English People.
> Chap. 5*)

THOMAS À KEMPIS
[1380–1471]

Be not angry that you cannot make
others as you wish them to be, since you
cannot make yourself as you wish to be.
> *Imitation of Christ. Book I,
> Chap. 16* (*Quoted by* DR. JOHN-
> SON [1778]: *Boswell's Life of
> Dr. Johnson, Vol. II, Page 165,
> Everyman Edition*)

Man proposes, but God disposes.[3]
> *Ibid. Chap. 19*

All, as they say, that glitters is not gold. —
DRYDEN: *The Hind and the Panther.*
  Que tout n'est pas or c'on voit luire (Everything is not gold that one sees shining). —
Li Diz de freire Denise Cordelier [*circa* 1300]
  [1] Many small make a great. — HEYWOOD:
Proverbes, Part I, Chap. XI
  [2] Written for his ten-year-old boy — and
while hardly a "Familiar Quotation" it has
sure power to touch the thoughtful mind.
Also quoted by SIR ARTHUR QUILLER-COUCH
in his admirable *Oxford Book of English
Prose* [1925]
  [3] This expression is of much greater antiquity. It appears in the *Chronicle of Battel Ab-*

What canst thou see elsewhere which thou canst not see here? Behold the heaven and the earth and all the elements; for of these are all things created.

> *Imitation of Christ. Book I.*
> *Chap. 20*

It is easier not to speak a word at all than to speak more words than we should.

> *Ibid.*

No man ruleth safely but he that is willingly ruled.

> *Ibid.*

And when he is out of sight, quickly also is he out of mind.[1]

> *Ibid. Chap. 23*

Of two evils, the less is alway to be chosen.[2]

> *Ibid. Book III, Chap. 12*

JOHN FORTESCUE
[*Circa* 1395–1476]

Moche Crye and no Wull.[3]

> *De Laudibus Legum Angliae.*
> *Chap. 10*

Comparisons are odious.[4]

> *Ibid. Chap. 19*

---

bey, *P. 27* (Lower's translation), and in *The Vision of Piers Ploughman, Line 13994* ed. 1550. HERBERT: *Jacula Prudentum*
A man's heart deviseth his way; but the Lord directeth his steps. — *Proverbs, XVI, 9*
[1] Out of syght, out of mynd.—GOOGE: *Eglogs.* [1563]
  And out of mind as soon as out of sight.
> LORD BROOKE: *Sonnet LVI.*
  Fer from eze, fer from herte,
  Quoth Hendyng.
> HENDYNG: *Proverbs, MSS* [*circa* 1320]
I do perceive that the old proverbis be not alwaies trew, for I do finde that the absence of my Nath. doth breede in me the more continuall remembrance of him. — *Ann Lady Bacon to Jane Lady Cornwallis* [1613]
On page 19 of *The Private Correspondence of Lady Cornwallis*, Sir Nathaniel Bacon speaks of the owlde proverbe, "Out of sighte, out of mynde."
  Out of sight and out of mind. — ROBERT BROWNING: *The Inn Album, I*
[2] See Chaucer, page 4.
[3] All cry and no wool. — BUTLER: *Hudibras, Pt. I, C. I, L. 852*
[4] CERVANTES: *Don Quixote* (Lockhart's ed.), *Part II, Chap. I.* LYLY: *Euphues* [1580]. MARLOWE: *Lust's Dominion, Act III, Sc. 4.* BURTON: *Anatomy of Melancholy, Part III,*

HENRY VI
[1421–1471]

Kingdoms are but cares,
  State is devoid of stay;
Riches are ready snares,
  And hasten to decay.

> *From* SIR JOHN HARRINGTON's
> *Nugae Antiquae* (*Quoted in* ED-
> WARD BULWER LYTTON's *novel,*
> *The Last of the Barons, Book*
> *III, Chap. 5*)

SIR RICHARD HOLLAND
[*Floruit* 1450]

O Douglas, O Douglas!
Tendir and trewe.

> *The Buke of the Howlat.*[1]
> *Stanza XXXI*

JOHN SKELTON
[*Circa* 1460–1529]

There is nothynge that more dyspleaseth God,
Than from theyr children to spare the rod.[2]

> *Magnyfycence. Line 1954*

He ruleth all the roste.[3]

> *Why Come Ye Not to Courte.*
> *Line 198*

Sec. 3. THOMAS HEYWOOD: *A Woman Killed with Kindness* [first ed. in 1607], *Act I, Sc. 1.* DONNE: *Elegy, VIII.* HERBERT: *Jacula Prudentum.* GRANGE: *Golden Aphrodite*
Comparisons are odorous. — SHAKESPEARE: *Much Ado about Nothing, Act III, Sc. 5, L. 18*
[1] The allegorical poem of *The Howlat* was composed about the middle of the fifteenth century. The author was a Scottish poet, an adherent of the Douglases. *The Buke of the Howlat,* edited by David Laing, was printed by the Bannatyne Club [1823].
  Do you know the truth now up in heaven, Douglas, Douglas, tender and true?
> DINAH MULOCK CRAIK: *Too Late, St. 3*
[2] He that spareth the rod hateth his son. — *Proverbs, XIII, 24*
  They spare the rod and spoyl the child. — RALPH VENNING: *Mysteries and Revelations* (second ed.), *P. 5.* [1649]
  Spare the rod and spoil the child. — BUTLER: *Hudibras, Part II, C. I, L. 843*
[3] Rule the rost. — HEYWOOD: *Proverbes, Part I, Chap. V*
  Her that ruled the rost. — THOMAS HEYWOOD: *History of Women*
  Rules the roast. — JONSON, CHAPMAN, MAR-

In the spight of his teeth.[1]
> *Colyn Cloute. Line 939*

He knew what is what.[2]
> *Ibid. Line 1106*

By hoke ne by croke.[3]
> *Ibid. Line 1240*

The wolfe from the dore.
> *Ibid. Line 1531*

Old proverbe says,
That byrd ys not honest
That fyleth hys owne nest.[4]
> *Poems against Garnesche*

Maide, wydowe, or wyffe.
> *Philip Sparrow*

Stedfast of thought,
Well made, well wrought,
Far may be sought,
Ere you can find
So courteous, so kind,
As merry Margaret,
This midsummer flower,
Gentle as falcon,
Or hawk of the tower.
> *To Mistress Margaret Hussey*

SIR THOMAS MORE [5]
[1478–1535]

The Utopians wonder how any man
should be so much taken with the glaring doubtful lustre of a jewel or stone,
that can look up to a star, or to the sun
himself.
> *Utopia: Of Jewels and Wealth*

They wonder much to hear that gold,
which in itself is so useless a thing,
should be everywhere so much esteemed, that even men for whom it was
made, and by whom it has its value,
should yet be thought of less value than
it is.
> *Ibid.*

They have no lawyers among them,
for they consider them as a sort of people whose profession it is to disguise
matters.
> *Ibid. Of Law and Magistrates*

Plato by a goodly similitude declar-
eth, why wise men refraine to medle in
the commonwealthe. For when they see
the people swarme into the stretes, and
daily wet to the skinne with rayne, and
yet can not persuade them to goe out
of the rayne, they do kepe them selfes
within their houses, seeinge they cannot
remedye the follye of the people.[1]
> *Ibid. Concerning the Best
> State of a Commonwealth*

Assist me up, and in coming down I
will shift for myself.
> *Said at the scaffold, on the way
> to execution*

Wait till I put aside my beard, for
that never committed treason.
> *To the headsman on the scaffold*

HUGH LATIMER
[1485 1555]

Play the man, Master Ridley; we
shall this day light such a candle, by
God's grace, in England, as I trust
shall never be put out.[2]
> *Addressed to Nicholas Ridley
> [1500–1555] as they were being
> burned alive at Oxford, for her-*

---

ston: *Eastward Ho, Act II, Sc. 1.* Shakespeare: *2 Henry VI, Part II, Act I, Sc. 1,
L. 110*

His wife "ruled the roast."—Washington
Irving: *Knickerbocker's History of New
York, Book IV, Chap. 4*

Rules the roast. — Robert Browning: *Mr.
Sludge, "the Medium."* Also *The Ring and the
Book, VI,* and *Prince Hohenstiel-Schwangau.*
Alexander Smith: *Dreamthorp — Christmas*

[1] In spite of my teeth. — Middleton: *A
Trick to Catch the Old One, Act I, Sc. 2.*
Fielding: *Eurydice Hissed*

[2] He knew what's what. — Butler: *Hudibras, Pt. I, C. I, L. 149*

[3] In hope her to attaine by hooke or crooke.
— Spenser: *Faerie Queene, Book III, C. I, St.
17*

The spoile of peoples evill gotten good,
The which her sire had scrap't by hooke or
    crooke.
> *Ibid. Book V, C. II, St. 27*

[4] It is a foule byrd that fyleth his owne nest.
— Heywood: *Proverbes, Part II, Chap. V*

[5] Canonized by Pope Pius XI [1935].

[1] In the modern phrase, "not sense enough
to come in out of the rain."

[2] I shall light a candle of understanding in
thine heart, which shall not be put out. — *2
Esdras, XIV, 25*

esy, *October 16, 1555* [1] *(Quoted by* J. R. GREEN: *A Short History of the English People, Chap. 7)*

SIR DAVID LYNDSAY
[1490–1555]

They gave me first ane thing they call
  citandum;
Within aucht days I gat but *libellan-*
  dum;
Within ane month I gat *ad opponen-*
  dum;
In ane half year I gat *inter loquendum;*
An syne I gat — how call ye it? — *ad*
  replicandum;
But, I could never ane word yet under-
  stand him.
  The Exactions and Delay of the Law
But or they came half gate to *con-*
  cludendum,
The fient a plack was left for to defend
  him.
                                   Ibid.
Thus they postponed me twa year, with
  their train,
Syne, *hodie ad octo,* bade me come
  again.
                                   Ibid.
Of *pronunciandum* they made we won-
  der fain;
But I gat ne'er my gude grey meir again.
                                   Ibid.

JOHN HEYWOOD [2]
[1497–1580]

The loss of wealth is loss of dirt,
As sages in all times assert;

The happy man's without a shirt. [1]
                          Be Merry Friends
Let the world slide, [2] let the world go;
A fig for care, and a fig for woe!
If I can't pay, why I can owe,
And death makes equal the high and
  low.
                                   Ibid.
All a green willow is my garland.
                          The Green Willow
Haste maketh waste.
                Proverbes. Part I, Chap. II
Beware of, Had I wist. [3]
                                   Ibid.
Good to be merie and wise. [4]
                                   Ibid.
Beaten with his owne rod.
                                   Ibid.
Look ere ye leape. [5]
                                   Ibid.
He that will not when he may,
When he would he shall have nay. [6]
                                   Ibid.

---

[1] See Latimer and Ridley in the might
  Of Faith stand coupled for a common
  flight!
    WORDSWORTH: *Ecclesiastical Sonnets,
    Part II, XXXIV, Latimer and Ridley*
[2] The *Proverbes of* JOHN HEYWOOD is the
earliest collection of English colloquial sayings. It was first printed in 1546. The title
of the edition of 1562 is *John Heywoodes
Woorkes. A Dialogue conteyning the number
in effect of all the proverbes in the English
tounge, compact in a matter concernynge two
maner of Maryages,* etc. The selection here
given is from the edition of 1874 (a reprint
of 1598), edited by JULIAN SHARMAN. See also
the *Oxford Dictionary of English Proverbs*
compiled by W. G. SMITH [1935].

[1] This line is the theme of many poems,
e. g. SIR WALTER SCOTT: *The Search after
Happiness; or, the Quest of Sultaun Solimaun.*
JOHN HAY: *The Enchanted Shirt.* EDWIN
MARKHAM: *The Shoes of Happiness.* EDGAR
A. GUEST: *Envy*
  In a footnote to his poem, Scott says the
hint for it came from a novel, *La Camiscia
Magica,* by GIAM BATTISTA CASTI. A similar
work is *The Seven Wives of Bluebeard,* by
ANATOLE FRANCE.
[2] Let the world slide. — *Towneley Mysteries, P. 101* [1420]. SHAKESPEARE: *Taming of
the Shrew, induc. 1.* BEAUMONT AND FLETCH-
ER: *Wit without Money, Act V, Sc. 2*
[3] A common exclamation of regret occurring
in Spenser, Harrington, and the older writers.
An earlier instance of the phrase occurs in the
Towneley Mysteries.
[4] 'Tis good to be merry and wise. — JON-
SON, CHAPMAN, MARSTON: *Eastward Ho, Act
I, Sc. 1.* BURNS: *Here's a health to them that's
awa'*
[5] Look ere thou leap. — *Tottel's Miscellany* [1557] and Tusser's *Five Hundred Points
of Good Husbandry, Of Wiving and Thriving*
[1573]
  Thou shouldst have looked before thou
hadst leapt. — JONSON, CHAPMAN, MARSTON:
Eastward Ho, Act V, Sc. 1
  Look before you ere you leap. — BUTLER:
Hudibras, Pt. II, C. II, L. 502
[6] He that will not when he may,
  When he will he shall have nay.
    BURTON: *Anatomy of Melancholy,
    Pt. III, Sec. 2, Memb. 5, Subsect. 5*

The fat is in the fire.[1]
>   *Proverbes. Part I, Chap. II*

When the sunne shineth, make hay.
>   *Ibid.*

When the iron is hot, strike.[2]
>   *Ibid.*

The tide tarrieth no man.[3]
>   *Ibid.*

Than catch and hold while I may, fast
binde, fast finde.[4]
>   *Ibid.*

And while I at length debate and beate
the bush,
There shall steppe in other men and
catch the burdes.[5]
>   *Ibid.*

While betweene two stooles my taile goe
to the ground.[6]
>   *Ibid.*

So many heads so many wits.[7]
>   *Ibid.*

He that wold not when he might,
He shall not when he wolda.
>   PERCY: *Reliques, The Baffled Knight*

[1] All the fatt's in the fire. — MARSTON:
What You Will [1607]

[2] You should hammer your iron when it is
glowing hot. — PUBLIUS SYRUS: *Maxim 262*
Strike whilst the iron is hot.—RABELAIS:
Book II, Chap. XXXI. WEBSTER: *Westward
Hoe, Tom A'Lincolne*. FARQUHAR: *The Beaux'
Stratagem, IV, 1*

[3] Hoist up saile while gale doth last,
Tide and wind stay no man's pleasure.
>   ROBERT SOUTHWELL: *St. Peter's
>   Complaint* [1595]
Nae man can tether time or tide. — BURNS:
Tam O'Shanter.

[4] Fast bind, fast find;
A proverb never stale in thrifty mind.
>   SHAKESPEARE: *Merchant of Venice,
>   Act II, Sc. 5, L. 54*
Also in *Jests of Scogin* [1565]

[5] It is this proverb which Henry V is reported to have uttered at the siege of Orleans.
"Shall I beat the bush and another take the
bird?" said King Henry.

[6] Entre deux arcouns chet cul à terre (Between two stools one sits on the ground. —
Les Proverbes del Vilain, MS. Bodleian [circa
1303]
S'asseoir entre deux selles le cul à terre (One
falls to the ground in trying to sit on two
stools). — RABELAIS: *Book I, Chap. II*

[7] As many men, so many mindes. — TER-
ENCE: *Phormio, II, 4*
As the saying is, So many heades, so many
wittes. — QUEEN ELIZABETH: *Godly Medita-
cyon of the Christian Sowle* [1548]

Wedding is destiny,
And hanging likewise.[1]
>   *Proverbes. Part I, Chap. II*

Happy man, happy dole.[2]
>   *Ibid.*

God never sends th' mouth but he sendeth meat.
>   *Ibid. Chap. IV*

Like will to like.
>   *Ibid.*

A hard beginning maketh a good ending.
>   *Ibid.*

When the skie falth we shall have
Larkes.[3]
>   *Ibid.*

More frayd then hurt.
>   *Ibid.*

Feare may force a man to cast beyond
the moone.[4]
>   *Ibid.*

Nothing is impossible to a willing hart.
>   *Ibid.*

The wise man sayth, store is no sore.
>   *Ibid. Chap. V*

Let the world wagge,[5] and take mine
ease in myne Inne.[6]
>   *Ibid.*

So many men so many mindes. — GAS-
COIGNE: *Glass of Government*

[1] Hanging and wiving go by destiny. —
The Schole-hous for Women [1541]. SHAKE-
SPEARE: *Merchant of Venice, Act II, Sc. 9,
L. 83*
Marriage and hanging go by destiny;
matches are made in heaven. — BURTON:
*Anatomy of Melancholy, Part III, Sec. 2,
Memb. 5, Subsect. 5*

[2] Happy man be his dole. — SHAKESPEARE:
*Merry Wives, Act III, Sc. 4, L. 68; Winter's
Tale, Act I, Sc. 2, L. 163*. BUTLER: *Hudibras,
P. I, C. III, L. 168*

[3] Si les nues tomboyent esperoyt prendre
les alouettes (If the clouds fall, one may hope
to catch larks). — RABELAIS: *Book I, Chap.
XI*

[4] To "cast beyond the moon" is a phrase in
frequent use by the old writers. LYLY: *Euphues, P. 78*. THOMAS HEYWOOD: *A Woman
Killed with Kindness*

[5] Let the world slide. — SHAKESPEARE:
Taming of the Shrew, Ind. 1, L. 6, and, Let
the world slip, *Ind. 2, L. 146*

[6] Shall I not take mine ease in mine inn? —
SHAKESPEARE: *Henry IV, Part I, Act III,
Sc. 3, L. 91*

Rule the rost.[1]
> *Proverbes. Part I, Chap. V*

Hold their noses to grinstone.[2]
> *Ibid.*

Better to give then to take.[3]
> *Ibid.*

When all candles bee out, all cats be gray.
> *Ibid.*

No man ought to looke a given horse in the mouth.[4]
> *Ibid.*

I perfectly feele even at my fingers end.[5]
> *Ibid. Chap. VI*

A sleveless errand.[6]
> *Ibid. Chap. VII*

We both be at our wittes end.[7]
> *Ibid. Chap. VIII*

Reckeners without their host must recken twice.
> *Ibid.*

A day after the faire.[8]
> *Ibid.*

Cut my cote after my cloth.[1]
> *Proverbes. Part I, Chap. VIII*

The neer to the church, the further from God.[2]
> *Ibid. Chap. IX*

Now for good lucke, cast an old shooe after me.
> *Ibid.*

Better is to bow then breake.[3]
> *Ibid.*

It hurteth not the toung to give faire words.[4]
> *Ibid.*

Two heads are better then one.
> *Ibid.*

A short horse is soone currid.[5]
> *Ibid. Chap. X*

To tell tales out of schoole.
> *Ibid.*

To hold with the hare and run with the hound.[6]
> *Ibid.*

She is nether fish nor flesh, nor good red herring.[7]
> *Ibid.*

All is well that endes well.[8]
> *Ibid.*

---

[1] See Skelton, page 9. SHAKESPEARE: *Henry VI, Part II, Act I, Sc. 1, L. 110.* THOMAS HEYWOOD: *History of Women*

[2] Hold their noses to the grindstone. — MIDDLETON: *Blurt, Master-Constable, Act III, Sc. 3*
See Burton, page 125.

[3] It is more blessed to give than to receive. — *Acts, XX, 35*

[4] This proverb occurs in Rabelais, *Book I, Chap. XI;* in *Vulgaria Stambrigi [circa* 1510]; in Butler, *Part I, Canto I, Line 490.* Archbishop Trench says this proverb is certainly as old as Jerome of the fourth century, who, when some found fault with certain writings of his, replied that they were free-will offerings, and that it did not behove to look a gift horse in the mouth.

[5] RABELAIS: *Book IV, Chap. LIV.* At my fingers' ends. — SHAKESPEARE: *Twelfth-Night, Act I, Sc. 3, L. 85*

[6] The origin of the word "sleveless," in the sense of unprofitable, has defied the most careful research. It is frequently found allied to other substantives. Bishop Hall speaks of the "sleveless tale of transubstantiation," and Milton writes of a "sleveless reason." Chaucer uses it in the *Testament of Love.* — SHARMAN
On a sleveless errand. — SHAKESPEARE: *Troilus and Cressida, Act V, Sc. 4, L. 9*
Sending every one of her children upon some sleveless errand, as she terms it. JOSEPH ADDISON: *The Spectator, No. 47* [April 24, 1711] (referring to April Fool errands).

[7] At their wit's end. — *Psalm CVII, 27*

[8] THOMAS HEYWOOD: *If you know not me, etc.* [1605]. TARLTON: *Jests* [1611]

[1] A relic of the Sumptuary Laws. One of the earliest instances occurs, 1530, in the interlude of *Godly Queene Hester.*

[2] Qui est près de l'église est souvent loin de Dieu (He who is near the Church is often far from God). — *Les Proverbes Communs [circa* 1500]

[3] Rather to bowe than breke is profitable; Humylite is a thing commendable.
> *The Morale Proverbs of Cristyne,* translated from the French [1390] by Earl Rivers, and printed by Caxton in 1478

[4] Fair words never hurt the tongue. — JONSON, CHAPMAN, MARSTON: *Eastward Ho, Act IV, Sc. 1*

[5] FLETCHER: *Valentinian, Act II, Sc. 1*

[6] HUMPHREY ROBERT: *Complaint for Reformation* [1572]. LYLY: *Euphues* [1579] (Arber's reprint), *P. 107*

[7] Neither fish nor flesh, nor good red herring. — SIR H. SHEERES: *Satyr on the Sea Officers.* TOM BROWN: *Æneus Sylvius's Letter.* DRYDEN: *Epilogue to the Duke of Guise*

[8] Si finis bonus est, totum bonum erit (If the end be well, all will be well). — *Gesta Romanorum, Tale LXVII*
SHAKESPEARE: *All's Well that Ends Well, Act IV, Sc. 4, L. 35,* and *Act V, Sc. 1, L. 25*

Of a good beginning cometh a good
end.[1]
> *Proverbes. Part I, Chap. X*

Shee had seene far in a milstone.[2]
> *Ibid.*

Better late than never.[3]
> *Ibid.*

When the steede is stolne, shut the stable durre.[4]
> *Ibid.*

Pryde will have a fall;
For pryde goeth before and shame com-
meth after.[5]
> *Ibid.*

She looketh as butter would not melt in
her mouth.[6]
> *Ibid.*

The still sowe eats up all the draffe.[7]
> *Ibid.*

Ill weede growth fast.[8]
> *Ibid.*

It is a deere collop
That is cut out of th' owne flesh.[9]
> *Ibid.*

Beggars should be no choosers.[1]
> *Proverbes. Part I, Chap. X*

Every cocke is proud on his owne dunghill.[2]
> *Ibid. Chap. XI*

The rolling stone never gathereth
mosse.[3]
> *Ibid.*

To robbe Peter and pay Poule.[4]
> *Ibid.*

A man may well bring a horse to the
water,
But he cannot make him drinke without he will.
> *Ibid.*

Men say, kinde will creepe where it may
not goe.[5]
> *Ibid.*

The cat would eate fish, and would not
wet her feete.[6]
> *Ibid.*

While the grasse groweth the horse
starveth.[7]
> *Ibid.*

---

[1] Who that well his warke beginneth,
The rather a good ende he winneth.
GOWER: *Confessio Amantis*
[2] LYLY: *Euphues* (Arber's reprint), *P. 288*
[3] TUSSER: *Five Hundred Points of Good
Husbandry, An Habitation Enforced.* BUN-
YAN: *Pilgrim's Progress.* MATHEW HENRY:
Commentaries, Matthew XXI. MURPHY: *The
School for Guardians*
Potius sero quam nunquam (Rather late
than never). — LIVY: *IV, II, 14*
[4] Quant le cheval est emblé dounke ferme
fols l'estable (When the horse has been stolen,
the fool shuts the stable). — *Les Proverbes
del Vilain*
[5] Pride goeth before destruction, and a
haughty spirit before a fall. — *Proverbs, XVI,
18*
Pryde goeth before, and shame cometh be-
hynde. — *Treatise of a Gallant* [*circa* 1510]
[6] She looks as if butter would not melt in
her mouth. — SWIFT: *Polite Conversation*
[7] 'Tis old, but true, still swine eat all the
draff. — SHAKESPEARE: *Merry Wives of Windsor, Act IV, Sc. 2, L. 112*
[8] Ewyl weed ys sone y-growe. — *MS. Har-
leian* [*circa* 1490]
An ill weed grows apace. — CHAPMAN: *An
Humorous Day's Mirth*
Great weeds do grow apace. — SHAKE-
SPEARE: *Richard III, Act II, Sc. 4, L. 13.*
BEAUMONT AND FLETCHER: *The Coxcomb, Act
IV, Sc. 4*
[9] God knows thou art a collop of my flesh.
— SHAKESPEARE: *1 Henry VI, Act V, Sc. 4,
L. 18*

[1] Beggars must be no choosers. — BEAU-
MONT AND FLETCHER: *The Scornful Lady,
Act V, Sc. 3*
[2] Þet coc is kene on his owne mixenne. —
Þe Ancren Riwle [*circa* 1250]
[3] The stone that is rolling can gather no
moss. — TUSSER: *Five Hundred Points of
Good Husbandry*
A rolling stone gathers no moss. — PUBLIUS
SYRUS: *Maxim 524.* GOSSON: *Ephemerides of
Phialo.* MARSTON: *The Fawn*
Pierre volage ne queult mousse (A rolling
stone gathers no moss). — *De l'hermite qui
se désespéra pour le larron que ala en paradis
avant que lui* [13th century]
[4] To rob Peter and pay Paul is said to have
derived its origin when, in the reign of Edward VI, the lands of St. Peter at Westminster
were appropriated to raise money for the re-
pair of St. Paul's in London. Also found in
Wycliffe's Works, Vol. III, page 174. See
Herbert, page 138.
[5] You know that love
Will creep in service when it cannot go.
SHAKESPEARE: *Two Gentlemen of Verona, Act IV, Sc. 2, L. 19*
[6] Shakespeare alludes to this proverb in
Macbeth, Act I, Sc. 7, L. 44:
Letting I dare not wait upon I would,
Like the poor cat i' the adage.
Cat lufat visch, ac he nele his feth wete. —
MS. Trinity College, Cambridge [*circa* 1250]
[7] Whylst grass doth grow, oft sterves the
seely steede. — WHETSTONE: *Promos and Cas-
sandra* [1578]

Better one byrde in hand than ten in the wood.[1]

Proverbes. Part I, Chap. XI

Rome was not built in one day.

Ibid.

Yee have many strings to your bowe.[2]

Ibid.

Many small make a great.[3]

Ibid.

Children learne to creepe ere they can learne to goe.

Ibid.

Better is halfe a lofe than no bread.

Ibid.

Nought venter nought have.[4]

Ibid.

Children and fooles cannot lye.[5]

Ibid.

Set all at sixe and seven.[6]

Ibid.

All is fish that comth to net.[7]

Ibid.

Who is worse shod than the shoemaker's wife?[8]

Ibid.

While the grass grows —
The proverb is something musty.
SHAKESPEARE: *Hamlet, Act III, Sc. 2, L. 365*

[1] An earlier instance occurs in Heywood, in his *Dialogue on Wit and Folly* [*circa* 1530]. See Herbert, page 137.

[2] Two strings to his bow. — HOOKER: *Polity, Book V, Chap. LXXX.* CHAPMAN: *D'Ambois, Act II, Sc. 3.* BUTLER: *Hudibras, Part III, Canto I, Line 1.* CHURCHILL: *The Ghost, Book IV.* FIELDING: *Love in Several Masques, Sc. 13*

[3] See Chaucer, page 8.

[4] Naught venture naught have. — TUSSER: *Five Hundred Points of Good Husbandry, October Abstract*

[5] 'Tis an old saw, Children and fooles speake true. — LYLY: *Endymion*

[6] Set all on sex and seven. — CHAUCER: *Troilus and Criseyde, Book IV, Line 622;* also *Towneley Mysteries*
At six and seven. — SHAKESPEARE: *Richard II, Act II, Sc. 2, L. 121*
Things going on at sixes and sevens. — GOLDSMITH: *The Good-Natur'd Man, Act I*

[7] All's fish they get that cometh to net. — TUSSER: *Five Hundred Points of Good Husbandry, February Abstract*
Where all is fish that cometh to net. — GASCOIGNE: *Steele Glas.* [1575]

[8] Him that makes shoes go barefoot himself. — BURTON: *Anatomy of Melancholy, Democritus to the Reader*

One good turne asketh another.

Proverbes. Part I, Chap. XI

By hooke or crooke.[1]

Ibid.

She frieth in her owne grease.[2]

Ibid.

Who waite for dead men shall goe long barefoote.

Ibid.

I pray thee let me and my fellow have
A haire of the dog that bit us last night.[3]

Ibid.

But in deede,
A friend is never knowne till a man have neede.

Ibid.

This wonder (as wonders last) lasted nine daies.[4]

Ibid. Part II, Chap. I

New brome swepth cleene.[5]

Ibid.

All thing is the woorse for the wearing.

Ibid.

Burnt child fire dredth.[6]

Ibid. Chap. II

All is not Gospell that thou doest speake.[7]

Ibid.

[1] This phrase derives its origin from the custom of certain manors where tenants are authorized to take fire-bote *by hook or by crook;* that is, so much of the underwood as may be cut with a crook, and so much of the loose timber as may be collected from the boughs by means of a hook. One of the earliest citations of this proverb occurs in John Wycliffe's *Controversial Tracts* [*circa* 1370]. See Skelton, page 9. RABELAIS: *Book V, Chap. XIII.* DU BARTAS: *The Map of Man.* SPENSER: *Faerie Queene, Book III, Canto I, St. 17.* BEAUMONT AND FLETCHER: *Women Pleased, Act I, Sc. 3*

[2] See Chaucer, page 7.

[3] In old receipt books we find it invariably advised that an inebriate should drink sparingly in the morning some of the same liquor which he had drunk to excess over night.

[4] See Chaucer, page 4.

[5] Ah, well I wot that a new broome sweepeth cleane. — LYLY: *Euphues* (Arber's reprint), *P. 89*

[6] Brend child fur dredth,
Quoth Hendyng.
Proverbs of Hendyng, MSS.
A burnt child dreadeth the fire. — LYLY: *Euphues* (Arber's reprint), *P. 319*

[7] You do not speak gospel. — RABELAIS: *Book I, Chap. XIII*

Love me litle, love me long.[1]
>> *Proverbes. Part II, Chap. II*

A fooles bolt is soone shot.[2]
>> *Ibid. Chap. III*

A woman hath nine lives like a cat.[3]
>> *Ibid. Chap. IV*

A peny for your thought.[4]
>> *Ibid.*

You stand in your owne light.
>> *Ibid.*

Though chaunge be no robbry.
>> *Ibid.*

Might have gone further and have fared worse.
>> *Ibid.*

The grey mare is the better horse.[5]
>> *Ibid.*

Three may keepe counsayle, if two be away.[6]
>> *Ibid. Chap. V*

Small pitchers have wyde eares.[7]
>> *Ibid.*

Many hands make light warke.
>> *Ibid.*

The greatest Clerkes be not the wisest men.[1]
>> *Proverbes. Part II, Chap. V*

Out of Gods blessing into the warme Sunne.[2]
>> *Ibid.*

There is no fire without some smoke.[3]
>> *Ibid.*

One swallow maketh not summer.[4]
>> *Ibid.*

Fieldes have eies and woods have eares.[5]
>> *Ibid.*

A cat may looke on a King.
>> *Ibid.*

It is a foule byrd that fyleth his owne nest.[6]
>> *Ibid.*

Have yee him on the hip.[7]
>> *Ibid.*

Hee must have a long spoone, shall eat with the devill.[8]
>> *Ibid.*

It had need to bee
A wylie mouse that should breed in the cats eare.[9]
>> *Ibid.*

Leape out of the frying pan into the fyre.[10]
>> *Ibid*

---

[1] MARLOWE: *Jew of Malta, Act IV, Sc. 6.* BACON: *Formularies.* See Herrick, page 133.

[2] Sottes bolt is sone shote. — *Proverbs of Hendyng, MSS.*
A fool's bolt is soon shot. — SHAKESPEARE: *King Henry V, Act III, Sc. 7, L. 137*

[3] It has been the Providence of Nature to give this creature nine lives instead of one. — BIDPAY: *The Greedy and Ambitious Cat, Fable III* [B. C.]

[4] LYLY: *Euphues* (Arber's reprint), *P. 80*

[5] *Pryde and Abuse of Women* [1550]. *The Marriage of True Wit and Science.* BUTLER: *Hudibras, P. II, C. I, L. 698.* FIELDING: *The Grub Street Opera, Act II, Sc. 4.* PRIOR: *Epilogue to Lucius.*
Lord Macaulay (*History of England, Vol. I, Chap. III*) thinks that this proverb originated in the preference generally given to the gray mares of Flanders over the finest coach-horses of England. Macaulay, however, is writing of the latter half of the seventeenth century, while the proverb was used a century earlier.

[6] Two may keep counsel when the third's away. — SHAKESPEARE: *Titus Andronicus, Act IV, Sc. 2, L. 145*
Three can hold their peace if two be away. — HERBERT: *Jacula Prudentum*

[7] Pitchers have ears. — SHAKESPEARE: *The Taming of the Shrew, Act IV, Sc. 4, L. 52; Richard III, Act II, Sc. 4, L. 37*
Little pitchers have wide ears. — HERBERT: *Jacula Prudentum*

[1] See Chaucer, page 6.
[2] Thou shalt come out of a warme sunne into Gods blessing. — LYLY: *Euphues*
Thou out of Heaven's benediction comest
To the warm sun.
>> SHAKESPEARE: *King Lear, Act II, Sc. 2, L. 168*
[3] There can no great smoke arise, but there must be some fire. — LYLY: *Euphues* (Arber's reprint), *P. 153*
[4] One swallowe prouveth not that summer is neare. — NORTHBROOKE: *Treatise against Dancing* [1577]
[5] See Chaucer, page 6.
[6] See Skelton, page 10.
[7] I have thee on the hip. — SHAKESPEARE: *Merchant of Venice, Act IV, Sc. 1, L. 335; Othello, Act II, Sc. 1, L. 317*
[8] See Chaucer, page 7.
[9] A hardy mouse that is bold to breede
In cattis eeris.
>> *Order of Foles* [MS. *circa* 1450]
[10] The same in *Don Quixote* (Lockhart's ed.), *Part I, Book III, Chap. IV.* BUNYAN: *Pilgrim's Progress.* FLETCHER: *The Wild-Goose Chase, Act IV, Sc. 3*

Time trieth troth in every doubt.[1]
> *Proverbes. Part II, Chap. V*

Mad as a march hare.[2]
> *Ibid.*

Much water goeth by the mill
That the miller knoweth not of.[3]
> *Ibid.*

He must needes goe whom the devill
doth drive.[4]
> *Ibid. Chap. VI*

Set the cart before the horse.[5]
> *Ibid.*

The moe the merrier.[6]
> *Ibid.*

To th' end of a shot and beginning of a
fray.[7]
> *Ibid.*

It is better to be
An old man's derling than a yong man's
werling.
> *Ibid.*

Be the day never so long,
Evermore at last they ring to evensong.[8]
> *Ibid.*

The moone is made of a greene cheese.[1]
> *Proverbes. Part II, Chap. VII*

I know on which side my bread is but-
tred.
> *Ibid.*

It will not out of the flesh that is bred
in the bone.[2]
> *Ibid. Chap. VIII*

Who is so deafe or so blinde as is hee
That wilfully will neither heare nor
see?[3]
> *Ibid. Chap. IX*

The wrong sow by th' eare.[4]
> *Ibid.*

Went in at the tone eare and out at the
tother.[5]
> *Ibid.*

Love me, love my dog.[6]
> *Ibid.*

An ill winde that bloweth no man to
good.[7]
> *Ibid.*

For when I gave you an inch, you tooke
an ell.[8]
> *Ibid.*

---

[1] Time trieth truth. — *Tottel's Miscellany* [reprint, 1867], *P. 221*
Time tries the troth in everything. — TUS-SER: *Five Hundred Points of Good Husbandry, Author's Epistle, Chap. I*
[2] I saye, thou madde March hare. — SKELTON: *Replycation against certayne yong scolers*
[3] More water glideth by the mill
Than wots the miller of.
SHAKESPEARE: *Titus Andronicus, Act II, Sc. 1, L. 85*
[4] An earlier instance of this proverb occurs in Heywood's *Johan the Husbande* [1533].
He must needs go whom the devil drives. — SHAKESPEARE: *All's Well that Ends Well, Act I, Sc. 3, L. 32.* CERVANTES: *Don Quixote, Part I, Book IV, Chap. IV.* GOSSON: *Ephemerides of Phialo.* PEELE: *Edward I*
[5] Others set carts before the horses. — RABELAIS: *Book V, Chap. XXII*
I run before my horse to market. — SHAKESPEARE: *King Richard III, Act I, Sc. 1, L. 159*
[6] GASCOIGNE: *Roses* [1575]. Title of a book of epigrams [1608]. BEAUMONT AND FLETCHER: *The Scornful Lady, Act I, Sc. 1; The Sea Voyage, Act I, Sc. 2*
[7] To the latter end of a fray and the beginning of a feast. — SHAKESPEARE: *Henry IV, Part II, Act IV, Sc. 2, L. 86*
[8] Be the day short or never so long,
At length it ringeth to even song.
FOXE: *Book of Martyrs, Chap. VII, P. 346*
Quoted at the stake by George Tankerfield [1555].

[1] *Jack Jugler, P. 46.* RABELAIS: *Book I, Chap. XI.* BLACKLOCH: *Hatchet of Heresies* [1565]. BUTLER: *Hudibras, Part II, C. III, L. 263*
[2] What is bred in the bone will never come out of the flesh. — BIDPAY: *The Two Fishermen, Fable XIV*
It will never out of the flesh that's bred in the bone. — JONSON: *Every Man in his Humour, Act I, Sc. 1*
[3] None so deaf as those that will not hear. — MATHEW HENRY: *Commentaries, Psalm LVIII*
[4] He has the wrong sow by the ear. — JONSON: *Every Man in his Humour, Act II, Sc. 1*
[5] See Chaucer, page 4.
[6] CHAPMAN: *Widow's Tears* [1612]
A proverb in the time of Saint Bernard was, Qui me amat, amet et canem meum (Who loves me will love my dog also). — *Sermo Primus*
The old Sicilian proverb, Love me, love my dog. — JOSEPH ADDISON: *The Spectator, No. 579* [August 11, 1714]
[7] *Falstaff.* What wind blew you hither, Pistol?
Pistol. Not the ill wind which blows no man to good.
SHAKESPEARE: *Henry IV, Part II, Act V, Sc. 3, L. 87*
[8] Give an inch, he'll take an ell. — WEBSTER: *Sir Thomas Wyatt*

Would yee both eat your cake and have your cake? [1]
> *Proverbes. Part II, Chap. IX*

Every man for himselfe and God for us all.[2]
> *Ibid.*

Though he love not to buy the pig in the poke.[3]
> *Ibid.*

This hitteth the naile on the hed.[4]
> *Ibid. Chap. XI*

Enough is as good as a feast.[5]
> *Ibid.*

SIR THOMAS WYATT
[1503–1542]

Noli me tangere, for Caesar's I am,
And wild to hold, though I seem tame.
> *To Anne Boleyn*

JOHN BRADFORD
[1510–1555]

The familiar story, that, on seeing evil-doers taken to the place of execution, he was wont to exclaim: "But for the grace of God there goes John Bradford," is a universal tradition, which has overcome the lapse of time.[6]
> *Biographical Notice, Parker So-*

---

[1] Wouldst thou both eat thy cake and have it? — HERBERT: *The Size*

[2] Every man for himself, his own ends, the Devil for all. — BURTON: *Anatomy of Melancholy, Part III, Sect. I, Memb. III*

[3] For buying or selling of pig in a poke. — TUSSER: *Five Hundred Points of Good Husbandry, September Abstract*

[4] You have there hit the nail on the head. — RABELAIS: *Bk. III, Ch. XXXI*

[5] *Dives and Pauper* [1493]. GASCOIGNE: *Poesies* [1575]. POPE: *Horace, Book I, Ep. VII, L. 24.* FIELDING: *Covent Garden Tragedy, Act V, Sc. 1.* BICKERSTAFF: *Love in a Village, Act III, Sc. 1*

[6] . . . Quoting an English divine . . . , by the grace of God I am not what I was. — WILLIAM G. SCHAUFFLER [1798–1893]: *Autobiography* [1887]
Did not Philip Neri [1515–1595] say to Philip, as he saw a criminal haled to execution: There thou goest, Philip, but for the grace of God! — PATRICK AUGUSTINE SHEEHAN [1852–1913]: *Under the Cedars and Stars* [1903], *Part II, Chap. 20, P. 97*
"I never hear of such a case as this that I do not think of Baxter's words, and say,

ciety edition, The Writings of John Bradford, Page XLIII [1853]

RICHARD GRAFTON
[?–1572]

Thirty dayes hath Nouember,
Aprill, June, and September,
February hath xxviii alone,
And all the rest have xxxi.[1]
> *Chronicles of England* [1562]

'There, but for the grace of God, goes Sherlock Holmes'." — SIR ARTHUR CONAN DOYLE [1859–1930]: *The Boscombe Valley Mystery, P. 106.* (The reference is to RICHARD BAXTER [1615–1691], author of *The Saint's Everlasting Rest* and *The Call to the Unconverted*.)
The saying is also attributed to the REVEREND JOHN NEWTON [1725–1807], and is said to be preserved in the epitaph he composed for the cenotaph of the Church of Saint Mary Woolnoth, London, of which he was rector.
"I say, Mayor — but for the grace of God, there go we." — JOHN GALSWORTHY: *A Family Man, Act III*

[1] Junius, Aprilis, Septémq; Nouemq; tricenos,
Vnum plus reliqui, Februs tenet octo vicenos,
At si bissextus fuerit superadditur vnus.

WILLIAM HARRISON: *Description of Britain*, prefixed to Holinshed's *Chronicle* [1577].
Thirty days hath September,
April, June, and November,
February has twenty-eight alone,
All the rest have thirty-one;
Excepting leap year, — that's the time
When February's days are twenty-nine.
> *The Return from Parnassus* [London, 1606]

Thirty days hath September,
April, June, and November;
All the rest have thirty-one,
Excepting February alone,
Which hath but twenty-eight, in fine,
Till leap year gives it twenty-nine.
> *Common in the New England states*

Fourth, eleventh, ninth, and sixth,
Thirty days to each affix;
Every other thirty-one
Except the second month alone.
> *Common in Chester County, Pennsylvania, among the Friends*

Compare the old Latin-class mnemonic: —
In March, July, October, May,
The Ides are on the fifteenth day,
The Nones the seventh; all other months besides
Have two days less for Nones and Ides.

SIR THOMAS VAUX
[1510–1556]

Companion none is like
Unto the mind alone;
For many have been harmed by specch,
Through thinking, few or none.
Of a Contented Mind. Stanza 3

RICHARD EDWARDS
[1523–1566]

The fallyng out of faithfull frends
renuyng is of loue.[1]
The Paradise of Dainty Devices

THOMAS TUSSER
[1524–1580]

God sendeth and giveth both mouth and
the meat.[2]
*Five Hundred Points of Good
Husbandry*
Except wind stands as never it stood,
It is an ill wind turns none to good.
*A Description of the Properties
of Wind*
At Christmas play and make good
cheer,
For Christmas comes but once a year.
The Farmer's Daily Diet
Such mistress, such Nan,
Such master, such man.[3]
*Five Hundred Points of Good
Husbandry, April's Abstract*

---

[1] The anger of lovers renews the strength of love. — PUBLIUS SYRUS: *Maxim 24*
Let the falling out of friends be a renewing of affection. — LYLY: *Euphues*
The falling out of lovers is the renewing of love. — BURTON: *Anatomy of Melancholy, Pt. III, Sect. 2*
Amantium iræ amoris integratio est (The quarrels of lovers are the renewal of love). — TERENCE: *Andria, Act III, Sc. 3, L. 23*
[2] God sends meat, and the Devil sends cooks. — JOHN TAYLOR: *Works, Vol. II, P. 85* [1630]. RAY: *Proverbs.* GARRICK: *Epigram on Goldsmith, Retaliation.*
Persian couplet: —
The holy prophet Zoroaster said,
The Lord who made thy teeth shall give thee bread.
[3] On the authority of M. Cimber, of the Bibliothèque Royale, we owe this proverb to Chevalier Bayard: "Tel maître, tel valet."

Who goeth a borrowing
Goeth a sorrowing.
*Five Hundred Points of Good
Husbandry, June's Abstract*
'T is merry in hall
Where beards wag all.[1]
Ibid. August's Abstract
Naught venture naught have.[2]
Ibid. October's Abstract
Dry sun, dry wind;
Safe bind, safe find.[3]
Washing
Hast thou a friend, as heart may wish at
will?
Then use him so, to have his friendship
still.
Wouldst have a friend, wouldst know
what friend is best?
Have God thy friend, who passeth all
the rest.
Posies for a Parlour
To Death we must stoop, be we high,
be we low,
But how, and how suddenly, few be
that know;
What carry we then but a sheet to the
grave,
To cover this carcass, of all that we
have?
Tenants of God's Farmstead

ELIZABETH, QUEEN OF ENGLAND
[1533–1603]

The use of the sea and air is common
to all; neither can a title to the ocean
belong to any people or private persons,
forasmuch as neither nature nor public
use and custom permit any possession thereof.

To the Spanish Ambassador [1580]

---

[1] Merry swithe it is in halle,
When the beards waveth alle.
Life of Alexander [1312]
This has been wrongly attributed to Adam Davie. There the line runs, —
Swithe mury hit is in halle,
When burdes waiven alle.
[2] See Heywood, page 15.
[3] See Heywood, page 12. SHAKESPEARE: *Merchant of Venice, Act II, Sc. 5, L. 54*

My care is like my shadow in the sun —
Follows me flying — flies when I pursue it.

On the Departure of Alençon
[1582]

Monarchs ought to put to death the authors and instigators of war, as their sworn enemies and as dangers to their states.

To Fénélon

I am no lover of pompous title, but only desire that my name may be recorded in a line or two, which shall briefly express my name, my virginity, the years of my reign, the reformation of religion under it, and my preservation of peace.

To her ladies, discussing her epitaph

EDWARD DYER
[Circa 1540–1607]

My mind to me a kingdom is;
　Such present joys therein I find,
　That it excels all other bliss
　That earth affords or grows by kind:
Though much I want which most would have,
Yet still my mind forbids to crave.
　　　　　MS. Rawl. 85, P. 17 [1]

Some have too much, yet still do crave;
　I little have, and seek no more:
They are but poor, though much they have,
　And I am rich with little store:

[1] There is a very similar but anonymous copy in the British Museum. Additional MS. 15225, P. 85. And there is an imitation in J. Sylvester's Works, P. 651. — HANNAH: Courtly Poets
My mind to me a kingdom is;
　Such perfect joy therein I find,
　As far exceeds all earthly bliss
　That God and Nature hath assigned.
Though much I want that most would have,
Yet still my mind forbids to crave.
　BYRD: Psalmes, Sonnets, etc. [1588]
My mind to me an empire is,
While grace affordeth health.
　ROBERT SOUTHWELL [1561–1595]:
　　　　　Look Home
Mens regnum bona possidet (A good mind possesses a kingdom). — SENECA: Thyestes, II, 380

They poor, I rich; they beg, I give;
They lack, I have; they pine, I live.
　　　　　MS. Rawl. 85, P. 17

MARY STUART, QUEEN OF SCOTS
[1542–1587]

O Master and Maker! my hope is in thee.
My Jesus, dear Saviour! now set my soul free.
From this my hard prison, my spirit uprisen,
　Soars upward to thee.
Thus moaning and groaning, and bending the knee,
I adore, and implore that thou liberate me.[1]

Prayer written before her execution, translated by the REVEREND JAMES FREEMAN CLARKE
[1810–1888]

BISHOP JOHN STILL
[1543–1608]

I cannot eat but little meat,
　My stomach is not good;
But sure I think that I can drink
　With him that wears a hood.
　Gammer Gurton's Needle,
　　Drinking Song, Act V [2]

Now let them drink till they nod and wink,
　Even as good fellows should do;
They shall not miss to have the bliss
　Good ale doth bring men to.
　　　　　Ibid. Stanza 4

Back and side go bare, go bare,
　Both foot and hand go cold;
But, belly, God send thee good ale enough,
　Whether it be new or old.
　　　　　Ibid. Refrain

[1] O Domine Deus, speravi in Te,
　O care mi Jesu, nunc libera me,
　In dura catena, in misera poena,
　　Desidero Te.
Languendo, gemendo, et genuflectendo,
　Adoro, imploro, ut liberes me!
[2] Stated by Dyce to be from a MS. of older date than Gammer Gurton's Needle. See Skelton's Works (Dyce's ed.), Vol. I, Pp. vii-x, note

GILES FLETCHER
[1549–1611]

He is a path, if any be misled;
He is a robe, if any naked be;
If any chance to hunger, he is bread;
If any be a bondman, he is free;
If any be but weak, how strong is he!
To dead men life is he, to sick men,
   health;
To blind men, sight, and to the needy,
   wealth;
A pleasure without loss, a treasure with-
   out stealth.
Excellency of Christ

WILLIAM CAMDEN
[1551–1623]

Betwixt the stirrup and the ground,
Mercy I ask'd; mercy I found.
Remains Concerning Britain [1605]

SIR EDWARD COKE
[1552–1634]

The gladsome light of jurisprudence.
First Institute

Reason is the life of the law; nay, the
common law itself is nothing else but
reason. . . . The law, which is perfection of reason.[1]
Ibid.

For a man's house is his castle, *et
domus sua cuique tutissimum refu-
gium.*[2]
Third Institute. Page 162

The house of every one is to him as
his castle and fortress, as well for his
defence against injury and violence as
for his repose.
Semayne's Case. 5 Rep. 91

They (corporations) cannot commit
treason, nor be outlawed nor excommu-
nicate, for they have no souls.
Case of Sutton's Hospital. 10 Rep. 32

[1] Let us consider the reason of the case. For
nothing is law that is not reason. — SIR JOHN
POWELL: *Coggs* vs. *Bernard, 2 Ld. Raym.
Rep. P. 911*
[2] One's home is the safest refuge to everyone. — *Pandects, Lib. II, Tit. IV, De in Jus
vocando*

Magna Charta is such a fellow that
he will have no sovereign.
Debate in the Commons
[May 17, 1628]

Six hours in sleep, in law's grave study
   six,
Four spend in prayer, the rest on Nature fix.[1]
Translation of lines quoted by COKE

SIR WALTER RALEIGH
[1552–1618]

If all the world and love were young,
And truth in every shepherd's tongue,
These pretty pleasures might me move
To live with thee, and be thy love.
*The Nymph's Reply to the Pas-
sionate Shepherd.*[2] *Stanza 1*

Fain would I, but I dare not; I dare,
   and yet I may not;
I may, although I care not, for pleasure
   when I play not.
Fain Would I

Passions are likened best to floods and
   streams:
The shallow murmur, but the deep are
   dumb.[3]
The Silent Lover, Prelude

Silence in love bewrays more woe
Than words, though ne'er so witty:
A beggar that is dumb, you know,
   May challenge double pity.
Ibid. Stanza 7

Go, Soul, the body's guest,
   Upon a thankless arrant:
Fear not to touch the best,
   The truth shall be thy warrant:

[1] Seven hours to law, to soothing slumber
      seven;
   Ten to the world allot, and all to heaven.
                        SIR WILLIAM JONES
[2] An answer to CHRISTOPHER MARLOWE'S
poem, *The Passionate Shepherd to His Love.*
[3] Altissima quæque flumina minimo sono
labi (The deepest rivers flow with the least
sound). — Q. CURTIUS, *VII, 4, 13*
   Smooth runs the water where the brook is
deep. — SHAKESPEARE: *Henry VI, Part II,
Act III, Sc. I, L. 53*
   Take heed of still waters, the quick pass
away. — HERBERT: *Jacula Prudentum*

Go, since I needs must die,
And give the world the lie.
    The Lie. Stanza 1 [1] *(Printed in
    Poetical Rhapsody* [*1608*];
    manuscript copy traced to 1593)

Give me my scallop-shell of quiet,
My staff of faith to walk upon,
My scrip of joy, immortal diet,
My bottle of salvation,
My gown of glory, hope's true gage,
And thus I'll take my pilgrimage.
                    His Pilgrimage

Methought I saw the grave where Laura
    lay.[2]
                Verses to Edmund Spenser

Cowards [may] fear to die; but cour-
    age stout,
Rather than live in snuff, will be put
    out.
    Remains, Page 258 [*ed. 1661*],
    *On the snuff of a candle the
    night before he died.*

Even such is time, that takes in trust
Our youth, our joys, our all we have,
And pays us but with age and dust;
Who in the dark and silent grave,
When we have wandered all our ways,
Shuts up the story of our days.
But from this earth, this grave, this
    dust,
My God shall raise me up, I trust!
    *Written the night before his
    death; found in his Bible in the
    Gate-house at Westminster*

Shall I, like a hermit, dwell
On a rock or in a cell?
                            Poem

If she undervalue me,
What care I how fair she be? [3]
                            Ibid.

If she seem not chaste to me,
What care I how chaste she be?
                            Ibid.

---

[1] This poem is included in the Works of
JOSHUA SYLVESTER [1563-1618], where the
title is *The Soul's Errand*. It has also been at-
tributed to FRANCIS DAVISON [*fl.* 1602].
    [2] Methought I saw my late espoused saint.
— MILTON: *Sonnet XXIII*
    Methought I saw the footsteps of a throne.
— WORDSWORTH: *Sonnet*
    [3] If she be not so to me,
    What care I how fair she be?
GEORGE WITHER: *The Shepherd's Resolution*

Fain would I climb, yet fear I to fall.[1]

[History] hath triumphed over time,
which besides it nothing but eternity
hath triumphed over.
            Historie of the World, Preface

O eloquent, just, and mightie Death!
whom none could advise, thou hast per-
swaded; what none hath dared, thou
hast done; and whom all the world
hath flattered, thou only hast cast out
of the world and despised. Thou hast
drawne together all the farre stretchèd
greatnesse, all the pride, crueltie, and
ambition of man, and covered it all
over with these two narrow words, *Hic
jacet!*
                    Ibid. Book V, Part I

RICHARD HOOKER
[1553–1600]

Of Law there can be no less acknowledged than that her seat is the bosom of
God, her voice the harmony of the
world. All things in heaven and earth
do her homage, — the very least as feeling her care, and the greatest as not exempted from her power.
                Ecclesiastical Polity. Book I

That to live by one man's will became
the cause of all men's misery.
                            Ibid.

GEORGE KEITH, FIFTH
EARL MARISCHAL
[1553–1623]

Thai half said. Quhat say thai? Let
    thame say.[2]
            *Family motto, Mitchell Tower,
            Marischal College, Aberdeen,
            Scotland, founded in 1593*

---

[1] Written in a glass window obvious to the
Queen's eye. "Her Majesty, either espying or
being shown it, did under-write, 'If thy heart
fails thee, climb not at all.'" — FULLER:
Worthies of England, Vol. I, P. 419
    [2] They say. What say they? Let them say.
— *Motto over the fireplace in George Bernard Shaw's home*

JOHN LYLY
[*Circa* 1553–1606]

Cupid and my Campaspe play'd
At cards for kisses: Cupid paid.
Alexander and Campaspe. Act III,
Sc. 5

How at heaven's gates she claps her
wings,
The morne not waking til she sings.[1]
Ibid. Act V, Sc. 1

Be valyaunt, but not too venturous.
Let thy attyre bee comely, but not
costly.[2]
Euphues [*1579*] (*Arber's reprint*).
Page 39

Though the Camomill, the more it is
trodden and pressed downe the more it
spreadeth.[3]
Ibid. Page 46

The finest edge is made with the
blunt whetstone.
Ibid. Page 47

I cast before the Moone.[4]
Ibid. Page 78

It seems to me (said she) that you
are in some brown study.[5]
Ibid. Page 80

The soft droppes of rain perce the
hard marble; [6] many strokes overthrow
the tallest oaks.[7]
Ibid. Page 81

[1] Hark, hark! the lark at heaven's gate
sings,
And Phœbus 'gins arise.
SHAKESPEARE: *Cymbeline, Act II,*
Sc. 3, L. 22
[2] Costly thy habit as thy purse can buy,
But not express'd in fancy; rich, not
gaudy.
SHAKESPEARE: *Hamlet, Act I, Sc. 3, L. 70*
[3] The camomile, the more it is trodden on
the faster it grows. — SHAKESPEARE: *Henry*
IV, Part I, Act II, Sc. 4, L. 446
[4] See Heywood, page 12.
[5] A brown study. — SWIFT: *Polite Con-*
versation
[6] Water continually dropping will wear
hard rocks hollow. — PLUTARCH: *Of the*
Training of Children
Stillicidi casus lapidem cavat (Continual
dropping wears away a stone). LUCRETIUS:
I, 314
[7] Many strokes, though with a little axe,
Hew down and fell the hardest-timber'd
oak.
SHAKESPEARE: *Henry VI, Part III, Act II,*
Sc. 1, L. 54

He reckoneth without his Hostesse.[1]
Love knoweth no lawes.
Euphues [*1579*] (*Arber's reprint*).
Page 84

Did not Jupiter transforme himselfe
into the shape of Amphitrio to embrace
Alcmæna; into the form of a swan to
enjoy Leda; into a Bull to beguile Io;
into a showre of gold to win Danae? [2]
Ibid. Page 93

Lette me stande to the maine chance.[3]
Ibid. Page 104

I mean not to run with the Hare and
holde with the Hounde.[4]
Ibid. Page 107

It is a world to see.[5]
Ibid. Page 116

There can no great smoke arise, but
there must be some fire.[6]
Euphues and his Euphœbus.
Page 153

A clere conscience is a sure carde.[7]
Euphues. Page 207

As lyke as one pease is to another.
Ibid. Page 215

Goe to bed with the Lambe, and rise
with the Larke.[8]
Euphues and his England. Page 229

A comely olde man as busie as a bee.
Ibid. Page 252

Maydens, be they never so foolyshe,
yet beeing fayre they are commonly fortunate.
Ibid. Page 279

[1] See Heywood, page 13.
[2] Jupiter himself was turned into a satyr,
a shepherd, a bull, a swan, a golden shower,
and what not for love. — BURTON: *Anatomy*
of Melancholy, Pt. III, Sect. II, Memb. I,
Subsect. I
[3] The main chance. — SHAKESPEARE: *Hen-*
ry VI, Part II, Act I, Sc. 1, L. 213. BUTLER:
Hudibras, Part II, Canto II. DRYDEN: *Persius,*
Satire VI
[4] See Heywood, page 13.
[5] 'Tis a world to see. — SHAKESPEARE:
Taming of the Shrew, Act II, Sc. 1, L. 305
[6] See Heywood, page 16.
[7] This is a sure card. — *Thersytes* [*circa*
1550]
[8] To rise with the lark and go to bed with
the lamb. — BRETON: *Court and Country*
[*1618*], *reprint, page 182*
Rise with the lark, and with the lark to bed.
— HURDIS: *The Village Curate*

Where the streame runneth smoothest, the water is deepest.[1]

Euphues and his England. Page 287

Your eyes are so sharpe that you cannot onely looke through a Milstone, but cleane through the minde.

Ibid. Page 289

I am glad that my Adonis hath a sweete tooth in his head.

Ibid. Page 308

A Rose is sweeter in the budde than full blowne.[2]

Ibid. Page 314

EDMUND SPENSER
[1553?–1599]

From the text of J. C. Smith and E. De Selincourt.[3]

Fierce warres and faithfull loves shall moralize my song.[4]

The Faerie Queene. Introduction, Stanza 1

A Gentle Knight was pricking on the plaine.

Ibid. Book I, Canto 1, Stanza 1

A bold bad man.[5]

Ibid. Stanza 37

Her angels face
As the great eye of heaven shyned bright,
And made a sunshine in the shadie place.

Ibid. Canto 3, Stanza 4

Ay me, how many perils doe enfold
The righteous man, to make him daily fall.[6]

Ibid. Canto 8, Stanza 1

As great a noyse, as when in Cymbrian plaine
An heard of Bulles, whom kindly rage doth sting,
Do for the milkie mothers [7] want complaine,

And fill the fields with troublous bellowing.

The Faerie Queene. Book I, Canto 8, Stanza 11

Is not short paine well borne, that brings long ease,
And layes the soule to sleepe in quiet grave?
Sleepe after toyle, port after stormie seas,
Ease after warre, death after life does greatly please.[1]

Ibid. Canto 9, Stanza 40

O happie earth,
Whereon thy innocent feet doe ever tread.

Ibid. Canto 10, Stanza 9

All for love, and nothing for reward.

Ibid. Book II, Canto 8, Stanza 2

Yet gold all is not, that doth golden seeme.[2]

Ibid. Stanza 14

Through thicke and thin, both over banke and bush.[3]

In hope her to attaine by hooke or crooke.[4]

Ibid. Book III, Canto 1, Stanza 17

Her berth was of the wombe of Morning dew,[5]
And her conception of the joyous Prime.

Ibid. Canto 6, Stanza 3

Roses red and violets blew,
And all the sweetest flowres, that in the forrest grew.

Ibid. Stanza 6

All that in this delightfull Gardin growes,
Should happie be, and have immortall blis.

Ibid. Stanza 41

That Squire of Dames.

Ibid. Canto 8, Stanza 44

How over that same dore was likewise writ,

---

[1] See Raleigh, page 21.
[2] The rose is fairest when 'tis budding new.
— SCOTT: *Lady of the Lake, Canto III, St. 1*
[3] Oxford University Press [1932].
[4] And moralized his song. — POPE: *Epistle to Dr. Arbuthnot, Line 340*
[5] This bold bad man. — SHAKESPEARE: *Henry VIII, Act II, Sc. 2, L. 44.* MASSINGER: *A New Way to Pay Old Debts, Act IV, Sc. 2*
[6] Ay me! what perils do environ
The man that meddles with cold iron!
     BUTLER: *Hudibras, Pt. I, C. III, L. 1*
[7] Milky Mothers. — POPE: *The Dunciad,*

Book II, L. 247. SCOTT: *The Monastery, Chap. XXVIII*
[1] The last two lines are cut on Joseph Conrad's gravestone at Canterbury, England.
[2] See Chaucer, page 8.
[3] *Ibid.*, page 6.
[4] See Skelton, page 10.
[5] The young men come to thee as dew from the womb of the morning.
     Psalm 110, 3; Book of Common Prayer, American Revision [1928]

Be bold, be bold, and every where *Be bold.*[1]

> *The Faerie Queene. Book III,*
> *Canto 11, Stanza 54*

Another yron dore, on which was writ,
Be not too bold.

> *Ibid.*

Dan Chaucer, well of English undefyled,
On Fames eternall beadroll worthie to
be fyled.

> *Ibid. Book IV, Canto 2, Stanza 32*

For all that nature by her mother wit [2]
Could frame in earth.

> *Ibid. Canto 10, Stanza 21*

Me seemes the world is runne quite out
of square,
From the first point of his appointed
sourse,
And being once amisse growes daily
wourse and wourse.

> *Ibid. Book V, Introduction,*
> *Stanza 1*

For from the golden age,[3] that first was
named,
It's now at earst become a stonie one.

> *Ibid. Stanza 2*

Ill can he rule the great, that cannot
reach the small.

> *Ibid. Canto 2, Stanza 43*

Who will not mercie unto others shew,
How can he mercy ever hope to have? [4]

> *Ibid. Book VI, Canto 1, Stanza 42*

The gentle minde by gentle deeds is
knowne.

[1] De l'audace, encore de l'audace, et tou-
jours de l'audace (Boldness, again boldness,
and ever boldness). — DANTON: *Speech in the
Legislative Assembly* [1792]
Write on your doors the saying wise and old,
"Be bold! be bold!" and everywhere — "Be
bold;
Be not too bold!"
     LONGFELLOW: *Morituri Salutamus*
[2] Mother wit. — MARLOWE: *Prologue to
Tamberlaine the Great, Part I.* MIDDLETON:
Your Five Gallants, Act I, Sc. 1. SHAKESPEARE:
Taming of the Shrew, Act II, Sc. 1, L. 258
[3] To excel the golden age. — SHAKESPEARE:
The Tempest, Act II, Sc. 1, L. 175
   Time will run back and fetch the Age of
Gold. — MILTON: *On the Morning of Christ's
Nativity*
[4] Blessed are the merciful, for they shall ob-
tain mercy. — *Matthew, V, 7*

For a man by nothing is so well bewrayed,
As by his manners.

> *The Faerie Queene. Book VI,*
> *Canto 3, Stanza 1*

That here on earth is no sure happiness.

> *Ibid. Canto 11, Stanza 1*

The ever-whirling wheele
Of *Change,* the which all mortall things
doth sway.

> *Ibid. Book VII, Canto 6, Stanza 1*

Warres and allarums unto Nations
wide.

> *Ibid. Stanza 3*

But Times do change and move continually.

> *Ibid. Stanza 47*

But of all burdens, that a man can
beare,
Moste is, a fooles talke to beare and to
heare.

> *The Shepheardes Calender.*
> *Maye, Line 140*

To Kerke the narre, from God more
farre,[1]
Has bene an old sayd sawe.
And he that strives to touch the starre,
Oft stombles at a strawe.

> *Ibid. July, Line 97*

For deeds doe die, how ever noblie
donne,
And thoughts of men do as themselves
decay,
But wise wordes taught in numbers for
to runne,
Recorded by the Muses, live for ay.

> *The Ruines of Time. Line 400*

Full little knowest thou that hast not
tride,
What hell it is, in suing long to bide:
To loose good dayes, that might be
better spent;
To wast long nights in pensive discontent;
To speed to-day, to be put back to-
morrow;
To feed on hope, to pine with feare and
sorrow.

> *Mother Hubberds Tale. Line 895*

To fret thy soule with crosses and with
cares;

[1] See Heywood, page 13.

To eate thy heart through comfortlesse
   dispaires; [1]
To fawne, to crowche, to waite, to ride,
   to ronne,
To spend, to give, to want, to be undonne.
Unhappie wight, born to desastrous
   end,
That doth his life in so long tendance
   spend.
> *Mother Hubberds Tale. Line 903*

Hereby I learned have, not to despise,
What ever thing seemes small in common eyes.[2]
> *Visions of the Worlds Vanitie. Line 69*

What more felicitie can fall to creature,
Than to enjoy delight with libertie.
> *Muiopotmos: or The Fate of
> the Butterflie. Line 209*

I hate the day, because it lendeth light
To see all things, and not my love to
   see.
> *Daphnaida. Line 407*

A sweet attractive kinde of grace,
A full assurance given by lookes,
Continuall comfort in a face,
The lineaments of Gospell bookes,
  I trowe that countenance cannot lie,
  Whose thoughts are legible in the eie.
> *An Elegie, or Friends Passion,
> for his Astrophill* (SIR PHILIP
> SIDNEY). *Line 103* [3]

Was never eie, did see that face,
Was never eare, did heare that tong,
Was never minde, did minde his grace,
That ever thought the travell long,
  But eies, and eares, and ev'ry
    thought,
  Were with his sweete perfections
    caught.
> *Ibid. Line 109*

---

[1] Eat not thy heart; which forbids to afflict
our souls, and waste them with vexatious
cares. — PLUTARCH: *Of the Training of Children*
        But suffered idleness
  To eat his heart away.
  BRYANT: *Homer's Iliad, Book I, Line 319*
[2] Who hath despised the day of small
things. — ZECHARIAH, *IV, 10*
[3] This elegy was printed anonymously in a
miscellany, *The Phoenix' Next* [1593]. It has
been erroneously ascribed to Mathew Roydon
[1580-1622].

Death slue not him, but he made death
   his ladder to the skies.
> *An Epitaph upon Sir Philip Sidney.
> Line 20*

And drizling drops that often doe redound,
The firmest flint doth in continuance
   weare.[1]
> *Amoretti. Sonnet 18*

Tell her the joyous time wil not be
   staid
Unlesse she doe him by the forelock
   take.[2]
> *Ibid. Sonnet 70*

Behold whiles she before the altar
   stands
Hearing the holy priest that to her
   speakes
And blesseth her with his two happy
   hands.
> *Epithalamion. Line 223*

For of the soule the bodie forme doth
   take:
For soule is forme, and doth the bodie
   make.
> *An Hymne in Honour of Beautie.
> Line 132*

For all that faire is, is by nature good; [3]
That is a signe to know the gentle blood.
> *Ibid. Line 139*

Sweete Themmes runne softly, till I
   end my Song.
> *Prothalamion. Refrain*

It was the time when rest the gift of
   Gods
Sweetely sliding into the eyes of men,
Doth drowne in the forgetfulnesse of
   slepe,
The carefull travailes of the painefull
   day.
> *Sonnet 1*

I was promised on a time
To have reason for my rhyme;
From that time unto this season,

---

[1] See Lyly, page 23.
[2] Take Time by the forelock. — THALES of
Miletus [636-546 B.C.]
[3] The hand that hath made you fair hath
made you good. — SHAKESPEARE: *Measure
for Measure, Act III, Sc. 1, L. 182*

I received nor rhyme nor reason.[1]
> *Lines on his Promised Pension*
> (*Quoted by* THOMAS FULLER *in*
> *Worthies of England* [*1662*],
> *Vol. 2, Page 379*)

FULKE GREVILLE,
LORD BROOKE
[1554–1628]

O wearisome condition of humanity!
> *Mustapha. Act V, Sc. 4*
And out of mind as soon as out of sight.[2]
> *Sonnet LVI*

SIR PHILIP SIDNEY
[1554–1586]

Sweet food of sweetly uttered knowledge.
> *Defence of Poesy*
He cometh unto you with a tale which holdeth children from play, and old men from the chimney-corner.
> *Ibid.*
I never heard the old song of Percy and Douglas that I found not my heart moved more than with a trumpet.
> *Ibid.*
High-erected thoughts seated in the heart of courtesy.[3]
> *Arcadia. Book I*
They are never alone that are accompanied with noble thoughts.[4]
> *Ibid.*

---

[1] Rhyme nor reason. — BLANCHET: *Pierre Patelin,* quoted by Tyndale in 1530. *Farce du Vendeur des Lieures,* sixteenth century. PEELE: *Edward I.* SHAKESPEARE: *Merry Wives of Windsor, Act V, Sc. 5, L. 135; Comedy of Errors, Act II, Sc. 2, L. 49; As You Like It, Act III, Sc. 2, L. 424*

Sir Thomas More advised an author, who had sent him his manuscript to read, "to put it in rhyme." Which being done, Sir Thomas said, "Yea, marry, now it is somewhat, for now it is rhyme; before it was neither rhyme nor reason."

[2] See Thomas à Kempis, page 9.

Out of sight and out of mind. — ROBERT BROWNING: *The Inn Album, Canto I*

[3] Great thoughts come from the heart. — VAUVENARGUES: *Maxim CXXVII*

[4] He never is alone that is accompanied with noble thoughts. — FLETCHER: *Love's Cure, Act III, Sc. 3*

Many-headed multitude.[1]
> *Arcadia. Book II*
My dear, my better half.
> *Ibid. Book III*
"Fool!" said my muse to me, "look in thy heart, and write." [2]
> *Astrophel and Stella*
With how sad steps, O Moon, thou climb'st the skies!
> *Ibid.*
Have I caught my heav'nly jewel.[3]
> *Ibid. Second Song*
My true-love hath my heart, and I have his,
By just exchange one for the other given:
I hold his dear, and mine he cannot miss,
There never was a better bargain driven.
> *The Bargain. Stanza 1*

THOMAS LODGE
[1558?–1625]

Love in my bosom like a bee
  Doth suck his sweet.
> *Rosalind*
Her paps are centres of delight,
Her breasts are orbs of heavenly frame.
> *Ibid.*

GEORGE PEELE
[1558–1597]

His golden locks time hath to silver turned;
  O time too swift! O swiftness never ceasing!
His youth 'gainst time and age hath ever spurned,
  But spurned in vain; youth waneth by encreasing.
> *Polyhymnia. The Aged Man-at-Arms, Stanza 1*

---

[1] Many-headed multitude. — SHAKESPEARE: *Coriolanus, Act II, Sc. 3, L. 18*

This many-headed monster, Multitude. — DANIEL: *History of the Civil War, Book II, St. 13*

[2] Look, then, into thine heart and write. — LONGFELLOW: *Voices of the Night, Prelude*

[3] Quoted by Shakespeare in *Merry Wives of Windsor, Act III, Sc. 3, L. 45*

His helmet now shall make a hive for
    bees,
    And lovers' songs be turned to holy
      psalms;
A man-at-arms must now serve on his
    knees,
    And feed on prayers, which are old
      age's alms.
      Polyhymnia. The Aged Man-at-
        Arms, Stanza 2
My merry, merry, merry roundelay
Concludes with Cupid's curse:
They that do change old love for new,
  Pray gods, they change for worse!
            Cupid's Curse

GEORGE CHAPMAN
[1559–1634]

None ever loved but at first sight they
  loved.[1]
      The Blind Beggar of Alexandria
An ill weed grows apace.[2]
       An Humorous Day's Mirth
Black is a pearl in a woman's eye.[3]
            Ibid.
Exceeding fair she was not; and yet fair
In that she never studied to be fairer
Than Nature made her.
        All Fools. Act I, Sc. 1
I tell thee Love is Nature's second sun,
Causing a spring of virtues where he
  shines.
            Ibid.
Cornelia. What flowers are these?
Gazetta. The pansy this.
Cornelia. Oh, that's for lovers'
    thoughts.[4]
        Ibid. Act II, Sc. 1
Fortune, the great commandress of the
  world,
Hath divers ways to advance her fol-
  lowers:

---

[1] Who ever loved that loved not at first
sight? — MARLOWE: *Hero and Leander*
  SHAKESPEARE: *As You Like It, Act III,
Sc. 5, L. 82*
  I saw and loved. — GIBBON: *Memoirs, Vol.
I, P. 106*
[2] See Heywood, page 14.
[3] Black men are pearls in beauteous ladies'
eyes. — SHAKESPEARE: *Two Gentlemen of Verona, Act V, Sc. 2, L. 12*
[4] There is pansies, that's for thoughts. —
SHAKESPEARE: *Hamlet, Act IV, Sc. 5, L. 175*

To some she gives honour without de-
  serving,
To other some, deserving without hon-
  our.
        All Fools. Act V, Sc. 1
Young men think old men are fools;
but old men know young men are fools.
            Ibid.
For one heat, all know, doth drive out
  another,
One passion doth expel another still.[1]
    Monsieur D'Olive. Act V, Sc. 1
To put a girdle round about the world.[2]
    Bussy D'Ambois. Act I, Sc. 1
His deeds inimitable, like the sea
That shuts still as it opes, and leaves no
  tracts
Nor prints of precedent for poor men's
  facts.
            Ibid.
        So our lives
In acts exemplary, not only win
Ourselves good names, but doth to
  others give
Matter for virtuous deeds, by which we
  live.[3]
            Ibid.
Who to himself is law no law doth need,
Offends no law, and is a king indeed.
        Ibid. Act II, Sc. 1
Give me a spirit that on this life's rough
  sea
Loves t' have his sails fill'd with a lusty
  wind,
Even till his sail-yards tremble, his
  masts crack,
And his rapt ship run on her side so
  low
That she drinks water, and her keel
  plows air.
    Conspiracy of Charles, Duke of
      Byron. Act III, Sc. 1

---

[1] One fire burns out another's burning,
  One pain is lessened by another's anguish.
  SHAKESPEARE: *Romeo and Juliet, Act I,
                  Sc. 2, L. 47*
[2] I'll put a girdle round about the earth. —
SHAKESPEARE: *Midsummer-Night's Dream,
Act II, Sc. 1, L. 175*
[3] Lives of great men all remind us
  We can make our lives sublime.
  LONGFELLOW: *A Psalm of Life*

Words writ in waters.[1]
Revenge for Honour. Act V, Sc. 2
They're only truly great who are truly
good.[2]
Ibid.
Keep thy shop, and thy shop will
keep thee.[3] Light gains make heavy
purses. 'Tis good to be merry and wise.[4]
Eastward Ho.[5] Act I, Sc. 1
Make ducks and drakes with shillings.
Ibid.
Only a few industrious Scots perhaps,
who indeed are dispersed over the face
of the whole earth. But as for them,
there are no greater friends to Englishmen and England, when they are out
on't, in the world, than they are. And
for my own part, I would a hundred
thousand of them were there [Vir-
ginia]; for we are all one countrymen
now, ye know, and we should find ten
times more comfort of them there than
we do here.[6]
Ibid. Act III, Sc. 2
Enough's as good as a feast.[7]
Ibid.
Fair words never hurt the tongue.[8]
Ibid. Act IV, Sc. 1
Let pride go afore, shame will follow
after.[9]
. *Ibid.*

[1] All your better deeds shall be in water
writ, but this in marble. — BEAUMONT AND
FLETCHER: *Philaster, Act V, Sc. 3*
Here lies one whose name was writ in water.
— *Keats's own Epitaph*
[2] To be noble we'll be good. — *Winifreda*
(Percy's *Reliques*)
'T is only noble to be good. — TENNYSON:
Lady Clara Vere de Vere, Stanza 7
[3] The same in Franklin's *Poor Richard*
[4] See Heywood, page 11.
[5] By Chapman, Jonson, and Marston.
[6] This is the famous passage that gave offence to James I., and caused the imprisonment of the authors. The leaves containing it
were cancelled and reprinted, and it only occurs in a few of the original copies. — RICH-
ARD HERNE SHEPHERD
[7] *Dives and Pauper* [1493]. GASCOIGNE:
Memories [1575]. FIELDING: *Covent Garden
Tragedy, Act II, Sc. 6.* BICKERSTAFF: *Love in
a Village, Act III, Sc. 1.* See Heywood, page
18.
[8] See Heywood, page 13.
[9] *Ibid.*, page 14.

I will neither yield to the song of the
siren nor the voice of the hyena, the
tears of the crocodile [1] nor the howling
of the wolf.
Eastward Ho. Act V, Sc. 1
Promise is most given when the least
is said.
Musæus of Hero and Leander

SIR JOHN HARRINGTON
[1561–1612]

Treason doth never prosper; what's the
reason?
Why, if it prosper, none dare call it
treason.[2]
Epigrams. Of Treason
Fortune, men say, doth give too much
to many,
But yet she never gave enough to any.
Ibid. Of Fortune
The readers and the hearers like my
books,
But yet some writers cannot them di-
gest;
But what care I? for when I make a
feast
I would my guests should praise it, not
the cooks.
*Ibid. Of Writers who Carp at
Other Men's Books*

ROBERT SOUTHWELL
[1561–1595]

What thought can think, another
thought can mend.
Look Home
Let this suffice, by this conceive the
rest,
He should, he could, he would, he did
the best.
Ibid.

[1] These crocodile tears. — BURTON: *Anat-
omy of Melancholy, Part III, Sect. 2, Memb.
2, Subsect. 4*
She's false, false as the tears of crocodiles.
— SIR JOHN SUCKLING: *The Sad One, Act IV,
Sc. 5*
[2] Prosperum ac felix scelus
Virtus vocatur
(Successful and fortunate crime is called vir-
tue).
SENECA: *Herc. Furens, II, 250*

Time goes by turns, and chances change
    by course,
From foul to fair, from better hap to
    worse.
Times Go by Turns

No joy so great but runneth to an end,
No hap so hard but may in time amend.
Ibid.

When sun is set the little stars will
    shine.
Scorn Not the Least

He that high growth on cedars did be-
    stow,
Gave also lowly mushrumps leave to
    grow.
Ibid.

May never was the month of love,
    For May is full of flowers;
But rather April, wet by kind,
    For love is full of showers.
Love's Servile Lot

All states with others' ruin built
    To ruin run amain.
No chance of Fortune's calms
Can cast my fortune down.
When Fortune smiles, I smile to think
How quickly she will frown.
I Envy Not Their Hap

As I in hoary winter night stood shiver-
    ing in the snow,
Surprised was I with sudden heat which
    made my heart to glow;
And lifting up a fearful eye to view
    what fire was near
A pretty Babe all burning bright did
    in the air appear.
*The Burning Babe. (A Christ-
mas poem praised by* BEN JON-
SON)

SAMUEL DANIEL
[1562–1619]

And for the few that only lend their ear,
That few is all the world.
Musophilus [*1599*]. *Stanza 97*

This is the thing that I was born to do.
Ibid. Stanza 100

And who (in time) knows whither we
    may vent
The treasure of our tongue? To what
    strange shores
This gain of our best glory shall be sent

T' enrich unknowing nations with
    our stores?
What worlds in the yet unformed Oc-
    cident
May come refin'd with th' accents
    that are ours? [1]
Musophilus [*1599*]. *Stanza 163*

As that the walls worn thin, permit the
    mind
To look out thorough, and his frailty
    find.[2]
History of the Civil War. [*1609*].
Book IV, Stanza 84

Unless above himself he can
Erect himself, how poor a thing is man!
*To the Countess of Cumberland.
Stanza 12*

Care-charmer Sleep, son of the sable
    Night,
Brother to Death, in silent darkness
    born.
Sonnet: To Delia

Make me to say when all my griefs are
    gone,
Happy the heart that sighed for such a
    one!
Sonnet: I Must Not Grieve

Love is a sickness full of woes,
    All remedies refusing.
Hymen's Triumph

MICHAEL DRAYTON
[1563–1631]

Had in him those brave translunary
    things
That the first poets had.
(*Said of* MARLOWE) *To Henry
Reynolds, of Poets and Poesy*

For that fine madness still he did re-
    tain
Which rightly should possess a poet's
    brain.
Ibid.

---

[1] Westward the course of empire takes its
way. — BERKELEY: *On the Prospect of Planting Arts and Learning in America*

[2] The soul's dark cottage, batter'd and de-
    cay'd,
  Lets in new light through chinks that
    Time has made.
  WALLER: *Verses upon his Divine Poesy*

The coast was clear.[1]

Nymphidia

Battles so bravely won
Have ever to the sun
  By fame been raised.

The Ballad of Agincourt. Stanza 4

O, when shall Englishmen
With such acts fill a pen,
Or England breed again
  Such a King Harry?

Ibid. Stanza 15

Since there's no help, come let us kiss
  and part.

Sonnet: Love's Farewell

When faith is kneeling by his bed of
  death,
And innocence is closing up his eyes,
Now if thou wouldst, when all have
  given him over,
From death to life thou might'st him
  yet recover.

Ibid.

CHRISTOPHER MARLOWE
[1564–1593]

Comparisons are odious.[2]

Lust's Dominion. Act III, Sc. 4

I'm armed with more than complete
  steel, —
The justice of my quarrel.[3]

Ibid.

Who ever loved that loved not at first
  sight?[4]

Hero and Leander

Come live with me, and be my love;
And we will all the pleasures prove
That hills and valleys, dales and fields,
Woods or steepy mountain yields.

The Passionate Shepherd to his Love

---

[1] SOMERVILLE: *The Night-Walker.*
[2] See Fortescue, page 9.
[3] Thrice is he armed that hath his quarrel
  just,
  And he but naked, though locked up in
    steel,
  Whose conscience with injustice is cor-
    rupted.
SHAKESPEARE: *Henry VI, Part II, Act III,*
  Sc. 2, L. 233
[4] Quoted in Shakespeare's *As You Like It,*
Act III, Sc. 5, L. 82
Compare Chapman, page 28.

By shallow rivers, to whose falls [1]
Melodious birds sing madrigals.

The Passionate Shepherd to his Love

And I will make thee beds of roses
And a thousand fragrant posies.[1]

Ibid.

Infinite riches in a little room.

The Jew of Malta. Act I

Excess of wealth is cause of covetousness.

Ibid.

Now will I show myself to have more
of the serpent than the dove; [2] that is,
more knave than fool.

Ibid. Act II

Love me little, love me long.[3]

Ibid. Act IV

Hell hath no limits, nor is circumscribed
In one self-place; for where we are is
  Hell,
And where Hell is, there must we ever
  be.

Faustus [1616]

When all the world dissolves,
And every creature shall be purified,
All places shall be hell that are not
  heaven.

Ibid.

Was this the face that launch'd a thousand ships,
And burnt the topless towers of Ilium? [4]
Sweet Helen, make me immortal with a
  kiss!
Her lips suck forth my soul: [5] see,
  where it flies!

Ibid.

---

[1] To shallow rivers, to whose falls
  Melodious birds sing madrigals;
  There will we make our peds of roses,
  And a thousand fragrant posies.
SHAKESPEARE: *Merry Wives of Windsor,*
  Act III, Sc. 1, L. 17 (Sung by Evans).
[2] Be ye therefore wise as serpents, and
harmless as doves. — *Matthew, X, 16*
[3] See Heywood, page 16.
[4] Was this fair face the cause, quoth she,
  Why the Grecians sacked Troy?
SHAKESPEARE: *All's Well that Ends Well,*
  Act I, Sc. 3, L. 75
[5]   Once he drew
With one long kiss my whole soul through
My lips.
  TENNYSON: *Fatima, Stanza 3*

O, thou art fairer than the evening air
Clad in the beauty of a thousand stars.
Faustus [1616]
Stand still, you ever moving spheres of
heaven,
That time may cease, and midnight
never come.
Ibid.
Cut is the branch that might have
grown full straight,
And burnèd is Apollo's laurel bough,[1]
That sometime grew within this
learnèd man.
Ibid.
Yet should there hover in their restless
heads
One thought, one grace, one wonder, at
the least,
Which into words no virtue can digest.
Tamburlaine the Great, I.
Act 5, Sc. 2
My men, like satyrs grazing on the
lawn,
Shall with their goat feet dance the
antic hay.
Edward II. Act 1, Sc. 1

WILLIAM SHAKESPEARE
[1564–1616]

From the text of W. J. Craig,
M.A.[2]

Now would I give a thousand fur-
longs of sea for an acre of barren
ground.
The Tempest. Act I, Sc. 1, Line 70
I would fain die a dry death.
Ibid. Line 73
What seest thou else
In the dark backward and abysm of
time?
Ibid. Sc. 2, Line 49
I, thus neglecting worldly ends, all ded-
icated
To closeness and the bettering of my
mind.
Ibid. Line 89

---

[1] O, withered is the garland of the war!
The soldier's pole is fallen.
SHAKESPEARE: *Antony and Cleopatra, Act*
IV, Sc. 13, L. 64
[2] *The Complete Works of Shakespeare.* Ox-
ford University Press.

By telling of it,
Made such a sinner of his memory,
To credit his own lie.
The Tempest. Act I, Sc. 2, Line 99
My library
Was dukedom large enough.
Ibid. Line 109
The very rats
Instinctively have quit it.
Ibid. Line 147
Knowing I lov'd my books, he furnish'd
me
From mine own library with volumes
that
I prize above my dukedom.
Ibid. Line 166
From the still-vexed Bermoothes.
Ibid. Line 229
I will be correspondent to command,
And do my spiriting gently.
Ibid. Line 297
Come unto these yellow sands,
And then take hands:
Courtsied when you have, and kiss'd
The wild waves whist.
Ibid. Line 375
Full fathom five thy father lies;
Of his bones are coral made;
Those are pearls that were his eyes:
Nothing of him that doth fade
But doth suffer a sea-change
Into something rich and strange.[1]
Ibid. Line 394
The fringed curtains of thine eye ad-
vance.
Ibid. Act I, Sc. 2, Line 405
Lest too light winning
Make the prize light.
Ibid. Line 448
He receives comfort like cold porridge.
Ibid. Act II, Sc. 1, Line 10
Gonzalo. Here is everything advanta-
geous to life.
Antonio. True; save means to live.
Ibid. Line 52
The golden age.[2]
Ibid. Line 175
A very ancient and fish-like smell.
Ibid. Sc. 2, Line 27

---

[1] The last three lines are inscribed on Shelley's gravestone.
[2] See Spenser, page 25.

Misery acquaints a man with strange bedfellows.
The Tempest. Act II, Sc. 2, Line 42

I shall laugh myself to death.
Ibid. Line 167

Ferdinand. Here's my hand.
Miranda. And mine, with my heart in't.
Ibid. Act III, Sc. 1, Line 89

Moon-calf.
Ibid. Sc. 2, Line 25

I am in case to justle a constable.
Ibid. Line 30

Keep a good tongue in your head.
Ibid. Line 41

He that dies pays all debts.
Ibid. Line 143

A kind
Of excellent dumb discourse.
Ibid. Sc. 3, Line 38

Do not give dalliance
Too much rein.
Ibid. Act IV, Sc. 1, Line 51

Our revels now are ended. These our actors,
As I foretold you, were all spirits, and
Are melted into air, into thin air;
And, like the baseless fabric of this vision,
The cloud-capp'd towers, the gorgeous palaces,
The solemn temples, the great globe itself,
Yea, all which it inherit, shall dissolve;
And, like this insubstantial pageant faded,
Leave not a rack behind. We are such stuff
As dreams are made on, and our little life
Is rounded with a sleep.
Ibid. Line 148

With foreheads villanous low.
Ibid. Line 252

Deeper than did ever plummet sound
I'll drown my book.
Ibid. Act V, Sc. 1, Line 56

Where the bee sucks, there suck I;
In a cowslip's bell I lie.
Ibid. Line 88

Merrily, merrily shall I live now,
Under the blossom that hangs on the bough.
The Tempest. Act V, Sc. 1, Line 93

'Tis a chronicle of day by day.
Ibid. Line 163

O brave new world,
That has such people in't!
Ibid. Line 183

Let us not burden our remembrances
With a heaviness that's gone.
Ibid. Line 199

I have been in such a pickle since I saw you last.
Ibid. Line 282

My ending is despair.
Ibid. Epilogue, Line 15

Home-keeping youth have ever homely wits.
*The Two Gentlemen of Verona.
Act I, Sc. 1, Line 2*

I have no other but a woman's reason:
I think him so, because I think him so.
Ibid. Sc. 2, Line 23

They do not love that do not show their love.
Ibid. Line 31

O! they love least that let men know their love.
Ibid. Line 32

Since maids, in modesty, say "No" to that
Which they would have the profferer construe "Ay."
Ibid. Line 53

What is't that you took up so gingerly?
Ibid. Line 68

O! how this spring of love resembleth
The uncertain glory of an April day!
Ibid. Sc. 3, Line 84

O jest unseen, inscrutable, invisible,
As a nose on a man's face,[1] or a weather-cock on a steeple.
Ibid. Act II, Sc. 1, Line 145

He makes sweet music with th' enamell'd stones,
Giving a gentle kiss to every sedge
He overtaketh in his pilgrimage.
Ibid. Sc. 7, Line 28

---

[1] As clear and as manifest as the nose in a man's face. — BURTON: *Anatomy of Melancholy, Part III, Sect. 3, Memb. 4, Subsect. 1*

That man that hath a tongue, I say, is
no man,
If with his tongue he cannot win a
woman.
> *The Two Gentlemen of Verona.*
> *Act III, Sc. 1, Line 104*

To make a virtue of necessity.[1]
> *Ibid. Act IV, Sc. 1, Line 62*

Who is Sylvia? what is she?
That all our swains commend her?
> *Ibid. Sc. 2, Line 40*

How use doth breed a habit in a man! [2]
> *Ibid. Act V, Sc. 4, Line 1*

I will make a Star-chamber matter of it.
> *The Merry Wives of Windsor.*
> *Act I, Sc. 1, Line 2*

All his successors gone before him
have done 't; and all his ancestors that
come after him may.
> *Ibid. Line 14*

Seven hundred pounds and possibilities
is goot gifts.
> *Ibid. Line 65*

Mine host of the Garter.
> *Ibid. Line 146*

I had rather than forty shillings I
had my Book of Songs and Sonnets
here.
> *Ibid. Line 205*

If there be no great love in the beginning, yet heaven may decrease it
upon better acquaintance, when we are
married and have more occasion to
know one another: I hope, upon familiarity will grow more contempt.[3]
> *Ibid. Line 255*

O base Hungarian wight! wilt thou the
spigot wield?
> *Ibid. Sc. 3, Line 21*

"Convey," the wise it call. "Steal!"
foh! a fico for the phrase!
> *Ibid. Line 30*

I am almost out at heels.
> *Ibid. Line 32*

Thou art the Mars of malcontents.
> *Ibid. Line 111*

Here will be an old abusing of God's
patience and the king's English.
> *The Merry Wives of Windsor.*
> *Act I, Sc. 4, Line 5*

Thereby hangs a tale.[1]
> *Ibid. Line 155*

Dispense with trifles.
> *Ibid. Act II, Sc. 1, Line 47*

We burn daylight.[2]
> *Ibid. Line 54*

There's the humour of it.
> *Ibid. Line 139*

Faith, thou hast some crotchets in thy
head now.
> *Ibid. Line 158*

Why, then the world's mine oyster,
Which I with sword will open.
> *Ibid. Sc. 2, Line 2*

This is the short and the long of it.
> *Ibid. Line 62*

Unless experience be a jewel.
> *Ibid. Line 216*

Like a fair house built on another
man's ground.
> *Ibid. Line 229*

Better three hours too soon than a minute too late.
> *Ibid. Line 332*

We have some salt of our youth in us.
> *Ibid. Sc. 3, Line 50*

I cannot tell what the dickens his name
is.[3]
> *Ibid. Act III, Sc. 2, Line 20*

What a taking was he in, when your
husband asked who was in the basket!
> *Ibid. Sc. 3, Line 190*

O, what a world of vile ill-favour'd
faults
Looks handsome in three hundred
pounds a year!
> *Ibid. Sc. 4, Line 32*

A woman would run through fire and
water for such a kind heart.
> *Ibid. Line 106*

---

[1] See Chaucer, page 4.
[2] Custom is almost second nature. — PLU-
TARCH: *Preservation of Health*
[3] Familiarity breeds contempt. — PUBLIUS
SYRUS: *Maxim 640*

[1] Also in *As You Like It, Act II, Sc. 7,
L. 26; The Taming of the Shrew, Act IV,
Sc. 1, L. 60; Othello, Act III, Sc. 1, L. 8;*
RABELAIS: *Book V, Chap. 4*
[2] Also in *Romeo and Juliet, Act I, Sc. 4,
L. 43*
Burn daylight. — DRYDEN: *The Maiden
Queen, Act II, Sc. 1*
[3] What the dickens! — THOMAS HEYWOOD:
Edward IV, Act III, Sc. 1

I have a kind of alacrity in sinking.
The Merry Wives of Windsor.
Act III, Sc. 5, Line 13
As good luck would have it.[1]
Ibid. Line 86
The rankest compound of villanous
smell that ever offended nostril.
Ibid. Line 95
A man of my kidney.
Ibid. Line 119
So curses all Eve's daughters, of what
complexion soever.
Ibid. Act IV, Sc. 2, Line 24
Wives may be merry, and yet honest
too.
Ibid. Line 110
There is an old tale goes that Herne the
hunter
Sometime a keeper here in Windsor
forest,
Doth all the winter-time, at still mid-
night,
Walk round about an oak, with great
ragg'd horns.[2]
Ibid. Sc. 4, Line 29
This is the third time; I hope good
luck lies in odd numbers. . . . There
is divinity in odd numbers, either in
nativity, chance, or death.
Ibid. Act V, Sc. 1, Line 2
Life is a shuttle.
Ibid. Line 25
Cry "mum."
Ibid. Sc. 2, Line 6
Better a little chiding than a great deal
of heartbreak.
Ibid. Sc. 3, Line 10
Honi soit qui mal y pense.[3]
Ibid. Sc. 5, Line 75

[1] As ill luck would have it. — CERVANTES:
Don Quixote, Pt. I, Bk. I, Ch. II
[2] There is a tradition that Herne ranged
near a tree, known as Herne's Oak, in Windsor Park. The tree was blown down in 1863,
when its age was estimated as 650 years.
Queen Victoria planted a young oak in its
place. The novel, *Windsor Castle*, by WIL-
LIAM HARRISON AINSWORTH [1805–1882] tells
of various appearances of Herne.
[3] Shamed be he who thinks evil of it. —
Motto of the Order of the Garter, founded by
Edward III in 1348
St. George he was for England; St. Dennis
  was for France;
Sing, *Honi soit qui mal y pense.*

Spirits are not finely touch'd
But to fine issues, nor Nature never
lends
The smallest scruple of her excellence
But, like a thrifty goddess, she deter-
mines
Herself the glory of a creditor,
Both thanks and use.
Measure for Measure. Act I,
Sc. 1, Line 35
He was ever precise in promise-keeping.
Ibid. Sc. 2, Line 80
Good counsellors lack no clients.
Ibid. Line 115
Who may, in the ambush of my name,
strike home.
Ibid. Sc. 3, Line 41
I hold you as a thing ensky'd and
sainted.
Ibid. Sc. 4, Line 34
A man whose blood
Is very snow-broth; one who never feels
The wanton stings and motions of the
sense.
Ibid. Line 57
He arrests him on it;
And follows close the rigour of the
statute,
To make him an example.
Ibid. Line 66
Our doubts are traitors,
And make us lose the good we oft might
win
By fearing to attempt.
Ibid. Line 78
The jury, passing on the prisoner's life,
May in the sworn twelve have a thief
or two
Guiltier than him they try.
Ibid. Act II, Sc. 1, Line 19
Some rise by sin, and some by virtue
fall.
Ibid. Line 38
Great with child, and longing for stewed
prunes.
Ibid. Line 94
They are not China dishes, but very
good dishes.
Ibid. Line 100

St. George for England, in PERCY: *Reliques*
of Ancient Poetry, Third Series, Book III

This will last out a night in Russia,[1]
When nights are longest there.
> *Measure for Measure. Act II,*
>   *Sc. 1, Line 144*

His face is the worst thing about him.
>   *Ibid. Line 167*

Condemn the fault, and not the actor
of it?
>   *Ibid. Sc. 2, Line 37*

No ceremony that to great ones 'longs,
Not the king's crown, nor the deputed
sword,
The marshal's truncheon, nor the
judge's robe,
Become them with one half so good a
grace
As mercy does.[2]
>   *Ibid. Line 59*

Why, all the souls that were, were forfeit once;
And He that might the vantage best
have took
Found out the remedy. How would you
be,
If He, which is the top of judgment,
should
But judge you as you are?
>   *Ibid. Line 73*

The law hath not been dead, though it
hath slept.
>   *Ibid. Line 90*

O, it is excellent
To have a giant's strength; but it is
tyrannous
To use it like a giant.
>   *Ibid. Line 107*

But man, proud man,
Drest in a little brief authority,
Most ignorant of what he's most as-
sured,
His glassy essence, like an angry ape,
Plays such fantastic tricks before high
heaven
As make the angels weep.
>   *Ibid. Sc. 2, Line 117*

That in the captain's but a choleric
word
Which in the soldier is flat blasphemy.
>   *Ibid. Line 130*

It oft falls out,
To have what we would have, we speak
not what we mean.
>   *Measure for Measure. Act II,*
>   *Sc. 4, Line 118*

I'll tell the world.[1]
>   *Ibid. Line 154*

The miserable have no other medicine,
But only hope.
>   *Ibid. Act III, Sc. 1, Line 2*

A breath thou art,
Servile to all the skyey influences.
>   *Ibid. Line 8*

Palsied eld.
>   *Ibid. Line 36*

The sense of death is most in appre-
hension;
And the poor beetle, that we tread upon,
In corporal sufferance finds a pang as
great
As when a giant dies.
>   *Ibid. Line 76*

The cunning livery of hell.
>   *Ibid. Line 93*

Ay, but to die, and go we know not
where;
To lie in cold obstruction and to rot;
This sensible warm motion to become
A kneaded clod; and the delighted
spirit
To bathe in fiery floods, or to reside
In thrilling region of thick-ribbed ice;
To be imprison'd in the viewless winds,
And blown with restless violence round
about
The pendent world.
>   *Ibid. Line 116*

The weariest and most loathed worldly
life
That age, ache, penury, and imprison-
ment
Can lay on nature, is a paradise
To what we fear of death.
>   *Ibid. Line 127*

I have no superfluous leisure.
>   *Ibid. Line 156*

---

[1] Will burn a Poland winter. — *The Comedy of Errors, Act III, Sc. 2, L. 101*
[2] Compare Portia's words in *The Merchant
of Venice, Act IV, Sc. 4, Lines 184–202*

[1] Let me tell the world. — *King Henry IV,
Part I, Act V, Sc. 2, L. 65*
Ay, tell the world! — BROWNING: *Paracel-
sus, Part II*

The hand that hath made you fair hath made you good.[1]
> *Measure for Measure. Act III,*
> *Sc. 1, Line 182*

Virtue is bold, and goodness never fearful.
> *Ibid. Line 214*

There, at the moated grange, resides this dejected Mariana.[2]
> *Ibid. Line 279*

Pygmalion's images, newly made woman.
> *Ibid. Sc. 2, Line 48*

This news is old enough, yet it is every day's news.
> *Ibid. Line 249*

He who the sword of heaven will bear
Should be as holy as severe.
> *Ibid. Line 283*

O, what may man within him hide,
Though angel on the outward side!
> *Ibid. Line 293*

Take, O take those lips away,
That so sweetly were forsworn;
And those eyes, the break of day,
Lights that do mislead the morn:
But my kisses bring again, bring again;
Seals of love, but sealed in vain, sealed in vain.[3]
> *Ibid. Act IV, Sc. 1, Line 1*

Every true man's apparel fits your thief.
> *Ibid. Sc. 2, Line 46*

Death's a great disguiser.
> *Ibid. Line 185*

We would, and we would not.
> *Ibid. Sc. 4, Line 37*

A forted residence 'gainst the tooth of time
And razure of oblivion.
> *Ibid. Act V, Sc. 1, Line 12*

---

[1] See Spenser, page 26.
[2] "Mariana in the moated grange." — The motto used by TENNYSON for the poem *Mariana*.
[3] This song occurs in *Act V, Sc. 2* of BEAUMONT AND FLETCHER'S *Bloody Brother*, with the following additional stanza: —
> Hide, O hide those hills of snow,
>   Which thy frozen bosom bears,
> On whose tops the pinks that grow
>   Are of those that April wears!
> But first set my poor heart free,
> Bound in those icy chains by thee.

Truth is truth
To the end of reckoning.
> *Measure for Measure. Act V,*
> *Sc. 1, Line 45*

Neither maid, widow, nor wife.
> *Ibid. Line 173*

They say best men are moulded out of faults.
And, for the most, become much more the better
For being a little bad.
> *Ibid. Line 440*

What's mine is yours, and what is yours is mine.
> *Ibid. Line 539*

The pleasing punishment that women bear.
> *The Comedy of Errors. Act I,*
> *Sc. 1, Line 46*

We may pity, though not pardon thee.
> *Ibid. Line 97*

To tell sad stories of my own mishaps.
> *Ibid. Line 120*

A wretched soul, bruised with adversity.
> *Ibid. Act II, Sc. 1, Line 34*

Every why hath a wherefore.[1]
> *Ibid. Sc. 2, Line 45*

Neither rhyme nor reason.[2]
> *Ibid. Line 49*

There's a time for all things.[3]
> *Ibid. Line 67*

There's no time for a man to recover his hair that grows bald by nature.
> *Ibid. Line 74*

What he hath scanted men in hair, he hath given them in wit.
> *Ibid. Line 83*

Time himself is bald, and therefore to the world's end will have bald followers.
> *Ibid. Line 109*

Small cheer and great welcome makes a merry feast.
> *Ibid. Act III, Sc. 1, Line 26*

There is something in the wind.
> *Ibid. Line 69*

We'll pluck a crow together.
> *Ibid. Line 83*

---

[1] For every why he had a wherefore. — BUTLER: *Hudibras, Pt. I, C. I, L. 132*
[2] See Spenser, page 26.
[3] To every thing there is a season, and a time to every purpose under the heaven — *Ecclesiastes, III, 1*

For slander lives upon succession,
For ever housed where it gets posses-
sion.
The Comedy of Errors.
Act III, Sc. 1, Line 105
Be not thy tongue thy own shame's ora-
tor.
Ibid. Sc. 2, Line 10
Ill deeds are doubled with an evil word.
Ibid. Line 20
A back-friend, a shoulder-clapper.
Ibid. Act IV, Sc. 2, Line 37
Give me your hand and let me feel your
pulse.
Ibid. Sc. 4, Line 54
Unquiet meals make ill digestions.
Ibid. Act V, Sc. 1, Line 74
One Pinch, a hungry lean-faced villain,
A mere anatomy.[1]
Ibid. Line 238
A needy, hollow-eyed, sharp-looking
wretch,
A living-dead man.
Ibid. Line 241
I hope I shall have leisure to make good.
Ibid. Line 378
He hath indeed better bettered expecta-
tion.
Much Ado about Nothing. Act I,
Sc. 1, Line 16
How much better is it to weep at joy
than to joy at weeping.
Ibid. Line 28
A very valiant trencher-man.
Ibid. Line 52
There's a skirmish of wit between them.
Ibid. Line 64
He wears his faith but as the fashion of
his hat.
Ibid. Line 76
The gentleman is not in your books.
Ibid. Line 79
What! my dear Lady Disdain! are you
yet living?
Ibid. Line 123
I would my horse had the speed of
your tongue, and so good a continuer.
Ibid. Line 151
Shall I never see a bachelor of three-
score again?
Ibid. Line 209

[1] See Burton, page 123.

Benedick the married man.
Much Ado about Nothing.
Act I, Sc. 1, Line 278
He is of a very melancholy disposition.
Ibid. Act II, Sc. 1, Line 6
I could not endure a husband with
a beard on his face: I had rather lie in
the woollen.
Ibid. Line 31
He that hath a beard is more than a
youth, and he that hath no beard is less
than a man.
Ibid. Line 38
As merry as the day is long.
Ibid. Line 52
I have a good eye, uncle; I can see a
church by daylight.
Ibid. Line 86
Speak low, if you speak love.
Ibid. Line 104
Friendship is constant in all other things
Save in the office and affairs of love:
Therefore, all hearts in love use their
own tongues;
Let every eye negotiate for itself,
And trust no agent.
Ibid. Line 184
Silence is the perfectest herald of
joy: I were but little happy, if I could
say how much.
Ibid. Line 319
It keeps on the windy side of care.[1]
Ibid. Line 328
There was a star danced, and under
that was I born.
Ibid. Line 351
I will tell you my drift.[2]
Ibid. Line 406
He was wont to speak plain and to
the purpose.
Ibid. Sc. 3, Line 19
Her hair shall be of what colour it
please God.
Ibid. Line 36
Sigh no more, ladies, sigh no more,
Men were deceivers ever;
One foot in sea and one on shore;
To one thing constant never.
Ibid. Line 65

[1] The windy side of the law. — *Twelfth-
Night, Act III, Sc. 4, L. 183*
[2] We know your drift. — *Coriolanus, Act
III, Sc. 3, L. 114*

Sits the wind in that corner?
> *Much Ado about Nothing.*
> *Act II, Sc. 3, Line 108*

Bait the hook well: this fish will bite.
> *Ibid. Line 121*

Happy are they that hear their detractions, and can put them to mending.
> *Ibid. Line 248*

Shall quips and sentences and these paper bullets of the brain awe a man from the career of his humour? No; the world must be peopled. When I said I would die a bachelor, I did not think I should live till I were married.
> *Ibid. Line 260*

The pleasant'st angling is to see the fish
Cut with her golden oars the silver stream,
And greedily devour the treacherous bait.
> *Ibid. Act III, Sc. 1, Line 26*

From the crown of his head to the sole of his foot,[1] he is all mirth.
> *Ibid. Sc. 2, Line 9*

He hath a heart as sound as a bell.
> *Ibid. Line 12*

Every one can master a grief but he that has it.
> *Ibid. Line 28*

Are you good men and true?
> *Ibid. Sc. 3, Line 1*

To be a well-favoured man is the gift of fortune; but to write and read comes by nature.
> *Ibid. Line 14*

You shall comprehend all vagrom men.
> *Ibid. Line 25*

2 Watch. How, if a' will not stand?
Dogberry. Why, then, take no note of him, but let him go; and presently call the rest of the watch together, and thank God you are rid of a knave.
> *Ibid. Line 28*

If they make you not then the better answer, you may say they are not the men you took them for.
> *Ibid. Line 49*

[1] From the crown of his head to the sole of the foot. — PLINY: *Natural History, Book VII, Chap. XVII.* BEAUMONT AND FLETCHER: *The Honest Man's Fortune, Act II, Sc. 2.* MIDDLETON: *A Mad World, etc.*

They that touch pitch will be defiled.[1]
> *Much Ado about Nothing.*
> *Act III, Sc. 3, Line 61*

The most peaceable way for you if you do take a thief, is to let him show himself what he is and steal out of your company.
> *Ibid. Line 62*

The fashion wears out more apparel than the man.
> *Ibid. Line 147*

I thank God, I am as honest as any man living, that is an old man and no honester than I.
> *Ibid. Sc. 5, Line 15*

Comparisons are odorous.
> *Ibid. Line 18*

A good old man, sir; he will be talking: as they say, When the age is in, the wit is out.
> *Ibid. Line 36*

O! what men dare do! what men may do! what men daily do, not knowing what they do!
> *Ibid. Act IV, Sc. 1, Line 19*

O! what authority and show of truth
Can cunning sin cover itself withal!
> *Ibid. Line 35*

> I have mark'd
A thousand blushing apparitions
To start into her face; a thousand innocent shames
In angel whiteness beat away those blushes.
> *Ibid. Line 160*

> For it so falls out
That what we have we prize not to the worth
Whiles we enjoy it, but being lack'd and lost,
Why, then we rack the value; then we find
The virtue that possession would not show us
Whiles it was ours.
> *Ibid. Line 219*

[1] He that toucheth pitch shall be defiled therewith. — *Apocrypha: Ecclesiasticus, XIII, 1*
This pitch, as ancient writers do report, doth defile; so doth the company thou keepest. — *King Henry IV, Part I, Act II, Sc. 4, L. 460*

The idea of her life shall sweetly creep
Into his study of imagination,
And every lovely organ of her life,
Shall come apparell'd in more precious
habit,
More moving-delicate, and full of life
Into the eye and prospect of his soul.
Much Ado about Nothing.
Act IV, Sc. 1, Line 226

Masters, it is proved already that you
are little better than false knaves; and
it will go near to be thought so shortly.
Ibid. Sc. 2, Line 23

Flat burglary as ever was committed.
Ibid. Line 54

Condemned into everlasting redemption.
Ibid. Line 60

O that he were here to write me down an
ass!
Ibid. Line 80

A fellow that hath had losses, and one
that hath two gowns, and every thing
handsome about him.
Ibid. Line 90

Patch grief with proverbs.
Ibid. Act V, Sc. 1, Line 17

Men
Can counsel and speak comfort to that
grief
Which they themselves not feel.
Ibid. Line 20

Charm ache with air, and agony with
words.
Ibid. Line 26

'Tis all men's office to speak patience
To those that wring under the load of
sorrow;
But no man's virtue nor sufficiency
To be so moral when he shall endure
The like himself.
Ibid. Line 27

For there was never yet philosopher
That could endure the toothache pa-
tiently.
Ibid. Line 35

Some of us will smart for it.
Ibid. Line 108

What though care killed a cat.[1]
Much Ado about Nothing.
Act V, Sc. 1, Line 135

I was not born under a rhyming planet.
Ibid. Sc. 2, Line 40

Done to death by slanderous tongues.
Ibid. Sc. 3, Line 3

Make us heirs of all eternity.
Love's Labour's Lost.
Act I, Sc. 1, Line 7

The huge army of the world's desires.
Ibid. Line 10

Or, having sworn too hard-a-keeping
oath,
Study to break it, and not break my
troth.
Ibid. Line 65

Light seeking light doth light of light
beguile.
Ibid. Line 77

Small have continual plodders ever won,
Save base authority from others'
books.
These earthly godfathers of heaven's
lights
That give a name to every fixed star,
Have no more profit of their shining
nights
That those that walk and wot not
what they are.
Ibid. Line 86

At Christmas I no more desire a rose
Than wish a snow in May's new-
fangled mirth;
But like of each thing that in season
grows.
Ibid. Line 105

A man in all the world's new fashion
planted,
That hath a mint of phrases in his brain.
Ibid. Line 163

And men sit down to that nourishment which is called supper.
Ibid. Line 237

That unlettered small-knowing soul.
Ibid. Line 251

[1] Care 'll kill a cat. — BEN JONSON: *Every Man in his Humour, Act I, Sc. 1*
Care will kill a cat. — GEORGE WITHER: *Poem* on *Christmas*

A child of our grandmother Eve, a female; or, for thy more sweet understanding, a woman.
Love's Labour's Lost.
Act I, Sc. 1, Line 263
Affliction may one day smile again; and till then, sit thee down, sorrow!
Ibid. Line 312
The world was very guilty of such a ballad some three ages since; but I think now 'tis not to be found.
Ibid. Sc. 2, Line 117
Devise, wit; write, pen; for I am for whole volumes in folio.
Ibid. Line 194
A man of sovereign parts he is esteem'd;
Well fitted in arts, glorious in arms:
Nothing becomes him ill that he would well.
Ibid. Act II, Sc. 1, Line 44
A merrier man,
Within the limit of becoming mirth,
I never spent an hour's talk withal.
Ibid. Line 66
Delivers in such apt and gracious words
That aged ears play truant at his tales,
And younger hearings are quite ravished;
So sweet and voluble is his discourse.
Ibid. Line 73
Remuneration! O! that's the Latin word for three farthings.
Ibid. Act III, Sc. 1, Line 143
A very beadle to a humorous sigh.
Ibid. Line 185
This senior-junior, giant-dwarf, Dan Cupid;
Regent of love-rhymes, lord of folded arms,
The anointed sovereign of sighs and groans,
Liege of all loiterers and malcontents.
Ibid. Line 190
A buck of the first head.
Ibid. Act IV, Sc. 2, Line 10
He hath not fed of the dainties that are bred in a book; he hath not eat paper, as it were; he hath not drunk ink.
Ibid. Line 25
Many can brook the weather that love not the wind.
Ibid. Line 34

You two are book-men.
Love's Labour's Lost.
Act IV, Sc. 2, Line 35
These are begot in the ventricle of memory, nourished in the womb of pia mater, and delivered upon the mellowing of occasion.
Ibid. Line 70
As upright as the cedar.
Ibid. Sc. 3, Line 89
For where is any author in the world
Teaches such beauty as a woman's eye?
Learning is but an adjunct to ourself.
Ibid. Line 312
It adds a precious seeing to the eye.
Ibid. Line 333
As sweet and musical
As bright Apollo's lute, strung with his hair;
And when Love speaks, the voice of all the gods
Makes heaven drowsy with the harmony.
Ibid. Line 342
From women's eyes this doctrine I derive:
They sparkle still the right Promethean fire;
They are the books, the arts, the academes,
That show, contain, and nourish all the world.
Ibid. Line 350
He draweth out the thread of his verbosity finer than the staple of his argument.
Ibid. Act V, Sc. 1, Line 18
They have been at a great feast of languages, and stolen the scraps.
Ibid. Line 39
In the posteriors of this day, which the rude multitude call the afternoon.
Ibid. Line 96
Let me take you a button-hole lower.
Ibid. Sc. 2, Line 705
The naked truth.
Ibid. Line 715
A jest's prosperity lies in the ear
Of him that hears it, never in the tongue
Of him that makes it.
Ibid. Line 869
When daisies pied and violets blue,
And lady-smocks all silver-white,

And cuckoo-buds of yellow hue
  Do paint the meadows with delight,
The cuckoo then, on every tree,
Mocks married men.

> *Love's Labour's Lost.*
> *Act V, Sc. 2, Line 902*

The words of Mercury are harsh after
the songs of Apollo.

> *Ibid. Line 938*

The moon, like to a silver bow
New-bent in heaven.

> *A Midsummer-Night's Dream.*
> *Act I, Sc. 1, Line 9*

But earthlier happy is the rose distill'd
Than that which withering on the virgin
  thorn [1]
Grows, lives, and dies in single blessedness.

> *Ibid. Line 76*

For aught that I could ever read,
Could ever hear by tale or history,
The course of true love never did run
  smooth.

> *Ibid. Line 132*

Swift as a shadow, short as any dream,
Brief as the lightning in the collied
  night,
That, in a spleen, unfolds both heaven
  and earth,
And ere a man hath power to say, "Be-
  hold!"
The jaws of darkness do devour it up:
So quick bright things come to confu-
  sion.

> *Ibid. Line 144*

Love looks not with the eyes, but with
  the mind,
And therefore is winged Cupid painted
  blind.

> *Ibid. Line 234*

Masters, spread yourselves.

> *Ibid. Sc. 2, Line 16*

This is Ercles' vein.

> *Ibid. Line 43*

I'll speak in a monstrous little voice.

> *Ibid. Line 55*

I am slow of study.

> *Ibid. Line 70*

[1] Maidens withering on the stalk. — WORDS-
WORTH: *Personal Talk, Stanza 1*

That would hang us, every mother's
  son.

> *A Midsummer-Night's Dream.*
> *Act I, Sc. 2, Line 81*

I will roar you as gently as any sucking dove; I will roar you, as 'twere any
nightingale.

> *Ibid. Line 85*

A proper man, as one shall see in a summer's day.

> *Ibid. Line 89*

The human mortals.

> *Ibid. Act II, Sc. 1, Line 101*

Knows not which is which.

> *Ibid. Line 114*

The rude sea grew civil at her song,
And certain stars shot madly from their
  spheres
To hear the sea-maid's music.

> *Ibid. Line 152*

And the imperial votaress passed on,
In maiden meditation, fancy-free.
Yet mark'd I where the bolt of Cupid
  fell:
It fell upon a little western flower,
Before milk-white, now purple with
  love's wound,
And maidens call it Love-in-idleness.

> *Ibid. Line 163*

I'll put a girdle round about the earth
In forty minutes.[1]

> *Ibid. Line 175*

                My heart
Is true as steel.[2]

> *Ibid. Line 196*

It is not night when I do see your face.

> *Ibid. Line 221*

For you in my respect are all the world:
Then how can it be said I am alone.

> *Ibid. Line 224*

We cannot fight for love, as men may
  do;
We should be woo'd and were not made
  to woo.

> *Ibid. Line 241*

I know a bank whereon the wild thyme
  blows.

> *Ibid. Line 249*

[1] See Chapman, page 28.
[2] Trewe as steel. — CHAUCER: *Troilus and
Criseyde, Book V, L. 831.* SHAKESPEARE: *Troilus and Cressida, Act III, Sc. 2, L. 184; Romeo
and Juliet, Act II, Sc. 4, L. 212*

As a surfeit of the sweetest things
The deepest loathing to the stomach
brings.
A Midsummer-Night's Dream.
Act II, Sc. 2, Line 137
A lion among ladies is a most dreadful
thing.
Ibid. Act III, Sc. 1, Line 32
A calendar, a calendar! look in the
almanack; find out moonshine.
Ibid. Line 55
Bless thee, Bottom! bless thee! thou art
translated.
Ibid. Line 124
Lord, what fools these mortals be!
Ibid. Sc. 2, Line 115
So we grew together,
Like to a double cherry, seeming parted,
But yet an union in partition—
Two lovely berries moulded on one
stem.
Ibid. Line 208
Though she be but little, she is fierce.
Ibid. Line 325
I have an exposition of sleep come upon
me.
Ibid. Act IV, Sc. 1, Line 44
I have had a dream, past the wit of
man to say what dream it was.
Ibid. Line 211
The eye of man hath not heard, the
ear of man hath not seen,[1] man's hand is
not able to taste, his tongue to conceive,
nor his heart to report, what my dream
was.
Ibid. Line 218
A paramour is, God bless us! a thing of
naught.
Ibid. Sc. 2, Line 14
Eat no onions nor garlic, for we are to
utter sweet breath.
Ibid. Line 44
The lunatic, the lover, and the poet
Are of imagination all compact:
One sees more devils than vast hell can
hold,
That is, the madman: the lover, all as
frantic,
Sees Helen's beauty in a brow of Egypt:
The poet's eye, in a fine frenzy rolling,

Doth glance from heaven to earth, from
earth to heaven;
And as imagination bodies forth
The forms of things unknown, the poet's
pen
Turns them to shapes, and gives to airy
nothing
A local habitation and a name.
Such tricks hath strong imagination,
That if it would but apprehend some
joy,
It comprehends some bringer of that
joy;
Or in the night, imagining some fear,
How easy is a bush supposed a bear!
A Midsummer-Night's Dream.
Act V, Sc. 1, Line 7
The true beginning of our end.[1]
Ibid. Line 111
The best in this kind are but shadows.
Ibid. Line 215
A very gentle beast, and of a good con-
science.
Ibid. Line 232
This passion, and the death of a dear
friend, would go near to make a man
look sad.
Ibid. Line 295
With the help of a surgeon, he might
yet recover.
Ibid. Line 318
The iron tongue of midnight hath told
twelve.
Ibid. Line 372
My ventures are not in one bottom
trusted,
Nor to one place.
The Merchant of Venice.
Act I, Sc. 1, Line 42
Now, by two-headed Janus,
Nature hath framed strange fellows in
her time.
Ibid. Line 50
Though Nestor swear the jest be laugh-
able.
Ibid. Line 56
You have too much respect upon the
world:
They lose it that do buy it with much
care.
Ibid. Line 74

---

[1] Eye hath not seen, nor ear heard. —
1 *Corinthians, II, 9*

[1] I see the beginning of my end. — MAS-
SINGER: *The Virgin Martyr, Act III, Sc. 3*

I hold the world but as the world, Grati-
ano, —
A stage, where every man must play a
part;
And mine a sad one.
The Merchant of Venice.
Act I, Sc. 1, Line 77

Why should a man, whose blood is
warm within,
Sit like his grandsire cut in alabaster?
Ibid. Line 83

There are a sort of men whose visages
Do cream and mantle like a standing
pond.
Ibid. Line 88

        I am Sir Oracle,
And when I ope my lips, let no dog
bark!
Ibid. Line 93

        I do know of these
That therefore only are reputed wise
For saying nothing.
Ibid. Line 95

Fish not, with this melancholy bait,
For this fool gudgeon, this opinion.
Ibid. Line 101

Gratiano speaks an infinite deal of
nothing, more than any man in all Venice. His reasons are as two grains of
wheat hid in two bushels of chaff: you
shall seek all day ere you find them, and
when you have them, they are not worth
the search.
Ibid. Line 114

In my school-days, when I had lost one
shaft,
I shot his fellow of the selfsame flight
The selfsame way, with more advised
watch,
To find the other forth; and by adven-
turing both,
I oft found both.
Ibid. Line 141

They are as sick that surfeit with too
much, as they that starve with nothing.
Ibid. Sc. 2, Line 5

Superfluity comes sooner by white
hairs, but competency lives longer.
Ibid. Line 9

If to do were easy as to know what
were good to do, chapels had been

churches, and poor men's cottages
princes' palaces.
The Merchant of Venice.
Act I, Sc. 2, Line 13

The brain may devise laws for the
blood, but a hot temper leaps o'er a cold
decree.
Ibid. Line 19

He doth nothing but talk of his horse.
Ibid. Line 43

God made him, and therefore let him
pass for a man.
Ibid. Line 59

When he is best, he is a little worse
than a man; and when he is worst, he is
little better than a beast.
Ibid. Line 93

I dote on his very absence.
Ibid. Line 118

My meaning in saying he is a good
man, is to have you understand me that
he is sufficient.
Ibid. Sc. 3, Line 15

Ships are but boards, sailors but
men: there be land-rats and water-rats,
water-thieves and land-thieves.
Ibid. Line 22

I will buy with you, sell with you,
talk with you, walk with you, and so
following; but I will not eat with you,
drink with you, nor pray with you.
What news on the Rialto?
Ibid. Line 36

I will feed fat the ancient grudge I bear
him.
He hates our sacred nation; and he
rails,
Even there where merchants most do
congregate.
Ibid. Line 48

The devil can cite Scripture for his purpose.
Ibid. Line 99

A goodly apple rotten at the heart:
O, what a goodly outside falsehood
hath!
Ibid. Line 102

For sufferance is the badge of all our
tribe.
Ibid. Line 110

You call me misbeliever, cut-throat dog,
And spet upon my Jewish gaberdine.
Ibid. Line 111

Shall I bend low, and in a bondman's key,
With bated breath and whispering humbleness.
> *The Merchant of Venice.*
> *Act I, Sc. 3, Line 124*

O father Abram! what these Christians are,
Whose own hard dealings teaches them suspect
The thoughts of others!
> *Ibid. Line 161*

Mislike me not for my complexion,
The shadow'd livery of the burnish'd sun.
> *Ibid. Act II, Sc. 1, Line 1*

An honest, exceeding poor man.
> *Ibid. Line 54*

The young gentleman, according to Fates and Destinies and such odd sayings, the Sisters Three and such branches of learning, is indeed deceased; or, as you would say in plain terms, gone to heaven.
> *Ibid. Sc. 2, Line 66*

The very staff of my age, my very prop.
> *Ibid. Line 71*

It is a wise father that knows his own child.
> *Ibid. Line 83*

Truth will come to light; murder cannot be hid long.[1]
> *Ibid. Line 86*

In the twinkling of an eye.
> *Ibid. Line 183*

And the vile squealing of the wry-necked fife.
> *Ibid. Sc. 5, Line 30*

Who risest from a feast
With that keen appetite that he sits down?
> *Ibid. Sc. 6, Line 8*

All things that are,
Are with more spirit chased than enjoy'd.
> *Ibid. Line 12*

But love is blind, and lovers cannot see
The pretty follies that themselves commit.
> *Ibid. Line 36*

[1] See Chaucer, page 6.

Must I hold a candle to my shames?
> *The Merchant of Venice.*
> *Act II, Sc. 6, Line 41*

A golden mind stoops not to show of dross.
> *Ibid. Sc. 7, Line 20*

All that glisters is not gold.[1]
> *Ibid. Line 65*

Young in limbs, in judgment old.
> *Ibid. Line 71*

Even in the force and road of casualty.
> *Ibid. Sc. 9, Line 30*

Hanging and wiving goes by destiny.[2]
> *Ibid. Line 83*

I am a Jew. Hath not a Jew eyes? Hath not a Jew hands, organs, dimensions, senses, affections, passions?
> *Ibid. Act III, Sc. 1, Line 62*

The villany you teach me I will execute, and it shall go hard, but I will better the instruction.
> *Ibid. Line 76*

I would not have given it for a wilderness of monkeys.
> *Ibid. Line 130*

There's something tells me.
> *Ibid. Sc. 2, Line 4*

Makes a swan-like end,
Fading in music.[3]
> *Ibid. Line 44*

Tell me where is fancy bred,
Or in the heart or in the head?
How begot, how nourished?
Reply, reply.
> *Ibid. Line 63*

[1] See Chaucer, page 8.
[2] See Heywood, page 12. See Burton, page 240.
[3] See Chaucer, page 4.
I will play the swan and die in music.— *Othello, Act V, Sc. 2, L. 245*
I am the cygnet to this pale faint swan,
Who chants a doleful hymn to his own death.
> *King John, Act V, Sc. 7, L. 21*
There, swan-like, let me sing and die.— BYRON: *Don Juan, Canto III, St. 86*
You think that upon the score of foreknowledge and divining I am infinitely inferior to the swans. When they perceive approaching death they sing more merrily than before, because of the joy they have in going to the God they serve. — SOCRATES: In *Phaedo, 77*

In law, what plea so tainted and corrupt
But being season'd with a gracious
voice,
Obscures the show of evil?
> *The Merchant of Venice.*
> *Act III, Sc. 2, Line 75*

There is no vice so simple but assumes
Some mark of virtue on his outward
parts.
> *Ibid. Line 81*

Thus ornament is but the guiled shore
To a most dangerous sea.
> *Ibid. Line 97*

The seeming truth which cunning times
put on
To entrap the wisest.
> *Ibid. Line 100*

An unlesson'd girl, unschool'd, unprac-
tised;
Happy in this, she is not yet so old
But she may learn.[1]
> *Ibid. Line 160*

Here are a few of the unpleasant'st
words
That ever blotted paper!
> *Ibid. Line 252*

> The kindest man,
The best-condition'd and unwearied
spirit
In doing courtesies.
> *Ibid. Line 293*

The sins of the father are to be laid
upon the children.
> *Ibid. Sc. 5, Line 1*

Thus when I shun Scylla, your father, I fall into Charybdis, your
mother.[2]
> *Ibid. Line 17*

Let it serve for table-talk.
> *Ibid. Line 95*

A harmless necessary cat.
> *Ibid. Act IV, Sc. 1, Line 55*

What! wouldst thou have a serpent
sting thee twice?
> *Ibid. Line 69*

I am a tainted wether of the flock,
Meetest for death: the weakest kind of
fruit
Drops earliest to the ground.
> *The Merchant of Venice.*
> *Act IV, Sc. 1, Line 114*

To hold opinion with Pythagoras
That souls of animals infuse themselves
Into the trunks of men.[1]
> *Ibid. Line 131*

I never knew so young a body with so
old a head.[2]
> *Ibid. Line 163*

The quality of mercy is not strain'd,
It droppeth as the gentle rain from
heaven
Upon the place beneath. It is twice
bless'd:
It blesseth him that gives and him that
takes.
'T is mightiest in the mightiest: it be-
comes
The throned monarch better than his
crown;
His sceptre shows the force of temporal
power,
The attribute to awe and majesty,
Wherein doth sit the dread and fear of
kings;
But mercy is above this sceptred
sway,
It is enthroned in the hearts of kings,
It is an attribute to God himself;
And earthly power doth then show lik-
est God's,
When mercy seasons justice. Therefore,
Jew,
Though justice be thy plea, consider
this,
That in the course of justice, none of us
Should see salvation: we do pray for
mercy;

---

[1] It is better to learn late than never. —
PUBLIUS SYRUS: *Maxim 864*
[2] Incidis in Scyllam cupiens vitare Charyb-
dim (One falls into Scylla in seeking to avoid
Charybdis). — PHILIPPE GUALTIER: *Alexan-
dreis, Book V, Line 301 [circa 1300.]*

[1] *Clown.* What is the opinion of Pythagoras
concerning wild fowl?
Malvolio. That the soul of our grandam
might haply inhabit a bird.
> *Twelfth-Night, Act IV, Sc. 2, L. 55*
[2] He is young, but, take it from me, a very
staid head. — THOMAS WENTWORTH [1593-
1641], EARL OF STRAFFORD: Letter, commend-
ing the Earl of Ormond to Charles I for
appointment as Councillor. *Gentleman's Magazine*, London, October, 1854, page 328.

And that same prayer doth teach us all
to render
The deeds of mercy.
The Merchant of Venice.
Act IV, Sc. 1, Line 184

To do a great right, do a little wrong.
Ibid. Line 216

A Daniel come to judgment! yea, a
Daniel!
Ibid. Line 223

How much more elder art thou than thy
looks.
Ibid. Line 251

Is it so nominated in the bond?
Ibid. Line 260

'Tis not in the bond.
Ibid. Line 263

Speak me fair in death.
Ibid. Line 276

An upright judge, a learned judge!
Ibid. Line 324

A second Daniel, a Daniel, Jew!
Now, infidel, I have thee on the hip.[1]
Ibid. Line 335

I thank thee, Jew, for teaching me that
word.
Ibid. Line 342

You take my house, when you do take
the prop
That doth sustain my house; you take
my life,
When you do take the means whereby
I live.
Ibid. Line 376

He is well paid that is well satisfied.
Ibid. Line 416

How sweet the moonlight sleeps upon
this bank!
Here we will sit and let the sounds of
music
Creep in our ears: soft stillness and the
night
Become the touches of sweet harmony.
Sit, Jessica. Look how the floor of
heaven
Is thick inlaid with patines of bright
gold:
There 's not the smallest orb which
thou behold'st
But in his motion like an angel sings,

---

[1] See Heywood, page 16.

Still quiring to the young-eyed cheru-
bins.
Such harmony is in immortal souls;
But whilst this muddy vesture of decay
Doth grossly close it in, we cannot hear
it.
The Merchant of Venice.
Act V, Sc. 1, Line 54

I am never merry when I hear sweet
music.
Ibid. Line 69

The man that hath no music in himself,
Nor is not moved with concord of sweet
sounds,
Is fit for treasons, stratagems, and
spoils;
The motions of his spirit are dull as
night,
And his affections dark as Erebus.
Let no such man be trusted.
Ibid. Line 83

How far that little candle throws his
beams!
So shines a good deed in a naughty
world.
Ibid. Line 90

How many things by season season'd
are
To their right praise and true perfection!
Ibid. Line 107

This night, methinks, is but the daylight sick.
Ibid. Line 124

A light wife doth make a heavy husband.
Ibid. Line 130

These blessed candles of the night.
Ibid. Line 220

Fleet the time carelessly, as they did in
the golden world.
As You Like It. Act I, Sc. 1, Line 126

Always the dulness of the fool is the
whetstone of the wits.
Ibid. Sc. 2, Line 59

The little foolery that wise men have
makes a great show.
Ibid. Line 97

Well said: that was laid on with a
trowel.
Ibid. Line 113

In the world I fill up a place, which

may be better supplied when I have
made it empty.
As You Like It. Act I, Sc. 2, Line 206
Your heart's desires be with you!
Ibid. Line 214
One out of suits with fortune.
Ibid. Line 263
My pride fell with my fortunes.
Ibid. Line 269
Hereafter, in a better world than this,
I shall desire more love and knowledge
of you.
Ibid. Line 301
Celia. Not a word?
Rosalind. Not one to throw at a dog.
Ibid. Sc. 3, Line 2
O, how full of briers is this working-
day world!
Ibid. Line 12
Beauty provoketh thieves sooner than
gold.
Ibid. Line 113
We 'll have a swashing and a martial
outside,
As many other mannish cowards have.
Ibid. Line 123
Sweet are the uses of adversity;
Which, like the toad, ugly and venom-
ous,
Wears yet a precious jewel in his head;
And this our life, exempt from public
haunt,
Finds tongues in trees, books in the run-
ning brooks,
Sermons in stones, and good in every
thing.
Ibid. Act II, Sc. 1, Line 12
The big round tears
Coursed one another down his innocent
nose
In piteous chase.
Ibid. Line 38
"Poor deer," quoth he, "thou mak'st a
testament
As worldlings do, giving thy sum of
more
To that which had too much."
Ibid. Line 47
Sweep on, you fat and greasy citizens.
Ibid. Line 55
And He that doth the ravens feed,
Yea, providently caters for the sparrow,

Be comfort to my age!
As You Like It. Act II, Sc. 3, Line 43
For in my youth I never did apply
Hot and rebellious liquors in my blood.
Ibid. Line 48
Therefore my age is as a lusty winter,
Frosty, but kindly.
Ibid. Line 52
O, good old man; how well in thee ap-
pears
The constant service of the antique
world,
When service sweat for duty, not for
meed!
Thou art not for the fashion of these
times,
Where none will sweat but for promo-
tion.
Ibid. Line 56
I will follow thee
To the last gasp [1] with truth and loy-
alty.
Ibid. Line 69
Ay, now am I in Arden: the more
fool I. When I was at home I was in a
better place; but travellers must be con-
tent.
Ibid. Sc. 4, Line 16
If you remember'st not the slightest
folly
That ever love did make thee run into,
Thou hast not lov'd.
Ibid. Line 34
Thou speakest wiser than thou art ware
of.
Ibid. Line 57
I shall ne'er be 'ware of mine own
wit, till I break my shins against it.
Ibid. Line 59
Under the greenwood tree
Who loves to lie with me.
Ibid. Sc. 5, Line 1
What's that "ducdame"?
'Tis a Greek invocation to call fools
into a circle. [2]
Ibid. Line 58

---

[1] Fight till the last gasp. — *King Henry VI,
Part I, Act I, Sc. 2, L. 127*
[2] Your name, even in life, was, alas! a kind
of *ducdame* to bring people of no very great
sense into your circle. — ANDREW LANG: *Letters to Dead Authors, To Percy Bysshe Shelley*

I met a fool i' the forest,
A motley fool.
As You Like It. Act II, Sc. 7, Line 12
And rail'd on Lady Fortune in good
terms,
In good set terms.
Ibid. Line 16
And then he drew a dial from his poke,
And looking on it with lack-lustre eye,
Says, very wisely, "It is ten o'clock:
Thus we may see," quoth he, "how the
world wags." [1]
Ibid. Line 20
And so from hour to hour we ripe and
ripe,
And then from hour to hour we rot and
rot;
And thereby hangs a tale. [2]
Ibid. Line 26
My lungs began to crow like chanti-
cleer,
That fools should be so deep-contem-
plative;
And I did laugh sans intermission
An hour by his dial.
Ibid. Line 30
Motley 's the only wear.
Ibid. Line 34
If ladies be but young and fair,
They have the gift to know it; and in
his brain,
Which is as dry as the remainder bis-
cuit
After a voyage, he hath strange places
cramm'd
With observation, the which he vents
In mangled forms.
Ibid. Line 37
I must have liberty
Withal, as large a charter as the wind,
To blow on whom I please.
Ibid. Line 47
The "why" is plain as way to parish
church.
Ibid. Line 52
Under the shade of melancholy boughs,
Lose and neglect the creeping hours of
time;
If ever you have look'd on better days,

If ever been where bells have knoll'd to
church,
If ever sat at any good man's feast.
*As You Like It. Act II,
Sc. 7, Line 111*
True is it that we have seen better days.
Ibid. Line 120
And wiped our eyes
Of drops that sacred pity hath engen-
der'd.
Ibid. Line 122
Oppress'd with two weak evils, age and
hunger.
Ibid. Line 132
The wide and universal theatre.
Ibid. Line 137
All the world 's a stage,
And all the men and women merely
players. [1]
They have their exits and their en-
trances;
And one man in his time plays many
parts,
His acts being seven ages. At first the
infant,
Mewling and puking in the nurse's
arms.
And then the whining school-boy, with
his satchel
And shining morning face, creeping like
snail
Unwillingly to school. And then the
lover,
Sighing like furnace, with a woful bal-
lad
Made to his mistress' eyebrow. Then a
soldier,
Full of strange oaths, and bearded like
the pard;
Jealous in honour, sudden and quick in
quarrel,
Seeking the bubble reputation
Even in the cannon's mouth. And then
the justice,

---

[1] So wags the world. — SCOTT: *Ivanhoe,*
Chap. 37
[2] See Shakespeare, page 34.

[1] The world's a theatre, the earth a stage,
Which God and Nature do with actors fill.
THOMAS HEYWOOD: *Apology for Actors*
[1612]
A noble farce, wherein kings, republics, and
emperors have for so many ages played their
parts, and to which the whole vast universe
serves for a theatre. — MONTAIGNE: *Of the
most Excellent Men*
See Middleton, page 117.

In fair round belly with good capon
   lined,
With eyes severe and beard of formal
   cut,
Full of wise saws and modern in-
   stances;
And so he plays his part. The sixth age
   shifts
Into the lean and slipper'd pantaloon,
With spectacles on nose and pouch on
   side;
His youthful hose, well saved, a world
   too wide
For his shrunk shank; and his big
   manly voice,
Turning again toward childish treble,
   pipes
And whistles in his sound. Last scene of
   all,
That ends this strange eventful histo-
   ry,
Is second childishness, and mere obliv-
   ion,
Sans teeth, sans eyes, sans taste, sans
   everything.
   As You Like It. Act II,
   Sc. 7, Line 139

Blow, blow, thou winter wind!
Thou art not so unkind
   As man's ingratitude.
   Ibid. Line 174

These trees shall be my books.
   Ibid. Act III, Sc. 2, Line 5

The fair, the chaste, and unexpressive
she.
   Ibid. Line 10

It goes much against my stomach.
Hast any philosophy in thee, shepherd?
   Ibid. Line 21

He that wants money, means, and
content is without three good friends.
   Ibid. Line 25

I am a true labourer: I earn that I
eat, get that I wear, owe no man hate,
envy no man's happiness, glad of other
men's good.
   Ibid. Line 78

This is the very false gallop of verses.
   Ibid. Line 120

Let us make an honourable retreat.
   Ibid. Line 170

With bag and baggage.[1]
   As You Like It. Act III,
   Sc. 2, Line 171

O, wonderful, wonderful, and most
wonderful wonderful! and yet again
wonderful, and after that out of all
hooping.
   Ibid. Line 202

Answer me in one word.
   Ibid. Line 238

Do you not know I am a woman?
when I think, I must speak.
   Ibid. Line 265

I do desire we may be better strangers.
   Ibid. Line 276

Jacques. What stature is she of?
Orlando. Just as high as my heart.
   Ibid. Line 286

Time travels in divers paces with
divers persons. I'll tell you who Time
ambles withal, who Time trots withal,
who Time gallops withal, and who he
stands still withal.
   Ibid. Line 328

Every one fault seeming monstrous
till his fellow fault came to match it.
   Ibid. Line 377

Everything about you demonstrating
a careless desolation.
   Ibid. Line 405

Neither rhyme nor reason.[2]
   Ibid. Line 424

I would the gods had made thee poetical.
   Ibid. Sc. 3, Line 16

The common executioner,
Whose heart the accustom'd sight of
   death makes hard,
Falls not the axe upon the humbled
   neck
But first begs pardon.
   Ibid. Sc. 5, Line 3

The wounds invisible
That love's keen arrows make.
   Ibid. Line 30

   Down on your knees,
And thank Heaven, fasting, for a good
   man's love.
   Ibid. Line 57

---

[1] And since "bag and baggage" is a phrase.
— ROBERT BROWNING: *The Inn Album,* V
[2] See Spenser, page 26.

I am falser than vows made in wine.
*As You Like It. Act III,
Sc. 5, Line 73*

It is a melancholy of mine own, compounded of many simples, extracted from many objects, and indeed the sundry contemplation of my travels, in which my often rumination wraps me in a most humorous sadness.
Ibid. Act IV, Sc. 1, Line 16

I had rather have a fool to make me merry than experience to make me sad.
Ibid. Line 28

I'll warrant him heart-whole.
Ibid. Line 51

Good orators, when they are out, they will spit.
Ibid. Line 77

Men have died from time to time, and worms have eaten them, but not for love.
Ibid. Line 110

Can one desire too much of a good thing? [1]
Ibid. Line 128

For ever and a day.
Ibid. Line 151

Men are April when they woo, December when they wed: maids are May when they are maids, but the sky changes when they are wives.
Ibid. Line 153

My affection hath an unknown bottom, like the bay of Portugal.
Ibid. Line 219

The horn, the horn, the lusty horn
Is not a thing to laugh to scorn.
Ibid. Sc. 2, Line 17

Chewing the food of sweet and bitter fancy.
Ibid. Sc. 3, Line 103

It is meat and drink to me to see a clown.
Ibid. Act V, Sc. 1, Line 11

"So so" is good, very good, very excellent good; and yet it is not; it is but so so.
Ibid. Line 30

The fool doth think he is wise, but the wise man knows himself to be a fool.
Ibid. Line 35

---

[1] Too much of a good thing. — CERVANTES: *Don Quixote*, Pt. I, Book I, Chap. VI

No sooner met but they looked; no sooner looked but they loved; no sooner loved but they sighed; no sooner sighed but they asked one another the reason; no sooner knew the reason but they sought the remedy.
As You Like It. Act V, Sc. 2, Line 37

How bitter a thing it is to look into happiness through another man's eyes!
Ibid. Line 48

Here comes a pair of very strange beasts, which in all tongues are called fools.
Ibid. Sc. 4, Line 36

An ill-favoured thing, sir, but mine own. [1]
Ibid. Line 60

Rich honesty dwells like a miser, sir, in a poor house; as your pearl in your foul oyster.
Ibid. Line 62

The Retort Courteous; . . . the Quip Modest; . . . the Reply Churlish; . . . the Reproof Valiant; . . . the Countercheck Quarrelsome; . . . the Lie with Circumstance; . . . the Lie Direct.
Ibid. Line 75

Your "If" is the only peacemaker; much virtue in "If."
Ibid. Line 108

Good wine needs no bush. [2]
Ibid. Epilogue, Line 4

What a case am I in.
Ibid. Line 7

Look in the chronicles; we came in with Richard Conqueror.
*The Taming of the Shrew.
Induc., Sc. 1, Line 4*

Let the world slide. [3]
Ibid. Line 5

I'll not budge an inch. [4]
Ibid. Line 14

---

[1] My glass is not large, but I drink out of my own. — ALFRED DE MUSSET

[2] You need not hang up the ivy branch over the wine that will sell. — PUBLIUS SYRUS: *Maxim 968*

[3] See Heywood, page 11. BEAUMONT AND FLETCHER: *Wit without Money.*

[4] The same in *King Henry VI, Part III*, Act V, Sc. 4, L. 66; *Romeo and Juliet*, Act III, Sc. 1, L. 60; *Hamlet*, Act III, Sc. 4, L. 18.

And if the boy have not a woman's gift
To rain a shower of commanded tears,
An onion will do well for such a shift.
The Taming of the Shrew.
Induc. Sc. 1, Line 124

As Stephen Sly and old John Naps of
Greece,
And Peter Turf and Henry Pimpernell,
And twenty more such names and men
as these
Which never were, nor no man ever
saw.
Ibid. Sc. 2, Line 95

Let the world slip: we shall ne'er be
younger.
Ibid. Line 147

No profit grows where is no pleasure
ta'en;
In brief, sir, study what you most affect.
Ibid. Act I, Sc. 1, Line 39

There's small choice in rotten apples.
Ibid. Line 137

Whom should I knock?
Ibid. Sc. 2, Line 6

To seek their fortunes further than at
home,
Where small experience grows.
Ibid. Line 51

As curst and shrewd
As Socrates' Xanthippe.
Ibid. Line 70

Nothing comes amiss, so money comes
withal.
Ibid. Line 82

Tush, tush! fear boys with bugs.
Ibid. Line 214

And do as adversaries do in law,
Strive mightily, but eat and drink as
friends.
Ibid. Line 281

Old fashions please me best.
Ibid. Act III, Sc. 1, Line 81

Who wooed in haste and means to wed
at leisure.[1]
Ibid. Sc. 2, Line 11

A little pot and soon hot.[2]
Ibid. Act IV, Sc. 1, Line 6

A cold world, Curtis, in every office
but thine; and therefore fire.
The Taming of the Shrew.
Act IV, Sc. 1, Line 37

It was the friar of orders grey,
As he forth walked on his way.[1]
Ibid. Line 148

Sits as one new-risen from a dream.
Ibid. Line 189

To kill a wife with kindness.
Ibid. Line 211

Kindness in women, not their beauteous
looks,
Shall win my love.
Ibid. Sc. 2, Line 41

Our purses shall be proud, our garments
poor:
For 'tis the mind that makes the body
rich.
Ibid. Sc. 3, Line 173

And as the sun breaks through the dark-
est clouds,
So honour peereth in the meanest habit.
Ibid. Line 175

Pitchers have ears.[2]
Ibid. Sc. 4, Line 52

So bedazzled with the sun
That everything I look on seemeth
green.
Ibid. Sc. 5, Line 46

My cake is dough.
Ibid. Act V, Sc. 1, Line 146

He that is giddy thinks the world turns
round.
Ibid. Sc. 2, Line 20

A woman moved is like a fountain
troubled,
Muddy, ill-seeming, thick, bereft of
beauty.
Ibid. Line 143

Such duty as the subject owes the
prince,
Even such a woman oweth to her husband.
Ibid. Line 156

Love all, trust a few,
Do wrong to none: be able for thine
enemy

---

[1] Married in haste, we may repent at leisure.
— CONGREVE: *The Old Bachelor, Act V, Sc. 1*
[2] A little chimney heated hot in a moment.
— H. W. LONGFELLOW: *The Courtship of Myles Standish*

[1] THOMAS PERCY [1728–1811] composed his ballad, *The Friar of Orders Grey*, of various ancient fragments found in Shakespeare's plays.
[2] See Heywood, page 16.

Rather in power than use, and keep
thy friend
Under thine own life's key: be check'd
for silence,
But never tax'd for speech.
All's Well that Ends Well.
Act I, Sc. 1, Line 74
It were all one
That I should love a bright particular
star
And think to wed it.
Ibid. Line 97
The hind that would be mated by the
lion
Must die for love.
Ibid. Line 103
Our remedies oft in ourselves do lie,
Which we ascribe to Heaven.
Ibid. Line 235
Service is no heritage.
Ibid. Sc. 3, Line 25
He must needs go that the devil drives.[1]
Ibid. Line 32
My friends were poor, but honest.
Ibid. Line 203
Great floods have flown
From simple sources.
Ibid. Act II, Sc. 1, Line 142
Oft expectation fails, and most oft
there
Where most it promises.
Ibid. Line 145
The horses of the sun.[2]
Ibid. Line 164
I will show myself highly fed and lowly
taught.
Ibid. Sc. 2, Line 3
They say miracles are past.
Ibid. Sc. 3, Line 1
All the learned and authentic fellows.
Ibid. Line 14
From lowest place when virtuous things
proceed,
The place is dignified by the doer's
deed.
Ibid. Line 132

A young man married is a man that's
marr'd.
All's Well that Ends Well.
Act II, Sc. 3, Line 315
Make the coming hour o'erflow with
joy,
And pleasure drown the brim.
Ibid. Sc. 4, Line 48
No legacy is so rich as honesty.
Ibid. Act III, Sc. 5, Line 13
The web of our life is of a mingled
yarn, good and ill together.
Ibid. Act IV, Sc. 3, Line 83
All's well that ends well.[1]
Ibid. Sc. 4, Line 35
I am a man whom Fortune hath cruelly
scratched.
Ibid. Act V, Sc. 2, Line 28
Whose words all ears took captive.
Ibid. Sc. 3, Line 17
Praising what is lost
Makes the remembrance dear.
Ibid. Line 19
The inaudible and noiseless foot of
Time.[2]
Ibid. Line 41
Love that comes too late,
Like a remorseful pardon slowly carried.
Ibid. Line 57
All impediments in fancy's course
Are motives of more fancy.
Ibid. Line 216
The bitter past, more welcome is the
sweet.
Ibid. Line 339
If music be the food of love,[3] play on;
Give me excess of it, that, surfeiting,
The appetite may sicken, and so die.
That strain again! it had a dying fall:
O! it came o'er my ear like the sweet
sound
That breathes upon a bank of violets,
Stealing and giving odour!
Twelfth-Night. Act I, Sc. 1,
Line 1

[1] See Heywood, page 17.
[2] Who drives the horses of the sun
Shall lord it but a day.
JOHN VANCE CHENEY [1848–1922]: *The Happiest Heart*

[1] Also in *Act V, Sc. 1, Line 25.* See Heywood, page 13.
[2] How noiseless falls the foot of time! —
W. R. SPENCER: *Lines to Lady A. Hamilton*
[3] Is not music the food of love? — R. B. SHERIDAN: *The Rivals, Act II, Sc. 1*

When my tongue blabs, then let mine
eyes not see.
                    Twelfth-Night. Act I,
                    Sc. 2, Line 61
I am sure care's an enemy to life.
                    Ibid. Sc. 3, Line 2
Let them hang themselves in their own
straps.
                    Ibid. Line 13
At my fingers' ends.[1]
                    Ibid. Line 85
I am a great eater of beef, and I be-
lieve that does harm to my wit.
                    Ibid. Line 92
Wherefore are these things hid?
                    Ibid. Line 135
Is it a world to hide virtues in?
                    Ibid. Line 142
God give them wisdom that have it;
and those that are fools, let them use
their talents.
                    Ibid. Sc. 4, Line 14
One draught above heat makes him
a fool, the second mads him, and a third
drowns him.
                    Ibid. Sc. 5, Line 139
What manner of man? [2]
                    Ibid. Line 162
We will draw the curtain and show you
the picture.
                    Ibid. Line 252
'Tis beauty truly blent, whose red and
white
Nature's own sweet and cunning hand
laid on:
Lady, you are the cruell'st she alive
If you will lead these graces to the
grave
And leave the world no copy.
                    Ibid. Line 259
Holla your name to the reverberate
hills,
And make the babbling gossip of the air
Cry out.
                    Ibid. Line 293
Journeys end in lovers meeting,
Every wise man's son doth know.
                    Ibid. Act II, Sc. 3, Line 46

[1] See Heywood, page 13.
[2] What manner of man is this? — *Mark,*
IV, 41

Then come kiss me, sweet and twenty,
Youth's a stuff will not endure.
                    Twelfth-Night. Act II,
                    Sc. 3, Line 54
He does it with a better grace, but
I do it more natural.
                    Ibid. Line 91
Is there no respect of place, persons,
nor time in you?
                    Ibid. Line 100
Sir Toby. Dost thou think, because
thou art virtuous, there shall be no more
cakes and ale? [1]
Clown. Yes, by Saint Anne, and gin-
ger shall be hot i' the mouth too.
                    Ibid. Line 124
My purpose is, indeed, a horse of that
colour.
                    Ibid. Line 184
Sport royal.
                    Ibid. Line 190
That old and antique song we heard
last night.
                    Ibid. Sc. 4, Line 3
These most brisk and giddy-paced
times.
                    Ibid. Line 6
            Let still the woman take
An elder than herself: so wears she to
him,
So sways she level in her husband's
heart:
For, boy, however we do praise our-
selves,
Our fancies are more giddy and unfirm,
More longing, wavering, sooner lost and
worn,
Than women's are.
                    Ibid. Line 29
Then let thy love be younger than thy-
self,
Or thy affection cannot hold the bent.
                    Ibid. Line 36
The spinsters and the knitters in the
sun
And the free maids that weave their
thread with bones,
Do use to chant it: it is silly sooth,

[1] There are cakes, there is ale —ay, and
      ginger
    Shall be hot in the mouth, as of old.
    ANDREW LANG: *A Remonstrance with the*
                    Fair, St. 6

And dallies with the innocence of love,
Like the old age.
*Twelfth-Night. Act II,
Sc. 4, Line 44*

Duke. And what's her history?
Viola. A blank, my lord. She never told her love,
But let concealment, like a worm i' the bud,
Feed on her damask cheek: she pined in thought,
And with a green and yellow melancholy
She sat like patience on a monument,
Smiling at grief.
Ibid. Line 112

I am all the daughters of my father's house,
And all the brothers too.
Ibid. Line 122

I know my place, as I would they should do theirs.
Ibid. Sc. 5, Line 61

Some are born great, some achieve greatness, and some have greatness thrust upon them.
Ibid. Line 159

Foolery, sir, does walk about the orb like the sun; it shines everywhere.
Ibid. Act III, Sc. 1, Line 44

Music from the spheres.[1]
Ibid. Line 122

How apt the poor are to be proud.
Ibid. Line 141

Then westward-ho!
Ibid. Line 148

Oh, what a deal of scorn looks beautiful
In the contempt and anger of his lip!
Ibid. Line 159

Love sought is good, but given unsought, is better.
Ibid. Line 170

You will hang like an icicle on a Dutchman's beard.
Ibid. Sc. 2, Line 30

Let there be gall enough in thy ink; though thou write with a goose-pen, no matter.
*Twelfth-Night. Act III,
Sc. 2, Line 54*

Laugh yourself into stitches.
Ibid. Line 75

I can no other answer make but thanks,
And thanks, and ever thanks.
Ibid. Sc. 3, Line 14

Haply your eye shall light upon some toy
You have desire to purchase.
Ibid. Line 44

I think we do know the sweet Roman hand.
Ibid. Sc. 4, Line 31

This is very midsummer madness.
Ibid. Line 62

Put thyself into the trick of singularity.
Ibid. Line 80

What, man! defy the Devil: consider, he's an enemy to mankind.
Ibid. Line 109

'Tis not for gravity to play at cherry-pit with Satan.
Ibid. Line 131

If this were played upon a stage now, I could condemn it as an improbable fiction.
Ibid. Line 142

More matter for a May morning.
Ibid. Line 158

Still you keep o' the windy side of the law.[1]
Ibid. Line 183

My remembrance is very free and clear from any image of offence done to any man.
Ibid. Line 251

Hob, nob, is his word: give 't or take 't.
Ibid. Line 265

I have heard of some kind of men that put quarrels purposely on others to taste their valour.
Ibid. Line 269

He's a very devil.
Ibid. Line 304

An I thought he had been valiant, and so cunning in fence, I'd have seen

---

[1] The music of the spheres. *Pericles, Act V, Sc. 1, L. 231*
We may maintain the music of the spheres. — SIR THOMAS BROWNE: *Religio Medici, Part II, Sect. 9*

[1] The windy side of care. — *Much Ado About Nothing, Act II, Sc. 1, L. 328*

him damned ere I'd have challenged
him.
Twelfth-Night. Act III,
Sc. 4, Line 314
Out of my lean and low ability
I'll lend you something.
Ibid. Line 380
I hate ingratitude more in a man
Than lying, vainness, babbling drunk-
enness,
Or any taint of vice whose strong cor-
ruption
Inhabits our frail blood.
Ibid. Line 390
Out of the jaws of death.[1]
Ibid. Line 396
   As the old hermit of Prague, that
never saw pen and ink, very wittily said
to a niece of King Gorboduc, "That
that is, is."
Ibid. Act IV, Sc. 2, Line 14
Thus the whirligig of time brings in his
revenges.
Ibid. Act V, Sc. 1, Line 388
For the rain it raineth every day.[2]
Ibid. Line 404
   You pay a great deal too dear for
what's given freely.
The Winter's Tale. Act I, Sc. 1,
Line 18
   One good deed, dying tongueless,
Slaughters a thousand waiting upon
that.
Ibid. Sc. 2, Line 92
            They say we are
Almost as like as eggs.
Ibid. Line 130
He makes a July's day short as De-
cember.
Ibid. Line 169
   Black brows, they say,
Become some women best, so that there
be not
Too much hair there, but in a semi-
circle,
Or a half-moon made with a pen.
Ibid. Act II, Sc. 1, Line 8

A sad tale's best for winter.
The Winter's Tale. Act II,
Sc. 1, Line 24
There's some ill planet reigns:
I must be patient till the heavens look
With an aspect more favourable.
Ibid. Line 104
The silence often of pure innocence
Persuades when speaking fails.
Ibid. Sc. 2, Line 41
Not so hot.[1]
Ibid. Sc. 3, Line 32
I am a feather for each wind that blows.
Ibid. Line 153
   What's gone and what's past help
Should be past grief.
Ibid. Act III, Sc. 2, Line 223
I am gone for ever. [*Exit, pursued by*
a bear.][2]
Ibid. Sc. 3, Line 57
This is fairy gold.
Ibid. Line 127
Then comes in the sweet o' the year.
Ibid. Act IV, Sc. 2, Line 3
A snapper-up of unconsidered trifles.
Ibid. Line 26
A merry heart goes all the day,
   Your sad tires in a mile-a.
Ibid. Line 135
There's rosemary and rue; these keep
Seeming and savour all the winter long.
Ibid. Sc. 3, Line 74
The marigold, that goes to bed wi' the
   sun . . .
They are given to men of middle age.
Ibid. Line 105
            Daffodils,
That come before the swallow dares,
   and take
The winds of March with beauty.
Ibid. Line 118
         What you do
Still betters what is done.
Ibid. Line 135
   When you do dance, I wish you
A wave o' the sea, that you might ever
   do

---

[1] Into the jaws of death. — TENNYSON:
The Charge of the Light Brigade, Stanza 3
   In the jaws of death. — DU BARTAS: *Divine*
Weekes and Workes, Second Week, First Day,
Part IV
[2] Also in *King Lear, Act III, Sc. 2, L. 77*

[1] *King Lear, Act V, Sc. 2, L. 67*
   SAMUEL PEPYS: *Diary,* April 26, 1664.
[2] Lightly we follow our cue,
   "Exit, pursued by a bear."
   ARTHUR GUITERMAN: *The Shakespearean*
Bear, Envoi

Nothing but that.
> *The Winter's Tale. Act IV,*
> *Sc. 3, Line 140*

I love a ballad in print, a-life, for then we are sure they are true.
> *Ibid. Line 262*

The self-same sun that shines upon his court
Hides not his visage from our cottage, but
Looks on alike.
> *Ibid. Line 457*

To unpathed waters, undreamed shores.
> *Ibid. Line 580*

Let me have no lying; it becomes none but tradesmen.
> *Ibid. Line 747*

To purge melancholy.
> *Ibid. Line 792*

Stars, stars! And all eyes else dead coals.
> *Ibid. Act V, Sc. 1, Line 67*

Where's Bohemia? [1]
> *Ibid. Line 185*

I was no gentleman born.
> *Ibid. Sc. 2, Line 146*

What fine chisel
Could ever yet cut breath?
> *Ibid. Sc. 3, Line 78*

There's time enough for that.
> *Ibid. Line 128*

Lord of thy presence and no land beside.
> *King John. Act I, Sc. 1, Line 137*

And if his name be George, I'll call him Peter;
For new-made honour doth forget men's names.
> *Ibid. Line 186*

For he is but a bastard to the time
That doth not smack of observation.
> *Ibid. Line 207*

Sweet, sweet, sweet poison for the age's tooth.
> *Ibid. Line 213*

Heaven lay not my transgression to my charge.
> *Ibid. Line 256*

[1] A desert Country near the Sea. — *Act III, Sc. 3*

A hazard of new fortunes. [1]
> *King John. Act II, Sc. 1, Line 71*

For courage mounteth with occasion.
> *Ibid. Line 82*

Saint George, that swing'd the dragon, and e'er since
Sits on his horse back at mine hostess' door.
> *Ibid. Line 288*

He is the half part of a blessed man,
Left to be finished by such a she;
And she a fair divided excellence,
Whose fulness of perfection lies in him.
> *Ibid. Line 437*

Talks as familiarly of roaring lions
As maids of thirteen do of puppy-dogs!
> *Ibid. Line 459*

Zounds! I was never so bethump'd with words,
Since I first call'd my brother's father dad.
> *Ibid. Line 466*

I will instruct my sorrows to be proud;
For grief is proud, and makes his owner stoop.
> *Ibid. Act III, Sc. 1, Line 68*

What hath this day deserved? what hath it done
That it in golden letters should be set
Among the high tides in the calendar?
> *Ibid. Line 84*

Thou ever strong upon the stronger side!
Thou Fortune's champion that dost never fight
But when her humorous ladyship is by
To teach thee safety.
> *Ibid. Line 117*

Thou wear a lion's hide! doff it for shame,
And hang a calf's-skin on those recreant limbs.
> *Ibid. Line 128*

I had a thing to say,
But I will fit it with some better time.
> *Ibid. Sc. 3, Line 25*

[1] Title of a novel [1889] by WILLIAM DEAN HOWELLS, who used Shakespearean quotations in this way probably more often than any other novelist.

O, amiable lovely death! [1]
King John. Act III, Sc. 4, Line 25
Grief fills the room up of my absent child,
Lies in his bed, walks up and down with me,
Puts on his pretty looks, repeats his words,
Remembers me of all his gracious parts,
Stuffs out his vacant garments with his form.
Ibid. Line 93
Life is as tedious as a twice-told tale,
Vexing the dull ear of a drowsy man.
Ibid. Line 108
When Fortune means to men most good,[2]
She looks upon them with a threatening eye.
Ibid. Line 119
And he that stands upon a slippery place
Makes nice of no vile hold to stay him up.
Ibid. Line 137
To gild refined gold, to paint the lily,
To throw a perfume on the violet,
To smooth the ice, or add another hue
Unto the rainbow, or with taper-light
To seek the beauteous eye of heaven to garnish,
Is wasteful and ridiculous excess.
Ibid. Act IV, Sc. 2, Line 11
And oftentimes excusing of a fault
Doth make the fault the worse by the excuse.[3]
Ibid. Line 30
We cannot hold mortality's strong hand.
Ibid. Line 82
There is no sure foundation set on blood,
No certain life achiev'd by others' death.
Ibid. Line 104

Make haste; the better foot before.[1]
King John. Act IV, Sc. 2, Line 170
I saw a smith stand with his hammer, thus,
The whilst his iron did on the anvil cool,
With open mouth swallowing a tailor's news.
Ibid. Line 193
Another lean unwashed artificer.
Ibid. Line 201
How oft the sight of means to do ill deeds
Makes ill deeds done!
Ibid. Line 219
Heaven take my soul, and England keep my bones.
Ibid. Sc. 3, Line 10
Mocking the air with colours idly spread.
Ibid. Act V, Sc. 1, Line 72
The day shall not be up so soon as I,
To try the fair adventure of to-morrow.
Ibid. Sc. 5, Line 21
'Tis strange that death should sing.
I am the cygnet to this pale faint swan,
Who chants a doleful hymn to his own death,[2]
And from the organ-pipe of frailty sings
His soul and body to their lasting rest.
Ibid. Sc. 7, Line 20
Now my soul hath elbow-room.
Ibid. Line 28
This England never did, nor never shall,
Lie at the proud foot of a conqueror.
Ibid. Line 112
Come the three corners of the world in arms,
And we shall shock them. Nought shall make us rue,
If England to itself do rest but true.
Ibid. Line 116
Old John of Gaunt, time-honoured Lancaster.
King Richard II. Act I, Sc. 1, Line 1
Mine honour is my life; both grow in one;

---

[1] Lovely and soothing death. — WALT WHITMAN: *When Lilacs Last in the Dooryard Bloom'd, Sect. 14*
[2] When fortune flatters, she does it to betray. — PUBLIUS SYRUS: *Maxim 278*
[3] Qui s'excuse, s'accuse (He who excuses himself accuses himself). — GABRIEL MEURIER: *Trésor des Sentences* [1530–1601]

[1] Come on, my lords, the better foot before. — *Titus Andronicus, Act II, Sc. 3, L. 192*
Put forward your best foot. — ROBERT BROWNING: *Respectability, St. 3*
[2] See Note 3, page 45.

Take honour from me, and my life is
done.
>> *King Richard II. Act I,*
>> *Sc. 1, Line 182*

The daintiest last, to make the end
most sweet.
>> *Ibid. Sc. 3, Line 68*

Truth hath a quiet breast.
>> *Ibid. Line 96*

How long a time lies in one little word!
>> *Ibid. Line 213*

Things sweet to taste prove in digestion
sour.
>> *Ibid. Line 236*

All places that the eye of heaven visits
Are to a wise man ports and happy
havens.
>> *Ibid. Line 275*

O, who can hold a fire in his hand
By thinking on the frosty Caucasus?
Or cloy the hungry edge of appetite
By bare imagination of a feast?
Or wallow naked in December snow
By thinking on fantastic summer's
heat?
O, no! the apprehension of the good
Gives but the greater feeling to the
worse.
>> *Ibid. Line 294*

>> The tongues of dying men
Enforce attention like deep harmony.
>> *Ibid. Act II, Sc. 1, Line 5*

The setting sun, and music at the close,
As the last taste of sweets, is sweetest
last,
Writ in remembrance, more than things
long past.
>> *Ibid. Line 12*

Small showers last long, but sudden
storms are short.
>> *Ibid. Line 35*

This royal throne of kings, this sceptred
isle,
This earth of majesty, this seat of Mars,
This other Eden, demi-paradise,
This fortress built by Nature for her-
self
Against infection and the hand of war,
This happy breed of men, this little
world,
This precious stone set in the silver sea,
Which serves it in the office of a wall
Or as a moat defensive to a house,

Against the envy of less happier lands,
This blessed plot, this earth, this realm,
this England.
>> *King Richard II. Act II,*
>> *Sc. 1, Line 40*

The ripest fruit first falls.
>> *Ibid. Line 154*

Your fair discourse hath been as sugar,
Making the hard way sweet and delectable.
>> *Ibid. Sc. 3, Line 6*

I count myself in nothing else so happy
As in a soul remembering my good
friends.
>> *Ibid. Line 46*

Evermore thanks, the exchequer of the
poor.
>> *Ibid. Line 65*

The caterpillars of the commonwealth,
Which I have sworn to weed and pluck
away.
>> *Ibid. Line 166*

Things past redress are now with me
past care.
>> *Ibid. Line 171*

I see thy glory like a shooting star
Fall to the base earth from the firmament.
>> *Ibid. Sc. 4, Line 19*

Eating the bitter bread of banishment.
>> *Ibid. Act III, Sc. 1, Line 21*

Fires the proud tops of the eastern
pines.
>> *Ibid. Sc. 2, Line 42*

Not all the water in the rough rude sea
Can wash the balm off from an anointed
king.
>> *Ibid. Line 55*

O, call back yesterday, bid time return!
>> *Ibid. Line 69*

Let's talk of graves, of worms, and
epitaphs.
>> *Ibid. Line 145*

Let's choose executors and talk of wills.
>> *Ibid. Line 148*

And nothing can we call our own but
death;
And that small model of the barren
earth,
Which serves as paste and cover to our
bones.
For God's sake, let us sit upon the
ground,

And tell sad stories of the death of kings.

King Richard II. Act III, Sc. 2, Line 152

Comes at the last, and with a little pin Bores through his castle wall, and farewell king!

Ibid. Line 169

Men judge by the complexion of the sky The state and inclination of the day.

Ibid. Line 194

He is come to open The purple testament of bleeding war.

Ibid. Sc. 3, Line 93

And my large kingdom for a little grave, A little little grave, an obscure grave.

Ibid. Line 153

The noisome weeds, that without profit suck The soil's fertility from wholesome flowers.

Ibid. Sc. 4, Line 38

Superfluous branches We lop away that bearing boughs may live.

Ibid. Line 63

Gave His body to that pleasant country's earth, And his pure soul unto his captain Christ, Under whose colours he had fought so long.

Ibid. Act IV, Sc. 1, Line 97

So Judas did to Christ: but he, in twelve, Found truth in all but one; I, in twelve thousand, none.

Ibid. Line 170

Some of you with Pilate wash your hands [1] Showing an outward pity.

Ibid. Line 239

A mockery king of snow.

Ibid. Line 260

Come home with me to supper.

Ibid. Line 333

As in a theatre, the eyes of men, After a well-graced actor leaves the stage,

---

[1] Pilate . . . took water, and washed his hands. — *Matthew, XXVII, 24*

Are idly bent on him that enters next, Thinking his prattle to be tedious.

King Richard II. Act V, Sc. 2, Line 23

No word like "pardon."

Ibid. Sc. 3, Line 118

As hard to come as for a camel To thread the postern of a small needle's eye.[1]

Ibid. Sc. 5, Line 16

How sour sweet music is When time is broke and no proportion kept! So is it in the music of men's lives.

Ibid. Line 42

So shaken as we are, so wan with care.

King Henry IV, Part I. Act I, Sc. 1, Line 1

In those holy fields Over whose acres walked those blessed feet Which fourteen hundred years ago were nail'd For our advantage on the bitter cross.

Ibid. Line 24

Here is a dear and true industrious friend.

Ibid. Line 62

Diana's foresters, gentlemen of the shade, minions of the moon.

Ibid. Sc. 2, Line 29

So far as my coin would stretch; and where it would not, I have used my credit.

Ibid. Line 61

Old father antic the law.

Ibid. Line 69

I would to God thou and I knew where a commodity of good names were to be bought.

Ibid. Line 92

Thou hast damnable iteration, and art indeed able to corrupt a saint.

Ibid. Line 101

'Tis my vocation, Hal; 'tis no sin for a man to labour in his vocation.

Ibid. Line 116

---

[1] It is easier for a camel to go through the eye of a needle, than for a rich man to enter into the kingdom of God. — *Matthew, XIX, 24*

He will give the devil his due.[1]
> *King Henry IV, Part I.*
> *Act I, Sc. 2, Line 132*

There's neither honesty, manhood, nor good fellowship in thee.
> *Ibid. Line 154*

If all the year were playing holidays,
To sport would be as tedious as to work.
> *Ibid. Line 226*

You tread upon my patience.
> *Ibid. Sc. 3, Line 4*

That title of respect
Which the proud soul ne'er pays but to the proud.
> *Ibid. Line 8*

Fresh as a bridegroom; and his chin new reap'd,
Showed like a stubble-land at harvest-home;
He was perfumed like a milliner,
And 'twixt his finger and his thumb he held
A pouncet-box, which ever and anon
He gave his nose and took 't away again.
> *Ibid. Line 34*

And as the soldiers bore dead bodies by,
He called them untaught knaves, unmannerly,
To bring a slovenly unhandsome corse
Betwixt the wind and his nobility.
> *Ibid. Line 42*

God save the mark.
> *Ibid. Line 56*

And telling me, the sovereign'st thing on earth
Was parmaceti for an inward bruise;
And that it was great pity, so it was,
This villanous saltpetre should be digg'd
Out of the bowels of the harmless earth,
Which many a good tall fellow had destroy'd
So cowardly; and but for these vile guns,
He would himself have been a soldier.
> *Ibid. Line 57*

The blood more stirs
To rouse a lion than to start a hare!
> *King Henry IV, Part I.*
> *Act I, Sc. 3, Line 197*

By heaven, methinks it were an easy leap
To pluck bright honour from the pale-faced moon,
Or dive into the bottom of the deep,
Where fathom-line could never touch the ground,
And pluck up drowned honour by the locks.
> *Ibid. Line 201*

This house is turned upside down.
> *Ibid. Act II, Sc. 1, Line 11*

What's o'clock?
> *Ibid. Line 36*

I know a trick worth two of that.[1]
> *Ibid. Line 40*

If the rascal have not given me medicines to make me love him, I'll be hanged.
> *Ibid. Sc. 2, Line 20*

It would be argument for a week, laughter for a month, and a good jest for ever.
> *Ibid. Line 104*

Falstaff sweats to death,
And lards the lean earth as he walks along.
> *Ibid. Line 119*

Out of this nettle, danger, we pluck this flower, safety.
> *Ibid. Sc. 3, Line 11*

Brain him with his lady's fan.
> *Ibid. Line 26*

A Corinthian, a lad of mettle, a good boy.
> *Ibid. Sc. 4, Line 13*

A plague of all cowards, I say.
> *Ibid. Line 129*

There live not three good men unhanged in England, and one of them is fat and grows old.
> *Ibid. Line 146*

Call you that backing of your friends? A plague upon such backing!
> *Ibid. Line 168*

I have peppered two of them: two

---

[1] THOMAS NASH: *Have with you to Saffron Walden.* DRYDEN: *Epilogue to the Duke of Guise*

[1] We know a trick worth two of that. — W. M. THACKERAY: *The Newcomes, Vol. I, Chap. 1*

I am sure I have paid, two rogues in
buckram suits. I tell thee what, Hal,
if I tell thee a lie, spit in my face; call
me horse. Thou knowest my old ward;
— here I lay, and thus I bore my point.
Four rogues in buckram let drive at
me —

> *King Henry IV, Part I.*
> *Act II, Sc. 4, Line 215*

Three misbegotten knaves in Kendal
green.

> *Ibid. Line 249*

Give you a reason on compulsion!
If reasons were as plentiful as blackberries, I would give no man a reason
upon compulsion, I.

> *Ibid. Line 267*

Mark now, how a plain tale shall put
you down.

> *Ibid. Line 285*

No more of that, Hal, an thou lovest
me!

> *Ibid. Line 316*

What doth gravity out of his bed at
midnight?

> *Ibid. Line 328*

A plague of sighing and grief! It
blows a man up like a bladder.

> *Ibid. Line 370*

You may buy land now as cheap as
stinking mackerel.

> *Ibid. Line 399*

That reverend vice, that grey iniquity, that father ruffian, that vanity
in years.

> *Ibid. Line 505*

Banish plump Jack, and banish all
the world.

> *Ibid. Line 534*

Play out the play.

> *Ibid. Line 539*

O, monstrous! but one half-pennyworth of bread to this intolerable deal
of sack!

> *Ibid. Line 597*

Diseased Nature oftentimes breaks
forth
In strange eruptions.

> *Ibid. Act III, Sc. 1, Line 27*

I am not in the roll of common men.

> *Ibid. Line 43*

Glendower. I can call spirits from the
vasty deep.

Hotspur. Why, so can I, or so can any
man;
But will they come when you do call
for them?

> *King Henry IV, Part I.*
> *Act III, Sc. 1, Line 53*

While you live, tell truth and shame
the devil! [1]

> *Ibid. Line 58*

I had rather be a kitten and cry mew,
Than one of these same metre ballad-
mongers.

> *Ibid. Line 128*

But in the way of bargain, mark ye me,
I'll cavil on the ninth part of a hair.

> *Ibid. Line 138*

A deal of skimble-skamble stuff.

> *Ibid. Line 153*

Exceedingly well read.

> *Ibid. Line 165*

Those musicians that shall play to you
Hang in the air a thousand leagues from
hence. [2]

> *Ibid. Line 226*

A good mouth-filling oath.

> *Ibid. Line 258*

A fellow of no mark nor likelihood.

> *Ibid. Sc. 2, Line 45*

To loathe the taste of sweetness,
whereof a little
More than a little is by much too much.

> *Ibid. Line 72*

The end of life cancels all bands.

> *Ibid. Line 157*

An I have not forgotten what the inside of a church is made of, I am a
pepper-corn.

> *Ibid. Sc. 3, Line 8*

---

[1] BEAUMONT AND FLETCHER: *Wit without
Money, Act IV, Sc. 1.* SWIFT: *Mary the Cook-
maid's Letter*
  Speak the truth and shame the devil. —
RABELAIS: *Works, Author's Prologue to the
Fifth Book*
  I'd tell the truth, and shame the devil. —
JOHNSON: *Boswell's Life of Dr. Johnson*
(Everyman edition), Vol. I, page 460
    Truth being truth,
    Tell it and shame the devil.
  BROWNING: *The Ring and the Book,*
        III, The Other Half-Rome
[2] A good motto for a broadcasting com-
pany. Or Walt Whitman: "Broadcast doings
of the day and night." [1855 Preface.]

Company, villanous company, hath been the spoil of me.
King Henry IV, Part I.
Act III, Sc. 3, Line 10

Shall I not take mine ease in mine inn? [1]
Ibid. Line 91

Rob me the exchequer.
Ibid. Line 204

How has he the leisure to be sick
In such a justling time?
Ibid. Act IV, Sc. 1, Line 17

This sickness doth infect
The very life-blood of our enterprise.
Ibid. Line 28

That daffed the world aside,
And bid it pass.
Ibid. Line 96

Baited like eagles having lately bathed. . . .
As full of spirit as the month of May,
And gorgeous as the sun at midsummer.
Ibid. Line 99

The cankers of a calm world and a long peace.
Ibid. Sc. 2, Line 32

There's but a shirt and a half in all my company; and the half-shirt is two napkins tacked together and thrown over the shoulders like an herald's coat without sleeves.
Ibid. Line 46

Food for powder, food for powder; they'll fill a pit as well as better.
Ibid. Line 72

To the latter end of a fray and the beginning of a feast
Fits a dull fighter and a keen guest.[2]
Ibid. Line 86

I could be well content
To entertain the lag-end of my life
With quiet hours.
Ibid. Act V, Sc. 1, Line 23

I would 't were bedtime, Hal, and all well.
Ibid. Line 126

Honour pricks me on. Yea, but how if honour prick me off when I come on, — how then? Can honour set to a leg? no: or an arm? no: or take away the grief of a wound? no. Honour hath no skill in surgery, then? no. What is hon-

our? a word. What is in that word honour; what is that honour? air. A trim reckoning! Who hath it? he that died o' Wednesday.[1] Doth he feel it? no. Doth he hear it? no. It is insensible, then? yea, to the dead. But will it not live with the living? no. Why? detraction will not suffer it. Therefore I'll none of it. Honour is a mere scutcheon. And so ends my catechism.
King Henry IV, Part I.
Act V, Sc. 1, Line 131

The time of life is short;
To spend that shortness basely were too long.
Ibid. Sc. 2, Line 81

Two stars keep not their motion in one sphere.
Ibid. Sc. 4, Line 65

This earth, that bears thee dead,
Bears not alive so stout a gentleman.
Ibid. Line 92

Thy ignominy sleep with thee in the grave,
But not remember'd in thy epitaph!
Ibid. Line 100

I could have better spared a better man.
Ibid. Line 104

The better part of valour is discretion.[2]
Ibid. Line 120

Full bravely hast thou fleshed
Thy maiden sword.
Ibid. Line 132

Lord, Lord, how this world is given to lying! I grant you I was down and out of breath; and so was he. But we rose both at an instant, and fought a long hour by Shrewsbury clock.
Ibid. Line 148

I'll purge, and leave sack, and live cleanly.
Ibid. Line 168

Even such a man, so faint, so spiritless,
So dull, so dead in look, so woe-begone,
Drew Priam's curtain in the dead of night,

---

[1] See Heywood, page 12.
[2] *Ibid.*, page 17.

[1] Where 's he that died o' Wednesday? — E. C. STEDMAN: *Falstaff's Song, St. 1*
[2] It show'd discretion the best part of valour. — BEAUMONT AND FLETCHER: *A King and no King, Act II, Sc. 3*

And would have told him half his Troy was burnt.

King Henry IV, Part II.
Act I, Sc. 1, Line 70

Yet the first bringer of unwelcome news
Hath but a losing office, and his tongue
Sounds ever after as a sullen bell,
Remember'd knolling a departing friend.

Ibid. Line 100

I am not only witty in myself, but the cause that wit is in other men.[1]

Ibid. Sc. 2, Line 10

A rascally yea-forsooth knave.

Ibid. Line 40

You lie in your throat if you say I am any other than an honest man.

Ibid. Line 97

Some smack of age in you, some relish of the saltness of time.

Ibid. Line 112

It is the disease of not listening, the malady of not marking, that I am troubled withal.

Ibid. Line 139

We that are in the vaward of our youth.

Ibid. Line 201

For my voice, I have lost it with hollaing and singing of anthems.

Ibid. Line 215

Pray that our armies join not in a hot day; for, by the Lord, I take but two shirts out with me, and I mean not to sweat extraordinarily.

Ibid. Line 237

It was always yet the trick of our English nation, if they have a good thing, to make it too common.

Ibid. Line 244

I were better to be eaten to death with rust than to be scoured to nothing with perpetual motion.

Ibid. Line 249

If I do, fillip me with a three-man beetle.

Ibid. Line 259

Who lined himself with hope,
Eating the air on promise of supply.

Ibid. Sc. 3, Line 27

[1] See Johnson, page 238.

When we mean to build,
We first survey the plot, then draw the model;
And when we see the figure of the house,
Then must we rate the cost of the erection.[1]

King Henry IV, Part II
Act I, Sc. 3, Line 41

A habitation giddy and unsure
Hath he that buildeth on the vulgar heart.

Ibid. Line 89

Past and to come seem best; things present worst.

Ibid. Line 108

A poor lone woman.

Ibid. Act II, Sc. 1, Line 37

I'll tickle your catastrophe.

Ibid. Line 68

He hath eaten me out of house and home.

Ibid. Line 82

Thou didst swear to me upon a parcel-gilt goblet, sitting in my Dolphin-chamber, at the round table, by a sea-coal fire, upon Wednesday in Wheeson week.

Ibid. Line 96

I do now remember the poor creature, small beer.[2]

Ibid. Sc. 2, Line 12

Let the end try the man.

Ibid. Line 52

Thus we play the fools with the time, and the spirits of the wise sit in the clouds and mock us.

Ibid. Line 155

He was indeed the glass
Wherein the noble youth did dress themselves.

Ibid. Sc. 3, Line 21

A good heart's worth gold.

Ibid. Sc. 4, Line 34

[1] Which of you, intending to build a tower, sitteth not down first, and counteth the cost, whether he have sufficient to finish it? — *Luke, XIV, 28*

[2] Doth it not show vilely in me to desire small beer? — *King Henry IV, Part II, Act II, Sc. 2, L. 7*

To suckle fools and chronicle small beer. — *Othello, Act II, Sc. 1, L. 160*

That questionable superfluity — small beer. — DOUGLAS JERROLD [1803–1857]: *The Tragedy of the Till*

Aggravate your choler.
King Henry IV, Part II.
Act II, Sc. 4, Line 174

Is it not strange that desire should so many years outlive performance?
Ibid. Line 283

Now comes in the sweetest morsel of the night, and we must hence and leave it unpicked.
Ibid. Line 401

O sleep, O gentle sleep,[1]
Nature's soft nurse! how have I frighted thee,
That thou no more wilt weigh my eyelids down
And steep my senses in forgetfulness?
Ibid. Act III, Sc. 1, Line 5

With all appliances and means to boot.
Ibid. Line 29

Uneasy lies the head that wears a crown.
Ibid. Line 31

There is a history in all men's lives.
Ibid. Line 80

How many of mine old acquaintance are dead!
Ibid. Sc. 2, Line 37

Death, as the Psalmist saith, is certain to all; all shall die. How a good yoke of bullocks at Stamford fair?
Ibid. Line 41

Accommodated; that is, when a man is, as they say, accommodated; or when a man is, being, whereby a' may be thought to be accommodated, — which is an excellent thing.
Ibid. Line 86

Most forcible Feeble.
Ibid. Line 181

We have heard the chimes at midnight.
Ibid. Line 231

A man can die but once.
Ibid. Line 253

We are ready to try our fortunes
To the last man.
Ibid. Act IV, Sc. 2, Line 43

I may justly say, with the hook-nosed fellow of Rome,[1] "I came, saw, and overcame."
King Henry IV, Part II.
Act IV, Sc. 3, Line 44

If I had a thousand sons, the first human principle I would teach them should be, to forswear thin potations and to addict themselves to sack.
Ibid. Line 133

Will Fortune never come with both hands full
But write her fair words still in foulest letters?
She either gives a stomach and no food;
Such are the poor, in health; or else a feast
And takes away the stomach.
Ibid. Sc. 4, Line 103

Golden care!
That keep'st the ports of slumber open wide
To many a watchful night!
Ibid. Sc. 5, Line 22

Thy wish was father, Harry, to that thought.
Ibid. Line 91

Commit
The oldest sins the newest kind of ways.
Ibid. Line 124

A joint of mutton, and any pretty little tiny kickshaws, tell William cook.
Ibid. Act V, Sc. 1, Line 28

His cares are now all ended.
Ibid. Sc. 2, Line 3

I hope to see London once ere I die.
Ibid. Sc. 3, Line 61

Falstaff. What wind blew you hither, Pistol?
Pistol. Not the ill wind which blows no man to good.[2]
Ibid. Line 87

A foutra for the world and worldlings base!
I speak of Africa and golden joys.
Ibid. Line 100

---

[1] Sleep, most gentle sleep. — Ovid: *Metamorphoses, Book II, L. 624*

[1] After he routed Pharnaces Ponticus at the first assault, Caesar wrote thus to his friends: "I came, I saw, I conquered" (Veni, vidi, vici). — Plutarch's *Lives: Cæsar*
[2] See Heywood, page 17.
Ill blows the wind that profits nobody. — *King Henry VI, Part III, Act 2, Sc. 5, L. 55*

Under which king, Bezonian? speak, or die!

> *King Henry IV, Part II.*
> *Act V, Sc. 3, Line 116*

Falstaff. What! is the old king dead?
Pistol. As nail in door.[1]

> *Ibid. Line 123*

How ill white hairs become a fool and jester.

> *Ibid. Sc. 4, Line 53*

O! for a Muse of fire, that would ascend
The brightest heaven of invention!

> *King Henry V. Prologue, Line 1*

Consideration like an angel came,
And whipped the offending Adam out of him.

> *Ibid. Act I, Sc. 1, Line 28*

Hear him debate of commonwealth affairs,
You would say it hath been all in all his study.

> *Ibid. Line 41*

Turn him to any cause of policy,
The Gordian knot of it he will unloose,
Familiar as his garter: that when he speaks,
The air, a chartered libertine, is still.

> *Ibid. Line 45*

Wholesome berries thrive and ripen best
Neighbour'd by fruit of baser quality.

> *Ibid. Line 61*

'Tis ever common
That men are merriest when they are from home.

> *Ibid. Sc. 2, Line 271*

O England! model to thy inward greatness,
Like little body with a mighty heart,
What mightst thou do, that honour would thee do,
Were all thy children kind and natural!

> *Ibid. Act II, Prologue, Line 16*

Even at the turning o' the tide.

> *Ibid. Act II, Sc. 3, Line 13*

---

[1] As dead as a door nail. — WILLIAM LANGLAND: *The Vision of Piers Plowman, Part 2,* L. *183*
As dead as a door-nail. — *King Henry VI, Part II, Act 4, Sc. 10, L. 43*
Old Marley was as dead as a door-nail. — CHARLES DICKENS: *A Christmas Carol, Stave One*

His nose was as sharp as a pen, and a' babbled of green fields.

> *King Henry V. Act II, Sc. 3, Line 17*

As cold as any stone.

> *Ibid. Line 26*

Self-love, my liege, is not so vile a sin
As self-neglecting.

> *Ibid. Sc. 4, Line 74*

Once more unto the breach, dear friends, once more;
Or close the wall up with our English dead!
In peace there's nothing so becomes a man
As modest stillness and humility;
But when the blast of war blows in our ears,
Then imitate the action of the tiger:
Stiffen the sinews, summon up the blood.

> *Ibid. Act III, Sc. 1, Line 1*

And sheathed their swords for lack of argument.

> *Ibid. Line 21*

The mettle of your pasture.

> *Ibid. Line 27*

I see you stand like greyhounds in the slips,
Straining upon the start.

> *Ibid. Line 31*

I would give all my fame for a pot of ale and safety.

> *Ibid. Sc. 2, Line 14*

Men of few words are the best men.

> *Ibid. Line 40*

He will maintain his argument as well as any military man in the world.

> *Ibid. Line 89*

I know the disciplines of wars.

> *Ibid. Line 156*

Impious war,
Array'd in flames like to the prince of fiends,
Do, with his smirch'd complexion, all fell feats
Enlink'd to waste and desolation.

> *Ibid. Sc. 3, Line 15*

A man that I love and honour with my soul, and my heart, and my duty, and my life, and my living, and my uttermost power.

> *Ibid. Sc. 6, Line 7*

Giddy Fortune's furious fickle wheel,
That goddess blind,
That stands upon the rolling restless
stone.
King Henry V. Act III, Sc. 6, Line 28
I thought upon one pair of English legs
Did march three Frenchmen.
Ibid. Line 161
We are in God's hand.
Ibid. Line 181
That island of England breeds very
valiant creatures: their mastiffs are of
unmatchable courage.
Ibid. Sc. 7, Line 155
You may as well say that's a val-
iant flea that dare eat his breakfast on
the lip of a lion.
Ibid. Line 160
The hum of either army stilly sounds,
That the fixed sentinels almost receive
The secret whispers of each other's
watch;
Fire answers fire, and through their
paly flames
Each battle sees the other's umbered
face;
Steed threatens steed, in high and boast-
ful neighs
Piercing the night's dull ear; and from
the tents
The armourers, accomplishing the
knights,
With busy hammers closing rivets up,[1]
Give dreadful note of preparation.
Ibid. Act IV, Prologue, Line 5
There is some soul of goodness in things
evil,
Would men observingly distil it out.
Ibid. Act IV, Sc. 1, Line 4
When blood is their argument.
Ibid. Line 151
Every subject's duty is the king's;
but every subject's soul is his own.
Ibid. Line 189
Who with a body filled and vacant mind
Gets him to rest, crammed with distress-
ful bread.
Ibid. Line 289
Winding up days with toil and nights
with sleep.
Ibid. Line 299

He is as full of valour as of kindness;
Princely in both.
King Henry V. Act IV, Sc. 3, Line 15
But if it be a sin to covet honour,
I am the most offending soul alive.
Ibid. Line 28
This day is called the feast of Crispian:
He that outlives this day, and comes
safe home,
Will stand a tip-toe when this day is
named,
And rouse him at the name of Crispian.
Ibid. Line 40
Then shall our names,
Familiar in his mouth as household
words,
Harry the King, Bedford and Exeter,
Warwick and Talbot, Salisbury and
Gloucester, —
Be in their flowing cups freshly remem-
bered.
Ibid. Line 51
We few, we happy few, we band of
brothers.
Ibid. Line 60
Those that leave their valiant bones in
France,
Dying like men, . . .
They shall be fam'd; for there the sun
shall greet them,
And draw their honours reeking up to
heaven.
Ibid. Line 98
The saying is true, "The empty ves-
sel makes the greatest sound."
Ibid. Sc. 4, Line 72
There is a river in Macedon, and
there is also moreover a river at Mon-
mouth; . . . and there is salmons in
both.
Ibid. Sc. 7, Line 28
There is occasions and causes why
and wherefore [1] in all things.
Ibid. Act V, Sc. 1, Line 3
By this leek, I will most horribly re-
venge. I eat and eat, I swear.
Ibid. Line 49
All hell shall stir for this.
Ibid. Line 72

---

[1] With clink of hammers closing rivets up.
— CIBBER: *Richard III (altered), Act V, Sc. 3*

[1] Every why hath a wherefore. — *The Comedy of Errors, Act II, Sc. 2, L. 45*
See Samuel Butler, page 142.

A fellow of plain and uncoined constancy.
King Henry V. Act V, Sc. 2, Line 160

My comfort is, that old age, that ill layer-up of beauty, can do no more spoil upon my face.
Ibid. Line 246

If he be not fellow with the best king, thou shalt find the best king of good fellows.[1]
Ibid. Line 259

Hung be the heavens with black, yield day to night!
King Henry VI, Part I. Act I, Sc. 1, Line 1

Fight till the last gasp.[2]
Ibid. Sc. 2, Line 127

Halcyon days.
Ibid. Line 131

Glory is like a circle in the water,
Which never ceaseth to enlarge itself,
Till by broad spreading it disperse to nought.
Ibid. Line 133

The sun with one eye vieweth all the world.
Ibid. Sc. 4, Line 84

Between two hawks, which flies the higher pitch;
Between two dogs, which hath the deeper mouth;
Between two blades, which bears the better temper;
Between two horses, which doth bear him best;
Between two girls, which hath the merriest eye;
I have perhaps, some shallow spirit of judgment;
But in these nice sharp quillets of the law,
Good faith, I am no wiser than a daw.
Ibid. Act II, Sc. 4, Line 12

I'll note you in my book of memory.
Ibid. Line 101

Just death, kind umpire of men's miseries.
Ibid. Sc. 5, Line 29

---

[1] He was a good felawe. — CHAUCER: *The Canterbury Tales, Prologue, L. 395*
[2] To the last gasp. — *As You Like It, Act II, Sc. 3, L. 69*

Fair be all thy hopes,
And prosperous be thy life in peace and war!
King Henry VI, Part I. Act II, Sc. 5, Line 113

Chok'd with ambition of the meaner sort.
Ibid. Line 123

Friendly counsel cuts off many foes.
Ibid. Act III, Sc. 1, Line 184

Delays have dangerous ends.[1]
Ibid. Sc. 2, Line 33

Care is no cure, but rather corrosive,
For things that are not to be remedied.
Ibid. Sc. 3, Line 3

Of all base passions, fear is most accurs'd.
Ibid. Act V, Sc. 2, Line 18

She's beautiful and therefore to be wooed,
She is a woman, therefore to be won.
Ibid. Sc. 3, Line 78

For what is wedlock forced, but a hell,
An age of discord and continual strife?
Whereas the contrary bringeth bliss,
And is a pattern of celestial peace.
Ibid. Sc. 5, Line 62

O Lord! that lends me life,
Lend me a heart replete with thankfulness!
Ibid. Part II. Act I, Sc. 1, Line 19

Whose large style
Agrees not with the leanness of his purse.
Ibid. Line 112

'Tis not my speeches that you do mislike,
But 'tis my presence that doth trouble ye.
Rancour will out.
Ibid. Line 141

Main chance.[2]
Ibid. Line 213

Could I come near your beauty with my nails

---

[1] All delays are dangerous in war. — DRYDEN: *Tyrannic Love, Act I, Sc. 1*
[2] Let me stande to the maine chance. — JOHN LYLY: *Euphues* [1579], *page 104*
Have a care o' th' main chance. — BUTLER: *Hudibras, Part II, Canto II*
Be careful still of the main chance. — DRYDEN: *Persius, Satire VI*

I'd set my ten commandments in your face.

King Henry VI, Part II.
Act I, Sc. 3, Line 144

Blessed are the peacemakers on earth.[1]

Ibid. Act II, Sc. 1, Line 34

God be prais'd, that to believing souls
Gives light in darkness, comfort in despair!

Ibid. Line 66

God defend the right!

Ibid. Sc. 3, Line 55

Sometimes hath the brightest day a cloud;
And after summer evermore succeeds
Barren winter, with his wrathful nipping cold:
So cares and joys abound, as seasons fleet.

Ibid. Sc. 4, Line 1

Now 'tis the spring, and weeds are shallow-rooted;
Suffer them now and they'll o'ergrow the garden.

Ibid. Act III, Sc. 1, Line 31

Smooth runs the water where the brook is deep.[2]

Ibid. Line 53

In thy face I see
The map of honour, truth, and loyalty.

Ibid. Line 202

What stronger breastplate than a heart untainted!
Thrice is he armed that hath his quarrel just,
And he but naked, though locked up in steel,
Whose conscience with injustice is corrupted.[3]

Ibid. Sc. 2, Line 232

For wheresoe'er thou art in this world's globe.
I'll have an Iris that shall find thee out.

Ibid. Line 406

He dies, and makes no sign.

Ibid. Sc. 3, Line 29

[1] Blessed are the peacemakers. — *Matthew,* V, 9
[2] See Raleigh, page 21, and Lyly, page 24.
[3] I'm armed with more than complete steel, —
The justice of my quarrel. —
CHRISTOPHER MARLOWE: *Lust's Dominion, Act III, Sc. 4*

Close up his eyes and draw the curtain close;
And let us all to meditation.

King Henry VI, Part II.
Act III, Sc. 3, Line 32

The gaudy, blabbing, and remorseful day
Is crept into the bosom of the sea.

Ibid. Act IV, Sc. 1, Line 1

Small things make base men proud.

Ibid. Line 106

True nobility is exempt from fear.

Ibid. Line 129

There shall be in England seven halfpenny loaves sold for a penny; the three-hooped pot shall have ten hoops; and I will make it felony to drink small beer.

Ibid. Sc. 2, Line 73

The first thing we do, let's kill all the lawyers.

Ibid. Line 86

Is not this a lamentable thing, that of the skin of an innocent lamb should be made parchment? that parchment, being scribbled o'er, should undo a man?

Ibid. Line 88

Sir, he made a chimney in my father's house, and the bricks are alive at this day to testify it.

Ibid. Line 160

Thou hast most traitorously corrupted the youth of the realm in erecting a grammar-school; and whereas, before, our forefathers had no other books but the score and the tally, thou hast caused printing to be used; and, contrary to the king, his crown, and dignity, thou hast built a paper-mill.

Ibid. Sc. 7, Line 35

Beggars mounted run their horse to death.

Ibid. Part III. Act I, Sc. 4, Line 127

O tiger's heart wrapp'd in a woman's hide![1]

Ibid. Line 137

And many strokes, though with a little axe,

[1] ROBERT GREENE in his famous attack on Shakespeare, *A Groats-Worth of Wit* [1592], burlesques this line: "Tyger's hart wrapt in a Player's hide."

Hew down and fell the hardest-timbered
oak.
> *King Henry VI, Part III.*
> *Act II, Sc. 1, Line 54*

To weep is to make less the depth of
grief.
> *Ibid. Line 85*

The smallest worm will turn, being
trodden on.
> *Ibid. Sc. 2, Line 17*

Didst thou never hear
That things ill got had ever bad suc-
cess?
And happy always was it for that son
Whose father for his hoarding went to
hell?
> *Ibid. Line 45*

Thou setter up and plucker down of
kings.[1]
> *Ibid. Sc. 3, Line 37*

And what makes robbers bold but too
much lenity?
> *Ibid. Sc. 6, Line 22*

My crown is in my heart, not on my
head;
Not deck'd with diamonds and Indian
stones,
Nor to be seen: my crown is call'd content;
A crown it is that seldom kings enjoy.
> *Ibid. Act III, Sc. 1, Line 62*

'Tis a happy thing
To be the father unto many sons.
> *Ibid. Sc. 2, Line 104*

Gloucester. That would be ten days'
wonder at the least.
Clarence. That's a day longer than a
wonder lasts.[2]
> *Ibid. Line 113*

Like one that stands upon a promontory,
And spies a far-off shore where he would
tread,
Wishing his foot were equal with his
eye.
> *Ibid. Line 135*

Yield not thy neck
To fortune's yoke, but let thy dauntless
mind

---

[1] Proud setter up and puller down of kings.
— *Act III, Sc. 3, L. 156*
[2] See Chaucer, page 4.

Still ride in triumph over all mischance.
> *King Henry VI, Part III.*
> *Act III, Sc. 3, Line 16*

For how can tyrants safely govern
home,
Unless abroad they purchase great alliance?
> *Ibid. Line 69*

Having nothing, nothing can he lose.
> *Ibid. Line 152*

Both of you are birds of self-same
feather.
> *Ibid. Line 161*

Hasty marriage seldom proveth well.
> *Ibid. Act IV, Sc. 1, Line 18*

Let us be back'd with God and with the
seas
Which he hath given for fence impregnable,
And with their helps only defend ourselves:
In them and in ourselves our safety lies.
> *Ibid. Line 43*

What fates impose, that men must
needs abide;
It boots not to resist both wind and tide.
> *Ibid. Sc. 3, Line 57*

'Tis no time to talk.
> *Ibid. Sc. 5, Line 24*

Now join your hands, and with your
hands your hearts.
> *Ibid. Sc. 6, Line 39*

For many men that stumble at the
threshold
Are well foretold that danger lurks
within.
> *Ibid. Sc. 7, Line 11*

A little fire is quickly trodden out;
Which, being suffered, rivers cannot
quench.
> *Ibid. Sc. 8, Line 7*

When the lion fawns upon the lamb,
The lamb will never cease to follow
him.
> *Ibid. Line 49*

What is pomp, rule, reign, but earth and
dust?
And, live we how we can, yet die we
must.
> *Ibid. Act V, Sc. 2, Line 27*

Every cloud engenders not a storm.
> *Ibid. Sc. 3, Line 12*

We are advertis'd by our loving friends.
King Henry VI, Part III.
Act V, Sc. 3, Line 18
What though the mast be now blown over-board,
The cable broke, the holding anchor lost,
And half our sailors swallow'd in the flood?
Yet lives our pilot still.
Ibid. Sc. 4, Line 3
So part we sadly in this troublous world
To meet with joy in sweet Jerusalem.
Ibid. Sc. 5, Line 7
Men ne'er spend their fury on a child.
Ibid. Line 57
He's sudden if a thing comes in his head.
Ibid. Line 86
Suspicion always haunts the guilty mind;
The thief doth fear each bush an officer.
Ibid. Sc. 6, Line 11
This word "love," which greybeards call divine.
Ibid. Line 81
Mirthful comic shows.
Ibid. Sc. 7, Line 43
Now is the winter of our discontent
Made glorious summer by this sun of York.
King Richard III. Act I, Sc. 1,
Line 1
Grim-visaged war hath smoothed his wrinkled front.
Ibid. Line 9
To leave this keen encounter of our wits.
Ibid. Sc. 2, Line 116
His better doth not breathe upon the earth.
Ibid. Line 141
Look, how my ring encompasseth thy finger,
Even so thy breast encloseth my poor heart;
Wear both of them, for both of them are thine.
Ibid. Line 204
Was ever woman in this humour wooed?
Was ever woman in this humour won?
Ibid. Line 229
Framed in the prodigality of nature.
Ibid. Line 245

The world is grown so bad,
That wrens make prey where eagles dare not perch.[1]
King Richard III. Act I,
Sc. 3, Line 70
They that stand high have many blasts to shake them.
Ibid. Line 259
And thus I clothe my naked villany
With odd old ends stolen forth of holy writ,
And seem a saint when most I play the devil.
Ibid. Line 336
Talkers are no good doers.
Ibid. Line 351
O, I have passed a miserable night,
So full of ugly sights, of ghastly dreams,
That, as I am a Christian faithful man,
I would not spend another such a night,
Though 'twere to buy a world of happy days.
Ibid. Sc. 4, Line 2
Lord, Lord! methought, what pain it was to drown:
What dreadful noise of waters in mine ears!
What ugly sights of death within mine eyes!
Ibid. Line 21
I pass'd, methought, the melancholy flood,
With that grim ferryman which poets write of,
Unto the kingdom of perpetual night.
Ibid. Line 45
Sorrow breaks seasons and reposing hours,
Makes the night morning, and the noon-tide night.
Ibid. Line 76
Thou art a widow; yet thou art a mother,
And hast the comfort of thy children left thee.
Ibid. Act II, Sc. 2, Line 55
A parlous boy.
Ibid. Sc. 4, Line 35

[1] For fools rush in where angels fear to tread. — POPE: *Essay on Criticism, Part III,* L. 66

So wise so young, they say, do never
live long.[1]
> *King Richard III. Act III,*
> *Sc. 1, Line 79*

Off with his head! [2]
> *Ibid. Sc. 4, Line 75*

Lives like a drunken sailor on a mast,
Ready with every nod to tumble down.
> *Ibid. Line 98*

Even in the afternoon of her best days.
> *Ibid. Sc. 7, Line 185*

Thou troublest me: I am not in the vein.
> *Ibid. Act IV, Sc. 2, Line 117*

Their lips were four red roses on a stalk.
> *Ibid. Sc. 3, Line 12*

The sons of Edward sleep in Abraham's
bosom.
> *Ibid. Line 38*

Let not the heavens hear these tell-tale
women
Rail on the Lord's anointed.
> *Ibid. Sc. 4, Line 150*

Tetchy and wayward.
> *Ibid. Line 169*

An honest tale speeds best being plainly
told.
> *Ibid. Line 359*

Harp not on that string.
> *Ibid. Line 365*

Thus far into the bowels of the land
Have we marched on without impediment.
> *Ibid. Act V, Sc. 2, Line 3*

True hope is swift, and flies with swallow's wings;
Kings it makes gods, and meaner creatures kings.
> *Ibid. Line 23*

The king's name is a tower of strength.
> *Ibid. Sc. 3, Line 12*

Give me another horse! bind up my
wounds!
> *Ibid. Line 178*

O coward conscience, how dost thou afflict me!
> *Ibid. Line 180*

My conscience hath a thousand several
tongues,

And every tongue brings in a several
tale,
And every tale condemns me for a villain.
> *King Richard III. Act V,*
> *Sc. 3, Line 194*

The early village cock
Hath twice done salutation to the morn
> *Ibid. Line 210*

By the apostle Paul, shadows to-night
Have struck more terror to the soul of
Richard
Than can the substance of ten thousand
soldiers.
> *Ibid. Line 217*

A horse! a horse! my kingdom for a
horse!
> *Ibid. Sc. 4, Line 7*

I have set my life upon a cast,
And I will stand the hazard of the die:
I think there be six Richmonds in the
field.
> *Ibid. Line 9*

Order gave each thing view.
> *King Henry VIII. Act I, Sc. 1,*
> *Line 44*

No man's pie is freed
From his ambitious finger.
> *Ibid. Line 52*

The force of his own merit makes his
way.
> *Ibid. Line 64*

Anger is like
A full-hot horse, who being allow'd his
way,
Self-mettle tires him.
> *Ibid. Line 132*

Heat not a furnace for your foe so hot
That it do singe yourself.
> *Ibid. Line 140*

New customs,
Though they be never so ridiculous,
Nay, let 'em be unmanly, yet are fol-
low'd.
> *Ibid. Sc. 3, Line 2*

The mirror of all courtesy.
> *Ibid. Act II, Sc. 1, Line 53*

This bold bad man.[1]
> *Ibid. Sc. 2, Line 44*

---

[1] A little too wise, they say, do ne'er live
long. — MIDDLETON: *The Phœnix, Act I, Sc. 1*
[2] Off with his head! so much for Buckingham! — CIBBER: *Richard III (altered), Act
IV, Sc. 3*

[1] See Spenser, page 24.

'Tis better to be lowly born,
And range with humble livers in content,
Than to be perked up in a glistering grief
And wear a golden sorrow.
*King Henry VIII. Act II,
Sc. 3, Line 19*

Orpheus with his lute made trees,
And the mountain-tops that freeze,
Bow themselves when he did sing.
Ibid. Act III, Sc. 1, Line 3

Heaven is above all yet; there sits a judge
That no king can corrupt.
Ibid. Line 99

'Tis well said again;
And 'tis a kind of good deed to say well:
And yet words are no deeds.
Ibid. Sc. 2, Line 153

And then to breakfast with
What appetite you have.
Ibid. Line 203

I have touched the highest point of all my greatness;
And from that full meridian of my glory,
I haste now to my setting: I shall fall
Like a bright exhalation in the evening,
And no man see me more.
Ibid. Line 224

Press not a falling man too far!
Ibid. Line 334

Farewell! a long farewell, to all my greatness!
This is the state of man: to-day he puts forth
The tender leaves of hopes; to-morrow blossoms,
And bears his blushing honours thick upon him;
The third day comes a frost, a killing frost;
And, when he thinks, good easy man, full surely
His greatness is a-ripening, nips his root,
And then he falls, as I do. I have ventured,
Like little wanton boys that swim on bladders,
This many summers in a sea of glory,
But far beyond my depth: my high-blown pride
At length broke under me, and now has left me,
Weary and old with service, to the mercy
Of a rude stream, that must forever hide me.
Vain pomp and glory of this world, I hate ye:
I feel my heart new opened. O! how wretched
Is that poor man that hangs on princes' favours!
There is, betwixt that smile we would aspire to,
That sweet aspect of princes, and their ruin,
More pangs and fears than wars or women have —
And when he falls, he falls like Lucifer,
Never to hope again.
*King Henry VIII. Act III,
Sc. 2, Line 352*

A peace above all earthly dignities,
A still and quiet conscience.
Ibid. Line 380

A load would sink a navy.
Ibid. Line 384

And sleep in dull cold marble.
Ibid. Line 434

Say, Wolsey, that once trod the ways of glory,
And sounded all the depths and shoals of honour,
Found thee a way, out of his wrack, to rise in;
A sure and safe one, though thy master missed it.
Ibid. Line 436

I charge thee, fling away ambition:
By that sin fell the angels.
Ibid. Line 441

Love thyself last: cherish those hearts that hate thee;
Corruption wins not more than honesty.
Still in thy right hand carry gentle peace,
To silence envious tongues: be just, and fear not:
Let all the ends thou aim'st at be thy country's,

Thy God's, and truth's; then if thou
　　fall'st, O Cromwell,
Thou fall'st a blessed martyr!
　　　　　King Henry VIII. Act III,
　　　　　　　　　Sc. 2, Line 444
Had I but served my God with half the
　　zeal [1]
I served my king, he would not in mine
　　age
Have left me naked to mine enemies.
　　　　　　　　Ibid. Line 456
A royal train, believe me.
　　　　　Ibid. Act IV, Sc. 1, Line 37
An old man, broken with the storms of
　　state,
Is come to lay his weary bones among
　　ye;
Give him a little earth for charity!
　　　　　　　　Ibid. Sc. 2, Line 21
He gave his honours to the world again,
His blessed part to heaven, and slept in
　　peace.
　　　　　　　　Ibid. Line 29
So may he rest; his faults lie gently on
　　him!
　　　　　　　　Ibid. Line 31
　　　　　He was a man
Of an unbounded stomach.
　　　　　　　　Ibid. Line 33
Men's evil manners live in brass; their
　　virtues
We write in water.[2]
　　　　　　　　Ibid. Line 45
He was a scholar, and a ripe and good
　　one;

[1] Had I served God as well in every part
　　As I did serve my king and master still,
My scope had not this season been so short,
Nor would have had the power to do me
　　ill.
　　　　THOMAS CHURCHYARD [1520–1604]:
　　　　Death of Morton [written in 1593]
[2] For men use, if they have an evil tourne,
to write it in marble: and whoso doth us a
good tourne we write it in duste. — SIR
THOMAS MORE: *Richard III and his Miserable
End*
　　　　　　　　All your better deeds
Shall be in water writ, but this in marble.
　　BEAUMONT AND FLETCHER: *Philaster,*
　　　　　　　　Act V, Sc. 3
L'injure se grave en métal; et le bienfait
s'escrit en l'onde.
(An injury graves itself in metal, but a bene-
　　fit writes itself in water.)
　　　　　JEAN BERTAUT [*circa* 1611]

Exceeding wise, fair-spoken, and per-
　　suading;
Lofty and sour to them that loved him
　　not,
But to those men that sought him sweet
　　as summer.
　　　　　King Henry VIII. Act IV,
　　　　　　　　　Sc. 2, Line 51
　　　　Yet in bestowing, madam,
He was most princely.
　　　　　　　　Ibid. Line 56
After my death I wish no other herald,
No other speaker of my living actions,
To keep mine honour from corruption,
But such an honest chronicler as Grif-
　　fith.
　　　　　　　　Ibid. Line 69
To dance attendance on their lordships'
　　pleasures.
　　　　　Ibid. Act V, Sc. 2, Line 30
　　　　　'Tis a cruelty
To load a falling man.
　　　　　　　　Ibid. Sc. 3, Line 76
You were ever good at sudden commen-
　　dations.
　　　　　　　　Ibid. Line 122
　　　　Those about her
From her shall read the perfect ways of
　　honour.
　　　　　　　　Ibid. Sc. 5, Line 37
Wherever the bright sun of heaven shall
　　shine,
His honour and the greatness of his
　　name
Shall be, and make new nations.
　　　　　　　　Ibid. Line 51
A most unspotted lily shall she pass
To the ground, and all the world shall
　　mourn her.
　　　　　　　　Ibid. Line 62
I have had my labour for my travail.[1]
　　　　　Troilus and Cressida. Act I,
　　　　　　　　　Sc. 1, Line 73
Men prize the thing ungain'd more than
　　it is.
　　　　　　　　Ibid. Sc. 2, Line 313
Take but degree away, untune that
　　string,

[1] Labour for his pains. — EDWARD MOORE.
The Boy and his Rainbow
　　Labour for their pains. — CERVANTES: *Don
Quixote, The Author's Preface*

And, hark! what discord follows; each
thing meets
In mere oppugnancy.[1]

> *Troilus and Cressida. Act I,*
> *Sc. 3, Line 109*

Appetite, a universal wolf.

> *Ibid. Line 121*

To hear the wooden dialogue.

> *Ibid. Line 155*

The baby figure of the giant mass
Of things to come.

> *Ibid. Line 345*

Modest doubt is call'd
The beacon of the wise, the tent that
searches
To the bottom of the worst.

> *Ibid. Act II, Sc. 2, Line 15*

'Tis mad idolatry
To make the service greater than the
god.

> *Ibid. Line 56*

The remainder viands
We do not throw in unrespective sink
Because we now are full.

> *Ibid. Line 70*

The elephant hath joints, but none
for courtesy: his legs are legs for necessity, not for flexure.

> *Ibid. Sc. 3, Line 114*

He that is proud eats up himself;
pride is his own glass, his own trumpet,
his own chronicle.

> *Ibid. Line 165*

Light boats sail swift, though greater
hulks draw deep.

> *Ibid. Line 280*

Words pay no debts.

> *Ibid. Act III, Sc. 2, Line 56*

To fear the worst oft cures the worse.

> *Ibid. Line 77*

All lovers swear more performance
than they are able, and yet reserve an
ability that they never perform; vowing more than the perfection of ten, and
discharging less than the tenth part of
one.

> *Ibid. Line 89*

---

[1] Unless degree is preserved, the first place
is safe for no one. — PUBLIUS SYRUS: *Maxim
1042*

For to be wise, and love,
Exceeds man's might; that dwells with
gods above.

> *Troilus and Cressida. Act III,*
> *Sc. 2, Line 163*

Time hath, my lord, a wallet at his
back,
Wherein he puts alms for oblivion.

> *Ibid. Sc. 3, Line 145*

Welcome ever smiles,
And farewell goes out sighing.

> *Ibid. Line 168*

One touch of nature makes the whole
world kin

> *Ibid. Line 175*

And give to dust that is a little gilt
More laud than gilt o'er-dusted.

> *Ibid. Line 178*

And, like a dew-drop from the lion's
mane,
Be shook to air.

> *Ibid. Line 225*

My mind is troubled, like a fountain
stirr'd;
And I myself see not the bottom of it.

> *Ibid. Line 314*

Be moderate, be moderate.

> *Ibid. Act IV, Sc. 4, Line 1*

As many farewells as be stars in heaven.

> *Ibid. Line 44*

The kiss you take is better than you
give.

> *Ibid. Sc. 5, Line 38*

There's language in her eye, her cheek,
her lip.

> *Ibid. Line 55*

Daughters of the game.

> *Ibid. Line 63*

The end crowns all,
And that old common arbitrator, Time,
Will one day end it.

> *Ibid. Line 223*

He has not so much brain as ear-wax.

> *Ibid. Act V, Sc. 1, Line 58*

A sleeveless errand.

> *Ibid. Sc. 4, Line 9*

O world! world! world! thus is the poor
agent despised.

> *Ibid. Sc. 10, Line 36*

Rubbing the poor itch of your opinion,
Make yourselves scabs.

> *Coriolanus. Act I, Sc. 1, Line 171*

The gods sent not
Corn for the rich men only.
Coriolanus. Act I, Sc. 1,
Line 213

Had I a dozen sons, each in my love
alike and none less dear than thine and
my good Marcius, I had rather eleven
die nobly for their country than one
voluptuously surfeit out of action.
Ibid. Sc. 3, Line 24

All the yarn she spun in Ulysses' absence did but fill Ithaca full of moths.
Ibid. Line 93

Nature teaches beasts to know their
friends.
Ibid. Act II, Sc. 1, Line 6

A cup of hot wine with not a drop of
allaying Tiber in't.[1]
Ibid. Line 52

Bid them wash their faces,
And keep their teeth clean.
Ibid. Sc. 3, Line 65

I thank you for your voices: thank you,
Your most sweet voices.
Ibid. Line 179

The mutable, rank-scented many.
Ibid. Act III, Sc. 1, Line 65

Hear you this Triton of the minnows?
Mark you
His absolute "shall"?
Ibid. Line 88

Enough, with over-measure.
Ibid. Line 139

What is the city but the people?
Ibid. Line 198

His nature is too noble for the world:
He would not flatter Neptune for his
trident,
Or Jove for 's power to thunder.
Ibid. Line 254

That it shall hold companionship in
peace
With honour, as in war.
Ibid. Sc. 2, Line 49

I do love
My country's good with a respect more
tender,

[1] When flowing cups pass swiftly round
With no allaying Thames.
RICHARD LOVELACE: *To Althea from*
Prison, St. 2

More holy, more profound, than mine
own life.
Coriolanus. Act III, Sc. 3,
Line 109

3 Servant. Where dwellest thou?
Coriolanus. Under the canopy.
Ibid. Act IV, Sc. 5, Line 40

You know the very road into his kind-
ness,
And cannot lose your way.
Ibid. Act V, Sc. 1, Line 60

Chaste as the icicle
That's curdied by the frost from purest
snow
And hangs on Dian's temple.
Ibid. Sc. 3, Line 65

Is't possible that so short a time can
alter the condition of a man?
Ibid. Sc. 4, Line 10

They'll give him death by inches.
Ibid. Line 43

Splitting the air with noise.
Ibid. Sc. 5, Line 52

If you have writ your annals true, 'tis
there
That, like an eagle in a dove-cote, I
Flutter'd your Volscians in Corioli:
Alone I did it. Boy!
Ibid. Line 114

Thou hast done a deed whereat valour
will weep.
Ibid. Line 135

He shall have a noble memory.
Ibid. Line 155

Sleep in peace, slain in your country's
wars!
Titus Andronicus. Act I, Sc. 1,
Line 91

Sweet mercy is nobility's true badge.
Ibid. Line 119

In peace and honour rest you here, my
sons;
. . . repose you here in rest,
Secure from worldly chances and mishaps!
Ibid. Line 150

These words are razors to my wounded
heart.
Ibid. Line 314

He lives in fame that died in virtue's
cause.
Ibid. Line 390

These dreary dumps.[1]

> *Titus Andronicus. Act I,*
> *Sc. 1, Line 391*

She is a woman, therefore may be woo'd;
She is a woman, therefore may be won;
She is Lavinia, therefore must be loved.
What, man! more water glideth by the mill
Than wots the miller of;[2] and easy it is
Of a cut loaf to steal a shive.

> *Ibid. Act II, Sc. 1, Line 82*

What you cannot as you would achieve,
You must perforce accomplish as you may.

> *Ibid. Line 106*

How easily murder is discovered!

> *Ibid. Sc. 3, Line 287*

Poor harmless fly.

> *Ibid. Act III, Sc. 2, Line 63*

Two may keep counsel when the third's away.[3]

> *Ibid. Act IV, Sc. 2, Line 145*

The eagle suffers little birds to sing.

> *Ibid. Sc. 4, Line 82*

A pair of star-cross'd lovers.

> *Romeo and Juliet. Act I, Pro-*
> *logue, Line 6*

The weakest goes to the wall.

> *Romeo and Juliet. Act I, Sc. 1,*
> *Line 17*

Gregory, remember thy swashing blow.

> *Ibid. Line 68*

An hour before the worshipp'd sun
Peered forth the golden window of the east.

> *Ibid. Line 124*

As is the bud bit with an envious worm,
Ere he can spread his sweet leaves to the air,
Or dedicate his beauty to the sun.

> *Ibid. Line 156*

Saint-seducing gold.

> *Ibid. Line 220*

He that is strucken blind cannot forget
The precious treasure of his eyesight lost.

> *Ibid. Line 238*

One fire burns out another's burning,[1]
One pain is lessen'd by another's anguish.

> *Romeo and Juliet. Act I,*
> *Sc. 1, Line 47*

I will make thee think thy swan a crow.

> *Ibid. Line 92*

One fairer than my love! the all-seeing sun
Ne'er saw her match since first the world begun.

> *Ibid. Line 97*

That book in many eyes doth share the glory
That in gold clasps locks in the golden story.

> *Ibid. Sc. 3, Line 91*

Beetle brows.

> *Ibid. Sc. 4, Line 32*

For I am proverb'd with a grandsire phrase.

> *Ibid. Line 37*

Benvolio. O! then, I see Queen Mab hath been with you! . . .
Mercutio. She is the fairies' midwife, and she comes
In shape no bigger than an agate-stone
On the fore-finger of an alderman,
Drawn with a team of little atomies
Athwart men's noses as they lie asleep.

> *Ibid. Line 53*

True, I talk of dreams,
Which are the children of an idle brain,
Begot of nothing but vain fantasy.

> *Ibid. Line 97*

Toes unplagu'd with corns.

> *Ibid. Sc. 5, Line 21*

For you and I are past our dancing days.[2]

> *Ibid. Line 35*

It seems she hangs upon the cheek of night
Like a rich jewel in an Ethiop's ear.

> *Ibid. Line 49*

Too early seen unknown, and known too late!

> *Ibid. Line 143*

Young Adam Cupid, he that shot so trim

---

[1] And doleful dumps the mind oppress. — *Romeo and Juliet, Act IV, Sc. 5, L. 130*
[2] See Heywood, page 17.
[3] *Ibid.*, page 16.

[1] See Chapman, page 28.
[2] My dancing days are done. — BEAUMONT AND FLETCHER: *The Scornful Lady, Act V, Sc. 3*

When King Cophetua loved the beggar maid.
>*Romeo and Juliet. Act II,*
>*Sc. 1, Line 13*

He jests at scars, that never felt a wound.

But, soft! what light through yonder window breaks?

It is the east, and Juliet is the sun.
>*Ibid. Sc. 2, Line 1*

She speaks, yet she says nothing.
>*Ibid. Line 12*

See, how she leans her cheek upon her hand.

O! that I were a glove upon that hand,
That I might touch that cheek.
>*Ibid. Line 23*

O Romeo, Romeo! wherefore art thou Romeo?
>*Ibid. Line 33*

What's in a name? That which we call a rose
By any other name would smell as sweet.
>*Ibid. Line 43*

For stony limits cannot hold love out.
>*Ibid. Line 67*

Alack! there lies more peril in thine eye
Than twenty of their swords.
>*Ibid. Line 71*

At lovers' perjuries,[1]
They say, Jove laughs.
>*Ibid. Line 92*

Romeo. Lady, by yonder blessed moon I swear,
That tips with silver all these fruit-tree tops, —

Juliet. O! swear not by the moon, the inconstant moon,
That monthly changes in her circled orb,
Lest that thy love prove likewise variable.
>*Ibid. Line 107*

The god of my idolatry.
>*Ibid. Line 114*

Too like the lightning, which doth cease to be
Ere one can say it lightens.
>*Ibid. Line 119*

[1] Perjuria ridet amantium Jupiter (Jupiter laughs at the perjuries of lovers). — TIBULLUS, III, 6, 49

This bud of love, by summer's ripening breath,
May prove a beauteous flower when next we meet.
>*Romeo and Juliet. Act II,*
>*Sc. 2, Line 121*

A thousand times good-night!
>*Ibid. Line 154*

Love goes toward love, as schoolboys from their books;
But love from love, toward school with heavy looks.
>*Ibid. Line 156*

How silver-sweet sound lovers' tongues by night,
Like softest music to attending ears!
>*Ibid. Line 165*

Good night, good night! parting is such sweet sorrow,
That I shall say good night till it be morrow.
>*Ibid. Line 184*

O! mickle is the powerful grace that lies
In herbs, plants, stones, and their true qualities:
For nought so vile that on the earth doth live
But to the earth some special good doth give,
Nor aught so good but strain'd from that fair use
Revolts from true birth, stumbling on abuse,
Virtue itself turns vice, being misapplied;
And vice sometime's by action dignified.
>*Ibid. Sc. 3, Line 15*

Care keeps his watch in every old man's eye,
And where care lodges, sleep will never lie.
>*Ibid. Line 35*

Wisely and slow; they stumble that run fast.
>*Ibid. Line 94*

Stabbed with a white wench's black eye.
>*Ibid. Sc. 4, Line 14*

The courageous captain of compliments.
>*Ibid. Line 21*

One, two, and the third in your bosom.
>*Ibid. Line 24*

O flesh, flesh, how art thou fishified!
Romeo and Juliet. Act II,
Sc. 4, Line 41

I am the very pink of courtesy.
Ibid. Line 63

If thy wits run the wild-goose chase, I
have done.
Ibid. Line 77

A gentleman, nurse, that loves to hear
himself talk, and will speak more in a
minute than he will stand to in a month.
Ibid. Line 155

A fool's paradise.[1]
Ibid. Line 176

My man's as true as steel.[2]
Ibid. Line 212

Love's heralds should be thoughts,
Which ten times faster glide than the
sun's beams.
Ibid. Sc. 5, Line 4

I wouldst thou hadst my bones, and I
thy news.
Ibid. Line 27

The excuse that thou dost make in this
delay
Is longer than the tale thou dost excuse.
Ibid. Line 33

These violent delights have violent
ends.
Ibid. Sc. 6, Line 9

Too swift arrives as tardy as too slow.
Ibid. Line 15

Here comes the lady: O! so light a foot
Will ne'er wear out the everlasting flint.
Ibid. Line 16

---

[1] The earliest instance of this expression
is found in the *Paston Letters* [1462], *No.
457.* Also WILLIAM BULLEIN's *Dialogue, P. 28*
[1573]
A fool's paradise. — GILES FLETCHER: *The
Sorcerer of Vain Delights, St. 3*
The Paradise of Fools, to few unknown. —
MILTON: *Paradise Lost, Book III, L. 496*
Hence the fool's paradise. — ALEXANDER
POPE: *The Dunciad, Book III, L. 9*
In this fool's paradise he drank delight. —
GEORGE CRABBE: *The Borough, Letter XII,
Players*
Used also by Middleton and Fielding.
[2] Trewe as steel. — CHAUCER: *Troilus and
Criseyde, Book V, L. 831*
As true as steel. — SHAKESPEARE: *Troilus
and Cressida, Act III, Sc. 2, L. 184*

Thy head is as full of quarrels as an
egg is full of meat.[1]
Romeo and Juliet. Act III,
Sc. 1, Line 23

A word and a blow.[2]
Ibid. Line 44

A plague o' both your houses!
Ibid. Line 96

Romeo. Courage, man; the hurt cannot be much.
Mercutio. No, 'tis not so deep as a
well, nor so wide as a church-door; but
'tis enough, 'twill serve.
Ibid. Line 100

When he shall die,
Take him and cut him out in little stars,
And he will make the face of heaven so
fine
That all the world will be in love with
night,
And pay no worship to the garish sun.
Ibid. Sc. 2, Line 21

Was ever book containing such vile
matter
So fairly bound? O! that deceit should
dwell
In such a gorgeous palace.
Ibid. Line 83

They may seize
On the white wonder of dear Juliet's
hand,
And steal immortal blessing from her
lips,
Who, even in pure and vestal modesty,
Still blush, as thinking their own kisses
sin.
Ibid. Sc. 3, Line 35

Adversity's sweet milk, philosophy.
Ibid. Line 54

The lark, the herald of the morn.
Ibid. Sc. 5, Line 6

Night's candles are burnt out, and joc-
und day
Stands tiptoe on the misty mountain-
tops.
Ibid. Line 9

---

[1] It's as full of good-nature as an egg's full
of meat. — R. B. SHERIDAN: *A Trip to Scar-
borough, Act III, Sc. 4*
[2] Word and a blow. — DRYDEN: *Amphitryon, Act I, Sc. 1.* BUNYAN: *Pilgrim's Progress, Part I*

Straining harsh discords and unpleasing sharps.
> *Romeo and Juliet. Act III, Sc. 5, Line 28*

All these woes shall serve
For sweet discourses in our time to come.
> *Ibid. Line 52*

Thank me no thankings, nor proud me no prouds.
> *Ibid. Line 153*

In that dim monument where Tybalt lies.[1]
> *Ibid. Line 203*

Past hope, past cure, past help!
> *Ibid. Act IV, Sc. 1, Line 45*

Not stepping o'er the bounds of modesty.
> *Ibid. Sc. 2, Line 28*

My dismal scene I needs must act alone.
> *Ibid. Sc. 3, Line 19*

My bosom's lord sits lightly in his throne.
> *Ibid. Act V, Sc. 1, Line 3*

Meagre were his looks,
Sharp misery had worn him to the bones.
> *Ibid. Line 40*

A beggarly account of empty boxes.
> *Ibid. Line 45*

Famine is in thy cheeks.
> *Ibid. Line 69*

The world is not thy friend nor the world's law.
> *Ibid. Line 72*

Apothecary. My poverty, but not my will, consents.
Romeo. I pay thy poverty, and not thy will.
> *Ibid. Line 75*

The strength
Of twenty men.
> *Ibid. Line 78*

One writ with me in sour misfortune's book.
> *Ibid. Sc. 3, Line 82*

Her beauty makes
This vault a feasting presence full of light.
> *Romeo and Juliet. Act V, Sc. 3, Line 85*

How oft when men are at the point of death
Have they been merry!
> *Ibid. Line 88*

Beauty's ensign yet
Is crimson in thy lips and in thy cheeks,
And death's pale flag is not advanced there.
> *Ibid. Line 94*

Eyes, look your last!
Arms, take your last embrace!
> *Ibid. Line 112*

O true apothecary!
Thy drugs are quick.
> *Ibid. Line 119*

'Tis not enough to help the feeble up,
But to support him after.
> *Timon of Athens. Act I, Sc. 1, Line 108*

I call the gods to witness.
> *Ibid. Line 138*

Satiety of commendations.
> *Ibid. Line 167*

Ceremony was but devis'd at first
To set a gloss on faint deeds, hollow welcomes,
Recanting goodness, sorry ere 'tis shown;
But where there is true friendship, there needs none.
> *Ibid. Sc. 2, Line 15*

Here's that which is too weak to be a sinner,
Honest water, which ne'er left man i' the mire.[1]
> *Ibid. Line 60*

Immortal gods, I crave no pelf;
I pray for no man but myself:
Grant I may never prove so fond,
To trust man on his oath or bond.
> *Ibid. Line 64*

Men shut their doors against a setting sun.
> *Ibid. Line 152*

---

[1] In that dim monument where Tybalt lies
I would that we lay sleeping side by side.
ARTHUR DAVISON FICKE: *Sonnet*

[1] Inscribed on the drinking fountain in the market-square of Stratford-on-Avon.

Every room
Hath blazed with lights and bray'd with
minstrelsy.
Timon of Athens. Act II,
Sc. 2, Line 170
Every man has his fault, and honesty is
his.
Ibid. Act III, Sc. 1, Line 30
Policy sits above conscience.
Ibid. Sc. 2, Line 95
We have seen better days.
Ibid. Act IV, Sc. 2, Line 27
I am Misanthropos, and hate mankind.
Ibid. Sc. 3, Line 53
I'll example you with thievery:
The sun's a thief, and with his great
attraction
Rob's the vast sea; the moon's an ar-
rant thief,
And her pale fire she snatches from the
sun;
The sea's a thief, whose liquid surge re-
solves
The moon into salt tears; the earth's a
thief,
That feeds and breeds by a composture
stolen
From general excrement, each thing's
a thief.
Ibid. Line 441
Life's uncertain voyage.
Ibid. Act V, Sc. 1, Line 207
A mender of bad soles . . . a surgeon
to old shoes.
Julius Caesar. Act I, Sc. 1, Line 15
As proper men as ever trod upon neat's
leather.
Ibid. Line 27
The live-long day.
Ibid. Line 45
Beware the ides of March.
Ibid. Sc. 2, Line 18
Well, honour is the subject of my story.
I cannot tell what you and other men
Think of this life; but, for my single
self,
I had as lief not be as live to be
In awe of such a thing as I myself.
Ibid. Line 92
"Darest thou, Cassius, now
Leap in with me into this angry flood,
And swim to yonder point?" Upon the
word,

Accoutred as I was, I plunged in
And bade him follow.
Julius Caesar. Act I, Sc. 2, Line 102
Help me, Cassius, or I sink!
Ibid. Line 111
Ye gods, it doth amaze me,
A man of such a feeble temper should
So get the start of the majestic world
And bear the palm alone.
Ibid. Line 128
Why, man, he doth bestride the narrow
world
Like a Colossus; and we petty men
Walk under his huge legs, and peep
about
To find ourselves dishonourable graves.
Men at some time are masters of their
fates:
The fault, dear Brutus, is not in our
stars,
But in ourselves, that we are underlings.
Ibid. Line 134
Upon what meat doth this our Caesar
feed,
That he is grown so great? Age, thou
art shamed!
Rome, thou hast lost the breed of noble
bloods!
Ibid. Line 148
There was a Brutus once that would
have brook'd
The eternal devil to keep his state in
Rome
As easily as a king.
Ibid. Line 158
Let me have men about me that are fat;
Sleek-headed men, and such as sleep o'
nights.
Yond Cassius has a lean and hungry
look;
He thinks too much: such men are dan-
gerous.
Ibid. Line 191
He reads much;
He is a great observer, and he looks
Quite through the deeds of men.
Ibid. Line 200
Seldom he smiles, and smiles in such a
sort
As if he mock'd himself, and scorn'd his
spirit

That could be moved to smile at anything.
>
> *Julius Caesar. Act I,*
> *Sc. 2, Line 204*

But, for my own part, it was Greek to
me.
>
> *Ibid. Line 288*

'Tis a common proof,
That lowliness is young ambition's lad-
der,
Whereto the climber-upward turns his
face;
But when he once attains the upmost
round,
He then unto the ladder turns his back,
Looks in the clouds, scorning the base
degrees
By which he did ascend.
>
> *Ibid. Act II, Sc. 1, Line 21*

Between the acting of a dreadful thing
And the first motion, all the interim is
Like a phantasma, or a hideous dream:
The Genius and the mortal instruments
Are then in council; and the state of
man,
Like to a little kingdom, suffers then
The nature of an insurrection.
>
> *Ibid. Line 63*

A dish fit for the gods.
>
> *Ibid. Line 173*

But when I tell him he hates flatterers,
He says he does, being then most flattered.
>
> *Ibid. Line 207*

Boy! Lucius! Fast asleep? It is no mat-
ter;
Enjoy the honey-heavy dew of slumber:
Thou hast no figures nor no fantasies
Which busy care draws in the brains of
men;
Therefore thou sleep'st so sound.
>
> *Ibid. Line 229*

You are my true and honourable wife,
As dear to me as are the ruddy drops
That visit my sad heart.[1]
>
> *Ibid. Line 288*

Think you I am no stronger than my
sex,
Being so father'd and so husbanded?
>
> *Ibid. Line 296*

[1] Dear as the ruddy drops that warm my
heart. — GRAY: *The Bard, I, 3, L. 12*

Cowards die many times before their
deaths;
The valiant never taste of death but
once.
Of all the wonders that I yet have
heard,
It seems to me most strange that men
should fear;
Seeing that death, a necessary end,
Will come when it will come.
>
> *Julius Caesar. Act II,*
> *Sc. 2, Line 32*

How hard it is for women to keep counsel.
>
> *Ibid. Sc. 4, Line 9*

But I am constant as the northern star,
Of whose true-fix'd and resting quality
There is no fellow in the firmament.
>
> *Ibid. Act III, Sc. 1, Line 60*

Et tu, Brute!
>
> *Ibid. Line 77*

How many ages hence
Shall this our lofty scene be acted o'er,
In states unborn and accents yet un-
known!
>
> *Ibid. Line 111*

The choice and master spirits of this
age.
>
> *Ibid. Line 163*

Though last, not least in love.[1]
>
> *Ibid. Line 189*

O! pardon me, thou bleeding piece of
earth,
That I am meek and gentle with these
butchers!
Thou art the ruins of the noblest man
That ever lived in the tide of times.
>
> *Ibid. Line 254*

Cry "Havoc!" and let slip the dogs of
war.
>
> *Ibid. Line 273*

Romans, countrymen, and lovers!
hear me for my cause; and be silent,
that you may hear.
>
> *Ibid. Sc. 2, Line 13*

[1] Though last not least. — SPENSER: *Colin
Clouts Come Home Againe, L. 444*
Although our last, not least. — *King Lear,
Act I, Sc. 1, L. 85*
The last, not least in honour or applause. —
ALEXANDER POPE: *The Dunciad, Book IV,
L. 577*

Not that I loved Caesar less, but that I loved Rome more.

Julius Caesar. Act III, Sc. 2, Line 22

If any, speak; for him have I offended. I pause for a reply.

Ibid. Line 36

Friends, Romans, countrymen, lend me your ears;
I come to bury Caesar, not to praise him.
The evil that men do lives after them,
The good is oft interred with their bones.

Ibid. Line 79

For Brutus is an honourable man;
So are they all, all honourable men.

Ibid. Line 88

Ambition should be made of sterner stuff.

Ibid. Line 98

O judgment! thou art fled to brutish beasts,
And men have lost their reason.

Ibid. Line 110

But yesterday the word of Caesar might
Have stood against the world; now lies he there,
And none so poor to do him reverence.

Ibid. Line 124

If you have tears, prepare to shed them now.

Ibid. Line 174

See what a rent the envious Casca made.

Ibid. Line 180

This was the most unkindest cut of all.

Ibid. Line 188

Great Caesar fell.
O! what a fall was there, my countrymen;
Then I, and you, and all of us fell down,
Whilst bloody treason flourish'd over us.

Ibid. Line 194

What private griefs they have, alas! I know not.

Ibid. Line 217

I come not, friends, to steal away your hearts:
I am no orator, as Brutus is;

But, as you know me all, a plain blunt man.

Julius Caesar. Act III, Sc. 2, Line 220

I only speak right on.

Ibid. Line 227

Put a tongue
In every wound of Caesar, that should move
The stones of Rome to rise and mutiny.

Ibid. Line 232

When love begins to sicken and decay,
It useth an enforced ceremony.
There are no tricks in plain and simple faith.

Ibid. Act IV, Sc. 2, Line 20

You yourself
Are much condemn'd to have an itching palm.

Ibid. Sc. 3, Line 9

The foremost man of all this world.

Ibid. Line 22

I had rather be a dog, and bay the moon,
Than such a Roman.

Ibid. Line 27

There is no terror, Cassius, in your threats;
For I am arm'd so strong in honesty
That they pass by me as the idle wind,
Which I respect not.

Ibid. Line 66

A friend should bear his friend's infirmities,
But Brutus makes mine greater than they are.

Ibid. Line 85

All his faults observed,
Set in a note-book, learn'd, and conn'd by rote.

Ibid. Line 96

There is a tide in the affairs of men,
Which, taken at the flood, leads on to fortune;
Omitted, all the voyage of their life
Is bound in shallows and in miseries.

Ibid. Line 217

We must take the current when it serves,
Or lose our ventures.

Ibid. Line 222

The deep of night is crept upon our talk,

And nature must obey necessity.
>> *Julius Caesar. Act IV,*
>> *Sc. 3, Line 225*

Brutus. Then I shall see thee again?
Ghost. Ay, at Philippi.
Brutus. Why, I will see thee at Philippi, then.
>> *Ibid. Line 283*

But for your words, they rob the Hybla bees,
And leave them honeyless.
>> *Ibid. Act V, Sc. 1, Line 34*

Forever, and forever, farewell, Cassius!
If we do meet again, why, we shall smile;
If not, why then, this parting was well made.
>> *Ibid. Line 117*

O, that a man might know
The end of this day's business, ere it come.
>> *Ibid. Line 123*

The last of all the Romans, fare thee well!
>> *Ibid. Sc. 3, Line 99*

This was the noblest Roman of them all.
>> *Ibid. Sc. 5, Line 68*

His life was gentle, and the elements
So mix'd in him that Nature might stand up
And say to all the world, "This was a man!"
>> *Ibid. Line 73*

1 Witch. When shall we three meet again
>> In thunder, lightning, or in rain?
2 Witch. When the hurlyburly's done,
>> When the battle's lost and won.
>> *Macbeth. Act I, Sc. 1, Line 1*

Sleep shall neither night nor day
Hang upon his pent-house lid.
>> *Ibid. Sc. 3, Line 19*

Dwindle, peak, and pine.
>> *Ibid. Line 23*

If you can look into the seeds of time,
And say which grain will grow and which will not.
>> *Ibid. Line 58*

Stands not within the prospect of belief.
>> *Ibid. Line 74*

The earth hath bubbles, as the water has,

And these are of them.
>> *Macbeth. Act I, Sc. 3, Line 79*

The insane root
That takes the reason prisoner.
>> *Ibid. Line 84*

And oftentimes, to win us to our harm,
The instruments of darkness tell us truths,
Win us with honest trifles, to betray 's
In deepest consequence.
>> *Ibid. Line 123*

Come what come may,
Time and the hour runs through the roughest day.
>> *Ibid. Line 146*

Nothing in his life
Became him like the leaving it; he died
As one that had been studied in his death
To throw away the dearest thing he owed,
As 'twere a careless trifle.
>> *Ibid. Sc. 4, Line 7*

There's no art
To find the mind's construction in the face:
He was a gentleman on whom I built
An absolute trust.
>> *Ibid. Line 11*

More is thy due than more than all can pay.
>> *Ibid. Line 21*

Yet do I fear thy nature;
It is too full o' the milk of human kindness.[1]
>> *Ibid. Sc. 5, Line 17*

That no compunctious visitings of nature
Shake my fell purpose.
>> *Ibid. Line 46*

Your face, my thane, is as a book where men
May read strange matters. To beguile the time,
Look like the time; bear welcome in your eye,
Your hand, your tongue: look like the innocent flower,
But be the serpent under 't.
>> *Ibid. Line 63*

---

[1] The thunder of your words has soured the milk of human kindness in my heart. — R. B. SHERIDAN: *The Rivals. Act III, Sc. 4*

This castle hath a pleasant seat; the air
Nimbly and sweetly recommends itself
Unto our gentle senses.

Macbeth. Act I, Sc. 6, Line 1

The heaven's breath
Smells wooingly here: no jutty, frieze,
Buttress, nor coign of vantage, but this
bird
Hath made his pendent bed and procre-
ant cradle:
Where they most breed and haunt, I
have observed
The air is delicate.

Ibid. Line 5

If it were done when 'tis done, then
'twere well
It were done quickly; if the assassina-
tion
Could trammel up the consequence,
and catch
With his surcease success; that but this
blow
Might be the be-all and the end-all here,
But here, upon this bank and shoal of
time,
We'd jump the life to come. But in
these cases
We still have judgment here; that we
but teach
Bloody instructions, which, being
taught, return
To plague the inventor; this even-
handed justice
Commends the ingredients of our poi-
son'd chalice
To our own lips.

Ibid. Sc. 7, Line 1

Besides, this Duncan
Hath borne his faculties so meek, hath
been
So clear in his great office, that his vir-
tues
Will plead like angels, trumpet-tongued
against
The deep damnation of his taking-off;
And pity, like a naked new-born babe,
Striding the blast, or heaven's cheru-
bim, horsed
Upon the sightless couriers of the air,
Shall blow the horrid deed in every eye,
That tears shall drown the wind. I have
no spur
To prick the sides of my intent, but only

Vaulting ambition, which o'erleaps itself
And falls on the other.

Macbeth. Act I, Sc. 7, Line 16

I have bought
Golden opinions from all sorts of people.

Ibid. Line 32

Letting "I dare not" wait upon "I
would,"
Like the poor cat i' the adage.[1]

Ibid. Line 44

I dare do all that may become a man;
Who dares do more is none.

Ibid. Line 46

Nor time nor place
Did then adhere.

Ibid. Line 51

Macbeth. If we should fail, —
Lady Macbeth.   We fail!
But screw your courage to the sticking-
place,
And we'll not fail.

Ibid. Line 59

Memory, the warder of the brain.

Ibid. Line 65

There's husbandry in heaven;
Their candles are all out.

Ibid. Act II, Sc. 1, Line 4

Shut up
In measureless content.

Ibid. Line 16

Is this a dagger which I see before me,
The handle toward my hand? Come, let
me clutch thee:
I have thee not, and yet I see thee still.
Art thou not, fatal vision, sensible
To feeling as to sight? or art thou but
A dagger of the mind, a false creation,
Proceeding from the heat-oppressed
brain?

Ibid. Line 33

Now o'er the one half-world
Nature seems dead.

Ibid. Line 49

Thou sure and firm-set earth,
Hear not my steps, which way they
walk, for fear
Thy very stones prate of my whereabout.

Ibid. Line 56

[1] See Heywood, page 14.

The bell invites me.
Hear it not, Duncan; for it is a knell
That summons thee to heaven or to hell.
Macbeth. Act II, Sc. 1, Line 62

It was the owl that shriek'd, the fatal bellman,
Which gives the stern'st good-night.
Ibid. Sc. 2, Line 4

The attempt and not the deed
Confounds us.
Ibid. Line 12

I had most need of blessing, and "Amen"
Stuck in my throat.
Ibid. Line 33

Methought I heard a voice cry, "Sleep no more!
Macbeth does murder sleep!" the innocent sleep,
Sleep that knits up the ravell'd sleave of care,
The death of each day's life, sore labour's bath,
Balm of hurt minds, great nature's second course,
Chief nourisher in life's feast.
Ibid. Line 36

Infirm of purpose!
Ibid. Line 53

Will all great Neptune's ocean wash this blood
Clean from my hand? No, this my hand will rather
The multitudinous seas incarnadine,
Making the green one red.
Ibid. Line 61

Go the primrose way to the everlasting bonfire.
Ibid. Sc. 3, Line 22

It [drink] provokes the desire, but it takes away the performance.
Ibid. Line 34

The labour we delight in physics pain.
Ibid. Line 56

Tongue nor heart
Cannot conceive nor name thee!
Ibid. Line 70

Confusion now hath made his masterpiece!
Most sacrilegious murder hath broke ope

The Lord's anointed temple, and stole thence
The life o' the building!
Macbeth. Act II, Sc. 3, Line 72

Downy sleep, death's counterfeit.
Ibid. Line 83

The wine of life is drawn, and the mere lees
Is left this vault to brag of.
Ibid. Line 102

Who can be wise, amazed, temperate and furious,
Loyal and neutral, in a moment?
Ibid. Line 115

To show an unfelt sorrow is an office
Which the false man does easy.
Ibid. Line 143

A falcon, towering in her pride of place,
Was by a mousing owl hawk'd at and kill'd.
Ibid. Sc. 4, Line 12

I must become a borrower of the night
For a dark hour or twain.
Ibid. Act III, Sc. 1, Line 27

Let every man be master of his time
Till seven at night.
Ibid. Line 41

Murderer. We are men, my liege.
Macbeth. Ay, in the catalogue ye go for men.
Ibid. Line 91

I am one, my liege,
Whom the vile blows and buffets of the world
Have so incensed that I am reckless what
I do to spite the world.
Ibid. Line 108

So weary with disasters, tugg'd with fortune,
That I would set my life on any chance,
To mend it or be rid on 't.
Ibid. Line 112

Things without all remedy
Should be without regard; what's done is done.
Ibid. Sc. 2, Line 11

We have scotch'd the snake, not kill'd it.
Ibid. Line 13

Duncan is in his grave;
After life's fitful fever he sleeps well;

Treason has done his worst: nor steel, nor poison,
Malice domestic, foreign levy, nothing
Can touch him further.
Macbeth. Act III, Sc. 2, Line 22
In them Nature's copy's not eterne.
Ibid. Line 38
Now spurs the lated traveller apace
To gain the timely inn.
Ibid. Sc. 3, Line 6
But now I am cabin'd, cribb'd, confined, bound in
To saucy doubts and fears.
Ibid. Sc. 4, Line 24
Now, good digestion wait on appetite,
And health on both!
Ibid. Line 38
Thou canst not say I did it; never shake
Thy gory locks at me.
Ibid. Line 50
The air-drawn dagger.
Ibid. Line 62
The times have been
That, when the brains were out, the man would die,
And there an end; but now they rise again,
With twenty mortal murders on their crowns,
And push us from our stools.
Ibid. Line 78
I drink to the general joy of the whole table.
Ibid. Line 89
Thou hast no speculation in those eyes
Which thou dost glare with!
Ibid. Line 95
A thing of custom: 'tis no other;
Only it spoils the pleasure of the time.
Ibid. Line 97
What man dare, I dare:
Approach thou like the rugged Russian bear,
The arm'd rhinoceros, or the Hyrcan tiger,
Take any shape but that, and my firm nerves
Shall never tremble.
Ibid. Line 99
Hence, horrible shadow!
Unreal mockery, hence!
Ibid. Line 106

Stand not upon the order of your going,
But go at once.
Macbeth. Act III, Sc. 4, Line 119
Macbeth. What is the night?
Lady Macbeth. Almost at odds with morning, which is which.
Ibid. Line 126
I am in blood
Stepp'd in so far, that, should I wade no more,
Returning were as tedious as go o'er.
Ibid. Line 136
My little spirit, see,
Sits in a foggy cloud, and stays for me.
Ibid. Sc. 5, Line 35
Double, double toil and trouble;
Fire burn and cauldron bubble.
Ibid. Act IV, Sc. 1, Line 10
Eye of newt, and toe of frog,
Wool of bat, and tongue of dog.
Ibid. Line 14
By the pricking of my thumbs,
Something wicked this way comes.
Open, locks,
Whoever knocks!
Ibid. Line 44
How now, you secret, black, and midnight hags!
Ibid. Line 48
I'll make assurance double sure,
And take a bond of fate.
Ibid. Line 83
Macbeth shall never vanquish'd be until
Great Birnam wood to high Dunsinane hill
Shall come against him.[1]
Ibid. Line 92
Show his eyes, and grieve his heart;
Come like shadows, so depart!
Ibid. Line 110
What! will the line stretch out to the crack of doom?
Ibid. Line 117
The weird sisters.
Ibid. Line 136
When our actions do not,
Our fears do make us traitors.
Ibid. Sc. 2, Line 3

---

[1] Till Birnam wood remove to Dunsinane I cannot taint with fear.
Act V, Sc. 2, Line 2

Things at the worst will cease, or else
climb upward
To what they were before.
Macbeth. Act IV, Sc. 2, Line 24
Angels are bright still, though the
brightest fell.
Ibid. Sc. 3, Line 22
Pour the sweet milk of concord into
hell,
Uproar the universal peace, confound
All unity on earth.
Ibid. Line 98
Stands Scotland where it did?
Ibid. Line 164
Give sorrow words; the grief that does
not speak
Whispers the o'er-fraught heart and
bids it break.
Ibid. Line 209
What! all my pretty chickens and their
dam
At one fell swoop?
Ibid. Line 218
O! I could play the woman with mine
eyes
And braggart with my tongue.
Ibid. Line 229
Out, damned spot! out, I say!
Ibid. Act V, Sc. 1, Line 38
Fie, my lord, fie! a soldier, and afeard?
Ibid. Line 40
Yet who would have thought the old
man to have had so much blood in him?
Ibid. Line 42
All the perfumes of Arabia will not
sweeten this little hand.
Ibid. Line 56
My way of life
Is fall'n into the sere, the yellow leaf;
And that which should accompany old
age,
As honour, love, obedience, troops of
friends,
I must not look to have.
Ibid. Sc. 3, Line 22
Doctor. Not so sick, my lord,
As she is troubled with thick-coming
fancies,
That keep her from her rest.
Macbeth. Cure her of that:
Canst thou not minister to a mind dis-
eas'd,

Pluck from the memory a rooted sor-
row,
Raze out the written troubles of the
brain,
And with some sweet oblivious antidote
Cleanse the stuff'd bosom of that peril-
ous stuff
Which weighs upon the heart?
Doctor. Therein the patient
Must minister to himself.
Macbeth. Throw physic to the dogs:
I'll none of it.
Macbeth. Act V, Sc. 3, Line 37
I would applaud thee to the very echo,
That should applaud again.
Ibid. Line 53
Hang out our banners on the outward
walls;
The cry is still, "They come"; our
castle's strength
Will laugh a siege to scorn.
Ibid. Sc. 5, Line 1
My fell of hair
Would at a dismal treatise rouse and
stir
As life were in 't. I have supp'd full with
horrors.
Ibid. Line 11
To-morrow, and to-morrow, and to-
morrow,
Creeps in this petty pace from day to
day,
To the last syllable of recorded time;
And all our yesterdays have lighted
fools
The way to dusty death. Out, out, brief
candle!
Life's but a walking shadow, a poor
player
That struts and frets his hour upon the
stage
And then is heard no more: it is a tale
Told by an idiot, full of sound and fury,
Signifying nothing.
Ibid. Line 19
I 'gin to be aweary of the sun.
Ibid. Line 49
Blow, wind! come, wrack!
At least we'll die with harness on our
back.
Ibid. Line 51
I bear a charmed life.
Ibid. Sc. 7, Line 41

And be these juggling fiends no more
believ'd,
That palter with us in a double sense;
That keep the word of promise to our
ear
And break it to our hope.
> *Macbeth. Act V, Sc. 7, Line 48*

Live to be the show and gaze o' the time.
> *Ibid. Line 53*
> Lay on, Macduff,

And damn'd be him that first cries,
"Hold, enough!"
> *Ibid. Line 62*

For this relief much thanks; 'tis bitter
cold,
And I am sick at heart.
> *Hamlet. Act I, Sc. 1, Line 8*

Not a mouse stirring.
> *Ibid. Line 10*

But in the gross and scope of my opinion,
This bodes some strange eruption to
our state.
> *Ibid. Line 68*
> Whose sore task

Does not divide the Sunday from the
week.
> *Ibid. Line 75*
> This sweaty haste

Doth make the night joint-labourer
with the day.
> *Ibid. Line 77*

In the most high and palmy state of
Rome,
A little ere the mightiest Julius fell,
The graves stood tenantless and the
sheeted dead
Did squeal and gibber in the Roman
streets.
> *Ibid. Line 113*

And then it started like a guilty thing
Upon a fearful summons.
> *Ibid. Line 148*

The cock, that is the trumpet of the
morn.
> *Ibid. Line 150*

Whether in sea or fire, in earth or air,
The extravagant and erring spirit hies
To his confine.
> *Ibid. Line 153*

It faded on the crowing of the cock.
Some say that ever 'gainst that season
comes

Wherein our Saviour's birth is celebrated,
The bird of dawning singeth all night
long:
And then, they say, no spirit can walk
abroad;
The nights are wholesome; then no
planets strike,
No fairy takes, nor witch hath power to
charm,
So hallow'd and so gracious is the time.
> *Hamlet. Act I, Sc. 1, Line 157*

So have I heard, and do in part believe
it.
But, look, the morn in russet mantle
clad,
Walks o'er the dew of yon high eastern
hill.
> *Ibid. Line 165*

The memory be green.[1]
> *Ibid. Sc. 2, Line 2*

With one auspicious and one dropping
eye,
With mirth in funeral and with dirge
in marriage,
In equal scale weighing delight and
dole.
> *Ibid. Line 11*

A little more than kin, and less than
kind.
> *Ibid. Line 65*
> All that live must die,

Passing through nature to eternity.
> *Ibid. Line 72*

Seems, madam! Nay, it is; I know not
"seems."
'Tis not alone my inky cloak, good
mother,
Nor customary suits of solemn black.
> *Ibid. Line 76*

But I have that within which passeth
show;
These but the trappings and the suits
of woe.
> *Ibid. Line 85*

O! that this too too solid flesh would
melt,
Thaw and resolve itself into a dew;
Or that the Everlasting had not fix'd

---

[1] Keep his memory green. — MOORE: *Oh,
Breathe Not His name*
  Lord, keep my memory green. — CHARLES
DICKENS: *The Haunted Man, last line*

His canon 'gainst self-slaughter! O
　God! O God!
How weary, stale, flat, and unprofitable
Seem to me all the uses of this world.
　　　Hamlet. Act I, Sc. 2, Line 129
That it should come to this!
　　　　　Ibid. Line 137
Hyperion to a satyr; so loving to my
　mother
That he might not beteem the winds of
heaven
Visit her face too roughly.
　　　　　Ibid. Line 140
　　　Why, she would hang on him,
As if increase of appetite had grown
By what it fed on.
　　　　　Ibid. Line 143
Frailty, thy name is woman!
　　　　　Ibid. Line 146
Like Niobe, all tears.
　　　　　Ibid. Line 149
A beast, that wants discourse of reason.
　　　　　Ibid. Line 150
It is not nor it cannot come to good.
　　　　　Ibid. Line 158
Thrift, thrift, Horatio! the funeral
　baked meats
Did coldly furnish forth the marriage
tables.
　　　　　Ibid. Line 180
In my mind's eye, Horatio.
　　　　　Ibid. Line 185
He was a man, take him for all in all,
I shall not look upon his like again.
　　　　　Ibid. Line 187
Season your admiration for a while.
　　　　　Ibid. Line 192
In the dead vast and middle of the
　night.
　　　　　Ibid. Line 198
Arm'd at points exactly, cap-a-pe.
　　　　　Ibid. Line 200
　　　　Distill'd
Almost to jelly with the act of fear.
　　　　　Ibid. Line 204
A countenance more in sorrow than in
　anger.
　　　　　Ibid. Line 231
While one with moderate haste might
　tell a hundred.
　　　　　Ibid. Line 237
Hamlet. His beard was grizzled, no?

Horatio. It was, as I have seen it in
　his life,
A sable silver'd.
　　　Hamlet. Act I, Sc. 2, Line 239
Give it an understanding, but no
　tongue.
　　　　　Ibid. Line 249
Foul play.
　　　　　Ibid. Line 255
The chariest maid is prodigal enough
If she unmask her beauty to the moon:
Virtue itself 'scapes not calumnious
　strokes;
The canker galls the infants of the
　spring
Too oft before their buttons be dis-
　closed,
And in the morn and liquid dew of
　youth
Contagious blastments are most im-
　minent.
　　　　　Ibid. Sc. 3, Line 36
Do not, as some ungracious pastors do,
Show me the steep and thorny way to
　heaven,
Whiles, like a puff'd and reckless liber-
　tine,
Himself the primrose path of dalliance
　treads,[1]
And recks not his own rede.[2]
　　　　　Ibid. Line 47
Give thy thoughts no tongue.
　　　　　Ibid. Line 59
Be thou familiar, but by no means vul-
　gar;
Those friends thou hast, and their adop-
　tion tried,
Grapple them to thy soul with hoops
　of steel.
　　　　　Ibid. Line 61
　　　　Beware
Of entrance to a quarrel, but, being in,
Bear 't that the opposed may beware of
　thee.

[1] See *Macbeth, Act II, Sc. 3, L. 22* (p. 86).
[2] Wel oghte a preest ensample for to yive,
　By his clennesse, how that his sheep shold
　　live.
　CHAUCER: *Canterbury Tales, Prologue,*
　　　　　　　　　　L. 504
And may you better reck the rede,
Than ever did the adviser.
　ROBERT BURNS: *Epistle to a Young
　　　　　　　　　　Friend*

Give every man thy ear, but few thy
    voice;
Take each man's censure, but reserve
    thy judgment.
Costly thy habit as thy purse can buy,
But not express'd in fancy; rich, not
    gaudy;
For the apparel oft proclaims the man.
      Hamlet. Act I, Sc. 3, Line 65
Neither a borrower, nor a lender be;
For loan oft loses both itself and friend,
And borrowing dulls the edge of hus-
    bandry.
This above all: to thine own self be true,
And it must follow, as the night the day,
Thou canst not then be false to any
    man.
             Ibid. Line 75
Springes to catch woodcocks.
            Ibid. Line 115
When the blood burns, how prodigal the
    soul
Lends the tongue vows.
            Ibid. Line 116
Be somewhat scanter of your maiden
    presence.
            Ibid. Line 121
Hamlet. The air bites shrewdly; it is
    very cold.
Horatio. It is a nipping and an eager
    air.
          Ibid. Sc. 4, Line 1
But to my mind, though I am native
    here
And to the manner born, — it is a cus-
    tom
More honoured in the breach than the
    observance.
            Ibid. Line 14
Angels and ministers of grace defend
    us!
            Ibid. Line 39
Be thy intents wicked or charitable,
Thou comest in such a questionable
    shape
That I will speak to thee.
            Ibid. Line 42
Hath oped his ponderous and marble
    jaws.
            Ibid. Line 50
        What may this mean,
That thou, dead corse, again in com-
    plete steel

Revisit'st thus the glimpses of the
    moon,
Making night hideous,[1] and we fools of
    nature
So horridly to shake our disposition
With thoughts beyond the reaches of
    our souls?
      Hamlet. Act I, Sc. 4, Line 51
I do not set my life at a pin's fee.
            Ibid. Line 65
      My fate cries out,
And makes each petty artery in this
    body
As hardy as the Nemean lion's nerve.
            Ibid. Line 81
      Unhand me, gentlemen,
By heaven! I'll make a ghost of him
    that lets me!
            Ibid. Line 84
Something is rotten in the state of Den-
    mark.
            Ibid. Line 90
I could a tale unfold whose lightest word
Would harrow up thy soul, freeze thy
    young blood,
Make thy two eyes, like stars, start
    from their spheres,
Thy knotted and combined locks to
    part,
And each particular hair to stand an
    end,
Like quills upon the fretful porpentine.
          Ibid. Sc. 5, Line 15
And duller shouldst thou be than the fat
    weed
That rots itself in ease on Lethe wharf.
            Ibid. Line 32
      O my prophetic soul!
My uncle!
            Ibid. Line 40
O Hamlet, what a falling-off was there!
            Ibid. Line 47
But, soft! methinks I scent the morning
    air;
Brief let me be. Sleeping within my
    orchard,
My custom always of the afternoon.
            Ibid. Line 58
Cut off even in the blossoms of my sin,
Unhousel'd, disappointed, unaneled,

[1] And makes night hideous. — POPE: *The
Dunciad, Book III, L. 166*

No reckoning made, but sent to my ac-
count
With all my imperfections on my head.
Hamlet. Act I, Sc. 5, Line 76
Leave her to heaven
And to those thorns that in her bosom
lodge,
To prick and sting her.
Ibid. Line 86
The glow-worm shows the matin to be
near,
And 'gins to pale his uneffectual fire.
Ibid. Line 89
While memory holds a seat
In this distracted globe. Remember
thee!
Yea, from the table of my memory
I'll wipe away all trivial fond records.
Ibid. Line 96
Within the book and volume of my
brain.
Ibid. Line 103
O villain, villain, smiling, damned vil-
lain!
My tables, — meet it is I set it down,
That one may smile, and smile, and be
a villain;
At least I'm sure it may be so in Den-
mark.
Ibid. Line 106
There are more things in heaven and
earth, Horatio,
Than are dreamt of in your philosophy.
Ibid. Line 166
Rest, rest, perturbed spirit!
Ibid. Line 182
The time is out of joint; O cursed spite,
That ever I was born to set it right!
Ibid. Line 188
Brevity is the soul of wit.
Ibid. Act II, Sc. 2, Line 90
More matter, with less art.
Ibid. Line 95
That he is mad, 'tis true; 'tis true 'tis
pity;
And pity 'tis 'tis true.
Ibid. Line 97
Find out the cause of this effect,
Or rather say, the cause of this defect,
For this effect defective comes by cause.
Ibid. Line 101
Doubt thou the stars are fire;
Doubt that the sun doth move;

Doubt truth to be a liar;
But never doubt I love.
Hamlet. Act II, Sc. 2, Line 115
To be honest, as this world goes, is
to be one man picked out of ten thou-
sand.
Ibid. Line 179
Still harping on my daughter.
Ibid. Line 190
Polonius. What do you read, my lord?
Hamlet. Words, words, words.
Ibid. Line 195
They have a plentiful lack of wit.
Ibid. Line 204
Though this be madness, yet there is
method in 't.
Ibid. Line 211
There is nothing either good or bad,
but thinking makes it so.
Ibid. Line 259
This goodly frame, the earth, seems
to me a sterile promontory; this most
excellent canopy, the air, look you, this
brave o'erhanging firmament, this ma-
jestical roof fretted with golden fire,
why, it appears no other thing to me
than a foul and pestilent congregation
of vapours. What a piece of work is a
man! how noble in reason! how infinite
in faculty! in form and moving how
express and admirable! in action how
like an angel! in apprehension how like
a god!
Ibid. Line 317
Man delights not me; no, nor woman
neither.
Ibid. Line 330
There is something in this more than
natural, if philosophy could find it out.
Ibid. Line 392
I know a hawk from a handsaw.
Ibid. Line 406
They say an old man is twice a child.
Ibid. Line 413
O Jephthah, judge of Israel, what a
treasure hadst thou!
Ibid. Line 431
One fair daughter and no more,
The which he loved passing well.
Ibid. Line 435
Come, give us a taste of your quality.
Ibid. Line 460

The play, I remember, pleased not the million; 'twas caviare to the general.

Hamlet. Act II, Sc. 2, Line 465

They are the abstracts and brief chronicles of the time: after your death you were better have a bad epitaph than their ill report while you live.

Ibid. Line 555

Use every man after his desert, and who should 'scape whipping?

Ibid. Line 561

What's Hecuba to him or he to Hecuba,
That he should weep for her?

Ibid. Line 593

Unpack my heart with words,
And fall a-cursing, like a very dràb.

Ibid. Line 622

The play's the thing
Wherein I'll catch the conscience of the king.

Ibid. Line 641

With devotion's visage
And pious action we do sugar o'er
The devil himself.

Ibid. Act III, Sc. 1, Line 47

To be, or not to be: that is the question:
Whether 'tis nobler in the mind to suffer
The slings and arrows of outrageous fortune,
Or to take arms against a sea of troubles,
And by opposing end them? To die: to sleep:
No more; and by a sleep to say we end
The heartache and the thousand natural shocks
That flesh is heir to, 'tis a consummation
Devoutly to be wish'd. To die, to sleep;
To sleep: perchance to dream: ay, there's the rub:
For in that sleep of death what dreams may come,
When we have shuffled off this mortal coil,
Must give us pause. There's the respect
That makes calamity of so long life;
For who would bear the whips and scorns of time,
The oppressor's wrong, the proud man's contumely,
The pangs of dispriz'd love, the law's delay,
The insolence of office and the spurns
That patient merit of the unworthy takes,
When he himself might his quietus make
With a bare bodkin? who would fardels bear,
To grunt and sweat under a weary life,
But that the dread of something after death,
The undiscover'd country from whose bourn
No traveller returns, puzzles the will
And makes us rather bear those ills we have
Than fly to others that we know not of?
Thus conscience does make cowards of us all;
And thus the native hue of resolution
Is sicklied o'er with the pale cast of thought,
And enterprises of great pith and moment
With this regard their currents turn awry,
And lose the name of action.

Hamlet. Act III, Sc. 1, Line 56

Nymph, in thy orisons
Be all my sins remember'd.

Ibid. Line 89

Rich gifts wax poor when givers prove unkind.

Ibid. Line 101

Be thou as chaste as ice, as pure as snow, thou shalt not escape calumny. Get thee to a nunnery, go.

Ibid. Line 142

I have heard of your paintings too, well enough; God has given you one face, and you make yourselves another.

Ibid. Line 150

O! what a noble mind is here o'erthrown:
The courtier's, soldier's, scholar's eye, tongue, sword.

Ibid. Line 159

The glass of fashion and the mould of form,

The observed of all observers!
　　　Hamlet. Act III, Sc. 1, Line 162
Now see that noble and most sovereign
　reason,
Like sweet bells jangled, out of tune and
　harsh.
　　　　　　　　Ibid. Line 166
　　　　　　　O, woe is me,
To have seen what I have seen, see what
　I see!
　　　　　　　　Ibid. Line 169
Nor do not saw the air too much with
your hand, thus; but use all gently: for
in the very torrent, tempest, and as I
may say the whirlwind of passion, you
must acquire and beget a temperance,
that may give it smoothness. Oh, it offends me to the soul to hear a robustious
periwig-pated fellow tear a passion to
tatters, to very rags, to split the ears of
the groundlings, who for the most part
are capable of nothing but inexplicable
dumb-shows and noise. I would have
such a fellow whipped for o'erdoing
Termagant; it out-herods Herod.
　　　　　Ibid. Sc. 2, Line 4
Suit the action to the word, the word
to the action; with this special observance, that you o'erstep not the modesty of nature.
　　　　　　　　Ibid. Line 20
To hold, as 'twere, the mirror up to
　nature.
　　　　　　　　Ibid. Line 25
To show the very age and body of
the time his form and pressure.
　　　　　　　　Ibid. Line 27
Though it make the unskilful laugh,
cannot but make the judicious grieve.
　　　　　　　　Ibid. Line 29
Not to speak it profanely.
　　　　　　　　Ibid. Line 35
I have thought some of Nature's
journeymen had made men and not
made them well, they imitated human-
ity so abominably.
　　　　　　　　Ibid. Line 38
First Player. I hope we have reformed
that indifferently with us, sir.
Hamlet. O, reform it altogether.
　　　　　　　　Ibid. Line 41
No; let the candied tongue lick absurd
　pomp,

And crook the pregnant hinges of the
　knee
Where thrift may follow fawning.
　　　Hamlet. Act III, Sc. 2, Line 65
A man that fortune's buffets and re-
　wards
Hast ta'en with equal thanks.
　　　　　　　　Ibid. Line 72
They are not a pipe for fortune's finger
To sound what stop she please. Give me
　that man
That is not passion's slave, and I will
　wear him
In my heart's core, ay, in my heart of
　heart,
As I do thee. Something too much of
　this.
　　　　　　　　Ibid. Line 75
And my imaginations are as foul
As Vulcan's stithy.
　　　　　　　　Ibid. Line 88
Nay, then, let the devil wear black,
for I'll have a suit of sables.
　　　　　　　　Ibid. Line 138
There's hope a great man's memory
may outlive his life half a year.
　　　　　　　　Ibid. Line 141
This is miching mallecho; it means mis-
　chief.
　　　　　　　　Ibid. Line 149
The lady doth protest too much, me-
　thinks.
　　　　　　　　Ibid. Line 242
Let the galled jade wince, our withers
　are unwrung.
　　　　　　　　Ibid. Line 256
Why, let the stricken deer [1] go weep,
　The hart ungalled play;
For some must watch, while some must
　sleep:
So runs the world away.
　　　　　　　　Ibid. Line 287
Pluck out the heart of my mystery.
　　　　　　　　Ibid. Line 389
Do you think I am easier to be played
　on than a pipe?
　　　　　　　　Ibid. Line 393
Hamlet. Do you see yonder cloud
that's almost in shape of a camel?
Polonius. By the mass, and 'tis like
a camel, indeed.

[1] I was a stricken deer. — WILLIAM COW-
PER: *The Task, Book III*

Hamlet. Methinks it is like a weasel.
Polonius. It is backed like a weasel.
Hamlet. Or like a whale?
Polonius. Very like a whale.
> *Hamlet. Act III, Sc. 2, Line 400*

They fool me to the top of my bent.
> *Ibid. Line 408*

By and by is easily said.
> *Ibid. Line 411*

'Tis now the very witching time of night,
When churchyards yawn and hell itself breathes out
Contagion to this world.
> *Ibid. Line 413*

I will speak daggers to her, but use none.
> *Ibid. Line 421*

O! my offence is rank, it smells to heaven;
It hath the primal eldest curse upon 't,
A brother's murder.
> *Ibid. Sc. 3, Line 36*

With all his crimes broad blown, as flush as May.
> *Ibid. Line 81*

My words fly up, my thoughts remain below:
Words without thoughts never to heaven go.
> *Ibid. Line 97*

Dead, for a ducat, dead!
> *Ibid. Sc. 4, Line 23*

And let me wring your heart; for so I shall,
If it be made of penetrable stuff.
> *Ibid. Line 35*

False as dicers' oaths.
> *Ibid. Line 45*

A rhapsody of words.
> *Ibid. Line 48*

What act
That roars so loud and thunders in the index?
> *Ibid. Line 51*

Look here, upon this picture, and on this,
The counterfeit presentment of two brothers.
See, what a grace was seated on this brow;
Hyperion's curls; the front of Jove himself;

An eye like Mars, to threaten and command,
A station like the herald Mercury
New-lighted on a heaven-kissing hill,
A combination and a form indeed,
Where every god did seem to set his seal,
To give the world assurance of a man.
> *Hamlet. Act III, Sc. 4, Line 53*

At your age
The hey-day in the blood is tame, it's humble.
> *Ibid. Line 68*

O shame! where is thy blush? Rebellious hell,
If thou canst mutine in a matron's bones,
To flaming youth let virtue be as wax,
And melt in her own fire: proclaim no shame
When the compulsive ardour gives the charge,
Since frost itself as actively doth burn,
And reason panders will.
> *Ibid. Line 82*

A king of shreds and patches.[1]
> *Ibid. Line 102*

How is 't with you,
That you do bend your eye on vacancy?
> *Ibid. Line 115*

This is the very coinage of your brain:
This bodiless creation ecstasy
Is very cunning in.
> *Ibid. Line 136*

Lay not that flattering unction to your soul.
> *Ibid. Line 145*

Assume a virtue, if you have it not.
> *Ibid. Line 160*

Refrain to-night,
And that shall lend a kind of easiness
To the next abstinence: the next more easy;
For use almost can change the stamp of nature.
> *Ibid. Line 165*

I must be cruel, only to be kind.
> *Ibid. Line 178*

---

[1] A wandering minstrel I—
A thing of shreds and patches.
WILLIAM SCHWENCK GILBERT:
The Mikado, Act 1

For 'tis the sport to have the enginer
Hoist with his own petar.
>   *Hamlet. Act III, Sc. 4, Line 206*
Diseases desperate grown
By desperate appliance are relieved,
Or not at all.[1]
>   *Ibid. Act IV, Sc. 3, Line 9*
A man may fish with the worm that
hath eat of a king, and eat of the fish
that hath fed of that worm.
>   *Ibid. Line 29*
Sure, he that made us with such large
    discourse,
Looking before and after, gave us not
That capability and godlike reason
To fust in us unused.
>   *Ibid. Line 36*
Rightly to be great
Is not to stir without great argument,
But greatly to find quarrel in a straw
When honour's at the stake.
>   *Ibid. Line 53*
So full of artless jealousy is guilt,
It spills itself in fearing to be spilt.
>   *Ibid. Sc. 5, Line 19*
We know what we are, but know not
    what we may be.
>   *Ibid. Line 43*
Come, my coach! Good night, sweet
    ladies; good night.
>   *Ibid. Line 72*
When sorrows come, they come not
    single spies,
But in battalions.
>   *Ibid. Line 78*
There's such divinity doth hedge a
    king,
That treason can but peep to what it
    would.
>   *Ibid. Line 123*
There's rosemary, that's for remem-
brance; . . . and there is pansies,
that's for thoughts.
>   *Ibid. Line 174*
You must wear your rue with a dif-
ference. There's a daisy; I would give
you some violets, but they withered.
>   *Ibid. Line 181*

[1] Extreme remedies are very appropriate
for extreme diseases. — HIPPOCRATES: *Aphorism I*

See Dryden, page 175, and Montaigne,
page 1028.

A very riband in the cap of youth.
>   *Hamlet. Act IV, Sc. 7, Line 77*
One woe doth tread upon another's
    heel,
So fast they follow.[1]
>   *Ibid. Line 164*
Nature her custom holds,
Let shame say what it will.
>   *Ibid. Line 188*
1 Clown. Argal, he that is not guilty
of his own death shortens not his own
life.
2 Clown. But is this law?
1 Clown. Ay marry, is 't; crowner's
quest law.
>   *Ibid. Act V, Sc. 1, Line 20*
There is no ancient gentlemen but
gardeners . . . they hold up Adam's
profession.[2]
>   *Ibid. Line 32*
Cudgel thy brains no more about it.
>   *Ibid. Line 61*
Has this fellow no feeling of his busi-
    ness?
>   *Ibid. Line 71*
Custom hath made it in him a property
    of easiness.
>   *Ibid. Line 73*
The hand of little employment hath the
    daintier sense.
>   *Ibid. Line 75*
But age, with his stealing steps,
Hath claw'd me in his clutch.
>   *Ibid. Line 77*
A politician, . . . one that would cir-
    cumvent God.
>   *Ibid. Line 84*
Why may not that be the skull of a
lawyer? Where be his quiddities now,
his quillets, his cases, his tenures, and
his tricks?
>   *Ibid. Line 104*

[1] Thus woe succeeds a woe, as wave a wave.
— HERRICK: *Sorrows Succeed*
Woes cluster; rare are solitary woes;
They love a train, they tread each other's heel.
        YOUNG: *Night Thoughts, Night III, L. 63*
And woe succeeds to woe. — POPE: *The
Iliad, Book XVI, L. 139*
[2] Oh, Adam was a gardener, and God who
    made him sees
That half a proper gardener's work is done
    upon his knees.
    RUDYARD KIPLING: *The Glory of the
                        Garden, St. 8*

One that was a woman, sir; but, rest her soul, she's dead.

Hamlet. Act V, Sc. 1, Line 145

How absolute the knave is! we must speak by the card, or equivocation will undo us.

Ibid. Line 147

The age is grown so picked that the toe of the peasant comes so near the heel of the courtier, he galls his kibe.

Ibid. Line 150

Alas, poor Yorick! I knew him, Horatio: a fellow of infinite jest, of most excellent fancy; he hath borne me on his back a thousand times; and now, how abhorred in my imagination it is! my gorge rises at it. Here hung those lips that I have kissed I know not how oft. Where be your gibes now? your gambols? your songs? your flashes of merriment, that were wont to set the table on a roar? Not one now, to mock your own grinning? quite chap-fallen? Now get you to my lady's chamber, and tell her, let her paint an inch thick, to this favour she must come.

Ibid. Line 201

To what base uses we may return, Horatio! Why may not imagination trace the noble dust of Alexander, till he find it stopping a bung-hole?

Ibid. Line 222

'Twere to consider too curiously, to consider so.

Ibid. Line 226

Imperious Caesar, dead and turn'd to clay,
Might stop a hole to keep the wind away.

Ibid. Line 235

Lay her i' the earth;
And from her fair and unpolluted flesh May violets spring! [1]

Ibid. Line 260

A ministering angel shall my sister be.[2]

Ibid. Line 263

Sweets to the sweet: farewell!

Ibid. Line 265

---

[1] And from his ashes may be made
The violet of his native land.
TENNYSON: *In Memoriam, XVIII*
[2] A ministering angel thou. — SCOTT: *Marmion, Canto VI, St. 30*

I thought thy bride-bed to have deck'd, sweet maid,
And not have strew'd thy grave.

Hamlet. Act V, Sc. 1, Line 267

Though I am not splenetive and rash, Yet have I in me something dangerous.

Ibid. Line 283

Forty thousand brothers
Could not, with all their quantity of love,
Make up my sum.

Ibid. Line 291

Nay, an thou'lt mouth,
I'll rant as well as thou.

Ibid. Line 305

Let Hercules himself do what he may, The cat will mew and dog will have his day.

Ibid. Line 313

There's a divinity that shapes our ends, Rough-hew them how we will.

Ibid. Sc. 2, Line 10

I once did hold it, as our statists do, A baseness to write fair.

Ibid. Line 33

It did me yeoman's service.

Ibid. Line 36

Popp'd in between the election and my hopes.

Ibid. Line 65

The bravery of his grief did put me Into a towering passion.

Ibid. Line 79

What imports the nomination of this gentleman?

Ibid. Line 134

'Tis the breathing time of day with me.

Ibid. Line 181

Winnowed opinions.

Ibid. Line 201

There's a special providence in the fall of a sparrow. If it be now, 'tis not to come; if it be not to come, it will be now; if it be not now, yet it will come: the readiness is all. Since no man has aught of what he leaves, what is 't to leave betimes?

Ibid. Line 232

A hit, a very palpable hit.

Ibid. Line 295

This fell sergeant, death,
Is strict in his arrest.

Ibid. Line 350

Report me and my cause aright.
> *Hamlet. Act V, Sc. 2, Line 353*

I am more an antique Roman than a Dane.
> *Ibid. Line 355*

Absent thee from felicity awhile.
> *Ibid. Line 361*

The rest is silence.[1]
> *Ibid. Line 372*

Now cracks a noble heart.
> *Ibid. Line 373*

My love's
More richer than my tongue.
> *King Lear. Act I, Sc. 1, Line 79*

Nothing will come of nothing.
> *Ibid. Line 92*

Mend your speech a little,
Lest you may mar your fortunes.
> *Ibid. Line 96*

I want that glib and oily art,
To speak and purpose not.
> *Ibid. Line 227*

A still-soliciting eye, and such a tongue
That I am glad I have not.
> *Ibid. Line 234*

As if we were villains by necessity;
fools by heavenly compulsion.
> *Ibid. Sc. 2, Line 136*

Some villain hath done me wrong.[2]
> *Ibid. Line 186*

That which ordinary men are fit for,
I am qualified in; and the best of me
is diligence.
> *Ibid. Sc. 4, Line 36*

Have more than thou showest,
Speak less than thou knowest.
> *Ibid. Line 133*

A little to disquantity your train.[3]
> *Ibid. Line 272*

Ingratitude, thou marble-hearted fiend!
> *Ibid. Line 283*

How sharper than a serpent's tooth it is
To have a thankless child!
> *Ibid. Line 312*

Striving to better, oft we mar what's well.
> *Ibid. Line 371*

[1] The rest is silence. — JOHN RUSKIN: *The Crown of Wild Olive, Traffic, Sect. 84*
[2] See page 107.
[3] A line often murmured by Long Island commuters about 5 P.M.

The son and heir of a mongrel bitch.
> *King Lear. Act II, Sc. 2, Line 23*

I have seen better faces in my time
Than stands on any shoulder that I see
Before me at this instant.
> *Ibid. Line 99*

Fortune, good night, smile once more;
turn thy wheel.
> *Ibid. Line 180*

Hysterica passio! down, thou climbing sorrow!
Thy element's below.
> *Ibid. Sc. 4, Line 57*

That sir which serves and seeks for gain,
And follows but for form,
Will pack when it begins to rain,
And leave thee in the storm.
> *Ibid. Line 79*

Nature in you stands on the very verge
Of her confine.
> *Ibid. Line 149*

Necessity's sharp pinch!
> *Ibid. Line 214*

Let not women's weapons, water-drops,
Stain my man's cheeks!
> *Ibid. Line 280*

Blow, winds, and crack your cheeks!
rage! blow!
> *Ibid. Act III, Sc. 2, Line 1*

I tax not you, you elements, with unkindness.
> *Ibid. Line 16*

A poor, infirm, weak, and despised old man.
> *Ibid. Line 20*

There was never yet fair woman but
she made mouths in a glass.
> *Ibid. Line 35*

I will be the pattern of all patience.
> *Ibid. Line 37*

I am a man,
More sinn'd against than sinning.
> *Ibid. Line 59*

Oh! that way madness lies; let me shun that.
> *Ibid. Sc. 4, Line 21*

Poor naked wretches, wheresoe'er you are,
That bide the pelting of this pitiless storm,

How shall your houseless heads and un-
    fed sides,
Your looped and windowed raggedness,
    defend you
From seasons such as these?
> *King Lear. Act. III, Sc. 4, Line 28*
> Take physic, pomp;
Expose thyself to feel what wretches
    feel.
> *Ibid. Line 33*
Out-paramoured the Turk.
> *Ibid. Line 91*
'Tis a naughty night to swim in.
> *Ibid. Line 113*
The green mantle of the standing pool.
> *Ibid. Line 137*
But mice and rats and such small deer
Have been Tom's food for seven long
    year.
> *Ibid. Line 142*
The prince of darkness is a gentleman.[1]
> *Ibid. Line 147*
Poor Tom's a-cold.
> *Ibid. Line 151*
I'll talk a word with this same learned
    Theban.
> *Ibid. Line 161*
Child Rowland to the dark tower came.[2]
His word was still, Fie, foh, and fum,
I smell the blood of a British man.
> *Ibid. Line 185*
> The little dogs and all,
Tray, Blanch, and Sweetheart, see, they
    bark at me.
> *Ibid. Sc. 6, Line 65*
Mastiff, greyhound, mongrel grim,
Hound or spaniel, brach or lym;
Or bobtail tike or trundle-tail.
> *Ibid. Line 71*
I am tied to the stake, and I must stand
    the course.
> *Ibid. Sc. 7, Line 54*

[1] The Prince of Darkness is a gentleman. —
SIR JOHN SUCKLING: *The Goblins, Act III*
The Devil is a gentleman. — SHELLEY: *Peter
Bell the Third, Part II, St. 2*
[2] Child Roland to the dark tower came. —
SCOTT: *The Bridal of Triermain*
Dauntless the slug-horn to my lips I set,
And blew. *"Childe Roland to the Dark
Tower came."*
    ROBERT BROWNING: *Childe Roland
    to the Dark Tower Came, St. 34*

The lowest and most dejected thing of
    fortune.
> *King Lear. Act IV, Sc. 1, Line 3*
> The worst is not
So long as we can say, "This is the
    worst."
> *Ibid. Line 27*
Sunshine and rain at once; her smiles
    and tears.
> *Ibid. Sc. 3, Line 20*
> It is the stars,
The stars above us, govern our con-
    ditions.
> *Ibid. Line 34*
Our foster-nurse of nature is repose.
> *Ibid. Sc. 4, Line 12*
> In nothing am I chang'd
But in my garments.
> *Ibid. Sc. 6, Line 9*
> Half way down
Hangs one that gathers samphire,
    dreadful trade!
Methinks he seems no bigger than his
    head:
The fishermen that walk upon the beach
Appear like mice.
> *Ibid. Line 15*
Nature's above art in that respect.
> *Ibid. Line 87*
Ay, every inch a king.
> *Ibid. Line 110*
Give me an ounce of civet, good
apothecary, to sweeten my imagination.
> *Ibid. Line 133*
A man may see how this world goes
with no eyes. Look with thine ears: see
how yond justice rails upon yon simple
thief. Hark, in thine ear: change places;
and, handy-dandy, which is the justice,
which is the thief?
> *Ibid. Line 154*
Through tatter'd clothes small vices do
    appear;
Robes and furr'd gowns hide all.
> *Ibid. Line 169*
> Mine enemy's dog,
Though he had bit me, should have
    stood that night
Against my fire.
> *Ibid. Sc. 7, Line 36*
Pray you now, forget and forgive.
> *Ibid. Line 84*

Men must endure
Their going hence, even as their com-
ing hither.
King Lear. Act V, Sc. 2, Line 9
Upon such sacrifices, my Cordelia,
The gods themselves throw incense.
Ibid. Sc. 3, Line 20
The gods are just, and of our pleasant
vices
Make instruments to plague us.
Ibid. Line 172
Her voice was ever soft,
Gentle, and low, an excellent thing in
woman.
Ibid. Line 274
Vex not his ghost: O! let him pass! he
hates him
That would upon the rack of this tough
world
Stretch him out longer.
Ibid. Line 315
That never set a squadron in the field,
Nor the division of a battle knows
More than a spinster.
Othello. Act I, Sc. 1, Line 22
The bookish theoric.
Ibid. Line 24
'Tis the curse of service,
Preferment goes by letter and affection,
And not by old gradation, where each
second
Stood heir to the first.
Ibid. Line 35
We cannot all be masters.
Ibid. Line 43
I will wear my heart upon my sleeve
For daws to peck at.
Ibid. Line 64
Trust not your daughters' minds
By what you see them act.
Ibid. Line 171
The wealthy curled darlings of our na-
tion.
Ibid. Sc. 2, Line 68
Most potent, grave, and reverend si-
gniors,
My very noble and approv'd good
masters.
Ibid. Sc. 3, Line 76
The very head and front of my offend-
ing
Hath this extent, no more.
Ibid. Line 80

Rude am I in my speech,
And little bless'd with the soft phrase
of peace:
For since these arms of mine had seven
years' pith,
Till now some nine moons wasted, they
have used
Their dearest action in the tented field.
Othello. Act I, Sc. 3, Line 81
Little shall I grace my cause
In speaking for myself. Yet, by your
gracious patience,
I will a round unvarnish'd tale deliver
Of my whole course of love.
Ibid. Line 88
Still question'd me the story of my life
From year to year, the battles, sieges,
fortunes
That I have passed.
Ibid. Line 129
Wherein I spake of most disastrous
chances,
Of moving accidents by flood and field,
Of hair-breadth 'scapes i' the imminent
deadly breach.
Ibid. Line 134
Hills whose heads touch heaven.
Ibid. Line 141
And of the Cannibals that each other
eat,
The Anthropophagi, and men whose
heads
Do grow beneath their shoulders.
Ibid. Line 143
My story being done,
She gave me for my pains a world of
sighs:
She swore, in faith, 'twas strange, 'twas
passing strange,
'Twas pitiful, 'twas wondrous pitiful:
She wish'd she had not heard it, yet
she wish'd
That Heaven had made her such a man;
she thank'd me,
And bade me, if I had a friend that
loved her,
I should but teach him how to tell my
story,
And that would woo her. Upon this hint
I spake:
She loved me for the dangers I had
pass'd,
And I loved her that she did pity them.

This only is the witchcraft I have used.
Othello. Act I, Sc. 1, Line 158
I do perceive here a divided duty.
Ibid. Line 181
The robb'd that smiles, steals something from the thief.
Ibid. Line 208
Our bodies are our gardens, to the which our wills are gardeners; . . . either to have it sterile with idleness or manured with industry.
Ibid. Line 324
Put money in thy purse.
Ibid. Line 345
The food that to him now is as luscious as locusts, shall be to him shortly as bitter as coloquintida.
Ibid. Line 354
Framed to make women false.
Ibid. Line 404
One that excels the quirks of blazoning pens.
Ibid. Act II, Sc. 1, Line 63
For I am nothing if not critical.
Ibid. Line 119
I am not merry; but I do beguile
The thing I am, by seeming otherwise.
Ibid. Line 122
She that was ever fair and never proud,
Had tongue at will and yet was never loud.
Ibid. Line 148
Iago. She was a wight, if ever such wight were, —
Desdemona. To do what?
Iago. To suckle fools and chronicle small beer.
Desdemona. O most lame and impotent conclusion!
Ibid. Line 158
You may relish him more in the soldier than in the scholar.
Ibid. Line 165
Base men being in love have then a nobility in their natures more than is native to them.
Ibid. Line 218
Egregiously an ass.
Ibid. Line 321
I have very poor and unhappy brains for drinking.
Ibid. Sc. 3, Line 34

Potations pottle-deep.
Othello. Act II, Sc. 3, Line 57
King Stephen was a worthy peer,
His breeches cost him but a crown;
He held them sixpence all too dear,
With that he called the tailor lown.[1]
Ibid. Line 93
Silence that dreadful bell! it frights the isle
From her propriety.
Ibid. Line 177
Your name is great
In mouths of wisest censure.
Ibid. Line 194
But men are men; the best sometimes forget.
Ibid. Line 243
Thy honesty and love doth mince this matter.[2]
Ibid. Line 249
Cassio, I love thee;
But never more be officer of mine.
Ibid. Line 250
Iago. What! are you hurt, lieutenant?
Cassio. Ay; past all surgery.
Ibid. Line 261
Reputation, reputation, reputation! Oh! I have lost my reputation. I have lost the immortal part of myself, and what remains is bestial.
Ibid. Line 264
Reputation is an idle and most false imposition; oft got without merit, and lost without deserving.
Ibid. Line 270
O thou invisible spirit of wine! if thou hast no name to be known by, let us call thee devil!
Ibid. Line 285
O God! that men should put an enemy in their mouths to steal away their brains!
Ibid. Line 293

---

[1] These lines are from an old ballad, Take Thy Old Cloak About Thee, found in PERCY's *Reliques:* —
King Stephen was a worthy peere,
　His breeches cost him but a crowne,
He held them sixpence all too deere;
　Therefore he called the taylor Lowne [rascal].
[2] Mince the matter. — CERVANTES: *Don Quixote, Author's Preface.* WILLIAM KING: *Ulysses and Teresias*

Good wine is a good familiar creature if it be well used.

Othello. Act II, Sc. 3, Line 315

How poor are they that have not patience!

Ibid. Line 379

Excellent wretch! Perdition catch my soul,
But I do love thee! and when I love thee not,
Chaos is come again.[1]

Ibid. Act III, Sc. 3, Line 90

Men should be what they seem.

Ibid. Line 126

Speak to me as to thy thinkings,
As thou dost ruminate, and give thy worst of thoughts
The worst of words.

Ibid. Line 131

Good name in man and woman, dear my lord,
Is the immediate jewel of their souls:
Who steals my purse steals trash; 'tis something, nothing;
'Twas mine, 'tis his, and has been slave to thousands;
But he that filches from me my good name
Robs me of that which not enriches him,
And makes me poor indeed.

Ibid. Line 155

O! beware, my lord, of jealousy;
It is the green-eyed monster which doth mock
The meat it feeds on.

Ibid. Line 165

Poor and content is rich, and rich enough.

Ibid. Line 172

If I do prove her haggard,
Though that her jesses were my dear heart-strings,
I'd whistle her off and let her down the wind,
To prey at fortune.

Ibid. Line 260

[1] For he being dead, with him is beauty slain,
And, beauty dead, black chaos comes again.
Venus and Adonis, L. 1019

I am declined
Into the vale of years.

Othello. Act III, Sc. 3, Line 265

O curse of marriage!
That we can call these delicate creatures ours,
And not their appetites. I had rather be a toad,
And live upon the vapour of a dungeon,
Than keep a corner in the thing I love
For others' uses.

Ibid. Line 268

Trifles light as air
Are to the jealous confirmations strong
As proofs of holy writ.

Ibid. Line 323

Not poppy, nor mandragora,
Nor all the drowsy syrups of the world,
Shall ever medicine thee to that sweet sleep
Which thou ow'dst yesterday.

Ibid. Line 331

I swear 'tis better to be much abused
Than but to know 't a little.

Ibid. Line 337

He that is robb'd, not wanting what is stolen,
Let him not know 't and he's not robb'd at all.

Ibid. Line 343

O! now, for ever
Farewell the tranquil mind; farewell content!
Farewell the plumed troop and the big wars
That make ambition virtue! O, farewell!
Farewell the neighing steed, and the shrill trump,
The spirit-stirring drum, the ear-piercing fife,
The royal banner, and all quality,
Pride, pomp, and circumstance of glorious war!
And, O you mortal engines, whose rude throats
The immortal Jove's dread clamours counterfeit,
Farewell! Othello's occupation's gone!

Ibid. Line 348

Be sure of it; give me the ocular proof.

Ibid. Line 361

No hinge nor loop
To hang a doubt on.
Othello. Act III, Sc. 3, Line 366
On horror's head horrors accumulate.
Ibid. Line 371
Take note, take note, O world!
To be direct and honest is not safe.
Ibid. Line 378
But this denoted a foregone conclusion.
Ibid. Line 429
Swell, bosom, with thy fraught,
For 'tis of aspics' tongues!
Ibid. Line 450
Like to the Pontick sea,
Whose icy current and compulsive course
Ne'er feels retiring ebb, but keeps due on
To the Propontic and the Hellespont,
Even so my bloody thoughts, with violent pace,
Shall ne'er look back, ne'er ebb to humble love,
Till that a capable and wide revenge
Swallow them up.
Ibid. Line 454
Our new heraldry is hands, not hearts.
Ibid. Sc. 4, Line 48
Fetch me the handkerchief.
Ibid. Line 89
To beguile many, and be beguil'd by one.
Ibid. Act IV, Sc. 1, Line 98
They laugh that win.
Ibid. Line 123
But yet the pity of it, Iago! O! Iago, the pity of it, Iago!
Ibid. Line 205
I understand a fury in your words,
But not the words.
Ibid. Sc. 2, Line 31
Steep'd me in poverty to the very lips.
Ibid. Line 49
But, alas! to make me
A fixed figure for the time of scorn
To point his slow and moving finger at!
Ibid. Line 52
Patience, thou young and rose-lipp'd cherubin.
Ibid. Line 62
O thou weed!
Who art so lovely fair and smell'st so sweet

That the sense aches at thee, would thou hadst ne'er been born.
Othello. Act IV, Sc. 2, Line 66
O Heaven! that such companions thou'dst unfold,
And put in every honest hand a whip
To lash the rascals naked through the world.
Ibid. Line 141
'Tis neither here nor there.
Ibid. Sc. 3, Line 60
It makes us, or it mars us.
Ibid. Act V, Sc. 1, Line 4
Every way makes my gain.
Ibid. Line 14
He hath a daily beauty in his life.
Ibid. Line 19
This is the night
That either makes me or fordoes me quite.
Ibid. Line 128
And smooth as monumental alabaster.
Ibid. Sc. 2, Line 5
Put out the light, and then put out the light:
If I quench thee, thou flaming minister,
I can again thy former light restore
Should I repent me; but once put out thy light,
Thou cunning'st pattern of excelling nature,
I know not where is that Promethean heat
That can thy light relume.
Ibid. Line 7
Curse his better angel from his side,
And fall to reprobation.
Ibid. Line 206
I have done the state some service, and they know 't;
No more of that. I pray you, in your letters,
When you shall these unlucky deeds relate,
Speak of me as I am; nothing extenuate,
Nor set down aught in malice: then, must you speak
Of one that loved not wisely but too well;
Of one not easily jealous, but, being wrought,

Perplex'd in the extreme; of one whose
hand,
Like the base Indian, threw a pearl
away
Richer than all his tribe; of one whose
subdued eyes
Albeit unused to the melting mood,
Drop tears as fast as the Arabian trees
Their medicinal gum.

> *Othello. Act V, Sc. 2, Line 338*

I took by the throat the circumcised
dog,
And smote him thus.

> *Ibid. Line 354*

There's beggary in the love that can
be reckon'd.

> *Antony and Cleopatra. Act I,*
> *Sc. 1, Line 15*

In nature's infinite book of secrecy
A little I can read.

> *Ibid. Sc. 2, Line 11*

On the sudden
A Roman thought hath struck him.

> *Ibid. Line 90*

Give me to drink mandragora.

> *Ibid. Sc. 5, Line 4*

Where's my serpent of old Nile?

> *Ibid. Line 25*

A morsel for a monarch.

> *Ibid. Line 31*

My salad days,
When I was green in judgment.

> *Ibid. Line 73*

We, ignorant of ourselves,
Beg often our own harms, which the
wise powers
Deny us for our good; so find we profit
By losing of our prayers.

> *Ibid. Act II, Sc. 1, Line 5*

Epicurean cooks
Sharpen with cloyless sauce his appetite.

> *Ibid. Line 24*

You patch'd up your excuses.

> *Ibid. Sc. 2, Line 60*

The barge she sat in, like a burnish'd
throne,
Burn'd on the water; the poop was
beaten gold,
Purple the sails, and so perfumed that
The winds were love-sick with them;
the oars were silver,

Which to the tune of flutes kept stroke,
and made
The water which they beat to follow
faster,
As amorous of their strokes. For her
own person,
It beggar'd all description.

> *Antony and Cleopatra. Act II,*
> *Sc. 2, Line 199*

Age cannot wither her, nor custom stale
Her infinite variety.

> *Ibid. Line 243*

I have not kept my square; but that to
come
Shall all be done by the rule.

> *Ibid. Sc. 3, Line 6*

'Twas merry when
You wager'd on your angling; when
your diver
Did hang a salt-fish on his hook, which
he
With fervency drew up.

> *Ibid. Sc. 5, Line 15*

Though it be honest, it is never good
To bring bad news.

> *Ibid. Line 85*

Come, thou monarch of the vine,
Plumpy Bacchus with pink eyne!

> *Ibid. Sc. 7, Line 120*

Who does i' the wars more than his
captain can
Becomes his captain's captain.

> *Ibid. Act III, Sc. 1, Line 21*

Celerity is never more admir'd
Than by the negligent.

> *Ibid. Sc. 7, Line 7*

He wears the rose
Of youth upon him.

> *Ibid. Sc. 11, Line 20*

Men's judgments are
A parcel of their fortunes, and things
outward
Do draw the inward quality after them,
To suffer all alike.

> *Ibid. Line 31*

Let's have one other gaudy night.

> *Ibid. Line 182*

To business that we love we rise be-
time,
And go to 't with delight.

> *Ibid. Act IV, Sc. 4, Line 20*

This morning, like the spirit of a youth
That means to be of note, begins betimes.
> *Antony and Cleopatra. Act IV,*
> *Sc. 4, Line 26*

I have yet
Room for six scotches more.
> *Ibid. Sc. 7, Line 9*

The shirt of Nessus is upon me.
> *Ibid. Sc. 10, Line 56*

Sometimes we see a cloud that's drag-
onish;
A vapour sometime like a bear or lion,
A tower'd citadel, a pendant rock,
A forked mountain, or blue promontory
With trees upon 't.
> *Ibid. Sc. 12, Line 2*

That which is now a horse, even with
a thought
The rack dislimns, and makes it indistinct,
As water is in water.
> *Ibid. Line 9*

I am dying, Egypt, dying.
> *Ibid. Sc. 13, Line 18*

There is nothing left remarkable
Beneath the visiting moon.
> *Ibid. Line 67*

Let's do it after the high Roman fashion.
> *Ibid. Line 87*

For his bounty,
There was no winter in 't; an autumn
'twas
That grew the more by reaping.
> *Ibid. Act V, Sc. 2, Line 86*

If there be, or ever were, one such,
It's past the size of dreaming.
> *Ibid. Line 96*

The bright day is done,
And we are for the dark.
> *Ibid. Line 192*

Mechanic slaves
With greasy aprons, rules, and hammers.
> *Ibid. Line 208*

A woman is a dish for the gods.
> *Ibid. Line 274*

I have
Immortal longings in me.
> *Ibid. Line 282*

Dost thou not see my baby at my
breast,

That sucks the nurse asleep?
> *Antony and Cleopatra. Act V,*
> *Sc. 2, Line 311*

Lest the bargain should catch cold and
starve.
> *Cymbeline. Act I, Sc. 4, Line 186*

Hath his bellyful of fighting.
> *Ibid. Act II, Sc. 1, Line 24*

How bravely thou becomest thy bed!
> *Ibid. Sc. 2, Line 15*

The most patient man in loss, the
most coldest that ever turned up ace.
> *Ibid. Sc. 3, Line 1*

Hark! hark! the lark at heaven's gate
sings,
And Phœbus 'gins arise,[1]
His steeds to water at those springs
On chaliced flowers that lies;
And winking Mary-buds begin
To ope their golden eyes:
With everything that pretty is,
My lady sweet, arise.
> *Ibid. Line 22*

As chaste as unsunn'd snow.
> *Ibid. Sc. 5, Line 13*

A kind of conquest
Caesar made here, but made not here
his brag
Of "came, and saw, and overcame."[2]
> *Ibid. Act III, Sc. 1, Line 22*

Some griefs are med'cinable.
> *Ibid. Sc. 2, Line 33*

Prouder than rustling in unpaid-for
silk.
> *Ibid. Sc. 3, Line 24*

So slippery that
The fear's as bad as falling.
> *Ibid. Line 48*

The game is up.
> *Ibid. Line 107*

Slander,
Whose edge is sharper than the sword,
whose tongue
Outvenoms all the worms of Nile,
whose breath
Rides on the posting winds and doth
belie
All corners of the world.
> *Ibid. Sc. 4, Line 35*

Against self-slaughter
There is a prohibition so divine

[1] See Lyly, page 23.
[2] See page 65.

That cravens my weak hand.
> *Cymbeline. Act III, Sc. 4, Line 78*

It is no act of common passage, but
A strain of rareness.
> *Ibid. Line 94*

I have not slept one wink.
> *Ibid. Line 103*

Weariness
Can snore upon the flint when resty
  sloth
Finds the down pillow hard.
> *Ibid. Sc. 6, Line 33*

An angel! or, if not,
An earthly paragon!
> *Ibid. Line 42*

Society is no comfort
To one not sociable.
> *Ibid. Act IV, Sc. 2, Line 12*

I wear not
My dagger in my mouth.
> *Ibid. Line 78*

And put
My clouted brogues from off my feet.
> *Ibid. Line 213*

Fear no more the heat o' the sun,
  Nor the furious winter's rages;
Thou thy worldly task hast done,
  Home art gone, and ta'en thy wages.
> *Ibid. Line 258*

Golden lads and girls all must,
As chimney-sweepers, come to dust.
> *Ibid. Line 262*

Fortune brings in some boats that are
  not steer'd.
> *Ibid. Sc. 3, Line 46*

By medicine life may be prolong'd, yet
  death
Will seize the doctor too.
> *Ibid. Act V, Sc. 5, Line 29*

As an arrow shot
From a well-experienc'd archer hits the
  mark
His eye doth level at.
> *Pericles. Act I, Sc. 1, Line 163*

3 Fisherman. Master, I marvel how
the fishes live in the sea.
1 Fisherman. Why, as men do aland;
the great ones eat up the little ones.[1]
> *Ibid. Act II, Sc. 1, Line 29*

[1] See Algernon Sidney, page 170.

My good will is great, though the gift
  small.
> *Pericles. Act III, Sc. 4, Line 18*

Bid me discourse, I will enchant thine
  ear.
> *Venus and Adonis. Line 145*

Love is a spirit all compact of fire.
> *Ibid. Line 149*

A red morn, that ever yet betoken'd
Wrack to the seaman, tempest to the
  field.
> *Ibid. Line 453*

The owl, night's herald.
> *Ibid. Line 531*

The path is smooth that leadeth on to
  danger.
> *Ibid. Line 788*

Love comforteth like sunshine after
  rain.
> *Ibid. Line 799*

The text is old, the orator too green.
> *Ibid. Line 806*

Lo! here the gentle lark, weary of rest,
From his moist cabinet mounts up on
  high,
And wakes the morning.
> *Ibid. Line 853*

For he being dead, with him is beauty
  slain,
And, beauty dead, black chaos comes
  again.
> *Ibid. Line 1019*

The grass stoops not, she treads on it so
  light.
> *Ibid. Line 1028*

Beauty itself doth of itself persuade
The eyes of men without an orator.
> *The Rape of Lucrece. Line 29*

Those that much covet are with gain so
  fond,
For what they have not, that which they
  possess
They scatter and unloose it from their
  bond,
And so, by hoping more, they have but
  less.
> *Ibid. Line 134*

One for all, or all for one we gage.[1]
> *Ibid. Line 144*

[1] All for one, one for all, that is our device.
— ALEXANDRE DUMAS [1802–1870]: *The
Three Musketeers, Chap. 9*

For greatest scandal waits on greatest state.

> *The Rape of Lucrece. Line 1006*

For men have marble, women waxen minds.

> *Ibid. Line 1240*

To see sad sights moves more than hear them told.

> *Ibid. Line 1324*

Lucrece swears he did her wrong.[1]

> *Ibid. Line 1462*

To the onlie begetter.

> *Sonnets, Dedication*

Thou art thy mother's glass, and she in thee
Calls back the lovely April of her prime.

> *Sonnet 3*

And stretched metre of an antique song.

> *Sonnet 17*

Shall I compare thee to a summer's day?

> *Sonnet 18*

But thy eternal summer shall not fade.

> *Ibid.*

The painful warrior famoused for fight,
After a thousand victories, once foil'd,
Is from the books of honour razed quite,
And all the rest forgot for which he toil'd.

> *Sonnet 25*

When in disgrace with fortune and men's eyes
I all alone beweep my outcast state.

> *Sonnet 29*

For thy sweet love remember'd such wealth brings
That then I scorn to change my state with kings.

> *Ibid.*

When to the sessions of sweet silent thought
I summon up remembrance of things past,
I sigh the lack of many a thing I sought,
And with old woes new wail my dear times' waste.

> *Sonnet 30*

While I think on thee, dear friend,
All losses are restor'd and sorrows end.

> *Ibid.*

[1] See page 98.

Full many a glorious morning have I seen.

> *Sonnet 33*

Nimble thought can jump both sea and land.

> *Sonnet 44*

My grief lies onward, and my joy behind.

> *Sonnet 50*

Blunting the fine point of seldom pleasure.

> *Sonnet 52*

Like stones of worth they thinly placed are,
Or captain jewels in the carconet.

> *Ibid.*

The rose looks fair, but fairer we it deem
For that sweet odour which doth in it live.

> *Sonnet 54*

Not marble, nor the gilded monuments
Of princes, shall outlive this powerful rhyme.

> *Sonnet 55*

Like as the waves make towards the pebbled shore,
So do our minutes hasten to their end

> *Sonnet 60*

Ruin hath taught me thus to ruminate.

> *Sonnet 64*

Since brass, nor stone, nor earth, nor boundless sea,
But sad mortality o'ersways their power,
How with this rage shall beauty hold a plea,
Whose action is no stronger than a flower?

> *Sonnet 65*

And art made tongue-tied by authority.

> *Sonnet 66*

And simple truth miscall'd simplicity,
And captive good attending captain ill.

> *Ibid.*

That time of year thou may'st in me behold
When yellow leaves, or none, or few, do hang
Upon those boughs which shake against the cold,

Bare ruin'd choirs, where late the sweet birds sang.

Sonnet 73

Clean starved for a look.

Sonnet 75

Your monument shall be my gentle verse,
Which eyes not yet created shall o'er-read;
And tongues to be your being shall re-hearse,
When all the breathers of this world are dead;
You still shall live — such virtue hath my pen —
Where breath most breathes, — even in the mouths of men.

Sonnet 81

Who is it that says most? which can say more
Than this rich praise, — that you alone are you?

Sonnet 84

Farewell! thou art too dear for my possessing.

Sonnet 87

Do not, when my heart hath 'scap'd this sorrow,
Come in the rearward of a conquer'd woe;
Give not a windy night a rainy morrow,
To linger out a purpos'd overthrow.

Sonnet 90

The summer's flower is to the summer sweet,
Though to itself it only live and die.

Sonnet 94

The hardest knife ill-used doth lose his edge.

Sonnet 95

From you I have been absent in the spring,
When proud-pied April, dress'd in all his trim,
Hath put a spirit of youth in everything.

Sonnet 98

That love is merchandiz'd whose rich esteeming
The owner's tongue doth publish every where.

Sonnet 102

Sweets grown common lose their dear delight.

Sonnet 102

To me, fair friend, you never can be old,
For as you were when first your eye I ey'd
Such seems your beauty still.

Sonnet 104

Still constant is a wondrous excellence.

Sonnet 105

The chronicle of wasted time.

Sonnet 106

And beauty, making beautiful old rhyme.

Ibid.

Peace proclaims olives of endless age.

Sonnet 107

That is my home of love; if I have ranged,
Like him that travels, I return again.

Sonnet 109

Made myself a motley to the view.

Sonnet 110

My nature is subdu'd
To what it works in, like the dyer's hand.

Sonnet 111

Let me not to the marriage of true minds
Admit impediments. Love is not love
Which alters when it alteration finds.

Sonnet 116

And ruin'd love, when it is built anew,
Grows fairer than at first, more strong, far greater.

Sonnet 119

'Tis better to be vile than vile esteem'd,
When not to be receives reproach of being;
And the just pleasure lost, which is so deem'd,
Not by our feeling, but by others' seeing.

Sonnet 121

No, I am that I am, and they that level
At my abuses reckon up their own.

Ibid.

To kiss the tender inward of thy hand.

Sonnet 128

That full star that ushers in the even.

Sonnet 132

So on the tip of his subduing tongue
All kind of arguments and question
deep,
All replication prompt, and reason
strong,
For his advantage still did wake and
sleep:
To make the weeper laugh, the laugher
weep,
He had the dialect and different skill,
Catching all passions in his craft of will.

A Lover's Complaint. Line 120

O father! what a hell of witchcraft lies
In the small orb of one particular tear.

Ibid. Line 288

When my love swears that she is made
of truth,
I do believe her, though I know she lies.

The Passionate Pilgrim, I

Love's best habit is a soothing tongue.

Ibid.

Bad in the best, though excellent in
neither.

Ibid. VII

Crabbed age and youth cannot live together.
Youth is full of pleasure, age is full of
care.

Ibid. XII

When as thine eye hath chose the
dame. . . .
Plainly say thou lov'st her well,
And set thy person forth to sell.

*Sonnets to Sundry Notes of
Music. IV*

The strongest castle, tower, and town,
The golden bullet beats it down.

Ibid.

Have you not heard it said full oft,
A woman's nay doth stand for naught?

Ibid.

Cursed be he that moves my bones.

Shakespeare's Epitaph

FRANCIS BACON
[1561–1626]

I hold every man a debtor to his profession; from the which as men of
course do seek to receive countenance
and profit, so ought they of duty to endeavour themselves by way of amends
to be a help and ornament thereunto.

Maxims of the Law. Preface

Come home to men's business and
bosoms.

*Dedication to the Essays
[Edition 1625]*

No pleasure is comparable to the
standing upon the vantage-ground of
truth.

Of Truth

Men fear death as children fear to go
in the dark; and as that natural fear in
children is increased with tales, so is the
other.

Of Death

Revenge is a kind of wild justice,
which the more man's nature runs to,
the more ought law to weed it out.

Of Revenge

It was a high speech of Seneca (after
the manner of the Stoics), that "The
good things which belong to prosperity
are to be wished, but the good things
that belong to adversity are to be admired."

Of Adversity

It is yet a higher speech of his than
the other, "It is true greatness to have
in one the frailty of a man and the security of a god."

Ibid.

Prosperity is the blessing of the Old
Testament; adversity is the blessing of
the New.

Ibid.

Prosperity is not without many fears
and distastes; and adversity is not without comforts and hopes.

Ibid.

Virtue is like precious odours,—
most fragrant when they are incensed
or crushed.[1]

Ibid.

He that hath wife and children hath
given hostages to fortune; for they are

---

[1] As aromatic plants bestow
No spicy fragrance while they grow;
But crushed or trodden to the ground,
Diffuse their balmy sweets around.
    GOLDSMITH: *The Captivity, Act I*
The good are better made by ill,
As odours crushed are sweeter still.
    ROGERS: *Jacqueline, Stanza 3*

impediments to great enterprises, either of virtue or mischief.

Of Marriage and Single Life

Wives are young men's mistresses, companions for middle age, and old men's nurses.[1]

Ibid.

The monuments of wit survive the monuments of power.

Essex's Device [1595]

A good name is like a precious ointment; it filleth all around about, and will not easily away; for the odors of ointments are more durable than those of flowers.[2]

Of Praise

Men in great place are thrice servants, — servants of the sovereign or state, servants of fame, and servants of business.

Of Great Place

Mahomet made the people believe that he would call a hill to him, and from the top of it offer up his prayers for the observers of his law. The people assembled. Mahomet called the hill to come to him, again and again; and when the hill stood still he was never a whit abashed, but said, "If the hill will not come to Mahomet, Mahomet will go to the hill."

Of Boldness

The desire of power in excess caused the angels to fall; the desire of knowledge in excess caused man to fall.[3]

Of Goodness

The remedy is worse than the disease.[4]

Of Seditions

I had rather believe all the fables in the legends and the Talmud and the Alcoran, than that this universal frame is without a mind.

Of Atheism

A little philosophy inclineth man's mind to atheism, but depth in philosophy bringeth men's minds about to religion.[1]

Of Atheism

Travel, in the younger sort, is a part of education; in the elder, a part of experience. He that travelleth into a country before he hath some entrance into the language, goeth to school, and not to travel.

Of Travel

Princes are like to heavenly bodies, which cause good or evil times, and which have much veneration but no rest.[2]

Of Empire

Fortune is like the market, where many times, if you can stay a little, the price will fall.

Of Delays

In things that a man would not be seen in himself, it is a point of cunning to borrow the name of the world; as to say, "The world says," or "There is a speech abroad."

Of Cunning

There is a cunning which we in England call "the turning of the cat in the pan"; which is, when that which a man says to another, he lays it as if another had said it to him.

Ibid.

It is a good point of cunning for a man to shape the answer he would have in his own words and propositions, for it makes the other party stick the less.

Ibid.

It hath been an opinion that the French are wiser than they seem, and the Spaniards seem wiser than they are; but howsoever it be between nations,

---

[1] BURTON (quoted): *Anatomy of Melancholy, Part III, Sect. 2, Memb. 5, Subsect. 5*
[2] A good name is better than precious ointment. — *Ecclesiastes, VII, 1*
[3] Pride still is aiming at the blest abodes;
Men would be angels, angels would be gods.
Aspiring to be gods if angels fell,
Aspiring to be angels men rebel.
POPE: *Essay on Man, Ep. I, L. 125*
[4] There are some remedies worse than the disease. — PUBLIUS SYRUS: *Maxim 301*

[1] Who are a little wise the best fools be. — DONNE: *Triple Fool*
A little skill in antiquity inclines a man to Popery; but depth in that study brings him about again to our religion. — FULLER: *The Holy State, The True Church Antiquary*
A little learning is a dangerous thing. — POPE: *Essay on Criticism, Part II, L. 15*
[2] Kings are like stars: they rise and set; they have
The worship of the world, but no repose. SHELLEY: *Hellas*

certainly it is so between man and man.
Of Seeming Wise

There is a wisdom in this beyond the rules of physic. A man's own observation, what he finds good of and what he finds hurt of, is the best physic to preserve health.
Of Regimen of Health

Discretion of speech is more than eloquence; and to speak agreeably to him with whom we deal is more than to speak in good words or in good order.
Of Discourse

Men's thoughts are much according to their inclination,[1] their discourse and speeches according to their learning and infused opinions.
Of Custom and Education

Chiefly the mould of a man's fortune is in his own hands.[2]
Of Fortune

If a man look sharply and attentively, he shall see Fortune; for though she is blind, she is not invisible.[3]
Ibid.

Young men are fitter to invent than to judge, fitter for execution than for counsel, and fitter for new projects than for settled business.
Of Youth and Age

Virtue is like a rich stone, — best plain set.
Of Beauty

There is no excellent beauty that hath not some strangeness in the proportion.
Ibid.

God Almighty first planted a garden.[4]
Of Gardens

And because the breath of flowers is far sweeter in the air (where it comes and goes, like the warbling of music) than in the hand, therefore nothing is more fit for that delight than to know what be the flowers and plants that do best perfume the air.
Of Gardens

It is generally better to deal by speech than by letter.
Of Negotiating

Some books are to be tasted, others to be swallowed, and some few to be chewed and digested.
Of Studies

Reading maketh a full man, conference a ready man, and writing an exact man.
Ibid.

Histories make men wise; poets, witty; the mathematics, subtile; natural philosophy, deep; moral, grave; logic and rhetoric, able to contend.
Ibid.

The greatest vicissitude of things amongst men is the vicissitude of sects and religions.[1]
Of Vicissitude of Things

Books must follow sciences, and not sciences books.
Proposition touching Amendment of Laws

Knowledge is power. — Nam et ipsa scientia potestas est.[2]
Meditationes Sacræ, De Hæresibus

Whence we see spiders, flies, or ants entombed and preserved forever in amber, a more than royal tomb.[3]
Historia Vitæ et Mortis, Sylva Sylvarum, Cent. I. Exper., 100

---

[1] Thy wish was father, Harry, to that thought. — SHAKESPEARE: *King Henry IV, Part II, Act IV, Sc. 5, L. 91*

[2] Every man is the architect of his own fortune. — PSEUDO-SALLUST: *Epist. de Rep. Ordin., I, 2*

His own character is the arbiter of every one's fortune. — PUBLIUS SYRUS: *Maxim 283*

[3] Fortune is painted blind, with a muffler afore her eyes, to signify to you that Fortune is blind. — SHAKESPEARE: *Henry V, Act III, Sc. 6, L. 31*

[4] And the Lord God planted a garden eastward in Eden. — *Genesis, II, 8*

God the first garden made, and the first city Cain.
COWLEY: *The Garden, Essay V*

God made the country, and man made the town.
COWPER: *The Task, Book I, L. 749*

Divina natura dedit agros, ars humana ædificavit urbes (Divine Nature gave the fields, human art built the cities). — VARRO: *De Re Rustica, III, 1*

[1] The vicissitude of things. — STERNE: *Sermon XVI.* GIFFORD: *Contemplation*

[2] A wise man is strong; yea, a man of knowledge increaseth strength. — *Proverbs, XXIV, 5*

Knowledge is more than equivalent to force. — JOHNSON: *Rasselas, Chap. XIII*

[3] The bee enclosed and through the amber shown,

When you wander, as you often delight to do, you wander indeed, and give never such satisfaction as the curious time requires. This is not caused by any natural defect, but first for want of election, when you, having a large and fruitful mind, should not so much labour what to speak as to find what to leave unspoken. Rich soils are often to be weeded.

Letter of Expostulation to Coke

"Antiquitas sæculi juventus mundi." These times are the ancient times, when the world is ancient, and not those which we account ancient *ordine retrogrado,* by a computation backward from ourselves.[1]

Advancement of Learning.
Book I [*1605*]

For the glory of the Creator and the relief of man's estate.

Ibid.

Seems buried in the juice which was his own.
MARTIAL: *Book IV, 32, VI, 15*
(Hay's translation)
I saw a flie within a beade
Of amber cleanly buried.
HERRICK: *On a Fly buried in Amber*
Pretty! in amber to observe the forms
Of hairs, or straws, or dirt, or grubs, or worms.
POPE: *Epistle to Dr. Arbuthnot, L. 169*
[1] As in the little, so in the great world, reason will tell you that old age or antiquity is to be accounted by the farther distance from the beginning and the nearer approach to the end, — the times wherein we now live being in propriety of speech the most ancient since the world's creation. — GEORGE HAKEWILL: *An Apologie or Declaration of the Power and Providence of God in the Government of the World* [London, 1627]
For as old age is that period of life most remote from infancy, who does not see that old age in this universal man ought not to be sought in the times nearest his birth, but in those most remote from it? — PASCAL: *Preface to the Treatise on Vacuum*
It is worthy of remark that a thought which is often quoted from Francis Bacon occurs in [Giordano] Bruno's "Cena di Cenere," published in 1584: I mean the notion that the later times are more aged than the earlier. — WHEWELL: *Philosophy of the Inductive Sciences, Vol. II, P. 198* [London, 1847]
We are Ancients of the earth,
And in the morning of the times.
TENNYSON: *The Day Dream, L'Envoi*

The sun, which passeth through pollutions and itself remains as pure as before.[1]

Advancement of Learning. Book II

It [Poesy] was ever thought to have some participation of divineness, because it doth raise and erect the mind by submitting the shews of things to the desires of the mind.

Ibid.

Sacred and inspired divinity, the sabaoth and port of all men's labours and peregrinations.

Ibid.

Cleanness of body was ever deemed to proceed from a due reverence to God.[2]

Ibid.

States as great engines move slowly.

Ibid.

The world's a bubble, and the life of man
Less than a span.[3]

The World

[1] The sun, though it passes through dirty places, yet remains as pure as before. — *Advancement of Learning* (ed. Dewey)
The sun, too, shines into cesspools and is not polluted. — DIOGENES LAERTIUS, *Lib. VI, Sect. 63*
Spiritalis enim virtus sacramenti ita est ut lux: etsi per immundos transeat, non inquinatur (The spiritual virtue of a sacrament is like light: although it passes among the impure, it is not polluted). — SAINT AUGUSTINE: *Works, Vol. III, in Johannis Evang., Cap. I, Tr. V, Sect. 15*
The sun shineth upon the dunghill, and is not corrupted. — LYLY: *Euphues* (Arber's reprint), *P. 43*
The sun reflecting upon the mud of strands and shores is unpolluted in his beam. — TAYLOR: *Holy Living, Chap. I, P. 3*
Truth is as impossible to be soiled by any outward touch as the sun-beam. — MILTON: *The Doctrine and Discipline of Divorce*
[2] Cleanliness is indeed next to godliness. — JOHN WESLEY (quoted): *Sermon XCII, On Dress*
According to Dr. A. S. Bettelheim, rabbi, this is found in the Hebrew fathers. He cites Phinehas ben Yair, as follows: "The doctrines of religion are resolved into carefulness; carefulness into vigorousness; vigorousness into guiltlessness; guiltlessness into abstemiousness; abstemiousness into cleanliness; cleanliness into godliness," — literally, next to godliness.
[3] Whose life is a bubble, and in length a span. — BROWNE: *Pastoral II*

Who then to frail mortality shall trust
But limns on water, or but writes in
   dust.
                                    The World
What then remains but that we still
   should cry
For being born, and, being born, to
   die? [1]
                                    Ibid.
My Lord St. Albans said that Nature
did never put her precious jewels into a
garret four stories high, and therefore
that exceeding tall men had ever very
empty heads.[2]
                       Apothegms. No. 17
Like the strawberry wives, that laid
two or three great strawberries at the
mouth of their pot, and all the rest were
little ones.[3]
                       Ibid. No. 54
Sir Henry Wotton used to say that
critics are like brushers of noblemen's
clothes.
                       Ibid. No. 64
Sir Amice Pawlet, when he saw too
much haste made in any matter, was
wont to say, "Stay a while, that we may
make an end the sooner."
                       Ibid. No. 76
Alonso of Aragon was wont to say in
commendation of age, that age appears
to be best in four things, — old wood
best to burn, old wine to drink, old
friends to trust, and old authors to
read.[4]
                       Ibid. No. 97

Pyrrhus, when his friends congratu-
lated to him his victory over the Romans under Fabricius, but with great
slaughter of his own side, said to them,
"Yes; but if we have such another victory, we are undone." [1]
                       Apothegms. No. 193
Cosmus, Duke of Florence, was wont
to say of perfidious friends, that "We
read that we ought to forgive our enemies; but we do not read that we ought
to forgive our friends."
                       Ibid. No. 206
Cato said the best way to keep good
acts in memory was to refresh them
with new.
                       Ibid. No. 247
I do plainly and ingenuously confess
that I am guilty of corruption, and do
renounce all defense. I beseech your
Lordships to be merciful to a broken
reed.[2]
           *On being charged by Parliament
           with corruption in the exercise
           of his office*
I bequeath my soul to God. . . . My
body to be buried obscurely. For my

Our life is but a span. — *New England
Primer*
[1] This line frequently occurs in almost ex-
actly the same shape among the minor poems
of the time: "Not to be born, or, being born,
to die." — DRUMMOND: *Poems, P. 44.* BISHOP
KING: *Poems, etc.* [1657], *P. 145*
[2] Tall men are like houses of four stories,
wherein commonly the uppermost room is
worst furnished. — HOWELL (quoted): *Letter
I, Book I, Sect. II* [1621]
   Often the cockloft is empty in those whom
Nature hath built many stories high. — FUL-
LER: *Andronicus, Sect. VI, Par. 18, 1*
   Such as take lodgings in a head
   That's to be let unfurnished.
      BUTLER: *Hudibras, Part I, Canto I,
                                       L. 161*
[3] The custom is not altogether obsolete.
[4] Is not old wine wholesomest, old pippins
toothsomest, old wood burns brightest, old

linen wash whitest? Old soldiers, sweetheart,
are surest, and old lovers are soundest. —
WEBSTER: *Westward Hoe, Act II, Sc. 2*
   Old friends are best. King James used to
call for his old shoes; they were easiest for
his feet. — SELDEN: *Table Talk, Friends*
   Old wood to burn! Old wine to drink! Old
friends to trust! Old authors to read! — Alonso of Aragon was wont to say in commendation of age, that age appeared to be best in
these four things. — MELCHIOR: *Floresta
Española de Apothegmas o sentencias, etc.,
II, 1, 20*
   What find you better or more honourable
than age? Take the preheminence of it in
everything, — in an old friend, in old wine, in
an old pedigree. — SHACKERLEY MARMION:
[1603-1639]: *The Antiquary*
   I love everything that's old, — old friends,
old times, old manners, old books, old wine. —
GOLDSMITH: *She Stoops to Conquer, Act I*
   Old books, old wine, old Nankin blue. —
AUSTIN DOBSON: *Rondeau, To Richard Watson Gilder*
[1] There are some defeats more triumphant
than victories. — MONTAIGNE: *Of Cannibals,
Chap. XXX*
[2] Thou trustest in the staff of this broken
reed. — *Isaiah, XXXVI, 6*
   A bruised reed shall he not break. — *Isaiah,
XLII, 3*

name and memory, I leave it to men's charitable speeches, and to foreign nations, and the next age.

From his Will

SIR HENRY WOTTON
[1568–1639]

Love lodged in a woman's breast
Is but a guest.

A Woman's Heart

How happy is he born and taught,
That serveth not another's will;
Whose armour is his honest thought,
And simple truth his utmost skill!

The Character of a Happy Life.
Stanza 1

Who God doth late and early pray
More of his grace than gifts to lend;
And entertains the harmless day
With a religious book or friend.

Ibid. Stanza 5

Lord of himself, though not of lands;
And having nothing, yet hath all.[1]

Ibid. Stanza 6

You meaner beauties of the night,
That poorly satisfy our eyes
More by your number than your light;
You common people of the skies,—
What are you when the moon [2] shall rise?

On his Mistress, the Queen of
Bohemia.[3] Stanza 1

He first deceased; she for a little tried
To live without him, liked it not, and died.

Upon the Death of Sir Albert
Morton's Wife

I am but a gatherer and disposer of other men's stuff.[4]

Preface to the Elements of
Architecture

Hanging was the worst use a man could be put to.

The Disparity between Buck-
ingham and Essex

An ambassador is an honest man sent to lie abroad for the commonwealth.[1]

Reliquiæ Wottonianæ

The itch of disputing will prove the scab of churches.[2]

A Panegyric to King Charles

SIR JOHN DAVIES
[1569–1626]

What can we know? or what can we discern,
When error chokes the windows of the mind?

The Vanity of Human Learning.
Stanza 15

For this the wisest of all moral men
Said he knew nought, but that he nought did know,
And the great mocking-master mock'd not then,
When he said, Truth was buried deep below.[3]

Ibid. Stanza 20

We that acquaint ourselves with ev'ry zone,
And pass both tropics, and behold each pole,
When we come home are to ourselves unknown,
And unacquainted still with our own soul.

Ibid. Stanza 25

I know my soul hath power to know all things,
Yet is she blind and ignorant in all:
I know I'm one of Nature's little kings,

---

[1] As having nothing, and yet possessing all things. — *2 Corinthians, VI, 10*

[2] "Sun" in *Reliquiæ Wottonianæ* [eds. 1651, 1654, 1672, 1685]

[3] This was printed with music as early as 1624, in Est's "Sixth Set of Books," etc., and is found in many MSS. — JOHN HANNAH [1818–1888]: *The Courtly Poets* [1870]

[4] I have here only made a nosegay of culled flowers, and have brought nothing of my own but the thread that ties them together. — MICHEL DE MONTAIGNE: *Of Physiognomy*

[1] In a letter to Velserus [1612] Wotton says, "This merry definition of an ambassador I had chanced to set down at my friend's, Mr. Christopher Fleckamore, in his Album."

[2] He directed the stone over his grave to be inscribed: —
Hic jacet hujus sententiæ primus auctor:
DISPUTANDI PRURITUS ECCLESIARUM SCABIES.
Nomen alias quære
(Here lies the author of this phrase: "The itch for disputing is the sore of churches." Seek his name elsewhere). — IZAAK WALTON: *Life of Wotton* [1651]

[3] See Diogenes Laertius, page 1014.

Yet to the least and vilest things am
thrall.
> *The Vanity of Human Learning.*
> *Ibid. Stanza 44*

I know my life's a pain, and but a span;
I know my sense is mock'd in ev'ry
thing:
And to conclude, I know myself a man,
Which is a proud, and yet a wretched
thing.
> *Ibid. Stanza 45*

Much like a subtle spider which doth
sit
In middle of her web, which spreadeth
wide;
If aught do touch the utmost thread of
it
She feels it instantly on every side.[1]
> *The Immortality of the Soul*

Wedlock, indeed, hath oft compared
been
To public feasts, where meet a public
rout, —
Where they that are without would fain
go in,
And they that are within would fain
go out.[2]
> *Contention Betwixt a Wife, etc.*

---

[1] As spiders touch'd, seek their web's in-
most part. — DAVIES: *The Vanity of Human
Learning*, St. 37
Our souls sit close and silently within,
And their own webs from their own entrails
spin;
And when eyes meet far off, our sense is such
That, spider-like, we feel the tenderest touch.
DRYDEN: *Mariage à la Mode, Act II, Sc. 1*
The spider's touch, how exquisitely fine!
Feels at each thread, and lives along the line.
POPE: *An Essay on Man, Epistle I, L. 217*
[2] 'Tis just like a summer bird-cage in a
garden: the birds that are without despair to
get in, and the birds that are within despair
and are in a consumption for fear they shall
never get out. — WEBSTER: *The White Devil,
Act I, Sc. 2*
Le mariage est comme une forteresse as-
siégée; ceux qui sont dehors veulent y entrer,
et ceux qui sont dedans veulent en sortir
(Marriage is like a beleaguered fortress: those
who are outside want to get in, and those inside want to get out). — QUITARD: *Études sur
les Proverbes Français, P. 102*
It happens as with cages: the birds without
despair to get in, and those within despair of
getting out. — MONTAIGNE: *Upon some Verses
of Virgil, Chap. V*
Is not marriage an open question, when it is

MARTYN PARKER
[? –1656]

Ye gentlemen of England
 That live at home at ease,
Ah! little do you think upon
 The dangers of the seas.
> *Song*

When the stormy winds do blow.[1]
> *Ibid.*

THOMAS DEKKER
[1570?–1641]

The reason why fond women love to buy
Adulterate complexion: here 'tis
read, —
False colours last after the true be dead.
> *A Description of a Lady by Her
> Lover*

This age thinks better of a gilded fool
Than of a threadbare saint in wisdom's
school.
> *Old Fortunatus*

The best of men
That e'er wore earth about him was a
sufferer;
A soft, meek, patient, humble, tranquil
spirit,
The first true gentleman that ever
breathed.[2]
> *The Honest Whore. Part I,
> Act I, Sc. 12*

I was ne'er so thrummed since I was a
gentleman.[3]
> *Ibid. Act IV, Sc. 2*

---

alleged, from the beginning of the world, that
such as are in the institution wish to get out,
and such as are out wish to get in? — EMER-
SON: *Representative Men: Montaigne*
[1] When the battle rages loud and long,
 And the stormy winds do blow.
 CAMPBELL: *Ye Mariners of England*
[2] Of the offspring of the gentilman Jafeth
come Habraham, Moyses, Aron, and the
profettys; also the Kyng of the right lyne of
Mary, of whom that gentilman Jhesus was
borne. — JULIANA BERNERS: *Heraldic Blazonry* [1486]
[3] I was never so bethump'd with words,
 Since I first call'd my brother's father dad.
 SHAKESPEARE: *King John, Act II,
 Sc. 1, L. 466*

This principle is old, but true as fate, —
Kings may love treason, but the traitor
hate.[1]
The Honest Whore. Part I,
Act IV, Sc. 4
We are ne'er like angels till our passion
dies.
Ibid. Part II, Act I, Sc. 2
Turn over a new leaf.[2]
Ibid. Act II, Sc. 1
To add to golden numbers, golden num-
bers.
Patient Grissell. Act I, Sc. 1
Honest labour bears a lovely face.
Ibid.

THOMAS MIDDLETON
[1570–1627]

As the case stands.[3]
The Old Law. Act II, Sc. 1
On his last legs.
Ibid. Act V, Sc. 1
Hold their noses to the grindstone.[4]
Blurt, Master-Constable.
Act III, Sc. 3
I smell a rat.[5]
Ibid.
A little too wise, they say, do ne'er live
long.[6]
The Phœnix. Act I, Sc. 1
The better day, the better deed.[7]
Ibid. Act III, Sc. 1
The worst comes to the worst.[8]
Ibid.

'Tis slight, not strength, that gives the
greatest lift.[1]
Michaelmas Term. Act IV, Sc. 1
From thousands of our undone widows
One may derive some wit.[2]
A Trick to Catch the Old One.
Act I, Sc. 2
Ground not upon dreams; you know
they are ever contrary.[3]
The Family of Love. Act IV, Sc. 3
Spick and span new.[4]
Ibid.
A flat case as plain as a pack-staff.[5]
Ibid. Act V, Sc. 3
Have you summoned your wits from
wool-gathering?
Ibid.
As true as I live.
Ibid.
From the crown of our head to the sole
of our foot.[6]
A Mad World, my Masters.
Act I, Sc. 3
That disease
Of which all old men sicken, — ava-
rice.[7]
The Roaring Girl. Act I, Sc. 1
Beat all your feathers as flat down as
pancakes.
Ibid.

[1] Cæsar said he loved the treason, but hated
the traitor. — PLUTARCH: *Life of Romulus*
[2] Also in THOMAS MIDDLETON: *Anything for
a Quiet Life, Act III, Sc. 3*
[3] As the case stands. — MATHEW HENRY:
Commentaries, Psalm CXIX
[4] Hold their noses to grinstone. — JOHN
HEYWOOD: *Proverbes, Part I, Chap. 5*
[5] I smell a rat. — BEN JONSON: *Tale of a
Tub, Act IV, Sc. 3*. BUTLER: *Hudibras, Part
I, Canto I, L. 281*
I begin to smell a rat. — CERVANTES: *Don
Quixote, Book IV, Chap. X*
[6] So wise so young, they say, do never live
long. — SHAKESPEARE: *King Richard III, Act
III, Sc. 1, L. 79*
[7] The better day, the worse deed. — HENRY:
Commentaries, Genesis III
[8] Worst comes to the worst. — CERVANTES:
Don Quixote, Part I, Book III, Chap. V.
MARSTON: *The Dutch Courtezan, Act III, Sc. 1*

[1] It is not strength, but art, obtains the
prize. — POPE: *The Iliad, Book XXIII, L. 383*
[2] Some undone widow sits upon mine arm.
— MASSINGER: *A New Way to Pay Old Debts,
Act V, Sc. 1*
[3] The visions of the night do often chance
contrary. — APULEIUS: *The Golden Ass, Book
IV*
Dhrames always go by contrairies, my dear!
— SAMUEL LOVER: *Rory O'More, St. 2*
[4] Spick and span new. — CERVANTES: *Don
Quixote, Part II, Chap. 58.* JOHN FORD: *The
Lover's Melancholy* [1629], *Act I, Sc. 1.* BUT-
LER: *Hudibras, Part I, Canto III, L. 399.*
GEORGE FARQUHAR: *Preface to his Works*
[5] Plain as a pike-staff. — *Terence in Eng-
lish* [1641]. BUCKINGHAM: *Speech in the
House of Lords* [1675]. *Gil Blas* (Smollett's
translation), *Book XII, Chap. VIII.* BYROM:
Epistle to a Friend
[6] From the crown of his head to the sole
of his foot, he is all mirth. — SHAKESPEARE:
Much Ado about Nothing, Act III, Sc. 2, L. 9
[7] So for a good old-gentlemanly vice
I think I must take up with avarice.
BYRON: *Don Juan, Canto I, Stanza 216*

There is no hate lost between us.[1]
The Witch. Act IV, Sc. 3

Black spirits and white, red spirits and
gray,
Mingle, mingle, mingle, you that mingle
may.[2]
Ibid. Act V, Sc. 2

All is not gold that glisteneth.[3]
A Fair Quarrel. Act V, Sc. 1

As old Chaucer was wont to say, that
broad famous English poet.
*More Dissemblers besides Women.
Act I, Sc. 4*

'Tis a stinger.[4]
Ibid. Act III, Sc. 2

The world's a stage on which all parts
are played.[5]
A Game of Chess. Act V, Sc. 1

Anything for a quiet life.
Title of play [1662]

Turn over a new leaf.[6]
*Anything for a Quiet Life.
Act II, Sc. 3*

My nearest
And dearest enemy.[7]
Ibid. Act V, Sc. 1

This was a good week's labour.
Ibid. Sc. 3

---

[1] There is no love lost between us. — CER-
VANTES: *Don Quixote, Book IV, Chap. XXIII.*
BEN JONSON: *Every Man Out of His Humour,
Act II, Sc. 1.* GOLDSMITH: *She Stoops to
Conquer, Act IV.* GARRICK: *Correspondence*
[1759]. FIELDING: *The Grub Street Opera,
Act I, Sc. 4*

[2] These lines are introduced into *Macbeth,
Act IV, Sc. 1.* According to Steevens, "the
song was, in all probability, a traditional
one." Collier says, "Doubtless it does not be-
long to Middleton more than to Shakespeare."
Dyce says, "There seems to be little doubt that
'Macbeth' is of an earlier date than 'The
Witch.'"

[3] See Chaucer, page 8.

[4] He 'as had a stinger. — BEAUMONT AND
FLETCHER: *Wit without Money, Act IV, Sc. 1*

[5] All the world's a stage. — SHAKESPEARE:
As You Like It, Act II, Sc. 7, L. 139
See Thomas Heywood, page 129.

[6] *A Health to the Gentlemanly Profession
of Servingmen* [1598]. Turn over a new leaf.
— DEKKER: *The Honest Whore, Part II,
Act I, Sc. 2.* BURKE: *Letter to Mrs. Haviland*

[7] My dearest foe. — SHAKESPEARE: *Hamlet,
Act I, Sc. 2, L. 182*

How many honest words have suf-
fered corruption since Chaucer's days!
*No Wit, no Help, Like a Woman's.
Act II, Sc. 1*

By many a happy accident.[1]
Ibid. Sc. 2

JOHN DONNE
[1573–1631]

I have done one braver thing
Than all the Worthies did;
And yet a braver thence doth spring,
Which is, to keep that hid.
The Undertaking, Stanza 1

Stay, O sweet, and do not rise!
The light that shines comes from thine
eyes;
The day breaks not: it is my heart,
Because that you and I must part.
Daybreak, Stanza 1

She and comparisons are odious.[2]
Elegie VIII, The Comparison

No spring nor summer beauty hath such
grace
As I have seen in one autumnal face.
*Elegie IX, The Autumnal:
To Lady Magdalen Herbert
(mother of George Herbert)*

The snail, which everywhere doth
roam
Carrying his own house still, still is at
home,
Follow (for he is easy paced) this snail,
Be thine own palace, or the world's thy
jail.
Verse Letter to Sir Henry Wotton

Pictures in our eyes to get
Was all our propagation.
The Ecstasy

Go and catch a falling star,
Get with child a mandrake root.
Song

I long to talk with some old lover's
ghost,
Who died before the god of love was
born.
Love's Deity

---

[1] A happy accident. — MADAME DE STAËL:
L'Allemagne, Chap. XVI. CERVANTES: *Don
Quixote, Book IV, Part II, Chap. LVII*

[2] See Fortescue, page 9.

His office was indulgently to fit
Actives to passives.
Love's Deity
'Twere profanation of our joys
To tell the laity our love.
A Valediction, Forbidding Mourning

Our two souls, therefore, which are one,
  Though I must go, endure not yet
A breach, but an expansion,
  Like gold to airy thinness beat.
Ibid.

A compassionate turquoise which
  doth tell
By looking pale, the wearer is not well.
An Anatomy of the World

I observe the physician with the same
diligence as he the disease.
Devotions, VI

The flea, though he kill none, he does
all the harm he can.
Ibid. XII

He was the Word, that spake it:
He took the bread and brake it;
And what that Word did make it,
I do believe and take it.[1]
Divine Poems. On the Sacrament

      Her pure and eloquent blood
Spoke in her cheeks, and so distinctly
  wrought
That one might almost say her body
  thought.
*Funeral Elegies. On the Death of
Mistress Drury*

Who are a little wise the best fools be.[2]
The Triple Fool

Death, be not proud, though some have
  called thee
Mighty and dreadful, for thou art not
  so;
For those whom thou think'st thou dost
  overthrow
Die not, poor Death; nor yet canst thou
  kill me.
Sonnet: Death

One short sleep past, we wake eternally;

And death shall be no more; death, thou
  shalt die.
Sonnet: Death

The Sea is as deepe in a calme, as in a
  storme.
Sermons. Mundus Mare

BEN JONSON [1]
[1573?–1637]

He despises me, I suppose, because I
live in an alley: tell him his soul lives
in an alley.
*Of James I. Quoted in Leigh Hunt's
essay, Coaches*

The dignity of truth is lost with much
  protesting.
Catiline's Conspiracy. Act III, Sc. 2

It was a mighty while ago.
*Every Man in his Humour. Act I,
Sc. 3*

Hang sorrow! care'll kill a cat.[2]
Ibid.

As he brews, so shall he drink.
Ibid. Act II, Sc. 1

Get money; still get money, boy,
No matter by what means.[3]
Ibid. Sc. 3

Have paid scot and lot there any time
this eighteen years.
Ibid. Act III, Sc. 3

It must be done like lightning.
Ibid. Act IV, Sc. 5

There shall be no love lost.[4]
*Every Man out of his Humour.
Act II, Sc. 1*

---

[1] Attributed by many writers to Princess
Elizabeth. It is not in the original edition of
Donne, but first appears in the edition of 1654,
P. 352.
  [2] See Bacon, page 110.

[1] O rare Ben Jonson! — SIR JOHN YOUNG:
Epitaph. (Which was donne at the charge of
Jack Young, who, walking there when the
grave was covering, gave the fellow 18 pence
to cutt it. — JOHN AUBREY: [1626–1697]
Brief Lives)
  [2] What though care killed a cat. — SHAKE-
SPEARE: *Much Ado about Nothing, Act V,
Sc. 1, L. 135*
  Hang sorrow! care will kill a cat. — GEORGE
WITHER: *Poem on Christmas*
  [3] O cives, cives, quaerenda pecunia primum,
  Virtus post nummos: haec Janus summus
    ab imo
  Perdocet.
  HORACE: *Epistles, Book I, Epistle 1, L. 53*
Get place and wealth, if possible with grace;
If not, by any means get wealth and place.
  Translation by ALEXANDER POPE, *L. 103*
  [4] See Middleton, page 117.

Still to be neat, still to be drest,
As you were going to a feast.[1]
  Epicœne; Or, the Silent Woman.
       Act I, Sc. 1
Give me a look, give me a face,
That makes simplicity a grace;
Robes loosely flowing, hair as free,
Such sweet neglect more taketh me
Than all the adulteries of art:
They strike mine eyes, but not my
 heart.
         Ibid.

Truth is the trial of itself
 And needs no other touch,
And purer than the purest gold,
 Refine it ne'er so much.
      On Truth, Stanza 1
Follow a shadow, it still flies you;
 Seem to fly it, it will pursue:
So court a mistress, she denies you;
 Let her alone, she will court you.
    Follow a Shadow, Stanza 1
That old bald cheater, Time.
    The Poetaster. Act I, Sc. 1
The world knows only two, — that's
 Rome and I.
     Sejanus. Act V, Sc. 1
Preserving the sweetness of propor-
tion and expressing itself beyond ex-
pression.
    The Masque of Hymen
Underneath this stone doth lie
As much beauty as could die;
Which in life did harbour give
To more virtue than doth live.
    Epitaph on Elizabeth, L. H.
Whilst that for which all virtue now is
 sold,
And almost every vice, — almighty
 gold.[2]
  *Epistle to Elizabeth, Countess of
          Rutland*
God wisheth none should wreck on a
 strange shelf:
To him man's dearer than to himself.
  The Forest: To Sir Robert Wroth
Drink to me only with thine eyes,
 And I will pledge with mine;

Or leave a kiss but in the cup
 And I'll not look for wine.[1]
   The Forest: To Celia, Stanza 1
I sent thee late a rosy wreath,
 Not so much honouring thee
As giving it a hope that there
 It could not wither'd be.
      Ibid. Stanza 2
Have you seen but a bright lily grow,
 Before rude hands have touched it?
Have you marked but the fall o' the
 snow
 Before the soil hath smutched it?
    Her Triumph. Stanza 3
  Reader, look,
Not at his picture, but his book.
  *On the Portrait of Shakespeare
  Prefixed to the First Folio [1623]*
   Soul of the age!
The applause, delight, the wonder of
 our stage!
My Shakespeare, rise! I will not lodge
 thee by
Chaucer or Spenser, or bid Beaumont
 lie
A little further, to make thee a room.[2]
  To the Memory of Shakespeare
Marlowe's mighty line.
         Ibid.
Small Latin and less Greek.
         Ibid.
He was not of an age but for all time.
         Ibid.
Who casts to write a living line, must
 sweat.
         Ibid.
For a good poet's made, as well as born.
         Ibid.
Sweet Swan of Avon!
         Ibid.
Underneath this sable hearse
Lies the subject of all verse, —
Sidney's sister, Pembroke's mother.

---

[1] Drink to me with your eyes alone. . . .
And if you will, take the cup to your lips
and fill it with kisses, and give it so to me. —
PHILOSTRATUS: *Letter XXIV*
[2] Renowned Spenser, lie a thought more nigh
To learned Chaucer, and rare Beaumont lie
A little nearer Spenser, to make room
For Shakespeare in your threefold, fourfold
 tomb.
  WILLIAM BASSE: *On Shakespeare*

---

[1] A translation from Bonnefonius.
[2] The flattering, mighty, nay, almighty
gold. — WOLCOT: *To Kien Long, Ode IV*
 Almighty dollar. — IRVING: *The Creole Village*

Death, ere thou hast slain another,
Learn'd and fair and good as she,
Time shall throw a dart at thee.

> *Epitaph on the Countess of*
> *Pembroke* [1]

Let those that merely talk and never
    think,
That live in the wild anarchy of drink.[2]

> *Underwoods. An Epistle, an-*
> *swering to One that asked to*
> *be sealed of the Tribe of Ben*

Still may syllabes jar with time,
Still may reason war with rhyme,
                    Resting never!

> *Ibid. Fit of Rhyme against Rhyme*

In small proportions we just beauties
    see,
And in short measures life may perfect
    be.

> *Ibid. To the immortal Memory*
> *of Sir Lucius Cary and Sir*
> *Henry Morison, III*

He seemed to me ever by his work
one of the greatest men, and most
worthy of admiration. In his adversity
I ever prayed that God would give him
strength; for greatness he could not
want.

> *Of Francis Bacon*

The players have often mentioned it
as an honor to Shakespeare, that in his
writing he never blotted out a line. My
answer hath been, Would he had blotted a thousand.

> *Timber, or Discoveries Made*
> *Upon Men and Matter*

I loved the man [Shakespeare] and
do honor his memory, on this side idolatry, as much as any.

> *Ibid.*

Greatness of name in the father ofttimes overwhelms the son; they stand
too near one another. The shadow kills

the growth: so much, that we see the
grandchild come more and oftener to
be heir of the first.

> *Timber, or Discoveries Made*
> *Upon Men and Matter*

Though the most be players, some
must be spectators.

> *Ibid.*

Whom the disease of talking once
possesseth, he can never hold his peace.
Nay, rather than he will not discourse
he will hire men to hear him.

> *Ibid.*

RICHARD BARNFIELD
[1574–1627]

As it fell upon a day
In the merry month of May,
Sitting in a pleasant shade
Which a grove of myrtles made.

> *Address to the Nightingale* [1]

King Pandion he is dead.[2]

> *Ibid.*

Every one that flatters thee
Is no friend in misery.
Words are easy, like the wind;
Faithful friends are hard to find.
Every man will be thy friend
Whilst thou hast wherewith to spend:
But, if store of crowns be scant,
No man will supply thy want.

> *Ibid.*

He that is thy friend indeed,
He will help thee in thy need.

> *Ibid.*

JOSEPH HALL, BISHOP
OF NORWICH
[1574–1656]

In bonds of love united, man and wife,
Long, yet too short, they spent a happy
    life.

> *Elegy on Sir Edward and Lady*
> *Lewkenor*

---

[1] This epitaph is generally ascribed to Ben
Jonson. It appears in the editions of his
works; but in a manuscript collection of
Browne's poems preserved amongst the Lansdowne MS. No. 777, in the British Museum, it
is ascribed to Browne, and awarded to him by
Sir Egerton Brydges in his edition of Browne's
poems.

[2] They never taste who always drink;
    They always talk who never think.

PRIOR: *Upon a Passage in the Scaligerana*

[1] This song, attributed to Shakespeare and
included in his *Sonnets to Sundry Notes of
Music,* is found in BARNFIELD'S *Poems in Divers Humours,* published in 1598, while Shakespeare's *Passionate Pilgrim,* etc. appeared in
1599. See *Specimens of Early English Romances in Meter,* by George Ellis [1753–1815],
Vol. 2, P. 316

[2] Used as refrain in a ballade by Don
Marquis.

So little in his purse, so much upon his
back.
Portrait of a Poor Gallant
'Mongst all these stirs of discontented
strife,
O, let me lead an academic life;
To know much, and to think for noth-
ing, know
Nothing to have, yet think we have
enow.
*Discontent of Men with their
Condition*
Moderation is the silken string run-
ning through the pearl chain of all vir-
tues.
Christian Moderation. Introduction
Death borders upon our birth, and
our cradle stands in the grave.[1]
Epistles. Dec. III, Ep. 2
There is many a rich stone laid up
in the bowels of the earth, many a fair
pearl laid up in the bosom of the sea,
that never was seen, nor never shall be.[2]
*Contemplations. Book IV, The
Veil of Moses*

THOMAS CAMPION
[1575?–1620?]

Good thoughts his only friends,
His wealth a well-spent age,
The earth his sober inn
And quiet pilgrimage.
*Integer Vitae, after Horace.
Stanza 6*
Never love unless you can
Bear with all the faults of man:
Men will sometimes jealous be,
Though but little cause they see;
And hang the head, as discontent,
And speak what straight they will re-
pent.
Never Love. Stanza 1
There is a garden in her face
Where roses and white lilies blow;
A heavenly paradise that place,
Wherein all pleasant fruits do grow;

---

[1] And cradles rock us nearer to the tomb.
Our birth is nothing but our death begun.
YOUNG: *Night Thoughts, Night V, L. 718*
[2] Full many a gem of purest ray serene
The dark, unfathomed caves of ocean bear.
GRAY: *Elegy, Stanza 14*

There cherries grow that none may buy,
Till Cherry-Ripe themselves do cry.
Cherry-Ripe.[1] Stanza 1
Those cherries fairly do enclose
Of orient pearl a double row,
Which when her lovely laughter shows,
They look like rosebuds fill'd with
snow.
Ibid. Stanza 2
The summer hath his joys,
And winter his delights;
Though love and all his pleasures are
but toys,
They shorten tedious nights.
Winter Nights. Stanza 2

ROBERT BURTON
[1577–1640]

Naught so sweet as melancholy.[2]
*Anatomy of Melancholy.[3] The
Author's Abstract*
I would help others, out of a fellow-
feeling.[4]
Ibid. Democritus to the Reader
They lard their lean books with the
fat of others' works.[5]
Ibid.
We can say nothing but what hath
been said.[6] Our poets steal from Homer.

---

[1] See Robert Herrick, page 133.
[2] See Strode, page 144.
There's not a string attuned to mirth
But has its chord in melancholy.
HOOD: *Ode to Melancholy*
[3] Burton's 'Anatomy of Melancholy,' he
said, was the only book that ever took him out
of bed two hours sooner than he wished to
rise. — JAMES BOSWELL: *The Life of Dr.
Johnson, Everyman Ed., Vol. I, P. 389*
If the reader has patience to go through his
volumes, he will be more improved for literary
conversation than by the perusal of any
twenty other works with which I am acquainted. — BYRON: *Works, Vol. I, P. 144*
[4] A fellow-feeling makes one wondrous
kind. — GARRICK: *Prologue on quitting the
stage*
Non ignara mali, miseris succurrere disco
(Being not unacquainted with woe, I learn
to help the unfortunate). — VIRGIL: *Æneid,
Lib. I, L. 630*
[5] And lards the lean earth as he walks along.
— SHAKESPEARE: *King Henry IV, Part I, Act
II, Sc. 2, L. 120*
[6] Nullum est jam dictum, quod non dictum
sit prius (There is nothing said, which has
not been said before). — TERENCE: *Eunuchus,
Prol., L. 41*

. . . Our story-dressers do as much; he that comes last is commonly best.

Anatomy of Melancholy.
Democritus to the Reader

I say with Didacus Stella, a dwarf standing on the shoulders of a giant may see farther than a giant himself.[1]

Ibid.

It is most true, *stylus virum arguit,* — our style bewrays us.[2]

Ibid.

I had not time to lick it into form, as a bear doth her young ones.[3]

Ibid.

As that great captain, Ziska, would have a drum made of his skin when he was dead, because he thought the very noise of it would put his enemies to flight.

Ibid.

Like the watermen that row one way and look another.[4]

Ibid.

Smile with an intent to do mischief, or cozen him whom he salutes.

Ibid.

Him that makes shoes go barefoot himself.[5]

Ibid.

---

[1] A dwarf on a giant's shoulders sees farther of the two. — HERBERT: *Jacula Prudentum*

A dwarf sees farther than the giant when he has the giant's shoulders to mount on. — COLERIDGE: *The Friend, Sect. I, Essay VIII*

Pigmæi gigantum humeris impositi plusquam ipsi gigantes vident (Pigmies placed on the shoulders of giants see more than the giants themselves). — *Didacus Stella in Lucan, 10, Tom. II*

[2] Le style est l'homme même (The style is the man himself). — COMTE DE BUFFON [1707–1788]: *Discours sur le Style,* on admission to the French Academy [1753]

[3] Arts and sciences are not cast in a mould, but are formed and perfected by degrees, by often handling and polishing, as bears leisurely lick their cubs into form. — MONTAIGNE: *Apology for Raimond Sebond, Book II, Chap. XII*

[4] Like watermen who look astern while they row the boat ahead. — PLUTARCH: *Whether 'twas rightfully said, Live concealed*

Like rowers, who advance backward. — MONTAIGNE: *Of Profit and Honour, Book III, Chap. I*

[5] Who is worse shod than the shoemaker's wife? — HEYWOOD: *Proverbes, Part I, Chap. II*

Rob Peter, and pay Paul.[1]

Anatomy of Melancholy.
Democritus to the Reader

Penny wise, pound foolish.

Ibid.

Women wear the breeches.

Ibid.

Like Æsop's fox, when he had lost his tail, would have all his fellow foxes cut off theirs.[2]

Ibid.

Hannibal, as he had mighty virtues, so had he many vices; he had two distinct persons in him.

Ibid.

Carcasses bleed at the sight of the murderer.[3]

Ibid. Part I, Sect. 1, Memb. 2, Subsect. 5

Every man hath a good and a bad angel attending on him in particular, all his life long.

Ibid. Sect. 2, Memb. 1, Subsect. 2

[Witches] steal young children out of their cradles, *ministerio dœmonum,* and put deformed in their rooms, which we call changelings.

Ibid. Subsect. 3

Can build castles in the air.

Ibid.

That which Pythagoras said to his scholars of old, may be for ever applied to melancholy men, *A fabis abstinete,* eat no beans.[4]

Ibid. Memb. 2, Subsect. 1

Joh. Mayor, in the first book of his "History of Scotland," contends much for the wholesomeness of oaten bread; it was objected to him, then living at Paris, that his countrymen fed on oats and base grain. . . . And yet Wecker out of Galen calls it horse-meat, and fitter juments than men to feed on.[5]

Ibid.

---

[1] To robbe Peter and pay Poule. — HEYWOOD: *Proverbes, Part I, Chap. II*

RABELAIS: *Book I, Chap. II*

[2] Aesop: *Fables, Book V, Fable 5*

[3] See Chaucer, page 6.

[4] There will be no beans in the Almost Perfect State. — DON MARQUIS: *The Almost Perfect State*

[5] Oats, — a grain which is generally given to horses, but in Scotland supports the people.

Cookery is become an art, a noble science; cooks are gentlemen.

Anatomy of Melancholy. Part I, Sect. 2, Memb. 2, Subsect. 2

As much valour is to be found in feasting as in fighting, and some of our city captains and carpet knights will make this good, and prove it.[1]

Ibid.

No rule is so general, which admits not some exception.

Ibid. Subsect. 3

Idleness is an appendix to nobility.

Ibid. Subsect. 6

Why doth one man's yawning make another yawn?

Ibid. Memb. 3, Subsect. 2

A nightingale dies for shame if another bird sings better.

Ibid. Subsect. 6

They do not live but linger.

Ibid. Subsect. 10

[Diseases] crucify the soul of man, attenuate our bodies, dry them, wither them, shrivel them up like old apples, make them so many anatomies.

Ibid.

[Desire] is a perpetual rack, or horsemill, according to Austin, still going round as in a ring.

Ibid. Subsect. 11

[The rich] are indeed rather possessed by their money than possessors.

Ibid. Subsect. 12

Like a hog, or dog in the manger, he doth only keep it because it shall do nobody else good, hurting himself and others.

Ibid.

Were it not that they are loath to lay out money on a rope, they would be hanged forthwith, and sometimes die to save charges.

Ibid.

— SAMUEL JOHNSON: *Dictionary of the English Language*
[1] Carpet knights are men who are by the prince's grace and favour made knights at home. . . . They are called carpet knights because they receive their honours in the court and upon carpets. — GERVASE MARKHAM [1568–1637]: *Booke of Honour* [1625]
Carpet knights. — DU BARTAS [ed. 1621], P. 311

A mere madness, to live like a wretch and die rich.

Anatomy of Melancholy. Part I, Sect. 2, Memb. 3, Subsect. 12

I may not here omit those two main plagues and common dotages of human kind, wine and women, which have infatuated and besotted myriads of people; they go commonly together.

Ibid. Subsect. 13

All our geese are swans.[1]

Ibid. Subsect. 14

Though they [philosophers] write *contemptu gloriæ*, yet as Hieron observes, they will put their names to their books.

Ibid.

They are proud in humility; proud in that they are not proud.[2]

Ibid.

We can make majors and officers every year, but not scholars; kings can invest knights and barons, as Sigismund the emperor confessed.[3]

Ibid. Subsect. 15

Hinc quam sic calamus sævior ense, patet. The pen worse than the sword.[4]

Ibid. Memb. 4, Subsect. 4

Homer himself must beg if he want means, and as by report sometimes he did "go from door to door and sing ballads, with a company of boys about him."[5]

Ibid. Subsect. 6

[1] Every man thinks his own geese swans. — DICKENS: *The Cricket on the Hearth, Chirp the Second*
[2]   His favourite sin
     Is pride that apes humility.
          SOUTHEY: *The Devil's Walk*
[3] When Abraham Lincoln heard of the death of a private, he said he was sorry it was not a general: "I could make more of them."
[4] Tant la plume a eu sous le roi d'avantage sur l'épée (So far had the pen under the king the superiority over the sword). — LOUIS DE ROUVROY SAINT SIMON: [1675–1755]: *Mémoires, Vol. III, P. 517* (1702) [ed. 1856]
The pen is mightier than the sword. — BULWER LYTTON: *Richelieu, Act II, Sc. 2*
Pyrrhus was used to say that Cineas had taken more towns with his words than he with his arms. — PLUTARCH: *Pyrrhus*
[5] Seven wealthy towns contend for Homer dead,

See one promontory (said Socrates of old), one mountain, one sea, one river, and see all.[1]

Anatomy of Melancholy. Part I,
Sect. 2, Memb. 4, Subsect. 7

Felix Plater notes of some young physicians, that study to cure diseases, catch them themselves, will be sick, and appropriate all symptoms they find related of others to their own persons.

Ibid. Sect. 3, Memb. 1, Subsect. 2

Aristotle said melancholy men of all others are most witty.

Ibid. Subsect. 3

Like him in Æsop, he whipped his horses withal, and put his shoulder to the wheel.[2]

Ibid. Part II, Sect. 1, Memb. 2

Fabricius finds certain spots and clouds in the sun.

Ibid. Sect. 2, Memb. 3

If the heavens then be penetrable, and no lets, it were not amiss to make wings and fly up; and some new-fangled wits, methinks, should some time or other find out.

Ibid.

Seneca thinks the gods are well pleased when they see great men contending with adversity.

Ibid. Sect. 2, Memb. 1, Subsect. 1

Machiavel says virtue and riches seldom settle on one man.

Ibid. Memb. 2

Almost in every kingdom the most ancient families have been at first princes' bastards; their worthiest captains, best wits, greatest scholars, brav-

est spirits in all our annals, have been base [born].

Anatomy of Melancholy. Part II,
Sect. 2, Memb. 2

As he said in Machiavel, *omnes eodem patre nati,* Adam's sons, conceived all and born in sin, etc. "We are by nature all as one, all alike, if you see us naked; let us wear theirs and they our clothes, and what is the difference?"

Ibid.

Set a beggar on horseback and he will ride a gallop.[1]

Ibid.

Christ himself was poor. . . . And as he was himself, so he informed his apostles and disciples, they were all poor, prophets poor, apostles poor.[2]

Ibid. Memb. 3

Who cannot give good counsel? 'Tis cheap, it costs them nothing.

Ibid.

Many things happen between the cup and the lip.[3]

Ibid.

What can't be cured must be endured.

Ibid.

Everything, saith Epictetus, hath two handles, — the one to be held by, the other not.

Ibid.

All places are distant from heaven alike.

Ibid. Memb. 4

How much are we bound to those munificent Ptolemies, bountiful Maecenates, heroical patrons, divine spirits,

---

Through which the living Homer begged his bread.
                                        ANONYMOUS
Great Homer's birthplace seven rival cities claim,
Too mighty such monopoly of Fame.
    THOMAS SEWARD [1708–1790]: *On Shakespeare's Monument at Stratford-upon-Avon*
Seven cities warred for Homer being dead;
Who living had no roofe to shrowd his head.
    THOMAS HEYWOOD: *Hierarchie of the Blessed Angells*
Seven cities claimed him. — ROBERT BROWNING: *Development*
    [1] A blade of grass is always a blade of grass, whether in one country or another. — JOHNSON: *Piozzi, 52*
    [2] ÆSOP: *Hercules and the Waggoner*

[1] Beggars mounted run their horse to death. — SHAKESPEARE: *King Henry VI, Part III, Act I, Sc. 4, L. 127*
Set a beggar on horseback, and he'll outride the Devil. — BOHN: *Foreign Proverbs, German*
    [2] See Wotton, page 114.
    [3] There is many a slip 'twixt the cup and the lip. — HAZLITT: *English Proverbs*
Though men determine, the gods doo dispose; and oft times many things fall out betweene the cup and the lip. — ROBERT GREENE [1560–1592]: *Perimedes the Blacke-Smith* [1588]
See Edward Bulwer Lytton, page 425.

that have provided for us so many well-furnished libraries.

Anatomy of Melancholy. Part II,
Sect. 2, Memb. 4

The commonwealth of Venice in their armoury have this inscription: "Happy is that city which in time of peace thinks of war."

Ibid. Memb. 6

Every man, as the saying is, can tame a shrew but he that hath her.

Ibid.

Divers have been relieved [of melancholy] by exonerating themselves to a faithful friend.

Ibid.

Tobacco, divine, rare, superexcellent tobacco, which goes far beyond all the panaceas, potable gold and philosopher's stones, a sovereign remedy to all diseases.

Ibid. Sect. 4, Memb. 2, Subsect. 2

"Let me not live," said Aretine's Antonia, "if I had not rather hear thy discourse than see a play."

Ibid. Part III, Sect. 1, Memb. 1,
Subsect. 1

Every schoolboy hath that famous testament of Grunnius Corocotta Porcellus at his fingers' end.

Ibid.

Birds of a feather will gather together.

Ibid. Subsect. 2

And hold one another's noses to the grindstone hard.[1]

Ibid. Memb. 3

Every man for himself, his own ends, the Devil for all.[2]

Ibid.

No cord nor cable can so forcibly draw, or hold so fast, as love can do with a twined thread.[3]

Ibid. Sect. 2, Memb. 1, Subsect. 2

To enlarge or illustrate this power and effect of love is to set a candle in the sun.

Anatomy of Melancholy. Part III,
Sect. 2, Memb. 1, Subsect. 2

He is only fantastical that is not in fashion.

Ibid. Memb. 2, Subsect. 3

[Quoting Seneca] Cornelia kept her in talk till her children came from school, "and these," said she, "are my jewels."

Ibid.

To these crocodile tears [1] they will add sobs, fiery sighs, and sorrowful countenance.

Ibid. Subsect. 4

Marriage and hanging go by destiny; matches are made in heaven.[2]

Ibid. Subsect. 5

Diogenes struck the father when the son swore.

Ibid.

Though it rain daggers with their points downward.

Ibid. Memb. 3

Going as if he trod upon eggs.

Ibid.

I light my candle from their torches.

Ibid. Memb. 5, Subsect. 1

England is a paradise for women and hell for horses; Italy a paradise for horses, hell for women, as the diverb goes.

Ibid. Sect. 3, Memb. 1, Subsect. 2

The miller sees not all the water that goes by his mill.[3]

Ibid. Memb. 4, Subsect. 1

As clear and as manifest as the nose in a man's face.[4]

Ibid.

Make a virtue of necessity.[5]

Ibid.

---

[1] See Heywood, page 13, and Middleton, page 116.
[2] See Heywood, page 18.
[3] One hair of a woman can draw more than a hundred pair of oxen. — JAMES HOWELL [1594–1666]: *Letters, Book II, IV* [1621]
She knows her man, and when you rant and swear,
Can draw you to her with a single hair.
DRYDEN: *Persius, Satire V, L. 246*

Beauty draws us with a single hair. —
POPE: *The Rape of the Lock, Canto II, L. 27*
And from that luckless hour my tyrant fair
Has led and turned me by a single hair.
ROBERT BLAND [1779–1825]: *Anthology,*
P. 20 [ed. 1813]

[1] See Chapman, page 29.
[2] See Heywood, page 12, and Shakespeare, page 45.
[3] See Heywood, page 17.
[4] See Shakespeare, page 33.
[5] See Chaucer, page 4.

Where God hath a temple, the Devil will have a chapel.[1]
Anatomy of Melancholy. Part III, Sect. 4, Memb. 1, Subsect. 1

If the world will be gulled, let it be gulled.
Ibid. Subsect. 2

For "ignorance is the mother of devotion," as all the world knows.[2]
Ibid.

The fear of some divine and supreme powers keeps men in obedience.[3]
Ibid.

Out of too much learning become mad.
Ibid.

The Devil himself, which is the author of confusion and lies.
Ibid. Subsect. 3

Isocrates adviseth Demonicus, when he came to a strange city, to worship by all means the gods of the place.
Ibid. Subsect. 5

When they are at Rome, they do there as they see done.[4]
Ibid. Memb. 2, Subsect. 1

---

[1] For where God built a church, there the Devil would also build a chapel. — MARTIN LUTHER: *Table Talk, LXVII*
God never had a church but there, men say,
The Devil a chapel hath raised by some wyles.
WILLIAM DRUMMOND [1585–1649]: *Posthumous Poems*
No sooner is a temple built to God but the Devil builds a chapel hard by. — HERBERT: *Jacula Prudentum*
Wherever God erects a house of prayer,
The Devil always builds a chapel there.
DANIEL DEFOE [1661–1731]: *The Trueborn Englishman, Part I, L. 1*
[2] Ignorance is the mother of devotion. — JEREMY TAYLOR [1613–1667]: *To a Person Newly Converted* [1657]
Your ignorance is the mother of your devotion to me. — DRYDEN: *The Maiden Queen, Act I, Sc. 2*
[3] The fear o' hell's a hangman's whip
To haud the wretch in order.
BURNS: *Epistle to a Young Friend*
[4] Saint Augustine was in the habit of dining upon Saturday as upon Sunday; but being puzzled with the different practices then prevailing (for they had begun to fast at Rome on Saturday), consulted Saint Ambrose on the subject. Now at Milan they did not fast on Saturday, and the answer of the Milan saint was this: "Quando hic sum, non jejuno Sabbato; quando Romæ sum, jejuno Sabbato" (When I am here, I do not fast on Saturday; when at Rome, I do fast on Saturday). — *Epistle XXXVI, to Casulanus*

One religion is as true as another.
Anatomy of Melancholy. Part III, Sect. 4, Memb. 2, Subsect. 1

They have cheveril consciences that will stretch.
Ibid. Subsect. 3

THOMAS WARD
[1577–1639]

Where to elect there is but one,
'Tis Hobson's choice, — take that or none.[1]
England's Reformation. Chapter IV, Page 326

JOHN FLETCHER
[1579–1625]

Man is his own star; and the soul that can
Render an honest and a perfect man
Commands all light, all influence, all fate.
Nothing to him falls early, or too late.
Our acts our angels are, or good or ill,
Our fatal shadows that walk by us still.
Upon an "Honest Man's Fortune"

Man is his own star; and that soul that can
Be honest is the only perfect man.[2]
Ibid.

---

[1] Thomas Hobson [1544–1631], of whom Steele wrote in *The Spectator, No. 509* [October 14, 1712]:
Mr. Tobias Hobson, from whom we have the expression, . . . was a carrier, . . . the first in this Island who let out hackney-horses. He lived in Cambridge, and observing that the scholars rid hard, his manner was to keep a large stable of horses, with boots, bridles, and whips. . . . When a man came for an horse, he was led into the stable, where there was great choice, but he obliged him to take the horse which stood next to the stable-door; so that every customer was alike well served according to his chance, and every horse ridden with the same justice. From whence it became a proverb, when what ought to be your election was forced upon you, to say Hobson's Choice.
[2] An honest man's the noblest work of God. — POPE: *Essay on Man, Epistle IV, L. 248*. BURNS: *The Cotter's Saturday Night*

Weep no more, nor sigh, nor groan,
Sorrow calls no time that's gone;
Violets plucked, the sweetest rain
Makes not fresh nor grow again.[1]
> *The Queen of Corinth. Act III,*
> *Sc. 2*

Hence, all you vain delights,
As short as are the nights
Wherein you spend your folly!
There's naught in this life sweet
But only melancholy.
> *Melancholy* [2]

O woman, perfect woman! what distraction
Was meant to mankind when thou wast
made a devil!
> *Monsieur Thomas. Act. III, Sc. 1*

Let us do or die.[3]
> *The Island Princess. Act II, Sc. 4*

Hit the nail on the head.
> *Love's Cure. Act II, Sc. 1*

I find the medicine worse than the
malady.[4]
> *Ibid. Act III, Sc. 2*

He went away with a flea in 's ear.
> *Ibid. Sc. 3*

Drink to-day, and drown all sorrow;
You shall perhaps not do 't to-morrow.
> *The Bloody Brother. Act II, Sc. 2*

And he that will to bed go sober
Falls with the leaf still in October.[5]
> *Ibid.*

Three merry boys, and three merry
boys,

---

[1] Weep no more, Lady! weep no more,
   Thy sorrow is in vain;
For violets plucked, the sweetest showers
   Will ne'er make grow again.
PERCY: *Reliques, The Friar of Orders Gray*
[2] See William Strode, page 144.
[3] Let us do or die. — BURNS: *Bannockburn.*
CAMPBELL: *Gertrude of Wyoming, Part III,*
St. 37
   This expression is a kind of common prop-
erty, being the motto, we believe, of a Scottish
family. — SIR WALTER SCOTT: *Miscellanies,*
Vol. I, P. 153, Review of Gertrude
[4] See Bacon, page 110.
[5] The following well-known catch, or glee,
is formed on this song: —
   He who goes to bed, and goes to bed sober,
   Falls as the leaves do, and dies in October;
   But he who goes to bed, and goes to bed
      mellow,
   Lives as he ought to do, and dies an honest
      fellow.

And three merry boys are we,[1]
As ever did sing in a hempen string
Under the gallows-tree.
> *The Bloody Brother. Act III, Sc. 2*

Hide, oh, hide those hills of snow
Which thy frozen bosom bears,
On whose tops the pinks that grow
Are of those that April wears!
But first set my poor heart free,
Bound in icy chains by thee.[2]
> *Ibid. Act V, Sc. 2*

Something given that way.
> *The Lover's Progress. Act I, Sc. 1*

Deeds, not words.[3]
> *Ibid. Act III, Sc. 4*

JOHN TAYLOR
("THE WATER POET")
[1580–1625]

Laugh and be fat.
> *Title of a tract*

God sends meat, and the Devil sends
cooks.[4]
> *Works, Vol. II, Page 85 [ed. 1630.]*

JOHN WEBSTER
[1580–1625]

Glories, like glow-worms, afar off shine
bright,
But look'd too near have neither heat
nor light.[5]
> *Duchess of Malfi. Act IV, Sc. 2*

I know death hath ten thousand several doors
For men to take their exit.[6]
> *Ibid.*

---

[1] Three merry men be we. — PEELE: *Old
Wives' Tale* [1595]. WEBSTER (quoted):
Westward Hoe [1607]
[2] See Shakespeare, page 37.
[3] Deeds, not words. — BUTLER: *Hudibras,*
Part I, Canto I, L. 867
[4] See Tusser, page 19.
[5] Love is like a landscape which doth stand
   Smooth at a distance, rough at hand.
      ROBERT HEGGE [1599–1629]: *On Love*
'Tis distance lends enchantment to the view,
And robes the mountain in its azure hue.
   CAMPBELL: *Pleasures of Hope, Part I, L. 7*
[6] Death hath a thousand doors to let out
life. — PHILIP MASSINGER: *A Very Woman,*
Act V, Sc. 4
   Death hath so many doors to let out life.
— BEAUMONT AND FLETCHER: *The Custom of
the Country, Act II, Sc. 2*

Heaven-gates are not so highly arch'd
As princes' palaces; they that enter
    there
Must go upon their knees.
> *Duchess of Malfi. Act IV, Sc. 2*

Other sins only speak; murder shrieks
out.[1]
> *Ibid.*

'Tis just like a summer bird-cage in
a garden, — the birds that are without despair to get in, and the birds that
are within despair and are in a consumption for fear they shall never get
out.[2]
> *The White Devil. Act I, Sc. 2*

Condemn you me for that the duke did
    love me?
So may you blame some fair and crystal
    river
For that some melancholic, distracted
    man
Hath drown'd himself in 't.
> *Ibid. Act III, Sc. 2*

We cease to grieve, cease to be fortune's
    slaves,
Yes, cease to die, by dying.
> *Ibid. Sc. 6*

Vain the ambition of kings
Who seek by trophies and dead things
To leave a living name behind,
And weave but nets to catch the wind.
> *The Devil's Law Case. Song*

The chiefest action for a man of great
    spirit
Is never to be out of action.
The soul was never put into the body,
Which has so many rare and curious
    pieces
Of mathematical motion, to stand still.
> *Honorable Employment*

Is not old wine wholesomest, old
pippins toothsomest, old wood burns
brightest, old linen wash whitest? Old
soldiers, sweetheart, are surest, and old
lovers are soundest.[3]
> *Westward Hoe. Act II, Sc. 2*

The thousand doors that lead to death. —
BROWNE: *Religio Medici, Part I, Sect. XLIV*
[1] See Chaucer, page 6.
[2] See Davies, page 115.
[3] See Bacon, page 113.

I saw him now going the way of all
flesh.
> *Westward Hoe. Act II, Sc. 2*

SIR THOMAS OVERBURY
[1581–1613]

Give me, next good, an understanding
    wife,
By nature wise, not learnèd much by
    art;
Some knowledge on her part will, all
    her life,
More scope of conversation impart.
> *The Wife*

In part to blame is she,
Which hath without consent been only
    tried:
He comes too near that comes to be de-
    nied.[1]
> *Ibid.*

Books are a part of man's prerogative;
In formal ink they thoughts and voices
    hold,
That we to them our solitude may give,
And make time present travel that of
    old.
> *Ibid.*

BISHOP RICHARD CORBET
[1582–1635]

Farewell rewards and fairies,
    Good housewives now may say.
> *Farewell to the Fairies. Stanza 1*

Nor too much wealth nor wit come to
    thee,
So much of either may undo thee.
> *To His Son, Vincent Corbet*

I wish thee all thy mother's graces,
Thy father's fortunes and his places.
> *Ibid.*

PHILIP MASSINGER
[1583–1640]

To be nobly born
Is now a crime.
> *The Roman Actor. Act I, Sc. 1*
> [1629]

---

[1] In part she is to blame that has been tried:
    He comes too near that comes to be de-
    nied.
    LADY MARY WORTLEY MONTAGU [1689–
    1762]: *The Lady's Resolve*

I in mine own house am an emperor [1]
And will defend what's mine.
>   *The Roman Actor. Act I, Sc. 2*

Whose wealth
Arithmetic cannot number.
>   *Ibid. Sc. 3*

This many-headed monster.[2]
>   *Ibid. Act III, Sc. 2*

Grim death.[3]
>   *Ibid. Act IV, Sc. 2*

Good kings are mourned for after life;
but ill,
And such as governed only by their will
And not their reason, unlamented
fall, —
No good man's tear shed at their funeral.
>   *Ibid. Act V, Sc. 2*

Some undone widow sits upon mine
arm,
And takes away the use of it; [4] and my
sword,
Glued to my scabbard with wronged
orphans' tears,
Will not be drawn.
>   *A New Way to Pay Old Debts.*
>   *Act V, Sc. 1 [1632]*

Death hath a thousand doors to let out
life.[5]
>   *A Very Woman. Act V, Sc. 4*

THOMAS HEYWOOD
[? –1649]

The world's a theatre, the earth a stage
Which God and Nature do with actors
fill.[6]
>   *Apology for Actors [1612]*

---

[1] A man's house is his castle. — SIR ED-
WARD COKE: *Third Institute, P. 162*
[2] Many-headed multitude. — SIR PHILIP
SIDNEY: *Arcadia, Book II*
Many-headed monster. — SCOTT: *The Lady
of the Lake, Canto V, St. 30*
[3] Grim death, my son and foe. — MILTON:
Paradise Lost, Book II, L. 804
[4] See Middleton, page 116.
[5] See John Webster, page 127.
[6]   All the world's a stage,
    And all the men and women merely play-
    ers.
SHAKESPEARE: *As You Like It, Act II,
                    Sc. 7, L. 139*
The world's a stage on which all parts are

Pack clouds away, and welcome day,
With night we banish sorrow.
>   *Pack Clouds Away, Stanza 1*

I hold he loves me best that calls me
Tom.
>   *Hierarchie of the Blessed Angells*

Seven cities warred for Homer being
dead,
Who living had no roofe to shrowd his
head.[1]
>   *Ibid.*

Fear and amazement beat upon my
heart,
Even as a madman beats upon a drum.[2]
>   *A Woman Killed with Kindness.*
>   *Act IV, Sc. 1*

Her that ruled the rost in the kitchen.[3]
>   *History of Women. Page 286*
>   *[ed. 1624]*

FRANCIS BEAUMONT
[1584–1616]

What things have we seen
Done at the Mermaid! heard words that
have been
So nimble and so full of subtile flame
As if that every one from whence they
came
Had meant to put his whole wit in a
jest,
And resolved to live a fool the rest
Of his dull life.
>   *Letter to Ben Jonson*

Mortality, behold and fear!
What a change of flesh is here!
>   *On the Tombs in Westminster*
>   *Abbey*

Here are sands, ignoble things,
Dropt from the ruined sides of kings.
>   *Ibid.*

It is always good
When a man has two irons in the fire.
>   *The Faithful Friends. Act I, Sc. 2*

---

played. — MIDDLETON: *A Game at Chess,
Act V, Sc. 1*
[1] See Burton, page 123. See Browning, page
493.
[2] A madman beating on a drum. — OSCAR
WILDE: *Ballad of Reading Gaol*
[3] See Skelton, page 9.

JOHN SELDEN
[1584–1654]

Equity is a roguish thing. For Law we have a measure, know what to trust to; Equity is according to the conscience of him that is Chancellor, and as that is larger or narrower, so is Equity. 'Tis all one as if they should make the standard for the measure we call a "foot" a Chancellor's foot; what an uncertain measure would this be! One Chancellor has a long foot, another a short foot, a third an indifferent foot. 'Tis the same thing in the Chancellor's conscience.

Table Talk. Equity

Old friends are best. King James used to call for his old shoes; they were easiest for his feet.[1]

Ibid. Friends

Humility is a virtue all preach, none practise; and yet everybody is content to hear.

Ibid. Humility

'Tis not the drinking that is to be blamed, but the excess.

Ibid.

Commonly we say a judgment falls upon a man for something in him we cannot abide.

Ibid. Judgments

Ignorance of the law excuses no man; not that all men know the law, but because 'tis an excuse every man will plead, and no man can tell how to refute him.

Ibid. Law

No man is the wiser for his learning.

Ibid. Learning

Wit and wisdom are born with a man.

Ibid.

Few men make themselves masters of the things they write or speak.

Ibid.

Take a straw and throw it up into the air, — you may see by that which way the wind is.

Ibid. Libels

Philosophy is nothing but discretion.

Ibid. Philosophy

[1] See Bacon, page 113.

Marriage is a desperate thing.

Table Talk. Marriage

Thou little thinkest what a little foolery governs the world.[1]

Ibid. Pope

They that govern the most make the least noise.

Ibid. Power

Syllables govern the world.

Ibid.

Never king dropped out of the clouds.

Ibid.

Never tell your resolution beforehand.

Ibid. Wisdom

Wise men say nothing in dangerous times.

Ibid.

Pleasures are all alike, simply considered in themselves. He that takes pleasure to hear sermons enjoys himself as much as he that hears plays.

Ibid. Pleasure

A King is a thing men have made for their own sakes, for quietness' sake. Just as in a Family one man is appointed to buy the meat.

Ibid. Of a King

BEAUMONT AND FLETCHER [2]
FRANCIS BEAUMONT [1584–1616] AND JOHN FLETCHER [1579–1625]

All your better deeds
Shall be in water writ, but this in marble.[3]

Philaster. Act V, Sc. 3

Upon my burned body lie lightly, gentle earth.

The Maid's Tragedy. Act I, Sc. 2

[1] Behold, my son, with how little wisdom the world is governed. — AXEL OXENSTIERN [1583–1654]

[2] Of whose partnership John Aubrey [1626–1697] said: "There was a wonderfull consimility of phansey. They lived together not far from the Play-house, had one wench in the house between them, the same cloathes and cloake, &c."

[3] See Shakespeare, page 74.

Then, my good girls, be more than
    women wise;
At least be more than I was; and be
    sure
You credit any thing the light gives
    life to,
Before a man.
    The Maid's Tragedy. Act II, Sc. 2

A soul as white as heaven.
    Ibid. Act IV, Sc. 1

It shrew'd discretion, the best part of
    valour.[1]
    A King and No King. Act IV, Sc. 3

There is a method in man's wicked-
    ness, —
It grows up by degrees.[2]
    Ibid. Act V, Sc. 4

As cold as cucumbers.
    Cupid's Revenge. Act I, Sc. 1

Calamity is man's true touchstone.[3]
    Four Plays in One. The Triumph
    of Honour, Sc. 1

Kiss till the cow comes home.
    Scornful Lady. Act III, Sc. 1

It would talk, —
    Lord! how it talked!
    Ibid. Act V, Sc. 1

Beggars must be no choosers.
    Ibid. Sc. 3

No better than you should be.[4]
    The Coxcomb. Act IV, Sc. 3

From the crown of the head to the sole
    of the foot.[5]
    The Honest Man's Fortune.
    Act. II, Sc. 2

One foot in the grave.[6]
    The Little French Lawyer.
    Act I, Sc. 1

Go to grass.
    The Little French Lawyer.
    Act IV, Sc. 7

There is no jesting with edge tools.[1]
    Ibid.

Though I say it that should not say it.
    Wit at Several Weapons. Act II,
    Sc. 2

I name no parties.[2]
    Ibid. Sc. 3

Whistle, and she'll come to you.[3]
    Wit Without Money. Act IV, Sc. 4

Let the world slide.[4]
    Ibid. Act V, Sc. 2

The fit's upon me now!
Come quickly, gentle lady;
The fit's upon me now.
    Ibid. Sc. 4

He comes not in my books.[5]
    The Widow. Act I, Sc. 1

Death hath so many doors to let out
    life.[6]
    The Custom of the Country.
    Act II, Sc. 2

Of all the paths [that] lead to a
    woman's love
Pity's the straightest.[7]
    The Knight of Malta. Act I, Sc. 1

Nothing can cover his high fame but
    heaven;
No pyramids set off his memories,
But the eternal substance of his great-
    ness, —
To which I leave him.
    The False One. Act II, Sc. 1

---

[1] See Shakespeare, page 63.
[2] Nemo repente fuit turpissimus (No man ever became extremely wicked all at once). — JUVENAL: *II, 83*
Ainsi que la vertu, le crime a ses degrés (As virtue has its degrees, so has vice). — RACINE: *Phédre, Act IV, Sc. 2*
[3] Ignis aurum probat, miseria fortes viros (Fire is the test of gold; adversity, of strong men). — SENECA: *De Providentia, V, 9*
[4] She is no better than she should be. — HENRY FIELDING: *The Temple Beau, Act IV, Sc. 3*
[5] See Shakespeare, page 39.
[6] An old doting fool, with one foot already in the grave. — PLUTARCH: *On the Training of Children*

[1] It is no jesting with edge tools. — *The True Tragedy of Richard III* [1594]
[2] The use of "party" in the sense of "person" occurs in the *Book of Common Prayer*, More's *Utopia*, Shakespeare, Ben Jonson, Fuller, and other old English writers.
[3] Whistle, and I'll come to ye. — BURNS: *Whistle, etc.*
[4] See Shakespeare, page 52.
[5] See Shakespeare, page 38.
[6] See Webster, page 127.
[7] Pity's akin to love. — THOMAS SOUTHERNE [1660–1746]: *Oroonoko, Act II, Sc. 1* [1696]
Pity swells the tide of love. — YOUNG: *Night Thoughts, Night III, L. 107*

Thou wilt scarce be a man before thy
    mother.[1]
Love's Cure. Act II, Sc. 2

What's one man's poison, signor,
Is another's meat or drink.[2]
Ibid. Act III, Sc. 2

Primrose, first-born child of Ver,
Merry springtime's harbinger.
The Two Noble Kinsmen. Act I,
Sc. 1

O great corrector of enormous times,
Shaker of o'er-rank states, thou grand
    decider
Of dusty and old titles, that healest with
    blood
The earth when it is sick, and curest
    the world
O' the pleurisy of people!
Ibid. Act V, Sc. 1

JOHN FORD
[1586–1639]

Diamond cut diamond.
The Lover's Melancholy. Act I,
Sc. 1 [1629]

NATHANIEL FIELD
[1587–1633]

Needle in a bottle of hay.
A Woman's a Weathercock.

THOMAS HOBBES
[1588–1679]

Words are wise men's counters,—
they do but reckon by them; but they
are the money of fools.
Leviathan. Part I, Chap. IV

The privilege of absurdity; to which
no living creature is subject but man
only.
Ibid. Chap. V

Sudden glory is the passion which
maketh those grimaces called laughter.
Ibid. Chap. VI

The secret thoughts of a man run
over all things, holy, profane, clean, ob-

scene, grave, and light, without shame
or blame.
Leviathan. Part I, Chap. VIII

As the nature of foul weather lieth
not in a shower or two of rain but in
an inclination thereto of many days together, so the nature of war consisteth
not in actual fighting but in the known
disposition thereto during all the time
there is no assurance to the contrary.
All other time is peace.
Ibid. Chap. XIII

[In a state of nature] No arts, no
letters, no society, and, which is worst
of all, continual fear and danger of
violent death, and the life of man solitary, poor, nasty, brutish, and short.
Ibid.

The praise of ancient authors proceeds not from the reverence of the
dead, but from the competition and mutual envy of the living.
Ibid. Review and Conclusion

Such truth as opposeth no man's
profit nor pleasure is to all men welcome.
Ibid.

GEORGE WITHER
[1588–1667]

Shall I, wasting in despair,
Die because a woman's fair?
Or make pale my cheeks with care,
'Cause another's rosy are?
Be she fairer than the day,
Or the flowery meads in May,
  If she be not so to me,
  What care I how fair she be?
The Author's Resolution. Stanza 1

If she love me, this believe,
I will die, ere she shall grieve.
If she slight me when I woo,
I can scorn and let her go.
  For if she be not for me,
  What care I for whom she be?
Ibid. Stanza 5

Her waist exceeding small,
  The fives did fit her shoe:
But now alas she's left me,
  Falero, lero, loo!
I Loved a Lass

---

[1] But strive still to be a man before your
mother. — COWPER: *Connoisseur, Motto of
No. III*

[2] Quod ali cibus est aliis fiat acre venenum
(What is food to one may be fierce poison to
others). — LUCRETIUS: *IV, 637*

Hang sorrow! care will kill a cat,[1]
And therefore let's be merry.
                    Poem on Christmas
'Twas I that beat the bush,
The bird to others flew.
                    A Love Sonnet. Stanza 11
Though I am young, I scorn to flit
On the wings of borrowed wit.
                    The Shepherd's Hunting
And I oft have heard defended, —
Little said is soonest mended.
                    Ibid.

WILLIAM BROWNE
[1591–1643]

For her gait, if she be walking;
    Be she sitting, I desire her
For her state's sake; and admire her
    For her wit if she be talking.
                    Song
Whose life is a bubble, and in length a
    span.[2]
                    Britannia's Pastorals. Book I,
                    Song
There is no season such delight can
    bring,
As summer, autumn, winter, and the
    spring.
                    Variety

ROBERT HERRICK
[1591–1674]

What is a kiss? Why this, as some ap-
    prove:
The sure, sweet cement, glue, and lime
    of love.
                    A Kiss
Bid me to live, and I will live
    Thy Protestant to be,
Or bid me love, and I will give
    A loving heart to thee.
                    To Anthea. Stanza 1
Cherry ripe, ripe, ripe, I cry,
Full and fair ones, — come and buy!
If so be you ask me where
They do grow, I answer, there,
Where my Julia's lips do smile, —

---

¹ See Jonson, page 118.
² See Bacon, page 112.

There's the land, or cherry-isle.
                    Cherry Ripe ¹
Some asked me where the rubies grew,
    And nothing I did say;
But with my finger pointed to
    The lips of Julia.
                    The Rock of Rubies, and the
                    Quarrie of Pearls
Some asked how pearls did grow, and
    where?
    Then spoke I to my girl
To part her lips, and showed them
    there
    The quarelets of pearl.²
                    Ibid.
A sweet disorder in the dress
Kindles in clothes a wantonness.
                    Delight in Disorder
A winning wave, deserving note,
In the tempestuous petticoat;
A careless shoe-string, in whose tie
I see a wild civility, —
Do more bewitch me than when art
Is too precise in every part.
                    Ibid.
You say to me-wards your affection's
    strong;
Pray love me little, so you love me long.³
                    Love me Little, Love me Long
Gather ye rosebuds while ye may,
    Old Time is still a-flying,
And this same flower that smiles to-
    day
    To-morrow will be dying.⁴
                    To the Virgins to make much
                    of Time
Fair daffadills, we weep to see
    You haste away so soon.
                    To Daffadills

---

¹ "Cherry ripe" was a familiar street-cry of
the time. Compare THOMAS CAMPION:
    There cherries grow that none may buy
    Till cherry-ripe themselves do cry.
² Those cherries fairly do enclose
    Of orient pearl a double row.
                    THOMAS CAMPION: *Cherry-Ripe*
³ See Heywood, page 16, and Marlowe,
page 31.
⁴ Let us crown ourselves with rose-buds,
before they be withered. — *Wisdom of Solomon, II, 8*
    Gather the rose of love, whilest yet is time.
— SPENSER: *The Faerie Queene, Book II,*
Canto XII, St. 75

Thus woe succeeds a woe, as wave a wave.[1]
> *Sorrows Succeed*

Her pretty feet, like snails, did creep
  A little out, and then,[2]
As if they played at bo-peep,
  Did soon draw in again.
> *To Mistress Susanna Southwell*

Her eyes the glow-worm lend thee,
The shooting-stars attend thee;
  And the elves also,
  Whose little eyes glow
Like the sparks of fire, befriend thee.
> *The Night Piece to Julia*

Thus times do shift, — each thing his
  turn does hold;
New things succeed, as former things
  grow old.
> *Ceremonies for Candlemas Eve*

Out-did the meat, out-did the frolick
  wine.
> *Ode for Ben Jonson*

Attempt the end, and never stand to
  doubt;
Nothing's so hard but search will find
  it out.
> *Seek and Find*

But ne'er the rose without the thorn.
> *The Rose*

Here a little child I stand
Heaving up my either hand.
Cold as paddocks though they be,
Here I lift them up to Thee,
For a benison to fall
On our meat, and on us all.
> *A Child's Grace*

Smell of the lamp.
> *His Farewell to Sack*

Her legs were such Diana shows
When tuckt up she a-hunting goes
With Buskins shortned to descrie
The happy dawning of her thigh.
> *The Vision*

Get up, sweet Slug-a-bed, and see
The Dew bespangling Herbe and Tree.
> *Corinna's Going a-Maying*

[1] See Shakespeare, page 96.
[2] Her feet beneath her petticoat,
  Like little mice, stole in and out.
    SIR JOHN SUCKLING: *Ballad upon a
    Wedding.* St. 8

Wash, dresse, be brief in praying:
Few Beads are best, when once we goe
  a-Maying.
> *Corinna's Going a-Maying*

Whenas in silks my Julia goes,
Then, then (methinks) how sweetly
  flowes
That liquefaction of her clothes.
> *Upon Julia's Clothes*

HENRY KING, BISHOP OF CHICHESTER
[1592–1669]

And that tame Lover who unlocks his
  heart
Unto his mistress, teaching her an art
To plague himself, shows her the secret
  way
How she may tyrannize another day!
> *The Steed that Comes to
> Understand*

Thou art the book, —
The library whereon I look.
> *Exequy on the Death of a
> Beloved Wife*

Then we shall rise
And view ourselves with clearer eyes
In that calm region where no night
Can hide us from each other's sight.
> *Ibid.*

Stay for me there; I will not fail
To meet thee in that hollow vale.
> *Ibid.*

FRANCIS QUARLES
[1592–1644]

Death aims with fouler spite
At fairer marks.[1]
> *Divine Poems* [ed. *1669*]

Sweet Phosphor, bring the day!
Light will repay
The wrongs of night;
Sweet Phosphor, bring the day!
> *Emblems. Book I, Emblem 14*

Be wisely worldly, be not worldly wise.
> *Ibid. Book II, Emblem 2*

This house is to be let for life or years;
Her rent is sorrow, and her income
  tears.

[1] Death loves a shining mark, a signal blow.
— YOUNG: *Night Thoughts, Night V, L. 1011*

Cupid, 't has long stood void; her bills
    make known,
She must be dearly let, or let alone.
                    Emblems. Book II,
                    Emblem 10, Ep. 10

The slender debt to Nature's quickly
    paid,[1]
Discharged, perchance, with greater
    ease than made.
                    Ibid. Emblem 13

The next way home's the farthest way
    about.[2]
    Ibid. Book IV, Emblem 2, Ep. 2

It is the lot of man but once to die.
                    Ibid. Book V, Emblem 7

And what's a life? — a weary pilgrim-
    age,
Whose glory in one day doth fill the
    stage
With childhood, manhood, and decrepit
    age.
                    What is Life? Stanza 1

Let all thy joys be as the month of
    May,
And all thy days be as a marriage day:
Let sorrow, sickness, and a troubled
    mind
Be stranger to thee, let them never find
Thy heart at home.
                    To a Bride

THOMAS RAVENSCROFT
[1592–1635]

Nose, nose, nose, nose!
And who gave thee that jolly red nose?
Sinament and Ginger, Nutmegs and
    Cloves,
And that gave me my jolly red nose.
                    Deuteromelia. Song No. 7[3]
                    [1609]

---

[1] To die is a debt we must all of us discharge. — EURIPIDES: *Alcestis, L. 418*

[2] The longest way round is the shortest way
home. — BOHN: *Foreign Proverbs, Italian*

[3] Interpolated in BEAUMONT AND FLETCH-
ER's *The Knight of the Burning Pestle, Act I,
Sc. 3.* RAVENSCROFT's *Deuteromelia* was a sup-
plement to his *Pammelia,* which was the earliest collection of rounds, catches, and canons
printed in England.

GEORGE HERBERT
[1593–1632]

To write a verse or two is all the praise
    That I can raise.
                    Praise. Stanza 1

Sweet day, so cool, so calm, so bright,
The bridal of the earth and sky.[1]
                    Virtue. Stanza 1

Sweet spring, full of sweet days and
    • roses,
A box where sweets compacted lie.
                    Ibid. Stanza 3

Only a sweet and virtuous soul,
Like seasoned timber, never gives.
                    Ibid. Stanza 4

                    Like summer friends,[2]
Flies of estate and sunneshine.
                    The Answer

A servant with this clause
    Makes drudgery divine;
Who sweeps a room, as for Thy laws,
    Makes that and th' action fine.
                    The Elixir. Stanza 5

'You must sit down,' says Love, 'and
    taste my meat.'
So I did sit and eat.
        Love Bade Me Welcome. Stanza 3

A verse may find him who a sermon
    flies,[3]
And turn delight into a sacrifice.
                    The Church Porch. Stanza 1

Drink not the third glass, which thou
    canst not tame,
When once it is within thee.
                    Ibid. Stanza 5

Dare to be true: nothing can need a
    lie;
A fault which needs it most, grows two
    thereby.[4]
                    Ibid. Stanza 13

---

[1] Quoted in IZAAK WALTON's *The Compleat
Angler*

[2] Summer friends. — GRAY: *Hymn on Adversity*

[3] That many people read a song
    Who will not read a sermon.
    WINTHROP MACKWORTH PRAED [1802–
    1839]: *The Chant of the Brazenhead,
    St. 1*

[4] And he that does one fault at first,
    And lies to hide it, makes it two.
    ISAAC WATTS: *Song XV*

Look to thy mouth: diseases enter there.

The Church Porch. Stanza 22

By all means use sometimes to be alone.

Ibid. Stanza 25

By no means run in debt: take thine own measure.

Who cannot live on twenty pound a year,
Cannot on forty.

Ibid. Stanza 30

Wit's an unruly engine, wildly striking
Sometimes a friend, sometimes the engineer.

Ibid. Stanza 41

Be useful where thou livest.

Ibid. Stanza 55

Sum up at night, what thou hast done by day.

Ibid. Stanza 76

For thirty pence he did my death devise,[1]
Who at three hundred did the ointment prize.[2]

The Sacrifice. Stanza 5

Most things move th' under-jaw, the Crocodile not.[3]

Most things sleep lying, th' Elephant leans or stands.[4]

Providence. Stanza 35

Bibles laid open, millions of surprises.

Sinne. Stanza 2

Religion stands on tiptoe in our land,
Ready to pass to the American strand.

The Church Militant

If goodness lead him not, yet weariness
May toss him to my breast.

The Pulley. Stanza 4

---

[1] For thirty pence our Saviour was sold.
PERCY's *Reliques, King John and the Abbot of Canterbury, St. 21*
Still as of old men by themselves are priced —
For thirty pieces Judas sold himself, not Christ.
HESTER H. CHOLMONDELEY [19th century]
[2] Why was not this ointment sold for three hundred pence, and given to the poor? — *John, XII, 4*
[3] The crocodile does not move the lower jaw, but is the only animal that brings down its upper jaw to the under one. — HERODOTUS, *Customs of the Egyptians*
[4] Leans the huge elephant. — JAMES THOMSON: *The Seasons, Summer, L. 725*

The fineness which a hymn or psalm affords
Is, when the soul unto the lines accords.

A True Hymn. Stanza 2

Wouldst thou both eat thy cake and have it?[1]

The Size. Stanza 3

Do well and right, and let the world sink.[2]

The Country Parson, Chapter 29

Man proposeth, God disposeth.[3]

Jacula Prudentum [1640]

Pleasing ware is half sold.

Ibid.

Love, and a cough, cannot be hid.

Ibid.

A dwarf on a giant's shoulder, sees further of the two.[4]

Ibid.

Who is so deaf as he that will not hear?

Ibid.

Praise day at night,[5] and life at the end.

Ibid.

---

[1] Would yee both eat your cake and have your cake? — JOHN HEYWOOD: *Proverbes, Part II, Chap. 9.* ISAAC BICKERSTAFF: *Thomas and Sally*
[2] Ruat cœlum, fiat voluntas tua (Though the sky fall, let Thy will be done). — SIR T. BROWNE: *Religio Medici, Sect. XI*
Fiat justitia ruat cœlum (Let justice be done though the heavens should fall). — WILLIAM WATSON [1559–1603]: *Ten Quodlibeticall Questions Concerning Religion and State* [1601]. WILLIAM PRYNNE [1600–1669]: *Fresh Discovery of Prodigious New Wandering-Blazing Stars* [2d ed., London, 1646]. NATHANIEL WARD [1578–1652]: *Simple Cobbler of Agawam in America* [1647]
Fiat Justitia et ruat Mundus (Let justice be done and let the world perish). — [1552], *P. 25,* Camden Society [1840]. LUCY AIKIN [1781–1864]: *Court and Times of James I, Vol. II, P. 500* [1625].
January 31, 1642, the House of Lords used these words: *Regnet Justitia et ruat Cœlum.* — *Old Parliamentary History, Vol. X, P. 28*
[3] See Thomas à Kempis, page 8.
[4] See Burton, page 122.
[5] Thou shalt not praise the day till night is falling,
However fair its dawn and noon may be;
Ofttimes at eventide come storms appalling,
Setting the lightning and the thunder free.
ANONYMOUS

Deceive not thy physician, confessor, nor lawyer.

Jacula Prudentum [*1640*]

Who would do ill ne'er wants occasion.

Ibid.

A snow year, a rich year.

Ibid.

The fox, when he cannot reach the grapes, says they are not ripe.

Ibid.

Love your neighbour, yet pull not down your hedge.

Ibid.

The mill cannot grind with water that's past.[1]

Ibid.

Good words are worth much, and cost little.

Ibid.

Hell is full of good meanings and wishings.[2]

Ibid.

Whose house is of glass, must not throw stones at another.

Ibid.

By suppers more have been killed than Galen ever cured.

Ibid.

The lion is not so fierce as they paint him.[3]

Ibid.

Go not for every grief to the physician, nor for every quarrel to the lawyer, nor for every thirst to the pot.

Ibid.

The best mirror is an old friend.

Ibid.

Stay till the lame messenger come, if you will know the truth of the thing.

Ibid.

When you are an anvil, hold you still; when you are a hammer, strike your fill.

Jacula Prudentum [*1640*]

He that lies with the dogs, riseth with fleas.

Ibid.

He that is not handsome at twenty, nor strong at thirty, nor rich at forty, nor wise at fifty, will never be handsome, strong, rich, or wise.

Ibid.

The buyer needs a hundred eyes, the seller not one.

Ibid.

My house, my house, though thou art small, thou art to me the Escurial.

Ibid.

Trust not one night's ice.

Ibid.

The back door robs the house.

Ibid.

The wearer knows where the shoe wrings.[1]

Ibid.

For want of a nail the shoe is lost, for want of a shoe the horse is lost, for want of a horse the rider is lost.[2]

Ibid.

Pension never enriched a young man.

Ibid.

One flower makes no garland.

Ibid.

One enemy is too much.

Ibid.

The offender never pardons.[3]

Ibid.

Help thyself, and God will help thee.[4]

Ibid.

A feather in hand is better than a bird in the air.[5]

Ibid.

---

[1] The mill cannot grind
  With the water that is past.
SARAH DOUDNEY [1843–1926]: *The Lesson of the Water-Mill* [1864]
The mill will never grind again with water that is past. DANIEL CRAIG McCALLUM [1815–1878]:*The Water-Mill* [1870]
See BURTON E. STEVENSON: *Famous Single Poems* [1923].

[2] Sir, Hell is paved with good intentions. — SAMUEL JOHNSON [1775]: *Boswell's Life of Dr. Johnson, Everyman ed., Vol. I, P. 555*

[3] The lion is not so fierce as painted. — FULLER: *Expecting Preferment*

[1] See Plutarch, page 997, and Cervantes, page 1037.

[2] A little neglect may breed mischief: for want of a nail, etc. — BENJAMIN FRANKLIN: *Maxim prefixed to Poor Richard's Almanac* [1757]

[3] They ne'er pardon who have done the wrong. — DRYDEN: *The Conquest of Granada*

[4] God helps those who help themselves. — SIDNEY: *Discourses on Government, Sect. XXIII.* FRANKLIN: *Poor Richard's Almanac*

[5] See Heywood, page 15, Plutarch, page 1005, and Cervantes, page 1037.

Thursday come, and the week is gone.

Jacula Prudentum [*1640*]

Time is the rider that breaks youth.

Ibid.

You may bring a horse to the river, but he will drink when and what he pleaseth.

Ibid.

Before you make a friend, eat a bushel of salt with him.

Ibid.

Show me a liar, and I will show thee a thief.

Ibid.

No sooner is a temple built to God, but the Devil builds a chapel hard by.[1]

Ibid.

One father is more than a hundred school-masters.

Ibid.

Reason lies between the spur and the bridle.

Ibid.

One sword keeps another in the sheath.

Ibid.

God's mill grinds slow, but sure.[2]

Ibid.

Every one thinks his sack heaviest.

Ibid.

It is a poor sport that is not worth the candle.

Ibid.

Give not Saint Peter so much, to leave Saint Paul nothing.[3]

Ibid.

He that lends, gives.

Ibid.

Poverty is no sin.

Ibid.

Words are women, deeds are men.[4]

Ibid.

[1] See Burton, page 126.
[2] Though the mills of God grind slowly, yet they grind exceeding small. — F. VON LOGAU [1604–1655]: *Retribution* (translated by LONGFELLOW)
[3] See Heywood, page 14.
[4] Words are men's daughters, but God's sons are things. — SAMUEL MADDEN [1686–1765]: *Boulter's Monument* (supposed to have been inserted by Dr. Johnson in 1745)
See Johnson, page 232.

To a close shorn sheep, God gives wind by measure.[1]

Jacula Prudentum [*1640*]

None knows the weight of another's burthen.

Ibid.

One hour's sleep before midnight is worth three after.

Ibid.

He hath no leisure who useth it not.

Ibid.

Half the world knows not how the other half lives.

Ibid.

Life is half spent before we know what it is.

Ibid.

All are presumed good till they are found in a fault.

Ibid.

Every mile is two in winter.

Ibid.

Pains to get, care to keep, fear to lose.

Ibid.

The eye is bigger than the belly.

Ibid.

His bark is worse than his bite.

Ibid.

To build castles in Spain.

Jacula Prudentum [*second edition, 1651*]

Whatsoever was the father of a disease, an ill diet was the mother.

Ibid.

He that steals an egg will steal an ox.

Ibid.

Those that God loves do not live long.[2]

Ibid.

Of a pig's tail you can never make a good shaft.[3]

Ibid.

[1] Dieu mésure le froid à la brebis tondue (God proportions the wind to the shorn sheep). — HENRI ESTIENNE: *Prémices* [1594]
"God tempers the wind," said Maria, "to the shorn lamb." LAURENCE STERNE: *A Sentimental Journey, Maria*
[2] See Byron, page 354, and Wordsworth, page 302.
[3] You cannot make, my Lord, I fear,
A velvet purse of a sow's ear.
JOHN WOLCOT ("Peter Pindar") [1738–1819]: *Lord B. and His Notions*

The mouse that hath but one hole is quickly taken.[1]

Jacula Prudentum [*second edition, 1651*]

There is an hour wherein a man might be happy all his life could he find it.

Ibid.

Woe be to him who reads but one book.[2]

Ibid.

IZAAK WALTON
[1593-1683]

Of which, if thou be a severe, sour-complexioned man, then I here disallow thee to be a competent judge.

The Compleat Angler. Author's Preface

I have laid aside business, and gone a-fishing.

Ibid.

Angling may be said to be so like the mathematics that it can never be fully learnt.

Ibid.

As no man is born an artist, so no man is born an angler.

Ibid.

I shall stay him no longer than to wish him a rainy evening to read this following discourse; and that if he be an honest angler, the east wind may never blow when he goes a fishing.

Ibid.

As the Italians say, Good company in a journey makes the way to seem the shorter.

Ibid. Part I, Chap. I

I am, sir, a Brother of the Angle.

The Compleat Angler. Part I, Chap. I

Doubt not but angling will prove to be so pleasant that it will prove to be, like virtue, a reward to itself.[1]

Ibid.

Sir Henry Wotton was a most dear lover and a frequent practiser of the Art of Angling; of which he would say, " 'Twas an employment for his idle time, which was then not idly spent, a rest to his mind, a cheerer of his spirits, a diverter of sadness, a calmer of unquiet thoughts, a moderator of passions, a procurer of contentedness"; and "that it begat habits of peace and patience in those that professed and practised it."

Ibid.

You will find angling to be like the virtue of humility, which has a calmness of spirit and a world of other blessings attending upon it.[2]

Ibid.

I remember that a wise friend of mine did usually say, "That which is everybody's business is nobody's business."

Ibid. Chap. II

An honest Ale-house where we shall find a cleanly room, Lavender in the Windows, and twenty Ballads stuck about the wall.

Ibid.

---

[1] Virtue is her own reward. — DRYDEN: *Tyrannic Love, Act III, Sc. 1*

That virtue is her own reward, is but a cold principle. — SIR THOMAS BROWNE: *Religio Medici, Part I, Sect. XLVII.*

Virtue is to herself the best reward. — HENRY MORE [1614-1687]: *Cupid's Conflict*

Virtue is its own reward. — PRIOR: *Imitations of Horace, Book III, Ode 2.* GAY: *Epistle to Methuen.* JOHN HOME [1722-1808]: *Douglas, Act III, Sc. 1*

Virtue was sufficient of herself for happiness. — DIOGENES LAERTIUS: *Plato, XLII*

Ipsa quidem virtus sibimet pulcherrima merces (Virtue herself is her own fairest reward). — SILIUS ITALICUS [25?-99]: *Punica, Lib. XIII, L. 663*

[2] There is certainly something in angling . . . that tends to produce a gentleness of spirit, and a pure serenity of mind. — WASHINGTON IRVING: *The Sketch-Book, The Angler*

You can't make a silk purse out of a sow's ear. — JONATHAN SWIFT: *Polite Conversation, Dialogue II*

As certainly as you can make a velvet cap out of a sow's ear. — STERNE: *Tristram Shandy, Book IV*

The proverb says you can't make a silk purse out of a sow's ear. — DICKENS: *David Copperfield, Chap. 30*

[1] See Chaucer, page 7.

[2] When St. Thomas Aquinas was asked in what manner a man might best become learned, he answered, "By reading one book." The *homo unius libri* is indeed proverbially formidable to all conversational figurantes. — SOUTHEY: *The Doctor, P. 164*

Good company and good discourse are the very sinews of virtue.
> *The Compleat Angler.*
> *Part I, Chap. II*

The Chavender or Chub.
> *Ibid. Chap. III*

An excellent angler, and now with God.
> *Ibid. Chap. IV*

Old-fashioned poetry, but choicely good.
> *Ibid.*

A draught of Red Cow's milk.
> *Ibid.*

No man can lose what he never had.
> *Ibid. Chap. V*

We may say of angling as Dr. Boteler [1] said of strawberries: "Doubtless God could have made a better berry, but doubtless God never did"; and so, if I might be judge, God never did make a more calm, quiet, innocent recreation than angling.
> *Ibid.*

Thus use your frog: put your hook through his mouth and out at his gills, and then with a fine needle and silk sew the upper part of his leg with only one stitch to the arming wire of your hook, or tie the frog's leg above the upper joint to the armed wire; and in so doing use him as though you loved him.
> *Ibid. Chap. VIII*

This dish of meat is too good for any but anglers, or very honest men.
> *Ibid.*

Health is the second blessing that we mortals are capable of, — a blessing that money cannot buy.
> *The Compleat Angler.*
> *Part I, Chap. XXI*

And upon all that are lovers of virtue, and dare trust in his Providence, and be quiet and go a-angling.
> *Ibid.*

I in these flowery meads would be;
These crystal springs should solace me;
To whose harmonious bubbling noise,
I with my angle would rejoice.
> *The Angler's Wish. Stanza 1*

But God, who is able to prevail, wrestled with him; marked him for his own.[1]
> *Life of Donne*

The great secretary of Nature, — Sir Francis Bacon.[2]
> *Life of Herbert*

Oh, the gallant fisher's life!
It is the best of any;
'Tis full of pleasure, void of strife,
And 'tis beloved by many.
> *The Angler (John Chalkhill)* [3]

THOMAS CAREW
[1595-1639]

Ask me no more where Jove bestows,
When June is past, the fading rose.
> *To Celia. Stanza 1*

Ask me no more if East or West
The phoenix builds her spicy nest.
> *Ibid. Stanza 5*

He that loves a rosy cheek,
Or a coral lip admires,
Or from star-like eyes doth seek
Fuel to maintain in his fires; —

---

[1] William Butler [1535-1618], styled by Dr. Thomas Fuller in his *Worthies of England, Suffolk*, the "Aesculapius of our age." He attended Prince Henry [1612]. This praise of the strawberry first appeared in the second edition of *The Angler*, [1655]. Roger Williams, in his *Key into the Language of America*, [1643] *P. 98*, says: "One of the chiefest doctors of England was wont to say, that God could have made, but God never did make, a better berry."

I know one person who is simular enough to think Cambridge the very best spot on the habitable globe. "Doubtless God *could* have made a better, but doubtless he never did." — James Russell Lowell: *On a Certain Condescension in Foreigners*

[1] Melancholy marked him for her own. — Gray: *The Epitaph*

[2] Plato, Aristotle, and Socrates are secretaries of Nature. — James Howell [1594-1666]: *Letters, Book II, Letter XI*

[3] In 1683, the year in which he died, Walton prefixed a preface to a work edited by him: "Thealma and Clearchus, a Pastoral History, in smooth and easy verse; written long since by John Chalkhill Esq., an acquaintant and friend of Edmund Spenser."

Chalkhill, — a name unappropriated, a verbal phantom, a shadow of a shade. Chalkhill is no other than our old piscatory friend incognito. — Thomas Zouch [1737-1815]: *Life of Izaak Walton*

As old Time makes these decay,
So his flames must waste away.
   Disdain Returned. Stanza 1
The firstling of the infant year.
     The Primrose
Then fly betimes, for only they
Conquer Love that run away.
     Conquest by Flight
An untimely grave.[1]
   On the Duke of Buckingham
The magic of a face.
   Epitaph on the Lady S——

JAMES SHIRLEY
[1596–1666]

The glories of our blood and state
 Are shadows, not substantial things;
There is no armour against fate;
 Death lays his icy hand on kings.
  Contention of Ajax and Ulysses.
    Scene 3 [1659]
The garlands wither on your brow;
Then boast no more your mighty deeds.
       Ibid.
Only the actions of the just
Smell sweet and blossom in their dust.[2]
       Ibid.
Death calls ye to the crowd of common
 men.
    Cupid and Death

OLIVER CROMWELL
[1599–1658]

The State, in choosing men to serve
it, takes no notice of their opinions. If
they be willing faithfully to serve it,
that satisfies.
  Before the Battle of Marston
    Moor [July 2, 1644]
A few honest men are better than
numbers. If you choose godly, honest
men to be captains of horse, honest men
will follow them.
  Reorganization of the Army
      [1645]

----

[1] An untimely grave. — Nahum Tate
[1652–1715] and Nicholas Brady [1659–
1726]: *Metrical Version of Psalm VII*
[2] The sweet remembrance of the just
 Shall flourish when he sleeps in dust.
 Tate and Brady: *Psalm CXXXII, 6*

I would have been glad to have lived
under my woodside, and to have kept
a flock of sheep, rather than to have
undertaken this government.
    To Parliament [1658]
I would be willing to live to be further serviceable to God and His people,
but my work is done! Yet God will be
with His people!
   [September 1, 1658, two days
    before his death]

SAMUEL BUTLER
[1600–1680]

And pulpit, drum ecclesiastick,[1]
Was beat with fist instead of a stick.
  Hudibras. Part I, Canto I, Line 11
We grant, although he had much wit,
He was very shy of using it.
     Ibid. Line 45
Beside, 'tis known he could speak
 Greek
As naturally as pigs squeak;[2]
That Latin was no more difficile
Than to a blackbird 'tis to whistle.
     Ibid. Line 51
He could distinguish and divide
A hair 'twixt south and southwest side.
     Ibid. Line 67
For rhetoric, he could not ope
His mouth, but out there flew a trope.
     Ibid. Line 81
For all a rhetorician's rules
Teach nothing but to name his tools.
     Ibid. Line 89
A Babylonish dialect
Which learned pedants much affect.
     Ibid. Line 93
For he by geometric scale
Could take the size of pots of ale.
     Ibid. Line 121
And wisely tell what hour o' the day
The clock does strike, by algebra.
     Ibid. Line 125

----

[1] This is the first we hear of the "drum ecclesiastic" beating up for recruits in worldly
warfare in our country. — Washington Irving: *Knickerbocker's History of New York,
Book V, Chap. 7*
[2] He Greek and Latin speaks with greater ease
 Than hogs eat acorns, and tame pigeons peas.
 Lionel Cranfield, Earl of Middlesex
  [1575–1645]: *Panegyric on Tom
       Coriate*

Whatever sceptic could inquire for,
For every why he had a wherefore.[1]
    Hudibras. Part I, Canto I, Line 131
Where entity and quiddity,
The ghosts of defunct bodies, fly.
                    Ibid. Line 145
He knew what's what,[2] and that's as
    high
As metaphysic wit can fly.
                    Ibid. Line 149
Such as take lodgings in a head
That's to be let unfurnished.[3]
                    Ibid. Line 161
'Twas Presbyterian true blue.
                    Ibid. Line 191
And prove their doctrine orthodox,
By apostolic blows and knocks.
                    Ibid. Line 199
Compound for sins they are inclined to,
By damning those they have no mind
    to.
                    Ibid. Line 215
The trenchant blade, Toledo trusty,
For want of fighting was grown rusty,
And ate into itself, for lack
Of somebody to hew and hack.
                    Ibid. Line 359
For rhyme the rudder is of verses,
With which, like ships, they steer their
    courses.
                    Ibid. Line 463
He ne'er consider'd it, as loth
To look a gift-horse in the mouth.[4]
                    Ibid. Line 489
And force them, though it was in spite
Of Nature and their stars, to write.
                    Ibid. Line 647
Quoth Hudibras, "I smell a rat![5]
Ralpho, thou dost prevaricate."
                    Ibid. Line 821
Or shear swine, all cry and no wool.[6]
                    Ibid. Line 852
And bid the devil take the hin'most.[7]
                    Ibid. Canto II, Line 633

---

[1] See Shakespeare, pages 37, 67.
[2] See Skelton, page 10.
[3] See Bacon, page 113.
[4] See Heywood, page 13.
[5] See Middleton, page 116.
[6] See Fortescue, page 9.
[7] Bid the Devil take the slowest. — PRIOR:
On the Taking of Namur
Deil tak the hindmost. — BURNS: *To a
Haggis*

I'll make the fur
Fly 'bout the ears of the old cur.
    *Hudibras. Part I, Canto III,
                    Line 277*
These reasons made his mouth to water.
                    Ibid. Line 379
I am not now in fortune's power:
He that is down can fall no lower.[1]
                    Ibid. Line 871
Cheer'd up himself with ends of verse
And sayings of philosophers.
                    Ibid. Line 1011
But those that write in rhyme still
    make
The one verse for the other's sake;
For one for sense, and one for rhyme,
I think's sufficient at one time.
    Ibid. Part II, Canto I, Line 23
Some have been beaten till they know
What wood a cudgel's of by th' blow;
Some kick'd until they can feel whether
A shoe be Spanish or neat's leather.
                    Ibid. Line 221
Quoth she, I've heard old cunning
    stagers
Say fools for arguments use wagers.
                    Ibid. Line 297
For what is worth in anything
But so much money as 'twill bring?
                    Ibid. Line 465
Love is a boy by poets styl'd;
Then spare the rod and spoil the child.[2]
                    Ibid. Line 843
The sun had long since in the lap
Of Thetis taken out his nap,
And, like a lobster boil'd the morn
From black to red began to turn.
                    Ibid. Canto II, Line 29
For truth is precious and divine, —
Too rich a pearl for carnal swine.
                    Ibid. Line 257
He that imposes an oath makes it,
Not he that for convenience takes it;
Then how can any man be said
To break an oath he never made?
                    Ibid. Line 377

The Devil may take the hindmost. —
SOUTHEY: *The March to Moscow*
[1] He that is down needs fear no fall. —
BUNYAN: *Pilgrim's Progress, Part II*
[2] See Skelton, page 9.

As the ancients
Say wisely, have a care o' th' main
    chance,[1]
And look before you ere you leap;[2]
For as you sow, ye are like to reap.[3]
Hudibras. Part II, Canto II,
Line 501

Doubtless the pleasure is as great
Of being cheated as to cheat.[4]
Ibid. Canto III, Line 1

He made an instrument to know
If the moon shine at full or no.
Ibid. Line 261

To swallow gudgeons ere they're
    catch'd,
And count their chickens ere they're
    hatch'd.[5]
Ibid. Line 923

But Hudibras gave him a twitch
As quick as lightning in the breech,
Just in the place where honour's lodg'd,
As wise philosophers have judg'd;
Because a kick in that part more
Hurts honour than deep wounds before.
Ibid. Line 1065

As men of inward light are wont
To turn their optics in upon 't.
Ibid. Part III, Canto I, Line 481

What makes all doctrines plain and
    clear?
About two hundred pounds a year.
And that which was prov'd true before
Prove false again? Two hundred more.
Ibid. Line 1277

Nick Machiavel had ne'er a trick,
Though he gave his name to our Old
    Nick.[6]
Ibid. Line 1313

With crosses, relics, crucifixes,

Beads, pictures, rosaries, and pixes, —
The tools of working our salvation
By mere mechanic operation.
Hudibras. Part III, Canto I,
Line 1495

True as the dial to the sun,[1]
Although it be not shin'd upon.
Ibid. Canto II, Line 175

For those that fly may fight again,
Which he can never do that's slain.[2]
Ibid. Canto III, Line 243

---

[1] See Lyly, page 23.
See Shakespeare, page 68.
[2] See Heywood, page 11.
[3] Whatsoever a man soweth, that shall he
also reap. — *Galatians, VI, 7*
[4] This couplet is enlarged on by SWIFT in
his *Tale of a Tub,* where he says that the
happiness of life consists in being well deceived.
[5] Many count their chickens before they
are hatched. — CERVANTES: *Don Quixote, Part
II, Chap. 55*
Reckon not on your chickens before they are
hatched. — JEFFERYS TAYLOR: [1792–1853]:
The Milkmaid
[6] See Macaulay, page 397.

---

[1] True as the needle to the pole,
    Or as the dial to the sun.
        BARTON BOOTH [1681–1733]: *Song*
[2] Sed omissis quidem divinis exhortationibus
illum magis Græcum versiculum secularis
sententiæ sibi adhibent, "Qui fugiebat, rursus
prœliabitur": ut et rursus forsitan fugiat (But
overlooking the divine exhortations, they act
rather upon that Greek verse of worldly
significance, "He who flees will fight again,"
and that perhaps to betake himself again to
flight). — TERTULLIAN: *De Fuga in Persecutione, C. 10*
A corresponding Greek passage is ascribed
to Menander. See *Fragments* (appended to
Aristophanes in Didot's *Bibliothèque des au-
teurs Grecs, P. 91*).
    That same man that runnith awaie
    Maie again fight an other daie.
        ERASMUS: *Apothegms* [1542], trans-
            lated by Udall
    Celuy qui fuit de bonne heure
    Peut combattre derechef
(He who flies at the right time can fight
again).
                Satyre Menippée [1594]
    Qui fuit peut revenir aussi;
    Qui meurt, il n'en est pas ainsi
(He who flies can also return; but it is not so
    with him who dies).
        PAUL SCARRON [1610–1660]
    He that fights and runs away
    May turn and fight another day;
    But he that is in battle slain
    Will never rise to fight again.
        JAMES RAY: *History of the Rebellion*
            [1752], *P. 48*
    For he who fights and runs away
    May live to fight another day;
    But he who is in battle slain
    Can never rise and fight again.
        GOLDSMITH: *The Art of Poetry on a*
            New Plan [1761], *Vol. II, P. 147*
    But since the man that runs away
    Lives to die another day,
    And cowards' funerals, when they come,
    Are not wept so well at home,
    Therefore, though the best is bad,
    Stand and do the best, my lad.
        A. E. HOUSMAN: *The Day of Battle*

He that complies against his will
Is of his own opinion still.
Hudibras. Part III, Canto III,
Line 547

And poets by their sufferings grow,[1]
As if there were no more to do,
To make a poet excellent,
But only want and discontent.
Fragments

WILLIAM STRODE
[1602–1645]

There's naught in this life sweet,
If man were wise to see 't,
But only melancholy;
O sweetest Melancholy! [2]
A Song in Praise of Melancholy

Fountain heads and pathless groves,
Places which pale passion loves.
Ibid.

SIR KENELM DIGBY
[1603–1665]

The hot water is to remain upon it
[the tea] no longer than whiles you can
say the Miserere Psalm very leisurely.
The Closet Opened. Tea with Eggs

Before the Deer be killed, he ought
to be hunted and chafed as much as
may be.
Ibid. To Bake Venison

All Matter is indifferent to Form.
Of the Vegetation of Plants

If she [the soul after death] be built
up again to a whole Man, out of the
general Magazine of Matter.
Ibid.

---

1   Most wretched men
Are cradled into poetry by wrong;
They learn in suffering what they teach in
song.
SHELLEY: *Julian and Maddalo*
2 JOHN FLETCHER introduced this song in his
play, *The Nice Valour, Act III, Sc. 3,* and it
has also been attributed to him.
Naught so sweet as melancholy. — BURTON:
Anatomy of Melancholy, Author's Abstract

SIR THOMAS BROWNE
[1605–1682]

Too rashly charged the troops of
error, and remain as trophies unto the
enemies of truth.
Religio Medici. Part I,
Sect. VI [1642]

I love to lose myself in a mystery, to
pursue my Reason to an *O altitudo!*
Ibid. Sect. IX

Rich with the spoils of Nature.[1]
Ibid. Sect. XIII

Nature is the art of God.[2]
Ibid. Sect. XVI

The thousand doors that lead to
death.[3]
Ibid. Sect. XLIV

The heart of man is the place the
Devil dwells in: I feel sometimes a hell
within myself.[4]
Ibid. Sect. LI

There is no road or ready way to
virtue.
Ibid. Sect. LV

It is the common wonder of all men,
how among so many millions of faces
there should be none alike.[5]
Ibid. Part II, Sect. II

That worldly principle, *Charity be-*
gins at home.
Ibid. Sect. V

---

[1] Rich with the spoils of time. — GRAY:
Elegy, St. 13
[2] The course of Nature is the art of God. —
YOUNG: *Night Thoughts, Night IX, L. 1267*
[3] See John Webster, page 127.
[4] The mind is its own place, and in itself
    Can make a heaven of hell, a hell of
    heaven.
    MILTON: *Paradise Lost, Book I, L. 253*
[5] The human features and countenance, although composed of but some ten parts or
little more, are so fashioned that among so
many thousands of men there are no two
in existence who cannot be distinguished
from one another. — PLINY: *Natural History,*
Book VII, Chap. I
Of a thousand shavers, two do not shave so
much alike as not to be distinguished. —
JOHNSON [1777]: *Boswell's Life, Vol. II,*
P. 120, Everyman ed.
There never were in the world two opinions
alike, no more than two hairs or two grains;
the most universal quality is diversity. —
MONTAIGNE: *Of the Resemblance of Children
to their Fathers, Book I, Chap. XXXVII*

There is music even in the beauty, and the silent note which Cupid strikes, far sweeter than the sound of an instrument; for there is music wherever there is harmony, order, or proportion; and thus far we may maintain the music of the spheres.[1]

> *Religio Medici. Part II,*
> *Sect. IX*

Ruat cœlum, fiat voluntas tua.[2]

> *Ibid. Sect. XI*

Sleep is a death; oh, make me try
By sleeping, what it is to die,
And as gently lay my head
On my grave, as now my bed!

> *Ibid. Sect. XII*

This is the dormitive I take to bedward.

> *Ibid.*

Times before you, when even living men were antiquities, — when the living might exceed the dead, and to depart this world could not be properly said to go unto the greater number.[3]

> *Dedication to Urn-Burial*

I look upon you as a gem of the old rock.[4]

> *Ibid.*

Quietly rested under the drums and tramplings of three conquests.

> *Urn-Burial. Chapter 5*

What song the Sirens sang, or what name Achilles assumed when he hid himself among women.

> *Ibid.*

The iniquity of oblivion blindly scattereth her poppy.

> *Ibid.*

Herostratus lives that burnt the temple of Diana; he is almost lost that built it.[5]

> *Ibid.*

[1] See Shakespeare, page 55.
Oh, could you view the melody
  Of every grace
  And music of her face.
  LOVELACE: *Orpheus to Beasts*
[2] See Herbert, page 136.
[3] 'Tis long since Death had the majority. —
BLAIR: *The Grave, Part II, L. 449*
[4] Adamas de rupe præstantissimus (A most excellent diamond from the rock).
A chip of the old block. — PRIOR: *Life of Burke*
[5] The aspiring youth that fired the Ephesian dome

Oblivion is not to be hired: the greater part must be content to be as though they had not been.

> *Urn-Burial. Chapter 5*

Man is a noble animal, splendid in ashes and pompous in the grave.

> *Ibid.*

When we desire to confine our words, we commonly say they are spoken under the rose.[1]

> *Vulgar Errors*

An old and gray-headed error.

> *Ibid.*

EDMUND WALLER
[1605–1687]

The yielding marble of her snowy breast.

> *On a Lady Passing through a*
> *Crowd of People*

That eagle's fate and mine are one,
  Which on the shaft that made him die
Espied a feather of his own,
  Wherewith he wont to soar so high.[2]

> *To a Lady Singing a Song*
> *of his Composing*

To man, that was in th' evening made,
  Stars gave the first delight;
Admiring, in the gloomy shade,
  Those little drops of light.

> *An Apology for Having Loved*
> *Before*

Outlives in fame the pious fool that raised it.
  CIBBER: *Richard III, Act III, Sc. 1*
[1] "Sub rosa."
[2] So in the Libyan fable it is told
That once an eagle, stricken with a dart,
Said, when he saw the fashion of the shaft,
"With our own feathers, not by others' hands,
Are we now smitten."
  ÆSCHYLUS: *Fragm. 123* (Plumptre's translation)
So the struck eagle, stretch'd upon the plain,
No more through rolling clouds to soar again,
View'd his own feather on the fatal dart,
And wing'd the shaft that quiver'd in his heart.
  BYRON: *English Bards and Scotch Reviewers, L. 826*
Like a young eagle, who has lent his plume
To fledge the shaft by which he meets his doom,
See their own feathers pluck'd to wing the dart
Which rank corruption destines for their heart.
  THOMAS MOORE: *Corruption*

A narrow compass! and yet there
Dwelt all that's good, and all that's
    fair;
Give me but what this riband bound,
Take all the rest the sun goes round!
    On a Girdle. Stanza 3

    For all we know
Of what the blessed do above
Is, that they sing, and that they love.
        While I Listen to thy Voice

Poets that lasting marble seek
Must come in Latin or in Greek.
        Of English Verse

Under the tropic is our language spoke,
And part of Flanders hath receiv'd our
    yoke.
    *Upon the Death of the Lord
        Protector*

Go, lovely rose!
Tell her that wastes her time and me
    That now she knows,
When I resemble her to thee,
How sweet and fair she seems to be.
        Go, Lovely Rose. Stanza 1

How small a part of time they share
That are so wondrous sweet and fair!
        Ibid. Stanza 4

Illustrious acts high raptures do infuse,
And every conqueror creates a muse.
        Panegyric on Cromwell

In such green palaces the first kings
    reign'd,
Slept in their shades, and angels enter-
    tain'd;
With such old counsellors they did ad-
    vise,
And by frequenting sacred groves grew
    wise.
        On St. James's Park

And keeps the palace of the soul.[1]
        Of Tea

Poets lose half the praise they should
    have got,
Could it be known what they discreetly
    blot.
    *Upon Roscommon's Translation
        of Horace, De Arte Poetica*

The soul's dark cottage, batter'd and
    decay'd,

[1] The dome of thought, the palace of the
soul. — BYRON: *Childe Harold, Canto II, St. 6*

Lets in new light through chinks that
    Time has made.[1]
Stronger by weakness, wiser men be-
    come
As they draw near to their eternal
    home:
Leaving the old, both worlds at once
    they view
That stand upon the threshold of the
    new.
        On the Divine Poems

SIR WILLIAM DAVENANT
[1606–1668]

The lark now leaves his wat'ry nest
And, climbing, shakes his dewy wings.
        Who Look for Day. Stanza 1

For angling-rod he took a sturdy oake; [2]
For line, a cable that in storm ne'er
    broke;
His hooke was such as heads the end
    of pole
To pluck down house ere fire consumes
    it whole;
The hook was baited with a dragon's
    tale,—
And then on rock he stood to bob for
    whale.
        *Britannia Triumphans. Page 15
            [1637]*

The assembled souls of all that men
    held wise.
        *Gondibert. Book II, Canto V,
            Stanza 37 [1651]*

[1] See Daniel, page 30.
    To vanish in the chinks that Time has
made. — ROGERS: *Pæstum*
[2] For angling rod he took a sturdy oak;
    For line, a cable that in storm ne'er
        broke; . . .
    His hook was baited with a dragon's tail, —
    And then on rock he stood to bob for whale.
        From *The Mock Romance,* a rhapsody
        attached to *The Loves of Hero and
        Leander,* published in London in the
        years 1653 and 1677. CHAMBERS's
        Book of Days, Vol. I, P. 173. DANIEL:
        Rural Sports, Supplement, P. 57
His angle-rod made of a sturdy oak;
His line, a cable which in storms ne'er broke;
His hook he baited with a dragon's tail, —
And sat upon a rock, and bobb'd for whale.
        WILLIAM KING [1663–1712]: *Upon a
        Giant's Angling* (In CHALMERS's *British
        Poets* ascribed to King)

Since knowledge is but sorrow's spy,
It is not safe to know.[1]

> *The Just Italian. Act V, Sc. 1*

How much pleasure they lose (and even the pleasures of heroic poesy are not unprofitable) who take away the liberty of a poet, and fetter his feet in the shackles of a historian.

> *Prefatory Letter to Thomas Hobbes (Quoted in Biographia Literaria by S. T. Coleridge, Chapter 22)*

I shall ask leave to desist, when I am interrupted by so great an experiment as dying.

> *His apology, in illness, for not having finished Gondibert*

THOMAS FULLER
[1608–1661]

Drawing near her death, she sent most pious thoughts as harbingers to heaven; and her soul saw a glimpse of happiness through the chinks of her sickness-broken body.

> *Life of Monica*

He was one of a lean body and visage, as if his eager soul, biting for anger at the clog of his body, desired to fret a passage through it.[2]

> *Life of the Duke of Alva*

She commandeth her husband, in any equal matter, by constant obeying him.

> *Holy and Profane State. The Good Wife*

He knows little who will tell his wife all he knows.

> *Ibid. The Good Husband*

One that will not plead that cause wherein his tongue must be confuted by his conscience.

> *Ibid. The Good Advocate*

---

[1] From ignorance our comfort flows. —
PRIOR: *To the Hon. Charles Montague*
Where ignorance is bliss,
'Tis folly to be wise.
GRAY: *Eton College, St. 10*
[2] A fiery soul, which, working out its way,
Fretted the pygmy-body to decay,
And o'er-inform'd the tenement of clay.
DRYDEN: *Absalom and Achitophel, Part I, L. 156*

Who durst be so bold with a few crooked boards nailed together, a stick standing upright, and a rag tied to it, to adventure into the ocean?

> *Holy and Profane State. The Good Sea-Captain*

To smell to a turf of fresh earth is wholesome for the body; no less are thoughts of mortality cordial to the soul.

> *Ibid. The Virtuous Lady*

The lion is not so fierce as painted.[1]

> *Ibid. Of Preferment*

Their heads sometimes so little that there is no room for wit; sometimes so long that there is no wit for so much room.

> *Ibid. Of Natural Fools*

The Pyramids themselves, doting with age, have forgotten the names of their founders.

> *Ibid. Of Tombs*

Learning hath gained most by those books by which the printers have lost.

> *Ibid. Of Books*

Deceive not thy self by overexpecting happiness in the married estate. Remember the nightingales which sing only some months in the spring, but commonly are silent when they have hatched their eggs.

> *Ibid. Of Marriage*

They that marry ancient people, merely in expectation to bury them, hang themselves in hope that one will come and cut the halter.

> *Ibid.*

Fame sometimes hath created something of nothing.

> *Ibid. Fame*

Anger is one of the sinews of the soul; he that wants it hath a maimed mind.

> *Ibid. Of Anger*

Light, God's eldest daughter, is a principal beauty in a building.

> *Ibid. Of Building*

In Building, rather believe any man than an Artificer for matter of charges. Should they tell thee all the cost at the first, it would blast a young Builder in the budding.

> *Ibid.*

---

[1] See Herbert, page 137.

Often the cockloft is empty in those whom Nature hath built many stories high.[1]

Andronicus. Sect. VI, Par. 18, 1

JOHN MILTON
[1608–1674]

Of Man's first disobedience, and the fruit
Of that forbidden tree whose mortal taste
Brought death into the world, and all our woe.

Paradise Lost. Book I, Line 1

Things unattempted yet in prose or rhyme.

Ibid. Line 16

What in me is dark
Illumine, what is low raise and support;
That to the height of this great argument
I may assert eternal Providence,
And justify the ways of God to men.[2]

Ibid. Line 22

As far as angels' ken.

Ibid. Line 59

Where peace
And rest can never dwell, hope never comes
That comes to all.

Ibid. Line 65

What though the field be lost?
All is not lost — th' unconquerable will,
And study of revenge, immortal hate,
And courage never to submit or yield.

Ibid. Line 105

To be weak is miserable,
Doing or suffering.

Ibid. Line 157

And out of good still to find means of evil.

Ibid. Line 165

A mind not to be chang'd by place or time.
The mind is its own place, and in itself

Can make a heaven of hell, a hell of heaven.[1]

Paradise Lost. Book I, Line 253

Better to reign in hell than serve in heaven.

Ibid. Line 263

Heard so oft
In worst extremes, and on the perilous edge
Of battle.

Ibid. Line 275

His spear, to equal which the tallest pine
Hewn on Norwegian hills to be the mast
Of some great ammiral, were but a wand
He walk'd with, to support uneasy steps
Over the burning marle.

Ibid. Line 292

Thick as autumnal leaves that strow the brooks
In Vallombrosa.

Ibid. Line 302

Awake, arise, or be forever fallen!

Ibid. Line 330

Spirits, when they please,
Can either sex assume, or both.

Ibid. Line 423

When night
Darkens the streets, then wander forth the sons
Of Belial, flown with insolence and wine.

Ibid. Line 500

Th' imperial ensign, which, full high advanc'd,
Shone like a meteor, streaming to the wind.[2]

Ibid. Line 536

Sonorous metal blowing martial sounds:
At which the universal host up sent
A shout that tore hell's concave, and beyond
Frighted the reign of Chaos and old Night.

Ibid. Line 540

---

[1] See Bacon, page 113.
[2] But vindicate the ways of God to man. —
POPE: *Essay on Man, Epistle I, L. 16*

[1] Which way I fly is Hell; myself am Hell.
— *Book IV, L. 75*
[2] Stream'd like a meteor to the troubled air. — GRAY: *The Bard, I, 2, L. 6*

Anon they move
In perfect phalanx, to the Dorian mood
Of flutes and soft recorders.
Paradise Lost. Book I, Line 549
     His form had yet not lost
All her original brightness, nor appear'd
Less than archangel ruin'd, and th' excess
Of glory obscur'd.
Ibid. Line 591
In dim eclipse, disastrous twilight sheds
On half the nations, and with fear of change
Perplexes monarchs.
Ibid. Line 597
Thrice he assay'd, and thrice, in spite of scorn,
Tears, such as angels weep, burst forth.
Ibid. Line 619
     Who overcomes
By force hath overcome but half his foe.
Ibid. Line 648
Mammon, the least erected spirit that fell
From heaven; for ev'n in heaven his looks and thoughts
Were always downward bent, admiring more
The riches of heaven's pavement, trodden gold,
Than aught divine or holy else enjoy'd
In vision beatific.
Ibid. Line 679
     Let none admire
That riches grow in hell: that soil may best
Deserve the precious bane.
Ibid. Line 690
     From morn
To noon he fell, from noon to dewy eve,
A summer's day; and with the setting sun
Dropp'd from the Zenith, like a falling star.
Ibid. Line 742
     Fairy elves,
Whose midnight revels, by a forest side
Or fountain, some belated peasant sees,
Or dreams he sees, while overhead the moon

Sits arbitress.
Paradise Lost. Book I, Line 781
High on a throne of royal state, which far
Outshone the wealth of Ormus and of Ind,
Or where the gorgeous East with richest hand
Showers on her kings barbaric pearl and gold,
Satan exalted sat, by merit rais'd
To that bad eminence.
Ibid. Book II, Line 1
The strongest and the fiercest spirit
That fought in heaven, now fiercer by despair.
Ibid. Line 44
     Rather than be less,
Car'd not to be at all.
Ibid. Line 47
My sentence is for open war.
Ibid. Line 51
Which, if not victory, is yet revenge.
Ibid. Line 105
But all was false and hollow; though his tongue
Dropp'd manna, and could make the worse appear
The better reason,[1] to perplex and dash
Maturest counsels.
Ibid. Line 112
     Th' ethereal mould,
Incapable of stain, would soon expel
Her mischief, and purge off the baser fire,
Victorious. Thus repuls'd, our final hope
Is flat despair.[2]
Ibid. Line 139
     For who would lose,
Though full of pain, this intellectual being,
Those thoughts that wander through eternity,
To perish rather, swallow'd up and lost
In the wide womb of uncreated night?
Ibid. Line 146

---

[1] Aristophanes turns Socrates into ridicule . . . as making the worse appear the better reason. — DIOGENES LAERTIUS: *Socrates, V*

[2] Our hap is loss, our hope but sad despair. —SHAKESPEARE: *Henry VI, Part III, Act II, Sc. 3 L o*

His red right hand.[1]
> *Paradise Lost. Book II, Line 174*

Unrespited, unpitied, unrepriev'd.
> *Ibid. Line 185*

The never-ending flight
Of future days.
> *Ibid. Line 221*

With grave
Aspect he rose, and in his rising seem'd
A pillar of state; deep on his front en-
graven
Deliberation sat, and public care;
And princely counsel in his face yet
shone,
Majestic though in ruin: sage he stood,
With Atlantean shoulders, fit to bear
The weight of mightiest monarchies;
his look
Drew audience and attention still as
night
Or summer's noontide air.
> *Ibid. Line 300*

The palpable obscure.
> *Ibid. Line 406*

Long is the way
And hard, that out of hell leads up to
light.
> *Ibid. Line 432*

Their rising all at once was as the
sound
Of thunder heard remote.
> *Ibid. Line 476*

Others apart sat on a hill retir'd,
In thoughts more elevate, and reason'd
high
Of providence, foreknowledge, will, and
fate,
Fix'd fate, free-will, foreknowledge absolute;
And found no end, in wand'ring mazes
lost.
> *Ibid. Line 557*

Arm th' obdur'd breast
With stubborn patience as with triple
steel.
> *Ibid. Line 568*

Far off from these a slow and silent
stream,
Lethe the River of Oblivion.
> *Ibid. Line 582*

[1] Rubente dextera. — HORACE: *Ode I, 2, 2, To Caesar Augustus*

A gulf profound as that Serbonian bog
Betwixt Damiata and Mount Casius
old,
Where armies whole have sunk: the
parching air
Burns frore, and cold performs th' ef-
fect of fire.
Thither by harpy-footed Furies hail'd,
At certain revolutions all the damn'd
Are brought: and feel by turns the bit-
ter change
Of fierce extremes, — extremes by
change more fierce;
From beds of raging fire to starve in
ice
Their soft ethereal warmth, and there
to pine
Immovable, infix'd, and frozen round,
Periods of time; thence hurried back
to fire.
> *Paradise Lost. Book II, Line 592*

O'er many a frozen, many a fiery Alp,
Rocks, caves, lakes, fens, bogs, dens,
and shades of death.
> *Ibid. Line 620*

Gorgons and Hydras and Chimæras
dire.
> *Ibid. Line 628*

The other shape,
If shape it might be call'd that shape
had none
Distinguishable in member, joint, or
limb;
Or substance might be call'd that
shadow seem'd,
For each seem'd either, — black it
stood as night,
Fierce as ten furies, terrible as hell,
And shook a dreadful dart; what
seem'd his head
The likeness of a kingly crown had on.
Satan was now at hand.
> *Ibid. Line 666*

Whence and what art thou, execrable
shape?
> *Ibid. Line 681*

Before mine eyes in opposition sits
Grim Death, my son and foe.
> *Ibid. Line 803*

Hot, cold, moist, and dry, four champions fierce,
Strive here for mast'ry.
> *Ibid. Line 898*

To compare
Great things with small.[1]

Paradise Lost. Book II, Line 921

With ruin upon ruin, rout on rout,
Confusion worse confounded.

Ibid. Line 995

And fast by, hanging in a golden chain,
This pendent world, in bigness as a
star
Of smallest magnitude close by the
moon.

Ibid. Line 1051

Hail, holy light! offspring of heav'n
first-born.

Ibid. Book III, Line 1

The rising world of waters dark and
deep.

Ibid. Line 11

Thus with the year
Seasons return; but not to me returns
Day, or the sweet approach of even or
morn,
Or sight of vernal bloom or summer's
rose,
Or flocks, or herds, or human face di-
vine;
But cloud instead, and ever-during dark
Surrounds me; from the cheerful ways
of men
Cut off, and for the book of knowledge
fair
Presented with a universal blank
Of Nature's works, to me expung'd and
raz'd,
And wisdom at one entrance quite shut
out.

Ibid. Line 40

See golden days, fruitful of golden
deeds,
With joy and love triumphing.

Ibid. Line 337

Dark with excessive bright.

Ibid. Line 380

Since call'd
The Paradise of Fools,[1] to few unknown.

Paradise Lost. Book III, Line 495

The hell within him.

Ibid. Book IV, Line 20

Now conscience wakes despair
That slumber'd, — wakes the bitter
memory
Of what he was, what is, and what must
be
Worse.

Ibid. Line 23

At whose sight all the stars
Hide their diminish'd heads.[2]

Ibid. Line 34

A grateful mind
By owing owes not, but still pays, at
once
Indebted and discharg'd.

Ibid. Line 55

Which way shall I fly
Infinite wrath and infinite despair?
Which way I fly is hell; myself am
hell;
And in the lowest deep a lower deep,
Still threat'ning to devour me, opens
wide,
To which the hell I suffer seems a
heaven.

Ibid. Line 73

Ease would recant
Vows made in pain, as violent and void.

Ibid. Book IV, Line 96

So farewell hope, and, with hope, fare-
well fear,
Farewell remorse; all good to me is lost.
Evil, be thou my good.

Ibid. Line 108

Sabean odours from the spicy shore
Of Araby the Blest.

Ibid. Line 162

And on the Tree of Life,
The middle tree and highest there that
grew,
Sat like a cormorant.

Ibid. Line 194

A heaven on earth.

Ibid. Line 208

---

[1] Compare great things with small. — VIR-
GIL: *Eclogues, I, 24; Georgics, IV, 176.* COW-
LEY: *The Motto.* DRYDEN: *Ovid, Metamor-
phoses, Book I, L. 727.* TICKELL: *Poem on
Hunting.* POPE: *Windsor Forest*
  To compare
Small things with greatest. — *Paradise Re-
gained, Book IV, L. 563*

[1] See Shakespeare, page 79.
[2] Ye little stars! hide your diminished rays.
— POPE: *Moral Essays, Epistle III, L. 282*

Flowers of all hue, and without thorn
     the rose.[1]
     Paradise Lost. Book IV, Line 256
For contemplation he and valour
     form'd,
For softness she and sweet attractive
     grace;
He for God only, she for God in him.
          Ibid. Line 297
          Implied
Subjection, but requir'd with gentle
     sway,
And by her yielded, by him best re-
     ceiv'd, —
Yielded with coy submission, modest
     pride,
And sweet, reluctant, amorous delay.
          Ibid. Line 307
Adam the goodliest man of men since
     born
His sons, the fairest of her daughters
     Eve.
          Ibid. Line 323
          And with necessity,
The tyrant's plea,[2] excus'd his devilish
     deeds.
          Ibid. Line 393
Imparadis'd in one another's arms.
          Ibid. Line 506
          Live while ye may,
Yet happy pair.
          Ibid. Line 533
Now came still evening on, and twilight
     gray
Had in her sober livery all things clad.
          Ibid. Line 598
          Now glow'd the firmament
With living sapphires; Hesperus, that
     led
The starry host, rode brightest, till the
     moon,
Rising in clouded majesty, at length
Apparent queen, unveil'd her peerless
     light,
And o'er the dark her silver mantle
     threw.
          Ibid. Line 604
The timely dew of sleep.
          Ibid. Line 614

With thee conversing I forget all time,
All seasons, and their change; all please
     alike.
Sweet is the breath of morn, her rising
     sweet,
With charm of earliest birds; pleasant
     the sun
When first on this delightful land he
     spreads
His orient beams on herb, tree, fruit,
     and flower,
Glist'ring with dew; fragrant the fertile
     earth
After soft showers; and sweet the com-
     ing on
Of grateful ev'ning mild, then silent
     night
With this her solemn bird, and this fair
     moon,
And these the gems of heaven, her
     starry train:
     Paradise Lost. Book IV, Line 639
Millions of spiritual creatures walk the
     earth
Unseen, both when we wake, and when
     we sleep.
          Ibid. Line 677
          In naked beauty more adorn'd,
More lovely, than Pandora.[1]
          Ibid. Line 713
          Eas'd the putting off
These troublesome disguises which we
     wear.
          Ibid. Line 739
Hail, wedded love, mysterious law, true
     source
Of human offspring.
          Ibid. Line 750
Squat like a toad, close at the ear of
     Eve.
          Ibid. Line 800
Him thus intent Ithuriel with his spear
Touch'd lightly; for no falsehood can
     endure
Touch of celestial temper.
          Ibid. Line 810
Not to know me argues yourselves un-
     known.
          Ibid. Line 830

---

[1] See Herrick, page 134.
[2] Necessity is the argument of tyrants, it is the creed of slaves. — WILLIAM PITT: *Speech on the India Bill* [November, 1783]

[1] When unadorned, adorned the most. — THOMSON: *Autumn, L. 204*

Abash'd the devil stood,
And felt how awful goodness is, and
saw
Virtue in her shape how lovely.
Paradise Lost. Book IV, Line 846

All hell broke loose.
Ibid. Line 918

Like Teneriff or Atlas unremoved.
Ibid. Line 987

The starry cope
Of heaven.
Ibid. Line 992

Now morn, her rosy steps in th' eastern
clime
Advancing, sow'd the earth with orient
pearl,
When Adam wak'd, so custom'd; for
his sleep
Was aery light, from pure digestion
bred.
Ibid. Book V, Line 1

Hung over her enamour'd, and beheld
Beauty, which, whether waking or
asleep,
Shot forth peculiar graces.
Ibid. Line 13

My latest found,
Heaven's last, best gift, my ever-new
delight!
Ibid. Line 18

Good, the more
Communicated, more abundant grows.
Ibid. Line 71

These are thy glorious works, Parent
of good!
Ibid. Line 153

A wilderness of sweets.
Ibid. Line 294

So saying, with despatchful looks in
haste
She turns, on hospitable thoughts intent.
Ibid. Line 331

Nor jealousy
Was understood, the injur'd lover's hell.
Ibid. Line 449

The bright consummate flower.
Ibid. Line 481

Thrones, Dominations, Princedoms,
Virtues, Powers.
Ibid. Line 601

They eat, they drink, and in communion
sweet

Quaff immortality and joy.
Paradise Lost. Book V, Line 637

Midnight brought on the dusky hour
Friendliest to sleep and silence.
Ibid. Line 667

Innumerable as the stars of night,
Or stars of morning, dewdrops which
the sun
Impearls on every leaf and every
flower.
Ibid. Line 745

So spake the seraph Abdiel, faithful
found;
Among the faithless, faithful only he.
Ibid. Line 896

Morn,
Wak'd by the circling hours, with rosy
hand
Unbarr'd the gates of light.
Ibid. Book VI, Line 2

Servant of God, well done! Well hast
thou fought
The better fight.
Ibid. Line 29

How vain
Against the Omnipotent to rise in arms.
Ibid. Line 135

Arms on armour clashing bray'd
Horrible discord, and the madding
wheels
Of brazen chariots rag'd: dire was the
noise
Of conflict.
Ibid. Line 209

Far off his coming shone.
Ibid. Line 768

Let it profit thee to have heard,
By terrible example, the reward
Of disobedience.
Ibid. Line 909

More safe I sing with mortal voice, un-
chang'd
To hoarse or mute, though fall'n on
evil days,
On evil days though fall'n, and evil
tongues.
Ibid. Book VII, Line 24

Still govern thou my song,
Urania, and fit audience find, though
few.
Ibid. Line 30

Out of one man a race
Of men innumerable.
Paradise Lost. Book VII, Line 155
Heaven open'd wide
Her ever-during gates, harmonious
sound,
On golden hinges moving.
Ibid. Line 205
God saw the Light was good;
And light from darkness by the hemi-
sphere
Divided: Light the Day, and Darkness
Night,
He named. Thus was the first Day even
and morn.
Ibid. Line 249
Endued
With sanctity of reason.
Ibid. Line 507
The breath of life.
Ibid. Line 526
A broad and ample road, whose dust
is gold,
And pavement stars, as stars to thee ap-
pear
Seen in the galaxy, that milky way
Which nightly as a circling zone thou
seest
Powder'd with stars.
Ibid. Line 577
The Angel ended, and in Adam's ear
So charming left his voice that he awhile
Thought him still speaking, still stood
fix'd to hear.
Ibid. Book VIII, Line 1
And grace that won who saw to wish
her stay.
Ibid. Line 43
To know
That which before us lies in daily life
Is the prime wisdom.
Ibid. Line 192
Liquid lapse of murmuring streams.
Ibid. Line 263
And feel that I am happier than I know.
Ibid. Line 282
Among unequals what society
Can sort, what harmony or true de-
light?
Ibid. Line 383
Her virtue, and the conscience of her
worth,

That would be woo'd, and not unsought
be won.
Paradise Lost. Book VIII, Line 502
She what was honour knew,
And with obsequious majesty approv'd
My pleaded reason. To the nuptial
bower
I led her blushing like the morn; all
heaven
And happy constellations, on that hour
Shed their selectest influence.
Ibid. Line 508
The sum of earthly bliss.
Ibid. Line 522
Accuse not Nature! she hath done her
part;
Do thou but thine!
Ibid. Line 561
Oft times nothing profits more
Than self-esteem, grounded on just and
right.
Ibid. Line 571
Those graceful acts,
Those thousand decencies that daily
flow
From all her words and actions.
Ibid. Line 600
My unpremeditated verse.
Ibid. Book IX, Line 24
Pleas'd me, long choosing and begin-
ning late.
Ibid. Line 26
Unless an age too late, or cold
Climate, or years, damp my intended
wing.
Ibid. Line 44
Revenge, at first though sweet,
Bitter ere long back on itself recoils.
Ibid. Line 171
For solitude sometimes is best society,
And short retirement urges sweet re-
turn.
Ibid. Line 249
At shut of evening flowers.
Ibid. Line 278
As one who long in populous city pent,
Where houses thick and sewers annoy
the air.
Ibid. Line 445
So gloz'd the tempter.
Ibid. Line 549
Led Eve, our credulous mother, to the
Tree

Of Prohibition, root of all our woe.
Paradise Lost. Book IX, Line 644
Left that command
Sole daughter of his voice.[1]
Ibid. Line 652
His words, replete with guile,
Into her heart too easy entrance won.
Ibid. Line 733
Earth felt the wound, and Nature from her seat,
Sighing through all her works, gave signs of woe
That all was lost.
Ibid. Line 782
So dear I love him that with him all deaths
I could endure, without him live no life.
Ibid. Line 832
In her face excuse
Came prologue, and apology too prompt.
Ibid. Line 853
O fairest of Creation, last and best
Of all God's works, creature in whom excelled
Whatever can to sight or thought be formed,
Holy, divine, good, amiable, or sweet!
Ibid. Line 896
Yet I shall temper so
Justice with mercy, as may illustrate most
Them fully satisfy'd, and thee appease.
Ibid. Book X, Line 77
She gave me of the tree, and I did eat.
Ibid. Line 143
Dust thou art, and shalt to dust return.
Ibid. Line 208
So scented the grim Feature, and up-turn'd
His nostril wide into the murky air,
Sagacious of his quarry from so far.
Ibid. Line 279
Pandemonium, city and proud seat
Of Lucifer.
Ibid. Line 424
A dismal universal hiss, the sound
Of public scorn.
Ibid. Line 508
Death . . . on his pale horse.
Ibid. Line 588

[1] Stern daughter of the voice of God. —
WORDSWORTH: *Ode to Duty*

Whatever thing
The scythe of Time mows down.
Paradise Lost. Book X, Line 606
How gladly would I meet
Mortality, my sentence, and be earth
Insensible! how glad would lay me down
As in my mother's lap!
Ibid. Line 775
Morn,
All concerned with out unrest, begins
Her rosy progress smiling.
Ibid. Book XI, Line 173
Must I thus leave thee, Paradise? thus leave
Thee, native soil? these happy walks and shades?
Ibid. Line 269
Then purg'd with euphrasy and rue
The visual nerve, for he had much to see.
Ibid. Line 414
Moping melancholy,
And moon-struck madness.
Ibid. Line 485
And over them triumphant Death his dart
Shook, but delay'd to strike, though oft invok'd.
Ibid. Line 491
The rule of *Not too much.*
Ibid. Line 531
So may'st thou live, till, like ripe fruit, thou drop
Into thy mother's lap.
Ibid. Line 535
Nor love thy life, nor hate; but what thou liv'st
Live well; how long or short permit to Heaven.[1]
Ibid. Line 553
A bevy of fair women.
Ibid. Line 582
The evening star,
Love's harbinger.
Ibid. Line 588
The brazen throat of war.
Ibid. Line 713
An olive-leaf he brings, pacific sign.
Ibid. Line 860

[1] Summum nec metuas diem, nec optes
(Neither fear nor wish for your last day). —
MARTIAL: *Lib. X, Epigram 47, L. 13*

The world was all before them, where
 to choose
Their place of rest, and Providence
 their guide.
They hand in hand, with wand'ring
 steps and slow,
Through Eden took their solitary way.
  Paradise Lost. Book XII, Line 646
  Most men admire
Virtue who follow not her lore.
  Paradise Regained. Book I, Line 482
   Beauty stands
In the admiration only of weak minds
Led captive.
   Ibid. Book II, Line 220
Rocks whereon greatest men have oft-
 est wreck'd.
    Ibid. Line 228
Of whom to be disprais'd were no small
 praise.
   Ibid. Book III, Line 56
What honour that,
But tedious waste of time, to sit and
 hear
So many hollow compliments and lies,
Outlandish flatteries?
    Ibid. Line 122
Elephants indorsed with towers.
    Ibid. Line 329
Syene, and where the shadow both way
 falls,
Meroë, Nilotic isle.
   Ibid. Book IV, Line 70
Dusk faces with white silken turbants
 wreath'd.
    Ibid. Line 76
  The childhood shows the man,
As morning shows the day.[1]
    Ibid. Line 220
Athens, the eye of Greece, mother of arts
And eloquence.
    Ibid. Line 240
  The olive grove of Academe,
Plato's retirement, where the Attic bird
Trills her thick-warbled notes the sum-
 mer long.
    Ibid. Line 244
Thence to the famous orators repair,
Those ancient whose resistless elo-
 quence
Wielded at will that fierce democratie,

[1] The child is father of the man. — WORDS-
WORTH: *My Heart Leaps Up*

Shook the arsenal, and fulmin'd over
 Greece,
To Macedon, and Artaxerxes' throne.
  Paradise Regained. Book IV,
    Line 267
Socrates . . .
Whom, well inspir'd, the oracle pro-
 nounc'd
Wisest of men.
    Ibid. Line 274
Deep vers'd in books, and shallow in
 himself.
    Ibid. Line 327
As children gath'ring pebbles on the
 shore.
Or, if I would delight my private hours
With music or with poem, where so soon
As in our native language can I find
That solace?
    Ibid. Line 330
  Till morning fair
Came forth with pilgrim steps, in amice
 gray.
    Ibid. Line 426
O loss of sight, of thee I most complain!
  Samson Agonistes. Line 68
O dark, dark, dark, amid the blaze of
 noon,
Irrecoverably dark, total eclipse
Without all hope of day!
    Ibid. Line 80
The sun to me is dark
And silent as the moon,
When she deserts the night,
Hid in her vacant interlunar cave.
    Ibid. Line 86
Ran on embattled armies clad in iron,
And, weaponless himself,
Made arms ridiculous.
    Ibid. Line 129
Just are the ways of God,
And justifiable to men;
Unless there be who think not God at
 all.
    Ibid. Line 293
A grain of manhood.
    Ibid. Line 408
What boots it at one gate to make de-
 fence,
And at another to let in the foe?
    Ibid. Line 560
But who is this, what thing of sea or
 land, —

Female of sex it seems —
That so bedeck'd, ornate, and gay,
Comes this way sailing
Like a stately ship
Of Tarsus, bound for th' isles
Of Javan or Gadire,
With all her bravery on, and tackle
  trim,
Sails fill'd, and streamers waving,
Courted by all the winds that hold them
  play,
An amber scent of odorous perfume
Her harbinger?
           Samson Agonistes. Line 710
In argument with men a woman ever
Goes by the worse, whatever be her
  cause.
For want of words, no doubt, or lack
  of breath!
           Ibid. Line 903
Fame, if not double-faced, is double-
  mouthed,
And with contrary blast proclaims most
  deeds;
On both his wings, one black, the other
  white,
Bears greatest names in his wild aery
  flight.
           Ibid. Line 971
Yet beauty, though injurious, hath
  strange power,
After offence returning, to regain
Love once possess'd.
           Ibid. Line 1003
Love-quarrels oft in pleasing concord
  end;
Not wedlock-treachery.
           Ibid. Line 1008
Boast not of what thou would'st have
  done, but do
What then thou would'st.
           Ibid. Line 1104
He's gone, and who knows how he may
  report
Thy words by adding fuel to the flame?
           Ibid. Line 1350
For evil news rides post, while good
  news baits.
           Ibid. Line 1538
Suspense in news is torture.
           Ibid. Line 1569
Nothing is here for tears, nothing to
  wail

Or knock the breast; no weakness, no
  contempt,
Dispraise, or blame; nothing but well
  and fair,
And what may quiet us in a death so
  noble.
           Samson Agonistes. Line 1721
All is best, though we oft doubt
What the unsearchable dispose
Of Highest Wisdom brings about.
           Ibid. Line 1745
Calm of mind, all passion spent.
           Ibid. Line 1758
Above the smoke and stir of this dim
  spot
Which men call earth.
           Comus. Line 5
Bacchus, that first from out the purple
  grape
Crush'd the sweet poison of misusèd
  wine.
           Ibid. Line 46
These my sky-robes, spun out of Iris'
  woof.
           Ibid. Line 83
The star that bids the shepherd fold.
           Ibid. Line 93
Midnight shout and revelry,
Tipsy dance and jollity.
           Ibid. Line 103
Ere the blabbing eastern scout,
The nice morn, on th' Indian steep,
From her cabin'd loop-hole peep.
           Ibid. Line 138
       When the gray-hooded Even,
Like a sad votarist in palmer's weed,
Rose from the hindmost wheels of
  Phœbus' wain.
           Ibid. Line 188
       A thousand fantasies
Begin to throng into my memory,
Of calling shapes, and beck'ning shad-
  ows dire,
And airy tongues that syllable men's
  names
On sands and shores and desert wilder-
  nesses.
           Ibid. Line 205
Was I deceiv'd, or did a sable cloud
Turn forth her silver lining on the
  night?
           Ibid. Line 221

How sweetly did they float upon the wings
Of silence, through the empty-vaulted night,
At every fall smoothing the raven down
Of darkness till it smil'd!
> *Comus. Line 249*

Who, as they sung, would take the prison'd soul
And lap it in Elysium.
> *Ibid. Line 256*

Such sober certainty of waking bliss.
> *Ibid. Line 263*

I took it for a faery vision
Of some gay creatures of the element,
That in the colours of the rainbow live,
And play i' th' plighted clouds.
> *Ibid. Line 298*

With thy long levell'd rule of streaming light.
> *Ibid. Line 340*

Virtue could see to do what Virtue would
By her own radiant light, though sun and moon
Were in the flat sea sunk. And Wisdom's self
Oft seeks to sweet retired solitude,
Where, with her best nurse Contemplation,
She plumes her feathers, and lets grow her wings.
> *Ibid. Line 373*

> The unsunn'd heaps
Of miser's treasure.
> *Ibid. Line 398*

Some say no evil thing that walks by night,
In fog or fire, by lake or moorish fen,
Blue meagre hag, or stubborn unlaid ghost,
That breaks his magic chains at curfew time,
No goblin, or swart faery of the mine,
Hath hurtful power o'er true virginity.
> *Ibid. Line 432*

How charming is divine philosophy!
Not harsh and crabbed, as dull fools suppose,

But musical as is Apollo's lute,[1]
And a perpetual feast of nectar'd sweets
Where no crude surfeit reigns.
> *Comus. Line 476*

Fill'd the air with barbarous dissonance.
> *Ibid. Line 550*

> That power
Which erring men call Chance.
> *Ibid. Line 587*

> This cordial julep here,
That flames and dances in his crystal bounds.
> *Ibid. Line 672*

Budge doctors of the Stoic fur.
> *Ibid. Line 707*

And live like Nature's bastards, not her sons.
> *Ibid. Line 727*

It is for homely features to keep home, —
They had their name thence; coarse complexions
And cheeks of sorry grain will serve to ply
The sampler, and to tease the huswife's wool.
What need a vermeil-tinctur'd lip for that,
Love-darting eyes, or tresses like the morn?
> *Ibid. Line 748*

Enjoy your dear wit, and gay rhetoric,
That hath so well been taught her dazzling fence.
> *Ibid. Line 790*

Sabrina fair,
  Listen where thou art sitting
Under the glassy, cool, translucent wave,
  In twisted braids of lilies knitting
The loose train of thy amber-dropping hair.
> *Ibid. Line 859*

But now my task is smoothly done:
I can fly, or I can run.
> *Ibid. Line 1012*

---

[1]   As sweet and musical
As bright Apollo's lute.
  SHAKESPEARE: *Love's Labour's Lost,*
    Act IV, Sc. 3, L. 342

Or, if Virtue feeble were,
Heav'n itself would stoop to her.
Comus. Line 1022

I come to pluck your berries harsh and
crude,
And with forc'd fingers rude
Shatter your leaves before the mellow-
ing year.
Lycidas. Line 3

He knew
Himself to sing, and build the lofty
rhyme.
Ibid. Line 10

Without the meed of some melodious
tear.
Ibid. Line 14

Hence with denial vain, and coy excuse.
Ibid. Line 18

Under the opening eyelids of the morn.
Ibid. Line 26

But oh the heavy change, now thou art
gone,
Now thou art gone and never must return!
Ibid. Line 37

The gadding vine.
Ibid. Line 40

And strictly meditate the thankless
Muse.
Ibid. Line 66

To sport with Amaryllis in the shade,
Or with the tangles of Neæra's hair.
Ibid. Line 68

Fame is the spur that the clear spirit
doth raise [1]
(That last infirmity of noble mind) [2]
To scorn delights, and live laborious
days;
But the fair guerdon when we hope to
find,
And think to burst out into sudden
blaze,

---

[1] Erant quibus appetentior famæ videretur,
quando etiam sapientibus cupido gloriæ novis-
sima exuitur (Some might consider him as too
fond of fame, for the desire of glory clings
even to the best of men longer than any other
passion) [said of Helvidius Priscus]. — TACI-
TUS: *Historia, IV, 6*

[2] That thirst (for applause), if the last infirmity of noble minds, is also the first infirmity of weak ones; and, on the whole, the
strongest impulsive influence of average humanity. — RUSKIN: *Sesame and Lilies, Of
Kings' Treasuries, 3*

Comes the blind Fury with th' abhorred
shears
And slits the thin-spun life.
Lycidas. Line 70

Fame is no plant that grows on mortal
soil.
Ibid. Line 78

It was that fatal and perfidious bark,
Built in th' eclipse, and rigg'd with
curses dark.
Ibid. Line 100

The Pilot of the Galilean lake;
Two massy keys he bore of metals
twain
(The golden opes, the iron shuts
amain).
Ibid. Line 109

The hungry sheep look up, and are not
fed.
Ibid. Line 123

But that two-handed engine at the
door
Stands ready to smite once, and smite
no more.
Ibid. Line 130

Throw hither all your quaint enamell'd
eyes,
That on the green turf suck the honied
showers,
And purple all the ground with vernal
flowers.
Bring the rathe primrose that forsaken
dies,
The tufted crow-toe, and pale jessa-
mine,
The white pink, and the pansy freaked
with jet,
The glowing violet,
The musk-rose, and the well-attir'd
woodbine,
With cowslips wan that hang the pen-
sive head,
And every flower that sad embroidery
wears.
Ibid. Line 139

So sinks the day-star in the ocean bed,
And yet anon repairs his drooping head,
And tricks his beams, and with new-
spangled ore
Flames in the forehead of the morning
sky.
Ibid. Line 168

He touch'd the tender stops of various quills,
With eager thought warbling his Doric lay.
Lycidas. Line 188

To-morrow to fresh woods, and pastures new.
Ibid. Line 193

Hence, loathed Melancholy,
Of Cerberus and blackest Midnight born.
L'Allegro. Line 1

Haste thee, Nymph, and bring with thee
Jest, and youthful Jollity,
Quips and Cranks and wanton Wiles,
Nods and Becks and wreathèd Smiles.
Ibid. Line 25

Sport, that wrinkled Care derides,
And Laughter holding both his sides.
Come, and trip it, as you go,
On the light fantastic toe.
Ibid. Line 31

The mountain nymph, sweet Liberty.
Ibid. Line 36

And every shepherd tells his tale
Under the hawthorn in the dale.
Ibid. Line 67

Meadows trim, with daisies pied,
Shallow brooks, and rivers wide;
Towers and battlements it sees
Bosom'd high in tufted trees,
Where perhaps some beauty lies,
The cynosure of neighboring eyes.
Ibid. Line 75

Then to the spicy nut-brown ale.
Ibid. Line 100

Tower'd cities please us then,
And the busy hum of men.
Ibid. Line 117

Ladies, whose bright eyes
Rain influence, and judge the prize.
Ibid. Line 121

Such sights as youthful poets dream
On summer eves by haunted stream.
Then to the well-trod stage anon,
If Jonson's learned sock be on,
Or sweetest Shakespeare, Fancy's child,
Warble his native wood-notes wild.
Ibid. Line 129

And ever, against eating cares,
Lap me in soft Lydian airs,

Married to immortal verse,[1]
Such as the meeting soul may pierce,
In notes with many a winding bout
Of linkèd sweetness long drawn out.
L'Allegro. Line 135

Untwisting all the chains that tie
The hidden soul of harmony.
Ibid. Line 143

Vain deluding Joys,
The brood of Folly without father bred!
Il Penseroso. Line 1

The gay motes that people the sunbeams.
Ibid. Line 8

Sober, stedfast, and demure.
Ibid. Line 32

And looks commercing with the skies,
Thy rapt soul sitting in thine eyes.
Ibid. Line 39

Forget thyself to marble.
Ibid. Line 42

And join with thee, calm Peace and Quiet,
Spare Fast, that oft with gods doth diet.
Ibid. Line 45

And add to these retired Leisure,
That in trim gardens takes his pleasure.
Ibid. Line 49

Sweet bird, that shun'st the noise of folly,
Most musical, most melancholy!
Ibid. Line 61

I walk unseen
On the dry smooth-shaven green,
To behold the wandering moon,
Riding near her highest noon,
Like one that had been led astray
Through the heav'n's wide pathless way,
And oft, as if her head she bow'd,
Stooping through a fleecy cloud.
Ibid. Line 65

Where glowing embers through the room
Teach light to counterfeit a gloom.
Ibid. Line 79

Far from all resort of mirth,
Save the cricket on the hearth.
Ibid. Line 81

[1] Wisdom married to immortal verse. —
WORDSWORTH: *The Excursion, Book VII*

Sometime let gorgeous Tragedy
In sceptred pall come sweeping by,
Presenting Thebes, or Pelops' line,
Or the tale of Troy divine.
Il Penseroso. Line 97

Or bid the soul of Orpheus sing
Such notes as, warbled to the string,
Drew iron tears down Pluto's cheek.
Ibid. Line 105

Or call up him that left half told
The story of Cambuscan bold.[1]
Ibid. Line 109

Where more is meant than meets the
ear.
Ibid. Line 120

When the gust hath blown his fill,
Ending on the rustling leaves,
With minute-drops from off the eaves.
Ibid. Line 128

Hide me from day's garish eye.
Ibid. Line 141

And storied windows richly dight,
Casting a dim religious light.
Ibid. Line 159

Till old experience do attain
To something like prophetic strain.
Ibid. Line 173

This is the month, and this the happy
morn,
Wherein the Son of Heaven's eternal
King,
Of wedded maid and virgin mother
born,
Our great redemption from above did
bring.
*On the Morning of Christ's Na-
tivity. Stanza 1, Line 1*

No war, or battle's sound
Was heard the world around.
Ibid. Stanza 4, Line 53

Time will run back and fetch the Age
of Gold.[2]
Ibid. Stanza 14, Line 135

The Oracles are dumb;
No voice or hideous hum
Runs through the archèd roof in words
deceiving.
Ibid. Stanza 19, Line 173

From haunted spring and dale
Edg'd with poplar pale

The parting genius is with sighing sent.
*On the Morning of Christ's Na-
tivity. Stanza 20, Line 184*

Peor and Baälim
Forsake their temples dim.
Ibid. Stanza 22, Line 197

The lazy leaden-stepping Hours,
Whose speed is but the heavy plum-
met's pace.
On Time

All this earthy grossness quit,
Attired with stars we shall for ever sit,
Triumphing over Death, and Chance,
and thee, O Time.
Ibid.

What needs my Shakespeare for his
honour'd bones
The labour of an age in pilèd stones?
Or that his hallow'd relics should be
hid
Under a star-ypointing pyramid?
Dear son of memory, great heir of fame,
What need'st thou such weak witness
of thy name?
On Shakespeare

And so sepúlchred in such pomp dost
lie,
That kings for such a tomb would wish
to die.
Ibid.

Thy liquid notes that close the eye of
day.[1]
Sonnet: To the Nightingale

Time, the subtle thief of youth.
*On His Having Arrived at
the Age of Twenty-three*

As ever in my great Taskmaster's eye.
Ibid.

That old man eloquent.
To the Lady Margaret Ley

That would have made Quintilian stare
and gasp.
*On the Detraction which followed
upon my writing certain Treatises*

License they mean when they cry Liberty;
For who loves that must first be wise
and good.
Ibid. II

---

[1] CHAUCER: *The Squieres Tale*
[2] See Spenser, page 25.

[1] Ye of day. — CHAUCER: *The Legend of
Good Women, Prologue, L. 184*

Peace hath her victories
No less renown'd than war.

To the Lord General Cromwell

Ev'n them who kept thy truth so pure
of old,
When all our fathers worshipp'd stocks
and stones.

On the late Massacre in Piedmont

Thousands at his bidding speed,
And post o'er land and ocean without
rest;

They also serve who only stand and
wait.

On his Blindness

What neat repast shall feast us, light
and choice,
Of Attic taste?

To Mr. Lawrence

In mirth that after no repenting draws.

Sonnet XXI: To Cyriac Skinner

For other things mild Heav'n a time
ordains,
And disapproves that care, though wise
in show,
That with superfluous burden loads the
day,
And, when God sends a cheerful hour,
refrains.

Ibid.

Yet I argue not
Against Heav'n's hand or will, nor bate
a jot
Of heart or hope; but still bear up and
steer
Right onward.

Sonnet XXII

Of which all Europe rings from side
to side.

Ibid.

But oh! as to embrace me she inclin'd,
I wak'd, she fled, and day brought back
my night.

On his Deceased Wife

For such kind of borrowing as this,
if it be not bettered by the borrower,
among good authors is accounted Plagiarè.

Iconoclastes, XXIII

Truth is as impossible to be soiled by
any outward touch as the sunbeam.[1]

*Doctrine and Discipline of
Divorce*

[1] See Bacon, page 112.

A poet soaring in the high reason of
his fancies, with his garland and singing robes about him.

*The Reason of Church Govern-
ment. Book II, Introduction*

By labour and intent study (which
I take to be my portion in this life),
joined with the strong propensity of
nature, I might perhaps leave something so written to after times as they
should not willingly let it die.

Ibid.

Beholding the bright countenance of
truth in the quiet and still air of delightful studies.

Ibid.

He who would not be frustrate of his
hope to write well hereafter in laudable
things ought himself to be a true poem.

Apology for Smectymnuus

His words, like so many nimble and
airy servitors, trip about him at command.

Ibid.

Litigious terms, fat contentions, and
flowing fees.

Tractate of Education

Enflamed with the study of learning
and the admiration of virtue; stirred up
with high hopes of living to be brave
men and worthy patriots, dear to God,
and famous to all ages.

Ibid.

Ornate rhetorick taught out of the
rule of Plato. . . . To which poetry
would be made subsequent, or indeed
rather precedent, as being less suttle
and fine, but more simple, sensuous,
and passionate.

Ibid.

In those vernal seasons of the year,
when the air is calm and pleasant, it
were an injury and sullenness against
Nature not to go out and see her riches,
and partake in her rejoicing with
heaven and earth.

Ibid.

Attic tragedies of stateliest and most
regal argument.

Ibid.

As good almost kill a man as kill a
good book: who kills a man kills a
reasonable creature, God's image; but

he who destroys a good book kills reason itself.

Areopagitica

A good book is the precious life-blood of a master-spirit, embalmed and treasured up on purpose to a life beyond life.

Ibid.

I cannot praise a fugitive and cloistered virtue, unexercised and unbreathed, that never sallies out and sees her adversary, but slinks out of the race where that immortal garland is to be run for, not without dust and heat.

Ibid.

Who shall silence all the airs and madrigals that whisper softness in chambers?

Ibid.

Methinks I see in my mind a noble and puissant nation rousing herself like a strong man after sleep, and shaking her invincible locks: methinks I see her as an eagle mewing her mighty youth, and kindling her undazzled eyes at the full midday beam.

Ibid.

Though all the winds of doctrine [1] were let loose to play upon the earth, so Truth be in the field, we do ingloriously, by licensing and prohibiting, to misdoubt her strength. Let her and Falsehood grapple: who ever knew Truth put to the worse in a free and open encounter? [2]

Ibid.

Men of most renowned virtue have sometimes by transgressing most truly kept the law.

Tetrachordon

Such bickerings to recount, met often in these our writers, what more worth is it than to chronicle the wars of kites or crows flocking and fighting in the air?

The History of England. Book IV

[1] *Winds of Doctrine: used as title of a book by* GEORGE SANTAYANA [1913]
[2] Error of opinion may be tolerated where reason is left free to combat it. — JEFFERSON: *Inaugural Address* [March 4, 1801]

SIR JOHN SUCKLING
[1609-1642]

Her feet beneath her petticoat
Like little mice, stole in and out,[1]
  As if they feared the light;
But oh, she dances such a way!
No sun upon an Easter-day
  Is half so fine a sight.
A Ballad upon a Wedding.
Stanza 8

Her lips were red, and one was thin,
Compared with that was next her chin,
Some bee had stung it newly.
Ibid. Stanza 11

Why so pale and wan, fond lover?
  Prithee, why so pale?
Will, when looking well can't move her,
  Looking ill prevail?
Song. Stanza 1

'Tis not the meat, but 'tis the appetite
  Makes eating a delight.
Of Thee, Kind Boy. Stanza 3

Long graces do
But keep good stomachs off, that would
  fall to.
To Lord Lepington

Spare diet is the cause love lasts,
For surfeits sooner kill than fasts.
Against Absence

Out upon it, I have loved
  Three whole days together;
And am like to love three more,
  If it prove fair weather.
A Poem with the Answer.
Stanza 1

'Tis expectation makes a blessing dear,
Heaven were not heaven, if we knew
  what it were.
Against Fruition. Stanza 4

Women are the baggage of life: they
  are
Troublesome, and hinder us in the great
  march,
And yet we cannot be without 'em.
The Tragedy of Brennoralt.
Act I, Sc. 1

Success is a rare paint, hides all the
  ugliness.
Ibid.

[1] Her pretty feet, like snails, did creep
    A little out.
ROBERT HERRICK: *To Mistress*
Susanna Southwell

Nipped i' the bud.
> *The Tragedy of Brennoralt.*
> *Act. I, Sc. 1*

Sleep is as nice as woman;
The more I court it, the more it flies me.
> *Ibid. Act II, Sc. 1*

She is pretty to walk with,
And witty to talk with,
And pleasant, too, to think on.
> *Ibid.*

Her face is like the milky way [1] i' the
sky, —
A meeting of gentle lights without
name.
> *Ibid. Act III, Sc. 1*

Death's no punishment: it is the sense,
The pains and fears afore, that makes
a death.
> *Aglaura. Act V, Sc. 1*

But as when an authentic watch is
shown,
Each man winds up and rectifies his
own,
So in our very judgments.[2]
> *Ibid. Epilogue*

The Prince of Darkness is a gentleman.[3]
> *The Goblins. Act III*

I' th' very nick of time!
> *Ibid. Act V*

High characters (cries one), and he
would see
Things that ne'er were, nor are, nor
ne'er will be.[4]
> *Ibid. Epilogue*

---

[1] The milkie way. — GEORGE HERBERT: *Prayer, St. 3*
[2] 'Tis with our judgments as our watches, none Go just alike, yet each believes his own.
POPE: *An Essay on Criticism, Part I, L. 9*
[3] See Shakespeare, page 99.
[4] Whoever thinks a faultless piece to see, Thinks what ne'er was, nor is, nor e'er shall be.
POPE: *An Essay on Criticism, Part II, L. 53*
There's no such thing in Nature, and you'll draw
A faultless monster which the world ne'er saw.
JOHN SHEFFIELD, DUKE OF BUCKINGHAMSHIRE [1648–1721]: *Essay on Poetry*

WILLIAM CARTWRIGHT
[1611–1643]

St. Francis and St. Benedight,
Bless this house from wicked wight,
From the nightmare and the Goblin
That is hight Good Fellow Robin.
Keep it from all evil spiretes,
Fairies, Wezles, Bats, and Ferrytes
From Curfew Time to the next Prime.
> *A House Blessing* [1]

JAMES GRAHAM, FIRST MARQUIS OF MONTROSE
[1612–1650]

He either fears his fate too much,
Or his deserts are small,
That dares not put it to the touch
To gain or lose it all.[2]
> *My Dear and Only Love.*
> *Stanza 2*

I'll make thee glorious by my pen,
And famous by my sword.[3]
> *Ibid. Stanza 5*

THOMAS JORDAN
[1612–1685]

Let us drink and be merry, dance, joke,
and rejoice,
With claret and sherry, theorbo and
voice!
> *Coronemus nos Rosis Antequam*
> *Marcescant.*[4] *Stanza 1*

Fish dinners will make a man spring
like a flea.
> *Ibid. Stanza 2*

Though now she be pleasant and sweet
to the sense,

---

[1] Matthew, Mark, Luke, and John, The bed be blest that I lye on.
THOMAS ADY: *A Candle in the Dark, P. 58* [London, 1656]
[2] That puts it not unto the touch To win or lose it all.
MARK NAPIER [1798–1879]: *Montrose and the Covenanters, Vol. II, P. 566*
[3] I'll make thee famous by my pen, And glorious by my sword.
SCOTT: *Legend of Montrose, Chap. XV*
[4] One of the songs of Sir Henry Morgan's buccaneers was an adaptation of this poem.

Will be damnable mouldy a hundred
years hence.
> *Coronemus nos Rosis Antequam*
> *Marcescant. Stanza 3*

For health, wealth and beauty, wit,
learning, and sense,
Must all come to nothing a hundred
years hence.
> *Ibid. Stanza 4*

RICHARD CRASHAW
[1613–1649]

The conscious water saw its God and
blushed.[1]
> *Epigrammata Sacra. Aquae in*
> *Vinum Versae*

Two went to pray? Oh, rather say
One went to brag, the other to pray;
One stands up close and treads on high
Where the other dares not send his eye;
One nearer to God's altar trod,
The other to the altar's God.
> *Two Went up to the Temple to*
> *Pray*

What wilt thou do
To entertain this starry stranger?
> *The Shepherds' Hymn*

Whoe'er she be,
That not impossible she,
That shall command my heart and me.
> *Wishes to his Supposed Mistress*

Where'er she lie,
Locked up from mortal eye,
In shady leaves of destiny.
> *Ibid.*

Days that need borrow
No part of their good morrow

[1] Nympha pudica Deum vidit et erubuit. —
Quoted by SAMUEL JOHNSON [1778], *Bos-*
well's Life of Dr. Johnson, Vol. II, P. 218,
Everyman ed. A footnote states that this line
has frequently been attributed to Dryden, but
appeared in Crashaw's *Epigrammata Sacra*
[1634]. Though many writers have translated the epigram, only the last line has survived.
> The bashful stream hath seen its God and
> blushed.
> > AARON HILL [1685–1750]

> The water hears thy faintest word,
> And blushes into wine.
> > JOHN SAMUEL BEWLEY MONSELL
> > [1811–1875]: *Mysterious is Thy*
> > *Presence, Lord, St. 1*

From a fore-spent night of sorrow.
> *Wishes to his Supposed Mistress*

Life that dares send
A challenge to his end,
And when it comes, say, Welcome,
friend!
> *Ibid.*

Sydneian showers
Of sweet discourse, whose powers
Can crown old Winter's head with
flowers.
> *Ibid.*

A happy soul, that all the way
To heaven hath a summer's day.
> *In Praise of Lessius's Rule of*
> *Health*

The modest front of this small floor,
Believe me, reader, can say more
Than many a braver marble can, —
"Here lies a truly honest man!"
> *Epitaph upon Mr. Ashton*

JEREMY TAYLOR
[1613–1667]

I end with a story which I find in the
Jews'[1] Books. When Abraham sat at

[1] In the Latin dedication to the Senate of
Hamburg of a Rabbinical work, *The Rod of*
Judah, the translator, George Genz, gives the
story substantially as found in Jeremy Taylor's *Liberty of Prophesying.* The work of
Genz was published at Amsterdam in 1651,
and the parable was credited to "a most noble
author Sadus." It was afterward found in
the *Bostan,* or *Flower Garden,* of Saadi, the
Persian poet of the twelfth century.
    Henry Home, Lord Kames [1696–1782],
published the *Parable on Persecution* in Volume II of his *Sketches of the History of Man*
in 1774, saying it had been communicated to
him by Benjamin Franklin.
    From Lord Kames' book the parable was
taken for the first English edition of Franklin's
writings, edited by Benjamin Vaughan [1751–
1835], published in London in 1779. Franklin had a copy of the parable bound in his
Bible as an added chapter to the Book of
Genesis.
    The Reverend Sydney Smith read the apo-
logue before the Mayor and Corporation of
Bristol, England, November 5, 1828, and it
is included in Chapter 8 of *A Memoir of the*
Reverend Sydney Smith by his daughter, Lady
Holland, 1855, where it is followed by a letter
from Edward Everett, giving information concerning the parable.
    No. 8 of Edward Everett's *Mount Vernon*
Papers, a series first published in *The New*

his tent-door, according to his custom, waiting to entertain strangers, he espied an old man stooping and leaning on his staffe, weary with age and travelle, coming toward him, who was an hundred years of age; he received him kindly, washed his feet, provided supper, caused him to sit down; but observing that the old man eat and prayed not, nor begged for a blessing on his meat, asked him why he did not worship the God of heaven. The old man told him that he worshiped the fire only, and acknowledged no other God: at which answer Abraham grew so zealously angry, that he thrust the old man out of his tent, and exposed him to all the evils of the night and an unguarded condition. When the old man was gone, God called to him and asked him where the stranger was; he replied, "I thrust him away because he did not worship thee"; God answered him, "I have suffered him these hundred years, although he dishonored me, and couldst thou not endure him one night, when he gave thee no trouble?" Upon this, saith the story, Abraham fetcht him back again, and gave him hospitable entertainment and wise instruction. Go thou and do likewise, and thy charity will be rewarded by the God of Abraham.

The Liberty of Prophesying.
Page 606 [*1657*]

He that is most knowing hath a capacity to become happy, which a lesse knowing prince or a rich person hath not.

XXVIII Sermons [*1651*]

We long for perishing meat, and fill our stomachs with corruption; we look after white and red, and the weaker beauties of the night; we are passionate after rings and seals, and enraged at

the breaking of a Crystall . . . our hearts are hard and inflexible, having no loves for anything but strange flesh, and heaps of money, and popular noises; and therefore we are a huge way off from the Kingdome of God.

XXV Sermons [*1653*]

No man ever repented that he arose from the table sober, healthfull, and with his wits about him.

Ibid.

Every man hath in his own life sins enough, in his own minde trouble enough: so that curiositie after the affairs of others cannot be without envy and an evil minde. What is it to me if my Neighbours Grandfather were a Syrian, or his Grandmother illegitimate, or that another is indebted five thousand pounds, or whether his wife be expensive?

Holy Living

Here is no place to sit down in, but you must rise as soon as you are set: for we have gnats in our chambers, and worms in our gardens, and spiders and flies in the palaces of the greatest Kings.

Holy Dying

RICHARD BAXTER
[1615–1691]

I preached as never sure to preach again,
And as a dying man to dying men.
Love Breathing Thanks and Praise

SIR JOHN DENHAM
[1615–1669]

Though with those streams he [1] no resemblance hold,
Whose foam is amber, and their gravel gold:
His genuine and less guilty wealth t' explore,

York Ledger and brought out in book form in 1860, is devoted to the history of the *Parable on Persecution* and includes the three versions, — those by Jeremy Taylor, Lord Kames, and Benjamin Franklin.

For a happy introduction to Jeremy Taylor's "Atlantic roll of English prose," see Logan Pearsall Smith: *The Golden Grove* [Oxford, 1930].

[1] Viz. the River Thames; described in the same poem as "Thames, the most loved of all the ocean's sons."

Search not his bottom, but survey his shore.
> *Cooper's Hill.*[1] *Line 165* [*1642*]

Oh, could I flow like thee, and make thy stream
My great example, as it is my theme!
Though deep, yet clear, though gentle yet not dull;
Strong without rage, without o'erflowing full.
> *Ibid. Line 189*

I can no more believe old Homer blind,
Than those who say the sun hath never shined:
The age wherein he lived was dark, but he
Could not want sight who taught the world to see.
> *Progress of Learning*

But whither am I strayed? I need not raise
Trophies to thee from other men's dispraise;
Nor is thy fame on lesser ruins built;
Nor needs thy juster title the foul guilt
Of Eastern kings, who, to secure their reign,
Must have their brothers, sons, and kindred slain.[2]
> *On Mr. John Fletcher's Works*

SIR ROGER L'ESTRANGE
[1616–1704]

Though this may be play to you,
'Tis death to us.
> *Fables from Several Authors.*
> *Fable 398*

ABRAHAM COWLEY
[1618–1667]

What shall I do to be forever known,
And make the age to come my own?
> *The Motto*

His time is forever, everywhere his place.
> *Friendship in Absence*

We spent them not in toys, in lusts, or wine,
But search of deep philosophy,
Wit, eloquence, and poetry;
Arts which I lov'd, for they, my friend, were thine.
> *On the Death of Mr. William Harvey*

Ye fields of Cambridge, our dear Cambridge, say
Have ye not seen us walking every day?
> *Ibid.*

His *faith*, perhaps, in some nice tenets might
Be wrong; his *life*, I'm sure, was in the right.[1]
> *On the Death of Crashaw*

The thirsty earth soaks up the rain,
And drinks, and gapes for drink again.
The plants suck in the earth, and are
With constant drinking fresh and fair.
> *From Anacreon, II. Drinking*

Fill all the glasses there, for why
Should every creature drink but I?
Why, man of morals, tell me why?
> *Ibid.*

A mighty pain to love it is,
And 'tis a pain that pain to miss;
But of all pains, the greatest pain
It is to love, but love in vain.
> *Ibid. VII. Gold*

Th' adorning thee with so much art
Is but a barb'rous skill;
'Tis like the pois'ning of a dart,
Too apt before to kill.
> *The Waiting Maid*

Nothing is there to come, and nothing past,
But an eternal now does always last.[2]
> *Davideis. Book I, Line 25*

---

[1] After Edgehill fight, his poem called Cowper's Hill was printed at Oxford in a sort of browne paper, for then they could gett no better. — JOHN AUBREY: *Brief Lives*

[2] Poets are sultans, if they had their will;
For every author would his brother kill.
ROGER BOYLE, first Earl of Orrery
[1621–1679]
Should such a man, too fond to rule alone,

Bear, like the Turk, no brother near the throne.
POPE: *Prologue to the Satires, L. 197*

[1] For modes of faith let graceless zealots fight,
He can't be wrong whose life is in the right.
POPE: *Essay on Man, Epistle III, L. 305*

[2] One of our poets (which is it?) speaks of an everlasting now. — SOUTHEY: *The Doctor, Chap. XXV, P. 1*

When Israel was from bondage led,
  Led by the Almighty's hand
  From out of foreign land,
The great sea beheld and fled.
            Davideis. Book I, Line 41

Let but thy wicked men from out thee
    go,
And all the fools that crowd thee so,
Even thou, who dost thy millions boast,
A village less than Islington wilt grow,
A solitude almost.
              Of Solitude. VII

The monster London laugh at me.
              Ibid. XI

The fairest garden in her looks,
And in her mind the wisest books.
              The Garden. I

God the first garden made, and the first
  city Cain.[1]
              Ibid. II

Hence, ye profane! I hate ye all,
Both the great vulgar and the small.
          Horace. Book III, Ode 1

Charm'd with the foolish whistling of a
  name.[2]
    Virgil, Georgics. Book II, Line 72

Words that weep and tears that speak.[3]
              The Prophet

We griev'd, we sigh'd, we wept; we
  never blush'd before.
  *Discourse concerning the Govern-
      ment of Oliver Cromwell*

Thus would I double my life's fading
  space;
For he that runs it well, runs twice his
  race.[4]
        *Discourse XI, Of Myself.
              Stanza XI*

To-morrow let my sun his beams display,
Or in clouds hide them; I have lived
  my day.[5]
              Ibid.

Well then! I now do plainly see

---

[1] See Bacon, page 111.
[2] Ravish'd with the whistling of a name. —
POPE: *Essay on Man, Epistle IV, L. 283*
[3] Thoughts that breathe, and words that
burn. — GRAY: *Progress of Poesy, III, 3, 4*
[4] For he lives twice who can at once employ
The present well, and ev'n the past enjoy.
    POPE: *Imitation of Martial, L. 10*
[5] See Dryden, page 177.

This busy world and I shall ne'er agree.
              The Wish

Ah yet, ere I descend to the grave
May I a small house and large garden
    have;
And a few friends, and many books,
    both true,
Both wise, and both delightful too!
              Ibid.

A mistress moderately fair.
              Ibid.

RICHARD LOVELACE
[1618–1658]

Oh, could you view the melody
  Of every grace
  And music of her face,[1]
You'd drop a tear;
  Seeing more harmony
  In her bright eye
Than now you hear.
          Orpheus to Beasts

I could not love thee, dear, so much,
  Lov'd I not honour more.
    *To Lucasta, on Going to the Wars.
              Stanza 3*

When flowing cups run swiftly round
With no allaying Thames.[2]
    To Althea from Prison. Stanza 2

Fishes that tipple in the deep,
  Know no such liberty.
              Ibid.

Stone walls do not a prison make,[3]
  Nor iron bars a cage;
Minds innocent and quiet take
  That for an hermitage;
If I have freedom in my love,
  And in my soul am free,
Angels alone that soar above
  Enjoy such liberty.
          Ibid. Stanza 4

---

[1] See Browne, page 145.
The mind, the music breathing from her
face. — BYRON: *Bride of Abydos, Canto I,
St. 6*
[2] Not a drop of allaying Tiber in 't. —
SHAKESPEARE: *Coriolanus, Act II, Sc. 2, L. 52*
[3] Stone walls a prisoner make, but not a
slave. — WORDSWORTH: *Humanity*

ANDREW MARVELL
[1620–1678]

> Orange bright,
> Like golden lamps in a green night.
> > *The Emigrants in Bermudas*

And all the way, to guide their chime,
With falling oars they kept the time.[1]
> > *Ibid.*

Had we but world enough, and time,
This coyness, lady, were no crime.
> > *To His Coy Mistress*

But at my back I always hear
Time's wingèd chariot hurrying near;
And yonder all before us lie
Deserts of vast eternity.
> > *Ibid.*

Though we cannot make our sun
Stand still, yet we will make him run.
> > *Ibid.*

Annihilating all that's made
To a green thought in a green shade.
> > *The Garden*

Casting the body's vest aside,
My soul into the boughs does glide.
> > *Ibid.*

The world in all doth but two nations
> bear, —
The good, the bad; and these mixed
everywhere.
> > *The Loyal Scot*

The inglorious arts of peace.
> > *Upon Cromwell's return from*
> > *Ireland* [1650]

He [2] nothing common did, or mean,
Upon that memorable scene.
> > *Ibid.*

So much one man can do,
That does both act and know.
> > *Ibid.*

As lines, so loves oblique, may well
Themselves in every angle greet;
But ours, so truly parallel,
Though infinite, can never meet.
> > *The Definition of Love*

---

[1] Faintly as tolls the evening chime
Our voices keep tune and our oars keep time.
THOMAS MOORE: *A Canadian Boat
Song, St. 1*

[2] King Charles I.

RALPH VENNING
[1621–1674]

All the beauty of the world, 'tis but
skin deep.[1]
> > *Orthodoxe Paradoxes* [3d ed.,
> > *1650*], *The Triumph of Assur-*
> > *ance, Page 41*

They spare the rod, and spoyle the
child.[2]
> > *Mysteries and Revelations,*
> > *Page 5*   [1649]

RICHARD RUMBOLD
[1622–1685]

I never could believe that Providence had sent a few men into the
world, ready booted and spurred to
ride, and millions ready saddled and
bridled to be ridden.
> > *On the scaffold* [1685], (*Ma-*
> > *caulay's History of England,*
> > *Chapter 1*)

ALGERNON SIDNEY
[1622–1683]

Manus haec, inimica tyrannis,
Ense petit placidam sub libertate
quietem.[3]
> > *Life and Memoirs of Algernon*
> > *Sidney*

Liars ought to have good memories.[4]
> > *Discourses on Government.*
> > *Chap. 2, Sect. XV* [1698]

---

[1] Many a dangerous temptation comes to
us in fine gay colours that are but skin-deep.
— HENRY: *Commentaries. Genesis, III*

[2] See Skelton, page 9.

[3] This hand, unfriendly to tyrants,
Seeks with the sword placid repose under
liberty.
His father writes to him [August 30, 1660]:
"It is said that the University of Copenhagen
brought their album unto you, desiring you to
write something; and that you did *scribere in
albo* these words." It is said that the first line
is to be found in a patent granted in 1616 by
Camden (Clarencieux). — *Notes and Queries*
[March 10, 1866]
The second line is the motto of the Commonwealth of Massachusetts.

[4] Il faut bonne mémoire, après qu'on a
menti. — PIERRE CORNEILLE: *Le Menteur*
[1642], *Act IV, Sc. 5*
He who has not a good memory should

Men lived like fishes; the great ones devoured the small.[1]

Discourses on Government.
Chap. 2, Sect. XVIII

God helps those who help themselves.[2]

Ibid. Sect. XXIII

It is not necessary to light a candle in the sun.[3]

Ibid.

HENRY VAUGHAN
[1622–1695]

My soul, there is a country
Afar beyond the stars.

Peace. Stanza 1

Search well another world; who studies this,
Travels in clouds, seeks manna, where none is.

The Search

I saw Eternity the other night
Like a great ring of pure and endless light.

The World

The darksome Statesman, hung with weights and woe,
Like a thick midnight fog, moved there so slow. . . .
And clouds of crying witnesses without
Pursued him with one shout.

Ibid.

But felt through all this fleshly dress
Bright shoots of everlastingness.

The Retreat

I see them walking in an air of glory
  Whose light doth trample on my days, —
My days, which are at best but dull and hoary,
  Mere glimmering and decays.

Departed Friends. Stanza 3

---

never take upon him the trade of lying. —
MONTAIGNE: *Book I, Chap. IX, Of Liars*

[1] See Shakespeare, page 106.

[2] See Herbert, page 137.
Heaven ne'er helps the men who will not act. — SOPHOCLES: *Fragment 288* (Plumptre's translation)
Help thyself, Heaven will help thee. — LA FONTAINE: *Book VI, Fable 18*

[3] Like his that lights a candle to the sun. — FLETCHER: *Letter to Sir Walter Aston*
And hold their farthing candle to the sun. — YOUNG: *Satire VII, L. 56*

Dear, beauteous death, the jewel of the just!
Shining nowhere but in the dark;
What mysteries do lie beyond thy dust,
Could man outlook that mark!

Departed Friends. Stanza 5

Then bless thy secret growth, nor catch
At noise, but thrive unseen and dumb;
Keep clean, bear fruit, earn life, and watch
Till the white-wing'd reapers come!

The Seed Growing Secretly

JOHN PLAYFORD
[1623–1686]

Begone, dull Care! I prithee begone from me!
Begone, dull Care! thou and I shall never agree.

Musical Companion [1687]

WILLIAM WALKER
[1623–1684]

Learn to read slow: all other graces
Will follow in their proper places.[1]

The Art of Reading

GEORGE FOX [2]
[1624–1691]

I used in my dealings the word *verily,* and it was a common saying among people that knew me, if George says *verily* there is no altering him.

Journal

The Lord opened unto me that being bred at Oxford or Cambridge was not enough to fit and qualify men to be ministers of Christ.

Ibid.

My relations were much troubled at me that I would not go with them to hear the priest; for I would get into the orchard or the fields with my Bible by myself.

Ibid.

---

[1] Take time enough; all other graces
Will soon fill up their proper places.
JOHN BYROM [1692–1763]: *Advice to Preach Slow*

[2] The founder of the Society of Friends ("Quakers").

When the Lord sent me forth into the world, He forbade me to put off my hat to any, high or low.

Journal

Justice Bennet of Derby, was the first that called us Quakers, because I bid them tremble at the word of the Lord. This was in the year 1650.

Ibid.

He [Oliver Cromwell] said: 'I see there is a people risen, that I cannot win either with gifts, honours, offices or places; but all other sects and people I can.'

Ibid. [*1654*]

RICHARD FRANCK
[1624–1708]

Art imitates Nature, and necessity is the mother of invention.[1]

Northern Memoirs, edited by Scott [written in 1658, published in 1694]

JOHN AUBREY
[1626–1697]

From the Brief Lives, edited by Andrew Clark [1898]

He [Thomas Hobbes] walked much and contemplated, and he had in the head of his staffe a pen and ink-horne, carried alwayes a note-booke in his pocket, and as soon as a thought darted, he presently entred it into his booke, or otherwise he might perhaps have lost it.

Ibid. I, 334

He [Hobbes] had read much, but his contemplation was much more than his reading. He was wont to say that

[1] Necessity, mother of invention. — WILLIAM WYCHERLY [1640–1716]: *Love in a Wood* [1671], Act III, Sc. 3
Necessity, the mother of invention. — GEORGE FARQUHAR [1678–1707]: *The Twin Rivals* [1702], Act I
Magister artis ingenique largitor
Venter
(Hunger is the teacher of the arts and the bestower of invention).
PERSIUS: *Prolog., L. 10*
Sheer necessity, — the proper parent of an art so nearly allied to invention. — R. B. SHERIDAN: *The Critic, Act I, Sc. 2*

if he had read as much as other men, he should have knowne no more than other men.

From the Brief Lives. I, 349

[William Oughtred, mathematician] His wife was a penurious woman, and would not allow him to burne candle after supper, by which means many a good notion is lost.

Ibid. II, 110

Mr. William Shakespear was borne at Stratford upon Avon in the county of Warwick. His father was a butcher, and I have been told heretofore by some of the neighbours, that when he was a boy he exercised his father's trade, but when he killed a calfe he would doe it in a high style and make a speech.

Ben Johnson and he did gather humours of men dayly where ever they came.

Brief Lives. II, 225

JOHN BUNYAN
[1628–1688]

And so I penned
It down, until at last it came to be,
For length and breadth, the bigness which you see.

Pilgrim's Progress. Apology for His Book

Some said, "John, print it"; others said, "Not so."
Some said, "It might do good"; others said, "No."

Ibid.

The name of the slough was Despond.

Ibid. Part I

Every fat must stand upon his bottom.[1]

Ibid.

Dark as pitch.[2]

Ibid.

He came to the house of the Interpreter.

Ibid.

The palace Beautiful.

Ibid.

[1] Every tub must stand upon its bottom. — CHARLES MACKLIN [1697?–1797]: *The Man of the World* [1781], Act I, Sc. 2
[2] RAY: *Proverbs*
GAY: *The Shepherd's Week, Wednesday*

The pilgrim they laid in a large upper chamber, whose window opened toward the sun-rising; the name of the chamber was Peace.

Pilgrim's Progress. Part I

I will talk of things heavenly, or things earthly; things moral, or things evangelical; things sacred, or things profane; things past, or things to come; things foreign, or things at home; things more essential, or things circumstantial.

Ibid.

It beareth the name of Vanity Fair, because the town where 'tis kept is lighter than vanity.

Ibid.

A castle called Doubting Castle, the owner whereof was Giant Despair.

Ibid.

They came to the Delectable Mountains.

Ibid.

Some things are of that nature as to make

One's fancy chuckle, while his heart doth ache.

Ibid. The Author's Way of Sending Forth His Second Part of the Pilgrim

A man that could look no way but downwards with a muck-rake in his hand.

Ibid. Part II

He that is down needs fear no fall.[1]

Ibid. The Shepherd Boy's Song

The first string that the musician usually touches is the bass, when he intends to put all in tune. God also plays upon this string first, when he sets the soul in tune for himself.

Ibid.

My sword I give to him that shall succeed me in my pilgrimage, and my courage and skill to him that can get it. My marks and scars I carry with me, to be a witness for me, that I have fought his battles who now will be my rewarder.

Ibid.

[1] He that is down can fall no lower. — SAMUEL BUTLER: *Hudibras, Part I, Canto 3, L. 878*

So he passed over, and all the trumpets sounded for him on the other side.

Pilgrim's Progress. Part II

The captain of all these men of death that came against him to take him away, was the Consumption, for it was that that brought him down to the grave.

The Life and Death of Mr. Badman

SIR WILLIAM TEMPLE
[1628–1699]

Books, like proverbs, receive their chief value from the stamp and esteem of ages through which they have passed.

Ancient and Modern Learning

No clap of thunder in a fair frosty day could more astonish the world than our declaration of war against Holland in 1672.

Memoirs. Vol. II, Page 255

When all is done, human life is, at the greatest and the best, but like a froward child, that must be played with and humoured a little to keep it quiet till it falls asleep, and then the care is over.

Miscellanea. Part II, Of Poetry

WALTER POPE
[1630?–1714]

May I govern my passions with absolute sway,

And grow wiser and better, as strength wears away,

Without gout or stone, by a gentle decay.

The Old Man's Wish

JOHN TILLOTSON
[1630–1694]

If God were not a necessary Being of himself, he might almost seem to be made for the use and benefit of men.[1]

Sermon

[1] If God did not exist, it would be necessary to invent him. — VOLTAIRE: *A l'Auteur du Livre des trois Imposteurs, Épitre CXL*

They who are in highest places, and have the most power, have the least liberty, because they are most observed.
Reflections

JOHN DRYDEN
[1631–1700]

Above any Greek or Roman name.[1]
Upon the Death of Lord Hastings.
Line 76

And threat'ning France, plac'd like a painted Jove,
Kept idle thunder in his lifted hand.
Annus Mirabilis. Stanza 39

Whate'er he did was done with so much ease,
In him alone, 'twas natural to please.
Absalom and Achitophel. Part I,
Line 27

A name to all succeeding ages curst.
Ibid. Line 151

A fiery soul, which, working out its way,
Fretted the pygmy-body to decay:
And o'er-inform'd the tenement of clay.[2]
A daring pilot in extremity;
Pleas'd with the danger, when the waves went high
He sought the storms.
Ibid. Line 156

Great wits are sure to madness near allied,
And thin partitions do their bounds divide.[3]
Ibid. Line 163

And all to leave what with his toil he won
To that unfeather'd two-legged thing, a son.
Ibid. Line 169

Resolv'd to ruin or to rule the state.
Absalom and Achitophel.
Part I, Line 174

And heaven had wanted one immortal song.
Ibid. Line 197

But wild Ambition loves to slide, not stand,
And Fortune's ice prefers to Virtue's land.[1]
Ibid. Line 198

The people's prayer, the glad diviner's theme,
The young men's vision, and the old men's dream! [2]
Ibid. Line 238

Behold him setting in his western skies,
The shadows lengthening as the vapours rise.[3]
Ibid. Line 268

Than a successive title long and dark,
Drawn from the mouldy rolls of Noah's ark.
Ibid. Line 301

His courage foes, his friends his truth proclaim.
Ibid. Line 357

Let him give on till he can give no more.
Ibid. Line 389

All empire is no more than power in trust.
Ibid. Line 411

Not only hating David, but the king.
Ibid. Line 512

Who think too little, and who talk too much.[4]
Ibid. Line 534

A man so various, that he seem'd to be
Not one, but all mankind's epitome;
Stiff in opinions, always in the wrong,

---

[1] Above all Greek, above all Roman fame.
— POPE: *Epistle I, Book II, L. 26*
[2] See Thomas Fuller, page 147.
[3] No excellent soul is exempt from a mixture of madness. — ARISTOTLE: *Problem, Sect. 30*
Nullum magnum ingenium sine mixtura dementiæ (There is no great genius without a tincture of madness). — SENECA: *De Tranquillitate Animi, 15*
What thin partitions sense from thought divide! — POPE: *Essay on Man, Epistle I, L. 226*

[1] Greatnesse on Goodnesse loves to slide, not stand,
And leaves, for Fortune's ice, Vertue's ferme land.
RICHARD KNOLLES [1550–1610]: *History of the Turks (under a portrait of Mustapha I)*
[2] Your old men shall dream dreams, your young men shall see visions. — *Joel, II, 28*
[3] Like our shadows,
Our wishes lengthen as our sun declines.
YOUNG: *Night Thoughts, Night V, L. 661*
[4] They always talk who never think.—
PRIOR: *Upon a Passage in the Scaligerana*

Was everything by starts, and nothing
   long;
But, in the course of one revolving
   moon
Was chymist, fiddler, statesman, and
   buffoon.[1]
     Absalom and Achitophel.
       Part I, Line 545
So over violent, or over civil,
That every man with him was God or
   Devil.
     Ibid. Line 557
His tribe were God Almighty's gentle-
   men.[2]
     Ibid. Line 645
Large was his wealth, but larger was
   his heart.
     Ibid. Line 826
Him of the western dome, whose
   weighty sense
Flows in fit words and heavenly elo-
   quence.
     Ibid. Line 868
Of ancient race by birth, but nobler yet
In his own worth.
     Ibid. Line 900
Beware the fury of a patient man.[3]
     Ibid. Line 1005
Made still a blund'ring kind of melody;
Spurr'd boldly on, and dashed through
   thick and thin,[4]
Through sense and nonsense, never out
   nor in.
     Ibid. Part II, Line 413
For every inch that is not fool is rogue.
     Ibid. Line 463
Men met each other with erected look,
The steps were higher that they took;

[1] Grammaticus, rhetor, geometres, pictor,
   aliptes,
  Augur, schœnobates, medicus, magus, omnia
   novit
(Grammarian, orator, geometrician; painter,
gymnastic teacher, fortune-teller, rope-dancer,
physician, conjurer, — he knew everything).
— JUVENAL: *Satire III, L. 76*
[2] A Christian is God Almighty's gentleman.
— JULIUS CHARLES HARE [1795-1855]:
Guesses at Truth
  A Christian is the highest style of man. —
YOUNG: *Night Thoughts, Night IV, L. 788*
[3] Furor fit læsa sæpius patientia (An overtaxed patience gives way to fierce anger). —
PUBLIUS SYRUS: *Maxim 289*
[4] See Chaucer, page 6.

Friends to congratulate their friends
   made haste,
And long inveterate foes saluted as they
   pass'd.
     Threnodia Augustalis. Line 124
For truth has such a face and such a
   mien,
As to be lov'd needs only to be seen.[1]
     The Hind and the Panther.
       Part I, Line 33
Of all the tyrannies on human kind
The worst is that which persecutes
   the mind.
     Ibid. Line 239
And kind as kings upon their coronation
   day.
     Ibid. Line 271
Too black for heaven, and yet too white
   for hell.
     Ibid. Line 343
And leaves the private conscience for
   the guide.
     Ibid. Line 478
Eternal house, not built with mortal
   hands!
     Ibid. Line 494
Who can believe what varies every day,
Nor ever was, nor will be at a stay?
     Ibid. Part II, Line 36
All have not the gift of martyrdom.
     Ibid. Line 59
That men may err was never yet de-
   nied.[2]
     Ibid. Line 61
All, as they say, that glitters is not
   gold.[3]
     Ibid. Line 215
When the cause goes hard, the guilty
   man
Excepts, and thins his jury all he can.
     Ibid. Line 242
War seldom enters but where wealth
   allures.
     Ibid. Line 706
Jealousy, the jaundice of the soul.
     Ibid. Part III, Line 73

[1] Vice is a monster of so frightful mien,
  As to be hated needs but to be seen.
  POPE: *Essay on Man, Epistle II, L. 217*
[2] To err is human. — POPE: *Essay on Criticism, Part II, L. 325*
[3] See Chaucer, page 8.

Let the guiltless person throw the stone.[1]

The Hind and the Panther.
Part III, Line 684

Secret guilt by silence is betrayed.

Ibid. Line 763

Possess your soul with patience.

Ibid. Line 839

For those whom God to ruin has design'd,

He fits for fate, and first destroys their
mind.[2]

Ibid. Line 1093

Desperate cures must be to desperate
ills applied.[3]

Ibid. Line 1111

But Shadwell never deviates into sense.

MacFlecknoe. Line 20

And torture one poor word ten thousand ways.

Ibid. Line 208

Our vows are heard betimes! and
Heaven takes care

To grant, before we can conclude the
prayer:

Preventing angels met it half the way,

And sent us back to praise, who came
to pray.[4]

Britannia Rediviva. Line 1

Genius must be born, and never can be
taught.

Epistle to Congreve. Line 60

Be kind to my remains; and oh defend,

---

[1] He that is without sin among you, let him
first cast a stone at her. — *John, VIII, 7*

[2] Quos Deus vult perdere prius dementat
(Whom God wishes to destroy he first de-
prives of reason). The author of this saying
is unknown. It has been ascribed to Euripides
by James Boswell in his *Life of Dr. Johnson,*
Everyman ed., II, p. 443.
When Divine power plans evils for a man,
it first injures his mind. — Sophocles: *Anti-
gone*
When falls on man the anger of the gods,
First from his mind they banish understanding.
Lycurgus
Whom the Gods would destroy they first
make mad. — Longfellow: *The Masque of
Pandora, VI*

[3] See Shakespeare, page 96, and Montaigne,
page 1028.

[4] And fools who came to scoff remain'd to
pray. — Goldsmith: *The Deserted Village,*
l. 180

Against your judgment, your departed
friend!

Epistle to Congreve. Line 72

Better to hunt in fields, for health unbought,

Than fee the doctor for a nauseous
draught.

The wise, for cure, on exercise depend;

God never made his work for man to
mend.

*Epistle to John Dryden of Ches-
terton. Line 92*

Words, once my stock, are wanting to
commend

So great a poet and so good a friend.

*Epistle to Peter Antony Mot-
teux. Line 54*

Wit will shine

Through the harsh cadence of a rugged
line.

To the Memory of Mr. Oldham
Line 15

So softly death succeeded life in her,

She did but dream of heaven, and she
was there.

Eleonora. Line 315

Since heaven's eternal year is thine.

Elegy on Mrs. Killegrew. Line 15

O gracious God! how far have we

Profan'd thy heavenly gift of poesy!

Ibid. Line 56

Her wit was more than man, her innocence a child.[1]

Ibid. Line 70

He was exhal'd; his great Creator drew

His spirit, as the sun the morning dew.[2]

On the Death of a Very Young
Gentleman

Three poets, in three distant ages born,

Greece, Italy, and England did adorn.

The first in loftiness of thought surpass'd;

The next, in majesty; in both the last.

The force of Nature could no further
go,

---

[1] Of manners gentle, of affections mild,
In wit a man; simplicity a child.
Pope: *Epitaph on Gay*

[2] Early, bright, transient, chaste as morning
dew,
She sparkl'd, was exhal'd, and went to
heaven.
Young: *Night Thoughts, Night V, L. 60*

To make a third, she join'd the former
two.[1]
Under Mr. Milton's Picture

From harmony, from heavenly har-
mony,
This universal frame began:
From harmony to harmony
Through all the compass of the notes
it ran,
The diapason closing full in Man.
A Song for St. Cecilia's Day.
Line 11

None but the brave deserves the fair.
Alexander's Feast. Line 15

With ravish'd ears
The monarch hears;
Assumes the god,
Affects to nod,
And seems to shake the spheres.
Ibid. Line 37

Bacchus, ever fair and ever young.
Ibid. Line 54

Rich the treasure,
Sweet the pleasure, —
Sweet is pleasure after pain.
Ibid. Line 58

Sooth'd with the sound, the king grew
vain;
Fought all his battles o'er again;
And thrice he routed all his foes, and
thrice he slew the slain.
Ibid. Line 66

Fallen from his high estate,
And welt'ring in his blood;
Deserted, at his utmost need,
By those his former bounty fed,
On the bare earth expos'd he lies,
With not a friend to close his eyes.
Ibid. Line 78

For pity melts the mind to love.[2]
Ibid. Line 96

Softly sweet, in Lydian measures,
Soon he sooth'd his soul to pleasures.
War, he sung, his toil and trouble;

[1] Græcia Mæonidam, jactet sibi Roma Maro-
nem,
Anglia Miltonum jactat utrique parem
(Greece boasts her Homer, Rome can Virgil
claim;
England can either match in Milton's fame).
SELVAGGI [fl. 1650]: *Ad Joannem*
Miltonum
[2] See Beaumont and Fletcher, page 131.

Honour but an empty bubble;
Never ending, still beginning,
Fighting still, and still destroying.
If all the world be worth thy win-
ning,
Think, oh think it worth enjoying:
Lovely Thais sits beside thee,
Take the good the gods provide thee.
Alexander's Feast. Line 97

Sigh'd and look'd, and sigh'd again.
Ibid. Line 120

And, like another Helen, fir'd another
Troy.
Ibid. Line 154

Could swell the soul to rage, or kindle
soft desire.
Ibid. Line 160

He rais'd a mortal to the skies,
She drew an angel down.
Ibid. Line 169

A very merry, dancing, drinking,
Laughing, quaffing, and unthinking
time.
The Secular Masque. Line 38

The sword within the scabbard keep,
And let mankind agree.
Ibid. Line 61

Fool, not to know that love endures no
tie,
And Jove but laughs at lovers' perjury.[1]
Palamon and Arcite. Book II,
Line 758

For Art may err, but Nature cannot
miss.
The Cock and the Fox. Line 452

Old as I am, for ladies' love unfit,
The power of beauty I remember yet.
Cymon and Iphigenia. Line 1

He trudg'd along unknowing what he
sought,
And whistled as he went, for want of
thought.
Ibid. Line 84

Love taught him shame; and shame,
with love at strife,
Soon taught the sweet civilities of life.
Ibid. Line 133

[1] Dryden repeats this proverb in *Amphi-*
tryon, Act I, Sc. 2
See Shakespeare, page 78.

She hugg'd the offender, and forgave
  the offence:
Sex to the last.[1]

Cymon and Iphigenia. Line 367

And raw in fields the rude militia
  swarms,
Mouths without hands; maintain'd at
  vast expense,
In peace a charge, in war a weak defence;
Stout once a month they march, a blustering band,
And ever but in times of need at hand.

Ibid. Line 400

Of seeming arms to make a short essay,
Then hasten to be drunk, — the business of the day.

Ibid. Line 407

Happy who in his verse can gently steer
From grave to light, from pleasant to
  severe.[2]

*The Art of Poetry. Canto I,
  Line 75*

Happy the man, and happy he alone,
  He who can call to-day his own;
  He who, secure within, can say,
To-morrow, do thy worst, for I have
  liv'd to-day.[3]

*Imitation of Horace. Book III,
  Ode 29, Line 65*

Not heaven itself upon the past has
  power;
But what has been, has been, and I have
  had my hour.

Ibid. Line 71

I can enjoy her while she's kind;
  But when she dances in the wind,
And shakes the wings and will not stay,
I puff the prostitute away.

Ibid. Line 81

---

[1] And love the offender, yet detest the offence. — POPE: *Eloisa to Abelard, L. 192*
[2] Heureux qui, dans ses vers, sait d'une voix
  légère,
  Passer du grave au doux, du plaisant au
  sévère.
      BOILEAU: *L'Art Poétique, Chant 1*
Formed by thy converse, happily to steer
From grave to gay, from lively to severe.
      POPE: *Essay on Man, Epistle IV, L. 379*
[3] See Cowley, page 168.
Serenely full, the epicure would say,
Fate cannot harm me; I have dined to-day.
      SYDNEY SMITH: *Recipe for Salad*

And virtue, though in rags, will keep me
  warm.

*Imitation of Horace. Book III,
  Ode 29, Line 87*

Arms and the man I sing, who, forced
  by fate
And haughty Juno's unrelenting hate.

Virgil, Æneid. Line 1

And new-laid eggs, which Baucis' busy
  care
Turn'd by a gentle fire and roasted
  rare.[1]

*Ovid, Metamorphoses. Book VIII
  Baucis and Philemon, Line 97*

Ill habits gather by unseen degrees, —
As brooks make rivers, rivers run to
  seas.

*Ibid. Book XV, The Worship of
  Æsculapius, Line 155*

She knows her man, and when you rant
  and swear,
Can draw you to her with a single hair.[2]

Persius. Satire V, Line 246

Look round the habitable world: how
  few
Know their own good, or knowing it,
  pursue.

Juvenal. Satire X

Our souls sit close and silently within,
And their own web from their own entrails spin;
And when eyes meet far off, our sense is
  such,
That, spider-like, we feel the tenderest
  touch.[3]

Mariage à la Mode. Act II, Sc. 1

Thespis, the first professor of our art,
At country wakes sung ballads from a
  cart.

Prologue to Lee's Sophonisba

Errors, like straws, upon the surface
  flow;
He who would search for pearls must
  dive below.

All for Love. Prologue

Men are but children of a larger growth.

Ibid. Act IV, Sc. 1

---

[1] Our scanty mutton scrags on Fridays, and
rather more savoury, but grudging, portions of
the same flesh, rotten-roasted or rare, on the
Tuesdays. — CHARLES LAMB: *Christ's Hospital Five-and-thirty Years Ago*
[2] See Burton, page 125.
[3] See Davies, page 115.

Your ignorance is the mother of your
devotion to me.[1]
The Maiden Queen. Act I, Sc. 2
Burn daylight.[2]
Ibid. Act II, Sc. 1
I am resolved to grow fat, and look
young till forty.[3]
Ibid. Act III, Sc. 1
But Shakespeare's magic could not cop-
ied be;
Within that circle none durst walk but
he.
The Tempest. Prologue
I am as free as Nature first made man,
Ere the base laws of servitude began,
When wild in woods the noble savage
ran.
The Conquest of Granada.
Part I, Act I, Sc. 1
Forgiveness to the injured does belong;
But they ne'er pardon who have done
the wrong.[4]
Ibid. Part II, Act I, Sc. 2
What precious drops are those
Which silently each other's track pur-
sue,
Bright as young diamonds in their in-
fant dew?
Ibid. Act III, Sc. 1
Fame then was cheap, and the first
comer sped;
And they have kept it since by being
dead.
Ibid. Epilogue
Death in itself is nothing; but we fear
To be we know not what, we know not
where.
Aurengzebe. Act IV, Sc. 1

When I consider life, 'tis all a cheat.
Yet fool'd with hope, men favour the
deceit;
Trust on, and think to-morrow will re-
pay.
To-morrow's falser than the former
day;
Lies worse, and while it says we shall be
blest
With some new joys, cuts off what we
possest.
Strange cozenage! none would live past
years again,
Yet all hope pleasure in what yet re-
main;[1]
And from the dregs of life think to re-
ceive
What the first sprightly running could
not give.
Aurengzebe. Act IV, Sc. 1
'Tis not for nothing that we life pur-
sue;
It pays our hopes with something still
that's new.
Ibid.
All delays are dangerous in war.
Tyrannic Love. Act I, Sc. 1
Pains of love be sweeter far
Than all other pleasures are.
Ibid. Act IV, Sc. 1
Whatever is, is in its causes just.[2]
Œdipus. Act III, Sc. 1
His hair just grizzled,
As in a green old age.[3]
Ibid.
Of no distemper, of no blast he died,
But fell like autumn fruit that mellow'd
long, —
Even wonder'd at, because he dropp'd
no sooner.
Fate seem'd to wind him up for four-
score years,
Yet freshly ran he on ten winters more;
Till like a clock worn out with eating
time,

---

[1] See Burton, page 126.
[2] See Shakespeare, page 34.
[3] Fat, fair, and forty. — SCOTT: *St. Ronan's Well, Chap. VII*
Lord —— is going to marry Lady ——,
a fat, fair, and fifty card-playing resident of
the Crescent. — MRS. MELESINA TRENCH
[1768–1827], in a letter [Feb. 18, 1816]
[4] Quos læserunt et oderunt (Whom they
have injured they also hate). — SENECA: *De Ira, Lib. II, Cap. 33*
Proprium humani ingenii est odisse quem
læseris (It belongs to human nature to hate
those you have injured). — TACITUS: *Agricola, 42, 15*
Chi fa ingiuria non perdona mai (He never
pardons those he injures). — *Italian Proverb*

[1] There are not eight finer lines in Lucretius. — MACAULAY: *History of England, Chap. XVIII*
[2] Whatever is, is right. — POPE: *Essay on Man, Epistle I, L. 294*
[3] A green old age unconscious of decays. —
POPE: *The Iliad, Book XXIII, L. 929*

The wheels of weary life at last stood
still.
Œdipus. Act IV, Sc. 1
She, though in full-blown flower of glo-
rious beauty,
Grows cold even in the summer of her
age.
Ibid.
There is a pleasure sure
In being mad which none but madmen
know.[1]
The Spanish Friar. Act II, Sc. 1
Lord of humankind.[2]
Ibid.
Bless the hand that gave the blow.[3]
Ibid.
Second thoughts, they say, are best.[4]
Ibid. Sc. 2
He's a sure card.
Ibid.
As sure as a gun.
Ibid. Act III, Sc. 2
This is the porcelain clay of human-
kind.[5]
Don Sebastian. Act I, Sc. 1
I have a soul that like an ample shield
Can take in all, and verge enough for
more.[6]
Ibid.
A knock-down argument: 'tis but a
word and a blow.
Amphitryon. Act I, Sc. 1
Whistling to keep myself from being
afraid.[7]
Ibid. Act III, Sc. 1
The true Amphitryon.[8]
Ibid. Act IV, Sc. 1

[1] There is a pleasure in poetic pains.
Which only poets know.
COWPER: *The Timepiece, L. 285*
[2] Lords of humankind. — GOLDSMITH: *The
Traveller, L. 327*
[3] Adore the hand that gives the blow. —
POMFRET: *Verses to His Friend*
[4] Among mortals second thoughts are the
wisest. — EURIPIDES: *Hippolytus, 438*
[5] The precious porcelain of human clay. —
BYRON: *Don Juan, Canto IV, St. 11*
[6] Give ample room and verge enough. —
GRAY: *The Bard, II, 1*
[7] Whistling aloud to bear his courage up. —
BLAIR: *The Grave, L. 58*
[8] Le véritable Amphitryon
Est l'Amphitryon où l'on dîne

He [Shakespeare] was the man who
of all Modern, and perhaps Ancient
Poets, had the largest and most compre-
hensive soul.
Essay of Dramatic Poesy [1668]
He needed not the spectacles of
Books to read Nature; he looked in-
wards, and found her there.
Ibid.
[Of Chaucer's *Canterbury Tales*]
Here is God's plenty.[1]
Preface to the Fables [1699]

WILLIAM STOUGHTON
[1631–1701]

God sifted a whole nation that he
might send choice grain over into this
wilderness.[2]
*Election Sermon at Boston
[April 29, 1669]*

BISHOP RICHARD
CUMBERLAND
[1632–1718]

It is better to wear out than to rust out.
*Quoted by Bishop George Horne
[1730–1792]: Sermon on the
Duty of Contending for the
Truth*

SIR CHRISTOPHER WREN
[1632–1723]

Whereas, among labourers and others, that ungodly custom of swearing is
too frequently heard, to the dishonour
of God and contempt of authority; and
to the end that such impiety may be utterly banished from these works, which
are intended for the service of God and
the honour of religion, it is ordered that

(The true Amphitryon is the Amphitryon
where we dine).
MOLIÈRE: *Amphitryon, Act III, Sc. 5*
[1] Dryden was buried in the same grave with
Chaucer, in Westminster Abbey.
[2] God had sifted three kingdoms to find the
wheat for this planting. — LONGFELLOW:
Courtship of Miles Standish, IV

profane swearing shall be a sufficient crime to dismiss any labourer.

> *Notice to workmen employed during the building of St. Paul's Cathedral*

WENTWORTH DILLON, EARL OF ROSCOMMON
[1633–1685]

Men ever had, and ever will have, leave
To coin new words well suited to the
    age.
Words are like leaves, some wither ev'ry
    year,
And ev'ry year a younger race succeeds.

> *Translation of Horace's Ars Poetica* [1680] *Line 73*

For Nature forms, and softens us
    within,
And writes our fortune's changes in our
    face.

> *Ibid. Line 130*

The lab'ring mountain scarce brings
    forth a mouse.

> *Ibid. Line 168*

Old men are only walking hospitals.

> *Ibid. Line 202*

Five acts are the just measure of a play.

> *Ibid. Line 226*

And in one scene no more than three
    should speak.

> *Ibid. Line 229*

A string may jar in the best master's
    hand,
And the most skilful archer miss his
    aim.

> *Ibid. Line 387*

Homer himself hath been observ'd to
    nod.

> *Ibid. Line 402*

But words once spoke can never be re-
    call'd.[1]

> *Ibid. Line 438*

[1] Thoughts unexpressed may sometimes fall
    back dead;
    But God himself can't kill them when they're
    said.
        WILL CARLETON [1845–1912]: *The
            First Settler's Story*
Never shall thy spoken word
Be again unsaid, unheard.
        ROSE TERRY COOKE [1827–1892]:
            Unreturning
Four things come not back:

'Tis hard to find a man of great estate,
That can distinguish flatterers from
    friends.

> *Translation of Horace's Ars Poetica* [1680] *Line 478*

True friends appear less mov'd than
    counterfeit;
As men that truly grieve at funerals
Are not so loud, as those that cry for
    hire.

> *Ibid. Line 484*

Remember Milo's end,
Wedged in that timber which he strove
    to rend.

> *Essay on Translated Verse* [1684]. *Line 87*

And choose an author as you choose a
    friend.

> *Ibid. Line 96*

Immodest words admit of no defence,
For want of decency is want of sense.

> *Ibid. Line 113*

The multitude is always in the wrong.

> *Ibid. Line 184*

My God, my Father, and my Friend,
Do not forsake me in my end.

> *Translation of Dies Iræ*

SAMUEL PEPYS
[1633–1703]

I pray God to keep me from being
proud.

> *Diary.*[1] *March 22, 1660*

This morning came home my fine
camlet cloak, with gold buttons, and a
silk suit, which cost me much money,
and I pray God to make me able to
pay for it.

> *Ibid. July 1, 1660*

And so to bed.

> *Ibid. July 22, 1660; December 7, 1660; May 19, 1662; etc.*

The spoken word;
The sped arrow;
Time past;
The neglected opportunity.
        OMAR IBN AL-HALIF: *Aphorism*
[1] So artless in its vanity,
    So fleeting, so eternal,
    So packed with "poor Humanity" —
    We know as Pepys his Journal.
        AUSTIN DOBSON: *Pepys' Diary*, St. 6

I am unwilling to mix my fortune with him that is going down the wind.

Diary. September 6, 1660

I did give ten shillings and no more, though I believe most of the rest did give more, and did believe that I did so too.

Ibid. November 5, 1660

One, by his own confession to me, that can put on two several faces, and look his enemies in the face with as much love as his friends. But, good God! what an age is this, and what a world is this! that a man cannot live without playing the knave and dissimulation.

Ibid. September 1, 1661

Though he be a fool, yet he keeps much company, and will tell all he sees or hears, so a man may understand what the common talk of the town is.

Ibid. September 2, 1661

Besides us and my uncle Fenner's family, there was none of any quality, but poor and rascally people.

Ibid. September 15, 1661

My wife, poor wretch.

Ibid. September 18, 1661;
December 19, 1662; etc.

To the paynter's, and sat and had more of my picture done, but it do not please me, for I fear it will not be like me.

Ibid. December 3, 1661

Thanks be to God, since my leaving drinking of wine, I do find myself much better, and do mind my business better, and do spend less money, and less time lost in idle company.

Ibid. January 26, 1662

Mr. Coventry had already feathered his nest.[1]

Ibid. June 7, 1662

As happy a man as any in the world, for the whole world seems to smile upon me.

Ibid. October 31, 1662

Great talk among people how some of the Fanatiques do say that the end

of the world is at hand, and that next Tuesday is to be the day. Against which, whenever it shall be, good God fit us all!

Diary. November 25, 1662

Bought Hudibras again, it being certainly some ill humour to be so against that which all the world cries up to be the example of wit; for which I am resolved once more to read him, and see whether I can find it or no.[1]

Ibid. February 6, 1663

Got my father, brother Tom, and myself together, and I advised my father to good husbandry, and to be living within the compass of £50 a year, and all in such kind words, as not only made both them but myself to weep.

Ibid. May 1, 1663

No high-flyer.

Ibid. May 27, 1663

Troubled to see my wife forced to sit in the back of the coach, though pleased to see her company none but women and one parson.

Ibid. June 15, 1663

Find myself £43 worse than I was the last month . . . chiefly arisen from my layings-out in clothes for myself and wife; viz., for her about £12, and for myself £55.

Ibid. October 31, 1663

Home, and dined, where I found an excellent mastiffe — his name Towser — sent me by a surgeon.

Ibid. February 17, 1664

To the Trinity House, where a very good dinner among the old soakers.

Ibid. February 15, 1665

I am at a loss to know whether it be my hare's foot which is my preservative, or my taking of a pill of turpentine every morning.

Ibid. March 26, 1665

Thus I ended this month with the greatest joy that ever I did any in my life, because I have spent the greatest part of it with abundance of joy, and honour, and pleasant journeys, and

---

[1] How well I feathered my nest. — RABE-LAIS: *Book II, Chap. 17*

Feather'd well her nest. — DRYDEN: *The Hind and the Panther, Part III, L. 436*

[1] Pepys had bought *Hudibras*, December 26, 1662, but thought it "so silly an abuse of the Presbyter Knight going to the wars" that he sold it the same day.

brave entertainments, and without cost of money.

Diary. July 31, 1665

But Lord! how everybody's looks, and discourse in the street, is of death, and nothing else; and few people going up and down, that the town is like a place distressed and forsaken.[1]

Ibid. August 30, 1665

Saw a wedding in the church; and strange to see what delight we married people have to see these poor fools decoyed into our condition.

Ibid. December 25, 1665

Musick and women I cannot but give way to, whatever my business is.

Ibid. March 9, 1666

The truth is, I do indulge myself a little the more in pleasure, knowing that this is the proper age of my life to do it; and, out of my observation that most men that do thrive in the world do forget to take pleasure during the time that they are getting their estate, but reserve that till they have got one, and then it is too late for them to enjoy it.

Ibid. March 10, 1666

Home, and, being washing-day, dined upon cold meat.

Ibid. April 4, 1666

Anon comes home my wife from Brampton, not looked for till Saturday, which will hinder me of a little pleasure, but I am glad of her coming.

Ibid. April 19, 1666

Musick is the thing of the world that I love most.

Ibid. July 30, 1666

Thus ends this year of publick wonder and mischief to this nation, and, therefore, generally wished by all people to have an end.

Ibid. December 31, 1666

Busy till night, pleasing myself mightily to see what a deal of business goes off a man's hands when he stays by it.

Ibid. January 14, 1667

Did satisfy myself mighty fair in the truth of the saying that the world do not grow old at all, but is in as good

[1] The time of the Great Plague.

condition in all respects as ever it was.

Diary. February 3, 1667

This day I am, by the blessing of God, 34 years old, in very good health and mind's content, and in condition of estate much beyond whatever my friends could expect of a child of their's, this day 34 years. The Lord's name be praised! and may I be thankful for it.

Ibid. February 23, 1667

To church; and with my mourning, very handsome, and new periwigg, make a great show.

Ibid. March 31, 1667

But to think of the clatter they make with his coach, and their own fine cloathes, and yet how meanly they live within doors, and nastily, and borrowing everything of neighbours.

Ibid. April 1, 1667

I have had it much in my thoughts lately that it is not too much for me now, in degree or cost, to keep a coach, but contrarily, that I am almost ashamed to be seen in a hackney.

Ibid. April 21, 1667

Whose red nose makes me ashamed to be seen with him.

Ibid. May 3, 1667

I staid talking below, while my wife dressed herself, which vexed me that she was so long about it.[1]

Ibid. July 14, 1667

Gives me some kind of content to remember how painful it is sometimes to keep money, as well as to get it.

Ibid. October 11, 1667

And there all my Fellow-Officers, and all the world that was within hearing, did congratulate me, and cry my speech as the best thing they ever heard.

Ibid. March 5, 1668

Not to make any more speech, which, while my fame is good, I will avoid, for fear of losing it.

Ibid. March 13, 1668

I find my wife hath something in her gizzard, that only waits an opportunity

[1] In fairness to Mrs. Pepys, it should be added that they were rising at 4 A. M. that warm morning, for a picnic in the country. The account of the day's adventures is so delightful it should be read in full.

of being provoked to bring up; but I will not, for my content-sake, give it.

Diary. June 17, 1668

I by little words find that she hath heard of my going to plays, and carrying people abroad every day, in her absence; and that I cannot but help the storm will break out in a little time.

Ibid. June 18, 1668

In appearance, at least, he being on all occasions glad to be at friendship with me, though we hate one another, and know it on both sides.

Ibid. September 22, 1668

I do hate to be unquiet at home.

Ibid. January 22, 1669

And so I betake myself to that course, which is almost as much as to see myself go into my grave; for which, and all the discomforts that will accompany my being blind, the good God prepare me!

Ibid. May 31, 1669 (final entry)

SIR GEORGE SAVILE, MARQUIS OF HALIFAX
[1633–1695]

Popularity is a crime from the moment it is sought; it is only a virtue where men have it whether they will or no.

Moral Thoughts and Reflections

Misspending a man's time is a kind of self-homicide.

Ibid.

Children and fools want everything, because they want wit to distinguish; there is no stronger evidence of a crazy understanding than the making too large a catalogue of things necessary.

Advice to a Daughter

ROBERT SOUTH
[1634–1716]

Lucid interval.[1]

Sermons. Vol. VIII, Page 403

[1] Lucid interval. — BACON: *Henry VII.* SIDNEY: *On Government, Vol. I, Chap. II, Sect. 24.* FULLER: *A Pisgah Sight of Palestine, Book IV, Chap. II.* PENN: *Some Fruits of Solitude, Preface.* DRYDEN: *MacFlecknoe.* MATHEW HENRY: *Commentaries, Psalm LXXXVIII.*

Speech was given to the ordinary sort of men whereby to communicate their mind; but to wise men, whereby to conceal it.[1]

Sermon [April 30, 1676]

BISHOP THOMAS KEN
[1637–1711]

Teach me to live, that I may dread
The grave as little as my bed.

Morning and Evening Hymn.
Stanza 3

Praise God, from whom all blessings flow!
Praise Him, all creatures here below!
Praise Him above, ye heavenly host!
Praise Father, Son, and Holy Ghost!

Ibid. Stanza 10

SIR CHARLES SEDLEY
[1639–1701]

When change itself can give no more,
'Tis easy to be true.

Reasons for Constancy. Stanza 4

JOHNSON: *Life of Lyttelton.* BURKE: *On the French Revolution*
[1] Speech was made to open man to man, and not to hide him; to promote commerce, and not betray it. — DAVID LLOYD [1635–1692]: *The Statesmen and Favourites of England since the Reformation* [1665, edited by Whitworth], *Vol. I, P. 503*
Men talk only to conceal the mind. — YOUNG: *Love of Fame, Satire II, L. 298*
The true use of speech is not so much to express our wants as to conceal them. — GOLDSMITH: *The Bee, No. 3* [Oct. 20, 1759]
Ils ne se servent de la pensée que pour autoriser leurs injustices, et emploient les paroles que pour déguiser leurs pensées (Men use thought only to justify their wrong doings, and employ speech only to conceal their thoughts). — VOLTAIRE: *Dialogue XIV, Le Chapon et la Poularde* [1766].
When Harel wished to put a joke or witticism into circulation, he was in the habit of connecting it with some celebrated name, on the chance of reclaiming it if it took. Thus he assigned to Talleyrand, in the "Nain Jaune," the phrase, "Speech was given to man to disguise his thoughts." — EDOUARD FOURNIER [1819–1880]: *L'Esprit dans l'Histoire*

SIR EUSTACE PEACHTREE
[*Floruit* 1640]

Among the notionable dictes of antique Rome was the fancy that when men heard thunder on the left the gods had somewhat of special advertisement to impart. Then did the prudent pause and lay down their affaire to study what omen Jove intended.

The Dangers of This Mortall Life

SIR ISAAC NEWTON
[1642–1727]

I do not know what I may appear to the world; but to myself I seem to have been only like a boy playing on the seashore, and diverting myself in now and then finding a smoother pebble or a prettier shell than ordinary, whilst the great ocean of truth lay all undiscovered before me.

Brewster's Memoirs of Newton.
Vol. II, Chap. XXVII

WILLIAM PENN
[1644–1718]

From Fruits of Solitude [*1693*]

A copy of this little book, wrote Robert Louis Stevenson, "I carried in my pocket all about the San Francisco streets, read in street-cars and ferry-boats when I was sick unto death, and found in all times and places a peaceful and sweet companion."

The receipts of cookery are swelled to a volume; but a good stomach excels them all.

Truth often suffers more by the heat of its defenders, than from the arguments of its opposers.

Men are generally more careful of the breed of their horses and dogs than of their children.

It were endless to dispute upon everything that is disputable.

Have a care where there is more sail than ballast.

Passion is a sort of fever in the mind, which ever leaves us weaker than it found us.

The public must and will be served.
Fruits of Solitude

Much reading is an oppression of the mind, and extinguishes the natural candle, which is the reason of so many senseless scholars in the world.

Advice to His Children [*1699*]

HENRY ALDRICH
[1647–1710]

If all be true that I do think,
There are five reasons we should drink:
Good wine — a friend — or being dry —
Or lest we should be by and by —
Or any other reason why.

Five Reasons for Drinking.
From Causae Bibendi,[1] *by John Sirmond* [*1589–1649*]

JOHN WILMOT, EARL OF ROCHESTER
[1647–1680]

Here lies our sovereign lord the king,
Whose word no man relies on;
He never says a foolish thing,
Nor ever does a wise one.

Written on the Bedchamber Door of Charles II

For pointed satire I would Buckhurst choose,
The best good man with the worst-natured muse.[2]

An Allusion to Horace. Satire X, Book I

A merry monarch, scandalous and poor.
On the King

The world appears like a great family,
Whose lord, oppressed with pride and poverty,

---

[1] Si bene commemini, causae sunt quinque bibendi:
   Hospitis adventus; praesens sitis atque futura;
   Et vini bonitas, et quaelibet altera causa.
   Ménagiana [1693], compiled by Giles Ménage [1613–1692], French philologist, who attributed the epigram to Sirmond.

[2] Thou best-humour'd man with the worst-humour'd muse! — GOLDSMITH: *Retaliation, Postscript*

(That to the few great bounty he may
show)
Is fain to starve the numerous train
below.
Like a Great Family
There's not a thing on earth that I can
name,
So foolish, and so false, as common
fame.
Did E'er This Saucy World
Reason, which fifty times to one does
err,
Reason, an ignis fatuus of the mind.
Then Old Age and Experience
Books bear him up a while, and make
him try
To swim with bladders of philosophy.
Ibid.
Then Old Age and Experience, hand in
hand,
Lead him to death, and make him un-
derstand,
After a search so painful and so long,
That all his life he has been in the
wrong.
Ibid.
Dead, we become the lumber of the
world.
After Death
It is a very good world to live in,
To lend, or to spend, or to give in;
But to beg or to borrow, or to get a
man's own,
It is the very worst world that ever was
known.[1]
Epigram

JOHN SHEFFIELD, DUKE OF BUCKINGHAMSHIRE
[1648–1721]

Of all those arts in which the wise excel,
Nature's chief masterpiece is writing
well.
Essay on Poetry
Read Homer once, and you can read no
more;

[1] These four lines are attributed to Rochester, and also to John Bromfield. They were included in a collection of epigrams in 1737.
Washington Irving gave them the title, *Lines
from an Inn Window* and used them on the
flyleaf of the story, *Buckthorne and His
Friends* in *Tales of a Traveller.*

For all books else appear so mean, so
poor,
Verse will seem prose; but still persist
to read,
And Homer will be all the books you
need.
Essay on Poetry
And when I feigned an angry look,
Alas! I loved you best.
The Reconcilement

THOMAS OTWAY
[1651–1685]

O woman! lovely woman! Nature made
thee
To temper man: we had been brutes
without you.
Venice Preserved. Act I, Sc. 1
What mighty ills have not been done by
woman!
Who was 't betrayed the Capital? — A
woman!
Who lost Mark Antony the world? —
A woman!
Who was the cause of a long ten years'
war,
And laid at last old Troy in ashes? —
Woman!
Destructive,   damnable,   deceitful
woman!
The Orphan. Act III, Sc. 1
Let us embrace, and from this very
moment vow an eternal misery together.
Ibid. Act IV, Sc. 2

NAHUM TATE
[1652–1715]
AND
NICHOLAS BRADY
[1659–1726]

Untimely grave.[1]
Psalms. VII
And though he promise to his loss,
He makes his promise good.
Ibid. XV, 5
The sweet remembrance of the just
Shall flourish when he sleeps in dust.
Ibid. CXII, 6
Permit the transports of a British Muse,

[1] An untimely grave. — THOMAS CAREW:
On the Duke of Buckingham

And pardon raptures that yourselves infuse.

NAHUM TATE, *as Poet Laureate, to the Parliament* [*1701*]

THOMAS D'URFEY
[1653–1723]

Of ancient modes and former ways
I'll teach you, Sirs, the manner,
In good Queen Bess's golden days,
When I was a Dame of Honor.

The Dame of Honor [*1706*]. *The World Turned Upside Down*

O'er the hills and far away.

Pills to Purge Melancholy

ANDREW FLETCHER
OF SALTOUN
[1655–1716]

Give me the making of the songs of a nation, and I care not who makes its laws.[1]

Conversation Concerning a Right Regulation of Government for the Common Good of Mankind [*1703*]

NATHANIEL LEE
[1655–1692]

Then he will talk — good gods! how he will talk! [2]

Alexander the Great. Act I, Sc. 3

Vows with so much passion, swears with so much grace,
That 'tis a kind of heaven to be deluded by him.

Ibid.

When Greeks joined Greeks, then was the tug of war.

Ibid. Act IV, Sc. 2

'Tis beauty calls, and glory shows the way.[3]

Ibid.

---

[1] Fletcher's aphorism . . . "Let me make the songs of a people," said he, "and you shall make its laws." — CARLYLE: *Essay on Robert Burns*

[2] See Beaumont and Fletcher, page 131.

[3] "Leads the way" in the stage editions, which contain various interpolations, among them —

Man, false man, smiling, destructive man!

Theodosius. Act III, Sc. 2

JOHN DENNIS
[1657–1734]

A man who could make so vile a pun would not scruple to pick a pocket.

The Gentleman's Magazine. Vol. LI, Page 324

They will not let my play run; and yet they steal my thunder.[1]

JOHN NORRIS
[1657–1711]

How fading are the joys we dote upon!
Like apparitions seen and gone.
But those which soonest take their flight
Are the most exquisite and strong, —
Like angels' visits, short and bright; [2]
Mortality's too weak to bear them long.

The Parting

When after some delays, some dying strife,
The soul stands shivering on the ridge of life;
With what a dreadful curiosity

See the conquering hero comes!
Sound the trumpet, beat the drums! — which was first used by Handel in *Joshua*, and afterwards transferred to *Judas Maccabæus*. The text of both oratorios was written by Dr. Thomas Morell [1703–1784], a clergyman.

[1] Our author, for the advantage of this play ("Appius and Virginia"), had invented a new species of thunder, which was approved of by the actors, and is the very sort that at present is used in the theatre. The tragedy however was coldly received, notwithstanding such assistance, and was acted but a short time. Some nights after, Mr. Dennis, being in the pit at the representation of "Macbeth," heard his own thunder made use of; upon which he rose in a violent passion, and exclaimed, with an oath, that it was his thunder. "See," said he, "how the rascals use me! They will not let my play run, and yet they steal my thunder!" — *Biographia Britannica, Vol. V, P. 103*

[2] Like those of angels, short and far between. — ROBERT BLAIR [1699–1746]: *The Grave* [1743], *L. 588*

Like angel visits, few and far between. — CAMPBELL: *Pleasures of Hope, Part II, L. 378*

Does she launch out into the sea of vast
eternity.

The Meditation

DANIEL DEFOE
[1661-1731]

Wherever God erects a house of prayer,
The Devil always builds a chapel
there;[1]
And 'twill be found, upon examination,
The latter has the largest congregation.

*The True-Born Englishman.
Part I, Line 1* [1701]

He bade me observe it, and I should
always find, that the calamities of life
were shared among the upper and lower
part of mankind; but that the middle
station had the fewest disasters.

Robinson Crusoe. Page 23
[1719]

One day, about noon, going towards
my boat, I was exceedingly surprised
with the print of a man's naked foot on
the shore, which was very plain to be
seen on the sand.

Ibid. Page 179

I let him know his name should be
Friday, which was the day I saved his
life.

Ibid. Page 234

I took my man Friday with me.

Ibid.

SIR SAMUEL GARTH [2]
[1661-1719]

To die is landing on some silent shore
Where billows never break, nor tempests roar;
Ere well we feel the friendly stroke, 'tis
o'er.

*The Dispensary. Canto III,
Line 225* [1699]

I see the right, and I approve it too,

Condemn the wrong, and yet the wrong
pursue.[1]

*Ovid, Metamorphoses, VII, 20
(translated by Tate and Stone-
street, edited by Garth)*

For all their luxury was doing good.[2]

Claremont. Line 149

RICHARD BENTLEY
[1662-1742]

It is a maxim with me that no man
was ever written out of reputation but
by himself.

MONK's *Life of Bentley. Page 90*

The fortuitous or casual concourse of
atoms.[3]

*Works, Vol. III, Sermon VII,
Page 147* [1692]

MATHEW HENRY
[1662-1714]

Many a dangerous temptation comes
to us in fine gay colours that are but
skin-deep.

Commentaries. Genesis, III

To their own second thoughts.

Ibid. Job, VI

He rolls it under his tongue as a sweet
morsel.

Ibid. Psalm XXXVI

Our creature comforts.

Ibid. Psalm XXXVII

None so deaf as those that will not
hear.[4]

Ibid. Psalm LVIII

They that die by famine die by inches.

Ibid. Psalm LIX

---

[1] I know and love the good, yet, ah! the
worst pursue. — PETRARCH: *Sonnet CCXXV,
Canzone XXI, To Laura in Life*
See Shakespeare, page 44.
[2] And learn the luxury of doing good. —
GOLDSMITH: *The Traveller, L. 22.* CRABBE:
Tales of the Hall, Book III. GRAVES: *The Epicure*
[3] That fortuitous concourse of atoms. —
*Review of Sir Robert Peel's Address, in Quar-
terly Review, Vol. LIII, P. 270* [1835]
In this article a party was described as a
fortuitous concourse of atoms, — a phrase
supposed to have been used for the first time
many years afterwards by Lord John Russell.
— *Croker Papers, Vol. II, P. 54*
[4] See Heywood, page 17.

---

[1] See Burton, page 126.
[2] Thou hast no faults, or I no faults can
spy;
Thou art all beauty, or all blindness I.
CHRISTOPHER CODRINGTON [1668-1710]:
Lines Addressed to Garth on His Dispensary

To fish in troubled waters.
> *Commentaries. Psalm LX*

Here is bread, which strengthens man's heart, and therefore called the staff of life.[1]
> *Ibid. Psalm CIV*

Hearkners, we say, seldom hear good of themselves.
> *Ibid. Ecclesiastes, VII*

It was a common saying among the Puritans, "Brown bread and the Gospel is good fare."
> *Ibid. Isaiah, XXX*

Blushing is the colour of virtue.[2]
> *Ibid. Jeremiah III*

None so blind as those that will not see.
> *Ibid. Jeremiah, XX*

Not lost, but gone before.[3]
> *Ibid. Matthew, II*

Better late than never.
> *Ibid. Matthew, XXI*

Judas had given them the slip.
> *Ibid. Matthew, XXII*

After a storm comes a calm.
> *Ibid. Acts, IX*

It is good news, worthy of all acceptation; and yet not too good to be true.
> *Ibid. Timothy, I*

It is not fit the public trusts should be lodged in the hands of any, till they are first proved and found fit for the business they are to be entrusted with.[4]
> *Ibid. Timothy, III*

[1] Bread is the staff of life. — SWIFT: *Tale of a Tub*
Corne, which is the staffe of life. — EDWARD WINSLOW [1595–1655]: *Good Newes from New England, P. 47* [London, 1624]
The stay and the staff, the whole staff of bread. — *Isaiah, III, 1*
[2] Diogenes once saw a youth blushing, and said: "Courage, my boy, that is the complexion of virtue." — DIOGENES LAERTIUS: *Diogenes, VI*
[3] Literally from SENECA: *Non amittuntur sed praemittuntur.* — *Epistola LXIII, 16*
Not dead, but gone before. — SAMUEL ROGERS: *Human Life* [1819]
[4] To execute laws is a royal office; to execute orders is not to be a king. However, a political executive magistracy, though merely such, is a great trust. — BURKE: *On the French Revolution*
When a man assumes a public trust, he should consider himself as public property. — THOMAS JEFFERSON ("Winter in Washington, 1807"), in a conversation with Baron Hum-

THOMAS (TOM) BROWN
[1663–1704]

I do not love thee, Doctor Fell,
The reason why I cannot tell;
But this alone I know full well,
I do not love thee, Doctor Fell.[1]
> *Written while a student at Christ Church, Oxford*

To treat a poor wretch with a bottle of Burgundy, and fill his snuff-box, is like giving a pair of laced ruffles to a man that has never a shirt on his back.[2]
> *Laconics*

In the reign of Charles II. a certain worthy divine at Whitehall thus addressed himself to the auditory at the conclusion of his sermon: "In short, if you don't live up to the precepts of the Gospel, but abandon yourselves to your irregular appetites, you must expect to receive your reward in a certain place which 'tis not good manners to mention here."[3]
> *Ibid.*

boldt. See RAYNER's *Life of Jefferson, P. 356* [Boston, 1834].
The very essence of a free government consists in considering offices as public trusts, bestowed for the good of the country, and not for the benefit of an individual or a party. — JOHN C. CALHOUN: *Speech,* [July 13, 1835]
The phrase, "public office is a public trust," has of late become common property. — CHARLES SUMNER [May 31, 1872]
[1] A slightly different version is found in Brown's *Works,* collected and published in 1707. Dr. John Fell [1625–1686] was Dean of Christ Church and later Bishop of Oxford, and a notable patron of the Oxford University Press. The famous verse is a translation of Martial: —
> Non amo te, Sabidi, nec possum dicere quare;
> Hoc tantum possum dicere, non amo te.
(I do not love thee, Sabidius, nor can I say why; this only I can say, I do not love thee). — MARTIAL: *Epigram I, 33*
> Je ne vous aime pas, Hylas;
> Je n'en saurois dire la cause,
> Je sais seulement une chose;
> C'est que je ne vous aime pas.
COMTE DE BUSSY RABUTIN [1618–1693]
[2] Like sending them ruffles, when wanting a shirt. — SORBIENNE [1610–1670]
GOLDSMITH: *The Haunch of Venison*
[3] Who never mentions hell to ears polite. — POPE: *Moral Essays, Epistle IV, L. 149*

HENRY CAREY
[1663-1743]

God save our gracious king!
Long live our noble king!
  God save the king!
                God Save the King

Namby Pamby's little rhymes,
Little jingle, little rhymes.
       Namby Pamby [1] (*Ambrose*
                 Phillips)

Aldeborontiphoscophornio!
Where left you Chrononhotonthologos?
  Chrononhotonthologos. Act I, Sc. 1

His cogitative faculties immersed
In cogibundity of cogitation.
                   Ibid.

      Let the singing singers
With vocal voices, most vociferous,
In sweet vociferation out-vociferize
Even sound itself.
                   Ibid.

To thee, and gentle Rigdom Funnidos,
Our gratulations flow in streams unbounded.
             Ibid. Sc. 3

What a monstrous tail our cat has got!
     The Dragon of Wantley.
           Act II, Sc. 1

Of all the girls that are so smart,
  There's none like pretty Sally.
She is the darling of my heart,
  And she lives in our alley.
     Sally in Our Alley. Stanza 1

Of all the days that's in the week
  I dearly love but one day,
And that's the day that comes betwixt
  A Saturday and Monday.
        Ibid. Stanza 4

WILLIAM WALSH
[1663-1708]

Of all the plagues a lover bears,
  Sure rivals are the worst.
                Song

I can endure my own despair,
  But not another's hope.
                Ibid.

[1] See Macaulay, page 400.

MATTHEW PRIOR
[1664-1721]

All jargon of the schools.[1]
    I Am That I Am, An Ode

Our hopes, like towering falcons, aim
  At objects in an airy height;
The little pleasure of the game
  Is from afar to view the flight.
    To the Hon. Charles Montague

Odds life! must one swear to the truth
  of a song?
       A Better Answer

Be to her virtues very kind;
Be to her faults a little blind.
      An English Padlock

That if weak women went astray,
Their stars were more in fault than
  they.
         Hans Carvel

The end must justify the means.
             Ibid.

And thought the nation ne'er would
  thrive
Till all the whores were burnt alive.
       Paulo Purganti

They never taste who always drink;
They always talk who never think.[2]
  Upon a Passage in the Scaligerana

And often took leave, but was loth to
  depart.[3]
    The Thief and the Cordelier

Nobles and heralds, by your leave,
  Here lies what once was Matthew
  Prior;

[1] Noisy jargon of the schools. — POMFRET: *Reason*
  The sounding jargon of the schools. — COWPER: *Truth, L. 367*
[2] See Jonson, page 120, and Dryden, page 173.
[3] As men that be lothe to departe do often take their leff [John Clerk to Wolsey.] — HENRY ELLIS [1777-1869]: *Letters, Third Series, Vol. I, P. 262*
"A loth to depart" was the common term for a song, or a tune played, on taking leave of friends. TARLTON: *News Out of Purgatory* [about 1689]. CHAPMAN: *Widow's Tears*. MIDDLETON: *The Old Law, Act IV, Sc. 1*. BEAUMONT AND FLETCHER: *Wit at Several Weapons, Act II, Sc. 2*

The son of Adam and of Eve:
  Can Stuart or Nassau claim higher? [1]
              Epitaph. Extempore
Lays the rough paths of peevish Nature
    even,
And opens in each heart a little heaven.
                        Charity
His noble negligences teach
What others' toils despair to reach.
            Alma. Canto II, Line 7
Till their own dreams at length deceive
    'em,
And oft repeating, they believe 'em.
          Ibid. Canto III, Line 13
Abra was ready ere I called her name;
And though I called another, Abra
    came.
    *Solomon on the Vanity of the
        World. Book II, Line 364*
Who breathes must suffer, and who
    thinks must mourn;
And he alone is bless'd who ne'er was
    born.
        Ibid. Book III, Line 240
A Rechabite poor Will must live,
And drink of Adam's ale. [2]
        The Wandering Pilgrim
In public employments industrious and
    grave,
And alone with his friends, Lord! how
    merry was he!
        For My Own Monument

SIR JOHN VANBRUGH
[1664–1726]
Much of a Muchness.
        *The Provoked Husband.
            Act I, Sc. 1*

SUSANNAH CENTLIVRE
[1667–1723]
The real Simon Pure.
    *A Bold Stroke for a Wife.
            Act V, Sc. 1*

---

[1] The following epitaph was written long
before the time of Prior: —
    Johnnie Carnegie lais heer.
        Descendit of Adam and Eve.
        Gif ony con gang hieher,
        Ise willing give him leve.
[2] A cup of cold Adam from the next purling
stream. — TOM BROWN: *Works, Vol. IV,
P. 11*

JOHN POMFRET
[1667–1702]
We bear it calmly, though a ponderous
    woe,
And still adore the hand that gives the
    blow. [1]
    *Verses to His Friend under
            Affliction*
Heaven is not always angry when he
    strikes,
But most chastises those whom most
    he likes.
                        Ibid.

JONATHAN SWIFT
[1667–1745]
So geographers, in Afric maps,
With savage pictures fill their gaps,
And o'er unhabitable downs
Place elephants for want of towns. [2]
        On Poetry, a Rhapsody
Hobbes clearly proves that every crea-
    ture
Lives in a state of war by nature.
                        Ibid.
So, naturalists observe, a flea
Hath smaller fleas that on him prey;
And these have smaller still to bite
    'em;
And so proceed *ad infinitum.* [3]
                        Ibid.
A college joke to cure the dumps.
            Cassinus and Peter
'Tis an old maxim in the schools,
That flattery's the food of fools;

---

[1] Bless the hand that gave the blow. —
DRYDEN: *The Spanish Friar, Act II, Sc. 1*
[2] As geographers, Sosius, crowd into the
edges of their maps parts of the world which
they do not know about, adding notes in the
margin to the effect that beyond this lies nothing but sandy deserts full of wild beasts and
unapproachable bogs. — PLUTARCH: *Theseus*
[3] Great fleas have little fleas upon their
        backs to bite 'em,
    And little fleas have lesser fleas, and so
        ad infinitum.
    And the great fleas themselves, in turn,
        have greater fleas to go on;
    While these again have greater still, and
        greater still, and so on.
    AUGUSTUS DE MORGAN [1806–1871]:
    A Budget of Paradoxes [1872], *P. 377*

Yet now and then your men of wit
Will condescend to take a bit.
Cadenus and Vanessa
Hail fellow, well met.
My Lady's Lamentation
Conversation is but carving!
Give no more to every guest
Than he's able to digest.
Give him always of the prime,
And but little at a time.
Carve to all but just enough,
Let them neither starve nor stuff,
And that you may have your due,
Let your neighbour carve for you.
Conversation
Under this window in stormy weather
I marry this man and woman together;
Let none but Him who rules the thunder
Put this man and woman asunder.
*Marriage Service from His
Chamber Window*
He [the Emperor] is taller by almost
the breadth of my nail, than any of his
court, which alone is enough to strike
an awe into the beholders.
*Gulliver's Travels. Part I,
Chap. II, Voyage to Lilliput*
Big-endians and small-endians.[1]
Ibid. Chap. IV
It is computed, that eleven thousand
persons have, at several times, suffered
death, rather than submit to break their
eggs at the smaller end.
Ibid.
And he gave it for his opinion, that
whoever could make two ears of corn, or
two blades of grass, to grow upon a spot
of ground where only one grew before,
would deserve better of mankind, and
do more essential service to his country,
than the whole race of politicians put
together.[2]
*Ibid. Part II, Chap. VII,
Voyage to Brobdingnag*

He had been eight years upon a proj-
ect for extracting sunbeams out of cucumbers, which were to be put in phials
hermetically sealed, and let out to warm
the air in raw inclement summers.
*Gulliver's Travels. Part III,
Chap. V, Voyage to Laputa*
Seamen have a custom, when they
meet a whale, to fling him out an empty
tub by way of amusement, to divert him
from laying violent hands upon the
ship.[1]
Tale of a Tub. Preface
Bread is the staff of life.[2]
Ibid.
Books, the children of the brain.
Ibid. Sect. I
As boys do sparrows, with flinging salt
upon their tails.
Ibid. Sect. VII
The two noblest things, which are
sweetness and light.
Battle of the Books
Censure is the tax a man pays to the
public for being eminent.
Thoughts on Various Subjects
Every man desires to live long, but
no man would be old.
Ibid.
If Heaven had looked upon riches to
be a valuable thing, it would not have
given them to such a scoundrel.
*Letter to Miss Vanhomrigh
[August 12, 1720]*
Not die here in a rage, like a poisoned
rat in a hole.
*Letter to Bolingbroke
[March 21, 1729]*
A penny for your thoughts.[3]
Polite Conversation, Introduction
The sight of you is good for sore eyes.[4]
Ibid. Dialogue I

[1] As the political parties of Whig and Tory
are pointed out by the high and low heels of
the Lilliputians (Framecksan and Hameck-
san), those of Papist and Protestant are designated under the Big-endians and Small-endians.
[2] He who makes two blades of grass grow
in place of one renders a service to the State.
— VOLTAIRE: *Letter to M. Moreau* [1765]

[1] In Sebastian Munster's "Cosmography"
there is a cut of a ship to which a whale was
coming too close for her safety, and of the
sailors throwing a tub to the whale, evidently
to play with. This practice is also mentioned
in an old prose translation of the "Ship of
Fools." — SIR JAMES MACKINTOSH: *Appendix
to the Life of Sir Thomas More*
[2] See Mathew Henry, page 188.
[3] See Heywood, page 16.
[4] The sight of me *is* good for sore eyes, as
the Scotch say. — DICKENS: *David Copperfield, Chap. 28*

'Tis as cheap sitting as standing.
Polite Conversation. Dialogue I

I hate nobody: I am in charity with the world.
Ibid.

I won't quarrel with my bread and butter.
Ibid.

She's no chicken; she's on the wrong side of thirty, if she be a day.
Ibid.

She looks as if butter wou'dn't melt in her mouth.[1]
Ibid.

She wears her clothes as if they were thrown on with a pitchfork.
Ibid.

He was a bold man that first eat an oyster.
Ibid. Dialogue II

That is as well said as if I had said it myself.
Ibid.

You must take the will for the deed.
Ibid.

Fingers were made before forks, and hands before knives.
Ibid.

She has more goodness in her little finger than he has in his whole body.
Ibid.

Lord! I wonder what fool it was that first invented kissing.
Ibid.

They say a carpenter's known by his chips.
Ibid.

The best doctors in the world are Doctor Diet, Doctor Quiet, and Doctor Merryman.[2]
Ibid.

I'll give you leave to call me anything, if you don't call me "spade."
Ibid.

---

[1] See Heywood, page 14.
[2] Use three physicians
First, Dr. Quiet;
Next, Dr. Merryman,
And Dr. Dyet.
Regimen Sanitatis Salernitanum
[edition 1607]

May you live all the days of your life.
Polite Conversation. Dialogue II

I have fed like a farmer: I shall grow as fat as a porpoise.
Ibid.

I always like to begin a journey on Sundays, because I shall have the prayers of the Church to preserve all that travel by land or by water.
Ibid.

I know Sir John will go, though he was sure it would rain cats and dogs.
Ibid.

I thought you and he were hand-in-glove.
Ibid.

There is none so blind as they that won't see.
Ibid. Dialogue III

She watches him as a cat would watch a mouse.
Ibid.

She pays him in his own coin.
Ibid.

There was all the world and his wife.
Ibid.

Only a woman's hair.[1]
Written upon a paper that wrapped a lock of hair, found among Swift's effects

I shall be like that tree, — I shall die at the top.
Sir Walter Scott's *Life of Swift* [2]

Ubi saeva indignatio ulterius cor lacerare nequit:

---

[1] "Only a woman's hair!" We may not guess
If 'twere a mocking sneer or the sharp cry
Of a great heart's o'ermastering agony
That spake in these four words.
James Ashcroft Noble [1844–1896]:
Sonnet, Only a Woman's Hair
[2] When the poem of "Cadenus and Vanessa" was the general topic of conversation, some one said, "Surely that Vanessa must be an extraordinary woman that could inspire the Dean to write so finely upon her." Mrs. Johnson smiled, and answered that "she thought that point not quite so clear; for it was well known the Dean could write finely upon a broomstick." — Johnson: *Life of Swift*

"Where savage indignation can no
longer tear his heart."
> *Inscription on Swift's grave,
> St. Patrick's, Dublin*

UNKNOWN
[*Floruit* 1700?]

Sabina has a thousand charms
  To captivate my heart;
Her lovely eyes are Cupid's arms,
  And every look a dart:
But when the beauteous idiot speaks,
  She cures me of my pain;
Her tongue the servile fetters breaks
  And frees her slave again.
> *From Amphion Anglicus* [*1700*].
> *Published in* NORMAN AULT:
> *Seventeenth Century Lyrics*
> [*1928*]

WILLIAM CONGREVE
[1670–1729]

Thus grief still treads upon the heels
  of pleasure;
Married in haste, we may repent at
  leisure.[1]
> *The Old Bachelor. Act V, Sc. 1*

Thou liar of the first magnitude.
> *Love for Love. Act II, Sc. 2*
> [*1695*]

Music hath charms to soothe the savage
  breast,
To soften rocks, or bend a knotted oak.
> *The Mourning Bride. Act I, Sc. 1*
> [*1697*]

By magic numbers and persuasive
  sound.
> *Ibid.*

Heaven has no rage like love to hatred
  turned,
Nor hell a fury like a woman scorned.
> *Ibid. Act III, Sc. 8*

Love's but a frailty of the mind,
When 'tis not with ambition joined:
A sickly flame, which, if not fed, ex-
  pires,

[1] Who wooed in haste and means to repent
at leisure. — SHAKESPEARE: *The Taming of
the Shrew, Act III, Sc. 2, L. 11*

And feeding, wastes in self-consuming
fires.
> *The Way of the World. Act III,
> Sc. 12* [*1700*]

Thou art a Retailer of Phrases, and
dost deal in Remnants of Remnants.
> *Ibid. Act IV, Sc. 9*

If there's delight in love, 'tis when I
  see
That heart which others bleed for, bleed
  for me.
> *Ibid.*

Defer not till to-morrow to be wise,
To-morrow's sun to thee may never
rise.
> *Letter to Cobham*

RICHARD LEVERIDGE
[1670–1758]

When mighty roast beef was the Englishman's food,
It ennobled our hearts, and enriched
  our blood,
Our soldiers were brave and our courtiers were good.
  Oh! the roast beef of old England!
> *The Roast Beef of Old England.
> Stanza 1*

COLLEY CIBBER
[1671–1757]

The aspiring youth that fired the
  Ephesian dome
Outlives in fame the pious fool that
  rais'd it.[1]
> *Richard III (altered).
> Act III, Sc. 1*

As good be out of the world as out of
  the fashion.
> *Love's Last Shift. Act II*

We shall find no fiend in hell can
match the fury of a disappointed
woman.
> *Ibid. Act IV*

Old houses mended,
Cost little less than new before they're
  ended.
> *The Double Gallant. Prologue*

Possession is eleven points in the law.
> *Woman's Wit. Act 1*

[1] See Sir Thomas Browne, page 145.

Words are but empty thanks.
                  Woman's Wit. Act V
This business will never hold water.
      She Wou'd and She Wou'd Not.
                              Act IV
Stolen sweets are best.
              The Rival Fools. Act I
The will for the deed.[1]
                      Ibid. Act III

JOSEPH ADDISON
[1672–1719]

Unbounded courage and compassion
    join'd,
Tempering each other in the victor's
    mind,
Alternately proclaim him good and
    great,
And make the hero and the man com-
    plete.
            The Campaign [2] *[1704]*
                          Line 219
So when an angel, by divine command,
With rising tempests shakes a guilty
    land
(Such as of late o'er pale Britannia
    passed); [3]
Calm and serene he drives the furious
    blast,
And, pleased the Almighty's orders to
    perform,
Rides in the whirlwind and directs the
    storm.[4]
                      Ibid. Line 287
The spacious firmament on high,
With all the blue ethereal sky,
And spangled heavens, a shining frame,
Their great Original proclaim.
      Ode [in The Spectator, No. 465,
                  August 23, 1712]
Soon as the evening shades prevail,
The moon takes up the wondrous tale,
And nightly to the listening earth
Repeats the story of her birth;

---

[1] See Swift, page 192.
[2] Addison wrote *The Campaign* on commission, in honor of Blenheim.
[3] The reference is to the great tempest of
November, 1703, which was the occasion of a
parliamentary address and a public fast.
[4] This line is frequently ascribed to Pope,
as it is repeated in his *Dunciad, Book III,
L. 264.*

While all the stars that round her burn,
And all the planets in their turn,
Confirm the tidings as they roll,
And spread the truth from pole to pole.
      Ode [in the Spectator, No. 465,
                  August 23, 1712]
For ever singing as they shine,
The hand that made us is divine.
                              Ibid.
Should the whole frame of Nature
    round him break,
In ruin and confusion hurled,
He, unconcerned, would hear the
    mighty crack,
And stand secure amidst a falling
    world.
          Horace. Ode III, Book III
The dawn is overcast, the morning
    lowers,
And heavily in clouds brings on the day,
The great, the important day, big with
    the fate
Of Cato and of Rome.
          Cato.[1] Act I, Sc. 1 [1713]
Thy steady temper, Portius,
Can look on guilt, rebellion, fraud, and
    Caesar,
In the calm lights of mild philosophy.
                              Ibid.
'Tis not in mortals to command success,
But we'll do more, Sempronius, — we'll
    deserve it.
                      Ibid. Sc. 2
Blesses his stars and thinks it luxury.
                      Ibid. Sc. 4
'T's pride, rank pride, and haughtiness
    of soul;
I think the Romans call it stoicism.
                              Ibid.
Were you with these, my prince, you'd
    soon forget
The pale, unripened beauties of the
    north.
                              Ibid.
Beauty soon grows familiar to the lover,
Fades in his eye, and palls upon the
    sense.

---

[1] The *Massachusetts Spy* used the following
lines from *Cato* as its motto from November
22, 1771 to April 6, 1775, inclusive:
Do thou Great Liberty inspire our Souls —
    and make our Lives in thy Possession
    happy —
Or, our Deaths glorious in thy just Defence.

The virtuous Marcia towers above her
sex.
Cato. Act I, Sc. 4

My voice is still for war.
Gods! can a Roman senate long debate
Which of the two to choose, slavery or
death?
Ibid. Act II, Sc. 1

The woman that deliberates is lost.
Ibid. Act IV, Sc. 1

Curse on his virtues! they've undone
his country.
Ibid. Sc. 4

What pity is it
That we can die but once to save our
country! [1]
Ibid.

When vice prevails, and impious men
bear sway,
The post of honour is a private station.[2]
Ibid.

It must be so, — Plato, thou reasonest
well!
Else whence this pleasing hope, this
fond desire,
This longing after immortality?
Or whence this secret dread, and in-
ward horror
Of falling into naught? Why shrinks
the soul
Back on herself, and startles at destruc-
tion?
'Tis the divinity that stirs within us;
'Tis Heaven itself that points out an
hereafter,
And intimates eternity to man.
Eternity! thou pleasing, dreadful
thought!
Ibid. Act V, Sc. 1

I'm weary of conjectures, — this must
end 'em.
Thus am I doubly armed: my death
and life,
My bane and antidote, are both before
me:

---

[1] I only regret that I have but one life to
lose for my country. — NATHAN HALE [before
his execution, 1775]

[2] Give me, kind Heaven, a private station,
A mind serene for contemplation!
Title and profit I resign;
The post of honour shall be mine.
GAY: *Fables, Part II, The Vulture, the
Sparrow, and other Birds*

This in a moment brings me to an end;
But this informs me I shall never die.
The soul, secure in her existence, smiles
At the drawn dagger, and defies its
point.
The stars shall fade away, the sun him-
self
Grow dim with age, and Nature sink in
years;
But thou shalt flourish in immortal
youth,[1]
Unhurt amidst the war of elements,
The wreck of matter, and the crush of
worlds.
Cato. Act V, Sc. 1

Sweet are the slumbers of the virtuous
man.
Ibid. Sc. 4

From hence, let fierce contending nations know
What dire effects from civil discord
flow.
Ibid.

For wheresoe'er I turn my ravish'd
eyes,
Gay gilded scenes and shining prospects
rise,
Poetic fields encompass me around,
And still I seem to tread on classic
ground.[2]
A Letter from Italy

Round-heads and wooden-shoes are
standing jokes.
The Drummer. Prologue, Line 8

I shall endeavour to enliven morality
with wit, and to temper wit with morality.
*The Spectator. No. 10,
March 11, 1711*

True happiness is of a retired nature,
and an enemy to pomp and noise; it
arises, in the first place, from the enjoyment of one's self; and, in the next,
from the friendship and conversation of
a few select companions.
Ibid. No. 15, March 17, 1711

---

[1] Smiling always with a never fading serenity of countenance, and flourishing in an immortal youth. — ISAAC BARROW [1630–1677]:
Works, Vol. I, P. 66, Duty of Thanksgiving

[2] Edmund Malone [1741–1812] states that
this was the first time the phrase "classic
ground," since so common, was ever used.

In all thy humours, whether grave or
mellow,
Thou'rt such a touchy, testy, pleasant
fellow;
Hast so much wit, and mirth, and
spleen about thee,
There is no living with thee, nor without thee.[1]

> *The Spectator. No. 68,*
> *May 18, 1711*

There is not a more unhappy being
than a superannuated idol.

> *Ibid. No. 73, May 24, 1711*

The stage might be made a perpetual source of the most noble and
useful entertainments, were it under
proper regulations.

> *Ibid. No. 93, June 16, 1711*

A man that has a taste of musick,
painting, or architecture, is like one
that has another sense, when compared
with such as have no relish of those
arts.

> *Ibid.*

Of all the diversions of life, there is
none so proper to fill up its empty
spaces as the reading of useful and entertaining authors.

> *Ibid.*

There is not so variable thing in nature as a lady's head-dress.

> *Ibid. No. 98, June 21, 1711*

There is no defence against reproach
but obscurity.

> *Ibid. No. 101, June 26, 1711*

Much may be said on both sides.[2]

> *Ibid. No. 122, July 20, 1711*

Authors have established it as a kind
of rule, that a man ought to be dull
sometimes; as the most severe reader
makes allowances for many rests and
nodding-places in a voluminous writer.

> *Ibid. No. 124, July 23, 1711*

Books are the legacies that a great
genius leaves to mankind, which are
delivered down from generation to generation, as presents to the posterity of
those who are yet unborn.

> *The Spectator. No. 166,*
> *September 10, 1711*

Good-nature is more agreeable in
conversation than wit, and gives a certain air to the countenance which is
more amiable than beauty.

> *Ibid. No. 169, September 13, 1711*

Were I to prescribe a rule for drinking, it should be formed upon a saying
quoted by Sir William Temple: the first
glass for myself, the second for my
friends, the third for good humour, and
the fourth for mine enemies.

> *Ibid. No. 195, October 13, 1711*

Physick, for the most part, is nothing else but the substitute of exercise
or temperance.

> *Ibid.*

A salamander is a kind of heroine in
chastity, that treads upon fire, and lives
in the midst of flames without being
hurt.

> *Ibid. No. 198, October 17, 1711*

I consider an human soul without
education like marble in the quarry,
which shows none of its inherent beauties till the skill of the polisher fetches
out the colours, makes the surface
shine, and discovers every ornamental
cloud, spot and vein that runs through
the body of it.

> *Ibid. No. 215, November 6, 1711*

I consider time as an immense ocean,
in which many noble authors are entirely swallowed up.

> *Ibid. No. 223, November 15, 1711*

Those marriages generally abound
most with love and constancy that are
preceded by a long courtship.

> *Ibid. No. 261, December 29, 1711*

A true critick ought to dwell rather
upon excellencies than imperfections, to
discover the concealed beauties of a
writer, and communicate to the world
such things as are worth their observation.

> *Ibid. No. 291, February 2, 1712*

Death only closes a man's reputation,
and determines it as good or bad.

> *Ibid. No. 349, April 10, 1712*

---

[1] A translation of MARTIAL, *XII, 47*, who
imitated Ovid, *Amores, III, 11, 39.*
[2] Much may be said on both sides. — FIELD-
ING: *The Covent Garden Tragedy, Act I, Sc. 8*

Mirth is like a flash of lightning, that breaks through a gloom of clouds, and glitters for a moment; cheerfulness keeps up a kind of daylight in the mind, and fills it with a steady and perpetual serenity.

The Spectator. No. 381,
May 17, 1712

Sir Roger made several reflections on the greatness of the British Nation; as, that one Englishman could beat three Frenchmen; that we could never be in danger of Popery so long as we took care of our fleet; that the Thames was the noblest river in Europe . . . with many other honest prejudices which naturally cleave to the heart of a true Englishman.

Ibid. No. 383, May 20, 1712

Could I transport myself with a wish from one country to another, I should choose to pass my winter in Spain, my spring in Italy, my summer in England, and my autumn in France.

Ibid. No. 393, May 31, 1712

The Fraternity of the Henpeck'd.[1]

Ibid. No. 482, September 12, 1712

It is a celebrated thought of Socrates, that if all the misfortunes of mankind were cast into a publick stock, in order to be equally distributed among the whole species, those who now think themselves the most unhappy would prefer the share they are already possessed of.

Ibid. No. 558, June 23, 1714

Perhaps the most eminent Egotist that ever appeared in the world was Montaigne, the author of the celebrated Essays.

Ibid. No. 562, July 2, 1714

A man should always consider how much he has more than he wants, and how much more unhappy he might be than he really is.

Ibid. No. 574, July 30, 1714

We are always doing something for Posterity, but I would fain see Posterity do something for us.

Ibid. No. 587, August 20, 1714

[1] See Byron, page 358.

EDMOND HOYLE [1]
[1672–1769]

When in doubt, win the trick.
Twenty-four Rules for Learners.
Rule 12

SIR RICHARD STEELE
[1672–1729]

Though her mien carries much more invitation than command, to behold her is an immediate check to loose behaviour; to love her was a liberal education.[2]

Tatler. No. 49

Every rich man has usually some sly way of jesting, which would make no great figure were he not a rich man.

The Spectator. No. 2,
March 2, 1711

When you fall into a man's conversation, the first thing you should consider is, whether he has a greater inclination to hear you, or that you should hear him.

Ibid. No. 49, April 26, 1711

Of all the affections which attend human life, the love of glory is the most ardent.

Ibid. No. 139, August 9, 1711

If we would consider how little of this vicissitude of motion and rest, which we call life, is spent with satisfaction, we should be more tender of our friends, than to bring them little sorrows which do not belong to them.

Ibid. No. 143, August 14, 1711

An old gentleman t'other day in discourse with a friend of his, (reflecting upon some adventures they had in youth together) cry'd out, Oh Jack, those were happy days!

Ibid. No. 153, August 25, 1711

Age in a virtuous person, of either sex, carries in it an authority which

[1] Hoyle published [1742] a *Short Treatise on Whist,* which, in subsequent editions, added rules for playing piquet, backgammon, chess, and other games. His *Laws* [1760] ruled whist-playing until 1864. Hence the saying, "according to Hoyle." His book on chess was reissued in 1808.

[2] Lady Elizabeth Hastings [1682–1739]

makes it preferable to all the pleasures of youth.

The Spectator. No. 153,
August 25, 1711

Among all the diseases of the mind there is not one more epidemical or more pernicious than the love of flattery.

Ibid. No. 238, December 3, 1711

Will Honeycomb calls these over-offended ladies the outrageously virtuous.

Ibid. No. 266, January 4, 1712

I beg of you to burn it when you've read it.

Ibid. No. 274, January 14, 1712

That sex which is therefore called fair.

Ibid. No. 302, February 15, 1712

They that live in a trading street are not disturbed at the passage of carts.

Ibid. No. 479, September 9, 1712

A favour well bestowed is almost as great an honour to him who confers it as to him who receives it.

Ibid. No. 497, September 30, 1712

From the Letters to His Wife [1]

I am come to a tavern alone to eat a stake, after which I shall return to the office.

October 28, 1707

I have partly succeeded in my businesse today, and enclose two guineas. Dear Prue, I can't come home to dinner.

January 3, 1708

I was going home two hours ago, but was met by Mr. Griffith, who has kept me ever since. I will come within a pint of wine.

Eleven at Night, January 5, 1708

A little in drink, but at all times yr. faithfull husband.

September 27, 1708

I am busy about the main chance.

October 13, 1708

---

[1] Selected and collated by R. BRIMLEY JOHNSON [1927]. The letters to Prue (his wife) are a classic of matrimonial humors; the perfect wedding present; what O. Henry would have called "A Handbook of Hymen."

If you do not hear of me before three tomorrow afternoon, believe I am too fuddled to take care to observe yr. orders.

October 25, 1708

The finest woman in nature should not detain me an hour from you; but you must sometimes suffer the rivalship of the wisest men.

September 17, 1712

NICHOLAS ROWE
[1673–1718]

As if Misfortune made the throne her seat,
And none could be unhappy but the great.[1]

The Fair Penitent. Prologue

At length the morn and cold indifference came.[2]

Ibid. Act I, Sc. 1

Is this that haughty gallant, gay Lothario?

Ibid. Act V, Sc. 1

ISAAC WATTS
[1674–1748]

Let dogs delight to bark and bite,
For God hath made them so;
Let bears and lions growl and fight,
For 'tis their nature too.

Divine Songs. XVI

But, children, you should never let
Such angry passions rise;
Your little hands were never made
To tear each other's eyes.

Ibid.

Birds in their little nests agree;
And 'tis a shameful sight
When children of one family
Fall out, and chide, and fight.

Ibid. XVII

---

[1] None think the great unhappy, but the great. — YOUNG: *The Love of Fame, Satire 1,* L. 238

[2] But with the morning cool reflection came. — SCOTT: *Chronicles of the Canongate, Chap. IV*

Scott also quotes it in his notes to *The Monastery, Chap. III, note 11;* and with "calm" substituted for "cool" in *The Antiquary, Chap. V;* and with "repentance" for "reflection" in *Rob Roy, Chap. XII.*

How doth the little busy bee
  Improve each shining hour,
And gather honey all the day
  From every opening flower!
Divine Songs. XX

For Satan finds some mischief still
  For idle hands to do.
Ibid.

Hush, my dear, lie still and slumber!
  Holy angels guard thy bed!
Heavenly blessings without number
  Gently falling on thy head.
A Cradle Hymn

How they served the Lord of Glory
Makes me angry while I sing.
Ibid.

'Tis the voice of the sluggard; I heard
  him complain,
"You have wak'd me too soon, I must
  slumber again."
The Sluggard. Stanza 1

But thanks to my friends for their care
  in my breeding,
Who taught me betimes to love working and reading.
Ibid. Stanza 5

How proud we are! how fond to shew
Our clothes, and call them rich and
  new!
When the poor sheep and silkworm
  wore
That very clothing long before.
Against Pride in Clothes.
Stanza 3

Lord, in the morning thou shalt hear
My voice ascending high.
Psalm V

And while the lamp holds out to burn,
The vilest sinner may return.
Hymns and Spiritual Songs.
Book I, Hymn 88

Strange that a harp of thousand strings
Should keep in tune so long!
Ibid. Book II, Hymn 19

Hark! from the tombs a doleful sound.
Ibid. Hymn 63

The tall, the wise, the reverend head
Must lie as low as ours.
Ibid.

When I can read my title clear
  To mansions in the skies,

I'll bid farewell to every fear,
  And wipe my weeping eyes.
Hymns and Spiritual Songs.
Book II, Hymn 65

There is a land of pure delight,
  Where saints immortal reign;
Infinite day excludes the night,
  And pleasures banish pain.
Ibid. Hymn 66

So, when a raging fever burns,
We shift from side to side by turns;
And 'tis a poor relief we gain
To change the place, but keep the pain.
Ibid. Hymn 146

Were I so tall to reach the pole,
  Or grasp the ocean with my span,
I must be measured by my soul:
  The mind's the standard of the man.
Horæ Lyricæ. Book II,
False Greatness

To God the Father, God the Son,
And God the Spirit, Three in One,
Be honour, praise, and glory given
By all on earth, and all in heaven.
Doxology

WILLIAM SOMERVILLE [1]
[1675–1742]

How humble, and how complaisant
Is the proud man reduced to want!
With what a silly, hanging face
He bears his unforeseen disgrace!
Ready Money

Let all the learned say what they can,
'Tis ready money makes the man.
Ibid.

There is something in a face,
An air, and a peculiar grace,
Which boldest painters cannot trace.
The Lucky Hit

So in each action 'tis success
That gives it all its comeliness.
Ibid.

For what is virtue, courage, wit,
In all men, but a lucky hit?
Ibid.

So, safe on shore the pensioned sailor
  lies,
And all the malice of the storm defies;

[1] Of whom DR. JOHNSON, in his *Lives of the Poets*, made the famous remark: "He writes very well for a gentleman."

With ease of body blest and peace of
mind
Pities the restless crew he left behind;
Whilst, in his cell, he meditates alone
On his great voyage to the world un-
known.
The Author, an Old Man, to
His Arm-chair

JOHN PHILIPS
[1676–1709]

My galligaskins, that have long with-
stood
The winter's fury, and encroaching
frosts,
By time subdued (what will not time
subdue!),
A horrid chasm disclosed.
The Splendid Shilling [1701].
Line 121

SIR ROBERT WALPOLE
[1676–1745]

The balance of power.
Speech [1741]

Flowery oratory he despised. He ascribed to the interested views of themselves or their relatives the declarations of pretended patriots, of whom he
said, "All those men have their price." [1]
WILLIAM COXE [1747–1828]:
Memoirs of Walpole [1798],
Vol. IV, P. 369

Anything but history, for history
must be false.
Walpoliana. No. 141

The gratitude of place-expectants is
a lively sense of future favours.[2]

[1] "All men have their price" is commonly
ascribed to Walpole. See Bulwer Lytton, page
425.
  All who prove that each man has his price.
— AKENSIDE: *An Epistle to Curio*
[2] HAZLITT, in his *Wit and Humour*, says,
"This is Walpole's phrase."
  The gratitude of most men is but a secret
desire of receiving greater benefits. — ROCHE-
FOUCAULD: *Maxim 298*

HENRY ST. JOHN,
VISCOUNT BOLINGBROKE
[1678–1751]

I have read somewhere or other, —
in Dionysius of Halicarnassus, I think,
— that history is philosophy teaching
by examples.[1]
On the Study and Use of History.
Letter 2

The dignity of history.[2]
Ibid. Letter 5

It is the modest, not the presumptuous, inquirer who makes a real and safe
progress in the discovery of divine
truths. One follows Nature and Nature's God; that is, he follows God in
his works and in his word.[3]
Letter to Mr. Pope

GEORGE FARQUHAR
[1678–1707]

Like hungry guests, a sitting audience
looks.
The Inconstant [1702]. *Prologue*

The prologue is the grace,
Each act, a course, each scene, a dif-
ferent dish.
Ibid.

Necessity, the mother of invention.[4]
The Twin Rivals [1702]. *Act I*

Cos. Pray now, what may be that
same bed of honour?
Kite. Oh, a mighty large bed! bigger
by half than the great bed at Ware:
ten thousand people may lie in it together, and never feel one another.
The Recruiting Officer [1706].
Act I, Sc. 1

[1] The contact with manners then is education; and this Thucydides appears to assert
when he says history is philosophy learned
from examples. — DIONYSIUS OF HALICARNAS-
SUS: *Ars Rhet. XI, 2*
[2] HENRY FIELDING: *Tom Jones, Book XI,
Chap. II.* HORACE WALPOLE: *Advertisement to
Letter to Sir Horace Mann.* MACAULAY: *History of England, Vol. I, Chap. I*
[3] Slave to no sect, who takes no private
road,
  But looks through Nature up to Nature's
God.
  POPE: *Essay on Man, Epistle IV, L. 331*
[4] See Richard Franck, page 171.

I believe they talked of me, for they laughed consumedly.

> *The Beaux' Stratagem* [1707].
> *Act III, Sc. 1*

'Twas for the good of my country that I should be abroad.[1]

> *Ibid. Sc. 2*

THOMAS PARNELL
[1679–1718]

Still an angel appear to each lover beside,
But still be a woman to you.

> *When Thy Beauty Appears.*
> *Stanza 3*

Remote from man, with God he passed
the days;
Prayer all his business, all his pleasure
praise.

> *The Hermit. Line 5*

We call it only pretty Fanny's way.

> *An Elegy to an Old Beauty.*
> *Stanza 4*

My days have been so wondrous free
The little birds that fly
With careless ease from tree to tree,
Were but as bless'd as I.

> *Song.[2] Stanza 1*

Let those love now who never loved before;
Let those who always loved, now love
the more.

> *Translation of the Pervigilium*
> *Veneris* [3]

---

[1] Leaving his country for his country's sake.
— CHARLES FITZ-GEFFREY [1575–1638]: *The Life and Death of Sir Francis Drake, St. 213* [1596]
True patriots all; for, be it understood,
We left our country for our country's good.
   GEORGE BARRINGTON [1755–1804]: *New South Wales, P. 152, Prologue Written for the Opening of the Play-house at New South Wales, Jan. 16, 1796*

[2] Set to music by Francis Hopkinson; one of the earliest American songs.

[3] Written in the time of Julius Caesar, and by some ascribed to Catullus:
   Cras amet qui nunquam amavit;
   Quique amavit, cras amet
(Let him love to-morrow who never loved be-fore; and he who has loved, let him love to-morrow).
   Love he to-morrow, who loved never;

EDWARD YOUNG
[1683–1765]

Tired nature's sweet restorer, balmy
sleep!

> *Night Thoughts. Night I, Line 1*

Night, sable goddess! from her ebon
throne,
In rayless majesty, now stretches forth
Her leaden sceptre o'er a slumbering
world.

> *Ibid. Line 18*

Creation sleeps! 'Tis as the general
pulse
Of life stood still, and Nature made a
pause, —
An awful pause! prophetic of her end.

> *Ibid. Line 23*

Poor pensioner on the bounties of an
hour.

> *Ibid. Line 67*

Be wise to-day; 'tis madness to defer.[1]

> *Ibid. Line 390*

Procrastination is the thief of time.

> *Ibid. Line 393*

At thirty, man suspects himself a fool;
Knows it at forty, and reforms his plan;
At fifty chides his infamous delay,
Pushes his prudent purpose to resolve;
In all the magnanimity of thought
Resolves, and re-resolves; then dies the
same.

> *Ibid. Line 417*

All men think all men mortal but themselves.

> *Ibid. Line 424*

Thy purpose firm is equal to the deed:
Who does the best his circumstance allows
Does well, acts nobly; angels could no
more.

> *Ibid. Night II, Line 90*

"I've lost a day!" — the prince who
nobly cried,

To-morrow, who hath loved, persever.
   Translation by THOMAS STANLEY
                              [1625–1678]
Love, oh love upon the morrow,
   You who never loved before;
And if you have loved in old days,
   On the morrow love once more.
   Translation by ZECHARIAH CHAFEE, JR.
[b. 1885], in *The Brunonian*, Brown Uni-
versity [1906]

[1] See Congreve, page 193.

Had been an emperor without his crown.[1]

Night Thoughts. Night II, Line 99

Ah, how unjust to Nature and himself
Is thoughtless, thankless, inconsistent man!

Ibid. Line 112

Whose yesterdays look backwards with a smile.

Ibid. Line 334

Thoughts shut up want air,
And spoil, like bales unopen'd to the sun.

Ibid. Line 466

How blessings brighten as they take their flight!

Ibid. Line 602

Heaven's Sovereign saves all beings but himself
That hideous sight, — a naked human heart.

Ibid. Night III, Line 226

Man wants but little, nor that little long.[2]

Ibid. Night IV, Line 118

A Christian is the highest style of man.[3]

Ibid. Line 788

By night an atheist half believes a God.

Ibid. Night V, Line 177

Early, bright, transient, chaste as morning dew,

---

[1] Once at supper, reflecting that he [Emperor Titus] had done nothing for any that day, he broke out into that memorable and justly admired saying, "My friends, I have lost 'a day!" — SUETONIUS: *Lives of the Twelve Cæsars* (translation by Alexander Thomson)

In the preface to Mr. Nichols's work on autographs, among other albums noticed by him as being in the British Museum is that of David Krieg, with Jacob Bobart's autograph [Dec. 8, 1697] and the verses, —
Virtus sui gloria.
Think that day lost whose descending sun
Views from thy hand no noble action done.
Bobart died in 1719.
Count that day lost whose low descending sun
Views from thy hand no worthy action done.
Staniford: *Art of Reading*, 3d. ed., P. 27 [Boston, 1803]

[2] Man wants but little here below,
Nor wants that little long.
GOLDSMITH: *Edwin and Angelina* [*The Hermit*], St. 8

[3] See Dryden, page 174.

She sparkled, was exhal'd and went to heaven.[1]

Night Thoughts. Night V, Line 600

We see time's furrows on another's brow,
And death intrench'd, preparing his assault;
How few themselves in that just mirror see!

Ibid. Line 627

Like our shadows,
Our wishes lengthen as our sun declines.[2]

Ibid. Line 661

Our birth is nothing but our death begun.[3]

Ibid. Line 719

That life is long which answers life's great end.

Ibid. Line 773

Death loves a shining mark, a signal blow.[4]

Ibid. Line 1011

And all may do what has by man been done.

Ibid. Night VI, Line 606

The man that blushes is not quite a brute.

Ibid. Night VII, Line 496

Too low they build, who build beneath the stars.[5]

Ibid. Night VIII, Line 215

Final Ruin fiercely drives
Her ploughshare o'er creation.[6]

Ibid. Night IX, Line 167

An undevout astronomer is mad.

Ibid. Line 771

The course of Nature is the art of God.[7]

Ibid. Line 1267

The love of praise, howe'er conceal'd by art,
Reigns more or less, and glows in ev'ry heart.

Love of Fame. Satire I, Line 51

---

[1] See Dryden, page 175.
[2] See Dryden, page 173.
[3] See Bishop Joseph Hall, page 121.
[4] See Quarles, page 134.
[5] Inscription on a wall of the Library of Congress, Washington, D. C.
[6] Stern Ruin's ploughshare drives elate
Full on thy bloom.
ROBERT BURNS: *To a Mountain Daisy*
[7] See Sir Thomas Browne, page 144.

Some for renown, on scraps of learning dote,
And think they grow immortal as they quote.
> *Love of Fame. Satire I, Line 89*

They that on glorious ancestors enlarge,
Produce their debt instead of their discharge.
> *Ibid. Line 147*

Unlearned men of books assume the care,
As eunuchs are the guardians of the fair.
> *Ibid. Satire II, Line 83*

Where Nature's end of language is declin'd,
And men talk only to conceal the mind.
> *Ibid. Line 207*

Be wise with speed;
A fool at forty is a fool indeed.
> *Ibid. Line 282*

For her own breakfast she'll project a scheme,
Nor take her tea without a stratagem.
> *Ibid. Satire VI, Line 190*

Think naught a trifle, though it small appear,
Small sands the mountain, moments make the year.
> *Ibid. Line 208*

One to destroy is murder by the law,
And gibbets keep the lifted hand in awe;
To murder thousands takes a specious name,
War's glorious art, and gives immortal fame.
> *Ibid. Satire VII, Line 55*

How commentators each dark passage shun,
And hold their farthing candle to the sun.[1]
> *Ibid. Line 97*

The man that makes a character makes foes.
> *To Mr. Pope. Epistle I, Line 28*

Their feet through faithless leather met the dirt,

[1] See Crabbe, page 280.

And oftener chang'd their principles than shirt.
> *To Mr. Pope. Epistle I, Line 277*

Accept a miracle instead of wit, —
See two dull lines with Stanhope's pencil writ.
> *Lines Written with the Diamond Pencil of Lord Chesterfield* [1]

In records that defy the tooth of time.
> *The Statesman's Creed*

And friend received with thumps upon the back.[2]
> *Universal Passion*

SIR WILLIAM PULTENEY [3]
[1684-1764]

For twelve honest men have decided the cause,
Who are judges alike of the facts and the laws.
> *The Honest Jury*

GEORGE BERKELEY, BISHOP OF CLOYNE
[1685-1753]

Westward the course of empire takes its way; [1]
The four first acts already past,
A fifth shall close the drama with the day:
Time's noblest offspring is the last.
> *On the Prospect of Planting Arts and Learning in America. Stanza 6*

Our youth we can have but to-day,
We may always find time to grow old.
> *Can Love Be Controlled by Advice?* [5]

[Tar water] is of a nature so mild and benign and proportioned to the

[1] Attributed to Alexander Pope by John Taylor [1757-1832].
[2] The man that hails you Tom or Jack,
   And proves, by thumping on your back.
      COWPER: *On Friendship*
[3] One of "the three grand allies," the others being Stanhope and Walpole. Walpole said that he feared Pulteney's tongue more than another man's sword.
[4] See Samuel Daniel, page 30.
   Westward the star of empire takes its way.
— JOHN QUINCY ADAMS [1767-1848]: *Oration at Plymouth* [1802]
[5] In AIKEN: *Vocal Poetry* [London, 1810]

human constitution, as to warm without heating, to cheer but not inebriate.[1]

Siris. Par. 217

He who says there is no such thing
as an honest man, you may be sure is
himself a knave.

Maxims Concerning Patriotism

Ferments of the worst kind succeed
to perfect inaction.

Ibid.

JANE BRERETON
[1685–1740]

The picture placed the busts between
　Adds to the thought much strength;
Wisdom and Wit are little seen,
　But Folly's at full length.

*On Beau Nash's Picture at Full
Length between the Busts of Sir
Isaac Newton and Mr. Pope.*[2]

AARON HILL
[1685–1750]

When Christ at Cana's feast by power
　divine
Inspired cold water with the warmth
　of wine,
"See," cried they, while in redding tide
　it gushed,
"The bashful stream hath seen its God
　and blushed."[3]

Translation from the Latin

First, then, a woman will or won't, de-
　pend on 't;
If she will do 't she will; and there's
　an end on 't.
But if she won't, since safe and sound
　your trust is,
Fear is affront, and jealousy injustice.[4]

Zara. Epilogue

[1]　　　　　　　　Cups
　That cheer but not inebriate.
　　　　COWPER: *The Task, Book IV*
[2] In ALEXANDER DYCE [1798–1869]: *Specimens of British Poetesses.* (This epigram is
generally ascribed to Chesterfield. See CAMP-
BELL: *English Poets, note, P. 521.*)
[3] See Crashaw, page 165.
[4] The following lines are copied from the
pillar erected on the mount in the Dane John
Field, Canterbury: —
Where is the man who has the power and
　skill
To stem the torrent of a woman's will?

Tender-handed stroke a nettle,
　And it stings you for your pains;
Grasp it like a man of mettle,
　And it soft as silk remains.

'Tis the same with common natures:
　Use 'em kindly, they rebel;
But be rough as nutmeg-graters,
　And the rogues obey you well.

*Verses Written on a Window
in Scotland*

SAMUEL MADDEN
[1686–1765]

Some write their wrongs in marble: he
　more just,
Stoop'd down serene and wrote them
　in the dust, —
Trod under foot, the sport of every
　wind,
Swept from the earth and blotted from
　his mind.
There, secret in the grave, he bade
　them lie,
And grieved they could not 'scape the
　Almighty eye.

Boulter's Monument

Words are men's daughters, but God's
　sons are things.[1]

Ibid.

In an orchard there should be enough
to eat, enough to lay up, enough to be
stolen, and enough to rot upon the
ground.

*Quoted by Samuel Johnson
(Boswell's Life of Dr. Johnson,
Vol. II, Page 457, Everyman
edition)*

ALLAN RAMSAY
[1686–1758]

My Peggy is a young thing,
　Just entered in her teens.

Peggy

Farewell to Lochaber, farewell to my
　Jean,

For if she will, she will, you may depend on 't;
And if she won't, she won't; so there's an
　end on 't.
　　　　　The Examiner [May 31, 1829]
[1] Words are women, deeds are men. —
GEORGE HERBERT: *Jacula Prudentum*
See Johnson, page 232.

Where heartsome wi' thee I hae mony
  days been;
For Lochaber no more, Lochaber no
  more,
We'll maybe return to Lochaber no
  more.
        Lochaber No More. Stanza 1

THOMAS TICKELL
[1686–1740]

Just men, by whom impartial laws were
  given;
And saints who taught and led the way
  to heaven.
        On the Death of Mr. Addison.
        Line 41
Nor e'er was to the bowers of bliss con-
  veyed
A fairer spirit or more welcome shade.
        Ibid. Line 45
There taught us how to live; and (oh,
  too high
The price for knowledge!) taught us
  how to die.[1]
        Ibid. Line 81
The sweetest garland to the sweetest
  maid.
        To a Lady with a Present of
        Flowers
I hear a voice you cannot hear,
  Which says I must not stay;
I see a hand you cannot see,
  Which beckons me away.[2]
        Colin and Lucy. Stanza 7

LAURENCE EUSDEN
[1688–1730]

A woman's work, grave sirs, is never
  done.[3]
        At a Cambridge Commencement
        [second edition, 1714]

[1] He who should teach men to die, would
at the same time teach them to live. — MON-
TAIGNE: *Essays, Book I, Chap. 9*
  I have taught you, my dear flock, for above
thirty years how to live, and I will show you
in a very short time how to die. — SIR EDWIN
SANDYS [1561–1629]: *Anglorum Speculum,
P. 903*
  [2] Scott used this as a heading for Chapter
17 of *Rob Roy.*
  [3] Man may work from sun to sun
    But woman's work is never done.
        Traditional version; origin unknown.

JOHN GAY
[1688–1732]

'Twas when the sea was roaring
With hollow blasts of wind,
A damsel lay deploring,
All on a rock reclin'd.
        The What d'ye Call It.
        Act II, Sc. 8
So comes a reckoning when the ban-
  quet's o'er, —
The dreadful reckoning, and men smile
  no more.[1]
        Ibid. Sc. 9
'Tis woman that seduces all mankind;
By her we first were taught the whee-
  dling arts.
        The Beggar's Opera. Act I, Sc. 1
Over the hills and far away.
        Ibid.
If the heart of a man is depress'd with
  cares,
The mist is dispell'd when a woman
  appears.
        Ibid. Act II, Sc. 1
The fly that sips treacle is lost in the
  sweets.
        Ibid. Sc. 2
How happy could I be with either,
Were t'other dear charmer away!
        Ibid.
The charge is prepar'd, the lawyers are
  met,
The judges all ranged, — a terrible
  show!
        Ibid. Act III, Sc. 2
All in the Downs the fleet was moor'd.
        Sweet William's Farewell to
        Black-eyed Susan
Adieu, she cried, and waved her lily
  hand.
        Ibid.
My lodging is on the cold ground,
  And hard, very hard, is my fare,
But that which grieves me more
  Is the coldness of my dear.
        My Lodging is on the Cold
        Ground. Stanza 1

[1] The time of paying a shot in a tavern
among good fellows, or Pantagruelists, is still
called in France a "quart d'heure de Rabelais,"
— that is, Rabelais's quarter of an hour, when
a man is uneasy or melancholy. — *Life of
Rabelais* (Bohn's edition), *P. 13*

Remote from cities liv'd a swain,
Unvex'd with all the cares of gain;
His head was silver'd o'er with age,
And long experience made him sage.
> *Fables. Part I, The Shepherd*
> *and the Philosopher*

Whence is thy learning? Hath thy toil
O'er books consum'd the midnight oil? [1]
> *Ibid.*

Where yet was ever found a mother
Who'd give her booby for another?
> *The Mother, the Nurse, and*
> *the Fairy*

When we risk no contradiction,
It prompts the tongue to deal in fiction.
> *The Elephant and the Bookseller*

Lest men suspect your tale untrue,
Keep probability in view.
> *The Painter who Pleased No-*
> *body and Everybody*

In ev'ry age and clime we see
Two of a trade can never agree. [2]
> *The Rat-catcher and Cats*

Is there no hope? the sick man said;
The silent doctor shook his head.
> *The Sick Man and the Angel*

While there is life there's hope, he
cried. [3]
> *Ibid.*

Those who in quarrels interpose
Must often wipe a bloody nose.
> *The Mastiffs*

That raven on yon left-hand oak
(Curse on his ill-betiding croak!)
  Bodes me no good. [4]
> *The Farmer's Wife and the Raven*

---

[1] "Midnight oil," — a common phrase, used by Quarles, Shenstone, Cowper, Lloyd, and others.

[2] Potter is jealous of potter, and craftsman of craftsman; and poor man has a grudge against poor man, and poet against poet. — HESIOD: *Works and Days, 24*

Le potier au potier porte envie (The potter envies the potter). — BOHN: *Handbook of Proverbs.*

[3] For the living there is hope, but for the dead there is none. — THEOCRITUS: *Idyl IV, 42*

Ægroto, dum anima est, spes est (While the sick man has life, there is hope). — CICERO: *Epistolarum ad Atticum, IX, 10*

[4] It wasn't for nothing that the raven was just now croaking on my left hand. — PLAUTUS: *Aulularia, Act IV, Sc. 3*

I hate the man who builds his name
On ruins of another's fame.
> *The Poet and the Rose*

The child whom many fathers share
Hath seldom known a father's care.
> *Fables. Part I, The Hare and*
> *Many Friends*

And when a lady's in the case,
You know all other things give place.
> *Ibid.*

Give me, kind Heaven, a private sta-
tion,
A mind serene for contemplation:
Title and profit I resign;
The post of honour shall be mine. [1]
> *Ibid. Part II, The Vulture, the*
> *Sparrow, and Other Birds*

From wine what sudden friendship
springs!
> *The Squire and His Cur*

Life is a jest, and all things show it;
I thought so once, but now I know it.
> *My Own Epitaph*

ALEXANDER POPE [2]
[1688–1744]

Awake, my St. John! leave all meaner
things
To low ambition and the pride of kings.
Let us, since life can little more supply
Than just to look about us, and to die,
Expatiate free o'er all this scene of
man;
A mighty maze! but not without a
plan.
> *Essay on Man. Epistle I, Line 1*

Eye Nature's walks, shoot folly as it
flies,
And catch the manners living as they
rise;
Laugh where we must, be candid where
we can,
But vindicate the ways of God to man.
> *Ibid. Line 13*

---

[1] When vice prevails, and impious men bear
sway,
  The post of honour is a private station.
> ADDISON: *Cato, Act IV, Sc. 4*

[2] A thousand years may elapse before there shall appear another man with a power of versification equal to that of Pope. — DR JOHNSON

Say first, of God above or man below,
What can we reason but from what we
know?
Essay on Man. Epistle I, Line 17

Heaven from all creatures hides the
book of Fate,
All but the page prescrib'd, their present state.
Ibid. Line 77

Pleased to the last, he crops the flowery
food,
And licks the hand just raised to shed
his blood.
Ibid. Line 83

Who sees with equal eye, as God of all,
A hero perish or a sparrow fall,
Atoms or systems into ruin hurl'd,
And now a bubble burst, and now a
world.
Ibid. Line 87

Hope springs eternal in the human
breast:
Man never is, but always to be, blest.
Ibid. Line 95

Lo, the poor Indian! whose untutor'd
mind
Sees God in clouds, or hears him in the
wind;
His soul proud Science never taught to
stray
Far as the solar walk or milky way.
Ibid. Line 99

But thinks, admitted to that equal sky,
His faithful dog shall bear him com-
pany.
Ibid. Line 111

Seas roll to waft me, suns to light me
rise;
My footstool earth, my canopy the
skies.[1]
Ibid. Line 139

Die of a rose in aromatic pain.
Ibid. Line 200

The spider's touch, how exquisitely
fine,

[1] All the parts of the universe I have an
interest in: the earth serves me to walk upon;
the sun to light me; the stars have their influence upon me. — MONTAIGNE: *Apology for
Raimond Sebond*

Feels at each thread, and lives along
the line.[1]
Essay on Man. Epistle I, Line 217

Remembrance and reflection how allied!
What thin partitions sense from
thought divide! [2]
Ibid. Line 225

All are but parts of one stupendous
whole,
Whose body Nature is, and God the
soul.
Ibid. Line 267

As full, as perfect, in vile man that
mourns
As the rapt seraph that adores and
burns.
To Him no high, no low, no great, no
small; [3]
He fills, he bounds, connects, and equals
all!
Ibid. Line 277

All nature is but art, unknown to thee;
All chance, direction, which thou canst
not see;
All discord, harmony not understood;
All partial evil, universal good;
And spite of pride, in erring reason's
spite,
One truth is clear, Whatever is, is
right.[4]
Ibid. Line 289

Know then thyself, presume not God
to scan;
The proper study of mankind is man.[5]
Ibid. Epistle II, Line 1

Chaos of thought and passion, all con-
fused;
Still by himself abused or disabused;
Created half to rise, and half to fall;
Great lord of all things, yet a prey to
all;

[1] See Sir John Davies, page 115.
[2] See Dryden, page 173.
[3] There is no great and no small. — EMER-
SON: *Epigraph to History*
[4] See Dryden, page 178.
[5] La vray science et le vray étude de
l'homme, c'est l'homme (The true science and
the true study of man is man). — PIERRE
CHARRON [1541-1603]: *Traité de la Sagesse*
[1601], *Book I, Preface*
  Trees and fields tell me nothing: men are
my teachers. — PLATO: *Phædrus*

Sole judge of truth, in endless error
hurled;
The glory, jest, and riddle of the world.
Essay on Man. Epistle II, Line 13
Fix'd like a plant on his peculiar spot,
To draw nutrition, propagate, and rot.
Ibid. Line 63
On life's vast ocean diversely we sail,
Reason the card, but passion is the gale.
Ibid. Line 107
And hence one master-passion in the
breast,
Like Aaron's serpent, swallows up the
rest.[1]
Ibid. Line 131
The young disease, that must subdue
at length,
Grows with his growth, and strength-
ens with his strength.
Ibid. Line 135
Vice is a monster of so frightful mien,
As to be hated needs but to be seen;
Yet seen too oft, familiar with her face,
We first endure, then pity, then em-
brace.
Ibid. Line 217
Behold the child, by Nature's kindly
law,
Pleased with a rattle, tickled with a
straw:
Some livelier plaything gives his youth
delight,
A little louder, but as empty quite:
Scarfs, garters, gold, amuse his riper
stage,
And beads and prayer-books are the
toys of age.
Pleased with this bauble still, as that
before,
Till tired he sleeps, and life's poor play
is o'er.
Ibid. Line 274
Learn of the little nautilus to sail,
Spread the thin oar, and catch the driv-
ing gale.
Ibid. Epistle III, Line 177
For forms of government let fools con-
test;
Whate'er is best administer'd is best:

[1] For they cast down every man his rod,
and they became serpents: but Aaron's rod
swallowed up their rods. — Exodus, VII, 12

For modes of faith let graceless zealots
fight;
His can't be wrong whose life is in the
right.
In faith and hope the world will dis-
agree,
But all mankind's concern is charity.
Essay on Man. Epistle III, Line 303
O happiness! our being's end and aim!
Good, pleasure, ease, content! whate'er
thy name:
That something still which prompts the
eternal sigh,
For which we bear to live, or dare to
die.
Ibid. Epistle IV, Line 1
Reason's whole pleasure, all the joys of
sense,
Lie in three words — health, peace, and
competence.
Ibid. Line 79
Worth makes the man, and want of it
the fellow;
The rest is all but leather or prunella.
Ibid. Line 203
What can ennoble sots or slaves or
cowards?
Alas! not all the blood of all the How-
ards.
Ibid. Line 215
A wit's a feather, and a chief a rod;
An honest man's the noblest work of
God.
Ibid. Line 247
One self-approving hour whole years
outweighs
Of stupid starers and of loud huzzas:
And more true joy Marcellus exil'd feels
Than Caesar with a senate at his heels.
Ibid. Line 255
If parts allure thee, think how Bacon
shin'd,
The wisest, brightest, meanest of man-
kind!
Or ravish'd with the whistling of a
name,
See Cromwell, damn'd to everlasting
fame!
Ibid. Line 281
Slave to no sect, who takes no private
road,

But looks through Nature up to Nature's God.[1]

Essay on Man. Epistle IV, Line 331

Form'd by thy converse, happily to steer
From grave to gay, from lively to severe.[2]

Ibid. Line 379

Say, shall my little bark attendant sail,
Pursue the triumph and partake the gale?

Ibid. Line 385

Thou wert my guide, philosopher, and friend.[3]

Ibid. Line 390

The fate of all extremes is such:
Men may be read, as well as books, too much.

Moral Essays. Epistle I, Line 9

To observations which ourselves we make,
We grow more partial for th' observer's sake.

Ibid. Line 11

Like following life through creatures you dissect,
You lose it in the moment you detect.

Ibid. Line 29

Not always actions show the man; we find
Who does a kindness is not therefore kind.

Ibid. Line 109

Who combats bravely is not therefore brave,
He dreads a death-bed like the meanest slave

Who reasons wisely is not therefore wise;
His pride in reasoning, not in acting, lies.

Ibid. Line 115

'Tis education forms the common mind:
Just as the twig is bent the tree's inclined.

Ibid. Line 149

Manners with fortunes, humours turn with climes,

Tenets with books, and principles with times.[1]

Moral Essays. Epistle I, Line 172

"Odious! in woollen! 'twould a saint provoke,"
Were the last words that poor Narcissa spoke.

Ibid. Line 246

Give this cheek a little red.

Ibid. Line 251

And you, brave Cobham! to the latest breath
Shall feel your ruling passion strong in death.

Ibid. Line 262

Most women have no characters at all.

Ibid. Epistle II, Line 2

Whether the charmer sinner it or saint it,
If folly grow romantic, I must paint it.

Ibid. Line 15

Choose a firm cloud before it fall, and in it
Catch, ere she change, the Cynthia of this minute.

Ibid. Line 19

Fine by defect, and delicately weak.

Ibid. Line 43

With too much quickness ever to be taught;
With too much thinking to have common thought.

Ibid. Line 97

Men, some to business, some to pleasure take;
But every woman is at heart a rake.

Ibid. Line 215

She who ne'er answers till a husband cools,
Or if she rules him, never shows she rules.

Ibid. Line 261

And mistress of herself though china fall.

Ibid. Line 268

Woman's at best a contradiction still.

Ibid. Line 270

---

[1] See Bolingbroke, page 200.
[2] See Dryden, page 177.
[3] Is this my guide, philosopher, and friend?
— POPE: *Epistle I, Book I, L. 177*

[1] Omnia mutantur, nos et mutamur in illis (All things change, and we change with them). — MATTHIAS BORBONIUS: *Deliciæ Poetarum Germanorum, I, 685*

Who shall decide when doctors dis-
agree?
  Moral Essays. Epistle III, Line 1
Blest paper-credit! last and best sup-
ply!
That lends corruption lighter wings to
fly!
     Ibid. Line 39
But thousands die without or this or
that,
Die, and endow a college or a cat.
     Ibid. Line 95
The ruling passion, be it what it will,
The ruling passion conquers reason
still.
     Ibid. Line 153
Ye little stars! hide your diminish'd
rays.[1]
     Ibid. Line 282
Who builds a church to God, and not
to fame,
Will never mark the marble with his
name.
     Ibid. Line 285
Where London's column, pointing at
the skies,
Like a tall bully, lifts the head and lies.[2]
     Ibid. Line 339
Satan now is wiser than of yore,
And tempts by making rich, not mak-
ing poor.
     Ibid. Line 351
Good sense, which only is the gift of
Heaven,
And though no science, fairly worth the
seven.
    Ibid. Epistle IV, Line 43
To rest, the cushion and soft dean in-
vite,
Who never mentions hell to ears polite.[3]
     Ibid. Line 149
Statesman, yet friend to truth; of soul
sincere,
In action faithful, and in honour clear;
Who broke no promise, serv'd no pri-
vate end,

Who gain'd no title, and who lost no
friend.
    Moral Essays. Epistle V,
     To Mr. Addison, Line 67
'Tis with our judgments as our watches,
none
Go just alike, yet each believes his
own.[1]
   Essay on Criticism. Part I, Line 9
One science only will one genius fit;
So vast is art, so narrow human wit.
     Ibid. Line 60
Be Homer's works your study and de-
light,
Read them by day, and meditate by
night.
     Ibid. Line 124
Music resembles poetry; in each
Are nameless graces which no methods
teach,
And which a master-hand alone can
reach.
     Ibid. Line 143
Those oft are stratagems which errors
seem,
Nor is it Homer nods, but we that
dream.[2]
     Ibid. Line 177
Of all the causes which conspire to
blind
Man's erring judgment, and misguide
the mind,
What the weak head with strongest
bias rules,
Is pride, the never-failing vice of fools.
     Ibid. Part II, Line 1
A little learning is a dangerous thing; [3]
Drink deep, or taste not the Pierian
spring:
There shallow draughts intoxicate the
brain,
And drinking largely sobers us again.
     Ibid. Line 15
Hills peep o'er hills, and Alps on Alps
arise!
     Ibid. Line 32
Whoever thinks a faultless piece to see,

---

[1] See Milton, page 151.
[2] Viz. the monument (near London Bridge)
built in memory of the great fire of 1666,
with an inscription attributing the disaster
to a Popish plot.
[3] See Tom Brown, page 188.

[1] See Suckling, page 164.
[2] Quandoque bonus dormitat Homerus
(Even the worthy Homer some times nods).
—HORACE: *De Arte Poetica, 359*
[3] See Bacon, page 110.

Thinks what ne'er was, nor is, nor e'er shall be.[1]

Essay on Criticism. Part II, Line 53

True wit is Nature to advantage dress'd,
What oft was thought, but ne'er so well express'd.

Ibid. Line 97

Words are like leaves; and where they most abound,
Much fruit of sense beneath is rarely found.

Ibid. Line 109

Such labour'd nothings, in so strange a style,
Amaze th' unlearn'd, and make the learned smile.

Ibid. Line 126

In words, as fashions, the same rule will hold,
Alike fantastic if too new or old:
Be not the first by whom the new are tried,
Nor yet the last to lay the old aside.

Ibid. Line 133

Some to church repair,
Not for the doctrine, but the music there.
These equal syllables alone require,
Though oft the ear the open vowels tire;
While expletives their feeble aid do join,
And ten low words oft creep in one dull line.

Ibid. Line 142

A needless Alexandrine ends the song,
That like a wounded snake, drags its slow length along.

Ibid. Line 156

True ease in writing comes from art, not chance,[1]
As those move easiest who have learn'd to dance.
'Tis not enough no harshness gives offence;
The sound must seem an echo to the sense.

Ibid. Line 162

[1] See Suckling, page 164.
[2] Also in *Epistle II, Book II, L. 178*

Soft is the strain when zephyr gently blows,
And the smooth stream in smoother numbers flows;
But when loud surges lash the sounding shore,
The hoarse rough verse should like the torrent roar.
When Ajax strives some rock's vast weight to throw,
The line, too, labours, and the words move slow:
Not so when swift Camilla scours the plain,
Flies o'er th' unbending corn, and skims along the main.

Essay on Criticism. Part II, Line 166

At ev'ry trifle scorn to take offence.

Ibid. Line 186

Yet let not each gay turn thy rapture move;
For fools admire, but men of sense approve.

Ibid. Line 190

Some judge of authors' names, not works, and then
Nor praise nor blame the writings, but the men.

Ibid. Line 212

But let a lord once own the happy lines,
How the wit brightens! how the style refines!

Ibid. Line 220

Some praise at morning what they blame at night,
But always think the last opinion right.

Ibid. Line 230

Envy will merit as its shade pursue,
But like a shadow proves the substance true.

Ibid. Line 266

To err is human, to forgive divine.[1]

Ibid. Line 325

All seems infected that th' infected spy,
As all looks yellow to the jaundic'd eye.

Ibid. Line 358

[1] See Royall Tyler, page 283.
Then gently scan your brother man,
  Still gentler sister woman;
Though they may gang a kennin' wrang,
  To step aside is human.
        BURNS: *Address to the Unco Guid*
See also C. T. Copeland, page 753.

Men must be taught as if you taught them not,
And things unknown propos'd as things forgot.
Essay on Criticism. Part III, Line 15

The bookful blockhead, ignorantly read,
With loads of learned lumber in his head.
Ibid. Line 53

For fools rush in where angels fear to tread.[1]
Ibid. Line 66

What dire offence from amorous causes springs!
What mighty contests rise from trivial things!
The Rape of the Lock. Canto I, Line 1

And all Arabia breathes from yonder box.
Ibid. Line 134

On her white breast a sparkling cross she wore,
Which Jews might kiss, and infidels adore.
Ibid. Canto II, Line 7

If to her share some female errors fall,
Look on her face, and you'll forget 'em all.
Ibid. Line 17

Fair tresses man's imperial race ensnare,
And beauty draws us with a single hair.[2]
Ibid. Line 27

Here thou, great Anna! whom three realms obey,
Dost sometimes counsel take — and sometimes tea.
Ibid. Canto III, Line 7

At every word a reputation dies.
Ibid. Line 16

The hungry judges soon the sentence sign,
And wretches hang that jurymen may dine.
Ibid. Line 21

Coffee, which makes the politician wise.
The Rape of the Lock.
Canto III, Line 117

But when to mischief mortals bend their will,
How soon they find fit instruments of ill!
Ibid. Line 125

The meeting points the sacred hair dissever
From the fair head, forever, and forever!
Ibid. Line 153

Steel could the labour of the gods destroy,
And strike to dust th' imperial towers of Troy;
Steel could the works of mortal pride confound
And hew triumphal arches to the ground.
Ibid. Line 173

Sir Plume, of amber snuff-box justly vain,
And the nice conduct of a clouded cane.
Ibid. Canto IV, Line 123

Charms strike the sight, but merit wins the soul.
Ibid. Canto V, Line 34

"Shut, shut the door, good John!" fatigued, I said;
"Tie up the knocker! say I'm sick, I'm dead."
Epistle to Dr. Arbuthnot, Prologue to the Satires, Line 1

Fire in each eye, and papers in each hand,
They rave, recite, and madden round the land.
Ibid. Line 5

Is there a parson much bemused in beer,
A maudlin poetess, a rhyming peer,
A clerk foredoom'd his father's soul to cross,
Who pens a stanza when he should engross?
Ibid. Line 15

Fired that the house [1] reject him,
" 'Sdeath, I'll print it,
And shame the fools."
Ibid. Line 61

---

[1] Wrens make prey where eagles dare not perch. — SHAKESPEARE: *King Richard III, Act I, Sc. 3, L. 71*
[2] See Burton, page 125.

[1] The theatre.

No creature smarts so little as a fool.
*Epistle to Dr. Arbuthnot, Prologue
to the Satires, Line 84*
As yet a child, nor yet a fool to fame,
I lisp'd in numbers, for the numbers
came.
Ibid. Line 127
This long disease, my life.
Ibid. Line 132
Means not, but blunders round about
a meaning;
And he whose fustian's so sublimely
bad,
It is not poetry, but prose run mad.
Ibid. Line 186
Should such a man, too fond to rule
alone,
Bear, like the Turk, no brother near
the throne.[1]
Ibid. Line 197
Damn with faint praise, assent with
civil leer,
And without sneering teach the rest to
sneer; [2]
Willing to wound, and yet afraid to
strike,
Just hint a fault, and hesitate dislike.
Ibid. Line 201
By flatterers besieg'd,
And so obliging that he ne'er oblig'd;
Like Cato, give his little senate laws,[3]
And sit attentive to his own applause.
Ibid. Line 207
Who but must laugh, if such a man
there be?
Who would not weep, if Atticus were
he?
Ibid. Line 213

[1] See Denham, page 167.
[2] When needs he must, yet faintly then he
   praises;
   Somewhat the deed, much more the means
   he raises:
   So marreth what he makes, and praising
   most, dispraises.
   PHINEAS FLETCHER [1582-1650]: *The
   Purple Island* [1633], *Canto VII*
   Even in the church, where boredom is
   prolific
   I hail thee first, Episcopalian bore:
   Who else could serve as social soporific,
   And without snoring, teach the rest to snore.
   CHRISTOPHER MORLEY: *On a Certain
   Cleric*
[3] While Cato gives his little senate laws. —
Prologue to Mr. Addison's Cato, L. 23

Cursed be the verse, how well so e'er
it flow,
That tends to make one worthy man my
foe.
*Epistle to Dr. Arbuthnot, Prologue
to the Satires, Line 283*
Satire or sense, alas! can Sporus feel?
Who breaks a butterfly upon a wheel?
Ibid. Line 307
Eternal smiles his emptiness betray,
As shallow streams run dimpling all the
way.
Ibid. Line 315
Wit that can creep, and pride that licks
the dust.
Ibid. Line 333
Unlearn'd, he knew no schoolman's
subtle art,
No language but the language of the
heart.
Ibid. Line 398
Me, let the tender office long engage
To rock the cradle of reposing age;
With lenient arts extend a mother's
breath,
Make languor smile, and smooth the
bed of death;
Explore the thought, explain the asking
eye,
And keep awhile one parent from the
sky.
Ibid. Line 408
I cannot sleep a wink.
*Satires, Epistles, and Odes of Horace.
Satire I, Book II, Line 12*
Satire's my weapon, but I'm too dis-
creet
To run amuck, and tilt at all I meet.
Ibid. Line 69
But touch me, and no minister so sore.
Ibid. Line 76
There St. John mingles with my
friendly bowl,
The feast of reason and the flow of soul.
Ibid. Line 127
For I, who hold sage Homer's rule the
best,
Welcome the coming, speed the going
guest.[1]
Ibid. Satire II, Book II, Line 159

[1] This line is repeated in the translation of
the *Odyssey, Book XV, L. 83,* with "parting"
instead of "going."

I've often wish'd that I had clear,
For life, six hundred pounds a year;
A handsome house to lodge a friend,
A river at my garden's end,
A terrace walk, and half a rood
Of land set out to plant a wood.

Satires, Epistles, and Odes of Horace.
Satire VI, Book II, Line 1

Give me again my hollow tree,
A crust of bread, and liberty.

Ibid. Line 220

A patriot is a fool in ev'ry age.

Epilogue to the Satires. Dialogue I,
Line 41

Laugh then at any but at fools or foes;
These you but anger, and you mend not
those.
Laugh at your friends, and if your
friends are sore,
So much the better, you may laugh the
more.

Ibid. Line 53

Do good by stealth, and blush to find
it fame.

Ibid. Line 136

Never gallop Pegasus to death.

Epistle I. Book I, Line 14

When the brisk minor pants for twenty-
one.

Ibid. Line 38

Not to go back is somewhat to advance.

Ibid. Line 53

He's armed without that's innocent
within.

Ibid. Line 94

Get place and wealth, if possible, with
grace;
If not, by any means get wealth and
place.[1]

Ibid. Line 103

Above all Greek, above all Roman
fame.[2]

Ibid. Book II, Line 26

The mob of gentlemen who wrote with
ease.

Ibid. Line 108

One simile that solitary shines
In the dry desert of a thousand lines.

Ibid. Line 111

Then marble, soften'd into life, grew
warm,

[1] See Ben Jonson, page 118.
[2] See Dryden, page 173.

And yielding metal flow'd to human
form.[1]

Epistle I. Book II, Line 147

Who says in verse what others say in
prose.

Ibid. Line 202

What will a child learn sooner than a
song?

Ibid. Line 205

Ev'n copious Dryden wanted, or forgot,
The last and greatest art — the art to
blot.

Ibid. Line 280

There still remains, to mortify a wit,
The many-headed monster of the pit.[2]

Ibid. Line 304

We poets are (upon a poet's word)
Of all mankind the creatures most absurd:
The season when to come, and when to
go,
To sing, or cease to sing, we never
know.

Ibid. Line 358

Call, if you will, bad rhyming a disease,
It gives men happiness, or leaves them
ease.

Epistle II. Book II, Line 182

The worst of madmen is a saint run
mad.

Epistle VI. Book I, Line 27

Vain was the chief's, the sage's pride!
They had no poet, and they died.

Odes. Book IV, Ode 9, Stanza 4

Nature and Nature's laws lay hid in
night:
God said, Let Newton be! and all was
light.

Epitaph Intended for Sir
Isaac Newton

Whether thou choose Cervantes' serious air,
Or laugh and shake in Rabelais' easy-
chair.

The Dunciad. Book I, Line 21

[1] The canvas glow'd beyond ev'n Nature
warm;
The pregnant quarry teem'd with human
form.
          GOLDSMITH: *The Traveller, L. 137*
[2] See Sidney, page 27.

Poetic Justice, with her lifted scale,
Where in nice balance truth with gold
she weighs,
And solid pudding against empty
praise.
      The Dunciad. Book I, Line 52
While pensive poets painful vigils keep,
Sleepless themselves to give their read-
ers sleep.
                  Ibid. Line 93
Next o'er his books his eyes begin to
roll,
In pleasing memory of all he stole.
                  Ibid. Line 127
Or where the pictures for the page
atone,
And Quarles is sav'd by beauties not his
own.
                  Ibid. Line 139
How index-learning turns no student
pale,
Yet holds the eel of science by the tail.
                  Ibid. Line 279
And gentle Dulness ever loves a joke.
            Ibid. Book II, Line 34
A brain of feathers, and a heart of lead.
                  Ibid. Line 44
Another, yet the same.[1]
            Ibid. Book III, Line 40
Makes night hideous.[2]
                  Ibid. Line 166
And proud his mistress' order to per-
form,
Rides in the whirlwind and directs the
storm.[3]
                  Ibid. Line 263
A wit with dunces, and a dunce with
wits.[4]
      Ibid. Book IV, Line 90

[1] Another, yet the same. — TICKELL: *From
a Lady in England.* JOHNSON: *Life of Dryden.*
DARWIN: *Botanic Garden, Part I, Canto IV,
L. 380.* WORDSWORTH: *The Excursion, Book
IX.* SCOTT: *The Abbot, Chap. I.* HORACE:
Carmen Saeculare, L. 10 (Aliusque et idem)
[2] See Shakespeare, page 91.
[3] See Addison, page 194.
[4] See Shakespeare, page 68.
This man [Chesterfield], I thought, had
been a lord among wits; but I find he is only
a wit among lords. — JOHNSON (*Boswell's
Life, Vol. I, P. 159, Everyman ed.*)
A fool with judges, amongst fools a judge.
— COWPER: *Conversation, L. 298*
Although too much of a soldier among

The right divine of kings to govern
wrong.
      The Dunciad. Book IV, Line 188
            Stuff the head
With all such reading as was never
read:
For thee explain a thing till all men
doubt it,
And write about it, goddess, and about
it.
                  Ibid. Line 249
To happy convents, bosom'd deep in
vines,
Where slumber abbots purple as their
wines.
                  Ibid. Line 301
Led by my hand, he saunter'd Europe
round,
And gather'd every vice on Christian
ground.
                  Ibid. Line 311
Ev'n Palinurus nodded at the helm.
                  Ibid. Line 614
Religion, blushing, veils her sacred
fires,
And unawares Morality expires.
Nor public flame nor private dares to
shine;
Nor human spark is left, nor glimpse
divine!
Lo! thy dread empire Chaos! is re-
stor'd,
Light dies before thy uncreating word:

sovereigns, no one could claim with better
right to be a sovereign among soldiers. —
WALTER SCOTT: *Life of Napoleon*
      He [Steele] was a rake among scholars,
and a scholar among rakes. — MACAULAY:
Review of Aikin's Life of Addison
      Temple was a man of the world among
men of letters, a man of letters among men
of the world. — MACAULAY: *Review of Life
and Writings of Sir William Temple*
      Greswell in his *Memoirs of Politian* says
that Sannazarius himself, inscribing to this
lady [Cassandra Marchesia] an edition of his
Italian poems, terms her "delle belle eruditis-
sima, delle erudite bellissima" (most learned
of the fair; fairest of the learned).
      Qui stultis videri eruditi volunt stulti erudi-
tis videntur (Those who wish to appear wise
among fools, among the wise seem foolish).
— QUINTILIAN, *X, 7, 22*

Thy hand, great Anarch! lets the curtain fall,
And universal darkness buries all.
The Dunciad. Book IV, Line 649
How vast a memory has Love!
Sappho to Phaon. Line 52
Speed the soft intercourse from soul to soul,
And waft a sigh from Indus to the Pole.
Eloisa to Abelard. Line 57
Curse on all laws but those which love has made!
Love, free as air at sight of human ties,
Spreads his light wings, and in a moment flies.
Ibid. Line 74
And love the offender, yet detest the offence.[1]
Ibid. Line 192
How happy is the blameless vestal's lot!
The world forgetting, by the world forgot.
Ibid. Line 207
One thought of thee puts all the pomp to flight,
Priests, tapers, temples, swim before my sight.[2]
Ibid. Line 273
He best can paint them who shall feel them most.
Ibid. Line 366 (last line)
Not chaos-like together crush'd and bruis'd,
But, as the world, harmoniously confus'd:
Where order in variety we see,
And where, though all things differ, all agree.
Windsor Forest. Line 13
Ye Gods! annihilate but space and time,
And make two lovers happy.
Martinus Scriblerus on the Art of Sinking in Poetry. Chap. XI
Nor Fame I slight, nor for her favours call;

[1] See Dryden, page 177.
[2] Priests, altars, victims, swam before my sight. — EDMUND SMITH [1672–1710]: *Phædra and Hippolytus, adapted from Racine, Act I, Sc. 1* [1707]

She comes unlooked for, if she comes at all.
The Temple of Fame. Line 513
Unblemish'd let me live or die unknown;
Oh, grant an honest fame or grant me none!
Ibid. Line 523 (last lines)
I am his Highness'[1] dog at Kew;
Pray tell me, sir, whose dog are you?
On the Collar of a Dog
There, take (says Justice), take ye each a shell:
We thrive at Westminster on fools like you;
'Twas a fat oyster — live in peace, — adieu.[2]
Verbatim from Boileau
Father of all! in every age,
In every clime adored,
By saint, by savage, and by sage,
Jehovah, Jove, or Lord!
The Universal Prayer. Stanza 1
And binding Nature fast in fate,
Left free the human will.
Ibid. Stanza 3
And deal damnation round the land.
Ibid. Stanza 7
Teach me to feel another's woe,
To hide the fault I see;
That mercy I to others show,
That mercy show to me.[3]
Ibid. Stanza 10
Happy the man whose wish and care
A few paternal acres bound.
Ode on Solitude. Stanza 1
Thus let me live, unseen, unknown,
Thus unlamented let me die;
Steal from the world, and not a stone
Tell where I lie.
Ibid. Stanza 5
Vital spark of heavenly flame,
Quit, Oh quit, this mortal frame!
The Dying Christian to His Soul. Stanza 1

[1] Frederick, Prince of Wales.
[2] "Tenez voilà," dit-elle, "à chacun une écaille, Des sottises d'autrui nous vivons au Palais; Messieurs, l'huître étoit bonne. Adieu. Vivez en paix."
BOILEAU: *Epître II (à M. l'Abbé des Roches)*
[3] See Spenser, page 25.

Is there no bright reversion in the sky
For those who greatly think, or bravely
die?
*To the Memory of an Unfortunate
Lady. Line 9*
By foreign hands thy dying eyes were
clos'd,
By foreign hands thy decent limbs com-
pos'd,
By foreign hands thy humble grave
adorn'd,
By strangers honoured, and by stran-
gers mourn'd!
Ibid. Line 51
How lov'd, how honour'd once, avails
thee not,
To whom related, or by whom begot;
A heap of dust alone remains of thee:
'Tis all thou art, and all the proud shall
be!
Ibid. Line 71
The saint sustain'd it, but the woman
died.
Epitaph on Mrs. Corbet
Of manners gentle, of affections mild;
In wit a man, simplicity a child.
Epitaph on Gay
Curtain lectures made a restless night.
*Paraphrases from Chaucer. The
Wife of Bath, Her Prologue,
Line 165*
A glutted market makes provision
cheap.
Ibid. Line 262
To see, be seen, to tell, and gather
tales.[1]
Ibid. Line 282
The wasting moth ne'er spoil'd my best
array;
The cause was this, I wore it every day.
Ibid. Line 288
Whoe'er it be
That tells my faults, I hate him mor-
tally!
Ibid. Line 351
Love seldom haunts the breast where
learning lies,
And Venus sets ere Mercury can rise.
Ibid. Line 369
You beat your pate, and fancy wit will
come;

[1] See Chaucer, page 7.

Knock as you please, there's nobody
at home.
Epigram: An Empty House
For he lives twice who can at once em-
ploy
The present well, and ev'n the past en-
joy.[1]
Imitation of Martial
Who dare to love their country, and
be poor.
On His Grotto at Twickenham
Party is the madness of many for the
gain of a few.
Thoughts on Various Subjects
I never knew any man in my life
who could not bear another's misfor-
tunes perfectly like a Christian.
Ibid.
A man should never be ashamed to
own he has been in the wrong, which is
but saying, in other words, that he is
wiser to-day than he was yesterday.
Ibid.
It is with narrow-souled people as
with narrow-necked bottles; the less
they have in them the more noise they
make in pouring out.
Ibid.
When men grow virtuous in their old
age, they only make a sacrifice to God
of the devil's leavings.[2]
Ibid.
True disputants are like true sportsmen, their whole delight is in the pursuit.
Ibid.
No literal Translation can be just to
an excellent Original: but it is a great
Mistake to imagine that a rash Paraphrase can make amends for this general Defect.
Preface to the Iliad

[1] Ampliat ætatis spatium sibi vir bonus; hoc
est
Vivere bis vita posse priore frui
(The good man prolongs his life; to be able
to enjoy one's past life is to live twice). —
MARTIAL, X, 237
See Cowley, page 168.
[2] Now their sins are all committed,
Lord, how virtuous they are!
WILHELM BUSCH [1832–1908]: *Die
fromme Helene* (translation by Chris-
topher Morley)

Simplicity is the Mean between Ostentation and Rusticity.

Preface to the Iliad

Achilles' wrath, to Greece the direful spring
Of woes unnumber'd, heavenly goddess, sing!

The Iliad of Homer.[1] *Book I, Line 1*

The distant Trojans never injur'd me.

Ibid. Line 200

Words sweet as honey from his lips distill'd.

Ibid. Line 332

Shakes his ambrosial curls, and gives the nod, —
The stamp of fate, and sanction of the god.

Ibid. Line 684

And unextinguish'd laughter shakes the skies.[2]

Ibid. Line 771

The man who acts the least, upbraids the most.

Ibid. Book II, Line 311

Thick as autumnal leaves or driving sand.

Ibid. Line 970

Chiefs, who no more in bloody fights engage,
But, wise through time, and narrative with age,
In summer-days like grasshoppers rejoice,
A bloodless race, that send a feeble voice.

Ibid. Book III, Line 199

She moves a goddess, and she looks a queen.

Ibid. Line 208

But when he speaks, what elocution flows!
Soft as the fleeces of descending snows
The copious accents fall, with easy art;
Melting they fall, and sink into the heart.

Ibid. Line 283

[1] A very pretty poem, Mr. Pope, but it's not Homer. — RICHARD BENTLEY, great classical scholar
[2] The same line occurs in the translation of the *Odyssey, Book VIII, L. 366.*

Ajax the great . . .
Himself a host.

The Iliad of Homer. Book III, Line 293

Wrapt in the cold embraces of the tomb.

Ibid. Line 312

Plough the watery deep.

Ibid. Line 357

And joyful nations join in leagues of peace.

Ibid. Line 401

The day shall come, the great avenging day,
Which Troy's proud glories in the dust shall lay,
When Priam's powers and Priam's self shall fall,
And one prodigious ruin swallow all.

Ibid. Book IV, Line 196

The first in banquets, but the last in fight.

Ibid. Line 401

Gods! How the son degenerates from the sire!

Ibid. Line 451

Not two strong men the enormous weight could raise, —
Such men as live in these degenerate days.[1]

Ibid. Book V, Line 371

Whose little body lodg'd a mighty mind.

Ibid. Line 999

He held his seat; a friend to human race.
Fast by the road, his ever-open door
Obliged the wealthy, and reliev'd the poor.[2]

Ibid. Book VI, Line 18

Like leaves on trees the race of man is found,
Now green in youth, now withering on the ground:

[1] A mass enormous! which in modern days
No two of earth's degenerate sons could raise.
Book XX, L. 337

[2] Let me live in my house by the side of the road
And be a friend of man.
SAM WALTER FOSS [1858–1911]: *The House by the Side of the Road, St. 5*

Another race the following spring supplies:
They fall successive, and successive rise.
The Iliad of Homer. Book VI,
Line 181
Inflaming wine, pernicious to mankind.
Ibid. Line 330
If yet, not lost to all the sense of shame.
Ibid. Line 350
He, from whose lips divine persuasion flows.
Ibid. Book VII, Line 143
Short is my date, but deathless my renown.
Ibid. Book IX, Line 535
Content to follow when we lead the way.
Ibid. Book X, Line 141
He serves me most, who serves his country best.
Ibid. Line 201
Praise from a friend, or censure from a foe,
Are lost on hearers that our merits know.
Ibid. Line 293
The rest were vulgar deaths, unknown to fame.
Ibid. Book XI, Line 394
Without a sign, his sword the brave man draws,
And asks no omen but his country's cause.
Ibid. Book XII, Line 283
A day to fire the brave, and warm the cold,
To gain new glories, or augment the old.
Ibid. Line 321
And seem to walk on wings, and tread in air.
Ibid. Book XIII, Line 106
Not vain the weakest, if their force unite.
Ibid. Line 311
The best of things, beyond their measure, cloy.
Ibid. Line 795
Heroes as great have died, and yet shall fall.
Ibid. Book XV, Line 157

And for our country 'tis a bliss to die.[1]
The Iliad of Homer. Book XV,
Line 583
Like strength is felt from hope, and from despair.
Ibid. Line 852
Two friends, two bodies with one soul inspir'd.[2]
Ibid. Book XVI, Line 267
Sleep and Death, two twins of winged race,
Of matchless swiftness, but of silent pace.
Ibid. Line 831
How vain, without the merit, is the name!
Ibid. Book XVII, Line 158
Achilles absent was Achilles still.
Ibid. Book XXII, Line 418
Forever honour'd, and forever mourn'd.
Ibid. Line 422
Unwept, unhonour'd, uninterr'd he lies![3]
Ibid. Line 484
It is not strength, but art, obtains the prize,[4]
And to be swift is less than to be wise.
'Tis more by art, than force of num'rous strokes.
Ibid. Book XXIII, Line 383
A green old age,[5] unconscious of decays.
Ibid. Line 929
An honest business never blush to tell.
The Odyssey of Homer.[6] Book III,
Line 20

---

[1] Dulce et decorum est pro patria mori (It is sweet and honourable to die for one's country). — HORACE: *Odes, Book III, 2, L. 13*
[2] A friend is one soul abiding in two bodies. — DIOGENES LAERTIUS: *On Aristotle*
Two souls with but a single thought,
Two hearts that beat as one.
VON MÜNCH BELLINGHAUSEN [1806–1871]: *Ingomar the Barbarian, Act II*
[3] Unwept, unhonoured, and unsung. — SCOTT: *Lay of the Last Minstrel*
Unknelled, uncoffined, and unknown. — BYRON: *Childe Harold, Canto IV, St. 179*
[4] See Middleton, page 116.
[5] See Dryden, page 178.
[6] Pope engaged two friends, ELIJAH FENTON [1683–1730] and WILLIAM BROOME [1689–1745], to translate certain books of *The Odyssey* of Homer for him. The division of the work was: — Pope: Books III, V, VII, IX, XIII, XIV, XVII, XXI, XXII, XXIV,

Urge him with truth to frame his fair
  replies;
And sure he will: for Wisdom never
  lies.
> *The Odyssey of Homer. Book III,*
> *Line 25*

The lot of man; to suffer and to die.
> *Ibid. Line 117*

A faultless body and a blameless mind.
> *Ibid. Line 138*

The long historian of my country's
  woes.
> *Ibid. Line 142*

When now Aurora, daughter of the
  dawn,
With rosy lustre purpled o'er the lawn.
> *Ibid. Line 516* [1]

Wise to resolve, and patient to perform.
> *Ibid. Book IV (Fenton transla-*
> *tion), Line 372*

The leader, mingling with the vulgar
  host,
Is in the common mass of matter lost.
> *Ibid. Line 397*

The people's parent, he protected all.
> *Ibid. Line 921*

The big round tear stands trembling in
  her eye.
> *Ibid. Line 936*

The windy satisfaction of the tongue.
> *Ibid. Line 1092*

No more was seen the human form
  divine.[2]
> *Ibid. Book X, Line 278*

Oh woman, woman! when to ill thy
  mind
Is bent, all hell contains no fouler
  fiend.[3]
> *Ibid. Book XI (Broome transla-*
> *tion), Line 531*

And what so tedious as a twice-told
  tale.[4]
> *Ibid. Book XII (Broome transla-*
> *tion), Line 538*

He ceas'd; but left so pleasing on their
  ear

His voice, that list'ning still they
  seem'd to hear.
> *The Odyssey of Homer. Book XIII,*
> *Line 1*

His native home deep imag'd in his
  soul.
> *Ibid. Line 38*

The sex is ever to a soldier kind.
> *Ibid. Book XIV, Line 246*

True friendship's laws are by this rule
  express'd,
Welcome the coming, speed the parting
  guest.[1]
> *Ibid. Book XV, Line 83*

For too much rest itself becomes a pain.
> *Ibid. Line 429*

He knew his lord; he knew, and strove
  to meet;
In vain he strove to crawl and kiss his
  feet;
Yet (all he could) his tail, his ears, his
  eyes
Salute his master, and confess his
  joys. . . .
The dog, whom Fate had granted to
  behold
His lord, when twenty tedious years
  had roll'd,
Takes a last look, and, having seen him,
  dies:
So closed forever faithful Argus' eyes!
> *Ibid. Book XVII, Line 359*

Unbless'd thy hand, if, in this low disguise,
Wander, perhaps, some inmate of the
  skies.[2]
> *Ibid. Line 576*

Impatient straight to flesh his virgin
  sword.
> *Ibid. Book XX (Fenton transla-*
> *tion), Line 461*

So ends the bloody business of the day.
> *Ibid. Book XXII, Line 516*

Blessed is he who expects nothing,
for he shall never be disappointed.[3]
> *Letter to Gay [October 6, 1727]*

---

and most of X and XV; Fenton: Books I, IV,
XIX, and XX; Broome: Books II, VI, VIII,
XI, XII, XVI, XVIII, XXIII.
  [1] Also *Line 623*
  [2] Human face divine. — MILTON: *Paradise
Lost, Book III, L. 44*
  [3] See Otway, page 185.
  [4] See Shakespeare, page 58.

[1] See Pope, page 213.
[2] Be not forgetful to entertain strangers, for
thereby some have entertained angels unawares. — *Hebrews, XIII, 2*
[3] Pope calls this the eighth beatitude (Roscoe's edition of Pope, *Vol. X, P. 184*).
  See Wolcot, page 272.

This is the Jew
That Shakespeare drew.[1]

LEWIS THEOBALD [2]
[1688–1744]

None but himself can be his parallel.[3]
The Double Falsehood

LADY MARY WORTLEY MONTAGU
[1690–1762]

Let this great maxim be my virtue's guide, —
In part she is to blame that has been tried:
He comes too near that comes to be denied.
The Lady's Resolve [4]

And we meet, with champagne and a chicken, at last.[5]
The Lover

Be plain in dress, and sober in your diet;
In short, my deary, kiss me, and be quiet.
A Summary of Lord Lyttelton's Advice

Satire should, like a polished razor keen,

[1] On the 14th of February, 1741, Macklin established his fame as an actor in the character of Shylock, in the "Merchant of Venice." . . . Macklin's performance of this character so forcibly struck a gentleman in the pit that he, as it were involuntarily, exclaimed, —
"This is the Jew
That Shakespeare drew!"
It has been said that this gentleman was Mr. Pope, and that he meant his panegyric on Macklin as a satire against Lord Lansdowne. — *Biographia Dramatica, Vol. I, Part II, P. 469*

[2] Editor of Shakespeare, and hero of Pope's *Dunciad.*

[3]   Quæris Alcidæ parem?
Nemo est nisi ipse
(Do you see Alcides' equal? None is, except himself). — SENECA: *Hercules Furens, I, I; 84.*
And but herself admits no parallel. — MASSINGER: *Duke of Milan, Act IV, Sc. 3.*

[4] A fugitive piece, written on a window by Lady Montagu, after her marriage [1713]. See Overbury, page 128.

[5] What say you to such a supper with such a woman? — BYRON: *Note to a Second Letter on Bowles*

Wound with a touch that's scarcely felt or seen.
To the Imitator of the First Satire of Horace. Book II

But the fruit that can fall without shaking
Indeed is too mellow for me.
The Answer

JOHN BYROM
[1692–1763]

God bless the King, — I mean the faith's defender!
God bless — no harm in blessing — the Pretender!
But who pretender is, or who is king, —
God bless us all! — that's quite another thing.[1]
*Miscellaneous Poems [1773].
To an Officer of the Army, extempore*

Take time enough: all other graces
Will soon fill up their proper places.[2]
Advice to Preach Slow

Some say, compar'd to Bononcini,
That Mynheer Handel's but a ninny;
Others aver that he to Handel
Is scarcely fit to hold a candle.
Strange all this difference should be
'Twixt Tweedledum and Tweedledee.
On the Feuds between Handel and Bononcini [3]

As clear as a whistle.
Epistle to Lloyd

The point is plain as a pike-staff.[4]
Epistle to a Friend

Bone and Skin, two millers thin,
Would starve us all, or near it:
But be it known to Skin and Bone
That Flesh and Blood can't bear it.
Epigram on Two Monopolists

[1] Quoted by SIR WALTER SCOTT in *Redgauntlet, Vol. II, Chap. I*, Edinburgh edition [1832].
[2] See Walker, page 170.
[3] Nourse asked me if I had seen the verses upon Handel and Bononcini, not knowing that they were mine. — *Byrom's Remains, Vol. I, P. 173* (Chetham Soc.)
The last two lines have been attributed to Swift and Pope (see Scott's edition of Swift, and Dyce's edition of Pope).
[4] See Middleton, page 116.

Thus adorned, the two heroes, 'twixt
shoulder and elbow,
Shook hands and went to 't; and the
word it was bilbow.
*Upon a Trial of Skill between
the Great Masters of the Noble
Science of Defence, Messrs.
Figg and Sutton*

PHILIP DORMER STANHOPE, EARL OF CHESTERFIELD
[1694–1773]

Whatever is worth doing at all, is
worth doing well.
Letters. March 10, 1746
Do as you would be done by, is the
surest method of pleasing.
Ibid. October 16, 1747
I knew once a very covetous, sordid
fellow,[1] who used to say, "Take care
of the pence, for the pounds will take
care of themselves."
Ibid. November 6, 1747
Sacrifice to the Graces.[2]
Ibid. March 9, 1748
Manners must adorn knowledge, and
smooth its way through the world. Like
a great rough diamond, it may do very
well in a closet by way of curiosity, and
also for its intrinsic value.
Ibid. July 1, 1748
Without some dissimulation no busi-
ness can be carried on at all.
Ibid. May 22, 1749
Style is the dress of thoughts.
Ibid. November 24, 1749
Religion must still be allowed to be
a collateral security to Virtue.
Ibid. January 8, 1750
Despatch is the soul of business.
Ibid. February 5, 1750

---

[1] William Lowndes [1652–1724], Secretary
of the Treasury in the Reigns of King William, Queen Anne, and King George the First.
He is credited with originating the phrase
"ways and means."
[2] Plato was continually saying to Xenocrates, "Sacrifice to the Graces." — DIOGENES
LAERTIUS: *Xenocrates, Book IV, Sect. 2*
 Let us sacrifice to the Muses. — PLUTARCH:
The Banquet of the Seven Wise Men. (A saying of Solon.)

Chapter of accidents.[1]
Letters. February 16, 1753
I assisted at the birth of that most
significant word "flirtation," which
dropped from the most beautiful mouth
in the world.
The World. No. 101
Unlike my subject now shall be my
song;
It shall be witty, and it sha'n't be long.
Impromptu Lines
The dews of the evening most carefully
shun, —
Those tears of the sky for the loss of
the sun.
Advice to a Lady in Autumn
The nation looked upon him as a de-
serter, and he shrunk into insignifi-
cancy and an earldom.
Character of Pulteney
He adorned whatever subject he
either spoke or wrote upon, by the most
splendid eloquence.[2]
Character of Bolingbroke
Women, and young men, are very
apt to tell what secrets they know,
from the vanity of having been trusted.
Letters to His Son

FRANCIS HUTCHESON
[1694–1746]

That action is best which procures
the greatest happiness for the greatest
numbers.[3]
*Inquiry Concerning Moral Good
and Evil. Sect. 3* [1720]

---

[1] Chapter of accidents. — BURKE: *Notes
for Speeches* [ed. 1852], Vol. II, P. 426
 John Wilkes said that "the Chapter of Accidents is the longest chapter in the book."
— SOUTHEY: *The Doctor, Chap. CXVIII*
[2] Who left scarcely any style of writing untouched,
And touched nothing that he did not adorn.
 JOHNSON: *Epitaph on Goldsmith*
 Il embellit tout ce qu'il touche (He adorns
whatever he touches). — FÉNELON [1651–
1715]: *Lettre sur les Occupations de l'Aca-
démie Française, Sect. IV*
[3] Priestley was the first (unless it was Beccaria) who taught my lips to pronounce this
sacred truth, — that the greatest happiness of
the greatest number is the foundation of

MATTHEW GREEN
[1696–1737]

Fling but a stone, the giant dies.
> *The Spleen. Line 93*

Laugh and be well.
> *Ibid. Line 94*

Life's moving-pictures, well-wrought
plays,
To others' grief attention raise.
> *Ibid. Line 131*

Music hath charms,[1] we all may find,
Ingratiate deeply with the mind.
> *Ibid. Line 141*

Happy the man, who, innocent,
Grieves not at ills he can't prevent;
His skiff does with the current glide,
Not puffing pulled against the tide.
> *Ibid. Line 365*

Though pleased to see the dolphins
play,
I mind my compass and my way.
> *Ibid. Line 826*

WILLIAM OLDYS
[1696–1761]

Busy, curious, thirsty fly,
Drink with me, and drink as I.
> *On a Fly Drinking out of a Cup
> of Ale. Stanza 1*

Three-score summers, when they're
gone,
Will appear as short as one.
> *Ibid. Stanza 2*

RICHARD SAVAGE
[1698–1743]

He lives to build, not boast, a generous
race;
No tenth transmitter of a foolish face.
> *The Bastard. Line 7*

May see thee now, though late, redeem
thy name,

And glorify what else is damn'd to
fame.
> *Character of Foster*

WILLIAM WARBURTON,
BISHOP OF GLOUCESTER
[1698–1779]

Orthodoxy is my doxy — heterodoxy
is another man's doxy.[1]
> *Quoted by* JOSEPH PRIESTLEY
> [1733–1804]: *Memoirs, Vol. I,
> Page 572*

JOHN DYER
[1700–1758]

A little rule, a little sway,
A sunbeam in a winter's day,
Is all the proud and mighty have
Between the cradle and the grave.
> *Grongar Hill. Line 89*

Sisyphus, with toil and sweat,
And muscles strain'd, striving to get
Up a steep hill a ponderous stone,
Which near the top recoils, and rolls
impetuous down.[2]
> *Epistle to a Famous Painter.
> Line 58*

JAMES THOMSON
[1700–1748]

As those we love decay, we die in part,
String after string is severed from the
heart;
Till loosen'd life, at last but breathing
clay,
Without one pang is glad to fall away.
> *On the Death of Mr. Aikman.*[3]

---

[1] Priestley relates that, in a debate on the
Test Laws, Lord Sandwich said: "I have heard
frequent use of the words 'orthodoxy' and
'heterodoxy' but I confess myself at a loss
to know precisely what they mean." Bishop
Warburton whispered his definition to him.

[2] Optat supremo collocare Sisyphus
In monte saxum: sed vetant leges Jovis.

(Sisyphus endeavors to place the stone on
the summit of the mountain, but the decrees
of Jove forbid).
> HORACE: *Epodes, XVIII, 68*

[3] William Aikman [1682–1731], portrait
painter.

---

morals and legislation. — JEREMY BENTHAM
[1748–1832]: *Works, Vol. X, P. 142*

The expression is used by CESARE BONEN-
SANO BECCARIA [1735–1794] in the introduction to his *Essay on Crimes and Punishments*
[1764].

[1] Music hath charms to soothe the savage
breast. — CONGREVE: *The Mourning Bride,
Act I, Sc. I*

Come, gentle Spring! ethereal Mildness! come.

The Seasons. Spring, Line 1

But who can paint
Like Nature? Can imagination boast,
Amid its gay creation, hues like hers?

Ibid. Line 465

Delightful task! to rear the tender thought,
To teach the young idea how to shoot.

Ibid. Line 1149

An elegant sufficiency, content,
Retirement, rural quiet, friendship, books.

Ibid. Line 1158

The meek-ey'd Morn appears, mother of dews.

Ibid. Summer, Line 47

Falsely luxurious, will not man awake?

Ibid. Line 67

Ships dim-discover'd dropping from the clouds.

Ibid. Line 946

And Mecca saddens at the long delay.

Ibid. Line 979

For many a day, and many a dreadful night,
Incessant lab'ring round the stormy cape.

Ibid. Line 1003

Sigh'd and look'd unutterable things.

Ibid. Line 1188

Who stemm'd the torrent of a downward age.

Ibid. Line 1505

Autumn nodding o'er the yellow plain.

Ibid. Autumn, Line 2

Loveliness
Needs not the foreign aid of ornament,
But is when unadorn'd, adorn'd the most.[1]

Ibid. Line 204

He saw her charming, but he saw not half
The charms her downcast modesty conceal'd.

Ibid. Line 229

For still the world prevail'd, and its dread laugh,

[1] See Milton, page 152.

Which scarce the firm philosopher can scorn.

The Seasons. Autumn, Line 233

See, Winter comes to rule the varied year.[1]

Ibid. Winter, Line 1

Cruel as death, and hungry as the grave.

Ibid. Line 393

There studious let me sit,
And hold high converse with the mighty dead.

Ibid. Line 431

The kiss, snatch'd hasty from the sidelong maid.

Ibid. Line 625

These as they change, Almighty Father! these
Are but the varied God. The rolling year
Is full of Thee.

Hymn. Line 1

Shade, unperceiv'd, so softening into shade.

Ibid. Line 25

From seeming evil still educing good.

Ibid. Line 114

Come then, expressive silence, muse His praise.

Ibid. Line 118

A pleasing land of drowsy head it was,
Of dreams that wave before the halfshut eye;
And of gay castles in the clouds that pass,
Forever flushing round a summer sky:
There eke the soft delights that witchingly
Instil a wanton sweetness through the breast,
And the calm pleasures always hover'd nigh;
But whate'er smack'd of noyance or unrest
Was far, far off expell'd from this delicious nest.

The Castle of Indolence. Canto I, Stanza 6

O fair undress, best dress! it checks no vein,

[1] O Winter, ruler of the inverted year. —
COWPER: *The Task, Book IV, Winter Evening. L. 34*

But every flowing limb in pleasure drowns,
And heightens ease with grace.
> *The Castle of Indolence.*
> *Canto I, Stanza 26*

Plac'd far amid the melancholy main.
> *Ibid. Stanza 30*

Scoundrel maxim.
> *Ibid. Stanza 50*

A bard here dwelt, more fat than bard beseems.
> *Ibid. Stanza 68*

A little round, fat, oily man of God.
> *Ibid. Stanza 69*

I care not, Fortune, what you me deny:
You cannot rob me of free Nature's grace,
You cannot shut the windows of the sky
Through which Aurora shows her brightening face;
You cannot bar my constant feet to trace
The woods and lawns, by living stream, at eve:
Let health my nerves and finer fibres brace,
And I their toys to the great children leave:
Of fancy, reason, virtue, naught can me bereave.
> *Ibid. Canto II, Stanza 3*

Health is the vital principle of bliss,
And exercise, of health.
> *Ibid. Stanza 55*

Forever, Fortune, wilt thou prove
An unrelenting foe to love;
And when we meet a mutual heart,
Come in between and bid us part?
> *To Fortune*

O Sophonisba! Sophonisba, O! [1]
> *Sophonisba. Act III, Sc. 2*

When Britain first, at Heaven's command,
  Arose from out the azure main,
This was the charter of her land,
  And guardian angels sung the strain:

Rule, Britannia! Britannia rules the waves!
Britons never shall be slaves.
> *Alfred. Act II, Sc. 5 [1740]*

PHILIP DODDRIDGE
[1702–1751]

Live while you live, the epicure would say,
And seize the pleasures of the present day;
Live while you live, the sacred preacher cries,
And give to God each moment as it flies.
Lord, in my views, let both united be:
I live in pleasure when I live to thee.
> *Epigram on His Family Arms* [1]

Awake, my soul! stretch every nerve,
  And press with vigour on;
A heavenly race demands thy zeal,
  And an immortal crown.
> *Zeal and Vigour in the Christian*
> *Race. Stanza 1*

ROBERT DODSLEY
[1703–1764]

One kind kiss before we part,
  Drop a tear and bid adieu;
Though we sever, my fond heart
  Till we meet shall pant for you.[2]
> *The Parting Kiss*

No state of life but must to patience bow:
  The tradesman must have patience for his bill;
He must have patience who to law will go;
  And should he lose his right, more patience still;
Yea, to prevent or heal full many a strife,
How oft, how long must man have patience with his wife.
> *To Patience*

---

[1] The line was altered after the second edition to
"O Sophonisba! I am wholly thine."

[1] A Latin proverb by Junius, — Dum vivimus, vivamus (Let us live while we live). — JOB ORTON [1717–1783]: *Memoirs of Doddridge* [1766]

[2] Ae fond kiss, and then we sever!
Ae farewell, and then for ever!
ROBERT BURNS: *Ae Fond Kiss, St. 1*

JONATHAN EDWARDS
[1703–1758]

Resolved, never to do anything which I should be afraid to do if it were the last hour of my life.

Seventy Resolutions

Intend to live in continual mortification, and never to expect or desire any worldly ease or pleasure.

Diary. 1723

I assert that nothing ever comes to pass without a cause.

The Freedom of the Will [1754]

This dictate of common sense.

Ibid.

JOHN WESLEY
[1703–1791]

That execrable sum of all villanies, commonly called the Slave Trade.

Journal. February 12, 1772

Certainly this is a duty, not a sin. "Cleanliness is indeed next to godliness." [1]

Sermon XCIII, On Dress

Though I am always in haste, I am never in a hurry.

Letters. December 10, 1777

Do all the good you can,
By all the means you can,
In all the ways you can,
In all the places you can,
At all the times you can,
To all the people you can,
As long as ever you can.

John Wesley's Rule

SOAME JENYNS
[1704–1787]

Let each fair maid, who fears to be disgraced,
Ever be sure to tie her garters fast,
Lest the loosed string, amidst the public hall,
A wished-for prize to some proud fop should fall.

The Art of Dancing

Ever let my lovely pupils fear

[1] See Bacon, page 112.

To chill their mantling blood with cold small beer:
Destruction lurks within the poisonous dose,
A fatal fever or a pimpled nose.

The Art of Dancing

NATHANIEL COTTON
[1705–1788]

If solid happiness we prize,
Within our breasts this jewel lies,
And they are fools who roam.
The world has nothing to bestow;
From our own selves our joys must flow,
And that dear hut, our home.

The Fireside. Stanza 3

To be resign'd when ills betide,
Patient when favours are deni'd,
And pleas'd with favours given, —
Dear Chloe, this is wisdom's part;
This is that incense of the heart [1]
Whose fragrance smells to heaven.

Ibid. Stanza 11

Yet still we hug the dear deceit.

Content. Vision IV

Hold the fleet angel fast until he bless thee.[2]

To-morrow

BENJAMIN FRANKLIN [3]
[1706–1790]

They that can give up essential liberty to obtain a little temporary safety deserve neither liberty nor safety.[4]

Historical Review of Pennsylvania

[1] The incense of the heart may rise. — JOHN PIERPONT [1785–1866]: *Every Place a Temple*

[2] I will not let thee go, except thou bless me. — *Genesis, XXXII, 26*
Like the patriarch's angel hold it fast
Till it gives its blessing.
WHITTIER: *My Soul and I, St. 34*

[3] Eripuit cœlo fulmen sceptrumque tyrannis (He snatched the lightning from heaven, and the sceptre from tyrants), — a line attributed to Turgot, and inscribed on Houdon's bust of Franklin. Frederick von der Trenck [1726–1794] asserted at his trial [1794] that he was the author of this line.

[4] This sentence was much used in the Revolutionary period. It occurs even so early as November, 1755, in an answer by the Assembly of Pennsylvania to the Governor, and forms the motto of Franklin's "Historical Re-

We are a kind of posterity in respect to them.[1]

Letter to William Strahan [*1745*]

Remember that time is money.

Advice to a Young Tradesman [*1748*]

God helps them that help themselves.

Maxims prefixed to Poor Richard's Almanac [*1757*]

Dost thou love life? Then do not squander time, for that is the stuff life is made of.

Ibid.

Early to bed and early to rise,
Makes a man healthy, wealthy, and wise.[2]

Ibid.

Plough deep while sluggards sleep.

Ibid.

Never leave that till to-morrow which you can do to-day.

Ibid.

Three removes are as bad as a fire.

Ibid.

Little strokes fell great oaks.

Ibid.

A little neglect may breed mischief: for want of a nail the shoe was lost; for want of a shoe the horse was lost; and for want of a horse the rider was lost.

Ibid.

He that goes a borrowing goes a sorrowing.

Ibid.

A man may, if he knows not how to save as he gets, keep his nose to the grindstone.

Ibid.

Vessels large may venture more,
But little boats should keep near shore.

Ibid.

It is hard for an empty sack to stand upright.

Maxims prefixed to Poor Richard's Almanac [*1757*]

Experience keeps a dear school, but fools will learn in no other.

Ibid.

Idleness and pride tax with a heavier hand than kings and parliaments. If we can get rid of the former, we may easily bear the latter.

Letter on the Stamp Act [*July 1, 1765*]

Here Skugg lies snug
As a bug in a rug.[1]

Letter to Miss Georgiana Shipley [*September, 1772*]

There never was a good war or a bad peace.[2]

Letter to Josiah Quincy [*September 11, 1773*]

You and I were long friends: you are now my enemy, and I am yours. B. Franklin.

Letter to William Strahan [*July 5, 1775*]

We must all hang together, or assuredly we shall all hang separately.

At the signing of the Declaration of Independence [*July 4, 1776*]

He has paid dear, very dear, for his whistle.

The Whistle [*November, 1779*]

Here you would know and enjoy what posterity will say of Washington. For a thousand leagues have nearly the same effect with a thousand years.

Letter to Washington [*March 5, 1780*]

Our Constitution is in actual operation; everything appears to promise

---

view," 1759, appearing also in the body of the work. — RICHARD FROTHINGHAM [1812–1880]: *Rise of the Republic of the United States, P. 413*

[1] Byron's European fame is the best earnest of his immortality, for a foreign nation is a kind of contemporaneous posterity. — HORACE BINNEY WALLACE [1817–1856]: *Stanley, or the Recollections of a Man of the World, Vol. II, P. 89*

[2] JOHN CLARKE: *Parœmiolgia* [1639].
My hour is eight o'clock, though it is an

infallible rule, "Sanat, sanctificat, et ditat, surgere mane" (That he may be healthy, happy, and wise, let him rise early). — *A Health to the Gentle Profession of Serving-men* [1598], *P. 121* (reprinted in Roxburghe Library)

[1] Snug as a bug in a rug. — *The Stratford Jubilee, II, 1* [1779]

[2] It hath been said that an unjust peace is to be preferred before a just war. — SAMUEL BUTLER: *Butler's Remains, Speeches in the Rump Parliament*

that it will last; but in this world nothing is certain but death and taxes.

Letter to M. Leroy [*1789*]

George Washington, Commander of the American armies, who, like Joshua of old, commanded the sun and the moon to stand still, and they obeyed him.

A Toast at a Dinner in Versailles. The British Minister had proposed a toast to George III, in which he likened him to the sun, and the French Minister had toasted Louis XVI, comparing him with the moon.

The next thing most like living one's life over again seems to be a recollection of that life, and to make that recollection as durable as possible by putting it down in writing.

Autobiography. Page 6 (Everyman Edition)

Often I sat up in my room reading the greatest part of the night, when the book was borrowed in the evening and to be returned early in the morning, lest it should be missed or wanted.

Ibid. Page 16

Persons of good sense, I have since observed, seldom fall into disputation, except lawyers, university men, and men of all sorts that have been bred at Edinborough.

Ibid. Page 17

An advantage itinerant preachers have over those who are stationary, the latter cannot well improve their delivery of a sermon by so many rehearsals.

Ibid. Page 129

I shall never ask, never refuse, nor ever resign an office.

Ibid. Page 134

Human felicity is produc'd not so much by great pieces of good fortune that seldom happen, as by little advantages that occur every day.

Ibid. Page 154

When men are employed, they are best contented; for on the days they worked they were good-natured and cheerful, and, with the consciousness of having done a good day's work, they spent the evening jollily; but on our idle days they were mutinous and quarrelsome.

Autobiography. Page 177

8th and lastly. They are so grateful!!

Reasons for Preferring an Elderly Mistress [1] [*1745*]

And God said, Have I not borne with him these hundred ninety and eight years, and nourished him, and clothed him, notwithstanding his rebellion against me: and couldst not thou, that art thyself a sinner, bear with him one night?

An Added Chapter to the Book of Genesis. [2] *Verse 11* [*1763*]

The grand leap of the Whale up the Fall of Niagara is esteemed, by all who have seen it, as one of the finest Spectacles in Nature.

To the Editor of a London newspaper [*1765*], *intended to chaff the English for their ignorance of America*

I wish the Bald Eagle had not been chosen as the Representative of our Country; he is a Bird of bad moral Character; like those among Men who live by Sharping and Robbing, he is generally poor, and often very lousy.

The Turky is a much more respectable Bird, and withal a true original Native of America.

Letter to Sarah Bache [*January 26, 1784*]

He [the sun] gives light as soon as he rises.

An Economical Project [3] [*1784*]

HENRY FIELDING
[1707–1754]

All Nature wears one universal grin.

Tom Thumb the Great. Act I, Sc. 1

To-day it is our pleasure to be drunk;

---

[1] Quoted by Dr. A. S. W. Rosenbach, owner of the original MS., in his *The All-Embracing Doctor Franklin* [1932].

[2] Founded on *The Liberty of Prophesying*, by Jeremy Taylor [1657]. See Taylor, page 165.

[3] A letter to the *Journal de Paris* advocating daylight saving.

And this our queen shall be as drunk as we.
Tom Thumb the Great. Act I, Sc. 2

When I'm not thank'd at all, I'm thank'd enough;
I've done my duty, and I've done no more.
Ibid. Sc. 3

Lo, when two dogs are fighting in the streets,
With a third dog one of the two dogs meets;
With angry teeth he bites him to the bone,
And this dog smarts for what that dog has done.[1]
Ibid. Sc. 6

I am as sober as a judge.
Don Quixote in England. Act III, Sc. 14

Much may be said on both sides.
The Covent Garden Tragedy. Act I, Sc. 8

Enough is equal to a feast.
Ibid. Act V, Sc. 1

We must eat to live and live to eat.[2]
The Miser. Act III, Sc. 3

Penny saved is a penny got.
Ibid. Sc. 12

Oh, the roast beef of England,
And old England's roast beef![3]
The Grub Street Opera. Act III, Sc. 2

This story will not go down.
Tumble-down Dick

The dusky night rides down the sky,
And ushers in the morn;
The hounds all join in glorious cry,
The huntsman winds his horn,
And a-hunting we will go.
A-hunting We Will Go. Stanza 1[1]

Can any man have a higher notion of the rule of right and the eternal fitness of things?
The History of Tom Jones. Book IV, Chap. 4

Wisdom, whose lessons have been represented as so hard to learn by those who never were at her school, only teaches us to extend a simple maxim universally known. And this is, not to buy at too dear a price.
Ibid. Book VI, Chap. 3

Distinction without a difference.
Ibid. Chap. 13

Amiable weakness.[2]
Ibid. Book X, Chap. 8

The dignity of history.[3]
Ibid. Book XI, Chap. 2

Nothing more aggravates ill success than the near approach to good.
Ibid. Book XIII, Chap. 2

Hairbreadth missings of happiness look like the insults of Fortune.
Ibid.

Republic of letters.[4]
Ibid. Book XIV, Chap. 1

---

[1] Thus when a barber and a collier fight,
The barber beats the luckless collier —
white;
The dusty collier heaves his ponderous sack,
And big with vengeance beats the barber —
black.
In comes the brick-dust man, with grime o'erspread,
And beats the collier and the barber — red:
Black, red, and white in various clouds are tost,
And in the dust they raise the combatants are lost.
CHRISTOPHER SMART [1722–1770]: *The Trip to Cambridge*
[2] Socrates said, Bad men live that they may eat and drink, whereas good men eat and drink that they may live. — PLUTARCH: *How a Young Man Ought to Hear Poems*
We should eat to live, not live to eat. — MOLIÈRE: *L'Avare, Act III, Sc. 5*
[3] See Richard Leveridge, page 193.

[1] A southerly wind and a cloudy sky
Proclaim a hunting morning;
Before the sun rises we nimbly fly,
Dull sleep and a downy bed scorning.
Hunting Song in *The Sportsmen's Vocal Library* [London, 1811]
It's of three jovial huntsmen, and a-hunting they did go;
And they hunted, and they hollo'd, and they blew their horns also;
Look ye there!
The Three Jovial Huntsmen (old English ballad), *St. 1*
[2] Amiable weaknesses of human nature. — GIBBON: *Decline and Fall of the Roman Empire, Chap. XIV*. Modern Library Giant, Vol. 1, P. 375.
[3] The dignity of history. — BOLINGBROKE: *Letter 5*
[4] Republic of letters. — STERNE: *Tristram Shandy, Book I, Chap. 20*. WASHINGTON IRVING: *Tales of a Traveller, Notoriety*

Illustrious predecessors.[1]
Covent Garden Journal
[January 11, 1752]
Perhaps there is more of Ostentation than of real Utility in ships of this vast and unwieldy Burthen.
Journal of a Voyage to Lisbon

WILLIAM PITT, EARL OF CHATHAM
[1708–1778]

Confidence is a plant of slow growth in an aged bosom.
Speech [January 14, 1766]
Where laws ends, tyranny begins.
Case of Wilkes. Speech
[January 9, 1770]
A long train of these practices has at length unwillingly convinced me that there is something behind the throne greater than the King himself.[2]
Chatham Correspondence. Speech
[March 2, 1770]
Reparation for our rights at home, and security against the like future violations.[3]
Letter to the Earl of Shelburne
[September 29, 1770]
You cannot conquer America.
Speech [November 18, 1777]
If I were an American, as I am an Englishman, while a foreign troop was landed in my country I never would lay down my arms, — never! never! never!
Ibid.
The poorest man may in his cottage bid defiance to all the force of the Crown. It may be frail; its roof may shake; the wind may blow through it;

the storms may enter, the rain may enter, — but the King of England cannot enter; all his forces dare not cross the threshold of the ruined tenement!
Speech on the Excise Bill

SAMUEL JOHNSON
[1709–1784]

Let observation with extensive view
Survey mankind, from China to Peru.[1]
Vanity of Human Wishes. Line 1
Deign on the passing world to turn thine eyes,
And pause a while from learning to be wise.
Ibid. Line 157
There mark what ills the scholar's life assail, —
Toil, envy, want, the patron, and the jail.
Ibid. Line 159
He left the name at which the world grew pale,
To point a moral, or adorn a tale.[2]
Ibid. Line 221
Hides from himself his state, and shuns to know
That life protracted is protracted woe.
Ibid. Line 257
Superfluous lags the veteran on the stage.
Ibid. Line 308
Must helpless man, in ignorance sedate,
Roll darkling down the torrent of his fate?
Ibid. Line 345
Of all the griefs that harass the distrest,
Sure the most bitter is a scornful jest.[3]
London. Line 166

---

[1] Illustrious predecessor. — BURKE: *The Present Discontents*
I tread in the footsteps of illustrious men. . . . In receiving from the people the sacred trust twice confided to my illustrious predecessor [Andrew Jackson]. — MARTIN VAN BUREN [1782–1862]: *Inaugural Address* [March 4, 1837]
[2] Quoted by Lord Mahon [1805–1875], "greater than the throne itself," in his *History of England, Vol. V, P. 258*
[3] Indemnity for the past and security for the future. — RUSSELL: *Memoir of Fox, Vol. III, P. 345, Letter to the Hon. T. Maitland*

[1] All human race, from China to Peru,
Pleasure, howe'er disguised by art, pursue.
THOMAS WARTON: *Universal Love of Pleasure*
DE QUINCEY (*Works, Vol. X, P. 72*) quotes the criticism of some writer, who contends with some reason that this high-sounding couplet of Dr. Johnson amounts in effect to this: Let observation with extensive observation observe mankind extensively.
[2] Quoted by SIR WALTER SCOTT at the end of *Ivanhoe*.
[3] Nil habet infelix paupertas durius in se,
Quam quod ridiculos homines facit.
JUVENAL: *Satires, III, 133*
Nothing in poverty so ill is borne

This mournful truth is ev'rywhere con-
fess'd, —
Slow rises worth, by poverty depress'd.[1]
London. Line 176

Call the Betsies, Kates, and Jennies,
All the names that banish care.
One-and-Twenty

In vain the surge's angry shock,
In vain the drifting sands;
Unharmed, upon the Eternal Rock,
The Eternal City stands.
The City of God. Stanza 5

Studious to please, yet not ashamed to
fail.
Prologue to the Tragedy of Irene

Each change of many-colour'd life he
drew,
Exhausted worlds, and then imagin'd
new.
*Prologue on the Opening of Drury
Lane Theatre*

And panting Time toil'd after him in
vain.
Ibid.

Declamation roar'd, while Passion
slept.
Ibid.

The wild vicissitudes of taste.
Ibid.

For we that live to please must please
to live.
Ibid.

Catch, then, oh catch the transient
hour;
Improve each moment as it flies!
Life's a short summer, man a flower;
He dies — alas! how soon he dies!
Winter, An Ode

Officious, innocent, sincere,
Of every friendless name the friend.
*Verses on the Death of Mr. Robert
Levet. Stanza 2*

In misery's darkest cavern known,
His useful care was ever nigh.[2]
Where hopeless anguish pour'd his
groan,

And lonely want retir'd to die.
*Verses on the Death of Mr. Robert
Levet. Stanza 5*

And sure th' Eternal Master found
His single talent well employ'd.
Ibid. Stanza 7

Then, with no throbs of fiery pain,[1]
No cold gradations of decay,
Death broke at once the vital chain,
And freed his soul the nearest way.
Ibid. Stanza 9

That saw the manners in the face.
Lines on the Death of Hogarth

A Poet, Naturalist, and Historian,
Who left scarcely any style of writing
untouched,
And touched nothing that he did not
adorn.[2]
Epitaph on Goldsmith

How small of all that human hearts
endure,
That part which laws or kings can cause
or cure!
Still to ourselves in every place con-
signed,
Our own felicity we make or find.
*Lines Added to Goldsmith's
Traveller*

From thee, great God, we spring, to
thee we tend, —
Path, motive, guide, original and end.[3]
Motto to The Rambler, No. 7

Curiosity is one of the permanent
and certain characteristics of a vigorous
mind.
The Rambler [March 12, 1751]

No place affords a more striking conviction of the vanity of human hopes,
than a public library.
Ibid. [March 23, 1751]

Parnassus has its flowers of transient
fragrance, as well as its oaks of towering height, and its laurels of eternal
verdure.
Ibid.

As its exposing men to grinning scorn.
JOHN OLDHAM [1653–1683]:
translation
[1] Three years later Johnson wrote, "Mere
unassisted merit advances slowly, if — what
is not very common — it advances at all."
[2] Variant, — His ready help was always
nigh.

[1] Variant, — Then with no fiery throbbing
pain.
[2] Qui nullum fere scribendi genus
Non tetigit,
Nullum quod tetigit non ornavit.
See Chesterfield, page 222.
[3] A translation of Boethius's *De Consolatione Philosophiæ*, III, 9, 27.

Life is surely given us for higher purposes than to gather what our ancestors have wisely thrown away.

The Rambler [May 14, 1751]

It is one of the maxims of the civil law, that definitions are hazardous.

Ibid. [May 28, 1751]

Praise like gold and diamonds owes its value only to its scarcity.

Ibid. [June 6, 1751]

Almost all absurdity of conduct arises from the imitation of those whom we can not resemble.

Ibid. [July 2, 1751]

Ye who listen with credulity to the whispers of fancy, and pursue with eagerness the phantoms of hope; who expect that age will perform the promises of youth, and that the deficiencies of the present day will be supplied by the morrow, — attend to the history of Rasselas, Prince of Abyssinia.

Rasselas. Chap. I

"I fly from pleasure," said the prince, "because pleasure has ceased to please; I am lonely because I am miserable, and am unwilling to cloud with my presence the happiness of others."

Ibid. Chap. III

Ingenious contrivances to facilitate motion, and unite levity with strength.

Ibid. Chap. VI, A Dissertation on the Art of Flying

A man used to vicissitudes is not easily dejected.

Ibid. Chap. XII

Few things are impossible to diligence and skill.

Ibid.

Knowledge is more than equivalent to force.[1]

Ibid. Chap. XIII

I live in the crowd of jollity, not so much to enjoy company as to shun myself.

Ibid. Chap. XVI

Many things difficult to design prove easy to performance.

Ibid.

[1] See Bacon, page 111.

The first years of man must make provision for the last.

Rasselas. Chap. XVII

Example is always more efficacious than precept.

Ibid. Chap. XXX

The endearing elegance of female friendship.

Ibid. Chap. XLVI

Words are men's daughters, but God's sons are things.

Supposed to have been inserted by Dr. Johnson in Samuel Madden's work, Boulter's Monument [1745]

I am not so lost in lexicography as to forget that *words are the daughters of earth, and that things are the sons of heaven.*[1]

Preface to His Dictionary [1755]

I dismiss it with frigid tranquillity, having little to fear or hope from censure or from praise.

Ibid.

CLUB — An assembly of good fellows, meeting under certain conditions.

Definition in the Dictionary

ESSAY — A loose sally of the mind; an irregular indigested piece; not a regular and orderly composition.

Ibid.

EXCISE — A hateful tax levied upon commodities, and adjudged not by the common judges of property, but wretches hired by those to whom excise is paid.

Ibid.

GRUBSTREET — The name of a street near Moorsfield, London, much inhabited by writers of small histories, dictionaries, and temporary poems.

Ibid.

OATS — A grain which in England is generally given to horses, but in Scotland supports the people.[2]

Ibid.

[1] See Herbert, page 138. See Samuel Madden, page 204.

[2] It was pleasant to me to find, that "Oats," the "food of horses," were so much used as the food of the people in Dr. Johnson's own

PENSION — An allowance made to any one without an equivalent. In England, it is generally understood to mean pay given to a state hireling for treason to his country.
Definition in the Dictionary

PIRATE — A sea robber, any robber; particularly a bookseller who seizes the copies of other men.
Ibid.

Whoever wishes to attain an English style, familiar but not coarse, and elegant but not ostentatious, must give his days and nights to the volumes of Addison.
Life of Addison

To be of no church is dangerous. Religion, of which the rewards are distant, and which is animated only by faith and hope, will glide by degrees out of the mind unless it be invigorated and reimpressed by external ordinances, by stated calls to worship, and the salutary influence of example.
Life of Milton

His death eclipsed the gayety of nations, and impoverished the public stock of harmless pleasure.[1]
Life of Edmund Smith (referring to the death of Garrick)

That man is little to be envied whose patriotism would not gain force upon the plain of Marathon, or whose piety would not grow warmer among the ruins of Iona.
Journey to the Western Islands. Inch Kenneth

He is no wise man that will quit a certainty for an uncertainty.
The Idler. No. 57

What is read twice is commonly better remembered than what is transcribed.
Ibid. No. 74

Boswell. That, Sir, was great fortitude of mind.

town. — BOSWELL: *Life of Dr. Johnson, Everyman ed., Vol. I, P. 628*
I own that by my definition of *oats* I meant to vex them [the Scotch]. — *Ibid., Vol. II, P. 434*
[1] Quoted by BOSWELL, *Vol. I, P. 39* and *Vol. II, P. 275.*

Johnson. No, Sir; stark insensibility.
Boswell's Life of Dr. Johnson.[1]
Vol. I, Page 28

On clean-shirt-day he went abroad, and paid visits.
Ibid. Page 56

Tom Birch is as brisk as a bee in conversation; but no sooner does he take a pen in his hand, than it becomes a torpedo to him, and benumbs all his faculties.
Ibid. Page 92

I'll come no more behind your scenes, David; for the silk stockings and white bosoms of your actresses excite my amorous propensities.[2]
Ibid. Page 117

Wretched un-idea'd girls.
Ibid. Page 148

Is not a patron, my lord [Chesterfield], one who looks with unconcern on a man struggling for life in the water, and when he has reached ground encumbers him with help?[3]
Ibid. Page 156

Sir, he [Bolingbroke] was a scoundrel and a coward: a scoundrel for charging a blunderbuss against religion and morality; a coward, because he had not resolution to fire it off himself, but left half a crown to a beggarly Scotchman to draw the trigger at his death.
Ibid. Page 160

If a man does not make new acquaintances as he advances through life, he will soon find himself left alone. A man, sir, should keep his friendship in a constant repair.
Ibid. Page 182

Towering in the confidence of twenty-one.[4]
Ibid. Page 197

[1] Everyman edition, 2 volumes.
The Life of Johnson is assuredly a great, a very great work. Homer is not more decidedly the first of heroic poets, Shakespeare is not more decidedly the first of dramatists, Demosthenes is not more decidedly the first of orators, than Boswell is the first of biographers. He has no second. — MACAULAY: *Samuel Johnson* [September, 1831]
[2] To David Garrick [1749].
[3] Letter to Chesterfield [Feb. 7, 1755].
[4] Letter to Bennet Langton [Jan. 9, 1758].

Being in a ship is being in a jail, with the chance of being drowned.

Boswell's Life of Dr. Johnson.
Vol. I, Page 215

A short letter to a distant friend is, in my opinion, an insult like that of a slight bow or cursory salutation.[1]

Ibid. Page 223

Nothing is little to him that feels it with great sensibility.[2]

Ibid. Page 230

Bounty always receives part of its value from the manner in which it is bestowed.[3]

Ibid. Page 233

Every man's affairs, however little, are important to himself.[4]

Ibid. Page 235

A man of genius has been seldom ruined but by himself.[5]

Ibid. Page 236

Sir, I think all Christians, whether Papists or Protestants, agree in the essential articles, and that their differences are trivial, and rather political than religious.[6]

Ibid. Page 251

The noblest prospect which a Scotchman ever sees, is the high-road that leads him to England.

Ibid. Page 264

A man ought to read just as inclination leads him; for what he reads as a task will do him little good.[7] A young

man should read five hours in a day, and so may acquire a great deal of knowledge.

Boswell's Life of Dr. Johnson.
Vol. I, Page 266

If he does really think that there is no distinction between virtue and vice, why, sir, when he leaves our houses let us count our spoons.

Ibid. Page 268

If I accustom a servant to tell a lie for *me,* have I not reason to apprehend that he will tell many lies for *himself?*

Ibid. Page 270

Sir, your levellers wish to level *down* as far as themselves; but they cannot bear levelling *up* to themselves.

Ibid. Page 277

Sherry[1] is dull, naturally dull; but it must have taken him a great deal of pains to become what we now see him. Such an excess of stupidity, sir, is not in Nature.

Ibid. Page 280

Sir, a woman preaching is like a dog's walking on his hind legs. It is not done well; but you are surprised to find it done at all.

Ibid. Page 287

I look upon it, that he who does not mind his belly will hardly mind anything else.

Ibid. Page 290

This was a good dinner enough, to be sure, but it was not a dinner to *ask* a man to.

Ibid. Page 291

Gloomy calm of idle vacancy.[2]

Ibid. Page 294

A very unclubable man.

Ibid. Page 298

He[3] is one of the many who have made themselves *publick,* without making themselves *known.*

Ibid. Page 310

---

[1] Letter to Joseph Baretti [June 10, 1761].
[2] To the same [July 20, 1762].
[3] Letter to the Earl of Bute [July 20, 1762].
[4] To the same [Nov. 3, 1762].
[5] Letter to Joseph Baretti [Dec. 21, 1762].
[6] All denominations of Christians have really little difference in point of doctrine, though they may differ widely in external forms. — *Vol. I, P. 411* [1772]
I do not find that the age or country makes the least difference; no, nor the language the actor spoke, nor the religion which they professed, — whether Arab in the desert, or Frenchman in the Academy. I see that sensible men and conscientious men all over the world were of one religion of well-doing and daring. — EMERSON: *Lectures and Biographical Sketches, The Preacher, P. 215*
See Benjamin Disraeli, page 421.
[7] The book which you read from a sense of duty, or because for any reason you must, does not commonly make friends with you. —

WILLIAM DEAN HOWELLS: *My Literary Passions, Chap. 7*
[1] Thomas Sheridan [1719–1788], actor, lecturer, and author.
[2] Letter to Boswell [Dec. 8, 1763]. See Cowper, page 266.
[3] William Kenrick [1725–1779], a writer who attacked Goldsmith, Garrick, Fielding, Johnson, and Colman.

I cannot see that lectures can do so much good as reading the books from which the lectures are taken.

Boswell's Life of Dr. Johnson.
Vol. I, Page 315

Life is not long, and too much of it must not pass in idle deliberation how it shall be spent.[1]

Ibid. Page 325

Were he not to marry again, it might be concluded that his first wife had given him a disgust to marriage; but by taking a second wife he pays the highest compliment to the first, by showing that she made him so happy as a married man, that he wishes to be so a second time.

Ibid. Page 360

I do not know, sir, that the fellow is an infidel; but if he be an infidel, he is an infidel as a dog is an infidel; that is to say, he has never thought upon the subject.

Ibid. Page 370

It matters not how a man dies, but how he lives.

Ibid. Page 378

That fellow seems to me to possess but one idea, and that is a wrong one.

Ibid. Page 393

The triumph of hope over experience.

Ibid. Page 394

A decent provision for the poor is the true test of civilization.

Ibid. Page 396

A fallible being will fail somewhere.

Ibid. Page 397

Whatever philosophy may determine of material nature, it is certainly true of intellectual nature, that it abhors a vacuum.

Ibid. Page 403

A common prejudice should not be found in one whose trade it is to rectify error.

Ibid. Page 409

Nobody can write the life of a man, but those who have eat and drunk and lived in social intercourse with him.[2]

Ibid. Page 422

The way to make sure of power and influence is by lending money confidentially to your neighbours at a small interest, or perhaps no interest at all, and having their bonds in your possession.

Boswell's Life of Dr. Johnson.
Vol. I, Page 422

I am a great friend to public amusements; for they keep people from vice.

Ibid. Page 424

A cow is a very good animal in the field; but we turn her out of a garden.

Ibid. Page 436

Much may be made of a Scotchman if he be caught young.

Ibid. Page 440

For my part, I'd tell the truth, and shame the devil.[1]

Ibid.

There is nothing, I think, in which the power of art is shown so much as in playing on the fiddle. In all other things we can do something at first.

Ibid. Page 462

The way to spread a work is to sell it at a low price. No man will send to buy a thing that costs even sixpence, without an intention to read it.

Ibid. Page 465

When people find a man of the most distinguished abilities as a writer, their inferior while he is with them, it must be highly gratifying to them.

Ibid. Page 469

An old tutor of a college said to one of his pupils: Read over your compositions, and wherever you meet with a passage which you think is particularly fine, strike it out.[2]

Ibid. Page 470

You are the most unscottified of your countrymen.

Ibid. Page 473

Was ever poet so trusted before?[3]

Ibid. Page 502

---

[1] Letter to Boswell [Aug. 21, 1766].

[2] They only who live with a man can write his life with any genuine exactness and dis-

crimination; and few people who have lived with a man know what to remark about him. —*Vol. I, P. 617*

[1] See Shakespeare, page 62.

[2] See Sydney Smith, page 313.

[3] Of Oliver Goldsmith in a letter to Boswell [July 4, 1774].

Mum, it is a secret.
Boswell's Life of Dr. Johnson.
Vol. I, Page 511
Attack is the reaction. I never think
I have hit hard unless it rebounds.
Ibid. Page 540
A man will turn over half a library
to make one book.
Ibid. Page 545
Patriotism is the last refuge of a
scoundrel.
Ibid. Page 547
Hell is paved with good intentions.[1]
Ibid. Page 555
Knowledge is of two kinds: we know
a subject ourselves, or we know where
we can find information upon it.
Ibid. Page 558
I never take a nap after dinner but
when I have had a bad night; and then
the nap takes me.
Ibid. Page 589
In lapidary inscriptions a man is not
upon oath.
Ibid.
There is now less flogging in our great
schools than formerly, but then less is
learned there; so that what the boys
get at one end they lose at the other.
Ibid.
There is nothing which has yet been
contrived by man by which so much
happiness is produced as by a good
tavern or inn.[2]
Ibid. Page 620
Questioning is not the mode of conversation among gentlemen.
Ibid. Page 635
A man is very apt to complain of the
ingratitude of those who have risen
far above him.
Ibid. Vol. II, Page 5
If a man could say nothing against
a character but what he can prove, history could not be written.
Ibid. Page 13

[1] See Herbert, page 137.
[2] Whoe'er has travell'd life's dull round,
    Where'er his stages may have been,
    May sigh to think he still has found
    His warmest welcome at an inn.
    WILLIAM SHENSTONE [1714-1763]: *Writ-
    ten on a Window of an Inn at Henley*

No man but a blockhead ever wrote
except for money.
Boswell's Life of Dr. Johnson.
Vol. II, Page 16
While grief is fresh, every attempt
to divert only irritates.
Ibid. Page 21
We would not be at the trouble to
learn a language, if we could have all
that is written in it just as well in a
translation.
Ibid. Page 26
Life is a progress from want to want,
not from enjoyment to enjoyment.
Ibid. Page 36
Life admits not of delays; when
pleasure can be had, it is fit to catch
it. Every hour takes away part of the
things that please us, and perhaps part
of our disposition to be pleased.[1]
Ibid. Page 98
In every volume of poems something
good may be found.
Ibid. Page 117
When a man is tired of London, he
is tired of life; for there is in London
all that life can afford.
Ibid. Page 131
He was so generally civil, that no-
body thanked him for it.
Ibid. Page 134
To *make* money is to *coin* it; you
should say *get* money.
Ibid. Page 143
Everything that enlarges the sphere
of human powers, that shows man he
can do what he thought he could not
do, is valuable.
Ibid. Page 168
Goldsmith, however, was a man, who,
whatever he wrote, did it better than
any other man could do.
Ibid. Page 182
It is a man's own fault, it is from
want of use, if his mind grows torpid in
old age.
Ibid. Page 183
Johnson had said that he could repeat a complete chapter of "The Natural History of Iceland," from the Danish of Horrebow, the whole of which

[1] Letter to Boswell [Sept. 1, 1777].

was exactly (Ch. LXXII. *Concerning snakes*) thus: "There are no snakes to be met with throughout the whole island." [1]

Boswell's Life of Dr. Johnson.
Vol. II, Page 201

As the Spanish proverb says, "He, who would bring home the wealth of the Indies, must carry the wealth of the Indies with him," so it is in travelling, a man must carry knowledge with him if he would bring home knowledge.

Ibid. Page 216

It is amazing how little literature there is in the world.

Ibid. Page 217

It is better to live rich, than to die rich.

Ibid. Page 218

I have known what it was to have a wife, and . . . I have known what it was to lose a wife.

Ibid. Page 219

I would rather be attacked than unnoticed. For the worst thing you can do to an author is to be silent as to his works.

Ibid. Page 257

I remember a passage in Goldsmith's "Vicar of Wakefield," which he was afterwards fool enough to expunge: "I do not love a man who is zealous for nothing."

Ibid. Page 267

Claret is the liquor for boys, port for men; but he who aspires to be a hero must drink brandy.

Ibid. Page 271

Worth seeing? yes; but not worth going to see.

Ibid. Page 291

You see in him vulgar prosperity.

Ibid.

He that outlives a wife whom he has long loved, sees himself disjoined from the only mind that has the same hopes, and fears, and interest; from the only companion with whom he has shared much good and evil; and with whom he could set his mind at liberty, to re-

trace the past or anticipate the future.

Boswell's Life of Dr. Johnson.
Vol. II, Page 298

A Frenchman must be always talking, whether he knows anything of the matter or not; an Englishman is content to say nothing, when he has nothing to say.

Ibid. Page 326

Of Dr. Goldsmith he said, "No man was more foolish when he had not a pen in his hand, or more wise when he had."

Ibid. Page 336

The applause of a single human being is of great consequence.

Ibid. Page 338

Come to me, my dear Bozzy, and let us be as happy as we can. [1]

Ibid. Page 366

The potentiality of growing rich beyond the dreams of avarice. [2]

Ibid. Page 376

Classical quotation is the *parole* of literary men all over the world.

Ibid. Page 386

My friend was of opinion that when a man of rank appeared in that character [as an author], he deserved to have his merits handsomely allowed. [3]

Ibid. Page 393

A jest breaks no bones.

Ibid. Page 405

To let friendship die away by negligence and silence, is certainly not wise. It is voluntarily to throw away one of the greatest comforts of this weary pilgrimage.

Ibid. Page 417

Whatever you have, spend less. [4]

Ibid. Page 427

I never have sought the world; the world was not to seek me. [5]

Ibid. Page 436

---

[1] Letter to Boswell [March 14, 1781].

[2] I am rich beyond the dreams of avarice. — EDWARD MOORE [1712–1757]: *The Gamester, Act II, Sc. 2* [1753]

[3] Usually quoted as "When a nobleman writes a book, he ought to be encouraged."

[4] Letter to Boswell [Dec. 7, 1782].

[5] I have not loved the world, nor the world me. — BYRON: *Childe Harold, Canto III, St. 113*

---

[1] Chapter XLII is still shorter: "There are no owls of any kind in the whole island."

He is not only dull himself, but the cause of dullness in others.[1]

> *Boswell's Life of Dr. Johnson.*
> *Vol. II, Page 441*

Clear your mind of cant.

> *Ibid. Page 469*

He thought it unnecessary to collect many editions of a book, which were all the same, except as to the paper and print; he would have the original, and all the translations, and all the editions which had any variations in the text.

> *Ibid. Page 512*

Every man should try to collect one book in that manner and present it to a publick library.

> *Ibid.*

You see they'd have fitted him to a T.[2]

> *Ibid. Page 518*

Who drives fat oxen should himself be fat.[3]

> *Ibid. Page 535*

I have found you an argument; I am not obliged to find you an understanding.

> *Ibid. Page 536*

Blown about with every wind of criticism.[4]

> *Ibid. Page 539*

Don't *attitudenize.*

> *Ibid. Page 541*

We now know a method of mounting into the air [balloons], and, I think, are not likely to know more. The vehicles can serve no use till we can guide them; and they can gratify no curiosity till we mount with them to greater heights than we can reach without; till we rise above the tops of the highest mountains, which we have not yet done.

> *Ibid. Page 566*

[1] See Shakespeare, page 64.
[2] We could manage this matter to a T. — STERNE: *Tristram Shandy, Book II, Chap.* 5
You will find it shall echo my speech to a T. — THOMAS MOORE: *Occasional Address for the Opening of the New Theatre of St. Stephen*
[3] A parody on "Who rules o'er freemen should himself be free," from BROOKE's *Gustavus Vasa, first edition.*
[4] Carried about with every wind of doctrine. — *Ephesians, IV, 14*

I look upon every day to be lost, in which I do not make a new acquaintance.

> *Boswell's Life of Dr. Johnson.*
> *Vol. II, Page 579*

Life is very short, and very uncertain; let us spend it as well as we can.

> *Ibid. Page 583*

God bless you, my dear.

> *Ibid. Page 609 (His last words)*

If the man who turnips cries
Cry not when his father dies,
'Tis a proof that he had rather
Have a turnip than his father.

> *Johnsoniana. Piozzi, 30*

He was a very good hater.

> *Ibid. 39*

The law is the last result of human wisdom acting upon human experience for the benefit of the public.

> *Ibid. 58*

The use of travelling is to regulate imagination by reality, and instead of thinking how things may be, to see them as they are.

> *Ibid. 154*

Dictionaries are like watches; the worst is better than none, and the best cannot be expected to go quite true.

> *Ibid. 178*

Books that you may carry to the fire and hold readily in your hand, are the most useful after all.

> *Ibid. Hawkins, 197*

Round numbers are always false.

> *Ibid. 235*

As with my hat[1] upon my head
I walk'd along the Strand,
I there did meet another man
With his hat in his hand.[2]

> *Ibid. George Steevens, 310*

Abstinence is as easy to me as temperance would be difficult.

> *Ibid. Hannah More, 467*

The limbs will quiver and move after the soul is gone.

> *Ibid. Northcote, 487*

Hawkesworth said of Johnson, "You have a memory that would convict any

[1] Elsewhere found, "I put my hat."
[2] A parody on PERCY's ballad, *The Hermit of Warkworth.*

author of plagiarism in any court of literature in the world."

Johnsoniana. Kearsley, 600

His conversation does not show the minute-hand, but he strikes the hour very correctly.

Ibid. 604

Hunting was the labour of the savages of North America, but the amusement of the gentlemen of England.

Ibid. 606

I am very fond of the company of ladies. I like their beauty, I like their delicacy, I like their vivacity, and I like their silence.

Ibid. Seward, 617

Tomorrow I purpose to regulate my room.

Prayers and Meditations. 1764

Preserve me from unseasonable and immoderate sleep.

ibid. 1767

Every man naturally persuades himself that he can keep his resolutions, nor is he convinced of his imbecility but by length of time and frequency of experiment.

Ibid. 1770

This world, where much is to be done and little to be known.

Ibid. Against Inquisitive and Perplexing Thoughts

Gratitude is a fruit of great cultivation; you do not find it among gross people.

Tour to the Hebrides.
[September 20, 1773]

A fellow that makes no figure in company, and has a mind as narrow as the neck of a vinegar-cruet.

Ibid. [September 30, 1773]

The atrocious crime of being a young man, which the honourable gentleman has with such spirit and decency charged upon me, I shall neither attempt to palliate nor deny; but content myself with wishing that I may be one of those whose follies may cease with their youth, and not of that number who are ignorant in spite of experience.[1]

Pitt's Reply to Walpole, a Speech
[March 6, 1741]

The hoary Sage replied,
Come, my lad, and drink some beer.

Quoted by MRS. PIOZZI: *Anecdotes*
of Samuel Johnson

Wharton quotes Johnson as saying of Dr. Campbell, "He is the richest author that ever grazed the common of literature."

GEORGE, LORD LYTTELTON
[1709-1773]

For his chaste Muse employ'd her heaven-taught lyre
None but the noblest passions to inspire,
Not one immoral, one corrupted thought,
One line which, dying, he could wish to blot.

Prologue to Thomson's Coriolanus

Women, like princes, find few real friends.

Advice to a Lady

What is your sex's earliest, latest care,
Your heart's supreme ambition? To be fair.

Ibid.

The lover in the husband may be lost.

Ibid.

How much the wife is dearer than the bride.

An Irregular Ode

None without hope e'er lov'd the brightest fair,
But love can hope where reason would despair.

Epigram

Where none admire, 'tis useless to excel;
Where none are beaux, 'tis vain to be a belle.

Soliloquy on a Beauty in the Country

[1] This is the composition of Johnson, founded on some note or statement of the actual speech. Johnson said, "That speech I wrote in a garret, in Exeter Street." — BOSWELL: *Life of Dr. Johnson, 1741*

ALICIA [1] RUTHERFORD COCKBURN
[1712–1794]

I've seen the smiling
Of Fortune beguiling,
I've felt all her favours and found her
　　decay;
Sweet was her blessing,
Kind her caressing:
But now they are fled, are fled far away.
　　　　The Flowers of the Forest.
　　　　　　　　Stanza 1

Thy frown cannot fear me,
Thy smile cannot cheer me —
Since the Flowers o' the Forest are a'
wede away.[2]
　　　　　　　Ibid. Stanza 4

RICHARD GLOVER
[1712–1785]

As near Porto-Bello lying
On the gently swelling flood,
At midnight with streamers flying
Our triumphant navy rode.
　　Admiral Hosier's Ghost.[3] *Stanza 1*
I am Hosier's injur'd ghost.
　　　　　　　Ibid. Stanza 4

GEORGE GRENVILLE
[1712–1770]

A wise Government knows how to
enforce with temper or to conciliate
with dignity.
　　*Speech against the Expulsion of
　　John Wilkes, House of Parliament
　　[1769]*

EDWARD MOORE
[1712–1757]

Can't I another's face commend,
And to her virtues be a friend,
But instantly your forehead lowers,

---

[1] Sometimes given as Alison.
[2] The flowers of the forest are a' wide awae.
— JANE ELLIOTT [1727–1805]: *The Flowers
of the Forest* (written before Mrs. Cockburn's
poem). Also known as *The Lament for
Flodden.*
[3] Written on the taking of Porto-Bello from
the Spaniards by Admiral Vernon [Nov. 22,
1739]. The ballad is in PERCY's *Reliques,
Series II, Book III.*

As if *her* merit lessen'd *yours?*
　　*The Farmer, the Spaniel, and
　　　　　　　　　the Cat*
The maid who modestly conceals
Her beauties, while she hides, reveals;
Give but a glimpse, and fancy draws
Whate'er the Grecian Venus was.
　　　　The Spider and the Bee
But from the hoop's bewitching round,
Her very shoe has power to wound.
　　　　　　　　　Ibid.
Time still, as he flies, brings increase
　　to her truth,
And gives to her mind what he steals
　　from her youth.
　　　　The Happy Marriage

JOSIAH TUCKER, DEAN OF GLOUCESTER
[1712–1799]

What is true of a shopkeeper is true
of a shopkeeping nation.[1]
　　*Tract Against Going to War for
　　　　the Sake of Trade [1763]*

---

[1] Men who content themselves with the
semblance of truth and a display of words
talk much of our obligations to Great Britain
for protection. Had she a single eye to our
advantage? A nation of shopkeepers are [sic]
very seldom so disinterested. — From an oration purporting to have been delivered by
SAMUEL ADAMS [1722–1803] at the State
House in Philadelphia, Aug. 1, 1776. (Philadelphia, printed; London, reprinted for E.
Johnson, No. 4 Ludgate Hill, 1776.) W. V.
Wells, in his *Life of Adams,* says: "No such
American edition has ever been seen, but at
least four copies are known of the London
issue. A German translation of this oration
was printed in 1778, perhaps at Berne; the
place of publication is not given."
　　To found a great empire for the sole purpose of raising up a people of customers may
at first sight appear a project fit only for a
nation of shopkeepers. It is, however, a project
altogether unfit for a nation of shopkeepers;
but extremely fit for a nation whose Government is influenced by shopkeepers. — ADAM
SMITH [1723–1790]: *Wealth of Nations, Vol.
II, Book IV, Chap. 7, Part 3 [1776]*
　　Let Pitt then boast of his victory to his
nation of shopkeepers. — BERTRAND BARÈRE
[1755–1841]: *Speech* [June 11, 1794]
　　But it may be said as a rule, that every
Englishman in the Duke of Wellington's army
paid his way. The remembrance of such a
fact surely becomes a nation of shopkeepers.

LAURENCE STERNE
[1713–1768]

So long as a man rides his hobby-horse peaceably and quietly along the King's highway, and neither compels you or me to get up behind him, — pray, Sir, what have either you or I to do with it?

Tristram Shandy. Book I, Chap. 7

For every ten jokes, thou hast got an hundred enemies.

Ibid. Chap. 12

Whistled up to London, upon a Tom Fool's errand.

Ibid. Chap. 16

'Tis known by the name of perseverance in a good cause, — and of obstinacy in a bad one.

Ibid. Chap. 17

The Republic of letters.[1]

Ibid. Chap. 20

The history of a soldier's wound beguiles the pain of it.

Ibid. Chap. 25

We could manage this matter to a T.[2]

Ibid. Book II, Chap. 5

Splashing and plunging like a devil thro' thick and thin.[3]

Ibid. Chap. 9

Writing, when properly managed (as you may be sure I think mine is) is but a different name for conversation.

Ibid. Chap. 11

Go, poor devil, get thee gone! Why should I hurt thee? This world surely is wide enough to hold both thee and me. [Uncle Toby to the fly]

Ibid. Chap 12

That's another story,[4] replied my father.

Ibid. Chap. 17

Good — bad — indifferent.[5]

Ibid. Book III, Chap. 2

Great wits jump.

Tristram Shandy.
Book III, Chap. 9

"Our armies swore terribly in Flanders," cried my Uncle Toby, "but nothing to this."

Ibid. Chap. 11

Of all the cants which are canted in this canting world, though the cant of hypocrites may be the worst, the cant of criticism is the most tormenting![1]

Ibid. Chap. 12

When Ernulphus[2] cursed — no part escaped him.

Ibid.

Angels and ministers of grace defend us.

Ibid. Chap. 20

'Twould be as much as my life was worth.

Ibid.

Before an affliction is digested, consolation ever comes too soon; and after it is digested, it comes too late.

Ibid. Chap. 29

The sweat of a man's brows, and the exudations of a man's brains, are as much a man's own property as the breeches upon his backside.

Ibid. Chap. 34

As certainly as you can make a velvet cap out of a sow's ear.[3]

Ibid. Book IV, Slawkenbergius's Tale

One of the two horns of my dilemma.

Ibid. Chap. 26

The feather put into his cap of having been abroad.

Ibid. Chap. 31

Now or never was the time.

Ibid.

— W. M. THACKERAY [1811–1863]: *Vanity Fair, Vol. I, Chap. 28*

[1] See Fielding, page 229.

[2] See Johnson, page 238.

[3] See Chaucer, page 6.

[4] But that is another story. — KIPLING: *Plain Tales from the Hills, Three and — an Extra*

[5] See Joel Barlow, page 280.

[1] Clear your mind of cant. — JOHNSON: *Boswell's Life of Dr. Johnson, Vol. II, P. 469, Everyman edition*

[2] Ernulph or Arnulph [1040–1124], French Benedictine and Bishop of Rochester.
May all the curses of the good Bishop Ernulphus light on the borrower-and-not-returner or upon the stealer of this book [Sir William Osler's inscription on the fly-leaf of his own copy of his *Textbook on the Principles and Practice of Medicine*]. — HARVEY CUSHING: *Life of Sir William Osler, Vol. I, Chap. 14*

[3] See Herbert, page 138.

The Accusing Spirit, which flew up
to heaven's chancery with the oath,
blushed as he gave it in; and the Re-
cording Angel, as he wrote it down,
dropped a tear upon the word and blot-
ted it out forever.[1]
Tristram Shandy.
Book VI, Chap. 8
A man should know something of
his own country, too, before he goes
abroad.
Ibid. Book VII, Chap. 2
I am sick as a horse.
Ibid.
Ho! 'tis the time of salads.
Ibid. Chap. 17
"They order," said I, "this matter
better in France."
A Sentimental Journey. Page 1
I pity the man who can travel from
Dan to Beersheba and cry, " 'Tis all
barren!"
Ibid. In the Street, Calais
Tant pis and *tant mieux*,[2] being two
of the great hinges in French conver-
sation, a stranger would do well to
set himself right in the use of them
before he gets to Paris.[3]
Ibid. Montreuil
Hail, ye small, sweet courtesies of
life! for smooth do ye make the road
of it.
Ibid. The Pulse, Paris
"Disguise thyself as thou wilt, still,
Slavery," said I, "still thou art a bit-
ter draught."
Ibid. The Passport, The Hotel
at Paris
"God tempers the wind," said Maria,
"to the shorn lamb." [4]
Ibid. Maria

[1] But sad as angels for the good man's sin,
  Weep to record, and blush to give it in.
  CAMPBELL: *Pleasures of Hope, Part II,*
   L. 357
[2] So much the worse; so much the better.
[3] Never go to France
  Unless you know the lingo.
  THOMAS HOOD: *French and English,*
   St. 1
[4] Dieu mésure le froid à la brebis tondue
(God measures the cold to the shorn lamb).
— HENRI ESTIENNE [1594]: *Prémices, etc.,*
P. 47
  See Herbert, page 138.

The sad vicissitude of things.[1]
Sermon 16, The Character of
Shimei

WILLIAM SHENSTONE
[1714–1763]

Whoe'er has travell'd life's dull round,
  Where'er his stages may have been,
May sigh to think he still has found
  The warmest welcome at an inn.[2]
Written on a Window of an Inn
at Henley. Stanza 5
Her cap, far whiter than the driven
  snow,
Emblems right meet of decency does
  yield.
The Schoolmistress. Stanza 6

WILLIAM WHITEHEAD
[1715–1785]

With indignation I survey
Such skill and judgment thrown away;
The time profusely squandered there
On vulgar arts beneath thy care,
If well employed at less expense
Had taught thee honour, virtue, sense.
The Youth and the Philosopher

DAVID GARRICK
[1716–1779]

A fellow-feeling makes one wondrous
  kind.[3]
Prologue on Quitting the Stage in
1776
Let others hail the rising sun:
I bow to that whose course is run.
On the Death of Mr. Pelham
Hearts of oak are our ships,
Gallant tars are our men,
  We always are ready,
  Steady, boys, steady,

[1] Revolves the sad vicissitudes of things. —
RICHARD GIFFORD [1725–1807]: *Contempla-*
tion
[2] See Johnson, page 236.
ROBERT LEIGHTON [1611–1684], Archbishop
of Glasgow, often said that if he were to
choose a place to die in, it should be an inn. —
Works, Vol. I, P. 76
[3] See Burton, page 121.

We'll fight, and we'll conquer again and again.
Hearts of Oak

Here lies James Quinn. Deign, reader, to be taught,
Whate'er thy strength of body, force of thought,
In Nature's happiest mould however cast,
To this complexion thou must come at last.
Epitaph on Quinn (in MURPHY's *Life of Garrick. Vol. II, Page 38)*

Are these the choice dishes the Doctor has sent us?
Is this the great poet whose works so content us?
This Goldsmith's fine feast, who has written fine books?
Heaven sends us good meat, but the Devil sends cooks? [1]
Epigram on Goldsmith's Retaliation (Ibid., Page 157)

Here lies Nolly Goldsmith, for shortness called Noll,
Who wrote like an angel, and talk'd like poor Poll.
Impromptu Epitaph on Goldsmith

THOMAS GRAY
[1716–1771]

What female heart can gold despise?
What cat's averse to fish?
On the Death of a Favourite Cat. Stanza 4

A fav'rite has no friend!
Ibid. Stanza 6

Ye distant spires, ye antique towers.
On a Distant Prospect of Eton College. Stanza 1

Ah, happy hills! ah, pleasing shade!
Ah, fields beloved in vain!
Where once my careless childhood stray'd,
A stranger yet to pain:
I feel the gales that from ye blow
A momentary bliss bestow.
Ibid. Stanza 2

[1] See Tusser, page 19.

They hear a voice in every wind,
And snatch a fearful joy.
On a Distant Prospect of Eton College. Stanza 4

Alas! regardless of their doom,
The little victims play;
No sense have they of ills to come,
Nor care beyond to-day.
Ibid. Stanza 6

To each his suff'rings; all are men,
Condemn'd alike to groan, —
The tender for another's pain,
Th' unfeeling for his own.

Yet ah! why should they know their fate,
Since sorrow never comes too late,
And happiness too swiftly flies?
Thought would destroy their paradise.
No more; where ignorance is bliss,
'Tis folly to be wise.[1]
Ibid. Stanza 10

Daughter of Jove, relentless power,
Thou tamer of the human breast,
Whose iron scourge and torturing hour
The bad affright, afflict the best!
Hymn to Adversity. Stanza 1

From Helicon's harmonious springs
A thousand rills their mazy progress take.
The Progress of Poesy. I, 1, Line 3

Glance their many-twinkling feet.
Ibid. 3, Line 11

O'er her warm cheek and rising bosom move
The bloom of young Desire and purple light of Love.
Ibid. Line 16

Or ope the sacred source of sympathetic tears.
Ibid. III, 1, Line 12

He [2] pass'd the flaming bounds of place and time:
The living throne, the sapphire-blaze,
Where angels tremble while they gaze,
He saw; but blasted with excess of light,
Closed his eyes in endless night.
Ibid. 2, Line 4

[1] See Davenant, page 147.
He that increaseth knowledge increaseth sorrow. — *Ecclesiastes, I, 18*
[2] Milton.

Bright-eyed Fancy, hov'ring o'er,
Scatters from her pictured urn
Thoughts that breathe and words that
burn.

The Progress of Poesy.
III, 3, Line 2

Ruin seize thee, ruthless king,
Confusion on thy banners wait;
Though fann'd by Conquest's crimson
wing,
They mock the air with idle state.

The Bard. I, 1, Line 1

Loose his beard, and hoary hair
Stream'd, like a meteor, to the troubled
air.[1]

Ibid. 2, Line 5

Dear as the light that visits these sad
eyes,
Dear as the ruddy drops that warm
my heart.[2]

Ibid. 3, Line 12

Weave the warp, and weave the woof,
The winding-sheet of Edward's race.
Give ample room and verge enough.[3]
The characters of hell to trace.

Ibid. II, 1, Line 1

Fair laughs the morn, and soft the
zephyr blows,
While proudly riding o'er the azure
realm,
In gallant trim the gilded vessel goes,
Youth on the prow, and Pleasure at
the helm;
Regardless of the sweeping whirlwind's
sway,
That, hush'd in grim repose, expects
his evening prey.

Ibid. 2, Line 9

Ye towers of Julius, London's lasting
shame,
With many a foul and midnight murder fed.

Ibid. 3, Line 11

Visions of glory, spare my aching
sight;
Ye unborn ages, crowd not on my soul!

Ibid. III, 1, Line 11

And truth severe, by fairy fiction drest.

Ibid. 3, Line 3

[1] See Milton, page 148.
[2] See Shakespeare, page 82.
[3] See Dryden, page 179.

While bright-eyed Science watches
round.

Ode for Music. Chorus, Line 3

The still small voice of gratitude.

Ibid. V, Line 8

Iron sleet of arrowy shower
Hurtles in the darken'd air.

The Fatal Sisters. Line 3

The curfew tolls the knell of parting
day,
The lowing herd wind slowly o'er the
lea,
The ploughman homeward plods his
weary way,
And leaves the world to darkness
and to me.

Elegy in a Country Churchyard.
Stanza 1

Each in his narrow cell forever laid,
The rude forefathers of the hamlet
sleep.

Ibid. Stanza 4

Nor grandeur hear with a disdainful
smile
The short and simple annals of the
poor.

Ibid. Stanza 8

The boast of heraldry, the pomp of
pow'r,
And all that beauty, all that wealth
e'er gave,
Await alike the inevitable hour:
The paths of glory lead but to the
grave.

Ibid. Stanza 9

Can storied urn, or animated bust
Back to its mansion call the fleeting
breath?
Can honour's voice provoke the silent
dust,
Or flatt'ry soothe the dull cold ear
of death?

Ibid. Stanza 11

Hands, that the rod of empire might
have sway'd,
Or waked to ecstasy the living lyre.

Ibid. Stanza 12

But Knowledge to their eyes her ample
page
Rich with the spoils of time did ne'er
unroll;[1]

[1] See Sir Thomas Browne, page 144.

Chill penury repress'd their noble rage,
  And froze the genial current of the soul.

  Elegy in a Country Churchyard.
    Stanza 13

Full many a gem of purest ray serene
  The dark unfathom'd caves of ocean bear:
Full many a flower is born to blush unseen,
  And waste its sweetness on the desert air.[1]

    Ibid. Stanza 14

Some village Hampden, that with dauntless breast
  The little tyrant of his fields withstood,
Some mute inglorious Milton here may rest,
  Some Cromwell guiltless of his country's blood.

    Ibid. Stanza 15

Forbade to wade through slaughter to a throne,
  And shut the gates of mercy on mankind.

    Ibid. Stanza 17

Far from the madding crowd's ignoble strife
  Their sober wishes never learn'd to stray;
Along the cool sequester'd vale of life
  They kept the noiseless tenor of their way.[2]

    Ibid. Stanza 19

Implores the passing tribute of a sigh.

    Ibid. Stanza 20

For who, to dumb forgetfulness a prey,
  This pleasing anxious being e'er resign'd,
Left the warm precincts of the cheerful day,
  Nor cast one longing ling'ring look behind?

    Ibid. Stanza 22

E'en from the tomb the voice of nature cries,

E'en in our ashes live their wonted fires.[1]

  Elegy in a Country Churchyard.
    Stanza 23

One morn I miss'd him on the custom'd hill,
  Along the heath, and near his fav'rite tree;
Another came; nor yet beside the rill,
  Nor up the lawn, nor at the wood was he.

    Ibid. Stanza 28

Here rests his head upon the lap of earth,
  A youth to fortune and to fame unknown.
Fair Science frown'd not on his humble birth,
  And Melancholy mark'd him for her own.[2]

    Ibid. The Epitaph, Stanza 1

Large was his bounty, and his soul sincere,
  Heaven did a recompense as largely send:
He gave to mis'ry (all he had) a tear,
  He gained from Heav'n ('twas all he wish'd) a friend.

    Ibid. Stanza 2

No farther seek his merits to disclose,
  Or draw his frailties from their dread abode,
(There they alike in trembling hope repose),
  The bosom of his Father and his God.

    Ibid. Stanza 3

The hues of bliss more brightly glow,
Chastised by sabler tints of woe.

  Ode on the Pleasure Arising from Vicissitude. Line 45

The meanest floweret of the vale,
The simplest note that swells the gale,
The common sun, the air, the skies,
To him are opening paradise.

    Ibid. Line 53

And hie him home, at evening's close,
To sweet repast and calm repose.

    Ibid. Line 87

---

[1] Nor waste their sweetness in the desert air. — CHURCHILL: *Gotham, Book II, L. 20*
[2] Usually quoted "even tenor of their way." See Porteus, page 268.

[1] See Chaucer, page 6.
[2] See Walton, page 140.

The social smile, the sympathetic tear.
Education and Government

When love could teach a monarch to be wise,
And gospel-light first dawn'd from Bullen's eyes.
Ibid.

Too poor for a bribe, and too proud to importune;
He had not the method of making a fortune.
On His Own Character

Now as the Paradisiacal pleasures of the Mahometans consist in playing upon the flute and lying with Houris, be mine to read eternal new romances of Marivaux and Crebillon.
Letters. Third Series, No. IV, To Mr. West

HORACE WALPOLE
[1717–1797]

Harry Vane, Pulteney's toad-eater,
Letter to Sir Horace Mann [1742]

The world is a comedy to those that think, a tragedy to those who feel.
Ibid. [1770]

A careless song, with a little nonsense in it now and then, does not misbecome a monarch.[1]
Ibid. [1774]

The whole [Scotch] nation hitherto has been void of wit and humour, and even incapable of relishing it.[2]
Ibid. [1778]

SAMUEL FOOTE
[1720–1777]

He made him a hut, wherein he did put
The carcass of Robinson Crusoe.
O poor Robinson Crusoe!
The Mayor of Garratt. Act I, Sc. 1

[1] A little nonsense now and then
Is relished by the wisest men.
ANONYMOUS
[2] It requires a surgical operation to get a joke well into a Scotch understanding. — SYDNEY SMITH: *Lady Holland's Memoir, Vol. I, Chap. 2*

Born in a cellar, and living in a garret.[1]
The Author. Act II

Matt Minikin won't set fire to the Thames though he lives near the Bridge.
Trip to Calais [1776]

So she went into the garden to cut a cabbage leaf to make an apple pie; and at the same time a great she-bear, coming up the street, pops its head into the shop. "What! no soap?" So he died, and she very imprudently married the barber; and there were present the Picninnies, and the Joblillies, and the Garyulies, and the Grand Panjandrum himself, with the little round button at top, and they all fell to playing the game of catch as catch can, till the gunpowder ran out at the heels of their boots.
Nonsense written to test the boasted memory of Charles Macklin, The Quarterly Review, London [September, 1854], Page 516. Quoted in Harry and Lucy, Concluded, Volume II, by MARIA EDGEWORTH

THOMAS GIBBONS
[1720–1785]

That man may last, but never lives,
Who much receives, but nothing gives;
Whom none can love, whom none can thank, —
Creation's blot, creation's blank.
When Jesus Dwelt

DENNIS O'KELLY
[1720–1787]

It will be Eclipse first, the rest nowhere.[2]
Declaration at Epsom [May 3, 1769] when the great racehorse, Eclipse, was to run his first race. Annals of Sporting, Volume II, Page 271

[1] Born in the garret, in the kitchen bred. — BYRON: *A Sketch*
[2] He [Boswell] has distanced all his competitors so decidedly that it is not worth while to place them. Eclipse is first, and the rest nowhere. — MACAULAY: *Samuel Johnson* [September, 1831]

GEORGE A. STEVENS
[1720–1784]

Cease, rude Boreas, blustering railer!
  List, ye landsmen all, to me;
Messmates, hear a brother sailor
  Sing the dangers of the sea.
The Storm

JOHN WOOLMAN
[1720–1772]

On the outside of that part of the
ship where the cabin was, I observed
sundry sorts of carved work and imagery, and in the cabin some superfluity of workmanship. . . . I felt a
scruple with regard to paying my
money to defray such expenses.
Journal. Chapter 11 [1772]

Though the change from day to
night is by a motion so gradual as
scarcely to be perceived, yet when
night is come we behold it very different
from the day; and thus as people become wise in their own eyes, and prudent in their own sight, customs rise
up from the spirit of this world, and
spread by little, and little, till a departure from the simplicity that there is
in Christ becomes as distinguishable
as light from darkness, to such who are
crucified to the world.
*Considerations on the True Har-
mony of Mankind*

Friends in early time refused, on a
religious principle, to make or trade in
Superfluities; but for want of Faithfulness some gave way, and thus Dimness of Sight came over many.
On Trading in Superfluities

GILBERT WHITE
[1720–1793]

The tortoise, like other reptiles, has
an arbitrary stomach as well as lungs;
and can refrain from eating as well as
breathing for a great part of the year.
*Natural History of Selborne.
April 12, 1772*

When one reflects on the state of
this strange being, it is a matter of
wonder that Providence should bestow
such a profusion of days, such a seeming waste of longevity, on a reptile that
appears to relish it so little as to squander more than two-thirds of its existence in a joyless stupor, and be lost
to all sensation for months together in
the profoundest of slumbers.
*Natural History of Selborne.
April 21, 1780*

WILLIAM COLLINS
[1721–1759]

In numbers warmly pure and sweetly
  strong.
Ode to Simplicity. Stanza 1

Well may your hearts believe the truths
  I tell:
'Tis virtue makes the bliss, where'er
  we dwell.
*Oriental Eclogues. I, Selim, or
The Shepherd's Moral, Line 5*

Curst be the gold and silver which per-
  suade
Weak men to follow far-fatiguing
  trade.
*Ibid. II, Hassan, or The Camel
Driver, Line 31*

Now air is hush'd, save where the weak-
  eyed bat,
With short shrill shriek, flits by on
  leathern wing,
  Or where the beetle winds
  His small but sullen horn.
Ode to Evening. Stanza 3

How sleep the brave, who sink to rest
By all their country's wishes bless'd!
*Ode Written in the Year 1746.
Stanza 1*

By fairy hands their knell is rung;
By forms unseen their dirge is sung.[1]
Ibid. Stanza 2

When Music, heavenly maid, was
  young,
While yet in early Greece she sung.
The Passions. Line 1

[1] Variant:
      By hands unseen the knell is rung;
      By fairy forms their dirge is sung.

'Twas sad by fits, by starts 'twas wild.
The Passions. Line 28

In notes by distance made more sweet.
Ibid. Line 60

In hollow murmurs died away.
Ibid. Line 68

O Music, sphere-descended maid,
Friend of Pleasure, Wisdom's aid!
Ibid. Line 95

TOBIAS SMOLLETT
[1721–1771]

Thy spirit, Independence, let me share,
Lord of the lion-heart and eagle-eye,[1]
Thy steps I follow, with my bosom
bare,
Nor heed the storm that howls along
the sky.
Ode to Independence. Strophe 1

Thy fatal shafts unerring move,
I bow before thine altar, Love!
Roderick Random. Chap. XL

Facts are stubborn things.[2]
*Translation of Gil Blas. Book X,
Chap. 1*

CHRISTOPHER SMART
[1722–1770]

O servant of God's holiest charge,
The minister of praise at large.
A Song to David. Stanza 3

Great, valiant, pious, good, and clean,
Sublime, contemplative, serene,
Strong, constant, pleasant, wise!
Ibid. Stanza 4

Strong is the lion — like a coal
His eyeball, — like a bastion's mole
His chest against the foes.
Ibid. Stanza 76

SIR WILLIAM BLACKSTONE
[1723–1780]

The royal navy of England hath ever
been its greatest defence and ornament;

it is its ancient and natural strength, —
the floating bulwark of our island.
*Commentaries. Vol. I, Book I,
Chap. XIII, § 418*

Time whereof the memory of man
runneth not to the contrary.[1]
Ibid. Chap. XVIII, § 472

MRS. GREVILLE [2]
[*Floruit* 1753]

Nor ease, nor peace, that heart can
know,
That like the needle true,
Turns at the touch of joy or woe,
But, turning, trembles too.
*Prayer for Indifference.
Stanza 6*

O! haste to shed the sovereign balm,
My shatter'd nerves new-string;
And for my guest, serenely calm,
The nymph Indifference bring.
Ibid. Stanza 9

JOHN HOME
[1724–1808]

In the first days
Of my distracting grief, I found myself
As women wish to be who love their
lords.
Douglas. Act I, Sc. 1

I'll woo her as the lion woos his brides.
Ibid.

My name is Norval; on the Grampian
hills
My father feeds his flocks; a frugal
swain,
Whose constant cares were to increase
his store,
And keep his only son, myself, at home.
Ibid. Act III, Sc. 1

A rude and boisterous captain of the
sea.
Ibid. Act IV, Sc. 1

Like Douglas conquer, or like Douglas
die.
Ibid. Act V, Sc. 1

---

[1] Quoted by THOMAS CARLYLE in his essay
on Boswell's *Life of Dr. Johnson.*
[2] Facts are stubborn things. — ELLIOT:
Essay on Field Husbandry, P. 35 [1747]

[1] See Emerson, page 413.
[2] The pretty Fanny Macartney. — HORACE
WALPOLE: *Memoirs*

RICHARD GIFFORD
[1725–1807]

Verse sweetens toil, however rude the
    sound;
    She feels no biting pang the while
        she sings;
Nor, as she turns the giddy wheel
    around,[1]
    Revolves the sad vicissitudes of
        things.[2]

Contemplation

LOGAN, MINGO CHIEF
[1725–1780]

I appeal to any white man to say if
he ever entered Logan's cabin hungry
and he gave him not meat; if ever he
came cold and naked and he clothed
him not?

*Message to Lord Dunmore,
Governor of Virginia [Novem-
ber 11, 1774], in Notes on Virginia, by* THOMAS JEFFERSON

WILLIAM MASON
[1725–1797]

The fattest hog in Epicurus' sty.[3]

Heroic Epistle

OLIVER GOLDSMITH
[1728–1774]

Remote, unfriended, melancholy, slow,
Or by the lazy Scheldt, or wandering
    Po.

The Traveller. Line 1

Where'er I roam, whatever realms to
    see,
My heart untravell'd fondly turns to
    thee;
Still to my brother turns, with cease-
less pain,

---

[1] Thus altered by Johnson, —
All at her work the village maiden sings,
Nor, while she turns the giddy wheel around.
[2] See Sterne, page 242.
[3] Me pinguem et nitidum bene curata cute
    vises,
    . . . Epicuri de grege porcum
(You may see me, fat and shining, with well-
cared for hide, — . . . a hog from Epicurus'
herd). — HORACE: *Epistolæ, Lib. I, IV, 15, 16*

And drags at each remove a lengthening chain.

The Traveller. Line 7

And learn the luxury of doing good.[1]

Ibid. Line 22

Such is the patriot's boast, where'er we
    roam,
His first, best country ever is, at home.

Ibid. Line 73

Where wealth and freedom reign contentment fails,
And honour sinks where commerce
    long prevails.

Ibid. Line 91

Man seems the only growth that
    dwindles here.

Ibid. Line 126

By sports like these are all their cares
    beguil'd,
The sports of children satisfy the child.

Ibid. Line 153

But winter lingering chills the lap of
    May.

Ibid. Line 172

Cheerful at morn, he wakes from short
    repose,
Breasts the keen air, and carols as he
    goes.

Ibid. Line 185

So the loud torrent, and the whirl-
    wind's roar,
But bind him to his native mountains
    more.

Ibid. Line 217

They please, are pleas'd, they give to
    get esteem,
Till, seeming blest, they grow to what
    they seem.[2]

Ibid. Line 266

Embosom'd in the deep where Holland
    lies.
Methinks her patient sons before me
    stand,
Where the broad ocean leans against
    the land.

Ibid. Line 282

---

[1] CRABBE: *Tales of the Hall, Book III*
RICHARD GRAVES: *The Epicure.* See Garth,
page 187.
[2] The character of the French.

Pride in their port, defiance in their
eye,
I see the lords of humankind pass by.[1]
The Traveller. Line 327

The land of scholars, and the nurse of
arms.
Ibid. Line 356

For just experience tells, in every soil,
That those that think must govern
those that toil.
Ibid. Line 372

Laws grind the poor, and rich men rule
the law.
Ibid. Line 386

Forc'd from their homes, a melancholy
train,
To traverse climes beyond the western
main;
Where wild Oswego spreads her swamps
around,
And Niagara stuns with thundering
sound.
Ibid. Line 409

Vain, very vain, my weary search to
find
That bliss which only centres in the
mind.
Ibid. Line 423

Sweet Auburn! loveliest village of the
plain.
The Deserted Village. Line 1

The hawthorn bush, with seats beneath the shade,
For talking age and whispering lovers
made.
Ibid. Line 13

The bashful virgin's sidelong looks of
love.
Ibid. Line 29

Ill fares the land, to hastening ills a
prey,
Where wealth accumulates, and men
decay;
Princes and lords may flourish or may
fade;
A breath can make them, as a breath
has made;[2]

But a bold peasantry, their country's
pride,
When once destroy'd, can never be supplied.
The Deserted Village. Line 51

His best companions, innocence and
health;
And his best riches, ignorance of
wealth.
Ibid. Line 61

How blest is he who crowns in shades
like these,
A youth of labour with an age of ease!
Ibid. Line 99

While Resignation gently slopes the
way,
And all his prospects brightening to
the last,
His heaven commences ere the world
be past.
Ibid. Line 110

The watch-dog's voice that bay'd the
whispering wind,
And the loud laugh that spoke the vacant mind.
Ibid. Line 121

A man he was to all the country dear,
And passing rich with forty pounds a
year.
Ibid. Line 141

Careless their merits or their faults to
scan,
His pity gave ere charity began.
Thus to relieve the wretched was his
pride,
And even his failings lean'd to Virtue's
side.
Ibid. Line 161

And as a bird each fond endearment
tries
To tempt its new-fledg'd offspring to
the skies,
He tried each art, reprov'd each dull
delay,
Allur'd to brighter worlds, and led the
way.
Ibid. Line 167

Truth from his lips prevail'd with
double sway,

---

[1] See Dryden, page 179.
[2]   C'est un verre qui luit,
Qu'un souffle peut détruire, et qu'un souffle a
produit
(It is a shining glass, which a breath may

destroy, and which a breath has produced).
— GILLES DE CAUX [1682–1733], comparing
the world to his hour-glass.

And fools, who came to scoff, remain'd
  to pray.[1]
   The Deserted Village. Line 179
Even children follow'd with endearing
  wile,
And pluck'd his gown, to share the good
  man's smile.
             Ibid. Line 183
As some tall cliff, that lifts its awful
  form,
Swells from the vale, and midway
  leaves the storm,
Though round its breast the rolling
  clouds are spread,
Eternal sunshine settles on its head.
             Ibid. Line 189
Well had the boding tremblers learn'd
  to trace
The day's disasters in his morning
  face;
Full well they laugh'd, with counter-
  feited glee,
At all his jokes, for many a joke had
  he;
Full well the busy whisper, circling
  round,
Convey'd the dismal tidings when he
  frown'd.
Yet was he kind; or if severe in aught,
The love he bore to learning was in
  fault;
The village all declar'd how much he
  knew;
'Twas certain he could write, and
  cipher too.
             Ibid. Line 199
In arguing too, the parson own'd his
  skill,
For e'en though vanquished, he could
  argue still;
While words of learned length and
  thundering sound
Amaz'd the gazing rustics rang'd
  around,
And still they gaz'd, and still the wonder grew,
That one small head could carry all he
  knew.
             Ibid. Line 209
Where village statesmen talk'd with
  looks profound,

[1] See Dryden, page 175.

And news much older than their ale
  went round.
   The Deserted Village. Line 223
The whitewash'd wall, the nicely sanded
  floor,
The varnish'd clock that click'd be-
  hind the door;
The chest contriv'd a double debt to
  pay, —
A bed by night, a chest of drawers by
  day.[1]
             Ibid. Line 227
The twelve good rules, the royal game
  of goose.[2]
             Ibid. Line 232
To me more dear, congenial to my
  heart,
One native charm, than all the gloss
  of art.
             Ibid. Line 253
And, ev'n while fashion's brightest arts
  decoy,
The heart distrusting asks, if this be
  joy.
             Ibid. Line 263
Her modest looks the cottage might
  adorn,
Sweet as the primrose peeps beneath
  the thorn.
             Ibid. Line 329
Through torrid tracts with fainting
  steps they go,
Where wild Altama [3] murmurs to their
  woe.
             Ibid. Line 344
In all the silent manliness of grief.
             Ibid. Line 384
O Luxury! thou curst by Heaven's de-
  cree!
             Ibid. Line 385
Thou source of all my bliss and all my
  woe,

[1] A cap by night, a stocking all the day. —
Description of an Author's Bed-Chamber. See
page 253.
[2] The twelve good rules were ascribed to
King Charles I: 1. Urge no healths. 2. Profane no divine ordinances. 3. Touch no state
matters. 4. Reveal no secrets. 5. Pick no
quarrels. 6. Make no comparisons. 7. Maintain no ill opinions. 8. Keep no bad company.
9. Encourage no vice. 10. Make no long meals.
11. Repeat no grievances. 12. Lay no wagers.
[3] Altamaha River, Georgia.

That found'st me poor at first, and
keep'st me so.
>   *The Deserted Village. Line 413*

Such dainties to them, their health it
might hurt;
It's like sending them ruffles, when
wanting a shirt.[1]
>   *The Haunch of Venison*

That strain once more; it bids remembrance rise.
>   *The Captivity, An Oratorio.*
>   *Act I*

O Memory! thou fond deceiver.
>   *Ibid.*

As aromatic plants bestow
No spicy fragrance while they grow;
But crush'd, or trodden to the ground,
Diffuse their balmy sweets around.[2]
>   *Ibid.*

To the last moment of his breath,
  On hope the wretch relies;
And even the pang preceding death
  Bids expectation rise.[3]
>   *Ibid. Act II*

Hope, like the gleaming taper's light,
  Adorns and cheers our way; [4]
And still, as darker grows the night,
  Emits a brighter ray.
>   *Ibid.*

Our Garrick's a salad; for in him we
  see
Oil, vinegar, sugar, and saltness agree!
>   *Retaliation. Line 11*

Who, born for the universe, narrow'd
his mind,
And to party gave up what was meant
for mankind . . .
Who, too deep for his hearers, still went
on refining,
And thought of convincing, while they
thought of dining:
Though equal to all things, for all
things unfit;

---

[1] See Tom Brown, page 188.
[2] See Bacon, page 109.
[3] The wretch condemn'd with life to part
  Still, still on hope relies;
And every pang that rends the heart
  Bids expectation rise.
>   *Original MS.*
[4] Hope, like the taper's gleamy light,
  Adorns the wretch's way.
>   *Original MS.*

Too nice for a statesman, too proud for
a wit.
>   *Retaliation. Line 31*

His conduct still right, with his argument wrong.
>   *Ibid. Line 46*

A flattering painter, who made it his
care
To draw men as they ought to be, not
as they are.
>   *Ibid. Line 63*

Here lies David Garrick, describe me,
who can,
An abridgment of all that was pleasant
in man.
>   *Ibid. Line 93*

As a wit, if not first, in the very first
line.
>   *Ibid. Line 96*

On the stage he was natural, simple,
affecting;
'Twas only that when he was off he was
acting.
>   *Ibid. Line 101*

He cast off his friends, as a huntsman
his pack,
For he knew when he pleas'd he could
whistle them back.
>   *Ibid. Line 107*

Who pepper'd the highest was surest
to please.
>   *Ibid. Line 112*

When they talk'd of their Raphaels,
Correggios, and stuff,
He shifted his trumpet and only took
snuff.
>   *Ibid. Line 145*

Thou best-humour'd man, with the
worst-humour'd Muse.[1]
>   *Ibid. Postscript*

Good people all, with one accord,
  Lament for Madam Blaize,
Who never wanted a good word —
  From those who spoke her praise.
>   *Elegy on Mrs. Mary Blaize.[2]*
>   *Stanza 1*

---

[1] See Rochester, page 184.
[2] Written in imitation of *Chanson sur le
fameux La Palisse,* which is attributed to
BERNARD DE LA MONNOYE: —
>   On dit que dans ses amours
>   Il fut caressé des belles,
>   Qui le suivirent toujours,

A night-cap deck'd his brows instead
of bay,
A cap by night, a stocking all the day.[1]
*Description of an Author's
Bed-chamber*

This same philosophy is a good horse
in the stable, but an arrant jade on a
journey.[2]
The Good-Natur'd Man. Act I

He calls his extravagance, generosity; and his trusting everybody, universal benevolence.
Ibid.

All his faults were such that one
loves him still the better for them.
Ibid.

Friendship is a disinterested commerce between equals; love, an abject
intercourse between tyrants and slaves.
Ibid.

Silence gives consent.[3]
Ibid. Act II

Measures, not men, have always been
my mark.[4]
Ibid.

I love everything that's old: old
friends, old times, old manners, old
books, old wine.[5]
She Stoops to Conquer. Act I

The very pink of perfection.
Ibid.

Let school-masters puzzle their brain,
With grammar, and nonsense, and
learning;
Good liquor, I stoutly maintain,
Gives *genus* a better discerning.
Ibid.

The genteel thing is the genteel thing
at any time. If so be that a gentleman
bees in a concatenation accordingly.
Ibid.

I'll be with you in the squeezing of a
lemon.
She Stoops to Conquer. Act I

A modest woman, dressed out in all
her finery, is the most tremendous object of the whole creation.
Ibid. Act II

This is Liberty Hall.[1]
Ibid.

They liked the book the better the
more it made them cry.
Ibid.

Ask me no questions, and I'll tell you
no fibs.[2]
Ibid. Act III

There's no love lost between us.[3]
Ibid. Act IV

The very pink of courtesy and circumspection.
Ibid.

I . . . chose my wife, as she did her
wedding-gown, not for a fine glossy
surface, but such qualities as would
wear well.
The Vicar of Wakefield. Chap. 1

We sometimes had those little rubs
which Providence sends to enhance the
value of its favours.
Ibid.

Handsome is that handsome does.[4]
Ibid.

When lovely woman stoops to folly,
And finds too late that men betray,
What charm can soothe her melancholy?
What art can wash her guilt away?[5]
Ibid. Chap 5, Song, Stanza 1

The only art her guilt to cover,

Tant qu'il marcha devant elles
(They say that in his love affairs he was petted
by beauties, who always followed him as long
as he walked before them).

[1] See page 251.
[2] Philosophy triumphs easily over past evils
and future evils, but present evils triumph
over it. — ROCHEFOUCAULD: *Maxim 22*
[3] RAY: *Proverbs.* FULLER: *Wise Sentences.*
EURIPIDES: *Iph. Aul.,* 1142
[4] Measures, not men. — CHESTERFIELD: *Letters,* March 6, 1742. Not men, but measures.
— BURKE: *Present Discontents*
[5] See Bacon, page 113.

[1] 'Tis a palace of no mortal architect's art,
For Liberty Hall's an American's heart.
Liberty Hall, St. 6 [Revolutionary
War period]
[2] Them that asks no questions isn't told a
lie. — KIPLING: *A Smuggler's Song, St. 6*
[3] See Middleton, page 117.
[4] See Chaucer, page 7.
[5] Lorsqu'une femme, après trop de tendresse,
D'une homme sent la trahison,
Comment, pour cette si douce foiblesse,
Peut-elle trouver une guérison?
SEGUR, an obscure French poet [Paris,
1719], in *Philadelphia Press* [Feb. 20,
1889], credited to St. James Gazette.

To hide her shame from every eye,
To give repentance to her lover,
And wring his bosom, is — to die.[1]
The Vicar of Wakefield. Chap. 5,
Song, Stanza 2

I find you want me to furnish you
with argument and intellects too.
Ibid. Chap. 7

Man wants but little here below,
Nor wants that little long.
Ibid. Chap. 8, The Hermit (Edwin
and Angelina), Stanza 8

She was all of a muck of sweat.
Ibid. Chap. 9

They would talk of nothing but high
life, and high-lived company, with
other fashionable topics, such as pictures, taste, Shakespeare, and the musical glasses.[2]
Ibid.

It has been a thousand times observed, and I must observe it once
more, that the hours we pass with
happy prospects in view, are more
pleasing than those crowned with fruition.[3]
Ibid. Chap. 10

A kind and gentle heart he had,
To comfort friends and foes;
The naked every day he clad
When he put on his clothes.
Ibid. Chap. 17, An Elegy on the
Death of a Mad Dog, Stanza 3

And in that town a dog was found,
As many dogs there be,
Both mongrel, puppy, whelp, and
hound,

And curs of low degree.
The Vicar of Wakefield. Chap. 17,
An Elegy on the Death of a
Mad Dog, Stanza 4

The dog, to gain some private ends,
Went mad, and bit the man.
Ibid. Stanza 5

The man recovered of the bite —
The dog it was that died.[1]
Ibid. Stanza 8

To what happy accident [2] is it that
we owe so unexpected a visit?
Ibid. Chap. 19

To what fortuitous concurrence do
we not owe every pleasure and convenience of our lives.
Ibid. Chap. 31

You may all go to pot.
Verses in Reply to an Invitation
to Dinner at Dr. Baker's

For he who fights and runs away
May live to fight another day;
But he who is in battle slain
Can never rise and fight again.[3]
The Art of Poetry on a New
Plan [1761]. Vol. II, Page 147

One writer, for instance, excels at a
plan or a title-page, another works
away the body of the book, and a third
is a dab at an index.[4]
The Bee. No. 1, October 6, 1759

The true use of speech is not so
much to express our wants as to conceal them.[5]
Ibid. No. 3, October 20, 1759

[To Dr. Johnson] If you were to

---

[1] While Fell was reposing himself in the hay,
A reptile concealed bit his leg as he lay;
But, all venom himself, of the wound he
made light,
And got well, while the scorpion died of the
bite.
GOTTHOLD EPHRAIM LESSING [1729–
1781]: *Paraphrase of a Greek Epi-*
gram by Demodocus

[2] See Middleton, page 117.

[3] See Butler, page 143.

[4] There are two things which I am confident
I can do very well: one is an introduction to
any literary work, stating what it is to contain, and how it should be executed in the
most perfect manner. — BOSWELL: *Life of*
Dr. Johnson, 1755. Vol. I, Page 179, Everyman Edition

[5] See South, page 183.

---

[1] Le seul remède qu'elle peut ressentir,
La seule revanche pour son tort,
Pour faire trop tard l'amant repentir,
Helas! trop tard! — est la mort.
SEGUR [Paris, 1719]

[2] Chat pleasantly to her of Shakespeare,
also the musical glasses. — SIR ARTHUR WING
PINERO [1855-1934:] *The Notorious Mrs.*
Ebbsmith, Act I
"Shall we talk about Shakespeare?" he
asked sarcastically. "Or the musical glasses?"
— ALDOUS HUXLEY [1894-   ]: *Point Coun-*
ter Point, Chap. 21

[3] An object in possession seldom retains the
same charm that it had in pursuit. — PLINY
THE YOUNGER: *Letters, Book II, Letter*
XV, 1

make little fishes talk, they would talk like whales.

> *Boswell's Life of Dr. Johnson. Vol. I, Page 466, Everyman Edition*

I consider an author's literary reputation to be alive only while his name will insure a good price for his copy from the bookseller's.

> *Quoted, Ibid., Page 468*

There is no arguing with Johnson: for if his pistol misses fire, he knocks you down with the butt end of it.

> *Quoted, Ibid., Vol. II, Page 509*

THOMAS PERCY
[1728–1811]

Though only an indifferent poet himself, Bishop Percy is immortal for the "Reliques of Ancient English Poetry," 1765, which collected many of the old ballads and songs. This work has been a feeding-place for poets ever since, and the inspiration of SIR WALTER SCOTT'S "Minstrelsy of the Scottish Border."

Everye white will have its blacke,
And everye sweete its sowre.

> *Reliques of Ancient English Poetry. Sir Cauline, Part II, Stanza 1*

Late, late yestreen I saw the new moone
Wi' the auld moone in hir arme.

> *Ibid. Sir Patrick Spence (Spens),[1] Stanza 7*

I think it was never man's destinye
To dye before his day.

> *Ibid. Robin Hood and Guy of Gisborne, Stanza 40*

Have you not heard, these many years ago,
Jephthah was judge of Israel?
He had one only daughter and no mo,
  The which he loved passing well;
  And, as by lott,

[1] From *Minstrelsy of the Scottish Border.*

God wot,
It so came to pass,
As God's will was.[1]

> *Reliques of Ancient English Poetry. Jephthah, Judge of Israel,[2] Stanza 1*

A Robyn,
Jolly Robyn,
Tell me how thy leman doeth,
And thou shalt know of myn.[3]

> *Ibid. A Robyn Jolly Robyn, Stanza 1*

Where gripinge grefes the hart would wounde
And dolefulle dumps the mynde oppresse,
There musicke with her silver sound
  With spede is wont to send redressc.[4]

> *Ibid. A Song to the Lute in Musicke,[5] Stanza 1*

The blinded boy that shootes so trim,
From heaven downe did hie.[6]

> *Ibid. King Cophetua and the Beggar-maid, Stanza 2*

"What is thy name, faire maid?" quoth he.
"Penelophon, O King!" quoth she.[7]

> *Ibid. Stanza 6*

A poore soule sat sighing under a sicamore tree;
  O willow, willow, willow!

---

[1] "As by lot, God wot"; and then you know, "It came to pass, as most like it was." — SHAKESPEARE: *Hamlet, Act II, Sc. 2, L. 444*

[2] *Judges, XI, 34 et seq.*

[3] Clown's song, "Hey Robin, jolly Robin." — SHAKESPEARE: *Twelfth-Night, Act IV, Sc. 2, L. 79*

[4] Quoted in *Romeo and Juliet, Act IV, Sc. 5, Lines 129 and 146.*

[5] The author is thought by Percy to have been Richard Edwards [1523–1566].

[6] Young Adam Cupid, he that shot so trim, When King Cophetua loved the beggar-maid! SHAKESPEARE: *Romeo and Juliet, Act II, Sc. 1, L. 13*

[7] Shakespeare, who alludes to this ballad in *Love's Labour's Lost, Act IV, Sc. 1*, gives Zenelophon as the beggar-maid's name (*L. 67*). The ballad is also referred to in *King Richard the Second, Act V, Sc. 3, L. 80.* See Tennyson, page 465.

With his hand on his bosom, his head
on his knee.
*Reliques of Ancient English Po-
etry. Willow, Willow, Willow,*[1]
Stanza 1
O that beauty should harbour a heart
that's so hard!
Ibid. Stanza 8
When Arthur first in court began,
And was approved king,
By force of armes great victorys
wanne,
And conquest home did bring.
Ibid. Sir Lancelot du Lake,[2]
Stanza 1
Shall I bid her goe? What, and if I doe?
Shall I bid her goe, and spare not?
O no, no, no, I dare not.[3]
*Ibid. Corydon's Farewell to
Phillis, Stanza 2*
And this shall be the forfeyture; of
your owne fleshe a pound.
*Ibid. Gernutus the Jew of
Venice,*[4] *Couplet 14*
It was a friar of orders gray[5]
Walkt forth to tell his beades.
Ibid. The Friar of Orders Gray,[6]
Stanza 1
And how should I know your true love
From many another one?
Oh, by his cockle hat, and staff,
And by his sandal shoone.[7]
Ibid. Stanza 3

[1] Quoted in *Othello, Act IV, Sc. 3, Lines
41, 49, 51, 56.*
On a tree by a river a little tom-tit
Sang "Willow, titwillow, titwillow!"
    WILLIAM SCHWENCK GILBERT: *The
    Mikado, Act II, Ko-Ko's song*
[2] The subject of this ballad is taken from
the ancient romance of *Morte d'Arthur, Chap.
108–110.*
[3] Quoted by Shakespeare in *Twelfth-Night,
Act II, Sc. 3, L. 119.*
[4] The story in this ballad is taken from an
Italian novel of the fourteenth century, *Peco-
rone.* Shakespeare is believed to have taken
the episode of Shylock and Antonio in *The
Merchant of Venice* from this ballad.
[5] SHAKESPEARE: *The Taming of the Shrew,
Act IV, Sc. 1, L. 148.*
[6] Chiefly composed of fragments of old
ballads dispersed through Shakespeare's plays,
especially those sung by Ophelia in *Hamlet.*
An excellent specimen of mosaic-work.
[7] The distinguishing marks of a pilgrim.
The chief places of devotion being beyond the

O Lady, he is dead and gone!
Lady, he's dead and gone!
And at his head a green grass turfe,
And at his heels a stone.[1]
*Reliques of Ancient English
Poetry. The Friar of Orders
Gray, Stanza 5*
Weep no more, lady, weep no more,
Thy sorrowe is in vaine;
For violets pluckt, the sweetest show-
ers
Will ne'er make grow againe.[2]
Ibid. Stanza 12
Our joys as wingèd dreams doe flye;
Why then should sorrow last?
Since grief but aggravates thy losse,
Grieve not for what is past.
Ibid. Stanza 13
Sigh no more, ladies, sigh no more!
Men were deceivers ever;
One foot in sea and one on shore,
To one thing constant never.[3]
Ibid. Stanza 17
King Stephen was a worthy peere,
His breeches cost him but a crowne.
*Ibid. Take Thy Old Coat About
Thee,*[4] *Stanza 7*
Itt's pride that putts this countrye
downe;
Man, take thine old cloake about thee.
Ibid.
Fight on, my merry men all;
For why, my life is at an end.[5]
*Ibid. The More Modern Ballad
of Chevy-Chace, Couplet 40*

sea, pilgrims put cockle-shells in their hats to
denote the intention or performance of their
devotion.
[1] Quoted in *Hamlet, Act IV, Sc. 5.*
[2] See Fletcher, page 127.
[3] SHAKESPEARE: *Much Ado About Nothing, Act II, Sc. 3, L. 65.*
[4] This stanza of eight lines is quoted in full
in *Othello, Act II, Sc. 3, L. 93.*
[5] "Fight on, my men," Sir Andrew sayes,
    "A little Ime hurt, but yett not slaine;
    Ile but lye downe and bleede awhile,
    And then Ile rise and fight againe."
Sir Andrew Barton, Part 2, St. 16 (PERCY'S
    Reliques, Series II, Book II)
Says Johnnie, "Fight on, my merry men all,
I'm a little wounded, but I am not slain;
I will lay me down for to bleed a while,
Then I'll rise and fight with you again."
*Johnnie Armstrong's Last Good-night,
St. 18* (DRYDEN'S *Miscellanies* [1702])

We'll shine in more substantial hon-
ours,
And to be noble we'll be good.
*Reliques of Ancient English Poetry.
Winifreda,*[1] *Stanza 2*

And when with envy Time, trans-
ported,
Shall think to rob us of our joys,
You'll in your girls again be courted,
And I'll go wooing in my boys.
Ibid. Stanza 8

Shall never be sayd, the Not-browne
Mayd
Was to her love unkynde.[2]
*Ibid. The Not-Browne Mayd,
Stanza 8*

A fairer ladye there never was seene
Than the blind beggar's daughter of
Bednall-greene.
*Ibid. The Beggar's Daughter of
Bednall-Green,*[3] *Stanza 33*

When captaines couragious,[4] whom
death cold not daunte,
Did march to the siege of the citty of
Gaunt,
They mustred their souldiers by two
and by three,
And the formost in battle was Mary
Ambree.
Ibid. Mary Ambree,[5] *Stanza 1*

[1] See Chapman, page 29.
Nobilitas sola est atque unica virtus (Nobility is the one only virtue). — JUVENAL:
Satire VIII, L. 20
"Winifreda" appeared in LEWIS's *Collection*
[1726]
[2] First published in ARNOLD's *Chronicle*, a
miscellany, about 1521.
[3] This very house was built by the blind
beggar of Bednall Green, so much talked of
and sang in ballads. — SAMUEL PEPYS: *Diary,
June 26, 1663*
The ballad was written in the reign of
Elizabeth.
[4] Source of the title of RUDYARD KIPLING's
book, *Captains Courageous.*
[5] This ballad was probably occasioned by
the attempt to regain Ghent, in 1584, when the
Spaniards, commanded by the Prince of Parma, took many fortresses and cities in Flanders and Brabant.
BEN JONSON calls any virago Mary Ambree,
and JOHN FLETCHER mentions Mary Ambree
in *The Scornful Lady* [1616].

Will you hear a Spanish lady,
How shee wooed an English man?
*Reliques of Ancient English
Poetry. The Spanish Lady's
Love,*[1] *Stanza 1*

Then let Jane Shore with sorrowe sing,
That was belovèd of a king.
Ibid. Jane Shore, Stanza 1

"I'll rest," sayd hee, "but thou shalt
walke";
So doth this wandring Jew
From place to place, but cannot rest
For seeing countries newe.
*Ibid. The Wandering Jew,
Stanza 9*

For thirty pence our Saviour was sold
Amonge the false Jewes, as I have bin
told;
And twenty-nine is the worth of thee,
For I thinke thou art one penny worser
than hee.
*Ibid. King John and the Abbot
of Canterbury, Stanza 21*

But in vayne shee did conjure him
To depart her presence soe;
Having a thousand tongues to allure
him,
And but one to bid him goe.
Ibid. Dulcina,[2] *Stanza 2*

Glasgerion swore a full great othe,
By oake, and ashe and thorne.
Ibid. Glasgerion,[3] *Stanza 19*

He that would not when he might,
He shall not when he wolda.[4]
*Ibid. The Baffled Knight,
Stanza 14*

In Scarlet towne, where I was borne,
There was a fair maid dwellin,
Made every youth crye, Wel-awaye!
Her name was Barbara Allen.
*Ibid. Barbara Allen's Cruelty,
Stanza 1*

[1] Founded on the capture of Cadiz by Lord
Essex in 1596.
[2] This song is mentioned as very popular by
IZAAK WALTON in *The Compleat Angler.* It has
been ascribed to Raleigh, on very doubtful
authority.
[3] CHARLES KINGSLEY refers to the oath of
Glasgerion in *Westward Ho, Chap. 2;* and
RUDYARD KIPLING, in *Puck of Pook's Hill.*
CHAUCER refers to the "harper Bret Glas-
curion" in *The House of Fame, Book III,
L. 1208.*
[4] See Heywood, page 11.

No burial this pretty pair
Of any man receives,
Till Robin Red-breast piously
Did cover them with leaves.
> *Reliques of Ancient English
> Poetry. The Children in the
> Wood,*[1] *Stanza 16*

Under floods that are deepest,
Which Neptune obey;
Over rocks that are steepest,
Love will find out the way.
> *Ibid. Love Will Find Out the
> Way,*[2] *Stanza 1*

For without money, George,
A man is but a beast:
But bringing money, thou shalt be
Always my welcome guest.
> *Ibid. George Barnwell,*[3] *Part II,
> Stanza 25*

And let all women strive to be
As constant as Penelope.
> *Ibid. Constant Penelope,
> Stanza 18*

St. George he was for England; St.
Dennis was for France;
Sing, *Honi soit qui mal y pense.*[4]
> *Ibid. St. George for England,
> Refrain*

Dark was the night, and wild the storm,
And loud the torrent's roar;
And loud the sea was heard to dash
Against the distant shore.
> *The Hermit of Warkworth,*[5]
> *Part I, Stanza 1*

THOMAS WARTON
[1728–1790]

All human race, from China to Peru,[6]
Pleasure, howe'er disguis'd by art, pursue.
> *Universal Love of Pleasure*

---

[1] Addison called this ballad one of the darling songs of the common people. It was first published in 1595.
[2] Modernized from an ancient song.
[3] Inspired by GEORGE LILLO's play, *The London Merchant, or the History of George Barnwell,* first acted in 1731.
[4] See Shakespeare, page 35.
[5] Percy's own composition, comprising 213 stanzas.
[6] See Johnson, page 230.

Nor rough, nor barren, are the winding ways
Of hoar antiquity, but strewn with flowers.
> *Written on a Blank Leaf of
> Dugdale's Monasticon*

All-powerful Ale! whose sorrow-soothing sweets
Oft I repeat in vacant afternoon.
> *A Panegyric on Oxford Ale*[1]

With British ale improving British worth.
> *Ibid.*

Thus too, the matchless bard, whose lay resounds
The Splendid Shilling's praise, in nightly gloom
Of lonesome garret, pined for cheerful ale.[2]
> *Ibid.*

EDMUND BURKE
[1729–1797]

The writers against religion, whilst they oppose every system, are wisely careful never to set up any of their own.
> *Works. Vol. I, Preface, A Vindication of Natural Society*

"War," says Machiavel, "ought to be the only study of a prince"; and by a prince he means every sort of state, however constituted. "He ought," says this great political doctor, "to consider peace only as a breathing-time, which gives him leisure to contrive, and furnishes ability to execute military plans." A meditation on the conduct of political societies made old Hobbes imagine that war was the state of nature.
> *Ibid.*

---

[1] From *The Oxford Sausage* [1764], a famous miscellany of 'varsity rhymes and satires, reprinted in several subsequent editions.
[2] Happy the man who, void of care and strife,
In silken or in leathern purse retains
A splendid shilling. He nor hears with pain
New oysters cried, nor sighs for cheerful ale.
JOHN PHILIPS [1676–1709]: *The Splendid Shilling* [1705]

I am convinced that we have a degree of delight, and that no small one, in the real misfortunes and pains of others.[1]

*On the Sublime and Beautiful.
Sect. XIV*

Custom reconciles us to everything.

Ibid. Sect. XVIII

There is, however, a limit at which forbearance ceases to be a virtue.

Observations on a Late Publication on the Present State of the Nation [1769]

The wisdom of our ancestors.[2]

Ibid. Also in the Discussion on the Traitorous Correspondence Bill [1793]

Illustrious predecessor.[3]

Thoughts on the Cause of the Present Discontents [April 23, 1770]

When bad men combine, the good must associate; else they will fall one by one, an unpitied sacrifice in a contemptible struggle.

Ibid.

Of this stamp is the cant of, Not men, but measures.[4]

Ibid.

So to be patriots as not to forget we are gentlemen.

Ibid.

Public life is a situation of power and energy; he trespasses against his duty who sleeps upon his watch, as well as he that goes over to the enemy.

Ibid.

It ought to be the happiness and glory of a representative to live in the strictest union, the closest correspondence, and the most unreserved communication with his constituents. Their wishes ought to have great weight with him; their opinion high respect; their business unremitted attention. It is his duty to sacrifice his repose, his pleasures, his satisfaction, to theirs; and above all, ever, and in all cases, to prefer their interests to his own.

*Speech to the Electors of Bristol.
[November 3, 1774]*

Your representative owes you, not his industry only, but his judgment; and he betrays instead of serving you if he sacrifices it to your opinion.

Ibid.

The concessions of the weak are the concessions of fear.

Speech on Conciliation with America [March 22, 1775]

There is America, which at this day serves for little more than to amuse you with stories of savage men and uncouth manners, yet shall, before you taste of death, show itself equal to the whole of that commerce which now attracts the envy of the world.

Ibid.

Fiction lags after truth, invention is unfruitful, and imagination cold and barren.

Ibid.

A people who are still, as it were, but in the gristle, and not yet hardened into the bone of manhood.

Ibid.

A wise and salutary neglect.

Ibid.

The religion most prevalent in our northern colonies is a refinement on the principles of resistance: it is the dissidence of dissent, and the protestantism of the Protestant religion.

Ibid.

I do not know the method of drawing up an indictment against an whole people.

Ibid.

The march of the human mind is slow.[1]

Ibid.

---

[1] In the adversity of our best friends we always find something which is not wholly displeasing to us. — ROCHEFOUCAULD: *Reflections, XV*

[2] Lord Brougham says of Bacon, "He it was who first employed the well-known phrase of 'the wisdom of our ancestors.'" SYDNEY SMITH: *Plymley's Letters, Letter V.* LORD ELDON: *On Sir Samuel Romilly's Bill* [1815]. CICERO: *De Legibus, II, 2, 3*

[3] See Fielding, page 230.

[4] See Goldsmith, page 253.

[1] The march of intellect. — SOUTHEY: *Progress and Prospects of Society, Vol. II, P. 360*

All government, — indeed, every human benefit and enjoyment, every virtue and every prudent act, — is founded on compromise and barter.

*Speech on Conciliation with
America [March 22, 1775]*

The worthy gentleman [Mr. Coombe] who has been snatched from us at the moment of the election, and in the middle of the contest, whilst his desires were as warm and his hopes as eager as ours, has feelingly told us what shadows we are, and what shadows we pursue.

*Speech at Bristol on Declining
the Poll [September 9, 1780]*

They made and recorded a sort of institute and digest of anarchy, called the Rights of Man.

*On the Army Estimates
[February 9, 1790]*

People will not look forward to posterity who never look backward to their ancestors.[1]

*Reflections on the Revolution
in France [1790]*

You had that action and counter-action which, in the natural and in the political world, from the reciprocal struggle of discordant powers draws out the harmony of the universe.[2]

Ibid.

It is now sixteen or seventeen years since I saw the Queen of France, then the Dauphiness, at Versailles; and surely never lighted on this orb, which she hardly seemed to touch, a more delightful vision. I saw her just above the horizon, decorating and cheering the elevated sphere she just began to move in, — glittering like the morning star full of life and splendour and joy. . . . Little did I dream that I should have lived to see such disasters fallen upon her in a nation of gallant men, — in a nation of men of honour

and of cavaliers. I thought ten thousand swords must have leaped from their scabbards to avenge even a look that threatened her with insult. But the age of chivalry is gone; that of sophisters, economists, and calculators has succeeded.

*Reflections on the Revolution
in France [1790]*

The unbought grace of life, the cheap defence of nations, the nurse of manly sentiment and heroic enterprise is gone.

Ibid.

That chastity of honour which felt a stain like a wound.

Ibid.

Vice itself lost half its evil by losing all its grossness.

Ibid.

Kings will be tyrants from policy, when subjects are rebels from principle.[1]

Ibid.

Learning will be cast into the mire and trodden down under the hoofs of a swinish multitude.

Ibid.

Because half-a-dozen grasshoppers under a fern make the field ring with their importunate chink, whilst thousands of great cattle, reposed beneath the shadow of the British oak, chew the cud and are silent, pray do not imagine that those who make the noise are the only inhabitants of the field; that of course they are many in number; or that, after all, they are other than the little shrivelled, meagre, hopping, though loud and troublesome insects of the hour.

Ibid.

---

[1] The Democratic Party is like a mule — without pride of ancestry or hope of posterity. — IGNATIUS DONNELLY [1831–1901]: *Speech in the Minnesota Legislature*

[2] Quid velit et possit rerum concordia discors (What the discordant harmony of circumstances would and could effect). — HORACE: *Epistle I, 12, 19*

[1] Rebellion to tyrants is obedience to God. —

From an inscription on the cannon near which the ashes of President John Bradshaw were lodged, on the top of a high hill near Martha Bay in Jamaica. — STILES: *History of the Three Judges of King Charles I*

This supposititious epitaph was found among the papers of Mr. Jefferson, and in his handwriting. It was supposed to be one of Dr. Franklin's spirit-stirring inspirations. — RANDALL: *Life of Jefferson, Vol. III, P. 585*

In their nomination to office they will not appoint to the exercise of authority as to a pitiful job, but as to a holy function.

Reflections on the Revolution in France [1790]

The men of England, — the men, I mean, of light and leading in England.

Ibid.

He that wrestles with us strengthens our nerves and sharpens our skill. Our antagonist is our helper.

Ibid.

To execute laws is a royal office; to execute orders is not to be a king. However, a political executive magistracy, though merely such, is a great trust.[1]

Ibid.

You can never plan the future by the past.[2]

Letter to a Member of the National Assembly

The cold neutrality of an impartial judge.

Preface to Brissot's Address

And having looked to Government for bread, on the very first scarcity they will turn and bite the hand that fed them.

Thoughts and Details on Scarcity

All men that are ruined, are ruined on the side of their natural propensities.

Letter I, On a Regicide Peace

Example is the school of mankind, and they will learn at no other.

Ibid.

The people never give up their liberties but under some delusion.

Speech at County Meeting of Bucks [1784]

There never was a bad man that had ability for good service.

Speech in Opening the Impeachment of Warren Hastings [1788, Third Day]

Mere parsimony is not economy. . . . Expense, and great expense, may be essential part of true economy.

Letter to a Noble Lord [1796]

Economy is a distributive virtue, and consists not in saving but in selection. Parsimony requires no providence, no sagacity, no powers of combination, no comparison, no judgment.

Ibid.

I would rather sleep in the southern corner of a little country churchyard than in the tomb of the Capulets.

Letter to Matthew Smith

It has all the contortions of the sibyl without the inspiration.[1]

Prior's Life of Burke

He was not merely a chip of the old block, but the old block itself.[2]

On Pitt's First Speech [February 26, 1781]. From Wraxall's Memoirs, First Series, Vol. I, Page 342

WILLIAM GERARD HAMILTON
[1729–1796]

He has made a chasm which not only nothing can fill up, but which nothing has a tendency to fill up. Johnson is dead. — Let us go to the next best: — there is nobody; no man can be said to put you in mind of Johnson.

Quoted in Boswell's Life of Dr. Johnson, Vol. II, Page 611, Everyman Edition

JOHN SCOTT
[1730–1783]

I hate the drum's discordant sound,
Parading round, and round, and round:

---

[1] See Mathew Henry, page 188.
[2] I know no way of judging of the future but by the past. — PATRICK HENRY: *Speech in the Virginia Convention* [March, 1775]

[1] When Croft's "Life of Dr. Young" was spoken of as a good imitation of Dr. Johnson's style, "No, no," said he, "it is not a good imitation of Johnson; it has all his pomp without his force; it has all the nodosities of the oak, without its strength; it has all the contortions of the sibyl, without the inspiration." — JAMES PRIOR [1790–1869]: *Life of Burke*

The gloomy companions of a disturbed imagination; the melancholy madness of poetry, without the inspiration. — JUNIUS: *Letter No. VII* [March 3, 1769], *To Sir W. Draper*

[2] See Sir Thomas Browne, page 145.

To me it talks of ravaged plains,
And burning towns, and ruined swains,
And mangled limbs, and dying groans,
And widows' tears, and orphans'
    moans;
And all that Misery's hand bestows
To fill the catalogue of human woes.

> *I Hate the Drum's Discordant*
> *Sound. Stanza 2*

CHARLES CHURCHILL
[1731–1764]

He mouths a sentence as curs mouth a
bone.

> *The Rosciad. Line 322*

But, spite of all the criticising elves,
Those who would make us feel — must
feel themselves.[1]

> *Ibid. Line 961*

Like gypsies, lest the stolen brat be
known,
Defacing first, then claiming for his
own.[2]

> *The Apology. Line 232*

Apt alliteration's artful aid.

> *The Prophecy of Famine.*
> *Line 86*

There webs were spread of more than
common size,
And half-starved spiders prey'd on
half-starved flies.

> *Ibid. Line 327*

With curious art the brain, too finely
wrought,
Preys on herself, and is destroyed by
thought.

> *Epistle to William Hogarth.*
> *Line 645*

Men the most infamous are fond of
fame,
And those who fear not guilt yet start
at shame.

> *The Author. Line 233*

1   Si vis me flere, dolendum est
    Primum ipsi tibi
(If you wish me to weep, you yourself must
first feel grief).

> HORACE: *Ars Poetica, L. 102*

2 Steal! to be sure they may; and, egad,
serve your best thoughts as gypsies do stolen
children, — disguise them to make 'em pass
for their own. — SHERIDAN: *The Critic, Act I,
Sc. 1*

Be England what she will,
With all her faults she is my country
still.[1]

> *The Farewell. Line 27*

WILLIAM COWPER
[1731–1800]

Happiness depends, as Nature shows,
Less on exterior things than most suppose.

> *Table Talk. Line 246*

Freedom has a thousand charms to
show,
That slaves, howe'er contented, never
know.

> *Ibid. Line 260*

Manner is all in all, whate'er is writ,
The substitute for genius, sense, and
wit.

> *Ibid. Line 542*

Ages elapsed ere Homer's lamp appear'd,
And ages ere the Mantuan swan was
heard:
To carry nature lengths unknown before,
To give a Milton birth, ask'd ages
more.

> *Ibid. Line 556*

Low ambition and the thirst of praise.[2]

> *Ibid. Line 591*

Made poetry a mere mechanic art.

> *Ibid. Line 654*

Lights of the world, and stars of human race.

> *The Progress of Error. Line 97*

How much a dunce that has been sent
to roam
Excels a dunce that has been kept at
home!

> *Ibid. Line 415*

1 England, with all thy faults I love thee
    still,
    My country!
    COWPER: *The Task, Book II, The Time-
                                        piece, L. 206*
Our country! In her intercourse with foreign nations may she always be in the right;
but our country, right or wrong.
    STEPHEN DECATUR [1779–1820]: *Toast
        given at Norfolk,* [April, 1816]
2 See Pope, page 206.

Just knows, and knows no more, her
  Bible true, —
A truth the brilliant Frenchman never
  knew.
                    Truth. Line 327
The sounding jargon of the schools.[1]
                    Ibid. Line 367
A fool must now and then be right by
  chance.
                  Conversation. Line 96
He would not, with a peremptory tone,
Assert the nose upon his face his own.
                    Ibid. Line 121
A moral, sensible, and well-bred man
Will not affront me, — and no other
  can.
                    Ibid. Line 193
Pernicious weed! whose scent the fair
  annoys,
Unfriendly to society's chief joys:
Thy worst effect is banishing for hours
The sex whose presence civilizes ours.
                    Ibid. Line 251
I cannot talk with civet in the room,
A fine puss-gentleman that's all per-
  fume.
                    Ibid. Line 283
The solemn fop; significant and budge;
A fool with judges, amongst fools a
  judge.[2]
                    Ibid. Line 299
His wit invites you by his looks to
  come,
But when you knock, it never is at
  home.[3]
                    Ibid. Line 303
Our wasted oil unprofitably burns,
Like hidden lamps in old sepulchral
  urns.[4]
                    Ibid. Line 357
A business with an income at its heels

---

[1] See Prior, page 189.
[2] See Pope, page 215.
[3] *Ibid.*, page 217.
[4] That lamp shall burn unquenchably,
    Until the eternal doom shall be.
        SIR WALTER SCOTT: *The Lay of the
        Last Minstrel, Canto II, St. 17*
The story of a lamp which was supposed to
have burned about fifteen hundred years in
the sepulchre of Tullia, the daughter of Cicero,
is told by Pancirollus and others.

Furnishes always oil for its own
  wheels.
                    Retirement. Line 615
Absence of occupation is not rest,
A mind quite vacant is a mind dis-
  tress'd.
                    Ibid. Line 623
An idler is a watch that wants both
  hands,
As useless if it goes as if it stands.
                    Ibid. Line 681
Built God a church, and laugh'd His
  word to scorn.
                    Ibid. Line 688
          Philologists, who chase
A panting syllable through time and
  space,
Start it at home, and hunt it in the
  dark
To Gaul, to Greece, and into Noah's
  ark.
                    Ibid. Line 691
I praise the Frenchman,[1] his remark
  was shrewd, —
How sweet, how passing sweet, is soli-
  tude!
But grant me still a friend in my re-
  treat,
Whom I may whisper, Solitude is
  sweet.
                    Ibid. Line 739
Regions Caesar never knew
  Thy posterity shall sway;
Where his eagles never flew,
  None invincible as they!
                    Boadicea
And still to love, though prest with ill,
In wintry age to feel no chill,
With me is to be lovely still,
          My Mary!
                  To Mary. Stanza 11
A kick that scarce would move a horse
May kill a sound divine.
          The Yearly Distress. Stanza 16
I am monarch of all I survey,
  My right there is none to dispute.
      *Verses Supposed to be Written
      by Alexander Selkirk. Stanza 1*
O Solitude! where are the charms
  That sages have seen in thy face?
                    Ibid.

---

[1] Jean de La Bruyère [1645–1696].

But the sound of the church-going bell
  These valleys and rocks never heard,
Ne'er sigh'd at the sound of a knell,
  Or smiled when a Sabbath appear'd.

  Verses Supposed to be Written
  by Alexander Selkirk. Stanza 4

How fleet is a glance of the mind!
  Compared with the speed of its
    flight
The tempest itself lags behind,
  And the swift-winged arrows of light.

  Ibid. Stanza 6

There goes the parson, O illustrious
    spark!
And there, scarce less illustrious, goes
    the clerk.

  On Observing Some Names of
  Little Note

But oars alone can ne'er prevail
  To reach the distant coast;
The breath of heaven must swell the
    sail,
  Or all the toil is lost.

  Human Frailty. Stanza 6

And the tear that is wiped with a little
    address,
May be follow'd perhaps by a smile.

  The Rose. Stanza 5

I shall not ask Jean Jacques Rousseau
If birds confabulate or no.

  Pairing Time Anticipated

Misses! the tale that I relate
  This lesson seems to carry, —
Choose not alone a proper mate,
  But proper time to marry.

  Ibid. Moral

That though on pleasure she was bent,
  She had a frugal mind.

  History of John Gilpin. Stanza 8

A hat not much the worse for wear.

  Ibid. Stanza 46

Now let us sing, Long live the king,
  And Gilpin, Long live he;
And when he next doth ride abroad,
  May I be there to see!

  Ibid. Stanza 63

The path of sorrow, and that path
    alone,
Leads to the land where sorrow is un-
    known.

  To an Afflicted Protestant
  Lady in France

God made the country, and man made
    the town.[1]

  The Task. Book I, The Sofa,
  Line 749

Oh for a lodge in some vast wilder-
    ness,[2]
Some boundless contiguity of shade,
Where rumour of oppression and de-
    ceit,
Of unsuccessful or successful war,
Might never reach me more.

  Ibid. Book II, The Timepiece,
  Line 1

      Mountains interposed
Make enemies of nations, who had else
Like kindred drops been mingled into
    one.

  Ibid. Line 17

Slaves cannot breathe in England; if
    their lungs
Receive our air, that moment they are
    free!
They touch our country, and their
    shackles fall.[3]

  Ibid. Line 40

Fast-anchor'd isle.

  Ibid. Line 151

England, with all thy faults I love thee
    still,
My country![4]

  Ibid. Line 206

Presume to lay their hand upon the
    ark[5]

[1] See Bacon, page 111.

[2] Oh that I had in the wilderness a lodging-place of wayfaring men! — *Jeremiah, IX, 2*

Oh that the desert were my dwelling-place!
— BYRON: *Childe Harold, Canto IV, St. 177*

[3] Servi peregrini, ut primum Galliæ fines penetraverint eodem momento liberi sunt (Foreign slaves, as soon as they come within the limits of Gaul, that moment they are free).
— BODINUS: *Liber I, 5*

Lord Campbell ("Lives of the Chief Justices," vol. ii, p. 418) says that "Lord Mansfield first established the grand doctrine that the air of England is too pure to be breathed by a slave." The words attributed to Lord Mansfield, however, are not found in his judgment. They are in Hargrave's argument, May 14, 1772, where he speaks of England as "a soil whose air is deemed too pure for slaves to breathe in." — LOFFT: *Reports, P. 2*

[4] See Churchill, page 262.

[5] Uzzah put forth his hand to the ark of God, and took hold of it . . . and the anger

Of her magnificent and awful cause.
> *The Task. Book II, The Time-*
> *piece, Line 231*

There is a pleasure in poetic pains
Which only poets know.[1]
> *Ibid. Line 285*

Transforms old print
To zigzag manuscript, and cheats the
eyes
Of gallery critics by a thousand arts.
> *Ibid. Line 363*

Reading what they never wrote,
Just fifteen minutes, huddle up their
work,
And with a well-bred whisper close the
scene!
> *Ibid. Line 411*

Whoe'er was edified, themselves were
not.
> *Ibid. Line 444*

Variety's the very spice of life.
> *Ibid. Line 606*

She that asks
Her dear five hundred friends.
> *Ibid. Line 642*

His head,
Not yet by time completely silver'd
o'er,
Bespoke him past the bounds of freakish youth,
But strong for service still, and un-
impair'd.
> *Ibid. Line 702*

Guilty splendour.
> *Ibid. Book III, The Garden,*
> *Line 70*

I was a stricken deer.[2]
> *Ibid. Line 108*

Great contest follows, and much
learned dust.
> *Ibid. Line 161*

From reveries so airy, from the toil
Of dropping buckets into empty wells,

And growing old in drawing nothing
up.[1]
> *The Task. Book III, The Garden,*
> *Line 188*

Riches have wings,[2] and grandeur is a
dream.
> *Ibid. Line 265*

How various his employments, whom
the world
Calls idle, and who justly in return
Esteems that busy world an idler too!
> *Ibid. Line 352*

Who loves a garden loves a greenhouse
too.
> *Ibid. Line 566*

Now stir the fire, and close the shutters
fast,
Let fall the curtains, wheel the sofa
round,
And while the bubbling and loud-hissing urn
Throws up a steamy column, and the
cups
That cheer but not inebriate [3] wait on
each,
So let us welcome peaceful evening in.
> *Ibid. Book IV, The Winter*
> *Evening, Line 36*

What is it, but a map of busy life,
Its fluctuations, and its vast concerns?
> *Ibid. Line 55*

'Tis pleasant, through the loopholes of
retreat,
To peep at such a world, to see the stir
Of the great Babel; and not feel the
crowd.
> *Ibid. Line 88*

While fancy, like the finger of a clock,
Runs the great circuit, and is still at
home.
> *Ibid. Line 118*

O Winter, ruler of the inverted year! [4]
> *Ibid. Line 120*

---

of the Lord was kindled against Uzzah. —
2 Samuel, VI, 6 and 7
   [1] See Dryden, page 179.
   [2] Let the stricken deer go weep. — SHAKE-
SPEARE: Hamlet, Act III, Sc. 2, L. 287
   Lord David Cecil gave his biography of
Cowper [1930] the title, *The Stricken Deer.*

   [1] He has spent all his life in letting down
buckets into empty wells; and he is frittering
away his age in trying to draw them up again.
— *Lady Holland's Memoir of Sydney Smith,*
Vol. I, Chap. 9
   [2] Riches certainly make themselves wings.
— *Proverbs, XXIII, 5*
   [3] To cheer but not inebriate. — BISHOP
BERKELEY: *Siris* [1744] *Par. 217*
   [4] See Thomson, page 224.

With spots quadrangular of diamond
form,
Ensanguined hearts, clubs typical of
strife,
And spades, the emblems of untimely
graves.
*The Task. Book IV, The Winter
Evening, Line 217*
In indolent vacuity of thought.[1]
Ibid. Line 297
It seems the part of wisdom.
Ibid. Line 336
All learned, and all drunk!
Ibid. Line 478
Gloriously drunk, obey the important
call.
Ibid. Line 510
Those golden times
And those Arcadian scenes that Maro
sings,
And Sidney, warbler of poetic prose.
Ibid. Line 514
The Frenchman's darling.[2]
Ibid. Line 765
Silently as a dream the fabric rose;
No sound of hammer or of saw was
there.[3]
*Ibid. Book V, The Winter
Morning Walk, Line 144*
But war's a game, which, were their
subjects wise,
Kings would not play at.
Ibid. Line 187
There is in souls a sympathy with
sounds;
And as the mind is pitch'd the ear is
pleased
With melting airs or martial, brisk or
grave;
Some chord in unison with what we
hear
Is touch'd within us, and the heart
replies.

[1] Gloomy calm of idle vacancy. — DR.
JOHNSON: *Letter to Boswell* [Dec. 8, 1763]
[2] It was Cowper who gave this now common name to the mignonette.
[3] No hammers fell, no ponderous axes rung,
Like some tall palm the mystic fabric
sprung.
REGINALD HEBER [1783–1826]: *Palestine*
So that there was neither hammer nor axe,
nor any tool of iron heard in the house while
it was in building. — *1 Kings, VI, 7*

How soft the music of those village
bells
Falling at intervals upon the ear
In cadence sweet!
*The Task. Book VI, Winter Walk
at Noon, Line 1*
Here the heart
May give a useful lesson to the head,
And Learning wiser grow without his
books.
Ibid. Line 85
Knowledge is proud that he has learn'd
so much;
Wisdom is humble that he knows no
more.
Ibid. Line 96
Some to the fascination of a name,
Surrender judgment hoodwink'd.
Ibid. Line 101
I would not enter on my list of friends,
(Though graced with polish'd manners
and fine sense,
Yet wanting sensibility), the man
Who needlessly sets foot upon a worm.
Ibid. Line 560
An honest man, close-button'd to the
chin,
Broadcloth without, and a warm heart
within.
Epistle to Joseph Hill
Shine by the side of every path we
tread
With such a lustre, he that runs may
read.[1]
Tirocinium. Line 79
What peaceful hours I once enjoy'd!
How sweet their memory still!
But they have left an ach'ng void
The world can never fill.
Walking with God
God moves in a mysterious way
His wonders to perform;
He plants his footsteps in the sea
And rides upon the storm.
Light Shining out of Darkness
Behind a frowning providence
He hides a shining face.
Ibid.

[1] Write the vision, and make it plain, upon
tables, that he may run that readeth it. —
Habakkuk, II, 2
He that runs may read. — TENNYSON: *The
Flower*

Beware of desperate steps! The darkest day,
Live till to-morrow, will have pass'd away.
The Needless Alarm. Moral
Oh that those lips had language! Life has pass'd
With me but roughly since I heard thee last.
On the Receipt of My Mother's Picture
The man that hails you Tom or Jack,
And proves, by thumping on your back,[1]
His sense of your great merit,[2]
Is such a friend that one had need
Be very much his friend indeed
To pardon or to bear it.
On Friendship. Stanza 26
Toll for the brave!
The brave that are no more,
All sunk beneath the wave,
Fast by their native shore!
*On the Loss of the Royal George.[3]
Stanza 1*
There is a bird who by his coat,
And by the hoarseness of his note,
Might be supposed a crow.
The Jackdaw (Translation from Vincent Bourne).[4] Stanza 1
He sees that this great roundabout
The world, with all its motley rout,
Church, army, physic, law,
Its customs and its businesses,
Is no concern at all of his,
And says — what says he? — Caw.
Ibid. Stanza 5
For 'tis a truth well known to most,
That whatsoever thing is lost,
We seek it, ere it come to light,
In every cranny but the right.
The Retired Cat

1 See Young, page 203.
2 Variant, — How he esteems your merit.
3 The *Royal George* was an English man-of-war of 108 guns, which suddenly heeled over, under the strain caused by the shifting of her guns, while being refitted at Spithead [August 29, 1782]. The commander, Admiral Kempenfeldt, and 800 of the sailors, marines, and visitors on board, were drowned.
4 VINCENT BOURNE [1695–1747], a Latin poet. Cowper was one of his pupils at Westminster School, where Bourne was Master.

He that holds fast the golden mean,[1]
And lives contentedly between
The little and the great,
Feels not the wants that pinch the poor,
Nor plagues that haunt the rich man's door.
Translation of Horace. Book II, Ode X, To Licinius, Stanza 2
If Fortune fill thy sail
With more than a propitious gale,
Take half thy canvas in.
Ibid. Stanza 6
But strive still to be a man before your mother.[2]
Connoisseur. Motto of No. III

ERASMUS DARWIN
[1731–1802]

Soon shall thy arm, unconquer'd steam! afar
Drag the slow barge, or drive the rapid car;
Or on wide-waving wings expanded bear
The flying chariot through the field of air.
The Botanic Garden. Part I, Canto I, Line 289
No radiant pearl which crested Fortune wears,
No gem that twinkling hangs from Beauty's ears,
Not the bright stars which Night's blue arch adorn,
Nor rising suns that gild the vernal morn,
Shine with such lustre as the tear that flows
Down Virtue's manly cheek for others' woes.
Ibid. Part II, Canto III, Line 459

CHARLES LEE
[1731–1782]

Beware that your Northern laurels do not change to Southern willows.
To General Horatio Gates [1728–1806] after surrender of

1 Keep the golden mean. — PUBLIUS SYRUS: *Maxim 1072*
2 See Beaumont and Fletcher, page 132.

Burgoyne at Saratoga [October 17, 1777]. Gates was later defeated by Lord Cornwallis at Camden, South Carolina [August 16, 1780] and was relieved of his command.

BEILBY PORTEUS
[1731–1808]

In sober state,
Through the sequestered vale of rural life,
The venerable patriarch guileless held
The tenor of his way.[1]
Death. Line 108
One murder made a villain,
Millions, a hero. Princes were privileged
To kill, and numbers sanctified the crime.[2]
Ibid. Line 154
War its thousands slays, Peace, its ten thousands.
Ibid. Line 178
Teach him how to live,
And, oh still harder lesson! how to die.[3]
Ibid. Line 316
Love is something so divine,
Description would but make it less;
'Tis what I feel, but can't define,
'Tis what I know, but can't express.
On Love

GEORGE WASHINGTON
[1732–1799]

Labour to keep alive in your breast that little spark of celestial fire, — conscience.
Rule from the copy-book of Washington when a schoolboy
That unmeaning and abominable custom, swearing.
Orders Against Profanity in the Army
Almighty God, we make our earnest prayer that Thou wilt keep the United States in Thy holy protection; that

[1] See Gray, page 245.
[2] See Young, page 203.
[3] See Tickell, page 205.

Thou wilt incline the hearts of the citizens to cultivate a spirit of subordination and obedience to government; to entertain a brotherly affection and love for one another and for their fellow-citizens of the United States at large.
Prayer after Inauguration (from copy in his pew, St. Paul's Chapel, New York)
To be prepared for war is one of the most effectual means of preserving peace.[1]
First Annual Address, to both Houses of Congress [January 8, 1790]
It is our true policy to steer clear of permanent alliances with any portion of the foreign world.
Farewell Address [September 17, 1796]

JOHN ADAMS
[1735–1826]

Yesterday the greatest question was decided which ever was debated in America; and a greater perhaps never was, nor will be, decided among men. A resolution was passed without one dissenting colony, that those United Colonies are, and of right ought to be, free and independent States.
Letter to Mrs. Adams [July 3, 1776]
The second day of July, 1776, will be the most memorable epocha in the history of America. I am apt to believe that it will be celebrated by succeeding generations as the great anniversary festival. It ought to be commemorated as the day of deliverance, by solemn acts of devotion to God Almighty. It ought to be solemnized with pomp and parade, with shows, games, sports, guns, bells, bonfires, and illuminations, from one end of this continent to the

[1] Qui desiderat pacem præparet bellum (Who would desire peace should be prepared for war). — VEGETIUS: *Rei Militari 3, Prolog*
In pace, ut sapiens, aptarit idonea bello (In peace, as a wise man, he should make suitable preparation for war). — HORACE: *Book II Satire II, Line 111*

other, from this time forward for evermore.

Letter to Mrs. Adams
[July 3, 1776]

JAMES BEATTIE
[1735–1803]

Mine be the breezy hill that skirts the
down,
Where a green grassy turf is all I crave,
With here and there a violet bestrewn,
Fast by a brook or fountain's murmur-
ing wave;
And many an evening sun shine sweetly
on my grave!
The Minstrel. Book II [1774],
Stanza 17
At the close of the day when the ham-
let is still,
And mortals the sweets of forgetful-
ness prove,
When naught but the torrent is heard
on the hill,
And naught but the nightingale's song
in the grove.
The Hermit
He thought as a sage, though he felt
as a man.
Ibid.

ISAAC BICKERSTAFF
[1735–1812?]

There was a jolly miller once lived on
the River Dee;
He worked and sung from morn till
night, no lark so blithe as he.
Love in a Village. Act I, Sc. 2
And this the burden of his song forever
used to be, —
"I care for nobody, no, not I, if no-
body cares for me." [1]
Ibid.

[1] Naebody cares for me,
I care for naebody.
ROBERT BURNS: *I Hae a Wife o' My Ain,*
St. 4
I envy none, no, no, not I,
And no one envies me.
CHARLES MACKAY: *The King and the Miller*

JOHN LANGHORNE
[1735–1779]

Cold on Canadian hills or Minden's
plain,
Perhaps that parent mourned her sol-
dier slain;
Bent o'er her babe, her eye dissolved
in dew,
The big drops mingling with the milk
he drew
Gave the sad presage of his future
years, —
The child of misery, baptized in tears. [1]
The Country Justice. Part I

WILLIAM JULIUS MICKLE
[1735–1788]

The dews of summer nights did fall,
The moon (sweet regent of the sky) [2]
Silvered the walls of Cumnor Hall
And many an oak that grew thereby.
Cumnor Hall.[3] Stanza 1
For know, when sickening grief doth
prey,
And tender love's repaid with scorn,
The sweetest beauty will decay:
What floweret can endure the storm?
Ibid. Stanza 10
For there's nae luck about the house,
There's nae luck at a';
There's little pleasure in the house
When our gudeman's awa.
The Mariner's Wife.[4] Stanza 1

[1] This allusion to the dead soldier and his
widow on the field of battle was made the
subject of a print by Bunbury, under which
were engraved the pathetic lines of Langhorne. Sir Walter Scott has mentioned that
the only time he saw Burns this picture was in
the room. Burns shed tears over it; and Scott,
then a lad of fifteen, was the only person present who could tell him where the lines were
to be found. — LOCKHART: *Life of Scott, Vol.
I, Chap. IV*
[2] Jove, thou regent of the skies. — POPE:
The Odyssey, Book II, L. 42
Now Cynthia, named fair regent of the
night. — GAY: *Trivia, Book III.*
And hail their queen, fair regent of the
night. — DARWIN: *The Botanic Garden, Part
I, Canto II, L. 90*
[3] This ballad is said to have suggested to
SIR WALTER SCOTT the writing of *Kenilworth.*
[4] *The Mariner's Wife* is now given "by
common consent," says Sarah Tytler, to Jean

Sae true his heart, sae smooth his
speech,
His breath like caller air;
His very foot has music in 't
As he comes up the stair.
The Mariner's Wife. Stanza 5

PATRICK HENRY
[1736–1799]

Tarquin and Caesar each had his
Brutus, Charles the First his Cromwell,
and George the Third ["Treason!"
cried the Speaker] — *may profit by
their example.* If *this* be treason, make
the most of it.
*Speech on the Stamp Act,
House of Burgesses, Richmond,
Virginia [May 29, 1765]*

I am not a Virginian, but an American.
*Speech in First Continental
Congress, Philadelphia [Oc-
tober 14, 1774]*

I have but one lamp by which my
feet are guided, and that is the lamp
of experience. I know of no way of
judging of the future but by the past.[1]
*Speech in Virginia Convention,
St. John's Episcopal Church,
Richmond, Virginia [March 23,
1775]*

We are not weak if we make a
proper use of those means which the
God of Nature has placed in our
power. . . . The battle, sir, is not to
the strong alone;[2] it is to the vigilant,
the active, the brave.
Ibid.

Adam [1710–1765], who published poems by
subscription, later opened a girls' school, and
died in Glasgow poorhouse. The *Dictionary
of National Biography* states that there is
small foundation for crediting the poem to
her. A shorter version of *The Mariner's Wife*,
entitled *There's Nae Luck About the House*,
is in the *Herd Collection of Ancient and Modern Scottish Songs, Heroic Ballads, etc.*

[1] See Burke, page 261.
[2] The race is not to the swift, nor the battle
to the strong. — *Ecclesiastes, IX, 11*
The race is not to the swift, nor the battle
to the strong; but the betting is best that
way. — FRANKLIN P. ADAMS: *The Conning
Tower*

Is life so dear, or peace so sweet, as
to be purchased at the price of chains
and slavery? Forbid it, Almighty God!
I know not what course others may
take, but as for me, give me liberty, or
give me death!
*Speech in Virginia Convention,
St. John's Episcopal Church,
Richmond, Virginia [March 23,
1775]*

EDWARD GIBBON
[1737–1794]

The reign of Antoninus is marked by
the rare advantage of furnishing very
few materials for history; which is indeed little more than the register of the
crimes, follies, and misfortunes of
mankind.[1]
*Decline and Fall of the Roman
Empire [1776]. Chap. 3. Modern Library Giant, Vol. I,
Page 69*

It has been calculated by the ablest
politicians that no State, without being soon exhausted, can maintain above
the hundredth part of its members in
arms and idleness.
Ibid. Chap. 5, Page 90

Amiable weaknesses of human nature.[2]
Ibid. Chap. 14, Page 375

In every deed of mischief he [Adroni-
cus] had a heart to resolve, a head to
contrive, and a hand to execute.[3]
Ibid. Chap. 48, Vol. II, Page 569

Our sympathy is cold to the relation
of distant misery.
Ibid. Chap. 49, Page 597

---

[1] L'histoire n'est que le tableau des crimes
et des malheurs (History is but the record of
crimes and misfortunes). — VOLTAIRE: *L'Ingénu, Chap. X*
[2] See Fielding, page 229 and Sheridan,
page 279.
[3] He [Hampden] had a head to contrive, a
tongue to persuade, and a hand to execute any
mischief. — EDWARD HYDE CLARENDON [1608–
1674]: *History of the Rebellion, Vol. III,
Book 7, Sect. 84*
Heart to conceive, the understanding to direct, or the hand to execute. — JUNIUS: *Letter XXXVII* [March 19, 1770]

The winds and waves are always on the side of the ablest navigators.[1]

Decline and Fall of the Roman Empire [*1776*]. *Vol. II, Chap. 68, Page 1343*

Vicissitudes of fortune, which spares neither man nor the proudest of his works, which buries empires and cities in a common grave.

Ibid. Chap. 71, Page 1438

All that is human must retrograde if it do not advance.

Ibid. Page 1440

I saw and loved.

Memoirs. Vol. I, Page 106

On the approach of spring I withdrew without reluctance from the noisy and extensive scene of crowds without company, and dissipation without pleasure.

Ibid. Page 116

I was never less alone than when by myself.[2]

Ibid. Page 117

THOMAS PAINE
[1737–1809]

And the final event to himself [Mr. Burke] has been, that, as he rose like a rocket, he fell like the stick.

Letter to the Addressers

These are the times that try men's souls.

The American Crisis. No. 1. In Pennsylvania Journal [*December 19, 1776*]

What we obtain too cheap, we esteem too lightly; it is dearness only that gives everything its value.

Ibid.

Panics, in some cases, have their uses; they produce as much good as hurt. Their duration is always short; the mind soon grows through them,

and acquires a firmer habit than before.

The American Crisis. No. 1. In Pennsylvania Journal [*December 19, 1776*]

Not a place upon earth might be so happy as America. Her situation is remote from all the wrangling world, and she has nothing to do but to trade with them.

Ibid.

In a chariot of light from the region of day
The Goddess of Liberty came.
Ten thousand celestials directed the way
And hither conducted the dame.
A fair budding branch from the gardens above,
Where millions with millions agree,
She brought in her hand as a pledge of her love,
And the plant she named Liberty Tree.

The Liberty Tree. Stanza 1. In Pennsylvania Magazine [*July, 1775*]

From the east to the west blow the trumpet to arms!
Through the land let the sound of it flee;
Let the far and the near all unite, with a cheer,
In defence of our Liberty Tree.

Ibid. Stanza 4

War involves in its progress such a train of unforeseen and unsupposed circumstances that no human wisdom can calculate the end. It has but one thing certain, and that is to increase taxes.

Prospects on the Rubicon [*1787*]

The world is my country,
All mankind are my brethren,[1]
To do good is my religion,
I believe in one God and no more.

The Rights of Man. Chap. 5

The sublime and the ridiculous are often so nearly related, that it is difficult to class them separately. One step above the sublime makes the ridicu-

---

[1] On dit que Dieu est toujours pour les gros bataillons (It is said that God is always on the side of the heaviest battalions). VOLTAIRE: *Letter to M. le Riche* [1770]

[2] Never less alone than when alone. — SAMUEL ROGERS [1763–1855]: *Human Life* [1819]

[1] See William Lloyd Garrison, page 424.

lous, and one step above the ridiculous makes the sublime again.[1]

Age of Reason. Part II, Note

JOHN WOLCOT ("PETER PINDAR") [1738–1819]

Blessed are those that nought expect,
For they shall not be disappointed.[2]

Ode to Pitt

You cannot make, my Lord, I fear,
A velvet purse of a sow's ear.[3]

Lord B. and His Notions

What rage for fame attends both great and small!
Better be damned than mentioned not at all.

To the Royal Academicians

Care to our coffin adds a nail, no doubt,
And every grin so merry draws one out.

Expostulatory Odes. XV

HESTER LYNCH THRALE (PIOZZI) [1739–1821]

The tree of deepest root is found
Least willing still to quit the ground:
'Twas therefore said by ancient sages,
  That love of life increased with years
So much, that in our latter stages,
When pain grows sharp and sickness rages,
  The greatest love of life appears.

Three Warnings

Johnson's conversation was by much too strong for a person accustomed to obsequiousness and flattery; it was mustard in a young child's mouth.

Quoted in Boswell's Life of Dr. Johnson, Vol. II, Page 396, Everyman Edition

---

DANIEL BLISS [1740–1806]

God wills us free, man wills us slaves,
I will as God wills, God's will be done.

Epitaph on gravestone of John Jack, "A Native of Africa, who died March 1773, aged about 60 years. Tho' born in a land of slavery he was born free." [1]

JAMES BOSWELL [1740–1795]

See also under SAMUEL JOHNSON

That favourite subject, Myself.

Letter to Temple [July 26, 1763]

Citizen of the world,[2] as I hold myself to be.

Life of Dr. Johnson, Everyman Edition, Page 521 (1775) Vol. I

We cannot tell the precise moment when friendship is formed. As in filling a vessel drop by drop, there is at last a drop which makes it run over; so in a series of kindnesses there is at last one which makes the heart run over.

Ibid. Vol. II, Page 122 (1777)

I think no innocent species of wit or pleasantry should be suppressed; and that a good pun may be admitted among the smaller excellencies of lively conversation.

Ibid. Page 537 (1784)

AUGUSTUS MONTAGUE TOPLADY [1740–1778]

Rock of Ages, cleft for me,
Let me hide myself in thee.

Rock of Ages [1775]. Stanza 1

ANNA LETITIA (AIKEN) BARBAULD [1743–1825]

Life! we've been long together
Through pleasant and through cloudy weather;

'Tis hard to part when friends are
   dear, —
Perhaps 'twill cost a sigh, a tear;
Then steal away, give little warning,
   Choose thine own time;
Say not "Good night," but in some
   brighter clime
   Bid me "Good morning."
           Life. Stanza 3

So fades a summer cloud away;
   So sinks the gale when storms are
   o'er;
So gently shuts the eye of day;
   So dies a wave along the shore.
     The Death of the Virtuous

This dead of midnight is the noon of
   thought.
    A Summer's Evening Meditation

THOMAS JEFFERSON
[1743–1826]

A lively and lasting sense of filial
duty is more effectually impressed on
the mind of a son or daughter by reading King Lear, than by all the dry volumes of ethics, and divinity, that ever
were written.
    Letter to Robert Skipwith
         [August 3, 1771]

The God who gave us life, gave us
liberty at the same time.
   Summary View of the Rights of
          British America

When, in the course of human events,
it becomes necessary for one people to
dissolve the political bands which have
connected them with another, and to
assume among the powers of the earth
the separate and equal station to which
the laws of nature and of nature's God[1]
entitle them, a decent respect to the
opinions of mankind requires that they
should declare the causes which impel
them to the separation.
    Declaration of Independence

We hold these truths to be self-
evident, — that all men are created
equal; that they are endowed by their
Creator with certain unalienable

[1] See Bolingbroke, page 200.

rights;[1] that among these are life,
liberty, and the pursuit of happiness.
    Declaration of Independence

We mutually pledge to each other
our lives, our fortunes, and our sacred
honour.
              Ibid.

What country before ever existed a
century and a half without a rebellion? . . . The tree of liberty must be
refreshed from time to time with the
blood of patriots and tyrants. It is its
natural manure.
   Letter to William Stevens Smith
         [November 13, 1787]

Error of opinion may be tolerated
where reason is left free to combat it.
    First Inaugural Address
         [March 4, 1801]

Equal and exact justice to all men,
of whatever state or persuasion, religious or political; peace, commerce,
and honest friendship with all nations,
— entangling alliances with none; the
support of the State governments in
all their rights, as the most competent
administrations for our domestic concerns, and the surest bulwarks against
anti-republican tendencies; the preservation of the general government in its
whole constitutional vigour, as the
sheet anchor of our peace at home and
safety abroad; . . . freedom of religion; freedom of the press; freedom
of person under the protection of the
habeas corpus; and trial by juries impartially selected, — these principles
form the bright constellation which has
gone before us, and guided our steps
through an age of revolution and reformation.
              Ibid.

In the full tide of successful experiment.
              Ibid.

Of the various executive abilities, no
one excited more anxious concern than
that of placing the interests of our

[1] All men are born free and equal, and have
certain natural, essential and unalienable
rights. — *Constitution of Massachusetts*
   The phrase is frequently misquoted "in-
alienable."

fellow-citizens in the hands of honest men, with understanding sufficient for their stations.[1]

Letter to Elias Shipman and Others of New Haven [*July 12, 1801*]

If a due participation of office is a matter of right, how are vacancies to be obtained? Those by death are few; by resignation, none.[2]

Ibid.

When a man assumes a public trust, he should consider himself as public property.[3]

RAYNER's *Life of Jefferson.*
Page 356

Indeed, I tremble for my country when I reflect that God is just.

Notes on Virginia. Query XVIII,
Manners

WILLIAM PALEY
[1743–1805]

Who can refute a sneer?

Moral Philosophy. Vol. II, Book V,
Chap. 9

ROWLAND HILL
[1744–1833]

Why should the Devil have all the good tunes?

JOSIAH QUINCY
[1744–1775]

Blandishments will not fascinate us, nor will threats of a "halter" intimidate. For, under God, we are determined that wheresoever, whensoever, or howsoever we shall be called to make our exit, we will die free men.

Observations on the Boston Port
Bill [*1774*]

---

[1] This passage is thus paraphrased by JOHN B. McMASTER in his *History of the People of the United States, Vol. II, P. 586:* "One sentence will undoubtedly be remembered till our republic ceases to exist. 'No duty the Executive had to perform was so trying,' he observed, 'as to put the right man in the right place.'"
[2] Usually quoted, "Few die and none resign."
[3] See Mathew Henry, page 188.

CHARLES DIBDIN
[1745–1814]

There's a sweet little cherub that sits up aloft,
To keep watch for the life of poor Jack.

Poor Jack

Did you ever hear of Captain Wattle?
He was all for love, and a little for the bottle.

Captain Wattle and Miss Roe

Here, a sheer hulk, lies poor Tom Bowling,
　The darling of our crew;
No more he'll hear the tempest howling,
　For death has broach'd him to.
His form was of the manliest beauty,
　His heart was kind and soft;
Faithful below he did his duty,
　But now he's gone aloft.

Tom Bowling

For though his body's under hatches,
　His soul has gone aloft.

Ibid.

But were it to my fancy given
To rate her charms, I'd call them heaven;
For though a mortal made of clay,
Angels must love Ann Hathaway;
She hath a way so to control,
To rapture the imprisoned soul,
And sweetest heaven on earth display,
That to be heaven Ann hath a way;
　She hath a way,
　Ann Hathaway, —
To be heaven's self Ann hath a way.

A Love Dittie, in the novel,
Hannah Hewit [*1792*]

Spanking Jack was so comely, so pleasant, so jolly,
　Though winds blew great guns, still he'd whistle and sing;
Jack loved his friend, and was true to his Molly,
　And if honour gives greatness, was great as a king.

The Sailor's Consolation

WILLIAM PITT
[? –1840]

One night came on a hurricane,
　The sea was mountains rolling,
When Barney Buntline turned his quid,

And said to Billy Bowling:
"A strong nor-wester's blowing, Bill;
Hark! don't ye hear it roar, now?
Lord help 'em, how I pities all
Unhappy folks on shore now!"
The Sailor's Consolation.[1] *Stanza 1*

HANNAH MORE
[1745–1833]

To those who know thee not, no words
    can paint!
And those who know thee, know all
    words are faint!
Sensibility
Since trifles make the sum of human
    things,
And half our misery from our foibles
    springs.
Ibid.
In men this blunder still you find, —
All think their little set mankind.
Florio and His Friend
Small habits well pursued betimes
May reach the dignity of crimes.
Ibid.
Some phrase that with the public took
Was all he read of any book.
Ibid.

WILLIAM SCOTT, LORD STOWELL
[1745–1836]

A dinner lubricates business.
Quoted in BOSWELL'S *Life of
Dr. Johnson, London edition
[1835], Vol. VIII, Page 67,
Note*
The elegant simplicity of the three per
cents.[2]
Quoted in CAMPBELL'S *Lives of
the Lord Chancellors, Vol. X,
Chap. 212*

[1] This song, because of a duplication of
title, has been ascribed to Charles Dibdin. Sir
Harold Boulton, after research, found that
William Pitt wrote it. He was Master Attendant at Jamaica Dockyard, and afterward went
to Malta, where he died. The song is ascribed
to Pitt in CHARLES MACKAY'S *Book of Songs*
and in the sheet music (A. M. Goodhart, composer) published by Boosey and Company.
[2] The sweet simplicity of the three per
cents. — DISRAELI (EARL OF BEACONSFIELD):
Endymion

JAMES HOOK
[1746–1827]

A little farm well tilled,
A little barn well filled,
A little wife well willed,
    Give me, give me.
The Soldier's Return. Stanza 1

I like the farm well tilled,
And I like the house well filled,
But no wife at all
    Give me, give me.
Ibid. Stanza 3

SIR WILLIAM JONES
[1746–1794]

Than all Bocara's vaunted gold,
Than all the gems of Samarcand.
A Persian Song of Hafiz

Go boldly forth, my simple lay,
Whose accents flow with artless
    ease,
Like orient pearls at random strung.[1]
Ibid.

On parent knees, a naked new-born
    child,
Weeping thou sat'st while all around
    thee smiled;
So live, that sinking in thy last long
    sleep,
Calm thou mayst smile, while all
    around thee weep.
From the Persian

Seven hours to law, to soothing slum-
    ber seven,
Ten to the world allot, and all to
    heaven.[2]
Epigram

[1] 'Twas he that ranged the words at ran-
    dom flung,
    Pierced the fair pearls and them together
    strung.
    EDWARD BACKHOUSE EASTWICK
    [1814–1833]: *Anvari Suhaili*
    (translated from Firdusi)
[2] See Coke, page 21.

CHARLES COTESWORTH PINCKNEY
[1746–1825]

Millions for defence, but not one cent
  for tribute.[1]
*When Ambassador to the French
  Republic [1796]*

JOHN O'KEEFFE
[1747–1833]

A glass is good, and a lass is good,
  And a pipe to smoke in cold weather;
The world is good, and the people are
  good,
  And we're all good fellows together.
Sprigs of Laurel. Act II, Sc. 1
And why I'm so plump the reason I
  tell, —
Who leads a good life is sure to live
  well.
*Merry Sherwood. A Friar of Orders
  Gray, Stanza 1*
A Rose Tree full in bearing
  Had sweet flowers fair to see;
One rose, without comparing,
  For beauty attracted me.
Though eager once to win it,
  Lovely, blooming, fresh and gay,
I find a canker in it
  And now throw it far away.
*The Poor Soldier [1783]. The
  Rose Tree (set to an earlier air)*

SAMUEL PARR [2]
[1747–1825]

Now that the old lion is dead, every
ass thinks he may kick at him.
*While dining with Sir Joshua
  Reynolds, after the death of Dr.
  Johnson. Quoted in* BOSWELL'S
  *Life of Dr. Johnson, Vol. II,
  Page 612, Everyman Edition*

JOHN LOGAN
[1748–1788]

Thou hast no sorrow in thy song,
  No winter in thy year.
        To the Cuckoo
Oh could I fly, I'd fly with thee!
  We'd make with joyful wing
Our annual visit o'er the globe,
  Companions of the spring.
                    Ibid.

JONATHAN M. SEWALL
[1748–1808]

No pent-up Utica contracts your powers,
But the whole boundless continent is
  yours.
          Epilogue to Cato [1]

JOHN EDWIN
[1749–1790]

A man's ingress into the world is naked
  and bare,
His progress through the world is
  trouble and care;
And lastly, his egress out of the world,
  is nobody knows where.
If we do well here, we shall do well
  there:
I can tell you no more if I preach a
  whole year.[2]
*The Eccentricities of John Ed-
  win [second edition, London,
  1791], Vol. I, Page 74*

EDWARD JENNER
[1749–1823]

The hollow winds begin to blow;
The clouds look black, the glass is low;
The soot falls down, the spaniels sleep,
And spiders from their cobwebs peep.
        Forty Signs of Rain

---

[1] Inscribed on the cenotaph in his memory
in St. Michael's Church, Charleston, South
Carolina. What Pinckney really said was more
forcible, — "not *a damned penny* for tribute."
[2] Dr. Parr composed the Latin epitaph for
the monument to Dr. Johnson, placed in St.
Paul's Cathedral, London, February, 1790.

[1] Written for the Bow Street Theatre, Ports-
mouth, New Hampshire.
[2] These lines Edwin offers as heads of a
"sermon." Longfellow places them in the
mouth of the Cobbler of Hagenau, as a "familiar tune." See *The Wayside Inn, Part II,
The Student's Tale.*

'Twill surely rain; I see with sorrow
Our jaunt must be put off to-morrow.
Forty Signs of Rain

LADY ANNE BARNARD
(née LINDSAY)
[1750–1825]

When the sheep are in the fauld, and
   the kye's come hame,
And a' the weary warld to rest are gone,
The waes o' my heart fall in showers
   frae my ee,
Unkenn'd by my gudeman, who sleeps
   sound by me.
Auld Robin Gray. Stanza 1
So I will do my best a gude wife to be,
For Auld Robin Gray he is kind to me.
Ibid. Stanza 9

JOHN PHILPOT CURRAN
[1750–1817]

It is the common fate of the indolent
to see their rights become a prey to the
active. The condition upon which God
hath given liberty to man is eternal
vigilance; [1] which condition if he break,
servitude is at once the consequence of
his crime and the punishment of his
guilt.
Speech upon the Right of Election
[1790]

JOHN LOWE
[1750–1798]

The moon had climb'd the highest hill
   Which rises o'er the source of Dee,
And from the eastern summit shed
   Her silver light on tower and tree,
When Mary laid her down to sleep,
   Her thoughts on Sandy far at sea,
When, soft and low, a voice was heard,
   Saying, "Mary, weep no more for
   me!"
Mary's Dream. Stanza 1

[1] Commonly quoted, — Eternal vigilance is
the price of liberty.
   There is one safeguard known generally to
the wise, which is an advantage and security
to all, but especially to democracies as against
despots. What is it? Distrust. — DEMOSTHE-
NES: *Philippic 2, Sect. 24*

JOHN TRUMBULL
[1750–1831]

But optics sharp it needs, I ween,
To see what is not to be seen.
McFingal. Canto I, Line 67
But as some muskets so contrive it
As oft to miss the mark they drive at,
And though well aimed at duck or
   plover,
Bear wide, and kick their owners over.
Ibid. Line 93
   As though there were a tie
And obligation to posterity.
We get them, bear them, breed, and
   nurse:
What has posterity done for us?
Ibid. Canto II, Line 121
No man e'er felt the halter draw,
With good opinion of the law.
Ibid. Canto III, Line 489

RICHARD BRINSLEY
SHERIDAN
[1751–1816]

Mrs. Malaprop. Illiterate him, I say,
   quite from your memory.
The Rivals. Act I, Sc. 2
'Tis safest in matrimony to begin with
   a little aversion.
Ibid.
   A circulating library in a town is as
an evergreen tree of diabolical knowl-
edge.
Ibid.
A progeny of learning.
Ibid.
Don't let your simplicity be imposed
   on.
Ibid.
Never say more than is necessary.
Ibid. Act II, Sc. 1
I know you are laughing in your sleeve.
Ibid.
He is the very pine-apple of politeness!
Ibid. Act III, Sc. 3
   If I reprehend anything in this world,
it is the use of my oracular tongue,
and a nice derangement of epitaphs!
Ibid.

As headstrong as an allegory on the banks of the Nile.

The Rivals. Act III, Sc. 3

Too civil by half.[1]

Ibid. Sc. 4

Our ancestors are very good kind of folks; but they are the last people I should choose to have a visiting acquaintance with.

Ibid. Act IV, Sc. 1

No caparisons, miss, if you please. Caparisons don't become a young woman.

Ibid. Sc. 2

We will not anticipate the past; so mind, young people, — our retrospection will be all to the future.

Ibid.

You are not like Cerberus, three gentlemen at once, are you?

Ibid.

The quarrel is a very pretty quarrel as it stands; we should only spoil it by trying to explain it.

Ibid. Sc. 3

You're our envoy; lead the way, and we'll precede.

Ibid. Act V, Sc. 1

There's nothing like being used to a thing.

Ibid. Sc. 3

As there are three of us come on purpose for the game, you won't be so cantankerous as to spoil the party by sitting out.

Ibid.

My valour is certainly going! it is sneaking off! I feel it oozing out, as it were, at the palm of my hands!

Ibid.

I own the soft impeachment.

Ibid.

Love gilds the scene, and women guide the plot.

Ibid. Epilogue

An apothecary should never be out of spirits.

St. Patrick's Day. Act I, Sc. 1

A fluent tongue is the only thing a

---

[1] Also in *The School for Scandal, Act V, Sc. 1.*

mother don't like her daughter to resemble her in.

St. Patrick's Day. Act I, Sc. 2

Death's a debt; his mandamus binds all alike — no bail, no demurrer.

Ibid. Act II, Sc. 4

I had rather follow you to your grave than see you owe your life to any but a regular-bred physician.

Ibid.

There is not a passion so strongly rooted in the human heart as envy.

The Critic. Act I, Sc. 1

Steal! to be sure they may; and, egad, serve your best thoughts as gypsies do stolen children, — disfigure them to make 'em pass for their own.[1]

Ibid.

The newspapers! Sir, they are the most villainous, licentious, abominable, infernal — Not that I ever read them! No, I make it a rule never to look into a newspaper.

Ibid.

Egad, I think the interpreter is the hardest to be understood of the two!

Ibid. Sc. 2

A practitioner in panegyric, or, to speak more plainly, a professor of the art of puffing.

Ibid.

Sheer necessity, — the proper parent of an art so nearly allied to invention.[2]

Ibid.

The number of those who undergo the fatigue of judging for themselves is very small indeed.[3]

Ibid.

---

[1] See Churchill, page 262.

[2] See Richard Franck, page 171.

[3] To the vast majority of mankind nothing is more agreeable than to escape the need for mental exertion. . . . To most people nothing is more troublesome than the effort of thinking. — JAMES BRYCE [1838-1922]: *Studies in History and Jurisprudence, Vol. 2, P. 7 and 8, Obedience*

We must view with profound respect the infinite capacity of the human mind to resist the introduction of useful knowledge. — THOMAS RAYNESFORD LOUNSBURY [1838-1915]: Quoted in *The Freshman and His College* [1913], by FRANCIS CUMMINS LOCKWOOD, *P. 44*

No scandal about Queen Elizabeth, I hope?

The Critic. Act II, Sc. 1

Certainly nothing is unnatural that is not physically impossible.

Ibid.

The Spanish fleet thou canst not see — because
— It is not yet in sight.[1]

Ibid.

Though hopeless love finds comfort in despair,
It never can endure a rival's bliss![2]

Ibid. Act III, Sc. 1

An oyster may be crossed in love.[3]

Ibid.

I ne'er could any lustre see
In eyes that would not look on me;
I ne'er saw nectar on a lip
But where my own did hope to sip.

The Duenna. Act I, Sc. 2

I loved him for himself alone.

Ibid. Sc. 3

I was struck all of a heap.

Ibid. Act II, Sc. 2

A bumper of good liquor
Will end a contest quicker
Than justice, judge, or vicar.[4]

Ibid. Sc. 3

Conscience has no more to do with gallantry than it has with politics.

Ibid. Sc. 4

Tale-bearers are as bad as the tale-makers.

The School for Scandal. Act I, Sc. 1

You shall see them on a beautiful quarto page, where a neat rivulet of text shall meander through a meadow of margin.

Ibid.

You had no taste when you married me.

Ibid. Sc. 2

Here's to the maiden of bashful fifteen;
Here's to the widow of fifty;
Here's to the flaunting, extravagant quean,
And here's to the housewife that's thrifty!
Let the toast pass;
Drink to the lass;
I'll warrant she'll prove an excuse for the glass.

The School for Scandal. Act III, Sc. 3

An unforgiving eye, and a damned disinheriting countenance.

Ibid. Act IV, Sc. 1

Be just before you're generous.

Ibid.

There is no sentiment he has such faith in as that Charity begins at home.[1]

Ibid. Act V, Sc. 1

It was an amiable weakness.[2]

Ibid.

The Right Honorable gentleman is indebted to his memory for his jests, and to his imagination for his facts.

Sheridaniana. Speech in Reply to Mr. Dundas

You write with ease to show your breeding,
But easy writing's curst hard reading.

Clio's Protest. In MOORE's Life of Sheridan, Vol. I, Page 155

PHILIP FRENEAU
[1752–1832]

From Susquehanna's utmost springs
Where savage tribes pursue their game,
His blanket tied with yellow strings,
A shepherd of the forest came.

The Indian Student. Stanza 1

In spite of all the learned have said,
I still my old opinion keep;
The posture that we give the dead
Points out the soul's eternal sleep.

*The Indian Burying-Ground.
Stanza 1*

---

[1] From the interpolated tragedy, *The Spanish Armada.*
[2] The same.
[3] The same.
[4] The government of a nation is often decided over a cup of coffee, or the fate of empires changed by an extra bottle of Johannisberg. — GEORGE PAYNE RAINSFORD JAMES [1801–1860]: *Richelieu, Chap. 16*

[1] See Sir Thomas Browne, page 144.
[2] See Fielding, page 229 and Gibbon, page 270.

Then rushed to meet the insulting foe;
They took the spear, but left the
  shield.[1]

To the Memory of the Ameri-
cans who Fell at Eutaw [Sep-
tember 8, 1781]

LEONARD McNALLY
[1752–1820]

On Richmond Hill there lived a lass
More bright than May-day morn;
Whose smiles all other maids' surpass,
A rose without a thorn.

The Lass of Richmond Hill.
Stanza 1

ROBERT HAWKER [2]
[1753–1827]

Lord, dismiss us with thy blessing,
  Hope, and comfort from above;
Let us each, thy peace possessing,
  Triumph in redeeming love.

Benediction

JOEL BARLOW [3]
[1754–1813]

E'en Hasty-Pudding, purest of all food,
May still be bad, indifferent, or good,[4]
As sage experience the short process
  guides,
Or want of skill, or want of care pre-
  sides.

Hasty-Pudding

The laws of husking every wight can
  tell —
And sure no laws he ever keeps so
  well:
For each red ear a general kiss he gains.

Ibid.

GEORGE CRABBE
[1754–1832]

Oh, rather give me commentators plain,
Who with no deep researches vex the
  brain;

Who from the dark and doubtful love
  to run,
And hold their glimmering tapers to
  the sun.[1]

The Parish Register. Part I,
Introduction

In this fool's paradise he drank delight.[2]

The Borough. Letter XII, Players

Books cannot always please, however
  good;
Minds are not ever craving for their
  food.

Ibid. Letter XXIV, Schools

In idle wishes fools supinely stay;
Be there a will, and wisdom finds a way.

The Birth of Flattery

Cut and come again.

Tales. VII, The Widow's Tale

Better to love amiss than nothing to
  have loved.[3]

Ibid. XIV, The Struggles of
Conscience

But 'twas a maxim he had often tried,
That right was right, and there he
  would abide.

Ibid. XV, The Squire and the
Priest

He tried the luxury of doing good.[4]

Tales of the Hall. Book III,
Boys at School

And took for truth the test of ridicule.[5]

Ibid. Book VIII, The Sisters

Time has touched me gently in his race,
And left no odious furrows in my face.

Ibid. Book XVII, The Widow

The ring, so worn as you behold,
So thin, so pale, is yet of gold.

A Marriage Ring

GEORGE BARRINGTON
[1755–1804]

True patriots all; for be it understood

---

[1] When Prussia hurried to the field,
  And snatched the spear, but left the shield.
  SCOTT: *Marmion, Introduction to Canto III*
[2] Not to be confused with Robert Stephen
Hawker [1803–1875].
[3] One of the (so-called) Hartford Wits.
[4] Good — bad — indifferent. — LAURENCE
STERNE: *Tristram Shandy, Book III, Chap. 2*

[1] See Young, page 203.
[2] See Shakespeare, page 79.
[3] 'Tis better to have loved and lost,
  Than never to have loved at all.
    TENNYSON: *In Memoriam, St. 27*
[4] See Goldsmith, page 249.
[5] See Thomas Carlyle, page 377.

We left our country for our country's
good.[1]

> *Prologue Written for the Open-*
> *ing of the Play-house at New*
> *South Wales [January 16, 1796]*

HENRY LEE
[1756–1818]

To the memory of the Man, first in
war, first in peace, and first in the
hearts of his countrymen.

> *Memoirs of Lee. Eulogy on Wash-*
> *ington [December 26, 1799]* [2]

WILLIAM BLAKE
[1757–1827]

Little lamb, who made thee?
Dost thou know who made thee,
Gave thee life, and bid thee feed
By the streams and o'er the mead?

> *The Lamb. Stanza 1*

Piping down the valleys wild,
Piping songs of pleasant glee,
On a cloud I saw a child.

> *Songs of Innocence. Introduction*

And I wrote my happy songs
Every child may joy to hear.

> *Ibid.*

My mother bore me in the southern
wild,
And I am black, but O my soul is white!

> *The Little Black Boy. Stanza 1*

---

[1] See Farquhar, page 201. According to the
Oxford Companion to English Literature,
"Barrington" was the adopted name of a notorious pickpocket who was transported to
the penal settlement at Botany Bay.

[2] To the memory of the Man, first in war,
first in peace, and first in the hearts of his
fellow-citizens. — *Resolutions Presented to
the United States' House of Representatives,
on the Death of Washington* [December, 1799]
The eulogy was delivered a week later. Marshall, in his *Life of Washington, Vol. V,
P. 767,* says in a note that these resolutions
were prepared by Colonel Henry Lee, who
was then not in his place to read them. General Robert E. Lee, in the life of his father
[1869] prefixed to the Report of his father's
Memoirs of the War of the Revolution, gives
[P. 5] the expression "fellow-citizens"; but on
P. 52 he says: "But there is a line, a single line,
in the Works of Lee which would hand him
over to immortality, though he had never
written another: 'First in war, first in peace,
and first in the hearts of his countrymen' will
last while language lasts."

And we are put on earth a little space
That we may learn to bear the beams
of love.

> *The Little Black Boy. Stanza 4*

The moon, like a flower
In heaven's high bower,
With silent delight
Sits and smiles on the night.

> *Night. Stanza 1*

Love seeketh not itself to please,
Nor for itself hath any care,
But for another gives its ease,
And builds a heaven in hell's despair.

> *The Clod and the Pebble. Stanza 1*

Tiger, tiger, burning bright
In the forests of the night,
What immortal hand or eye
Could frame thy fearful symmetry?

> *The Tiger. Stanza 1*

To see the world in a grain of sand,
And a heaven in a wild flower;
Hold infinity in the palm of your hand,
And eternity in an hour.

> *Auguries of Innocence. Stanza 1*

He who doubts from what he sees
Will ne'er believe, do what you please.
If the Sun and Moon should doubt,
They'd immediately go out.

> *Ibid. Stanza 6*

He who bends to himself a Joy
Doth the wingèd life destroy;
But he who kisses the Joy as it flies
Lives in Eternity's sunrise.

> *Eternity*

I was angry with my friend:
I told my wrath, my wrath did end.
I was angry with my foe:
I told it not, my wrath did grow.

> *A Poison Tree. Stanza 1*

He who desires but acts not, breeds
pestilence.

> *The Marriage of Heaven and Hell*

He who has suffer'd you to impose on
him, knows you.

> *Ibid.*

A Robin Redbreast in a cage
Puts all heaven in a rage.

> *Proverbs. Line 1*

A dog starved at his master's gate
Predicts the ruin of the state.

> *Ibid. Line 5*

A horse misused upon the road
Calls to heaven for human blood.
Proverbs. Line 9
Tools were made, and born were hands,
Every farmer understands.
Ibid. Line 83
A truth that's told with bad intent
Beats all the lies you can invent.
Ibid. Line 95
Every night and every morn
Some to misery are born;
Every morn and every night
Some are born to sweet delight.
Ibid. Line 101
For the tear is an intellectual thing,
And a sigh is the sword of an Angel
King;
And the bitter groan of a martyr's woe
Is an arrow from the Almighty's bow.
The Grey Monk. Stanza 10
When I saw that rage was vain
And to sulk would nothing gain,
Turning many a trick and wile
I began to soothe and smile.
Infant Sorrow. Stanza 3
The Vision of Christ that thou dost see,
Is my vision's greatest enemy.
Thine is the friend of all Mankind,
Mine speaks in Parables to the blind.
The Everlasting Gospel
Seek Love in the pity of others' woe,
In the gentle relief of another's care,
In the darkness of night and the win-
ter's snow,
With the naked and outcast — see
Love there.
William Bond. Stanza 13
Never seek to tell thy love.
Love's Secret. Stanza 1
The door of Death is made of gold,
That mortal eyes cannot behold.
Dedication of the Designs for
BLAIR'S *"Grave." To Queen
Charlotte*
The Angel that presided at my birth
Said: "Little creature, formed of joy
and mirth,
Go, love without the help of any thing
on earth."
Couplets and Fragments. 15
Great things are done when men and
mountains meet;

This is not done by jostling in the
street.
Gnomic Verses
The lineaments of gratified desire.
Ibid.
The Human Form Divine.[1]
The Divine Image
The busy bee has no time for sorrow.
Proverbs of Hell
Think in the morning, act in the
noon, eat in the evening, sleep in the
night.
Ibid.
The weak in courage is strong in cun-
ning.
Ibid.
Improvement makes straight roads,
but the crooked roads without improve-
ment are roads of genius.
Ibid.
Poetry fettered, fetters the human
race. Nations are destroyed or flourish
in proportion as their poetry, painting,
and music are destroyed or flourish.[2]
Jerusalem. Preface to Chapter 1
A man's worst enemies are those
Of his own house and family.
Ibid. Preface to Chapter 2, Stanza 21
I give you the end of a golden string:
Only wind it into a ball, —
It will lead you in at Heaven's gate,
Built in Jerusalem's wall.
Ibid. Preface to Chapter 4
And did those feet in ancient time
Walk upon England's mountain
green?
And was the holy Lamb of God
On England's pleasant pastures seen?
Milton
Bring me my bow of burning gold!
Bring me my arrows of desire!
Ibid.

[1] This phrase is used several times by Blake.
See also Pope, page 220.
[2] Vain was the chief's, the sage's pride!
They had no poet, and they died.
ALEXANDER POPE: *Odes of Horace, Book IV,
Ode IX, St. 4*
They built with bronze and gold and brawn,
The inner Vision still denied;
Their conquests . . . Ask oblivion! . . .
"They had no poet, and they died."
DON MARQUIS: *"They Had No Poet . . ."
St. 6*

I will not cease from mental fight,
  Nor shall my sword sleep in my
    hand,
Till we have built Jerusalem
  In England's green and pleasant
    land.
                              Milton

JOHN PHILIP KEMBLE
[1757–1823]

Perhaps it was right to dissemble your
    love,
But — why did you kick me down
    stairs? [1]
            The Panel. Act I, Sc. 1

ROYALL TYLER
[1757–1826]

Why should our thoughts to distant
    countries roam,
When each refinement may be found
    at home?
            The Contrast. Prologue
We all are mortals, and as mortals err.[2]
                              Ibid.
This outlandish lingo.
            Ibid. Act II, Sc. 2
  By the living jingo, you look so top-
ping, I took you for one of the agents
to Congress.
                              Ibid.
  Since General Shays has sneaked off
and given us the bag to hold.
                              Ibid.
Father and I went to camp,
Along with Captain Goodwin;
And there we saw the men and boys
As thick as hasty pudding,
    Yankee Doodle do.
            Ibid. Act III, Sc. 1
I am at the end of my tether.
                              Ibid.
  Every possible display of jocularity,
from an *affettuoso* smile to a *piano* tit-
ter, or full chorus *fortissimo* ha, ha, ha!
            Ibid. Act V, Sc. 1

---

[1] Altered from BICKERSTAFF's *'Tis Well 'tis
no Worse.* The lines are also found in DE-
BRETT's *Asylum for Fugitive Pieces, Vol. I,
P. 15*
[2] To err is human. — POPE: *Essay on Criticism, Part II, L. 325*

JAMES MONROE [1]
[1758–1831]

National honor is national property
of the highest value.
      *First Inaugural Address [March 4,
                              1817]*

  The American continents . . . are
henceforth not to be considered as subjects for future colonization by any European powers.
      *Annual Message to Congress
      [December, 1823] (The Mon-
      roe Doctrine)*

  We owe it, therefore, to candor, and
to the amicable relations existing between the United States and those powers to declare that we should consider
any attempt on their part to extend
their system to any portion of this
hemisphere as dangerous to our peace
and safety. With the existing colonies
or dependencies of any European power
we . . . shall not interfere. But with
the governments . . . whose independence we have . . . acknowledged, we
could not view any interposition for
the purpose of oppressing them, or controlling, in any other manner, their
destiny, by any European power, in any
other light than as a manifestation of
an unfriendly disposition towards the
United States.
                              Ibid.

HORATIO NELSON
[1758–1805]

  In the battle off Cape St. Vincent,
Nelson gave orders for boarding the
"San Josef," exclaiming "Westminster
Abbey, or victory!"
      SOUTHEY's *Life of Nelson. Vol. I,
                              Page 93*

---

[1] Monroe's administration was called the
"Era of Good Feeling" (title of an article in
the *Boston Centinel, July 12, 1817*) because
he had practically no opposition, the Federalist party having passed out of existence, and
because the declaration of his "Doctrine" did
much to keep the United States clear of European politics.

England expects every man to do his duty.[1]

SOUTHEY's *Life of Nelson.*
Vol. II, Page 131

May the great God, whom I worship, grant to my country and for the benefit of Europe in general, a great and glorious victory, and may no misconduct in anyone tarnish it, and may humanity after the victory be the predominant feature in the British fleet.

Prayer written in his diary [October 21, 1805]

ROBERT BURNS
[1759–1796]

Auld Nature swears the lovely dears
Her noblest work she classes, O;
Her 'prentice han' she tried on man,
And then she made the lasses, O!

Green Grow the Rashes. Stanza 5

Some books are lies frae end to end.

Death and Dr. Hornbook. Stanza 1

Some wee short hour ayont the twal.

Ibid. Stanza 31

The best laid schemes o' mice and men
Gang aft a-gley;
An' lea'e us nought but grief and pain,
For promis'd joy.

To a Mouse. Stanza 7

When chill November's surly blast
Made fields and forests bare.

Man Was Made to Mourn. Stanza 1

Man's inhumanity to man
Makes countless thousands mourn.

Ibid. Stanza 7

Gars auld claes look amaist as weel's
the new.

*The Cotter's Saturday Night.
Stanza 5*

Beneath the milk-white thorn that
scents the evening gale.

Ibid. Stanza 9

He wales a portion with judicious care;

---

[1] This famous sentence is thus first reported: "Say to the fleet, England confides that every man will do his duty." Captain Pasco, Nelson's flag-lieutenant, suggested substituting "expects" for "confides," which was adopted. Captain Blackwood, who commanded the *Euryalus,* says that the correction suggested was from "Nelson expects" to "England expects."

And "Let us worship God," he says,
with solemn air.

*The Cotter's Saturday Night.
Stanza 12*

From scenes like these, old Scotia's
grandeur springs,
That makes her loved at home, revered abroad:
Princes and lords are but the breath
of kings,
"An honest man's the noblest work
of God."[1]

Ibid. Stanza 19

For a' that, and a' that,
An' twice as muckle 's a' that.

The Jolly Beggars

John Barleycorn got up again,
And sore surpris'd them all.

John Barleycorn. Stanza 3

Life is but a day at most,
Sprung from night, — in darkness lost:
Hope not sunshine ev'ry hour,
Fear not clouds will always lour.

*Written in Friars Carse Hermitage.
Stanza 2*

Gie me ae spark o' Nature's fire,
That's a' the learning I desire.

First Epistle to J. Lapraik. Stanza 13

Gif ye want ae friend that's true,
I'm on your list.

Ibid. Stanza 15

I winna blaw about mysel,
As ill I like my fauts to tell.

Ibid. Stanza 16

My worthy friend, ne'er grudge an'
carp,
Tho' Fortune use you hard an' sharp.

*Second Epistle to J. Lapraik.
Stanza 8*

The social, friendly, honest man,
Whate'er he be,
'Tis he fulfils great Nature's plan,
And none but he.

Ibid. Stanza 15

Morality, thou deadly bane,
Thy tens o' thousands thou hast slain!

A Dedication to Gavin Hamilton

It's hardly in a body's pow'r,
To keep, at times, frae being sour.

Epistle to Davie. Stanza 2

---

[1] See Fletcher, page 126.

The mair they talk, I'm kend the better;
E'en let them clash.
A Poet's Welcome to His Love-Begotten Daughter. Stanza 2

God knows, I'm no the thing I should be,
Nor am I even the thing I could be.
To the Reverend John M'Math, Stanza 8

O Life! how pleasant, in thy morning,
Young Fancy's rays the hills adorning!
Cold-pausing Caution's lesson scorning,
  We frisk away,
Like schoolboys, at th' expected warning,
  To joy an' play.
Epistle to James Smith. Stanza 15

Misled by fancy's meteor ray,
  By passion driven;
But yet the light that led astray
  Was light from heaven.
The Vision. II, Stanza 18

And, like a passing thought, she fled
  In light away.
Ibid. Stanza 24

Affliction's sons are brothers in distress;
A brother to relieve, — how exquisite
  the bliss!
A Winter Night. Stanza 8

His lockèd, lettered, braw brass collar
Showed him the gentleman an' scholar.
The Twa Dogs. Stanza 3

An' there began a lang digression
About the lords o' the creation.
Ibid. Stanza 6

Oh wad some power the giftie gie us
To see oursels as others see us!
It wad frae monie a blunder free us,
  An' foolish notion.
To a Louse. Stanza 8

A dear loved lad, convenience snug,
  A treacherous inclination —
But, let me whisper i' your lug,
  Ye're aiblins nae temptation.
Address to the Unco Guid. Stanza 6

Then gently scan your brother man,
  Still gentler sister woman;
Though they may gang a kennin
  wrang,

To step aside is human.
Address to the Unco Guid. Stanza 7

What's done we partly may compute,
But know not what's resisted.
Ibid. Stanza 8

Stern Ruin's ploughshare drives elate,
  Full on thy bloom.
To a Mountain Daisy. Stanza 9

O life! thou art a galling load,
Along a rough, a weary road,
  To wretches such as I!
Despondency. Stanza 1

Perhaps it may turn out a sang,
Perhaps turn out a sermon.
Epistle to a Young Friend. Stanza 1

A man may tak a neebor's part,
  Yet hae nae cash to spare him.
Ibid. Stanza 4

I waive the quantum o' the sin,
  The hazard of concealing;
But, och! it hardens a' within,
  And petrifies the feeling!
Ibid. Stanza 6

To catch Dame Fortune's golden smile,
  Assiduous wait upon her;
And gather gear by ev'ry wile
  That's justified by honor:
Not for to hide it in a hedge,
  Nor for a train-attendant;
But for the glorious privilege
  Of being independent.
Ibid. Stanza 7

The fear o' hell's a hangman's whip
  To haud the wretch in order;
But where ye feel your honour grip,
  Let that ay be your border.
Ibid. Stanza 8

An atheist's laugh's a poor exchange
  For Deity offended!
Ibid. Stanza 9

And may ye better reck the rede,
  Than ever did the adviser!
Ibid. Stanza 11

If there's another world, he lives in
  bliss;
If there is none, he made the best of
  this.
Epitaph on William Muir

Shall I like a fool, quoth he,
  For a haughty hizzie die?
She may gae to — France for me! —
  Ha, ha, the wooing o't!
Duncan Gray. Stanza 3

When Nature her great masterpiece
    design'd,
And fram'd her last, best work, the hu-
    man mind,
Her eye intent on all the wondrous
    plan,
She form'd of various stuff the various
    Man.
        To Robert Graham. Stanza 1
Flow gently, sweet Afton, among thy
    green braes;
Flow gently, I'll sing thee a song in thy
    praise.
    Flow Gently, Sweet Afton. Stanza 1
Oh whistle, and I'll come to ye, my lad.[1]
Whistle, and I'll Come to Ye. Chorus
Naebody cares for me,
I care for naebody.
    I Hae a Wife o' my Ain. Stanza 4
Should auld acquaintance be forgot,
    And never brought to mind?
Should auld acquaintance be forgot,
    And auld lang syne?
        Auld Lang Syne. Stanza 1
We twa hae run about the braes,
    And pou'd the gowans fine.
            Ibid. Stanza 3
We'll tak a cup o' kindness yet
    For auld lang syne!
            Ibid. Stanza 5
To make a happy fireside clime
    To weans and wife,
That's the true pathos and sublime
    Of human life.
    Epistle to Dr. Blacklock. Stanza 9
If there's a hole in a' your coats,
    I rede you tent it;
A chiel's amang you takin' notes,
    And faith he'll prent it.
    *On the Late Captain Grose's
    Peregrinations thro' Scotland.
    Stanza 1*
John Anderson my jo, John,
    When we were first acquent,
Your locks were like the raven,
    Your bonny brow was brent.
        John Anderson. Stanza 1
This day Time winds th' exhausted
    chain,
To run the twelvemonth's length again.
    New Year's Day, 1791. Stanza 1

The voice of Nature loudly cries,
And many a message from the skies,
That something in us never dies.
    New Year's Day, 1791. Stanza 3
My heart's in the Highlands, my heart
    is not here;
My heart's in the Highlands a-chasing
    the deer.[1]
    *My Heart's in the Highlands.
        Chorus*
She is a winsome wee thing,
She is a handsome wee thing,
She is a lo'esome wee thing,
This sweet wee wife o' mine.
    *My Wife's a Winsome Wee Thing.
        Chorus*
The golden hours on angel wings
    Flew o'er me and my dearie;
For dear to me as light and life
    Was my sweet Highland Mary.
        Highland Mary. Stanza 2
But, oh! fell death's untimely frost,
    That nipt my flower sae ear.y.
            Ibid. Stanza 3
It's guid to be merry and wise,
It's guid to be honest and true,
It's guid to support Caledonia's cause
And bide by the buff and the blue.
    *Here's a Health to Them that's
        Awa'. Stanza 1*
Scots, wha hae wi' Wallace bled,
Scots, wham Bruce has aften led,
Welcome to your gory bed,
        Or to victory!
Now's the day and now's the hour;
See the front o' battle lour.
    *Scots, Wha Hae [Bannockburn].
        Stanzas 1 and 2*
Liberty's in every blow!
    Let us do, or die.[2]
            Ibid. Stanza 6
In durance vile [3] here must I wake and
    weep,
And all my frowsy couch in sorrow
    steep.
    Epistle from Esopus to Maria

---

[1] See Beaumont and Fletcher, page 131.

[1] These lines, from an old ballad, entitled
The Strong Walls of Derry, Burns made a
basis for his own beautiful song.
[2] See Fletcher, page 127.
[3] Durance vile. — W. KENRICK [1766]:
Falstaff's Wedding, Act I, Sc. 2. BURKE: *The
Present Discontents*

Oh, my luve is like a red, red rose,
    That's newly sprung in June;
Oh, my luve is like the melodie,
    That's sweetly played in tune.
                A Red, Red Rose. Stanza 1
Contented wi' little, and cantie wi'
    mair.
            Contented wi' Little. Stanza 1
Whare sits our sulky, sullen dame,
Gathering her brows like gathering
    storm,
Nursing her wrath to keep it warm.
                Tam o' Shanter. Stanza 1
Ah, gentle dames! it gars me greet
To think how monie counsels sweet,
How monie lengthened, sage advices,
The husband frae the wife despises.
                Ibid. Stanza 4
His ancient, trusty, drouthy cronie;
Tam lo'ed him like a vera brither, —
They had been fou for weeks thegither.
                Ibid. Stanza 5
The landlady and Tam grew gracious
Wi' secret favours, sweet and precious.
                Ibid.
The landlord's laugh was ready chorus.
                Ibid.
Kings may be blest, but Tam was
    glorious,
O'er a' the ills o' life victorious.
                Ibid. Stanza 6
But pleasures are like poppies spread,
You seize the flower, its bloom is shed;
Or like the snow falls in the river,
A moment white, then melts forever.
                Ibid. Stanza 7
That hour, o' night's black arch the
    keystane.
                Ibid.
Inspiring bold John Barleycorn,
What dangers thou canst make us
    scorn!
                Ibid. Stanza 11
As Tammie glow'red, amazed, and curi-
    ous,
The mirth and fun grew fast and furi-
    ous.
                Ibid. Stanza 13
Her cutty sark,[1] o' Paisley harn,
That while a lassie she had worn,

[1] The famous tea clipper, *Cutty Sark*, designed by Hercules Linton, and built in 1869,
had the story of Tam o' Shanter carved upon

In longitude tho' sorely scanty,
It was her best, and she was vauntie.
                Tam o' Shanter. Stanza 16
But to see her was to love her,
Love but her, and love forever.
                Ae Fond Kiss. Stanza 2
Had we never loved sae kindly,
Had we never loved sae blindly,
Never met — or never parted —
We had ne'er been broken-hearted!
                Ibid.
Ye banks and braes o' bonny Doon,
    How can ye bloom sae fresh and fair?
How can ye chant, ye little birds,
    And I sae weary fu' o' care?
                The Banks o' Doon. Stanza 1
Chords that vibrate sweetest pleasure
Thrill the deepest notes of woe.
Sensibility How Charming. Stanza 4
The rank is but the guinea's stamp,
    The man's the gowd for a' that.
            Is There for Honest Poverty.
                        Stanza 1
A prince can mak a belted knight,
    A marquis, duke, and a' that;
But an honest man's aboon his might,
    Guid faith, he mauna fa' that.
                Ibid. Stanza 4
Some hae meat and canna eat,
    And some wad eat that want it;
But we hae meat, and we can eat,
    And sae the Lord be thankit.
                The Selkirk Grace.[1]
It was a' for our rightfu' King
    We left fair Scotland's strand.
    It Was a' for Our Rightful King.[2]
                        Stanza 1
Now a' is done that men can do,
    And a' is done in vain.
                Ibid. Stanza 2
He turn'd him right and round about
    Upon the Irish shore,
And gae his bridle reins a shake,

her bow and counter. Nannie with flying locks
and scanty chemise was the figurehead.
[1] A note prefacing the verse says: "Allan
Cunningham records that this very characteristic 'Grace before meat' was uttered at the
table of the Earl of Selkirk, while on his tour
through Galloway with his friend Syme in
July, 1793. — William Scott Douglas."
[2] This ballad first appeared in JOHNSON'S
Museum [1796]. Sir Walter Scott was never
tired of hearing it sung.

With adieu for evermore,
  My dear —
And adieu for evermore! [1]
    It Was a' for Our Rightful King.
                 Stanza 3

JOHN FERRIAR
[1761–1815]

The princeps copy, clad in blue and
  gold.
    *Illustrations of Sterne. Biblio-
        mania, Line 6*
Now cheaply bought for thrice their
  weight in gold.
             Ibid. Line 65
How pure the joy, when first my hands
  unfold
The small, rare volume, black with tarnished gold!
             Ibid. Line 137

JOANNA BAILLIE
[1762–1851]

Oh, swiftly glides the bonnie boat,
  Just parted from the shore,
And to the fisher's chorus-note
  Soft moves the dipping oar.[2]
    *Oh, Swiftly Glides the Bonnie
                   Boat*
The wild-fire dances on the fen,
  The red star sheds its ray;
Uprouse ye then, my merry men!
  It is our op'ning day.
    The Outlaw's Song. Stanza 1
The gowan glitters on the sward,
  The laverock's in the sky,
And Collie on my plaid keeps ward,
  And time is passing by.
    *The Gowan Glitters on the Sward.
                 Stanza 1*

---

[1] Under the impression that this stanza is
ancient, SCOTT has made very free use of it,
first in *Rokeby* [1813], and then in *The Monastery* [1816]. In *Rokeby* he thus introduces
the verse: —
  He turn'd his charger as he spake,
    Upon the river shore,
  He gave his bridle reins a shake,
    Said, "Adieu for evermore, my love,
    And adieu for evermore."
[2] Our voices keep tune and our oars keep
time. — THOMAS MOORE: *Canadian Boat
Song, St. 1*

Oh, who shall lightly say that fame
Is nothing but an empty name,
When but for those, our mighty dead,
All ages past a blank would be.
    The Worth of Fame. Stanza 2
Good-morrow to thy sable beak
And glossy plumage dark and sleek,
Thy crimson moon and azure eye,
Cock of the heath, so wildly shy.
    The Heath-Cock. Stanza 1

ANDREW CHERRY
[1762–1812]

Loud roared the dreadful thunder,
  The rain a deluge showers.
        The Bay of Biscay
As she lay, on that day,
In the bay of Biscay, O!
                    Ibid.

GEORGE COLMAN, THE
YOUNGER
[1762–1836]

On their own merits modest men are
  dumb.
    Epilogue to the Heir at Law
And what's impossible can't be,
And never, never comes to pass.
    The Maid of the Moor
Three stories high, long, dull, and old,
As great lords' stories often are.
                  Ibid.
    But when ill indeed,
E'en dismissing the doctor don't always
  succeed.
    Lodgings for Single Gentlemen
When taken,
  To be well shaken.
    The Newcastle Apothecary
                O Miss Bailey!
Unfortunate Miss Bailey!
    *Love Laughs at Locksmiths.
               Act II, Song*
'Tis a very fine thing to be father-in-
  law
To a very magnificent three-tailed Ba-
  shaw!
    Blue Beard. Act II, Sc. 5
I had a soul above buttons.
    *Sylvester Daggerwood, or New
      Hay at the Old Market. Sc. 1*

Mynheer Vandunck, though he never
  was drunk,
Sipped brandy and water gayly.
> *Mynheer Vandunck*

SAMUEL ROGERS
[1763–1855]

Sweet Memory! wafted by thy gentle
  gale,
Oft up the stream of Time I turn my
  sail.
> *The Pleasures of Memory. Part II, 1*

She was good as she was fair,
None — none on earth above her!
As pure in thought as angels are:
To know her was to love her.[1]
> *Jacqueline.*[2] *Stanza 1*

The good arc better made by ill,
As odours crushed are sweeter still.[3]
> *Ibid. Stanza 3*

A guardian angel o'er his life presiding,
Doubling his pleasures, and his cares
  dividing.
> *Human Life*

To fireside happiness, to hours of ease
Blest with that charm, the certainty to
  please.
> *Ibid.*

The soul of music slumbers in the shell
Till waked and kindled by the master's
  spell;
And feeling hearts, touch them but
  rightly, pour
A thousand melodies unheard before!
> *Ibid.*

Then never less alone than when alone.[4]
> *Ibid.*

Those whom he loved so long and sees
  no more,

[1] See Burns, page 287.
  None knew thee but to love thee. — HAL-
LECK: *On the Death of Joseph Rodman Drake.*
[2] First published in the same volume with
Byron's *Lara* [1813], neither author append-
ing his name to his work.
[3] See Bacon, page 109.
[4] See Gibbon, page 271.
  Numquam se minus otiosum esse, quam
quum otiosus, nec minus solum, quam quum
solus esset (He is never less at leisure than
when at leisure, not less alone than when he is
alone). — CICERO: *De Officiis, Liber III, C. 1,*
quoting Publius Scipio

Loved and still loves, — not dead, but
  gone before.[1]
> *Human Life*

Mine be a cot beside the hill;
  A beehive's hum shall soothe my
    ear;
A willowy brook that turns a mill,
  With many a fall shall linger near.
> *A Wish. Stanza 1*

That very law which moulds a tear
And bids it trickle from its source, —
That law preserves the earth a sphere,
And guides the planets in their course.
> *On a Tear. Stanza 6*

Go! you may call it madness, folly;
  You shall not chase my gloom away!
There's such a charm in melancholy
  I would not if I could be gay.
> *To ———. Stanza 1*

There is a glorious city in the sea,
The sea is in the broad, the narrow
  streets,
Ebbing and flowing; and the salt sea-
  weed
Clings to the marble of her palaces.
> *Italy. Venice*

Lo, a skeleton,
With here and there a pearl, an em-
  erald stone,
A golden clasp, clasping a shred of
  gold;
All else had perished — save a nuptial
  ring,
And a small seal, her mother's legacy,
Engraven with a name, the name of
  both, "Ginevra."
> *Ibid. Ginevra* [2] *[Modena]*

To vanish in the chinks that Time has
  made.[3]
> *Ibid. Pæstum*

Ward has no heart, they say, but I
  deny it:
He has a heart, and gets his speeches
  by it.
> *Epigram*

[1] This is literally from SENECA, *Epistola
LXIII,* 16. See Mathew Henry, page 188.
[2] THOMAS HAYNES BAYLY's poem, *The Mistletoe Bough,* relates the same legend of the
bride accidentally imprisoned in a chest on her
wedding night.
[3] See Waller, page 146.

ROBERT HALL
[1764–1831]

His [Burke's] imperial fancy has laid all Nature under tribute, and has collected riches from every scene of the creation and every walk of art.
Apology for the Freedom of the Press

He [Kippis] might be a very clever man by nature for aught I know, but he laid so many books upon his head that his brains could not move.
GREGORY's *Life of Hall*

Call things by their right names. . . . Glass of brandy and water! That is the current but not the appropriate name: ask for a glass of liquid fire and distilled damnation.
Ibid.

THOMAS MORTON
[1764–1838]

What will Mrs. Grundy say? What will Mrs. Grundy think?
Speed the Plough [1798]. Act I, Sc. 1

Push on, — keep moving.
A Cure for the Heartache. Act II, Sc. 1

Approbation from Sir Hubert Stanley is praise indeed.
Ibid. Act V, Sc. 2

ANN RADCLIFFE
[1764–1823]

Fate sits on these dark battlements and frowns,
And as the portal opens to receive me,
A voice in hollow murmurs through the courts
Tells of a nameless deed.
Motto of her novel, The Mysteries of Udolpho, and presumably of her own composition

HELEN D'ARCY CRANSTOUN (MRS. DUGALD STEWART)
[1765–1838]

I weep not for the silent dead,
Their pains are past, their sorrows o'er.[1]
The Song of Genius

CATHERINE MARIA FANSHAWE
[1765–1834]

'Twas whisper'd in heaven, 'twas mutter'd in hell,
And echo caught faintly the sound as it fell;
On the confines of earth 'twas permitted to rest,
And the depths of the ocean its presence confess'd.
Enigma: The Letter H

MARY LAMB
[1765–1847]

Thou straggler into loving arms,
Young climber-up of knees.
A Child. Stanza 3

SIR JAMES MACKINTOSH
[1765–1832]

Diffused knowledge immortalizes itself.
Vindiciæ Gallicæ

The Commons, faithful to their system, remained in a wise and masterly inactivity.
Ibid

Disciplined inaction.
Causes of the Revolution of 1688. Chap. VII

The frivolous work of polished idleness
Dissertation on Ethical Philosophy. Remarks on Thomas Brown

[1] Quoted by SIR WALTER SCOTT in *The Talisman, Chap. 26.*

ISAAC DISRAELI
[1766–1848]

They [the early writers] looked with alarm upon the halo of immortality that encircled the printing-press.

Amenities of Literature. Vol. II, Page 278 [1840]

Whatever is felicitously expressed risks being worse expressed: it is a wretched taste to be gratified with mediocrity when the excellent lies before us.

Curiosities of Literature. On Quotation.

CAROLINA OLIPHANT, LADY NAIRNE
[1766–1845]

Sweet's the laverock's note and lang,
  Lilting wildly up the glen;
But aye to me he sings ae sang,
  Will ye no come back again?

Will Ye No Come Back Again? Stanza 5

Would you be young again?
  So would not I —
One tear to memory given,
  Onward I'd hie.

Would You Be Young Again?
[Looking Backward]. Stanza 1

I'm wearin' awa'
  To the land o' the leal.
There's nae sorrow there, John,
There's neither cauld nor care, John,
  The day is aye fair
  In the land o' the leal.

The Land o' the Leal. Stanza 1

Gude nicht, and joy be wi' you a'.

Gude Nicht.[1]

Oh, we're a' noddin', nid, nid, noddin';
Oh, we're a' noddin' at our house at hame.

We're a' Noddin'

A penniless lass wi' a lang pedigree.

The Laird o' Cockpen. Stanza 2

Oh! for ane I'll get better, it's waur I'll get ten,

---

[1] SIR ALEXANDER BOSWELL [1775–1822], eldest son of James Boswell, biographer of Dr. Johnson, composed a version of this song.

I was daft to refuse the Laird o' Cockpen.

The Laird o' Cockpen. Stanza 8

NANCY DENNIS SPROAT
[1766–1826]

Why, Phoebe, are you come so soon?
  Where are your berries, child?
You cannot, sure, have sold them all,
  You had your basket piled.

The Blackberry Girl.[1] Stanza 1

How pleasant is Saturday night,
  When I've tried all the week to be good,
And not spoke a word that was bad,
  And obliged every one that I could.

Lullabies for Children [1818].
Saturday Night,[2] Stanza 1

To-morrow our holy day comes,
  Which our merciful Father has given,
That we may rest from our work
  And prepare for His beautiful heaven.

Ibid. Stanza 2

JOHN QUINCY ADAMS
[1767–1848]

Think of your forefathers! Think of your posterity! [3]

Speech at Plymouth [December 22, 1802]

In charity to all mankind, bearing no malice or ill-will to any human being, and even compassionating those who hold in bondage their fellow-men, not knowing what they do.[4]

Letter to A. Bronson [July 30, 1838]

My wants are many, and, if told,
  Would muster many a score;

---

[1] From Salem Town's *Third Reader*.
[2] Pierpont's *Reader* [1831].
[3] Et majores vestros et posteros cogitate. — TACITUS: *Agricola, C. 32, 26*
[4] With malice towards none, with charity for all, with firmness in the right, as God gives us to see the right. — ABRAHAM LINCOLN: *Second Inaugural Address*

And were each wish a mint of gold,
I still should long for more.
> *The Wants of Man, Stanza 1.*
> *In The Quincy [Massachu-*
> *setts] Patriot, September 25,*
> *1841*

In days of yore, the poet's pen
From wing of bird was plundered,
Perhaps of goose, but now and then
From Jove's own eagle sundered.
But now, metallic pens disclose
Alone the poet's numbers;
In iron inspiration glows,
Or with the poet slumbers.
> *The Pen*

This is the last of earth! I am content.
> *His Last Words [February 21,*
> *1848]*

ANDREW JACKSON
[1767–1845]

Our Federal Union: it must be preserved.
> *Toast given on the Jefferson Birth-*
> *day Celebration [1830]*

You are uneasy; you never sailed
with *me* before, I see.[1]
> PARTON's *Life of Jackson. Vol. III,*
> *Page 493*

DAVID EVERETT
[1769–1813]

You'd scarce expect one of my age
To speak in public on the stage;
And if I chance to fall below
Demosthenes or Cicero,
Don't view me with a critic's eye,
But pass my imperfections by.
Large streams from little fountains
flow,
Tall oaks from little acorns grow.[2]
> *Lines written for a school dec-*
> *lamation for Ephraim H. Far-*
> *rar, aged seven, New Ipswich,*
> *New Hampshire [1791]*

---

[1] A remark made to an elderly gentleman who was sailing with Jackson down Chesapeake Bay in an old steamboat, and who exhibited a little fear.

[2] The lofty oak from a small acorn grows. — LEWIS DUNCOMBE [1711–1730]: *De Minimis Maxima* (translation)
Parvis e glandibus quercus. — Latin motto

These thoughts inspire my youthful
mind
To be the greatest of mankind;
Great, not like Caesar, stained with
blood,
But only great as I am good.
> *Lines written for a school dec-*
> *lamation. [1791]*

JOHN HOOKHAM FRERE
[1769–1846]

And don't confound the language of
the nation
With long-tailed words in *osity* and
ation.
> *The Monks and the Giants. Canto I,*
> *Line 6*

A sudden thought strikes me, — let
us swear an eternal friendship.[1]
> *The Rovers. Act I, Sc. 1*

Despair in vain sits brooding over
the putrid eggs of hope.
> *Ibid. Sc. 2*

I've often wished that I could write a
book,
Such as all English people might peruse;
I never should regret the pains it took,
That's just the sort of fame that I
should chuse.
> *Prospectus and Specimen of an*
> *Intended National Work. Proem,*
> *Stanza 1*

It grieves me much, that names that
were respected
In former ages, persons of such mark
And countrymen of ours, should lie
neglected,
Just like old portraits, lumbering in
the dark.
> *Ibid. Stanza 10*

ARTHUR WELLESLEY,
DUKE OF WELLINGTON
[1769–1852]

Nothing except a battle lost can be
half so melancholy as a battle won.
> *Despatch [1815*

---

[1] See Otway, page 185, and Sydney Smith, page 313.
My fair one, let us swear an eternal friendship. — MOLIÈRE: *Le Bourgeois Gentilhomme. Act IV, Sc. 1*

It is very true that I have said that I considered Napoleon's presence in the field equal to forty thousand men in the balance. This is a very loose way of talking; but the idea is a very different one from that of his presence at a battle being equal to a reinforcement of forty thousand men.

Memoir [1] [*September 18, 1836*]

Circumstances over which I have no control.[2]

I never saw so many shocking bad hats in my life.[3]

Upon seeing the first Reformed Parliament

There is no mistake; there has been no mistake; and there shall be no mistake.

Letter to Mr. Huskisson

I care not one two-penny damn.[4]

The battle of Waterloo was won on the playing fields of Eton.

Attributed to the Duke of Wellington

GEORGE CANNING
[1770–1827]

Weary knife-grinder! little think the proud ones,
Who in their coaches roll along the turnpike-road,
What hard work 'tis crying all day "Knives and
Scissors to grind, oh!"

The Friend of Humanity and the Knife-Grinder. Stanza 2

[1] PHILIP HENRY STANHOPE [1805–1875]: *Notes of Conversations with Wellington* [1888], *P. 81*

[2] This phrase was first used by the Duke of Wellington in a letter, about 1839 or 1840. — SALA: *Echoes of the Week,* in *London Illustrated News, Aug. 23, 1884.* GREVILLE, *Memoirs, Ch. II* [1823], gives an earlier instance.

[3] SIR WILLIAM FRASER, in *Words on Wellington* [1889], *P. 12,* says this phrase originated with the Duke. CAPTAIN GRONOW, in his *Recollections,* says it originated with the Duke of York, second son of George III, about 1817.

[4] It was the Duke of Wellington who invented this oath, so disproportionated to the greatness of its author. — GEORGE OTTO TREVELYAN: *Life and Letters of Lord Macaulay, Vol. II, P. 221*

Story! God bless you! I have none to tell, sir.

The Friend of Humanity and the Knife-Grinder. Stanza 6

I give thee sixpence! I will see thee damned first.

Ibid. Stanza 9

And finds, with keen, discriminating sight,
Black's not so black, — nor white so *very* white.

New Morality

Give me the avowed, the erect, the manly foe,
Bold I can meet, — perhaps may turn his blow!
But of all plagues, good Heaven, thy wrath can send,
Save, save, oh save me from the *candid friend!* [1]

Ibid.

I think of those companions true
Who studied with me at the U-
-niversity of Göttingen.

Song sung by Rogero in the burlesque play, The Rover. Stanza 1

Here rests, and let no saucy knave
Presume to sneer and laugh,
To learn that mouldering in the grave
Is laid a British Calf.

Epitaph on the Tombstone Erected over the Marquis of Anglesea's Leg, Lost at the Battle of Waterloo. Stanza 1

She saw two legs were lost on him
Who never meant to run.

Ibid. Stanza 9

In matters of commerce the fault of the Dutch
Is offering too little and asking too much.

Dispatch to Sir Charles Bagot, British Minister at The Hague [*January 31, 1826*]

I called the New World into existence to redress the balance of the Old.

The King's Message [*December 12, 1826*]

[1] "Defend me from my friends; I can defend myself from my enemies." The French *Ana* assign to Maréchal Villars this aphorism when taking leave of Louis XIV.

So down thy hill, romantic Ashbourn,
    glides
The Derby dilly, carrying *three* IN-
    SIDES.
> *The Loves of the Triangles.*
> *Line 178*

Here's to the pilot that weathered the
    storm!
> *The Pilot that Weathered the*
> *Storm*

JAMES HOGG [1]
[1770–1835]

Blest be the day Kilmeny was born!
Now shall the land of the spirits see,
Now shall it ken what a woman may
    be!
> *Kilmeny*

She left this world of sorrow and pain,
And returned to the Land of Thought
    again.
> *Ibid.*

Charlie is my darling,
The young Chevalier.
> *Charlie is My Darling. Refrain*

Bird of the wilderness,
Blithesome and cumberless.
> *The Skylark*

Love is like a dizziness,
It winna let a poor body
Gang about his bizziness.
> *Love is Like a Dizziness. Stanza 1*

JOSEPH HOPKINSON
[1770–1842]

Hail, Columbia! happy land!
Hail, ye heroes! heaven-born band!
    Who fought and bled in Freedom's
        cause,
    Who fought and bled in Freedom's
        cause,
And when the storm of war was gone,
Enjoyed the peace your valor won.
    Let independence be our boast,
    Ever mindful what it cost;
    Ever grateful for the prize,
    Let its altar reach the skies!
> *Hail, Columbia.* [2] *Stanza 1*

[1] The "Ettrick Shepherd."
[2] The musical setting of *Hail, Columbia*,
generally attributed to Philip Phile, was orig-

GEORGE NUGENT
REYNOLDS
[1770–1802]

Every night
The cottage rung,
As they sung:
"Oh! Dulce, dulce domum!" [1]
> *Dulce Domum. Stanza 1*

WILLIAM ROBERT
SPENCER
[1770–1834]

Too late I stayed, — forgive the crime!
    Unheeded flew the hours;
How noiseless falls the foot of time
    That only treads on flowers.
> *Lines to Lady Anne Hamilton.*
> *Stanza 1*

When the black-lettered list to the gods
    was presented,
(The list of what Fate for each mor-
    tal intends,)
At the long string of ills a kind god-
    dess relented,
And slipped in three blessings — wife,
    children, and friends.
> *Wife, Children, and Friends.*
> *Stanza 1*

Oh! where does faithful Gêlert roam,
    The flow'r of all his race?
So true, so brave; a lamb at home,
    A lion in the chase!
> *Beth-Gêlert. Stanza 4*

His gallant hound the wolf had slain,
    To save Llewellyn's heir.
> *Ibid. Stanza 19*

---

inally *The President's March*, written in 1789
as an inaugural march for George Washington.
In 1798, Joseph Hopkinson was asked by Mr
Fox, a young actor-singer, to write verses to
the music of the march, to introduce at a
benefit performance. The song was repeated
eight times, and when sung the ninth time
the audience stood and joined in the chorus.
    At the Republican Festival, in Boston, July
4, 1803, an ode, set to the same music, was
sung, the refrain being:
> By yon orb of living light,
> Swear to guard your native right;
> Sooner let it cease to shine,
> Than your liberties resign.

[1] Sweet, sweet home.

JOHN TOBIN
[1770–1804]

The man that lays his hand upon a woman,
Save in the way of kindness, is a wretch
Whom 'twere gross flattery to name a coward.
The Honeymoon [1805]. Act II, Sc. 1

She's adorned
Amply that in her husband's eye looks lovely, —
The truest mirror that an honest wife
Can see her beauty in.
Ibid. Act III, Sc. 4

WILLIAM WORDSWORTH [1]
[1770–1850]

Poetry is the breath and finer spirit of all knowledge; it is the impassioned expression which is in the countenance of all Science.
Lyrical Ballads, Second Edition. Preface

In spite of difference of soil and climate, of language and manners, of laws and customs, — in spite of things silently gone out of mind, and things violently destroyed, the Poet binds together by passion and knowledge the vast empire of human society, as it is spread over the whole earth, and over all time.
Ibid.

All men feel something of an honorable bigotry for the objects which have long continued to please them.
Ibid.

And homeless near a thousand homes I stood,
And near a thousand tables pined and wanted food.
Guilt and Sorrow. Part II, Stanza 41

A simple child,
That lightly draws its breath,
And feels its life in every limb,
What should it know of death?
We are Seven. Stanza 1

[1] Coleridge said to Wordsworth (*Memoirs* by his nephew, *Vol. II, P. 74*), "Since Milton, I know of no poet with so many *felicities* and unforgettable lines and stanzas as you."

O Reader! had you in your mind
Such stores as silent thought can bring,
O gentle Reader! you would find
A tale in everything.
Simon Lee. Stanza 9

In that sweet mood when pleasant thoughts
Bring sad thoughts to the mind.
Lines Written in Early Spring. Stanza 1

And 'tis my faith, that every flower
Enjoys the air it breathes.
Ibid. Stanza 3

Nor less I deem that there are Powers
Which of themselves our minds impress;
That we can feed this mind of ours
In a wise passiveness.
Expostulation and Reply. Stanza 6

Up! up! my friend, and quit your books;
Or surely you'll grow double:
Up! up! my friend, and clear your looks;
Why all this toil and trouble?
The Tables Turned. Stanza 1

Come forth into the light of things,
Let Nature be your teacher.
Ibid. Stanza 4

One impulse from a vernal wood
May teach you more of man,
Of moral evil and of good,
Than all the sages can.
Ibid. Stanza 6

Sensations sweet,
Felt in the blood, and felt along the heart.
Lines Composed a Few Miles Above Tintern Abbey

That best portion of a good man's life, —
His little, nameless, unremembered, acts
Of kindness and of love.
Ibid.

That blessed mood,
In which the burthen of the mystery,
In which the heavy and the weary weight
Of all this unintelligible world,
Is lightened.
Ibid.

The sounding cataract
Haunted me like a passion; the tall rock,
The mountain, and the deep and gloomy wood,
Their colours and their forms, were then to me
An appetite; a feeling and a love,
That had no need of a remoter charm,
By thoughts supplied, nor any interest
Unborrowed from the eye.
*Lines Composed a Few Miles
Above Tintern Abbey*
But hearing oftentimes
The still, sad music of humanity.
Ibid.
A sense sublime
Of something far more deeply interfused,
Whose dwelling is the light of setting suns,
And the round ocean and the living air,
And the blue sky, and in the mind of man;
A motion and a spirit, that impels
All thinking things, all objects of all thought,
And rolls through all things.
Ibid.
Knowing that Nature never did betray
The heart that loved her.
Ibid.
Men who can hear the Decalogue and feel
No self-reproach.
The Old Cumberland Beggar
As in the eye of Nature he has lived,
So in the eye of Nature let him die!
Ibid.
Full twenty times was Peter feared,
For once that Peter was respected.
Peter Bell. Part I, Stanza 3
A primrose by a river's brim
A yellow primrose was to him,
And it was nothing more.
Ibid. Stanza 12
The soft blue sky did never melt
Into his heart; he never felt
The witchery of the soft blue sky!
Ibid. Stanza 15
On a fair prospect some have looked,
And felt, as I have heard them say,
As if the moving time had been

A thing as steadfast as the scene
On which they gazed themselves away.
Peter Bell. Part I, Stanza 16
As if the man had fixed his face,
In many a solitary place,
Against the wind and open sky!
Ibid. Stanza 26 [1]
One of those heavenly days that cannot die.
Nutting
What fond and wayward thoughts will slide
Into a lover's head!
"O mercy!" to myself I cried,
"If Lucy should be dead!"
*Strange Fits of Passion Have I
Known. Stanza 7*
She dwelt among the untrodden ways
Beside the springs of Dove,
A maid whom there were none to praise
And very few to love.[2]
Lucy: She Dwelt Among the Untrodden Ways. Stanza 1
A violet by a mossy stone
Half hidden from the eye! —
Fair as a star, when only one
Is shining in the sky.
Ibid. Stanza 2
She lived unknown, and few could know
When Lucy ceased to be;
But she is in her grave, and, oh
The difference to me!
Ibid. Stanza 3
The stars of midnight shall be dear
To her; and she shall lean her ear
In many a secret place

[1] The original edition [London, 1819] had the following as the fourth stanza from the end of Part I, which was omitted in all subsequent editions: —
Is it a party in a parlour?
Crammed just as they on earth were crammed, —
Some sipping punch, some sipping tea,
But, as you by their faces see,
All silent and all damned.

[2] He lived amidst th' untrodden ways
To Rydal Lake that lead;
A bard whom there were none to praise,
And very few to read.
Unread his works — his "Milk White Doe"
With dust is dark and dim;
It's still in Longmans' shop, and oh!
The difference to him!
— *Parody by Hartley Coleridge.*

Where rivulets dance their wayward round,
And beauty born of murmuring sound
Shall pass into her face.
> *Lucy: Three Years She Grew in Sun and Shower. Stanza 5*

May no rude hand deface it,
And its forlorn *hic jacet!*
> *Ellen Irwin. Stanza 7*

She gave me eyes, she gave me ears;
And humble cares, and delicate fears;
A heart, the fountain of sweet tears;
And love, and thought, and joy.
> *The Sparrow's Nest. Stanza 2*

The child is father of the man.[1]
> *My Heart Leaps Up When I Behold*

The cattle are grazing,
Their heads never raising;
There are forty feeding like one!
> *The Cock Is Crowing. Stanza 1*

Sweet childish days, that were as long
As twenty days are now.
> *To a Butterfly. Part II, I've Watched You Now a Full Half-hour, Stanza 2*

Often have I sighed to measure
By myself a lonely pleasure,
Sighed to think, I read a book
Only read, perhaps, by me.
> *To the Small Celandine. Part II, Stanza 4*

I thought of Chatterton, the marvellous boy,
The sleepless soul that perished in his pride;
Of him who walked in glory and in joy
Following his plough, along the mountain-side:
By our own spirits are we deified:
We Poets in our youth begin in gladness;
But thereof come in the end despondency and madness.
> *Resolution and Independence [The Leech Gatherer]. Stanza 7*

That heareth not the loud winds when they call,
And moveth all together, if it moves at all.
> *Ibid. Stanza 11*

[1] See Milton, page 156.

Choice word and measured phrase, above the reach
Of ordinary men.
> *Resolution and Independence [The Leech Gatherer]. Stanza 14*

And mighty poets in their misery dead.
> *Ibid. Stanza 17*

Ne'er saw I, never felt, a calm so deep!
The river glideth at his own sweet will;
Dear God! the very houses seem asleep;
And all that mighty heart is lying still!
> *Lines Composed Upon Westminster Bridge*

The holy time is quiet as a nun
Breathless with adoration.
> *It is a Beauteous Evening*

Men are we, and must grieve when even the shade
Of that which once was great, is passed away.
> *On the Extinction of the Venetian Republic*

Thou hast left behind
Powers that will work for thee; air, earth, and skies;
There's not a breathing of the common wind
That will forget thee; thou hast great allies;
Thy friends are exultations, agonies,
And love, and man's unconquerable mind.
> *To Toussaint L'Ouverture* [1]

One that would peep and botanize
Upon his mother's grave.
> *A Poet's Epitaph. Stanza 5*

And you must love him, ere to you
He will seem worthy of your love.
> *Ibid. Stanza 11*

The harvest of a quiet eye.
> *Ibid. Stanza 13*

Yet sometimes, when the secret cup
Of still and serious thought went round,

[1] Sleep calmly in thy dungeon-tomb,
Beneath Besançon's alien sky,
Dark Haytien! — for the time shall come,
Yea, even now is nigh, —
When, everywhere, thy name shall be
Redeemed from color's infamy.
WHITTIER: *Toussaint L'Ouverture*

It seemed as if he drank it up —
He felt with spirit so profound.
Matthew. Stanza 7
The sweetest thing that ever grew
Beside a human door.
Lucy Gray. Stanza 2
A youth to whom was given
So much of earth — so much of heaven.
Ruth. Stanza 21
Something between a hindrance and a
help.
Michael
Drink, pretty creature, drink!
The Pet Lamb. Stanza 1
Plain living and high thinking are no
more: [1]
The homely beauty of the good old
cause
Is gone; our peace, our fearful inno-
cence,
And pure religion breathing household
laws.
*O Friend! I Know Not Which
Way I Must Look*
Milton! thou should'st be living at this
hour:
England hath need of thee! . . .
Thy soul was like a star, and dwelt
apart: . . .
So didst thou travel on life's common
way,
In cheerful godliness.
London, 1802
We must be free or die, who speak the
tongue
That Shakespeare spake; the faith and
morals hold
Which Milton held.
It Is Not To Be Thought Of
We meet thee, like a pleasant thought,
When such are wanted.
To the Daisy. Part I, Stanza 3
The poet's darling.
Ibid. Stanza 4
Thou unassuming commonplace
Of Nature.
Ibid. Part II, Stanza 1
Oft on the dappled turf at ease
I sit, and play with similes,

---

[1] Plain living and high thinking. — R. W.
EMERSON: *Domestic Life*

Loose type of things through all de-
grees.
To the Daisy. Part II, Stanza 2
Sweet Mercy! to the gates of heaven
This minstrel lead, his sins forgiven;
The rueful conflict, the heart riven
With vain endeavour,
And memory of Earth's bitter leaven
Effaced forever.
*Thoughts Suggested on the Banks
of the Nith. Stanza 10*
And stepping westward seemed to be
A kind of heavenly destiny.
Stepping Westward. Stanza 2
For old, unhappy, far-off things,
And battles long ago.
The Solitary Reaper. Stanza 3
Some natural sorrow, loss, or pain,
That has been, and may be again.
Ibid.
The music in my heart I bore
Long after it was heard no more.
Ibid. Stanza 4
Because the good old rule
Sufficeth them, the simple plan,
That they should take, who have the
power,
And they should keep who can.
Rob Roy's Grave. Stanza 9
Yon foaming flood seems motionless as
ice;
Its dizzy turbulence eludes the eye,
Frozen by distance.
Address to Kilchurn Castle
A brotherhood of venerable trees.
Sonnet composed at —— Castle
Let beeves and home-bred kine par-
take
The sweets of Burn-mill meadow;
The swan on still St. Mary's Lake
Float double, swan and shadow!
Yarrow Unvisited. Stanza 6
A remnant of uneasy light.
The Matron of Jedborough
Oh for a single hour of that Dundee
Who on that day the word of onset
gave! [1]
Sonnet, in the Pass of Killicranky

---

[1] It was on this occasion [the failure in
energy of Lord Mar at the battle of Sheriff-
muir] that Gordon of Glenbucket made the
celebrated exclamation, "Oh for an hour of

O Cuckoo! shall I call thee bird,
Or but a wandering voice?
To the Cuckoo. Stanza 1

She was a phantom of delight
When first she gleamed upon my sight;
A lovely apparition, sent
To be a moment's ornament;
Her eyes as stars of twilight fair,
Like twilight's, too, her dusky hair,
But all things else about her drawn
From May-time and the cheerful dawn.
*She Was a Phantom of Delight.
Stanza 1*

A creature not too bright or good
For human nature's daily food;
For transient sorrows, simple wiles,
Praise, blame, love, kisses, tears, and
smiles.
Ibid. Stanza 2

And now I see with eye serene
The very pulse of the machine.
Ibid. Stanza 3

The reason firm, the temperate will,
Endurance, foresight, strength, and
skill;
A perfect woman, nobly planned,
To warn, to comfort, and command.
Ibid.

I saw a crowd,
A host, of golden daffodils.
*I Wandered Lonely as a Cloud.
Stanza 1*

That inward eye
Which is the bliss of solitude.
Ibid. Stanza 4

Stern Daughter of the Voice of God! [1]
Ode to Duty. Stanza 1

A light to guide, a rod
To check the erring, and reprove.
Ibid.

Thou dost preserve the stars from
wrong;
And the most ancient heavens, through
Thee, are fresh and strong.
Ibid. Stanza 6

The light that never was, on sea or
land;
The consecration, and the Poet's
dream.
*Suggested by a Picture of Peele
Castle in a Storm. Stanza 4*

Shalt show us how divine a thing
A woman may be made.
*To a Young Lady. Dear Child
of Nature, Stanza 2*

But an old age serene and bright,
And lovely as a Lapland night,
Shall lead thee to thy grave.
Ibid. Stanza 3

Many are our joys
In youth, but oh! what happiness to
live
When every hour brings palpable ac-
cess
Of knowledge, when all knowledge is
delight,
And sorrow is not there!
The Prelude. Book II

Where the statue stood
Of Newton with his prism and silent
face,
The marble index of a mind forever
Voyaging through strange seas of
thought, alone.
Ibid. Book III

There's not a man
That lives who hath not known his god-
like hours.
Ibid.

When from our better selves we have
too long
Been parted by the hurrying world,
and droop,
Sick of its business, of its pleasures
tired,
How gracious, how benign, is Solitude.
Ibid. Book IV

Oh! give us once again the wishing-cap
Of Fortunatus, and the invisible coat
Of Jack the Giant-Killer, Robin Hood,
And Sabra in the forest with St.
George!
The child, whose love is here, at least,
doth reap
One precious gain, that he forgets him-
self.
The Prelude. Book V

Dundee!" — MAHON: *History of England,
Vol. I, P. 184*
Oh for one hour of blind old Dandolo,
The octogenarian chief, Byzantium's conquer-
ing foe!
BYRON: *Childe Harold, Canto IV, St. 12*
[1] See Milton, page 155.

'Tis told by one whom stormy waters threw,
With fellow-sufferers by the shipwreck spared,
Upon a desert coast, that having brought
To land a single volume, saved by chance,
A treatise on Geometry.
The Prelude. Book VI

Multitudes of hours
Pilfered away, by what the Bard who sang
Of the Enchanter Indolence [1] hath called
"Good-natured lounging," and behold a map
Of my collegiate life.
Ibid.

How men lived
Even next-door neighbours, as we say, yet still
Strangers, not knowing each the other's name.
Ibid. Book VII

Bliss was it in that dawn to be alive,
But to be young was very heaven!
Ibid. Book XI

There is
One great society alone on earth:
The noble living and the noble dead.
Ibid.

Who is the happy Warrior? Who is he
That every man in arms would wish to be?
Character of the Happy Warrior

Who, doomed to go in company with Pain,
And Fear, and Bloodshed, miserable train!
Turns his necessity to glorious gain.
Ibid.

Controls them and subdues, transmutes, bereaves
Of their bad influence, and their good receives.
Ibid.

But who, if he be called upon to face
Some awful moment to which Heaven has joined

[1] THOMSON'S *Castle of Indolence.*

Great issues, good or bad for humankind,
Is happy as a lover.
Character of the Happy Warrior

And, through the heat of conflict, keeps the law
In calmness made, and sees what he foresaw.
Ibid.

Whom neither shape of danger can dismay,
Nor thought of tender happiness betray.
Ibid.

Like, — but oh how different!
Yes, It Was the Mountain Echo

The world is too much with us; late and soon,
Getting and spending, we lay waste our powers:
Little we see in Nature that is ours.
The World Is Too Much With Us

Great God! I'd rather be
A Pagan suckled in a creed outworn; [1]
So might I, standing on this pleasant lea,
Have glimpses that would make me less forlorn;
Have sight of Proteus rising from the sea;
Or hear old Triton blow his wreathed horn.
Ibid.

Where lies the land to which yon Ship must go? [2]
Fresh as a lark mounting at break of day,
Festively she puts forth in trim array.
Where Lies the Land

A flock of sheep that leisurely pass by, [3]

[1]   Good Lord! I'd rather be
Quite unacquainted with the A.B.C.
Than write such hopeless rubbish as thy worst.
JAMES KENNETH STEPHEN [1859–1892]:
Sonnet, Wordsworth
[2] Where lies the land to which the ship would go?
Far, far ahead, is all her seamen know.
ARTHUR HUGH CLOUGH [1819–1861]:
Songs of Absence
[3]   An old half-witted sheep
Which bleats articulate monotony,
And indicates that two and one are three.
JAMES KENNETH STEPHEN: *Sonnet,
Wordsworth*

One after one; the sound of rain, and
  bees
Murmuring; the fall of rivers, winds
  and seas,
Smooth fields, white sheets of water,
  and pure sky;
I have thought of all by turns, and yet
  do lie
Sleepless!
> *To Sleep. II, A Flock of Sheep*

Blessed barrier between day and day.
> *Ibid.*

Maidens withering on the stalk.[1]
> *Personal Talk. Sonnet 1*

Dreams, books, are each a world; and
  books, we know,
Are a substantial world, both pure and
  good.
Round these, with tendrils strong as
  flesh and blood,
Our pastime and our happiness will
  grow.
> *Ibid. Sonnet 3*

The gentle Lady married to the Moor,
And heavenly Una with her milk-white
  lamb.
> *Ibid.*

A power is passing from the earth.
> *Lines on the Expected Dissolu-*
> *tion of Mr. Fox. Stanza 5*

An unexampled voice of awful memory.
> *On the Death of George III*

Look for the stars, you'll say that there
  are none;
Look up a second time, and, one by
  one,
You mark them twinkling out with silvery light,
And wonder how they could elude the
  sight!
> *Calm Is the Fragrant Air*

The rainbow comes and goes,
And lovely is the rose.
> *Intimations of Immortality.*[2]
> *Stanza 2*

The sunshine is a glorious birth;
But yet I know, where'er I go,

---

[1] Withering on the virgin thorn. — SHAKE-
SPEARE: *A Midsummer-Night's Dream*, Act I,
Sc. 1, L. 77
[2] The Ode on Immortality is the high water
mark which the intellect has reached in this
age. — R. W. EMERSON: *English Traits*

That there hath passed away a glory
  from the earth.
> *Intimations of Immortality.*
> *Stanza 2*

Where is it now, the glory and the
  dream?
> *Ibid. Stanza 4*

Our birth is but a sleep and a forget-
  ting:
The soul that rises with us, our life's
  star,
  Hath had elsewhere its setting,
  And cometh from afar:
  Not in entire forgetfulness,
  And not in utter nakedness,
But trailing clouds of glory do we
  come
From God, who is our home:
Heaven lies about us in our infancy!
> *Ibid. Stanza 5*

At length the man perceives it die
  away,
And fade into the light of common day.
> *Ibid.*

As if his whole vocation
Were endless imitation.
> *Ibid. Stanza 7*

  Those obstinate questionings
  Of sense and outward things,
  Fallings from us, vanishings;
  Blank misgivings of a creature
Moving about in worlds not realized,
High instincts before which our mortal
  nature
Did tremble like a guilty thing sur-
  prised.
> *Ibid. Stanza 9*

  Truths that wake,
To perish never.
> *Ibid.*

  Though inland far we be,
Our souls have sight of that immortal
  sea
  Which brought us hither.
> *Ibid.*

Though nothing can bring back the
  hour
Of splendour in the grass, of glory in
  the flower.
> *Ibid. Stanza 10*

In years that bring the philosophic
  mind.
> *Ibid.*

The clouds that gather round the setting sun
Do take a sober colouring from an eye
That hath kept watch o'er man's mortality.

Intimations of Immortality.
Stanza 11

To me the meanest flower that blows can give
Thoughts that do often lie too deep for tears.

Ibid.

The silence that is in the starry sky,
The sleep that is among the lonely hills.

Song at the Feast of Brougham Castle.

The monumental pomp of age
Was with this goodly personage;
A stature undepressed in size,
Unbent, which rather seemed to rise,
In open victory o'er the weight
Of seventy years, to loftier height.

The White Doe of Rylstone.
Canto III

A few strong instincts, and a few plain rules.

Alas! What Boots the Long Laborious Quest?

Strongest minds
Are often those of whom the noisy world
Hears least.

The Excursion. Book I

The imperfect offices of prayer and praise.

Ibid.

That mighty orb of song,
The divine Milton.

Ibid.

The good die first,[1]
And they whose hearts are dry as summer dust
Burn to the socket.

Ibid.

---

[1] Heaven gives its favourites — early death.
— BYRON: *Childe Harold, Canto IV, St. 102.*
Also *Don Juan, Canto IV, St. 12.*
Quem Di diligunt
Adolescens moritur
(He whom the gods favor dies in youth).
PLAUTUS: *Bacchides, Act IV, Sc. 7*

Wrongs unredressed, or insults unavenged.

The Excursion. Book III

Society became my glittering bride.

Ibid.

There is a luxury in self-dispraise;
And inward self-disparagement affords
To meditative spleen a grateful feast.

Ibid. Book IV

I have seen
A curious child, who dwelt upon a tract
Of inland ground, applying to his ear
The convolutions of a smooth-lipped shell,
To which, in silence hushed, his very soul
Listened intensely; and his countenance soon
Brightened with joy, for from within were heard
Murmurings, whereby the monitor expressed
Mysterious union with its native sea.[1]

Ibid.

One in whom persuasion and belief
Had ripened into faith, and faith become
A passionate intuition.

Ibid.

Spires whose "silent finger points to heaven."[2]

Ibid. Book VI

Ah! what a warning for a thoughtless man,

---

[1] But I have sinuous shells of pearly hue . . .
Shake one, and it awakens; then apply
Its polisht lips to your attentive ear,
And it remembers its august abodes,
And murmurs as the ocean murmurs there.
WALTER SAVAGE LANDOR: *Gebir, Book V*
Upon a mountain height, far from the sea,
I found a shell,
And to my listening ear the lonely thing
Ever a song of ocean seemed to sing,
Ever a tale of ocean seemed to tell.
EUGENE FIELD: *The Wanderer, St. 1*

[2] An instinctive taste teaches men to build their churches in flat countries with spire steeples, which, as they cannot be referred to any other object, point as with silent finger to the sky and stars. — COLERIDGE: *The Friend, No. 14*

Could field or grove, could any spot of
    earth,
Show to his eye an image of the pangs
Which it hath witnessed; render back
    an echo
Of the sad steps by which it hath been
    trod!
            The Excursion. Book VI
            And, when the stream
Which overflowed the soul was passed
    away,
A consciousness remained that it had
    left,
Deposited upon the silent shore
Of memory, images and precious
    thoughts,
That shall not die, and cannot be de-
    stroyed.
            Ibid. Book VII

Wisdom married to immortal verse.
            Ibid.

A man he seems of cheerful yesterdays
And confident to-morrows.
            Ibid.

Her bosom heaves and spreads, her
    stature grows;
And she expects the issue in repose.
            Laodamia. Stanza 2
            The gods approve
The depth, and not the tumult, of the
    soul.
            Ibid. Stanza 13
            Mightier far
Than strength of nerve and sinew, or
    the sway
Of magic potent over sun and star,
Is Love, though oft to agony distrest,
And though his favorite seat be feeble
    woman's breast.
            Ibid. Stanza 15

Elysian beauty, melancholy grace,
Brought from a pensive though a happy
    place.
            Ibid. Stanza 16

He spake of love, such love as spirits
    feel
In worlds whose course is equable and
    pure;
No fears to beat away — no strife to
    heal, —

The past unsighed for, and the future
    sure.
            Laodamia. Stanza 17
An ampler ether, a diviner air.
            Ibid. Stanza 18
But thou that didst appear so fair
    To fond imagination,
Dost rival in the light of day
    Her delicate creation.
            Yarrow Visited. Stanza 6
We bow our heads before Thee, and we
    laud
And magnify thy name, Almighty God!
But man is thy most awful instrument,
In working out a pure intent.
        *Ode, Imagination Ne'er Before
                    Content. IV*
That kill the bloom before its time;
And blanch, without the owner's crime,
The most resplendent hair.
        *Lament of Mary Queen of Scots.
                    Stanza 6*
The sightless Milton, with his hair
Around his placid temples curled;
And Shakespeare at his side, — a
    freight,
If clay could think and mind were
    weight,
For him who bore the world!
            The Italian Itinerant. Part I, 1
Meek Nature's evening comment on
    the shows
That for oblivion take their daily birth
From all the fuming vanities of earth.
        *Sky-Prospect from the Plain of
                    France*
As thou these ashes, little brook, wilt
    bear
Into the Avon, Avon to the tide
Of Severn, Severn to the narrow seas,
Into main ocean they, this deed ac-
    cursed
An emblem yields to friends and en-
    emies
How the bold teacher's doctrine, sanc-
    tified
By truth, shall spread, throughout the
    world dispersed.[1]
        *Ecclesiastical Sonnets. Part II,
                    XVII, To Wickliffe*

[1] In obedience to the order of the Council of
Constance (1415), the remains of Wickliffe
were exhumed and burned to ashes, and these

The feather, whence the pen
Was shaped that traced the lives of
these good men,
Dropped from an angel's wing.[1]
> *Ecclesiastical Sonnets. Part III,*
> *V, Walton's Book of Lives*

Give all thou canst; high Heaven rejects the lore
Of nicely-calculated less or more.
> *Ibid. XLIII, Inside of King's*
> *College Chapel, Cambridge*

Where music dwells
Lingering — and wandering on as loth
to die.
> *Ibid.*

Two voices are there: one is of the
sea,[2]
One of the mountains; each a mighty
voice.
> *Thought of a Briton on the*
> *Subjugation of Switzerland*

Or, shipwrecked, kindles on the coast
False fires, that others may be lost.
> *To the Lady Fleming. Stanza 7*

But hushed be every thought that
springs

---

cast into the Swift, a neighbouring brook running hard by; and "thus this brook hath conveyed his ashes into Avon, Avon into Severn,
Severn into the narrow seas, they into the
main ocean. And thus the ashes of Wickliffe
are the emblem of his doctrine, which is now
dispersed all the world over." — FULLER:
Church History, Sect. II, Book IV, Par. 53

What Heraclitus would not laugh, or
what Democritus would not weep? . . . For
though they digged up his body, burned his
bones, and drowned his ashes, yet the word of
God and truth of his doctrine, with the fruit
and success thereof, they could not burn. —
FOXE: *Book of Martyrs, Vol. I, P. 606* [ed.
1641]

Some prophet of that day said, —
"The Avon to the Severn runs,
　The Severn to the sea;
And Wickliffe's dust shall spread abroad
　Wide as the waters be."
DANIEL WEBSTER: *Address before the Sons*
　　　of New Hampshire [*1849*]
[1] The pen wherewith thou dost so heavenly
　sing
Made of a quill from an angel's wing.
　HENRY CONSTABLE [1562–1613]: *Sonnet*
[2] Two voices are there: one is of the deep.
And one is of an old half-witted sheep.
JAMES KENNETH STEPHEN: *Sonnet, Words-*
　　　worth (See footnote, page 300.)

From out the bitterness of things.
> *Elegiac Stanzas, Addressed to*
> *Sir G. H. B. Stanza 7*

Ethereal minstrel! pilgrim of the sky!
> *To a Skylark. Stanza 1*

Type of the wise who soar, but never
roam,
True to the kindred points of heaven
and home.
> *Ibid. Stanza 2*

A Briton, even in love, should be
A subject, not a slave!
> *Ere with Cold Beads of Midnight*
> *Dew. Stanza 5*

Scorn not the sonnet. Critic, you have
frowned,
Mindless of its just honours; with this
key
Shakespeare unlocked his heart.[1]
> *Scorn Not the Sonnet*

And, when a damp
Fell round the path of Milton, in his
hand
The thing became a trumpet; whence
he blew
Soul-animating strains, — alas, too
few!
> *Ibid.*

The bosom-weight, your stubborn gift,
That no philosophy can lift.
> *Presentiments. Stanza 5*

Nature's old felicities.
> *The Trosachs*

Myriads of daisies have shone forth in
flower
Near the lark's nest, and in their natural hour
Have passed away; less happy than
the one
That by the unwilling ploughshare,
died to prove
The tender charm of poetry and love.
> *Poems Composed During a Tour*
> *in the Summer of 1833. XXXVII,*
> *Mosgiel*

Small service is true service while it
lasts.
Of humblest friends, bright creature!
scorn not one:

---

[1]　　　　With this same key
Shakespeare unlocked his heart.
　ROBERT BROWNING: *House, St. 10*

The daisy, by the shadow that it casts,
Protects the lingering dewdrop from the sun.
> *To a Child, Written in her Album*

Since every mortal power of Coleridge
Was frozen at its marvellous source;
The rapt one, of the godlike forehead,
The heaven-eyed creature sleeps in earth:
And Lamb, the frolic and the gentle,
Has vanished from his lonely hearth.
> *Extempore Effusion upon the Death of James Hogg. Stanzas 4 and 5*

How fast has brother followed brother,
From sunshine to the sunless land!
> *Ibid. Stanza 6*

Enough if something from our hands have power
To live, and act, and serve the future hour.
> *Sonnet to the River Duddon*

We feel that we are greater than we know.
> *Ibid.*

They called thee Merry England in old time; [1]
A happy people won for thee that name
With envy heard in many a distant clime.
> *They Called Thee Merry England*

Wouldst thou be gathered to Christ's chosen flock,
Shun the broad way too easily explored,
And let thy path be hewn out of the Rock,
The living Rock of God's Eternal Word.
> *Inscription on a Rock at Rydal Mount*

How does the meadow-flower its bloom unfold?
Because the lovely little flower is free
Down to its root, and, in that freedom, bold.
> *A Poet! He Hath Put His Heart to School*

[1] England was merry England, when
Old Christmas brought his sports again.
SIR WALTER SCOTT: *Marmion, Introd. to Canto VI, St. 3*

Minds that have nothing to confer
Find little to perceive.
> *Yes, Thou art Fair. Stanza 2*

THOMAS DIBDIN
[1771–1841]

Oh, it's a snug little island!
A right little, tight little island.
> *The Snug Little Island*

JAMES MONTGOMERY
[1771–1854]

To-morrow — oh, 'twill never be,
If we should live a thousand years!
Our time is all to-day, to-day,
The same, though changed; and while it flies
With still small voice the moments say:
"To-day, to-day, be wise, be wise."
> *To-day*

Give me the hand that is honest and hearty,
Free as the breeze and unshackled by party.
> *Give Me Thy Hand. Stanza 2*

The rose has but a summer reign,
The daisy never dies.
> *The Daisy. Stanza 10*

Servant of God! well done; [1]
Rest from thy loved employ;
The battle fought, the victory won,
Enter thy Master's joy.
> *The Christian Soldier. Stanza 1*

"The Press! — What is the Press?" I cried;
When thus a wondrous voice replied:
"In me all human knowledge dwells;
The oracle of oracles,
Past, present, future, I reveal,
Or in oblivion's silence seal;
What I preserve can perish never,
What I forego is lost forever."
> *The Press. Stanza 1*

All that philosophers have sought,
Science discovered, genius wrought;
All that reflective memory stores,
Or rich imagination pours;
All that the wit of man conceives,
All that he wishes, hopes, believes;

[1] See Milton, page 153.

All that he loves, or fears, or hates,
All that to heaven and earth relates,
— These are the lessons that I teach
In speaking silence, silent speech.
The Press. Stanza 4

Counts his sure gains, and hurries back
  for more.
The West Indies. Part III

Hope against hope, and ask till ye re-
  ceive.
*The World before the Flood.
Canto V, Stanza 10*

Joys too exquisite to last,
And yet *more* exquisite when past.
The Little Cloud. Stanza 9

Bliss in possession will not last;
Remembered joys are never past;
At once the fountain, stream, and sea,
They were, they are, they yet shall be.
Ibid. Stanza 10

Friend after friend departs;
  Who hath not lost a friend?
There is no union here of hearts
  That finds not here an end.
Friends. Stanza 1

Nor sink those stars in empty night:
But hide themselves in heaven's own
  light.
Ibid. Stanza 4

'Tis not the whole of life to live,
  Nor all of death to die.
*The Issues of Life and Death.
Stanza 2*

Beyond this vale of tears
  There is a life above,
Unmeasured by the flight of years;
  And all that life is love.
Ibid. Stanza 3

Who, that hath ever been,
  Could bear to be no more?
Yet who would tread again the scene
  He trod through life before?
The Falling Leaf. Stanza 7

Here in the body pent,
  Absent from Him I roam,
Yet nightly pitch my moving tent
  A day's march nearer home.
At Home in Heaven

Prayer is the soul's sincere desire,
  Uttered or unexpressed;
The motion of a hidden fire
  That trembles in the breast.
What is Prayer? Stanza 1

Prayer is the burden of a sigh,
  The falling of a tear;
The upward glancing of an eye,
  When none but God is near.
What is Prayer? Stanza 2

ROBERT OWEN
[1771–1858]

All the world is queer save thee and
me, and even thou art a little queer.[1]
*On severing business relations
with his partner, William Allen
[1828]*

SIR WALTER SCOTT
[1771–1832]

His withered cheek, and tresses gray,
Seem'd to have known a better day.
*The Lay of the Last Minstrel.
Introduction*

Such is the custom of Branksome Hall.
Ibid. Canto I, Stanza 7

Your mountains shall bend,
And your streams ascend,
Ere Margaret be our foeman's bride!
Ibid. Stanza 18

If thou would'st view fair Melrose
  aright,
Go visit it by the pale moonlight.
Ibid. Canto II, Stanza 1

I cannot tell how the truth may be;
I say the tale as 'twas said to me.
Ibid. Stanza 22

In peace, Love tunes the shepherd's
  reed;
In war, he mounts the warrior's steed;
In halls, in gay attire is seen;
In hamlets, dances on the green.
Love rules the court, the camp, the
  grove,
And men below, and saints above;
For love is heaven, and heaven is love.
Ibid. Canto III, Stanza 2

Her blue eyes sought the west afar,
For lovers love the western star.
Ibid. Stanza 24

---

[1] Priests is queer people, and I don't know
who isn't. — JOHN MILLINGTON SYNGE [1871–
1909]: *The Aran Islands* [Luce ed. 1911],
P. 122

Ne'er
Was flattery lost on poet's ear;
A simple race! they waste their toil
For the vain tribute of a smile.

> *The Lay of the Last Min-*
> *strel. Canto IV, Interlude after*
> *Stanza 35*

Call it not vain: they do not err
Who say, that when the poet dies,
Mute Nature mourns her worshipper,
And celebrates his obsequies.

> *Ibid. Canto V, Stanza 1*

True love's the gift which God has
given
To man alone beneath the heaven:
  It is not fantasy's hot fire,
    Whose wishes, soon as granted,
    fly;
  It liveth not in fierce desire,
    With dead desire it doth not die;
It is the secret sympathy,
The silver link, the silken tie,
Which heart to heart and mind to mind
In body and in soul can bind.

> *Ibid. Stanza 13*

Breathes there the man, with soul so
dead,
Who never to himself hath said,
  This is my own, my native land!
Whose heart hath ne'er within him
burn'd [1]
As home his footsteps he hath turn'd,
  From wandering on a foreign strand?
If such there breathe, go, mark him
well;
For him no minstrel raptures swell;
High though his titles, proud his name,
Boundless his wealth as wish can
claim, —
Despite those titles, power, and pelf,
The wretch, concentred all in self,
Living, shall forfeit fair renown,
And, doubly dying, shall go down
To the vile dust, from whence he
sprung,
Unwept, unhonour'd, and unsung.[2]

> *Ibid. Canto VI, Stanza 1*

O Caledonia! stern and wild,
Meet nurse for a poetic child!

---

[1] Did not our heart burn within us while
he talked with us by the way? — *Luke,*
XXIV, 32

[2] See Pope, page 219.

Land of brown heath and shaggy
wood;
Land of the mountain and the flood!

> *The Lay of the Last Minstrel.*
> *Canto VI, Stanza 2*

Stood for his country's glory fast,
And nail'd her colors to the mast!

> *Marmion. Introduction to*
> *Canto I, Stanza 10*

Just at the age 'twixt boy and youth,
When thought is speech, and speech is
truth.

> *Ibid. Introduction to Canto II,*
> *Stanza 4*

When, musing on companions gone,
We doubly feel ourselves alone.

> *Ibid. Stanza 5*

When Prussia hurried to the field,
And snatch'd the spear, but left the
shield.[1]

> *Ibid. Introduction to Canto III,*
> *Stanza 3*

To bring my tribute to his grave: —
'Tis little — but 'tis all I have.

> *Ibid. Introduction to Canto IV,*
> *Stanza 5*

Where's the coward that would not
dare
  To fight for such a land?

> *Ibid. Canto IV, Stanza 30*

Lightly from fair to fair he flew,
And loved to plead, lament, and sue;
Suit lightly won, and short-lived pain,
For monarchs seldom sigh in vain.

> *Ibid. Canto V, Stanza 9*

Young Lochinvar is come out of the
West.

> *Ibid. Stanza 12 [Lochinvar.*
> *Stanza 1]*

So faithful in love, and so dauntless in
war,
There never was knight like the young
Lochinvar.

> *Ibid.*

With a smile on her lips, and a tear in
her eye.[2]

> *Ibid. Stanza 5*

Heap on more wood! — the wind is
chill;

---

[1] See Freneau, page 280.
[2] Reproof on her lips, but a smile in her eye.
SAMUEL LOVER: *Rory O'More, St. 1*

But let it whistle as it will,
We'll keep our Christmas merry still.
> *Marmion. Introduction to*
> *Canto VI, Stanza 1*

Still linger, in our northern clime,
Some remnants of the good old time.
> *Ibid. Stanza 4*

And dar'st thou, then,
To beard the lion in his den,
The Douglas in his hall?
> *Ibid. Canto VI, Stanza 14*

Oh, what a tangled web we weave,
When first we practise to deceive!
> *Ibid. Stanza 17*

O woman! in our hours of ease,
Uncertain, coy, and hard to please,
And variable as the shade
By the light quivering aspen made;
When pain and anguish wring the
brow,
A ministering angel thou! [1]
> *Ibid. Stanza 30*

"Charge, Chester, charge! on, Stanley,
on!"
Were the last words of Marmion.
> *Ibid. Stanza 32*

To all, to each, a fair good-night,
And pleasing dreams, and slumbers
light.
> *Ibid. L'Envoy, To the Reader*

In listening mood she seemed to stand,
The guardian Naiad of the strand.
> *The Lady of the Lake. Canto I,*
> *Stanza 17*

And ne'er did Grecian chisel trace
A Nymph, a Naiad, or a Grace

---

[1] A ministering angel shall my sister be. —
SHAKESPEARE: *Hamlet, Act V, Sc. 1, L. 263*

Scott, writing to Southey in 1810, said: "A witty rogue the other day, who sent me a letter signed Detector, proved me guilty of stealing a passage from one of Vida's Latin poems, which I had never seen or heard of." The passage alleged to be stolen ends with, —
　When pain and anguish wring the brow,
　A ministering angel thou!
which in Vida "ad Eranen," El. ii. v. 21, ran, —
　Cum dolor atque supercilio gravis imminet
　　angor,
　Fungeris angelico sola ministerio.
"It is almost needless to add," says LOCK-HART, "there are no such lines." — *Life of Scott, Vol. III, P. 294* (American edition)

Of finer form, or lovelier face.
> *The Lady of the Lake.*
> *Canto I, Stanza 18*

A foot more light, a step more true,
Ne'er from the heath-flower dash'd the
dew.
> *Ibid.*

On his bold visage middle age
Had slightly press'd its signet sage,
Yet had not quench'd the open truth
And fiery vehemence of youth:
Forward and frolic glee was there,
The will to do, the soul to dare.
> *Ibid. Stanza 21*

Soldier, rest! thy warfare o'er.
> *Ibid. Stanza 31*

Sleep the sleep that knows not breaking,
Morn of toil, nor night of waking.
> *Ibid.*

Hail to the chief who in triumph advances!
> *Ibid. Canto II, Stanza 19*

Some feelings are to mortals given,
With less of earth in them than heaven.
> *Ibid. Stanza 22*

Like the dew on the mountain,
　Like the foam on the river,
Like the bubble on the fountain,
　Thou art gone, and forever!
> *Ibid. Canto III, Stanza 16*
> *[Coronach. Stanza 3]*

Come one, come all! this rock shall fly
From its firm base as soon as I.
> *Ibid. Canto V, Stanza 10*

And the stern joy which warriors feel
In foemen worthy of their steel.
> *Ibid.*

Who o'er the herd would wish to reign,
Fantastic, fickle, fierce, and vain!
Vain as the leaf upon the stream,
And fickle as a changeful dream;
Fantastic as a woman's mood,
And fierce as Frenzy's fever'd blood.
Thou many-headed monster [1] thing,
Oh who would wish to be thy king!
> *Stanza 30*

Where, where was Roderick then!
One blast upon his bugle horn
Were worth a thousand men!
> *Ibid. Canto VI, Stanza 18*

---

[1] See Massinger, page 129.

Oh, many a shaft at random sent
Finds mark the archer little meant!
And many a word, at random spoken,
May soothe or wound a heart that's
  broken!
  The Lord of the Isles. Canto V,
  Stanza 18
Randolph, thy wreath has lost a rose.[1]
  Ibid. Canto VI, Stanza 18
There was — and O! how many sor-
rows crowd
Into these two brief words!
  Ibid. Conclusion
Where lives the man that has not tried
How mirth can into folly glide,
  And folly into sin!
  The Bridal of Triermain. Canto I,
  Stanza 21
Long loved, long woo'd, and lately won,
My life's best hope, and now mine
  own.
  Ibid. Introduction to Canto II,
  Stanza 1
List how she tells, in notes of flame,
"Child Roland to the dark tower
  came." [2]
  Ibid. Stanza 6
Two sisters by the goal are set,
Cold Disappointment and Regret;
One disenchants the winner's eyes,
And strips of all its worth the prize,
While one augments its gaudy show,
More to enhance the loser's woe.
  Rokeby. Canto I, Stanza 31
Still are the thoughts to memory dear.
  Ibid. Stanza 33
A mother's pride, a father's joy.
  Ibid. Canto III, Stanza 15
Oh, Brignall banks are wild and fair,
  And Greta woods are green,
And you may gather garlands there
  Would grace a summer's queen.
  Ibid. Stanza 16
The tear down childhood's check that
  flows,
Is like the dewdrop on the rose;

When next the summer breeze comes
  by,
And waves the bush, the flower is dry.
  Rokeby. Canto IV, Stanza 11
Thus aged men, full loth and slow,
The vanities of life forego,
And count their youthful follies o'er,
Till Memory lends her light no more.
  Ibid. Canto V, Stanza 1
No pale gradations quench his ray,
No twilight dews his wrath allay.
  Ibid. Canto VI, Stanza 21
Time will rust the sharpest sword,
Time will consume the strongest cord;
That which moulders hemp and steel,
Mortal arm and nerve must feel.
  Harold the Dauntless. Canto I,
  Stanza 4
Then strip, lads, and to it, though
  sharp be the weather,
  And if, by mischance, you should
  happen to fall,
There are worse things in life than a
  tumble on heather,
  And life is itself but a game at foot-
  ball.
  Song.[1] Stanza 5
Vacant heart, and hand, and eye,
Easy live and quiet die.
  Lucy Ashton's Song (in The Bride
  of Lammermoor, Chap. 3).
  Cursed war and racking tax
Have left us scarcely raiment to our
  backs.
  The Search after Happiness.[2]
  Stanza 16
Paddy had not — a shirt to his back!
  Ibid. Stanza 22
Come as the winds come, when
  Forests are rended;
Come as the waves come, when
  Navies are stranded.
  Pibroch of Donald Dhu. Stanza 4
A lawyer without history or litera-
ture is a mechanic, a mere working

---

[1] A rose hath fallen from thy chaplet. —
Halidon Hall, Act II, Sc. 2
  Robert Bruce's censure of Randolph for
permitting an English body of cavalry to pass
his flank on the day preceding the battle of
Bannockburn [June 24, 1314].
[2] See Shakespeare, page 99.

[1] On the lifting of the banner of the House
of Buccleuch at a great football match on
Carterhaugh [December 5, 1815].
[2] JOHN HAY in his poem, *The Enchanted
Shirt,* and EDWIN MARKHAM in *The Shoes of
Happiness,* have the same theme, — a monarch's search for the garment of an absolutely
happy man, and the discovery, when such a
man is found, that he does not possess one.

mason; if he possesses some knowledge of these, he may venture to call himself an architect.

Guy Mannering. Chap. 37

Bluid is thicker than water.[1]

Ibid. Chap. 38

It's no fish ye're buying, it's men's lives.[2]

The Antiquary. Chap. 11

So wags the world.[3]

Ivanhoe. Chap. 37

When Israel, of the Lord belov'd,
Out of the land of bondage came,
Her fathers' God before her mov'd,
An awful guide, in smoke and flame.

Ibid. Chap. 39 [Rebecca's Song. Stanza 1]

Sea of upturned faces.[4]

Rob Roy. Chap. 20

Lochow and the adjacent districts formed the original seat of the Campbells. The expression of "a far cry to Lochow" was proverbial.

Ibid. Chap. 29, Note

There's a gude time coming.[5]

Ibid. Chap. 32

My foot is on my native heath, and my name is MacGregor.

Ibid. Chap. 34

Scared out of his seven senses.[6]

Ibid.

Sound, sound the clarion, fill the fife!
To all the sensual world proclaim,
One crowded hour of glorious life
Is worth an age without a name.[7]

Old Mortality. Chap. 34

The happy combination of fortuitous circumstances.[1]

The Monastery. Answer of the Author of Waverley to the Letter of Captain Clutterbuck

Within that awful volume [2] lies
The mystery of mysteries!

The Monastery. Chap. 12

And better had they ne'er been born,
Who read to doubt, or read to scorn.

Ibid.

When we are handfasted, as we term it, we are man and wife for a year and day; that space gone by, each may choose another mate, or, at their pleasure, may call the priest to marry them for life; and this we call handfasting.[3]

Ibid. Chap. 25

Spur not an unbroken horse; put not your ploughshare too deep into new land.

Ibid.

Meat eaten without either mirth or music is ill of digestion.

Ibid.

I am she, O most bucolical juvenal, under whose charge are placed the milky mothers of the herd.[4]

Ibid. Chap. 28

But with the morning cool reflection came.[5]

Chronicles of the Canongate. Chap. 4

Ah, County Guy, the hour is nigh,
The sun has left the lea.
The orange flower perfumes the bower,
The breeze is on the sea.

Quentin Durward. Chap. 4

---

[1] This is a seventeenth-century proverb, found in RAY's *Collection* and elsewhere.
Blood is thicker, sir, than water, now as then.
    WALLACE RICE [1859–   ]: *Blood is Thicker than Water, St. 9*
See Whittier, page 443.
[2] It is not linen you're wearing out,
    But human creatures' lives.
THOMAS HOOD: *The Song of the Shirt, St. 4*
[3] See Shakespeare, page 49.
[4] DANIEL WEBSTER: *Speech* [Sept. 30, 1842]
[5] There's a good time coming. — CHARLES MACKAY: *The Good Time Coming*
[6] Huzza'd out of my seven senses. — *The Spectator, No. 616, Nov. 5, 1774*
[7] See page 311.

[1] Fearful concatenation of circumstances. — DANIEL WEBSTER: *Argument on the Murder of Captain White* [1830]
Fortuitous combination of circumstances. — DICKENS: *Our Mutual Friend, Vol. II, Chap. VII* (American ed.)
[2] The Bible.
[3] This custom of handfasting actually prevailed in the upland days. It arose partly from the want of priests. While the convents subsisted, monks were detached on regular circuits through the wilder districts, to marry those who had lived in this species of connexion. — ANDREW LANG: *Note* in his edition of *The Monastery*
[4] See Spenser, page 24.
[5] See Rowe, page 198.

But patience, cousin, and shuffle the cards,[1] till our hand is a stronger one.
Quentin Durward. Chap. 8

Too much rest is rust.[2]
The Betrothed. Chap. 13

If you keep a thing seven years, you are sure to find a use for it.
Woodstock. Chap. 28

What can they see in the longest kingly line in Europe, save that it runs back to a successful soldier?[3]
Ibid. Chap. 37

The playbill, which is said to have announced the tragedy of Hamlet, the character of the Prince of Denmark being left out.
The Talisman. Introduction

Rouse the lion from his lair.
Ibid. Heading, Chap. 6

Recollect that the Almighty, who gave the dog to be companion of our pleasures and our toils, hath invested him with a nature noble and incapable of deceit.
Ibid. Chap. 24

Jock, when ye hae naething else to do, ye may be aye sticking in a tree; it will be growing, Jock, when ye're sleeping.[4]
The Heart of Midlothian. Chap. 8

One hour of life, crowded to the full with glorious action, and filled with noble risks, is worth whole years of

those mean observances of paltry decorum.[1]
Count Robert of Paris. Chap. 25

Heaven knows its time; the bullet has its billet.
Ibid.

Fat, fair, and forty.[2]
St. Ronan's Well. Chap. 7

Good wine needs neither bush nor preface
To make it welcome.[3]
Peveril of the Peak. Chap. 4

When I hae a saxpence under my thumb,
Then I get credit in ilka town;
But when I am poor, they bid me gae by,
O, poverty parts good company.
The Abbot. Chap. 7

The jolly old landlord said, "Nothing's to pay."
The Pirate. Chap. 23

Tell that to the marines — the sailors won't believe it.[4]
Redgauntlet. Vol. II, Chap. 7

Although too much of a soldier among sovereigns, no one could claim with better right to be a sovereign among soldiers.[5]
Life of Napoleon

The sun never sets on the immense empire of Charles V.[6]
Ibid. [February, 1807]

---

[1] Patience, and shuffle the cards. — CERVANTES: *Don Quixote, Part II, Chap. 23*
Cut the fiercest quarrels short
With "Patience, gentlemen, and shuffle."
W. M. PRAED [1802–1839]: *Quince, St. 5*
Men disappoint me so, I disappoint myself so, yet courage, patience, shuffle the cards.
MARGARET FULLER OSSOLI [1810–1850]: *Letter to the Reverend W. H. Channing.* Quoted in HIGGINSON's *biography of Margaret Fuller*, page 112.

[2] German proverb: Rast ich, so rost ich (when I rest, I rust).

[3] Le premier qui fut roi, fut un soldat heureux:
Qui sert bien son pays, n'a pas besoin d'aïeux
(The first who was king was a successful soldier. He who serves well his country has no need of ancestors). — VOLTAIRE: *Mérope, Act I, Sc. 3*

[4] The words of a Highland laird, while on his death-bed, to his son.

[1] See page 310.

[2] See Dryden, page 178.

[3] Good wine needs no bush. — SHAKESPEARE: *As You Like It, Epilogue*

[4] "Right," quoth Ben, "that will do for the marines." — BYRON: *The Island, Canto II, last line*. A footnote states: "'That will do for the marines, but the sailors won't believe it,' is an old saying; and one of the few fragments of former jealousies which still survive (in jest only) between these gallant services."
When they talk about making your fortune all I can say is tell it to the marines. — JOHN GALSWORTHY [1867–1933]: *The Silver Spoon, Part II, Chap. 4*

[5] See Pope, page 215.

[6] A power which has dotted over the surface of the whole globe with her possessions and military posts, whose morning drumbeat, following the sun, and keeping company with the hours, circles the earth with one continuous and unbroken strain of the martial

[Miss Austen] had a talent for describing the involvements and feelings and characters of ordinary life which is to me the most wonderful I ever met with. The Big Bow-wow strain [1] I can do myself like any now going; but the exquisite touch which renders ordinary, commonplace things and characters interesting, from the truth of the description and the sentiment is denied to me.

Journal. March 14, 1826

SYDNEY SMITH
[1771–1845]

It requires a surgical operation to get a joke well into a Scotch understanding.[2]

*Lady Holland's Memoir. Vol. I,
Chap. 2*

That knuckle-end of England,—that land of Calvin, oat-cakes, and sulphur.

Ibid.

No one minds what Jeffrey says: . . . it is not more than a week ago that I heard him speak disrespectfully of the equator.

Ibid.

We cultivate literature on a little oatmeal.[3]

Ibid.

---

airs of England. — DANIEL WEBSTER: *Speech* [May 7, 1834]

Why should the brave Spanish soldier brag the sun never sets in the Spanish dominions, but ever shineth on one part or other we have conquered for our king? — CAPTAIN JOHN SMITH: *Advertisements for the Unexperienced, &c.* (Mass. Hist. Soc. Coll., Third Series, Vol. III, P. 49)

It may be said of them (the Hollanders) as of the Spaniards, that the sun never sets on their dominions. — GAGE: *New Survey of the West Indies, Epistle Dedicatory* [London, 1648]

[1] He had the most atrocious bow-wow public park manner. — JAMES M. BARRIE [1860–1937]: *What Every Woman Knows, Act 3*

[2] See Walpole, page 246.

[3] Sydney Smith, with reference to the *Edinburgh Review,* says: "The motto I proposed for the 'Review' was 'Tenui musam meditamur avena'; but this was too near the truth to be admitted; so we took our present grave

Preaching has become a by-word for long and dull conversation of any kind; and whoever wishes to imply, in any piece of writing, the absence of everything agreeable and inviting, calls it a sermon.

*Lady Holland's Memoir. Vol. I,
Chap. 3*

It is always right that a man should be able to render a reason for the faith that is within him.

Ibid.

The sense of sight is indeed the highest bodily privilege, the purest physical pleasure, which man has derived from his Creator.

Ibid.

Avoid shame, but do not seek glory,—nothing so expensive as glory.

Ibid. Chap. 4

It is no part of the duty of a clergyman to preach upon subjects purely political, but it is not therefore his duty to avoid religious subjects which have been distorted into political subjects.

Ibid.

What would have become of us had it pleased Providence to make the weather unchangeable? Think of the state of destitution of the morning callers.

Ibid.

Take short views, hope for the best, and trust in God.

Ibid. Chap. 6

Hope is the belief, more or less strong, that joy will come; desire is the wish it may come. There is no word to designate the remembrance of joys past.

Ibid.

Looked as if she had walked straight out of the ark.

Ibid. Chap. 7

Great men hallow a whole people, and lift up all who live in their time.

Ibid.

The Smiths never had any arms,

---

motto from Publius Syrus, of whom none of us had, I am sure, read a single line."

and have invariably sealed their letters with their thumbs.

Lady Holland's Memoir. Vol. I, Chap. 9

Madam, I have been looking for a person who disliked gravy all my life; let us swear eternal friendship.[1]

Ibid.

Not body enough to cover his mind decently with; his intellect is improperly exposed.

Ibid.

He has spent all his life in letting down empty buckets into empty wells; and he is frittering away his age in trying to draw them up again.[2]

Ibid.

You find people ready enough to do the Samaritan, without the oil and twopence.

Ibid.

Ah, you flavour everything; you are the vanilla of society.

Ibid.

My living in Yorkshire was so far out of the way, that it was actually twelve miles from a lemon.

Ibid.

As the French say, there are three sexes, — men, women, and clergymen.[3]

Ibid.

To take Macaulay out of literature and society, and put him in the House of Commons, is like taking the chief physician out of London during a pestilence.

Ibid.

Daniel Webster struck me much like a steam-engine in trousers.

Ibid.

"Heat, ma'am!" I said; "it was so dreadful here, that I found there was nothing left for it but to take off my flesh and sit in my bones."

Ibid.

[1] See Frere, page 292.
[2] See Cowper, page 265.
[3] Lord Wharncliffe says, "The well-known sentence, almost a proverb, that 'this world consists of men, women, and Herveys,' was originally Lady Montagu's." — *Montagu Letters, Vol. I, P. 64*

I have gout, asthma, and seven other maladies, but am otherwise very well.

Lady Holland's Memoir. Vol. I, Chap. 10

When you rise in the morning, form a resolution to make the day a happy one to a fellow-creature.

Ibid.

Live always in the best company when you read.

Ibid.

Never give way to melancholy; resist it steadily, for the habit will encroach.

Ibid.

I first gave it a dose of castor-oil, and then I christened it; so now the poor child is ready for either world.

Ibid. Chap. 11

He was a one-book man. Some men have only one book in them; others, a library.

Ibid.

Marriage resembles a pair of shears, so joined that they can not be separated; often moving in opposite directions, yet always punishing anyone who comes between them.[1]

Ibid.

Macaulay is like a book in breeches. . . . He has occasional flashes of silence, that make his conversation perfectly delightful.

Ibid.

Let onion atoms lurk within the bowl And, half suspected, animate the whole.

Ibid. Recipe for Salad

Serenely full, the epicure would say, Fate cannot harm me, — I have dined to-day.[2]

Ibid.

Don't tell me of facts, I never believe facts; you know Canning said nothing was so fallacious as facts, except figures.

Ibid.

What you don't know would make a great book.

Ibid.

In composing, as a general rule, run your pen through every other word you

[1] See Dickens, page 495.
[2] See Dryden, page 177.

have written; you have no idea what vigor it will give your style.[1]

> *Lady Holland's Memoir. Vol. I,*
> *Chap. 11*

Thank God for tea! What would the world do without tea? — how did it exist? I am glad I was not born before tea.

> *Ibid.*

That sign of old age, extolling the past at the expense of the present.

> *Ibid.*

We know nothing of to-morrow; our business is to be good and happy to-day.

> *Ibid. Chap. 12*

Light, dust, contradiction, an absurd remark, the sight of a Dissenter — anything, sets me sneezing; and if I begin sneezing at twelve, I don't leave off till two o'clock, and am heard distinctly in Taunton, when the wind sets that way — a distance of six miles. Turn your mind to this little curse.

> *To Dr. Holland, about Hay*
> *Fever [June, 1835]*

Correspondences are like small-clothes before the invention of suspenders; it is impossible to keep them up.

> *Letter to Mrs. Crowe*
> *[January 31, 1841]*

If you choose to represent the various parts in life by holes upon a table, of different shapes, — some circular, some triangular, some square, some oblong, — and the persons acting these parts by bits of wood of similar shapes, we shall generally find that the triangular person has got into the square hole, the oblong into the triangular, and a square person has squeezed himself into the round hole. The officer and the office, the doer and the thing done, seldom fit so exactly that we can say they were almost made for each other.[2]

> *Sketches of Moral Philosophy*

The schoolboy whips his taxed top; the beardless youth manages his taxed horse with a taxed bridle on a taxed road; and the dying Englishman, pouring his medicine, which has paid seven per cent, into a spoon that has paid fifteen per cent, flings himself back upon his chintz bed which has paid twenty-two per cent, and expires in the arms of an apothecary who has paid a license of a hundred pounds for the privilege of putting him to death.

> *Review of Seybert's Annals of*
> *the United States [1820]*

In the four quarters of the globe, who reads an American book, or goes to an American play, or looks at an American picture or statue?

> *Ibid.*

Magnificent spectacle of human happiness.

> *America. In Edinburgh Review,*
> *July, 1824*

In the midst of this sublime and terrible storm [at Sidmouth], Dame Partington, who lived upon the beach, was seen at the door of her house with mop and pattens, trundling her mop, squeezing out the sea-water, and vigorously pushing away the Atlantic Ocean. The Atlantic was roused; Mrs. Partington's spirit was up. But I need not tell you that the contest was unequal; the Atlantic Ocean beat Mrs. Partington.

> *Speech at Taunton [1813]*

Men who prefer any load of infamy, however great, to any pressure of taxation, however light.

> *On American Debts*

SAMUEL TAYLOR
COLERIDGE
[1772–1834]

He holds him with his glittering
    eye, . . .
And listens like a three years' child.[1]

> *The Ancient Mariner. Part I,*
> *Stanza 4*

Red as a rose is she.

> *Ibid. Stanza 9*

---

[1] See Samuel Johnson, page 235.
[2] Generally accepted as the origin of the phrase "A square peg in a round hole."

[1] WORDSWORTH, in his notes to *We Are Seven*, claims to have written this line.

We were the first that ever burst
Into that silent sea.

The Ancient Mariner.
Part II, Stanza 5

As idle as a painted ship
Upon a painted ocean.

Ibid. Stanza 8

Water, water, everywhere,
Nor any drop to drink.

Ibid. Stanza 9

Without a breeze, without a tide,
She steadies with upright keel.

Ibid. Part III, Stanza 6

The nightmare Life-in-Death was she.

Ibid. Stanza 11

The sun's rim dips, the stars rush out:
At one stride comes the dark;
With far-heard whisper o'er the sea
Off shot the spectre-bark.

Ibid. Stanza 13

We listen'd and look'd sideways up!
Fear at my heart, as at a cup,
My life-blood seem'd to sip.

Ibid. Stanza 14

And thou art long, and lank, and
brown,
As is the ribbed sea-sand.[1]

Ibid. Part IV, Stanza 1

Alone, alone, all, all alone;
Alone on a wide, wide sea.

Ibid. Stanza 3

The moving moon went up the sky,
And nowhere did abide;
Softly she was going up,
And a star or two beside.

Ibid. Stanza 10

A spring of love gush'd from my heart,
And I bless'd them unaware.

Ibid. Stanza 14

Oh sleep! it is a gentle thing,
Beloved from pole to pole.

Ibid. Part V, Stanza 1

A noise like of a hidden brook
In the leafy month of June,
That to the sleeping woods all night
Singeth a quiet tune.

Ibid. Stanza 17

Like one that on a lonesome road
Doth walk in fear and dread,
And having once turned round, walks
on,

[1] Coleridge says: "For these lines I am indebted to Mr. Wordsworth."

And turns no more his head;
Because he knows a frightful fiend
Doth close behind him tread.

The Ancient Mariner.
Part VI, Stanza 10

Is this the hill? is this the kirk?
Is this mine own countree?

Ibid. Stanza 14

So lonely 'twas, that God himself
Scarce seemed there to be.

Ibid. Part VII, Stanza 19

He prayeth well who loveth well
Both man and bird and beast.

Ibid. Stanza 22

He prayeth best who loveth best
All things both great and small.

Ibid. Stanza 23

A sadder and a wiser man
He rose the morrow morn.

Ibid. Stanza 25

And the spring comes slowly up this
way.

Christabel. Part I

Her gentle limbs did she undress,
And lay down in her loveliness.

Ibid.

A sight to dream of, not to tell!

Ibid.

That saints will aid if men will call;
For the blue sky bends over all!

Ibid. Conclusion

To be wroth with one we love
Doth work like madness in the brain.

Ibid. Part II

In Xanadu did Kubla Khan
A stately pleasure-dome decree;
Where Alph, the sacred river, ran
Through caverns measureless to man,
Down to a sunless sea.

Kubla Khan

A savage place! as holy and enchanted
As e'er beneath a waning moon was
haunted
By woman wailing for her demon
lover!

Ibid.

Ancestral voices prophesying war.

Ibid.

A damsel with a dulcimer
In a vision once I saw:
It was an Abyssinian maid,

And on her dulcimer she played,
Singing of Mount Abora.
Kubla Khan
For he on honey-dew hath fed,
And drunk the milk of Paradise.
Ibid.
What is an Epigram? A dwarfish whole,
Its body brevity, and wit its soul.[1]
An Epigram
The Eighth Commandment was not
made for bards.
The Reproof and Reply
Ere sin could blight or sorrow fade,
Death came with friendly care;
The opening bud to heaven conveyed,
And bade it blossom there.
Epitaph on an Infant
When France in wrath her giant limbs
up-rear'd.
France: An Ode. I.
Yes, while I stood and gazed, my temples bare,
And shot my being through earth, sea,
and air,
Possessing all things with intensest
love,
O Liberty! my spirit felt thee there.
Ibid. V.
Forth from his dark and lonely hiding-place
(Portentous sight!) the owlet Atheism,
Sailing on obscene wings athwart the
noon,
Drops his blue-fring'd lids, and holds
them close,
And hooting at the glorious sun in
heaven
Cries out, "Where is it?"
Fears in Solitude
And the Devil did grin, for his darling
sin
Is pride that apes humility.[2]
The Devil's Thoughts. Stanza 6

[1] See Shakespeare, page 92.
[2]   His favourite sin
Is pride that apes humility.
SOUTHEY: *The Devil's Walk*
ALEXANDER SMITH, in his essay on William
Dunbar, in *Dreamthorp,* says that Dunbar's
satire, *The Devil's Inquest,* probably gave
Coleridge the hint of his poem. Two lines
from Dunbar are:
The Devil said then, withouten mair,
"Renounce your God, and cum to me."

All thoughts, all passions, all delights,
Whatever stirs this mortal frame,
All are but ministers of Love,
And feed his sacred flame.
Love. Stanza 1
Saved from outrage worse than death.
Ibid. Stanza 14
Blest hour! it was a luxury — to be!
*Reflections on Having Left a
Place of Retirement*
A charm
For thee, my gentle-hearted Charles,[1]
to whom
No sound is dissonant which tells of
life.
This Lime-tree Bower My Prison
Hast thou a charm to stay the morning
star
In his steep course?
Hymn in the Vale of Chamouni
Risest from forth thy silent sea of
pines.
Ibid.
Motionless torrents! silent cataracts!
Ibid.
Ye living flowers that skirt the eternal
frost.
Ibid.
Earth, with her thousand voices, praises
God.
Ibid.
Tranquillity! thou better name
Than all the family of Fame.
Ode to Tranquillity
Aloof with hermit-eye I scan
The present work of present man —
A wild and dream-like trade of blood
and guile,
Too foolish for a tear, too wicked for a
smile.
Ibid.
The grand old ballad of Sir Patrick
Spence.[2]
Dejection, An Ode. Stanza 1
A mother is a mother still,
The holiest thing alive.
The Three Graves
The knight's bones are dust,

[1] Charles Lamb. See Lamb, page 325.
[2] The King sits in Dumferling toune,
Drinking the blude-reid wine.
PERCY: *Reliques, Sir Patrick Spence*

And his good sword rust;
His soul is with the saints, I trust.
                    The Knight's Tomb

How seldom, friend! a good great man
    inherits
Honor or wealth, with all his worth and
    pains!
It sounds like stories from the land of
    spirits
If any man obtains that which he mer-
    its,
Or any merit that which he obtains.

.   .   .   .   .

Greatness and goodness are not means,
    but ends!
Hath he not always treasures, always
    friends,
The good great man? Three treasures,
    — love, and light,
And calm thoughts, regular as infant's
    breath; —
And three firm friends, more sure than
    day and night, —
Himself, his Maker, and the angel
    Death.
        *Complaint [Edition of 1852]
        — The Good Great Man [Edi-
        tion of 1893]*

My eyes make pictures, when they are
    shut.
                    A Day-Dream. Stanza 1

Nought cared this body for wind or
    weather,
When youth and I lived in 't together.
                    Youth and Age. Stanza 1

Flowers are lovely; love is flower-like;
Friendship is a sheltering tree;
Oh the joys that came down shower-
    like,
Of friendship, love, and liberty,
    Ere I was old!
                    Ibid. Stanza 2

I have heard of reasons manifold
    Why Love must needs be blind,
But this the best of all I hold, —
    His eyes are in his mind.[1]
        *To a Lady, Offended by a
        Sportive Observation*

[1] Love looks not with the eyes, but with
the mind. — SHAKESPEARE: *A Midsummer-
Night's Dream, Act I, Sc. 1, L. 234*

What outward form and feature are
    He guesseth but in part;
But what within is good and fair
    He seeth with the heart.
        *To a Lady, Offended by a
        Sportive Observation*

Be that blind bard, who on the Chian
    strand,
By those deep sounds possessed with
    inward light,
Beheld the Iliad and the Odyssey
Rise to the swelling of the voiceful sea.[1]
                    Fancy in Nubibus

In many ways doth the full heart reveal
The presence of the love it would con-
    ceal.
        *Motto to Poems Written in
                    Later Life*

I counted two-and-seventy stenches,
All well defined, and several stinks.
                    Cologne

The river Rhine, it is well known,
Doth wash your city of Cologne;
But tell me, nymphs! what power di-
    vine
Shall henceforth wash the river Rhine?
                    Ibid.

Trochee trips from long to short;
From long to long in solemn sort
Slow Spondee stalks.
                    Metrical Feet

Strongly it bears us along in swelling
    and limitless billows;
Nothing before and nothing behind but
    the sky and the ocean.
        *The Homeric Hexameter
        (translated from Schiller)*

In the hexameter rises the fountain's
    silvery column,
In the pentameter aye falling in melody
    back.
        *The Ovidian Elegiac Metre
                    (from Schiller)*

The intelligible forms of ancient poets,
The fair humanities of old religion,
The power, the beauty, and the majesty
That had their haunts in dale or piny
    mountain,

[1] And Iliad and Odyssey
    Rose to the music of the sea.
        CHRISTIAN STOLBERG [1748–1821]:
        Thalatta, P. 132 (From the German)

Or forest by slow stream, or pebbly
   spring,
Or chasms and watery depths, — all
   these have vanished;
They live no longer in the faith of
   reason.
> *Wallenstein. Part I, Piccolo-*
> *mini, Act II, Sc. 4 (translated*
> *from Schiller)*

Clothing the palpable and familiar
With golden exhalations of the dawn.
> *Ibid. Part II, The Death of*
> *Wallenstein, Act V, Sc. 1*

     Often do the spirits
Of great events stride on before the
   events,
And in to-day already walks to-
   morrow.[1]
> *Ibid.*

The happiness of life is made up of
minute fractions — the little soon forgotten charities of a kiss or smile, a
kind look, a heartfelt compliment, and
the countless infinitesimals of pleasurable and genial feeling.
> *The Friend. The Improvisatore*

A dwarf sees farther than the giant
when he has the giant's shoulder to
mount on.[2]
> *Ibid. Sect. I, Essay 8*

An instinctive taste teaches men to
build their churches in flat countries,
with spire steeples, which, as they cannot be referred to any other object,
point as with silent finger to the sky
and star.[3]
> *Ibid. Essay 14*

Not the poem which we have *read,*
but that to which we *return,* with the
greatest pleasure, possesses the genuine power, and claims the name of *es-*
sential poetry.
> *Biographia Literaria. Chap. 1*

Every reform, however necessary,
will by weak minds be carried to an
excess, that itself will need reforming.
> *Ibid.*

Experience informs us that the first
defence of weak minds is to recriminate.
> *Ibid. Chap. 2*

Through all the works of Chaucer,
there reigns a cheerfulness, a manly hilarity, which makes it almost impossible to doubt a correspondent habit of
feeling in the author himself.
> *Ibid.*

Men whose dearest wishes are fixed
on objects wholly out of their own
power, become in all cases more or less
impatient and prone to anger.
> *Ibid.*

Veracity does not consist in *saying,*
but in the intention of *communicating*
truth.
> *Ibid. Chap. 9*

The lamentable difficulty I have always experienced in saying "No."
> *Ibid. Chap. 10*

To have lived in vain must be a painful thought to any man, and especially
so to him who has made literature his
profession.
> *Ibid.*

Never pursue literature as a trade.
> *Ibid. Chap. 11*

The first range of hills that encircles
the scanty vale of human life is the
horizon for the majority of its inhabitants. On *its* ridges the common sun is
born and departs. From *them* the stars
rise, and touching *them,* they vanish.
> *Ibid. Chap. 12*

Good sense is the body of poetic
genius, fancy its drapery, motion its
life, and imagination the soul.
> *Ibid. Chap. 14*

Our myriad-minded Shakespeare.[1]
> *Ibid. Chap. 15*

---

[1] Sed ita a principio inchoatum esse mun-
dum ut certis rebus certa signa præcurrerent
(Thus in the beginning the world was so made
that certain signs come before certain events).
— CICERO: *Divinatione, Liber I, Cap. 52*
   Coming events cast their shadows before. —
CAMPBELL: *Lochiel's Warning*
   Poets are the hierophants of an unapprehended inspiration; the mirrors of the gigantic shadows which futurity casts upon the
present. — SHELLEY: *A Defence of Poetry*
[2] See Burton, page 122.
[3] See Wordsworth, page 302.

[1] "A phrase," says Coleridge, "which I have
borrowed from a Greek monk, who applies it
to a patriarch of Constantinople."

Polysyllabic (or what the common people call, *dictionary*) words.
> *Biographia Literaria. Chap. 20*

The infallible test of a blameless style: namely, its untranslatableness in words of the same language, without injury to the meaning.
> *Ibid. Chap. 22*

A poem is not necessarily obscure, because it does not aim to be popular. It is enough if a work be perspicuous to those for whom it is written.
> *Ibid.*

Talk of the devil, and his horns appear, says the proverb.
> *Ibid. Chap. 23*

Reviewers are usually people who would have been poets, historians, biographers, if they could; they have tried their talents at one or the other, and have failed; therefore they turn critics.[1]
> *Lectures on Shakespeare and*
> *Milton [1811–1812]. Page 36*

Schiller has the material sublime.
> *Table Talk*

I wish our clever young poets would remember my homely definitions of prose and poetry; that is, prose, — words in their best order; poetry, — the best words in their best order.
> *Ibid.*

That passage is what I call the sublime dashed to pieces by cutting too close with the fiery four-in-hand round the corner of nonsense.
> *Ibid.*

Iago's soliloquy, the motive-hunting of a motiveless malignity — how awful it is!
> *Notes on Some Other Plays of*
> *Shakespeare*

Beneath this sod
A poet lies, or that which once seemed he —
Oh, lift a thought in prayer for S.T.C.!

---

[1] Reviewers, with some rare exceptions, are a most stupid and malignant race. As a bankrupt thief turns thief-taker in despair, so an unsuccessful author turns critic. — SHELLEY: *Fragments of Adonais*
You know who critics are? The men who have failed in literature and art. — DISRAELI: *Lothair, Chap. XXXV*

That he, who many a year, with toil of breath,
Found death in life, may here find life in death.
> *Epitaph written for himself*

JOSIAH QUINCY, JR.
[1772–1864]

If this bill [for the admission of Orleans Territory as a State] passes, it is my deliberate opinion that it is virtually a dissolution of the Union; that it will free the States from their moral obligation; and, as it will be the right of all, so it will be the duty of some, definitely to prepare for a separation, — amicably if they can, violently if they must.[1]
> *Abridged Congressional Debates.*
> *Vol. IV, Page 327, Jan. 14, 1811*

WILLIAM BARNES RHODES
[1772–1826]

Who dares this pair of boots displace,
Must meet Bombastes face to face.[2]
> *Bombastes Furioso. Act I, Sc. 4*

Bombastes. So have I heard on Afric's burning shore
A hungry lion give a grievous roar;
The grievous roar echoed along the shore.
Artaxaminous. So have I heard on Afric's burning shore
Another lion give a grievous roar;
And the first lion thought the last a bore.
> *Ibid.*

WILLIAM HENRY HARRISON
[1773–1841]

We admit of no government by divine right . . . the only legitimate

---

[1] The gentleman [Mr. Quincy] cannot have forgotten his own sentiment, uttered even on the floor of this House, "Peaceably if we can, forcibly if we must." — HENRY CLAY: *Speech* [Jan. 8, 1813]
[2] Let none but he these arms displace,
Who dares Orlando's fury face.
CERVANTES: *Don Quixote, Part II, Chap. LXVI;* RAY: *Proverbs*

right to govern is an express grant of power from the governed.

Inaugural Address [*March 4, 1841*]

Never with my consent shall an officer of the people, compensated for his services out of their pockets, become the pliant instrument of the Executive will.

Ibid.

A decent and manly examination of the acts of Government should be not only tolerated, but encouraged.

Ibid.

The delicate duty of devising schemes of revenue should be left where the Constitution has placed it — with the immediate representatives of the people.

Ibid.

If parties in a republic are necessary to secure a degree of vigilance sufficient to keep the public functionaries within the bounds of law and duty, at that point their usefulness ends.

Ibid.

JOHN RANDOLPH
[1773–1833]

The surest way to prevent war is not to fear it.

Speech before Committee of Whole, U. S. House of Representatives [*March 5, 1806*]

So brilliant, yet so corrupt, which, like a rotten mackerel by moonlight, shines and stinks.[1]

Of Henry Clay

SAMUEL JAMES ARNOLD
[1774–1852]

Along the line our signal ran:
"England expects that every man
This day will do his duty." [2]

The Death of Nelson. Stanza 1

[1] Quoted by JOHN McCONAUGHY in *Who Owns America?*
    'Tis vain for present fame to wish.
    Our persons first must be forgotten;
    For poets are like stinking fish,
    They never shine until they're rotten.
        MACDONALD CLARKE [1798–1842]:
        Epigram

[2] See Nelson, page 284.

ROBERT SOUTHEY
[1774–1843]

"You are old, Father William," the young man cried,
    "The few locks which are left you are gray;
You are hale, Father William, a hearty old man, —
    Now tell me the reason I pray."

The Old Man's Comforts, and How He Gained Them.[1] Stanza 1

"In the days of my youth," Father William replied,
    "I remembered that youth could not last;
I thought of the future, whatever I did,
    That I never might grieve for the past."

Ibid. Stanza 4

Bishop Hatto fearfully hastened away,
And he crossed the Rhine without delay,
And reached his tower, and barred with care
All the windows, and doors, and loopholes there.

God's Judgment on a Wicked Bishop.[2] Stanza 12

[1] Of several parodies of this poem, the one by "Lewis Carroll" is probably better known than the original.
    "You are old, father William," the young man said,
        "And your hair has become very white;
    And yet you incessantly stand on your head —
        Do you think, at your age, it is right?"
            "LEWIS CARROLL": *You Are Old, Father William, St. 1*
    "You are old, Father William, and though one would think
        All the veins in your body were dry,
    Yet the end of your nose is red as a pink;
        I beg your indulgence, but why?"
            LEE O. HARRIS AND JAMES WHITCOMB RILEY: *Father William, St. 1*

[2] Hatto, in the time of the great famine of 914, when he saw the poor exceedingly oppressed by famine, assembled a great company of them together into a barn at Kaub and burnt them . . . because he thought the famine would sooner cease if those poor folks were despatched out of the world. . . . But God . . . sent against him a plague of mice . . . and the prelate retreated to a tower in the Rhine . . . but the mice chased him continually . . . and at last he was most miser-

Who is yonder poor maniac, whose
  wildly fixed eyes
  Seem a heart overcharged to express?
She weeps not, yet often and deeply
  she sighs;
She never complains, but her silence
  implies
  The composure of settled distress.
      Mary, the Maid of the Inn.[1]
          Stanza 1

One dreadful sound could the Rover
  hear,
A sound as if with the Inchcape Bell
The Devil below was ringing his knell.
      The Inchcape Rock.[2] *Stanza 17*

Where Washington hath left
  His awful memory
  A light for after times!
      *Ode Written during the War
          with America [1814]*

The march of intellect.[3]
      *Colloquies on the Progress and
      Prospects of Society. Vol. II,
      The Doctor, Chap. Extraordi-
      nary, Page 360*

The laws are with us, and God on
our side.
      *On the Rise and Progress of
      Popular Disaffection [1817].
      Vol. II, Essay VIII, Page 107*

Agreed to differ.
          Life of Wesley.

My days among the dead are passed;
  Around me I behold,
Where'er these casual eyes are cast,
  The mighty minds of old;
My never-failing friends are they,
  With whom I converse night and day.
      Occasional Pieces. The Library

---

ably devoured. — Thomas Coryat [1577–
1617]: *Crudities* [1611], *P. 571*

[1] This poem was dramatized by George
Soane [1790–1860] as *The Innkeeper's Daughter, or The Smuggler's Fate,* and produced at
the Boston Museum [May 10, 1852].

[2] A rock in the North Sea, off the Firth of
Tay, Scotland, dangerous to navigators because it is covered with every tide. There is a
tradition that a warning bell was fixed on
the rock by the Abbot of Aberbrothok, which
was stolen by a sea pirate, who perished on
the rock a year later. Southey's ballad deals
with this tradition.

[3] See Burke, page 259.

So I told them in rhyme,
For of rhymes I had store.
      The Cataract of Lodore
          Helter-skelter,
          Hurry-scurry.
                  Ibid.

And so never ending, but always descending.
                  Ibid.

And this way the water comes down at
  Lodore.
                  Ibid.

"And wherefore do the poor com-
  plain?"
  The rich man asked of me —
"Come walk abroad with me," I said,
  "And I will answer thee."
      The Complaints of the Poor.
          Stanza 1

From his brimstone bed, at break of
  day,
A-walking the Devil is gone,
To look at his little snug farm of the
  World,
And see how his stock went on.
      The Devil's Walk. Stanza 1

How then was the Devil dressed?
O, he was in his Sunday's best;
His coat was red, and his breeches were
  blue,
And there was a hole where his tail
  came through.
              Ibid. Stanza 3

He passed a cottage with a double
  coach-house, —
  A cottage of gentility;
    And he owned with a grin,
    That his favourite sin
  Is pride that apes humility.[1]
              Ibid. Stanza 8

He was always found
Among your ten and twenty pound
  subscribers,
Your benefactors in the newspapers.
His alms were money put to interest
In the other world.
      The Alderman's Funeral

There is not a wife in the west country
But has heard of the well of St. Keyne.
      The Well of St. Keyne. Stanza 1

---

[1] See Coleridge, page 316.

If the husband, of this gifted well
Shall drink before his wife,
A happy man thenceforth is he,
For he shall be master for life.
> *The Well of St. Keyne. Stanza 10*

As frozen as charity.[1]
> *The Soldier's Wife. Stanza 4*

"But what good came of it at last?"
Quoth little Peterkin.
"Why, that I cannot tell," said he;
"But 'twas a famous victory."
> *The Battle of Blenheim. Stanza 11*

Blue, darkly, deeply, beautifully blue.[2]
> *Madoc in Wales. Part I, 5*

What will not woman, gentle woman
dare,
When strong affection stirs her spirit
up?
> *Ibid. Part II, 2*

How beautiful is night!
A dewy freshness fills the silent air;
No mist obscures, nor cloud, nor speck,
nor stain,
Breaks the serene of heaven:
In full-orbed glory yonder moon di-
vine
Rolls through the dark blue depths;
Beneath her steady ray
The desert circle spreads,
Like the round ocean, girdled with the
sky.
How beautiful is night!
> *Thalaba. Book I, Stanza 1*

And last of all an Admiral came,
A terrible man with a terrible
name, —
A name which you all know by sight
very well,
But which no one can speak, and no
one can spell.
> *The March to Moscow. Stanza 8*

The Devil may take the hindmost.[3]
> *Ibid. Stanza 10*

They sin who tell us love can die;
With life all other passions fly,
All others are but vanity. . . .
Love is indestructible,

Its holy flame forever burneth;
From heaven it came, to heaven re-
turneth. . . .
It soweth here with toil and care,
But the harvest-time of love is there
> *The Curse of Kehama. Canto X
Stanza 10*

Oh, when a mother meets on high
The babe she lost in infancy,
Hath she not then for pains and fears,
The day of woe, the watchful night
For all her sorrow, all her tears,
An over-payment of delight?
> *Ibid. Stanza 11*

Thou hast been called, O sleep! the
friend of woe;
But 'tis the happy that have called
thee so.
> *Ibid. Canto XV, Stanza 11*

The Satanic school.
> *Vision of Judgment. Original
Preface*

Snips and snails and puppy dog tails
And such are little boys made of.
> *What All the World is Made of.*

Sugar and spice and all things nice.
> *Ibid.*

JANE AUSTEN
[1775–1817]

Everything nourishes what is strong
already.
> *Pride and Prejudice. Chap. 9*

My dear, I have two small favours
to request. First, that you will allow
me the free use of my understanding
on the present occasion; and secondly,
of my room. I shall be glad to have the
library to myself as soon as may be.[1]
> *Ibid. Chap. 20*

Those who do not complain are never
pitied.
> *Ibid.*

Mrs. Bennet was restored to her
usual querulous serenity.
> *Ibid. Chap. 42*

---

[1] See Hood, page 392.
[2] "Darkly, deeply, beautifully blue,"
　As some one somewhere sings about the
　　sky.
　　BYRON: *Don Juan, Canto IV, St. 110*
[3] See Butler, page 142.

[1] Rather your room as your company.
　ANONYMOUS: *Marriage of Wit and Wis-
　　dom* [circa 1570]

What dreadful hot weather we have! It keeps me in a continual state of inelegance.

Letters to her sister Cassandra.
September 18, 1796

Miss Blachford is agreeable enough. I do not want people to be very agreeable, as it saves me the trouble of liking them a great deal.

Ibid. December 24, 1798

She was highly rouged, and looked rather quietly and contentedly silly than anything else.

Ibid. May 12, 1801

"Only a novel" . . . in short, only some work in which the greatest powers of the mind are displayed, in which the most thorough knowledge of human nature, the happiest delineation of its varieties, are conveyed to the world in the best chosen language.

Northanger Abbey. Chap. 5

CHARLES LAMB
[1775–1834]

The red-letter days, now become, to all intents and purposes, dead-letter days.

Oxford in the Vacation [1]

The human species, according to the best theory I can form of it, is composed of two distinct races, the men who borrow, and the men who lend.[2]

The Two Races of Men

Borrowers of books — those mutilators of collections, spoilers of the symmetry of shelves, and creators of odd volumes.

Ibid.

Of all sound of all bells — (bells, the music nighest bordering upon heaven) — most solemn and touching is the peal which rings out the Old Year.

New Year's Eve

[1] Which, it has been pointed out, was actually written at Cambridge. See E. V. LUCAS: *Lamb and the Universities.*
[2] Compare Max Beerbohm's delightful essay, "Hosts and Guests," in "And Even Now."

A clear fire, a clean hearth, and the rigour of the game.

Mrs. Battle's Opinions on Whist

Sentimentally I am disposed to harmony; but organically I am incapable of a tune.

A Chapter on Ears

Not if I know myself at all.

The Old and New Schoolmaster

Credulity is the man's weakness, but the child's strength.

Witches, and Other Night Fears

Parents do not know what they do when they leave tender babes alone to go to sleep in the dark.

Ibid.

Not many sounds in life, and I include all urban and all rural sounds, exceed in interest a knock at the door.[1]

Valentine's Day

A God-send, as our familiarly pious ancestors termed a benefit received where the benefactor was unknown.

Ibid.

The custom of saying grace at meals had, probably, its origin in the early times of the world, and the hunter-state of man, when dinners were precarious things, and a full meal was something more than a common blessing.

Grace Before Meat

Sassafras wood boiled down to a kind of tea, and tempered with an infusion of milk and sugar, hath to some tastes a delicacy beyond the China luxury.[2]

The Praise of Chimney-Sweepers

A fair sepulchre in the grateful stomach of the judicious epicure.

A Dissertation upon Roast Pig

Presents, I often say, endear absents.

Ibid.

[1] Doorbells are like a magic game,
  Or the grab-bag at a fair —
You never know when you hear one ring
  Who may be waiting there.
        RACHEL FIELD [1894–   ]:
                Doorbells

[2] Sassafras, oh, sassafras,
  Thou art the stuff for me,
And in the Spring I love to sing,
  Sweet sassafras, of thee!
        EDWARD EGGLESTON [1837–1902]:
                Sassafras

It argues an insensibility.

A Dissertation upon Roast Pig

Nothing is to me more distasteful than that entire complacency and satisfaction which beam in the countenances of a new-married couple.

The Behaviour of Married People

He has left off reading altogether, to the great improvement of his originality.

Detached Thoughts on Books and Reading

Books think for me.

Ibid.

Books which are no books.

Ibid.

To be strong-backed and neat-bound is the desideratum of a volume. Magnificence comes after.

Ibid.

Newspapers always excite curiosity. No one ever lays one down without a feeling of disappointment.

Ibid.

If there be a regal solitude, it is a sick bed.

The Convalescent

How sickness enlarges the dimensions of a man's self to himself.

Ibid.

Let me caution persons grown old in active business, not lightly, nor without weighing their own resources, to forego their customary employment all at once, for there may be danger in it.

The Superannuated Man

Your absence of mind we have borne, till your presence of body came to be called in question by it.

Amicus Redivivus

A pun is a pistol let off at the ear; not a feather to tickle the intellect.

Popular Fallacies. IX, That the Worst Puns are the Best

A presentation copy . . . is a copy of a book which does not sell, sent you by the author, with his foolish autograph at the beginning of it; for which, if a stranger, he only demands your friendship; if a brother author, he ex-

pects from you a book of yours, which does not sell, in return.

Popular Fallacies. XI, That We Must Not Look a Gift-Horse in the Mouth

The growing infirmities of age manifest themselves in nothing more strongly, than in an inveterate dislike of interruption.

Ibid. XII, That Home is Home Though it is Never so Homely

The good things of life are not to be had singly, but come to us with a mixture.

Ibid. XIII, That You Must Love Me and Love My Dog

It has happened not seldom that one work of some author has so transcendently surpassed in execution the rest of his compositions, that the world has agreed to pass a sentence of dismissal upon the latter, and to consign them to total neglect and oblivion.

Eliana. Estimate of Defoe's Secondary Novels

Cannot the heart in the midst of crowds feel frightfully alone?

Ibid.

The greatest pleasure I know is to do a good action by stealth, and to have it found out by accident.

Table Talk. In the Athenaeum [*1834*]

Reputation said: "If once we sever, Our chance of future meeting is but vain:
Who parts from me, must look to part for ever,
For Reputation lost comes not again."

Love, Death, and Reputation. Stanza 4

Some cry up Haydn, some Mozart,
Just as the whim bites. For my part,
I do not care a farthing candle
For either of them, nor for Handel.

Free Thoughts on Several Eminent Composers

A bird appears a thoughtless thing . . .
No doubt he has his little cares,
And very hard he often fares,
The which so patiently he bears.

Crumbs to the Birds

Gone before
To that unknown and silent shore.
Hester. Stanza 7
I have had playmates, I have had com-
panions,
In my days of childhood, in my joyful
school-days.
All, all are gone, the old familiar faces.
Old Familiar Faces
For thy sake, tobacco, I
Would do anything but die.
A Farewell to Tobacco
And half had staggered that stout Stag-
irite.
Written at Cambridge
Who first invented work, and bound
the free
And holiday-rejoicing spirit down . . .
To that dry drudgery at the desk's dead
wood?
Work
The economy of Heaven is dark
And wisest clerks have missed the
mark.
*On an Infant Dying as Soon
as Born*
I have something more to do than feel.
*Letter to Coleridge after the
death of Lamb's mother* [*1796*]
The not unpeaceful evening of a day
Made black by morning storms.
Poem-letter to Coleridge [*1797*]
A good-natured woman, which is as
much as you can expect from a friend's
wife, whom you got acquainted with a
bachelor.
Letter to Hazlitt [*1805*]
Anything awful makes me laugh. I
misbehaved once at a funeral.
Letter to Southey [*1815*]
Fanny Kelly's divine plain face.
Letter to Mrs. Wordsworth
[*1818*]
I have confessed to you my utter inability to remember in any compre-
hensive way what I read. I can vehemently applaud, or perversely stickle,
at *parts;* but I cannot grasp at a whole.
Letter to Godwin [*1803*]
For God's sake (I never was more
serious) don't make me ridiculous any
more by terming me gentle-hearted

in print [1] . . . substitute drunken dog,
ragged head, seld-shaven, odd-eyed,
stuttering, or any other epithet which
truly and properly belongs to the gen-
tleman in question.
To Coleridge [*August, 1800*]
An archangel a little damaged.
His description of Coleridge
He might have proved a useful ad-
junct, if not an ornament to society.
Captain Starkey
Separate from the pleasure of your
company, I don't much care if I never
see a mountain in my life.
Letter to Wordsworth [*1801*]
Neat, not gaudy.[2]
Ibid. [*1806*]
Martin, if dirt was trumps, what
hands you would hold!
Lamb's Suppers
I came home for ever!
Letter to Bernard Barton
[*1825*], *on leaving his "33
years' desk" at the East India
House*

WALTER SAVAGE
LANDOR
[1775–1864]

Rose Aylmer, whom these wakeful eyes
  May weep, but never see,
A night of memories and of sighs
  I consecrate to thee.
Rose Aylmer
But I have sinuous shells of pearly hue
Within, and they that lustre have im-
  bibed
In the sun's palace-porch, where when
  unyoked
His chariot-wheel stands midway in the
  wave:
Shake one, and it awakens; then apply
Its polisht lips to your attentive ear,
And it remembers its august abodes,
And murmurs as the ocean murmurs
  there.[3]
Gebir. Book I [*1798*]

[1] See Coleridge, page 316.
[2] Rich, not gaudy. — SHAKESPEARE: *Hamlet, Act I, Sc. 3, L. 71*
[3] See Wordsworth, page 302.

Past are three summers since she first
    beheld
The ocean; all around the child await
Some exclamation of amazement here.
She coldly said, her long-lasht eyes
    abased,
Is this the mighty ocean? is this all?
           Gebir. Book II

Shakespeare is not our poet, but the
    world's,[1] —
Therefore on him no speech! And brief
    for thee,
Browning! Since Chaucer was alive
    and hale,
No man hath walk'd along our roads
    with step
So active, so inquiring eye, or tongue
So varied in discourse.
        To Robert Browning

The Siren waits thee, singing song for
    song.
                Ibid.

Around the child bend all the three
Sweet Graces — Faith, Hope, Charity.
Around the man bend other faces —
Pride, Envy, Malice, are his Graces.
          Around the Child

Children are what the mothers are.
No fondest father's fondest care
Can fashion so the infant heart.
              Children

When we play the fool, how wide
The theatre expands! beside,
How long the audience sits before us!
How many prompters! what a chorus!
         Plays. Stanza 2

I strove with none, for none was worth
    my strife;
    Nature I loved; and next to Nature,
    Art.
I warm'd both hands against the fire of
    life;
    It sinks, and I am ready to depart.
   Dying Speech of an Old Philosopher

There are no fields of amaranth on
this side of the grave; there are no
voices, O Rhodopè, that are not soon
mute, however tuneful; there is no
name, with whatever emphasis of pas-

sionate love repeated, of which the
echo is not faint at last.
      Imaginary Conversations.
        Aesop and Rhodopè, I

Elegance in prose composition is
mainly this: a just admission of topics
and of words; neither too many nor
too few of either; enough of sweetness
in the sound to induce us to enter and
sit still; enough of illustration and reflection to change the posture of our
minds when they would tire; and
enough of sound matter in the complex
to repay us for our attendance.
   Ibid. Chesterfield and Chatham

Of all failures, to fail in a witticism
is the worst, and the mishap is the
more calamitous in a drawn out and
detailed one.
               Ibid.

Stand close around, ye Stygian set,
   With Dirce in one boat convey'd!
Or Charon, seeing, may forget
   That he is old, and she a shade.
              Dirce

    'Tis verse that gives
Immortal youth to mortal maids.
              Verse

JOSEPH BLANCO WHITE
[1775–1841]

Mysterious Night! when our first par-
    ent knew
Thee from report divine, and heard
    thy name,
Did he not tremble for this lovely
    frame,
This glorious canopy of light and blue?
          Sonnet, Night

Hesperus with the host of heaven came,
And lo! creation widened in man's
    view.
              Ibid.

Why do we, then, shun Death with anx-
    ious strife?
If Light can thus deceive, wherefore
    not Life?
              Ibid.

---

[1] Nor sequent centuries could hit
  Orbit and sum of Shakespeare's wit.
     R. W. EMERSON: *Solution*

THOMAS CAMPBELL
[1777-1844]

'Tis distance lends enchantment to the view,
And robes the mountain in its azure hue.[1]
> *Pleasures of Hope. Part I, Line 7*

Hope, for a season, bade the world farewell,
And Freedom shriek'd as Kosciusko fell!
> *Ibid. Line 381*

Who hath not own'd, with rapture-smitten frame,
The power of grace, the magic of a name?
> *Ibid. Part II, Line 5*

The world was sad, the garden was a wild,
And man, the hermit, sigh'd — till woman smiled.
> *Ibid. Line 37*

While Memory watches o'er the sad review
Of joys that faded like the morning dew.
> *Ibid. Line 45*

There shall he love, when genial morn appears,
Like pensive Beauty smiling in her tears.
> *Ibid. Line 95*

And muse on Nature with a poet's eye.
> *Ibid. Line 98*

That gems the starry girdle of the year.
> *Ibid. Line 194*

Melt, and dispel, ye spectre-doubts, that roll
Cimmerian darkness o'er the parting soul!
> *Ibid. Line 263*

O star-eyed Science! hast thou wandered there,

---

[1] See John Webster, page 127.
The mountains too, at a distance, appear airy masses and smooth, but seen near at hand they are rough. — DIOGENES LAERTIUS: *Pyrrho, IX*

> O distance! thou dear enchanter,
> Still hold in thy magic veil
> The glory of far-off mountains,
> The gleam of the far-off sail.
> CARLOTTA PERRY [1848-1914]: *Distance, the Enchantress, St. 5*

To waft us home the message of despair?
> *Pleasures of Hope. Part II, Line 325*

But, sad as angels for the good man's sin,
Weep to record, and blush to give it in.[1]
> *Ibid. Line 357*

Cease, every joy, to glimmer on my mind,
But leave, oh leave the light of Hope behind!
What though my wingèd hours of bliss have been
Like angel visits, few and far between.[2]
> *Ibid. Line 375*

Oh! once the harp of Innisfail
Was strung full high to notes of gladness;
But yet it often told a tale
Of more prevailing sadness.
> *O'Connor's Child. Stanza 1*

'Tis the sunset of life gives me mystical lore,
And coming events cast their shadows before.[3]
> *Lochiel's Warning*

Shall victor exult, or in death be laid low,
With his back to the field and his feet to the foe,
And leaving in battle no blot on his name,
Look proudly to heaven from the death-bed of fame.
> *Ibid.*

And rustic life and poverty
Grow beautiful beneath his touch.
> *Ode to the Memory of Burns.*
> *Stanza 5*

Whose lines are mottoes of the heart,
Whose truths electrify the sage.
> *Ibid. Stanza 14*

Ye mariners of England,
That guard our native seas;
Whose flag has braved, a thousand years,
The battle and the breeze!
> *Ye Mariners of England. Stanza 1*

Britannia needs no bulwarks,
No towers along the steep;

---

[1] See Sterne, page 242.
[2] See Norris, page 186.
[3] See Coleridge, page 318.

Her march is o'er the mountain waves,
Her home is on the deep.
> *Ye Mariners of England. Stanza 3*

When the battle rages loud and long,
And the stormy winds do blow.
> *Ibid.*

The meteor flag of England
Shall yet terrific burn,
Till danger's troubled night depart,
And the star of peace return.
> *Ibid. Stanza 4*

There was silence deep as death,
And the boldest held his breath,
For a time.
> *Battle of the Baltic. Stanza 2*

The combat deepens. On, ye brave,
Who rush to glory or the grave!
Wave, Munich! all thy banners wave,
And charge with all thy chivalry!
> *Hohenlinden. Stanza 7*

Few, few shall part where many meet!
The snow shall be their winding-sheet
And every turf beneath their feet
Shall be a soldier's sepulchre.
> *Ibid. Stanza 8*

All worldly shapes shall melt in gloom,
The Sun himself must die,
Before this mortal shall assume
Its Immortality!
> *The Last Man. Stanza 1*

I saw the last of human mould
That shall Creation's death behold,
As Adam saw her prime!
> *Ibid.*

There came to the beach a poor exile
of Erin,
The dew on his thin robe was heavy
and chill;
For his country he sigh'd, when at twilight repairing
To wander alone by the wind-beaten
hill.
> *The Exile of Erin. Stanza 1*

On the green banks of Shannon, when
Sheelah was nigh,
No blithe Irish lad was so happy as I;
No harp like my own could so cheerily
play,

And wherever I went was my poor dog
Tray.[1]
> *The Harper. Stanza 1*

Star that bringeth home the bee,
And sett'st the weary labourer free!
> *Song to the Evening Star. Stanza 1*

Oh, how hard it is to find
The one just suited to our mind!
> *Song. Stanza 1*

Triumphal arch, that fill'st the sky
When storms prepare to part,
I ask not proud Philosophy
To teach me what thou art.
> *To the Rainbow. Stanza 1*

To live in hearts we leave behind
Is not to die.
> *Hallowed Ground. Stanza 6*

Oh leave this barren spot to me!
Spare, woodman, spare the beechen
tree![2]
> *The Beech-Tree's Petition. Stanza 1*

Drink ye to her that each loves best!
And if you nurse a flame
That's told but to her mutual breast,
We will not ask her name.
> *Drink Ye to Her. Stanza 1*

A stoic of the woods,— a man without
a tear.
> *Gertrude of Wyoming. Part I*
> *Stanza 23*

HENRY CLAY
[1777–1852]

Sir, the gentleman soils the spot he
stands upon.
> *On the proposal to impeach*
> *Thomas Jefferson*

If you wish to avoid foreign collision
you had better abandon the ocean.
> *Speech on the Increase of the*
> *Navy, U. S. House of Repre-*
> *sentatives [January 22, 1812]*

It would not be thought very just or
wise to arraign the honorable professions of law and physic because the one

---

[1] Old dog Tray's ever faithful,
Grief cannot drive him away.
> STEPHEN COLLINS FOSTER [1826–
> 1864]: *Old Dog Tray*

[2] Woodman, spare that tree!
Touch not a single bough!
> GEORGE POPE MORRIS [1802–1864]:
> *Woodman, Spare That Tree, St. 1*

produces the pettifogger and the other the quack.

> *Speech on the Protection of Home Industry, U. S. House of Representatives [April 26, 1820]*

I have doubtless committed many errors and indiscretions, over which you have thrown the broad mantle of charity. But I can say, and in the presence of my God and of this assembled multitude I do say, that I have honestly served my country — that I have never wronged it — and that, however unprepared I lament that I am to appear in the Divine Presence on other accounts, I invoke the justice of His judgment on my official conduct without the smallest apprehension of His displeasure.

> *Speech at Lexington, Kentucky [1829]*

Government is a trust, and the officers of the government are trustees; and both the trust and the trustees are created for the benefit of the people.

> *Speech at •Ashland, Kentucky [March, 1829]*

The arts of power and its minions are the same in all countries and in all ages. It marks its victim; denounces it; and excites the public odium and the public hatred, to conceal its own abuses and encroachments.

> *Speech on the State of the Country, U. S. Senate [March 14, 1834]*

Precedents deliberately established by wise men are entitled to great weight. They are evidence of truth, but *only* evidence. . . . But a solitary precedent . . . which has never been re-examined, can not be conclusive.

> *Speech on Appointments and Removals, U. S. Senate [February 18, 1835]*

I have heard something said about allegiance to the South. I know no South, no North, no East, no West, to which I owe any allegiance.

> *Speech [1848]*

Sir, I would rather be right than be President.

> *Speech [1850], referring to the compromise measures*

General Alexander Smyth, a tedious speaker in Congress, observed: "You, sir, speak for the present generation; but I speak for posterity."

"Yes," said Mr. Clay, "and you seem resolved to speak until the arrival of your audience."

> *Quoted by* Epes Sargent *in Life of Henry Clay*

HENRY ELLIS
[1777–1869]

To make a mountain of a mole-hill.

> *Original Letters. Second Series, Page 312*

COLONEL VALENTINE BLACKER
[1778–1823]

Put your trust in God, my boys, and keep your powder dry! [1]

> *Oliver's Advice [1834]*

ROBERT EMMET
[1778–1803]

Let there be no inscription upon my tomb; let no man write my epitaph: no man can write my epitaph.

> *Speech on His Trial and Conviction for High Treason [September, 1803]*

WILLIAM HAZLITT
[1778–1830]

One of the pleasantest things in the world is going a journey; but I like to go by myself.

> *On Going a Journey*

---

[1] There is a well-authenticated anecdote of Cromwell. On a certain occasion, when his troops were about to cross a river to attack the enemy, he concluded an address, with these words: "Put your trust in God; but mind to keep your powder dry!" — Hayes: *Ballads of Ireland, Vol. I, P. 191*

The soul of a journey is liberty, perfect liberty, to think, feel, do just as one pleases.

On Going a Journey

Oh! it is great to shake off the trammels of the world and of public opinion — to lose our importunate, tormenting, everlasting personal identity and become the creature of the moment, clear of all ties . . . to be known by no other title than *the Gentleman in the parlour!*

Ibid.

What I mean by living to one's self is living in the world, as in it, not of it. . . . It is to be a silent spectator of the mighty scene of things; . . . to take a thoughtful, anxious interest or curiosity in what is passing in the world, but not to feel the slightest inclination to make or meddle with it.

On Living to One's Self

Even in the common affairs of life, in love, friendship, and marriage, how little security have we when we trust our happiness in the hands of others!

Ibid.

There is not a more mean, stupid, dastardly, pitiful, selfish, spiteful, envious, ungrateful animal than the Public. It is the greatest of cowards, for it is afraid of itself.

Ibid.

When a man is dead, they put money in his coffin, erect monuments to his memory, and celebrate the anniversary of his birthday in set speeches. Would they take any notice of him if he were living? No!

Ibid.

What a sight for sore eyes that would be! [1]

Of Persons One Would Have Seen

Horas non numero nisi serenas [2] — is the motto of a sun-dial near Venice. [3]

[1] See Swift, page 191.
[2] I count only the sunny hours.
[3] There stands in the garden of old St. Mark
A sun-dial quaint and gray.
WILLIAM CROSWELL DOANE [1832–1913]: *Horas Non Numero*

There is a softness and a harmony in the words and in the thought unparalleled.

On a Sun-Dial

If our hours were all serene, we might probably take almost as little note of them, as the dial does of those that are clouded.

Ibid

No young man believes he shall ever die.

The Feeling of Immortality in Youth

There is a feeling of Eternity in youth, which makes us amends for everything. To be young is to be as one of the Immortal Gods.

Ibid.

The young are prodigal of life from a superabundance of it; the old are tenacious on the same score, because they have little left, and cannot enjoy even what remains of it.

Ibid.

As we advance in life, we acquire a keener sense of the value of time. Nothing else, indeed, seems of any consequence; and we become misers in this respect.

Ibid.

The only true retirement is that of the heart; the only true leisure is the repose of the passions. To such persons it makes little difference whether they are young or old; and they die as they have lived, with graceful resignation.

Ibid.

If I have not read a book before, it is, to all intents and purposes, new to me, whether it was printed yesterday or three hundred years ago.

On Reading New Books

When I take up a work that I have read before (the oftener the better) I know what I have to expect. The satisfaction is not lessened by being anticipated.

On Reading Old Books

Persons without education certainly do not want either acuteness or strength of mind in what concerns themselves, or in things immediately within their observation; but they have no power

f abstraction, no general standard of
aste, or scale of opinion. They see their
bjects always near, and never in the
orizon. Hence arises that egotism
vhich has been remarked as the char-
cteristic of self-taught men.
The Round Table. I, 26

It is better to be able neither to read
or write than to be able to do nothing
lse.

On the Ignorance of the Learned

Men of genius do not excel in any
rofession because they labour in it,
ut they labour in it, because they excel.
Characteristics

We are not hypocrites in our sleep.
On Dreams

"The English," says Froissart,
amused themselves sadly after the
ashion of their country." They have in-
eed a way of their own. Their mirth is
relaxation from gravity, a challenge to
ull care to be gone; and one is not
lways clear at first, whether the ap-
eal is successful.
Merry England

Takes up the meanest subjects with
ne same tenderness that we do an in-
ct's wing, and would not kill a fly.
Lectures on the Comic Writers.
Shakespeare

When a person dies who does any
ne thing better than any one else in
ne world, it leaves a gap in society.
Table Talk (On the death of John
Cavanagh, famous player of
"fives," a kind of hand-ball)

HENRY PETER,
LORD BROUGHAM
[1779–1868]

Let the soldier be abroad if he will,
e can do nothing in this age. There is
nother personage, — a personage less
nposing in the eyes of some, perhaps
nsignificant. The schoolmaster is
oroad,[1] and I trust to him, armed with

[1] At the first meeting of the London Me-
nanics' Institution, 1825, John Reynolds,
ead of a school in Clerkenwell, acted as
cretary of the meeting. Lord Brougham,
ho spoke at this meeting, said in the course
his remarks, "Look out, gentlemen, the

his primer, against the soldier in full
military array.
Speech, Opening of Parliament
[January 29, 1828]

In my mind, he was guilty of no
error, he was chargeable with no exaggeration, he was betrayed by his fancy
into no metaphor, who once said that
all we see about us, kings, lords, and
Commons, the whole machinery of the
State, all the apparatus of the system,
and its varied workings, end in simply
bringing twelve good men into a box.
Present State of the Law
[February 7, 1828]

Pursuit of knowledge under difficulties.[1]

Death was now armed with a new
terror.[2]

THOMAS, LORD DENMAN
[1779–1854]

A delusion, a mockery, and a snare.[3]
O'Connell v. The Queen (in 11
Clark and Finnelly Reports)

The mere repetition of the *Cantilena*
of lawyers cannot make it law, unless
it can be traced to some competent authority; and if it be irreconcilable, to
some clear legal principle.
Ibid.

---

schoolmaster is abroad." The phrase attracted
little attention at that time, but when used
in a speech three years later, it at once became popular.

[1] The title given by Lord Brougham to a
book published in 1830.

[2] Brougham delivered a very warm panegyric upon the ex-Chancellor, and expressed
a hope that he would make a good end, although to an expiring Chancellor death was
now armed with a new terror. — CAMPBELL:
Lives of the Chancellors, Vol. VII, P. 163

Lord St. Leonards attributes this phrase to
Sir Charles Wetherell, who used it on the occasion referred to by Lord Campbell.

From Edmund Curll's practice of issuing
miserable catch-penny lives of every eminent
person immediately after his decease, Arbuthnot wittily styled him "one of the new terrors
of death." — CARRUTHERS: *Life of Pope* (2d
ed.), *P. 149*

[3] Franklin P. Adams; of a beautiful Spanish woman: "A snare Andalusian."

FRANCIS SCOTT KEY
[1779–1843]

And the star-spangled banner, oh long
    may it wave
O'er the land of the free and the home of
    the brave!
> *The Star-Spangled Banner.*
> *Stanza 2 [September 14, 1814]*

O! thus be it ever when freemen shall
    stand
Between their loved homes and the foe's
    desolation;
Bless'd with victory and peace, may our
    Heaven-rescued land
Praise the Power that hath made and
    preserved us a nation.[1]
> *Ibid. Stanza 4*

Then conquer we must, for our cause
    it is just, —
And this be our motto, — "In God is
    our trust!"
> *Ibid.*

WILLIAM LAMB,
VISCOUNT MELBOURNE
[1779–1848]

I wish that I could be as cocksure of
anything as Tom Macaulay is of everything.
> *Quoted. Attributed also to William*
> *Windham [1750–1810]*

CLEMENT CLARKE MOORE
[1779–1863]

'Twas the night before Christmas, when
    all through the house
Not a creature was stirring, — not even
    a mouse;[2]
The stockings were hung by the chim-
    ney with care,
In hopes that St. Nicholas soon would
    be there.
> *A Visit from St. Nicholas*
> *[December, 1823]*

"Happy Christmas to all, and to all
    good-night!"
> *A Visit from St. Nichol*
> *[December, 182*

HORACE SMITH
[1779–1849]

Thinking is but an idle waste (
    thought,
And nought is everything, and every
    thing is nought.
> *Rejected Addresses. Cui Bon*
> *Stanza*

In the name of the Prophet — figs.
> *Johnson's Gho.*

And thou hast walked about (ho
    strange a story!)
  In Thebes's streets three thousan
    years ago,
When the Memnonium was in all i
    glory.
> *Address to the Mummy at Be*
> *zoni's Exhibition.[1] Stanza*

Although corruption may our fram
    consume.
The immortal spirit in the skies ma
    bloom.
> *Ibid. Stanza*

JOSEPH STORY
[1779–1845]

Whene'er you speak, remember eve
    cause
Stands not on eloquence, but stands (
    laws;
Pregnant in matter, in expression bri
Let every sentence stand with bold r
    lief;
On trifling points not time nor talen
    waste,
A sad offence to learning and to tast
Nor deal with pompous phrase, nor e'
    suppose
Poetic flights belong to reasoning pros
> *Advice to Young Lawye*
> *Stanza*

---

[1] It made and preserves us a nation. —
GEORGE POPE MORRIS: *The Flag of Our
Union*, St. 1

[2] Not a mouse stirring. — SHAKESPEARE:
Hamlet, Act I, Sc. 1, L. 10

[1] Giovanni Battista Belzoni [1778–182.
Italian traveler and explorer, opened t
sepulcher of Seti I, in 1817, and the seco
pyramid of Gizeh. He brought the bust
the "Young Memnon" from Thebes to t
British Museum.

Here shall the Press the People's right maintain,
Unaw'd by influence and unbrib'd by gain;
Here patriot Truth her glorious precepts draw,
Pledg'd to Religion, Liberty, and Law.
Motto of the Salem Register
(In Life of Story, Vol. I, Page 127)

WILLIAM ELLERY CHANNING
[1780–1842]

The office of government is not to confer happiness, but to give men opportunity to work out happiness for themselves.
The Life and Character of Napoleon Bonaparte

I see the marks of God in the heavens and the earth; but how much more in a liberal intellect, in magnanimity, in unconquerable rectitude, in a philanthropy which forgives every wrong, and which never despairs of the cause of Christ and human virtue: I do and I must reverence human nature. I bless it for its kind affections. I honor it for its achievements in science and art, and still more for its examples of heroic and saintly virtue. These are marks of a divine origin and the pledges of a celestial inheritance; and I thank God that my own lot is bound up with that of the human race.
Inscription, from his writings, on Channing Memorial, Public Garden, Boston

CHARLES CALEB COLTON
[1780–1832]

Imitation is the sincerest flattery.
The Lacon

JOHN MARRIOTT
[1780–1825]

In a Devonshire lane, as I tottered along,
The other day, much in want of a subject for song,
Thinks I to myself, I have hit on a strain —
That marriage is much like a Devonshire lane.
How Marriage is Like a Devonshire Lane. Stanza 1
And the conjugal fence, which forbids us to roam,
Looks lovely when decked with the comforts of home.
Ibid. Stanza 6

CHARLES MINER
[1780–1865]

When I see a merchant over-polite to his customers, begging them to taste a little brandy and throwing half his goods on the counter, — thinks I, that man has an axe to grind.
Who'll Turn Grindstones[1]

THOMAS MOORE
[1780–1852]

Weep on! and, as thy sorrows flow,
I'll taste the luxury of woe.
Anacreontic. Press the Grape, Stanza 2
How shall we rank thee upon glory's page?
Thou more than soldier and just less than sage!
To Thomas Hume. Stanza 6
I knew by the smoke, that so gracefully curl'd
Above the green elms, that a cottage was near;
And I said, "If there's peace to be found in the world,
A heart that was humble might hope for it here!"
Ballad Stanzas. 1
They made her a grave, too cold and damp
For a soul so warm and true;
And she's gone to the Lake of the Dismal Swamp,

[1] From *Essays from the Desk of Poor Robert the Scribe* [Doylestown, Pennsylvania, 1815]. It first appeared in the Wilkes-Barre Gleaner in 1911.

Where, all night long, by a firefly lamp,
She paddles her white canoe.
The Lake of the Dismal Swamp.
Stanza 1

Faintly as tolls the evening chime,
Our voices keep tune and our oars keep
time.[1]
A Canadian Boat-Song. Stanza 1

Row, brothers, row, the stream runs
fast,
The rapids are near, and the daylight's
past.
Ibid.

The minds of some of our statesmen,
like the pupil of the human eye, contract themselves the more, the stronger
light there is shed upon them.
Preface to Corruption and
Intolerance

Like a young eagle who has lent his
plume
To fledge the shaft by which he meets
his doom.[2]
Corruption

Young Love may go,
For aught I care,
To Jericho!
When Love is Kind. Stanza 6

A Persian's heaven is easily made:
'Tis but black eyes and lemonade.
Intercepted Letters. VI

There was a little man, and he had a
little soul;
And he said, Little Soul, let us try, try,
try!
Little Man and Little Soul.
Stanza 1

Go where glory waits thee! [3]
But while fame elates thee,
Oh, still remember me!
Go Where Glory Waits Thee.
Stanza 1

Oh, breathe not his name! let it sleep
in the shade,
Where cold and unhonour'd his relics
are laid,
Oh Breathe Not His Name.
Stanza 1

And the tear that we shed, though in
secret it rolls,
Shall long keep his memory green in our
souls.[1]
Oh Breathe Not His Name
Stanza 2

The harp that once through Tara's halls
The soul of music shed,
Now hangs as mute on Tara's walls
As if that soul were fled.
So sleeps the pride of former days,
So glory's thrill is o'er;
And hearts that once beat high for
praise
Now feel that pulse no more.
The Harp That Once Through
Tara's Halls. Stanza 1

Whose wit in the combat, as gentle as
bright,
Ne'er carried a heart-stain away on its
blade.
On the Death of Sheridan.
Stanza 11

Good at a fight, but better at a play;
Godlike in giving, but the devil to pay.
Life of Sheridan. On a Cast of
Sheridan's Hand

Fly not yet, — 'tis just the hour,
When pleasure, like the midnight flower
That scorns the eye of vulgar light,
Begins to bloom for sons of night,
And maids who love the moon.
Fly Not Yet. Stanza 1

Oh stay! oh stay!
Joy so seldom weaves a chain
Like this to-night, that oh, 'tis pain
To break its links so soon.
Ibid.

And the heart that is soonest awake to
the flowers
Is always the first to be touch'd by the
thorns.
Oh, Think Not My Spirits Are
Always as Light. Stanza 1

Rich and rare were the gems she wore,
And a bright gold ring on her wand
she bore.
Rich and Rare Were the Gems She
Wore. Stanza 1

There is not in the wide world a valley
so sweet

---

[1] See Marvell, page 169.
[2] See Waller, page 145.
[3] This goin ware glory waits ye haint one
agreeable feetur. — LOWELL: *The Biglow Pa-*
pers, First Series, No. 11

[1] See Shakespeare, page 89.

As that vale in whose bosom the bright
waters meet.[1]
*The Meeting of the Waters.
Stanza 1*

Come, send round the wine, and leave
points of belief
To simpleton sages, and reasoning fools.
*Come, Send Round the Wine.
Stanza 1*

Shall I ask the brave soldier, who fights
by my side
In the cause of mankind, if our creeds
agree?
Shall I give up the friend I have valued
and tried,
If he kneel not before the same altar
with me?
Ibid. Stanza 2

Beauty lies
In many eyes,
But Love in yours, my Nora Creina.
*Lesbia Hath a Beaming Eye.
Stanza 1*

So Life's year begins and closes;
Days though shortening still can
shine;
What though youth gave love and roses,
Age still leaves us friends and wine.
Spring and Autumn. Stanza 1

Ah! little they think who delight in her
strains,
How the heart of the Minstrel is breaking.
She is Far from the Land. Stanza 2

No, the heart that has truly lov'd never
forgets,
But as truly loves on to the close;
As the sunflower turns on her god, when
he sets,
The same look which she turn'd when
he rose.
*Believe Me, if All Those Endearing
Young Charms. Stanza 2*

The moon looks
On many brooks,
"The brook can see no moon but this." [2]
*When Gazing on the Moon's Light.
Stanza 2*

And when once the young heart of a
maiden is stolen,
The maiden herself will steal after
it soon.
Ill Omens. Stanza 1

'Tis sweet to think, that, where'er we
rove,
We are sure to find something blissful and dear;
And that when we're far from the lips
we love,
We've but to make love to the lips
we are near.
'Tis Sweet to Think. Stanza 1

Give smiles to those who love you less,
But keep your tears for me.[1]
*When Midst the Gay I Meet.
Stanza 1*

Though wooed by flattering friends,
And fed with fame (if fame it be),
This heart, my own dear mother, bends,
With love's true instinct, back to thee!
To My Mother. Stanza 2

'Tis believ'd that this harp which I
wake now for thee
Was a siren of old who sung under the
sea.
The Origin of the Harp

But there's nothing half so sweet in life
As love's young dream.
Love's Young Dream. Stanza 1

To live with them is far less sweet,
Than to remember thee.[2]
I Saw Thy Form. Stanza 3

Eyes of unholy blue.
*By That Lake Whose Gloomy
Shore. Stanza 2*

'Tis the last rose of summer.
Left blooming alone.
*The Last Rose of Summer.
Stanza 1*

When true hearts lie wither'd
And fond ones are flown,

---

[1] The vale of Avoca, County Wicklow, Ireland, where the Avonmore and Avonbeg meet
to form the river Avoca.

[2] This image was suggested by the following
thought, which occurs somewhere in SIR WIL-

LIAM JONES's *Works:* "The moon looks upon
many night-flowers; the night-flower sees but
one moon."

[1] Give other friends your lighted face,
The laughter of the years;
I come to crave a greater grace —
Bring me your tears.
EDWIN MARKHAM: *Your Tears, St. 1*

[2] In imitation of SHENSTONE's inscription,
"Heu! quanto minus est cum reliquis versari
quam tui meminisse."

Oh, who would inhabit
  This bleak world alone?
          The Last Rose of Summer.
                      Stanza 3

And the best of all ways
  To lengthen our days
Is to steal a few hours from the night,
  my dear.
      The Young May Moon. Stanza 1

You may break, you may shatter the
  vase if you will,
But the scent of the roses will hang
  round it still.
                          Ibid.

No eye to watch, and no tongue to
  wound us,
All earth forgot, and all heaven around
  us.
          Come O'er the Sea. Stanza 2

The light that lies [1]
In woman's eyes.
      The Time I've Lost in Wooing.
                      Stanza 1

My only books
  Were woman's looks,
And folly's all they've taught me.
                          Ibid.

I know not, I ask not, if guilt's in that
  heart,
I but know that I love thee, whatever
  thou art.
          Come, Rest in This Bosom.
                      Stanza 2

Oft in the stilly night,
  Ere slumber's chain has bound me,
Fond memory brings the light
  Of other days around me;
    The smiles, the tears,
    Of boyhood's years,
The words of love then spoken;
    The eyes that shone
    Now dimmed and gone,
The cheerful hearts now broken.
      Oft in the Stilly Night. Stanza 1

I feel like one,
  Who treads alone
Some banquet-hall deserted,
  Whose lights are fled,

[1]   O dreamy eyes,
  They tell sweet lies of Paradise;
  And in those eyes the love-light lies
  And lies — and lies — and lies!
      ANITA OWEN: *Dreamy Eyes*

Whose garlands dead,
And all but he departed.
      Oft in the Stilly Night. Stanza 2

Came but for Friendship and took away
  Love.
      A Temple to Friendship. Stanza 2

As half in shade and half in sun
  This world along its path advances,
May that side the sun's upon
  Be all that e'er shall meet thy
    glances!
      Peace Be Around Thee. Stanza 2

If I speak to thee in friendship's name,
  Thou think'st I speak too coldly;
If I mention love's devoted flame,
  Thou say'st I speak too boldly.
          How Shall I Woo? Stanza 1

A friendship that like love is warm;
  A love like friendship steady.
                  Ibid. Stanza 3

The bird, let loose in Eastern skies,
  When hastening fondly home,
Ne'er stoops to earth her wing, nor flies
  Where idle warblers roam;
But high she shoots through air and
  light,
  Above all low delay,
Where nothing earthly bounds her
  flight,
  Nor shadow dims her way.
      The Bird Let Loose. Stanza 1

This world is all a fleeting show,
  For man's illusion given;
The smiles of joy, the tears of woe,
Deceitful shine, deceitful flow, —
  There's nothing true but Heaven.
      This World is All a Fleeting Show.
                      Stanza 1

Sound the loud timbrel o'er Egypt's
  dark sea!
Jehovah has triumph'd, — his people
  are free.
              Sound the Loud Timbrel

As down in the sunless retreats of the
  ocean
  Sweet flowers are springing no mortal
    can see,
So, deep in my soul the still prayer of
  devotion,
  Unheard by the world, rises silent to
    Thee.
      As Down in the Sunless Retreats.
                      Stanza 1

As still to the star of its worship, though
    clouded,
  The needle points faithfully o'er the
    dim sea,
So, dark as I roam, in this wintry
    world shrouded,
  The hope of my spirit turns trembling
    to Thee.
    As Down in the Sunless Retreats.
                 Stanza 2

Ask a woman's advice, and, whate'er
    she advise,
Do the very reverse and you're sure to
    be wise.
   How to Make a Good Politician.
                 Stanza 1

How oft we sigh
When histories charm to think that his-
    tories lie! [1]
                 The Sceptic

That best of fame, a rival's praise.
        Rhymes of the Road. XV

Scarce a sail
Is whiskt from England by the gale,
But bears on board some authors, shipt
For foreign shores, all well equipt
With proper book-making machinery,
To sketch the morals, manners, scenery,
Of all such lands as they shall see,
Or not see, as the case may be.
    Thoughts on Patrons. Stanza 3

'Twas nuts to the Father of Lies.
    A Case of Libel. Stanza 16

Oh, call it by some better name,
  For friendship sounds too cold.
   Oh, Call It by Some Better Name.
                 Stanza 1

Who has not felt how sadly sweet
  The dream of home, the dream of
    home,
Steals o'er the heart, too soon to fleet,
  When far o'er sea or land we roam?
    The Dream of Home. Stanza 1

When thus the heart is in a vein
Of tender thought, the simplest strain
Can touch it with peculiar power.
    Evenings in Greece. First Evening,
                 Stanza 20

---

[1] On the breast of that huge Mississippi of
falsehood called history. — MATTHEW AR-
NOLD: *Literary Influence of Academies*
  History is a fable agreed upon. — NAPOLEON
  History is bunk. — HENRY FORD (1863–)

If thou would'st have me sing and play
  As once I play'd and sung,
First take this time-worn lute away,
  And bring one freshly strung.
  If Thou Would'st Have Me Sing
         and Play. Stanza 1

To sigh, yet feel no pain;
  To weep, yet scarce know why;
To sport an hour with Beauty's chain,
  Then throw it idly by.
   M.P., The Blue Stocking. VI

And from the lips of Truth one mighty
    breath
Shall like a whirlwind scatter in its
    breeze
That whole dark pile of human mock-
    eries: —
Then shall the reign of mind commence
    on earth,
And starting fresh as from a second
    birth,
Man in the sunshine of the world's new
    spring
Shall walk transparent like some holy
    thing!
   Lalla Rookh. The Veiled Prophet
         of Khorassan, Part I

The heaven of each is but what each
    desires.
                   Ibid.

This narrow isthmus 'twixt two bound-
    less seas,
The past, the future, — two eternities!
             Ibid. Part II

There's a bower of roses by Bende-
    meer's stream.[1]
                   Ibid.

Like the stained web that whitens in the
    sun,
Grow pure by being purely shone upon.
                   Ibid.

But Faith, fanatic Faith, once wedded
    fast
To some dear falsehood, hugs it to the
    last.
            Ibid. Part III

One morn a Peri at the gate
Of Eden stood disconsolate.
  Ibid. Part IV, Paradise and the Peri

---

[1] As I recall them the roses bloom again,
and the nightingales sing by the calm Bendemeer. — W. M. THACKERAY: *The Newcomes,*
Chap. 1

Take all the pleasures of all the spheres
And multiply each through endless
    years, —
One minute of heaven is worth them
    all.
*Lalla Rookh. The Veiled Prophet
of Khorassan, Part IV*
But the trail of the serpent is over them
    all.
                                    Ibid.

Oh! ever thus, from childhood's hour,
    I've seen my fondest hope decay;
I never loved a tree or flower,
    But 'twas the first to fade away.
I never nurs'd a dear gazelle
    To glad me with its soft black eye,
But when it came to know me well
    And love me it was sure to die.[1]
            *Ibid. Part V, The Fire-
                    Worshippers*

Paradise itself were dim
And joyless, if not shared with him!
                        Ibid. Part VI

Alas! how light a cause may move
Dissension between hearts that love!
Hearts that the world in vain had tried,
And sorrow but more closely tied;
That stood the storm when waves were
    rough
Yet in a sunny hour fall off,
Like ships that have gone down at sea
When heaven was all tranquillity.
        *Ibid. Part VIII, The Light of the
                    Haram*

Like that celestial bird whose nest
    Is found beneath far Eastern skies,
Whose wings though radiant when at
    rest
    Lose all their glory when he flies.[2]
                                    Ibid.

Fly to the desert, fly with me,
Our Arab tents are rude for thee.[3]
                                    Ibid.

---

[1] See Calverley, page 590.
[2] A species of goldfinch, which sings so
melodiously that it is called the Celestial Bird.
Its wings, when it is perched, appear varie-
gated with beautiful colors, but when it flies
they lose all their splendor.
[3] It is thought that the popular song of
the 1840s, known as *Ossian's Serenade*, was
inspired by the lines of *Fly to the Desert*.
See Calder Campbell, page 395.

Humility, that low, sweet root
From which all heavenly virtues shoot.
                        *The Loves of the Angels.
                            Third Angel's Story*

EBENEZER ELLIOTT
[1781–1849]

When wilt Thou save the people?
    O God of mercy, when?
Not kings and lords, but nations!
    Not thrones and crowns, but men!
Flowers of Thy heart, O God are they;
Let them not pass, like weeds, away —
    God save the people!
        *Corn Law Rhymes. When Wilt
            Thou Save the People?, Stanza 1*

What pensioned slave of Attila
    Leads in the rear?
                            Battle Song
Dark and still, we inly glow,
    Condensed in ire!
                                    Ibid.

ANNA JANE VARDHILL
[1781–1852]

Behold this ruin! 'Twas a skull
Once of ethereal spirit full;
This narrow cell was Life's retreat,
This space was Thought's mysterious
    seat.
            Lines on a Skeleton. Stanza 1

THOMAS HART BENTON
[1782–1858]

This new page opened in the book of
our public expenditures, and this new
departure taken, which leads into the
bottomless gulf of civil pensions and
family gratuities.
        *Speech, U. S. Senate, against a
            Grant to President Harrison's
            Widow [April, 1841]*

JOHN C. CALHOUN
[1782–1850]

Protection and patriotism are reciprocal.
        *Speech, U. S. House of Representa-
            tives [December 12, 1811]*

The very essence of a free government consists in considering offices as public trusts,[1] bestowed for the good of the country, and not for the benefit of an individual or a party.

Speech [February 13, 1835]

A power has risen up in the government greater than the people themselves, consisting of many and various and powerful interests, combined into one mass, and held together by the cohesive power of the vast surplus in the banks.[2]

Speech [May 27, 1836]

The surrender of life is nothing to sinking down into acknowledgment of inferiority.

Speech, U. S. Senate [February 19, 1847]

SIR CHARLES JAMES NAPIER
[1782–1853]

Peccavi [I have Sind].

Message to the British War Office [February 17, 1843] after the surrender of Hyderabad, Province of Sind

ANN TAYLOR
[1782–1866]

See also her sister Jane Taylor [1783–1824]

Oh, that it were my chief delight
  To do the things I ought!
Then let me try with all my might
  To mind what I am taught.

For a Very Little Child

There's hardly anything so small,
  So trifling or so mean,
That we may never want at all,
  For service unforeseen;
And wilful waste, depend upon 't,
Brings, almost always, woeful want!

The Pin. Stanza 6

'Twas fancied by some, who but slightly
  had seen them,

There was not a pin to be chosen between them.

Jane and Eliza. Stanza 2

One ugly trick has often spoiled
  The sweetest and the best;
Matilda, though a pleasant child,
  One ugly trick possessed,
Which, like a cloud before the skies,
Hid all her better qualities.

Meddlesome Matty. Stanza 1

DANIEL WEBSTER
[1782–1852]

Whatever makes men good Christians, makes them good citizens.

Speech at Plymouth, Massachusetts [December 22, 1820] [1]

We wish that this column, rising towards heaven among the pointed spires of so many temples dedicated to God, may contribute also to produce in all minds a pious feeling of dependence and gratitude. We wish, finally, that the last object to the sight of him who leaves his native shore, and the first to gladden his who revisits it, may be something which shall remind him of the liberty and the glory of his country. Let it rise! let it rise, till it meet the sun in his coming; let the earliest light of the morning gild it, and parting day linger and play on its summit!

Address on Laying the Corner-Stone of the Bunker Hill Monument [June 17, 1825]

Venerable men! you have come down to us from a former generation. Heaven has bounteously lengthened out your lives, that you might behold this joyous day.

Ibid.

Mind is the great lever of all things; human thought is the process by which human ends are ultimately answered.

Ibid.

---

[1] See Mathew Henry, page 188.

[2] From this speech comes the phrase, "Cohesive power of public plunder."

[1] This oration will be read five hundred years hence with as much rapture as it was heard. It ought to be read at the end of every century, and indeed at the end of every year, forever and ever. — JOHN ADAMS: *Letter to Webster* [Dec. 23, 1821]

Knowledge, in truth, is the great sun in the firmament. Life and power are scattered with all its beams.

> *Address on Laying the Corner-Stone of the Bunker Hill Monument* [*June 17, 1825*]

Let our object be our country, our whole country, and nothing but our country.

> *Ibid.*

The staff on which my years should lean
Is broken ere those years come o'er me;
My funeral rites thou shouldst have seen,
But thou art in the tomb before me.

> *On the Death of His Son, Charles, 1826. Stanza 1*

Sink or swim, live or die, survive or perish, I give my hand and my heart to this vote.[1]

> *Eulogy on Adams and Jefferson, Faneuil Hall, Boston* [*August 2, 1826*]

It is my living sentiment, and by the blessing of God it shall be my dying sentiment, — Independence now and Independence forever.[2]

> *Ibid.*

Washington is in the clear upper sky.[3]

> *Ibid.*

He smote the rock of the national resources, and abundant streams of revenue gushed forth. He touched the

dead corpse of Public Credit, and it sprung upon its feet.[1]

> *Speech on Hamilton* [*March 10, 1831*]

One country, one constitution, one destiny.

> *Speech* [*March 15, 1837*]

There are persons who constantly clamor. They complain of oppression, speculation, and pernicious influence of wealth. They cry out loudly against all banks and corporations, and a means by which small capitalists become united in order to produce important and beneficial results. They carry on mad hostility against all established institutions. They would choke the fountain of industry and dry all streams.

> *Speech, U. S. Senate* [*March 12, 1838*]

When tillage begins, other arts follow. The farmers therefore are the founders of human civilization.

> *Remarks on Agriculture* [*January 13, 1840*]

Sea of upturned faces.[2]

> *Speech* [*September 30, 1842*]

America has furnished to the world the character of Washington. And if our American institutions had done nothing else, that alone would have entitled them to the respect of mankind.

> *Completion of Bunker Hill Monument* [*June 17, 1843*]

Thank God! I — I also — am an American!

> *Ibid.*

Justice, sir, is the great interest of man on earth.

> *On Mr. Justice Story* [*September 12, 1845*]

Liberty exists in proportion to wholesome restraint.

> *Speech at the Charleston Bar Dinner* [*May 10, 1847*]

---

[1] Mr. Adams, describing a conversation with Jonathan Sewall in 1774, says: "I answered that the die was now cast; I had passed the Rubicon. Swim or sink, live or die, survive or perish with my country was my unalterable determination." — JOHN ADAMS: *Works, Vol. IV, P. 8*
Live or die, sink or swim. — GEORGE PEELE [1558–1597]: *Edward I* [1584?]
[2] Mr. Webster says of Mr. Adams: "On the day of his death, hearing the noise of bells and cannon, he asked the occasion. On being reminded that it was 'Independent Day,' he replied, 'Independence forever'" — *Webster's Works, Vol. I, P. 150.* BANCROFT: *History of the United States, Vol. VII, P. 65*
[3] We shall be strong to run the race,
And climb the upper sky.
WATTS: *Spiritual Hymns, XXIV*

[1] He it was that first gave to the law the air of a science. He found it a skeleton, and clothed it with life, colour, and complexion; he embraced the cold statue, and by his touch it grew into youth, health, and beauty. — BARRY YELVERTON, LORD AVONMORE [1736–1805]: *On Blackstone*
[2] See Scott, page 310.

The law: It has honored us; may we honor it.

Toast at the Charleston Bar Dinner [May 10, 1847]

I have read their platform, and though I think there are some unsound places in it, I can stand upon it pretty well. But I see nothing in it both new and valuable. "What is valuable is not new, and what is new is not valuable."

Speech at Marshfield, Massachusetts [September 1, 1848]

Labor in this country is independent and proud. It has not to ask the patronage of capital, but capital solicits the aid of labor.

Speech [April 2, 1824]

The gentleman has not seen how to reply to this, otherwise than by supposing me to have advanced the doctrine that a national debt is a national blessing.[1]

Second Speech on Foote's Resolution [January 26, 1830][2]

I shall enter on no encomium upon Massachusetts; she needs none. There she is. Behold her, and judge for yourselves. There is her history; the world knows it by heart. The past, at least, is secure. There is Boston and Concord and Lexington and Bunker Hill; and there they will remain forever.

Ibid.

The people's government, made for the people, made by the people, and answerable to the people.[3]

Ibid.

When my eyes shall be turned to behold for the last time the sun in heaven, may I not see him shining on the broken and dishonored fragments of a once glorious Union; on States dissevered, discordant, belligerent; on a land rent with civil feuds, or drenched, it may be, in fraternal blood.

Second Speech on Foote's Resolution [January 26, 1830]

Liberty and Union, now and forever, one and inseparable.

Ibid.

God grants liberty only to those who love it, and are always ready to guard and defend it.

Speech [June 3, 1834]

On this question of principle, while actual suffering was yet afar off, they [the Colonies] raised their flag against a power to which, for purposes of foreign conquest and subjugation, Rome in the height of her glory is not to be compared, — a power which has dotted over the surface of the whole globe with her possessions and military posts, whose morning drum-beat, following the sun,[1] and keeping company with the hours, circles the earth with one continuous and unbroken strain of the martial airs of England.[2]

Speech [May 7, 1834]

Inconsistencies of opinion, arising from changes of circumstances, are often justifiable.[3]

Speech [July 25 and 27, 1846]

---

[1] A national debt, if it is not excessive, will be to us a national blessing. — ALEXANDER HAMILTON

[2] The resolution introduced into the United States Senate, Dec. 29, 1829, by Samuel Augustus Foote [1780–1846], Senator from Connecticut, which occasioned the famous debate in the Senate between Webster and Senator Robert Young Hayne of South Carolina, was that the Committee on Public Affairs should inquire into the expediency of limiting the sale of public lands for a certain period to those which had already been offered for sale.

[3] Our sovereign, the people. — CHARLES JAMES FOX [1749–1806]: Toast [1798], for which his name was erased from the Privy Council.

When the State of Pennsylvania held its convention to consider the Constitution of the United States, Judge Wilson said of the introductory clause, "We, the people, do ordain and establish," etc.: "It is not an unmeaning flourish. The expressions declare in a practical manner the principle of this Constitution. It is ordained and established by the people themselves." This was regarded as an authoritative exposition. — *The Nation*

That government of the people, by the people, for the people, shall not perish from the earth. — ABRAHAM LINCOLN: *Speech at Gettysburg* [Nov. 19, 1863]

[1] See Scott, page 311.

[2] The martial airs of England
Encircle still the earth.
AMELIA BLANFORD EDWARDS [1831–1892]: *The Martial Airs of England*

[3] L'homme absurde est celui qui ne change jamais (The absurd man is he who never

I was born an American; I will live an American; I shall die an American.[1]
Speech [*July 17, 1850*]

There is no refuge from confession but suicide; and suicide is confession.
Argument on the Murder of Captain White [*April 6, 1830*]

There is nothing so powerful as truth, — and often nothing so strange.
Ibid.

Fearful concatenation of circumstances.[2]
Works, Vol. VI, Page 88

A sense of duty pursues us ever. It is omnipresent, like the Deity. If we take to ourselves the wings of the morning, and dwell in the uttermost parts of the sea, duty performed or duty violated is still with us, for our happiness or our misery. If we say the darkness shall cover us, in the darkness as in the light our obligations are yet with us.
Ibid. Page 105

I shall defer my visit to Faneuil Hall, the cradle of American liberty, until its doors shall fly open on golden hinges to lovers of Union as well as lovers of liberty.[3]
Letter [*April, 1851*]

Men hang out their signs indicative of their respective trades: shoemakers hang out a gigantic shoe; jewelers, a monster watch; and the dentist hangs out a gold tooth; but up in the mountains of New Hampshire, God Almighty has hung out a sign to show that there He makes men.
The Old Man of the Mountain

Philosophical argument, especially that drawn from the vastness of the universe, in comparison with the apparent insignificance of this globe, has sometimes shaken my reason for the faith which is in me; but my heart has always assured and reassured me that

the gospel of Jesus Christ must be Divine Reality. The Sermon on the Mount cannot be a mere human production. This belief enters into the very depth of my conscience. The whole history of man proves it.
Epitaph (dictated day before his death) on his tombstone, Marshfield, Massachusetts

I still live.
Last words [*October 24, 1852*]

PRINCESS AMELIA [1]
[1783–1810]

Unthinking, idle, wild, and young,
I laugh'd and danc'd and talk'd and sung.
Fragment

REGINALD HEBER
[1783–1826]

Failed the bright promise of your early day.
Palestine

No hammers fell, no ponderous axes rung;
Like some tall palm the mystic fabric sprung.[2]
Majestic silence!
Ibid.

Brightest and best of the sons of the morning,
Dawn on our darkness, and lend us thine aid.
Epiphany. Stanza 1

By cool Siloam's shady rill
How sweet the lily grows!
First Sunday after Epiphany. No. II

When Spring unlocks the flowers to paint the laughing soil.
Seventh Sunday after Trinity

Death rides on every passing breeze,
He lurks in every flower.
Each season has its own disease,
Its peril every hour!
At a Funeral. No. I, Stanza 3

---

changes). — AUGUSTE MARSEILLE BARTHÉLEMY [1796–1867]: *Ma Justification* [1832]

[1] See Patrick Henry, page 270.

[2] See Scott, page 310.

[3] Webster's reply to the invitation of his friends, who had been refused the use of Faneuil Hall by the Mayor and Aldermen of Boston.

---

[1] Youngest daughter of George III.

[2] Altered in later editions to —
No workman's steel, no ponderous axes rung,
Like some tall palm the noiseless fabric sprung.
See Cowper, page 266.

Thou art gone to the grave; but we will
    not deplore thee,
Though sorrows and darkness encom-
    pass the tomb.
          At a Funeral. No. 11

Where, in creation's wide domains,
Can perfect bliss be found?
          Happiness. Stanza 3

The Son of God goes forth to war,
  A kingly crown to gain;
His blood-red banner streams afar,
  Who follows in His train?
    The Son of God Goes Forth to
              War. Stanza 1

From Greenland's icy mountains,
  From India's coral strand,
Where Afric's sunny fountains
  Roll down their golden sand.
        Missionary Hymn. Stanza 1

Though every prospect pleases,
  And only man is vile.
          Ibid. Stanza 2

Thus heavenly hope is all serene,
But earthly hope, how bright soe'er,
Still fluctuates o'er this changing scene,
As false and fleeting as 'tis fair.
    On Heavenly Hope and Earthly
              Hope

When hands are linked that dread to
  part,
And heart is met by throbbing heart —
Oh! bitter, bitter is the smart
  Of them that bid farewell!
        Farewell. Stanza 1

WASHINGTON IRVING
[1783–1859]

How convenient it would be to many
of our great men and great families of
doubtful origin, could they have the
privilege of the heroes of yore, who,
whenever their origin was involved in
obscurity, modestly announced themselves descended from a god.
    Knickerbocker's History of New
      York. Book II, Chap. 3

Who ever hears of fat men heading a
riot, or herding together in turbulent
mobs? — no — no, 'tis your lean, hungry men who are continually worrying

society, and setting the whole community by the ears.
    Knickerbocker's History of New
      York. Book III, Chap. 2

Your true dull minds are generally
preferred for public employ, and especially promoted to city honors; your
keen intellects, like razors, being considered too sharp for common service.
            Ibid.

His wife "ruled the roast," [1] and in
governing the governor, governed the
province, which might thus be said to
be under petticoat government.
      Ibid. Book IV, Chap. 4

The most glorious hero that ever desolated nations might have mouldered
into oblivion among the rubbish of his
own monument, did not some historian
take him into favor, and benevolently
transmit his name to posterity.
       Ibid. Book V, Chap. 1

Whenever a man's friends begin to
compliment him about looking young,
he may be sure that they think he is
growing old.
    Bracebridge Hall. Bachelors

The almighty dollar,[2] that great
object of universal devotion throughout our land, seems to have no genuine
devotees in these peculiar villages.
    Wolfert's Roost. The Creole
              Village

Those calm, sunny seasons in the
commercial world, which are known by
the name of "times of unexampled prosperity."
    Ibid. "A Time of Unexampled
           Prosperity"

The constant interchange of those
thousand little courtesies which imper-
ceptibly sweeten life, has a happy effect
upon the features, and spreads a mellow
evening charm over the wrinkles of old
age.
    Ibid. A Contented Man

There is in every true woman's heart
a spark of heavenly fire, which lies
dormant in the broad daylight of prosperity; but which kindles up, and beams

[1] See Heywood, page 9.
[2] See Jonson, page 119.

and blazes in the dark hour of adversity.

The Sketch-Book. The Wife

Those men are most apt to be obsequious and conciliating abroad, who are under the discipline of shrews at home.

Ibid. Rip Van Winkle

A curtain lecture is worth all the sermons in the world for teaching the virtues of patience and long-suffering.

Ibid.

A sharp tongue is the only edge tool that grows keener with constant use.

Ibid.

That happy age when a man can be idle with impunity.

Ibid.

Language gradually varies, and with it fade away the writings of authors who have flourished their allotted time.

Ibid. The Mutabilities of Literature

There rise authors now and then, who seem proof against the mutability of language, because they have rooted themselves in the unchanging principles of human nature.

Ibid.

His [the author's] renown has been purchased, not by deeds of violence and blood, but by the diligent dispensation of pleasure.

Ibid. Westminster Abbey [The Poets' Corner]

The sorrow for the dead is the only sorrow from which we refuse to be divorced. Every other wound we seek to heal, every other affliction to forget; but this wound we consider it a duty to keep open; this affliction we cherish and brood over in solitude.

Ibid. Rural Funerals

There is certainly something in angling . . . that tends to produce a gentleness of spirit, and a pure serenity of mind.[1]

Ibid. The Angler

"The literary world," said he, "is made up of little confederacies, each looking upon its own members as the

lights of the universe; and considering all others as mere transient meteors, doomed soon to fall and be forgotten, while its own luminaries are to shine steadily on to immortality."

Tales of a Traveller. Literary Life

The land of literature is a fairy land to those who view it at a distance, but, like all other landscapes, the charm fades on a nearer approach, and the thorns and briars become visible. The republic of letters [1] is the most factious and discordant of all republics, ancient or modern.

Ibid. Notoriety

[Captain Delaplace [2]] gazed at [Ethan] Allen in bewildered astonishment. "By whose authority do you act?" exclaimed he. "In the name of the great Jehovah, and the Continental Congress!" replied Allen.

Life of Washington. Vol. I, Chap. 38

SELLECK OSBORN
[1783–1826]

"My father's trade! — why, blockhead, art thou mad?
My father, sir, did never stoop so low;
He was a Gentleman, I'd have you know."
"Excuse the liberty I take,"
Modestus said, with archness on his brow —
"Pray, why did not your father make
A Gentleman of you?"

The Modest Retort

JANE TAYLOR
[1783–1824]

See also her sister Ann Taylor [1782–1866]

Though man a thinking being is defined,
Few use the grand prerogative of mind.

---

[1] See Walton, page 139.

[1] See Fielding, page 229.
[2] Commandant at Fort Ticonderoga, New York, May 10, 1775.

How few think justly of the thinking
  few!
How many never think, who think they
  do!
  *Essays in Rhyme. On Morals and
  Manners, Prejudice, Essay I,
  Stanza 45*

Far from mortal cares retreating,
  Sordid hopes and vain desires,
Here, our willing footsteps meeting,
  Every heart to heaven aspires.
  Hymn

I thank the goodness and the grace
  Which on my birth have smiled,
And made me, in these Christian days,
  A happy Christian child.
  *A Child's Hymn of Praise.
  Stanza 1*

Who ran to help me when I fell,
And would some pretty story tell,
Or kiss the place to make it well?
  My mother.
  My Mother. Stanza 6

One honest John Tompkins, a hedger
  and ditcher,
Although he was poor, did not want to
  be richer;
For all such vain wishes in him were
  prevented
By a fortunate habit of being contented.
  *Contented John [Honest John
  Tompkins]. Stanza 1*

The lark is up to greet the sun,
  The bee is on the wing;
The ant its labor has begun,
  The woods with music ring.
  The Sun Is Up. Stanza 1

But success is secure, unless energy
  fails;
And at last he produced the Philosopher's Scales.
  The Philosopher's Scales. Stanza 2

The first thing he weighed was the head
  of Voltaire,
Which retained all the wit that had
  ever been there.
  Ibid. Stanza 5

"Take a seat," said the cow, gently
  waving her hand;
"By no means, dear madam," said he,
  "while you stand."
  The Cow and the Ass. Stanza 4

Twinkle, twinkle, little star,
How I wonder what you are,
Up above the world so high,
Like a diamond in the sky.[1]
  *The Star [with ANN TAYLOR].
  Stanza 1*

ALLAN CUNNINGHAM
[1784-1842]

A wet sheet and a flowing sea,
  A wind that follows fast,
And fills the white and rustling sail,
  And bends the gallant mast;
And bends the gallant mast, my boys,
  While, like the eagle free,
Away the good ship flies, and leaves
  Old England on the lee.
  *A Wet Sheet and a Flowing Sea.
  Stanza 1*

While the hollow oak our palace is,
  Our heritage the sea.
  Ibid. Stanza 3

When looks were fond and words were
  few.
  Poet's Bridal-day Song. Stanza 2

John Grumlie swore by the light o' the
  moon,
And the green leaves on the tree,
That he could do more work in a day
Than his wife could do in three.
  *John Grumlie (adapted from
  the old ballad, The Wife of
  Auchtermuchty).[2] Stanza 1*

But henceforth I maun mind the plow,
And ye maun bide at hame.
  Ibid. Stanza 6

The sun rises bright in France,
  And fair sets he;
But he has tint[3] the blythe blink he
  had

---

[1] Scintillate, scintillate, globule vivific,
  Fain would I fathom thy nature specific,
  Loftily poised in ether capacious,
  Strongly resembling a gem carbonaceous.
  — Anonymous Boston version
[2] Another adaptation of the old ballad is
Darby and Joan, by ST. JOHN HONEYWOOD
[1763-1798]. —
  When Darby saw the setting sun,
  He swung his scythe and home he run,
  Sat down, drank off his quart, and said:
  "My work is done, I'll go to bed."
[3] Lost.

In my ain countree.
The Sun Rises Bright in France.
Stanza 1
Hame, hame, hame, to my ain coun-
tree.
Hame, Hame, Hame

LEIGH HUNT
[1784–1859]

Abou Ben Adhem (may his tribe in-
crease!)
Awoke one night from a deep dream of
peace.
Abou Ben Adhem
An angel writing in a book of gold.[1]
Ibid.
Write me as one who loves his fellow-
men.
Ibid.
And lo! Ben Adhem's name led all the
rest.
Ibid.
Oh for a seat in some poetic nook,
Just hid with trees and sparkling with
a brook!
Politics and Poetics. Line 72
With spots of sunny openings, and with
nooks
To lie and read in, sloping into brooks.
The Story of Rimini. Canto III,
Line 418
The world was all forgot, the struggle
o'er,
Desperate the joy. — That day they
read no more.
Ibid. Line 607
His lady to remove the toll that makes
the land forlorn,
Will surely ride through Coventry,
naked as she was born.
Godiva. Stanza 1
"No love," quoth he, "but vanity, sets
love a task like that."
The Glove and the Lions.[2]
Stanza 4

---

[1] I am God's messenger, employed to write
Within this book the pious deeds of men.
J. G. SAXE: *Hassan and the Angel*
[2] SCHILLER wrote a poem on the same
theme. In *The Glove*, ROBERT BROWNING
gives a new version of the familiar legend.

Say I'm weary, say I'm sad,
Say that health and wealth have missed
me,
Say I'm growing old, but add,
Jenny kissed me.[1]
Rondeau
Learn the right
Of coining words in the quick mint of
joy.
A Rustic Walk and Dinner. Line 33
Some people say it is a very easy
thing to get up of a cold morning. You
have only, they tell you, to take the
resolution; and the thing is done.
Getting Up on Cold Mornings
Our Old Gentleman, in order to be
exclusively himself, must be either a
widower or a bachelor.
The Old Gentleman
The pocket-book, among other
things, contains a receipt for a cough,
and some verses cut out of an odd sheet
of an old magazine. . . . He intends
this for a commonplace book which he
keeps, consisting of passages in verse
and prose, cut out of newspapers and
magazines, and pasted in columns;
some of them rather gay.
Ibid.
She thinks the young women of the
present day too forward, and the men
not respectful enough; but hopes her
grandchildren will be better; though
she differs with her daughter in several points respecting their management.
The Old Lady
Those who have lost an infant are
never, as it were, without an infant
child. They are the only persons who,
in one sense, retain it always.
Deaths of Little Children
The groundwork of all happiness is
health.
Ibid.
A fireside is a great opiate.
A Few Thoughts on Sleep

---

[1] The "Jenny" was Mrs. Thomas Carlyle,
who kissed Hunt when he brought Carlyle
good news.

The Irish Shilelah, which a friend has well defined to be "a stick with two butt-ends."

Of Sticks

It has been said of ladies when they write letters, that they put their minds in their postscripts — let out the real objects of their writing, as if it were a second thought, or a thing comparatively indifferent.

Anacreon

The only place a new hat can be carried into with safety is a church, for there is plenty of room there.

A Chapter on Hats

The maid-servant, the sailor, and the schoolboy, are the three beings that enjoy a holiday beyond all the rest of the world.

The Maid-Servant

JAMES SHERIDAN KNOWLES
[1784–1862]

A sound so fine, there's nothing lives 'Twixt it and silence.

Virginius. Act V, Sc. 2

THOMAS DE QUINCEY
[1785–1859]

If once a man indulges himself in murder, very soon he comes to think little of robbing; and from robbing he next comes to drinking and Sabbath-breaking, and from that to incivility and procrastination.

On Murder

It is notorious that the memory strengthens as you lay burdens upon it, and becomes trustworthy as you trust it.

Confessions of an English Opium-Eater (Everyman Edition). Page 30

Call for the grandest of all earthly spectacles, what is that? It is the sun going to his rest. Call for the grandest of all human sentiments, what is that? It is that man should forget his anger before he lies down to sleep.

Ibid. Page 86

If in this world there is one misery having no relief, it is the pressure on the heart from the Incommunicable.

Confessions of an English Opium-Eater (Everyman Edition). Page 110

The reception one meets with from the women of a family generally determines the tenor of one's whole entertainment.

Ibid. Page 132

Mails from the North — the East — the West — the South — whence, according to some curious etymologists, comes the magical word NEWS.

Ibid. Page 145

Oxford Street, stony-hearted stepmother, thou that listenest to the sighs of orphans, and drinkest the tears of children.

Ibid. Page 174

The morning was come of a mighty day — a day of crisis and of ultimate hope for human nature, then suffering mysterious eclipse, and labouring in some dread extremity. . . . Some greater interest was at stake, some mightier cause, than ever yet the sword had pleaded, or trumpet had proclaimed.

Ibid. Page 245

Worlds of fine thinking lie buried in that vast abyss [newspapers], never to be disentombed or restored to human admiration.

Reminiscences of the English Lake Poets. Coleridge

Dyspepsy is the ruin of most things: empires, expeditions, and everything else.

Letter to Hessey [1823]

THOMAS LOVE PEACOCK
[1785–1866]

Seamen three! what men be ye?
Gotham's three Wise Men we be.
Whither in your bowl so free?
To rake the moon from out the sea.
The bowl goes trim. The moon doth shine,
And our ballast is old wine.

Three Men of Gotham. Stanza 1

How troublesome is day!
It calls us from our sleep away;
It bids us from our pleasant dreams
    awake,
And sends us forth to keep or break
Our promises to pay.
                How Troublesome Is Day
None better knew the feast to sway,
    Or keep mirth's boat in better trim;
For Nature had but little clay
    Like that of which she moulded him.
The meanest guest that graced his board
    Was there the freest of the free,
His bumper toast when Peter poured
    And passed it round with three times
    three.
        In His Last Binn Sir Peter Lies.
                            Stanza 2
A heeltap! a heeltap! I never could
    bear it!
So fill me a bumper, a bumper of
    claret!
                Headlong Hall. Chap. 5
Not drunk is he who from the floor
Can rise alone and still drink more;
But drunk is he, who prostrate lies,
Without the power to drink or rise.
        The Misfortunes of Elphin
        [1829]. Heading, Chap. 3,
        translated from the Welsh
The mountain sheep are sweeter,
But the valley sheep are fatter;
We therefore deemed it meeter
To carry off the latter.
                    Ibid. Chap. 11

OLIVER HAZARD PERRY
[1785–1820]

We have met the enemy, and they are
    ours.
        Letter to General Harrison
        [dated "United States Brig Ni-
        agara. Off the Western Sisters.
        Sept. 10, 1813, 4 P. M."]

JOHN PIERPONT
[1785–1866]

A weapon that comes down as still
    As snowflakes fall upon the sod;
But executes a freeman's will,
    As lightning does the will of God;

And from its force nor doors nor locks
Can shield you, — 'tis the ballot-box.
                A Word from a Petitioner
The Yankee boy, before he's sent to
    school,
Well knows the mystery of that magic
    tool,
The pocket-knife.
        Whittling, A Yankee Portrait.
                            Stanza 1

HENRY KIRKE WHITE
[1785–1806]

What is this passing scene?
    A peevish April day!
A little sun, a little rain,
And then night sweeps along the plain,
    And all things fade away;
        Man (soon discuss't)
        Yields up his trust,
And all his hopes and fears lie with him
    in the dust.
        Ode to Disappointment. Stanza 3

SAMUEL WOODWORTH
[1785–1842]

How dear to this heart are the scenes
    of my childhood,
When fond recollection presents them
    to view.
                The Old Oaken Bucket
Then soon with the emblem of truth
    overflowing,
And dripping with coolness, it rose from
    the well.
                                Ibid.
The old oaken bucket, the iron-bound
    bucket,
The moss-covered bucket, which hung
    in the well.
                                Ibid.
Pickaxe, shovel, spade, crowbar, hoe,
    and barrow,
Better not invade, Yankees have the
    marrow.
        The Patriotic Diggers [1814].
                            Stanza 1
We'll show him that Kentucky boys
    Are Alligator-horses.
    The Hunters of Kentucky.[1] *Stanza 2*

[1] This ballad, having the sub-title, *Half
Horse and Half Alligator,* celebrates the par-

So Pakenham he made his brags
  If he in fight was lucky,
He'd have their gals and cotton bags,
  In spite of old Kentucky.
    The Hunters of Kentucky. Stanza 4

EATON STANNARD BARRETT
[1786–1820]

Not she with trait'rous kiss her Saviour
    stung,
Not she denied him with unholy
    tongue;
She, while apostles shrank, could dan-
    ger brave,
Last at his cross, and earliest at his
    grave.[1]
    Woman. Part I [1822]

DAVID CROCKETT
[1786–1836]

I leave this rule for others when I'm
    dead,
Be always sure you're right — then go
    ahead.[2]
    Autobiography [1834]
Don't shoot, colonel, I'll come down:
I know I'm a gone coon.[3]
    *Story told by Crockett of a treed
    raccoon*

---

ticipation of the Kentuckians, under the command of General John Coffee, in the Battle
of New Orleans, January 8, 1815. It was
published as a broadside in Boston, and, in
1826, collected in a volume, *Melodies, Duets,
Trios, Songs, and Ballads,* by JAMES M.
CAMPBELL.
  [1] In another edition, the lines read, —
Not she with trait'rous kiss her Master stung,
Not she denied Him with unfaithful tongue;
She, when apostles fled, could danger brave,
Last at His cross, and earliest at His grave.
  [2] Crockett's motto in the War of 1812.
  [3] The expression, "gone coon," was current
during the Revolutionary War, originating in
the plea of a spy, dressed in raccoon-skins, to
his discoverer, an English rifleman. — *Century
Cyclopedia of Names*

WILLIAM LEARNED MARCY
[1786–1857]

They see nothing wrong in the rule
that to the victors belong the spoils of
the enemy.
    Speech, U. S. Senate [*January,
    1832*]

WINFIELD SCOTT
[1786–1861]

Say to the seceded States, "Wayward
sisters, depart in peace."[1]
    Letter to W. H. Seward [*March 3,
    1861*]

CAROLINE ANNE BOWLES SOUTHEY
[1786–1854]

All day the low-hung clouds have
    dropped
  Their garnered fullness down;
All day that soft gray mist hath
    wrapped
  Hill, valley, grove, and town.
    An April Day. Stanza 1
Tread softly; bow the head,
  In reverent silence bow;
No passing bell doth toll,
Yet an immortal soul
  Is passing now.
    The Pauper's Death-bed. Stanza 1
Come not in terrors clad, to claim
An unresisting prey.
    To Death
Dashed with a little sweet at best.
    Ibid.

RICHARD HENRY DANA
[1787–1879]

Of thousands, thou, both sepulchre
    and pall,
Old Ocean!
    The Little Beach-Bird. Stanza 4

---

  [1] The North would not allow itself to consider seriously of coercing the seceding states;
and there was a party willing to bid them,
with unavailing tears, "Erring sisters, go in
peace," as if the seceding states, being thus
delicately entreated, could not have the heart
to go, even in peace. — WILLIAM DEAN HOW-
ELLS: *Years of My Youth, IV, XI*

A voice within us speaks the startling
  word,
"Man, thou shalt never die!"
                    Immortality

Patient endurance of sufferings, bold
resistance of power, forgiveness of injuries, hard-tried and faithful friendship, and self-sacrificing love, are seen
in beautiful relief over the flat uniformity of life, or stand out in steady and
bright grandeur in the midst of the
dark deeds of men.
                The Man of Ideality

It is an impression, of which we can
not rid ourselves if we would, when
sitting by the body of a friend, that
he has still a consciousness of our
presence; that, though he no longer has
a concern in the common things of the
world, love and thought are still there.
The face which we had been familiar
with so long, when it was all life and
motion, seems only in a state of rest.
We know not how to make it real to
ourselves that in the body before us
there is not a something still alive.
                    Mother and Son

ELIZA LEE CABOT FOLLEN
[1787–1860]

Dear mother, how pretty
  The moon looks to-night!
She was never so cunning before:
  Her two little horns
  Are so sharp and so bright,
I hope she'll not grow any more.
              The New Moon. Stanza 1

BRYAN WALLER PROCTER
("BARRY CORNWALL")
[1787–1874]

We know not alway who are kings by
  day,
But the king of the night is the bold
  brown owl.
                    The Owl. Stanza 3
A thousand miles from land are we,
Tossing about on the roaring sea.
                  The Stormy Petrel
Humanity's poor sum and story:

Life — Death — and all that is of
  Glory.
              The History of a Life. Stanza 5
The sea! the sea! the open sea!
The blue, the fresh, the ever free!
                        The Sea. Stanza 1
I'm on the sea! I'm on the sea!
I am where I would ever be,
With the blue above and the blue be-
  low,
And silence wheresoe'er I go.
                        Ibid. Stanza 2
I never was on the dull, tame shore,
But I loved the great sea more and
  more.
                        Ibid. Stanza 4
Touch us gently, Time! [1]
  Let us glide adown thy stream
Gently, — as we sometimes glide
  Through a quiet dream.
              A Petition to Time. Stanza 1
Humble voyagers are we,
O'er life's dim, unsounded sea.
                        Ibid. Stanza 2

EMMA WILLARD
[1787–1870]

Rocked in the cradle of the deep,
I lay me down in peace to sleep.
                  The Cradle of the Deep

RICHARD HARRIS BARHAM
[1788–1845]

The Lady Jane was tall and slim,
The Lady Jane was fair.
          *Ingoldsby Legends. The Knight
                        and the Lady*
My Lord Tomnoddy got up one day;
It was half after two; he had nothing
  to do,
So his lordship rang for his cabriolet.
                    Ibid. The Execution
Right as a trivet.
                    Ibid. Auto-da-fè
A Franklyn's dogge leped over a style,
And hys name was littel Byngo.
B with a Y, — Y with an N,
N with a G, — G with an O,
They call'd hym littel Byngo!
              A Lay of St. Gengulphus

----

[1] See Crabbe, page 280.

The Devil must be in that little Jackdaw!

The Jackdaw of Rheims

The Cardinal rose with a dignified look,
He call'd for his candle, his bell, and
his book!
In holy anger, and pious grief,
He solemnly cursed that rascally
thief!
He cursed him at board, he cursed
him in bed;
From the sole of his foot to the
crown of his head;
He cursed him in sleeping, that every
night
He should dream of the devil, and
wake in a fright;
He cursed him in living, he cursed
him in drinking,
He cursed him in coughing, in sneez-
ing, in winking;
He cursed him in sitting, in stand-
ing, in lying;
He cursed him in walking, in riding,
in flying,
He cursed him in living, he cursed
him dying! —
Never was heard such a terrible curse!
But what gave rise to no little
surprise,
Nobody seem'd one penny the worse!

Ibid.

Heedless of grammar, they all cried,
THAT'S HIM!

Ibid.

GEORGE NOEL GORDON, LORD BYRON
[1788–1824]

Farewell! if ever fondest prayer
For other's weal avail'd on high,
Mine will not all be lost in air,
But waft thy name beyond the sky.

*Farewell! If Ever Fondest Prayer.
Stanza 1*

I only know we loved in vain;
I only feel — farewell! farewell!

Ibid. Stanza 2

When we two parted
In silence and tears,

Half broken-hearted,
To sever for years.

When We Two Parted. Stanza 1

Fools are my theme, let satire be my
song.

*English Bards and Scotch Reviewers.
Line 6*

'Tis pleasant, sure, to see one's name
in print;
A book's a book, although there's nothin 't.

Ibid. Line 51

With just enough of learning to misquote.

Ibid. Line 66

As soon
Seek roses in December, ice in June;
Hope constancy in wind, or corn in
chaff;
Believe a woman or an epitaph,
Or any other thing that's false, before
You trust in critics.

Ibid. Line 75

So the struck eagle, stretch'd upon the
plain,
No more through rolling clouds to soar
again,
View'd his own feather on the fatal
dart,
And wing'd the shaft that quiver'd in
his heart.[1]

Ibid. Line 826

Yet truth sometimes will lend her
noblest fires,
And decorate the verse herself inspires:
This fact, in virtue's name, let Crabbe
attest, —
Though Nature's sternest painter, yet
the best.

Ibid. Line 839

Maid of Athens, ere we part,
Give, oh give me back my heart!

Maid of Athens. Stanza 1

Near this spot are deposited the remains of one who possessed Beauty
without Vanity, Strength without Insolence, Courage without Ferocity, and
all the Virtues of Man, without his
Vices. This Praise, which would be unmeaning Flattery if inscribed over hu-

[1] See Waller, page 145.

man ashes, is but a just tribute to the Memory of Boatswain, a Dog.

Inscription on the Monument of a Newfoundland Dog

The poor dog, in life the firmest friend, The first to welcome, foremost to defend.[1]

Ibid.

Vex'd with mirth the drowsy ear of night.

Childe Harold's Pilgrimage. Canto I, Stanza 2

Had sigh'd to many, though he loved but one.

Ibid. Stanza 5

If ancient tales say true, nor wrong these holy men.

Ibid. Stanza 7

Maidens, like moths, are ever caught by glare, And Mammon wins his way where seraphs might despair.

Ibid. Stanza 9

Might shake the saintship of an anchorite.

Ibid. Stanza 11

Adieu! adieu! my native shore Fades o'er the waters blue.

Ibid. Stanza 13

My native land, good night!

Ibid.

In hope to merit heaven by making earth a hell.

Ibid. Stanza 20

Still from the fount of joy's delicious springs Some bitter o'er the flowers its bubbling venom flings.[2]

Ibid. Stanza 82

---

[1] The one absolutely unselfish friend that man can have in this selfish world, the one that never deserts him, the one that never proves ungrateful or treacherous, is his dog. A man's dog stands by him in prosperity and in poverty, in health and in sickness. — GEORGE GRAHAM VEST [1830–1904]: *Eulogy on the Dog*, in Johnson County Circuit Court, Warrensburg, Missouri

[2]   Medio de fonte leporum Surgit amari aliquid quod in ipsis floribus angat

(In the midst of the fountain of wit there arises something bitter, which stings in the very flowers). — LUCRETIUS: *IV, 1133*

War, war is still the cry, — "war even to the knife!"[1]

Childe Harold's Pilgrimage. Canto I, Stanza 86

Gone, glimmering through the dream of things that were.

Ibid. Canto II, Stanza 2

The dome of thought, the palace of the soul.[2]

Ibid. Stanza 6

There was a sound of revelry by night, And Belgium's capital had gather'd then Her beauty and her chivalry, and bright The lamps shone o'er fair women and brave men. A thousand hearts beat happily; and when Music arose with its voluptuous swell, Soft eyes look'd love to eyes which spake again, And all went merry as a marriage bell. But hush! hark! a deep sound strikes like a rising knell!

Ibid. Canto III, Stanza 21

Did ye not hear it? — No! 'twas but the wind, Or the car rattling o'er the stony street. On with the dance! let joy be unconfined; No sleep till morn, when Youth and Pleasure meet To chase the glowing hours with flying feet.

Ibid. Stanza 22

And there was mounting in hot haste.

Ibid. Stanza 25

Or whispering, with white lips, "The foe! They come! they come!"

Ibid.

Like to the apples on the Dead Sea's shore, All ashes to the taste.

Ibid. Stanza 34

He who ascends to mountain-tops, shall find The loftiest peaks most wrapt in clouds and snow;

---

[1] "War even to the knife" was the reply of Palafox, the governor of Saragossa, when summoned to surrender by the French, who besieged that city in 1808.

[2] See Waller, page 146.

He who surpasses or subdues mankind
Must look down on the hate of those
below.
>*Childe Harold's Pilgrimage.*
>*Canto III, Stanza 45*

All tenantless, save to the crannying
wind.
>*Ibid. Stanza 47*

History's purchased page to call them
great.
>*Ibid. Stanza 48*

The castled crag of Drachenfels
Frowns o'er the wide and winding
Rhine.
>*Ibid. Stanza 55*

To fly from need not be to hate mankind.
>*Ibid. Stanza 69*

By the blue rushing of the arrowy
Rhone.
>*Ibid. Stanza 71*

I live not in myself, but I become
Portion of that around me: [1] and to me
High mountains are a feeling, but the
hum
Of human cities torture.
>*Ibid. Stanza 72*

For his mind
Had grown Suspicion's sanctuary.
>*Ibid. Stanza 80*

This quiet sail is as a noiseless wing
To waft me from distraction.
>*Ibid. Stanza 85*

On the ear
Drops the light drip of the suspended
oar.
>*Ibid. Stanza 86*

All is concentr'd in a life intense,
Where not a beam, nor air, nor leaf is
lost,
But hath a part of being.
>*Ibid. Stanza 89*

In solitude, where we are least alone.[2]
>*Ibid. Stanza 90*

The sky is changed, — and such a
change! O night
And storm, and darkness! ye are
wondrous strong,
Yet lovely in your strength, as is the
light

[1] I am a part of all that I have met. —
TENNYSON: *Ulysses*
[2] See Gibbon, page 271.

Of a dark eye in woman! Far along,
From peak to peak, the rattling crags
among,
Leaps the live thunder.
>*Childe Harold's Pilgrimage.*
>*Canto III, Stanza 92*

The morn is up again, the dewy morn,
With breath all incense.[1]
>*Ibid. Stanza 98*

Exhausting thought,
And hiving wisdom with each studious
year.
>*Ibid. Stanza 107*

Sapping a solemn creed with solemn
sneer.
>*Ibid.*

Fame is the thirst of youth.
>*Ibid. Stanza 112*

I have not loved the world, nor the
world me.[2]
>*Ibid. Stanza 113*

I stood
Among them, but not of them; in a
shroud
Of thoughts which were not their
thoughts.
>*Ibid.*

I stood in Venice on the Bridge of
Sighs,
A palace and a prison on each hand.
>*Ibid. Canto IV, Stanza 1*

Where Venice sate in state, throned on
her hundred isles.
>*Ibid.*

The thorns which I have reap'd are of
the tree
I planted; they have torn me, and I
bleed.
I should have known what fruit would
spring from such a seed.
>*Ibid. Stanza 10*

Oh for one hour of blind old Dandolo,
The octogenarian chief, Byzantium's
conquering foe! [3]
>*Ibid. Stanza 12*

[1] Incense-breathing morn. — GRAY: *Elegy,*
St. 5
[2] Good-bye, proud world; I'm going home.
Thou art not my friend, and I'm not thine.
R. W. EMERSON: *Good-bye, Proud World*
See Johnson, page 237.
[3] See Wordsworth, page 298.

Parting day
Dies like the dolphin, whom each pang
    imbues
With a new colour as it gasps away,
The last still loveliest, till — 'tis gone,
    and all is gray.
                    Childe Harold's Pilgrimage.
                        Canto IV, Stanza 29
The Ariosto of the North.
                        Ibid. Stanza 40
Italia! O Italia! thou who hast
The fatal gift of beauty.[1]
                        Ibid. Stanza 42
                    Fills
The air around with beauty.
                        Ibid. Stanza 49
Let these describe the undescribable.
                        Ibid. Stanza 53
The starry Galileo, with his woes.
                        Ibid. Stanza 54
Ungrateful Florence! Dante sleeps
    afar,
Like Scipio, buried by the upbraiding
    shore.
                        Ibid. Stanza 57
The poetry of speech.
                        Ibid. Stanza 58
Then farewell Horace, whom I hated
    so,
Not for thy faults, but mine.
                        Ibid. Stanza 77
O Rome! my country! city of the soul!
                        Ibid. Stanza 78
The Niobe of nations! there she stands.
                        Ibid. Stanza 79
I speak not of men's creeds — they
    rest between
Man and his Maker.
                        Ibid. Stanza 95
Yet, Freedom! yet thy banner, torn,
    but flying,
Streams like the thunder-storm against
    the wind.
                        Ibid. Stanza 98
Heaven gives its favourites — early
    death.[2]
                        Ibid. Stanza 102

'Tis but the same rehearsal of the
    past . . .
And History, with all her volumes vast,
Hath but one page.
                    Childe Harold's Pilgrimage.
                        Canto IV, Stanza 108
Egeria! sweet creation of some heart
Which found no mortal resting-place
    so fair
As thine ideal breast.
                        Ibid. Stanza 115
The nympholepsy of some fond des-
    pair.
                                Ibid.
Death, the sable smoke where vanishes
    the flame.
                        Ibid. Stanza 124
Butcher'd to make a Roman holiday!
                        Ibid. Stanza 141
"While stands the Coliseum, Rome
    shall stand;
When falls the Coliseum, Rome shall
    fall;
And when Rome falls — the world." [1]
                        Ibid. Stanza 145
Oh! that the desert were my dwelling-
    place,[2]
With one fair spirit for my minister,
That I might all forget the human
    race,
And, hating no one, love but only her!
                        Ibid. Stanza 177
There is a pleasure in the pathless
    woods,
There is a rapture on the lonely shore,
There is society, where none intrudes,
By the deep sea, and music in its roar:
I love not man the less, but Nature
    more.
                        Ibid. Stanza 178
Roll on, thou deep and dark blue ocean,
    roll!
Ten thousand fleets sweep over thee in
    vain;
Man marks the earth with ruin, — his
    control
Stops with the shore.
                        Ibid. Stanza 179

[1] A translation of the famous sonnet of
VINCENZO DA FILICAJA [1642–1707]:
        Italia, Italia! O tu cui feo la sorte.
[2] See Herbert, page 138.
    See Wordsworth, page 302.

[1] The saying of the ancient pilgrims.
Quoted from Bede by Gibbon: *The Decline
and Fall of the Roman Empire, Chap. LXXI.
Modern Library Giant, Vol. II, P. 1451.*
    [2] See Cowper, page 264.

He sinks into thy depths with bubbling
  groan,
Without a grave, unknell'd, uncoffin'd,
  and unknown.[1]
> *Childe Harold's Pilgrimage.*
> *Canto IV, Stanza 179*

Time writes no wrinkle on thine azure
  brow —
Such as creation's dawn beheld, thou
  rollest now.[2]
> *Ibid. Stanza 182*

Thou glorious mirror, where the Almighty's form
Glasses itself in tempests.
> *Ibid. Stanza 183*

And I have loved thee, Ocean! and my
  joy
Of youthful sports was on thy breast
  to be
Borne, like thy bubbles, onward; from
  a boy
I wantoned with thy breakers, . . .
And trusted to thy billows far and near,
And laid my hand upon thy mane, —
  as I do here.
> *Ibid. Stanza 184*

  Hands promiscuously applied,
Round the slight waist, or down the
  glowing side.
> *The Waltz*

He who hath bent him o'er the dead,
Ere the first day of death is fled,
The first dark day of nothingness,
The last of danger and distress,
Before decay's effacing fingers
Have swept the lines where beauty
  lingers.
> *The Giaour. Line 68*

Such is the aspect of this shore;
'Tis Greece, but living Greece no more!
So coldly sweet, so deadly fair,
We start, for soul is wanting there.
> *Ibid. Line 90*

Shrine of the mighty! can it be
That this is all remains of thee?
> *Ibid. Line 106*

[1] See Pope, page 219.
[2] And thou vast ocean, on whose awful face
Time's iron feet can print no ruin-trace.
  ROBERT MONTGOMERY: *The Omnipresence of the Deity*

For freedom's battle, once begun,
Bequeath'd by bleeding sire to son,
Though baffled oft, is ever won.
> *The Giaour. Line 123*

And lovelier things have mercy shown
To every failing but their own;
And every woe a tear can claim,
Except an erring sister's shame.
> *Ibid. Line 418*

The keenest pangs the wretched find
  Are rapture to the dreary void,
The leafless desert of the mind,
  The waste of feelings unemployed.
> *Ibid. Line 957*

Better to sink beneath the shock
Than moulder piecemeal on the rock.
> *Ibid. Line 969*

The cold in clime are cold in blood,
Their love can scarce deserve the name.
> *Ibid. Line 1099*

I die, — but first I have possess'd,
And come what may, I *have been*
  bless'd.
> *Ibid. Line 1114*

She was a form of life and light
That, seen, became a part of sight,
And rose, where'er I turn'd mine eye,
The morning-star of memory!
> *Ibid. Line 1127*

Know ye the land where the cypress
  and myrtle
  Are emblems of deeds that are done
  in their clime;
Where the rage of the vulture, the love
  of the turtle,
  Now melt into sorrow, now madden
  to crime? [1]
> *The Bride of Abydos. Canto I,*
> *Stanza 1*

Where the virgins are soft as the roses
  they twine,
And all save the spirit of man is divine?
> *Ibid.*

[1] Know'st thou the land where the lemon-
    trees bloom,
  Where the gold orange glows in the deep
    thicket's gloom,
  Where a wind ever soft from the blue
    heaven blows,
  And the groves are of laurel and myrtle
    and rose!
    GOETHE: *Wilhelm Meister's Appren-
    ticeship, Book III, Chap. 1, Heading*

Who hath not proved how feebly words essay
To fix one spark of beauty's heavenly ray?
Who doth not feel, until his failing sight
Faints into dimness with its own delight,
His changing cheek, his sinking heart, confess
The might, the majesty of loveliness?

> *The Bride of Abydos. Canto I,*
> *Stanza 6*

The light of love, the purity of grace,
The mind, the music breathing from her face,
The heart whose softness harmonized the whole, —
And oh, that eye was in itself a soul!

> *Ibid.*

He makes a solitude, and calls it — peace! [1]

> *Ibid. Canto II, Stanza 20*

Hark! to the hurried question of despair:
"Where is my child?" — an echo answers, "Where?" [2]

> *Ibid. Stanza 27*

The fatal facility of the octosyllabic verse.

> *The Corsair. Dedication*

He left a corsair's name to other times,
Link'd with one virtue, and a thousand crimes. [3]

> *Ibid. Canto III, Stanza 24*

She walks in beauty, like the night
Of cloudless climes and starry skies;
And all that's best of dark and bright
Meet in her aspect and her eyes;
Thus mellow'd to that tender light
Which Heaven to gaudy day denies.

> *Hebrew Melodies. She Walks in*
> *Beauty, Stanza 1*

The Assyrian came down like the wolf on the fold,

And his cohorts were gleaming in purple and gold.

> *The Destruction of Sennacherib.*[1]
> *Stanza 1*

Lord of himself, — that heritage of woe!

> *Lara. Canto I, Stanza 2*

The hand that kindles cannot quench the flame.

> *Ibid. Canto II, Stanza 11*

Fare thee well! and if forever,
Still forever, fare thee well.

> *Fare Thee Well. Stanza 1*

Sighing that Nature form'd but one such man,
And broke the die, in moulding Sheridan.[2]

> *Monody on the Death of Sheridan.*
> *Line 117*

O God! it is a fearful thing
To see the human soul take wing
In any shape, in any mood.

> *The Prisoner of Chillon. Stanza 8*

A light broke in upon my brain, —
It was the carol of a bird;
It ceased, and then it came again,
The sweetest song ear ever heard.

> *Ibid. Stanza 10*

I had a dream which was not all a dream.

> *Darkness*

My boat is on the shore,
And my bark is on the sea;
But, before I go, Tom Moore,
Here's a double health to thee!

> *To Thomas Moore. Stanza 1*

Here's a sigh to those who love me,
And a smile to those who hate;

---

[1] Solitudinem faciunt, pacem appellant (They make solitude, which they call peace). — TACITUS: *Agricola, C. 30*

[2] I came to the place of my birth, and cried, "The friends of my youth, where are they?" And echo answered, "Where are they?" — *Arabic MS.*

[3] See Burton, page 122.

---

[1] And it came to pass that night, that the angel of the Lord went out, and smote in the camp of the Assyrians an hundred fourscore and five thousand: and when they arose early in the morning, behold, they were all dead corpses. — *Isaiah, XXXVII, 36. 2 Kings, XIX, 35*

[2] Natura il fece, e poi ruppe la stampa (Nature made him, and then broke the mould). — ARIOSTO: *Orlando Furioso, Canto X, St. 84*

The idea that Nature lost the perfect mould has been a favorite one with all song-writers and poets, and is found in the literature of all European nations. — *Book of English Songs, P. 28*

And, whatever sky's above me,
Here's a heart for every fate.[1]
To Thomas Moore. Stanza 2

So we'll go no more a-roving
So late into the night.
Letter to Thomas Moore [February 26, 1817]

Mont Blanc is the monarch of mountains;
They crowned him long ago
On a throne of rocks, in a robe of clouds,
With a diadem of snow.
Manfred. Act I, Sc. 1

All farewells should be sudden.
Sardanapalus. Act V

She was not old, nor young, nor at the years
Which certain people call a "certain age,"
Which yet the most uncertain age appears.
Beppo. Stanza 22

For most men (till by losing rendered sager)
Will back their own opinions by a wager.
Ibid. Stanza 27

His heart was one of those which most enamour us, —
Wax to receive, and marble to retain.[2]
Ibid. Stanza 34

Besides, they always smell of bread and butter.
Ibid. Stanza 39

That soft bastard Latin,
Which melts like kisses from a female mouth.
Ibid. Stanza 44

One hates an author that's all author.
Ibid. Stanza 75

O Mirth and Innocence! O milk and water!
Ye happy mixtures of more happy days.
Ibid. Stanza 80

[1] With a heart for any fate. — LONGFELLOW: *A Psalm of Life*
[2] My heart is wax to be moulded as she pleases, but enduring as marble to retain. — CERVANTES: *The Little Gypsy*

By fair exchange, not robbery.[1]
The Deformed Transformed. Act I, Sc. 1

What's drinking?
A mere pause from thinking!
Ibid. Act III, Sc. 1

He seems
To have seen better days, as who has not
Who has seen yesterday?
Werner. Act I, Sc. 1

The Cincinnatus of the West,
Whom envy dared not hate,
Bequeathed the name of Washington
To make man blush there was but one! [2]
Ode to Napoleon Bonaparte. II

And if we do but watch the hour,
There never yet was human power
Which could evade, if unforgiven,
The patient search and vigil long
Of him who treasures up a wrong.
Mazeppa. Stanza 10

The "good old times" — all times when old are good.
The Age of Bronze. Stanza 1

Whose game was empires and whose stakes were thrones,
Whose table earth, whose dice were human bones.
Ibid. Stanza 3

While Franklin's quiet memory climbs to heaven,
Calming the lightning which he thence had riven,
Or drawing from the no less kindled earth
Freedom and peace to that which boasts his birth.
Ibid. Stanza 5

[1] Chaunge be no robbry. — HEYWOOD: *Proverbs, Part II, Chap. 4*
[2] Washington's a watchword, such as ne'er
Shall sink while there's an echo left to air.
The Age of Bronze, St. 5
Washington,
Whose every battle field is holy ground.
Don Juan, Canto VIII, St. 5
George Washington had thanks and nought beside,
Except the all-cloudless glory (which few men's is)
To free his country.
Ibid. Canto IX, St. 8

How often we forget all time, when
  lone,
Admiring Nature's universal throne,
Her woods, her wilds, her waters, the
  intense
Reply of hers to our intelligence.
      The Island. Canto II, Stanza 16
Sublime tobacco! which from east to
  west
Cheers the tar's labour or the Turk-
  man's rest.[1]
            Ibid. Stanza 19
Divine in hookas, glorious in a pipe
When tipp'd with amber, mellow, rich,
  and ripe;
Like other charmers, wooing the caress
More dazzlingly when daring in full
  dress;
Yet thy true lovers more admire by far
Thy naked beauties — give me a cigar!
                    Ibid.
"That will do for the marines." [2]
            Ibid. Stanza 21
My days are in the yellow leaf;
  The flowers and fruits of love are
    gone;
The worm, the canker, and the grief
  Are mine alone!
      On My Thirty-sixth Year. Stanza 2
Brave men were living before Agamem-
  non.[3]
      Don Juan. Canto I, Stanza 5
In virtues nothing earthly could sur-
  pass her,
Save thine "incomparable oil," Macas-
  sar!
            Ibid. Stanza 17
But, oh! ye lords of ladies intellectual,
Inform us truly, — have they not hen-
  peck'd you all? [4]
            Ibid. Stanza 22

The languages, especially the dead,
  The sciences, and most of all the
    abstruse,
The arts, at least all such as could be
  said
  To be the most remote from com-
    mon use.
      Don Juan. Canto I, Stanza 40
Her maids were old, and if she took a
  new one,
You might be sure she was a perfect
  fright.
            Ibid. Stanza 48
Her stature tall, — I hate a dumpy
  woman.
            Ibid. Stanza 61
What men call gallantry, and gods
  adultery.
            Ibid. Stanza 63
Christians have burnt each other, quite
  persuaded
That all the Apostles would have done
  as they did.
            Ibid. Stanza 83
And whispering, "I will ne'er consent,"
  — consented.
            Ibid. Stanza 117
'Tis sweet to hear the watch-dog's hon-
  est bark
  Bay deep-mouth'd welcome as we
    draw near home;
'Tis sweet to know there is an eye will
  mark
  Our coming, and look brighter when
    we come.
            Ibid. Stanza 123
Sweet is revenge — especially to
  women.
            Ibid. Stanza 124
And truant husband should return and
  say,
"My dear, I was the first who came
  away."
            Ibid. Stanza 141
Man's love is of man's life a thing
  apart;
'Tis woman's whole existence.
            Ibid. Stanza 194
In my hot youth, when George the
  Third was king.[1]
            Ibid. Stanza 212

---

[1] Whatever Aristotle, and his worthy cabal,
    may say of it,
  Tobacco is divine, there is nothing to
    equal it.
      THOMAS CORNEILLE [1625–1709]:
        Le Festin de Pierre, Act I, Sc. 1
        [1673]
[2] See Scott, page 311.
[3] Vixere fortes ante Agamemnona
  Multi.
      HORACE: *Book IV, Ode 9, L. 25*
[4] The Fraternity of the Henpeck'd. —
JOSEPH ADDISON: *The Spectator, No. 482,
Sept. 12, 1712*

[1] Non ego hoc ferrem, callidus juventa,
  Consule Planco

So for a good old-gentlemanly vice
I think I must take up with avarice.[1]
 Don Juan. Canto I, Stanza 216
There's nought, no doubt, so much the spirit calms
As rum and true religion.
 Ibid. Canto II, Stanza 34
A solitary shriek, the bubbling cry
Of some strong swimmer in his agony.
 Ibid. Stanza 53
'Tis very certain the desire of life
Prolongs it.
 Ibid. Stanza 64
'Tis said that persons living on annuities
Are longer lived than others.
 Ibid. Stanza 65
  All who joy would win
Must share it, — happiness was born a twin.
 Ibid. Stanza 172
Let us have wine and women, mirth and laughter,
Sermons and soda-water the day after.[2]
 Ibid. Stanza 178
In her first passion woman loves her lover,
  In all the others, all she loves is love.[3]
 Ibid. Canto III, Stanza 3
All tragedies are finished by a death,
All comedies are ended by a marriage.
 Ibid. Stanza 9
He was the mildest manner'd man
That ever scuttled ship or cut a throat.
 Ibid. Stanza 41
Even good men like to make the public stare.
 Ibid. Stanza 81
The isles of Greece, the isles of Greece!
Where burning Sappho loved and sung. . . .
Eternal summer gilds them yet,

(I would not have borne this in my flaming youth while Plancus was consul). — HORACE: *Book III, Ode 14, Ad Populum Romanum, St. 7*
[1] See Middleton, page 116.
[2] See Browning, page 495.
It is no time for mirth and laughter,
The cold, gray dawn of the morning after!
 GEORGE ADE: *The Sultan of Sulu, Remorse*
[3] Dans les premières passions les femmes aiment l'amant, et dans les autres elles aiment l'amour. — ROCHEFOUCAULD: *Maxim 471*

But all, except their sun, is set.
 Don Juan. Canto III, Stanza 86, 1
The mountains look on Marathon,
  And Marathon looks on the sea;
And musing there an hour alone,
  I dreamed that Greece might still be free.
 Ibid. Stanza 86, 3
Earth! render back from out thy breast
A remnant of our Spartan dead!
Of the three hundred grant but three,
To make a new Thermopylæ.
 Ibid. Stanza 86, 7
You have the Pyrrhic dance as yet,
  Where is the Pyrrhic phalanx gone?
Of two such lessons, why forget
  The nobler and the manlier one?
You have the letters Cadmus gave —
Think ye he meant them for a slave?
 Ibid. Stanza 86, 10
Fill high the bowl with Samian wine!
 Ibid. Stanza 86, 11
To think such breasts must suckle slaves.
 Ibid. Stanza 86, 15
Place me on Sunium's marble steep,
  Where nothing save the waves and I
May hear our mutual murmurs sweep;
  There, swan-like, let me sing and die.[1]
 Ibid. Stanza 86, 16
But words are things, and a small drop of ink,
  Falling like dew upon a thought, produces
That which makes thousands, perhaps millions, think.
 Ibid. Stanza 88
And glory long has made the sages smile,
  'Tis something, nothing, words, illusion, wind —
Depending more upon the historian's style
Than on the name a person leaves behind.
 Ibid. Stanza 90
Ah, surely nothing dies but something mourns.
 Ibid. Stanza 108

[1] See Shakespeare, page 45.

And if I laugh at any mortal thing,
'Tis that I may not weep.[1]
Don Juan. Canto IV, Stanza 4

The precious porcelain of human clay.[2]
Ibid. Stanza 11

"Whom the gods love die young," was
said of yore.[3]
Ibid. Stanza 12

And her face so fair
Stirr'd with her dream, as rose-leaves
with the air.[4]
Ibid. Stanza 29

These two hated with a hate
Found only on the stage.
Ibid. Stanza 93

"Arcades ambo," — id est, blackguards
both.
Ibid.

I've stood upon Achilles' tomb,
And heard Troy doubted: time will
doubt of Rome.
Ibid. Stanza 101

There's not a sea the passenger e'er
pukes in,
Turns up more dangerous breakers than
the Euxine.
Ibid. Canto V, Stanza 5

And put himself upon his good behaviour.
Ibid. Stanza 47

That all-softening, overpowering knell,
The tocsin of the soul — the dinner
bell.
Ibid. Stanza 49

The women pardon'd all except her
face.
Ibid. Stanza 113

Heroic, stoic Cato, the sententious,
Who lent his lady to his friend Hor-
tensius.
Ibid. Canto VI, Stanza 7

---

[1] I make haste to laugh at everything, for
fear of being obliged to weep. — PIERRE BEAU-
MARCHAIS [1732–1799]: The Barber of Seville, Act I, Sc. 2 [1775]

He jested, that he might not weep. — ALEX-
ANDER SMITH: Dreamthorp, Of Vagabonds.
(The reference is to Charles Lamb.)

[2] See Dryden, page 179.

[3] See Wordsworth, page 302.

[4] All her innocent thoughts
Like rose-leaves scatter'd.
JOHN WILSON ("CHRISTOPHER NORTH")
[1785–1854]: On the Death of a Child
[1812]

Polygamy may well be held in dread,
Not only as a sin, but as a bore.
Don Juan. Canto VI, Stanza 12

A "strange coincidence," to use a
phrase
By which such things are settled nowadays.
Ibid. Stanza 78

He scratch'd his ear, the infallible resource
To which embarrass'd people have recourse.
Ibid. Stanza 100

'Mongst them were several Englishmen of pith,
Sixteen were called Thompson and
nineteen Smith.
Ibid. Canto VII, Stanza 18

The drying up a single tear has more
Of honest fame than shedding seas of
gore.
Ibid. Canto VIII, Stanza 3

Half-pay for life makes mankind worth
destroying.
Ibid. Stanza 14

Neck or nothing.
Ibid. Stanza 45

Indigestion is — that inward fate
Which makes all Styx through one
small liver flow.
Ibid. Canto IX, Stanza 15

"Gentlemen farmers" — a race worn
out quite.
Ibid. Stanza 32

He said
Little, but to the purpose.
Ibid. Stanza 83

And wrinkles (the damned democrats)
won't flatter.
Ibid. Canto X, Stanza 24

What a delightful thing's a turnpike
road.
Ibid. Stanza 78

When Bishop Berkeley said "there was
no matter,"
And proved it, — 'twas no matter
what he said.[1]
Ibid. Canto XI, Stanza 1

---

[1] What is mind? No matter. What is matter? Never mind. — THOMAS HEWITT KEY
[1799–1875], once Head Master of University College School. Quoted by F. J. Furnivall.

So prime, so swell, so nutty, and so knowing.
> *Don Juan. Canto XI, Stanza 19*

'Tis strange the mind, that very fiery particle,
Should let itself be snuff'd out by an article.
> *Ibid. Stanza 60*

Ready money is Aladdin's lamp.
> *Ibid. Canto XII, Stanza 12*

Cervantes smil'd Spain's chivalry away.
> *Ibid. Canto XIII, Stanza 11*

Society is now one polish'd horde,
Formed of two mighty tribes, the *Bores* and *Bored*.
> *Ibid. Stanza 95*

All human history attests
That happiness for man, — the hungry sinner! —
Since Eve ate apples, much depends on dinner.[1]
> *Ibid. Stanza 99*

Death, so called, is a thing which makes men weep,
And yet a third of life is passed in sleep.
> *Ibid. Canto XIV, Stanza 3*

'Tis strange, but true; for truth is always strange, —
Stranger than fiction.[2]
> *Ibid. Stanza 101*

The Devil hath not, in all his quiver's choice,
An arrow for the heart like a sweet voice.
> *Ibid. Canto XV, Stanza 13*

A lovely being, scarcely formed or moulded,
A rose with all its sweetest leaves yet folded.
> *Ibid. Stanza 43*

The antique Persians taught three useful things, —

To draw the bow, to ride, and speak the truth.[1]
> *Don Juan. Canto XVI, Stanza 1*

Heart ballads of Green Erin or Gray Highlands,
That bring Lochaber back to eyes that roam
O'er far Atlantic continents or islands.
> *Ibid. Stanza 46*

Friendship is Love without his wings.
> *L'Amitié est l'Amour sans Ailes*

I awoke one morning and found myself famous.
> *Entry in Memoranda after publication of first two cantos of Childe Harold's Pilgrimage. Quoted by* THOMAS MOORE *in his* Life of Byron, *Chap. 14*

The best of prophets of the future is the past.
> *Letter [January 28, 1821]*

What say you to such a supper with such a woman? [2]
> *Note to a Letter to Mr. Murray on the Reverend W. L. Bowles' Strictures on Pope [March 25, 1821]*

The world is a bundle of hay,
Mankind are the asses that pull,
Each tugs in a different way, —
And the greatest of all is John Bull!
> *Letter to Thomas Moore [June 22, 1821]*

SIR WILLIAM HENRY MAULE
[1788–1858]

My lords, we are vertebrate animals, we are mammalia! My learned friend's manner would be intolerable in Almighty God to a black beetle.
> *Appeal to the court in a case where the opposing counsel, Sir Cresswell Cresswell, was lofty and offensive in manner. Reported by Lord Coleridge*

---

[1] For a man seldom thinks with more earnestness of anything than he does of his dinner. — PIOZZI: *Anecdotes of Samuel Johnson, P. 149*

[2] Le vrai peut quelquefois n'être pas vraisemblable
(Truth may sometimes be improbable).
NICHOLAS BOILEAU-DESPRÉAUX: *L'Art Poétique, III, L. 48*

[1] To ride, shoot straight, and speak the truth —
This was the ancient Law of Youth.
Old times are past, old days are done;
But the Law runs true, O little son!
CHARLES T. DAVIS: *For a Little Boy, St. 1*

[2] See Lady Montagu, page 221.

WILLIAM MEE
[1788–1862]

She's all my fancy painted her;
She's lovely, she's divine.
Alice Gray

HANNAH FLAGG GOULD
[1789–1865]

Alone I walked the ocean strand;
A pearly shell was in my hand;
I stooped and wrote upon the sand
My name — the year — the day.
A Name on the Sand. Stanza 1

"Now, just to set them a-thinking,
I'll bite this basket of fruit," said he,
"This costly pitcher I'll burst in three;
And the glass of water they've left for
me
Shall 'tchick!' to tell them I'm drink-
ing!"
The Frost. Stanza 4

Wisdom, Power and Goodness meet
In the bounteous field of wheat.
The Wheatfield. Stanza 4

WILLIAM KNOX
[1789–1825]

Oh why should the spirit of mortal be
proud?
Like a fast-flitting meteor, a fast-flying
cloud,
A flash of the lightning, a break of the
wave,
He passes from life to his rest in the
grave.
Songs of Israel [1824]. Mortality,[1]
Stanza 1

'Tis the wink of an eye, 'tis the draught
of a breath,
From the blossom of health to the paleness of death.
Ibid. Stanza 14

The fool hath said: There is no God!
No God! Who lights the morning
sun,

[1] This poem was a favorite of Abraham
Lincoln.

And sends him on his heavenly road,
A far and brilliant course to run?
The Atheist. Stanza 1

CHARLES PHILLIPS
[1789–1859]

Grand, gloomy, and peculiar, he sat
upon the throne a sceptred hermit,
wrapped in the solitude of his own
originality.
The Character of Napoleon

SARAH JOSEPHA HALE
[1790–1879]

Mary had a little lamb,
Its fleece was white as snow,
And everywhere that Mary went
The lamb was sure to go;
He followed her to school one day,
That was against the rule;
It made the children laugh and play
To see a lamb in school.
Mary's Lamb. In the Juvenile Mis-
cellany [September, 1830]

"It snows!" cries the school-boy, "Hur-
rah!" and his shout
Is ringing through parlor and hall,
While swift as the wing of a swallow,
he's out,
And his playmates have answered
his call.
It Snows. Stanza 1

FITZ-GREENE HALLECK
[1790–1867]

Strike — till the last armed foe ex-
pires;
Strike — for your altars and your fires;
Strike — for the green graves of your
sires;
God — and your native land!
Marco Bozzaris.[1] *Stanza 3*

Come to the bridal chamber, Death!
Come to the mother, when she feels
For the first time her first-born's
breath;
Come when the blessed seals

[1] A Greek patriot, born about 1788, killed
in a night attack against the Turks, near
Missolonghi, Greece, August 20, 1823.

Which close the pestilence are broke,
And crowded cities wail its stroke;
Come in consumption's ghastly form,
The earthquake's shock, the ocean
    storm;
Come when the heart beats high and
    warm
    With banquet song, and dance, and
    wine,
And thou art terrible: the tear,
The groan, the knell, the pall, the bier,
And all we know, or dream, or fear
    Of agony are thine.
                Marco Bozzaris. Stanza 5
But to the hero, when his sword
    Has won the battle for the free,
Thy voice sounds like a prophet's word,
And in its hollow tones are heard
    The thanks of millions yet to be.
                Ibid. Stanza 6
One of the few, the immortal names
    That were not born to die.
                Ibid. Stanza 7
Such graves as his are pilgrim shrines,
    Shrines to no code or creed con-
    fined, —
The Delphian vales, the Palestines,
    The Meccas of the mind.
                Burns. Stanza 32
Green be the turf above thee,
    Friend of my better days!
None knew thee but to love thee,[1]
    Nor named thee but to praise.
    *On the Death of Joseph Rodman
                            Drake*
There is an evening twilight of the
    heart,
When its wild passion-waves are lulled
    to rest.
                Twilight
They love their land because it is their
    own,
    And scorn to give aught other rea-
    son why;
Would shake hands with a king upon
    his throne,
    And think it kindness to his Majesty.
                Connecticut
This bank-note world.
                Alnwick Castle. Stanza 7

[1] See Rogers, page 289.

Lord Stafford mines for coal and salt,
The Duke of Norfolk deals in malt,
    The Douglas in red herrings.
                Alnwick Castle. Stanza 8

SAMUEL GILMAN
[1791–1858]

Fair Harvard! Thy sons to thy Jubilee
    throng,
    And with blessings surrender thee
    o'er,
By these festival rites, from the age
    that is past,
    To the age that is waiting before.
    *Ode, Bicentennial, Harvard Uni-
    versity [September 8, 1836].
    Stanza 1*
Thou wert our parent, the nurse of our
    souls,
    We were moulded to manhood by
    thee,
Till freighted with treasure-thoughts,
    friendships, and hopes,
    Thou didst launch us on Destiny's
    sea.
                Ibid. Stanza 2

HENRY HART MILMAN
[1791–1868]

And the cold marble leapt to life a
    god.
                The Belvedere Apollo
Too fair to worship, too divine to love.
                Ibid.
And more than wisdom, more than
    wealth, —
A merry heart that laughs at care.
                The Merry Heart. Stanza 1

LYDIA HUNTLY SIGOURNEY
[1791–1865]

Toll for the queenly boat, wrecked on
    rocky shore!
Sea-weed is in her palace halls; she
    rides the surge no more.
                The Bell of the Atlantic.[1]

[1] The *Atlantic* was wrecked on an island
near New London, Connecticut, in 1846. The
bell, on a portion of the wreck, tolled for
many days until salvaged. It later hung at
the Seamen's Church Institute, South Street,
New York.

Ye say that all have passed away —
  That noble race and brave . . .
But their name is on your waters [1] —
  Ye may not wash it out.
        Indian Names. Stanza 1
Old Massachusetts wears it
  Upon her lordly crown.
        Ibid. Stanza 4
Your mountains build their monu-
  ment,
  Though ye destroy their dust.
        Ibid. Stanza 5
Through the open window's space
Behold, a camel thrust his face.
"My nose is cold," he meekly cried,
"Oh, let me warm it by thy side."
        The Camel's Nose. Stanza 1
To evil habit's earliest wile
Lend neither ear, nor glance, nor
  smile —
Choke the dark fountain ere it flows,
Nor e'en admit the camel's nose.
        Ibid. Stanza 4

CHARLES SPRAGUE
[1791–1875]

  Gay, guiltless pair,
What seek ye from the fields of heaven?
  Ye have no need of prayer,
Ye have no sins to be forgiven.
        The Winged Worshippers.[2]
        Stanza 1
It is not often thus around
Our old familiar hearth we're found.
Bless, then, the meeting and the spot;
For once be every care forgot;
Let gentle Peace assert her power,
And kind Affection rule the hour.
  We're all — all here.
        The Family Meeting. Stanza 1
Then Shakespeare rose!
Across the trembling strings
His daring hand he flings,
And lo! a new creation glows!
      Ode, Shakespeare Celebration
        [Boston, 1823]

[1] We will give the names of our fearless race
  To each bright river whose course we
    trace.
  Felicia D. Hemans: *Song of Emigra-*
          tion
[2] Two swallows that flew into the Chauncy
Place Church, Boston, during a service.

In fields of air, he writes his name,
And treads the chambers of the sky.
        Ode, Art
Yes, social friend, I love thee well,
  In learned doctors' spite;
Thy clouds all other clouds dispel,
  And lap me in delight.
        To My Cigar
Through life's dark road his sordid way
  he wends,
An incarnation of fat dividends.
    Phi Beta Kappa Ode, Curiosity
  Here lived and loved another race
of beings. Beneath the same sun that
rolls over your heads the Indian hunter
pursued the panting deer. . . . The
Indian of falcon glance and lion bear-
ing, the theme of the touching ballad,
the hero of the pathetic tale, is gone.
        The American Indian

CHARLES WOLFE
[1791–1823]

Not a drum was heard, not a funeral
  note,
  As his corse to the rampart we hur-
    ried.
    The Burial of Sir John Moore
       at Corunna.[1] *Stanza 1*
But he lay like a warrior taking his
  rest
  With his martial cloak around him.
        Ibid. Stanza 3
Slowly and sadly we laid him down,
  From the field of his fame fresh and
    gory;
We carved not a line, and we raised
  not a stone,
  But we left him alone with his glory.
        Ibid. Stanza 8
If I had thought thou couldst have
  died,
  I might not weep for thee;
But I forgot, when by thy side,
  That thou couldst mortal be.
        To Mary. Stanza 1
Yet there was round thee such a dawn
  Of light ne'er seen before,

[1] First published in the *Newry Telegraph*
[1817].

As fancy never could have drawn,
And never can restore.
To Mary. Stanza 4

Go, forget me! why should sorrow
O'er that brow a shadow fling?
Go, forget me, and to-morrow
Brightly smile and sweetly sing!
Smile, — though I shall not be near
thee;
Sing, — though I shall never hear
thee!
Go, Forget Me!

WILLIAM HOWITT
[1792–1879]

The Wind one morning sprang up from
sleep,
Saying, "Now for a frolic, now for a
leap!
Now for a madcap galloping chase!
I'll make a commotion in every place!"
The Wind in a Frolic

JOHN KEBLE
[1792–1866]

The trivial round, the common task,
Would furnish all we ought to ask.
Morning. Stanza 10

Why should we faint and fear to live
alone,
Since all alone, so Heaven has willed,
we die?
Nor even the tenderest heart, and next
our own,
Knows half the reasons why we
smile and sigh.
*The Christian Year. Twenty-
fourth Sunday after Trinity*

'Tis sweet, as year by year we lose
Friends out of sight, in faith to muse
How grows in Paradise our store.
Burial of the Dead

Abide with me from morn till eve,
For without Thee I cannot live;
Abide with me when night is nigh,
For without Thee I dare not die.
Evening. Stanza 4

JOHN HOWARD PAYNE
[1792–1852]

'Mid pleasures and palaces though we
may roam,
Be it ever so humble, there's no place
like home; [1]
A charm from the skies seems to hallow us there,
Which sought through the world is
ne'er met with elsewhere.

An exile from home splendour dazzles
in vain,
Oh give me my lowly thatched cottage
again;
The birds singing gayly, that came at
my call,
Give me them, and that peace of mind
dearer than all.
*Home, Sweet Home.[2] (From
the opera Clari, the Maid of
Milan)*

PERCY BYSSHE SHELLEY
[1792–1822]

With hue like that when some great
painter dips
His pencil in the gloom of earthquake
and eclipse.
*The Revolt of Islam. Canto V,
Stanza 23*

The awful shadow of some unseen
Power
Floats tho' unseen amongst us.
*Hymn to Intellectual Beauty.
Stanza 1*

As long as skies are blue, and fields
are green,
Evening must usher night, night urge
the morrow,
Month follow month with woe, and
year wake year to sorrow.
Adonais. XXI

[1] Home is home, though it be never so
homely. — CLARK: *Parœmiologia, P. 101*
[1639]
[2] See Reynolds, page 294.
The Latin song *Dulce Domum,* words
anonymous, was set to music by John Reading, organist of Winchester Cathedral [1675–
1681] and of Winchester College [1681–
1692]. The refrain of the song is:
Domum, domum, dulce domum,
Dulce, dulce, dulce domum.

I would give
All that I am to be as thou now art!
But I am chained to Time, and can
    not thence depart!
                        Adonais. XXVI
The Pilgrim of Eternity,[1] whose fame
Over his living head like heaven is
    bent,
An early but enduring monument,
Came, veiling all the lightnings of his
    song
In sorrow.
                        Ibid. XXX
A pard-like spirit, beautiful and swift.
                        Ibid. XXXII
In mockery of monumental stone.
                        Ibid. XXXV
Peace, peace! he is not dead, he doth
    not sleep —
He hath awakened from the dream of
    life.
                        Ibid. XXXIX
He has outsoared the shadow of our
    night;
Envy and calumny and hate and pain,
And that unrest which men miscall de-
    light
Can touch him not and torture not
    again;
From the contagion of the world's
    slow stain
He is secure, and now can never mourn
A heart grown cold, a head grown gray
    in vain.
                        Ibid. XL
He is made one with Nature: there is
    heard
His voice in all her music, from the
    moan
Of thunder to the song of night's sweet
    bird.
                        Ibid. XLII
He is a portion of the loveliness
Which once he made more lovely.
                        Ibid. XLIII
And many more, whose names on
    Earth are dark,
But whose transmitted effluence can
    not die
So long as fire outlives the parent
    spark,

[1] The allusion is to Byron.

Rose, robed in dazzling immortality.
                        Adonais. XLVI
Life, like a dome of many-coloured
    glass,
Stains the white radiance of eternity.
                        Ibid. LII
The soul of Adonais, like a star,
Beacons from the abode where the
    Eternal are.
                        Ibid. LV
Some say that gleams of a remoter
    world
Visit the soul in sleep, — that death is
    slumber,
And that its shapes the busy thoughts
    outnumber
Of those who wake and live.
                        Mont Blanc. III
I fall upon the thorns of life! I bleed!
                        Ode to the West Wind. IV
O, wind,
If Winter comes, can Spring be far be-
    hind?
                        Ibid. V
Chameleons feed on light and air:
Poets' food is love and fame.
                        An Exhortation. Stanza 1
I bring fresh showers for the thirsting
    flowers,
From the seas and the streams.
                        The Cloud. Stanza 1
That orbèd maiden with white fire
    laden,
Whom mortals call the moon.
                        Ibid. Stanza 4
I am the daughter of Earth and Water,
And the nursling of the Sky;
I pass through the pores of the ocean
    and shores,
I change, but I cannot die.
                        Ibid. Stanza 6
Hail to thee, blithe spirit!
Bird thou never wert.
                        To a Skylark. Stanza 1
We look before and after,
    And pine for what is not;
Our sincerest laughter
    With some pain is fraught;
Our sweetest songs are those that tell
    of saddest thought.
                        Ibid. Stanza 18
Teach me half the gladness
    That thy brain must know,

Such harmonious madness
From my lips would flow,
The world should listen then, as I am
listening now.
To a Skylark. Stanza 21

Kings are like stars — they rise and
set, they have
The worship of the world, but no repose.[1]
Hellas. Line 195

The moon of Mahomet
Arose, and it shall set; ·
While, blazoned as on heaven's im-
mortal noon,
The cross leads generations on.
Ibid. Line 221

The world's great age begins anew,
The golden years return,
The earth doth like a snake renew
Her winter weeds outworn.
Ibid. Line 1060

The world is weary of the past,
Oh, might it die or rest at last!
Ibid. Final Chorus

What! alive, and so bold, O earth?
*Written on Hearing the News of
the Death of Napoleon. Stanza 1*

Forms more real than living man,
Nurslings of immortality!
Prometheus Unbound. Act I

Like stars half quencht in mists of silver dew.
Ibid. Act II, Sc. 1

All love is sweet,
Given or returned. Common as light
is love,
And its familiar voice wearies not
ever. . . .
They who inspire it most are fortunate,
As I am now; but those who feel it
most
Are happier still.[2]
Ibid. Sc. 5

Death is the veil which those who live
call life;
They sleep, and it is lifted.
Ibid. Act III, Sc. 3

Good, great and joyous, beautiful and
free;
This is alone Life, Joy, Empire, and
Victory.
*Prometheus Unbound. Act IV,
Closing lines*

Most wretched men
Are cradled into poetry by wrong,
They learn in suffering what they
teach in song.[1]
Julian and Maddalo. Line 544

I could lie down like a tired child,
And weep away the life of care
Which I have borne and yet must bear.
*Stanzas Written in Dejection,
near Naples. Stanza 4*

Jealousy's eyes are green.
Swellfoot the Tyrant. Act II, Sc. 1

Round the decay
Of that colossal wreck, boundless and
bare
The lone and level sands stretch far
away.
Ozymandias

The Devil is a gentleman.[2]
*Peter Bell the Third. Part II,
Stanza 2*

Hell is a city much like London —
A populous and smoky city.
Ibid. Part III, Stanza 1

Teas,
Where small talk dies in agonies.
Ibid. Stanza 12

He had as much imagination
As a pint-pot.
Ibid. Part IV, Stanza 8

Peter was dull — he was at first
Dull — oh so dull — so very dull!
Whether he talked, wrote, or re-
hearsed —
Still with this dulness was he cursed —
Dull — beyond all conception —
dull.
Ibid. Part VII, Stanza 11

A lovely lady, garmented in light
From her own beauty.
The Witch of Atlas. Stanza 5

Music, when soft voices die,
Vibrates in the memory —

---

[1] See Bacon, page 110.
[2] The pleasure of love is in loving. We are
much happier in the passion we feel than in
that we inspire. — ROCHEFOUCAULD: *Maxim
259*

[1] See Butler, page 144.
[2] See Shakespeare, page 99.

Odours, when sweet violets sicken,
Live within the sense they quicken.
*To — : Music, When Soft
Voices Die. Stanza 1*

Rarely, rarely, comest thou,
Spirit of Delight! [1]
*Song: Rarely, Rarely, Comest
Thou. Stanza 1*

I love tranquil solitude
And such society
As is quiet, wise, and good.
Ibid. Stanza 7

Sing again, with your dear voice revealing
A tone
Of some world far from ours,
Where music and moonlight and feeling
Are one.
*To Jane: The Keen Stars Were
Twinkling. Stanza 4*

The desire of the moth for the star,
Of the night for the morrow,
The devotion to something afar
From the sphere of our sorrow.
*To — : One Word Is Too Often
Profaned. Stanza 2*

The seed ye sow, another reaps;
The wealth ye find, another keeps;
The robes ye weave, another wears;
The arms ye forge, another bears.
*Song to the Men of England.
Stanza 5*

Nothing in the world is single,
All things by a law divine
In one spirit meet and mingle.
Love's Philosophy. Stanza 1

I arise from dreams of thee
In the first sweet sleep of night,
When the winds are breathing low,
And the stars are shining bright.
The Indian Serenade. Stanza 1

The Champak odours pine,
Like sweet thoughts in a dream.
Ibid. Stanza 2

A Sensitive Plant in a garden grew,
And the young winds fed it with silver
dew.
The Sensitive Plant. I, Stanza 1

[1] Motto of Symphony No. 2 in E-flat, Opus 63, by SIR EDWARD ELGAR [1857–1934].

For love and beauty and delight,
There is no death nor change.
*The Sensitive Plant.
Conclusion, Stanza 6*

We rest. A dream has power to poison
sleep;
We rise. One wandering thought pollutes the day.
Mutability. I, Stanza 3

Man's yesterday may ne'er be like his
morrow;
Naught may endure but Mutability.
Ibid. Stanza 4

The flower that smiles to-day
To-morrow dies;
All that we wish to stay
Tempts and then flies.
What is this world's delight?
Lightning that mocks the night,
Brief even as bright.
Ibid. II, Stanza 1

There is no sport in hate when all the
rage
Is on one side.
Lines to a Reviewer

The weary Day turned to his rest,
Lingering like an unloved guest.
To Night. Stanza 3

When the lamp is shattered
The light in the dust lies dead: —
When the cloud is scattered
The rainbow's glory is shed.
*When the Lamp Is Shattered.
Stanza 1*

Once, early in the morning,
Beelzebub arose,
With care his sweet person adorning,
He put on his Sunday clothes.[1]
*The Devil's Walk, A Ballad.
Stanza 1*

How wonderful is Death,
Death and his brother Sleep.
Queen Mab. I

Power, like a desolating pestilence,
Pollutes whate'er it touches; and obedience,
Bane of all genius, virtue, freedom,
truth,
Makes slaves of men, and, of the human frame,
A mechanized automaton.
Ibid. III

[1] See Southey, page 321.

Heaven's ebon vault,
Studded with stars unutterably bright,
Through which the moon's unclouded
    grandeur rolls,
Seems like a canopy which love had
    spread
To curtain her sleeping world.
                    Queen Mab. IV

Poets are the hierophants of an unapprehended inspiration; the mirrors
of the gigantic shadows which futurity
casts upon the present.[1]
                    A Defence of Poetry

Poetry is the record of the best and
happiest moments of the happiest and
best minds.
                    Ibid.

Poets are the unacknowledged legislators of the world.
                    Ibid.

SEBA SMITH ("MAJOR JACK DOWNING")
[1792–1868]

The cold winds swept the mountain-
    height,
And pathless was the dreary wild,
And 'mid the cheerless hours of night
A mother wandered with her child:
As through the drifting snows she
    press'd,
The babe was sleeping on her breast.
            The Snow Storm. Stanza 1

'Twas autumn, and the leaves were
    dry,
And rustled on the ground;
And chilly winds went whistling by
With low and pensive sound.
            Three Little Graves. Stanza 1

JEFFERYS TAYLOR
[1792–1853]

This moral, I think, may be safely at-
    tached;
Reckon not on your chickens before
    they are hatched.[2]
                    The Milkmaid. Moral

[1] See Coleridge, page 318.
[2] See Butler, page 143.

JOHN CLARE
[1793–1864]

I am! yet what I am who cares, or
    knows?
My friends forsake me like a memory
    lost.
            *Written in Northampton
            County Asylum*

The daisy lives, and strikes its little
    root
Into the lap of time: centuries may
    come,
And pass away into the silent tomb,
And still the child, hid in the womb of
    time,
Shall smile and pluck them, when this
    simple rhyme
Shall be forgotten.
            The Daisy's Eternity

With its little brimming eye
    And its yellow rims so pale
    And its crimp and curdled leaf,
Who can pass its beauties by?
            The Primrose Bank

The world was on thy page
Of victories but a comma.
            To Napoleon

The wind and clouds, now here, now
    there,
    Hold no such strange dominion
As woman's cold, perverted will,
    And soon estranged opinion.
            When Lovers Part

If life had a second edition, how
I would correct the proofs.[1]
            Quoted by DANIEL BERKELEY
            UPDIKE *in History of the
            Merrymount Press, Introduc-
            tion*

SAMUEL GRISWOLD GOODRICH ("PETER PARLEY")
[1793–1860]

The earth is round, and like a ball
    Seems swinging in the air;
A sky extends around it all,

[1] Compare the epitaph written for himself
(at the age of 22) by Benjamin Franklin:
"Benjamin Franklin, Printer. . . . Will Appear Once More, In a New and More Elegant Edition, Revised and Corrected by the
Author."

And stars are shining there.
Water and land upon the face
Of this round world we see;
The land is man's safe dwelling place,
But ships sail on the sea.
The Earth

FELICIA DOROTHEA HEMANS
[1793–1835]

The stately homes of England!
How beautiful they stand,
Amidst their tall ancestral trees,
O'er all the pleasant land!
The Homes of England. Stanza 1

The breaking waves dashed high
On a stern and rock-bound coast,
And the woods, against a stormy sky,
Their giant branches tossed.
*The Landing of the Pilgrim
Fathers. Stanza 1*

A band of exiles moored their bark
On a wild New England shore.
Ibid. Stanza 2

What sought they thus afar?
Bright jewels of the mine?
The wealth of seas, the spoils of
war? —
They sought a faith's pure shrine.
Ibid. Stanza 9

Ay, call it holy ground,
The soil where first they trod!
They have left unstained what there
they found —
Freedom to worship God.
Ibid. Stanza 10

The boy [1] stood on the burning deck,
Whence all but he had fled; [2]

---

[1] Giacomo Casabianca, whose father, Louis, was an officer in the Comte de Grasse's command at the siege of Yorktown. At the battle of the Nile, in August, 1798, Louis Casabianca commanded the *Orient*, flagship of Admiral Brueys, who was killed, Louis then taking supreme command. The flagship took fire and blew up, the commander was mortally wounded, and when most of the crew fled, Giacomo remained aboard, in an effort to help his gallant father.

[2] The first American edition of Mrs. Hemans' *Poems* [1826] gave this line "whence all but him had fled." English editions and subsequent American editions seem evenly divided between "but him" and "but he." The

---

The flame that lit the battle's wreck
Shone round him o'er the dead.
Casabianca. Stanza 1

There came a burst of thunder sound;
The boy, — oh! where was he?
Ibid. Stanza 9

Leaves have their time to fall,
And flowers to wither at the north-
wind's breath,
And stars to set; — but all,
Thou hast *all* seasons for thine own,
O Death!
The Hour of Death. Stanza 1

Come to the sunset tree!
The day is past and gone;
The woodman's axe lies free,
And the reaper's work is done.
Tyrolese Evening Song. Stanza 1

In the busy haunts of men.
*Tale of the Secret Tribunal.
Part I*

Oh, call my brother back to me!
I cannot play alone:
The summer comes with flower and
bee, —
Where is my brother gone?
The Child's First Grief. Stanza 1

I have looked o'er the hills of the
stormy North,
And the larch has hung all his tassels
forth.
The Voice of Spring. Stanza 3

But tell us, thou bird of the solemn
strain!
Can those who have loved forget?
We call — and they answer not
again —
Do they love — do they love us yet?
The Messenger Bird

Wave may not foam nor wild wind
sweep
Where rest not England's Dead.
England's Dead

'Twas a lovely thought to mark the
hours
As they floated in light away,

---

last edition published while Mrs. Hemans was still living and presumably approved the contents (Blackwood, Edinburgh, 1829, P. 243), gives "but he."

By the opening and the folding flowers,
That laugh to the summer's day.
The Dial of Flowers [of Linnaeus]

So moved they calmly to the field,
Thence never to return,
Save bearing back the Spartan shield,
Or on it proudly borne.
The Spartans' March. Stanza 9

The bark that held a prince went down,
The sweeping waves rolled on;
And what was England's glorious crown
To him that wept a son?

He lived — for life may long be borne
Ere sorrow break its chain; —
Why comes not death to those who mourn? —
He never smiled again! [1]
He Never Smiled Again [2]

EDWARD T. TAYLOR ("FATHER TAYLOR") [3]
[1793–1871]

Simon Stone, he spied a boat,
"Oh, here is a boat," cried Simon Stone.
"I've a mind to see if this boat will float,
I'll fish a spell, if I go alone."
Simon Stone (a Ballad of the Disciple, Simon Peter). Stanza 1

WILLIAM CULLEN BRYANT
[1794–1878]

Here the free spirit of mankind, at length,
Throws its last fetters off; and who shall place

A limit to the giant's unchained strength,
Or curb his swiftness in the forward race?
The Ages. Stanza 33

To him who in the love of Nature holds
Communion with her visible forms, she speaks
A various language.
Thanatopsis

Go forth, under the open sky, and list
To Nature's teachings.
Ibid.

The hills,
Rock-ribbed, and ancient as the sun.
Ibid.

Old ocean's gray and melancholy waste.
Ibid.

All that tread
The globe are but a handful to the tribes
That slumber in its bosom.
Ibid.

So live, that when thy summons comes to join
The innumerable caravan which moves [1]
To that mysterious realm, where each shall take
His chamber in the silent halls of death,
Thou go not, like the quarry-slave at night,
Scourged to his dungeon, but, sustained and soothed

---

[1] Prince William, son of King Henry I, perished, in 1120, when the *White Ship* of the royal fleet struck a rock and sank instantly. J. R. GREEN, in *A Short History of the English People*, says: "It was not till the morning that the fatal news reached the King. He fell unconscious to the ground, and rose never to smile again."
[2] D. G. ROSSETTI'S ballad, *The White Ship*, deals with the same theme.
[3] CHARLES DICKENS wrote of Father Taylor in *American Notes, Chap. 3* [1842]; and WALT WHITMAN included a three-page sketch about him in *November Boughs*. Father Taylor was known as the "seaman's preacher."

---

[1] The edition of 1821 read, —
The innumerable caravan that moves
To the pale realms of shade, where each shall take.

So live, that when the mighty caravan,
Which halts one night-time in the vale of death,
Shall strike its white tents for the morning march,
Thou shalt mount onward to the Eternal Hills,
Thy foot unwearied, and thy strength renewed,
Like the strong eagle's, for its upward flight.
EDWARD PAYSON WESTON [1819–1879]: *A Vision of Immortality, A Reply to Thanatopsis*

By an unfaltering trust, approach thy
    grave,
Like one that wraps the drapery of his
    couch
About him, and lies down to pleasant
    dreams.
                    Thanatopsis

He who, from zone to zone,
Guides through the boundless sky thy
    certain flight,
In the long way that I must tread alone,
    Will lead my steps aright.
            To a Waterfowl. Stanza 8

God made his grave, to men unknown,
    Where Moab's rocks a vale infold,
And laid the aged seer alone
    To slumber while the world grows
    old.
    *"No Man Knoweth His Sepul-
        chre."* [1] *Stanza 2*

The stormy March has come at last,
With wind, and cloud, and changing
    skies;
I hear the rushing of the blast,
That through the snowy valley flies.
                March. Stanza 1

But 'neath yon crimson tree
Lover to listening maid might breathe
    his flame,
Nor mark, within its roseate canopy,
    Her blush of maiden shame.
            Autumn Woods. Stanza 9

The groves were God's first temples.
                A Forest Hymn

Thou com'st from Jersey meadows,
    fresh and green.
            To a Mosquito. Stanza 3

Rogue's Island once — but when the
    rogues were dead,

Rhode Island was the name it took
    instead.[1]
    *A Meditation on Rhode Island
                    Coal. Stanza 1*

The melancholy days are come, the
    saddest of the year,
Of wailing winds, and naked woods,
    and meadows brown and sere.
            *The Death of the Flowers.
                        Stanza 1*
And sighs to find them in the wood and
    by the stream no more.
                Ibid. Stanza 4
Chained in the market-place he stood,
    A man of giant frame,
Amid the gathering multitude
    That shrunk to hear his name.
            The African Chief. Stanza 1
Loveliest of lovely things are they,
On earth, that soonest pass away.
The rose that lives its little hour
Is prized beyond the sculptured flower.
    *A Scene on the Banks of the
                    Hudson. Stanza 3*
Thou blossom bright with autumn dew,
And colored with the heaven's own
    blue,
That openest when the quiet light
Succeeds the keen and frosty night.
        To the Fringed Gentian. Stanza 1
These are the gardens of the Desert,
    these
The unshorn fields, boundless and
    beautiful,
For which the speech of England has
    no name —
The Prairies.
                    The Prairies
Well knows the fair and friendly moon
    The band that Marion leads —
The glitter of their rifles,
    The scampering of their steeds.
            Song of Marion's [2] *Men.
                        Stanza 4*

---

[1] So Moses the servant of the Lord died
there in the land of Moab, according to the
word of the Lord. And he buried him in a
valley in the Land of Moab, over against
Bethpeor; but no man knoweth of his sepulchre unto this day. — *Deuteronomy, XXXIV,
5, 6*
    And no man knows that sepulchre,
        And no man saw it e'er,
    For the angels of God upturned the sod,
        And laid the dead man there.
        CECIL FRANCES ALEXANDER [1830–
        1895]: *The Burial of Moses, St. 1*

[1] EDWARD EVERETT HALE, in *New England
History in Ballads,* prefaces a ballad, *Roses
Island,* with the suggestion that Rhode Island
was thus named because of the glory of the
rhododendron, blooming in profusion when
Adrian Block landed and gave the island a
name.
[2] Francis Marion [1732–1795], of South
Carolina, a General in the Revolutionary War,
known as the "Swamp Fox."

The praise of those who sleep in earth,
The pleasant memory of their worth,
The hope to meet when life is past,
Shall heal the tortured mind at last.

The Living Lost. Stanza 3

Truth, crushed to earth, shall rise again; [1]
The eternal years of God are hers;
But Error, wounded, writhes in pain,
And dies among his worshippers.

The Battle-Field. Stanza 9

How shall I know thee in the sphere which keeps
The disembodied spirits of the dead,
When all of thee that time could wither sleeps
And perishes among the dust we tread?

The Future Life. Stanza 1

Robert of Lincoln is telling his name:
Bob-o'-link, bob-o'-link.

Robert of Lincoln. Stanza 1

Beside a massive gateway built up in years gone by,
Upon whose top the clouds in eternal shadow lie,
While streams the evening sunshine on quiet wood and lea,
I stand and calmly wait till the hinges turn for me.

Waiting by the Gate. Stanza 1

I grieve for life's bright promise, just shown and then withdrawn.

Ibid. Stanza 7

The fiercest agonies have shortest reign.

Mutation

Tender pauses speak
The overflow of gladness, when words are all too weak.

The Damsel of Peru. Stanza 7

Let no maid nor matron grieve,
To see her locks of an unlovely hue,
Frouzy or thin, for liberal art shall give
Such piles of curls as Nature never knew.

Spring in Town. Stanza 7

Oh mother of a mighty race,
Yet lovely in thy youthful grace!

Oh Mother of a Mighty Race. Stanza 1

[1] Truth, crushed to earth, burrows out of sight. — J. MISTLETOE

Man foretells afar
The courses of the stars; the very hour
He knows when they shall darken or grow bright;
Yet doth the eclipse of Sorrow and of Death
Come unforewarned.

An Evening Revery

We plant, upon the sunny lea,
A shadow for the noontide hour,
A shelter from the summer shower,
When we plant the apple-tree.

The Planting of the Apple-Tree. Stanza 2

The horrid tale of perjury and strife,
Murder and spoil, which men call history.

Earth

Oh, slow to smite and swift to spare,
Gentle and merciful and just!
Who, in the fear of God, didst bear
The sword of power, a nation's trust!

The Death of Lincoln. Stanza 1

When the blind suppliant in the way,
By friendly hands to Jesus led,
Prayed to behold the light of day,
"Receive thy sight," the Saviour said.[1]

"Receive Thy Sight." Stanza 1

Lord, who ordainest for mankind
Benignant toils and tender cares!
We thank Thee for the ties that bind
The mother to the child she bears.

The Mother's Hymn. Stanza 1

As one who, dwelling in the distant fields,
Without a neighbor near him, hides a brand
In the dark ashes, keeping carefully
The seeds of fire alive, lest he, perforce,
To light his hearth must bring them from afar.

Translation of the Odyssey of Homer. Book V

[1] And Jesus said unto him, Receive thy sight: thy faith hath saved thee. — *Luke, XVIII, 42*

EDWARD EVERETT
[1794–1865]

When I am dead, no pageant train
  Shall waste their sorrows at my bier,
Nor worthless pomp of homage vain
  Stain it with hypocritic tear.
      Alaric the Visigoth. Stanza 1

Ye shall not pile, with servile toil,
  Your monuments upon my breast,
Nor yet within the common soil
 ˙Lay down the wreck of power to
        rest,
Where man can boast that he has trod
On him that was "the scourge of God."
      Ibid. Stanza 2

But ye the mountain-stream shall turn,
  And lay its secret channel bare
And hollow, for your sovereign's urn,
  A resting-place forever there.
      Ibid. Stanza 3

As a work of art, I know few things
more pleasing to the eye, or more capable of affording scope and gratification to a taste for the beautiful, than
a well-situated, well-cultivated farm.
      Address at Buffalo, New York
      [October 9, 1857]

No gilded dome swells from the
lowly roof to catch the morning or evening beam; but the love and gratitude
of united America settle upon it in one
eternal sunshine. From beneath that
humble roof went forth the intrepid
and unselfish warrior, the magistrate
who knew no glory but his country's
good; to that he returned, happiest
when his work was done. There he
lived in noble simplicity, there he died
in glory and peace. While it stands, the
latest generations of the grateful children of America will make this pilgrimage to it as to a shrine; and when it
shall fall, if fall it must, the memory
and the name of Washington shall shed
an eternal glory on the spot.
      Oration on the Character of
      Washington

I am no aristocrat. I do not own a
quadruped larger than a cat, and she
an indifferent mouser; nor any kind of
vehicle, with the exception, possibly, of
a wheelbarrow.
      Mount Vernon Papers. No. 7

The days of palmy prosperity are
not those most favorable to the display
of public virtue or the influence of wise
and good men. In hard, doubtful, unprosperous, and dangerous times, the
disinterested and patriotic find their
way, by a species of public instinct, un-
opposed, joyfully welcomed, to the
control of affairs.
      Ibid. No. 14

When I contemplate the extent to
which the moral sentiments, the intelligence, the affections of so many millions of people, — sealed up by a sacred charm within the cover of a letter,
— daily circulate through a country, I
am compelled to regard the Post-office,
next to Christianity, as the right arm
of our modern civilization.
      Ibid. No. 27

CAROLINE HOWARD
GILMAN
[1794–1888]

You must know I've resolved and
    agreed
My books from my room not to lend,
But you may sit by my fire and read.
      One Good Turn Deserves
      Another. Stanza 2

My bellows I never will lend,
But you may sit at my fire and blow.
      Ibid. Stanza 4

JOHN GIBSON LOCKHART
[1794–1854]

Rise up, rise up, Xarifa! lay your
    golden cushion down;
Rise up! come to the window, and gaze
    with all the town.
      The Bridal of Andalla. Stanza 1

There was crying in Granada when the
    sun was going down;
Some calling on the Trinity — some
    calling on Mahoun.

Here passed away the Koran — there
   in the Cross was borne —
And here was heard the Christian bell
   — and there the Moorish horn.
                The Flight from Granada.
                            Stanza 1

A tower is fallen! a star is set! — Alas,
   alas for Celin.
                The Lamentation for Celin.
                            Stanza 1

Beyond the sphere of Time,
   And sin, and Fate's control,
Serene in changeless prime
   Of body and of soul.
                            Beyond

MICHAEL MORAN
[1794–1846]

In Egypt's land, contagious to the
   Nile,
King Pharaoh's daughter went to bathe
   in style.
She tuk her dip, then walked unto the
   land,
To dry her royal pelt she ran along the
   strand.
A bulrush tripped her, whereupon she
   saw
A smiling babby in a wad o' straw.
She tuk it up, and said with accents
   mild,
"Tare-and-agers, girls, which av yez
   owns the child?"
                His parody of his poem, Moses.
                Quoted by W. B. YEATS *in his*
                essay, The Last Gleeman

WILLIAM WHEWELL
[1794–1866]

   And so no force, however great, can
stretch a cord, however fine, into a
horizontal line which shall be absolutely straight.[1]
                Elementary Treatise on Me-
                chanics (1st ed.), *The Equili-*
                brium of Forces on a Point

[1] Reputed to be an example of unconscious
but perfect rhyme.

JOHN GARDINER CALKINS
BRAINARD
[1795–1828]

Death has shaken out the sands of thy
   glass.
                Lament for Long Tom
At the piping of all hands,
When the judgment-signal's spread —
When the islands and the lands
And the seas give up their dead,
And the South and North shall come;
   When the sinner is dismayed,
   And the just man is afraid,
   Then Heaven be thy aid,
      Poor Tom.
                            Ibid.
   Far beneath the tainted foam
That frets above our peaceful home,
We dream in joy and wake in love
Nor know the rage that yells above.[1]
                            The Deep
I saw two clouds at morning,
   Tinged with the rising sun,
And in the dawn they floated on,
   And mingled into one.
I thought that morning cloud was
   blest,
It moved so sweetly to the West.
                Epithalamium. Stanza 1

MARIA GOWEN BROOKS
("MARIA DEL OCCIDENTE")
[1795–1845]

Day in melting purple dying,
Blossoms all around me sighing,
Fragrance from the lilies straying,
Zephyr with my ringlets playing,
Ye but waken my distress:
I am sick of loneliness.
                Song of Egla. Stanza 1

THOMAS CARLYLE
[1795–1881]

   May blessings be upon the head of
Cadmus or the Phoenicians, or whoever invented books! . . . An art that
carries the voice of man to the extrem-

[1] When winds are raging o'er the upper
ocean. — HARRIET BEECHER STOWE

ities of the earth, and to the latest generations.

Early Letters. To Mr. R. Mitchell

Except by name, Jean Paul Friedrich Richter is little known out of Germany. The only thing connected with him, we think, that has reached this country is his saying, — imported by Madame de Staël, and thankfully pocketed by most newspaper critics, — "Providence has given to the French the empire of the land; to the English that of the sea; to the Germans that of — the air!"

Richter (In Edinburgh Review, June, 1827)

True humour springs not more from the head than from the heart; it is not contempt, its essence is love; it issues not in laughter, but in still smiles, which lie far deeper.

Ibid.

The great law of culture is: Let each become all that he was created capable of being; expand, if possible, to his full growth; resisting all impediments, casting off all foreign, especially all noxious adhesions; and show himself at length in his own shape and stature, be these what they may.

Ibid.

He who would write heroic poems should make his whole life a heroic poem.

Life of Schiller

Literary men are . . . a perpetual priesthood.

State of German Literature [1827]. Fichte

I came hither [Craigenputtoch] solely with the design to simplify my way of life and to secure the independence through which I could be enabled to remain true to myself.

Letter to Goethe [1828]

Fame, we may understand, is no sure test of merit, but only a probability of such.

Goethe (In Edinburgh Review, 1828)

In every man's writings, the character of the writer must lie recorded.

Ibid.

Clever men are good, but they are not the best.

Goethe (In Edinburgh Review, 1828)

We are firm believers in the maxim that, for all right judgment of any man or thing, it is useful, nay essential, to see his good qualities before pronouncing on his bad.

Ibid.

If an individual is really of consequence enough to have his life and character recorded for public remembrance, we have always been of the opinion that the public ought to be made acquainted with all the inward springs and relations of his character.

Burns [1828]

An educated man stands, as it were, in the midst of a boundless arsenal and magazine, filled with all the weapons and engines which man's skill has been able to devise from the earliest time.

Ibid.

How does the poet speak to men, with power, but by being still more a man than they?

Ibid.

A poet without love were a physical and metaphysical impossibility.

Ibid.

His religion, at best, is an anxious wish; — like that of Rabelais, "a great Perhaps." [1]

Ibid.

Aesop's Fly, sitting on the axle of the chariot, has been much laughed at for exclaiming: What a dust I do raise!

On Boswell's Life of Johnson [1832]

Whoso belongs only to his own age, and reverences only its gilt Popinjays or soot-smeared Mumbojumbos, must needs die with it.

Ibid.

There is tolerable travelling on the beaten road, run how it may; only on the new road not yet levelled and paved, and on the old road all broken

---

[1] The grand Perhaps. — ROBERT BROWNING: *Bishop Blougram's Apology*

into ruts and quagmires, is the travelling bad or impracticable.

On Boswell's Life of Johnson.
[*1832*]

The stupendous Fourth Estate, whose wide world-embracing influences what eye can take in? [1]

Ibid.

Of all outward evils Obscurity is perhaps in itself the least.

Ibid.

Loud clamor is always more or less insane.

Ibid.

All work is as seed sown; it grows and spreads, and sows itself anew.

Ibid.

We have oftener than once endeavoured to attach some meaning to that aphorism, vulgarly imputed to Shaftesbury, which however we can find nowhere in his works, that "ridicule is the test of truth." [2]

Voltaire (In Foreign Review, 1829)

Man makes the circumstances, and spiritually as well as economically is the artificer of his own fortune. . . . Man's circumstances are the element he is appointed to live and work in; . . . so that in another no less genuine

sense, it can be said circumstances make the man.[1]

Diderot

There is no heroic poem in the world but is at bottom a biography, the life of a man; also, it may be said, there is no life of a man, faithfully recorded, but is a heroic poem of its sort, rhymed or unrhymed.

Sir Walter Scott (In London and Westminster Review. No. 12, 1838)

There is a great discovery still to be made in Literature, that of paying literary men by the quantity they do not write.

Ibid.

Silence is deep as Eternity; speech is shallow as Time.

Ibid.

No man lives without jostling and being jostled; in all ways he has to elbow himself through the world, giving and receiving offence.

Ibid.

The biographer has this problem set before him: to delineate a likeness of the earthly pilgrimage of a man.

Ibid.

All greatness is unconscious, or it is little and naught.

Ibid.

To the very last, he [Napoleon] had a kind of idea; that, namely, of *la carrière ouverte aux talens,* — the tools to him that can handle them.[2]

Ibid.

Blessed is the healthy nature; it is the coherent, sweetly co-operative, not incoherent, self-distracting, self-destructive one!

Ibid.

The uttered part of a man's life, let us always repeat, bears to the unuttered, unconscious part a small unknown proportion. He himself never knows it, much less do others.

Ibid.

---

[1] The gallery in which the reporters sit has become a fourth estate of the realm. — T. B. MACAULAY: *On Hallam's Constitutional History* [1828]
See pages 380 and 381 for other references by Carlyle to the Fourth Estate.
[2] How comes it to pass, then, that we appear such cowards in reasoning, and are so afraid to stand the test of ridicule? — SHAFTESBURY [1671–1713]: *Characteristics, A Letter concerning Enthusiasm, Sect. 2*
Truth, 'tis supposed, may bear all lights; and one of those principal lights or natural mediums by which things are to be viewed in order to a thorough recognition is ridicule itself. — SHAFTESBURY: *Essay on the Freedom of Wit and Humour, Sect. 1*
'Twas the saying of an ancient sage (Gorgias Leontinus, *apud* Aristotle's "Rhetoric," lib. iii. c. 18), that humour was the only test of gravity, and gravity of humour. For a subject which would not bear raillery was suspicious; and a jest which would not bear a serious examination was certainly false wit. — *Ibid., Sect. 5*
See Crabbe, page 280.

---

[1] See Benjamin Disraeli, page 420.
[2] Carlyle in his essay on Mirabeau [1837] quotes this from a "New England book." This was his *Sartor Resartus,* first published in America.

Ill-health, of body or of mind, is defeat. . . . Health alone is victory. Let all men, if they can manage it, contrive to be healthy!

> Sir Walter Scott (*In London and Westminster Review. No. 12, 1838*)

It can be said of him, when he departed he took a Man's life along with him. No sounder piece of British manhood was put together in that eighteenth century of Time.

> *Ibid.*

The lightning-spark of Thought, generated or say rather heaven-kindled, in the solitary mind, awakens its express likeness in another mind, in a thousand other minds, and all blaze up together in combined fire.

> *Ibid.*

Considered as a whole, the Christian religion of late ages has been continually dissipating itself into Metaphysics; and threatens now to disappear, as some rivers do, in deserts of barren sand.

> *Ibid.*

Nothing that was worthy in the past departs; no truth or goodness realized by man ever dies, or can die; but is all still here, and, recognized or not, lives and works through endless changes.

> *Ibid.*

The barrenest of all mortals is the sentimentalist.

> *Ibid.*

Love is ever the beginning of Knowledge, as fire is of light.

> *Essays. Death of Goethe [May, 1832]*

Music is well said to be the speech of angels.

> *Ibid. The Opera*

A mystic bond of brotherhood makes all men one.

> *Ibid. Goethe's Works [1832]*

Everywhere the human soul stands between a hemisphere of light and another of darkness on the confines of two everlasting hostile empires, — Necessity and Free Will.

> *Ibid.*

Democracy is, by the nature of it, a self-cancelling business; and gives in the long run a net result of zero.

> *Chartism. Chap. 6, Laissez-Faire*

What is Aristocracy? A corporation of the best, of the bravest.

> *Ibid.*

He that works and *does* some Poem, not he that merely *says* one, is worthy of the name of Poet.

> *Introduction to Cromwell's Letters and Speeches*

History is the essence of innumerable biographies.

> *On History*

The Public is an old woman. Let her maunder and mumble.

> *Journal [1835]*

It is now almost my sole rule of life to clear myself of cants and formulas, as of poisonous Nessus shirts.

> *Letter to His Wife [1835]*

The eye of the intellect "sees in all objects what it brought with it the means of seeing."

> *Varnhagen von Ense's Memoirs (In London and Westminster Review, No. 62, 1838)*

There is endless merit in a man's knowing when to have done.

> *Francia [1845]*

"A fair day's-wages for a fair day's-work": it is as just a demand as governed men ever made of governing. It is the everlasting right of man.

> *Past and Present. Book I, Chap. 3*

Fire is the best of servants; but what a master! [1]

> *Ibid. Book II, Chap. 9*

All work, even cotton-spinning, is noble; work is alone noble. . . . A life of ease is not for any man, nor for any god.

> *Ibid. Book III, Chap. 4*

Every noble crown is, and on earth will forever be, a crown of thorns.

> *Ibid. Chap. 7*

Even in the meanest sorts of Labor, the whole soul of a man is composed

---

[1] Mammon is like fire: the usefulest of all servants, if the frightfulest of all masters! — *Book IV, Chap. 7*

into a kind of real harmony the instant he sets himself to work.
Past and Present. Book III, Chap. 11
Blessed is he who has found his work; let him ask no other blessedness.
Ibid.

To make some nook of God's Creation a little fruitfuler, better, more worthy of God; to make some human hearts a little wiser, manfuler, happier, — more blessed, less accursed! It is work for a God.
Ibid. Book IV, Chap. 8
Respectable Professors of the Dismal Science.[1]
Latter Day Pamphlets. No. 1 [1850]
A Parliament speaking through reporters to Buncombe and the twenty-seven millions, mostly fools.
Ibid. No. 6
The fine arts once divorcing themselves from *truth* are quite certain to fall mad, if they do not die.
Ibid. No. 8
A healthy hatred of scoundrels.
Ibid. No. 12
Genius . . . which is the transcendent capacity for taking trouble first of all.[2]
Life of Frederick the Great. Book IV, Chap. III
Happy the people whose annals are blank in history-books.[3]
Ibid. Book XVI, Chap. I

[1] Referring to political economy and social science, Carlyle also in his essay on *The Nigger Question* [1849] speaks of "What we might call, by way of Eminence, the Dismal Science."
[2] La génie n'est autre chose qu'une grande aptitude à la patience (Genius is nothing else than a great aptitude for patience). — BUFFON [1707–1788]
This is quoted by MATTHEW ARNOLD in his *Essays in Criticism, A French Coleridge*. There is also a popular proverb: "Genius is patience." DISRAELI, *The Young Duke*: "Patience is a necessary ingredient of genius." LESLIE STEPHEN: "Genius is a capacity for taking trouble." JAN WALÆUS also says: "Genius is an intuitive talent for labor." LORD SYDENHAM [1799–1841] defined genius as a consummate sense of proportion. The more recent version of Carlyle's sentence is "an infinite capacity for taking pains."
[3] MONTESQUIEU: *Aphorism*

No man who has once heartily and wholly laughed can be altogether irreclaimably bad.
Sartor Resartus. Book I, Chap. 4
The man who cannot laugh is not only fit for treasons, stratagems and spoils; but his whole life is already a treason and a stratagem.
Ibid.

He who first shortened the labor of Copyists by device of *Movable Types* was disbanding hired Armies, and cashiering most Kings and Senates, and creating a whole new Democratic world: he had invented the Art of printing.
Ibid. Chap. 5
Be not the slave of Words.
Ibid. Chap. 8
The Philosopher is he to whom the Highest has descended, and the Lowest has mounted up; who is the equal and kindly brother of all.
Ibid. Chap. 10
Wonder is the basis of Worship.
Ibid.
Biography is by nature the most universally profitable, universally pleasant of all things: especially biography of distinguished individuals.
Ibid. Chap. 11
What you see, yet can not see over, is as good as infinite.
Ibid. Book II, Chap. 1
To each is given a certain inward talent, a certain outward environment of Fortune; to each, by wisest combination of these two, a certain maximum of capability.
Ibid. Chap. 4
Sarcasm I now see to be, in general, the language of the Devil; for which reason I have, long since, as good as renounced it.
Ibid.
To consume your own choler, as some chimneys consume their own smoke;[1]

[1] See page 381.
Burn your own smoke and the world will go well.
CHRISTOPHER PEARSE CRANCH [1813–1892]: *Life's Sunny Side, St. 6*

to keep a whole Satanic School spouting, if it must spout, inaudibly, is a negative yet no slight virtue, nor one of the commonest in these times.

Sartor Resartus. Book II, Chap. 6

Alas! the fearful Unbelief is unbelief in yourself.

Ibid. Chap. 7

O thou who art able to write a book, which once in the two centuries or oftener there is a man gifted to do, envy not him whom they name Citybuilder, and inexpressibly pity him whom they name Conqueror or Cityburner. Thou too art a Conqueror and Victor.

Ibid. Chap. 8

Produce! Were it but the pitifulest infinitesimal fraction of a product, produce it in God's name.

Ibid. Chap. 9

As the Swiss inscription says: *Sprechen ist silbern, Schweigen ist golden,* — "Speech is silvern, Silence is golden"; or, as I might rather express it, Speech is of Time, Silence is of Eternity.[1]

Ibid. Book III, Chap. 3

Wouldst thou plant for Eternity, then plant into the deep infinite faculties of man.

Ibid.

Two men I honour, and no third. First, the toilworn craftsman that with earth-made implement laboriously conquers the earth, and makes her man's. . . . A second man I honour, and still more highly: Him who is seen toiling for the spiritually indispensable; not daily bread, but the bread of life.

Ibid. Chap. 4

That there should one man die ignorant who had capacity for knowledge, this I call a tragedy.

Ibid.

Consume your own smoke. — BROWNING: *Pacchiarotto,* XXV; Would that he consumed his own smoke. — HERMAN MELVILLE [1819–1891]: Moby Dick, Chap. XCVI; Consume your own smoke with an extra draught of hard work. — SIR WILLIAM OSLER [1849–1919] (in HARVEY CUSHING'S *Life of Sir William Osler, Vol. I, P. 619*).

[1] Quoted also in Carlyle's essay on Boswell's *Life of Dr. Johnson.*

In good-breeding, which differs, if at all, from high-breeding, only as it gracefully remembers the rights of others, rather than gracefully insists on its own rights, I discern no special connection with wealth or birth.

Sartor Resartus. Book III, Chap. 6

Trust not the heart of that man for whom old clothes are not venerable.

Ibid.

Does it not stand on record that the English Queen Elizabeth, receiving a deputation of eighteen tailors, addressed them with a "Good morning, gentlemen both!"[1]

Ibid. Chap. 11

No sadder proof can be given by a man of his own littleness than disbelief in great men.

Heroes and Hero-Worship. The Hero as Divinity

The history of the world is but the biography of great men.[2]

Ibid.

We must get rid of Fear.

Ibid.

The greatest of faults, I should say, is to be conscious of none.[3]

Ibid. The Hero as Prophet

A vein of poetry exists in the hearts of all men.

Ibid. The Hero as Poet

The Age of Miracles is forever here!

Ibid. The Hero as Priest

Burke said there were Three Estates in Parliament; but, in the Reporters' Gallery yonder, there sat a Fourth Estate more important far than they all. It is not a figure of speech, or witty saying; it is a literal fact, — very momentous to us in these times.[4]

Ibid. The Hero as a Man of Letters

In books lies the soul of the whole Past Time: the articulate audible voice of the Past, when the body and ma-

---

[1] Nine tailors make a man. — Old Proverb (the origin of which is said to be nine *tellers* or strokes of the church bell, indicating that the deceased was a man). See *Oxford Dictionary of English Proverbs.*

[2] See Emerson, page 411.

[3] His only fault is that he has none. — PLINY THE YOUNGER: *Book IX, Letter 26*

[4] See page 377.

terial substance of it has altogether vanished like a dream.

Heroes and Hero-Worship.
The Hero as a Man of Letters

All that mankind has done, thought, gained or been: it is lying as in magic preservation in the pages of books.

Ibid.

The true University of these days is a Collection of Books.

Ibid.

The suffering man ought really to consume his own smoke; there is no good in emitting smoke till you have made it into fire.[1]

Ibid.

Adversity is sometimes hard upon a man; but for one man who can stand prosperity, there are a hundred that will stand adversity.

Ibid.

The oak grows silently, in the forest, a thousand years; only in the thousandth year, when the woodman arrives with his axe is there heard an echoing through the solitudes; and the oak announces itself when, with far-sounding crash, it falls.

The French Revolution. Vol. I,
Book II, Chap. 1

No lie you can speak or act but it will come, after longer or shorter circulation, like a bill drawn on Nature's Reality, and be presented there for payment, — with the answer, No effects.

Ibid. Book III, Chap. 1

To a shower of gold most things are penetrable.

Ibid. Chap. 7

"The people may eat grass": [2] hasty words, which fly abroad irrevocable, — and will send back tidings.

Ibid. Chap. 9

O poor mortals, how ye make this earth bitter for each other.

Ibid. Book V, Chap. 5

A Fourth Estate, of able editors,

springs up; increases and multiplies; irrepressible, incalculable.[1]

The French Revolution. Vol. I,
Book VI, Chap. 5

Men that can have communion in nothing else, can sympathetically eat together, can still rise into some glow of brotherhood over food and wine.

Ibid. Book VII, Chap. 2

Battles, in these ages, are transacted by mechanism; with the slightest possible development of human individuality or spontaneity; men now even die, and kill one another, in an artificial manner.

Ibid. Chap. 4

There were certain runaways whom Fritz the Great bullied back into the battle with a: "*R* —, *wollt ihr ewig leben,* Unprintable Offscouring of Scoundrels, would ye live forever!" [2]

Ibid. Vol. II, Book I, Chap. 4

Flying for life, one does not stickle about the vehicle.

Ibid. Book IV, Chap. 5

Governing persons, were they never so insignificant intrinsically, have for most part plenty of memoir-writers.

Ibid. Vol. III, Book I, Chap. 1

Looking at the Statue of Liberty which stands there, she says bitterly: "O Liberty, what things are done in thy name!" [3]

Ibid. Book V, Chap. 2

Is man's civilization only a wrappage, through which the savage nature of him can still burst, infernal as ever?

Ibid. Chap. 7

"Thou wilt show my head to the people: it is worth showing." [4]

Ibid. Book VI, Chap. 2

So here hath been dawning
Another blue day:
Think, wilt thou let it
Slip useless away?

To-day

What is Man? A foolish baby,
Vainly strives, and fights, and frets.

---

[1] See page 379.
[2] The remark of Foulon, when his finance scheme raised the question: What will the people do?

[1] See Carlyle, page 377.
[2] A similar exclamation was current during the World War.
[3] Madame Roland on the scaffold [Nov. 8, 1793].
[4] Danton's last words [April 5, 1794].

Demanding all, deserving nothing,
   One small grave is what he gets.
                    Cui Bono. Stanza 3
My whinstone house my castle is;
   I have my own four walls.
                    My Own Four Walls
Lord Bacon could as easily have
created the planets as he could have
written Hamlet.
                    Remark in discussion
The unspeakable Turk.
                    In public letter [1877]

GEORGE DARLEY
[1795–1846]

Last night we saw the stars arise,
But clouds soon dimmed the ether
   blue:
And when we sought each other's eyes
   Tears dimmed them too!
                    Last Night. Stanza 2
A little cross
To tell my loss;
A little bed
To rest my head;
A little tear is all I crave
Under my very little grave.
                    Robin's Cross. Stanza 1
With nothing more upon it than —
Here lies the Little Friend of Man!
                    Ibid. Stanza 2

JOSEPH RODMAN DRAKE
[1795–1820]

When Freedom from her mountain-
   height
   Unfurled her standard to the air,
She tore the azure robe of night,
   And set the stars of glory there.
She mingled with its gorgeous dyes
The milky baldric of the skies,
And striped its pure, celestial white
With streakings of the morning light.
                    The American Flag. Stanza 1
                    (In New York Evening Post,
                    May 29, 1819)
Flag of the free heart's hope and home!
   By angel hands to valour given;
Thy stars have lit the welkin dome,
   And all thy hues were born in
      heaven.

Forever float that standard sheet!
   Where breathes the foe but falls be-
      fore us,
With Freedom's soil beneath our feet,
   And Freedom's banner streaming
      o'er us?
                    The American Flag. Stanza 5
Go! kneel a worshiper at Nature's
   shrine!
For you her fields are green, and fair
   her skies!
For you her rivers flow, her hills arise!
                    The Culprit Fay. Stanza 14

JOHN KEATS
[1795–1821]

There is not a fiercer hell than the failure in a great object.
                    Preface to Endymion

A thing of beauty is a joy forever:
Its loveliness increases; it will never
Pass into nothingness.
                    Endymion. Book I, Line 1
         Time, that aged nurse,
Rock'd me to patience.
                    Ibid. Line 705
A hope beyond the shadow of a dream.
                    Ibid. Line 857
Pleasure is oft a visitant; but pain
Clings cruelly to us.
                    Ibid. Line 906
            He ne'er is crown'd
With immortality, who fears to follow
Where airy voices lead.
                    Ibid. Book II, Line 211
'Tis the pest
Of love, that fairest joys give most un-
   rest.
                    Ibid. Line 365
   To sorrow,
   I bade good-morrow,
And thought to leave her far away
   behind;
   But cheerly, cheerly,
   She loves me dearly;
She is so constant to me, and so kind.
                    Ibid. Book IV, Line 173

Love in a hut, with water and a crust,
Is — Love, forgive us! — cinders,
ashes, dust.
Lamia. Part II, Line 1
There was an awful rainbow once in
heaven:
We know her woof, her texture; she is
given
In the dull catalogue of common
things.
Philosophy will clip an angel's wings.
Ibid. Line 231
St. Agnes' Eve — Ah, bitter chill it
was!
The owl, for all his feathers, was a-cold.
The Eve of St. Agnes. Stanza 1
　　　Music's golden tongue
Flatter'd to tears this aged man and
poor.
Ibid. Stanza 3
The silver, snarling trumpets 'gan to
chide.
Ibid. Stanza 4
Asleep in lap of legends old.
Ibid. Stanza 15
Sudden a thought came like a full-
blown rose,
Flushing his brow.
Ibid. Stanza 16
A poor, weak, palsy-stricken, church-
yard thing.
Ibid. Stanza 18
Her rich attire creeps rustling to her
knees.
Ibid. Stanza 26
As though a rose should shut, and be
a bud again.
Ibid. Stanza 27
He play'd an ancient ditty long since
mute,
In Provence call'd, "La belle dame sans
mercy."
Ibid. Stanza 33
Dance, and Provençal song, and sun-
burnt mirth!
O for a beaker full of the warm South,
Full of the true, the blushful Hippo-
crene,
With beaded bubbles winking at the
brim,
And purple-stainèd mouth.
Ode to a Nightingale. Stanza 2

I cannot see what flowers are at my
feet,
Nor what soft incense hangs upon the
boughs.
Ode to a Nightingale. Stanza 5
I have been half in love with easeful
Death,
Call'd him soft names in many a mused
rhyme.
Ibid. Stanza 6
The self-same song that found a path
Through the sad heart of Ruth, when,
sick for home,
She stood in tears amid the alien corn;
　The same that oft-times hath
Charm'd magic casements, opening on
the foam
Of perilous seas, in faery lands forlorn.
Ibid. Stanza 7
Thou foster-child of Silence and slow
Time.
Ode on a Grecian Urn. Stanza 1
Heard melodies are sweet, but those
unheard
Are sweeter.
Ibid. Stanza 2
For ever wilt thou love, and she be fair!
Ibid.
O Attic shape! fair attitude!
Ibid. Stanza 5
Beauty is truth, truth beauty, — that
is all
Ye know on earth, and all ye need
to know.
Ibid.
　In a drear-nighted December
　　Too happy, happy tree
　Thy branches ne'er remember
　　Their green felicity.
Stanzas
　　　Hear ye not the hum
Of mighty workings?
Sonnet 14, Addressed to Haydon
To one who has been long in city pent,
'Tis very sweet to look into the fair
And open face of heaven.
*Sonnet, To One Who Has Been
Long in City Pent*
E'en like the passage of an angel's tear
That falls through the clear ether si-
lently.
Ibid.

Much have I travell'd in the realms of
  gold,
  And many goodly states and king-
    doms seen.
        Sonnet, On First Looking Into
            Chapman's Homer
Then felt I like some watcher of the
  skies
  When a new planet swims into his
    ken;
Or like stout Cortez when with eagle
  eyes
  He stared at the Pacific and all his
    men
Look'd at each other with a wild sur-
  mise
  Silent, upon a peak in Darien.
                            Ibid.
When I have fears that I may cease to
  be.
        Sonnet, When I Have Fears
Huge cloudy symbols of a high ro-
  mance.
                            Ibid.
Fair creature of an hour!
                            Ibid.
      Life is but a day;
A fragile dewdrop on its perilous way
From a tree's summit.
        Sleep and Poetry. Line 85
Life is the rose's hope while yet un-
  blown.
              Ibid. Line 90
Too many tears for lovers have been
  shed,
Too many sighs give we to them in fee,
Too much of pity after they are dead,
Too many doleful stories do we see,
Whose matter in bright gold were best
  be read.
      Isabella [The Pot of Basil].
                      Stanza 12
She wrapp'd it up; and for its tomb did
  choose
A garden-pot, wherein she laid it by,
And cover'd it with mould, and o'er it
  set
Sweet Basil, which her tears kept ever
  wet.
              Ibid. Stanza 52
Ever let the Fancy roam,
Pleasure never is at home.
        Fancy. Line 1

Where's the eye, however blue,
Doth not weary? Where's the face
One would meet in every place?
Where's the voice, however soft,
One would hear so very oft?
              Fancy. Line 72
Souls of Poets dead and gone,
What Elysium have ye known,
Happy field or mossy cavern,
Choicer than the Mermaid Tavern?
      Lines on the Mermaid Tavern.
                      Line 23
Bards of Passion and of Mirth,
Ye have left your souls on earth!
Have ye souls in heaven too?
        Ode (written in a volume of
        Beaumont and Fletcher). Line 1
Season of mists and mellow fruitful-
  ness,
  Close bosom-friend of the maturing
    sun;
Conspiring with him how to load and
  bless
  With fruit the vines.
              To Autumn. Stanza 1
Their lips touched not, but had not
  bade adieu.
              Ode to Psyche
        All soft delight
That shadowy thought can win,
A bright torch, and a casement ope at
  night
To let the warm Love in!
                            Ibid.
Emprison her soft hand, and let her
  rave,
And feed deep, deep upon her peerless
  eyes.
        Ode on Melancholy. Stanza 2
Ay, in the very temple of Delight
Veil'd Melancholy has her sovran
  shrine.
              Ibid. Stanza 3
That large utterance of the early gods!
        Hyperion. Book I, Line 51
Those green-robed senators of mighty
  woods,
Tall oaks, branch-charmed by the
  earnest stars,
Dream, and so dream all night without
  a stir.
              Ibid. Line 73

Verse, Fame, and Beauty are intense
indeed,
But Death intenser — Death is Life's
high meed.
Sonnet, Why Did I Laugh To-night?
Fame, like a wayward girl, will still be
coy
To those who woo her with too slavish
knees.
Sonnet on Fame
The day is gone, and all its sweets are
gone!
Sweet voice, sweet lips, soft hand,
and softer breast.
Sonnet, The Day Is Gone
Mortality
Weighs heavily on me like unwilling
sleep.
Sonnet, On Seeing the Elgin Marbles
Shed no tear — O shed no tear!
The flower will bloom another year.
Weep no more — O weep no more!
Young buds sleep in the root's white
core.
Faery Songs. I
Sweet Hope, ethereal balm upon me
shed,
And wave thy silver pinions o'er my
head.
To Hope. Stanza 1
Disappointment, parent of Despair.
Ibid. Stanza 3
I stood tip-toe upon a little hill,
The air was cooling, and so very still.
I Stood Tip-toe. Line 1
Open afresh your round of starry folds,
Ye ardent marigolds!
Ibid. Line 47
The moon lifting her silver rim
Above a cloud, and with a gradual swim
Coming into the blue with all her light.
Ibid. Line 113
Nought but a lovely sighing of the
wind
Along the reedy stream; a half-heard
strain,
Full of sweet desolation — balmy pain.
Ibid. Line 160
And no birds sing.
La Belle Dame Sans Merci. Stanza 1
Bright star, would I were stedfast as
thou art —

Not in lone splendour hung aloft the
night
And watching, with eternal lids apart,
Like nature's patient, sleepless Ere-
mite,
The moving waters at their priestlike
task
Of pure ablution round earth's hu-
man shores.
The Last Sonnet
Pillow'd upon my fair love's ripening
breast,
To feel for ever its soft fall and swell,
Awake for ever in a sweet unrest.
Ibid.
The poetry of earth is never dead.
*Sonnet, On the Grasshopper and
Cricket*
Four Seasons fill the measure of the
year;
There are four seasons in the mind of
man.
Sonnet, The Human Seasons
Blue! Gentle cousin of the forest-green,
Married to green in all the sweetest
flowers, —
Forget-me-not, — the blue bell, —
and, that Queen
Of secrecy, the violet.
Sonnet, Blue
It keeps eternal whisperings around
Desolate shores, and with its mighty
swell
Gluts twice ten thousand caverns.
Sonnet, On the Sea
I am certain of nothing but of the
holiness of the heart's affections, and
the truth of Imagination. What the
Imagination seizes as Beauty must be
Truth.
Letter [November 22, 1817]
Poetry should surprise by a fine ex-
cess, and not by singularity; it should
strike the reader as a wording of his
own highest thoughts, and appear al-
most a remembrance.
Letter [February 27, 1818]
A man's life of any worth is a con-
tinual Allegory, and very few eyes can
see the Mystery of his life.
Letter [February 18, 1819]
I have loved the principle of beauty
in all things, and if I had had time I

would have made myself remembered.
Letter [*1820*]
Here lies one whose name was writ
in water.[1]

Epitaph for himself

JAMES GATES PERCIVAL
[1795–1856]

Hail to the land whereon we tread,
  Our fondest boast!
The sepulchres of mighty dead,
The truest hearts that ever bled,
Who sleep on glory's brightest bed,
  A fearless host:
No slave is here: — our unchained feet,
Walk freely as the waves that beat
  Our coast.

New England

On thy fair bosom, silver lake,
  The wild swan spreads his snowy
    sail,
And round his breast the ripples break,
  As down he bears before the gale.

To Seneca Lake. Stanza 1

SIR THOMAS NOON
TALFOURD
[1795–1854]

  'Tis a little thing
To give a cup of water; yet its draught
Of cool refreshment, drained by fev-
  ered lips,
May give a shock of pleasure to the
  frame
More exquisite than when nectarean
  juice
Renews the life of joy in happiest
  hours.

Ion. Act I, Sc. 2

[1] Words writ in waters. — GEORGE CHAP-
MAN: *Revenge for Honour, Act V, Sc. 2*
  Below lies one whose name was traced in
sand. — DAVID GRAY
  Among the many things he has requested of
me to-night, this is the principal, — that on his
gravestone shall be this inscription. — RICH-
ARD MONCKTON MILNES: *Life, Letters, and
Literary Remains of John Keats, Vol. II,
P. 91, Letter to Severn*

  Fill the seats of justice
With good men, not so absolute in
  goodness
As to forget what human frailty is.

Ion. Act V

WILLIAM SIDNEY WALKER
[1795–1846]

Too solemn for day, too sweet for night,
Come not in darkness, come not in
  light;
But come in some twilight interim,
When the gloom is soft, and the light
  is dim.

*From the Oxford Book of
English Verse*

ALFRED BUNN
[1796–1860]

I dreamt that I dwelt in marble halls,
With vassals and serfs at my side.

The Bohemian Girl. Act 2, Song

But — I also dreamt, which pleas'd me
  most,
That you loved me still the same.

Ibid.

HARTLEY COLERIDGE
[1796–1849]

Be not afraid to pray; to pray is right.
Pray, if thou canst, with hope, but ever
  pray,
Though hope be weak, or sick with
  long delay.
Pray in the darkness if there be no
  light.

Prayer

The soul of man is larger than the sky,
  Deeper than ocean, or the abysmal
    dark
Of the unfathomed center.

To Shakespeare

  On this hapless earth
There's small sincerity of mirth,
And laughter oft is but an art
To drown the outcry of the heart.

Address to Certain Gold-fishes

She is not fair to outward view
  As many maidens be;
Her loveliness I never knew
  Until she smiled on me:

Oh! then I saw her eye was bright,
A well of love, a spring of light.
Song, She Is Not Fair
Her very frowns are fairer far
Than smiles of other maidens are.
Ibid.

THOMAS CHANDLER HALI-BURTON ("SAM SLICK")
[1796–1865]

I want you to see Peel, Stanley, Graham, Sheil, Russell, Macaulay, Old Joe, and soon. They are all upper-crust here.[1]
Sam Slick in England.[2] *Chap. XXIV*
Circumstances alter cases.
The Old Judge. Chap. XV
We reckon hours and minutes to be dollars and cents.[3]
The Clockmaker
We can do without any article of luxury we have never had; but when once obtained, it is not in human natur' to surrender it voluntarily.
Ibid.

HORACE MANN [4]
[1796–1859]

Lost, yesterday, somewhere between sunrise and sunset, two golden hours, each set with sixty diamond minutes. No reward is offered for they are gone forever.
Aphorism

[1] Those families, you know, are our upper-crust, — not upper ten thousand. — JAMES FENIMORE COOPER [1789–1851]: *The Ways of the Hour, Chap. VI* [1850]
At present there is no distinction among the upper ten thousand of the city. — N. P. WILLIS: *Necessity for a Promenade Drive*
[2] The "Sam Slick" papers first appeared in a weekly paper in Nova Scotia in 1836.
[3] Remember that time is money. — BENJAMIN FRANKLIN: *Advice to a Young Tradesman* [1748]
[4] American educator. Not to be confused with Sir Horace Mann [1701–1786], the correspondent of Horace Walpole.

WILLIAM AUGUSTUS MUHLENBERG
[1796–1877]

I would not live alway: I ask not to stay
Where storm after storm rises dark o'er the way.
I Would Not Live Alway. Stanza 2
That heavenly music! what is it I hear?
The notes of the harpers ring sweet in mine ear.
And, see, soft unfolding those portals of gold,
The King all arrayed in his beauty behold!
Ibid. Stanza 6

JAMES ROBINSON PLANCHÉ
[1796–1880]

Gentle Zitella, whither away?
Love's ritornella list, while I play.
The Brigand. Love's Ritornella

WILLIAM HICKLING PRESCOTT
[1796–1859]

The surest test of the civilization of a people — at least, as sure as any — afforded by mechanical art is to be found in their architecture, which presents so noble a field for the display of the grand and the beautiful, and which, at the same time, is so intimately connected with the essential comforts of life.
The Conquest of Peru. Book I, Chap. 5
Where there is no free agency, there can be no morality. Where there is no temptation, there can be little claim to virtue.[1] Where the routine is rigorously proscribed by law, the law, and not the man, must have the credit of the conduct.
Ibid.

[1] There's many a life of sweet content Whose virtue is environment. — WALTER LEARNED [1847–1915]: *On the Fly-Leaf of Manon Lescaut*

Drawing his sword he traced a line with it on the sand from East to West. Then, turning towards the South, "Friends and comrades!" he said, "on that side are toil, hunger, nakedness, the drenching storm, desertion, and death; on this side ease and pleasure. There lies Peru with its riches; here, Panama and its poverty. Choose, each man, what best becomes a brave Castilian. For my part, I go to the South." So saying, he stepped across the line.

The Conquest of Peru.
Book II, Chap. 4

RICHARD RYAN
[1796–1849]

O, saw ye the lass wi' the bonnie blue een?
Her smile is the sweetest that ever was seen,
Her cheek like the rose is, but fresher, I ween,
She's the loveliest lassie that trips on the green.

O, Saw Ye the Lass

JOSEPH AUGUSTINE WADE
[1796–1845]

Meet me by moonlight alone,
  And then I will tell you a tale
Must be told by the moonlight alone,
  In the grove at the end of the vale!
You must promise to come, for I said
  I would show the night-flowers their queen.
Nay, turn not away that sweet head,
  'Tis the loveliest ever was seen.

Meet Me by Moonlight

THOMAS HAYNES BAYLY
[1797–1839]

I'd be a butterfly born in a bower,
  Where roses and lilies and violets meet.

I'd Be a Butterfly. Stanza 1

Those who have wealth must be watchful and wary,
  Power, alas! naught but misery brings!

Ibid. Stanza 2

Oh no! we never mention her, — [1]
Her name is never heard;
My lips are now forbid to speak
That once familiar word.

Oh No! We Never Mention Her

We met, — 'twas in a crowd. [2]

We Met

Gayly the troubadour
  Touched his guitar.

Welcome Me Home. Stanza 1

Why don't the men propose, Mamma?
Why don't the men propose?

Why Don't the Men Propose?

She wore a wreath of roses
The first night that we met.

She Wore a Wreath

Friends depart, and memory takes them
  To her caverns, pure and deep.

Teach Me to Forget

Tell me the tales that to me were so dear,
  Long, long ago, long, long ago.

Long, Long Ago [3]

The rose that all are praising
  Is not the rose for me.

The Rose That All Are Praising

Oh pilot, 'tis a fearful night!
There's danger on the deep.

The Pilot

Absence makes the heart grow fonder: [4]
Isle of Beauty, fare thee well!

Isle of Beauty

Oh, I have roamed o'er many lands,
  And many friends I've met;
Not one fair scene or kindly smile
  Can this fond heart forget.

Oh, Steer My Bark to Erin's Isle

My fond affection thou hast seen,
  Then judge of my regret

---

[1] Variant: "Oh, no, we never mention him."

[2] Parodied by THOMAS HOOD: "We met, — 'twas in a mob."

[3] A temperance song, sung in the meetings held by John B. Gough, was adapted by Mrs. M. LINDSAY BLISS from Bayly's *Long, Long Ago,* and became as popular as the original.
Where are the friends that to me were so dear?

[4] I find that absence still increases love. — CHARLES HOPKINS [1664–1700]: *To C. C.* [1694]
Distance sometimes endears friendship, and absence sweeteneth it. — JAMES HOWELL [1594–1666]: *Familiar Letters, Book I, Sect. 1, No. 6*

To think more happy thou hadst been
If we had never met.
To My Wife

I'm saddest when I sing.[1]
You Think I Have a Merry Heart

SAMUEL LOVER
[1797–1868]

A baby was sleeping,
Its mother was weeping,
For her husband was far on the wild-
raging sea.
The Angel's Whisper

Reproof on her lip, but a smile in her
eye.
Rory O'More. Stanza 1

For dhrames always go by contrairies,
my dear.
Ibid. Stanza 2

"That's eight times to-day that you've
kissed me before."
"Then here goes another," says he, "to
make sure,
For there's luck in odd numbers," says
Rory O'More.[2]
Ibid. Stanza 3

As she sat in the low-backed car
The man at the turn-pike bar
Never asked for the toll
But just rubbed his old poll
And looked after the low-backed car.
The Low-Backed Car. Stanza 1

Sure my love is all crost
Like a bud in the frost
And there's no use at all in my going
to bed,
For 'tis dhrames and not slape that
comes into my head!
Molly Carew

And with my advice, faith I wish you'd
take me.
Widow Machree

Sure the shovel and tongs
To each other belongs.
Ibid.

[1] I am saddest when I sing. — CHARLES FAR-
RAR BROWNE. *Artemus Ward's Lecture*
[2] Also said VIRGIL, *Eclogue VIII, 75:
Numero Deus impare gaudet* (God delights
in an odd number).

WILLIAM MOTHERWELL
[1797–1835]

I've wandered east, I've wandered west,
Through mony a weary way;
But never, never can forget
The luve o' life's young day!
Jeannie Morrison. Stanza 1

'Twas then we luvit ilk ither weel,
'Twas then we twa did part:
Sweet time — sad time! twa bairns at
scule —
Twa bairns and but ae heart.[1]
Ibid. Stanza 3

MARY WOLLSTONECRAFT
SHELLEY
[1797–1851]

I beheld the wretch — the miserable
monster whom I had created.
Frankenstein. Chap. 5

MACDONALD CLARKE
[1798–1842]

Whilst twilight's curtain spreading far,
Was pinned with a single star.[2]
*Death in Disguise. Line 227
[Boston edition, 1833]*

Ha! see where the wild-blazing Grog-
shop appears,
As the red waves of wretchedness
swell;
How it burns on the edge of tempestu-
ous years —
The horrible Light-house of Hell!
The Rum-hole

[1] See Alexander Pope, page 219.
[2] *Variant:* While twilight's curtain gathering far
Is pinned with a single diamond
star

Mrs. L. M. Child says: "He thus describes
the closing day: —
'Now twilight lets her curtain down,
And pins it with a star.' "

The moon is a silver pinhead vast
That holds the heavens tent-hangings fast.
WILLIAM ROUNSEVILLE ALGER [1822–
1905]: *The Use of the Moon*
When the curtains of night are pinned back
by the stars. — Old song: *I'll Remember You,
Love, in My Prayers*

JOHN ADAMS DIX
[1798–1879]

If any one attempts to haul down the American flag, shoot him on the spot.

An Official Despatch
[January 29, 1861]

ROBERT GILFILLAN
[1798–1850]

There's a hope for every woe,
  And a balm for every pain,[1]
But the first joys of our heart
  Come never back again!

The Exile's Song. Stanza 4

In the days of langsyne we were happy and free,
Proud lords on the land, and kings on the sea!
To our foes we were fierce, to our friends we were kind,
And where battle raged loudest, you ever did find
The banner o' Scotland float high in the wind!

In the Days o' Langsyne. Stanza 2

THOMAS HOOD
[1798–1845]

There is a silence where hath been no sound,
There is a silence where no sound may be,
In the cold grave — under the deep, deep sea,
Or in wide desert where no life is found.

Sonnet, Silence

We watched her breathing through the night,
  Her breathing soft and low,
As in her breast the wave of life
  Kept heaving to and fro.

The Death-Bed. Stanza 1

Our very hopes belied our fears,
  Our fears our hopes belied; —
We thought her dying when she slept,
  And sleeping when she died.

Ibid. Stanza 3

Never go to France
  Unless you know the lingo,

If you do, like me,
  You will repent, by jingo.

French and English. Stanza 1

Never, from folly or urbanity,
Praise people thus profusely to their faces,
Till quite in love with their own graces,
They're eaten up by vanity!

The Turtles. Moral

My life was like a London fog —
What d'ye think of that, my Cat?
What d'ye think of that, my Dog?

The Bachelor's Dream. Stanza 8

I remember, I remember
The house where I was born,
The little window where the sun
Came peeping in at morn;
He never came a wink too soon
Nor brought too long a day.

I Remember, I Remember. Stanza 1

I remember, I remember
The fir-trees dark and high;
I used to think their slender tops
Were close against the sky:
It was a childish ignorance,
But now 'tis little joy
To know I'm farther off from heaven
Than when I was a boy.

Ibid. Stanza 4

She stood breast-high amid the corn,[1]
Clasped by the golden light of morn,
Like the sweetheart of the sun,
Who many a glowing kiss had won.

Ruth. Stanza 1

Thus she stood amid the stooks,
Praising God with sweetest looks.

Ibid. Stanza 4

When he's forsaken,
  Withered and shaken,
What can an old man do but die?

Spring It Is Cheery. Stanza 1

And there is even a happiness
That makes the heart afraid.

Ode to Melancholy

There's not a string attuned to mirth
But has its chord in melancholy.

Ibid.

But evil is wrought by want of thought,
As well as want of heart.

The Lady's Dream. Stanza 16

---

[1] There are balms for all our pain. — R. H. STODDARD: *The Flight of Youth*

[1] She stood in tears amid the alien corn. — KEATS: *Ode to a Nightingale*

Oh! would I were dead now,
Or up in my bed now,
To cover my head now,
   And have a good cry!
         A Table of Errata. Stanza 15
Straight down the Crooked Lane,
And all round the Square.
         A Plain Direction. Stanza 1
Be contented. Thou hast got
The most of heaven in thy young lot;
There's sky-blue in thy cup.
      Ode on a Distant Prospect of
            Clapham College
Two stern-faced men set out from Lynn
   through the cold and heavy mist,
And Eugene Aram walked between
   with gyves upon his wrist.
      The Dream of Eugene Aram.
            Stanza 36
No sun — no moon!
No morn — no noon —
No dawn — no dusk — no proper time
   of day —
No sky — no earthly view —
No distance looking blue —
No road — no street — no "t'other
   side the way."
                        No
No warmth, no cheerfulness, no health-
   ful ease,
   No comfortable feel in any mem-
   ber —
No shade, no shine, no butterflies, no
   bees,
   No fruits, no flowers, no leaves, no
   birds,
            November!
                     Ibid.
Seem'd washing his hands with invis-
   ible soap
In imperceptible water.
      Miss Kilmansegg and Her Pre-
      cious Leg. Her Christening,
            Stanza 10
O bed! O bed! delicious bed!
That heaven upon earth to the weary
   head!
      Ibid. Her Dream, Stanzas 7, 8
He lies like a hedgehog rolled up the
   wrong way,
   Tormenting himself with his prick-
   les.
            Ibid. Stanza 14

There's a double beauty whenever a
   swan
Swims on a lake, with her double
   thereon.[1]
      Miss Kilmansegg and Her Pre-
      cious Leg. Her Honeymoon,
            Stanza 9
Home-made dishes that drive one from
   home.
            Ibid. Her Misery, Stanza 1
Gold! Gold! Gold! Gold!
Bright and yellow, hard and cold.
            Ibid. Her Moral
Spurned by the young, but hugged by
   the old
To the very verge of the churchyard
   mould.
                     Ibid.
How widely its agencies vary, —
To save — to ruin — to curse — to
   bless, —
As even its minted coins express,
Now stamped with the image of Good
   Queen Bess,
And now of a Bloody Mary.
                     Ibid.
Another tumble! — that's his precious
   nose!
      Parental Ode to My Infant Son.
            Stanza 3
Boughs are daily rifled
   By the gusty thieves,
And the book of Nature
   Getteth short of leaves.
            The Season. Stanza 2
With fingers weary and worn,
   With eyelids heavy and red,
A woman sat in unwomanly rags
   Plying her needle and thread —
Stitch! stitch! stitch!
      The Song of the Shirt. Stanza 1
O men, with sisters dear!
O men, with mothers and wives!
It is not linen you're wearing out,
   But human creatures' lives![2]
            Ibid. Stanza 4

---

[1] The swan on still St. Mary's lake
   Float double, swan and shadow!
   WORDSWORTH: *Yarrow Unvisited,*
                              St. 6

[2] It's no fish ye're buying, it's men's lives. —
   SCOTT: *The Antiquary, Chap.* 11

Sewing at once with a double thread,
A shroud as well as a shirt.
>*The Song of the Shirt. Stanza 4*

O God! that bread should be so dear,
And flesh and blood so cheap!
>*Ibid. Stanza 5*

No blessed leisure for love or hope,
But only time for grief.
>*Ibid. Stanza 10*

My tears must stop, for every drop
Hinders needle and thread.
>*Ibid.*

A wife who preaches in her gown,
And lectures in her night-dress.
>*The Surplice Question. Stanza 2*

I saw old Autumn in the misty morn
Stand shadowless like silence, listening
To silence.
>*Ode, Autumn. Stanza 1*

Peace and rest at length have come
All the day's long toil is past,
And each heart is whispering, "Home,
Home at last."
>*Home at Last*

Ben Battle was a soldier bold,
And used to war's alarms;
But a cannon-ball took off his legs,
So he laid down his arms!
>*Faithless Nellie Gray. Stanza 1*

One more unfortunate,
Weary of breath,
Rashly importunate,
Gone to her death!
>*The Bridge of Sighs. Stanza 1*

Take her up tenderly,
Lift her with care;
Fashioned so slenderly,
Young, and so fair!
>*Ibid. Stanza 2*

Alas for the rarity
Of Christian charity
Under the sun! [1]
>*Ibid. Stanza 9*

No solemn sanctimonious face I pull,
Nor think I'm pious when I'm only
bilious;
Nor study in my sanctum supercilious,

[1] See Southey, page 322.
The organized charity, scrimped and iced,
In the name of a cautious, statistical Christ.
>JOHN BOYLE O'REILLY: *In Bohemia, St. 5*

To frame a Sabbath Bill or forge a
Bull.
>*Ode to Rae Wilson*

His death, which happened in his
berth,
At forty-odd befell:
They went and told the sexton, and
The sexton tolled the bell.
>*Faithless Sally Brown. Stanza 17*

That fierce thing
They call a conscience.
>*Lamia. Scene VII*

O'er the earth there comes a bloom;
Sunny light for sullen gloom;
Warm perfume for vapour cold —
I smell the rose above the mould!
>*Farewell, Life*

GEORGE LINLEY
[1798–1865]

Among our ancient mountains,
And from our lovely vales,
Oh, let the prayer re-echo:
"God bless the Prince of Wales!"
>*God Bless the Prince of Wales.*
>*Stanza 1*

Above the throne of England
May fortune's star long shine,
And round its sacred bulwarks
The olive branches twine.
>*Ibid. Stanza 4*

Thou art gone from my gaze like a
beautiful dream,
And I seek thee in vain by the meadow
and stream.
>*Thou Art Gone*

Tho' lost to sight, to memory dear
Thou ever wilt remain;
One only hope my heart can cheer, —
The hope to meet again.
>*Song* [1]

[1] This song was written and composed by Linley for Mr. Augustus Braham, and sung by him. It is not known when it was written, — probably about 1830.
Another song, entitled *Though Lost to Sight, to Memory Dear,* was published in London in 1880, purporting to have been written by Ruthven Jenkyns in 1703 and published in the *Magazine for Mariners.* That magazine, however, never existed, and the composer of the music acknowledged, in a private letter, that he copied the words from an American newspaper. The reputed author, Ruthven Jen-

DAVID MACBETH MOIR
("DELTA")
[1798–1851]

To me, through every season dearest;
  In every scene, by day, by night,
Thou, present to my mind appearest
  A quenchless star, forever bright;
  My solitary sole delight:
Where'er I am, by shore, at sea,
  I think of thee.
                    When Thou at Eve

Were life spun out a thousand years,
It could not match Langsyne.
                    Langsyne. Stanza 1

ROBERT POLLOK
[1798–1827]

Sorrows remembered sweeten present
  joy.
  The Course of Time. Book I, Line 464

Most wondrous book! bright candle of
  the Lord!
Star of Eternity! The only star
By which the bark of man could navi-
  gate
The sea of life, and gain the coast of
  bliss
Securely.
                    Ibid. Book II, Line 270

He touched his harp, and nations
  heard, entranced,
As some vast river of unfailing source,
Rapid, exhaustless, deep, his numbers
  flowed,
And opened new fountains in the human heart.
                    Ibid. Book IV, Line 684

He laid his hand upon "the Ocean's
  mane," [1]
And played familiar with his hoary
  locks.
                    Ibid. Line 689

kyns, was living, under another name, in Cali-
fornia in 1882.
  Absent or dead, still let a friend be dear. —
ALEXANDER POPE: *Epistle to Robert, Earl of
Oxford and Mortimer*
[1] See Byron, page 355.

HENRY SCOTT RIDDELL
[1798–1870]

Then Scotland's dales and Scotland's
  vales,
  And Scotland's hills for me;
I'll drink a cup to Scotland yet,
  Wi' a' the honours three.
                    Scotland Yet. Stanza 2

AMOS BRONSON ALCOTT
[1799–1888]

Greater is he who is above temptation than he who being tempted overcomes.
                    Orphic Sayings. No. 12
The true teacher defends his pupils
against his own personal influence. He
inspires self-distrust. He guides their
eyes from himself to the spirit that
quickens him. He will have no disciple.
                    Ibid. The Teacher
Who loves a garden still his Eden keeps,
Perennial pleasures plants, and wholesome harvests reaps.
                    Tablets. Page 6
Nature is thought immersed in matter.
                    Ibid. Page 176
I press thee to my heart as Duty's
  faithful child.
                    Sonnet to Louisa May Alcott

RUFUS CHOATE
[1799–1859]

The courage of New England was
the "courage of Conscience." It did
not rise to that insane and awful passion, the love of war for itself.
                    *Address at Ipswich Centennial
                    [1834]*
The final end of Government is not
to exert restraint but to do good.
                    *Speech, The Necessity of Com-
                    promise in American Politics,
                    U. S. Senate [July 2, 1841]*
There was a state without king or
nobles; there was a church without a
bishop; [1] there was a people governed

[1] The Americans equally detest the pageantry of a king and the supercilious hypocrisy
of a bishop. — JUNIUS: *Letter XXXV [Dec.*

by grave magistrates which it had selected, and by equal laws which it had framed.

Speech before the New England Society [December 22, 1843]

We join ourselves to no party that does not carry the flag and keep step to the music of the Union.

Letter to the Whig Convention, Worcester [October 1, 1855]

Its constitution the glittering and sounding generalities [1] of natural right which make up the Declaration of Independence.

Letter to the Maine Whig Committee [1856]

GEORGE DUBOURG
[1799–1882]

A lady help wanted — genteel and refined,
Obliging and cheerful, industrious and kind.

Wanted, a Lady Help

An orphan or destitute lady would find
In return for her services treatment most kind.[2]

Ibid.

19, 1769]. Compare the anonymous poem, *The Puritans' Mistake*, published by Oliver Ditson in 1844: —

Oh, we are weary pilgrims; to this wilderness we bring
A Church without a bishop, a State without a King.

It [Calvinism] established a religion without a prelate, a government without a king. — GEORGE BANCROFT: *History of the United States, Vol. III, Chap. VI*

[1] Six years earlier, Choate gave a lecture in Providence, a review of which, by FRANKLIN J. DICKMAN, appeared in the *Journal* of Dec. 14, 1849. Unless Choate used the words "glittering generalities," and Dickman made reference to them, it would seem as if Dickman must have the credit of inventing the phrase. He wrote: "We fear that the glittering generalities of the speaker have left an impression more delightful than permanent."

[2] This doggerel somehow recalls *The Accomplished Female Friend*, by the Rev. CORNELIUS WHAURR, one stanza of which concludes: —

What lasting joys the man attend
Who has a Polished Female Friend.

MARY HOWITT
[1799–1888]

Old England is our home, and Englishmen are we;
Our tongue is known in every clime, our flag in every sea.

Old England Is Our Home

"Will you walk into my parlour?" said the spider to the fly;
" 'Tis the prettiest little parlour that ever you did spy."

The Spider and the Fly

"Arise, my maiden Mabel,"
Her mother said, "arise!
For the golden sun of midsummer
Is shining in the skies."

Mabel on Midsummer Day. Stanza 1

Little Gretchen, little Gretchen,
Wanders up and down the street.

The Little Match Girl.[1] Stanza 1

God might have bade the earth bring forth
Enough for great and small,
The oak-tree and the cedar-tree,
Without a flower at all.

The Use of Flowers. Stanza 1

GEORGE PAYNE RAINSFORD JAMES
[1799–1860]

I envy them, those monks of old;
Their books they read, and their beads they told.

The Monks of Old

Thou'rt an ass, Robin, thou'rt an ass,
To think that great men be
More gay than I that lie on the grass
Under the greenwood tree.
I tell thee no, I tell thee no,
The Great are slaves to their gilded show.

Richelieu. Chap. 3, Robber's Song, Stanza 1

The best happiness a woman can boast is that of being most carefully deceived.

Ibid. Chap. 4

[1] From the Danish of Hans Christian Andersen [1805–1875].

Turning over a page or two in the book of Nature, I found that the most brilliant actions and the greatest events were generally brought about from the meanest motives and most petty causes.

Richelieu. Chap. 5

Dirty fingers soil no gold.

Ibid.

A single word has sometimes lost or won an empire — even less than a single word, if we may believe the history of Darius's horse, who proclaimed his master emperor without speaking.[1]

Ibid. Chap. 6

A great bad man is worse than one of less talents, for he has the extended capability of doing harm.

Ibid.

Age is the most terrible misfortune that can happen to any man; other evils will mend, this is every day getting worse.

Ibid. Chap. 14

JOHN MOULTRIE
[1799–1874]

"Forget thee?" — If to dream by night
  and muse on thee by day,
If all the worship, deep and wild, a
  poet's heart can pay,
If prayers in absence breathed for thee
  to Heaven's protecting power,
If wingèd thoughts that flit to thee —
  a thousand in an hour,
If busy Fancy blending thee with all
  my future lot —
If this thou call'st forgetting, thou indeed shalt be forgot.

Forget Thee. Stanza 1

[1] The seven candidates for the throne of Persia agreed that he should be king whose horse neighed first. The horse of Darius was the first.

Who found more sweetness in his horse's
  neighing
Than all the Phrygian, Dorian, Lydian playing.

FULKE GREVILLE, LORD BROOKE
[1554–1628]

THOMAS NOEL
[1799–1861]

Rattle his bones over the stones!
He's only a pauper, whom nobody
  owns!

The Pauper's Drive. Stanza 1

By the waters of Life we sat together,
  Hand in hand, in the golden days
Of the beautiful early summer weather,
  When skies were purple and breath
  was praise.

An Old Man's Idyll

MISS WROTHER

Hope tells a flattering tale,
  Delusive, vain, and hollow.
Ah! let not hope prevail,
  Lest disappointment follow.[1]

The Universal Songster. Vol. II,
Page 86

JOSEPH ADDISON ALEXANDER
[1800–1860]

There is a time, we know not when,
  A point we know not where,
That marks the destiny of men,
  For glory or despair.

The Doomed Man. Stanza 1

There is a line, by us unseen,
  That crosses every path;
The hidden boundary between
  God's patience and His wrath.

Ibid. Stanza 2

CALDER CAMPBELL
[*Floruit* 1840]

I'll chase the antelope over the plain,
The tiger's cub I'll bind with a chain,
And the wild gazelle with its silvery
  feet
I'll give thee for a playmate sweet.

Ossian's Serenade.[2] *Refrain*

[1] Hope told a flattering tale,
    That Joy would soon return;
  Ah! naught my sighs avail,
    For Love is doomed to mourn.
  ANONYMOUS, air by Giovanni Paisiello [1741–1816]: *Universal Songster, Vol. I, P. 320*

[2] This song was published in *Godey's Lady's Book, Nov., 1840*. The sheet music was

Then come with me in my light canoe,
Where the sea is calm and the sky is
blue.
Ibid. Stanza 2

JULIA CRAWFORD
[1800–1885]

Kathleen mavourneen! the grey dawn
is breaking,
The horn of the hunter is heard on the
hill.
Kathleen Mavourneen. Stanza 1
Hast thou forgotten how soon we must
sever?
Oh! hast thou forgotten this day we
must part?
It may be for years, and it may be for-
ever;
Then why art thou silent, thou voice
of my heart?
Ibid.
We parted in silence, we parted by
night,
On the banks of that lonely river;
Where the fragrant limes their boughs
unite,
We met — and we parted forever!
We Parted in Silence.
Stanza 1
Rest, thou troubled heart,
Within this captive bosom swelling;
Rest, thou troubled heart,
No more of love or glory telling.
Now no more by wrongs or tyrant
power oppressed,
From a thousand woes,
Ah, what sweet repose
Soon will seal these eyes in everlasting
rest.
Pestal's Lay.[1] Rest, Troubled
Heart

---

brought out by Oliver Ditson Company, Boston, in 1850. The song was known as *Ossian's
Serenade,* as it was sung by Ossian E. Dodge,
a popular entertainer of the period. He
achieved fame, or notoriety, when he purchased the first ticket sold for Jenny Lind's
first Boston concert under the auspices of
P. T. Barnum, paying $625 for it.
See Thomas Moore, page 338.
[1] Paul Pestal [1794–1826], a Russian colonel of infantry, is said to have scratched the
words and music of a song on the wall of his

KENELM HENRY DIGBY
[1800–1880]

Island of Saints, still constant, still al-
lied
To the great truths opposed to human
pride;
Island of ruins, towers, cloisters grey,
Whence palmer kings with pontiffs
once did stray
To Rome and Sion, or to kindle fire
Which amid later darkness can inspire
Lands that in fondest memory and
song
Thy pristine glory fearlessly prolong.
Erin

MILLARD FILLMORE
[1800–1874]

Let us remember that revolutions do
not always establish freedom.
Third Annual Address
[December 6, 1852]
It is not strange . . . that such an
exuberance of enterprise should cause
some individuals to mistake change for
progress, and the invasion of the rights
of others for national prowess and
glory.
Ibid.

JOHN WOODCOCK GRAVES
[*Circa* 1800]

Do ye ken John Peel with his coat so
gay?
Do ye ken John Peel at the break of
day?
John Peel. Old Hunting Song
[1832]

---

prison cell while awaiting execution. There
are at least two other versions of his song,
both anonymous:
Yes! it comes at last,
And from a troubled dream awaking,
Death will soon be past,
And brighter worlds around me breaking.
Pestal's Lay, St. 1
Yes! the die is cast!
The turbid dream of life is waning,
The gulf will soon be past,
The soul immortal joy attaining.
In *The Silver Bell* [a school
songbook, 1864]

'Twas the sound of his horn brought
    me from my bed,
And the cry of his hounds, which he
    oft-times led,
For Peel's view-hallo would waken the
    dead,
Or the fox from his lair in the morn-
    ing.

    John Peel. Old Hunting Song
        [1832]. Refrain

JAMES GILBORNE LYONS
[1800–1868]

Now gather all our Saxon bards — let
    harps and hearts be strung,
To celebrate the triumphs of our own
    good Saxon tongue!
For stronger far than hosts that march
    with battle-flags unfurled,
It goes with freedom, thought, and
    truth to rouse and rule the world.

    The Triumphs of the English
        Language

THOMAS BABINGTON,
LORD MACAULAY
[1800–1859]

That is the best government which
desires to make the people happy, and
knows how to make them happy.

    On Mitford's History of Greece
    (In Knight's Quarterly, No-
    vember, 1824)

Free trade, one of the greatest blessings which a government can confer on
a people, is in almost every country unpopular.

    Ibid.

Wherever literature consoles sorrow
or assuages pain; wherever it brings
gladness to eyes which fail with wakefulness and tears, and ache for the dark
house and the long sleep, — there is
exhibited in its noblest form the immortal influence of Athens.

    Ibid.

Out of his surname they have coined
an epithet for a knave, and out of his

Christian name a synonym for the
Devil.[1]

    On Niccolo de Machiavelli (In
    Edinburgh Review, March,
    1825)

Nothing is so useless as a general
maxim.

    Ibid.

We hold that the most wonderful and
splendid proof of genius is a great
poem produced in a civilized age.

    On Milton (In Edinburgh Re-
    view, August, 1825)

Nobles by the right of an earlier
creation, and priests by the imposition
of a mightier hand.

    Ibid.

Our academical Pharisees.

    Ibid.

The dust and silence of the upper
shelf.

    Ibid.

Perhaps no person can be a poet, or
even can enjoy poetry, without a certain unsoundness of mind.

    Ibid.

The English Bible, — a book which
if everything else in our language
should perish, would alone suffice to
show the whole extent of its beauty
and power.

    On John Dryden (In Edin-
    burgh Review, January, 1828)

His imagination resembled the wings
of an ostrich. It enabled him to run,
though not to soar.

    Ibid.

A man possessed of splendid talents,
which he often abused, and of a sound
judgment, the admonitions of which he
often neglected; a man who succeeded
only in an inferior department of his
art, but who, in that department, succeeded pre-eminently.

    Ibid.

The gallery in which the reporters
sit has become a fourth estate of the
realm.[2]

    On Hallam's Constitutional
    History [September, 1828]

---

[1] Nick Machiavel had ne'er a trick,
  Though he gave his name to our Old Nick.
    SAMUEL BUTLER: *Hudibras, III, I, 1313*
[2] See Carlyle, pages 377, 380, 381.

Men are never so likely to settle a question rightly as when they discuss it freely.

Southey's Colloquies [*January, 1830*]

Nothing is so galling to a people, not broken in from the birth, as a paternal or, in other words, a meddling government, a government which tells them what to read and say and eat and drink and wear.

Ibid.

I have not the Chancellor's [Brougham] encyclopedic mind. He is indeed a kind of semi-Solomon. He *half* knows everything, from the cedar to the hyssop.[1]

Letter to Macvey Napier [*December 17, 1830*]

He had a head which statuaries loved to copy, and a foot the deformity of which the beggars in the streets mimicked.

On Moore's Life of Lord Byron [*June, 1831*]

We know no spectacle so ridiculous as the British public in one of its periodical fits of morality.

Ibid.

From the poetry of Lord Byron they drew a system of ethics compounded of misanthropy and voluptuousness, — a system in which the two great commandments were to hate your neighbour and to love your neighbour's wife.

Ibid.

What a singular destiny has been that of this remarkable man! — To be regarded in his own age as a classic, and in ours as a companion! To receive from his contemporaries that full homage which men of genius have in general received only from posterity; to be more intimately known to posterity than other men are known to their contemporaries!

On Boswell's Life of Johnson [*September, 1831*]

That wonderful book, while it obtains admiration from the most fastidious critics, is loved by those who are too simple to admire it.

On Bunyan's Pilgrim's Progress [*December, 1831*]

The conformation of his mind was such that whatever was little seemed to him great, and whatever was great seemed to him little.

On Horace Walpole [*1833*]

An acre in Middlesex is better than a principality in Utopia.[1]

On Lord Bacon

Temple was a man of the world among men of letters, a man of letters among men of the world.[2]

On Sir William Temple [*October, 1838*]

She [the Roman Catholic Church] may still exist in undiminished vigour when some traveller from New Zealand shall, in the midst of a vast solitude, take his stand on a broken arch of London Bridge to sketch the ruins of St. Paul's.[3]

On Ranke's History of the Popes [*October, 1840*]

[1] I wish I were as sure of anything as Macaulay is of everything. — WILLIAM WINDHAM [1750-1810]. Attributed also to William Lamb, Viscount Melbourne [1779-1848].

[1] Utopia, from the Greek, *no-place*. In Sir Thomas More's political romance, Utopia was an imaginary island, where the laws, the politics, the morals, and the institutions were perfect.
Better fifty years of Europe than a cycle of Cathay. — TENNYSON: *Locksley Hall, L. 184*
[2] See Pope, page 215.
[3] The same image was employed by Macaulay in 1824 in the concluding paragraph of a review of MITFORD'S *Greece*, and he repeated it in his review of MILL'S *Essay on Government* in 1829.
What cities, as great as this, have . . . promised themselves immortality! Posterity can hardly trace the situation of some. The sorrowful traveller wanders over the awful ruins of others. . . . Here stood their citadel, but now grown over with weeds; there their senate-house, but now the haunt of every noxious reptile; temples and theatres stood here, now only an undistinguished heap of ruins. — GOLDSMITH: *The Bee, No. IV* [1759], *A City Night-Piece*
Who knows but that hereafter some traveller like myself will sit down upon the banks of the Seine, the Thames, or the Zuyder Zee, where now, in the tumult of enjoyment, the heart and the eyes are too slow to take in the multitude of sensations? Who knows but he

She [the Catholic Church] thoroughly understands what no other Church has ever understood, how to deal with enthusiasts.

On Ranke's History of the Popes
[October, 1840]

He [Warren Hastings] was a man for whom nature had done much of what the Stoic philosophy pretended. *"Mens aequa in arduis"* [1] is the inscription under his picture in the Government house at Calcutta, and never was there a more appropriate motto.

Letter to Macvey Napier
[January 11, 1841]

The chief-justice was rich, quiet, and infamous.

On Warren Hastings [October, 1841]

In that temple of silence and reconciliation where the enmities of twenty generations lie buried, in the Great Abbey which has during many ages afforded a quiet resting-place to those

---

will sit down solitary amid silent ruins, and weep a people inurned and their greatness changed into an empty name? — CONSTANTIN DE VOLNEY [1757–1820]: *Ruins, Chap. II*

The next Augustan age will dawn on the other side of the Atlantic. There will, perhaps, be a Thucydides at Boston, a Xenophon at New York, in time a Virgil at Mexico, and a Newton at Peru. At last some curious traveller from Lima will visit England, and give a description of the ruins of St. Paul's, like the editions of Balbec and Palmyra. — HORACE WALPOLE: *Letter to Sir Horace Mann [Nov. 24, 1774]*

Where now is Britain? . . .
Even as the savage sits upon the stone
That marks where stood her capitols, and hears
The bittern booming in the weeds, he shrinks
From the dismaying solitude.
HENRY KIRKE WHITE [1785–1806]: *Time*

In the firm expectation that when London shall be a habitation of bitterns, when St. Paul and Westminster Abbey shall stand shapeless and nameless ruins in the midst of an unpeopled marsh, when the piers of Waterloo Bridge shall become the nuclei of islets of reeds and osiers, and cast the jagged shadows of their broken arches on the solitary stream, some Transatlantic commentator will be weighing in the scales of some new and now unimagined system of criticism the respective merits of the Bells and the Fudges and their historians. — SHELLEY: *Dedication to Peter Bell the Third*
[1] An even mind in difficulties.

whose minds and bodies have been shattered by the contentions of the Great Hall.

On Warren Hastings [October, 1841]

I shall not be satisfied unless I produce something which shall for a few days supersede the last fashionable novel on the tables of young ladies.

Letter to Macvey Napier
[November 5, 1841]

In order that he might rob a neighbour whom he had promised to defend, black men fought on the coast of Coromandel and red men scalped each other by the great lakes of North America.

On Frederic the Great
[April, 1842]

We hardly know an instance of the strength and weakness of human nature so striking and so grotesque as the character of this haughty, vigilant, resolute, sagacious blue-stocking,[1] half Mithridates and half Trissotin, bearing up against a world in arms, with an ounce of poison in one pocket and a quire of bad verses in the other.

Ibid.

A man who has never looked on Niagara has but a faint idea of a cataract; and he who has not read Barère's Memoirs may be said not to know what it is to lie.

Mémoires de Bertrand Barère
[1843]

Ambrose Phillips . . . who had the honour of bringing into fashion a species of composition which has been

---

[1] About 1748, Benjamin Stillingfleet [1702–1771] was a member of an assembly of men and women meeting to discuss literature, etc. He wore blue stockings. Such was the excellence of his conversation that his absence was felt to be so great a loss that it was said, "We can do nothing without the blue-stockings." Miss Hannah More has admirably described a Blue-stocking Club, in her *Bas Bleu*, a poem in which many of the persons who were most conspicuous there are mentioned.

From a discussion by BOSWELL in his *Life of Dr. Johnson, Vol. II, P. 390, Everyman ed.* Boswell's account is in 1781, but the *Dictionary of National Biography* gives the year as "C. 1748."

See Mrs. Browning, page 430.

called, after his name, Namby Pamby.[1]
Review of Aikin's Life of Addison
[July, 1843]

He [Steele] was a rake among scholars and a scholar among rakes.
Ibid.

The highest proof of virtue is to possess boundless power without abusing it.
Ibid.

There you sit, doing penance for the disingenuousness of years.[2]
Speech, House of Commons
[April 14, 1845]

Your Constitution is all sail and no anchor.
Letter to H. S. Randall, author of a Life of Thomas Jefferson
[May 23, 1857]

Those who compare the age in which their lot has fallen with a golden age which exists only in imagination, may talk of degeneracy and decay; but no man who is correctly informed as to the past, will be disposed to take a morose or desponding view of the present.
History of England. Vol. I,
Chap. 1

I shall cheerfully bear the reproach of having descended below the dignity of history [3] if I can succeed in placing before the English of the nineteenth century a true picture of the life of their ancestors.
Ibid.

The Puritan hated bear-baiting, not because it gave pain to the bear, but because it gave pleasure to the spectators.[4]
Ibid. Chap. 2

There were gentlemen and there were seamen in the navy of Charles II. But the seamen were not gentlemen, and the gentlemen were not seamen.
Ibid. Chap. 3

---

[1] See Henry Carey, page 189.
[2] Macaulay refers to Sir Robert Peel.
[3] The dignity of history. — BOLINGBROKE: *On the Study and Use of History, Letter V*
[4] Even bear-baiting was esteemed heathenish and unchristian: the sport of it, not the inhumanity, gave offence. — HUME: *History of England, Vol. I, Chap. LXII*

The ambassador [of Russia] and the grandees who accompanied him were so gorgeous that all London crowded to stare at them, and so filthy that nobody dared to touch them. They came to the court balls dropping pearls and vermin.
History of England. Vol. V,
Chap. 23

I met Sir Bulwer Lytton, or Lytton Bulwer. He is anxious about some scheme for some association of literary men. I detest all such associations. I hate the notion of gregarious authors. The less we have to do with each other, the better.
Quoted in GEORGE OTTO TRE-VELYAN: *Life and Letters of Lord Macaulay. Vol. II, Page 245 [Harper, 1877]*

Friends, how goes the fight?
The Battle of the Lake Regillus.
Stanza 16

These be the great Twin Brethren
To whom the Dorians pray.
Ibid. Stanza 40

To every man upon this earth
Death cometh soon or late;
And how can man die better
Than facing fearful odds
For the ashes of his fathers,
And the temples of his gods?
Lays of Ancient Rome. Horatius,
Stanza 27

The Romans were like brothers
In the brave days of old.
Ibid. Stanza 32

Those behind cried "Forward!"
And those before cried "Back!"
Ibid. Stanza 50

Oh, Tiber! father Tiber!
To whom the Romans pray,
A Roman's life, a Roman's arms,
Take thou in charge this day.
Ibid. Stanza 59

How well Horatius kept the bridge.
Ibid. Stanza 70

Press where ye see my white plume shine, amidst the ranks of war,
And be your oriflamme to-day the helmet of Navarre.
Ivry. Line 29

Such night in England ne'er had been,
    nor ne'er again shall be.
                    The Armada. Line 34

Oh! wherefore come ye forth, in tri-
    umph from the North,
With your hands, and your feet, and
    your raiment all red?
And wherefore doth your rout send
    forth a joyous shout?
And whence be the grapes of the
    wine-press which ye tread?
        The Battle of Naseby. Stanza 1

From a shore no search hath found,
    from a gulf no line can sound,
Without rudder or needle we steer;
Above, below, our bark dies the sea-
    fowl and the shark,
As we fly by the last Buccaneer.
        The Last Buccaneer. Stanza 3

April's ivory moonlight.
    The Prophecy of Capys. Stanza 18

The mighty name of Rome.
            Ibid. Stanza 31

Soon fades the spell, soon comes the
    night;
Say will it not be then the same,
Whether we played the black or white,
Whether we lost or won the game?
    Sermon in a Churchyard. Stanza 8

The sweeter sound of woman's praise.
    Lines Written July 30, 1847.
                    Stanza 20

Forget all feuds, and shed one English
    tear
O'er English dust. A broken heart lies
    here.
    Epitaph on a Jacobite [*1845*]

Ye diners-out from whom we guard
    our spoons.[1]
            Political Georgics

Who never forgot that the end of
Government is the happiness of the
governed.
    *Inscription for the Statue of
    Lord William Bentinck*

[1] I sent these lines to the "Times" about
three years ago. — *Letter* [June 29, 1831]
    The louder he talked of his honor, the
faster we counted our spoons. — EMERSON:
Conduct of Life, Worship

LUCIUS O'BRIEN
[? –1841]

To our old Alma Mater, our rock-
    bound Highland home,
We'll cast back many a fond regret, as
    o'er life's sea we roam,
Until on our last battlefield the lights
    of heaven shall glow,
We'll never fail to drink to her and
    Benny Havens, oh!
        West Point Song [1] [*1838*]

SIR HENRY TAYLOR
[1800–1886]

                    His food
Was glory, which was poison to his
    mind
And peril to his body.
    Philip Van Artevelde. Part I,
                Act I, Sc. 5

The world knows nothing of its great-
    est men.
                    Ibid.

An unreflected light did never yet
Dazzle the vision feminine.
                    Ibid.

He that lacks time to mourn, lacks
    time to mend.
Eternity mourns that. 'Tis an ill cure
For life's worst ills, to have no time to
    feel them.
Where sorrow's held intrusive and
    turned out,
There wisdom will not enter, nor true
    power,
Nor aught that dignifies humanity.
                    Ibid.

            We figure to ourselves
The thing we like; and then we build
    it up,
As chance will have it, on the rock or
    sand, —
For thought is tired of wandering o'er
    the world,
And homebound Fancy runs her bark
    ashore.
                    Ibid.

[1] Benny Havens had a shop on the academy
grounds. He died in 1877, at the age of 89,
and was buried in Highland Union Cemetery.
    Dr. O'Brien was appointed Second Lieu-
tenant, 8th U. S. Infantry, and promoted to
First Lieutenant, December 1, 1839.

Such souls,
Whose sudden visitations daze the
world,
Vanish like lightning, but they leave
behind
A voice that in the distance far away
Wakens the slumbering ages.
Philip Van Artevelde. Part I,
Act. I, Sc. 5

RICHARD BETHELL, LORD WESTBURY
[1800–1873]

A solicitor, after hearing Lord Westbury's opinion, ventured to say that he
had turned the matter over in his mind,
and thought that something might be
said on the other side; to which he replied, "Then, sir, you will turn it over
once more in what you are *pleased to
call your mind.*"
NASH: *Life of Lord Westbury.*
Vol. II, Page 292

JANE WELSH CARLYLE (MRS. THOMAS CARLYLE) [1]
[1801–1866]

Medical men all over the world having merely entered into a tacit agreement to call all sorts of maladies people are liable to, in cold weather, by
one name; so that one sort of treatment may serve for all, and their practice be thereby greatly simplified.
Letter to John Welsh
[March 4, 1837]
Some new neighbours, that came a
month or two ago, brought with them
an accumulation of all the things to
be guarded against in a London neighbourhood, viz., a pianoforte, a lap-dog,
and a parrot.
Letter to Mrs. Carlyle [May 6,
1839]

[1] I have read your glorious letters,
Where you threw aside all fetters,
Spoke your thoughts and mind out freely
In your own delightful style.
BESSIE CHANDLER: *To Mrs. Carlyle,*
St. 1 (In *Century Magazine, Nov.,*
1883)

Never does one feel oneself so utterly helpless as in trying to speak
comfort for great bereavement. I will
not try it. Time is the only comforter
for the loss of a mother.
Letter to Thomas Carlyle
[December 27, 1853]
If peace and quietness be not in one's
own power, one can always give one-
self at least bodily fatigue — no such
bad succedaneum after all.
Journal. October 23, 1855
When one has been threatened with
a great injustice, one accepts a smaller
as a favour.
Ibid. November 21, 1855
Of all God's creatures, man
Alone is poor.
To a Swallow Building Under
Our Eaves

GEORGE WASHINGTON CUTTER
[1801–1865]

Harness me down with your iron
bands,
Be sure of your curb and rein:
For I scorn the power of your puny
hands,
As the tempest scorns a chain.
Song of Steam. Stanza 1

JOHN ELLERTON

Now the labourer's task is o'er;
Now the battle day is past;
Now upon the farther shore
Lands the voyager at last.
Father, in Thy gracious keeping
Leave we now Thy servant sleeping.
Now the Labourer's Task Is
O'er. Stanza 1

DAVID GLASGOW FARRAGUT
[1801–1870]

Damn the torpedoes! Go ahead!
At Mobile Bay [August 5, 1864]

JOHN HENRY, CARDINAL NEWMAN
[1801–1890]

Time hath a taming hand.
> *Persecution. Stanza 3 [1832]*

Lead, kindly Light, amid the encircling gloom;
  Lead thou me on!
The night is dark, and I am far from home;
  Lead thou me on!
Keep thou my feet: I do not ask to see
The distant scene; one step enough for me.
> *The Pillar of the Cloud.*
> *Stanza 1 [1833]*

And with the morn, those angel faces smile
Which I have loved long since, and lost awhile.
> *Ibid. Stanza 3*

It is thy very energy of thought
Which keeps thee from thy God.
> *Dream of Gerontius. Part III*

Who lets his feelings run
In soft luxurious flow,
Shrinks when hard service must be done,
And faints at every woe.
> *Flowers Without Fruit*

Living Nature, not dull Art
Shall plan my ways and rule my heart.
> *Nature and Art. Stanza 12*

Mine, the Unseen to display
In the crowded public way,
Where life's busy arts combine
To shut out the Hand Divine.
> *Snapdragon*

Weep not for me;
Be blithe as wont, nor tinge with gloom
The stream of love that circles home,
  Light hearts and free!
Joy in the gifts Heaven's bounty lends,
Nor miss my face, dear friends!
  I still am near.
> *A Voice from Afar [Knowledge]. Stanza 1*

Growth is the only evidence of life.
> *Dr. Scott, cited by Cardinal Newman*

It is almost a definition of a gentleman to say he is one who never inflicts pain.
> *Idea of a University. The Man of the World*

If he be an unbeliever, he will be too profound and large-minded to ridicule religion or to act against it; he is too wise to be a dogmatist or fanatic in his infidelity. He respects piety and devotion; he even supports institutions as venerable, beautiful, or useful, to which he does not assent; he honours the ministers of religion, and it contents him to decline its mysteries without assailing or denouncing them.
> *Ibid.*

A great memory does not make a philosopher, any more than a dictionary can be called a grammar.
> *Ibid. Knowledge in Relation to Learning*

Ex Umbris et Imaginibus in Veritatem! (From shadows and symbols into the truth.)
> *Epitaph at Edgbaston, composed by himself.*

ALDEN C. SPOONER
[*Floruit* 1846]

I mused upon the Pilgrim flock
  Whose luck it was to land
Upon almost the only rock
  Among the Plymouth sand.[1]
> *Old Times and New. Stanza 2 (Written for the New England Society Festival, New York, December 22, 1846)*

LYDIA MARIA CHILD
[1802–1880]

Pillars are falling at thy feet,
  Fanes quiver in the air,
A prostrate city is thy seat,
  And thou alone art there.
> *Marius Amid the Ruins of Carthage*

---

[1] How much better if Plymouth Rock had landed on the Pilgrims. — Modern saying, origin dubious.

Genius hath electric power
Which earth can never tame,
Bright suns may scorch and dark
    clouds lower,
Its flash is still the same.
                Marius Amid the Ruins of
                                Carthage

Over the river and through the wood,
To grandfather's house we'll go;
    The horse knows the way
    To carry the sleigh,
Through the white and drifted snow.
                Thanksgiving Day. Stanza 1

ALBERT GORTON GREENE
[1802–1868]

Old Grimes is dead, that good old man
We never shall see more;
He used to wear a long black coat
All buttoned down before.[1]
                Old Grimes. Stanza 1

He had no malice in his mind,
No ruffles on his shirt.
                Ibid. Stanza 8

His knowledge hid from public gaze,
He did not bring to view,
Nor made a noise town-meeting days,
As many people do.
                Ibid. Stanza 10

His worldly goods he never threw
In trust to fortune's chances.
                Ibid. Stanza 11

Fill every beaker up, my men, pour
    forth the cheering wine:
There's life and strength in every drop,
    — thanksgiving to the vine!
                The Baron's Last Banquet.
                                Stanza 7

1 John Lee is dead, that good old man, —
    We ne'er shall see him more;
    He used to wear an old drab coat
    All buttoned down before.
To the memory of John Lee, who died
    May 21, 1823.
    An Inscription in Matherne Churchyard
Old Abram Brown is dead and gone, —
    You'll never see him more;
    He used to wear a long brown coat
    That buttoned down before.
    HALLIWELL: *Nursery Rhymes of
                England, P. 60*

LETITIA ELIZABETH LANDON
[1802–1838]

As beautiful as woman's blush, —
As evanescent too.
                Apple Blossoms

Were it not better to forget
Than but remember and regret?
                Despondency

GEORGE POPE MORRIS
[1802–1864]

Woodman, spare that tree!
    Touch not a single bough! [1]
In youth it sheltered me,
    And I'll protect it now.
                *Woodman, Spare That Tree.
                        Stanza 1 [1830]*

The iron-armed soldier, the true-
    hearted soldier,
The gallant old soldier of Tippecanoe.[2]
                *Campaign Song for William
                        Henry Harrison [1840]*

A song for our banner! The watchword
    recall
    Which gave the Republic her sta-
        tion:
"United we stand, divided we fall!" [3]
    It made and preserves us a nation! [4]
                *The Flag of Our Union.
                                Stanza 1*

The union of lakes, the union of lands,
    The union of States none can sever,

1 See Campbell, page 328. — It is interesting
to remember that the elm tree for which Morris pleaded stood just about where is now the
crossing of 98th Street and West End Avenue,
New York. See RIDER's *Guide to New York
City, P. 346.*
2 Harrison had distinguished himself in a
victorious battle with Indians, near Tippecanoe River [Indiana], November 7, 1811.
Morris's words, sung to the tune of "The Old
Oaken Bucket," were immensely popular. For
the first time in our land the power of song
was invoked to aid a Presidential candidate.
— BENJAMIN PERLEY POORE [1820–1887]:
Reminiscences, Vol. I, P. 233
3 Then join hand in hand, brave Americans
all!
    By uniting we stand, by dividing we fall.
                JOHN DICKINSON [1732–1808]:
                        The Liberty Song (1768)
4 See Key, page 332.

The union of hearts, the union of
    hands,
And the flag of our Union forever!
            The Flag of Our Union.
                        Refrain

Old Ironsides at anchor lay,
    In the harbor of Mahon;
A dead calm rested on the bay, —
    The waves to sleep had gone;
When little Hal, the captain's son,
    A lad both brave and good,
In sport, up shroud and rigging ran,
    And on the main truck stood!
        *The Main Truck, A Leap for
                Life. Stanza 1*

The land of the heart is the land of
    the West.
        *The West. Stanza 1 (In Lit-
        tell's Magazine, April 5, 1851)*

In other countries, when I heard
    The language of my own,
How fondly each familiar word
    Awoke an answering tone.
        *I'm With You Once Again.
                        Stanza 3*

'Tis ever thus, when in life's storm
    Hope's star to man grows dim,
An angel kneels, in woman's form,
    And breathes a prayer for him.
        Pocahontas. Stanza 3

Near the lake where drooped the wil-
    low,
            Long time ago!
                    Near the Lake

In teaching me the way to live
    It taught me how to die.
            *My Mother's Bible.
                        Stanza 4*

EDWARD COOTE PINKNEY
[1802–1828]

I fill this cup to one made up
    Of loveliness alone,
A woman, of her gentle sex
    The seeming paragon;
To whom the better elements
    And kindly stars have given
A form so fair, that, like the air,
    'Tis less of earth than heaven.
                        A Health

Her every tone is music's own,
    Like those of morning birds,
And something more than melody
    Dwells ever in her words.
                        A Health

Look out upon the stars, my love,
    And shame them with thine eyes.
                        A Serenade

WINTHROP MACKWORTH
PRAED
[1802–1839]

And oh! I shall find how, day by day,
    All thoughts and things look older;
How the laugh of pleasure grows less
    gay,
    And the heart of friendship colder.
        Twenty-eight and Twenty-nine

She was our queen, our rose, our star;
    And then she danced — O Heaven,
    her dancing!
                The Belle of the Ball

I remember, I remember [1]
    How my childhood fleeted by, —
The mirth of its December
    And the warmth of its July.
            I Remember, I Remember

I think, whatever mortals crave,
    With impotent endeavor,
A wreath, a rank, a throne, a grave —
    The world goes round forever;
I think that life is not too long,
    And therefore I determine
That many people read a song
    Who will not read a sermon. [2]
        *The Chant of the Brazen Head.
                        Stanza 1*

His talk was like a stream which runs
    With rapid change from rocks to
    roses,
It slipped from politics to puns;
    It passed from Mahomet to Moses.
                The Vicar. Stanza 5

Events are writ by History's pen:
    Though causes are too much to care
    for: —
Fame talks about the where and when,

[1] See Thomas Hood, page 390.
[2] See Herbert, page 135.

While folly asks the why and wherefore.
>Epitaph on the Late King of
>the Sandwich Islands. Stanza 4

There are tones that will haunt us,
though lonely
Our path be o'er mountain or sea;
There are looks that will part from us
only
When memory ceases to be.
>Good-Night. Stanza 5

His partners at the whist-club said
That he was faultless in his dealings.
>Quince. Stanza 3

And cut the fiercest quarrel short
With "Patience, gentlemen, and
shuffle." [1]
>Ibid. Stanza 5

My debts are paid; but Nature's debt
Almost escaped my recollection:
Tom! we shall meet again; and yet
I cannot leave you my direction.
>Ibid. Stanza 13

Dame Fortune is a fickle gipsy,
And always blind, and often tipsy;
Sometimes for years and years to-
gether,
She'll bless you with the sunniest
weather,
Bestowing honour, pudding, pence,
You can't imagine why or whence; —
Then in a moment — Presto, pass! —
Your joys are withered like the grass.
>The Haunted Tree

John Bull was beat at Waterloo!
They'll swear to that in France.
>Waterloo

Of science and logic he chatters,
As fine and as fast as he can;
Though I am no judge of such matters,
I'm sure he's a talented man.
>The Talented Man

MARIAN DIX SULLIVAN
[1802–1860]

Wild roved an Indian girl, bright Al-
farata,
Where sweep the waters of the blue
Juniata.
Swift as an antelope, through the for-
ests going,

[1] See Scott, page 311.

Loose were her jetty locks, in wavy
tresses flowing.
>The Blue Juniata [1850].
>Stanza 1

THOMAS LOVELL BEDDOES
[1803–1849]

The anchor heaves, the ship swings
free,
The sails swell full. To sea, to sea!
>Sailor's Song. Stanza 2

If there were dreams to sell,
What would you buy? [1]
Some cost a passing-bell;
Some a light sigh.
>Dream-Pedlary

Tell me how many beads there are
In a silver chain
Of evening rain,
Unravell'd from the tumbling main,
And threading the eye of a yellow star:
So many times do I love, again.
>Song. Stanza 2

That divinest hope, which none can
know of
Who have not laid their dearest in the
grave.
>Death's Jest Book

LAMAN BLANCHARD
[1803–1845]

Sooth 'twere a pleasant life to lead,
With nothing in the world to do
But just to blow a shepherd's reed,
The silent season thro'
And just to drive a flock to feed, —
Sheep — quiet, fond and few!
>Dolce far Niente. Stanza 1

Give me to live with Love alone
And let the world go dine and dress;
For Love hath lowly haunts. . . .
If life's a flower, I choose my own —
'Tis "love in Idleness."
>Ibid. Stanza 4

[1] If there were dreams to sell,
Do I not know full well
What I would buy?
Hope's dear delusive spell,
It's happy tale to tell,
Joy's fleeting sigh.
LOUISE CHANDLER MOULTON
[1835–1908]: *If There Were
Dreams to Sell, St. 1*

Pleasures lie thickest where no pleas-
    ures seem:
  There's not a leaf that falls upon the
    ground
  But holds some joy of silence or of
    sound,
Some sprite begotten of a summer
    dream.
                Sonnet, Hidden Joys

GEORGE BORROW
[1803–1881]

O England! long, long may it be ere
the sun of thy glory sink beneath the
wave of darkness! Though gloomy and
portentous clouds are now gathering
rapidly around thee, still, still may it
please the Almighty to disperse them,
and to grant thee a futurity longer in
duration and still brighter in renown
than thy past! Or, if thy doom be at
hand, may that doom be a noble one,
and worthy of her who has been styled
the Old Queen of the waters! May thou
sink, if thou dost sink, amidst blood
and flame, with a mighty noise, causing more than one nation to participate
in thy downfall!
            The Bible in Spain [*1842*]
  O ye gifted ones, follow your calling,
for, however various your talents may
be, ye can have but one calling capable
of leading ye to eminence and renown;
follow resolutely the one straight path
before you, it is that of your good
angel, let neither obstacles nor temptations induce ye to leave it; bound along
if you can; if not, on hands and knees
follow in it, perish in it, if needful; but
ye need not fear that; no one ever yet
died in the true path of his calling before he had attained the pinnacle.
Turn into other paths, and for a momentary advantage or gratification ye
have sold your inheritance, your immortality. Ye will never be heard of
after death.
            Lavengro. Chap. 21 [*1851*]
  Trust not a man's words if you
please, or you may come to very erroneous conclusions; but at all times
place implicit confidence in a man's
countenance in which there is no deceit;

and of necessity there can be none. If
people would but look each other more
in the face, we should have less cause to
complain of the deception of the world;
nothing so easy as physiognomy nor so
useful.
                Lavengro. Chap. 22
  Translation is at best an echo.
                    Ibid. Chap. 25
  There's night and day, brother, both
sweet things; sun, moon, and stars,
brother, all sweet things; there's likewise a wind on the heath.[1] Life is very
sweet, brother; who would wish to
die?
                            Ibid.
  I have known the time when a pugilistic encounter between two noted
champions was almost considered in
the light of a national affair; when tens
of thousands of individuals, high and
low, meditated and brooded upon it,
the first thing in the morning and the
last at night, until the great event was
decided.
                    Ibid. Chap. 26
  I learnt . . . to fear God, and to
take my own part.
                    Ibid. Chap. 86
  Youth is the only season for enjoyment, and the first twenty-five years
of one's life are worth all the rest of
the longest life of man, even though
those five-and-twenty be spent in penury and contempt, and the rest in the
possession of wealth, honours, respectability.
    The Romany Rye. Chap. 30 [*1857*]

WILLIAM DRIVER
[1803–1886]

I name thee Old Glory.[2]

---

[1] He built life well, the gypsy-man
    In those days gone by —
  "There's the wind on the heath, brother,
    And a quiet sky."
        MARGARET WIDDEMER: *Gypsy Wis-
                        dom, St. 1*
[2] On August 10, 1831, a large American flag
was presented to Captain William Driver of
the brig *Charles Doggett* by a band of women,

RALPH WALDO EMERSON
[1803–1882]

Nor knowest thou what argument
Thy life to thy neighbor's creed has
　　lent.
All are needed by each one;
Nothing is fair or good alone.
Each and All. Stanza 1

I wiped away the weeds and foam,
I fetched my sea-born treasures home;
But the poor, unsightly, noisome things
Had left their beauty on the shore,
With the sun and the sand and the wild
　　uproar.
Ibid. Stanza 3

I like a church; I like a cowl;
I love a prophet of the soul;
And on my heart monastic aisles
Fall like sweet strains or pensive
　　smiles;
Yet not for all his faith can see
Would I that cowléd churchman be.
The Problem. Stanza 1

Not from a vain or shallow thought
His awful Jove young Phidias brought.
Ibid. Stanza 2

The hand that rounded Peter's dome,
And groined the aisles of Christian
　　Rome,
Wrought in a sad sincerity;
Himself from God he could not free;
He builded better than he knew; —
The conscious stone to beauty grew.
Ibid.

Earth proudly wears the Parthenon
As the best gem upon her zone.
Ibid. Stanza 3

---

in recognition of his humane service in bringing back the British mutineers of the ship
Bounty from Tahiti to their former home, Pit-
cairn Island. As the flag was hoisted to the
masthead, Captain Driver proclaimed, "I
name thee Old Glory." The flag is now in the
Smithsonian Institution, Washington, D. C.

Who gave you, Old Glory, the name that you
　　bear
With such pride everywhere
As you cast yourself free to the rapturous air
And leap out full-length?
　　JAMES WHITCOMB RILEY [1849–1916]:
　　The Name of Old Glory, St. 1 [1898]

The passive Master lent his hand
To the vast soul that o'er him planned.[1]
The Problem. Stanza 3

Enclosed
In a tumultuous privacy of storm.
The Snow-Storm

Life is too short to waste
In critic peep or cynic bark,
Quarrel or reprimand:
'Twill soon be dark;
Up! mind thine own aim, and
God speed the mark!
To J. W.

There's no rood has not a star above it.
Musketaquid

All sorts of things and weather
Must be taken in together,
To make up a year
And a Sphere.
Fable, The Mountain and the
Squirrel

Good-bye, proud world! I'm going
　　home;
Thou art not my friend and I'm not
　　thine.[2]
Good-bye. Stanza 1

Oh, when I am safe in my sylvan home,
I tread on the pride of Greece and
　　Rome;
And when I am stretched beneath the
　　pines
Where the evening star so holy shines,
I laugh at the lore and the pride of
　　man,
At the sophist schools, and the learned
　　clan;
For what are they all in their high con-
　　ceit,
When man in the bush with God may
　　meet.[3]
Ibid. Stanza 4

Let me go where'er I will,
I hear a sky-born music still.
Fragments

---

[1] This couplet is inscribed on the boulder
marking Emerson's grave in Sleepy Hollow
Cemetery, Concord, Massachusetts.
[2] See Byron, page 353.
[3] Inscribed on the boulder, a memorial to
Emerson, Schoolmaster's Hill, Franklin Park,
Boston.

But in the mud and scum of things
There alway, alway something sings.
Fragments

If eyes were made for seeing,
Then Beauty is its own excuse for be-
ing.[1]
The Rhodora

Things are in the saddle,
And ride mankind.[2]
Ode Inscribed to W. H. Chan-
ning

Olympian bards who sung
Divine ideas below,
Which always find us young,
And always keep us so.
The Poet. Ode to Beauty

Heartily know,
When half-gods go,
The gods arrive.
Give All to Love. Stanza 4

Love not the flower they pluck, and
know it not,
And all their botany is Latin names.
Blight

By the rude bridge that arched the
flood,
Their flag to April's breeze unfurled,
Here once the embattled farmers
stood,
And fired the shot heard round the
world.[3]
Hymn sung at the Completion
of the Battle Monument, Con-
cord [April 19, 1836].
Stanza 1

Hast thou named all the birds without
a gun; [4]

[1] The beautiful seems right,
By force of beauty.
E. B. BROWNING: *Aurora Leigh, Book I*
[2] I never could believe that Providence had
sent a few men into the world ready booted
and spurred to ride, and millions ready saddled and bridled to be ridden. — RICHARD
RUMBOLD [1622–1685], colonel of horse regiment, Argyll's expedition to Scotland: *State-*
ment on the scaffold
[3] No war or battle sound
Was heard the world around.
MILTON: *Hymn of Christ's*
Nativity, L. 31
[4] To the hunters who hunt for the gunless
game

Loved the wood-rose, and left it on its
stalk?
Forbearance

And striving to be man, the worm
Mounts through all the spires of form.
May-Day

God said, I am tired of kings,
I suffer them no more.
Boston Hymn [January 1, 1863].
Stanza 1

Oh, tenderly the haughty day
Fills his blue urn with fire.
Ode, Concord [July 4, 1857].
Stanza 1

Go put your creed into your deed,
Nor speak with double tongue.
Ibid. Stanza 5

I think no virtue goes with size.
The Titmouse

For well the soul, if stout within,
Can arm impregnably the skin.
Ibid.

So nigh is grandeur to our dust,
So near is God to man,
When Duty whispers low, *Thou must,*
The youth replies, *I can.*
Voluntaries. III

Nor sequent centuries could hit
Orbit and sum of Shakespeare's wit.
Solution

Born for success he seemed,
With grace to win, with heart to hold,
With shining gifts that took all eyes.
In Memoriam

Nor mourn the unalterable Days
That Genius goes and Folly stays.
Ibid.

Fear not, then, thou child infirm,
There's no god dare wrong a worm.
Compensation. I

He thought it happier to be dead,
To die for Beauty, than live for bread.
Beauty

Wilt thou seal up the avenues of ill?
Pay every debt, as if God wrote the
bill.
"Suum Cuique"

Too busied with the crowded hour to
fear to live or die.
Nature

The streams and the woods belong.
SAM WALTER FOSS [1858–1911]:
The Bloodless Sportsman, St. 3

Damsels of Time, the hypocritic Days,
Muffled and dumb like Barefoot dervishes,
And marching single in an endless file,
Bring diadems and fagots in their hands.

Days

I, too late,
Under her solemn fillet saw the scorn.

Ibid.

It is time to be old,
To take in sail.

Terminus

Obey the voice at eve obeyed at prime.

Ibid.

Though love repine, and reason chafe,
There came a voice without reply, —
" 'Tis man's perdition to be safe,
When for the truth he ought to die."

Sacrifice

For what avail the plough or sail,
Or land or life, if freedom fail?

Boston. Stanza 5

What care though rival cities soar
Along the stormy coast,
Penn's town, New York, and Baltimore,
If Boston knew the most!

Ibid. Stanza 9

If the red slayer think he slays,
Or if the slain think he is slain,
They know not well the subtle ways
I keep, and pass, and turn again.

Brahma

They reckon ill who leave me out;
When me they fly, I am the wings;
I am the doubter and the doubt,
And I the hymn the Brahmin sings.

Ibid.

Draw, if thou canst, the mystic line,
Severing rightly his from thine,
Which is human, which divine.

Worship

Nor scour the seas, nor sift mankind,
A poet or a friend to find:
Behold, he watches at the door!
Behold his shadow on the floor!

Saadi

Go where he will, the wise man is at home,
His hearth the earth, — his hall the azure dome.

Wood-Notes. I, 3

That book is good
Which puts me in a working mood.
Unless to Thought is added Will,
Apollo is an imbecile.

The Poet

In the vaunted works of Art
The master-stroke is Nature's part.[1]

Art

There is no great and no small [2]
To the Soul that maketh all:
And where it cometh, all things are;
And it cometh everywhere.

History

I am the owner of the sphere,
Of the seven stars and the solar year,
Of Caesar's hand, and Plato's brain,
Of Lord Christ's heart, and Shakespeare's strain.

Ibid.

Ever from one who comes to-morrow
Men wait their good and truth to borrow.

Merlin's Wisdom

The music that can deepest reach,
And cure all ill, is cordial speech.

Ibid.

A day for toil, an hour for sport,
But for a friend is life too short.

Ibid.

Some of your hurts you have cured,
And the sharpest you still have survived,
But what torments of grief you endured
From evils which never arrived!

Borrowing [From the French]

He who has a thousand friends has not
a friend to spare,
And he who has one enemy will meet
him everywhere.

Translation [3]

A ruddy drop of manly blood
The surging sea outweighs,

---

[1] Nature paints the best part of a picture, carves the best part of the statue, builds the best part of the house, and speaks the best part of the oration. — *Society and Solitude, Art*

[2] No great, no small. — POPE: *Essay on Man, Epistle 1, L. 279*

[3] In his essay, *Considerations by the Way*, Emerson credits this couplet to "an Eastern poet, Ali Ben Abu Taleb," and changes *will* to *shall* in the second line.

The world uncertain comes and goes,
  The lover rooted stays.
                                    Friendship
Me too thy nobleness has taught
  To master my despair;
The fountains of my hidden life
  Are through thy friendship fair.
                                    Ibid.
Time dissipates to shining ether the solid angularity of facts.
                                    History
There is properly no History; only Biography.[1]
                                    Ibid.
Nature is a mutable cloud, which is always and never the same.
                                    Ibid.
A man is a bundle of relations, a knot of roots, whose flower and fruitage is the world.
                                    Ibid.
The virtue in most request is conformity. Self-reliance is its aversion. It loves not realities and creators, but names and customs.
                                    Self-Reliance
Whoso would be a man must be a non-conformist.
                                    Ibid.
A foolish consistency is the hobgoblin of little minds, adored by little statesmen and philosophers and divines.
                                    Ibid.
To be great is to be misunderstood.
                                    Ibid.
An institution is the lengthened shadow of one man.
                                    Ibid.
Nothing can bring you peace but yourself.
                                    Ibid.
Every sweet has its sour; every evil its good.
                                    Compensation
For every thing you have missed, you have gained something else; and for every thing you gain, you lose something.
                                    Ibid.

[1] See Carlyle, page 380.

Everything in Nature contains all the powers of Nature. Everything is made of one hidden stuff.
                                    Compensation
It is as impossible for a man to be cheated by any one but himself, as for a thing to be, and not to be, at the same time.
                                    Ibid.
There is no luck in literary reputation. They who make up the final verdict upon every book are not the partial and noisy readers of the hour when it appears; but a court as of angels, a public not to be bribed, not to be entreated, and not to be overawed, decides upon every man's title to fame.
                                    Spiritual Laws
All mankind love a lover.
                                    Love
No man ever forgot the visitations of that power to his heart and brain, which created all things new; which was the dawn in him of music, poetry, and art.
                                    Ibid.
Thou art to me a delicious torment.
                                    Friendship
Happy is the house that shelters a friend.
                                    Ibid.
A friend is a person with whom I may be sincere. Before him, I may think aloud.
                                    Ibid.
A friend may well be reckoned the masterpiece of Nature.
                                    Ibid.
Two may talk and one may hear, but three cannot take part in a conversation of the most sincere and searching sort.
                                    Ibid.
The only reward of virtue is virtue; the only way to have a friend is to be one.
                                    Ibid.
I do then with my friends as I do with my books. I would have them where I can find them, but I seldom use them.
                                    Ibid.

Do what we can, summer will have its flies. If we walk in the woods, we must feed mosquitoes.

Prudence

In skating over thin ice our safety is our speed.

Ibid.

Heroism feels and never reasons and therefore is always right.

Heroism

Nothing great was ever achieved without enthusiasm.

Circles

Nothing astonishes men so much as common sense and plain dealing.

Art

Nature and Books belong to the eyes that see them.

Experience

No house, though it were the Tuileries, or the Escurial, is good for anything without a master.

Manners

The only gift is a portion of thyself.

Gifts

The less government we have, the better — the fewer laws, and the less confided power.

Politics

Money, which represents the prose of life, and which is hardly spoken of in parlors without an apology, is, in its effects and laws, as beautiful as roses.

Nominalist and Realist

Every man is wanted, and no man is wanted much.

Ibid.

And with Cæsar to take in his hand the army, the empire, and Cleopatra, and say, "All these will I relinquish if you will show me the fountains of the Nile."

New England Reformers

The reward of a thing well done, is to have done it.

Ibid.

Poetry teaches the enormous force of a few words, and, in proportion to the inspiration, checks loquacity.

Parnassus. Preface

There are two classes of poets, — the poets by education and practice, these we respect; and poets by nature, these we love.

Parnassus. Preface

No lover of poetry can spare Chaucer, or should grudge the short study required to command the archaisms of his English, and the skill to read the melody of his verse.[1]

Ibid.

He is great who is what he is from Nature, and who never reminds us of others.

Representative Men. Uses of Great Men

Cecil's saying of Sir Walter Raleigh, "I know that he can toil terribly," is an electric touch.

Ibid.

When nature removes a great man, people explore the horizon for a successor; but none comes, and none will. His class is extinguished with him. In some other and quite different field, the next man will appear.

Ibid.

Every hero becomes a bore at last.

Ibid.

Great geniuses have the shortest biographies.

Ibid. Plato; or, The Philosopher

Keep cool: it will be all one a hundred years hence.

Ibid. Montaigne; or, The Skeptic

Is not marriage an open question, when it is alleged, from the beginning of the world, that such as are in the institution wish to get out, and such as are out wish to get in?[2]

Ibid.

Thought is the property of him who can entertain it, and of him who can adequately place it.

Ibid. Shakespeare; or, The Poet

[1] The influence of Chaucer is conspicuous in all our early literature; and, more recently, . . . in the whole society of English writers, a large unacknowledged debt is easily traced. One is charmed with the opulence which feeds so many pensioners. — *Representative Men, Shakespeare*

[2] See Sir John Davies, page 115.

"There shall be no Alps," he said.
*Representative Men. Napoleon;
or, The Man of the World*

[Napoleon] directed Bourrienne to leave all his letters unopened for three weeks, and then observed with satisfaction how large a part of the correspondence had thus disposed of itself, and no longer required an answer.
Ibid.

Classics which at home are drowsily read have a strange charm in a country inn, or in the transom of a merchant brig.
English Traits

The favorite phrase of their law is "a custom whereof the memory of man runneth not back to the contrary." [1]
Ibid.

The hearing ear is always found close to the speaking tongue.
Ibid. Race

I find the Englishman to be him of all men who stands firmest in his shoes.
Ibid. Manners

A creative economy is the fuel of magnificence.
Ibid. Aristocracy

Coal is a portable climate.
Conduct of Life. Wealth

The world is his, who has money to go over it.
Ibid.

The farmer is covetous of his dollar, and with reason. . . . He knows how many strokes of labor it represents. His bones ache with the day's work that earned it.
Ibid.

Art is a jealous mistress,[2] and, if a man have a genius for painting, poetry, music, architecture, or philosophy, he makes a bad husband, and an ill-provider.
Ibid.

[1] See Blackstone, page 248.
[2] Blackstone's confession of his own original preference for literature, and his perception that the law was "a jealous mistress," who would suffer no rival in his affections. — W. D. HOWELLS: *My Literary Passions, Chap. 19*

One of the benefits of a college education is to show the boy its little avail.
Conduct of Life. Culture

All educated Americans, first or last, go to Europe.
Ibid.

Solitude, the safeguard of mediocrity, is to genius the stern friend.
Ibid.

A man known to us only as a celebrity in politics or in trade, gains largely in our esteem if we discover that he has some intellectual taste or skill.
Ibid.

There is always a best way of doing everything, if it be to boil an egg. Manners are the happy ways of doing things.
Ibid. Behavior

Your manners are always under examination, and by committees little suspected, — a police in citizens' clothes, — but are awarding or denying you very high prizes when you least think of it.
Ibid.

The alleged power to charm down insanity, or ferocity in beasts, is a power behind the eye.
Ibid.

Fine manners need the support of fine manners in others.
Ibid.

The highest compact we can make with our fellow is, — "Let there be truth between us two forevermore."
Ibid.

It is sublime to feel and say of another, I need never meet, or speak, or write to him: we need not reinforce ourselves, or send tokens of remembrance: I rely on him as on myself: if he did thus or thus, I know it was right.
Ibid.

There is no beautifier of complexion, or form, or behavior, like the wish to scatter joy and not pain around us.
Ibid.

We must be as courteous to a man as we are to a picture, which we are willing to give the advantage of a good light.
Ibid.

There is one topic peremptorily forbidden to all well-bred, to all rational mortals, namely, their distempers. If you have not slept, or if you have slept, or if you have headache, or sciatica, or leprosy, or thunder-stroke, I beseech you, by all angels, to hold your peace.

Conduct of Life. Behavior

Shallow men believe in luck.[1]

Ibid. Worship

'Tis a Dutch proverb, that "paint costs nothing," such are its preserving qualities in damp climates.

Ibid. Considerations by the Way

Our chief want in life is somebody who shall make us do what we can.

Ibid.

Make yourself necessary to somebody.

Ibid.

Beauty without grace is the hook without the bait.

Ibid. Beauty

Never read any book that is not a year old.

Ibid. In Praise of Books

I should as soon think of swimming across Charles River, when I wish to go to Boston, as of reading all my books in originals, when I have them rendered for me in my mother tongue.

Ibid.

He who has mastered any law in his private thoughts, is master to that extent of all men whose language he speaks, and of all into whose language his own can be translated.

The American Scholar

Wherever Macdonald sits, there is the head of the table.[2]

Ibid.

If the single man plant himself indomitably on his instincts, and there abide, the huge world will come round to him.[1]

The American Scholar

Give me health and a day, and I will make the pomp of emperors ridiculous.

Nature, Addresses and Lectures.
Chap. 3, Beauty

Men grind and grind in the mill of a truism, and nothing comes out but what was put in. But the moment they desert the tradition for a spontaneous thought, then poetry, wit, hope, virtue, learning, anecdote, all flock to their aid.

Literary Ethics

God may forgive sins, he said, but awkwardness has no forgiveness in heaven or earth.

Society and Solitude

The most advanced nations are always those who navigate the most.

Ibid. Civilization

Hitch your wagon to a star.

Ibid.

The true test of civilization is, not the census, nor the size of cities, nor the crops — no, but the kind of man the country turns out.

Ibid.

Raphael paints wisdom; Handel sings it, Phidias carves it, Shakespeare writes it, Wren builds it, Columbus sails it, Luther preaches it, Washington arms it, Watt mechanizes it.

Ibid. Art

Every genuine work of art has as much reason for being as the earth and the sun.

Ibid.

We boil at different degrees.

Ibid. Eloquence

The ornament of a house is the friends who frequent it.

Ibid. Domestic Life

---

[1] Luck is infatuated with the efficient. *Persian proverb.*

[2] Let me sit wherever I will, that will still be the upper end. — CERVANTES: *Don Quixote, Part II, Chap. 31*

Emerson's sentence is usually quoted with the substitution of "Macgregor" for "Macdonald." When Theodore Parker quoted it, he said "Highlander" in place of "Macdonald."

[1] Everything comes if a man will only wait. — DISRAELI: *Tancred, Book IV, Chap. 8*

Everything comes to him who waits
If he waits in a place that's meet,
But never wait for an uptown car
On the downtown side of the street.
Modern jingle.

We have the newspaper, which does its best to make every square acre of land and sea give an account of itself at your breakfast-table.[1]

Society and Solitude.
Works and Days

Can anybody remember when the times were not hard and money not scarce?

Ibid.

A man builds a fine house; and now he has a master, and a task for life; he is to furnish, watch, show it, and keep it in repair the rest of his days.

Ibid.

We do not count a man's years until he has nothing else to count.

Ibid. Old Age

The establishment of Christianity in the world does not rest on any miracle but the miracle of being the broadest and most humane doctrine.

Miscellanies. Character

Life is not so short but that there is always time enough for courtesy.

Letters and Social Aims. Social Aims

I have heard with admiring submission the experience of the lady who declared that the sense of being well-dressed gives a feeling of inward tranquillity which religion is powerless to bestow.[2]

Ibid.

Do not say things. What you are stands over you the while, and thunders so that I cannot hear what you say to the contrary.

Ibid.

Abraham Lincoln . . . who was at home and welcome with the humblest, and with a spirit and a practical vein in the times of terror that commanded the admiration of the wisest. His heart was as great as the world, but there was no room in it to hold the memory of a wrong.

Greatness

Next to the originator of a good sentence is the first quoter of it.[1]

Quotation and Originality

When Shakespeare is charged with debts to his authors, Landor replies, "Yet he was more original than his originals. He breathed upon dead bodies and brought them into life."

Ibid.

In fact, it is as difficult to appropriate the thoughts of others as it is to invent.

Ibid.

By necessity, by proclivity, and by delight, we all quote.

Ibid.

Every good poem that I know I recall by its rhythm also. Rhyme is a pretty good measure of the latitude and opulence of a writer. If unskilled, he is at once detected by the poverty of his chimes.

Poetry and Imagination

A good poem goes about the world offering itself to reasonable men, who read it with joy and carry it to their reasonable neighbors.

Morals

Wit makes its own welcome, and levels all distinctions.

The Comic

The perception of the comic is a tie of sympathy with other men.

Ibid.

All thoughts of a turtle are turtles, and of a rabbit, rabbits.

The Natural History of Intellect

What is a weed? A plant whose virtues have not yet been discovered.

Fortune of the Republic

---

[1] The news! Our morning, noon and evening cry;
Day unto day repeats it till we die.
CHARLES SPRAGUE: *Curiosity*
[2] The lady was Miss Cornelia Frances Forbes [1817–1911] of Milton, Massachusetts.

[1] There is not less wit nor less invention in applying rightly a thought one finds in a book, than in being the first author of that thought. Cardinal du Perron has been heard to say that the happy application of a verse of Virgil has deserved a talent. — BAYLE: *Vol. II, P. 779*
Though old the thought and oft exprest,
'Tis his at last who says it best.
LOWELL: *For an Autograph*
He who first praises a book becomingly, is next in merit to the author. — WALTER SAVAGE LANDOR

Great men are they who see that spiritual is stronger than any material force; that thoughts rule the world.

Progress of Culture, Phi Beta Kappa
Address [July 18, 1867]

I wish to write such rhymes as shall not suggest a restraint, but contrariwise the wildest freedom.

Journal. June 27, 1839

I trust a good deal to common fame, as we all must. If a man has good corn, or wood, or boards, or pigs to sell, or can make better chairs or knives, crucibles or church organs than anybody else, you will find a broad, hard-beaten road to his house, though it be in the woods.[1]

Journals, edited by Edward
Waldo Emerson and Waldo
Emerson Forbes [1912], *Vol. 8,*
P. 528–529, 1855

[1] The editors appended a footnote: "There has been much inquiry in the newspapers recently as to whether Mr. Emerson wrote a sentence very like the above, which has been attributed to him in print. The editors do not find the latter in his works, but there can be little doubt that it was a memory quotation by some hearer, or quite probably correctly reported from one of his lectures — the same image in differing words."

The West Publishing Company, St. Paul, Minnesota, in an advertisement of the National Reporting System, adapted the Emerson passage to read: "If you write a better book, or preach a better sermon, or build a better mousetrap than your neighbor, the world will make a beaten path to your door."

In *Borrowings,* compiled by Mrs. SARAH S. B. YULE and MARY S. KEENE [Dodge Publishing Company, 1889], Mrs. Yule includes the "mousetrap quotation" as written in her notebook, copied from an address heard many years before, this being the first known definite credit to Emerson.

In a Roycroft publication, *The Philistine, July, 1912,* H. T. MORGAN claimed the authorship for Elbert Hubbard [1859–1915], but did not state where and when Mr. Hubbard had printed the "modern proverb," as he termed it. In an earlier Roycroft periodical, *The Fra, May, 1911,* it is said that Mr. Hubbard wrote the "mousetrap" paragraph, and to give it "specific gravity," attributed it to Ralph Waldo Emerson.

A New York shoe store proprietor claimed that Mr. Hubbard wrote the paragraph for his store, and exhibits a framed copy of it.

The *Boston Evening Transcript, Notes and Queries Department, October 14, 1922,* printed

GERALD GRIFFIN
[1803–1840]

A place in thy memory, dearest,
    Is all that I claim;
To pause and look back when thou hearest
    The sound of my name.
        A Place in Thy Memory. Stanza 1

When, like the rising day,
    Eileen aroon!
Love sends his early ray,
    Eileen aroon!
What makes his dawning glow
Changeless through joy or woe?
Only the constant know! —
    Eileen aroon!
        Eileen Aroon. Stanza 3

On the ocean that hollows the rocks
    where ye dwell,
A shadowy land has appeared, as they tell;
Men thought it a region of sunshine and rest,
And they called it Hy-Brasail, the isle of the blest.
        Hy-Brasail, Isle of the Blest.
        Stanza 1

ROBERT STEPHEN HAWKER
[1803–1875]

And shall Trelawny die?
Here's twenty thousand Cornish men
Will know the reason why.[1]
        The Song of the Western Men.
        Stanza 1

a compilation of information concerning this famous quotation; and *The Colophon, First Series, XIX,* and *New Series, I, 1,* contains monographs on the subject by BURTON E. STEVENSON.

If a man builds a better mousetrap than his neighbor, the world will not only beat a path to his door, it will make newsreels of him and his wife in beach pajamas, it will discuss his diet and his health, it will publish heart-throb stories of his love life, it will publicize him, analyze him, photograph him, and make his life thoroughly miserable by feeding to the palpitant public intimate details of things that are none of its damned business. — NEWMAN LEVY: [1888–   ] *The Right To Be Alone* (In *American Mercury, June, 1935*)

[1] This ballad commemorates the commitment to the Tower of London of Sir Jonathan Trelawny [1650–1721], with six other

RICHARD HENRY HENGIST HORNE
[1803–1884]

'Tis always morning somewhere in the world.[1]
> *Orion. Book III, Canto II [1843]*

A sweet content
Passing all wisdom or its fairest flower.
> *Ibid.*

The wisdom of mankind creeps slowly on,
Subject to every doubt that can retard
Or fling it back upon an earlier time.
> *Ibid.*

Ye rigid Plowmen! Bear in mind
Your labor is for future hours.
Advance! spare not! nor look behind!
Plow deep and straight with all your powers!
> *The Plow*

DOUGLAS JERROLD
[1803–1857]

He is one of those wise philanthropists who in a time of famine would vote for nothing but a supply of toothpicks.
> *Douglas Jerrold's Wit*

Dogmatism is puppyism come to its full growth.
> *Ibid.*

The surest way to hit a woman's heart is to take aim kneeling.
> *Ibid.*

That fellow would vulgarize the day of judgment.
> *A Comic Author*

The best thing I know between France and England is the sea.
> *The Anglo-French Alliance*

The life of the husbandman, — a life fed by the bounty of earth and sweetened by the airs of heaven.
> *The Husbandman's Life*

Some people are so fond of ill-luck that they run half-way to meet it.
> *Meeting Troubles Half-Way*

Earth is here [Australia] so kind, that just tickle her with a hoe and she laughs with a harvest.
> *A Land of Plenty*

The ugliest of trades have their moments of pleasure. Now, if I were a grave-digger, or even a hangman, there are some people I could work for with a great deal of enjoyment.
> *Ugly Trades*

He was so good he would pour rosewater on a toad.
> *A Charitable Man*

As for the brandy, "nothing extenuate"; and the water, put nought in in malice.
> *Shakespeare Grog*

Talk to him of Jacob's ladder, and he would ask the number of the steps.
> *A Matter-of-fact Man*

That questionable superfluity — small beer.[1]
> *The Tragedy of the Till*

JAMES CLARENCE MANGAN
[1803–1849]

I see thee ever in my dreams,
    Karaman!
Thy hundred hills, thy thousand streams,
    Karaman, O Karaman!
As when thy gold-bright morning gleams,
As when the deepening sunset seams
With lines of light thy hills and streams,
    Karaman!
> *The Karamanian Exile.[2] Stanza 1*

---

prelates, in 1688, for refusing to recognize the Declaration of Indulgence issued by King James II. Hawker wrote the ballad in 1825, and it was praised by Sir Walter Scott and Macaulay, under the impression that it was an ancient song. "And shall Trelawny die?" has been a popular phrase throughout Cornwall since the imprisonment of the seven bishops.

[1] 'Tis always morning somewhere. — LONGFELLOW: *Tales of a Wayside Inn, The Birds of Killingworth*

[1] Small beer. — SHAKESPEARE: *King Henry IV, Part II, Act II, Sc. 2, L. 8 and 13; Othello, Act II, Sc. 1, L. 160*

[2] JAMES RYDER RANDALL used this poem as a pattern when writing *Maryland, my Maryland.*

He too had tears for all souls in trouble,
Here and in hell.
The Nameless One. Stanza 14

CHARLES SWAIN
[1803–1874]

Let to-morrow take care of to-
morrow, —
Leave things of the future to fate;
What's the use to anticipate sorrow? —
Life's troubles come never too late!
Imaginary Evils. Stanza 1

Though poor be our purse, and though
narrow our span,
Let us all try to do a good turn when
we can.
Do a Good Turn When You Can

For there's a heart for every one,
If every one could find it!
A Heart for Every One. Stanza 1

Home's not merely four square walls,
Though with pictures hung and
gilded;
Home is where Affection calls, —
Filled with shrines the Heart hath
builded.
Home. Stanza 1

SARAH HELEN POWER WHITMAN
[1803–1878]

Star of resplendent front! Thy glorious
eye
Shines on me still from out yon clouded
sky.
Arcturus (To Edgar Allan Poe)

Tell him I lingered alone on the shore,
Where we parted, in sorrow, to meet
nevermore;
The night-wind blew cold on my deso-
late heart
But colder those wild words of doom,
— "Ye must part."
Our Island of Dreams

The sweet imperious mouth, whose
haughty valor
Defied all portents of impending doom.
The Portrait [of Poe]

Warm lights are on the sleepy uplands
waning
Beneath soft clouds along the horizon
rolled,

Till the slant sunbeams through the
fringes raining
Bathe all the hills in melancholy gold.
A Still Day in Autumn. Stanza 4

Enchantress of the stormy seas,
Priestess of Night's high mysteries.
Moonrise in May

The summer skies are darkly blue,
The days are still and bright,
And Evening trails her robes of gold
Through the dim halls of Night.[1]
Summer's Call

Raven from the dim dominions
On the Night's Plutonian shore,[2]
Oft I hear thy dusky pinions
Wave and flutter round my door —
See the shadow of thy pinions
Float along the moonlit floor.
The Raven

BENJAMIN DISRAELI, EARL OF BEACONSFIELD
[1804–1881]

Yes, I am a Jew, and when the ancestors of the right honourable gentleman were brutal savages in an unknown
island, mine were priests in the temple
of Solomon.[3]
Reply to a taunt by
Daniel O'Connell [4]

---

[1] I heard the trailing garments of the Night
Sweep through her marble halls.
    LONGFELLOW: *Hymn to the Night.
Stanza 1*

[2] Night's Plutonian shore. — POE: *The Raven, St. 8*

[3] You called me a damned Jew. My race
was old when you were all savages. I am
proud to be a Jew.
    JOHN GALSWORTHY: *Loyalties, Act II, Sc. 1*
[Quoting a Hungarian friend] We Magyars
are a very old race; we have a civilization of
a thousand years. A thousand years ago, at a
time when your ancestors were savages hunting in the swamps of what is now London,
my ancestors had discovered that a man who
tells the truth is very likely to be disagreeable.
    A. EDWARD NEWTON: *Derby Day, Chap. 14*

[4] Disraeli's name shows he is by descent
a Jew. His father became a convert. He is the
better for that in this world, and I hope he
will be the better for it in the next. I have the
happiness of being acquainted with some Jewish families in London, and among them more
accomplished ladies, or more humane, cordial,
high-minded, or better-educated gentlemen I

I will sit down now, but the time will come when you will hear me.[1]

Maiden Speech in the House of Commons [1837]

Free trade is not a principle, it is an expedient.[2]

On Import Duties [April 25, 1843]

The noble lord [3] is the Rupert of debate.[4]

Speech [April, 1844]

The Right Honorable gentleman [5] caught the Whigs bathing and walked away with their clothes.

Speech, House of Commons [February 28, 1845]

A conservative government is an organized hypocrisy.

Speech on Agricultural Interests [March 17, 1845]

A precedent embalms a principle.

Speech on the Expenditures of the Country [February 22, 1848]

Justice is truth in action.

Speech [February 11, 1851]

It is much easier to be critical than to be correct.

Speech [January 24, 1860]

Posterity is a most limited assembly. Those gentlemen who reach posterity are not much more numerous than the planets.

Speech [June 3, 1862]

The characteristic of the present age is craving credulity.

Speech at Oxford Diocesan Conference [November 25, 1864]

What is the question now placed before society with the glib assurance which to me is most astonishing? That question is this: Is man an ape or an angel? [1] I, my lord, I am on the side of the angels. I repudiate with indignation and abhorrence those new fangled theories.

Ibid.

There are rare instances when the sympathy of a nation approaches those tenderer feelings which are generally supposed to be peculiar to the individual and to be the happy privilege of private life; and this is one.

Address, House of Commons [May 1, 1865]

In the character of the victim [Lincoln], and even in the accessories of his last moments, there is something so homely and innocent that it takes the question, as it were, out of all the pomp of history and the ceremonial of diplomacy — it touches the heart of nations and appeals to the domestic sentiment of mankind.

Ibid.

Ignorance never settles a question.

Ibid. [May 14, 1866]

Individualities may form communities, but it is institutions alone that can create a nation.

Speech at Manchester [1866]

However gradual may be the growth of confidence, that of credit requires still more time to arrive at maturity.

Speech [November 9, 1867]

The secret of success is constancy to purpose.

Speech [June 24, 1870]

The author who speaks about his own books is almost as bad as a mother who talks about her own children.

Speech [November 19, 1870]

Increased means and increased leisure are the two civilizers of man.

Speech to the Conservatives of Manchester [April 3, 1872]

---

have never met. It will not be supposed, therefore, that when I speak of Disraeli as the descendant of a Jew, that I mean to tarnish him on that account. They were once the chosen people of God. There were miscreants among them, however, also, and it must certainly have been from one of these that Disraeli descended. He possesses just the qualities of the impenitent thief who died upon the Cross, whose name, I verily believe, must have been Disraeli.

DANIEL O'CONNELL [1775–1847]: *Speech*, at trades union meeting in Dublin [1835]

[1] I will be heard! — WILLIAM LLOYD GARRISON: *Salutatory* of his paper, *The Liberator*, January 1, 1831

[2] It is a condition which confronts us, not a theory. — GROVER CLEVELAND: *Annual Message* [1887], referring to the tariff

[3] Lord Stanley.

[4] See Bulwer Lytton, page 425.

[5] Sir Robert Peel.

[1] See C. R. Darwin, page 448.

A university should be a place of light, of liberty, and of learning.
Speech, House of Commons
[March 8, 1873]

The health of the people is really the foundation upon which all their happiness and all their powers as a State depend.
Speech [July 24, 1877]

A sophisticated rhetorician [Gladstone], inebriated with the exuberance of his own verbosity, and gifted with an egotistical imagination that can at all times command an interminable and inconsistent series of arguments to malign an opponent and to glorify himself.
Speech at Riding School, London
[July 27, 1878]

A series of congratulatory regrets.
Lord Hartington's Resolution on the Berlin Treaty [July 30, 1878]

The hare-brained chatter of irresponsible frivolity.
Speech, Guildhall, London
[November 9, 1878]

The microcosm of a public school.
Vivian Grey. Book I, Chap. II
[1826]

I hate definitions.
Ibid. Book II, Chap. VI

Experience is the child of Thought, and Thought is the child of Action. We can not learn men from books.
Ibid. Book V, Chap. I

Variety is the mother of Enjoyment.
Ibid. Chap. IV

There is moderation even in excess.
Ibid. Book VI, Chap. I

I repeat . . . that all power is a trust; that we are accountable for its exercise; that from the people and for the people all springs, and all must exist.[1]
Ibid. Chap. VII

Man is not the creature of circumstances. Circumstances are the creatures of men.[2]
Ibid.

The disappointment of manhood succeeds to the delusion of youth: let us hope that the heritage of old age is not despair.
Vivian Grey. Book VIII,
Chap. IV

A dark horse [1] which had never been thought of, and which the careless St. James had never even observed in the list, rushed past the grand stand in sweeping triumph.
The Young Duke. Book I, Chap. V
[1831]

What we anticipate seldom occurs; [2] what we least expected generally happens.
Henrietta Temple. Book II,
Chap. IV [1837]

Nature has given us two ears but only one mouth.
Ibid. Book VI, Chap. XXIV

Youth is a blunder; manhood a struggle; old age a regret.
Coningsby. Book III, Chap. I
[1844]

Property has its duties as well as its rights.[3]
Sybil. Book II, Chap. XI [1845]

Little things affect little minds.
Ibid. Book III, Chap. II

We all of us live too much in a circle.[4]
Ibid. Chap. VII

Mr. Kremlin was distinguished for ignorance; for he had only one idea, and that was wrong.[5]
Ibid. Book IV, Chap. V

---

[1] A political phrase common in the United States, drawn from racing cant, referring to a little-known competitor who comes to the fore unexpectedly.

[2] What torments of grief you endured
From evils which never arrived.
EMERSON: *Borrowing*

[3] Property has its duties as well as its rights.
— CAPTAIN THOMAS DRUMMOND [1797-1840], inventor of the Drummond light: *Letter to the Landlords of Tipperary* [May 22, 1838]

[4] The life of man is a self-evolving circle. —
EMERSON: *Essays, First Series, Circles*

[5] See Johnson, page 235.

---

[1] See Webster, page 341, Lincoln, page 456, and Parker, page 477.

[2] See Carlyle, page 377.

He was fresh and full of faith that "something would turn up." [1]

> *Tancred. Book III, Chap. VI*
> *[1847]*

Everything comes if a man will only wait.[2]

> *Ibid. Book IV, Chap. VIII*

That when a man fell into his anecdotage, it was a sign for him to retire.

> *Lothair. Chap. XXVIII [1870]*

Every woman should marry — and no man.

> *Ibid. Chap. XXX*

You know who critics are? — the men who have failed in literature and art.[3]

> *Ibid. Chap. XXXV*

"My idea of an agreeable person," said Hugo Bohun, "is a person who agrees with me."

> *Ibid.*

His Christianity was muscular.

> *Endymion. Chap. XIV [1880]*

The Athanasian Creed is the most splendid ecclesiastical lyric ever poured forth by the genius of man.

> *Ibid. Chap. LII*

The world is a wheel, and it will all come round right.

> *Ibid. Chap. LXX*

"As for that," said Waldenshare, "sensible men are all of the same religion." "Pray, what is that?" inquired the Prince. "Sensible men never tell." [4]

> *Ibid. Chap. LXXXI*

The sweet simplicity of the three per cents.[5]

> *Ibid. Chap. XCVI*

[1] The perpetual state of Wilkins Micawber in *David Copperfield*. See Dickens, page 496.

[2] See Emerson, page 414.

All things come round to him who will but wait. — LONGFELLOW: *Tales of a Wayside Inn, The Student's Tale* [1862]

[3] See Coleridge, page 319.

[4] See Johnson, page 234.

An anecdote is related of Sir Anthony Ashley Cooper [1621–1683], who, in speaking of religion, said, "People differ in their discourse and profession about these matters, but men of sense are really but of one religion." To the inquiry of "What religion?" the Earl said, "Men of sense never tell it." — BURNET: *History of My Own Times, Vol. I, P. 175, note* [ed. 1833].

[5] See Lord Stowell, page 275.

NATHANIEL HAWTHORNE
[1804–1864]

Sleeping or waking, we hear not the airy footsteps of the strange things that almost happen.

> *Twice-Told Tales. David Swan*

The sky, now gloomy as an author's prospects.

> *Ibid. Sights from a Steeple*

Our Creator would never have made such lovely days, and have given us the deep hearts to enjoy them, above and beyond all thought, unless we were meant to be immortal.

> *Mosses from an Old Manse.*
> *The Old Manse*

With that rich perfume of her breath, she blasted the very air.

> *Ibid. Rappaccini's Daughter*

That lack of energy that distinguishes the occupants of almshouses, and all other human beings who depend for subsistence on charity, on monopolized labor, or anything else, but their own independent exertions.

> *The Scarlet Letter. The Custom-House*

Human nature will not flourish, any more than a potato, if it be planted and replanted, for too long a series of generations, in the same worn-out soil.

> *Ibid.*

Neither the front nor the back entrance of the Custom-House opens on the road to Paradise.

> *Ibid.*

It is a good lesson — though it may often be a hard one — for a man who has dreamed of literary fame, and of making for himself a rank among the world's dignitaries by such means, to step aside out of the narrow circle in which his claims are recognized, and to find how utterly devoid of significance, beyond that circle, is all that he achieves, and all he aims at.

> *Ibid.*

The black flower of civilized society, a prison.

> *Ibid. Chap. I*

On the breast of her gown, in red cloth, surrounded with an elaborate

embroidery and fantastic flourishes of gold-thread, appeared the letter A.
The Scarlet Letter. Chap. 2
She named the infant "Pearl," as being of great price, — purchased with all she had.[1]
Ibid. Chap. 6
It is to the credit of human nature, that, except where its selfishness is brought into play, it loves more readily than it hates.
Ibid. Chap. 13
Let men tremble to win the hand of woman, unless they win along with it the utmost passion of her heart.
Ibid. Chap. 15
No man, for any considerable period, can wear one face to himself, and another to the multitude, without finally getting bewildered as to which may be the true.
Ibid. Chap. 20
Life is made up of marble and mud.
The House of the Seven Gables. Chap. 2
Providence seldom vouchsafes to mortals any more than just that degree of encouragement which suffices to keep them at a reasonably full exertion of their powers.
Ibid. Chap. 3
A stale article, if you dip it in a good, warm, sunny smile, will go off better than a fresh one that you've scowled upon.
Ibid. Chap. 4
Life, within doors, has few pleasanter prospects than a neatly arranged and well-provisioned breakfast-table.
Ibid. Chap. 7
What other dungeon is so dark as one's own heart! What jailer so inexorable as one's self!
Ibid. Chap. 11
There is no greater bugbear than a strong-willed relative, in the circle of his own connections.
Ibid.
Once in every half-century, at longest, a family should be merged into the

great, obscure mass of humanity, and forget all about its ancestors.
The House of the Seven Gables. Chap. 12
The world owes all its onward impulses to men ill at ease. The happy man inevitably confines himself within ancient limits.
Ibid. Chap. 20
Of all the events which constitute a person's biography, there is scarcely one . . . to which the world so easily reconciles itself as to his death.
Ibid. Chap. 21
A revolution, or anything that interrupts social order, may afford opportunities for the individual display of eminent virtues; but its effects are pernicious to general morality.
The Snow Image. Old News, Chap. 3
It is a token of healthy and gentle characteristics, when women of high thoughts and accomplishments love to sew; especially as they are never more at home with their own hearts than while so occupied.
The Marble Faun. Chap. 5
Rome? The city of all time, and of all the world!
Ibid. Chap. 12
Every young sculptor seems to think that he must give the world some specimen of indecorous womanhood, and call it Eve, Venus, a Nymph, or any name that may apologize for a lack of decent clothing.
Ibid. Chap. 14
The public, in whose good graces lie the sculptor's or the painter's prospects of success, is infinitely smaller than the public to which literary men make their appeal.
Ibid. Chap. 15
At no time are people so sedulously careful to keep their trifling appointments, attend to their ordinary occupations, and thus put a commonplace aspect on life, as when conscious of some secret that if suspected would make them look monstrous in the general eye.
Ibid. Chap. 20

---

[1] Pearl of great price. — *Matthew, XIII, 46*

Nobody, I think, ought to read poetry, or look at pictures or statues, who cannot find a great deal more in them than the poet or artist has actually expressed.[1]

The Marble Faun. Chap. 41

Caskets! — a vile modern phrase, which compels a person of sense and good taste to shrink more disgustfully than ever before from the idea of being buried at all.

Our Old Home. About Warwick

That odd state of mind wherein we fitfully and teasingly remember some previous scene or incident, of which the one now passing appears to be but the echo and reduplication.

Ibid. Near Oxford

Old soldiers, I know not why, seem to be more accostable than old sailors.

Ibid. Up the Thames

It is not the statesman, the warrior, or the monarch that survives, but the despised poet, whom they may have fed with their crumbs, and to whom they owe all that they now are or have — a name.

Ibid.

Mountains are earth's undecaying monuments.

Sketches from Memory: The Notch of the White Mountains

THOMAS KIBBLE HERVEY
[1804–1859]

The tomb of him who would have made
The world too glad and free.

The Devil's Progress

A love that took an early root,
And had an early doom.

Ibid.

Like ships, that sailed for sunny isles,
But never came to shore.

Ibid.

---

[1] Every book is written with a constant secret reference to the few intelligent persons whom the writer believes to exist in the million. . . . The artist has always the masters in his eye. — EMERSON: *Progress of Culture*

FRANCIS SYLVESTER MAHONY ("FATHER PROUT")
[1804–1866]

With deep affection
And recollection
I often think of
Those Shandon Bells.

The Bells of Shandon. Stanza 1

The bells of Shandon
That sound so grand on
The pleasant waters
Of the river Lee.

Ibid. Stanza 2

SARAH FLOWER ADAMS
[1805–1848]

Though like the wanderer,
   The sun gone down,
Darkness be over me,
   My rest a stone;
Yet in my dreams I'd be
Nearer, my God, to Thee,
   Nearer to Thee.

Nearer, My God, to Thee. Stanza 2

He sendeth sun, he sendeth shower,
Alike they're needful to the flower;
And joys and tears alike are sent
To give the soul fit nourishment.
As comes to me or cloud or sun,
Father! thy will, not mine, be done.

He Sendeth Sun, He Sendeth Shower

Once have a priest for enemy, good bye
To peace.

Vivia Perpetua. Act III, Sc. II

WILLIAM HARRISON AINSWORTH
[1805–1884]

She must be seen to be appreciated.

Old Saint Paul's. Book I, Chap. 3

HENRY GLASSFORD BELL
[1805–1874]

I looked far back into other years, and lo! in bright array
I saw as in a dream the forms of ages passed away.
It was a stately convent, with its old and lofty walls

And gardens with their broad green
walks, where soft the footstep falls.
Mary, Queen of Scots

The scene was changed. It was a bark
that slowly held its way
And o'er its lee the coast of France in
the light of evening lay;
And on its deck a lady sat, who gazed
with tearful eyes
Upon the fast receding hills that dim
and distant rise.
Ibid.

The blood of beauty, wealth, and power
— the heart-blood of a Queen,
The noblest of the Stuart race — the
fairest earth has seen —
Lapped by a dog! Go think of it in
silence and alone!
Then weigh against a grain of sand the
glories of a throne.
Ibid.

WILLIAM LLOYD GARRISON
[1805–1879]

My country is the world; my countrymen are mankind.[1]
Prospectus of the Public Liberator
[1830]

I am in earnest. I will not equivocate;
I will not excuse; I will not retreat a
single inch; and I will be heard![2]
Salutatory of the Liberator
[January 1, 1831]

---

[1] Socrates said he was not an Athenian or a
Greek, but a citizen of the world. — PLU-
TARCH: *On Banishment*
Diogenes, when asked from what country
he came, replied, "I am a citizen of the world."
— DIOGENES LAERTIUS
My country is the world, and my religion
is to do good. — THOMAS PAINE: *Rights of
Man, Chap. V*
See Boswell, page 272.
This famous motto of Garrison's appears in
several different forms. On the first number
of the *Liberator* in 1831, the *my* was changed
to *our*. In the *Prospectus* of Dec. 15, 1837, it
read: Our country is the world; our countrymen are all mankind.
[2] Inscription on the Garrison monument,
Commonwealth Avenue, Boston.
The time will come when you will hear
me. — DISRAELI: *Maiden Speech in the House
of Commons* [1837]

I will be as harsh as truth and as
uncompromising as justice.
The Liberator. Vol. I, No. 1
[1831]

The compact which exists between
the North and the South is a covenant
with death and an agreement with hell.[1]
Resolution adopted by the Anti-
slavery Society [January 27, 1843]

With reasonable men, I will reason;
with humane men I will plead; but to
tyrants I will give no quarter, nor waste
arguments where they will certainly be
lost.
Life. Vol. I, Page 188

Since the creation of the world there
has been no tyrant like Intemperance,
and no slaves so cruelly treated as his.
Ibid. Page 268

We may be personally defeated, but
our principles never.
Ibid. Page 402

Wherever there is a human being, I
see God-given rights inherent in that
being, whatever may be the sex or complexion.
Ibid. Vol. III, Page 390

The success of any great moral enterprise does not depend upon numbers.
Ibid. Page 473

You can not possibly have a broader
basis for any government than that
which includes all the people, with all
their rights in their hands, and with an
equal power to maintain their rights.
Ibid. Vol. IV, Page 224

'Tis up before the sun, roaming afar,
And in its watches wearies every star.
The Free Mind

Though woman never can be man,
By change of sex and a' that,
To social rights, 'gainst class and clan,
Her claim is just, for a' that.
For a' that, and a' that,
Her Eden slip, and a' that,
In all that makes a living soul
She matches man, for a' that.
An Autograph [January 3, 1875]

---

[1] We have made a covenant with death, and
with hell are we at agreement. — *Isaiah,
XXVIII, 15*

EDWARD BULWER LYTTON
[1805–1873]

Rank is a great beautifier.
 The Lady of Lyons. Act II, Sc. 1
       [1838]

Love, like Death,
Levels all ranks,[1] and lays the shepherd's crook
Beside the sceptre.
 Ibid. Act III, Sc. 2

 Curse away!
And let me tell thee, Beauseant, a wise proverb
The Arabs have, — "Curses are like young chickens,
And still come home to roost."
 Ibid. Act V, Sc. 2

Every man has his price,[2] I will bribe left and right.
 Walpole. Act II, Sc. 2

'Tis at sixty man learns how to value home.
 Ibid. Sc. 5

 Bear up.
There is many a slip 'twixt the lip and the cup.[3]
 Ibid. Sc. 9

 You speak
As one who fed on poetry.
 Richelieu. [1839] Act I, Sc. 1

The mate for beauty
Should be a man, and not a money-chest.
 Ibid. Sc. 2

Great men gain doubly when they make foes their friends.
 Ibid.

Beneath the rule of men entirely great,
The pen is mightier than the sword.[4]
 Ibid. Act II, Sc. 2

---

[1] Love levels all ranks. — *Walpole, Act II, Sc. 5*

[2] See Sir Robert Walpole, page 200.

[3] See Burton, page 124.
"Many's the slip,"
Hath the proverb well said, " 'twixt the cup and the lip."
 ROBERT, LORD LYTTON ("Owen Meredith"): *Lucile, Part I, Canto V, Sect. 1*

[4] See Burton, page 123.
Eloquence a hundred times has turned the scale of war and peace at will. — EMERSON: *Progress of Culture*

 Take away the sword;
States can be saved without it.
 Richelieu. [1839] Act II, Sc. 2

In the lexicon of youth, which fate reserves
For a bright manhood, there is no such word
As "fail."
 Ibid.

Ambition has no risk.
 Ibid. Act III, Sc. 1

Our glories float between the earth and heaven
Like clouds which seem pavilions of the sun.
 Ibid. Act V, Sc. 3

 To what a reed
We bind our destinies, when man we love.
 The Duchess de la Vallière.
    Act III, Sc. 3

What's affection, but the power we give another to torment us?
 Darnley. Act II, Sc. 1

A good cigar is as great a comfort to a man as a good cry to a woman.
 Ibid. Act III, Sc. 2

The brilliant chief, irregularly great,
Frank, haughty, rash, — the Rupert of debate! [1]
 The New Timon [1847]. Part I

Next cool, and all unconscious of reproach,
Comes the calm "Johnny who upset the coach." [2]
 Ibid.

Alone! — that worn-out word,
So idly spoken, and so coldly heard;
Yet all that poets sing and grief hath known
Of hopes laid waste, knells in that word
ALONE!
 Ibid. Part II

Two lives that once part are as ships that divide
When, moment on moment, there rushes between
The one and the other a sea; — [3]

---

[1] See Disraeli, page 419. The reference is to Edward, Lord Stanley [1799–1869].

[2] Lord John Russell [1792–1878].

[3] Ships that pass in the night. — LONGFELLOW: *Tales of a Wayside Inn, Part III, The Theologian's Tale, Elizabeth*

Ah, never can fall from the days that
have been
A gleam on the years that shall be!
A Lament
Memory, no less than hope, owes its
charm to "the far away." [1]
Ibid.
When stars are in the quiet skies,
Then most I pine for thee;
Bend on me then thy tender eyes,
As stars look on the sea.
When Stars Are in the Quiet Skies
A good heart is better than all the
heads in the world.
The Disowned. Chap. 33 [1828]
The easiest person to deceive is one's
own self.
Ibid. Chap. 42
The magic of the tongue is the most
dangerous of all spells.
*Eugene Aram. Book I, Chap. 7
[1832]*
Fate laughs at probabilities.
Ibid. Chap. 10
He who has little silver in his pouch
must have the more silk on his tongue.
*The Last of the Barons.
Book I, Chap. 3 [1843]*
Happy is the man who hath never
known what it is to taste of fame — to
have it is a purgatory, to want it is a
hell.
Ibid. Book V, Chap. 1
That should be a warning to you
never again to fall into the error of
the would-be scholar — namely, quote
second-hand.
My Novel [1853]. Chap. 19
There are times when the mirth of
others only saddens us, especially the
mirth of children with high spirits, that
jar on our own quiet mood.
Kenelm Chillingly [1873]
The man who smokes, thinks like a
sage and acts like a Samaritan.
Night and Morning. Chap. 6
The worst part of an eminent man's
conversation is, nine times out of ten,

[1] *The Pathos of Distance*—title of book of
essays (1913) by James Huneker [1860–1921].
The phrase is translated from Nietzsche.

to be found in that part which he means
to be clever.
*Caxtonia. Differences Between the
Urban and Rural Temperament*
If the whole be greater than a part,
a whole man must be greater than that
part of him which is found in a book.
Ibid. Hints on Mental Culture
In science, read, by preference, the
newest works; in literature, the oldest.
The classic literature is always modern.
Ibid.
Rhetorically, yes; conscientiously,
no.
Ibid. Motive Power
In science, address the few, in literature the many. In science, the few must
dictate opinion to the many; in literature, the many, sooner or later, force
their judgment on the few.
Ibid. Readers and Writers
Doubt the permanent fame of any
work of science which makes immediate reputation with the ignorant multitude; doubt the permanent fame of any
work of imagination which is at once
applauded by a conventional clique that
styles itself "the critical few."
Ibid.

PHILIP HENRY STANHOPE, LORD MAHON
[1805–1875]

The island of Sardinia, consisting
chiefly of marshes and mountains, has
from the earliest period to the present
been cursed with a noxious air, an ill-
cultivated soil, and a scanty population.
The convulsions produced by its poisonous plants gave rise to the expression
of sardonic smile, which is as old as
Homer (Odyssey, xx. 302). [1]
*History of England. Vol. I,
Page 287*

[1] The explanation given by Mahon of the
meaning of "sardonic smile" is to be sure the
traditional one, and was believed in by the
late classical writers. But in the Homeric passage referred to, the word is "sardanion"
(σαρδάνιον), not "sardonion." There is no evidence that Sardinia was known to the composers of what we call Homer. It looks as
though the word was to be connected with the

HERMAN MILLER

Think not the beautiful doings of thy
    soul
Shall perish unremembered. They abide
With thee forever; and alone the good
Thou doest nobly, Truth and Love ap-
    prove.
Each pure and gentle deed of mercy
    brings
An honest recompense, and from it
    looms
That sovereign knowledge of thy duty
    done —
A joy beyond all dignities of earth.
        The Doings of Thy Soul [1]

WILLIAM PITT PALMER
[1805–1884]

I couldn't stand it, sir, at all,
But up and kissed her on the spot!
I know — boo-hoo — I ought to not,
But, somehow, from her looks — boo-
    hoo —
I thought she kind o' wished me to!
        The Smack in School

ELIZA LEWIS HENING
SCHERMERHORN
[*Floruit* 1840]

Thou are crumbling to the dust, old
    pile!
Thou art hastening to thy fall,
And around thee in thy loneliness
Clings the ivy to thy wall.
Old Blandford Church, Petersburg,
        Virginia [1840] [2]

---

verb σαίρω, "show the teeth;" "grin like a
dog;" hence that the "sardonic smile" was a
"grim laugh."—MORRIS HICKEY MORGAN
[1859–1910].
[1] Inscription on the wall above the main entrance of the old Medico-Chirurgical Hospital,
now a part of the Graduate Hospital, University of Pennsylvania, Philadelphia.
[2] This poem was long attributed to Tyrone
Power [1797–1841], Irish comedian, who
toured the United States several times, and
visited Old Blandford Church.

COLONEL SIDNEY SHERMAN
[1805–1873]

Remember the Alamo!
        Battle-cry, San Jacinto
            [*April 21, 1836*]

WILLIAM ALLEN
[1806–1879]

Fifty-four forty, or fight.[1]

ELIZABETH BARRETT
BROWNING
[1806–1861]

Of all the thoughts of God that are
Borne inward into souls afar,
Along the Psalmist's music deep,
Now tell me if that any is,
For gift or grace, surpassing this:
"He giveth his belovèd — sleep?" [2]
        The Sleep. Stanza 1
    A child's kiss
Set on thy sighing lips shall make thee
    glad;
A poor man served by thee shall make
    thee rich;
A sick man helped by thee shall make
    thee strong;
Thou shalt be served thyself by every
    sense
Of service which thou renderest.
        A Drama of Exile. Line 1869
Thou large-brained woman and large-
    hearted man.
        To George Sand, A Desire
Or from Browning some "Pome-
    granate," which, if cut deep down
    the middle,

---

[1] The challenge of Senator Allen (of Ohio)
became the slogan of the expansionists who
claimed for the United States the region, now
Oregon, as far north as the southern boundary
of Alaska, latitude 50° 40'. As the campaign
cry of James K. Polk, who was elected President, it is an early example of the popularity
of slogans, such as: "Free soil, free men, free
speech, Frémont" in 1856; "He kept us out of
war" in 1916; "A chicken in every pot, two
cars in every garage" in 1932; "The New
Deal" and "The forgotten man" in the early
days of Franklin D. Roosevelt's presidency.
[2] *Psalm CXXVII, 2*

Shows a heart within blood-tinctured,
of a veined humanity.
Lady Geraldine's Courtship.
Stanza 41

Poets ever fail in reading their own
verses to their worth.
Ibid. Stanza 42

There Shakespeare, on whose forehead
climb
The crowns o' the world; O eyes sub-
lime
With tears and laughters for all time!
A Vision of Poets. Line 298

And Chaucer, with his infantine
Familiar clasp of things divine.
Ibid. Line 388

And Marlowe, Webster, Fletcher, Ben,
Whose fire-hearts sowed our furrows
when
The world was worthy of such men.
Ibid. Line 400

And poor, proud Byron, sad as grave
And salt as life; forlornly brave.
Ibid. Line 412

Life treads on life, and heart on heart;
We press too close in church and mart
To keep a dream or grave apart.
Ibid. Conclusion, Line 820

Knowledge by suffering entereth,
And life is perfected by death.
Ibid. Line 929; also 1005

And I smiled to think God's greatness
flowed around our incomplete-
ness, —
Round our restlessness, His rest.
Rhyme of the Duchess May.
Conclusion, Stanza 11

Do ye hear the children weeping, O my
brothers,
Ere the sorrow comes with years?
The Cry of the Children. Stanza 1

The child's sob in the silence curses
deeper
Than the strong man in his wrath.
Ibid. Stanza 13

Therefore to this dog will I,
Tenderly not scornfully,
Render praise and favor:
With my hand upon his head,
Is my benediction said
Therefore and for ever.
To Flush, My Dog. Stanza 14

The Flushes have their laurels as
well as the Caesars.
Author's note appended to the
foregoing

And lips say "God be pitiful,"
Who ne'er said "God be praised."
The Cry of the Human. Stanza 1

But since he had
The genius to be loved, why let him have
The justice to be honoured in his grave.
Crowned and Buried. Stanza 27

By thunders of white silence.
Hiram Powers's Greek Slave

Unless you can muse in a crowd all day
On the absent face that fixed you;
Unless you can love, as the angels may,
With the breadth of heaven betwixt
you;
Unless you can dream that his faith is
fast,
Through behoving and unbehoving;
Unless you can die when the dream is
past —
Oh, never call it loving!
A Woman's Shortcomings.
Stanza 5

And that dismal cry rose slowly
And sank slowly through the air,
Full of spirit's melancholy
And eternity's despair!
And they heard the words it said —
"Pan is dead — great Pan is dead —
Pan, Pan is dead!" [1]
The Dead Pan. Stanza 26

"Yes," I answered you last night;
"No," this morning, sir, I say:
Colors seen by candle-light
Will not look the same by day. [2]
The Lady's "Yes." Stanza 1

"Guess now who holds thee?" —
"Death," I said. But there
The silver answer rang, — "Not Death,
but Love."
Sonnets from the Portuguese. I

[1] Thamus . . . uttered with a loud voice his
message, "The great Pan is dead." — PLU-
TARCH: *Why the Oracles Cease to Give An-*
swers

[2] And if I loved you Wednesday,
Well, what is that to you?
I do not love you Thursday —
So much is true.
EDNA ST. VINCENT MILLAY: *Thursday*

Go from me. Yet I feel that I shall stand
Henceforward in thy shadow.
> *Sonnets from the Portuguese. VI*

The widest land
Doom takes to part us, leaves thy hand
in mine
With pulses that beat double. What I do
And what I dream include thee, as the
wine
Must taste of its own grapes.
> *Ibid.*

If thou must love me, let it be for
nought
Except for love's sake only.
> *Ibid. XIV*

When our two souls stand up erect and
strong,
Face to face, silent.
> *Ibid. XXII*

To drop some golden orb of perfect song
Into our deep, dear silence.
> *Ibid.*

God only, who made us rich, can make
us poor.
> *Ibid. XXIV*

How do I love thee? Let me count the
ways.
> *Ibid. XLIII*

I shall but love thee better after death.
> *Ibid.*

When the dust of death has choked
A great man's voice, the common words
he said
Turn oracles.
> *Casa Guidi Windows. Part I,*
> *Line 250*

She has seen the mystery hid
Under Egypt's pyramid:
By those eyelids pale and close
Now she knows what Rhamses knows.
> *Little Mattie. Stanza 2*

But so fair,
She takes the breath of men away
Who gaze upon her unaware.
> *Bianca Among the Nightingales.*
> *Stanza 12*

She never found fault with you, never
implied
Your wrong by her right; and yet men
at her side
Grew nobler, girls purer, as through the
whole town

The children were gladder that pulled
at her gown —
My Kate.
> *My Kate. Stanza 5*

We walked too straight for fortune's
end,
We loved too true to keep a friend;
At last we're tired, my heart and I.
> *My Heart and I. Stanza 2*

Grief may be joy misunderstood;
Only the Good discerns the good.
> *De Profundis. Stanza 21*

Women know
The way to rear up children (to be
just),
They know a simple, merry, tender
knack
Of tying sashes, fitting baby-shoes,
And stringing pretty words that make
no sense.
> *Aurora Leigh. Book I, Line 47*

God laughs in heaven when any man
Says "Here I'm learned; this I understand;
In that, I am never caught at fault or
doubt."
> *Ibid. Line 191*

Life, struck sharp on death,
Makes awful lightning.
> *Ibid. Line 210*

The book-club, guarded from your modern trick
Of shaking dangerous questions from
the crease,
Preserved her intellectual.
> *Ibid. Line 302*

Alas, a mother never is afraid
Of speaking angerly to any child,
Since love, she knows, is justified of
love.
> *Ibid. Line 369*

We get no good
By being ungenerous, even to a book,
And calculating profits, — so much
help
By so much reading. It is rather when
We gloriously forget ourselves and
plunge
Soul-forward, headlong, into a book's
profound,
Impassioned for its beauty and salt of
truth —

'Tis then we get the right good from a
book.
 Aurora Leigh. Book I, Line 702
The beautiful seems right
By force of Beauty, and the feeble
wrong
Because of weakness.
 Ibid. Line 753
As sings the lark when sucked up out
of sight
In vortices of glory and blue air.
 Ibid. Line 1055
A woman's always younger than a man
At equal years.
 Ibid. Book II, Line 329
Men do not think
Of sons and daughters, when they fall
in love.
 Ibid. Line 608
Dreams of doing good
To good-for-nothing people.
 Ibid. Line 645
I should not dare to call my soul my
own.
 Ibid. Line 786
God answers sharp and sudden on some
prayers,
And thrusts the thing we have prayed
for in our face,
A gauntlet with a gift in 't.
 Ibid. Line 952
Every wish
Is like a prayer, with God.[1]
 Ibid. Line 954
Girls have curious minds
And fain would know the end of every-
thing.
 Ibid. Line 1194
I learnt the use
Of the editorial "we" in a review.
 Ibid. Book III, Line 312
Is the blue in eyes
As awful as in stockings?[2]
 Ibid. Line 379
Pay the income-tax
And break your heart upon 't.
 Ibid. Line 566
How many desolate creatures on the
earth

---

[1] Prayer is the soul's sincere desire. — JAMES
MONTGOMERY: *What is Prayer?, St. 1*
[2] See Macaulay, page 399.

Have learnt the simple dues of fellow-
ship
And social comfort, in a hospital.
 Aurora Leigh. Book III, Line 1122
A good neighbour, even in this,
Is fatal sometimes, — cuts your morn-
ing up
To mincemeat of the very smallest talk,
Then helps to sugar her bohea at night
With your reputation.
 Ibid. Book IV, Line 488
Good critics who have stamped out
poet's hope,
Good statesmen, who pulled ruin on the
state,
Good patriots who for a theory risked
a cause.
 Ibid. Line 499
A little sunburnt by the glare of life.
 Ibid. Line 1140
Let no one till his death
Be called unhappy. Measure not the
work
Until the day's out and the labor done.
 Ibid. Book V, Line 76
Every age
Appears to souls who live in 't (ask
Carlyle)
Most unheroic.
 Ibid. Line 155
The growing drama has outgrown such
toys
Of stimulated stature, face, and speech,
It also peradventure may outgrow
The simulation of the painted scene,
Boards, actors, prompters, gaslight, and
costume,
And take for a worthier stage the soul
itself,
Its shifting fancies and celestial lights,
With all its grand orchestral silences
To keep the pauses of its rhythmic
sounds.
 Ibid. Line 335
Men get opinions as boys learn to spell,
By reiteration chiefly.
 Ibid. Book VI, Line 6
Surgeons . . .
Spend raptures upon perfect specimens
Of indurated veins, distorted joints,
Or beautiful new cases of curved spine.
 Ibid. Line 173

Since when was genius found respectable?
Aurora Leigh. Book VI, Line 275

Earth's crammed with heaven,
And every common bush afire with
God; [1]
And only he who sees takes off his
shoes —
The rest sit round it and pluck black-
berries.
Ibid. Book VII, Line 820

LADY FLORA HASTINGS
[1806–1839]

Get up; for when all things are merry
and glad,
Good children should never be lazy and
sad;
For God gives us daylight, dear sister,
that we
May rejoice like the lark and may work
like the bee.
Early Rising. A Spring Morning

CHARLES FENNO HOFFMAN
[1806–1884]

Sparkling and bright in liquid light
Does the wine our goblets gleam in;
With hue as red as the rosy bed
Which a bee would choose to dream
in.
Then fill to-night, with hearts as light
To loves as gay and fleeting
As bubbles that swim on the beaker's
brim
And break on the lips while meeting.
Sparkling and Bright

We were not many — we who stood
Before the iron sleet that day;
Yet many a gallant spirit would
Give half his years, if he but could
Have been with us at Monterey.
Monterey. Stanza 1

[1] The still small voice in autumn's hush,
Yon maple wood the burning bush.
WHITTIER: *The Chapel of the
Hermits, St. 16*

WILLIAM GILMORE SIMMS
[1806–1870]

Lithe and long as the serpent train,
Springing and clinging from tree to
tree,
Now darting upward, now down again,
With a twist and a twirl that are
strange to see.
The Grape-Vine Swing.[1] Stanza 1

NATHANIEL PARKER WILLIS
[1806–1867]

The shadows lay along Broadway,
'Twas near the twilight tide.
Unseen Spirits. Stanza 1
The sin forgiven by Christ in Heaven
By man is cursed alway.
Ibid. Stanza 5
Let us weep, in our darkness, but weep
not for him!
Not for him who, departing, leaves mil-
lions in tears!
Not for him who has died full of honor
and years!
Not for him who ascended Fame's
ladder so high:
From the round at the top he has
stepped to the sky.
The Death of Harrison. Stanza 5

CHARLES FRANCIS ADAMS
[1807–1886]

It would be superfluous in me to point
out to your Lordship that this is war.
*Despatch to Earl Russell
[September 5, 1863]*

THOMAS HOLLEY CHIVERS
[1807–1858]

Many mellow Cydonian suckets
Sweet apples, anthosmial, divine,
From the ruby-rimmed beryline buckets
Star-gemmed, lily-shaped, hyaline;
Like the sweet golden goblet found
growing
On the wild emerald cucumber-tree,

[1] It was on a grapevine swing that man first
teetered a little nearer the stars. — CAMERON
ROGERS (ed.): *Full and By*

Rich, brilliant, like chrysoprase glow-
ing
Was my beautiful Rosalie Lee.
Rosalie Lee
On the beryl-rimmed rebecs of Ruby
Brought fresh from the hyaline
streams,
She played on the banks of the Yuba
Such songs as she heard in her
dreams.
Lily Adair
Thus she stood on the arabesque bor-
ders
Of the beautiful blossoms that blew
On the banks of the crystalline waters,
Every morn, in the diaphane dew.
The flowers, they were radiant with
glory,
And shed such perfume on the air,
That my soul, now to want them, feels
sorry,
And bleeds for my Lily Adair.
Ibid.
As the diamond is the crystalline
Revelator of the achromatic white light
of Heaven, so is a perfect poem the
crystalline revelation of the Divine
Idea.
Preface to Eonchs of Ruby
In the music of the morns
Blown through the Conchimarian
horns,
Down the dark vistas of the reboantic
Norns,
To the Genius of Eternity
Crying, "Come to me! Come to me!"
The Poet's Vacation
As an egg, when broken, never
Can be mended, but must ever
Be the same crushed egg for ever —
So shall this dark heart of mine!
To Allegra Florence in Heaven

HELEN SELINA SHERIDAN, LADY DUFFERIN
[1807–1867]

I'm very lonely now, Mary,
For the poor make no new friends;
But, oh! they love the better still
The few our Father sends!
Lament of the Irish Emigrant.
Stanza 4

They say there's bread and work for
all,
And the sun shines always there;
But I'll not forget old Ireland,
Were it fifty times as fair.
Lament of the Irish Emigrant.
Stanza 7

JAMES HENRY HAMMOND
[1807–1864]

The very mudsills of society. . . .
We call them slaves. . . . But I will
not characterize that class at the North
with that term; but you have it. It is
there, it is everywhere; it is eternal.
Speech, U. S. Senate
[March, 1858]
Cotton is King.[1]
Ibid.

CHARLES JEFFERYS
[1807–1865]

It matters not how dear the spot,
How proud or poor the dome,
Love still retains some deathless chains
That bind the heart to home.
Song of Blanche Alpen. Stanza 3
Oh! if I were Queen of France, or still
better, Pope of Rome,
I'd have no fighting men abroad, no
weeping maids at home;
All should be at peace; or, if kings must
show their might,
Why, let them who make the quarrel be
the only men to fight.
Jeannette and Jeannot. Stanza 4
Why, since the world began, the surest
road to fame
Has been the field where men unknown
might win themselves a name;
And well I know the brightest eyes have
all the brighter shone,
When looking at some warrior bold, re-
turned from battle won.
Jeannot's Answer. Stanza 1

[1] DAVID CHRISTY: *Cotton is King; or, Slavery in the Light of Political Economy* [1855]
Take away *time is money*, and what is left
of England? take away *cotton is king*, and
what is left of America? — VICTOR HUGO: *Les
Misérables, Marius, Book IV, Chap. 4*

Were only kings themselves to fight,
  there'd be an end of war.
              Jeannot's Answer. Stanza 4

HENRY WADSWORTH LONGFELLOW
[1807–1882]

Look, then, into thine heart, and write! [1]
              Voices of the Night. Prelude,
              Stanza 19

I heard the trailing garments of the Night [2]
Sweep through her marble halls.
              Hymn to Night. Stanza 1

Tell me not, in mournful numbers,
  Life is but an empty dream!
For the soul is dead that slumbers,
  And things are not what they seem. [3]
              A Psalm of Life. Stanza 1

Life is real! Life is earnest!
  And the grave is not its goal;
Dust thou art, to dust returnest,
  Was not spoken of the soul.
              Ibid. Stanza 2

Art is long, and Time is fleeting, [4]
  And our hearts, though stout and brave,
Still, like muffled drums, are beating
  Funeral marches to the grave. [5]
              Ibid. Stanza 4

Trust no Future, howe'er pleasant!
  Let the dead Past bury its dead!
Act, act in the living present!
  Heart within, and God o'erhead!
              Ibid. Stanza 6

Lives of great men all remind us
  We can make our lives sublime,

[1] See Sir Philip Sidney, page 27.
[2] See Mrs. Whitman, page 418.
[3] Non semper ea sunt quae videntur (Things are not always what they seem). — PHAEDRUS: *Fables, Book IV, Fable 2, L. 5*
[4] The lyf so short, the craft so long to lerne. — CHAUCER: *The Parlement of Foules, L. 1*
  Art is long, life is short. — GOETHE: *Wilhelm Meister, VII, 9.* Hippocrates is supposed to have originated this saying, which is better known in Latin: Ars longa, vita brevis est.
  Art's long, though time is short. — BROWNING: *The Ring and the Book, IX, Juris Doctor Johannes-Baptista Bottinius*
[5] Our lives are but our marches to the grave. — BEAUMONT AND FLETCHER: *The Humorous Lieutenant, Act III, Sc. 5*

And, departing, leave behind us
  Footprints on the sands of time.
              A Psalm of Life. Stanza 7

Let us, then, be up and doing,
  With a heart for any fate; [1]
Still achieving, still pursuing,
  Learn to labour and to wait.
              Ibid. Stanza 9

There is a Reaper whose name is Death, [2]
  And, with his sickle keen,
He reaps the bearded grain at a breath,
  And the flowers that grow between.
              The Reaper and the Flowers.
              Stanza 1

Spake full well, in language quaint and olden,
  One who dwelleth by the castled Rhine,
When he called the flowers, so blue and golden,
  Stars, that in earth's firmament do shine. [3]
              Flowers. Stanza 1

The hooded clouds, like friars,
  Tell their beads in drops of rain.
              Midnight Mass for the Dying
              Year. Stanza 4

Blue were her eyes as the fairy-flax.
              The Wreck of the Hesperus.
              Stanza 2

Christ save us all from a death like this,
  On the reef of Norman's Woe!
              Ibid. Stanza 22

If this glass doth fall,
  Farewell then, O Luck of Edenhall.
              The Luck of Edenhall.[4] Stanza 4

His brow is wet with honest sweat,
  He earns whate'er he can,
And looks the whole world in the face,
  For he owes not any man.
              The Village Blacksmith. Stanza 2

[1] Here's a heart for every fate. — BYRON: *To Thomas Moore, St. 1*
[2] There is a Reaper whose name is death. — ARNIM AND BRENTANO: *Erntelied* (from *Des Knaben Wunderhorn,* ed. 1857, *Vol. I, P. 59*)
[3] Flowerets that shine as blue stars in the green firmament of the earth. — FREDERICK WILHELM CAROVÉ [1789–1852]: *A Story Without an End.* Carové lived in Coblenz on the Rhine.
[4] From the German of UHLAND.

Something attempted, something done,
Has earned a night's repose.
                The Village Blacksmith. Stanza 7

No one is so accursed by fate,
No one so utterly desolate,
    But some heart, though unknown,
    Responds unto his own.
                        Endymion. Stanza 8

For Time will teach thee soon the truth,
    There are no birds in last year's
    nest! [1]
                It Is Not Always May. Stanza 6

Into each life some rain must fall,
    Some days must be dark and dreary.
                    The Rainy Day. Stanza 3

I like that ancient Saxon phrase, which calls
The burial-ground God's-Acre!
                        God's-Acre. Stanza 1

Thou hast taught me, Silent River!
    Many a lesson, deep and long;
Thou hast been a generous giver;
    I can give thee but a song.
                To the River Charles. Stanza 3

The prayer of Ajax was for light.[2]
                The Goblet of Life. Stanza 9

Standing with reluctant feet,
Where the brook and river meet,
Womanhood and childhood fleet!
                    Maidenhood. Stanza 3

A banner with the strange device,
            Excelsior!
                    Excelsior. Stanza 1

Stars of the summer night!
    Far in yon azure deeps,
Hide, hide your golden light!
    She sleeps.
        *The Spanish Student. Act I, Sc. 3,
                            Serenade*

---

[1] En los nidos de antaño
    No hay pajaros hogano
    (In last year's nests
    This year no sparrow rests).
                Cervantes: *Don Quixote,
                    Part II, Chap. LXXIV*
See François Villon:
    Mais où sont les neiges d'antan?
    (Where are the snows of yester year?)
                        Rossetti's translation
There is no bird in any last year's nest! —
Austin Dobson: *The Dying of Tanneguy du Bois*
[2]   The light of Heaven restore;
    Give me to see, and Ajax asks no more.
        Pope: *The Iliad, Book XVII, L. 730*
More light. — Goethe's last words

She floats upon the river of his
    thoughts.[1]
                The Spanish Student. Act II, Sc. 3

Heaven gives almonds
To those who have no teeth. That's nuts
    to crack.
                    Ibid. Act III, Sc. 5

Were half the power, that fills the world
    with terror,
    Were half the wealth, bestowed on
    camps and courts,
Given to redeem the human mind from
    error,
    There were no need of arsenals or
    forts.
                *The Arsenal at Springfield.
                            Stanza 9*

Between the dark and the daylight,
    When the night is beginning to lower,
Comes a pause in the day's occupations,
    That is known as the Children's
    Hour.
            The Children's Hour. Stanza 1

The day is done, and the darkness
    Falls from the wings of Night,
As a feather is wafted downward
    From an eagle in his flight.
                The Day Is Done. Stanza 1

A feeling of sadness and longing
    That is not akin to pain,
And resembles sorrow only
    As the mist resembles the rain.
                        Ibid. Stanza 3

And the night shall be filled with music,
    And the cares, that infest the day,
Shall fold their tents, like the Arabs,
    And as silently steal away.
                        Ibid. Stanza 11

The horologe of Eternity
Sayeth this incessantly, —
    "Forever — never!
    Never — forever!"
                *The Old Clock on the Stairs.
                            Stanza 9*

I shot an arrow into the air,
It fell to earth, I knew not where.
                The Arrow and the Song. Stanza 1

---

[1] The river of his thoughts. — Byron: *The Dream, St. 2*

Joy and Temperance and Repose
Slam the door on the doctor's nose.
The Best Medicines [1]

Man-like is it to fall into sin,
Fiend-like is it to dwell therein,
Christ-like is it for sin to grieve,
God-like is it all sin to leave.
Sin [2]

Though the mills of God grind slowly,
  yet they grind exceeding small; [3]
Though with patience He stands waiting, with exactness grinds He all.
Retribution [4]

This is the forest primeval.
Evangeline. Prelude

Alike were they free from
Fear, that reigns with the tyrant, and
  envy, the vice of republics.
Ibid. Part I, 1

Neither locks had they to their doors,
  nor bars to their windows;
But their dwellings were open as day
  and the hearts of the owners;
There the richest was poor, and the
  poorest lived in abundance.
Ibid.

When she had passed, it seemed like
  the ceasing of exquisite music.
Ibid.

Silently one by one, in the infinite
  meadows of heaven
Blossomed the lovely stars, the forget-
  me-nots of the angels.
Ibid. 3

Talk not of wasted affection! affection
  never was wasted;
If it enrich not the heart of another, its
  waters, returning

---

[1] From the German of FRIEDRICH VON LO-
GAU [1604–1655].

[2] From the German of FRIEDRICH VON LO-
GAU.

[3] God's mill grinds slow, but sure. — HER-
BERT: *Jacula Prudentum*
᾿Οψὲ θεοῦ μύλοι ἀλέουσι τὸ λεπτὸν ἄλευρον. —
Oracula Sibylliana, VIII, 14
᾿Οψὲ θεῶν ἀλέουσι μύλοι, ἀλέουσι δὲ λεπτά. —
LEUTSCH AND SCHNEIDEWIN: *Corpus Parœmi-
ographorum Grœcorum, Vol. I, P. 444*
Sextus Empiricus is the first writer who has
presented the whole of the adage cited by
Plutarch in his treatise *Concerning such whom
God is slow to punish.*

[4] From the German of FRIEDRICH VON
LOGAU.

Back to their springs, like the rain, shall
  fill them full of refreshment:
That which the fountain sends forth
  returns again to the fountain.
Evangeline. Part II, 1

This is the compass-flower,[1] that the
  finger of God has planted
Here in the houseless wild, to direct the
  traveller's journey
Over the sea-like, pathless, limitless
  waste of the desert.
Ibid. 4

We shall sail securely, and safely reach
The Fortunate Isles.[2]
The Building of the Ship

Sail on, O Ship of State!
Sail on, O Union, strong and great!
Humanity with all its fears,
With all the hopes of future years,
Is hanging breathless on thy fate!
Ibid.

Our hearts, our hopes, are all with thee,
Our hearts, our hopes, our prayers, our
  tears,
Our faith triumphant o'er our fears,
Are all with thee, — are all with thee!
Ibid.

There is no flock, however watched and
  tended,
  But one dead lamb is there!
There is no fireside, howsoe'er de-
  fended,
  But has one vacant chair! [3]
Resignation. Stanza 1

There is no Death! [4] What seems so
  is transition;

---

[1] Known also as the pilot-weed and polar
plant.
  Look at this delicate plant that lifts its
    head from the meadow;
  See how its leaves all point to the north as
    true as a magnet.
NELTJE BLANCHAN (DOUBLEDAY)
[1865–1918]: *Nature's Garden*

[2] You sail and you seek for the Fortunate
    Isles,
  The old Greek Isles of the yellow bird's
    song.
JOAQUIN MILLER: *The Fortunate Isles*

[3] We shall meet, but we shall miss him,
  There will be one vacant chair.
HENRY STEVENSON WASHBURN [1813–
1903]: *The Vacant Chair*

[4] There is no death! The stars go down
  To rise upon some other shore.
JOHN LUCKEY McCREERY [1835–
1906]: *There Is no Death*

This life of mortal breath
Is but a suburb of the life elysian,
Whose portal we call Death.
Resignation. Stanza 5

Nothing useless is, or low;
Each thing in its place is best;
And what seems but idle show
Strengthens and supports the rest.
The Builders. Stanza 2

In the elder days of Art,
Builders wrought with greatest care
Each minute and unseen part;
For the Gods see everywhere.
Ibid. Stanza 5

God sent his Singers upon earth
With songs of sadness and of mirth.
The Singers. Stanza 1

But the great Master said, "I see
No best in kind, but in degree;
I gave a various gift to each,
To charm, to strengthen, and to teach."
Ibid. Stanza 6

All your strength is in your union.
All your danger is in discord;
Therefore be at peace henceforward,
And as brothers live together.
The Song of Hiawatha. Part I

As unto the bow the cord is,
So unto the man is woman,
Though she bends him, she obeys him,
Though she draws him, yet she follows,
Useless each without the other!
Ibid. Part X

Oh the long and dreary Winter!
Oh the cold and cruel Winter!
Ibid. Part XX

If I am not worth the wooing, I surely
am not worth the winning.
*The Courtship of Miles Standish.
Part III*

"Why don't you speak for yourself,
John?"
Ibid.

God had sifted three kingdoms to find
the wheat for this planting.[1]
Ibid. Part IV

He is a little chimney, and heated hot
in a moment.[2]
Ibid. Part VI

[1] See Stoughton, page 179.
[2] A little pot and soon hot. — SHAKESPEARE:
The Taming of the Shrew, Act IV, Sc. 1, L. 6

Saint Augustine! well hast thou said,
That of our vices we can frame
A ladder, if we will but tread
Beneath our feet each deed of shame.[1]
*The Ladder of Saint Augustine.
Stanza 1*

The heights by great men reached and
kept
Were not attained by sudden flight,
But they, while their companions slept,
Were toiling upward in the night.
Ibid. Stanza 10

All houses wherein men have lived and
died
Are haunted houses.
Haunted Houses. Stanza 1

The long mysterious Exodus of death.
*The Jewish Cemetery at Newport.
Stanza 1*

Pride and humiliation hand in hand
Walked with them through the world
where'er they went;
Trampled and beaten were they as the
sand,
And yet unshaken as the continent.
Ibid. Stanza 12

A boy's will is the wind's will,
And the thoughts of youth are long,
long thoughts.
My Lost Youth. Stanza 1

Spanish sailors with bearded lips,
And the beauty and mystery of the
ships,
And the magic of the sea.
Ibid. Stanza 3

Whene'er a noble deed is wrought,
Whene'er is spoken a noble thought,
Our hearts, in glad surprise,
To higher levels rise.
Santa Filomena. Stanza 1

A Lady with a Lamp [2] shall stand
In the great history of the land,
A noble type of good,
Heroic womanhood.
Ibid. Stanza 10

[1] I held it truth, with him who sings
To one clear harp in divers tones,
That men may rise on stepping-stones
Of their dead selves to higher things.
TENNYSON: *In Memoriam, I*
[2] Florence Nightingale [1820–1910], nurse
at Scutari during the Crimean War [1854–
1856].

And Nature, the old nurse, took
 The child upon her knee,
Saying: "Here is a story-book
 Thy Father has written for thee."
   The Fiftieth Birthday of Agassiz.
       Stanza 2

Ye are better than all the ballads
 That ever were sung or said;
For ye are living poems,
 And all the rest are dead.
     Children. Stanza 9

So it happens with the poets:
 Every province hath its own;
Camaralzaman is famous
 Where Badoura is unknown.
    Vox Populi. Stanza 3

Listen, my children, and you shall hear.
  *Tales of a Wayside Inn. Paul
  Revere's Ride, Stanza 1*

One if by land, and two if by sea;
And I on the opposite shore will be.
    Ibid. Stanza 2

The fate of a nation was riding that
 night.
    Ibid. Stanza 8

A voice in the darkness, a knock at the
 door,
And a word that shall echo forevermore!
    Ibid. Stanza 14

A town that boasts inhabitants like me
Can have no lack of good society.
  *Ibid. The Birds of Killingworth,
      Stanza 6*

His form was ponderous, and his step
 was slow;
 There never was so wise a man before;
He seemed the incarnate "Well, I told
 you so!"
    Ibid. Stanza 9

For after all, the best thing one can do
When it is raining, is to let it rain.
    Ibid. Stanza 26

Moons waxed and waned, the lilacs
 bloomed and died,
In the broad river ebbed and flowed the
 tide,
Ships went to sea, and ships came home
 from sea,
And the slow years sailed by and ceased
 to be.
  Ibid. Lady Wentworth, Stanza 7

A maid of all work, whether coarse or
 fine,
A servant who made service seem divine! [1]
    *Tales of a Wayside Inn.
   Lady Wentworth, Stanza 7*

How can I tell the signals and the signs
By which one heart another heart di-
 vines?
How can I tell the many thousand ways
By which it keeps the secret it betrays?
  Ibid. Emma and Eginhard, Stanza 8

Ships that pass in the night, and speak
 each other in passing,
Only a signal shown and a distant voice
 in the darkness;
So on the ocean of life we pass and
 speak one another,[2]
Only a look and a voice; then darkness
 again and a silence.
    Ibid. Elizabeth, IV

The unfinished window in Aladdin's
 tower
Unfinished must remain!
    Hawthorne. Stanza 9

No endeavor is in vain;
Its reward is in the doing,
And the rapture of pursuing
Is the prize the vanquished gain.
   *The Wind Over the Chimney.
       Stanza 10*

Let nothing disturb thee,
Nothing affright thee;
All things are passing;

---

[1] See Herbert, page 135.
[2] And soon, too soon, we part with pain,
  To sail o'er silent seas again.
  THOMAS MOORE: *Meeting of the Ships*
Two lives that once part are as ships that
 divide.
  EDWARD BULWER LYTTON: *A Lament*
We twain have met like the ships upon the sea.
  ALEXANDER SMITH: *A Life Drama*
As two floating planks meet and part on the
 sea,
O friend! so I met and then parted from thee.
  W. R. ALGER: *The Brief Chance Encounter*
Like as a plank of driftwood, tossed on a
 stormy sea,
Another plank encounters, meets, touches,
 parts again.
  SIR EDWIN ARNOLD: *Driftwood*
As vessels starting from ports thousands of
miles apart pass close to each other in the
naked breadths of the ocean, nay, sometimes
even touch in the dark.
  HOLMES: *Professor at the Breakfast Table*

God never changeth;
Patient endurance
Attaineth to all things;
Who God possesseth
In nothing is wanting;
Alone God sufficeth.
　　　　Santa Teresa's Book-Mark [1]
He speaketh not; and yet there lies
A conversation in his eyes.
　　　The Hanging of the Crane. III
"O Caesar, we who are about to die
Salute you!" was the gladiators' cry
In the arena, standing face to face
With death and with the Roman popu-
　　lace.
　　　Morituri Salutamus. Stanza 1
Let him not boast who puts his armor on
As he who puts it off, the battle done.
　　　　　Ibid. Stanza 9
Write on your doors the saying wise
　　and old,
"Be bold! be bold!" and everywhere
　— "Be bold;
Be not too bold!" [2]
　　　　　Ibid. Stanza 10
Better like Hector in the field to die,
Than like a perfumed Paris turn and
　　fly.
　　　　　　　　Ibid.
Ye, against whose familiar names not
　　yet
The fatal asterisk of death is set.
　　　　　Ibid. Stanza 11
The love of learning, the sequestered
　　nooks,
And all the sweet serenity of books.
　　　　　Ibid. Stanza 21
　　Ah, nothing is too late,
Till the tired heart shall cease to palpi-
　　tate.
Cato learned Greek at eighty; Sopho-
　　cles
Wrote his grand Oedipus, and Simoni-
　　des

---

[1] From the Spanish of Santa Teresa. 1515–
1582.
　[2] See Spenser, page 25.
　One would say, he had read the inscription
on the gates of Busyrane, — "Be bold"; and
on the second gate, — "Be bold, be bold, and
evermore be bold": and then again had paused
well at the third gate, — "Be not too bold." —
EMERSON: *Plato; or, the Philosopher*

Bore off the prize of verse from his
　　compeers,
When each had numbered more than
　　fourscore years.
　　　Morituri Salutamus. Stanza 22
Chaucer, at Woodstock with the night-
　　ingales,
At sixty wrote the Canterbury Tales;
Goethe at Weimar, toiling to the last,
Completed Faust when eighty years
　　were past.
　　　　　　　　Ibid.
For age is opportunity no less
Than youth itself, though in another
　　dress,
And as the evening twilight fades away
The sky is filled with stars, invisible
　　by day.
　　　　　Ibid. Stanza 24
So when a great man dies,
For years beyond our ken,
The light he leaves behind him lies
Upon the paths of men.
　　　Charles Sumner. Stanza 9
Sweet the memory is to me
Of a land beyond the sea,
Where the waves and mountains meet,
Where, amid her mulberry-trees
Sits Amalfi in the heat.
　　　　　Amalfi. Stanza 1
The birds, God's poor who cannot wait.
　　　The Sermon of St. Francis.
　　　　　　　　Stanza 3
Be not like a stream that brawls
Loud with shallow waterfalls,
But in quiet self-control
Link together soul and soul.
　　　Songo River. Stanza 11
　Nothing that is can pause or stay;
The moon will wax, the moon will wane,
The mist and cloud will turn to rain,
The rain to mist and cloud again,
　To-morrow be to-day.
　　　　　　　Kéramos
Thine was the prophet's vision, thine
The exaltation, the divine
Insanity of noble minds,
That never falters nor abates,
But labors and endures and waits,
Till all that it foresees it finds,
Or what it can not find creates!
　　　　　　　　Ibid.

Turn, turn, my wheel! 'Tis nature's plan
The child should grow into the man.
Kéramos

The willow pattern, that we knew
In childhood, with its bridge of blue.
Ibid.

He has singed the beard of the king of Spain.[1]
A Dutch Picture. Stanza 1

She knew the life-long martyrdom,
The weariness, the endless pain
Of waiting for some one to come
Who nevermore would come again.
Vittoria Colonna. Stanza 6

Three Kings came riding from far away,
Melchior and Gaspar and Baltasar;
Three Wise Men out of the East were they,
And they travelled by night and they slept by day,
For their guide was a beautiful, wonderful star.
The Three Kings. Stanza 1

Stay, stay at home, my heart, and rest;
Home-keeping hearts are happiest.
Song. Stanza 1

So Nature deals with us, and takes away
Our playthings one by one, and by the hand
Leads us to rest.
Nature

Not in the clamor of the crowded street,
Not in the shouts and plaudits of the throng,
But in ourselves, are triumph and defeat.
The Poets

Three Silences there are: the first of speech,
The second of desire, the third of thought;
This is the lore a Spanish monk, distraught

With dreams and visions, was the first to teach.
The Three Silences of Molinos [1]

The holiest of all holidays are those
Kept by ourselves in silence and apart;
The secret anniversaries of the heart.
Holidays

His presence haunts this room to-night,
A form of mingled mist and light
From that far coast.
Welcome beneath this roof of mine!
Welcome! this vacant chair is thine,
Dear guest and ghost!
Robert Burns. Stanza 9

Your silent tents of green [2]
We deck with fragrant flowers;
Yours has the suffering been,
The memory shall be ours.
Decoration Day. Stanza 6

Great is the art of beginning, but greater the art is of ending;
Many a poem is marred by a superfluous verse.
Elegiac Verse. Stanza 14

Out of the shadows of night
The world rolls into light;
It is daybreak everywhere.
The Bells of San Blas. [3] *Stanza 11*

Who ne'er his bread in sorrow ate,
Who ne'er the mournful midnight hours
Weeping upon his bed has sate,
He knows you not, ye Heavenly Powers.[4]
Hyperion. Book I, Motto

Alas! it is not till time, with reckless hand, has torn out half the leaves from the Book of Human Life to light the

[1] Sir Francis Drake entered the harbour of Cadiz, April 19, 1587, and destroyed shipping to the amount of ten thousand tons lading. To use his own expressive phrase, he had "singed the Spanish king's beard." — CHARLES KNIGHT [1791–1873]: *Pictorial History of England, Vol. III, P. 215*

[1] Miguel Molinos [1640–1696], a Spanish mystic, founder of the Quietists.
[2] The low green tent
  Whose curtain never outward swings.
WHITTIER: *Snow-Bound*
  The little green tent is a country's shrine where patriots kneel and pray. — WALT MASON: *The Little Green Tents*
[3] The last poem written by Longfellow. It is dated March 15, 1882. He died March 24, 1882.
[4] Wer nie sein Brod mit Thränen ass,
  Wer nicht die kummervollen Nächte
  Auf seinem Bette weinend sass,
  Der kennt euch nicht, ihr himmlischen Mächte.
GOETHE: *Wilhelm Meister's Apprenticeship, Book II, Chap. 13*

fires of passion with from day to day,
that man begins to see that the leaves
which remain are few in number.

Hyperion. Book IV, Chap. 8

Look not mournfully into the Past.
It comes not back again. Wisely improve the Present. It is thine. Go forth
to meet the shadowy Future, without
fear, and with a manly heart.[1]

Ibid.

Time has laid his hand
Upon my heart, gently, not smiting it,
But as a harper lays his open palm
Upon his harp to deaden its vibrations.

The Golden Legend. IV, The Cloisters

The grave itself is but a covered bridge
Leading from light to light, through a
brief darkness.[2]

Ibid. V, A Covered Bridge at Lucerne

Don't cross the bridge till you come
to it,
Is a proverb old, and of excellent wit.

Ibid. VI, The School of Salerno

If we could read the secret history
of our enemies, we should find in each
man's life sorrow and suffering enough
to disarm all hostility.

Driftwood

Music is the universal language of
mankind, — poetry their universal
pastime and delight.

Outre-Mer

Hold the fleet angel fast until he bless
thee.[3]

Kavanagh

Give what you have. To some one,
it may be better than you dare to think.

Ibid.

[1] The original inscription on the wall of the
chapel of St. Gilgen, a small village in the Austrian Alps, near Salzburg, thus translated by
Longfellow, is:
  Blicke nicht trauernd in die Vergangenheit,
  Sie kommt nicht wieder, nutze weise die
    Gegenwart,
  Sie ist dein, der düsteren Zukunft geh ohne
  Furcht mit männlichem Sinne entgegen.
Bayard Taylor's translation duplicates Longfellow's.

[2] See Whittier, page 443.

[3] Quoted from *To-morrow*, by NATHANIEL
COTTON [1705–1788].
I will not let thee go, except thou bless me.
— *Genesis, XXXII, 26*

There is no greater sorrow
Than to be mindful of the happy time
In misery.[1]

Inferno. Canto V, Line 121

There was a little girl
Who had a little curl
Right in the middle of her forehead;
  And when she was good
She was very, very good,
But when she was bad she was horrid.

There Was a Little Girl[2]

ROBERT MONTGOMERY
[1807–1855]

And thou, vast ocean! on whose awful
  face
Time's iron feet can print no ruin-
  trace.[3]

*The Omnipresence of the Deity.
Part I*

The soul aspiring pants its source to
  mount,
As streams meander level with their
  fount.[4]

Ibid.

[1]   Nessun maggior dolore
     Che ricordarsi del tempo felice
     Nella miseria.
In omni adversitate fortunæ, infelicissimum
genus est infortunii fuisse felicem (In every
adversity of fortune, to have been happy is
the most unhappy kind of misfortune). —
BOETHIUS: *De Consolatione Philosophiæ, II*
     This is truth the poet sings,
That a sorrow's crown of sorrow is remembering happier things.
     TENNYSON: *Locksley Hall, L. 75*
See Chaucer, page 4.

[2] BLANCHE ROOSEVELT TUCKER, in *The
Home Life of Henry W. Longfellow* [1882],
states that these lines were written by the poet
for his children on a day when Edith did not
want to have her hair curled.

[3] Time writes no wrinkle on thine azure
brow. — BYRON: *Childe Harold's Pilgrimage,
Canto IV, St. 182*

[4] We take this to be, on the whole, the worst
similitude in the world. In the first place, no
stream meanders or can possibly meander
level with the fount. In the next place, if
streams did meander level with their founts,
no two motions can be less like each other
than that of meandering level and that of
mounting upwards. — MACAULAY: *Review of
Montgomery's Poems* (Eleventh Edition), in
Edinburgh Review, April, 1830.
These lines were omitted in the subsequent
edition of the poem.

RICHARD CHEVENIX TRENCH
[1807–1886]

True servant's title he may wear,
  He only who has not
For his lord's gifts, how rich soe'er,
  His lord himself forgot.
The Spilt Pearls. Stanza 8

Lord, what a change within us one
    short hour
Spent in Thy presence will prevail to
    make!
Prayer

We kneel, how weak! we rise, how full
    of power!
Ibid.

I say to thee, — do thou repeat
To the first man thou mayest meet
In lane, highway, or open street,
That he and we and all men move
Under a canopy of love
As broad as the blue sky above.
The Kingdom of God. Stanzas 1 and 2

To leave unseen so many a glorious
    sight,
  To leave so many lands unvisited,
To leave so many worthiest books un-
    read,
  Unrealized so many visions bright: —
Oh! wretched yet inevitable spite
  Of our brief span.
Here and Hereafter

Make channels for the stream of love
Where they may broadly run,
And love has overflowing streams
To fill them every one.
The Law of Love

Thou hast said that mine my life is,
  Till the water of that cup
I have drained; then bid thy servants
  That spilled water gather up!
Harmosan

Bring another cup, and straightway
  To the noble Persian give:
Drink, I said before, and perish, —
  Now I bid thee drink and live!
Ibid.

JOHN GREENLEAF WHITTIER
[1807–1892]

The Present, the Present is all thou hast
  For thy sure possessing;
Like the patriarch's angel hold it fast
  Till it gives its blessing.[1]
My Soul and I. Stanza 34

Pluck one thread, and the web ye mar;
  Break but one
Of a thousand keys, and the paining
    jar
  Through all will run.
Ibid. Stanza 38

The Night is mother of the Day,
  The Winter of the Spring,
And ever upon old Decay
  The greenest mosses cling.
A Dream of Summer. Stanza 4

Art's perfect forms no moral need,
  And beauty is its own excuse;[2]
But for the dull and flowerless weed
Some healing virtue still must plead.
Songs of Labor. Dedication, Stanza 5

Heap high the farmer's wintry hoard!
  Heap high the golden corn!
No richer gift has Autumn poured
  From out her lavish horn!
The Corn-Song. Stanza 1

Speak, Ximena, speak and tell us, who
  has lost, and who has won?
The Angels of Buena Vista. Stanza 6

What calls back the past, like the rich
  pumpkin pie?
The Pumpkin. Stanza 3

And the prayer, which my mouth is
  too full to express,
Swells my heart that thy shadow may
  never be less.
Ibid. Stanza 5

The tissue of the Life to be
  We weave with colors all our own,
And in the field of Destiny
  We reap as we have sown.
Raphael. Stanza 16

God blesses still the generous thought,
  And still the fitting word He speeds,

[1] See Cotton, page 226.
[2] In a footnote, Whittier acknowledges his
indebtedness for this line to EMERSON'S *The
Rhodora.*

And Truth, at His requiring taught,
He quickens into deeds.
Channing. Stanza 23

So fallen! so lost! the light withdrawn
Which once he wore!
The glory from his gray hairs gone
For evermore!
Ichabod. Stanza 1

When faith is lost, when honor dies
The man is dead!
Ibid. Stanza 8

Through the shadowy lens of even
The eye looks farthest into heaven
On gleams of star and depths of blue
The glaring sunshine never knew!
All's Well

Yet sometimes glimpses on my sight,
Through present wrong the eternal
right;
And, step by step, since time began,
I see the steady gain of man.
The Chapel of the Hermits. Stanza 11

We lack but open eye and ear
To find the Orient's marvels here;
The still small voice in autumn's hush,
Yon maple wood the burning bush.[1]
Ibid. Stanza 16

Search thine own heart. What paineth
thee
In others in thyself may be.
Ibid. Stanza 85

The Beauty which old Greece or Rome
Sung, painted, wrought, lies close at
home.
To —, *Lines Written after
a Summer Day's Excursion.
Stanza 7*

Give lettered pomp to teeth of Time,
So "Bonnie Doon" but tarry;
Blot out the Epic's stately rhyme,
But spare his "Highland Mary!"
*Burns: On Receiving a Sprig of
Heather in Blossom. Stanza 29*

We seemed to see our flag unfurled,
Our champion waiting in his place
For the last battle of the world, —
The Armageddon of the race.
Rantoul. Stanza 6

O for a knight like Bayard,
Without reproach or fear.[1]
The Hero. Stanza 1

Blessings on thee, little man,
Barefoot boy, with cheek of tan!
The Barefoot Boy. Stanza 1

Health that mocks the doctor's rules,
Knowledge never learned of schools.
Ibid. Stanza 2

The age is dull and mean. Men creep,
Not walk.
*Lines Inscribed to Friends under
Arrest for Treason Against the
Slave Power. Stanza 1*

God's ways seem dark, but, soon or
late,
They touch the shining hills of day.
Ibid. Stanza 5

Nature speaks in symbols and in signs.
To Charles Sumner

We cross the prairie as of old
The pilgrims crossed the sea,
To make the West, as they the East,
The homestead of the free!
The Kansas Emigrants. Stanza 1

Tradition wears a snowy beard, romance is always young.
Mary Garvin. Stanza 4

Better heresy of doctrine, than heresy
of heart.
Ibid. Stanza 22

For of all sad words of tongue or pen,
The saddest are these: "It might have
been!"[2]
Maud Muller. Stanza 53

Ah, well! for us all some sweet hope
lies
Deeply buried from human eyes.
Ibid. Stanza 54

I know not how, in other lands,
The changing seasons come and go;
What splendors fall on Syrian sands,
What purple lights on Alpine snow.
The Last Walk in Autumn. Stanza 7

I pray the prayer of Plato old:
God make thee beautiful within.
My Namesake. Stanza 40

---

[1] Every common bush afire with God. —
MRS. BROWNING: *Aurora Leigh, Book VII,
L. 821*

[1] Bayard [1476–1524], "le Chevalier sans
peur et sans reproche," a French national
hero.

[2] More sad are these we daily see:
It is, but hadn't ought to be.
FRANCIS BRET HARTE: *Mrs. Judge
Jenkins*

The great eventful Present hides the
Past; but through the din
Of its loud life hints and echoes from
the life behind steal in.
The Garrison of Cape Ann. Stanza 5
And the white magnolia-blossoms star
the twilight of the pines.
Ibid. Stanza 11
Soon or late to all our dwellings come
the spectres of the mind.
Ibid. Stanza 22
True and tender and brave and just,
That man might honor and woman
trust.
*The Prophecy of Samuel Sewall.
Stanza 1*
Old roads winding, as old roads will.
Ibid. Stanza 6
Old Floyd Ireson, for his hard heart,
Tarred and feathered and carried in a
cart
By the women of Marblehead.
Skipper Ireson's Ride. Stanza 1
Round the silver domes of Lucknow,
Moslem mosque and Pagan shrine,
Breathed the air to Britons dearest,
The air of Auld Lang Syne.[1]
The Pipes at Lucknow. Stanza 9
The windows of my soul I throw
Wide open to the sun.
My Psalm. Stanza 2
No longer forward nor behind
I look in hope or fear;
But, grateful, take the good I find,
The best of now and here.
Ibid. Stanza 3
Death seems but a covered way
Which opens into light.[2]
Ibid. Stanza 14
Dead Petra in her hill-tomb sleeps,
Her stones of emptiness remain;
Around her sculptured mystery sweeps
The lonely waste of Edom's plain.[3]
"The Rock" in El Ghor. Stanza 1

[1] It was the pipes of the Highlanders,
And now they played "Auld Lang Syne."
ROBERT TRAILL SPENCE LOWELL [1816–
1891]: *The Relief of Lucknow, September 25, 1857*
[2] See Longfellow, page 440.
[3] A rose-red city, half as old as time.
JOHN WILLIAM BURGON [1813–1888]:
Petra [Newdigate Prize Poem, 1845]

Who never wins can rarely lose,
Who never climbs as rarely falls.
To James T. Fields. Stanza 13
Happy is he who heareth
The signal of his release
In the bells of the Holy City,
The chimes of eternal peace!
The Red River Voyageur. Stanza 10
Perish with him the folly that seeks
through evil good.
Brown of Ossawatomie. Stanza 6
Once more the liberal year laughs out
O'er richer stores than gems or gold;
Once more with harvest-song and shout
Is Nature's bloodless triumph told.
For an Autumn Festival. Stanza 5
Strike, Thou the Master, we Thy keys,
The anthem of the destinies!
The minor of Thy loftier strain,
Our hearts shall breathe the old refrain,
Thy will be done!
Thy Will Be Done. Stanza 7
O Englishmen! — in hope and creed,
In blood and tongue our brothers!
We too are heirs of Runnymede;
And Shakespeare's fame and Crom-
well's deed
Are not alone our mother's.
To Englishmen. Stanza 5
"Thicker than water,"[1] in one rill
Through centuries of story
Our Saxon blood has flowed, and still
We share with you its good and ill,
The shadow and the glory.
Ibid. Stanza 6
"Shoot, if you must, this old gray head,
But spare your country's flag," she said.
Barbara Frietchie. Stanza 18
O, rank is good, and gold is fair,
And high and low mate ill;
But love has never known a law
Beyond its own sweet will!
Amy Wentworth
Shut in from all the world without,
We sat the clean-winged hearth about.
Snow-Bound
Melt not in an acid sect
The Christian pearl of charity.
Ibid.
Angel of the backward look.
Ibid.

[1] See Sir Walter Scott, page 310.

Yet Love will dream, and Faith will
  trust,
(Since He who knows our need is just,)
That somehow, somewhere, meet we
  must.
Alas for him who never sees
The stars shine through his cypress-
  trees!
Who, hopeless, lays his dead away,
Nor looks to see the breaking day
Across the mournful marbles play!
                          Snow-Bound

Life is ever lord of Death
And Love can never lose its own.
                          Ibid.

To eat the lotus of the Nile
  And drink the poppies of Cathay.
      The Tent on the Beach. Stanza 4
    The life to be
Is still the unguessed mystery:
Unscaled, unpierced the cloudy walls
  remain,
We beat with dream and wish the
  soundless doors in vain.
    *Ibid. Interlude after The Grave by
                          the Lake*

And so beside the Silent Sea
  I wait the muffled oar.
      The Eternal Goodness. Stanza 19

I know not where His islands lift
  Their fronded palms in air;
I only know I cannot drift
  Beyond His love and care.
                  Ibid. Stanza 20

Flowers spring to blossom where she
  walks
  The careful ways of duty;
Our hard, stiff lines of life with her
Are flowing curves of beauty.[1]
          Among the Hills. Stanza 52

If woman lost us Eden, such
  As she alone restore it.
                  Ibid. Stanza 60

Heaven's gate is shut to him who comes
  alone;

---

[1] Straight is the line of Duty,
  Curved is the line of Beauty,
  Follow the straight line, thou shalt see
  The curved line ever follow thee.
    WILLIAM MACCALL [1812–1888]: *Duty*
See Ellen Sturgis Hooper, page 508.

Save thou a soul, and it shall save thy
  own!
                      The Two Rabbis

And so, I find it well to come
For deeper rest to this still room,
For here the habit of the soul
Feels less the outer world's control.
                        The Meeting

The world that time and sense have
  known
Falls off and leaves us God alone.
                              Ibid.

He lives to learn, in life's hard school,
  How few who pass above him
Lament their triumph and his loss,
  Like her, — because they love him.
          In School-Days. Stanza 11

Let the thick curtain fall;
I better know than all
How little I have gained,
How vast the unattained.
              My Triumph. Stanza 7

Sweeter than any sung
My songs that found no tongue;
Nobler than any fact
My wish that failed of act.
                  Ibid. Stanza 9

Others shall sing the song,
Others shall right the wrong, —
Finish what I begin,
And all I fail of win.
                  Ibid. Stanza 10

God is and all is well.[1]
                My Birthday. Stanza 2

He brings cool dew in his little bill,
  And lets it fall on the souls of sin:
You can see the mark on his red breast
  still
  Of fires that scorch as he drops it in.[2]
                  The Robin. Stanza 4

One language held his heart and lip,
  Straight onward to his goal he trod,

---

[1] God's in his heaven:
  All's right with the world.
    ROBERT BROWNING: *Pippa Passes,
                              Part I*
[2] Far, far away, is a land of woe and darkness, spirits of evil and fire. Day after day a
little bird flies there, bearing in his bill a drop
of water to quench the flame. So near the
burning stream does he fly that his feathers
are scorched by it, and hence he is named
"Bron-rhuddyn" — breast-burned. —Carmar-
thenshire Legend of the Robin

And proved the highest statesmanship
Obedience to the voice of God.
Charles Sumner. Stanza 17

With fifty years between you and your
well-kept wedding vow,
The Golden Age, old friends of mine,
is not a fable now.
*The Golden Wedding at Longwood.
Stanza 1*

Still, as at Cana's marriage-feast, the
best wine is the last.[1]
Ibid. Stanza 2

The holiest task by Heaven decreed,
An errand all divine,
The burden of our common need
To render less is thine.
The Healer.[2] Stanza 4

Touched by a light that hath no name,
A glory never sung,
Aloft on sky and mountain wall
Are God's great pictures hung.
Sunset on the Bearcamp. Stanza 2

Our fathers' God! from out whose hand
The centuries fall like grains of sand.
Centennial Hymn. Stanza 1

Behold in the bloom of apples
And the violets in the sward
A hint of the old, lost beauty
Of the Garden of the Lord!
The Minister's Daughter. Stanza 7

If any words of mine,
Through right of life divine,
Remain, what matters it
Whose hand the message writ?
An Autograph. Stanza 5

Whate'er his life's defeatures,
He loved his fellow-creatures.
Ibid. Stanza 10

Hater of din and riot
He lived in days unquiet;
And, lover of all beauty,
Trod the hard ways of duty.
Ibid. Stanza 15

---

[1] Thou hast kept the good wine until now.
— *John, II, 10*

[2] A well trained sensible family doctor is
one of the most valuable assets in a community, worth to-day, as in Homer's time,
many another man. . . . Few men live lives
of more devoted self-sacrifice. — Sir William
Osler: *Aequanimitas and Other Addresses,
XIV, Chauvinism in Medicine*

Our first and best! — his ashes lie
Beneath his own Virginian sky.
The Vow of Washington. Stanza 14

Close to my heart I fold each lovely
thing
The sweet day yields; and, not dis-
consolate,
With the calm patience of the woods
I wait
For leaf and blossom when God gives
us Spring!
A Day. Stanza 6

HORATIUS BONAR
[1808–1889]

In the still air the music lies unheard;
In the rough marble beauty lies un-
seen;
To wake the music and the beauty
needs
The master's touch, the sculptor's
chisel keen.
The Master's Touch. Stanza 1

The star is not extinguished when it
sets
Upon the dull horizon; it but goes
To shine in other skies, then reappear
In ours, as fresh as when it first
arose.
Life from Death. Stanza 1

Calm me, my God, and keep me calm,
While these hot breezes blow;
Be like the night-dew's cooling balm
Upon earth's fevered brow.
Calm Me, My God. Stanza 1

Beyond the smiling and the weeping
I shall be soon;
Beyond the waking and the sleeping,
Beyond the sowing and the reaping.
A Little While. Stanza 1

We have no time to sport away the
hours;
All must be earnest in a world like ours.
Our One Life. Stanza 1

SALMON PORTLAND CHASE
[1808–1873]

The Constitution, in all its provisions, looks to an indestructible Union
composed of indestructible States.
*Decision in Texas v. White,
7 Wallace, 725*

The only way to resumption is to resume.

Letter to Horace Greeley
[March 17, 1866]

HENRY FOTHERGILL CHORLEY
[1808–1872]

A song to the oak, the brave old oak,
  Who hath ruled in the greenwood
    long!

The Brave Old Oak. Stanza 1

Then here's to the oak, the brave old
  oak,
Who stands in his pride alone!
And still flourish he, a hale green tree,
When a hundred years are gone!

Ibid. Refrain

Go to the dreamless bed
  Where grief reposes;
Thy book of toil is read;
  The long day closes.

The Long Day Closes. Stanza 3

FRANCES DANA GAGE
[1808–1884]

The home we first knew on this beautiful earth,
The friends of our childhood, the place
  of our birth,
In the heart's inner chamber sung always will be,
As the shell ever sings of its home in
  the sea! [1]

Home

Wife, mother, nurse, seamstress, cook,
  housekeeper, chambermaid, laun-

---

[1] As a sea-shell of the sea
  Ever shall I sing of thee.
    GEORGE MEREDITH: *Love Within*
                the Lover's Breast
Listen thou well, for my shell hath speech.
    CHARLES HENRY WEBB: *With a*
                 Nantucket Shell
One song it sang, —
Sang of the awful mysteries of the tide,
Sang of the misty sea, profound and wide, —
  Ever with echoes of the ocean rang.
    EUGENE FIELD: *The Wanderer*

dress, dairy-woman, and scrub
  generally, doing the work of six,
For the sake of being supported.

The Housekeeper's Soliloquy.
Stanza 10

ANDREW JOHNSON
[1808–1875]

We are swinging round the circle.

On the Presidential Reconstruction
Tour [August, 1866]

THOMAS MILLER
[1808–1874]

What though upon his hoary head
Have fallen many a winter's snow?
His wreath is still as green and red
As 'twas a thousand years ago.
For what has he to do with care!
His wassail-bowl and old arm-chair
Are ever standing ready there,
For Christmas comes but once a year.

Christmas Comes but Once a Year

CAROLINE ELIZABETH SHERIDAN NORTON, LADY MAXWELL
[1808–1877]

We have been friends together,
  In sunshine and in shade,
Since first beneath the chestnut-tree
  In infancy we played.
But coldness dwells within thine heart
  A cloud is on thy brow;
We have been friends together,
  Shall a light word part us now?

We Have Been Friends. Stanza 1

I am listening for the voices
Which I heard in days of old.

The Lonely Harp

Love not! love not! ye hopeless sons
  of clay;
  Hope's gayest wreaths are made of
    earthly flowers —
Things that are made to fade and fall
  away,
  Ere they have blossomed for a few
    short hours.

Love Not

I need no squire, no page with bended
    knee,
To bear my baby through the wild-
    wood track,
Where Allan Percy used to roam with
    me.
                    Allan Percy. Stanza 3
A soldier of the Legion lay dying in
    Algiers;
There was lack of woman's nursing,
    there was dearth of woman's tears.
        Bingen on the Rhine. Stanza 1
Too innocent for coquetry, too fond for
    idle scorning, —
Oh friend! I fear the lightest heart
    makes sometimes heaviest mourn-
    ing.
                    Ibid. Stanza 5
Every poet hopes that after-times
Shall set some value on his votive lay.
        To the Duchess of Sutherland
O Twilight! Spirit that dost render
    birth
To dim enchantments; melting heaven
    with earth,
Leaving on craggy hills and running
    streams
A softness like the atmosphere of
    dreams.
                    The Winter's Walk
For death and life, in ceaseless strife,
    Beat wild on this world's shore,
And all our calm is in that balm —
    Not lost but gone before.
            Not Lost but Gone Before

GEORGE WASHINGTON PATTEN
[1808–1882]

Blaze, with your serried columns!
    I will not bend the knee!
The shackles ne'er again shall bind
    The arm which now is free.
        The Seminole's Reply. Stanza 1
I scorn your proffered treaty!
    The paleface I defy,
Revenge is stamped upon my spear,
    And blood my battle-cry!
                    Ibid. Stanza 2
I'll taunt ye with my latest breath,
    And fight ye till I die!
                    Ibid. Stanza 5

Keep honor, like your sabre, bright,
    Shame coward fear — and then,
If we must perish in the fight,
    Oh! let us die like men.
        Oh, Let Us Die Like Men. Stanza 4
Joys that we've tasted
    May sometimes return,
But the torch when once wasted,
    Ah! how can it burn?
Splendors now clouded,
    Say, when will ye shine?
Broke is the goblet,
    And wasted the wine.
        Joys That We've Tasted. Stanza 1

SAMUEL FRANCIS SMITH
[1808–1895]

My country, 'tis of thee,
Sweet land of liberty,
    Of thee I sing:
Land where my fathers died,
Land of the pilgrims' pride,
From every mountain-side
    Let freedom ring.
                    America
Our fathers' God, to thee,
Author of liberty,
    To thee I sing;
Long may our land be bright
With freedom's holy light;
Protect us by thy might,
    Great God, our King!
                    Ibid.
Our glorious land to-day,
'Neath Education's sway,
    Soars upward still.
Its halls of learning fair,
Whose bounties all may share,
Behold them everywhere,
    On vale and hill.
        Ibid. (Discarded stanza)

CHARLES TENNYSON-TURNER
[1808–1879]

The shadow of our travelling earth
Hung on the silver moon.
                Eclipse of the Moon
And while she hid all England with a
    kiss,

Bright over Europe fell her golden hair.
Letty's Globe

The little moulted feathers, saffron-
tipt,
The perches, which his faltering feet
embraced,
All these remain — not even his bath
removed —
But where's the spray and flutter that
we loved?
The Vacant Cage

FREDERICK WILLIAM
THOMAS
[1808–1866]

'Tis said that absence conquers love;
But oh believe it not!
I've tried, alas! its power to prove,
But thou art not forgot.
Absence Conquers Love

PARK BENJAMIN
[1809–1864]

I'm king of the dead — and I make my
throne
On a monument slab of marble cold;
And my scepter of rule is the spade I
hold:
Come they from cottage or come they
from hall,
Mankind are my subjects, all, all, all!
Let them loiter in pleasure or toilfully
spin —
I gather them in, I gather them in! [1]
The Old Sexton

CHARLES ROBERT DARWIN
[1809–1882]

I have called this principle, by which
each slight variation, if useful, is preserved, by the term Natural Selection.
The Origin of Species. Chap. 3

The expression often used by Mr.
Herbert Spencer, of the Survival of the

[1] These words came from his lips so thin:
"I gather them in — I gather them in!"
EUGENE FIELD: *The Old Sexton*
(a parody)

Fittest, is more accurate, and is sometimes equally convenient.[1]
The Origin of Species. Chap. 3

We will now discuss in a little more
detail the Struggle for Existence.[2]
Ibid.

Even when we are quite alone, how
often do we think with pleasure or pain
of what others think of us — of their
imagined approbation or disapprobation.
The Descent of Man. Chap. 4

The highest possible stage in moral
culture is when we recognize that we
ought to control our thoughts.
Ibid.

The presence of a body of well-
instructed men, who have not to labor
for their daily bread, is important to a
degree which cannot be overestimated;
as all high intellectual work is carried
on by them, and on such work material
progress of all kinds mainly depends,
not to mention other and higher advantages.
Ibid. Chap. 5

Progress has been much more general
than retrogression.
Ibid.

The Simiadae then branched off into
two great stems, the New World and
Old World monkeys; and from the latter at a remote period, Man, the wonder and the glory of the universe, proceeded.[3]
Ibid. Chap. 6

[1] This survival of the fittest which I have
here sought to express in mechanical terms, is
that which Mr. Darwin has called "natural selection, or the preservation of favoured races
in the struggle for life." — HERBERT SPENCER:
Principles of Biology, Indirect Equilibration

[2] The perpetual struggle for room and food.
— MALTHUS: *On Population, Chap. III, P. 48*
[1798]

[3] Pouter, tumbler and fantail are from the
same source;
The racer and hack may be traced to one
horse;
So men were developed from monkeys,
of course,
Which nobody can deny.
LORD CHARLES NEAVES [1800–1876]:
The Origin of Species

See Benjamin Disraeli, page 419.

False facts are highly injurious to the progress of science, for they often endure long; but false views, if supported by some evidence, do little harm, for every one takes a salutary pleasure in proving their falseness.

The Descent of Man. Chap. 21

Physiological experiment on animals is justifiable for real investigation, but not for mere damnable and detestable curiosity.[1]

Letter to E. Ray Lankester

I love fools' experiments. I am always making them.

Remark cited in Life of Darwin

As for a future life, every man must judge for himself between conflicting vague probabilities.

Life and Letters

Believing as I do that man in the distant future will be a far more perfect creature than he now is, it is an intolerable thought that he and all other sentient beings are doomed to complete annihilation after such long-continued slow progress. To those who fully admit the immortality of the human soul, the destruction of our world will not appear so dreadful.

Ibid.

Among the scenes which are deeply impressed on my mind, none exceed in sublimity the primeval forests undefaced by the hand of man. No one can stand in these solitudes unmoved, and not feel that there is more in man than the mere breath of his body.

Journal during the Voyage of H. M. S. Beagle. Chap. 21

---

[1] The main cause of this unparalleled progress in physiology, pathology, medicine and surgery has been the fruitful application of the experimental method of research, just the same method which has been the great lever of all scientific advance in modern times. — DR. WILLIAM H. WELCH [1850–1934]: *Argument against Antivivisection Bill* (Senate No. 34), Fifty-sixth Congress, First Session, February 21, 1900. Quoted in HARVEY CUSHING: *Life of Sir William Osler, Vol. I, P. 521.*

EDWARD FITZGERALD [1]
[1809–1883]

Whether we wake or we sleep,
Whether we carol or weep,
The Sun with his Planets in chime,
Marketh the going of Time.

Chronomoros

The King in a carriage may ride,
And the Beggar may crawl at his side;
But in the general race,
They are traveling all the same pace.

Ibid.

Mrs. Browning's death was rather a relief to me, I must say; no more Aurora Leighs, thank God!

Letter [July 15, 1861] [2]

The soul indeed is far away,
But we would reverence the clay
In which she made so long a stay.

On the Death of Bernard Barton

I have heard tell of another Poet's saying that he knew of no human outlook so solemn as that from an Infant's Eyes.

Euphranor

'Tis a dull sight
To see the year dying,
When winter winds
Set the yellow wood sighing.

Literary Remains: Old Song, Stanza 1

---

[1] For translation of *The Rubaiyat* of Omar Khayyám, see Translations.

[2] I chanced upon a new book yesterday;
I opened it, and where my fingers lay
'Twixt page and uncut page these words I read —
Some six or seven at most — and learned thereby
That you, Fitzgerald, whom by ear and eye
She never knew, thanked God my wife was dead.
Aye, dead! and were yourself alive, good Fitz,
How to return your thanks would pass my wits.
Kicking you seems the common lot of curs,
While more appropriate greeting lends you grace.
Surely to spit there glorifies your face,
Spitting with lips once sanctified by hers.
ROBERT BROWNING in *The Athenaeum, London, July 13, 1889.* Quoted by E. F. BENSON: *As We Were, a Victorian Peep-Show, P. 126*

WILLIAM EWART GLADSTONE
[1809–1898]

To be engaged in opposing wrong affords, under the conditions of our mental constitution, but a slender guarantee for being right.
> *Time and Place of Homer.*
> *Introduction*

Decision by majorities is as much an expedient as lighting by gas.
> *Speech, House of Commons* [*1858*]

The disease of an evil conscience is beyond the practice of all the physicians of all the countries in the world.
> *Speech, Plumstead* [*1878*]

National injustice is the surest road to national downfall.
> *Ibid.*

I have always regarded that Constitution as the most remarkable work known to me in modern times to have been produced by the human intellect, at a single stroke (so to speak), in its application to political affairs.[1]
> *Letter to the Committee in charge of the celebration of the Centennial Anniversary of the American Constitution* [*July 20 1887*]

Selfishness is the greatest curse of the human race.
> *Speech, Hawarden* [*May 28, 1890*]

Tell him, O gracious Lord, if it may be, how much I love him and miss him and long to see him again; and if there be ways in which he may come, vouchsafe him to me as a guide and guard, and grant me a sense of his nearness, in such degree as Thy laws permit.
> *A Prayer for a Friend Out of Sight*

Within the short and narrow bound,
From morn to eventide
In quick, successive train,

---

[1] As the British Constitution is the most subtle organism which has proceeded from progressive history, so the American Constitution is the most wonderful work ever struck off at a given time by the brain and purpose of man. — *Kin Beyond the Sea* (in *The North American Review, September, 1878*)

An infant lived and died
And lived again.
> *On an Infant Who Was Born, Was Baptized, and Died on the Same Day* [*1836*]. *Stanza 12*

Lord, as Thy temple's portals close
Behind the outward-parting throng,
So shut my spirit in repose,
So bind it there, Thy flock among.
The fickle wanderer else will stray
Back to the world's wide parchèd way.
> *Holy Communion. Stanza 1*

OLIVER WENDELL HOLMES [1]
[1809–1894]

Ay, tear her tattered ensign down!
Long has it waved on high,
And many an eye has danced to see
That banner in the sky.
> *Old Ironsides. Stanza 1*

Nail to the mast her holy flag,
Set every threadbare sail,
And give her to the god of storms,
The lightning and the gale!
> *Ibid. Stanza 3*

The mossy marbles rest
On the lips that he has prest
In their bloom —
And the names he loved to hear
Have been carved for many a year
On the tomb.
> *The Last Leaf. Stanza 4*

I know it is a sin
For me to sit and grin
At him here;
But the old three-cornered hat,
And the breeches, and all that,
Are so queer!
> *Ibid. Stanza 7*

And if I should live to be
The last leaf upon the tree
In the spring,
Let them smile, as I do now,
At the old forsaken bough [2]
Where I cling.
> *Ibid. Stanza 8*

---

[1] The most successful combination the world has ever seen, of physician and man of letters. — Sir William Osler. Quoted in Harvey Cushing: *Life of Sir William Osler, Vol. 1, Chap. 15*

[2] A forsaken bough. — *Isaiah, XVII, 9*

Thou say'st an undisputed thing
  In such a solemn way.
            To an Insect. Stanza 7
One sad, ungathered rose
On my ancestral tree.
            My Aunt. Stanza 6
You think they are crusaders, sent
  From some infernal clime,
To pluck the eyes of Sentiment
  And dock the tail of Rhyme,
To crack the voice of Melody
  And break the legs of Time.
      The Music Grinders. Stanza 9
And silence, like a poultice, comes
  To heal the blows of sound.
            Ibid. Stanza 10
I'm not a chicken; I have seen
Full many a chill September.
      The September Gale. Stanza 1
And since, I never dare to write
  As funny as I can.
      The Height of the Ridiculous.
            Stanza 8
Little I ask; my wants are few,
  I only wish a hut of stone,
(A *very plain* brownstone will do,)
  That I may call my own.[1]
            Contentment. Stanza 1
When the last reader reads no more.
            The Last Reader
The freeman, casting with unpurchased
    hand,
The vote that shakes the turret of the
    land.
    Poetry, a Metrical Essay. Proem
Age, like distance, lends a double
    charm.[2]
      A Rhymed Lesson. Urania
And when you stick on conversation's
    burs,
Don't strew your pathway with those
    dreadful *urs.*
                  Ibid.
Be sure your tailor is a man of sense.
                  Ibid.
Wear seemly gloves; not black, nor yet
    to light,
And least of all the pair that once was
    white.
                  Ibid.

Have a good hat; the secret of your
    looks
Lives with the beaver in Canadian
    brooks;
Virtue may flourish in an old cravat,
But man and nature scorn the shock-
    ing hat.[1]
      A Rhymed Lesson. Urania
Learn the sweet magic of a cheerful
    face;
Not always smiling, but at least serene.
            The Morning Visit
There was a young man in Boston town,
  He bought him a stethoscope nice
    and new,
All mounted and finished and polished
    down,
  With an ivory cap and a stopper too.
      The Stethoscope Song. Stanza 1
Now when a doctor's patients are per-
    plexed,
A consultation comes in order next —
You know what that is? In a certain
    place
Meet certain doctors to discuss a case
And other matters, such as weather,
    crops,
Potatoes, pumpkins, lager-beer, and
    hops.
            Rip Van Winkle, M.D.
Wake in our breast the living fires,
The holy faith that warmed our sires;
Thy hand hath made our Nation free;
To die for her is serving Thee.
            Army Hymn. Stanza 2
Thine eye was on the censer,
  And not the hand that bore it.
      Lines by a Clerk. Stanza 5
Where go the poet's lines?
  Answer, ye evening tapers!
Ye auburn locks, ye golden curls,
  Speak from your folded papers!
            The Poet's Lot. Stanza 3
A few can touch the magic string,
  And noisy Fame is proud to win
    them: —
Alas for those that never sing,
  But die with all their music in them!
            The Voiceless. Stanza 1

[1] See Goldsmith, page 254.
[2] See Campbell, page 327.

[1] See page 454.

O hearts that break and give no sign
  Save whitening lip and fading
    tresses.
           The Voiceless. Stanza 3

When darkness gathers over all,
And the last tottering pillars fall,
Take the poor dust thy mercy warms,
And mould it into heavenly forms!
      The Living Temple [Anatomist's
          Hymn]. Stanza 7

We will not speak of years to-night, —
  For what have years to bring
But larger floods of love and light,
  And sweeter songs to sing?
      At a Birthday Festival [for
      James Russell Lowell]. Stanza 1

And faith that sees the ring of light
  Round nature's last eclipse!
             Ibid. Stanza 6

The lusty days of long ago,
When you were Bill and I was Joe.
          Bill and Joe. Stanza 1

Where are the Marys, and Anns, and
  Elizas,
  Loving and lovely of yore?
    Questions and Answers. Stanza 3

Oh for one hour of youthful joy!
Give back my twentieth spring!
      The Old Man Dreams. Stanza 1

Old Time is a liar! We're twenty to-
  night!
          The Boys. Stanza 1

Where the snow-flakes fall thickest
  there's nothing can freeze!
             Ibid. Stanza 2

You hear that boy laughing? [1] — You
  think he's all fun;
But the angels laugh, too, at the good
  he has done;
The children laugh loud as they troop
  to his call,
And the poor man that knows him
  laughs loudest of all.
             Ibid. Stanza 9

One flag, one land, one heart, one hand,
  One Nation, evermore!
    Voyage of the Good Ship Union.
             Stanza 12

Good to the heels the well-worn slipper
  feels

---

[1] The Reverend Samuel May, abolitionist.

When the tired player shuffles off the
  buskin;
A page of Hood may do a fellow good
  After a scolding from Carlyle or
    Ruskin.
      How Not to Settle It. Stanza 3

Build thee more stately mansions, O
  my soul,
As the swift seasons roll!
Leave thy low-vaulted past!
Let each new temple, nobler than the
  last,
Shut thee from heaven with a dome
  more vast,
Till thou at length art free,
Leaving thine outgrown shell by life's
  unresting sea!
    The Chambered Nautilus. Stanza 5

One unquestioned text we read,
All doubt beyond, all fear above, —
Nor crackling pile nor cursing creed
  Can burn or blot it: God is love.[1]
     What We All Think. Stanza 10

When lawyers take what they would
  give
And doctors give what they would take.
     Latter-day Warnings. Stanza 4

His home! — the Western giant smiles,
  And twirls the spotty globe to find
    it; —
This little speck, the British Isles?
  'Tis but a freckle, — never mind it!
     A Good Time Going (to Charles
          Mackay). Stanza 3

But Memory blushes at the sneer,
  And Honor turns with frown defiant,
And Freedom, leaning on her spear,
  Laughs louder than the laughing
    giant.
             Ibid. Stanza 4

Have you heard of the wonderful one-
  hoss shay,
That was built in such a logical way
It ran a hundred years to a day?
    The Deacon's Masterpiece. Stanza 1

A general flavor of mild decay.
            Ibid. Stanza 10

---

[1] God is love. — *1 John, IV, 8*
God! Thou art love! I build my faith on
that. — Robert Browning: *Paracelsus, V*

It went to pieces all at once, —
All at once, and nothing first,
Just as bubbles do when they burst.
The Deacon's Masterpiece. Stanza 11

Learn to give
Money to colleges while you live.
Don't be silly and think you'll try
To bother the colleges, when you die,
With codicil this, and codicil that,
That Knowledge may starve while Law
grows fat;
For there never was pitcher that
wouldn't spill,
And there's always a flaw in a donkey's
will.
Parson Turell's Legacy

Our truest steps are human still, —
To walk unswerving were divine.
The Crooked Footpath. Stanza 8

The living fountain overflows
For every flock, for every lamb,
Nor heeds, though angry creeds oppose
With Luther's dike or Calvin's dam.
Robinson of Leyden. Stanza 6

Where we love is home,
Home that our feet may leave, but not
our hearts.
Homesick in Heaven. Stanza 5

And from two things left behind him, —
(Be sure they'll try to find him,)
The tax-bill and assessor, —
Heaven keep the great Professor!
A Farewell to Agassiz

The brightest blade grows dim with
rust,
The fairest meadow white with snow.
Chanson Without Music. Stanza 3

There is no time like the old time, when
you and I were young.[1]
No Time Like the Old Time. Stanza 1

Fame is the scentless sunflower, with
gaudy crown of gold;
But friendship is the breathing rose,
with sweets in every fold.
Ibid. Stanza 3

'Tis like stirring living embers when,
at eighty, one remembers

All the achings and the quaking of "the
times that tried men's souls." [1]
*Grandmother's Story of Bunker-Hill
Battle. Stanza 1*

Trained in the holy art whose lifted
shield
Wards off the darts a never-slumbering
foe,
By hearth and wayside lurking, waits
to throw.[2]
Sonnet, Joseph Warren, M.D.

The style's the man, so books avow;
The style's the woman, anyhow.
*How the Old Horse Won the Bet.
Stanza 2*

I come not here your morning hour to
sadden,
A limping pilgrim, leaning on his
staff, —
I, who have never deemed it sin to
gladden
This vale of sorrows with a wholesome laugh.
The Iron Gate. Stanza 16

I read it in the story-book, that, for to
kiss his dear,
Leander swam the Hellespont, — and
I will swim this here.
*The Ballad of the Oysterman.
Stanza 3*

Lean, hungry, savage, anti-everythings.
A Modest Request. The Speech.

This body in which we journey
across the isthmus between the two
oceans is not a private carriage, but an
omnibus.
The Guardian Angel. Chap. 3

He comes of the Brahmin caste of
New England. This is the harmless, in-
offensive, untitled aristocracy.
The Brahmin Caste of New England [3]

A thought is often original, though
you have uttered it a hundred times.
*The Autocrat of the Breakfast-
Table. I*

Everybody likes and respects self-
made men. It is a great deal better to

---

[1] There are no days like the good old days,
The days when we were youthful!
Eugene Field: *Old Times, Old
Friends, Old Love*

[1] See Thomas Paine, page 271.
[2] Amid an eternal heritage of sorrow and
suffering our work is laid. — **Sir William Osler:** *Aequanimitas* [1906], XX, *The Student
Life.*
[3] In *The Atlantic Monthly, January, 1860.*

be made in that way than not to be made at all.

The Autocrat of the Breakfast-Table. I

Insanity is often the logic of an accurate mind overtaxed.

Ibid.

Put not your trust in money, but put your money in trust.

Ibid. II

Sin has many tools, but a lie is the handle which fits them all.

Ibid. VI

There is that glorious epicurean paradox uttered by my friend the historian,[1] in one of his flashing moments: "Give us the luxuries of life, and we will dispense with its necessaries." To this must certainly be added that other saying of one of the wittiest of men: [2] "Good Americans, when they die, go to Paris."

Ibid.

Boston State-house is the hub of the solar system. You couldn't pry that out of a Boston man, if you had the tire of all creation straightened out for a crowbar.

Ibid.

The axis of the earth sticks out visibly through the centre of each and every town or city.

Ibid.

The world's great men have not commonly been great scholars, nor its great scholars great men.

Ibid.

Knowledge and timber shouldn't be much used till they are seasoned.

Ibid.

The hat is the *ultimum moriens* of respectability.[3]

Ibid. XIII

I firmly believe that if the whole *materia medica* as now used could be sunk to the bottom of the sea, it would be all the better for mankind — and all the worse for the fishes.[1]

Address, Massachusetts Medical Society [May 30, 1860]

To be seventy years young is sometimes far more cheerful and hopeful than to be forty years old.

On the Seventieth Birthday of Julia Ward Howe [May 27, 1889]

FRANCES ANNE KEMBLE
[1809–1893]

What shall I do with all the days and hours
  That must be counted ere I see thy face?
How shall I charm the interval that lowers
  Between this time and that sweet time of grace?

Absence. Stanza 1

Maids must be wives and mothers to fulfil
The entire and holiest end of woman's being.

Woman's Heart

A sacred burden is this life ye bear:
Look on it, lift it, bear it solemnly,
Stand up and walk beneath it steadfastly.
Fail not for sorrow, falter not for sin,
But onward, upward, till the goal ye win.

Lines addressed to the Young Gentleman leaving the Lenox Academy, Massachusetts

MARK LEMON
[1809–1870]

Oh would I were a boy again,
  When life seemed formed of sunny years,

[1] Stir the mixture well
  Lest it prove inferior,
  Then put half a drop
  Into Lake Superior.

Every other day
  Take a drop in water,
You'll be better soon
  Or at least you oughter.
BISHOP WILLIAM CROSWELL
DOANE [1832–1913]: *Lines on Homœopathy*

---

[1] John Lothrop Motley [1814–1877].
Said Scopas of Thessaly, "We rich men count our felicity and happiness to lie in these superfluities, and not in those necessary things." — PLUTARCH: *On the Love of Wealth*
[2] Thomas Gold Appleton [1812–1884]
[3] See Holmes, page 451.

And all the heart then knew of pain
Was wept away in transient tears!
When every tale Hope whispered then,
My fancy deemed was only truth.
Oh, would that I could know again,
The happy visions of my youth.

Oh Would I Were a Boy Again

Forth we went, a gallant band —
Youth, Love, Gold and Pleasure.

Last Song

ABRAHAM LINCOLN
[1809–1865]

If the good people, in their wisdom, shall see fit to keep me in the background, I have been too familiar with disappointments to be very much chagrined.

*Address, New Salem, Illinois
[March 9, 1832]*

I go for all sharing the privileges of the government who assist in bearing its burden.

Letter to Editor of the Sangamo Journal, New Salem, Illinois [June 13, 1835]

There is no grievance that is a fit object of redress by mob law.

Address, Young Men's Lyceum, Springfield, Illinois [January 27, 1837]

Whether or not the world would be vastly benefited by a total and final banishment from it of all intoxicating drinks seems to me not now an open question. Three-fourths of mankind confess the affirmative with their tongues, and, I believe, all the rest acknowledge it in their hearts. Ought any, then, to refuse their aid in doing what good the good of the whole demands?

Speech, Washingtonian Temperance Society, Springfield, Illinois [February 22, 1842]

I believe this government cannot endure permanently half slave and half free.

Speech, Republican State Convention, Springfield, Illinois [June 16, 1858]

Nobody has ever expected me to be president. In my poor, lean lank face nobody has ever seen that any cabbages were sprouting.

Second Campaign Speech against Douglas,[1] Springfield, Illinois [July 17, 1858]

As I would not be a slave, so I would not be a master. This expresses my idea of democracy. Whatever differs from this, to the extent of the difference, is no democracy.

Letter [August 1 (?), 1858]

Let us have faith that right makes might; and in that faith let us to the end, dare to do our duty as we understand it.

Address, Cooper Union, New York [February 27, 1860]

Trusting to Him who can go with me, and remains with you, and be everywhere for good, let us confidently hope that all will yet be well.

Farewell Address, Springfield, Illinois [February 11, 1861]

If we do not make common cause to save the good old ship of the Union on this voyage, nobody will have a chance to pilot her on another voyage.

Address, Cleveland, Ohio [February 15, 1861]

Why should there not be a patient confidence in the ultimate justice of the people? Is there any better or equal hope in the world?

First Inaugural Address [March 4, 1861]

No government proper ever had a provision in its organic law for its own termination.

Ibid.

While the people retain their virtue and vigilance, no administration, by any extreme of wickedness or folly, can very seriously injure the government in the short space of four years.

Ibid.

[1] They have seen in his [Douglas's] round, jolly fruitful face, post-offices, landoffices, marshalships and cabinet-appointments, charge-ships and foreign missions, bursting and sprouting out in wonderful exuberance, ready to be laid hold of by their greedy hands. — *Ibid.*

Labor is prior to, and independent of, capital. Capital is only the fruit of labor, and could never have existed if labor had not first existed.

First Annual Message to Congress
[December 3, 1861]

It is difficult to make a man miserable while he feels he is worthy of himself and claims kindred to the great God who made him.

Address on Colonization to a
Deputation of Colored Men
[August 14, 1862]

My paramount object in this struggle is to save the Union, and is not either to save or destroy slavery. If I could save the Union without freeing any slave, I would do it; and if I could do it by freeing all the slaves, I would do it; and if I could save it by freeing some and leaving others alone, I would also do that.

Letter to Horace Greeley
[August 22, 1862]

I shall try to correct errors where shown to be errors, and I shall adopt new views as fast as they shall appear to be true views.

Ibid.

In giving freedom to the slave we assure freedom to the free, — honorable alike in what we give and what we preserve.

Second Annual Message to Congress
[December 1, 1862]

Beware of rashness, but with energy and sleepless vigilance go forward and give us victories.

Letter to Major-General Joseph
Hooker [January 26, 1863]

The Father of Waters [1] again goes unvexed to the sea.

Letter to James C. Conkling
[August 26, 1863]

Among freemen there can be no successful appeal from the ballot to the bullet, and . . . they who take such appeal are sure to lose their case and pay the cost.

Ibid.

---

[1] Ol' Man River [Mississippi] . . . he keeps on rollin' along. — Song by OSCAR HAMMERSTEIN 2ND., music by JEROME KERN. (1927).

I have endured a great deal of ridicule without much malice; and have received a great deal of kindness, not quite free from ridicule.

Letter to J. H. Hackett
[November 2, 1863]

But, in a larger sense, we cannot dedicate, we cannot consecrate, we cannot hallow this ground. The brave men, living and dead, who struggled here, have consecrated it, far above our poor power to add or to detract. The world will little note nor long remember what we say here, but it can never forget what they did here.

Address, Gettysburg
[November 19, 1863]

It is rather for us to be here dedicated to the great task remaining before us; that from these honored dead we take increased devotion to that cause for which they gave the last full measure of devotion.

Ibid.

That this nation, under God, shall have a new birth of freedom, and that government of the people, by the people, for the people, shall not perish from the earth.[1]

Ibid.

The world has never had a good definition of the word liberty, and the American people, just now, are much in want of one.

Address, Sanitary Fair, Baltimore
[April 18, 1864]

It is no fault in others that the Methodist Church sends more soldiers to the field, more nurses to the hospital, and more prayers to heaven than any. God bless the Methodist Church. Bless all the churches, and blessed be God, who, in this our great trial, giveth us the churches.

To a Methodist Delegation
[May 14, 1864]

I have not permitted myself, gentlemen, to conclude that I am the best man in the country; but I am reminded in this connection of a story of an old Dutch farmer, who remarked to a com-

---

[1] See Daniel Webster, page 341, and Theodore Parker, page 477.

panion once that it was not best to swap horses when crossing a stream.

Reply to National Union League
[June 9, 1864]

Truth is generally the best vindication against slander.

Letter to Secretary Stanton, refusing to dismiss Postmaster-General Montgomery Blair [July 18, 1864]

It has long been a grave question whether any government, not too strong for the liberties of its people, can be strong enough to maintain its existence in great emergencies.

Response to a Serenade
[November 10, 1864]

Human nature will not change. In any future great national trial, compared with the men of this, we shall have as weak and as strong, as silly and as wise, as bad and as good.

Ibid.

I pray that our Heavenly Father may assuage the anguish of your bereavement and leave you only the cherished memory of the loved and lost, and the solemn pride that must be yours to have laid so costly a sacrifice upon the altar of freedom.

Letter to Mrs. Bixby, whose five sons were reported killed in battle [November 21, 1864]

The religion that sets men to rebel and fight against their Government, because, as they think, that Government does not sufficiently help some men to eat their bread in the sweat of other men's faces, is not the sort of religion upon which people can get to heaven.

Reply to two women who had pleaded for the release of their husbands [Washington Chronicle, December 7, 1864]

The Almighty has His own purposes.

Second Inaugural Address
[March 4, 1865]

Fondly do we hope, fervently do we pray, that this mighty scourge of war may speedily pass away. Yet, if God wills that it continue until all the wealth piled by the bondman's two-hundred and fifty years of unrequited toil shall be sunk, and until every drop of blood drawn with the lash shall be paid by another drawn with the sword, as was said three thousand years ago, so still it must be said, that the judgments of the Lord are true and righteous altogether.

Second Inaugural Address
[March 4, 1865]

With malice toward none; with charity for all; with firmness in the right, as God gives us to see the right,[1] let us strive on to finish the work we are in; to bind up the nation's wounds; to care for him who shall have borne the battle, and for his widow and his orphan — to do all which may achieve and cherish a just and lasting peace among ourselves and with all nations.

Ibid.

Men are not flattered by being shown that there has been a difference of purpose between the Almighty and them.

Letter to Thurlow Weed
[March 15, 1865]

Important principles may and must be flexible.

Last public address, Washington [April 11, 1865]

If you once forfeit the confidence of your fellow citizens, you can never regain their respect and esteem. It is true that you may fool all the people some of the time; you can even fool some of the people all the time; but you can't fool all of the people all the time.

To a caller at the White House.
In ALEXANDER K. MCCLURE: *Lincoln's Yarns and Stories, Page 124*

One night he dreamed that he was in a crowd, when someone recognized him as the President, and exclaimed in surprise, "He is a very common-looking man." Whereupon he answered, "Friend, the Lord prefers common-looking people. That is the reason he makes so many of them."

JAMES MORGAN: *Our Presidents, Chap. 6*

[1] See J. Q. Adams, page 291.

If I were to try to read, much less answer, all the attacks made on me, this shop might as well be closed for any other business. I do the very best I know how — the very best I can; and I mean to keep doing so until the end. If the end brings me out all right, what is said against me won't amount to anything. If the end brings me out wrong, ten angels swearing I was right would make no difference.

> *Conversation at the White House, reported by Frank B. Carpenter*

As thin as the homœopathic soup that was made by boiling the shadow of a pigeon that had been starved to death.

> *Quoted by* ALONZO ROTHS-CHILD: *Lincoln, Master of Men, Chap. 3*

Conceited whelp! we laugh at thee,
  Nor mind that not a few
Of pompous, two-legged dogs there be
  Conceited quite as you.

> *The Bear Hunt (Original manuscript in the J. Pierpont Morgan Library, New York)*

I don't s'pose anybody on earth likes gingerbread better'n I do — and gets less'n I do.

> *Quoted by* CARL SANDBURG: *Abraham Lincoln: The Prairie Years, II, 290*

If you call a tail a leg, how many legs has a dog? Five? No; calling a tail a leg don't *make* it a leg.

> *Traditionally attributed to Lincoln*

RICHARD MONCKTON MILNES (LORD HOUGH-TON)[1]
[1809–1885]

But on and up, where Nature's heart
Beats strong amid the hills.
> *Tragedy of the Lac de Gaube. Stanza 2*

[1] George Otto Trevelyan referred to Lord Houghton as "he whom men name Baron Houghton, but the gods call Dicky Milnes." Another friend said of him: "Plenty of people

Great thoughts, great feelings, came to them,
  Like instincts unawares.
> *The Men of Old. Stanza 5*

A man's best things are nearest him,
  Lie close about his feet.
> *Ibid. Stanza 7*

I wandered by the brookside,
  I wandered by the mill;
I could not hear the brook flow,
  The noisy wheel was still.
> *The Brookside. Stanza 1*

The beating of my own heart
Was all the sound I heard.
> *Ibid.*

The hills of manhood wear a noble face
  When seen from far;
The mist of light from which they take their grace
  Hides what they are.
> *Carpe Diem*

Oh glory, that we wrestle
  So valiantly with Time!
> *The Ela*

Heaven was not Heaven if Phaon was not there.
> *A Dream of Sappho*

A poet's Mistress is a hallowed thing.
> *Tempe*

Mohammed's truth lay in a holy Book,
  Christ's in a sacred Life.
> *Mohammedanism*

A fair little girl sat under a tree,
Sewing as long as her eyes could see;
Then smoothed her work, and folded it right,
And said, "Dear work, good-night good-night."
> *Good-Night and Good-Morning Stanza 1*

If what shone afar so grand
Turn to nothing in thy hand,
On again! the virtue lies
In the struggle, not the prize.
> *The World to the Soul*

Heart of the people! Workingmen!
  Marrow and nerve of human powers;
Who on your sturdy backs sustain

will visit you in misfortune, but Milnes is the only one who will visit you in disgrace." — Unidentified newspaper clipping

Through streaming time this world
of ours.
Labor. Stanza 1

Thus all must work: with head or
hand,
For self or others, good or ill;
Life is ordained to bear, like land,
Some fruit, be fallow as it will.
Ibid. Stanza 6

O little fleet that on thy quest divine
Sailest from Palos one bright autumn
morn,
Say, has old ocean's bosom ever borne
A freight of faith and hope to match
with thine?
*Columbus and the Mayflower.
Stanza 1*

They who have steeped their souls in
prayer
Can every anguish calmly bear.
The Sayings of Rabia. IV

Lady Moon, Lady Moon, where are
you roving?
Over the sea.
Lady Moon, Lady Moon, whom are
you loving?
All that love me!
A Child's Song

The sense of humour is the just balance of all the faculties of man, the
best security against the pride of
knowledge and the conceits of the
imagination, the strongest inducement
to submit with a wise and pious patience to the vicissitudes of human
existence.
Memoir of Thomas Hood

ALBERT PIKE
[1809–1891]

The spring has less of brightness,
Every year;
And the snow a ghastlier whiteness,
Every year;
Nor do summer flowers quicken,
Nor the autumn fruitage thicken,
As they once did, for they sicken,
Every year.
Every Year.[1] Stanza 1

[1] A very similar poem, with the title, *The
Old Bachelor's New Year*, is included in *The
Poetical Works* of CHARLES GRAHAM HALPINE

EDGAR ALLAN POE
[1809–1849]

All that we see or seem
Is but a dream within a dream.
*A Dream within a Dream.
Stanza 1*

Sound loves to revel in a summer night.
Al Aaraaf. Part II

Years of love have been forgot
In the hatred of a minute.
To ——

The viol, the violet, and the vine.
The City in the Sea. Stanza 2

From a proud tower in the town
Death looks gigantically down.
Ibid.

The play is the tragedy, "Man,"
And its Hero the Conqueror Worm.
*Ligeia. The Conqueror Worm,
Stanza 5*

Vastness! and Age! and Memories of
Eld!
Silence! and Desolation! and dim
Night!
The Coliseum. Stanza 2

This — all this — was in the olden
Time long ago.
The Haunted Palace. Stanza 2

Unthought-like thoughts that are the
souls of thought.
To Marie Louise

This maiden she lived with no other
thought
Than to love and be loved by me.
Annabel Lee. Stanza 1

I was a child and she was a child,
In this kingdom by the sea,
But we loved with a love that was more
than love—
I and my Annabel Lee—
With a love that the winged seraphs
of heaven
Coveted her and me.
Ibid. Stanza 2

Keeping time, time, time,
In a sort of Runic rhyme,
To the tintinnabulation that so musi-
cally wells
From the bells.
The Bells. Stanza 1

(MILES O'REILLY), compiled and published
after his death, in 1869.

Hear the mellow wedding bells,
　　Golden bells!
What a world of happiness their har-
　　mony foretells!
　　Through the balmy air of night
　　How they ring out their delight!
　　　　　　The Bells. Stanza 2
Thou wast all that to me, love,
　　For which my soul did pine—
A green isle in the sea, love,
　　A fountain and a shrine,
All wreathed with fairy fruits and flow-
　　ers,
　　And all the flowers were mine.
　　　　　　To One in Paradise. Stanza 1
And all my days are trances,
　　And all my nightly dreams
Are where thy dark eye glances
　　And where thy footstep gleams —
In what ethereal dances,
　　By what eternal streams!
　　　　　　Ibid. Stanza 4
I feel that, in the Heavens above,
　　The angels, whispering to one an-
　　　　other,
Can find, among their burning terms
　　of love,
　　None so devotional as that of
　　　　"Mother."
　　　　　　To My Mother [*Mrs. Clemm*]
The fever called "Living"
　　Is conquered at last.
　　　　　　For Annie. Stanza 1
O'er his heart a shadow
　　Fell as he found
　　No spot of ground
That looked like Eldorado.
　　　　　　Eldorado. Stanza 2
A dirge for her, the doubly dead in that
　　she died so young.
　　　　　　Lenore. Stanza 1
O, human love! thou spirit given,
On Earth, of all we hope in Heaven!
　　　　　　Tamerlane. Stanza 15
In Heaven a spirit doth dwell
　　"Whose heart-strings are a lute"; [1]
None sing so wildly well
　　As the angel Israfel.
　　　　　　Israfel. Stanza 1

---

[1] And the angel Israfel, whose heart-strings
are a lute, and who has the sweetest voice of
all God's creatures. — *The Koran*

Once upon a midnight dreary, while
　　pondered, weak and weary,
Over many a quaint and curious vol
　　ume of forgotten lore —
While I nodded, nearly napping, sud
　　denly there came a tapping,
As of some one gently rapping.
　　　　　　The Raven. Stanza
Ah, distinctly I remember, it was in th
　　bleak December,
And each separate dying embe
　　wrought its ghost upon the floor.
　　　　　　Ibid. Stanza
And the silken sad uncertain rustling o
　　each purple curtain
Thrilled me — filled me with fantasti
　　terrors never felt before.
　　　　　　Ibid. Stanza
Deep into that darkness peering, lon
　　I stood there, wondering, fearing,
Doubting, dreaming dreams no morta
　　ever dared to dream before.
　　　　　　Ibid. Stanza
Perched upon a bust of Pallas jus
　　above my chamber door —
　　Perched, and sat, and nothing more
　　　　　　Ibid. Stanza
　　Whom unmerciful Disaster
Followed fast and followed faster.
　　　　　　Ibid. Stanza 1
Take thy beak from out my heart, an
　　take thy form from off my door!
Quoth the Raven, "Nevermore."
　　　　　　Ibid. Stanza 1
And my soul from out that shadow tha
　　lies floating on the floor
Shall be lifted — Nevermore!
　　　　　　Ibid. Stanza 1
Helen, thy beauty is to me
　　Like those Nicæan barks of yore,
That gently, o'er a perfumed sea,
　　The weary, wayworn wanderer bor
　　To his own native shore.
　　　　　　To Helen. Stanza
To the glory that was Greece,
And the grandeur that was Rome.
　　　　　　Ibid. Stanza
The skies they were ashen and sober;
　　The leaves they were crispèd an
　　　　sere —
　　The leaves they were withering an
　　　　sere;

It was night in the lonesome October
Of my most immemorial year.
Ulalume. Stanza 1

It was down by the dank tarn of
Auber,
In the ghoul-haunted woodland of
Weir.
Ibid.

Here once, through an alley Titanic,
Of cypress, I roamed with my
soul —
Of cypress, with Psyche, my soul.
Ibid. Stanza 2

And now, as the night was senescent
And star-dials pointed to morn. . . .
At the end of our path a liquescent
And nebulous lustre was born.
Ibid. Stanza 4

Thus I pacified Psyche and kissed her,
And tempted her out of her gloom.
Ibid. Stanza 8

It is with literature as with law or
empire — an established name is an
estate in tenure, or a throne in possession.
*Poems [1831], Introduction,
Letter to Mr. B——*

With me poetry has been not a purpose, but a passion; and the passions
should be held in reverence: they must
not — they can not at will be excited,
with an eye to the paltry compensations, or the more paltry commendations, of mankind.
Poems [1845], Preface

The object Truth, or the satisfaction
of the intellect, and the object Passion,
or the excitement of the heart, are, although attainable, to a certain extent,
in poetry, far more readily attainable
in prose.
The Philosophy of Composition

I would define, in brief, the Poetry
of words as the Rhythmical Creation of
Beauty. Its sole arbiter is Taste.
The Poetic Principle

Can it be fancied that Deity ever vindictively

Made in his image a mannikin merely
to madden it? [1]
The Rationale of Verse

A Quixotic sense of the honorable —
of the chivalrous.
*Letter to Mrs. Whitman
[October 18, 1848]*

Glitter — and in that one word how
much of all that is detestable do we
express!
Philosophy of Furniture

There is something in the unselfish
and self-sacrificing love of a brute,
which goes directly to the heart of him
who has had frequent occasion to test
the paltry friendship and gossamer
fidelity of mere Man.
The Black Cat

Perverseness is one of the primitive
impulses of the human heart.
Ibid.

There are chords in the hearts of the
most reckless which can not be touched
without emotion. Even with the utterly
lost, to whom life and death are equally
jests, there are matters of which no
jest can be made.
The Masque of the Red Death

The boundaries which divide Life
from Death are at best shadowy and
vague. Who shall say where the one
ends, and where the other begins?
The Premature Burial

The question is not yet settled,
whether madness is or is not the loftiest
intelligence — whether much that is
glorious — whether all that is profound — does not spring from disease
of thought — from moods of mind exalted at the expense of the general intellect.
Eleonora

Those who dream by day are cognizant of many things which escape
those who dream only by night.
Ibid.

---

[1] What! out of senseless Nothing to provoke
A conscious Something to resent the yoke.
FITZGERALD: *The Rubáiyát of Omar
Khayyám, 78*

ALFRED, LORD TENNYSON
[1809–1892]

This laurel greener from the brows
Of him that uttered nothing base.
> *To the Queen. Stanza 2*

And statesmen at her council met
  Who knew the seasons when to take
  Occasion by the hand, and make
The bounds of freedom wider yet.
> *Ibid. Stanza 8*

Broad based upon her people's will,
And compassed by the inviolate sea.
> *Ibid. Stanza 9*

For it was in the golden prime
  Of good Haroun Alraschid.
> *Recollections of the Arabian*
> *Nights. Stanza 2*

A still small voice spake unto me,
"Thou art so full of misery,
Were it not better not to be?"
> *The Two Voices. Stanza 1*

This truth within thy mind rehearse,
That in a boundless universe
Is boundless better, boundless worse.
> *Ibid. Stanza 9*

Tho' thou wert scattered to the wind,
Yet is there plenty of the kind.[1]
> *Ibid. Stanza 11*

I know that age to age succeeds,
Blowing a noise of tongues and deeds,
A dust of systems and of creeds.
> *Ibid. Stanza 69*

Like glimpses of forgotten dreams.
> *Ibid. Stanza 127*

No life that breathes with human
  breath
Has ever truly longed for death.
> *Ibid. Stanza 132*

'Tis life, whereof our nerves are scant,
Oh life, not death, for which we pant;
More life, and fuller, that I want.
> *Ibid. Stanza 133*

Across the walnuts and the wine.
> *The Miller's Daughter. Stanza 4*

---

[1] And fear not lest Existence closing *your*
Account, and mine, should know the like
no more.
The Eternal Sáki from that Bowl has
pour'd
Millions of Bubbles like us, and will pour.
FITZGERALD: *The Rubáiyát of Omar*
Khayyám [1889], *XLVI*

Dowered with the hate of hate, the
  scorn of scorn,
The love of love.
> *The Poet. Stanza 1*

O love, O fire! once he drew
With one long kiss my whole soul
  through
My lips, as sunlight drinketh dew.[1]
> *Fatima. Stanza 3*

Self-reverence, self-knowledge, self-
  control,
These three alone lead life to sovereign
  power.
> *Œnone. Stanza 12*

I built my soul a lordly pleasure-house,
  Wherein at ease for aye to dwell.
> *The Palace of Art. Stanza 1*

The daughter of a hundred Earls.
> *Lady Clara Vere de Vere.*
> *Stanza 1*

A simple maiden in her flower
  Is worth a hundred coats-of-arms.
> *Ibid. Stanza 2*

The lion on your old stone gates
  Is not more cold to you than I.
> *Ibid. Stanza 3*

Her manners had not that repose
  Which stamps the caste of Vere de
  Vere.
> *Ibid. Stanza 5*

From yon blue heavens above us
  bent,
The grand old gardener and his wife [2]
  Smile at the claims of long descent.
> *Ibid. Stanza 7*

Howe'er it be, it seems to me,
  'Tis only noble to be good.[3]
Kind hearts are more than coronets,
  And simple faith than Norman
  blood.
> *Ibid.*

If time be heavy on your hands,
Are there no beggars at your gate,
  Nor any poor about your lands?

---

[1] See Marlowe, page 31.
[2] This line stands in Moxon's edition of
1842, —
  "The gardener Adam and his wife,"—
and was restored by the author in his edition
of 1873.
[3] See Chapman, page 29.

Oh! teach the orphan-boy to read,
  Or teach the orphan-girl to sew.
            Lady Clara Vere de Vere.
                        Stanza 9

You must wake and call me early, call
    me early, mother dear;
To-morrow 'ill be the happiest time of
    all the glad New Year, —
Of all the glad New Year, mother, the
    maddest, merriest day;
For I'm to be Queen o' the May,
    mother, I'm to be Queen o' the
    May.
            The May Queen. Stanza 1

There is sweet music here that softer
    falls
Than petals from blown roses on the
    grass.
        The Lotos-Eaters. Choric Song,
                        Stanza 1

Music that gentlier on the spirit lies,
Than tir'd eyelids upon tir'd eyes;
Music that brings sweet sleep down
    from the blissful skies.
                            Ibid.

            Ah, why
Should life all labour be?
            Ibid. Stanza 4

Time driveth onward fast,
And in a little while our lips are dumb.
Let us alone. What is it that will last?
All things are taken from us, and be-
    come
Portions and parcels of the dreadful
    Past.
                            Ibid.

Give us long rest or death, dark death
    or dreamful ease.
                            Ibid.

The spacious times of great Elizabeth.
        A Dream of Fair Women.
                        Stanza 2

A daughter of the gods, divinely tall,
    And most divinely fair.
            Ibid. Stanza 22

God gives us love. Something to love
    He lends us; but when love is grown
To ripeness, that on which it throve
    Falls off, and love is left alone.
            To J. S. Stanza 4

Sleep sweetly, tender heart, in peace;
    Sleep, holy spirit, blessed soul,

While the stars burn, the moons in-
    crease,
    And the great ages onward roll.
            To J. S. Stanza 18

Sleep till the end, true soul and sweet!
    Nothing comes to thee new or
    strange.
Sleep full of rest from head to feet;
    Lie still, dry dust, secure of change.
            Ibid. Stanza 19

The old order changeth, yielding place
    to new; [1]
And God fulfils himself in many ways,
Lest one good custom should corrupt
    the world.
        Morte D'Arthur. Line 408

More things are wrought by prayer
Than this world dreams of. Wherefore,
    let thy voice
Rise like a fountain for me night and
    day.
                Ibid. Line 415

        I am going a long way
With these thou seest — if indeed I
    go —
(For all my mind is clouded with a
    doubt)
To the island-valley of Avilion,
Where falls not hail, or rain, or any
    snow,
Nor ever wind blows loudly; but it
    lies
Deep-meadowed, happy, fair with or-
    chard lawns
And bowery hollows crowned with
    summer sea,
Where I will heal me of my grievous
    wound.
                Ibid. Line 424

My first, last love; the idol of my
    youth,
The darling of my manhood, and, alas!
Now the most blessed memory of mine
    age!
            The Gardener's Daughter

The long mechanic pacings to and fro,
The set gray life, and apathetic end.
                    Love and Duty

    Ah! when shall all men's good
Be each man's rule, and universal peace
Lie like a shaft of light across the land,

1 Also in *The Coming of Arthur, L. 508.*

And like a lane of beams athwart the
    sea,
Thro' all the circle of the golden year?
                  The Golden Year

Much have I seen and known; cities of
    men
And manners, climates, councils, gov-
    ernments,
Myself not least, but honour'd of them
    all;
And drunk delight of battle with my
    peers,
Far on the ringing plains of windy
    Troy.
                        Ulysses

I am a part of all that I have met.[1]
                        Ibid.

How dull it is to pause, to make an end,
To rust unburnished, not to shine in
    use,
As tho' to breathe were life!
                        Ibid.

       The deep
Moans round with many voices. Come,
    my friends,
'Tis not too late to seek a newer world.
                        Ibid.

It may be we shall touch the Happy
    Isles,
And see the great Achilles, whom we
    knew.
                        Ibid.

To strive, to seek, to find, and not to
    yield.[2]
                        Ibid.

Here at the quiet limit of the world.
                    Tithonus

In the spring a livelier iris changes on
    the burnished dove;
In the spring a young man's fancy
    lightly turns to thoughts of love.
          Locksley Hall. Line 19

He will hold thee, when his passion
    shall have spent its novel force,
Something better than his dog, a little
    dearer than his horse.
                Ibid. Line 49

     This is truth the poet sings,
That a sorrow's crown of sorrow is re-
    membering happier things.[1]
          Locksley Hall. Line 75

Like a dog, he hunts in dreams.
                Ibid. Line 79

With a little hoard of maxims preach-
    ing down a daughter's heart.
                Ibid. Line 94

But the jingling of the guinea helps the
    hurt that Honour feels.
               Ibid. Line 105

For I dipt into the future, far as hu-
    man eye could see,
Saw the Vision of the world, and all
    the wonder that would be;
Saw the heavens fill with commerce,
    argosies of magic sails,
Pilots of the purple twilight, dropping
    down with costly bales;
Heard the heavens fill with shouting,
    and there rain'd a ghastly dew
From the nations' airy navies grappling
    in the central blue.
               Ibid. Line 119

Till the war drum throbbed no longer
    and the battle flags were furled
In the Parliament of Man, the Federa-
    tion of the world.
               Ibid. Line 127

Yet I doubt not through the ages one
    increasing purpose runs,
And the thoughts of men are widened
    with the process of the suns.
               Ibid. Line 137

Knowledge comes, but wisdom lingers.
               Ibid. Line 141

Woman is the lesser man.
               Ibid. Line 151

I will take some savage woman, she
    shall rear my dusky race.
               Ibid. Line 168

I the heir of all the ages in the fore-
    most files of time.
               Ibid. Line 178

Let the great world spin forever down
    the ringing grooves of change.
               Ibid. Line 182

---

[1] See Byron, page 353.
[2] Inscribed on the memorial cross erected
to the memory of Captain Robert Falcon
Scott and his men at Hut Point in the Antarctic.

---

[1] See Longfellow, page 440.
The remembrance of past happiness adds an
insupportable weight to our ills. — VOLTAIRE:
L'Enfant Prodigue, Act III, Sc. 1

Better fifty years of Europe than a
cycle of Cathay.
> *Locksley Hall. Line 184*

And on her lover's arm she leant,
And round her waist she felt it fold,
And far across the hills they went
In that new world which is the old.
> *The Day-Dream. The Departure,*
> *Stanza 1*

And o'er the hills, and far away
Beyond their utmost purple rim,
Beyond the night, across the day,
Thro' all the world she followed him.
> *Ibid. Stanza 4*

We are Ancients of the earth,
And in the morning of the times.
> *Ibid. L'Envoi, Stanza 1*

My strength is as the strength of ten,
Because my heart is pure.
> *Sir Galahad. Stanza 1*

Others' follies teach us not,
Nor much their wisdom teaches;
And most, of sterling worth, is what
Our own experience preaches.
> *Will Waterproof's Lyrical Mon-*
> *ologue. Stanza 22*

And wheresoe'r thou move, good luck
Shall fling her old shoe after.
> *Ibid. Stanza 27*

As she fled fast through sun and shade
The happy winds upon her played,
Blowing the ringlet from the braid.
> *Sir Launcelot and Queen Guine-*
> *vere. Stanza 5*

Cophetua sware a royal oath;
"This beggar maid shall be my
queen!" [1]
> *The Beggar Maid. Stanza 2*

For now the poet can not die,
Nor leave his music as of old,
But round him ere he scarce be cold
Begins the scandal and the cry.
> *To —— , after Reading a Life and*
> *Letters. Stanza 4*

He gave the people of his best:
His worst he kept, his best he gave.
> *Ibid. Stanza 7*

But O for the touch of a vanished
hand,

[1] See Percy, page 255.

And the sound of a voice that is
still!
> *Break, Break, Break. Stanza 3*

But the tender grace of a day that is
dead
Will never come back to me.
> *Ibid. Stanza 4*

Cast all your cares on God; that anchor holds.
> *Enoch Arden*

For men may come and men may go,
But I go on forever.
> *The Brook*

Insipid as the queen upon a card.
> *Aylmer's Field*

Marriages are made in Heaven.
> *Ibid.*

Mastering the lawless science of our
law,
That codeless myriad of precedent,
That wilderness of single instances.
> *Ibid.*

He cursed his credulousness,
And that one unctuous mouth which
lured him, rogue,
To buy strange shares in some Peruvian mine.[1]
> *Sea Dreams*

Is it so true that second thoughts are
best? [2]
> *Ibid.*

He that wrongs his friend
Wrongs himself more, and ever bears
about
A silent court of justice in his breast,
Himself the judge and jury, and him-
self
The prisoner at the bar, ever con-
demn'd.
> *Ibid.*

The worst is yet to come.
> *Ibid.*

Veneer'd with sanctimonious theory.
> *The Princess. Prologue, Line 117*

[1] Money invested in a library gives much
better returns than mining stock. — SIR WIL-
LIAM OSLER: *Letter* [Feb. 11, 1908], quoted in
CUSHING: *Life of Sir William Osler, Vol. II,
Chap. 28*
[2] Second thoughts, they say, are best. —
DRYDEN: *The Spanish Friar, Act II, Sc. 2*
Second thoughts are ever wiser. — EURIPI-
DES: *Hippolytus, Fragment 436*

With prudes for proctors, dowagers for deans,
And sweet girl-graduates in their golden hair.

The Princess. Prologue, Line 141

A rosebud set with little wilful thorns,
And sweet as English air could make her, she.

Ibid. Line 153

A little street half garden and half house.

Ibid. Part I, Line 211

When we fall out with those we love
And kiss again with tears.

Ibid. Part II, Song

Two heads in council, two beside the hearth,
Two in the tangled business of the world,
Two in the liberal offices of life.

Ibid. Line 154

Jewels five-words-long
That on the stretched forefinger of all Time
Sparkle forever.

Ibid. Line 355

Sweet and low,
Wind of the western sea.

Ibid. Part III, Song

The splendour falls on castle walls
And snowy summits old in story.

Ibid. Part IV, Song, Stanza 1

Blow, bugle, blow, set the wild echoes flying,
Blow, bugle; answer, echoes, dying, dying, dying.

Ibid.

The horns of Elfland faintly blowing.

Ibid. Stanza 2

O Love, they die in yon rich sky,
They faint on hill or field or river:
Our echoes roll from soul to soul,
And grow forever and forever.

Ibid. Stanza 3

There sinks the nebulous star we call the sun.

Ibid. Part IV, Line 1

Tears, idle tears, I know not what they mean.
Tears from the depth of some divine despair
Rise in the heart, and gather to the eyes,

In looking on the happy autumn-fields,
And thinking of the days that are no more.

The Princess. Part IV, Song, Stanza 1

Unto dying eyes
The casement slowly grows a glimmering square.

Ibid. Stanza 3

Dear as remembered kisses after death,
And sweet as those by hopeless fancy feigned
On lips that are for others; deep as love,
Deep as first love, and wild with all regret;
Oh death in life, the days that are no more.

Ibid. Stanza 4

Sweet is every sound,
Sweeter thy voice, but every sound is sweet;
Myriads of rivulets hurrying thro' the lawn,
The moan of doves in immemorial elms,
And murmuring of innumerable bees.

Ibid. Part VII, Line 203

Happy he
With such a mother! faith in womankind
Beats with his blood, and trust in all things high
Comes easy to him; and tho' he trip and fall,
He shall not blind his soul with clay.

Ibid. Line 308

Some sense of duty, something of a faith,
Some reverence for the laws ourselves have made,
Some patient force to change them when we will,
Some civic manhood firm against the crowd.

Ibid. Conclusion, Line 54

Rich in saving common-sense,
And, as the greatest only are,
In his simplicity sublime.

Ode on the Death of the Duke of Wellington. Stanza 4

Oh good gray head which all men knew!

Ode on the Death of the Duke of Wellington. Stanza 4

O iron nerve to true occasion true,
O fall'n at length, that tower of strength
Which stood four-square to all the winds that blew.

Ibid.

Not once or twice in our rough island story
The path of duty was the way to glory.[1]

Ibid. Stanza 8

We are not cotton-spinners all.

The Third of February, 1852. Stanza 8

All in the valley of death
  Rode the six hundred.

The Charge of the Light Brigade. Stanza 1

Some one had blundered:
Theirs not to make reply,
Theirs not to reason why,
Theirs but to do and die.

Ibid. Stanza 2

Cannon to right of them,
Cannon to left of them,
Cannon in front of them. . . .
  Into the jaws of death,[2]
  Into the mouth of hell
  Rode the six hundred.

Ibid. Stanza 3

That a lie which is half a truth is ever the blackest of lies,
That a lie which is all a lie may be met and fought with outright,
But a lie which is part a truth is a harder matter to fight.

The Grandmother. Stanza 8

Doänt thou marry for munny, but goä wheer munny is!

Northern Farmer: New Style. Stanza 5

Read my little fable:
  He that runs may read.[1]
Most can raise the flowers now,
  For all have got the seed.

The Flower. Stanza 5

Speak to Him thou for He hears, and Spirit with Spirit can meet —
Closer is He than breathing, and nearer than hands and feet.

The Higher Pantheism. Stanza 6

Flower in the crannied wall,
I pluck you out of the crannies,
I hold you here, root and all, in my hand,
Little flower — but if I could understand
What you are, root and all, and all in all,
I should know what God and man is.

Flower in the Crannied Wall

Dear, near and true — no truer Time himself
Can prove you, tho' he make you evermore
Dearer and nearer, as the rapid of life
Shoots to the fall.

A Dedication

Our little systems have their day.

In Memoriam. Prologue, Stanza 5

Let knowledge grow from more to more.

Ibid. Stanza 7

I held it truth, with him who sings [2]
  To one clear harp in divers tones,
  That men may rise on stepping-stones
Of their dead selves to higher things.[3]

Ibid. Part I, Stanza 1

I sometimes hold it half a sin
  To put in words the grief I feel.

Ibid. Part V, Stanza 1

But, for the unquiet heart and brain
  A use in measured language lies;

---

[1] The paths of glory lead but to the grave. — GRAY: *Elegy Written in a Country Churchyard, St. 9.*
[2] Jaws of death. — SHAKESPEARE: *Twelfth-Night, Act III, Sc. 4, L. 396*
DU BARTAS: *Weekes and Workes, Day I, Part 4.*

[1] He that runs may read. — COWPER: *Tirocinium, Line 79*
[2] The poet alluded to is Goethe. I know this from Lord Tennyson himself, although he could not identify the passage; and when I submitted to him a small book of mine on his marvellous poem, he wrote, "It is Goethe's creed," on this very passage. — REV. DR. GETTY (Vicar of Ecclesfield, Yorkshire)
[3] See Longfellow, page 436.

The sad mechanic exercise,
Like dull narcotics numbing pain.
    In Memoriam. Part V, Stanza 2
Never morning wore
To evening, but some heart did break.
    Ibid. Part VI, Stanza 2
And topples round the dreary west
A looming bastion fringed with fire.
    Ibid. Part XV, Stanza 5
And from his ashes may be made
The violet of his native land.[1]
    Ibid. Part XVIII, Stanza 1
I do but sing because I must,
And pipe but as the linnets sing.[2]
    Ibid. Part XXI, Stanza 6
The shadow cloaked from head to foot.
    Ibid. Part XXIII, Stanza 1
Who keeps the keys of all the creeds.
    Ibid. Stanza 2
And Thought leapt out to wed with
    Thought
Ere Thought could wed itself with
    Speech.
    Ibid. Stanza 4
And round us all the thicket rang
To many a flute of Arcady.
    Ibid. Stanza 6
'Tis better to have loved and lost
Than never to have loved at all.[3]
    Ibid. Part XXVII. Stanza 4;
    Part LXXXV, Stanza 1

---

[1] From her fair and unpolluted flesh
  May violets spring.
    SHAKESPEARE: *Hamlet, Act V,*
        Sc. 1, L. 261
That every Hyacinth the Garden wears
Dropt in her Lap from some once lovely Head.
    FITZGERALD: *The Rubáiyát of*
        Omar Khayyám, XIX
[2] Ich singe, wie der Vogel singt
  Der in den Zweigen wohnet.
    GOETHE: *Wilhelm Meister's Appren-*
        ticeship, Book II, Chap. 11
[3] Say what you will, 'tis better to be left
  Than never to have loved.
    CONGREVE: *The Way of the World,*
        Act II, Sc. 1
  Better to love amiss than nothing to have
    loved.
    CRABBE: *Tale 14, The Struggles of*
        Conscience
What voice did on my spirit fall,
  Peschiera, when thy bridge I crost?
  'Tis better to have fought and lost
Than never to have fought at all.
    ARTHUR HUGH CLOUGH: *Peschiera*

Her eyes are homes of silent prayer.
    In Memoriam. Part XXXII,
        Stanza 1
Whose faith has centre everywhere,
Nor cares to fix itself to form.
    Ibid. Part XXXIII, Stanza 1
How fares it with the happy dead?
    Ibid. Part XLIV, Stanza 1
Short swallow-flights of song, that dip
Their wings in tears, and skim away.
    Ibid. Part XLVIII, Stanza 4
Be near me when my light is low.
    Ibid. Part L, Stanza 1
Do we indeed desire the dead
  Should still be near us at our side?
    Ibid. Part LI, Stanza 1
Hold thou the good; define it well;
  For fear divine Philosophy
Should push beyond her mark, and
  be
Procuress to the Lords of Hell.
    Ibid. Part LIII, Stanza 4
Oh yet we trust that somehow good
  Will be the final goal of ill.
    Ibid. Part LIV, Stanza 1
But what am I?
  An infant crying in the night:
  An infant crying for the light:
And with no language but a cry.
    Ibid. Stanza 5
So careful of the type she seems,
So careless of the single life.
    Ibid. Part LV, Stanza 2
The great world's altar-stairs,
That slope through darkness up to
  God.
    Ibid. Stanza 4
Who battled for the True, the Just.
    Ibid. Part LVI, Stanza 5
The sweetest soul
That ever look'd with human eyes.
    Ibid. Part LVII, Stanza 3
Who breaks his birth's invidious bar,
And grasps the skirts of happy chance,
And breasts the blows of circumstance.
    Ibid. Part LXIV, Stanza 2
And lives to clutch the golden keys,
To mould a mighty state's decrees,
And shape the whisper of the throne.
    Ibid. Stanza 3
Sleep, Death's twin-brother.
    Ibid. Part LXVIII, Stanza 1

So many worlds, so much to do,
So little done, such things to be.[1]
In Memoriam. Part LXXIII,
Stanza 1

Thy leaf has perished in the green,
And, while we breathe beneath the
sun,
The world which credits what is done
Is cold to all that might have been.
Ibid. Part LXXV, Stanza 4

O last regret, regret can die!
Ibid. Part LXXVIII, Stanza 5

The little speedwell's darling blue.
Ibid. Part LXXXIII, Stanza 2

God's fingers touch'd him, and he
slept.
Ibid. Part LXXXV, Stanza 5

There lives more faith in honest doubt,[2]
Believe me, than in half the creeds.
Ibid. Part XCVI, Stanza 3

He seems so near, and yet so far.
Ibid. Part XCVII, Stanza 6

Ring out, wild bells, to the wild sky!
Ibid. Part CVI, Stanza 1

Ring out the old, ring in the new,
Ring, happy bells, across the snow!
Ibid. Stanza 2

Ring in the nobler modes of life
With sweeter manners, purer laws.
Ibid. Stanza 4

Ring out old shapes of foul disease,
Ring out the narrowing lust of gold;
Ring out the thousand wars of old, ·
Ring in the thousand years of peace!
Ibid. Stanza 7

Ring in the valiant man and free,
The larger heart, the kindlier hand!
Ring out the darkness of the land,
Ring in the Christ that is to be!
Ibid. Stanza 8

The blind hysterics of the Celt.
Ibid. Part CIX, Stanza 4

And thus he bore without abuse
The grand old name of gentleman,
Defamed by every charlatan,
And soiled with all ignoble use.
Ibid. Part CXI, Stanza 6

Wearing all that weight
Of learning lightly like a flower.
In Memoriam. Conclusion,
Stanza 10

One God, one law, one element,
And one far-off divine event,
To which the whole creation moves.
Ibid. Stanza 36

Faultily faultless, icily regular, splendidly null.
Maud. Part I, II

That jewelled mass of millinery,
That oiled and curled Assyrian Bull.
Ibid. VI, Stanza 6

One still strong man in a blatant land.
Ibid. X, Stanza 5

Gorgonized me from head to foot,
With a stony British stare.
Ibid. XIII, Stanza 2

Come into the garden, Maud,
For the black bat, night, has flown,
Come into the garden, Maud,
I am here at the gate alone.
Ibid. XXII, Stanza 1

Queen rose of the rosebud garden of
girls.
Ibid. Stanza 9

She is coming, my own, my sweet;
Were it ever so airy a tread,
My heart would hear her and beat,
Were it earth in an earthy bed;
My dust would hear her and beat,
Had I lain for a century dead.
Ibid. Stanza 11

Ah Christ, that it were possible
For one short hour to see
The souls we loved, that they might
tell us
What and where they be.
Ibid. Part II, IV, Stanza 3

Wearing the white flower of a blame-
less life,
Before a thousand peering littlenesses,
In that fierce light which beats upon a
throne.
Idylls of the King. Dedication,
Line 24

Large divine and comfortable words.[1]
Ibid. The Coming of Arthur,
Line 267

---

[1] How little I have gained,
How vast the unattained.
WHITTIER: *My Triumph, St. 7*
[2] Who never doubted never half believed.
P. J. BAILEY: *Festus: A Country Town*

[1] Hear what comfortable words our Saviour
Christ saith unto all who truly turn to him. —
Book of Common Prayer, Holy Communion

Live pure, speak true, right wrong, fol-
low the King —
Else, wherefore born?
>> *Idylls of the King. Gareth and
Lynette, Line 117*

Eyes of pure women, wholesome stars
of love.
>> *Ibid. Line 367*

A damsel of high lineage, and a brow
May-blossom, and a cheek of apple-
blossom,
Hawk-eyes; and lightly was her slen-
der nose
Tip-tilted like the petal of a flower.
>> *Ibid. Line 574*

Our hoard is little, but our hearts are
great.
>> *Ibid. Geraint and Enid, I,
Line 352*

For man is man and master of his fate.[1]
>> *Ibid. Line 355*

The useful trouble of the rain.
>> *Ibid. II, Line 770*

The world will not believe a man repents;
And this wise world of ours is mainly
right.
>> *Ibid. Line 899*

The whole wood-world is one full peal
of praise.
>> *Ibid. Balin and Balan, Line 444*

Mere white truth in simple nakedness.
>> *Ibid. Line 509*

Woods have tongues
As walls have ears.[2]
>> *Ibid. Line 522*

As love, if love be perfect, casts out
fear,
So hate, if hate be perfect, casts out
fear.
>> *Ibid. Merlin and Vivien, Line 41*

[1] I am the master of my fate:
I am the captain of my soul.
W. E. HENLEY: *To R. T. Hamilton Bruce*
(Invictus)
Be the proud captain still of thine own fate.
JAMES BENJAMIN KENYON [1858–1924]:
A Challenge
Dux atque imperator vitae mortalium ani-
mus est (The soul is the captain and ruler of
the life of mortals). — SALLUST: *Jugurtha,
Chap. 1*
[2] That feeld hath eyen, and the wode hath
eres.
CHAUCER: *The Knightes Tale, L. 1522*

Faith and unfaith can ne'er be equal
powers:
Unfaith in aught is want of faith in all.
>> *Idylls of the King. Merlin and
Vivien, Line 384*

It is the little rift within the lute,
That by and by will make the music
mute,
And ever widening slowly silence all.
>> *Ibid. Line 386*

Blind and naked Ignorance
Delivers brawling judgments, un-
ashamed,
On all things all day long.
>> *Ibid. Line 662*

For men at most differ as heaven and
earth,
But women, worst and best, as heaven
and hell.
>> *Ibid. Line 812*

I know the Table Round, my friends of
old;
All brave, and many generous, and
some chaste.
>> *Ibid. Line 814*

There must be now no passages of love
Betwixt us twain henceforward evermore.
>> *Ibid. Line 911*

Elaine, the lily maid of Astolat.
>> *Ibid. Lancelot and Elaine. Line 2*

But, friend, to me
He is all fault who hath no fault at all.
For who loves me must have a touch
of earth.
>> *Ibid. Line 132*

In me there dwells
No greatness, save it be some far-off
touch
Of greatness to know well I am not
great.
>> *Ibid. Line 447*

The shackles of an old love straitened
him,
His honour rooted in dishonour stood,
And faith unfaithful kept him falsely
true.
>> *Ibid. Line 870*

Sweet is true love tho' given in vain,
in vain;
And sweet is death who puts an end
to pain.
>> *Ibid. Line 1000*

As when we dwell upon a word we
know,
Repeating, till the word we know so
well
Becomes a wonder, and we know not
why,
So dwelt the father on her face, and
thought
"Is this Elaine?"
> *Idylls of the King. Lancelot and
> Elaine. Line 1020*

He makes no friend who never made
a foe.
> *Ibid. Line 1082*

Figs out of thistles.
> *Ibid. The Last Tournament,
> Line 356*

The greater man the greater courtesy.
> *Ibid. Line 628*

The vow that binds too strictly snaps
itself.
> *Ibid. Line 652*

For courtesy wins woman all as well
As valor may.
> *Ibid. Line 702*

For manners are not idle, but the fruit
Of loyal nature and of noble mind.
> *Ibid. Guinevere, Line 333*

To love one maiden only, cleave to her,
And worship her by years of golden
deeds.
> *Ibid. Line 472*

No more subtle master under heaven
Than is the maiden passion for a maid,
Not only to keep down the base in man
But teach high thought, and amiable
words
And courtliness, and the desire of fame
And love of truth, and all that makes
a man.
> *Ibid. Line 475*

To where beyond these voices there is
peace.
> *Ibid. Last line*

I found Him in the shining of the stars,
I mark'd Him in the flowering of His
fields,
But in His ways with men I find Him
not.
> *Ibid. The Passing of Arthur,
> Line 9*

For why is all around us here
As if some lesser god had made the
world,
But had not force to shape it as he
would? [1]
> *Idylls of the King. The Passing
> of Arthur, Line 13*

The golden guess
Is morning-star to the full round of
truth.
> *Columbus*

Cleave ever to the sunnier side of
doubt,
And cling to Faith beyond the forms
of Faith.
> *The Ancient Sage*

The shell must break before the bird
can fly.
> *Ibid.*

All the charm of all the Muses often
flowering in a lonely word.
> *To Virgil*

Slav, Teuton, Kelt, I count them all
My friends and brother souls,
With all the peoples, great and small,
That wheel between the poles.
> *The Charge of the Heavy Brigade.
> Epilogue*

The song that nerves a nation's heart
Is in itself a deed.
> *Ibid.*

That man's the best Cosmopolite
Who loves his native country best.
> *Hands All Round*

Love your enemy, bless your haters,
said the Greatest of the great;
Christian love among the Churches
looked the twin of heathen hate.
> *Locksley Hall Sixty Years After.
> Line 85*

Charm us, orator, till the lion look no
larger than the cat.
> *Ibid. Line 112*

Authors — essayist, atheist, novelist,
realist, rhymester, play your part,

[1] Ah Love! could you and I with Him con-
spire
To grasp this sorry Scheme of Things en-
tire,
Would not we shatter it to bits — and
then
Re-mould it nearer to the Heart's Desire!
FITZGERALD: *The Rubáiyát of Omar
Khayyám, XCIX*

Paint the mortal shame of nature with
the living hues of art.
Locksley Hall Sixty Years After.
Line 139

Be patient. Our Playwright may show
In some fifth act what this wild Drama
means.
The Play

A mastiff dog
May love a puppy cur for no more
reason
Than that the twain have been tied up
together.
Queen Mary. Act I, Sc. 4

My lord, you know what Virgil sings—
Woman is various and most mutable.[1]
Ibid. Act III, Sc. 6

Come out, my lord, it is a world of
fools.[2]
Ibid. Act IV, Sc. 3

Unalterably and pesteringly fond.
Ibid. Act V, Sc. 1

Old men must die, or the world would
grow mouldy, would only breed
the past again.
Becket. Prologue

Not of the sunlight,
Not of the moonlight,
Not of the starlight!
O young Mariner,
Down to the haven,
Call your companions,
Launch your vessel
And crowd your canvas,
And, ere it vanishes
Over the margin,
After it, follow it,
Follow the Gleam.[3]
Merlin and the Gleam. Stanza 10

Sunset and evening star,
And one clear call for me!

---

[1] Varium et mutabile semper femina. —
VIRGIL: *Aeneid, IV, 569*
La donna è mobile. — *Rigoletto, Duke's
Song*
[2] Tous les hommes sont fous. — BOILEAU,
Satire IV
The twenty-seven millions, mostly fools.
— CARLYLE: *Latter Day Pamphlets, No. 6*
[3] The Gleam . . . signifies in my poem
the higher poetic imagination. — TENNYSON:
Memoir, Vol. II, P. 366

And may there be no moaning of the
bar,
When I put out to sea.
Crossing the Bar. Stanza 1

But such a tide as moving seems asleep,
Too full for sound and foam,
When that which drew from out the
boundless deep
Turns again home.
Ibid. Stanza 2

Twilight and evening bell,
And after that the dark.
Ibid. Stanza 3

I hope to meet my Pilot face to face
When I have crossed the bar.
Ibid. Stanza 4

ROBERT CHARLES WINTHROP
[1809–1894]

Our Country,[1] — whether bounded
by the St. John's and the Sabine, or
however otherwise bounded [2] or described, and be the measurements more
or less, — still our Country, to be
cherished in all our hearts, to be defended by all our hands.
*Toast at Faneuil Hall [Fourth of
July, 1845]*

A star for every State, and a State
for every star.
Address on Boston Common [1862]

The poor must be wisely visited and
liberally cared for, so that mendicity
shall not be tempted into mendacity,
nor want exasperated into crime.
Yorktown Oration [1881]

---

[1] With all her faults she is my country still.
— CHARLES CHURCHILL [1731–1764]: *The
Farewell, L. 27*
Our country! In her intercourse with foreign nations may she always be in the right;
but our country, right or wrong. — STEPHEN
DECATUR [1779–1820]: Toast, Norfolk, Virginia [April, 1816]
I hope to find my country in the right:
however, I will stand by her, right or wrong.
— JOHN JORDAN CRITTENDEN [1787–1863]:
On the Mexican War
[2] The United States — bounded on the
north by the Aurora Borealis, on the south by
the precession of the equinoxes, on the east by
the primeval chaos, and on the west by the
Day of Judgment. — JOHN FISKE [1842–
1901]: *Bounding the United States*

Slavery is but half abolished, emancipation is but half completed, while millions of freemen with votes in their hands are left without education. Justice to them, the welfare of the States in which they live, the safety of the whole Republic, the dignity of the elective franchise, — all alike demand that the still remaining bonds of ignorance shall be unloosed and broken, and the minds as well as the bodies of the emancipated go free.

Yorktown Oration [*1881*]

JAMES ALDRICH
[1810–1856]

Her suffering ended with the day,
  Yet lived she at its close,
And breathed the long, long night away
  In statue-like repose.
A Death-Bed. Stanza 1

But when the sun in all his state
  Illumed the eastern skies,
She passed through Glory's morning-
    gate,
  And walked in Paradise.[1]
Ibid. Stanza 2

HENRY ALFORD
[1810–1871]

My bark is wafted to the strand
  By breath divine;
And on the helm there rests a hand
  Other than mine.
I Know Not if the Dark or Bright.
Stanza 4

Life is so short, so fast the lone hours
    fly,
We ought to be together, you and I.
You and I. Stanza 4

DAVID BATES [2]
[1810–1876]

Speak gently; it is better far
  To rule by love than fear.

Speak gently; let no harsh word mar
  The good we may do here.
Speak Gently.[1] *Stanza 1*

The tooth is out; once more again
  The throbbing, jumping nerves are
    stilled;
Reader, would you avoid this pain?
  Then have your crumbling teeth well
    filled.
The Toothache. Stanza 11

PAKENHAM BEATTY
[*Floruit* 1881]

By thine own soul's law learn to live,
And if men thwart thee, take no heed,
And if men hate thee, have no care;
Sing thou thy song, and do thy deed,
Hope thou thy hope, and pray thy
    prayer.
Self-Reliance. Stanza 1

WILLIAM HENRY CHANNING
[1810–1884]

To live content with small means; to seek elegance rather than luxury, and refinement rather than fashion; to be worthy, not respectable, and wealthy, not rich; to study hard, think quietly, talk gently, act frankly; to listen to stars and birds, to babes and sages, with open heart; to bear all cheerfully, do all bravely, await occasions, hurry never. In a word, to let the spiritual, unbidden and unconscious, grow up through the common. This is to be my symphony.

My Symphony

JAMES FREEMAN CLARKE
[1810–1888]

Beneath the shadow of the Great Protection,
  The soul sits, hushed and calm.
The Shadow. Stanza 2
Nought that He has made, below,
    above,
  Can part us from His love.
Ibid. Stanza 3

---

[1] Parodied by PHOEBE CARY. See page 557.
[2] A Philadelphian, known as "Old Mortality."

[1] Wrongly attributed to G. W. Langford and others.

Dear friend, whose presence in the
house,
Whose gracious word benign,
Could once, at Cana's wedding feast,
Change water into wine,
Come, visit us and when dull work
Grows weary, line on line,
Revive our souls, and let us see
Life's water turned to wine.

Cana

Every inmost aspiration is God's angel
undefiled;
And in every "O my Father!" slumbers
deep a "Here, my child!"[1]

*Prayer Its Own Answer (translated from Jelal-el-Deen).
Couplet 8*

DANIEL CLEMENT
COLESWORTHY
[1810–1893]

Ay, soon upon the stage of life,
Sweet, happy children, you will rise,
To mingle in its care and strife,
Or early find the peaceful skies.
Then be it yours, while you pursue
The golden moments, quick to haste
Some noble work of love to do,
Nor suffer one bright hour to waste.

School is Out

A little word in kindness spoken,
A motion or a tear,
Has often healed the heart that's
broken,
And made a friend sincere.

A Little Word. Stanza 1

Then deem it not an idle thing
A pleasant word to speak;
The face you wear — the thoughts you
bring —
The heart may heal or break.

Ibid. Stanza 3

[1] Thy love is but a girdle of the love I bear
to thee,
And sleeping in thy "Come, O Lord!"
there lies "Here, son!" from me.
WILLIAM ROUNSEVILLE ALGER [1822–
1905]: *The Contents of Piety*

MARY STANLEY BUNCE
DANA
[1810–1883]

I saw the young bride in her beauty and
pride,
Bedecked in her snowy array.

Pass Under the Rod. Stanza 1

'Twas the voice of her God:
"I love thee, I love thee — pass under
the rod."

Ibid.

SAMUEL DODGE
[*Floruit* 1868]

You may go through this world, but
'twill be very slow
If you listen to all that is said as you
go;
You'll be worried and fretted and kept
in a stew,
For meddlesome tongues must have
something to do,
For people will talk, you know.

People Will Talk. Stanza 1

SIR FRANCIS HASTINGS
DOYLE
[1810–1888]

Last night, among his fellow roughs,
He jested, quaffed, and swore;
A drunken private of the Buffs,
Who never looked before.
To-day, beneath the foeman's frown,
He stands in Elgin's place,
Ambassador from Britain's crown,
And type of all her race.

The Private of the Buffs.[1] Stanza 1

[1] Doyle's poem is prefaced by the following
news item from the London *Times,* correspondence from China:

Some Seiks, and a private of the Buffs, East
Kent Regiment, having remained behind with
the grog-carts, fell into the hands of the Chinese. On the next morning they were brought
before the authorities, and commanded to perform the kotou. The Seiks obeyed; but Moyse,
the English soldier, declaring that he would
not prostrate himself before any Chinaman
alive, was immediately knocked upon the
head, and his body thrown on a dunghill.

In JOHN GALSWORTHY'S novel, *Flowering
Wilderness,* Wilfrid Desert becomes a Mohammedan in order to save his life when taken
prisoner by a band of fanatical Arabs.

Vain, mightiest fleets of iron framed;
  Vain, those all-shattering guns;
Unless proud England keep, untamed,
  The strong heart of her sons.
    The Private of the Buffs. Stanza 5

So we made women with their children
    go,
  The oars ply back again, and yet
    again;
Whilst, inch by inch, the drowning
    ship sank low,
  Still, under steadfast men.
    The Loss of the "Birkenhead." [1]
                          Stanza 10

Not hopeless, round this calm sepul-
    chral spot,
  A wreath, presaging life, we twine;
If God be love, what sleeps below was
    not
  Without a spark divine.
    Epitaph on a Favourite Dog

ELIZABETH CLEGHORN
GASKELL
[1810–1865]

A man is *so* in the way in the house.
    Cranford. Chap. 1

Correspondence, which bears much
the same relation to personal intercourse that the books of dried plants I
sometimes see ("Hortus Siccus," I
think they call the thing) do to the
living and fresh flowers in the lanes
and meadows.
    Ibid. Chap. 3

People talk a great deal about idealizing nowadays, whatever that may
mean.
    Ibid. Chap. 5

One gives people in grief their own
way.
    Ibid. Chap. 6

A little credulity helps one on
through life very smoothly.
    Ibid. Chap. 11

I'll not listen to reason. . . . Reason always means what some one else
has got to say.
    Ibid. Chap. 14

[1] Origin of the Birkenhead Drill, "women
and children first" [Feb. 26, 1852].

JAMES SLOANE GIBBONS
[1810–1892]

We are coming, Father Abraham, three
    hundred thousand more,
From Mississippi's winding stream and
    from New England's shore;
We leave our ploughs and workshops,
    our wives and children dear,
With hearts too full for utterance, with
    but a silent tear.
    Three Hundred Thousand More. [1]
                          Stanza 1

ORRIN GOODRICH
[*Floruit* 1855]

A stranger preached last Sunday,
  And crowds of people came
To hear a two-hour sermon
  On a theme I scarce can name.
'Twas all about some heathen,
  Thousands of miles afar,
Who lived in a land of darkness
  Called Borrioboola Gha.
    Borrioboola Gha. [2] *Stanza 1*

Alas, for the cold and hungry
  That met me every day,
While all my tears were given
  To the suffering far away!
    Ibid. Stanza 8

WILLIAM MILLER
[1810–1872]

Wee Willie Winkie rins through the
    toun,
Upstairs and dounstairs, in his nicht-
    goun,
Tirlin' at the window, cryin' at the
    lock,
"Are the weans in their bed? for it's
    nou ten o'clock."
    Willie Winkie

(SARAH) MARGARET FULLER
OSSOLI
[1810–1850]

What I mean by the Muse is that
unimpeded clearness of the intuitive

[1] First printed in the *New York Evening
Post* [July 16, 1862].
[2] *Knickerbocker Magazine, Vol. 45* [1855].

powers, which a perfectly truthful adherence to every admonition of the higher instincts would bring to a finely organized human being. . . . Should these faculties have free play, I believe they will open new, deeper and purer sources of joyous inspiration than have yet refreshed the earth.

Woman in the 19th Century
[circa 1832]

It does not follow because many books are written by persons born in America that there exists an American literature. Books which imitate or represent the thoughts and life of Europe do not constitute an American literature. Before such can exist, an original idea must animate this nation and fresh currents of life must call into life fresh thoughts along its shores.

In the New York Tribune [1833]

Truth is the nursing mother of genius. No man can be absolutely true to himself, eschewing cant, compromise, servile imitation, and complaisance, without becoming original for there is in every creature a fountain of life which, if not choked back by stones and other dead rubbish, will create a fresh atmosphere, and bring to life fresh beauty.

Ibid.

When an immortal poet was secure only of a few copyists to circulate his works, there were princes and nobles to patronize literature and the arts. Here is only the public, and the public must learn how to cherish the nobler and rarer plants, and to plant the aloe, able to wait a hundred years for its bloom, or its garden will contain, presently, nothing but potatoes and pot-herbs.

Ibid.

Beware of over-great pleasure in being popular or even beloved. As far as an amiable disposition and powers of entertainment make you so, it is happiness, but if there is one grain of plausibility, it is a poison.

Letter to her brother Arthur
[December 20, 1840]

I myself am more divine than any I see.

Letter to R. W. Emerson
[March 1, 1838]

Put up at the moment of greatest suffering a prayer, not for thy own escape, but for the enfranchisement of some being dear to thee, and the sovereign spirit will accept thy ransom.

Recipe to prevent the cold of January from utterly destroying life [January 30, 1841]

The golden-rod is one of the fairy, magical flowers; it grows not up to seek human love amid the light of day, but to mark to the discerning what wealth lies hid in the secret caves of earth.

Journal. September, 1840

This was one of the rye-bread days, all dull and damp without.

Diary. Quoted by Thomas Wentworth Higginson: *Life of Margaret Fuller Ossoli, Chap. 7*

For precocity some great price is always demanded sooner or later in life.

Ibid. Chap. 18

Genius will live and thrive without training, but it does not the less reward the watering-pot and pruning-knife.

Ibid.

It does not follow, because the United States print and read more books, magazines, and newspapers than all the rest of the world, that they really have therefore a literature.

Quoted by Walt Whitman *in an article on American National Literature*

THEODORE PARKER
[1810–1860]

Truth never yet fell dead in the streets; it has such affinity with the soul of man, the seed however broadcast will catch somewhere and produce its hundredfold.

A Discourse of Matters Pertaining to Religion

Truth stood on one side and Ease on the other; it has often been so.

Ibid.

Man never falls so low that he can see nothing higher than himself.

Essay, A Lesson for the Day

A democracy, — that is a government of all the people, by all the people, for all the people;[1] of course, a government of the principles of eternal justice, the unchanging law of God; for shortness' sake I will call it the idea of Freedom.

The American Idea[2]

All men desire to be immortal.

A Sermon on the Immortal Life
[September 20, 1846]

We look to Thee; Thy truth is still the Light
Which guides the nations, groping on their way,
Stumbling and falling in disastrous night,
Yet hoping ever for the perfect day.

The Way, the Truth, and the Life.
Stanza 2

EDMUND HAMILTON SEARS
[1810–1876]

Calm on the listening ear of night
Come Heaven's melodious strains,
Where wild Judea stretches far
Her silver-mantled plains.

Christmas Song

It came upon the midnight clear,
That glorious song of old.

The Angels' Song

For lo! the days are hastening on,
By prophet-bards foretold,
When with the ever-circling years,
Comes round the age of gold;

[1] See Daniel Webster, page 341, and Lincoln, page 456.

Parker used the same phrase in a speech delivered in Boston [May 31, 1854] and in a sermon in Music Hall, Boston [July 4, 1858]. WILLIAM H. HERNDON visited Boston and on his return to Springfield, Illinois, took with him some of Parker's sermons and addresses. In his *Abraham Lincoln, Vol. 2, P. 65*, Herndon says that Lincoln marked with pencil the portion of the Music Hall address, "Democracy is direct self-government, over all the people, by all the people, for all the people."

[2] Speech at the New England Anti-Slavery Convention, Boston [May 29, 1850].

When Peace shall over all the earth
Its ancient splendors fling
And the whole world send back the song
Which now the angels sing.

The Angels' Song

GEORGE SHARSWOOD
[1810–1883]

It is not uncommon to hear the expression, "The law is a jealous mistress." It is true that this profession, like all others, demands of those who would succeed in it an earnest and entire devotion.[1]

Memoir of William Blackstone,
Blackstone's Commentaries
[1860]

MARTIN FARQUHAR TUPPER
[1810–1889]

A babe in a house is a well-spring of pleasure.

Of Education

Analogy is milk for babes, but abstract truths are strong meat.

Ibid.

God, from a beautiful necessity, is Love.

Of Immortality

Error is a hardy plant: it flourisheth in every soil.

Of Truth in Things False

Wait, thou child of hope, for Time shall teach thee all things.

Of Good in Things Evil

Clamorous pauperism feasteth
While honest Labor, pining, hideth his sharp ribs.

Of Discretion

[1] I have never regretted reading a first volume of Blackstone through, or not going on to the second; his frank declaration that the law was a jealous mistress and would brook no divided love, was upon reflection quite enough for one whose heart was given to a different muse. — WILLIAM DEAN HOWELLS: *Years of My Youth, II, XI*

A similar passage occurs in HOWELLS: *My Literary Passions, Chap. 19.*

Well-timed silence hath more elo-
quence than speech.
Of Discretion
It is well to lie fallow for a while.
Of Recreation
A good book is the best of friends,
the same to-day and for ever.
Of Reading
Who can wrestle against Sleep? —
Yet is that giant very gentleness.
Of Beauty
Never give up! — if adversity presses,
  Providence wisely has mingled the
    cup,
And the best counsel, in all your dis-
    tresses,
  Is the stout watchword of "Never
    give up!"
Never Give Up. Stanza 3
Nature's own Nobleman, friendly and
    frank,
Is a man with his heart in his hand!
Nature's Nobleman. Stanza 1
Hope and be happy that all's for the
    best!
All's for the Best. Stanza 3
Never go gloomily, man with a mind!
Hope is a better companion than fear.
Cheer Up. Stanza 1

JOHN FRANCIS WALLER
[1810–1894]

Near the city of Sevilla,
  Years and years ago,
Dwelt a lady in a villa,
  Years and years ago.
Magdalena, or the Spanish Duel [1]

JOHN BRIGHT
[1811–1889]

And even if I were alone, if mine
were a solitary voice, raised amid the
din of arms and the clamours of a venal
press, I should have the consolation I

---

have to-night — and which I trust will
be mine to the last moment of my existence — the priceless consolation that
no word of mine has tended to the
squandering of my country's treasure
or the spilling of one single drop of my
country's blood.
*Speech on the Crimean War;
House of Commons [December
22, 1854]*
The Angel of Death has been abroad
throughout the land; you may almost
hear the beating of his wing.
*Speech, House of Commons
[February 23, 1855]*
The right honorable gentleman
[Robert Lowe, Viscount Sherbrooke]
is the first of the new party who has retired into his political cave of Adullam [1]
and he has called about him everyone
that was in distress and everyone that
was discontented.
Speech [March, 1866]
Force is no remedy.
On the Irish Troubles [1880]
Had they [the Tories] been in the
wilderness they would have complained
of the Ten Commandments.
Remark

ALFRED DOMETT [2]
[1811–1887]

It was the calm and silent night!
  Seven hundred years and fifty-three
Had Rome been growing up to might,
  And now was queen of land and sea.
No sound was heard of clashing wars,
  Peace brooded o'er the hushed do-
    main;

---

[1] Read her Waller's "Magdalena" —
  She had Magdalena's grace.
  Read her of the Spanish duel,
  Of the brother, courtly, cruel,
  Who between the British wooer
  And the Seville lady came.
  HENRY CUYLER BUNNER [1855–1896]:
    "*Magdalena*"

[1] I Samuel, XXII, 1.
  I Chronicles, XI, 15.
[2] An early friend of ROBERT BROWNING and
subject of his poem, *Waring:*
  What's become of Waring
  Since he gave us all the slip,
  Chose land-travel or seafaring,
  Boots and chest or staff and scrip,
  Rather than pace up and down
  Any longer London town?
An account of Domett's life and work will
be found in the Appendix to the Cambridge
Edition of ROBERT BROWNING'S *Complete
Poetical Works, Pp. 1019–1020.*

Apollo, Pallas, Jove, and Mars
Held undisturbed their ancient reign,
In the solemn midnight,
Centuries ago.
Christmas Hymn

HORACE GREELEY
[1811–1872]

The illusion that times that were are better than those that are, has probably pervaded all ages.
The American Conflict
A widow of doubtful age will marry almost any sort of a white man.
Letter to Dr. Rufus Wilmot Griswold
And now, having fully expressed our conviction that the punishment of death is one which should sometimes be inflicted, we may add that we would have it resorted to as unfrequently as possible. Nothing, in our view, but cold-blooded, premeditated, unpalliated murder, can fully justify it. Let this continue to be visited with the sternest penalty.
The New Yorker [June, 1836]
If, on a full and final review, my life and practice shall be found unworthy my principles, let due infamy be heaped on my memory; but let none be thereby led to distrust the principles to which I proved recreant, nor yet the ability of some to adorn them by a suitable life and conversation. To unerring time be all this committed.
Statement [1846] quoted on the first page of Life of Horace Greeley [1855] by JAMES PARTON *[1822–1891]*
The best business you can go into you will find on your father's farm or in his workshop. If you have no family or friends to aid you, and no prospect opened to you there, turn your face to the great West,[1] and there build up a home and fortune.
To Aspiring Young Men (Ibid. Page 414)

[1] See J. B. L. Soule, page 505.

Wisdom is never dear, provided the article be genuine.
Address on Agriculture, Houston, Texas [May 23, 1871]
The Niagara of edifices.
Of St. Peter's, Rome (PARTON, *Page 370*)
'Twas the voice of the Press — on the startled ear breaking
In giant-born prowess, like Pallas of old;
'Twas the flash of Intelligence, gloriously waking
A glow on the cheek of the noble and bold.
Ode to the Press. Stanza 2

ROBERT LOWE, VISCOUNT SHERBROOKE
[1811–1892]

Soft lies the turf on those who find their rest
Beneath our common mother's ample breast,
Unstained by meanness, avarice, or pride;
They never cheated, and they never lied;
They ne'er intrigued a rival to dispose;
They ran, but never betted on the race;
Content with harmless sport and simple food,
Boundless in faith and love and gratitude;
Happy the man, if there be any such —
Of whom his epitaph can say as much.
A Horse's Epitaph

WENDELL PHILLIPS
[1811–1884]

Revolutions are not made; they come.
Speech [January 28, 1852]
What the Puritans gave the world was not thought, but action.
Speech [December 21, 1855]
One on God's side is a majority.
Speech [November 1, 1859]
Every man meets his Waterloo at last.
Ibid.

Revolutions never go backward.
Speech [February 12, 1861]
Some doubt the courage of the Negro. Go to Haiti and stand on those fifty thousand graves of the best soldiers France ever had, and ask them what they think of the Negro's sword.
Address on Toussaint L'Ouverture
[1861]
Aristocracy is always cruel.
Ibid.

Take the whole range of imaginative literature, and we are all wholesale borrowers. In every matter that relates to invention, to use, or beauty or form, we are borrowers.
Lecture, The Lost Arts

JANE CROSS SIMPSON
[1811–1886]

Go, when the morning shineth;
Go, when the noon is bright;
Go, when the eve declineth;
Go, in the high of night;
Go with pure mind and feeling,
Fling earthly cares away,
And in thy chamber kneeling,
Do thou in secret pray.
Prayer

HARRIET BEECHER STOWE [1]
[1811–1896]

It lies around us like a cloud,
A world we do not see;
Yet the sweet closing of an eye
May bring us there to be.
The Other World. Stanza 1
Let death between us be as naught,
A dried and vanished stream;
Your joy be the reality —
Our suffering life the dream!
Ibid. Stanza 10
Still, still with Thee, when purple morning breaketh,

When the bird waketh and the shadows flee.
Still, Still with Thee. Stanza 1
When winds are raging o'er the upper ocean,
And billows wild contend with angry roar,
'Tis said, far down beneath the wild commotion,
That peaceful stillness reigneth, evermore.
Hymn. Stanza 1
Far, far beneath, the noise of tempests dieth,
And silver waves chime ever peacefully,
And no rude storm, how fierce soe'er it flieth,
Disturbs the Sabbath of that deeper sea.[1]
Ibid. Stanza 2
Eliza made her desperate retreat across the river just in the dusk of twilight. The grey mist of evening, rising slowly from the river, enveloped her as she disappeared up the bank, and the swollen current and floundering masses of ice presented a hopeless barrier between her and her pursuer.
Uncle Tom's Cabin. Chap. 8
I 'spect I growed. Don't think nobody never made me.
Ibid. Chap. 20
I's wicked — I is. I's mighty wicked, anyhow. I can't help it.
Ibid.
Whipping and abuse are like laudanum: you have to double the dose as the sensibilities decline.
Ibid.
Legree, taking up a cow hide, and striking Tom a heavy blow across the cheek, and following up the infliction by a shower of blows.
Ibid. Chap. 33

CHARLES SUMNER
[1811–1874]

There is the National flag. He must be cold, indeed, who can look upon its

---

[1] We have seen an American woman write a novel of which a million copies were sold in all languages, and which had one merit, of speaking to the universal heart, and was read with equal interest to three audiences, namely, in the parlor, in the kitchen, and in the nursery of every house. — R. W. EMERSON: *Society and Solitude, Success*

[1] See J. G. C. Brainard, page 375, and F. W. H. Myers, page 667.

folds rippling in the breeze without pride of country. If in a foreign land, the flag is companionship, and country itself, with all its endearments.

Are We a Nation? [*November 19, 1867*]

White is for purity; red, for valor; blue for justice. And altogether, bunting, stripes, stars, and colors, blazing in the sky, make the flag of our country, to be cherished by all our hearts, to be upheld by all our hands.

Ibid.

The phrase, "public office is a public trust," has of late become common property.[1]

Statement [*May 31, 1872*]

WILLIAM MAKEPEACE THACKERAY
[1811–1863]

Although I enter not,
Yet round about the spot
  Ofttimes I hover;
And near the sacred gate,
With longing eyes I wait,
  Expectant of her.

At the Church Gate [2]

The play is done; the curtain drops,
  Slow falling to the prompter's bell:
A moment yet the actor stops,
  And looks around, to say farewell.
It is an irksome word and task;
  And when he's laughed and said his say,
He shows, as he removes the mask,
  A face that's anything but gay.

Doctor Birch and His Young Friends. Epilogue, The End of the Play, Stanza 1

Christmas is here:
Winds whistle shrill,
Icy and chill,
Little care we;
Little we fear
Weather without,

Shelter about
The Mahogany Tree.

The Mahogany Tree. Stanza 1

Though more than half the world was his,
He [1] died without a rood his own;
And borrow'd from his enemies
Six foot of ground to lie upon.

The Chronicle of the Drum. Part II

Werther had a love for Charlotte
  Such as words could never utter;
Would you know how first he met her?
  She was cutting bread and butter.[2]

Sorrows of Werther. Stanza 1

Charlotte, having seen his body
  Borne before her on a shutter,
Like a well-conducted person,
  Went on cutting bread and butter.

Ibid. Stanza 4

Though small was your allowance,
  You saved a little store;
And those who save a little
  Shall get a plenty more.

*The King of Brentford's Testament.
Stanza 22*

This Bouillabaisse a noble dish is —
  A sort of soup, or broth, or brew.

The Ballad of Bouillabaisse. Stanza 2

Ho, pretty page, with the dimpled chin,
That never has known the barber's shear,
All your wish is woman to win,
This is the way that boys begin, —
  Wait till you come to Forty Year.

*Rebecca and Rowena. The Age of
Wisdom, Stanza 1*

Then sing as Martin Luther sang:
"Who loves not wine, woman, and song,
He is a fool his whole life long!"

*The Adventures of Philip. A Credo,
Stanza 1*

Away from the world and its toils and
  its cares,

---

[1] See Mathew Henry, page 188.
[2] In *Pendennis, Vol. I, Chap. 31,* the third and fourth lines read:
      Sometimes I hover,
      And at the sacred gate.

[1] Napoleon Bonaparte. The ballad was written in Paris at the time of the second funeral of Napoleon [1841].
[2] Charlotte held a brown loaf in her hand, and was cutting slices for the little ones all round in proportion to their age and appetite. — GOETHE: *The Sorrows of Werther, June 16th*

I've a snug little kingdom up four pair of stairs.

The Cane-Bottom'd Chair. Stanza 1

A man — I let the truth out —
Who's had almost every tooth out,
Cannot sing as once he sung,
When he was young as you are young,
When he was young and lutes were strung,
And love-lamps in the casement hung.

Mrs. Katherine's Lantern. Stanza 6

The rose upon my balcony the morning air perfuming,
Was leafless all the winter time and pining for the spring.

The Rose Upon My Balcony.
Stanza 1

There lived a sage in days of yore,
And he a handsome pigtail wore;
But wondered much and sorrowed more
Because it hung behind him.

A Tragic Story (from von Chamisso).
Stanza 1

In the brave days when I was twenty-one.

The Garret. Refrain

Always remember to take the door-key.

The Willow-Tree. Stanza 9

As we go on the downhill journey, the milestones are gravestones, and on each more and more names are written; unless haply you live beyond man's common age, when friends have dropped off, and, tottering, and feeble, and unpitied, you reach the terminus alone.

The Roundabout Papers.
On Letts' Diary

I'm no angel.

Vanity Fair. Vol. I, Chap. 2

This I set down as a positive truth. A woman with fair opportunities, and without an absolute hump, may marry whom she likes.[1]

Ibid. Chap. 4

Them's my sentiments.[1]

Vanity Fair. Vol. I, Chap. 21

Everybody in Vanity Fair must have remarked how well those live who are comfortably and thoroughly in debt; how they deny themselves nothing; how jolly and easy they are in their minds.

Ibid. Chap. 22

When we say of a gentleman that he lives elegantly on nothing a year, we use the word "nothing" to signify something unknown; meaning, simply, that we don't know how the gentleman in question defrays the expenses of his establishment.

Ibid. Chap. 35

Mother is the name for God in the lips and hearts of little children.

Ibid. Chap. 37

I think I could be a good woman if I had five thousand a year.[2]

Ibid. Vol. II, Chap. 1

A comfortable career of prosperity, if it does not make people honest, at least keeps them so.

Ibid.

By economy and good management, — by a sparing use of ready money and by paying scarcely anybody, — people can manage, for a time at least, to make a great show with very little means.

Ibid. Chap. 11

Ah! Vanitas Vanitatum! which of us is happy in this world? Which of us has his desire? or, having it, is satisfied?

Ibid. Chap. 27

'Tis strange what a man may do and a woman yet think him an angel.

Henry Esmond. Chap. 7

The book of female logic is blotted all over with tears, and Justice in their courts is forever in a passion.

The Virginians. Chap. 4

Heaven does not choose its elect from among the great and wealthy.

Ibid. Chap. 5

Women like not only to conquer, but to be conquered.

Ibid.

---

[1] I should like to see any kind of a man, distinguishable from a gorilla, that some good and even pretty woman could not shape a husband out of. — O. W. HOLMES: *The Professor at the Breakfast Table*
The whole world is strewn with snares, traps, gins and pitfalls for the capture of men by women. — BERNARD SHAW: *Man and Superman, Epistle Dedicatory*

[1] Them's my sentiments, tew. — WILL CARLETON [1845–1912]: *The Schoolmaster's Guests*

[2] See Huxley, page 563.

George sat down at the harpsichord and played and sang "Malbrook s'en va t'en guerre; Mironton, mironton, mirontaine." [1]

The Virginians. Chap. 8

Next to the very young, I suppose the very old are the most selfish.

Ibid. Chap. 61

'Tis hard with respect to Beauty, that its possessor should not have even a life-enjoyment of it, but be compelled to resign it after, at the most, some forty years' lease.

Ibid. Chap. 73

For a steady self-esteem and indomitable confidence in our own courage, greatness, magnanimity, who can compare with Britons, except their children across the Atlantic?

Ibid. Chap. 89

Through all the doubt and darkness, the danger and long tempest of the war, I think it was only the American leader's [2] indomitable soul that remained entirely steady.

Ibid. Chap. 90

To endure is greater than to dare; to tire out hostile fortune; to be daunted by no difficulty; to keep heart when all have lost it; to go through intrigue spotless; to forego even ambition when the end is gained — who can say this is not greatness?

Ibid. Chap. 92

Remember, it's as easy to marry a rich woman as a poor woman.

Pendennis. Chap. 28

Of the Corporation of the Goose-quill — of the Press, . . . of the fourth estate.[1] . . . There she is — the great engine — she never sleeps. She has her ambassadors in every quarter of the world — her courtiers upon every road. Her officers march along with armies, and her envoys walk into statesmen's cabinets. They are ubiquitous.

Pendennis. Chap. 30

The best way is to make your letters safe. I never wrote a letter in all my life that would commit me, and demmy, sir, I have had some experience of women.

Ibid. Chap. 64

How hard it is to make an Englishman acknowledge that he is happy!

Ibid. Chap. 69

The true pleasure of life is to live with your inferiors.

The Newcomes. Chap. 9

The wicked are wicked, no doubt, and they go astray and they fall, and they come by their deserts; but who can tell the mischief which the very virtuous do?

Ibid. Chap. 20

Just as the last bell struck, a peculiar sweet smile shone over his face, and he lifted up his head a little, and quickly said "Adsum!" and fell back. It was the word we used at school, when names were called; and lo, he, whose heart was as that of a little child, had answered to his name, and stood in the presence of The Master.[2]

Ibid. Chap. 80

Certain opuscules, denominated "Christmas Books," with the ostensible intention of swelling the tide of exhilaration, or other expansive emotions, incident upon the exodus of the old and the inauguration of the new year.

The Kickleburys on the Rhine.
Preface to Second Edition

A pedigree reaching as far back as the Deluge.

The Rose and the Ring. Chap. 2

---

[1] Malbrouk has gone to the war —
    Mironton, mironton, mirontaine! —
Malbrouk has gone to war,
    Ah, when will he return?
He will be back at Easter —
    Mironton, mironton, mirontaine! —
He will be back at Easter,
    Or else at Trinity.

This French ballad, sometimes thought to refer to the Duke of Marlborough, is said to have originated at the time of the Crusades. See DAVID GRAHAM ADEE: *The Story of a Song*, in *Harper's Monthly, September, 1895.*

[2] George Washington.

[1] For Carlyle's references to the fourth estate, see pages 377, 380, and 381.

[2] He answered, "I am here."
R. H. STODDARD: *Adsum (On the Death of Thackeray, December 23–24, 1863)*

Bravery never goes out of fashion.
> *The Four Georges. George II*

Fiction carries a greater amount of truth in solution than the volume which purports to be all true.
> *The English Humourists. Steele*

Harlequin without his mask is known to present a very sober countenance, and was himself, the story goes, the melancholy patient whom the Doctor advised to go and see Harlequin.[1]
> *Ibid. Swift*

ROBERT BROWNING
[1812–1889]

Sun-treader,[2] life and light be thine forever!
> *Pauline*

I am a watcher whose eyes have grown dim
With looking for some star which breaks on him
Altered and worn and weak and full of tears.
> *Ibid.*

For music (which is earnest of a heaven,
Seeing we know emotions strange by it,
Not else to be revealed,) is like a voice,
A low voice calling fancy, as a friend,
To the green woods in the gay summer time.
> *Ibid.*

I go to prove my soul!
I see my way as birds their trackless way.
I shall arrive! what time, what circuit first,
I ask not; but unless God send his hail
Or blinding fire-balls, sleet or stifling snow,
In some time, his good time, I shall arrive:
He guides me and the bird. In his good time!
> *Paracelsus. Part I*

Are there not, dear Michal,
Two points in the adventure of the diver,
One — when, a beggar, he prepares to plunge,

[1] See Lombroso, page 1077.   [2] Shelley.

One — when, a prince, he rises with his pearl?
Festus, I plunge!
> *Paracelsus. Part I*

Ay, tell the world! [1]
> *Ibid. Part II*

Heap logs and let the blaze laugh out!
> *Ibid. Part III*

Respect all such as sing when all alone!
> *Ibid.*

I detest all change,
And most a change in aught I loved long since.[2]
> *Ibid.*

Every joy is gain
And gain is gain, however small.
> *Ibid. Part IV*

Over the sea our galleys went.
> *Ibid.*

The sad rhyme of the men who proudly clung
To their first fault, and withered in their pride.
> *Ibid.*

Jove strikes the Titans down
Not when they set about their mountain-piling
But when another rock would crown the work.
> *Ibid. Part V*

I give the fight up: let there be an end,
A privacy, an obscure nook for me.
I want to be forgotten even by God.
> *Ibid.*

Would you have your songs endure?
Build on the human heart.
> *Sordello. II*

Thoughts may be
Over-poetical for poetry.
> *Ibid. III*

'Twere too absurd to slight
For the hereafter the to-day's delight!
> *Ibid. VI*

Any nose
May ravage with impunity a rose.
> *Ibid.*

Day!
Faster and more fast,

[1] See Shakespeare, page 36.
[2] Which I have loved long since. — CARDINAL NEWMAN: *The Pillar of the Cloud* [*Lead, Kindly Light*]

O'er night's brim, day boils at last.
Pippa Passes. Introduction
Say not "a small event!" Why "small"?
Costs it more pain that this, ye call
A "great event," should come to pass,
Than that?
Ibid.
The year's at the spring
And day's at the morn.
Ibid. Part I
God's in his heaven:
All's right with the world.[1]
Ibid.
One may do whate'er one likes
In Art: the only thing is, to make sure
That one does like it.
Ibid. Part II
Some unsuspected isle in far-off seas.
Ibid.
May's warm slow yellow moonlit summer nights —
Gone are they, but I have them in my soul!
Ibid. Part III
In the morning of the world,
When earth was nigher heaven than now.
Ibid.
June reared that bunch of flowers you carry,
From seeds of April's sowing.
Ibid.
All service ranks the same with God:
With God, whose puppets, best and worst,
Are we; there is no last nor first.
Ibid. Part IV
Great-hearted gentlemen, singing this song.
Cavalier Tunes. I, Marching Along
King Charles, and who'll do him right now?
Ibid. II, Give a Rouse
Boot, saddle, to horse, and away!
Ibid. III, Boot and Saddle
Just for a handful of silver he left us,
Just for a riband to stick in his coat.
The Lost Leader [2]

We shall march prospering, — not thro' his presence;
Songs may inspirit us, — not from his lyre;
Deeds will be done, — while he boasts his quiescence,
Still bidding crouch whom the rest bade aspire.
The Lost Leader
Never glad confident morning again.
Ibid.
And into the midnight we galloped abreast.
How They Brought the Good News from Ghent to Aix. Stanza 1
Round the cape of a sudden came the sea,
And the sun looked over the mountain's rim:
And straight was a path of gold for him,
And the need of a world of men for me.
Parting at Morning
Where the apple reddens
Never pry —
Lest we lose our Edens,
Eve and I.
A Woman's Last Word. Stanza 5
Be a god and hold me
With a charm!
Be a man and fold me
With thine arm!
Ibid. Stanza 6
Teach me, only teach, Love!
As I ought
I will speak thy speech, Love,
Think thy thought.
Ibid. Stanza 7
Just because I was thrice as old
And our paths in the world diverged so wide,
Each was naught to each, must I be told?
We were fellow mortals, naught beside?
Evelyn Hope. Stanza 3
No, indeed! for God above
Is great to grant, as mighty to make,

---

[1] See O. W. Holmes, page 452.
[2] Written in reference to Wordsworth's abandonment of the Liberal cause, with perhaps a thought of Southey, but it is applicable to any popular apostasy. — ARTHUR

SYMONS: *An Introduction to the Study of Browning* [1906], *P. 77*.

And creates the love to reward the
　love;
　I claim you still, for my own love's
　　sake!
　　　　　　　　Evelyn Hope. Stanza 4
Dear dead women.
　　　A Toccata of Galuppi's.[1] *Stanza 15*
This world, and the wrong it does.
　　　Old Pictures in Florence. Stanza 7
What a man's work comes to! So he
　plans it,
Performs it, perfects it, makes amends
For the toiling and moiling, and then,
　sic transit!
　　　　　　　　　Ibid. Stanza 10
They are perfect — how else? — they
　shall never change:
　We are faulty — why not? — we
　have time in store.
　　　　　　　　　Ibid. Stanza 16
What's come to perfection perishes.
Things learned on earth, we shall prac-
　tise in heaven:
　Works done least rapidly, Art most
　cherishes.
　　　　　　　　　Ibid. Stanza 17
Italy, my Italy!
Queen Mary's saying serves for me—
　(When fortune's malice
　Lost her, Calais):
　Open my heart, and you will see
Graved inside of it, "Italy."
　　　　　　　　　　　De Gustibus
Oh, to be in England,
Now that April's there.
　　　Home-Thoughts from Abroad.
　　　　　　　　　　　Stanza 1
That's the wise thrush; he sings each
　song twice over,
Lest you should think he never could
　recapture
The first fine careless rapture!
　　　　　　　　　Ibid. Stanza 2
God made all the creatures, and gave
　them our love and our fear,

To give sign, we and they are his chil-
　dren, one family here.
　　　　　　　　　　　Saul. VI
How good is man's life, the mere liv-
　ing! how fit to employ
All the heart and the soul and the senses
　forever in joy!
　　　　　　　　　　　Ibid. IX
I have lived, seen God's hand through
　a lifetime, and all was for best.
　　　　　　　　　　　Ibid.
　　God is seen God
In the star, in the stone, in the flesh,
　in the soul and the clod.[1]
　　　　　　　　　　　Saul. XVII
'Tis not what man Does which exalts
　him, but what man Would do!
　　　　　　　　　　　Ibid. XVIII
How well I know what I mean to do
When the long dark evenings come.
　　　　　　　By the Fireside. Stanza 1
O woman-country![2] wooed not wed,
　Loved all the more by earth's male-
　lands,
Laid to their hearts instead.
　　　　　　　　　　Ibid. Stanza 6
When earth breaks up and heaven ex-
　pands,
　How will the change strike me and
　you
In the house not made with hands?
　　　　　　　　　Ibid. Stanza 27
Oh, the little more, and how much it is!
　And the little less, and what worlds
　away!
　　　　　　　　　Ibid. Stanza 39
If two lives join, there is oft a scar.
　They are one and one, with a shad-
　owy third;
One near one is too far.
　　　　　　　　　Ibid. Stanza 46
　　　　Only I discern
Infinite passion, and the pain
Of finite hearts that yearn.
　　　　Two in the Campagna. Stanza 12

---

[1] Baldassarre Galuppi, surnamed Buranello
[1706–1785], a Venetian composer.
　He was an immensely prolific composer,
and abounded in melody, tender, pathetic,
brilliant, which in its extreme simplicity and
slightness occasionally rose to the highest
beauty. — VERNON LEE (Violet Paget):
[1856–1935]: *Studies of the Eighteenth Century in Italy* [1880], *P. 101*

[1] God sleeps in the stone, breathes in the
plant, moves in the animal, and wakes to
consciousness in the man. — Quoted, as from
the German, by JONATHAN BRIERLEY in
Studies of the Soul, Chap. 1, and as from
the Greek in BENJAMIN RAND's *Modern Classical Philosophers.* It has also been attributed
to Hindu theosophy.
[2] Italy.

This is a spray the Bird clung to,
Making it blossom with pleasure.
> *Misconceptions. Stanza 1*

Room after room,
I hunt the house through
We inhabit together.
> *Love in a Life. Stanza 1*

Escape me?
Never —
Beloved!
While I am I, and you are you.
> *Life in a Love. Stanza 1*

To dry one's eyes and laugh at a fall,
And baffled, get up and begin again.
> *Ibid. Stanza 2*

Ah, did you once see Shelley plain,
  And did he stop and speak to you,
And did you speak to him again?
  How strange it seems and new! [1]
> *Memorabilia. I*

There's a woman like a dewdrop, she's
  so purer than the purest.
> *A Blot in the 'Scutcheon. Act I,*
> *Sc. 3*

When is man strong until he feels
  alone? [2]
> *Colombe's Birthday. Act III*

"You're wounded!" "Nay," the sol-
dier's pride
Touched to the quick, he said:
"I'm killed, Sire!" And his chief be-
side,
Smiling the boy fell dead.
> *Incident of the French Camp.*
> *Stanza 5*

The lie was dead,
And damned, and truth stood up instead.
> *Count Gismond. Stanza 13*

Over my head his arm he flung
Against the world.
> *Ibid. Stanza 19*

Morning, evening, noon and night,
"Praise God!" sang Theocrite.
> *The Boy and the Angel*

---

[1] And did you once find Browning plain?
  And did he really seem quite clear?
And did you read the book again?
  How strange it seems and queer.
CHARLES WILLIAM STUBBS [1845–1912]:
> *Parody*

[2] The strongest man on earth is he who
stands most alone. — HENRIK IBSEN: *The
Enemy of the People, Act V*

Just my vengeance complete,
  The man sprang to his feet,
Stood erect, caught at God's skirts, and
  prayed!
—So, *I* was afraid!
> *Instans Tyrannus. Stanza 7*

When a man's busy, why, leisure
Strikes him as wonderful pleasure:
'Faith, and at leisure once is he?
Straightway he wants to be busy.
> *The Glove.* [1] *Stanza 1*

Fail I alone, in words and deeds?
Why, all men strive, and who succeeds?
> *The Last Ride Together. Stanza 5*

All labor, yet no less
Bear up beneath their unsuccess.
Look at the end of the work, contrast
The petty done, the undone vast,
This present of theirs with the hopeful
  past!
> *Ibid.*

What hand and brain went ever paired?
What heart alike conceived and dared?
What act proved all its thought had
  been?
> *Ibid. Stanza 6*

Sing, riding's a joy! For me I ride.
> *Ibid. Stanza 7*

Earth being so good, would heaven
  seem best?
> *Ibid. Stanza 9*

Changed not in kind, but in degree.
> *Ibid. Stanza 10*

A thousand guilders! Come, take fifty!
> *The Pied Piper of Hamelin.*
> *Stanza 9*

If we've promised them aught, let us
  keep our promise!
> *Ibid. Stanza 15*

When the liquor's out, why clink the
  cannikin?
> *The Flight of the Duchess. XVI*

It's a long lane that knows no turnings.
> *Ibid. XVII*

That low man seeks a little thing to do,
  Sees it and does it;
This high man, with a great thing to
  pursue,
  Dies ere he knows it.

---

[1] Another version of the legend forming
the theme of SCHILLER'S *The Glove* and
LEIGH HUNT'S *The Glove and the Lions.*

That low man goes on adding one to
one,
  His hundred's soon hit;
This high man, aiming at a million,
  Misses an unit.
That has the world here — should he
  need the next.
  Let the world mind him!
This throws himself on God, and un-
perplexed
  Seeking shall find him.
             A Grammarian's Funeral.
The sin I impute to each frustrate ghost
Is — the unlit lamp and the ungirt loin.
            The Statue and the Bust.
                Stanza 83
And inasmuch as feeling, the East's
  gift,
Is quick and transient, — comes, and
  lo, is gone —
While Northern thought is slow and
  durable.
                Luria. Act V
Ah, but a man's reach should exceed
  his grasp,
Or what's a heaven for?
             Andrea del Sarto.[1]
How I shall lie through centuries,
And hear the blessed mutter of the
  mass,
And see God made and eaten all day
  long,
And feel the steady candle-flame, and
  taste
Good strong thick stupefying incense-
  smoke!
    *The Bishop Orders His Tomb at
        Saint Praxed's Church*
The common problem, yours, mine,
  every one's,
Is — not to fancy what were fair in life
Provided it could be, — but, finding
  first
What may be, then find how to make it
  fair
Up to our means.
      Bishop Blougram's Apology [2]

Just when we are safest, there's a sun-
  set-touch,
A fancy from a flower-bell, some one's
  death,
A chorus-ending from Euripides.
      Bishop Blougram's Apology
One wise man's verdict outweighs all
  the fools'.
                  Ibid.
    You call for faith:
I show you doubt, to prove that faith
  exists.
The more of doubt, the stronger faith,
  I say,
If faith o'ercomes doubt.
                  Ibid.
When the fight begins within himself,
A man's worth something.
                  Ibid.
    The sprinkled isles,
Lily on lily, that o'erlace the sea.
                Cleon
And I have written three books on the
  soul,
Proving absurd all written hitherto,
And putting us to ignorance again.
                  Ibid.
Rafael made a century of sonnets.
        One Word More. II
Does he paint? he fain would write a
  poem, —
Does he write? he fain would paint a
  picture.
             Ibid. VIII
God be thanked, the meanest of his
  creatures
Boasts two soul-sides, one to face the
  world with,
One to show a woman when he loves
  her!
             Ibid. XVII
Oh, their Rafael of the dear Madonnas,
Oh, their Dante of the dread Inferno,
Wrote one song — and in my brain I
  sing it,
Drew one angel — borne, see, on my
  bosom!
             Ibid. XIX

---

[1] The poem is based on the account of
the artist given in VASARI'S *Lives of the Painters.*

[2] It is no secret that Blougram himself is,
in the main, modelled after and meant for
Cardinal Wiseman, who, it is said, was the
writer of a good-humoured review of the
poem in the Catholic Journal, The Rambler
(January, 1856). —ARTHUR SYMONS: *An Introduction to the Study of Browning* [1906],
P. 112.

Was there naught better than to enjoy?
  No feat which, done, would make
    time break,
  And let us pent-up creatures through
Into eternity, our due?
No forcing earth teach heaven's em-
  ploy?
        Dis Aliter Visum. Stanza 24

That out of three sounds he frame, not
  a fourth sound, but a star.
        Abt Vogler.[1] *Stanza 7*

There shall never be one lost good!
  What was, shall live as before;
  The evil is null, is naught, is silence
    implying sound;
What was good shall be good, with for
  evil so much good more;
  On the earth the broken arcs; in the
    heaven, a perfect round.
        Ibid. Stanza 9

The high that proved too high, the heroic for earth too hard,
The passion that left the ground to lose
  itself in the sky.
        Ibid. Stanza 10

Sorrow is hard to bear, and doubt is
  slow to clear,
  Each sufferer says his say, his scheme
    of the weal and woe:
But God has a few of us whom he whis-
  pers in the ear;
  The rest may reason and welcome:
    'tis we musicians know.
        Ibid. Stanza 12

Grow old along with me!
The best is yet to be,
The last of life, for which the first was
  made.
Our times are in his hand.
        Rabbi Ben Ezra.[2] *Stanza 1*

Then welcome each rebuff
  That turns earth's smoothness
    rough,
Each sting that bids nor sit nor stand,
  but go!
  Be our joys three-parts pain!
  Strive, and hold cheap the
    strain;
Learn, nor account the pang; dare,
  never grudge the throe!
      Rabbi Ben Ezra. Stanza 6

What I aspired to be,
And was not, comforts me.
        Ibid. Stanza 7

Therefore I summon age
To grant youth's heritage.
        Ibid. Stanza 13

Thou waitedst age: wait death nor be
  afraid!
        Ibid. Stanza 19

Look not thou down but up!
        Ibid. Stanza 30

Progress, man's distinctive mark alone,
Not God's, and not the beasts': God is,
  they are;
Man partly is, and wholly hopes to be.
      A Death in the Desert.

    The ultimate, angels' law,
Indulging every instinct of the soul
There where law, life, joy, impulse are
  one thing!
        Ibid.

How sad and bad and mad it was — [1]
  But then, how it was sweet!
      Confessions. Stanza 9

Fear death? — to feel the fog in my
  throat,
    The mist in my face.
        Prospice

No! let me taste the whole of it, fare
  like my peers,
    The heroes of old,
Bear the brunt, in a minute pay glad
  life's arrears
    Of pain, darkness, and cold.
        Ibid.

Hold me but safe again within the bond
  Of one immortal look.
      Eurydice to Orpheus

---

[1] The Abt or Abbé George Joseph Vogler was born at Würzburg, Bavaria, in 1749, and died at Darmstadt in 1824. He was a composer, professor, Kapellmeister, and writer on music. Weber and Meyerbeer were among his pupils. He invented a musical instrument, a type of organ, called an orchestrion.

[2] Rabbi ben Ezra was a universal genius and wanderer, whose travels brought him as far as England. — SIR WILLIAM OSLER: *Address*, Jewish Historical Society of England [April 27, 1914], quoted in CUSHING: *Life of Sir William Osler, Vol. II, Chap. 34, P. 404*

---

[1] Villon, our sad bad glad mad brother's name.
   SWINBURNE: *A Ballad of François Villon, Refrain*

This could but have happened once, —
And we missed it, lost it forever.
                    Youth and Art. Stanza 17

All that I own is a print,
An etching, a mezzotint.
                    A Likeness

He never saw, never before to-day,
What was able to take his breath away,
A face to lose youth for, to occupy age
With the dream of, meet death with.[1]
                    Ibid.

We find great things are made of little
        things,
And little things go lessening till at last
Comes God behind them.
                Mr. Sludge, "the Medium"

I'm — now the President, now Jenny
        Lind,
Now Emerson, now the Benicia Boy
        —[2]
With all the civilized world a-wonder-
        ing
And worshipping.
                    Ibid.

It's wiser being good than bad;
    It's safer being meek than fierce;
    It's fitter being sane than mad.
    My own hope is, a sun will pierce
The thickest cloud earth ever stretched;
    That, after Last, returns the First,
    Though a wide compass round be
        fetched;
    That what began best can't end
        worst,
    Nor what God blessed once, prove
        accurst.
                Apparent Failure. Stanza 7

O Lyric Love, half angel and half bird,
And all a wonder and a wild desire.
                The Ring and the Book. I

Call in law when a neighbor breaks
        your fence,
Cribs from your field, tampers with
        rent or lease,
Touches the purse or pocket, — but
        woos your wife?

No: take the old way trod when men
        were men!
                The Ring and the Book.
                    II, Half-Rome

Years make men restless — they needs
        must spy
Some certainty, some sort of end
        assured,
Some sparkle, though from topmost
        beacon-tip,
That warrants life a harbor through
        the haze.
            Ibid. III, The Other Half-Rome

There is but one way to browbeat this
        world,
Dumb-founder doubt, and repay scorn
        in kind, —
To go on trusting, namely, till faith
        move
Mountains.
                    Ibid.

"The serpent tempted me and I did
        eat."
So much of paradisal nature, Eve's!
Her daughters ever since prefer to urge
"Adam so starved me I was fain accept
The apple any serpent pushed my
        way."
                Ibid. IV, Tertium Quid

The truth was felt by instinct here,
— Process which serves a world of
        trouble and time.
                    Ibid.

Justinian's Pandects only make precise
What simply sparkled in men's eyes
        before,
Twitched in their brow or quivered on
        their lip,
Waited the speech they called but
        would not come.
            Ibid. V, Count Guido Franceschini

'Twas a thief that said the last kind
        word to Christ:
Christ took the kindness and forgave
        the theft.
            Ibid. VI, Giuseppe Caponsacchi

Read the little prayer
To Raphael, proper for us travellers![1]
                    Ibid.

---

[1] A face that a man might die for. — SIR
ARTHUR CONAN DOYLE: *The Adventures of
Sherlock Holmes. A Scandal in Bohemia*
[1892], *P. 16.*
[2] The Benicia Boy was John C. Heenan, an
American pugilist, of Benicia, Solano County,
California.

[1] Raphael, the archangel, in the guise of a
traveller, accompanied Tobias on his journey.
The account is given in the *Apocrypha:
Tobit, V.*

All human plans and projects come to naught.
The Ring and the Book.
VII, Pompilia

All poetry is difficult to read,
— The sense of it is, anyhow.
Ibid.

No work begun shall ever pause for death!
Ibid.

So, let him wait God's instant men call years;
Meantime hold hard by truth and his great soul,
Do out the duty! Through such souls alone
God stooping shows sufficient of his light
For us i' the dark to rise by.
Ibid.

There's a blessing on the hearth,
A special providence for fatherhood!
Ibid. VIII, Dominus Hyacinthus de Archangelis

How it disgusts when weakness, false-refined,
Censures the honest rude effective strength, —
When sickly dreamers of the impossible
Decry plain sturdiness which does the feat
With eyes wide open.
Ibid. IX, Juris Doctor Johannes-Baptista Bottinius

Steep horsehair certain weeks,
In water, there will be produced a snake;
Spontaneous product of the horse.
Ibid.

The curious crime, the fine
Felicity and flower of wickedness.
Ibid. X, The Pope

What I call God,
And fools call Nature.[1]
Ibid.

Why comes temptation, but for man to meet
And master and make crouch beneath his foot,

[1] Some of us call it Autumn,
And others call it God.
WILLIAM HERBERT CARRUTH [1859–1924]:
Each in His Own Tongue, St. 2

And so be pedestaled in triumph?
The Ring and the Book.
X, The Pope

White shall not neutralize the black, nor good
Compensate bad in man, absolve him so:
Life's business being just the terrible choice.
Ibid.

You never know what life means till you die:
Even throughout life, 'tis death that makes life live,
Gives it whatever the significance.
Ibid. XI, Guido

A man in armor is his armor's slave.
Herakles

Life's a little thing!
Such as it is, then, pass life pleasantly
From day to night, nor once grieve all the while.
Ibid.

I recognize
Power passing mine, immeasurable, God.
Prince Hohenstiel-Schwangau [1]

In God's good time,
Which does not always fall on Saturday
When the world looks for wages.[2]
Ibid.

The great mind knows the power of gentleness,
Only tries force, because persuasion fails.
Ibid.

'Tis the great gardener grafts the excellence
On wildings where he will.
Ibid.

'Twas not for every Gawain to gaze upon the Grail!
Fifine at the Fair. IV

[1] Louis Napoleon. The name, Hohenstiel-Schwangau, is formed from Hohenschwangau, one of the castles of the King of Bavaria.
[2] The old Tuscan proverb, "*Iddio non paga sabato*"; "God does not pay Saturdays." — *Life in Letters of William Dean Howells, Vol. II, P. 169, Letter to Mrs. James T. Fields* [Feb. 23, 1903]

No creature's made so mean
But that, some way, it boasts, could we
    investigate,
Its supreme worth.
            Fifine at the Fair. XXIX

So absolutely good is truth, truth never
    hurts
The teller.
            Ibid. XXXII

Death reads the title clear —
What each soul for itself conquered
    from out things here.
            Ibid. LV

Clash forth life's common chord,
    whence, list how there ascend
Harmonics far and faint, till our per-
    ception end.
            Ibid. LXII

That far land we dream about,
Where every man is his own architect.
        *Red Cotton Night-Cap Coun-
                try. II*

Who is a poet needs must apprehend
Alike both speech and thoughts which
    prompt to speak.
Part these, and thought withdraws to
    poetry:
Speech is reported in the newspaper.
            Ibid. IV

A secret's safe
'Twixt you, me, and the gate-post!
            The Inn Album. II

Better have failed in the high aim, as I,
Than vulgarly in the low aim suc-
    ceed, —
As, God be thanked, I do not!
            Ibid. IV

Earth's a mill where we grind and wear
    mufflers:
A whip awaits shirkers and shufflers
Who slacken their pace, sick of lugging
At what don't advance for their tug-
    ging.
            Pacchiarotto. XXI

Things rarely go smooth at Rehearsal.
            Ibid. XXII

No ear! or if ear, so tough-gristled —
He thought that he sung while he whis-
    tled.
            Ibid. XXVI

Have you found your life distasteful?
    My life did and does smack sweet.
Was your youth of pleasure wasteful?

Mine I saved and hold complete.
Do your joys with age diminish?
    When mine fail me, I'll complain.
Must in death your daylight finish?
    My sun sets to rise again.
        At the "Mermaid." Stanza 10

I find earth not gray but rosy,
    Heaven not grim but fair of hue.
Do I stoop? I pluck a posy.
    Do I stand and stare? [1] All's blue.
            Ibid. Stanza 12

"With this same key
Shakespeare unlocked his heart" [2] once
    more!
Did Shakespeare? If so, the less Shake-
    speare he!
            House. Stanza 10

Because a man has shop to mind
In time and place, since flesh must
    live,
Needs spirit lack all life behind,
    All stray thoughts, fancies fugitive,
    All love except what trade can give?
            Shop. Stanza 20

Save the squadron, honor France, love
    thy wife the Belle Aurore!
            Hervé Riel.[3] Stanza 11

Good, to forgive;
    Best, to forget!
Living, we fret;
    Dying, we live.
        La Saisiaz. Introduction, Stanza 1

Can we love but on condition that the
    thing we love must die?
            Ibid.

Such a starved bank of moss
    Till, that May-morn,

---

[1] What is this life if, full of care,
    We have no time to stand and stare.
            W. H. DAVIES: *Leisure*
[2] The line is quoted from *Scorn not the
Sonnet*, by WORDSWORTH.
[3] The ballad of "Hervé Riel" which has no
rival but Tennyson's "Revenge" among modern sea-ballads, was written at Croisic, 30th
September, 1867, and was published in the
Cornhill Magazine for March, 1871, in order
that the hundred pounds which had been
offered for it might be sent to the Paris
Relief Fund. — ARTHUR SYMONS: *An Introduction to the Study of Browning* [1906]
P. 200

Blue ran the flash across:
Violets were born!
The Two Poets of Croisic.
Introduction, Stanza 1

Sky — what a scowl of cloud
Till, near and far,
Ray on ray split the shroud:
Splendid, a star!
Ibid. Stanza 2

As if true pride
Were not also humble!
In an Album

Wanting is — what?
Summer redundant,
Blueness abundant,
— Where is the blot?
Wanting is — What? [1]

Out of the wreck I rise.[2]
Ixion

Climb the rounds
Of life's long ladder, one by slippery
one.
Jochanan Hakkadosh. Stanza 27

The way of all flesh.[3]
Ibid. Stanza 48

What Youth deemed crystal, Age finds
out was dew
Morn set a-sparkle, but which noon
quick dried.
Ibid. Stanza 101

Never the time and the place
And the loved one all together!
Never the Time and the Place

Help me with knowledge — for Life's
Old — Death's New!
Epitaph on Levi Lincoln Thaxter
[1824–1884] [4]

But little do or can the best of us:
That little is achieved through Lib-
erty.
Why I Am a Liberal

What if the rose-streak of morning
Pale and depart in a passion of tears?
Once to have hoped is no matter for
scorning!
Love once — e'en love's disappoint-
ment endears!
A minute's success pays the failure of
years.
Apollo and the Fates. Stanza 42

Cease from anger at the fates
Which thwart themselves so madly.
Live and learn,[1]
Not first learn and then live.
Parleyings with Certain People.
With Christopher Smart, IX

There is no truer truth obtainable
By Man than comes of music.
Ibid. With Charles Avison, VI

Oh, fancies that might be, oh, facts
that are!
Asolando. [2] *Inapprehensiveness*

What most moved him was a certain
meal on beans.
Ibid. The Bean-Feast, Stanza 1

That I have appetite, digest, and thrive
— that boon's for me.[3]
Ibid. Stanza 11

Songs, Spring thought perfection,
Summer criticizes:
What in May escaped detection,
August, past surprises,
Notes, and names each blunder.
Ibid. Flute-Music, with an
Accompaniment, Stanza 11

Homer, all the world knows: of his life
Doubtless some facts exist: it's every-
where:
We have not settled, though, his place
of birth:
He begged, for certain, and was blind
beside:
Seven cities claimed him.[4]
Ibid. Development

---

[1] Browning is — what?
Riddle redundant,
Baldness abundant,
Sense, who can spot?
ANONYMOUS, in *Punch, April 21, 1883*

[2] Title of a novel [1912] by BEATRICE HAR-
RADEN.

[3] Title of a novel by SAMUEL BUTLER
[1835–1902]. Also in JOHN WEBSTER: *Westward Hoe!* II, 2 (1603).

[4] Carved on the boulder marking Thaxter's
grave at Kittery Point, Maine.

[1] It is good to live and learn. — CERVANTES:
Don Quixote, Part II, Chap. 32

[2] Asolando (a name taken from the invented verb *Asolare,* "to disport in the open
air") was published on the day of Browning's
death. — ARTHUR SYMONS: *An Introduction
to the Study of Browning* [1906], *P. 231*

[3] To eat is human; to digest, divine. —
CHARLES TOWNSEND COPELAND: *Epigram*

[4] See Thomas Heywood, page 129.

One who never turned his back but
  marched breast forward,
Never doubted clouds would break,
Never dreamed, though right were
  worsted, wrong would triumph,
Held we fall to rise, are baffled to fight
  better,
Sleep to wake.
            Asolando. Epilogue, Stanza 3
No, at noonday in the bustle of man's
  work-time
Greet the unseen with a cheer!
            Ibid. Stanza 4

SAMUEL DICKINSON
BURCHARD
[1812–1891]

We are Republicans, and don't propose to leave our party and identify
ourselves with the party whose ante-
cedents have been Rum, Romanism,
and Rebellion.
    *Speaking for a deputation of
    clergymen calling upon James
    G. Blaine, the Republican Pres-
    idential candidate, New York
    [October 29, 1884]*

CHARLES DICKENS
[1812–1870]

He had used the word in its Pickwickian sense.
            Pickwick Papers. Chap. 1
Did it ever strike you on such a
morning as this that drowning would
be happiness and peace?
            Ibid. Chap. 5
Be wery careful o' vidders all your
life.
            Ibid. Chap. 20
The wictim o' connubiality.
            Ibid.
Despair seldom comes with the first
severe shock of misfortune. A man has
confidence in untried friends, he remembers the many offers of service so
freely made by his boon companions
when he wanted them not; he has hope
— the hope of happy inexperience.
            Ibid. Chap. 21

I have heerd how many ord'nary
women one vidder's equal to, in pint
o' comin' over you. I think it's five-and-
twenty, but I don't rightly know vether
it a'n't more.
        Pickwick Papers. Chap. 23
As grand a personage as the fastest
walker would find out, between sunrise and sunset, on the twenty-first of
June.
            Ibid. Chap. 24
Bold Turpin vunce, on Hounslow
  Heath,
His bold mare Bess bestrode.
        Ibid. Chap. 43, Romance
Please, sir, I want some more.
        Oliver Twist. Chap. 2
There are books of which the backs
and covers are by far the best parts.
            Ibid. Chap. 14
There is something about a roused
woman, especially if she add to all
her other strong passions, the fierce
impulses of recklessness and despair,
which few men like to provoke.
            Ibid. Chap. 16
There's light enough for wot I've
got to do.
            Ibid. Chap. 47
"If the law supposes that," said Mr.
Bumble, . . . "the law is a ass, a
idiot."
            Ibid. Chap. 51
A demd, damp, moist, unpleasant
body!
        Nicholas Nickleby. Chap. 34
He has gone to the demnition bow-
wows.
            Ibid. Chap. 64
My life is one demd horrid grind.
            Ibid.
What is the odds, so long as the
wing of friendship never moults a
feather . . . and the present moment
is the least happiest of our existence.
        The Old Curiosity Shop. Chap. 2
She's the ornament of her sex.
            Ibid. Chap. 5
In love of home, the love of country
has its rise.
            Ibid. Chap. 38

That vague kind of penitence which holidays awaken next morning.[1]

The Old Curiosity Shop. Chap. 40

The memory of those who lie below passes away so soon. At first they tend them, morning, noon, and night; they soon begin to come less frequently; from once a day, to once a week; from once a week to once a month; then at long and uncertain intervals; then, not at all.

Ibid. Chap. 54

When Death strikes down the innocent and young, for every fragile form from which he lets the panting spirit free, a hundred virtues rise, in shapes of mercy, charity, and love, to walk the world, and bless it.

Ibid. Chap. 72

Any man may be in good spirits and good temper when he's well dressed. There ain't much credit in that.

Martin Chuzzlewit. Chap. 5

Regrets are the natural property of gray hairs.

Ibid. Chap. 10

Keep up appearances whatever you do.

Ibid. Chap. 11

We are the two halves of a pair of scissors, when apart, Pecksniff, but together we are something.[2]

Ibid.

Buy an annuity cheap, and make your life interesting to yourself and everybody else that watches the speculation.

Ibid. Chap. 18

Leave the bottle on the chimley-piece, and don't ask me to take none, but let me put my lips to it when I am so disposed.

Ibid. Chap. 19

What we've got to do, is to keep up our spirits, and be neighbourly. We shall come all right in the end, never fear.

Ibid. Chap. 33

A man ain't got no right to be a public man, unless he meets the public views.

Martin Chuzzlewit. Chap. 34

Here are all kinds of employers wanting all sorts of servants, and all sorts of servants wanting all kinds of employers, and they never seem to come together.

Ibid. Chap. 36

Oh Sairey, Sairey, little do we know wot lays afore us!

Ibid. Chap. 40

I don't believe there's no sich a person!

Ibid. Chap. 49

Old Marley was as dead as a doornail.[1] . . . The wisdom of our ancestors is in the simile.

A Christmas Carol. Stave One

Secret, and self-contained, and solitary as an oyster.

Ibid.

I wear the chain I forged in life.

Ibid.

In came Mrs. Fezziwig, one vast substantial smile.

Ibid. Stave Two

As good as gold.

Ibid. Stave Three

"God bless us every one!" said Tiny Tim.

Ibid.

It was always said of him, that he knew how to keep Christmas well.

Ibid. Stave Five

The good old times, the grand old times, the great old times! [2]

The Chimes. First Quarter

Facts and Figures! Put 'em down!

Ibid.

The New Year, like an Infant Heir to the whole world, was waited for, with welcomes, presents, and rejoicings.

Ibid. Second Quarter

O let us love our occupations,
Bless the squire and his relations,
Live upon our daily rations,
And always know our proper stations.

Ibid.

[1] See Byron, page 359.
[2] See Sydney Smith, Page 313.

[1] See Shakespeare, page 66.
[2] See Holmes, page 453.

Oh the nerves, the nerves; the mysteries of this machine called Man! Oh the little that unhinges it: poor creatures that we are!
The Chimes. Third Quarter
Give us, in mercy, better homes when we're a-lying in our cradles; give us better food when we're a-working for our lives; give us kinder laws to bring us back when we're a-going wrong; and don't set Jail, Jail, Jail afore us, everywhere we turn.
Ibid.

I know that our inheritance is held in store for us by Time. I know there is a sea of Time to rise one day, before which all who wrong us or oppress us will be swept away like leaves. I see it, on the flow!
Ibid. Fourth Quarter
He's tough, ma'am, tough is J. B.; tough and devilish sly.
Dombey and Son. Chap. 7
I want to know what it says. . . . The sea, Floy, what it is that it keeps on saying.[1]
Ibid. Chap. 8
When found, make a note of.
Ibid. Chap. 15
A mind equal to any undertaking that he puts it alongside of.
Ibid. Chap. 23
The bearings of this observation lays in the application on it.
Ibid.
Lord, keep my memory green.[2]
The Haunted Man. Last line
You'll find us rough, Sir, but you'll find us ready.
David Copperfield. Chap. 3
I am a lone lorn creetur . . . and everythink goes contrairy with me.
Ibid.
Barkis is willin'.
Ibid. Chap. 5
That he may be ready — in case of anything turning up.[3]
Ibid. Chap. 12
I never will desert Mr. Micawber.
Ibid.

[1] See Joseph Edwards Carpenter, page 500.
[2] See Shakespeare, page 89.
[3] See Disraeli, page 421.

Annual income twenty pounds, annual expenditure nineteen nineteen six, result happiness. Annual income twenty pounds, annual expenditure twenty pounds ought and six, result misery.
David Copperfield. Chap. 12
It's a mad world. Mad as Bedlam.
Ibid. Chap. 14
"Did he [Mr. Dick] say anything to you about King Charles the First, child?"
"Yes, aunt."
"Ah!" said my aunt, rubbing her nose as if she were a little vexed. "That's his allegorical way of expressing it. He connects his illness with great disturbance and agitation, naturally, and that's the figure, or the simile, or whatever it's called, which he chooses to use. And why shouldn't he, if he thinks proper?"[1]
Ibid.
I'm a very umble person.[2]
Ibid. Chap. 16
The winds you are going to tempt, have wafted thousands upon thousands to fortune, and brought thousands upon thousands happily back.
Ibid.
I only ask for information.
Ibid. Chap. 20
It was as true . . . as turnips is. It was as true . . . as taxes is. And nothing's truer than them.
Ibid. Chap. 21
Ain't I volatile?
Ibid. Chap. 22
Nobody's enemy but his own.
Ibid. Chap. 25
Accidents will occur in the best regulated families.
Ibid. Chap. 28
Ride on! Rough-shod if need be, smooth-shod if that will do, but ride

[1] "King Charles's Head" has passed into common use in the English language as a phrase meaning some whimsical obsession. — G. B. STERN: *Monogram*
[2] Not only humble but umble, which I look upon to be the comparative, or, indeed, superlative degree. — ANTHONY TROLLOPE: *Doctor Thorne, Chap. 4*

on! Ride on over all obstacles, and win the race!

> *David Copperfield. Chap. 28*

A long pull, and a strong pull, and a pull altogether.

> *Ibid. Chap. 30*

People can't die, along the coast . . . except when the tide's pretty nigh out. They can't be born, unless it's pretty nigh in — not properly born, till flood. He's going out with the tide.

> *Ibid.*

There wasn't room to swing a cat there.[1]

> *Ibid. Chap. 35*

I ate umble pie with an appetite.

> *Ibid. Chap. 39*

Let sleeping dogs lie.

> *Ibid.*

Skewered through and through with office-pens, and bound hand and foot with red tape.

> *Ibid. Chap. 43*

A man must take the fat with the lean.

> *Ibid. Chap. 51*

Least said, soonest mended.

> *Ibid. Chap. 52*

Trifles make the sum of life.

> *Ibid. Chap. 53*

The seamen said it blew great guns.

> *Ibid. Chap. 55*

Our distinguished guest, the ornament of our town. May he never leave us but to better himself, and may his success among us be such as to render his bettering himself impossible.

> *Ibid. Chap. 63*

So may thy face be by me when I close my life indeed; so may I, when realities are melting from me like the shadows which I now dismiss, still find thee near me, pointing upward!

> *Ibid. Chap. 64, Closing lines*

Not to put too fine a point upon it.

> *Bleak House. Chap. 32*

The dreams of childhood — its airy fables; its graceful, beautiful, humane, impossible adornments of the world beyond: so good to be believed in once,

so good to be remembered when outgrown.

> *Hard Times. Book II, Chap. 9*

One always begins to forgive a place as soon as it's left behind.

> *Little Dorrit. Book I, Chap. 2*

Whatever was required to be done, the Circumlocution Office was beforehand with all the public departments in the art of perceiving HOW NOT TO DO IT.

> *Ibid. Chap. 10*

A person who can't pay, gets another person who can't pay, to guarantee that he can pay.

> *Ibid. Chap. 23*

Papa, potatoes, poultry, prunes, and prism, are all very good words for the lips: especially prunes and prism.

> *Ibid. Book II, Chap. 5*

It is at least as difficult to stay a moral infection as a physical one.

> *Ibid. Chap. 13*

It was the best of times, it was the worst of times, it was the age of wisdom, it was the age of foolishness, it was the epoch of belief, it was the epoch of incredulity, it was the season of Light, it was the season of Darkness, it was the spring of hope, it was the winter of despair.

> *A Tale of Two Cities. Book I, Chap. 1*

A wonderful fact to reflect upon, that every human creature is constituted to be that profound secret and mystery to every other.

> *Ibid. Chap. 3*

The calm that must follow all storms — emblem to humanity of the rest and silence into which the storm called Life must hush at last.

> *Ibid. Chap. 6*

Detestation of the high is the involuntary homage of the low.

> *Ibid. Book II, Chap. 9*

Dead as mutton.

> *Ibid. Chap. 14*

He's as thin as a lath.

> *Ibid.*

The murmuring of many voices, the upturning of many faces, the pressing on of many footsteps in the outskirts of the crowd, so that it swells forward

---

[1] You can swing a cat here. — JOHN GALSWORTHY: *The Man of Property*, Part I, Chap. 8

in a mass, like one great heave of water, all flashes away. Twenty-three.
> *A Tale of Two Cities. Book III, Chap. 15*

It is a far, far better thing that I do, than I have ever done; it is a far, far better rest that I go to, than I have ever known.
> *Ibid.*

I have known a vast quantity of nonsense talked about bad men not looking you in the face. Don't trust that conventional idea. Dishonesty will stare honesty out of countenance, any day in the week, if there is anything to be got by it.
> *Hunted Down. Chap. 2*

In the little world in which children have their existence, whosoever brings them up, there is nothing so finely perceived and so finely felt, as injustice.
> *Great Expectations. Chap. 9*

Probably every new and eagerly expected garment ever put on since clothes came in, fell a trifle short of the wearer's expectation.
> *Ibid. Chap. 19*

Heaven knows we need never be ashamed of our tears, for they are rain upon the blinding dust of earth, overlying our hard hearts.
> *Ibid.*

Throughout life, our worst weaknesses and meannesses are usually committed for the sake of the people whom we most despise.
> *Ibid. Chap. 27*

The Bigwig family (composed of all the stateliest people thereabouts, and all the noisiest).
> *Nobody's Story*

And I *do* come home at Christmas. We all do, or we all should. We all come home, or ought to come home, for a short holiday — the longer, the better — from the great boarding-school, where we are forever working at our arithmetical slates, to take, and give a rest.
> *A Christmas Tree*

My best of wishes for your merry Christmases and your happy New Years, your long lives and your true prosperities. Worth twenty pound good if they are delivered as I send them. Remember! Here's a final prescription added, "To be taken for life."
> *Doctor Marigold. Chap. 1*

EDWARD LEAR
[1812–1888]

They went to sea in a sieve, they did;
  In a sieve they went to sea;
In spite of all their friends could say.
> *The Jumblies. Stanza 1*

Far and few, far and few,
  Are the lands where the Jumblies live:
Their heads are green, and their hands are blue
And they went to sea in a sieve.
> *Ibid.*

The Pobble who has no toes
  Swam across the Bristol Channel;
But before he set out he wrapped his nose
  In a piece of scarlet flannel.
> *The Pobble Who Has No Toes. Stanza 2*

On the top of the Crumpetty Tree
  The Quangle Wangle sat,
But his face you could not see,
  On account of his Beaver Hat.
> *The Quangle Wangle's Hat. Stanza 1*

On the coast of Coromandel
  Where the early pumpkins blow,
    In the middle of the woods
Lived the Yonghy-Bonghy-Bò.
Two old chairs, and half a candle,
One old jug without a handle, —
  These were all his worldly goods.
> *The Courtship of the Yonghy-Bonghy-Bò. Stanza 1*

The Owl and the Pussy-Cat went to sea
  In a beautiful pea-green boat.
> *The Owl and the Pussy-Cat. Stanza 1*

They sailed away, for a year and a day,
  To the land where the bong-tree grows.
> *Ibid. Stanza 2*

When awful darkness and silence reign
Over the great Gromboolian plain,

Through the long, long wintry nights.
The Dong with the Luminous Nose. Stanza 1

Who, or why, or which, or *what*,
Is the Akond of Swat?
The Akond of Swat [1] [September, 1873]

Does he study the wants of his own dominion?
Or doesn't he care for public opinion?
Ibid.

Some one, or nobody, knows I wot
Who or which or why or what.
Ibid.

There was an old man at a Station,
Who made a promiscuous oration.
Limerick

He made them a book
And with laughter they shook.
Limerick

There was an Old Man with a beard,
Who said: "It is just as I feared!
  Two Owls and a Hen,
  Four Larks and a Wren
Have all built their nests in my beard."
Limerick

He weareth a runcible hat.
How Pleasant to Know Mr. Lear. Stanza 5

Ere the days of his pilgrimage vanish,
How pleasant to know Mr. Lear!
Ibid. Stanza 8

Ploffskin, Pluffskin, Pelican jee!
We think no Birds so happy as we!
Plumpskin, Ploshkin, Pelican jill!
We think so then, and we thought so still.
The Pelican Chorus.

WILLIAM JAMES LINTON
[1812–1898]

He boasts nor wealth nor high descent,
  yet he may claim to be
A gentleman to match the best of any
  pedigree:

His blood hath run in peasant veins
  through many a noteless year;
Yet, search in every prince's court,
  you'll rarely find his peer.
For he's one of Nature's Gentlemen,
  the best of every time.
Nature's Gentleman. Stanza 1

Be patient, O be patient! Put your ear
  against the earth;
Listen there how noiselessly the germ
  o' the seed has birth;
How noiselessly and gently it upheaves
  its little way
Till it parts the scarcely broken ground,
  and the blade stands up in day.
Patience [1]

NORMAN MACLEOD
[1812–1872]

Courage, brother! do not stumble,
  Though thy path be dark as night;
There's a star to guide the humble,
  Trust in God and do the Right.
Trust in God. Stanza 1

FRANCES SARGENT OSGOOD
[1812–1850]

Work — for some good, be it ever so slowly;
Cherish some flower, be it ever so lowly;
Labor! — all labor is noble and holy!
  Let thy great deeds be thy prayer to thy God!
Laborare est Orare. [2] *Stanza 6*

A whisper woke the air —
A soft, light tone, and low,
Yet barbed with shame and woe.
Calumny. Stanza 1

From ear to lip, from lip to ear,
Until it reached a gentle heart
That throbbed from all the world apart
  And that — it broke!
Ibid. Stanza 2

---

[1] The Ahkoond is dead! — GEORGE THOMAS LANIGAN [1845–1886]: *A Threnody, St. 1* [January, 1878]
   It borders upon Swat. — G. T. LANIGAN: *Dirge of the Moolla of Kotal, Rival of the Ahkoond of Swat, St. 1*

[1] From LINTON's *Poems of Freedom.* This poem is attributed to R. C. TRENCH in some anthologies.
[2] To labor is to pray. — Motto of BENEDICT [480–543], founder of the Benedictine Order.

WILLIAM EDMONDSTOUNE AYTOUN
[1813–1865]

News of battle! — news of battle!
  Hark! 'tis ringing down the street;
And the archways and the pavement
  Bear the clang of hurrying feet.
*Edinburgh after Flodden.
Stanza 1*

The German heart is stout and true,
  the German arm is strong,
The German foot goes seldom back
  where armed foemen throng;
But never had they faced in field so
  stern a charge before,
And never had they felt the sweep of
  Scotland's broad claymore.
The Island of the Scots

'Twas I that led the Highland host
  through wild Lochaber's snows,
What time the plaided clans came
  down to battle with Montrose.
*The Execution of Montrose.
Stanza 2*

Had I been there with sword in hand,
  and fifty Camerons by,
That day through high Dunedin's
  streets had pealed the slogan cry.
Ibid. Stanza 6

HENRY WARD BEECHER
[1813–1887]

If there were no religion, if that vast
sphere, out of which glow all the super-
eminent truths of the Bible, was a mere
emptiness and void, yet, methinks, the
very idea of Fatherland, the exceeding
preciousness of the laws and liberties of
a great people, would enkindle such a
high and noble enthusiasm that all
baser feelings would be consumed.
The Dishonest Politician

A thoughtful mind, when it sees a
Nation's flag, sees not the flag only,
but the Nation itself; and whatever
may be its symbols, its insignia, he
reads chiefly in the flag the Government, the principles, the truths, the
history which belongs to the Nation
that sets it forth.
The American Flag

Nothing marks the increasing wealth
of our times and the growth of the public mind toward refinement, more than
the demand for books.
*Star Papers. Subtleties of Book
Buyers*

Where is human nature so weak as
in the book-store!
Ibid.

No subtle manager or broker ever
saw through a maze of financial embarrassments half so quick as a poor bookbuyer sees his way clear to pay for
what he *must* have.
Ibid.

You cannot forget if you would,
those golden kisses all over the cheeks
of the meadow, queerly called dandelions.
Ibid. A Discourse on Flowers

JOHN WILLIAM BURGON
[1813–1888]

It seems no work of man's creative
  hand
By labor wrought as wavering fancy
  planned,
But from the rock as if by magic
  grown,
Eternal, silent, beautiful, alone!
Petra [1] [*Newdigate Prize Poem,
1845*]

Match me such marvel save in Eastern
  clime,
A rose-red city half as old as time.
Ibid.

JOSEPH EDWARDS CARPENTER
[1813–1885]

What are the wild waves saying,[2]
  Sister, the whole day long,
That ever amid our playing
  I hear but their low, lone song?
*What Are the Wild Waves
Saying? Stanza 1*

Yes, but the waves seem ever
  Singing the same sad thing,

---

[1] See Whittier, page 443.
[2] See Dickens, page 496.

And vain is my weak endeavor
 To guess what the surges sing.
   What Are the Wild Waves
    Saying? Stanza 3
Yes! but there's something greater
 That speaks to the heart alone:
'Tis the voice of the great Creator
 Dwells in that mighty tone.
     Ibid. Refrain
For her voice lives on the breeze,
 And her spirit comes at will,
In the midnight on the seas,
 Her bright smile haunts me still.
   Her Bright Smile Haunts Me
    Still. Stanza 1

WILLIAM LORENZO CARTER
[1813–1860]

Young Charlotte lived by a mountain-
 side in a wild and lonely spot,
There was no village for miles around
 except her father's cot;
And yet on many a wintry night young
 boys would gather there, —
Her father kept a social board, and she
 was very fair.
   Young [or Fair] Charlotte.[1]
     Stanza 1
"O daughter, dear," her mother said,
 "this blanket round you fold,
'Tis such a dreadful night abroad you
 will catch your death of cold."
    Ibid. Stanza 3
Young ladies, think of this fair girl and
 always dress aright,
And never venture thinly clad on such
 a wintry night.
    Ibid. Last stanza

CHRISTOPHER PEARSE
CRANCH
[1813–1892]

Thought is deeper than all speech,
 Feeling deeper than all thought;

---

[1] Carter was a Vermont man, but his ballad has become a folk-song of the South and a cowboy song of the West. There is a sketch, *William Carter, the Bensontown Homer*, by Phillips Barry, in the *Journal of American Folk-Lore*, April–June, 1912. The ballad is included in the published collections of Lomax, Spaeth, Cox, Pound, and others.

Souls to souls can never teach
 What unto themselves was taught.
   Thought [Gnosis]. Stanza 1
We are spirits clad in veils;
 Man by man was never seen;
All our deep communing fails
 To remove the shadowy screen.
     Ibid. Stanza 2
We are columns left alone
 Of a temple once complete.
     Ibid. Stanza 3
No night so wild but brings the con-
 stant sun
With love and power untold;
No time so dark but through its woof
 there run
Some blessed threads of gold.
    Oh, Love Supreme
O Light divine! we need no fuller test
 That all is ordered well;
We know enough to trust that all is
 best
Where Love and Wisdom dwell.
     Ibid.

JOHN SULLIVAN DWIGHT
[1813–1893]

Is not true leisure
 One with true toil? [1]
    Rest.[2] *Stanza 1*
Rest is not quitting
 The busy career,
Rest is the fitting
 Of self to its sphere.
     Ibid. Stanza 4
'Tis the brook's motion,
 Clear without strife,
Fleeing to ocean
 After its life.
     Ibid. Stanza 5
'Tis loving and serving
 The Highest and Best!
'Tis onwards! unswerving,
 And that is true rest.
     Ibid. Stanza 7
Work, and thou wilt bless the day
 Ere the toil be done;
They that work not, can not pray,
 Can not feel the sun.

---

[1] Absence of occupation is not rest.
   Cowper: *Retirement, L. 615*
[2] Wrongly attributed to Goethe.

God is living, working still,
All things work and move;
Work, or lose the power to will,
Lose the power to love.
Working

JOSEPH HOOKER
[1813-1879]

Well, General, we have not had many
dead cavalrymen lying about lately.
*Remark to General William
Woods Averell, of the Cavalry
[November, 1862]*

JESSE HUTCHINSON, JR. [1]
[1813-1853]

Of all the mighty nations
In the east or in the west,
O this glorious Yankee nation
Is the greatest and the best.
We have room for all creation,
And our banner is unfurled,
Here's a general invitation
To the people of the world.
Uncle Sam's Farm. Stanza 1
Uncle Sam is rich enough
To give us all a farm.
Ibid. Refrain
Then ho, brothers, ho,
To California go;
There's plenty of gold in the world
we're told
On the banks of the Sacramento.
Ho for California [1849]. Refrain
The gold is thar, most anywhar,
And they dig it out with an iron bar.
Ibid. Stanza 3

ELIJAH KELLOGG
[1813-1901]

If ye are men, follow me! Strike
down your guard, gain the mountain
passes, and then do bloody work, as
did your sires at old Thermopylae! Is
Sparta dead? Is the old Grecian spirit
frozen in your brains, that you do
cower like a belabored hound beneath
his master's lash? O comrades, war-

[1] A member of the famous Hutchinson
Family of Singers, of Lynn, Massachusetts,
which toured the country in the 1860s.

riors, Thracians! If we must fight, let
us fight for ourselves. If we must
slaughter, let it be under the clear sky,
by the bright waters, in noble, honorable battle!
Spartacus to the Gladiators

EPES SARGENT
[1813-1881]

A life on the ocean wave,
A home on the rolling deep;
Where the scattered waters rave,
And the winds their revels keep!
Like an eagle caged I pine
On this dull, unchanging shore:
Oh, give me the flashing brine,
The spray and the tempest's roar!
*A Life on the Ocean Wave.
Stanza 1*

JONES VERY
[1813-1880]

'Tis all a great show,
The world that we're in ―
None can tell when 'twas finished ―
None saw it begin.
The World. Stanza 1

HENRY STEVENSON · WASHBURN
[1813-1903]

We shall meet, but we shall miss him,
There will be one vacant chair;
We shall linger to caress him
When we breathe our evening
prayer.[1]
The Vacant Chair. Stanza 1

THOMAS OSBORNE DAVIS
[1814-1845]

Come in the evening, or come in the
morning,
Come when you're looked for, or come
without warning.
The Welcome. Stanza 1
The starlight of heaven above us shall
quiver

[1] See Longfellow, page 435.

As our souls flow in one down eternity's
river.
The Welcome. Stanza 3

AUBREY THOMAS DE VERE
[1814–1902]

Count each affliction, whether light or
grave,
God's messenger sent down to thee; do
thou
With courtesy receive him.
Sorrow

Grief should be
Like joy, majestic, equable, sedate,
Confirming, cleansing, raising, making
free;
Strong to consume small troubles; to
commend
Great thoughts, grave thoughts,
thoughts lasting to the end.
Ibid.

Sad is our youth, for it is ever going,
Crumbling away beneath our very
feet;
Sad is our life, for onward it is flowing
In current unperceived, because so
fleet.
Sad Is Our Youth. Stanza 1

Of all great Nature's tones that sweep
Earth's resonant bosom, far or near,
Low-breathed or loudest, shrill or deep,
How few are grasped by mortal ear.
Implicit Faith. Stanza 1

In holy music's golden speech
Remotest notes to notes respond:
Each octave is a world: yet each
Vibrates to worlds its own beyond.
Ibid. Stanza 4

FREDERICK WILLIAM
FABER
[1814–1863]

For right is right, since God is God,
And right the day must win;
To doubt would be disloyalty,
To falter would be sin.
On the Field

The sea, unmated creature, tired and
lone.

Makes on its desolate sands eternal
moan.
The Sorrowful World

O majesty unspeakable and dread!
Wert thou less mighty than Thou
art,
Thou wert, O Lord, too great for our
belief,
Too little for our heart.
The Greatness of God

Hark! Hark! my soul, angelic songs
are swelling
O'er earth's green fields, and ocean's
wave-beat shore;
How sweet the truth those blessed
strains are telling
Of that new life when sin shall be
no more!
Pilgrims of the Night

O Paradise! O Paradise!
Who doth not crave for rest?
Who would not seek the happy land
Where they that love are blest?
Paradise

CHARLES MACKAY
[1814–1889]

Cleon hath a million acres, — ne'er a
one have I;
Cleon dwelleth in a palace, — in a cottage I.
Cleon and I. Stanza 1

But the sunshine aye shall light the
sky,
As round and round we run;
And the truth shall ever come upper-
most,
And justice shall be done.
Eternal Justice. Stanza 4

Men of thought and men of action,
Clear the way!
Clear the Way. Stanza 1

Aid the dawning, tongue and pen;
Aid it, hopes of honest men!
Ibid. Stanza 2

Some love to roam o'er the dark sea's
foam,
Where the shrill winds whistle free.
Some Love to Roam

There's a good time coming, boys! [1]
  A good time coming.
      The Good Time Coming. Stanza 1
Cannon-balls may aid the truth,
  But thought's a weapon stronger;
We'll win our battles by its aid; —
  Wait a little longer.
                              Ibid.
The smallest effort is not lost,
Each wavelet on the ocean tost
Aids in the ebb-tide or the flow;
Each rain-drop makes some floweret
    blow;
Each struggle lessens human woe.
              The Old and the New
There is no such thing as death.
  In Nature nothing dies.
From each sad remnant of decay
  Some forms of life arise.
      There Is No Such Thing as Death
To every dungeon comes a ray
Of God's interminable day.
          The Ivy in the Dungeon.
                          Stanza 10
Whenever a rascal strove to pass,
Instead of silver, a coin of brass,
He took his hammer, and said, with a
    frown,
"The coin is spurious, nail it down." [2]
        The Coin Is Spurious. Stanza 1
Old Tubal Cain was a man of might,
In the days when earth was young.
            Tubal Cain. Stanza 1
Not alone for the blade was the bright
    steel made, .
And he fashioned the first plowshare. [3]
              Ibid. Stanza 4
To the West! to the West! to the land
    of the free,
Where the mighty Missouri rolls down
    to the sea.
            To the West. Stanza 1
Where the prairies, like seas where the
    billows have rolled,

----

[1] See Scott, page 310.
[2] There was an old custom that all counterfeit coins taken in a shop should be nailed to the counter, door-frame, or any solid woodwork, so that they could not be passed again.
[3] Tubal fashioned the hand-flung spears
  And showed his neighbours peace.
      KIPLING: *Jubal and Tubal Cain, St. 3*

Are broad as the kingdoms and empires of old.
              To the West. Stanza 2
A traveler through a dusty road
    strewed acorns on the lea,
And one took root and sprouted up,
    and grew into a tree.
          Small Beginnings. Stanza 1
A nameless man, amid a crowd that
    thronged the daily mart,
Let fall a word of Hope and Love, unstudied, from the heart;
A whisper on the tumult thrown, — a
    transitory breath, —
It raised a brother from the dust; it
    saved a soul from death.
                Ibid. Stanza 4
Croesus! hast thou riches
  That with mine can vie?
Pope! hast thou dominion
  Absolute as I?
                  Day Dreams
Make my coffee strong!
                  The Quarrel
The king can drink the best of wine —
    So can I;
And has enough when he would dine —
    So have I;
And can not order rain or shine —
    Nor can I.
Then where's the difference — let me
    see —
Betwixt my lord the king and me?
                  Differences
If happy I and wretched he,
Perhaps the king would change with
    me.
                      Ibid.
You have no enemies, you say?
  Alas! my friend, the boast is poor —
He who has mingled in the fray
  Of duty, that the brave endure,
Must have made foes! If you have
    none,
Small is the work that you have done;
You've hit no traitor on the hip;
You've dashed no cup from perjured
    lip;
You've never turned the wrong to
    right —

You've been a coward in the fight! [1]
> Quoted by MARIE CORELLI
> (*Mackay's adopted daughter*)
> in *Free Opinions: The Happy
> Life, Page 369*

THOMAS WESTWOOD
[1814–1888]

Storm upon the mountain, night upon
    its throne!
And the little snow-white lamb left
    alone — alone!
> *The Pet Lamb. Stanza 1*

MICHAEL WENTWORTH
BECK
[1815–1843]

This world is not so bad a world
    As some would like to make it;
Though whether good, or whether bad,
    Depends on how we take it.
> *The World as It Is. Stanza 1*

RICHARD HENRY DANA
[1815–1882]

Six days shalt thou labor and do all
    thou art able,
And on the seventh — holystone the
    decks and scrape the cable.
> *Two Years Before the Mast.
> Chap. 3, Philadelphia Cate-
> chism*

Like a true ship, committed to her
element once for all at her Launching,
she perished at sea.
> *Ibid. Twenty-Four Years After*
> *[1869]*

DANIEL DECATUR EMMET
[1815–1904]

In Dixie land, I'll took my stand,
To lib an' die in Dixie,
    Away, away,
Away down South in Dixie.
> *I Wish I Was in Dixie's Land*
> *[1859]*

[1] From the German of ANASTASIUS GRUEN
(COUNT VON AUERSPERG) [1806–1876].

JOHN BABSONE LANE SOULE
[1815–1891]

Go west, young man.[1]
> *Article in the Terre Haute,
> Indiana, Express [1851]*

ANTHONY TROLLOPE [2]
[1815–1882]

He argued that the principal duty
which a parent owed to a child was to
make him happy.
> *Doctor Thorne. Chap. 3*

In these days a man is nobody unless his biography is kept so far posted
up that it may be ready for the national
breakfast-table on the morning after
his demise.
> *Ibid. Chap. 25*

How I do hate those words, "an excellent marriage." In them is contained
more of wicked worldliness than any
other words one ever hears spoken.
> *The Small House at Allington.
> Chap. 39*

Those who offend us are generally
punished for the offence they give; but
we so frequently miss the satisfaction
of knowing that we are avenged!
> *Ibid. Chap. 50*

She understood how much louder a
cock can crow in its own farmyard than
elsewhere.
> *The Last Chronicle of Barset.
> Vol. I, Chap. 17*

Always remember that when you go
into an attorney's office door, you will
have to pay for it, first or last.
> *Ibid. Chap. 20*

[1] Horace Greeley [1811–1872] was attracted by the expression, and used it in an
editorial in *The New York Tribune*. As the
saying, "Go west, young man, and grow up
with the country," gained popularity, Greeley
printed Soule's article, to show the source of
his inspiration.
    Many men have stated that the advice was
given to them by Greeley, among them William S. Verity [1837–1934], who said Greeley
had given it to him in 1859.
    [2] I proclaim the fact that Anthony Trollope
has written a greater number of first-class
novels than Dickens or Thackeray or George
Eliot. — A. EDWARD NEWTON: *The Trollope
Society* (1934).

It is a comfortable feeling to know
that you stand on your own ground.
Land is about the only thing that can't
fly away.
The Last Chronicle of Barset.
Vol. II, Chap. 58

It's dogged as does it.
Ibid. Chap. 61
Nothing reopens the springs of love
so fully as absence, and no absence so
thoroughly as that which must needs
be endless.
Ibid. Chap. 67

PHILIP JAMES BAILEY
[1816–1902]

Let each man think himself an act of
God,
His mind a thought, his life a breath of
God;
And let each try, by great thoughts and
good deeds,
To show the most of Heaven he hath
in him.
Festus. Proem
Evil and good are God's right hand
and left.
Ibid.
Art is man's nature; nature is God's
art.
Ibid.
It matters not how long we live, but
how.
Ibid. Wood and Water
The world must have great minds, even
as great spheres
Or suns, to govern lesser restless minds.
Ibid. Water and Wood
I loved her for that she was beautiful.
Ibid.
Men might be better if we better
deemed
Of them. The worst way to improve the
world
Is to condemn it.[1]
Ibid. A Mountain, Sunrise

[1] The surest plan to make a Man
Is, think him so.
J. R. LOWELL: *The Biglow Papers,*
Jonathan to John, St. 9

It is much less what we do
Than what we think, which fits us for
the future.
Festus. Alcove and Garden
The first and worst of all frauds is to
cheat
Oneself.
Ibid. Anywhere
Who never doubted never half be-
lieved.[1]
Where doubt there truth is — 'tis her
shadow.
Ibid. A Country Town
We live in deeds, not years; in
thoughts, not breaths;
In feelings, not in figures on a dial.
We should count time by heart-throbs.
He most lives
Who thinks most — feels the noblest
— acts the best.
Life's but a means unto an end; that
end
Beginning, mean, and end to all things
— God.
Ibid.
Envy's a coal comes hissing hot from
hell.
Ibid.
The sole equality on earth is death.
Ibid.
I should like to macadamize the world;
The road to Hell wants mending.
Ibid.
America, half-brother of the world!
With something good and bad of every
land.
Ibid. The Surface
Beauty, but skin deep.
Ibid. A Village Feast
Worthy books
Are not companions — they are soli-
tudes:
We lose ourselves in them and all our
cares.
Ibid.
Music tells no truths.
Ibid.
Respect is what we owe; love, what we
give.
Ibid.

[1] There lives more faith in honest doubt,
Believe me, than in half the creeds.
TENNYSON: *In Memoriam, XCVI, 3*

Who can mistake great thoughts?
They seize upon the mind — arrest,
  and search,
And shake it.
> *Festus. A Village Feast*

The worst men often give the best advice.
> *Ibid.*

Man is a military animal,
Glories in gunpowder, and loves parade.
> *Ibid. A Metropolis*

Poets are all who love, who feel great
  truths,
And tell them; and the truth of truths
  is love.
> *Ibid. Another and a Better World*

The great ancients' writings, beside
  ours,
Look like illuminated manuscripts
Before plain press print.
> *Ibid. Home*

There is no disappointment we endure
One half so great as that we are to ourselves.[1]
> *Ibid. The Sun*

There are some hearts, aloe-like flower
  once, and die.[2]
> *Ibid. A Gathering of Kings and
> People*

It is folly to tell women truth!
They would rather live on lies, so they
  be sweet.
> *The Devil's Advice on Love-
> Making*

DAVID BARKER
[1816–1874]

One night, as old St. Peter slept,
  He left the door of Heaven ajar,
When through, a little angel crept,
  And came down with a falling star.
> *My Child's Origin. Stanza 1*

---

[1] Every really able man, if you talk sincerely with him, considers his work, however much admired, as far short of what it should be. — R. W. EMERSON: *Immortality*
[2] Have you heard the tale of the aloe plant,
  Away in the sunny clime?
By humble growth of an hundred years
  It reaches its blooming time.
  HENRY HARBAUGH [1817–1867]:
  Through Death to Life

CHARLOTTE BRONTË
[1816–1855]

Life, believe, is not a dream
  So dark as sages say;
Oft a little morning rain
  Foretells a pleasant day.
> *Life. Stanza 1*

The human heart has hidden treasures,
  In secret kept, in silence sealed; —
The thoughts, the hopes, the dreams,
  the pleasures,
  Whose charms were broken if revealed.
> *Evening Solace. Stanza 1*

An abundant shower of curates has
fallen upon the north of England.
> *Shirley, Chap. I*

FRANCES BROWN
[1816–1864]

Sad losses have ye met,
  But mine is heavier yet,
For a believing heart hath gone from
  me.
> *Losses. Stanza 5*

The age is weary with work and gold;
  And high hopes wither,[1] and memories wane,
On hearths and altars the fires are
  dead;
  But that brave faith hath not lived
  in vain.
> *Is It Come? Stanza 6*

Oh! those blessed times of old! with
  their chivalry and state;
I love to read their chronicles, which
  such brave deeds relate;
I love to sing their ancient rhymes, to
  hear their legends told —
But, Heaven be thanked! I live not in
  those blessed times of old!
> *Oh! the Pleasant Days of Old.
> Stanza 7*

JOSIAH DEAN CANNING
[1816–1892]

O'er the ruins of home, o'er my heart's
  desolation,

---

[1] High hopes faint on a warm hearth stone.
  KIPLING: *The Winners, St. 2*

No more shalt thou hear my unblest
  lamentation,
For death's dark encounter I make
  preparation,
  He hears the last cry of the wild
    Cherokee.
    The Lament of the Cherokee.[1]
    Stanza 5

CHARLOTTE CUSHMAN
[1816–1876]

God conceived the world, that was
  poetry;
He formed it, that was sculpture;
He colored it; that was painting;
He peopled it with living beings; that
  was the grand, divine, eternal
  drama.
  *On the Curtain of Ford's Opera
  House, Baltimore, Maryland*

JAMES THOMAS FIELDS
[1816–1881]

How sweet and gracious, even in com-
  mon speech,
Is that fine sense which men call Cour-
  tesy!
    Courtesy
It transmutes aliens into trusting
  friends,
And gives its owner passport round the
  globe.
    Ibid.
No wonder skies upon you frown;
You've nailed the horse-shoe upside
  down!
Just turn it round, and soon you'll see
How you and Fortune will agree.
    The Lucky Horse-shoe. Stanza 6
"Paint me as I am," said Cromwell,
  Rough with age and gashed with
    wars;
"Show my visage as you find it, —
  Less than truth my soul abhors."
    *On a Portrait of Cromwell.
    Stanza 1*

Oh, to be home again, home again,
  home again![1]
Under the apple-boughs, down by
  the mill!
    In a Strange Land
Just then, with a wink and a sly normal
  lurch,
The owl, very gravely, got down from
  his perch,
Walked round, and regarded his fault-
  finding critic
(Who thought he was stuffed) with a
  glance analytic.
    The Owl-Critic
"I'm an owl; you're another. Sir Critic,
  good day!"
And the barber kept on shaving.
    Ibid.
The skipper stormed, and tore his hair,
  Hauled on his boots and roared to
    Marden,
"Nantucket's sunk, and here we are
  Right over old Marm Hackett's gar-
    den!"
    The Nantucket Skipper. Stanza 10
'Tis a fearful thing in winter
  To be shattered in the blast,
And to hear the rattling trumpet
  Thunder, "Cut away the mast!"
    Ballad of the Tempest. Stanza 2
Is not God upon the ocean,
  Just the same as on the land?[2]
    Ibid. Stanza 5

ELLEN STURGIS HOOPER [3]
[1816–1841]

I slept and dreamed that life was
  beauty.

---

[1] So it's home again, and home again,
    America for me.
  My heart is turning home again, and
    there I long to be.
  HENRY VAN DYKE: *America for Me, St. 2*
[2] Sir Humphrey Gilbert [1539 ?–1583], on
  embarking on his ill-fated voyage homeward,
  — "We are as near to Heaven by sea as by
  land." — J. R. GREEN: *A Short History of
  the English People, Chap. 8*
  "Do not fear! Heaven is as near,"
  He said, "by water as by land!"
  LONGFELLOW: *Sir Humphrey Gilbert, St. 6*
[3] Mrs. Ellen Hooper, wife of Dr. R. W.
  Hooper, — a woman of genius, who gave our
  literature a classic in the lines beginning, —

---

[1] This poem has been attributed erroneously to John Howard Payne. It is in Canning's early book, *Harp and Plow,* and a later
book, *Connecticut River Reeds.*

I woke — and found that life was
    duty; [1]
Was my dream, then, a shadowy lie?
Toil on, sad heart, courageously,
And thou shalt find thy dream shall be
A noonday light and truth to thee.
                    Beauty and Duty

ROBERT TRAILL SPENCE LOWELL
[1816–1891]

It was the pipes of the Highlanders,
    And now they played "Auld Lang
    Syne."
It came to our men like the voice of
    God,
    And they shouted along the line.
            The Relief of Lucknow,[2]
                September 25, 1857

JOHN GODFREY SAXE
[1816–1887]

There's a castle in Spain, very charm-
    ing to see,
    Though built without money or toil;
Of this handsome estate I am owner in
    fee,
    And paramount lord of the soil.
            My Castle in Spain. Stanza 1
There is a saying of the ancient sages:
    No noble human thought,
However buried in the dust of ages,
    Can ever come to naught.
                Spes est Vates. Stanza 1
The saying is wise, though it sounds
    like a jest,
    That "the gods don't allow us to be
    in their debt,"
For though we may think we are spe-
    cially blest,
We are certain to pay for the favors
    we get!
            The Gifts of the Gods. Stanza 1
When skies are clear, expect the cloud;
    In darkness, wait the coming light;

"I slept, and dreamed that life was beauty."
— THOMAS WENTWORTH HIGGINSON: *Margaret Fuller Ossoli, Chap. 10*
[1] See Whittier, page 444.
[2] *Ibid.*, page 443.

Whatever be thy fate to-day,
    Remember, "This will pass away!" [1]
        The Old Man's Motto. Stanza 6
Of all amusements for the mind,
    From logic down to fishing,
There isn't one that you can find
    So very cheap as "wishing."
                Wishing. Stanza 1
I wish that practising was not
    So different from preaching.
                Ibid. Stanza 4
I'm growing fonder of my staff;
    I'm growing dimmer in the eyes;
I'm growing fainter in my laugh;
    I'm growing deeper in my sighs;
I'm growing careless of my dress;

---

[1] At the time of his trial in England, Warren Hastings related to his friends an Indian
tale which had given him much comfort: A
monarch, who suffered many hours of dis-
couragement, urged his courtiers to devise a
motto, short enough to be engraved on a ring,
which should be suitable alike in prosperity
and in adversity. After many suggestions had
been rejected, his daughter offered an emerald
bearing the inscription in Arabic, "This, too,
will pass."

This greatest mortal consolation, which we
derive from the transitoriness of all things —
from the right of saying, in every conjunc-
ture, — "This, too, will pass away."
    NATHANIEL HAWTHORNE: *The Marble
                        Faun, Chap. 16*
Whate'er thou art, where'er thy footsteps
        stray,
Heed these wise words: This, too, shall pass
    away.
        PAUL HAMILTON HAYNE: *This, Too,
                        Shall Pass Away*
Solemn words, and these were they:
"Even this shall pass away."
        THEODORE TILTON: *All Things Shall
                        Pass Away*
"Even this will pass away."
    THOMAS BAILEY ALDRICH: Title of sonnet
Lo! characters of glory play
'Mid shades — "This, too, shall pass away."
        BENJAMIN DAVIS WINSLOW [1815–
                1839]: *This, Too, Shall Pass Away*
Many the maxims sent the king, men say;
The one he chose, "This, too, shall pass
    away."
        ELLA WHEELER WILCOX: *This, Too,
                        Shall Pass Away*
Let these few words their fullest import bear:
"This, too, will pass away."
    MRS. LANTA WILSON SMITH [1856–   ]:
                This, Too, Shall Pass Away
This, Too, Shall Pass Away.
        JAMIE SEXTON HOLME: Title of poem

I'm growing frugal of my gold;
I'm growing wise; I'm growing —
yes, —
I'm growing old!
        I'm Growing Old. Stanza 3

For she was rich, and he was poor
And so it might not be.
        The Way of the World. Stanza 1

Of all the notable things on earth,
The queerest one is pride of birth,
        Among our "fierce Democracie"!
A bridge across a hundred years,
Without a prop to save it from
        sneers, —
Not even a couple of rotten Peers, —
A thing for laughter, fleers, and jeers,
        Is American aristocracy.
        The Proud Miss MacBride.
        Stanza 13

Depend upon it, my snobbish friend,
Your family thread you can't ascend,
Without good reason to apprehend
You may find it waxed at the farther
        end
By some plebeian vocation;
Or, worse than that, your boasted Line
May end in a loop of stronger twine,
        That plagued some worthy relation!
        Ibid. Stanza 15

He takes the strangest liberties, —
        But never takes his leave!
        My Familiar. Stanza 2

A frown is no extinguisher —
        It does not put him out!
        Ibid. Stanza 6

Bless me! this is pleasant
        Riding on the Rail.
        Rhyme of the Rail. Stanza 1

In battle or business, whatever the
        game,
In law or in love, it is ever the same;
In the struggle for power, or the scram-
        ble for pelf,
Let this be your motto, — Rely on
        yourself!
For, whether the prize be a ribbon or
        throne,
The victor is he who can go it alone![1]
        The Game of Life. Stanza 7

[1] He travels the fastest who travels alone.
        KIPLING: *The Winners*

"Got any boys," the Marshal said
To a lady from over the Rhine;
And the lady shook her flaxen head,
And civilly answered, *"Nein!"*
        The Puzzled Census-Taker.
        Stanza 1

I'll find a way, or make it![1]
        Where There's a Will There's a
        Way. Stanza 2

"God bless the man who first invented
        sleep!"
        So Sancho Panza said, and so say I.
        Early Rising. Stanza 1

I like the lad, who when his father
        thought
To clip his morning nap by hackneyed
        phrase
Of vagrant worm by early songster
        caught,
Cried, "Served him right! It's not at all
        surprising;
The worm was punished, Sir, for early
        rising!"
        Ibid. Stanza 8

How goes the Money? — Sure,
I wish the ways were something fewer;
It goes for wages, taxes, debts;
It goes for presents, goes for bets,
For paint, pomade, and eau de rose, —
And that's the way the Money goes![2]
        How the Money Goes. Stanza 3

I know a girl with teeth of pearl,
And shoulders white as snow;
        She lives, — ah! well,
        I must not tell, —
Wouldn't you like to know?
        Wouldn't You Like to Know?
        Stanza 1

It was six men of Indostan
        To learning much inclined,
Who went to see the Elephant
        (Though all of them were blind),

[1] Aut viam inveniam, aut faciam. — Latin
motto
[2] Up and down the City Road,
        In and out the Eagle,
    That's the way the money goes —
        Pop goes the weasel!
        Popular song in London [1852–1853]
The Eagle was a music-hall, in which
drinks were sold, on the City Road, London.
The weasel was a tool used by hatters, often
pawned on Saturday night, "pop" being
equivalent to "hock".

That each by observation
Might satisfy his mind.
The Blind Men and the Elephant.
Stanza 1
"Whose very charming grounds are
these?
And — pardon me — be pleased to tell
Who in this splendid house may dwell?"
To which, in Dutch, the puzzled man
Replied what seemed like *"Nick Van*
Stann." [1]
The Romance of Nick Van Stann
With sudden anger, Hassan looked
around,
And saw an angel standing on the
ground,
With wings of gold, and robe of purest
white.
"I am God's messenger, employed to
write
Within this book the pious deeds of
men;
I have revised thy reckoning: look
again." [2]
Hassan and the Angel
"Whose work is this?" Murillo said,
The while he bent his eager gaze
Upon a sketch (a Virgin's head)
That filled the painter with amaze. [3]
Murillo and His Slave. [4] *Stanza 1*
'Tis wise to learn; 'tis God-like to
create.
The Library
I asked of Echo, 't other day
(Whose words are few and often
funny),
What to a novice she could say
Of courtship, love, and matrimony?

Quoth Echo, plainly: — "Matter-o'-
money."
Echo. Stanza 1
Young ladies! — beware of hasty con-
nections;
And don't marry suitors of swarthy
complexions;
For though they may chance to be cap-
ital fellows,
Depend upon it, they're apt to be jeal-
ous!
Othello, the Moor. Moral

MICHAEL JOSEPH BARRY
[1817–1889]

Death is a common friend or foe,
As different men may hold,
And at his summons each must go,
The timid and the bold;
But when the spirit, free and warm,
Deserts it, as it must,
What matter where the lifeless form
Dissolves again to dust?
The Place Where Men Should
Die. [1] *Stanza 2*
But whether on the scaffold high
Or in the battle's van, [2]
The fittest place where man can die
Is where he dies for man!
Ibid. Stanza 5

ELIZA COOK
[1817–1889]

There's a magical tie to the land of our
home,
Which the heart cannot break, though
the footsteps may roam. [3]
The Land of My Birth. Stanza 1
Whom do we dub as Gentlemen? The
knave, the fool, the brute —
If they but own full tithe of gold, and
wear a courtly suit.
Nature's Gentleman. Stanza 1

---

[1] "I say, whose house is that there here?"
"House! *Je vous n'entends pas, Mon-*
sieur."
"What, Nongtongpaw again!" cries John;
"This fellow is some mighty Don."
CHARLES DIBDIN [1745–1814]:
Nongtongpaw
[2] See Leigh Hunt, page 346.
[3] "Who is your master, boy?"
"You, Señor," said the trembling slave;
"Nay, who, I mean, instruction gave,
Before that Virgin's head you drew?"
SUSAN WILSON: *The Painter of Seville*
[4] The incident related in the poem occurred
about 1630. The slave was Sebastian Gómez.
See DOLORES BACON [1870–1934]: *Pictures*
Every Child Should Know. P. 219.

[1] Printed in *The Dublin Nation, Sept. 28,*
1844, Vol. II, P. 809.
[2] Whether on the scaffold high, or the battlefield we die,
O what matter, when for Erin dear we
fall!
TIMOTHY DANIEL SULLIVAN [1827–
1914]: *God Save Ireland*
[3] See Holmes, page 453.

They hold the rank no king can give,
　　no station can disgrace;
Nature puts forth her Gentleman, and
　　monarchs must give place.[1]
　　　　Nature's Gentleman. Stanza 6
There's a land that bears a well-known
　　name,
Though it is but a little spot;
I say 'tis first on the scroll of Fame,
And who shall say it is not?
　　　　The Englishman. Stanza 1
There's a star in the West that shall
　　never go down
Till the records of Valour decay;
We must worship its light, though it is
　　not our own,
For liberty burst in its ray.
　　　　There's a Star in the West.[2]
　　　　　　Stanza 1
I love it, I love it; and who shall dare
To chide me for loving that old arm-
　　chair?
　　　　The Old Arm-Chair
How cruelly sweet are the echoes that
　　start
When memory plays an old tune on the
　　heart!
　　　　Old Dobbin. Stanza 16
Better build schoolrooms for "the boy"
Than cells and gibbets for "the man."[3]
　　　　A Song for the Ragged Schools.
　　　　　　Stanza 12
"God speed the plough!" be this a
　　prayer
To find its echo everywhere.
　　　　God Speed the Plough. Stanza 1
How busy we are on Tom Tidler's
　　ground
　　Looking for gold and silver.[4]
　　　　Tom Tidler's Ground. Stanza 1

---

[1] See Linton, page 499.
[2] The poem is in praise of George Washington.
[3] Give them a chance — if you stint them
　　now, to-morrow you'll have to pay
A larger bill for a darker ill.
　　DENIS A. MCCARTHY [1870–1931]:
　　　Give Them a Place to Play, St. 4
[4] Here we are on Tom Tidler's ground,
picking up gold and silver. — A children's
game

"And why Tom Tidler's ground?" asked
the Traveller.

Whenever you find your heart despair
Of doing some goodly thing,
Con over this strain, try bravely again,
And remember the Spider and King.[1]
　　　　Try Again. Stanza 16

JOHN BALLANTINE GOUGH
[1817–1886]

What is a minority? The chosen heroes of this earth have been in a minority. There is not a social, political, or
religious privilege that you enjoy to-
day that was not bought for you by the
blood and tears and patient suffering
of the minority. It is the minority that
have stood in the van of every moral
conflict, and achieved all that is noble
in the history of the world.
　　　　What Is a Minority?

Everywhere water is a thing of
beauty, gleaming in the dewdrop; singing in the summer rain; shining in the
ice-gems till the leaves all seem to turn
to living jewels; spreading a golden
veil over the setting sun; or a white
gauze around the midnight moon.
　　　　A Glass of Water

My old gray mare run up the hill,
and as she turned the top, she waved
her tail back at me, seemingly to say —
fare ye well, brother Watkins.
　　　　Brother Watkins

"Because he scatters halfpence to Tramps
and such-like." — DICKENS: *Christmas Stories, Tom Tidler's Ground*
[1] Bruce, banned and hunted on his native
　　soil,
With curious eyes surveyed a spider's
　　toil;
Six times the little climber strove and
　　failed;
Six times the chief before his foe had
　　quailed.
"Once more," he cried, "in thine my doom
　　I read,
Once more I dare the fight if thou suc-
　　ceed."
'Twas done; the insect's fate he made his
　　own;
Once more the battle waged, and gained
　　a throne.
CHARLES SPRAGUE [1791–1875]: *Curiosity*

FRANCIS DE HAES JANVIER
[1817–1885]

The woes of thirty millions filled his
burdened heart with grief,
Embattled hosts on land and sea acknowledged him their chief,
And yet amid the din of war he heard
the plaintive cry
Of that poor soldier as he lay in prison,
doomed to die.

The Sleeping Sentinel.[1] *Stanza 10*

SIR AUSTEN HENRY
LAYARD
[1817–1894]

I have always believed that success
would be the inevitable result if the
two services, the army and the navy,
had fair play, and if we sent the right
man to fill the right place.

Speech in Parliament [2]
[January 15, 1855]

TOM TAYLOR
[1817–1880]

You lay a wreath on murdered Lincoln's bier,
You, who, with mocking pencil,
wont to trace,
Broad for self-complacent British
sneer,
His length of shambling limb, his
furrowed face.

*Abraham Lincoln Foully
Assassinated.*[3] *Stanza 1*

[1] A poem, largely romance, on President
Lincoln's pardoning a Vermont soldier, William Scott, who slept while on guard duty.
President Lincoln did not pardon Scott, according to a paper, *The Element of Romance
in Military History*, by COLONEL GEORGE G.
BENEDICT, read before the Vermont Com-
mandery, Loyal Legion, March 14, 1893.

In 1936 the Vermont Historical Society
published a book on the subject by WALDO
F. GLOVER, presenting various documents in
Scott's case.

There are other versions of the legend, in
both verse and prose, one being *The Soldier's
Reprieve: The Generous Soldier Saved* in
Tiffany's Gems for the Fireside.

[2] Reported in T. C. HANSARD's *Parliamentary Debates, Third Series, Vol. 138, P. 2077.*

[3] Printed in *Punch*, London, May 6, 1865.
(Taylor became editor of *Punch* in 1874.) It
was at a performance of Taylor's play, *Our
American Cousin*, that Lincoln was shot.

Yes: he had lived to shame me from
my sneer,
To lame my pencil, and confute my
pen;
To make me own this hind of Princes
peer,
This rail-splitter a true-born king of
men.

*Abraham Lincoln Foully
Assassinated. Stanza 5*

How his quaint wit made home-truth
seem more true.

Ibid. Stanza 6

He went about his work — such work
as few
Ever had laid on head and heart and
hand —
As one who knows, where there's a task
to do,
Man's honest will must Heaven's
good grace command.

Ibid. Stanza 8

The Old World and the New, from sea
to sea,
Utter one voice of sympathy and
shame.
Sore heart, so stopped when it at last
beat high!
Sad life, cut short, just as its triumph
came!

Ibid. Stanza 17

HENRY DAVID THOREAU
[1817–1862]

My life is like a stroll upon the beach,
As near the ocean's edge as I can go.

The Fisher's Boy.[1] *Stanza 1*

I have but few companions on the
shore, —
They scorn the strand who sail upon
the sea;
Yet oft I think the ocean they've sailed
o'er
Is deeper down upon the strand to
me.

Ibid. Stanza 3

Whate'er we leave to God, God does
And blesses us.

Inspiration. Proem

[1] Entitled *The Fisher's Son* in Thoreau's
Journal [1840] and *Upon the Beach* in some
anthologies.

I hear beyond the range of sound,
I see beyond the range of sight,
New earths and skies and seas around,
And in my day the sun doth pale his
light.

Inspiration. Stanza 7

She with one breath attunes the
spheres,
And also my poor human heart.

Ibid. Stanza 15

I am a parcel of vain strivings tied
By a chance bond together.

Sic Vita.[1] *Stanza 1*

Great God, I ask thee for no meaner
pelf
Than that I may not disappoint myself,
That in my action I may soar as high
As I can now discern with this clear
eye.

A Prayer.[2] *Stanza 1*

Any man more right than his neighbors, constitutes a majority of one.

The Duty of Civil Disobedience

I have travelled a good deal in Concord.

Walden. I, Economy

What a man thinks of himself, that
it is which determines, or rather indicates, his fate.

Ibid.

As if you could kill time without
injuring eternity.

Ibid.

Most of the luxuries, and many of
the so-called comforts, of life are not
only not indispensable, but positive hindrances to the elevation of mankind.

Ibid.

It is true, I never assisted the sun ma-
terially in his rising; but, doubt not, it
was of the last importance only to be
present at it.

Ibid.

For many years I was self-appointed
inspector of snow-storms and rain-
storms, and did my duty faithfully.

Ibid.

Beware of all enterprises that require
new clothes.

Ibid.

[1] Published [July, 1841] in *The Dial,*
edited by Margaret Fuller.
[2] *The Dial* [July, 1842].

The swiftest traveller is he that goes
afoot.

Walden. I, Economy

The man who goes alone can start to-
day; but he who travels with another
must wait till that other is ready.

Ibid.

There is no odor so bad as that which
arises from goodness tainted.

Ibid. Philanthropy

There are a thousand hacking at the
branches of evil to one who is striking
at the root.

Ibid.

Philanthropy is almost the only virtue which is sufficiently appreciated by
mankind.

Ibid.

To him whose elastic and vigorous
thought keeps pace with the sun, the
day is a perpetual morning.

Ibid. II, What I Lived For

To be awake is to be alive.

Ibid.

I went to the woods because I wished
to live deliberately, to front only the
essential facts of life, and see if I could
not learn what it had to teach, and not,
when I came to die, discover that I had
not lived.

Ibid.

Our life is frittered away by detail.
. . . Simplify, simplify.

Ibid.

Time is but the stream I go a-fishing
in.

Ibid.

Books must be read as deliberately
and reservedly as they were written.

Ibid. III, Reading

The works of the great poets have
never yet been read by mankind, for
only great poets can read them.

Ibid.

I love a broad margin to my life.

Ibid. IV, Sounds

Our horizon is never quite at our
elbows.

Ibid. V, Solitude

I never found the companion that
was so companionable as solitude.

Ibid.

Society is commonly too cheap. We meet at very short intervals, not having had time to acquire any new value for each other.

Walden. V, Solitude

I had three chairs in my house: one for solitude, two for friendship, three for society.

Ibid. VI, Visitors

I was determined to know beans.

Ibid. VII, The Beanfield

If the day and the night are such that you greet them with joy, and life emits a fragrance like flowers and sweet-scented herbs, is more elastic, more starry, more immortal, — that is your success.

Ibid. XI, Higher Laws

There is never an instant's truce between virtue and vice. Goodness is the only investment that never fails.

Ibid.

Every man is the builder of a temple, called his body.

Ibid.

While men believe in the infinite, some ponds will be thought to be bottomless.

Ibid. XVI, The Pond in Winter

Through our own recovered innocence we discern the innocence of our neighbors.

Ibid. XVII, Spring

If one advances confidently in the direction of his dreams, and endeavors to live the life which he has imagined, he will meet with a success unexpected in common hours.

Ibid. XVIII, Conclusion

If a man does not keep pace with his companions,[1] perhaps it is because he hears a different drummer. Let him step to the music which he hears, however measured or far away.

Ibid.

Love your life, poor as it is. You may perhaps have some pleasant, thrilling, glorious hours, even in a poorhouse. The setting sun is reflected from the windows of the almshouse as brightly as from the rich man's abode.

Walden. XVIII, Conclusion

It is life near the bone where it is sweetest.

Ibid.

Rather than love, than money, than fame, give me truth.

Ibid.

Only that day dawns to which we are awake. There is more day to dawn. The sun is but a morning star.

Ibid.

I saw a delicate flower had grown up two feet high between the horses' feet and the wheel track. An inch more to right or left had sealed its fate, or an inch higher. Yet it lived to flourish, and never knew the danger it incurred. It did not borrow trouble, nor invite an evil fate by apprehending it.

Journal. September, 1850

The blue-bird carries the sky on his back.

Ibid. April 3, 1852

The perception of beauty is a moral test.

Ibid. June 21, 1852

The youth gets together his materials to build a bridge to the moon, or, perchance, a palace or temple on the earth, and, at length, the middle-aged man concludes to build a woodshed with them.[1]

Ibid. July 14, 1852

Fire is the most tolerable third party.

Ibid. January 2, 1853

Some circumstantial evidence is very strong, as when you find a trout in the milk.

Ibid. November 11, 1854

That man is the richest whose pleasures are the cheapest.

Ibid. March 11, 1856

---

[1] This reminds the editor of the old cockney story of the infatuated mother who saw her hobbledehoy marching in a company of recruits. "All out of step but Bill!" she exclaimed proudly.

[1] At noon he bounded out for food, and nothing less than roast lion would content him. But by suppertime milk toast would do. — Quoted without provenance in *We Accept With Pleasure*, by BERNARD DE VOTO (1897–).

When the playful breeze drops in the pool, it springs to right and left, quick as a kitten playing with dead leaves.[1]
Journal. April 9, 1859

CECIL FRANCES ALEXANDER
[1818–1895]

By Nebo's lonely mountain,
  On this side Jordan's wave,
In a vale in the land of Moab,
  There lies a lonely grave.[2]
  The Burial of Moses. Stanza 1
Noiselessly as the spring-time
  Her crown of verdure weaves,
And all the trees on all the hills
  Open their thousand leaves.
  Ibid. Stanza 3
This was the truest warrior
  That ever buckled sword;
This the most gifted poet
  That ever breathed a word;
And never earth's philosopher
  Traced with his golden pen
On the deathless page, truths half so sage
  As he wrote down for men.
  Ibid. Stanza 7
The roseate hues of early dawn,
  The brightness of the day,
The crimson of the sunset sky,
  How fast they fade away!
  The Roseate Hues of Early Dawn. Stanza 1
There was no other good enough
  To pay the price of sin;
He only could unlock the gate
  Of heaven and let us in.
  There Is a Green Hill Far Away. Stanza 4

EMILY BRONTË
[1818–1848]

Sleep not, dream not; this bright day
Will not, cannot last for aye;

Bliss like thine is bought by years
Dark with torment and with tears.
  Sleep Not. Stanza 1
The Bluebell is the sweetest flower
  That waves in summer air:
Its blossoms have the mightiest power
  To soothe my spirit's care.
  The Bluebell. Stanza 1
Love is like the wild rose-briar;
  Friendship like the holly-tree.
The holly is dark when the rose-briar blooms,
  But which will bloom most constantly?
  Love and Friendship. Stanza 1
I'll walk where my own nature would be leading —
It vexes me to choose another guide —
Where the grey flocks in ferny glens are feeding,
Where the wild wind blows on the mountain-side.
  Often Rebuked. Stanza 4
Cold in the earth — and fifteen wild Decembers
From those brown hills have melted into spring:
Faithful, indeed, is the spirit that remembers
After such years of change and suffering!
  Remembrance
No coward soul is mine,
  No trembler in the world's storm-troubled sphere:
I see Heaven's glories shine,
  And faith shines equal, arming me from fear.
  Last Lines. Stanza 1
There is not room for Death.
  Ibid. Stanza 7

BENJAMIN FRANKLIN BUTLER
[1818–1893]

There is no need for me to answer the gentleman from New York. Every negro minstrel just now is singing the

---

[1] See the kitten on the wall,
  Sporting with the leaves that fall.
    WORDSWORTH: *The Kitten and the Falling Leaves*
[2] See Bryant, page 372.

answer, and the hand-organs are playing the tune, "Shoo, Fly, Don't Bodder Me." [1]

Debate. House of Representatives

WILLIAM ELLERY CHANNING
[1818–1901]

Habitant of castle gray,
Creeping thing in sober way,
Visible sage mechanician,
Skilfulest arithmetician.
The Spider. [2]

It is not far beyond the village church,
After we pass the wood that skirts the road,
A lake, — the blue-eyed Walden, that doth smile
Most tenderly upon its neighbor pines.
Walden Lake, Concord

Beneath the endless surges of the deep,
Whose green content o'erlaps them evermore,
A host of mariners perpetual sleep,
Too hushed to heed the wild commotion's roar.
Death. Stanza 1

I laugh, for hope hath happy place with me, —
If my bark sinks, 'tis to another sea.
A Poet's Hope

I sing New England, as she lights her fire

In every Prairie's midst; and where the bright
Enchanting stars shine pure through Southern night,
She still is there, the guardian on the tower,
To open for the world a purer hour.
New England

Most joyful let the Poet be;
It is through him that all men see.
The Poet of the Old and New Times

My highway is unfeatured air,
My consorts are the sleepless stars,
And men my giant arms upbear —
My arms unstained and free from scars.
The Earth. Stanza 1

A wail in the wind is all I hear;
A voice of woe for a lover's loss.
Tears in Spring. Lament for Thoreau, Stanza 3

The hills are reared, the seas are scooped in vain
If learning's altar vanish from the plain.
Inscription for the Alcott House, Concord [1]

ARTHUR CLEVELAND COXE
[1818–1896]

I never can see the old churchyard
But I breathe to God a prayer,
That, sleep as I may in this fevered life,
I may rest when I slumber there.
St. George's Churchyard, Hempstead, Long Island

WILLIAM MAXWELL EVARTS
[1818–1901]

The pious ones of Plymouth, who, reaching the Rock, first fell upon their

---

[1] In his *Autobiography of Seventy Years*, GEORGE FRISBIE HOAR [1826–1904] tells of a five-minute debate in the House of Representatives. Samuel Sullivan ("Sunset") Cox [1824–1889], Democratic member from New York, had attacked Butler savagely. In his reply, Butler took no notice of Cox until the close of his argument.

The song, *Shoo Fly, Don't Bodder Me*, was written by THOMAS BRIGHAM BISHOP, set to music by FRANK CAMPBELL, popularized by Billy Reeves, in the late 1860s.

It would get to running through his head, like the "shoo-fly" song which Butler sings in the House.

CHARLES DUDLEY WARNER: *My Summer in a Garden, Eighth Week*

[2] His first poem, published in *The New England Magazine* [Oct., 1835].

[1] This couplet remains over the mantelpiece in Alcott House, Concord, Massachusetts, just as it was painted by May Alcott. Ellery Channing, the poet, who supplied the motto, was a nephew of the clergyman of the same name.

own knees and then upon the aborigines.[1]

Quoted by HENRY WATTERSON
*in The Louisville Courier-
Journal* [*July 4, 1913*]

JOHN JAMES ROBERT MANNERS, DUKE OF RUTLAND
[1818–1906]

No: by the names inscribed in History's page,
Names that are England's noblest heritage,
Names that shall live for yet unnumbered years
Shrined in our hearts with Cressy and Poictiers;
Let wealth and commerce, laws and learning die,
But leave us still our old nobility.

England's Trust. Part III, Line 227

JOHN MASON NEALE
[1818–1866]

There must in every cause be some first Martyr
To suffer and to fall;
There must be also those content to barter
Their victory for their all.

Abraham Lincoln. Stanza 1

Jerusalem the golden, with milk and honey blest,
Beneath thy contemplation sink heart and voice oppressed.

*Hymn (paraphrased from the
Latin of Bernard de Cluny)*

Brief life is here our portion.

Hymn

HENRY PETERSON
[1818–1891]

Sing, bird, on green Missouri's plain,
The saddest song of sorrow.

Lyon.[2] *Stanza 1*

HENRY WHEELER SHAW
("JOSH BILLINGS")
[1818–1885]

It is better to know nothing than to know what ain't so.[1]

Proverb [*1874*]

A sekret ceases tew be a sekret if it iz once confided — it iz like a dollar bill, once broken, it iz never a dollar agin.

Affurisms [2]

Love iz like the meazles; we kant have it bad but onst, and the later in life we have it the tuffer it goes with us.

Ibid.

Put an Englishman into the garden of Eden, and he would find fault with the whole blarsted consarn; — put a Yankee in, and he would see where he could alter it to advantage; — put an Irishman in, and he would want tew boss the thing; — put a Dutchman in, and he would proceed tew plant it.

Ibid.

Better make a weak man your enemy than your friend.

Ibid.

I never knu a man trubbled with melankolly, who had plenty to dew, and did it.

Ibid.

Poverty iz the step-mother ov genius.

Ibid.

Manifest destiny iz the science ov going tew bust, or enny other place before yu git thare.

Manifest Destiny

Thare iz such a thing az manifest destiny, but when it occurs it iz like the number ov rings on the rakoon's tale, ov no great consequense only for ornament.

Ibid.

The wheel that squeaks the loudest
Is the one that gets the grease.

The Kicker

---

[1] This pun has been attributed to Oliver Wendell Holmes, Bill Nye, and George Frisbie Hoar. See Guiterman, page 815.
[2] General Nathaniel Lyon [1818–1861], killed in battle at Wilson's Creek, Missouri, August 10, 1861.

[1] Better know nothing than half-know many things. — NIETZSCHE: *Thus Spake Zarathustra, Part IV, 64*
[2] From *Josh Billings: His Sayings.*

ARTHUR HUGH CLOUGH
[1819–1861]

It fortifies my soul to know
That, though I perish, Truth is so:
That, howsoe'er I stray and range,
Whate'er I do, Thou dost not change.
I steadier step when I recall
That, if I slip, Thou dost not fall.
"With Whom Is no Variableness" [1]

Because we can't do all we would,
Does it follow, to do nothing's good?
Dipsychus. Part I, Sc. 4

And almost every one when age,
  Disease, or sorrows strike him,
Inclines to think there is a God,
  Or something very like Him.
Ibid. Sc. 5

This world is very odd we see,
  We do not comprehend it;
But in one fact we all agree,
  God won't, and we can't, mend it.
Ibid. Part II, Sc. 2

How pleasant it is to have money!
Ibid.

In light things
Prove thou the arms thou long'st to
  glorify,
Nor fear to work up from the lowest
  ranks
Whence come great Nature's Captains.
  And high deeds
Haunt not the fringy edges of the fight
But the pell-mell of men.
Ibid. Sc. 4

Grace is given of God, but knowledge
  is bought in the market.
*The Bothie of Tober-na-Vuolich.
  Part IV*

A world where nothing is had for nothing.
Ibid. Part VIII

There is a great Field-Marshal, my
  friend, who arrays our battalions;
Let us to Providence trust, and abide
  and work in our stations.
Ibid. Part IX

Where lies the land to which the ship
  would go?

[1] *James, I, 17.*

Far, far ahead, is all her seamen
  know.
Songs of Absence

That out of sight is out of mind [1]
Is true of most we leave behind;
It is not sure, nor can be true,
My own and only love, of you.
Ibid.

How in God's name did Columbus get
    over
  Is a pure wonder to me.
Columbus. Stanza 1

What if wise men had, as far back as
    Ptolemy,
  Judged that the earth, like an orange
    was round,
None of them ever said, Come along,
    follow me,
  Sail to the West, and the East will be
    found.
Ibid. Stanza 3

Say not, the struggle naught availeth,
  The labor and the wounds are vain,
The enemy faints not, nor faileth,
  And as things have been they remain.
*Say Not the Struggle Naught
    Availeth. Stanza 1*

For while the tired waves, vainly break-
    ing,
  Seem here no painful inch to gain,
Far back, through creeks and inlets
    making,
  Comes silent, flooding in, the main.
Ibid. Stanza 3

And not by eastern windows only,
  When daylight comes, comes in the
    light;
In front, the sun climbs slow, how
    slowly,
  But westward, look, the land is
    bright.
Ibid. Stanza 4

As ships, becalmed at eve, that lay
  With canvas drooping, side by side,
Two towers of sail, at dawn of day
  Are scarce long leagues apart de-
    scried.
Qua Cursum Ventus. Stanza 1

[1] See Thomas à Kempis, page 9.

MARIAN EVANS CROSS ("GEORGE ELIOT")
[1819–1880]

'Tis God gives skill,
But not without men's hands: He could
    not make
Antonio Stradivari's violins
Without Antonio.

Stradivarius

O may I join the choir invisible
Of those immortal dead who live again
In minds made better by their presence.
    O May I Join the Choir Invisible
    May I reach
That purest heaven, be to other souls
The cup of strength in some great
    agony.

Ibid.

Boots and shoes are the greatest
trouble of my life. Everything else one
can turn and turn about, and make old
look like new; but there's no coaxing
boots and shoes to look better than
they are.

Amos Barton. Chap. 2

It's no trifle at her time of life to
part with a doctor who knows her constitution.

Janet's Repentance. Chap. 3

Any coward can fight a battle when
he's sure of winning; but give me the
man who has pluck to fight when he's
sure of losing. That's my way, sir; and
there are many victories worse than a
defeat.

Ibid. Chap. 6

Opposition may become sweet to a
man when he has christened it persecution.

Ibid. Chap. 8

It's but little good you'll do watering last year's crops.

Adam Bede. Chap. 18

He was like a cock who thought the
sun had risen to hear him crow.

Ibid. Chap. 33

We all have a chance of meeting
with some pity, some tenderness, some
charity, when we are dead; it is the
living only who cannot be forgiven.

The Lifted Veil

I've never any pity for conceited
people, because I think they carry their
comfort about with them.[1]

The Mill on the Floss.
Book V, Chap. 4

Below their names it was written:
"In their death they were not divided." [2]

Ibid. Last line of book

Blessed is the man who, having nothing to say, abstains from giving in
words evidence of the fact.

Impressions of Theophrastus Such

Life is too precious to be spent in
this weaving and unweaving of false
impressions, and it is better to live
quietly under some degree of misrepresentation than to attempt to remove it
by the uncertain process of letter-
writing.

Life and Letters.[3] Letter to
Mrs. Peter Taylor [June 8, 1856]

The years seem to rush by now, and
I think of death as a fast approaching
end of a journey — [4] double and treble
reason for loving as well as working
while it is day.

Ibid. Letter to Miss Sara Hen-
nell [November 22, 1861]

It seems to me much better to read
a man's own writing than to read what
others say about him, especially when
the man is first-rate and the "others"
are third-rate.

Ibid. To Miss Hennell
[October 28, 1865]

I have the conviction that excessive
literary production is a social offence.

Ibid. Letter to Alexander Main
[September 11, 1871]

To hear of a friend's illness after he

---

[1] There is not enough of love and goodness in the world to throw any of it away
on conceited people.
NIETZSCHE: *Human, All Too Human, 129*
[2] *2 Samuel I, 23.*
[3] Edited [1884] by J. W. CROSS.
[4] I think of death as some delightful jour-
    ney
That I shall take when all my tasks are
    done.
ELLA WHEELER WILCOX: *The Journey,*
St. 1

has got well through it, is the least painful way of learning the bad news.

Life and Letters. Letter to John Blackwood [*February 21, 1872*]

I like not only to be loved, but also to be told that I am loved. I am not sure that you are of the same kind. But the realm of silence is large enough beyond the grave. This is the world of light and speech, and I shall take leave to tell you that you are very dear.

Ibid. Letter to Mrs. Burne-Jones [*May 11, 1875*]

All biography diminishes in interest when the subject has won celebrity — or some reputation that hardly comes up to a celebrity. But autobiography at least saves a man or woman that the world is curious about from the publication of a string of mistakes called "Memoirs."

Ibid. Letter to Miss Sara Hennell [*November 22, 1876*]

THOMAS DUNN ENGLISH
[1819–1902]

Don't you remember sweet Alice, Ben Bolt?
  Sweet Alice, whose hair was so brown;
Who wept with delight when you gave her a smile,
  And trembled with fear at your frown!

Ben Bolt [1]

Your eyes were filled with love, Kate Vane;
Ah, would that we were young again!

Kate Vane

Up with three cheers and a tiger!
  Let the flags wave as they come!
Give them the blare of the trumpet!
  Give them the roll of the drum!

*The Charge by the Ford.
Stanza 11*

[1] First published in *The New York Mirror*, Sept. 2, 1843. It was set to music, an adaptation of an old German melody, by NELSON KNEASS, and sung in a play, *The Battle of Buena Vista*. In 1894, GEORGE DU MAURIER used the song in his novel, *Trilby*, and it became popular at once.

For one on the ocean of crime long tossed,
Who loves his mother, is not quite lost.

Smiting the Rock

Less good from genius we may find
  Than that from perseverance flowing;
So have good grist at hand to grind,
  And keep the mill a-going.

Keep the Mill a-Going. Stanza 7

Though little dangers they may fear,
When greater dangers men environ
Then women show a front of iron;
And, gentle in their manner, they
Do bold things in a quiet way.

Betty Zane. [1] *Stanza 1*

Not one has lineage prouder than
(Be he poor or rich) the man
Who boasts that in his spotless strain
Mingles the blood of Betty Zane.

Ibid. Stanza 10

JOSIAH GILBERT HOLLAND
[1819–1881]

Heaven is not reached at a single bound;
  But we build the ladder by which we rise
From the lowly earth to the vaulted skies,
And we mount to its summit round by round. [2]

Gradatim. Stanza 1

Wings for the angels, but feet for men.

Ibid. Stanza 6

Only in dreams is a ladder thrown
  From the weary earth to the sapphire walls;
But the dreams depart, and the vision falls,
And the sleeper wakes on his pillow of stone.

Ibid. Stanza 7

[1] Fort Henry (now Wheeling, West Virginia) was attacked by Simon Girty and a band of Wyandot Indians, September 27–28, 1777. Betty Zane ran from the blockhouse to the log hut on the hill, and returned with a cask of gunpowder wrapped in her apron. Zanesville, Ohio, is named for the Zane family.

[2] Step after step the ladder is ascended. — HERBERT: *Jacula Prudentum*

He could see naught but vanity in
　　beauty,
　　And naught but weakness in a fond
　　　　caress,
And pitied men whose views of Chris-
　　tian duty
　　Allowed indulgence in such foolish-
　　　　ness.
　　　　　　　　Daniel Gray. Stanza 9

More human, more divine than we —
In truth, half human, half divine
Is woman when good stars agree
To temper with their beams benign
The hour of her nativity.
　　　　　　　　　　　　Kathrina

Who can tell what a baby thinks?
　　　　　　Cradle Song. Stanza 2

My dear dumb friend, low lying there,
　　A willing vassal at my feet —
Glad partner of my home and fare,
　　My shadow in the street.
　　　　To My Dog, Blanco. Stanza 1

God give us men! A time like this de-
　　mands
　　Strong minds, great hearts, true
　　　　faith, and ready hands;
Men whom the lust of office does not
　　kill;
　　Men whom the spoils of office can-
　　　　not buy;
Men who possess opinions and a will;
　　Men who have honor; men who will
　　　　not lie;
Men who can stand before a demagogue
　　And damn his treacherous flatteries
　　　　without winking;
Tall men, sun-crowned, who live above
　　the fog
　　In public duty and in private think-
　　　　ing.
　　　　　　　　　　The Day's Demand

Hearts, like apples, are hard and sour,
Till crushed by Pain's resistless power.
　　　　　Bitter-Sweet. First Episode

Nay, Whittier, thou art not old;
Thy register a lie hath told,
For lives devote to love and truth
Do only multiply their youth.
　　　　　Ten Times Seven.[1] Stanza 3

[1] Written for Whittier's seventieth birthday, December 17, 1877.

Where shall the baby's dimple be,
Cheek, chin, knuckle or knee?
　　　　　　　　*Where Shall the Baby's
　　　　　　　　　　　　Dimple Be?*

JULIA WARD HOWE
[1819–1910]

Mine eyes have seen the glory of the
　　coming of the Lord;
He is trampling out the vintage where
　　the grapes of wrath are stored;
He hath loosed the fateful lightning of
　　His terrible, swift sword;
　　His truth is marching on.
　　　　*Battle Hymn of the Republic.
　　　　　　　　　　　　Stanza 1*

In the beauty of the lilies Christ was
　　born across the sea,
With a glory in His bosom that trans-
　　figures you and me;
As He died to make men holy, let us die
　　to make men free.
　　　　　　　　　Ibid. Stanza 5

Weave no more silks, ye Lyons looms,
　　To deck our girls for gay delights!
The crimson flower of battle blooms,
　　And solemn marches fill the nights.
　　　　　　　　　　　Our Orders

I gave my son a palace
　　And a kingdom to control:
The palace of his body,
　　The kingdom of his soul.
　　　　　　Palace and Kingdom

Don't trouble more to celebrate this
　　natal day of mine,
But keep the grasp of fellowship which
　　warms us more than wine.
Let us thank the lavish hand that gives
　　world beauty to our eyes,
And bless the days that saw us young,
　　and years that make us wise.
　　　　　　　　　　　Growing Old

I have made a voyage upon a golden
　　river,
　　'Neath clouds of opal and of ame-
　　　　thyst;
Along its banks bright shapes were
　　moving ever,
　　And threatening shadows melted
　　　　into mist.
　　Reminiscences [1899]. At the end

CHARLES KINGSLEY
[1819–1875]

O Mary, go and call the cattle home,
  And call the cattle home,
  And call the cattle home,
Across the sands o' Dee!
          The Sands of Dee. Stanza 1
The cruel crawling foam.
                    Ibid. Stanza 4
Men must work, and women must
    weep,
And there's little to earn and many to
    keep,
Though the harbor bar be moaning.
          The Three Fishers. Stanza 1
Be good, sweet maid, and let who can
    be clever;
  Do lovely things, not dream them,
    all day long;
And so make Life, Death, and that vast
    Forever
      One grand sweet song.
            A Farewell. Stanza 3
O haud your hands frae inkhorns,
    though a' the Muses woo;
For critics lie, like saumon fry, to mak'
    their meals o' you.
            The Oubit. Stanza 3
Oh green is the colour of faith and
    truth,
And rose the colour of love and youth,
And brown of the fruitful clay.
              Dartside, 1849
Oh! that we two were Maying.
          The Saint's Tragedy.
                Act II, Sc. 9
Oh! that we two lay sleeping
  In our nest in the churchyard sod,
With our limbs at rest on the quiet
    earth's breast,
  And our souls at home with God.
                      Ibid.
The world goes up and the world goes
    down,
  And the sunshine follows the rain;
And yesterday's sneer and yesterday's
    frown
    Can never come over again.
              Dolcino to Margaret
Oh England is a pleasant place for
    them that's rich and high,

But England is a cruel place for such
    poor folks as I.
          The Last Buccanier. Stanza 1
In the light of fuller day,
  Of purer science, holier laws.[1]
          *On the Death of a Certain
              Journal.[2] Stanza 5*
Young blood must have its course, lad,
  And every dog his day.[3]
          Water Babies. Song II, Stanza 1
When all the world is old, lad,
  And all the trees are brown;
And all the sport is stale, lad,
  And all the wheels run down.
                    Ibid. Stanza 2
God grant you find one face there
  You loved when all was young!
                      Ibid.
I once had a sweet little doll, dears,
  The prettiest doll in the world;
Her cheeks were so red and so white,
    dears,
  And her hair was so charmingly
    curled.
          Ibid. Song IV, Stanza 1
So fleet the works of men, back to their
    earth again;
Ancient and holy things fade like a
    dream.
          Old and New: A Parable.
                    Stanza 1

Do the work that's nearest,
  Though it's dull at whiles,
Helping, when you meet them,
  Lame dogs over stiles;
See in every hedgerow
  Marks of angels' feet,
Epics in each pebble
  Underneath our feet.
        The Invitation to Tom Hughes
We were crawling slowly along, look-
ing out for Virgin Garda; the first of
those numberless isles which Colum-
bus, so goes the tale, discovered on St.
Ursula's day, and named them after
the saint and her eleven thousand
mythical virgins. Unfortunately, Eng-
lish buccaneers have since given to
most of them less poetic names. The

---

[1] See Tennyson, page 469.
[2] *The Christian Socialist.*
[3] Dog will have his day. — SHAKESPEARE:
Hamlet. Act V. Sc. 1, L. 314

Dutchman's Cap, Broken Jerusalem, The Dead Man's Chest,[1] Rum Island, and so forth, mark a time and race more prosaic.

At Last [*1870*]. *Chap. 1*

A lone man's companion, a bachelor's friend, a hungry man's food, a sad man's cordial, a wakeful man's sleep, and a chilly man's fire . . . there's no herb like unto it under the canopy of heaven.

[*Tobacco*] *Westward Ho, Chap. 7*

Thank God every morning when you get up that you have something to do that day which must be done, whether you like it or not. Being forced to work, and forced to do your best, will breed in you temperance and self-control, diligence and strength of will, cheerfulness and content, and a hundred virtues which the idle never know.

Letter

To be discontented with the divine discontent, and to be ashamed with the noble shame, is the very germ of the first upgrowth of all virtue.

Health and Education. The Science of Health [*1874*]

"What is the secret of your life?" asked Mrs. Browning of Charles Kingsley. "Tell me, that I may make mine beautiful, too." He replied: "I had a friend."

Related by WILLIAM CHANNING GANNETT

JAMES RUSSELL LOWELL
[1819–1891]

She doeth little kindnesses
Which most leave undone, or despise.

My Love. Stanza 4

Be noble! and the nobleness that lies
In other men, sleeping, but never dead,
Will rise in majesty to meet thine own.

Sonnet IV

Great Truths are portions of the soul of man;

---

¹ Treasure Island came out of Kingsley's "At Last," where I got the Dead Man's Chest — and that was the seed. — R. L. STEVENSON in a letter to Sidney Colvin

Great souls are portions of Eternity.

Sonnet VI

To win the secrets of a weed's plain heart.

Sonnet XXV

Who speaks the truth stabs Falsehood to the heart.

L'Envoi

His words were simple words enough,
And yet he used them so,
That what in other mouths was rough
In his seemed musical and low.

The Shepherd of King Admetus. Stanza 5

All thoughts that mould the age begin
Deep down within the primitive soul.

An Incident in a Railroad Car. Stanza 13

It may be glorious to write
Thoughts that shall glad the two or three
High souls, like those far stars that come in sight
Once in a century.

Ibid. Stanza 19

No man is born into the world whose work
Is not born with him; there is always work,
And tools to work withal, for those who will;
And blessèd are the horny hands of toil.

A Glance Behind the Curtain

They are slaves who fear to speak
For the fallen and the weak. . . .
They are slaves who dare not be
In the right with two or three.

Stanzas on Freedom. IV

The nurse of full-grown souls is solitude.

Columbus

And I believed the poets; it is they
Who utter wisdom from the central deep,
And, listening to the inner flow of things,
Speak to the age out of eternity.

Ibid.

Once to every man and nation comes the moment to decide,
In the strife of Truth with Falsehood, for the good or evil side.

The Present Crisis. Stanza 5

Truth forever on the scaffold, Wrong
    forever on the throne.[1]
        The Present Crisis. Stanza 8
Then to side with Truth is noble when
    we share her wretched crust,
Ere her cause bring fame and profit,
    and 'tis prosperous to be just;
Then it is the brave man chooses, while
    the coward stands aside,
Doubting in his abject spirit, till his
    Lord is crucified.
        Ibid. Stanza 11
New occasions teach new duties; Time
    makes ancient good uncouth;
They must upward still, and onward,
    who would keep abreast of Truth.
        Ibid. Stanza 18
The birch, most shy and ladylike of
    trees.
      An Indian-Summer Reverie.
            Stanza 8
Dear common flower, that grow'st be-
    side the way,
Fringing the dusty road with harmless
    gold.
      To the Dandelion. Stanza 1
They came three thousand miles, and
    died,
To keep the Past upon its throne;
Unheard, beyond the ocean tide,
Their English mother made her moan.[2]
    Graves of Two English Soldiers
    on   Concord   Battle-ground.
              Stanza 3
Slowly the Bible of the race is writ,
And not on paper leaves nor leaves of
    stone;
Each age, each kindred, adds a verse
    to it,
Texts of despair or hope, of joy or
    moan.
       Bibliolatres. Stanza 6
Thou art not idle: in thy higher sphere
    Thy spirit bends itself to loving
    tasks,

And strength to perfect what it
    dreamed of here
Is all the crown and glory that it
    asks.
        Elegy on the Death of
      Dr. Channing. Stanza 12
Not only around our infancy
Doth heaven with all its splendors lie;
Daily, with souls that cringe and plot,
We Sinais climb and know it not.
      The Vision of Sir Launfal.
      Part I, Prelude, Stanza 2
'Tis heaven alone that is given away;
'Tis only God may be had for the ask-
    ing.
           Ibid. Stanza 4
And what is so rare as a day in June?
Then, if ever, come perfect days;
Then Heaven tries the earth if it be in
    tune,
And over it softly her warm ear lays.
           Ibid. Stanza 5
He gives only the worthless gold
Who gives from a sense of duty.
        Ibid. Part I, Stanza 6
The gift without the giver is bare;[1]
Who gives himself with his alms feeds
    three, —
Himself, his hungering neighbor, and
    me.
        Ibid. Part II, Stanza 8
Got the ill name of augurs, because
    they were bores.
        A Fable for Critics
A weed is no more than a flower in dis-
    guise.[2]
              Ibid.
For reading new books is like eating
    new bread,
One can bear it at first, but by gradual
    steps he
Is brought to death's door of a mental
    dyspepsy.
              Ibid.

---

[1] Worth on foot, and rascals in the coach.
    DRYDEN: *Art of Poetry, L. 376*
  Wrong rules the land, and waiting Jus-
    tice sleeps.
    J. G. HOLLAND: *The Day's Demand*
[2] Inscribed on the memorial to the two
British soldiers, Concord, Massachusetts.

[1] The only gift is a portion of thyself. —
EMERSON: *Gifts*
  See Walt Whitman, page 535.
  [2] And what is a weed? A plant whose vir-
tues have not yet been discovered. — EMER-
SON: *Fortune of the Republic*
  A weed is but an unloved flower!
  ELLA WHEELER WILCOX: *The Weed, St. 1*

A reading-machine, always wound up
    and going,
He mastered whatever was not worth
    the knowing.
                    A Fable for Critics
I've thought very often 'twould be a
    good thing
In all public collections of books, if a
    wing
Were set off by itself, like the seas from
    the dry lands,
Marked *Literature suited to desolate
    islands.*
                    Ibid.
There comes Emerson first, whose rich
    words, every one,
Are like gold nails in temples to hang
    trophies on;
Whose prose is grand verse, while his
    verse, the Lord knows,
Is some of it pr — No, 'tis not even
    prose.[1]
                    Ibid.
And I honor the man who is willing to
    sink
Half his present repute for the freedom
    to think,
And, when he has thought, be his cause
    strong or weak,
Will risk t' other half for the freedom
    to speak.
                    Ibid.
There comes Poe, with his raven, like
    Barnaby Rudge,
Three fifths of him genius and two
    fifths sheer fudge.
                    Ibid.
Nature fits all her children with some-
    thing to do,
He who would write and can't write,
    can surely review.
                    Ibid.
Ez fer war, I call it murder, —
    There you hev it plain an' flat;
I don't want to go no furder
    Than my Testament fer that. . . .
An' you've gut to git up airly
Ef you want to take in God.
                    *The Biglow Papers. Series I,
                        No. 1, Stanza 5*

Laborin' man an' laborin' woman
    Hev one glory an' one shame;
Ev'y thin' thet's done inhuman
    Injers all on 'em the same.
                    *The Biglow Papers. Series I,
                        No. 1, Stanza 10*
This goin' ware glory waits ye haint
    one agreeable feetur.[1]
                    Ibid. No. 2, Stanza 6
Gineral C. is a dreffle smart man:
    He's ben on all sides thet give places
        or pelf;
But consistency still wuz a part of his
        plan, —
    He's ben true to *one* party, — an'
        thet is himself.
                    Ibid. No. 3, Stanza 3
We kind o' thought Christ went agin
    war an' pillage.
                    Ibid. Stanza 5
        But John P.
        Robinson, he
Sez they didn't know everythin' down
    in Judee.
                    Ibid. Stanza 8
A marciful Providunce fashioned us
        holler
O' purpose thet we might our princi-
        ples swaller.
                    Ibid. No. 4, Stanza 2
I should like to shoot
The holl gang, by the gret horn spoon! [2]
                    Ibid. No. 5, Stanza 2
I du believe with all my soul
    In the gret Press's freedom,[3]
To pint the people to the goal
    An' in the traces lead 'em.
                    Ibid. No. 6, Stanza 7
I *don't* believe in princerple,
    But oh I *du* in interest.
                    Ibid. Stanza 9
It ain't my princerples nor men
    My preudunt course is steadied, —
I scent which pays the best, an' then
    Go into it baldheaded.
                    Ibid. Stanza 10

---

[1] Meredith is only a prose Browning — and
so was Browning. — Impromptu by OSCAR
WILDE.

[1] Go where glory waits thee. — THOMAS
MOORE: Poem of same title
[2] He vow'd by the great horn spoon.
    French Claim, St. 5 (an anonymous
    song of the Revolutionary War pe-
    riod)
[3] See Herbert Clark Hoover, page 830.

Of my merit
On thet pint you yourself may jedge;
All is, I never drink no sperit,
Nor I haint never signed no pledge.
The Biglow Papers. Series I,
No. 7, Stanza 9

Ez to my princerples, I glory
In hevin' nothin' o' the sort.
Ibid. Stanza 10

God makes sech nights, all white and still,
Fur'z you can look or listen.
Ibid. Series II, The Courtin',
Stanza 1

His heart kep' goin' pity-pat,
But hern went pity-Zekle.
Ibid. Stanza 15

To say why gals acts so or so,
Or don't, 'ould be presumin';
Mebby to mean *yes* an' say *no*
Comes nateral to women.[1]
Ibid. Stanza 18

All kin' o' smily round the lips,
An' teary round the lashes.
Ibid. Stanza 21

My gran'ther's rule was safer 'n 'tis to crow:
Don't never prophesy — onless ye know.
Ibid. No. 2

It's 'most enough to make a deacon swear.
Ibid.

The one thet fust gits mad's most ol-lers wrong.
Ibid.

Folks never understand the folks they hate.
Ibid.

Ef you want peace, the thing you've gut tu du
Is jes' to show you're up to fightin', tu.
Ibid.

Bad work follers ye ez long's ye live.
Ibid.

Don't give up afore the ship goes down.[2]
Ibid.

Our papers don't purtend to print on'y wut Guv'ment choose,
An' thet insures us all to git the very best o' noose.
The Biglow Papers. Series II,
No. 3

The thing's a gone coon.[1]
Ibid. No. 4

Facts are contrary 'z mules.[2]
Ibid.

No, never say nothin' without you're compelled tu,
An' then don't say nothin' thet you can be held tu.
Ibid. No. 5

Our lives in sleep are some like streams that glide
'Twixt flesh an' sperrit boundin' on each side,
Where both shores' shadders kind o' mix an' mingle
In sunthin' thet ain't jes' like either single.
Ibid. No. 6, Sunthin' in the
Pastoral Line

Wut's words to them whose faith an' truth
On War's red techstone rang true metal,
Who ventered life an' love an' youth
For the gret prize o' death in battle?
Ibid. No. 10, Stanza 17

What public, were they new to-day, would ever stop to read
The Iliad, the Shanàmeh, or the Nibelungenlied?
Fragments of an Unfinished Poem

Each year to ancient friendships adds a ring,
As to an oak.
Under the Willows

I thought of a mound in sweet Auburn
Where a little headstone stood;
How the flakes were folding it gently,
As did robins the babes in the wood.[3]
The First Snowfall. Stanza 5

---

[1] See Mrs. Browning, page 428.
[2] Tell the men to fire faster and not to give up the ship; fight her till she sinks. — COMMANDER JAMES LAWRENCE, U.S.N. [1781–1813] on board the *Chesapeake,* June 1, 1813.

[1] See David Crockett, page 349.
[2] See Smollett, page 248.
Facts are stubborn things. — LE SAGE: *Gil Blas, X, 1*
[3] See Percy, page 258.

The shell disdained a soul had gained,
The lyre had been discovered.
        The Finding of the Lyre.
                Stanza 4

Though old the thought and oft ex-
        prest,
'Tis his at last who says it best.[1]
        For an Autograph. Stanza 1

Not failure, but low aim, is crime.
                Ibid. Stanza 5

When I was a beggarly boy,
        And lived in a cellar damp,
I had not a friend nor a toy,
        But I had Aladdin's lamp.
                Aladdin. Stanza 1

Granting our wish one of Fate's sad-
        dest jokes is! [2]
        *Two Scenes from the Life of
        Blondel.[3] Sc. II, Stanza 2*

For somehow the poor old Earth blun-
        ders along,
    Each son of hers adding his mite of
        unfitness,
And, choosing the sure way of coming
        out wrong,
    Gets to port as the next generation
        will witness.
                Ibid. Stanza 4

What men call treasure and the Gods
        call dross.
        *Ode Recited at the Harvard
        Commemoration, 1865. IV*

Here was a type of the true elder race,
And one of Plutarch's men talked with
        us face to face.
                Ibid. VI

Safe in the hallowed quiets of the past.
        The Cathedral.[4] Stanza 9

[1] See Emerson, page 415.
[2] Beware, my lord! Beware lest stern
Heaven hate you enough to hear your
prayers! — ANATOLE FRANCE: *The Crime of
Sylvestre Bonnard, Part II, Chap. 4*
    See Oscar Wilde, page 724.
        The fates are not quite obdurate;
        They have a grim, sardonic way
    Of granting men who supplicate
        The things they wanted — yesterday.
        ROSELLE MERCIER MONTGOMERY:
                The Fates
[3] See Ingelow, page 541.
[4] Chartres.

The one thing finished in this hasty
        world.
                The Cathedral. Stanza 9

The unmotived herd that only sleep and
        feed.[1]
        *Under the Old Elm. Part VII,
                Stanza 3*

These pearls of thought in Persian gulfs
        were bred,
Each softly lucent as a rounded moon;
The diver Omar plucked them from
        their bed,
Fitzgerald strung them on an English
        thread.
        *In a Copy of Omar Khayyàm.
                Stanza 1*

The wisest man could ask no more of
        Fate
Than to be simple, modest, manly, true,
Safe from the Many, honored by the
        Few;
To count as naught in World, or
        Church, or State;
But inwardly in secret to be great.
        Sonnet, Jeffries Wyman

But life is sweet, though all that makes
        it sweet
Lessen like sound of friends' departing
        feet;
And Death is beautiful as feet of friend
Coming with welcome at our journey's
        end.
        *Epistle to George William Curtis,
                Postscript.*

For me Fate gave, whate'er she else
        denied,
A nature sloping to the southern side;
I thank her for it, though when clouds
        arise
Such Natures double-darken gloomy
        skies.
                Ibid.

Like him who, in the desert's awful
        frame,
Notches his cockney initials on the
        Sphinx.
        *Sonnet on Being Asked for an
                Autograph in Venice*

[1] What is a man,
    If his chief good and market of his time
    Be but to sleep and feed? a beast, no
        more.
    SHAKESPEARE: *Hamlet, Act IV, Sc. 4, l. 33*

The Maple puts her corals on in May.
The Maple

As brief
As a dragon-fly's repose.
Scherzo. Stanza 3

In life's small things be resolute and
great
To keep thy muscle trained: know'st
thou when Fate
Thy measure takes, or when she'll say
to thee,
"I find thee worthy; do this deed for
me"?
Sayings. I

In vain we call old notions fudge,
And bend our conscience to our deal-
ing;
The Ten Commandments will not
budge,
And stealing will continue stealing.
*Motto of the American Copyright
League [November 20, 1885]*

As life runs on, the road grows strange
With faces new, and near the end
The milestones into headstones change,
'Neath every one a friend.
Sixty-Eighth Birthday

The story of any one man's real experience finds its startling parallel in
that of every one of us.
Spenser

Solitude is as needful to the imagination as society is wholesome for the
character.
Dryden

Men have their intellectual ancestry,
and the likeness of some one of them
is forever unexpectedly flashing out in
the features of a descendant, it may be
after a gap of several generations. In
the parliament of the present every man
represents a constituency of the past.
Keats

From the days of the first grandfather, everybody has remembered a
golden age behind him!
Carlyle

Notoriety may be achieved in a narrow sphere, but fame demands for its
evidence a more distant and prolonged
reverberation.
A Great Public Character

A wise scepticism is the first attribute
of a good critic.
Shakespeare Once More

Truly there is a tide in the affairs of
men, but there is no gulf-stream setting forever in one direction.
New England Two Centuries Ago

There is no better ballast for keeping
the mind steady on its keel, and saving
it from all risk of crankiness, than business.
Ibid.

Puritanism, believing itself quick
with the seed of religious liberty, laid,
without knowing it, the egg of democracy.
Ibid.

It was in making education not only
common to all, but in some sense compulsory on all, that the destiny of the
free republics of America was practically settled.
Ibid.

Talent is that which is in a man's
power; genius is that in whose power
a man is.
Rousseau and the Sentimentalists

There is no work of genius which has
not been the delight of mankind, no
word of genius to which the human
heart and soul have not sooner or later
responded.
Ibid.

Every man feels instinctively that all
the beautiful sentiments in the world
weigh less than a single lovely action.
Ibid.

It is singular how impatient men are
with over-praise of others, how patient
with over-praise of themselves; and yet
the one does them no injury, while the
other may be their ruin.
*Literary Remains of the
Rev. Homer Wilbur*

Things always seem fairer when we
look back at them, and it is out of that
inaccessible tower of the past that
Longing leans and beckons.
A Few Bits of Roman Mosaic

There is nothing so desperately monotonous as the sea, and I no longer
wonder at the cruelty of pirates.
Fireside Travels. At Sea

An umbrella is of no avail against a Scotch Mist.

On a Certain Condescension in Foreigners

It is by presence of mind in untried emergencies that the native metal of a man is tested.

Abraham Lincoln [1864]

The soil out of which such men as he are made is good to be born on, good to live on, good to die for and to be buried in.

Garfield

Mishaps are like knives, that either serve us or cut us, as we grasp them by the blade or the handle.

Cambridge Thirty Years Ago

No man, I suspect, ever lived long in the country without being bitten by these meteorological ambitions. He likes to be hotter and colder, to have been more deeply snowed up, to have more trees and larger blown down than his neighbors.

My Garden Acquaintance

As if old age were never kindly as well as frosty; as if it had no reverend graces of its own as good in their way as the noisy impertinence of childhood, the elbowing self-conceit of youth, or the pompous mediocrity of middle life!

A Good Word for Winter

What a sense of security in an old book which Time has criticised for us!

A Library of Old Authors

There is no good in arguing with the inevitable. The only argument available with an east wind is to put on your overcoat.

Democracy and Addresses

Let us be of good cheer, however, remembering that the misfortunes hardest to bear are those which never come.[1]

Ibid.

It is curious how tyrannical the habit of reading is, and what shifts we make to escape thinking.[2] There is no bore

[1] See Emerson, page 410, and Foss, page 733.
[2] See Sheridan, page 278.

we dread being left alone with so much as our own minds.

A Moosehead Journal

There are few brains that would not be better for living on their own fat a little while.

Ibid.

If I were asked what book is better than a cheap book, I should answer that there is one book better than a cheap book, — and that is a book honestly come by.

Before the U. S. Senate Committee on Patents [January 29, 1886]

HERMAN MELVILLE [1]
[1819–1891]

Thou belongest to that hopeless, sallow tribe which no wine of this world will ever warm; and for whom even Pale Sherry would be too rosy-strong; but with whom one sometimes loves to sit, and feel poor-devilish, too; and grow convivial upon tears; and say to them bluntly, with full eyes and empty glasses, and in not altogether unpleasant sadness — Give it up, Sub-Subs! For by how much the more pains ye

[1] May one cry of human distress interpolate here? The editors of BARTLETT confess the complete inadequacy of these few quotations from *Moby Dick*. For that great book there is no substitute; it cannot be represented in excerpts; to attempt that would require (as we have said before) a Moby Dictionary.

"He sank without a ripple of renown" was the fine valediction of RAYMOND M. WEAVER in his *Herman Melville, Mariner and Mystic* (1921). Melville died the same year that John Bartlett completed the Ninth Edition of this work. Neither then, nor in Dole's Tenth Edition (1914) was Melville's name mentioned. It was his centennial in 1919, coming in the general quickening and disgust of After-War, that brought him alive for a new generation. But he is too dense with intuition to be parcelled out in clippings.

"To read *Moby Dick* and absorb it is the crown of one's reading life." — VIOLA MEYNELL, introduction to World's Classics Edition.

We forward the problem to the editor of the Twelfth Edition, which should be due about 1960.

take to please the world, by so much the more shall ye for ever go thankless!

Moby Dick: Preface, the Sub-
Sub-Librarian

The Nantucketer, out of sight of land, furls his sails and lays him to his rest, while under his very pillow rush herds of walruses and whales.

Ibid. Chap. 14

A whale ship was my Yale College and my Harvard.

Ibid. Chap. 24

Thou great democratic God! who didst not refuse to the swart convict, Bunyan, the pale poetic pearl; Thou who didst clothe with doubly hammered leaves of finest gold, the stumped and paupered arm of old Cervantes; Thou who didst pick up Andrew Jackson from the pebbles; who didst hurl him upon a warhorse; who didst thunder him higher than a throne!

Ibid. Chap. 26

The starred and stately nights seemed haughty dames in jewelled velvets, nursing at home in lonely pride the memory of their absent conquering Earls, the golden helmeted suns!

Ibid. Chap. 29

The choice hidden handful of the Divine Inert.

Ibid. Chap. 33

Give me a condor's quill! Give me Vesuvius' crater for an inkstand! . . . To produce a mighty book you must choose a mighty theme.

Ibid. Chap. 104

Where lies the final harbour, whence we unmoor no more?

Ibid. Chap. 114

Sailor or landsman, there is some sort of Cape Horn for all. Boys! beware of it; prepare for it in time. Greybeards! thank God it is passed.

White-Jacket. Chap. 26

All dies! and not alone
The aspiring trees and men and grass;
The poets' forms of beauty pass,
And noblest deeds they are undone,
Even truth itself decays, and lo,
From truth's sad ashes pain and false-
    hood grow.

The Lake

There is no faith, and no stoicism, and no philosophy, that a mortal man can possibly evoke, which will stand the final test in a real impassioned onset of Life and Passion upon him. Faith and philosophy are air, but events are brass.

Pierre

THOMAS WILLIAM PARSONS
[1819–1892]

Sorrow and the scarlet leaf,
    Sad thoughts and sunny weather:
Ah me, this glory and this grief
    Agree not well together!

A Song for September

We have forgot what we have been,
And what we are we little know;
We fancy new events begin,
But all has happened long ago.

Stanzas. 1

To larger sight the rim of shadow is the line of light.

Inscription for a sundial at
Milton, Massachusetts

JOHN RUSKIN
[1819–1900]

He is the greatest artist who has embodied, in the sum of his works, the greatest number of the greatest ideas.

Modern Painters. Vol. I, Part I,
Chap. 2, Sect. 9

The greatest thing a human soul ever does in this world is to *see* something, and tell what it *saw* in a plain way. Hundreds of people can talk for one who can think, but thousands can think for one who can see. To see clearly is poetry, prophecy, and religion, all in one.

Ibid. Vol. III, Part IV, Chap. 16,
Sect. 28

In order that people may be happy in their work, these three things are needed: They must be fit for it: They must not do too much of it: And they must have a sense of success in it.

Pre-Raphaelitism

No great intellectual thing was ever done by great effort; a great thing can only be done by a great man, and he does it *without* effort.

Pre-Raphaelitism

It is chiefly by private, not by public, effort that your city must be adorned.

Lectures on Architecture and Painting.[1] *I*

Blue colour is everlastingly appointed by the Deity to be a source of delight.

Ibid.

Whenever men have become skillful architects at all, there has been a tendency in them to build high.

Ibid.

Life being very short, and the quiet hours of it few, we ought to waste none of them in reading valueless books.[2]

Sesame and Lilies. Preface

The greatest efforts of the race have always been traceable to the love of praise, as its greatest catastrophes to the love of pleasure.

Ibid. Of Kings' Treasuries, Sect. 3

At the portières of that silent Faubourg St. Germain, there is but brief question, "Do you deserve to enter? Pass. Do you ask to be the companion of nobles? Make yourself noble, and you shall be. Do you long for the conversation of the wise? Learn to understand it, and you shall hear it. But on other terms? — no. If you will not rise to us, we cannot stoop to you."

Ibid. Sect. 12

There are masked words abroad, I say, which nobody understands, but which everybody uses, and most people will also fight for, live for, or even die for, fancying they mean this, or that, or the other, of things dear to them.

Ibid. Sect. 16

The very cheapness of literature is making even wise people forget that if a book is worth reading, it is worth buying. No book is worth anything which is not worth *much;* nor is it serviceable, until it has been read, and

[1] At Edinburgh, November, 1853.
[2] Life is too short for reading inferior books. — JAMES BRYCE [1838–1922]: *Address* at Rutgers College, Nov. 10, 1911

re-read, and loved, and loved again; and marked, so that you can refer to the passages you want in it.

Sesame and Lilies.
Of King's Treasuries, Sect. 32

The power of the press in the hands of highly-educated men, in independent position, and of honest purpose, may indeed become all that it has been hitherto vainly vaunted to be.

Ibid. Sect. 37, Footnote

When men are rightly occupied, their amusement grows out of their work, as the colour-petals out of a fruitful flower.

Ibid. Sect. 39

He only is advancing in life, whose heart is getting softer, whose blood warmer, whose brain quicker, whose spirit is entering into Living peace. And the men who have this life in them are the true lords or kings of the earth — they, and they only.

Ibid. Sect. 42

This is the true nature of home — it is the place of Peace; the shelter, not only from all injury, but from all terror, doubt, and division.

Ibid. Of Queens' Gardens, Sect. 68

Borrowers are nearly always ill-spenders, and it is with lent money that all evil is mainly done, and all unjust war protracted.

The Crown of Wild Olive.
Work, Sect. 34

Give a little love to a child, and you get a great deal back.

Ibid. Sect. 49

There's no music in a "rest," Katie, that I know of: but there's the making of music in it.[1] And people are always missing that part of the life-melody.

Ethics of the Dust. Lecture 4,
The Crystal Orders

That treacherous phantom which men call Liberty.

Seven Lamps of Architecture.
Chap. 7, The Lamp of Obedience, Sect. 1

[1] "There is no music in a rest,
But there is music's making";

Life without industry is guilt, industry without art is brutality.

Lectures on Art. III, The Relation of Art to Morals

Engraving, then, is, in brief terms, the Art of Scratch.

Ariadne Florentina. Lecture I

Wealth, therefore, is "the possession of the valuable by the valiant."

Unto This Last. Sect. 64

There is no Wealth but Life.

Ibid. Sect. 77

That country is the richest which nourishes the greatest number of noble and happy human beings; that man is richest who, having perfected the functions of his own life to the utmost, has also the widest helpful influence, both personal, and by means of his possessions, over the lives of others.

Ibid.

Trust thou thy Love: if she be proud,
    is she not sweet?
Trust thou thy Love: if she be mute,
    is she not pure?
Lay thou thy soul full in her hands,
    low at her feet;
Fail, Sun and Breath! — yet, for thy
    peace, she shall endure.

Trust Thou Thy Love

WILLIAM WETMORE STORY
[1819–1895]

I sing the hymn of the conquered, who
    fell in the Battle of Life,[1] —
The hymn of the wounded, the beaten,
    who died overwhelmed in the
    strife.

A Poet's Portfolio. Io Victis

The hymn of the low and the humble,
    the weary, the broken in heart,
Who strove and who failed, acting
    bravely a silent and desperate
    part.

Ibid.

For melody is best expressed
    By pause and re-awaking.
    MARY E. WISEWELL: *Rests, St. 1* [1872]
[1] It seems to me, when it cannot be help'd,
    that defeat is great.
    WALT WHITMAN: *Leaves of Grass, To
    a Foil'd European Revolutionaire*

Speak, History! Who are life's victors?
    Unroll thy long annals and say;
Are they those whom the world calls
    the victors, who won the success of
    a day?
The martyrs, or Nero? The Spartans
    who fell at Thermopylae's tryst,
Or the Persians and Xerxes? Pilate, or
    Christ?

A Poet's Portfolio. Io Victis

Give me the old enthusiasms back,
Give me the ardent longings that I
    lack, —
The glorious dreams that fooled me in
    my youth,
The sweet mirage that lured me on its
    track, —
And take away the bitter, barren truth.
Ah, yes! Success, I fear, has come too
    late!

Girolamo, Detto il Fiorentino

Mosquito critics with a poisonous sting.

Ibid.

A picture is not wrought
By hands alone, good Padre, but by
    thought.
In the interior life it first must start,
And grow to form and colour in the
    soul;
There once conceived and rounded to
    a whole,
The rest is but the handicraft of art.

Padre Bandelli Proses

Of every noble work the silent part is
    best,
Of all expression that which can not be
    expressed.

The Unexpressed

What looks like swindling with a petty
    sum,
Is on a grand and speculative scale
Honest enough, so it be large enough.

Baron Fisco at Home

Man is content to know that he is
    loved,
And tires the constant phrase "I love"
    to hear;
But woman doubts the instrument is
    broke
Unless she daily hear the sweet refrain.

Ginevra da Siena

We live as much in all that we have
lost
As what we own.
> *Sonnet, After Long Days of
> Dull Perpetual Rain*

All Arts are one, howe'er distributed
they stand;
Verse, tone, shape, color, form, are
fingers on one hand.
> *Couplets. V*

QUEEN VICTORIA
[1819–1901]

We are not amused.
> *Comment, upon seeing an imi-
> tation of herself by the Hon-
> orable Alexander Grantham
> Yorke, Groom-in-Waiting to
> the Queen [1884–1901]*

WILLIAM ROSS WALLACE
[1819–1881]

They say that man is mighty, he governs land and sea;
He wields a mighty sceptre o'er lesser
powers that be.
> *The Hand That Rules the World.
> Stanza 1*

The hand that rocks the cradle is the
hand that rules the world.
> *Ibid.*

WALT WHITMAN [1]
[1819–1892]

Once fully enslaved, no nation, state,
city of this earth, ever afterward
resumes its liberty.
> *To the States*

I hear America singing, the varied
carols I hear.
> *I Hear America Singing*

Shut not your doors to me proud libraries,
For that which was lacking on all your

[1] In a certain sense, Whitman interpreted
America to Europe; and to America he tried
to interpret the universe. — WILLIAM LYON
PHELPS: *Howells, James, Bryant and Other
Essays* [1924]

well-fill'd shelves, yet needed
most, I bring.
> *Shut Not Your Doors*

I will write the evangel-poem of comrades and of love.
> *Starting from Paumanok. 6*

I say the whole earth and all the
stars in the sky are for religion's sake.
> *Ibid. 7*

None has begun to think how divine
he himself is, and how certain the future is.
> *Ibid.*

I say the real and permanent grandeur of these States must be their religion.
> *Ibid.*

Nothing can happen more beautiful
than death.[1]
> *Ibid. 12*

Whoever you are, to you endless announcements!
> *Ibid. 14*

I celebrate myself and sing myself,
And what I assume you shall assume.
> *Song of Myself. 1*

I loafe and invite my soul.
> *Ibid.*

Creeds and schools in abeyance.
> *Ibid.*

I have no mockings or arguments; I
witness and wait.
> *Ibid. 4*

It [grass] is the handkerchief of the
Lord.
> *Ibid. 6*

[1] Why fear death? Death is only a beautiful adventure. — CHARLES FROHMAN [1860–
1915]: Last words to a group of friends as
the *Lusitania* was sinking [May 7, 1915].
Report of conversation with Rita Jolivet, a
survivor, in a letter from C. Haddon Chambers to Alfred Hayman [May 18, 1915].

Why should I fear Death's call? Can there
    e'er be
In life more beautiful adventure than
To re-embark upon that unknown sea?
> JAMES TERRY WHITE [1845–1920]:
> *Why Fear? St. 1*

"A beautiful adventure" — to be dead;
Or, in long pauses of one's dying breath,
To turn some splendid compliment to
    death.
> RICHARD LeGALLIENNE: *Charles Froh-
> man, St. 3*

All goes onward and outward, nothing collapses,
And to die is different from what any one supposed, and luckier.
Song of Myself. 6

Whether I come to my own [1] to-day or in ten thousand or ten million years,
I can cheerfully take it now, or with equal cheerfulness I can wait.
Ibid. 20

I hear the violoncello, ('tis the young man's heart's complaint).
Ibid. 26

The orchestra whirls me wider than Uranus flies,
It wrenches such ardors from me I did not know I possess'd them.
Ibid.

I believe a leaf of grass is no less than the journey-work of the stars.
Ibid. 31

And the tree-toad is a chef-d'oeuvre for the highest. . . .
And a mouse is miracle enough to stagger sextillions of infidels.
Ibid.

I think I could turn and live with animals, they are so placid and self-contain'd.
Ibid. 32

Behold, I do not give lectures or a little charity,
When I give I give myself.[2]
Ibid. 40

And when you rise in the morning you will find what I tell you is so.
Ibid.

The clock indicates the moment — but what does eternity indicate?
Ibid. 44

In the faces of men and women I see God.
Ibid. 48

I sound my barbaric yawp over the roofs of the world.
Ibid. 52

[1] Nor time, nor space, nor deep, nor high,
Can keep my own away from me.
JOHN BURROUGHS [1837–1931]: *Waiting, St. 6*

[2] See Lowell, page 525.

If any thing is sacred the human body is sacred.
Children of Adam. 8

I hear it was charged against me that I sought to destroy institutions,
But really I am neither for nor against institutions.
I Hear It Was Charged Against Me

When I peruse the conquer'd fame of heroes and the victories of mighty generals, I do not envy the generals.
When I Peruse the Conquer'd Fame

Henceforth I ask not good-fortune, I myself am good-fortune,
Henceforth I whimper no more, postpone no more, need nothing,
Done with indoor complaints, libraries, querulous criticisms,
Strong and content I travel the open road.
Song of the Open Road. 1

A great city is that which has the greatest men and women.
Song of the Broad-Axe. 4

All architecture is what you do to it when you look upon it.
A Song for Occupations. 4

All music is what awakes from you when you are reminded by the instruments.
Ibid.

In this broad earth of ours,
Amid the measureless grossness and the slag,
Enclosed and safe within its central heart,
Nestles the seed perfection.
Song of the Universal. 1

All, all for immortality,
Love like the light silently wrapping all.
Ibid. 4

Through the battle, through defeat, moving yet and never stopping,
Pioneers! O pioneers!
Pioneers! O Pioneers! 13

Youth, large, lusty, loving — Youth, full of grace, force, fascination,
Do you know that Old Age may come

after you, with equal grace, force, fascination?
Youth, Day, Old Age and Night. 1

Out of the cradle endlessly rocking,
Out of the mocking-bird's throat, the musical shuttle.
Out of the Cradle Endlessly Rocking. 1

A pennant universal, subtly waving all time, o'er all brave sailors,
All seas, all ships.
Song for All Seas, All Ships. 2

Roaming in thought over the Universe, I saw the little that is Good steadily hastening towards immortality,
And the vast that is Evil I saw hastening to merge itself and become lost and dead.[1]
Roaming in Thought After Reading Hegel

Over all the sky — the sky! far, far out of reach, studded, breaking out, the eternal stars.
Bivouac on a Mountain Side

Long, too long America,
Traveling roads all even and peaceful you learn'd from joys and prosperity only,
But now, ah now, to learn from crises of anguish, advancing, grappling with direst fate and recoiling not.
Long, Too Long America

Give me the splendid silent sun, with all his beams full-dazzling!
Give Me the Splendid Silent Sun. 1

Lo, the moon ascending,
Up from the East, the silvery round moon,
Beautiful over the house-tops, ghastly, phantom moon,
Immense and silent moon.
Dirge for Two Veterans. 2

Beautiful that war and all its deeds of carnage must in time be utterly lost,
That the hands of the sisters Death and Night incessantly softly wash

[1] Evil perpetually tends to disappear. — HERBERT SPENCER: *The Evanescence of Evil*

again and ever again, this soiled world.
Reconciliation

When lilacs last in the door-yard bloom'd,
And the great star early droop'd in the western sky in the night,
I mourn'd, and yet shall mourn with ever-returning spring.
When Lilacs Last in the Door-yard Bloom'd. 1

Come lovely and soothing death,
Undulate round the world, serenely arriving, arriving,
In the day, in the night, to all, to each,
Sooner or later, delicate death.
Ibid. 14

Prais'd be the fathomless universe,
For life and joy, and for objects and knowledge curious,
And for love, sweet love — But praise! praise! praise!
For the sure-enwinding arms of cool-enfolding Death.
Ibid.

O Captain! my Captain! our fearful trip is done!
The ship has weather'd every wrack, the prize we sought is won,
The port is near, the bells I hear, the people all exulting.
O Captain! My Captain! 1

The ship is anchor'd safe and sound, its voyage closed and done,
From fearful trip the victor ship comes in with object won.
Ibid. 3

I with mournful tread,
Walk the deck my Captain lies,
Fallen cold and dead.
Ibid.

No more for him life's stormy conflicts,
Nor victory, nor defeat — no more time's dark events,
Charging like ceaseless clouds across the sky.
Hush'd be the Camps To-day. 2

This dust was once the man,
Gentle, plain, just and resolute.
This Dust Was Once the Man

He or she is greatest who contributes the greatest original practical example.

By Blue Ontario's Shore. 13

The whole theory of the universe is directed unerringly to one single individual — namely to You.

Ibid. 15

Not till the sun excludes you do I exclude you.

To a Common Prostitute

Liberty is to be subserved whatever occurs.

To a Foil'd European Revolutionaire. 1

I do not think seventy years is the time of a man or woman, . . .

Nor that years will ever stop the existence of me, or any one else.

Who Learns My Lesson Complete?

Joyous we too launch out on trackless seas,

Fearless for unknown shores.

Passage to India. 8

My terminus near,

The clouds already closing in upon me,

The voyage balk'd, the course disputed, lost,

I yield my ships to Thee.

Prayer of Columbus. 9

What do you suppose will satisfy the soul, except to walk free and own no superior?

Laws for Creations. 3

To me every hour of the light and dark is a miracle,

Every cubic inch of space is a miracle.

Miracles. 2

Whispers of heavenly death murmur'd I hear.

Whispers of Heavenly Death

I was thinking the day most splendid till I saw what the not-day exhibited,

I was thinking this globe enough till there sprang out so noiseless around me myriads of other globes.

Night on the Prairies

I swear I think there is nothing but immortality!

To Think of Time. 9

The paths to the house I seek to make,

But leave to those to come the house itself.

Thou Mother with Thy Equal Brood. 1

As a strong bird on pinions free,

Joyous, the amplest spaces heavenward cleaving,

Such be the thought I'd think of thee, America,

Such be the recitative I'd bring for thee.

Ibid. 2

Sail, sail thy best, ship of Democracy.

Of value is thy freight, 'tis not the Present only,

The Past is also stored in thee.

Ibid. 4

This is thy hour O Soul, thy free flight into the wordless,

Away from books, away from art, the day erased, the lesson done,

Thee fully forth emerging, silent, gazing, pondering the themes thou lovest best,

Night, sleep, death and the stars.

A Clear Midnight

Society waits unform'd, and is for a while between things ended and things begun.

Thoughts. 1

Our life is closed, our life begins,

The long, long anchorage we leave,

The ship is clear at last, she leaps!

She swiftly courses from the shore,

Joy, shipmate, joy.

Joy, Shipmate, Joy!

Now obey thy cherished secret wish,

Embrace thy friends, leave all in order,

To port and hawser's tie no more returning,

Depart upon thy endless cruise, old Sailor.

Now Finalè to the Shore [1]

I announce the great individual, fluid as Nature, chaste, affectionate, compassionate, fully armed;

I announce a life that shall be copious, vehement, spiritual, bold,

And I announce an end that shall

[1] To Tennyson.

lightly and joyfully meet its trans-
lation.
So Long!
Camerado, this is no book,
Who touches this touches a man.
Ibid.
The world, the race, the soul — in
space and time the universes,
All bound as is befitting each — all
surely going somewhere.
Going Somewhere
Thanks in old age — thanks ere I go,
For health, the midday sun, the impal-
pable air — for life, mere life,
For precious ever-lingering memories.
Thanks in Old Age
I am the Poem of Earth, said the voice
of the rain,
Eternal I rise impalpable out of the
land and the bottomless sea.
The Voice of the Rain
Have you not learn'd great lessons
from those who reject you, and
brace themselves against you? or
who treat you with contempt, or
dispute the passage with you?
Stronger Lessons
Soon to be lost for aye in the darkness
— loth, O so loth to depart!
Garrulous to the very last.
After the Supper and Talk
No one will ever get at my verses
who insists upon viewing them as a literary performance.
*A Backward Glance O'er
Travel'd Roads*
None of the artists or pictures has
caught the deep, though subtle and indirect expression of this man's face.
There is something else there. One of
the great portrait painters of two or
three centuries ago is needed.
*Specimen Days. Of Lincoln,
August 12, 1863*
I never see that man without feeling
that he is one to become personally attach'd to, for his combination of purest, heartiest tenderness, and native
western form of manliness.
Ibid. The Inauguration [*of
Lincoln*] *March 4, 1865*
He leaves for America's history and
biography, so far, not only its most

dramatic reminiscence — he leaves, in
my opinion, the greatest, best, most
characteristic, artistic, moral personality.
*Specimen Days. Death of President
Lincoln, April 16, 1865*
The real war will never get in the
books.
Ibid. The Real War, etc.
Tone your wants and tastes down
low enough, and make much of negatives, and of mere daylight and the
skies.
Ibid. An Interregnum Paragraph
After you have exhausted what
there is in business, politics, conviviality, and so on — have found that none
of these finally satisfy, or permanently
wear — what remains? Nature remains.
Ibid. New Themes Entered Upon
Hast Thou, pellucid, in Thy azure
depths, medicine for case like mine?
Ibid. The Sky. October 20, 1876
One is never entirely without the instinct of looking around.
Ibid. One of the Human Kinks
You must not know too much, or be
too precise or scientific about birds and
trees and flowers and water-craft; a
certain free margin, and even vagueness — perhaps ignorance, credulity —
helps your enjoyment of these things.
Ibid. Birds. May 14, 1881
In the civilization of to-day it is undeniable that, over all the arts, literature dominates, serves beyond all.
Democratic Vistas
The main social, political spine-
character of the States will probably
run along the Ohio, Missouri and Mississippi rivers, and west and north of
them, including Canada.
Ibid.
Political democracy, as it exists and
practically works in America, with all
its threatening evils, supplies a training-
school for making first-class men. It is
life's gymnasium, not of good only, but
of all.
Ibid.
It is native personality, and that
alone, that endows a man to stand be-

fore presidents or generals, or in any distinguish'd collection, with *aplomb* — and *not* culture, or any knowledge or intellect whatever.

Democratic Vistas

If the United States haven't grown poets, on any scale of grandeur, it is certain they import, print, and read more poetry than any equal number of people elsewhere — probably more than all the rest of the world combined.

Notes Left Over. Ventures, on an Old Theme

To have great poets, there must be great audiences, too.

Ibid.

No really great song can ever attain full purport till long after the death of its singer — till it has accrued and incorporated the many passions, many joys and sorrows, it has itself aroused.

November Boughs. The Bible as Poetry

The United States themselves are essentially the greatest poem. . . . Here at last is something in the doings of man that corresponds with the broadcast doings of the day and night.

Preface to Leaves of Grass [*1855*]

The proof of a poet is that his country absorbs him as affectionately as he has absorbed it.

Ibid.

URANIA LOCKE STOUGHTON BAILEY ("JULIA GILL")
[1820–1882]

I want to be an angel,
  And with the angels stand,
A crown upon my forehead,
  A harp within my hand.

I Want to Be an Angel. Stanza 1

WILLIAM COX BENNETT
[1820–1895]

"God wills but ill," the doubter said,
  "Lo, time doth evil only bear;
Give me a sign His love to prove,
  His vaunted goodness to declare!"
The poet pointed where a flower,
  A simple daisy, starred the sod,

And answered, "Proof of love and power
Behold, behold a smile of God!"

A Thought [1]

Man of the Future, what shall be
The life of Earth that you shall see?
What strange new facts the years will show?
What wonders rare your eyes shall know?
To what new realms of marvel, say,
Will conquering science war its way?

To a Boy. Stanza 1

Oh! come you from the Indies, and, soldier, can you tell
Aught of the gallant Ninetieth, and who are safe and well?
O soldier, say my son is safe — for nothing else I care,
And you shall have a mother's thanks — shall have a widow's prayer.

From India. Stanza 1

HENRY HOWARD BROWNELL
[1820–1872]

As vonce I valked by a dismal svamp,
There sot an Old Cove in the dark and damp,
And at everybody as passed that road
A stick or a stone this Old Cove throwed.
And venever he flung his stick or his stone,
He'd set up a song of "Let me alone." [2]

Let Us Alone

A head how sober; a heart how spacious;
  A manner equal with high or low;
Rough but gentle, uncouth but gracious,
  And still inclining to lips of woe.

Abraham Lincoln. Stanza 24

Patient when saddest, calm when sternest,
  Grieved when rigid for justice sake;
Given to jest, yet ever in earnest

---

[1] Nathaniel Hawthorne copied this verse in an autograph album in 1853.
[2] All we ask is to be let alone. — JEFFERSON DAVIS [1808–1889] in his first message to the Confederate Congress [March, 1861]

If aught of right or truth were at
stake.
Abraham Lincoln. Stanza 25

ALICE CARY
[1820–1871]

There must be rough, cold weather,
And winds and rains so wild;
Not all good things together
Come to us here, my child.
November

So when some dear joy loses
Its beauteous summer glow,
Think how the roots of roses
Are kept alive in the snow.
Ibid.

Kiss me, though you make believe;
Kiss me, though I almost know
You are kissing to deceive.
Make Believe. Stanza 1

My soul is full of whispered song, —
My blindness is my sight;
The shadows that I feared so long
Are full of life and light.
Dying Hymn

Three little bugs in a basket,
And hardly room for two.
Three Bugs. Stanza 1

JAMES ORCHARD
HALLIWELL
[1820–1889]

A warke it ys as easie to be done
As tys to saye *Jacke robyson.*[1]
*Archaeological Dictionary
(cited from an old play)*

JEAN INGELOW
[1820–1897]

But two are walking apart forever,
And wave their hands for a mute
farewell.
Divided. VI, 5

---

[1] The current phrase, "Before you could
say Jack Robinson," is said to be derived
from a humorous song by Hudson, a tobac-
conist in Shoe Lane, London. He was a professional song-writer and vocalist, who used
to be engaged to sing at supper-rooms and
theatrical houses.

If there be memory in the world to
come,
If thought recur to some things silenced here,
Then shall the deep heart be no longer
dumb,
But find expression in that happier
sphere.
The Star's Monument. Stanza 1

Play uppe, play uppe, O Boston bells!
Ply all your changes, all your swells,
Play uppe "The Brides of Enderby."
*High Tide on the Coast of
Lincolnshire, 1571. Stanza 1*

"Cusha! Cusha! Cusha!" calling,
Ere the early dews were falling.
Ibid. Stanza 4

Come uppe, Whitefoot! come uppe,
Lightfoot!
Come uppe, Jetty! rise and follow,
Jetty, to the milking shed.
Ibid.

A sweeter woman ne'er drew breath
Than my sonne's wife, Elizabeth.
Ibid. Stanza 11

Man dwells apart, though not alone,
He walks among his peers unread;
The best of thoughts which he hath
known
For lack of listeners are not said.
Afterthought. Stanza 1

It is a comely fashion to be glad, —
Joy is the grace we say to God.
Dominion

Many fair tombs in the glorious glooms
At Westminster they show;
The brave and the great lie there in
state:
Winstanley lieth low.
Winstanley.[1] Stanza 77

Like coral insects multitudinous
The minutes are whereof our life is
made.
Work

---

[1] Henry Winstanley [1644–1703] designed
the Eddystone Lighthouse, 1696. While su-
perintending its construction, he was captured by a French privateer in 1697, and
later released. He completed the lighthouse,
but lost his life in a storm which demolished
the structure in 1703.

Blondel, when his lay
Pierced the strong tower, and Richard
  answered it.[1]
                                    Wishing
I marked my love by candle-light
Sewing her long white seam.
  The Long White Seam. Stanza 1
A land where all the men are stones,
  Or all the stones are men.
  *A Land That Living Warmth
                        Disowns*

THEODORE O'HARA
[1820–1867]

On Fame's eternal camping-ground
  Their silent tents are spread,
And Glory guards, with solemn round,
  The bivouac of the dead.
    The Bivouac of the Dead.[2]
                        Stanza 1
Sons of the Dark and Bloody ground,[3]
  Ye must not slumber there,
Where stranger steps and tongues re-
  sound
  Along the heedless air.
                Ibid. Stanza 9

MARGARET JUNKIN PRESTON
[1820–1897]

You have read of the Moslem palace,
  The marvelous fane that stands
On the banks of the distant Jumna,
  The wonder of all the lands.[4]
        For Love's Sake. Stanza 1

---

[1] There is a tradition that Blondel, a French troubadour, attendant and friend of Richard Coeur de Lion, discovered Richard, imprisoned in the castle of Dürrenstein, by singing beneath the tower window a song which they had composed and to which the king responded.

Blondel were royal himself, if he knew it!
    J. R. Lowell: *Two Scenes from the
              Life of Blondel, II, 6*
[2] Written in August, 1847, to commemorate the Americans slain in the battle of Buena Vista, Feb. 22–23, 1847.
[3] Translation of the Indian name, Kentucky.
[4] The Taj Mahal.

If from his home the lad that day
  His five small loaves had failed to
    take,
Would Christ have wrought — can any
    say —
  This miracle beside the lake?
    A Store of Loaves. Stanza 7
And therefore, I, William Bradford
  (by the grace of God to-day,
And the franchise of this good people),
  governor of Plymouth, say —
Through virtue of vested power — ye
  shall gather with one accord,
And hold in the month of November,
  thanksgiving unto the Lord.
    *The First Thanksgiving Day,
            1622. Stanza 2*
What use for the rope if it be not flung
Till the swimmer's grasp to the rock
  has clung?
                What Use?
What worth is eulogy's blandest breath,
When whispered in ears that are hushed
  in death?
                        Ibid.

GEORGE FREDERICK ROOT
[1820–1895]

And the hollow eye grows bright,
  And the poor heart almost gay,
As we think of seeing home and friends
  once more.
    Tramp, Tramp, Tramp. Stanza 3
Rally round the flag, boys,
  Rally once again,
Shouting the battle-cry of Freedom.
        *The Battle-cry of Freedom.
                        Stanza 1*

SIR WILLIAM HOWARD RUSSELL
[1820–1907]

The Russians dashed on towards
that thin red-line [1] streak tipped with a
line of steel.
    *Correspondence to the London
    Times from the Crimea, describ-*

---

[1] Soon the men of the column began to see that though the scarlet line was slender,

ing the British infantry at Balaclava [October 25, 1854] [1]

WILLIAM TECUMSEH SHERMAN
[1820–1891]

War is cruel and you cannot refine it.
Reply to the protest of the Atlanta, Georgia, city government on invasion [1864]
Hold the fort! I am coming!
Signaled to General Corse in Allatoona from the top of Kenesaw [October 5, 1864]
War at best is barbarism.
Letter to General Steele
I am tired and sick of war. Its glory is all moonshine. It is only those who have neither fired a shot nor heard the shrieks and groans of the wounded who cry aloud for blood, more vengeance, more desolation. War is hell.[2]
Attributed to an address before the graduating class, Michigan Military Academy [June 19, 1879], in a letter published in The National Tribune, Washington, D. C., November 26, 1914

JOHN TYNDALL
[1820–1893]

It is one of the disadvantages of reading books about natural scenery that they fill the mind with pictures, often exaggerated, often distorted,

often blurred, and, even when well drawn, injurious to the freshness of first impressions.
Fragments of Science. Vol. I, Niagara
It is not my habit of mind to think otherwise than solemnly of the feeling which prompts prayer. It is a power which I should like to see guided, not extinguished — devoted to practicable objects instead of wasted upon air.
Ibid. Vol. II, Prayer as a Form of Physical Energy
Life is a wave, which in no two consecutive moments of its existence is composed of the same particles.
Ibid. Vitality
We are truly heirs of all the ages; but as honest men it behooves us to learn the extent of our inheritance, and as brave ones not to whimper if it should prove less than we had supposed.
Ibid. Matter and Force
The mind of man may be compared to a musical instrument with a certain range of notes, beyond which in both directions we have an infinitude of silence.
Ibid.
The brightest flashes in the world of thought are incomplete until they have been proved to have their counterparts in the world of fact.
Ibid. Scientific Materialism
The formation of right habits is essential to your permanent security. They diminish your chance of falling when assailed, and they augment your chance of recovery when overthrown.
Ibid. An Address to Students
"Two things," said Immanuel Kant, "fill me with awe: the starry heavens, and the sense of moral responsibility in man."
Ibid. Scientific Use of the Imagination
Believing, as I do, in the continuity of nature, I cannot stop abruptly where

---

it was very rigid and exact. — A. W. KINGLAKE [1809–1891]: *Invasion of the Crimea, Vol. III, P. 455*
The spruce beauty of the slender red line. — *Ibid.* (sixth edition), *P. 248*
It's "Thin red line of 'eroes" when the drums begin to roll.
      KIPLING: *Tommy, St. 3*
Robert Gibb [1845–1932], Scottish artist, painted *The Thin Red Line,* which was exhibited at the Royal Scottish Academy Exposition in 1881.
   [1] Later included in Russell's book, *The British Expedition to the Crimea* (revised edition), *P. 187.*
   [2] This is the soldier brave enough to tell
      The glory-dazzled world that "war is hell":
   Lover of peace, he looks beyond the strife,

And rides through hell to save his country's life.
   HENRY VAN DYKE: *The Statue of Sherman by St. Gaudens*

our microscopes cease to be of use. Here the vision of the mind authoritatively supplements the vision of the eye. By a necessity engendered and justified by science I cross the boundary of the experimental evidence, and discern in that Matter which we, in our ignorance of its latent powers, and notwithstanding our professed reverence for its Creator, have hitherto covered with opprobrium, the promise and potency of all terrestrial Life.[1]

Fragments of Science. Address at Belfast [August 19, 1874]

Accept, if the choice be forced upon you, commotion before stagnation, the breezy leap of the torrent before the fetid stillness of the swamp.

Ibid.

To look at his picture as a whole, a painter requires distance; and to judge of the total scientific achievement of any age, the standpoint of a succeeding age is desirable.

Ibid. Science and Man

It is not given to any man, however endowed, to rise spontaneously into intellectual splendor without the parentage of antecedent thought.

Ibid.

It is as fatal as it is cowardly to blink facts because they are not to our taste.

Ibid.

Charles Darwin, the Abraham of scientific men — a searcher as obedient to the command of truth as was the patriarch to the command of God.

Ibid.

Superstition may be defined as constructive religion which has grown incongruous with intelligence.

Ibid.

Religious feeling is as much a verity as any other part of human consciousness; and against it, on the subjective side, the waves of science beat in vain.

Ibid. Professor Virchow and Evolution

[1] This statement aroused much bitterness, and Tyndall was subjected to lively abuse.

GEORGE LINNAEUS BANKS
[1821–1881]

I live for those who love me,
  Whose hearts are kind and true;
For the Heaven that smiles above me,
  And awaits my spirit too;
For all human ties that bind me,
For the task by God assigned me,
For the bright hopes yet to find me,
  And the good that I can do.

What I Live For. Stanza 1

For the cause that lacks assistance,
For the wrong that needs resistance,
For the future in the distance.

Ibid. Stanza 5

GEORGE SHEPARD BURLEIGH
[1821–1903]

Behold the mansion reared by daedal Jack.
See the malt stored in many a plethoric sack,
In the proud cirque of Ivan's bivouac.
Mark how the rat's felonious fangs invade
The golden stores in John's pavilion laid.

The Domicile Erected by John [1857]

Here walks forlorn the damsel crowned with rue.

Ibid.

That horned brute morose
That tossed the dog that worried the cat that kilt
The rat that ate the malt that lay in the house that Jack built.

Ibid.

SIR RICHARD FRANCIS BURTON
[1821–1890]

Why meet we on the bridge of Time to 'change one greeting and to part?

The Kasidah of Haji Abdu El-Yazdi. I, 11

Why must we meet, why must we part, why must we bear this yoke of MUST,

Without our leave or asked or given,
by tyrant Fate on victim thrust?
The Kasidah of Haji Abdu.
El-Yazdi. I, 13

Friends of my youth, a last adieu!
haply some day we meet again;
Yet ne'er the selfsame men shall meet;
the years shall make us other men.
Ibid. 16

What endless questions vex the
thought, of Whence and Whither,
When and How?
Ibid. II, 3

How short this Life, how long withal;
how false its weal, how true its
woes,
This fever-fit with paroxysms to mark
its opening and its close.
Ibid. III, 23

Hardly we learn to wield the blade be-
fore the wrist grows stiff and old;
Hardly we learn to ply the pen ere
Thought and Fancy faint with
cold.
Ibid. 32

Life, atom of that Infinite Space that
stretcheth, 'twixt the Here and
There.
Ibid. 36

All Faith is false, all Faith is true:
Truth is the shattered mirror
strown
In myriad bits; while each believes
his little bit the whole to own.
Ibid. VI, 1

Indeed he knows not how to know who
knows not also how to un-know.
Ibid. 18

What men are pleased to call their
souls was in the hog and dog begun.
Ibid. VII, 6

Life is a ladder infinite-stepped, that
hides its rungs from human eyes;
Planted its foot in chaos-gloom, its
head soars high above the skies.
Ibid. 7

Our hearts, affections, hopes and fears
for Life-to-be shall ever crave.
Ibid. VIII, 5

Mankind a future life must have to
balance life's unequal lot.
Ibid. 9

When doctors differ [1] who decides amid
the milliard-headed throng? [2]
The Kasidah of Haji Abdu.
El-Yazdi. VIII, 29

Do what thy manhood bids thee do,
from none but self expect applause;
He noblest lives and noblest dies who
makes and keeps his self-made
laws.
Ibid. 37

With Ignorance wage eternal war, to
know thyself for ever strain, [3]
Thine ignorance of thine ignorance is
thy fiercest foe, thy deadliest bane.
Ibid. IX, 14

Enough to thee the small still voice [4]
aye thundering in thine inner ear.
Ibid. 19

Wend now thy way with brow serene,
fear not thy humble tale to tell:
The whispers of the Desert-wind; the
tinkling of the Camel's-bell. [5]
Ibid. 45

JOSEPH WARREN FABENS
[1821–1875]

I've seen the land of all I love
Fade in the distance dim;
I've watched above the blighted heart,
Where once proud hope had been;
But I've never known a sorrow
That could with that compare,
When off the blue Canaries
I smoked my last cigar.
My Last Cigar. Stanza 4

DORA GREENWELL
[1821–1882]

A world of care without,
A world of strife shut out,
A world of love shut in.
Home. Stanza 2

---

[1] Who shall decide when doctors disagree?
POPE: *Moral Essays, Epistle III, L. 1*
[2] See Sidney, page 27.
[3] See Chaucer, page 6.
Make it thy business to know thyself,
which is the most difficult lesson in the
world. — CERVANTES: *Don Quixote, Part II,
Book III, Chap. 42*
[4] A still, small voice. — *1 Kings, XIX, 12*
[5] Death rides a camel. — Arabian legend

FREDERICK LOCKER-
LAMPSON
[1821–1895]

"Vanitas vanitatum" has rung in the
  ears
Of gentle and simple for thousands of
  years;
The wail still is heard, yet its notes
  never scare
Either simple or gentle from Vanity
  Fair.
Vanity Fair

This rhyme is the commonplace pas-
  sion
  That glows in a fond woman's heart;
Lay it by in some sacred deposit
  For relics, — we all have a few!
Love, some day they'll print it, be-
  cause it
  Was written to you.
A Nice Correspondent. Stanza 7

What an arm — what a waist
  For an arm!
To My Grandmother

The world's as ugly, ay, as Sin, —
  And almost as delightful.
The Jester's Plea

If you lift a guinea-pig up by the tail
  His eyes drop out!
A Garden Lyric. Stanza 5

GEORGE JOHN WHYTE-
MELVILLE
[1821–1878]

When you sleep in your cloak there's
  no lodging to pay.
Boots and Saddles

For everything created
  In the bounds of earth and sky
Has such longing to be mated,
  It must couple or must die.
Like to Like

Ah, better to love in the lowliest cot
  Than pine in a palace alone.
Chastelar

There are men both good and wise who
  hold that in a future state
Dumb creatures we have cherished here
  below

Shall give us joyous greeting when we
  pass the golden gate.
*The Place Where the
Old Horse Died*

In the choice of a horse and a wife,
a man must please himself, ignoring
the opinion and advice of friends.
Riding Recollections

Education should be as gradual as
the moonrise, perceptible not in progress but in result.
Ibid.

Pluck takes us into a difficulty,
nerve brings us out of it. Both are com-
prised in the noble quality we call
valor.
Ibid.

MATTHEW ARNOLD
[1822–1888]

One lesson, Nature, let me learn of thee.
Sonnet 1, Quiet Work

  Be his
My special thanks, whose even-
  balanced soul,
From first youth tested up to extreme
  old age,
Business could not make dull, nor Pas-
  sion wild:
Who saw life steadily and saw it whole.
Sonnet 2, To a Friend

Others abide our question. Thou art
  free.
We ask and ask: Thou smilest and art
  still,
Out-topping knowledge.
Sonnet 3, Shakespeare

  The will is free:
Strong is the Soul, and wise, and beau-
  tiful:
The seeds of godlike power are in us
  still:
Gods are we, Bards, Saints, Heroes, if
  we will.
*Sonnet 4, Written in
Emerson's Essays*

France, famed in all great arts, in none
  supreme.
*Sonnet 10, To a Republican
Friend, 1848*

To its own impulse every creature stirs:
Live by thy light, and Earth will live
  by hers.
       Sonnet 11, Religious Isolation

Strew on her roses, roses,
  And never a spray of yew.
In quiet she reposes:
  Ah! would that I did too.
       Requiescat. Stanza 1

Tonight it doth inherit
  The vasty Hall of Death.
       Ibid. Stanza 4

Ennobling this dull pomp, the life of
  kings,
By contemplation of diviner things.
       Mycerinus. Stanza 2

From grief, that is but passion;
From mirth, that is but feigning;
From tears, that bring no healing;
From wild and weak complaining;
Thine old strength revealing;
    Save, oh, save.
       Stagirius

Fate gave, what Chance shall not control,
His sad lucidity of soul.
       Resignation

Yet they, believe me, who await
No gifts from Chance, have conquered
  Fate.
       Ibid.

Resolve to be thyself: and know, that
  he
Who finds himself, loses his misery.
       Self-Dependence. Stanza 8

We cannot kindle when we will
The fire that in the heart resides.
       Morality. Stanza 1

But tasks in hours of insight will'd
Can be through hours of gloom fulfill'd.
       Ibid.

With aching hands and bleeding feet
  We dig and heap, lay stone on stone;
We bear the burden and the heat
  Of the long day, and wish 'twere
  done.
Not till the hours of light return
All we have built do we discern.
       Ibid. Stanza 2

Calm Soul of all things! make it mine
  To feel, amid the city's jar,
That there abides a peace of thine,

Man did not make, and can not mar.
      Lines Written in Kensington
           Gardens. Stanza 10

Eternal Passion,
Eternal Pain!
       Philomela

So Tiberius might have sat,
Had Tiberius been a cat.
       Poor Matthias

Physician of the Iron Age,
Goethe has done his pilgrimage.
He took the suffering human race,
He read each wound, each weakness
  clear —
And struck his finger on the place
And said — Thou ailest here, and here.
       Memorial Verses. Stanza 3

Time may restore us in his course
Goethe's sage mind and Byron's force;
But where will Europe's latter hour
Again find Wordsworth's healing
  power?
       Ibid. Stanza 5

Wandering between two worlds, one
  dead,
The other powerless to be born.
      Stanzas from the Grande Char-
           treuse. Stanza 15

The kings of modern thought are
  dumb.
       Ibid. Stanza 20

Children of men! not that your age
  excel
  In pride of life the ages of your sires;
But that you too feel deeply, bear fruit
  well,
  The Friend of man desires.
       Progress

Ah, love, let us be true
To one another!
       Dover Beach

  And we are here as on a darkling
  plain
Swept with confused alarms of struggle
  and flight,
  Where ignorant armies clash by
  night.
       Ibid.

People who lived here long ago
Did by this stone, it seems, intend
To name for future times to know

The dachs-hound, Geist, their little friend.
> *Geist's Grave. Stanza 20*

The foot less prompt to meet the morning dew,
The heart less bounding to emotion new,
And hope, once crush'd, less quick to spring again.
> *Thyrsis. Stanza 14*

We do not what we ought;
  What we ought not, we do;
And lean upon the thought
  That Chance will bring us through.
> *Empedocles on Etna*

Is it so small a thing
To have enjoy'd the sun,
To have lived light in the spring,
To have loved, to have thought, to have done;
To have advanced true friends, and beat down baffling foes?
> *Ibid.*

The day in its hotness,
The strife with the palm;
The night in its silence,
The stars in their calm.
> *Ibid. Callicles' Song*

Peace, peace is what I seek, and public calm;
Endless extinction of unhappy hates.
> *Merope*

With women the heart argues, not the mind.
> *Ibid.*

This strange disease of modern life.
> *The Scholar Gypsy. Stanza 21*

Still nursing the unconquerable hope,
  Still clutching the inviolable shade.
> *Ibid. Stanza 22*

Most men eddy about
Here and there — eat and drink,
Chatter and love and hate,
Gather and squander, are raised
Aloft, are hurl'd in the dust,
Striving blindly, achieving
Nothing; and then they die.
> *Rugby Chapel*

Radiant with ardour divine,
Beacons of Hope ye appear!
Languor is not in your heart,

Weakness is not in your word,
Weariness not on your brow.
> *Rugby Chapel*

What shelter to grow ripe is ours?
  What leisure to grow wise?
> *Stanzas in Memory of the Author*
> *of "Obermann." [1] Stanza 18*

We, in some unknown Power's employ,
  Move on a rigorous line;
Can neither, when we will, enjoy;
  Nor, when we will, resign.
> *Ibid. Stanza 34*

The East bow'd low before the blast
In patient deep disdain;
She let the legions thunder past
And plunged in thought again.
> *"Obermann" Once More.*
> *Stanza 28*

Hath man no second life? *Pitch this one high!*
Sits there no judge in Heaven, our sin to see?
More strictly then the inward judge obey!
Was Christ a man like us? *Oh, let us try*
If we then, too, can be such men as he!
> *The Better Part*

Let the long contention cease!
Geese are swans, and swans are geese. [2]
> *The Last Word. Stanza 2*

When the forts of folly fall,
Find thy body by the wall!
> *Ibid. Stanza 4*

Spare me the whispering, crowded room,
  The friends who come and gape and go,
The ceremonious air of gloom —
  All, which makes death a hideous show.
> *A Wish*

Below the surface stream, shallow and light,
Of what we say and feel — below the stream,

---

[1] Étienne Pivert de Sénancour, born at Paris [1770], died at St. Cloud [1846], French author, much influenced by Rousseau. His most notable work, *Obermann,* in two volumes, was published in 1804.

[2] See Burton, page 123.

As light, of what we think we feel, there
    flows
With noiseless current, strong, obscure
    and deep,
The central stream of what we feel in-
    deed.
                *Essays. St. Paul and
                    Protestantism* [1]
Poetry is simply the most beautiful,
impressive and widely effective mode
of saying things, and hence its importance.
                Ibid. Heinrich Heine
Philistine must have originally
meant, in the mind of those who invented the nickname, a strong, dogged,
unenlightened opponent of the children
of the light.
                                Ibid.
On the breast of that huge Mississippi of falsehood called history, a
foam-bell more or less is of no consequence.[2]
                *Ibid. Literary Influence of
                        Academies*
The pursuit of the perfect, then, is
the pursuit of sweetness and light.
                Ibid. Culture and Anarchy
There is no better motto which it
[culture] can have than these words of
Bishop Wilson, "To make reason and
the will of God prevail."
                                Ibid.
Whispering from her towers the last
enchantments of the Middle Age . . .

[1] For admission of Arnold's authorship of
this interpolated verse, see his *Letters, Vol. II,
P. 32, Feb. 21, 1870.*
    [2]   The fretful foam
Of vehement actions without scope or term,
Called History.
    ARNOLD: *Sonnet to the Duke of Wellington*
With so little knowledge is history written,
and thus doth each chattering brook of a
"Life" swell with its tribute "that great Mis-
sissippi of falsehood," Biography. — ANDREW
LANG: *Letters to Dead Authors, To Pierre de
Ronsard*
    See Thomas Moore, page 337.
    History is nothing more than the belief in
the senses, the belief in falsehood. — NIETZ-
SCHE: *The Twilight of the Idols, "Reason" in
Philosophy, 1*
    History never embraces more than a small
part of reality.—LA ROCHEFOUCAULD: *Paul
Sabatier*

home of lost causes, and forsaken beliefs, and unpopular names, and impossible loyalties!
                Essays in Criticism. Oxford

DION BOUCICAULT
[1822–1890]

Then take the shamrock from your hat
    and cast it on the sod,
It will take root and flourish still,
    though under foot it's trod.
                The Wearing of the Green. [1]
                                Stanza 2
I have another life I long to meet,
Without which life my life is incom-
    plete,
Oh, sweeter self! Like me, art thou
    astray?
Trying with all thy heart to find the
    way
To mine? Straying, like mine, to find
    the breast
On which alone can weary heart find
    rest?
                    Led Astray [*1873*]

MARGARET COURTNEY
[1822–1862]

Be kind to thy father, for when thou
    wert young,
Who loved thee so fondly as he?
He caught the first accents that fell
    from thy tongue,
And joined in thy innocent glee.
                    Be Kind. Stanza 1

MARY BAKER EDDY
[1822–1910]

The prayer that reforms the sinner
and heals the sick is an absolute faith
that all things are possible to God, —
a spiritual understanding of Him, an
unselfed love.
                *Science and Health with Key to
                        the Scriptures. Page 1*
The basis of all health, sinlessness,
and immortality is the great fact that
God is the only Mind; and this Mind

[1] Adapted, from the traditional Irish ballad,
for Boucicault's play *Arrah-na-Pogue.* [1865]

must be not merely believed, but it must be understood.

Science and Health with Key to the Scriptures. Page 339

Being is holiness, harmony, immortality. It is already proved that a knowledge of this, even in small degree, will uplift the physical and moral standard of mortals, will increase longevity, will purify and elevate character. Thus progress will finally destroy all error, and bring immortality to light.

Ibid. Page 492

Divine Love always has met and always will meet every human need.

Ibid. Page 494

How would you define Christian Science?

As the law of God, the law of good, interpreting and demonstrating the divine Principle and rule of universal harmony.

Rudimental Divine Science. Page 1

To live and let live, without clamor for distinction or recognition; to wait on divine Love; to write truth first on the tablet of one's own heart, — this is the sanity and perfection of living, and my human ideal.

Message to the Mother Church for 1902. Page 2

To live so as to keep human consciousness in constant relation with the divine, the spiritual, and the eternal, is to individualize infinite power; and this is Christian Science.

The First Church of Christ, Scientist, and Miscellany. Page 160

It matters not what be thy lot,
So Love doth guide;
For storm or shine, pure peace is thine,
Whate'er betide.

Satisfied. Stanza 1

Blest Christmas morn, though murky clouds
Pursue thy way,
Thy light was born where storm enshrouds
Nor dawn nor day!

Christmas Morn. Stanza 1

Shepherd, show me how to go
O'er the hillside steep,
How to gather, how to sow,
How to feed Thy sheep;
I will listen for Thy voice,
Lest my footsteps stray,
I will follow and rejoice
All the rugged way.

Shepherd, Show Me How to Go. Stanza 1

O'er waiting harp-strings of the mind
There sweeps a strain,
Low, sad, and sweet, whose measures bind
The pow'r of pain.

O'er Waiting Harp-strings of the Mind. Stanza 1

My prayer, some daily good to do
To Thine, for Thee —
An off'ring pure of Love, whereto
God leadeth me.

Ibid. Stanza 7

ULYSSES S. GRANT
[1822–1885]

No terms except an unconditional and immediate surrender can be accepted. I propose to move immediately upon your works.

To General S. B. Buckner, Fort Donelson [February 16, 1862]

I propose to fight it out on this line, if it takes all summer.

Despatch to Washington, Before Spottsylvania Court House [May 11, 1864]

Let us have peace.

Accepting a Nomination for the Presidency [May 29, 1868]

I know no method to secure the repeal of bad or obnoxious laws so effective as their stringent execution.

Inaugural Address [March 4, 1869]

Let no guilty man escape, if it can be avoided. No personal considerations should stand in the way of performing a public duty.

Indorsement of a Letter relating to the Whiskey Ring [July 29, 1875]

Leave the matter of religion to the family altar, the church, and the private school, supported entirely by private contributions. Keep the church and the State for ever separate.

Speech at Des Moines, Iowa
[1875]

Labor disgraces no man; unfortunately you occasionally find men disgrace labor.

Speech at Midland International
Arbitration Union, Birmingham,
England [1877]

They [the Pilgrim Fathers] fell upon an ungenial climate, where there were nine months of winter and three months of cold weather and that called out the best energies of the men, and of the women too, to get a mere subsistence out of the soil, with such a climate. In their efforts to do that they cultivated industry and frugality at the same time — which is the real foundation of the greatness of the Pilgrims.

Speech at New England Society
Dinner [December 22, 1880]

EDWARD EVERETT HALE
[1822–1909]

To look up and not down,
To look forward and not back,
To look out and not in, and
To lend a hand.[1]

Ten Times One Is Ten [1870]

I am only one,
But still I am one.
I cannot do everything,
But still I can do something;
And because I cannot do everything
I will not refuse to do the something
that I can do.

For the Lend-a-Hand Society

Let the scroll
Fill as it may as years unroll;
But when again she calls her youth
To serve her in the ranks of Truth,
May she find all one heart, one soul —
At home or on some distant shore —
"All present, or accounted for!"

Alma Mater's Roll [For a
Harvard dinner, 1875]

[1] Rule of the Harry Wadsworth Club.

Its pink and white are everywhere,
A ray of sun — and all the slope
Laughs with its white and red.
"It is the Mayflower of our hope;
The spring is come."

The Finding of the First May-
flower. Stanza 3

Behind all these men you have to do with, behind officers, and government, and people even, there is the Country Herself, your Country, and . . . you belong to Her as you belong to your own mother. Stand by Her, boy, as you would stand by your mother.

The Man Without a Country

He loved his country as no other man has loved her, but no man deserved less at her hands.

Ibid. Epitaph of Philip Nolan

I taught him four speeches. . . .
1. "Very well, thank you. And you?" This for an answer to casual salutations.
2. "I am very glad you liked it."
3. "There has been so much said, and, on the whole, so well said, that I will not occupy the time."
4. "I agree, in general, with my friend the other side of the room."

My Double and How He
Undid Me

It is not necessary to finish your sentences in a crowd, but by a sort of mumble, omitting sibilants and dentals. This, indeed, if your words fail you, answers even in public extempore speech, but better where other talking is going on.

Ibid.

THOMAS HUGHES
[1822–1896]

Throo aal the waarld owld Gaarge
would bwoast,
Commend me to merry owld England
mwoast;
While vools gwoes prating vur and
nigh,
We stwops at whum, my dog and I.

Tom Brown's School-days.
Chap. 1 [1]

[1] The verse is ascribed to "Gaarge Ridler, old west-country yeoman."

Life isn't all beer and skittles; [1] but beer and skittles, or something better of the same sort, must form a good part of every Englishman's education.

Tom Brown's School-days.
Chap. 2

ROBERT LEIGHTON
[1822–1869]

I have a thought that, as we live elsewhere,
  So will those dear creations of the
  brain;
That what I lose unread, I'll find, and
  there
    Take up my joy again.

Books. Stanza 2

With liberty and endless time to read
  The libraries of Heaven!

Ibid. Stanza 3

GEORGE LIPPARD
[1822–1854]

There was tumult in the city,
  In the quaint old Quaker town,
And the streets were rife with people
  Pacing restless up and down.

Independence Bell. Stanza 1

When a nation's life's at hazard,
  We've no time to think of men!

Ibid. Stanza 3

DONALD GRANT MITCHELL
("IK. MARVEL")
[1822–1908]

Ashes follow blaze inevitably as death follows life. Misery treads on the

---

[1] It's a regular holiday to them — all porter and skittles. . . . Down-hearted fellers as can't svig away at the beer, nor play at skittles neither. — DICKENS: *Pickwick Papers, Chap. 41*
Life is with such all beer and skittles. — C. S. CALVERLEY: *Contentment*
  That it should not be all beer and skittles with us, and therefore apt to pall, my cousins and I had to work pretty hard. — GEORGE DU MAURIER: *Peter Ibbetson, P. 47*
  And though life's not all beer and skittles,
    Yet the sun, on occasion, can shine.
      ANDREW LANG: *A Remonstrance with the Fair*

heels of joy; anguish rides swift after pleasure.

Reveries of a Bachelor. First
Reverie, Part III

Blessed be letters — they are the monitors, they are also the comforters, and they are the only true heart-talkers.

Ibid. Second Reverie

Coquetry whets the appetite; flirtation depraves it. Coquetry is the thorn that guards the rose — easily trimmed off when once plucked. Flirtation is like the slime on water-plants, making them hard to handle, and when caught, only to be cherished in slimy waters.

Ibid.

A man without some sort of religion is at best, a poor reprobate, the football of destiny, with no tie linking him to infinity, and the wondrous eternity that is begun with him; but a woman without it is even worse — a flame without heat, a rainbow without color, a flower without perfume!

Ibid.

JOHN TYLER PETTEE
[1822–1907]

Pray for peace and grace and spiritual
  food,
For wisdom and guidance, for all these
  are good,
    But don't forget the potatoes.

Prayer and Potatoes

EDWARD JOHN PHELPS
[1822–1900]

Waiting for that delusive train
That, always coming, never comes,
Till weary and worn, cold and forlorn,
And paralyzed in every function,
  I hope in hell
  Their souls may dwell
Who first invented Essex Junction.

Essex Junction. Stanza 1

THOMAS BUCHANAN READ
[1822–1872]

Within his sober realm of leafless trees,
  The russet year inhaled the dreamy
  air;

Like some tanned reaper in his hour of
  ease,
  When all the fields are lying brown
    and bare.
        The Closing Scene. Stanza 1
My soul to-day
Is far away
Sailing the Vesuvian Bay.
            Drifting. Stanza 1
With dreamful eyes
My spirit lies
Under the walls of Paradise.
            Ibid. Stanza 5
There is the shaded doorway still,
But a stranger's foot has crossed the
  sill.
    The Stranger on the Sill. Stanza 1
The old, old sea, as one in tears,
  Comes murmuring with its foamy
    lips,
And knocking at the vacant piers,
  Calls for its long-lost multitude of
    ships.[1]
        Come, Gentle Trembler,
                Stanza 5
I stood by the open casement
  And looked upon the night,
And saw the westward-going stars
  Pass slowly out of sight.
      The Celestial Army. Stanza 1
Now begins
The housewife's happiest season of the
  year.
The ground, already broken by the
  spade —
The beds, made level by the passing
  rake.
      The New Pastoral. Book V
Boone, the pioneer,
Whose statue, in the eternal niche of
  fame,
Leans on his gleaming rifle; and whose
  name
Is carved so deep in the Kentuckian
  rocks,
It may not be effaced.
        Ibid. Book XXVII
The terrible grumble, and rumble, and
  roar,
Telling the battle was on once more,

---

[1] Misquoted by MARK TWAIN: *Life on the
Mississippi, Chap.* 22.

And Sheridan twenty miles away.
        Sheridan's Ride. Stanza 1
I hate the sin, but I love the sinner.
        What a Word May Do.
               Stanza 1

BERNARD ELLIOTT BEE
[1823–1861]

  See, there is Jackson, standing like
a stone-wall.
    *Of General T. J. Jackson, at the
    Battle of Bull Run* [1] *[July 21,
    1861]*

GEORGE HENRY BOKER
[1823–1890]

"Freedom!" their battle-cry, —
"Freedom! or leave to die!"
    The Black Regiment. Stanza 5
Lay him low, lay him low,
In the clover or the snow!
What cares he? he cannot know.
    Dirge for a Soldier. [2] *Stanza 1*
"Give me but two brigades," said
  Hooker, frowning at fortified
  Lookout.
    Battle of Lookout Mountain. [3]
               Stanza 1
All through the long, long polar day,
  The vessels westward sped;
And wherever the sail of Sir John was
  blown,
  The ice gave way and fled.
    *The Ballad of Sir John Frank-
             lin.* [4] *Stanza 7*
And there, while thread shall hang to
  thread,
  Oh, let that ensign fly!
The noblest constellation set
  Against the Northern sky.
      The Cumberland. [5] *Stanza 37*

---

[1] Bee was killed in this battle.
[2] General Philip Kearny [1815–1862], killed
near Chantilly, Virginia [Sept. 1, 1862].
[3] Chattanooga, Tennessee [Nov. 24, 1863].
[4] Arctic explorer [1786–1847].
[5] Sunk by the *Merrimac,* off Hampton
Roads, Virginia [March 8, 1862]. Commanded
by Lieutenant George U. Morris, she went
down with all on board and colors flying.
Most of the crew were lost.

I am that blessing which men fly from
— Death.
Countess Laura. Stanza 13

Love is that orbit of the restless soul
  Whose circle grazes the confines of
    space,
  Bounding within the limits of its
    race
Utmost extremes.
Sonnet, Love

WILLIAM BRIGHTY RANDS ("MATTHEW BROWNE")
[1823–1880]

Never do to-day what you can
Put off till to-morrow.
Lilliput Levee

Great wide, beautiful, wonderful world,
With the wonderful waters round you
  curled,
And the wonderful grass upon your
  breast,
World, you are beautifully drest.
The Child's World. Stanza 1

You are more than the earth, though
  you are such a dot;
You can love and think, and the earth
  cannot!
Ibid. Stanza 5

JULIA A. FLETCHER CARNEY
[1823–1908]

Little drops of water, little grains of
  sand,
Make the mighty ocean and the pleas-
  ant land.
So the little moments, humble though
  they be,
Make the mighty ages of eternity.
Little Things [1845]

Little deeds of kindness, little words of
  love,
Help to make earth happy like the
  heaven above.
Ibid.

ROBERT COLLIER
[1823–1912]

Steadily steering, eagerly peering,
  Trusting in God, your fathers came,

Pilgrims and strangers, fronting all
  dangers,
  Cool-headed Saxons, with hearts
    aflame.
Saxon Grit. Stanza 7

WILLIAM JOHNSON CORY
[1823–1892]

All beauteous things for which we live
By laws of time and space decay.
But oh, the very reason why
I clasp them, is because they die.
Mimnermus in Church. Stanza 4

Somewhere beneath the sun,
These quivering heart-strings prove it,
Somewhere there must be one
Made for this soul, to move it.
Amaturus

Oh, earlier shall the rosebuds blow,
In after years, those happier years;
And children weep, when we lie low,
Far fewer tears, far softer tears.
A Song. Stanza 1

For waste of scheme and toil we grieve,
For snowflakes on the wave we sigh,
For writings on the sand that leave
Naught for to-morrow's passer-by.
On Livermead Sands. Stanza 1

You come not, as aforetime, to the
  headstone every day,
And I, who died, I do not chide because, my friend, you play;
Only, in playing, think of him who once
  was kind and dear,
And, if you see a beauteous thing, just
  say, he is not here.
Remember

They told me, Heraclitus, they told me
  you were dead;
They brought me bitter news to hear
  and bitter tears to shed.
I wept, as I remembered, how often you
  and I
Had tired the sun with talking and sent
  him down the sky.
And now that thou art lying, my dear
  old Carian guest,
A handful of grey ashes, long long ago
  at rest,

Still are thy pleasant voices, thy Night-
ingales,[1] awake,
For Death, he taketh all away, but
them he cannot take.
Heraclitus,[2] *Paraphrase from*
Callimachus [3]

BARTHOLOMEW DOWLING
[1823–1863]

We meet 'neath the sounding rafter,
And the walls around are bare;
As they shout back our peals of laugh-
ter
It seems that the dead are there.
Then stand to your glasses, steady!
We drink in our comrades' eyes:
One cup to the dead already —
Hurrah for the next that dies!
The Revel.[4] *Stanza 1*

[1] *The Nightingales* was the title of the
poems left by Heraclitus.
[2] They told me, Herakleitos, thou wast dead.
  What tears I shed!
  As I remembered how we two as one
    Talked down the sun.
  Well, Halicarnessian friend, long since
      thou must
    Have turned to dust;
  Yet live thy Nightingales, and Hades, who
    Doth all subdue,
  Shall never until Time itself shall close
  Lay hand on those.
    Translation by BASIL LANNEAU GILDER-
      SLEEVE [1831–1924]
One told me, Heraclitus, of thy fate;
He brought me tears, he brought me memo-
  ries;
Alas, my Carian friend, how oft, how late,
We twain have talked the sun adown the skies,
And somewhere thou art dust without a date!
But of thy songs death maketh not his prize,
In death's despite, that stealeth all, they wait,
The new year's nightingale that never dies!
    ANDREW LANG [1844–1912]: *Heraclitus*
They tell me, Heraclitus, thou art dead,
And many are the tears for thee I shed,
With memories of those summer nights op-
  prest
When we together talked the sun to rest.
Alas! my guest, my friend! no more art thou;
Long, long ago wert ashes, and yet now
Thy Nightingales live on, I hear them sing,
E'en death spares them, who spares not any-
    thing.
    LILLA CABOT PERRY [1848–1933]:
      translated from Callimachus, *Greek*
      Anthology, Book VII, Epigram 80
[3] ? —A. D. 240.
[4] Commemorating those who died in a great
cholera epidemic in India.

There's a mist on the glass congealing,
  'Tis the hurricane's sultry breath;
And thus does the warmth of feeling
  Turn ice in the grasp of Death.
    The Revel. Stanza 6
Who dreads to the dust returning?
Who shrinks from the sable shore,
Where the high and haughty yearning
  Of the soul can sting no more?
    Ibid. Stanza 7

AUGUSTINE JOSEPH HICKEY
DUGANNE
[1823–1884]

"Heimgang!" So the German people
  Whisper when they hear the bell
Tolling from some gray old steeple,
  Death's familiar tale to tell;
When they hear the organ surges
  Swelling out from chapel dome,
And the singers chanting dirges,
  "Heimgang!" Always going home.
    Heimgang. Stanza 1

THOMAS WENTWORTH
HIGGINSON
[1823–1911]

To be parochial is to turn away from
the great and look at the little. . . .
To look out of the little world into the
great, that is enlargement; all else is
parochialism.
    Margaret Fuller Ossoli.
    Chap. 9
The test of an author is not to be
found merely in the number of his
phrases that pass current in the corner
of newspapers . . . but in the number
of passages that have really taken root
in younger minds.
    Ibid. Chap. 18
When a thought takes one's breath
away, a lesson on grammar seems an
impertinence.
    Preface to EMILY DICKINSON'S
    Poems, First Series
An easy thing, O Power Divine,
To thank Thee for these gifts of Thine,
For summer's sunshine, winter's snow,
For hearts that kindle, thoughts that
    glow;

But when shall I attain to this —
To thank Thee for the things I miss?
The Things I Miss
Age, I make light of it,
Fear not the sight of it,
Time's but our playmate, whose toys
are divine.
Sixty and Six: A Fountain
of Youth

WILLIAM WALSHAM HOW
[1823–1897]

For all the saints who from their la-
bours rest,
Who Thee by faith before the world
confest,
Thy name, O Jesus, be forever blest.
For All the Saints [1864].
Stanza 1

JOHN KELLS INGRAM
[1823–1907]

Who fears to speak of Ninety-eight?
Who blushes at the name?
When cowards mock the patriot's fate,
Who hangs his head for shame?
The Memory of the Dead.[1]
Stanza 1

GEORGE MARTIN LANE
[1823–1897]

The waiter he to him doth call,
And gently whispers — "One Fish-
ball."
The waiter roars it through the hall,
The guests they start at "One Fish-
ball!"
The guest then says, quite ill at ease,
"A piece of bread, sir, if you please."
The waiter roars it through the hall:
"We don't give bread with one Fish-
ball!"
One Fish-ball.[2] *Couplets 7–10*
[The Drawer, Harper's
Monthly, July, 1855]

[1] First published anonymously in *The Dublin Nation, April 1, 1843.*
[2] The author was Professor of Latin at Harvard; in a memoir of him by PROFESSOR MOR-
GAN, it is stated that the embarrassment of the
"lone fish-ball" was an actual experience.
The ballad was translated into Italian by

JAMES MATTHEWS LEGARÉ
[1823–1859]

Go bow thy head in gentle spite,
Thou lily white,
For she who spies thee waving here,
With thee in beauty can compare
As day with night.
To a Lily
Thou in thy lake dost see
Thyself: so she
Beholds her image in her eyes
Reflected. Thus did Venus rise
From out the sea.
Ibid.

CAROLINE ATHERTON
BRIGGS MASON
[1823–1890]

Do they miss me at home — do they
miss me?
'Twould be an assurance most dear,
To know that this moment some loved
one
Were saying, "I wish he were here."
Do They Miss Me at Home?
Stanza 1
His grave a nation's heart shall be,
His monument a people free!
President Lincoln's Grave
Whichever way the wind doth blow,
Some heart is glad to have it so;
Then, blow it east, or blow it west,
The wind that blows, that wind is best.
En Voyage. Stanza 1
When I am old, and oh, how soon
Will life's sweet morning yield to noon,
And noon's broad, fervid, earnest light
Be shaded in the solemn night,
Till, like a story well-nigh told,
Will seem my life — when I am old.
When I Am Old. Stanza 1

EDWARD HAZEN PARKER
[1823–1896]

Life's race well run,
Life's work well done,

PROFESSOR FRANCIS J. CHILD, who, with
JAMES RUSSELL LOWELL, made a one-act opera, Il Pesceballo, based upon it, which was
produced at Harvard in 1862.
See *The Bibelot, Vol. 17, No. 11,* published
by Thomas Bird Mosher.

Life's victory won,
  Now cometh rest.
      Funeral Ode on James A. Garfield.
          Stanza 1

COVENTRY KERSEY
DIGHTON PATMORE
[1823–1896]

The sunshine dreaming upon Salmon's
    height
Is not so sweet and white
As the most heretofore sin-spotted Soul
That darts to its delight
Straight from the absolution of a faith-
    ful fight.
          Peace
Life is not life at all without delight.
          Victory in Defeat
  To have nought
Is to have all things without care or
    thought!
          Legem Tuam Dilexi
For want of me the world's course will
    not fail;
When all its work is done, the lie shall
    rot;
The truth is great, and shall prevail
When none cares whether it prevail or
    not.
          Magna est Veritas
None thrives for long upon the happiest
    dream.
          Tired Memory
The flower of olden sanctities.
          1867
Ah, wasteful woman! she who may
  On her sweet self set her own price,
Knowing he cannot choose but pay,
  How has she cheapened Paradise!
How given for nought her priceless gift,
  How spoiled the bread and spilled the
    wine,
Which, spent with due respective thrift,
  Had made brutes men and men
    divine! [1]
  The Angel in the House. Preludes,
          Unthrift
Love wakes men, once a lifetime each;
They lift their heavy lids, and look;

---

[1] Quoted by JOHN RUSKIN in *Sesame and
Lilies.*

And, lo, what one sweet page can teach
They read with joy, then shut the book.
    The Angel in the House. Canto 8,
        Prelude 2, The Revelation
Love's perfect blossom only blows
  Where noble manners veil defect.
Angels may be familiar; those
  Who err each other must respect.
          Thoughts. V, Courtesy
Be not amazed at life; 'tis still
  The mode of God with his elect
Their hopes exactly to fulfil,
  In times and ways they least expect.
          The Heart's Prophecies
He that but once too nearly hears
The music of forefended spheres,
Is thenceforth lonely.
          He That But Once
If I were dead, you'd sometimes say,
  "Poor Child!"
          If I Were Dead
It is not true that Love will do no
    wrong.
          Ibid.
Thou rememberest of what toys
We made our joys,
How weakly understood,
Thy great commanded good.
          The Toys
Some who do not consider that
Christianity has proved a failure, do,
nevertheless, hold that it is open to
question whether the race, as a race,
has been much affected by it, and
whether the external and visible evil
and good which have come of it do not
pretty nearly balance one another.
          Christianity and Progress
Atheism in art, as well as in life, has
only to be pressed to its last consequences in order to become ridiculous.
          Emotional Art
The poet, as a rule, should avoid religion altogether as a direct subject.
          Bad Morality Is Bad Art
It is a great consolation to reflect that,
among all the bewildering changes to
which the world is subject, the character of woman cannot be altered.
          Ibid.
A Woman is a foreign land,
  Of which, though there he settle
    young,

A man will ne'er quite understand
  The customs, politics, and tongue.
                              Woman

EDWARD POLLOCK
[1823–1858]

There's something in the parting hour
  Will chill the warmest heart,
Yet kindred, comrades, lovers, friends,
  Are fated all to part.
              The Parting Hour
The one who goes is happier
  Than those he leaves behind.
                              Ibid.

JOHN R. THOMPSON
[1823–1873]

No unresponsive soul had heard
  That plaintive note's appealing,
So deeply "Home, Sweet Home" had
  stirred
The hidden founts of feeling.
        Music in Camp. Stanza 14
Never have I seen Carcassonne.[1]
  From the French of GUSTAVE
      NADAUD [*1820–1893*]

PHOEBE CARY
[1824–1874]

I think true love is never blind,
  But rather brings an added light,
An inner vision quick to find
  The beauties hid from common sight.
              True Love. Stanza 1
Give plenty of what is given to you,
  And listen to pity's call;
Don't think the little you give is great
  And the much you get is small.
    A Legend of the Northland. I,
                        Stanza 8
Sometimes, I think, the things we see
Are shadows of the things to be;
  That what we plan we build;
That every hope that hath been crossed,
And every dream we thought was lost,
  In heaven shall be fulfilled.
    Dreams and Realities.[2] *Stanza 7*

---

[1] See Julia C. R. Dorr, page 562.
[2] Her last poem.

I'm done gone, Massa — step on me,
  And you can scale the wall!
              The Hero of Fort Wagner
And though hard be the task,
"Keep a stiff upper lip."
              Keep a Stiff Upper Lip
One sweetly solemn thought
  Comes to me o'er and o'er;
I am nearer home to-day
  Than I ever have been before.
              Nearer Home. Stanza 1
Kate Ketcham on a Winter's night
Went to a party dressed in white.
    Kate Ketcham (Parody on
        WHITTIER'S *Maud Muller)*
For of all the hard things to bear and
  grin,
The hardest is being taken in.
                              Ibid.
Her washing ended with the day,
  Yet lived she at its close,
And passed the long, long night away
  In darning ragged hose.
    The Wife (Parody on JAMES
        ALDRICH'S *A Death-Bed)* [1]
But when the sun in all its state
  Illumed the Eastern skies,
She passed about the kitchen grate
  And went to making pies.
                              Ibid.

PHILA HENRIETTA CASE
[*Floruit* 1864]

Oh! why does the wind blow upon me
  so wild?
Is it because I'm nobody's child?
              Nobody's Child. Stanza 1

ELIZABETH HANNAH
JOCELYN CLEAVELAND
[1824–1911]

I'm bound for heaven and when I'm
  there
I shall want my Book of Common
  Prayer,
And though I put on a starry crown,
I should feel quite lost without my
  gown.
      No Sects in Heaven [*1860*].
                        Stanza 4

---

[1] See James Aldrich, page 473.

Side by side, for the way was one,
The toilsome journey of life was done,
And priest and Quaker, and all who
    died,
Came out alike on the other side;
No forms or crosses, or books had they,
No gowns of silk, or suits of gray.

No Sects in Heaven [*1860*]
Stanza 23

GEORGE WILLIAM CURTIS
[1824–1892]

I walked beside the evening sea
And dreamed a dream that could not
    be;
The waves that plunged along the
    shore
Said only: "Dreamer, dream no more!"

Ebb and Flow. Stanza 1

In that calm Syrian afternoon, memory, a pensive Ruth, went gleaning the silent fields of childhood and found the scattered grain still golden and the morning sunlight fresh and fair.

The Howadji in Syria. Ave Maria

While we read history we make history.

The Call of Freedom

Every great crisis of human history is a pass of Thermopylae, and there is always a Leonidas and his three hundred to die in it, if they can not conquer.

Ibid.

Gentlemen, this is the convention of free speech, and I have been given the floor. I have only a few words to say to you, but I shall say them if I stand here until to-morrow morning.

At the Republican National Convention [*1860*]

Imagination is as good as many voyages — and how much cheaper.

Prue and I. Preface

Every mother who has lost an infant, has gained a child of immortal youth.

Ibid. Chap. 3

I think that to have known one good old man — one man who, through the chances and rubs of a long life, has carried his heart in his hand, like a palm branch, waving all discords into peace, helps our faith in God, in ourselves, and in each other, more than many sermons.

Prue and I. Chap. 4

Happiness is speechless.

Ibid.

It is not observed in history that families improve with time. It is rather discovered that the whole matter is like a comet, of which the brightest part is the head; and the tail, although long and luminous, is gradually shaded into obscurity.

Ibid. Chap. 6

The pride of ancestry increases in the ratio of distance.

Ibid.

It is a great pity that men and women forget that they have been children. Parents are apt to be foreigners to their sons and daughters. Maturity is the gate of Paradise which shuts behind us; and our memories are gradually weaned from the glories in which our nativity was cradled.

Ibid. Chap. 7

Love is the coldest of critics.

Ibid.

SYDNEY THOMPSON DOBELL
[1824–1874]

Children brave and free
Of the great Mother-tongue, and ye
    shall be
Lords of an empire wide as Shakespeare's soul,
Sublime as Milton's immemorial theme,
And rich as Chaucer's speech, and fair
    as Spenser's dream.

Sonnets on America

AMANDA M. EDMOND
[1824–1862]

Give me three grains of corn, mother,
Only three grains of corn;

Citizens! God reigns, and the Government at Washington still lives!

Address in Wall Street,
New York [April 15, 1865]

For mere vengeance I would do nothing. This nation is too great to look for mere revenge. But for the security of the future I would do everything.

Ibid.

I am not willing that this discussion should close without mention of the value of a true teacher. Give me a log hut, with only a simple bench, Mark Hopkins [1] on one end and I on the other, and you may have all the buildings, apparatus and libraries without him.

Address to Williams College
Alumni, New York [December
28, 1871] [2]

ROWLAND HOWARD
[Floruit 1876]

Waste not, want not, is a maxim I would teach.
Let your watchword be dispatch, and practise what you preach;
Do not let your chances like sunbeams pass you by,
For you never miss the water till the well runs dry.

You Never Miss the Water [3]

HELEN HUNT JACKSON
("SAXE HOLM")
[1831–1885]

O suns and skies and clouds of June,
And flowers of June together,
Ye cannot rival for one hour
October's bright blue weather.

October's Bright Blue Weather.
Stanza 1

The lesson of St. Christopher,
Who spent his strength for others,
And saved his soul by working hard

To help and save his brothers.

The Parable of St. Christopher.[1]
Stanza 54

Only a night from old to new,
Only a sleep from night to morn.
The new is but the old come true,
Each sunrise sees a new year born.

New Year's Morning. Stanza 3

Find me the men on earth who care
Enough for faith or creed to-day
To seek a barren wilderness
For simple liberty to pray.

The Pilgrim Forefathers. Stanza 5

Like a blind spinner in the sun,
I tread my days;
I know that all the threads will run
Appointed ways;
I know each day will bring its task,
And, being blind, no more I ask.

Spinning. Stanza 1

On the king's gate the moss grew gray;
The king came not. They called him dead
And made his eldest son one day
Slave in his father's stead.

Coronation. Stanza 10

Oh, write of me, not "Died in bitter pains,"
But "Emigrated to another star!"

Emigravit [2]

Father, I scarcely dare to pray,
So clear I see, now it is done,
How I have wasted half my day,
And left my work but just begun.

A Last Prayer. Stanza 1

My body, eh. Friend Death, how now?
Why all this tedious pomp of writ?
Thou hast reclaimed it sure and slow
For half a century, bit by bit.

Habeas Corpus.[3] Stanza 1

There is nothing so skilful in its own defence as imperious pride.

Ramona. Chap. 13

Wounded vanity knows when it is mortally hurt; and limps off the field, piteous, all disguises thrown away. But pride carries its banner to the last.

Ibid.

---

[1] Mark Hopkins [1802–1887], president of Williams College [1836–1872], and president of the American Board of Commissioners for Foreign Missions [1857–1881]. See Guiterman, page 815.

[2] In BURKE A. HINSDALE: *President Garfield and Education* [1882], P. 43.

[3] In *Peterson's Magazine*, 1876.

[1] In *St. Nicholas, January, 1876.*

[2] Emigravit is the inscription on the tombstone where he [Dürer] lies;
Dead he is not, but departed, — for the artist never dies.

LONGFELLOW: *Nuremberg, St. 13*

[3] Her last poem, left unfinished.

There cannot be found in the animal kingdom a bat, or any other creature, so blind in its own range of circumstance and connection, as the greater majority of human beings are in the bosoms of their families.

Ramona. Chap. 13

That indescribable expression peculiar to people who hope they have not been asleep, but know they have.

Ibid. Chap. 14

EDWARD ROBERT BULWER LYTTON, EARL OF LYTTON ("OWEN MEREDITH")
[1831–1891]

Since we parted yester eve,
I do love thee, love, believe,
Twelve times dearer, twelve hours longer —
One dream deeper, one night stronger,
One sun surer — thus much more
Than I loved thee, love, before.

Since We Parted

Death comes at last to all mankind;
Yet ere I die, I know not where,
I know not how, but I must find
Fair Yoland with the yellow hair.

Fair Yoland with the Yellow Hair. Stanza 13

The heart of a man's like that delicate weed
Which requires to be trampled on, boldly indeed,
Ere it gives forth the fragrance you wish to extract.[1]

Lucile.[2] Part I, Canto 1, IV

A dwarf on a dead giant's shoulders sees more
Than the 'live giant's eyesight availed to explore.[3]

Ibid. Canto 2, III

The man who seeks one thing in life, and but one,
May hope to achieve it before life be done;

But he who seeks all things, wherever he goes
Only reaps from the hopes which around him he sows
A harvest of barren regrets.

Lucile. Part I, Canto 2, IV

Let any man once show the world that he feels
Afraid of its bark, and 'twill fly at his heels:
Let him fearlessly face it, 'twill leave him alone:
But 'twill fawn at his feet if he flings it a bone.

Ibid. VII

The Italians have voices like peacocks; the Spanish
Smell, I fancy, of garlic; the Swedish and Danish
Have something too Runic, too rough and unshod, in
Their accent for mouths not descended from Odin;
German gives me a cold in the head, sets me wheezing
And coughing; and Russian is nothing but sneezing.

Ibid. XII

Whene'er I hear French spoken as I approve,
I feel myself quietly falling in love.

Ibid.

We may live without poetry, music and art;
We may live without conscience and live without heart;
We may live without friends; we may live without books;
But civilized man can not live without cooks.
He may live without books, — what is knowledge but grieving?
He may live without hope, — what is hope but deceiving?
He may live without love, — what is passion but pining?
But where is the man that can live without dining?

Ibid. XIX

The world is a nettle; disturb it, it stings:

---

[1] See Lyly, page 23.
[2] Lord Lytton, the Viceroy, who still lives in the literary hall of fame as the author of Lucile — a vast, stale Victorian piece of poetry. — WILLIAM E. WOODWARD: *Meet General Grant, Part 4, Chap. 30*
[3] See Burton, page 122.

Grasp it firmly, it stings not.[1]

Lucile. Part I, Canto 3, II

The face the most fair to our vision
allowed
Is the face we encounter and lose in the
crowd.
The thought that most thrills our existence is one
Which, before we can frame it in language, is gone.

Ibid. Canto 5, I

Having largely invested
Not only where treasure is never molested
By thieves, moth, or rust; but on this
earthly ball
Where interest was high, and security
small.

Ibid. Canto 6, XX

In Rome, — in the Forum, — there
opened one night
A gulf. All the augurs turned pale at
the sight.
In this omen the anger of Heaven they
read.
Men consulted the gods: then the
oracle said: —
"Ever open this gulf shall endure, till
at last
That which Rome hath most precious
within it be cast."
The Romans threw in their corn and
their stuff,
But the gulf yawned as wide. Rome
seemed likely enough
To be ruined ere this rent in her heart
she could choke.
Then Curtius, revering the oracle,
spoke:
"O Quirites! to this Heaven's question
has come:
What to Rome is most precious? The
manhood of Rome."
He plunged, and the gulf closed.[2]

Ibid. Part II, Canto 1, XVI

[1] See Aaron Hill, page 204.
[2] Marcus Curtius, legendary hero of Rome.
In 362 B. C., a chasm having been formed in
the Forum by an earthquake, the soothsayers
announced that it could be closed only by the
sacrifice of Rome's greatest treasure. Marcus
Curtius, a noble youth, declared that the state
possessed no greater treasure than a brave citizen in arms, and, in full armor, mounted on

There's no weapon that slays
Its victim so surely (if well aimed) as
praise.

Lucile. Part II, Canto 1, XX

A wink is as good as a nod to the wise.

Ibid. Canto 2, I

Those true eyes
Too pure and too honest in aught to
disguise
The sweet soul shining through them.[1]

Ibid. III

Thought alone is eternal.

Ibid. Canto 5, XV

A nun hath no nation.
Wherever man suffers or woman may
soothe,
There her land! there her kindred!

Ibid. Canto 6, XII

Love thou the rose, yet leave it on its
stem.

*The Wanderer, Prologue,
Part I, 19*

Oh, moment of sweet peril, perilous
sweet!
When woman joins herself to man.

Ibid. 27

I will not cant that commonplace of
friends,
Which never yet hath dried one
mourner's tears,
Nor say that grief's slow wisdom makes
amends
For broken hearts and desolated
years.

*The Wanderer in Italy.
A Love-Letter, 29*

I would that this woman's head
Were less golden about the hair:
I would her lips were less red,
And her face less deadly fair.

Ibid. The Vampire, 5

But I am sick of all the din
That's made in praising Verdi,
Who only know a violin
Is not a hurdy-gurdy.

*The Wanderer in France.
"Prensus in Aegaeo"*

his steed, leaped into the chasm, which closed
after him.
[1] Ils sont si transparents qu'ils laissent voir
votre âme.

THÉOPHILE GAUTIER: *The Two
Beautiful Eyes*

Could we find out her heart through
　　that velvet and lace!
　Can it beat without ruffling her sump-
　　tuous dress?
She will show us her shoulder, her
　　bosom, her face;
　But what the heart's like, we must
　　guess.
　　　　　The Wanderer in France.
　　　　　Madame La Marquise, 12
Of all the operas that Verdi wrote,
　The best, to my taste, is the Trova-
　　tore.
　　　　　Ibid. Aux Italiens, 2
And I think, in the lives of most women
　　and men,
　There's a moment when all would
　　go smooth and even,
If only the dead could find out when
　To come back, and be forgiven.
　　　　　Ibid. 27
Who knows how sculptor on sculptor
　　starved
With the thought in the head by the
　　hand uncarved?
And he that spread out in its ample
　　repose
That grand, indifferent, godlike brow,
How vainly his own may have ached,
　　who knows,
'Twixt the laurel above and the wrinkle
　　below?
　　　　　The Wanderer in England.
　　　　　Babylonia
　　　　The ages roll
Forward; and forward with them draw
　　my soul
Into Time's infinite sea.
And to be glad, or sad, I care no more;
But to have done and to have been, be-
　　fore
　I cease to do and be!
　　　　The Wanderer in Switzerland.
　　　　A Confession and Apology, 9
My life is a torn book. But at the end
A little page, quite fair, is saved, my
　　friend,
Where thou didst write thy name.
　　　　　The Wanderer in Holland.
　　　　　Jacqueline
Nor shall I leave thee wholly. I shall be
An evening thought, — a morning
　　dream to thee, —

A silence in thy life when, through the
　　night,
The bell strikes, or the sun, with sink-
　　ing light,
Smites all the empty windows.
　　　　　The Wanderer in Holland.
　　　　　Jacqueline
Death is no evil, since it comes to all.[1]
　　　　Palingenesis. Epilogue, Part I, 12
Ay, there are some good things in life,
　　that fall not away with the rest.
And, of all best things upon earth, I
　　hold that a faithful friend is the
　　best.
　　　　　Last Words
Talk not of genius baffled. Genius is
　　master of man.
Genius does what it must, and talent
　　does what it can.
　　　　　Ibid.
When Richelieu learned that Wallen-
　　stein was dead,
His thin face sharpened to an edge. He
　　said,
"Soon as the great tree falls, the rabble
　　run
To strip him of his branches one by
　　one."
　　　　　Wallenstein's Death

PHILIP HENRY SHERIDAN
[1831–1888]

The only good Indians I ever saw
were dead.[2]
　　　　Remark at Fort Cobb, Indian
　　　　Territory [January, 1869]

LOUISA MAY ALCOTT
[1832–1888]

A little kingdom I possess,
　Where thoughts and feelings dwell;

---

[1] That must be somehow best that comes
to all.
　　　　C. P. CRANCH: *Life and Death*
[2] Edward Sylvester Ellis [1840–1916] reported that after Custer's fight with Black
Kettle's band of Cheyenne Indians, the Co-
manche Chief Toch-a-way (Turtle Dove)
was presented to General Sheridan. The Indian
said: "Me Toch-a-way, me good Indian." The
General's reply has become a familiar quotation.

And very hard the task I find
Of governing it well.
> *Life, Letters and Journals.*
> *Chap. 3, My Kingdom,*[1] *Stanza 1*

I do not ask for any crown
But that which all may win;
Nor try to conquer any world
Except the one within.
> *Ibid. Stanza 4*

I had a pleasant time with my mind,
for it was happy.
> *Ibid.*

I know what death means, — a liberator for her, a teacher for us.[2]
> *Ibid. Chap. 5*

Resolved to take Fate by the throat
and shake a living out of her.
> *Ibid.*

Life is my college. May I graduate
well, and earn some honors!
> *Ibid.*

For such as he there is no death; —
His life the eternal life commands;
Above man's aims his nature rose.
The wisdom of a just content
Made one small spot a continent,
And tuned to poetry Life's prose.[3]
> *Life, Letters and Journals.*
> *Chap. 7, Thoreau's Flute,*[4] *Stanza 2*

My definition [of a philosopher] is
of a man up in a balloon, with his family and friends holding the ropes which
confine him to earth and trying to haul
him down.
> *Ibid. Chap. 10*

To smooth the rough and thorny way
Where other feet begin to tread;
To feed some hungry soul each day
With sympathy's sustaining bread.
> *Ibid. Chap. 11, My Prayer,*
> *Stanza 4*

Now I am beginning to live a little,
and feel less like a sick oyster at low
tide.
> *Ibid. Chap. 11*

A child her wayward pencil drew
On margins of her book:

---

[1] Written at the age of thirteen years.
[2] Miss Alcott's sister Beth.
[3] The word "tuned" is frequently misprinted
as "turned."
[4] In *The Atlantic Monthly, September,*
1863.

Garlands of flowers, dancing elves,
Bird, butterfly and brook.
Lessons undone, and play forgot,
Seeking with hand and heart
The teacher whom she learned to love
Before she knew 'twas Art.
> *Our Madonna.*[1] *Stanza 1*

Death, the stern sculptor, with a touch
No earthly power can stay,
Changes to marble in an hour
The beautiful, pale clay.
> *Ibid. Stanza 6*

Philosophers sit in their sylvan hall
And talk of the duties of man,
Of Chaos and Cosmos, Hegel and Kant,
With the Oversoul well in the van;
All on their hobbies they amble away
And a terrible dust they make;
Disciples devout both gaze and adore,
As daily they listen and bake.
> *Philosophers*[2]

ELIZABETH AKERS ALLEN
[1832–1911]

Backward, turn backward, O Time, in
your flight,
Make me a child again just for tonight!
> *Rock Me to Sleep.*[3] *Stanza 1*

Backward, flow backward, O tide of
the years!
I am so weary of toil and of tears —
Toil without recompense, tears all in
vain —
Take them and give me my childhood
again!
> *Ibid. Stanza 2*

Over my heart in the days that have
flown,
No love like mother-love ever has
shone;
No other worship abides and endures,

---

[1] May Alcott Neiriker, youngest of the Alcott sisters.
[2] Quoted by MRS. FLORENCE WHITING
BROWN: *Alcott and the Concord School of*
Philosophy [1926], *P. 46.*
[3] Written by Elizabeth Akers in May, 1860,
and sent to *The Saturday Evening Post* under
her pen-name, "Florence Percy." The poem
was published in that periodical on June 9,
1860.

Faithful, unselfish, and patient, like
yours.
                Rock Me to Sleep. Stanza 4

How much the heart may bear, and yet
    not break!
How much the flesh may suffer and not
    die!
I question much if any pain or ache
Of soul or body brings our end more
    nigh:
Death chooses his own time.
                Endurance. Stanza 1

Behold, we live through all things —
    famine, thirst,
Bereavement, pain; all grief and
    misery,
All woe and sorrow; life inflicts its
    worst
On soul and body — but we can not die,
Though we be sick, and tired, and faint,
    and worn, —
Lo, all things can be borne!
                Ibid. Stanza 5

Unremembered and afar
I watched you as I watched a star,
Through darkness struggling into view,
And loved you better than you knew.
                Left Behind. Stanza 5

And all the pain of lonely days,
    And nights with sleepless sorrow
        wild,
Hides in the quaint and stilted phrase,
    "An amiable child."
                "An Amiable Child." [1] *Stanza 15*

Let all unselfish spirits heed
The story of Johnny Appleseed.
He had another and prouder name
In far New England, whence he came,
But by this title, and this alone,

[1] On the stone marking the grave of St. Clair
Pollock, near Grant's Tomb, on Riverside
Drive, New York, is inscribed: "Erected to
the memory of an amiable child." The boy
died July 15, 1797, at the age of five years.
    At Riverside, on the slow hill-slant,
        Two memoried graves are seen;
    A granite dome is over Grant,
        And over a child the green.
            ANNA CATHERINE MARKHAM:
                An Amiable Child

Was the kindly wanderer loved and
    known.
                Johnny Appleseed. [1] *Stanza 1*
Carve not upon a stone when I am dead
    The praises which remorseful mourn-
        ers give
To women's graves — a tardy recom-
    pense —
    But speak them while I live.
                Till Death. Stanza 6

SIR EDWIN ARNOLD
[1832–1904]

He who died at Azan sends
This to comfort all his friends: —
Faithful friends! It lies I know
Pale and white and cold as snow;
And ye say, "Abdallah's dead!"
Weeping at the feet and head.
I can see your falling tears,
I can hear your sighs and prayers;
Yet I smile and whisper this:
I am not the thing you kiss.
Cease your tears and let it lie;
It was mine — it is not I.
                After Death in Arabia
Farewell, friends! Yet not farewell;
Where I am, ye too shall dwell.
I am gone before your face,
A moment's time, a little space.
                Ibid.
Ay! it will come, — the bitter hour! —
    but bringing
    A better love beyond, more subtle-
        sweet;
A higher road to tread, with happier
    singing,
    And no cross-ways to part familiar
        feet!
                The New Lucian
Not a face below the sun
But is precious — unto one!

[1] John Chapman [1775–1847].

One pouch with hoarded seed was packed,
From Penn-land cider-presses.
            WILLIAM HENRY VENABLE:
                Johnny Appleseed, St. 11
Long, long after,
When settlers put up beam and rafter,
They asked of the birds: "Who gave this
    fruit?"
            VACHEL LINDSAY: *Johnny
                Appleseed, Part III*

Not an eye, however dull,
But seems — somewhere — beautiful.
Facies non Omnibus Una
We are they who will not take
From palace, priest, or code,
A meaner Law than "Brotherhood" —
A lower Lord than God.
*Armageddon: A War Song of
the Future. Stanza 4*

And richer than red gold that dull
bronze seems,
Since it was bought with lavish waste
of worth
Whereto the wealth of Earth's gold-
sanded streams
Were but a lack, and dearth.
*The First Distribution of the
Victoria Cross, 1856. Stanza 4*

Don't poets know
Better than others?
God can't be always everywhere: and,
so,
Invented Mothers.
Mothers. Stanza 6

Somewhere there waiteth in this world
of ours
For one lone soul, another lonely
soul —
Each chasing each through all the
weary hours,
And meeting strangely at one sud-
den goal;
Then blend they — like green leaves
with golden flowers,
Into one beautiful and perfect
whole —
And life's long night is ended, and the
way
Lies open onward to eternal day.[1]
Destiny

[1] A sublime hope cheers ever the faithful
heart, that elsewhere, in other regions of the
universal powers, souls are now acting, enduring and daring, which can love us, and which
we can love.
R. W. EMERSON: *Friendship*

Two shall be born the whole wide world apart
And speak in different tongues and have no
thought
Each of the other's being and no heed.
And these o'er unknown seas to unknown
lands
Shall cross, escaping wreck, defying death;
And all unconsciously shape every act
And bend each wandering step to this one end,

We are the voices of the wandering
wind,
Which moan for rest and rest can never
find;
Lo! as the wind is, so is mortal life,
A moan, a sigh, a sob, a storm, a strife.
The Deva's Song

Never the spirit was born; the spirit
shall cease to be never;
Never was time it was not; End and
Beginning are dreams!
Birthless and deathless and changeless
remaineth the spirit for ever;
Death hath not touched it at all, dead
though the house of it seems.
*The Song Celestial (Translated
from The Bhagavad-Gita)*

The end of birth is death; the end of
death is birth: this is ordained.
Ibid.

WILLIAM CROSWELL DOANE
[1832–1913]

Their Lent is over, and their Easter
won.
Death

There stands in the garden of old St.
Mark
A sun-dial quaint and gray.
*"Horas non Numero Nisi Serenas."
Stanza 1*

"I number none but the cloudless
hours," [1]
Its motto the live day long.
Ibid. Stanza 2

I am quite sure he thinks that I am
God —
Since he is God on whom each one de-
pends
For life and all things that His bounty
sends —
My dear old dog, most constant of all
friends.
Cluny

He had lived out his life, but not his
love;

That one day out of darkness they shall meet
And read life's meaning in each other's eyes.
SUSAN MARR SPALDING [1841–1908]:
Fate, St. 1

[1] See Hazlitt, page 330.

Daily up steep and weary stair he
   came,
His big heart bursting with the strain,
   to prove
His loneliness without me.
                In Memory of Cluny,
                   May 24–25, 1902

CHARLES LUTWIDGE DODG-SON ("LEWIS CARROLL")
[1832–1898]

Alice! a childish story take
   And with a gentle hand
Lay it where childhood's dreams are
   twined
   In Memory's mystic band,
Like pilgrim's withered wreath of flow-
   ers
   Plucked in a far-off land.
         Alice's Adventures in Wonder-
            land. Introduction
"You are old, Father William," the
   young man said,
   "And your hair has become very
   white;
And yet you incessantly stand on your
   head —
   Do you think, at your age, it is
   right?" [1]
                Ibid. Chap. 5
"Really, now you ask me," said
Alice, very much confused, "I don't
think — "
"Then you shouldn't talk," said the
Hatter.
                Ibid. Chap. 7
"Tut, tut, child," said the Duchess.
"Everything's got a moral if only you
can find it."
                Ibid. Chap. 9
Take care of the sense and the sounds
will take care of themselves.
                Ibid.
"Reeling and Writhing, of course, to
begin with," the Mock Turtle replied,
"and the different branches of Arith-
metic — Ambition, Distraction, Uglifi-
cation, and Derision."
                Ibid.
Child of the pure, unclouded brow
   And dreaming eyes of wonder!

[1] See Southey, page 320.

Though time be fleet and I and thou
   Are half a life asunder,
Thy loving smile will surely hail
The love-gift of a fairy-tale.
         Through the Looking-Glass and
            What Alice Found There. In-
            troduction
'Twas brillig, and the slithy toves
   Did gyre and gimble in the wabe;
All mimsy were the borogoves,
   And the mome raths outgrabe.
         Ibid. Chap. 1 (Jabberwocky.
                Stanza 1)
He chortled in his joy.
                Ibid. (Stanza 6)
"The horror of that moment," the
King went on, "I shall never, *never* for-
get!"
"You will, though," the Queen said,
"if you don't make a memorandum of
it."
                Ibid.
"A slow sort of country," said the
Queen. "Now, *here,* you see, it takes all
the running you can do, to keep in the
same place. If you want to get some-
where else, you must run at least twice
as fast as that!"
                Ibid. Chap. 2
"The time has come," the Walrus said,
   "To talk of many things:
Of shoes — and ships — and sealing-
   wax —
Of cabbages — and kings —
And why the sea is boiling hot —
   And whether pigs have wings."
         Ibid. Chap. 4, The Walrus and
            the Carpenter, Stanza 11
"The rule is, jam to-morrow, and
jam yesterday — but never jam *to-*
day."
"It *must* come sometimes to 'jam to-
day,' " Alice objected.
"No, it can't," said the Queen. "It's
jam every *other* day: to-day isn't any
other day, you know."
                Ibid. Chap. 5
"When I use a word," Humpty-
Dumpty said, "it means just what I
choose it to mean — neither more nor
less."
                Ibid. Chap. 6

As large as life and twice as natural.
*Through the Looking Glass and
What Alice Found There.
Chap. 7*

He had bought a large map represent-
ing the sea,
Without the least vestige of land:
And the crew were much pleased when
they found it to be
A map they could all understand.
*The Hunting of the Snark.
Fit the Second, Stanza 2*

"What's the good of Mercator's North
Poles and Equators,
Tropics, Zones and Meridian Lines?"
So the Bellman would cry: and the
crew would reply
"They are merely conventional
signs!"
Ibid. Stanza 3

It is this, it is this that oppresses my
soul.
Ibid. Fit the Third, Stanza 11

And my heart is like nothing so much
as a bowl
Brimming over with quivering curds.
Ibid.

You may charge me with murder — or
want of sense —
(We are all of us weak at times):
But the slightest approach to a false
pretence
Was never among my crimes!
Ibid. Fit the Fourth, Stanza 4

And summed it so well that it came to
far more
Than the Witnesses ever had said!
Ibid. Fit the Sixth, Stanza 11

There are certain things — as, a spider,
a ghost,
The income-tax, gout, an umbrella
for three —
That I hate, but the thing that I hate
the most
Is a thing they call the Sea.
A Sea Dirge. Stanza 1

Then, if you'd be impressive,
Remember what I say,
That abstract qualities begin
With capitals alway:

The Good, the True, the Beautiful, —
Those are the things that pay!
*Poeta Fit, non Nascitur.
Stanza 5*

Such epithets, like pepper,
Give zest to what you write;
And, if you strew them sparely,
They whet the appetite:
But if you lay them on too thick,
You spoil the matter quite!
Ibid. Stanza 10

Where Life becomes a Spasm,
And History a Whiz:
If that is not Sensation,
I don't know what it is.
Ibid. Stanza 16

And I said "This is scrumptious!" —
a phrase I had learned from the
Devonshire shrimpers.
*Atalanta in Camden-Town.
Stanza 4*

What *you* call healthy appetite
I feel as Hunger's savage tooth:
And, when no dinner is in sight,
The dinner-bell's a sound of ruth! [1]
Peter and Paul. Stanza 17

BENJAMIN H. HILL
[1832–1882]

He was a foe without hate, a friend
without treachery, a soldier without
cruelty, and a victim without murmuring. He was a public officer without
vices, a private citizen without wrong,
a neighbor without reproach, a Christian without hypocrisy, and a man without guilt. He was Caesar without his
ambition, Frederick without his tyranny, Napoleon without his selfishness,
and Washington without his reward.
Tribute to Robert E. Lee. [2]

[1] Noon. As the Texas darky said: "Dinner-
time fur some folks; but just twelve o'clock
fur me!" — IRVIN SHREWSBURY COBB: *Paths
of Glory* [1915], *Chap. 5*
[2] Quoted in *General Lee* by FITZHUGH LEE
and in *Robert E. Lee* by THOMAS NELSON
PAGE.

NORA PERRY
[1832–1896]

Tying her bonnet under her chin,
She tied her raven ringlets in;
But not alone in the silken snare
Did she catch her lovely floating hair,
For, tying her bonnet under her chin,
She tied a young man's heart within.
The Love-Knot. Stanza 1

O, did you see him riding down,
And riding down, while all the town
Came out to see, came out to see,
And all the bells rang mad with glee?
Riding Down. Stanza 1

What silences we keep, year after year,
With those who are most near to us,
and dear! [1]
Too Late. Stanza 1

Some day of days, threading the street
With idle, heedless pace,
Unlooking for such grace,
I shall behold your face!
Some Day of Days. Stanza 1

Who knows the thoughts of a child?
Who Knows? Stanza 1

Gayly and gayly rang the gay music,
The blithe merry music of harp and of
horn,
The mad, merry music, that set us a-
dancing
Till over the midnight came stealing
the morn.
That Waltz of von Weber's.
Stanza 1

They sat and combed their beautiful
hair,
Their long, bright tresses, one by
one,
As they laughed and talked in the
chamber there,
After the revel was done.
After the Ball. Stanza 1

---

[1] Often, the sayings which are dearest to our hearts are least frequent on our lips; and those great ideas which cheer men in their direst struggles are not things which they are likely to inflict by frequent repetition upon those they live with. There is a certain reticence with us as regards anything we deeply love. — SIR ARTHUR HELPS [1813–1875]: *Friends in Council*

THEODORE WATTS-DUNTON
[1832–1914]

Love's old songs shall never die
Yet the new shall suffer proof:
Love's old drink of Yule brew I,
Wassail for new love's behoof.
Christmas at the Mermaid Tavern

A sonnet is a wave of melody.
The Sonnet's Voice

HENRY CLAY WORK
[1832–1884]

At the captain's forequarters they said
he would pass —
They'd train him up well in the in-
fantry class —
So they've grafted him into the
Army.
Grafted into the Army. Stanza 1

So we made a thoroughfare for Free-
dom and her train,
Sixty miles in latitude; three hundred
to the main.
Marching through Georgia.
Stanza 5

It mus' be now de kingdom coming,
An' de year ob Jubilo!
Kingdom Coming. Chorus

O don't you know dat
Babylon is fallen,
An' we's gwine to occupy de land?
Babylon Is Fallen. Chorus

Nicodemus, the slave, was of African
birth,
And was bought for a bag full of
gold:
He was reckoned as part of the salt of
the earth,
But he died, years ago, very old.
Wake Nicodemus. Stanza 1

There's a good time coming, it's almost
here,
'Twas a long, long time on the way.
Ibid. Chorus

Father, dear father, come home with
me now,
The clock in the steeple strikes one;
You said you were coming right home
from the shop
As soon as your day's work was done.
Come Home, Father. Stanza 1

My grandfather's clock was too large
    for the shelf,
So it stood ninety years on the floor.
                    Grandfather's Clock
But it stopped short — never to go
    again —
When the old man died.
                    Ibid.

ISAAC HILL BROMLEY
[1833–1898]

Listen! John A. Logan is the Head
Center, the Hub, the King Pin, the
Main Spring, Mogul and Mugwump [1]
of the final plot by which partisanship
was installed in the Commission.
                Editorial in New York Tribune
                    [February 16, 1877]
Bring me honey of Hymettus, bring me
    stores of Attic salt;
I am weary of the commonplace, to dul-
    ness call a halt!
These dinner speeches tire me, they are
    tedious, flat, and stale:
From a hundred thousand banquet ta-
    bles comes a melancholy wail,
As a hundred thousand banqueters sit
    up in evening dress
And salute each mouldy chestnut with
    a signal of distress.
                Our Chauncey.[2] *Stanza 2*

RICHARD WATSON DIXON
[1833–1900]

Forth comes the moon, the sweet sur-
    prise of heaven,
And her footfall light
Drops on the multiplied wave.
                    The Spirit Wooed
I must have love in my degree,
    A human heart, a human hand.
For oh! 'tis better far to share,
    Though life all dark and bitter be,
With human bosoms human care.
                    The Wanderer

[1] A mugwump is a person educated beyond
his intellect.
        HORACE PORTER [1837–1921] in the
        Cleveland-Blaine campaign [1884].
[2] In praise of Chauncey M. Depew. Read at
the annual dinner of the New York Yale
Alumni Association [Jan. 23, 1891].

There is a soul above the soul of each,
A mightier soul, which yet to each be-
    longs:
There is a sound made of all human
    speech,
And numerous as the concourse of all
    songs.
                    Humanity

ADAM LINDSAY GORDON
[1833–1870]

Question not, but live and labour
    Till yon goal be won,
Helping every feeble neighbour,
    Seeking help from none;
Life is mostly froth and bubble,
    Two things stand like stone —
Kindness in another's trouble,
    Courage in our own.
                    Ye Wearie Wayfarer.
                Finis Exoptatus, Stanza 8
For good undone and gifts misspent
    and resolutions vain,
    'Tis somewhat late to trouble. This
        I know —
I should live the same life over, if I had
    to live again;
    And the chances are I go where most
        men go.
                    The Sick Stockrider
A little season of love and laughter,
    Of light and life, and pleasure and
        pain,
And a horror of outer darkness after,
    And dust returneth to dust again.
                    The Swimmer
In a thousand years we shall all forget
The things that trouble us now.
                    After the Quarrel
On earth there's little worth a sigh,
    And nothing worth a tear!
                To My Sister. Stanza 8
Lay me low, my work is done,
    I am weary. Lay me low.
                    Valedictory

JOHN JAMES INGALLS
[1833–1900]

The purification of politics is an iridescent dream.
                    Epigram

Every man is the center of a circle, whose fatal circumference he can not pass.

Eulogy on Benjamin Hill, United States Senate [January 23, 1882]

In the democracy of the dead, all men at last are equal. There is neither rank nor station nor prerogative in the republic of the grave.

On the Death of Senator Barnes

Next in profusion to the divine profusion of water, light and air, those three physical facts which render existence possible, may be reckoned the universal beneficence of grass.

Blue Grass

Grass is the forgiveness of nature — her constant benediction. Fields trampled with battle, saturated with blood, torn with the ruts of the cannon, grow green again with grass, and carnage is forgotten. Forests decay, harvests perish, flowers vanish, but grass is immortal.

Ibid.

It bears no blazonry of bloom to charm the senses with fragrance or splendor, but its homely hue is more enchanting than the lily or the rose. It yields no fruit in earth or air, and yet, should its harvest fail for a single year, famine would depopulate the world.

Ibid.

I knock unbidden once at every gate!
If sleeping, wake; if feasting, rise before
I turn away. It is the hour of fate.

Opportunity

ROBERT GREEN INGERSOLL
[1833–1899]

These heroes are dead. They died for liberty — they died for us. They are at rest. They sleep in the land they made free, under the flag they rendered stainless, under the solemn pines, the sad hemlocks, the tearful willows, the embracing vines. They sleep beneath the shadows of the clouds, careless alike of sunshine or storm, each in the windowless palace of rest. Earth may run red with other wars — they are at peace. In the midst of battles, in the roar of conflict, they found the serenity of death.

Vision of War [Speech at Indianapolis, Indiana, September 21, 1876; repeated by request in the Metropolitan Opera House, New York, May 30, 1888]

Life is a narrow vale between the cold and barren peaks of two eternities. We strive in vain to look beyond the heights. We cry aloud — and the only answer is the echo of our wailing cry. From the voiceless lips of the unreplying dead there comes no word. But in the night of Death Hope sees a star and listening Love can hear the rustling of a wing.

At the Grave of his Brother, Ebon Clark Ingersoll [June, 1879] [1]

He added to the sum of human joy, and were every one to whom he did some loving service to bring a blossom to his grave, he would sleep to-night beneath a wilderness of flowers.

Ibid.

I am the inferior of any man whose rights I trample under foot. Men are not superior by reason of the accidents of race or color. They are superior who have the best heart — the best brain.

Liberty

The superior man is the providence of the inferior. He is eyes for the blind, strength for the weak, and a shield for the defenseless. He stands erect by bending above the fallen. He rises by lifting others.

Ibid.

Every cradle asks us, "Whence?" and every coffin, "Whither?" The poor barbarian, weeping above his dead, can answer these questions as intelligently as the robed priest of the most authentic creed.

Address at a Little Boy's Grave

[1] Read at the service for Luther Burbank [April 14, 1926].

We, too, have our religion, and it is this: Help for the living, hope for the dead.

Address at a Little Boy's Grave

I would rather have been a French peasant and worn wooden shoes. I would rather have lived in a hut with a vine growing over the door and the grapes growing purple in the kisses of the Autumn sun. I would rather have been that poor peasant with my loving wife by my side, knitting as the day died out of the sky, with my children upon my knee and their arms about me. I would rather have been that man and gone down to the tongueless silence of the dreamless dust than to have been that imperial impersonation of force and murder known as Napoleon the Great.

At the Tomb of Napoleon

And will there, some time, be another world? We have our dream. The idea of immortality, that like a sea has ebbed and flowed in the human heart, beating with its countless waves against the sands and rocks of time and fate, was not born of any creed, nor of any book, nor of any religion. It was born of human affection, and it will continue to ebb and flow beneath the mists and clouds of doubt and darkness, as long as love kisses the lips of death.

At the Bier of a Friend

Few rich men own their own property. The property owns them.

Address to the McKinley League, Carnegie Hall, New York [October 29, 1896]

An honest God is the noblest work of man.

Epigram

Though Scotland boasts a thousand names,
  Of patriot, king and peer,
The noblest, grandest of them all
  Was loved and cradled here.

The Birthplace of Burns, Ayr [1]
[*August 19, 1878*]

[1] This poem hangs in the Burns birthplace, Ayr.

And here the world, through all the years,
  As long as day returns,
The tribute of its love and tears
  Will pay to Robert Burns.

The Birthplace of Burns, Ayr
[*August 19, 1878*]

Justice is the only worship.
Love is the only priest.
Ignorance is the only slavery.
Happiness is the only good.
The time to be happy is now,
The place to be happy is here,
The way to be happy is to make others so.

Creed

Is there beyond the silent night
  An endless day?
Is death a door that leads to light?
  We cannot say.

Declaration of the Free. Stanza 16

DAVID ROSS LOCKE
("PETROLEUM V. NASBY")
[1833–1888]

The contract 'twixt Hannah, God and me,
Was not for one or twenty years, but for eternity.

Hannah Jane. [1] *Stanza 29*

JULIA HARRIS MAY
[1833–1912]

Slower, sweet June,
Each step more slow;
Linger and loiter as you go.

Slower, Sweet June. Stanza 1

If we could know
Which of us, darling, would be first to go,
Which would be first to breast the swelling tide,
And step alone upon the other side,
  If we could know!

If We Could Know. Stanza 1

[1] In *Harper's Monthly, October, 1871.*

EMILY HUNTINGTON MILLER
[1833–1913]

Hang up the baby's stocking;
  Be sure you don't forget
The dear little dimpled darling!
  She ne'er saw Christmas yet.
      Hang Up the Baby's Stocking

SIR LEWIS MORRIS
[1833–1907]

The wind that sighs before the dawn
  Chases the gloom of night,
The curtains of the East are drawn,
  And suddenly — 'tis light.
      Le Vent de l'Esprit. Stanza 1

There shall rise from this confused
    sound of voices
  A firmer faith than that our fathers
    knew,
A deep religion which alone rejoices
  In worship of the Infinitely True.
      Brotherhood. Stanza 1

Call no faith false which e'er hath
    brought
  Relief to any laden life,
Cessation from the pain of thought,
  Refreshment 'mid the dust of strife.
      Tolerance. Stanza 1

CHARLES CARROLL SAWYER
[1833– ?]

When this cruel war is over,
Praying that we meet again.
      *Weeping, Sad and Lonely (When
      This Cruel War is Over)*

EDMUND CLARENCE STEDMAN
[1833–1908]

Prison-mate and dock-yard fellow,
  Blades to Meg and Molly dear,
Off to capture Porto Bello
Sailed with Morgan the Buccaneer!
      Morgan.[1] Stanza 1

[1] The old bold mate of Henry Morgan.
    JOHN MASEFIELD: *Captain Stratton's
      Fancy*

Where's he that died o' Wednesday?[1]
What place on earth hath he?
      Falstaff's Song. Stanza 1

Just where the Treasury's marble front
  Looks over Wall Street's mingled na-
    tions;
Where Jews and Gentiles most are wont
  To throng for trade and last quota-
    tions.
      Pan in Wall Street. Stanza 1

Give me to die unwitting of the day,
And stricken in Life's brave heat, with
    senses clear!
      Sonnet, Mors Benefica

Crops failed; wealth took a flight;
    house, treasure, land,
  Slipped from my hold — thus plenty
    comes and goes.
One friend I had, but he too loosed his
    hand
  (Or was it I?) the year I met with
    Rose.
      The World Well Lost. Stanza 2

Not braver he that leaps the wall
  By level musket-flashes litten,
Than I, who stepped before them all,
  Who longed to see me get the mitten.
      On the Doorstep. Stanza 2

"Oh, anywhere! Forward! 'Tis all the
    same, Colonel:
You'll find lovely fighting along the
    whole line!"
      Kearny[2] at Seven Pines. Stanza 3

Look on this cast, and know the hand
  That bore a nation in its hold:
From this mute witness understand
  What Lincoln was, — how large of
    mould.
      The Hand of Lincoln. Stanza 1

Give us a man of God's own mould,
  Born to marshal his fellow-men;
One whose fame is not bought and sold
  At the stroke of a politician's pen.
      Wanted — a Man. Stanza 2

Not thou, not thou — 'tis we
Are deaf, are dumb, are blind!
      Helen Keller. Stanza 4

[1] See Shakespeare, page 63.
[2] General Philip Kearny [1815–1862].

JULIA LOUISE MATILDA WOODRUFF
("W. M. L. JAY")
[1833–1909]

Out of the strain of the doing,
Into the peace of the done.

Gone

HORATIO ALGER
[1834–1899]

'Twas on Lake Erie's broad expanse,
  One bright midsummer day,
The gallant steamer Ocean Queen
  Swept proudly on her way.

John Maynard.[1] Stanza 1

Three hundred grateful voices rise
  In praise to God that He
Hath saved them from the fearful fire,
  And from the engulfing sea.

Ibid. Stanza 11

GEORGE ARNOLD
[1834–1865]

"Learn while you're young," he often said,
"There is much to enjoy down here below;
Life for the living, and rest for the dead!"
Said the jolly old pedagogue, long ago.

The Jolly Old Pedagogue. Stanza 2

"The living need charity more than the dead."

Ibid. Stanza 3

"I need so little," he often said,
"And my friends and relatives here below

[1] John Maynard was a pilot on a steamboat plying between Detroit and Buffalo. The steamer did not carry boats, and one summer afternoon, when proceeding with large quantities of resin and tar on board, it caught fire, seven miles from Buffalo. Passengers and crew crowded the forward part of the ship. John Maynard stayed at the helm and beached the ship, all lives being saved except his own. — JOHN B. GOUGH [1817–1886]: *Sermon*

And, sure's you're born, they all got off
  Afore the smokestacks fell, —
And Bludso's ghost went up alone
  In the smoke of the Prairie Belle.
JOHN HAY [1838–1905]:
Jim Bludso, St. 6

Won't litigate over me when I am dead."

The Jolly Old Pedagogue. Stanza 4

I,
Being dry,
Sit, idly sipping here
My Beer.

Beer

O, finer far
Than fame, or riches, are
The graceful smoke-wreaths of this free cigar!

Ibid.

Gray distance hid each shining sail,
  By ruthless breezes borne from me;
And lessening, fading, faint, and pale
  My ships went forth to sea.

Jubilate. Stanza 1

SIR JOHN LUBBOCK, LORD AVEBURY
[1834–1913]

The world would be better and brighter if our teachers would dwell on the Duty of Happiness as well as on the Happiness of Duty, for we ought to be as cheerful as we can, if only because to be happy ourselves is a most effectual contribution to the happiness of others.

The Pleasures of Life. Page 2

As the sun colors flowers, so does art color life.

Ibid. Page 177

The idle man does not know what it is to enjoy rest. Hard work, moreover, not only tends to give us rest for the body, but, what is even more important, peace to the mind.

Ibid. Page 316

SABINE BARING-GOULD
[1834–1924]

Crowns and thrones may perish,
  Kingdoms rise and wane,
But the church of Jesus
  Constant will remain.

Onward, Christian Soldiers

Now the day is over,
  Night is drawing nigh;

Shadows of the evening
Steal across the sky.
　　　Now the Day Is Over. Stanza 1
Comfort every sufferer
Watching late in pain;
Those who plan some evil,
From their sin restrain.
　　　Ibid. Stanza 5

CHARLES FARRAR BROWNE ("ARTEMUS WARD")
[1834–1867]

My pollertics, like my religion, being of an exceedin' accommodatin' character.
　　　The Crisis
The fack can't be no longer disgised that a Krysis is onto us.
　　　Ibid.
I am not a politician, and my other habits are good.
　　　Fourth of July Oration
The prevailin' weakness of most public men is to Slop over. G. Washington never slopt over.
　　　Ibid.
I can't sing. As a singist I am not a success. I am saddest when I sing. So are those who hear me. They are sadder even than I am.
　　　Artemus Ward's Lecture
N. B. This is rote Sarcastikul.
　　　A Visit to Brigham Young
Did you ever have the measels, and if so, how many?
　　　The Census
I have alreddy given Two cousins to the war, & I stand reddy to sacrifiss my wife's brother ruther 'n not see the rebelyin krusht. And if wuss comes to wuss, I'll shed ev'ry drop of blud my able-bodid relations has got.
　　　To the Prince of Wales
Why is this thus? What is the reason of this thusness?
　　　Moses, the Sassy
He is dreadfully married. "He's the most married man I ever saw in my life."
　　　Ibid.

Let us all be happy and live within our means, even if we have to borrow the money to do it with.
　　　Natural History
The sun has a right to "set" where it wants to, and so, I may add, has a hen.
　　　A Morman Romance. IV
They cherish his mem'ry, and them as sell picturs of his birth-place, etc., make it prof'tible cherishin' it.
　　　At the Tomb of Shakespeare

GEORGE LOUIS PALMELLA BUSSON DU MAURIER
[1834–1896]

He had never heard such music as this, never dreamt such music was possible. He was conscious, while it lasted, that he saw deeper into the beauty, the sadness of things, the very heart of them, and their pathetic evanescence, as with a new inner eye — even into eternity itself, beyond the veil.
　　　Trilby.[1] Part I
Meat so dressed and sauced and seasoned that you didn't know whether it was beef or mutton — flesh, fowl, or good red herring.[2]
　　　Ibid.
Lovely female shapes are terrible complicators of the difficulties and dangers of this earthly life, especially for their owner.
　　　Ibid.
A wave of religious emotion rolled over Little Billee and submerged him; swept him off his little legs, swept him out of his little self, drowned him in a great seething surge of love — love of his kind, love of love, love of life, love of death, love of all that is and ever was and ever will be.
　　　Ibid. Part III
That is the worst of those dear people who have charm; they are so terrible to do without, when once you

[1] *Trilby* was published serially in *Harper's Monthly,* beginning with the January, 1894 issue.
[2] See Heywood, page 13.

have got accustomed to them and all their ways.

Trilby. Part V

Every single phrase is a string of perfect gems, of purest ray serene,[1] strung together on a loose golden thread.

Ibid. Part VI

She was one of those rarely gifted beings who cannot look or speak or even stir without waking up (and satisfying) some vague longing that lies dormant in the hearts of most of us.

Ibid. Part VII

There can be prayers without words just as well as songs, I suppose.

Ibid. Part VIII

Grief tires more than anything, and brings a deeper slumber.

Ibid.

A little work, a little play,
To keep us going — and so, good-day!

A little warmth, a little light,
Of love's bestowing — and so, good-night![2]

---

[1] Full many a gem of purest ray serene.
THOMAS GRAY: *Elegy in a Country Churchyard, St. 14*

[2]   La vie est vaine:
Un peu d'amour,
Un peu de haine, . . .
Et puis — Bonjour!

La vie est brève:
Un peu d'espoir,
Un peu de rêve
Et puis — Bon soir!
LEON MONTENAEKEN [1859–   ]:
Peu de Chose
Ah, brief is Life,
Love's short sweet way,
With dreamings rife,
And then — Good-day!

And Life is vain —
Hope's vague delight,
Grief's transient pain,
And then — Good-night.
Translation by LOUISE
CHANDLER MOULTON

In *The London Daily Express, July 3, 1902,* a third stanza by Montenaeken was published with a somewhat imperfect translation:
La vie est telle
Que Dieu le fit;

A little fun, to match the sorrow
Of each day's growing — and so, good-morrow!

A little trust that when we die
We reap our sowing! and so — good-by!

Trilby. Part VIII

That aristocratic flavor, so grateful and comforting to scholar and ignoramus alike, which the costly British public-school system (and the British accent) alone can impart to a dead language.

Peter Ibbetson. Page 49

The wretcheder one is, the more one smokes; and the more one smokes, the wretcheder one gets — a vicious circle![1]

Ibid. Page 135

I do not know if little dogs cause as large griefs when they die as big ones.

Ibid. Page 152

There is an old French air,
A little song of loneliness and grief —
Simple as nature, sweet beyond compare —
And sad — past all belief!

Ibid. Page 153 (The Chime. Stanza 1)

Songs without words are best.

Ibid. Page 162

What matter if it be a fool's paradise?[2] Paradise is paradise, for whoever owns it!

Ibid. Page 265

What matters what anybody thinks? "It will be all the same a hundred years hence." That is the most sensible proverb ever invented.

Ibid. Page 268

Et telle quelle —
Elle suffit!

Life is but such
As wrought God's will;
'Tis naught, and still —
'Tis oft too much!

[1] Bobus, you are in a vicious circle, rounder than one of your own sausages. — THOMAS CARLYLE: *Past and Present, Book I, Chap. 5.*

[2] See Shakespeare, page 79.

I have no talent for making new friends, but oh, such a genius for fidelity to old ones!

Peter Ibbetson. Page 276

There is both an impertinence and a lack of taste in any man's laying bare to the public eye — to any eye — the bliss that has come to him through the love of a devoted woman, with whose life his own has been bound up.

Ibid. Page 305

Happiness is like time and space — we make and measure it ourselves; it is a fancy — as big, as little, as you please; just a thing of contrasts and comparisons.

Ibid. Page 399

All will be well for us all, and of such a kind that all who do not sigh for the moon will be well content.

Ibid. Page 415

CHARLES WILLIAM ELIOT
[1834–1926]

Carrier of news and knowledge
Instrument of trade and commerce
Promoter of mutual acquaintance
Among men and nations and hence
Of peace and good will.

Carrier of love and sympathy
Messenger of friendship
Consoler of the lonely
Servant of the scattered family
Enlarger of the public life.

Inscriptions for the East and West Pavilions, Post Office, Washington, D. C.[1]

[1] These inscriptions were edited by Woodrow Wilson, to read:

Carrier of news and knowledge
Instrument of trade and
Promoter of mutual acquaintance
Of peace and good will
Among men and nations.

Messenger of sympathy and love
Servant of parted friends
Consoler of the lonely
Bond of the scattered family
Enlarger of the common life.

MARY ANNE HEARN
("MARIANNE FARNING-HAM")
[1834–1909]

I cannot tell why there should come to me
A thought of someone miles and years away.

Unforgotten. Stanza 1

Will any one there, at the beautiful gate,
Be waiting and watching for me?

Waiting and Watching for Me. Stanza 1

WALTER KITTREDGE
[1834–1905]

We're tenting to-night on the old camp-ground,
Give us a song to cheer
Our weary hearts, a song of home
And friends we love so dear.

Tenting on the Old Camp-ground. Stanza 1

WILLIAM MORRIS
[1834–1896]

I know a little garden-close,
Set thick with lily and red rose,
Where I would wander if I might
From dewy morn to dewy night.

The Life and Death of Jason. A Garden by the Sea, Stanza 1

The idle singer of an empty day.

The Earthly Paradise. An Apology, Stanza 1

Dreamer of dreams, born out of my due time,
Why should I strive to set the crooked straight?

Ibid. Stanza 4

Masters, I have to tell a tale of woe,
A tale of folly and of wasted life,
Hope against hope, the bitter dregs of strife,
Ending, where all things end, in death at last.

Ibid. Prologue

Forget six counties overhung with smoke,

Forget the snorting steam and piston
    stroke,
Forget the spreading of the hideous
    town;
Think rather of the pack-horse on the
    down,
And dream of London, small, and white,
    and clean.
      The Earthly Paradise. Prologue
Love is enough, though the world be
    a-waning.
               Love Is Enough

RODEN BERKELEY
WRIOTHESLEY NOEL
[1834–1894]

After battle sleep is best,
    After noise, tranquillity.
                   The Old
The bass eternal of the sea.
                   Beatrice
Ah! what if some unshamed iconoclast
Crumbling old fetish raiments of the
    past,
Rises from dead cerements the Christ
    at last?
What if men take to following where
    He leads,
Weary of mumbling Athanasian creeds?
               The Red Flag

RICHARD REALF
[1834–1878]

Back of the canvas that throbs, the
    painter is hinted and hidden;
Into the statue that breathes, the soul
    of the sculptor is bidden.
          Indirection. Stanza 3
Back of the sound broods the silence,
    back of the gift stands the giving;
Back of the hand that receives thrill
    the sensitive nerves of receiving.
             Ibid. Stanza 4
Harms of the world have come unto us,
    Cups of sorrow we yet shall drain;
But we have a secret that doth show us
    Wonderful rainbows in the rain.
       An Old Man's Idyl. Stanza 7
Here, gathered from all places and all
    time,

The waifs of wisdom and of folly meet.
             In a Scrap-Book

ABRAM JOSEPH RYAN
[1834–1886]

But far on the deep there are billows
That never shall break on the beach;
And I have heard songs in the Silence
That never shall float into speech.
      Song of the Mystic. Stanza 9
I wish I were the little key
That locks Love's Captive in.
    A Child's Wish Before an Altar.
                   Stanza 1
When falls the soldier brave,
Dead at the feet of wrong,
The poet sings and guards his grave
With sentinels of song.
        Sentinel Songs. Stanza 1
Hearts that are great are always lone,
They never will manifest their best;
Their greatest greatness is unknown —
Earth knows a little — God, the rest.
          A Thought. Stanza 3
A land without ruins is a land with-
out memories — a land without mem-
ories is a land without history.
         A Land Without Ruins.
                  Foreword
Crowns of roses fade — crowns of
thorns endure. Calvaries and crucifixions take deepest hold of humanity —
the triumphs of might are transient —
they pass and are forgotten — the sufferings of right are graven deepest on
the chronicle of nations.
                   Ibid.

HENRY THOMPSON STANTON
[1834–1898]

Ah, search the wide world wherever
    you can,
There is no open door for the money-
    less man!
      The Moneyless Man. Stanza 1

FRANK RICHARD STOCKTON
[1834–1902]

He could open either door he pleased.
. . . If he opened the one, there came
out of it a hungry tiger, the fiercest and

most cruel that could be procured, which immediately sprang upon him, and tore him to pieces, as a punishment for his guilt. . . . But if the accused person opened the other door, there came forth from it a lady, the most suitable to his years and station that his Majesty could select among his fair subjects. . . . So I leave it with all of you: Which came out of the opened door — the lady or the tiger?

The Lady or the Tiger?

JAMES THOMSON
[1834–1882]

The wine of Love is music,
    And the feast of Love is song:
And when Love sits down to the banquet,
    Love sits long.

The Vine. Stanza 1

Let my voice ring out and over the earth
    Through all the grief and strife,
With a golden joy in a silver mirth,
    Thank God for life!

Life, Love and You. Stanza 1

Give a man a horse he can ride,
    Give a man a boat he can sail;
And his rank and wealth, his strength and health
    On sea nor shore shall fail.

Gifts. Stanza 1

Give a man a pipe he can smoke,
    Give a man a book he can read:
And his home is bright with a calm delight,
    Though the room be poor indeed.

Ibid. Stanza 2

Singing is sweet, but be sure of this,
Lips only sing when they cannot kiss.

Art

Statues and pictures and verse may be grand,
But they are not the Life for which they stand.

Ibid.

He came to the desert of London town
    Grey miles long.

William Blake. Stanza 1

Be assured; no secret can be told
To any who divined it not before:

None uninitiate by many a presage
Will comprehend the language of the message,
    Although proclaimed aloud for evermore.

The City of Dreadful Night.
Proem.

As I came through the desert thus it was
As I came through the desert. . . .
    But I rode on austere;
    No hope could have no fear.

Ibid. IV

Dateless oblivion and divine repose.

Ibid. XIII

CHARLES HENRY WEBB
("JOHN PAUL")
[1834–1905]

Turn out more ale, turn up the light;
I will not go to bed to-night.
Of all the foes that man should dread
The first and worst one is a bed.

Dum Vivimus Vigilamus.
Stanza 1

Friends I have had both old and young,
And ale we drank and songs we sung:
Enough you know when this is said,
That, one and all, — they died in bed.
    In bed they died and I'll not go
    Where all my friends have perished so.

Ibid.

For I've been born and I've been wed —
All of man's peril comes of bed.

Ibid. Stanza 2

I care not a pin what the world may say
    In regard to the wrong or right;
My money goes as well as my song
    For the dog that keeps out of the fight!

The Outside Dog in the Fight.
Stanza 3

The King and the Pope together
    Have sent a letter to me;
It is signed with a golden sceptre,
    It is sealed with a golden key.

The King wants me out of his eye-
sight;
The Pope wants me out of his See.
*The King and the Pope.
Stanza 1*
That 'tis well to be off with the old
love
Before one is on with the new
Has somehow passed into a proverb,[1]
But who follows its teaching may
rue.
Proverbum Sap. Stanza 1
Were the proverb not wiser if mended,
And the fickle and wavering told
To be sure that they're on with the new
love
Before being off with the old?
Ibid. Stanza 3
Of Christian souls more have been
wrecked on shore
Than ever were lost at sea.
With a Nantucket Shell. Stanza 3

JAMES McNEILL WHISTLER
[1834–1903]

The rare Few, who, early in Life,
have rid Themselves of the Friendship
of the Many.
*The Gentle Art of Making
Enemies. Dedication*
To say of a picture, as is often said
in its praise, that it shows great and
earnest labour, is to say that it is incomplete and unfit for view.
Ibid. Propositions, 2
Industry in Art is a necessity — not
a virtue — and any evidence of the
same, in the production, is a blemish,
not a quality; a proof, not of achievement, but of absolutely insufficient
work, for work alone will efface the
footsteps of work.
Ibid.

[1] It's gude to be merry and wise,
It's gude to be honest and true;
It's gude to be off with the old love,
Before you are on with the new.
ANONYMOUS [1816]. Quoted by AN-
THONY TROLLOPE in *Barchester Tow-
ers, Chap. 46.*
See G. B. Shaw, page 720.

The work of the master reeks not of
the sweat of the brow — suggests no
effort and is finished from the beginning.
*The Gentle Art of Making
Enemies. Propositions, 2*

The masterpiece should appear as
the flower to the painter — perfect in
its bud as in its bloom — with no reason
to explain its presence — no mission to
fulfil — a joy to the artist, a delusion
to the philanthropist — a puzzle to the
botanist — an accident of sentiment
and alliteration to the literary man.
Ibid.

Art should be independent of all
clap-trap — should stand alone, and
appeal to the artistic sense of eye and
ear, without confounding this with
emotions entirely foreign to it, as devotion, pity, love, patriotism, and the
like. All these have no kind of concern
with it.
Ibid.

The imitator is a poor kind of creature. If the man who paints only the
tree, or flower, or other surface he sees
before him were an artist, the king of
artists would be the photographer. It
is for the artist to do something beyond
this: in portrait painting to put on canvas something more than the face the
model wears for that one day; to paint
the man, in short, as well as his features.
Ibid.

Nature sings her exquisite song to the
artist alone, her son and her master —
her son in that he loves her, her master
in that he knows her.
Ibid. Ten O'Clock

Two and two continue to make four,
in spite of the whine of the amateur for
three, or the cry of the critic for five.
Ibid. Whistler vs. Ruskin [1]

[1] In the law-suit for libel [1878]. Ruskin
had written of Whistler's *Nocturne in Black
and Gold,* "I never expected to hear a coxcomb ask two hundred guineas for flinging a
pot of paint in the public's face."

One cannot continually disappoint a
Continent
> *The Gentle Art of Making
> Enemies. (Of a contemplated
> visit to the U. S.)*

Wilde. I wish I'd said that.
Whistler. You will, Oscar, you will.
> *Traditional Dialogue*

I am not arguing with you — I am telling you.
> *Quoted by* ELIZABETH ROBINS
> PENNELL *in Art of Whistler*

Why drag in Velasquez?
> *Traditional (quoted by
> Mrs. Pennell)*

ALFRED AUSTIN
[1835–1913]

So long as Faith with Freedom reigns,
  And loyal Hope survives,
And gracious Charity remains
  To leaven lowly lives;
While there is one untrodden tract
  For intellect or will,
And men are free to think and act,
  Life is worth living still.
> *Is Life Worth Living?* [1]

Why should we lodge in marble or in
  bronze
Spirits more vast than earth, or sea, or
  sky?
Wiser the silent worshiper who cons
Their page for Wisdom that will never
  die.
> *On the Proposal to Erect a Statue
> to Shakespeare in London*

Gods for themselves are monuments
  enough.
> *Ibid.*

Kinsmen, hail!
We severed have been too long.
Now let us have done with a worn-out
  tale —
The tale of an ancient wrong —
And our friendship last long as our love
  doth, and be stronger than death
  is strong.
> *To America*

Who say we cherish far-off feud,
  Still nurse the ancient grudges?
Show me the title of this brood
  Of self-appointed judges;

[1] See William James, page 663.

Their name, their race, their nation,
  clan,
  And we will teach them whether
We do not, as none others can,
  Feel, think and work together.
> *Together*

THOMAS BRIGHAM BISHOP
[1835–1905]

John Brown's body lies a-mouldering in
  the grave,
His soul goes marching on.
> *John Brown's Body*

Shoo, fly! don't bodder me! I belong
  to Company G,
  I feel like a morning star.
> *Shoo, Fly.* [1] *Refrain*

MARY EMILY BRADLEY
[1835–1898]

Of all the bonny buds that blow
  In bright or cloudy weather,
Of all the flowers that come and go
  The whole twelve months together,
This little purple pansy brings
Thoughts of the sweetest, saddest
  things.
> *Heart's Ease. Stanza 1*

PHILLIPS BROOKS
[1835–1893]

O little town of Bethlehem!
  How still we see thee lie;
Above thy deep and dreamless sleep
  The silent stars go by;
Yet in thy dark streets shineth
  The everlasting Light;
The hopes and fears of all the years
  Are met in thee to-night.
> *O Little Town of Bethlehem.
> Stanza 1*

Everywhere, everywhere, Christmas to-
  night!
Christmas in lands of the fir-tree and
  pine,
Christmas in lands of the palm-tree and
  vine;
Christmas where snow-peaks stand
  solemn and white,

[1] See B. F. Butler, page 516.

Christmas where corn-fields lie sunny
and bright.

A Christmas Carol. Stanza 1

Life comes before literature, as the
material always comes before the work.
The hills are full of marble before the
world blooms with statues.

Literature and Life

Do not pray for easy lives. Pray to
be stronger men! Do not pray for tasks
equal to your powers. Pray for powers
equal to your tasks.

*Twenty Sermons. 18, Going up
to Jerusalem*

May I try to tell you again where
your only comfort lies? It is not in forgetting the happy past. People bring
us well-meant but miserable consolation when they tell what time will do
to help our grief. We do not want to
lose our grief, because our grief is
bound up with our love and we could
not cease to mourn without being
robbed of our affections.

*Letter to a friend on the death
of his mother [November 19,
1891]*

SAMUEL BUTLER
[1835–1902]

It is far safer to know too little than
too much. People will condemn the one,
though they will resent being called
upon to exert themselves to follow the
other.

The Way of All Flesh.[1] Chap. 5

Adversity, if a man is set down to it
by degrees, is more supportable with
equanimity by most people than any
great prosperity arrived at in a single
lifetime.

Ibid.

It is our less conscious thoughts and
our less conscious actions which mainly
mould our lives and the lives of those
who spring from us.

Ibid.

To me it seems that youth is like
spring, an over-praised season — de-

[1] I saw him now going the way of all flesh.
— JOHN WEBSTER: *Westward Hoe, Act II,
Sc. 2*

lightful if it happen to be a favoured
one, but in practice very rarely favoured and more remarkable, as a general rule, for biting east winds than
genial breezes.

The Way of All Flesh. Chap. 6

In old age we live under the shadow
of Death, which, like a sword of Damocles, may descend at any moment,
but we have so long found life to be
an affair of being rather frightened than
hurt that we have become like the people who live under Vesuvius, and chance
it without much misgiving.

Ibid.

A pair of lovers are like sunset and
sunrise: there are such things every day
but we very seldom see them.

Ibid. Chap. 11

Every man's work, whether it be
literature or music or pictures or architecture or anything else, is always a
portrait of himself, and the more he
tries to conceal himself the more clearly
will his character appear in spite of
him.

Ibid. Chap. 14

A virtue, to be serviceable, must,
like gold, be alloyed with some commoner but more durable metal.

Ibid. Chap. 19

One great reason why clergymen's
households are generally unhappy is
because the clergyman is so much at
home and close about the house.

Ibid. Chap. 24

The best liar is he who makes the
smallest amount of lying go the longest way — who husbands it too carefully to waste it where it can be dis-
pensed with.

Ibid. Chap. 39

If people would dare to speak to one
another unreservedly, there would be a
good deal less sorrow in the world a
hundred years hence.

Ibid. Chap. 44

Everyone has a mass of bad work in
him which he will have to work off and
get rid of before he can do better —
and indeed, the more lasting a man's
ultimate good work, the more sure he
is to pass through a time, and perhaps

a very long one, in which there seems very little hope for him at all. We must all sow our spiritual wild oats.

The Way of All Flesh. Chap. 51

It is in the uncompromisingness with which dogma is held and not in the dogma or want of dogma that the danger lies.

Ibid. Chap. 68

When people get it into their heads that they are being specially favoured by the Almighty, they had better as a general rule mind their p's and q's.

Ibid. Chap. 71

An empty house is like a stray dog or a body from which life has departed.[1]

Ibid. Chap. 72

A man's friendships are, like his will, invalidated by marriage — but they are also no less invalidated by the marriage of his friends.

Ibid. Chap. 75

I reckon being ill as one of the great pleasures of life, provided one is not too ill and is not obliged to work till one is better.

Ibid. Chap. 80

A hen is only an egg's way of making another egg.

Life and Habit. Chap. 8

Stowed away in a Montreal lumber room
The Discobolus standeth and turneth his face to the wall;
Dusty, cobweb-covered, maimed and set at naught,
Beauty crieth in an attic and no man regardeth.
O God! O Montreal!

A Psalm of Montreal.[2] Stanza 1

The Discobolus is put here because he is vulgar —
He has neither vest nor pants with which to cover his limbs;
I, Sir, am a person of most respectable connections. —

[1] I suppose I've passed it a hundred times, but I always stop for a minute
And look at the house, the tragic house, the house with nobody in it.
JOYCE KILMER: *The House with Nobody in It*
[2] In *The London Spectator, May 18, 1878.*

My brother-in-law is haberdasher to Mr. Spurgeon.
O God! O Montreal!

A Psalm of Montreal. Stanza 5

Life is the art of drawing sufficient conclusions from insufficient premises.

Note-Books. Lord, What Is Man?

All progress is based upon a universal innate desire on the part of every organism to live beyond its income.

Ibid.

Though analogy is often misleading, it is the least misleading thing we have.

Ibid. Music, Pictures, and Books

I have gone in for posthumous fame. . . . Posterity will give a man a fair hearing; his own times will not do so if he is attacking vested interests, and I have attacked two powerful sets of vested interests at once — the Church and Science.

Ibid. Homo Unius Libri [1883]

Ideas and opinions, like living organisms, have a normal rate of growth which cannot be either checked or forced beyond a certain point. The more unpopular an opinion is, the more necessary is it that the holder should be somewhat punctilious in his observance of conventionalities generally.

Ibid. The Art of Propagating Opinion

I do not think America is a good place in which to be a genius. A genius can never expect to have a good time anywhere, but America is about the last place in which life will be endurable at all for an inspired writer.

Ibid. Cash and Credit

The Ancient Mariner would not have taken so well if it had been called *The Old Sailor.*

Ibid. Titles and Subjects

The public buys its opinions as it buys its meat, or takes in its milk, on the principle that it is cheaper to do this than to keep a cow. So it is, but the milk is more likely to be watered.

Ibid. Sequel to "Alps and Sanctuaries"

How holy people look when they are sea-sick!

Ibid. The Channel Passage

The man who lets himself be bored is even more contemptible than the bore.[1]

The Fair Haven. Memoir, Chap. 3

O Critics, Cultured Critics!
Who will praise me after I am dead,
Who will see in me both more and less
    than I intended,
But who will swear that whatever it was
    it was all perfectly right;
You will think you are better than the
    people who, when I was alive,
    swore that whatever I did was
    wrong,
And damned my books for me as fast as
    I could write them;
But you will not be better, you will be
    just the same, neither better nor
    worse,
And you will go for some future Butler
    as your fathers have gone for me;
Oh, how I should have hated you!

To Critics and Others

SAMUEL LANGHORNE CLEMENS
("MARK TWAIN") [2]
[1835–1910]

This is petrified truth.

*A Complaint about Corre-
    spondents*

This poor little one-horse town.

The Undertaker's Story

[1] See, on this topic, an exquisitely humorous essay by HILAIRE BELLOC, "A Guide to Boring," in his volume *A Conversation with a Cat, etc.* (1931).

[2] I was a fresh, new journalist, and needed a *nom de guerre;* so I confiscated the ancient mariner's discarded one ["Mark Twain"], and have done my best to make it remain what it was in his hands — a sign and symbol and warrant that whatever is found in its company may be gambled on as being the petrified truth. — MARK TWAIN: *Life on the Mississippi, Chap. 50.* (The earlier use of the penname was by Captain Isaiah Sellers, in *The New Orleans Picayune.*)

By American literature in the proper sense we ought to mean literature written in an American way, with an American turn of language and an American cast of thought. The test is that it couldn't have been written anywhere else. — STEPHEN LEACOCK: *Mark Twain as a National Asset*

They spell it Vinci and pronounce it Vinchy; foreigners always spell better than they pronounce.

The Innocents Abroad

He is now fast rising from affluence to poverty.

Henry Ward Beecher's Farm

I'll resk forty dollars that he can outjump any frog in Calaveras county.

The Notorious Jumping Frog

There is no red outside the arteries of an archangel that can compare with it.[1]

*Lotos Club Speech [January 11,
    1908]*

A classic is something that everybody wants to have read and nobody wants to read.

The Disappearance of Literature

A powerful agent is the right word. Whenever we come upon one of those intensely right words in a book or a newspaper the resulting effect is physical as well as spiritual, and electrically prompt.

Essay on William Dean Howells

Work consists of whatever a body is *obliged* to do, and Play consists of whatever a body is not obliged to do.

*The Adventures of Tom Sawyer.
    Chap. 2*

Pilgrim's Progress, about a man that left his family, it didn't say why. The statement was interesting but tough.

*The Adventures of Huckleberry
    Finn. Chap. 17*

But soft you, the fair Ophelia:
Ope not thy ponderous and marble jaws,
But get thee to a nunnery — go!

*Ibid. Chap. 21 (The Duke's
    version of Hamlet's soliloquy)*

Cauliflower is nothing but cabbage with a college education.

Pudd'nhead Wilson's Calendar

If you pick up a starving dog and make him prosperous, he will not bite you. This is the principal difference between a dog and a man.

Ibid.

[1] His scarlet Doctor's gown from Oxford.

It is difference of opinion that makes horse races.

Pudd'nhead Wilson's Calendar

Why is it that we rejoice at a birth and grieve at a funeral? It is because we are not the person involved.

Ibid.

The reports of my death are greatly exaggerated.

Cable from Europe to the Associated Press

Barring that natural expression of villainy which we all have, the man looked honest enough.

A Mysterious Visit

An experienced, industrious, ambitious, and often quite picturesque liar.

My Military Campaign

I will set down a tale as it was told to me by one who had it of his father, which latter had it of *his* father, this last having in like manner had it of *his* father.

The Prince and the Pauper. Foreword

The world and the books are so accustomed to use, and over-use, the word "new" in connection with our country, that we early get and permanently retain the impression that there is nothing old about it.

Life on the Mississippi.[1] Chap. 1

When I'm playful I use the meridians of longitude and parallels of latitude for a seine, and drag the Atlantic Ocean for whales. I scratch my head with the lightning and purr myself to sleep with the thunder.

Ibid. Chap. 3

The Child of Calamity.

Ibid.

I was gratified to be able to answer promptly, and I did. I said I didn't know.

Ibid. Chap. 6

A limb of Satan.[1]

Life on the Mississippi. Chap. 8

The first time I ever saw St. Louis I could have bought it for six million dollars, and it was the mistake of my life that I did not do it.

Ibid. Chap. 22

Give an Irishman lager for a month, and he's a dead man. An Irishman is lined with copper, and the beer corrodes it. But whiskey polishes the copper and is the saving of him.

Ibid. Chap. 23

Spread open on the rack, where the plaintive singer had left it, *Ro*-holl on, silver *moo*-hoon, guide the *trav*-el-lerr his *way*.[2]

Ibid. Chap. 38

All the modern inconveniences.

Ibid. Chap. 43

The educated Southerner has no use for an *r*, except at the beginning of a word.

Ibid. Chap. 44

The Northern word "guess" —imported from England, where it used to be common, and now regarded by satirical Englishmen as a Yankee original — is but little used among Southerners. They say "reckon."

Ibid.

War talk by men who have been in a war is always interesting; whereas moon talk by a poet who has not been in the moon is likely to be dull.

Ibid. Chap. 45

It was without a compeer among swindles. It was perfect, it was rounded, symmetrical, complete, colossal.

Ibid. Chap. 52

When I retired from the rebel army in '61 I retired upon Louisiana in good order; at least in good enough order for a person who had not yet learned how

---

[1] If it's your Mississippi in dry time,
    If it's yours, Uncle Sam, when it's wet,
If it's your Mississippi in fly time,
    In flood time it's your Mississippi yet.
       ANONYMOUS: *Whose is the Mississippi? St. 6*, printed in *The Helena (Arkansas) World* [1913]

[1] Also in *The Prince and the Pauper*, Chap. 13.
[2] Roll on, silver moon, point the traveler his way. — Popular song of the 1840s. The words were old English, and the music by Joseph W. Turner, who later became musical editor of *The Waverly Magazine*.

to retreat according to the rules of war, and had to trust to native genius.

Life on the Mississippi. Chap. 53

Weather is a literary speciality, and no untrained hand can turn out a good article on it.

An American Claimant. Foreword

In Boston they ask, How much does he know? In New York, How much is he worth? In Philadelphia, Who were his parents?

What Paul Blouet [1] *Thinks of Us*

There's millions in it!

The Gilded Age [2]

There is a sumptuous variety about the New England weather that compels the stranger's admiration — and regret. The weather is always doing something there; always attending strictly to business; always getting up new designs and trying them on people to see how they will go. But it gets through more business in Spring than in any other season. In the Spring I have counted one hundred and thirty-six different kinds of weather inside of twenty-four hours.

New England Weather, Speech at dinner of New England Society, New York [*December 22, 1876*]

Probable nor'-east to sou'-west winds, varying to the southard and westard and eastard and points between; high and low barometer, sweeping round from place to place; probable areas of rain, snow, hail, and drought, succeeded or preceded by earthquakes with thunder and lightning.

Ibid.

We haven't all had the good fortune to be ladies; we haven't all been generals, or poets, or statesmen; but when the toast works down to the babies, we stand on common ground.

Answering a Toast to the Babies, Banquet in honor of Gen-

eral *U. S. Grant, Palmer House, Chicago* [*November 14, 1879*]

Among the three or four million cradles now rocking in the land are some which this nation would preserve for ages as sacred things, if we could know which ones they are.

Ibid.

RICHARD GARNETT
[1835–1906]

Man and Woman may only enter Paradise hand in hand. Together, the myth tells us, they left it and together must they return.

De Flagello Myrteo. Preface, XII

Have patience with the jealousies and petulances of actors, for their hour is their eternity.

Ibid. Preface, XV

Evergreens are said to be associated with Death as emblems of immortality, and this is true. But there is another and perhaps a deeper symbol: that all seasons are alike to him, as to them.

Ibid. Preface, XXXI

The three eldest children of Necessity: God, the World, and Love.

Ibid. I

Love is God's essence; Power but his attribute; therefore is his love greater than his power.

Ibid. IV

To become Love, Friendship needs what Morality needs to become Religion — the fire of emotion.

Ibid. LV

Perfect Love casts out Prudery together with Fear.

Ibid. LIX

Joy to forgive and joy to be forgiven Hang level in the balances of Love.

Ibid. LXII

Sleep, if thou wilt, with thy Love's picture or letter under thy pillow, but remember not to leave them there.

Ibid. LXXXVII

When Silence speaks for Love she has much to say.

Ibid. XCIX

Is life worth living? This if thou inquire,

---

[1] "Max O'Rell" [1848–1903], French author and lecturer.

[2] Written in collaboration with CHARLES DUDLEY WARNER.

'Tis probable that thou hast never
    lived,
And palpable that thou hast never
    loved.
        De Flagello Myrteo. CCVII
The thought that would delight thy
Love must first have delighted thyself.
        Ibid. CCXLIII
Sweet are the words of Love, sweeter
    his thoughts:
Sweetest of all what Love nor says nor
    thinks.
        Ibid. CCL
  Ascend above the restrictions and
conventions of the World, but not so
high as to lose sight of them.
        Ibid. CCCXXXIII
"Let the man that woos to win
Woo with an unhairy chin;"
Thus she said, and as she bid
Each devoted Vizier did.
        The Fair Circassian. Stanza 3

SIR ALFRED COMYN LYALL
[1835–1911]

"I think till I'm weary of thinking,"
    Said the sad-eyed Hindu King,
"And I see but shadows around me,
    Illusion in everything."
      The Hindu King's Reply to the
                Missionary
All the world over, I wonder, in lands
    that I never have trod,
Are the people eternally seeking for the
    signs and the steps of a God?
      Meditations of a Hindu Prince
                and Sceptic
Is life, then, a dream and delusion, and
    where shall the dreamer awake?
Is the world seen like shadows on water,
    and what if the mirror break?
Shall it pass a camp that is struck, as a
    tent that is gathered and gone
From the sands that were lamplit at
    eve, and at morning are level and
    lone?
        Ibid.

JOHN LUCKEY McCREERY
[1835–1906]

There is no death! The stars go down
    To rise upon some other shore,

And bright in heaven's jeweled crown
    They shine for evermore.
        There Is No Death.[1] *Stanza 1*
And ever near us, though unseen,
    The dear immortal spirits tread;
For all the boundless universe
    Is Life — there are no dead!
        Ibid. Stanza 10
Machines, that equity demands
    Should benefit the human race,
But serve, in heartless owners' hands,
    Competing workmen to displace;
So every great invention means
    Another multi-millionaire,
Whose hirelings — also his machines —
    Subsist on less than prison fare.
      Decoration Day [*1903*]. *Stanza 7*

ADAH ISAACS MENKEN [2]
[1835–1868]

Where is the promise of my years,
    Once written on my brow?
Ere errors, agonies, and fears
Brought with them all that speaks in
    tears,
Ere I had sunk beneath my peers; —
    Where sleeps that promise now?
        El Suspiro (*Infelix*)
I stand a wreck on Error's shore,
A spectre not within the door,
A houseless shadow evermore,
    An exile lingering here.
        Ibid.

AGNES E. MITCHELL
[*Floruit* 1880]

Klingle, klangle, klingle,
Far down the dusky dingle,
The cows are coming home;
Now sweet and clear, and faint and
    low,
The airy tinklings come and go,
Like chimings from the far-off tower,
Or patterings of an April shower
That makes the daisies grow.
      When the Cows Come Home.
           Stanza 1

[1] In *Arthur's Home Magazine* (Philadelphia), *July, 1863.*
[2] This is she that was the world's delight.
    SWINBURNE: *Laus Veneris, St. 2*

LOUISE CHANDLER MOULTON
[1835–1908]

Bend low, O dusky Night,
　And give my spirit rest,
　Hold me to your deep breast,
And put old cares to flight.
Give back the lost delight
　That once my soul possest,
　When Love was loveliest.
　　　　　　To-night

I hied me off to Arcady —
　The month it was the month of May,
　And all along the pleasant way,
The morning birds were mad with glee,
And all the flowers sprang up to see,
As I went on to Arcady.[1]
　　　The Secret of Arcady

HENRY CODMAN POTTER
[1835–1908]

We have exchanged the Washingtonian dignity for the Jeffersonian simplicity, which was in truth only another name for the Jacksonian vulgarity.
　　Address at the Washington Centennial Service in St. Paul's Chapel, New York [April 30, 1889]

If there be no nobility of descent, all the more indispensable is it that there should be nobility of ascent, — a character in them that bear rule so fine and high and pure that as men come within the circle of its influence they involuntarily pay homage to that which is the one preeminent distinction, the royalty of virtue.
　　　　　　Ibid.

W. S. RALPH
[*Floruit* 1880]

Unless there's a boy there a-whistling,
　Its music will not be complete.
　　Whistling in Heaven. Stanza 1

[1] See H. C. Bunner, page 715.

HARRIET PRESCOTT SPOFFORD
[1835–1921]

The awful phantom of the hungry poor.
　　Sonnet, A Winter's Night

Ah, happy world, where all things live
Creatures of one great law, indeed;
Bound by strong roots, the splendid
　flower, —
　Swept by great seas, the drifting
　　seed!
　　　The Story of the Flower

Dear the people coming home,
　Dear glad faces long away,
Dear the merry cries, and dear
　All the glad and happy play.
Dear the thanks, too, that we give
　For all of this, Thanksgiving Day.
　　Every Day Thanksgiving Day.
　　　　　　Stanza 3

CELIA LAIGHTON THAXTER
[1835–1894]

Sad soul, take comfort, nor forget
That sunrise never failed us yet.
　　The Sunrise Never Failed
　　　　Us Yet. Stanza 4

I have so loved thee, but cannot, cannot hold thee!
Fading like a dream, the shadows fold
　thee.
Slowly thy perfect beauty fades away,
Good-bye, sweet day.
　　Good-bye, Sweet Day. Stanza 1

Already the dandelions
　Are changed into vanishing ghosts.
　　　　　　Already

Staunch friends are we, well tried and
　strong,
　The little sandpiper and I.
　　The Sandpiper. Stanza 3

From wind to wind, earth has one tale
　to tell;
All other sounds are dulled, and
　drowned, and lost,
　In this one cry, "Farewell."
　　Farewell. Stanza 6

THEODORE TILTON
[1835–1907]

I won a noble fame,
But, with a sudden frown,
The people snatched my crown,
And in the mire trod down
    My lofty name.
        Sir Marmaduke's Musings
            [*1871*]. *Stanza 1*

So, lest I be inclined
    To render ill for ill —
Henceforth in me instil,
O God, a sweet good-will
To all mankind.
            Ibid. Stanza 7

Once in Persia reigned a king,
Who upon his signet ring
Graved a maxim true and wise,
Which, if held before the eyes,
Gave him counsel at a glance
Fit for every change and chance;
Solemn words, and these are they:
"Even this shall pass away." [1]
        Even This Shall Pass Away.
                Stanza 1

    Toll! Roland, toll!
In old St. Bavon's Tower.
At midnight hour
The great Bell Roland spoke,
And all who slept in Ghent awoke.
        The Great Bell Roland [2]

THOMAS BAILEY ALDRICH
[1836–1907]

Somewhere — in desolate wind-swept
    space —
In   Twilight-land — in   No-man's
    land —
Two hurrying Shapes met face to face,
    And bade each other stand.
            Identity. Stanza 1

"And who are you?" cried one agape,
    Shuddering in the gloaming light.
"I know not," said the second Shape,
    "I only died last night."
            Ibid. Stanza 2

[1] See J. G. Saxe, page 509.
[2] This poem was written the day on which
President Lincoln issued his proclamation calling for volunteers, and was distributed to the
first regiments and at public meetings, to stir
patriotism.

So precious life is! Even to the old
    The hours are as a miser's coins!
            Broken Music. Stanza 4
A man should live in a garret aloof,
    And have few friends, and go poorly
        clad,
With an old hat stopping a chink in the
        roof,
    To keep the Goddess constant and glad.
        The Flight of the Goddess.
                Stanza 1
We knew it would rain, for the poplars
        showed
        The white of their leaves.
            Before the Rain. Stanza 3
You do poets and their song
        A grievous wrong,
If your own soul does not bring
    To their high imagining
As much beauty as they sing.
            Appreciation. Stanza 2
I would be the Lyric
        Ever on the lip,
Rather than the Epic
        Memory lets slip.
            Lyrics and Epics
When were December and May known
    to be happy together?
            Thalia. Stanza 4
It has become almost an honor
        Not to be crowned.
                Popularity
Black Tragedy lets slip her grim dis-
        guise
And shows you laughing lips and ro-
        guish eyes;
But when, unmasked, gay Comedy ap-
        pears,
How wan her cheeks are, and what
        heavy tears!
                Masks
Some weep because they part,
    And languish broken-hearted,
And others — O my heart! —
    Because they never parted.
                The Difference
Sweet courtesy has done its most
If you have made each guest forget
That he himself is not the host.
                Hospitality
'Tis said the seeds wrapped up among
    the balms
And hieroglyphics of Egyptian kings

Hold strange vitality, and, planted, grow
After the lapse of thrice a thousand years.[1]
At the Funeral of a Minor Poet

My mind lets go a thousand things,
Like dates of wars and deaths of kings.
Memory

The folk who lived in Shakespeare's day
And saw that gentle figure pass
By London Bridge, his frequent way —
They little knew what man he was.
Guilielmus Rex. Stanza 1

Enamored architect of airy rhyme,
Build as thou wilt, heed not what each man says.
Enamored Architect of Airy Rhyme

They fail, and they alone, who have not striven.
Ibid.

From the dead Danish sculptor let us learn
To make Occasion, not to be denied:
Against the sheer precipitous mountain-side
Thorwaldsen carved his Lion at Lucerne.
Thorwaldsen

I vex me not with brooding on the years
That were ere I drew breath: why should I then
Distrust the darkness that may fall again
When life is done?
I Vex Me Not

What is more cheerful, now, in the fall of the year, than an open-wood-fire? Do you hear those little chirps and twitters coming out of that piece of apple-wood? Those are the ghosts of the robins and blue-birds that sang upon the bough when it was in blossom last Spring. In Summer whole flocks of them come fluttering about

the fruit-trees under the window: so I have singing birds all the year round.
Miss Mehitabel's Son

It was very pleasant to me to get a letter from you the other day. Perhaps I should have found it pleasanter if I had been able to decipher it. I don't think that I mastered anything beyond the date (which I knew) and the signature (which I guessed at). There's a singular and a perpetual charm in a letter of yours; it never grows old, it never loses its novelty. . . . Other letters are read and thrown away and forgotten, but yours are kept forever — unread. One of them will last a reasonable man a lifetime.
Letter to Professor Edward Sylvester Morse

EDWARD ERNEST BOWEN
[1836–1901]

Forty years on, when afar and asunder
Parted are those who are singing to-day,
When you look back, and forgetfully wonder
What you were like in your work and your play;
Then, it may be, there will often come o'er you
Glimpses of notes like the catch of a song —
Visions of boyhood shall float them before you,
Echoes of dreamland shall bear them along.
Forty Years On, Harrow Football Song [1872]

JOSEPH CHAMBERLAIN
[1836–1914]

I never like being hit without striking back.
Speech on Tariff Reform, Greenock, Scotland [October 7, 1903]

London is the clearing-house of the world.
Speech, Guildhall, London [January 19, 1904]

---

[1] In Cairo, I secured a few grains of wheat that had slumbered for more than three thousand years in an Egyptian tomb. — WILLIAM JENNINGS BRYAN: *The Prince of Peace*

The day of small nations has passed
away; the day of Empires has come.
Speech, Birmingham
[May 13, 1904]

JOHN CLIFFORD
[1836–1923]

Last evening I paused beside a black-
smith's door
And heard the anvil ring the vesper
chime.
Hammer and Anvil. Stanza 1
"How many anvils have you had,"
said I,
"To wear and batter all these ham-
mers so?"
"Just one," said he; then said with
twinkling eye,
"The anvil wears the hammers out,
you know."
Ibid. Stanza 2
And so, I thought, the anvil of God's
Word
For ages skeptic blows have beat
upon;
Yet, though the noise of falling blows
was heard,
The anvil is unharmed — the ham-
mers gone.
Ibid. Stanza 3

WILLIAM SCHWENCK
GILBERT [1]
[1836–1911]

Of all the ships upon the blue,
No ship contain'd a better crew
Than that of worthy Captain Reece,
Commanding of The Mantelpiece.
Captain Reece. Stanza 1
The Times and Saturday Review
Beguiled the leisure of the crew.
Ibid. Stanza 7
I write the pretty mottoes which you
find inside the crackers.
Ferdinando and Elvira
The Ballyshannon foundered off the
coast of Cariboo,

[1] His foe was folly and his weapon wit. —
Inscription by ANTHONY HOPE HAWKINS on
Gilbert memorial, Victoria Embankment,
London.

And down in fathoms many went the
captain and the crew;
Down went the owners — greedy men
whom hope of gain allured:
Oh, dry the starting tear, for they were
heavily insured.
Etiquette. Stanza 1
These passengers, by reason of their
clinging to a mast,
Upon a desert island were eventually
cast.
They hunted for their meals, as Alex-
ander Selkirk used,
But they couldn't chat together — they
had not been introduced.
Ibid. Stanza 3
Oh, I am a cook and a captain bold
And the mate of the *Nancy* brig,
And a bo'sun tight, and a midshipmite,
And the crew of the captain's gig.
The Yarn of the "Nancy Bell."
Stanza 3
Roll on, thou ball, roll on
Through pathless realms of Space,
Roll on!
To the Terrestrial Globe. Stanza 1
It's true I've got no shirts to wear;
It's true my butcher's bill is due;
It's true my prospects all look blue,
But don't let that unsettle you!
Never *you* mind!
Roll on!   (*It rolls on.*)
Ibid. Stanza 2
As innocent as a new-laid egg.
Engaged. Act I [1877]
Bad language or abuse,
I never, never use,
Whatever the emergency;
Though "Bother it" I may
Occasionally say,
I never never use a big, big D.
H.M.S. Pinafore. Act I,
I Am the Captain
What, never?
Hardly ever.
Ibid.
And so do his sisters, and his cousins,
and his aunts.
Ibid. I Am the Monarch of the Sea
Now landsmen all, whoever you may be,
If you want to rise to the top of the tree
If your soul isn't fettered to an office
stool,

Be careful to be guided by this golden
   rule —
Stick close to your desks and *never go
   to sea,*
And you all may be Rulers of the
   Queen's Navee!
> *H.M.S. Pinafore*
> *Act I, When I Was a Lad*

Say, why is everything
Either at sixes or at sevens? [1]
> *Ibid. Act II, Fair Moon*

Things are seldom what they seem,
Skim milk masquerades as cream.
> *Ibid. Duet, Buttercup and Captain*

He is an Englishman!
   For he himself has said it,
   And it's greatly to his credit,
That he is an Englishman!
> *Ibid. Boatswain's Song*

   For he might have been a Roosian,
   A French or Turk or Proosian,
Or perhaps Itali-an.
   But in spite of all temptations
   To belong to other nations,
He remains an Englishman.
> *Ibid.*

I know the Kings of England, and I
   quote the fights historical,
From Marathon to Waterloo, in order
   categorical.
> *The Pirates of Penzance. Act I,*
> *Major-General's Song*

Ah, take one consideration with another —
A policeman's lot is not a happy one!
> *Ibid. Act II, Sergeant's Song*

Come, friends, who plough the sea,[2]
   Truce to navigation,
   Take another station;
Let's vary piracee
With a little burglaree.
> *Ibid. Pirates' Chorus*

The enemy of one
The enemy of all is.
> *Patience. Act I, Dragoons' Chorus*

[1] See Heywood, page 15.
Let things go at sixes and sevens. — CER-
VANTES: *Don Quixote, Part I, Book IV,
Chap. 3*
[2] The roystering chorus, "Hail, hail, the
gang's all here," is sung to Sir Arthur Sullivan's music for these lines.

The pluck of Lord Nelson on board of
   the *Victory.*
> *Patience. Act I, Colonel's Song*

Set them to simmer and take off the
   scum,
And a Heavy Dragoon is the residuum!
> *Ibid.*

It's one to a million
That any civilian
My figure and form'll surpass.
> *Ibid. When I First Put This*
> *Uniform On*

I am not fond of uttering platitudes
In stained-glass attitudes.
> *Ibid. Bunthorne's Song*

If he's content with a vegetable love
   which would certainly not suit *me,*
Why, what a most particularly pure
   young man this pure young man
   must be!
> *Ibid.*

"High diddle diddle"
Will rank as an idyll,
If I pronounce it chaste!
> *Ibid. Duet, Bunthorne and*
> *Grosvenor*

None shall part us from each other,
   One in life and death are we:
All in all to one another —
   I to thee and thou to me!
Thou the tree and I the flower —
   Thou the idol; I the throng —
Thou the day and I the hour —
   Thou the singer; I the song!
> *Iolanthe. Act I, Duet, Strephon*
> *and Phyllis*

The Law is the true embodiment
Of everything that's excellent.
It has no kind of fault or flaw,
And I, my Lords, embody the Law.
> *Ibid. Lord Chancellor's Song*

Here's a pretty kettle of fish!
> *Ibid. Act II, Peers' Chorus*

Did nothing in particular
And did it very well.
> *Ibid. Lord Mountararat*

I love my fellow-creatures — I do all
   the good I can —
Yet everybody says I'm such a disagreeable man!
   And I can't think why!
> *Princess Ida. Act I, King Gama's*
> *Song*

Darwinian Man, though well-behaved,
At best is only a monkey shaved!
> *Princess Ida. Act II,*
> *Psyche's Song*

As some day it may happen that a victim must be found,
   I've got a little list — I've got a little list.
Of society offenders who might well be under ground,
   And who never would be missed — who never would be missed.
> *The Mikado. Act I, KoKo's Song*

The people who eat peppermint and puff it in your face.
> *Ibid.*

The idiot who praises, with enthusiastic tone,
All centuries but this, and every country but his own.
> *Ibid.*

Here's a pretty state of things!
Here's a pretty how-de-do.
> *Ibid. Duet, Yum Yum and*
> *Nanki-Poo*

My object all sublime
I shall achieve in time —
To let the punishment fit the crime.
> *Ibid. Mikado's Song*

"Is it weakness of intellect, birdie?" I cried,
"Or a rather tough worm in your little inside?"
With a shake of his poor little head he replied,
"Oh, Willow, titwillow, titwillow!"
> *Ibid. Act II, KoKo's Song*

Hail the Bridegroom — hail the Bride!
When the nuptial knot is tied.
> *Ruddigore. Act I, Chorus of*
> *Bridesmaids*

He led his regiment from behind —
He found it less exciting.
> *The Gondoliers. Act I,*
> *Duke of Plaza-Toro*

No soldier in that gallant band
   Hid half as well as he did.
He lay concealed throughout the war,
   And this preserved his gore, O!
> *Ibid.*

Of that there is no manner of doubt —
No probable, possible shadow of doubt —

No possible doubt whatever.
> *The Gondoliers. Act I,*
> *Don Alhambra's Song*

Life's a pudding full of plums;
Care's a canker that benumbs,
Wherefore waste our elocution
On impossible solution?
Life's a pleasant institution,
Let us take it as it comes!
> *Ibid. Life's Tangled Skein*

Life's perhaps the only riddle
That we shrink from giving up.
> *Ibid.*

The gratifying feeling that our duty has been done.
> *Ibid. Giuseppe's Song*

Go search the world and search the sea,
Then come you home and sing with me
There's no such gold and no such pearl
As a bright and beautiful English girl!
> *Utopia Limited. Act II,*
> *Mr. Goldbury's Song*

Here they come, the couple plighted —
   On life's journey gaily start them.
Soon to be for aye united,
   Till divorce or death shall part them.
> *The Grand Duke. Act I, Chorus*

Old wine is a true panacea
   For ev'ry conceivable ill,
When you cherish the soothing idea
   That somebody else pays the bill!
> *Ibid. Act II, Baroness' Song*

Quixotic is his enterprise and hopeless his adventure is,
Who seeks for jocularities that haven't yet been said.
The world has joked incessantly for over fifty centuries,
And every joke that's possible has long ago been made.
> *His Excellency. The Played-Out*
> *Humorist [1894]*

Humour is a drug which it's the fashion to abuse.
> *Ibid.*

WASHINGTON GLADDEN
[1836–1918]

When the anchors that faith has cast
   Are dragging in the gale,

I am quietly holding fast
  To the things that cannot fail.
          Ultima Veritas. Stanza 1
In the darkest night of the year,
  When the stars have all gone out,
That courage is better than fear,
  That faith is truer than doubt.
          Ibid. Stanza 4

FRANCES RIDLEY HAVERGAL
[1836–1879]

Silence is no certain token
  That no secret grief is there;
Sorrow which is never spoken
  Is the heaviest load to bear.
          Misunderstood. Stanza 15
Seldom can the heart be lonely,
  If it seek a lonelier still;
Self-forgetting, seeking only
  Emptier cups of love to fill.
          Ibid. Stanza 16

CHARLES FREDERICK JOHNSON
[1836–1931]

Surely, the ups and downs of this world
  are past calculation.
          The Modern Romans
Persian and Arab, and Greek, and Hun,
  and Roman, and Vandal,
Master the world in turn and then disappear in the darkness,
Leaving a remnant as hewers of wood
  and drawers of water.
          Ibid.
Genius finds in our every-day words
The music of the woodland birds,
Discloses hidden beauty furled
In the commonplace stuff of the everyday world,
And for her highest vision looks
To the world of men, not the world of
  books.
          The Shakespearean Phrase

FITZHUGH LUDLOW
[1836–1870]

When we want, we have for our pains
The promise that if we but wait

Till the want has burnt out of our brains,
Every means shall be present to sate;
While we wait for the napkin, the soup gets cold,
While the bonnet is trimming, the face grows old,
When we've matched our buttons, the pattern is sold,
And everything comes too late — too late.
          Too Late. Stanza 2

SARAH MORGAN BRYANT PIATT
[1836–1919]

My mother says I must not pass
Too near that glass;
She is afraid that I will see
A little witch that looks like me,
With a red mouth to whisper low
The very thing I should not know.
          The Witch in the Glass
Other suns will shine as golden,
  Other skies be just as blue;
Other south winds blow as softly,
  Gently drinking up the dew.
          To-day. Stanza 1
All the glories of the sunset
  In the sunrise one may see;
That which others call the dawning
  Is the night for you and me.
          Ibid. Stanza 3
You did not sing to Shelley such a song
  As Shelley sang to you.
          A Word with a Skylark

WILLIAM JEFFREY PROWSE
[1836–1870]

How we laughed as we laboured together!
          The City of Prague. Stanza 3 [1]
Though the latitude's rather uncertain,
And the longitude likewise is vague,
Still the people I pity who know not the City,
The beautiful City of Prague.
          Ibid. Stanza 5

[1] Stanza 3 is used by Leonard Merrick as a chapter heading in his novel, *Conrad in Quest of His Youth*.

MARY ASHLEY TOWNSEND
[1836–1901]

I believe if I should die
And you should kiss my eyelids when I
  lie
Cold, dead, and dumb to all the world
  contains,
The folded orbs would open at thy
  breath,
And, from its exile in the isles of death,
Life would come gladly back along my
  veins.
Creed. Stanza 1

To every life there comes a time supreme;
One day, one night, one morning, or one
  noon,
One freighted hour, one moment opportune,
One rift through which sublime fulfilments gleam.
Sonnet, Opportunity

WILLIAM HENRY VENABLE
[1836–1918]

Remember Johnny Appleseed,[1]
  All ye who love the apple;
He served his kind by Word and Deed,
  In God's grand greenwood chapel.
Johnny Appleseed. Stanza 25

WILLIAM WINTER
[1836–1917]

Who cares for nothing alone is free, —
Sit down, good fellow, and drink with
  me!
Orgia

Though all the bards of earth were
  dead,
  And all their music passed away,
What Nature wishes should be said
  She'll find the rightful voice to say!
The Golden Silence

There is not anything of human trial
  That ever love deplored or sorrow
  knew,
No glad fulfilment and no sad denial,

[1] See E. A. Allen, page 596.

Beyond the pictured truth that
Shakespeare drew.
Ashes

On wings of deeds the soul must mount!
  When we are summoned from afar,
Ourselves, and not our words, will
  count —
Not what we said, but what we are!
George Fawcett Rowe

The golden time of Long Ago.
I. H. Bromley

His love was like the liberal air, —
  Embracing all, to cheer and bless;
And every grief that mortals share
  Found pity in his tenderness.
Ibid.

Fierce for the right, he bore his part
  In strife with many a valiant foe;
But Laughter winged his polished dart,
  And kindness tempered every blow.
Ibid.

Cold the stars are, cold the earth is,
  Everything is grim and cold!
Strange and drear the sound of mirth is
  — Life and I are old.
Age

One other bitter drop to drink,
  And then — no more!
One little pause upon the brink,
  And then — go o'er!
The Rubicon

And, lucid in that second birth,
  I shall discern
What all the sages of the earth
  Have died to learn.
Ibid.

MARY GARDINER
BRAINARD
[1837–1905]

I see not a step before me as I tread on
  another year;
But I've left the Past in God's keeping,
  — the Future His mercy shall
  clear;
And what looks dark in the distance,
  may brighten as I draw near.
Not Knowing. Stanza 2

RICHARD MAURICE BUCKE
[1837–1892]

Only a little while now and we shall be again together and with us those other noble and well-beloved souls gone before. I am sure I shall meet you and them; that you and I shall talk of a thousand things and of that unforgettable day and of all that followed it; and that we shall clearly see that all were parts of an infinite plan which was wholly wise and good.

Cosmic Consciousness. Dedication

SIR FRANCIS COWLEY BURNAND
[1837–1917]

In the very earliest and darkest ages of our ancient earth, before even the Grand Primeval forests could boast the promise of an incipient bud, there existed in the inexhaustible self-inexhausting Possible, innumerable types. . . .

Burlesque philosophical treatise in Happy Thoughts [1866]

JOHN BURROUGHS
[1837–1921]

In sorrow he learned this truth —
One may return to the place of his birth,
He cannot go back to his youth.

The Return. Stanza 3

Serene, I fold my hands and wait,
  Nor care for wind, nor tide, nor sea;
I rave no more 'gainst time or fate,
  For lo! my own shall come to me.

Waiting. Stanza 1 [1862]

Nor time, nor space, nor deep, nor high,
Can keep my own away from me.

Ibid. Stanza 6

I was born with a chronic anxiety about the weather.

Is It Going to Rain?

Literature is an investment of genius which pays dividends to all subsequent times.

Literary Fame

It is always easier to believe than to deny. Our minds are naturally affirmative.

The Light of Day. The Modern Skeptic

Time does not become sacred to us until we have lived it.

The Spell of the Past

Nature teaches more than she preaches. There are no sermons in stones. It is easier to get a spark out of a stone than a moral.

Time and Change. The Gospel of Nature

I go to books and to nature as a bee goes to the flower, for a nectar that I can make into my own honey.

The Summit of the Years

Life is a struggle, but not a warfare.

Ibid.

How far are we from home?

Last words [March 29, 1921], on a train crossing Ohio, homeward bound from California

GROVER CLEVELAND
[1837–1908]

Public officers are the servants and agents of the people, to execute the laws which the people have made.

Letter accepting the nomination for Governor of New York [October, 1882]

Your every voter, as surely as your chief magistrate, exercises a public trust.[1]

Inaugural Address [March 4, 1885]

However plenty silver dollars may become, they will not be distributed as gifts among the people.

First Annual Message [December 8, 1885]

The so-called debtor class . . . are not dishonest because they are in debt.

Ibid.

After an existence of nearly twenty years of almost innocuous desuetude these laws are brought forth.

Message [March 1, 1886]

[1] The familiar saying "Public office is a public trust" seems to have been paraphrased from various campaign speeches by Cleveland in 1884.

When more of the people's sustenance is exacted through the form of taxation than is necessary to meet the just obligations of Government and expenses of its economical administration, such exaction becomes ruthless extortion and a violation of the fundamental principles of a free Government.

Second Annual Message
[December, 1886]

It is a condition which confronts us — not a theory.[1]

Third Annual Message
[December 6, 1887]

The lessons of paternalism ought to be unlearned and the better lesson taught that while the people should patriotically and cheerfully support their Government, its functions do not include the support of the people.

Inaugural Address [March 4, 1893]

I have tried so hard to do the right.

Last Words

MARY KYLE DALLAS
[1837–1897]

Man never quite forgets his very first love,
   Unless she's true.
     After Ten Years. Stanza 4

He'd nothing but his violin,
   I'd nothing but my song;
But we were wed when skies were blue,
   And summer days were long.
     Brave Love

But those who wait for gold or gear,
   For houses or for kine,
Till youth's sweet spring grows brown and sere,
   And love and beauty tine,
Will never know the joy of hearts
   That met without a fear.
     Ibid.

JOHN RICHARD GREEN
[1837–1883]

The words of consecration, *"Hoc est corpus,"* were travestied into a nick-

name for jugglery, as "Hocus-pocus."[1]
A Short History of the English
People. Chap. VII, Sect. 1

CLARA B. SAWYER HEATH
[1837–1911]

Four-score! yet softly the years have swept by thee,
   Touching thee lightly with tenderest care;
Sorrow and death they have often brought nigh thee,
   Yet they have left thee but beauty to wear,
Growing old gracefully, graceful and fair.[2]
     Growing Old Gracefully

WILLIAM DEAN HOWELLS [3]
[1837–1920]

We live, but a world has passed away
With the years that perished to make us men.
     The Mulberries

Lord, for the erring thought
Not into evil wrought:
Lord, for the wicked will
Betrayed and baffled still:
For the heart from itself kept,
Our thanksgiving accept.
     Thanksgiving

Though I move with leaden feet,
Light itself is not so fleet;
And before you know me gone
Eternity and I are one.
     Time

---

[1] The law is a sort of hocus-pocus science. — CHARLES MACKLIN [1690–1797]: *Love à la Mode, Act II, Sc. 1*

Hocus was an old cunning attorney. — DR. JOHN ARBUTHNOT [1667–1735]: *Law is a Bottomless Pit: or, History of John Bull, Chap. 5* [1712]

[2] Let me grow lovely, growing old —
   So many fine things do.
     KARLE WILSON BAKER: *Old Lace,*
     Let Me Grow Lovely

[3] No tribute to his art would be complete without a tribute to the beauty of his character. I never met a better man than Mr. Howells, I never saw one who was more generous, more sincere, more genuine, more essentially noble. — WILLIAM LYON PHELPS: *Howells, James, Bryant and Other Essays* [1924]

---

[1] See Disraeli, page 419.

I know his name, I know his note,
That so with rapture takes my soul;
Like flame the gold beneath his throat,
His glossy cope is black as coal.
The Song the Oriole Sings

He who sleeps in continual noise is wakened by silence.
Pordenone. IV

It shall belong hereafter to all who per-
ceive and enjoy it,
Rather than him who made it.
Ibid.

See how to-day's achievement is only
to-morrow's confusion;
See how possession always cheapens the
thing that was precious.
Ibid.

Yes, death is at the bottom of the cup,
And every one that lives must drink it
up;
And yet between the sparkle at the top
And the black lees where lurks that bit-
ter drop,
There swims enough good liquor,
Heaven knows,
To ease our hearts of all their other
woes.
If

The first night, when at night I went
about
Locking the doors and windows every-
where,
After she died, I seemed to lock her out
In the starred silence and the homeless
air.
Experience

Tossing his mane of snows in wildest
eddies and tangles,
Lion-like March cometh in, hoarse,
with tempestuous breath.
Earliest Spring. Stanza 1

Rapture of life ineffable, perfect — as
if in the brier,
Leafless there by my door, trembled a
sense of the rose.
Ibid. Stanza 3

The Bostonian who leaves Boston
ought to be condemned to perpetual
exile.
The Rise of Silas Lapham. Chap. 5

The book which you read from a
sense of duty, or because for any reason

you must, does not commonly make
friends with you. It may happen that it
will yield you an unexpected delight,
but this will be in its own unentreated
way and in spite of your good intentions.
My Literary Passions. Chap. 7

Does it afflict you to find your books
wearing out? I mean literally. . . .
The mortality of all inanimate things is
terrible to me, but that of books most
of all.
*Letter to Charles Eliot Norton
[April 6, 1903] (Life in Letters,
Vol. II, Page 171)*

I am not sorry for having wrought in
common, crude material so much; that
is the right American stuff; and perhaps hereafter, when my din is done,
if any one is curious to know what that
noise was, it will be found to have proceeded from a small insect which was
scraping about on the surface of our
life and trying to get into its meaning
for the sake of the other insects larger
or smaller. That is, such has been my
unconscious work; consciously, I was
always, as I still am, trying to fashion
a piece of literature out of the life next
at hand.
*Letter to Charles Eliot Norton
[April 26, 1903] (Ibid., Page
173)*

Last night, after I got back from my
Balfour tailor, I expressed my surprise
that B. should go to such a simple shop.
"Well, I don't think, sir, Mr. Balfour
cares much for his clothes, sir. Them
distinguished men can't, sir. Their
thoughts soars to 'igher things, sir."
*Letter to Mrs. Howells [April
12, 1904], quoting his London
landlord (Ibid., Page 191)*

Spain, where most of my boyhood
was past while I was working at case in
my father's printing-office in Northern
Ohio.
*Letter to Brander Matthews
[July 22, 1911], referring to his
love for Don Quixote (Ibid.,
Page 301)*

HENRY SAMBROOKE LEIGH
[1837–1883]

A tiny paper, tightly rolled
   About some Latakia,
Contains within its magic fold
   A mighty panacea.
            My Three Loves. Stanza 3

In form and feature, face and limb,
   I grew so like my brother,
That folks got taking me for him
   And each for one another.
            The Twins. Stanza 1

And when I died the neighbors came
   And buried brother John.
            Ibid. Stanza 5

My love she is a kitten,
   And my heart's a ball of string.
            My Love and My Heart. Stanza 1

Said I, "What is it makes you bad?
How many apples have you had?"
   She answered, "Only seven!"
            *Only Seven (Parody of
                  Wordsworth)*

JOHN L. PARKER
[1837–1917]

The little brown button,
The sacred bronze button,
The Grand Army button
He wears on his coat.
            The Little Bronze Button [1]

INNES RANDOLPH
[1837–1887]

I am a good old rebel —
   Yes; that's just what I am —
And for this land of freedom
   I do not give a dam'.
I'm glad I fit agin 'em,
   And I only wish we'd won;
And I don't ax no pardon
   For anything I've done.
      *A Good Old Rebel (Unrecon-
            structed).* [2] *Stanza 1*

[1] The highly prized button, the dearly
   bought button,
   That binds us together in bonds so true.
      SAMUEL C. LAMBERT: *The Little
                        Bronze Button*
[2] An adaptation of this ballad became a
popular cowboy song in the Southwest.

I cotch the rheumatism
   A-campin' in the snow,
But I killed a chance of Yankees,
   I'd like to kill some mo'.
      *A Good Old Rebel (Unrecon-
            structed). Stanza 4*

I won't be reconstructed.
            Ibid. Stanza 6

The *tours de force* of the great Paganini
Have never found favor in Old Virginny.
            A Fish Story

The waves settled placidly over his
   head,
And his last remark was a bubble.
            Ibid.

ALGERNON CHARLES
SWINBURNE
[1837–1909]

Lo, this is she that was the world's delight.
            Laus Veneris. Stanza 3

Ah yet would God this flesh of mine
   might be
Where air might wash and long leaves
   cover me,
Where tides of grass break into foam of
   flowers,
Or where the wind's feet shine along the
   sea.
            Ibid. Stanza 14

And lo, between the sundawn and the
   sun,
His day's work and his night's work
   are undone;
And lo, between the nightfall and the
   light,
He is not, and none knoweth of such
   an one.
            Ibid. Stanza 19

O sad kissed mouth, how sorrowful it
   is!
            Ibid. Stanza 79

To have known love, how bitter a
   thing it is.
            Ibid. Stanza 103

There will no man do for your sake, I
   think,
   What I would have done for the
   least word said.

I had wrung life dry for your lips to
    drink,
    Broken it up for your daily bread.
         The Triumph of Time. Stanza 12

I wish we were dead together to-day,
    Lost sight of, hidden away out of
    sight,
Clasped and clothed in the cloven clay,
    Out of the world's way, out of the
    light.
         Ibid. Stanza 15

At the door of life, by the gate of breath,
There are worse things waiting for men
    than death.
         Ibid. Stanza 20

I will go back to the great sweet mother,
    Mother and lover of men, the sea.
         Ibid. Stanza 33

There lived a singer in France of old,
    By the tideless dolorous midland sea.
In a land of sand and ruin and gold
    There shone one woman, and none
    but she.
And finding life for her love's sake fail,
Being fain to see her, he bade set sail,
Touched land, and saw her as life grew
    cold,
    And praised God, seeing; and so died
    he.
         Ibid. Stanza 41

O brother, the gods were good to you.
    Sleep, and be glad while the world en-
    dures.
Be well content as the years wear
    through;
    Give thanks for life, and the loves
    and lures.
         Ibid. Stanza 43

I shall never be friends again with
    roses;
    I shall loathe sweet tunes.
         Ibid. Stanza 45

Marvellous mercies and infinite love.
         Les Noyades. Stanza 1

I am sick of singing; the bays burn deep
    and chafe: I am fain
To rest a little from praise and grievous
    pleasure and pain.
      Hymn to Proserpine: After the
      Proclamation in Rome of the
      Christian Faith

Thou hast conquered, O pale Galilean;
    the world has grown grey from thy
    breath;
We have drunken of things Lethean,
    and fed on the fulness of death.
Laurel is green for a season, and love is
    sweet for a day;
But love grows bitter with treason, and
    laurel outlives not May.
Sleep, shall we sleep after all? for the
    world is not sweet in the end;
For the old faiths loosen and fall, the
    new years ruin and rend.
        Hymn to Proserpine: Ibid.

I shall die as my fathers died, and sleep
    as they sleep; even so.
For the glass of the years is brittle
    wherein we gaze for a span.
             Ibid.

For there is no God found stronger than
    death; and death is a sleep.
             Ibid.

If you loved me ever so little,
    I could bear the bonds that gall,
I could dream the bonds were brittle;
    You do not love me at all.
      Satia te Sanguine. Stanza 1

While he lives let a man be glad,
For none hath joy of his death.
        A Lamentation. I, 4

If love were what the rose is,
    And I were like the leaf,
Our lives would grow together
In sad or singing weather.
         A Match. Stanza 1

If you were April's lady,
    And I were lord in May.
         Ibid. Stanza 5

If you were queen of pleasure,
    And I were king of pain,
We'd hunt down love together,
Pluck out his flying feather,
    And teach his feet a measure,
    And find his mouth a rein.
         Ibid. Stanza 6

For in the time we know not of
    Did fate begin
Weaving the web of days that wove
    Your doom, Faustine.
        Faustine. Stanza 24

A love machine
With clockwork joints of supple gold —
No more, Faustine.

Faustine. Stanza 36

Take hand and part with laughter;
  Touch lips and part with tears;
Once more and no more after,
  Whatever comes with years.

Rococo. Stanza 1

Forget that I remember,
  And dream that I forget.

Ibid. Stanza 2

The burden of long living. Thou shalt
    fear
  Waking, and sleeping mourn upon
    thy bed;
And say at night "Would God the day
    were here,"
  And say at dawn "Would God the
    day were dead." [1]

A Ballad of Burdens. Stanza 4

For life is sweet, but after life is death.
  This is the end of every man's desire.

Ibid. L'Envoy

O love, O lover, loose or hold me fast,
I had thee first, whoever have thee last.

Erotion

I shall remember while the light lives
    yet.
And in the night-time I shall not forget.
Though (as thou wilt) thou leave me
    ere life leave,
I will not, for thy love I will not, grieve.

Ibid.

O wise among women, and wisest,
  Our Lady of Pain.

Dolores. Stanza 5

Despair the twin-born of devotion.

Ibid. Stanza 14

I have passed from the outermost portal
  To the shrine where a sin is a prayer.

Ibid. Stanza 17

What ailed us, O gods, to desert you
  For creeds that refuse and restrain?
Come down and redeem us from virtue,
  Our Lady of Pain.

Ibid. Stanza 35

[1] In the morning thou shalt say, Would God
it were even! and at even thou shalt say,
Would God it were morning! for the fear of
thine heart wherewith thou shalt fear, and for
the sight of thine eyes which thou shalt see. —
Deuteronomy, XXVIII, 27

Then love was the pearl of his oyster,
  And Venus rose red out of wine.

Dolores. Stanza 39

Time stoops to no man's lure;
  And love, grown faint and fretful,
  With lips but half regretful
  Sighs, and with eyes forgetful
Weeps that no loves endure.

*The Garden of Proserpine.
Stanza 10*

From too much love of living,
  From hope and fear set free,
We thank with brief thanksgiving
  Whatever gods may be
That no life lives forever;
That dead men rise up never;
That even the weariest river
  Winds somewhere safe to sea.

Ibid. Stanza 11

The sweetest name that ever love
Waxed weary of.

Félise. Stanza 18

Ah that such sweet things should be
    fleet,
Such fleet things sweet!

Ibid. Stanza 22

Those eyes the greenest of things blue,
  The bluest of things grey.

Ibid. Stanza 24

Eyes colored like a water-flower,
  And deeper than the green sea's
    glass;
Eyes that remember one sweet hour —
  In vain we swore it should not pass.

Ibid. Stanza 36

Two gifts perforce he has given us yet,
  Though sad things stay and glad
    things fly;
Two gifts he has given us, to forget
  All glad and sad things that go by,
    And then to die.

Ibid. Stanza 56

We know not whether death be good,
  But life at least it will not be:
Men will stand saddening as we stood,
  Watch the same fields and skies as we
    And the same sea.

Ibid. Stanza 57

Live and let live, as I will do,
  Love and let love, and so will I.
But, sweet, for me no more with you:

Not while I live, not though I die.
Good-night, good-bye.
Félise. Stanza 59

I remember the way we parted,
The day and the way we met;
You hoped we were both broken-
hearted
And knew we should both forget.
An Interlude. Stanza 11

And the best and the worst of this is
That neither is most to blame,
If you have forgotten my kisses
And I have forgotten your name.
Ibid. Stanza 14

By the waters of Babylon we sat down
and wept,
Remembering thee.
*Super Flumina Babylonis.
Stanza 1*

A creed is a rod,
And a crown is of night;
But this thing is God,
To be man with thy might,
To grow straight in the strength of thy
spirit, and to live out thy life as the
light.
Hertha. Stanza 15

In the grey beginning of years, in the
twilight of things that began,
The word of the earth in the ears of
the world, was it God? was it man?
Hymn of Man

O strong-winged soul with prophetic
Lips hot with the bloodbeats of song,
With tremor of heartstrings magnetic,
With thoughts as thunders in throng.
*To Walt Whitman in America.
Stanza 3*

Ask nothing more of me, sweet,
All I can give you I give;
Heart of my heart, were it more,
More would be laid at your feet:
Love that should help you to live,
Song that should spur you to soar.
The Oblation. Stanza 1

Poor splendid wings so frayed and
soiled and torn!
*A Ballad of François Villon.
Stanza 3*

Many loves of many a mood and many
a kind

Fill the life of man, and mould the
secret mind.
Erechtheus

For the shades are about us that hover
When darkness is half withdrawn,
And the skirts of the dead night cover
The face of the live new dawn.
The Last Oracle

Is the sun yet cast out of heaven?
Is the song yet cast out of man?
Life that had song for its leaven
To quicken the blood that ran.
Ibid.

Out of heaven they shall cast not the
day,
They shall cast not out song from the
world.
Ibid.

In a coign of the cliff between lowland
and highland,
At the sea-down's edge between
windward and lee,
Walled round with rocks as an inland
island,
The ghost of a garden fronts the sea.[1]
The Forsaken Garden. Stanza 1

The year of the rose is brief;
From the first blade blown to the sheaf,
From the thin green leaf to the gold,
It has time to be sweet and grow old.
The Year of the Rose. Stanza 1

A rain and ruin of roses
Over the red rose-land.
Ibid. Stanza 9

When the hounds of spring are on winter's traces.
Atalanta in Calydon. Chorus

For winter's rains and ruins are over,
And all the season of snows and sins;
The days dividing lover and lover,
The light that loses, the night that
wins.
Ibid.

Before the beginning of years
There came to the making of man
Time with a gift of tears,
Grief with a glass that ran.
Ibid.

---

[1] On the grass of the cliff, at the edge of the
steep,
God planted a garden, a garden of sleep.
CLEMENT W. SCOTT [1841–1904]: *The
Garden of Sleep* (Cromer, England)

He weaves, and is clothed with derision;
　Sows, and he shall not reap;
His life is a watch or a vision
　Between a sleep and a sleep.
　　　　Atalanta in Calydon. Chorus

A little while and I shall laugh; and
　then
I shall weep never and laugh not any
　more.
　　　　Ibid.

And through the trumpet of a child of
　Rome
Rang the pure music of the flutes of
　Greece.
　　　　*Song for the Centenary
　　　　of Walter Savage Landor.
　　　　Stanza 17*

No sweeter thing than children's ways
　and wiles,
　Surely, we say, can gladden eyes and
　　ears:
Yet sometimes sweeter than their words
　or smiles
　Are even their tears.
　　　　A Child's Pity. Stanza 1

All the bells of heaven may ring,
All the birds of heaven may sing,
All the wells on earth may spring,
All the winds on earth may bring
　All sweet sounds together.
　　　　A Child's Laughter. Stanza 1

Faith in faith established evermore
Stands a sea-mark in the tides of time.
　　　　A Sea-Mark. Stanza 5

Not with dreams, but with blood and
　with iron,
　Shall a nation be moulded to last.
　　　　A Word for the Country. Stanza 13

Is not Precedent indeed a King of men?
　　　　A Word from the Psalmist. Stanza 4

Stately, kindly, lordly friend
　Condescend
Here to sit by me.
　　　　To a Cat

There is no help for these things;
　none to mend,
And none to mar; not all our songs,
　O friend,
Will make death clear or make life dur-
　able.
　　　　*Ave atque Vale: In Memory of
　　　　Charles Baudelaire. Stanza 16*

A little soul scarce fledged for earth
Takes wing with heaven again for goal
Even while we hailed as fresh from
　birth
　A little soul.
　　　　A Baby's Death. I, 1

Who knows but on their sleep may rise
Such light as never heaven let through
To lighten earth from Paradise?
　　　　Ibid. IV, 2

A baby's feet, like sea-shells pink,
　Might tempt, should heaven see meet,
An angel's lips to kiss, we think,
　A baby's feet.
　　　　Étude Réaliste. I, 1

The sweetest flowers in all the world —
　A baby's hands.
　　　　Ibid. II, 3

All our past acclaims our future: Shake-
　speare's voice and Nelson's hand,
Milton's faith and Wordsworth's trust
　in this our chosen and chainless
　land,
Bear as witness: come the world against
　her, England yet shall stand.
　　　　England, An Ode. II, 5

Shelley, lyric lord of England's lordliest
　singers, here first heard
Ring from lips of poets crowned and
　dead the Promethean word
Whence his soul took fire, and power to
　outsoar the sunward-soaring bird.
　　　　Eton, An Ode. III

Body and spirit are twins: God only
　knows which is which.
　　　　*The Higher Pantheism in a Nut-
　　　　shell (Imitation of Tennyson).
　　　　Stanza 7*

God, whom we see not, is: and God,
　who is not, we see:
Fiddle, we know, is diddle: and diddle,
　we take it, is dee.
　　　　Ibid. Stanza 12

The most BEAUT—iful babbie ever be-
　held by mortal eyes.
　　　　Quoted by MAX BEERBOHM, *in
　　　　No. 2, The Pines*

It is long since Mr. Carlyle expressed
his opinion that if any poet or other literary creature could really be "killed
off by one critique" or many, the sooner
he was so despatched the better; a sen-

timent in which I for one humbly but heartily concur.

Under the Microscope

A blatant Bassarid of Boston, a rampant Maenad of Massachusetts.

Ibid.

To wipe off the froth of falsehood from the foaming lips of inebriated virtue, when fresh from the sexless orgies of morality and reeling from the delirious riot of religion, may doubtless be a charitable office.

Ibid.

The more congenial page of some tenth-rate poeticule worn out with failure after failure and now squat in his hole like the tailless fox, he is curled up to snarl and whimper beneath the inaccessible vine of song.

Ibid.

The tadpole poet will never grow into anything bigger than a frog; not though in that stage of development he should puff and blow himself till he bursts with windy adulation at the heels of the laureled ox.

Ibid.

FORCEYTHE WILLSON
[1837–1867]

And I heard a Bugle sounding, as from
  some celestial Tower;
And the same mysterious voice said:
  "It is the Eleventh Hour!
Orderly Sergeant — Robert Burton —
  it is the Eleventh Hour!"

The Old Sergeant.[1] *Stanza 9*

HENRY BROOKS ADAMS
[1838–1918]

Accident counts for much in companionship as in marriage.

*The Education of Henry Adams.
Chap. 4*

---

[1] In *The Louisville* (Kentucky) *Journal,
Jan. 1, 1863.*

Forceythe Willson, whose poem of "The Old Sergeant" Doctor Holmes used to read publicly in the closing year of the civil war, was of a Western altitude of figure, and of an extraordinary beauty of face in an oriental sort. — W. D. HOWELLS: *Literary Friends and Acquaintance, Part VIII, Chap. 8*

Women have, commonly, a very positive moral sense; that which they will, is right; that which they reject, is wrong; and their will, in most cases, ends by settling the moral.

*The Education of Henry Adams.
Chap. 6*

All experience is an arch, to build upon.[1]

Ibid.

Only on the edge of the grave can man conclude anything.

Ibid.

Although the Senate is much given to admiring in its members a superiority less obvious or quite invisible to outsiders, one Senator seldom proclaims his own inferiority to another, and still more seldom likes to be told of it.

Ibid. Chap. 7

Friends are born, not made.

Ibid.

A friend in power is a friend lost.

Ibid. (Also in Chap. 16)

The effect of power and publicity on all men is the aggravation of self, a sort of tumor that ends by killing the victim's sympathies.

Ibid. Chap. 10

Young men have a passion for regarding their elders as senile.

Ibid. Chap. 11

Knowledge of human nature is the beginning and end of political education.

Ibid. Chap. 12

These questions of taste, of feeling, of inheritance, need no settlement. Everyone carries his own inch-rule of taste, and amuses himself by applying it, triumphantly, wherever he travels.

Ibid.

Intimates are predestined.

Ibid. Chap. 13

His first struggle with a sleeping-car made him doubt the value — to him — of a Pullman civilization.

Ibid. Chap. 16

---

[1] Yet all experience is an arch wherethrough
Gleams that untraveled world.
TENNYSON: *Ulysses*

Chaos often breeds life, when order breeds habit.
> *The Education of Henry Adams.*
> *Chap. 16*

At best, the renewal of broken relations is a nervous matter.
> *Ibid.*

Sumner's[1] mind had reached the calm of water which receives and reflects images without absorbing them; it contained nothing but itself.
> *Ibid.*

The difference is slight, to the influence of an author, whether he is read by five hundred readers, or by five hundred thousand; if he can select the five hundred, he reaches the five hundred thousand.
> *Ibid. Chap. 17*

The newspaper-man is, more than most men, a double personality; and his person feels best satisfied in its double instincts when writing in one sense and thinking in another.
> *Ibid.*

A teacher affects eternity; he can never tell where his influence stops.
> *Ibid. Chap. 20*

One friend in a lifetime is much; two are many; three are hardly possible. Friendship needs a certain parallelism of life, a community of thought, a rivalry of aim.
> *Ibid.*

What one knows is, in youth, of little moment; they know enough who know how to learn.
> *Ibid. Chap. 21*

He had often noticed that six months' oblivion amounts to newspaper-death, and that resurrection is rare. Nothing is easier, if a man wants it, than rest, profound as the grave.
> *Ibid. Chap. 22*

Morality is a private and costly luxury.
> *Ibid.*

Nothing is more tiresome than a superannuated pedagogue.
> *Ibid. Chap. 23*

[1] Charles Sumner [1811-1874].

The study of history is useful to the historian by teaching him his ignorance of women. . . . The woman who is known only through a man is known wrong.
> *The Education of Henry Adams.*
> *Chap. 23*

He too serves a certain purpose who only stands and cheers.[1]
> *Ibid. Chap. 24*

Practical politics consists in ignoring facts.
> *Ibid.*

Nothing in education is so astonishing as the amount of ignorance it accumulates in the form of inert facts.
> *Ibid. Chap. 25*

Power when wielded by abnormal energy is the most serious of facts.
> *Ibid. Chap. 28*

Those who seek education in the paths of duty are always deceived by the illusion that power in the hands of friends is an advantage to them.
> *Ibid.*

Power is poison. Its effect on Presidents had been always tragic, chiefly as an almost insane excitement at first, and a worse reaction afterwards; but also because no mind is so well balanced as to bear the strain of seizing unlimited force without habit or knowledge of it; and finding it disputed with him by hungry packs of wolves and hounds whose lives depend on snatching the carrion.
> *Ibid.*

A certain chronic irritability — a sort of Bostonitis — which, in its primitive Puritan forms, seemed due to knowing too much of his neighbors and thinking too much of himself.
> *Ibid.*

Modern politics is, at bottom, a struggle not of men but of forces.
> *Ibid.*

We combat obstacles in order to get repose, and, when got, the repose is insupportable.
> *Ibid. Chap. 29*

[1] And if I should lose, let me stand by the road
And cheer as the winners go by!
BERTON BRALEY: *Prayer of a Sportsman*

Simplicity is the most deceitful mistress that ever betrayed man.
*The Education of Henry Adams.
Chap. 30*
No one means all he says, and yet very few say all they mean, for words are slippery and thought is viscous.
Ibid. Chap. 31
The movement from unity into multiplicity, between 1200 and 1900, was unbroken in sequence, and rapid in acceleration. Prolonged one generation longer, it would require a new social mind.
*Ibid. Chap. 34
(A Law of Acceleration)*
Even in America, the Indian Summer of life should be a little sunny and a little sad, like the season, and infinite in wealth and depth of tone — but never hustled.
Ibid. Chap. 35
Perhaps some day — say 1938, their centenary — . . . they would find a world that sensitive and timid natures could regard without a shudder.
Ibid. Closing words

JOSEPH ASHBY-STERRY
[1838–1917]

When the glass is at ninety a man is a fool
Who directs not his efforts to try to keep cool.
Ninety in the Shade
Half-hidden in its grassy bed
You'll find that slender silver thread —
The tiny Thames; which, here set free,
Begins its journey to the sea!
The Source of the Thames
The ruddy ripe tomata
In china bowl of ice,
And grouse worth a sonata
Undoubtedly are nice.
The Riparian Philosopher
It's much too hot for reason,
And far too warm for rhyme.
Ibid.
There are people, I'm told — some say there are heaps —
Who speak of the talkative Samuel as Peeps;

And some so precise and pedantic their step is,
Who call the delightful old diarist Pepys;
But those I think right, and I follow their steps,
Ever mention the garrulous gossip as Pepys.
Pepys

JAMES BRYCE [1]
[1838–1922]

The greatest liberty that man has taken with Nature.
*South America [Of the
Panama Canal]*
What you want [in Washington] is to have a city which every one who comes from Maine, Texas, Florida, Arkansas, or Oregon can admire as being something finer and more beautiful than he had ever dreamed of before; something which makes him even more proud to be an American.
The Nation's Capital [2]
You have never sufficiently foreseen how enormously rich and populous a nation you are going to be.
Ibid.
Medicine, the only profession that labours incessantly to destroy the reason for its own existence.
*Address at dinner for General
W. C. Gorgas [March 23,
1914]*
To most people nothing is more troublesome than the effort of thinking.
Studies in History and Jurisprudence, Vol. 2, Page 7

GEORGE COOPER
[1838–1927]

October gave a party;
The leaves by hundreds came:
The ashes, oaks, and maples,
And those of every name.
October's Party. Stanza 1

[1] Ambassador from Great Britain to the United States, 1906–1913.
[2] In *The National Geographic Magazine*, 1913.

After the shower, the tranquil sun;
  After the snow, the emerald leaves;
Silver stars when the day is done;
  After the harvest, golden sheaves.
                After. Stanza 1

Brave your storm with firm endeavor,
  Let your vain repinings go!
Hopeful hearts will find forever
  Roses underneath the snow!
        Roses Underneath the Snow.
                Stanza 1

Sweet Genevieve,
The days may come, the days may go,
But still the hands of memory weave
The blissful dreams of long ago.
                Sweet Genevieve

GEORGE DEWEY
[1838–1917]

You may fire when ready, Gridley.
        At battle of Manila Bay
                [May 1, 1898]

I am convinced that the office of the President is not such a very difficult one to fill, his duties being mainly to execute the laws of Congress.
        Interview in The New York World,
                April 4, 1900

MARY ABIGAIL DODGE
("GAIL HAMILTON")
[1838–1896]

Whatever an author puts between the two covers of his book is public property; whatever of himself he does not put there is his private property, as much as if he had never written a word.
        Country Living and Country
                Thinking. Preface

The moment an audacious head is lifted one inch above the general level, pop! goes the unerring rifle of some biographical sharpshooter, and it is all over with the unhappy owner.
        Skirmishes and Sketches. The
                New School of Biography

What's virtue in man can't be vice in a cat.
                Both Sides

MARY MAPES DODGE
[1838–1905]

Grandma told me all about it,
Told me, so I couldn't doubt it,
How she danced — my Grandma
    danced! —
        Long ago.
                The Minuet. Stanza 1

Whimpy, little Whimpy,
  Cried so much one day,
His grandma couldn't stand it,
  And his mother ran away.
                Little Whimpy. Stanza 1

Whenever a snowflake leaves the sky,
It turns and turns to say "Good-by!
Good-by, dear clouds, so cool and
    gray!"
Then lightly travels on its way.
                Snowflakes

Life is a mystery as deep as ever death
    can be;
Yet oh, how sweet it is to us, this life
    we live and see!
        The Two Mysteries. Stanza 3

But I believe that God is overhead;
And as life is to the living, so death is to
    the dead.
                Ibid. Stanza 5

KATE FIELD
[1838–1896]

My faithful cavalier,
At dusk he draweth near,
  To wait outside my wicket.
I hear him draw his bow,
He playeth soft and low,
  My dusky little cricket.
                My Serenade. Stanza 3

They talk about a woman's sphere as
    though it had a limit;
There's not a place in earth or heaven,
There's not a task to mankind given,
There's not a blessing or a woe,
There's not a whispered "yes" or "no,"
There's not a life, or death, or birth,
That has a feather's weight of worth
Without a woman in it.
                Woman's Sphere

JOHN HAY [1]
[1838–1905]

A keerless man in his talk was Jim,
  And an awkward hand in a row,
He never flunked, and he never lied, —
  I reckon he never knowed how.
                    Jim Bludso

"I'll hold her nozzle agin the bank
  Till the last galoot's ashore."
                    Ibid.

And they all had trust in his cussedness,
  And knowed he would keep his word.
                    Ibid.

He weren't no saint — but at jedgment
  I'd run my chance with Jim,
'Longside of some pious gentlemen
  That wouldn't shook hands with him.
He seen his duty, a dead-sure thing, —
  And went for it thar and then;
And Christ ain't a-going to be too hard
  On a man that died for men.
                    Ibid.

I don't go much on religion,
  I never ain't had no show;
But I've got a middlin' tight grip, sir,
  On the handful o' things I know.
I don't pan out on the prophets
  And free-will, and that sort of
    thing, —
But I b'lieve in God and the angels
  Ever sence one night last spring.
                    Little Breeches

And I think that saving a little child,
  And fotching him to his own,
Is a derned sight better business
  Than loafing around The Throne.
                    Ibid.

He trumped Death's ace for me that
    day,
  And I'm not goin' back on him!
                    Banty Tim

He was hard on women and rough on
    his friends;
  And he didn't have many, I'll let you
    know.
                    Golyer

But I never seed nothing that could or
    can
Jest get all the good from the heart of a
    man
  Like the hands of a little child.
                    Golyer

The King will be well if he sleeps one
    night
  In the Shirt of a Happy Man.
            The Enchanted Shirt.[1] Part 1

"An idle man has so much to do
  That he never has time to be sad."
                    Ibid. Part 2

"I would do it, God wot," and he roared
    with the fun,
  "But I haven't a shirt to my back."
                    Ibid.

The night comes down, the lights burn
    blue;
And at my door the Pale Horse stands,[2]
To bear me forth to unknown lands.
                    The Stirrup Cup

Bring me to-night a lotus tied
With thread from a house where none
    has died.[3]
                    The Law of Death

There stands not by the Ganges' side
A house where none hath ever died.
                    Ibid.

I know not what this man may be,
Sinner or saint; but as for me,
One thing I know, — that I am he
Who once was blind, and now I see.[4]
            Religion and Doctrine

Good Luck is the gayest of all gay girls,
  Long in one place she will not stay,
Back from your brow she strokes the
    curls,
  Kisses you quick and flies away.

---

[1] See Sir Walter Scott, page 309.
[2] A pale horse: and his name that sat on him
was Death. — *Revelation, VI, 8*
[3] "A grain of mustard-seed," the sage re-
    plied,
  "Found where none old or young has ever
      died,
  Will cure the pain you carry in your
      side."
                    JOHN WHITE CHADWICK:
                        Buddha's Lesson
[4] Whether he be a sinner or no, I know not:
one thing I know, that, whereas I was blind,
now I see. — *John, IX, 25*

---

[1] It is strange how the memory of a man
may float to posterity on what he would have
himself regarded as the most trifling of his
works. — SIR WILLIAM OSLER, quoted by
HARVEY CUSHING: *Life of Sir William Osler*,
Vol. II, Chap. 31, P. 301

But Madame Bad Luck soberly
    comes . . .
  And sits by your bed, and brings her
    knitting.
      Good and Bad Luck (After Heine)
There are three species of creatures who
    when they seem coming are going,
When they seem going they come:
    Diplomats, women, and crabs.
      Distichs. II
When you break up housekeeping, you
    learn the extent of your treasures.
      Ibid. IX
Who would succeed in the world should
    be wise in the use of his pronouns.
Utter the You twenty times, where you
    once utter the I.
      Ibid. XIII
True luck consists not in holding the
    best of the cards at the table:
Luckiest he who knows just when to rise
    and go home.
      Ibid. XV
Try not to beat back the current, yet be
    not drowned in its waters;
Speak with the speech of the world,
    think with the thoughts of the few.
      Ibid. XVII

GEORGE WASHINGTON JOHNSON
[1838–1917]

I wandered to-day to the hill, Maggie,
  To watch the scene below,
The creek and the creaking old mill,
    Maggie,[1]
  As we used to, long ago.
    When You and I Were Young,
      Maggie. Stanza 1
To me you're as fair as you were, Mag-
    gie,
  When you and I were young.
      Ibid. Stanza 3

WILLIAM EDWARD HARTPOLE LECKY
[1838–1903]

Offspring of an idle hour,
Whence has come thy lasting power?
      On an Old Song

[1] The mill was situated on the bank of
Twenty Mile Creek, Glanford, Ontario, Canada. It is now owned by Henry Ford.

The stately ship is seen no more,
The fragile skiff attains the shore;
And while the great and wise decay,
And all their trophies pass away,
Some sudden thought, some careless
    rhyme,
Still floats above the wrecks of Time.
      On an Old Song

EMMA A. LENT
[*Floruit* 1885]

They said, "The Master is coming
  To honor the town to-day,
And none can tell at whose house or
    home
  The Master will choose to stay."
And I thought, while my heart beat
    wildly,
  What if He should come to mine?
How would I strive to entertain
  And honor the Guest divine?
      The Master Is Coming

GEORGE LEYBOURNE
[? –1884]

He'd fly through the air with the great-
    est of ease,
This handsome young man on the fly-
    ing trapeze;
His movements were graceful, all girls
    he could please,
  And my love he purloined away!
    The Man on the Flying Trapeze
      [*1865*]

JOSEPH MALINS [1]
[*Floruit* 1895]

Better put a strong fence 'round the
    top of the cliff,
  Than an ambulance down in the
    valley.
    A Fence or an Ambulance.
      Stanza 7

[1] Editor of *The Reciter*, an English publication.

JOHN, VISCOUNT MORLEY
[1838-1923]

Evolution is not a force but a process; not a cause but a law.
On Compromise

It is not enough to do good; one must do it the right way.
Ibid.

You have not converted a man because you have silenced him.
Ibid.

The great business of life is to be, to do, to do without, and to depart.
Address on Aphorisms [1887]

The gravity and concision of Thucydides are of specially wholesome example in these days of over-coloured and over-voluminous narrative.
Ibid.

Those who would treat politics and morality apart will never understand the one or the other.
Rousseau

You can not demonstrate an emotion or prove an aspiration.
Ibid.

Literature — the most seductive, the most deceiving, the most dangerous of professions.
Burke

No man can climb out beyond the limitations of his own character.
Robespierre

A great interpreter of life ought not himself to need interpretation.
Emerson

The most frightful idea that has ever corroded human nature — the idea of eternal punishment.
Vauvenargues

Where it is a duty to worship the sun it is pretty sure to be a crime to examine the laws of heat.
Voltaire

A man will already be in no mean Paradise if at the hour of sunset a ray of good hope may fall upon him like harmonies of music.
Ibid.

Simplicity of character is no hindrance to subtlety of intellect.
Life of Gladstone

Every man of us has all the centuries in him.
Life of Gladstone

Great economic and social forces flow with a tidal sweep over communities that are only half conscious of that which is befalling them. Wise statesmen are those who foresee what time is thus bringing, and endeavor to shape institutions and to mold men's thought and purpose in accordance with the change that is silently surrounding them.
Life of Richard Cobden.
Closing paragraph

There are some books which cannot be adequately reviewed for twenty or thirty years after they come out.
Recollections. Vol. I, Book 2,
Chap. 8

The proper memory for a politician is one that knows what to remember and what to forget.
Ibid. Vol. II, Book 4, Chap. 2

Men bound to make their watches keep time in two longitudes at once.
Ibid. Book 5, Chap. 1

In my creed, waste of public money is like the sin against the Holy Ghost.
Ibid. Chap. 3

Success depends on three things: who says it, what he says, how he says it; and of these three things, what he says is the least important.
Ibid. Chap. 4

Excess of severity is not the path to order. On the contrary, it is the path to the bomb.
Ibid.

MOSES OWEN
[1838-1878]

Nothing but flags! but simple flags,
Tattered and torn and hanging in rags;
And we walk beneath them with careless tread,
Nor think of the hosts of the mighty dead

Who have marched beneath them in days gone by.

> *The Returned Maine Battle Flags.*[1] *Stanza 1*

EMILY REBECCA PAGE
[1838–1860]

Where the rocks are gray and the shore is steep,
And the waters below look dark and deep,
Where the rugged pine, in its lonely pride
Leans gloomily over the murky tide; . . .
Where the shadow is heavy the whole day through,
There lies at its moorings the old canoe.

> *The Old Canoe.*[2] *Stanza 1*

EDNA DEAN PROCTOR
[1838–1923]

The rose may bloom for England,
  The lily for France unfold;
Ireland may honor the shamrock,
  Scotland her thistle bold;
But the shield of the great Republic,
  The glory of the West,
Shall bear a stalk of the tasselled corn —
  The sun's supreme bequest!

> *Columbia's Emblem*

Good-night! and sweetest dreams be thine
Through all their shining way,
Till darkness goes, and bird and rose
With rapture greet the day.

> *Good-Night. Stanza 6*

[1] Written on hearing a visitor exclaim, "Nothing but flags!" as she passed through a room in the State Capitol, Augusta, Maine.

[2] Miss Page lived at Bradford, Vermont, on the Connecticut River, where her father was tollkeeper of the bridge.

The authorship of the poem has been ascribed to Thomas J. Worthen, of Little Rock, Arkansas. Earlier the poem had been credited to Albert Pike, who denied that he had either written or claimed the poem.

MARGARET ELIZABETH SANGSTER
[1838–1912]

I know — yet my arms are empty,
  That fondly folded seven,
And the mother heart within me
  Is almost starved for heaven.

> *Are the Children at Home?*

Never yet was a springtime,
  Late though lingered the snow,
That the sap stirred not at the whisper
  Of the southwind, sweet and low;
Never yet was a springtime
  When the buds forgot to blow.

> *Awakening*

A tiny flower, pale and sweet,
  That blooms o'er breath of ice;
And glad are they, on any day,
  Who find the edelweiss.

> *The Edelweiss. Stanza 1*

There's joy in sailing outward —
  Though we leave upon the pier,
With faces grieved and wistful,
  Our very dearest dear.

> *The Joy of Coming Home.*
> *Stanza 1*

There's nothing half so pleasant
  As coming home again.

> *Ibid. Stanza 3*

We have careful thought for the stranger,
  And smiles for the sometime guest,
But oft for our own the bitter tone,
  Though we love our own the best.

> *Our Own. Stanza 3*

The tender word forgotten,
  The letter you did not write,
The flower you might have sent, dear,
  Are your haunting ghosts to-night.

> *At Sunset (The Sin of Omission).*
> *Stanza 1*

Child of the boundless prairie, son of the virgin soil,
Heir to the bearing of burdens, brother to them that toil;
God and Nature together shaped him to lead in the van,
In the stress of the wildest weather, when the nation needed a man.

> *Abraham Lincoln. Stanza 1*

FREDERICK WHITTAKER
[1838-1917]

Dead! Is it possible? He, the bold
    rider;
Custer, our hero, the first in the fight,
Charming the bullets of yore to fly
    wider,
Shunning our battle-king's ringlets of
    light!
    Custer's Last Charge. Stanza 1

HEZEKIAH BUTTERWORTH
[1839-1905]

The bird with the broken pinion
    Never soared as high again.
    The Bird with a Broken Wing
One taper lights a thousand,
    Yet shines as it has shone;
And the humblest light may kindle
    A brighter than its own.
    The Taper. Stanza 10
Methinks when I stand in life's sunset,
    As I stood when we parted at school,
I shall see the bright faces of children
    I loved in the village of Yule.
    The Beautiful Village of Yule.
    Stanza 9

FRANCIS PHARCELLUS
CHURCH
[1839-1906]

Virginia, your little friends are wrong.
They have been affected by the skepticism of a skeptical age. They do not believe except they see. They think that
nothing can be which is not compre-
hensible by their little minds. All minds,
Virginia, whether they be men's or children's, are little. In this great universe
of ours man is a mere insect, an ant,
in his intellect, as compared with the
boundless world about him, as measured by the intelligence capable of
grasping the whole of truth and knowledge.
    Editorial: Is There a Santa Claus? [1]

[1] First published in *The New York Sun,*
Sept. 21, 1897, in reply to an inquiry from Virginia O'Hanlon. These extracts are included by
permission of *The New York Sun.*

Not believe in Santa Claus? You
might as well not believe in fairies.
    Is There a Santa Claus?
No Santa Claus! Thank God, he
lives, and he lives forever. A thousand
years from now, Virginia, nay, ten
times ten thousand years from now, he
will continue to make glad the heart of
childhood.
    Ibid.

FRANCIS BRET HARTE [1]
[1839-1902]

The patient stars
Lean from their lattices, content to wait.
All is illusion till the morning bars
Slip from the levels of the Eastern gate.
Night is too young, O friend! day is too
    near;
Wait for the day that maketh all things
    clear.
Not yet, O friend, not yet!
    Cadet Grey. Song, Not Yet.
    All is not true,
All is not ever as it seemeth now.
    Ibid.
What lieth dark, O love, bright day will
    fill;
Wait for thy morning, be it good or ill.
    Ibid.
Fades the light,
    And afar
Goeth day, cometh night;
    And a star
      Leadeth all,
      Speedeth all
        To their rest.[2]

    Ibid. Bugle Song

[1] Yon yellow sun melts in the sea;
  A sombre ship sweeps silently
  Past Alcatraz tow'rd Orient skies —
  A mist is rising to the eyes —
  Good-bye, Bret Harte, good-night, good-
    night.
    JOAQUIN MILLER: *Good-Bye, Bret Harte*
        [May, 1902], *Stanza 1*
[2] Fading light
  Dims the sight,
    And the stars gem the sky,
  Gleaming bright,
    From afar drawing nigh,
  Falls the night.
    JOSEPH BERG ESENWEIN [1867-   ]:
        Taps, St. 1

Love, good-night!
  Must thou go
  When the day
And the light
  Need thee so?
            Cadet Grey. Bugle Song

Bells of the Past, whose long-forgotten
    music
  Still fills the wide expanse,
Tingeing the sober twilight of the Pres-
    ent
  With color of romance!
        The Angelus Heard at the
          Mission Dolores, 1868

Until points of gravest import yielded
    slowly one by one,
And by Love was consummated what
    Diplomacy begun.
            Concepcion de Arguello

Never a tear bedims the eye
That time and patience will not dry;
Never a lip is curved with pain
That can't be kissed into smiles again.
            The Lost Galleon

And the way to look for a thing is plain,
To go where you lost it, back again.
            Ibid.

Which I wish to remark,
  And my language is plain,
That for ways that are dark
  And for tricks that are vain,
The heathen Chinee is peculiar.
        Plain Language from Truthful
          James. Stanza 1

Ah Sin was his name.
            Ibid. Stanza 2

With the smile that was childlike and
    bland.
            Ibid. Stanza 4

We are ruined by Chinese cheap labor.[1]
            Ibid. Stanza 7

But still, when the mists of Doubt pre-
    vail,
And we lie becalmed by the shores of
    Age,
We hear from the misty troubled
    shore
The voice of the children gone before,
  Drawing the soul to its anchorage.
            A Greyport Legend. Stanza 6

[1] Not a Chinaman's chance. — This saying
originated when the Californians were opposing the introduction of Chinese labor.

And ever since then, when the clock
    strikes two,
  She walks unbidden from room to
    room,
And the air is filled that she passes
    through
  With a subtle, sad perfume.
            A Newport Romance. Stanza 6

He read aloud wherein the Master
  Had writ of "Little Nell."
            Dickens in Camp. Stanza 4

And on that grave where English oak
    and holly
  And laurel wreaths entwine,
Deem it not all a too presumptuous
    folly,
  This spray of Western pine!
            Ibid. Stanza 10

These things are managed so well in
    France.[1]
            The Tale of a Pony

Brief words, when actions wait, are
    well:
The prompter's hand is on his bell;
The coming heroes, lovers, kings,
Are idly lounging in the wings;
Behind the curtain's mystic fold
The glowing future lies unrolled.
        Address at opening of the Cali-
          fornia Theatre, San Francisco
          [January 19, 1870]

What was it the Engines said,
Pilots touching, — head to head
Facing on the single track,
Half a world behind each back?
        What the Engines Said (Opening
          of the Pacific Railroad) [2]

I reside at Table Mountain, and my
    name is Truthful James;
I am not up to small deceit, or any sin-
    ful games.
            The Society upon the Stanislaus

He smiled a kind of sickly smile, and
    curled up on the floor

[1] "They order," said I, "this matter better in
France." — LAURENCE STERNE: *A Sentimental
Journey, P. 1*
[2] Drill, ye tarriers, drill,
  And it's work all day
  Without sugar in your tay,
  When you're working for the U.P. Rail-
    way.
    Laborers' song during the construc-
    tion of the Union Pacific Railway

And the subsequent proceedings interested him no more.
> *The Society upon the Stanislaus*

For there be women, fair as she,
Whose verbs and nouns do more agree.
> *Mrs. Judge Jenkins*

Oh, yer's yer good old whiskey,
Drink it down.
> *Two Men of Sandy Bar. Act IV*

One big vice in a man is apt to keep
out a great many smaller ones.
> *Ibid.*

Give me a man that is capable of a
devotion to anything, rather than a
cold, calculating average of all the virtues!
> *Ibid.*

I'm acquainted with affliction,
Chiefly in the form of fiction,
As 'tis offered up by strangers
At the consul's open door.
> *At the Consul's Open Door.*[1]

I think I know all fancy
Styles of active mendicancy.
> *Ibid.*

I know the worthy tourist,
Who by accident the purest,
Lost his letters, watch and wallet,
From the cold deck coming o'er.
> *Ibid.*

JAMES PROCTOR KNOTT
[1839–1911]

Duluth! The word fell upon my ear
with a peculiar and indescribable
charm, like the gentle murmur of a low
fountain stealing forth in the midst of
roses, or the soft sweet accent of an
angel's whisper in the bright, joyous
dream of sleeping innocence. 'Twas the
name for which my soul had panted for
years, as the hart panteth for the water-
brooks.
> *Speech on the St. Croix and Bay-
> field Railroad Bill [January 27,
> 1871]*

[1] Written while Harte was a U. S. Consul at
Glasgow, after receiving a note of warning
from Bristol, England, that an impostor had
been pretending to be a destitute American
and procuring money from United States con-
suls.

SIBYL F. PARTRIDGE
(SISTER MARY XAVIER)

Lord, for to-morrow and its needs,
I do not pray;
Keep me, my God, from stain of sin,
Just for to-day.
> *Just for To-day [1877]*

WALTER PATER
[1839–1894]

Every intellectual product must be
judged from the point of view of the
age and the people in which it was produced.
> *The Renaissance. Mirandola*

Its generous belief that nothing which
had ever interested the human mind
could wholly lose its vitality.
> *Ibid.*

That sweet look of devotion which
men have never been able altogether to
love, and which still makes the born
saint an object almost of suspicion to
his earthly brethren.
> *Ibid. Botticelli*

The sunless pleasures of weary people, whose care for external things is
slackening.
> *Ibid. Michelangelo*

Hers is the head upon which all "the
ends of the world are come," and the
eyelids are a little weary. It is a beauty
wrought out from within upon the flesh,
the deposit, little cell by cell, of strange
thoughts and fantastic reveries and exquisite passions.
> *Ibid. Leonardo da Vinci.
> [Monna Lisa]*

All art constantly aspires towards the
condition of music.
> *Ibid. Giorgione*

A circle which in an age of great troubles, losses, anxieties, can amuse itself
with art, poetry, intrigue.
> *Ibid. Du Bellay*

Religions, as they grow by natural
laws out of man's life, are modified by
whatever modifies his life.
> *Ibid. Winckelmann*

Let us understand by poetry all literary production which attains the power

of giving pleasure by its form, as distinct from its matter.

The Renaissance. Winckelmann

What we have to do is to be for ever curiously testing new opinions and courting new impressions.

Ibid. Conclusion

Art comes to you proposing frankly to give nothing but the highest quality to your moments as they pass.

Ibid.

A book, like a person, has its fortunes with one; is lucky or unlucky in the precise moment of its falling in our way, and often by some happy accident counts with us for something more than its independent value.

Marius the Epicurean. Chap. 6

To know when one's self is interested, is the first condition of interesting other people.

Ibid.

Given the hardest terms, supposing our days are indeed but a shadow, even so, we may well adorn and beautify, in scrupulous self-respect, our souls, and whatever our souls touch upon.

Ibid. Chap. 8

Certainly, flowers were pleasant to the eye. Such things had even their sober use, as making the outside of human life superficially attractive, and thereby promoting the first steps towards friendship and social amity.

Ibid. Chap. 12

By the attainment of a true philosophy to attain happiness; or, having missed both, to perish, as one of the vulgar herd.

Ibid. Chap. 24

There is but one road that leads to Corinth.[1]

Ibid.

[1] Non cuivis homini contingit adire Corinthum
(It is not every man's lot to gain Corinth).
HORACE: *Epistles, Book I, XVII, To Scaeva, L. 36*
'Tis not every one who can afford to go to Corinth. — PLUTARCH: *Parallel Lives, Aristophanes*
"There is but one way to Corinth," as of old. — ANDREW LANG: *Letters to Dead Authors, To Lucian of Samosata*

I hardly know wherein philosophy and wine are alike unless it be in this, that the philosophers exchange their ware for money, like the wine-merchants; some of them with a mixture of water or worse, or giving short measure.

Marius the Epicurean. Chap. 24

We need some imaginative stimulus, some not impossible ideal such as may shape vague hope, and transform it into effective desire, to carry us year after year, without disgust, through the routine-work which is so large a part of life.

Ibid. Chap. 25

The aim of a true philosophy must lie, not in futile efforts towards the complete accommodation of man to the circumstances in which he chances to find himself, but in the maintenance of a kind of candid discontent, in the face of the very highest achievement.

Ibid.

Through the survival of their children, happy parents are able to think calmly, and with a very practical affection, of a world in which they are to have no direct share.

Ibid.

JAMES RYDER RANDALL
[1839–1908]

Hark to an exiled son's appeal,
Maryland, my Maryland!
My Mother State, to thee I kneel.[1]

Maryland, My Maryland. Stanza 2

From hill to hill, from creek to creek,
Potomac calls to Chesapeake,
Maryland, my Maryland.

Ibid. Stanza 7

Hushed in the alabaster arms of Death
Our young Marcellus sleeps.

John Pelham

After a little while,
The birds will serenade in bush and tree,
But not for me;

[1] Randall, a native of Baltimore, was working on *The New Orleans Sunday Delta* when he wrote this song in April, 1861.

On billows duskier than the gloomy
   Nile
My barque must be —
After a little while.
       After a Little While. Stanza 5
Teach me, my God, to bear my cross
   As Thine was borne;
Teach me to make of every loss
   A crown of thorn.
               Resurgam
The Robin wears his silver vest
   In panoplies of red.
   Why the Robin's Breast Is Red [1]

SAMUEL JOHN STONE
[1839–1900]

Where did I come from, then? Ah,
   where indeed?
This is a riddle monstrous hard to read.
I have it! Why, of course,
All things are moulded by some plastic
   force
Out of some atoms somewhere up in
   space,
Fortuitously concurrent anyhow —
There, now!
That's plain as is the beak upon my
   face.
       *Soliloquy of a Rationalistic
              Chicken* [2]
What I can't see, I never will believe in!
                  Ibid.

G. W. BELLAMY

Old Simon, the cellarer, keeps a rare
   store
Of Malmsey and Malvoisie,
And Cyprus, and who can say how
   many more?
       Simon, the Cellarer. Stanza 1

WILFRID SCAWEN BLUNT
[1840–1922]

He who has once been happy is for aye
   Out of destruction's reach.
        Sonnet, With Esther
Nor has the world a better thing,
   Though one should search it round,

Than thus to live one's own sole king,
   Upon one's own sole ground.
        The Old Squire. Stanza 14
Ay, this is the famed rock, which Her-
   cules
And Goth and Moor bequeathed us. At
   this door
England stands sentry.
          Sonnet, Gibraltar

HENRY BURTON
[1840–1930]

Have you had a kindness shown?
   Pass it on.
         Pass It On. [1] *Stanza 1*
Hold thy lighted lamp on high,
Be a star in someone's sky.
         Ibid. Stanza 4

HENRY BERNARD
CARPENTER
[1840–1887]

Oh, there are moments in man's mortal
   years
When for an instant that which long
   has lain
Beyond our reach is on a sudden found
In things of smallest compass, and we
   hold
The unbounded shut in one small min-
   ute's space,
And worlds within the hollow of our
   hand, —
A world of music in one word of love,
A world of love in one quick wordless
   look,
A world of thought in one translucent
   phrase,
A world of memory in one mournful
   chord,
A world of sorrow in one little song.
            Liber Amoris
The time will come when this, our Holy
   Church,
Shall melt away in ever widening walls,
And be for all mankind. And in its
   place
Shall rise another church, whose cove-
   nant word

---

[1] See P. H. Hayne, page 586.
[2] In *Harper's Monthly, Sept., 1875.*

[1] Official poem of the International Sunshine Society.

Shall be the act of love. Not *Credo* then
But *Amo* shall be the watchword
  through its gate.
Liber Amoris

LIZZIE YORK CASE
[1840–1911]

There is no unbelief;
Whoever plants a seed beneath the sod
And waits to see it push away the clod,
  He trusts in God.
Unbelief. Stanza 1

Whoever says "To-morrow," "The un-
  known,"
"The future," trusts the Power alone
  He dares disown.
Ibid. Stanza 5

JOHN WHITE CHADWICK
[1840–1904]

If good men were only better,
  Would the wicked be so bad?
A Timely Question. Stanza 1

It singeth low in every heart,
  We hear it each and all, —
A song of those who answer not,
  However we may call.
Auld Lang Syne. Stanza 1

They cannot be where God is not,
  On any sea or shore.
Ibid. Stanza 3

HENRY AUSTIN DOBSON
[1840–1921]

Once at the Angelus
  (Ere I was dead),
Angels all glorious
  Came to my bed.
"Good-Night, Babette!"

I am so old! . . . Good-night, Babette!
Ibid.

For lo! the same old myths that made
  The early "stage successes,"
Still "hold the boards," and still are
  played,
  "With new effects and dresses."
*The Drama of the Doctor's
Window. Prologue, Stanza 6*

I am a Shade: a Shadowe too arte thou:
I marke the Time: saye, Gossip, dost
  thou soe?
The Sundial. Stanza 2

He had played for his lordship's levee,
  He had played for her ladyship's
  whim,
Till the poor little head was heavy,
  And the poor little brain would swim.
The Child-Musician. Stanza 1

Time goes, you say? Ah no!
Alas, Time stays, *we* go.
The Paradox of Time. Stanza 1

O Poet, then, forbear
  The loosely-sandalled verse,
Choose rather thou to wear
  The buskin — strait and terse.
*Ars Victrix (Imitated from
Théophile Gautier). Stanza 2*

All passes. Art alone
  Enduring stays to us;
The Bust outlasts the throne, —
  The Coin, Tiberius.
Ibid. Stanza 8

Paint, chisel, then, or write;
  But, that the work surpass,
With the hard fashion fight, —
  With the resisting mass.
Ibid. Stanza 10

The ladies of St. James's!
  They're painted to the eyes;
Their white it stays for ever,
  Their red it never dies:
But Phyllida, my Phyllida!
  Her color comes and goes;
It trembles to a lily, —
  It wavers to a rose.
The Ladies of St. James's. Stanza 4

Far better, in some nook unknown,
  To sleep for once — and soundly —
Than still survive in wistful stone,
  Forgotten more profoundly.
*To an Unknown Bust in the
British Museum. Stanza 6*

Yet would to-day when Courtesy grows
  chill,
And life's fine loyalties are turned to
  jest,
Some fire of thine might burn within us
  still!
Ah, would but one might lay his lance
  in rest, ·

And charge in earnest . . . were it but
a mill!
Don Quixote

I grant you freely that he sought his
Ends
Not always wisely — but he lov'd his
Friends.
*A Dialogue to the Memory of
Mr. Alexander Pope*

Ye gods! how he talk'd! What a torrent of sound,
His hearers invaded, encompass'd and
— drown'd!
A Postscript to "Retaliation"

He made little fishes talk vastly like
whales.[1]
Ibid.

Read him for Style.
Ibid.

"Not to be tuneless in old age!"[2]
*Henry Wadsworth Longfellow.
Stanza 1*

Rather we count thee one
Who, when his race is run,
Layeth him down,
Calm — through all coming days,
Filled with a nation's praise,
Filled with renown.
Alfred, Lord Tennyson. Stanza 6

Form is the Cage and Sense the Bird.
The Poet twirls them in his Mind,
And wins the Trick with both combined.
The Toyman

He praised the Thing he understood;
'Twere well if every Critic would.
The 'Squire at Vauxhall. Moral 2

What is a Patron? Johnson knew,
And well that lifelike portrait drew.
He is a Patron who looks down
With careless eye on men who drown;
But if they chance to reach the land,
Encumbers them with helping hand.[3]
The Noble Patron

But little lore of loving can any flagon
teach,

[1] See Goldsmith, page 254.
[2] Nec turpem senectam
Degere, nec cithara carentem
(That in age I may not drift
Long years, my lyre forgot!)
HORACE: *Odes, Book I, XXXI,
To Apollo, L. 19*
[3] See Johnson, page 233.

For when my tongue is loosèd most,
then most I lose my speech.
*The Maltworm's Madrigal.
Stanza 6*

I intended an Ode,
And it turned to a Sonnet.
Urceus Exit

Love comes back to his vacant dwelling, —
The old, old Love that we knew of
yore!
The Wanderer. Stanza 1

This is the Actor's gift; to share
All moods, all passions, nor to care
One whit for scene, so he without
Can lead men's minds the round-
about,
Stirred as of old those hearers were
When Burbadge played!
When Burbadge Played. Stanza 3

What flaws! what faults! — on every
page,
When *Finis* comes.
When Finis Comes. Stanza 2

O Singer of the field and fold,
Theocritus! Pan's pipe was thine, —
Thine was the happier Age of Gold.
*For a Copy of Theocritus.
Stanza 1*

Life, — 'tis of thee they fable so.
Thou bidd'st us eat, and still denied,
Still fasting, from thy board we go: —
"Where is *thy* feast, O Barmecide?"
*The Ballad of the Barmecide.
Envoy*

Dear Critics, whose verdicts are always
so new! —
One word in your ear. There were Critics before . . .
And the man who plants cabbages imitates, too![1]
The Ballad of Imitation

In the work-a-day world, — for its
needs and woes,
There is place and enough for the pains
of prose;
But whenever the May-bells clash and
chime,

[1] C'est imiter quelqu'un que de planter des
choux (We are imitating someone even when
planting cabbages). — ALFRED DE MUSSET:
Namouna, Canto 2, St. 9

Then hey! — for the ripple of laughing rhyme!
> *The Ballad of Prose and Rhyme.*
> *Envoy*

Old books, old wine, old Nankin blue; —
All things, in short, to which belong
The charm, the grace that Time makes strong, —
All these I prize, but (*entre nous*)
> Old friends are best!
> *To Richard Watson Gilder.*
> *Stanza 3*

So artless in its vanity,
So fleeting, so eternal,
So packed with "poor Humanity" —
We know as Pepys his Journal.
> *Pepys' Diary. Stanza 6*

Fame is a food that dead men eat, —
I have no stomach for such meat.
> *Fame Is a Food that Dead Men*
> *Eat. Stanza 1*

The Press is too much with us: small and great;
We are undone of chatter and *on dit*,
Report, retort, rejoinder, repartee,
Mole-hill and mare's nest, fiction up-to-date.
> *A Pleasant Invective Against*
> *Printing*

I shall not see the morning sky;
I shall not hear the night-wind sigh;
I shall be mute, as all men must
In after days!
> *In After Days*

He held his pen in trust
To Art, not serving shame or lust.
> *Ibid.*

WILLIAM CHANNING GANNETT
[1840–1923]

The poem hangs on the berry bush
When comes the poet's eye;
The street begins to masquerade
When Shakespeare passes by.
The Christ sees white in Judas's heart
And loves His traitor well;
The God, to angel His new heaven,
Explores His lowest hell.
> *We See as We Are*

MRS. C. GILDERSLEEVE (LONGSTREET)
[*Floruit* 1885]

Mrs. Lofty keeps a carriage,
> So do I;
She has dappled grays to draw it,
> None have I;
She's no prouder with her coachman
> Than am I
With my blue-eyed, laughing baby
> Trundling by.
> *Mrs. Lofty and I. Stanza 1*

THOMAS HARDY
[1840–1928]

When false things are brought low,
And swift things have grown slow,
Feigning like froth shall go,
> Faith be for aye.
> *Between Us Now*

Whence comes solace? Not from seeing,
What is doing, suffering, being;
Not from noting Life's conditions,
Not from heeding Time's monitions;
> But in cleaving to the Dream
> And in gazing at the Gleam
Whereby gray things golden seem.[1]
> *On a Fine Morning*

Why doth IT so and so, and ever so,
This viewless, voiceless Turner of the Wheel?
> *The Dynasts. Fore Scene,*
> *Spirit of the Pities*

A local thing called Christianity.
> *Ibid. Spirit of the Years, Sc. 6*

Aggressive Fancy working spells
Upon a mind o'erwrought.
> *Ibid. Act I, Sc. 6, Napoleon*

Ere systemed suns were globed and lit
The slaughters of the race were writ.
> *Ibid. Act II, Sc. 5, Semi-chorus*

My argument is that War makes rattling good history; but Peace is poor reading.
> *Ibid. Spirit Sinister*

Like the British Constitution, she owes her success in practice to her inconsistencies in principle.
> *The Hand of Ethelberta*

---

[1] No longer a shadow,
But clothed with the Gleam.
TENNYSON: *Merlin and the Gleam, L. 93*

' A lover without indiscretion is no lover at all.

The Hand of Ethelberta

That cold accretion called the world, which, so terrible in the mass, is so unformidable, even pitiable, in its units.

Tess of the D'Urbervilles.
Chap. 13

That shabby corner of God's allotment where He lets the nettles grow, and where all unbaptized infants, notorious drunkards, suicides, and others of the conjecturally damned are laid.

Ibid. Chap. 14

The chronic melancholy which is taking hold of the civilized races with the decline of belief in a beneficent power.

Ibid. Chap. 18

The debatable land between predilection and love.

Ibid. Chap. 20

Patience, that blending of moral courage with physical timidity.

Ibid. Chap. 43

"Justice" was done, and the President of the Immortals (in Aeschylean phrase) had ended his sport with Tess.

Ibid. Chap. 59

We have triumphed: this achievement
    turns the bane to antidote,
Unsuccesses to success,
Many thought-worn eves and morrows
    to a morrow free of thought.

Friends Beyond. Stanza 4

No more need we corn and clothing,
    feel of old terrestrial stress;
Chill detraction stirs no sigh;
Fear of death has even bygone us:
    death gave all that we possess.

Ibid. Stanza 5

A bird sings the selfsame song,
With never a fault in its flow,
That we listened to here those long
    Long years ago.

The Selfsame Song. Stanza 1

I heard a Voice from I knew not
    where: —
"The Great Adjustment is taking
    place!"

"There Seemed a Strangeness,"
A Phantasy. Stanza 1

And they shall see what is, ere long,
Not through a glass, but face to face;
And Right shall disestablish Wrong.

"There Seemed a Strangeness,"
A Phantasy. Stanza 4

That faiths by which my comrades
    stand
    Seem fantasies to me,
And mirage-mists their Shining Land,
    Is a strange destiny.

The Impercipient at a Cathedral
Service. Stanza 1

He who breathes All's-Well to these
Breathes no All's-Well to me.

Ibid. Stanza 3

Let me enjoy the earth no less
Because the all-enacting Might
That fashioned forth its loveliness
Had other aims than my delight.

Let Me Enjoy. Minor Key,
Stanza 1

There trembled through
His happy good-night air
Some blessed Hope, whereof he knew
And I was unaware.

The Darkling Thrush. By the
Century's Death-Bed, Stanza 4

To see stand weeping by
A woman once embraced, will try
The tension of a man the most austere.

The Contretemps. Stanza 6

One pairing is as good as another
Where all is venture!

Ibid. Stanza 10

You have not known
Men's lives, deaths, toils, and teens;
You are but a heap of stick and stone:
A new house has no sense of the have-
    beens.[1]

The Two Houses. Stanza 5

"Yes; quaint and curious war is!
You shoot a fellow down
You'd treat if met where any bar is,
Or help to half-a-crown."

The Man He Killed. Stanza 5

We have lost somewhat, afar and near,
    Gentlemen,

---

[1] There's nothing mournful about it; it cannot be sad and lone
For the lack of something within it that it has never known.
JOYCE KILMER: *The House with Nobody in It, St. 5*

The thinning of our ranks each year
Affords a hint we are nigh undone,
That we shall not be ever again
The marked of many, loved of one.
An Ancient to Ancients. Stanza 3

We who met sunrise sanguine-souled,
  Gentlemen,
Are wearing weary. We are old;
These younger press; we feel our rout
Is imminent to Aïdes' den, —
The evening shades are stretching out.
Ibid. Stanza 7

Much is there waits you we have
  missed;
Much lore we leave you worth the
  knowing;
Much, much has lain outside our ken.
Nay, rush not: time serves; we are go-
  ing.
Ibid. Stanza 10

You have dropped your dusty cloak and
  taken your wondrous wings
  To another sphere,
Where no pain is.
"Why Do I?" Stanza 2

A star looks down at me,
And says: "Here I and you
Stand, each in our degree:
What do you mean to do?"
Waiting Both. Stanza 1

We two kept house, the Past and I,
  The Past and I;
I tended while it hovered nigh,
Leaving me never alone.
The Ghost of the Past. Stanza 1

Do you think of me at all,
  Wistful ones?
Do you think of me at all
  As if nigh?
*Dead "Wessex," the Dog, to the
  Household. Stanza 1*

You may hear a jump or trot
On the stair or path or plot;
But I shall cause it not,
  Be not there.
Ibid. Stanza 3

Further and further still
Through the world's vaporous vitiate
  air
His words wing on — as strong words
  will.
*George Meredith, 1828–1909.
  Stanza 6*

Yes, yes; I am old. In me appears
The history of a hundred years.
Empires', kings', captives' births and
  deaths;
Strange faiths and fleeting shibboleths;
Tragedy, comedy, through my pages
Beyond all mummed on any stages;
Cold hearts beat hot, hot hearts beat
  cold,
And I beat on.
*The Newspaper Soliloquizes:
  London Observer, March 14,
  1926*

I traversed a dominion
  Whose spokesmen spake out strong
Their purpose and opinion
  Through pulpit, press, and song.

I saw, in web unbroken
  Its history outwrought
Not as the loud had spoken
  But as the mute had thought.
I Traversed a Dominion

ROSSITER JOHNSON
[1840–1931]

O for a lodge in a garden of cucumbers!
  O for an iceberg or two at control!
O for a vale which at mid-day the dew
  cumbers!
  O for a pleasure trip up to the Pole!
Ninety-nine in the Shade. Stanza 1

Then O for a draught from a cup of
  cold pizen,
  And O for a resting-place in the cold
  grave!
With a bath in the Styx where the thick
  shadow lies on
  And deepens the chill of its dark-
  running wave.
Ibid. Stanza 6

SAMUEL ALROY JONAS
[?–1915]

Representing nothing on God's earth
  now,
And naught in the waters below it,
As a pledge of a nation that's dead and
  gone,
Keep it, dear friend, and show it.
*Lines on the Back of a
  Confederate Note*

COSMO MONKHOUSE
[1840–1901]

So we must part, my body, you and I
   Who've spent so many pleasant years
     together.
'Tis sorry work to lose your company
   Who clove to me so close.
          Any Soul to Any Body

M. T. MORRISON
[*Circa* 1840– ?]

A foolish little maiden bought a foolish
   little bonnet,
With a ribbon and a feather and a bit
   of lace upon it;
And that all the other maidens in the
   little town might know it,
She thought she'd go to meeting the
   next Sunday, just to show it.
    *What the Choir Sang about the
      New Bonnet. Stanza 1*

"Alleluia, Alleluia!" sang the choir
   above her head;
"Hardly knew you, hardly knew you!"
   were the words she thought they
   said.
          Ibid. Stanza 3

WILLIAM HENRY HARRISON ("ADIRONDACK") MURRAY
[1840–1904]

Ah, friends, dear friends, as years go on
   and heads get gray, how fast the
   guests do go!
Touch hands, touch hands, with those
   that stay.
Strong hands to weak, old hands to
   young, around the Christmas
   board, touch hands.
The false forget, the foe forgive, for
   every guest will go and every fire
   burn low and cabin empty stand.
Forget, forgive, for who may say that
   Christmas day may ever come to
   host or guest again.
Touch hands!
        John Norton's Vagabond

MINNA PAULL
[*Floruit* 1890]

From an old English parsonage,
   Down by the sea,
There came in the twilight
   A message to me;
Its quaint Saxon legend,
   Deeply engraven,
Hath, as it seems to me,
   Teaching from Heaven;
And through the hours
   The quiet words ring,
Like a low inspiration,
   "Doe ye nexte thynge."
      *"Doe Ye Nexte Thynge."
          Stanza 1*

ROSSITER WORTHINGTON RAYMOND
[1840–1918]

In Paestum's ancient fanes I trod,
   And mused on those strange men of
   old,
Whose dark religion could unfold
   So many gods, and yet no God.
    Ramblings in Greece. Stanza 1

Life is eternal; and love is immortal;
and death is only a horizon; and a
horizon is nothing save the limit of our
sight.
      A Commendatory Prayer

BENJAMIN SCOVILLE
[*Floruit* 1890]

Some day I'll pass by the Great Gates
   of Gold,
And see a man pass through unquestioned and bold.
"A Saint?" I'll ask, and old Peter'll
   reply:
"No, he carries a pass — he's a newspaper guy."
    The Newspaper Guy. Stanza 4

SIR HENRY M. STANLEY
[1840–1904]

Dr. Livingstone, I presume?
   *On meeting Livingstone in Ujiji,
   Central Africa [November 10,
   1871]*

WILLIAM GRAHAM SUMNER
[1840–1910]

The Forgotten Man [1] works and
votes — generally he prays — but his
chief business in life is to pay. . . .
Who and where is the Forgotten Man
in this case, who will have to pay for it
all?
Essay, The Forgotten Man [1883]

JOHN ADDINGTON SYMONDS
[1840–1893]

No seed shall perish which the soul hath
sown.
Sonnet, Versöhnung, A Belief
Gods fade; but God abides and in
man's heart
Speaks with the clear unconquerable
cry
Of energies and hopes that can not
die.
Sonnet, On the Sacro Monte
She smiled, and the shadows departed;
She shone, and the snows were rain;
And he who was frozen-hearted
Bloomed up into love again.
Eyebright
These things shall be, — a loftier race
Than e'er the world hath known shall
rise
With flame of freedom in the souls,
And light of knowledge in their eyes.
The Days That Are to Be

KATHARINE KENT CHILD
(MRS. EDWARD ASHLEY)
WALKER
[1840–1916]

However divinity schools may refuse
to "skip" in unison, and may butt and
butter each other about the doctrine
and origin of human depravity, all will
join devoutly in the credo, I believe

in the total depravity of inanimate
things.[1]
*The Total Depravity of
Inanimate Things.*[2]
There is melancholy pleasure in the
knowledge that a great soul has gone
mourning before me in the path I am
now pursuing. It was only to-day that
in glancing over the pages of Victor
Hugo's greatest work I chanced upon
the following: "Everyone will have noticed with what skill a coin let fall upon
the ground runs to hide itself, and what
art it has in rendering itself invisible."
Ibid.
Stern necessity, proverbially known
as "the mother of invention," and practically the stepmother of ministers'
daughters.
Ibid.
The elusiveness of soap, the knottiness of strings, the transitory nature of
buttons, the inclination of suspenders
to twist and of hooks to forsake their
lawful eyes, and cleave only unto the
hairs of their hapless owner's head.
Ibid.

HENRY WATTERSON
[1840–1921]

Things have come to a heluva pass
When a man can't cudgel his own jackass.
*Reply when rebuked for criticiz-
ing the Governor of Kentucky*

JOHN WILSON [3]
[?–1889]

O for a Booke and a shadie nooke,
eyther in-a-doore or out;
With the grene leaves whisp'ring overhede, or the Streete cryes all about.
Where I maie Reade all at my ease,
both of the Newe and Olde;

[1] The forgotten man at the bottom of
the economic pyramid. — FRANKLIN DELANO
ROOSEVELT: Radio address [April 7, 1932]

[1] Outrage from lifeless things. — MILTON:
Paradise Lost, X, 707
[2] In *The Atlantic Monthly, Sept., 1864*
(Vol. XIV, Pp. 357–364).
[3] A London bookseller, friend of Austin
Dobson.

For a jollie goode Booke whereon to
  looke is better to me than Golde.
    *For a Catalogue of Second-
        hand Books*

MATHILDE BLIND
[1841–1896]

We are so tired; my heart and I.
Of all things here beneath the sky
Only one thing would please us best —
Endless, unfathomable rest.
              Rest. Stanza 1

ROBERT BUCHANAN
[1841–1901]

        Alone at nights,
I read my Bible more and Euclid less.
        An Old Dominie's Story
Beauty and Truth, tho' never found,
  are worthy to be sought.
              To David in Heaven
I saw the starry Tree
Eternity
Put forth the blossom Time.
                    Proteus
Full of a sweet indifference.
                    Charmian
I say, the world is lovely,
  And that loveliness is enough.
              Artist and Model
        A race that binds
Its body in chains and calls them Lib-
  erty,
And calls each fresh link Progress.
              Political Mystics.
              Titan and Avatar

CHARLES EDWARD CARRYL
[1841–1920]

The night was thick and hazy
When the *Piccadilly Daisy*
Carried down the crew and Captain in
  the sea;
And I think the water drowned 'em,
For they never, never found 'em,
And I know they didn't come ashore
  with me.
        Robinson Crusoe. Stanza 1

I had that fellow Friday [1]
Just to keep the tavern tidy.
              Robinson Crusoe. Stanza 3
Canary birds feed on sugar and seed,
  Parrots have crackers to crunch;
And as for the poodles, they tell me the
    noodles
  Have chicken and cream for their
    lunch.
        But there's never a question
        About my digestion —
Anything does for me!
              The Camel's Complaint.
                    Stanza 1
A capital ship for an ocean trip
  Was the "Walloping Window-blind."
No gale that blew dismayed her crew
  Or troubled the Captain's mind.
The man at the wheel was taught to feel
  Contempt for the wildest blow,
And it often appeared, when the
    weather had cleared,
  That he'd been in his bunk below.
      *Davy and the Goblin, A Nautical
              Ballad. Stanza 1*

OLIVER WENDELL HOLMES (JR.)
[1841–1935]

The riders in a race do not stop short
when they reach the goal. There is a
little finishing canter before coming to
a standstill. There is time to hear the
kind voice of friends and to say to one's
self: "The work is done." But just as
one says that, the answer comes: "The
race is over, but the work never is done
while the power to work remains." The
canter that brings you to a standstill
need not be only coming to rest. It
cannot be, while you still live. For to
live is to function. That is all there is
in living.
      *Radio address on his ninetieth
          birthday [March 8, 1931]*

WILLIAM HENRY HUDSON
[1841–1922]

When I meet with a falsehood, I care
not who the great persons who proclaim

[1] I took my man Friday with me. — DANIEL
DEFOE: *Robinson Crusoe*

it may be, I do not try to like it or believe it or mimic the fashionable prattle of the world about it.

The Purple Land. Chap. 28

When I hear people say they have not found the world and life so agreeable or interesting as to be in love with it, or that they look with equanimity to its end, I am apt to think they have never been properly alive nor seen with clear vision the world they think so meanly of, or anything in it — not a blade of grass. Only I know that mine is an exceptional case, that the visible world is to me more beautiful and interesting than to most persons, that the delight I experienced in my communings with Nature did not pass away, leaving nothing but a recollection of vanished happiness to intensify a present pain. The happiness was never lost, but owing to that faculty I have spoken of, had a cumulative effect on the mind and was mine again, so that in my worst times, when I was compelled to exist shut out from Nature in London for long periods, sick and poor and friendless, I could yet always feel that it was infinitely better to be than not to be.

Far Away and Long Ago. Chap. 24

SIR RICHARD CLAVER-HOUSE JEBB
[1841–1905]

At the middle point of the [Greek] stage, some steps — known as "Charon's staircase," because the ghost sometimes comes up by them — lead down into what we should call the pit.

Greek Literature. Page 76

JOHN ALEXANDER JOYCE
[*Floruit* 1885]

You must leave your many millions
And the gay and festive crowd;
Though you roll in royal billions,
There's no pocket in a shroud.

There's No Pocket in a Shroud.
Stanza 1

I shall love you in December
With the love I gave in May!

Question and Answer. Stanza 8

For the sake of the almighty dollar [1]
And whatever else he could gain.

The Sutler

MARY ARTEMISIA LATHBURY [2]
[1841–1913]

Day is dying in the west;
Heaven is touching earth with rest.

Day Is Dying in the West
[1877]. Stanza 1

Children of yesterday,
  Heirs of to-morrow,
What are you weaving?
  Labor and sorrow?
Look to your looms again,
  Faster and faster
Fly the great shuttles
  Prepared by the Master.
Life's in the loom,
Room for it — room!

Song of Hope. Stanza 1

BREWER MATTOCKS
[1841–1934]

The parish priest
Of Austerity
Climbed up in a high church steeple
To be nearer God,
So that he might hand
His word down to His people.

The Preacher's Mistake. Stanza 1

In his age God said —
"Come down and die!"
And he cried out from the steeple,
"Where art Thou, Lord?"
And the Lord replied,
"Down here among my people."

Ibid. Stanza 5

[1] Almighty gold. — BEN JONSON: *Epistle to Elizabeth, Countess of Rutland*
The almighty dollar. — IRVING: *Bracebridge Hall, The Stout Gentleman*
[2] Miss Lathbury was known as the Chautauqua Laureate.

CINCINNATUS HEINE ("JOAQUIN")[1] MILLER
[1841–1913]

Is it worth while that we jostle a brother
  Bearing his load on the rough road of life?
Is it worth while that we jeer at each other
  In blackness of heart? — that we war to the knife?
God pity us all in our pitiful strife.
                    Is It Worth While? Stanza 1

That man who lives for self alone
Lives for the meanest mortal known.
            *Walker in Nicaragua. Chant I,
                              Stanza 1*

Who harvests what his hand hath sown,
Does more for God, for man, his own —
Dares more than all mad heroes dare.
                    Ibid. Stanza 3

I do not question school nor creed
Of Christian, Protestant, or Priest;[2]
I only know that creeds to me
Are but new names for mystery,
That good is good from east to east,
And more I do not know nor need
To know, to love my neighbor well.
            The Tale of the Tall Alcalde

It is not wise to be a poet now,
For, oh, the world it has so modest grown
It will not praise a poet to his face,
But waits till he is dead some hundred years,

---

[1] In a paper, *How I Came to be a Writer of Books,* contributed to *Lippincott's Magazine* in 1886, and quoted in STUART P. SHERMAN's introduction to *The Poetical Works of Joaquin Miller* (G. P. Putnam's Sons, 1923), Miller explains the origin of his pen-name. His first writing was a public letter in defense of Joaquin Murietta, the outlaw. A Sacramento newspaper banteringly identified him with the outlaw, and friends continued the banter. The name "Joaquin" clung to him, so Miller accepted it and used it in the title of his first book and thereafter.

[2] Shall I give up the friend I have valued and tried,
  If he kneel not before the same altar with me?
            THOMAS MOORE: *Come, Send
                              Round the Wine*

Then uprears marbles cold and stupid as itself.
                    Bits from Ina, a Drama. Sc. 4

In men whom men condemn as ill
I find so much of goodness still,
In men whom men pronounce divine
I find so much of sin and blot,
I do not dare to draw a line[1]
Between the two, where God has not.
                    Byron

Lo! Christ himself chose only twelve,
Yet one of these turned out a thief.
            *A Song of the South. Part II,
                              Canto 3*

Who taught you tender Bible tales
Of honey-lands, of milk and wine?
Of happy, peaceful Palestine?
Of Jordan's holy harvest vales?
Who gave the patient Christ? I say
Who gave your Christian creed? Yea, yea,
Who gave your very God to you?
Your Jew! Your Jew! Your hated Jew!
                    To Russia. Stanza 3

The bravest battle that ever was fought;
  Shall I tell you where and when?
On the maps of the world you will find it not;
  It was fought by the mothers of men.
                    The Bravest Battle. Stanza 1

Man's books are but man's alphabet,
Beyond and on his lessons lie —
The lessons of the violet,
The large gold letters of the sky.
            *The Larger College
            [Man's Books]. Stanza 7*

The soul that feeds on books alone —
I count that soul exceeding small
That lives alone by book and creed, —
A soul that has not learned to read.
                    Ibid. Stanza 10

Honor and glory forever more
  To this good man gone to rest;

---

[1] There is so much good in the worst of us,
  And so much bad in the best of us,
  That it hardly behooves any of us
  To talk about the rest of us.
    First printed in *The Marion* (Kansas) *Record,* owned by Governor Edward Wallis Hoch [1849–1925], and assumed to have been written by him.

Peace on the dim Plutonian shore; [1]
  Rest in the land of the blest.
          Peter Cooper, April, 1883. [2]
                    Stanza 1
Aye, wisest he is in this whole wide
    land,
  Of hoarding till bent and gray;
For all you can hold in your cold, dead
    hand
  Is what you have given away.
              Ibid. [3] *Stanza 3*
The biggest dog has been a pup.
        William Brown of Oregon.
                    Stanza 5
Behind him lay the gray Azores,
  Behind the Gates of Hercules;
Before him not the ghost of shores,
  Before him only shoreless seas.
              Columbus. Stanza 1
He gained a world; he gave that world
Its grandest lesson: "On! sail on!"
              Ibid. Stanza 5
The Lightning reached a fiery rod,
And on Death's fearful forehead wrote
The autograph of God.
        With Love to You and Yours.
                Part I, Canto III

KATE PUTNAM OSGOOD
[1841–1910]

The great tears sprang to their meeting
    eyes,
  For the heart must speak when the
    lips are dumb;
And under the silent evening skies
  Together they followed the cattle
    home.
            Driving Home the Cows. [4]
                    Stanza 12

[1] Night's Plutonian shore. — POE: *The Raven, St. 8*
  See Lytle, page 568.
[2] In his autobiography, *My Life and Memories,* JOSEPH I. C. CLARKE [1846–1925] devotes several pages to an account of Miller bringing this poem to the office of *The New York Herald* on the night of Peter Cooper's death in April, 1883.
[3] The world did not want all I had to say of this gentle old man and kept only the three little verses. — MILLER: Comment on the poem
[4] In *Harper's Monthly Magazine*, March, 1865.

EMILY BRUCE ROELOFSON
[1841–1921]

When to the flowers so beautiful
  The Father gave a name,
Back came a little blue-eyed one
  (All timidly it came);
And standing at its Father's feet
  And gazing in His face,
It said, in low and trembling tone,
  "Dear God, the name Thou gavest
    me,
Alas! I have forgot!"
  Kindly the Father looked Him down
And said: "Forget-me-not."
        The Origin of the Forget-me-not

MINOT JUDSON SAVAGE
[1841–1918]

Oh, where is the sea? the fishes cried,
As they swam its crystal clearness
    through.
            Where Is God? Stanza 1
A man's truest monument must be a
    man.
            The Song of a Man
        (Phillips Brooks). Stanza 8

CLEMENT WILLIAM SCOTT
[1841–1904]

Bring, novelist, your notebook! Bring,
    dramatist, your pen!
And I'll tell you a simple story of what
    women do for men.
It's only a tale of a lifeboat, of the dy-
    ing and the dead,
Of the terrible storm and shipwreck
    that happened off Mumbles Head!
        The Women of Mumbles Head.
                    Stanza 1
Be this our covenant, apart, alone,
Carve thou this sign upon Love's altar-
    stone,
    Mizpah! [1]

                Mizpah. Stanza 1

[1] Mizpah . . . The Lord watch between thee and me, when we are absent one from another. — *Genesis, XXXI, 49*

KATE BROWNLEE SHERWOOD
[1841–1914]

Washington rode from the bloody fray
Up to the gun that a woman manned.
"Molly Pitcher, you saved the day,"
He said, as he gave her a hero's hand.
Molly Pitcher.[1] Stanza 5

EDWARD ROWLAND SILL
[1841–1887]

At the punch-bowl's brink
Let the thirsty think
What they say in Japan:
"First the man takes a drink,
Then the drink takes a drink,
Then the drink takes the man!"
An Adage from the Orient

I would be satisfied if I might tell,
Before I go,
That one warm word, — how I have
loved them well,
Could they but know.
A Foolish Wish

The light we almost had
Shall make them glad;
The words we waited long
Shall run in music from their voice
and song.
Field Notes.[2] XII

Then came the king's son, wounded,
sore bestead,
And weaponless, and saw the broken
sword,
Hilt-buried in the dry and trodden
sand,
And ran and snatched it, and with
battle-shout
Lifted afresh he hewed his enemy
down,
And saved a great cause that heroic day.
Opportunity

[1] Molly Pitcher was the wife of a Revolutionary soldier, and after he had been killed, she took his place at the cannon in the Battle of Monmouth [June 28, 1778].
Sure, honor's name will aye be richer
For the bright name of Molly Pitcher.
LAURA ELIZABETH RICHARDS:
Molly Pitcher
[2] For the class of 1882, Smith College.

No pity, Lord, could change the heart
From red with wrong to white as
wool;
The rod must heal the sin: but Lord,
Be merciful to me, a fool!
The Fool's Prayer

'Tis by our follies that so long
We hold the earth from heaven away.
Ibid.

The ill-timed truth we might have
kept —
Who knows how sharp it pierced and
stung?
The word we had not sense to say —
Who knows how grandly it had rung?
Ibid.

Earth bears no balsam for mistakes;
Men crown the knave, and scourge
the tool
That did his will.[1]
Ibid.

What may we take into the vast forever?
That marble door
Admits no fruit of all our long endeavor,
No fame-wreathed crown we wore,
No garnered lore.
The Future

What if some morning, when the stars
were paling,
And the dawn whitened, and the East
was clear,
Strange peace and rest fell on me from
the presence
Of a benignant Spirit standing near.
A Morning Thought

And what if then, while the still morning brightened,
And freshened in the elm the Summer's breath,
Should gravely smile on me the gentle
angel
And take my hand and say, "My
name is Death."
Ibid.

[1] The law locks up both man and woman
Who steals the goose from off the common,
But lets the greater felon loose
Who steals the common from the goose.
Anonymous. Quoted by EDWARD POTTS
CHEYNEY: *Social and Industrial History of England* [1901], *Introduction*

You need not think to palm yourself
off as a freakish young zephyr, just born
of yonder snow-streak and the sun-
warmed rock; you have been roaming
this planet ever since its birth. You
have whirled in cyclones and danced
with the streamers of the aurora; it was
you that breathed Job's curses, and the
love vows of the first lover that was
ever forsworn.

> *The Mountain Wind,*
> *Sierra Nevadas*

GEORGE ALFRED
TOWNSEND ("GATH")
[1841–1914]

Here a suffering animal lies,
  Faithful, trusty, and true;
If she lives, she lives — if she dies, she
    dies;
  And nothing more can I do.

> *The Cow and the Bishop*

EUGENE FITCH WARE
("IRONQUILL")
[1841–1911]

When back into the alphabet
The critic's satires shall have crumbled,
When into dust his hand is humbled,
  One verse of mine may linger yet.

> *The Rhymes of Ironquill. Preface*

In the suds and in the soap,
Worked a woman full of hope;
Working, singing, all alone,
In a sort of undertone:
  "With the Savior for a friend,
  He will keep me to the end."

> *The Washerwoman's Song*

Human hopes and human creeds
Have their root in human needs.

> *Ibid.*

The charm of a love is its telling, the
    telling that goes with the giving;
The charm of a deed is its doing; the
    charm of a life is its living;
The soul of the thing is the thought;
    the charm of the act is the actor;

The soul of the fact is its truth, and the
    NOW is its principal factor.

> *The Now*

Man builds no structure which outlives
    a book.

> *The Book*

Of all the States, but three will live in
    story:
Old Massachusetts with her Plymouth
    Rock
And old Virginia with her noble stock,
And sunny Kansas with her woes and
    glory.

> *Three States*

O Dewey was the morning
  Upon the first of May,
And Dewey was the Admiral
  Down in Manila Bay;
And Dewey were the Regent's eyes,
  "Them" orbs of royal blue!
And Dewey feel discouraged?
  I Dew not think we Dew.

> *In The Topeka (Kansas) Daily*
> *Capital, May 3, 1898*

Work brings its own relief;
He who most idle is
Has most of grief.

> *To-day*

No evil deed live oN.

> *The Palindrome.*

No matter how long the river, the river
    will reach the sea.

> *The Blizzard*

Hour after hour the cards were fairly
    shuffled
  And fairly dealt, but still I got no
    hand.

> *Whist*

I like the game and want to play;
And through the long, long night will I,
    unruffled,
  Play what I get until the break of
    day.

> *Ibid.*

I'm ignorant of music, but still, in spite
    of that,
I always drop a quarter in an organ-
    grinder's hat.

> *The Organ-Grinder*

The ballads of the people are the bul-
    warks of the State.

> *Ibid.*

The highest of renown
Are the surest stricken down;
But the stupid and the clown
They remain.
Paresis

The Turks,
Becoming somewhat sad,
Surrendered every
Consonant they had.
The Siege of Djklxprwbz

We fixed him up an epitaph,
"Death loves a mining shark."
A Shining Mark

Oft the statesman and the saint
Think they're doing good, but ain't.
Aesop's Fables. No. 17

The days of long-haired poets now are
o'er;
The short-haired poet seems to have the
floor.
The Short-Haired Poet. Stanza 3

No town can hope prosperity and trade,
Unless the Press shall vigorously aid.
Ibid. Stanza 63

The farmer works the soil,
The agriculturist works the farmer.
The Kansas Bandit

When a person knows a story that he
thinks he ought to tell,
If he doesn't get to tell it, why of course
he don't feel well;
And if no one stops to listen, why of
course a man will feel
All broke up and dislocated, and uneasy as an eel.
A Romance. Preface.

Human beings are like boilers, and the
same rules, it would seem,
Have an equal application to affection
and to steam.
Making love and putting steam on will
entail the same mishaps —
When you get on too much pressure, all
is lost by a collapse.
Ibid. Chap. IV

SARAH WILLIAMS
[1841–1868]

Is it so, O Christ in heaven, that the
highest suffer most?
That the strongest wander farthest and
most hopelessly are lost?

That the mark of rank in nature is ca-
pacity for pain,
And the anguish of the singer makes the
sweetness of the strain?
"I have many things to tell you, but ye
cannot bear them now." [1]
Is It So, O Christ in Heaven?
Stanza 3

Though my soul may set in darkness, it
will rise in perfect light,
I have loved the stars too fondly to be
fearful of the night.
The Old Astronomer. Stanza 4

CHARLES FOLLEN ADAMS
[1842–1918]

I haf von funny leedle poy
Vot gomes schust to mine knee;
Der queerest schap, der createst rogue,
As efer you dit see.
He runs, und schumps, und schmashes
dings
In all barts off der house:
But vot off dot? He vas mine son,
Mine leedle Yawcob Strauss.
Yawcob Strauss. Stanza 1

I schtill vill remember dot oldt country
kitchen
Und dot long-handled dipper, dot hangs
py der sink.
Dot Long-Handled Dipper.

I vants to gondradict dot shap
Dot made dis leedle shoke:
"A voman vas der glinging vine,
Und man der shturdy oak."
Der Oak und der Vine. Stanza 1

AMBROSE BIERCE
[1842–1914 ?]

Whose laws, imperfect and unjust,
Thy just and perfect purpose serve;
The needle, howsoe'er it swerve,
Still warranting the sailor's trust.
Invocation

Cynic, perforce, from study of mankind
In the false volume of his single mind,
He damned his fellows for his own un-
worth,
And, bad himself, thought nothing good
on earth.

[1] *John, XVI, 12*

He yearned to squander what he lived
    to save
And did not, for he could not, cheat the
    grave.
                  An Epitaph

To men a man is but a mind. Who cares
What face he carries or what form he
    wears?
But woman's body is the woman. O
Stay thou, my sweetheart, and do never
    go.
          The Devil's Dictionary

Bore: a person who talks when you wish
    him to listen.
                      Ibid.

Garter: an elastic band intended to
keep a woman from coming out of
her stockings and desolating the country.
                      Ibid.

Labor: one of the processes by which A
acquires property for B.
                      Ibid.

Marriage: a community consisting of a
master, a mistress, and two slaves,
making in all, two.
                      Ibid.

Woman would be more charming if
one could fall into her arms without
falling into her hands.
                  Epigrams

You are not permitted to kill a
woman who has injured you, but nothing forbids you to reflect that she is
growing older every minute. You are
avenged 1440 times a day.
                      Ibid.

Self-denial is indulgence of a propensity to forego.
                      Ibid.

CHARLES MONROE
DICKINSON [1]
[1842–1924]

If the days grow dark, if care and pain
Press close and sharp on heart and
    brain,

[1] Mr. Dickinson, who was the editor and
publisher of *The Binghamton* (New York)
Republican for many years, suggested and initiated the Associated Press in 1892.

Then lovely pictures still shall bloom
Upon the walls of memory's room.
                  My Burdens

When the lessons and tasks are all
    ended,
    And the school for the day is dis-
      missed,
And the little ones gather around me
    To bid me "good-night" and be
    kissed.
         The Children.[1] *Stanza 1*

Within an ancient hollow oak
  That stood beside the road,
Just on the border of a wood,
  An aged Owl abode.
         A Sharp Trade. Stanza 1

WILLIAM JAMES
[1842–1910]

Habit is thus the enormous fly-wheel
of society, its most precious conservative agent. It alone is what keeps us all
within the bounds of ordinance.
      Psychology. Chap. 10 [*1892*]

It is well for the world that in most of
us, by the age of thirty, the character
has set like plaster, and will never
soften again.
                      Ibid.

There is no more miserable human
being than one in whom nothing is
habitual but indecision.
                      Ibid.

No matter how full a reservoir of
maxims one may possess, and no matter
how good one's *sentiments* may be, if
one have not taken advantage of every
concrete opportunity to *act,* one's character may remain entirely unaffected
for the better. With mere good intentions, hell is proverbially paved.[2]
                      Ibid.

Keep the faculty of effort alive in you
by a little gratuitous exercise every day.
That is, be systematically ascetic or heroic in little unnecessary points, do

[1] This poem is frequently attributed to
Charles Dickens, because of the similarity of
names.
[2] See Johnson, page 236.
The road to hell is paved with good intentions. — KARL MARX: *Capital,* Modern Library ed. (abridged), *P. 42.*

every day or two something for no other reason than that you would rather not do it, so that when the hour of dire need draws nigh, it may find you not unnerved and untrained to stand the test.

Psychology. Chap. 10 [*1892*]

The hell to be endured hereafter, of which theology tells, is no worse than the hell we make for ourselves in this world by habitually fashioning our characters in the wrong way.

Ibid.

No state [of mind] once gone can recur and be identical with what it was before.

Ibid. Chap. 11

We are not only gregarious animals, liking to be in sight of our fellows, but we have an innate propensity to get ourselves noticed, and noticed favorably, by our kind. No more fiendish punishment could be devised, were such a thing physically possible, than that one should be turned loose in society and remain absolutely unnoticed by all the members thereof.

Ibid. Chap. 12

In the practical as in the theoretic life, the man whose acquisitions *stick* is the man who is always achieving and advancing, whilst his neighbors, spending most of their time in relearning what they once knew but have forgotten, simply hold their own.

Ibid. Chap. 18

Genius, in truth, means little more than the faculty of perceiving in an unhabitual way.

Ibid. Chap. 20

The great source of terror to infancy is solitude.

Ibid. Chap. 25

The deepest thing in our nature is this dumb region of the heart in which we dwell alone with our willingnesses and our unwillingnesses, our faiths and our fears.

The Will to Believe [*1897*]

Be not afraid of life. Believe that life *is* worth living, and your belief will help create the fact.[1]

Ibid.

[1] See Alfred Austin, page 612.

The whole drift of my education goes to persuade me that the world of our present consciousness is only one out of many worlds of consciousness that exist.

The Varieties of Religious Experience [*1902*]. *Lecture XX*

SIDNEY LANIER
[1842–1881]

The sun is a-wait at the ponderous gate of the West.

The Marshes of Glynn. IV, 3

Ye marshes, how candid and simple and
    nothing-withholding and free
Ye publish yourselves to the sky and
    offer yourselves to the sea!
Tolerant plains, that suffer the sea and
    the rains and the sun,
Ye spread and span like the catholic
    man who hath mightily won
God out of knowledge and good out of
    infinite pain
And sight out of blindness and purity
    out of a stain.

Ibid. 6

As the marsh-hen secretly builds on the
    watery sod,
Behold I will build me a nest on the
    greatness of God:
I will fly in the greatness of God as the
    marsh-hen flies
In the freedom that fills all the space
    'twixt the marsh and the skies:
By so many roots as the marsh-grass
    sends in the sod
I will heartily lay me a-hold on the
    greatness of God:
Oh, like to the greatness of God is the
    greatness within
The range of the marshes, the liberal
    marshes of Glynn.

Ibid. 7

Out of the hills of Habersham,
Down the valleys of Hall.

Song of the Chattahoochee.
Stanza 1

Downward the voices of Duty call —
Downward, to toil and be mixed with
    the main,

The dry fields burn, and the mills are to turn.
Song of the Chattahoochee.
Stanza 5

Death, thou'rt a cordial old and rare:
Look how compounded, with what care!
Time got his wrinkles reaping thee
Sweet herbs from all antiquity.
The Stirrup-Cup. Stanza 1

The incalculable Up-and-Down of Time.
Clover

Life! thou sea-fugue, writ from east to west,
Love, Love alone can pore
On thy dissolving score
Of harsh half-phrasings,
Blotted ere writ,
And double erasings
Of chords most fit.
The Symphony

Music is Love in search of a word.
Ibid.

Into the woods my Master went,
Clean forspent.
A Ballad of Trees and the Master. Stanza 1

'Twas on a tree they slew Him — last
When out of the woods He came.
Ibid. Stanza 2

Now in the sea's red vintage melts the sun,
As Egypt's pearl dissolved in rosy wine,
And Cleopatra night drinks all.
Evening Song. Stanza 2

A rainbow span of fifty years,
Painted upon a cloud of tears,
In blue for hopes and red for fears,
Finds end in a golden hour to-day.
The Golden Wedding of Sterling and Sarah Lanier. Stanza 1

Through seas of dreams and seas of phantasies,
Through seas of solitudes and vacancies,
And through my Self, the deepest of the seas,
I strive to thee, Nirvâna.
Nirvâna. Stanza 1

My soul is sailing through the sea,
But the Past is heavy and hindereth me.
Barnacles. Stanza 1

T. MACLAGAN
[*Floruit* 1870]

I'm Captain Jinks of the Horse Marines,
I give my horse good corn and beans;
Of course 'tis quite beyond my means,
Though a Captain in the army.
Captain Jinks. Refrain

ARTHUR MACY
[1842–1904]

Cheers for the sailors that fought on the wave for it,
Cheers for the soldiers that always were brave for it,
Tears for the men that went down to the grave for it,
Here comes the Flag!
The Flag. Stanza 4

A little cat played on a silver flute,
And a big cat sat and listened;
The little cat's strains gave the big cat pains,
And a tear on his eyelids glistened.
The Boston Cats

Sit closer, friends, around the board!
Death grants us yet a little time.
Now let the cheering cup be poured,
And welcome song and jest and rhyme;
Enjoy the gifts that fortune sends,
Sit closer, friends.
Sit Closer, Friends: To the Papyrus Club, Boston. Stanza 1

Dear Omar, should you chance to meet
Our Brother Somewhere in the Gloom,
Pray give to Him a Message Sweet,
For Brothers in the Tavern Room.
He will not ask who 'tis that sends,
For We were Friends.
Ibid. Stanza 6

DAVID LAW PROUDFIT
("PELEG ARKWRIGHT")
[1842–1897]

A man sat on a rock and sought
Refreshment from his thumb;
A dinotherium wandered by
And scared him some.
His name was Smith. The kind of rock

He sat upon was shale.
One feature quite distinguished him —
He had a tail.
Prehistoric Smith
Nature abhors imperfect work
And on it lays her ban;
And all creation must despise
A tailless man.
Ibid.

ANNIE DOUGLAS GREEN ROBINSON ("MARION DOUGLAS")
[1842–1913]

Said old Gentleman Gay, "On a Thanksgiving Day,
If you want a good time, then give something away."
A Good Thanksgiving
There was once a pretty chicken, but his friends were pretty few,
For he thought that there was nothing in the world but what he knew.
The Ugly Duckling

DEXTER SMITH
[1842– ?]

Ring the bell softly, there's crape on the door.
Ring the Bell Softly

MAY RILEY (MRS. ALBERT) SMITH
[1842–1927]

Strange we never prize the music
Till the sweet-voiced bird has flown,
Strange that we should slight the violets
Till the lovely flowers are gone.
If We Knew [1]
The sweetest face in all the world to me,
Set in a frame of shining golden hair,
With eyes whose language is fidelity:
This is my mother. Is she not most fair?
Dedication in Cradle and Arm Chair

[1] First published in *The Rochester*, New York, *Union and Advertiser, Feb. 23, 1867.*

I wonder so that mothers ever fret
At little children clinging to their gown;
Or that the footprints, when the days are wet,
Are ever black enough to make them frown.
Tired Mothers. Stanza 3
Life's sweetest joys are hidden
In unsubstantial things;
An April rain, a fragrance,
A vision of blue wings.
The Treetop Road. Stanza 2
My life's swift river widens to the sea,
The careless babble of the brook is past;
A few late roses blossom still for me,
But spring is gone, and summer cannot last.
If I Could Choose. Stanza 6

RUSSELL HERMAN CONWELL
[1843–1925]

I ask not for a larger garden,
But for finer seeds.
My Prayer. Stanza 1
Acres of diamonds.
Title of lecture

HUGH ANTOINE D'ARCY
[1843–1925]

With chalk in hand the vagabond began
To sketch a face that well might buy the soul of any man.
Then as he placed another lock upon the shapely head,
With a fearful shriek he leaped and fell across the picture — dead!
The Face Upon the Floor [1887] [1]

SARAH DOUDNEY
[1843–1926]

The pure, the beautiful, the bright,
That stirred our hearts in youth,
The impulse to a wordless prayer,
The dreams of love and truth,
The longings after something lost,

[1] Often misquoted as "The Face on the Barroom Floor."

The spirit's yearning cry,
The strivings after better hopes, —
These things can never die.
Things That Never Die

Listen to the water-mill
Through the livelong day,
How the clicking of its wheel
Wears the hours away. . . .
And a proverb haunts my mind
As a spell is cast —
"The mill cannot grind
With the water that is past."
The Lesson of the Water-Mill [1]
[*1864*]

Oh, the wasted hours of life
That have drifted by!
Oh, the good that might have been,
Lost without a sigh!
Ibid.

Sleep on, beloved, sleep, and take thy
rest;
Lay down thy head upon thy Saviour's
breast;
We love thee well, but Jesus loves thee
best —
Good-night!
Good-Night. [2] *Stanza 1*

EDWARD DOWDEN
[1843–1913]

I said, "I will find God," and forth I
went
To seek him in the clearness of the sky,

[1] In 1870, Major-General DANIEL CRAIG
MCCALLUM [1815–1878] published a book of
verse, *The Water-Mill, and Other Poems,* in
which the first poem was practically the same
as Miss Doudney's, and caused international
dispute. His poem contained the following
lines:
Oh! listen to the water-mill, through all the
live-long day,
As the clicking of the wheel, wears hour by
hour away. . . .
The mill will never grind again with water
that is past. . . .
Oh! the wasted hours of life, that have swiftly
drifted by,
Alas! the good we might have done, all gone
without a sigh.

Miss Doudney's poem was first published in
1864. See Burton E. Stevenson: *Famous Single Poems* [1923].

[2] Ira D. Sankey composed music for this
poem, and sang it at the funeral of the Reverend Charles H. Spurgeon, Feb., 1892.

But he over me, stood unendurably
Only a pitiless sapphire firmament
Ringing the world — blank splendor.
Sonnet, Seeking God

ANNA E. HAMILTON
[1843–1876]

This learned I from the shadow of a
tree,
That to and fro did sway against a
wall,
Our shadow selves, our influence,
may fall
Where we ourselves can never be.
Influence

ALPHONSO ALVA HOPKINS
[1843–1918]

'Tis the joys the most prized that are
fleetest,
And that soonest creep out from the
heart,
As perfumes that are richest and sweetest
Are the earliest ones to depart.
Flitting Away

Flitting away, flitting away,
All that we cherished most dear;
There is nothing on earth that will stay,
Roses must die with the year.
Ibid.

HENRY JAMES
[1843–1916]

There are few hours in life more
agreeable than the hour dedicated to
the ceremony known as afternoon tea.
The Portrait of a Lady. I

At moments she discovered she was
grotesquely wrong, and then she treated
herself to a week of passionate humility.
Ibid. VI

The time-honored bread-sauce of the
happy ending.
Theatricals: Second Series

It's a complex fate, being an American, and one of the responsibilities it entails is fighting against a superstitious
valuation of Europe.
*Letter, 1872. (Quoted by Van
Wyck Brooks: The Pilgrimage
of Henry James)*

Try to be one of the people on whom nothing is lost.

The Art of Fiction

There are few things more exciting to me than a psychological reason.

Ibid.

The chances and changes, the personal history of any absolute genius, draw us to watch his adventure with curiosity and inquiry, lead us on to win more of his secret and borrow more of his experience (I mean, needless to say, when we are at all critically minded); but there is something in the clear safe arrival of the poetic nature, in a given case, at the point of its free and happy exercise, that provokes, if not the cold impulse to challenge or cross-question it, at least the need of understanding so far as possible how, in a world in which difficulty and disaster are frequent, the most wavering and flickering of all fine flames has escaped extinction.

*Preface to Rupert Brooke's
Letters from America (1916)*

FREDERIC WILLIAM
HENRY MYERS
[1843–1901]

Look when the clouds are blowing
    And all the winds are free:
In fury of their going
    They fall upon the sea.
But though the blast is frantic,
    And though the tempest raves,
The deep immense Atlantic
    Is still beneath the waves.

Wind, Moon, and Tides

Christ, I am Christ's, and let the name
    suffice you;
Aye, for me, too, it greatly hath suf-
    ficed.
Lo, with no winning words would I en-
    tice you,
Paul hath no honor and no friend but
    Christ.

Saint Paul

Coldly sublime, intolerably just.

Ibid.

Whoso has felt the Spirit of the Highest
    Cannot confound nor doubt Him nor
        deny:
Yea, with one voice, O world, though
        thou deniest,
Stand thou on that side, for on this
        am I.

The Inner Light

In no single act or passion can salvation stand; far hence, beyond Orion
and Andromeda, the cosmic process
works and shall work forever through
unbegotten souls.

Human Personality. Chap. X

JOSEPHINE POLLARD
[1843–1892]

Though he has Eden to live in,
    Man cannot be happy alone.

*We Cannot Be Happy Alone.
Stanza 5*

Miss Annabel McCarty
Was invited to a party,
"Your company from four to ten," the
        invitation said;
And the maiden was delighted
To think she was invited
To sit up till the hour when the big
        folks went to bed.

The First Party. Stanza 1

She screamed: "I want my supper —
        and I want to go to bed!"

Ibid. Stanza 7

I knew a man and his name was Horner,
Who used to live in Grumble Corner;
Grumble Corner in Cross Patch Town,
And he never was seen without a frown.

Grumble Corner

And many a discontented mourner
Is spending his days in Grumble Cor-
        ner;
Sour and sad, whom I long to entreat
To take a house in Thanks-giving
        Street.

Ibid.

CHARLES WARREN
STODDARD
[1843–1909]

And every note of every bell
Sang Gabriel! rang Gabriel!

In the tower that is left the tale to tell
Of Gabriel, the Archangel.
                    The Bells of San Gabriel
My heart to thy heart,
    My lips to thine,
In the dew of the cornfield
    The blood of the vine.
The last sigh at leaving,
    The word as we part
Is, my lips to thy lips,
    We two, heart to heart.
                    Lines on a Loving Cup

GEORGE BIRDSEYE
[1844–1919]

The longest day is in June, they say;
    The shortest in December.
They did not come to me that way:
    The shortest I remember
You came a day with me to stay,
    And filled my heart with laughter;
The longest day — you were away —
    The very next day after.
                    Shortest and Longest [1]
A Hindoo died — a happy thing to do
When twenty years united to a shrew.
                    The Hindoo's Paradise
"He has married been,
And so on earth has suffered for all sin."
"Married? 'Tis well; for I've been married twice!"
"Begone! We'll have no fools in Paradise."
                    Ibid.

ROBERT BRIDGES [2]
[1844–1930]

Beneath the crisp and wintry carpet hid
    A million buds but stay their blossoming;
    And trustful birds have built their nests amid
The shuddering boughs, and only wait to sing
    Till one soft shower from the south shall bid,
    And hither tempt the pilgrim steps of Spring.
                    The Growth of Love. Sonnet 6

[1] In *The Century Magazine, June, 1889.*
[2] Appointed Poet Laureate in 1913.

Beauty being the best of all we know
Sums up the unsearchable and secret aims
Of nature.
                    The Growth of Love. Sonnet 8
I live on hope and that I think do all
Who come into this world.
                    Ibid. Sonnet 63
Behind the western bars
The shrouded day retreats,
And unperceived the stars
Steal to their sovran seats.
                    The Clouds Have Left the Sky.
                    Stanza 3
And whiter grows the foam,
The small moon lightens more;
And as I turn me home,
My shadow walks before.
                    Ibid. Stanza 4
Whither, O splendid ship, thy white sails crowding,
    Leaning across the bosom of the urgent West,
That fearest nor sea rising, nor sky clouding,
    Whither away, fair rover, and what thy quest?
                    A Passer-By. Stanza 1
I have loved flowers that fade,
    Within whose magic tents
Rich hues have marriage made
    With sweet unmemoried scents.
                    I Have Loved Flowers that Fade.
                    Stanza 1
Ah! little at best can all our hopes avail us
    To lift this sorrow, or cheer us, when in the dark,
        Unwilling, alone we embark,
And the things we have seen and have known and have heard of, fail us.
                    On a Dead Child. Stanza 7
Gird on thy sword, O man, thy strength endue,
In fair desire thine earth-born joy renew.
Live thou thy life beneath the making sun
Till Beauty, Truth, and Love in thee are one.
                    A Hymn of Nature. VII, Stanza 1

When first we met we did not guess
That Love would prove so hard a mas-
 ter.
Of more than common friendliness
When first we met we did not guess.
Triolet

So sweet love seemed that April morn,
When first we kissed beside the thorn,
So strangely sweet, it was not strange
We thought that love could never
 change.
Shorter Poems. Book V, 5

Now learn, love, have, do, be the best;
Each in one thing excel the rest:
Strive; and hold fast this truth of
 heaven —
To him that hath shall more be given.
*Ode on the Ninth Jubilee of
Eton College*

My delight and thy delight
Walking, like two angels white,
In the gardens of the night.
New Poems. Number 9

Love, from whom the world begun,
Hath the secret of the sun.
Love can tell, and love alone,
Whence the million stars were strewn,
Why each atom knows its own.
Ibid.

The nightingale
as amorous of his art as of his brooding
 mate
practiseth every phrase of his espousal
 lay,
and still provoketh envy of the lesser
 songsters
with the same notes that woke poetic
 eloquence
alike in Sophocles and the sick heart of
 Keats.
The Testament of Beauty

Wisdom will repudiate thee, if thou
 think to enquire
WHY things are as they are or whence
 they came: thy task
is first to learn WHAT IS, and in pur-
 suant knowledge
pure intellect will find pure pleasure
 and the only ground
for a philosophy conformable to truth.
Ibid.

Sickening thought itself engendereth
 corporal pain.
The Testament of Beauty
Our hope is ever livelier than despair,
 our joy
livelier and more abiding than our sorrows are.
Ibid.

For what were pleasure if never contemplation gave
a spiritual significance to objects of
 sense,
nor in thought's atmosphere poet vision
 arose?
Ibid.

Man, in the unsearchable darkness,
 knoweth one thing
that as he is, so was he made: and if
 the Essence
and characteristic faculty of humanity
is our conscient Reason and our desire
 of knowledge,
that was Nature's Purpose in the making of man.
Ibid.

ROBERT JONES BURDETTE
[1844–1914]

I love the man who knows it all,
 From east to west, from north to
 south,
Who knows all things, both great and
 small,
 And tells it with his tiresome mouth.
He Knows It All. Stanza 1
Since she went home —
The evening shadows linger longer
 here, —
The winter days fill so much of the year,
And even summer winds are chill and
 drear.
Since She Went Home. Stanza 1
I would receive my sight; my clouded
 eyes
 Miss the glad radiance of the morn-
 ing sun,
The changing tints that glorify the skies
 With roseate splendors when the day
 is done;
The shadows soft and gray, the pearly
 light

Of summer twilight deep'ning into night.

Bartimeus.[1] *Stanza 1*

There are two days in the week about which and upon which I never worry. Two carefree days, kept sacredly free from fear and apprehension. One of these days is Yesterday. . . . And the other day I do not worry about is To-morrow.

The Golden Day

GEORGE WASHINGTON CABLE
[1844–1925]

There came to port last Sunday night
 The queerest little craft,
Without an inch of rigging on;
 I looked and looked — and laughed!

The New Arrival. Stanza 1

She has no manifest but this,
 No flag floats o'er the water;
She's too new for the British Lloyd's —
 My daughter! O my daughter!

Ibid. Stanza 2

EDWARD CARPENTER
[1844–1929]

So thin a veil divides
Us from such joy, past words,
Walking in daily life — the business of
 the hour, each detail seen to;
Yet carried, rapt away, on what sweet
 floods of other Being:
Swift streams of music flowing, light far
 back through all Creation shining,
Loved faces looking.

So Thin a Veil

Newer ways are ours,
New thoughts, new fancies, and we
 deem our lives
New-fashioned in a mould of vaster
 powers;
But as of old with flesh the spirit strives.

The World-Spirit. Stanza 14

It should be as easy to expel an obnoxious thought from your mind as to shake a stone out of your shoe.

A Visit to a Gnani. Chap. 3

---

[1] The blind man said unto him, Lord, that I might receive my sight. — *Mark, X, 51*

(*Also in From Adam's Peak to Elephanta*)

Motherhood is, after all, woman's great and incomparable work.

Love's Coming-of-Age.
Woman in Freedom

Each one thinks that the current in which he lives is the whole ocean.

Ibid. The Free Society

There is nothing that is evil except because a man has not mastery over it; and there is no good thing that is not evil if it have a mastery over a man.

Towards Democracy. The
Secret of Time and Satan

When Death comes, breaking into the circle of our friends, words fail us, our mental machinery ceases to operate, all our little stores of wit and wisdom, our maxims, our mottoes, accumulated from daily experience, evaporate and are of no avail. These things do not seem to touch or illuminate in any effective way the strange vast Presence whose wings darken the world for us.

The Drama of Love and Death.
Chap. 1

Love is an Art, and the greatest of the Arts.

Ibid. Chap. 4

Nothing is more certain than that worlds on worlds, and spheres on spheres, stretch behind and beyond the actually seen.

Ibid. Chap. 7

Every new movement or manifestation of human activity, when unfamiliar to people's minds, is sure to be misrepresented and misunderstood.

Ibid. Chap. 8, Note

In Man, the positive content of religion is the instinctive sense — whether conscious or subconscious — of an inner unity and continuity with the world around. This is the stuff out of which religion is made.

Pagan and Christian Creeds.
Chap. 4

The first condition of social happiness and prosperity must be the sense of the Common Life.

Ibid. Chap. 17

There is a presence and an influence in Nature and the Open which expands the mind and causes brigand cares and worries to drop off — whereas in confined places foolish and futile thoughts of all kinds swarm like microbes and cloud and conceal the soul.

Lecture I, The Teaching of the Upanishads. Rest

EDWARD A. CHURCH
[1844–1929]

Friends, whom the softest whistle of my call
  Brought to my side in love that knew no doubt,
Would I not seek to cross the jasper wall
  If haply I might find you there "without"?

Without Are Dogs.[1] Stanza 3

Of all the words the Evangelists record,
To comfort souls perplexèd and distressed,
This ever seems to me divinest, best —
The thought that Peter spoke — "Thou knowest, Lord."

Sonnet, Thou Knowest

Come, holy fire, consume this clay,
  Ashes to ashes now return;
An outworn garment here we lay,
  As on thine Altar, Lord, to burn.

Cremation Hymn. Stanza 1

Not to corruption and the worm
  Our shrinking spirits yield the claim,
But give this well-beloved form
  The cleanly burial of the flame.

Ibid. Stanza 2

From duty's path, however steep, we ask
  For no ill-timed release;
Only — for strength to finish well our task —
  Grant us thy peace!

A Prayer. Stanza 6

Bragging of crests and pedigrees —
  And all most noble through and through!
Cadets of Gascony are these
  With Carbon de Castel Jaloux.

Gasconade. Stanza 1

[1] Revelation, XXII, 15.

I strike at close of the Envoy.

Ballade of the Duel, Cyrano de Bergerac

INA DONNA COOLBRITH
[1844–1928]

He walks with God upon the hills!
And sees, each morn, the world arise
New-bathed in light of paradise.

The Poet

It must be sweet, O thou my dead, to lie
  With hands that folded are from every task,
Sealed with the seal of that great mystery,
  The lips that nothing answer, nothing ask,
The lifelong struggle ended.

Beside the Dead

MARY AINGE DE VERE ("MADELINE BRIDGES")
[1844–1920]

There are loyal hearts, there are spirits brave,
  There are souls that are pure and true;
Then give to the world the best you have,
  And the best will come back to you.

Life's Mirror. Stanza 1

For life is the mirror of king and slave,
  'Tis just what we are and do.

Ibid. Stanza 5

God keep you, dearest, all this lonely night:
  The winds are still,
The moon drops down behind the western hill;
God keep you, dearest, till the light.

God Keep You. Stanza 1

RICHARD WATSON GILDER
[1844–1909]

Not from the whole wide world I chose thee,
  Sweetheart, light of the land and the sea!
The wide, wide world could not enclose thee,

For thou art the whole wide world
  to me.
                      Song

Through love to light! Oh wonderful
  the way
That leads from darkness to the perfect day!
                After-song

I am a woman — therefore I may not
Call to him, cry to him,
Fly to him,
Bid him delay not.
          A Woman's Thought

How to the singer comes the song?
How to the summer fields
Come flowers? How yields
Darkness to happy morn? How doth
  the night
Bring stars?
     How to the Singer Comes the
            Song? Stanza 4

This house that looks to east, to west,
This, dear one, is our home, our rest;
Yonder the stormy sea, and here
The woods that bring the sunset near.
     The Woods that Bring the
        Sunset Near. Stanza 3

What is a sonnet? 'Tis a pearly shell
  That murmurs of the far-off mur-
    muring sea;
  A precious jewel carved most curi-
    ously;
It is a little picture painted well.
              The Sonnet

This is the poet's triumph, his high
  doom!
After life's stress —
For him the silent, dark, o'ershadowing
  tomb
  Is shadowless.
And this the miracle and mystery —
  In that he gives
His soul away, magnificently free,
  By this he lives.
     On Reading of a Poet's Death

I count my time by times that I meet
  thee;
These are my yesterdays, my morrows,
  noons
And nights; these my old moons and
  my new moons.
       The New Day. Book IV, 6

GERARD MANLEY HOPKINS [1]
[1844–1889]

The world is charged with the grandeur
  of God. . . .
There lives the dearest freshness deep
  down things.
           God's Grandeur

Glory be to God for dappled things —
For skies as couple-colored as a brindled
  cow;
For rose-moles all in stipple upon trout
  that swim.
            Pied Beauty

Elected Silence, sing to me
And beat upon my whorlèd ear,
Pipe me to pastures still and be
The music that I care to hear.
     The Habit of Perfection

I say that we are wound
With mercy round and round
As if with air.
    Mary Mother of Divine Grace

World-mothering air, air wild,
Wound with thee, in thee isled,
Fold home, fast fold thy child.
                Ibid.

Summer ends now; now, barbarous in
  beauty, the stooks rise
Around; up above, what wind-walks!
  what lovely behavior
Of silk-sack clouds! Has wilder,
  willful-wavier
Meal-drift molded ever and melted
  across skies?
       Hurrahing in Harvest

I have asked to be
  Where no storms come,
Where the green swell is in the havens
  dumb
  And out of the swing of the sea.
          Heaven-Haven

I kiss my hand
To the stars, lovely-asunder
Starlight, wafting him out of it; and
Glow, glory in thunder. . . .

[1] He has left us only 90 poems — but so essential that they will colour and convert the development of English poetry for many decades to come. — HERBERT READ (1893–) in *The Criterion, April, 1931.*

Since though he is under the world's
  splendour and wonder,
His mystery must be instressed,
  stressed;
For I greet him the days I meet him,
  and bless when I understand.
  The Wreck of the Deutschland.
  Stanza 5
To lift up the hands in prayer gives
God glory, but a man with a dungfork
in his hand, a woman with a slop-pail,
give him glory too. He is so great that
all things give him glory if you mean
they should. So then, my brethren, live.
  An Address on St. Ignatius

ANDREW LANG
[1844–1912]

My mind is gay but my soul is mel-
ancholy.
  Quoted by MRS. LANG *in Pref-
  ace, The Poetical Works of
  Andrew Lang*
St. Andrews by the northern sea,
A haunted town it is to me!
A little city, worn and gray,
The gray North Ocean girds it round.
  *Almae Matres (St. Andrews,
  1862; Oxford, 1865). Stanza 1*
You can cover a great deal of country
in books.
  To the Gentle Reader. Stanza 5
Such is the fate of borrowed books:
  they're lost,
Or not the book returneth, but its
  ghost!
  From Colletet
Here stand my books, line upon line
They reach the roof, and row by row,
They speak of faded tastes of mine,
And things I did, but do not, know.
  Ballade of His Books. Stanza 1
The watches of the night reveal
The books that never can be mine!
  Ballade of the Unattainable.
  Stanza 3
One gift the fairies gave me: (three
They commonly bestowed of yore)
The love of books, the golden key
That opens the enchanted door.
  Ballade of the Bookworm.
  Stanza 2

When others fail him, the wise man
  looks
To the sure companionship of books.
  Old Friends
Prince, you may storm and ban —
Joe Millers *are* a pest,
Suppress me if you can!
I am a Merry Jest!
  Ballade of the Primitive Jest.
  Envoy
Why, why are rhymes so rare to *love?*
  Ballade of Difficult Rhymes
There's a joy without canker or cark,
  There's a pleasure eternally new,
'Tis to gloat on the glaze and the mark
Of china that's ancient and blue.
  Ballade of Blue China. Stanza 1
Here's a pot with a cot in a park
  In a park where the peach-blossoms
  blew;
Where the lovers eloped in the dark,
  Lived, died, and were changed into
  two
Bright birds that eternally flew
Through the boughs of the may, as they
  sang;
'Tis a tale was undoubtedly true
In the reign of the Emperor Hwang.
  Ibid. Stanza 3
We marvel, now we look behind:
Life's more amusing than we thought!
  Ballade of Middle Age. Stanza 1
Prince, 'tis a melancholy lay!
For youth, for life we both regret!
How fair they seem, how far away;
With Aucassin and Nicolete.
  Ballade of Aucassin. Envoy
The windy lights of Autumn flare:
  I watch the moonlit sails go by;
I marvel how men toil and fare,
  The weary business that they ply!
  Their voyaging is vanity,
And fairy gold is all their gain,
  And all the winds of winter cry,
"My Love returns no more again."
  Ballade of Autumn. Stanza 2
I'd leave all the hurry, the noise, and
  the fray,
For a house full of books, and a garden
  of flowers.
  Ballade of True Wisdom. Stanza 3
Sleep, that giv'st what Life denies,
Shadowy bounties and supreme,

Bring the dearest face that flies
Following darkness like a dream!
Ballade of the Dream. Envoy
O bargains in books that they send us,
Ye come through the Ivory Gate!
Ballade of the Real and Ideal.
Stanza 2
So gladly, from the songs of modern
speech
Men turn, and see the stars, and feel
the free
Shrill wind beyond the close of
heavy flowers;
And, through the music of the
languid hours,
They hear like ocean on a western
beach
The surge and thunder of the Odys-
sey.
Sonnet, The Odyssey
The Angler hath a jolly life
Who by the rail runs down,
And leaves his business and his wife,
And all the din of town.
The wind down stream is blowing
straight,
And nowhere cast can he:
Then lo, he doth but sit and wait
In kindly company.
The Contented Angler. Stanza 1
When we have cut each other's throats
And robbed each other's land;
And turned, and changed, and lost our
coats,
Till progress is at stand;
When every "programme's" been gone
through
This good old world will wake anew!
An Aspiration. Stanza 1
A land where newspapers were dumb
From scandal and from scare.[1]
Ibid. Stanza 6

[1] In 1895, a New York paper was carrying
a series of comic strips, "Hogan's Alley," by
Richard Felton Outcault [1863-1928]. In
1896, a rival paper engaged the artist to begin
a new series portraying "The Yellow Kid."
The quarrel of the two newspapers over the
right to run the cartoons, together with the
similarity in the manner in which the two
newspapers displayed sensational news, led to
the coining of the term, "Yellow Journalism."
— Condensed from *The New York Sun, May
15, 1898*

Why ladies read what they *do* read
Is a thing that no man may explain.
A Remonstrance with the Fair.
Stanza 1
From the damp sheiling on the draggled
island
Mountains divide you, and no end of
seas.
But, though your heart is genuinely
Highland,
Still, you're in luck to be away from
these! [1]
*To Fiona, Parody of Canadian
Boat Song*
Had cigarettes no ashes,
And roses ne'er a thorn,
The big trout would not ever
Escape into the river.
*A Highly Valuable Chain of
Thoughts. Stanza 2*
We meet him first in Homer's verse,
The dog by the Aegean seas;
He barks at strangers, ay, and worse,
He bites! We learn, in language terse,
That even Argos has the curse
Of fleas! [2]
The Friend of Man. Stanza 3

[1] From the lone sheiling of the misty island
Mountains divide us, and the waste of
seas —
Yet still the blood is strong, the heart is
Highland,
And we in dreams behold the Hebrides.
Canadian Boat Song, St. 2
This poem appeared in *Noctes Ambrosiana,*
No. 46, in *Blackwood's Magazine, Vol. 26,
P. 400, Sept., 1829.* It is generally credited to
JOHN GALT [1779-1839], but JOHN WILSON
("Christopher North"), who won the first
Newdigate Prize, founded in 1805, has been
suggested as the author. John Gibson Lock-
hart, son-in-law of Sir Walter Scott, noted, on
a copy of the poem in his own handwriting,
that the song had been sent to him by a friend
in Upper Canada. Galt, author of *Annals of
the Parish,* was in Canada in 1824 and 1826.
The poem was likewise found in the handwriting of Hugh Montgomerie [1739-1819],
twelfth Earl of Eglinton, ascribed to a Gaelic
origin.
Robert Louis Stevenson misquotes the second stanza of the song in *The Silverado
Squatters,* Chap. 4. Joseph Chamberlain, the
British statesman, gave Stevenson's version in
a speech at Inverness.
[2] There lay the old dog, Argos, full of fleas!
THOMAS HOBBES [1588-1679]: *Odyssey*

Who wins his love shall lose her,
  Who loses her shall gain.
        Lost Love. Stanza 1

In dreams she grows not older
  The lands of dream among;
Though all the world wax colder,
  Though all the songs be sung,
In dreams doth he behold her
  Still fair and kind and young.
        Ibid. Stanza 4

And, if one Rag of Character they
  spare,
Comes the Biographer, and strips it
  bare!
    Letters to Dead Authors. Epistle
        to Mr. Alexander Pope

'Tis the fault of all art to seem antiquated and faded in the eyes of the succeeding generation.
        Ibid. To Jane Austen

Contemporary spites do not harm
true genius.
        Ibid. To M. Chapelain

Perchance for poets dead there is
prepared a place more beautiful than
their dreams.
        Ibid. To Theocritus

The dusty and stony ways of contemporary criticism.
        Ibid. To Edgar Allan Poe

About the writers of his own generation a leader of that generation should
hold his peace.
        Ibid.

Great minds should only criticize the
great who have passed beyond the
reach of eulogy or fault-finding.
        Ibid.

The eye of each man sees but what
it has the power of seeing.
        Ibid. To Homer

JAMES HILARY MULLIGAN
[1844–1916]

The moonlight is the softest, in Ken-
  tucky,
Summer days come oftest, in Kentucky,
Friendship is the strongest,
Love's fires glow the longest,
Yet a wrong is always wrongest,
  In Kentucky.
        In Kentucky. Stanza 1

Songbirds are sweetest, in Kentucky,
Thoroughbreds the fleetest, in Ken-
  tucky;
  The mountains tower proudest,
  Thunder peals the loudest,
  The landscape is the grandest,
  And politics the damnedest,
    In Kentucky.
        In Kentucky. Stanza 7

JOHN BOYLE O'REILLY
[1844–1890]

Though it lash the shallows that line
  the beach,
  Afar from the great sea-deeps,
There is never a storm whose might can
  reach
  Where the vast leviathan sleeps.
Like a mighty thought in a mighty
  mind
  In the clear cold depths he swims;
Whilst above him the pettiest form of
  his kind
  With a dash o'er the surface skims.
        Prelude to the Amber Whale

They who see the Flying Dutchman
  never, never reach the shore.
        The Flying Dutchman

Doubt is brother-devil to Despair.
        Prometheus

The world is large when weary leagues
  two loving hearts divide
But the world is small when your enemy
  is loose on the other side.
        Distance

The red rose whispers of passion
  And the white rose breathes of love;
O, the red rose is a falcon,
  And the white rose is a dove.
        A White Rose. Stanza 1

You may grind their souls in the self-
  same mill,
  You may bind them, heart and brow;
But the poet will follow the rainbow
  still,
  And his brother will follow the plow.
        The Rainbow's Treasure.
        Stanza 5

There are times when a dream delicious
  Steals into a musing hour,

Like a face with love capricious,
    That peeps from a woodland bower.
        An Old Picture. Stanza 1

You gave me the key to your heart, my
    love;
    Then why do you make me knock?
"Oh, that was yesterday; Saints above,
    Last night I changed the lock!"
        Constancy

First across the gulf we cast
Kite-borne threads, till lines are passed,
And habit builds the bridge at last!
    A Builder's Lesson. Stanza 3

He draws no rein, but he shakes the
    street
With a shout and the ring of the gal-
    loping feet;
And this the cry he flings to the wind:
"To the hills for your lives, the flood
    is behind!" [1]
    The Ride of Collins Graves

The wealth of mankind is the wisdom
    they leave.
        Rules of the Road

Be silent and safe — silence never be-
    trays you.
        Ibid.

"I had" is a heartache, "I have" is a
    fountain,
You're worth what you saved, not the
    million you made.
        Ibid.

This truth keep in sight, — every man
    on the planet
Has just as much right as yourself to
    the road.
        Ibid.

The organized charity, scrimped and
    iced,
In the name of a cautious, statistical
    Christ. [2]
        In Bohemia. Stanza 5

Oh, I long for the glow of a kindly
    heart and the grasp of a friendly
    hand!
And I'd rather live in Bohemia than in
    any other land.
        Ibid. Stanza 6

---

[1] The breaking of the dam over Mill River,
Williamsburg, Massachusetts, May 16, 1874.
[2] See Southey, page 322, and Hood, page
392.

Well blest is he who has a dear one
    dead;
A friend he has whose face will never
    change —
A dear communion that will not grow
    strange;
The anchor of a love is death.
        Forever. Stanza 3

ARTHUR WILLIAM EDGAR O'SHAUGHNESSY
[1844–1881]

What man is able to master
And stem the great Fountain of Tears?
    The Fountain of Tears.
        Stanza 8

We are the music-makers,
    And we are the dreamers of dreams,
Wandering by lone sea-breakers,
    And sitting by desolate streams;
World-losers and world-forsakers,
    On whom the pale moon gleams:
Yet we are the movers and shakers
    Of the world forever, it seems.
        Ode. Stanza 1

One man with a dream, at pleasure,
    Shall go forth and conquer a crown;
And three with a new song's measure
    Can trample an empire down.
        Ibid. Stanza 2

For each age is a dream that is dying,
    Or one that is coming to birth.
        Ibid. Stanza 3

MAURICE THOMPSON
[1844–1901]

May one who fought in honor for the
    South
Uncovered stand and sing by Lincoln's
    grave?
        At Lincoln's Grave

A soft Kentucky strain was in his voice,
And the Ohio's deeper boom was there,
With some wild accents of old Wabash
    days,
    And winds of Illinois;
And when he spoke he took us unaware,
With his high courage and unselfish
    ways.
        Ibid.

The sky is like a woman's love,
  The ocean like a man's;
Oh, neither knows, below, above,
  The measure that it spans!
        Love's Horizon. Stanza 1

ELIZABETH STUART PHELPS WARD
[1844–1911]

O tender arms that meet and clasp!
Gather and cherish while ye may.
The morrow knoweth God. Ye know
Your own are yours to-day.
        Gloucester Harbor. Stanza 7
There breaks in every Gloucester wave
A widowed woman's heart.
              Ibid. Stanza 8
There is no vacant chair. To love is
    still
To have.
        Afterward. Stanza 5
Our souls are like the sparrows
  Imprisoned in the clay;
Bless Him who came to give them
    wings,
Upon a Christmas Day.
        *A Jewish Legend: The Clay
        Sparrows. Stanza 10*

JOHN B. BOGART [1]
[1845–1921]

When a dog bites a man, that is not
news, because it happens so often. But
if a man bites a dog, that is news.
        Quoted by FRANK M. O'BRIEN
        in The Story of The Sun [*1918*]

JOHN HENRY BONER
[1845–1903]

Ah, we fondly cherish
  Faded things
That had better perish.
  Memory clings
To each leaf it saves.
        Gather Leaves and Grasses
Here lived the soul enchanted
  By melody of song;

---

[1] City Editor of *The Sun*, New York, 1873–1890.

Here dwelt the spirit haunted
  By a demoniac throng.
        Poe's Cottage at Fordham

WILL CARLETON
[1845–1912]

Worm or beetle — drought or tempest
  — on a farmer's land may fall,
Each is loaded full o' ruin, but a mort-
  gage beats 'em all.
        The Tramp's Story
I've watched my duty, straight an'
    true,
  An' tried to do it well;
Part of the time kept heaven in view,
  An' part steered clear of hell.
        *The New Church Doctrine.
                    Stanza 2*
My business on the jury's done — the
  quibblin' all is through —
I've watched the lawyers, right and
  left, and give my verdict true.
        Goin' Home To-day. Stanza 1
If there's a heaven upon the earth, a
    fellow knows it when
He's been away from home a week, and
  then gets back again.
              Ibid. Stanza 7
"There is nothing worth the doing that
  it does not pay to try,"
Thought the little black-eyed rebel,
  with a twinkle in her eye.
        *The Little Black-Eyed Rebel.
                    Stanza 11*
Boys flying kites haul in their white-
  winged birds;
You can't do that way when you're fly-
  ing words.
"Careful with fire," is good advice, we
  know:
"Careful with words," is ten times
  doubly so.
Thoughts unexpressed may sometimes
  fall back dead;
But God himself can't kill them when
  they're said.
        The First Settler's Story
Not a log in this buildin' but its memories has got,

And not a nail in this old floor but touches a tender spot.
Out of the Old House, Nancy.
Stanza 17

Fare you well, old house! you're naught that can feel or see,
But you seem like a human being — a dear old friend to me;
And we never will have a better home, if *my* opinion stands,
Until we commence a-keepin' house in the house not made with hands.
Ibid. Stanza 20

The kind old country doctor
Whom the populace considered with a mingled love and dread.
The Country Doctor. Stanza 1

He has seen old views and patients disappearing, one by one,
He has learned that Death is master both of Science and of Art.
Ibid. Stanza 3

Them's my sentiments, tew.[1]
The Schoolmaster's Guests.
Canto 3

If we who have sailed together
Flit out of each other's view,
The world will sail on, I think,
Just as it used to do.
One and Two. Stanza 3

But ships long time together
Can better the tempest weather
Than any other two.
Ibid.

Things at home are crossways, and Betsey and I are out.
Betsey and I Are Out. Stanza 1

I have talked with Betsey, and Betsey has talked with me,
And so we've agreed together that we can't never agree.
Ibid. Stanza 3

Betsey, like all good women, had a temper of her own.
Ibid. Stanza 4

The more we arg'ed the question the more we didn't agree.
Ibid. Stanza 5

I don't complain of Betsey, or any of her acts,

[1] See Thackeray, page 482.

Exceptin' when we've quarreled, and told each other facts.
Betsey and I Are Out. Stanza 18

You see, when we came to division, there was things that wouldn't divide.
Betsey Destroys the Paper.
Stanza 6

Now he didn't give you that baby, by a hundred thousand mile;
He just think you need some sunshine, and he lent him for a while.
The Funeral. Stanza 6

I'm going away to-day with a handsomer man than you.
Gone with a Handsomer Man.
Stanza 4

To appreciate heaven well
'Tis good for a man to have some fifteen minutes of hell.
Ibid. Stanza 20

Over the hill to the poor-house I'm trudgin' my weary way.
Over the Hill to the Poor-House. Stanza 1

She had an education, an' that was good for her;
But when she twitted me on mine, 'twas carryin' things too fur.
Ibid. Stanza 14

WILLIAM ULICK O'CONNOR CUFFE (LORD DESART)
[1845–1898]

Mother Hubbard, you see, was old: there being no mention of others, we may presume she was alone; a widow — a friendless, old, solitary widow. Yet did she despair? Did she sit down and weep, or read a novel, or wring her hands? No! She went to the cupboard.
Mock Sermon: Old Mother Hubbard [1877]

CHARLES FLETCHER DOLE
[1845–1927]

Good Will is the mightiest practical force in the universe.
Cleveland Address

The Golden Rule works like gravitation.

Cleveland Address

Democracy is on trial in the world, on a more colossal scale than ever before.

The Spirit of Democracy

EDWARD HARRIGAN
[1845–1911]

The best of luck is always waiting on you
If you pick up on the road a horse's shoe.

Never Take the Horseshoe from the Door. Stanza 1

The drums and fifes, how sweetly they did play,
As we march'd, march'd, march'd in the Mulligan Guard.

The Mulligan Guard [1873]

As I walk the street each friend I meet
Says, "There goes Muldoon. He's a solid man."

Muldoon, the Solid Man

DANIEL WEBSTER HOYT
[1845–1936]

If you have a friend worth loving,
Love him. Yes, and let him know
That you love him, ere life's evening
Tinge his brow with sunset glow.
Why should good words ne'er be said
Of a friend till he is dead?

A Sermon in Rhyme [1878].
Stanza 1

If you hear a song that thrills you,
Sung by any child of song,
Praise it. Do not let the singer
Wait deservèd praises long.
Why should one who thrills your heart
Lack the joy you may impart?

Ibid. Stanza 2

MARGARET THOMSON JANVIER ("MARGARET VANDEGRIFT")
[1845–1913]

You needn't be trying to comfort me —
I tell you my dolly is dead!

There's no use in saying she isn't, with a crack like that in her head.

The Dead Doll. Stanza 1

GEORGE THOMAS LANIGAN
[1845–1886]

What, what, what,
What's the news from Swat?
Sad news,
Bad news,
Comes by cable led
Through the Indian Ocean's bed,
Through the Persian Gulf, the Red
Sea and the Med-
Iterranean — he's dead;
The Ahkoond is dead! [1]

A Threnody [*January, 1878*].
Stanza 1

Alas, unhappy land; ill-fated spot
Kotal — though where or what
On earth Kotal is, the bard has forgot;
Further than this indeed he knoweth not —
It borders upon Swat.

Dirge of the Moolla of Kotal, Rival of the Ahkoond of Swat. Stanza 1

EUGENE LEE-HAMILTON
[1845–1907]

The hollow sea-shell, which for years hath stood
On dusty shelves, when held against the ear
Proclaims its stormy parent, and we hear
The faint, far murmur of the breaking flood.
We hear the sea.[2] The Sea? It is the blood
In our own veins, impetuous and near.

Sonnet, Sea-shell Murmurs

---

[1] See Lear, page 499.
Now the Ahkoond of Swat is a vague sort of man
  Who lives in a country far over the sea;
Pray tell me, good reader, if tell me you can,
  What's the Ahkoond of Swat to you folks or to me?
    EUGENE FIELD: *The Ahkoond of Swat*
      [Sept. 19, 1884]

[2] See F. D. Gage, page 446.

It is the pure white diamond Dante
brought
  To Beatrice; the sapphire Laura
  wore
When Petrarch cut it sparkling out of
thought;
  The ruby Shakespeare hewed from
  his heart's core;
The dark, deep emerald that Rossetti
wrought
  For his own soul, to wear for evermore.

What Is a Sonnet?

Things bygone are the only things that
last:
The present is mere grass, quick-mown
away;
The past is stone, and stands for ever
fast.

Roman Baths

GEORGE SAINTSBURY
[1845–1933]

It must be remembered that the
point of honour which decrees that a
man must not under any circumstances
accept money from a woman with
whom he is on certain terms, is of very
modern growth, and is still tempered
by the proviso that he may take as
much as he likes or can get from his
wife.

Preface to FIELDING'S *Tom Jones*

I have myself a great admiration for
nice fine points of honour — I don't
think you can make them too nice or
too fine.

Ibid.

One of the commonest but most uncritical faults of criticism — the refusal
to consider what it is that the author
intended to give us.

Ibid.

Criticism is the endeavor to find, to
know, to love, to recommend, not only
the best, but all the good, that has been
known and thought and written in the
world.

A History of Criticism

It is the first duty of the novelist to
let himself be read — anything else

that he gives you is a bonus, a trimming, a dessert.

History of the English Novel

I have never tried to be in the fashion
for the sake of being in it, and seldom,
I think, to be out of it for the sake of
being out of it. Logic and history have
been the only external guides I have
accepted in temporal things, except
where pure taste has reigned alone.

Notes on a Cellar Book. Preface

When they [wines] were good they
pleased my sense, cheered my spirits,
improved my moral and intellectual
powers, besides enabling me to confer
the same benefits on other people.

Ibid.

Men will try to persuade themselves,
or at least others, that they read poetry
because it is a criticism of life, because
it expresses the doubts and fears and
thoughts and hopes of the time, because it is a substitution for religion,
because it is a relief from serious work,
because and because and because. As a
matter of fact, they (that is to say,
those of them who like it generally)
read it because they like it, because it
communicates an experience of half-
sensual, half-intellectual pleasure to
them.

Corrected Impressions.
Tennyson

R. L. SHARPE

Each is given a bag of tools,
A shapeless mass,
A book of rules;
And each must make,
Ere life is flown,
A stumbling-block
Or a stepping-stone.

Stumbling-Block or Stepping-
Stone. Stanza 2

ARABELLA EUGENIA SMITH
[1845–1916]

If I should die to-night,
My friends would look upon my quiet
face,
Before they laid it in its resting place,

And deem that death had left it almost
    fair.
If I Should Die To-night.[1]
    Stanza 1
Keep not your kisses for my dead, cold
    brow;
The way is lonely, let me feel them now.
    Ibid. Stanza 4
When dreamless rest is mine, I shall not
    need
The tenderness for which I long to-
    night.
    Ibid.

CHARLES WILLIAM STUBBS
[1845–1912]

I sat alone with my conscience
    In a place where time had ceased,
And we talked of my former living
    In the land where the years increased.
Conscience and Future
    Judgment [1876]
The ghost of forgotten actions
    Came floating before my sight,
And things that I thought were dead
    things
Were alive with a terrible might.
    Ibid.
To sit alone with my conscience
    Will be judgment enough for me.[2]
    Ibid.

JOHN BANISTER TABB
[1845–1909]

When Christ was taken from the rood,
    One thorn upon the ground,
Still moistened with the Precious
    Blood,
    An early robin found,

[1] First printed in *The Christian Union, June
18, 1873.*
  The parody by BEN KING [1857–1894] has
become better known than the original. See
page 729.
[2] There's just ae thing I cannae bear,
    An' that's my conscience.
    R. L. STEVENSON: *In Scots, XIV,*
    My Conscience
Conscience allus welts it to me with a mighty
    cuttin' rod,
When thar ain't nobody near me, 'ceptin' God.
    JAMES BARTON ADAMS: *A Cowboy*
    Alone with His Conscience

And wove it crosswise in his nest,
Where, lo, it reddened all his breast! [1]
    Robin Redbreast
The ghost am I
  Of winds that die
Alike on land or sea.
    The Fog. Stanza 1
No more the battle or the chase
    The phantom tribes pursue,
But each in its accustomed place
    The Autumn hails anew;
And still from solemn councils set
    On every hill and plain,
The smoke of many a calumet
    Ascends to heaven again.
    Indian Summer
Before a clock was in the tower
    Or e'er a watch was worn,
I knew of night the passing hour
    And prophesied the morn;
To man of every age and clime
The oldest chronicler of time.
    The Cock
How many an acorn falls to die
    For one that makes a tree!
How many a heart must pass me by
    For one that cleaves to me!
    Compensation. Stanza 1
Out of the dusk a shadow,
    Then a spark;
Out of the cloud a silence,
    Then a lark;
Out of the heart a rapture,
    Then a pain;
Out of the dead, cold ashes,
    Life again.
    Evolution
A little Boy of heavenly birth,
    But far from home to-day,
Comes down to find His ball, the earth,
    That sin has cast away.
O comrades, let us one and all
Join in to get Him back His ball!
    Out of Bounds
With locks of gold to-day;
To-morrow silver-gray;
Then blossom-bald. Behold,
O man, thy fortune told!
    The Dandelion
Why should I stay? Nor seed nor fruit
    have I,

[1] See Hayne, page 586.

But, sprung at once to beauty's perfect
  round,
Nor loss nor gain nor change in me is
  found, —
A life-complete in death-complete to
  die.
                        The Bubble

Back to the primal gloom
  Where life began.
                        Going Blind

And in the School of Darkness learn
  What mean
  "The things unseen."
                        Ibid.

Well, chile, de slip may come to all,
  But den de diff'ence foller;
For, if you watch him when he fall,
  De jus' man do not *waller*.
            The Difference. Stanza 2

ELLEN H. UNDERWOOD
[1845–1930]

The bread that bringeth strength I want
  to give,
The water pure that bids the thirsty
  live;
I want to help the fainting day by day;
I'm sure I shall not pass again this
  way.[1]
          I Shall Not Pass Again This
                        Way. Stanza 1

JAMES TERRY WHITE
[1845–1920]

And when I face the dark, and must resign
Love's tender, human touch; must dis-
  entwine
Its dear, detaining clasp; when fears
  depress,
Those mortal fears I cannot quite repress,

[1] I shall pass through this world but once.
— Attributed to Etienne de Grellet [1773–
1855]
      I shall not pass this way again —
      Although it bordered be with flowers.
        Eva Rose York [1858–   ]: *I Shall*
                Not Pass This Way Again, St. 1

For all my faith and trust — O Love
  divine,
  Hold thou my hands!
          Hold Thou My Hands. Stanza 3
If thou of fortune be bereft
And in thy store there be but left
Two loaves, sell one and with the dole
Buy hyacinths to feed thy soul.
                Not by Bread Alone [1]

SARAH CHAUNCEY WOOLSEY
("SUSAN COOLIDGE")
[1845–1905]

Every day is a fresh beginning,
  Every morn is the world made new.[2]
            New Every Morning. Stanza 1
The tasks are done and the tears are
  shed.
Yesterday's errors let yesterday cover;
Yesterday's wounds, which smarted and
  bled,
Are healed with the healing that night
  has shed.
                        Ibid. Stanza 2
A little rudely sculptured bed,
  With the shadowing folds of marble
  lace,
And quilt of marble, primly spread,
  And folded round a baby's face.
              The "Cradle Tomb" at
                        Westminster
Men die, but sorrow never dies.
                        Ibid.
These are weighty secrets, and we must
  whisper them.
                        Secrets
"A commonplace life," we say, and we
  sigh;
  But why should we sigh as we say?
The commonplace sun in the common-
  place sky
  Makes up the commonplace day.
                        Commonplace
And God, who studies each common-
  place soul,

[1] In *The Century Magazine, Aug., 1907.*
Adaptation of a Persian theme.
[2] Every step is an end, and every step is a
fresh beginning. — Goethe: *Elective Affini-*
ties, Book I, Chap. 10

Out of commonplace things makes His
beautiful whole.
Commonplace

"MICHAEL FIELD"
(KATHARINE BRADLEY)
[1846–1914]
(EDITH COOPER)
[1862–1913]

The enchanting miracles of change.
Renewal

Come, mete out my loneliness, O wind,
For I would know
How far the living who must stay be-
hind
Are from the dead who go.
Mete Out My Loneliness

Praying and sighing through the Lon-
don streets
While my heart beats
To do some miracle, when suddenly
At curve of Regent Circus I espy,
Set 'mid a jeweller's trays of spangle-
glitter,
A tiny metal insect-pin, a fly.
This utter trifle for my love I buy,
And thinking of it on her breast
My heart has rest.
A Miracle [1]

Among the hills I trace the path that I
must wend;
I watch, not bidding him farewell, the
sun descend.
Sweet and of their nature vacant are
the days I spend —
Quiet as a plough laid by at the furrow's end.
Old Age

JOSEPH IGNATIUS
CONSTANTINE CLARKE
[1846–1925]

"Here's to the Maine, and I'm sorry for
Spain,"
Said Kelly and Burke and Shea.
The Fighting Race. Stanza 1
"Wherever there's Kellys there's trou-
ble," said Burke.
"Wherever fighting's the game,

[1] Surely the prettiest poem on shopping
in our language. — LOGAN PEARSALL SMITH

Or a spice of danger in grown man's
work,"
Said Kelly, "you'll find my name."
The Fighting Race. Stanza 2
"Oh, the fighting races don't die out,
If they seldom die in bed."
Ibid. Stanza 5

GRANVILLE STANLEY HALL
[1846–1924]

The mother's face and voice are the
first conscious objects as the infant soul
unfolds, and she soon comes to stand in
the very place of God to her child.[1]
*Article in Pedagogical Seminary,
June, 1891, Page 199*

HAMILTON WRIGHT MABIE
[1846–1916]

The peculiarity of the New England
hermit has not been his desire to get
near to God, but his anxiety to get away
from man.
*Backgrounds of Literature.
Emerson and Concord*
There will come another era when it
shall be light and man will awaken from
his lofty dreams, and find his dreams
all there, and nothing is gone save his
sleep.
The Awakening

LLOYD MIFFLIN
[1846–1921]

Inscrutable, colossal, and alone.
Sesostris
The affrighted ostrich dare not dust her
wings
Anear this Presence.
Ibid.

RICHARD LEWIS
NETTLESHIP
[1846–1892]

The only strength for me is to be
found in the sense of a personal presence everywhere, it scarcely matters
whether it be called human or divine; a

[1] Mother is the name for God in the lips
and hearts of little children. — THACKERAY:
Vanity Fair, Vol. I, Chap. 37

presence which only makes itself felt at first in this and that particular form and feature.

Lectures and Memories. I, 72

Into this presence we come, not by leaving behind what are usually called earthly things, or by loving them less, but by living more intensely in them, and loving more what is really lovable in them.

Ibid.

It is literally true that this world *is* everything to us, if only we choose to make it so, if only we "live in the present" *because* it is eternity.

Ibid.

ALEXANDER MacGREGOR ROSE
[1846–1898]

Der Kaiser auf der Vaterland
Und Gott on high, all dings gommand,
Ve two, ach, don'd you understandt?
Meinself — und Gott.
Hoch! Der Kaiser (Kaiser &
Co.).[1] *Stanza 1*
Gott pulls mit me, und I mit him.
Ibid. Stanza 16

JOHN PETER ALTGELD [2]
[1847–1902]

In writing "Progress and Poverty," he dipped his pen into the tears of the human race, and with celestial clearness wrote down what he conceived to be eternal truths.

Memorial Address on Henry
George [1897]

When he died, there was nowhere a soul that cried out: "There is one iron hand less to grind us, one wolf less to

tear our flesh," but everywhere a feeling that a friend of the race had gone.

Memorial Address on Henry
George [1897]

HENRY AUGUSTIN BEERS
[1847–1926]

He sang one song and died — no more but that;
A single song and carelessly complete.
The Singer of One Song [1]
So through the poets' orchestra, which weaves
One music from a thousand stops and strings,
Pierces the note of that immortal song:
"High over all the lonely bugle grieves." [2]
Ibid.

CHARLES HEBER CLARK
("MAX ADELER")
[1847–1915]

Willie had a purple monkey climbing on a yellow stick,
And when he sucked the paint all off it made him deathly sick.
The Purple Monkey. Stanza 1
We have lost our little Hanner in a very painful manner.
Little Hanner. Stanza 1

JOHN WALLACE
("CAPTAIN JACK")
CRAWFORD
[1847–1917]

When a bit of sunshine hits ye,
After passing of a cloud,
When a fit of laughter gits ye
An' yer spine is feelin' proud,
Don't fergit to up and fling it
At a soul that's feelin' blue,
For the minute that ye sling it,
It's a boomerang to you.
The Boomerang

---

[1] The verses were first published in *The Montreal*, Canada, *Herald*, in 1897. They created a stir when recited by Captain Joseph Bullock Coghlan [1844–1908] at a dinner given in his honor at the Union League Club, New York, April 21, 1899. Captain Coghlan (later Rear Admiral) had commanded the United States Cruiser *Raleigh* of Admiral Dewey's squadron, Manila Bay, May 1, 1898.
[2] Eagle forgotten.
　　VACHEL LINDSAY: *The Eagle That Is*
　　　　　　　　　　Forgotten

[1] Grenville Mellen [1799–1841].
[2] And high above the fight the lonely bugle grieves!
　　GRENVILLE MELLEN: *Ode on the Celebration of the Battle of Bunker Hill, June 17, 1825*

EDGAR FAWCETT
[1847–1904]

She remembers so many graves
That no one else will remember.
> *The Grass. Stanza 3*

In some blithe moment, was it Nature's
    choice
To dower a scrap of sunset with a
    voice?
> *To an Oriole*

Two haggard shapes in robes of mist
  For longer years than each will tell,
Joined by a stern gyve, wrist to wrist,
  Have roamed the courts of hell.
Their blank eyes know each other
    not —
  Their cold hearts hate the union
    drear;
Yet one poor ghost was Lancelot,
  And one was Guinevere.
> *Lancelot and Guinevere*

WALTER LEARNED
[1847–1915]

To you whose temperate pulses flow
With measured beat, serene and slow,
The even tenor of whose way
Is undisturbed by passion's sway,
This tale of wayward love may seem
The record of a fevered dream.
> *On the Flyleaf of "Manon Lescaut"*

A lure more strong, a wish more faint,
Makes one a monster, one a saint.[1]
> *Ibid.*

There's many a life of sweet content
Whose virtue is environment.
> *Ibid.*

O carping world! If there's an age
  Where youth and manhood keep
An equal poise, alas! I must
  Have passed it in my sleep.
> *To Critics. Stanza 3*

Her lips were so near
That — what else could I do?
> *An Explanation*

This world is a difficult world, indeed,
  And people are hard to suit,

And the man who plays on the violin
Is a bore to the man with the flute.
> *Consolation. Stanza 4*

JOHN LOCKE [1]
[1847–1889]

O Ireland, isn't it grand you look —
Like a bride in her rich adornin'?
And with all the pent-up love of my
    heart
I bid you the top o' the mornin'!
> *The Exile's Return (Dawn on*
> *the Irish Coast). Stanza 1*

JULIA A. MOORE [2]
[1847–1920]

Dear Friends, I write for money,
  With a kind heart and hand,
I wish to make no Enemies
  Throughout my native land.
Kind friends, now I close my rhyme,
  And lay my pen aside,
Between me and my critics
  I leave you to decide.
> *To My Friends and Critics.*
> *Stanza 6*

Leave off the agony, leave off style,
Unless you've got money by you all the
    while.
If you look about you you'll often have
    to smile
To see so many poor people putting on
    style.
> *Leave Off the Agony in Style*

"Lord Byron" was an Englishman
  A poet I believe,
His first works in old England
  Was poorly received.
Perhaps it was "Lord Byron's" fault
  And perhaps it was not.
His life was full of misfortunes,
  Ah, strange was his lot.
> *Sketch of Lord Byron's Life.*
> *Stanza 1*

---

[1] If you take temptations into account, who
is to say that he is better than his neighbor?
— THACKERAY: *Vanity Fair, Vol. II, Chap. 1*

[1] Known as "The Southern Gael."
[2] "The Sweet Singer of Michigan."

MILTON NOBLES
[1847–1924]

The villain still pursued her.
The Phœnix. Act I, Sc. 3 [1875]

JAMES JEFFREY ROCHE
[1847–1908]

A brave endeavor
To do thy duty, whate'er its worth,
Is better than life with love for-
ever —
And love is the sweetest thing on earth.
Sir Hugo's Choice

The love of man and woman is as fire
To warm, to light, but surely to con-
sume
And self-consuming die . . .
But comrade-love is as a welding blast
Of candid flame and ardent tempera-
ture:
Glowing more fervent, it doth bind
more fast.
My Comrade

What gain is it to the people that a God
laid down His life,
If twenty centuries after, His world be
a world of strife?
For the People. Stanza 4

What matter if king or consul or presi-
dent holds the rein,
If crime and poverty ever be links in the
bondsman's chain?
What careth the burden-bearer that
Liberty packed his load,
If Hunger presseth behind him with a
sharp and ready goad?
Ibid. Stanza 6

The slaves of Pilate have washed his
hands
As white as a king's might be.
Barabbas with wrists unfettered stands,
For the world has made him free.
But Thy palms toil-worn by nails are
torn,
O Christ, on Calvary.
The Way of the World. Stanza 2

For all knew Davy Crockett, blithe and
generous and bold,
And strong and rugged as the quartz
that hides its heart of gold.

His simple creed for word or deed true
as the bullet sped,
And rung the target straight: "Be sure
you're right, then go ahead." [1]
The Men of the Alamo

Yea, the gateway shall be free
Unto all, from sea to sea;
And no fratricidal slaughter
Shall defile its sacred water;
But — the hand that ope'd the gate
shall forever hold the key!
Panama

"No enemies! Can such a grace
To any erring mortal fall?"
A smile lit up the grim old face:
"None, padre, none; I slew them all."
Carvajal the Thorough

I'd rather be handsome than homely;
I'd rather be youthful than old;
If I can't have a bushel of silver
I'll do with a barrel of gold.
Contentment

All loved Art in a seemly way
With an earnest soul and a capital A.
The V-A-S-E

Baby's brain is tired of thinking
On the Wherefore and the Whence;
Baby's precious eyes are blinking
With incipient somnolence.
A Boston Lullaby. Stanza 1

The stranger wrote. I read the scrawl
The sacred page engrossed on;
The name was nought, the place was
all, —
"J. Winthrop Wiggins, Boston."
A Title Clear

ARCHIBALD PHILIP PRIM-
ROSE, EARL OF ROSEBERY
[1847–1929]

Few speeches which have produced
an electrical effect on an audience can
bear the colorless photography of a
printed record.
Life of Pitt

It is beginning to be hinted that we
are a.nation of amateurs.
Rectorial Address, Glasgow
[November 16, 1900]

[1] See Crockett, page 349.

GEORGE ROBERT SIMS
[1847–1922]

Lor', but women's rum cattle to deal
with, the first man found that to
his cost,
And I reckon it's just through a woman
the last man on earth'll be lost.
Moll Jarvis o' Morley

O gleaming lamps of London, that gem
the city's crown,
What fortunes lie within you, O Lights
of London Town?
The Lights of London Town.
Stanza 1

You come here to see how paupers the
season of Christmas spend;
You come here to watch us feeding, as
they watch the captured beast.
Christmas Day in the Workhouse.
Stanza 8

EDWARD NOYES
WESTCOTT
[1847–1898]

Yes, an' no, an' mebbe, an' mebbe
not.
David Harum. Chap. 1

Do unto the other feller the way he'd
like to do unto you an' do it fust.
Ibid. Chap. 20

They say a reasonable number of
fleas is good fer a dog — keeps him
from broodin' over bein' a dog.
Ibid. Chap. 32

The' ain't nothin' truer in the Bible
'n that sayin' thet them that has gits.
Ibid. Chap. 35

I've often had to notice that a man'll
sometimes do the foolishest thing or
meanest thing in his hull life after he's
dead.
Ibid.

ARTHUR JAMES BALFOUR
[1848–1930]

The energies of our system will decay; the glory of the sun will be
dimmed, and the earth, tideless and inert, will no longer tolerate the race
which has for a moment disturbed its
solitude. Man will go down into the pit
and all his thoughts will perish.
The Foundations of Belief

Biography should be written by an
acute enemy.
Quoted by S. K. RATCLIFFE *in*
The London Observer, January
30, 1927

JOHN VANCE CHENEY
[1848–1922]

Who drives the horses of the sun
Shall lord it but a day;
Better the lowly deed were done,
And kept the humble way.
The Happiest Heart. Stanza 1

The happiest heart that ever beat
Was in some quiet breast
That found the common daylight sweet,
And left to Heaven the rest.
Ibid. Stanza 3

DIGBY MACKWORTH
DOLBEN
[1848–1867]

The world is young to-day:
Forget the gods are old,
Forget the years of gold
When all the months were May.
A Song

Poetry, the hand that wrings,
Bruised albeit at the strings,
Music from the soul of things.
Core

As fresh as when the first sunrise
Awoke the lark in Paradise.
The Shrine

W. G. ELMSLIE
[1848–1889]

He held the lamp of Truth that day
So low that none could miss the way;
And yet so high to bring in sight
That picture fair — the World's Great
Light —
That gazing up — the lamp between —
The hand that held it scarce was seen.
The Hand That Held It. Stanza 1

WILLIAM DUDLEY FOULKE
[1848–1935]

What makes a city great? [1] Huge piles
 of stone
Heaped heavenward? Vast multitudes
 who dwell
Within wide circling walls?
The City's Crown

True glory dwells where glorious deeds
 are done,
Where great men rise whose names
 athwart the dusk
Of misty centuries gleam like the sun!
Ibid.

So may the city that I love be great
Till every stone shall be articulate.
Ibid.

SAMUEL MILLER HAGEMAN
[1848–1905]

Slowly climb the moon-touched mountains up their stairway to the sky,
Slowly each white cloud ascending,
 seems a soul that passed on high.
Silence. Stanza 1 [1876]

Every sound shall end in silence, but
 the silence never dies.
Ibid. Stanza 10

Earth is but the frozen echo of the silent voice of God.
Ibid. Stanza 19

Every sound that breaks the silence
 only makes it more profound,
Like a crash of deafening thunder in
 the sweet blue stillness drowned;
Let thy soul walk slowly in thee, as a
 saint in heaven unshod,
For to be alone with Silence is to be.
 alone with God.
Ibid. Stanza 23

Somewhere in the far-off silence, I shall
 feel a vanished hand. [2]
Ibid. Stanza 46

---

[1] Why build these cities glorious
 If man unbuilded goes?
 In vain we build the world, unless
  The builder also grows.
   EDWIN MARKHAM: *Man-Making*
[2] O for the touch of a vanished hand.
  TENNYSON: *Break, Break, Break*

Faith is but an idle canvas, flapping on
 an idle mast,
If it be not found within thee as the
 work of life at last.
Silence. Stanza 70

Tamper not with idle rumor, lest the
 truth appear to lie,
Carve thy life to hilted silence, wrong
 shall fall on it, and die:
Tamper not with accusation, harvest
 not what thou hast heard,
Christ stood in the court of Pilate, but
 he answered not a word.
Ibid. Stanza 74

Creature in Creator meeting, crystal-
 lizing into one,
As stalactite meets stalagmite, standing
 pillared where they run.
Ibid. Stanza 92

JOEL CHANDLER HARRIS
[1848–1908]

Brer Fox, he lay low.
Legends of the Old Plantation

Ez soshubble ez a baskit er kittens.
Ibid.

Lazy fokes's stummucks don't git
tired.
Plantation Proverbs

Jay-bird don't rob his own nes'.
Ibid.

Licker talks mighty loud w'en it gits
loose from de jug.
Ibid.

Hungry rooster don't cackle w'en he
fine a wum.
Ibid.

Youk'n hide de fier, but w'at you
gwine do wid de smoke?
Ibid.

Dogs don't bite at de front gate.
Ibid.

Watch out w'en youer gittin' all you
want. Fattenin' hogs ain't in luck.
Ibid.

De place wharbouts you spill de grease,
 Right dar youer boun' ter slide,
An' whar you fine a bunch er ha'r,
 You'll sholy fine de hide.
Uncle Remus

Bred en bawn in a brier-patch, Brer
Fox.
Uncle Remus

You do de pullin', Sis Cow, en I'll do
de gruntin'.
Ibid.

He diggy, diggy, diggy, but no meat
dar!
Ibid.

W'en ole man Rabbit say 'scoot,' dey
scooted, en w'en ole Miss Rabbit say
'scat,' dey scatted.
Ibid.

Hop light, ladies,
  Oh, Miss Loo!
Oh, swing dat yaller gal!
  Do, boys, do!
Plantation Play Song

How many po' sinners'll be kotched
  out late
En fin' no latch ter de golden gate?
No use fer ter wait twell ter-morrer,
De sun mus'n't set on yo' sorrer, —
Sin's ez sharp ez a bamboo-brier, —
O Lord! fetch de mo'ners up higher!
Negro Revival Hymn. Stanza 1

When you've got a thing to say,
Say it! Don't take half a day.
When your tale's got little in it,
Crowd the whole thing in a minute!
Life is short — a fleeting vapor —
Don't you fill the whole blamed paper
With a tale which, at a pinch,
Could be cornered in an inch!
Boil her down until she simmers,
Polish her until she glimmers.
Advice to Writers for the
Daily Press

RICHARD JEFFERIES
[1848–1887]

Give me fulness of life like to the sea
and the sun; give me fulness of physical
life, mind equal and beyond their fulness; give me a greatness and perfection
of soul higher than all things; give me
my inexpressible desire.
The Story of My Heart. Chap. VI
No thought which I have ever had
has satisfied my soul.
Ibid.
The most extraordinary spectacle is

the vast expenditure of labor and time
wasted in obtaining mere subsistence.
The Story of My Heart. Chap. X
The world works only for today, as
the world worked twelve thousand
years ago, and our children's children
will still have to toil and slave for the
bare necessities of life.
Ibid.
I hope succeeding generations will be
able to be idle. I hope that nine-tenths
of their time will be leisure time; that
they may enjoy their days, and the
earth, and the beauty of this beautiful
world; that they may rest by the sea
and dream; that they may dance and
sing, and eat and drink.
Ibid. Chap. XI
Let me exhort everyone to do their
utmost to think outside and beyond our
present circle of ideas. For every idea
gained is a hundred years of slavery
remitted.
Ibid.

CHARLOTTE AUGUSTA ("CARLOTTA") PERRY
[1848–1914]

If you have gifts and I have none,
If I have shade and you have sun,
'Tis yours with freer hand to give,
'Tis yours with truer grace to live,
Than I, who giftless, sunless, stand
With barren life and hand.
Noblesse Oblige. Stanza 1
The sails we see on the ocean
  Are as white as white can be;
But never one in the harbor,
  As white as the sails at sea.
Distance, the Enchantress.
Stanza 1
It was only a glad "Good morning,"
  As she passed along the way,
But it spread the morning's glory
  Over the livelong day.
Good Morning

LILLA CABOT PERRY
[1848–1933]

Forgive me not! Hate me and I shall
  know

Some of Love's fire still burns in your
breast!
Forgiveness finds its home in hearts
at rest,
On dead volcanoes only lies the snow.
Forgive Me Not
I turn to you, who have known pain and
fear
And failure and despair, and in your
eyes
I read companionship; and though your
cloak
Be threadbare, half of it is mine.
You are my friend.
A Friend. Stanza 2
Death is Love's friend: it sets a holy
seal
On all the past that never can be
broken;
Its beautifying touch knows to reveal
On lips long silent eloquence un-
spoken.
Love's Not Death's Slave.
Stanza 2

EBEN EUGENE REXFORD
[1848–1916]

Love can never more grow old,
Locks may lose their brown and gold,
Cheeks may fade and hollow grow,
But the hearts that love will know
Never winter's frost and chill,
Summer's warmth is in them still.
Silver Threads Among the Gold

WILL HENRY THOMPSON
[1848–   ]

Then at the brief command of Lee
Moved out that matchless infantry,
With Pickett leading grandly down,
To rush against the roaring crown
Of those dread heights of destiny.[1]
The High Tide at Gettysburg.[2]
Stanza 2
The voice that rang through Shiloh's
woods
And Chickamauga's solitudes,
The fierce South cheering on her sons!
Ibid. Stanza 3

[1] See Cone, page 737.
[2] In *The Century Magazine, July, 1888.*

The brave went down! Without dis-
grace
They leaped to Ruin's red embrace;
They only heard Fame's thunders wake,
And saw the dazzling sunburst break
In smiles on Glory's bloody face!
The High Tide at Gettysburg.
Stanza 11
Fold up the banners! Smelt the guns!
Love rules. Her gentle purpose runs;
A mighty mother turns in tears
The pages of her battle years,
Lamenting all her fallen sons!
Ibid. Stanza 15

FREDERIC EDWARD WEATHERLY
[1848–1929]

Playing all my heart remembers,
Old, old songs from far away;
Golden Junes and bleak Decembers
Rise around me as I play.
Fiddle and I. Stanza 2
Always the same, Darby, my own,
Always the same to your old wife Joan.
Darby and Joan.[1] Stanza 1
The sailor's wife the sailor's star shall
be.
Nancy Lee
Ah, Lisette! my pretty Lisette!
Do not listen! do not care!
Lips are laughing, but eyes are wet,
Hearts are breaking in Vanity Fair.
Lisette
Back to the joyless duties,
Back to the fruitless tears,
Loving, and yet divided,
All through the empty years.
Parted. Stanza 1

ROLLIN JOHN WELLS
[1848–1923]

A little more tired at close of day,
A little less anxious to have our way;
A little less ready to scold and blame,
A little more care of a brother's name;
And so we are nearing our journey's
end,
Where time and eternity meet and
blend.
Growing Old. Stanza 1

[1] See Cunningham, page 345.

A little more laughter, a few more tears,
And we shall have told our increasing
  years;
The book is closed and the prayers are
  said,
And we are part of the countless dead.
Thrice happy if then some soul can say,
"I live because he has passed my way."
Growing Old. Stanza 5

JAMES LANE ALLEN
[1849–1925]

Good friend, around these hearthstones speak no evil word of any creature.
A Kentucky Cardinal

The finest music in the room is that
which streams out to the ear of the
spirit in many an exquisite strain from
the little shelf of books on the opposite
wall. Every volume there is an instrument which some melodist of the mind
created and set vibrating with music.
Ibid.

The birds are moulting. If man could
only moult also — his mind once a year
its errors, his heart once a year its useless passions.
Ibid.

I have yet to encounter that common
myth of weak men, an insurmountable
barrier.
The Choir Invisible. Chap. 3

By degrees the comforting light of
what you may actually do and be in an
imperfect world will shine close to you
and all around you, more and more. It
is this that will lead you never to perfection, but always toward it.
Ibid. Chap. 20

JOSEPH GREEN FRANCIS
[1849–1930]

But the kittens were rude and grabbed
  their food,
And treated the Dolls with jeers;
Which caused their Mother an aching
  heart
And seven or eight large tears.
*A Little Girl Asked Some Kittens
to Tea*

A Tam o' Shanter Dog
And a plaintive piping Frog,
With a Cat whose one extravagance was
  clothes,
Went to see a Bounding Bug
Dance a jig upon a rug,
While a Beetle balanced bottles on his
  nose.
The Book of Cheerful Cats

" 'Tis a perfect picnic day!" the little
  dog did say.
Ibid.

A Raging, Roaring Lion, of a Lamb-
  devouring kind,
Reformed and led a sweet, submissive
  life.
For with face all steeped in smiles
He propelled a Lamb for miles
And he wed a woolly Spinster for a
  wife.
Ibid.

EDMUND GOSSE
[1849–1928]

It is a curious reflection, that the ordinary private person who collects objects of a modest luxury, has nothing
about him so old as his books.
Gossip in a Library

The girls nowadays display a shocking freedom; but they were partly led
into it by the relative laxity of their
mothers, who, in their turn, gave great
anxiety to a still earlier generation.
The Whole Duty of Woman

There never, we suppose, from the
beginning of the world, was a man-
preacher who did not warn the women
of his congregation against the vanity
of fair raiment.
Ibid.

Where are the cities of old time?
The Ballade of Dead Cities

The wizard silence of the hours of dew.
The White Throat

Canst thou not wait for Love one flying
  hour,
O heart of little faith?
Dejection and Delay

The Past is like a funeral gone by,
The Future comes like an unwelcome
guest.
                              May-Day
I do not hunger for a well-stored mind,
I only wish to live my life, and find
My heart in unison with all mankind.
                        Lying in the Grass
To all at length an end!
All sailors to some unseen harbour
float.
Farewell, mysterious, happy, twilight
boat.
Farewell, my friend!
                        The Vanishing Boat

MARGARET JOHNSTON GRAFFLIN
[1849–1925]

None other can pain me as you, dear,
can do;
None other can please me or praise me
as you.
                        To My Son. Stanza 1
"Like mother, like son," is the saying
so true,
The world will judge largely of
"Mother" by you.
                        Ibid. Stanza 2

THOMAS CHALMERS HARBAUGH
[1849–1924]

I've sung the Psalms of David for
nearly eighty years,
They've been my staff and comfort and
calmed life's many fears;
I'm sorry I disturb the choir, perhaps
I'm doing wrong,
But when my heart is filled with praise
I can't keep back a song.
                Trouble in the "Amen Corner."
                        Stanza 15

WILLIAM ERNEST HENLEY
[1849–1903]

The Hospital, grey, quiet, old,
Where Life and Death like friendly
chafferers meet.
                In Hospital. Enter Patient

Life is (I think) a blunder and a shame.
                In Hospital. Waiting
Far in the stillness a cat
Languishes loudly.
                        Ibid. Vigil
A well-bred silence always at command.
                Ibid. Lady-Probationer
From the winter's gray despair,
From the summer's golden languor,
Death, the lover of Life,
Frees us for ever.
                        Ibid. Ave, Caesar
His wise, rare smile is sweet with cer-
tainties,
And seems in all his patients to compel
Such love and faith as failure cannot
quell.
                Ibid. "The Chief" (Lister)
Bland as a Jesuit, sober as a hymn.
                Ibid. House-Surgeon
  I know
That in the shade of Fujisan,
What time the cherry-orchards blow,
I loved you once in old Japan.
                Ballade of a Toyokuni
                        Colour-Print
As dust that drives, as straws that blow,
Into the night go one and all.
                Ballade of Dead Actors
Fate's a fiddler, Life's a dance.
                Double Ballade of Life and Fate
Let us break out, and taste the morning
prime . . .
        Let us be drunk.
                        To F. W.
The ways of Death are soothing and
serene,
And all the words of Death are grave
and sweet.
                In Memoriam R. G. C. B.
What is to come we know not. But we
know
That what has been was good.
                        What Is to Come
Out of the night that covers me,
  Black as the Pit from pole to pole,
I thank whatever gods may be
  For my unconquerable soul.
        Echoes. IV, In Memoriam R. T.
        Hamilton Bruce ["Invictus"]
Under the bludgeonings of chance
My head is bloody, but unbowed.
                        Ibid.

It matters not how strait the gate,
How charged with punishments the
scroll,
I am the master of my fate;
I am the captain of my soul.[1]
Echoes. IV, In Memoriam R. T.
Hamilton Bruce ["Invictus"]

Praise the generous gods for giving
In a world of wrath and strife,
With a little time for living,
Unto all the joy of life.
Ibid. VI

We'll go no more a-roving by the light
of the moon.[2]
November glooms are barren beside the
dusk of June.
Ibid. VIII

The nightingale has a lyre of gold,
The lark's is a clarion call,
And the blackbird plays but a boxwood
flute,
But I love him best of all.
Ibid. XVIII, To A. D.

Tired of experience, he turns
To the friendly and comforting breast
Of the old nurse, Death.
Ibid. XXIX, To R. L. S.

A late lark twitters from the quiet skies.
Ibid. XXXV, In Memoriam
Margaritae Sorori

Night with her train of stars
And her great gift of sleep.
Ibid.

So be my passing!
My task accomplished and the long day
done,
My wages taken, and in my heart
Some late lark singing.
Ibid.

Or ever the knightly years were gone
With the old world to the grave,
I was a King in Babylon
And you were a Christian Slave.
Ibid. XXXVII, To W. A.

[1] Dux atque imperator vitae mortalium animus est (The soul is the captain and master of the life of mortals). — SALLUST: *Jugurtha, Chap. 1*
Be the proud captain still of thine own fate.
JAMES BENJAMIN KENYON
[1858-1924]: *A Challenge*
[2] So we'll go no more a-roving.
BYRON: *Letter to Thomas Moore*

The Spirit of Wine
Sang in my glass, and I listened
With love to his odorous music,
His flushed and magnificent song.
Echoes. XLI, To R. A. M. S.

These poor Might-Have-Beens,
These fatuous, ineffectual Yesterdays!
To James McNeill Whistler

For Death and Time bring on the prime
Of God's own chosen weather,
And we lie in the peace of the Great
Release
As once in the grass together.
In Memoriam R. L. S.

What have I done for you,
England, my England?
Rhymes and Rhythms. XXV

In the street of By-and-By
Stands the hostelry of Never,
Dream from deed he must dissever
Who his fortune here would try.
In the Street of By-and-By

With what a genius for administration
We rearrange the rumbling universe,
And map the course of man's regenera-
tion
Over a pipe.
Inter Sodales

SARAH ORNE JEWETT
[1849-1909]

A harbor, even if it is a little harbor,
is a good thing, since adventurers come
into it as well as go out, and the life in
it grows strong, because it takes something from the world and has something
to give in return.
Country By-Ways. River
Driftwood

God bless them all who die at sea!
If they must sleep in restless waves,
God make them dream they are ashore,
With grass above their graves.
The Gloucester Mother.[1] Stanza 3

Look bravely up into the sky,
And be content with knowing
That God wished for a buttercup
Just here, where you are growing.
Discontent. Stanza 9

[1] In *McClure's Magazine, Oct., 1908.*

FREDERICK LANGBRIDGE
[1849–1923]

Yield thy poor best, and muse not how
    or why,
Lest one day, seeing all about thee
    spread,
A mighty crowd and marvellously fed,
Thy heart break out into a bitter cry:
"I might have furnished, I, yea, even I,
The two small fishes and the barley
    bread." [1]
    A Cluster of Quiet Thoughts

EMMA LAZARUS
[1849–1887]

Give me your tired, your poor,
Your huddled masses yearning to
    breathe free,
The wretched refuse of your teeming
    shore,
Send these, the homeless, tempest-
    tossed, to me:
I lift my lamp beside the golden door.
    The New Colossus: Inscription
    for the Statue of Liberty, New
    York harbor

GRACE DENIO LITCHFIELD
[1849–   ]

We have no dearer word for our
    heart's friend,
For him who journeys to the world's
    far end,
And scars our soul with going; thus we
    say,
As unto him who steps but o'er the
    way —
"Good-by."
    Good-by. Stanza 2

SIR WILLIAM OSLER
[1849–1919]

Speck in cornea, 50¢.
    Entry in his account-book, first
    fee as a practicing physician.
    From Life of Sir William Osler
    by HARVEY CUSHING, *Vol. I,*
    Chap. 6

[1] *Luke, IX, 16.*

After all, there is no such literature
as a Dictionary.
    Life of Sir William Osler.
    Vol. I, Chap. 11

The desire to take medicine is perhaps the greatest feature which distinguishes man from animals.
    Ibid. Chap. 14

This is yet the childhood of the world,
and a supine credulity is still the most
charming characteristic of man.
    Ibid.

We are here to add what we can *to,*
not to get what we can *from,* Life. [1]
    Ibid.

To have striven, to have made an effort, to have been true to certain ideals
— this alone is worth the struggle.
    Ibid. Chap. 16

Humanity has but three great enemies: fever, famine and war; of these
by far the greatest, by far the most
terrible, is fever.
    Ibid.

Though a little one, the master-word
[Work] looms large in meaning. It is
the open sesame to every portal, the
great equalizer in the world, the true
philosopher's stone which transmutes
all the base metal of humanity into
gold. [2]
    Ibid. Chap. 22

Things cannot always go your way.
Learn to accept in silence the minor
aggravations, cultivate the gift of taciturnity and consume your own smoke [3]
with an extra draught of hard work, so
that those about you may not be an-
noyed with the dust and soot of your
complaints.
    Ibid.

We are here not to get all we can out
of life for ourselves, but to try to make
the lives of others happier.
    Ibid.

Take the sum of human achieve-
ment in action, in science, in art, in lit-

[1] Also in *Doctor and Nurse,* Paper II in
Aequanimitas and Other Addresses.
[2] Lecture, *The Master-Word in Medicine,*
Toronto, Oct. 1, 1903. Paper XVIII in *Aequanimitas.*
[3] See Carlyle, page 379.

erature — subtract the work of the men above forty, and while we should miss great treasures, even priceless treasures, we would practically be where we are to-day. . . . The effective, moving, vitalizing work of the world is done between the ages of twenty-five and forty.[1]

Life of Sir William Osler.
Vol. I, Chap. 24

My second fixed idea is the uselessness of men above sixty years of age, and the incalculable benefit it would be in commercial, political, and in professional life if, as a matter of course, men stopped work at this age.

Ibid.

In that charming novel, "The Fixed Period," [by] Anthony Trollope, . . . the plot hinges upon the admirable scheme of a college into which at sixty men retired for a year of contemplation before a peaceful departure by chloroform. That incalculable benefits might follow such a scheme is apparent to anyone who, like myself, is nearing the limit, and who has made a careful study of the calamities which may befall men during the seventh and eighth decades.[2]

Ibid.

Nothing will sustain you more potently than the power to recognize in your humdrum routine, as perhaps it may be thought, the true poetry of life — the poetry of the commonplace, of the ordinary man, of the plain, toil-worn woman. with their loves and their joys, their sorrows and their griefs.

Ibid. (The Student Life)

Lift up one hand to heaven and thank your stars if they have given you the proper sense to enable you to appreciate the inconceivably droll situations in which we catch our fellow creatures.

Ibid.

I have three personal ideals. One, to

do the day's work well and not to bother about to-morrow. . . . The second ideal has been to act the Golden Rule, as far as in me lay, toward my professional brethren and toward the patients committed to my care. And the third has been to cultivate such a measure of equanimity as would enable me to bear success with humility, the affection of my friends without pride, and to be ready when the day of sorrow and grief came to meet it with the courage befitting a man.

Life of Sir William Osler. (Farewell Dinner, May 2, 1905)

Throw all the beer and spirits into the Irish Channel, the English Channel, and the North Sea for a year, and people in England would be infinitely better. It would certainly solve all the problems with which the philanthropists, the physicians, and the politicians have to deal.[1]

Ibid. Vol. II, Chap. 26

No man is really happy or safe without a hobby, and it makes precious little difference what the outside interest may be — botany, beetles or butterflies, roses, tulips or irises; fishing, mountaineering or antiquities — anything will do so long as he straddles a hobby and rides it hard.[2]

Ibid. Chap. 29

Nothing in life is more wonderful than faith — the one great moving force which we can neither weigh in the balance nor test in the crucible.[3]

Ibid. Chap. 30

In the life of a young man the most essential thing for happiness is the gift of friendship.

Ibid. Chap. 31

No bubble is so iridescent or floats longer than that blown by the successful teacher.

Ibid.

[1] Address, *The Fixed Period*, Johns Hopkins University, Baltimore, Feb. 22, 1905.
[2] This valedictory address caused much discussion and misquotation. It was headlined in the press, "Osler Recommends Chloroform at Sixty," and occasioned many columns of letters, caustic cartoons, etc., until to "Oslerize" became a byword.

[1] Address at Working Men's College, Camden Town, Nov. 17, 1906.
[2] Address, Medical Library Association, Belfast, July 28, 1909.
[3] The Faith That Heals.

The nation's Valhalla [Westminster Abbey].[1]

Life of Sir William Osler.
Vol. II, Chap. 32

It is one of the greatest blessings that so many women are so full of tact. The calamity happens when a woman who has all the other riches of life just lacks that one thing.[2]

Ibid. Chap. 33

It is the prime duty of a woman of this terrestrial world to look well. Neatness is the asepsis of clothes.

Ibid.

The quest for righteousness is Oriental, the quest for knowledge, Occidental.[3]

Ibid. Chap. 34

In science the credit goes to the man who convinces the world, not to the man to whom the idea first occurs.[4]

Ibid. Chap. 38

JAMES WHITCOMB RILEY
[1849–1916]

O'er folded blooms
  On swirls of musk,
The beetle booms adown the glooms
  And bumps along the dusk.
The Beetle. Stanza 7

The ripest peach is highest on the tree.
The Ripest Peach. Stanza 1

An' the Gobble-uns'll git you
  Ef you don't watch out.
Little Orphant Annie. Stanza 1

His Mammy heered him holler, an' his Daddy heered him bawl,
An' when they turn't the kivvers down, he wasn't there at all!
Ibid. Stanza 2

I cannot say, and I will not say
That he is dead. — He is just away!
Away

Heaven holds all for which you sigh —
There! little girl; don't cry!
A Life-Lesson. Stanza 3

[1] See Beaumont, page 129.
[2] Commencement Address, Johns Hopkins Hospital School of Nursing, May 7, 1913.
[3] Address, Jewish Historical Society of England, April 27, 1914.
[4] Address, Royal Society of Medicine, Historical Section, May 15, 1918.

I can see the pink sunbonnet and the little checkered dress
She wore when first I kissed her and she answered the caress
With the written declaration that, "as surely as the vine
Grew 'round the stump," she loved me
  — that old sweetheart of mine.
An Old Sweetheart of Mine.
Stanza 12

How the grand band-wagon shone with a splendor all its own,
And glittered with a glory that our dreams had never known!
The Circus-Day Parade. Stanza 2

When over the fair fame of friend or foe
  The shadow of disgrace shall fall, instead
Of words of blame, or proof of thus and so,
  Let something good be said.
Let Something Good Be Said.
Stanza 1

Forget not that no fellow-being yet
  May fall so low but love may lift his head.
Ibid. Stanza 2

You think them "out of reach," your dead?
Nay, by my own dead, I deny
Your "out of reach." — Be comforted:
  'Tis not so far to die.
"Out of Reach." Stanza 1

"God bless us every one!" prayed Tiny Tim.[1]
God Bless Us Every One. Stanza 1

"Well, good-by, Jim:
Take keer of yourse'f!"
The Old Man and Jim. Stanza 1

Fer the world is full of roses, and the roses full of dew,
And the dew is full of heavenly love that drips fer me and you.
Thoughts fer the Discuraged Farmer. Stanza 5

'Long about knee-deep in June,
'Bout the time strawberries melts
On the vine.
Knee-deep in June. Stanza 1

Oh! the old swimmin'-hole! When I last saw the place,

[1] See Dickens, page 495.

The scene was all changed, like the change in my face.
The Old Swimmin'-Hole. Stanza 5
Work is the least o' my idees
When the green, you know, gits back in the trees!
When the Green Gits Back in the Trees. Stanza 1
O, the Raggedy Man he works fer Pa,
An' he's the goodest man ever you saw!
The Raggedy Man. Stanza 1
There's a boil on his ear and a corn on his chin, —
He calls it a dimple — but dimples stick in.
The Man in the Moon. Stanza 3
A pictur' that no painter has the colorin' to mock —
When the frost is on the punkin and the fodder's in the shock.
When the Frost Is on the Punkin. Stanza 2
Le's go a-visitin' back to Griggsby's Station —
Back where we ust to be so happy and so pore!
Griggsby's Station. Stanza 1
And thus, borne to me o'er the seas between
 Thy land and mine, thy song of certain wing
Circles above me.
Reply to Rudyard Kipling.[1]
Stanza 3

EDWARD BELLAMY [2]
[1850–1898]

If we could have devised an arrangement for providing everybody with music in their homes, perfect in quality, unlimited in quantity, suited to every mood, and beginning and ceasing at will, we should have considered the limit of human felicity already attained.
Looking Backward [*1887*]
Your system was liable to periodical convulsions, overwhelming alike the wise and unwise, the successful cutthroat as well as his victim. I refer to the business crises at intervals of five to ten years, which wrecked the industries of the nation.
Ibid.

AUGUSTINE BIRRELL
[1850–1933]

Libraries are not made; they grow.
Obiter Dicta. Book-Buying
Good as it is to inherit a library, it is better to collect one.
Ibid.

FLORENCE EARLE COATES
[1850–1927]

Far, far the mountain peak from me
Where lone He stands, with look caressing;
I lift my dreaming eyes and see
His hand stretched forth in blessing.
The Christ of the Andes.[1] *Stanza 1*
The messenger of sure and swift relief,
Welcomed with wailings and reproachful grief;
The friend of those that have no friend but me,
I break all chains, and set all captives free.
Death. Stanza 2
There is always room for beauty: memory
 A myriad lovely blossoms may enclose,
But, whatsoe'er hath been, there still must be
Room for another rose.
The Poetry of Earth. Stanza 1
How living are the dead!
 Enshrined, but not apart,

---

[1] Your trail runs to the westward,
  And mine to my own place;
 There is water between our lodges
  And I have not seen your face.
  RUDYARD KIPLING: *To J. W. R., St. 1*
[2] There is at least a fair chance that another fifty years will confirm Edward Bellamy's position as one of the most authentic prophets of our age. — HEYWOOD BROUN [1931]

[1] The statue, The Christ of the Andes, by the Argentine sculptor, Mateo Alonso, commemorates the peaceful settlement of boundary disputes between Chile and Argentina. It was cast in bronze from melted cannon, and dedicated in March, 1904.

How safe within the heart
  We hold them still — our dead,
  Whatever else be fled!
                Immortal. Stanza 1
Think not of love as a debt —
  Due in May [1] or in December.
                Mother-Love. Stanza 1

EUGENE FIELD
[1850–1895]

I feel a sort of yearnin' 'nd a chokin' in
  my throat
When I think of Red Hoss Mountain
  'nd of Casey's tabble dote!
        Casey's Table d'Hôte. Stanza 1
He could whip his weight in wildcats.
        Modjesky as Cameel. Stanza 10
Let my temptation be a book,
  Which I shall purchase, hold, and keep.
              The Bibliomaniac's Prayer.
                Stanza 2
No matter what conditions
  Dyspeptic come to feaze,
The best of all physicians
  Is Apple-pie and cheese!
        Apple-Pie and Cheese. Stanza 5
A little peach in the orchard grew, —
A little peach of emerald hue;
Warmed by the sun and wet by the dew
  It grew.
          The Little Peach. Stanza 1
And God had set upon his head a crown
  uv silver hair
In promise uv the golden crown He
  meaneth him to wear.
So, uv us boys that met him out'n Den-
  ver, there wuz none
But fell in love with Dana uv the Noo
  York Sun.[2]
      Mr. Dana, of the New York Sun.
                Stanza 5
You'll need no epitaph but this: "Here
  sleeps the man who run
That best 'nd brightest paper, the Noo
  York Sun."
                Ibid. Stanza 9
I like the Anglo-Saxon speech
  With its direct revealings;

  [1] "Mother's Day," the second Sunday in
May.
  [2] Charles Anderson Dana [1819–1897].

It takes a hold, and seems to reach
  'Way down into your feelings.
      "Good-by — God Bless You!"
                Stanza 1
I'm sure no human heart goes wrong
  That's told "Good-by — God bless
  you!"
                Ibid. Stanza 2
Conjectures obtain that for language
  profane
There is no such place as Flanders.[1]
              In Flanders. Stanza 5
I never lost a little fish — yes, I am free
  to say
It always was the biggest fish I caught
  that got away.
        Our Biggest Fish. Stanza 2
How gracious those dews of solace that
  over my senses fall
At the clink of the ice in the pitcher the
  boy brings up the hall!
        The Clink of the Ice. Stanza 1
When one's all right, he's prone to spite
  The doctor's peaceful mission;
But when he's sick, it's loud and quick
  He bawls for a physician.[2]
              Doctors. Stanza 2
          We twain
Discussed with buoyant hearts
The various things that appertain
To bibliomaniac arts.
          Dibdin's Ghost. Stanza 2
When I demanded of my friend what
  viands he preferred,

  [1] Our armies swore terribly in Flanders. —
STERNE: *Tristram Shandy, Book 3, Chap. 11*
  [2] Three faces wears the doctor: when first
      sought
    An Angel's; and a god's the cure half-
      wrought;
    But when, the cure complete, he seeks his
      fee,
    The Devil looks less terrible than he.
                Anonymous
    God and the soldier
    All men adore
    In time of trouble
    And no more;
    For when war is over
    And all things righted,
    God is neglected —
    The old soldier slighted.
        Lines found on an old stone sentry-
      box in Gibraltar. They have been
      adapted to read "God and the doc-
      tor."

He quoth: "A large cold bottle, and a
small hot bird!"
  The Bottle and the Bird. Stanza 1
Have you ever heard of the Sugar-Plum
Tree?
  'Tis a marvel of great renown!
It blooms on the shore of the Lollipop
  sea
  In the garden of Shut-Eye Town.
      The Sugar-Plum Tree. Stanza 1
I pray that, risen from the dead,
  I may in glory stand —
A crown, perhaps, upon my head,
  But a needle in my hand.
      Grandma's Prayer. Stanza 1
Wynken, Blynken, and Nod one night
  Sailed off in a wooden shoe —
Sailed on a river of crystal light
  Into a sea of dew.
      Wynken, Blynken, and Nod.
          Stanza 1
The little toy dog is covered with dust,
  But sturdy and stanch he stands;
And the little toy soldier is red with
  rust,
  And his musket moulds in his hands;
Time was when the little toy dog was
  new,
  And the soldier was passing fair;
And that was the time when our Little
  Boy Blue
  Kissed them and put them there
      Little Boy Blue. Stanza 1
The Rock-a-By Lady from Hushaby
  street
  Comes stealing; comes creeping.
      The Rock-a-By Lady. Stanza 1
Have you ever heard the wind go
  "Yooooo"?
  'Tis a pitiful sound to hear!
It seems to chill you through and
  through
  With a strange and speechless fear.
      The Night Wind. Stanza 1
The Dinkey-Bird goes singing
  In the amfalula tree!
      The Dinkey-Bird. Stanza 1
The gingham dog went "Bow-wow-
  wow!"
And the calico cat replied "Mee-ow!"
The air was littered, an hour or so,
With bits of gingham and calico.
      The Duel. Stanza 2

We all hev our choice, an' you, like the
  rest,
Allow that the dorg which you've got
  is the best;
I wouldn't give much for the boy 'at
  grows up
With no friendship subsistin' 'tween
  him an' a pup!
      The Bench-Legged Fyce.
          Stanza 7
Father calls me William, sister calls me
  Will,
Mother calls me Willie, but the fellers
  call me Bill!
      Jest 'Fore Christmas. Stanza 1
'Most all the time, the whole year
  round, there ain't no flies on me,
But jest 'fore Christmas I'm as good
  as I kin be!
          Ibid.
Shuffle-Shoon and Amber-Locks
Sit together, building blocks;
Shuffle-Shoon is old and gray,
Amber-Locks a little child,
But together at their play
Age and Youth are reconciled.
      Shuffle-Shoon and Amber-Locks.
          Stanza 1
Mother tells me "Happy dreams!" and
  takes away the light,
An' leaves me lyin' all alone an' seein'
  things at night.
      Seein' Things. Stanza 1
Over the hills and far away,
A little boy steals from his morning
  play
And under the blossoming apple-tree
He lies and he dreams of the things
  to be.
      Over the Hills and Far Away.
          Stanza 1
That the troubles of the little boy pur-
  sue the man through life;
That here and there along the course
  wherein we hoped to glide
Some envious hand has sprinkled ashes
  just to spoil our slide!
      Ashes on the Slide. Stanza 5
Strive not to hew your path through
  life — it really doesn't pay;
Be sure the salve of flattery soaps all
  you do and say;

Herein the only royal road to fame and
 fortune lies:
Put not your trust in vinegar — molasses catches flies!
> *Uncle Eph. Stanza 4*

And speechless pride and rapture ineffable shall fill
The beatific bosom of Penn Yan Bill.
> *Penn Yan Bill. Stanza 9*

The sturdiest peak is Fame's!
And there be many on its very height,
Who strut in pride and vaunt their
 empty claims,
 While those poor human asses who
 delight
To place them there have unremem-
 bered names!
> *Pike's Peak. Stanza 4*

JOHN CHEEVER GOODWIN
[1850–1912]

For that elephant ate all night,
 And that elephant ate all day;
Do what he could to furnish him food,
 The cry was still *more hay*.
> *Wang: The Man with an Ele-*
> *phant on His Hands* [*1891*]

JANE ELLEN HARRISON
[1850–1928]

Language is as much an art and as
sure a refuge as painting or music or
literature.
> *Reminiscences of a Student's*
> *Life. Chap. 2*

Old age, believe me, is a good and
pleasant time. It is true that you are
gently shouldered off the stage, but
then you are given such a comfortable
front stall as spectator, and, if you have
really played your part, you are more
content to sit down and watch.
> *Ibid. Conclusion*

Life does not cease when you are old,
it only suffers a rich change. You go
on loving, only your love, instead of a
burning, fiery furnace, is the mellow
glow of an autumn sun.
> *Ibid.*

ROSE HENNIKER HEATON

She answered by return of post
The invitation of her host.
She caught the train she said she would,
And changed at junctions as she should.
She brought a light and smallish box
And keys belonging to the locks.
> *The Perfect Guest*

She left no little things behind
Excepting loving thoughts and kind.
> *Ibid.*

HENRY CABOT LODGE
[1850–1924]

New England has a harsh climate, a
barren soil, a rough and stormy coast,
and yet we love it, even with a love
passing that of dwellers in more favored regions.
> *Address, New England Society*
> *of New York* [*December 22,*
> *1884*]

Of "Americanism" of the right sort
we cannot have too much. Mere vapor-
ing and boasting become a nation as
little as a man. But honest, outspoken
pride and faith in our country are infinitely better and more to be respected
than the cultivated reserve which sets
it down as ill-bred and in bad taste ever
to refer to our country except by way
of deprecation, criticism, or general negation.
> *Ibid.*

Let every man honor and love the
land of his birth and the race from
which he springs and keep their memory green. It is a pious and honorable
duty. But let us have done with British-Americans and Irish-Americans and
German-Americans, and so on, and all
be Americans. . . . If a man is going
to be an American at all let him be so
without any qualifying adjectives; and
if he is going to be something else, let
him drop the word American from his
personal description.[1]
> *The Day We Celebrate (Fore-*
> *fathers' Day), Address, New*
> *England Society of Brooklyn*
> [*December 21, 1888*]

[1] See Theodore Roosevelt, page 734.

There was no hour down to the end when he would not turn aside from everything else to preach the doctrine of Americanism, of the principles and the faith upon which American government rested, and which all true Americans should wear in their heart of hearts. He was a great patriot, a great man; above all, a great American. His country was the ruling, mastering passion of his life from the beginning even unto the end.

Theodore Roosevelt, Address before Congress [February 9, 1919]

PHILIP BOURKE MARSTON
[1850–1887]

A little time for laughter,
  A little time to sing,
  A little time to kiss and cling,
And no more kissing after.
        After. Stanza 1

ALICE MEYNELL
[1850 1922]

My heart shall be thy garden. Come, my own,
  Into thy garden; thine be happy hours
  Among my fairest thoughts, my tallest flowers,
From root to crowning petal thine alone.
        Sonnet, The Garden
She walks — the lady of my delight —
  A shepherdess of sheep.
Her flocks are thoughts. She keeps them white;
  She guards them from the steep.
        The Shepherdess. Stanza 1
I must not think of thee; and, tired yet strong,
  I shun the thought that lurks in all delight —
The thought of thee — and in the blue heaven's height
And in the sweetest passage of a song.
        Sonnet, Renouncement
With the first dream that comes with the first sleep

I run, I run, I am gathered to thy heart.
        Sonnet, Renouncement
O heavenly colour, London town
  Has blurred it from her skies;
And, hooded in an earthly brown,
  Unheaven'd the city lies.
        November Blue. Stanza 1
Blue comes to earth, it walks the street,
  It dyes the wide air through;
A mimic sky about their feet,
  The throng go crowned with blue.
        Ibid. Stanza 2
It is principally for the sake of the leg that a change in the dress of man is so much to be desired. . . . The leg is the best part of the figure . . . and the best leg is the man's. Man should no longer disguise the long lines, the strong forms, in those lengths of piping or tubing that are of all garments the most stupid.[1]
        Essays. Unstable Equilibrium

LAURA ELIZABETH RICHARDS
[1850–   ]

Great is truth and shall prevail,
Therefore must we weep and wail.
        The Mameluke and the Hospodar
Every little wave had its nightcap on.
        A Song for Hal
"Trifles are trifles, but serious matters,
They must be seen to," says little Prince Tatters.
        Prince Tatters. Stanza 3
Ponsonby Perks,
He fought with Turks,
Performing many wonderful works.
        Nonsense Verses. Stanza 2
The branches of the pencil-tree
  Are pointed every one.
        Song of the Mother whose Children Are Fond of Drawing. Stanza 2

---

[1]   In creased and flapping bags,
  Dull parallels of cloth from cush to kibe,
  Where is your mannish limb? For lack of praise
It atrophies and shrivels.
        — Shakespeare in Modern Dress (C. M.)

The fairest spot to me,
On the land or on the sea,
Is the charming little cupboard where
the jam-pots grow.
Master Jack's Song
Baby said
When she smelt the rose,
"Oh! what a pity
I've only one nose!"
The Difference. Stanza 1

ROBERT RICHARDSON
[1850–1901]

Warm summer sun, shine friendly
here;
Warm western wind, blow kindly here;
Green sod above, rest light, rest light —
Good-night, Annette! Sweetheart, good-
night.[1]
To Annette

ROBERT LOUIS STEVENSON
[1850–1894]

In winter I get up at night
And dress by yellow candle-light.
In summer, quite the other way,
I have to go to bed by day.
Bed in Summer. Stanza 1
A child should always say what's true
And speak when he is spoken to,
And behave mannerly at table;
At least as far as he is able.
Whole Duty of Children
Dark brown is the river,
Golden is the sand.
It flows along for ever,
With trees on either hand.
Where Go the Boats? Stanza 1
The pleasant land of counterpane.
The Land of Counterpane.
Stanza 4
I have a little shadow that goes in and
out with me,

[1] Mark Twain adapted this verse, by an
Australian poet, for the stone marking the
grave of his daughter, Olivia Susan Clemens,
who died August 18, 1896, aged 24 years:
Warm summer sun, shine kindly here;
Warm southern wind, blow softly here;
Green sod above, lie light, lie light —
Good-night, dear heart, good-night, good-
night.

And what can be the use of him is more
than I can see.
My Shadow. Stanza 1
The world is so full of a number of
things,
I'm sure we should all be as happy as
kings.
Happy Thought
The eternal dawn, beyond a doubt,
Shall break on hill and plain,
And put all stars and candles out
Ere we be young again.
To Minnie
All that I could think of, in the dark-
ness and the cold,
Was just that I was leaving home and
my folks were growing old.
Christmas at Sea. Stanza 11
There are men and classes of men
that stand above the common herd: the
soldier, the sailor, and the shepherd not
infrequently; the artist rarely; rarelier
still, the clergyman; the physician almost as a rule. He is the flower (such as
it is) of our civilization.
Underwoods. Dedication
Generosity he has, such as is possible
to those who practise an art, never to
those who drive a trade; discretion,
tested by a hundred secrets; tact, tried
in a thousand embarrassments; and
what are more important, Heraclean
cheerfulness and courage.
Ibid.
Gratitude is but a lame sentiment;
thanks, when they are expressed, are
often more embarrassing than welcome.
Ibid.
Go, little book, and wish to all
Flowers in the garden, meat in the hall,
A bin of wine, a spice of wit,
A house with lawns enclosing it,
A living river by the door,
A nightingale in the sycamore!
Ibid. Envoy
Youth now flees on feathered foot.
Ibid. To Will H. Low [1]
Life is over, life was gay:
We have come the primrose way.
Ibid.

[1] American painter [1853–1932], whose wife
translated Stevenson's fable, *The Strange
Case of Dr. Jekyll and Mr. Hyde,* into French.

Dear Andrew, with the brindled hair.[1]
Underwoods. To Andrew Lang

Under the wide and starry sky,
Dig the grave and let me lie.
Glad did I live and gladly die,
And I laid me down with a will.
Ibid. Requiem,[2] Stanza 1

This be the verse you grave for me:
Here he lies where he longed to be;
Home is the sailor, home from sea,
And the hunter home from the hill.
Ibid. Stanza 2

If I have faltered more or less
In my great task of happiness.
Ibid. The Celestial Surgeon

If beams from happy human eyes
Have moved me not; if morning skies,
Books, and my food, and summer rain
Knocked on my sullen heart in vain: —
Lord, thy most pointed pleasure take
And stab my spirit broad awake.
Ibid.

Yet, O stricken heart, remember, O remember
How of human days he lived the better part.
April came to bloom and never dim December
Breathed its killing chills upon the head or heart.
Ibid. In Memoriam F. A. Sitwell[3]
[*1881*]

Let first the onion flourish there,
Rose among roots, the maiden-fair
Wine-scented and poetic soul
Of the capacious salad bowl.
Ibid. To a Gardener

In the highlands, in the country places,
Where the old plain men have rosy faces,

And the young fair maidens
Quiet eyes.
Underwoods. XVI

My body, which my dungeon is,
And yet my parks and palaces.
Ibid. XXXVII

There are kind hearts still, for friends to fill
And fools to take and break them;
But the nearest friends are the auldest friends
And the grave's the place to seek them.
Ibid. In Scots, XVI, Stanza 3

Wealth I ask not, hope nor love,
Nor a friend to know me;
All I ask, the heaven above
And the road below me.
The Vagabond. Stanza 4

And this shall be for music when no one else is near,
The fine song for singing, the rare song to hear!
Romance (I Will Make You Brooches). Stanza 3

God, if this were enough,
That I see things bare to the buff.
If This Were Faith

For all the story-books you read:
For all the pains you comforted:
For all you pitied, all you bore,
In sad and happy days of yore . . .
Take, nurse, the little book you hold!
To Alison Cunningham from Her Boy

Bright is the ring of words
When the right man rings them.
Songs of Travel. XV

I have trod the upward and the downward slope;
I have endured and done in days before;
I have longed for all, and bid farewell to hope;
And I have lived and loved and closed the door.
Ibid. XXII

Be it granted me to behold you again in dying,
Hills of home!
Ibid. XLIII, To S. R. Crockett

Trusty, dusky, vivid, true,
With eyes of gold and bramble-dew,

---

[1] Dear Louis of the awful cheek!
  Who told you it was right to speak,
  Where all the world might hear and stare,
  Of other fellows' "brindled hair"?
        ANDREW LANG: *To R. L. S.*
[2] As originally written, *Requiem* had as a second stanza:
  Here may the winds about me blow;
  Here the clouds may come and go;
  Here shall be rest for evermo',
    And the heart for aye shall be still.
[3] Lady Colvin's son by her first marriage; he died at the age of eighteen.

Steel-true and blade-straight
The great artificer made my mate.
> *To My Wife. Stanza 1*

I am in the habit of looking not so much to the nature of a gift as to the spirit in which it is offered.
> *New Arabian Nights. The Suicide Club*

I was a great solitary when I was young.
> *The Pavilion on the Links*

I have played the sedulous ape to Hazlitt, to Lamb, to Wordsworth, to Sir Thomas Browne, to Defoe, to Hawthorne, to Montaigne, to Baudelaire and to Obermann.
> *A College Magazine*

Mankind was never so happily inspired as when it made a cathedral.
> *An Inland Voyage. Noyon Cathedral*

Every man is his own doctor of divinity, in the last resort.
> *Ibid.*

To love is the great Amulet that makes this world a garden.
> *Travels with a Donkey. The Heart of the Country*

The cruellest lies are often told in silence.
> *Virginibus Puerisque. IV, Truth of Intercourse*

Old and young, we are all on our last cruise.
> *Ibid. Crabbed Age and Youth*

Give me the young man who has brains enough to make a fool of himself.
> *Ibid.*

Books are good enough in their own way, but they are a mighty bloodless substitute for life.
> *Ibid. An Apology for Idlers*

Perpetual devotion to what a man calls his business, is only to be sustained by perpetual neglect of many other things.
> *Ibid.*

There is no duty we underrate so much as the duty of being happy.
> *Ibid.*

To travel hopefully is a better thing than to arrive.
> *Virginibus Puerisque. El Dorado*

To be what we are, and to become what we are capable of becoming, is the only end of life.
> *Familiar Studies of Men and Books*

Science carries us into zones of speculation, where there is no habitable city for the mind of man.
> *Pulvis et Umbra*

In the harsh face of life faith can read a bracing gospel.
> *Ibid.*

You cannot run away from a weakness; you must some time fight it out or perish; and if that be so, why not now, and where you stand?
> *The Amateur Emigrant*

Youth is wholly experimental.
> *A Letter to a Young Gentleman*

Fifteen men on the Dead Man's Chest — [1]
Yo-ho-ho, and a bottle of rum! [2]
Drink and the devil had done for the rest —
Yo-ho-ho, and a bottle of rum!
> *Treasure Island*

Doctors is all swabs.
> *Ibid. Billy Bones, Chap. 3*

Many's the long night I've dreamed of cheese — toasted, mostly.
> *Ibid. Ben Gunn, Chap. 15*

There's no music like a little river's. It plays the same tune (and that's the favourite) over and over again, and yet does not weary of it like men fiddlers. It takes the mind out of doors; and though we should be grateful for good houses, there is, after all, no house like God's out-of-doors.
> *Prince Otto. Chap. 2*

I feel very strongly about putting questions; it partakes too much of the style of the day of judgment. You start a question, and it's like starting a stone.

[1] See Charles Kingsley, page 524.
[2] While we shared all by the rule of thumb —
Yo-ho-ho and a bottle of rum!
YOUNG EWING ALLISON [1853–1932]: *Derelict*

You sit quietly on the top of a hill; and away the stone goes, starting others.

The Strange Case of Dr. Jekyll and Mr. Hyde

"A Penny Plain and Twopence Coloured."

Memories and Portraits. Essay about Skelt's Juvenile Drama

Let any man speak long enough, he will get believers.

The Master of Ballantrae. Summary of Events

Not every man is so great a coward as he thinks he is — nor yet so good a Christian.

Ibid. Mr. Mackellar's Journey

Am I no a bonny fighter?

Alan Breck. Kidnapped. Chap. 10

If I have at all learned the trade of using words to convey truth and to arouse emotion, you have at last furnished me with a subject.

An Open Letter on Father Damien [1]

The kingdom of heaven is of the childlike, of those who are easy to please, who love and give pleasure.

Across the Plains. A Christmas Sermon

So long as we love we serve; so long as we are loved by others, I would almost say that we are indispensable; and no man is useless while he has a friend.

Lay Morals

To be honest, to be kind — to earn a little and spend a little less, to make upon the whole a family happier for his presence, to renounce when that shall be necessary and not to be embittered, to keep a few friends, but these without capitulation — above all, on the same grim conditions, to keep friends with himself — here is a task for all that a man has of fortitude and delicacy.

A Christmas Sermon

Chiefs! Our road is not built to last a thousand years, yet in a sense it is. When a road is once built, it is a strange thing how it collects traffic, how every year as it goes on, more and more people are found to walk thereon, and others are raised up to repair and perpetuate it, and keep it alive.[1]

Vailima Letters. Address to the Chiefs on the Opening of the Road of Gratitude, October, 1894

Give us grace and strength to forbear and to persevere. Give us courage and gaiety and the quiet mind, spare to us our friends, soften to us our enemies.

Prayer [2]

ROSA HARTWICK THORPE

[1850–   ]

England's sun was slowly setting o'er the hilltops far away,
Filling all the land with beauty at the close of one sad day.

Curfew Must Not Ring To-night. Stanza 1

Long, long years I've rung the curfew from that gloomy, shadowed tower;
Every evening, just at sunset, it has told the twilight hour;
I have done my duty ever, tried to do it just and right,
Now I'm old I will not falter, — Curfew it must ring to-night.

Ibid. Stanza 3

Out she swung — far out; the city seemed a speck of light below,
There 'twixt heaven and earth suspended as the bell swung to and fro.

Ibid. Stanza 7

---

[1] Robert Louis Stevenson was a roadmender. . . . Ay, and with more than his pen. . . . I wonder was he ever so truly great, so entirely the man we know and love, as when he inspired the chiefs to make a highway in the wilderness. Surely no more fitting monument could exist to his memory than the Road of Gratitude, cut, laid, and kept by the pureblood tribe kings of Samoa. — MICHAEL FAIRLESS (Margaret Fairless Barber) [1869–1901]: *The Roadmender, Chap. 5*

[2] On the bronze memorial to Stevenson in St. Giles Cathedral, Edinburgh, Scotland.

[1] And Molokai's lord of love
And tenderness, and piteous tears
For stricken man!

JOAQUIN MILLER: *With Love to You and Yours, III, 3*

SAMUEL VALENTINE COLE
[1851–1925]

Why fret you at your work because
    The deaf world does not hear and
    praise?
Were it so bad, O workman true,
    To work in silence all your days?
                In Silence. Stanza 1
"Hammer away, ye hostile hands,
Your hammers break, God's anvil
    stands." [1]
                Hammer and Anvil
Where'er men go, in heaven, or earth,
    or hell,
They find themselves, and that is all
    they find.
                The Difference
The man who knows and knows he
    knows,[2]
    To him your homage bring;
He wields the power that waits and
    wins,
    And he is rightful king.
                An Old Saw Reset. Stanza 1
He who walked in our common ways,
With the seal of a king on his brow;
Who lived as a man among men his
    days,
And "belongs to the ages" now.[3]
                Lincoln
In April Rome was founded; Shakes-
    peare died;
    The shot whose sound rang out from
    Concord town
And brought an avalanche of echoes
    down,
Shaking all thrones of tyranny and
    pride,
Was fired in April; Sumter far and
    wide

[1] Inscription on a memorial to the Hugue-
nots, Rue de Rivoli, Paris.
[2] He who knows not, and knows not that
    he knows not, is a fool. Shun him.
    He who knows not, and knows that he
        knows not, is simple. Teach him.
    He who knows, and knows not that he
        knows, is asleep. Waken him.
    He who knows, and knows that he knows,
        is wise. Follow him.
                Arabic apothegm
[3] Now he belongs to the ages. — EDWIN M.
STANTON [1814–1869], Secretary of War, at
the deathbed of President Lincoln.

Lifted a voice the years will never
    drown;
'Twas April when they laid the
    martyr's crown
On Lincoln's brow.
                In April

SIR WILLIAM ROBERTSON
NICOLL
[1851–1923]

He is, if we may be allowed the expression, a typical John Bull, and it is
his John Bullism in religion that has
made him so popular with all classes of
the community.
                Said of the Reverend Charles
                Haddon Spurgeon [1834–1892]

LOUIS SHREVE OSBORNE
[1851–1912]

Maiden's hair is tumbled,
    And then and there appeared
Cunning little ear-ring
    Caught in student's beard.
                In the Tunnel.[1] Stanza 6

MARIANA GRISWOLD
(MRS. SCHUYLER)
VAN RENSSELAER
[1851–1934]

Sorrow is mine, but there is no more
    dread.
The word has come — On the field of
    battle, dead.
                It Is Well with the Child

BENJAMIN BRECKINRIDGE
WARFIELD
[1851–1921]

"There is a place for everything,
    In earth, or sky, or sea,
Where it may find its proper use,
    And of advantage be,"
    Quoth Augustine, the saint.
                Augustine's Philosophy. Stanza 1

[1] In *The Harvard Advocate, Nov. 10, 1871.*

FRANCIS WILLIAM BOURDILLON
[1852–1921]

The night has a thousand eyes,
  And the day but one;
Yet the light of the bright world dies,
  With the dying sun.
                    Light. Stanza 1

The mind has a thousand eyes,
  And the heart but one;
Yet the light of a whole life dies,
  When love is done.
                    Ibid. Stanza 2

Upon the valley's lap
  The dewy morning throws
A thousand pearly drops
  To wash a single rose.
So, often in the course
  Of life's few fleeting years,
A single pleasure costs
  The soul a thousand tears.
                Upon the Valley's Lap

MOLLIE E. MOORE (MRS. THOMAS E.) DAVIS
[1852–1909]

If thou shouldst bid thy friend farewell,
  But for one night though that farewell should be,
Press thou his hand in thine; how canst thou tell
  How far from thee
Fate, or caprice, may lead his feet
  Ere that to-morrow come? Men have been known
Lightly to turn the corner of a street,[1]
  And days have grown
To months, and months to lagging years,
  Before they looked in loving eyes again.
                    Counsel [2]

[1] Round the corner of the street
    Who can say what waits for us?
        JAMES WHITCOMB RILEY: *Reach
            Your Hand to Me*
[2] Frequently attributed to Coventry Patmore.

NATHAN HASKELL DOLE [1]
[1852–1935]

We have no leas, no larks, no rooks,
No swains, no nightingales,
No singing milkmaids (save in
  books) —
The poet does his best,
It is the rhyme that fails!
          Larks and Nightingales. Stanza 6

What other State compares with Maine
  In glorious coasts, where ocean tides
Have for long ages beat in vain
  To storm the coves where safety hides;
Where pillared cliffs like sentries stand
To guard the entries to the land,
    From Kittery to Calais!
              The State of Maine. Stanza 1

ROBERT BONTINE CUNNINGHAME GRAHAM
[1852–1936]

Success, which touches nothing that it does not vulgarize, should be its own reward . . . the odium of success is hard enough to bear, without the added ignominy of popular applause.
                    Success

The ancient seat of pedantry [Oxford], where they manufacture prigs as fast as butchers in Chicago handle hogs.
          With the North-West Wind

Every American child should learn at school the history of the conquest of the West. The names of Kit Carson, of General Custer and of Colonel Cody should be as household words to them. These men as truly helped to form an empire as did the Spanish conquistadores. Nor should Sitting Bull, the Short Wolf, Crazy Horse, and Rain-in-the-Face be forgotten. They too were Americans, and showed the same heroic qualities as did their conquerors.
          Letter to Theodore Roosevelt
                    [*1917*]

[1] Editor of the tenth edition of *Bartlett's Familiar Quotations* (1914).

God forbid that I should go to any heaven in which there are no horses.

Letter to Theodore Roosevelt
[1917]

The rain had cleared and the sun poured down upon us, as in procession, headed by the acolytes and priests, we bore the coffin to the grave. A semicircle of Scotch firs formed, as it were, a little harbour for him. The breeze blew freshly, south-west by south a little westerly — a good wind, as I thought, to steer up Channel by, and one that he who would no longer feel it on his cheek, looking aloft to see if all the sails were drawing properly, must have been glad to carry when he struck soundings, passing the Wolf Rock or the Smalls after foul weather in the Bay.

Handsomely, as he who lay in it might well have said, they lowered the coffin down. The priest had left his Latin and said a prayer or two in English, and I was glad of it, for English surely was the speech the Master Mariner most loved, and honoured in the loving with new graces of his own.

Harboured [The burial of
Joseph Conrad, 1924]

EDWIN MARKHAM
[1852–   ]

Bowed by the weight of centuries he leans
Upon his hoe and gazes on the ground,
The emptiness of ages in his face,
And on his back the burden of the world.

The Man with the Hoe.[1] Stanza 1

O masters, lords and rulers in all lands,
Is this the handiwork you give to God?

Ibid. Stanza 3

Here was a man to hold against the world,
A man to match the mountains[2] and the sea.

Lincoln, the Man of the People.
Stanza 1

The color of the ground was in him, the red earth,
The smack and tang of elemental things.

Lincoln, the Man of the People.
Stanza 2

So came the Captain with the mighty heart;
And when the judgment thunders split the house,
Wrenching the rafters from their ancient rest,
He held the ridgepole up, and spiked again
The rafters of the Home.

Ibid. Stanza 4

And when he fell in whirlwind, he went down
As when a lordly cedar, green with boughs,
Goes down with a great shout upon the hills,
And leaves a loncsome place against the sky.

Ibid.

Three times I came to your friendly door;
Three times my shadow was on your floor.
I was the beggar with bruisèd feet;
I was the woman you gave to eat;
I was the child on the homeless street.

How the Great Guest Came

He drew a circle that shut me out —
Heretic, rebel, a thing to flout.
But Love and I had the wit to win:
We drew a circle that took him in.

Outwitted

For all your days prepare,
And meet them ever alike:
When you are the anvil, bear —
When you are the hammer, strike.[1]

Preparedness

---

[1] Millet's painting.
[2] A man to match his mountains, not to creep

Dwarfed and abased below them.
WHITTIER: *Among the Hills, Prelude*
Bring me men to match my mountains.
SAM WALTER FOSS: *The Coming American*
[1] Stand like an anvil when it is beaten upon.
ST. IGNATIUS THEOPHORUS, Bishop of Antioch [A. D. 104]
See George Herbert, page 137.

GEORGE MOORE
[1852–1933]

After all there is but one race — humanity.
The Bending of the Bough. Act III
The difficulty in life is the choice.
Act IV
The wrong way always seems the more reasonable.
Ibid.

A quotation, a chance word heard in an unexpected quarter, puts me on the trail of the book destined to achieve some intellectual advancement in me.
Confessions of a Young Man. XII
A constant and careful invocation of meaning that was a little aside of the common comprehension, and also a sweet depravity of ear for unexpected falls of phrase.
Ibid.
English, Scotchmen, Jews, do well in Ireland — Irishmen never; even the patriot has to leave Ireland to get a hearing.
Ave. Overture
Within the oftentimes bombastic and truculent appearance that I present to the world, trembles a heart shy as a wren in the hedgerow or a mouse along the wainscoting.
Ibid. Chap. 2
My one claim to originality among Irishmen is that I have never made a speech.
Ibid. Chap. 4
Modern painting is uninteresting because there is no innocency left in it.
Ibid. Chap. 6
As the moon is more interested in the earth than in any other thing, there is always some woman more interested in a man's mind than in anything else, who is willing to follow it sentence by sentence.
Ibid. Chap. 10
It is the plain duty of every Irishman to disassociate himself from all memories of Ireland — Ireland being a fatal disease, fatal to Englishmen and doubly fatal to Irishmen.
Ibid. Chap. 11

Death is in such strange contradiction to life that it is no matter for wonder that we recoil from it, and turn to remembrances, and find recompense in perceiving that those we have loved live in our memories as intensely as if they were still before our eyes.
Ave. Chap. 13
A man travels the world over in search of what he needs and returns home to find it.
The Brook Kerith. Chap. 11
My definition of pure poetry, something that the poet creates outside of his own personality.
Anthology of Pure Poetry. Introduction

HENRY VAN DYKE
[1852–1933]

If all the skies were sunshine,
  Our faces would be fain
To feel once more upon them
  The cooling plash of rain.
If All the Skies. Stanza 1
Men have dulled their eyes with sin,
  And dimmed the light of heaven with doubt,
And built their temple-walls to shut thee in,
  And framed their iron creeds to shut thee out.
God of the Open Air. Stanza 3
"Raise the stone, and thou shalt find me; cleave the wood and there am I." [1]
The Toiling of Felix. Part I, Prelude
This is the gospel of labour, ring it, ye bells of the kirk!
The Lord of Love came down from above, to live with the men who work;
This is the rose that He planted, here in the thorn-curst soil:
Heaven is blest with perfect rest, but the blessing of Earth is toil.
Ibid. Envoy, Stanza 5
Oh, London is a man's town, there's power in the air;

[1] *Oxyrhynchus Logia (Agrapha), the Unwritten Sayings of Jesus, Fifth Logion.*

And Paris is a woman's town, with
  flowers in her hair.
      "America for Me." Stanza 3
It's home again, and home again, Amer-
  ica for me!
I want a ship that's westward bound to
  plough the rolling sea,
To the blessèd Land of Room Enough
  beyond the ocean bars,
Where the air is full of sunlight and the
  flag is full of stars.
                  Ibid. Stanza 6
This is my work; my blessing, not my
  doom;
Of all who live, I am the one by whom
This work can best be done in the right
  way.
    The Three Best Things. I, Work
Not to the swift, the race:
Not to the strong, the fight: [1]
Not to the righteous, perfect grace:
Not to the wise, the light.
              Reliance. Stanza 1
Oh, was I born too soon, my dear, or
  were you born too late,
That I am going out the door while you
  come in the gate?
          Rencontre. Stanza 1
The lintel low enough to keep out pomp
  and pride:
The threshold high enough to turn de-
  ceit aside.
    For the Friends at Hurstmont.
                    The Door
Self is the only prison that can ever
  bind the soul.
        The Prison and the Angel
He that planteth a tree is a servant of
  God,
He provideth a kindness for many gen-
  erations,
And faces that he hath not seen shall
  bless him.
    The Friendly Trees. Stanza 10
The heavenly hills of Holland —
  How wondrously they rise
Above the smooth green pastures
  Into the azure skies!

[1] In anguish we uplift
    A new unhallowed song:
    The race is to the swift;
    The battle to the strong.
        JOHN DAVIDSON: *War-Song, St. 1*

With blue and purple hollows,
  With peaks of dazzling snow,
Along the far horizon
  The clouds are marching slow.
    The Heavenly Hills of Holland.
                    Stanza 1
Individuality is the salt of common
life. You may have to live in a crowd,
but you do not have to live like it, nor
subsist on its food.
      The School of Life. Page 33
It is with rivers as it is with people:
the greatest are not always the most
agreeable nor the best to live with.
        Little Rivers. Chap. 2
The first day of spring is one thing,
and the first spring day is another. The
difference between them is sometimes
as great as a month.
      Fisherman's Luck. Chap. 5

YOUNG EWING ALLISON
[1853–1932]

The mate was fixed by the bos'n's pike,
The bos'n brained with a marlinspike,
And Cookey's throat was marked belike
      It had been gripped
        By fingers ten;
      And there they lay,
        All good dead men,
Like break-o'-day in a boozing ken —
Yo-ho-ho and a bottle of rum! [1]
      Derelict, A Reminiscence of
                Treasure Island

The very texture of every enduring
work of art must imbed the glowing life
of its own times and the embers of the
past. If it does not cover space as history it must plumb the depths of emo-

[1] See Stevenson, page 704.
Fifteen men on the dead man's chest —
    Yo-ho-ho and a bottle of rum!
Young E. Allison done all the rest —
    Yo-ho-ho and a bottle of rum!
He's sung this song for you and me,
    Jest as it wuz — or it ort to be —
Clean through time and eternity.
    Yo-ho-ho and a bottle of rum!
        JAMES WHITCOMB RILEY: *To Young
                          E. Allison*
See *Y. E. A. and a Bottle of Rum* in *Buried
Caesars* by Vincent Starrett [1923].

tion in an individual to reach the universal perception.

"My Old Kentucky Home"
[Stephen] Foster's songs have been received into the world's choir. His music lives and has become universal, but the name and memory of the man who created it lie dead amidst the singing crowds awaiting resurrection in the world that owes him so much of pleasure and profound solace.

> *Ibid.*

HALL CAINE
[1853–1931]

I reject the monstrous theory that while a man may redeem the past a woman never can.

> *The Eternal City. Part VI,*
> *Chap. 18*

A great outrage on the spirit of Justice breaks down all barriers of race and nationality.

> *Ibid. Part VII, Chap. 5*

FRANK DESPREZ
[1853–1916]

Lasca used to ride
On a mouse-gray mustang close to my side.

> *Lasca*

And I wonder why I do not care
For the things that are, like the things that were.
Does half my heart lie buried there,
In Texas, down by the Rio Grande?

> *Ibid.*

EDGAR WATSON HOWE
[1853–1937]

A really busy person never knows how much he weighs.

> *Country Town Sayings*

What people say behind your back is your standing in the community.

> *Ibid.*

There is nothing so well known as that we should not expect something for nothing — but we all do and call it Hope.

> *Ibid.*

ROBERT UNDERWOOD JOHNSON
[1853–1937]

In tears I tossed my coin from Trevi's edge, —
A coin unsordid as a bond of love, —
And, with the instinct of the homing dove,
I gave to Rome my rendezvous and pledge.

> *Italian Rhapsody. Stanza 18*

For lover or nightingale who can wait?
Whenever he cometh he cometh late.

> *Spring at the Villa Conti*

Song's but solace for a day;
Wine's a traitor not to trust;
Love's a kiss and then away;
Time's a peddler deals in dust.

> *Hearth-Song. Stanza 2*

"Gridley," says the Commodore,
"You may fire when ready."

> *Dewey at Manila. Stanza 12*

EMILIE POULSSON
[1853–   ]

"Now put in one thing more; I give you leave to try."
The mousie chuckled to himself; and then he softly stole
Right to the stocking's crowded toe, and gnawed a little hole!

> *Santa Claus and the Mouse*

The essence of Boston, now grown somewhat rare,
Still lends its aroma to Louisburg Square.

> *Louisburg Square. Stanza 1*

Books are keys to wisdom's treasure;
Books are gates to lands of pleasure;
Books are paths that upward lead;
Books are friends. Come, let us read.

> *Inscription for the Children's*
> *Reading Room, Hopkinton,*
> *Massachusetts*

CECIL JOHN RHODES
[1853–1902]

I desire to encourage and foster an appreciation of the advantages which will result from the union of the English-speaking peoples throughout the world, and to encourage in the students from the United States of America an attachment to the country from which they have sprung without I hope withdrawing them or their sympathies from the land of their adoption or birth.

Will, establishing the Rhodes Scholarships

Educational relations make the strongest tie.

Ibid.

So little done — so much to do.

Last words

IRWIN RUSSELL [1]
[1853–1879]

De man what keeps pullin' de grape-vine shakes down a few bunches at leas'.

Precepts at Parting. Stanza 3

You mus' reason with a mule.

Nebuchadnezzar. Stanza 3

You bless us, please sah, eben ef we's doin' wrong to-night,
Kase den we'll need de blessin' more'n ef we's doin' right;
An' let de blessin' stay wid us untel we comes to die
An' goes to keep our Christmas wid dem sheriffs in de sky.

Christmas Night in the Quarters.
Blessing the Dance

"Dar's gwine to be a overflow," said Noah, lookin' solemn —
Fur Noah tuk de *Herald,* an' he read de ribber column —
An' so he sot his hands to wuk a-clarin' timber-patches,
An' 'lowed he's gwine to build a boat to beat de steamah *Natchez.*

De Fust Banjo. Stanza 2

MARION COUTHOUY SMITH
[1853–1931]

Go, then, and plant a tree, lovely in sun and shadow,

[1] Among the first — if not the very first — of Southern writers to appreciate the literary possibilities of the negro character. — JOEL CHANDLER HARRIS

Gracious in every kind — maple and oak and pine.
Peace of the forest glade, wealth of the fruitful meadow,
Blessings of dew and shade, hereafter shall be thine.

The Planting of a Tree.
Stanza 4

FRANCIS MARION CRAWFORD
[1854–1909]

The sea is Death's garden, and he sows dead men in the loam,
When the breast of the waters is ploughed like a field by the gale,
When the ocean is turned up and rent in long furrows of foam
By the coulter and share of the wind and the harrow of hail.

The Song of the Sirens. [1]
Stanza 7

JULIAN STEARNS CUTLER
[1854–1930]

A common thing is a grass blade small,
Crushed by the feet that pass,
But all the dwarfs and giants tall,
Working till doomsday shadows fall
Can't make a blade of grass.

Wonderful. Stanza 1

You're only a dog, old fellow; a dog, and you've had your day;
But never a friend of all my friends has been truer than you alway.

Roger and I. Stanza 1

Never a heaven shall harbor me, where they won't let Roger in. [2]

Ibid. Stanza 4

WILLIAM HENRY DRUMMOND
[1854–1907]

De win' can blow lak hurricane
An' s'pose she blow some more,

[1] At the close of the novel, *With the Immortals* [1888].

[2] If there is no God for thee
Then there is no God for me.
ANNA HEMPSTEAD BRANCH:
To a Dog, St. 1

You can't get drown on Lac St. Pierre
So long you stay on shore.
> *The Wreck of the "Julie Plante."*
> *Stanza 6*

Do w'at you lak wit' your old gran-
'pere
For w'en you're beeg feller he won't be
dere —
Leetle Bateese!
> *Little Bateese. Stanza 7*

To the hut of the peasant, or lordly
hall,
To the heart of the king, or humblest
thrall,
Sooner or late, love comes to all.
> *The Grand Seigneur. Stanza 1*

SIR JAMES GEORGE FRAZER
[1854–   ]

The wine-coloured amethyst received
its name, which means "not drunken,"
because it was supposed to keep the
wearer of it sober.
> *The Golden Bough.*[1] *Chap. 3*

Dwellers by the sea cannot fail to be
impressed by the sight of its ceaseless
ebb and flow, and are apt, on the principles of that rude philosophy of sympathy and resemblance . . . to trace a
subtle relation, a secret harmony, between its tides and the life of man. . . .
The belief that most deaths happen at
ebb tide is said to be held along the
east coast of England from Northum-
berland to Kent.[2]
> *Ibid.*

The heaviest calamity in English
history, the breach with America,
might never have occurred if George
the Third had not been an honest dullard.
> *Ibid.*

By religion, then, I understand a
propitiation or conciliation of powers
superior to man which are believed to
direct and control the course of nature
and of human life.
> *The Golden Bough. Chap. 4*

It is a common rule with primitive
people not to waken a sleeper, because
his soul is away and might not have
time to get back.
> *Ibid. Chap. 18*

The awe and dread with which the
untutored savage contemplates his
mother-in-law are amongst the most
familiar facts of anthropology.
> *Ibid.*

The world cannot live at the level of
its great men.
> *Ibid. Chap. 37*

QUINCY KILBY
[1854–1931]

Here in my library I sit,
Amid rare volumes richly bound,
A mine of cleverness and wit,
From authors everywhere renowned.
To-night their words seem flat and
stale,
Their weakness fills me with disgust,
I want that crude, hard-fisted tale,[1]
Where *seven more redskins bit the dust*.
> *"And Seven More Redskins Bit*
> *the Dust."*[2] *Stanza 4*

He who has quickened multitudes to
mirth,
Who won their frank applause, their
hearty laughter,
Has bade a final long farewell to earth,
And sought the pathway to the
Grand Hereafter.
> *Henry Clay Barnabee [1917]*

---

[1] Abridged one-volume edition, The Mac-
millan Company [1922].
[2] Just between twelve and one, even at the
turning o' the tide. — SHAKESPEARE: *King
Henry V*, Act II, Sc. 3 (Falstaff's death)
See Dickens, page 497.

[1] Hugo, Huxley, Darwin, too,
   And twenty score beside,
   They lined his book-shelves while he read
"Proud Poll, the Pirate's Bride."
   WILBUR DICK NESBIT [1871–1927]:
   Mr. Bluff, St. 1
[2] A line familiar to readers of Western
stories by "Ned Buntline" (EDWARD Z. C.
JUDSON [1822–1886]).

THOMAS RILEY MARSHALL
[1854–1925]

What this country needs is a good five-cent cigar.[1]

Remark to John Crockett, Chief Clerk of the United States Senate

EVA MARCH TAPPAN
[1854–1930]

We drove the Indians out of the land,
But a dire revenge these redmen planned,
For they fastened a name to every nook,
And every boy with a spelling-book
Will have to toil till his hair turns gray
Before he can spell them the proper way.[2]

On the Cape. Stanza 1

EDITH MATILDA THOMAS
[1854–1925]

I come to the velvet, imperial crowd,
The wine-red, the gold, the crimson, the pied, —
The dahlias that reign by the garden-side.

"Frost To-night." Stanza 2

In my garden of Life with its all-late flowers,
I heed a Voice in the shrinking hours:
"Frost to-night — so clear and dead-still" . . .

Ibid. Stanza 4

The god of music dwelleth out of doors.

Music

The love of my life came not
As love unto others is cast;
For mine was a secret wound —
But the wound grew a pearl, at last.

The Deep-Sea Pearl. Stanza 1

And they are with us at Life's farthest reach,
A light when into shadow all else dips,

As, in the stranger's land, their native speech
Returns to dying lips.

The Triumph of Forgotten Things. Stanza 6

WILLARD DUNCAN VANDIVER
[1854–1932]

I come from a State that raises corn and cotton and cockleburs and Democrats, and frothy eloquence neither convinces nor satisfies me. I am from Missouri. You have got to show me.[1]

Speech at a naval banquet in Philadelphia, while a Representative in Congress from Missouri, and a member of the House Committee on Naval Affairs [1899]

WILLIAM COWPER BRANN [2]
[1855–1898]

Boston runs to brains as well as to beans and brown bread. But she is cursed with an army of cranks whom nothing short of a straight-jacket or a swamp-elm club will ever control.

The Iconoclast. Beans and Blood

No man can be a patriot on an empty stomach.

Ibid. Old Glory [July 4, 1893]

It has the subtle flavor of an old pair of sox.

Ibid. Godey's Magazine

The Lydian notes of Andrew Carnegie as he warbles a riant roundelay in praise of poverty, or laments in pathetic spondees the woes of the man with spondulix.

Ibid. Our American Czars

---

[1] What this country needs is a good five-cent nickel. — FRANKLIN P. ADAMS [1932].

[2] See Mrs. Sigourney, page 364.

[1] *Festus:* Angel bosoms know no jealousy.
Helen: Show me.
PHILIP JAMES BAILEY: *Festus, A Visit*

[2] Known as "The Iconoclast," from the name of his paper, first published in Austin, Texas, and later in Waco. He was shot by an outraged reader.

Every few years our industrial system gets the jim-jams. Capital flies to cover, factories close and labor goes tramping across the country seeking honest employment and receiving a warm welcome — from militia companies with shotted guns. Cheerful idiots begin to prattle of "over-production," the economic M. D.'s to refurbish all the old remedies, from conjure-bags to communism. They all know exactly what caused the "crisis" and what to do for it; but despite the doctors the patient usually — survives. And the M. D. who succeeds in cramming his pet panacea down its throat claims all the credit for the recovery. We are slowly emerging from the crash of '93, and the cuckoos are cock-sure that a country fairly bursting with wealth was saved from the demnition bowwows by the blessed expedient of going into debt.

Slave or Sovereign
[*Speech, August 10, 1895*]

GERALD BRENNAN
[*Floruit* 1899]

Th' mem'ry comes like a banshee meself an' me wealth between,
An' I long for a mornin's mornin' in Shanahan's ould shebeen.
Shanahan's Ould Shebeen.[1]
Stanza 4

If you couldn't afford good whiskey, he'd take you on trust for beer.
Ibid. Stanza 5

MARY DOW BRINE

She's somebody's mother, boys, you know,
For all she's aged and poor and slow.
Somebody's Mother

HENRY CUYLER BUNNER
[1855–1896]

Love must kiss that mortal's eyes
Who hopes to see fair Arcady.
The Way to Arcady

[1] Published in *Puck* [1899].

That pitcher of mignonette
Is a garden in heaven set
To the little sick child in the basement.
A Pitcher of Mignonette

Off with your hat as the flag goes by!
And let the heart have its say;
You're man enough for a tear in your eye
That you will not wipe away.
The Old Flag. Stanza 1

It was an old, old, old, old lady,
And a boy that was half-past three;
And the way that they played together
Was beautiful to see.
"One, Two, Three." Stanza 1

What does he plant who plants a tree?
He plants the friend of sun and sky;
He plants the flag of breezes free;
The shaft of beauty towering high.
The Heart of the Tree. Stanza 1

Happy the mortal free and independent,
Master of the mainspring of his own volition!
Look on us with the eye of sweet compassion:
We are Cook's Tourists.
The Wail of the "Personally Conducted." Stanza 6

I have a bookcase, which is what
Many much better men have not.
There are no books inside, for books,
I am afraid, might spoil its looks.
But I've three busts, all second-hand,
Upon the top. You understand
I could not put them underneath —
Shake, Mulleary and Go-ethe.
Shake, Mulleary and Go-ethe.
Stanza 1

I of my landlady am lockèd in
For being short on this sad Saturday,
Nor having shekels of silver wherewith to pay:
She turned and is departed with my key.
Behold the Deeds! Stanza 1

Behold the deeds that are done of Mrs. Jones!
Ibid.

HEINRICH CONRIED
[1855–1909]

These words no Shakespeare wrote,
These words no Byron penned,
Nor poet classical, with fancy free;
It is an honest heart speaks to a precious friend,
And yet it sounds like purest poetry.

Interpolated Song [1]

BETH DAY
[*Circa* 1855]

If you are tempted to reveal
A tale to you someone has told
About another, make it pass,
Before you speak, three gates of gold:
These narrow gates. First, "Is it true?"
Then, "Is it needful?" In your mind
Give truthful answer. And the next
Is last and narrowest, "Is it kind?"
And if to reach your lips at last
It passes through these gateways three,
Then you may tell the tale, nor fear
What the result of speech may be. [2]

Three Gates of Gold

FRANK FRANKFORT
MOORE
[1855–1931]

He knew that to offer a man friendship when love is in his heart is like giving a loaf of bread to one who is dying of thirst.

The Jessamy Bride.[3] *Chap. 9*

---

[1] Written, with B. F. Roeder, for the American production of a Viennese opera, *The King's Fool* (*Der Hofnarr*), presented at the Hollis Street Theatre, Boston, March, 1890. The song is not in the German libretto by H. Wittman and J. Bauer.

[2] If your lips would keep from slips,
Five things observe with care:
To whom you speak; of whom you speak;
And how, and when, and where.
　　Nursery rhyme quoted by WILLIAM
　　EDWARD NORRIS [1847–1925] in
　　Thirlby Hall

[3] This age of ours
But marks your grass-grown headstone now
By Goldsmith's jasmine flowers!
　　AUSTIN DOBSON: *On a Picture by
　　Hoppner, St. 6* (Mrs. Gwyn, Oliver
　　Goldsmith's "Jessamy Bride")

No man of letters is deserving of an eulogy who is scared by a detraction.

The Jessamy Bride. Chap. 16

Happy it is for mankind that Heaven has laid on few men the curse of being poets.

Ibid. Chap. 18

To strike at a serpent that hisses may only cause it to spring.

Ibid. Chap. 19

Destiny has more resources than the most imaginative composer of fiction.

Ibid. Chap. 22

Patchwork should not only be made, it should be used by the blind.

Ibid. Chap. 26

WALTER HINES PAGE
[1855–1918]

There is one thing better than good government, and that is government in which all the people have a part.

Life and Letters. Vol. 3, Page 31

Every letter of declination ought to be written by a skilful man — a diplomatist who can write an unpleasant truth without offence.

A Publisher's Confession [*1905*]

SIR ARTHUR WING PINERO
[1855–1934]

It is to laugh.

The Amazons

You may dive into many waters, but there is one social Dead Sea.

The Second Mrs. Tanqueray.
Act I

From forty to fifty a man is at heart either a stoic or a satyr.

Ibid.

There are two sorts of affection — the love of a woman you respect, and the love for the woman you love.

Ibid. Act II

It is only one step from toleration to forgiveness.

Ibid.

I believe the future is only the past again, entered through another gate.

Ibid. Act IV

I've heard what doctors' consultations consist of. After looking at the pictures you talk about whist.
The Notorious Mrs. Ebbsmith.
Act I
How many "coming men" has one known! Where on earth do they all go to?
Ibid.
There's only one hour in a woman's life. . . . One supreme hour. Her poor life is like the arch of a crescent; so many years lead up to that hour, so many weary years decline from it.
Ibid. Act III
Vanity is the cause of a great deal of virtue in men; the vainest are those who like to be thought respectable.
Ibid. Act IV

OLIVE SCHREINER
("RALPH IRON")
[1855–1920]

It came to pass that after a time the artist was forgotten, but the work lived.
Dreams. The Artist's Secret
At last they came to where Reflection sits, — that strange old woman, who had always one elbow on her knee, and her chin in her hand, and who steals light out of the past to shed it on the future.
Ibid. The Lost Joy
There's something so beautiful in coming on one's very own inmost thoughts in another. In one way it's one of the greatest pleasures one has.
Letter to Havelock Ellis
[March 2, 1885]
A thoughtful life, in which one might read and creep into the hearts of books, as they can only be crept into when the wheels of the daily life are grinding soft and low.
From Man to Man. Chap. 1
If you are an artist, may no love of wealth or fame or admiration and no fear of blame or misunderstanding make you ever paint, with pen or brush, an ideal or a picture of external life otherwise than as you see it.
Ibid. Chap. 7

Man individually and as a race is possible on earth only because, not for weeks or months but for years, love and the guardianship of the strong over the weak has existed.
From Man to Man. Chap. 7
The higher the flame has leaped, the colder and deader the ashes.
Ibid. Chap. 8

WILLIAM SHARP
("FIONA MACLEOD")
[1855–1905]

My heart is a lonely hunter that hunts
   on a lonely hill.
The Lonely Hunter. Stanza 6
But sometimes, through the Soul of
   Man,
   Slow moving o'er his pain,
The moonlight of a perfect peace
   Floods heart and brain.
The White Peace. Stanza 2
Across the silent stream
Where the slumber-shadows go,
From the dim blue Hills of Dream
I have heard the west wind blow.
From the Hills of Dream. Stanza 1
I hear the little children of the wind
Crying solitary in lonely places.
Little Children of the Wind

CY WARMAN
[1855–1914]

Every daisy in the dell knows my secret, knows it well,
And yet I dare not tell, sweet Marie.
Sweet Marie. Stanza 1
Oft when I feel my engine swerve,
   As o'er strange rails we fare,
I strain my eyes around the curve
   For what awaits us there.
When swift and free she carries me
   Through yards unknown at night,
I look along the line to see
   That all the lamps are white.
Will the Lights be White? Stanza 1
Swift towards life's terminal I trend,
   The run seems short to-night;
God only knows what's at the end —
   I hope the lamps are white.
Ibid. Stanza 3

ELLA WHEELER WILCOX
[1855-1919]

Talk happiness. The world is sad
    enough
Without your woe. No path is wholly
    rough.
Speech. Stanza 1

Talk faith. The world is better off with-
    out
Your uttered ignorance and morbid
    doubt.
Ibid. Stanza 2

Talk health. The dreary, never-ending
    tale
Of mortal maladies is more than stale;
You cannot charm or interest or please
By harping on that minor chord, dis-
    ease.
Say you are well, or all is well with you,
And God shall hear your words and
    make them true.
Ibid. Stanza 3

The two kinds of people on earth that
    I mean
Are the people who lift and the people
    who lean.
To Lift or to Lean

It ever has been since time began,
    And ever will be, till time lose breath,
That love is a mood — no more — to
    man,
    And love to woman is life or death.
Blind. Stanza 1

Since life is short, we need to make it
    broad;
Since life is brief, we need to make it
    bright;
Then keep the old king's motto well in
    sight,
And let its meaning permeate each day
Whatever comes — "This, too, shall
    pass away." [1]
This, Too, Shall Pass Away.
Stanza 7

It is easy to sit in the sunshine
    And talk to the man in the shade;
It is easy to float in a well-trimmed
    boat,
    And point out the places to wade.
Practice vs. Preaching. Stanza 1

[1] See J. G. Saxe, page 509.

Laugh, and the world laughs with you;
    Weep, and you weep alone;
For the sad old earth must borrow its
    mirth,
    But has trouble enough of its own.
Solitude. Stanza 1

Feast, and your halls are crowded;
    Fast, and the world goes by.
Ibid. Stanza 3

So many gods, so many creeds,
    So many paths that wind and wind,
    When just the art of being kind
Is all this sad world needs.
The World's Need

No question is ever settled
    Until it is settled right.
Settle the Question Right

We flatter those we scarcely know,
    We please the fleeting guest,
And deal full many a thoughtless blow
    To those who love us best.
Life's Scars. Stanza 3

GEORGE EDWARD WOODBERRY
[1855-1930]

O, inexpressible as sweet,
    Love takes my voice away;
I cannot tell thee when we meet
    What most I long to say.
Song

Where are the friends that I knew in my
    Maying,
In the days of my youth, in the first of
    my roaming?
We were dear; we were leal; oh, far we
    went straying,
Now never a heart to my heart comes
    homing!
Comrades. Stanza 1

FRANCIS M. BELLAMY
[1856-1931]

I pledge allegiance to the flag of the
United States and to the republic for
which it stands, one nation, indivisible,
with liberty and justice for all.
The Pledge of Allegiance to the
Flag [1892]

KENYON COX
[1856–1919]

Work thou for pleasure — paint, or
    sing, or carve
The thing thou lovest, though the body
    starve —
Who works for glory misses oft the
    goal;
Who works for money coins his very
    soul.
Work for the work's sake, then, and it
    may be
That these things shall be added unto
    thee.
                       Work

SARAH PRATT McLEAN GREENE
[1856–1935]

De massa ob de sheepfol',
Dat guards de sheepfol' bin,
Look out in de gloomerin' meadows
Wha'r de long night rain begin;
So he call to de hirelin' shepa'd —
"Is my sheep, is dey all come in?"
        De Sheepfol'. Stanza 1
            [Towhead, 1883]

EDWARD SANDFORD MARTIN
[1856–   ]

Within my earthly temple there's a
    crowd.
There's one of us that's humble; one
    that's proud.
There's one that's broken-hearted for
    his sins,
And one who, unrepentant, sits and
    grins.
There's one who loves his neighbor as
    himself,
And one who cares for naught but fame
    and pelf.
From much corroding care would I be
    free
If once I could determine which is Me.
                    Mixed

ROBERT EDWIN PEARY
[1856–1920]

We returned from the Pole to Cape
Columbia in only sixteen days . . . the
exhilaration of success lent wings to our
sorely battered feet. But Ootah, the
Eskimo, had his own explanation. Said
he: "The devil is asleep or having trouble with his wife, or we should never
have come back so easily."
             The North Pole

LIZETTE WOODWORTH REESE
[1856–1935]

When I consider Life and its few
    years —
A wisp of fog betwixt us and the sun;
A call to battle, and the battle done
Ere the last echo dies within our ears.
                   Tears
The burst of music down an unlistening
    street.
                   Ibid.
How each hath back what once he
    stayed to weep;
Homer his sight, David his little lad!
                   Ibid.
Creeds grow so thick along the way,
Their boughs hide God.
                  Doubt
Glad that I live am I;
That the sky is blue;
Glad for the country lanes,
And the fall of dew.
     A Little Song of Life. Stanza 1
An apple orchard smells like wine;
    A succory flower is blue;
Until Grief touched these eyes of mine,
    Such things I never knew.
             Wise. Stanza 1

GEORGE BERNARD SHAW
[1856–   ]

My method is to take the utmost
trouble to find the right thing to say,
and then to say it with the utmost levity.
       Answers to Nine Questions
We have no more right to consume
happiness without producing it than to
consume wealth without producing it.
            Candida. Act I

A prosperous man of business, who probably never read anything but a newspaper since he left school.

Cashel Byron's Profession. Chap. 5

All this struggling and striving to make the world better is a great mistake; not because it isn't a good thing to improve the world if you know how to do it, but because striving and struggling is the worst way you could set about doing anything.

Ibid. Chap. 6

We don't bother much about dress and manners in England, because, as a nation we don't dress well and we've no manners.

You Never Can Tell. Act I

A family enjoying the unspeakable peace and freedom of being orphans.

Ibid. Act II

The great advantage of a hotel is that it's a refuge from home life.

Ibid.

It's well to be off with the Old Woman before you're on with the New.[1]

The Philanderer. Act II

The fickleness of women I love is only equaled by the infernal constancy of the women who love me.

Ibid.

The test of a man or woman's breeding is how they behave in a quarrel.

Ibid. Act IV

People are always blaming their circumstances for what they are. I don't believe in circumstances. The people who get on in this world are the people who get up and look for the circumstances they want, and, if they can't find them, make them.

Mrs. Warren's Profession. Act II

There are no secrets better kept than the secrets that everybody guesses.

Ibid. Act III

A great devotee of the Gospel of Getting On.

Ibid. Act IV

This is the true joy in life, the being used for a purpose recognized by yourself as a mighty one; the being thoroughly worn out before you are thrown on the scrap heap; the being a force of Nature instead of a feverish selfish little clod of ailments and grievances complaining that the world will not devote itself to making you happy.

Man and Superman. Epistle Dedicatory

A lifetime of happiness! No man alive could bear it: it would be hell on earth.

Man and Superman. Act I

The more things a man is ashamed of, the more respectable he is.

Ibid.

You think that you are Ann's suitor: that you are the pursuer and she the pursued; that it is your part to woo, to persuade, to prevail, to overcome. Fool: it is you who are the pursued, the marked-down quarry, the destined prey.

Ibid. Act II

Marry Ann and at the end of a week you'll find no more inspiration in her than in a plate of muffins.

Ibid.

Home life as we understand it is no more natural to us than a cage is natural to a cockatoo.

Getting Married. Preface

In the extreme instances of reaction against convention, female murderers get sheaves of offers of marriage.

Ibid.

When two people are under the influence of the most violent, most insane, most delusive, and most transient of passions, they are required to swear that they will remain in that excited, abnormal, and exhausting condition continuously until death do them part.

Ibid.

A man is like a phonograph with half-a-dozen records. You soon get tired of them all; and yet you have to sit at table whilst he reels them off to every new visitor.

Ibid. (The Play)

In England we always let an institution strain itself until it breaks.

Ibid.

---

[1] See Charles Henry Webb, page 611.

The whole strength of England lies in the fact that the enormous majority of the English people are snobs.

Getting Married (The Play)

You don't learn to hold your own in the world by standing on guard, but by attacking, and getting well hammered yourself.

Ibid.

Religion is a great force — the only real motive force in the world; but what you fellows don't understand is that you must get at a man through his own religion and not through yours.

Ibid.

The modest cough of a minor poet.

The Dark Lady of the Sonnets

This writing of plays is a great matter, forming as it does the minds and affections of men in such sort that whatsoever they see done in show on the stage, they will presently be doing in earnest in the world, which is but a larger stage.

Ibid.

I like a bit of a mongrel myself, whether it's a man or a dog; they're the best for every day.

Misalliance. Episode I

If parents would only realize how they bore their children!

Ibid.

He's a gentleman: look at his boots.

Pygmalion. Act I

Women upset everything. When you let them into your life, you find that the woman is driving at one thing and you're driving at another.

Ibid. Act II

I have to live for others and not for myself; that's middle class morality.

Ibid. Act V

The great secret, Eliza, is not having bad manners or good manners or any other particular sort of manners, but having the same manner for all human souls: in short, behaving as if you were in Heaven, where there are no third-class carriages, and one soul is as good as another.

Ibid.

Independence? That's middle class blasphemy. We are all dependent on one another, every soul of us on earth.

Pygmalion. Act V

The nauseous sham goodfellowship our democratic public men get up for shop use.

Back to Methuselah. Gospel of the Brothers Barnabas

Life is a disease; and the only difference between one man and another is the stage of the disease at which he lives.

Ibid.

I enjoy convalescence. It is the part that makes the illness worth while.

Ibid.

A nap, my friend, is a brief period of sleep which overtakes superannuated persons when they endeavor to entertain unwelcome visitors or to listen to scientific lectures.

Ibid. Tragedy of an Elderly Gentleman

Everything happens to everybody sooner or later if there is time enough.

Ibid. As Far As Thought Can Reach

Silence is the most perfect expression of scorn.

Ibid.

The worst cliques are those which consist of one man.

Ibid.

The Jews generally give value. They make you pay; but they deliver the goods. In my experience the men who want something for nothing are invariably Christians.

Saint Joan. Scene IV

Kings are not born: they are made by universal hallucination.

The Revolutionist's Handbook

At last I went to Ireland,
'Twas raining cats and dogs:
I found no music in the glens,
Nor purple in the bogs.
And as far as angels' laughter in the
  smelly Liffy's tide —
Well, my Irish daddy said it, but the
  dear old humbug lied.

Envoi added to a song, My Irish

Daddy, by Miss MAISIE HURL
[*May, 1931*]

Every person who owes his life to civilized society and who has enjoyed since his childhood its very costly protections and advantages should appear at reasonable intervals before a properly qualified jury to justify his existence, which should be summarily and painlessly terminated if he fails to justify it and it develops that he is a positive nuisance and more trouble than he is worth. Nothing less will really make people responsible citizens.

Radio address from London to America [*October 11, 1931*]

You put up in New York Harbor a monstrous idol which you called "Liberty." [1]

Speech, Metropolitan Opera House, [2] *New York* [*April 11, 1933*]

You in America should trust to that volcanic political instinct which I have divined in you.

Ibid.

KATE DOUGLAS WIGGIN
[1856–1923]

My heart is open wide to-night
For stranger, kith or kin.
I would not bar a single door
Where Love might enter in.
The Romance of a Christmas Card

OSCAR FINGAL O'FLAHERTIE WILLS WILDE
[1856–1900]

Tread lightly, she is near
Under the snow,

---

[1] "I see," said he, speaking to some American friends, "that you too put up monuments to your great dead!" — Story of a distinguished Frenchman on a visit to the United States during Prohibition; related by RALPH NEVILL: *Paris of To-day* [1924]

[2] Made before the Academy of Political Science, and broadcast by radio.

Speak gently, she can hear
The daisies grow.
Requiescat. Stanza 1

Thy name was writ in water [1] — it shall stand:
And tears like mine will keep thy memory green,
As Isabella did her Basil-tree.
The Grave of Keats

Think of all
The suns that go to make one speedwell blue!
Quia Multum Amavi. Stanza 4

These are the letters which Endymion wrote
To one he loved in secret, and apart.
And now the brawlers of the auction mart
Bargain and bid for each poor blotted note.
On the Sale by Auction of Keats' Love Letters

Yet each man kills the thing he loves,
By each let this be heard,
Some do it with a bitter look,
Some with a flattering word,
The coward does it with a kiss,
The brave man with a sword!
The Ballad of Reading Gaol. I, 7

I never saw a man who looked
With such a wistful eye
Upon that little tent of blue
Which prisoners call the sky,
And at every wandering cloud that trailed
Its ravelled fleeces by.
Ibid. II, 2

For he that lives more lives than one
More deaths than one must die.
Ibid. III, 37

All that we know who lie in gaol
Is that the wall is strong;
And that each day is like a year,
A year whose days are long.
Ibid. V, 1

The vilest deeds like poison-weeds
Bloom well in prison-air:
It is only what is good in Man
That wastes and withers there:

---

[1] See Keats, page 386.

Pale Anguish keeps the heavy gate
And the Warder is Despair.
The Ballad of Reading Gaol. V, 5
Down the long and silent street,
The dawn, with silver-sandaled feet,
Crept like a frightened girl.
The Harlot's House
A poet can survive everything but a misprint.
The Children of the Poets
Most modern calendars mar the sweet simplicity of our lives by reminding us that each day that passes is the anniversary of some perfectly uninteresting event.
A Poetic Calendar
Though it would be dangerous to make calendars the basis of Culture, we should all be much improved if we began each day with a fine passage of English poetry.[1]
Ibid.
To say "mither" instead of "mother" seems to many the acme of romance.
Romantic Poems and Ballads
An age that has no criticism is either an age in which art is immobile, hieratic, and confined to the reproduction of formal types, or an age that possesses no art at all.
The Critic as Artist. Part I
It is through Art, and through Art only, that we can realize our perfection; through Art and Art only that we can shield ourselves from the sordid perils of actual existence.
Ibid. Part II
As long as war is regarded as wicked, it will always have its fascination. When it is looked upon as vulgar, it will cease to be popular.
Ibid.
There is no sin except stupidity.
Ibid.
Where there is sorrow there is holy ground.
De Profundis
There is no such thing as a moral or an immoral book. Books are well written, or badly written. That is all.
*The Picture of Dorian Gray.
Preface*

[1] See Charles Eliot Norton, page 572.

All art is quite useless.
*The Picture of Dorian Gray.
Preface*
There is only one thing in the world worse than being talked about, and that is not being talked about.
Ibid. Chap. 1
Conscience and cowardice are really the same things.
Ibid.
Laughter is not at all a bad beginning for a friendship, and it is far the best ending for one.
Ibid.
The only way to get rid of a temptation is to yield to it.
Ibid. Chap. 2
He knew the precise psychological moment [1] when to say nothing.
Ibid.
The only difference between a caprice and a lifelong passion is that the caprice lasts a little longer.
Ibid.
Children begin by loving their parents; as they grow older they judge them; sometimes they forgive them.
Ibid. Chap. 5
Conscience makes egotists of us all.
Ibid. Chap. 8
When a woman marries again it is because she detested her first husband. When a man marries again, it is because he adored his first wife.[2] Women try their luck; men risk theirs.
Ibid. Chap. 15

[1] In all considerations the psychological momentum or factor must be allowed to play a prominent part, for without its co-operation, there is little to be hoped from the work of the artillery. — The *Neue Preussische Kreuz-Zeitung, Dec. 16, 1870,* commenting upon the siege of Paris.
An error in translation gave us "psychological moment" (i. e., the critical moment). Attributed to German pedantry, the Parisians ridiculed the phrase, but it speedily became universal.

Felt the psychologic moment.
KIPLING: *Et Dona Ferentes, St. 4*
[1896]

[2] See Samuel Johnson, page 235.

Over the piano was printed a notice: Please do not shoot the pianist. He is doing his best.

Impressions of America. Leadville

Now-a-days we are all of us so hard up, that the only pleasant things to pay are compliments. They're the only things we *can* pay.

Lady Windermere's Fan. Act I

I can resist everything except temptation.

Ibid.

History is merely gossip.

Ibid. Act III

In this world there are only two tragedies. One is not getting what one wants, and the other is getting it.

Ibid.

What is a cynic? A man who knows the price of everything, and the value of nothing.

Ibid.

Experience is the name everyone gives to his mistakes.

Ibid.

They say that when good Americans die they go to Paris.

A Woman of No Importance. Act I

Nothing spoils a romance so much as a sense of humour in the woman.

Ibid.

Men always want to be a woman's first love. That is their clumsy vanity. We women have a more subtle instinct about things. What we like is to be a man's last romance.

Ibid. Act II

Discontent is the first step in the progress of a man or a nation.

Ibid.

Talk to every woman as if you loved her, and to every man as if he bored you, and at the end of your first season you will have the reputation of possessing the most perfect social tact.

Ibid. Act III

I delight in men over seventy. They always offer one the devotion of a lifetime.

Ibid. Act IV

I have invented an invaluable invalid called Bunbury, in order that I may be able to go down into the country whenever I choose.

The Importance of Being Earnest. Act I

Memory is the diary that we all carry about with us.

Ibid. Act II

No woman should ever be quite accurate about her age. It looks so calculating.

Ibid. Act III

An acquaintance that begins with a compliment is sure to develop into a real friendship.

An Ideal Husband. Act I

Nothing produces such an effect as a good platitude.[1]

Ibid.

Private information is practically the source of every large modern fortune.

Ibid. Act II

When the gods wish to punish us they answer our prayers.[2]

Ibid.

To love oneself is the beginning of a lifelong romance.

Ibid. Act III

As for borrowing Mr. Whistler's ideas about art, the only thoroughly original ideas I have ever heard him express have had reference to his own superiority as a painter over painters greater than himself.

Reply to an attack by James McNeill Whistler, Truth [January 9, 1890]

WOODROW WILSON
[1856–1924]

You deal in the raw material of opinion, and, if my convictions have any validity, opinion ultimately governs the world.

Address to the Associated Press [April 20, 1915]

There is such a thing as a man being too proud to fight.

Address to Foreign-Born Citizens [May 10, 1915]

---

[1] Stroke a platitude until it purrs like an epigram. — DON MARQUIS: *The Sun Dial.*

[2] See James Russell Lowell, page 528.

The things that the flag stands for were created by the experiences of a great people. Everything that it stands for was written by their lives. The flag is the embodiment, not of sentiment, but of history. It represents the experiences made by men and women, the experiences of those who do and live under that flag.

Address [June 14, 1915]

There must be, not a balance of power, but a community of power; not organized rivalries, but an organized common peace.

*Address to the Senate
[January 22, 1917]*

I am seeking only to face realities and to face them without soft concealments.

Ibid.

A little group of willful men, representing no opinion but their own.

Of certain members of the United States Senate [March 4, 1917]

To such a task we dedicate our lives, our fortunes, everything that we are and everything that we have, with the pride of those who know that the day has come when America is privileged to spend her blood and her might for the principles that gave her birth and happiness and the peace which she has treasured. God helping her, she can do no other.

Address to Congress, asking for a declaration of war [April 2, 1917]

The world must be made safe for democracy.

Ibid.

Open covenants of peace, openly arrived at.

*Address to Congress
[January 8, 1918]*

GERTRUDE FRANKLIN ATHERTON
[1857–   ]

Women love the lie that saves their pride, but never an unflattering truth.

The Conqueror. Book III, Chap. 6

To put a tempting face aside when duty demands every faculty, it is a lesson which takes most men longest to learn.

The Conqueror. Book III, Chap. 6

The perfect friendship of two men is the deepest and highest sentiment of which the finite mind is capable; women miss the best in life.

Ibid. Chap. 12

No matter how hard a man may labour, some woman is always in the background of his mind. She is the one reward of virtue.

Ibid. Book IV, Chap. 3

ALICE BROWN
[1857–   ]

Praise not the critic, lest he think
You crave the shelter of his ink;
But pray his halo, when he dies,
May tip the steelyards of the skies.

The Critic

Yet thou, O banqueter on worms,
  Who wilt not let corruption pass! —
Dost search out mildew, mould and stain,
  Beneath a magnifying-glass.

The Slanderer

Of this round earth whereon I stand,
I do not own one inch of land; [1]
I shall not lose upon the day
When Gaffer Death drags me away.

Autolycus. Stanza 1

Whip of toil no more shall touch you,
  nor din of turmoil hinder,
Nor fate affright your quiet with his
  grisly mask of doom.
You shall lie by living waters, you shall
  walk with laughing heroes,
You are garnered up in safety in a large
  and lofty room.

*On the Death of Louise Imogen
Guiney [2]*

He holds his spear benignant, sceptrewise,
And strikes out flame from the adoring hills.

Sunrise on Mansfield Mountain

[1] I do not own an inch of land,
  But all I see is mine.
    LUCY LARCOM: *A Strip of Blue*
[2] In *The Atlantic Monthly, March, 1921.*

JOSEPH CONRAD
[1857–1924]

A work that aspires, however humbly, to the condition of art should carry its justification in every line.

*The Nigger of the Narcissus.
Preface*

But the artist appeals to that part of our being which is not dependent on wisdom; to that in us which is a gift and not an acquisition — and, therefore, more permanently enduring. He speaks to our capacity for delight and wonder, to the sense of mystery surrounding our lives: to our sense of pity, and beauty, and pain.

Ibid.

The ship, a fragment detached from the earth, went on lonely and swift like a small planet.

Ibid. Chap. 2

Goodbye, brothers! You were a good crowd. As good a crowd as ever fisted with wild cries the beating canvas of a heavy foresail; or tossing aloft, invisible in the night, gave back yell for yell to a westerly gale.

Ibid. Chap. 5

She strode like a grenadier, was strong and upright like an obelisk, had a beautiful face, a candid brow, pure eyes, and not a thought of her own in her head.

Tales of Unrest. The Return

What greatness had not floated on the ebb of that river [the Thames] into the mystery of an unknown earth! . . . The dreams of men, the seed of commonwealths, the germs of empires.

Heart of Darkness

Running all over the sea trying to get behind the weather.

Typhoon. Chap. 2

The sea never changes and its works, for all the talk of men, are wrapped in mystery.

Ibid. Falk: A Reminiscence

I have known the sea too long to believe in its respect for decency.

Ibid.

An elemental force is ruthlessly frank.

Typhoon. Falk: A Reminiscence

Efficiency of a practically flawless kind may be reached naturally in the struggle for bread. But there is something beyond — a higher point, a subtle and unmistakable touch of love and pride beyond mere skill; almost an inspiration which gives to all work that finish which is almost art — which *is* art.

*The Mirror of the Sea.
The Fine Art*

The East Wind, an interloper in the dominions of Westerly Weather, is an impassive-faced tyrant with a sharp poniard held behind his back for a treacherous stab.

Ibid. Rulers of East and West

The autocratic sway of the West Wind, whether forty north or forty south of the equator, is characterized by an open, generous, frank, barbarous recklessness. For he is a great autocrat, and to be a great autocrat you must be a great barbarian.

Ibid.

The air of the New World seems favorable to the art of declamation.

Nostromo. Chap. 6

There are on earth no actors too humble and obscure not to have a gallery; that gallery which envenoms the play by stealthy jeers, counsels of anger, amused comments, or words of perfidious compassion.

Chance. Part II, Chap. 4

What all men are really after is some form, or perhaps only some formula, of peace.

Under Western Eyes. Part 1

A man's real life is that accorded to him in the thoughts of other men by reason of respect or natural love.

Ibid. 1

Let a fool be made serviceable according to his folly.

Ibid. 3

The belief in a supernatural source of evil is not necessary; men alone are quite capable of every wickedness.

Ibid. Part II, 4

Why should a man certain of immortality think of his life at all?

Under Western Eyes. Part II, 4

No woman is an absolute fool. . . . No woman is ever completely deceived.

Ibid. 5

That strange impulse of indiscretion, common to men who lead secret lives, and accounting for the invariable existence of "compromising documents" in all the plots and conspiracies of history.

Ibid. Part III, 1

You can't ignore the importance of a good digestion. The joy of life . . . depends on a sound stomach, whereas a bad digestion inclines one to skepticism, incredulity, breeds black fancies and thoughts of death.

Ibid. 3

All ambitions are lawful except those which climb upward on the miseries or credulities of mankind.

A Personal Record. Preface

The sight of human affairs deserves admiration and pity. And he is not insensible who pays them the undemonstrative tribute of a sigh which is not a sob, and of a smile which is not a grin.

Ibid.

Only in men's imagination does every truth find an effective and undeniable existence. Imagination, not invention, is the supreme master of art as of life.

Ibid. Chap. 1

For Englishmen especially, of all the races of the earth, a task, any task, undertaken in an adventurous spirit acquires the merit of romance.

Ibid. Chap. 5

Only a moment; a moment of strength, of romance, of glamour — of youth! . . . A flick of sunshine upon a strange shore, the time to remember, the time for a sigh, and — goodbye! — Night — Goodbye . . . !

Youth

There is no rest for a messenger till the message is delivered.

The Rescue. Part VI, 8

I am a great foe of favouritism in public life, in private life, and even in the delicate relationship of an author to his works.

Lord Jim. Author's Note

There is a weird power in a spoken word. . . . And a word carries far — very far — deals destruction through time as the bullets go flying through space.

Ibid. Chap. 15

That faculty of beholding at a hint the face of his desire and the shape of his dream, without which the earth would know no lover and no adventurer.

Ibid. Chap. 16

Felicity, felicity — how shall I say it? — is quaffed out of a golden cup in every latitude: the flavour is with you — with you alone, and you can make it as intoxicating as you please.

Ibid.

It is when we try to grapple with another man's intimate need that we perceive how incomprehensible, wavering, and misty are the beings that share with us the sight of the stars and the warmth of the sun.

Ibid.

We wander in our thousands over the face of the earth, the illustrious and the obscure, earning beyond the seas our fame, our money, or only a crust of bread; but it seems to me that for each of us going home must be like going to render an account. We return to face our superiors, our kindred, our friends — those whom we obey, and those whom we love.

Ibid. Chap. 21

You shall judge of a man by his foes as well as by his friends.

Ibid. Chap. 34

Vanity plays lurid tricks with our memory.

Ibid. Chap. 41

Some great men owe most of their greatness to the ability of detecting in those they destine for their tools the exact quality of strength that matters for their work.

Ibid. Chap. 42

In plucking the fruit of memory one runs the risk of spoiling its bloom.
> *The Arrow of Gold.*
> *Author's Note*

Historian of fine consciences.
> *Notes on Life and Letters.*
> *Henry James, An Appreciation*

Most of us, if you will pardon me for betraying the universal secret, have, at some time or other, discovered in ourselves a readiness to stray far, ever so far, on the wrong road.
> *Ibid. A Happy Wanderer*

What humanity needs is not the promise of scientific immortality, but compassionate pity in this life and infinite mercy on the Day of Judgment.
> *Ibid. The Life Beyond*

JOHN DAVIDSON
[1857–1909]

That minister of ministers,
  Imagination, gathers up
The undiscovered Universe,
  Like jewels in a jasper cup.
> *There Is a Dish to Hold the Sea*

My feet are heavy now but on I go,
My head erect beneath the tragic years.
> *I Felt the World A-spinning*

Fame is the breath of power:
What valid work was ever for itself
Wrought solely, be it war, art, statesmanship?
> *Smith*

Our language is too worn, too much abused,
Jaded and over-spurred, wind-broken, lame, —
The hackneyed roadster every bagman mounts.
> *Ibid.*

Dance and sing, we are eternal;
  Let us still be mad with drinking:
'Tis a madness less infernal
  Than the madness caused by thinking.
> *Song of Bacchantes and Satyrs.*
> *Stanza 1*

Nothing is lost that's wrought with tears:

The music that you made below
Is now the music of the spheres.
> *A Ballad of Heaven. Stanza 26*

I leave the righteous God behind;
I go to worship sinful man.
> *A Ballad of a Nun. Stanza 16*

A vagrant bee twanged like an airy lyre
Of one rich-hearted chord.
> *The Ordeal*

The lowliest men would sooner face
A thousand dreadful deaths, than come
Before their loved ones in disgrace.
> *A Ballad of a Coward. Stanza 12*

Some diplomat no doubt
Will launch a heedless word,
And lurking war leap out.
> *War-Song*

And blood in torrents pour
In vain — always in vain,
For war breeds war again.
> *Ibid.*

The hostess of the sky, the moon.
> *Afternoon. Stanza 1*

Do I believe in Heaven and Hell? I do;
We have them here; the world is nothing else.
> *Dedication to the Generation*
> *Knocking at the Door*

Men should no longer degrade themselves under such appellations as Christian, Mohammedan, Agnostic, Monist, etc. Men are the Universe become conscious: the simplest man should consider himself too great to be called after any name.
> *Fleet Street and Other Poems.*[1]
> *Foreword [1909]*

MARGARET WADE DELAND
[1857–   ]

By one great Heart the Universe is stirred:
  By its strong pulse, stars climb the darkening blue;
  It throbs in each fresh sunset's changing hue,

---

[1] Davidson was never seen alive after he left his home to mail the manuscript of this book to his publisher. Six months later his body was found in the English Channel.

And thrills through low sweet song of
    every bird.
Life. Stanza 1

Alas! that men must see
    Love, before Death!
Else they content might be
    With their short breath.
Love and Death

HENRY BLAKE FULLER
[1857–1929]

The martyrdom involved in a fort-
night's entertainment of anybody
whomsoever.
*The Chevalier of Pensieri-Vani.
Chap. 10*

GEORGE GISSING
[1857–1903]

It is because nations tend to stupidity and baseness that mankind moves
so slowly; it is because individuals have
a capacity for better things that it
moves at all.
*The Private Papers of Henry
Ryecroft. I, 16*

It is a joy to go through booksellers'
catalogues, ticking here and there a possible purchase.
Ibid. 17

Greater still is the happiness of unpacking volumes which one has bought
without seeing them. . . . The first
glimpse of bindings when the inmost
protective wrapper has been folded
back! The first scent of books! The
first gleam of a gilded title!
Ibid.

The mind which renounces, once and
for ever, a futile hope, has its compensation in ever-growing calm.
Ibid. 20

Education is a thing of which only
the few are capable; teach as you will
only a small percentage will profit by
your most zealous energy.
Ibid. 22

For the man sound in body and serene of mind there is no such thing as
bad weather; every sky has its beauty,

and storms which whip the blood do but
make it pulse more vigorously.
*The Private Papers of Henry
Ryecroft. IV, 1*

In the days to come, as through all
time that is past, man will lord it over
his fellow, and earth will be stained red
from veins of young and old. That
sweet and sounding name of *patria* becomes an illusion and a curse.
By the Ionian Sea. XVIII

I wished it were mine to wander endlessly amid the silence of the ancient
world, today and all its sounds forgotten.
Ibid.

BENJAMIN FRANKLIN
KING, JR.
[1857–1894]

Old friends are most too home-like now.
They know your age, and when
You got expelled from school, and lots
Of other things.
Like the New Friends Best

Nothing to do but work,
    Nothing to eat but food,
Nothing to wear but clothes
    To keep one from going nude.
*The Pessimist (The Sum of Life).
Stanza 1*

Nowhere to go but out,
    Nowhere to come but back.
Ibid. Stanza 4

If I should die to-night [1]
And you should come in deepest grief
    and woe —
And say: "Here's that ten dollars that
    I owe,"
I might arise in my large white cravat
And say, "What's that?"
If I Should Die. Stanza 1

MARY HANNAH KROUT
[1857–1927]

Those who toil bravely are strongest;
    The humble and poor become great;
And so from these brown-handed chil-
    dren
    Shall grow mighty rulers of state.

[1] See Arabella E. Smith, page 681.

The pen of the author and statesman —
  The noble and wise of the land —
The sword, and the chisel, and palette
  Shall be held in the little brown hand.
    Little Brown Hands. Stanza 4

AGNES MARY FRANCES ROBINSON
[1857–   ]

To think the face we love shall ever die,
  And be the indifferent earth, and
    know us not!
To think that one of us shall live to cry
  On one long buried in a distant spot!
    Etruscan Tombs. I
Let us forget we ever loved each other
    much,
  Let us forget we ever have to part,
Let us forget that any look or touch
  Once let in either to the other's heart.
    Tuscan Cypress. XII
You hail from Dream-land, Dragon-
    fly?
A stranger hither? So am I,
And (sooth to say) I wonder why
  We either of us came!
    To a Dragon-fly
In the cup of life, 'tis true,
Dwells a draught of bitter dew . . .
Yet no other cup I know
Where such radiant waters glow.
    Epilogue

EDGAR SMITH
[1857–1938]

You may tempt the upper classes
With your villainous demi-tasses,
But Heaven will protect the Working
    Girl.
    *Heaven Will Protect the
      Working Girl* [1]

FRANK LEBBY STANTON
[1857–1927]

Jest a-wearyin' fer you —
All the time a-feelin' blue;

[1] Sung by Marie Dressler [1873–1934] in
Tillie's Nightmare.

Wishin' fer you — wonderin' when
You'll be comin' home again.
    Wearyin' for You. Stanza 1
Sweetes' li'l' feller —
  Everybody knows;
Dunno what ter call 'im,
  But he mighty lak' a rose!
    Sweetes' Li'l' Feller. Stanza 1
Year ain't been the very best;
Purty hard by trouble pressed;
But the rough way leads to rest —
  Here's hopin'!
    Here's Hopin'. Stanza 1
If you strike a thorn or rose,
  Keep a-goin'!
    Keep a-Goin'. Stanza 1
This world that we're a-livin' in
  Is mighty hard to beat;
You get a thorn with every rose,
  But ain't the roses sweet!
    The World

THORSTEIN VEBLEN
[1857–1929]

With the exception of the instinct of
self-preservation, the propensity for
emulation is probably the strongest and
most alert and persistent of the economic motives proper.
    *The Theory of the Leisure Class.
      Chap. 5*
The dog commends himself to our
favour by affording play to our propensity for mastery, and as he is also an
item of expense, and commonly serves
no industrial purpose, he holds a well-
assured place in men's regard as a thing
of good repute.
    Ibid. Chap 6
The visible imperfections of the hand-
wrought goods, being honorific, are
accounted marks of superiority in point
of beauty, or serviceability, or both.
Hence has arisen that exaltation of the
defective, of which John Ruskin and
William Morris were such eager spokesmen in their time. . . . The Kelmscott
Press reduced the matter to an absurdity by issuing books for modern use,
edited with the obsolete spelling,

printed in black-letter, and bound in limp vellum fitted with thongs.

The Theory of the Leisure Class.
Chap. 6

The womanliness of woman's apparel resolves itself into the more effective hindrance to useful exertion offered by the garments peculiar to women.

Ibid. Chap. 7

Priestly vestments show, in accentuated form, all the features that have been shown to be evidence of a servile status and a vicarious life.

Ibid.

The walking-stick serves the purpose of an advertisement that the bearer's hands are employed otherwise than in useful effort, and it therefore has utility as an evidence of leisure.

Ibid. Chap. 10

The sporting man's sense of luck and chance is an inarticulate or inchoate animism . . . it implies the possibility of propitiating, or of deceiving and cajoling, or otherwise disturbing the unfolding of propensities resident in the objects which constitute the apparatus and accessories of any game of skill or chance. There are few sporting men who are not in the habit of wearing charms or talismans.

Ibid. Chap. 11

To meet the requirements of the highest economic efficiency under modern conditions, the world process must habitually be apprehended in terms of quantitative, dispassionate force and sequence.

Ibid. Chap. 12

The adoption of the cap and gown is one of the striking atavistic features of modern college life.

Ibid. Chap. 14

The classics have scarcely lost in absolute value as a voucher of scholastic respectability, since for this purpose it is only necessary that the scholar should be able to put in evidence some learning which is conventionally recognized as evidence of wasted time.

Ibid.

As felicitous an instance of futile classicism as can well be found is the conventional spelling of the English language. English orthography satisfies all the requirements of the canons of reputability under the law of conspicuous waste. It is archaic, cumbrous, and ineffective; its acquisition consumes much time and effort; failure to acquire it is easy of detection.

The Theory of the Leisure Class.
Chap. 14

HENRY WILLARD AUSTIN
[1858–1912]

Genius, that power which dazzles mortal eyes,
Is oft but perseverance in disguise.

Perseverance Conquers All

MALTBIE DAVENPORT BABCOCK
[1858–1901]

Back of the loaf is the snowy flour,
  And back of the flour the mill,
And back of the mill is the wheat and
    the shower,
  And the sun and the Father's will.

"Give Us this Day Our
Daily Bread"

HENRY A. BARNHART
[1858–1934]

A message from home to-day stating that old Bob, deaf and decrepit, but the family pet and pride and protector for fifteen years, had died, halted interest in all else with me save memory of the past; and while he was only a fox terrier dog, no affair of state nor burst of congressional eloquence, nor dream of future glory attracts my attention.

Congressional Record,
April 29, 1912

EDITH NESBIT
(MRS. HUBERT BLAND)
[1858–1924]

Dear Mother, in whose eyes I see
All that I would and cannot be,
Let thy pure light forever shine,

Though dimly, through this life of mine.

> *To Our Lady: For a Picture by Giovanni Bellini*

The chestnut's proud, and the lilac's pretty,
The poplar's gentle and tall,
But the plane tree's kind to the poor dull city —
I love him best of all!

> *Child's Song in Spring*

JAMES BUCKHAM ("PAUL PASTNOR") [1858–1908]

King Hassan, well beloved, was wont to say
When aught went wrong, or any project failed:
"To-morrow, friends, will be another day!"
And in that faith he slept and so prevailed.

> *To-morrow. Stanza 1*

WILLISTON FISH [1858–]

A will is a solemn matter, even with men whose life is given up to business, and who are by habit mindful of the future.

> *A Last Will* [1]

I, Charles Lounsbury, being of sound and disposing mind and memory [he lingered on the word memory], do now make and publish this my last will and testament, in order, as justly as I may, to distribute my interests in the world among succeeding men.

> *Ibid.*

I leave to children exclusively, but only for the life of their childhood, all and every the dandelions of the fields and the daisies thereof, with the right to play among them freely.

> *Ibid.*

And I devise to children the yellow shores of creeks and the golden sands

[1] In *Harper's Weekly, Sept. 3, 1898,* and repeated by request of many readers, *Dec. 12, 1908.*

beneath the waters thereof, with the dragon-flies that skim the surface of said waters.

> *A Last Will*

To lovers I devise their imaginary world, with whatever they may need, as the stars of the sky, the red, red roses by the wall, the snow of the hawthorn, the sweet strains of music, or aught else they may desire to figure to each other the lastingness and beauty of their love.

> *Ibid.*

To those who are no longer children, or youths, or lovers, I leave, too, the knowledge of what a rare, rare world it is.

> *Ibid.*

SAM WALTER FOSS [1858–1911]

We are waiting for you there — for you, the man!
Come up from the jostle as soon as you can;
Come up from the crowd there, for you are the man,
The man who comes up from the crowd.

> *The Man from the Crowd. Stanza 4*

Bring me men to match my mountains, [1]
Bring me men to match my plains,
Men with empires in their purpose,
And new eras in their brains.

> *The Coming American. Stanza 1*

The plain man is the basic clod
From which we grow the demigod;
And in the average man is curled
The hero stuff that rules the world.

> *In Memoriam. Stanza 2*

Strew gladness on the paths of men —
You will not pass this way again.

> *I Shall Not Pass This Way Again* [2]

A voice came o'er the waters far:
"Just drop your bucket where you are."
And then they dipped and drank their fill

[1] A man to match his mountains, not to creep
Dwarfed and abased below them.
  WHITTIER: *Among the Hills, Prelude*
[2] See Underwood, page 682.

Of water fresh from mead and hill;
And then they knew they sailed upon
The broad mouth of the Amazon.
*Drop Your Bucket Where You
Are. Stanza 1*

No financial throe volcanic
  Ever yet was known to scare it;
Never yet was any panic
  Scared the firm of Grin and Barrett.
*The Firm of Grin and Barrett.
Stanza 1*

A hundred thousand men were led
By one calf near three centuries dead.
They followed still his crooked way,
And lost one hundred years a day;
For thus such reverence is lent
To well-established precedent.
The Calf-Path

A rodless Walton of the brooks,
A bloodless sportsman, I.[1]
The Bloodless Sportsman

There are plenty of fish still left in the
  streams
For the angler who has no rod.
Ibid.

The path that leads to a Loaf of Bread
  Winds through the Swamps of Toil,
And the path that leads to a Suit of
  Clothes
  Goes through a flowerless soil,
And the paths that lead to a Loaf of
  Bread
And the Suit of Clothes are hard to
  tread.
Paths. Stanza 1

Let me live in my house by the side of
  the road
  Where the race of men go by;
They are good, they are bad, they are
  weak, they are strong,
  Wise, foolish — so am I.
Then why should I sit in the scorner's
  seat,
  Or hurl the cynic's ban?
Let me live in my house by the side of
  the road
  And be a friend of man.
*The House by the Side of the
Road.[2] Stanza 5*

[1] See R. W. Emerson, page 409.
[2] See Alexander Pope, page 218.
  And greatly was he loved, for courteously

On the thirty-second day of the thir-
  teenth month of the eighth day of
  the week,
On the twenty-fifth hour and the sixty-
  first minute, we'll find all things
  that we seek.
The Eighth Day of the Week

I say the very things that make the
  greatest Stir
An' the most interestin' things, are
  things that didn't occur.[1]
Things That Didn't Occur

He had a startling genius, but somehow it didn't emerge;
  Always on the evolution of things
  that wouldn't evolve;
Always verging toward some climax,
  but he never reached the verge;
Always nearing the solution of some
  theme he could not solve.
The Inventor [2]

JOHN TROTWOOD MOORE
[1858–1929]

Only the game fish swims up stream.[3]
The Unafraid

I sing softly to myse'f dat good ole
hymn, sung by Moses an' de profets so
long ergo:
"Baptis', Baptis' is my name,
  I'm Baptis' till I die.
I've been baptized in de Baptis' church,
  Gwin' ter eat all de Baptis' pie!"
*Old Mistis. How the Bishop
Broke the Record*

He welcomed to his house beside the way
  All comers.
    HOMER: *Iliad, Book VI,* translated by
      WILLIAM CULLEN BRYANT
[1] What torments of grief you endured
  From evils which never arrived.
    R. W. EMERSON: *Borrowing*
  See Lowell, page 530; Waterman, page
750.
[2] Ef you want to be sick of your life,
  Jest come and change places with me a
    spell — for I'm an inventor's wife.
    MRS. E. T. CORBETT: *The Inventor's
      Wife* [1883]
[3] See Grantland Rice, page 865.

THEODORE ROOSEVELT
[1858–1919]

I wish to preach, not the doctrine of ignoble ease,[1] but the doctrine of the strenuous life.

Speech before the Hamilton Club, Chicago [April 10, 1899]

Far better it is to dare mighty things, to win glorious triumphs, even though checkered by failure, than to take rank with those poor spirits who neither enjoy much nor suffer much, because they live in the gray twilight that knows not victory nor defeat.

Ibid.

We must remember not to judge any public servant by any one act, and especially should we beware of attacking the men who are merely the occasions and not the causes of disaster.

Ibid.

I am as strong as a bull moose.

Letter to Mark Hanna, 1900

There is a homely adage which runs, "Speak softly and carry a big stick; you will go far." If the American nation will speak softly and yet build and keep at a pitch of the highest training a thoroughly efficient navy, the Monroe Doctrine will go far.

Speech at Minnesota State Fair [September 2, 1901]

A man who is good enough to shed his blood for his country is good enough to be given a square deal afterward. More than that no man is entitled to, and less than that no man shall have.

Speech at Springfield, Illinois [July 4, 1903]

Men with the muck-rake [2] are often indispensable to the well-being of society, but only if they know when to stop raking the muck.

Address, Laying of the Corner Stone, Office Building of House of Representatives, Washington [April 14, 1906]

1   Me . . . dulcis alebat
Parthenope, studiis florentem ignobilis otii (Sweet Parthenope [Naples] nourished me flourishing in the studies of ignoble ease). VIRGIL: *Georgics, Book 4, L. 563.*
    2 See John Bunyan, page 172.

Malefactors of great wealth.

Speech at Provincetown, August 20, 1907

Nature-faker.

Everybody's Magazine, September, 1907

We have room for but one language here, and that is the English language, for we intend to see that the crucible turns our people out as Americans, and not as dwellers in a polyglot boarding house.

Letter read at the All American Festival, New York [January 5, 1919]

The lunatic fringe in all reform movements.

Autobiography. Chap. 7

LANGDON SMITH
[1858–1908]

When you were a tadpole and I was a fish,
In the Paleozoic time.

Evolution. Stanza 1 [1895]

And that was a million years ago,
In a time that no man knows;
Yet here to-night in the mellow light,
We sit at Delmonico's.

Ibid. Stanza 11

CLARENCE URMY
[1858–1923]

Old songs are best — how sweet to hear
The strains to home and memory dear!
Old books are best — how tale and rhyme
Float with us down the stream of time!

Old Songs Are Best

Not what we have, but what we use;
Not what we see, but what we choose —
These are the things that mar or bless
The sum of human happiness.

The Things that Count. Stanza 1

BOOKER TALIAFERRO WASHINGTON
[1858–1915]

No race can prosper till it learns that there is as much dignity in tilling a field as in writing a poem.

Up From Slavery

SIR WILLIAM WATSON
[1858–1935]

April, April,
Laugh thy girlish laughter;
Then, the moment after,
Weep thy girlish tears.
Song

And though circuitous and obscure
The feet of Nemesis how sure!
Europe at the Play

O let me leave the plains behind,
  And let me leave the vales below!
Into the highlands of the mind,
  Into the mountains let me go.
Shakespeare. Stanza 1

Here are the heights, crest beyond
  crest,
  With Himalayan dews impearled;
And I will watch from Everest
  The long heave of the surging world.
Ibid. Stanza 3

All the rapturous heart of things
Throbs through his own.
Shelley's Centenary. Stanza 17

Where is the singer whose large notes
  and clear
  Can heal and arm and plenish and
    sustain?
Lo, one with empty music floods the
  ear,
  And one, the heart refreshing, tires
    the brain.
Wordsworth's Grave. V, Stanza 2

But he preserved from chance control
The fortress of his 'stablisht soul;
In all things sought to see the Whole;
  Brooked no disguise;
And set his heart upon the goal,
  Not on the prize.
In Laleham Churchyard.[1]
Stanza 11

What is so sweet and dear
As a prosperous morn in May,
The confident prime of the day,
And the dauntless youth of the year,
When nothing that asks for bliss,
Asking aright, is denied,
And half of the world a bridegroom is,
And half of the world a bride.
Ode in May. Stanza 2

[1] Matthew Arnold's grave.

He[1] hath fared forth, beyond these
  suns and showers.
Lachrymae Musarum. Stanza 2

The seasons change, the winds they
  shift and veer;
The grass of yesteryear
Is dead; the birds depart, the groves
  decay:
Empires dissolve and peoples disap-
  pear:
Song passes not away.
Captains and conquerors leave a little
  dust,
And kings a dubious legend of their
  reign;
The swords of Caesars, they are less
  than rust:
The poet doth remain.
Ibid. Stanza 9

Master who crown'st our immelodious
  days
With flower of perfect speech.
Ibid.

The Poet gathers fruit from every tree,
Yea, grapes from thorns, and figs from
  thistles, he.
Epigram

Love, like a bird, hath perch'd upon a
  spray
  For thee and me to hearken what he
    sings.
Contented, he forgets to fly away;
  But hush! . . . remind not Eros of
    his wings.
Epigram

Too long the gulf betwixt
This man and that man fixt
  Yawns yet unspanned.
Too long, that some may rest,
Tired millions toil unblessed.
A New National Anthem.
Stanza 3

His delicate ears and superfine long
  nose,
With that last triumph, his distin-
  guished tail,
In their collective glory spoke his race
The flower of Collie aristocracy.
A Study in Contrasts. Part I

His friends he loved. His fellest earthly
  foes —

[1] Tennyson.

Cats — I believe he did but feign to hate.
My hand will miss the insinuated nose,
Mine eyes the tail that wagg'd contempt at Fate.
An Epitaph

I count him wise
Who loves so well Man's noble memories
He needs must love Man's nobler hopes yet more.
To a Friend

Momentous to himself, as I to me,
Hath each man been that ever woman bore;
Once, in a lightning-flash of sympathy,
I *felt* this truth, an instant, and no more.
Epigram

Say what thou wilt, the young are happy never.
Give me bless'd Age, beyond the fire and fever, —
Past the delight that shatters, hope that stings,
And eager flutt'ring of life's ignorant wings.
Epigram

Too avid of earth's bliss, he was of those
Whom Delight flies because they give her chase.
Only the odour of her wild hair blows
Back in their faces hungering for her face.
Byron the Voluptuary

Strange the world about me lies,
Never yet familiar grown —
Still disturbs me with surprise,
Haunts me like a face half known.
World-Strangeness. Stanza 1

Five-and-thirty black slaves,
Half-a-hundred white,
All their duty but to sing
For their Queen's delight.
The Key-board. Stanza 1

Hate and mistrust are the children of blindness, —
Could we but see one another, 'twere well!
Knowledge is sympathy, charity, kindness,
Ignorance only is maker of hell.

Could we but gaze for an hour, for a minute,
Deep in each other's unfaltering eyes,
Love were begun — for that look would begin it —
Born in the flash of a mighty surprise.
England to Ireland. Stanza 3

For still the ancient riddles mar
Our joy in man, in leaf, in star.
The Whence and Whither give no rest,
The Wherefore is a hopeless quest.
An Epistle to N. A. Stanza 4

And whether, stepping forth, my soul shall see
New prospects, or fall sheer — a blinded thing!
There is, O grave, thy hourly victory,
And there, O death, thy sting.
The Great Misgiving. Stanza 5

To dress, to call, to dine, to break
No canon of the social code,
The little laws that lacqueys make,
The futile decalogue of Mode, —
How many a soul for these things lives,
With pious passion, grave intent!
While Nature careless-handed gives
The things that are more excellent.
The Things that Are More Excellent. Stanza 6

The sense of greatness keeps a nation great.
Our Eastern Treasure

Yet do the songsmiths
Quit not their forges;
Still on life's anvil
Forge they the rhyme.
England My Mother. Part I, Stanza 5

Lo, with the ancient
Roots of man's nature,
Twines the eternal
Passion of song.
Ibid. Part II, Stanza 1

Ever Love fans it,
Ever Life feeds it,
Time cannot age it,
Death cannot slay.
Ibid. Stanza 2

Trees in their blooming,
Tides in their flowing,

Stars in their circling,
  Tremble with song.
        England My Mother. Part II,
                Stanza 5
She is not old, she is not young,
The woman with the serpent's tongue.
    *The Woman with the Serpent's
                Tongue* [1]

Who half makes love to you to-day,
To-morrow gives her guest away.
                Ibid.

KATHARINE LEE BATES
[1859–1929]

O beautiful for patriot dream
  That sees beyond the years
Thine alabaster cities gleam
  Undimmed by human tears!
    America! America!
  God shed His grace on thee,
And crown thy good with brotherhood
  From sea to shining sea!
    America the Beautiful. Stanza 4
Because the years are few, I must be
        glad;
Because the silence is so near, I sing;
'Twere ill to quit an inn where I have
        had
  Such bounteous fare nor pay my
        reckoning.
                The Debt. Stanza 1

WILLIAM HERBERT
CARRUTH
[1859–1924]

Some call it Evolution,
  And others call it God.
    Each in His Own Tongue. Stanza 1
A haze on the far horizon,
  The infinite, tender sky,
The ripe, rich tint of the cornfields,
  And the wild geese sailing high —
And all over upland and lowland
  The charm of the golden-rod,

---

[1] Was he a "guest" — who dares to wrong
  His hostess in so foul a song?
  O poet with the coward's tongue!
    RICHARD LEGALLIENNE: *The Poet with
        a Coward's Tongue*

Some of us call it Autumn,
  And others call it God.[1]
    Each in His Own Tongue. Stanza 2

HELEN GRAY CONE
[1859–1934]

Pickett's Virginians were passing
        through;
  Supple as steel and brown as leather,
Rusty and dusty of hat and shoe,
  Wonted to hunger and war and
        weather;
Peerless, fearless, an army's flower!
  Sterner soldiers the world saw never,
Marching lightly, that summer hour,
  To death and failure and fame for-
        ever.[2]
        Greencastle Jenny. Stanza 4
Dash the bomb on the dome of
        Paul's, —
Deem ye the fame of the Admiral falls?
Pry the stone from the chancel floor, —
Dream ye that Shakespeare shall live
        no more?
Where is the giant shot that kills
Wordsworth walking the old green
        hills?
        A Chant of Love for England

SIR ARTHUR CONAN DOYLE
[1859–1930]

Come, Watson, come! The game is
afoot.
    The Adventure of the Abbey Grange
To Sherlock Holmes she is always *the*
woman.
        A Scandal in Bohemia
I [Sherlock Holmes] abhor the dull
routine of existence. I crave for mental exaltation.
        The Sign of The Four
Elementary, my dear Watson.
        The Crooked Man
It is a great thing to start life with
a small number of really good books
which are your very own.
    Through the Magic Door [*1908*]
No British autobiography has ever
been frank, and consequently no Brit-

---

[1] See Browning, page 491.
[2] See Will Henry Thompson, page 690.

ish autobiography has ever been good. Of all forms of literature it is the one least adapted to the national genius. You could not imagine a British Rousseau, still less a British Benvenuto Cellini.

Through the Magic Door [*1908*]

Several incidents in my life have convinced me of spiritual interposition — of the promptings of some beneficent force outside ourselves, which tries to help us where it can.

Ibid.

The bow was made in England,
Of true wood, of yew wood.
The Song of the Bow. Stanza 1

My life is gliding downward, it speeds swifter to the day
When it shoots the last dark canyon to the Plains of Faraway;
But while its streams are running through the years that are to be,
The mighty voice of Canada will ever call to me.
The Athabasca Trail

The Grenadiers of Austria are proper men and tall;
The Grenadiers of Austria have scaled the city wall;
They have marched from far away
Ere the dawning of the day,
And the morning saw them masters of Cremona.
Cremona. Stanza 1

One favor we entreat,
We were called a little early, and our toilet's not complete.
We've no quarrel with the shirt,
But the breeches wouldn't hurt,
For the evening air is chilly in Cremona.[1]
Ibid. Stanza 20

[1] In the surprise attack on Cremona, Feb. 1, 1702, the Irish Brigade rushed out to resist the invaders, without waiting to dress.

Through the naked battalions the cuirassiers go; —
But the man, not the dress, makes the soldier, I trow.
THOMAS OSBORNE DAVIS [1814–1845]:
The Surprise of Cremona, St. 6

ARTHUR WENTWORTH HAMILTON EATON
[1859–1937]

O give me a place in the garden of song,
I would linger and labor there all summer long,
There are corners to care for, stray beds to make bloom,
I ask not for wages, I only seek room
In the garden of song.
The Garden of Song. Stanza 1

Pity the man who has no gift of speech
For those compelling thoughts, that peace and pain,
That press unsought from the remoter reach
Of mind and soul to the near heart and brain.
Compelling Thoughts. Stanza 1

His heart was breaking, breaking,
'Neath loads of care and wrong;
Who blames the man for taking
What life denied so long?
The Suicide.[1] Stanza 1

HAVELOCK ELLIS
[1859–   ]

To be a leader of men one must turn one's back on men.
Introduction to J. K. HUYS-
MANS' *Against the Grain*

The text of the Bible is but a feeble symbol of the Revelation held in the text of Men and Women.
Impressions and Comments

God is an Unutterable Sigh in the Human Heart, said the old German mystic.
Ibid.

[1] There is a justice according to which we may deprive a man of life, but none that permits us to deprive him of death: this is merely cruelty. — NIETZSCHE: *Human, All Too Human, Prevention of Suicide*

When he went blundering back to God,
His songs half written, his work half done,
Who knows what paths his bruised feet trod,
What hills of peace or pain he won?
CHARLES HANSON TOWNE: *Of One Self-Slain, St. 1*

See Charlotte P. S. Gilman, page 754.

Without an element of the obscene there can be no true and deep aesthetic or moral conception of life. . . . It is only the great men who are truly obscene. If they had not dared to be obscene they could never have dared to be great.

Impressions and Comments

The omnipresent process of sex, as it is woven into the whole texture of our man's or woman's body, is the pattern of all the process of our life.

The New Spirit

The Normans who came over to England with William the Conqueror and constituted the proud English nobility were simply a miscellaneous set of adventurers, professional fighting men, of unknown, and no doubt for the most part undistinguished, lineage. William the Conqueror himself was the son of a woman of the people.

The Task of Social Hygiene.
Introduction

If men and women are to understand each other, to enter into each other's nature with mutual sympathy, and to become capable of genuine comradeship, the foundation must be laid in youth.

Ibid. Chap. 1

The larger our great cities grow, the more irresistible becomes the attraction which they exert on the children of the country, who are fascinated by them, as the birds are fascinated by the lighthouse or the moths by the candle.[1]

Ibid. Chap. 5

An urban life saps that calm and stolid strength which is necessary for all great effort and stress, physical or intellectual.

Ibid.

Prosperity and civilization are far from being synonymous terms. The working community that is suddenly glutted by an afflux of work and wages is in exactly the same position as the savage who is suddenly enabled to fill himself with a rich mass of decaying blubber. It is prosperity, it is not civilization.

The Task of Social Hygiene.
Chap. 5

There are few among us who have not suffered from too early familiarity with the Bible and the conceptions of religion.

Ibid. Chap. 7

The German feels nothing of that sensitive jealousy with which the French seek to guard private life and the rights of the individual.

Ibid. Chap. 9

The Englishman's reverence for the individual's rights goes beyond the Frenchman's, for in France there is a tendency to subordinate the individual to the family, and in England the interests of the individual predominate.

Ibid.

Holland is one of the traditional lands of freedom; it was the home of independent intellect, of free religion, of autonomous morals, when every other country in Europe was closed to these manifestations of the spirit.

Ibid.

When Charles V retired in weariness from the greatest throne in the world to the solitude of the monastery at Yuste, he occupied his leisure for some weeks in trying to regulate two clocks. It proved very difficult. One day, it is recorded, he turned to his assistant and said: "To think that I attempted to force the reason and conscience of thousands of men into one mould, and I cannot make two clocks agree!"

Ibid.

The extension of trade is a matter of tariffs rather than of war, and in any case the trade of a country with its own acquisitions by conquest is a comparatively insignificant portion of its total trade.

Ibid. Chap. 10

---

[1] It is well known that a number of eminent men have been born in London; but, in the course of a somewhat elaborate study of the origins of British men of genius, I have not been able to find that any were genuinely Londoners by descent. — *A Study of British Genius*

So far as business and money are concerned, a country gains nothing by a successful war, even though that war involves the acquisition of immense new provinces.

The Task of Social Hygiene.
Chap. 10

Conquest brings self-conceit and intolerance, the reckless inflation and dissipation of energies. Defeat brings prudence and concentration; it ennobles and fortifies.

Ibid.

A nation's art-products and its scientific activities are not mere national property; they are international possessions, for the joy and service of the whole world. The nations hold them in trust for humanity.

Ibid.

There has never been any country at every moment so virtuous and so wise that it has not sometimes needed to be saved from itself.

Ibid.

Those persons who are burning to display heroism may rest assured that the course of social evolution will offer them every opportunity.

Ibid.

The immense value of becoming acquainted with a foreign language is that we are thereby led into a new world of tradition and thought and feeling.

Ibid. Chap. 11

While some would claim for the English the supreme poetic literature, there can be no doubt that the French own the supreme prose literature of modern Europe.

Ibid.

The family only represents one aspect, however important an aspect, of a human being's functions and activities. . . . A life is beautiful and ideal, or the reverse, only when we have taken into our consideration the social as well as the family relationship.

Little Essays of Love and Virtue.
Chap. 1

One can know nothing of giving aught that is worthy to give unless one also knows how to take.

Little Essays of Love and Virtue.
Chap. 1

That indeed were a world fit to perish, wherein the moralist had set up the ignoble maxim: Safety first.

Ibid. Chap. 2

The by-product is sometimes more valuable than the product.

Ibid. Chap. 3

It has taken God — or Nature, if we will — unknown millions of years of painful struggle to evolve Man, and to raise the human species above that helpless bondage to reproduction which marks the lower animals.

Ibid.

All civilization has from time to time become a thin crust over a volcano of revolution.

Ibid. Chap. 7

The greatest task before civilization at present is to make machines what they ought to be, the slaves, instead of the masters of men.

Ibid.

The art of dancing stands at the source of all the arts that express themselves first in the human person. The art of building, or architecture, is the beginning of all the arts that lie outside the person; and in the end they unite.

The Dance of Life. Chap. 2

Dancing is the loftiest, the most moving, the most beautiful of the arts, because it is no mere translation or abstraction from life; it is life itself.

Ibid.

The place where optimism most flourishes is the lunatic asylum.

Ibid. Chap. 3

He who would walk sanely amid the opposing perils in the path of life always needs a little optimism; he also needs a little pessimism.

Ibid.

Thinking in its lower grades is comparable to paper money, and in its higher forms it is a kind of poetry.

Ibid.

In philosophy, it is not the attainment of the goal that matters, it is the things that are met with by the way.

The Dance of Life. Chap. 2

Every man of genius sees the world at a different angle from his fellows, and there is his tragedy.

Ibid.

The mathematician has reached the highest rung on the ladder of human thought.

Ibid.

The verse of every young poet, however original he may afterwards grow, usually has plainly written across it the rhythmic signature of some great master. . . . The same thing happens with prose, but the rhythm of the signature is less easy to hear.

Ibid. Chap. 4

The most obviously beautiful things in the world of Nature are birds and flowers and the stones we call precious.

Ibid.

All the conventional rules of the construction of speech may be put aside if a writer is thereby enabled to follow more closely and lucidly the form and process of his thought.

Ibid.

If at some period in the course of civilization we seriously find that our science and our religion are antagonistic, then there must be something wrong either with our science or with our religion.

Ibid. Chap. 5

A man must not swallow more beliefs than he can digest.

Ibid.

The Promised Land always lies on the other side of a wilderness.

Ibid.

What we call "morals" is simply blind obedience to words of command.

Ibid. Chap. 6

There is no occasion for any one who is told that he has written a "moral" book to be unduly elated, or when he is told that his book is "immoral" to be unduly cast down. The significance of these adjectives is strictly limited. Neither the one nor the other can have more than the faintest effect on the march of the great compact majority of the social army.

The Dance of Life. Chap. 6

The world's greatest thinkers have often been amateurs; for high thinking is the outcome of fine and independent living, and for that a professorial chair offers no special opportunities.

Ibid.

For the artist life is always a discipline, and no discipline can be without pain. That is so even of dancing, which of all the arts is most associated in the popular mind with pleasure. To learn to dance is the most austere of disciplines.

Ibid.

The methods of statistics are so variable and uncertain, so apt to be influenced by circumstance, that it is never possible to be sure that one is operating with figures of equal weight.

Ibid. Chap. 7

The prevalence of suicide, without doubt, is a test of height in civilization; it means that the population is winding up its nervous and intellectual system to the utmost point of tension and that sometimes it snaps.[1]

Ibid.

The more rapidly a civilization progresses, the sooner it dies for another to arise in its place.

Ibid.

The sun and the moon and the stars would have disappeared long ago — as even their infinitely more numerous analogues on the earth beneath are likely to disappear — had they happened to be within the reach of predatory human hands.

Ibid.

Had there been a Lunatic Asylum in the suburbs of Jerusalem, Jesus Christ would infallibly have been shut up in it at the outset of his public career. That interview with Satan on a pinnacle of the Temple would alone have damned him, and everything that happened after could but have confirmed

[1] See Eaton, page 738.

the diagnosis. The whole religious complexion of the modern world is due to the absence from Jerusalem of a Lunatic Asylum.

Impressions and Comments.
Series III, Page 130

KENNETH GRAHAME
[1859–1932]

As a rule, indeed, grown-up people are fairly correct on matters of fact; it is in the higher gift of imagination that they are so sadly to seek.

The Golden Age. The Finding of
the Princess

A man can stand very much in the cause of love: poverty, aunts, rivals, barriers of every sort, — all these only serve to fan the flame. But personal ridicule is a shaft that reaches the very vitals.

Ibid. "Young Adam Cupid"

The year was in its yellowing time, and the face of Nature a study in old gold.

Ibid. A Harvesting

Those who painfully and with bleeding feet have scaled the crags of mastery over musical instruments have yet their loss in this, — that the wild joy of strumming has become a vanished sense.

Ibid.

I began to like this man. He answered your questions briefly and to the point, and never tried to be funny. I felt I could be confidential with him.

Ibid. The Roman Road

Monkeys, who very sensibly refrain from speech, lest they should be set to earn their livings.

Ibid. "Lusisti Satis"

Grown-up people really ought to be more careful. Among themselves it may seem but a small thing to give their word and take back their word.

The Magic Ring

There is nothing — absolutely nothing — half so much worth doing as simply messing about in boats, . . . or

with boats. . . . In or out of 'em, it doesn't matter.

The Wind in the Willows. Chap. 1

Villagers all, this frosty tide,
Let your doors swing open wide,
Though wind may follow, and snow beside,
Yet draw us in by your fire to bide;
Joy shall be yours in the morning!

Ibid. Chap. 5 (Carol)

ALFRED EDWARD
HOUSMAN
[1859–1936]

Loveliest of trees, the cherry now
Is hung with bloom along the bough.

A Shropshire Lad. II

Now, of my threescore years and ten,
Twenty will not come again,
And take from seventy springs a score,
It only leaves me fifty more.

Ibid.

Clay lies still, but blood's a rover;
Breath's a ware that will not keep.
Up, lad: when the journey's over
There'll be time enough to sleep.

Ibid. IV, Reveille

The sun moves always west;
The road one treads to labour
Will lead one home to rest,
And that will be the best.

Ibid. VII

If the heats of hate and lust
In the house of flesh are strong,
Let me mind the house of dust
Where my sojourn shall be long.

Ibid. XII

When I was one-and-twenty
I heard a wise man say,
"Give crowns and pounds and guineas
But not your heart away;
Give pearls away and rubies
But keep your fancy free."
But I was one-and-twenty,
No use to talk to me.

Ibid. XIII

"The heart out of the bosom
Was never given in vain;
'Tis paid with sighs a-plenty
And sold for endless rue."

And I am two-and-twenty,
And Oh, 'tis true, 'tis true.
A Shropshire Lad. XIII

His folly has not fellow
Beneath the blue of day
That gives to man or woman
His heart and soul away.
Ibid. XIV

To-day, the road all runners come,
Shoulder-high, we bring you home,
And set you at your threshold down,
Townsman of a stiller town.
*Ibid. XIX, To an Athlete
Dying Young*

And silence sounds no worse than
cheers
After earth has stopped the ears.
Ibid.

That is the land of lost content,
I see it shining plain,
The happy highways where I went
And cannot come again.
Ibid. XL

Oh, 'tis jesting, dancing, drinking
Spins the heavy world around.
If young hearts were not so clever,
Oh, they would be young for ever:
Think no more; 'tis only thinking
Lays lads underground.
Ibid. XLIX

With rue my heart is laden
For golden friends I had,
For many a rose-lipt maiden
And many a lightfoot lad.
Ibid. LIV

By brooks too broad for leaping
The lightfoot boys are laid.
Ibid.

And cowards' funerals, when they
come,
Are not wept so well at home,
Therefore, though the best is bad,
Stand and do the best, my lad.
Ibid. LVI, The Day of Battle

Why, if 'tis dancing you would be,
There's brisker pipes than poetry.
Ibid. LXII

Oh many a peer of England brews
Livelier liquor than the Muse,
And malt does more than Milton can
To justify God's ways to man.

Ale, man, ale's the stuff to drink
For fellows whom it hurts to think.
A Shropshire Lad. LXII

Oh, I have been to Ludlow fair
And left my necktie God knows where,
And carried half way home, or near,
Pints and quarts of Ludlow beer.
Ibid.

Luck's a chance, but trouble's sure,
I'd face it as a wise man would,
And train for ill and not for good.
Ibid.

Mithridates, he died old.
Ibid.

We'll to the woods no more,
The laurels all are cut,[1]
The bowers are bare of bay
That once the Muses wore.
Last Poems. Foreword

The troubles of our proud and angry
dust
Are from eternity, and shall not fail.
Bear them we can, and if we can we
must.
Shoulder the sky, my lad, and drink
your ale.
Ibid. IX

Could man be drunk for ever
With liquor, love, or fights,
Lief should I rouse at morning
And lief lie down of nights.
Ibid. X

The laws of God, the laws of man,
He may keep that will and can;
Not I: let God and man decree
Laws for themselves and not for me.
Ibid. XII

And how am I to face the odds
Of man's bedevilment and God's?
I, a stranger and afraid
In a world I never made.
Ibid.

And then the clock collected in the
tower
Its strength, and struck.
Ibid. XV, Eight O'Clock

These, in the day when heaven was
falling,

[1] Nous n'irons plus au bois, les lauriers sont
coupés (We'll go no longer to the woods, the
laurel trees are clipped).
THÉODORE DE BANVILLE [1823-1891], based
on an old French folksong, Tiersot collection

The hour when earth's foundations
  fled,
Followed their mercenary calling
And took their wages and are dead.
    *Last Poems. XXXVII, Epitaph
      on an Army of Mercenaries* [1]
Oh stay with company and mirth
And daylight and the air;
Too full already is the grave
Of fellows that were good and brave
And died because they were.
        Ibid. XXXVIII
They say my verse is sad: no wonder;
  Its narrow measure spans
Tears of eternity, and sorrow,
  Not mine, but man's.
      More Poems [*1936*]
The thoughts of others
  Were light and fleeting,
  Of lovers' meeting
    Or luck or fame;
Mine were of trouble
  And mine were steady,
  So I was ready
    When trouble came.
        Ibid. VI
The rainy Pleiads wester,
  Orion plunges prone,
And midnight strikes and hastens,
  And I lie down alone.
        Ibid. XI
Oh, the pearl seas are yonder,
  The gold and amber shore;
Shires where the girls are fonder,
  Towns where the pots hold more.
       Ibid. XXXIII
Silent hills indenting
The orange band of eve.
          Ibid.
We now to peace and darkness
  And earth and thee restore
Thy creature that thou madest
  And wilt cast forth no more.
    Ibid. XLVII, For My Funeral
Good night. Ensured release,
Imperishable peace,
  Have these for yours. [2]
While sky and sea and land

[1] To the British who made the retreat from
Mons.
[2] These three lines are on a tablet over
Housman's grave in the parish church at
Ludlow (Shropshire).

And earth's foundations stand
And heaven endures.
      More Poems [*1936*]
      XLVIII, Alta Quies
  I was brought up in the Church of
England and in the High Church party,
which is much the best religion I have
ever come across. But Lemprière's
"Classical Dictionary," read when I
was eight, made me prefer paganism
to Christianity; I abandoned Christianity at thirteen, and became an
atheist at twenty-one.
    *Autobiographical note written
    for a French translation of his
    poems*
  I am not a pessimist but a pejorist
(as George Eliot said she was not an
optimist but a meliorist); and that
philosophy is founded on my observation of the world, not on anything so
trivial and irrelevant as personal history. Secondly, I did not begin to write
poetry in earnest until the really emotional part of my life was over; and
my poetry, so far as I could make out,
sprang chiefly from physical causes,
such as a relaxed sore throat during
my most prolific period, the first five
months of 1895.
              Ibid.
  Good literature continually read for
pleasure must, let us hope, do some
good to the reader: must quicken his
perception though dull, and sharpen
his discrimination though blunt, and
mellow the rawness of his personal opinions.
    The Name and Nature of Poetry [1]
  Poems very seldom consist of poetry
and nothing else; and pleasure can be
derived also from their other ingredients.
              Ibid.
  Good religious poetry, whether in
Keble or Dante or Job, is likely to be
most justly appreciated and most dis-
criminatingly relished by the undevout.
              Ibid.

[1] The Leslie Stephen Lecture, delivered at
Cambridge University, May 9, 1933.

Even when poetry has a meaning, as it usually has, it may be inadvisable to draw it out. . . . Perfect understanding will sometimes almost extinguish pleasure.

The Name and Nature of Poetry

Experience has taught me, when I am shaving of a morning, to keep watch over my thoughts, because, if a line of poetry strays into my memory, my skin bristles so that the razor ceases to act. . . . The seat of this sensation is the pit of the stomach.

Ibid.

I have seldom written poetry unless I was rather out of health, and the experience, though pleasurable, was generally agitating and exhausting.

Ibid.

I can no longer expect to be revisited by the continuous excitement under which in the early months of 1895 I wrote the greater part of my other book [*A Shropshire Lad*].

Last Poems, Preface [1922]

ELBERT HUBBARD
[1859–1915]

It is not book learning young men need, nor instruction about this and that, but a stiffening of the vertebrae which will cause them to be loyal to a trust, to act promptly, concentrate their energies, do a thing — "carry a message to Garcia." [1]

A Message to Garcia [2]

The man who is anybody and who does anything is surely going to be criticized, vilified, and misunderstood. This is a part of the penalty for greatness, and every great man understands it; and understands, too, that it is no proof of greatness. The final proof of

greatness lies in being able to endure contumely without resentment.

Get Out or Get in Line

If you work for a man, in heaven's name work for him! If he pays you wages that supply you your bread and butter, work for him — speak well of him, think well of him, stand by him and stand by the institution he represents.

Ibid.

JEROME KLAPKA JEROME
[1859–1927]

Let your boat of life be light, packed with only what you need — a homely home and simple pleasures, one or two friends, worth the name, some one to love and some one to love you,[1] a cat, a dog, and a pipe or two, enough to eat and enough to wear, and a little more than enough to drink; for thirst is a dangerous thing.

Three Men in a Boat. Chap. 3

Fox-terriers are born with about four times as much original sin in them as other dogs.

Ibid. Chap. 13

They [bagpipes] appear to be a trying instrument to perform upon. You have to get enough breath for the whole tune before you start.

Ibid. Chap. 14

It is in the circumstantial detail, the embellishing touches of probability, the general air of scrupulous — almost of pedantic — veracity, that the experienced angler is seen.

Ibid. Chap. 17

"Nothing, so it seems to me," said the stranger, "is more beautiful than the love that has weathered the storms of life. . . . The love of the young for the young, that is the beginning of life. But the love of the old for the old, that is the beginning of—of things longer."

The Passing of the Third Floor Back

---

[1] After the declaration of the Spanish-American War, Andrew Summers Rowan, then Lieutenant, United States Bureau of Military Intelligence, was sent to communicate with General Calixto Garcia. He landed in an open boat near Turquino Peak, April 24, 1898, executed the mission, and brought back information regarding the insurgent army.

[2] In *The Philistine, March, 1900.*

[1] Find someone to love . . . and, oh, some-one to love you. — SACHA GUITRY: *Deburau*, translated by H. GRANVILLE BARKER.

There is a certain satisfaction in feeling you are bearing with heroic resignation the irritating folly of others.
The Passing of the Third Floor Back

Leave-takings are but wasted sadness. Let me pass out quietly.
Ibid.

WILLIAM JAMES LAMPTON
[1859–1917]

Same old slippers,
  Same old rice,
Same old glimpse of
  Paradise.
June Weddings. Stanza 10

Where the corn is full of kernels
And the colonels full of corn.
Kentucky

ALBERT EDWARD LANCASTER
[*Floruit* 1890]

An "unelected infant" sighed out its
  little breath,
And wandered through the darkness
  along the shores of death,
Until the gates of heaven, a-gleam with
  pearl, it spied.
The Unelected Infant. Stanza 1

"Who are you, thus to hallow my unelected brow?"
"Dear child, my name was Calvin, —
  but I see things better now."
Ibid. Stanza 2

EDWIN GORDON LAWRENCE
[1859–   ]

Take these two messengers
With you o'er land or seas
To close and ope the doors:
"Thank you" and "If you please." [1]
Two Messengers. Stanza 1

---

[1] Hearts, like doors, will ope with ease
   To very, very little keys;
   And don't forget that two of these
   Are "I thank you" and "If you please."
   Nursery Rhyme

CHARLES FLETCHER LUMMIS
[1859–1928]

I am bigger than anything that can happen to me. All these things, sorrow, misfortune, and suffering, are outside my door. I am in the house and I have the key.
Epigram

My cigarette! The amulet
  That charms afar unrest and sorrow,
The magic wand that, far beyond
  To-day, can conjure up to-morrow.
My Cigarette. Stanza 1

ERNEST RHYS
[1859–   ]

Wales England wed; so I was bred.
  'Twas merry London gave me
  breath.
I dreamt of love, and fame: I strove.
But Ireland taught me love was best.
And Irish eyes, and London cries, and
  streams of Wales may tell the rest.
What more than these I asked of Life
  I am content to have from Death.
An Autobiography

WALLACE RICE
[1859–   ]

Ebbs and flows the muddy Pei-Ho by
  the Gulf of Pechili,
  Idly floats beside the stream the
  dragon-flag;
Past the batteries of China, looking
  westward still you see
  Lazy junks along the lazy river lag.
Let the long, long years drip slowly
  on that lost and ancient land,
  Ever dear one scene to hearts of gal-
  lant men;
There's a hand-clasp and a heart-throb,
  there's a word we understand:
  Blood is thicker, sir, than water, now
  as then.
"Blood Is Thicker Than Water." [1]
Stanza 9

---

[1] See Scott, page 310.

In 1857, Commodore Josiah Tatnall [1795–1871] went to the rescue of an English ship in trouble in the Pei-Ho River, China,

NORA ARCHIBALD SMITH
[1859–1934]

They'd knock on a tree and would tim-
    idly say
To the Spirit who might be within
    there that day:
"Fairy fair, Fairy fair, wish thou me
    well;
'Gainst evil witcheries weave me a
    spell!"
        Knocking on Wood. Stanza 3
An e'en to this day is the practice made
    good
When, to ward off disaster, we knock
    upon wood.
        Ibid. Stanza 4

SIR CECIL ARTHUR
SPRING-RICE
[1859–1918]

I vow to thee, my country — all earthly
    things above —
Entire and whole and perfect, the serv-
    ice of my love.
The love that asks no questions; the
    love that stands the test,
That lays upon the altar the dearest
    and the best;
The love that never falters, the love
    that pays the price,
The love that makes undaunted the
    final sacrifice.
        I Vow to Thee, My Country [1]
And there's another country, I've heard
    of long ago —
Most dear to them that love her, most
    great to them that know —
We may not count her armies; we may
    not see her King;
Her fortress is a faithful heart, her
    pride is suffering —
And soul by soul and silently her shin-
    ing bounds increase,
And her ways are ways of gentleness,
    and all her paths are peace.
        Ibid.

---

while China was at war with the English and
French.
  [1] Written Jan. 12, 1918, on his last night as
British Ambassador in Washington.

CHARLES E. STANTON [1]
[1859–1933]

America has joined forces with the
Allied Powers, and what we have of
blood and treasure are yours. Therefore it is that with loving pride we
drape the colors in tribute of respect
to this citizen of your great republic.
And here and now in the presence of
the illustrious dead we pledge our
hearts and our honor in carrying this
war to a successful issue. Lafayette,
we are here.
        *Address at the Tomb of Lafayette,
        Picpus Cemetery, Paris* [July 4,
        1917]

JAMES KENNETH STEPHEN
[1859–1892]

Searching an infinite Where,
Probing a bottomless When,
  Dreamfully wandering,
  Ceaselessly pondering,
What is the Wherefore of men.
        *Lapsus Calami. The Philosopher
        and the Philanthropist, Stanza 1*
If all the harm that women have done
Were put in a bundle and rolled into
    one,
  Earth would not hold it,
  The sky could not enfold it,
It could not be lighted nor warmed by
    the sun.
        Ibid. A Thought, Stanza 1
An old half-witted sheep
Which bleats articulate monotony,
And indicates that two and one are
    three.
        *Ibid. Sonnet (Parody of Words-
        worth's Two Voices)*
Of sentences that stir my bile,
  Of phrases I detest,
There's one beyond all others vile:
  "He did it for the best."
        *Ibid. The Malefactor's Plea,
        Stanza 1*

---

  [1] Nephew of Edwin M. Stanton, Secretary
of War in President Lincoln's Cabinet. He
was chief disbursing officer of the American
Expeditionary Forces in France, and was
deputed by General John J. Pershing to speak
on behalf of the A. E. F. on this occasion.

No cat so sweet a mistress owned;
No mistress owned so sweet a cat.
*Lapsus Calami. Elegy on
De Marsay, Stanza 9*

Once there was a famous nation
With a long and glorious past:
Very splendid was its station,
And its territory vast.
A Political Allegory

To the nation now occurred an
Opportunity of saying
What they thought about the burden
Which the government was laying
On their shoulders: and they said it
In uncompromising terms.
Ibid.

But the nation — mark the moral,
For its value is untold —
During each successive quarrel
Grew and prospered as of old.
Ibid.

FRANCIS THOMPSON
[1859–1907]

The fairest things have fleetest end,
Their scent survives their close:
But the rose's scent is bitterness
To him that loved the rose.
Daisy. Stanza 10

She went her unremembering way,
She went and left in me
The pang of all the partings gone,
And partings yet to be.
Ibid. Stanza 12

Nothing begins, and nothing ends,
That is not paid with moan;
For we are born in other's pain,
And perish in our own.
Ibid. Stanza 15

Look for me in the nurseries of
Heaven.[1]
To My Godchild

The innocent moon, that nothing does
but shine,
Moves all the labouring surges of the
world.
Sister Songs. Part II

We speak a lesson taught we know not
how,

---

[1] This line is inscribed on Thompson's
tombstone in Kensal Green.

And what it is that from us flows
The hearer better than the utterer
knows.
Sister Songs. Part II

O Captain of the wars, whence won Ye
so great scars?
In what fight did Ye smite, and what
manner was the foe?
Was it on a day of rout they compassed
Thee about,
Or gat Ye these adornings when Ye
wrought their overthrow?
The Veteran of Heaven. Stanza 1

I fear to love thee, Sweet, because
Love's the ambassador of loss.
To Olivia

Little Jesus, wast Thou shy
Once, and just so small as I?
And what did it feel like to be
Out of Heaven, and just like me?
Little Jesus

I fled Him, down the nights and down
the days;
I fled Him, down the arches of the
years;
I fled Him, down the labyrinthine ways
Of my own mind; and in the mist
of tears
I hid from Him, and under running
laughter.
The Hound of Heaven

Across the margent of the world I fled,
And troubled the gold gateways of
the stars,
Smiting for shelter on their clangèd
bars;
Fretted to dulcet jars
And silvern chatter the pale ports o'
the moon.
Ibid.

Still with unhurrying chase,
And unperturbèd pace,
Deliberate speed, majestic instancy,
Came on the following Feet,
And a Voice above their beat —
"Naught shelters thee, who wilt not
shelter Me."
Ibid.

I stand amid the dust o' the mounded
years —
My mangled youth lies dead beneath
the heap.

My days have crackled and gone up in
    smoke,
Have puffed and burst as sun-starts on
    a stream.
The Hound of Heaven

Ever and anon a trumpet sounds
From the hid battlements of Eternity.
Ibid.

All which I took from thee I did but
    take,
  Not only for thy harms,
  But just that thou might'st seek it
    in My arms.
All which thy child's mistake
Fancies as lost, I have stored for thee
    at home.
Ibid.

There is no expeditious road
To pack and label men for God,
And save them by the barrel-load.
Epilogue, A Judgment in Heaven

Thou canst not stir a flower
Without troubling of a star.
The Mistress of Vision

When thy seeing blindeth thee
To what thy fellow-mortals see;
When their sight to thee is sightless;
Their living, death; their light, most
    lightless;
Search no more —
Pass the gates of Luthany, tread the
    region Elenore.
Ibid.

From stones and poets you may know,
Nothing so active is, as that which least
    seems so.
Contemplation

Happiness is the shadow of things past,
Which fools still take for that which is
    to be!
From the Night of Forebeing

O world invisible, we view thee,
O world intangible, we touch thee,
O world unknowable, we know thee.
The Kingdom of God ("In No
* Strange Land"). Stanza 1*

The drift of pinions, would we hearken,
Beats at our own clay-shuttered doors.
Ibid. Stanza 3

The angels keep their ancient places; —
Turn but a stone, and start a wing!

'Tis ye, 'tis your estrangèd faces,
That miss the many-splendoured thing.
The Kingdom of God.
Stanza 4

Upon thy so sore loss
Shall shine the traffic of Jacob's ladder
Pitched betwixt Heaven and Charing
    Cross.
Ibid. Stanza 5

And lo, Christ walking on the water
Not of Gennesareth, but Thames!
Ibid. Stanza 6

Short arm needs man to reach to
    Heaven
So ready is Heaven to stoop to him.
Grace of the Way. Stanza 6

Know you what it is to be a child?
It is to be something very different
from the man of to-day. It is to have
a spirit yet streaming from the waters
of baptism; it is to believe in love, to
believe in loveliness, to believe in belief; it is to be so little that the elves
can reach to whisper in your ear; it is to
turn pumpkins into coaches, and mice
into horses, lowness into loftiness, and
nothing into everything, for each child
has its fairy godmother in its soul.
Shelley [1]

Children's griefs are little, certainly;
but so is the child, so is its endurance,
so is its field of vision, while its nervous
impressionability is keener than ours.
Grief is a matter of relativity; the sorrow should be estimated by its proportion to the sorrower; a gash is as painful to one as an amputation to another.
Ibid.

Few poets were so mated before, and
no poet was so mated afterwards, until
Browning stooped and picked up a fair-
coined soul that lay rusting in a pool
of tears.
Ibid.

The designs of his bright imagination were never etched by the sharp
fumes of necessity.
Ibid.

A poet must to some extent be a
chameleon, and feed on air. But it need

[1] In *The Dublin Review, July, 1908.*

not be the musty breath of the multitude.

Shelley

Mighty meat for little guests, when the heart of Shelley was laid in the cemetery of Caius Cestius!

Ibid.

NIXON WATERMAN
[1859–   ]

We shall do so much in the years to
    come,
But what have we done to-day?
We shall give our gold in a princely
    sum,
But what did we give to-day?
    What Have We Done To-day?
No man can feel himself alone
    The while he bravely stands
Between the best friends ever known —
    His two good, honest hands.
    Interludes
Though life is made up of mere bubbles,
  'Tis better than many aver,
For while we've a whole lot of troubles,
  The most of them never occur.[1]
    Why Worry?

JANE ADDAMS
[1860–1935]

Private beneficence is totally inadequate to deal with the vast numbers of the city's disinherited.

Twenty Years at Hull House

The common stock of intellectual enjoyment should not be difficult of access because of the economic position of him who would approach it.

Ibid.

JAMES MATTHEW BARRIE
[1860–1937]

The life of every man is a diary in which he means to write one story, and writes another; and his humblest hour is when he compares the volume as it is with what he vowed to make it.

The Little Minister. Chap. 1

[1] See Emerson, page 410; Lowell, page 530; Foss, page 733.

The most gladsome thing in the world is that few of us fall very low; the saddest that, with such capabilities, we seldom rise high.

The Little Minister. Chap. 3

If it's heaven for climate, it's hell for company.

Ibid.

It's a weary warld, and nobody bides in't.

Ibid. Chap. 4

Has it ever struck you that the trouts bite best on the Sabbath? God's critters tempting decent men.

Ibid. Chap. 8

We should be slower to think that the man at his worst is the real man, and certain that the better we are ourselves the less likely is he to be at his worst in our company. Every time he talks away his own character before us he is signifying contempt for ours.

Ibid. Chap. 9

You canna expect to be baith grand and comfortable.

Ibid. Chap. 10

A house is never still in darkness to those who listen intently; there is a whispering in distant chambers, an unearthly hand presses the snib of the window, the latch rises. Ghosts were created when the first man woke in the night.

Ibid. Chap. 22

Let no one who loves be called altogether unhappy. Even love unreturned has its rainbow.

Ibid. Chap. 24

Them that has china plates themsels is the maist careful no to break the china plates of others.

Ibid. Chap. 26

The humourist's like a man firin' at a target — he doesna ken whether he hits or no till them at the target tells 'im.

A Window in Thrums. Chap. 5

Those who bring sunshine to the lives of others cannot keep it from themselves.

Ibid. Chap. 18

Though it was really one laugh with a tear in the middle I counted it as two.

Margaret Ogilvy. Chap. 1

So much of what is great in Scotland has sprung from the closeness of the family ties.

Ibid. Chap. 2

We never understand how little we need in this world until we know the loss of it.

Ibid. Chap. 8

In dinner talk it is perhaps allowable to fling on any faggot rather than let the fire go out.

Tommy and Grizel. Chap. 3

Do you believe in fairies?

Peter and Wendy. Chap. 13

Eyes that say you never must, nose that says why don't you? and a mouth that says I rather wish you could: such is the portrait of Mary A——.

The Little White Bird. Chap. 1

Shall we make a new rule of life from tonight: always to try to be a little kinder than is necessary?

Ibid. Chap. 4

The only ghosts, I believe, who creep into this world, are dead young mothers, returned to see how their children fare. There is no other inducement great enough to bring the departed back.

Ibid.

She was the thing we call romance, which lives in the little hut beyond the blue haze of the pine-woods.

Ibid. Chap. 9

I am in danger, I see, of being included among the whimsical fellows.

Ibid.

Every maid, I say, is for him who can know her. The others had but followed the glamour in which she walked, but I had pierced it and found the woman.

Ibid.

The reason birds can fly and we can't is simply that they have perfect faith, for to have faith is to have wings.

Ibid. Chap. 14

Poets are people who despise money except what you need for today.

Ibid. Chap. 15

When a great man dies — and this was one of the greatest since Shakespeare — the immortals await him at the top of the nearest hill.

George Meredith [1]

When you come to write my epitaph, Charles, let it be in these delicious words, "She had a long twenty-nine." [2]

Rosalind

One's religion is whatever he is most interested in, and yours is Success.

The Twelve-Pound Look

Alick: What *is* charm, exactly, Maggie?

Maggie: Oh, it's — it's a sort of bloom on a woman. If you have it, you don't need to have anything else; and if you don't have it, it doesn't much matter what else you have. Some women, the few, have charm for all; and most have charm for one. But some have charm for none. [3]

What Every Woman Knows. Act I

The tragedy of a man who has found himself out.

Ibid. Act IV

Every man who is high up loves to think that he has done it all himself; and the wife smiles, and lets it go at that.

Ibid.

The greatest glory that has ever come to me was to be swallowed up in London, not knowing a soul, with no means of subsistence, and the fun of

---

[1] In *The Westminster Gazette, May 26, 1909.*

[2] I have never admitted that I am more than twenty-nine, or thirty at the most. Twenty-nine when there are pink shades, thirty when there are not. — Oscar Wilde: *Lady Windermere's Fan, Act IV*

She had said she was twenty-eight years old when she came, and she was twenty-eight still; and she sometimes speculated as to when she would have another birthday. — Olive Schreiner: *From Man to Man, Chap. 6*

[3] What is charm? It is what the violet has and the camellia has not. — Francis Marion Crawford: *Children of the King, Chap. 5*

"Charm" — which means the power to effect work without employing brute force — is indispensable to women. Charm is a woman's strength just as strength is a man's charm. — Havelock Ellis: *The Task of Social Hygiene, Chap. 3*

working till the stars went out. To have known any one would have spoilt it. I did not even quite know the language.
Courage, Rectorial Address at St. Andrews [May 3, 1922]

Do you keep to the old topics? King Charles's head;[1] and Bacon wrote Shakespeare, or if he did not he missed the opportunity of his life. Don't forget to speak scornfully of the Victorian age; there will be time for meekness when you try to better it.
Ibid.

Mighty are the Universities of Scotland, and they will prevail. But even in your highest exultations never forget that they are not four, but five. The greatest of them is the poor, proud homes you come out of, which said so long ago: "There shall be education in this land."
Ibid.

For several days after my first book was published I carried it about in my pocket, and took surreptitious peeps at it to make sure that the ink had not faded.
Speech at the Critics' Circle, London [1922]

JOHN COLLINS BOSSIDY
[1860–1928]

And this is good old Boston,
  The home of the bean and the cod,
Where the Lowells talk only to Cabots
  And the Cabots talk only to God.[2]
Toast, Midwinter Dinner, Holy Cross Alumni [1910]

[1] See Dickens, page 496.
[2] Patterned on the toast given at the twenty-fifth anniversary dinner of the Harvard Class of 1880, by a Western man:
Here's to old Massachusetts,
  The home of the sacred cod,
Where the Adamses vote for Douglas,
  And the Cabots walk with God.

Here's to the town of New Haven,
  The home of the Truth and the Light,
Where God talks to Jones
  In the very same tones
That he uses with Hadley and Dwight.
  FREDERICK SCHEETZ JONES [1862–   ]:
    A Toast for New Haven: Lux et Veritas,
at a dinner of the Yale Alumni Associ-

HAROLD EDWIN BOULTON
[1859–1935]

Speed, bonnie boat, like a bird on the wing;
  Onward, the sailors cry:
Carry the lad that's born to be King
  Over the sea to Skye.
Skye Boat Song. Stanza 1

PAULINE CARRINGTON RUST BOUVÉ
[1860–1928]

In the land of the Island Kingdom,
  'Mid Shinto temple and shrine,
Where the lights of a thousand altars
  To a thousand false gods shine,
There is carved an odd, quaint lesson,
  Wondrously cut in the wood —
The three wise monkeys of Nikko,
  Who see, speak, hear, but the good!
The Three Wise Monkeys.[1] Stanza 1

WILLIAM JENNINGS BRYAN
[1860–1925]

The humblest citizen of all the land, when clad in the armor of a righteous cause is stronger than all the hosts of Error.
Speech at the National Democratic Convention,[2] Chicago [1896]

tion, Waterbury, Connecticut, Feb. 5, 1915
Here's to the town of Hanover,
  The home of the "Indian voice,"
  Where God talks to all
  Who will hark to His call —
Words of wisdom, and does it from choice.
  CHARLES THEODORE GALLAGHER [1851–1919]: *Dartmouth College Toast*
Here's to New Haven and Boston,
  And the turf that the Puritans trod,
In the rest of mankind little virtue they find,
  But they feel quite chummy with God.
  WALTER FOSTER ANGELL [1858–   ]:
    Brown University Toast
[1] Mizaru, Kikazaru, and Iwazaru.
In a temple at Kioto in far-away Japan,
  The little Apes of Nikko are sitting, wondrous wise.
  FLORENCE BOYCE DAVIS: *The Three Wise Monkeys*
[2] After Bryan made his "cross of gold" speech at the convention, a railroad president offered him the use of a private car for cam-

You shall not press down upon the brow of labor this crown of thorn. You shall not crucify mankind upon a cross of gold.

Speech at the National Democratic Convention [*1896*]

If the Father deigns to touch with divine power the cold and pulseless heart of the buried acorn and to make it burst forth from its prison walls, will He leave neglected in the earth the soul of man made in the image of his Creator?

The Prince of Peace

If matter mute and inanimate, though changed by the forces of Nature into a multitude of forms, can never die, will the spirit of man suffer annihilation when it has paid a brief visit, like a royal guest, to this tenement of clay? No. I am as sure that there is another life as I am that I live to-day.

Ibid.

If this invisible germ of life in the grain of wheat can thus pass unimpaired through three thousand resurrections, I shall not doubt that my soul has power to clothe itself with a new body, suited to its new existence, when this early frame has crumbled into dust.

Ibid.

CHARLES TOWNSEND COPELAND
[1860–]

For the common man, the best memorial is some beneficent thing or function that shall bear his name.

Tribute to Nathaniel Southgate Shaler [*July, 1906*]
Copeland Reader

A man is always better than a book.

Ibid.

To blame him were absurd; to pity were profane.

Not "Poor Charles Lamb." Copeland Reader Introduction

Whenever we encounter the typical essayist, he is found to be a tatler, a spectator, a rambler, a lounger, and, in the best sense, a citizen of the world.

Copeland Reader Introduction

Where novelists are concerned, because with lyric poets novelists are the most personal of writers, the question of the best book is likely to be as alluring as it is ultimately futile.

Ibid.

To eat is human; to digest, divine.[1]

Epigram

HAMLIN GARLAND
[1860–]

Do you fear the force of the wind,
  The slash of the rain?
Go face them and fight them,
  Be savage again.

Do You Fear the Wind?

The palms of your hands will thicken,
  The skin of your cheek will tan,
You'll go ragged and weary and swarthy,
  But you'll walk like a man!

Ibid.

CHARLOTTE PERKINS STETSON GILMAN
[1860–1935]

Said the little Eohippus,
  "I am going to be a horse!"

Similar Cases

Cried all, "Before such things can come,
You idiotic child,
You must alter Human Nature!"
And they all sat back and smiled.

Ibid.

Said I, in scorn all burning hot,
  In rage and anger high,
"You ignominious idiot!
  Those wings are made to fly!"

A Conservative. Stanza 5

"I do not want to be a fly!
I want to be a worm!"

Ibid. Stanza 6

---

paign travel. Willis John Abbot [1863–1934], present when the offer was made, advised Bryan not to accept, saying: "You are the Great Commoner."

[1] See Pope, page 211 and Robert Browning, page 493.

I ran against a Prejudice
    That quite cut off the view.
                An Obstacle. Stanza 1
I walked directly through him,
    As if he wasn't there.
                Ibid. Stanza 8
There's a whining at the threshold —
    There's a scratching at the floor —
To work! To work! In Heaven's name!
    The wolf is at the door!
        The Wolf at the Door. Stanza 6
Shall you complain who feed the world?
    Who clothe the world?
    Who house the world?
Shall you complain who are the world,
    Of what the world may do?
        As from this hour
        You use your power,
    The world must follow you!
                To Labor. Stanza 1
The people people work with best
    Are sometimes very queer;
The people people own by birth
    Quite shock your first idea.
The people people have for friends
    Your common sense appal,
But the people people marry
    Are the queerest folk of all.
                Queer People
If fifty men did all the work,
    And gave the price to five,
And let those five make all the rules —
You'd say the fifty men were fools,
    Unfit to be alive.
                Five and Fifty. Stanza 1
Below my window goes the cattle train,
    And stands for hours along the river
        park,
Fear, cold, exhaustion, hunger, thirst,
        and pain;
    Dumb brutes we call them — Hark!
        The Cattle Train. Stanza 1
We kill these weary creatures, sore and
        worn,
    And eat them — with our friends.
                Ibid. Stanza 4
Human life consists in mutual service. No grief, pain, misfortune, or
"broken heart," is excuse for cutting
off one's life while any power of service
remains. But when all usefulness is
over, when one is assured of an un-
avoidable and imminent death, it is the
simplest of human rights to choose a
quick and easy death in place of a slow
and horrible one.[1]
    Note written before her suicide
        [August 17, 1935]

HENRY LAWSON
[*Floruit* 1896]

When you wear a cloudy collar and a
        shirt that isn't white,
And you cannot sleep for thinking how
        you'll reach tomorrow night,
You may be a man of sorrows, and on
        speaking terms with Care,
And as yet be unacquainted with the
        Demon of Despair;
But I rather think that nothing heaps
        the trouble on your mind
Like the knowledge that your trousers
        badly need a patch behind.
    When Your Pants Begin to Go.[2]
                Stanza 1
A man's an awful coward when his
        pants begin to go.
                Ibid.

MISS L. M. LITTLE
[*Floruit* 1905]

There will be always one or two who
        hold
Earth's coin of less account than fairy
        gold;
Their treasure, not the spoil of crowds
        and kings,
But the dim beauty at the heart of
        things.
                Fairy Gold[3]

JAMES BALL NAYLOR
[1860–   ]

King David and King Solomon
    Led merry, merry lives,

[1] Asthma and other annoyances I have tolerated for years; but I cannot put up with
cancer.
    JOHN DAVIDSON: *Fleet Street and Other
            Poems*, Preface [1909]
[2] From *In the Days When the World Was
Wide*, published by Angus & Robertson,
Sydney, Australia, 1896.
[3] Thomas Bird Mosher printed these lines
on the fly-leaf of *A Little Garland of Celtic
Verse* in 1905. He had no biographical infor-

With many, many lady friends
  And many, many wives;
But when old age crept over them —
  With many, many qualms,
King Solomon wrote the Proverbs
  And King David wrote the Psalms.
                Ancient Authors

BLISS PERRY
[1860–   ]

The permanent vitality of a work of art does consist in its capacity for stimulating and transmitting pleasure.
                A Study of Poetry. Chap. 1
You and I may never see it, but ultimately nothing is so certain as the triumph of the things of the spirit over the gross material forces of American civilization.
                A Study of Prose Fiction. Chap. 13
The fact is, we are not a book-reading people. The vast majority of our ninety-odd millions of population have no literary appetites which cannot be supplied by the newspapers, the magazines, and an occasional "best-seller" novel.
        *The Praise of Folly. Criticism in
                American Periodicals*

CHARLES GEORGE
DOUGLAS ROBERTS
[1860–   ]

Comes the lure of green things growing,
Comes the call of waters flowing —
  And the wayfarer desire
Moves and wakes and would be going.
                Afoot. Stanza 1

HARRY ROMAINE
[*Floruit* 1895]

At the muezzin's call for prayer,
The kneeling faithful thronged the square.
                Ad Coelum
The one great God looked down and smiled,
And counted each His loving child;
For Turk and Brahmin, monk and Jew,

Had reached Him through the gods they knew.
                Ad Coelum
The little lonely souls go by,
Seeking their God who lives on high,
With conscious step and hat and all,
As if on Him they meant to call
In some sad ceremonial.
                The Sabbath. Stanza 1
The man who idly sits and thinks,
  May sow a nobler crop than corn,
For thoughts are seeds of future deeds,
  And when God thought — the world was born!
                Inaction

CLINTON SCOLLARD
[1860–1932]

Don't you hear the flutes of April calling clear and calling cool
From the crests that front the morning, from the hidden valley pool,
Runes of rapture half forgotten, tunes wherein old passions rule?
        The Flutes of April. Stanza 1
So Farmer Johnson shouldered his gun,
And left his scythe in the rain and the sun.
        The Scythe Tree.[1] *Stanza 2*

FRED NEWTON SCOTT
[1860–1931]

I am the hero of this little tale;
  I'm Romeo, Romeo.
I am that sadly susceptible male;
  I'm Romeo, Romeo.
Scarce did a lover e'er do as I did,
When his best girl to eternity slided;
I took cold poison and I suicided.
  I'm Romeo, Romeo.
        Glee Club Song. Stanza 2
I am the heroine of this tale of woe.
  I'm Juliet, I'm Juliet.
I am the darling that mashed Romeo.
  I'm Juliet, I'm Juliet.

---

mation concerning the author except that she lived in Ireland.

[1] Farmer Tyler J. Snyder hung his scythe in the crotch of a tree near Geneva, New York, as he left his hayfield in August, 1862, to answer President Lincoln's call for volunteers. He never returned, and the scythe remains in the tree as a mute memorial.

Locked in a tomb with no pickaxe to
    force it,
Gloomy old hole without room to stand
    or sit,
I up and stabbed myself right in the
    corset.
    I'm Juliet, I'm Juliet.
Glee Club Song. Stanza 3

How dear to my heart are the scenes of
    Ann Arbor,
    The ramshackled sidewalks, the one
        lonesome cop,
The beauties of Dutchtown, the fat col-
    ored barber,
    And e'en the gay widow I took to the
        hop,
That tough-hearted widow, that frisky
    old widow,
    That gay college widow I took to the
        hop.
College Days. Stanza 1

FRANK DEMPSTER
SHERMAN
[1860–1916]

Of all the threads of rhyme
    Which I have spun,
I shall be glad if Time
    Save only one.
His Desire

A land-flower broken from the stem,
And few indeed there be of them
Fitted so perfectly to gem
    The blue Atlantic.
Nantucket

Out of the scabbard of the night,
    By God's hand drawn,
Flashes his shining sword of light,
    And lo, — the dawn!
Dawn

Here in their bright metropolis of
    flowers
The banker bees are busy with their
    gold.
In a Garden

Hark to the noisy caravans of brown,
Intrepid Sparrows, — Arabs of the air!
City Sparrows

Give me the room whose every nook
Is dedicated to a book.
The Library

. . . Such be the library; and take
This motto of a Latin make
To grace the door through which I
    pass:
Hic habitat Felicitas!
The Library

And now, behold him dead, alas!
    Where he made joy so long:
A bit of blue amid the grass, —
    A tiny, broken song.
A Bird's Elegy

GEORGE MEASON WHICHER
[1860–1937]

How are the mighty withered! You are
    now
    Become your book, and that (O last
        of woes!)
Shrunk to a school-room bogey. Ped-
    ants plow
    With salt your fields; and there no
        harvest grows
Save juiceless weeds of grammar.
Ave Caesar! Stanza 3

Butchered to make the school-girl's ex-
    ercise!
Ibid.

Two thousand years ago! O god that
    gave
The power divine that saved his[1] song
    from death. . . .
O save this praise thus shapen by my
    breath:
Link deathless to his name one word of
    mine — one word!
A Prayer to Apollo

OWEN WISTER
[1860–   ]

When you call me that, *smile!*
The Virginian. Chap. 2 [*1902*]

RICHARD BURTON
[1861–   ]

From their folded mates they wander
    far,
Their ways seem harsh and wild;
They follow the beck of a baleful star,
    Their paths are dream-beguiled.
Black Sheep

[1] Horace.

How often in the summer-tide,
His graver business set aside,
Has stripling Will, the thoughtful-
eyed,
As to the pipe of Pan,
Stepped blithesomely with lover's pride
Across the fields to Anne.
Across the Fields to Anne. Stanza 1
I sit in mine house at ease,
  Moving nor foot nor hand;
Yet sail through uncharted seas
  And wander from land to land.
Travel

BLISS CARMAN
[1861–1929]

Have little care that life is brief,
And less that art is long.
Success is in the silences
Though fame is in the song.
Songs from Vagabondia. Foreword
An open hand, an easy shoe,
And a hope to make the day go through.
The Joys of the Road
A comrade neither glum nor merry.
Ibid.
No fidget and no reformer, just
A calm observer of ought and must.
Ibid.
And two brown arms at the journey's
end!
Ibid.
These are the joys of the open road —
For him who travels without a load.
Ibid.
Make me over, mother April,
When the sap begins to stir!
Spring Song. Stanza 1
Make me over in the morning
From the rag-bag of the world!
Scraps of dream and duds of daring,
Home-brought stuff from far sea-faring.
Ibid. Stanza 12
O foolish ones, put by your cares!
Where wants are many, joys are few;
And at the wilding springs of peace
God keeps an open house for you.
The Mendicants. Stanza 5
Over the shoulders and slopes of the
dune

I saw the white daisies go down to the
sea.
Daisies. Stanza 1
And all of their singing was, "Earth, it
is well!"
And all of their dancing was, "Life,
thou art good!"
Ibid. Stanza 2
The scarlet of the maples can shake me
like a cry
Of bugles going by.
A Vagabond Song. Stanza 2
There is something in October sets the
gypsy blood astir.
Ibid. Stanza 3
Hack and Hew were the sons of God
In the earlier earth than now;
One at his right hand, one at his left,
To obey as he taught them how.
Hack and Hew. Stanza 1
Hem and Haw were the sons of sin,
Created to shally and shirk;
Hem lay 'round and Haw looked on
While God did all the work.
Hem and Haw. Stanza 1
Lord of the far horizons,
  Give us the eyes to see
Over the verge of the sundown
  The beauty that is to be.
Lord of the Far Horizons. Stanza 1
We are the roadside flowers,
Straying from garden grounds, —
Lovers of idle hours,
Breakers of ordered bounds.
Roadside Flowers. Stanza 1
Here we came when love was young.
Now that love is old,
Shall we leave the floor unswept
And the hearth acold?
The Homestead. Stanza 1
Heaven is no larger than Connecticut;
No larger than Fairfield County.
A Measure of Heaven
There is virtue in the open; there is
healing out of doors;
The great Physician makes his rounds
along the forest floors.
An Open Letter, Christmas, 1920.[1]
Stanza 4

---

[1] Written at Lake Placid, New York, while
Carman was a patient there.

I took a day to search for God,
And found Him not. But as I trod
  By rocky ledge, through woods un-
    tamed,
  Just where one scarlet lily flamed,
I saw His footprint in the sod.
Vestigia. Stanza 1

LOUISE IMOGEN GUINEY
[1861–1920]

He has done with roofs and men,
Open, Time, and let him pass.
Ballad of Kenelm
A short life in the saddle, Lord!
Not long life by the fire.
The Knight Errant. Stanza 2
To fear not sensible failure,
  Nor covet the game at all,
But fighting, fighting, fighting,
  Die, driven against the wall!
The Kings. Stanza 9
Cowley said it engagingly: *Bene qui
latuit, bene vixit:* he lives well, that has
lain well hidden. The pleasantest con-
dition of life is in incognito.
*Patrins. On the Delights of an
Incognito*
"Isn't there heaven,"
  (She was but seven)
"Isn't there" (sobbing), "for dogs?"
she said.
Davy. Stanza 1
Man is immortal, sage or fool;
Animals end by different rule.
Ibid. Stanza 2
Use me in honor; cherish me
As ivy from a sacred tree:
Mine in the winds of war to close
Around the armor of Montrose,
And kiss the death-wound of Dundee.
The Graham Tartan to a Graham
A passing salute to this world and her
  pitiful beauty.
The Wild Ride. Stanza 5
We spur to a land of no name, outrac-
  ing the stormwind;
We leap to the infinite dark like sparks
  from the anvil.
Ibid. Stanza 7
A certain sesquipedalianism is nat-
ural to Americans: witness our press
editorials, our Fourth of July orations,
and the public messages of all our Presi-
dents since Lincoln.
*In Scribner's Magazine,
January, 1911*
Quotations (such as have point and
lack triteness) from the great old authors are an act of filial reverence on
the part of the quoter, and a blessing
to a public grown superficial and external.
Ibid.

KATHARINE TYNAN
HINKSON
[1861–1931]

All in the April evening,
  April airs were abroad,
I saw the sheep with their lambs,
  And thought on the Lamb of God.
Sheep and Lambs. Stanza 6
There's a lark in the noon sky, a thrush
  on the tree,
And a linnet sings wildly across the
  green lea,
And the finches are merry, the cuckoos
  still call,
But where is my Blackbird, the dearest
  of all?
The Blackbird.[1] *Stanza 1*
The Spring comes slowly up this way,[2]
Slowly, slowly!
A little nearer every day.
A New Old Song. Stanza 1
I served Christ Jesus and I bear
  His Cross upon my rough grey back.
Dear Christian people, pray you, spare
  The whip, for Jesus Christ His sake.
The Ass Speaks.[3] *Stanza 9*
Of all the birds from East to West
  That tuneful are and dear,
I love that farmyard bird the best,
  They call him Chanticleer.
Chanticleer. Stanza 1

---

[1] Mrs. Hinkson was called "the blackbird's
poet."
[2] A line from Coleridge's *Christabel, Part I*.
[3] Fools! For I also had my hour;
  One far fierce hour and sweet:
There was a shout about my ears,
  And palms before my feet.
GILBERT KEITH CHESTERTON:
The Donkey, St. 4

God made the country,
  Man made the town.[1]
God clad the country
  In a green gown.
                The Maker. Stanza 1
Lest Heaven be thronged with grey-
    beards hoary,
  God, who made boys for His delight,
Stoops in a day of grief and glory
  And calls them in, in from the night.
When they come trooping from the war
Our skies have many a young new star.
                Flower of Youth. Stanza 1

JOHN LUTHER LONG
[1861–1927]

To die with honour when one can no
longer live with honour.[2]
  *Madam Butterfly (inscription on
            Samurai blade)*

JUSTIN HUNTLY
McCARTHY
[1861–1936]

On level lines of woodwork stand
My books obedient to my hand.
                My Books
The playwrights mouth, the preachers
    jangle,
  The critics challenge and defend,
And Fiction turns the Muses' mangle —
  Of making books there is no end.
          *A Ballade of Book-Making.
                    Stanza 2*
A simple ballad, to a sylvan air,
  Of love that ever finds your face more
      fair;
I could not give you any goodlier thing
  If I were king.
          If I Were King. Stanza 2
Alas for lovers! Pair by pair
  The Wind has blown them all away;

The young and yare, the fond and fair;
Where are the Snows of Yesterday?
          *A Ballad of Dead Ladies: After
                    Villon. Envoy*

EDWARD MacDOWELL
[1861–1908]

A house of Dreams untold
That looks out over the whispering
    tree-tops
And faces the setting sun.
                House of Dreams [1]

BYRON RUFUS NEWTON
[1861–1938]

Vulgar of manner, overfed,
Overdressed and underbred;
Heartless, Godless, hell's delight,
Rude by day and lewd by night;
Bedwarfed the man, o'ergrown the
    brute,
Ruled by Jew and prostitute;
Purple-robed and pauper-clad,
Raving, rotting, money-mad;
A squirming herd in Mammon's mesh,
A wilderness of human flesh;
Crazed with avarice, lust, and rum,
New York, thy name's Delirium.
          Owed to New York [1906]

SIR WALTER RALEIGH
[1861–1922]

I wish I loved the Human Race;
I wish I loved its silly face;
I wish I liked the way it walks;
I wish I liked the way it talks;
And when I'm introduced to one
I wish I thought *What Jolly Fun!*
          *Wishes of an Elderly Man (Wished
              at a Garden-Party, June, 1914)*
Brief delight, eternal quiet,
How change these for endless riot
Broken by a single rest?
Well you know that sleep is best.
                My Last Will
Listen; you may be allowed
To hear my laughter from a cloud.
                Ibid.

---

[1] God made the country, and man made
  the town.
      COWPER: *The Task, Book I, L. 749*
[2] One should die proudly when it is no
longer possible to live proudly. — NIETZSCHE:
*The Twilight of the Idols, Skirmishes in a
War with the Age, 36,* translated by AN-
THONY M. LUDOVICI

[1] Preface to his composition, *From a Log
Cabin,* and inscribed on the memorial tablet
near his grave.

SIR OWEN SEAMAN
[1861–1936]

Whene'er I walk the public ways,
  How many poor that lack ablution
Do probe my heart with pensive gaze,
  And beg a trivial contribution!
      *The Bitter Cry of the Great
                    Unpaid*

O hearts of metal pure as finest gold!
  O great ensample, where our sons
    may trace,
Too proud for tears, their birthright
    from of old,
  Heirs of the Island Race!
  *In Memoriam: The Scott Antarctic
    Expedition, 1912. Stanza 4*

Ye that have faith to look with fearless
    eyes
  Beyond the tragedy of a world at
    strife,
And trust that out of night and death
    shall rise
  The dawn of ampler life;
Rejoice, whatever anguish rend your
    heart,
  That God has given you for a price-
    less dower,
To live in these great times and have
    your part
  In Freedom's crowning hour;
That you may tell your sons who see
    the light
  High in the heavens — their heritage
    to take —
"I saw the powers of Darkness put to
    flight,
  I saw the Morning break."
  Between Midnight and Morning [1]

Still where the countless ripples laugh
    above
  The blue of halcyon seas, long may
    you keep
Your course unbroken, buoyed upon a
    love
  Ten thousand fathoms deep!
      In Memoriam. Mark Twain [2]

[1] Written for *The Book of King Albert* of
Belgium.
[2] In *Punch* [1910].

WENDELL PHILLIPS
STAFFORD
[1861–   ]

My heart is where the hills fling up
  Green garlands to the day.
'Tis where the blue lake brims her cup,
  The sparkling rivers play.
My heart is on the mountain still,
  Where'er my steps may be,
Vermont, O maiden of the hills,
  My heart is there with thee!
      Vermont: A Song. Stanza 1

JOHN KENDRICK BANGS
[1862–1922]

Shakespeare was not accounted great
When good Queen Bess ruled Eng-
    land's state,
So why should I to-day repine
Because the laurel is not mine?
      Consolation. Stanza 1

He does not read at all, yet he doth
    hoard
Rich books. In exile on his shelves
    they're stored;
And many a volume, sweet and good
    and true,
Fails in the work that it was made to
    do.
      The Bibliomiser

Be sure to keep a mirror always nigh
  In some convenient, handy sort of
    place,
And now and then look squarely in
    thine eye,
  And with thyself keep ever face to
    face.
      Face to Face. Stanza 1

I think mankind by thee would be less
    bored
If only thou wert not thine own reward.
      A Hint to Virtue

I have no dog, but it must be
Somewhere there's one belongs to me —
A little chap with wagging tail,
And dark brown eyes that never quail,
      My Dog. Stanza 1

I never seen a night
So dark there wasn't light

Somewhere about if I took care
To strike a match an' find out where.
                My Philosophy. Stanza 5
I love to watch the rooster crow,
He's like so many men I know
Who brag and bluster, rant and shout
And beat their manly breasts, without
The first damn thing to crow about.
                        The Rooster
To dig and delve in nice clean dirt
Can do a mortal little hurt.
                        Gardening
"I'm just as big for me," said he,
    "As you are big for you!"
        The Little Elfman. Stanza 2

ARTHUR CHRISTOPHER
BENSON
[1862–1925]

Friend, of my infinite dreams
    Little enough endures;
Little howe'er it seems,
    It is yours, all yours.
Faith hath a fleeting breath,
    Hopes may be frail but fond,
But Love shall be Love till death,
    And perhaps beyond.
                        The Gift
If it be well with him,
If it be well, I say,
I will not try with a childish cry
To draw him thence away:
Only my day is dim,
Only I long for him,
Where is my friend to-day?
                        My Friend
Thy name is writ in water, ay, 'tis writ
    As when the moon, a chill and
        friendless thing,
    Passes and writes her will upon
        the tide,
And piles the ocean in a moving
    ring:
And every stagnant bay is brimmed
    with it,
    Each mast-fringed port, each estu-
        ary wide.
                        Keats
Land of Hope and Glory, Mother of
    the Free,
How shall we extol thee, who are born
    of thee?

Wider still and wider shall thy bounds
    be set;
God, who made thee mighty, make thee
    mightier yet.
        Land of Hope and Glory. Chorus
    Edward Fitzgerald said that he
wished we had more lives of obscure
persons; one wants to know what other
people are thinking and feeling about
it all. . . . If the dullest person in the
world would only put down sincerely
what he or she thought about his or her
life, about work and love, religion and
emotion, it would be a fascinating doc-
ument.
                From a College Window

JAMES W. BLAKE
[1862–1935]

East Side, West Side, all around the
    town,
The tots sang "Ring-a-rosie," "London
    Bridge is falling down";
Boys and girls together, me and Mamie
    Rorke,
Tripped the light fantastic on the side-
    walks of New York.
        The Sidewalks of New York [1]
                                [*1894*]

CARRIE JACOBS BOND
[1862–   ]

For Memory has painted this perfect
    day
With colors that never fade,
And we find at the end of a perfect day
The soul of a friend we've made.
                A Perfect Day. Stanza 2

NICHOLAS MURRAY BUTLER
[1862–   ]

    An expert is one who knows more and
more about less and less. [2]
                *Commencement Address,
                Columbia University*

---

[1] The music of the song was composed by
Charles B. Lawlor [1852–1925].
[2] An expert is a person who avoids the
small errors as he sweeps on to the grand
fallacy. — BENJAMIN STOLBERG [1891–   ]

JOHN ARMSTRONG CHALONER
[1862–1935]

Who's loony now?
*Message to his brother, Robert
Chanler [December, 1911]*

GOLDSWORTHY LOWES DICKINSON
[1862–1932]

Chinese poetry is of all poetry I know the most human and the least symbolic or romantic. It contemplates life just as it presents itself, without any veil of ideas, any rhetoric or sentiment; it simply clears away the obstruction which habit has built up between us and the beauty of things.
*An Essay on the Civilizations of
India, China, and Japan. Page 47*

Consider the American continent! How simple it is! How broad! How large! How grand in design! A strip of coast, a range of mountains, a plain, a second range, a second strip of coast! That is all! Contrast the complexity of Europe, its lack of symmetry, its variety, irregularity, disorder and caprice! The geography of the two continents already foreshadows the differences in their civilizations.
A Modern Symposium

The United States of America — the greatest potential force, material, moral, and spiritual, in the world.
The Choice Before Us. Chap. 1

To the man who has the religion of peace, the supreme value is love. To the man who has the religion of war, the supreme value is strife.
Ibid. Chap. 3

Government is everywhere to a great extent controlled by powerful minorities, with an interest distinct from that of the mass of the people.
Ibid. Chap. 4

The true way for one civilization to "conquer" another is for it to be so obviously superior in this or that point that others desire to imitate it.
Ibid. Chap. 5

War is not "inevitable," but proceeds from definite and removable causes.
The Choice Before Us. Chap. 9

Nations are quite capable of starving every other side of life — education, sanitation, housing, public health, everything that contributes to life, physical, intellectual, moral, and spiritual, in order to maintain their armaments.
Ibid. Chap. 11

Every kind of discrimination is a protection of the incompetent against the competent, with the result that the motive to become competent is taken away.
Ibid. Chap. 12

What we commonly have in our mind when we speak of religion is a definite set of doctrines, of a more or less metaphysical character, formulated in a creed and supported by an organization distinct from the state.
*The Greek View of Life. Chap. 1,
Sect. 1*

A fundamental, and as many believe, the most essential part of Christianity, is its doctrine of reward and punishment in the world beyond; and a religion which had nothing at all to say about this great enigma we should hardly feel to be a religion at all.
Ibid. Sect. 11

All modern societies aim, to this extent at least, at equality, that their tendency, so far as it is conscious and avowed, is not to separate off a privileged class of citizens, set free by the labour of others to live the perfect life, but rather to distribute impartially to all the burdens and advantages of the state, so that every one shall be at once a labourer for himself and a citizen of the state.
Ibid. Chap. 2, Sect. 12

Dissatisfaction with the world in which we live and determination to realize one that shall be better, are the prevailing characteristics of the modern spirit.
Ibid. Chap. 5

ANNIE JOHNSON FLINT
[1862–1932]

The thrones are rocking to their fall —
It is the twilight of the Kings!
The Twilight of the Kings [1]
Have you come to the Red Sea place
in your life,
Where, in spite of all you can do,
There is no way out, there is no way
back,
There is no other way but through?
At the Place of the Sea. Stanza 1

NORMAN GALE
[1862–   ]

Here in the country's heart
Where the grass is green,
Life is the same sweet life
As it e'er hath been.
The Country Faith. Stanza 1
God comes down in the rain,
And the crop grows tall —
This is the country faith,
And the best of all!
Ibid. Stanza 3
The cheated stockings lean and long,
The swift-descending petticoat,
The breasts that heave because they
ran,
The rounded arms, the brilliant limbs,
The pretty necklaces of tan.
The Shaded Pool
Write: — He had made a finer man
And left increased renown behind,
If he had only shut his books
To read the chapters of mankind!
Last Words. Stanza 10

ELLA HIGGINSON
[1862–   ]

Oh, every year hath its winter,
And every year hath its rain —

[1] This is the twilight of the kings. Western Europe of the people may be caught in this debacle, but never again. Eastern Europe of the kings will be remade and the name of God shall not give grace to a hundred square miles of broken bodies. If Divinity enters here it comes with a sword to deliver the people from the sword. It is the twilight of the kings. The republic marches east in Europe. — Editorial, *The Chicago Tribune, Aug. 2, 1914*

But a day is always coming
When the birds go north again.
*When the Birds Go North Again.
Stanza 1*
One leaf is for hope, and one is for
faith,
And one is for love, you know,
And God put another in for luck.
Four-Leaf Clover. Stanza 2
The low brown hills, the bare brown
hills
Of San Francisco Bay.
The Low Brown Hills. Stanza 1
Forgive you? — Oh, of course, dear,
A dozen times a week!
We women were created
Forgiveness but to speak.
Wearing Out Love. Stanza 1
It's what you do, unthinking,
That makes the quick tear start;
The tear may be forgotten —
But the hurt stays in the heart.
Ibid. Stanza 3

E. PAULINE JOHNSON
("TEKAHIONWAKE")
[1862–1913]

And down these nineteen centuries
anew
Comes the hoarse-throated, brutal-
ized refrain,
"Give us Barabbas, crucify the Jew!"
Once more a man must bear a na-
tion's stain.
"Give Us Barabbas." [1] *Stanza 3*

WALT MASON
[1862–   ]

The little green tents where the soldiers sleep and the sunbeams play and
the women weep, are covered with
flowers to-day.
The Little Green Tents

[1] Written after Captain Alfred Dreyfus [1859–1935] was exiled to Devil's Island, 1894.

In all ages the multitude has looked upon Barabbas as a less violent and dangerous disrupter of social laws than the Christ — not this man but Barabbas!
OLIVE SCHREINER: *From Man to Man, Chap. 7*

The statesman throws his shoulders
  back, and straightens out his tie,
And says, "My friends, unless it rains,
  the weather will be dry."
And when this thought into our brains
  has percolated through,
We common people nod our heads and
  loudly cry, "How true!"
                    The Statesman
  There's a man in the world who
is never turned down, wherever he
chances to stray; he gets the glad hand
in the populous town, out where the
farmers make hay; he's greeted with
pleasure on deserts of sand, and deep
in the aisles of the woods; wherever he
goes there's the welcoming hand —
he's the Man Who Delivers the Goods.
        The Man Who Delivers the Goods
  Little drops of water poured into the
milk, give the milkman's daughter
lovely gowns of silk. Little grains of
sugar mingled with the sand, make the
grocer's assets swell to beat the band.
                    Little Things
  Why taste the wormwood when the
prunes are wholesome, sweet and
cheap? The night is coming on eftsoons
when we lie down to sleep.
                    Why?

SIR HENRY NEWBOLT
[1862–1938]

To set the cause above renown,
  To love the game beyond the prize,
To honor, while you strike him down,
  The foe that comes with fearless
    eyes;
To count the life of battle good
  And dear the land that gave you
    birth,
And dearer yet the brotherhood
  That binds the brave of all the earth.
                Clifton Chapel. Stanza 2
Qui procul hinc, the legend's writ, —
  The frontier-grave is far away —
Qui ante diem periit:
  Sed miles, sed pro patria.[1]
                    Ibid. Stanza 4

---

[1] Who died far away, before his time; but
as a soldier, for his country.

      When the strong command
Obedience is best.
              A Ballad of John Nicholson
And now he saw with lifted eyes
The East like a great chancel rise,
And deep through all his senses drawn,
Received the sacred wine of dawn.
                    The Last Word
Like a sun bewitched in alien realms of
    night,
Mellow and yellow and rounded hangs
    the moon.
                    Moonset
April's anger is swift to fall,
April's wonder is worth it all.
              The Adventurers. Stanza 8
Beyond the book his teaching sped,
He left on whom he taught the trace
Of kinship with the deathless dead.
                    Ionicus
Admirals all, they went their way
  To the haven under the hill.
But they left us a kingdom none can
    take,
  The realm of the circling sea.
                    Admirals All
He's sailed in a hundred builds o' boat,
He's fought in a thousand kinds o' coat,
He's the senior flag of all that float,
  And his name's Admiral Death.
                    Admiral Death
      Craven spoke,
Spoke as he lived and fought, with a
    captain's pride,
"After you, Pilot": the pilot woke,
Down the ladder he went, and Craven
    died.[1]
        Craven: August 5, 1864. Stanza 6
Sidney thirsting a humbler need to
    slake,
Nelson waiting his turn for the sur-
    geon's hand,
Lucas crushed with chains for a com-
    rade's sake,
Outram coveting right before com-
    mand.
                    Ibid. Stanza 8

---

[1] Caught by the under-death,
  In the drawing of a breath
Down went dauntless Craven,
He and his hundred!
              HENRY HOWARD BROWNELL:
                    The Bay Fight

Princes of courtesy, merciful, proud
and strong.
Craven: August 5, 1864. Stanza 9

Their fame's on Torres Vedras, their
fame's on Vigo Bar,
Far-flashed to Cape St. Vincent; it
burns from Trafalgar;
Mark as ye go the beacons that woke
the world with light
When down their ancient highway your
fathers passed to fight.
The Sailing of the Long-ships

The sand of the desert is sodden red —
Red with the wreck of a square that
broke —
The gatling's jammed, and the colonel
dead,
And the regiment blind with the dust
and smoke:
The river of death has brimmed its
banks,
And England's far and honour a
name.
Vitaï Lampada

This they all with a joyful mind
Bear through life like a torch in
flame,
And, falling, fling to the hosts behind,
"Play up! play up! and play the
game!"
Ibid.

Come, boys, come!
You that mean to fight it out, wake and
take your load again,
Fall in! Fall in! Follow the fife and
drum!
The Toy Band

Drake he was a Devon man, an' ruled
the Devon seas.
Drake's Drum. Stanza 2

"Take my drum to England, hang et
by the shore,
Strike et when your powder's run-
nin' low;
If the Dons sight Devon, I'll quit the
port o' Heaven,
An' drum them up the Channel as we
drummed them long ago."
Ibid.

England! where the sacred flame
Burns before the inmost shrine,
Where the lips that love thy name
Consecrate their hopes and thine,

Where the banners of thy dead
Weave their shadows overhead,
Watch beside thine arms to-night,
Pray that God defend the Right.
The Vigil. Stanza 1

EDEN PHILLPOTTS
[1862–   ]

A sudden wakin', a sudden weepin',
A li'l suckin', a li'l sleepin';
A cheel's full joys an' a cheel's short
sorrows,
Wi' a power o' faith in gert to-morrows.
Man's Days. Stanza 1

A li'l dreamin', a li'l dyin':
A li'l lew corner o' airth to lie in.
Ibid. Stanza 3

'Tis here they say the journey ends
And little doubt it must be so;
But, as I tell my bestest friends,
I hate to go.
Lament. Stanza 1

By all the agonies of all the past,
By earth's cold dust and ashes at the
last,
By her return to the unconscious vast,
Oh, hear!
Litany to Pan. Stanza 7

WILLIAM MARION REEDY
[1862–1920]

Force is good and fire is good and
fancy is good in a poet, but if he have
not Love then he is as sounding brass
and tinkling cymbal. Love is best of
all. There is not, nor ever shall be, true
song without it.
A Nest of Singing Birds

ROBERT CAMERON ROGERS
[1862–1912]

The hours I spent with thee, dear heart,
Are as a string of pearls to me;
I count them over, every one apart,
My rosary, my rosary.
My Rosary

Oh memories that bless — and burn!
Oh barren gain — and bitter loss!
I kiss each bead and strive at last to
learn
To kiss the cross,

Sweetheart,
To kiss the cross.
My Rosary
Sage-brush to kindle with,
Quaking-asp to glow,
Pine-roots to last until the dawn-winds
blow.
Oh smoke full of fancies,
And dreams gone to smoke,
At the camp-fires dead long ago!
A Ballad of Dead Camp-Fires
Oh master mine, lo I remember thee, —
But I am old and weak and near to
death —
I cannot fawn and leap and be thy dog,
Thy dog of old — I cannot show the
love
That I have kept so long for one ca-
ress, —
But, master, I have not forgotten thee.
The Death of Argus [1]
Visions I no longer see,
And smoke is only smoke to me,
Now I am old.
The Old Smoker

EDITH WHARTON
[1862–1937]

There are two ways of spreading light:
to be
The candle or the mirror that reflects
it.
Vesalius in Zante
Somewhere I read, in an old book whose
name
Is gone from me, I read that when the
days
Of a man are counted, and his business
done,
There comes up the shore at evening,
with the tide,
To the place where he sits, a boat —
And in the boat, from the place where
he sits, he sees,
Dim in the dusk, dim and yet so fa-
miliar,
The faces of his friends long dead; and
knows
They come for him, brought in upon
the tide,

[1] See Pope, p. 220.

To take him where men go at set of
day.[1]
*With the Tide: Theodore
Roosevelt*
I was never allowed to read the popular American children's books of my
day because, as my mother said, the
children spoke bad English *without the
author's knowing it.*
A Backward Glance. Chap. 3
My parents and their group, though
they held literature in great esteem,
stood in nervous dread of those who
produced it. Washington Irving, Fitz-
Greene Halleck and William Dana were
the only representatives of the disquiet-
ing art who were deemed uncontaminated by it; though Longfellow, they
admitted, if a popular poet, was nevertheless a gentleman. As for Herman
Melville, a cousin of the Van Rens-
selaers, and qualified by birth to figure
in the best society, he was doubtless
excluded from it by his deplorable Bo-
hemianism, for I never heard his name
mentioned, or saw one of his books.
Ibid.
To [Henry] James's intimates, however, these elaborate hesitancies, far
from being an obstacle, were like a cobweb bridge flung from his mind to
theirs, an invisible passage over which
one knew that silver-footed ironies,
veiled jokes, tiptoe malices, were stealing to explode a huge laugh at one's
feet.
Ibid. Chap. 8
"Summer afternoon — summer afternoon; to me those have always been the
two most beautiful words in the English
language."
(*Said by* HENRY JAMES *to* E. W.)
Ibid. Chap. 10
One day when the Sultan was in his
palace at Damascus a beautiful youth
who was his favourite rushed into his
presence, crying out in great agitation

[1] Whenever a good Haida is about to die
he sees a canoe manned by some of his dead
friends, who come with the tide to bid him
welcome to the spirit land. — SIR JAMES G.
FRAZER: *The Golden Bough* (abridged edition), *Chap. 3*

that he must fly at once to Baghdad, and imploring leave to borrow his Majesty's swiftest horse.

The Sultan asked why he was in such haste to go to Baghdad. "Because," the youth answered, "as I passed through the garden of the Palace just now, Death was standing there, and when he saw me he stretched out his arms as if to threaten me, and I must lose no time in escaping from him."

The young man was given leave to take the Sultan's horse and fly; and when he was gone the Sultan went down indignantly into the garden, and found Death still there. "How dare you make threatening gestures at my favourite?" he cried; but Death, astonished, answered: "I assure your Majesty I did not threaten him. I only threw up my arms in surprise at seeing him here, because I have a tryst with him tonight in Baghdad." [1]

A Backward Glance. Chap. 11

HENRY HOLCOMB BENNETT
[1863–1924]

Hats off!
Along the street there comes
A blare of bugles, a ruffle of drums,
A flash of color beneath the sky:
    Hats off!
The flag is passing by.
            The Flag Goes By. Stanza 1

GAMALIEL BRADFORD
[1863–1932]

My art is the painting of soul,
    So fine, so exacting, so strange:
To blend in one tangible whole
    The manifold features of change.
            Soul. Stanza 1

My prose is decorous,
    Or strips other men,
Discreetly sonorous
    On things that have been.
My verse tears the curtain

From shuddering me,
Pale, haggard, uncertain,
    As souls should not be.
            My Art. Stanza 2

I sometimes wish that God were back
    In this dark world and wide;
For though some virtues he might lack,
    He had his pleasant side.
            Exit God

Youth is alive, and once we too were
        young,
    Dreamed we could make the world
        all over new,
Tossed eager projects lightly from the
        tongue,
    And hoped the hurrying years would
        prove them true.
        Wellesley at Fifty, 1881–1931

That odd, fantastic ass, Rousseau,
    Declared himself unique.
How men persist in doing so,
    Puzzles me more than Greek.
            Rousseau

The sins that tarnish whore and thief
    Beset me every day.
My most ethereal belief
    Inhabits common clay.
            Ibid.

JOSEPH HAYDEN
[*Floruit* 1896]

There'll be a hot time in the old town
    to-night.
    A Hot Time in the Old Town [1]
            [*1896*]

OLIVER HERFORD
[1863–1935]

God made Man
    Frail as a bubble;
God made Love,
    Love made Trouble.
God made the Vine,

---

[1] Story told E. W. by JEAN COCTEAU. The same fable was current many years later under the title *Appointment in Samarra*.

[1] Theodore August Metz [1848–1936] composed a march, *A Hot Time in the Old Town To-night*, in 1886 for the McIntyre and Heath minstrel show. In 1896 Joseph Hayden wrote words for the music, and the song was published. It became the favorite rallying song of Theodore Roosevelt's Rough Riders in Cuba, and later was the campaign song of Colonel Roosevelt.

Was it a sin
That Man made Wine
  To drown Trouble in?
                                  A Plea
The Gargoyle often makes his perch
On a cathedral or a church,
Where, mid ecclesiastic style,
He smiles an early-Gothic smile.
                             The Gargoyle
Children, behold the Chimpanzee:
He sits on the ancestral tree
From which we sprang in ages gone.
                           The Chimpanzee
It hath been writ that anye manne
May blameless kiss what mayde he
  canne
Nor anyone shall say hym "no"
Beneath the holye mistletoe.
              The Enchanted Oak. Stanza 5
Ermined and minked and Persian-
  lambed,
Be-puffed (be-painted, too, alas!)
Be-decked, be-diamonded — be-
  damned!
The women of the better class.
           The Women of the Better Class.
                                Stanza 4
It is not fair to visit all
The blame on Eve, for Adam's fall;
The most Eve did was to display
Contributory negligé.
                    Eve: Apropos de Rien
O Mongoose, where were you that day
When Mistress Eve was led astray?
If you'd but seen the serpent first,
Our parents would not have been
  cursed.
                  Child's Natural History.
                          The Mongoose

JOSEPH P. MacCARTHY
[1863–1934]

You must select the Puritans for
your ancestors. You must have a sheltered youth and be a graduate of Harvard. . . . Eat beans on Saturday
night and fish-balls on Sunday morning. . . . You must be a D.A.R., a
Colonial Dame, an S.A.R. or belong
to the Mayflower Society. . . . You
must read the Atlantic Monthly. . . .
You must make sure in advance that

your obituary appears in the Boston
Transcript. There is nothing else.
          To be Happy in New England,
          Letter to the Editor of The Chris-
          tian Register

ARTHUR MACHEN
[1863–   ]

It was better, he thought, to fail in
attempting exquisite things than to
succeed in the department of the utterly contemptible.
            The Hill of Dreams. Chap. 5

CLARENCE OUSLEY
[1863–   ]

When the mint is in the liquor and its
  fragrance on the glass,
It breathes a recollection that can
  never, never pass —
When the South was in the glory of a
  never-ending June,
The strings were on the banjo and the
  fiddle was in tune,
And we reveled in the plenty that we
  thought could never pass
And lingered at the julep in the ever-
  brimming glass.
          When the Mint Is in the Liquor.
                                Stanza 1

SIR ARTHUR THOMAS
QUILLER-COUCH
[1863–   ]

Literature is not an abstract science,
to which exact definitions can be applied. It is an art, the success of which
depends on personal persuasiveness, on
the author's skill to give as on ours to
receive.
          Inaugural Lecture at Cambridge
                     University [1913]

JAMES HARVEY ROBINSON
[1863–1935]

Political campaigns are designedly
made into emotional orgies which endeavor to distract attention from the
real issues involved, and they actually

paralyze what slight powers of cerebration man can normally muster.

The Human Comedy. Chap. 9

With supreme irony, the war to "make the world safe for democracy" [1] ended by leaving democracy more unsafe in the world than at any time since the collapse of the revolutions of 1848.

Ibid.

GEORGE SANTAYANA
[1863–   ]

He carries his English weather in his heart wherever he goes, and it becomes a cool spot in the desert, and a steady and sane oracle amongst all the delirium of mankind.

Soliloquies in England. The British Character

England is the paradise of individuality, eccentricity, heresy, anomalies, hobbies, and humours.

Ibid.

The world is a perpetual caricature of itself; at every moment it is the mockery and the contradiction of what it is pretending to be.

Ibid. Dickens

There is no cure for birth and death save to enjoy the interval.

Ibid. War Shrines

I like to walk about amidst the beautiful things that adorn the world; but private wealth I should decline, or any sort of personal possessions, because they would take away my liberty.

Ibid. The Irony of Liberalism

My atheism, like that of Spinoza, is true piety towards the universe and denies only gods fashioned by men in their own image, to be servants of their human interests.

Ibid. On My Friendly Critics

The human race, in its intellectual life, is organized like the bees: the masculine soul is a worker, sexually atrophied, and essentially dedicated to impersonal and universal arts; the feminine is a queen, infinitely fertile, omnipresent in its brooding industry, but passive and abounding in intuitions

[1] See Woodrow Wilson, page 725.

without method and passions without justice.

The Life of Reason. Vol. 2

Civilisation is perhaps approaching one of those long winters that overtake it from time to time. Romantic Christendom — picturesque, passionate, unhappy episode — may be coming to an end. Such a catastrophe would be no reason for despair.

Character and Opinion in the · United States [1922]

American life is a powerful solvent. It seems to neutralise every intellectual element, however tough and alien it may be, and to fuse it in the native good-will, complacency, thoughtlessness, and optimism.

Ibid.

All his life he [the American] jumps into the train after it has started and jumps out before it has stopped; and he never once gets left behind, or breaks a leg.

Ibid.

There is nothing impossible in the existence of the supernatural: its existence seems to me decidedly probable.

The Genteel Tradition at Bay

It is a great advantage for a system of philosophy to be substantially true.

The Unknowable

The young man who has not wept is a savage, and the old man who will not laugh is a fool.

Dialogues in Limbo. III

Beauty is pleasure regarded as the quality of a thing.

The Sense of Beauty. On Nature of Beauty

The infinity which moves us is the sense of multiplicity in uniformity. Accordingly, things which have enough multiplicity, as the lights of a city seen across water, have an effect similar to that of the stars, if less intense; whereas a star, if alone, because the multiplicity is lacking, makes a wholly different impression.

Ibid. On Form

Beauty as we feel it is something indescribable: what it is or what it means
can never be said.

The Sense of Beauty.
On Expression

Beauty is a pledge of the possible
conformity between the soul and nature, and consequently a ground of faith
in the supremacy of the good.

Ibid.

Let a man once overcome his selfish
terror at his own finitude, and his finitude is, in one sense, overcome.

Introduction to The Ethics of
Spinoza

Perhaps the only true dignity of man
is his capacity to despise himself.

Ibid.

Miracles are propitious accidents,
the natural causes of which are too
complicated to be readily understood.

Ibid.

The Bible is literature, not dogma.

Ibid.

O World, thou choosest not the better
  part!
  It is not wisdom to be only wise,
  And on the inward vision close the
    eyes,
But it is wisdom to believe the heart.

O World, Thou Choosest Not

Columbus found a world, and had no
  chart,
  Save one that faith deciphered in the
    skies;
  To trust the soul's invincible surmise
Was all his science and his only art.

Ibid.

Heaven is to be at peace with things;
Come chaos now, and in a whirlwind's
  rings
Engulf the planets. I have seen the best.

Sonnet 49

Old age, on tiptoe, lays her jeweled
  hand
Lightly in mine. Come, tread a stately
  measure,
Most gracious partner, nobly poised
  and bland.

A Minuet on Reaching the Age of
Fifty

ERNEST LAWRENCE THAYER
[1863–   ]

The outlook wasn't brilliant for the
  Mudville nine that day.

Casey at the Bat.[1] *Stanza 1*

There was ease in Casey's manner as he
  stepped into his place,
There was pride in Casey's bearing, and
  a smile lit Casey's face,
And when, responding to the cheers, he
  lightly doffed his hat,
No stranger in the crowd could doubt
  'twas Casey at the bat.

Ibid. Stanza 6

"Strike one," the umpire said.

Ibid. Stanza 8

From the benches dark with people
  there went up a muffled roar,
Like the beating of the storm-waves on
  a stern but distant shore.

Ibid. Stanza 9

With a smile of Christian charity great
  Casey's visage shone;
He stilled the rising tumult, he bade
  the game go on.

Ibid. Stanza 10

Oh, somewhere in this favored land the
  sun is shining bright;
The band is playing somewhere, and
  somewhere hearts are light,
And somewhere men are laughing and
  little children shout,
But there is no joy in Mudville, great
  Casey has struck out.

Ibid. Stanza 13

AMÉLIE RIVES TROUBETZKOY
[1863–   ]

Oh, my laddie, my laddie,
I lo'e your very plaidie,
I lo'e your very bonnet
Wi' the silver buckle on it.

My Laddie. Stanza 1

[1] First printed in *The San Francisco Exam-*
iner, June 3, 1888.

  Yet I'd take my chance with fame,
    Calmly let it go at that,
  With the right to sign my name
    Under "Casey at the Bat."

GRANTLAND RICE: *The Masterpiece*

SIR ROGER CASEMENT
[1864–1916]

All that was beautiful and just,
  All that was pure and sad,
Went in one little, moving plot of dust
  The world called bad.
    In the Streets of Catania. Stanza 1

It is gone from the hill and glen,
  The strong speech of our sires;
It is sunk in the mire and the fen
  Of our nameless desires.
    The Irish Language. Stanza 1

OSCAR W. FIRKINS
[1864–1932]

I should have enjoyed the country [Switzerland] more thoroughly if the poets and romancers had not corrupted my mind with their pestiferous superlatives.
    Letter [August 3, 1913] [1]

My state is contentment *within* despair.
    Letter [December 29, 1922]

The great art includes much that the small art excludes: humor, pain, and evil. Much that is repulsive when alone becomes beautiful in its relation. To find the ennobling relation is the task of life and of art.
    Lecture Notes

A classic is produced by the cooperation of the public with the author. A classic is a work which is fit to enter into permanent relations with a large section of mankind.
    Ibid.

RICHARD HOVEY
[1864–1900]

In all climes we pitch our tents,
Cronies of the elements,
With the secret lords of birth
Intimate and free.
    The Wander-lovers. Stanza 2

Comrades, pour the wine to-night
For the parting is with dawn!

[1] These quotations are from *Memoirs and Letters of O. W. Firkins,* University of Minnesota Press, 1934.

Oh, the clink of cups together,
With the daylight coming on!
    Comrades

For 'tis always fair weather
When good fellows get together
With a stein on the table and a good
  song ringing clear.
    A Stein Song. Stanza 1

The guns that spoke at Lexington
  Knew not that God was planning then
The trumpet word of Jefferson
  To bugle forth the rights of men.
    Unmanifest Destiny. Stanza 3

I do not know beneath what sky
  Nor on what seas shall be thy fate:
I only know it shall be high,
  I only know it shall be great.
    Ibid. Stanza 7

Whose furthest footstep never strayed
Beyond the village of his birth
Is but a lodger for the night
In this old wayside inn of earth.
    More Songs from Vagabondia.
    Envoy, Stanza 1

There are worser ills to face
  Than foemen in the fray;
And many a man has fought because —
  He feared to run away.
    The Marriage of Guenevere.
    Act IV, Sc. 3

I have need of the sky,
I have business with the grass;
I will up and get me away where the
  hawk is wheeling
Lone and high,
And the slow clouds go by.
I will get me away to the waters that
  glass
The clouds as they pass.
I will get me away to the woods.
    I Have Need of the Sky

MARK ANTONY DE WOLFE HOWE
[1864–   ]

The village sleeps, a name unknown, till men
  With life-blood stain its soil, and pay
  the due

That lifts it to eternal fame, — for then
'Tis grown a Gettysburg or Water-
loo.
Distinction

Not for the star-crowned heroes, the
men that conquer and slay,
But a song for those that bore them, the
mothers braver than they!
With never a blare of trumpets, with
never a surge of cheers,
They march to the unseen hazard —
pale, patient volunteers.
The Valiant

When morning broke, and day
Smiled up across the tide,
Here in the harbor safe she lay,
Her rescue by her side!
A Birthday Verse. Stanza 2

ROBERT LOVEMAN
[1864–1923]

It is not raining rain to me,
It's raining daffodils;
In every dimpled drop I see
Wild flowers on the hills.
April Rain.[1] *Stanza 1*

A health unto the happy!
A fig for him who frets! —
It is not raining rain to me,
It's raining violets.
Ibid. Stanza 4

PAUL ELMER MORE [2]
[1864–1937]

As our private memory is not a
merely passive retention of sensations,
so in literature the critical spirit is at
work as a conscious energy of selection. The function of criticism is far
removed from the surrender to luxurious revery.
Shelburne Essays. Criticism

Great music is a psychical storm,
agitating to fathomless depths the mystery of the past within us. Or we might

[1] In *Harper's Magazine, May, 1901.*
[2] To read him is to enter an austere and
elevated realm of ideas and to know a man
who, in the guise of a critic, is authentically
concerned with the first and last things of
human experience. — WALTER LIPPMANN, in
*The Saturday Review of Literature, March
15, 1930*

say that it is a prodigious incantation.
There are tones that call up all ghosts
of youth and joy and tenderness; —
there are tones that evoke all phantom
pains of perished passion; — there are
tones that revive all dead sensations of
majesty and might and glory, — all expired exultations, — all forgotten mag-
nanimities. Well may the influence of
music seem inexplicable to the man
who idly dreams that his life began
less than a hundred years ago! He who
has been initiated into the truth knows
that to every ripple of melody, to every billow of harmony, there answers
within him, out of the Sea of Death
and Birth, some eddying immeasurable
of ancient pleasure and pain.
Shelburne Essays. Lafcadio Hearn

All things are fleeting; nothing is our
own, not even this spark of life which
is owed to Death; but Oh, grant that
after our going some interposition of
human memory come between us and
utter obliteration!
Ibid. The Greek Anthology

A. EDWARD NEWTON
[1864–]

Young man, get a hobby; preferably
get two, one for indoors and one for
out; get a pair of hobby-horses that
can safely be ridden in opposite directions.
*Amenities of Book-Collecting.
Chap. 1*

I may as well confess that the envy
shown by our fellow collectors when we
display our treasures is not annoying to
us.
Ibid.

Possession is the grave of bliss. No
sooner do we own some great book than
we want another.
Ibid. Chap. 3

Only when a man is safely ensconced
under six feet of earth, with several
tons of enlauding granite upon his
chest, is he in a position to give advice
with any certainty, and then he is silent.
Ibid. Chap. 4

A good resolution is, never to be satisfied with a poor copy of a book at any price; a superlatively fine copy of a good book is always cheap.

This Book-Collecting Game.
Chap. 2

I wish that some one would give a course in how to live. It can't be taught in the colleges: that's perfectly obvious, for college professors don't know any better than the rest of us.

Ibid. Chap. 10

Gilbert White discovered the formula for complete happiness, but he died before making the announcement, leaving it for me to do so. It is to be very busy with the unimportant.

Ibid.

What a delight it is, at the end of a busy day, to throw one's self into an arm chair before a wood fire, and think. No, not think! muse is a better word. I am by no means sure that I've ever thought, and I'm not certain that I wish to; looking about me, I see thinkers, and it does not appear that they are any wiser or better or happier than I.

A Magnificent Farce. Chap. 7

From contemplation one may become wise, but knowledge comes only from study.

Ibid. Chap. 8

I read for pleasure, mark you. In general I like wedding bells at the end of novels. "They married and lived happily ever after" — why not? it has been done.

A Great Victorian

STEPHEN PHILLIPS
[1864–1915]

The moment deep
When we are conscious of the secret dawn,
Amid the darkness that we feel is green.
Marpessa

Thy face remembered is from other worlds,
It has been died for, though I know not when,

It has been sung of, though I know not where.
Marpessa

Women that remember in the night.
Ibid.

The half of music, I have heard men say,
Is to have grieved.
Ibid.

Out of our sadness have we made this world
So beautiful.
Ibid.

The constable with lifted hand
Conducting the orchestral Strand.
The Wife

O to recall!
What to recall?
Not the star in waters red,
 Not this:
Laughter of a girl that's dead,
 O this!
Lyrics. I Stanza 4

Thou shalt stand
Gazing for ever on the earth, and watch
How fast thy words incarnadine the world!
Christ in Hades

Who shall set a shore to love?
When hath it ever swerved from death, or when
Hath it not burned away all barriers,
Even dearest ties of mother and of son,
Even of brothers?
Paolo and Francesca. Act II, Sc. 1

We two rush
Together through the everlasting years.
Us, then, whose only pain can be to part,
How wilt Thou punish? For what ecstasy
Together to be blown about the globe!
What rapture in perpetual fire to burn
Together!
Ibid. Act IV

JOSEPH BERT SMILEY
[1864–1903]

Thirty years with that tongue so sharp?
Ho! Angel Gabriel! Give him a Harp!
St. Peter at the Gate (Thirty Years with a Shrew). Stanza 13

See that on finest ambrosia he feeds,
He's had about all the Hades he needs;
It isn't just hardly the thing to do
To roast him on earth and the future,
    too.
> *St. Peter at the Gate*
> *Stanza 14*

ISRAEL ZANGWILL
[1864–1926]

In how many lives does Love really play a dominant part? The average taxpayer is no more capable of a "grand passion" than of a grand opera.
> *Romeo and Juliet and Other Love*
> *Stories*

JOHN BENNETT
[1865–   ]

God made memory cruel, that men might know remorse; but the Devil devised forgetfulness, anodyne of regret.
> *Madame Margot. Page 82*

If Life's a lie, and Love's a cheat,
    As I have heard men say,
Then here's a health to fond deceit —
    God bless you, dear, to-day!
> *God Bless You, Dear, To-day.*
> *Stanza 3*

A hundred years from now, dear heart,
    We shall not care at all.
It will not matter then a whit,
    The honey or the gall.
> *In a Rose Garden. Stanza 1 [1895]*

I want men to remember,
    When gray Death sets me free,
I was a man who had many friends,
    And many friends had me.
> *I Want an Epitaph*

But, yet . . . he made a thousand
    friends.
Yes: and, by God! he kept them.
> *Ibid.*

We are all but fellow-travellers
    Along Life's weary way;
If any man can play the pipes,
    In God's name, let him play.
> *Year Book, Poetry Society of*
> *South Carolina [1921]*

MADISON JULIUS CAWEIN
[1865–1914]

Some reckon time by stars,
    And some by hours;
Some measure days by dreams, .
    And some by flowers;
My heart alone records
    My days and hours.
> *Some Reckon Time by Stars.*
> *Stanza 1*

Here is the place where Loveliness keeps
    house,
Between the river and the wooded hills.
> *Here Is the Place*

High as a star, yet lowly as a flower,
    Unknown she takes her unassuming
    place
At Earth's proud masquerade — the
    appointed hour
    Strikes, and, behold, the marvel of
    her face.
> *Beauty*

An old Spanish saying is that "a kiss without a moustache is like an egg without salt."
> *Nature-Notes. Page 119*

ROBERT WILLIAM CHAMBERS
[1865–1933]

Sez Corporal Madden to Private Mc-
    Fadden:
"Yer figger wants padd'n —
    Sure, man, ye've no shape!
Behind ye yer shoulders
Stick out like two bowlders;
Yer shins are as thin
As a pair of pen-holders!"
> *The Recruit. Stanza 3*

FRANK MOORE COLBY [1]
[1865–1925]

True satire is not the sneering substance that we know, but satire that includes the satirist.
> *Essays. Vol. 1*

---

[1] He possessed a sense of humor which for depth, comprehension, and incisiveness is unequalled in the whole range of American criticism. — JOHN ABBOT CLARK

Men will confess to treason, murder, arson, false teeth, or a wig. How many of them will own up to a lack of humor?
Essays. Vol. 1

Nobody can describe a fool to the life, without much patient self-inspection.
Ibid.

Every man ought to be inquisitive through every hour of his great adventure down to the day when he shall no longer cast a shadow in the sun. For if he dies without a question in his heart, what excuse is there for his continuance?
Ibid.

In spite of the large population of this planet, men and women remain to-day the most inaccessible things on it.
Ibid. Vol. 2

A new movement is not a stampede to some new object, but a stampede away from some old person.
Ibid.

The attempt to turn a complex problem of the head into a simple moral question for the heart to answer, is of course a necessary part of all political discussions.
Ibid.

I have found some of the best reasons I ever had for remaining at the bottom simply by looking at the men at the top.
Ibid.

A "new thinker," when studied closely, is merely a man who does not know what other people have thought.
The Margin of Hesitation

Were it not for the presence of the unwashed and the half-educated, the formless, queer and incomplete, the unreasonable and absurd, the infinite shapes of the delightful human tadpole, the horizon would not wear so wide a grin.
Imaginary Obligations

In public we say the race is to the strongest; in private we know that a lopsided man runs the fastest along the little side-hills of success.
Constrained Attitudes

Journalists have always been our most old-fashioned class, being too busy with the news of the day to lay aside the mental habits of fifty years before.
Constrained Attitudes

HOLMAN FRANCIS DAY
[1865–1935]

He pasted a sheet of postage stamps
    from snout clear down to tail,
Put on a quick delivery stamp, and
    sent the cod by mail.
Cure for Homesickness

The purest affection the heart can hold
Is the honest love of a nine-year-old.
That May-basket for Mabel Fry

If ye only knew the backaches in an
    old stun' wall!
An Old Stun' Wall

"LAURENCE HOPE"
(ADELA FLORENCE CORY NICOLSON)
[1865–1904]

Less than the dust, beneath thy Chariot
    wheel,
Less than the rust, that never stained
    thy Sword.
Less Than the Dust. Stanza 1

For this is Wisdom; to love, to live,
To take what Fate, or the Gods, may
    give.
The Teak Forest

To have, — to hold, — and, — in time,
    — let go!
Ibid.

Pale hands I loved beside the Shalimar,
    Where are you now? Who lies beneath your spell?
Whom do you lead on Rapture's roadway, far,
    Before you agonize them in farewell?
Kashmiri Song. Stanza 1

Yet I, this little while ere I go hence,
Love very lightly now, in self-defence.
Verse by Taj Mahomed

Men should be judged, not by their tint
    of skin,
    The Gods they serve, the Vintage
    that they drink,
Nor by the way they fight, or love, or
    sin,

But by the quality of thought they think.
Men Should Be Judged

Often devotion to virtue arises from sated desire.
I Arise and Go Down to the River. Stanza 6

RUDYARD KIPLING
[1865–1936]

I have eaten your bread and salt.
I have drunk your water and wine.
The deaths ye died I have watched beside
And the lives ye led were mine.
Departmental Ditties. Prelude, Stanza 1

Who shall doubt "the secret hid
Under Cheops' pyramid"
Was that the contractor did
Cheops out of several millions?
A General Summary. Stanza 4

Little Tin Gods on Wheels.
Public Waste. Stanza 4

Trust me, To-day's Most Indispensables,
Five hundred men can take your place or mine.
The Last Department. Stanza 8

The blush that flies at seventeen
Is fixed at forty-nine.
My Rival. Stanza 2

The toad beneath the harrow knows
Exactly where each tooth-point goes;
The butterfly upon the road
Preaches contentment to that toad.
Pagett, M.P.

Cross that rules the Southern Sky!
Stars that sweep, and turn, and fly,
Hear the Lovers' Litany: —
"Love like ours can never die!" [1]
The Lovers' Litany. Stanza 2

But seamen learnt — what landsmen know —
That neither gifts nor gain

Can hold a winking Light o' Love
Or Fancy's flight restrain.
The Ballad of Fisher's Boarding-House. Stanza 9

And a woman is only a woman, but a good cigar is a smoke.
The Betrothed. Stanza 25

The temper of chums, the love of your wife,[1] and a new piano's tune —
Which of the three will you trust at the end of an Indian June?
Certain Maxims of Hafiz. IV

Pleasant the snaffle of Courtship, improving the manners and carriage;
But the colt who is wise will abstain from the terrible thorn-bit of Marriage.
Ibid. XI

If She have spoken a word, remember thy lips are sealed,
And the Brand of the Dog is upon him by whom is the secret revealed.
If She have written a letter, delay not an instant but burn it.
Ibid. XV

If there be trouble to Herward, and a lie of the blackest can clear,
Lie, while thy lips can move or a man is alive to hear.
Ibid.

My Son, if a maiden deny thee and scufflingly bid thee give o'er,
Yet lip meets with lip at the lastward. Get out! She has been there before.
They are pecked on the ear and the chin and the nose who are lacking in lore.
Ibid. XVI

You'll never plumb the Oriental mind,
And if you did, it isn't worth the toil.
One Viceroy Resigns

How can I turn from any fire
On any man's hearthstone?
I know the wonder and desire
That went to build my own!
The Fires. Stanza 7

---

[1] The tender motto, writ so fair,
Upon his 'bacco box he views,
Nancy the poet, Love the muse:
"If you loves I as I loves you,
No pair so happy as we two."
CHARLES DIBDIN [1745–1814]:
The Token

[1] It is as foolish to make experiments upon the constancy of a friend, as upon the chastity of a wife. — DR. SAMUEL JOHNSON: Letter to James Boswell, Sept. 9, 1779

It may be that Fate will give me life
    and leave to row once more —
Set some strong man free for fighting
    as I take awhile his oar.
But to-day I leave the galley. Shall I
    curse her service then?
God be thanked! Whate'er comes after,
    I have lived and toiled with Men!
        The Galley-Slave. Stanza 10

I am sick of endless sunshine, sick of
    blossom-burdened bough.
Give me back the leafless woodlands
    where the winds of Springtime
    range —
Give me back one day in England, for
    it's Spring in England now!
        In Springtime. Stanza 1

They rise to their feet as He passes by,
    gentlemen unafraid.
        Barrack Room Ballads.
        Dedication, Stanza 5

He scarce had need to doff his pride or
    slough the dross of Earth —
E'en as he trod that day to God so
    walked he from his birth,
In simpleness and gentleness and hon-
    our and clean mirth.[1]
        Ibid. Stanza 7

Since spoken word Man's Spirit stirred
    Beyond his belly-need,
What is is Thine of fair design
    In Thought and Craft and Deed.
        To the True Romance. Stanza 3

It's like a book, I think, this bloomin'
    world,
Which you can read and care for just
    so long,
But presently you feel that you will die
Unless you get the page you're readin'
    done,
An' turn another — likely not so good;
But what you're after is to turn 'em all.
        Sestina of the Tramp-Royal.
        Stanza 6

And the tunes that mean so much to
    you alone —
Common tunes that make you choke
    and blow your nose,
Vulgar tunes that bring the laugh that
    brings the groan —

I can rip your very heartstrings out
    with those.
        The Song of the Banjo. Stanza 6
"Something hidden. Go and find it. Go
    and look behind the Ranges —
Something lost behind the Ranges.
    Lost and waiting for you. Go!"
        The Explorer. Stanza 2

Anybody might have found it but —
    His Whisper came to Me!
        Ibid. Stanza 18

Who hath desired the Sea? — the sight
    of salt water unbounded —
The heave and the halt and the hurl
    and the crash of the comber wind-
    hounded?
        The Sea and the Hills. Stanza 1

So and no otherwise — hillmen desire
    their Hills!
        Ibid.

Lord, send a man like Robbie Burns to
    sing the Song o' Steam!
        M'Andrew's Hymn

Interdependence absolute, foreseen, or-
    dained, decreed,
To work, ye'll note, at any tilt an' every
    rate o' speed.
        Ibid.

But I ha' lived an' I ha' worked. Be
    thanks to Thee, Most High!
An' I ha' done what I ha' done — judge
    Thou if ill or well.
        Ibid.

Absolute, unvarying rigidity, rigidity!
        The Ship that Found Herself

They copied all they could follow, but
    they couldn't copy my mind.
        The "Mary Gloster"

Overloaded, undermanned, meant to
    founder, we
Euchred God Almighty's storm, bluffed
    the Eternal Sea!
        The Ballad of the "Bolivar."
        Stanza 12

King Solomon drew merchantmen
    Because of his desire
For peacocks, apes, and ivory,
    From Tarshish unto Tyre.[1]
        The Merchantmen. Stanza 1

[1] Wolcott Balestier [1861–1891], Mrs. Kipling's brother.

[1] See Masefield, page 832.

The God of Fair Beginnings
  Hath prospered here my hand —
The cargoes of my lading,
  And the keels of my command.
            The Song of Diego Valdez.
                        Stanza 1
The Liner she's a lady, and if a war
  should come,
The Man-o'-War's 'er 'usband, and 'e'd
  bid 'er stay at home;
But, oh, the little cargo-boats that fill
  with every tide!
'E'd 'ave to up an' fight for them for
  they are England's pride.
      The Liner She's a Lady. Stanza 5
And it's time to turn on the old trail,
  our own trail, the out trail,
Pull out, pull out, on the Long Trail —
  the trail that is always new!
            The Long Trail. Stanza 1
There be triple ways to take, of the
  eagle or the snake,
Or the way of a man with a maid; [1]
But the sweetest way to me is a ship's
  upon the sea
In the heel of the North-East Trade.
                Ibid. Stanza 4
We have fed our sea for a thousand
  years
  And she calls us, still unfed,
Though there's never a wave of all her
  waves
  But marks our English dead.
      The Song of the Dead. II, Stanza 1
If blood be the price of admiralty,
  Lord God, we ha' paid in full!
                        Ibid.
Deeper than speech our love, stronger
  than life our tether,
But we do not fall on the neck nor kiss
  when we come together.
                England's Answer
So long as The Blood endures,
I shall know that your good is mine: ye
  shall feel that my strength is
  yours:
In the day of Armageddon, at the last
  great fight of all,
That Our House stand together and
  the pillars do not fall.
                        Ibid.

[1] See *Proverbs, XXX, 18 and 19.*

Go to your work and be strong, halting
  not in your ways,
Baulking the end half-won for an in-
  stant dole of praise.
Stand to your work and be wise — cer-
  tain of sword and pen,
Who are neither children nor God, but
  men in a world of men!
                England's Answer
Ever the wide world over, lass,
  Ever the trail held true,
Over the world and under the world,
  And back at the last to you.
            The Gipsy Trail. Stanza 2
The wild hawk to the wind-swept sky,
  The deer to the wholesome wold
And the heart of a man to the heart of
  a maid,
  As it was in the days of old.
                Ibid. Stanza 11
Daughter am I in my mother's house;
  But mistress in my own.
        Our Lady of the Snows.[1] *Stanza 1*
Enslaved, illogical, elate,
  He greets the embarrassed Gods, nor
  fears
To shake the iron hand of Fate
  Or match with Destiny for beers.
            An American. Stanza 13
Buy my English posies!
  Kent and Surrey may —
Violets of the Undercliff
  Wet with Channel spray;
Cowslips from a Devon combe —
  Midland furze afire.
                The Flowers. Stanza 1
They change their skies above them,
  But not their hearts that roam.
            The Native-born. Stanza 2
Last toast — and your foot on the
  table! —
A health to the Native-born!
                Ibid. Stanza 11
There's a Legion that never was 'listed,
  That carries no colours or crest.
            The Lost Legion. Stanza 1
Old Days! The wild geese are flighting,
  Head to the storm as they faced it
  before!
For where there are Irish there's loving
  and fighting,

[1] The Dominion of Canada.

And when we stop either, it's Ireland
no more!

The Irish Guards. Stanza 4

And he wrote for them wonderful verses
that swept the land like flame,
Till the fatted souls of the English were
scourged with the thing called
Shame.

The Last of the Light Brigade.
Stanza 8

God gives all men all earth to love,
But since man's heart is small,
Ordains for each one spot shall prove
Belovèd over all.

Sussex. Stanza 12

A fool there was and he made his prayer
(Even as you and I!)
To a rag and a bone and a hank of hair
(We called her the woman who did not
care)
But the fool he called her his lady
fair —
(Even as you and I!)

The Vampire. Stanza 1

Oh, the years we waste and the tears
we waste
And the work of our head and hand
Belong to the woman who did not
know . . .
And did not understand.

Ibid. Stanza 2

When Earth's last picture is painted,
and the tubes are twisted and
dried,
When the oldest colours have faded,
and the youngest critic has died,
We shall rest, and, faith, we shall need
it — lie down for an æon or two,
Till the Master of All Good Workmen
shall put us to work anew.

When Earth's Last Picture Is
Painted. Stanza 1

And only the Master shall praise us,
and only the Master shall blame;
And no one shall work for money, and
no one shall work for fame;
But each for the joy of the working,
and each, in his separate star,
Shall draw the Thing as he sees It for
the God of Things as They Are!

Ibid. Stanza 3

Oh, East is East, and West is West, and
never the twain shall meet,
Till Earth and Sky stand presently at
God's great Judgment Seat.
But there is neither East nor West, Border, nor Breed, nor Birth,
When two strong men stand face to
face, though they come from the
ends of the earth!

The Ballad of East and West

Send the road is clear before you when
old Spring-fret comes o'er you,
And the Red Gods call for you!

The Feet of the Young Men

Make ye no truce with Adam-zad —
the Bear that walks like a Man!

The Truce of the Bear. Stanza 2

The Goth and the shameless Hun!

The Rowers. Stanza 11

Cock the gun that is not loaded, cook
the frozen dynamite —
But oh, beware my Country, when my
Country grows polite!

Et Dona Ferentes. Stanza 11

A Tinker out of Bedford,
A vagrant oft in quod,
A private under Fairfax,
A minister of God, —
Two hundred years and thirty
Ere Armageddon came
His single hand portrayed it,
And Bunyan was his name!

The Holy War. Stanza 1

Broke to every known mischance, lifted
over all
By the light sane joy of life, the buckler
of the Gaul;
Furious in luxury, merciless in toil.

France [1913]

Strictest judge of her own worth, gentlest of man's mind,
First to face the Truth and last to leave
old Truths behind —
France, beloved of every soul that loves
or serves its kind!

Ibid.

All we have of freedom, all we use or
know —
This our fathers bought for us long and
long ago.

The Old Issue. Stanza 5

Ancient Right unnoticed as the breath
    we draw —
Leave to live by no man's leave, under-
    neath the law.
                    The Old Issue. Stanza 6
We have had a jolly good lesson, and it
    serves us jolly well right!
                    The Lesson [*1902*]. *Stanza 2*
We have forty million reasons for fail-
    ure, but not a single excuse.
                    Ibid. Stanza 8
With the flannelled fools at the wicket
    or the muddied oafs at the goals.
                    The Islanders [*1902*]
No doubt but ye are the People — ab-
    solute, strong, and wise;
Whatever your heart has desired ye
    have not withheld from your eyes.
On your own heads, in your own hands,
    the sin and the saving lies!
                    Ibid.
Creation's cry goes up on high
    From age to cheated age:
"Send us the men who do the work
    For which they draw the wage!"
                    The Wage-Slaves. Stanza 3
This is our lot if we live so long and
    labour unto the end —
That we outlive the impatient years
    and the much too patient friend:
And because we know we have breath
    in our mouth and think we have
    thoughts in our head,
We shall assume that we are alive,
    whereas we are really dead.
                    The Old Men. Stanza 1
Take up the White Man's burden.
                    The White Man's Burden.
                    Stanza 1
The tumult and the shouting dies;
    The Captains and the Kings depart:
Still stands Thine ancient sacrifice,
    An humble and a contrite heart.
                    Recessional. Stanza 2
Lest we forget — lest we forget! [1]
                    Ibid.

---

[1]   Best by remembering God, say some,
        We keep our high imperial lot.
    Fortune, I fear, hath oftenest come
        When we forgot — when we forgot.
                    SIR WILLIAM WATSON:
                    The Unknown God, St. 10

Lo, all our pomp of yesterday
    Is one with Nineveh and Tyre!
                    Recessional. Stanza 3
But, spite all modern notions, I've
    found her first and best —
The only certain packet for the Islands
    of the Blest.
                    The Three-Decker. Stanza 1
One was Admiral of the North from
    Solway Firth to Skye,
And one was Lord of the Wessex Coast
    and all the lands thereby,
And one was Master of the Thames
    from Limehouse to Blackwall,
And he was Chaplain of the Fleet —
    the bravest of them all.
                    The Rhyme of the Three Captains
                    [*1890*] [1]
The Devil whispered behind the leaves,
    "It's pretty, but is it Art?"
                    The Conundrum of the Workshops
Ah! what avails the classic bent
    And what the cultured word,
Against the undoctored incident
    That actually occurred?
                    The Benefactors. Stanza 1
It is not learning, grace nor gear,
    Nor easy meat and drink,
But bitter pinch of pain and fear
    That makes creation think.
                    Ibid. Stanza 3
There are nine and sixty ways of con-
    structing tribal lays,
And every single one of them is right.
                    In the Neolithic Age. Stanza 5
You must hack through much deposit
Ere you know for sure who was it
Came to burial with such honour in the
    Files
(Only seven seasons back beneath the
    Files).
"Very great our loss and grievous —
So our best and brightest leave us,
And it ends the Age of Giants," say
    the Files.
                    The Files
When your Imp of Blind Desire
Bids you set the Thames afire,

---

[1] William Black, Thomas Hardy, Walter
Besant. The poem is an elaborate satire on the
lack of copyright protection in the United
States at that time.

You'll remember men have done so —
in the Files.

The Files

And the naked soul of Tomlinson grew
white as a rain-washed bone.

Tomlinson

The sin they do by two and two they
must pay for one by one.

Ibid.

Those who have passed to the further
shore
May be hailed — at a price — on the
road to En-dor.[1]

En-Dor. Stanza 2

The female of the species is more
deadly than the male.

*The Female of the Species.
Stanza 1*

For as we come and as we go (and
deadly-soon go we!)
The people, Lord, Thy people, are
good enough for me!

A Pilgrim's Way. Stanza 1

And when they bore me overmuch, I
will not shake mine ears,
Recalling many thousand such whom I
have bored to tears.
And when they labour to impress, I will
not doubt nor scoff;
Since I myself have done no less and
— sometimes pulled it off.

Ibid. Stanza 3

"Goodbye, Romance" . . . and all unseen
Romance brought up the nine-fifteen.

The King

The Sons of Mary seldom bother, for
they have inherited that good
part;
But the Sons of Martha favour their
Mother of the careful soul and the
troubled heart.[2]

The Sons of Martha. Stanza 1

It is their care in all the ages to take
the buffet and cushion the shock.
It is their care that the gear engages; it
is their care that the switches lock.

Ibid. Stanza 2

Raise ye the stone or cleave the wood [1]
to make a path more fair or flat;
Lo, it is black already with blood some
Son of Martha spilled for that!
Not as a ladder from Earth to Heaven,
not as a witness to any creed,
But simple service simply given to his
own kind in their common need.

The Sons of Martha. Stanza 7

They have cast their burden upon the
Lord, — and the Lord He lays it
on Martha's Sons!

Ibid. Stanza 8

My son was killed while laughing at
some jest. I would I knew
What it was, and it might serve me in
a time when jests are few.

Epitaphs of the War. A Son

They've taken of his buttons off an' cut
his stripes away,
An' they're hangin' Danny Deever in
the mornin'.

Danny Deever. Stanza 5

We aren't no thin red 'eroes.[2]

Tommy. Stanza 4

Single men in barricks don't grow into
plaster saints.

Ibid.

It's Tommy this, an' Tommy that, an'
"Chuck 'im out, the brute!"
But it's "Savior of 'is country," when
the guns begin to shoot.

Ibid. Stanza 5

So 'ere's *to* you, Fuzzy-Wuzzy, at your
'ome in the Soudan;
You're a pore benighted 'eathen but a
first-class fightin' man.

"Fuzzy-Wuzzy." Stanza 1

'E's all 'ot sand an' ginger when alive,
An' 'e's generally shammin' when 'e's
dead.

Ibid. Stanza 4

Though I've belted you and flayed you,
By the livin' Gawd that made you,
You're a better man than I am, Gunga
Din!

Gunga Din. Stanza 5

---

[1] Behold there is a woman that hath a familiar spirit at En-dor.— *1 Samuel, XXVIII, 7*
[2] Martha, thou art careful and troubled
about many things. — *Luke, X, 41*

[1] See Henry van Dyke, page 709.
[2] See Russell, page 541.

'Ave you 'eard o' the Widow at Windsor
  With a hairy gold crown on 'er 'ead?
      The Widow at Windsor. Stanza 1

Walk wide o' the Widow at Windsor,
  For 'alf o' Creation she owns:
We 'ave bought 'er the same with the sword an' the flame,
  An' we've salted it down with our bones!
      Ibid. Stanza 2

On the road to Mandalay,
Where the flyin'-fishes play,
An' the dawn comes up like thunder outer China 'crost the Bay!
      Mandalay. Stanza 1

I've a neater, sweeter maiden in a cleaner, greener land.
      Ibid. Stanza 5

Ship me somewheres east of Suez, where the best is like the worst,
Where there aren't no Ten Commandments an' a man can raise a thirst.
      Ibid. Stanza 6

Back to the Army again, sergeant,
  Back to the Army again.
Out o' the cold an' the rain.
      "Back to the Army Again."
      Refrain

For there isn't a job on the top of the earth the beggar don't know, nor do.
      "Soldier an' Sailor Too." Stanza 2

'E's a sort of a bloomin' cosmopolouse — soldier an' sailor too.
      Ibid.

To stand an' be still to the Birken'ead drill [1] is a damn' tough bullet to chew.
      Ibid. Stanza 5

I've taken my fun where I've found it.
      The Ladies. Stanza 1

An' I learned about women from 'er.
      Ibid. Refrain

For the Colonel's Lady an' Judy O'Grady
Are sisters under their skins!
      Ibid. Stanza 8

We met upon the level an' we parted on the Square,

[1] See F. H. Doyle, page 475.

An' I was Junior Deacon in my Mother-Lodge out there!
      The Mother-Lodge. Refrain

The backbone of the Army is the Non-commissioned Man!
      The 'Eathen. Stanza 18

For to admire an' for to see,
For to be'old this world so wide —
It never done no good to me
But I can't drop it if I tried!
      "For to Admire." Refrain

He's an absent-minded beggar, but he heard his country's call,
And his reg'ment didn't need to send to find him!
      The Absent-minded Beggar.
      Stanza 3

A kopje is always a kopje,
And a Boojer is always a Boer!
      Two Kopjes. Stanza 2

Boots — boots — boots — boots — movin' up and down again!
There's no discharge in the war! [1]
      Boots. Stanza 1

The bachelor may risk 'is 'ide
  To 'elp you when you're downed;
But the married man will wait beside
  Till the ambulance comes round.
      The Married Man. Stanza 5

The married man must sink or swim
An' — 'e can't afford to sink!
      Ibid. Stanza 7

If England was what England seems,
An' not the England of our dreams,
But only putty, brass, an' paint,
'Ow quick we'd drop 'er! But she ain't.
      The Return. Refrain

Of all the trees that grow so fair,
  Old England to adorn,
Greater are none beneath the Sun,
  Than Oak, and Ash, and Thorn. [2]
      A Tree Song. Stanza 1

Take of English earth as much
As either hand may rightly clutch.
In the taking of it breathe
Prayer for all who lie beneath.
      A Charm. Stanza 1

[1] There is no discharge in that war. — *Ecclesiastes, VIII, 8*

[2] Glasgerion swore a full great othe,
  By oake, and ashe, and thorne.
    PERCY: *Reliques, Glasgerion, St. 19*

Ride with an idle whip, ride with an
    unused heel,
But, once in a way, there will come a
    day
When the colt must be taught to feel
The lash that falls, and the curb that
    galls, and the sting of the row-
    elled steel.
        *The Conversion of Aurelian
                McGoggin*
If there be good in that I wrought
Thy Hand compelled it, Master, Thine.
    "My New-cut Ashlar." Stanza 2
One stone the more swings into place
In that dread Temple of Thy worth.
It is enough that, through Thy Grace,
I saw nought common on Thy Earth.
              Ibid. Stanza 6
Help me to need no aid from men
That I may help such men as need!
              Ibid. Stanza 7
One man in a thousand, Solomon says,
Will stick more close than a brother.
    The Thousandth Man. Stanza 1
But the Thousandth Man will stand by
    your side
To the gallows-foot — and after!
              Ibid. Stanza 4
Down to Gehenna or up to the Throne,
He travels the fastest who travels alone.
        The Winners. Stanza 1
King over all the children of pride
Is the Press.
        The Press. Stanza 5
The end of the fight is a tombstone
    white with the name of the late de-
    ceased,
And the epitaph drear: "A Fool lies
    here who tried to hustle the East."
        The Naulahka. Chap. 5
"Let us now praise famous men" — [1]
Men of little showing —
For their work continueth,
Broad and deep continueth,
Greater than their knowing.
        A School Song. Stanza 1
When Pack meets with Pack in the
    Jungle, and neither will go from
    the trail,

[1] Let us now praise famous men. — *Apocrypha, Ecclesiasticus, XLIV, 1*

Lie down till the leaders have spoken
    — it may be fair words shall pre-
    vail.
    The Law of the Jungle. Stanza 6
Now these are the Laws of the Jungle,
    and many and mighty are they;
But the head and the hoof of the Law
    and the haunch and the hump is
    — Obey!
             Ibid. Refrain
Anything green that grew out of the
    mould
Was an excellent herb to our fathers of
    Old.
    "Our Fathers of Old." Stanza 1
Wonderful little our fathers knew,
Half their remedies cured you dead —
Most of their teaching was quite un-
    true.
              Ibid. Stanza 3
By — they are by with mirth and tears,
Wit or the works of Desire —
Cushioned about on the kindly years
Between the wall and the fire.
    "Our Fathers Also." Stanza 2
Land of our Birth, we pledge to thee
Our love and toil in the years to be.
    The Children's Song. Stanza 1
Teach us Delight in simple things,
And Mirth that has no bitter springs.
              Ibid. Stanza 7
If you can meet with Triumph and
    Disaster
    And treat those two impostors just
    the same.
              If. Stanza 2
If you can talk with crowds and keep
    your virtue,
    Or walk with Kings — nor lose the
    common touch.
              Ibid. Stanza 4
Yours is the Earth and everything that's
    in it,
    And — which is more — you'll be a
    Man, my son!
              Ibid.
And thrones on Shrieking Circumstance
The Sacredly Absurd.
    The Necessitarian. Stanza 3
When the body that lived at your single
    will,
With its whimper of welcome, is stilled
    (how still!)

When the spirit that answered your every mood
Is gone — wherever it goes — for good,
You will discover how much you care,
And will give your heart to a dog to tear.
>> *The Power of the Dog. Stanza 4*

The arrows of our anguish
Fly farther than we guess.
>> *The Rabbi's Song. Stanza 3*

I keep six honest serving-men
(They taught me all I knew);
Their names are What and Why and When
And How and Where and Who.
>> *The Elephant's Child. Stanza 1*

I'd love to roll to Rio
Some day before I'm old!
>> *The Beginning of the Armadilloes.*
>> *Stanza 4*

When the ship goes *wop* (with a wiggle between)
And the steward falls into the souptureen. . . .
Why, then you will know (if you haven't guessed)
You're "Fifty North and Forty West!"
>> *How the Whale Got His Throat*

We must go back with Policeman Day —
Back from the City of Sleep!
>> *The City of Sleep. Stanza 1*

Until thy feet have trod the Road
Advise not wayside folk.
>> *The Comforters. Stanza 1*

Roses red and roses white
Plucked I for my love's delight.
She would none of all my posies —
Bade me gather her blue roses.
>> *Blue Roses. Stanza 1*

Lo, I have wrought in common clay
Rude figures of a rough-hewn race.
>> *Soldiers Three. Dedication,*
>> *Stanza 2*

If I were damned of body and soul,
I know whose prayers would make me whole,
>> Mother o' mine.
>> *Mother o' Mine*

Them that asks no questions isn't told a lie.
>> *A Smuggler's Song. Stanza 6*

When the robust and Brass-bound Man
commissioned first for sea
His fragile raft, Poseidon laughed, and
"Mariner," said he . . .
"You the unhoodwinked wave shall test
— the immediate gulf condemn —
Except ye owe the Fates a jest, be slow
to jest with them."
>> *Poseidon's Law*

If once you have paid him the Danegeld
You never get rid of the Dane.
>> *Danegeld. Stanza 4*

Far — oh, very far behind,
So far she cannot call to him,
Comes Tegumai alone to find
The daughter that was all to him.
>> *Merrow Down. Stanza 11*

Say "we," "us" and "ours" when you're
talking instead of "you fellows"
and "I."
>> *Norman and Saxon. Stanza 6*

At Runnymede, at Runnymede,
What say the reeds at Runnymede?
>> *The Reeds of Runnymede.*
>> *Stanza 1*

When Crew and Captain understand
each other to the core,
It takes a gale and more than a gale to
put their ship ashore.
>> *Together. Stanza 2*

The snow lies thick on Valley Forge,
The ice on the Delaware,
But the poor dead soldiers of King George
They neither know nor care.
>> *The American Rebellion. II, After,*
>> *Stanza 1*

If you're off to Philadelphia in the morning,
You mustn't take my stories for a guide.
There's little left, indeed, of the city you will read of,
And all the folk I write about have died.
>> *Philadelphia. Stanza 1*

When 'Omer smote 'is blooming lyre,
He'd 'eard men sing by land an' sea;
An' what he thought 'e might require,
'E went an' took — the same as me!
>> *When 'Omer Smote 'is Bloomin'*
>> *Lyre. Stanza 1*

Our England is a garden, and such gar-
dens are not made
By singing: — "Oh, how beautiful!"
and sitting in the shade.
The Glory of the Garden. Stanza 5
Oh, Adam was a gardener, and God
who made him sees
That half a proper gardener's work is
done upon his knees.
Ibid. Stanza 8
Our realm is diminished
With Great-Heart away.
*Great-Heart (Theodore
Roosevelt). Stanza 1*
Zogbaum draws with a pencil,[1]
And I do things with a pen,
And you sit up in a conning tower
Bossing eight hundred men.
Inscription to Robley D. Evans
As I pass through my incarnations in
every age and race,
I make my proper prostrations to the
gods of the Market Place;
Peering through reverent fingers, I
watch them flourish and fall,
And the Gods of the Copybook Max-
ims, I notice, outlast them all.
*The Gods of the Copybook
Maxims. Stanza 1*
Master, this is Thy Servant.
He is rising eight weeks old.
He is mainly Head and Tummy.
His legs are uncontrolled.
His Apologies [Scottish terrier]
There rise her timeless capitals of em-
pires daily born,
Whose plinths are laid at midnight and
whose streets are packed at morn;
And here come tired youths and maids
that feign to love or sin
In tones like rusty razor blades to tunes
like smitten tin.
Naaman's Song [2]
It takes a great deal of Christianity
to wipe out uncivilized Eastern in-
stincts, such as falling in love at first
sight.
Plain Tales. Lispeth

After marriage arrives a reaction,
sometimes a big, sometimes a little,
one; but it comes sooner or later, and
must be tided over by both parties if
they desire the rest of their lives to go
with the current.
Plain Tales. Three and — an Extra
But that is another story.[1]
Ibid.
This is worth remembering. Speaking to, or crying over, a husband never
did any good yet.
Ibid.
A woman's guess is much more accurate than a man's certainty.
Ibid.
The silliest woman can manage a
clever man; but it needs a very clever
woman to manage a fool!
Ibid.
Never praise a sister to a sister, in
the hope of your compliments reaching
the proper ears.
Ibid. False Dawn
If you hit a pony over the nose at
the outset of your acquaintance, he may
not love you, but he will take a deep
interest in your movements ever after-
wards.
Ibid.
Meddling with another man's folly is
always thankless work.
Ibid. The Rescue of Pluffles
Many religious people are deeply
suspicious. They seem — for purely re-
ligious purposes, of course — to know
more about iniquity than the Unregen-
erate.
Ibid. Watches of the Night
She was as immutable as the Hills.
But not quite so green.
Ibid. Venus Annodomini
Youth had been a habit of hers for
so long, that she could not part with it.
Ibid.
Every one is more or less mad on one
point.[2]
*Ibid. On the Strength of a
Likeness*

[1] Rufus Fairchild Zogbaum [1849–1925],
artist and author.
[2] Interpreted as a description of Hollywood,
California.

[1] See Sterne, page 241.
[2] Semel insanivimus omnes (We have all
once been mad). — Latin proverb; attributed
to Virgil

Little Friend of All the World.
                    Kim. Chap. 1

The first proof a man gives of his interest in a woman is by talking to her about his own sweet self. If the woman listens without yawning, he begins to like her. If she flatters the animal's vanity, he ends by adoring her.
        Under the Deodars. The Education
                    of Otis Yeere

He wrapped himself in quotations [1] — as a beggar would enfold himself in the purple of Emperors.
        Many Inventions. The Finest
                    Story in the World

Man that is born of woman is small potatoes and few in a hill.
        Life's Handicap. The Head of the
                    District

I hold by the Ould Church, for she's the mother of them all — ay, an' the father, too. I like her bekase she's most remarkable regimental in her fittings. I may die in Honolulu, Nova Zambra, or Cape Cayenne, but wherever I die, me bein' fwhat I am, an' a priest handy, I go under the same orders an' the same words an' the same unction as tho' the pope himself come down from the dome av St. Peter's to see me off. There's neither high nor low, nor broad nor deep, nor betwixt nor between with her, an' that's what I like.
        Mine Own People. On Greenhow
                    Hill

More men are killed by overwork than the importance of the world justifies.
        The Phantom 'Rickshaw

For all we take we must pay, but the price is cruel high.
        The Courting of Dinah Shadd.
                    Chap. 1

Never show a woman that ye care the snap av a finger for her, an' begad she'll come bleatin' to your boot heels.
        Ibid. Chap. 2

As the day wears and the impetus of the morning dies away, there will come upon you an overwhelming sense of the uselessness of your toil. This must be striven against.
        The Judgment of Dungara

There aren't twelve hundred people in the world who understand pictures. The others pretend and don't care.
        The Light That Failed. Chap. 7

"What did the Governor of North Carolina say to the Governor of South Carolina?"
"Excellent notion. It *is* a long time between drinks." [1]
        Ibid. Chap. 8

'Tisn't beauty, so to speak, nor good talk necessarily. It's just It.
        Traffics and Discoveries.
                    Mrs. Bathurst

He who rebukes the world is rebuked by the world.
        Second Jungle Book.
                    The Undertakers

He had been, as the old law recommends, twenty years a youth, twenty years a fighter, though he had never carried a weapon in his life, and twenty years head of a household.
        Ibid. Miracle of Purun Bhagat

Hot and bothered.
        Independence [2]

If you have not your own rations you must feed out of your Tribe's hands — with all that that implies.
        Ibid.

---

[1] Of the several traditions relating to the origin of this remark, the most reasonable one traces it to John Motley Morehead [1796–1866], who was Governor of North Carolina 1841–1845. He was visited by James H. Hammond [1807–1864], who was Governor of South Carolina 1842–1844. They engaged in discussion and argument, and when the latter waxed hot, Governor Morehead was reported by a servant to have exclaimed: "It's a long time between drinks." — Personal letter from John Motley Morehead, Nov. 21, 1934

Do you know what the Governor of South Carolina said to the Governor of North Carolina? It's a long time between drinks, observed that powerful thinker. — R. L. Stevenson: *The Wrong Box, Chap. 8*
[2] Rectorial Address, St. Andrews, Oct. 10, 1923.

---

[1] In literature quotation is good only when the writer whom I follow goes my way, and, being better mounted than I, gives me a cast. — R. W. Emerson: *Quotation and Originality*

A man may be festooned with the whole haberdashery of success, and go to his grave a castaway.

Independence

Enough work to do, and strength enough to do the work.

A Doctor's Work [1]

That packet of assorted miseries which we call a Ship.

The First Sailor

For what there is of it — for such as it is — and for what it may be worth — will you drink to England and the English?

St. George's Day Dinner, 1920

An imperfectly denatured animal intermittently subject to the unpredictable reactions of an unlocated spiritual area.

Surgeons and The Soul [1923]. *(Definition of man)*

This new ship here, is fitted according to the reported increase of knowledge among mankind. Namely, she is cumbered, end to end, with bells and trumpets and clocks and wires which, it has been told to me, can call Voices out of the air or the waters to con the ship while her crew sleep. But sleep *Thou* lightly, O Nakhoda! [Captain]. It has not yet been told to me that the Sea has ceased to be the Sea.

Foreword to the Publisher [1935]

When your Daemon is in charge, do not try to think consciously. Drift, wait, and obey.

Something of Myself. Chap. 8 (Posthumous autobiography, 1937)

LOGAN PEARSALL SMITH
[1865–   ]

I rang the bell as of old; as of old I gazed at the great shining Door and waited. But, alas! that flutter and beat of the wild heart, that delicious Doorstep Terror — it was gone; and with it dear, fantastic, panic-stricken Youth

[1] Address, Oct., 1908, at Middlesex Hospital (where Kipling died in 1936).

had rung the bell, flitted around the corner and vanished for ever.

Trivia. On the Doorstep

'For the Pen,' said the Vicar; and in the sententious pause which followed I felt that I would offer any gifts of gold to avert or postpone the solemn, inevitable, and yet, as it seemed to me, perfectly appalling statement that 'the Pen is mightier than the Sword.'

Ibid. In Church

What a bore it is, waking up in the morning always the same person. I wish I were unflinching and emphatic, and had big, bushy eyebrows and a Message for the Age. I wish I were a deep Thinker, or a great Ventriloquist.

Ibid. Green Ivory

Enshrined in a box of white pasteboard I keep upstairs a black ceremonial object: it's my last link with Christendom and grave Custom: only on sacred occasions does it make its appearance, only at some great tribal dance of my race. To pageants of Woe I march with it, or of the hugest Felicity: at great Hallelujahs of Wedlock, or at last Valedictions, I hold it bareheaded as I bow before altars and tombs.

Ibid. The Fetish

But when in modern books, reviews, and thoughtful magazines I read about the Needs of the Age, its Complex Questions, its Dismays, Doubts, and Spiritual Agonies, I feel an impulse to go out and comfort that bewildered Epoch, to wipe away its tears, still its cries, and speak edifying words of Consolation to it.

Ibid. My Mission

And as at night I went past the Abbey, saw its walls towering high and solemn among the Autumn stars, I pictured to myself the white population in the vast darkness of its interior — all that hushed people of Heroes — ; not dead, I would think them, but animated with a still kind of life, and at last, after all their intolerable toils, the sounding tumult of battle, and perilous sea-paths, resting there, tranquil and satisfied and glorious, amid the epitaphs and allegorical figures of their tombs; — those high-piled, trophied, shapeless Abbey tombs, that long ago they toiled for, and laid down their gallant lives to win.

Trivia. The Abbey at Night

There are two things to aim at in life: first, to get what you want; and, after that, to enjoy it. Only the wisest of mankind achieve the second.

Afterthoughts [*1931*]

Happiness is a wine of the rarest vintage, and seems insipid to a vulgar taste.

Ibid.

How awful to reflect that what people say of us is true!

Ibid.

Solvency is entirely a matter of temperament and not of income.

Ibid.

That we should practise what we preach is generally admitted; but anyone who preaches what he and his hearers practise must incur the gravest moral disapprobation.

Ibid.

It is almost always worth while to be cheated; people's little frauds have an interest which more than repays what they cost us.

Ibid.

'Well, for my part,' they say, 'I cannot see the charm of Mrs. Jones.'
'Is it not just conceivable,' I feel inclined to answer, 'that Mrs. Jones hasn't tried to charm you?'

Ibid.

Why are happy people not afraid of Death, while the insatiable and the unhappy so abhor that grim feature?

Ibid.

When they come downstairs from their Ivory Towers, Idealists are apt to walk straight into the gutter.

Ibid.

The indefatigable pursuit of an unattainable Perfection, even though it consist in nothing more than in the pounding of an old piano, is what alone gives a meaning to our life on this unavailing star.

Ibid.

Eat with the Rich, but go to the play with the Poor, who are capable of Joy.

Afterthoughts [*1931*]

We need new friends; some of us are cannibals who have eaten their old friends up: others must have ever-renewed audiences before whom to re-enact an ideal version of their lives.

Ibid.

A best-seller is the gilded tomb of a mediocre talent.

Ibid.

What I like in a good author is not what he says, but what he whispers.

Ibid.

People say that life is the thing, but I prefer reading.

Ibid.

Most of all I envy the octogenarian poet [1] who joined three words —
'Go, lovely Rose' —
so happily together, that he left his name to float down through Time on the wings of a phrase and a flower.

Ibid.

Thank heavens, the sun has gone in, and I don't have to go out and enjoy it.

Ibid.

What with its crude awakenings can youth know of the rich returns of awareness to elderly people from their afternoon naps; of their ironic thoughts and long retrospections, and the sweetness they taste of not being dead?

Ibid.

How I should like to distil my disesteem of my contemporaries into prose so perfect that all of them would have to read it!

Ibid.

Unsaleability is almost the hallmark, in modern times, of quality in writing . . . the enormous and half-educated publics of present-day England and America, though welcoming the novels of our famous novelists, have as a rule acclaimed as masterpieces books that were soon forgotten, while ignoring at first all that was exquisite and rare.

Fine Writing

[1] Edmund Waller [1606–1687]. See page 146.

ARTHUR SYMONS
[1865–   ]

And I would have, now love is over,
  An end to all, an end:
I cannot, having been your lover,
  Stoop to become your friend!
            After Love. Stanza 3

As a perfume doth remain
In the folds where it hath lain,
So the thought of you, remaining
Deeply folded in my brain,
Will not leave me: all things leave me:
You remain.
            Memory. Stanza 1

Life is a dream in the night, a fear
  among fears,
A naked runner lost in a storm of spears.
      In the Wood of Finvara. Stanza 1

Saint Anthony of Padua, whom I bear
In effigy about me, hear my prayer:
Kind saint who findest what is lost, I
  pray,
Bring back her heart: I lost it yester-
  day.
      A Prayer to Saint Anthony of
                    Padua

Out of the eternal bronze and mortal
  breath,
  And to the glory of man, me Rodin
    wrought;
Before the gates of glory and of death
  I bear the burden of the pride of
    thought.
      For Le Penseur of Rodin [1905]

He knew that the whole mystery of
beauty can never be comprehended by
the crowd, and that while clearness is
a virtue of style, perfect explicitness is
not a necessary virtue.
      The Symbolist Movement in
      Literature. Gérard de Nerval

Without charm there can be no fine
literature, as there can be no perfect
flower without fragrance.
      Ibid. Stéphane Mallarmé

The mystic too full of God to speak
intelligibly to the world.
      Ibid. Arthur Rimbaud

Many excellent writers, very many
painters, and most musicians are so tedious on any subject but their own.
      Ibid.

I have ever held that the rod with
which popular fancy invests criticism
is properly the rod of divination: a
hazel-switch for the discovery of buried
treasure, not a birch-twig for the casti-
gation of offenders.
      An Introduction to the Study of
      Browning. Preface, first edition

HERBERT TRENCH
[1865–1923]

A circumnavigator of the soul.
      Shakespeare. Stanza 4

Last: if upon the cold green mantling
  sea
  Thou cling, alone with Truth, to the
    last spar —
  Both castaway,
And one must perish — let it not be he
  Whom thou art sworn to obey!
      A Charge. Stanza 4

JOHN E. WOODROW
[? –1905]

The Church should have a tapering
  spire,
To point to realms where sin's forgiven,
And lead men's thoughts from earth to
  heaven.
      Spire and Tower

  I like a tower,
It speaks of strength, of might, of
  power —
An emblem of the Church's strength
To overcome the world at length.
      Ibid.

WILLIAM BUTLER YEATS
[1865–   ]

The land of faery,
Where nobody gets old and godly and
  grave,
Where nobody gets old and crafty and
  wise,
Where nobody gets old and bitter of
  tongue.
      The Land of Heart's Desire

When we are young
We long to tread a way none trod before,

But find the excellent old way through love
And through the care of children to the hour
For bidding Fate and Time and Change good-bye.
The Land of Heart's Desire

I would mould a world of fire and dew
With no one bitter, grave, or over wise,
And nothing marred or old to do you wrong.
Ibid.

Land of Heart's Desire,
Where beauty has no ebb, decay no flood,
But joy is wisdom, Time an endless song.
Ibid.

Have I not seen the loveliest woman born
Out of the mouth of Plenty's horn,
Because of her opinionated mind
Barter that horn and every good
By quiet natures understood
For an old bellows full of angry wind?
A Prayer for My Daughter.
Stanza 8

Though I am old with wandering
Through hollow lands and hilly lands,
I will find out where she has gone,
And kiss her lips and take her hands;
And walk among long dappled grass,
And pluck till time and times are done
The silver apples of the moon,
The golden apples of the sun.
The Song of Wandering Aengus.
Stanza 3

All things uncomely and broken, all things worn out and old,
The cry of a child by the roadway, the creak of a lumbering cart,
The heavy steps of the ploughman, splashing the wintry mould,
Are wronging your image that blossoms a rose in the deeps of my heart.
The Lover Tells of the Rose in His Heart. Stanza 1

The wrong of unshapely things is a wrong too great to be told.
Ibid. Stanza 2

The years like great black oxen tread the world

And God, the herdsman, goads them on behind.
The Countess Cathleen

I find, under the boughs of love and hate,
In all poor foolish things that live a day,
Eternal beauty wandering on her way.
To the Rose upon the Rood of Time

Had I the heavens' embroidered cloths,
Enwrought with gold and silver light.
He Wishes for the Cloths of Heaven

But I, being poor, have only my dreams;
I have spread my dreams under your feet;
Tread softly because you tread on my dreams.
Ibid.

When you are old and gray and full of sleep,
And nodding by the fire, take down this book.
When You Are Old

How many loved your moments of glad grace,
And loved your beauty, with love false or true;
But one man loved the pilgrim soul in you,
And loved the sorrows of your changing face.
Ibid.

She bid me take life easy, as the grass grows on the weirs;
But I was young and foolish, and now am full of tears.
Down by the Salley Gardens

I will arise and go now, and go to Innisfree,
And a small cabin build there, of clay and wattles made;
Nine bean-rows will I have there, a hive for the honey-bee,
And live alone in the bee-loud glade.
The Lake Isle of Innisfree [1]

[1] I had still the ambition, formed in Sligo in my teens, of living in imitation of Thoreau on Innisfree, a little island in Lough Gill, and when walking through Fleet Street very homesick I heard a little tinkle of water and saw a fountain in a shop-window which balanced a little ball upon its jet, and began to

I hear it in the deep heart's core.

The Lake Isle of Innisfree

When I play on my fiddle in Dooney,
Folk dance like a wave of the sea.

The Fiddler of Dooney. Stanza 1

For the good are always the merry,
Save by an evil chance,
And the merry love the fiddle,
And the merry love to dance.

Ibid. Stanza 4

Romantic Ireland's dead and gone,
It's with O'Leary in the grave.

September, 1913. Stanza 1

GEORGE W. YOUNG

The word must be spoken that bids you
    depart —
Though the effort to speak it should
    shatter my heart —
Though in silence, with blighted affec-
    tion, I pine,
Yet the lips that touch liquor must
    never touch mine!

The Lips That Touch Liquor.
Stanza 5

GEORGE ADE
[1866–   ]

Last night at twelve I felt immense,
But now I feel like thirty cents.

The Sultan of Sulu. Remorse

But, R-E-M-O-R-S-E!
The water-wagon is the place for me;
It is no time for mirth and laughter,
The cold, gray dawn of the morning
    after! [1]

Ibid.

A good folly is worth what you pay
for it.

Fables in Slang. A Lot for Three
Dollars

In uplifting, get underneath.

Ibid. The Good Fairy

He had been kicked in the Head by
a Mule when young and believed everything he read in the Sunday Papers.

Ibid. The Slim Girl

Only the more rugged mortals should
attempt to keep up with current literature.

Fables in Slang. Didn't Care for
Story-books

Never put off until To-morrow what
should have been Done early in the
Seventies.

Forty Modern Fables. The Third
and Last Call

To insure Peace of Mind ignore the
Rules and Regulations.

Ibid. The Crustacean

If it were not for the Presents, an
Elopement would be Preferable.

Ibid. The General Manager of
the Love Affair

Stay with the Procession or you will
Never Catch up.

Ibid. The Old-Time Pedagogue

The Time to enjoy a European trip
is about Three Weeks after Unpacking.

Ibid. The Hungry Man

The Julep is built in a Tall Vase. It
consists of a Leafy Roof-Garden superimposed on a Display of Small Fruit,
the whole underlaid with a Nansen Ice-
Floe.

Ibid. The Brotherhood of States

Draw your Salary before Spending it.

Ibid. The People's Choice

The Man was a Pinhead in a good
many Respects, but he was Wise as a
Serpent.

Ibid. The Wise Piker

For Parlor Use the Vague Generality
is a Life-Saver.

Ibid.

GELETT BURGESS
[1866–   ]

I'd rather have Fingers than Toes,
I'd rather have Eyes than a Nose;
    And as for my Hair
    I'm glad it's all there,
I'll be awfully sad when it goes.

Nonsense Verses

He joyed of life's pleasures
    All he could find;
Yet richest the treasures
    He found in his mind.

Epitaph. Stanza 2

---

remember lake water. From the sudden remembrance came my poem Innisfree. — *The*
Trembling of the Veil (autobiography)

[1] See Byron, page 359, and Dickens, page
495.

Leave the lady, Willy, let the racket rip,
She is going to fool you, you have lost
    your grip,
Your brain is in a muddle, and your
    heart is in a whirl,
Come along with me, Willy, never mind
    the girl!
            Willy and the Lady. Stanza 1
I never saw a Purple Cow,
    I never hope to see one;
But I can tell you, anyhow,
    I'd rather see than be one.
            The Purple Cow
Ah, yes, I wrote the "Purple Cow" —
    I'm sorry, now, I wrote it!
But I can tell you, anyhow,
    I'll kill you if you quote it.
            Cinq Ans Après

"ETHNA CARBERY"
(MRS. SEUMAS MacMANUS)
[1866–1902]

Blow softly down the valley,
    O wind, and stir the fern
That waves its green fronds over
    The King of Ireland's Cairn.
            The King of Ireland's Cairn.
            Stanza 1
'Tis well he seeks no tidings —
    His heart would ache to know
That all is changed in Ireland,
    And Tara lieth low.[1]
            Ibid. Stanza 11

EDMUND VANCE COOKE
[1866–1932]

Well, did you hear? Tom Lincoln's wife
    to-day,
The devil's luck for folk as poor as
    they!
Poor Tom! poor Nance!
Poor youngun born without a chance!
            Born Without a Chance. Stanza 1
The Woman tempted me — and tempts
    me still!

[1] No more to chiefs and ladies bright
    The harp of Tara swells;
    The chord alone, that breaks at night,
        Its tale of ruin tells.
            THOMAS MOORE: *The Harp that*
            Once thro' Tara's Halls, St. 2

Lord God, I pray You that she ever
    will!
            Adam
'Tis not the weight of jewel or plate,
    Or the fondle of silk and fur;
'Tis the spirit in which the gift is rich,
    As the gifts of the wise ones were;
And we are not told whose gift was gold
    Or whose was the gift of myrrh.
            The Spirit of the Gift
Oh, a trouble's a ton, or a trouble's an
    ounce,
    Or a trouble is what you make it,
And it isn't the fact that you're hurt
    that counts,
    But only how did you take it.
            How Did You Die? Stanza 1
Now by the rood, as Hamlet says, it
    grieves me sore to say
The stage is not as once it was when
    I was wont to play.
            The Other One Was Booth.
            Stanza 1
True artists are a rare, rare breed; there
    were but two, forsooth,
In all my time, the stage's prime; and
    the other one was Booth.
            Ibid.
My pa held me up to the moo-cow-moo,
    So clost I could almost touch,
En' I fed him a couple of times or two,
    En' I wasn't a fraid-cat — much.
            The Moo-Cow-Moo. Stanza 1

RICHARD LE GALLIENNE
[1866–   ]

Yea, howso we dream,
    Or how bravely we do;
The end is the same,
    Be we traitor or true:
        And after the bloom
        And the passion is past,
Death cometh at last.
            An Old Man's Song. Stanza 4
There's too much beauty upon this
    earth
For lonely men to bear.
            A Ballad of Too Much Beauty.
            Stanza 1
One asked of Regret,
    And I made reply:

To have held the bird,
And let it fly.
Regret

Canst thou be true across so many miles,
So many days that keep us still apart?
Ah, canst thou live upon remembered smiles,
And ask no warmer comfort for thy heart?
Love Platonic. 17

Bear to-day whate'er To-day may bring,
'Tis the one way to make To-morrow sing.
Ibid. In Her Diary

She's somewhere in the sunlight strong,
Her tears are in the falling rain,
She calls me in the wind's soft song,
And with the flowers she comes again.
Song

Shadow and sun — so too our lives are made —
Here learn how great the sun, how small the shade!
For Sundials

How many friends I loved are gone!
Death delicately takes the best:
O Death, be careful of the rest!
I cannot spare another one.
How Many Friends

May is building her house. With apple blooms
She is roofing over the glimmering rooms.
May Is Building Her House. Stanza 1

I meant to do my work to-day —
But a brown bird sang in the apple-tree,
And a butterfly flitted across the field,
And all the leaves were calling me.
Transgression. Stanza 1

Poet of doom, dementia, and death.
For the Birthday of Edgar Allan Poe

Behind the times I know I am,
But what is a tired man to do?
I light my pipe, and read Charles Lamb.
Ballade of the Noisiness of the Times. Stanza 1

I would make a list against the evil days
Of lovely things to hold in memory.
A Ballade-Catalogue of Lovely Things. Stanza 1

None else can equal, by the Rood,
Dickens, Dumas, or Walter Scott.
A Bookman's Ballade of "The Big Three"

Ah London! London! our delight,
Great flower that opens but at night.
A Ballad of London

Leaping alight on either hand
The iron lilies of the Strand.
Ibid.

Yet all the while my Lord I meet
In every London lane and street.[1]
The Second Crucifixion

"Name your favorite writer" should be one of the first questions in the Engagement Catechism.
The Quest of the Golden Girl. Book II, Chap. 6

Wild oats will get sown some time, and one of the arts of life is to sow them at the right time.
Ibid. Book III, Chap. 9

WALTER MALONE
[1866–1915]

They do me wrong who say I come no more
When once I knock and fail to find you in;
For every day I stand outside your door,
And bid you wake, and rise to fight and win.
Opportunity. Stanza 1

And if a lowly singer dries one tear,
Or soothes one humble human heart in pain,
Be sure his homely verse to God is dear,
And not one stanza has been sung in vain.
The Humbler Poets. Stanza 3

---

[1] Mark Symons [1887–1935], an English artist, chose this couplet as the theme and title of his controversial painting of Christ preaching in the street to a modern crowd. The Royal Academy rejected the painting, which is now in a private collection in New York.

GILBERT MURRAY
[1866–   ]

Romantic plays with happy endings are almost of necessity inferior in artistic value to true tragedies. Not, one would hope, simply because they end happily; happiness in itself is certainly not less beautiful than grief; but because a tragedy in its great moments can generally afford to be sincere, while romantic plays live in an atmosphere of ingenuity and make-believe.

Preface to The Iphigenia in Tauris of Euripides

The enemy has no definite name, though in a certain degree we all know him. He who puts always the body before the spirit, the dead before the living; who makes things only in order to sell them; who has forgotten that there is such a thing as truth, and measures the world by advertisement or by money; who daily defiles the beauty that surrounds him and makes vulgar the tragedy.

Religio Grammatici [*1918*]

JOHN OXENHAM

Art thou lonely, O my brother?
Share thy little with another!
Stretch a hand to one unfriended,
And thy loneliness is ended.
Lonely Brother

Kneel always when you light a fire!
The Sacrament of Fire

Thank God for sleep!
And, when you cannot sleep,
Still thank Him that you live
To lie awake.
The Sacrament of Sleep

For ears to hear the heavenly harmonies;
For eyes to see the unseen in the seen;
For vision of The Worker in the work;
For hearts to apprehend Thee everywhere; —
We thank Thee, Lord!
A Little Te Deum of the Commonplace

JOHN JEROME ROONEY
[1866–1934]

Yea, "writ in water," child of earth and sky,
Sprung from the sod, yet winging from on high:
Untainted, blithe, in beauty's passion strong
And shimmering with the rainbow hues of song!
John Keats

DORA SIGERSON
(MRS. CLEMENT SHORTER)
[1866–1918]

For if thy charity be overstrained
And would bring slander where it cannot bless,
Give me but silence where good friendship waned,
Grant me the mercy of forgetfulness.
If You Should Pass. Stanza 5

All night the small feet of the rain
Within my garden ran,
And gentle fingers tapped the pane
Until the dawn began.
April. Stanza 1

BERT LESTON TAYLOR
[1866–1921]

Profitless others, and stale and flat —
There are no more books in the world like that.
"Treasure Island." Stanza 2

When quacks with pills political would dope us,
When politics absorbs the livelong day,
I like to think about the star Canopus,
So far, so far away!
Canopus. Stanza 1

I meditate on interstellar spaces,
And smoke a mild seegar.
Ibid. Stanza 4

A star that has no parallax to speak of,
Conduces to repose.
Ibid. Stanza 5

To free, what I am pleased to call my mind,[1]

[1] See Lord Westbury, page 402.

From matters that perplex it and embarrass,
I take a glass, and seek until I find,
Far in the heaven, southward from Polaris,
A wisp of cloud — a nebula by name,
Andromeda provides a starry frame.
Ataraxia. Stanza 1

Hate of the millions who've choked you down,
In country kitchen or house in town,
We love a thousand, we hate but one,
With a hate more hot than the hate of the Gun —
    Bread Pudding!
Chant of Hate for Bread Pudding.
Stanza 2

These scoffers, these obstructionists,
    These fossils — who are they?
The glad young, mad young futurists
    Who prance around to-day.
So Shall It Be. Stanza 6

Everywhere I look I see —
    Fact or fiction, life or play,
Still the little game of Three:
    B and C in love with A.
Old Stuff. Stanza 3

Consider, friends, this trio —
    How little fuss they made.
They didn't curse when it was worse
    Than ninety in the shade.
They moved about serenely
    Within the furnace bright,
And soon forgot that it was hot,
    With "no relief in sight."
A Hot Weather Classic: Shadrach,
Meshach, and Abed-nego. Stanza 4

When my sun of life is low,
    When the dewy shadows creep,
Say for me before I go,
    "Now I lay me down to sleep."
Sundown. Stanza 1

HERBERT GEORGE WELLS
[1866–   ]

The professional military mind is by necessity an inferior and unimaginative mind; no man of high intellectual quality would willingly imprison his gifts in such a calling.
The Outline of History. Chap. 40
[1920]

The Great War and the Petty Peace.
The Outline of History. Chap. 40
[1920]

Human history is in essence a history of ideas.
Ibid.

Every one of these hundreds of millions of human beings is in some form seeking happiness. . . . Not one is altogether noble nor altogether trustworthy nor altogether consistent; and not one is altogether vile. Not a single one but has at some time wept.
Ibid.

A federation of all humanity, together with a sufficient measure of social justice to ensure health, education, and a rough equality of opportunity, would mean such a release and increase of human energy as to open a new phase in human history.
Ibid. Chap. 41

Our true nationality is mankind.
Ibid.

While the poor little affairs of obscure, industrious men of letters are made the subject of intensive research, the far more romantic, thrilling and illuminating documents about the seekers and makers of great fortunes, are neither gathered nor cherished.
The Work, Wealth and Happiness of Mankind. Chap. 10 [1931]

In England we have come to rely upon a comfortable time-lag of fifty years or a century intervening between the perception that something ought to be done and a serious attempt to do it.
Ibid. Chap. 11

ERNEST DOWSON
[1867–1900]

They are not long, the weeping and the laughter,
    Love and desire and hate:
I think they have no portion in us after
    We pass the gate.
Vitae Summa Brevis. Stanza 1

I have been faithful to thee, Cynara!
　　in my fashion.
　　　　*Non Sum Qualis Eram Bonae
　　　　　　Sub Regno Cynarae* [1]
I cried for madder music and for
　　stronger wine.
　　　　　　　　　　Ibid.

You would have understood me, had
　　you waited;
　　I could have loved you, dear! as
　　　　well as he:
Had we not been impatient, dear! and
　　fated
　　　　Always to disagree.
　　　　*You Would Have Understood Me.
　　　　　　　　　　Stanza 1*

What is the use of speech? Silence were
　　fitter:
　　Lest we should still be wishing things
　　　　unsaid.
　　　　　　　　Ibid. Stanza 2

We have walked in Love's land a little
　　way,
　　We have learnt his lesson a little
　　　　while,
And shall we not part at the end of
　　day,
　　　　With a sigh, a smile?
　　　　　　April Love. Stanza 1

Always I know, how little severs me
From mine heart's country, that is yet
　　so far.
　　　　　　Terre Promise. Stanza 2

From troublous sights and sounds set
　　free;
　　In such a twilight hour of breath,
Shall one retrace his life, or see,
　　Through shadows, the true face of
　　　　death?
　　　　　　Extreme Unction. Stanza 3

When this, our rose, is faded,
　　And these, our days, are done,
In lands profoundly shaded
　　From tempest and from sun;
Ah, once more come together,
　　Shall we forgive the past,
And safe from worldly weather
　　Possess our souls at last?
　　　　　　Amantium Irae. Stanza 1

[1] I am not the man I was under the reign
　　of the good Cynara.
　　Horace: *Book 4, Ode 1, Ad Venerem*

Before my light goes out forever if God
　　should give me a choice of graces,
I would not reck of length of days, nor
　　crave for things to be;
But cry: "One day of the great lost
　　days, one face of all the faces,
Grant me to see and touch once more
　　and nothing more to see."
　　　　Impenitentia Ultima. Stanza 1

FINLEY PETER DUNNE
("MR. DOOLEY")
[1867–1936]

Th' dead ar-re always pop'lar. I
knowed a society wanst to vote a mon-
yment to a man an' refuse to help his
fam'ly, all in wan night.
　　　　　　　　　On Charity

Life'd not be worth livin' if we
didn't keep our inimies.
　　　　On New Year's Resolutions

No matther whether th' constitution
follows th' flag or not, th' Supreme
Coort follows th' iliction returns.
　　　　The Supreme Court's Decisions

Ivrything that's worth havin' goes
to th' city; th' counthry takes what's
left.
　　　　The City as a Summer Resort

I think a lie with a purpose is wan
iv th' worst kind an' th' mos' profitable.
　　　　　　　　　On Lying

Th' dimmycratic party ain't on
speakin' terms with itsilf.
　　　　*Mr. Dooley Discusses Party
　　　　　　　　　　Politics*

Th' raypublican party broke ye, but
now that ye're down we'll not turn a
cold shoulder to ye. Come in an' we'll
keep ye broke.
　　　　　　　　　　Ibid.

What's fame, afther all, me la-ad?
'Tis as apt to be what some wan writes
on ye'er tombstone.
　　　　　　　　　Fame

When ye build yer triumphal arch to
yer conquerin' hero, Hinnissey, build
it out of bricks so the people will have
somethin' convanient to throw at him
as he passes through.
　　　　　　　　　　Ibid.

Vice . . . is a creature of such hee-
jus mien, . . . that the more ye see it
th' better ye like it.
The Crusade Against Vice
"D'ye think th' colledges has much
to do with th' progress iv th' wurruld?"
asked Mr. Hennessy.
"D'ye think," said Mr. Dooley, " 'tis
th' mill that makes th' wather run?"
Colleges and Degrees

"Ye know a lot about marriage, but
ye niver marrid," said Mr. Hennessy.
"No," said Mr. Dooley. "No, say I,
givin' three cheers, I know about marriage th' way an astronomer knows
about th' stars."
Marriage
"It's too bad that th' goolden days
has passed. Capital still pats labor on
th' back, but on'y with an axe. Labor
rayfuses to be threated as a friend. It
wants to be threated as an inimy. It
thinks it gets more that way. They ar-re
still a happy fam'ly, but it's more like
an English fam'ly. They don't speak."
Labor and Capital

EDWIN FRANCIS EDGETT
[1867–   ]

He may have a message
For the world,
But he is welcome
To no editorial haunts
If he rolls his manuscript.
The Manuscript Roller

JOHN GALSWORTHY
[1867–1933]

Justice is a machine that, when some
one has once given it the starting push,
rolls on of itself.
Justice. Act II
There is nothing more tragic in life
than the utter impossibility of changing what you have done. •
Ibid.
You don't know what marriage is.
Day after day, year after year. It's no
use being sentimental — for people
brought up as we are to have different

manners is worse than to have differ-
ent souls. . . . It's the little things.
The Eldest Son. Act II
You called me a damned Jew. My
race was old when you were all savages. I am proud to be a Jew.[1]
Loyalties. Act II, Sc. 1
Public opinion's always in advance
of the Law.
Windows. Act I
The value of a sentiment is the
amount of sacrifice you are prepared
to make for it.
Ibid. Act II
For a man that can't see an inch
into human nature, give me a psychological novelist.
Ibid.
Love is no hot-house flower, but a
wild plant, born of a wet night, born
of an hour of sunshine; sprung from
wild seed, blown along the road by a
wild wind. A wild plant that, when it
blooms by chance within the hedge of
our gardens, we call a flower; and
when it blooms outside we call a weed;
but, flower or weed, whose scent and
colour are always wild!
*The Man of Property. Part II,
Chap. 4*
By the cigars they smoke, and the
composers they love, ye shall know the
texture of men's souls.
*Indian Summer of a Forsyte.
Chap. 1*
A man of action, forced into a state
of thought, is unhappy until he can get
out of it.
Maid in Waiting. Chap. 3

[1] In his *Reminiscences of Sixty Years in
the National Metropolis*, BENJAMIN PERLEY
POORE [1820–1887] quotes this reply of Senator Judah P. Benjamin [1181–1884] to a Senator of German extraction who taunted him
with being a Jew: "The gentleman will please
remember that when his half-civilized ancestors were hunting the wild boar in the forests
of Silesia, mine were the Princes of the earth."
See Disraeli, page 418.
We were running naked and staining ourselves with woad in our woods, when the
looms of India and China were producing
the delicate fabrics we seek now to imitate.
—OLIVE SCHREINER: *From Man to Man,
Chap. 7*

Politicians are marvels of energy and principle when they're out of office, but when they get in, they simply run behind the machine.

Maid in Waiting. Chap. 5

There's just one rule for politicians all over the world: Don't say in Power what you say in Opposition; if you do, you only have to carry out what the other fellows have found impossible.

Ibid. Chap. 7

One's eyes are what one is, one's mouth what one becomes.

Flowering Wilderness. Chap. 2

She had that peculiar feeling, experienced by all at times, of having once been someone else, which accounts for so much belief in the transmigration of souls.

Ibid. Chap. 11

The beginnings and endings of all human undertakings are untidy, the building of a house, the writing of a novel, the demolition of a bridge, and, eminently, the finish of a voyage.

Over the River. Chap. 1

He ordered himself a dozen oysters; but, suddenly remembering that the month contained no "r," changed them to a fried sole.[1]

The White Monkey. Part III, Chap. 7

It has often been remarked that the breakfast-tables of people who avow themselves indifferent to what the Press may say of them are garnished by all the newspapers on the morning when there is anything to say.

The Silver Spoon. Part II, Chap. 2

I've seen the moon, with lifted wing, A white hawk, over cypress tree,

---

[1] Is is unseasonable and unwholesome in all months that have not an *R* in their name to eat an oyster. — WILLIAM BUTLER [1535–1618]: *Dyet's Dry Dinner* [1599]
Let's sing a song of glory to Themistocles O'Shea,
Who ate a dozen oysters on the second day of May.
. STODDARD KING [1889–1933]: *The Man Who Dared*

The lover's star, the bloom of spring, And evening folded on Tennessee.

At Sunset. Stanza 1

I, who exulted in sunshine and laughter,
Dreamed not of dying — death is such waste of me!

Valley of the Shadow

LIONEL JOHNSON [1]
[1867–1902]

The splendid silence clings
Around me: and around
The saddest of all kings
Crowned, and again discrowned.

By the Statue of King Charles at Charing Cross. Stanza 2

Vanquished in life, his death
By beauty made amends.

Ibid. Stanza 8

I know you: solitary griefs,
Desolate passions, aching hours!
I know you: tremulous beliefs,
Agonized hopes, and ashen flowers!

The Precept of Silence. Stanza 1

Some players upon plaintive strings
Publish their wistfulness abroad;
I have not spoken of these things,
Save to one man, and unto God.

Ibid. Stanza 3

Dear, human books,
With kindly voices, winning looks!
Enchaunt me with your spells of art,
And draw me homeward to your heart.

Oxford Nights

ERNEST FENWICK JOHNSTONE
[1867–1938]

I dreamed that I went to the City of Gold,
To Heaven resplendent and fair,
And after I entered that beautiful fold
By one in authority there I was told
That not a Vermonter was there.

No Vermonters in Heaven. Stanza 1

---

[1] Inter Poetas Wiccamicos Haud Minimus Habebitur (Among the poets of Wykeham he will be held not least). — Tablet to Johnson in the cloisters of Winchester College.

We give them the best the Kingdom
 provides;
They have everything here that they
 want,
But not a Vermonter in Heaven abides;
A very brief period here he resides,
 Then hikes his way back to Ver-
 mont.
No Vermonters in Heaven.
Stanza 6

W. COMPTON LEITH

What song the Sirens sang? . . .
They sang of all that is above fulfilment and beyond clear vision; of the
immeasurable, the uncontained, the
half-imagined; of that which is touched
but never held, implored but unpos-
sessed. . . . They sang the vileness of
all who live contented upon an alms,
and are at ease in bonds, the slaves
whose servitude is made sweet by
habit.
Sirenica [*1913*]

The third hour after the meridian,
which is the day's autumn, the fatal
hour, unbearably steeped in sorrow.
Many, asked in what hour they have
perceived themselves most desolate
and under Medusa's eyes, would answer: "At this hour, and upon a summer's day."
Ibid.

JUDD MORTIMER LEWIS
[1867–   ]

If you know of a skeleton hidden away
In a closet and guarded and kept from
 the day
In the dark; and whose showing, whose
 sudden display
Would cause grief and sorrow and
 lifelong dismay,
 It's a pretty good plan to forget it.
Forget It. Stanza 2

CHARLES EDWARD
MONTAGUE
[1867–1928]

All authentic affection rests upon
vision . . . the state of mind and

heart which does not merely apprehend evidence but broods excitedly
over some completed and transfigured
image of an apprehended object.
The Right Place. Chap. 8

London on an early autumn afternoon of quiet sunshine, when all the
air is mysterious with a vaporous gold-
dust of illuminated motes and the hum
of the traffic seems to fall pensive and
muted round the big, benign London
policeman
 with uplifted hand
Conducting the orchestral Strand.[1]
Ibid. Chap. 14

A gifted small girl has explained
that pins are a great means of saving
life, "by not swallowing them."
Dramatic Values

Germany lay at our feet, a world's
wonder of downfall, a very Lucifer,
fallen, broken, bereaved beyond all the
retributive griefs which Greek tragedy
shows you afflicting the great who were
insolent, wilful, and proud. But it was
not enough for our small epicures of
revenge. They wanted to twist the enemy's wrists, where he lay bound, and
to run pins into his eyes. And they had
the upper hand of us now. The soldiers could only look on while the
scurvy performance dragged itself out
till the meanest of treaties was signed
at Versailles.
Disenchantment. Chap. 13 [*1922*]

"The freedom of Europe," "The
war to end war," "The overthrow of
militarism," "The cause of civilization" — most people believe so little
now in anything or anyone that they
would find it hard to understand the
simplicity and intensity of faith with
which these phrases were once taken
among our troops, or the certitude felt
by hundreds of thousands of men who
are now dead that if they were killed
their monument would be a new Europe not soured or soiled with the hates
and greeds of the old.
Ibid.

[1] Stephen Phillips, see page 773.

Among the mind's powers is one that comes of itself to many children and artists. It need not be lost, to the end of his days, by anyone who has ever had it. This is the power of taking delight in a thing, or rather in anything, everything, not as a means to some other end, but just because it is what it is, as the lover dotes on whatever may be the traits of the beloved object. A child in the full health of his mind will put his hand flat on the summer turf, feel it, and give a little shiver of private glee at the elastic firmness of the globe.

Disenchantment. Chap. 15

All dullness is in the mind; it comes out thence and diffuses itself over everything round the dull person, and then he terms everything dull, and thinks himself the victim of the impact of dull things. In stupid rich people, in boys and girls deadeningly taught at dead-alive schools, in all disappointed weaklings and in declining nations, this loss of power to shed anything but dullness upon what one sees and hears is common enough.

Ibid.

The paradoxes of conduct begin to twinkle into sight; sugar is good, but there is a time to refrain from taking it though you can; a lie will easily get you out of a scrape, and yet, strangely and beautifully, rapture possesses you when you have taken the scrape and left out the lie.

Ibid.

War hath no fury like a non-combatant.

Ibid.

Burgundy was the winiest wine, the central, essential, and typical wine, the soul and greatest common measure of all the kindly wines of the earth.

Judith

"I was born below par to th' extent of two whiskies."

Fiery Particles

WILLIAM SYDNEY PORTER ("O. HENRY")

[1867–1910]

Hard ye may be in the tumult,
    Red to your battle hilts,
Blow give for blow in the foray,
    Cunningly ride in the tilts;
But when the roaring is ended,
    Tenderly, unbeguiled,
Turn to a woman a woman's
    Heart, and a child's to a child.

The Crucible.[1] *Stanza 1*

Lost, your Excellency. Lost associations and societies. Lost right reverends and wrong reverends of every order. Lost reformers and lawmakers, born with heavenly compassion in your hearts, but with the reverence of money in your souls. And lost thus around us every day.[2]

Elsie in New York

He was outwardly decent and managed to preserve his aquarium, but inside he was impromptu and full of unexpectedness.

The Octopus Marooned

East is East, and West is San Francisco, according to Californians. Californians are a race of people; they are not merely inhabitants of a State. They are the Southerners of the West.

A Municipal Report

Take of London fog 30 parts; malaria 10 parts; gas leaks 20 parts; dewdrops gathered in a brick-yard at sunrise 25 parts; odor of honeysuckle 15 parts. Mix. The mixture will give you an approximate conception of a Nashville drizzle.

Ibid.

Most wonderful of all are words, and how they make friends one with another, being oft associated, until not even obituary notices them do part.

Calloway's Code

[1] Verses found among his MSS after his death.
[2] A paraphrase of the closing lines of Chap. 47, *Bleak House*, by Dickens.

If men knew how women pass the time when they are alone, they'd never marry.
Memoirs of a Yellow Dog

Ready to melt in the crucible of her ire a little more gold plating from the wrought steel chains of matrimony.
The Pendulum

He no longer saw a rabble, but his brothers seeking the ideal.
Brickdust Row

She would have made a splendid wife, for crying only made her eyes more bright.
No Story

A man asleep is certainly a sight to make angels weep. Now, a woman asleep you regard as different. No matter how she looks, you know it's better for all hands for her to be that way.
The Hiding of Black Bill

There was too much scenery and fresh air. What I need is a steam-heated flat with no ventilation or exercise.
Letter [April 15, 1910]

Turn up the lights; I don't want to go home in the dark.
Last words (quoted in the biography by C. ALPHONSO SMITH)

GEORGE W. RUSSELL ("AE")
[1867–1935]

Our hearts were drunk with a beauty
Our eyes could never see.
The Unknown God

Twilight, a timid fawn, went glimmering by,
And Night, the dark-blue hunter, followed fast.
Refuge

That blazing galleon the sun,
This dusky coracle I ride,
Both under secret orders sail,
And swim upon the selfsame tide.
Mutiny. Stanza 1

Its edges foamed with amethyst and rose,
Withers once more the old blue flower of day:

There where the ether like a diamond glows,
Its petals fade away.
The Great Breath. Stanza 1

When the breath of twilight blows to flame the misty skies,
All its vaporous sapphire, violet glow and silver gleam,
With their magic flood me through the gateway of the eyes;
I am one with the twilight's dream.
By the Margin of the Great Deep. Stanza 1

HARRY LEON WILSON
[1867–   ]

It would never do with us.
Ruggles of Red Gap

I can be pushed just so far.
Ibid.

She'd fight a rattlesnake and give it the first two bites.
Ibid.

MARY HUNTER AUSTIN
[1868–1934]

Whisper of the wind along the sage,
Only wait till I can get the word —
Never was it printed in a page,
Never was it spoken, never heard.
Whisper of the Wind

There are no fairy-folk in our Southwest,
The cactus spines would tear their filmy wings,
There's no dew anywhere for them to drink
And no green grass to make them fairy rings.
Western Magic. Stanza 1

What need has he of clocks who knows
When highest peaks are gilt and rose
Day has begun?
Clocks and Calendars. Stanza 1

At midnight drink no water,
For I have heard said
That on the stroke of midnight
All water goes dead.
Dead Water. New Mexico Legend, Stanza 1

I arise, facing east,
I am asking toward the light:
I am asking that my day
Shall be beautiful with light.
Morning Prayer

THOMAS WILLIAM HODGSON CROSLAND
[1868–1924]

God's infinite mercy, how that child did
cry,
In spite of bottle, bauble, peppermint,
nurse!
The Baby in the Ward
Unhonoured by his fellows he grew old
And trod the path to hell,
But there were many things he might
have sold
And did not sell.
Epitaph. Stanza 2
CHIDDEN still murmurs,
SLAPPED and RAPPED complain,
HURT, with a thousand tongues,
Whines out his pain.

This is the learning
Unto which we come:
PROPERLY WALLOPED
Is for ever dumb.
Recipe

GEORGE NORMAN DOUGLAS
[1868–   ]

You can tell the ideals of a nation by
its advertisements.
South Wind. Chap. 7
What a pity that Latin, as scholars'
language, for the definition and regis-
tration of ideas, was ever abandoned!
It has the incalculable advantage that
the meanings of words are irrevocably
fixed by authority.
Ibid. Chap. 8
Men have lost sight of distant horizons. Nobody writes for humanity, for
civilization; they write for their country, their sect; to amuse their friends
or annoy their enemies.
Ibid.

No one can expect a majority to be
stirred by motives other than ignoble.
South Wind. Chap. 10

A love-match is generally a failure
and a money-match is always a mistake. The heroes, the saints and sages —
they are those who face the world alone.
Ibid. Chap. 11

No great man is ever born too soon or
too late. When we say that the time is
not ripe for this or that celebrity, we
confess by implication that this very
man, and no other, is required.
Ibid. Chap. 13

Impoverished them to such an extent
that for three consecutive months they
could barely afford the most unnecessary luxuries of life.
Ibid. Chap. 20

Many a man who thinks to found a
home discovers that he has merely
opened a tavern for his friends.
Ibid. Chap. 24

WILLIAM EDWARD BURGHARDT DuBOIS
[1868–   ]

Herein lies the tragedy of the age:
not that men are poor — all men know
something of poverty; not that men are
wicked — who is good? Not that men
are ignorant — what is truth? Nay, but
that men know so little of men.
The Souls of Black Folk [1903]

GRENVILLE KLEISER
[1868–   ]

She gleans how long you wish to stay;
She lets you go without delay.
The Ideal Hostess

She is not difficult to please;
She can be silent as the trees.
She shuns all ostentatious show;
She knows exactly when to go.
The Ideal Guest

HERMAN W. KNICKERBOCKER
[1868–1934]

I believe that when you say one is a "dead game sport" you have reached the climax of human philosophy.

Eulogy at the funeral of Riley Grannan, Rawhide, Nevada [April 3, 1908]

If I had the power to-day by the simple turning of my hand to endow myself with personal immortality, in my infinite ignorance I would refuse to turn my hand. God knows best.

Ibid.

EDWARD VERRALL LUCAS
[1868–1938]

You ask me "why I like him." Nay,
I cannot; nay, I would not, say.
I think it vile to pigeonhole
The pros and cons of a kindred soul.

Friends. Stanza 1

A stamp's a tiny, flimsy thing,
No thicker than a beetle's wing,
And yet 'twill roam the world for you
Exactly where you tell it to.

*The Three-Halfpenny Traveller.
Stanza 1*

When clay has such red mouths to kiss,
    Firm hands to grasp, it is enough:
How can I take it aught amiss
    We are not made of rarer stuff?

Clay. Stanza 3

Has any reader ever found perfect accuracy in the newspaper account of any event of which he himself had inside knowledge?

Of Accuracy

The art of life is to be so well known at a good restaurant that you can pay by cheque.

Over Bemerton's

The art of life is to keep down acquaintances. One's friends one can manage, but one's acquaintances can be the devil.

Ibid.

The noise from good toast should reverberate in the head like the thunder of July.

A Word on Toast

O to hunt books in
    The Charing Cross Road!

The Friendly Town

Lamb's great discovery was that he himself was better worth laying bare than obscuring: that his memories, his impressions, his loyalties, his dislikes, his doubts, his beliefs, his prejudices, his enthusiasms, in short, everything that was his, were suitable material for literature. Pope said that the proper study of mankind was man; Lamb amended this to — the proper study of man is himself.

At the Shrine of Saint Charles

WILLIAM TYLER PAGE
[1868–   ]

I believe in the United States of America as a Government of the people, by the people, for the people; whose just powers are derived from the consent of the governed; a democracy in a republic, a sovereign Nation of many sovereign States; a perfect Union one and inseparable; established upon those principles of freedom, equality, justice and humanity for which American patriots sacrificed their lives and fortunes. I therefore believe it is my duty to my country to love it, to support its Constitution, to obey its laws, to respect its flag, and to defend it against all enemies.

The American's Creed.[1]

ROBERT FALCON SCOTT
[1868–1912]

Make the boy interested in natural history if you can; it is better than games; they encourage it at some schools.

Last Message to His Wife

He [Oates] [2] said: "I am just going outside, and may be some time." He went out into the blizzard, and we have not seen him since. . . . We knew that

[1] Adopted by the House of Representatives [April 3, 1918].
[2] Lawrence Edward Grace Oates [1880–1912], of the Inniskilling Dragoons, one of Scott's last Antarctic expedition.

poor Oates was walking to his death, but though we tried to dissuade him, we knew that it was the act of a brave man and an English gentleman. We all hope to meet the end with a similar spirit, and assuredly the end is not far.

Diary. March 16, 1912

Had we lived, I should have had a tale to tell of the hardihood, endurance, and courage of my companions which would have stirred the heart of every Englishman. These rough notes and our dead bodies must tell the tale.

Journal. Message to the Public.[1]

ARTHUR FREDERICK SHELDON
[1868–1935]

He profits most who serves best.

Motto for Rotary International

WILLIAM ALLEN WHITE
[1868–   ]

And thus the King of Boyville first set his light little foot upon the soil of an unknown country.

The King of Boyville [*1896*]

LAURENCE BINYON
[1869–   ]

O World, be nobler, for her sake!
  If she but knew thee what thou art,
What wrongs are borne, what deeds are done
In thee, beneath thy daily sun,
  Know'st thou not that her tender heart
For pain and very shame would break?
O World, be nobler, for her sake!

O World, Be Nobler

Our speech is spun from the pain
Of thought and heavy with years,
And dyed with an ancient stain
From passion and blood and tears.

One Year Old. Stanza 5

For Mercy, Courage, Kindness, Mirth,
There is no measure upon earth.
Nay, they wither, root and stem,
If an end be set to them.

A Song

They shall grow not old, as we that are
  left grow old:
Age shall not weary them, nor the years
  condemn.
At the going down of the sun and in the
  morning
We will remember them.

For the Fallen. Stanza 4

In the terrible hour of the dawn, when
  the veins are cold,
  They led her forth to the wall.
"I have loved my land," she said, "but
  it is not enough:
  Love requires of me all."

Edith Cavell.[1] *Stanza 5*

J. GORDON COOGLER
[1869–   ]

Alas! for the South, her books have
  grown fewer —
She never was much given to literature.

Purely Original Verse (*1897*)

From early youth to the frost of age
  Man's days have been a mixture
Of all that constitutes in life
  A dark and gloomy picture.

Ibid.

She died after the beautiful snow had
  melted
  And was buried beneath the slush.

Ibid. In Memorial

My style and my sentiments are MY
  OWN, purely original.

Ibid. Preface

ROBERT HOBART
("BOB") DAVIS
[1869–   ]

I am the printing-press, born of the mother earth. My heart is of steel, my limbs are of iron, and my fingers are of brass.

---

[1] Inscribed on the memorial to Captain Scott and his companions, Waterloo Place, London.

[1] Have pity on her. — BRAND WHITLOCK [1869–1934]: Letter to Baron von der Lancken, Civil Governor of Brussels

I sing the songs of the world, the oratorios of history, the symphonies of all time.

I am the voice of to-day, the herald of to-morrow. I weave into the warp of the past the woof of the future. I tell the stories of peace and war alike.

I make the human heart beat with passion or tenderness. I stir the pulse of nations, and make brave men do better deeds, and soldiers die. . . .

I am the laughter and tears of the world, and I shall never die until all things return to the immutable dust.

I am the printing-press.

I Am the Printing-Press
[*July, 1911*]

"MICHAEL FAIRLESS" (MARGARET FAIRLESS BARBER)
[1869–1901]

The people who make no roads are ruled out from intelligent participation in the world's brotherhood.

The Roadmender. I, 5

Necessity can set me helpless on my back, but she cannot keep me there; nor can four walls limit my vision.

Ibid. II, 6

Revelation is always measured by capacity.

Ibid. III, 3

STRICKLAND GILLILAN
[1869–   ]

Make 'em brief, Finnigin!

Finnigin to Flannigan. Stanza 3

Bilin' down his repoort, wuz Finnigin!
An' he writed this here: "*Muster Flannigan* —
Off ag'in, on ag'in,
Gone ag'in. — FINNIGIN."

Ibid. Stanza 6

Just stand aside and watch yourself go by;
Think of yourself as "he" instead of "I."

Watch Yourself Go By. Stanza 1

FREDERIC LAWRENCE KNOWLES
[1869–1905]

When navies are forgotten
  And fleets are useless things,
When the dove shall warm her bosom
  Beneath the eagle's wings.

The New Age. Stanza 1

In the conquest which is service,
  In the victory which is peace!

Ibid. Stanza 4

These are the best of him,
Pathos and jest of him;
Earth holds the rest of him.

On a Fly-Leaf of Burns's Songs.
Stanza 1

Each little lyrical
Grave or satirical
Musical miracle!

Ibid. Stanza 3

Helen's lips are drifting dust;
Ilion is consumed with lust;
All the galleons of Greece
Drink the ocean's dreamless peace;
Lost was Solomon's purple show
Restless centuries ago.

Love Triumphant

This body is my house — it is not I:
Triumphant in this faith I live and die.

The Tenant

Our crosses are hewn from different trees,
But we all must have our Calvaries.

Golgotha

STEPHEN LEACOCK
[1869–   ]

The classics are only primitive literature. They belong to the same class as primitive machinery and primitive music and primitive medicine.

Homer and Humbug

If I were founding a university I would found first a smoking room; then when I had a little more money in hand I would found a dormitory; then after that, or more probably with it, a decent reading room and a library. After that, if I still had more money that I couldn't use, I would hire a professor and get some textbooks.

Oxford As I See It

EDGAR LEE MASTERS
[1869–   ]

All, all are sleeping on the hill.
Spoon River Anthology. The Hill

Tick, tick, tick, what little iambics,
While Homer and Whitman roared in
the pines.
Ibid. Petit, the Poet.

Out of me unworthy and unknown
The vibrations of deathless music;
"With malice toward none, with charity
for all."
Ibid. Anne Rutledge

I am Anne Rutledge who sleep beneath
these weeds,
Beloved in life of Abraham Lincoln,
Wedded to him, not through union,
But through separation.
Bloom forever, O Republic,
From the dust of my bosom!
Ibid.

WILLIAM VAUGHN MOODY
[1869–1910]

Jill-o'er-the-ground is purple blue,
Blue is the quaker-maid,
The wild geranium holds its dew
Long in the boulder's shade.
Gloucester Moors. Stanza 2

This earth is not the steadfast place
We landsmen build upon;
From deep to deep she varies pace,
And while she comes is gone.
Ibid. Stanza 4

But on, but on does the old earth steer
As if her port she knew.
Ibid. Stanza 5

But thou, vast outbound ship of souls,
What harbor town for thee?
What shapes, when thy arriving tolls,
Shall crowd the banks to see?
Shall all the happy shipmates then
Stand singing brotherly?
Ibid. Stanza 10

Then not to kneel, almost
Seemed like a vulgar boast.
Good Friday. Stanza 9

Gigantic, wilful, young,
Chicago sitteth at the northwest gates,
With restless violent hands and casual
tongue
Moulding her mighty fates.
*An Ode in Time of Hesitation.
Stanza 3*

The wars we wage
Are noble, and our battles still are won
By justice for us, ere we lift the gage.
We have not sold our loftiest heritage.
The proud republic hath not stooped to
cheat
And scramble in the market-place of
war.
Ibid. Stanza 5

Our fluent men of place and conse-
quence
Fumble and fill their mouths with hol-
low phrase,
Or for the end-all of deep arguments
Intone their dull commercial liturgies.
Ibid. Stanza 7

Blindness we may forgive, but baseness
we will smite.
Ibid. Stanza 9

Praise, and never a whispered hint but
the fight he fought was good;
Never a word that the blood on his
sword was his country's own
heart's-blood.
*On a Soldier Fallen in the
Philippines. Stanza 2*

And souls are restless, plagued, impa-
tient things,
All dream and unaccountable desire;
Crawling, but pestered with the
thought of wings;
Spreading through every inch of earth's
old mire
Mystical hanker after something
higher.
The Menagerie. Stanza 19

Shrill and high, newsboys cry
The worst of the city's infamy.
In New York. Stanza 4

The roaring street is hung for miles
With fierce electric fire.
Ibid. Stanza 9

Of wounds and sore defeat
I made my battle stay;

Winged sandals for my feet
I wove of my delay.
The Fire-Bringer.
Pandora's Song, II

WILLIAM HENRY OGILVIE
[1869–   ]

Ragged, uncomely, and old and gray,
 A woman walked in a northern town,
And through the crowd as she wound
    her way
 One saw her loiter and then stoop
    down,
 Putting something away in her old
    torn gown.
A Royal Heart. Stanza 1

"It's broken glass,"
She said: "I hae lifted it frae the street
To be oot o' the road o' the bairnies'
    feet!"
Ibid. Stanza 3

The real ones, the right ones, the
    straight ones and the true,
The pukka, peerless sportsmen — their
    numbers are but few;
The men who keep on playing though
    the sun be in eclipse,
The men who go on losing with a laugh
    upon their lips.
The True Sportsman

When the last fence looms up, I am
    ready
And I hope when the rails of it crack,
There'll be nothing in front but the
    master,
 The huntsman, the fox and the pack.
The Last Fence. Stanza 1

EDWIN ARLINGTON
ROBINSON
[1869–1935]

We cannot know how much we learn
From those who never will return,
Until a flash of unforeseen
Remembrance falls on what has been.
Flammonde

To shake the tree
Of life itself and bring down fruit un-
    heard-of.
Ben Jonson Entertains a Man
from Stratford

I would have rid the earth of him
    Once, in my pride. . . .
I never knew the worth of him
    Until he died.
An Old Story

Life is the game that must be played:
    This truth at least, good friends, we
    know;
So live and laugh, nor be dismayed
    As one by one the phantoms go.
Ballade by the Fire. Envoy

The songs of one who strove to play
    The broken flutes of Arcady.
Ballade of Broken Flutes

There be two men of all mankind
    That I'm forever thinking on:
They chase me everywhere I go, —
    Melchizedek, Ucalegon.
Two Men

Like dead, remembered footsteps on old
    floors.
The Pity of the Leaves

Oh for a poet — for a beacon bright
To rift this changeless glimmer of dead
    gray;
To spirit back the Muses, long astray,
And flush Parnassus with a newer light.
Sonnet

Look at a branch, a bird, a child, a rose,
Or anything God ever made that
    grows, —
Nor let the smallest vision of it slip,
Till you may read, as on Belshazzar's
    wall,
The glory of eternal partnership.
Sonnet

        And thus we die,
Still searching, like poor old astrono-
    mers
Who totter off to bed and go to sleep
To dream of untriangulated stars.
Octaves. XI

Two kinds of gratitude: the sudden
    kind
We feel for what we take, the larger
    kind
We feel for what we give.
Captain Craig. Part I

    Friends
To borrow my books and set wet glasses
    on them.
Ibid. Part II

The saddest among kings of earth,
Bowed with a galling crown, this man
Met rancor with a cryptic mirth,
Laconic — and Olympian.
The Master: Lincoln

And have one Titan at a time.
Ibid.

Wearing upon his forehead, with no fear,
The laurel of approved iniquity.
Uncle Ananias

Miniver loved the Medici,
Albeit he had never seen one;
He would have sinned incessantly
Could he have been one.
Miniver Cheevy

Miniver Cheevy, born too late,
Scratched his head and kept on thinking;
Miniver coughed, and called it fate,
And kept on drinking.
Ibid.

Thrall to the gilded ease
Of every day,
Mocker of all degrees
And always gay,
Child of the Cyclades
And of Broadway.
Bon Voyage

Who of us, being what he is,
May scoff at others' ecstasies?
However we may shine to-day,
More-shining ones are on the way.
Atherton's Gambit

The forehead and the little ears
Have gone where Saturn keeps the years;
The breast where roses could not live
Has done with rising and with falling.
For a Dead Lady

Death, like a friend unseen, shall say to me
My toil is over and my work begun.
The Three Taverns

If I have loosed
A shaft of language that has flown sometimes
A little higher than the hearts and heads
Of nature's minions, it will yet be heard.
Ibid.

I shall have more to say when I am dead.
John Brown

Like a physician who can do no good,
But knows how soon another would have his fee
Were he to tell the truth.
Avon's Harvest

Art's long hazard, where no man may choose
Whether he play to win, or toil to lose.
Caput Mortuum

Love that's wise
Will not say all it means.
Tristram. Part VII

For when a woman is left too much alone,
Sooner or later she begins to think;
And no man knows what then she may discover.
Ibid.

There is a little watchman in my heart
Who is always telling me what time it is.
Ibid. Part VIII

Love must have wings to fly away from love,
And to fly back again.
Ibid.

I like rivers
Better than oceans, for we see both sides.
An ocean is forever asking questions
And writing them aloud along the shore.
Roman Bartholow. Part III

Once in a life, they tell us, and once only,
So great a thing as a great love may come —
To crown us, or to mark us with a scar
No craft or custom shall obliterate.
Ibid. Part IV

A thousand golden sheaves were lying there,
Shining and still, but not for long to stay —
As if a thousand girls with golden hair
Might rise from where they slept and go away.
The Sheaves

Of all small things
That have the most infernal power to
grow,
Few may be larger than a few small
words
That may not say themselves and be
forgotten.
Genevieve and Alexandra

Here where the wind is always north-
north-east
And children learn to walk on frozen
tocs.
New England

HERBERT SHIPMAN
[1869–1930]

Across the gateway of my heart
I wrote "No Thoroughfare,"
But love came laughing by, and cried:
"I enter everywhere."
No Thoroughfare. Stanza 1

GEORGE STERLING
[1869–1926]

Their hearts, contemptuous of death,
shall dare
His roads between the thunder and
the sun.
The Black Vulture

Thou art the star for which all evening
waits.
Aldebaran at Dusk

Like truant children going home
We turn to thee, the beautiful and best.
The Final Faith

Into a crystal cup the dusky wine
I pour, and, musing at so rich a shrine,
I watch the star that haunts its ruddy
gloom.
A Wine of Wizardry

Let us be just with life. Although it
bear
A thousand thorns for every perfect
rose,
And though the happy day have
mournful close,
Slumber awaits to house the mind from
care.
The Balance

NEWTON BOOTH
TARKINGTON
[1869–   ]

Penrod was doing something very unusual and rare, something almost never
accomplished except by coloured people or by a boy in school on a spring
day: he was doing really nothing at all.
He was merely a state of being.
Penrod. Chap. 8

There are two things that will be believed of any man whatsoever, and one
of them is that he has taken to drink.
Ibid. Chap. 10

They were upon their great theme:
"When I get to be a man!" Being human, though boys, they considered
their present estate too commonplace to
be dwelt upon. So, when the old men
gather, they say: "When I was a boy!"
It really is the land of nowadays that
we never discover.
Ibid. Chap. 26

HILAIRE BELLOC
[1870–   ]

The voyage which I was born to
make in the end, and to which my desire
has driven me, is towards a place in
which everything we have known is forgotten, except those things which, as we
knew them, reminded us of an original
joy.
The Harbour in the North

Child, do not throw this book about,
Refrain from the unholy pleasure
Of cutting all the pictures out,
Regard it as your choicest treasure.
A Bad Child's Book of Beasts.
Foreword

Balliol made me, Balliol fed me,
Whatever I had she gave me again:
And the best of Balliol loved and led
me.
God be with you, Balliol men.
To the Balliol Men Still in Africa
[1900]

Oh, he didn't believe in Adam and
    Eve —
He put no faith therein;
His doubts began with the fall of man,
    And he laughed at original sin.
          Song of the Pelagian Heresy

The Tipple's aboard and the night is
    young,
The door's ajar and the Barrel is
    sprung,
I am singing the best song ever was
    sung
    And it has a rousing chorus.
        West Sussex Drinking Song.
                    Chorus

A lovely river, all alone,
    She lingers in the hills and holds
A hundred little towns of stones,
    Forgotten in the western wolds.
                The Evenlode

Don poor at Bed and worse at Table,
Don pinched, Don starved, Don miser-
    able;
Don stuttering, Don with roving eyes,
Don nervous, Don of crudities. . . .
Don middle-class, Don sycophantic,
Don dull, Don brutish, Don pedantic;
Don hypocritical, Don bad,
Don furtive, Don three-quarters mad;
Don (since a man must make an end),
Don that shall never be my friend.
              Lines to a Don

The moon on the one hand, the dawn
    on the other:
The moon is my sister, the dawn is my
    brother.
The moon on my left and the dawn on
    my right.
My brother, good morning: my sister,
    good night.
           The Early Morning

The great hills of the South Country
    They stand along the sea;
And it's there walking in the high
    woods
    That I could wish to be,
And the men that were boys when I was
    a boy
    Walking along with me.
      The South Country. Stanza 2

If I ever become a rich man,
    Or if ever I grow to be old,
I will build a house with deep thatch

To shelter me from the cold,
And there shall the Sussex songs be
    sung
    And the story of Sussex told.
      The South Country. Stanza 9

And the men that were boys when I was
    a boy
    Shall sit and drink with me.
           Ibid. Stanza 10

He does not die that can bequeath
Some influence to the land he knows,
Or dares, persistent, interwreath
Love permanent with the wild hedge-
    rows;
    He does not die, but still remains
    Substantiate with his darling plains.
        Duncton Hill. Stanza 1

They say that in the unchanging place,
    Where all we loved is always dear,
We meet our mornings face to face
    And find at last our twentieth year.
            Dedicatory Ode

From quiet homes and first beginning,
    Out to the undiscovered ends,
There's nothing worth the wear of win-
    ning
    But laughter and the love of friends.
                    Ibid.

For no one, in our long decline,
    So dusty, spiteful and divided,
Had quite such pleasant friends as
    mine,
    Or loved them half as much as I did.
                    Ibid.

Of Courtesy, it is much less
Than Courage of Heart or Holiness,
Yet in my walks it seems to me
That the Grace of God is in Courtesy.
                  Courtesy

Drinking when I had a mind to,
Singing when I felt inclined to.
           The Path to Rome

Most holy Night, that still dost keep
The keys of all the doors of sleep,
To me when my tired eyelids close
    Give thou repose.
         The Night. Stanza 1

Do you remember an Inn,
Miranda?
Do you remember an Inn?
And the tedding and the spreading
Of the straw for a bedding,

And the fleas that tease in the High
  Pyrenees,
And the wine that tasted of the tar?
Tarantella
Noting one that brings
With careless step a mist of shadowy
  things:
Laughter and memories, and a few re-
  grets,
Some honour, and a quantity of debts,
A doubt or two of sorts, a trust in God,
And (what will seem to you extremely
  odd)
His father's granfer's father's father's
  name,
Unspoilt, untitled, even spelt the same;
Charon, who twenty thousand times be-
  fore
Has ferried Poets to the ulterior shore,
Will estimate the weight I bear, and
  cry —
"Comrade!"
To Dives
I said to Heart, "How goes it?" Heart
  replied:
"Right as a Ribstone Pippin!" But it
  lied.
The False Heart
When I am dead, I hope it may be said:
"His sins were scarlet, but his books
  were read."
On His Books

CHARLES T. DAVIS

To ride, shoot straight, and speak the
  truth — [1]
This was the ancient Law of Youth.
Old times are past, old days are done;
But the Law runs true, O little son!
For a Little Boy. Stanza 1

ANNA BUNSTON DE BARY

O little lark, you need not fly
To seek your Master in the sky,
  He treads our native sod;
Why should you sing aloft, apart?
Sing to the heaven of my heart;
  In me, in me, in me is God!
*A Basque Peasant Returning
from Church. Stanza 1*

[1] See Byron, page 361.

LORD ALFRED DOUGLAS
[1870–   ]

I have been profligate of happiness
And reckless of the world's hostility,
The blessèd part has not been given to
  me
Gladly to suffer fools.
To Olive
Trace
Under the common thing the hidden
  grace
And conjure wonder out of emptiness,
Till mean things put on beauty like a
  dress
And all the world was an enchanted
  place.
The Dead Poet

JAMES STANLEY GILBERT
[? –1906]

Close the door — across the river
  He has gone.
With an abscess on his liver
  He has gone.
Many years of rainy seasons
And malaria's countless treasons
Are among the many reasons
  Why he's gone.
*Panama Patchwork.
He Has Gone, Stanza 1*

DENIS ALOYSIUS McCARTHY
[1870–1931]

Proud is the city — she finds a place for
  many a fad to-day,
But she's more than blind if she fails
  to find a place for the boys to
  play! [1]
*Give Them a Place to Play.
Stanza 3*
The newspaper poet's a commonplace
  fellow —
  The humblest may know what his
  poetry means.
But clearness is treason, and so, for this
  reason,
  He never gets into the big magazines.
The Newspaper Poet. Stanza 1

[1] See Eliza Cook, page 512.

CHARLOTTE MEW
[1870–1928]

What shall we do with this strange
Summer, meant for you, —
Dear, if we see the Winter through
What shall be done with Spring — ?
To a Child in Death
Bury your heart in some deep green
hollow
Or hide it up in a kind old tree;
Better still, give it the swallow
When she goes over the sea.
Saturday Market

HECTOR HUGH MUNRO
("SAKI")
[1870–1916]

She took to telling the truth; she said
she was forty-two and five months. It
may have been pleasing to the angels,
but her elder sister was not gratified.
Reginald [1904]
The cook was a good cook, as cooks
go; and as cooks go she went.
Ibid.
Women and elephants never forget
an injury.
Ibid.
I might have been a gold-fish in a
glass bowl for all the privacy I got.
Ibid.
Hating anything in the way of ill-
natured gossip ourselves, we are always
grateful to those who do it for us.
Reginald in Russia
"It was their Silver Wedding; such
lots of silver presents, quite a show."
"We must not grudge them their
show of presents after twenty-five years
of married life; it is the silver lining to
their cloud."
The Unbearable Bassington
Sherard Blaw, the dramatist who had
discovered himself, and who had given
so ungrudgingly of his discovery to the
world.
Ibid.
Confront a child, a puppy, and a kitten with a sudden danger; the child will
turn instinctively for assistance, the
puppy will grovel in abject submission,
the kitten will brace its tiny body for a
frantic resistance.
The Achievement of the Cat

FRANK NORRIS
[1870–1902]

He's the kind of man that gets up a
reputation for being clever and artistic
by running down the very one particular thing that every one likes, and
cracking up some book or picture or
play that no one has ever heard of.
The Pit. Chap. 2

ALICE HEGAN RICE
[1870–   ]

"Was he a church member?" . . .
"Well, no, not exactly," admitted
Mrs. Wiggs, reluctantly. "But he was
what you might say a well-wisher."
Mrs. Wiggs of the Cabbage Patch

CAROLYN WELLS

Youth is a silly, vapid state;
Old age with fears and ills is rife;
This simple boon I beg of Fate —
A thousand years of Middle Life!
My Boon
"A noble theme!" the tyro cried,
And straightway scribbled off a son-
net.
"A noble theme," the poet sighed,
"I am not fit to write upon it."
Humility
I love the Christmas-tide, and yet,
I notice this, each year I live;
I always like the gifts I get,
But how I love the gifts I give!
A Thought
He laughs best who laughs last,
The wiseacres vow;
But I am impatient,
I want to laugh now.
Delays Are Dangerous. Stanza 1
The books we think we ought to read
are poky, dull and dry;
The books that would like to read
we are ashamed to buy;
The books that people talk about we
never can recall;

And the books that people give us, Oh,
   they're the worst of all.
On Books
They borrow books they will not buy,
   They have no ethics or religions;
I wish some kind Burbankian guy
   Could cross my books with homing
      pigeons.
Book-Borrowers
I don't believe the half I hear,
   Nor the quarter of what I see!
But I have one faith, sublime and true,
   That nothing can shake or slay;
Each spring I firmly believe anew
   All the seed catalogues say!
One Firm Faith
The smile that won't come off.
Winning slogan in a contest

STEPHEN CRANE
[1871–1900]

He had fought like a pagan who defends his religion.
The Red Badge of Courage.
Chap. 17

Within him, as he hurled himself forward, was born a love, a despairing fondness for this flag which was near him. It was a creation of beauty and invulnerability.
Ibid. Chap. 19

None of them knew the color of the sky.
The Open Boat

Presently, God said,
"And what did you do?"
The little blade answered, "Oh, my Lord,
Memory is bitter to me,
For, if I did good deeds,
I know not of them."
Then God, in all His splendor,
Arose from His throne.
"O best little blade of grass!" He said.
The Blades of Grass

A man said to the universe:
   "Sir, I exist!"
"However," replied the universe,
"That fact has not created in me
A sense of obligation."
War Is Kind. Fragment

THOMAS AUGUSTINE DALY
[1871–   ]

I gotta love for Angela,
   I love Carlotta, too.
I no can marry both o' dem,
   So w'at I gona do?
Between Two Loves. Stanza 1

Da spreeng ees com'; but oh, da joy
   Eet ees too late!
He was so cold, my leetla boy,
   He no could wait.
Da Leetla Boy. Stanza 1

When all is still within these walls
And Thy sweet sleep through darkness
     falls
On little hearts that trust in me,
However bitter toil may be,
For length of days, O Lord! on Thee
     My spirit calls.
The Man's Prayer

Kind Reader, here's a tip for you:
   Go buy, though skinny be your purse
And other books of yours be few,
   "The Oxford Book of English Verse."
Ballade of the Tempting Book.
L'Envoi

Up to the breeze of the morning I fling
   you,
   Blending your folds with the dawn in
     the sky;
There let the people behold you, and
   bring you
   Love and devotion that never shall
     die.
Proudly, agaze at your glory, I stand,
Flag o' my land! flag o' my land!
Flag o' My Land. Stanza 1

Flo was fond of Ebenezer —
   "Eb," for short, she called her beau.
Talk of tides of love, great Caesar!
   You should see them — Eb and Flo.
The Tides of Love

Sing clear, O! throstle,
Thou golden-tongued apostle
And little brown-frocked brother
   Of the loved Assisian!
To a Thrush

W'at good eesa wife eef she don'ta be
   fat?
Da Styleesha Wife

Giuseppe, da barber, ees greata for
  "mash,"
He gotta da bigga, da blacka moustache,
Good clo'es an' good styla an' playnta
  good cash.
Mia Carlotta

I'm Home's heart! Warmth I give and
  light,
  If you but feed me.
I blossom in the winter night,
  When most you need me.
Inscription for a Fireplace

WILLIAM HENRY DAVIES
[1871–   ]

A poor life this if, full of care,
We have no time to stand and stare.
Leisure

They sniffed, poor things, for their
  green fields,
  They cried so loud I could not sleep:
For fifty thousand shillings down
  I would not sail again with sheep.
Sheep. Stanza 5

So every time we passed it by,
  Sailing to England's slaughter-house,
Eight ragged sheep-men — tramps and
  thieves —
  Would stroke that sheep's black nose.
A Child's Pet. Stanza 5

What glorious sunsets have their birth
  In Cities fouled by smoke!
This tree — whose roots are in a
  drain —
  Becomes the greenest Oak!
Love's Rivals

Look, there's a rainbow now!
  See how that lovely rainbow throws
Her jewelled arm around
  This world, when the rain goes.
The Rainbow. Stanza 2

I turned my head and saw the wind,
  Not far from where I stood,
Dragging the corn by her golden hair
  Into a dark and lonely wood.
The Villain

I am as certain of my song,
  When first it warms the brain,
As woman of her unborn child,
  Or wind that carries rain.
The Birth of Song

Nature's real king, to whom the power
  was given
To make an inkdrop scent the world
  for ever.
Shakespeare

I had Ambition, by which sin
  The angels fell;
I climbed and, step by step, O Lord,
  Ascended into Hell.
Ambition

There was a battle in her face,
  Between a lily and a rose;
My love would have the lily win,
  And I the lily lose.
Song

I'll make my Joy a secret thing,
  My face shall wear a mask of care;
And those who hunt a Joy to death,
  Shall never know what sport is
    there!
Hunting Joy. Stanza 3

I see at last our great Lamorna Cove,
Which, danced on by ten thousand sil-
  ver feet,
Has all those waves that run like little
  lambs,
To draw the milk from many a rocky
  teat,
Spilt in white gallons all along the
  shore.
Lamorna Cove

The mind, with its own eyes and ears,
  May for these others have no care;
No matter where this body is,
  The mind is free to go elsewhere. . . .
And when I'm passing near St. Paul's,
  I see, beyond the dome and crowd,
Twm Barlum, that green pap in Gwent,
  With its dark nipple in a cloud.
The Mind's Liberty

Strive not for gold, for greedy fools
  Measure themselves by poor men
    never;
Their standards still being richer men,
  Makes them poor ever.
Songs of Joy. Stanza 3

LADY PAMELA WYNDHAM
GLENCONNER
[1871–1928]

Bitter are the tears of a child:
  Sweeten them.

Deep are the thoughts of a child:
  Quiet them.
Sharp is the grief of a child:
  Take it from him.
Soft is the heart of a child:
  Do not harden it.
                                    A Child

ARTHUR GUITERMAN
[1871–   ]

Hail Guest! We ask not what thou art:
If Friend, we greet thee, hand and
  heart;
If Stranger, such no longer be;
If Foe, our love shall conquer thee.
                                    Door Verse

The Antiseptic Baby and the Prophy-
  lactic Pup
Were playing in the garden when the
  Bunny gamboled up;
They looked upon the Creature with a
  loathing undisguised; —
It wasn't Disinfected and it wasn't Ster-
  ilized.
                          Strictly Germ-Proof. Stanza 1

The Pilgrims landed, worthy men,
  And saved from wreck on raging seas,
They fell upon their knees, and then
Upon the Aborigines.[1]
                          *The Pilgrims' Thanksgiving
                              Feast. Stanza 1*

The Cat on your hearthstone to this
  day presages,
By solemnly sneezing, the coming of
  rain! [2]
                          The First Cat. Stanza 7

Oh, the saddest of sights in a world of
  sin
Is a little lost pup with his tail tucked
  in!
                          Little Lost Pup. Stanza 1

He stood with his muzzle thrust out
  through the door
The whole forty days of that terrible
  pour!
Because of which drenching, the Sages
  unfold,

The Nose of a Healthy Dog always is
  Cold.[1]
                          The Dog's Cold Nose

The finest thing in London is the
  Bobby;
Benignant information is his hobby.
                          The Lyric Baedeker. London

Drab is the town as a shawl-hooded
  crone,
And dreary and cold with a chill all its
  own.
You ask them for bread and they give
  you a scone,
  In Glasgow.
                          Ibid. Glasgow, Stanza 2

For Education is, Making Men;
So is it now, so was it when
Mark Hopkins sat on one end of a log
And James Garfield sat on the other.[2]
                                    Education

Amoebas at the start
  Were not complex;
They tore themselves apart
  And started Sex.
                                    Sex. Stanza 1

The three-toed tree-toad
Sings his sweet ode
  To the moon.
                                    Nocturne

I breathed a song into the air;
That little song of beauty rare
Is flying still, for all I know,
Around the world by Radio.
                                    Radiolatry

They earned a name that lives in song,
  Those woodsmen stout and plucky
Whose hair and rifles both were long —
  The Hunters of Kentucky.[3]
                                    The Tall Men

Of all cold words of tongue or pen
The worst are these: "I knew him
  when — "
                          Prophets in Their Own Country

---

[1] See W. M. Evarts, page 517.
[2] While rain depends, the pensive cat gives
      o'er
    Her frolics, and pursues her tail no more.
    JONATHAN SWIFT: *Description of a
                        City Shower*

[1] Most frozen was his honest nose,
      And never could it lose again
    The dampness of that dreadful rain.
    MARGARET EYTINGE: *Why the Dog's
                        Nose Is Cold* [1883]
[2] See James A. Garfield, page 591.
[3] See Woodworth, page 348.

Much have I sorrowed,
  Learning to my cost
That a book that's borrowed
  Is a book that's lost!
          Lament in a Library. Stanza 3

My sword is Strength, my spear is
    Song;
· With these upon a stubborn field
I challenge Falsehood, Fear and
    Wrong;
  But Laughter is my shield.
          Re-armed. Stanza 1

Oh, the Brown Missouri Mule has a
    copper-plated throat
And the welkin splits apart when he
    hits an upper note.
          Mule Song. Stanza 1

Lightly we follow our cue,
  "Exit, pursued by a bear." [1]
          The Shakespearean Bear. Envoi

Then up he rose, and forth they went
Away from battleground, fortress, tent,
Mountain, wilderness, field and farm,
Death and the General, arm in arm.
  Death and General Putnam.
          Death and General Putnam.
          Stanza 8

RALPH HODGSON
[1871–   ]

'Twould ring the bells of Heaven
The wildest peal for years,
If Parson lost his senses
And people came to theirs,
And he and they together
Knelt down with angry prayers
For tamed and shabby tigers
And dancing dogs and bears,
And wretched, blind pit ponies,
And little hunted hares.
          The Bells of Heaven

God loves an idle rainbow
No less than labouring seas.
          A Wood Song

I saw with open eyes
Singing birds sweet
Sold in the shops
For the people to eat,

[1] Stage direction, *The Winter's Tale,* Act
III, Sc. 3.

Sold in the shops of
Stupidity Street.
          Stupidity Street. Stanza 1

Time, you old gipsy man,
  Will you not stay,
Put up your caravan
  Just for one day?
          Time, You Old Gipsy Man.
          Stanza 1

Pity him, this dupe of dream,
Leader of the herd again
Only in his daft old brain,
Once again the bull supreme.
          The Bull

Wondering, listening,
Listening, wondering,
Eve with a berry
Half-way to her lips.
          Eve. Stanza 4

Oh, had our simple Eve
Seen through the make-believe!
          Ibid. Stanza 5

I stared into the sky,
As wondering men have always done
Since beauty and the stars were one,
Though none so hard as I.
          The Song of Honor

I heard it all, I heard the whole
Harmonious hymn of being roll
Up through the chapel of my soul
And at the altar die,
And in the awful quiet then
Myself I heard, Amen, Amen,
Amen I heard me cry!
          Ibid.

Reason has moons, but moons not hers
  Lie mirrored on her sea,
Confounding her astronomers,
  But O! delighting me.
          Reason

JAMES WELDON JOHNSON
[1871–1938]

O black and unknown bards of long
    ago,
How came your lips to touch the sacred
    fire?
How, in your darkness, did you come to
    know
The power and beauty of the minstrel's
    lyre?
          O Black and Unknown Bards.
          Stanza 1

Weep not, weep not,
She is not dead;
She's resting in the bosom of Jesus.
Heart-broken   husband — weep   no
      more;
Grief-stricken son — weep no more;
Left-lonesome   daughter — weep   no
      more;
She's only just gone home.

> *Go Down Death: A Funeral
> Sermon. Stanza 1*

CHARLES RANN KENNEDY
[1871–   ]

A peculiar kind of fear they call courage.

> *The Terrible Meek*

The meek, the terrible meek, the fierce agonizing meek, are about to enter into their inheritance.

> *Ibid.*

AGNES LEE
(MRS. OTTO FREER)

Then she gazed down some wilder,
      darker hour,
And said — when Mary questioned,
      knowing not,
"Who art thou, mother of so sweet a
      son?" —
"I am the mother of Iscariot."

> *Motherhood. Stanza 6*

Bed is the boon for me!
   It's well to bake and sweep,
But hear the word of old Lizette:
   It's better than all to sleep.

> *Old Lizette on Sleep. Stanza 1*

There's nothing, nothing, nothing, I
      say,
That's worth the lying awake!

> *Ibid. Stanza 3*

EDDIE NEWTON AND
T. LAURENCE SEIBERG

Casey Jones! Orders in his hand.
Casey Jones! Mounted to the cabin,
Took his farewell journey to that promised land.

> *Casey Jones [1900] (Adapted*

from verses and melody by
WALLACE SAUNDERS) [1]

HERBERT GEORGE
PONTING
[1871–1935]

On the outside grows the furside, on the
      inside grows the skinside;
So the furside is the outside, and the
      skinside is the inside.

> *The Sleeping Bag* [2]

JOHN MILLINGTON
SYNGE
[1871–1909]

It's in a lonesome place you do have to be talking with someone, and looking for someone, in the evening of the day.

> *In the Shadow of the Glen*

What is the price of a thousand horses against a son where there is one son only?

> *Riders to the Sea*

Bartley will have a fine coffin out of the white boards, and a deep grave surely. What more can we want than that? No man at all can be living for ever, and we must be satisfied.

> *Ibid.*

When I was writing "The Shadow of the Glen" I got more aid than any learning could have given me from a chink in the floor of the old Wicklow house where I was staying, that let me hear what was being said by the servant girls in the kitchen.

> *The Playboy of the Western
> World. Preface*

[1] Of the many versions of this traditional ballad, the most familiar is printed in CARL SANDBURG'S *The American Songbag* [1927]. It begins:
Come all you rounders, for I want you to hear
The story of a brave engineer.
Casey Jones was the rounder's name,
On a big eight-wheeler of a mighty fame.

[2] For *The South Polar Times, Midwinter Day, June 22, 1911,* prepared by the men of Captain Robert Falcon Scott's last Antarctic expedition.

Drink a health to the wonders of the western world, the pirates, preachers, poteen-makers, with the jobbing jockies; parching peelers, and the juries fill their stomachs selling judgments of the English law.

The Playboy of the Western World. Act II

May I meet him with one tooth and it aching, and one eye to be seeing seven and seventy divils in the twists of the road, and one old timber leg on him to limp into the scalding grave. There he is now crossing the strands, and that the Lord God would send a high wave to wash him from the world.[1]

Ibid.

Aid me for to win her, and I'll be asking God to stretch a hand to you in the hour of death, and lead you short cuts through the Meadows of Ease, and up the floor of Heaven to the Footstool of the Virgin's Son.

Ibid.

A man who is not afraid of the sea will soon be drowned, he said, for he will be going out on a day he shouldn't. But we do be afraid of the sea, and we do only be drownded now and again.

The Aran Islands. Page 127

There is no language like the Irish for soothing and quieting.

Ibid. Page 180

A translation is no translation, he said, unless it will give you the music of a poem along with the words of it.

Ibid. Page 181

ALBERT EDWARD WIGGAM
[1871–   ]

Intelligence appears to be the thing that enables a man to get along without education. Education appears to be

---

[1] May the grass grow at your door and the fox build his nest on your hearthstone. May the light fade from your eyes, so you never see what you love. May your own blood rise against you, and the sweetest drink you take be the bitterest cup of sorrow. May you die without benefit of clergy; may there be none to shed a tear at your grave, and may the hearthstone of hell be your best bed forever. — Traditional Wexford curse

the thing that enables a man to get along without the use of his intelligence.

The New Decalogue of Science

Statesmanship should quickly learn the lesson of biology, as stated by Conklin, that "Wooden legs are not inherited, but wooden heads are."

Ibid.

If your father went crazy from a hit on the head with a brickbat, you do not inherit his cracked brain but only his inability to dodge brickbats.

Ibid.

JULIET WILBOR TOMPKINS
[1871–   ]

The hurrying footsteps came and went,
And the heart beat thick for the great
     event,
When the Minister came to tea.[1]

When the Minister Came to Tea.
Stanza 1

MAX BEERBOHM
[1872–   ]

I have known no man of genius who had not to pay, in some affliction or defect either physical or spiritual, for what the gods had given him.

No. 2, The Pines

It seems to be a law of nature that no man ever is loth to sit for his portrait. A man may be old, he may be ugly, he may be burdened with grave responsibilities to the nation, and that nation be at a crisis of its history; but none of these considerations, nor all of them together, will deter him from sitting for his portrait.

Quia Imperfectum

To say that a man is vain means merely that he is pleased with the effect he produces on other people. A conceited man is satisfied with the effect he produces on himself.

Ibid.

---

[1] Pa has shaved as slick as can be, and I'm
     rigged way up in G,
And it's all because we're goin' ter have
     the minister ter tea.
     JOSEPH CROSBY LINCOLN: *When the Minister Comes to Tea, St. 1*

Strange, when you come to think of it, that of all the countless folk who have lived before our time on this planet not one is known in history or in legend as having died of laughter.

Laughter

He was fond of quoting those incomparable poets, Homer.

Works

JAMES BONE
[1872–   ]

The mighty fleet of Wren, with their topgallants and mainsails of stone.

The nautical simile leaps to the mind at the sight of Wren's white spires and towers, and it is appropriate, too, to the material in which Wren worked. Portland stone is a marine deposit of the Jurassic period before Britain first at Heaven's command arose from out the azure main. Its beds are full of fossils of marine creatures, cockles, sea-urchins, starfish, and oysters. You can see shell imprints on the freshly cut whitbed stone on the top of the new Bush Building, and you can see 'horses' heads' — as certain shell fossils are called by masons — on the weather-beaten south parapet of St. Paul's. You can see and feel the shells projecting from the plinth of King Charles's statue at Charing Cross. It is a strange thought that the majesty of the capital of this sea-joined empire should come itself from beneath the sea. How could our poets have missed such a theme?

The London Perambulator

The City of Dreadful Height.

Description of New York [1]

CALVIN COOLIDGE
[1872–1933]

Have faith in Massachusetts. In some unimportant detail some other States may surpass her, but in the general results, there is no place on earth where the people secure, in larger measure, the blessings of organized govern-

[1] In *The Manchester Guardian.*

ment, and nowhere can those functions more properly be termed self-government.

Address to the Massachusetts Senate on being elected its president [January 7, 1914]

There is no right to strike against the public safety by anybody, anywhere, any time.

Telegram to Samuel Gompers, President of the American Federation of Labor [September 14, 1919], on the occasion of the Boston police strike

Vermont is a State I love. I could not look upon the peaks of Ascutney, Killington, Mansfield, and Equinox without being moved in a way that no other scene could move me. It was here that I first saw the light of day; here I received my bride; here my dead lie pillowed on the loving breast of our everlasting hills. I love Vermont because of her hills and valleys, her scenery and invigorating climate, but most of all because of her indomitable people. They are a race of pioneers who have almost beggared themselves to serve others. If the spirit of liberty should vanish in other parts of our Union and support of our institutions should languish, it could all be replenished from the generous store held by the people of this brave little State of Vermont.

Address from train platform, Bennington, Vermont [September 21, 1928]

To my friend, in recollection of his son, and my son, who, by the grace of God, have the privilege of being boys throughout Eternity.

Inscription in a friend's book, after the death of Calvin Coolidge, Jr.

JAMES B. DOLLARD
[1872–   ]

I'm sick o' New York City an' the roarin' o' the thrains
That rowl above the blessèd roofs an' underneath the dhrains;

Wid dust an' smoke an' divilmint I'm
moidhered head an' brains,
An' I'm thinkin' o' the skies of ould
Kilkinny!
Ould Kilkinny!

PAUL LAURENCE DUNBAR
[1872–1906]

Sometimes the sun, unkindly hot,
My garden makes a desert spot;
Sometimes a blight upon the tree
Takes all my fruit away from me;
And then with throes of bitter pain
Rebellious passions rise and swell;
But — life is more than fruit or grain,
And so I sing, and all is well.
The Poet and His Song

Folks ain't got no right to censuah otha
folks about dey habits;
Him dat giv' de squir'ls de bushtails
made de bobtails fu' de rabbits.
Accountability

You cain't sta't no notes a-flyin'
Lak de ones dat rants and rings
From de kitchen to de big woods
When Malindy sings.
When Malindy Sings

There is a heaven, for ever, day by day,
The upward longing of my soul doth
tell me so.
There is a hell, I'm quite as sure; for
pray,
If there were not, where would my
neighbours go?
Theology

An' you couldn't he'p f'om dancin' ef
yo' feet was boun' wif twine,
When Angelina Johnson comes a-swingin' down de line.
Angelina

Speak up, Ike, an' 'spress yo'se'f.
Encouragement

Sweetah den de music of a lovesick
mockin'-bird,
Comin' f'om de gal you loves better den
yo' kin,
"Howdy, honey, howdy, won't you step
right in?"
"Howdy, Honey, Howdy!"

Heish yo' mouf, I's only tu'nin' of de
chillun in de bed.
The Turning of the Babies in the Bed

It's easy 'nough to titter w'en de stew
is smokin' hot,
But hit's mighty ha'd to giggle w'en
dey's nuffin' in de pot.
Philosophy

EVA GORE-BOOTH
[1872–1926]

The little waves of Breffny go stumbling
through my soul.
The Little Waves of Breffny.
Stanza 3

MILDRED HOWELLS
[1872–   ]

Yet close, I feel, there wraps us all
around
Some mighty force, some mystery profound,
And through my doubts and ignorance, I trust
The power that bound with laws the
moon and tide
And hung the stars in heavenly spaces
wide,
Must, by their witness, be both wise
and just.
If This Be All. Stanza 3

Within a garden once there grew
A flower that seemed the very pattern
Of all propriety; none knew
She was at heart a wandering slattern.
A Very Wild Flower. Stanza 1

And so it criticized each flower,
This supercilious seed;
Until it woke one summer hour,
And found itself a weed.
The Difficult Seed. Stanza 5

JOHN McCRAE
[1872–1918]

In Flanders fields the poppies blow
Between the crosses, row on row.
In Flanders Fields. Stanza 1 [1]
Take up our quarrel with the foe:
To you from failing hands we throw
The torch; be yours to hold it high.

[1] In London *Punch, Dec. 8, 1915.*

If ye break faith with us who die
We shall not sleep, though poppies grow
In Flanders fields.
In Flanders Fields. Stanza 3

JOHN CLAIR MINOT
[1872–   ]

May the God we trust as a nation
Throw the light of His peace and
grace
On a flag with its stripes untarnished,
And with every star in place.
*The Flag of Fort McHenry.
Stanza 10*

PATRICK F. O'KEEFE
[1872–1934]

Say it with flowers.
Slogan for the Society of American Florists [1917]

BERTRAND ARTHUR WILLIAM RUSSELL
[1872–   ]

It is preoccupation with possession,
more than anything else, that prevents
men from living freely and nobly.
Principles of Social Reconstruction
Mathematics possesses not only
truth, but supreme beauty — a beauty
cold and austere, like that of sculpture,
without appeal to any part of our
weaker nature, sublimely pure, and capable
of a stern perfection such as only
the greatest art can show.
The Study of Mathematics
Mathematics takes us into the region
of absolute necessity, to which not only
the actual world, but every possible
world, must conform.
Ibid.

LEONORA SPEYER
[1872–   ]

Out of my sorrow
I'll build a stair,
And every to-morrow
Will climb to me there

With ashes of yesterday
In its hair.
Duet: I Sing with Myself.

HENRY NOEL BRAILSFORD
[1873–   ]

Music is neither secular nor religious.
It can at best suggest the beating of
the pulse, the rhythm of the blood that
accompanies a given order of ideas.
On Handel's Largo
The musician who tries to rival the
painter by describing external things,
is a magician who has thrown aside his
wand to wield a quarter-staff.
The Sea in Music

GUY WETMORE CARRYL
[1873–1904]

You call it a waste of time, this taste
For popular tunes, and yet
Good-bye to care when you whistle the
air
Of the song that you can't forget.
The Organ Man. Stanza 3
How imposing it would be
If pumpkins grew upon a tree!
*The Iconoclast and the Acorn.
Stanza 1*
And in his dim, uncertain sight
Whatever wasn't must be right,
From which it follows he had strong
Convictions that what was, was wrong.
Ibid. Stanza 2
In every new and smart disease,
From housemaid's knee to heart disease,
She recognized the symptoms as her
own!
*How Jack Found That Beans May
Go Back on a Chap. Stanza 2*

ARTHUR CHAPMAN
[1873–1935]

Out where the handclasp's a little
stronger,

Out where the smile dwells a little
   longer,
  That's where the West begins.
        Out Where the West Begins.[1]
               Stanza 1
Out where the skies are a trifle bluer,
Out where friendship's a little truer.
            Ibid. Stanza 2
Where there's more of singing and less
   of sighing,
Where there's more of giving and less of
   buying,
And a man makes friends without half
   trying.
            Ibid. Stanza 3
Oh, the quickly faded glory
Of the cowboy's brief, brief story!
How the old range beckons vainly in the
   sunshine and the rain!
      The Cow-Puncher's Elegy.
               Stanza 2
Plain duty's a term that is harsh to men
   In the country God forgot.
    The Border Riders. Stanza 1

WALTER DE LA MARE
[1873–   ]

Slowly, silently, now the moon
Walks the night in her silver shoon.
                Silver
Couched in his kennel, like a log,
With paws of silver sleeps the dog.
                Ibid.
When all at peace, two friends at ease
   alone
Talk out their hearts; yet still

  [1] Up where the north winds blow just a
     little keener,
  Up where the grasses grow just a little
     greener,
  Up where the mountain peaks rise a little
     higher,
  Up where the human kind draws a little
     nigher,
     That's where Vermont comes in.
     CHARLES HIAL DARLING [1859–   ]:
        Where Vermont Comes In

  Down where I fear there's a terrible lot
     o' me,
  Down where some people are hippopot-
     ami,
  In the department of laparotomy,
     That's where the vest begins.
     ARTHUR GUITERMAN: *Vulgar Lines*
      for a Distinguished Surgeon, St. 3

Between the grace notes of
The voice of love
From each to each
Trembles a rarer speech,
And with its presence every pause doth
   fill.
                Silence
"World of divine delight," heart whis-
   pereth,
Though all its all lie but 'twixt birth
   and death.
           Divine Delight
Softly along the road of evening,
  In a twilight dim with rose,
Wrinkled with age, and drenched with
   dew,
  Old Nod, the shepherd, goes.
           Nod. Stanza 1
Here lies a most beautiful lady,
Light of step and heart was she.
           An Epitaph
"Is there anybody there?" said the
   Traveller,
Knocking on the moonlit door;
And his horse in the silence champed
   the grasses
Of the forest's ferny floor.
         The Listeners
"Tell them that I came, and no one
   answered,
  That I kept my word," he said.
                Ibid.
If I were Lord of Tartary,
  Myself and me alone,
My bed should be of ivory,
  Of beaten gold my throne.
        Tartary. Stanza 1
I saw sweet Poetry turn troubled eyes
On shaggy Science nosing in the grass;
For by that way poor Poetry must pass
On her long pilgrimage to Paradise.
      The Happy Encounter
Look thy last on all things lovely
Every hour. Let no night
Seal thy sense in deathly slumber
Till to delight
Thou have paid thy utmost blessing.
       Farewell. Stanza 3
Here lies, but seven years old, our little
   maid,
Once of the darkness, oh, so sore afraid.
Light of the World — remember that
   small fear,

And when nor moon nor stars do shine
  — draw near!
                   An Epitaph

'Tis the immortal thought
  Whose passion still
Makes of the unchanging
  The unchangeable.
        When the Rose Is Faded.
                 Stanza 3

No lovelier hills than thine have laid
  My tired thoughts to rest:
No peace of lovelier valleys made
  Like peace within my breast.
           England. Stanza 1

My heart within me faints to roam
  In thought even far from thee:
Thine be the grave whereto I come,
  And thine my darkness be.
             Ibid. Stanza 4

Nay, nay, sweet England, do not
  grieve!
Not one of these poor men who died
But did within his soul believe
  That death for thee was glorified.
      "How Sleep the Brave." Stanza 1

And into Time's enormous nought,
  Sweet-fed, will flit away.
          Titmouse. Stanza 3

Hi! handsome hunting man,
Fire your little gun.
Bang! Now the animal
Is dead and dumb and done.
Nevermore to peep again, creep again,
  leap again,
Eat or sleep or drink again, oh, what
  fun!
                     Hi!

"Chariots of gold," says Timothy;
"Silvery wings," says Elaine;
"A bumpity ride in a wagon of hay
For me," says Jane.
        Bunches of Grapes. Stanza 3

Ann, Ann!
  Come! quick as you can!
There's a fish that *talks*
  In the frying pan.
             Alas, Alack

It's a very odd thing —
  As odd as can be —
That whatever Miss T. eats
  Turns into Miss T.
                Miss T.

Who said, "Ay, mum's the word";
  Sexton to willow:
Who said, "Green dusk for dreams,
  Moss for a pillow"?
Who said, "All Time's delight
  Hath she for narrow bed;
Life's troubled bubble broken"? —
  That's what I said.
      Song of the Mad Prince. Stanza 2

Be not too wildly amorous of the far,
  Nor lure thy fantasy to its utmost
  scope.
        The Imagination's Pride

But what can Miss Emily
  Want with a box
So long, narrow, shallow,
  And without any locks?
             Peeping Tom

At lip, miraculous, life's wine,
  At hand, its wondrous bread.
             The Sleeper

Never was sweeter seraph hid
  Within so small a house —
A tiny, inch-long, eager, ardent
  Feathered mouse.
             Jenny Wren

Grotesque, irrational, and sans
All law and order known as Man's.
        Dreams. Stanza 3

At his absence all elate,
His body's artisans sustain
Their toil in sinew, nerve, and brain:
Nothing recks he: he roves afar,
Past compass, chart, and calendar.
           Ibid. Stanza 4

The genius of William Hamilton
Sought the square root of *minus* one;
In vain; till — all thought of it leagues
  away —
The problem flowered from a dream one
  day.
         Ibid. Stanza 25

And Conscience less my mind indicts
For idle days than dreamless nights.
         Ibid. Stanza 37

FORD MADOX (HUEFFER) FORD

[1873–   ]

But we who remain shall grow old,
We shall know the cold
Of cheerless

Winter and the rain of Autumn and the
 sting
Of poverty, of love despised and of dis-
 graces,
And mirrors showing stained and aging
 faces,
And the long ranges of comfortless
 years
And the long gamut of human fears —
But for you — it shall be forever
 Spring.
       One Day's List

LENA GUILBERT FORD
[*Floruit* 1915]

Keep the home fires burning,
While your hearts are yearning,
Though your lads are far away
They dream of home.
There's a silver lining
Through the dark clouds shining,
Turn the dark clouds inside out,
Till the boys come home.
     Keep the Home Fires
      Burning [*1915*]

WILLIAM HERSCHELL
[1873–]

The Kid has gone to the Colors
 And we don't know what to say;
The Kid we have loved and cuddled
 Stepped out for the Flag to-day.
   The Kid Has Gone to the
    Colors [*1917*]. *Stanza 1*

What do little girls talk about?
 What is their mystic theme?
Those still too young for puppy love,
 Yet old enough to dream.
   What Do Little Girls Talk
    About? Stanza 1

Ain't God good to Indiana!
 Folks, a feller never knows
Just how close he is to Eden
 Till, sometime, he ups and goes
Seekin' fairer, greener pastures
 Than he has right here at home.
   Ain't God Good to Indiana!
    Stanza 1

DANIEL GREGORY MASON
[1873–]

The ideal of Independence requires
resistance to the herd spirit now so
widespread, to our workshop of quantity and indifference to quality, to our
unthinking devotion to organization,
standardization, propaganda, and advertising.
    Artistic Ideals. Page 3

Art of any profundity can be appreciated only slowly, gradually, in leisurely contemplation.
     Ibid. Page 105

JAMES JACKSON MONTAGUE
[1873–]

My beagle bit a Kleagle
Of the Ku Klux Klan.
    Doomed. Stanza 1

But no one ever is allowed in Sleepy-
 town, unless
He goes to bed in time to take the
 Sleepytown Express!
  The Sleepytown Express. Stanza 1

ELIZABETH CUTTER
(MRS. DWIGHT WHITNEY)
MORROW
[1873–]

My friend and I have built a wall
 Between us thick and wide:
The stones of it are laid in scorn
 And plastered high with pride.
    Wall. Stanza 1

There is no lover like an island shore
For lingering embrace;
No tryst so faithful as the turning tide
At its accustomed place.
    Islands. Stanza 1

He who has given
A hostage knows
All ways of dying
Terror shows.
     Hostage

H. M. TOMLINSON
[1873–]

The sea is at its best at London, near
midnight, when you are within the arms

of a capacious chair, before a glowing fire, selecting phases of the voyages you will never make.

The Sea and the Jungle

In the west was a steep range of cloudland rising from the sea, and against it was inclined the flame of a rainbow. The world's noble emblem was aloft. I demanded of the Skipper if he would run up our ensign in reply to it; but he only peered at me curiously.

Ibid.

How many grave speeches, which have surprised, shocked, and directed the nation, have been made by Great Men too soon after a noble dinner, words winged by the Press without an accompanying and explanatory wine list.

Waiting for Daylight

That figure of Nobody in sodden khaki, cumbered with ugly gear, its precious rifle wrapped in rags, no brightness anywhere about it except the light of its eyes, its face seamed with lines which might have been dolorous, which might have been ironic, with the sweat running from under its steel casque, looms now in the memory, huge, statuesque, silent but questioning, like an overshadowing challenge. . . .

What is that figure now? The ghost of what was fair, but was broken, and is lost.

Ibid. The Nobodies [*November 11, 1918*]

The reader who is illuminated is, in a real sense, the poem.

Between the Lines [1]

Bad and indifferent criticism of books is just as serious as a city's careless drainage.

Ibid.

It has to be a good book which can maintain its value beside the lamp of a ship's berth at midnight — the best time and place in all the world for reading.

South to Cadiz. Sea-Light

[1] Lecture at the Harvard Union, Oct. 14, 1927.

What was created in Concord, though in so airy a fashion, may be standing to America's credit when her vast engine shops are homes for spiders.

The Road to Concord [*1931*]

MAURICE BARING
[1874–   ]

Because of you we will be glad and gay,
    Remembering you, we will be brave
        and strong;
And hail the advent of each dangerous
        day,
    And meet the great adventure with
        a song.

Julian Grenfell (*1888–1915*) [1]

And you will speed us onward with a
        cheer,
    And wave beyond the stars that all is
        well.

Ibid.

All theories of what a good play is, or how a good play should be written, are futile. A good play is a play which when acted upon the boards makes an audience interested and pleased. A play that fails in this is a bad play.

Have You Anything to Declare?

DAVID WILLIAM BONE
[1874–   ]

"Ah wouldna go in them if ye wass t' gif me thirrty pounss a munss! Coaffins, Ah caall them!"

I thought of a ship staggering hard-pressed to windward of a ledge of cruel rocks, the breakers shrieking for a prey, and the old grey-haired Master of her slapping the rail and shouting, "Up t' it, m' beauty! T' windward, ye bitch!"

"Aye, coaffins," he repeated. "That iss what they are!"

I had no answer — he was a steamboat man, and would not have understood.

The Brassbounder. Chap. 26

[1] Julian Grenfell, Captain in the First Royal Dragoons, wounded near Ypres, March 13, 1915, died at Boulogne, May 26.

We sailors are jealous for our vessels. Abuse us if you will, but have a care for what you may say of our ships. We alone are entitled to call them bitches, wet brutes, stubborn craft, but we will stand for no such liberties from the beach.

Merchantmen-at-Arms

Nobly she has held afloat to the debarking of the last man. There is no further life in her. Evenly, steadily, as we had seen her leave the launching ways at Meadowside, she goes down.[1]

Ibid.

GORDON BOTTOMLEY
[1874–]

Many deaths have place in men
　Before they come to die;
Joys must be used and spent, and then
　Abandoned and passed by.

New Year's Eve, 1913

Poetry is founded on the hearts of men:
Though in Nirvana or the Heavenly
　courts
The principle of beauty shall persist,
Its body of poetry, as the body of man,
Is but a terrene form, a terrene use,
That swifter being will not loiter with;
And, when mankind is dead and the
　world cold,
Poetry's immortality will pass.

Atlantis

When you destroy a blade of grass
　You poison England at her roots.

To Iron Founders and Others

Your worship is your furnaces,
　Which, like old idols, lost obscenes,
Have molten bowels; your vision is
　Machines for making more machines.

Ibid.

GILBERT KEITH
CHESTERTON
[1874–1936]

Nothing sublimely artistic has ever arisen out of mere art, any more than anything essentially reasonable has ever arisen out of the pure reason. There

[1] Sinking of the *Cameronia*, torpedoed in the Mediterranean.

must always be a rich moral soil for any great aesthetic growth.

A Defence of Nonsense

Every great literature has always been allegorical — allegorical of some view of the whole universe.

Ibid.

The whole difference between construction and creation is exactly this: that a thing constructed can only be loved after it is constructed; but a thing created is loved before it exists.

Preface to DICKENS' *Pick-wick Papers*

A man knows what style of book he wants to write when he knows nothing else about it.

Ibid.

The book originated in the suggestion of a publisher; as many more good books have done than the arrogance of the man of letters is commonly inclined to admit.

Ibid.

A good joke is the one ultimate and sacred thing which cannot be criticized. Our relations with a good joke are direct and even divine relations.

Ibid.

The world will never starve for wonders; but only for want of wonder.

Inscription on General Motors Building, A Century of Progress Exposition, Chicago

But they that fought for England,
　Following a fallen star,
Alas, alas for England
　They have their graves afar.

Elegy in a Country Churchyard

If I ever go back to Baltimore,
The City of Maryland,
I shall miss again as I missed before
A thousand things of the world in store,
The story standing in every door
That beckons on every hand.

Memory

Like the white lock of Whistler, that lit
　our aimless gloom,
Men showed their own white feather as
　proudly as a plume.

*The Man Who Was Thursday.
Dedication, to Edmund Clerihew Bentley*

Far out of fish-shaped Paumanok some
    cry of cleaner things; [1]
And the Green Carnation withered, as
    in forest fires that pass.[2]
*   The Man Who Was Thursday.*
*   Dedication*

Truth out of Tusitala [3] spoke and
    pleasure out of pain.
*   Ibid.*

Thieves respect property. They
merely wish the property to become
their property that they may more perfectly respect it.
*   Ibid.*

Mr. Max Beerbohm attempted to
analyze the jokes at which the mob
laughs. He divided them into three sections: jokes about bodily humiliation,
jokes about things alien, such as foreigners, and jokes about bad cheese.
*   Cockneys and Their Jokes*

Art is limitation; the essence of every
picture is the frame.
*   Orthodoxy. Chap. 3*

You can free things from alien or accidental laws, but not from the laws of
their own nature. . . . Do not go
about as a demagogue, encouraging tri-
angles to break out of the prison of
their three sides. If a triangle breaks out
of its three sides, its life comes to a
lamentable end.
*   Ibid.*

The English poor, broken in every revolt, bullied by every fashion, long despoiled of property, and now being
despoiled of liberty, entered history
with a noise of trumpets, and turned
themselves in two years into one of the
iron armies of the world.
*   A Short History of England*
*   [1917]*

Don John of Austria is going to the war.
*   Lepanto*

The hidden room in a man's house
    where God sits all the year,

[1] Walt Whitman.
[2] Oscar Wilde.
[3] Robert Louis Stevenson.

The secret window whence the world
    looks small and very dear.
*   Lepanto*

Cervantes on his galley sets the sword
    back in the sheath
(Don John of Austria rides homeward
    with a wreath).
And he sees across a weary land a strag-
    gling road in Spain,
Up which a lean and foolish knight for-
    ever rides in vain.
*   Ibid.*

To an open house in the evening
Home shall men come,
To an older place than Eden
And a taller town than Rome.
*   The House of Christmas*

Burn from my brain and from my
    breast
Sloth, and the cowardice that clings,
And stiffness and the soul's arrest:
And feed my brain with better things.
*   A Ballade of a Book-Reviewer*

I think I will not hang myself to-day.
*   A Ballade of Suicide*

St. George he was for England,
And before he killed the dragon
He drank a pint of English ale
Out of an English flagon.
*   The Englishman*

Step softly, under snow or rain,
    To find the place where men can
      pray;
The way is all so very plain
    That we may lose the way.
*   The Wise Men*

And Noah he often said to his wife
    when he sat down to dine,
"I don't care where the water goes if
    it doesn't get into the wine."
*   Wine and Water*

Before the Roman came to Rye or out
    to Severn strode,
The rolling English drunkard made the
    rolling English road.
*   The Rolling English Road*

If an angel out of heaven
Brings you other things to drink,
Thank him for his kind attentions,
Go and pour them down the sink.
*   The Song of Right and Wrong*

Tea is like the East he grows in,
A great yellow Mandarin
With urbanity of manner
And unconsciousness of sin.
        The Song of Right and Wrong
And, like all the East he grows in,
He is Poison when he's strong.
                            Ibid.

Cocoa is a cad and coward.
                            Ibid.

Heaven sent us Soda Water
As a torment for our crimes.
                            Ibid.

For the great Gaels of Ireland
    Are the men that God made mad,
For all their wars are merry,
    And all their songs are sad.[1]
        *The Ballad of the White
                Horse. Book II*
And if ever ye ride in Ireland,
    The jest may yet be said,
There is the land of broken hearts,
    And the land of broken heads.
                    Ibid. Book V
I also had my hour;
One far fierce hour and sweet:
There was a shout about my ears,
And palms before my feet.[2]
                        The Donkey
The Yankee is a dab at electricity and
        crime,
He tells you how he hustles and it takes
        him quite a time,
I like his hospitality that's cordial and
        frank,
I do not mind his money but I do not
        like his swank.
                    A Song of Self-Esteem
The Faith of Tennessee has wafted
        o'er the sea,
The odour of its sanctity — and Golly
        how it stank![3]
                            Ibid.

---

[1] For the Young Gaels of Ireland
        Are the lads that drive me mad;
    For half their words need footnotes,
        And half their rhymes are bad.
            ARTHUR GUITERMAN: *The Young
                        Celtic Poets, St. 2*
[2] My shoulders were His throne.
            JOHN B. TABB: *The Burthen
                            of the Ass*
[3] The prosecution of John Thomas Scopes
in Dayton, Tennessee, July, 1925, for teach-

ISABEL FISKE CONANT
[1874–   ]

Give me but a tearing,
    A scrap of Beauty's cloth,
Warm from her wearing;
    A song, a shell, a moth,
Still faintly fragrant;
    Her glove, her torn veil,
And I will find vagrant
    Beauty's trail.
                Hound of Beauty. Stanza 1
He who loves an old house
Never loves in vain,
How can an old house
Used to sun and rain,
To lilac and larkspur,
And an elm above,
Ever fail to answer
The heart that gives it love?
                    Old House. Stanza 1
If haloed Christ still walked to-day
And made new saints again,
I'd have for mine, in bright array,
Old Ellen, down the lane.
                    Old Ellen. Stanza 1

CLARENCE DAY
[1874–1935]

A race of civilized beings descended
from the great cats would have been
rich in hermits and solitary thinkers.
The recluse would not have been stigmatized as peculiar, as he is by us
simians. They would not have been a
credulous people, or easily religious.
False prophets and swindlers would
have found few dupes. And what generals they would have made! what consummate politicians!
                    This Simian World. VI
Curiosity is a valuable trait. It will
make the simians learn many things.
But the curiosity of a simian is as excessive as the toil of an ant. Each
simian will wish to know more than his
head can hold, let alone ever deal with;
and those whose minds are active will
wish to know everything going. It would
stretch a god's skull to accomplish such

---

ing the theory of evolution in his classroom
at the Central High School.

an ambition, yet simians won't like to think it's beyond their powers. Even small tradesmen and clerks, no matter how thrifty, will be eager to buy costly encyclopedias, or books of all knowledge. Almost every simian family, even the dullest, will think it is due to themselves to keep all knowledge handy.

This Simian World. IX

Simians even believe, many of them, that knowledge is power. Unfortunate dupes of this saying will keep on reading, ambitiously, till they have stunned their native initiative, and made their thoughts weak; and will then wonder dazedly what in the world is the matter, and why the great power they were expecting to gain fails to appear. Again, if they ever forget what they read, they'll be worried. Those who *can* forget — those with fresh eyes who have swept from their minds such facts as the exact month and day that their children were born, or the numbers on houses, or the names (the mere meaningless labels) of the people they meet, — will be urged to go live in sanitariums or see memory doctors!

Ibid.

Huge seas of talk of every sort and kind, in print, speech, and writing, will roll unceasingly, involving an unbelievable waste in labor and time, and sapping the intelligence talk is supposed to upbuild. In a simian civilization, great halls will be erected for lectures, and great throngs will actually pay to go inside at night to hear some self-satisfied talk-maker chatter for hours. Almost any subject will do for a lecture, or talk; yet very few subjects will be counted important enough for the average man to do any *thinking* on them, off by himself.

Ibid. X

It is possible that our race may be an accident, in a meaningless universe, living its brief life uncared-for, on this dark, cooling star: but even so — and all the more — what marvelous creatures we are! What fairy story, what tale from the Arabian Nights of the jinns, is a hundredth part as wonderful as this true fairy story of simians! It is so much more heartening, too, than the tales we invent. A universe capable of giving birth to many such accidents is — blind or not — a good world to live in, a promising universe.

This Simian World. XIX

Father declared he was going to buy a new plot in the cemetery, a plot all for himself. "And I'll buy one on a corner," he added triumphantly, "where I can get out!"

Mother looked at him, startled but admiring, and whispered to me, "I almost believe he could do it."

Life with Father

JAMES WILLIAM FOLEY
[1874–   ]

It does a heap o' good sometimes, to go
   a little slow,
To say a word o' comfort to th' man
   that's stubbed his toe.

Stubbed His Toe. Stanza 2

I take a little bunch of words and set
   'em in a row,
I take a little bit of ink and mark 'em
   down just so.[1]

Technique

THEODOSIA GARRISON
[1874–   ]

I sicken of men's company,
   The crowded tavern's din,
Where all day long with oath and song
   Sit they who entrance win,
So come I out from noise and rout
   To rest in God's Green Inn.

The Green Inn. Stanza 1

ELLEN GLASGOW
[1874–   ]

I have observed with wonder so many intellectual and literary fashions that I have come at last to rely positively

---

[1] Webster has the words, and I
   Pick them up from where they lie,
   Twist and turn them one by one
   And give them places in "The Sun."
   DON MARQUIS: *On the Ease of Column
      Writing*

upon one conviction alone. No idea is so antiquated that it was not once modern. No idea is so modern that it will not some day be antiquated. . . . To seize the flying thought before it escapes us is our only touch with reality.

Address to the Modern Language Association [*1936*]

HARRY GRAHAM
[1874–1936]

Though the noblest disposition you inherit,
And your character with piety is pack'd,
All such qualities have very little merit,
Unaccompanied by Tact.

Tact. Stanza 1

HERBERT CLARK HOOVER
[1874–　　]

A great social and economic experiment, noble in motive and far-reaching in purpose.

[*Of National Prohibition.*] *Letter to Senator Borah, February 28, 1928*

We were challenged with a peacetime choice between the American system of rugged individualism and a European philosophy of diametrically opposed doctrines — doctrines of paternalism and state socialism.

Campaign speech, New York [*October 22, 1928*]

Absolute freedom of the press to discuss public questions is a foundation stone of American liberty.[1]

Address, Annual Luncheon of the Associated Press, New York [*April 22, 1929*]

[1] Where dwells the man that dare suppress
The noble freedom of the press?
Sure he who would attempt the thing,
On Haman's gallows ought to swing.
ANONYMOUS: *The Freedom of the Press, St. 1,* in *Freeman's Journal* (*North American Intelligencer*), *June 27, 1787*
See James Russell Lowell, page 526.

No economic equality can survive the working of biological inequality.

The Challenge to Liberty [*1934*]. *Chap. 3*

While I can make no claim for having introduced the term "rugged individualism," I should be proud to have invented it. It has been used by American leaders for over a half-century in eulogy of those God-fearing men and women of honesty whose stamina and character and fearless assertion of rights led them to make their own way in life.

Ibid. Chap. 5

When I comb over these accounts of the New Deal, my sympathy arises for the humble decimal point. His is a pathetic and hectic life, wandering around among regimented ciphers, trying to find some of the old places he used to know.

Address, John Marshall Republican Club, St. Louis, Missouri [*December 16, 1935*]

A good many things go around in the dark besides Santa Claus.

Ibid.

HENRY HERBERT KNIBBS
[1874–　　]

We'll dance a merry saraband from here to drowsy Samarcand;
Along the sea, across the land, the birds are flying South,
And you, my sweet Penelope, out there somewhere you wait for me,
With buds of roses in your hair and kisses on your mouth.

Out There Somewhere

I'm strong for the man who named it,
The Valley that God Forgot.

The Valley that God Forgot

Have ye dreamed of the mesa grass starred with the flower of blue;
Morning haze in the mountain-pass, sage in the silver dew?

Last of the Cavaliers

Sage a-shinin' in the sun that's just
a-breakin' cover;
All around the ranges loomin' high and
cold and still.
The Far and Lonely Hill
After the coffee things ain't so bad.
That Inside Song
You haven't whipped religion; just a
man.
The Fighting Parson
Far trails await me; valleys vast and
still,
Vistas undreamed-of, cañon-guarded
streams,
Lowland and range, fair meadow,
flower-girt hill,
Forests enchanted, filled with magic
dreams.
Make Me No Grave
The heart of a dog — and he love a
man — may never forget or
change.
The Dog-Star Pup
Roll a rock down when I slide into glory,
And say that I went like a ranger
should go.
Roll a Rock Down

AMY LOWELL
[1874–1925]

My words are little jars
For you to take and put upon a shelf.
Their shapes are quaint and beautiful,
And they have many pleasant colours
and lustres
To recommend them.
A Gift
Hung all over with mouse-traps of
metres, and cages
Of bright-plumaged rhythms, with
pages and pages
Of colours slit up into streaming confetti.
A Critical Fable [1] *(passage
describing herself)*
Hedges of England, peppered with
sloes; hedges of England, rows and rows
of thorn and brier raying out from the
fire where London burns with its steam-
ing lights, throwing a glare on the sky
o' nights. Hedges of England, road after

[1] First published anonymously.

road, lane after lane, and on again to
the sea at the North, to the sea at the
East, blackberry hedges, and man and
beast plod and trot and gallop between
hedges of England, clipped and clean;
beech, and laurel, and hornbeam, and
yew, wheels whirl under, and circle
through, tunnels of green to the sea at
the South; wind-blown hedges to mark
the mouth of Thames or Humber, the
Western rim. Star-point hedges, smooth
and trim.
Hedge Island
I walk down the garden paths,
And all the daffodils
Are blowing, and the bright blue squills.
Patterns
A pattern called a war.
Christ! What are patterns for?
Ibid.
All about us peal the loud, sweet *Te
Deums* of the Canterbury bells.
Madonna of the Evening Flowers
Heart-leaves of lilac all over New Eng-
land,[1]
Roots of lilac under all the soil of New
England,
Lilac in me because I am New England.
Lilacs
The sight of a white church above thin
trees in a city square
Amazes my eyes as though it were the
Parthenon.
Meeting-House Hill

JOHN MASEFIELD [2]
[1874–   ]

Not of the princes and prelates with
periwigged charioteers
Riding triumphantly laurelled to lap
the fat of the years, —
Rather the scorned — the rejected —
the men hemmed in with the
spears.
A Consecration. Stanza 1
Others may sing of the wine and the
wealth and the mirth,

[1] Stands the lilac-bush tall-growing with
heart-shaped leaves of rich green.
WALT WHITMAN: *When Lilacs Last
in the Dooryard Bloom'd*
[2] Appointed Poet Laureate, 1930.

The portly presence of potentates
  goodly in girth; —
Mine be the dirt and the dross, the dust
  and scum of the earth!
            A Consecration. Stanza 6
Theirs be the music, the colour, the
  glory, the gold;
Mine be a handful of ashes, a mouthful
  of mould.
Of the maimed, of the halt and the
  blind in the rain and the cold —
Of these shall my songs be fashioned,
  my tales be told.
            Ibid. Stanza 7
I must go down to the seas again, to
  the lonely sea and the sky,
And all I ask is a tall ship and a star
  to steer her by.
            Sea-Fever. Stanza 1
And all I ask is a merry yarn from a
  laughing fellow-rover,
And quiet sleep and a sweet dream when
  the long trick's over.
            Ibid. Stanza 3
The schooners and the merry crews are
  laid away to rest,
A little south the sunset in the Islands of
  the Blest.
            A Ballad of John Silver. Stanza 6
And he who gives a child a treat
Makes joy-bells ring in Heaven's street,
And he who gives a child a home
Builds palaces in Kingdom come.
            The Everlasting Mercy
To get the whole world out of bed
And washed, and dressed, and warmed,
  and fed,
To work, and back to bed again,
Believe me, Saul, costs worlds of pain.
            Ibid.
Whatever seems, God doth not slumber
Though he lets pass times without
  number.
He'll come with trump to call his own,
And this world's way'll be overthrown.
            Ibid.
O Christ who holds the open gate,
O Christ who drives the furrow straight,
O Christ, the plough, O Christ, the
  laughter
Of holy white birds flying after.
            Ibid.

The rain that makes things new,
The earth that hides things old.
            The Everlasting Mercy
When I am buried, all my thoughts and
  acts
Will be reduced to lists of dates and
  facts,
And long before this wandering flesh
  is rotten
The dates which made me will be all
  forgotten.
            Biography
O Time, bring back those midnights
  and those friends,
Those glittering moments that a spirit
  lends.
            Ibid.
The days that make us happy make us
  wise.
            Ibid.
Man with his burning soul
Has but an hour of breath
To build a ship of Truth
In which his soul may sail,
Sail on the sea of death,
For death takes toll
Of beauty, courage, youth,
Of all but Truth.
            Truth. Stanza 1
Spanish waters, Spanish waters, you
  are ringing in my ears,
Like a slow sweet piece of music from
  the grey forgotten years.
            Spanish Waters. Stanza 1
In the dark womb where I began
My mother's life made me a man.
Through all the months of human birth
Her beauty fed my common earth.
I cannot see, nor breathe, nor stir,
But through the death of some of her.
            C. L. M. Stanza 1
Quinquireme of Nineveh from distant
  Ophir,
Rowing home to haven in sunny Pales-
  tine,
With a cargo of ivory,
And apes and peacocks,[1]
Sandalwood, cedarwood, and sweet
  white wine.
            Cargoes. Stanza 1

[1] Once in three years came the navy of
Tharshish, bringing gold, and silver, ivory,
and apes and peacocks. — *I Kings, X, 22*
See Kipling, page 777.

But rum alone's the tipple, and the heart's delight
  Of the old bold mate of Henry Morgan.
  Captain Stratton's Fancy. Stanza 1
So I'm for drinking honestly, and dying in my boots.
  Ibid. Stanza 7
Oh London Town's a fine town, and London sights are rare,
And London ale is right ale, and brisk's the London air.
  London Town. Stanza 1
Laugh and be merry, remember, better the world with a song,
Better the world with a blow in the teeth of a wrong.
Laugh, for the time is brief, a thread the length of a span.
Laugh and be proud to belong to the old proud pageant of man.
  Laugh and Be Merry. Stanza 1
I hold that when a person dies
  His soul returns again to earth;
Arrayed in some new flesh-disguise
  Another mother gives him birth.
With sturdier limbs and brighter brain
The old soul takes the roads again.
  A Creed. Stanza 1
And may we find, when ended is the page,
Death but a tavern on our pilgrimage.
  The Word
For bitter moments given, bitter pay,
The time for payment comes, early or late,
No earthly debtor but accounts to Fate.
  The Widow in the Bye Street.
  Part 2
All the great things of life are swiftly done,
Creation, death, and love the double gate.
However much we dawdle in the sun
We have to hurry at the touch of Fate;
When Life knocks at the door no one can wait,
When Death makes his arrest we have to go.
  Ibid.
Love is a flame to burn out human wills,
Love is a flame to set the will on fire,
Love is a flame to cheat men into mire.

One of the three, we make Love what we choose.
  The Widow in the Bye Street.
  Part 2
What good can painting do to anyone?
I don't say never do it; far from that —
No harm in sometimes painting just for fun.
Keep it for fun, and stick to what you're at.
  Dauber. Part 2
Spit brown, my son, and get a hairy breast.
  Ibid.
All through the windless night the clipper rolled
In a great swell with oily gradual heaves
Which rolled her down until her time-bells tolled,
Clang, and the weltering water moaned like beeves,
The thundering rattle of slatting shook the sheaves,
Startles of water made the swing ports gush.
The sea was moaning and sighing and saying "Hush!"
  Ibid. Part 6
Then in the sunset's flush they went aloft,
And unbent sails in that most lovely hour,
When the light gentles and the wind is soft,
And beauty in the heart breaks like a flower.
  Ibid. Part 7
What am I, Life? A thing of watery salt
Held in cohesion by unresting cells,
Which work they know not why, which never halt,
Myself unwitting where their Master dwells?
  Sonnets. 14
Is there a great green commonwealth of Thought
Which ranks the yearly pageant, and decides
How Summer's royal progress shall be wrought,

By secret stir which in each plant abides?

Sonnets. 28

With such dumb loving of the Berkshire loam
As breaks the dumb hearts of the English kind.

August, 1914

If there be any life beyond the grave,
It must be near the men and things we love.

Ibid.

O beautiful is love and to be free
Is beautiful, and beautiful are friends.
Love, freedom, comrades, surely make amends
For all these thorns through which we walk to death.

Enslaved

O beautiful in this living that passes like the foam,
It is to go with sorrow, yet come with beauty home.

Ibid.

Perhaps, long since, there was a land beyond
Westward from death, some city, some calm place,
Where one could taste God's quiet and be fond
With the little beauty of a human face.

The Lemmings

Be with me Beauty for the fire is dying,
My dog and I are old, too old for roving,
Man, whose young passion sets the spindrift flying
Is soon too lame to march, too cold for loving.

On Growing Old. Sonnet 1

Bitter it is, indeed, in human Fate
When Life's supreme temptation comes too late.

The Woman Speaks

Go forth to seek: the quarry never found
Is still a fever to the questing hound,
The skyline is a promise, not a bound.

The Wanderer of Liverpool

I touch my country's mind, I come to grips
With half her purpose, thinking of these ships,

That art untouched by softness, all that line
Drawn ringing hard to stand the test of brine. . . .
That art of masts, sail crowded, fit to break,
Yet stayed to strength and backstayed into rake. . . .
They mark our passage as a race of men,
Earth will not see such ships as those again.

Ships

May shipwreck and collision, fog and fire,
Rock, shoal and other evils of the sea
Be kept from you; and may the heart's desire
Of those who speed your launching come to be.

Launching of the "Queen Mary,"
September 26, 1934. Stanza 7

When Custom presses on the souls apart,
Who seek a God not worshipped by the herd,
Forth, to the wilderness, the chosen start
Content with ruin, having but the Word.

Lines on the Tercentenary of
Harvard College [1936]

There was a preacher in that little band,
John Harvard, son of one from Stratford town,
Who may have shaken William Shakespeare's hand. . . .
Would that his human eyes, untimely dead,
Freed from that quiet where the generous are,
Might see this scene of living corn made bread
This Lamp of human hope become a star.

Ibid.

Commonplace people dislike tragedy, because they dare not suffer and cannot exult. The truth and rapture of man are holy things, not lightly to be scorned. A carelessness of life and beauty marks the glutton, the idler, and the fool in their deadly path across history.

The Tragedy of Nan. Preface

Man consists of body, mind, and imagination. His body is faulty, his mind untrustworthy, but his imagination has made him remarkable. In some centuries, his imagination had made life on this planet an intense practice of all the lovelier energies.

Shakespeare and Spiritual Life

There is another way to truth: by the minute examination of facts. That is the way of the scientist: a hard and noble and thankless way. It is not the way of the great poet, the rare unreasonable who comes once in ten generations. He apprehends truth by power: the truth which he apprehends cannot be defined, save by greater power, and there is no greater power.

Ibid.

WILLIAM SOMERSET MAUGHAM
[1874–]

Do you know that conversation is one of the greatest pleasures in life? But it wants leisure.

The Trembling of a Leaf. Chap. 3

The tragedy of love is indifference.

Ibid. Chap. 4

The mystic sees the ineffable, and the psycho-pathologist the unspeakable.

The Moon and Sixpence. Chap. 1

I forget who it was that recommended men for their soul's good to do each day two things they disliked: . . . it is a precept that I have followed scrupulously; for every day I have got up and I have gone to bed.

Ibid. Chap. 2

Impropriety is the soul of wit.

Ibid. Chap. 4

Conscience is the guardian in the individual of the rules which the community has evolved for its own preservation.

Ibid. Chap. 14

It is not true that suffering ennobles the character; happiness does that

sometimes, but suffering, for the most part, makes men petty and vindictive.

The Moon and Sixpence. Chap. 17

A woman can forgive a man for the harm he does her, but she can never forgive him for the sacrifices he makes on her account.

Ibid. Chap. 41

He made one laugh sometimes by speaking the truth, but this is a form of humour which gains its force only by its unusualness.

Ibid. Chap. 44

ROSELLE MERCIER MONTGOMERY
[1874–1933]

Companioned years have made them comprehend
The comradeship that lies beyond a kiss.
The young ask much of life — they ask but this,
To fare the road together to its end.

For a Wedding Anniversary

The fates are not quite obdurate;
They have a grim, sardonic way
Of granting men who supplicate
The things they wanted — yesterday.[1]

The Fates

JOSEPHINE PRESTON PEABODY (MRS. LIONEL MARKS)
[1874–1922]

Truly, one thing is sweet
Of things beneath the Sun;
This, that a man should earn his bread and eat
Rejoicing in his work which he hath done.

The Singing Man

[1] See J. R. Lowell, page 528, and Oscar Wilde, page 724.

A voice cried out to you, as to the imprudent Theseus: "Beware, my lord! Beware lest stern Heaven hate you enough to hear your prayers! Often 'tis in wrath that Heaven receives our sacrifices; its gifts are often the punishment of our crimes." — ANATOLE FRANCE: *The Crime of Sylvestre Bonnard*, trans. by LAFCADIO HEARN, *Part II, Chap. 4*

Flooding the waste of this dishonored
Star.
The Singing Man
Cry, from the deep of world-accusing
waves,
With longing more than all since
Light began,
Above the nations, — underneath the
graves, —
"Give back the Singing Man."
Ibid.

The little Road says, Go;
The little House says, Stay;
And oh, it's bonny here at home,
But I must go away.
The House and the Road. Stanza 1

EDWARD HERSEY
RICHARDS
[1874–   ]

A wise old owl sat on an oak,
The more he saw the less he spoke;
The less he spoke the more he heard;
Why aren't we like that wise old bird?
A Wise Old Owl

GERTRUDE STEIN [1]
[1874–   ]

Rose is a rose is a rose is a rose.
Sacred Emily
Pigeons in the grass alas.
Four Saints in Three Acts
Before the Flowers of Friendship Faded
Friendship Faded.
Title
In the United States there is more
space where nobody is than where any-
body is.
This is what makes America what
it is.
*The Geographical History
of America*

[1] There's a notable family called Stein:
  There's Gertrude, there's Ep, and there's
  Ein.
    Gert's writings are punk,
    Ep's statues are junk,
  And nobody understands Ein.
            ANONYMOUS: *Stein Song*
Ep = Jacob Epstein, sculptor.
Ein = Albert Einstein, mathematician.

ARTHUR STRINGER
[1874–   ]

Beauty is not immortal. In a day
Blossom and June and rapture pass
away.
*A Fragile Thing Is Beauty.
Stanza 2*
When my life has enough of love,
And my spirit enough of mirth,
When the ocean no longer beckons me,
When the roadway calls no more,
Oh, on the anvil of Thy wrath,
Remake me, God, that day!
A Wanderer's Litany. Stanza 1
Yea, It, the heart of her who bore
Him as a child, slimed Hell's worn floor.
On Its slow tears he slipped, and fell
On that bruised heart that knew him
well.
And It, ere he rose up to go,
Lay close to him and whispered low,
Whispered tenderly, whispered clear:
"Son of mine, did I hurt you, dear?"
Mother and Son (After Echegaray)

ROBERT GILBERT WELSH
[1874–1924]

His wings are gray and trailing,
Azrael, Angel of Death.
And yet the souls that Azrael brings
Across the dark and cold,
Look up beneath those folded wings,
And find them lined with gold.
Azrael. Stanza 2

H. J. WILLIAMS
[1874–1924]

Good-bye, Piccadilly,
Farewell, Leicester Square,
It's a long, long way to Tipperary,
But my heart's right there!
Tipperary

WILLIAM E. WOODWARD
[1874–   ]

In the queer mess of human destiny
the determining factor is Luck. For every important place in life there are
many men of fairly equal capacities.

Among them Luck decides who shall accomplish the great work, who shall be crowned with laurel, and who shall fall back into obscurity and silence.
George Washington.
Chap. 3, Part 2

The turning points of lives are not the great moments. The real crises are often concealed in occurrences so trivial in appearance that they pass unobserved.
Ibid.

Vanity as an impulse has without doubt been of far more benefit to civilization than modesty has ever been.
Ibid. Chap. 5, Part 1

In the face of opposition he [Charles Sumner] would support his theories with formidable citations from history, law, economics, belles-lettres, anthropology, chemistry and religion. He would quote Spinoza and the Boston Cooking School in the same breath. But he rarely, if ever, cited common sense.
Meet General Grant.
Chap. 25, Part 2

Here is another bead on the string of confusions.
Ibid. Chap. 27, Part 5

JOHN BUCHAN, LORD TWEEDSMUIR
[1875–   ]

In perfect honour, perfect truth,
And gentleness to all mankind,
You trod the golden paths of youth,
Then left the world and youth behind.
Ah, no! 'tis we who fade and fail —
And you, from Time's slow torments free,
Shall pass from strength to strength and scale
The steeps of immortality.
Fratri Dilectissimo, W.H.B.
Stanza 5

LOUISE DRISCOLL
[1875–   ]

Happy New Year! There's always hope, there's promise!

No sorrow ever held a crocus back.
The rigid earth revives, day breaks; to-morrow,
Deliberate, comes down the starry track.
New Year. Stanza 8

There you will find what
Every man needs,
Wild religion
Without any creeds.
Spring Market. Stanza 5

You can't forget a garden
When you have planted seed —
When you have watched the weather
And know a rose's need.
You Can't Forget a Garden

Villon among the birds is he,
A bold, bright rover, bad and free;
Yet not without such loveliness
As makes the curse upon him less.
The Blue Jay. Stanza 1

ELLEN THORNEYCROFT FOWLER
[1875–1929]

The inner half of every cloud
Is bright and shining;
I therefore turn my clouds about,
And always wear them inside out
To show the lining.
The Wisdom of Folly. Stanza 3

ROBERT FROST
[1875–   ]

Something there is that doesn't love a wall.
Mending Wall

My apple trees will never get across
And eat the cones under his pines, I tell him.
He only says, "Good fences make good neighbors."
Ibid.

I'd like to get away from earth awhile
And then come back to it and begin over.
May no fate wilfully misunderstand me
And half grant what I wish and snatch me away
Not to return. Earth's the right place for love:

I don't know where it's likely to go better.
Birches

The nearest friends can go
With anyone to death, comes so far short
They might as well not try to go at all.
No, from the time when one is sick to death,
One is alone, and he dies more alone.
Friends make pretence of following to the grave,
But before one is in it, their minds are turned
And making the best of their way back to life
And living people, and things they understand.
Home Burial

Nothing to look backward to with pride,
And nothing to look forward to with hope.
The Death of the Hired Man.

"Home is the place where, when you have to go there
They have to take you in." "I should have called it
Something you somehow haven't to deserve."
Ibid.

As a child misses the unsaid Goodnight,
And falls asleep with heartache.
The Black Cottage

Most of the change we think we see in life
Is due to truths being in and out of favour.
Ibid.

I shall be telling this with a sigh
Somewhere ages and ages hence:
Two roads diverged in a wood, and I —
I took the one less travelled by,
And that has made all the difference.
The Road Not Taken

The blue's but a mist from the breath of the wind,
A tarnish that goes at a touch of the hand.
Blueberries

The best way out is always through.
A Servant to Servants

Pressed into service means pressed out of shape.
The Self-Seeker

I have been one acquainted with the night.
Acquainted with the Night

I wonder about the trees:
Why do we wish to bear
Forever the noise of these
More than another noise
So close to our dwelling-place?
The Sound of Trees

I met a Californian who would
Talk California — a state so blessed,
He said, in climate none had ever died there
A natural death.
New Hampshire. Stanza 3

In the market with a climate.
Ibid.

Do you know,
Considering the market, there are more
Poems produced than any other thing?
No wonder poets sometimes have to seem
So much more business-like than business men.
Their wares are so much harder to get rid of.
Ibid. Stanza 17

She's one of the two best states in the Union.
Vermont's the other.
Ibid. Stanza 18

Anything I can say about New Hampshire
Will serve almost as well about Vermont,
Excepting that they differ in their mountains.
The Vermont mountains stretch extending straight;
New Hampshire mountains curl up in a coil.
Ibid. Stanza 19

The sun was warm but the wind was chill.
You know how it is with an April day:
When the sun is out and the wind is still,
You're one month on in the middle of May.
But if you so much as dare to speak,

A cloud comes over the sunlit arch,
A wind comes off a frozen peak,
And you're two months back in the middle of March.
                    Two Tramps in Mud Time
Don't join too many gangs. Join few if any.
Join the United States and join the family —
But not much in between unless a college.
                    Build Soil
Why make so much of fragmentary blue
In here and there a bird, or butterfly,
Or flower, or wearing-stone, or open eye,
When heaven presents in sheets the solid hue?
                    Fragmentary Blue. Stanza 1
Keep cold, young orchard. Good-bye and keep cold.
Dread fifty above more than fifty below.
                    Good-bye and Keep Cold
The woods are lovely, dark and deep.
But I have promises to keep,
And miles to go before I sleep.
                    Stopping by Woods on a Snowy Evening
Never ask of money spent
Where the spender thinks it went.
Nobody was ever meant
To remember or invent
What he did with every cent.
                    The Hardship of Accounting
If, as they say, some dust thrown in my eyes
Will keep my talk from getting over-wise,
I'm not the one for putting off the proof.
Let it be overwhelming.
                    Dust in the Eyes
No ship of all that under sail or steam
Has gathered people to us more and more
But Pilgrim-manned the Mayflower in a dream
Has been their anxious convoy in to shore.
                    Immigrants
Some say the world will end in fire,
Some say in ice.

From what I've tasted of desire
I hold with those who favor fire.
But if it had to perish twice,
I think I know enough of hate
To say that for destruction ice
Is also great
And would suffice.
                    Fire and Ice

FREDERICK PALMER LATIMER
[1875–   ]

I wish I were a little rock,
    A-sitting on a hill,
A-doing nothing, all day long,
    But just a-sitting still;
I wouldn't eat, I wouldn't sleep,
    I wouldn't even wash —
I'd sit and sit a thousand years,
    And rest myself, b' Gosh!
                    The Weary Wisher

PERCY MACKAYE
[1875–   ]

Because he never wore his sentient heart
For crows and jays to peck, ofttimes to such
He seemed a silent fellow, who o'er-much
Held from the general gossip-ground apart,
Or tersely-spoke, and tart.
                    Uriel. Stanza 11

A man went down to Panama
    Where many a man has died
To slit the sliding mountains
    And lift the eternal tide:
A man stood up in Panama,
    And the mountains stood aside.
                    Goethals. Stanza 1

            The lover,
And the young of soul, his friend,
And the artist, follow after
The children in their laughter,
And the daring half discover,
And the happy comprehend.
                    The Sybil

MOIRA O'NEILL
(MRS. N. H. SKRINE)

Youth's for an hour,
Beauty's a flower,
But love is the jewel that wins the
  world.
Beauty's a Flower

"If she was tall?" Like a king's own
  daughter.
"If she was fair?" Like a mornin' o'
  May.
A Broken Song. Stanza 2

Corrymeela an' the blue sky over it.
Corrymeela. Stanza 1

The memory's fairly spoilt on me
  Wid mindin' to forget.
"Forgettin'." Stanza 5

RAFAEL SABATINI
[1875-   ]

Born with the gift of laughter and a
sense that the world is mad.[1]
Scaramouche. Chap. 1

RIDGELY TORRENCE
[1875-   ]

God gave them Youth, God gave them
Love, and even God can give no
more.
The House of a Hundred Lights.
The Young Lovers

Of all the languages of earth in which
  the human kind confer
The Master Speaker is the Tear: it is
  the Great Interpreter.
Ibid. The Conclusion of the
Whole Matter

I was weak as a rained-on bee.
Eye-Witness. The Tramp Sings

It feels like frost was near —
His hair was curly.
The spring was late that year,
But the harvest early.
The Son. Stanza 4

---

[1] Inscribed on one of the new buildings at
Yale University under the misapprehension
that this sentiment was a translation of some
ancient classic.

EVELYN UNDERHILL
(MRS. STUART MOORE)
[1875-   ]

I come in the little things,
Saith the Lord:
My starry wings
I do forsake,
Love's highway of humility to take.
Immanence. Stanza 3

I shall achieve My Immemorial Plan,
Pass the low lintel of the human heart.
Ibid.

  I saw the race fulfil
The spiral of its steep ascent, predes-
  tined of the Will.
Yet not unled, but shepherded by one
  they may not see —
The one who walked with starry feet
  the western road by me!
Uxbridge Road. Stanza 5

THOMAS WALSH
[1875-1928]

A little world — we truly say
  While days are young and careless-
  hearted;
From clime to clime we speed to-day,
  Earth's paths are cleared and ocean's
  charted;
But ah, how large a world we stray
  When thou and I are parted!
Zither Song

Death sallied forth upon this fateful
  day
Through Spain and England for a
  mighty prey,
And struck two masters with a single
  blow
And laid Cervantes and Will Shakespeare low!
April Twenty-third

HAROLD MacDONALD
ANDERSON
[1876-   ]

Alone?
  Is he alone at whose right side rides
Courage, with Skill within the cockpit
and Faith upon the left? Does solitude
surround the brave when Adventure
leads the way and Ambition reads the

dials? Is there no company with him for whom the air is cleft by Daring and the darkness is made light by Emprise?

True, the fragile bodies of his fellows do not weigh down his plane; true, the fretful minds of weaker men are lacking from his crowded cabin; but as his airship keeps her course he holds communion with those rarer spirits that inspire to intrepidity and by their sustaining potency give strength to arm, resource to mind, content to soul.

Alone? With what other companions would that man fly to whom the choice were given?

> *"Lindbergh Flies Alone," Editorial, New York Sun, May 21, 1927* [1]

SHERWOOD ANDERSON
[1876–   ]

Everyone in the world is Christ and they are all crucified.

> *Winesburg, Ohio. The Philosopher*

I am a lover and have not found my thing to love.

> *Ibid. Tandy*

ANNA HEMPSTEAD BRANCH
[1875–1937]

Order is a lovely thing;
On disarray it lays its wing,
Teaching simplicity to sing.

> *The Monk in the Kitchen*

Shape, the strong and awful Spirit,
Laid his ancient hand on you.
He waste chaos doth inherit;
He can alter and subdue.

> *Ibid.*

His screaming stallions maned with whistling wind.

> *Nimrod Wars with the Angels*

God wove a web of loveliness,
Of clouds and stars and birds,

[1] Included by permission of Mr. Anderson and *The Sun*.

But made not anything at all
So beautiful as words.

> *Songs for My Mother: Her Words. Stanza 5*

If there is no God for thee
Then there is no God for me.

> *To a Dog*

WILLA SIBERT CATHER
[1876–   ]

Oh, this is the joy of the rose:
That it blows,
And goes.

> *In Rose-Time*

Where are the loves that we have loved before
When once we are alone, and shut the door?

> *L'Envoi*

Fireflies gleam in the damp and mould, —
All that is left of the Caesars' gold.

> *The Palatine. Stanza 3*

The old West, the old time,
The old wind singing through
The red, red grass a thousand miles,
And, Spanish Johnny, you!

> *Spanish Johnny. Stanza 1*

A Polack's brat
Joylessly torments a cat. . . .
To hurt and to be hurt; he knows
All he will know on earth, or need to know.

> *Street in Packingtown (Chicago)*

How smoothly the trains run beyond the Missouri.

> *Going Home, Burlington Route*

No one can build his security upon the nobleness of another person.

> *Alexander's Bridge. Chap. 8*

There are only two or three human stories, and they go on repeating themselves as fiercely as if they had never happened before.

> *O Pioneers! Part II, Chap. 4*

I like trees because they seem more resigned to the way they have to live than other things do.

> *Ibid. Chap. 8*

Winter lies too long in country towns; hangs on until it is stale and shabby, old and sullen.

> *My Ántonia. Book II, Chap. 7*

Old men are like that, you know. It makes them feel important to think they're in love with somebody.

My Ántonia. Book III, Chap. 4

We all like people who do things, even if we only see their faces on a cigar-box lid.

The Song of the Lark.
Part I, Chap. 18

That irregular and intimate quality of things made entirely by the human hand.

Death Comes for the Archbishop.
Book I, Chap. 3

The Miracles of the Church seem to me to rest not so much upon faces or voices or healing power coming suddenly near to us from afar off, but upon our perceptions being made finer, so that for a moment our eyes can see and our ears can hear what is there about us always.

Ibid. Chap. 4

The universal human yearning for something permanent, enduring, without shadow of change.

Ibid. Book III, Chap. 3

PATRICK REGINALD CHALMERS

Oh, bright as a berry,
    They're red and they're rare,
The setters from Kerry,
    And Cork and Kildare!

The Red Dogs

A year of philatelic fame,
    For — lest my point should miss
    you —
In eighteen forty-seven came
    The first Mauritius issue.

Tuppenny Blues: A Tale for
Philatelists. Stanza 3

"I find," said 'e, "things very much as 'ow I've always found,
For mostly they goes up and down or else goes round and round."

Roundabouts and Swings.
Stanza 2

What's lost upon the roundabout we pulls up on the swings!

Ibid.

If you'd move to a bygone measure,
    Or shape your heart to an ancient
    mould,
Maroons and schooners and buried
    treasure
Wrought on a page of gold, —

Then take the book in the dingy bind-
    ing,
    Still the magic comes, bearded, great,
And swaggering files of sea-thieves
    winding
    Back, with their ruffling cut-throat
    gait,
Reclaim an hour when we first went
    finding
    Pieces of Eight — of Eight.

"Treasure Island"

RICHARD BUTLER GLAENZER
[1876–1937]

Indian only in this:
    Your sudden way
Of stealing on us — but to kiss
    With peace, not slay!

Indian Summer. Stanza 1

NORAH MARY HOLLAND (MRS. LIONEL WILLIAM CLAXTON)
[1876–1925]

High up in the courts of Heaven to-day
    A little dog-angel waits;
With the other angels he will not play,
    But he sits alone at the gates.

The Little Dog-Angel

Yet, in that land of shadows, there are
    two
    Whose welcome will not fail me,
    though I stray
    Bewildered, lost, alone in that dim
    way
'Mid the unfriendly ghosts — my dog
    and you.[1]

Two

[1] See St. John Lucas, page 858.

WALLACE IRWIN
[1876–   ]

It's happy goes as lucky goes
To Romany in June.
Upon the Road to Romany.
Stanza 1

Of all the fish that swim or swish
In ocean's deep autocracy,
There's none possess such haughtiness
As the codfish aristocracy.
Codfish Aristocracy. Stanza 1

"Suppose that this here vessel," says
the skipper, with a groan,
"Should lose 'er bearin's, run away, and
bump upon a stone;
Suppose she'd shiver and go down,
when save ourselves we could-
n't — "
The mate replies, "O, blow me eyes,
suppose again she shouldn't."
The Sorrows of a Skipper.
Stanza 3

Better than years with Ibsen spent, I
said,
One Evening with my Friend, Boccac-
cio.
Rubáiyát of Omar Khayyám, Jr.
XXXVI

I ask to know.
Letters of a Japanese Schoolboy

"GORDON JOHNSTONE"
(JOSEPH SWEENEY)
[1876–1926]

Death's but an open door,
We move from room to room.
There is one life, no more,
No dying, and no tomb.
There Is No Death. Stanza 3

WILLIAM ELLERY LEONARD
[1876–   ]

The shriveled stalks of goldenrod are
sere,
And crisp and white their flashing old
racemes.
(. . . forever . . . forever . . . forever . . .)
This is the lonely season of the year,
This is the season of our lonely dreams.

(*O Earth-and-Autumn of the setting*
Sun,
She is not by, to know my task is
done!)
Two Lives. Indian Summer

And, ever wistful of the doom to come,
I built her many a fire for love . . . for
mirth. . . .
(When snows were falling on our oaks
outside,
Dear, many a winter fire upon the
hearth) . . .
(. . . farewell . . . farewell . . . farewell
. . .)
We dare not think too long on those
who died,
While still so many yet must come to
birth.
Ibid.

GRACE FALLOW NORTON
[1876–   ]

I have loved many, the more and the
few —
I have loved many, that I might love
you.
Song of the Sum of All. Stanza 1

TED OLSON

Honor and truth and manhood —
These are the things that stand,
Though the sneer and jibe of the cynic
tribe
Are loud through the width of the
land.
Things That Endure. Stanza 1

But a lie, whatever the guise it wears,
Is a lie as it was of yore,
And a truth that has lasted a million
years
Is good for a million more.
Ibid. Stanza 3

FRANK WARD O'MALLEY
[1876–1932]

Life is just one damned thing after
another.[1]
Quoted in The Literary Digest,
November 5, 1932

[1] Also attributed to Elbert Hubbard; probably precedes them both.

ABRAHAM S. WOLF ROSENBACH
[1876–   ]

On February 14, 1493, Columbus carefully prepared as complete an account of his marvelous voyage as was possible under the circumstances. He wrote the details of his journey on a stout piece of parchment, wrapped it carefully in a piece of waterproof cloth, then placed it in an iron-bound barrel and threw it into the raging ocean. . . . If I thought there were one chance in a million of finding it I would take my power boat, the *First Folio,* and cruise in the neighborhood of the Azores forever!

(1927) Page 269. Books and Bidders

After love, book collecting is the most exhilarating sport of all.

(1936) Page 106. A Book Hunter's Holiday

Brooklyn has the proud distinction of having had more distinguished bibliophiles than any other city of its size in the world.

Page 126. Ibid.

Lives of great men all remind us
  As their pages o'er we turn,
That we're apt to leave behind us
  Letters that we ought to burn.

Page 36. Ibid. Quoted by Dr. Rosenbach, *authorship unknown*

ROBERT WILLIAM SERVICE
[1876–   ]

This is the Law of the Yukon, that only
  the Strong shall thrive;
That surely the Weak shall perish, and
  only the Fit survive.[1]

The Law of the Yukon

Master, I've filled my contract, wrought
  in Thy many lands;

[1] An obvious echo of Kipling's *The Law of the Jungle:*
Now this is the Law of the Jungle — as old
    and as true as the sky;
And the Wolf that shall keep it may prosper,
    but the Wolf that shall break it must die.

Not by my sins wilt Thou judge me,
  but by the work of my hands.
Master, I've done Thy bidding, and the
  light is low in the west,
And the long, long shift is over . . .
  Master, I've earned it — Rest.

The Song of the Wage-Slave

Back of the bar, in a solo game, sat
  Dangerous Dan McGrew,
And watching his luck was his light-o'-
  love, the lady that's known as
  Lou.

The Shooting of Dan McGrew. Stanza 1

There's a race of men that don't fit in,
  A race that can't stay still;
So they break the hearts of kith and kin,
  And they roam the world at will.

The Men That Don't Fit In. Stanza 1

Fate has written a tragedy; its name is
  "The Human Heart."
The Theatre is the House of Life,
  Woman the mummer's part;
The Devil enters the prompter's box
  and the play is ready to start.

The Harpy. Stanza 12

God made a heart of gold, of gold,
  Shining and sweet and true;
Gave it a home of fairest mould,
  Blest it, and called it — You.

Sunshine. VI

I just think that dreams are best,
  Just to sit and fancy things;
Give your gold no acid test,
  Try not how your silver rings.

Dreams Are Best. Stanza 1

It's easy to cry that you're beaten —
  and die;
  It's easy to crawfish and crawl;
But to fight and to fight when hope's
  out of sight —
  Why, that's the best game of them
  all!

The Quitter. Stanza 3

A million stars are in the sky;
A million planets plunge and die;
A million million men are sped;
A million million wait ahead.
Each plays his part and has his day —
What ho! the World's all right, I say.

The World's All Right. Stanza 3

They talk o' England's glory and a-
   'oldin' of our trade,
Of Empire and 'igh destiny until we're
   fair flimflammed;
But if it's for the likes o' that that
   bloody war is made,
Then wot I say is: Empire and 'igh
   destiny be damned!
     A Song of the Sandbags. Stanza 5

Ah! the clock is always slow;
It is later than you think.
     It Is Later than You Think.
            Stanza 7

That classic that the world has lost,
The Little Book I Never Wrote.
     My Masterpiece. Stanza 2

I have some friends, some honest
   friends,
And honest friends are few;
My pipe of briar, my open fire,
A book that's not too new.
     I Have Some Friends. Stanza 2

When we, the Workers, all demand:
   "What are we fighting for?" . . .
Then, then we'll end that stupid crime,
   that devil's madness — War.
            Michael

EDGAR WALLACE
[1876–1932]

'E doesn't want no pass;
'E's journeying first-class;
'Is trav'ling rug's a Union Jack, which
   isn't bad at all;
The tune the drummers play
It ain't so very gay,
But a rather slow selection from a piece
   that's known as "Saul."
     Burial of Private Ginger Jones.
            Stanza 6

Oh God of Battles, Lord of Might — a
   sentry in the silent night —
I, 'oo've never prayed
Kneel on the dew-damp sands to say:
Oh, keep me through the coming day!
But, please remember, though I pray,
   That I am not afraid.
     The Prayer by Private Edgar
     Wallace, R.A.M.C. Stanza 1

GRACE NOLL
(MRS. NORMAN H.)
CROWELL
[1877–   ]

No day has ever failed me quite:
Before the grayest day is done
I find some misty purple bloom,
Or a late line of crimson sun.
     The Day. Stanza 3

I hold to my heart when the geese are
   flying —
A wavering wedge on the high, bright
   blue —
I tighten my lips to keep from crying:
"Beautiful birds, let me go with you."
     Wild Geese. Stanza 1

GEORGE ALLAN ENGLAND
[1877–1936]

He yawned, and laid his cigaret aside,
And on the baggage-check, grimly
   stamped "Body," wrote
Two simple words. Scrawled words,
   with careless fingers. Just a note
Of this poor shipment's worthlessness.
   She who had died,
Two days before, was sunshine, joy,
   and life
To all of us.
          "No Value"

"No Value!" And the world had ceased
   to turn:
And all the gold from here to Babylon
   might burn
To dross, unminded, for we bore our
   dead.
          Ibid.

ANTHONY EUWER
[1877–   ]

As a beauty I'm not a great star.
Others are handsomer far;
   But my face — I don't mind it
   Because I'm behind it;
It's the folks out in front that I jar.
          Limerick [1]

I like a good grouch when I get it,
Sea-deep and dark indigo blue.
     My Grouch. Stanza 1

[1] Often quoted by Woodrow Wilson.

ROSE FYLEMAN
[1877-   ]

The Fairies have never a penny to
    spend,
They haven't a thing put by,
But theirs is the dower of bird and of
    flower,
And theirs are the earth and the sky.
    *The Fairies Have Never a Penny
        to Spend. Stanza 1*

And though you be foolish or though
    you be wise,
With hair of silver or gold,
You could never be young as the fairies
    are,
And never as old.
    Ibid. Stanza 2

A fairy went a-marketing —
    She bought a little fish;
She put it in a crystal bowl
Upon a golden dish.
    *A Fairy Went A-Marketing.
        Stanza 1*

Cheerfully adorn the proudest table,
Since yours it is to bear the glorious
    label —
"Richest in Vitamines!"
    To an Orange. Stanza 4

SIR JAMES HOPWOOD JEANS
[1877-   ]

Hubble [1] estimates that about two
million such nebulae are visible in the
great 100-inch telescope at Mount Wilson, and that the whole universe has
about a thousand million times the volume of that part of space visible in this
telescope. Let us now multiply 1,000
million by 2 million, and the product by
1,000 million. The answer (2×10^{24})
gives some indication of the probable
number of stars in the universe; the
same number of grains of sand spread
over England would make a layer hundreds of yards in depth. Let us reflect
that our earth is one millionth part of
one such grain of sand, and our mun-
dane affairs, our troubles and our
achievements, begin to appear in their

    [1] Edwin Powell Hubble [1889-   ], dis-
tinguished American astronomer.

correct proportion to the universe as a
whole.
    *The Wider Aspects of Cosmog-
        ony [1928]*

Observation and theory agree in indicating that the universe is melting
away into radiation. Our position is
that of polar bears on an iceberg that
has broken loose from the icepack surrounding the pole, and is inexorably
melting away as the iceberg drifts to
warmer latitudes and ultimate extinction.
    Ibid.

Taking a very gloomy view of the
future of the human race, let us suppose that it can only expect to survive
for two thousand million years longer,
a period about equal to the past age of
the earth. Then, regarded as a being
destined to live for threescore years and
ten, humanity, although it has been
born in a house seventy years old, is itself only three days old.
    Ibid.

It does not at present look as though
Nature had designed the universe pri-
marily for life; the normal star and the
normal nebula have nothing to do with
life except making it impossible. Life is
the end of a chain of by-products; it
seems to be the accident, and torrential
deluges of life-destroying radiation the
essential.
    Ibid.

DOUGLAS MALLOCH
[1877-   ]

If you can't be a pine on the top of the
    hill,
Be a scrub in the valley — but be
The best little scrub by the side of the
    rill;
Be a bush if you can't be a tree.
    *Be the Best of Whatever You Are.
        Stanza 1*

The tree that never had to fight
For sun and sky and air and light;
That stood out in the open plain
And always got its share of rain,

Never became a forest king,
But lived and died a scrubby thing.
Good Timber. Stanza 1

Time brings not death, it brings but
changes;
I know he rides, but rides afar,
To-day some other planet ranges
And camps to-night upon a star
Where all his other comrades are.
*A Comrade Rides Ahead: To
the Memory of Emerson Hough
[1857-1923]. Stanza 1*

JESSIE BELLE RITTENHOUSE
(MRS. CLINTON SCOLLARD)

My debt to you, Belovèd,
Is one I cannot pay
In any coin of any realm
On any reckoning day.
Debt

I worked for a menial's hire,
Only to learn, dismayed,
That any wage I had asked of Life,
Life would have paid.
My Wage

LEONARD H. ROBBINS
[1877-   ]

Be true while there yet is time.
For this is the cry of a thousand souls
that down to the Pit have trod —
Who keeps the Truth from the people
stands in the way of God!
*The Truth and John Billington.
Stanza 8*

THEODORE GOODRIDGE
ROBERTS
[1877-   ]

The wide seas and the mountains called
to him
And gray dawn saw his campfires in the
rain.
A Vagrant's Epitaph. Stanza 1
Change was his mistress, Chance his
counselor.
The dark pines knew his whistle up the
trail.

Why tarries he to-day? And yester-
night
Adventure lit her stars without avail.
A Vagrant's Epitaph. Stanza 4

LAURA SIMMONS
[1877-   ]

What though you hide it in your
trunk —
Ere sailing hour has set?
Jammed down beneath your old blue
serge?
Don't think you can forget!
The face within that passport book
Will rise to haunt you yet.
Your Passport Picture

CHARLES HANSON TOWNE
[1877-   ]

Youth, there are countless stories
spread
By gentlemen whose hair is gray.
Believe them not, but me instead —
The 'Nineties were not really gay.
Ballade of Gentle Denial
Does the skylark, singing sweet and
clear,
Beg the cold world to hear?
*The Quiet Singer
(Francis Thompson)*
As if upon the breeze,
There came the teeming wonder of his
words —
A golden troop of birds,
Caged in a little volume made to love.
Ibid.

ARTHUR UPSON
[1877-1908]

My days are phantom days, each one
The shadow of a hope;
My real life never was begun
Nor any of my real deeds done.
Phantom Life
Late the fond tyrant who misrules our
land,
Bidding his serfs dig deep in marshes
old,
Trembled, not knowing wherefore, as
they drew

From out this swampy bed of ancient
  mould
A shattered torch held in a mighty
  hand.

> *The Statue of Liberty (New
>   York Harbour, A.D. 2900)*

All are folded now so peacefully
Within her breast whose glory was their
  dream —
From her own sanguine fields, from isles
  extreme,
From the long tumult of the land and
  sea —
Where lies the steel Potomac's jewelled
  stream
Like the surrendered sword of Memory.

> *Arlington*

Dig my life deep enough, you must
Find broken friendships round its inner
  wall —
Which once my careless hand let slip
  and fall —
Brave with faint memories, rich in
  rainbow-crust.

> *Octaves in an Oxford Garden.
>   XXV, Roman Glassware Pre-
>   served in the Ashmolean*

Wine that was spilt in haste
  Arising in fumes more precious;
Garlands that fell forgot
  Rooting to wondrous bloom;
Youth that would flow to waste
  Pausing in pool-green valleys —
And Passion that lasted not
  Surviving the voiceless Tomb!

> *After a Dolmetsch Concert.
>   Stanza 2*

McLANDBURGH WILSON

From out our crowded calendar
  One day we pluck to give;
It is the day the Dying pause
  To honor those who live.

> *Memorial Day*

Our hero is a man of peace,
  Preparedness he implores;
His sword within its scabbard sleeps,
  But mercy, how it snores!

> *Theodore Roosevelt*

LOUIS KAUFMAN
ANSPACHER
[1878–   ]

Marriage is that relation between
man and woman in which the independence is equal, the dependence mutual,
and the obligation reciprocal.

> *Address, Boston
>   [December 30, 1934]*

BERTHA ADAMS BACKUS
[*Floruit* 1911]

Build for yourself a strong-box,
  Fashion each part with care;
When it's strong as your hand can make
  it,
  Put all your troubles there;
Hide there all thought of your failures,
  And each bitter cup that you quaff;
Lock all your heartaches within it,
  Then sit on the lid and laugh.

> *Then Laugh.*[1] *Stanza 1*

KARLE WILSON
(MRS. THOMAS ELLIS)
BAKER
[1878–   ]

Masters have wrought in prisons,
  At peace in cells of stone:
From their thick walls I fashion
  Windows to light my own.

> *Prisons*

Brother, the creed would stifle me
  That shelters you.

> *Creeds. Stanza 2*

Let me grow lovely, growing old—[2]
  So many fine things do:
Laces, and ivory, and gold,
  And silks need not be new.

> *Old Lace: Let Me Grow Lovely*

To-day I have grown taller from walking with the trees.

> *Good Company*

I love the friendly faces of old sorrows;
I have no secrets that they do not know.

> *I Love the Friendly Faces.
>   Stanza 1*

---

[1] In *Munsey's Magazine*, Feb., 1911.
[2] See Heath, page 628.

HENRY SEIDEL CANBY
[1878–]

We can put our children on wheels to see the world, but we cannot give them the kind of home that any town provided in the nineties, not at any price.
The Age of Confidence. Chap. 14

Arrogance, pedantry, and dogmatism are the occupational diseases of those who spend their lives directing the intellects of the young.
Alma Mater

Poet who disdained to be just a poet and so fell something short of his powers [Walt Whitman], he belongs now in that Platonic world where republics never realized keep their power to enrich the imagination. . . . He remembered things impossible for us, impossible but intelligible, and which will become unintelligible at our peril.
Classic Americans. Walt Whitman

GEORGE MICHAEL COHAN
[1878–]

Hurried and worried until we're buried, and there's no curtain call,
Life's a very funny proposition, after all.
Life's a Funny Proposition

No matter what may happen, whatever may befall,
I only know I'm mighty glad I'm living, that is all.
I'm Mighty Glad I'm Living

You won't do any business, if you haven't got a band:
The folks expect a street parade and uniforms so grand.
You Won't Do Any Business

Always leave them laughing when you say good-bye.
Title of song

GRACE HAZARD CONKLING
[1878–]

I have an understanding with the hills
At evening when the slanted radiance fills
Their hollows, and the great winds let them be,

And they are quiet and look down at me.
After Sunset

Invisible beauty has a word so brief
A flower can say it or a shaken leaf,
But few may ever snare it in a song.
Ibid.

To build the trout a crystal stair.
The Whole Duty of Berkshire Brooks

Oh, cut me reeds to blow upon,
Or gather me a star,
But leave the sultry passion-flowers
Growing where they are.
Tampico

He who gives a passion-flower
Always asks it back.
Ibid.

ADELAIDE CRAPSEY
[1878–1914]

These be
Three silent things:
The falling snow . . . the hour
Before the dawn . . . the mouth of one
Just dead.
Cinquain: Triad

EDWARD JOHN MORETON DRAX PLUNKETT, LORD DUNSANY
[1878–]

We shall be with you in your distant time,
Shall lean towards you across many a year,
Shall bring you courage with a wayworn rhyme:
We were not wholly here.
To Those That Come After. Stanza 3

A new thing came and they could not see,
A new wind blew and they would not feel it.
In His Own Country. Stanza 1

May you go safe, my friend, across that dizzy way
No wider than a hair, by which your people go

From Earth to Paradise; may you go
    safe to-day
With stars and space above, and time
    and stars below.
       May You Go Safe: On the
       Death of a Muhammedan
       Friend. Stanza 1

All who write put me in mind of sailors hastily making rafts upon doomed
ships.

When we break up under the heavy
years and go down into eternity our
thoughts like small lost rafts float on
awhile upon Oblivion's sea. They will
not carry much over those tides, our
names and a phrase or two and little
else. . . .

See now Oblivion shimmering all
around us, its very tranquillity deadlier
than tempest. . . .

There goes the raft that Homer made
for Helen.
    Fifty-One Tales. The Raft Builders

WILFRID WILSON GIBSON
[1878–   ]

I did not write; and now I cannot
    write —
    Or, rather, it were useless; no king's
    head
That pence or pounds might purchase
    may secure
    Delivery in the region of the dead —
And all I meant to say remains unsaid.
       The Unwritten Letter
One song leads on to another,
One friend to another friend,
So I'll travel along
With a friend and a song —
I'll travel along
Ten thousand strong —
To the end.
       The Empty Purse. Stanza 1
All life moving to one measure —
Daily bread.
      All Life Moving to One Measure
And as I lingered, lost in divine delight,
My heart thanked God for the goodly
    gift of sight
And all youth's lively senses keen and
    quick —
When suddenly, behind me in the night,

I heard the tapping of a blind man's
    stick.
       Sight. Stanza 2
That night when she came home
Her arms were full of blossom.
She'd scarcely left a pot or pan
For me to cook a meal in.
       Holiday
Just what it meant to smile and smile
And let my son go cheerily —
My son . . . and wondering all the
    while
What stranger would come back to me.
       The Return. Stanza 2
Though now beyond earth's farthest
    hills you fare,
Song-crowned, immortal, sometimes it
    seems to me
That, if I listen very quietly,
Perhaps I'll hear a light foot on the
    stair
And see you, standing with your angel
    air,
Fresh from the uplands of eternity.
       Rupert Brooke
When I must breast the stiller sea
That stretches everlastingly
Beneath the starless unknown night,
The darkness round me falling,
May it be given me to hear
Life calling me as crystal-clear —
To glance back once through failing
    light
And answer that sweet calling.
       The Voice. Stanza 2

OLIVER ST. JOHN GOGARTY
[1878–   ]

O Boys, the times I've seen!
The things I've done and known!
If you knew where I have been
Or half the joys I've had,
You never would leave me alone;
But pester me to tell,
Swearing to keep it dark,
What . . . but I know quite well:
Every solicitor's clerk
Would break out and go mad;
And all the dogs would bark!
       O Boys! O Boys!
  No one believes in joys,
And Peace on Earth is a joke,

Which, anyhow, telling destroys;
So better go on with your work:
But Boys! O Boys! O Boys!
                    O Boys! O Boys!
Our friends go with us as we go
   Down the long path where Beauty
   wends,
Where all we love foregathers, so
   Why should we fear to join our
   friends?
                    Non Dolet
Only the Lion and the Cock,
As Galen says, withstand Love's shock.
So, Dearest, do not think me rude
If I yield now to lassitude,
But sympathize with me. I know
You would not have me roar, or crow.
                    After Galen

PERCY ADAMS HUTCHISON
[1878–   ]

Ay, down the years, behold, He rides,
   The lowly Christ, upon an ass;
But conquering? Ten shall heed the
   call,
A thousand idly watch Him pass.
           The Swordless Christ:
           Vicisti Galilæe. Stanza 1

DONALD ROBERT PERRY
MARQUIS
[1878–1937]

The saddest ones are those that wear
   The jester's motley garb.
           The Tavern of Despair
The world hath just one tale to tell, and
   it is very old,[1]
A little tale — a simple tale — a tale
   that's easy told:
"There was a youth in Babylon who
   greatly loved a maid!"
                    News from Babylon
Who storms the moss-grown walls of eld
   And beats some falsehood down
Shall pass the pallid gates of death
   Sans laurel, love, or crown;
For him who fain would teach the world
   The world holds hate in fee —

[1] See Kendall Banning, page 855.

For Socrates, the hemlock cup;
   For Christ, Gethsemane.
                    The Wages
No doubt the cherubs earn their wage
   Who wind each ticking star.
                    The Rebel
Still mounts the Dream on shining pin-
   ion . . .
   Still broods the dull distrust . . .
Which shall have ultimate dominion,
   Dream, or dust?
                    A Little While
A little while with grief and laughter,
   And then the day will close;
The shadows gather . . . what comes
   after
No man knows.
                    Ibid.
Let us not babble of eternity
Who stand upon this little edge of
   time!
Even old godheads sink in space and
   drown,
Their arks like foundered galleons
   sucked down.
                    Transient
Noah an' Jonah an' Cap'n John Smith,
Mariners, travelers, magazines of myth,
Settin' up in Heaven, chewin' and a-
   chawin'
Eatin' their terbaccy, talkin' and a-
   jawin'.
                Noah an' Jonah an'
                Cap'n John Smith [1]
Fill me with sassafras, nurse,
   And juniper juice!
Let me see if I'm still any use!
For I want to be young and to sing
   again,
   Sing again, sing again!
   Middle age is a curse! [2]
                    Spring Ode
For I want to hire out as the Skipper
   (Who dodges life's stress and its
   strains)

[1] In *The Sun* (New York), *July 28, 1919.*
[2] Of middle age the best that can be said is
that a middle-aged person has likely learned
how to have a little fun in spite of his troubles. — *The Almost Perfect State*

Of the Trolley, the Toonerville Trolley,
   The Trolley that Meets all the
   Trains.
       The Toonerville Trolley:
          To Fontaine Fox
A dollar a line,
The Uplifting stuff brings a dollar a
   line!
       Yes, Song Is Coming into Its
          Own Again
And similar goddamned phrases.
     Ballade of Goddamned Phrases [1]
A man has jest naturally got to have
something to cuss around and boss, so's
to keep himself from finding out he
don't amount to nothing.
        Danny's Own Story
It's a DEE-vice.
       The Old Soak. Act I
Jehovah. Did I ever mention publicly
how Hell got started? I don't think I
ever did. It was this way: I thought
I'd do something nice for a lot of theologians who had, after all, been doing
the best they could, according to their
lights; so I gave them an enormous
tract of Heaven to do what they pleased
with — set it apart for them to inhabit
and administer. I didn't pay any attention to it for a few thousand years, and
when I looked at it again, they'd made
it into Hell.
     Chapters for the Orthodox.
          Chap. 7
Dreadful things are just as apt to
happen when stupid people control a
situation as when definitely ill-natured
people are in charge.
        Ibid. Chap. 8
All religion, all life, all art, all expression come down to this: to the effort of the human soul to break through
its barrier of loneliness, of intolerable
loneliness, and make some contact with
another seeking soul, or with what all
souls seek, which is (by any name)
God.
        Ibid. Chap. 11

[1] Inspired by a protest from General Ian
Hamilton, Commander of the Mediterranean
Expeditionary Force [1915], against turning
his cables into hackneyed phrases.

procrastination is the
art of keeping
up with yesterday
    archy and mehitabel. certain
    maxims of archy. [1] *page 43*
    [*1927*]
dance mehitabel dance
caper and shake a leg
what little blood is left
will fizz like wine in a keg
    Ibid. mehitabel dances with
        boreas. page 140
but still her word
is toujours gai
    archys life of mehitabel: the
    life of mehitabel the cat. page 2
    [*1933*]
i have noticed that when chickens
quit quarrelling over their food they
often find that there is enough for all of
them i wonder if it might not be the
same way with the human race
    Ibid. random thoughts by archy.
        page 82
nowadays an author owns his stuff
only between air programs
    Ibid. archy on the radio. page 108
  so unlucky
that he runs into accidents
which started out to happen
to somebody else
    Ibid. archy says. page 146
theres life in the old dame yet
    Ibid. the retreat from hollywood.
        page 155
a suicide is a person who has
considered his own case and decided
that he is worthless and who acts
as his own judge jury and executioner
and he probably knows better
than anyone else whether there is jus-
    tice
in the verdict [2]
    archy does his part. now look at
        it. page 7 [*1935*]

[1] Archy, a cockroach, is unable to use the
shift-key on the typewriter; therefore he
cannot print capital letters and punctuation
marks.
[2] See Eaton, page 738, and Ellis, page
741.

it is a cheering thought to think
that god is on the side of the best di-
    gestion [1]
    *archy does his part. the
    big bad wolf. page 11*
there is bound to be a certain amount of
trouble running any country
if you are president the trouble happens
    to you
but if you are a tyrant you can arrange
    things so
that most of the trouble happens to
    other people
    Ibid. archy's newest deal. page 18
there is always
a comforting thought
in time of trouble when
it is not our trouble
    *Ibid. comforting thoughts.
    page 149*
too many creatures
both insects and humans
estimate their own value
by the amount of minor irritation
they are able to cause
to greater personalities than themselves
    Ibid. pride. page 171
the females of all species are most
dangerous when they appear to retreat
    Ibid. a farewell. page 252
Comet, shake out your locks and let
    them flare
Across the startled heaven of my soul!
Pluck out the hairpins, Sue, and let her
    roll!
Don't be so stingy with your blooming
    hair.
    Sonnets to a Red-Haired Lady. I
I love you as New Englanders love pie!
    Ibid. XII
Their names were . . . Ask oblivion!
"They had no poet, and they died." [2]
    "They Had No Poet"
Should chance strike out of me some
    human heat,
    Leap not at that and think to grasp
    my soul!

[1] Give me a good digestion, Lord,
    And also something to digest.
    A Pilgrim's Grace, St. 1 (From a sou-
    venir card given those who visit Ches-
    ter Cathedral, Cheshire, England)
[2] See Pope, page 214.

I flee new bonds. My self must still re-
    treat
    Down devious ways to keep me free
    and whole.
    A Gentleman of Fifty Soliloquizes
One boob may die, but deathless is
    The royal race of hicks —
When Ahab went to Ascalon
    They sold him gilded bricks.
    Boob Ballad
How often when they find a sage
    As sweet as Socrates or Plato
They hand him hemlock for his wage,
    Or bake him like a sweet potato!
    Taking the Longer View
There will be no beans in the Almost
Perfect State.
    The Almost Perfect State
For a territory the size of the United
States five millions of people would be
about right. . . . The human popula-
tion of the entire world should be kept
well under a hundred millions. . . . If
the world were not so full of people, and
most of them did not have to work so
hard, there would be more time for
them to get out and lie on the grass, and
there would be more grass for them to
lie on.
    Ibid.
"You go and find her Husband's name
    and other similar facks,"
Says the king to the Execushioner, "and
    measure his neck for an ax;
For the turtle doves is singing sweet —
    Oh, what the hell, it's Spring!
And just for the sake of argyment, I'll
    show 'em who is king."
    *David and Bathsheba
    (As Interpreted by the Old Soak)*
To stroke a platitude until it purrs
like an epigram.
    The Sun Dial
Publishing a volume of verse is like
dropping a rose-petal down the Grand
Cañon and waiting for the echo.
    Ibid.
Poetry is what Milton saw when he
went blind.
    Ibid.

If you make people think they're thinking, they'll love you. If you really make them think they'll hate you.

The Sun Dial

An Idea isn't responsible for the people who believe in it.

Ibid.

Speed, I bid you, speed the earth
Onward with a shout of mirth,
Fill your eager eyes with light,
Put my face and memory
Out of mind and out of sight.
Nothing I have caused or done,
But this gravestone, meets the sun:
Friends, a great simplicity
Comes at last to you and me.

Lines for a Gravestone

EDWIN MEADE ROBINSON
[1878–   ]

Write me a verse, my old machine —
I lack for an inspiration;
The skies are blue and the trees are green,
And I long for a long vacation.

The Typewriter's Song. Stanza 1

A start! A thrill! A rattle — and then
It pounds out, swift and hearty —
"Now is the time for all good men
To come to the aid of the party."

Ibid. Stanza 4

Dying and letting die, they call "living and letting live";
They do not even make mistakes for live ones to forgive;
Wouldst thou be Nothing? Then, my son, be a Conservative!

Conservatives

CARL SANDBURG
[1878–   ]

Pile the bodies high at Austerlitz and Waterloo,
Shovel them under and let me work —
I am the grass; I cover all.

Grass

The fog comes on little cat feet.

Fog

O prairie mother, I am one of your boys.

I have loved the prairie as a man with a heart shot full of pain over love.

Prairie

I tell you the past is a bucket of ashes.

Ibid.

The peace of great churches be for you,
Where the players of lofty pipe organs
Practice old lovely fragments, alone.

For You

The peace of great books be for you,
Stains of pressed clover leaves on pages,
Bleach of the light of years held in leather.

Ibid.

For the gladness here where the sun is shining at evening on the weeds of the river,
    Our prayer of thanks.

Our Prayer of Thanks

For the laughter of children who tumble barefooted and bareheaded in the summer grass.

Ibid.

The republic is a dream.
Nothing happens unless first a dream.

Washington Monument by Night

Death sends a radiogram every day:
When I want you I'll drop in — and then one day he comes with a master-key and lets himself in and says: We'll go now.

Death Snips Proud Men

That sergeant at Belleau Woods,
Walking into the drumfires, calling his men,
"Come on, you . . . Do you want to live forever?" [1]

Losers

When Abraham Lincoln was shoveled into the tombs, he forgot the copperheads and the assassin . . . in the dust, in the cool tombs.

Cool Tombs

Take any streetful of people buying clothes and groceries, cheering a hero or throwing confetti and blowing tin horns . . . tell me if the lovers are losers . . . tell me if any get more than the lovers . . . in the dust . . . in the cool tombs.

Ibid.

---

[1] See Thomas Carlyle, page 381.

Lay me on an anvil, O God.
Beat me and hammer me into a crow-
bar.
Let me pry loose old walls.
Let me lift and loosen old foundations.
Prayers of Steel
I won't take my religion from any man
who never works except with his
mouth and never cherishes any
memory except the face of the
woman on the American silver dol-
lar.
To a Contemporary Bunkshooter
Look out how you use proud words.
When you let proud words go, it is not
easy to call them back.
They wear long boots, hard boots. . . .
Look out how you use proud words.
Primer Lesson
Time is a sandpile we run our fingers in.
Hotel Girl
Hog Butcher for the World,
Tool Maker, Stacker of Wheat,
Player with Railroads and the Nation's
Freight Handler;
Stormy, husky, brawling,
City of the Big Shoulders.
Chicago
I know a Jew fish crier down on Max-
well Street, with a voice like a
north wind blowing over corn
stubble in January. . . .
His face is that of a man terribly glad
to be selling fish.
Fish Crier

LOUIS EDWIN THAYER
[1878–   ]

Here is a toast that I want to give
To a fellow I'll never know;
To the fellow who's going to take my
place
When it's time for me to go.
To My Successor. Stanza 1 [1909]
I fancy when I go to rest some one will
bring to light
Some kindly word or goodly act long
buried out of sight;
But, if it's all the same to you, just give
to me, instead,

The bouquets while I'm living and the
knocking when I'm dead.
Of Post-Mortem Praises. Stanza 1

EDWARD THOMAS
[1878–1917]

Out of the night, two cocks together
crow,
Cleaving the darkness with a silver
blow.
Cock-Crow
The swift with wings and tail as sharp
and narrow
As if the bow had flown off with the ar-
row.
Haymaking
If I should ever by chance grow rich
I'll buy Codham, Cockridden, and
Childerditch,
Roses, Pyrgo, and Lapwater,
And let them all to my elder daughter.
If I Should Ever by Chance

KENDALL BANNING
[1879–   ]

The world has but one song to sing,[1]
And it is ever new;
The first and last of all the songs,
For it is ever true;
A little song, a tender song,
The only song it hath:
"There was a youth of Ascalon
Who loved a girl of Gath."
Once on a Time. Stanza 2

GEORGE SANDS BRYAN
[1879–   ]

"What has upheld you on your way?
What has supported you when faint?
On what have you for strength relied?"
"My vittles," said the dear old saint.
Aunt Phoebe. Stanza 4

JAMES BRANCH CABELL
[1879–   ]

Why is the King of Hearts the only
one that hasn't a moustache?
The Rivet in Grandfather's Neck

[1] See Don Marquis, page 851.

Divers queens who die with Antony
But live a great while first with Julius.
Retractions. V

LEE WILSON DODD
[1879–1933]

You steal green apples from the Tree
Of Life, miscalling greenness pleasure.
To the Younger Generation

Much that I sought, I could not find;
Much that I found, I could not bind;
Much that I bound, I could not free;
Much that I freed returned to me.
Ronde Macabre

Furious Propaganda, with her brand,
Fires the dry prairies of our wide Waste
Land:
Making the Earth, Man's temporal sta-
tion, be
One stinking altar to Publicity.
The Great Enlightenment

JOHN ERSKINE
[1879–   ]

The Moral Obligation to Be Intelligent.
Title of book [1915]

And win, with simple gratitude and
wonder,
Peace in themselves, which is their sole
applause.
At the Front [1918]

EDWARD MORGAN FORSTER
[1879–   ]

The historian must have some conception of how men who are not historians behave.
*Abinger Harvest. Captain Ed-
ward Gibbon*

It is not that the Englishman can't
feel — it is that he is afraid to feel. He
has been taught at his public school
that feeling is bad form. He must not
express great joy or sorrow, or even
open his mouth too wide when he talks
— his pipe might fall out if he did.
Ibid. Notes on English Character

English literature is a flying fish. It
is a sample of the life that goes on day
after day beneath the surface; [1] it is a

[1] Viz. of the English character.

proof that beauty and emotion exist in
the salt, inhospitable sea.
*Abinger Harvest. Notes on
English Character*

How rare, how precious is frivolity!
How few writers can prostitute all their
powers! They are always implying "I
am capable of higher things."
Ibid. Ronald Firbank

NICHOLAS VACHEL LINDSAY
[1879–1931]

Man is a torch, then ashes soon,
May and June, then dead December,
Dead December, then again June.
Who shall end my dream's confusion?
Life is a loom, weaving illusion.
The Chinese Nightingale

They spoke, I think, of perils past.
They spoke, I think, of peace at last.
One thing I remember:
Spring came on forever,
Spring came on forever,
Said the Chinese nightingale.
Ibid.

The flower-fed buffaloes of the spring
In the days of long ago,
Ranged where the locomotives sing
And the prairie flowers lie low.
The Flower-Fed Buffaloes

Then you died on the prairie, and
scorned all disgraces,
O broncho that would not be broken of
dancing.
*The Broncho that Would Not
Be Broken. Stanza 5*

Booth died blind and still by faith he
trod,
Eyes still dazzled by the ways of God.
*General William Booth Enters
into Heaven*

Drabs and vixens in a flash made
whole!
Gone was the weasel-head, the snout,
the jowl; . . .
The banjos rattled, and the tambou-
rines
Jing-jing-jingled in the hands of
Queens!
Ibid.

Record it for the grandson of your
    son —
A city is not builded in a day;
Our little town cannot complete her
    soul
Till countless generations pass away.
        On the Building of Springfield.
                Stanza 2

A bronzed, lank man! His suit of an-
    cient black,
A famous high top-hat and plain worn
    shawl
Make him the quaint great figure that
    men love,
The prairie-lawyer, master of us all.
        Abraham Lincoln Walks at
                Midnight. Stanza 3

Sleep softly, . . . eagle forgotten, . . .
    under the stone,
Time has its way with you there and
    the clay has its own.
Sleep on, O brave-hearted, O wise man,
    that kindled the flame —
To live in mankind is far more than to
    live in a name,
To live in mankind, far, far more . . .
    than to live in a name.
        The Eagle That Is Forgotten.[1]
                Stanza 5

I look on the specious electrical light
Blatant, mechanical, crawling and
    white,
Wickedly red or malignantly green
Like the beads of a young Senegambian
    queen.
        A Rhyme About an Electrical
                Advertising Sign

See how the generations pass
Like sand through Heaven's blue hour-
    glass.
                        Shantung

I want live things in their pride to re-
    main.
I will not kill one grasshopper vain
Though he eats a hole in my shirt like
    a door.

[1] John Peter Altgeld [1847–1902], Governor of Illinois [1893–1897], widely criticized
for pardoning, in June, 1893, three anarchists
who were serving terms in prison for their
part in the Haymarket Riot at Chicago,
May 4, 1886. In 1896 and 1900 he supported
W. J. Bryan's candidacy for the Presidency.

I let him out, give him one chance more.
Perhaps, while he gnaws my hat in his
    whim,
Grasshopper lyrics occur to him.
                The Santa Fé Trail

Far away the Rachel-Jane
Not defeated by the horns
Sings amid a hedge of thorns: —
"Love and life,
Eternal youth —
Sweet, sweet, sweet, sweet,
Dew and glory,
Love and truth,
Sweet, sweet, sweet, sweet."
                        Ibid.

We shall see silver ships,
We shall see singing ships,
Valleys of spray today,
Mountains of foam.
We have been long away,
Far from our wonderland.
Here come the ships of love
Taking us home.
        The Lame Boy and the Fairy

The blood-fed captains nod. . . .
Rise, rise,
Take the sick dragons by surprise,
Highly establish
In the name of God,
The United States of Europe, Asia, and
    the World.
        Sew the Flags Together[1]

Fat black bucks in a wine-barrel room,
Barrel-house kings, with feet unstable,
Sagged and reeled and pounded on the
    table,
Pounded on the table,
Beat an empty barrel with the handle
    of a broom,
Hard as they were able,
Boom, boom, Boom,
With a silk umbrella and the handle of
    a broom,
Boomlay, boomlay, boomlay, Boom.
                The Congo. Part I

Then I saw the Congo, creeping through
    the black,
Cutting through the jungle with a
    golden track.
                        Ibid.

[1] Written November, 1918.

Mumbo-Jumbo is dead in the jungle,
Never again will he hoo-doo you.
                              The Congo. Part III

"I am your slave," said the Jinn.
                              Aladdin and the Jinn

God give such dawns as when, his venture o'er,
The Sailor looked upon San Salvador.
God lead us past the setting of the sun
To wizard islands, of august surprise;
God make our blunders wise.
                    Litany of the Heroes. Stanza 16

Come let us forget our ivory-towers,[1]
    brothers,
Come let us be bold with our songs.
            *Every Soul Is a Circus. Part IV,
              The Pontoon Bridge Miracle*

Planting the trees that would march
    and train

---

[1] Charles-Augustin Sainte-Beuve [1804–1869] is the first writer known to have likened a poet's retreat to an ivory tower. In his *Pensées d'Août, To M. Villemain, St. 3*, dated October, 1837, he wrote:

              Hugo, dur partisan
. . . combattit sous l'armure,
Et tint haut sa bannière au milieu du murmure:
Il la maintient encore; et Vigny, plus secret,
Comme en sa tour d'ivoire, avant midi, rentrait
              (Hugo, strong partisan
. . . fought in armor,
And held high his banner in the midst of the tumult:
He still holds it; and Vigny, more discreet,
As if in his tower of ivory, retired before noon).

The poet, retired in his Tower of Ivory, isolated, according to his desire, from the world of man, resembles, whether he so wishes or not, another solitary figure, the watcher enclosed for months at a time in a lighthouse at the head of a cliff. — JULES DE GAULTIER [1858–   ]: *La Guerre et les Destinées de l'Art*

The ivory tower awakened my desire;
    I longed to enclose myself in selfish bliss.
        RUBÉN DARIO [1867–1916]: *Portico,
                                        St. 13*

    A tower of ivory it is
    Beside a shoreless sea;
    I look out of my lattices
    And the saints appear to me.
WILFRED ROWLAND CHILDE [1890–   ]:
                        Turris Eburnea, St. 5

On, in his name to the great Pacific,
Like Birnam Wood to Dunsinane,[1]
Johnny Appleseed swept on.[2]
        *In Praise of Johnny Appleseed
                    (1775–1847)*

ST. JOHN LUCAS
[1879–1934]

The curate thinks you have no soul;
    I know that he has none.
                              My Dog

This prayer at least the gods fulfill:
    That when I pass the flood and see
Old Charon by the Stygian coast
    Take toll of all the shades who land,
Your little, faithful, barking ghost
    May leap to lick my phantom hand.[3]
                              Ibid.

I would resort to any method —
megaphones in the street, sonnets on
the partitions of third-class carriages,
and even the biograph — if by such
base uses I could really arouse an interest in things that are fine.
        The Rose-Winged Hours. Preface

HAROLD MONRO
[1879–1932]

How lonely we shall be!
What shall we do,
You without me,
I without you?
                    Midnight Lamentation

She nestles over the shining rim,
Buries her chin in the creamy sea;
Her tail hangs loose; each drowsy paw
Is doubled under each bending knee.
                              Milk for the Cat

We are going *Out*. You know the pitch
    of the word,
Probing the tone of thought as it comes
    through fog
And reaches by devious means (half-
    smelt, half-heard)
The four-legged brain of a walk-ecstatic
    dog.
                              Dog

---

[1] *Macbeth, Act V, Sc. 5.*
[2] See Allen, page 596.
[3] See Norah Holland, page 842.

PADRAIC H. PEARSE
[1879–1916]

Naked I saw thee,
O beauty of beauty!
And I blinded my eyes
For fear I should flinch.
Ideal. Stanza 1

Of wealth or of glory
I shall leave nothing behind me
(I think it, O God, enough!)
But my name in the heart of a child.
To Death. Stanza 2

FELIX RIESENBERG
[1879–   ]

City, lyric city. . . .
City kind to actresses; tolerant of
actors; city of independent handmaid-
ens. City of contraceptions, contrap-
tions, and curses thundered from a
thousand pulpits. City of unfortunate fortune tellers. City entered by
night. . . .
Reporters cover you, yet you are
never covered. . . .
City of carpenters without wood, of
plumbers without mercy. City of uncomfortable comfort stations. City of
clanging radiators, of supine superin-
tendents. City wherein there is no room
to die. . . .
City wrought in flame. City of arguments unending. City of terminals, city
of endings, city of the last attempt. City
wherein no one knows whether he is
coming or going. . . . City of oda-
lisques working in stores, of seraglios
seeking for sultans, of tired old women
scrubbing offices by night. Great glorious patriotic city, giving its canes to
crippled soldiers. Fairy city in those
magic hours of the passing night; the
pause before the dawn. . . .
Dress-suit city, for hire and for
keeps. . . .
City that breathes of things too large
for books, that is too beautiful for poets,
too terrible for drama, too true for
testimony. . . .

City worth visiting, if only for a
week.
East Side, West Side, 1919–1929

The sea has always been a seducer,
a careless lying fellow, not feminine, as
many writers imagine, but strongly
masculine in its allurement. The king
of the sea, with his whiskers of weed
and his trident and dolphins, truly represents the main and gives it character.
The sea, like a great sultan, supports
thousands of ships, his lawful wives.
These he caresses and chastises as the
case may be. This explains the feminine
gender of all proper vessels.
Vignettes of the Sea

Have you ever considered that if
every thumb print is different, perhaps
everything else is different? No two
people are alike. Yet originals, individu-
alists, bright intellects, and the gang
who lead the laughter and point the
way, are alarmed by an idea that we
are becoming standardized.
Endless River

If the ship is troubled with rats, place
a good deal of dry newspaper in the
sail locker for the rats to chew on.
Standard Seamanship

WILL ROGERS [1]
[1879–1935]

All I know is just what I read in the
papers.
Prefatory remark

I never met a man I didn't like.
*Address, Tremont Temple,
Boston [June, 1930]*

There is a lot of difference in pioneering for gold and pioneering for spinach.
*Last syndicated contribution to
the press, sent from Fairbanks,
Alaska, and published the day
after his death in an airplane
crash [August 15, 1935]*

[1] I worked with gum and grin and lariat
To entertain the proletariat,
And with my Oklahomely wit
I brightened up the earth a bit.
OGDEN NASH [1902–   ]

ROBERT HAVEN SCHAUFFLER
[1879–   ]

At the gate of the West I stand,
On the isle where the nations throng,
We call them "scum o' the earth."
Scum o' the Earth
Newcomers all from the eastern seas,
Help us incarnate dreams like these.
Forget, and forgive, that we did you
      wrong.
Help us to father a nation strong
In the comradeship of an equal birth,
In the wealth of the richest bloods of
      earth.
Ibid.

BESSIE ANDERSON
(MRS. ARTHUR J.) STANLEY
[1879–   ]

He has achieved success who has
lived well, laughed often and loved
much; who has enjoyed the trust of
pure women, the respect of intelligent
men and the love of little children; who
has filled his niche and accomplished his
task; who has left the world better than
he found it, whether by an improved
poppy, a perfect poem, or a rescued
soul; who has never lacked appreciation
of earth's beauty or failed to express it;
who has always looked for the best in
others and given them the best he had;
whose life was an inspiration; whose
memory a benediction.
*Success (prize-winning defini-
tion in a contest conducted by
the Brown Book Magazine, Boston, 1904)*

ROSE PASTOR STOKES
[1879–1933]

Some pray to marry the man they love,
   My prayer will somewhat vary:
I humbly pray to Heaven above
   That I love the man I marry.
My Prayer

SIMEON STRUNSKY
[1879–   ]

If you made a poll of newspaper editors, you might find a great many who
think that war is evil. But if you were
to take a census among pastors of fashionable metropolitan churches —
Professor Latimer's Progress
[1918]

We need a vindication of the night,
and especially of night in the city. . . .
The more you think of it the more you
will be persuaded that night is prima-
rily the time of the innocent industries,
and for the most part the primitive industries, employing simple, innocent,
primitive men — slow-speaking truck
farmers, husky red-faced slaughterers in
the abattoirs, solid German bakers, and
milkmen. The milkman alone is enough
to redeem the night from its undeserved
evil reputation. A cartload of pasteur-
ized milk for nurslings at four o'clock in
the morning represents more service to
civilization than a cartful of bullion on
its way from the Sub-treasury to the
vaults of a national bank five hours
later.
Belshazzar Court. Night Life

ROY ATWELL
[1880–   ]

In these days of indigestion
It is oftentimes a question
As to what to eat and what to leave
      alone;
For each microbe and bacillus
Has a different way to kill us,
And in time they always claim us for
      their own.
*Some Little Bug Is Going to
Find You Some Day. Stanza 1*

Some little bug is going to find you
   some day,
Some little bug will creep behind you
   some day.
Ibid. Stanza 3

HENRY HOWARTH BASHFORD
[1880–   ]

As I came down the Highgate Hill
  I met the sun's bravado,
And saw below me, fold on fold,
Grey to pearl and pearl to gold,
This London like a land of old,
  The land of Eldorado.
            Romance. Stanza 1

ALBERT JAY COOK

It's Heaven, Hell or Hoboken [1] before
  next Christmas Day.
        Heaven, Hell or Hoboken [2]

ROBERT BROWNING HAMILTON
[1880–   ]

I walked a mile with Pleasure.
  She chattered all the way,
But left me none the wiser
  For all she had to say.

I walked a mile with Sorrow,
  And ne'er a word said she;
But, oh, the things I learned from her
  When Sorrow walked with me!
            Along the Road

ROBERT CORTES HOLLIDAY
[1880–   ]

The best, the most exquisite automobile is a walking-stick; and one of the finest things in life is going a journey with it.
        Walking-Stick Papers [*1918*]

They [women] are too personal for the high enjoyment of going a journey. They must be forever thinking about you or about themselves; with them everything in the world is somehow tangled up in these matters; and when you are with them (you cannot help it, or if you could they would not allow it), you must be forever thinking about them or

yourself. Nothing on either side can be seen detached. They cannot rise to that philosophic plane of mind which is the very marrow of going a journey. One reason for this is that they can never escape from the idea of society. You are in their society, they are in yours.
        Walking-Stick Papers [*1918*]

There is not in the press any reading so improving as the "obits" . . . I doubt very much indeed whether any one could read obituaries every day for a year and remain a bad man or woman.
        Ibid. The Deceased

We go into the feature headed "Died," a department similar in design to that on the literary page headed "Books Received." We are arranged alphabetically according to the first letter of our surnames. We are set in small type with lines following the name line indented. It is difficult for me to tell with certainty from the printed page but I think we are set without leads.
                    Ibid.

HELEN KELLER [1]
[1880–   ]

Literature is my Utopia. Here I am not disfranchised. No barrier of the senses shuts me out from the sweet, gracious discourse of my book-friends. They talk to me without embarrassment or awkwardness.
        The Story of My Life

At first I was rather unwilling to study Latin grammar. It seemed absurd to waste time analyzing every word I came across — noun, genitive, singular, feminine — when its meaning was quite plain. I thought I might just as well describe my pet in order to know it — order, vertebrate; division, quadruped; class, mammalia; genus, filinus; species, cat; individual, Tabby. But as I got deeper into the subject, I became more interested, and the beauty of the language delighted me. I often amused myself by reading Latin passages, picking up words I understood and trying to

---

[1] Hoboken, New Jersey, was a port of embarkation and return for the American Expeditionary Forces during the World War.

[2] Published in *The Stars and Stripes* during the World War.

[1] Helen Keller has been blind and deaf since infancy.

make sense. I have never ceased to enjoy this pastime.

The Story of My Life

MARY ANTIN

So at last I was going to America!
Really, really going, at last! The boundaries burst. The arch of heaven soared.
A million suns shone out for every star.
The winds rushed in from outer space,
roaring in my ears, "America! America!"

The Promised Land

Spirit of all childhood! Forgive me,
forgive me, for so lightly betraying a
child's dream-secrets. I that smile so
scoffingly today at the unsophisticated
child that was myself, have I found any
nobler thing in life than my own longing to be noble? Would I not rather be
consumed by ambitions that can never
be realized than live in stupid accept-
ance of my neighbor's opinion of me?
The statue in the public square is less a
portrait of a mortal individual than a
symbol of the immortal aspiration of
humanity.

Ibid.

RUDOLPH CHAMBERS LEHMANN

When eight strong fellows are out to
row,
With a slip of a lad to guide them,
I warrant they'll make the light ship go,
Though the coach on the launch may
chide them,
With his "Six, get on to it! Five, you're
late!
Don't hurry the slides, and use your
weight!
You're bucketing, Bow; and, as to
Four,
The sight of his shoulders makes me
sore!"

At Putney. Stanza 1

They have slipped through Barnes;
they are round the bend;
And the chests of the eight are tightening.
"Now spend your strength, if you've
strength to spend,

And away with your hands like lightning!
Well rowed!" — and the coach is forced
to cheer —
"Now stick to it, all, for the post is
near!"
And, lo, they stop at the coxswain's call,
With its message of comfort, "Easy
all!"

At Putney. Stanza 4

HENRY LOUIS MENCKEN
[1880–   ]

The virulence of the national appetite for bogus revelation.

A Book of Prefaces. Chap. 1, Sect. 2

To the man with an ear for verbal
delicacies — the man who searches
painfully for the perfect word, and puts
the way of saying a thing above the
thing said — there is in writing the constant joy of sudden discovery, of happy
accident.

Ibid. Chap. 2, Sect. 2

Poverty is a soft pedal upon all
branches of human activity, not excepting the spiritual.

Ibid. Chap. 4, Sect. 3

Formalism is the hall-mark of the
national culture.

Ibid. Sect. 6

Time is a great legalizer, even in the
field of morals.

Ibid.

All successful newspapers are ceaselessly querulous and bellicose. They
never defend anyone or anything if they
can help it; if the job is forced upon
them, they tackle it by denouncing
someone or something else.

Prejudices, First Series. Chap. 13

The great artists of the world are
never Puritans, and seldom even ordinarily respectable.

Ibid. Chap. 16

To be in love is merely to be in a
state of perceptual anaesthesia — to
mistake an ordinary young man for a
Greek god or an ordinary young woman
for a goddess.

Ibid.

Here, more than anywhere else in the world, the daily panorama of human existence — the unending procession of governmental extortions and chicaneries, of commercial brigandages and throat-slittings, of theological buffooneries, of aesthetic ribaldries, of legal swindles and harlotries — is so inordinately extravagant, so perfectly brought up to the highest conceivable amperage, that only the man who was born with a petrified diaphragm can fail to go to bed every night grinning from ear to ear, and awake every morning with the eager, unflagging expectations of a Sunday-school superintendent touring the Paris peep-shows.

On Being an American [*1922*]

Human enterprises that, in all other countries, are resigned despairingly to an incurable dulness — things that seem devoid of exhilarating amusement by their very nature — are here lifted to such inordinate buffoonery that contemplating them tears the very midriff from its moorings.

Ibid.

To be happy one must be (*a*) well fed, unhounded by sordid cares, at ease in Zion, (*b*) full of a comfortable feeling of superiority to the masses of one's fellow men, and (*c*) delicately and unceasingly amused according to one's taste. It is my contention that, if this definition be accepted, there is no country in the world wherein a man constituted as I am — a man of my peculiar weakness, vanities, appetites, and aversions — can be so happy as he can be in the United States. Going further, I lay down the doctrine that it is a sheer physical impossibility for such a man to live in the United States and *not* be happy.

Ibid.

All the more pretentious American authors try to write chastely and elegantly; the typical literary product of the country is still a refined essay in the *Atlantic Monthly,* perhaps gently jocose but never rough — by Emerson, so to speak, out of Charles Lamb.

The American Language [*1919*]

Philadelphia is the most pecksniffian of American cities, and thus probably leads the world.

The American Language [*1919*]

MENCKEN AND NATHAN
[GEORGE JEAN NATHAN]
[1882–]

From the American Credo [*1920*]

That all one has to do to gather a large crowd in New York is to stand on the curb a few moments and gaze intently at the sky.

That the postmasters in small towns read all the postcards.

That all theater box-office employés are very impolite and hate to sell a prospective patron a ticket.

That all newspaper reporters carry notebooks.

That, when shaving on a railway train, a man invariably cuts himself.

That the jokes in *Punch* are never funny.

That nicotine keeps the teeth in a sound condition.

That the wife of a rich man always wistfully looks back into the past and wishes she had married a poor man.

That the quality of the champagne may be judged by the amount of noise the cork makes when it is popped.

That all French women are very passionate, and will sacrifice everything to love.

That beer is very fattening.

That the cloth used in suits made in England is so good that it never wears out.

That Philadelphia is a very sleepy town.

That if one swallows an ounce of olive oil before going to a banquet, one will not get drunk.

That the worst actress in the company is always the manager's wife.

That milking a cow is an operation demanding a special talent that is possessed only by yokels, and that a person born in a large city can never hope to acquire it.

ALFRED NOYES
[1880–   ]

There was music all about us, we were
    growing quite forgetful
We were only singing seamen from the
    dirt of Londontown.
        Forty Singing Seamen. Stanza 4
There's a magic in the distance, where
    the sea-line meets the sky.
            Ibid. Stanza 9
The music's not immortal, but the world
    has made it sweet.
        The Barrel-Organ. Stanza 1
Go down to Kew in lilac-time, in lilac-
    time, in lilac-time;
    Go down to Kew in lilac-time (it isn't
    far from London!)
And you shall wander hand in hand
    with love in summer's wonder-
    land;
    Go down to Kew in lilac-time (it isn't
    far from London!)
            Ibid. Stanza 5
Ye that follow the vision
    Of the world's weal afar,
Have ye met with derision
    And the red laugh of war?
Yet the thunder shall not hurt you
    Nor the battle storms dismay;
Tho' the sun in heaven desert you
    "Love will find out the way." [1]
        Love Will Find Out the Way
England, my mother,
    Lift to my Western Sweetheart
One full cup of English mead, breathing
    of the May!
Pledge the may-flower in her face that
    you and ah, none other,
        Sent her from the mother-land
        Across the dashing spray.
America, My Sweetheart. Stanza 1
(*prologue to the American edition
of Drake*)
The wind was a torrent of darkness
    among the gusty trees,
The moon was a ghostly galleon tossed
    upon cloudy seas,

---

[1] Under floods which are deepest,
    Which Neptune obey;
    Over rocks that are steepest,
    Love will find out the way.
        PERCY: *Reliques, Love Will Find
        Out the Way*

The road was a ribbon of moonlight
    over the purple moor,
And the highwayman came riding —
    Riding — riding —
The highwayman came riding, up to the
    old inn-door.
        The Highwayman. I, Stanza 1
I'll come to thee by moonlight, though
    hell should bar the way.
            Ibid. Stanza 5
The cymbals crash,
    And the dancers walk,
With long silk stockings
    And arms of chalk.
        A Victory Dance. Stanza 1
God how the dead men
    Grin by the wall,
Watching the fun
    Of the Victory Ball.
            Ibid. Stanza 9
Die to the little hatreds; die to greed;
    Die to the old ignoble selves we knew;
Die to the base contempts of sect and
    creed.
    A Victory Celebration. Sonnet VII
And that's not done by sword, or tongue,
    or pen,
There's but one way. God make us bet-
    ter men.
                Ibid.
Gardener of God, if wild and weak de-
    sires
Choke the true growth, and rob the
    soul of power,
Use thy sharp knife on wandering shoots
    and briars,
    Cut the weak stem hard back, and let
    it flower.
        The Rose and the Knife [*1934*]

VILDA SAUVAGE OWENS

If I ever have time for things that
    matter,
If ever I have the smallest chance,
I'm going to live in
Little Broom Gardens,
Moat-by-the-Castle,
Nettlecombe, Hants.
    *If I Ever Have Time for the Things
        That Matter. Stanza 1*

EDMUND LESTER PEARSON
[1880–1937]

The agile bookworm eats, conceal'd
from sight,
Also the prowling mouse abhors the
light,
But be assur'd that Philobiblos knows,
The hellish Cockroach is the chief of
foes.
The Old Librarian's Almanack [1]

Matrimony is no fit Diversion for the
Librarian. The dissipations of Time, the
vain Emptinesses of Amusement, the
general be-pesterment . . . agree to
harass the Librarian and woo him from
his legitimate tasks.
Ibid.

No agreement about books can make
us look upon another man with so
friendly an eye as the discovery that he
belonged to our period, and shared our
special enthusiasms about reading, in
the years that stretched between the
sixth birthday and the sixteenth.
Books in Black or Red

The eccentricities of collectors are as
merry as the cantrips of unicorns on a
grassy plain.
Ibid.

GRANTLAND RICE
[1880–   ]

Where the puddle is shallow, the weak-
fish stay
To drift along with the current's flow;
To take the tide as it moves each day
With the idle ripples that come and
go.
Ballade of the Gamefish
Where the far heights call through the
silver glow,

"Only the gamefish swims up
stream." [1]
Ballade of the Gamefish
Keep coming back for all they've got,
and take it with a grin
When disappointment trips you up or
failure barks your shin;
Keep coming back — and if at last you
lose the game of right
Let those who whipped you know at
least they, too, have had a fight.
Alumnus Football

GILES LYTTON STRACHEY
[1880–1932]

Bertie [2] seemed to display a deep-
seated repugnance to every form of
mental exertion.
Queen Victoria. Chap. 6
In women's hearts he [3] had always
read as in an open book. . . . He realised everything — the interacting com-
plexities of circumstance and character,
the pride of place mingled so inextric-
ably with personal arrogance, the super-
abundant emotionalism, the ingenuous-
ness of outlook, the solid, the laborious
respectability, shot through so incon-
gruously by temperamental cravings for
the coloured and the strange, the singular intellectual limitations, and the mys-
teriously essential female elements im-
pregnating every particle of the whole.
A smile hovered over his impassive features, and he dubbed Victoria "the
Faery."
Ibid. Chap. 8
The inconsistency of the Elizabethans exceeds the limits permitted to man.
Their elements fly off from one another
wildly; we seize them; we struggle hard
to shake them together into a single
compound, and the retort bursts. How
is it possible to give a coherent account

---

[1] An ingenious literary hoax. This "Almanack for the year 1774," purporting to have
been issued by "Jared Bean" in New Haven
in 1773, was published by Mr. Pearson in
1909, and successfully fooled many critics and
bibliophiles — even the late Sir William Osler.
See Pearson's *Books in Black or Red, Chap. 2.*

[1] See John Trotwood Moore, page 733.
Mr. Rice used this line in another poem, *Ex-
panding the Theme.*

Only the gamefish swims upstream,
But the sensible fish swims down.
OGDEN NASH [1902–   ]: *When You
Say That, Smile*
[2] King Edward VII as a child.
[3] Disraeli.

of their subtlety and their *naïveté*, their delicacy and their brutality, their piety and their lust?
> *Elizabeth and Essex. Chap. 2*

Perhaps of all the creations of man language is the most astonishing.
> *Words and Poetry*

RICHARD HENRY TAWNEY
[1880–   ]

The burden of our civilization is not merely, as many suppose, that the product of industry is ill-distributed, or its conduct tyrannical, or its operation interrupted by bitter disagreements. It is that industry itself has come to hold a position of exclusive predominance among human interests, which no single interest, and least of all the provision of the material means of existence, is fit to occupy. Like a hypochondriac who is so absorbed in the processes of his own digestion that he goes to the grave before he has begun to live, industrialized communities neglect the very objects for which it is worth while to acquire riches in their feverish preoccupation with the means by which riches can be acquired.

That obsession by economic issues is as local and transitory as it is repulsive and disturbing. To future generations it will appear as pitiable as the obsession of the seventeenth century by religious quarrels appears today.
> *The Acquisitive Society*

NANCY BYRD TURNER
[1880–   ]

The Bookshop has a thousand books,
All colors, hues, and tinges,
And every cover is a door
That turns on magic hinges.
> *The Bookshop. Stanza 2*

May I have eyes to see
Beauty in this plain room
Where I am called to be.
> *A Prayer for the Kitchen Wall*

Aisne-Marne, Chavignon, St. Mihiel,
  Meuse-Argonne — east and west —
The old strange names, familiar now as
  heart-beats in each breast,
And keen with memories of those they
  left to sleep alone,
Dust to dust in an alien land, yet still
  New England's Own.
> *New England's Own.*[1] *Stanza 3*

MARGARET WIDDEMER

I have shut my little sister in from life
  and light
(For a rose, for a ribbon, for a wreath
  across my hair),
I have made her restless feet still under
  the night,
Locked from sweets of summer and from
  wild spring air.
> *The Factories. Stanza 1*

The old road to Paradise
  Easy it is missed!
> *The Old Road to Paradise.*
> *Stanza 2*

Carnations and my first love! And he
  was seventeen,
And I was only twelve years — a stately
  gulf between.
> *Carnations. Stanza 1*

Well, if the thing is over, better it is
  for me,
The lad was ever a rover, loving and
  laughing and free.
> *Mary, Helper of Heartbreak.*
> *Stanza 1*

Mary, helper of heartbreak, send him
  to me to-night!
> *Ibid. Stanza 3*

The only work about writing —
  It's a very terrible thing —
Is wrapping your stuff and stamping it
  And tying it up with string.
> *Confession. Stanza 3*

WILLIAM W. WOOLLCOTT

I am a One Hundred Per-Cent American.
> *Refrain of ironical patriotic anthem*

---

[1] Commemorating the return of the Yankee Division from France, April 25, 1919.

I am an anti-Darwin intellectual:
The man that says any nice young boy
    or gal
Is a descendant of the ape
Shall never from Hell's fire escape.
Refrain of ironical patriotic anthem
In art I pull no high-brow stuff,
I know what I like, and that's enough.
                                    Ibid.

THOMAS R. YBARRA

Oh, the Roman was a rogue,
    He erat was, you bettum;
He ran his automobilus
    And smoked his cigarettum.
He wore a diamond studibus
    And elegant cravattum,
A maxima cum laude shirt,
    And such a stylish hattum.
                        Lay of Ancient Rome

LASCELLES ABERCROMBIE
[1881–]

But here's the happiest light can lie on
    ground,
Grass sloping under trees
Alive with yellow shine of daffodils!
                                Ryton Firs
These, who desired to live, went out to
    death:
Dark underground their golden youth is
    lying.
We live: and there is brightness in our
    breath
They could not know — the splendour
    of their dying.
                                Epitaph
No faith can last
That never sings.
                        The Stream's Song
The great blue ceremony of the air
Did a new morrow for the earth prepare.
                        Mary and the Bramble
    What is all
The world, but an awning scaffolded
    amid
The waste perilous Eternity, to lodge
This Heaven-wander'd princess, wom-
    an's beauty?
                                Vashti

FRANKLIN PIERCE ADAMS
("F.P.A.")
[1881–]

Christmas is over and Business is Busi-
ness.
                        For the Other 364 Days
"Up, to the office, . . . and so to bed."
        A Ballade of Mr. Samuel Pepys.
                                Refrain
"Oh, why do you gaze, my dear, my
    dear,
    And muse on the misty sky?"
"I'm afraid that it isn't going to clear,
    And we won't get the washing dry."
                        Sehnsucht. Stanza 5

If, my dear, you seek to slumber,
Count of stars an endless number;
If you still continue wakeful,
Count the drops that make a lakeful;
Then, if vigilance yet above you
Hover, count the times I love you;
And if slumber still repel you,
Count the times I do not tell you.
                                Lullaby

I've been from Banff to Painted Post,
    From Harrisburg to Monterey,
    From Cedarhurst to San José,
From Santa Cruz to Valley Forge,
    And yet, on all my witless way,
I've never called a waiter "George."
        A Ballade of Egregiousness.
                                Stanza 1

Ruthlessly pricking our gonfalon bub-
    ble,
Making a Giant hit into a double,
Words that are weighty with nothing
    but trouble:
"Tinker to Evers to Chance."
                        Baseball's Sad Lexicon

The rich man has his motor-car,
    His country and his town estate.
He smokes a fifty-cent cigar
    And jeers at Fate.
                        The Rich Man. Stanza 1
Yet though my lamp burn low and dim,
    Though I must slave for livelihood —
Think you that I would change with
    him?
You bet I would!
                        Ibid. Stanza 3

It is cold, O Thaliarchus, and Soracte's
    crest is white;
There is skating on the Tiber; there is
    No Relief in Sight.
Tell the janitor the radiator's absolutely
    cold. . . .
Let us crack a quart of Sabine; I've a
    case of four-year old.
            The Cold Wave of 32 B. C.
                (Horace, Odes I, 9)
The best you get is an even break.
        *Ballade of Schopenhauer's
                    Philosophy*

I shot a poem into the air,
It was reprinted everywhere
From Bangor to the Rocky Range
And always credited to
                — Exchange.
                Frequently

O bards of rhyme and metre free,
My gratitude goes out to ye
For all your deathless lines — ahem!
Let's see now. . . . What *is* one of
    them?
                To a Vers Librist

Of making many books there is no
    end —
So Sancho Panza said, and so say I.
Thou wert my guide, philosopher and
    friend
When only one is shining in the sky.
        *Lines on and from "Bartlett's
                    Familiar Quotations"*

Go, lovely Rose that lives its little hour!
Go, little booke! and let who will be
    clever!
Roll on! From yonder ivy-mantled
    tower
The moon and I could keep this up
    forever.
                Ibid.

WITTER BYNNER
[1881–   ]

Name me no names for my disease,
    With uninforming breath;
I tell you I am none of these,
    But homesick unto death.
        *The Patient to the Doctors.
                    Stanza 1*

Sometimes when people pity me,
    I tell them with no rancor
That for what it costs me to be free
    I might have bought an anchor.
            When People Pity Me

You must keep your goal in sight,
Labor toward it day and night,
Then at last arriving there —
You shall be too old to care.
                Wisdom

What's the use of a new-born
    child? [1] . . .
To raise the dead heart? — to set wild
The fettered hope?
                Poor Richard

The look in your eyes
Was as soft as the underside of soap in a
    soap-dish.
                I Evade

There is a solitude in seeing you,
Followed by your company when you
    are gone.
                Lightning

What is so nameless as beauty,
Which poets, who give it a name,
Are only unnaming forever? —
Content, though it go, that it came.
                Grass-Tops

JOSEPH CAMPBELL
[1881–   ]

As a white candle
In a holy place,
So is the beauty
Of an aged face.
            The Old Woman. Stanza 1

Her thoughts as still
As the waters
Under a ruined mill.
                Ibid. Stanza 3

---

[1] "What is the use of this new invention?"
some one asked Franklin. "What is the use
of a new-born child?" was his reply. — JAMES
PARTON: *The Life and Times of Benjamin
Franklin* [1864], *Vol. 2, Pp. 514-515.* (A footnote states that the anecdote is taken from the
memoirs of Baron de Grimm.)
    The economist of 1855 who asks, Of what
use are the lords? may learn of Franklin, Of
what use is a baby? — R. W. EMERSON: *English Traits*

FRANCIS CARLIN (JAMES FRANCIS CARLIN MacDONNELL)
[1881–   ]

My Love has crossed an Ocean
  O'er which no breezes blow,
And I would it had the motion
  Of but an ebb and flow.
          The Stilly Sea. Stanza 1
My Love is o'er a Water,
  A calm and tideless sea,
And I would that I had taught her
  To come in dreams to me.
          Ibid. Stanza 2
That which is in disorder
  Has neither rule nor rhyme,
Like the stars at Heaven's border
  And the troubled laughter of Time.
          The Ravelled Edge. Stanza 3

ROBERT WILLIAM CHAPMAN
[1881–   ]

A house is infinitely communicative,
and tells many things besides the figure
of its master's income. There are houses
that confess intellectual penury, and
houses that reek of enlightenment.
      The Portrait of a Scholar [1920]
All poetry, and all good prose, invite
me to utterance. I hope I do not sit
muttering in public places; but if I cannot give voice, my ear hearkens to unheard melodies . . . but I believe that
most readers are deaf. . . . This conspiracy of silence has much to answer
for in the general decay of writing and
the false notions of style now commonly
entertained.
            Ibid. Reading Aloud
A quotation, like a pun, should come
unsought, and then be welcomed only
for some propriety or felicity justifying
the intrusion.
        Ibid. The Art of Quotation
A collector should not be too careful
to be sure of what he buys, or the sporting spirit will atrophy; and he who collects that he may have the best collection, or a better than his friend's, is
little more than a miser.
          Ibid. Silver Spoons

When I dine out and find my soup
embellished by a notable spoon, as may
often happen to those who dine in Colleges or Inns of Court, my manners are
seldom proof against temptation. I contrive a furtive scrutiny of the underside.
          The Portrait of a Scholar.
          Silver Spoons

PADRAIC COLUM
[1881–   ]

Oh, to have a little house!
  To own the hearth and stool and all!
          An Old Woman of the Roads.
          Stanza 1
And I am praying God on high,
  And I am praying Him night and day,
For a little house — a house of my
    own —
  Out of the wind's and the rain's way.
          Ibid. Stanza 6
A tune is more lasting than the voice of
    the birds.
A song is more lasting than the riches of
    the world.
      Polonius and the Ballad-Singers

JOHN FREEMAN
[1881–1929]

Who may regret what was, since it has
    made
Himself himself? All that I was I am,
And the old childish joy now lives in
    me
At sight of a green field or a green tree.
          All That I Was I Am
I knew how beauty seen from unseen
    must rise,
  How the body's joy for more than
    body's use was made.
I knew then how the body is the body of
    the mind,
  And how the mind's own fire beneath
    the cool skin played.
          The Body
Knowing that beauty's self rose visible
    in the world
Over age that darkens, and griefs that
    destroy.
          Ibid.

HELEN GRANVILLE-BARKER

Night and the curtains drawn,
  The household still,
Fate, with appointed strength,
  Hath worked its will.
  Night and the Curtains Drawn
Dearest, the whole world ends,
  Ends well — in this —
Night — and the firelit dark,
  Your touch, your kiss.
  Ibid.

EDGAR ALBERT GUEST
[1881–   ]

Somebody said that it couldn't be done
  But he with a chuckle replied
That "maybe it couldn't," but he would
    be one
  Who wouldn't say so till he'd tried.
  It Couldn't Be Done
It takes a heap o' livin' in a house t'
    make it home,
A heap o' sun an' shadder, an' ye some-
    times have t' roam
Afore ye really 'preciate the things ye
    lef' behind,
An' hunger fer 'em somehow, with 'em
    allus on yer mind.
  Home
How do you tackle your work each day?
  Are you scared of the job you find?
Do you grapple the task that comes your
    way
  With a confident, easy mind?
  How Do You Tackle Your Work?
The things that haven't been done be-
    fore,
  Those are the things to try;
Columbus dreamed of an unknown
    shore
  At the rim of the far-flung sky.
  *The Things That Haven't Been
    Done Before*
I'd rather see a sermon than hear one
    any day;
I'd rather one should walk with me than
    merely tell the way.
  Sermons We See
In this bright little package, now isn't
    it odd?

You've a dime's worth of something
    known only to God!
  The Package of Seeds
Here is one of God's miracles soon to
    unfold,
Thus for ten cents an ounce is Divinity
    sold!
  Ibid.

JOHN EDWARD HAZZARD
[1881–1935]

It worries me to beat the band
To hear folks say our lives is grand;
Wish they'd try some one-night stand.
  Ain't it awful, Mabel!
  Ain't It Awful, Mabel!

WILLIAM McFEE
[1881–   ]

To those who live and toil and lowly die,
  Who pass beyond and leave no last-
    ing trace,
To those from whom our queen Pros-
    perity
  Has turned away her fair and fickle
    face.
  Casuals of the Sea. Dedication
A trouble is a trouble, and the gen-
eral idea, in the country, is to treat it
as such, rather than to snatch the
knotted cords from the hand of God and
deal out murderous blows.
  Ibid. Book I
It is extraordinary how many emo-
tional storms one may weather in safety
if one is ballasted with ever so little
gold.
  Ibid.
The world belongs to the Enthusiast
who keeps cool.
  Ibid. Book II
Terrible and sublime thought, that
every moment is supreme for some man
and woman, every hour the apotheosis
of some passion!
  Ibid.
Responsibility's like a string we can
only see the middle of. Both ends are
out of sight.
  Ibid.

And so, having sailed the seas for many years, having debauched the gifts of God, and the love of women, having avoided with incredible dexterity the esteem of man and the joy of accomplishment, Jan Ostade went out into the void.
Casuals of the Sea. Book III

A certain incomprehensible reticence of soul which is peculiar to the English.
Command. Chap. 6

The alluring yet ineluctable problem of human folly.
Aliens. Preface [*1917*]

It has become fashionable to blame America for sins that are the common heritage of mankind . . . it is amusing to witness the astonishment and even incredulity of Americans who learn that such outstanding and typical citizens as Edgar Guest, Father Coughlin, Bishop Manning and Aimee McPherson were all born British.
On Living in America

Steam engines are very human. Their very weaknesses are understandable. Steam engines do not flash back and blow your face in. They do not short-circuit and rive your heart with imponderable electric force. They have arms and legs and warm hearts and veins full of warm vapour. Give us steam every time. You know where you are with steam.
A Six-Hour Shift [*1917*]

High-brow communists affect vast interest in pictures of machinery as art. They discover aesthetic qualities in a photograph of a broken crankshaft or the gear-wheels of a power press. A couple of screws lying on a mirror will send them into toothy ecstasies of appreciation.
More Harbours of Memory.
Introduction [*1934*]

The bourgeois artist who retains his integrity is the only really happy man in the modern world. He is unable to envy anybody because nobody has anything he can use which is not his already.
Ibid.

Most of our nautical fictions seem to be caulked with hokum . . . it is almost impossible to get Americans to view the life of a seafaring man save as a chapter out of Jack London's *Sea Wolf* or some equally virile and odious fiction.
More Harbours of Memory.
Romance

JOHN GNEISENAU NEIHARDT
[1881–   ]

Come back and bring the summer in your eyes,
The peace of evening in your quiet ways;
Come back and lead again to Paradise
The errant days!
Come Back. Stanza 1

Let me live out my years in heat of blood!
Let me die drunken with the dreamer's wine!
Let me not see this soul-house built of mud
Go toppling to the dust — a vacant shrine!
Let Me Live Out My Years

Give me high noon — and let it then be night!
Ibid.

And grant me, when I face the grisly Thing,
One haughty cry to pierce the gray Perhaps!
O let me be a tune-swept fiddlestring
That feels the Master Melody — *and snaps!*
Ibid.

Glowing through the gray rack
Breaks the Day —
Like a burning haystack
Twenty farms away!
Break of Day. Stanza 13

STUART PRATT SHERMAN
[1881–1926]

Nine-tenths of our university teachers are more competent to discuss the literature of England than the literature of America.

> *Introduction* [*1923*] *to American Prose Masters by* W. C. BROWNELL

If a choice must be made, the American student should choose to be familiar with the Federalist rather than with the Letters of Junius, with Irving rather than Leigh Hunt, with Emerson rather than Carlyle, with Thoreau rather than Richard Jefferies, with Whitman rather than William Morris, with Mark Twain rather than Oscar Wilde, with Henry James rather than George Moore, and with Theodore Roosevelt rather than Queen Victoria.

> *Ibid.*

The delectable form which intelligence takes in its moments of surplus power — the form of wit.

> *Ibid.*

MARY (MRS. HENRY BERTRAM LAW) WEBB
[1881–1927]

The past is only the present become invisible and mute; and because it is invisible and mute, its memoried glances and its murmurs are infinitely precious. We are to-morrow's past.

> *Precious Bane.*[1] *Foreword*

It made me gladsome to be getting some education, it being like a big window opening.

> *Ibid. Book I, Chap. 5*

Saddle your dreams afore you ride 'em.

> *Ibid. Chap. 6*

If you stop to be kind, you must swerve often from your path.

> *Ibid. Book II, Chap. 3*

When you dwell in a house you mislike, you will look out of window a deal more than those that are content with their dwelling.

> *Ibid. Book III, Chap.5*

It's the folk that depend on us for this and for the other that we most do miss.

[1]   That soil may best
Deserve the precious bane.
MILTON: *Paradise Lost, Book I, L. 689*

So the mother is more let and hindered lacking the little creatures clinging to her skirt than she is when they be there, for she has no heart for her work.

> *Precious Bane. Book IV, Chap. 4*

BERTON BRALEY
[1882–   ]

Got any river they say isn't crossable?
   Got any mountains that can't be cut
      through?
We specialize in the wholly impossible,
   Doing things "nobody ever could do."

> *At Your Service. Stanza 2*

Trained by a task that's the biggest in
      history:
   Who has a job for this Panama Gang?

> *Ibid. Stanza 3*

The grammar has a rule absurd
   Which I would call an outworn myth:
"A preposition is a word
   You mustn't end a sentence with!"

> *No Rule to be Afraid of. Stanza 1*

And so they sailed away, these three,
      Mencken,
         Nathan
            And God.[1]

> *Three Minus One. Stanza 1*

With doubt and dismay you are smitten,
   You think there's no chance for you,
      son?
Why, the best books haven't been written,
   The best race hasn't been run.

> *Opportunity. Stanza 1*

If with pleasure you are viewing any
      work a man is doing,
   If you like him or you love him, tell
      him now.

> *Do It Now. Stanza 1*

Do not wait till life is over and he's
      underneath the clover,
   For he cannot read his tombstone
      when he's dead!

> *Ibid. Stanza 2*

[1] I shall name you the fishermen three:
         Wynken,
         Blynken,
         And Nod.
EUGENE FIELD: *Wynken, Blynken, and Nod, St. 3*

If neither cold poverty, famished and
    gaunt,
Nor sickness nor pain
Of body or brain
Can turn you away from the thing that
    you want,
If dogged and grim you besiege and be-
    set it,
You'll get it!
Success

Give the boy a dog and you've furnished
    him a playmate
Always true and faithful as can be.[1]
A Gift. Stanza 1

It's seldom any one bestows
    The praise that Father should have
    had,
But — here's the debt that one man
    owes,
    I sing a little song to Dad!
It's Only Fair. Envoy

Back of the beating hammer
    By which the steel is wrought,
Back of the workshop's clamor
    The seeker may find the Thought.
The Thinker. Stanza 1

Back of the Job — the Dreamer
    Who's making the dream come true!
Ibid. Stanza 4

JOHN DRINKWATER
[1882–1937]

This be my pilgrimage and goal,
    Daily to march and find
The secret phrases of the soul,
    The evangels of the mind.
Vocation

Great hills that fold above the sea,
    Ecstatic airs and sparkling skies,
Sing out your words to master me,
    Make me immoderately wise.
Invocation

And not a girl goes walking
    Along the Cotswold lanes
But knows men's eyes in April
    Are quicker than their brains.
Cotswold Love

---

[1] Dogs are faithful; they will stick to a bone
after everybody has deserted it. — HENRY
WHEELER SHAW ("Josh Billings"): *Animile
Statistix*

O Love, you happy wayfarer,
Be still my fond interpreter,
Of all the glory that can be
As once on starlight Winchelsea,
Finding upon my pilgrim way
A burning bush for every day.
The Burning Bush

Grant us the will to fashion as we feel,
Grant us the strength to labor as we
    know,
Grant us the purpose, ribbed and edged
    with steel,
    To strike the blow.
A Prayer. Stanza 9

When the high heart we magnify,
    And the clear vision celebrate,
And worship greatness passing by,
    Ourselves are great.
Abraham Lincoln

CECILY FOX-SMITH
[1882–   ]

Lord knows it's bitter in an open boat
    to see your shipmates die.
The Open Boat. Stanza 4

As I went down by Hastings Mill I
    lingered in my going
To smell the smell of piled-up deals and
    feel the salt wind blowing.
Hastings Mill. Stanza 1

Along the wharves in sailor town a sing-
    ing whisper goes
Of wind among the anchored ships, the
    wind that blows
Off a broad brimming water, where the
    summer day had died
Like a wounded whale a-sounding in
    the sunset tide.
Sailor Town. Stanza 1

When the long day's tramp is over, when
    the journey's done,
I shall dip down from some hill-top at
    the going down o' the sun,
And turn in at the open door, and lay
    down staff and load,
And wash me clean of the heat o' the
    day, and white dust o' the road.
Journey's End. Stanza 1

HERMANN HAGEDORN
[1882–   ]

Down the fair-chambered corridor of
years,
The quiet shutting, one by one, of doors.
Doors

You'll find us kindly on the whole,
though queer;
Not ever quite so bad as we appear,
And at our maddest not without our
graces.
"A Traveler from a Distant Land"

How like the stars are these white,
nameless faces —
These far innumerable burning coals!
This pale procession out of stellar
spaces,
This Milky Way of souls!
Each in its own bright nebulae enfurled,
Each face, dear God, a world!
Broadway

HUGH S. JOHNSON
[1882–   ]

There was never a war at arms that
was not merely the extension of a preceding war of commerce grown fiercer
until the weapons of commerce seemed
no longer sufficiently deadly.
*Radio broadcast for "World
Peaceways"* [1935]

It is some commercial stake or ambition that makes all wars, and we
haven't got enough commercial stake
or ambition in the whole of Europe to
be worth the life or heart's blood of one
single mother's son.
Ibid.

THOMAS SAMUEL JONES, JR.
[1882–1932]

Across the fields of yesterday
He sometimes comes to me,
A little lad just back from play —
The lad I used to be.
Sometimes. Stanza 1

I wonder if he hopes to see
The man I might have been.
Ibid. Stanza 2

There is an island in the silent sea,
Whose marge the wistful waves lap list-
lessly —
An isle of rest for those who used to be.
The Island [*For the painting,
The Isle of the Dead, by* ARNOLD
BOECKLIN, *1827–1901* [1]]

JAMES JOYCE
[1882–   ]

Pity is the feeling which arrests the
mind in the presence of whatsoever is
grave and constant in human sufferings
and unites it with the human sufferer.
*A Portrait of the Artist as a
Young Man. Chap. 5*

Welcome, O life! I go to encounter
for the millionth time the reality of experience and to forge in the smithy of
my soul the uncreated conscience of my
race. Old father, old artificer, stand me
now and ever in good stead.
*Ibid. Concluding words of
Stephen Dedalus* [2]

A man of genius makes no mistakes.
His errors are volitional and are the
portals of discovery.
Ulysses. Page 188 [*Random
House edition*] [3]

Let some meinherr from Almany
grope his life long for deephid meanings in the depth of the buckbasket.
Ibid. Page 202

He [Shakespeare] has hidden his own
name, a fair name, William, in the
plays, a super here, a clown there, as
a painter of old Italy set his face in a

---

[1] One of Boecklin's five versions of this subject was acquired by the Metropolitan Museum of Art, New York, in 1926. It was
painted in 1880.

[2] The reader must never forget the symbolism in the name Dedalus. — HERBERT GOR-
MAN: Introduction to Modern Library edition.

[3] In respect of the recurrent emergence of
the theme of sex in the minds of his characters, it must always be remembered that his
locale was Celtic and his season spring . . .
in many places the effect on the reader is
somewhat emetic, nowhere does it tend to be
an aphrodisiac. "Ulysses" may, therefore, be
admitted into the United States. — Judge
JOHN M. WOOLSEY: decision of U. S. District
Court [Dec. 6, 1933]

dark corner of his canvas. He has revealed it in the sonnets where there is Will in overplus. Like John O'Gaunt his name is dear to him, as dear as the coat of arms he toadied for, on a bend sable a spear or steeled argent, honorificabilitudinitatibus, dearer than his glory of greatest shakescene in the country. What's in a name? That is what we ask ourselves in childhood when we write the name that we are told is ours. A star, a daystar, a firedrake rose at his birth. It shone by day in the heavens alone, brighter than Venus in the night, and by night it shone over delta in Cassiopeia, the recumbent constellation which is the signature of his initial among the stars. His eyes watched it, lowlying on the horizon, eastward of the bear, as he walked by the slumberous summer fields at midnight, returning from Shottery and from her arms.

Ulysses. Page 207

Every life is many days, day after day. We walk through ourselves, meeting robbers, ghosts, giants, old men, young men, wives, widows, brothers-in-love. But always meeting ourselves.

Ibid. Page 210

WINIFRED MARY LETTS
[1882–   ]

I saw the spires of Oxford
　As I was passing by,
The gray spires of Oxford
　Against a pearl-gray sky.

The Spires of Oxford. Stanza 1

God rest you, happy gentlemen,
　Who laid your good lives down. . . .
God bring you to a fairer place
　Than even Oxford town.

Ibid. Stanza 4

That God once loved a garden
We learn in Holy writ.
And seeing gardens in the Spring
I well can credit it.
But if God walks in Dublin,
I think that He'd be seen
Pacing up and down the paths
That lead through Stephen's Green.

Stephen's Green. Stanza 1

I like the people who keep shops,
Busy and cheerful folk with friendly
　faces.

Shops. Stanza 1

To serve us seems their only aim,
Asking our wishes, quick to crave our
　pardon,
And yet I know in each of these shop
　people
There dwells a soul withdrawn from us,
　elusive,
The shop can never know — a secret
　garden.

Ibid. Stanza 4

Then God go with you, priest of God,
For all is well, and shall be well.
What though you tread the roads of
　Hell,
Your Captain these same ways has trod.
Above the anguish and the loss
Still floats the ensign of His Cross.

Chaplain to the Forces

I laugh when I hear thim make it plain
That dogs and men never meet again.
For all their talk, who'd listen to thim,
With the soul in the shining eyes of him?
Would God be wasting a dog like Tim?

Tim, an Irish Terrier. Stanza 4

RICHARD MIDDLETON
[1882–1911]

Servant of the eternal Must
　I lie here, here let me lie,
In the ashes and the dust,
　Dreaming, dreaming pleasantly.

Pagan Epitaph

Why are her eyes so bright, so bright,
　Why do her lips control
The kisses of a summer night
　When I would love her soul?

Any Lover, Any Lass

The Silver Girl she came to me
　When spring was dancing green,
She said "I've come to wait on you
　And keep your cabin clean;
To wash your face and hands and feet
　And keep your forehead cool —
I'll get you into Heaven yet,
　You damned old fool!"

The Silver Girl

ALAN ALEXANDER MILNE
[1882–   ]

Could we have some butter for
The Royal slice of bread?

The King's Breakfast

"Nobody, my darling,
Could call me
A fussy man —
  BUT
I do like a little bit of butter to my
  bread!"

Ibid.

It isn't really
Anywhere!
It's somewhere else
Instead!

Halfway Down. Stanza 2

If I were a bear,
  And a big bear, too,
I shouldn't much care
  If it froze or snew.

Furry Bear

What shall I call my dear little dormouse?
His eyes are small, but his tail is e-nor-
  mouse.

The Christening

Christopher Robin goes
Hoppity, hoppity,
Hoppity, hoppity, hop.
Whenever I tell him
Politely to stop it, he
Says he can't possibly stop.

Hoppity

James James
Morrison Morrison
Weatherby George Dupree
Took great
Care of his Mother
Though he was only three.
James James
Said to his Mother,
"Mother," he said, said he:
You must never go down to the end of
  the town, if you don't go down with
  me.

Disobedience

FRANKLIN DELANO
ROOSEVELT
[1882–   ]

The forgotten man [1] at the bottom of
the economic pyramid.

Radio address [April 7, 1932]

The only thing we have to fear is
fear itself.

*First Inaugural Address
[March 4, 1933]*

In the field of world policy I would
dedicate this nation to the policy of the
good neighbor.[2]

Ibid.

For the trust reposed in me I will return the courage and the devotion that
befit the time. I can do no less. We face
the arduous days that lie before us in
the warm courage of national unity;
with the clear consciousness of seeking
old and precious moral values; with the
clean satisfaction that comes from the
stern performance of duty by old and
young alike. We aim at the assurance of
a rounded and permanent national life.
We do not distrust the future of essential democracy.

Ibid.

Continued dependence upon relief in-
duces a spiritual and moral disintegra-
tion fundamentally destructive to the
national fibre. To dole out relief in this

[1] Wealth comes only from production, and
all that the wrangling grabbers, loafers and
jobbers get to deal with comes from somebody's toil and sacrifice. Who, then, is he who
provides it all? The Forgotten Man . . .
delving away in patient industry, supporting
his family, paying his taxes, casting his vote,
supporting the church and the school . . .
but he is the only one for whom there is no
provision in the great scramble and the big
divide. Such is the Forgotten Man. He works,
he votes, generally he prays — but he always
pays. . . . All the burdens fall on him, or on
her, for the Forgotten Man is not seldom a
woman. — WILLIAM GRAHAM SUMNER [1840–
1910], Professor of Political and Social Science
at Yale: *The Forgotten Man* [1883], a speech

[2] I am as desirous of being a good neighbor
as I am of being a bad subject. — HENRY
DAVID THOREAU: *On the Duty of Civil Disobedience* [1848]

way is to administer a narcotic, a subtle destroyer of the human spirit.

Message to Congress
[January 4, 1935]

I hope that calm counsel and constructive leadership will provide the steadying influence and the time necessary for the coming of new and more practical forms of representative government throughout the world wherein privilege will occupy a lesser place and welfare a greater.

Ibid.

Economic royalists.

Speech accepting renomination
[June 27, 1936]

This generation of Americans has a rendezvous with destiny.

Ibid.

We have always known that heedless self-interest was bad morals; we know now that it is bad economics.

Second Inaugural Address
[January 20, 1937]

The change in the moral climate of America.

Ibid.

The test of our progress is not whether we add more to the abundance of those who have much; it is whether we provide enough for those who have too little.

Ibid.

If they can take it, I can.

Replying to the suggestion that the inauguration ceremony be held indoors on account of bad weather [January 20, 1937]

JAMES STEPHENS
[1882–   ]

I hear a sudden cry of pain!
There is a rabbit in a snare.

The Snare

I saw God! Do you doubt it?
Do you dare to doubt it?
I saw the Almighty Man! His hand
Was resting on a mountain! And
He looked upon the World, and all
     about it.

What Tomas Said in a Pub.
Stanza 1

Forgive us all our trespasses,
Little creatures, everywhere!

Little Things. Stanza 5

Let the man who has and doesn't give
Break his neck, and cease to live!
Let him who gives without a care
Gather rubies from the air!

In the Imperative Mood

When you walk in a field,
Look down
Lest you tramp
On a daisy's crown!

When You Walk. Stanza 1

God help the horse, and the driver too!
And the people and beasts who have
     never a friend!

To the Four Courts, Please.
Stanza 3

In cloud and clod to sing
Of everything and anything.

The Pit of Bliss

Women are wiser than men because they know less and understand more.

The Crock of Gold. Chap. 2

Virtue is the performance of pleasant actions.

Ibid. Chap. 10

Women and birds are able to see without turning their heads, and that is indeed a necessary provision, for they are both surrounded by enemies.

The Demi-Gods. Chap. 2

If a person desires to be a humorist it is necessary that the people around him shall be at least as wise as he is, otherwise his humor will not be comprehended.

Ibid. Chap. 27

Something depressing comes on the mind when it has been too extensively occupied with the female sex.

In the Land of Youth. Chap. 28

VIRGINIA WOOLF [1]
[1882–   ]

Those comfortably padded lunatic asylums which are known, euphemistically, as the stately homes of England.

The Common Reader. Lady
Dorothy Nevill

[1] Virginia Woolf is the best living example of that sort of mind which had its innings

Trivial personalities decomposing in the eternity of print.

The Common Reader. The Modern Essay

There is no room for the impurities of literature in an essay.

Ibid.

That complete statement which is literature.

Ibid. How It Strikes a Contemporary

The word-coining genius, as if thought plunged into a sea of words and came up dripping.

Ibid. An Elizabethan Play

MORRIS BISHOP
[1883–   ]

After the day is over
  And the passers-by are rare
The lights burn low in the barber-shop
  And the shades are drawn with care
To hide the haughty barbers
  Cutting each other's hair.

The Tales the Barbers Tell

And on the pedestal these words appear:
"My name is Ozymandias, king of kings!
Look on my works, ye Mighty, and despair!"
Also the names of Emory P. Gray,
Mr. and Mrs. Dukes, and Oscar Baer,
Of 17 West 4th Street, Oyster Bay.

Ozymandias Revisited [1]

BADGER CLARK, JR.
[1883–   ]

I waste no thought on my neighbor's birth
Or the way he makes his prayer.

---

in letters in the eighteenth century — a mind partly critical, partly philosophical, highly imaginative, incapable of the vaster emotions but so subtle in its emotionalized intellectuality, so polished, that it makes most other contemporary writers appear to be parvenus of the intellect. — MARY M. COLUM in *The New York Herald-Tribune, May 8, 1927*

The talent of this generation which is most certain of survival. — REBECCA WEST: *Ending in Earnest* [1931]

[1] SHELLEY: *Ozymandias of Egypt.*

I grant him a white man's room on earth
If his game is only square.
While he plays it straight I'll call him mate;
If he cheats I drop him flat.

The Westerner. Stanza 3

O Lord, I've never lived where churches grow,
I love creation better as it stood
That day You finished it so long ago,
And looked upon Your work and called it good.

A Cowboy's Prayer. Stanza 1

I thank You, Lord, that I am placed so well,
That You have made my freedom so complete,
That I'm no slave of whistle, clock, or bell,
No weak-eyed prisoner of wall and street.

Ibid. Stanza 2

And guide me on the long, dim trail ahead
That stretches upward toward the Great Divide.

Ibid. Stanza 4

Oh, stranger, tell my pards below
I took a rampin' dream in tow,
And if I never lay him low,
  I'll never turn him loose!

The Glory Trail [*also known as High-Chin Bob*]

ARTHUR DAVISON FICKE
[1883–   ]

When this my mortal course is run
And I withdraw to far retreat
Among the angels, there is one
I hope with all my heart to meet —
That worthy prelate Dr. Donne
Strolling down the Celestial Street.

Soul in Torment. Stanza 1

Put up his spear, his knightly pennon furled,
And died of the unworthiness of the world.

Don Quixote. IV

O great Don Quixote! Let your reckless mood
Still be our light, through midnights of despair —

That we, though knowing all that once
  you knew,
Hopeless and grim, adventure forth with
  you!
 *Nocturne in a Library [Phi Beta
  Kappa Poem, Harvard, 1925]*

I am in love with high far-seeing places
 That look on plains half-sunlight and
  half-storm,
In love with hours when from the cir-
 cling faces
 Veils pass, and laughing fellowship
  glows warm.
 Sonnets of a Portrait-Painter. XIII

No man of elder years than fifty
Should be empowered with lands and
 gold.
It turns them shrewd and over-thrifty,
It makes them cruel and blind and cold.
 Youth and Age. Stanza 1

Old men in impotence can beget
New wars to kill the lusty young.
Young men can sing: old men forget
That any song was ever sung.
 Ibid. Stanza 3

Those great obscure momentous souls
Whom fame does not record,
Whose impulse still our fate controls
With deathless deed or word.
 Immortals in Exile. Stanza 2

. . . the snivelling servant maid
With injured peevish look,
Who on the lagging fire-coals laid
Carlyle's long-labored book.
 Ibid. Stanza 4

. . . The Man from Porlock strode
Whose visit broke the wizard song
Of Kubla Khan's abode.
 Ibid. Stanza 6

Men who perhaps down wells have
 thrown
Plays of Euripides.
 Ibid. Stanza 7

Or sold some budding Shakespeare
 drink,
Or shut in cells some Blake,
Or forced some Shelley to death's brink
For true religion's sake.
 Ibid. Stanza 8

LOUISA FLETCHER

I wish that there were some wonderful
 place
Called the Land of Beginning Again.
 *The Land of Beginning Again.
  Stanza 1*

I am the color of audacity,
 Of rhythmic tribal dance, of tropic
  love;
I am that tint released upon the air
 When cymbals kiss, or comets meet
  above.
 Mandarin Red. Stanza 1

KAHLIL GIBRAN
[1883–1931]

Let there be spaces in your togetherness.
 The Prophet. On Marriage
You are the bows from which your
children as living arrows are sent forth.
 Ibid. On Children
You give but little when you give of
your possessions. It is when you give of
yourself that you truly give.[1]
 Ibid. On Giving
Work is love made visible. And if you
cannot work with love but only with
distaste, it is better that you should
leave your work and sit at the gate of
the temple and take alms of those who
work with joy.
 Ibid. On Work.
The lust for comfort, that stealthy
thing that enters the house a guest, and
then becomes a host, and then a master.
 Ibid. On Houses
The master spirit of the earth shall
not sleep peacefully upon the wind till
the needs of the least of you are satisfied.
 Ibid. On Buying and Selling
When one of you falls down he falls
for those behind him, a caution against
the stumbling stone. Ay, and he falls
for those ahead of him, who though
faster and surer of foot, yet removed
not the stumbling stone.
 Ibid. On Crime and Punishment

[1] The gift without the giver is bare.
 LOWELL: *The Vision of Sir Launfal,
  Part II, VIII*

What is evil but good tortured by its own hunger and thirst.

The Prophet. On Good and Evil

You pray in your distress and in your need; would that you might pray also in the fullness of your joy and in your days of abundance.

Ibid. On Prayer

Beauty is eternity gazing at itself in a mirror.

Ibid. On Beauty

He who wears his morality but as his best garment were better naked.

Ibid. On Religion

What is it to cease breathing, but to free the breath from its restless tides, that it may rise and expand and seek God unencumbered?

Ibid. On Death

I have learned silence from the talkative, toleration from the intolerant, and kindness from the unkind; yet strange, I am ungrateful to those teachers.

Sand and Foam

An exaggeration is a truth that has lost its temper.

Ibid.

Sadness is a wall between two gardens.

Ibid.

We shall never understand one another until we reduce the language to seven words.

Ibid.

HARRY KEMP
[1883–   ]

I pitied him in his blindness;
But can I boast, "I see"?
Perhaps there walks a spirit
Close by, who pities me.

Blind. Stanza 2

Joses, the brother of Jesus, plodded from day to day,
With never a vision within him to glorify his clay;
Joses, the brother of Jesus, was one with the heavy clod,

But Christ was the soul of rapture and soared, like a lark, with God.

Joses, Brother of Jesus.[1] Stanza 1

GEOFFREY ANKETELL STUDDERT-KENNEDY ("WOODBINE WILLIE")[2]
[1883–1929]

When Jesus came to Birmingham, they simply passed Him by,
They never hurt a hair of Him, they only let Him die.

Indifference

HOWARD ARNOLD WALTER
[1883–1918]

I would be true, for there are those who trust me;
I would be pure, for there are those who care;
I would be strong, for there is much to suffer;
I would be brave, for there is much to dare.

My Creed

ANNA WICKHAM (MRS. PATRICK HEPBURN)
[1883–   ]

The true male never yet walked
Who liked to listen when his mate talked.

The Affinity

From a wealth of living I have proved
I must be silent, if I would be loved.

Ibid.

My mind is like a catacomb, where early Christians pray.

Ibid.

Because of the body's hunger are we born,
And by contriving hunger are we fed;
Because of hunger is our work well done,
And so our songs well sung, and things well said.

Sehnsucht

[1] Is not his mother called Mary? and his brethren, James, and Joses, and Simon, and Judas? — *Matthew, XIII, 55*
[2] The affectionate nickname given him by the soldiers to whom, while chaplain, he distributed cigarettes in the trenches.

For all the frittered days
That I have spent in shapeless ways,
Give me one perfect thing.
                              Envoi

LAURA BENÉT
[1884–   ]

Lost in the spiral of his conscience, he
    Detachedly takes rest.
                        The Snail. Stanza 1
He spoke: she teetered up
On pink rheumatic feet;
"Go forth, my dove," he said,
"That we may eat."
                        Noah's Dove. Stanza 6

JAMES ELROY FLECKER
[1884–1915]

I who am dead a thousand years,
    And wrote this sweet archaic song,
Send you my words for messengers
    The way I shall not pass along.
                    *To a Poet a Thousand Years
                              Hence. Stanza 1*
O friend unseen, unborn, unknown,
    Student of our sweet English tongue,
Read out my words at night, alone:
    I was a poet, I was young.
                        Ibid. Stanza 5
Since I can never see your face,
    And never shake you by the hand,
I send my soul through time and space
    To greet you. You will understand.
                        Ibid. Stanza 6
God be thy guide from camp to camp:
    God be thy shade from well to well;
God grant beneath the desert stars thou
    hear the Prophet's camel bell.
                        Gates of Damascus
Yet is not death the great adventure
    still,
And is it all loss to set ship clean anew,
When heart is young and life an eagle
    poised?
                    The Burial in England
I am Don Juan, curst from age to age
By priestly tract and sentimental stage:
Branded a villain or believed a fool,
Battered by hatred, seared by ridicule.
                        Don Juan Declaims

At last they knew that they had died
When they heard music in that land,
And some one there stole forth a hand
To draw a brother to his side.
            Tenebris Interlucentem. Stanza 2
The lean and swarthy poet of despair.
                              Envoy
I have seen old ships sail like swans
    asleep
Beyond the village which men still call
    Tyre.
                        The Old Ships
That talkative, bald-headed seaman
    came
(Twelve patient comrades sweating at
    the oar)
From Troy's doom-crimson shore,
And with great lies about his wooden
    horse
Set the crew laughing, and forgot his
    course.
                              Ibid.
My brother and good friend, the Sun.
            A Western Voyage
West of these out of seas colder than
    the Hebrides
        I must go
Where the fleet of stars is anchored and
    the young
        Star-captains glow.
                    The Dying Patriot
We who with songs beguile your pilgrim-
    age
    And swear that Beauty lives though
        lilies die,
We Poets of the proud old lineage
    Who sing to find your hearts, we know
        not why.
            *The Golden Journey to Samar-
                        kand. Prologue*
When even lovers find their peace at
    last,
    And Earth is but a star, that once had
        shone.
                              Ibid.
What would ye, ladies? It was ever
    thus;
Men are unwise and curiously
    planned.
*They have their dreams and do not
    think of us.*

We make the Golden Journey to
Samarkand.
*The Golden Journey to Samar-
kand. Epilogue*

Out he goes: the mirror strains to kiss
her darling; out he goes!
Since the flame is out, the water can
but freeze.
The water froze.
*The Hammam Name: Poem by
a Turkish Lady. Stanza 6*

A ship, an isle, a sickle moon —
With few but with how splendid stars.
A Ship, An Isle, A Sickle Moon

I am emptied of all my dreams:
I only hear Earth turning, only see
Ether's long bankless streams,
And only know I should drown if you
laid not your hand on me.
Stillness. Stanza 3

FANNY HEASLIP LEA
[1884–]

It's odd to think we might have been
Sun, moon and stars unto each
other —
Only, I turned down one little street
As you went up another.
Fate. Stanza 5

KEITH PRESTON
[1884–1927]

Imperial Caesar dead and turned to
clay
Estopped a hole to keep the wind away;
The great god Ra whose shrine once
covered acres
Is filler now for cross-word puzzle
makers.
The Destiny That Shapes Our Ends

Love, lay thy phobias to rest,
Inhibit thy taboo!
We twain shall share, forever blest,
A complex built for two.
Love Song, Freudian

Among our literary scenes,
Saddest this sight to me,
The graves of little magazines
That died to make verse free.
The Liberators

He must not laugh at his own wheeze:
A snuff box has no right to sneeze.
The Humorist

RUTH MASON RICE
[1884–1927]

A curve for the shore,
A line for the lea,
A tint for the sky —
Where the sunrise will be;
A stroke for a gull,
A sweep for the main;
The skill to do more,
With the will to refrain.
A Japanese Print

ODELL SHEPARD
[1884–]

October in New England,
And I not there to see
The glamour of the goldenrod,
The flame of the maple tree!
Home Thoughts. Stanza 1

SIR JOHN COLLINGS SQUIRE
[1884–]

Princess, inscribe beneath my name:
"He never begged, he never sighed,
He took his medicine as it came";
For this the poets lived — and died.
Ballade of the Poetic Life. Envoi

And stared, and saw, and did not under-
stand,
Columbus's doom-burdened caravels
Slant to the shore, and all their seamen
land.
Sonnet

SARA TEASDALE
[1884–1933]

When I am dead and over me bright
April
Shakes out her rain-drenched hair,
Though you should lean above me
broken-hearted,
I shall not care.
I Shall Not Care. Stanza 1

When I can look Life in the eyes,
Grown calm and very coldly wise,

Life will have given me the Truth,
And taken in exchange — my youth.
Wisdom

How many million Aprils came
  Before I ever knew
How white a cherry bough could be,
  A bed of squills, how blue!
Blue Squills. Stanza 1

Strephon's kiss was lost in jest,
  Robin's lost in play,
But the kiss in Colin's eyes
  Haunts me night and day.
The Look. Stanza 2

Let it be forgotten, as a flower is for-
  gotten,
  Forgotten as a fire that once was sing-
    ing gold,
Let it be forgotten for ever and ever,
  Time is a kind friend, he will make
    us old.
Let It Be Forgotten. Stanza 1

I must have passed the crest a while ago
  And now I am going down —
Strange to have crossed the crest and
    not to know,
  But the brambles were always catch-
    ing the hem of my gown.
The Long Hill. Stanza 1

Never think she loves him wholly,
Never believe her love is blind,
All his faults are locked securely
In a closet of her mind.
Appraisal

I make the most of all that comes,
  And the least of all that goes.
The Philosopher. Stanza 4

DAVID HERBERT
LAWRENCE
[1885–1930]

I never saw a wild thing
Sorry for itself.
Self-Pity

When I wish I was rich, then I know I
  am ill.
Riches

When I read Shakespeare I am struck
  with wonder

That such trivial people should muse
    and thunder
In such lovely language.
When I Read Shakespeare.
Stanza 1

And Hamlet, how boring, how boring to
    live with,
So mean and self-conscious, blowing
    and snoring
His wonderful speeches, full of other
    folks' whoring!
Ibid. Stanza 3

My mother was a superior soul
  A superior soul was she,
Cut out to play a superior rôle
  In the god-damn bourgeoisie.
Red-Herring. Stanza 2

Tell me a word
That you've often heard
Yet it makes you squint
If you see it in print!
Conundrums. Stanza 1

Tell me what's wrong
With words or with you
That you don't mind the thing
Yet the name is taboo.
Ibid. Stanza 4

Men are free when they are in a living homeland, not when they are straying and breaking away. . . . The most
unfree souls go west, and shout of freedom. Men are freest when they are most
unconscious of freedom. The shout is
a rattling of chains.
Studies in Classic American
Literature. Chap. 1

One realm we have never conquered
— the pure present. One great mystery
of time is terra incognita to us — the
instant. The most superb mystery we
have hardly recognized — the immediate, instant self. The quick of all time
is the instant. The quick of all the universe, of all creation, is the incarnate,
carnal self.
New Poems. Preface

It has been a savage enough pilgrimage.
Quoted by CATHERINE CARS-
WELL *in The Savage Pilgrimage,*
a biography

The dead don't die. They look on and help.

> *Quoted by* CATHERINE CARSWELL *in The Savage Pilgrimage, a biography*

RINGGOLD WILMER LARDNER
[1885–1933]

A good many young writers make the mistake of enclosing a stamped, self-addressed envelope, big enough for the manuscript to come back in. This is too much of a temptation to the editor.

Personally I have found it a good scheme to not even sign my name to the story, and when I have got it sealed up in its envelope and stamped and addressed, I take it to some town where I don't live and mail it from there. The editor has no idea who wrote the story, so how can he send it back? He is in a quandary.

> *How to Write Short Stories*

Mother set facing the front of the train, as it makes her giddy to ride backwards. I set facing her, which does not affect me.

> *The Golden Honeymoon*

Mother pointed out that she had the money.

"Well," I said, "we are in Washington and I could of borrowed from the United States Treasury. I would of pretended I was an Englishman."

> *Ibid.*

SINCLAIR LEWIS
[1885–   ]

Babbitt's spectacles had huge, circular, frameless lenses of the very best glass; the ear-pieces were thin bars of gold. In them he was the modern business man; one who gave orders to clerks and drove a car and played occasional golf and was scholarly in regard to Salesmanship . . . a Solid Citizen.

> *Babbitt. Chap. 1*

A sensational event was changing from the brown suit to the gray the contents of his pockets. He was earnest about these objects. They were of eternal importance, like baseball or the Republican Party. They included a fountain pen and a silver pencil (always lacking a supply of new leads) which belonged in the righthand upper vest pocket. Without them he would have felt naked. On his watch-chain were a gold penknife, silver cigar-cutter, seven keys (the use of two of which he had forgotten), and incidentally a good watch. Depending from the chain was a large, yellowish elk's-tooth — proclamation of his membership in the Brotherly and Protective Order of Elks. Most significant of all was his loose-leaf pocket note-book, that modern and efficient note-book which contained the addresses of people whom he had forgotten, prudent memoranda of postal money-orders which had reached their destinations months ago, stamps which had lost their mucilage, clippings of verses by T. Cholmondeley Frink and of the newspaper editorials from which Babbitt got his opinions and his polysyllables, notes to be sure and do things which he did not intend to do, and one curious inscription — D.S.S.D.M.Y.P.D.F.[1]

> *Babbitt. Chap. 1*

Not only Gopher Prairie, but ten thousand towns from Albany to San Diego . . . not a dozen buildings which suggested that, in the fifty years of Gopher Prairie's existence, the citizens had realized that it was either desirable or possible to make this, their common home, amusing or attractive.

> *Main Street. Chap. 4*

Pastoral visiting:
No partiality.
Don't neglect hired girls, be cordial.
Guard conversation, pleasing manner and laugh and maybe one funny story but no scandal or crit. of others.
Stay only 15–30 minutes.
Ask if like to pray with, not insist.

[1] Don't Smoke So Damn Much You Poor Damn Fool.

Rem gt opportunities during sickness, sorrow, marriage.

Ask jokingly why husband not oftener to church.

Elmer Gantry. Chap. 8, notes on Practical Theology lectures

Love:
a rainbow
AM & PM star
from cradle to tomb
inspires art etc. music voice of love
slam atheists etc. who not appreciate love

Ibid. Chap. 10, Elmer's notes for sermon

I can be whatever I will to be; I turn my opened eyes on my Self and possess whatever I desire.

I am God's child, God created all good things including wealth, and I will to inherit it.

I am resolute — I am utterly resolute — I fear no man, whether in offices or elsewhere.

Power is in me, encompassing you to my demands.

Hold fast, O Subconscious, the thought of Prosperity.

In the divine book of achievements my name is written in Gold. I am thus of the world's nobility and now, this moment, I take possession of my kingdom.

Ibid. Chap. 16, Elmer's incantation

Between the Pulitzer Prizes, the American Academy of Arts and Letters and its training-school the National Institute of Arts and Letters, amateur boards of censorship, and the inquisition of earnest literary ladies, every compulsion is put upon writers to become safe, polite, obedient, and sterile. In protest, I declined election to the National Institute of Arts and Letters some years ago, and now I must decline the Pulitzer Prize.

I invite other writers to consider the fact that by accepting the prizes and approval of these vague institutions, we are admitting their authority, publicly confirming them as the final judges of literary excellence, and I inquire whether any prize is worth that subservience.

Letter declining the Pulitzer Prize for his novel, Arrowsmith [1926]

To a true-blue professor of literature in an American university, literature is not something that a plain human being, living today, painfully sits down to produce. No; it is something dead; it is something magically produced by superhuman beings who must, if they are to be regarded as artists at all, have died at least one hundred years before the diabolical invention of the typewriter. To any authentic don, there is something slightly repulsive in the thought that literature could be created by any ordinary human being, still to be seen walking the streets, wearing quite commonplace trousers and coat and looking not so unlike a chauffeur or a farmer. Our American professors like their literature clear and cold and pure and very dead.

The American Fear of Literature, address given at Stockholm, on receiving the Nobel Prize for Literature [December 12, 1930]

WILLIAM ALEXANDER PERCY
[1885–   ]

I heard a bird at break of day
  Sing from the autumn trees
A song so mystical and calm,
  So full of certainties.

Overtones

EZRA POUND
[1885–   ]

Sing we for love and idleness,
Naught else is worth the having.

An Immorality

And I would rather have my sweet,
Though rose-leaves die of grieving,
Than do high deeds in Hungary
To pass all men's believing.

Ibid.

They'll no get him a' in a book I think
Though they write it cunningly;
No mouse of the scrolls was the Goodly
    Fere
But aye loved the open sea.
            Ballad of the Goodly Fere,[1]
                    Stanza 6
"Ye ha' seen me heal the lame and blind,
And wake the dead," says he.
"Ye shall see one thing to master all:
'Tis how a brave man dies on the tree."
            Ibid. Stanza 8
A master of men was the Goodly Fere,
A mate of the wind and sea.
If they think they ha' slain our Goodly
    Fere
They are fools eternally.
            Ibid. Stanza 13
For God, our God, is a gallant foe that
    playeth behind the veil.
Whom God deigns not to overthrow hath
    need of triple mail.
            Ballad for Gloom. Stanza 7
Winter is icummen in,
Lhude sing Goddamm,
Raineth drop and staineth slop,
And how the wind doth ramm!
        Sing: Goddamm.
                    Ancient Music
I beg you, my friendly critics,
Do not set about to procure me an
    audience.
I mate with my free kind upon the crags.
                    Tenzone
Go, my songs, to the lonely and the un-
    satisfied,
Go also to the nerve-wracked, go to the
    enslaved-by-convention,
Bear to them my contempt for their op-
    pressors.
                    Commission
Lovely thou art, to hold me close and
    kisst,
Now cry the birds out in the meadow
    mist,
Despite the cuckold, do thou as thou
    list,
So swiftly goes the night,
        And day comes on!
            Langue D'Oc. Vergier

[1] Companion.

They will come no more,
The old men with beautiful manners.
                    I Vecchii
Real education must ultimately be
limited to men who insist on knowing
the rest is mere sheep-herding.
        A, B, C of Reading. Page 70
                    [*1934*]
It is only after long experience that
most men are able to define a thing in
terms of its own genus, painting as
painting, writing as writing. You can
spot the bad critic when he starts by
discussing the poet and not the poem.
                Ibid. Page 71
There is no reason why the same man
should like the same book at 18 and at
48.
                Ibid. Page 72
Any one who is too lazy to master
the comparatively small glossary necessary to understand Chaucer deserves to
be shut out from the reading of good
books forever.
                Ibid. Page 87
Men do not understand books until
they have had a certain amount of life,
or at any rate no man understands a
deep book, until he has seen and lived
at least part of its contents.
                Ibid. Page 88

WILLIAM LEROY STIDGER
[1885–   ]

I saw God wash the world last night.
    Ah, would He had washed me
As clean of all my dust and dirt
    As that old white birch tree.
            I Saw God Wash the World.
                    Stanza 5

LOUIS UNTERMEYER
[1885–   ]

May nothing evil cross this door
    And may ill fortune never pry
About these windows; may the roar
    And rains go by.
        Prayer for a New House. Stanza 1
And though these shattering walls are
    thin,

May they be strong to keep hate out
  And hold love in.
    Prayer for a New House. Stanza 4
God, if You wish for our love,
  Fling us a handful of stars!
    Caliban in the Coal Mines.
      Stanza 4
God, though this life is but a wraith,
  Although we know not what we use,
Although we grope with little faith,
  Give me the heart to fight — and
    lose.
    Prayer. Stanza 1
Open my ears to music; let
  Me thrill with Spring's first flutes
    and drums —
But never let me dare forget
  The bitter ballads of the slums.
    Ibid. Stanza 4
God, keep me still unsatisfied.
    Ibid. Stanza 5
Is it a tribute or betrayal when
Turning from all the sweet, accustomed
    ways,
I leave your lips and eyes to see you in
Some other face?
    The Wanderer. Stanza 1
Why has our poetry eschewed
The rapture and response of food?
What hymns are sung, what praises said
For home-made miracles of bread?
    Food and Drink
Proverbial parsnips; muscular cheese.
    Ibid.
Eternity is thrust upon
A bit of earth, a senseless stone.
A grain of dust, a casual clod
Receives the greatest gift of God.
    Irony. Stanza 1
There is no kind of death to kill
The sands that lie so meek and still . . .
But Man is great and strong and wise —
  And so he dies.
    Ibid. Stanza 2

HUMBERT WOLFE
[1885–   ]

All I had, you thought, was given —
  Life and ladies, you were wrong;
In a poet's secret heaven
  There is always one last song.
    Heine's Last Song

Even he is half afraid of,
  Even he but hears in part,
For the stuff that it is made of,
  Ladies, is the poet's heart.
    Heine's Last Song
Who thought of the lilac?
"I," dew said,
"I made up the lilac
out of my head."
    The Lilac. Stanza 1
Like a small grey
coffee-pot
sits the squirrel.
    The Grey Squirrel. Stanza 1
What will they give me, when journey's
    done?
Your own room to be quiet in, Son!
    Journey's End

ZOË AKINS
[1886–   ]

So much do I love wandering,
  So much I love the sea and sky,
That it will be a piteous thing
  In one small grave to lie.
    The Wanderer. Stanza 2
  Nothing seems so tragic to one who
is old as the death of one who is young,
and this alone proves that life is a good
thing.
    The Portrait of Tiero

CLIFFORD BAX
[1886–   ]

Count me not with those that whine
  for what is over, —
All that once was good is good for ever-
    more.
    Musician. Stanza 12
All we had of joy endures, a joy within
    us;
All the rest of life is lovelier for those
    years.
    Ibid. Stanza 13

WILLIAM ROSE BENÉT
[1886–   ]

I flung my soul to the air like a falcon
  flying. . . .
  I shall start a heron soon

In the marsh beneath the moon —
A strange white heron rising with silver
   on its wings.
      The Falconer of God. Stanza 1

I beat forever
The fens and the sedges.
The pledge is still the same — for all
   disastrous pledges,
      All hopes resigned!
My soul still flies above me for the
   quarry it shall find.
          Ibid. Stanza 4

You are to me what the bowstring is
   to the shaft,
Speeding my purpose aloft and aflame
   and afar.
      Dedication. Stanza 2

Neither will I put myself forward as
   others may do,
Neither, if you wish me to flatter, will
   I flatter you;
I will look at you grimly, and so you
   will know I am true.
      Eternal Masculine. Stanza 1

Rain, with a silver flail;
   Sun, with a golden ball;
Ocean, wherein the whale
   Swims minnow-small.
        Whale. Stanza 1

"With flanged and battering tail,
   With huge and dark baleen,"
He said, "Let there be Whale
   In the Cold and Green!"
        Ibid. Stanza 3

For the Lord said, "Let Whale Be!"
And there was Whale!
        Ibid. Stanza 22

Monarch is night
Of all eldest things,
Pain and affright,
Rapturous wings.
        Night. Stanza 3

Times she'll be docile as the gentlest
   thing
That ever blinked in fur or folded wing,
And then, like lightning in the dead of
   night,
Fill with wild, crackling, intermitting
   light
My mind and soul and senses, — and
   next be
Aloof, askance as a dryad in a tree.
      The Woodcutter's Wife. Stanza 2

You cannot slay yourself in me,
Nor I — to all eternity —
Destroy my truest self in you.
All that our ingrate thought would do,
All senseless wounds we give and take,
Are powerless — for the other's sake.
      We Ask No Shield. Stanza 3

O Love, a thousand, thousand voices,
   From night to dawn, from dawn to
      night,
Have cried the passion of their choices
   To orb your name and keep it bright.
      The Name of Love. Stanza 1

In vast infant sagacity brooding.
        Mad Blake

Like a knight in glittering armor,
   Laughter
Stood up at his side.
        The Last Ally

Lay her sword by her,
Her steel of spirit,
Her phantom blade,
Lest the loud liar
In his hell inherit
What her soul made.
      For the Eyes Loved —

Time, the dark whale, spouts blithely
   from his spiracle
A jet of memory that makes glad the
   sun.
      Sonnets to My Father. III

Blue oblivion, largely lit, smiled and
   smiled at me.
        Mid-Ocean

Jesse James was a two-gun man
   (*Roll on, Missouri!*)
      Jesse James: American Myth

In seven states he cut up dadoes.
He's gone with the buffler an' the desperadoes.
           Ibid.

I know some force is mighty, some force
   I cannot reach.
I know that words are said to me that
   are not said with speech.
My heart has learned a lesson that I
   can never teach.
Only this I know, that I am overtaken
By a swifter runner Whose breath is
   never shaken,
That I follow on His pace, and that
   round me, as I waken,

Are the headlands of home and the blue
   sea swinging
And the flowers of the valleys their
   fresh scents flinging
And the prophets and the poets, with
   their singing — with their singing!
                Man Possessed

  Who writes poetry imbibes honey
from the poisoned lips of life.
                Ibid. Preface

Chilled Martini like Ithuriel's spear
Transfixing all dubiety within,
Oiled by an olive and shred of lemon-
   peel!
                The Martini

Like flame, like wine, across the still
   lagoon
The colors of the sunset stream.
Spectral in heaven as climbs the frail
   veiled moon,
So climbs my dream.
Out of the heart's eternal torture fire
No flaming Phœnix risen —
Only the naked soul, spent with desire,
Bursts its prison.
      Gaspara Stampa. Stanza 1

The gods returned to earth when Venice
   broke
Like Venus from the dawn-encircled
   sea.
Wide laughed the skies with light when
   Venice woke
Crowned of antiquity,
And like a spoil of gems unmined on
   earth
Art in her glorious mind
Jewelled all Italy for joy's rebirth
To all mankind.
            Ibid. Stanza 9

So let it be, let it be,
Fretting all the day!
What is this or that to me
Who talked it out in Tartary
Centuries away!

Yet a while with love I stroll
Bright streets of air,
Silver precincts few extol,
Mist-blue cities of the soul,
Countries here nor there.
     Smooth-Sliding Mincius.
         Stanzas 5 and 6

One speck within vast star-space lying
Awoke, arose, resumed its clothing,
And crawled another day toward dying.
        Animalcule. Stanza 7

Voice of the forum loud and harsh
Full of frog-rhetoric of the marsh;
Awful percipience whose small eye
Views art through ordure of the sty;
Apocalyptic commonplace
Whose every utterance is base —
Yearlong the nations cry to thee,
God of our gods, Stupidity!
        Hymn to Stupidity

You came to climb,
And you endure —
So turn your face to the rock of Time,
Make one more foothold sure!
     Because You Came to Climb

O there beloved, all loved, forever
As light you are, in light you move;
Pride of the father, tears of the mother,
Silver sister and golden brother —
The glowing mind of all endeavor,
The full irradiancy of love.
     Nebular Hypothesis. Stanza 5

Only madmen seize the story
With coals of fire upon their tongue.
        Ibid. Stanza 13

When at our history men stand
   amazed . . .
Our captains may have grown as quaint
And crazed as any medieval saint.
         Ode for an Epoch

VAN WYCK BROOKS
[1886–]

His wife not only edited his works
but edited him.
     The Ordeal of Mark Twain
         [1920]. Chap. 5

  Read, writers of America, the driven,
disenchanted, anxious faces of your
sensitive countrymen; remember the
splendid parts your confrères have
played in the human drama of other
times and other peoples, and ask yourselves whether the hour has not come
to put away childish things and walk
the stage as poets do.
         Ibid. Chap. 11

Even the Concord ice had bubbles in it. As wood and grass were its only staples, Emerson advised his fellow-townsmen to manufacture school-teachers and make them the best in the world.
The Flowering of New England.
Chap. 13

FRANCES CORNFORD
[1886–   ]

I had a little dog and my dog was very small;
He licked me in the face, and he answered to my call;
Of all the treasures that were mine I loved him most of all.
A Child's Dream. Stanza 1

His body covered thick with hair was very good to smell;
His little stomach underneath was pink as any shell;
And I loved him and honoured him, more than words can tell.
Ibid. Stanza 3

Deep in my heart I thought with pride, "I know a person who has died."
A Recollection

JOYCE KILMER
[1886–1918]

The midnight train is slow and old,
But of it let this thing be told,
To its high honor be it said,
It carries people home to bed.
My cottage lamp shines white and clear.
God bless the train that brought me here.
The Twelve-Forty-Five

I think that I shall never see
A poem lovely as a tree.
Trees [1]

A tree that may in Summer wear
A nest of robins in her hair.
Ibid.

Poems are made by fools like me,
But only God can make a tree.
Ibid.

[1] First published in *Poetry: A Magazine of Verse*, Chicago, *August, 1913*.

The pleasantest sort of poet
Is the poet who's old and wise.
Old Poets

The young poet screams forever
About his sex and his soul.
Ibid.

There is no peace to be taken
With poets who are young,
For they worry about the wars to be fought
And the songs that must be sung.
Ibid.

Her lips' remark was: "Oh, you kid!"
Her soul spoke thus (I know it did):
"O king of realms of endless joy,
My own, my golden grocer's boy."
Servant Girl and Grocer's Boy

Pile laurel wreaths upon his grave
Who did not gain, but was, success.
Martin

A house that has echoed a baby's laugh
and held up his stumbling feet,
Is the saddest sight, when it's left alone,
that ever your eyes could meet.
The House with Nobody in It

Main Street bordered with autumn leaves, it was a pleasant thing.
Main Street

But we who inherit the primal curse,
and labour for our bread,
Have yet, thank God, the gift of Home,
though Eden's gate is barred.
The Snowman in the Yard

For nothing keeps a poet
In his high singing mood
Like unappeasable hunger
For unattainable food.
Apology

It is stern work, it is perilous work, to thrust your hand in the sun
And pull out a spark of immortal flame to warm the hearts of men.
The Proud Poet

Unlock the door this evening
And let your gate swing wide,
Let all who ask for shelter
Come speedily inside.
What if your yard be narrow?
What if your house be small?
There is a Guest is coming
Will glorify it all.
Gates and Doors

In a wood they call the Rouge Bouquet
There is a new-made grave to-day,
Built by never a spade nor pick
Yet covered with earth ten metres thick.
Rouge Bouquet
My shoulders ache beneath my pack
(Lie easier, Cross, upon His back).
Prayer of a Soldier in France

DAVID MORTON
[1886–   ]

Corridors, like windy tulip beds,
Of swaying girls and lifted, tossing
heads.
In a Girls' School
Who walks with Beauty has no need of
fear;
The sun and moon and stars keep pace
with him;
Invisible hands restore the ruined year,
And time, itself, grows beautifully dim.
Who Walks with Beauty

SHAEMAS O'SHEEL
[1886–   ]

They went forth to battle, but they al-
ways fell;
Their eyes were fixed above the sul-
len shields;
Nobly they fought and bravely, but not
well,
And sank heart-wounded by a subtle
spell.
They Went Forth to Battle but
They Always Fell. Stanza 1
He whom a dream hath possessed
knoweth no more of doubting,
For mist and the blowing of winds and
the mouthing of words he scorns;
Not the sinuous speech of schools he
hears, but a knightly shouting,
And never comes darkness down, but he
greeteth a million morns.
He Whom a Dream Hath
Possessed. Stanza 1
The ruin of worlds that fall he views
from eternal arches,
And rides God's battlefield in a flashing
and golden car.
Ibid. Stanza 4

ELIZABETH MADOX ROBERTS
[1886–   ]

I used to think when I was a young-
one, Jasper, that all the things you read
about or hear came to pass in some
country, all in one country somewheres.
"Oh, Mary go and call the cattle home,"
and "Lady Nancy died like it might be
today," all in one country. . . . A country a far piece off. Off past Tennessee
somewheres. But now I know better
and know how the world is, a little.
The Time of Man

SIEGFRIED SASSOON
[1886–   ]

Soldiers are citizens of death's grey
land,
Drawing no dividend from time's to-
morrows.
In the great hour of destiny they stand,
Each with his feuds, and jealousies, and
sorrows.
Soldiers are sworn to action; they must
win
Some flaming, fatal climax with their
lives.
Soldiers are dreamers; when the guns
begin
They think of firelit homes, clean beds,
and wives.
Dreamers
Have you forgotten yet?
Look down and swear by the slain of
the War that you'll never forget.
Aftermath
Guest of those infinitely privileged ones
Whose lives are padded, petrified, and
pleasant.
On Reading the War Diary of a
Defunct Ambassador. Stanza 3
The visionless officialized fatuity
That once kept Europe safe for Per-
petuity.
Ibid. Stanza 6
Religion beats me. I'm amazed at folk
Drinking the gospels in and never
scratching
Their heads for questions.
The Old Huntsman

O Jesus, send me a wound today,
And I'll believe in Your bread and wine,
And get my bloody old sins washed
  white!
  Stand-to: Good Friday Morning [1]
"He's a cheery old card," grunted Harry
  to Jack
As they slogged up to Arras with rifle
  and pack. . . .
But he did for them both by his plan of
  attack.
  The General
In me the cave-man clasps the seer,
And garlanded Apollo goes
Chanting to Abraham's deaf ear.
In me the tiger sniffs the rose.
Look in my heart, kind friends, and
  tremble,
Since there your elements assemble.
  The Heart's Journey. VIII
Who will remember, passing through
  this Gate,
The unheroic Dead who fed the guns?
Who shall absolve the foulness of their
  fate, —
Those doomed, conscripted, unvictori-
  ous ones?
  On Passing the New Menin Gate
"Do you remember the five-thirty
from Paddington? What a dear old
train it was!"
  Memoirs of a Fox-Hunting Man
  (*homesick conversation in the
  trenches during the War*)

VINCENT STARRETT
[1886–   ]

Suicide . . . to the many is the final
proof of insanity, and, therefore, in a
writing man (or a painting man) of
genius.
  Buried Caesars. Two Suicides
The day before yesterday always has
been a glamor day. The present is sordid and prosaic. Time colors history as
it does a meerschaum pipe.
  *Ibid. Robert Neilson Stephens and
  The Costume Novel*

[1] In 1922 a New Zealand publisher was con-
victed of "blasphemous libel" for republish-
ing this poem in his paper.

Centenary celebrations are posterity's tributes to the favored children of
fame; sometimes they are tardy ac-
knowledgments to genius. Too often
does genius sup late, and sometimes it
does not sup at all.
  *Buried Caesars. "Black Beauty"
  and its Author, Anna Sewell*
Westminster Abbey is a mausoleum;
the book barrows in Charing Cross
Road are resurrection grounds.
  The Diamond in the Dust Heap
  [*1925*]
When we are collecting books, we are
collecting happiness.
  The A B C of First Editions
  [*1926*]

JOHN HALL WHEELOCK
[1886–   ]

There is a panther caged within my
  breast,
But what his name there is no breast
  shall know
Save mine, nor what it is that drives
  him so,
Backward and forward, in relentless
  quest.
  The Black Panther
When death has carved me to his stern
  design
And of this self only the shell endures,
If any face look down with love on
  mine,
Beloved, may it be yours.
  Finale. Stanza 1
For, as all flesh must die, so all
Now dust, shall live.
  This Quiet Dust
A bit of God Himself I keep
Between two vigils fallen asleep.
  Ibid.

LEONARD BACON
[1887–   ]

Technique! The very word is like the
  shriek
Of outraged Art. It is the idiot name
Given to effort by those who are too
  weak,

Too weary, or too dull to play the
  game.
The mighty have no theory of tech-
  nique.
                    Ph.D's. Sophia Trenton
Interpreting the simplest symbol
  wrong,
  Missing the gold and treasuring the
    tin,
Dwelling upon the trivial so long,
  And spinning allegory out so thin
That the line parts, and neither brawn
  nor brain
Can splice the mainbrace of the mind
  again.
                                        Ibid.
Men have laughed at me, that I jotted
  down
What was their only title to renown.
    Evening in Great Portland Street
              (James Boswell speaks)
Let 'em laugh at my notebooks. It was
  much
To have the ears of Midas — and the
  touch.
                                        Ibid.
O graven Imagist!
Was it then thou, grey Fancy's strang-
  est child?
Sweet Anarch, literary Nihilist
Thick warbling thy jaw-breaking
  woodnotes wild?
Was it then thou, delicious egotist?
Well of soft incoherence undefiled!
        The Banquet of the Poets
Those who dwell upon ivory towers
Have heads of the same material.
                        Tower of Ivory
Go forth, my book, and take whatever
  pounding
The heavy-fisted destinies prepare.
I know you are not anything astound-
  ing,
And, to be quite sincere, I don't much
  care.
Get off your overcoat. The gong is
  sounding.
The enemy has risen from his chair.
He doesn't look so overwhelming, but
His arm is long. Watch for an upper-
  cut.
                  Ulug Beg. Introduction

RUPERT BROOKE [1]
[1887–1915]

Somewhere, behind Space and Time,
Is wetter water, slimier slime!
                                    Heaven
And in that Heaven of all their wish,
There shall be no more land, say fish.
                                        Ibid.
Unkempt about those hedges blows
An English unofficial rose.
        The Old Vicarage, Grantchester
                                    [1912]
Curates, long dust, will come and go
On lissom, clerical, printless toe.
                                        Ibid.
  England's the one land, I know,
Where men with Splendid Hearts may
  go;
And Cambridgeshire, of all England,
The shire of Men who Understand.
                                        Ibid.
Say, is there Beauty yet to find?
And Certainty? and Quiet kind?
Deep meadows yet, for to forget
The lies, and truths, and pain? . . .
  oh! yet
Stands the Church clock at ten to three?
And is there honey still for tea?
                                        Ibid.
Breathless, we flung us on the windy
  hill,
Laughed in the sun, and kissed the
  lovely grass.
                                    The Hill
And then you suddenly cried, and
  turned away.
                                        Ibid.
For what they'd never told me of,
  And what I never knew,
It was that all the time, my love,
  Love would be merely you.
                                        Song
Spend in pure converse our eternal day;
  Think each in each, immediately
    wise;
Learn all we lacked before; hear, know,
  and say

---

[1] Among all who have been poets and died
young, it is hard to think of one who, both in
life and death, has so typified the ideal radiance of youth and poetry. — GILBERT MUR-
RAY [1915]

What this tumultuous body now denies;
And feel, who have laid our groping
hands away;
And see, no longer blinded by our
eyes.
Sonnet

I have been so great a lover: filled my
days
So proudly with the splendor of Love's
praise. . . .
These I have loved:
White plates and cups, clean-gleam-
ing . . .
The cool kindliness of sheets, that soon
Smooth away trouble; and the rough
male kiss
Of blankets; grainy wood; live hair that
is
Shining and free; blue-massing clouds;
the keen
Unpassioned beauty of a great machine;
The benison of hot water; furs to touch;
The good smell of old clothes.
The Great Lover

If I should die, think only this of me:
That there's some corner of a foreign
field
That is for ever England.
The Soldier

This heart, all evil shed away,
A pulse in the eternal mind, no less
Gives somewhere back the thoughts by
England given.
Ibid.

Now, God be thanked, who has matched
us with his hour,
And caught our youth, and wakened us
from sleeping.
Peace

The worst friend and enemy is but
Death.
Ibid.

Blow out, you bugles, over the rich
dead!
There's none of these so lonely and
poor of old,
But, dying, has made us rarer gifts
than gold.
The Dead. I

Honour has come back, as a king, to
earth,

And paid his subjects with a royal
wage;
And Nobleness walks in our ways
again;
And we have come into our heritage.
The Dead. I

ISAAC GOLDBERG
[1887–   ]

Diplomacy is to do and say
The nastiest thing in the nicest way.
The Reflex

JAMES NORMAN HALL
[1887–   ]

The thing that numbs the heart is this:
That men cannot devise
Some scheme of life to banish fear
That lurks in most men's eyes.
Fear

Fear of the lack of shelter, food,
And fire for winter's cold;
Fear of their children's lacking these,
This in a world so old.
Ibid.

This is my sure, my very firm belief:
That life, to one born whole, is worth
the living,
Well worth the taking, having, and the
giving.
A Starry Night at Arué

ROBINSON JEFFERS
[1887–   ]

The gulls, the cloud-calligraphers of
windy spirals before a storm.
The Cycle

Four pelicans went over the house,
Sculled their worn oars over the court-
yard:
I saw that ungainliness
Magnifies the idea of strength.
Pelicans

While this America settles in the mould
of its vulgarity, heavily thickening
to empire,
And protest, only a bubble in the molten
mass, pops and sighs out, and the
mass hardens. . . .
Shine, Perishing Republic.
Stanza 1

You make haste on decay: not blame-
worthy; life is good, be it stubbornly long or suddenly
A mortal splendor: meteors are not
needed less than mountains: shine,
perishing republic.

But for my children, I would have them
keep their distance from the thickening center; corruption
Never has been compulsory, when the
cities lie at the monster's feet there
are left the mountains.

Shine, Perishing Republic.
Stanzas 3 and 4

All these tidal gatherings, growth and
decay,
Shining and darkening, are forever
Renewed; and the whole cycle impenitently
Revolves, and all the past is future: ——
Make it a difficult world . . . for practical people.

Practical People

After all, after all we endured, who has
grown wise?
We take our mortal momentary hour
With too much gesture, the derisive
skies
Twinkle against our wrongs, our rights,
our power.
Look up the night, starlight's a steady-
ing draught
For nerves at angry tension.

The Truce and the Peace. 7 [1918]

"Loyal to your highest, sensitive, brave,
Sanguine, some few ways wise, you and
all men are drawn out of this
depth
Only to be these things you are, as
flowers for color, falcons for swiftness,
Mountains for mass and quiet. Each for
its quality
Is drawn out of this depth. Your tragic
quality
Required the huge delusion of some major purpose to produce it.
What, that the God of the stars needed
your help?" He said "This is my
last

Worst pain, the bitter enlightenment
that buys peace."

Woodrow Wilson [1924]

All the arts lose virtue
Against the essential reality
Of creatures going about their business
among the equally
Earnest elements of nature.

Boats in a Fog.

Singing to himself the fool south-border
couplet
"No tengo tabaco, no tengo papel,
No tengo dinero, God damn it to hell."

Tamar. VI

Grass that is made each year equals the
mountains in her past and future;
Fashionable and momentary things we
need not see nor speak of.

Point Joe

Lend me the stone strength of the past
and I will lend you
The wings of the future, for I have them.
How dear you will be to me when I too
grow old, old comrade.

To the Rock That Will Be a
Cornerstone

Divinely superfluous beauty
Rules the games, presides over destinies,
makes trees grow
And hills tower, waves fall.
The incredible beauty of joy.

Divinely Superfluous Beauty

The beauty of things was born before
eyes and sufficient to itself; the
heart-breaking beauty
Will remain when there is no heart to
break for it.

Credo

The heads of strong old age are beautiful
Beyond all grace of youth. They have
strange quiet,
Integrity, health, soundness, to the full
They've dealt with life and been atemp-
ered by it.

Promise of Peace

ORRICK JOHNS
[1887–   ]

There's nothing very beautiful and
nothing very gay

About the rush of faces in the town by
    day,
But a light tan cow in a pale green mead,
That is very beautiful, beautiful indeed.
                            Little Things
And better is a temple made of bark and
    thong
Than a tall stone temple that may stand
    too long.
                            Ibid.
Love is a proud and gentle thing, a bet-
    ter thing to own
Than all of the wide impossible stars
    over the heavens blown.
                            The Door
Yet maybe now there passes here,
    In reverential dream, a boy
Whose voice shall rise another year
    And rouse the sleeping lords of joy.
                            Second Avenue
He shall bring back the faded bays,
    The Muses to their ancient rule,
The temples to the market-place,
    The genius nearer to the fool.
                            Ibid.

SISTER MARY MADELEVA
[1887–   ]

Death is no foeman, we were born to-
    gether;
He dwells between the places of my
    breath.
Night vigil at my heart he keeps and
    whether
I sleep or no, he never slumbereth.
                            Knights-Errant
It was a bird first spoke to me at Ox-
    ford
Through the white fog a single, tenta-
    tive word.
                            I Enter Oxford
Oh! there are bells and there are spires
    at Oxford,
Ancient,   heart-breaking,   wordless,
    splendorous things;
Only to me belongs this simple, silver
Welcome on wings.
                            Ibid.
The day you do not write and silence
    follows, to be broken only by my
    life's end,

I shall know that you have not forgot-
    ten, that now you love me per-
    fectly,
For I shall understand that you are
    dead.
                        The Day No Letter Comes

Two doves I bring;
One broods all day;
One has a broken wing;
One is the prayer I have no words to
    say;
One is the song I have no words to sing.
                            Presentation

HARRY IRVING ("H.I.")
PHILLIPS
[1887–   ]

Horse-sense in an atmosphere of
Pomp and glory,
Self-effacement in a generation
Of self-salesmanship,
A Vermont Yankee in
King Ballyhoo's Court!
                            Calvin Coolidge

EDITH SITWELL
[1887–   ]

Down the horn
Of her ear-trumpet I convey
The news that: "It is Judgment Day!"
"Speak louder; I don't catch, my dear."
I roared: *"It is the Trump we hear!"*
"The *What?*" — "The TRUMP!" . . .
    "I shall complain —
Those boy-scouts practising again!"
                            Solo for Ear-Trumpet

    Every hundred years or so it becomes
necessary for a change to take place in
the body of poetry . . . a fresh movement appears and produces a few great
men, and once more the force and vigour die from the results of age; the
movement is carried on by weak and
worthless imitators, and a change becomes necessary again.
                    Poetry and Criticism [*1926*]

ALEXANDER WOOLLCOTT
[1887–   ]

The attitude of the professional players toward the amateurs is best summed up in a raffish story they delight in telling on all occasions. It begins with a touching picture of an old broken-down tragedian sharing a park bench with a bedraggled and unappetizing street-walker. "Ah, Madame," says the tragedian, "*quelle Ironie!* The two oldest professions in the world — ruined by amateurs."

The Knock at the Stage-Door

Beerbohm Tree said what we have all wanted to say of the extra-women in nearly every throne-room and ball-room and school-room scene since the theater began. "Ladies," said Tree, peering at them plaintively through his monocle, "just a little more virginity, if you don't mind."

Capsule Criticism

ELINOR HOYT WYLIE
[1887–1928]

We shall walk in velvet shoes:
    Wherever we go
Silence will fall like dews
    On white silence below.
We shall walk in the snow.
Velvet Shoes. Stanza 4

Avoid the reeking herd,
    Shun the polluted flock,
Live like that stoic bird
    The eagle of the rock.
The Eagle and the Mole. Stanza 1

If you would keep your soul
    From spotted sight or sound,
Live like the velvet mole;
    Go burrow underground.
Ibid. Stanza 5

She, whose song we loved the best,
    Is voiceless in a sudden night;
On your light limbs, O, Loveliest,
    May the dust be light!
On a Singing Girl. Stanza 2

I was, being human, born alone;
    I am, being woman, hard beset;

I live by squeezing from a stone
    The little nourishment I get.
Let No Charitable Hope. Stanza 2

In masks outrageous and austere
The years go by in single file;
But none has merited my fear,
And none has quite escaped my smile.
Ibid. Stanza 3

Farewell, sweet dust; I was never a
    miser:
    Once, for a minute, I made you mine:
Now you are gone, I am none the wiser,
    But the leaves of the willow are
    bright as wine.
Farewell, Sweet Dust. Stanza 4

I have believed that I prefer to live
Preoccupied by a Platonic mind;
I have believed me obdurate and blind
To those sharp ecstasies the pulses give:
The clever body five times sensitive
I never have discovered to be kind
As the poor soul, deceived and half-
    divined,
Whose hopes are water in a witch's
    sieve.
*Angels and Earthly Creatures.
Sonnet VI*

A subtle spirit has my path attended,
In likeness not a lion but a pard;
And when the arrows flew like hail, and
    hard,
He licked my wounds, and all my
    wounds were mended;
And happy I, who walked so well-
    defended,
With that translucid presence for a
    guard,
Under a sky reversed and evil-starred;
A woman by an archangel befriended.
Ibid. Sonnet IX

If any have a stone to throw
It is not I, ever or now.
The Pebble

Alembics turn to stranger things
Strange things, but never while we live
Shall magic turn this bronze that sings
To singing water in a sieve.
*Bronze Trumpets and Sea Wa-
ter (On Turning Latin into Eng-
lish). Stanza 1*

Pity the prickly star that frightens
    The Christ Child with its shattered
      spear;
Pity the midnight when it lightens;
    Pity me, my dear.
                Pity Me. Stanza 3

The worst and best are both inclined
To snap like vixens at the truth;
But, O, beware the middle mind
That purrs and never shows a tooth!
           Nonsense Rhyme. Stanza 2

Honied words like bees,
Gilded and sticky, with a little sting.
                Pretty Words

She'd give the shirt from off her back,
    except that
She doesn't wear a shirt, and most men
    do;
And often and most bitterly she's wept
    that
A starving tramp can't eat a silver shoe,
Or some poor beggar, slightly alcoholic,
Enjoy with Donne a metaphysical
    frolic.
        Portrait in Black Paint. Stanza 2

Farewell, incomparable element,
Whence man arose, where he shall not
    return;
And hail, imperfect urn
Of his last ashes, and his firstborn fruit;
Farewell, the long pursuit,
And all the adventures of his discontent.
            Hymn to Earth. Stanza 1

Hail, element of earth, receive thy own,
And cherish, at thy charitable breast,
This man, this mongrel beast:
He plows the sand, and, at his hardest
    need,
He sows himself for seed.
                Ibid. Stanza 6

Receive him as thy lover for an hour
Who will not weary, by a longer stay,
The kind embrace of clay.
                Ibid. Stanza 7

HEYWOOD CAMPBELL
BROUN
[1888–   ]

"You've got a kiss coming to you.
When you live up as far as 168th Street
you've got to do at least that much for
any fellow that takes you home. . . .

"And say, listen, next month I'm going to move to 242nd Street."
        The Boy Grew Older. Chap. 13

The ability to make love frivolously
is the chief characteristic which distinguishes human beings from the beasts.
      It Seems to Me. A Spring Sunday

I saw a money-changer in the neighborhood of the temple late yesterday
afternoon, and it did not seem to me
that he was on his way to catch an outbound train. On the contrary, he was
headed up the steps, cool as a cucumber. "I wonder if the old place has
changed," he remarked as we passed.
    Ibid. "The Worst Is Over" [1933]

"Trees" (if I have the name right) is
one of the most annoying pieces of verse
within my knowledge. The other one is
Kipling's "If," with third place reserved
for Henley's "Invictus."

"Trees" maddens me, because it contains the most insincere line ever written by mortal man. Surely the Kilmer
tongue must have been not far from the
Kilmer cheek when he wrote, "Poems
are made by fools like me."
    Ibid. "Trees," "If," and "Invictus"

It is a good trick when a writer can go
out and set down with accuracy some
living being whom he has observed with
fidelity. He holds the mirror up to Nature.

But that is not the furthest reach of
literature. There are a few who venture
forth and say with divine arrogance: "I
see it this way. Let Nature catch up
with my conception."

Life is a copycat and can be bullied
into following the master artist who
bids it come to heel.
        Ibid. Nature the Copycat

I have known people to stop and buy
an apple on the corner and then walk
away as if they had solved the whole
unemployment problem.
          Ibid. Chummy Charlie

The Irish are the cry-babies of the
Western world. Even the mildest quip
will set them off into resolutions and
protests.
    Ibid. The Piece That Got Me Fired

ANNE CAMPBELL
(MRS. GEORGE W. STARK)
[1888–   ]

You are the trip I did not take;
You are the pearls I cannot buy;
You are my blue Italian lake;
You are my piece of foreign sky.
To My Child

NORMAN DAVEY
[1888–   ]

By the canal in Flanders I watched a
   barge's prow
Creep slowly past the poplar-trees; and
   there I made a vow
That when these wars are over and I
   am home at last
However much I travel I shall not
   travel fast.

Horses and cars and yachts and planes:
   I've no more use for such:
For in three years of war's alarms I've
   hurried far too much;
And now I dream of something sure, si-
   lent and slow and large;
So when the War is over — why, I
   mean to buy a barge.
By the Canal in Flanders

By Charing Cross in London Town
There runs a road of high renown,
Where antique books are ranged on
   shelves
As dark and dusty as themselves.
And many booklovers have spent
Their substance there with great con-
   tent,
And vexed their wives and filled their
   homes
With faded prints and massive tomes.
The Booklover

THOMAS STEARNS ELIOT
[1888–   ]

April is the cruelest month, breeding
Lilacs out of dead land, mixing
Memory and desire, stirring
Dull roots with spring rain.
The Waste Land

But at my back from time to time I hear
The sound of horns and motors, which
   shall bring
Sweeney to Mrs. Porter in the spring.
O the moon shone bright on Mrs. Porter
And on her daughter
They wash their feet in soda water.
The Waste Land

When lovely woman stoops to folly and
Paces about her room again, alone,
She smooths her hair with automatic
   hand,
And puts a record on the gramophone.
Ibid.

We are the hollow men
We are the stuffed men
Leaning together
Headpiece filled with straw. Alas!
Our dried voices, when
We whisper together
Are quiet and meaningless
As wind in dry grass
Or rats' feet over broken glass
In our dry cellar.
The Hollow Men. I

Eyes I dare not meet in dreams
In death's dream kingdom
These do not appear:
There, the eyes are
Sunlight on a broken column
There, is a tree swinging
And voices are
In the wind's singing
More distant and more solemn
Than a fading star.
Ibid. II

This is the way the world ends
Not with a bang but a whimper.
Ibid. V

Where is the Life we have lost in living?
Where is the wisdom we have lost in
   knowledge?
Where is the knowledge we have lost in
   information?
The cycles of Heaven in twenty cen-
   turies
Bring us farther from God and nearer to
   the Dust.
The Rock

Donne, I suppose, was such another
Who found no substitute for sense.
Whispers of Immortality

Uncorseted, her friendly bust
Gives promise of pneumatic bliss.
Whispers of Immortality

Sweeney shifts from ham to ham
Stirring the water in his bath.
The masters of the subtle schools
Are controversial, polymath.
Sunday Morning Service

Reorganized upon the floor
She yawns and draws a stocking up.
Sweeney Among the Nightingales

The evening is spread out against the
sky
Like a patient etherized upon a table.
The Love Song of J. Alfred Prufrock

Should I, after tea and cakes and ices,
Have the strength to force the moment
to its crisis?
But though I have wept and fasted, wept
and prayed,
Though I have seen my head (grown
slightly bald) brought in upon a
platter,
I am no prophet — and here's no great
matter;
I have seen the moment of my greatness
flicker,
And I have seen the eternal Footman
hold my coat, and snicker,
And in short, I was afraid.
Ibid.

No! I am not Prince Hamlet, nor was
meant to be;
Am an attendant lord, one that will do
To swell a progress, start a scene or two
Advise the prince; no doubt, an easy
tool,
Deferential, glad to be of use,
Politic, cautious, and meticulous;
Full of high sentence, but a bit obtuse;
At times, indeed, almost ridiculous —
Almost, at times, the Fool.
Ibid.

I grow old. . . . I grow old. . . .
I shall wear the bottoms of my trousers
rolled.
Ibid.

The readers of the *Boston Evening
Transcript*
Sway in the wind like a field of ripe corn.
The Boston Evening Transcript

Upon the glazen shelves kept watch
Matthew and Waldo, guardians of the
faith,
The army of unalterable law.
Cousin Nancy

The broad-backed hippopotamus
Rests on his belly in the mud;
Although he seems so firm to us
He is merely flesh and blood.
The Hippopotamus

We have been, let us say, to hear the
latest Pole
Transmit the Preludes, through his hair
and finger-tips.
Portrait of a Lady. I

My smile falls heavily among the bric-
à-brac.
Ibid. III

I am aware of the damp souls of house-
maids
Sprouting despondently at area gates.
Morning at the Window

The new years walk, restoring
Through a bright cloud of tears, the
years, restoring
With a new verse the ancient rhyme.
Redeem
The time. Redeem
The unread vision in the higher dream
While jewelled unicorns draw by the
gilded hearse.
Ash-Wednesday. IV

JULIAN GRENFELL
[1888–1915]

All the bright company of Heaven
Hold him in their high comradeship,
The Dog-star, and the Sisters Seven,
Orion's Belt and sworded hip.
Into Battle. Stanza 3

But Day shall clasp him with strong
hands,
And Night shall fold him in soft
wings.
Ibid. Stanza 10

MOLLY ANDERSON (MRS. FRANK LeROY) HALEY
[1888–   ]

Between the tonics and the beauty-creams,
This shabby slowly-turning shelf of dreams!
Loan Library at the Corner Drug Store

ALINE (MRS. JOYCE) KILMER
[1888–   ]

I shall not be afraid any more,
Either by night or day;
What would it profit me to be afraid
With you away?
I Shall Not Be Afraid. Stanza 1

Deborah danced, when she was two,
As buttercups and daffodils do.
Experience

Smilingly, out of my pain,
I have woven a little song;
You may take it away with you.
I shall not sing it again.
Tour de Force

I'm sorry you are wiser,
I'm sorry you are taller;
I liked you better foolish,
And I liked you better smaller.
For the Birthday of a Middle-Aged Child. Stanza 1

My heart shall keep the child I knew,
When you are really gone from me,
And spend its life remembering you
As shells remember the lost sea.
Prevision (To a Child). Stanza 4

If I live till my fighting days are done
I must fasten my armour on my eldest son.
Against the Wall. Stanza 1

Things have a terrible permanence
When people die.
Things. Stanza 6

THOMAS EDWARD LAWRENCE [1]
[1888–1935]

I loved you, so I drew these tides of men
into my hands and wrote my will
across the sky in stars.
*Seven Pillars of Wisdom.
Dedication*

Arabs could be swung on an idea as on a cord; for the unpledged allegiance of their minds made them obedient servants. None of them would escape the bond till success had come, and with it responsibility and duty and engagements. Then the idea was gone and the work ended — in ruins. Without a creed they could be taken to the four corners of the world (but not to heaven) by being shown the riches of earth and the pleasures of it; but if on the road, led in this fashion, they met the prophet of an idea, who had nowhere to lay his head and who depended for his food on charity or birds, then they would all leave their wealth for his inspiration.
Ibid. Chap. 3

There could be no honour in a sure success, but much might be wrested from a sure defeat. Omnipotence and the Infinite were our two worthiest foemen, indeed the only ones for a full man to meet, they being monsters of his own spirit's making; and the stoutest enemies were always of the household. In fighting Omnipotence, honour was proudly to throw away the poor resources that we had, and dare Him empty-handed.
Revolt in the Desert. Chap. 19

I grew proud of the enemy [the Germans] who had killed my brothers. They were two thousand miles from home, without hope and without guides, in conditions mad enough to break the bravest nerves. Yet their sections held together in firm rank, sheering through the wrack of Turk and Arab like armoured ships, high-faced and silent. When attacked they halted, took position, fired to order. There was no haste,

[1] Changed his name to T. E. Shaw, 1927.

no crying, no hesitation. They were glorious.

Revolt in the Desert. Chap. 34

It came upon me freshly how the secret of uniform was to make a crowd solid, dignified, impersonal: to give it the singleness and tautness of an upstanding man. This death's livery which walled its bearers from ordinary life, was sign that they had sold their wills and bodies to the State: and contracted themselves into a service not the less abject for that its beginning was voluntary. Some of them had obeyed the instinct of lawlessness: some were hungry: others thirsted for glamour, for the supposed colour of a military life: but, of them all, those only received satisfaction who had sought to degrade themselves, for to the peace-eye they were below humanity.

Ibid. Chap. 35

Appearing first in the war news from Arabia as a personage rather more incredible than Prester John, and presently emerging into clear definition as the author of one of the great histories of the world, recording his own conquests at an age at which young company officers are hardly allowed to speak at the mess table.

BERNARD SHAW, in *The New York Evening Post, April 16, 1927*

NEWMAN LEVY
[1888–   ]

In Spain, where the courtly Castilian
    hidalgo twangs lightly each night
    his romantic guitar,
Where the castanets clink on the gay
    piazetta, and strains of fandangoes
    are heard from afar,
There lived, I am told, a bold hussy
    named Carmen, a pampered young
    vamp full of devil and guile.
Cigarette and cigar men were smitten
    with Carmen; from near and from
    far men were caught with her smile.

Opera Guyed. Carmen

But here's our friend José who seizes
    her bridle. A wild homicidal glint
    gleams in his eye.
He's mad and disgusted and cries out,
    "You've busted the heart that once
    trusted you. Wed me or die!"
Though Carmen is frightened at how
    this scene might end, I'm forced to
    admit she is game to the last.
She says to him "Banish the notion and
    vanish. *Vamos!*" which is Spanish
    for "run away fast."
A scream and a struggle! She reels and
    she staggers, for Don José's dag-
    ger's plunged deep in her breast.
No more will she flirt in her old way,
    that's certain. So ring down the
    curtain, poor Carmen's at rest.

Opera Guyed. Carmen

EUGENE O'NEILL
[1888–   ]

Dat ole davil, sea.

Anna Christie. Act I

We're all poor nuts and things happen, and we yust get mixed in wrong, that's all.

Ibid. Act IV

For de little stealin' dey gits you in jail soon or late. For de big stealin' dey makes you emperor and puts you in de Hall o' Fame when you croaks. If dey's one thing I learns in ten years on de Pullman cars listenin' to de white quality talk, it's dat same fact.

The Emperor Jones. Sc. 1

The child was diseased at birth, stricken with a hereditary ill that only the most vital men are able to shake off. I mean poverty — the most deadly and prevalent of all diseases.

Fog

He couldn't design a cathedral without it looking like the First Supernatural Bank!

The Great God Brown

Yank. Sure! Lock me up! Put me in a cage! Dat's de on'y answer yuh know. G'wan, lock me up!
Policeman. What you been doin'?
Yank. Enough to gimme life for! I was born, see? Sure, dat's de charge.

Write it in de blotter. I was born, get
me!
The Hairy Ape
Our lives are merely strange dark interludes in the electrical display of God
the Father!
Strange Interlude

JOHN CROWE RANSOM
[1888–   ]

Up once I rose, in a fury of heard-of
things,
To travel the splendid sphere and see
its fame;
But the wars and ships and towns and
the roaring kings
But flashed with the image of her!
and back I came.
Sonnet of a Sure Heart
Hands hold much of heat in little stor-
age.
They Hail the Sunrise
The lazy geese, like a snow cloud
Dripping their snow on the green grass,
Tricking and stopping, sleepy and
proud,
Who cried in goose, Alas.
*Bells for John Whitesides'
Daughter*
Here lies a lady of beauty and high de-
gree.
Of chills and fever she died, of fever and
chills,
The delight of her husband, her aunts,
an infant of three,
And of medicos marvelling sweetly on
her ills.
Here Lies a Lady
Two evils, monstrous either one apart,
Possessed me, and were long and loath
at going:
A cry of Absence, Absence, in the heart,
And in the wood the furious winter
blowing.
Winter Remembered
Do they not hear the burst of bells
Pealing at every step you take?
Are not their eyelids winking too,
Feeling your sudden brightness break?
O, too much glory shut with us,
O, walls too narrow and opaque!

O, come into the night with me
And let me speak, for Jesus' sake!
The Lover
Long, long before men die I sometimes
read
Their stoic backs as plain as graveyard
stones.
The Resurrection
And kept their blue eyes blue to any
weather.
Men
Mouth he remembered: the quaint ori-
fice
From which came heat that flamed
upon the kiss.
The Equilibrists
In Heaven you have heard no marriage
is,
No white flesh tinder to your lecheries,
Your male and female tissue sweetly
shaped
Sublimed away, and furious blood
escaped.
Ibid.
Equilibrists lie here; stranger, tread
light;
Close, but untouching in each other's
sight;
Mouldered the lips and ashy the tall
skull,
Let them lie perilous and beautiful.
Ibid.
He rose and was himself again.
Simply another morning, and simply
Jane.
Morning
God have mercy on the sinner
Who must write with no dinner,
No gravy and no grub,
No pewter and no pub,
No belly and no bowels,
Only consonants and vowels.
Survey of Literature
Athens, a fragile kingdom by the foam,
Assumed the stranger's yoke; but then
behold how meek
Those unbred Caesars grew, who spent
their fruits of Rome
Forever after, trying to be Greek.
Triumph

LEW SARETT
[1888–   ]

God, let me flower as I will!
For I am weary of the chill
Companionship of waxen vines
And hothouse-nurtured columbines.
Let Me Flower as I Will. Stanza 1

Walk softly, March, forbear the bitter
blow;
Her feet within a trap, her blood upon
the snow,
The four little foxes saw their mother
go —
Walk softly.
Four Little Foxes. Stanza 2

ALAN SEEGER
[1888–1916]

Whether I am on the winning or losing side is not the point with me: it is
being on the side where my sympathies
lie that matters, and I am ready to see
it through to the end. Success in life
means doing that thing than which
nothing else conceivable seems more noble or satisfying or remunerative, and
this enviable state I can truly say that
I enjoy, for had I the choice I would be
nowhere else in the world than where I
am.[1]
Letter to his mother [July 3, 1915]

I have a rendezvous with Death [2]
At some disputed barricade,
When Spring comes back with rustling
shade
And apple-blossoms fill the air.
I Have a Rendezvous with Death

[1] I think he would not wish himself any
where but where he is. — SHAKESPEARE: *King
Henry V, Act IV, Sc. 1, L. 125*
[2] We who have walked with Death in
France,
When all the world with death was rife,
Who came through all that devils' dance,
When life was but a circumstance,
A sniper's whim, a bullet's glance,
We have a rendezvous with life!
HERVEY ALLEN: *We, St. 2*
I have a rendezvous with Life,
When Spring's first heralds hum.
COUNTEE CULLEN: *I Have a Rendez-
vous with Life*

When Spring trips north again this year,
And I to my pledged word am true,
I shall not fail that rendezvous.
I Have a Rendezvous with Death

MRS. BERTYE YOUNG
WILLIAMS
[1888–   ]

The inn was full. There was no room.[1]
But certainly I could have done
Something if I had known for whom —
Ah, that my door should be the one
To shut out Mary and her Son!
*The Bethlehem Innkeeper Speaks.
Stanza 3*

CONRAD AIKEN
[1889–   ]

Music I heard with you was more than
music,
And bread I broke with you was more
than bread.
Music I Heard with You. Stanza 1

It is morning, Senlin says, and in the
morning
When the light drips through the shut-
ters like the dew,
I arise, I face the sunrise,
And do the things my fathers learned to
do.
Stars in the purple dusk above the roof-
tops
Pale in a saffron mist and seem to die,
And I myself on a swiftly tilting planet
Stand before a glass and tie my tie.
Senlin. Morning Song

One by one in the moonlight there,
Neighing far off on the haunted air,
The unicorns come down to the sea.
Ibid. Evening Song

Rock meeting rock can know love bet-
ter
Than eyes that stare or lips that touch.
All that we know in love is bitter,
And it is not much.
Annihilation. Stanza 8

When trout swim down Great Ormond
Street,
And sea-gulls cry above them lightly,

[1] There was no room for them in the inn. —
Luke, II, 7

And hawthorns heave cold flagstones
up
To blossom whitely. . . .
Priapus and the Pool. III

Then I shall hold my breath and die,
Swearing I never loved you; no,
"You were not lovely!" I shall cry,
"I never loved you so."
Ibid.

How shall we praise the magnificence of
the dead,
The great man humbled, the haughty
brought to dust?
Is there a horn we should not blow as
proudly
For the meanest of us all, who creeps
his days,
Guarding his heart from blows, to die
obscurely?
Tetélestai

HERVEY ALLEN
[1889–]

Christ Jesus, when I come to die
Grant me a clean, sweet, summer sky,
Without the mad wind's panther cry.
Send me a little garden breeze
To gossip in magnolia trees;
For I have heard, these fifty years,
Confessions muttered at my ears,
Till every mumble of the wind
Is like tired voices that have sinned.
*The Priest and the Pirate: A
Ballad of Theodosia Burr.[1]
Stanza 3*

Grow up as soon as you can. It pays.
The only time you really live fully is
from thirty to sixty. . . . The young
are slaves to dreams; the old servants
of regrets. Only the middle-aged have
all their five senses in the keeping of
their wits.
Anthony Adverse. Chap. 31

What is even a wise book but a blast
from the lungs made visible to the eyes?
Ibid.

[1] Theodosia Burr, daughter of Aaron Burr,
perished at sea while on a voyage from
Charleston, S. C., to New York, in January,
1813. The wreck was plundered by pirates.

Practise what I call a decent mammalian philosophy.
Anthony Adverse. Chap. 31

ROBERT CHARLES BENCHLEY
[1889–]

I haven't been abroad in so long that
I almost speak English without an ac-
cent.
The Old Sea Rover Speaks

Enter first Lady-in-Waiting (*Flour-
ish,[1] Hautboys[2] and[3] torches*).[4]
First Lady-in-Waiting—What[5] ho![6]
Where[7] is[8] the[9] music?[10]

NOTES

1. *Flourish:* The stage direction here
is obscure. Clarke claims it should read
"flarish," thus changing the meaning
of the passage to "flarish" (that is,
the King's), but most authorities have
agreed that it should remain "flourish,"
supplying the predicate which is to be
flourished. There was at this time a custom in the countryside of England to
flourish a mop as a signal to the passing vender of berries, signifying that
in that particular household there was a
consumer-demand for berries, and this
may have been meant in this instance.
That Shakespeare was cognizant of this
custom of flourishing the mop for berries is shown in a similar passage in the
second part of King Henry IV, where
he has the Third Page enter and say,
"Flourish." Cf. also Hamlet, IV, 7:4.
*Of All Things. Shakespeare
Explained*

CHARLES DIVINE
[1889–]

I wonder who is haunting the little snug
café,
That place, half restaurant and home,
since we have gone away;
The candled dimness, smoke and talk,
and tables brown and bare —
But no one thinks of tablecloths when
love and laughter's there.
At the Lavender Lantern. Stanza 1

Where hearts were high and fortunes
low, and onions in the stew.
At the Lavender Lantern. Stanza 3
A crooked street goes past my door, en-
twining love of every land;
It wanders, singing, round the world, to
Askelon and Samarkand.
The Crooked Street of Dreams.
Stanza 1

PHILIP GUEDALLA
[1889–   ]

Biography, like big game hunting, is
one of the recognized forms of sport,
and it is as unfair as only sport can be.
High on some far hill-side of politics or
history the amateur marks down his distant quarry. Follows an intensely distasteful period of furtive approach to
the subject which leads the deer-stalker
up gullies and ravines and the biographer through private letters and
washing-books. The burns grow deeper
and wetter, the letters take a more private and a less publishable turn, until
at last our sportsman, well within range,
turns to his publisher, who carries the
guns, and empties one, two, and (if the
public will stand it) three barrels into
his unprotesting victim: because it is a
cruel truth that the subjects of *Lives*
are rarely themselves alive.
Supers and Supermen
Whispering from its towers the last
enchantment of the middle-class, the
Foreign Office occupies an eligible central situation between Whitehall and
St. James's Park. The grateful taxpayer
provides it with an abundance of admirable stationery, and it is perhaps the
last place in London where everybody is
a gentleman.
Ibid.
Because the sporting England of
Queen Victoria could never understand
the unathletic France of President
Thiers, we have all in our time conjured
up delightful visions of legions of little
Frenchmen in flat-brimmed silk hats
going fox-shooting with packs of poodles. No picture of life in Calais was too
ludicrous to be believed in Dover; that

is one of the advantages of being an
Island Race.[1]
Supers and Supermen
There is no Gibbon but Gibbon, and
Gibbon is his prophet. The solemn
march of his cadences, the majestic im-
propriety of his innuendo are without
rivals in the respective annals of British
eloquence and British indelicacy.
Ibid.
The work of Henry James has al-
ways seemed divisible by a simple dy-
nastic arrangement into three reigns:
James I, James II, and the Old Pre-
tender.
Ibid.
An Englishman is a man who lives on
an island in the North Sea governed by
Scotsmen.
Ibid.
Walker . . . followed with the full
energy of a man born in Nashville, Tennessee, the high calling of a filibuster.
He was the son of an insurance manager, and he became almost mechanically a pirate. . . . Walker filiburst
(if that is the appropriate aorist).
General Walker
The cheerful clatter of Sir James Barrie's cans as he went round with the
milk of human kindness.
Some Critics
A somewhat disjointed series of stac-
cato notes which leave one with the misleading impression that Mr. Pound's
shirt-cuffs have been sent to the printer
instead of to the laundress.
Ibid.
Strange that pre-eminence in Germany has more than once been indi-
cated by an eccentric pattern in the hair
upon the upper lip.
The Hundred Years
The true history of the United States
is the history of transportation . . . in
which the names of railroad presidents
are more significant than those of Presidents of the United States.
Ibid.

---

[1] Cf. the immortal headline in the London
Times: TERRIBLE GALE IN THE CHANNEL —
CONTINENT ISOLATED.

His [Du Maurier's] incomparable duchesses drew together like tall galleons in mid-ocean, as the first American heiresses came brightly on the social scene.

The Hundred Years

STODDARD KING
[1889–1933]

A writer owned an Asterisk,
  And kept it in his den,
Where he wrote tales (which had large sales)
  Of frail and erring men;
And always, when he reached the point
  Where carping censors lurk,
He called upon the Asterisk
  To do his dirty work.

The Writer and the Asterisk.
Stanza 1

The books I read and the life I lead
  Are sensible, sane and mild.
I like calm hats and I don't wear spats,
  But I want my neckties wild!

The Tie That Blinds

Give me a wild tie, brother,
  One with a cosmic urge!
A tic that will swear and rip and tear
  When it sees my old blue serge.

Ibid.

But since I am not lord of the sun, nor yet of the realms below,
Would you care to be told that I have two seats for an elegant movie show?

A Matter-of-Fact Love Song.
Stanza 1

Of all the pestilences dire,
Including famine, flood, and fire,
By Satan and his imps rehearsed,
The neighbors' children are the worst.

Philosophy for Parents. Stanza 1

KATHERINE MANSFIELD
(MRS. JOHN MIDDLETON MURRY)
[1889–1923]

Oh, flock of thoughts with their shepherd Fear
Shivering, desolate, out in the cold,
That entered into my heart to fold!

Two Nocturnes. II, Stanza 3

Whenever I prepare for a journey I prepare as though for death. Should I never return, all is in order. This is what life has taught me.

Journal, 1922

I want, by understanding myself, to understand others. I want to be all that I am capable of becoming. . . . This all sounds very strenuous and serious. But now that I have wrestled with it, it's no longer so. I feel happy — deep down. *All is well.*

Ibid. (end of her journal)

WALTER JAMES TURNER
[1889–   ]

When I was but thirteen or so
  I went into a golden land,
Chimborazo, Cotopaxi
  Took me by the hand.

Romance. Stanza 1

Chimborazo, Cotopaxi,
  They had stolen my soul away!

Ibid. Stanza 7

T. P. CAMERON WILSON
[1889–1918]

Stare Sphinx-like into space,
Nor march the chalky floor all tousle-haired
  When bright boys mention with a cheerful face
That $(a + a)$ is written down a^2.

The Mathematical Master to
His Blackboard

God gives to each man, however beset he may be with the world, a few minutes at least daily, when he is utterly alone. I have read Shelley in a Public Lavatory, and learnt Rupert Brooke's war sonnets by heart while I was doing my morning duty to this body.

Waste Paper Philosophy. IX

WILLIAM BOLITHO
[1890–1930]

When the Poincarés and Ludendorffs have brought a man to death they have not finished with him. They use his body to slay others. The most precious gain of Nationalism from war and bloodshed (and they have many) is this profiteering in the dead.

Leviathan [*1923*]

The adventurer is within us, and he contests for our favour with the social man we are obliged to be. These two sorts of life are incompatibles; one we hanker after, the other we are obliged to. There is no other conflict so deep and bitter as this, whatever the pious say, for it derives from the very constitutions of human life, which so painfully separate us from all other beings. We, like the eagles, were born to be free. Yet we are obliged, in order to live at all, to make a cage of laws for ourselves and to stand on the perch. We are born as wasteful and unremorseful as tigers; we are obliged to be thrifty, or starve, or freeze. We are born to wander, and cursed to stay and dig.

Twelve Against the Gods [*1929*].
Introduction

He, and the world with him, — for Wilson's adventure was the world's, and one day the world will know it, even the fools — were not the victims of a vulgar trick, unless the dizziness that pulls down climbers from the peak is some cunning of the Alps. We fell there because the height was too great, because he saw all the countries of the world, the bare immensity of the mass of common people which he had worshipped all his life, but never imagined until that day he knew he had them, their lives, and all uncountable, future ages of them in his own two hands. Seeing, a great vertigo leapt on him. Those days have passed more utterly from memory than if a hundred years had gone since then; but a few who lived through them, and stood near where the pedestal of Wilson was standing can remember, vaguely, as if they had read it somewhere, something of the madness, the sheer panic, mixed with exaltation, of the times.

Ibid. Woodrow Wilson

Like Arthur and the legendary Alexander, and many other lesser men, he

[Woodrow Wilson] left, even though defeated, a hope, a promise, that League, which is as it were a symbol of his perished flesh and blood, a fragment torn out of his heart and left with us, to serve for one who will come after in a retaking up of his adventure.

Twelve Against the Gods [*1929*]
Woodrow Wilson

MARCUS COOK CONNELLY
[1890–   ]

Gangway for de Lawd God Jehovah!
The Green Pastures.[1]
God. I'll jest r'ar back an' pass a miracle.

Ibid.

Gabriel. How about cleanin' up de whole mess of 'em and sta'tin all over ag'in wid some new kind of animal?
God. An' admit I'm licked?

Ibid.

Even bein' Gawd ain't a bed of roses.
Ibid.

ALAN PATRICK HERBERT
[1890–   ]

When laughing Ann trips down the
        street
    The sun comes out as well,
The town is at her twinkling feet,
    The crier rings his bell,
The young men leap like little fish,
    Policemen stand and purr,
While husbands look behind and wish
    That they had married her.

Laughing Ann. Stanza 1

I wish I hadn't broke that dish,
    I wish I was a movie-star,
I wish a lot of things, I wish
    That life was like the movies are;
    It May Be Life, But Ain't It Slow?
Stanza 1

        If there's a dish
        For which I wish
    More frequent than the rest,
        If there's a food
        On which I brood
    When starving or depressed,

[1] First produced in 1930. Suggested by Roark Bradford's stories, *Ol' Man Adam an' His Chillun.*

If there's a thing that life can give
Which makes it worth our while to live,
   If there's an end
   On which I'd spend
My last remaining cash,
   It's sausage, friend,
   It's sausage, friend,
It's sausage, friend, and mash.
      Sausage and Mash. Stanza 1
   When Love is dead,
   Ambition fled,
And Pleasure, lad, and Pash,
   You'll still enjoy
   A sausage, boy,
A sausage, boy, and mash.
      Ibid. Stanza 3
Teetot'lers seem to die the same as oth-
   ers,
So what's the use of knocking off the
   beer?
      The Ladies' Bar. Refrain
The chameleon's life is confusing,
   He is used to adventure and pain;
But if ever he sat on Aunt Maggie's
   cretonne,
And noticed what curious colors he'd
   gone,
   I don't think he'd do it again.
      The Chameleon. Stanza 4
The sturgeon belongs to the King,
   And if in some desolate chasm,
You feloniously catch one or two on a
   string
You must see that His Majesty has
   'em.
      Caviare. Stanza 1
I regard the pub as a valuable insti-
tution.
   *Letter to the Electors of Oxford
      University [1935]* [1]
I shall examine with some suspicion
any proposals that may be made for
the distribution of the British Empire
among foreign countries, whatever their
birth-rate, insolence or inefficiency.
      Ibid.
I have no plan for the restoration of
world trade: there will be 613 members
of the new Parliament, who have.
      Ibid.

[1] Mr. Herbert was elected to the House of
Commons, November, 1935, as one of the two
representatives of Oxford University.

They tell us that capitalism is
doomed: Karl Marx, I believe, made
the same announcement 80 years ago.
He may still be right: but the old clock
ticks on; and it does not help very much
to throw stones at it. It would be surprising indeed if our system had survived quite unshaken the unprecedented upheaval of a World War. But
it is infinitely adaptable and has not, I
think, exhausted its resources.
   *Letter to the Electors of Oxford
      University [1935]*
We shall not produce equality by
turning everything upside-down. My
reason, such as it is, reluctantly rebels
when I am asked to believe that after
thousands of years of not wholly fruitless civilization the best and only way
of managing this complicated world has
been revealed to my old football captain, Sir Stafford Cripps.
      Ibid.
I know nothing about Agriculture.
      Ibid.
Holy Deadlock.
   *Title of novel [1934] satirizing the
      paradoxes of British divorce law*

SAMUEL HOFFENSTEIN
[1890–   ]

When trouble drives me into rhyme,
Which is two-thirds of all the time,
What peace a thought like this can
   give —
Great is the age in which we live!
      Songs to Break the Tedium. III
Oh, how various is the scene
Allowed to Man for his demesne!
   *Verses Demonstrating That No
      Man Can Be Unhappy*
You buy some flowers for your table;
You tend them tenderly as you're able;
You fetch them water from hither and
   thither —
What thanks do you get for it all? They
   wither.
    *Poems in Praise of Practically
      Nothing. I*

When the wind is in the tree,
It makes a noise just like the sea,
As if there were not noise enough
To bother one, without that stuff.
A Garden of Verses for the Lit-
tle Ones. XIII, The Wind in the
Tree

Loyal be to loyal friends;
Make them pay you dividends;
Work, like the industrious bee,
Your friends and foes impartially.
Ibid. XIX, For Little Boys
Destined for Big Business

I'd rather listen to a flute
In Gotham, than a band in Butte.
Songs about Life. VIII

The apple grows so bright and high,
And ends its days in apple pie.
Ibid. XXXIII

Of all the birds that sing and fly
Between the housetops and the sky,
The muddy sparrow, mean and small,
I like, by far, the best of all.
Ibid. LIII

I play with the bulls and the bears;
I'm the Bartlett of market quotations.
Songs for an Old-Fashioned
Lute. VI

The stars, like measles, fade at last.
The Mimic Muse. V

Babies haven't any hair;
Old men's heads are just as bare; —
Between the cradle and the grave
Lies a haircut and a shave.
Songs of Faith in the Year after
Next. VIII

The head that wears a crown may be
Inclined to some anxiety,
But, on the other hand, I know
A derby domes its meed of woe.
Ibid. XVI

Your little voice,
So soft and kind;
Your little soul,
Your little mind!
Love-songs. XIII

The countless cousins of the Czar,
Grand Duke or Duchess, every one,
As multitudinous as are
The spheres (who borrow from the
sun).
Invocation. Stanza 15

Blessings love disguise.
Serenades and Songs for a Pent-
House Window. III

My soul is dark with stormy riot,
Directly traceable to diet.
Out of the Everywhere into the
Here. XIII

Which six of the seven cities that
claimed Homer were liars?
The Moist Land. I

Little by little we subtract
Faith and Fallacy from Fact,
The Illusory from the True,
And starve upon the residue.
Rag-Bag, II. Observation,
Stanza 1

To You, oh, Goddess of Efficiency,
Your happy vassals bend the reverent
knee,
Save when arthritis, your benighted foe,
Sulks in the bones and sourly mumbles
"No!"
Hymn to Science

To all the starry host of Heaven they
cried,
But had no radio and of course they
died.
Ibid.

Smelling like a municipal budget.
Entr' Acte. VI

The heart's dead
Are never buried.
Summer Day

Though poor he lived among the throng,
And though obscure he died,
With a betrothal-ring of song
He made the world his bride.
To Genius, Dying Young.
Stanza 1

Greater than all my songs am I;
Much more have seen, have heard much
more —
For who shall fetch in a pitcher of sing-
ing
All that lies on the ocean's floor?
Apologia. Stanza 5

THEODORE MAYNARD
[1890–   ]

I know a sheaf of splendid songs by
heart

Which stir the blood or move the soul
to tears,
Of death or honour or of love's sweet
smart,
The runes and legends of a thousand
years;
And some of them go plaintively and
slow,
And some are jolly like the earth in
May —
But this is *really* the best song I know:
I-tiddly-iddly-i-ti-iddly-ay.
*Ballade of the Best Song in the
World. Stanza 1*

VIOLA MEYNELL

His kisses touch her marvelling eyes
And wander searching through her
thinking face;
And though so loved and near she lies
He knows he travels in a distant place.
A Girl Adoring. Prefatory verses
He does not know how far, how far;
Only she makes him think of some
strange land.
Beyond the earth his journeys are,
Touching that wild, wild heart and
thinking hand.
Ibid. Stanza 5

CHRISTOPHER MORLEY
[1890–   ]

There is no prince or prelate
I envy — no, not one.
No evil can befall me —
By God, I have a son!
Secret Laughter
And of all man's felicities
The very subtlest one, say I,
Is when for the first time he sees
His hearthfire smoke against the sky.
A Hallowe'en Memory. Stanza 5
Heaven is not built of country seats,
But little queer suburban streets.
To the Little House. Stanza 4
The man who never in his life
Has washed the dishes with his wife
Or polished up the silver plate —
He still is largely celibate.
Washing the Dishes. Stanza 4

The greatest poem ever known
Is one all poets have outgrown:
The poetry, innate, untold,
Of being only four years old.
To a Child

One good nocturne
Deserves another,
Said George Sand
When she met Chopin.
Reciprocation

Now fades the glossy, cherished anthra-
cite;
The radiators lose their temperature:
How ill avail, on such a frosty night,
The short and simple flannels of the
poor.[1]
*Elegy Written in a Country
Coal-Bin*

Unhappy lovers always should be
Frenchmen,
So sweet a tongue for any kind of pain!
Toulemonde. III

Such color as the curtained bee would
know
Drowsed in the bedstead of a crimson
rose,
Such color as the vineyard speck might
swim
Deepened in the full Burgundian glass,
Such color as the unborn Juliet felt
Nursed in the reddest vein of Shake-
speare's heart.
Ibid. V

Women all
Raiment themselves most brightly for
the dark
Which is, on information and belief,
Their true dominion.
Ibid. VI

Know, then, that I consider brown
For ladies' eyes, the only color;
And deem all other orbs in town
(Compared to yours) opaquer, duller.
To His Brown-Eyed Mistress

[1] Daily she came from Bromley to the City,
Pink underclothes of crêpe de Chine she
wore,
So that in each backyard she viewed with
pity
The short and simple flannels of the poor.
—OLIVER HERFORD? Quoted by
A. EDWARD NEWTON, in *Derby Day*

I bid you, mock not Eros;
  He knows not doubt or shame,
And, unaware of proverbs,
  The burnt child craves the flame.
          Of a Child That Had Fever

With pained surprise
Men learn that poetry's not just the
  skill
Of words long dead, but actual You's
  and I's —
And if you have not learned that yet,
  you will.
  Memoranda for a Sonnet Sequence

A human being: an ingenious assembly of portable plumbing.
          Human Being. Chap. 11

How great a bonfire the savages of
New York kindle for their evening
meal!
          Ibid. Chap. 33

Prophets were twice stoned — first in
anger; then, after their death, with a
handsome slab in the graveyard.
          Where the Blue Begins. Chap. 11

He is too experienced a parent ever
to make positive promises.
          Thunder on the Left. Chap. 5

Informal's what women always say
they're going to be and never are.
          Ibid.

As calmly detached as nurses in a
hospital who smile faintly at what the
patients say under ether.
          Ibid. Chap. 6

If you have to keep reminding yourself of a thing, perhaps it isn't so.
          Ibid. Chap. 9

Life is a foreign language: all men
mispronounce it.
          Ibid. Chap. 14

Poetry comes with anger, hunger and
dismay; it does not often visit groups
of citizens sitting down to be literary
together, and would appal them if it did.
          John Mistletoe. 7

April prepares her green traffic light
and the world thinks Go.
          Ibid. 8

JAMES RORTY
[1890–   ]

There is a peewee bird that cries
"La, sol, me
"La, sol, me" —
He is the only thing that sighs
Beside the western sea.
          California Dissonance. Stanza 1

The blue jays chatter, "Tcha! Tcha!
  Tcha!"
And cheer for California
The real estate men chortle "Whee!"
And tout the loud calliope.
The sky is blue, the land is glad —
The peewee bird alone is sad
And sings in minor key.
          Ibid. Stanza 2

It was a shock, I own, to see
Sedition sitting in a tree.
          Ibid. Stanza 3

FRANCIS LEDWIDGE
[1891–1917]

Had I a golden pound to spend,
My love should mend and sew no more.
And I would buy her a little quern,
Easy to turn on the kitchen floor.
          Had I a Golden Pound. Stanza 1

From its blue vase the rose of evening
  drops;
Upon the streams its petals float away.
          An Evening in England

IRENE RUTHERFORD
McLEOD (MRS. AUBREY
DE SELINCOURT)
[1891–   ]

I'm a lean dog, a keen dog, a wild dog,
  and lone;
I'm a rough dog, a tough dog, hunting
  on my own;
I'm a bad dog, a mad dog, teasing silly
  sheep;
I love to sit and bay the moon, to keep
  fat souls from sleep.
          Lone Dog. Stanza 1

I've hated all that's mean and cold,
All that's dusty, tame, and old,
Comfortable lies in books,
Pallid Virtue's sidelong looks,

Saints who wash their hands too clean,
And walk where only saints have been.
Rebel

HERBERT V. WILEY
[1891–   ]

Stand by to crash.
Last command to the crew of the falling U. S. Navy dirigible Akron [April 4, 1933]

RICHARD ALDINGTON
[1892–   ]

The moon,
With a rag of gauze about her loins.
Evening

PEARL SYDENSTRICKER BUCK
(MRS. RICHARD J. WALSH)
[1892–   ]

Be born anywhere, little embryo novelist, but do not be born under the shadow of a great creed, not under the burden of original sin, not under the doom of salvation. Go out and be born among gypsies or thieves or among happy workaday people who live in the sun and do not think about their souls.
Advice to Unborn Novelists

How could an actual person fit into the covers of a book? The book is not a continent, not a definite geographical measure, it cannot contain so huge a thing as an actual full-size person. Any person has to be scaled by eliminations to fit the book world.
Ibid.

STELLA BENSON (MRS. J. C. O 'GORMAN ANDERSON)
[1892–1933]

Call no man foe, but never love a stranger.
Build up no plan, nor any star pursue.
Go forth with crowds; in loneliness is danger.
Thus nothing God can send,

And nothing God can do
Shall pierce your peace, my friend.
To the Unborn. Stanza 3

Oh, bless your blindness, glory in your groping!
Mock at your betters with an upward chin!
And when the moment has gone by for hoping,
Sling your fifth stone, O son of mine, and win.

Grief do I give you, grief and dreadful laughter;
Sackcloth for banner, ashes in your wine.
Go forth, go forth, nor ask me what comes after;
The fifth stone shall not fail you, son of mine.

Go forth, go forth, and slay the Philistine.
*Five Smooth Stones.
Stanzas 12 and 13*

High and miraculous skies bless and astonish my eyes;
All my dead secrets arise, all my dead stories come true.
Here is the Gate to the Sea. Once you unlocked it for me;
Now, since you gave me the key, shall I unlock it for you?
This Is the End

Did Older and Wiser people ever shout and jump with joy in their pyjamas in the moonlight? Did they ever feel just drunk with being young? And were Older and Wiser people's jokes ever funny?
Ibid.

Family jokes, though rightly cursed by strangers, are the bond that keeps most families alive.
Pipers and a Dancer. Chap. 9

ELIZABETH ASQUITH BIBESCO

I have made a great discovery.
What I love belongs to me. Not the chairs and tables in my house, but the masterpieces of the world.

It is only a question of loving them enough.

Balloons

He is invariably in a hurry. Being in a hurry is one of the tributes he pays to life.

Ibid.

It is sometimes the man who opens the door who is the last to enter the room.

The Fir and the Palm. Chap. 13

You are such a wonderful Baedeker to life. All of the stars are in the right places.

Ibid.

It is never any good dwelling on good-byes. It is not the being together that it prolongs, it is the parting.

Ibid. Chap. 15

ROBERT PETER TRISTRAM COFFIN
[1892–   ]

If men could still be holy anywhere,
  It would be in towers such as these
That line the coasts with lamps and
    warn the ships —
  The holy towers of the silences.

Towers of Silence

A man should choose with careful eye
The things to be remembered by.

The Weather Vane

Life and death upon one tether
And running beautiful together.

Crystal Moment

FRANCIS E. FALKENBURY

As I came down to South Street by the
    soft sea-water,
  I saw long ships, their mast-heads
    ever bowing:
Sweet slender maids in clinging gowns
    of golden,
Curtseying stately in a fashion olden,
Bowing sweetly — each a king's fair
    daughter —
To me, their millionth, millionth lover,
I, the seventh son of the old sea-rover,
As I came down to South Street by the
    myriad moving water.

South Street

JOHN BURDON SANDERSON HALDANE
[1892–   ]

Science is vastly more stimulating to the imagination than are the classics.

Daedalus

ARCHIBALD MacLEISH
[1892–   ]

Sometimes within the brain's old
    ghostly house,
  I hear, far off, at some forgotten door,
A music and an eerie faint carouse,
  And stir of echoes down the creaking
    floor.

Chambers of Imagery. Stanza 1

Beauty is that Medusa's head
Which men go armed to seek and sever.
It is most deadly when most dead,
And dead will stare and sting forever.

Beauty

A poem should not mean
But be.

Ars Poetica

Here, face downward in the sun
To feel how swift, how secretly,
The shadow of the night comes on.

You, Andrew Marvell

There with vast wings across the can-
    celed skies,
There in the sudden blackness, the
    black pall
Of nothing, nothing, nothing — noth-
    ing at all.

The End of the World

The world was always yours: you would
    not take it.

Speech to a Crowd

Speaking alone for myself it's the steep
    hill and the
Toppling lift of the young men I am
    toward now —
Waiting for that as the wave for the
    next wave.
Let them go over us all I say with the
    thunder of
What's to be next in the world. It's we
    will be under it!

*"Dover Beach" — A Note to
That Poem*

Christ but this earth goes over to the
    squall of time!
Hi but she heels to it — rail down: ribs
    down: rolling
Dakotas under her hull! And the night
    climbing
Sucking the green from the ferns by
    these Berkshire boulders!
                 The Sunset Piece

EDNA ST. VINCENT MILLAY (MRS. EUGEN JAN BOISSEVAIN) [1892–   ]

And what are you that, missing you,
    I should be kept awake
As many nights as there are days
    With weeping for your sake?
                 The Philosopher

Death devours all lovely things;
    Lesbia with her sparrow
Shares the darkness, — presently
    Every bed is narrow.
       Passer Mortuus Est. Stanza 1

All I could see from where I stood
Was three long mountains and a wood.
           Renascence. Line 1

I would I were alive again
To kiss the fingers of the rain,
To drink into my eyes the shine
Of every slanting silver line,
To catch the freshened, fragrant breeze
From drenched and dripping apple-
    trees.
           Ibid. Line 119

I know not how such things can be,
I only know there came to me
A fragrance such as never clings
To aught save happy living things;
A sound as of some joyous elf
Singing sweet songs to please himself,
And, through and over everything,
A sense of glad awakening.
           Ibid. Line 143

The world stands out on either side
No wider than the heart is wide;
Above the world is stretched the sky, —
No higher than the soul is high.
The heart can push the sea and land
Farther away on either hand;

The soul can split the sky in two,
And let the face of God shine through.
         Renascence. Line 189

She that had no need of me,
Is a little lonely child
Lost in Hell. Persephone,
Take her head upon your knee,
Say to her: "My dear, my dear,
It is not so dreadful here."
        A Prayer to Persephone

I know I am but summer to your heart,
And not the full four seasons of the year.
        Two Seasons. Sonnet 1

I drank at every vine.
    The last was like the first.
I came upon no wine
    So wonderful as thirst.
          Feast. Stanza 1

I only know that summer sang in me
A little while, and in me sings no more.
    What Lips My Lips Have Kissed

    Euclid alone
Has looked on Beauty bare.[1] Fortunate
    they
Who, though once only and then but far
    away,
Have heard her massive sandal set on
    stone.
      Euclid Alone Has Looked on
              Beauty Bare

My candle burns at both ends;
    It will not last the night;
But, ah, my foes, and, oh, my friends —
    It gives a lovely light.[2]
      Figs from Thistles. First Fig

Safe upon the solid rock the ugly houses
    stand:
Come and see my shining palace built
    upon the sand!
         Ibid. Second Fig

---

[1] Mathematics possesses not only truth, but supreme beauty — a beauty cold and austere, like that of sculpture, without appeal to any part of our weaker nature, yet sublimely pure, and capable of a stern perfection such as only the greatest art can show. — BERTRAND RUSSELL [1872–   ]: *The Principles of Mathematics* [1903]

[2] I burned my candle at both ends,
    And now have neither foes nor friends.
    SAMUEL HOFFENSTEIN: *Songs of Fairly*
               Utter Despair, VIII

Oh, come again to Astolat!
　I will not ask you to be kind;
And you may go when you will go,
　And I will stay behind.
　　　　　Elaine. Stanza 1

Music my rampart, and my only one.
　　　On Hearing a Symphony of
　　　　　　　　　　Beethoven

Stranger, pause and look;
From the dust of ages
Lift this little book,
Turn the tattered pages,
Read me, do not let me die!
Search the fading letters, finding
Steadfast in the broken binding
All that once was I!
　　The Poet and His Book. Stanza 6

Weep him dead and mourn as you may,
　Me, I sing as I must:
Blessed be death, that cuts in marble
　What would have sunk in dust.
　　　　　Keen. Stanza 1

Who builds her a house with love for
　　timber,
　Builds her a house of foam;
And I'd rather be bride to a lad gone
　　down
　Than widow to one safe home.
　　　　　Ibid. Stanza 5

Spring rides no horses down the hill,
But comes on foot, a goose girl still.
And all the loveliest things there be
Come simply, so it seems to me.
If ever I said, in grief or pride,
I tired of honest things, I lied.
　　　　　The Goose Girl

I'll keep a little tavern
　Below the high hill's crest,
Wherein all gray-eyed people
　May sit them down and rest.
　　　The Little Tavern. Stanza 1

Aye, 'tis a curious fancy —
　But all the good I know
Was taught me out of two gray eyes
　A long time ago.
　　　　　Ibid. Stanza 4

O world, I cannot hold thee close
　enough!
Thy winds, thy wide gray skies!
Thy mists, that roll and rise!

Thy woods, this autumn day, that ache
　and sag
And all but cry with color.
　　　　God's World. Stanza 1
　Lord, I do fear
Thou'st made the world too beautiful
　this year.
My soul is all but out of me — let fall
No burning leaf; prithee, let no bird
　call.
　　　　　Ibid. Stanza 2

I will be the gladdest thing under the
　sun!
I will touch a hundred flowers and not
　pick one.
　　　　Afternoon on a Hill

And if I loved you Wednesday,
　Well, what is that to you?
I do not love you Thursday —
　So much is true.
　　　　Thursday. Stanza 1

There's little kind and little fair
　Is worth its weight in smoke
To me, that's grown so free from care
　Since my heart broke!
　　　The Merry Maid. Stanza 2

Love has gone, and left me and the days
　are all alike.
Eat I must, and sleep I will — and
　would that night were here!
But ah, to lie awake and hear the slow
　hours strike!
Would that it were day again, with
　twilight near!
　　　　Ashes of Life. Stanza 1

Life goes on forever like the gnawing of
　a mouse.
　　　　　Ibid. Stanza 3

Thanks be to God, the world is wide,
　And I am going far from home!
And I forgot in Camelot
　The man I loved in Rome.
　　　　Fugitive. Stanza 1

My heart is warm with the friends I
　make,
　And better friends I'll not be know-
　　ing;
Yet there isn't a train I wouldn't take,
　No matter where it's going.
　　　　Travel. Stanza 3

I know some poison I could drink;
　I've often thought I'd taste it;

But Mother bought it for the sink,
  And drinking it would waste it.
      The Cheerful Abstainer. Stanza 3

Men say the winter
  Was bad that year;
Fuel was scarce,
  And food was dear.
A wind with a wolf's head
  Howled about our door.
      *The Ballad of the Harp-Weaver.
          Stanzas 13, 14.*

I am not resigned to the shutting away
  of loving hearts in the hard ground.
So it is, and so it will be, for so it has
  been, time out of mind:
Into the darkness they go, the wise and
  the lovely. Crowned
With lilies and with laurel they go.
      Dirge Without Music. Stanza 1

Death is our master, — but his seat is
  shaken;
He rides victorious, — but his ranks are
  thinned.
      Not That It Matters

I had a little Sorrow,
  Born of a little Sin.
      The Penitent. Stanza 1

You leave me much against my will.
      To S. M.

Whether or not we find what we are
  seeking
Is idle, biologically speaking.
      *Sonnet: I Shall Forget You
          Presently*

Breathes but one mortal on the teeming
  globe
Could minister to my soul's or body's
  needs —
Physician minus physic, minus robe;
Confessor minus Latin, minus beads.
Yet should you bid me name him, I am
  dumb;
For though you summon him, he would
  not come.
      Fatal Interview. IV

Love in the open hand, nothing but
  that,
Ungemmed, unhidden, wishing not to
  hurt,
As one should bring you cowslips in a
  hat
Swung from the hand, or apples in her
  skirt,

I bring you, calling out as children do:
"Look what I have! — And these are
  all for you."
      Fatal Interview. XI

ELIZABETH J. COATSWORTH
(MRS. HENRY BESTON)
[1893–   ]

Let it be understood that I am Don
  Juan Gomez!
My saddle cloth is fringed with scalps
  of Indians I have slain,
And when I see a girl and knock upon
  her shutter,
Though it be dawn or dark, I need not
  knock again.
      Announcement. Stanza 2

And when I pray, the saints go hurrying
  to the Virgin,
And cry, "Don Juan is praying, and
  must not pray in vain!"
      Ibid. Stanza 3

Cat, if you go outdoors you must walk
  in the snow.
You will come back with little white
  shoes on your feet,
Little white slippers of snow that have
  heels of sleet.
Stay by the fire, my Cat. Lie still, do
  not go.
      On a Night of Snow

JAMES BRYANT CONANT
[1893–   ]

Behavior which appears superficially
correct but is intrinsically corrupt always irritates those who see below the
surface.
      *Baccalaureate Address, Harvard
          College [June 17, 1934]*

Slogans are both exciting and comforting, but they are also powerful opiates for the conscience.
      Ibid.

Some of mankind's most terrible misdeeds have been committed under the
spell of certain magic words or phrases.
      Ibid.

DOROTHY FRANCES BLOMFIELD (MRS. GERALD) GURNEY
[–1932]

The kiss of the sun for pardon,
  The song of the birds for mirth, —
One is nearer God's heart in a garden
  Than anywhere else on earth.[1]
    The Lord God Planted a Garden.
                Stanza 4

CECILY W. HALLACK

Lord of the pots and pipkins, since I
  have no time to be
A saint by doing lovely things and vig-
  illing with Thee,
By watching in the twilight dawn, and
  storming Heaven's gates,
Make me a saint by getting meals and
  washing up the plates!
    The Divine Office of the Kitchen.
                Stanza 1

ROBERT MALISE BOWYER NICHOLS
[1893–   ]

God, if Thou livest, Thine eye on me
  bend,
And stay my grief and bring my pain to
  end:
Pain for my lost, the deepest, rarest
  friend
  Man ever had, whence groweth this
  despair.
    Plaint of Friendship by Death
            Broken. Stanza 1
Beauty is its own reward,
Being a form of Peace.
    The Water-Lily. Stanza 2
Was there love once? I have forgotten
  her.
Was there grief once? grief yet is mine.
               Fulfilment

---

[1] Inscription at the Bok Singing Tower, Lake Wales, Florida.
  The garden seems the one spot on earth where history does not assert itself, and, no doubt, when Nero was fiddling over the blaze of Rome, there were florists counting the petals of rival roses at Paestum as peacefully and conscientiously as any gardeners of to-day.
    EDMUND GOSSE: *Gossip in a Library, Gerard's Herbal*

WILFRED OWEN
[1893–1918]

What passing-bells for these who died
  as cattle?
Only the monstrous anger of the guns.
Only the stuttering rifles' rapid rattle
Can patter out their hasty orisons.
    The Anthem for Doomed Youth
. . . . You would not tell with such
  high zest
To children ardent for some desperate
  glory,
The old lie: *Dulce et decorum est
Pro patria mori.*
        Dulce et Decorum Est

DOROTHY PARKER (MRS. ALAN CAMPBELL)
[1893–   ]

Where's the man could ease a heart
Like a satin gown?
    The Satin Dress. Stanza 1
Yet this the need of woman, this her
  curse:
To range her little gifts, and give, and
  give,
Because the throb of giving's sweet to
  bear.
    I Know I Have Been Happiest
Four be the things I am wiser to know:
Idleness, sorrow, a friend, and a foe.
              Inventory
Four be the things I'd been better
  without:
Love, curiosity, freckles, and doubt.
                 Ibid.
And this is the sum of a lasting lore:
Scratch a lover, and find a foe.
    Ballade of a Great Weariness.
                Stanza 1
Men seldom make passes
At girls who wear glasses.
             News Item
Razors pain you;
Rivers are damp;
Acids stain you;
And drugs cause cramp.
Guns aren't lawful;
Nooses give;

Gas smells awful;
You might as well live.
                                Résumé
Why is it no one ever sent me yet
    One perfect limousine, do you sup-
        pose?
Ah no, it's always just my luck to get
    One perfect rose.
                One Perfect Rose. Stanza 3
Then if my friendships break and bend,
    There's little need to cry
The while I know that every foe
    Is faithful till I die.
                        The Leal. Stanza 2
He lies below, correct in cypress wood,
And entertains the most exclusive
    worms.
            Epitaph for a Very Rich Man
I never saw a sweeter child —
    The little one, the darling one! —
I mind I told her, when he smiled
    You'd know he was his mother's son.
            *The Maid-Servant at the Inn.
                                Stanza 4*
It's queer that I should see them so —
    The time they came to Bethlehem
Was more than thirty years ago;
    I've prayed that all is well with them.
                        Ibid. Stanza 5
The man she had was kind and clean
    And well enough for every day,
But, oh, dear friends, you should have
    seen
The one that got away!
                        The Fisherwoman
There was nothing more fun than a
    man!
            *The Little Old Lady in
                        Lavender Silk*
Women and elephants never forget.
        *Ballade of Unfortunate Mammals.
                                Refrain*

HERBERT READ
[1893–   ]

The only literature which is at the
same time vital and popular is the literature of the music-hall.
            Phases of English Poetry
Poetry can never again become a popular art until the poet gives himself

wholly to "the cadence of consenting
feet." [1]
            Phases of English Poetry

DOROTHY L. SAYERS
[1893–   ]

To that still center where the spinning
    world
Sleeps on its axis, to the heart of rest.
        Gaudy Night. Chap. 18, Sonnet
    Death seems to provide the minds of
the Anglo-Saxon race with a greater
fund of innocent amusement than any
other single subject . . . the tale must
be about dead bodies or very wicked
people, preferably both, before the
Tired Business Man can feel really
happy.
            *The Third Omnibus of Crime.
                        Introduction*

SYLVIA TOWNSEND
WARNER
[1893–   ]

John Bird, a laborer, lies here,
Who served the earth for sixty year
With spade and mattock, drill and
    plough;
But never found it kind till now.
                            Epitaph

JOHN VAN ALSTYN
WEAVER
[1893–1938]

Don't you ever try to go there —
    It's to dream of, not to find.
Lovely things like that is always
    Mostly in your mind.
                    Legend. Stanza 7
Sure enough, the towers and castles
    Went like lightnin' out of sight —
Nothin' there but filthy Jersey
    On a drizzly night.
                    Ibid. Stanza 9

---

[1] The quotation is from Francis Barton
Gummere [1855–1919]: *The Beginnings of
Poetry.*

WINIFRED WELLES
[1893–   ]

My squirrel with his tail curved up
  Like half a silver lyre.
                Silver for Midas. Stanza 4
Oh all you safe and smooth of heart
  Listen to song from me,
Whose wooden throat was once a part
  Of the north side of a tree!
                The Violin. Stanza 4
Once, on a cliff, I saw perfection happen.
The full, gold moon was balanced on
    the sea
Just as the red sun rested on the moor.
The summer evening ripened and fell
    open;
And people walking through that fruit's
    rich core
Were suddenly what they were meant
    to be.
                The Heart of Light

DON BLANDING
[1894–   ]

When I have a house . . . as I some-
    time may . . .
I'll suit my fancy in every way.
I'll fill it with things that have caught
    my eye
In drifting from Iceland to Molokai.
                Vagabond's House. Stanza 1
There are times when only a dog will do
For a friend . . . when you're beaten
    sick and blue
And the world's all wrong, for he won't
    care
If you break and cry, or grouch and
    swear,
For he'll let you know as he licks your
    hands
That he's downright sorry . . . and
    understands.[1]
                Ibid. Stanza 5
And the thought will strike with a swift
    sharp pain
That I probably never will build again

[1] In the whole history of the world there is
but one thing that money can not buy — to
wit, the wag of a dog's tail. — HENRY
WHEELER SHAW ("Josh Billings"). Quoted in
KATE SANBORN'S *My Literary Zoo* [1896],
P. 69.

This house that I'll have in some far
    day.
Well . . . it's just a dream-house any-
    way.
                Vagabond's House. Stanza 21
Hollywood . . . Hollywood . . .
Fabulous Follywood . . .
Celluloid Babylon, glorious, glamorous.
                Hollywood. Stanza 1
It's more than just an easy word for
    casual good-bye;
It's gayer than a greeting, and it's sad-
    der than a sigh.
                Aloha Oe: Its Meaning
It's said a hundred different ways, in
    sadness and in joy,
Aloha means "I love you." So I say
    "Aloha Oe."
                Ibid.

EDWARD ESTLIN
CUMMINGS [1]
[1894–   ]

when the proficient poison of sure sleep
bereaves us of our slow tranquilities

and He without Whose favour nothing
    is
(being of men called Love) upward
    doth leap
from the mute hugeness of depriving
    deep,

with thunder of those hungering wings
    of His,

into the lucent and large signories
— i shall not smile beloved; i shall not
    weep.
                *When the Proficient Poison of
                    Sure Sleep*
while in an earthless hour my fond
soul seriously yearns beyond
this fern of sunset frond on frond
opening in a rare
Slowness of gloried air. . . .
                Always Before Your Voice

[1] "The terror of typesetters, an enigma to
book reviewers, and the special target of all
the world's literary philistines." — Publisher's
note, Modern Library edition of *The Enormous Room*.

nobody, not even the rain, has such
   small hands
              Somewhere I Have Never
                      Travelled

"next to of course god america i
love you land of the pilgrims' and so
   forth oh
say can you see by the dawn's early my
country 'tis of centuries come and go
and are no more what of it we should
   worry
in every language even deafanddumb
thy sons acclaim your glorious name by
   gorry
by jingo by gee by gosh by gum
why talk of beauty what could be more
   beaut-
iful, than these heroic happy dead
who rushed like lions to the roaring
   slaughter
they did not stop to think they died
   instead
then shall the voices of liberty be
   mute?"

He spoke. And drank rapidly a glass of
   water.
             Next To Of Course God

KING EDWARD VIII
[1894–   ]

I am better known to most of you as
the Prince of Wales, as the man who
during the war and since has had the
opportunity of getting to know the people of nearly every country of the world
under all conditions and circumstances.
And although I now speak to you as the
King, I am still the same man who has
had the experience, and whose constant
effort will be to continue to promote the
well-being of his fellow men.
      First broadcast to the Empire
      after ascending the throne
      [March 1, 1936]

At long last I am able to say a few
words of my own. I have never wanted
to withhold anything, but until now it
has not been constitutionally possible
for me to speak.

I have found it impossible to carry
the heavy burden of responsibility and
to discharge my duties as King as I
would wish to do without the help and
support of the woman I love.

I now quit altogether public affairs
and I lay down my burden.

It may be some time before I return
to my native land, but I shall always
follow the fortunes of the British race
and empire with profound interest and
if, at any time in the future, I can be
found of service to His Majesty in a
private station I shall not fail.

And now we all have a new King. I
wish him and you, his people, happiness
and prosperity with all my heart.

God bless you all! God save the
King!
      Farewell broadcast after abdication
               [December 11, 1936]

ALDOUS LEONARD HUXLEY
[1894–   ]

It is far easier to write ten passably
effective Sonnets, good enough to take
in the not too inquiring critic, than one
effective advertisement that will take in
a few thousand of the uncritical buying
public.
                    On the Margin

There are not enough *bon mots* in
existence to provide any industrious
conversationalist with a new stock for
every social occasion.[1]
      Point Counter Point. Chap. 7

A bad book is as much of a labour to
write as a good one; it comes as sincerely from the author's soul.
              Ibid. Chap. 13

---

[1] What horrors, when it flashed over him
that he had made this fine speech, word for
word, twice over! Yet it was not true, as the
lady might perhaps have fairly inferred, that
he had embellished his conversation with the
Huma daily during that whole interval of
years. — OLIVER WENDELL HOLMES: *The Autocrat of the Breakfast Table, Every Man His
Own Boswell*

There is no substitute for talent. Industry and all the virtues are of no
avail.
Point Counter Point. Chap. 13

Parodies and caricatures are the most
penetrating of criticisms.
Ibid. Chap. 28

Over her the swan shook slowly free
The folded glory of his wings, and made
A white-walled tent of soft and lumi-
nous shade.
Leda

Seated upon the convex mound
Of one vast kidney, Jonah prays
And sings his canticles and hymns,
Making the hollow vault resound
God's goodness and mysterious ways,
Till the great fish spouts music as he
swims.
Jonah

Blood of the world, time stanchless
flows;
The wound is mortal and is mine.
Seasons

Life is their madness, life that all night
long
Bids them to sing and sing, they know
not why;
Mad cause and senseless burden of their
song;
For life commands, and Life! is all their
cry.
The Cicadas. Stanza 5

Clueless we go; but I have heard thy
voice,
Divine Unreason! harping in the leaves,
And grieve no more; for wisdom never
grieves,
And thou hast taught me wisdom; I re-
joice.
Ibid. Stanza 14

A million million spermatozoa,
All of them alive:
Out of their cataclysm but one poor
Noah
Dare hope to survive.
And among that billion minus one
Might have chanced to be
Shakespeare, another Newton, a new
Donne —
But the One was Me.
Fifth Philosopher's Song

ROBERT NATHAN
[1894–   ]

Love hath no physic for a grief too deep.
A Cedar Box. Sonnet V

Because my grief seems quiet and apart,
Think not for such a reason it is less.
True sorrow makes a silence in the
heart,
Joy has its friends, but grief its lone-
liness.
Ibid. Sonnet VII

So we stand silent, having lost so soon
The best of us, the high and silver
flute;
The clearest melody, the happiest tune,
The loveliest voice of all our times is
mute.
For Elinor Wylie

Toward men and toward God, she
maintained a respectful attitude, lightened by the belief that in a crisis she
could deal adequately with either of
them.
The Road of Ages. Chap. 2

WESTBROOK PEGLER
[1894–   ]

The Era of Wonderful Nonsense.[1]
Mr. Gump Himself

For the fifth year in succession I
have pored over the catalogue of dogs
in the show at Madison Square Garden
without finding a dog named Rover,
Towser, Sport, Spot or Fido.

Who is the man who can call from his
back door at night: "Here, Champion
Alexander of Clane o' Wind-Holme!
Here, Champion Alexander of Clane o'
Wind-Holme"?
Here, Rover!

I am a member of the rabble in good
standing.
The Lynching Story

After a quiet study of the rules and
tools of civilized table warfare your
correspondent has decided that the
French combine the greatest simplicity
with the best results.

[1] Viz. the period of spending and speculation during what used to be called "Coolidge
Prosperity," before the depression of (approx-
imately) 1930–1935.

The Frenchman, like the old Scotch golfer, endeavors to do what there is to be done without superfluous weapons or fancy gestures. He sits down, ties his napkin behind his ears, picks up a knife and fork and goes to work with admirable directness. He dunks his bread in the juice of the snail, he chases fragments of steak and gravy with a piece of crust, he licks his fingers, says, "Ah!" and gets fed.

France in One Easy Lesson

The French avoid no hazards, they take food as it comes without false restrictions on style or stance, and they make their victuals holler "Uncle!"

Ibid.

H. PHELPS PUTNAM
[1894–   ]

We have insulted you as Lady Luck.
Hymn to Chance

Hard-boiled, unbroken egg, what can you care
For the enfolded passion of the Rose?
Hasbrouck and the Rose

In Springfield, Massachusetts, I devoured
The mystic, the improbable, the Rose.
Ibid.

MARGARET E. SANGSTER
(MRS. GERRIT VAN DETH)
[1894–   ]

Oh, cakes and friends we should choose with care,
Not always the fanciest cake that's there
Is the best to eat! And the plainest friend
Is sometimes the finest one in the end!
French Pastry. Stanza 3

I think that folk should carry bright umbrellas in the rain,
To smile into the sullen sky and make it glad again.
On a Rainy Day. Stanza 4

GENEVIEVE TAGGARD
[1894–   ]

Try tropic for your balm,
Try storm,
And after storm, calm.
Try snow of heaven, heavy, soft, and slow,
Brilliant and warm.
Nothing will help, and nothing do much harm.
Of the Properties of Nature for Healing an Illness. Stanza 1

Drink iron from rare springs; follow the sun;
Go far
To get the beam of some medicinal star;
Or in your anguish run
The gauntlet of all zones to an ultimate one.
Fever and chill
Punish you still,
Earth has no zone to work against your will.
Ibid. Stanza 2

Terror touches me when I
Dream I am touching a butterfly.
The Enamel Girl

Defiant even now, it tugs and moans
To be untangled from these mother's bones.
With Child. Stanza 3

MARK VAN DOREN
[1894–   ]

Grass nibbling inward
Like green fire.
Former Barn Lot. Stanza 3

The sun
Drew semicircles smooth and high.
A week was seven domes across a desert,
And any afternoon took long to die.
The Difference. Stanza 1

Wit is the only wall
Between us and the dark.
Wit. Stanza 1

Wit is the only breath
That keeps our eyelids warm,
Facing the driven ice
Of an old storm
That blows as ever it has blown
Against imperishable stone.
Ibid. Stanza 2

MARGARET L. FARRAND

A curve in the road and a hillside
Clear-cut against the sky;
A tall tree tossed by the Autumn wind,
And a white cloud riding high;
Ten men went along that road
And all but one passed by.
            The Seeing Eye. Stanza 1
And he put them down on canvas
For the other nine men to buy.
            Ibid. Stanza 2

ROBERT GRAVES
[1895–   ]

As you are woman, so be lovely:
As you are lovely, so be various,
Merciful as constant, constant as various,
So be mine, as I yours for ever.
            Pygmalion to Galatea
With a fork drive Nature out,
    She will ever yet return.[1]
            Marigolds
Look: the constant marigold
    Springs again from hidden roots.
Baffled gardener, you behold
    New beginnings and new shoots.
            Ibid.
Hate is a fear, and fear is rot
    That cankers root and fruit alike:
Fight cleanly then, hate not, fear not,
    Strike with no madness when you strike.
            Hate Not, Fear Not
"How is your trade, Aquarius,
This frosty night?"
"Complaints is many and various,
And my feet are cold," says Aquarius.
            Star Talk. Stanza 5
I do not love the Sabbath,
    The soapsuds and the starch,
The troops of solemn people
    Who to Salvation march.
            The Boy Out of Church
Resolved that church and Sabbath
Were never made for man.
            Ibid.

[1] Naturam expelles furca, tamen usque recurret.
            HORACE: *Epistles, I, 10, 24*

When a dream is born in you
    With a sudden clamorous pain,
When you know the dream is true
    And lovely, with no flaw nor stain,
O then, be careful, or with sudden clutch
You'll hurt the delicate thing you prize so much.
            A Pinch of Salt. Stanza 1
May the gift of heavenly peace
And glory for all time
Keep the boy Tom who, tending geese,
First made the nursery rhyme.
            A Ballad of Nursery Rhyme.
            Stanza 6
A well-chosen anthology is a complete dispensary of medicine for the more common mental disorders, and may be used as much for prevention as cure.[1]
            On English Poetry. XXIX

ROBERT HILLYER
[1895–   ]

As one who bears beneath his neighbor's roof
Some thrust that staggers his unready wit
And brooding through the night on such reproof
Too late conceives the apt reply to it,
So all our life is but an afterthought.
            Sonnet: As One Who Bears
Fate harries us; we answer not a word,
Or answering too late, we waste our breath;
Not even a belated quip is heard
From those who bore the final taunt of death.
            Ibid.

LEWIS MUMFORD
[1895–   ]

People have hesitated to call Whitman's poems poetry; it is useless to deny that they belong to sacred literature.
            The Golden Day. V

[1] The same idea has been admirably pursued in Robert Haven Schauffler's anthology, *The Poetry Cure: A Pocket Medicine Chest of Verse* [1925].

The jolly and comfortable bourgeois tradition of the Victorian age, a state of mind composed of felt slippers and warm bellywash.

The Golden Day. VIII

In Whitman and Melville letters again became as racy as the jabber of a waterside saloon; in all of Poe's poetry there is scarcely a line as good as pages of the best of Melville's prose.

Ibid.

E. MERRILL ROOT
[1895–   ]

Quietly I rise again
Over violence or chicane —
Defying from the deeper granite
The skin-diseases of the planet.

Scrub Oak. Stanza 5

Build on waste and desolation
Your green towers of affirmation.

Ibid. Stanza 6

JOHN RODERIGO
DOS PASSOS
[1896–   ]

All along the rails there were faces; in the portholes there were faces. Leeward a stale smell came from the tubby steamer that rode at anchor listed a little to one side with the yellow quarantine flag drooping at the foremast.

"I'd give a million dollars," said the old man resting on his oars, "to know what they come for."

"Just for that pop," said the young man who sat in the stern. "Ain't it the land of opportoonity?"

"One thing I do know," said the old man. "When I was a boy it was wild Irish came in the spring with the first run of shad. . . . Now there ain't no more shad, an them folks, Lord knows where they come from."

"It's the land of opportoonity."

Manhattan Transfer. Dollars

BEN RAY REDMAN
[1896–   ]

"What are you reading? . . . My dear! *not* a detective story!"

The delinquent hung her head. "Yes, it is," she murmured. Then, looking bravely up, she added: "But, you see, I am not reading to retain."

Reading at Random

DIXIE WILLSON

He may look just the same to you,
And he may be just as fine,
But the next-door dog is the next-door dog,
And mine — is — mine!

Next-Door Dog

DOROTHY KEELEY ALDIS
[1897–   ]

Why, when I was told the news,
I felt wings upon my shoes
And gallivanted down the street
Wanting to be indiscreet
And shout to all the world that I
Was about to multiply.

Maternity

JOSEPH AUSLANDER
[1897–   ]

This man is dead.
Everything you can say
Is now quite definitely said:
This man held up his head
And had his day,
Then turned his head a little to one way
And slept instead.

Steel

Spring had come
Like the silver needle-note of a fife,
Like a white plume and a green lance and a glittering knife
And a jubilant drum.

Ibid.

BERNARD DE VOTO
[1897–   ]

Much energy has been spent in an effort to determine where the West begins. The definitions of poetry and the luncheon clubs are unsatisfactory: vagueness should not be invoked when a precise answer is possible. The West begins where the average annual rainfall drops below twenty inches. When you reach the line which marks that drop — for convenience, the one hundredth meridian — you have reached the West.

The Plundered Province

Their [the Vermont highlanders'] ancestral religion told them that the world is a battleground whereon mankind is sentenced to defeat — an idea not inappropriate to the granite against which they must make their way. By the granite they have lived on for three centuries, tightening their belts and hanging on, by the sense of what is real. They are the base of the Yankee commonwealth, and America, staring apprehensively through fog that may not lift in this generation, may find their knowledge of hard things more than a little useful.

New England: There She Stands

New England is a finished place. Its destiny is that of Florence or Venice, not Milan, while the American empire careens onward toward its unpredicted end. . . . It is the first American section to be finished, to achieve stability in the conditions of its life. It is the first old civilization, the first permanent civilization in America.

Ibid.

Pessimism is only the name that men of weak nerves give to wisdom.

Mark Twain: The Ink of History

PHOEBE HOFFMAN
(MRS. SPENCER
BICKERTON)

In the long spring evening's twilight,
   when the sun is setting low,
And the smoke from all the engines
   flushes up, a rosy glow,
Then I come up to the bridge-head,
   watch the lights and net-work
   rails,
Think of when I rode the freighters —

engines   spouting   steam   like
   whales,
D.L.W., Jersey Central, old *Rock
   Island, Pere Marquette,*
Reading coal cars down from Scranton,
   piled with anthracite like jet.
      The Freight Yards. Stanza 1

N. and W., the *Great Northern, Lehigh Valley, B. and O.,*
Like a giant earth-worm twisting,
   slowly 'round the curve they flow.
Caravans of freight move westward,
   bearing eastern goods away —
To come back with hogs and cattle,
   bales of sweet Kentucky hay.
Brakemen walk along the roof-tops,
   lingering for a moment's chat:
There an engineer, while smoking, long
   and eloquently spat.
      Ibid. Stanza 2
*L. and N., D. L. and W., Erie, Reading,
   P.R.R.*
Riding on your sliding roof-tops, that's
   where joy and freedom are.
      Ibid. Stanza 4

BERNICE LESBIA KENYON
(MRS. WALTER GILKYSON)
[1897–   ]

Never return in August to what you
   love;
Along the leaves will be rust
And over the hedges dust,
And in the air vague thunder and silence burning . . .
Choose some happier time for your returning.
      Return. Stanza 1

DAVID T. W. McCORD
[1897–   ]

An old man sleeps. The house-fly goes,
Tasting the salt-lick of his nose.
      Salt Lick. Stanza 3
There were two engines: a great
Bull, his iron spouse,
Under the bridge in wait,
Breathing by Westinghouse.[1]
      8:15. Stanza 2

[1] George Westinghouse [1846–1914], inventor of the air-brake.

No sound, no cry: The longest aisle
Shows the deep colon rabbit-flight,
And where he went in pretty style,
As now his tracks go, out of sight.
>> *Tracks in the Snow. Stanza 5*

This bit of marmalade
which I've not ate,
this almost square of toast,
they'll save me yet.
>> *Moment in Marmalade*

By and by
God caught his eye.
>> *Epitaphs. The Waiter.*

THORNTON NIVEN WILDER
[1897–   ]

The whole purport of literature,
which is the notation of the heart. Style
is but the faintly contemptible vessel in
which the bitter liquid is recommended
to the world.
>> *The Bridge of San Luis Rey. II*

For what human ill does not dawn
seem to be an alleviation?
>> *Ibid. III*

We come from a world where we
have known incredible standards of excellence, and we dimly remember beauties which we have not seized again.
. . . The public for which masterpieces
are intended is not on this earth.
>> *Ibid. IV*

STEPHEN VINCENT BENÉT
[1898–   ]

I died in my boots like a pioneer
With the whole wide sky above me.
>> *The Ballad of William Sycamore*

He could fiddle all the bugs off a sweet-
potato-vine.
>> *The Mountain Whippoorwill.*
>> *Stanza 22*

Oh, Georgia booze is mighty fine booze,
The best yuh ever poured yuh,
But it eats the soles right offen yore
shoes,
For Hell's broke loose in Georgia.
>> *Ibid. Stanza 48*

He cleansed and anointed, took fresh
apparel,
And worshiped the Lord in a tuneful
carol.
>> *King David. Part VI, Stanza 5*

Down where the taproots of New England trees
Suck bare existence from the broken
stones.
>> *The Golden Corpse. Sonnet 4*

The years have hardier tasks
Than listening to a whisper or a sigh.
They creep among us with a bag of
masks
And fit them to our brows obsequiously.
Some are of iron, to affront the gay,
And some of bronze, to satirize the
brave,
But most are merely a compost of clay
Cut in the sleepy features of a slave.
>> *Ibid. Sonnet 5*

There are sorceries more excellent
Than the first conflagration of the dust,
But none are quite so single in intent
Or unsophisticated with distrust.
The ripened fruit is golden to the core.
But an enchantment fosters it no more.
>> *Ibid. Sonnet 6*

American Muse, whose strong and diverse heart
So many men have tried to understand
But only made it smaller with their
art,
Because you are as various as your
land.
>> *John Brown's Body. Invocation*

Thames and all the rivers of the kings
Ran into Mississippi and were drowned.
>> *Ibid.*

Lincoln, six feet one in his stocking feet,
The lank man, knotty and tough as a
hickory rail,
Whose hands were always too big for
white-kid gloves,
Whose wit was a coonskin sack of dry,
tall tales,
Whose weathered face was homely as
a plowed field.
>> *Ibid. Book 2*

Honesty rare as a man without self-
pity,
Kindness as large and plain as a prairie
wind.
>> *Ibid.*

The Union's too big a horse to keep
changing the saddle
Each time it pinches you. As long as
you're sure

The saddle fits, you're bound to put up
　　with the pinches
And not keep fussing the horse.
　　　　John Brown's Body. Book 2

The small, dim noises, thousand-fold,
That all old houses and forests hold.
　　　　　　　　Ibid.

So many letters come to a War Depart-
　　ment,
One can hardly bother the clerks to
　　answer them all.
　　　　　　Ibid. Book 3

The ladies remember Butler for fifty
　　years . . .
Make war on the men — the ladies
　　have too-long memories.
　　　　　　Ibid. Book 4

Broad-streeted Richmond. . . .
The trees in the streets are old trees
　　used to living with people,
Family-trees that remember your
　　grandfather's name.
　　　　　　　　Ibid.

A little galled by Jefferson Davis . . .
He is not from Virginia, we never knew
　　his grandfather.
　　　　　　　　Ibid.

Whitman, with his sack of tobacco and
　　comfits,
Passing along the terrible, crowded
　　wards,
Listening, writing letters, trying to
　　breathe
Strong life into lead-colored lips.
　　　　　　　　Ibid.

Stonewall Jackson, wrapped in his
　　beard and his silence.
　　　　　　　　Ibid.

Comes Traveller and his master [Lee].
　　. . . Such horses are
The jewels of the horseman's hands and
　　thighs,
They go by the word and hardly need
　　the rein.
They bred such horses in Virginia then,
Horses that were remembered after
　　death
And buried not so far from Christian
　　ground.
　　　　　　　　Ibid.

A great victor, in defeat as great,
No more, no less, always himself in
　　both.
　　　　John Brown's Body. Book 4

The ant finds kingdoms in a foot of
　　ground.
　　　　　　　　Ibid.

Grant . . .
There is no brilliant lamp in that dogged
　　mind
And no conceit of brilliance to shake
　　the hand,
But hand and mind can use the tools
　　they get.
. . . The quiet, equable, deadly holder-
　　on,
Faded-brown as a cinnamon-bear in
　　Spring.
　　　　　　Ibid. Book 6

"Let us cross the river," he said, "and
　　rest under the shade of the trees." [1]
　　　　　　　　Ibid.

So, when the crowd gives tongue
And prophets, old or young,
Bawl out their strange despair
Or fall in worship there,
Let them applaud the image or con-
　　demn
But keep your distance and your soul
　　from them,
And, if the heart within your breast
　　must burst
Like a cracked crucible and pour its
　　steel
White-hot before the white heat of the
　　wheel,
Strive to recast once more
That attar of the ore
In the strong mold of pain
Till it is whole again,
And while the prophets shudder or
　　adore
Before the flame, hoping it will give
　　ear,
If you at last must have a word to say,
Say neither, in their way,
"It is a deadly magic and accursed,"
Nor "It is blest," but only "It is here."
　　　　Ibid. Book 8. Conclusion

[1] General "Stonewall" Jackson's last words
[May 10, 1863].

It is so they die on the plains, the great, old buffalo,
The herd-leaders, the beasts with the kingly eyes,
Innocent, curly-browed,
They sink to the earth like mountains, hairy and silent,
And their tongues are cut by the hunter. Oh, singing tongue!
Great tongue of bronze and salt and the free grasses,
Tongue of America, speaking for the first time,
Must the hunter have you at last?

Now, face to face, you saw him
And lifted the right arm once, as a pilot lifts it,
Signalling with the bell,
In the passage at night, on the river known yet unknown,
— Perhaps to touch his shoulder, perhaps in pain —
Then the rain fell on the roof and the twilight darkened
And they said that in death you looked like a marvelous old, wise child.
                    Ode to Walt Whitman. I
You're still the giant lode we quarry
For gold, fools' gold and all the earthy metals,
The matchless mine.
Still the trail-breaker, still the rolling river.
                    Ode to Walt Whitman. IV
Far north, far north are the sources of the great river,
The headwaters, the cold lakes,
By the little sweet-tasting brooks of the blond country,
The country of snow and wheat,
Or west among the black mountains, the glacial springs.
Far North and West they lie and few come to them.
                    Ibid.
Rolling, rolling from Arkansas, Kansas, Iowa,
Rolling from Ohio, Wisconsin, Illinois,
Rolling and shouting:
Till, at last, it is Mississippi,
The Father of Waters; the matchless; the great flood

Dyed with the earth of States; with the dust and the sun and the seed of half the States.
                    Ode to Walt Whitman. IV
I have fallen in love with American names,
The sharp names that never get fat,
The snakeskin-titles of mining-claims,
The plumed war-bonnet of Medicine Hat,
Tucson and Deadwood and Lost Mule Flat.
                    American Names
Did they never watch for Nantucket Light?
                    Ibid.
I shall not rest quiet in Montparnasse.
I shall not lie easy at Winchelsea.
You may bury my body in Sussex grass,
You may bury my tongue at Champmédy.
I shall not be there. I shall rise and pass.
Bury my heart at Wounded Knee.
                    Ibid.
Now grimy April comes again,
Maketh bloom the fire-escapes,
Maketh silvers in the rain,
Maketh winter coats and capes
Suddenly all worn and shabby
Like the fur of winter bears,
Maketh kittens, maketh baby,
Maketh kissing on the stairs.
Maketh bug crawl out of crack,
Maketh ticklings down the back
As if sunlight stroked the spine
To a hurdy-gurdy's whine
And the shower ran white wine.
                    For City Spring
April hieth, April spieth
Everywhere a lover lieth,
Bringeth sweetness, bringeth fever,
Will not stop at "I would liever,"
Will not heed, "Now God a mercy!"
Turneth Moral topsy-versy,
Bringeth he and she to bed,
Bringeth ill to maidenhead,
Bringeth joyance in its stead.
                    Ibid.
"It is eighteen years," I cried. "You must come no more."
"We know your names. We know that you are the dead.

Must you march forever from France
and the last, blind war?"
"Fool! From the next!" they said.

1936

ERNEST HEMINGWAY
[1898–   ]

A growing ecstasy of ordered, formal,
passionate, increasing disregard for
death. . . .

It is impossible to believe the emotional and spiritual intensity and pure,
classic beauty that can be produced by
a man, an animal, and a piece of scarlet
serge draped over a stick.

Death in the Afternoon. Chap. 18

All modern American literature comes
from one book by Mark Twain called
Huckleberry Finn. If you read it you
must stop where the Nigger Jim is
stolen from the boys. That is the real
end. The rest is just cheating. But it's
the best book we've had. All American
writing comes from that. There was
nothing before. There has been nothing
as good since.

The Green Hills of Africa. Chap. 1

Not this August, nor this September;
you have this year to do in what you
like. Not next August, nor next September; that is still too soon; they are
still too prosperous from the way things
pick up when armament factories start
at near capacity; they never fight as
long as money can still be made without. . . . But the year after that or
the year after that they fight.

Notes on the Next War [1]

The first panacea for a mismanaged
nation is inflation of the currency; the
second is war. Both bring a temporary
prosperity; both bring a permanent
ruin. But both are the refuge of political
and economic opportunists.

Ibid.

They wrote in the old days that it
is sweet and fitting to die for one's
country. But in modern war there is
nothing sweet nor fitting in your dying.
You will die like a dog for no good
reason.

Ibid.

[1] In *Esquire, Sept., 1935.*

DONALD CULROSS PEATTIE
[1898–   ]

It is natural that women should like
the birds whose domestic affairs can be
observed under the eaves; they love the
sweetest singers, the brightest plumage,
the species not too shy to be seen at
close range. For them the waders and
swimmers, the awkward of leg, the
harsh of cry, the wild of soul, have
seldom the same appeal. But that
which flees from men, that will men
have. Women of all people ought to
understand this, but they do not, quite.

An Almanac for Moderns.
November 9

In Thomas Henry Huxley Darwinism
had a champion in invincible armor.
For sheer glitter his mind has seldom
had an equal in any land or age and
he laid waste about him with the
weapon of truth. "The cradle of every
science," he chuckled, "is surrounded
by dead theologians as that of Hercules
was with strangled serpents."

Ibid. February 13

The beauty of a butterfly's wing, the
beauty of all things, is not a slave to
purpose, a drudge sold to futurity. It
is excrescence, superabundance, random
ebullience, and sheer delightful waste
to be enjoyed in its own high right.

Ibid. March 13

Life is adventure in experience, and
when you are no longer greedy for the
last drop of it, it means no more than
that you have set your face, whether
you know it or not, to the day when you
shall depart without a backward look.
Those who look backward longingly to
the end die young, at whatever age.

Ibid. March 18

The time to hear bird music is between four and six in the morning.
Seven o'clock is not too late, but by
eight the fine rapture is over, due, I
suspect, to the contentment of the inner man that comes with breakfast; a
poet should always be hungry or have
a lost love.

Ibid. April 22

RUTH PITTER

Towns and noblemen are made
By silly fortune's dole,
But birds, and they who wield the
    spade,
They are green England's singing soul.
                    The Realm. Stanza 4

When we have buried her, made her
    unseen,
    We will lie down and weep;
Our part is done; we have found her a
    green
    Quiet place wherein to sleep.
                    The Burial. Stanza 1

It was the mystery and the dark way
    That made them weep so sore;
They knew not whether she were grave
    or gay
    Or peaceful, or no more.
                    Ibid. Stanza 2

You are afraid. You do not dare
Up to the Lion to lift your eyes,
And unashamed his beauty share
    As once in that lost Paradise.
                    Caged Lion. Stanza 1

His maned neck of massy girth
Only one Arm in love enfolds:
His beauty humbled to the earth
Only my wrathful God beholds.
                    Ibid. Stanza 3

DOROTHY E. REID

A goosegirl ermined is a goosegirl still
And geese will gabble everywhere she
    goes.
                    Not in Andersen

I'll spend my time till midnight, sewing
Red flannel drawers for leprechauns!
                    Concession

There was a sunrise falling like red
    blood. . . .
And men and women creeping through
    the red
Of the marvellous city, could not quite
    deny
All day the life that startled them: they
    said
Beautiful things, and wept, and won-
    dered why.
                    Poem Carried as a Banner

HELENE MULLINS
[1899–   ]

The anxious and distrustful constantly
Require that their companions speak
    their praise,
Holding it as a gross discourtesy
If any disagree with them.
                    Only the Self-Confident

Only the stern self-confident can hold
Their peace amidst the clamor, nor be-
    tray
Their capabilities; can sit unmoved,
With all around them trembling to have
    told
The utmost of their merits; only they
Can bear to leave their strength un-
    guessed, unproved.
                    Ibid.

ELWYN BROOKS WHITE
[1899–   ]

The critic leaves at curtain fall
    To find, in starting to review it,
He scarcely saw the play at all
    For watching his reaction to it.
                    Critic

All poets who, when reading from
their own works, experience a choked
feeling, are major. For that matter, all
poets who read from their own works
are major, whether they choke or not.
All women poets, dead or alive, who
smoke cigars are major. All poets who
have sold a sonnet for one hundred and
twenty-five dollars to a magazine with
a paid circulation of four hundred thousand are major. A sonnet is composed
of fourteen lines; thus the payment in
this case is eight dollars and ninety-
three cents a line, which constitutes a
poet's majority.
                    How to Tell a Major Poet
                    from a Minor Poet

The truth is, it is fairly easy to tell
the two types apart; it is only when
one sets about trying to decide whether
what they write is any good or not that
the thing really becomes complicated.
                    Ibid.

"It's broccoli, dear."

"I say it's spinach, and I say the hell with it."

In The New Yorker

RICHARD HUGHES
[1900–   ]

Puddings should be
Full of currants, for me:
Boiled in a pail,
Tied in the tail
Of an old bleached shirt:
So hot that they hurt.

Poets, Painters, Puddings

I saw the World's arches,
The spreading roots of light,
The high wordy pillars
That hold all upright,
The deep verbal fundament
Whereon rests sure
The world on thoughtful vaulting,
Interlocked, secure.

Ecstatic Ode on Vision

MARTHA OSTENSO
[1900–   ]

Pity the Unicorn,
Pity the Hippogriff,
Souls that were never born
Out of the land of If!

The Unicorn and the Hippogriff.
Stanza 1

THOMAS WOLFE
[1900–   ]

He awakes at morning in a foreign land, he draws his breath in labor in the wool-soft air of Europe: the wool-gray air is all about him like a living substance; it is in his heart, his stomach, and his entrails; it is in the slow and vital movements of the people; it soaks down from the sodden skies into the earth, into the heavy buildings, into the limbs and hearts and brains of living men. . . .

It was there now; it will always be there. They had it in Merry England and they had it in Gay Paree; and they were seldom merry, and they were rarely gay. The wet, woolen air is over Munich; it is over Paris; it is over Rouen and Madame Bovary; it soaks into England; it gets into boiled mutton and the Brussels sprouts; it gets into Hammersmith on Sunday; it broods over Bloomsbury and the private hotels and the British Museum; it soaks into the land of Europe and keeps the grass green.

Of Time and the River. Book VII

Where can you match the mighty music of their names? — The Monongahela, the Colorado, the Rio Grande, the Columbia, the Tennessee, the Hudson (Sweet Thames!); the Kennebec, the Rappahannock, the Delaware, the Penobscot, the Wabash, the Chesapeake, the Swannanoa, the Indian River, the Niagara (Sweet Afton!); the Saint Lawrence, the Susquehanna, the Tombigbee, the Nantahala, the French Broad, the Chattahoochee, the Arizona, and the Potomac (Father Tiber!) — these are a few of their princely names, these are a few of their great, proud, glittering names, fit for the immense and lonely land that they inhabit.

Oh, Tiber! Father Tiber! You'd only be a suckling in that mighty land! And as for you, sweet Thames, flow gently till I end my song: flow gently, gentle Thames, be well-behaved, sweet Thames, speak softly and politely, little Thames, flow gently till I end my song.

Ibid.

It is Europeans, for the most part, who have constructed these great ships, but without America they have no meaning. These ships are alive with the supreme ecstasy of the modern world, which is the voyage to America. There is no other experience that is remotely comparable to it, in its sense of joy, its exultancy, its drunken and magnificent hope which, against reason and knowledge, soars into a heaven of fabulous conviction, which believes in the miracle and sees it invariably achieved.

In this soft, this somewhat languid air, the ship glowed like an immense and brilliant jewel. All of her lights were on, they burned row by row straight across her 900 feet of length, with the small, hard twinkle of cut gems: it was as if the vast, black cliff of her hull, which strangely suggested the glittering night-time cliff of the fabulous city that was her destination, had been sown with diamonds.

Of Time and the River. Book VIII

Out of one darkness the travellers have come to be taken into another, but for a moment one sees their faces, awful and still, all uplifted towards the ship. This is all: their words have vanished, all memory of the movements they made then has also vanished: one remembers only their silence and their still faces lifted in the phantasmal light of lost time; one sees them ever, still and silent, as they slide from darkness on the river of time; one sees them waiting at the ship's great side, all silent and all damned to die, with their grave, white faces lifted in a single supplication to the ship, and towards the silent row of passengers along the deck, who for a moment return their gaze with the same grave and tranquil stare. That silent meeting is a summary of all the meetings of men's lives.

Ibid.

ALAN PORTER

Every countenance
That warms and lights the heart of the
  beholder
Shews, clear and true, the signature of
  pain.

The Signature of Pain

"Good men have bags of money
And blazoned shields.
I wonder how much money
My new play yields?"
This is what Shakespeare said,
Wagging his wicked head,
Walking from Aldermanbury
To Bunhill Fields.

The Poet's Journey

Not being versed in argument
They killed the herald heaven had sent,
Taking the trouble to invent
An instrument,

A golden mechanical hammer, such
In size, he could not suffer much.

But warned by heaven,
Hours before,
He had deposited a pamphlet under
  every door.

The Transit of Joy

Let him that beds a princess fear
To show himself too free,
And ceremoniously draw near:
There should between true lovers be
An excellent immodesty.

A Plea That Shame Be Forgotten

I am not one that would be thinned
Into an immaterial wind:
I have no longing to be seen
A part of April's fledge of green,
Or burn where summer suns have been.

Death. Stanza 2

Were death forgotten, days were white
Circles of unimpaired delight.

Ibid. Stanza 4

ROY CAMPBELL
[1902–   ]

You praise the firm restraint with
  which they write —
I'm with you there, of course:
They use the snaffle and the curb all
  right,
But where's the bloody horse?

On Some South African Novelists

We had no time for make-believe
So early each began
To wear his liver on his sleeve,
To snarl, and be an angry man:
Far in the desert we have been
Where Nature, still to poets kind,
Admits no vegetable green
To soften the determined mind.

Poets in Africa. Stanza 2

Each like a freezing salamander
Impervious and immune,
No snivelling sentiment shall pander
To our flirtations with the moon,
And though with gay batrachian chir-
  rup
Her poets thrill the swampy reach,
Not with so glutinous a syrup

As moonlight shall we grease our
speech.
                    Poets in Africa. Stanza 4
With white tails smoking free,
Long streaming manes, and arching
    necks, they show
Their kinship to their sisters of the
    sea —
And forward hurl their thunderbolts of
    snow.
Still out of hardship bred,
Spirits of power and beauty and de-
    light
Have ever on such frugal pastures fed
And loved to course with tempests
    through the night.
                    Horses on the Camargue
I love to see, when leaves depart,
The clear anatomy arrive,
Winter, the paragon of art,
That kills all forms of life and feeling
Save what is pure and will survive.
                    Autumn

LANGSTON HUGHES [1]
[1902–   ]

De railroad bridge's
A sad song in de air.
Ever' time de trains pass
I wants to go somewhere.
                    Homesick Blues. Stanza 1
A bright bowl of brass is beautiful to
    the Lord.
Bright polished brass like the cymbals
Of King David's dancers,
Like the wine cups of Solomon.
        Hey, boy!
A clean spittoon on the altar of the
    Lord.
A clean bright spittoon all newly pol-
    ished, —
At least I can offer that.
        Com'mere, boy!
                    Brass Spittoons

[1] Working as a busboy in Washington, he
was discovered by Vachel Lindsay, who read
several of his poems to a fashionable audience
in the very hotel in which Hughes carried
trays of dishes. This incident attracted the
attention of the press of the country, and people who never would have glanced at the
poetry for its own sake became interested in
the career of so strange a singer. — Louis
Untermeyer: *Modern American Poetry*

CHARLES AUGUSTUS LINDBERGH
[1902–   ]

We (that's my ship and I) took off
rather suddenly. We had a report somewhere around 4 o'clock in the afternoon
before that the weather would be fine,
so we thought we would try it.
        Lindbergh's Own Story [of his
        non-stop flight, Long Island to
        Paris], in The New York Times,
        May 23, 1927
I saw a fleet of fishing boats. . . .
I flew down almost touching the craft
and yelled at them, asking if I was on
the right road to Ireland.
    They just stared. Maybe they didn't
hear me. Maybe I didn't hear them.
Or maybe they thought I was just a
crazy fool. An hour later I saw land.
                    Ibid.

OGDEN NASH
[1902–   ]

They have such refined and delicate
    palates
That they can discover no one worthy
    of their ballots,
And then when some one terrible gets
    elected
They say, There, that's just what I ex-
    pected!
                    Election Day Is a Holiday
I think that I shall never see
A billboard lovely as a tree.[1]

[1] Another parody of Kilmer's poem, often
quoted in trade journals (authorship already
uncertain?) runs as follows: —
I think that I shall never see
Aught lovely as a pulpwood tree.

A tree that grows through sunny noons
To furnish sporting page cartoons.

A tree whose girth will prove its age
Is ample for a want ad page.

A tree with grace toward heaven rising,
Men macerate for advertising.

A tree that lifts its arms and laughs,
To be made into paragraphs.

A tree that falls before the saw,
A five-star final in the raw.

Perhaps, unless the billboards fall,
I'll never see a tree at all.
> *Song of the Open Road*

The season when ordinarily kind-
hearted business men fill up their
pockets with cartridges
And go prowling around the woods in
search of caribous and partridges.
> *Ode to the N.W. by W. Wind*

In the phalanx of hy-
Phenated names!
(Have you ever observed
That the name of Smith
Is the oftenest hy-
Phenated with?)
> *Pride Goeth Before a Raise*

They take a paper and they read the
headlines,
So they've heard of unemployment and
they've heard of breadlines,
And they philanthropically cure them
all
By getting up a costume charity ball.
> *Ibid.*

There are some people who are very
resourceful
At being remorseful,
And who apparently feel that the best
way to make friends
Is to do something terrible and then
make amends.
> *Hearts of Gold*

Candy is dandy
But liquor is quicker.
> *Reflection on Ice-Breaking*

Some one invented the telephone,
And interrupted a nation's slumbers,
Ringing wrong but similar numbers.
> *Look What You Did, Christopher*

I wonder if the citizens of New York
will ever get sufficiently wroth
To remember that Tammany cooks
spoil the broth.
> *Speculative Reflection*

A regular poet published a book,
And an excellent book it was,
But nobody gave it a second look,
As nobody often does.
> *A Parable for Sports Writers. III*

One would be in less danger
From the wiles of the stranger

If one's own kin and kith
Were more fun to be with.
> *Family Court*

O money, money, money, I am not necessarily one of those who think
thee holy,
But I often stop to wonder how thou
canst go out so fast when thou
comest in so slowly.
> *Hymn to the Thing That Makes
> the Wolf Go*

Thanksgiving, like ambassadors, cabinet-officers and others smeared
with political ointment,
Depends for its existence on Presidential appointment.
> *A Short Outline of Thanksgiving*

If you are grateful for anything on any
particular day,
By the time you wake up next morning it's probably been taken away.
> *Ibid.*

This is the sum total of Thanksgiving
lore:
Not to be thankful until you're tired of
what you're being thankful for.
> *Ibid.*

The old men know when an old man
dies.
> *Old Men*

Yours be the genial holly wreaths,
The stockings and the tree;
An aged world to you bequeaths
Its own forgotten glee.
> *A Carol for Children. Stanza 2*

God rest you, merry Innocents,
While innocence endures.
A sweeter Christmas than we to ours
May you bequeath to yours.
> *Ibid. Stanza 9*

COUNTEE CULLEN
[1903–   ]

Not for myself I make this prayer,
But for this race of mine
That stretches forth from shadowed
places
Dark hands for bread and wine.
> *Pagan Prayer. Stanza 1*

She thinks that even up in heaven
Her class lies late and snores,

While poor black cherubs rise at seven
To do celestial chores.
Epitaph: A Lady I Know

MERRILL MOORE
[1903–   ]

Talking about men who are richer than
    they are
And telling how things that are might
    be otherwise
And looking out of the corners of their
    eyes
Are what old men inordinately like to
    do,

Men not so old that they have lost all
    care
For matters they used to pride them-
    selves about
But certainly long since past the find-
    ing out
Of whether these matters were or were
    not true.
Old Men

WILLIAM PLOMER
[1903–   ]

We saw, heraldic in the heat,
A scorpion on a stone.
The Scorpion

MacKINLAY KANTOR
[1904–   ]

I was a dog of Gettysburg. I trotted
    near the train
And nosed among the officers who
    kicked me to my pain.
A man came by . . . I could not see.
    I howled. The light was dim,
But when I brushed against his legs, I
    liked the smell of him.
Abraham Lincoln at Gettysburg.
Stanza 9

CECIL DAY LEWIS
[1905–   ]

I've heard them lilting at loom and
    belting,
Lasses lilting before dawn of day:

But now they are silent, not gamesome
    and gallant —
The flowers of the town are rotting
    away.[1]

There was laughter and loving in the
    lanes at evening;
Handsome were the boys then, and
    girls were gay.
But lost in Flanders by medalled com-
    manders
The lads of the village are vanished
    away.
A Time to Dance

Come, live with me and be my love,[2]
And we will all the pleasures prove
Of peace and plenty, bed and board,
That chance employment may afford.

I'll handle dainties on the docks
And thou shalt read of summer frocks:
At evening by the sour canals
We'll hope to hear some madrigals.
Ibid.

Stake out your claim. Go downwards.
    Bore
Through the tough crust. Oh learn to
    feel
A way in darkness to good ore.
You are the magnet and the steel.

Out of that dark a new world flowers.
There in the womb, in the rich veins
Are tools, dynamos, bridges, towers,
Your tractors and your travelling-
    cranes.
The Magnetic Mountain. 28

Make us a wind
To shake the world out of this sleepy
    sickness
Where flesh has dwindled and bright-
    ness waned!
New life multiple in seed and cell
Mounts up to brace our slackness.

[1] I've heard them lilting at our ewe-milking,
    Lasses a-lilting before dawn o' day;
  But now they are moaning on ilka green
    loaning:
    "The Flowers of the Forest are a' wede
    away."
            JANE ELLIOTT [1727–1805]:
            A Lament for Flodden
            (September 9, 1513)
See Cockburn, page 240.
  [2] See Marlowe, page 31.

Oppression's passion, a full organ swell
Through our throats welling wild
Of angers in unison arise
And hunger haunted with a million
 sighs,
Make us a wind to shake the world!
> *The Magnetic Mountain. 31*

Spring through death's iron guard
Her million blades shall thrust;
Love that was sleeping, not extinct,
Throw off the nightmare crust.

Eyes, though not ours, shall see
Sky-high a signal flame,
The sun returned to power above
A world, but not the same.
> *Ibid. 35*

The Georgian poets, a sadly pedestrian rabble, flocked along the roads their fathers had built, pointing out to each other the beauty spots and ostentatiously drinking small-beer in a desperate effort to prove their virility. The winds blew, the floods came: for a moment a few of them showed on the crest of the seventh great wave; then they were rolled under and nothing marks their graves. One only rode the whirlwind: Wilfrid Owen, killed on the Sambre canal, spoke above the barrage and the gas-cloud, saying to us, 'The poetry is in the pity.' When it was all over, it was left to an American, T. S. Eliot, to pick up some of the fragments of civilization, place them end to end, and on that crazy pavement walk precariously through the waste land.
> *A Hope for Poetry* [*1934*]

Writers of my own generation are interested in politics to an extent unequalled among English writers since the French Revolution.
> *The Revolution in Literature*
> [*1936*]

WYSTAN HUGH AUDEN
[1907–   ]

A host of columbines and pathics
Who show the poor by mathematics
 In their defence
That wealth and poverty are merely
Mental pictures, so that clearly

Every tramp's a landlord really
 In mind-events.

Let fever sweat them till they tremble
Cramp rack their limbs till they resemble
 Cartoons by Goya:
Their daughters sterile be in rut,
May cancer rot their herring gut,
The circular madness on them shut,
 Or paranoia.
> *On This Island. XIV*

Cathedrals,
Luxury liners laden with souls,
Holding to the east their hulls of stone,
> *Ibid. XVII*

The poet reciting to Lady Diana
While the footmen whisper 'Have a
 banana,'
The judge enforcing the obsolete law,
The banker making the loan for the
 war,

The expert designing the long-range
 gun
To exterminate everyone under the sun,
Would like to get out but can only
 mutter; —
'What can I do? It's my bread and
 butter.'
> *Ibid. XVIII*

Underneath the abject willow,
 Lover, sulk no more;
Act from thought should quickly follow:
 What is thinking for?
Your unique and moping station
 Proves you cold;
 Stand up and fold
Your map of desolation.
> *Ibid. XXII*

O for doors to be open and an invite
 with gilded edges
To dine with Lord Lobcock and Count
 Asthma on the platinum benches,
With the somersaults and fireworks, the
 roast and the smacking kisses —
 Cried the cripples to the silent
 statue,
 The six beggared cripples.
> *Ibid. XXIV*

GEORGE DILLON
[1907–   ]

When love was false and I was full of
    care,
And friendship cold and I was sick with
    fear,
Music, the beautiful disturber of the
    air,
Drew near,
Saying: Come with me into my country
    of air
Out of the querulous and uncivil clay;
Fling down its aching members into a
    chair,
And come away.
The Constant One. Stanzas 1 and 2

EDWARD DORO
[1909–   ]

I was eleven, hardly more,
    When first I saw a crystal boar,
Stretched on the ground in self-admir-
    ing fettle,
With purple eyes and snout of golden
    metal —
Polished by digging roots — and bones
    of coral.
Looking, I deemed he was a thing im-
    moral,
Something a boy should never see.
I turned and ran, precipitously.
The Boar and Shibboleth. Stanza 1
I was thrown for ever in a riot
Of gold and purple thoughts. I wait in
    quiet.
    Sometimes I say beneath my breath
    The lovely name of Shibboleth.
Ibid. Stanza 10

STEPHEN SPENDER
[1909–   ]

Central 'I' is surrounded by 'I eating',
'I loving', 'I angry', 'I excreting',
And the 'great I' planted in him
Has nothing to do with all these,

It can never claim its true place
Resting in the forehead, and secure in
    his gaze.
The 'great I' is an unfortunate intruder

Quarrelling with 'I tiring' and 'I sleep-
    ing'
And all those other 'I's who long for
'We dying'.
Poems. 9

I think continually of those who were
    truly great.
Who, from the womb, remembered the
    soul's history
Through corridors of light where the
    hours are suns
Endless and singing. Whose lovely am-
    bition
Was that their lips, still touched with
    fire,
Should tell of the Spirit clothed from
    head to foot in song.
Ibid. 30

After the first powerful plain manifesto
The black statement of pistons, with-
    out more fuss
But gliding like a queen, she leaves the
    station.
Without bowing and with restrained
    unconcern
She passes the houses which humbly
    crowd outside,
The gasworks and at last the heavy
    page
Of death, printed by gravestones in the
    cemetery.
Beyond the town there lies the open
    country
Where, gathering speed, she acquires
    mystery,
The luminous self-possession of ships
    on ocean.
Ibid. 34, The Express

NATHALIA CRANE
[1913–   ]

Oh, I'm in love with the janitor's boy,
    And the janitor's boy loves me;
He's going to hunt for a desert isle
    In our geography.
The Janitor's Boy. Stanza 1
I linger on the flathouse roof, the moon-
    light is divine.
But my heart is all a-flutter like the
    washing on the line.
The Flathouse Roof. Stanza 1

Once a pallid vestal
  Doubted truth in blue;
Listed red as ruin,
  Harried every hue.
                    The Vestal. Stanza 1

Every gaudy color
  Is a bit of truth.
                    Ibid. Stanza 5

In the darkness, who would answer for
  the color of a rose,
Or the vestments of the May moth and
  the pilgrimage it goes?
                    The Blind Girl. Stanza 1

I sat down on a bumble bee,
  But I arose again;

And now I know the tenseness of
  Humiliating pain.
                    Suffering. Stanza 3

The steps of the paper-box factory,
As well as the gardens of kings
Are only the blue-print devices
Of love, and the commonplace things.
                    The Commonplace. Stanza 6

When the moon comes over Brooklyn
  On time with the borough clock,
'Tis the same that saw Palmyra
  And the walls of Antioch.
                    The Moon of Brooklyn. Stanza 1

There is a glory
  In a great mistake.
                    Imperfection

MISCELLANEOUS

WALTER DE MAP
[1140–1210]

Die I must, but let me die drinking in
an inn!
Hold the wine-cup to my lips sparkling
from the bin!
So, when angels flutter down to take
me from my sin,
"Ah, God have mercy on this sot," the
cherubs will begin.[1]

> *Quoted by* J. R. GREEN, *in A
> Short History of the English
> People, Chap. 3, Sect. 1 (There
> is also a translation by Leigh
> Hunt: "The Jovial Priest's Con-
> fession.")*

MARTHA ("MOTHER")
SHIPTON
[1488–1561]

Carriages without horses shall go,
And accidents fill the world with woe.
> *Prophecy*

Around the world thoughts shall fly
In the twinkling of an eye.
> *Ibid.*

Under water men shall walk,
Shall ride, shall sleep, and talk;
In the air men shall be seen
In white, in black, and in green.
> *Ibid.*

Iron in the water shall float
As easy as a wooden boat.
> *Ibid.*

WILLIAM, PRINCE OF
ORANGE
[1533–1584]

There is one certain means by which

I can be sure never to see my country's
ruin, — I will die in the last ditch.[1]
> HUME: *History of England
> [1622] and* J. R. GREEN: *A
> Short History of the English
> People, Chap. 9*

ROBERT GREENE
[1560–1592]

Sweet are the thoughts that savour of
content;
The quiet mind is richer than a
crown. . . .
A mind content both crown and kingdom is.
> *Farewell to Folly*

RICHARD BRATHWAITE
[1588–1673]

Hanging of his cat on Monday
For killing of a mouse on Sunday.[2]
> *Drunken Barnabee's Four Journeys.
> Page 5 [1805 edition]*

KING CHARLES II
[1630–1685]

Good as a play.[3]
> *Exclamation in Parliament, dur-
> ing the discussion of Lord Ross's
> Divorce Bill*

---

[1] Buckingham had urged the inevitable destruction which hung over the United Provinces, and asked the Prince whether he did not
see that the commonwealth was ruined.
[2] For killing of the Lord's own mouse
   Upon the Sabbath-day.
   ANONYMOUS: *The Cameronian Cat,*
   St. 4 (written between 1642 and 1684)
[3] The king remained in the House of Peers
while his speech was taken into consideration,
— a common practice with him; for the debates amused his sated mind, and were sometimes, he used to say, as good as a comedy. — MACAULAY: *Review of the Life and
Writings of Sir William Temple*
   Nullos his mallem ludos spectasse (No
plays would I prefer to have seen than
these). — HORACE: *Satires, II, 8, 79*

---

[1] The Latin version concludes:
   *Tunc cantabunt laetius angelorum chori
   Deus sit propitius isti potatori.*

JOHN DYER
[*Floruit* 1714]

While wine and friendship crown the
    board,
We'll sing the joys that both afford;
And he that won't with us comply,
Down among the dead men let him lie.
       Down Among the Dead Men.
                Stanza 3

LORD CHARLES HAY
[? –1760]

Gentlemen of the French guard, fire
first.[1]
    At the Battle of Fontenoy [*1745*]

JOSIAH WEDGWOOD
[1730–1795]

Am I not a man and brother?
      On a Medallion [2] [*1787*]

WILLIAM DRENNAN
[1754–1820]

Nor one feeling of vengeance presume
    to defile
The cause, or the men, of the Emerald
    Isle.[3]
      Erin. Stanza 3 [*1795*]

R. S. SHARPE
[1759–1835]

In two little words all the difference lies,
I always say "come," and you always
    say "go." . . .
You say "go" to your man, as you lay
    in your bed,
I say, "Come, Jack, with me," and I see
    the work done.
      Come and Go. Stanzas 7 and 8

---

[1] To which the Comte d'Auteroches replied,
"Sir, we never fire first; please to fire yourselves." — EDOUARD FOURNIER [1819–1880]:
L'Esprit dans l'Histoire
[2] Representing a Negro in chains, with one
knee on the ground and both hands lifted up
to heaven. This was adopted as a seal by the
Anti-Slavery Society of London.
[3] The first known use of this appellation for
Ireland.

MASON LOCKE WEEMS
[1759–1825]

"George," said his father, "do you
know who killed that beautiful little
cherry tree yonder in the garden?" . . .
Looking at his father with the sweet
face of youth brightened with the inexpressible charm of all-conquering
truth, he bravely cried out, "I can't tell
a lie, Pa; you know I can't tell a lie. I
did cut it with my hatchet."
      The Life of George Washing-
      ton: With Curious Anecdotes.
      Equally Honorable to Himself
      and Exemplary to His Young
      Countrymen

SCROPE DAVIES
[1771–1852]

Babylon in all its desolation is a sight
not so awful as that of the human mind
in ruins.
      Letter to Thomas Raikes
            [May 25, 1835]

JOHN SINCLAIR
[1791–1857]

A man, whose name was Johnny Sands,
    Had married Betty Haigh,
And though she brought him gold and
    lands,
    She proved a terrible plague.
      Johnny Sands. Stanza 1

JOHN HAMILTON REYNOLDS
("PETER CORCORAN")
[1796–1852]

Throw in his hat, and with a spring
Get gallantly within the ring.
      The Fancy: Poetry of the
            Pugilistic Club

HOWARD FISH

The good but pine; the order of the day
Is — prey on others, or become a
prey. . . .

With which, who will not readily comply,
But rates a vagrant, and as such may
die.
                The Wrongs of Man [1] *[1819]*

ALFRED AINGER
[1837–1904]

Our English critics their dull wits keep
straining,
When — Enter Taine! [2] — and all is
entertaining.
                                    Epigram

ELIZABETH WORDSWORTH
[1840– ?]

If all good people were clever,
  And all clever people were good,
The world would be nicer than ever
  We thought that it possibly could.

But somehow, 'tis seldom or never
  The two hit it off as they should;
The good are so harsh to the clever,
  The clever so rude to the good.
                The Clever and the Good

BARTLEY CAMPBELL
[1843–1888]

Rags are royal raiment when worn
for virtue's sake. [3]
                The White Slave [1882]

JARRETT AND PALMER
[*Flourished* 1866]

Legs are staple articles and will never
go out of fashion while the world lasts.
  *Of the original production [1866]
  of their Grand Magical Spectacu-
  lar Drama, The Black Crook, by
  Charles M. Barras*

[1] Painted by a vandal on Grant's Tomb,
New York, August 28, 1932.
[2] Hippolyte Taine [1828–1893], famous
French critic and historian of literature.
[3] The line is carved on Campbell's monument in St. Mary's Cemetery, Pittsburgh, Pa.

MRS. EDWARD CRASTER

The centipede was happy quite
  Until a toad in fun
Said, "Pray, which leg goes after
  which?"
That worked her mind to such a pitch,
She lay distracted in a ditch,
  Considering how to run.
        *Credited, in Cassell's Weekly, to
          Pinafore Poems* [1871]

LORD NANCY

To have a thing is nothing, if you've not
  the chance to show it,
And to know a thing is nothing, unless
  others know you know it.
                        Source unknown

KING GEORGE V
[1865–1936]

If I may be regarded as in some true
sense the head of this great and wide-
spread family, sharing its life and sustained by its affection, this will be a full
reward for the long and sometimes anxious labours of my reign.
        *Radio greeting to the British Em-
          pire [Christmas Day, 1934]*

THE REVEREND CORNELIUS
WHAURR

In this imperfect, gloomy scene
  Of complicated ill,
How rarely is a day serene,
  The throbbing bosom still!
Will not a beauteous landscape bright
  Or music's soothing sound,
Console the heart, afford delight,
  And throw sweet peace around?
They may; but never comfort lend
Like an Accomplished Female Friend!
        *The Female Friend. Stanza 1
        (Quoted by E. V. Lucas and
        J. C. Squire; source unknown)*

But lasting joys the man attend
Who has a Polished Female Friend!
                        Ibid. Stanza 3

BURTON J. HENDRICK
[1871–   ]

It is now a commonplace that the dissenting opinions of one generation become the prevailing interpretation of the next.

Bulwark of the Republic, Page 417

RUSSELL HILLARD LOINES
[1874–1922]

"Scorn not the sonnet," though its
  strength be sapped,
  Nor say malignant its inventor blundered:
The corpse that here in fourteen lines is
  wrapped
  Had otherwise been covered with a
  hundred.

On a Magazine Sonnet

FRANK ALOYSIUS ROBERT TINNEY
[1878–   ]

I ain't going to have more than three children, I read in an almanac that every fourth person born into the world is a Chinaman.

Vaudeville quip

BRUCE BAIRNSFATHER
[1887–   ]

If you know a better 'ole, go to it.

*Caption of famous cartoon
during the Great War*

ROBERT LEROY RIPLEY
[1893–   ]

Believe it or not.

*Title of syndicated
newspaper feature*

KING GEORGE VI
[1895–   ]

The highest of distinctions is service to others.

*Broadcast greeting to his em-
pire after his coronation, May
12, 1937*

In the years yet to come, some of you will travel from one part of the commonwealth to another and, moving thus within the family circle, will meet many whose thoughts are colored by the same memories, whose hearts unite in devotion to our common heritage.

Ibid.

G. L. HEMMINGER

Tobacco is a dirty weed. I like it.
It satisfies no normal need. I like it.
It makes you thin, it makes you lean,
It takes the hair right off your bean.
It's the worst darn stuff I've ever seen.
  I like it.

*First published in Penn State
Froth, November, 1915*

All the brothers were valiant,[1] and all the sisters virtuous.

*From the inscription on the tomb of
the Duchess of Newcastle in Westminster Abbey*

Art and part.

A Scottish law phrase, an accessory before and after the fact. A man is said to be *art and part* of a crime when he contrives the manner of the deed, and concurs with and encourages those who commit the crime, although he does not put his own hand to the actual execution of it. — SCOTT: *Tales of a Grand-father, Chap. 22* (Execution of Morton)

Art preservative of all arts.

From the inscription upon the façade of the house in Haarlem, Holland, formerly occupied by Laurens Koster (or Coster), who is credited, among others, with the invention of printing with movable types, about 1440 or 1446. Mention is first made of this inscription about 1628:

MEMORIAE SACRUM
TYPOGRAPHIA
ARS ARTIUM OMNIUM
CONSERVATRIX.
HIC PRIMUM INVENTA
CIRCUM ANNUM MCCCCXL.[2]

[1] Title of a novel [1919] by Ben Ames Williams.
[2] Compare inscription on the "Printer's Sun-Dial" at the Country Life Press (Doubleday, Doran and Company), Garden City,

Begging the question.

This is a common logical fallacy, *petitio principii;* and the first explanation of the phrase is to be found in Aristotle's *Topica, VIII, 13,* where the five ways of begging the question are set forth. The earliest English work in which the expression is found is *The Arte of Logike plainlie set forth in our English Tongue, &c.* [1584].

Bitter end.

This phrase is somewhat ambiguous as now used. The older form, "better end," was used to designate a crisis, or a moment of extremity. When in a gale a vessel has paid out all her cable, her cable has run out to the "better end," — the end which is secured within the vessel and little used. Robinson Crusoe, in describing the terrible storm in Yarmouth Roads, says: "We rode with two anchors ahead, and the cables veered out to the better end." CHAUCER, *Canterbury Tales, The Squieres Tale, Line 224,* says: "They demen gladly to the badder ende," Skeat's glossary giving "worse" as the definition for "badder."

Cockles of the heart.

R. G. Latham [1812–1888], English philologist, wrote that the most probable explanation of the phrase lies (1) in the likeness of the heart to a cockleshell, — the base of the former being compared to the hinge of the latter; (2) in the zoological name for the cockle and its congeners, *Cardium* (heart). A contemporary explanation [1936] is the comparison of the cockle, or fire chamber, of the furnace with the chambers (ventricles and auricles) of the heart, hence, to warm the cockles of the heart. See Cervantes, page 1039.

N. Y. Authorship uncertain, perhaps the late WALTER GILLISS:
O measure of Time! Thou merest mite
  Within the endless providence of God:
May thy unerring finger ever point
  To those who printed first the written word.

Consistency, thou art a jewel.

A popular saying, like "Be good, and you will be happy," or "Virtue is its own reward," that, like Topsy, just "growed." From the earliest times it has been the popular tendency to call this or that cardinal virtue, or bright and shining excellence, a jewel, by way of emphasis. For example, Iago says:
> "*Good name,* in man or woman, dear my lord,
>   Is the immediate *jewel* of their souls."

Shakespeare elsewhere calls experience a "jewel." Miranda says her modesty is the "jewel" in her dower; and in *All's Well that Ends Well,* Diana terms her chastity the "jewel" of her house. — R. A. WIGHT

O discretion, thou art a jewel! — *The Skylark, a Collection of Well-chosen Songs* [London, 1772]

Dead as Chelsea.

To get Chelsea, to obtain the benefit of that hospital (for old soldiers). "Dead as Chelsea, by God!" an exclamation uttered by a grenadier at Fontenoy, 1745, on having his leg carried away by a cannon-ball. — *Dictionary of the Vulgar Tongue,* quoted by BRADY in *Varieties of Literature* [1826]

Dirty work at the crossroads.

Notes and Queries (London) attributes this to WALTER MELVILLE's melodrama *The Girl Who Took the Wrong Turning, or No Wedding Bells for Him.*

Don't sell America short.

Modern Version of J. P. MORGAN's saying, "Never be a bear on the United States." See MARK SULLIVAN: *Our Times,* II, 318.

Doesn't amount to Hannah Cook.

A saying common in Maine and on Cape Cod, Massachusetts, variously explained as a character who once lived on Campobello Island; a corruption of a phrase in Indian dialect; and a comparison with the worthlessness (for navigation) of a cook on board ship.

Drive a coach and six through an Act of Parliament.

Credited to Sir Stephen Rice [1637–1715], who became Chief Baron of the Exchequer, by MACAULAY in *History of England, Chap. 12*

During good behaviour.

That after the said limitation shall take effect, . . . judge's commissions be made *quando se bene gesserit.* — *Statutes 12 and 13, William III, Chap. 2, Sect. 3*

FIFTH OF NOVEMBER
(GUY FAWKES' DAY)

Don't you remember
The fifth of November,
The Gunpowder treason and Plot?

Ballad, chanted on "Pope Day" in Boston [1774]. Quoted in *The History and Antiquities of Boston* by SAMUEL GARDNER DRAKE [1798–1875], from TUDOR'S *Life of Otis*.

Free soil, free men, free speech, Frémont.

Rallying cry of the Republican Party in 1856, when John Charles Frémont [1813–1890], "the Pathfinder," was the party's candidate for the presidency.

Gentle craft.

According to John Brady [died 1814], in *Clavis Calendaria* [1812], this designation arose from the fact that in an old romance, a prince named Crispin is made to exercise, in honour of his namesake, Saint Crispin, the trade of shoemaking. There is a tradition that King Edward IV, in one of his disguises, once drank with a party of shoemakers, and pledged them. The story is alluded to in the old play of *George a-Greene* [1599]:
Marry, because you have drank with the King,
And the King hath so graciously pledged you,
You shall no more be called shoemakers;

But you and yours, to the world's end,
Shall be called the trade of the gentle craft.

The goose hangs high.

Originally, perhaps, "the goose *honks* high," — it cries and flies high. Wild geese fly higher when the weather is fine or promises to be fine. Hence, the prospects are bright; everything is favourable. — *Century Dictionary*

Another explanation is that in some parts of the country a goose is hung high to season, and denotes that a feast of roast goose will soon be ready.

The Great White Way.

Title of a play (1901) by ALBERT BIGELOW PAINE [1861–1937], which was adopted as a name for Broadway and the theatrical district of New York.

Hot afternoons have been in Montana.

Title of a prize-winning poem by ELI SIEGEL, published in *The Nation*, New York, 1925.

The man on horseback.

Applied to General Georges Ernest Jean Marie Boulanger [1837–1891].

Nisi suadeat intervallis (Unless he recommends delays).

Used by Henry De Bracton [died 1268] in Folio 1243 and Folio 420 b; Register Original, 267 a.

Nothing succeeds like success.

A French proverb, *Rien ne réussit comme le succès,* quoted by DUMAS in *Ange Pitou, Vol. I, P. 72* [*1854*].

Paying through the nose.

Grimm says that Odin had a poll-tax which was called in Sweden a nose-tax; it was a penny per nose, or poll. — *Deutsche Rechts Alterthümer*

Rebellion to tyrants is obedience to God.

From an inscription on the cannon near which the ashes of President Bradshaw were lodged, on the top of a high hill near Martha Bay in Jamaica. — EZRA STILES: *History of the Three Judges of King Charles I*

This supposititious epitaph was found among the papers of Mr. Jefferson, and in his handwriting. It was supposed to be one of Dr. Franklin's spirit-stirring inspirations. — H. S. RANDALL: *Life of Jefferson, Vol. III, Page 585*

Rest and be thankful.

Inscription on a stone seat on the top of one of the Highlands in Scotland. It is the title of one of Wordsworth's poems.

Roland for an Oliver.

These were the two most famous of Charlemagne's paladins, and their exploits are rendered so ridiculously and equally extravagant by the old romancers, that from them arose the saying, to signify matching one incredible lie with another, giving tit for tat, as good as one receives. In *King Henry VI, Part I, Act I, Sc. 2, Line 30*, SHAKESPEARE says [in 1589]:
England all Olivers and Rowlands bred
During the time Edward the Third did
    reign.

Sister Anne, do you see any one coming?

The anxious cry of Fatima, one of the wives of Bluebeard.

The public be damned.

William H. Vanderbilt [1821–1885], reply to a newspaper reporter. There are various versions of the occasion of this remark. See MELVILLE E. STONE: *Fifty Years a Journalist, Page 116*, and GUSTAVUS MYERS: *History of the Great American Fortunes*, Modern Library Giant edition, *Page 344*.

The woods are full of them.

Alexander Wilson [1766–1813], in the Preface to his *American Ornithology* [1808], quotes these words and relates the story of a boy who had been gathering flowers. On bringing them to his mother, he said: "Look, my dear ma! What beautiful flowers I have found growing in our place! Why, all the woods are full of them!"

Wisdom of many and the wit of one.

Definition of a proverb which Lord John Russell gave one morning at breakfast at Mardock's, — "One man's wit, and all men's wisdom." — *Memoirs of Sir James Mackintosh* [1765–1832], *Vol. I, Page 473*

Wooden walls of England.

The credite of the Realme, by defending the same with our Wodden Walles, as Themistocles called the Ships of Athens. — Preface to the English translation of Linschoten (London).

Worry, the interest paid by those who borrow trouble.
    GEORGE WASHINGTON LYON
    [*1879–*   ], *in Judge, March 1, 1924*

But me no buts.
    FIELDING: *Rape upon Rape, Act II, Sc. 2.* AARON HILL: *Snake in the Grass, Sc. 1*
Cause me no causes.
    MASSINGER: *A New Way to Pay Old Debts, Act I, Sc. 3*
Clerk me no clerks.
    SCOTT: *Ivanhoe, Chap. XX*
Diamond me no diamonds! prize me no prizes!
    TENNYSON: *Idylls of the King. Elaine, Line 402*
Dick me no Dicks.
    F. FRANKFORT MOORE: *Nell Gwyn, in The Chap-Book, March 15, 1896*
End me no ends.
    MASSINGER: *A New Way to Pay Old Debts, Act V, Sc. 1*

Fool me no fools.
> BULWER: *Last Days of Pompeii,*
> *Book III, Chap. VI*

Front me no fronts.
> FORD: *The Lady's Trial,*
> *Act II, Sc. 1*

Grace me no grace, nor uncle me no uncle.
> SHAKESPEARE: *Richard II,*
> *Act II, Sc. 3, Line 87*

Madam me no madam.
> DRYDEN: *The Wild Gallant,*
> *Act II, Sc. 2*

Map me no maps.
> FIELDING: *Rape upon Rape,*
> *Act I, Sc. 5*

Midas me no Midas.
> DRYDEN: *The Wild Gallant,*
> *Act II, Sc. 1*

Miracle me no Miracles.
> CERVANTES: *Don Quixote,*
> *Part II, Book III, Chap. 3*

O me no O's.
> BEN JONSON: *The Case Is*
> *Altered, Act V, sc. 1*

Parish me no parishes.
> PEELE: *The Old Wives' Tale*

Petition me no petitions.
> FIELDING: *Tom Thumb, Act I, Sc. 2*

Play me no plays.
> FOOTE: *The Knight, Act II*

Plot me no plots.
> BEAUMONT AND FLETCHER: *The*
> *Knight of the Burning Pestle,*
> *Act II, Sc. 5*

Sirrah me no sirrahs.
> LONGFELLOW: *The New England*
> *Tragedies, Act III, Sc. 1*

Thank me no thankings, nor proud me no prouds.
> SHAKESPEARE: *Romeo and Juliet,*
> *Act III, Sc. 5, Line 153*

Virgin me no virgins.
> MASSINGER: *A New Way to Pay*
> *Old Debts, Act III, Sc. 3*

Vow me no vows.
> BEAUMONT AND FLETCHER: *Wit*
> *without Money, Act IV, Sc. 4*

THE NEW ENGLAND PRIMER [1]

In Adam's fall
We sinned all.

My Book and Heart
Must never part.

Young Obadias,
David, Josias, —
All were pious.

Peter denied
His Lord, and cryed.

Young Timothy
Learnt sin to fly.

Xerxes did die,
And so must I.

Zaccheus he
Did climb the tree
Our Lord to see.

Our days begin with trouble here,
  Our life is but a span,
And cruel death is always near,
  So frail a thing is man.

Now I lay me down to take my sleep,[2]
I pray the Lord my soul to keep;
If I should die before I wake,
I pray the Lord my soul to take.

His wife, with nine small children and one at the breast, following him to the stake.
> *Martyrdom of John Rogers,*
> *Burned at Smithfield, Febru-*
> *ary 14, 1554* [3]

[1] As early as 1691, Benjamin Harris, of Boston, advertised as in press the second impression of the *New England Primer*. The oldest copy known to be extant is dated 1737.

[2] The first record of this prayer is found in the *Enchiridion Leonis* [A. D. 1160]. In the earliest edition of the *Primer*, the prayer is given as above, which is copied from the reprint of 1777. In the edition of 1784 it is altered to read, "Now I lay me down to sleep." In the edition of 1814, the second line of the prayer reads, "I pray thee, Lord, my soul to keep."

[3] The correct date is Feb. 4, 1555.

EPITAPHS

A house she hath, 'tis made of such good
    fashion,
The tenant ne'er shall pay for repara-
    tion,
Nor will the landlord ever raise her rent
Or turn her out of doors for non-pay-
    ment;
From chimney-tax this cell is free,
To such a house who would not tenant
    be?
> *For Rebecca Bogess, Folkestone,*
> *August 22, 1688*

It is so soon that I am done for,
I wonder what I was begun for.
> *For a child aged three weeks,*
> *Cheltenham Churchyard*

She tasted of life's bitter cup,
Refused to drink the potion up;
She turned her little head aside,
Disgusted with the task and died.
> *For a child aged six months*

Here lies John Knott:
His father was Knott before him,
He lived Knott, died Knott,
Yet underneath this stone doth lie
Knott christened, Knott begot,
And here he lies and still is Knott.
> *Perthshire Churchyard*

Here lie I, Martin Elginbrodde:
Ha'e mercy o' my soul, Lord God,
As I wad do, were I Lord God
And ye were Martin Elginbrodde.
> *Aberdeen Churchyard (Quoted*
> *by* GEORGE MACDONALD *in his*
> *novel, David Elginbrod* [*1862*],
> *Chap. 13*)

A dying preacher I have been,
To dying hearers such as you.
Though dead, a preacher still I am
To such as come my grave to view.
Let this to you a warning be
That quickly you must follow me.
> *Elder Samuel Waldo, South*
> *Dover (Wingdale) Cemetery,*
> *Dutchess County, New York,*
> *September 10, 1798*

The Queene was brought by water to
    White-hall,
At every stroake the oares teares let
    fall:
More clung about the Barge, fish under
    water
Wept out their eyes of pearle, and
    swome blinde after.
I think the Barge-men might with eas-
    ier thighes
Have rowed her thither in her peoples
    eyes,
For how so ere, thus much my thoughts
    have scand,
She'd come by water, had she come by
    land.
> *Epitaph for Queen Elizabeth,*
> *who ended this transitory life at*
> *Richmond 24 of March, 1602,*
> *the 45 yeare of her Raigne, and*
> *seventy of her age.* WILLIAM
> CAMDEN [*1551–1623*]: *Re-*
> *maines Concerning Britaine, 5th*
> *edn.* [*1637*], *Page 393*

A zealous Lock-Smith dyed of late,
And did arrive at heaven gate,
He stood without and would not knocke,
Because he meant to picke the locke.
> *Epitaph upon a Puritanicall*
> *Lock-Smith. Ibid. Page 408*

Man is a glasse, life is as water
That's weakely wall'd about:
Sinne brings in death, death breakes the
    glasse,
So runnes the water out.
> *Mans Life. Ibid. Page 414*

Here lies Sir Jenkin Grout, who loved
his friend, and persuaded his enemy:
what his mouth ate, his hand paid for:
what his servants robbed, he restored:
if a woman gave him pleasure, he supported her in pain: he never forgot his
children: and whoso touched his finger,
drew after it his whole body.
> *Quoted by* RALPH WALDO EM-
> ERSON *in his Essay, Manners*

This is the grave of Mike O'Day
Who died maintaining his right of way.
His right was clear, his will was strong,
But he's just as dead as if he'd been
    wrong.
> *Modern*

OF UNKNOWN AUTHORSHIP

JUNIUS

One precedent creates another. They soon accumulate and constitute law. What yesterday was fact, to-day is doctrine.

> *The Letters of Junius.*[1] *Dedication to the English Nation*

The liberty of the press is the Palladium of all the civil, political, and religious rights of an Englishman.

> *Ibid.*

These are the gloomy companions of a disturbed imagination; the melancholy madness of poetry, without the inspiration.[2]

> *Ibid. VII, To Sir William Draper* [*March 3, 1769*]

There are some hereditary strokes of character by which a family may be as clearly distinguished as by the blackest features of the human face.

> *Ibid. XII, To the Duke of Grafton* [*May 30, 1769*]

I do not give you to posterity as a pattern to imitate, but as an example to deter.

> *Ibid.*

I believe there is yet a spirit of resistance in this country, which will not submit to be oppressed; but I am sure there is a fund of good sense in this country, which cannot be deceived.

> *Ibid. XVI, To the Printer of the Public Advertiser (H. S. Woodfall)* [*July 19, 1769*]

We owe it to our ancestors to preserve entire those rights, which they have delivered to our care: we owe it to our posterity, not to suffer their dearest inheritance to be destroyed.

> *The Letters of Junius. XX, To the Printer of the Public Advertiser* [*August 8, 1769*]

When the constitution is openly invaded, when the first original right of the people, from which all laws derive their authority, is directly attacked, inferior grievances naturally lose their force, and are suffered to pass by without punishment or observation.

> *Ibid. XXX, To the Printer of the Public Advertiser* [*October 17, 1769*]

There is a moment of difficulty and danger at which flattery and falsehood can no longer deceive, and simplicity itself can no longer be misled.

> *Ibid. XXXV,*[1] *To the Printer of the Public Advertiser* [*December 19, 1769*]

They [the Americans] equally detest the pageantry of a King, and the supercilious hypocrisy of a bishop.[2]

> *Ibid.*

The least considerable man among us has an interest equal to the proudest nobleman, in the laws and constitution of his country, and is equally called upon to make a generous contribution in support of them; — whether it be the heart to conceive, the understanding to direct, or the hand to execute.[3]

> *Ibid. XXXVII, To the Printer of the Public Advertiser* [*March 19, 1770*]

---

[1] Attributed, among others, to Sir Philip Francis, Lord Shelburne, Lord George Sackville, and Earl Temple.

[2] See Burke, page 261.

[1] This letter is of great significance in the history of the liberty of the press. The publisher was prosecuted for seditious libel, and the jury brought in a verdict of "guilty of printing and publishing only." After a second trial, Woodfall was freed on the payment of costs.

[2] See Rufus Choate, page 393.

[3] See Gibbon, page 270.

We lament the mistakes of a good man, and do not begin to detest him until he affects to renounce his principles.
The Letters of Junius. XLI, To Lord Mansfield [November 14, 1770]

The injustice to an individual is sometimes of service to the public. Facts are apt to alarm us more than the most dangerous principles.
Ibid.

An honest man, like the true religion, appeals to the understanding, or modestly confides in the internal evidence of his conscience. The impostor employs force instead of argument, imposes silence where he cannot convince, and propagates his character by the sword.
Ibid.

Private credit is wealth; — public honour is security. —The feather that adorns the royal bird, supports his flight. Strip him of his plumage, and you fix him to the earth.
Ibid. XLII, On the Falkland Islands [January 30, 1771]

If individuals have no virtues, their vices may be of use to us.
Ibid. LIX, To the Printer of the Public Advertiser [October 5, 1771]

The temple of fame is the shortest passage to riches and preferment.
Ibid.

Love not me for comely grace,
For my pleasing eye or face,
Nor for any outward part,
No, nor for a constant heart.
Included by JOHN WILBYE *[died 1614] in Second Set of Madrigals [1608]*

The King of France went up the hill
With twenty thousand men;
The King of France came down the hill,
And ne'er went up again.
Pigges Corantoe, or Newes from the North.[1] *Page 3*

[1] A quarto tract printed in London in 1642. This is called "Old Tarlton's Song."

Though little, I'll work as hard as a Turk,
If you'll give me employ,
To plow and sow, and reap and mow,
And be a farmer's boy.
The Farmer's Boy. Stanza 2 [before 1689]

The United Voice of all His Majesty's free and loyal Subjects in America — Liberty and Property, and no Stamps.
Motto of various American colonial newspapers [1765–1766]

Lost is our old simplicity of times,
The world abounds with laws, and teems with crimes.
On the Proceedings Against America.[1] *Stanza 1*

Our cargoes of meat, drink, and cloaths beat the Dutch.
Siege of Boston [1775]

Count that day lost whose low descending sun
Views from thy hand no worthy action done.[2]
Staniford's Art of Reading. Page 27 [Third edition, Boston, 1803]

No foe dare molest, where in union are join'd
The plough, loom, and chisel, with commerce combined.
Plough, Loom, and Chisel. Stanza 1 [Ode sung at the Triennial Festival of the Massachusetts Charitable Mechanic Association, Boston, 1810]

An Austrian army, awfully array'd,
Boldly by battery besiege Belgrade;
Cossack commanders cannonading come,
Deal devastation's dire destructive doom;

[1] In *The Pennsylvania Gazette*, Feb. 8, 1775, "from a late London Magazine."
[2] In the autograph album of David Krieg, in the British Museum, with the autograph of Jacob Bobart [Dec. 8, 1697] are the lines:
Virtus sui gloria.
Think that day lost whose descending sun
Views from thy hand no noble action done.
Bobart, son of a celebrated botanist, died in 1719.

Ev'ry endeavour engineers essay,
For fame, for freedom, fight, fierce furious fray.
Gen'rals 'gainst gen'rals grapple, — gracious God!
How honors Heav'n heroic hardihood!
Infuriate, indiscriminate in ill,
Just Jesus, instant innocence instill!
Kinsmen kill kinsmen, kindred kindred kill.
Labour low levels longest, loftiest lines;
Men march 'midst mounds, moats, mountains, murd'rous mines.
Now noisy, noxious numbers notice nought,
Of outward obstacles o'ercoming ought;
Poor patriots perish, persecution's pest!
Quite quiet Quakers "Quarter, quarter" quest;
Reason returns, religion, right, redounds,
Suwarrow stop such sanguinary sounds!
Truce to thee, Turkey, terror to thy train!
Unwise, unjust, unmerciful Ukraine!
Vanish vile vengeance, vanish victory vain!
Why wish we warfare? wherefore welcome won
Xerxes, Xantippus, Xavier, Xenophon?
Yield, ye young Yaghier yeomen, yield your yell!
Zimmerman's, Zoroaster's, Zeno's zeal
Again attract; arts against arms appeal.
All, all ambitious aims, avaunt, away!
Et cætera, et cætera, et cæterā.

Alliteration, or the Siege of Belgrade: a Rondeau [1]

When shall we three meet again? [2]

Parting Friends [Dartmouth College song, 1830]

[1] These lines having been incorrectly printed in a London publication, we have been favoured by the author with an authentic copy of them. — *Wheeler's Magazine* [Winchester, England, 1828], *Vol. I, P. 244*
In *The Trifler, 1817*. The lines have been attributed to the Reverend B. Poulton, of Winchester, England, and to Alaric Alexander Watts [1797–1864]. They were included in Bentley's *Miscellany* [1838], and in *Literary Frivolities*, compiled by William Dobson [1820–1884]. There are various versions of the *Alliteration*.
[2] *Macbeth, Act I, Sc. 1, Line 1.*

The cunning seldom gain their ends;
The wise are never without friends.

The Fox and the Hen. Moral [1]

A fox went out in a hungry plight
And he begged of the moon to give him light,
For he'd many miles to go that night
Before he could reach his den-O.

The Gray Goose. Stanza 1

The nox was lit by lux of Luna,
And 'twas a nox most opportuna
To catch a possum or a coona;
For nix was scattered o'er this mundus,
A shallow nix, et non profundus.

Carmen Possum

One night when the wind it blew cold,
  Blew bitter across the wild moor,
Young Mary she came with her child,
  Wandering home to her own father's door.

Mary of the Wild Moor. [2] *Stanza 1*

Physicians of the highest rank
(To pay their fees, we need a bank),
Combine all wisdom, art and skill,
Science and sense, in Calomel.

Calomel. Stanza 1 [before 1853]

Howe'er their patients may complain,
Of head, or heart, or nerve, or vein,
Of fever high, or parch, or swell,
The remedy is Calomel.

Ibid. Stanza 2

The sons of the prophet are brave men and bold,
  And quite unaccustomed to fear,
But the bravest by far in the ranks of the Shah
  Was Abdul the Bulbul Amir.

Abdul the Bulbul Amir. Stanza 1

Now the heroes were plenty and well known to fame
  In the troops that were led by the Czar,
And the bravest of these was a man by the name
  Of Ivan Petruski Skavar.

Ibid. Stanza 3

Oh, were you ne'er a school-boy,
  And did you never train,

[1] In John Pierpont's *Young Reader* [1843].
[2] Set to music by C. H. Keith and arranged for piano by Joseph W. Turner [1846].

And feel that swelling of the heart
 You ne'er can feel again?
                Young Soldiers.[1] *Stanza 1*

We charged upon a flock of geese
 And put them all to flight.
                Ibid. Stanza 3

Oh, the praties they are small —
 Over here, over here.
Oh, the praties they are small
When we dig 'em in the fall,
And we eat 'em, coats and all,
 Full of fear, full of fear.
      Irish Famine Song [1846–1847]

Oh, potatoes they grow small,
 In Kansas.
Oh, potatoes they grow small,
For they plant them in the fall,
And they eat 'em skins and all,
 In Kansas.
        Kansas version of famine song

Van Amburgh is the man who goes with
 all the shows,
He gets into the lion's cage, and tells
 you all he knows.
He puts his head in the lion's mouth,
 and keeps it there a while,
And when he takes it out again, he
 greets you with a smile.
       Menagerie, or Showman's Song [2]

Oh, ye'll tak' the high road an' I'll tak'
 the low road,
An' I'll be in Scotland before ye;
But trouble it is there an' mony hearts
 are sair,[3]
On the bonnie, bonnie banks of Loch
 Lomond.
        Scottish Ballad, Loch Lomond.[4]
        Refrain

So I said, "Old man, for whom digg'st
 thou this grave
 In the heart of London town?"

And the deep-toned voice of the digger
 replied —
 "We're laying a gas-pipe down!"
          *From the Sublime to the
             Ridiculous.*[1] *Stanza 3*

You-all means a race or section,
 Family, party, tribe, or clan;
You-all means the whole connection
 Of the individual man.
      *You-All. Stanza 2 [From The
      Richmond (Virginia) Times-
      Dispatch]*

In the singular it's never
 Used in this part of the land;
But we give up hope of ever
 Making others understand.
                Ibid. Stanza 4

The lady would remind you, please,
Her name is not Lost Angie Lees,
Nor Angie anything whatever.
She hopes her friends will be so clever
To share her fit historic pride,
The *g* shall not be jellified.
O long, *g* hard, and rhyme with "yes" —
That's all about Loce Ang-El-Ess.
                Los Angeles

Just after the death of the flowers,
 And before they are buried in snow,
There comes a festival season
 When Nature is all aglow.
     Indian Summer. Stanza 1 [1860]

Dreamer of dreams, we take the taunt
 with gladness,
Knowing that God beyond the years we
 see
Hath wrought the dreams that count
 with men for madness
Into the fabric of the world to be.
       *On the defeat by the London
       County Council of some ed-
       ucational plans; ascribed to
       F. W. H. Myers, but not
       found in his writings*

I pray the prayer the Easterners do,
May the peace of Allah abide with you;
Wherever you stay, wherever you go,
May the beautiful palms of Allah grow;
Through days of labor and nights of
 rest,

---

[1] In McGuffey's *Reader.*
[2] Popular at Eton and in American colleges
in the 1860s. There are various versions.
[3] A version more familiar than the one
given above changes the third line to
But I and my true love will never meet again.
[4] Found in *The Vocal Melodies of Scotland*
[1840] and *Christie's Traditional Ballad Airs*
[1876].

[1] Included in *Course of Composition and
Rhetoric* by GEORGE PAYN QUACKENBOS
[1826–1881].

The love of good Allah make you blest.
So I touch my heart as the Easterners
    do, —
May the peace of Allah abide with you.
            *Salaam Alaikum (Peace Be
                    with You)*
Listen to the Exhortation of the Dawn!
    Look to this Day!
For it is Life, the very Life of Life.
In its brief course lie all the Verities
        and Realities of your Existence:
    The Bliss of Growth,
    The Glory of Action,
    The Splendor of Beauty.
For Yesterday is but a Dream,
And To-morrow is only a Vision;
But To-day well-lived makes every
        Yesterday a Dream of Happiness,
And every To-morrow a Vision of Hope.
Look well therefore to this Day!
Such is the Salutation of the Dawn.
            *The Salutation of the Dawn,
                    from the Sanskrit*
The woman was not taken
    From Adam's head, you know,
So she must not command him,
    'Tis evidently so;
The woman was not taken
    From Adam's feet, you see,
So he must not abuse her —
    The meaning seems to be.
The woman she was taken
    From under Adam's arm,
Which shows he must protect her
    From injury and harm.
            *Old Scotch Nuptial Song
                [before 1860]*
Yestreen the Queen had four Maries,
    The night she'll hae but three;
There was Mary Seaton, and Mary
        Beaton,
    And Mary Carmichael, and me.
    *The Queen's Maries. Stanza 19
    (Oxford Book of English Verse,
    No. 375)*
In the days of old Rameses
That story had paresis.
    *Attributed to Ben King, but a
    familiar saying in the White-
    chapel Club, Chicago, before he
    became a member. Quoted by
    Kipling in The Ship That Found
    Herself.*

From the halls of Montezuma,
    To the shores of Tripoli,
We fight our country's battles
    On the land as on the sea.
        U. S. Marines' Song. Stanza 1

If the Army and the Navy
    Ever look on Heaven's scenes,
They will find the streets are guarded
        by
    The United States Marines.
            Ibid. Stanza 4

The beauty of the house is order;
The blessing of the house is content-
    ment;
The glory of the house is hospitality;
The crown of the house is godliness.
            Fireplace Motto

Men are only boys grown tall;
Hearts don't change much after all.
        *Katie Lee and Willie Gray.
                Stanza 6*

May I carry, if I will,
All your burdens up the hill?
And she answered with a laugh,
No, but you may carry half.
            Ibid. Stanza 8

"I drink to one," he said,
"Whose image never may depart,
Deep graven on this grateful heart,
Till memory be dead.
To one whose love for me shall last
When lighter passions long have passed,
So holy 'tis, and true."
        *The Knight's Toast (to his
        Mother). Stanzas 7 and 8*

Mr. Finney had a turnip,
    And it grew behind the barn,
And it grew, and it grew,
    And the turnip did no harm.
        Mr. Finney's Turnip.[1] *Stanza 1*

Of all the funny things that live, in
        woodland, marsh, or bog,
That creep the ground or fly the air, the
        funniest thing's a frog.
        *The Scientific Frog. Stanza 1
                [1860s]*

[1] Persistently attributed to H. W. Longfellow, who denied the authorship in a letter
to George Anderson, July 11, 1881.

I belong to that highly respectable tribe
Which is known as the Shabby Gen-
teel . . .
Too proud to beg, too honest to steal.
> *The Shabby Genteel. Stanza 1*
> *(Sung by Sol Smith Russell*
> *[1848–1901] in A Poor Rela-*
> *tion)*

Hands off! Stand back! Leave us alone!
You shall not rob us of our own;
We will be free! We will be free!
God and Right our standard be.
> *War-Song of the Boers.*
> *Stanza 1 [1881]*

I'm Terence O'Reilly, I'm a man of re-
nown . . .
If they'd let me be, I'd have Ireland
free,
On the railroads you'd not pay any fare,
I'd have the United States under my
thumb,
And I'd sleep in the President's chair.
> *Is That Mr. Reilly?* [1]
> *Stanza 1 [1882]*

Sow a Thought, and you reap an Act;
Sow an Act, and you reap a Habit;
Sow a Habit, and you reap a Character;
Sow a Character, and you reap a Des-
tiny.
> *Quoted by* SAMUEL SMILES
> *[1812–1904] in Life and La-*
> *bour [1887]*

The Monkey married the Baboon's sister,
Smacked his lips and then he kissed her.
> *The Monkey's Wedding. Stanza 1*
> *(Regimental March of the Ninth*
> *U.S. Cavalry)*

Three thousand miles of borderline, —
nor fort nor armèd host
On all this frontier neighbor-ground
from east to western coast;
A spectacle to conjure with — a thought
to stir the blood!
A living proof to all the world of faith
in brotherhood.
> *Our Borderline. Stanza 1*

God speed that surely dawning day,
that coming hour divine,

When all the nations of the earth shall
boast such borderline.
> *Our Borderline. Stanza 3*

King Arthur had three sons — that he
had;
He had three sons of yore,
And he kicked them out the door
Because they could not sing — that he
did.
> *King Arthur: English Folksong* [1]

In good old Colony times
When we lived under the King,
Three roguish chaps
Fell into mishaps
Because they could not sing.
> *Another version, once popular*
> *as an American college song, In*
> *Good Old Colony Times*

Reuben, I have long been thinking
What a good world this would be,
If the men were all transported
On this side the Northern Sea.
> *Reuben and Rachel.* [2] *Stanza 1*

Mankind looks forth with careful
glance,
Time steady plies the oar,
While old age calmly waits to hear
The keel upon the shore.
> *Life Voyage (on an engraving*
> *by F. T. Stuart from a painting*
> *by Clarence M. Dobell)*

There is never a daughter of earth but
once, ere the tale of her days is
done,
She will know the scent of the Eden
rose, just once beneath the sun!
And whatever else she may win or lose,
endure, or do, or dare,
She will never forget the enchantment
it gave to the common air;
For the world may give her content or
joy, fame, sorrow, or sacrifice,
But the hour that brought the scent of
the rose, she lived it in Paradise.
> *The Rose of Eden: Arabic*
> *Legend.* [3] *Stanza 3*

[1] Assumed to be the origin of the phrase,
"the life of Reilly."

[1] From *English County Songs,* collected
[1893] by LUCY E. BROADWOOD and J. A.
FULLER MAITLAND.
[2] An adaptation of this old song, entitled
"Reuben and Cynthia," was sung in Charles
Hoyt's play, *A Trip to Chinatown* [1890].
[3] Published in *All the Year Round,* a periodical edited by Charles Dickens and contin-

I loathe, abhor, despise,
Abominate dried apple pies.
I like good bread, I like good meat,
Or anything that's fit to eat,
But of all poor grub beneath the skies,
The poorest is dried apple pies.
Give me the toothache or sore eyes
In preference to such kind of pies.
Dried Apple Pies

Tread on my corns, or tell me lies,
But don't pass me dried apple pies!
Ibid.

If I had but a thousand a year, Gaffer
Green,
If I had but a thousand a year,
What a man I would be, and what
sights I would see.
Robin Ruff.[1] *Stanza 1*

There's a place that is better than this,
Robin Ruff,
And I hope in my heart you'll go
there,
Where the poor man's as great though
he hath no estate,
Aye, as if he'd a thousand a year.
Ibid. Stanza 6

It's the 'ammer, 'ammer, 'ammer
along the 'ard 'igh road.
*Under a drawing by John Leech
[1817-1874] in London Punch,
— a veterinary and horseman
discussing a horse's legs*

If any lift of mine may ease
The burden of another,
God give me love and care and strength
To help my ailing brother.
*If Any Little Word of Mine.
Stanza 2 [1880]*

There is a mystery in human hearts,
And though we be encircled by a host
Of those who love us well and are be-
loved,

To every one of us, from time to time,
There comes a sense of utter loneliness.
A Solitary Way. Stanza 1 [1885]

And those who walk with Him from day
to day
Can never have a solitary way.
Ibid. Stanza 3

In the first person, simply *shall* fore-
tells,
In *will* a threat or else a promise dwells;
Shall in the second and third does
threat,
Will then simply foretells a future feat.
Grammar, Irish National Schools

Much that well may be thought cannot
wisely be said.
*The Priest and the Mulberry-
Tree. Stanza 5 (In Epes Sargent's Standard Fourth Reader)*

Try what you will, there's nothing like
leather.
Nothing Like Leather

The sweetest lives are those to duty
wed,
Whose deeds, both great and small,
Are close-knit strands of an unbroken
thread,
Where love ennobles all.
The world may sound no trumpet, ring
no bells;
The book of life the shining record tells.
*Attributed to Elizabeth Barrett
Browning, but not found in her
writings*

The little cares that fretted me,
I lost them yesterday,
Among the fields above the sea,
Among the winds at play,
Among the lowing of the herds,
The rustling of the trees,
Among the singing of the birds,
The humming of the bees.
The foolish fears of what might pass
I cast them all away
Among the clover-scented grass
Among the new-mown hay,
Among the hushing of the corn
Where drowsy poppies nod,

---

ued by his son, Charles, after the death of the
elder Dickens in 1870. The poem appeared in
The St. Louis Globe-Democrat, July 13, 1878.
Rudyard Kipling quotes from this poem in
"Mrs. Hauksbee Sits Out," in *Under the De-
odars*.
[1] Set to music by Henry Russell [1812-
1900].

Where ill thoughts die and good are
    born —
Out in the fields with God.
> *Out in the Fields (Anony-*
> *mous, in St. Paul's Maga-*
> *zine, August 20, 1898, page*
> *307. Reprinted in The*
> *Boston Globe, April 30,*
> *1899)* [1]

Monday's child is fair of face,
Tuesday's child is full of grace,
Wednesday's child is loving and giving,
Thursday's child works hard for a liv-
    ing.
Friday's child is full of woe,
Saturday's child has far to go,
But the child that is born on the
    Sabbath-day
Is brave and bonny, and good and gay.
> *Birthdays (Quoted in Miser*
> *Farebrother by B. L. Farjeon,*
> *Harper's Weekly, September*
> *17, 1887)*

Cut your nails on Monday, cut them for
    wealth,
Cut them on Tuesday, cut them for
    health,
Cut them on Wednesday, cut them for
    news,
Cut them on Thursday, a new pair of
    shoes.
Cut them on Friday, cut them for sor-
    row,
Cut them on Saturday, see sweetheart
    to-morrow.
Cut them on Sunday, cut them for evil,
The whole of the week you'll be ruled
    by the devil.
> *Quoted as above*

Something old, something new,
Something borrowed, something blue.
> *Wedding Rhyme*

The Pyramids first, which in Egypt
    were laid;
Next Babylon's Garden, for Amytis
    made;
Then Mausolos' Tomb of affection and
    guilt;
Fourth, the Temple of Dian in Ephesus
    built;

[1] Also attributed to Mrs. Browning and to
Louise Imogen Guiney. There is no convincing proof of either authorship.

The Colossus of Rhodes, cast in brass,
    to the Sun;
Sixth, Jupiter's Statue, by Phidias
    done;
The Pharos of Egypt comes last, we are
    told,
Or the Palace of Cyrus, cemented with
    gold.
> *Seven Wonders of the*
> *Ancient World*

When every pool in Eden was a mirror
    That unto Eve her dainty charms
    proclaimed,
She went undraped without a single
    fear, or
Thought that she had need to be
    ashamed.
> *Needed Apples. Stanza 1*
> *(Printed in Philip Hale's col-*
> *umn, As the World Wags,*
> *Boston Herald, June 30,*
> *1924)*

'Twas only when she'd eaten of the ap-
    ple
    That she became inclined to be a
    prude. . . .
The snake should pass the apples 'round
    again.
> *Ibid. Stanzas 3 and 4*

Every time I come to town
The boys keep kicking my dawg
    around;
Makes no difference if he is a hound,
They've got to quit kicking my dawg
    around.
> *Champ Clark campaign song*
> *[1912]*

My granddad, viewing earth's worn
    cogs,
Said things were going to the dogs;
His granddad in his house of logs,
Said things were going to the dogs;
His granddad in the Flemish bogs
Said things were going to the dogs;
His granddad in his old skin togs,
Said things were going to the dogs;
There's one thing that I have to state —
The dogs have had a good long wait.
> *Perennial Journeys*

Lord, through this hour
  Be Thou our Guide,
So by Thy power
  No foot shall slide.
       Westminster Chimes

Climb high
Climb far
Your goal the sky
Your aim the star.
      Inscription on Hopkins Memo-
      rial Steps, Williams College,
      Williamstown, Massachusetts

Mother, may I go out to swim?
Yes, my darling daughter:
Hang your clothes on a hickory limb
And don't go near the water.
      Origin dubious.

See the happy moron,
  He doesn't give a damn.
I wish I were a moron —
  My God, perhaps I am!
      Incorrectly attributed to Dorothy
            Parker

Lizzie Borden took an axe
And gave her mother forty whacks;
When she saw what she had done
She gave her father forty-one.
      Ballad current after the Borden
      murder, Fall River, Massachu-
      setts [August 4, 1892] [1]

Work and pray, live on hay,
You'll get pie, in the sky,
When you die —
It's a lie!
      Song of the I.W.W. (Industrial
         Workers of the World)

Once aboard the lugger and the girl
is mine.
      Quotation from (or parody of)
      some Victorian melodrama? First
      four words used as title of novel
      by A. S. M. Hutchinson

Nunc scripsi totum: pro Christo da
  mihi potum.
      Monkish inscription at the end of
            medieval manuscripts

---

[1] EDMUND PEARSON, *The Trial of Lizzie Borden*, says the verse was frequently sung to the tune of *Ta-ra-ra-boom-de-ay*.

TRANSLATIONS

ANCIENT EGYPT

To resist him that is set in authority is evil.

The Instruction of Ptahhotep [1]
[Circa *2675 B.C.*]

There it o'ertook me that I fell down for thirst, I was parched, my throat burned, and I said: "This is the taste of death."

The Story of Sinuke [1]
[Circa *2000 B.C.*]

There is none that hath turned his shaft, there is none that hath bent his bow.

Ibid.

Then the ship perished, and of them that were in it not one survived. And I was cast on to an island by a wave of the sea.

The Story of the Shipwrecked Sailor [1] [Circa *1700 B.C.?*]

Everywhere he feels his Heart because its vessels run to all his limbs.

The Beginning of the Secret Book of the Physician [2] [Circa *1550 B.C.*]

Go not in and out in the court of justice, that thy name may not stink.

The Wisdom of Anii [1]
[Circa *900 B.C.*]

HAMMURABI
[Circa 1955–1913 B. C.] [3]

[*From* ROBERT FRANCIS HARPER's *The Code of Hammurabi King of Babylon about 2250 B.C., second edition*]

I established law and justice in the land.

Page 9 (Prologue)

[1] From ADOLF ERMAN [1854–]: *The Literature of the Ancient Egyptians,* translated [1927] by AYLWARD M. BLACKMAN.
[2] In *The Papyrus Ebers,* translated [1931] from the German version by CYRIL P. BRYAN.
[3] According to *Webster's New International Dictionary,* 2d ed. Authorities disagree on the probable dates.

If a man owe a debt and Adad [1] inundate his field and carry away the produce, or, through lack of water, grain have not grown in the field, in that year he shall not make any return of grain to the creditor, he shall alter his contract-tablet and he shall not pay the interest for that year.

Page 27 (Sect. 48)

If a man destroy the eye of another man, they shall destroy his eye.

Page 73 (Sect. 196)

HOMER [2]
[Circa 850 B. C.]

These things surely lie on the knees of the gods.

Odyssey.[3] *Book I, Line 267*

HESIOD
[Circa 720 B. C.?]

Translation by J. BANKS, M.A., *with a few alterations. Bohn Classical Library*

We know to tell many fictions like to truths, and we know, when we will, to speak what is true.

The Theogony. Line 27

On the tongue of such an one they shed a honeyed dew,[4] and from his lips drop gentle words.

Ibid. Line 82

Night, having Sleep, the brother of Death.[5]

Ibid. Line 754

[1] The storm god.
[2] For quotations from the *Iliad* and *Odyssey,* see Alexander Pope and William Cullen Bryant.
[3] Translated [1879] by BUTCHER AND LANG.
[4] He on honey-dew hath fed. — COLERIDGE: *Kubla Khan*
[5] Death and his brother Sleep. — SHELLEY: *Queen Mab, I*

From whose eyelids also as they gazed dropped love.
The Theogony. Line 910

Both potter is jealous of potter and craftsman of craftsman; and poor man has a grudge against poor man, and poet against poet.[1]
Works and Days. Line 25

Fools! they know not how much half exceeds the whole.[2]
Ibid. Line 40

For full indeed is earth of woes, and full the sea; and in the day as well as night diseases unbidden haunt mankind, silently bearing ills to men, for all-wise Zeus hath taken from them their voice. So utterly impossible is it to escape the will of Zeus.
Ibid. Line 101

Oft hath even a whole city reaped the evil fruit of a bad man.[3]
Ibid. Line 240

For himself doth a man work evil in working evils for another.
Ibid. Line 265

Badness, look you, you may choose easily in a heap: level is the path, and right near it dwells. But before Virtue the immortal gods have put the sweat of man's brow; and long and steep is the way to it, and rugged at the first.
Ibid. Line 287

Let it please thee to keep in order a moderate-sized farm, that so thy garners may be full of fruits in their season.
Ibid. Line 304

Invite the man that loves thee to a feast, but let alone thine enemy.
Ibid. Line 342

A bad neighbour is as great a misfortune as a good one is a great blessing.
Ibid. Line 346

Gain not base gains; base gains are the same as losses.
Ibid. Line 353

If thou shouldst lay up even a little upon a little, and shouldst do this often, soon would even this become great.
Works and Days. Line 360

At the beginning of the cask and at the end take thy fill, but be saving in the middle; for at the bottom saving comes too late. Let the price fixed with a friend be sufficient, and even dealing with a brother call in witnesses, but laughingly.
Ibid. Line 366

The morn, look you, furthers a man on his road, and furthers him too in his work.
Ibid. Line 579

Observe moderation. In all, the fitting season is best.
Ibid. Line 694

Neither make thy friend equal to a brother; but if thou shalt have made him so, be not the first to do him wrong.
Ibid. Line 707

MIMNERMUS
[*Floruit* 630–600 B. C.]

We are all clever enough at envying a famous man while he is yet alive, and at praising him when he is dead.
Fragment 1

STESICHORUS
[630–550 B. C.]
Loeb Classical Library, Lyra Graeca, Vol. 2

'Tis a vain and impotent thing to bewail the dead.
STOBAEUS: *Anthology*[1]

When a man dies, all his glory among men dies also.
Ibid.

ALCAEUS
[611–580 B. C.]
*Translation by J. M. Edmonds.
Loeb Classical Library, Lyra Graeca, Vol. 1*

Not houses finely roofed or the stones of walls well-builded, nay nor canals

---

[1] See Gay, page 206.
[2] Pittacus said that half was more than the whole. — DIOGENES LAERTIUS: *Pittacus, II*
[3] One man's wickedness may easily become all men's curse. — PUBLILIUS SYRUS: *Maxim 463*

[1] Translated by J. M. EDMONDS.

and dockyards, make the city, but men able to use their opportunity.

> ARISTIDES: *Rhodian Oration*

Painting a lion from the claw.

> PLUTARCH: *On the Cessation of Oracles*

'Tis said that wrath is the last thing in a man to grow old.

> *Scholiast on Sophocles*

One that hath wine as a chain about his wits, such an one lives no life at all.

> DEMETRIUS: *On Poems. Papyrus of the First Century B.C. found at Herculaneum*

In fleeing the ashes he's fallen into the coals.

> APOSTOLIUS: *Proverbs*

SAPPHO OF LESBOS [1]
[*Circa* 610 B. C.]

Art thou the topmost apple
The gatherers could not reach,
Reddening on the bough?

> *To Atthis, paraphrase by* BLISS CARMAN

I loved thee, Atthis, once — long, long ago;
Long, long ago — the memory still is dear.
Stand face to face, friend, and unveil thine eyes,
Look deep in mine and keep the dead past clear
Of all regret.

> *To Atthis, paraphrase by* ANNE BUNNER

For to whomsoever I do good they harm me most.

> *Fragment 11* [2]

Evening, thou that bringest all, whatever the light-giving dawn scattered; thou bringest the sheep, thou bringest the goat, thou bringest the child to its mother.

> *Fragment 93* [2]

---

[1] Some say the Muses are nine but how carelessly! Look at the tenth, Sappho from Lesbos. — PLATO (Loeb Classical Library, *Greek Anthology, Vol. 3, P. 281*)

[2] Translated by MARY MILLS PATRICK.

THEOGNIS
[570?–490? B. C.]

Wine is wont to show the mind of man.[1]

> *Maxims. Line 500*

No one goes to Hades with all his immense wealth.[2]

> *Ibid. Line 725*

ANACREON
[563–478 B. C.]

Translation by J. M. Edmonds.
Loeb Classical Library, Lyra Graeca, Vol. 2

Nor in those days did Persuasion shine all silver.

> *Scholiast on Pindar*

Doorkeepers that fight are a mischief.

> *Etymologicum Magnum*

Shining with desire and gleaming with unguents.

> PLUTARCH: *Amatorius*

SIMONIDES OF CEOS
[556–469 B. C.]

In silence also there's a worth that brings no risk.

> PLUTARCH: *Sayings of Emperors. Augustus Caesar*

There's no joy even in beautiful Wisdom, unless one have holy Health.

> SEXTUS EMPIRICUS: *Against the Mathematicians*

Whereas gold is the kindest of all hosts when it shines in the sky,
It comes an evil guest unto those that receive it in their hand.

> PLUTARCH: *The Malignity of Herodotus*

He that would live completely happy must before all things belong to a country that is of fair report.

> AMMIANUS MARCELLINUS: *History*

The city is the teacher of the man.

> PLUTARCH: *Should Old Men Govern?*

---

[1] In wine there is truth. — PLINY: *Natural History, Book XIV, Sect. 141.*

[2] For when he dieth he shall carry nothing away: his glory shall not descend after him. — *Psalm XLIX, 17*

Go tell the Spartans, thou that passeth
    by,
That here, obedient to their laws, we
    lie.[1]

> *Thermopylae* [2]

AESOP
[*Floruit* 550 B. C.]

Any excuse will serve a tyrant.

> *The Wolf and the Lamb*

Beware lest you lose the substance
by grasping at the shadow.

> *The Dog and the Shadow*

You may share the labours of the
great, but you will not share the spoil.

> *The Lion's Share*

You have put your head inside a
wolf's mouth and taken it out again in
safety. That ought to be reward enough
for you.

> *The Wolf and the Crane*

Better beans and bacon in peace than
cakes and ale in fear.

> *The Town Mouse and the Country
> Mouse*

Only cowards insult dying majesty.

> *The Sick Lion*

Little friends may prove great
friends.

> *The Lion and the Mouse*

Better no rule than cruel rule.

> *The Frogs Desiring a King*

A huge gap appeared in the side of
the mountains. At last a tiny mouse
poked its little head out of the gap.[3]

> *The Mountains in Labour*

Much outcry, little outcome.

> *The Mountains in Labour*

There is always someone worse off
than yourself.

> *The Hares and the Frogs*

It is easy to be brave from a safe
distance.

> *The Wolf and the Kid*

You will only injure yourself if you
take notice of despicable enemies.

> *The Bald Man and the Fly*

Outside show is a poor substitute for
inner worth.

> *The Fox and the Mask*

Borrowed plumes.

> *The Jay and the Peacock*

It is not only fine feathers that make
fine birds.

> *Ibid.*

Self-conceit may lead to self-destruc-
tion.

> *The Frog and the Ox*

Gratitude is the sign of noble souls.

> *Androcles*

We often despise what is most useful to us.

> *The Hart and the Hunter*

They found that even the Belly, in
its dull quiet way, was doing necessary
work for the Body, and that all must
work together or the Body will go to
pieces.

> *The Belly and the Members*

I am sure the grapes are sour.[1]

> *The Fox and the Grapes*

It is easy to despise what you cannot
get.

> *Ibid.*

Be content with your lot; one cannot be first in everything.

> *The Peacock and Juno*

Familiarity breeds contempt.[2]

> *The Fox and the Lion*

---

[1] Ruskin said of this epitaph that it was the
noblest group of words ever uttered by man.
In Luderitzbucht Cemetery, German Southwest Africa, the lines, adapted to read:
Tell England, ye who pass this monument,
    That we who rest here, die content,
mark the grave of Rex and Wilfred Wilmslow,
who fell in the battle of Stetting [Nov., 1914].
In Southport, England, the War Memorial
bears another adaptation of the epitaph:
Tell Britain, ye who mark this monument,
    Faithful to her we fell, and rest content.
[2] Translated by WILLIAM LISLE BOWLES
[1762–1850].
[3] A mountain was in labour, sending forth
dreadful groans, and there was in the region
the highest expectation. After all, it brought
forth a mouse. — PHAEDRUS: *Fable 22, 1*

The mountains are in labour, and a ridicu-

lous mouse will be born. — HORACE: *The Art
of Poetry, L. 139*
[1] See George Herbert, page 137. See also
La Fontaine, page 1045.
[2] This is Maxim 640 of Publilius Syrus.
Upon familiarity will grow more contempt.
  SHAKESPEARE: *The Merry Wives of
        Windsor, Act I, Sc. 1, L. 258*
See Cervantes, page 1035.

We can easily represent things as we wish them to be.
The Lion and the Statue
Then the Grasshopper knew it is best to prepare for the days of necessity.
The Ant and the Grasshopper
The little Reed, bending to the force of the wind, soon stood upright again when the storm had passed over.
The Tree and the Reed
Obscurity often brings safety.
Ibid.
The Lamb that belonged to the Sheep, whose skin the Wolf was wearing, began to follow the Wolf in the Sheep's clothing.
The Wolf in Sheep's Clothing
Appearances are deceptive.
Ibid.
The Dog barked at the Ox and attempted to bite it when it approached the manger in the hope of getting at the straw.
The Dog in the Manger [1]
People often grudge others what they cannot enjoy themselves.
Ibid.
The boy called out "Wolf, Wolf!" and the villagers came out to help him. A few days afterward he tried the same trick, and again they came to his help. Shortly after this a Wolf actually came, but this time the villagers thought the boy was deceiving them again and nobody came to his help.
The Shepherd's Boy
A liar will not be believed, even when he speaks the truth.
Ibid.
Never soar aloft on an enemy's pinions.
The Tortoise and the Birds
Do but set the example yourself, and I will follow you. Example is the best precept. [2]
The Two Crabs
Never trust a friend who deserts you at a pinch.
The Two Fellows and the Bear

[1] See Burton, page 123.
[2] Example is always more efficacious than precept. — JOHNSON: *Rasselas, Chap. 30*

United we stand, divided we fall. [1]
The Four Oxen and the Lion
A little thing in hand is worth more than a great thing in prospect. [2]
The Fisher and the Little Fish
Little by little does the trick.
The Crow and the Pitcher
I will have nought to do with a man who can blow hot and cold with the same breath.
The Man and the Satyr
Thinking to get at once all the gold the Goose could give, he killed it and opened it only to find, — nothing.
The Goose with the Golden Eggs
Put your shoulder to the wheel.
Hercules and the Waggoner
The gods help them that help themselves.
Ibid.
Please all, and you will please none.
The Man, the Boy, and the Donkey
Who is to bell the Cat? It is easy to propose impossible remedies.
Belling the Cat
When the Hare awoke from his nap, he saw the Tortoise just near the winning post. Plodding wins the race.
The Hare and the Tortoise
We would often be sorry if our wishes were gratified. [3]
The Old Man and Death
Union gives strength.
The Bundle of Sticks
While I see many hoof-marks going in, I see none coming out. It is easier to get into the enemy's toils than out again.
The Lion, the Fox, and the Beasts
The haft of the arrow had been feathered with one of the eagle's own plumes. We often give our enemies the means of our own destruction. [4]
The Eagle and the Arrow

[1] See George Pope Morris, page 404.
[2] Better one byrde in hande than ten in the wood. — HEYWOOD [1546]
[3] See Lowell, page 528.
[4] Viewed his own feather on the fatal dart.
BYRON: *English Bards and Scotch Reviewers, L. 828*
See Waller, page 145, and Aeschylus, page 964.

Nature will out.
> *The Cat-Maiden*

Do not count your chickens before they are hatched.[1]
> *The Milkmaid and Her Pail*

Men often applaud an imitation, and hiss the real thing.
> *The Buffoon and the Countryman*

Never trust the advice of a man in difficulties.
> *The Fox and the Goat*

IBYCUS

[*Floruit circa* 550 B. C.]

Translation by J. M. EDMONDS. *Loeb Classical Library, Lyra Graeca*

You cannot find a medicine for life when once a man is dead.
> CHRYSIPPUS: *Negatives*

Every reef may be safely let out so long as the sail clears the top of the wave.
> *Scholiast on the Iliad*

Contests allow no excuses, no more do friendships.
> ZENOBIUS: *Proverbs*

The cranes of Ibycus.[2]

AESCHYLUS

[525–456 B. C.]

I would far rather be ignorant than wise in the foreboding of evil.[3]
> *Suppliants.*[4] *Nauck's Edition, No. 453*

"Honour thy father and thy mother" stands written among the three laws of most revered righteousness.[5]
> *Ibid. No. 707*

1 See Samuel Butler, page 143.
2 According to legend, Ibycus was murdered at sea, and his murderers were discovered through cranes that followed the ship. Hence, the "cranes of Ibycus" became a proverb for the agency of the gods in revealing crime.
3 See Thomas Gray, page 243.
4 Translated by MORRIS HICKEY MORGAN.
5 The three great laws ascribed to Triptolemus are referred to, — namely, to honour parents; to worship the gods with the fruits of the earth; to hurt no living creature. The first two laws are also ascribed to the centaur Cheiron.

Words are the physicians of a mind diseased.[1]
> *Prometheus.*[2] *Nauck's Edition, No. 378*

Time as he grows old teaches many lessons.
> *Ibid. No. 981*

God's mouth knows not to utter falsehood, but he will perform each word.[3]
> *Ibid. No. 1032*

Too lightly opened are a woman's ears; Her fence downtrod by many trespassers.
> *Agamemnon.*[4] *Line 486*

I think the slain
Care little if they sleep or rise again;
And we, the living, wherefore should we ache
With counting all our lost ones?
> *Ibid. Line 595*

Sweet is a grief well ended.
> *Ibid. Line 805*

For not many men, the proverb saith, Can love a friend whom fortune prospereth
Unenvying.
> *Ibid. Line 832*

I know how men in exile feed on dreams.
> *Ibid. Line 1668*

Him who pitieth suffering men
Zeus pitieth, and his ways are sweet on earth.
> *The Eumenides.*[4] *Line 91*

Fortune is a god and rules men's life.[5]
> *The Choëphoroe.*[4] *Line 59*

Destiny
Waiteth alike for them that men call free,
And them by others mastered.
> *Ibid. Line 101*

Pleasantest
Of all ties is the tie of host and guest.
> *Ibid. Line 699*

1 Apt words have power to suage
The tumours of a troubl'd mind.
> MILTON: *Samson Agonistes*
2 Translated by MORRIS HICKEY MORGAN.
3 God is not a man that he should lie; . . . hath he said, and shall he not do it? — *Numbers, XXIII, 19.*
4 Translated by SIR GILBERT MURRAY.
5 Fortune commands men, and not men fortune. — HERODOTUS: *Book VII, Polymnia, Chap. 49*

So in the Libyan fable it is told
That once an eagle, stricken with a dart,
Said, when he saw the fashion of the
    shaft,
"With our own feathers, not by others'
    hands,
Are we now smitten." [1]

Fragment 135 [2]

O Death the Healer, scorn thou not, I
    pray,
To come to me: of cureless ills thou art
The one physician. Pain lays not its
    touch
Upon a corpse.

Fragment 250 [2]

A prosperous fool is a grievous burden.

Fragment 383

Bronze is the mirror of the form; wine,
    of the heart.

Fragment 384

It is not the oath that makes us believe
the man, but the man the oath.

Fragment 385

PINDAR
[518–438 B. C.]

Translation by Sir J. E. SANDYS.
Loeb Classical Library

The best of healers is good cheer.

Nemean Ode 4

Longer than deeds liveth the word.

Ibid.

It is the natal star that ruleth over
every deed.

Nemean Ode 5

For whatsoever one hath well said goeth forth with a voice that never dieth.

Isthmian Ode 4

Refrain from peering too far.

Olympian Ode 1

The word that is overbearing is a
spur unto strife.

Fragment from Hymns

To foolish men belongeth a love for
things afar.

Paean 4

[1] See Waller, page 145, and Aesop, page 962.
[2] Translated by PLUMPTRE.

Every noble deed dieth, if suppressed in silence.

*Eulogy on Alexander, Son of
Amyntas*

Whether the race of men on earth
mounteth a loftier tower by justice, or
by crooked wiles, my mind is divided
in telling clearly.

Fragment

SOPHOCLES
[496–406 B. C.]

The ship of state — the gods once more,
After much rocking on a stormy surge,
Set her on even keel.

Antigone [1]

That pilot of the state
Who sets no hand to the best policy,
But remains tongue-tied through some
    terror, seems
Vilest of men.

Ibid.

None love the messenger who brings
bad news. [2]

Ibid.

For money you would sell your soul.

Ibid.

A man of worth
In his own household will appear up-
    right
In the state also.

Ibid.

There lives no greater fiend than An-
    archy;
She ruins states, turns houses out of
    doors,
Breaks up in rout the embattled sol-
    diery.

Ibid.

Do not persist, then, to retain at heart
One sole idea, that the thing is right
Which your mouth utters, and nought
    else beside.

Ibid.

[1] Translated by SIR GEORGE YOUNG [1837–
1930].
[2] The first bringer of unwelcome news
    Hath but a losing office.
    SHAKESPEARE: *King Henry IV, Part II,
        Act I, Sc. 1, L. 100*

Though a man be wise,
It is no shame for him to live and
learn.[1]

Antigone

To err
From the right path is common to mankind.[2]

Ibid.

A day can prostrate and upraise again
All that is human.

Ajax [3]

To behold harms of our own hands'
doing,
Where none beside us wrought, causes
sharp ruing.

Ibid.

A woman should be seen, not heard.

Ibid.

I would not take the fellow at a gift
Who warms himself with unsubstantial
hopes;
But bravely to live on, or bravely end,[4]
Is due to gentle breeding.

Ibid.

In the ills of men
There is none sorer than Necessity.

Ibid.

Some mindfulness
A man should surely keep, of any thing
That pleased him once.

Ibid.

The happiest life consists in ignorance,
Before you learn to grieve and to rejoice.

Ibid.

Sleep, the universal vanquisher.

Ibid.

I for my own part, having learnt of
late
Those hateful to us we are not to hate
As though they might not soon be
friends again,
Intend to measure, now, the services
I render to my friend, as if not so

---

[1] See Browning, page 493.
[2] To err is human. — POPE: *Essay on Criticism, Part II, L. 325*
[3] Translated by SIR GEORGE YOUNG.
[4] Where life is more terrible than death, it
is then the truest valour to dare to live. —
SIR THOMAS BROWNE [1605–1682]: *Religio
Medici* (Everyman ed.), *P. 49*

To abide for ever; for of mortals most
Find friendship an unstable anchorage.[1]

Ajax

'Tis a long road knows no turning.

Ibid.

Men of perverse opinion do not know
The excellence of what is in their hands
Till some one dash it from them.

Ibid.

Death is not the worst; rather, in vain
To wish for death, and not to compass it.

Electra [3]

The flower
Of our young manhood.[3]

Oedipus Tyrannus [2]

Towers and ships are nothingness,
Void of our fellow men to inhabit them.

Ibid.

This dim-seen track-mark of an ancient
crime.

Ibid.

The Sphinx
With her enigma.

Ibid.

I benefit myself in aiding him.

Ibid.

Now am I hail-fellow-well-met with
all.[4]

Ibid.

Pride, when puffed up, vainly, with
many things

[1] I know, of late experience taught, that him
Who is my foe I must but hate as one
Whom I may yet call friend: and him who
loves me
Will I but serve and cherish as a man
Whose love is not abiding. Few be they
Who reaching friendship's port have there
found rest.
The Death of Ajax, translated by CHARLES
STUART CALVERLEY [1831–1884]

Long since I knew to treat my foe like one
Whom I hereafter as a friend might love
If he deserved it, and to love my friend
As if he still might one day be my foe:
For little is the trust we can repose
In human friendships.

Translator unknown

Love him so, as if you were one day to hate
him and hate him so, as you were one day to
love him. — Attributed to CHILO [flourished
556 B.C.] in MONTAIGNE's essay, *Of Friendship.*

[2] Translated by SIR GEORGE YOUNG.
[3] See Terence, page 979.
[4] See Swift, page 191.

Unseasonable, unfitting, mounts the wall,
Only to hurry to that fatal fall.[1]
Oedipus Tyrannus

That kindred only should behold and hear
The griefs of kin, fits best with decency.
Ibid.

Of no mortal say
"That man is happy," till
Vexed by no grievous ill
He pass Life's goal.[2]
Ibid. Closing lines

To know that all is well, even if late
We come to know it, is at least some gain.
Trachiniae [3]

There is occasion for the vigilant
To fear for one who prospers, lest he fall.
Ibid.

One must learn
By doing the thing; for though you think you know it
You have no certainty, until you try.
Ibid.

If any
Count on two days, or any more, to come,
He is a fool; for a man has no morrow,
Till with good luck he has got through to-day.
Ibid.

War never slays a bad man in its course,
But the good always!
Philoctetes [3]

Winds are fair always, when you fly from harm.
Ibid.

---

[1] See Heywood, page 14, and Chapman, page 29.
[2] Call no man happy till you know the nature of his death. — HERODOTUS: *Clio, Book I, 32*

'Tis an old well-known proverb of mankind,
"You cannot tell men's fortunes till they die,
In any case, if they be good or bad."
SOPHOCLES: *Trachiniae*

'Tis never seemly to felicitate
The fortunes of a man, as prosperous,
Before his life shall have been lived by him
Completely through.
SOPHOCLES: *Tyndareus, Fragment 572*
[3] Translated by SIR GEORGE YOUNG.

Who does not befriend himself
By doing good?
Oedipus Coloneus [1]

To the gods alone
Belongs it never to be old or die,
But all things else melt with all-powerful Time.
Ibid.

If a man to you
Refused a favour, when you begged for it,
And would give nothing, and then afterwards,
When you were satisfied of your desire,
And all the grace was graceless, proffered it,
Would not the pleasure so received be vain? [2]
Ibid.

Never to have been born is much the best;
And the next best, by far,
To return thence, by the way speediest,
Where our beginnings are.
Ibid.

This is our portion at the close of life,
Strengthless — companionless.
Ibid.

It is the merit of a general
To impart good news, and to conceal the bad.
Ibid.

The very hair on my head
Stands up for dread.[3]
Ibid.

A remedy too strong for the disease.
Tereus. Fragment 514 [4]

Truly, to tell lies is not honourable;
But when the truth entails tremendous ruin,
To speak dishonourably is pardonable.
Creusa. Fragment 323

Sons are the anchors of a mother's life.
Phaedra. Fragment 612

---

[1] Translated by SIR GEORGE YOUNG.
[2] See Samuel Johnson, page 233, and Dobson, page 649.
[3] The hair of all stood up for fear. — Later in same drama
[4] The fragments are from pages 311–377 of the Everyman Edition of *The Dramas of Sophocles.*

To him who is in fear everything rustles.

> *Acrisius. Fragment 58*

No falsehood lingers on into old age.

> *Ibid. Fragment 59*

Lady, cheer up; most of our ills, blowing loudly
In dreams by night, grow milder when 'tis day.

> *Ibid. Fragment 63*

No man loves life like him that's growing old.

> *Ibid. Fragment 64*

War loves to prey upon the young.[1]

> *Scyrian Women. Fragment 498*

A wise gamester ought to take the dice
Even as they fall, and pay down quietly,
Rather than grumble at his luck.

> *Unknown Dramas. Fragment 686*

Truth ever has most strength of what men say.

> *Ibid. Fragment 691*

A woman's vows I write upon the wave.

> *Ibid. Fragment 694*

The friends of the unlucky are far away.

> *Ibid. Fragment 773*

If I am Sophocles, I am not mad; and if I am mad, I am not Sophocles.

> *Vit. Anon.*[2], *P. 64*

EURIPIDES [3]
[484–406 B. C.]

Old men's prayers for death are lying prayers, in which they abuse old age and long extent of life. But when death draws near, not one is willing to die, and age no longer is a burden to them.

> *Alcestis.*[4] *Line 669*

I care for riches, to make gifts
To friends, or lead a sick man back to health
With ease and plenty. Else small aid is wealth
For daily gladness; once a man be done
With hunger, rich and poor are all as one.

> *Electra.*[1] *Line 539*

A hundred little things make likenesses
In brethren born, and show the father's blood.

> *Ibid. Line 642*

Danger gleams
Like sunshine to a brave man's eyes.

> *Iphigenia in Tauris.*[1] *Line 115*

How oft the darkest hour of ill
Breaks brightest into dawn.[2]

> *Ibid. Line 723*

I think that Fortune watcheth o'er our lives,
Surer than we. But well said: he who strives
Will find his gods strive for him equally.[3]

> *Ibid. Line 910*

The night
Is the safe time for robbers, as the light
For just men.

> *Ibid. Line 1024*

Put not thy faith in any Greek.[4]

> *Ibid. Line 1205*

The gifts of a bad man bring no good with them.

> *Medea.*[5] *Line 618*

Moderation, the noblest gift of Heaven.

> *Ibid. Line 636*

I know, indeed, the evil of that I purpose; but my inclination gets the better of my judgment.[6]

> *Ibid. Line 1078*

---

[1] In peace, children inter their parents; war violates the order of nature, and causes parents to inter their children. — HERODOTUS: *Book I, Clio, Chap. 87*

[2] Translated by PLUMPTRE.

[3] Our Euripides, the human,
With his droppings of warm tears,
And his touches of things common
Till they rose to touch the spheres.
  MRS. BROWNING: *Wine of Cyprus*

[4] Translated by MORRIS HICKEY MORGAN.

---

[1] Translated by SIR GILBERT MURRAY.

[2] The darkest hour is that before the dawn. — HAZLITT: *English Proverbs*

[3] See George Herbert, page 137.

[4] See Virgil, page 982.

[5] Translated by MORRIS HICKEY MORGAN.

[6] See Sir Samuel Garth, page 187, Ovid, page 986, and *Romans, VII, 19.*
I find my growing judgment daily instruct me how to be better, but my untamed affections and confirmed vitiosity makes me daily

Slowly but surely withal moveth the might of the gods.[1]

Bacchae.[2] Line 882

Slight not what's near through aiming at what's far.

Rhesus.[2] Line 482

Thou didst bring me forth for all the Greeks in common, not for thyself alone.

Iphigenia in Aulis.[2] Line 1386

The company of just and righteous men is better than wealth and a rich estate.

Aegeus.[2] Fragment 7

A bad beginning makes a bad ending.

Aeolus.[2] Fragment 32

Time will explain it all. He is a talker, and needs no questioning before he speaks.

Ibid. Fragment 38

Waste not fresh tears over old griefs.

Alexander.[2] Fragment 44

The nobly born must nobly meet his fate.[3]

Alcymene.[2] Fragment 100

Woman is woman's natural ally.

Alope.[2] Fragment 109

Man's best possession is a sympathetic wife.

Antigone.[2] Fragment 164

Try first thyself, and after call in God;
For to the worker God himself lends aid.[4]

Hippolytus. Fragment 435

Second thoughts are ever wiser.[5]

Ibid. Fragment 436

Toil, says the proverb, is the sire of fame.

Licymnius.[2] Fragment 477

Cowards do not count in battle; they are there, but not in it.

Meleager.[2] Fragment 523

A woman should be good for everything at home, but abroad good for nothing.

Meleager. Fragment 525

Silver and gold are not the only coin; virtue too passes current all over the world.

Oedipus.[1] Fragment 546

Where two discourse, if the one's anger rise,
The man who lets the contest fall is wise.

Protesilaus.[1] Fragment 656

When good men die their goodness does not perish,
But lives though they are gone. As for the bad,
All that was theirs dies and is buried with them.

Temenidae.[1] Fragment 734

Every man is like the company he is wont to keep.

Phoenix.[1] Fragment 809

Who knows but life be that which men call death,
And death what men call life?

Phrixus.[1] Fragment 830

Whoso neglects learning in his youth, loses the past and is dead for the future.

Ibid. Fragment 927

The gods visit the sins of the fathers upon the children.

Ibid. Fragment 970

In a case of dissension, never dare to judge till you've heard the other side.

*Heracleidae.[1] (Quoted by ARIS-
TOPHANES in The Wasps)*

Leave no stone unturned.[2]

Ibid. 1002

Those whom God wishes to destroy, he first deprives of their senses.[3]

Fragment, Greek Iambic

---

do worse. — SIR THOMAS BROWNE: *Religio Medici* (Everyman ed.), *P. 47*

We naturally know what is good, but naturally pursue what is evil. — *Ibid., P. 61*

[1] See George Herbert, page 138.
[2] Translated by MORRIS HICKEY MORGAN.
[3] Noblesse oblige (Nobility has its obligation). — BOHN: *Foreign Proverbs*
[4] See George Herbert, page 137.
[5] See Tennyson, page 465.

[1] Translated by MORRIS HICKEY MORGAN.
[2] This may be traced to a response of the Delphic oracle given to Polycrates, as the best means of finding a treasure buried by Xerxes' general, Mardonius, on the field of Plataea. The oracle replied, "Turn every stone." — LEUTSCH AND SCHNEIDEWIN: *Corpus Paraemiographorum Graecorum, Vol. I, P. 146*
[3] See Dryden, page 175.

Quos deus vult perdere, prius dementat.
In Boswell's *Life of Dr. Johnson* (Everyman ed.), *Vol. 2, Pp. 442–443,* this is quoted

These men won eight victories over the Syracusans when the favor of the gods was equal for both sides.

Epitaph for the Athenians Slain in Sicily

HERODOTUS
[484–424 B. C.]

Translation by William Beloe
[1756–1817]

Call no man happy till you know the nature of his death; he is at best but fortunate.[1]

Book I, Clio. Chap. 32

They [the Persians] are accustomed to deliberate on matters of the highest moment when warm with wine; but whatever they in this situation may determine is again proposed to them on the morrow, in their cooler moments, by the person in whose house they had before assembled. If at this time also it meet their approbation, it is executed; otherwise it is rejected. Whatever also they discuss when sober, is always a second time examined after they have been drinking.[2]

Ibid. Chap. 133

They joined battle, and the Phocaeans won, yet it was but a Cadmean victory.[3]

Ibid. Chap. 166

The art of medicine in Egypt is thus exercised: one physician is confined to the study and management of one disease; there are of course a great number who practice this art; some attend to the disorders of the eyes, others to those of the head, some take care of the teeth, others are conversant with all diseases of the bowels; whilst many attend to the cure of maladies which are less conspicuous.

Book II, Euterpe. Chap. 84

They who mutually injure the state, mutually support each other.

Book III, Thalia. Chap. 82

You may have observed how the thunderbolt of Heaven chastises the insolence of the more enormous animals, whilst it passes over without injury the weak and insignificant: before these weapons of the gods you must have seen how the proudest palaces and the loftiest trees fall and perish.[1]

Book VII, Polymnia. Chap. 10

Every measure undertaken with temerity is liable to be perplexed with error, and punished by misfortune.

Ibid.

The Persian messengers travel with a velocity which nothing human can equal. . . . Neither snow, nor rain, nor heat, nor darkness, are permitted to obstruct their speed.[2]

Book VIII, Urania. Chap. 98

Nothing in human life is more to be lamented, than that a wise man should have so little influence.

Book IX, Calliope. Chap. 16

THUCYDIDES
[471–401 B. C.]

Translation [1629] by Thomas Hobbes [1588–1679]

Because in the administration it hath respect not to the few but to the mul-

---

as a saying which everybody repeats, but nobody knows where to find.

[1] See Sophocles, page 966.

[2] The ancient Goths of Germany . . . had all of them a wise custom of debating every thing of importance to their state, twice; that is, — once drunk, and once sober: — Drunk — that their councils might not want vigour; and sober — that they might not want discretion. — STERNE: *Tristram Shandy, Book V, Chap. 17*

Appeal from Philip drunk to Philip sober. — VALERIUS MAXIMUS: *Book VI, Chap. 2*

[3] A Cadmean (or a Pyrrhic) victory was one in which the victors suffered as much as their enemies. "One more such victory," said Pyrrhus, "and I am lost."

[1] It is the lofty pine that by the storm
Is oftener tossed; towers fall with heavier crash
Which higher soar.
HORACE: *Odes, Book II, X, To Licinius, L. 9*

The bigger they come, the harder they fall. — ROBERT FITZSIMMONS [1862–1917], pugilist, before his fight with James J. Jeffries, a heavier man, in San Francisco [July 25, 1902]

[2] Not snow, nor rain, nor heat, nor gloom of night stays these couriers from the swift completion of their appointed rounds. — Inscription on the Main Post Office, New York City

titude, our form of government is called a democracy. Wherein there is not only an equality amongst all men in point of law for their private controversies, but in election to public offices we consider neither class nor rank, but each man is preferred according to his virtue or to the esteem in which he is held for some special excellence: nor is any one put back even through poverty, because of the obscurity of his person, so long as he can do good service to the commonwealth.

> *History. Book II, Chap. 37, Pericles' Funeral Oration over the Athenians who fell in the first year of the Peloponnesian War*

And when Athens shall appear great to you, consider then that her glories were purchased by valiant men, and by men that learned their duty; by men that were sensible of dishonour when they came to act; by such men as, though they failed in their attempt, yet would not be wanting to the city with their virtue, but made unto it a most honourable contribution.

> *Ibid.*

To famous men all the earth is a sepulchre.

> *Ibid.*

Their virtues shall be testified not only by the inscription on stone at home but in all lands wheresoever in the unwritten record of the mind, which far beyond any monument will remain with all men everlastingly.

> *Ibid.*

SIMPLICIUS

They [atoms] move in the void and catching each other up jostle together, and some recoil in any direction that may chance, and others become entangled with one another in various degrees according to the symmetry of their shapes and sizes and positions and order, and they remain together and thus the coming into being of composite things is effected.

> *De Caelo. 242, 15* [1]

SOCRATES
[470–399 B. C.]
Translation by BENJAMIN JOWETT

Either death is a state of nothingness and utter unconsciousness, or, as men say, there is a change and migration of the soul from this world to another.

> *Apology*

No evil can happen to a good man, either in life or after death.

> *Ibid.*

Man is a prisoner who has no right to open the door of his prison and run away. . . . A man should wait, and not take his own life until God summons him.

> *Dialogues of* PLATO. *Phaedo*

The partisan, when he is engaged in a dispute, cares nothing about the rights of the question, but is anxious only to convince his hearers of his own assertions.

> *Ibid.*

False words are not only evil in themselves, but they infect the soul with evil.

> *Ibid.*

The soul takes nothing with her to the other world but her education and culture; and these, it is said, are of the greatest service or of the greatest injury to the dead man, at the very beginning of his journey thither.

> *Ibid.*

I think that I had better bathe before I drink the poison, and not give the women the trouble of washing my dead body.

> *Ibid.*

I owe a cock to Asclepius; do not forget to pay it.

> *Ibid. (The last words of Socrates)*

[1] Quoted by CYRIL BAILEY: *The Greek Atomists and Epicurus.*

HIPPOCRATES
[460–377 B. C.]

Translation by WILLIAM HENRY RICH JONES [1817–1885]

I swear by Apollo Physician, by Asclepius, by Health, by Panacea, and by all the gods and goddesses, making them my witnesses, that I will carry out, according to my ability and judgment, this oath and this indenture. To hold my teacher in this art equal to my own parents; to make him partner in my livelihood; when he is in need of money to share mine with him; to consider his family as my own brothers, and to teach them this art, if they want to learn it, without fee or indenture. I will use treatment to help the sick according to my ability and judgment, but never with a view to injury and wrong doing. I will keep pure and holy both my life and my art. In whatsoever houses I enter, I will enter to help the sick, and I will abstain from all intentional wrong-doing and harm. And whatsoever I shall see or hear in the course of my profession in my intercourse with men, if it be what should not be published abroad, I will never divulge, holding such things to be holy secrets. Now if I carry out this oath, and break it not, may I gain forever reputation among all men for my life and for my art; but if I transgress it and forswear myself, may the opposite befall me.

The Physician's Oath

Healing is a matter of time, but it is sometimes also a matter of opportunity.

Precepts. Chap. 1

Sometimes give your services for nothing, calling to mind a previous benefaction or present satisfaction. And if there be an opportunity of serving one who is a stranger in financial straits, give full assistance to all such. For where there is love of man, there is also love of the art. For some patients, though conscious that their condition is perilous, recover their health simply through their contentment with the goodness of the physician. And it is well to superintend the sick to make them well, to care for the healthy to keep them well, but also to care for one's own self, so as to observe what is seemly.

Precepts. Chap. 6

In all abundance there is lack.

Ibid. Chap. 8

If for the sake of a crowded audience you do wish to hold a lecture, your ambition is no laudable one, and at least avoid all citations from the poets, for to quote them argues feeble industry.

Ibid. Chap. 12

Life is short and the art long.[1]

Aphorisms. Sect. I, 1

Extreme remedies are very appropriate for extreme diseases.[2]

Ibid. 6

ARISTOPHANES
[446–380 B. C.]

What heaps of things have bitten me
    to the heart!
A small few pleased me, very few, just
    four;
But those that vexed were sand-dune-
    hundredfold.

The Acharnians [3]

If a word
Our orators let fall, save what pertains
To peace, I'll raise a storm of words,
    and rain
A very tempest of abuse upon them!

Ibid.[4]

He works and blows the coals
And has plenty of other irons in the
    fire.[5]

Ibid.

---

[1] Life is short, art is long. — SENECA: *On the Shortness of Life, I, 1*

The lyf so short, the craft so long to lerne. — CHAUCER: *The Parlement of Foules, Proem, L. 1*

[2] See Shakespeare, page 96.

For a desperate disease a desperate cure. — MONTAIGNE: *The Custom of the Isle of Cea, Chap. 3*

[3] Translated by B. B. ROGERS.

[4] Translated by JOHN HOOKHAM FRERE [1769–1846].

[5] See Francis Beaumont, page 129.

Master, shall I begin with the usual
jokes
That the audience always laugh at?

The Frogs [1]

Lodgings, — free from bugs and fleas,
if possible,
If you know any such.

Ibid.

Brekeke-kesh, koash, koash. [2]

Ibid.

The men that stood for office, noted for
acknowledged worth,
And for manly deeds of honour, and
for honourable birth;
Train'd in exercise and art, in sacred
dances and in song,
All are ousted and supplanted by a base
ignoble throng.

Ibid.

He collected audiences about him,
And flourish'd, and exhibited, and ha-
rangued.

Ibid.

A vast expenditure of human voice.

Ibid.

Exalted ideas of fancy require
To be clothed in a suitable vesture of
phrase.

Ibid.

I laugh'd till I cried.

Ibid.

If we withdraw the confidence we
placed
In these our present statesmen, and
transfer it
To those whom we mistrusted heretofore,
This seems I think our fairest chance
for safety:
If with our present counsellors we fail,
Then with their opposites we might
succeed.

Ibid.

Shame is the apprehension of a vision
Reflected from the surface of opinion —
The opinion of the public.

Ibid.

Perhaps death is life, and life is death,
And victuals and drink an illusion of
the senses;
For what is Death but an eternal sleep?
And does not Life consist in sleeping
and eating?

The Frogs

Happy is the man possessing
The superior holy blessing
Of a judgment and a taste
Accurate, refined and chaste.

Ibid.

I commend the old proverb, "For we
must look about under every stone, lest
an orator bite us."

The Trial of Euripides [1]

When shall I see those halcyon days? [2]

The Clouds [3]

If you strike
Upon a thought that baffles you, break
off
From that entanglement and try another.
So shall your wits be fresh to start
again.

Ibid.

Old age is but a second childhood.

Ibid.

Throw fear to the wind.

The Wasps [4]

Rais'd and swell'd with honours great
(such on bard yet never sate)
With meekness and modesty he bore
him;
And while his laurels grew, he kept ever
in his view
The heights yet unconquer'd before
him.

Ibid.

[1] Translated by WILLIAM JAMES HICKIE.
[2] Halcyon days. — SHAKESPEARE: *King
Henry VI, Part I, Act I, Sc. 1, L. 131*
 The appellation of Halcyon-days, which
was applied to a rare and bloodless week of
repose. — GIBBON: *Decline and Fall of the
Roman Empire, Chap. 48*
[3] Translated by THOMAS MITCHELL [1783–
1845].
[4] Translated by RICHARD CUMBERLAND
[1732–1811].

[1] Translated by JOHN HOOKHAM FRERE
[1769–1846].
[2] Adapted in college cheer: Brekeke-kex,
koax, koax.

O the days that are gone by, O the days
that are no more,[1]
When my eye was bold and fearless,
and my hand was on the oar.
The Wasps
Bitt'rest stroke of all we feel it, that an
idle brood be fed
At our cost, who never handled oar or
jav'lin, never bled,
Nor so much as rais'd a blister in their
suff'ring country's stead.
Ibid.

DIONYSIUS THE ELDER
[430–367 B.C.]

Let thy speech be better than silence,
or be silent.
Fragment 6

PLATO
[427–347 B.C.]

Translation by BENJAMIN JOWETT.
Oxford University Press

He who is of a calm and happy nature
will hardly feel the pressure of age, but
to him who is of an opposite disposition
youth and age are equally a burden.
The Republic. Book I, 329-D

No physician, in so far as he is a
physician, considers his own good in
what he prescribes, but the good of his
patient; for the true physician is also a
ruler having the human body as a subject, and is not a mere money-maker.
Ibid. 342-D

When there is an income-tax, the just
man will pay more and the unjust less
on the same amount of income.
Ibid. 343-D

Mankind censure injustice, fearing
that they may be the victims of it and
not because they shrink from commit-
ting it.
Ibid. 344-C

[1] The golden olden glory of the days gone
by. — J. W. RILEY: *The Days Gone By*

The days that are no more.
TENNYSON: *The Princess. Tears, Idle Tears*

The beginning is the most important
part of the work.
The Republic. Book II, 377-B

A fit of laughter which has been indulged to excess almost always produces
a violent reaction.
Ibid. Book III, 388-E

Beauty of style and harmony and
grace and good rhythm depend on simplicity.
Ibid. 400-D

Musical training is a more potent instrument than any other, because
rhythm and harmony find their way
into the inward places of the soul.
Ibid. 401-D

Gymnastic as well as music should
begin in early years.
Ibid. 403-C

They do certainly give very strange
and new-fangled names to diseases.
Ibid. 405-C

The judge should not be young; he
should have learned to know evil, not
from his own soul, but from late and
long observation of the nature of evil
in others: knowledge should be his
guide, not personal experience.
Ibid. 409-B

Everything that deceives may be said
to enchant.
Ibid. 413-C

Under the influence either of poverty
or of wealth, workmen and their work
are equally liable to degenerate.
Ibid. Book IV, 421-E

Wealth is the parent of luxury and indolence, and poverty of meanness and
viciousness, and both of discontent.
Ibid. 422

The direction in which education
starts a man will determine his future
life.
Ibid. 425-B

What is the prime of life? May it not
be defined as a period of about twenty
years in a woman's life, and thirty in a
man's?
Ibid. Book V, 460-E

Let there be one man who has a city
obedient to his will, and he might bring

into existence the ideal polity about which the world is so incredulous.

The Republic. Book V, 502-B

Astronomy compels the soul to look upwards and leads us from this world to another.

Ibid. Book VII, 529

I have hardly ever known a mathematician who was capable of reasoning.

Ibid. 531-E

Solon was under a delusion when he said that a man when he grows old may learn many things — for he can no more learn much than he can run much; youth is the time for any extraordinary toil.

Ibid. 536-D

Bodily exercise, when compulsory, does no harm to the body; but knowledge which is acquired under compulsion obtains no hold on the mind.

Ibid. 536-E

Let early education be a sort of amusement; you will then be better able to find out the natural bent.

Ibid. 537

The character of the son begins to develop when he hears his mother complaining that her husband has no place in the government, of which the consequence is that she has no precedence among other women.

Ibid. Book VIII, 549-C

Oligarchy: A government resting on a valuation of property, in which the rich have power and the poor man is deprived of it.

Ibid. 550-C

Democracy, which is a charming form of government, full of variety and disorder, and dispensing a sort of equality to equals and unequals alike.[1]

Ibid. 558-C

The people have always some champion whom they set over them and nurse into greatness. . . . This and no other is the root from which a tyrant springs; when he first appears he is a protector.

Ibid. 565-C

[1] See Aristotle, page 975.

In the early days of his power, he is full of smiles, and he salutes every one whom he meets.

The Republic. Book VIII, 566-D

When the tyrant has disposed of foreign enemies by conquest or treaty, and there is nothing to fear from them, then he is always stirring up some war or other, in order that the people may require a leader.

Ibid. 566-E

Has he not also another object which is that they may be impoverished by payment of taxes, and thus compelled to devote themselves to their daily wants and therefore less likely to conspire against him?

Ibid. 567

What a poor appearance the tales of poets make when stripped of the colours which music puts upon them, and recited in simple prose.

Ibid. Book X, 601-B

There are three arts which are concerned with all things: one which uses, another which makes, a third which imitates them.

Ibid. 601-D

No human thing is of serious importance.

Ibid.

The soul of man is immortal and imperishable.

Ibid. 608-D

These are the Fates, daughters of Necessity . . . Lachesis singing of the past, Clotho of the present, Atropos of the future.

Ibid. 617-C

You are young, my son, and, as the years go by, time will change and even reverse many of your present opinions. Refrain therefore awhile from setting yourself up as a judge of the highest matters.[1]

Laws. 888

[1] I could never divide myself from any man upon the difference of an opinion, or be angry with his judgment for not agreeing with me in that from which perhaps within a few days I should dissent myself. — SIR THOMAS BROWNE: *Religio Medici* (Everyman ed.). P. 7

And this which you deem of no moment is the very highest of all: that is whether you have a right idea of the gods, whereby you may live your life well or ill.

Laws. 888

Not one of them who took up in his youth with this opinion that there are no gods, ever continued until old age faithful to his conviction.

Ibid.

ZEUXIS
[*Circa* 400 B.C.]

Criticism comes easier than craftsmanship.

Quoted by PLINY *in Natural History*

ARISTOTLE
[384–322 B.C.]

Poverty is the parent of revolution and crime.

Politics.[1] *Book II*

Even when laws have been written down, they ought not always to remain unaltered.

Ibid.

The law has no power to command obedience except that of habit, which can only be given by time, so that a readiness to change from old to new laws enfeebles the power of the law.

Ibid.

That judges of important causes should hold office for life is not a good thing, for the mind grows old as well as the body.

Ibid.

If liberty and equality, as is thought by some, are chiefly to be found in democracy, they will be best attained when all persons alike share in the government to the utmost.[2]

Ibid. Book IV

The best political community is formed by citizens of the middle class. Those States are likely to be well administered in which the middle class is large, and larger if possible than both

[1] Translated by BENJAMIN JOWETT.
[2] See Plato, page 974.

the other classes, or at any rate than either singly; for the addition of the middle class turns the scale and prevents either of the extremes from being dominant.

Politics. Book IV

Inferiors revolt in order that they may be equal, and equals that they may be superior. Such is the state of mind which creates revolutions.

Ibid. Book V

Revolutions break out when opposite parties, the rich and the poor, are equally balanced, and there is little or nothing between them; for, if either party were manifestly superior, the other would not risk an attack upon them.

Ibid.

All admit that in a certain sense the several kinds of character are bestowed by nature. Justice, a tendency to Temperance, Courage, and the other types of character are exhibited from the moment of birth.

Nicomachean Ethics. VI, 13, 1

In practical matters the end is not mere speculative knowledge of what is to be done, but rather the doing of it. It is not enough to know about Virtue, then, but we must endeavour to possess it, and to use it, or to take any other steps that may make us good.

Ibid. X, 9, 1

The generality of men are naturally apt to be swayed by fear rather than by reverence, and to refrain from evil rather because of the punishment that it brings, than because of its own foulness.

Ibid.

What makes men good is held by some to be nature, by others habit or training, by others instruction. As for the goodness that comes by nature, this is plainly not within our control, but is bestowed by some divine agency on certain people who truly deserve to be called fortunate.

Ibid. 9, 6

DEMOSTHENES
[384-322 B. C.]

I do not purchase regret at such a price.
Reply to Laïs

Though a man escape every other danger, he can never wholly escape those who do not want such a person as he is to exist.
De Falsa Legatione.[1] 228

Every advantage in the past is judged in the light of the final issue.
First Olynthiac.[1] 11

Like the diet prescribed by doctors, which neither restores the strength of the patient nor allows him to succumb, so these doles that you are now distributing neither suffice to ensure your safety nor allow you to renounce them and try something else.
Third Olynthiac.[1] 33

To remind the man of the good turns you have done him is very much like a reproach.
De Corona.[1] 269

MENANDER
[343-292 B. C.]

Translation by FRANCIS G. ALLINSON, *Loeb Classical Library*

You knew not how to live in clover.
The Girl from Samos. Act 2, Sc. 4

The man who first invented the art of supporting beggars made many wretched.
The Fishermen. Fragment

We live, not as we wish to, but as we can.
The Lady of Andros. Fragment

In many ways the saying "Know thyself" is not well said. It were more practical to say "Know other people."[2]
Thrasyleon. Fragment

I call a fig a fig, a spade a spade.[3]
Unidentified minor fragment

[1] Translation by C. A. AND J. H. VINCE, *Loeb Classical Library.*

[2] See Chaucer, page 6.

[3] Call a spade a spade. — PLUTARCH: *Philip*

A similar saying is credited to Aristophanes by LUCIAN, *Quom. Hist. sit conscrib.,* 41

Brought up like a rude Macedon, and taught

A woman is necessarily an evil, but he that gets the most tolerable one is lucky.[1]
Unidentified minor fragment

Manner, not gold, is woman's best adornment.
Fragment. Quoted in The Spectator, January 3, 1712

PILPAY OR BIDPAI[2]
[*Circa* 326 B. C.?]

We ought to do our neighbour all the good we can. If you do good, good will be done to you; but if you do evil, the same will be measured back to you again.[3]
Chap. 1. Dabschelim and Pilpay

It has been the providence of Nature to give this creature [the cat] nine lives instead of one.[4]
Ibid. Fable 3, The Greedy and Ambitious Cat

There is no gathering the rose without being pricked by the thorns.[5]
Chap. 2. Fable 6, The Two Travellers

Wise men say that there are three sorts of persons who are wholly deprived of judgment, — they who are ambitious of preferments in the courts of princes; they who make use of poison

---

to call a spade a spade. — STEPHEN GOSSON [1554-1624]: *Ephemerides of Phialo* [1579].

I think it good plain English, without fraud, To call a spade a spade, a bawd a bawd.
JOHN TAYLOR, the "Water Poet" [1580-1653]

[1] Marriage is an evil that most men welcome. — MENANDER: *Fragment, Monost. 102.* Motto of *The Spectator,* December 29, 1711

[2] Theodor Benfey [1809-1881], German Orientalist, in tracing the name Pilpay or Bidpai, found that it was an appellative applied to the chief pandit or court scholar of an Indian prince. The *Fables of Pilpay,* or *Kalilah and Dimnah,* are the Arabic translation of the Pahlavi translation of the Sanskrit original of the *Panchatantra.* The first English translation appeared in 1570.

[3] And with what measure ye mete, it shall be measured to you again. — *Matthew, VII, 2*

[4] Nine lives like a cat. — HEYWOOD: *Proverbes, Part II, Chap. 4*

[5] Ne'er the rose without the thorn. — HERRICK: *The Rose*

to show their skill in curing it; and they who intrust women with their secrets.

> *Chap. 2. Fable 6, The Two Travellers*

Men are used as they use others.

> *Ibid. Fable 9, The King Who Became Just*

What is bred in the bone will never come out of the flesh.[1]

> *Ibid. Fable 14, The Two Fishermen*

Guilty consciences always make people cowards.[2]

> *Chap. 3. Fable 3, The Prince and His Minister*

Whoever . . . prefers the service of princes before his duty to his Creator, will be sure, early or late, to repent in vain.

> *Ibid.*

There are some who bear a grudge even to those that do them good.

> *Ibid. Fable 6, A Religious Doctor*

There was once, in a remote part of the East, a man who was altogether void of knowledge and experience, yet presumed to call himself a physician.

> *Ibid. Fable 8, The Ignorant Physician*

He that plants thorns must never expect to gather roses.[3]

> *Ibid.*

Honest men esteem and value nothing so much in this world as a real friend. Such a one is as it were another self, to whom we impart our most secret thoughts, who partakes of our joy, and comforts us in our affliction; add to this, that his company is an everlasting pleasure to us.

> *Chap. 4. Choice of Friends*

---

[1] It will not out of the flesh that is bred in the bone. — HEYWOOD: *Proverbes, Part II, Chap. 8*

[2] Conscience does make cowards of us all. SHAKESPEARE: *Hamlet, Act III, Sc. 1, L. 83*

[3] Whatsoever a man soweth, that shall he also reap. — *Galatians, VI, 7*

As you sow, ye are like to reap.
BUTLER: *Hudibras, II, ii, 504*

That possession was the strongest tenure of the law.[1]

> *Chap. 5. Fable 4, The Cat and the Two Birds*

Wild elephants are caught by tame;
With money it is just the same.

> *The Panchatantra. Book I (Translation adapted from ARTHUR W. RYDER)*

EUCLID
[*Circa* 300 B. C.]

Pons asinorum (the bridge of asses).[2]

> *Elements. Book I, Proposition 5*

There is no royal road to geometry.[3]

> *Quoted by PROCLUS: Commentaria in Euclidem. Book 2, Chap. 4*

THEOCRITUS
[THIRD CENTURY B. C.]

Translation by J. M. EDMONDS, Loeb Classical Library

'Tis peace of mind, lad, we must find, and have a beldame nigh
To sit for us and spit for us and bid all ill go by.

> *The Harvest-Home. Line 126*

O cricket is to cricket dear, and ant for ant doth long,
The hawk's the darling of his fere, and o' me the Muse and her song.

> *The Third Country Singing-Match. Line 31*

O to be a frog, my lads, and live aloof from care.

> *The Reapers. Line 52*

Thou 'lt cut thy finger, niggard, a splitting caraway.

> *Ibid. Line 55*

A great love goes here with a little gift.

> *The Distaff. Line 24*

---

[1] Possession is eleven points in the law. — COLLEY CIBBER: *Woman's Wit, Act I*

[2] Too difficult for asses, or stupid boys, to get over.

[3] Ptolemy I, King of Egypt, wished to study geometry, without going over the thirteen parts of Euclid's *Elements*. He said that a short-cut would be agreeable, whereupon Euclid answered that there was no royal road to geometry. Often misquoted as "no royal road to learning."

PLAUTUS
[254–184 B. C.]

Translation by HENRY THOMAS
RILEY [1816–1878]. *The references are to the text of Ritschl's
second edition, Bohn Classical
Library*

What is yours is mine, and all mine
is yours.[1]

> *Trinummus. Act II, Sc. 2, Line 48
> (329)*

Not by years but by disposition is
wisdom acquired.

> *Ibid. Line 88 (367)*

He whom the gods favour dies in
youth.[2]

> *Bacchides. Act IV, Sc. 7, Line 18
> (816)*

You are seeking a knot in a bulrush.[3]

> *Menaechmi. Act II, Sc. 1, Line 22
> (247)*

In the one hand he is carrying a stone,
while he shows the bread in the other.[4]

> *Aulularia. Act II, Sc. 2, Line 18
> (195)*

It was not for nothing that the raven
was just now croaking on my left hand.[5]

> *Ibid. Act IV, Sc. 3, Line 1 (624)*

There are occasions when it is undoubtedly better to incur loss than to
make gain.

> *Captivi. Act II, Sc. 2, Line 77
> (327)*

Patience is the best remedy for every
trouble.[6]

> *Rudens. Act II, Sc. 5, Line 71*

[1] See Shakespeare, page 37.
[2] The good die first.
WORDSWORTH: *The Excursion, Book I*
[3] A proverbial expression implying a desire
to create doubts and difficulties where there
really are none. It occurs in TERENCE: *Andria, Act V, Sc. 4, L. 38;* also in ENNIUS:
Saturae, 46.
[4] What man is there of you, whom if his
son ask bread, will he give him a stone? —
Matthew, VII, 9
[5] See John Gay, page 206.
[6] Patience is a remedy for every sorrow.—
PUBLILIUS SYRUS: *Maxim 170*

Consider the little mouse, how sagacious an animal it is which never entrusts its life to one hole only.[1]

> *Truculentus. Act IV, Sc. 4, Line 15
> (868)*

Nothing is there more friendly to a
man than a friend in need.[2]

> *Epidicus. Act III, Sc. 3, Line 44
> (425)*

Things which you do not hope happen more frequently than things which
you do hope.[3]

> *Mostellaria. Act I, Sc. 3, Line 40
> (197)*

To blow and swallow at the same
moment is not easy.

> *Ibid. Act III, Sc. 2, Line 104 (791)*

QUINTUS ENNIUS
[239–169 B. C.]

No sooner said than done — so acts
your man of worth.

> *Annals. Book 9 (Quoted by*
> PRISCIANUS)

I never indulge in poetics
Unless I am down with rheumatics.

> *Fragment of a Satire (Quoted by*
> PRISCIANUS)

Let no one pay me honor with tears,
nor celebrate my funeral with mourning.[4]

> *Quoted by* CICERO *in
> De Senectute, XX*

CAECILIUS STATIUS
[220–168 B. C.]

Let him draw out his old age to dotage drop by drop.

> *Hymnis (Quoted by* FESTUS)

The facts will promptly blunt his
ardor.

> *The Changeling (Quoted by*
> CHARISIUS)

[1] See Chaucer, page 7.
[2] A friend in need is a friend indeed. — HAZ-
LITT: *English Proverbs*
[3] The unexpected always happens. — *A common saying*
[4] No funeral gloom, my dears, when I am
gone,
Corpse-gazings, tears, black raiment, graveyard grimness.
WILLIAM ALLINGHAM [1828–1889]: *Diary*

He plants trees to benefit another generation.

Synephebi (Quoted by CICERO in De Senectute, VII)

TERENCE
[185–159 B. C.]

Translation by HENRY THOMAS RILEY [*1816–1878*]. *The references are to the text of the Bohn Classical Library.*

Of surpassing beauty and in the bloom of youth.

Andria. Act I, Sc. 1, Line 45 (72)

Hence these tears.

Ibid. Line 99 (126)

That is a true proverb which is wont to be commonly quoted, that "all had rather it were well for themselves than for another."

Ibid. Act II, Sc. 5, Line 15 (426)

The quarrels of lovers are the renewal of love.[1]

Ibid. Act III, Sc. 3, Line 23 (555)

Look you, I am the most concerned in my own interests.[2]

Ibid. Act IV, Sc. 1, Line 12 (636)

In fine, nothing is said now that has not been said before.[3]

Eunuchus. The Prologue, Line 41

Immortal gods! how much does one man excel another! What a difference there is between a wise person and a fool!

Ibid. Act II, Sc. 2, Line 1 (232)

I have everything, yet have nothing; and although I possess nothing, still of nothing am I in want.[4]

Ibid. Line 12 (243)

There are vicissitudes in all things.

Ibid. Line 45 (276)

The very flower of youth.[5]

Ibid. Sc. 3, Line 27 (319)

I did not care one straw.

Eunuchus. Act III, Sc. 1, Line 21 (411)

Jupiter, now assuredly is the time when I could readily consent to be slain, lest life should sully this ecstasy with some disaster.[1]

Ibid. Sc. 5, Line 2 (550)

This and a great deal more like it I have had to put up with.

Ibid. Act IV, Sc. 6, Line 8 (746)

Take care and say this with presence of mind.[2]

Ibid. Line 31 (769)

It behooves a prudent person to make trial of everything before arms.

Ibid. Sc. 7, Line 19 (789)

I know the disposition of women: when you will, they won't; when you won't, they set their hearts upon you of their own inclination.

Ibid. Line 42 (812)

I took to my heels as fast as I could.

Ibid. Act V, Sc. 2, Line 5 (844)

Many a time, . . . from a bad beginning great friendships have sprung up.

Ibid. Line 34 (873)

I only wish I may see your head stroked down with a slipper.[3]

Ibid. Sc. 8, Line 1 (1028)

I am a man, and nothing that concerns a man do I deem a matter of indifference to me.[4]

Heauton Timoroumenos. Act I, Sc. 1, Line 25 (77)

This is a wise maxim, "to take warning from others of what may be to your own advantage."

Ibid. Sc. 2, Line 36 (210)

That saying which I hear commonly repeated, — that time assuages sorrow.

Ibid. Act III, Sc. 1, Line 12 (421)

---

[1] See Richard Edwards, page 19.

[2] Charity begins at home, is the voice of the World. — SIR THOMAS BROWNE: *Religio Medici* (Everyman ed.), P. 72

[3] See *Ecclesiastes, I, 10* on page 1109

[4] See Wotton, page 114.

[5] See Sophocles, page 965.

---

[1] If it were now to die, 'Twere now to be most happy. SHAKESPEARE: *Othello, Act. II, Sc. 1,* L. 192

[2] Literally, "with a present mind," — equivalent to CAESAR'S *praesentia animi* (*De Bello Gallico, V, 43, 4*).

[3] According to LUCIAN, there was a story that Omphale used to beat Hercules with her slipper or sandal.

[4] Quoted by CICERO in *De Officiis, I, 30.* In the Latin, Homo sum: humani nihil a me alienum puto.

Really, you have seen the old age of an eagle,[1] as the saying is.

> Heauton Timoroumenos. Act III, Sc. 2, Line 9 (520)

Many a time a man cannot be such as he would be, if circumstances do not admit of it.

> Ibid. Act IV, Sc. 1, Line 53 (666)

Nothing is so difficult but that it may be found out by seeking.

> Ibid. Sc. 2, Line 7 (675)

What now if the sky were to fall? [2]

> Ibid. Line 41 (719)

Rigorous law is often rigorous injustice.[3]

> Ibid. Sc. 4, Line 48 (796)

There is nothing so easy but that it becomes difficult when you do it with reluctance.

> Ibid. Sc. 5, Line 1 (805)

Fortune helps the brave.[4]

> Phormio. Act I, Sc. 4, Line 26 (203)

It is the duty of all persons, when affairs are the most prosperous,[5] then in especial to reflect within themselves in what way they are to endure adversity.

> Ibid. Act II, Sc. 1, Line 11 (241)

As many men, so many minds; [6] every one his own way.

> Ibid. Sc. 4, Line 14 (454)

---

[1] This was a proverbial expression, signifying a hale and vigorous old age.

[2] See Heywood, page 12.
Some ambassadors from the Celtae, being asked by Alexander what in the world they dreaded most, answered, that they feared lest the sky should fall upon them. — ARRIANUS: Book I, 4

[3] Extreme law, extreme injustice, is now become a stale proverb in discourse. — CICERO: De Officiis, I, 33
Une extrême justice est souvent une injure (Extreme justice is often injustice). — RACINE: Frères Ennemies, Act IV, Sc. 3
Mais l'extrême justice est une extrême injure. — VOLTAIRE: Oedipus, Act III, Sc. 3

[4] PLINY THE YOUNGER says (Book 6, Letter 16) that PLINY THE ELDER said this during the eruption of Vesuvius: "Fortune favours the brave."

[5] CICERO: Tusculan Questions, Book 3, 30

[6] Quot homines, tot sententiae.

As the saying is, I have got a wolf by the ears.[1]

> Phormio. Act III, Sc. 2, Line 21 (506)

I bid him look into the lives of men as though into a mirror, and from others to take an example for himself.

> Adelphoe. Act III, Sc. 3, Line 61 (415)

According as the man is, so must you humour him.

> Ibid. Line 77 (431)

It is a maxim of old that among themselves all things are common to friends.[2]

> Ibid. Act V, Sc. 3, Line 18 (803)

It is the common vice of all, in old age, to be too intent upon our interests.[3]

> Ibid. Sc. 8, Line 30 (953)

MARCUS TULLIUS CICERO
[106–43 B. C.]

For as lack of adornment is said to become some women, so this subtle oration, though without embellishment, gives delight.[4]

> De Oratore. 78

Thus in the beginning the world was so made that certain signs come before certain events.[5]

> De Divinatione. I, 118

He is never less at leisure than when at leisure.[6]

> De Officiis. IX, 10

What a time! What a civilization! [7]

> Catiline. I, 1

For how many things, which for our own sake we should never do, do we perform for the sake of our friends.

> De Amicitia.[8] XVI

---

[1] A proverbial expression, which, according to SUETONIUS, was frequently in the mouth of Tiberius Caesar.

[2] All things are in common among friends. — DIOGENES LAERTIUS: Diogenes, VI

[3] CICERO quotes this in Tusculan Questions, Book 3. The maxim was a favorite one with the Stoic philosophers.

[4] See Thomson, page 224.

[5] See Coleridge, page 318.

[6] See Samuel Rogers, page 289.

[7] O tempora! O mores!

[8] Translated by CYRUS R. EDMONDS.

Nothing can be more disgraceful than to be at war with him with whom you have lived on terms of friendship.

De Amicitia. XXI

He removes the greatest ornament of friendship, who takes away from it respect.

Ibid. XXII

There is no greater bane to friendship than adulation, fawning, and flattery.

Ibid. XXV

Crimes are not to be measured by the issue of events, but from the bad intentions of men.

Paradox III

There is no place more delightful than home.

Epistolae. IV, 8

While the sick man has life there is hope.[1]

Ibid. IX, 10

For as I like a young man in whom there is something of the old, so I like an old man in whom there is something of the young; and he who follows this maxim, in body will possibly be an old man, but he will never be an old man in mind.

De Senectute.[2] XI

Old age is by nature rather talkative.

Ibid. XVI

Old age, especially an honored old age, has so great authority, that this is of more value than all the pleasures of youth.

Ibid. XVII

Intelligence, and reflection, and judgment, reside in old men, and if there had been none of them, no states could exist at all.

Ibid. XIX

The short period of life is long enough for living well and honourably.[3]

Ibid.

The harvest of old age is the recollection and abundance of blessings previously secured.

De Senectute. XIX

Nor, in truth, would the honours of illustrious men continue after death, if their own spirits did not make us preserve a longer remembrance of them.

Ibid. XXII

Old age is the consummation of life, just as of a play.

Ibid. XXIII

LUCRETIUS
[95–55 B. C.]

Continual dropping wears away a stone.[1]

De Rerum Natura. I, 313

The swift runners who hand over the lamp of life.

Ibid. II, 279

What is food to one man may be fierce poison to others.[2]

Ibid. IV, 637

In the midst of the fountain of wit there arises something bitter, which stings in the very flowers.[3]

Ibid. 1133

SALLUST
[86–34 B. C.]

Translation by J. C. ROLFE

Experience has shown that to be true which Appius[4] says in his verses, that every man is the architect of his own fortune;[5] and this proverb is especially true of you, who have excelled others to such a degree that men are sooner wearied in singing the praises of your deeds than you in doing deeds worthy of praise.

Speech on the State, Addressed to Caesar in His Later Years. Chap. I, Sentence 2

---

[1] While there is life, there's hope. — JOHN GAY: *The Sick Man and the Angel*

[2] Translated by CYRUS R. EDMONDS.

[3] Life is amply long for him who orders it properly. — SENECA: *On the Shortness of Life, I, 4*

[1] See Lyly, page 23.

[2] See Beaumont and Fletcher, page 132.

[3] See Byron, page 352.

[4] Appius Claudius Caecus, consul in 307 B. C.

[5] See Bacon, page 111, and Publilius, Maxim 283.

CORNELIUS NEPOS
[*Floruit* 75 B. C.]

More brawn than brain.
> *Epaminondas. Chap. V, Line 21*

VIRGIL
[70–19 B. C.]

Age carries all things, even the mind, away.
> *Bucolics. IX, Line 51*

We have now made you for a time out of marble.
> *Eclogues. VII, Line 35*

Love conquers all.[1]
> *Ibid. X, Line 69*

Be favourable to bold beginnings.[2]
> *Georgics. I, Line 40*

Practice, by taking thought, might little by little hammer out divers arts.
> *Ibid. Line 133*

Let the fields and the gliding streams in the valleys delight me. Inglorious, let me court the rivers and forests.[3]
> *Ibid. II, Line 485*

Some trouble the dangerous seas with oars, others rush to arms.
> *Ibid. Line 503*

Happy they whose walls already rise.
> *Aeneid. Book I, Line 437*

While rivers run into the sea, while on the mountains shadows move over the slopes, while heaven feeds the stars, ever shall thy honour, thy name, and thy praises endure.
> *Ibid. Line 607*

I fear the Greeks, even when bringing gifts.[4]
> *Ibid. Book II, Line 49*

Do not commit your poems to pages alone. Sing them, I pray you.
> *Ibid. Book VI, Line 74*

Easy is the descent to Avernus.
> *Aeneid. Book VI, Line 126*

Fortunate isle, the abode of the blest.
> *Ibid. Line 639*

Faith in the tale is old, but its fame is everlasting.
> *Ibid. Book IX, Line 79*

It is enough to have perished once.
> *Ibid. Line 140*

I could not bear a mother's tears.
> *Ibid. Line 289*

Steep thyself in a bowl of summer-time.
> *Minor Poems. Copa: Syrisca, a Dancing Girl,[1] Line 29*

Here's Death, twitching my ear: "Live," says he, "for I'm coming."[2]
> *Ibid. Line 38*

These lines made I, another steals my honors;
So you for others, oxen, bear the yoke;
So you for others, bees, store up your honey;
So you for others, sheep, put on your fleece;
So you for others, birds, construct your nests.[3]

HORACE
[65–8 B. C.]

Everyman Edition

But if by thee place 'mid the bards I'm given,

---

[1] See Chaucer, page 5.

[2] For the reverse side of the Great Seal of the United States (first used on the silver dollar certificates, series of 1935) this line of Virgil has been adapted, changed from the imperative mood, *Audacibus annue coeptis,* to the indicative mood, *Annuit coeptis,* He smiles on our beginnings.

[3] These lines preface PHILIP FRENEAU'S poem, *The Indian Student.*

[4] See Euripides, page 967.

[1] Attributed to Virgil by CHARISIUS, the Grammarian, and by SUETONIUS, though modern scholars question the authenticity of all the minor poems.

[2] Quoted by Justice Oliver Wendell Holmes in a radio address on his ninetieth birthday [March 8, 1931].

[3] Virgil wrote a distich, praising Caesar, and Bathyllus claimed the lines. To expose him, Virgil wrote beneath the distich the following incomplete verses, and Caesar asked Bathyllus to finish the lines. He could not, and Virgil then supplied the missing words (italicized below):
Hos ego versiculos feci, tulit alter honores;
Sic vos non vobis, *fertis aratra boves;*
Sic vos non vobis, *mellificatis apes;*
Sic vos non vobis, *vellera fertis oves;*
Sic vos non vobis, *nidificatis aves.*

With soaring head I'll strike the stars of heaven.

> *Odes, Book I.*[1] *I, To Maecenas, Line 35*

No task's too steep for human wit.

> *Ibid. III, To a Ship Bearing Virgil Over Seas, Line 37*

With equal foot Pluto knocks at hovels of the poor,
And at the tyrant's towers.

> *Ibid. IV, Spring, Line 13*

To-night with wine drown care.

> *Ibid. VII, To Plancus, Line 30*

Melt me this cold, freely the firelogs throwing
On hearth, my Thaliarchus! And from crock
Two-eared, of Sabine make, unlock
Wine, with four years a-glowing! [2]

> *Ibid. IX, To Thaliarchus, Line 5*

What next morn's sun may bring, forebear to ask;
But count each day that comes by gift of chance
So much to the good.

> *Ibid. Line 13*

Seize now and here the hour that is, nor trust some later day! [3]

> *Ibid. XI, Leuconoé, Last line*

Daughter, than lovely mother lovelier still.[4]

> *Ibid. XVI, A Palinode or Song of Apology, To a Beloved Girl, Line 1*

Ills which Fate forbids to heal,
Are by endurance lighter made.

> *Ibid. XXIV, Quintilius, Line 19*

One night waits all; Death's road we all must go.

> *Ibid. XXVIII, Archytas, Line 16*

Grant that in age I may not drift
Long years, my lyre forgot! [5]

> *Ibid. XXXI, To Apollo, Line 19*

Brace thee, my friend, when times are hard, to show
A mind unmoved; nor less, when fair thy state,
A sober joy.

> *Odes, Book II.*[1] *III, To Dellius, Line 1*

It is the lofty pine that by the storm
Is oftener tossed; towers fall with heavier crash
Which higher soar.[2]

> *Ibid. X, To Licinius, Line 9*

Spring's flowers, howe'er they bloom, must fade again.

> *Ibid. XI, To Hirpinus Quinctius, Line 9*

And Sisyphus who bears the ban
Of labour without end.[3]

> *Ibid. XIV, To Postumus, Line 19*

Death's boatman takes no bribe, nor brings
Ev'n skilled Prometheus back from Hades' shore.

> *Ibid. XVIII, To a Miser, Line 35*

Good 'tis and fine, for fatherland to die! [4]

> *Ibid. Book III.*[5] *II, Of Roman Virtue, Line 13*

Our fathers' age, than their sires' not so good,
Bred us ev'n worse than they; a brood
We'll leave that's viler still.[6]

> *Ibid. VI, Of Rome's Degeneracy, Line 46*

Bandusia's fount, more bright than crystal.

> *Ibid. XIII, Bandusia's Fountain, Line 1*

Years with their whitening locks subdue the heart

---

[1] Translated by Dr. JOHN MARSHALL.
[2] Dissolve frigus, ligna super foco
Large reponens, atque benignius
Deprome quadrimum Sabina,
O Thaliarche, merum diota.
  Inscription over the fireplace of the
    Harvard Club of Boston
[3] Carpe diem, quam minimum credula postero.
[4] O matre pulchra filia pulchrior.
[5] See Austin Dobson, page 649.

[1] Translated by Dr. JOHN MARSHALL.
[2] See Herodotus, page 969.
[3] Sisyphus, by fate doomed to uplift from ground,
And uphill thrust the stone.
  HORACE: *Epodes, XVII, Horace and Canidia, L. 68* (translated by Dr. JOHN MARSHALL)
[4] Dulce et decorum est pro patria mori.
[5] Translated by Dr. JOHN MARSHALL.
[6] Few sons are like their father, many are worse,
Few, indeed, are better than the father.
  HOMER: *Odyssey, Book II*

Once keen for lawsuits and the reckless
    fray;
I had not taken thus the peaceful part
    In Plancus' day.[1]
> *Odes, Book III. XIV, Triumphal*
> *Ode to Augustus, Line 25*

As riches grow, care follows, and a
    thirst
For more and more.
> *Ibid. XVI, Of Riches and*
> *Contentment, Line 17*

Learn calm to face what's pressing.
> *Ibid. XXIX, To Maecenas,*
> *Line 33*

This day I've lived.
> *Ibid. Line 43*

I shall not wholly die. What's best of
    me
Shall 'scape the tomb.[2]
> *Ibid. XXX, To Melpomene,*
> *A Closing Song to His Muse,*
> *Line 6*

Ev'n though the Golden Age upon the
    earth
Once more may live.[3]
> *Ibid. Book IV.[4] II, To Iulus An-*
> *tonius, a Brother Poet, Line 39*

Summer treads
On heels of Spring.
> *Ibid. VII, To Torquatus, Line 9*

Brave men were living before Agamemnon.
> *Ibid. IX, To Lollius, Line 25*

At the fit hour 'tis sweet to unbend.
> *Ibid. XII, To Virgil, Line 28*

But now Lyciscus' beauty rules the
    roast.[5]
> *Epodes.[4] XI, To Pettius, Line 23*

The laugh will then be mine.
> *Ibid. XV, To Neaera, Line 24*

To bronze Jove changed Earth's golden
    time;

With bronze, then iron, stamped the
    age.
> *Epodes. XVI, Iron and Golden*
> *Age, Line 64*

Then, gods, to reverent youth grant
    purity,
Grant, gods, to quiet age a peaceful
    end.
> *Saecular Hymn.[1] Line 45*

The mountains are in labour, and a
ridiculous mouse will be born.[2]
> *The Art of Poetry.[3] Line 139*

In long works sleep will sometimes
surprise, Homer himself hath been observ'd to nod.[4]
> *Ibid. Line 359*

No one lives content with his condition, whether reason gave it him, or
chance threw it in his way.
> *Satires, Book I.[5] I, Line 1*

We rarely find a man who can say
he has lived happy, and content with
his life can retire from the world like
a satisfied guest.
> *Ibid. Line 117*

This is a fault common to all singers,
that among their friends they never are
inclined to sing when they are asked,
unasked they never desist.
> *Ibid. III, Line 1*

There are many who recite their
writings in the middle of the forum;
and who do it while bathing: the closeness of the place gives melody to the
voice.
> *Ibid. IV, Line 74*

Ridicule often decides matters of importance more effectually, and in a better manner, than severity.
> *Ibid. X, Line 14*

Carrying timber into a wood.[6]
> *Ibid. Line 34*

---

[1] See Byron, page 358.
[2] I shall have more to say when I am dead.
    EDWIN ARLINGTON ROBINSON [1869–
    1935]: *John Brown, last line*
[3] See Spenser, page 25.

The golden age, which a blind tradition has
hitherto placed in the past, is before us. —
C. A. SAINT-SIMON [1675–1755], quoted by
CARLYLE in *Sartor Resartus, Book 3, Chap. 5*
[4] Translated by DR. JOHN MARSHALL.
[5] See John Skelton, page 9.

[1] Translated by DR. JOHN MARSHALL.
[2] See Aesop, page 961.
[3] For other passages from *The Art of Poetry*,
see the Earl of Roscommon, page 180.
[4] *Indignor quandoque bonus dormitat Homerus* (I feel aggrieved whenever good Homer
nods). Generally translated as, "Even the
worthy Homer sometimes nods."
[5] Translated by CHRISTOPHER SMART [1722–
1770].
[6] Or, "Carrying coals to Newcastle." See
Diogenes Laertius, page 1014.

You that intend to write what is worthy to be read more than once, blot frequently: and take no pains to make the multitude admire you, content with a few judicious readers.

Satires, Book I. X, Line 72

Now learn what and how great benefits a temperate diet will bring along with it. In the first place you will enjoy good health.

Ibid. Book II.[1] II, Line 70

Provident for the future, like a wise man in time of peace, shall make the necessary preparations for war.

Ibid. Line 110

Live undaunted; and oppose gallant breasts against the strokes of adversity.[2]

Ibid. Line 135

At Rome, you long for the country; when you are in the country, fickle, you extol the absent city to the skies.

Ibid. VII, Line 28

He has half the deed done, who has made a beginning.

Epistles, Book I.[1] II, To Lollius, Line 40

The covetous man is ever in want.

Ibid. Line 56

Sicilian tyrants never invented a greater torment than envy.

Ibid. Line 58

In the midst of hope and care, in the midst of fears and disquietudes, think every day that shines upon you is the last. Thus the hour, which shall not be expected, will come upon you an agreeable addition.

Ibid. IV, To Albius Tibullus, Line 12

When you have a mind to laugh, you shall see me, fat and sleek with good keeping, a hog of Epicurus' herd.

Ibid. Line 15

As soon as a man perceives how much the things he has discarded excel those which he pursues, let him return

in time, and resume those which he relinquished.

Epistles, Book I. VII, To Maecenas, Line 96

You may drive out nature with a fork, yet still she will return.

Ibid. X, To Aristius Fuscus, Line 24

Whatever prosperous hour Providence bestows upon you, receive it with a thankful hand: and defer not the enjoyment of the comforts of life.

Ibid. XI, To Bullatius, Line 22

They change their climate, not their disposition, who run beyond the sea.

Ibid. Line 27

That man is by no means poor, who has the use of everything he wants. If it is well with your belly, your back, and your feet, regal wealth can add nothing greater.

Ibid. XII, To Iccius, Line 4

Joys are not the property of the rich alone: nor has he lived ill, who at his birth and at his death has passed unnoticed.

Ibid. XVII, To Scaeva, Line 9

To have been acceptable to the great is not the last of praises. It is not every man's lot to gain Corinth.[1]

Ibid. Line 35

The man who makes the experiment deservedly claims the honour and the reward.

Ibid. Line 42

A word, once sent abroad, flies irrevocably.[2]

Ibid. XVIII, To Lollius, Line 70

PROPERTIUS
[54 B.C.–A.D. 2]

Never change when love has found its home.

Book I. Elegy 1, Line 36

Let each man pass his days in that wherein his skill is greatest.

Book II. Elegy 1, Line 46

---

[1] Translated by CHRISTOPHER SMART.
[2] The company is Spartan; see how all their wounds are in front. — BASSUS: *The Greek Anthology, Book 9, Epigram 279*

[1] See Walter Pater, page 646.
[2] Words once spoke can never be recall'd. — HORACE: *De Arte Poetica, L. 390*

Scandal has ever been the doom of beauty.

> *Book II. Elegy 32, Line 26*

OVID
[43 b. c.–a. d. 18]

They come to see; they come that they themselves may be seen.[1]

> *The Art of Love. I, 99*

Nothing is stronger than custom.

> *Ibid. II, 345*

Then the omnipotent Father with his thunder made Olympus tremble, and from Ossa hurled Pelion.[2]

> *Metamorphoses. I, 154*

What you desire is not mortal.

> *Ibid. II, 55*

---

[1] See Chaucer, page 7, and Pope, page 217.
[2]   They were setting
Ossa upon Olympus, and upon
Steep Ossa leafy Pelius.
> CHAPMAN: *Homer's Odyssey,*
> *Book XI, 426*
Heav'd on Olympus tott'ring Ossa stood;
On Ossa Pelion nods with all his wood.
> POPE: *Odyssey, Book XI, 387*
Ossa on Olympus heave, on Ossa roll
Pelion with all his woods; so scale the starry pole.
> SOTHEBY: *Odyssey, Book XI, 315*
To the Olympian summit they essay'd
To heave up Ossa, and to Ossa's crown
Branch-waving Pelion.
> COWPER: *Odyssey, Book XI, 379*
They on Olympus Ossa fain would roll;
On Ossa Pelion's leaf-quivering hill.
> WORSLEY: *Odyssey, Book XI, 414*
> To fling
Ossa upon Olympus, and to pile
Pelion with all its growth of leafy woods
On Ossa.
> BRYANT: *Odyssey, Book XI, 390*
Ossa they pressed down with Pelion's weight,
And on them both impos'd Olympus' hill.
> FITZ-GEFFREY: *The Life and Death of*
> *Sir Francis Drake, St. 99* [1596]
Ter sunt conati imponere Pelio Ossam.
> — VIRGIL: *Georgics, I, 281*
I would have you call to mind the strength of the ancient giants, that undertook to lay the high mountain Pelion on the top of Ossa, and set among those the shady Olympus. —
RABELAIS: *Works, Book IV, Chap. 38*

I see the right, and I approve it, too,
Condemn the wrong and yet the wrong pursue.[1]

> *Metamorphoses. VII, 17*

Poetry comes fine spun from a mind at peace.

> *Tristia. Book I, Chap. 1, Line 39*

While fortune smiles you'll have a host of friends,
But they'll desert you when the storm descends.

> *Ibid. Chap. 9, Line 5*

Grateful must we be that the heart may go whithersoever it will.

> *Epistolae ex Ponto. Book III,*
> *Chap. 5, Line 48*

How little you know about the age you live in if you fancy that honey is sweeter than cash in hand.

> *Fasti. Book I, Line 191*

Janus: I bar the doors in time of peace, lest peace depart.

> *Ibid. Line 279*

The mind, conscious of rectitude, laughed to scorn the falsehood of report.[2]

> *Ibid. Book IV, Line 311*

PUBLILIUS SYRUS [3]
[*Circa* 42 b. c.]

Translation by DARIUS LYMAN. *The numbers are those of the translator.*

As men, we are all equal in the presence of death.

> *Maxim 1*

To do two things at once is to do neither.

> *Maxim 7*

We are interested in others when they are interested in us.[4]

> *Maxim 16*

---

[1] The better I see and approve, the worse I follow. — SPINOZA'S translation in *Ethics, Part IV*
See Euripides, page 967.
[2] The mind conscious of virtue may bring to thee suitable rewards. — VIRGIL: *Aeneid, Book I, L. 603*
[3] Commonly called Publius, but spelled Publilius by PLINY in his *Natural History, 35, Sect. 199.*
[4] We always like those who admire us. —
ROCHEFOUCAULD: *Maxim 294*

Every one excels in something in which another fails.

Maxim 17

The anger of lovers renews the strength of love.[1]

Maxim 24

A god could hardly love and be wise.[2]

Maxim 25

The loss which is unknown is no loss at all.[3]

Maxim 38

He sleeps well who knows not that he sleeps ill.

Maxim 77

A good reputation is more valuable than money.[4]

Maxim 108

It is well to moor your bark with two anchors.

Maxim 119

Learn to see in another's calamity the ills which you should avoid.[5]

Maxim 120

An agreeable companion on a journey is as good as a carriage.

Maxim 143

Society in shipwreck is a comfort to all.[6]

Maxim 144

Many receive advice, few profit by it.

Maxim 149

Patience is a remedy for every sorrow.[7]

Maxim 170

While we stop to think, we often miss our opportunity.

Maxim 185

Whatever you can lose, you should reckon of no account.

Maxim 191

Even a single hair casts its shadow.

Maxim 228

It is sometimes expedient to forget who we are.

Maxim 233

We may with advantage at times forget what we know.

Maxim 234

The end justifies the means.[1]

Maxim 244

You should hammer your iron when it is glowing hot.[2]

Maxim 262

What is left when honour is lost?

Maxim 265

A fair exterior is a silent recommendation.

Maxim 267

Fortune is not satisfied with inflicting one calamity.

Maxim 274

When Fortune is on our side, popular favour bears her company.

Maxim 275

When Fortune flatters, she does it to betray.

Maxim 277

Fortune is like glass, — the brighter the glitter, the more easily broken.

Maxim 280

It is more easy to get a favour from fortune than to keep it.

Maxim 282

His own character is the arbiter of every one's fortune.[3]

Maxim 283

There are some remedies worse than the disease.[4]

Maxim 301

Powerful indeed is the empire of habit.[5]

Maxim 305

---

[1] See Richard Edwards, page 19.

[2] It is impossible to love and be wise. — BACON: *Of Love*

[3] Let him not know 't and he's not robb'd at all.
SHAKESPEARE: *Othello, Act III, Sc. 3, L. 344*

[4] A good name is better than riches. — CERVANTES: *Don Quixote, Part II, Book II, Chap. 33*

[5] The best plan is, as the common proverb has it, to profit by the folly of others. — PLINY: *Natural History, 18, Sect. 31*

[6] See *Maxim 995*.

[7] See Plautus, page 978.

[1] A very free translation of Honesta turpitudo est pro causa bona (Crime is honest for a good cause).

The end must justify the means,
MATTHEW PRIOR: *Hans Carvel*

[2] See Heywood, page 12.

[3] See Bacon, page 111, and Sallust, page 981.

[4] See Bacon, page 110.

Marius said, "I see the cure is not worth the pain." — PLUTARCH: *Lives, Caius Marius*

[5] Habit is second nature. — MONTAIGNE: *Essays, Book III, Chap. 10*

Amid a multitude of projects, no plan is devised.[1]

Maxim 319

It is easy for men to talk one thing and think another.

Maxim 322

When two do the same thing, it is not the same thing after all.

Maxim 338

A cock has great influence on his own dunghill.[2]

Maxim 357

Any one can hold the helm when the sea is calm.[3]

Maxim 358

No tears are shed when an enemy dies.

Maxim 376

The bow too tensely strung is easily broken.

Maxim 388

Treat your friend as if he might become an enemy.

Maxim 402

No pleasure endures unseasoned by variety.[4]

Maxim 406

The judge is condemned when the criminal is absolved.[5]

Maxim 407

Practice is the best of all instructors.[6]

Maxim 439

He who is bent on doing evil can never want occasion.

Maxim 459

One man's wickedness may easily become all men's curse.

Maxim 463

Never find your delight in another's misfortune.

Maxim 467

It is a bad plan that admits of no modification.

Maxim 469

It is better to have a little than nothing.

Maxim 484

It is an unhappy lot which finds no enemies.

Maxim 499

The fear of death is more to be dreaded than death itself.[1]

Maxim 511

A rolling stone gathers no moss.[2]

Maxim 524

Never promise more than you can perform.

Maxim 528

A wise man never refuses anything to necessity.[3]

Maxim 540

No one should be judge in his own cause.[4]

Maxim 545

Necessity knows no law except to conquer.[5]

Maxim 553

Nothing can be done at once hastily and prudently.[6]

Maxim 557

We desire nothing so much as what we ought not to have.

Maxim 559

It is only the ignorant who despise education.

Maxim 571

Do not turn back when you are just at the goal.[7]

Maxim 580

---

[1] He that hath many irons in the fire, some of them will cool. — HAZLITT: *English Proverbs*

[2] See Heywood, page 14.

[3]   The sea being smooth, How many shallow bauble boats dare sail Upon her patient breast.
SHAKESPEARE: *Troilus and Cressida, Act I, Sc. 3, L. 34*

[4] See Cowper, page 265.

[5] Judex damnatur cum nocens absolvitur, — the motto adopted for the *Edinburgh Review*.

[6] Practice makes perfect. — *Proverb*

[1] The sense of death is most in apprehension. SHAKESPEARE: *Measure for Measure, Act III, Sc. 1, L. 76*

[2] See Heywood, page 14.

[3] Yet do I hold that mortal foolish who strives against the stress of necessity. — EURIPIDES: *Hercules Furens, L. 281*

[4] It is not permitted to the most equitable of men to be a judge in his own cause. — PASCAL: *Thoughts, Chap. 4, 1*

[5] See Milton, page 152.

[6] See Chaucer, page 7.

[7] When men are arrived at the goal, they should not turn back. — PLUTARCH: *Of the Training of Children*

It is not every question that deserves an answer.

Maxim 581

No man is happy who does not think himself so.[1]

Maxim 584

Never thrust your own sickle into another's corn.[2]

Maxim 593

You cannot put the same shoe on every foot.

Maxim 596

He bids fair to grow wise who has discovered that he is not so.

Maxim 598

A guilty conscience never feels secure.[3]

Maxim 617

Every day should be passed as if it were to be our last.[4]

Maxim 633

Familiarity breeds contempt.[5]

Maxim 640

Money alone sets all the world in motion.

Maxim 656

He who has plenty of pepper will pepper his cabbage.

Maxim 673

You should go to a pear-tree for pears, not to an elm.[6]

Maxim 674

It is a very hard undertaking to seek to please everybody.

Maxim 675

We should provide in peace what we need in war.[1]

Maxim 709

Look for a tough wedge for a tough log.

Maxim 723

How happy the life unembarrassed by the cares of business!

Maxim 725

They who plough the sea do not carry the winds in their hands.[2]

Maxim 759

He gets through too late who goes too fast.

Maxim 767

In every enterprise consider where you would come out.[3]

Maxim 777

It takes a long time to bring excellence to maturity.

Maxim 780

The highest condition takes rise in the lowest.

Maxim 781

It matters not what you are thought to be, but what you are.

Maxim 785

No one knows what he can do till he tries.

Maxim 786

The next day is never so good as the day before.

Maxim 815

He is truly wise who gains wisdom from another's mishap.

Maxim 825

Good health and good sense are two of life's greatest blessings.

Maxim 827

It matters not how long you live, but how well.

Maxim 829

It is vain to look for a defence against lightning.

Maxim 835

---

[1] No man can enjoy happiness without thinking that he enjoys it. — JOHNSON: *The Rambler, P. 150*

[2] Did thrust as now in others' corn his sickle. — DU BARTAS: *Divine Weekes and Workes, Part II, Second Weeke*

Not presuming to put my sickle in another man's corn. — NICHOLAS YONGE [died 1619]: *Musica Transalpini, Epistle Dedicatory* [1588]

[3] Conscience does make cowards of us all. SHAKESPEARE: *Hamlet, Act III, Sc. 1, L. 83*

[4] Thou wilt find rest from vain fancies if thou doest every act in life as though it were thy last. — MARCUS AURELIUS: *Meditations, II, 5*

[5] See Shakespeare, page 34.

[6] You may as well expect pears from an elm. — CERVANTES: *Don Quixote, Part II, Book II, Chap. 40*

[1] See Washington, page 268.

[2] The pilot cannot mitigate the billows or calm the winds. — PLUTARCH: *Of the Tranquillity of the Mind*

[3] In every affair, consider what precedes and what follows, and then undertake it. — EPICTETUS: *That Everything is to be Undertaken with Circumspection, Chap. 15*

No good man ever grew rich all at once.[1]

Maxim 837

Everything is worth what its purchaser will pay for it.[2]

Maxim 847

It is better to learn late than never.[3]

Maxim 864

Better be ignorant of a matter than half know it.[4]

Maxim 865

Better use medicines at the outset than at the last moment.

Maxim 866

Prosperity makes friends, adversity tries them.

Maxim 872

Whom Fortune wishes to destroy she first makes mad.[5]

Maxim 911

Let a fool hold his tongue and he will pass for a sage.

Maxim 914

He knows not when to be silent who knows not when to speak.

Maxim 930

You need not hang up the ivy-branch over the wine that will sell.[6]

Maxim 968

It is a consolation to the wretched to have companions in misery.[7]

Maxim 995

Unless degree is preserved, the first place is safe for no one.[8]

Maxim 1042

Confession of our faults is the next thing to innocency.

Maxim 1060

---

[1] No just man ever became rich all at once. — MENANDER: *Fragment*

[2]   What is worth in anything
But so much money as 'twill bring?
BUTLER: *Hudibras, Part I, Canto I, L. 465*

[3] See Shakespeare, page 46.

[4] See Bacon, page 110.

[5] See Dryden, page 175.

[6] Good wine needs no bush. — SHAKESPEARE: *As You Like It, Epilogue, L. 4*

[7] See *Maxim 144.*
See Cervantes, page 1036.
It is a comfort to the unhappy to have companions in misery. — SPINOZA: *Ethics, Part 4, Proposition 57, Note*

[8] See Shakespeare, page 75.

I have often regretted my speech, never my silence.[1]

Maxim 1070

Keep the golden mean [2] between saying too much and too little.

Maxim 1072

Speech is a mirror of the soul: as a man speaks, so is he.

Maxim 1073

SENECA
[8 B. C.–A. D. 65]

Translation by W. H. D. ROUSE,
Loeb Classical Library

What fools these mortals be.[3]

Epistles. 1, 3

It is not the man who has too little, but the man who craves more, that is poor.

Ibid. 2, 2

Love of bustle is not industry.

Ibid. 3, 5

Live among men as if God beheld you; speak to God as if men were listening.

Ibid. 10, 5

The best ideas are common property.

Ibid. 12, 11

Men do not care how nobly they live, but only how long, although it is within the reach of every man to live nobly, but within no man's power to live long.

Ibid. 22, 17

A great pilot can sail even when his canvas is rent.

Ibid. 30, 3

Man is a reasoning animal.

Ibid. 41, 8

That most knowing of persons, — gossip.

Ibid. 43, 1

---

[1] Simonides said "that he never repented that he held his tongue, but often that he had spoken." — PLUTARCH: *Rules for the Preservation of Health*

[2] The golden mean. — COWPER: *Translation of Horace's Odes, Book II, Ode 10, To Licinius, St. 2*

[3] Lord, what fools these mortals be. — SHAKESPEARE: *A Midsummer-Night's Dream, Act III, Sc. 2, L. 115*

It is quality rather than quantity that matters.

Epistles. 45, 1

You can tell the character of every man when you see how he receives praise.

Ibid. 52, 12

Not lost, but gone before.[1]

Ibid. 63, 16

All art is but imitation of nature.

Ibid. 65, 3

It is a rough road that leads to the heights of greatness.

Ibid. 84, 13

I was shipwrecked before I got aboard.

Ibid. 87, 1

It is better, of course, to know useless things than to know nothing.

Ibid. 88, 45

Do not ask for what you will wish you had not got.

Ibid. 95, 1

We are mad, not only individually, but nationally. We check manslaughter and isolated murders; but what of war and the much vaunted crime of slaughtering whole peoples?

Ibid. 95, 30

A great step towards independence is a good-humored stomach.

Ibid. 123, 3

Fire is the test of gold; adversity, of strong men.[2]

Moral Essays. On Providence, 5, 9

Whom they have injured they also hate.[3]

Ibid. On Anger, 2, 33

I do not distinguish by the eye, but by the mind, which is the proper judge of the man.

Ibid. On the Happy Life, 2, 2

There is no great genius without some touch of madness.[1]

Moral Essays. On Tranquillity of the Mind, 17, 10

A great fortune is a great slavery.

Ibid. To Polybius on Consolation, 6, 5

Wherever the Roman conquers, there he dwells.

Ibid. To Helvia on Consolation, 7, 7

He who receives a benefit with gratitude, repays the first instalment on his debt.

On Benefits. Book 2, 22, 1

You roll my log, and I will roll yours.

Apocolocyntosis. Chap. 9

Do you seek Alcides' equal? None is, except himself.[2]

Hercules Furens. 1, 1, 84

Successful and fortunate crime is called virtue.[3]

Ibid. 255

A good mind possesses a kingdom.[4]

Thyestes. 380

PHAEDRUS
[*Circa* A. D. 8]

Translation by HENRY THOMAS RILEY [*1816–1878*]. *Bohn Classical Library*

Submit to the present evil, lest a greater one befall you.

Book I. Fable 2, 31

He who covets what belongs to another deservedly loses his own.

Ibid. Fable 4, 1

That it is unwise to be heedless ourselves while we are giving advice to others, I will show in a few lines.

Ibid. Fable 9, 1

Whoever has even once become notorious by base fraud, even if he speaks the truth, gains no belief.

Ibid. Fable 10, 1

---

[1] Non amittuntur, sed praemittuntur. See Samuel Rogers, page 289.
[2] See Beaumont and Fletcher, page 131.
[3] See Dryden, page 178.

[1] An ancient commonplace, which Seneca says he quotes from ARISTOTLE: *Problemata, 30, 1.* It is also in PLATO: *Phaedrus, 245 A.* See Dryden, page 173, and Lombroso, page 1077.
[2] See Theobald, page 221.
[3] See Harrington, page 29.
[4] See Dyer, page 20.

By this story [The Fox and the Raven] it is shown how much ingenuity avails, and how wisdom is always an overmatch for strength.

Book I. Fable 13, 13

No one returns with good-will to the place which has done him a mischief.

Ibid. Fable 18, 1

It has been related that dogs drink at the river Nile running along, that they may not be seized by the crocodiles.[1]

Ibid. Fable 25, 3

Every one is bound to bear patiently the results of his own example.

Ibid. Fable 26, 12

Come of it what may, as Sinon said.

Book III. The Prologue, 27

Things are not always what they seem.[2]

Book IV. Fable 2, 5

Jupiter has loaded us with a couple of wallets: the one, filled with our own vices, he has placed at our backs; the other, heavy with those of others, he has hung before.[3]

Ibid. Fable 10, 1

A mountain was in labour, sending forth dreadful groans, and there was in the region the highest expectation. After all, it brought forth a mouse.[4]

Ibid. Fable 22, 1

A fly bit the bare pate of a bald man, who in endeavouring to crush it gave himself a hard slap. Then said the fly jeeringly, "You wanted to revenge the

---

[1] PLINY, in his *Natural History, Book 8, Sect. 148*, and AELIAN, in his *Various Histories*, relate the same fact as to the dogs drinking from the Nile. "To treat a thing as the dogs do the Nile" was a common proverb with the ancients, signifying to do it superficially.

[2] Non semper ea sunt quae videntur.
See Longfellow, page 433.

[3] Everybody has his own delusion assigned to him: but we do not see that part of the bag which hangs on our back. — CATULLUS: *Poem 22, L. 20*
Whosoever shall call me madman, shall hear as much from me, and shall learn to look back upon the bag that hangs behind him. — HORACE: *Satires, Book II, III*
All watch the wallet on the back that walks before. — PERSIUS: *4, 24*

[4] See Aesop, page 961, and Horace, page 984.

sting of a tiny insect with death; what will you do to yourself, who have added insult to injury?"[1]

Book V. Fable 3, 1

"I knew that before you were born." Let him who would instruct a wiser man consider this as said to himself.

Ibid. Fable 9, 4

PLINY THE ELDER
[A. D. 23–79]

With some alterations, from translations by JOHN BOSTOCK, M.D. *[1773–1846] and* HENRY THOMAS RILEY *[1816–1878]. Bohn Classical Library*

In comparing various authors with one another, I have discovered that some of the gravest and latest writers have transcribed, word for word, from former works, without making acknowledgment.

Natural History. Book I, Dedication, Sect. 22

The world, and whatever that be which we call the heavens, by the vault of which all things are enclosed, we must conceive to be a deity, to be eternal, without bounds, neither created nor subject at any time to destruction. To inquire what is beyond it is no concern of man; nor can the human mind form any conjecture concerning it.

Ibid. Book II, Sect. 1

It is ridiculous to suppose that the great head of things, whatever it be, pays any regard to human affairs.

Ibid. Sect. 20

Everything is soothed by oil, and this is the reason why divers send out small quantities of it from their mouths, because it smooths every part which is rough.[2]

Ibid. Sect. 234

---

[1] See Aesop, page 961.

[2] Why does pouring oil on the sea make it clear and calm? Is it for that the winds, slipping the smooth oil, have no force, nor cause any waves? — PLUTARCH: *Natural Questions, IX*
Bishop Adain [A. D. 651] gave to a company about to take a journey by sea "some holy oil,

It is far from easy to determine whether she [Nature] has proved to him a kind parent or a merciless step-mother.[1]

Natural History. Book VII, Sect. 1

Man alone at the very moment of his birth, cast naked upon the naked earth, does she abandon to cries and lamentations.[2]

Ibid. Sect. 2

To laugh, if but for an instant only, has never been granted to man before the fortieth day from his birth, and then it is looked upon as a miracle of precocity.[3]

Ibid.

Man is the only one that knows nothing, that can learn nothing without being taught. He can neither speak nor walk nor eat, and in short he can do nothing at the prompting of nature only, but weep.[4]

Ibid. Sect. 4

saying, 'I know that when you go abroad you will meet with a storm and contrary wind; but do you remember to cast this oil I give you into the sea, and the wind shall cease immediately.' " — BEDE: *Ecclesiastical History, Book III, Chap. 14*

In JARED SPARKS' edition of BENJAMIN FRANKLIN'S *Works, Vol. VI, P. 354,* there are letters between Franklin, Brownrigg, and Parish on the stilling of waves by means of oil.

[1] To man the earth seems altogether
No more a mother, but a step-dame rather.
  GUILLAUME DE SALLUSTE DU BARTAS [1544–1590]: *Divine Weekes and Workes, First Weeke, Third Day*

[2] He is born naked, and falls a-whining at the first. — BURTON: *Anatomy of Melancholy, Part I, Sect. 2, Memb. 3, Subsect. 10*

And when I was born, I drew in the common air, and fell upon the earth, which is of like nature; and the first voice which I uttered was crying, as all others do. — *The Wisdom of Solomon, VII, 3*

It was the custom among the ancients to place the new-born child upon the ground immediately after its birth

[3] This term of forty days is mentioned by ARISTOTLE in his *Natural History,* as also by some modern physiologists.

[4] No language but a cry. — TENNYSON: *In Memoriam, LIV, 5*

With man, most of his misfortunes are occasioned by man.[1]

Natural History. Book VII, Sect. 5

Indeed, what is there that does not appear marvellous when it comes to our knowledge for the first time?[2] How many things, too, are looked upon as quite impossible until they have been actually effected?

Ibid. Sect. 6

The human features and countenance, although composed of but some ten parts or little more, are so fashioned that among so many thousands of men there are no two in existence who cannot be distinguished from one another.[3]

Ibid. Sect. 8

All men possess in their bodies a poison which acts upon serpents; and the human saliva, it is said, makes them take to flight, as though they had been touched with boiling water. The same substance, it is said, destroys them the moment it enters their throat.[4]

Ibid. Sect. 15

It has been observed that the height of a man from the crown of the head to the sole of the foot is equal to the distance between the tips of the middle fingers of the two hands when extended in a straight line.

Ibid. Sect. 77

When a building is about to fall down, all the mice desert it.[5]

Ibid. Book VIII, Sect. 103

[1] Man's inhumanity to man. — BURNS: *Man Was Made to Mourn*

[2] Omne ignotum pro magnifico (Everything that is unknown is taken to be grand). — TACITUS: *Agricola, 30*

[3] See Sir Thomas Browne, page 144.

[4] Madame d'Abrantes relates that when Bonaparte was in Cairo he sent for a serpent-detecter (Psylli) to remove two serpents that had been seen in his house. He having enticed one of them from his hiding-place, caught it in one hand, just below the jaw-bone, in such a manner as to oblige the mouth to open. when spitting into it, the effect was like magic: the reptile appeared struck with instant death. — *Memoirs, Vol. I, Chap. 59*

[5] This is alluded to by CICERO in his letters to Atticus, and is mentioned by AELIAN (*Animated Nature, Book VI, Chap. 41*). Compare the modern proverb, "Rats desert a sinking ship."

Bears when first born are shapeless masses of white flesh a little larger than mice, their claws alone being prominent. The mother then licks them gradually into proper shape.[1]

Natural History. Book VIII,
Sect. 126

It has become quite a common proverb that in wine there is truth.

Ibid. Book XIV, Sect. 141

Cincinnatus was ploughing his four jugera of land upon the Vaticanian Hill, — the same that are still known as the Quintian Meadows, — when the messenger brought him the dictatorship, finding him, the tradition says, stripped to the work.

Ibid. Book XVIII, Sect. 20

The agricultural population, says Cato, produces the bravest men, the most valiant soldiers, and a class of citizens the least given of all to evil designs.

Ibid. Sect. 26

Why is it that we entertain the belief that for every purpose odd numbers are the most effectual?[2]

Ibid. Book XXVIII, Sect. 23

It was a custom with Apelles, to which he most tenaciously adhered, never to let any day pass, however busy he might be, without exercising himself by tracing some outline or other, — a practice which has now passed into a proverb.[3] It was also a practice with him, when he had completed a work, to exhibit it to the view of the passers-by in his studio, while he himself, con-

cealed behind the picture, would listen to the criticisms. . . . Under these circumstances, they say that he was censured by a shoemaker for having represented the shoes with one latchet too few. The next day, the shoemaker, quite proud at seeing the former error corrected, thanks to his advice, began to criticize the leg; upon which Apelles, full of indignation, popped his head out and reminded him that a shoemaker should give no opinion beyond the shoes,[1] — a piece of advice which has equally passed into a proverbial saying.

Natural History. Book XXXV,
Sect. 84

LUCAN
[A. D. 39–65]

Translation by J. D. DUFF. *Loeb Classical Library*

Poverty, the mother of manhood.

The Civil War. Book I, Line 165

Delay is ever fatal to those who are prepared.

Ibid. Line 281

When the whole world is nodding to its fall, happy the man who has been able to learn already the lowly place appointed for him.

Ibid. Book IV, Line 393

Boldness is a mask for fear, however great.

Ibid. Line 702

Yonder trouble concerns the sky and sea, but not our bark; for Caesar treads the deck.[2]

Ibid. Book V, Line 584

DIO CHRYSOSTOM
[A. D. 40–120]

Translation by J. W. COHOON. *Loeb Classical Library*

Diogenes: The man I know not, for I am not acquainted with his mind.

Fourth Discourse on Kingship.
Chap. 17

---

[1] See Burton, page 122, and Montaigne, page 1029.

Not unlike the bear which bringeth forth
In the end of thirty dayes a shapeless birth;
But after licking, it in shape she drawes,
And by degrees she fashions out the pawes,
The head, and neck, and finally doth bring
To a perfect beast that first deformed thing.
DU BARTAS: *Divine Weekes and Workes,*
First Weeke, First Day

[2] See Shakespeare, page 35, and Samuel Lover, page 389.

Numero deus impare gaudet (The god delights in an odd number). — VIRGIL: *Eclogues,* 8, 75

[3] Nulla dies abeat, quin linea ducta supersit. — ERASMUS. Generally quoted, Nulla dies sine linea (No day without a line).

[1] Ne supra crepidam sutor judicaret (Let not a shoemaker judge above his shoe), or, Let the cobbler stick to his last.

[2] See Plutarch, page 1000.

Idleness and lack of occupation are the best things in the world to ruin the foolish.

Tenth Discourse, On Servants.
Chap. 7

Like men with sore eyes: they find the light painful, while the darkness, which permits them to see nothing, is restful and agreeable.

Eleventh, or Trojan, Discourse.
Chap. 2

Most men are so completely corrupted by opinion that they would rather be notorious for the greatest calamities than suffer no ill and be unknown.

Ibid. Chap. 6

Generally speaking, men are too cowardly to be willing to undergo severe suffering, since they fear death and pain, but they highly prize being mentioned as having suffered.

Ibid. Chap. 10

MARTIAL
[A. D. 40–102]

To yield to the stronger is valor's second prize.

On the Spectacles. Epigram 32

I do not love thee, Sabidius, nor can I say why; this only I can say, I do not love thee.[1]

Epigrams. Book I, 32

I write long epigrams, you yourself write nothing. Yours are shorter.[2]

Ibid. 110

Nothing is more confident than a bad poet.[3]

Ibid. Book II, 63

He does not write at all whose poems no man reads.

Ibid. Book III, 9

The flaw which is hidden is deemed greater than it is.

Ibid. 52

The bee enclosed and through the amber shown

[1] See Tom Brown, page 188.
[2] An epigram of two lines has every merit, and if you exceed three lines it is rhapsody. — CYRILLUS: *The Greek Anthology, Book 9, Epigram 369*
[3] Quoted by MONTAIGNE in *Of Presumption.*

Seems buried in the juice which was his own.[1]

Epigrams. Book IV, 32

What is the use of brevity if it constitute a book?

Ibid. Book VIII, 29

The good man prolongs his life; to be able to enjoy one's past life is to live twice.[2]

Ibid. Book X, 23

Neither fear, nor wish for, your last day.[3]

Ibid. 47

There is no glory in outstripping donkeys.

Ibid. Book XII, 36

QUINTILIAN
[A. D. 42–118]

We give to necessity the praise of virtue.[4]

Institutiones Oratoriae.
Book I, 8, 14

A liar should have a good memory.[5]

Ibid. Book IV, 2, 91

Vain hopes are often like the dreams of those who wake.

Ibid. Book VI, 2, 30

Those who wish to appear wise among fools, among the wise seem foolish.[6]

Ibid. Book X, 7, 21

PLUTARCH
[A. D. 46–120]

Translation by JOHN DRYDEN, *revised by* ARTHUR HUGH CLOUGH.
Modern Library Giant Edition

As geographers, Sosius, crowd into the edges of their maps parts of the world which they do not know about, adding notes in the margin to the effect that beyond this lies nothing but sandy

[1] See Bacon, page 111.
[2] See Alexander Pope, page 217.
[3] See Milton, page 155.
[4] See Chaucer, page 4.
[5] See Algernon Sidney, page 169.
[6] See Pope, page 215.

deserts full of wild beasts, and unapproachable bogs.[1]

Lives. Theseus, Page 3

From Theseus began the saying, "He is a second Hercules."

Ibid. Page 19

The most perfect soul, says Heraclitus, is a dry light, which flies out of the body as lightning breaks from a cloud.

Ibid. Romulus, Page 45

Anacharsis, coming to Athens, knocked at Solon's door, and told him that he, being a stranger, was come to be his guest, and contract a friendship with him; and Solon replying, "It is better to make friends at home," Anacharsis replied, "Then you that are at home make friendship with me."

Ibid. Solon, Page 99

Themistocles said that he certainly could not make use of any stringed instrument; could only, were a small and obscure city put into his hands, make it great and glorious.

Ibid. Themistocles, Page 134

Eurybiades lifting up his staff as if he were going to strike, Themistocles said, "Strike, if you will, but hear." [2]

Ibid. Page 141

Themistocles said to Antiphates, . . . "Time, young man, has taught us both a lesson."

Ibid. Page 145

"You speak truth," said Themistocles; "I should never have been famous if I had been of Seriphus; [3] nor you, had you been of Athens."

Ibid.

Laughing at his own son, who got his mother, and, by his mother's means, his father also, to indulge him, he told him that he had the most power of any one in Greece: "For the Athenians command the rest of Greece, I command the Athenians, your mother commands me, and you command your mother." [4]

Ibid.

[1] See Jonathan Swift, page 190.
[2] "Strike," said he, "but hear me." — *Apophthegms of Kings and Great Commanders, Themistocles*
[3] An obscure island.
[4] "Men," said Marcus Cato, "usually command women; but we command all men, and

Of two who made love to his daughter, he preferred the man of worth to the one who was rich, saying he desired a man without riches, rather than riches without a man.

Lives. Themistocles, Page 145

Themistocles replied that a man's discourse was like to a rich Persian carpet, the beautiful figures and patterns of which can be shown only by spreading and extending it out; when it is contracted and folded up, they are obscure and lost.[1]

Ibid. Page 152

Moderation is best, and to avoid all extremes.

Ibid. Camillus, Page 159

Caesar once, seeing some wealthy strangers at Rome, carrying up and down with them in their arms and bosoms young puppy-dogs and monkeys, embracing and making much of them, took occasion not unnaturally to ask whether the women in their country were not used to bear children.

Ibid. Pericles, Page 182

He who busies himself in mean occupations produces, in the very pains he takes about things of little or no use, an evidence against himself of his negligence and indisposition to what is really good.

Ibid. Page 183

the women command us." But this, indeed, is borrowed from the sayings of Themistocles. — *Lives, Marcus Cato, P. 416*
Diophantus, the young son of Themistocles, made his boast often and in many companies, that whatsoever pleased him pleased also all Athens; for whatever he liked, his mother liked; and whatever his mother liked, Themistocles liked; and whatever Themistocles liked, all the Athenians liked. — *Of the Training of Children*
When the son of Themistocles was a little saucy toward his mother, he said that this boy had more power than all the Grecians; for the Athenians governed Greece, he the Athenians, his wife him, and his son his wife. — *Apophthegms of Kings and Great Commanders, Themistocles*
[1] Themistocles said speech was like to tapestry; and like it, when it was spread it showed its figures, but when it was folded up, hid and spoiled them. — *Apophthegms of Kings and Great Commanders, Themistocles*

So very difficult a matter is it to trace and find out the truth of anything by history.

Lives. Pericles, Page 194

Like a skilful physician, who, in a complicated and chronic disease, as he sees occasion, at one while allows his patient the moderate use of such things as please him, at another while gives him keen pains and drugs to work the cure.

Ibid. Page 195

Be ruled by time, the wisest counsellor of all.

Ibid. Page 198

Old women should not seek to be perfumed.

Ibid. Page 203

Trees, when they are lopped and cut, grow up again in a short time,[1] but men, being once lost, cannot easily be recovered.

Ibid. Page 207

To be turned from one's course by men's opinions, by blame, and by misrepresentation, shows a man unfit to hold an office.

Ibid. Fabius, Page 216

You know, Hannibal, how to gain a victory, but not how to use it.

Ibid. Page 224

One colour, indeed, they say the chameleon cannot assume: it cannot itself appear white; but Alcibiades, whether with good men or bad, could adapt himself to his company.

Ibid. Alcibiades, Page 249

Menenius Agrippa concluded, at length, with the celebrated fable: "It once happened that all the other members of a man mutinied against the stomach, which they accused as the only idle, uncontributing part in the whole body, while the rest were put to hardships and the expense of much labour to supply and minister to its appetites."[2]

Ibid. Coriolanus, Page 266

Men are usually more stung and galled by reproachful words than hostile actions.

Lives. Timoleon, Page 316

A Roman divorced from his wife, being highly blamed by his friends, who demanded, "Was she not chaste? Was she not fair? Was she not fruitful?" holding out his shoe, asked them whether it was not new and well made. "Yet," added he, "none of you can tell where it pinches me."[1]

Ibid. Aemilius Paulus, Page 322

Petty repeated annoyances, arising from unpleasantness or incongruity of character, have been the occasion of such estrangement as to make it impossible for man and wife to live together with any content.

Ibid.

A man without one scar to show on his skin, that is smooth and sleek with ease and home-keeping habits, will undertake to define the office and duties of a general.

Ibid. Page 340

The saying of old Antigonus, who when he was to fight at Andros, and one told him, "The enemy's ships are more than ours," replied, "For how many then wilt thou reckon me?"

Ibid. Pelopidas, Page 348

Archimedes had stated, that given the force, any given weight might be moved; and even boasted . . . that if there were another earth, by going into it he could remove this.

Ibid. Marcellus, Page 367

They named it Ovation, from the Latin *ovis* (a sheep).

Ibid. Page 382

Asking him if Aristides had ever done him any injury, "None at all," said he, "neither know I the man; but I am tired of hearing him everywhere called the Just."

Ibid. Aristides, Page 396

Nor are we to use living creatures like old shoes or dishes and throw them

---

[1] The lopped tree in time may grow again,
  Most naked plants renew both fruit and
    flower.
  ROBERT SOUTHWELL: *Times Go by Turns*
[2] See Aesop, page 961.

[1] See Herbert, page 137.
I can tell where my own shoe pinches me.
— CERVANTES: *Don Quixote, Part I, Book IV, Chap. 5*

away when they are worn out or broken with service.

Lives. Marcus Cato, Page 415

It is a difficult task, O citizens, to make speeches to the belly, which has no ears.[1]

Ibid. Page 416

Cato used to assert that wise men profited more by fools, than fools by wise men; for that wise men avoided the faults of fools, but that fools would not imitate the good examples of wise men.

Ibid. Page 417

He said that in his whole life he most repented of three things: one was that he had trusted a secret to a woman; another, that he went by water when he might have gone by land; the third, that he had remained one whole day without doing any business of moment.

Ibid. Page 418

It was hard for him who had lived with one generation of men, to plead now before another.

Ibid. Page 422

Carthage, methinks, ought utterly to be destroyed.

Ibid. Page 431

Marius said, "I see the cure is not worth the pain."[2]

Ibid. Caius Marius, Page 496

Extraordinary rains pretty generally fall after great battles.

Ibid. Page 507

Marius said that the law spoke too softly to be heard in such a noise of war.

Ibid. Page 511

Lycurgus . . . used to say that long hair made good-looking men more beautiful, and ill-looking men more terrible.

Ibid. Lysander, Page 525

Where the lion's skin will not reach, you must patch it out with the fox's.[1]

Lives. Lysander, Page 529

Moral habits, induced by public practices, are far quicker in making their way into men's private lives, than the failings and faults of individuals are in infecting the city at large.

Ibid. Page 535

As it is in the proverb, played Cretan against Cretan.[2]

Ibid. Page 537

Did you not know, then, that to-day Lucullus dines with Lucullus?

Ibid. Lucullus, Page 622

Lucullus' furnishing a library, however, deserves praise and record, for he collected very many choice manuscripts; and the use they were put to was even more magnificent than the purchase, the library being always open, and the walks and reading-rooms about it free to all Greeks.

Ibid. Page 623

Economy, which in things inanimate is but money-making, when exercised over men becomes policy.

Ibid. Crassus, Page 651

Whoever tries for great objects must suffer something.

Ibid. Page 669

It is no great wonder if in long process of time, while fortune takes her course hither and thither, numerous coincidences should spontaneously occur. If the number and variety of subjects to be wrought upon be infinite, it is all the more easy for fortune, with such an abundance of material, to effect this similarity of results.[3]

Ibid. Sertorius, Page 678

---

[1] The prince must be a lion, but he must also know how to play the fox. — NICOLO MACHIAVELLI: *The Prince*

[2] He only played the Cretan with the Cretans. — PLUTARCH: *Lives, Aemilius Paulus, P. 335*

Cheat against cheat. The Cretans were notorious as liars.

[3] History repeats itself. — *Proverb*

'Tis one and the same Nature that rolls on her course, and whoever has sufficiently considered the present state of things might certainly conclude as to both the future and

---

[1] The belly has no ears, nor is it to be filled with fair words. — RABELAIS: *Book IV, Chap. 67*

[2] See Bacon, page 110.

In treating wounds, the cure for pain is pain. CATO THE CENSOR [234–149 B.C.], *Book IV, Distich 40*

Perseverance is more prevailing than violence; and many things which cannot be overcome when they are together, yield themselves up when taken little by little.

Lives. Sertorius, Page 688

Good fortune will elevate even petty minds, and give them the appearance of a certain greatness and stateliness, as from their high place they look down upon the world; but the truly noble and resolved spirit raises itself, and becomes more conspicuous in times of disaster and ill fortune.

Ibid. Eumenes, Page 703

Agesilaus being invited once to hear a man who admirably imitated the nightingale, he declined, saying he had heard the nightingale itself.[1]

Ibid. Agesilaus, Page 726

If all the world were just, there would be no need of valour.

Ibid. Page 727

It is circumstance and proper measure that give an action its character, and make it either good or bad.

Ibid. Page 736

The old proverb was now made good, "the mountain had brought forth a mouse."[2]

Ibid.

No man ever asked a favour with less offence, or conferred one with a better grace. When he gave, it was without assumption; when he received, it was with dignity and honour.

Ibid. Pompey, Page 740

Pompey bade Sylla recollect that more worshipped the rising than the setting sun.[1]

Lives. Pompey, Page 749

A dead man cannot bite.

Ibid. Page 795

Whenever Alexander heard Philip had taken any town of importance, or won any signal victory, instead of rejoicing at it altogether, he would tell his companions that his father would anticipate everything, and leave him and them no opportunities of performing great and illustrious actions.[2]

Ibid. Alexander, Page 804

When Alexander asked Diogenes whether he wanted anything, "Yes," said he, "I would have you stand from between me and the sun."

Ibid. Page 810

Alexander finding himself unable to untie the Gordium knot, the ends of which were secretly twisted round and folded up within it, cut it asunder with his sword.

Ibid. Page 813

When asked why he parted with his wife, Caesar replied, "I wished my wife to be not so much as suspected."[3]

Ibid. Caesar, Page 860

For my part, I had rather be the first man among these fellows, than the second man in Rome.[4]

Ibid. Page 861

He who reflects on another man's want of breeding, shows he wants it as much himself.

Ibid. Page 865

Using the proverb frequently in their mouths who enter upon dangerous and

---

the past. — MONTAIGNE: *Essays, Book II, Chap. 12, Apology for Raimond Sebond*

I shall be content if those shall pronounce my History useful who desire to give a view of events as they did really happen, and as they are very likely, in accordance with human nature, to repeat themselves at some future time, — if not exactly the same, yet very similar. — THUCYDIDES: *History, I, 2, 2*

What is this day supported by precedents will hereafter become a precedent. — THUCYDIDES: *Annals, XI, 24*

[1] Agesilaus being exhorted to hear one that imitated the voice of a nightingale, "I have often," said he, "heard nightingales themselves." — *Apophthegms of Kings and Great Commanders, Agesilaus*

[2] See Aesop, page 961, and Horace, page 984.

[1] See David Garrick, page 242.

He [Tiberius] upbraided Macro in no obscure and indirect terms "with forsaking the setting sun and turning to the rising." — TACITUS: *Annals, Book IV, Chap. 47, 20*

[2] While Alexander was a boy, Philip had great success in his affairs, at which he did not rejoice, but told the children that were brought up with him, "My father will leave me nothing to do." — *Apophthegms of Kings and Great Commanders, Alexander*

[3] Caesar's wife ought to be above suspicion. — *Roman Apophthegms, Caesar*

[4] I had rather be the first in this town than second in Rome. — *Ibid.*

bold attempts, "The die is cast," he took the river.[1]

Lives. Caesar, Page 874

"And this," said Caesar, "you know, young man, is more disagreeable for me to say than to do."[2]

Ibid. Page 876

Go on, my friend, and fear nothing; you carry Caesar and his fortune in your boat.[3]

Ibid. Page 877

[Cleopatra] was at a loss how to get in undiscovered, till she thought of putting herself into the coverlet of a bed and lying at length, whilst Apollodorus tied up the bedding and carried it on his back through the gates to Caesar's apartment.

Ibid. Page 883

Caesar's barber, a busy listening fellow.

Ibid.

Caesar said to the soothsayer, "The ides of March are come"; who answered him calmly, "Yes, they are come, but they are not past."[4]

Ibid. Page 890

Phocion's oratory, like small coin of great value, was to be estimated, not by its bulk, but its intrinsic worth.

Ibid. Phocion, Page 898

Even a nod from a person who is esteemed is of more force than a thousand arguments or studied sentences from others.

Ibid.

Demosthenes told Phocion, "The Athenians will kill you some day when they once are in a rage." "And you,"

said he, "if they once are in their senses."[1]

Lives. Phocion, Page 901

Men, steered by popular applause, though they bear the name of governors, are in reality the mere underlings of the multitude. The man who is completely wise and virtuous has no need at all of glory, except so far as it disposes and eases his way of action by the greater trust that it procures him.

Ibid. Agis, Page 960

Pytheas once, scoffing at Demosthenes, said that his arguments smelt of the lamp.

Ibid. Demosthenes, Page 1026

Demosthenes overcame and rendered more distinct his inarticulate and stammering pronunciation by speaking with pebbles in his mouth.

Ibid. Page 1028

In his house he had a large looking-glass, before which he would stand and go through his exercises.

Ibid.

Cicero called Aristotle a river of flowing gold, and said of Plato's Dialogues, that if Jupiter were to speak, it would be in language like theirs.

Ibid. Cicero, Page 1054

Medicine, to produce health, has to examine disease, and music, to create harmony, must investigate discord.

Ibid. Demetrius, Page 1073

Once Antigonus was told his son was ill, and went to see him. At the door he met some young beauty. Going in, he sat down by the bed and took his pulse. "The fever," said Demetrius, "has just left me." "Oh, yes," replied the father, "I met it going out at the door."

Ibid. Page 1083

"It is not," said Caesar, "these well-fed, long-haired men that I fear, but the

---

[1] He passed the river Rubicon, saying, "Let every die be thrown." — *Ibid.*

[Caesar] merely uttered to those near him in Greek the words "Anerriphtho kubos" (let the die be cast), and led his army through the Rubicon. — *Lives, Pompey, P. 783*

[2] Caesar said to Metellus, "This, young man, is harder for me to say than do." — *Roman Apophthegms, Caesar*

[3] Trust Fortune, and know that you carry Caesar. — *Ibid.*

See Lucan, page 994.

[4] See Shakespeare, page 81.

---

[1] Demosthenes the orator told Phocion, "If the Athenians should be mad, they would kill you." "Like enough," said he, — "me if they were mad, but you if they were wise." — *Apophthegms of Kings and Great Commanders, Phocion*

pale and the hungry-looking"; meaning Brutus and Cassius, by whose conspiracy he afterwards fell.[1]

Lives. Antony, Page 1111

There was no man of his time like Antony for addressing a multitude, or for carrying soldiers with him by the force of words.

Ibid. Page 1127

From PLUTARCH'S *Morals, by various translators; revised by* WILLIAM WATSON GOODWIN [*1831–1912*]

For water continually dropping will wear hard rocks hollow.[2]

Of the Training of Children

It is a true proverb, that if you live with a lame man you will learn to halt.
Ibid.

The very spring and root of honesty and virtue lie in the felicity of lighting on good education.
Ibid.

It is indeed a desirable thing to be well descended, but the glory belongs to our ancestors.
Ibid.

Nothing made the horse so fat as the king's eye.
Ibid.

Democritus said, words are but the shadows of actions.
Ibid.

It is a point of wisdom to be silent when occasion requires, and better than to speak, though never so well.[3]
Ibid.

Abstain from beans; that is, keep out of public offices, for anciently the choice of the officers of state was made by beans.
Ibid.

[1] See Shakespeare, page 81.
This passage is repeated in *Marcus Brutus,* P. 1190.
[2] See Lyly, page 23.
[3] Closed lips hurt no one, speaking may. — CATO THE CENSOR, *Book I, Distich 12*

The whole life of man is but a point of time; let us enjoy it, therefore, while it lasts, and not spend it to no purpose.

Of the Training of Children

An old doting fool, with one foot already in the grave.[1]
Ibid.

Xenophanes said, "I confess myself the greatest coward in the world, for I dare not do an ill thing."

Of Bashfulness

One made the observation of the people of Asia that they were all slaves to one man, merely because they could not pronounce that syllable No.[2]
Ibid.

Euripides was wont to say, "Silence is an answer to a wise man."
Ibid.

Zeno first started that doctrine that knavery is the best defence against a knave.[3]
Ibid.

Alexander wept when he heard from Anaxarchus that there was an infinite number of worlds; and his friends asking him if any accident had befallen him, he returns this answer: "Do you not think it a matter worthy of lamentation that when there is such a vast multitude of them, we have not yet conquered one?"

On the Tranquillity of the Mind

Like the man who threw a stone at a bitch, but hit his step-mother, on which he exclaimed, "Not so bad!"
Ibid.

Pittacus said, "Every one of you hath his particular plague, and my wife is mine; and he is very happy who hath this only."
Ibid.

He was a man, which, as Plato saith, is a very inconstant creature.[4]
Ibid.

[1] See Beaumont and Fletcher, page 131.
[2] See S. T. Coleridge, page 318.
[3] Set a thief to catch a thief. — BOHN'S *Handbook of Proverbs*
[4] Man in sooth is a marvellous vain, fickle, and unstable subject. — MONTAIGNE: *Works, Book I, Chap. 1, That Men by Various Ways Arrive at the Same End*

The pilot cannot mitigate the billows or calm the winds.[1]

On the Tranquillity of the Mind

All men whilst they are awake are in one common world; but each of them, when he is asleep, is in a world of his own.[2]

Of Superstition

I, for my own part, had much rather people should say of me that there neither is nor ever was such a man as Plutarch, than that they should say, "Plutarch is an unsteady, fickle, froward, vindictive, and touchy fellow."

Ibid.

Scilurus on his death-bed, being about to leave four-score sons surviving, offered a bundle of darts to each of them, and bade them break them. When all refused, drawing out one by one, he easily broke them, — thus teaching them that if they held together, they would continue strong; but if they fell out and were divided, they would become weak.[3]

Apophthegms of Kings and Great Commanders.[4] Scilurus

Dionysius the Elder, being asked whether he was at leisure, he replied, "God forbid that it should ever befall me!"

Ibid. Dionysius

A prating barber asked Archelaus how he would be trimmed. He answered, "In silence."

Ibid. Archelaus

When Philip had news brought him of divers and eminent successes in one day, "O Fortune!" said he, "for all these so great kindnesses do me some small mischief."

Ibid. Philip

There were two brothers called Both and Either; perceiving Either was a good, understanding, busy fellow, and Both a silly fellow and good for little,

Philip said, "Either is both, and Both is neither."

Apophthegms of Kings and Great Commanders. Philip

Philip being arbitrator betwixt two wicked persons, he commanded one to fly out of Macedonia and the other to pursue him.

Ibid.

Being about to pitch his camp in a likely place, and hearing there was no hay to be had for the cattle, "What a life," said he, "is ours, since we must live according to the convenience of asses!"

Ibid.

"These Macedonians," said he, "are a rude and clownish people, that call a spade a spade."[1]

Ibid.

He made one of Antipater's recommendation a judge; and perceiving afterwards that his hair and beard were dyed, he removed him, saying, "I could not think one that was faithless in his hair could be trusty in his deeds."

Ibid.

Being nimble and light-footed, his father encouraged him to run in the Olympic race. "Yes," said he, "if there were any kings there to run with me."

Ibid. Alexander

Pyrrhus said, "If I should overcome the Romans in another fight, I were undone."

Ibid. Pyrrhus

Themistocles being asked whether he would rather be Achilles or Homer, said, "Which would you rather be, — a conqueror in the Olympic games, or the crier that proclaims who are conquerors?"

Ibid. Themistocles

Alcibiades had a very handsome dog, that cost him seven thousand drachmas; and he cut off his tail, "that," said he, "the Athenians may have this story to tell of me, and may concern themselves no further with me."

Ibid. Alcibiades

---

[1] See Publilius Syrus, *Maxim 759*.

[2] A saying attributed to HERACLITUS. Quoted by ADDISON in *The Spectator, No. 487, Sept. 18, 1712.*

[3] AESOP's fable, *The Bundle of Sticks,* has this theme.

[4] Rejected by some critics as not a genuine work of Plutarch.

[1] See Menander, page 976.

To Harmodius, descended from the ancient Harmodius, when he reviled Iphicrates [a shoemaker's son] for his mean birth, "My nobility," said he, "begins with me, but yours ends in you." [1]

Apophthegms of Kings and Great Commanders. Iphicrates

Once when Phocion had delivered an opinion which pleased the people, . . . he turned to his friend and said, "Have I not unawares spoken some mischievous thing or other?" [2]

Ibid. Phocion

Phocion compared the speeches of Leosthenes to cypress-trees. "They are tall," said he, "and comely, but bear no fruit."

Ibid.

King Agis said, "The Lacedaemonians are not wont to ask how many, but where the enemy are."

Ibid. Agis

To one that promised to give him hardy cocks that would die fighting, "Prithee," said Cleomenes, "give me cocks that will kill fighting."

Ibid. Cleomenes

A soldier told Pelopidas, "We are fallen among the enemies." Said he, "How are we fallen among them more than they among us?"

Ibid. Pelopidas

Cato the Elder wondered how that city was preserved wherein a fish was sold for more than an ox.

Roman Apophthegms. Cato the Elder

Cato instigated the magistrates to punish all offenders, saying that they that did not prevent crimes when they might, encouraged them.[3] Of young men, he liked them that blushed better than those who looked pale.

Ibid.

Cato requested old men not to add the disgrace of wickedness to old age,

which was accompanied with many other evils.

Roman Apophthegms. Cato the Elder

He said they that were serious in ridiculous matters would be ridiculous in serious affairs.

Ibid.

Cicero said loud-bawling orators were driven by their weakness to noise, as lame men to take horse.

Ibid. Cicero

After he routed Pharnaces Ponticus at the first assault, he wrote thus to his friends: "I came, I saw, I conquered." [1]

Ibid. Caesar

As Caesar was at supper the discourse was of death, — which sort was the best. "That," said he, "which is unexpected."

Ibid.

As Athenodorus was taking his leave of Caesar, "Remember," said he, "Caesar, whenever you are angry, to say or do nothing before you have repeated the four-and-twenty letters to yourself."

Ibid. Caesar Augustus

"Young men," said Caesar, "hear an old man to whom old men hearkened when he was young."

Ibid.

Custom is almost a second nature.

Rules for the Preservation of Health. 18

Epaminondas is reported wittily to have said of a good man that died about the time of the battle of Leuctra, "How came he to have so much leisure as to die, when there was so much stirring?"

Ibid. 25

Socrates thought that if all our misfortunes were laid in one common heap, whence every one must take an equal

---

[1] I am my own ancestor. — JUNOT, DUC D'ABRANTES [1771–1813], when asked about his ancestry.

[2] See Diogenes Laertius, page 1015.

[3] Pardon one offence, and you encourage the commission of many. — PUBLILIUS SYRUS: *Maxim 750*

[1] Veni, vidi, vici.

A severe critic might curtail that famous brevity of Caesar's by two thirds, drawing his pen through the supererogatory *veni* and *vidi*. — J. R. LOWELL: *The Biglow Papers, Series I, No. 7*

portion, most persons would be contented to take their own and depart.[1]

Consolation to Apollonius

Diogenes the Cynic, when a little before his death he fell into a slumber, and his physician rousing him out of it asked him whether anything ailed him, wisely answered, "Nothing, sir; only one brother anticipates another, — Sleep before Death."

Ibid.

About Pontus there are some creatures of such an extempore being that the whole term of their life is confined within the space of a day; for they are brought forth in the morning, are in the prime of their existence at noon, grow old at night, and then die.

Ibid.

There are two sentences inscribed upon the Delphic oracle, hugely accommodated to the usages of man's life: "Know thyself,"[2] and "Nothing too much"; and upon these all other precepts depend.

Ibid.

Agesilaus was very fond of his children; and it is reported that once toying with them he got astride upon a reed as upon a horse, and rode about the room; and being seen by one of his friends, he desired him not to speak of it till he had children of his own.

Laconic Apophthegms. Of Agesilaus the Great

Lysander, when Dionysius sent him two gowns, and bade him choose which he would carry to his daughter, said, "She can choose best," and so took both away with him.

Ibid. Of Lysander

And when the physician said, "Sir, you are an old man," "That happens," replied Pausanias, "because you never were my doctor."

Laconic Apophthegms. Of Pausanias

When one told Plistarchus that a notorious railer spoke well of him, "I'll lay my life," said he, "somebody hath told him I am dead, for he can speak well of no man living."

Ibid. Of Plistarchus

Said Periander, "Hesiod might as well have kept his breath to cool his pottage."[1]

The Banquet of the Seven Wise Men. 14

Socrates said, "Bad men live that they may eat and drink, whereas good men eat and drink that they may live."[2]

How a Young Man Ought to Hear Poems. 4

Archimedes, as he was washing, thought of a manner of computing the proportion of gold in King Hiero's crown by seeing the water flowing over the bathing-stool. He leaped up as one possessed or inspired, crying, "I have found it! Eureka!"

Pleasure Not Attainable, According to Epicurus. 11

That proverbial saying, "Ill news goes quick and far."

Of Inquisitiveness

Spintharus, speaking in commendation of Epaminondas, says he scarce ever met with any man who knew more and spoke less.

Of Hearing. 6

It is a thing of no great difficulty to raise objections against another man's oration, — nay, it is a very easy matter; but to produce a better in its place is a work extremely troublesome.

Ibid.

Antiphanes said merrily, that in a certain city the cold was so intense that

---

[1] ADDISON'S paper, *The Spectator, No. 558, June 23, 1714,* is on this theme.

The translation is somewhat ambiguous. Socrates meant that we would all prefer to bear our own lot rather than take the risk of an equal share in the world's total of grievances.

[2] See Alexander Pope, page 207. Plutarch ascribes this saying to Plato. It is also ascribed to Pythagoras, Chilo, Thales, Cleobulus, Bias, and Socrates; also to Phemonë, a mythical Greek poetess of the ante-Homeric period. JUVENAL (*Satire XI, 27*) says that this precept descended from heaven.

---

[1] Spare your breath to cool your porridge. — RABELAIS: *Works, Book V, Chap. 28*

[2] See Fielding, page 229.

He used to say that other men lived to eat, but that he ate to live. — DIOGENES LAERTIUS: *Socrates, 14*

words were congealed as soon as spoken, but that after some time they thawed and became audible; so that the words spoken in winter were articulated next summer.[1]

Of Man's Progress in Virtue

As those persons who despair of ever being rich make little account of small expenses, thinking that little added to a little will never make any great sum.

Ibid.

What is bigger than an elephant? But this also is become man's plaything, and a spectacle at public solemnities; and it learns to skip, dance, and kneel.

Of Fortune

No man ever wetted clay and then left it, as if there would be bricks by chance and fortune.

Ibid.

Alexander was wont to say, "Were I not Alexander, I would be Diogenes."

Of the Fortune or Virtue of Alexander the Great

When the candles are out all women are fair.[2]

Conjugal Precepts

Like watermen, who look astern while they row the boat ahead.[3]

Whether 'Twas Rightfully Said, Live Concealed

Socrates said he was not an Athenian or a Greek, but a citizen of the world.[4]

Of Banishment

Anaximander says that men were first produced in fishes, and when they were grown up and able to help themselves were thrown up, and so lived upon the land.

Symposiacs. Book VIII, Question 8

Athenodorus says hydrophobia,· or water-dread, was first discovered in the time of Asclepiades.

Ibid. Question 9

The great god Pan is dead.[1]

Why the Oracles Cease to Give Answers

I am whatever was, or is, or will be; and my veil no mortal ever took up.[2]

Of Isis and Osiris

When Hermodotus in his poems described Antigonus as the son of Helios, "My valet-de-chambre," said he, "is not aware of this."[3]

Ibid.

He is a fool who lets slip a bird in the hand for a bird in the bush.[4]

Of Garrulity

We are more sensible of what is done against custom than against Nature.

Of Eating of Flesh. Tract 1

When Demosthenes was asked what was the first part of oratory, he answered, "Action"; and which was the second, he replied, "Action"; and which was the third, he still answered, "Action."

Lives of the Ten Orators

Xenophon says that there is no sound more pleasing than one's own praises.

Whether an Aged Man Ought to Meddle in State Affairs

---

[1] Rabelais gives a somewhat similar account, referring to Antiphanes, in *Book IV, Chaps. 55 and 56.*
See Raspe (Baron Munchausen), page 1056.
[2] When all candles be out, all cats be gray.
— HEYWOOD: *Proverbes, Part 1, Chap. 5*
[3] See Burton, page 122.
[4] See Boswell, page 272, and W. L. Garrison, page 424.

[1] Great Pan is dead. — MRS. BROWNING: *The Dead Pan, St. 26*
Plutarch relates (*Isis and Osiris*) that a ship well laden with passengers drove with the tide near the Isles of Paxi, when a loud voice was heard by most of the passengers calling unto one Thanus. The voice then said aloud to him, "When you are arrived at Palodes, take care to make it known that the great god Pan is dead."
[2] I am the things that are, and those that are to be, and those that have been. No one ever lifted my skirts; the fruit which I bore was the sun. — PROCLUS: *On Plato's Timaeus, P. 30, D.* (Inscription in the temple of Neith at Sais, in Egypt.)
[3] No man is a hero to his valet-de-chambre. — MARSHAL CATINAT [1637–1712]
Few men have been admired by their domestics. — MONTAIGNE: *Essays, Book III, Chap. 2*
This phrase, "No man is a hero to his valet," is commonly attributed to Madame de Sévigné, but on the authority of Madame Aissé (*Letters*, edited by Jules Ravenal, 1853) it really belongs to Madame Cornuel.
[4] See Heywood, page 15, and Herbert, page 137.

Statesmen are not only liable to give an account of what they say or do in public, but there is a busy inquiry made into their very meals, beds, marriages, and every other sportive or serious action.

Political Precepts

Leo Byzantius said, "What would you do, if you saw my wife, who scarce reaches up to my knees? . . . Yet," went he on, "as little as we are, when we fall out with each other, the city of Byzantium is not big enough to hold us."

Ibid.

Cato said, "I had rather men should ask why my statue is not set up, than why it is."

Ibid.

It was the saying of Bion, that though the boys throw stones at frogs in sport, yet the frogs do not die in sport but in earnest.

Which Are the Most Crafty, Water or Land Animals? 7

Both Empedocles and Heraclitus held it for a truth that man could not be altogether cleared from injustice in dealing with beasts as he now does.

Ibid.

For to err in opinion, though it be not the part of wise men, is at least human.[1]

Against Colotes

Simonides calls painting silent poetry, and poetry, speaking painting.

Whether the Athenians Were More Warlike or Learned. 3

As Menander says, "For our mind is God"; and as Heraclitus, "Man's genius is a deity."

Platonic Questions

Pythagoras, when he was asked what time was, answered that it was the soul of this world.

Ibid.

JUVENAL
[A. D. 47–138]

Honesty is praised and starves.[2]

Satire I. Line 74

No man ever became extremely wicked all at once.[1]

Satire II. Line 83

Grammarian, orator, geometrician; painter, gymnastic teacher; fortune-teller, rope-dancer, physician, conjuror, — he knew everything.[2]

Satire III. Line 76

We all live in a state of ambitious poverty.

Ibid. Line 182

ONASANDER
[*Floruit* A. D. 49]

Translation by Illinois Greek Club. Loeb Classical Library

Vigor is found in the man who has not yet grown old, and discretion in the man who is not too young.

The General. Chap. I, Sect. 10

Envy is a pain of mind that successful men cause their neighbours.

Ibid. Chap. 42, Paragraph 25

TACITUS
[A. D. 54–119]

The Oxford Translation. Bohn Classical Library

The images of twenty of the most illustrious families — the Manlii, the Quinctii, and other names of equal splendour — were carried before it [the bier of Junia]. Those of Brutus and Cassius were not displayed; but for that very reason they shone with pre-eminent lustre.[3]

Annals. III, 76, 11

He had talents equal to business, and aspired no higher.

Ibid. VI, 39, 17

---

[1] See Pope, page 211.
[2] A favorite quotation of Linnaeus, Swedish botanist and naturalist.

[1] Nemo repente fit turpissimus. See Beaumont and Fletcher, page 131.
[2] See Dryden, page 174.
[3] Lord John Russell, alluding to an expression used by him ("Conspicuous by his absence") in his address to the electors of the city of London, said, "It is not an original expression of mine, but is taken from one of the greatest historians of antiquity."

Some might consider him as too fond of fame; for the desire of glory clings even to the best men longer than any other passion.[1]

History. IV, 6, 36

They make desolation, which they call peace.[2]

Agricola. 30

EPICTETUS
[*Circa* A. D. 60]

Translation [1865] by Thomas Wentworth Higginson [*1823–1911*], *based on that [1758] of* Elizabeth Carter [*1717–1806*]

To a reasonable creature, that alone is insupportable which is unreasonable; but everything reasonable may be supported.

Discourses. Chap. 2

When you have shut your doors, and darkened your room, remember never to say that you are alone, for you are not alone;[3] but God is within, and your genius is within, — and what need have they of light to see what you are doing?

Ibid. Chap. 14

No great thing is created suddenly, any more than a bunch of grapes or a fig. If you tell me that you desire a fig, I answer you that there must be time. Let it first blossom, then bear fruit, then ripen.

Ibid. Chap. 15

Any one thing in the creation is sufficient to demonstrate a Providence to an humble and grateful mind.

Ibid. Chap. 16

Were I a nightingale, I would act the part of a nightingale; were I a swan, the part of a swan.

Ibid.

Since it is Reason which shapes and regulates all other things, it ought not itself to be left in disorder.

Ibid. Chap. 17

---

[1] See Milton, page 159.
[2] See Byron, page 356.
[3] Though in a wilderness, a man is never alone. — Sir Thomas Browne: *Religio Medici* (Everyman ed.), *P. 82*

Practise yourself, for heaven's sake, in little things; and thence proceed to greater.

Discourses. Chap. 18

Why, then, do you walk as if you had swallowed a ramrod?

Ibid. Chap. 21

Difficulties are things that show what men are.

Ibid. Chap. 24

If we are not stupid or insincere when we say that the good or ill of man lies within his own will, and that all beside is nothing to us, why are we still troubled?

Ibid. Chap. 25

In theory there is nothing to hinder our following what we are taught; but in life there are many things to draw us aside.

Ibid. Chap. 26

Appearances to the mind are of four kinds. Things either are what they appear to be; or they neither are, nor appear to be; or they are, and do not appear to be; or they are not, and yet appear to be. Rightly to aim in all these cases is the wise man's task.

Ibid. Chap. 27

The appearance of things to the mind is the standard of every action to man.

That We Ought Not to Be Angry with Mankind. 27

For what constitutes a child? — Ignorance. What constitutes a child? — Want of instruction; for they are our equals so far as their degree of knowledge permits.

That Courage Is Not Inconsistent with Caution. Book II, 1

The materials of action are variable, but the use we make of them should be constant.

How Nobleness of Mind May Be Consistent with Prudence. 5

Shall I show you the muscular training of a philosopher? "What muscles are those?" — A will undisappointed; evils avoided; powers daily exercised; careful resolutions; unerring decisions.

Wherein Consists the Essence of Good. 8

What is the first business of one who studies philosophy? To part with self-conceit. For it is impossible for any one to begin to learn what he thinks that he already knows.

How to Apply General Principles to Particular Cases. 17

Every habit and faculty is preserved and increased by correspondent actions, — as the habit of walking, by walking; or running, by running.

How the Semblances of Things Are to Be Combated. 18

Whatever you would make habitual, practise it; and if you would not make a thing habitual, do not practise it, but habituate yourself to something else.

Ibid.

Reckon the days in which you have not been angry. I used to be angry every day; now every other day; then every third and fourth day; and if you miss it so long as thirty days, offer a sacrifice of thanksgiving to God.

Ibid.

Be not hurried away by excitement, but say, "Semblance, wait for me a little. Let me see what you are and what you represent. Let me try you."

Ibid.

There are some things which men confess with ease, and others with difficulty.

Of Inconsistency. 21

Who is there whom bright and agreeable children do not attract to play and creep and prattle with them?

Concerning a Person Whom He Treated with Disregard. 24

Two rules we should always have ready, — that there is nothing good or evil save in the will; and that we are not to lead events, but to follow them.

In What Manner We Ought to Bear Sickness. Book III, 10

In every affair consider what precedes and what follows, and then undertake it.[1]

That Everything Is to Be Undertaken with Circumspection. 15

¹ See Publilius Syrus, *Maxim 777.*

First say to yourself what you would be; and then do what you have to do.

Concerning Such as Read and Dispute Ostentatiously. 23

Let not another's disobedience to Nature become an ill to you; for you were not born to be depressed and unhappy with others, but to be happy with them. And if any is unhappy, remember that he is so for himself; for God made all men to enjoy felicity and peace.

That We Ought Not to Be Affected by Things Not in Our Own Power. 24

Everything has two handles, — one by which it may be borne; another by which it cannot.[1]

Enchiridion. 43

PLINY THE YOUNGER
[A. D. 61–105]

Translation [1746] by WILLIAM MELMOTH [1710–1799]. *Bohn Classical Library*

Modestus said of Regulus that he was "the biggest rascal that walks upon two legs."

Letters.[2] *Book I, Letter 5, 14*

There is nothing to write about, you say. Well, then, write and let me know just this, — that there *is* nothing to write about; or tell me in the good old style if you are well. That's right. I am quite well.[3]

Ibid. Letter 11, 1

An object in possession seldom retains the same charm that it had in pursuit.[4]

Ibid. Book II, Letter 15, 1

¹ See Raspe, page 1056.
² Book VI, Letter 16 contains the description of the eruption of Vesuvius, A. D. 79, as witnessed by Pliny the Elder.
³ This comes to inform you that I am in a perfect state of health, hoping you are in the same. Ay, that's the old beginning. — GEORGE COLMAN THE YOUNGER [1762–1836]: *The Heir at Law* [1797], *Act III, Sc. 2*
⁴ See Goldsmith, page 254.

He [Pliny the Elder] used to say that "no book was so bad but some good might be got out of it." [1]

Letters. Book III, Letter 5, 10

This expression of ours, "Father of a family."

Ibid. Book V, Letter 19, 2

That indolent but agreeable condition of doing nothing.[2]

Ibid. Book VIII, Letter 9, 3

Objects which are usually the motives of our travels by land and by sea are often overlooked and neglected if they lie under our eye. . . . We put off from time to time going and seeing what we know we have an opportunity of seeing when we please.

Ibid. Letter 20, 1

His only fault is that he has no fault.[3]

Ibid. Book IX, Letter 26, 1

EMPEROR HADRIAN
[A. D. 76–138]

Dear fleeting, sweeting, little soul,
My body's comrade and its guest,
What region now must be thy goal,
Poor little wan, numb, naked soul,
Unable, as of old, to jest? [4]

Dying Farewell to His Soul, to Honor the Tomb of His Friend, Voconius

I've no mind to be a Florus,
Strolling round among the drink-shops,
Skulking round among the cook-shops,
Victim of fat-gorged mosquitoes.

Retort to Florus [5]

---

[1] "There is no book so bad," said the bachelor, "but something good may be found in it." — CERVANTES: *Don Quixote, Part II, Chap. 3*

[2] Dolce far niente (Sweet doing-nothing). — *Italian proverb*

[3] See Thomas Carlyle, page 380.

[4] Animula, vagula, blandula
Hospes comesque corporis,
Quae nunc abibis in loca,
Pallidula, frigida, nudula,
Nec, ut soles, dabis joca.

[5] Florus, born in Africa [A. D. 74], Hadrian's friend, had addressed these lines to him. The third line has been lost.

I've no mind to be a Caesar,
Strolling round among the Britons
.   .   .   .
Victim of the Scythian hoar-frosts.

MARCUS AURELIUS ANTONINUS
[A. D. 121–180]

Translation by MORRIS HICKEY MORGAN [*1859–1910*]

This Being of mine, whatever it really is, consists of a little flesh, a little breath, and the part which governs.

Meditations. II, 2

The ways of the gods are full of providence.

Ibid. 3

Thou wilt find rest from vain fancies if thou doest every act in life as though it were thy last.[1]

Ibid. 5

Find time still to be learning somewhat good, and give up being desultory.

Ibid. 7

No state sorrier than that of the man who keeps up a continual round, and pries into "the secrets of the nether world," as saith the poet, and is curious in conjecture of what is in his neighbour's heart.

Ibid. 13

Though thou be destined to live three thousand years and as many myriads besides, yet remember that no man loseth other life than that which he liveth, nor liveth other than that which he loseth.

Ibid. 14

For a man can lose neither the past nor the future; for how can one take from him that which is not his? So remember these two points: first, that each thing is of like form from everlasting and comes round again in its cycle, and that it signifies not whether a man shall look upon the same things for a hundred years or two hundred, or for an infinity of time; second, that the longest lived and the shortest lived man, when they come to die, lose one and the same thing.

Ibid.

---

[1] See Publilius Syrus, *Maxim 633*.

As for life, it is a battle and a sojourning in a strange land; but the fame that comes after is oblivion.

Meditations. II, 17

Waste not the remnant of thy life in those imaginations touching other folk, whereby thou contributest not to the common weal.

Ibid. III, 4

A man should *be* upright, not be *kept* upright.

Ibid. 5

Never esteem anything as of advantage to thee that shall make thee break thy word or lose thy self-respect.

Ibid. 7

Let no act be done at haphazard, nor otherwise than according to the finished rules that govern its kind.

Ibid. IV, 2

By a tranquil mind I mean nothing else than a mind well ordered.

Ibid. 3

Think on this doctrine, — that reasoning beings were created for one another's sake; that to be patient is a branch of justice, and that men sin without intending it.

Ibid.

The universe is change; our life is what our thoughts make it.

Ibid.

Nothing can come out of nothing,[1] any more than a thing can go back to nothing.

Ibid. 4

Death, like generation, is a secret of Nature.

Ibid. 5

That which makes the man no worse than he was makes his life no worse: it has no power to harm, without or within.

Ibid. 8

Whatever happens at all happens as it should; thou wilt find this true, if thou shouldst watch narrowly.

Ibid. 10

How much time he gains who does not look to see what his neighbour says

---

[1] See Diogenes Laertius, page 1016.

or does or thinks, but only at what he does himself, to make it just and holy.

Meditations. IV, 18

Whatever is in any way beautiful hath its source of beauty in itself, and is complete in itself; praise forms no part of it. So it is none the worse nor the better for being praised.

Ibid. 20

All that is harmony for thee, O Universe, is in harmony with me as well. Nothing that comes at the right time for thee is too early or too late for me. Everything is fruit to me that thy seasons bring, O Nature. All things come of thee, have their being in thee, and return to thee.

Ibid. 23

"Let thine occupations be few," saith the sage,[1] "if thou wouldst lead a tranquil life."

Ibid. 24

Love the little trade which thou hast learned, and be content therewith.

Ibid. 31

Remember this, — that there is a proper dignity and proportion to be observed in the performance of every act of life.

Ibid. 32

All is ephemeral, — fame and the famous as well.

Ibid. 35

Observe always that everything is the result of a change, and get used to thinking that there is nothing Nature loves so well as to change existing forms and to make new ones like them.

Ibid. 36

Search men's governing principles, and consider the wise, what they shun and what they cleave to.

Ibid. 38

Time is a sort of river of passing events, and strong is its current; no sooner is a thing brought to sight than it is swept by and another takes its place, and this too will be swept away.

Ibid. 43

---

[1] DEMOCRITUS apud Senecam: *De Ira, III, 6; De Animi Tranquillitate, 13*

All that happens is as usual and familiar as the rose in spring and the crop in summer.

Meditations. IV, 44

That which comes after ever conforms to that which has gone before.

Ibid. 45

Mark how fleeting and paltry is the estate of man, — yesterday in embryo, to-morrow a mummy or ashes. So for the hair's-breadth of time assigned to thee live rationally, and part with life cheerfully, as drops the ripe olive, extolling the season that bore it and the tree that matured it.

Ibid. 48

Deem not life a thing of consequence. For look at the yawning void of the future, and at that other limitless space, the past.

Ibid. 50

Always take the short cut; and that is the rational one. Therefore say and do everything according to soundest reason.

Ibid. 51

In the morning, when thou art sluggish at rousing thee, let this thought be present; "I am rising to a man's work."

Ibid. V, 1

A man makes no noise over a good deed, but passes on to another as a vine to bear grapes again in season.

Ibid. 6

Nothing happens to anybody which he is not fitted by nature to bear.

Ibid. 18

Live with the gods.

Ibid. 27

Look beneath the surface; let not the several quality of a thing nor its worth escape thee.

Ibid. VI, 3

The controlling Intelligence understands its own nature, and what it does, and whereon it works.

Ibid. 5

Do not think that what is hard for thee to master is impossible for man; but if a thing is possible and proper to man, deem it attainable by thee.

Ibid. 19

If any man can convince me and bring home to me that I do not think or act aright, gladly will I change; for I search after truth, by which man never yet was harmed.

Meditations. VI, 21

What is not good for the swarm is not good for the bee.

Ibid. 54

How many, once lauded in song, are given over to the forgotten; and how many who sung their praises are clean gone long ago!

Ibid. VII, 6

One Universe made up of all that is; and one God in it all, and one principle of Being, and one Law, the Reason, shared by all thinking creatures, and one Truth.

Ibid. 9

Let not thy mind run on what thou lackest as much as on what thou hast already.

Ibid. 27

Just as the sand-dunes, heaped one upon another, hide each the first, so in life the former deeds are quickly hidden by those that follow after.

Ibid. 34

The art of living is more like wrestling than dancing, in so far as it stands ready against the accidental and the unforeseen, and is not apt to fall.

Ibid. 61

Remember this, — that very little is needed to make a happy life.

Ibid. 67

Remember that to change thy mind and to follow him that sets thee right, is to be none the less the free agent that thou wast before.

Ibid. VIII, 16

Look to the essence of a thing, whether it be a point of doctrine, of practice, or of interpretation.

Ibid. 22

Be not careless in deeds, nor confused in words, nor rambling in thought.

Ibid. 51

Think not disdainfully of death, but look on it with favour; for even death is one of the things that Nature wills.

Ibid. IX, 3

A wrong-doer is often a man that has left something undone, not always he that has done something.

Meditations. IX, 5

Blot out vain pomp; check impulse; quench appetite; keep reason under its own control.

Ibid. 7

Things that have a common quality ever quickly seek their kind.

Ibid. 9

All things are the same, — familiar in enterprise, momentary in endurance, coarse in substance. All things now are as they were in the day of those whom we have buried.

Ibid. 14

Everything is in a state of metamorphosis. Thou thyself art in everlasting change and in corruption to correspond; so is the whole universe.

Ibid. 19

Forward, as occasion offers. Never look round to see whether any shall note it. . . . Be satisfied with success in even the smallest matter, and think that even such a result is no trifle.

Ibid. 29

Whatever may befall thee, it was preordained for thee from everlasting.

Ibid. X, 5

"The earth loveth the shower," and "the holy ether knoweth what love is." [1] The Universe, too, loves to create whatsoever is destined to be made.

Ibid. 21

TERTULLIAN
[A. D. 160–240]

See how these Christians love one another.

Apologeticus. 39

Blood of the martyrs is the seed of the Church.

Ibid. 50

It is certain because it is impossible.[2]

De Carne Christi. 5

---

[1] *Fragmenta Euripidis,* apud Aristotelem, *N. A. VIII, 1, 6*
[2] Certum est, quia impossibile est. This is usually misquoted, "Credo quia impossibile"

He who flees will fight again.[1]

De Fuga in Persecutione. 10

ATHENAEUS
[*Circa* A. D. 200]

Translation by CHARLES DUKE YONGE [*1812–1891*]

It was a saying of Demetrius Phalereus, that "Men having often abandoned what was visible for the sake of what was uncertain, have not got what they expected, and have lost what they had, — being unfortunate by an enigmatical sort of calamity."

The Deipnosophists. VI, 23

Every investigation which is guided by principles of Nature fixes its ultimate aim entirely on gratifying the stomach.[2]

Ibid. VII, 11

Dorion, ridiculing the description of a tempest in the "Nautilus" of Timotheus, said that he had seen a more formidable storm in a boiling saucepan.[3]

Ibid. VIII, 19

On one occasion some one put a very little wine into a wine-cooler, and said that it was sixteen years old. "It is very small for its age," said Gnathaena.

Ibid. XIII, 47

DIOGENES LAERTIUS [4]
[*Circa* A. D. 200]

From The Lives and Opinions of Eminent Philosophers, translated by CHARLES DUKE YONGE [*1812–1891*]. *Bohn Classical Library*

When Thales was asked what was difficult, he said, "To know one's self."

(I believe it because it is impossible). Also attributed to St. Augustine in the form "Credo quia absurdum."
[1] See Butler, page 143.
[2] See Dr. Johnson, page 234.
[3] A tempest in a teapot. — *Proverb*
[4] There is scarce any Philosopher but dies twice or thrice in Laertius; nor almost any life without two or three deaths in Plutarch. — SIR THOMAS BROWNE: *Urn-Burial, Chap. 3*

And what was easy, "To advise another."

Thales. 9

The apophthegm "Know thyself" is his.[1]

Ibid. 13

Writers differ with respect to the apophthegms of the Seven Sages, attributing the same one to various authors.

Ibid. 14

Solon used to say that speech was the image of actions; . . . that laws were like cobwebs, — for that if any trifling or powerless thing fell into them, they held it fast; while if it were something weightier, it broke through them and was off.

Solon. 10

Solon gave the following advice: "Consider your honour, as a gentleman, of more weight than an oath."

Ibid. 12

As some say, Solon was the author of the apophthegm, "Nothing in excess."

Ibid. 16

Chilo advised, "not to speak evil of the dead."[2]

Chilo. 2

Pittacus said that half was more than the whole.[3]

Pittacus. 2

Heraclitus says that Pittacus, when he had got Alcaeus into his power, released him, saying, "Forgiveness is better than revenge."[4]

Ibid. 3

One of his sayings was, "Even the gods cannot strive against necessity."[1]

Pittacus. 4

Another was, "Watch your opportunity."[2]

Ibid. 7

Bias used to say that men ought to calculate life both as if they were fated to live a long and a short time, and that they ought to love one another as if at a future time they would come to hate one another; for that most men were bad.

Bias. 5

Ignorance plays the chief part among men, and the multitude of words.[3]

Cleobulus. 4

The saying, "Practice is everything," is Periander's.[4]

Periander. 6

Anarcharsis, on learning that the sides of a ship were four fingers thick, said that "the passengers were just that distance from death."[5]

Anarcharsis. 5

It was a common saying of Myson that men ought not to investigate things from words, but words from things; for that things are not made for the sake of words, but words for things.

Myson. 3

Epimenides was sent by his father into the field to look for a sheep, turned out of the road at mid-day and lay down in a certain cave and fell asleep, and slept there fifty-seven years; and after that, when awake, he went on looking for the sheep, thinking that he had been taking a short nap.[6]

Epimenides. 2

---

[1] See Pope, page 207, and Plutarch, page 1004.
'Tis said that Attic Solon wrote at Delphi: "Gnothi seauton," which in our tongue is "Know thyself." Many think this to be by Chilon the Laconian. — AUSONIUS DECIMUS MAGNUS [A. D. 310–394]: *The Masque of the Seven Sages, Poem 3, Chorus*
[2] De mortuis nil nisi bonum (Of the dead be nothing said but what is good).
[3] See Hesiod, page 959.
[4] Forgiveness is better than punishment; for the one is proof of a gentle, the other of a savage nature. — Quoted by EPICTETUS, *Fragment 62*

[1] Nature must obey necessity. — SHAKESPEARE: *Julius Caesar, Act IV, Sc. 3, L. 226*
[2] Observe the opportunity. — *Apocrypha: Ecclesiasticus, IV, 20*
[3] In the multitude of words there wanteth not sin. — *Proverbs, X, 19*
[4] See Publilius Syrus, *Maxim 439*.
[5] "How thick do you judge the planks of our ship to be?" "Some two good inches and upward," returned the pilot. "It seems, then, we are within two fingers' breadth of damnation." — RABELAIS: *Book IV, Chap. 23*
[6] The theme of IRVING's story of Rip Van Winkle.

Anaximander used to assert that the primary cause of all things was the Infinite, — not defining exactly whether he meant air or water or anything else.

Anaximander. 2

Anaxagoras said to a man who was grieving because he was dying in a foreign land, "The descent to Hades is the same from every place."

Anaxagoras. 6

Aristophanes turns Socrates into ridicule in his comedies, as making the worse appear the better reason.[1]

Socrates. 5

Often when he was looking on at auctions he would say, "How many things there are which I do not need!"[2]

Ibid. 10

Socrates said, "Those who want fewest things are nearest to the gods."

Ibid. 11

He said that there was one only good, namely, knowledge; and one only evil, namely, ignorance.

Ibid. 14

He declared that he knew nothing, except the fact of his ignorance.

Ibid. 16

Being asked whether it was better to marry or not, he replied, "Whichever you do, you will repent it."

Ibid.

Aristippus being asked what were the most necessary things for well-born boys to learn, said, "Those things which they will put in practice when they become men."

Aristippus. 4

Like sending owls to Athens, as the proverb goes.[3]

Plato. 32

[1] See Milton, page 149.
[2] Socrates once, it is said, was persuaded to go to a fair:
In his one poor cloak, in his wonted way, he stood musing there,
Stood long till a friend inquired what his thoughts might be about —
"How many things there are here that I could do better without."
EDITH M. THOMAS [1854–1925]:
The Burden of Possessions. St. 1
[3] See Horace, page 984.

Plato affirmed that the soul was immortal and clothed in many bodies successively.[1]

Plato. 40

Time is the image of eternity.

Ibid. 41

There is a written and an unwritten law. The one by which we regulate our constitutions in our cities is the written law; that which arises from custom is the unwritten law.

Ibid. 51

Plato was continually saying to Xenocrates, "Sacrifice to the Graces."[2]

Xenocrates. 3

Arcesilaus had a peculiar habit while conversing of using the expression, "My opinion is," and "So and so will not agree to this."

Arcesilaus. 12

Of a rich man who was niggardly he said, "That man does not own his estate, but his estate owns him."

Bion. 3

Very late in life, when he was studying geometry, some one said to Lacydes, "Is it then a time for you to be learning now?" "If it is not," he replied, "when will it be?"

Lacydes. 5

Aristotle was once asked what those who tell lies gain by it. Said he, "That when they speak truth they are not believed."

Aristotle. 11

The question was put to him, what hope is; and his answer was, "The dream of a waking man."

Ibid.

He used to say that personal beauty was a better introduction than any letter; but others say that it was Diogenes who gave this description of it, while Aristotle called beauty "the gift of God"; that Socrates called it "a short-lived tyranny"; Theophrastus, "a silent deceit"; Theocritus, "an ivory mischief."

Ibid.

[1] See Plato, page 974.
[2] See Chesterfield, page 222.

On one occasion Aristotle was asked how much educated men were superior to those uneducated: "As much," said he, "as the living are to the dead." [1]

Aristotle. 11

It was a saying of his that education was an ornament in prosperity and a refuge in adversity.

Ibid.

He was once asked what a friend is, and his answer was, "One soul abiding in two bodies." [2]

Ibid.

Asked what he gained from philosophy, he answered, "To do without being commanded what others do from fear of the laws."

Ibid.

The question was once put to him, how we ought to behave to our friends; and the answer he gave was, "As we should wish our friends to behave to us."

Ibid.

He used to define justice as "a virtue of the soul distributing that which each person deserved."

Ibid.

Another of his sayings was, that education was the best viaticum of old age.

Ibid.

It was a favourite expression of Theophrastus that time was the most valuable thing that a man could spend. [3]

Theophrastus. 10

Antisthenes used to say that envious people were devoured by their own disposition, just as iron is by rust.

Antisthenes. 4

When he was praised by some wicked men, he said, "I am sadly afraid that I must have done some wicked thing." [4]

Ibid.

When asked what learning was the most necessary, he said, "Not to unlearn what you have learned."

Antisthenes. 4

Diogenes would frequently praise those who were about to marry, and yet did not marry.

Diogenes. 4

"Bury me on my face," said Diogenes; and when he was asked why, he replied, "Because in a little while everything will be turned upside down."

Ibid. 6

All things are in common among friends.

Ibid.

Plato having defined man to be a two-legged animal without feathers, Diogenes plucked a cock and brought it into the Academy, and said, "This is Plato's man." On which account this addition was made to the definition, — "With broad flat nails."

Ibid.

A man once asked Diogenes what was the proper time for supper, and he made answer, "If you are a rich man, whenever you please; and if you are a poor man, whenever you can." [1]

Ibid.

Diogenes lighted a candle in the daytime, and went round saying, "I am looking for a man." [2]

Ibid.

When asked what he would take to let a man give him a blow on the head, he said, "A helmet."

Ibid.

Once he saw a youth blushing, and addressed him, "Courage, my boy! that is the complexion of virtue." [3]

Ibid.

When asked what wine he liked to drink, he replied, "That which belongs to another."

Ibid.

---

[1] Quoted with great warmth by Dr. Johnson (Boswell). — BENNET LANGTON [1737–1801]: *Collectanea*

[2] See Pope, page 219.

[3] Remember that time is money. — BENJAMIN FRANKLIN: *Advice to a Young Tradesman* [1748]

[4] See Plutarch, page 1003.

[1] The rich when he is hungry, the poor when he has anything to eat. — RABELAIS: *Book IV, Chap. 64*

[2] Told also of Aesop.

[3] See Mathew Henry, page 188.

Asked from what country he came, he replied, "I am a citizen of the world."[1]

Diogenes. 6

When a man reproached him for going into unclean places, he said, "The sun too penetrates into privies, but is not polluted by them."[2]

Ibid.

Diogenes said once to a person who was showing him a dial, "It is a very useful thing to save a man from being too late for supper."

Menedemus. 3

When Zeno was asked what a friend was, he replied, "Another I."[3]

Zeno. 19

They say that the first inclination which an animal has is to protect itself.

Ibid. 52

He calls drunkenness an expression identical with ruin.[4]

Pythagoras. 6

Among what he called his precepts were such as these: Do not stir the fire with a sword. Do not sit down on a bushel. Do not devour thy heart.[5]

Ibid. 17

In the time of Pythagoras that proverbial phrase "Ipse dixit"[6] was introduced into ordinary life.

Ibid. 25

It takes a wise man to discover a wise man.

Xenophanes. 3

Protagoras asserted that there were two sides to every question, exactly opposite to each other.

Protagoras. 3

Nothing can be produced out of nothing.[7]

Diogenes of Apollonia. 2

The chief good is the suspension of the judgment, which tranquillity of mind follows like its shadow.

Pyrrho. 11

[1] See Garrison, page 424.
[2] See Bacon, page 112.
[3] See page 1015.
[4] See Robert Hall, page 290.
[5] See Spenser, page 26.
[6] He, the master himself, said it, — an authoritative assertion.
[7] See Marcus Aurelius, page 1010.

Epicurus laid down the doctrine that pleasure was the chief good.

Epicurus. 6

ST. JEROME
[A. D. 345-420]
Translation by F. A. WRIGHT

Avoid, as you would the plague, a clergyman who is also a man of business.

Letter 52, To Nepotian

A fat paunch never breeds fine thoughts.

Ibid.

The best almoner is he who keeps back nothing for himself.

Ibid.

It is no fault of Christianity if a hypocrite falls into sin.

Letter 125, To Rusticus

Preferring to store her money in the stomachs of the needy rather than hide it in a purse.

Letter 127, To Principia

ST. AUGUSTINE
[A. D. 354-430]

When I am here, I do not fast on Saturday; when at Rome, I do fast on Saturday.[1]

Epistle 36, To Casulanus

The spiritual virtue of a sacrament is like light, — although it passes among the impure, it is not polluted.[2]

Tract on St. John. Chap. 5, 15

ST. BENEDICT[3]
[A. D. 480-543]

We are therefore about to establish a school of the Lord's service in which we hope to introduce nothing harsh or burdensome.

Rule of St. Benedict. Prologue

[1] See Burton, page 126.
[2] See Bacon, page 112, and Diogenes Laertius, page 1016.
[3] Founder of Western monasticism.

LONGUS
[Fifth Century]

There was never any yet that wholly could escape love, and never shall there be any, never so long as beauty shall be, never so long as eyes can see.

Daphnis and Chloe.[1] *Proem, Chap. 2*

He is so poor that he could not keep a dog.

Ibid. Chap. 15

ALI BEN ABOU TALEB [2]
[? –660]

Believe me, a thousand friends suffice thee not;
In a single enemy thou hast more than enough.[3]

MEIR BEN ISAAC NEHERAI
[*Circa* 1050]

Could we with ink the ocean fill,
Were every blade of grass a quill,
Were the world of parchment made,
And every man a scribe by trade,
  To write the love
  Of God above
Would drain the ocean dry;
  Nor would the scroll
  Contain the whole,
Though stretched from sky to sky.

A Book of Jewish Thoughts Selected for the Sailors and Soldiers of England

---

[1] The only known Greek prose romance (pastoral).

[2] Ali Ben Abou Taleb, son-in-law of Mahomet, and fourth caliph, who was for his courage called "The Lion of God," was murdered A.D. 660. He was the author of *A Hundred Sayings*.

[3] Translated by Ralph Waldo Emerson, and wrongly called by him a translation from Omar Khayyám.

Found in Dr. Hermann Tolowiez's *Polyglotte der Orientalischen Poesie*.

Translated by James Russell Lowell thus: —

He who has a thousand friends has not a friend to spare,
And he who has one enemy will meet him everywhere.

ABU MOHAMMED KASIM BEN ALI HARIRI
[1054–1122]

We praise Thee, O God,
For whatever perspicuity of language Thou hast taught us
And whatever eloquence Thou hast inspired us with.

Makamat. Prayer

And we beg Thee freely to bestow
Propitious succor to lead us aright
And a heart turning in unison with truth,
And a language adorned with veracity,
And style supported by conclusiveness,
And accuracy that may exclude incorrectness,
And firmness of purpose that may overcome caprice,
And sagacity whereby we may attain discrimination.

Ibid.

Guard us from error in narration,
And keep us from folly even in pleasantry,
So that we may be safe from the censure of sarcastic tongues.

Ibid.

BERNARD OF CLUNY
[Twelfth Century]

Brief life is here our portion,
  Brief sorrow, short-lived care;
The life that knows no ending,
  The tearless life, is there.

The Celestial Country[1]

For thee, O dear, dear country,
  Mine eyes their vigils keep.

Ibid.

Jerusalem, the Golden,
  With milk and honey blest.

Ibid.

---

[1] Translated by John Mason Neale [1818–1866]. See Neale, page 518.

OMAR KHAYYÁM
[1070–1123]

Translation by EDWARD FITZGER-
ALD [*1809–1883*]

Come, fill the Cup, and in the fire of
Spring
Your Winter-garment of Repentance
fling:
  The Bird of Time has but a little way
To flutter — and the Bird is on the
Wing.
              Rubáiyát.[1] *Stanza 7*

The Leaves of Life keep falling one by
one.
                Ibid. Stanza 8

Each Morn a thousand Roses brings,
you say:
Yes, but where leaves the Rose of Yesterday?
                Ibid. Stanza 9

The strip of Herbage strown
That just divides the desert from the
sown.
                Ibid. Stanza 11

A Book of Verses underneath the
Bough,
A Jug of Wine, a Loaf of Bread — and
Thou
  Beside me singing in the Wilder-
ness —
Oh, Wilderness were Paradise enow!
                Ibid. Stanza 12

Ah, take the Cash, and let the Credit go,
Nor heed the rumble of a distant Drum!
                Ibid. Stanza 13

The Worldly Hope men set their Hearts
upon
Turns Ashes — or it prospers; and
anon,
  Like Snow upon the Desert's dusty
Face,
Lighting a little hour or two — is gone.
                Ibid. Stanza 16

This batter'd Caravanserai
Whose Portals are alternate Night and
Day.
                Ibid. Stanza 17

I sometimes think that never blows so
red

---

[1] Fifth edition [1889].

The Rose as where some buried Caesar
bled;
  That every Hyacinth the Garden
wears
Dropt in her Lap from some once lovely
Head.
              Rubáiyát. Stanza 19

Ah, my Belovèd, fill the Cup that clears
TO-DAY of past Regrets and future
Fears:
  To-morrow! — Why, To-morrow I
may be
Myself with Yesterday's Sev'n thou-
sand Years.
              Ibid. Stanza 21

Myself when young did eagerly frequent
Doctor and Saint, and heard great argument
  About it and about: but evermore
Came out by the same door where in I
went.
              Ibid. Stanza 27

There was the Door to which I found no
Key;
  There was the Veil through which I
might not see.
              Ibid. Stanza 32

  "While you live,
Drink! — for, once dead, you never
shall return."
              Ibid. Stanza 35

To-morrow's tangle to the winds resign.
              Ibid. Stanza 41

So when that Angel of the darker Drink
At last shall find you by the river-brink,
  And, offering his Cup, invite your
Soul
Forth to your Lips to quaff — you shall
not shrink.
              Ibid. Stanza 43

And fear not lest Existence closing your
Account, and mine, should know the
like no more;
  The Eternal Sákí from that Bowl
has pour'd
Millions of Bubbles like us, and will
pour.
              Ibid. Stanza 46

A Moment's Halt — a momentary taste
Of BEING from the Well amid the
Waste —

And, Lo! — the phantom Caravan has reach'd
The NOTHING it set out from — Oh, make haste!
Rubáiyát. Stanza 48

A Hair perhaps divides the False and True.
Ibid. Stanza 49

Waste not your Hour, nor in the vain pursuit
Of This and That endeavour and dispute.
Ibid. Stanza 54

Striking from the Calendar
Unborn To-morrow and dead Yesterday.
Ibid. Stanza 57

The Grape that can with Logic absolute
The Two-and-Seventy jarring Sects confute.
Ibid. Stanza 59

The Flower that once has blown for ever dies.
Ibid. Stanza 63

Strange, is it not? that of the myriads who
Before us pass'd the door of Darkness through,
Not one returns to tell us of the Road,
Which to discover we must travel too.
Ibid. Stanza 64

I sent my Soul through the Invisible,
Some letter of that After-life to spell:
And by and by my Soul return'd to me,
And answer'd "I Myself am Heav'n and Hell."
Ibid. Stanza 66

Heav'n but the Vision of fulfill'd Desire,
And Hell the Shadow from a Soul on fire.
Ibid. Stanza 67

We are no other than a moving row
Of Magic Shadow-shapes that come and go.
Ibid. Stanza 68

This Chequer-board of Nights and Days.
Ibid. Stanza 69

The Moving Finger writes; and, having writ,
Moves on: nor all your Piety nor Wit
Shall lure it back to cancel half a Line,
Nor all your Tears wash out a Word of it.
Rubáiyát. Stanza 71

That inverted Bowl they call the Sky,
Whereunder crawling coop'd we live and die.
Ibid. Stanza 72

And this I know: whether the one True Light
Kindle to Love, or Wrath-consume me quite,
One Flash of It within the Tavern caught
Better than in the Temple lost outright.
Ibid. Stanza 77

"And He that with his hand the Vessel made
Will surely not in after Wrath destroy."
Ibid. Stanza 85

"Some there are who tell
Of one who threatens he will toss to Hell
The luckless Pots he marr'd in making — Pish!
He's a Good Fellow, and 'twill all be well."
Ibid. Stanza 88

Fill me with the old familiar Juice.
Ibid. Stanza 89

Indeed the Idols I have loved so long
Have done my credit in this World much wrong:
Have drown'd my Glory in a shallow Cup,
And sold my Reputation for a Song.
Ibid. Stanza 93

I wonder often what the Vintners buy
One half so precious as the stuff they sell.
Ibid. Stanza 95

Yet Ah, that Spring should vanish with the Rose!
That Youth's sweet-scented manuscript should close!
Ibid. Stanza 96

Ah Love! could you and I with Him conspire

To grasp this Sorry Scheme of Things
   entire,
    Would not we shatter it to bits —
    and then
Re-mould it nearer to the Heart's Desire!
           Rubáiyát. Stanza 99

Yon rising Moon that looks for us
   again —
How oft hereafter will she wax and
   wane;
    How oft hereafter rising look for us
Through this same Garden — and for
   one in vain!
           Ibid. Stanza 100

And when like her, O Sákí, you shall
   pass
Among the Guests Star-scatter'd on the
   Grass,
    And in your joyous errand reach the
   spot
Where I made One — turn down an
   empty Glass!
           Ibid. Stanza 101

MOSES BEN MAIMON (MAIMONIDES)
[1135–1204]

Anticipate charity by preventing
poverty; assist the reduced fellowman,
either by a considerable gift, or a sum
of money, or by teaching him a trade,
or by putting him in the way of business, so that he may earn an honest
livelihood, and not be forced to the
dreadful alternative of holding out his
hand for charity. This is the highest
step and the summit of charity's golden
ladder.
        Charity's Eight Degrees [1]

ALPHONSO THE LEARNED
[1221–1284]

Had I been present at the creation,
I would have given some useful hints
for the better ordering of the universe.[2]

---

[1] *New York Sun, Jan. 6, 1933.*
[2] CARLYLE says, in his *History of Frederick
the Great, Book II, Chap. 7,* that this saying
of Alphonso about Ptolemy's astronomy,
"that it seemed a crank machine; that it was

DANTE ALIGHIERI
[1265–1321]
Translation by HENRY FRANCIS
CARY [1772–1844]

All hope abandon, ye who enter here.
        Hell. Canto III, Line 9
The wretched souls of those who lived
Without or praise or blame.
           Ibid. Line 34
And to a part I come, where no light
   shines.
       Ibid. Canto IV, Line 148
Avarice, envy, pride,
Three fatal sparks.
       Ibid. Canto V, Line 74
No greater grief than to remember days
Of joy, when misery is at hand.[1]
          Ibid. Line 118
But to the pleasant world when thou
   returnest,
Of me make mention, I entreat thee,
   there.
       Ibid. Canto VI, Line 90
"If thou," he answered, "follow but thy
   star,
Thou canst not miss at last a glorious
   haven."
       Ibid. Canto XV, Line 55
Do Fortune as she list, I stand pre-
   pared.
           Ibid. Line 94
He listens to good purpose who takes
   note.
          Ibid. Line 100
   Think within thyself, so God
Fruit of thy reading give thee.
       Ibid. Canto XX, Line 18
   To fair request
Silent performance maketh best return.
       Ibid. Canto XXIV, Line 75
Though somewhat tardy I perchance
   arrive.
      Ibid. Canto XXVII, Line 19

---

pity the Creator had not taken advice," is still
remembered by mankind, — this and no other
of his many sayings.
[1]   It is the worst of woes
    That in them men look back with stream-
      ing eyes
    On bygone joy.
     Translation by JOHN JAY CHAPMAN
               [1862–1933]
See Longfellow, page 440.

The light bark of my genius lifts the sail.
> *Purgatory. Canto I, Line 2*

O clear conscience, and upright!
How doth a little failing wound thee sore.
> *Ibid. Canto III, Line 8*

Who knows most, him loss of time most grieves.
> *Ibid. Line 77*

So wide arms
Hath goodness infinite, that it receives
All who turn to it.
> *Ibid. Line 118*

If prayer do not aid me first,
That riseth up from heart which lives in grace,
What other kind avails, not heard in heaven?
> *Ibid. Canto IV, Line 129*

Be as a tower, that, firmly set,
Shakes not its top for any blast that blows.
> *Ibid. Canto V, Line 14*

I am Virgil; for no sin
Deprived of heaven, except for lack of faith.
> *Ibid. Canto VII, Line 6*

Now was the hour that wakens fond desire
In men at sea, and melts their thoughtful heart
Who in the morn have bid sweet friends farewell.
> *Ibid. Canto VIII, Line 1*

Grant us, this day,
Our daily manna.
> *Ibid. Canto XI,[1] Line 13*

The noise
Of worldly fame is but a blast of wind,
That blows from diverse points, and shifts its name,
Shifting the point it blows from.
> *Ibid. Line 97*

Consider that this day ne'er dawns again.
> *Ibid. Canto XII, Line 78*

God be with you.
I bear you company no more.
> *Ibid. Canto XVI, Line 145*

[1] Lines 1–24 of this canto give a paraphrase of the Lord's Prayer.

Mine eye
Was closed, and meditation changed to dream.
> *Purgatory. Canto XVIII, Line 142*

The woes
Of Midas, which his greedy wish ensued,
Marked for derision to all future times.
> *Ibid. Canto XX, Line 104*

Let its pure flame
From virtue flow, and love can never fail
To warm another's bosom, so the light
Shine manifestly forth.
> *Ibid. Canto XXII, Line 9*

If too secure, I loose
The rein with a friend's license, as a friend
Forgive me, and speak now as with a friend.
> *Ibid. Line 19*

Woman, the creature of an hour.
> *Ibid. Canto XXIX, Line 25*

Between two kinds of food, both equally
Remote and tempting, first a man might die
Of hunger, ere he one could freely choose.
> *Paradise. Canto IV, Line 1*

Nature, that is the seal to mortal wax.
> *Ibid. Canto VIII, Line 133*

Whose affirmation, or denial, is
Without distinction.
> *Ibid. Canto XIII, Line 111*

How salt the savor is of other's bread;
How hard the passage to descend and climb
By other's stairs.
> *Ibid. Canto XVII, Line 58*

As for the leaves, that in the garden bloom,
My love for them is great, as is the good
Dealt by the eternal hand, that tends them all.
> *Ibid. Canto XXVI, Line 62*

As one, who from a dream awaken'd, straight,
All he hath seen forgets; yet still retains
Impression of the feeling in his dream;

E'en such am I: for all the vision dies,
As 'twere, away.
Paradise. Canto XXXIII, Line 55

JEAN FROISSART
[1337-1410]

Above all flowers, I find the Daisy dear.
Above All Flowers [1]

FRANÇOIS VILLON
[1430-1484]

Where are the snows of yester-year? [2]
The Greater Testament. [3] *Ballad*
of Old-Time Ladies

All must come to the self-same bay;
Sons and servants, their days are told:
The wind carries their like away.
Ibid. Ballad of Old-Time Lords,
No. 2

Blonde or brunette, this rhyme applies,
Happy is he who knows them not.
Ibid. Double Ballad to the Like
Purport

O Virgin clean,
To whom all sinners lift their hands on
high,
Made whole in faith through Thee their
go-between.
In this belief I will to live and die.
Ibid. Ballad of Homage to Our
Lady

My heart shall not dissever aye from
thee
Nor thine from me, if it aright I read:
And to this end we twain together be.
Ibid. Ballad to a Newly Married
Gentleman

There's no right speech out of Paris
town.
Ibid. Ballad of the Women of
Paris

If you have money, it doth not stay,
But this way and that it wastes amain:
What does it profit you, anyway?
Ill-gotten good is nobody's gain.
Ibid. Seemly Lesson to the Good-
for-Noughts

[1] Translated by GRACE WARRACK.
[2] See J. H. McCarthy, page 759.
But where is last year's snow? This was the
greatest care that Villon, the Parisian poet,
took. — RABELAIS: *Book II, Chap. 14.*
[3] Translation by D. G. ROSSETTI.

I know all save myself alone.
Ballad of Things Known and
Unknown

For he deserves not any fortune fair
Who would wish ill unto the realm of
France.
Ballad Against Those Who Missay
of France

These traitorous thieves, accursèd and
unfair,
The vintners that put water in our wine.
A Merry Ballad of Vintners

In the amorous war
The wealthy gallant always gains the
day.
Ballad of Ladies' Love, No. 1

ALDUS (MANUTIUS)
[1450-1515]

Talk of nothing but business, and
despatch that business quickly.
Placard on the door of the Aldine
Press, Venice, established about
1490 [1]

LEONARDO DA VINCI
[1452-1519]

From his Note-Books, translated by
EDWARD McCURDY

In rivers, the water that you touch
is the last of what has passed and the
first of that which comes: so with time
present.

Whoever in discussion adduces authority uses not intellect but memory.

No counsel is more trustworthy than
that which is given upon ships that are
in peril.

Intellectual passion drives out sensuality.

Let the street be as wide as the height
of the houses.

No member needs so great a number
of muscles as the tongue; this exceeds
all the rest in the number of its movements.

[1] Quoted by Thomas Frognall Dibdin
[1776-1847] in *Introduction to the Knowl-*
edge of Rare and Valuable Editions of the
Greek and Latin Classics [1802], *Vol. I,*
P. 436.

It is of no small benefit on finding oneself in bed in the dark to go over again in the imagination the main outlines of the forms previously studied, or of other noteworthy things conceived by ingenious speculation.

As a well-spent day brings happy sleep, so life well used brings happy death.

DESIDERIUS ERASMUS
[1465–1536]

No one is injured save by himself.[1]
Adages

I know how busy you are in your library, which is your Paradise.[2]
Letter to Bishop Fisher [1524]

NICOLÒ MACHIAVELLI [3]
[1469–1527]

There is nothing more difficult to take in hand, more perilous to conduct, or more uncertain in its success, than to take the lead in the introduction of a new order of things.
The Prince.[4] Chap. 6

The chief foundations of all states, new as well as old or composite, are good laws and good arms; and as there cannot be good laws where the state is not well armed, it follows that where they are well armed they have good laws.
Ibid. Chap. 12

Among other evils which being unarmed brings you, it causes you to be despised.
Ibid. Chap. 14

When neither their property nor their honour is touched, the majority of men live content.
Ibid. Chap. 19

[1] No one can harm the man who does himself no wrong. — SAINT CHRYSOSTOM [327–407]:*Letter to Olympia*

[2] Nec me fugit quam assiduus sis in bibliotheca, quae tibi Paradisi loco est.
P. S. ALLEN: *Selections from Erasmus, P. 128*

[3] Every Country hath its Machiavel. — SIR THOMAS BROWNE: *Religio Medici* (Everyman ed.), *P. 24*

[4] *Translation by* W. K. MARRIOTT

There are three classes of intellects: one which comprehends by itself; another which appreciates what others comprehend; and a third which neither comprehends by itself nor by the showing of others; the first is the most excellent, the second is good, the third is useless.
The Prince. Chap. 22

Where the willingness is great, the difficulties cannot be great.
Ibid. Chap. 26

God is not willing to do everything, and thus take away our free will and that share of glory which belongs to us.
Ibid.

MICHELANGELO
[1474–1564]

The more the marble wastes,
The more the statue grows.
Sonnet

If it be true that any beauteous thing
Raises the pure and just desire of man
From earth to God, the eternal fount of all,
Such I believe my love.
Sonnet

The might of one fair face sublimes my love,
For it hath weaned my heart from low desires.
Sonnet

I live and love in God's peculiar light.
Ibid.

MARTIN LUTHER
[1483–1546]

A mighty fortress is our God,
A bulwark never failing;
Our helper He amid the flood
Of mortal ills prevailing.[1]
Psalm, Ein' Feste Burg [2]

[1] Great God! there is no safety here below;
Thou art my fortress, thou that seem'st my foe.
FRANCIS QUARLES [1592–1644]:
Divine Poems

[2] Translated by FREDERIC H. HEDGE.

Tell your master that if there were as many devils at Worms as tiles on its roofs, I would enter.[1]

On approaching Worms

Here I stand; I can do no otherwise. God help me. Amen![2]

Speech at the Diet of Worms

For where God built a church, there the Devil would also build a chapel.[3]

Table Talk. 67

A faithful and good servant is a real godsend; but truly 'tis a rare bird in the land.

Ibid. 156

It makes a difference whose ox is gored.[4]

Works [1854 edition]. Vol. 62, Page 449

ST. IGNATIUS LOYOLA [5]
[1491-1556]

Teach us, good Lord, to serve Thee as Thou deservest:
To give and not to count the cost;
To fight and not to heed the wounds;
To toil and not to seek for rest;
To labour and not ask for any reward

[1] On the 16th of April, 1521, Luther entered the imperial city [of Worms]. . . . On his approach . . . the Elector's chancellor entreated him, in the name of his master, not to enter a town where his death was decided. The answer which Luther returned was simply this. — BARON VON BUNSEN [1791-1860]: *Life of Luther*

I will go, though as many devils aim at me as there are tiles on the roofs of the houses. — LEOPOLD VON RANKE [1795-1886]: *History of the Reformation, Vol. I, P. 533,* translated by SARAH TAYLOR AUSTIN [1793-1867].

Luther it was who, when advised not to trust himself in Worms, declared, "Although there be as many devils in Worms as there are tiles on the house-tops, I will go." — ALEXANDER SMITH: *Dreamthorp, A Shelf in My Bookcase*

[2] [Luther] it was who, when brought to bay in the splendid assemblage, said, "It is neither safe nor prudent to do aught against conscience. Here stand I — I cannot do otherwise. God help me. Amen." — *Ibid.*

[3] See Burton, page 126.

[4] This is the moral of the fable of the lawyer, the farmer, and the farmer's ox, which was included in NOAH WEBSTER'S *American Spelling Book* [1802], entitled *The Partial Judge.*

[5] Founder of the Society of Jesus.

Save that of knowing that we do Thy will.

Prayer for Generosity

FRANCIS I
[1494-1547]

All is lost save honour and my life.[1]

Letter to his mother

FRANÇOIS RABELAIS
[1495-1553]

I am just going to leap into the dark.[2]

PETER ANTHONY MOTTEUX: *Life of Rabelais*

Let down the curtain: the farce is done.

Ibid.

He left a paper sealed up, wherein were found three articles as his last will: "I owe much; I have nothing; I give the rest to the poor."

Ibid.

One inch of joy surmounts of grief a span,
Because to laugh is proper to the man.

Works. To the Readers

To return to our wethers.[3]

Ibid. Book I, Chap. 1

I drink no more than a sponge.

Ibid. Chap. 5

[1] From the imperial camp near Pavia, Italy, after the battle of February 24, 1525, Francis I wrote to his mother: "Madame, pour vous faire savoir comme se porte le reste de mon infortune, de toutes choses ne m'est demeuré que l'honneur et la vie qui est sauvé."
— HENRI MARTIN: *History of France, Vol. 8*

SISMONDI [1773-1842], *Vol. 16, Pp. 241, 242,* corrected the expression which had become altered to "Tout est perdu fors l'honneur."

The letter itself is printed entire in *Histoire Civile, Physique et Morale de Paris* by JACQUES ANTOINE DULAURE [1755-1835]: "Pour vous avertir comment se porte le ressort de mon infortune, de toutes choses ne m'est demeuré que l'honneur et la vie, — qui est sauvé."

All gone but faith in God. — BISHOP JOHN McKIM [1852-1936]: Cabled message to the New York headquarters of the Episcopal Church after the destruction of the mission by the Japanese earthquake [1923].

[2] Je m'en vay chercher un grand Peut-estre (I am going to seek a great Perhaps).

[3] Revenons à nos moutons. — A proverb taken from the farce, *L'Avocat Pierre Patelin,* by BLANCHET [1459-1519], *P. 90* [1762 ed.].

Appetite comes with eating, says An-
geston.[1]
Works. Book I, Chap. 5
Thought the moon was made of green
cheese.[2]
Ibid. Chap. 11
He always looked a given horse in the
mouth.[3]
Ibid.
By robbing Peter he paid Paul,[4]
. . . and hoped to catch larks if ever
the heavens should fall.[5]
Ibid.
He laid him squat as a flounder.
Ibid. Chap. 27
Send them home as merry as crickets.
Ibid. Chap. 29
War begun without good provision of
money beforehand for going through
with it is but as a breathing of strength
and blast that will quickly pass away.
Coin is the sinews of war.[6]
Ibid. Chap. 46
How shall I be able to rule over
others, that have not full power and
command of myself?
Ibid. Chap. 52
Subject to a kind of disease, which
at that time they called lack of money.[7]
Ibid. Book II, Chap. 16

[1] My appetite comes to me while eating. —
MONTAIGNE: *Book III, Chap. 9, Of Vanity*
[2] See Heywood, page 17.
[3] See *Ibid.*, page 13, Butler, page 142, and
Cervantes, page 1042.
[4] See Heywood, page 14.
[5] See *Ibid.*, page 12.
[6] AESCHINES [389–314 B. C.] ascribes to Demosthenes the expression, "The sinews of affairs are cut" (*Adv. Ctesiphon, Chap. 53*).
DIOGENES LAERTIUS, in his *Life of Bion, Book
IV, Chap. 7, Sect. 3*, represents Bion as saying,
"Riches were the sinews of business," or, as
the phrase may mean, "of the state." Referring perhaps to this maxim of the philosopher
Bion, PLUTARCH says in his *Life of Cleomenes*,
"He that first said that money was the sinews
of affairs, seems especially in that saying to
refer to war" (*Modern Library Giant ed., P.
986*). Accordingly we find money called ex-
pressly "the sinews of war" in LIBANIUS, *Oration 46*, and by the scholiast on PINDAR,
Olymp., 1, 4, and in CICERO, *Philipp., V, 2*,
"nervos belli, infinitam pecuniam."
[7] Or that eternal want of pence,
Which vexes public men.
TENNYSON:
Will Waterproof's Lyrical Monologue, St. 6

He did not care a button for it.
Works. Book II, Chap. 16
How well I feathered my nest.[1]
Ibid. Chap. 17
So much is a man worth as he esteems
himself.
Ibid. Chap. 29
A good crier of green sauce.
Ibid. Chap. 31
Then I began to think that it is very
true which is commonly said, that the
one half of the world knoweth not how
the other half liveth.
Ibid. Chap. 32
This flea which I have in mine ear.
Ibid. Book III, Chap. 31
You have there hit the nail on the
head.[2]
Ibid. Chap. 34
Above the pitch, out of tune, and off
the hinges.
Ibid. Book IV, Chap. 19
I'll go his halves.
Ibid. Chap. 23
The Devil was sick, — the Devil a
monk would be;
The Devil was well, — the Devil a
monk was he.[3]
Ibid. Chap. 24
Do not believe what I tell you here
any more than if it were some tale of
a tub.[4]
Ibid. Chap. 38
I would have you call to mind the
strength of the ancient giants, that un-
dertook to lay the high mountain Pelion
on the top of Ossa, and set among those
the shady Olympus.[5]
Ibid.
Which was performed to a T.[6]
Ibid. Chap. 41
He that has patience may compass
anything.
Ibid. Chap. 48

[1] See Pepys, page 181.
[2] See Heywood, page 18.
[3] Quoted by SIR WALTER SCOTT in *The
Black Dwarf, Chap. 6*.
[4] Title of a religious satire by JONATHAN
SWIFT.
[5] See Ovid, page 986.
[6] See Johnson, page 238.

We will take the good will for the deed.[1]
> *Works. Book IV, Chap. 49*

You are Christians of the best edition, all picked and culled.
> *Ibid. Chap. 50*

Would you damn your precious soul?
> *Ibid. Chap. 54*

Let us fly and save our bacon.
> *Ibid. Chap. 55*

Needs must when the Devil drives.[2]
> *Ibid. Chap. 57*

Scampering as if the Devil drove them.
> *Ibid. Chap. 62*

He freshly and cheerfully asked him how a man should kill time.
> *Ibid.*

The belly has no ears, nor is it to be filled with fair words.[3]
> *Ibid.*

Whose cockloft is unfurnished.[4]
> *Ibid. Book V, Author's Prologue*

Speak the truth and shame the Devil.[5]
> *Ibid.*

Plain as a nose in a man's face.[6]
> *Ibid.*

Like hearts of oak.[7]
> *Ibid.*

You shall never want rope enough.
> *Ibid.*

Looking as like . . . as one pea does like another.[8]
> *Ibid. Chap. 2*

And thereby hangs a tale.[9]
> *Ibid. Chap. 4*

Nothing is so dear and precious as time.[10]
> *Ibid. Chap. 5*

It is meat, drink,[1] and cloth to us.
> *Works. Book V, Chap. 7*

And so on to the end of the chapter.
> *Ibid. Chap. 10*

What is got over the Devil's back is spent under the belly.[2]
> *Ibid. Chap. 11*

We have here other fish to fry.[3]
> *Ibid. Chap. 12*

What cannot be cured must be endured.[4]
> *Ibid. Chap. 15*

Thought I to myself, we shall never come off scot-free.
> *Ibid.*

It is enough to fright you out of your seven senses.[5]
> *Ibid.*

Necessity has no law.[6]
> *Ibid.*

Panurge had no sooner heard this, but he was upon the high-rope.
> *Ibid. Chap. 18*

We saw a knot of others, about a baker's dozen.
> *Ibid. Chap. 23*

Others made a virtue of necessity.[7]
> *Ibid.*

Spare your breath to cool your porridge.[8]
> *Ibid. Chap. 28*

I believe he would make three bites of a cherry.
> *Ibid.*

KENKO [9]
[FOURTEENTH CENTURY]

Too much furniture in one's living-room.

---

[1] See Swift, page 192.
[2] See Heywood, page 17.
[3] See Plutarch, page 998.
[4] See Bacon, page 113.
[5] See Shakespeare, page 62, and Johnson, page 235.
[6] See Shakespeare, page 33, and Cervantes, page 1034.
[7] See Garrick, page 242.
[8] See Lyly, page 23, Shakespeare, page 56, and Cervantes, page 1040.
[9] See Shakespeare, page 34, and Cervantes, page 1042.
[10] See Diogenes Laertius, page 1015.

[1] See Shakespeare, page 51.
[2] Isocrates was in the right to insinuate that what is got over the Devil's back is spent under his belly. — LE SAGE: *Gil Blas, Book 8, Chap. 9*
[3] I have other fish to fry. — CERVANTES: *Don Quixote, Part II, Chap. 35*
[4] See Burton, page 124.
[5] See Scott, page 310.
[6] See Diogenes Laertius, page 1013.
[7] See Chaucer, page 4, and Burton, page 125.
[8] See Plutarch, page 1004.
[9] A Japanese Buddhist.

Too many pens in a stand.
Too many Buddhas in a private shrine.
Too many rocks, trees, and herbs in a garden.
Too many children in a house.
Too many words when men meet.
Too many books in a bookcase there can never be,
Nor too much litter in a dust heap.

Fragment

GEORGIUS FABRICIUS
[1516–1571]

He doth raise his country's fame with his own
And in the mouths of nations yet unborn
His praises shall be sung; Death comes to all
But great achievements raise a monument
Which shall endure until the sun grows cold.

In Praise of Georgius Agricola [1494–1555]. Quoted by HERBERT CLARK HOOVER *and* LOU HENRY HOOVER *in their translation of Agricola's De Re Metallica, Page XXIV*

PIERRE DE RONSARD
[1524–1585]

When you are old, and in the candle light
Sit spinning by the fire at close of day,
You'll sing my songs in praise of you, and say:
"Thus Ronsard sang, whilst still my eyes were bright."[1]

Sonnet XLII,[2] *To Helen*[3]

[1] Compare WILLIAM BUTLER YEATS's adaptation: "When you are old and gray and full of sleep," page 790.
[2] Translated by WILLIAM A. DRAKE.
[3] Madame de Suggères.

MICHEL DE MONTAIGNE
[1533–1592]
Translation by CHARLES COTTON [1630–1687], *revised by* HAZLITT *and* WIGHT

Man in sooth is a marvellous vain, fickle, and unstable subject.[1]

Works.[2] *Book I, Chap. 1, That Men by Various Ways Arrive at the Same End*

All passions that suffer themselves to be relished and digested are but moderate.[3]

Ibid. Chap. 2, Of Sorrow

It is not without good reason said, that he who has not a good memory should never take upon him the trade of lying.[4]

Ibid. Chap. 9, Of Liars

He who should teach men to die would at the same time teach them to live.[5]

Ibid. Chap. 19, That to Study Philosophy Is to Learn to Die

The laws of conscience, which we pretend to be derived from nature, proceed from custom.

Ibid. Chap. 22, Of Custom

Accustom him to everything, that he may not be a Sir Paris, a carpet-knight,[6] but a sinewy, hardy, and vigorous young man.

Ibid. Chap. 25, On the Education of Children

It can be of no importance to me of what religion my physician or my lawyer is; this consideration has nothing in

[1] See Plutarch, page 1001.
[2] This book of Montaigne the world has indorsed by translating it into all tongues. — EMERSON: *Representative Men, Montaigne*
[3] See Raleigh, page 21.
Curae leves loquuntur ingentes stupent (Light griefs are loquacious, but the great are dumb). — SENECA: *Hippolytus, II, 3, 607.*
[4] See Sidney, page 169.
Mendacem memorem esse oportere (To be a liar, memory is necessary). — QUINTILIAN: *IV, 2, 91*
[5] See Tickell, page 205.
[6] See Burton, page 123, and Cervantes, page 1035.

common with the offices of friendship which they owe me.

> Works. Book I, Chap. 27,
> Of Friendship

We were halves throughout, and to that degree that methinks, by outliving him, I defraud him of his part.

> Ibid.

There are some defeats more triumphant than victories.[1]

> Ibid. Chap. 30, Of Cannibals

Nothing is so firmly believed as what we least know.

> Ibid. Chap. 31, Of Divine
> Ordinances

A wise man never loses anything if he have himself.

> Ibid. Chap. 38, Of Solitude

Even opinion is of force enough to make itself to be espoused at the expense of life.

> Ibid. Chap. 40, Of Good and Evil

Plato says, " 'Tis to no purpose for a sober man to knock at the door of the Muses"; and Aristotle says "that no excellent soul is exempt from a mixture of folly."[2]

> Ibid. Book II, Chap. 2, Of
> Drunkenness

For a desperate disease a desperate cure.[3]

> Ibid. Chap. 3, The Custom of the
> Isle of Cea

And not to serve for a table-talk.[4]

> Ibid.

To which we may add this other Aristotelian consideration, that he who confers a benefit on any one loves him better than he is beloved by him again.[5]

> Ibid. Chap. 8, Of the Affection of
> Fathers

The middle sort of historians (of which the most part are) spoil all; they will chew our meat for us.

> Ibid. Chap. 10, Of Books

The only good histories are those that have been written by the persons themselves who commanded in the affairs whereof they write.

> Works. Book II, Chap. 10,
> Of Books

She [virtue] requires a rough and stormy passage; she will have either outward difficulties to wrestle with, or internal difficulties.[1]

> Ibid. Chap. 11, Of Cruelty

There is, nevertheless, a certain respect, and a general duty of humanity, that ties us, not only to beasts that have life and sense, but even to trees and plants.

> Ibid.

Some impose upon the world that they believe that which they do not; others, more in number, make themselves believe that they believe, not being able to penetrate into what it is to believe.

> Ibid. Chap. 12, Apology for
> Raimond Sebond[2]

When I play with my cat, who knows whether I do not make her more sport than she makes me?

> Ibid.

'Tis one and the same Nature that rolls on her course, and whoever has sufficiently considered the present state of things might certainly conclude as to both the future and the past.[3]

> Ibid.

The souls of emperors and cobblers are cast in the same mould. . . . The same reason that makes us wrangle with a neighbour causes a war betwixt princes.

> Ibid.

Man is certainly stark mad; he cannot make a worm, and yet he will be making gods by dozens.

> Ibid.

Why may not a goose say thus: "All the parts of the universe I have an in-

---

[1] See Bacon, page 113.
[2] See Dryden, page 173.
[3] See Shakespeare, page 96, and Dryden, page 175.
[4] Let it serve for table-talk. — SHAKESPEARE: The Merchant of Venice, Act III, Sc. 5, L. 95
[5] ARISTOTLE: Ethics, 9, 7

[1] Let Truth and Falsehood grapple. — MILTON: Areopagitica
[2] Raimond Sebond, born at Barcelona in the 14th century, died in 1432, at Toulouse, where he had lived as professor of medicine and theology.
[3] See Plutarch, page 998.

terest in: the earth serves me to walk upon, the sun to light me; the stars have their influence upon me; I have such an advantage by the winds and such by the waters; there is nothing that you heavenly roof looks upon so favourably as me. I am the darling of Nature! Is it not man that keeps, lodges, and serves me?"

Works. Book II, Chap. 12,
Apology for Raimond Sebond

Arts and sciences are not cast in a mould, but are formed and perfected by degrees, by often handling and polishing, as bears leisurely lick their cubs into form.[1]

Ibid.

He that I am reading seems always to have the most force.

Ibid.

Apollo said that every one's true worship was that which he found in use in the place where he chanced to be.[2]

Ibid.

The mariner of old said thus to Neptune in a great tempest, "O God! thou mayest save me if thou wilt, and if thou wilt, thou mayest destroy me; but whether or no, I will steer my rudder true."[3]

Ibid. Chap. 16, Of Glory

How many worthy men have we known to survive their own reputation![4]

Ibid.

There is another sort of glory, which is the having too good an opinion of our own worth.

Ibid. Chap. 17, Of Presumption

One may be humble out of pride.

Ibid.

Nature has presented us with a large faculty of entertaining ourselves alone; and often calls us to it, to teach us that

we owe ourselves partly to society, but chiefly and mostly to ourselves.

Works. Book II, Chap. 18,
On Giving the Lie

I find that the best virtue I have has in it some tincture of vice.

Ibid. Chap. 20, That We Taste
Nothing Pure

Saying is one thing, and doing is another.

Ibid. Chap. 31, Of Anger

Is it not a noble farce, wherein kings, republics, and emperors have for so many ages played their parts, and to which the whole vast universe serves for a theatre?[1]

Ibid. Chap. 36, Of the Most
Excellent Men

Nature forms us for ourselves, not for others; to be, not to seem.

Ibid. Chap. 37, Of the Resemblance of Children to Their Brothers

There never was in the world two opinions alike, no more than two hairs or two grains; the most universal quality is diversity.[2]

Ibid. Of the Resemblance of Children to Their Fathers

The public weal requires that men should betray, and lie, and massacre.

Ibid. Book III, Chap. 1, Of
Profit and Honesty

I will follow the right side even to the fire, but excluding the fire if I can.

Ibid.

Does not he to whom you betray another, to whom you were as welcome as to himself, know that you will at another time do as much for him?

Ibid.

Like rowers, who advance backward.[3]

Ibid.

I speak truth, not so much as I would, but as much as I dare; and I dare a little the more, as I grow older.

Ibid. Chap. 2, Of Repentance

---

[1] See Burton, page 122, and Pliny, page 994.
[2] XENOPHON: *Mem. Socratis, I, 3, 1*
[3] The pilot . . . who has been able to say, "Neptune, you shall never sink this ship except on an even keel," has fulfilled the requirements of his art. — SENECA: *Epistle 85*
[4] See Bentley, page 187.

[1] See Shakespeare, page 49.
[2] See Browne, page 144, and Plato, page 974.
[3] See Burton, page 122.

Few men have been admired by their own domestics.[1]

> *Works. Book III, Chap. 2,*
> *Of Repentance*

It happens as with cages: the birds without despair to get in, and those within despair of getting out.[2]

> *Ibid. Chap. 5, Upon Some Verses*
> *of Virgil*

And to bring in a new word by the head and shoulders, they leave out the old one.

> *Ibid.*

All the world knows me in my book, and my book in me.

> *Ibid.*

'Tis so much to be a king, that he only is so by being so. The strange lustre that surrounds him conceals and shrouds him from us; our sight is there broken and dissipated, being stopped and filled by the prevailing light.[3]

> *Ibid. Chap. 7, Of the Inconven-*
> *ience of Greatness*

We are born to inquire after truth; it belongs to a greater power to possess it. It is not, as Democritus said, hid in the bottom of the deeps, but rather elevated to an infinite height in the divine knowledge.[4]

> *Ibid. Chap. 8, Of the Art of*
> *Conversation*

I moreover affirm that our wisdom itself, and wisest consultations, for the most part commit themselves to the conduct of chance.[5]

> *Ibid.*

What if he has borrowed the matter and spoiled the form, as it oft falls out?[6]

> *Ibid.*

---

[1] See Plutarch, page 1005.
[2] See Davies, page 115.
[3] That fierce light which beats upon a
throne.
    TENNYSON: *Idylls of the King, Dedication*
[4] LACTANTIUS [early 4th century]: *Divin.*
Inst., 3, 28
[5] Although men flatter themselves with their great actions, they are not so often the result of great design as of chance. — ROCHE-FOUCAULD: *Maxim 57*
[6] Defacing first, then claiming as his own.
    CHARLES CHURCHILL: *The Apology,*
    L. 235

The oldest and best known evil was ever more supportable than one that was new and untried.[1]

> *Works. Book III, Chap. 9,*
> *Of Vanity*

Not because Socrates said so, . . . I look upon all men as my compatriots.

> *Ibid.*

My appetite comes to me while eating.[2]

> *Ibid.*

There is no man so good, who, were he to submit all his thoughts and actions to the laws, would not deserve hanging ten times in his life.

> *Ibid.*

Saturninus said, "Comrades, you have lost a good captain to make him an ill general."

> *Ibid.*

A little folly is desirable in him that will not be guilty of stupidity.[3]

> *Ibid.*

Habit is a second nature.[4]

> *Ibid. Chap. 10*

We seek and offer ourselves to be gulled.

> *Ibid. Chap. 11, Of Cripples*

I have never seen a greater monster or miracle in the world than myself.

> *Ibid.*

Men are most apt to believe what they least understand.

> *Ibid.*

I have here only made a nosegay of culled flowers, and have brought nothing of my own but the thread that ties them together.

> *Ibid. Chap. 12, Of Physiognomy*

Amongst so many borrowed things, I am glad if I can steal one, disguising and altering it for some new service.

> *Ibid.*

I am further of opinion that it would be better for us to have [no laws] at

---

[1] LIVY: *23, 3*
[2] See Rabelais, page 1025.
[3] See Walpole, page 246.
[4] See Plutarch, page 1003.

all than to have them in so prodigious numbers as we have.

Works. Book III, Chap. 13, Of Experience

There is more ado to interpret interpretations than to interpret the things, and more books upon books than upon all other subjects; we do nothing but comment upon one another.

Ibid.

What can we do with those people who will not believe anything unless it is in print? . . . I would as soon quote one of my friends as I would Aulus Gellius or Macrobius.

Ibid.

For truth itself has not the privilege to be spoken at all times and in all sorts.

Ibid.

The diversity of physical arguments and opinions embraces all sorts of methods.

Ibid.

Let us a little permit Nature to take her own way; she better understands her own affairs than we.

Ibid.

I have ever loved to repose myself, whether sitting or lying, with my heels as high or higher than my head.

Ibid.

I, who have so much and so universally adored this "excellent mediocrity" of ancient times, and who have concluded the most moderate measure the most perfect, shall I pretend to an unreasonable and prodigious old age?

Ibid.

Que scais-je [1] (What do I know)?

Motto on his seal

I do not understand; I pause; I examine.

Inscription for his library [2]

---

[1] "Que scais-je?" was the motto of Montaigne.
    BYRON: *Don Juan, Canto IX, St. 17*
[2] Quoted by ALEXANDER SMITH: *Dreamthorp, On the Writing of Essays*

JAN ZAMOYSKI
[1541–1605]

The king reigns, but does not govern.[1]

Speech in the Polish Parliament [1605], referring to King Sigismund III

GUILLAUME DE SALLUSTE, SEIGNEUR DU BARTAS
[1544–1590]

From Divine Weekes and Workes, translated [1606] by J. SYLVESTER *[1563–1618]*

The world's a stage,[2] where God's omnipotence,
His justice, knowledge, love, and providence
Do act the parts.

First Week. First Day

And reads, though running,[3] all these needful motions.

Ibid.

Mercy and justice, marching cheek by joule.

Ibid.

Not unlike the bear which bringeth forth
In the end of thirty dayes a shapeless birth;
But after licking, it in shape she drawes,
And by degrees she fashions out the pawes,
The head, and neck, and finally doth bring
To a perfect beast that first deformed thing.[4]

Ibid.

What is well done is done soon enough.

Ibid.

And swans seem whiter if swart crowes be by.

Ibid.

---

[1] Louis Adolphe Thiers adopted the epigram as the motto for his journal, the *Nationale*, which he established with Mignet and Carrel in 1830.
[2] See Shakespeare, page 49, and Du Bartas, page 1033.
[3] See Cowper, page 266.
[4] See Montaigne, page 994.

Night's black mantle covers all alike.[1]
> *First Week. First Day*

Hot and cold, and moist and dry.[2]
> *Ibid. Second Day*

Much like the French (or like ourselves, their apes),
Who with strange habit do disguise their shapes;
Who loving novels, full of affectation,
Receive the manners of each other nation.[3]
> *Ibid.*

With tooth and nail.
> *Ibid.*

From the foure corners of the worlde doe haste.[4]
> *Ibid.*

Oft seen in forehead of the frowning skies.[5]
> *Ibid.*

Bright-flaming, heat-full fire,
The source of motion.[6]
> *Ibid.*

To man the earth seems altogether
No more a mother, but a step-dame rather.[7]
> *Ibid. Third Day*

For where's the state beneath the firmament
That doth excel the bees for government?[8]
> *Ibid. Fifth Day, Part 1*

---

[1] Night . . . with thy black mantle.
> SHAKESPEARE: *Romeo and Juliet,*
> *Act III, Sc. 2, L. 10 and 15*

[2] Hot, cold, moist, and dry, four champions fierce.
> MILTON: *Paradise Lost, Book 2, L. 898*

[3] Report of fashions in proud Italy,
Whose manners still our tardy apish nation
Limps after in base imitation.
> SHAKESPEARE: *King Richard II,*
> *Act II, Sc. 1, L. 21*

[4] Come the three corners of the world in arms.
> SHAKESPEARE: *King John,*
> *Act V, Sc. 7, L. 116*

[5] The forehead of the morning sky.
> MILTON: *Lycidas, L. 171*

[6] *Heat Considered as a Mode of Motion,* title of a treatise [1863] by JOHN TYNDALL [1820–1893].

[7] See Pliny, page 993.

[8]   So work the honey-bees,
Creatures that by a rule in Nature teach

These lovely lamps, these windows of the soul.[1]
> *First Week. Sixth Day*

Or almost like a spider, who, confin'd
In her web's centre, shakt with every winde,
Moves in an instant if the buzzing flie
Stir but a string of her lawn canapie.[2]
> *Ibid.*

Even as a surgeon, minding off to cut
Some cureless limb, — before in ure he put
His violent engins on the vicious member,
Bringeth his patient in a senseless slumber,
And grief-less then (guided by use and art),
To save the whole, sawes off th' infested part.
> *Ibid.*

Two souls in one, two hearts into one heart.[3]
> *Ibid.*

Which serves for cynosure[4]
To all that sail upon the sea obscure.
> *Ibid. Seventh Day*

Living from hand to mouth.
> *Second Week. First Day, Part 4*

In the jaws of death.[5]
> *Ibid.*

Will change the pebbles of our puddly thought
To orient pearls.[6]
> *Ibid. Third Day, Part 1*

Soft carpet-knights,[7] all scenting musk and amber.
> *Ibid.*

The act of order to a peopled kingdom.
> SHAKESPEARE: *King Henry V,*
> *Act I, Sc. 2, L. 187*

[1] The windows of mine eyes.
> SHAKESPEARE: *King Richard III,*
> *Act V, Sc. 3, L. 117*

[2] See Davies, page 115.

[3] See Pope, page 219.

[4] The cynosure of neighbouring eyes.
> MILTON: *L'Allegro, L. 80*

[5] See Shakespeare, page 56, and Tennyson, page 467.

[6] Sow'd the earth with orient pearl.
> MILTON: *Paradise Lost, Book 5, L. 2*
Orient pearls. — SHAKESPEARE: *A Midsummer-Night's Dream, Act IV, Sc. 1, L. 60*

[7] See Burton, page 123, and Montaigne, page 1027.

The will for deed I doe accept.[1]
Second Week. Third Day, Part 2
Only that he may conform
To tyrant custom.[2]
Ibid.
Who breaks his faith, no faith is held
with him.
Ibid. Fourth Day, Book 2
Who well lives, long lives; for this age
of ours
Should not be numbered by years, daies,
and hours.
Ibid.
My lovely living boy,
My hope, my hap, my love, my life, my
joy.[3]
Ibid.
Out of the book of Natur's learned
brest.[4]
Ibid.
Flesh of thy flesh, nor yet bone of thy
bone.
Ibid.
Through thick and thin, both over hill
and plain.[5]
Ibid. Book 4
Weakened and wasted to skin and
bone.[6]
Ibid.
I take the world to be but as a stage,
Where net-maskt men do play their
personage.[7]
*Dialogue Between Heraclitus and
Democritus*
Made no more bones.
The Maiden Blush

---

[1] See Swift, page 192.
[2] The tyrant custom.
  SHAKESPEARE: *Othello, Act I, Sc. 3, L. 230*
[3]   My fair son!
  My life, my joy, my food, my all the
  world.
      SHAKESPEARE: *King John,
        Act III, Sc. 4, L. 103*
[4] The book of Nature is that which the
physician must read; and to do so he must
walk over the leaves. — PARACELSUS [1493–
1541]. Quoted in *Encyclopaedia Britannica*
(9th ed.), *Vol. 18, P. 234*
[5] See Chaucer, page 6.
[6] See John Byrom, page 221.
[7] See Shakespeare, page 49, and Du Bartas,
page 1031.

MIGUEL DE CERVANTES
[1547–1616]

From Don Quixote, translated by
PETER ANTHONY MOTTEUX [*died
1718*]. *The page numbers are those
of the Modern Library Giant edition.*

You are a King by your own Fire-
side, as much as any Monarch in his
Throne.
The Author's Preface. Page XIX
I was so free with him as not to mince
the matter.[1]
Ibid. Page XX
They can expect nothing but their
labour for their pains.[2]
Ibid. Page XXIII
Time out of mind.[3]
Part I. Book I, Chap. 1, Page 4
As ill-luck would have it.[4]
Ibid. Chap. 2, Page 12
The brave man carves out his for-
tune, and every man is the son of his
own works.[5]
Ibid. Chap. 4, Page 22
Which I have earned with the sweat
of my brows.
Ibid.
By a small sample we may judge of
the whole piece.
Ibid. Page 25
Put you in this pickle.
Ibid. Chap. 5, Page 30
Can we ever have too much of a good
thing? [6]
Ibid. Chap. 6, Page 37
Fortune may have yet a better suc-
cess in reserve for you, and they who
lose to-day may win to-morrow.
Ibid. Chap. 7, Page 39
The charging of his enemy was but
the work of a moment.
Ibid. Chap. 8, Page 50

---

[1] You mince matters. — MOLIÈRE: *Tartuffe,
Act I, Sc. 1*
[2] See Shakespeare, page 74.
[3] Time out o' mind. — SHAKESPEARE: *Romeo and Juliet, Act I, Sc. 4, L. 70*
[4] As good luck would have it. — SHAKE-
SPEARE: *The Merry Wives of Windsor, Act III,
Sc. 5, L. 86*
[5] See Bacon, page 111.
[6] See Shakespeare, page 51.

I don't know that ever I saw one in my born days.[1]

> *Part I. Book II, Chap. 2, Page 57*

Those two fatal words, Mine and Thine.[2]

> *Ibid. Chap. 3, Page 63*

The eyes those silent tongues of Love.

> *Ibid. Page 65*

Ambrose and his friends will carry the day.

> *Ibid. Chap. 4, Page 67*

As good-natured a soul as e'er trod on shoe of leather.

> *Ibid. Page 69*

And had a face like a blessing.[3]

> *Ibid.*

He's a good man, I'll say that for him, and a true Christian every inch of him.

> *Ibid. Page 70*

There's not the least thing can be said or done, but people will talk and find fault.[4]

> *Ibid.*

Without a wink of sleep.[5]

> *Ibid. Page 72*

One swallow never makes a summer.[6]

> *Ibid. Page 77*

Everything disturbs an absent lover.

> *Ibid. Page 84*

It is a true saying, that a man must eat a peck of salt with his friend, before he knows him.

> *Ibid. Book III, Chap. 1, Page 92*

---

[1] Many of the phrases and proverbs are repeated elsewhere in *Don Quixote*. Only the first appearance is given here.
[2] See Boileau, page 1050.
[3] He had a face like a benediction. — JARVIS's translation
[4] See Samuel Dodge, page 474.

Take wife, or cowl; ride you, or walk:
Doubt not but tongues will have their talk.
     JEAN DE LA FONTAINE: *The Miller, His Son, and the Donkey*
Do you think you could keep people from talking? — MOLIÈRE: *Tartuffe, Act I, Sc. 1*
[5] I have not slept one wink. — SHAKESPEARE: *Cymbeline, Act III, Sc. 4, L. 103*
[6] See Heywood, page 16.

Fortune leaves always some door open to come at a remedy.

> *Part I. Book III, Chap. 1, Page 94*

Thank you for nothing.

> *Ibid.*

Fair and softly goes far.

> *Ibid. Chap. 2, Page 97*

May Old Nick[1] rock my cradle.

> *Ibid. Chap. 3, Page 103*

No limits but the sky.[2]

> *Ibid. Page 110*

To give the devil his due.[3]

> *Ibid. Page 111*

Plain as the nose on a man's face.[4]

> *Ibid. Chap. 4, Page 112*

A peck of troubles.

> *Ibid.*

The short and long is.

> *Ibid.*

Lest we leap out of the frying-pan into the fire;[5] or, out of God's blessing into the warm sun.[5]

> *Ibid.*

You're leaping over the hedge before you come to the stile.

> *Ibid. Page 117*

You're taking the wrong sow by the ear.[6]

> *Ibid.*

Paid him in his own coin.

> *Ibid. Page 119*

Bell, book, and candle.

> *Ibid. Page 120*

Every tooth in a man's head is more valuable than a diamond.

> *Ibid. Page 121*

The famous Don Quixote de la Mancha, otherwise called The Knight of the Woeful Figure.[7]

> *Ibid. Chap. 5, Page 126*

---

[1] Nick Machiavel had ne'er a trick,
Though he gave his name to our Old Nick.
     BUTLER: *Hudibras, Part 3, Canto 1, L. 1313*
[2] Modern saying: The sky's the limit.
[3] See Shakespeare, page 61.
[4] See *Ibid.*, page 33.
[5] See Heywood, page 16.
[6] See *Ibid.*, page 17.
[7] Elsewhere translated as Rueful Countenance.

Let the worst come to the worst.[1]
Part I. Book III, Chap. 5, Page 127

You are come off now with a whole skin.
Ibid.

Get out of harm's way.
Ibid. Chap. 6, Page 130

Fear is sharp-sighted, and can see things under ground, and much more in the skies.
Ibid. Page 131

One of those carpet-knights[2] that abandon themselves to sleep and lazy ease.
Ibid.

A finger in every pie.[3]
Ibid. Page 133

No better than she should be.
Ibid.

Every dog has his day.
Ibid.

That's the nature of women, . . . not to love when we love them, and to love when we love them not.
Ibid.

You may go whistle for the rest.
Ibid. Page 134

Ill-luck, you know, seldom comes alone.[4]
Ibid. Page 135

Why do you lead me a wild-goose chase?
Ibid. Page 136

I find my familiarity with thee has bred contempt.[5]
Ibid.

Experience, the universal Mother of Sciences.
Ibid. Chap. 7, Page 140

I tell thee, that's Mambrino's helmet.[1]
Part I. Book III, Chap. 7, Page 141

I give up the ghost.
Ibid. Page 143

Give me but that, and let the world rub, there I'll stick.
Ibid. Page 148

Ne'er cringe nor creep, for what you by force may reap.
Ibid. Page 149

'Tis an office of more trust to shave a man's beard than to saddle a horse.
Ibid. Page 151

Sing away sorrow, cast away care.
Ibid. Chap. 8, Page 153

After meat comes mustard; or, like money to a starving man at sea, when there are no victuals to be bought with it.
Ibid.

Of good natural parts, and of a liberal education.
Ibid. Page 154

A medley of kindred, that 'twould puzzle a convocation of casuists to resolve their degrees of consanguinity.
Ibid. Page 155

I know it all by heart.
Ibid. Page 157

Let every man mind his own business.
Ibid.

Murder will out.[2]
Ibid.

Those who'll play with cats must expect to be scratched.
Ibid. Page 159

The main chance.[3]
Ibid.

Raise a hue and cry.
Ibid.

Return to our flesh-pots of Egypt.
Ibid. Page 160

Nor do they care a straw.[4]
Ibid. Chap. 9, Page 161

---

[1] See Middleton, page 116.
[2] See Burton, page 123, and Montaigne, page 1027.
[3] No pie was baked at Castlewood but her little finger was in it. — THACKERAY: *The Virginians, Chap. 5*
[4] One woe doth tread upon another's heel.
SHAKESPEARE: *Hamlet, Act IV, Sc. 7, L. 164*
[5] See Shakespeare, page 34, and Aesop, page 961.

---

[1] Mambrino, a Saracen of great valour, who had a golden helmet, which Rinaldo took from him. — ARIOSTO [1474–1533]: *Orlando Furioso, Canto I*
[2] See Chaucer, page 6.
[3] See Lyly, page 23.
[4] See Terence, page 979.

'Tis the part of a wise man to keep himself to-day for to-morrow, and not venture all his eggs in one basket.

Part I. Book III, Chap. 9, Page 162

I know what's what.

Ibid.

The ease of my burdens, the staff of my life.

Ibid. Page 163

I'm almost frighted out of my seven senses.[1]

Ibid. Page 168

Within a stone's throw of it.

Ibid. Page 170

'Tis the only comfort of the miserable to have partners in their woes.[2]

Ibid. Chap. 10, Page 173

The very remembrance of my former misfortune proves a new one to me.

Ibid. Page 174

Absence, that common cure of love.

Ibid. Page 177

Lovers are commonly industrious to make themselves uneasy.

Ibid. Page 179

From pro's and con's they fell to a warmer way of disputing.

Ibid. Page 181

Make hay while the sun shines.[3]

Ibid. Chap. 11, Page 182

I never thrust my nose into other men's porridge. It is no bread and butter of mine; every man for himself, and God for us all.[4]

Ibid. Page 183

Naked came I into the world, and naked must I go out.

Ibid.

Little said is soon amended.[5]

Ibid. Page 184

A close mouth catches no flies.

Ibid.

She may guess what I should perform in the wet, if I do so much in the dry.[1]

Part I. Book III, Chap. 11, Page 186

Mere flim-flam stories,[2] and nothing but shams and lies.

Ibid. Page 187

To tell you the truth.

Ibid. Page 190

Thou hast seen nothing yet.

Ibid.

For goodness-sake.

Ibid.

Between jest and earnest.

Ibid.

Cutting the air as swift as a witch upon a broomstick.

Ibid. Page 191

My love and hers have always been purely Platonick.

Ibid. Page 192

'Tis ten to one.

Ibid. Page 193

As sure as I'm alive.

Ibid.

There's no need to make an enquiry about a woman's pedigree, as there is of us men, when some badge of honour is bestowed on us.

Ibid. Page 194

There are but two things that chiefly excite us to love a woman, an attractive beauty, and unspotted fame.

Ibid. Page 195

'Tis ill talking of halters in the house of a man that was hanged.

Ibid.

My memory is so bad, that many times I forget my own name!

Ibid.

You're a devil at everything; and there's no kind of thing in the versal world but what you can turn your hand to.

Ibid. Page 196

'Twill grieve me so to the heart, that I shall cry my eyes out.

Ibid. Page 197

---

[1] See Scott, page 310.
[2] See Publilius Syrus, *Maxim 995,* and Spinoza, page 1049.
[3] See Heywood, page 12.
[4] See *Ibid.,* page 18.
[5] Little said is soonest mended.
  GEORGE WITHER: *The Shepherd's Hunting*

[1] An allusion to *Luke, XXIII, 31,* — For if they do these things in a green tree, what shall be done in the dry?
[2] You must not think to put us off with a flim-flam story. — *Don Quixote, P. 203*

Without knowing why or wherefore.
Part I. Book III, Chap. 11, Page 197
Ready to split his sides with laughing.
Ibid. Chap. 13, Page 208
As much a fool as he was, he loved money, and knew how to keep it when he had it, and was wise enough to keep his own counsel.
Ibid.
What man has assurance enough to pretend to know thoroughly the riddle of a woman's mind, and who could ever hope to fix her mutable nature? [1]
Ibid. Page 216
Demonstrations of love are never altogether displeasing to women, and the most disdainful, in spite of all their coyness, reserve a little complaisance in their hearts for their admirers.
Ibid. Book IV, Chap. 1, Page 226
My honour is dearer to me than my life.
Ibid. Page 228
On the word of a gentleman, and a Christian.
Ibid. Chap. 2, Page 236
Delay always breeds danger.[2]
Ibid. Page 240
Higgledy-piggledy.
Ibid. Page 241
Let things go at sixes and sevens.[3]
Ibid. Chap. 3, Page 250
Think before thou speakest.
Ibid. Page 252
Let us forget and forgive injuries.
Ibid. Page 254
I must speak the truth, and nothing but the truth.
Ibid. Page 255
They must needs go whom the Devil drives.[4]
Ibid. Chap. 4, Page 259
A bird in hand is worth two in the bush.[5]
Ibid.

More knave than fool.[1]
Part I. Book IV, Chap. 4, Page 261
Mind your own business.
Ibid. Page 263
A fig for your great captain.
Ibid. Chap. 5, Page 267
I can tell where my own shoe pinches me; [2] and you must not think, sir, to catch old birds with chaff.
Ibid.
Within the bounds of possibility.
Ibid. Chap. 6, Page 283
The ornament of her sex.[3]
Ibid. Chap. 7, Page 287
He that gives quickly gives twice.[4]
Ibid. Page 291
Thank your stars.
Ibid. Page 292
Required in every good lover . . . the whole alphabet . . . Agreeable, Bountiful, Constant, Dutiful, Easy, Faithful, Gallant, Honourable, Ingenious, Kind, Loyal, Mild, Noble, Officious, Prudent, Quiet, Rich, Secret, True, Valiant, Wise . . . Young and Zealous.
Ibid.
Harp so on the same string.
Ibid. Chap. 8, Page 305
At his wit's end.[5]
Ibid. Page 306
She made a virtue of necessity.[6]
Ibid. Chap. 9, Page 313
Virtue is the truest nobility.
Ibid. Page 314
Here's the devil-and-all to pay.
Ibid. Chap. 10, Page 319
I begin to smell a rat.[7]
Ibid.
I'll take my corporal oath on 't.
Ibid. Page 321
The proof of the pudding is in the eating.
Ibid. Page 322

---

[1] A fickle and changeful thing is woman ever.
    VIRGIL: *Aeneid, Book 4, L. 569*
[2] See Shakespeare, page 68.
[3] See W. S. Gilbert, page 623.
[4] See Heywood, page 17.
[5] See *Ibid.*, page 15, and Plutarch, page 1005.

[1] More knave than fool. — CHRISTOPHER MARLOWE: *The Jew of Malta, Act 2*
[2] See Plutarch, page 997.
[3] She's the ornament of her sex. — DICKENS: *The Old Curiosity Shop, Chap. 5*
[4] Bis dat qui cito dat. — *Latin proverb*
[5] See Heywood, page 13.
[6] See Chaucer, page 4.
[7] See Middleton, page 116.

Let none presume to tell me that the pen is preferable to the sword.[1]

Part I. Book IV, Chap. 10, Page 325

By hook or by crook.[2]

Ibid. Page 328

It is past all controversy, that what costs dearest, is, and ought most to be valued.

Ibid. Chap. 11, Page 328

It seldom happens that any felicity comes so pure as not to be tempered and allayed by some mixture of sorrow.

Ibid. Chap. 14, Page 359

Stopped them in the nick.[3]

Ibid. Chap. 17, Page 383

There's no striving against the stream; and the weakest still goes to the wall.

Ibid. Chap. 20, Page 404

The bow cannot always stand bent, nor can human frailty subsist without some lawful recreation.

Ibid. Chap. 21, Page 412

Give them the slip.[4]

Ibid. Chap. 22, Page 415

Faith without good works is dead.

Ibid. Chap. 23, Page 423

I would have nobody to control me, I would be absolute; and who but I? Now, he that is absolute can do what he likes; he that can do what he likes, can take his pleasure; he that can take his pleasure, can be content; and he that can be content, 'has no more to desire. So the matter's over; and come what will come, I am satisfied.[5]

Ibid.

Even a worm when trod upon, will turn again.[1]

*Part II. Book III, Author's
Preface, Page 440*

It is not the hand, but the understanding of a man, that may be said to write.[2]

Ibid. Page 441

Had only now and then lucid intervals.[3]

Ibid. Chap. 1, Page 448

How blind must he be that can't see through a sieve.

Ibid. Page 450

Keep within bounds.

Ibid. Chap. 2, Page 455

When the head aches, all the members partake of the pains.[4]

Ibid.

While there's life there's hope.[5]

Ibid. Chap. 3, Page 463

Miracle me no miracles.

Ibid. Page 464

He has done like Orbaneja, the painter of Ubeda; who, being asked what he painted, answered, "As it may hit;" and when he had scrawled out a misshapen cock, was forced to write underneath in Gothic letters, "This is a cock."[6]

Ibid.

Youngsters read it, grown men understand it, and old people applaud it.

Ibid.

The most artful part in a play is the fool's.

Ibid. Page 465

---

[1] See Edward Bulwer Lytton, page 425.
Scholars' pens carry farther, and give a louder report than thunder. — SIR THOMAS BROWNE: *Religio Medici* (Everyman ed.), P. 70

[2] See Skelton, page 10.

[3] Nick of time. — SUCKLING: *The Goblins, Act 5*

[4] Judas had given them the slip. — MATHEW HENRY: *Commentaries, Matthew XXII*

[5] I would do what I pleased; and doing what I pleased, I should have my will; and having my will, I should be contented; and when one is contented, there is no more to be desired; and when there is no more to be desired, there is an end of it. — JARVIS's translation

[1] The smallest worm will turn, being trodden on.
SHAKESPEARE: *King Henry VI, Part III, Act II, Sc. 2, L. 17*

[2] Cervantes' left hand was maimed for life by gunshot wounds in the battle of Lepanto.

[3] See Robert South, page 183.

[4] For let our finger ache, and it indues
Our other healthful members even to that sense
Of pain.
SHAKESPEARE: *Othello, Act III, Sc. 4, L. 145*

[5] See Gay, page 206.

[6] The painter Orbaneja of Ubeda, if he chanced to draw a cock, he wrote under it, "This is a cock," lest the people should take it for a fox. — JARVIS's translation

There are men that will make you books, and turn 'em loose into the world, with as much dispatch as they would do a dish of fritters.

Part II. Book III, Chap. 3, Page 465

"There is no book so bad," said the bachelor, "but something good may be found in it." [1]

Ibid.

He that publishes a book runs a very great hazard, since nothing can be more impossible than to compose one that may secure the approbation of every reader.

Ibid. Page 466

Ready cash.

Ibid. Chap. 4, Page 468

Every man is as Heaven made him, and sometimes a great deal worse.

Ibid.

Rejoices the cockles of my heart. [2]

Ibid. Chap. 5, Page 472

There's no sauce in the world like hunger.

Ibid. Page 473

Birds of a feather flock together.

Ibid. Page 474

He casts a sheep's eye at the wench.

Ibid.

I ever loved to see everything upon the square.

Ibid. Page 475

Neither will I make myself anybody's laughing-stock.

Ibid.

That feather in their caps.

Ibid. Page 476

Stand in thy own light.

Ibid.

In the twinkling of an eye. [3]

Ibid.

Journey over all the universe in a map, without the expense and fatigue of travelling, without suffering the inconveniences of heat, cold, hunger, and thirst.

Ibid. Chap. 6, Page 479

Presume to put in her oar.

Ibid. Page 480

The fair sex. [1]

Part II. Book III, Chap. 6, Page 480

A little in one's own pocket is better than much in another man's purse. 'Tis good to keep a nest-egg. Every little makes a mickle.

Ibid. Chap. 7, Page 486

That's neither here nor there.

Ibid. Chap. 9, Page 498

Remember the old saying, "Faint heart ne'er won fair lady." [2]

Ibid. Chap. 10, Page 501

Fore-warned fore-armed.

Ibid. Page 502

As well look for a needle in a bottle of hay. [3]

Ibid.

Sleeveless errants. [4]

Ibid.

Are we to mark this day with a white or a black stone?

Ibid. Page 503

Spare your breath to cool your porridge. [5]

Ibid. Page 505

A great cry, but little wool. [6]

Ibid. Chap. 13, Page 520

The very pink of courtesy. [7]

Ibid. Page 521

Neither fish, flesh, nor good red-herring. [8]

Ibid.

I'll turn over a new leaf. [9]

Ibid. Page 524

Let every man look before he leaps. [10]

Ibid. Chap. 14, Page 528

---

[1] See Pliny the Younger, page 1009.
[2] See Miscellaneous, page 944.
[3] See Shakespeare, page 45.

[1] See Addison, page 198.
[2] SPENSER: *Britain's Ida, Canto V, St. 1.* ELLERTON: *George-a-Greene* (a ballad). WHETSTONE: *Rocke of Regard.* BURNS: *To Dr. Blacklock.* COLMAN: *Love Laughs at Locksmiths, Act I.* GILBERT: *Iolanthe, Act II*
[3] Needle in a bottle of hay. — NATHANIEL FIELD: *A Woman's a Weathercock* [1612]
[4] See Heywood, page 13.
[5] See Plutarch, page 1004.
[6] See John Fortescue, page 9.
[7] I am the very pink of courtesy.
    SHAKESPEARE: *Romeo and Juliet, Act II, Sc. 4, L. 63*
[8] See Heywood, page 13.
[9] See Middleton, page 117.
[10] See Heywood, page 11.

As one egg is like another.[1]
Part II. Book III, Chap. 14, Page 530
The pen is the tongue of the mind.
Ibid. Chap. 16, Page 543
Modesty is a virtue not often found among poets, for almost every one of them thinks himself the greatest in the world.
Ibid. Chap. 18, Page 555
Sings like a lark.
Ibid. Chap. 19, Page 564
Marriage is a noose.
Ibid.
She'll give Camacho the bag to hold.
Ibid. Page 565
There were but two families in the world, Have-much and Have-little.
Ibid. Chap. 20, Page 574
He preaches well that lives well, quoth Sancho, that's all the divinity I understand.
Ibid. Page 575
Love and War are the same thing, and stratagems and policy are as allowable in the one as in the other.
Ibid. Chap. 21, Page 580
A private sin is not so prejudicial in this world as a public indecency.
Ibid. Chap. 22, Page 582
He has an oar in every man's boat, and a finger in every pie.[2]
Ibid. Page 583
There is no love lost, sir.[3]
Ibid.
Come back sound, wind and limb.
Ibid. Page 587
Patience, and shuffle the cards.[4]
Ibid. Chap. 23, Page 592
Comparisons are odious.[5]
Ibid. Page 593
Tell me thy company, and I'll tell thee what thou art.[6]
Ibid. Page 594

---

[1] See Shakespeare, page 56, and Rabelais, page 1026.
[2] See Cervantes, page 1035.
[3] See Jonson, page 118.
[4] See Sir Walter Scott, page 311.
[5] See Fortescue, page 9. .
[6] Show me your garden and I shall tell you what you are. — ALFRED AUSTIN: *The Garden That I Love* [1905], *P. 98*
Tell me what you eat, and I will tell you

Returning the compliment.
Part II. Book III, Chap. 25, Page 606
To-morrow will be a new day.
Ibid. Chap. 26, Page 618
Like a man of mettle.[1]
Ibid. Chap. 27, Page 625
You can see farther into a millstone than he.[2]
Ibid. Chap. 28, Page 628
I can see with half an eye.
Ibid. Chap. 29, Page 632
Scum of the world.[3]
Ibid. Page 635
The apples of his eyes.[4]
Ibid. Chap. 30, Page 637
Old . . . that's an affront no woman can well bear.
Ibid. Chap. 31, Page 644
One of the most considerable advantages the great have over their inferiors, is to have servants as good as themselves.
Ibid. Page 645
Speak the truth and shame the devil.[5]
Ibid. Page 647
"Sit there, clod-patc!" cried he; "for let me sit wherever I will, that will still be the upper end, and the place of worship to thee."[6]
Ibid. Page 648
Building castles in the air.[7]
Ibid.
Upon second thoughts.[8]
Ibid. Chap. 32, Page 653
Made 'em pay dear for their frolic.
Ibid. Page 655

---

what you are. — ANTHELME BRILLAT-SAVARIN: *Physiologie du Goût, Aphorism 4*
[1] A lad of mettle. — SHAKESPEARE: *King Henry IV, Part I, Act II, Sc. 4, L. 13*
A man of mettle. — AARON HILL: *Verses Written on a Window in Scotland*
[2] See Heywood, page 14.
[3] See R. H. Schauffler, page 860.
[4] The apple of his eye. — *Deuteronomy, XXXII, 10*
The apple of the eye. — *Psalm XVII, 8*
[5] See Shakespeare, page 62.
[6] Sit thee down, chaff-threshing churl! for let me sit where I will, that is the upper end to thee. — JARVIS'S translation
See Emerson, page 414.
[7] See Burton, page 122.
[8] See Dryden, page 179.

'Tis good to live and learn.
Part II. Book III, Chap. 32, Page 655
Great persons are able to do great
kindnesses.
Ibid. Page 662
He's as mad as a March hare.[1]
Ibid. Chap. 33, Page 664
In the night all cats are gray.[2]
Ibid. Page 665
All is not gold that glisters.[3]
Ibid. Page 666
Honesty's the best policy.[4]
Ibid.
A good name is better than riches.[5]
Ibid. Page 668
An honest man's word is as good as
his bond.
Ibid. Book IV, Chap. 34, Page 674
Heaven's help is better than early
rising.
Ibid.
He would not budge an inch.[6]
Ibid. Page 677
A blot in thy scutcheon to all fu-
turity.
Ibid. Chap. 35, Page 681
This is no time for me to mind nice-
ties, and spelling of letters. I have other
fish to fry.[7]
Ibid. Page 682
There's a time for some things, and
a time for all things; a time for great
things, and a time for small things.[8]
Ibid.
The worst is still behind.[9]
Ibid. Page 683
'Twill do you a world of good.
Ibid.

[1] See Heywood, page 17.
[2] See *Ibid.*, page 13.
[3] See Chaucer, page 8.
[4] I hold the maxim no less applicable to
public than to private affairs, that honesty is
always the best policy. — GEORGE WASHING-
TON: *Farewell Address* [1796]
[5] See Publilius Syrus, *Maxim 108*, and Old
Testament, page 1109.
[6] See Shakespeare, page 51.
[7] See Rabelais, page 1026.
[8] To everything there is a season, and a time
to every purpose. — *Ecclesiastes, III, 1*
[9] Aun le falta la cola por desollar (The tail
still remains to be flayed). — Spanish proverb

But all in good time.
Part II. Book IV, Chap. 36, Page 686
With a grain of salt.
Ibid. Chap. 37, Page 690
They had best not stir the rice,
though it sticks to the pot.
Ibid. Page 691
They cover a dunghill with a piece of
tapestry when a procession goes by.
Ibid.
Good wits jump; [1] a word to the wise
is enough.
Ibid. Page 692
My understanding has forsook me,
and is gone a wool-gathering.[2]
Ibid. Chap. 38, Page 692
You may as well expect pears from
an elm.[3]
Ibid. Chap. 40, Page 704
Make it thy business to know thy-
self, which is the most difficult lesson
in the world.[4]
Ibid. Chap. 42, Page 719
You cannot eat your cake and have
your cake; [5] and store's no sore.[6]
Ibid. Chap. 43, Page 723
Diligence is the mother of good for-
tune.
Ibid. Page 724
What a man has, so much he's sure of.
Ibid. Page 725
When a man says, "Get out of my
house! what would you have with my
wife?" there's no answer to be made.
Ibid. Page 726
The pot calls the kettle black.
Ibid. Page 727
Mum's the word.[7]
Ibid. Chap. 44, Page 729
Walls have ears.[8]
Ibid. Chap. 48, Page 763
Set a beggar on horseback.[9]
Ibid. Chap. 50, Page 782

[1] See Laurence Sterne, page 241.
[2] My thoughts ran a wool-gathering; and
I did like the countryman, who looked for his
ass while he was mounted on his back. — *Don
Quixote, P. 827*
[3] See Publilius Syrus, *Maxim 674*.
[4] See Burton, page 544.
[5] See Heywood, page 18.
[6] See *Ibid.*, page 12.
[7] See Shakespeare, page 35.
[8] See Chaucer, page 6.
[9] See Burton, page 124.

I may at last hit the nail o' the head.[1]
Part II. Book IV, Chap. 51, Page 785
When thou art at Rome, do as they do at Rome.[2]
Ibid. Chap. 54, Page 806
Man appoints, and God disappoints.[3]
Ibid. Chap. 55, Page 816
Many count their chickens before they are hatched; and where they expect bacon meet with broken bones.
Ibid.
As they use to say, spick and span new.[4]
Ibid. Chap. 58, Page 829
I think it a very happy accident.[5]
Ibid. Page 831
He that proclaims the kindnesses he has received, shows his disposition to repay 'em if he could.
Ibid. Page 835
He that errs in so considerable a passage, may well be suspected to have committed many gross errors through the whole history.
Ibid. Chap. 59, Page 843
A gift-horse should not be looked in the mouth.[6]
Ibid. Chap. 62, Page 861
I shall be as secret as the grave.
Ibid. Page 862
Now blessings light on him that first invented this same sleep! It covers a man all over, thoughts and all, like a cloak; 'tis meat for the hungry, drink for the thirsty, heat for the cold, and cold for the hot. 'Tis the current coin that purchases all the pleasures of the world cheap; and the balance that sets the king and the shepherd, the fool and the wise man even.[7]
Ibid. Chap. 68, Page 898

All the fat shall be in the fire.[1]
Part II. Book IV, Chap. 69, Page 906
There is a thing called poetical license.
Ibid. Chap. 70, Page 913
Rome was not built in a day.[2]
Ibid. Chap. 71, Page 917
The ass will carry his load, but not a double load; ride not a free horse to death.
Ibid.
I thought it working for a dead horse, because I am paid beforehand.[3]
Ibid.
Nothing like striking while the iron is hot.[4]
Ibid. Page 919
Thereby hangs a tale.[5]
Ibid. Chap. 72, Page 923
He . . . got the better of himself, and that's the best kind of victory one can wish for.
Ibid. Page 924
Every man was not born with a silver spoon in his mouth.
Ibid. Chap. 73, Page 926
Die merely of the mulligrubs.
Ibid. Chap. 74, Page 932
Get out of your doleful dumps.[6]
Ibid.
Ne'er look for birds of this year in the nests of the last.[7]
Ibid. Page 933
There is a strange charm in the thoughts of a good legacy, or the hopes of an estate, which wondrously allevi-

---

[1] See Heywood, page 18, Fletcher, page 127, and Rabelais, page 1025.
[2] See Burton, page 126.
[3] See Thomas à Kempis, page 8.
[4] See Middleton, page 116.
[5] See *Ibid.*, page 117.
[6] See Heywood, page 13, Butler, page 142, and Rabelais, page 1025.
[7] Blessing on him who invented sleep, — the mantle that covers all human thoughts, the food that appeases hunger, the drink that quenches thirst, the fire that warms cold, the cold that moderates heat, and, lastly, the gen-

eral coin that purchases all things, the balance and weight that equals the shepherd with the king, and the simple with the wise. — JARVIS's translation
[1] See Heywood, page 12.
[2] See *Ibid.*, page 15.
[3] It is a heart-rending delusion and a cruel snare to be paid for your work before you accomplish it. As soon as once your work is finished you ought to be promptly paid; but to receive your lucre one minute before it is due, is to tempt Providence to make a Micawber of you. — EDMUND GOSSE: *Gossip in a Library, Beau Nash* [1891], P. 230
[4] See Heywood, page 12.
[5] See Shakespeare, page 34, and Rabelais, page 1026.
[6] See Shakespeare, page 77.
[7] See Longfellow, page 434.

ates the sorrow that men would otherwise feel for the death of friends.

Part II. Book IV, Chap. 74, Page 934

For if he like a madman lived,
At least he like a wise one died.

Ibid. Page 935 (Don Quixote's Epitaph)

Don't put too fine a point to your wit for fear it should get blunted.

*The Little Gypsy
(La Gitanilla)*

My heart is wax moulded as she pleases, but enduring as marble to retain.[1]

Ibid.

BARTHOLOMEW SCHIDONI
[1560–1616]

I, too, was born in Arcadia.[2]

Adopted by GOETHE *as the motto for his Travels in Italy* [1816]

PIERRE CORNEILLE
[1606–1684]

We easily believe that which we wish.

Le Baron. Act I, Sc. 3

Do your duty, and leave the rest to heaven.

Horace [1640]. Act II, Sc. 8

Who is all-powerful should fear everything.

Cinna [1640]. Act IV, Sc. 2

The manner of giving is worth more than the gift.

Le Menteur [1642]. Act I, Sc. 1

A kindness loses its grace by being
noised abroad,
Who desires it to be remembered should
forget it.

Théodore. Act I, Sc. 2

A service beyond all recompense
Weighs so heavy that it almost gives
offence.

Suréna [1674]. Act III, Sc. 1

---

[1] Wax to receive, and marble to retain.
BYRON: *Beppo, St. 34*
[2] Et ego in Arcadia vixi [I, too, have lived in Arcadia], motto used by Nicolas Poussin (1594–1665) for his famous painting *Les Bergers d'Arcadie*.

ISAAC DE BENSERADE
[1612–1691]

In bed we laugh, in bed we cry;
And, born in bed, in bed we die.
The near approach a bed may show
Of human bliss to human woe.

Translated by DR. SAMUEL
JOHNSON

FRANÇOIS, DUC DE LA ROCHEFOUCAULD
[1613–1680]

Reflections, or Sentences and Moral Maxims

Our virtues are most frequently but vices disguised.[1]

We have all sufficient strength to endure the misfortunes of others.

Maxim 19

Philosophy triumphs easily over past evils and future evils; but present evils triumph over it.[2]

Maxim 22

We need greater virtues to sustain good than evil fortune.

Maxim 25

Neither the sun nor death can be looked at with a steady eye.

Maxim 26

If we were without faults, we should not take so much pleasure in remarking them in others.

Maxim 31

Interest speaks all sorts of tongues, and plays all sorts of parts, even that of disinterestedness.

Maxim 39

We are never so happy nor so unhappy as we imagine.

Maxim 49

---

[1] This epigraph, which is the key to the system of La Rochefoucauld, is found in another form as No. 179 of the Maxims of the first edition, 1665; it is omitted from the second and third, and reappears for the first time in the fourth edition at the head of the Reflections. — AIME MARTIN
[2] See Goldsmith, page 253.

There are few people who would not be ashamed of being loved when they love no longer.

Maxim 71

True love is like ghosts, which everybody talks about and few have seen.

Maxim 76

The love of justice is simply, in the majority of men, the fear of suffering injustice.

Maxim 78

Silence is the best resolve for him who distrusts himself.

Maxim 79

Friendship is only a reciprocal conciliation of interests, and an exchange of good offices; it is a species of commerce out of which self-love always expects to gain something.

Maxim 83

Everyone complains of his memory, and no one complains of his judgment.

Maxim 89

A man who is ungrateful is often less to blame than his benefactor.

Maxim 96

The understanding is always the dupe of the heart.

Maxim 102

Nothing is given so profusely as advice.

Maxim 110

The true way to be deceived is to think oneself more knowing than others.

Maxim 127

Usually we praise only to be praised.

Maxim 146

Our repentance is not so much regret for the ill we have done as fear of the ill that may happen to us in consequence.

Maxim 180

Most people judge men only by success or by fortune.

Maxim 212

Hypocrisy is a homage vice pays to virtue.

Maxim 218

Too great haste to repay an obligation is a kind of ingratitude.

Maxim 226

There is great ability in knowing how to conceal one's ability.

Maxim 245

The pleasure of love is in loving. We are happier in the passion we feel than in that we inspire.[1]

Maxim 259

We always like those who admire us; we do not always like those whom we admire.

Maxim 294

The gratitude of most men is but a secret desire of receiving greater benefits.[2]

Maxim 298

Lovers are never tired of each other, though they always speak of themselves.

Maxim 312

We pardon in the degree that we love.

Maxim 330

We hardly find any persons of good sense save those who agree with us.[3]

Maxim 347

The greatest fault of a penetrating wit is to go beyond the mark.

Maxim 377

We may give advice, but we cannot inspire the conduct.

Maxim 378

The veracity which increases with old age is not far from folly.

Maxim 416

Nothing prevents our being natural so much as the desire to appear so.

Maxim 431

In their first passion women love their lovers, in all the others they love love.[4]

Maxim 471

Quarrels would not last long if the fault was only on one side.

Maxim 496

---

[1] See Shelley, page 367.

[2] See Walpole, page 200.

[3] "That was excellently observed," say I when I read a passage in another where his opinion agrees with mine. When we differ, then I pronounce him to be mistaken. — SWIFT: *Thoughts on Various Subjects*

[4] See Byron, page 359.

In the adversity of our best friends we often find something that is not exactly displeasing.[1]

To win that wonder of the world,
A smile from her bright eyes,
I fought my King, and would have hurled
The gods out of their skies.[2]
To Madame de Longueville

HANS JAKOB CHRISTOFFEL VON GRIMMELSHAUSEN
[*Circa* 1620–1676]

For gluttony and drunkenness, hunger and thirst, wenching and dicing and playing, riot and roaring, murdering and being murdered, slaying and being slain, torturing and being tortured, hunting and being hunted, harrying and being harried, robbing and being robbed, frighting and being frighted, causing trouble and suffering trouble, beating and being beaten: in a word, hurting and harming, and in turn being hurt and harmed — this was their [3] whole life. And in this career they let nothing hinder them: neither winter nor summer, snow nor ice, heat nor cold, rain nor wind, hill nor dale, wet nor dry; ditches, mountain-passes, ramparts and walls, fire and water, were all the same to them. Father nor mother, sister nor brother, no, nor the danger to their own bodies, souls, and consciences, nor even loss of life and of heaven itself, or aught else that can be named, will ever stand in their way, for ever they toil and moil at their own strange work, till at last, little by little, in battles, sieges, attacks, campaigns,

yea, and in their winter-quarters too (which are the soldiers' earthly paradise, if they can but happen upon fat peasants) they perish, they die, they rot and consume away, save but a few, who in their old age, unless they have been right thrifty reivers and robbers, do furnish us with the best of all beggars and vagabonds.
The Adventurous Simplicissimus.[1]
Book I, Chap. XVI

JEAN DE LA FONTAINE
[1621–1695]

The opinion of the strongest is always the best.
*Book I. Fable 10, The Wolf
and the Lamb*
By the work one knows the workman.
*Ibid. Fable 21, The Hornets
and the Bees*
It is a double pleasure to deceive the deceiver.
*Book II. Fable 15, The Cock
and the Fox*
It is impossible to please all the world and one's father.
*Book III. Fable 1, The Man,
the Boy, and the Donkey*
In everything one must consider the end.[2]
*Ibid. Fable 5, The Fox
and the Gnat*
"They are too green," he said, "and only good for fools."[3]
*Ibid. Fable 11, The Fox
and the Grapes*
Help thyself, and God will help thee.[4]
*Book VI. Fable 18, Hercules
and the Waggoner*
The sign brings customers.
*Book VII. Fable 15, The
Fortune-Tellers*

---

[1] This reflection, No. 99 in the edition of 1665, the author suppressed in the third edition.
In all distresses of our friends
We first consult our private ends;
While Nature, kindly bent to ease us,
Points out some circumstance to please us.
DEAN SWIFT: *A Paraphrase of
Rochefoucauld's Maxim*
[2] Quoted by EDMUND GOSSE in *Gossip in a Library, Pharamond* [1891].
[3] The *Landsknechte*, mercenary foot soldiers, of the Thirty Years' War.

[1] Translated by A. T. S. G.; published [1912] by Heinemann, London.
[2] Remember the end, and thou shalt never do amiss. — Apocrypha, *Ecclesiasticus III, 36*.
[3] Sour grapes. See George Herbert, page 137, and Aesop, page 961.
[4] See Herbert, page 137.

Let ignorance talk as it will, learning has its value.

> *Book VIII. Fable 19, The*
> *Use of Knowledge*

People who make no noise are dangerous.[1]

> *Ibid. Fable 23, The Current*
> *and the Stream*

No path of flowers leads to glory.

> *Book X. Fable 14*

JEAN BAPTISTE MOLIÈRE [2]
[1622–1673]

The world, dear Agnes, is a strange affair.

> *L'École des Femmes* [1662].
> *Act II, Sc. 6*

There are fagots and fagots.

> *Le Médecin Malgré Lui*
> [1666]. *Act I, Sc. 6*

We have changed all that.

> *Ibid. Act II, Sc. 6*

He's a wonderful talker, who has the art of telling you nothing in a great harangue.

> *Le Misanthrope* [1666].
> *Act II, Sc. 5*

He makes his cook his merit, and the world visits his dinners and not him.

> *Ibid.*

You see him in travail to produce *bons mots*.

> *Ibid.*

The more we love our friends, the less we flatter them; it is by excusing nothing that pure love shows itself.

> *Ibid.*

Doubts are more cruel than the worst of truths.

> *Ibid. Act III, Sc. 7*

Anyone may be an honourable man, and yet write verse badly.

> *Ibid. Act IV, Sc. 1*

---

[1] See Raleigh, page 21, and Lyly, page 24.

[2] Of all dramatists, ancient and modern, Molière is perhaps that one who has borne most constantly in mind the theory that the stage is a lay pulpit, and that its end is not merely amusement, but the reformation of manners by means of amusing spectacles. — GEORGE SAINTSBURY: *A Short History of French Literature* [1882], *P. 311*

If everyone were clothed with integrity, if every heart were just, frank, kindly, the other virtues would be well-nigh useless, since their chief purpose is to make us bear with patience the injustice of our fellows.

> *Le Misanthrope* [1666].
> *Act V, Sc. 1*

It is a wonderful seasoning of all enjoyments to think of those we love.

> *Ibid. Sc. 4*

There is no rampart that will hold out against malice.

> *Tartuffe* [1667]. *Act I, Sc. 1*

Those whose conduct gives room for talk are always the first to attack their neighbours.

> *Ibid.*

She is laughing in her sleeve at you.

> *Ibid. Sc. 6*

A woman always has her revenge ready.

> *Ibid. Act II, Sc. 2*

A heart that forgets us puts us on our mettle to forget just as quickly, and, if we don't succeed, at least we make believe to have succeeded.

> *Ibid. Sc. 4*

Although I am a pious man, I am not the less a man.

> *Ibid. Act III, Sc. 3*

The real Amphitryon is the Amphitryon who gives dinners.[1]

> *Amphitryon* [1668]. *Act III, Sc. 5*

Ah that I — You would have it so, you would have it so; George Dandin, you would have it so! [2] This suits you very nicely, and you are served right; you have precisely what you deserve.

> *Georges Dandin* [1668]. *Act I, Sc. 9*

Tell me to whom you are addressing yourself when you say that.

I am addressing myself — I am addressing myself to my cap.

> *L'Avare* [1668]. *Act I, Sc. 3*

The beautiful eyes of my cash-box.

> *Ibid. Act V, Sc. 3*

You are speaking before a man to whom all Naples is known.

> *Ibid. Sc. 5*

---

[1] See Dryden, page 179.
[2] Vous l'avez voulu, Georges Dandin.

My fair one, let us swear an eternal friendship.[1]

> *Le Bourgeois Gentilhomme*
> [*1670*]. *Act IV, Sc. 1*

I will maintain it before the whole world.

> *Ibid. Sc. 5*

What the devil did he want in that galley?[2]

> *Les Fourberies de Scapin*
> [*1671*]. *Act II, Sc. 11*

Grammar, which knows how to control even kings.[3]

> *Les Femmes Savantes* [*1672*].
> *Act II, Sc. 6*

It is seasoned throughout with Attic salt.

> *Ibid. Act III, Sc. 2*

Ah, there are no longer any children!
> *Le Malade Imaginaire* [*1673*].
> *Act II, Sc. 11*

Nearly all men die of their remedies, and not of their illnesses.

> *Ibid. Act III, Sc. 3*

BLAISE PASCAL
[1623–1662]

Translation by O. W. WIGHT

Man is but a reed, the weakest in nature, but he is a thinking reed.

> *Thoughts. Chap. 2, 10*

---

[1] See Sydney Smith, page 313.

[2] What the deuce did he want on board a Turk's galley? — CYRANO DE BERGERAC: *Le Pédant Joué, Act II, Sc. 4* [1654]

The saying of Molière came into his head: "But what the devil was he doing in that galley?" and he laughed at himself. — LYOF TOLSTOI: *War and Peace, Part IV, Chap. 6*

Often misquoted, "in that gallery," as in DICKENS's *A Tale of Two Cities, Book I, Chap. 5:* "What the devil do you do in that gallery there!"

[3] Sigismund [1361–1437], Emperor of the Holy Roman Empire, at the Council of Constance [1414], said to a prelate who had objected to his Majesty's grammar: "Ego sum rex Romanus, et supra grammaticam" (I am the Roman emperor, and am above grammar).

It is not permitted to the most equitable of men to be a judge in his own cause.

> *Thoughts. Chap. 4, 1*

Montaigne[1] is wrong in declaring that custom ought to be followed simply because it is custom, and not because it is reasonable or just.

> *Ibid. 6*

Thus we never live, but we hope to live; and always disposing ourselves to be happy, it is inevitable that we never become so.[2]

> *Ibid. Chap. 5, 2*

If the nose of Cleopatra had been shorter, the whole face of the earth would have been changed.

> *Ibid. Chap. 8, 29*

The last thing that we find in making a book is to know what we must put first.

> *Ibid. Chap. 9, 30*

Rivers are highways that move on, and bear us whither we wish to go.

> *Ibid. 38*

What a chimera, then, is man! what a novelty, what a monster, what a chaos, what a subject of contradiction, what a prodigy! A judge of all things, feeble worm of the earth, depositary of the truth, cloaca of uncertainty and error, the glory and the shame of the universe![3]

> *Ibid. Chap. 10, 1*

We know the truth, not only by the reason, but also by the heart.

> *Ibid.*

For as old age is that period of life most remote from infancy, who does not see that old age in this universal man ought not to be sought in the times nearest his birth, but in those most remote from it?[4]

> *Preface to the Treatise on Vacuum*

---

[1] Montaigne, Book I, Chap. 22.

[2] Man never is, but always to be, blest.
POPE: *Essay on Man, Epistle I, L. 96*

[3] See Pope, page 207.

[4] See Bacon, page 112.

JACQUES BÉNIGNE BOSSUET
[1627–1704]

Perfidious England.[1]
First Sermon on the Circumcision [2]

BENEDICT (BARUCH) SPINOZA [3]
[1632–1677]

Nature abhors a vacuum.
Ethics.[4] *Part I, Prop. XV, Note*

God and all the attributes of God are eternal.
Ibid. Prop. XIX

Nothing exists from whose nature some effect does not follow.
Ibid. Prop. XXXVI

He who would distinguish the true from the false must have an adequate idea of what is true and false.
Ibid. Part II, Prop. XLII, Proof

Will and Intellect are one and the same thing.
Ibid. Prop. XLIX, Corollary

He that can carp in the most eloquent or acute manner at the weakness of the human mind is held by his fellows as almost divine.
Ibid. Part III, Preface

Surely human affairs would be far happier if the power in men to be silent were the same as that to speak. But experience more than sufficiently teaches

that men govern nothing with more difficulty than their tongues.
Ethics. Part III, Prop. II, Note

Pride is therefore pleasure arising from a man's thinking too highly of himself.
Ibid. Prop. XXVI, Note

It may easily come to pass that a vain man may become proud and imagine himself pleasing to all when he is in reality a universal nuisance.
Ibid. Prop. XXX, Note

Sadness diminishes or hinders a man's power of action.
Ibid. Prop. XXXVII, Proof

Self-complacency is pleasure accompanied by the idea of oneself as cause.
Ibid. Prop. LI, Note

It therefore comes to pass that every one is fond of relating his own exploits and displaying the strength both of his body and his mind, and that men are on this account a nuisance one to the other.
Ibid. Prop. LIV, Note

I refer those actions which work out the good of the agent to courage, and those which work out the good of others to nobility. Therefore temperance, sobriety, and presence of mind in danger, etc., are species of courage; but modesty, clemency, etc., are species of nobility.
Ibid. Prop. LIX, Note

Fear cannot be without hope nor hope without fear.
Ibid. Definition XIII, Explanation

So long as a man imagines that he cannot do this or that, so long is he determined not to do it: and consequently, so long it is impossible to him that he should do it.
Ibid. Definition XXVIII, Explanation

Those who are believed to be most abject and humble are usually most ambitious and envious.
Ibid. Definition XXIX, Explanation

One and the same thing can at the same time be good, bad, and indifferent, e. g., music is good to the melancholy,

---

[1] Napoleon I in 1803 used the phrase, "perfidious Albion," which was taken up by the French press and pamphleteers, after the rupture of the Peace of Amiens.

[2] Edition Lefèvre, Paris [1836], *Vol. III, P. 687.*

[3] Ein Gottbetrunkener Mensch (A God-intoxicated man). — Novalis (Friedrich von Hardenberg) [1772–1801]
The Lord blot out his name under heaven. The Lord set him apart for destruction from all the tribes of Israel, with all the curses of the firmament which are written in the Book of the Law. . . . There shall no man speak to him, no man write to him, no man show him any kindness, no man stay under the same roof with him, no man come nigh him. — Amsterdam Synagogue's curse on Spinoza [1656]

[4] Everyman edition, translated by Andrew Boyle, M.A.

bad to those who mourn, and neither good nor bad to the deaf.

Ethics. Part IV, Preface

Those who commit suicide are powerless souls, and allow themselves to be conquered by external causes repugnant to their nature.

Ibid. Prop. XVIII, Note

Man is a social animal.

Ibid. Prop. XXXV, Note

Men will find that they can prepare with mutual aid far more easily what they need, and avoid far more easily the perils which beset them on all sides, by united forces.

Ibid.

Avarice, ambition, lust, etc., are nothing but species of madness, although not enumerated among diseases.[1]

Ibid. Prop. XLIV, Note

It is the part of a wise man to feed himself with moderate pleasant food and drink, and to take pleasure with perfumes, with the beauty of growing plants, dress, music, sports, and theatres, and other places of this kind which man may use without any hurt to his fellows.

Ibid. Prop. XLV, Note 2

It is a comfort to the unhappy to have companions in misery.[2]

Ibid. Prop. LVII, Note

He whose honour depends on the opinion of the mob must day by day strive with the greatest anxiety, act and scheme in order to retain his reputation. For the mob is varied and inconstant, and therefore if a reputation is not carefully preserved it dies quickly.

Ibid. Prop. LVIII, Note

In refusing benefits caution must be used lest we seem to despise or to refuse them for fear of having to repay them in kind.

Ibid. Prop. LXX, Note

To give aid to every poor man is far beyond the reach and power of every man. . . . Care of the poor is incumbent on society as a whole.

Ethics. Part IV, Appendix, XVII

None are more taken in by flattery than the proud, who wish to be the first and are not.

Ibid. XXI

Those are most desirous of honour and glory who cry out the loudest of its abuse and the vanity of the world.

Ibid. Part V, Prop. X, Note

We feel and know that we are eternal.

Ibid. Prop. XXIII, Note

All excellent things are as difficult as they are rare.

Ibid. Prop. XLII, Note

The things which . . . are esteemed as the greatest good of all, . . . can be reduced to these three headings: to wit, Riches, Fame, and Pleasure. With these three the mind is so engrossed that it cannot scarcely think of any other good.

Tractatus de Intellectus Emendatione. I, 3

Fame has also this great drawback, that if we pursue it we must direct our lives in such a way as to please the fancy of men, avoiding what they dislike and seeking what is pleasing to them.

Ibid. 5

The more intelligible a thing is, the more easily it is retained in the memory, and contrariwise, the less intelligible it is, the more easily we forget it.

Ibid. XI, 81

NICHOLAS BOILEAU-DESPRÉAUX
[1636–1711]

Happy who in his verse can gently steer
From grave to light, from pleasant to severe.[1]

The Art of Poetry. Canto I, Line 75

Every age has its pleasures, its style of wit, and its own ways.

Ibid. Canto III, Line 374

---

[1] To me, avarice seems not so much a vice, as a deplorable piece of madness. — SIR THOMAS BROWNE: *Religio Medici* (Everyman ed.), *P. 86*

[2] See Publilius Syrus, *Maxim 995*, and Cervantes, page 1036.

[1] See Dryden, page 177.

Plague on the fool who taught us to confine
The swelling thought within a measured line;
Who first in narrow thraldom fancy pent,
And chained in rhyme each pinioned sentiment.
Satire 2. Line 55

He [Molière] pleases all the world, but cannot please himself.
Ibid. Line 94

In spite of every sage whom Greece can show,
Unerring wisdom never dwelt below;
Folly in all of every age we see,
The only difference lies in the degree.
Satire 4. Line 37

Greatest fools are oft most satisfied.
Ibid. Line 128

If your descent is from heroic sires,
Show in your life a remnant of their fires.
Satire 5. Line 43

Of all the creatures that creep, swim, or fly,
Peopling the earth, the waters, and the sky,
From Rome to Iceland, Paris to Japan,
I really think the greatest fool is man.
Satire 8. Line 1

Follows his wife like fringe upon her gown.
Ibid. Line 47

A hero may be dragged in a romance
Through ten long volumes [1] by the laws of France.
Hence every year our books in torrents run,
And Paris counts an author in each son.
Satire 9. Line 103

But satire, ever moral, ever new,
Delights the reader and instructs him, too.
She, if good sense refine her sterling page,
Oft shakes some rooted folly of the age.
Ibid. Line 257

---

[1] Three-volume novels, those signs-manual of our British dulness and crafty disdain for literature. — EDMUND GOSSE: *Gossip in a Library, The Shaving of Shagpat*

Now two punctilious envoys, Thine and Mine,[1]
Embroil the earth about a fancied line;
And, dwelling much on right and much on wrong,
Prove how the right is chiefly with the strong.
Satire 11. Line 141

All Europe by conflicting Faiths was rent,
And e'en the Orthodox on carnage bent;
The blind avengers of Religion's cause
Forgot each precept of her peaceful laws.
Satire 12. Line 169

The terrible burden of having nothing to do.
Epistle XI

JEAN BAPTISTE RACINE
[1639–1699]

Crime like virtue has its degrees;
And timid innocence was never known
To blossom suddenly into extreme license.
Phèdre [1677]. Act IV, Sc. 2

According to ancient, sacred custom.
Athalie [1691]. Act I, Sc. 1

To repair the irreparable ravages of time.
Ibid. Act II, Sc. 5

JEAN DE LA BRUYERE
[1645–1696]

Liberality consists less in giving a great deal than in gifts well-timed.
Les Caractères. Du Cœur

To laugh at men of sense is the privilege of fools.
Ibid. De la Société

Everything has been said.
Ibid. Des Ouvrages de l'Esprit

Most men make use of the first part of their life to render the other part wretched.
Ibid. De l'Homme

If women were by nature what they make themselves by artifice, if their faces suddenly became as bright or as

---

[1] See Cervantes, page 1034.

leaden as they make them with paint and powder, they would be inconsolable.

Les Caractères. Des Femmes

JEANNE GUYON
[1648-1717]

A little bird I am,
Shut from the fields of air;
And in my cage I sit and sing
To Him who placed me there;
Well pleased a prisoner to be,
Because, my God, it pleases Thee.

A Prisoner's Song, Castle of
Vincennes, France. Stanza 1

But though my wing is closely bound,
My heart's at liberty;
My prison walls cannot control
The flight, the freedom of the soul.[1]

Ibid. Stanza 4

FRANÇOIS DE SALIGNAC DE LA MOTHE FÉNELON
[1651-1715]

That weary listlessness, which renders life unsupportable to the voluptuous and the indolent, is unknown to those who can employ themselves by reading.

Telemachus. Book II

Commerce is a kind of spring, which, diverted from its natural channel, ceases to flow. There are but two things which invite foreigners — profit and convenience. If you render commerce less convenient, or less gainful, they will insensibly forsake you.

Ibid. Book III

There were some who said that a man at the point of death was more free than all others, because death breaks every bond, and over the dead the united world has no power.

Ibid. Book V

Love is conquered only by flight. Against such an enemy, true courage consists in fear and retreat, in retreat without deliberation, and without looking back.

Ibid. Book VI

[1] See Lovelace, page 168.

By labor Wisdom gives poignancy to pleasure, and by pleasure she restores vigor to labor.

Telemachus. Book VII

Do not men die fast enough without being destroyed by each other? Can any man be insensible of the brevity of life? and can he who knows it, think life too long!

Ibid.

They that defy the tempest to gratify avarice and luxury, deserve shipwreck.

Ibid.

A kingdom is best fortified by justice, moderation, and good faith, by which neighbouring States are convinced that their territories will never be usurped.

Ibid. Book IX

Courage is a virtue only in proportion as it is directed by prudence.

Ibid. Book X

No distinction so little excites envy as that which is derived from ancestors by a long descent.

Ibid.

The art of cookery is the art of poisoning mankind, by rendering the appetite still importunate, when the wants of nature are supplied.

Ibid.

To be always ready for war, said Mentor, is the surest way to avoid it.

Ibid.

Some of the most dreadful mischiefs that afflict mankind proceed from wine; it is the cause of disease, quarrels, sedition, idleness, aversion to labour, and every species of domestic disorder.

Ibid.

The blood of a nation ought never to be shed except for its own preservation in the utmost extremity.

Ibid. Book XIII

The number of diseases is a disgrace to mankind.

Ibid.

Mankind, by the perverse depravity of their nature, esteem that which they have most desired as of no value the moment it is possessed, and torment themselves with fruitless wishes for that which is beyond their reach.

Telemachus. Book XVIII

ALAIN RENÉ LE SAGE
[1668–1747]

It may be said that his wit shines at the expense of his memory.[1]

Gil Blas. Book 3, Chap. 11

I wish you all sorts of prosperity with a little more taste.

Ibid. Book 7, Chap. 4

Isocrates was in the right to insinuate, in his elegant Greek expression, that what is got over the Devil's back is spent under his belly.[2]

Ibid. Book 8, Chap. 9

Facts are stubborn things.[3]

Ibid. Book 10, Chap. 1

Plain as a pike-staff.[4]

Ibid. Book 12, Chap. 8

BENJAMIN SCHMOLKE
[1672–1737]

The heavier cross, the heartier prayer;
The bruisèd herbs most fragrant are;
If wind and sky were always fair
The sailor would not watch the star,
And David's Psalms had ne'er been
    sung
If grief his heart had never wrung.

Bearing the Burden. Stanza 4

FRANÇOIS M. A. VOLTAIRE [5]
[1694–1778]

If there were no God, it would be necessary to invent him.[6]

Épître à l'Auteur du Livre des Trois Imposteurs. CXI

A witty saying proves nothing.

Le Dîner du Comte de Boulainvilliers

The king [Frederick the Great] has sent me some of his dirty linen to wash; I will wash yours another time.[1]

Reply to General Manstein

In this best of all possible worlds, the Baron's castle was the most magnificent of castles, and his lady the best of all possible Baronesses.

Candide [2] [1759]. Chap. 1

They who assert that all is well have said a foolish thing, they should have said all is for the best.

Ibid.

If this is best of possible worlds,[3] what then are the others?

Ibid. Chap. 6

Optimism is the madness of maintaining that everything is right when it is wrong.

Ibid. Chap. 19

For what end, then, has this world been formed? . . . To plague us to death.

Ibid. Chap. 21

In this country [England] it is found good, from time to time, to kill one Admiral to encourage the others.

Ibid. Chap. 23

This is the happiest of mortals, for he is above everything he possesses.

Ibid. Chap. 26

Labour preserves us from three great evils — weariness, vice, and want.

Ibid. Chap. 30

Let us work without disputing; it is the only way to render life tolerable.

Ibid.

Let us cultivate our garden.

Ibid.

Men use thought only as authority for their injustice, and employ speech only to conceal their thoughts.[4]

Dialogue 14, Le Chapon et la Poularde [1763]

---

[1] See Sheridan, page 279.
[2] See Rabelais, page 1026.
[3] See Smollett, page 248, and Lowell, page 527.
[4] See Middleton, page 116.
[5] Perhaps the only famous writer whose heart is preserved in a library — at the Bibliothèque Nationale in Paris.
[6] See Tillotson, page 172.

[1] Voilà le roi qui m'envoie son linge à blanchir. — VOLTAIRE: *Letter* to his niece, Mme. Denis [July 24, 1752]
See Bonaparte, page 1060.
[2] Modern Library ed.
[3] Referring to the philosophy of Leibnitz and his contemporaries.
[4] See Robert South, page 183.

History is little else than a picture of human crimes and misfortunes.[1]

  L'Ingénu [*1767*]. *Chap. 10*

The embarrassment of riches.[2]

  Le Droit du Seigneur. Act II, Sc. 6

The first who was king was a fortunate soldier:

Who serves his country well has no need of ancestors.[3]

  Mérope. Act I, Sc. 3

It is better to risk saving a guilty person than to condemn an innocent one.

  Zadig. Chap. 6

The superfluous, a very necessary thing.

  Le Mondain. Line 21

Love truth, but pardon error.

  Discours sur l'Homme. Discours 3

Crush the infamous thing [superstition].

  Letter to d'Alembert
   [*June 23, 1760*]

In the case of news, we should always wait for the sacrament of confirmation.

  Letter to Count d'Argental
   [*August 28, 1760*]

The first among languages is that which possesses the largest number of excellent works.

  Letter to Deodati de Tovazzi
   [*January 24, 1761*]

There are truths which are not for all men, nor for all times.

  Letter to Cardinal de Bernis
   [*April 23, 1761*]

The proper mean.[4]

  Letter to Count d'Argental
   [*November 28, 1765*]

It is said that God is always on the side of the heaviest battalions.[5]

  Letter to M. le Riche
   [*February 6, 1770*]

[1] See Gibbon, page 270.
[2] Title of a comedy by SOULAS D'ALLAINVAL, produced in 1725.
[3] See Scott, page 311.
Borrowed from LEFRANC DE POMPIGNAN's *Didon.*
[4] See Publilius Syrus, *Maxim 1072.*
[5] See Gibbon, page 271.
Napoleon said, "Providence is always on the side of the last reserve."
BUSSY RABUTIN: *Lettres, IV, 91;* SÉVIGNÉ: *Lettre à sa Fille, P. 202;* TACITUS: *Historia, IV, 17;* TERENCE: *Phormio, I, 4, 26*

It seems clear to me that God designed us to live in society — just as He has given the bees the honey; and as our social system could not subsist without the sense of justice and injustice, He has given us the power to acquire that sense.

  Letter to Frederick the Great.[1]

I advise you to go on living solely to enrage those who are paying your annuities. It is the only pleasure I have left.

  Letter to Madame du Deffand[1]

I disapprove of what you say, but I will defend to the death your right to say it.[2]

  To Helvetius[3]

Liberty of thought is the life of the soul.

  Essay on Epic Poetry
   (*written in English*)

Whoe'er thou art, behold thy master,
He is, or was, or is to be.

  On a Statuette of Cupid in the
   Cirey Gardens

MADAME DU DEFFAND
[1697–1784]

He [Voltaire] has invented history.

  Quoted by FOURNIER, *L'Esprit*
   dans l'Histoire, Page 191

It is only the first step which costs.[4]

  In reply to Cardinal de Polignac

[1] S. G. TALLENTYRE: *Voltaire in His Letters* [1919]
[2] I do not agree with a word that you say, but I will defend to the death your right to say it. — Variation given by WILL DURANT: *The Story of Philosophy, P. 271*
This quotation is not found *verbatim* in Voltaire's works. It seems to originate in S. G. TALLENTYRE (E. Beatrice Hall): *The Friends of Voltaire* [1907], where she employed it as a paraphrase of Voltaire's words in the *Essay on Tolerance:* "Think for yourselves and let others enjoy the privilege to do so too." The editors are under obligation to Mr. Harry Weinberger for establishing this point.
[3] S. G. TALLENTYRE: *The Friends of Voltaire, P. 199.*
[4] Voltaire wrote to Madame du Deffand [Jan., 1764] that one of her bon-mots was quoted in the notes of *La Pucelle, Canto I:* "Il n'y a que le premier pas qui coûte."

CARL LINNAEUS
[1707–1778]

To live by medicine is to live horribly.
> *Diaeta Naturalis. Introduction*

Mingle your joys sometimes with your earnest occupation.
> *Quoted in biography of Linnaeus by* BENJAMIN DAYDON JONES, *Chap. 9*

A professor can never better distinguish himself in his work than by encouraging a clever pupil, for the true discoverers are among them, as comets amongst the stars.
> *Ibid.*

Live innocently; God is here.
> *Ibid. Chap. 15 (Inscribed over the door of Linnaeus's bedchamber)*

If a tree dies, plant another in its place.
> *Ibid.*

JEAN JACQUES ROUSSEAU
[1712–1778]

Man is born free, and everywhere he is in irons.
> *The Social Contract* [1] *[1762]. Book I, Chap. 1*

The strongest is never strong enough to be always the master, unless he transforms strength into right, and obedience into duty.
> *Ibid. Chap. 3*

The right of conquest has no foundation other than the right of the strongest.
> *Ibid. Chap. 4*

As soon as public service ceases to be the chief business of the citizens, and they would rather serve with their money than with their persons, the State is not far from its fall.
> *Ibid. Book III, Chap. 15*

Good laws lead to the making of better ones; bad ones bring about worse. As soon as any man says of the affairs of the State, "What does it matter to me?" the State may be given up for lost.
> *The Social Contract* [1762]. *Book III, Chap. 15*

Never exceed your rights, and they will soon become unlimited.
> *A Discourse on Political Economy*

Money is the seed of money, and the first guinea is sometimes more difficult to acquire than the second million.
> *Ibid.*

God makes all things good; man meddles with them and they become evil.
> *Émile, or Education* [1] *[1762]. Book I*

Medicine is all the fashion in these days, and very naturally. It is the amusement of the idle and unemployed, who do not know what to do with their time in taking care of themselves. If by ill-luck they had happened to be born immortal, they would have been the most miserable of men; a life they could not lose would be of no value to them. Such men must have doctors to threaten and flatter them, to give them the only pleasure they can enjoy, the pleasure of not being dead.
> *Ibid.*

Hygiene is the only useful part of medicine, and hygiene is rather a virtue than a science. Temperance and industry are man's true remedies; work sharpens his appetite and temperance teaches him to control it.
> *Ibid.*

What wisdom can you find that is greater than kindness?
> *Ibid. Book II*

The happiest is he who suffers least; the most miserable is he who enjoys least. Ever more sorrow than joy,— this is the lot of all of us.
> *Ibid.*

Provided a man is not mad, he can be cured of every folly but vanity.
> *Ibid. Book IV*

---

[1] Everyman ed., translated by G. D. H. COLE.

[1] Everyman ed., translated by BARBARA FOXLEY.

I shall always maintain that whoso says in his heart, "There is no God," while he takes the name of God upon his lips, is either a liar or a madman.

Émile, or Education [*1762*].
Book I

People who know little are usually great talkers, while men who know much say little.

Ibid.

A man says what he knows, a woman says what will please.

Ibid. Book V

Where is the man who owes nothing to the land in which he lives? Whatever that land may be, he owes to it the most precious thing possessed by man, the morality of his actions and the love of virtue.

Ibid.

I have entered on a performance which is without precedent, and will have no imitator. I propose to show my fellow-mortals a man in all the integrity of nature; and this man shall be myself.

Confessions [*1782*].
Opening words

Hatred, as well as love, renders its votaries credulous.

Ibid. Book V

My third child was carried to the foundling hospital as well as the two former, and the next two were disposed of in the same manner, for I have had five children in all.

Ibid. Book VIII

The thirst after happiness is never extinguished in the heart of man.

Ibid. Book IX

To appear the friend of a man, when in reality we are no longer so, is to reserve to ourselves the means of doing him an injury by surprising honest men into an error.

Ibid. Book X

He thinks like a philosopher, and acts like a king.

Ibid. Book XII

Salaam aliakum, i. e., Peace be with you, the common Turkish salutation.

Ibid.

MICHEL JEAN SEDAINE
[1717–1797]

O Richard! O my king!
The universe forsakes thee!

Sung at the Dinner given to the French Soldiers in the Opera Salon at Versailles [*October 1, 1789*]

MADAME JEANNE DE POMPADOUR
[1721–1764]

After us the deluge.[1]

Reply to Louis XV [*November 5, 1757*] *after the defeat of the French and Austrian armies by Frederick the Great in the battle of Rossbach. Quoted by* MADAME DE HAUSSET *in Memoirs, Page 19*

PIERRE DE BEAUMARCHAIS
[1732–1799]

If you assure me that your intentions are honourable.

Le Barbier de Séville [*1775*].
Act IV, Sc. 6

CHARLES JOSEPH, PRINCE DE LIGNE
[1735–1814]

The congress of Vienna does not walk, but it dances.[2]

RUDOLF ERICH RASPE
[1737–1794]

What in the dark I had taken to be a stump of a little tree appearing above the snow, to which I had tied my horse, proved to have been the weathercock of the church steeple.

Travels of Baron Munchausen [*1785*]. *Chap. 2*

---

[1] LAROUSE, in *Fleurs Historiques*, credits the saying to Louis XV.
[2] One of the Prince de Ligne's speeches that will last forever. — *Edinburgh Review, July, 1890, P. 244*

We all did our duty, which, in the patriot's, soldier's, and gentleman's language, is a very comprehensive word, of great honour, meaning, and import.
>   *Travels of Baron Munchausen*
>   [*1785*]. *Chap. 5*

The sprigs took root in my horse's body, grew up, and formed a bower over me.
>   *Ibid.*

His tunes were frozen up in the horn, and came out now by thawing.[1]
>   *Ibid. Chap. 6*

If any of the company entertain a doubt of my veracity, I shall only say to such, I pity their want of faith.
>   *Ibid.*

I had the very sling in my pocket which assisted David in slaying Goliath.
>   *Ibid. Chap. 10*

Upon this island of cheese grows great plenty of corn, the ears of which produce loaves of bread, ready made.
>   *Ibid. Chap. 20*

I have ever confined myself to facts.
>   *Ibid.*

A traveller has a right to relate and embellish his adventures as he pleases, and it is very unpolite to refuse that deference and applause they deserve.
>   *Ibid. Chap. 21*

There is a right and wrong handle to everything.[2]
>   *Ibid. Chap. 30*

JACQUES DELILLE
[1738–1813]

Fate makes our relatives, choice makes our friends.[3]
>   *La Pitié* [*1803*]. *Canto I*

LOUIS SÉBASTIEN MERCIER
[1740–1814]

Extremes meet.
>   *Tableaux de Paris* [*1782*].
>   *Vol. IV, Chap. 348, Title*

[1] See Plutarch, page 1004.
[2] See Epictetus, page 1008.
[3] Friends, those relatives we make for ourselves. — ÉMILE DESCHAMPS [1791–1871]: *Epigram*

SÉBASTIEN R. N. CHAMFORT
[1741–1794]

The most useless day of all is that in which we have not laughed.
>   *Maxims and Thoughts. 1*

Chance is a sobriquet for Providence.
>   *Ibid. 62*

JOHANN KASPAR LAVATER
[1741–1801]

From the Aphorisms on Man [*London, 1788*] *much admired and privately annotated by* WILLIAM BLAKE. *See the one-volume edition of* BLAKE'S *Poetry and Prose, edited by* GEOFFREY KEYNES.

If you mean to know yourself, interline such of these aphorisms as affect you agreeably in reading, and set a mark to such as left a sense of uneasiness with you; and then shew your copy to whom you please.

Who has many wishes has generally but little will. Who has energy of will has few diverging wishes. Whose will is bent with energy on *one, must* renounce the wishes for *many* things.

Say not you know another entirely, till you have divided an inheritance with him.

He who, when called upon to speak a disagreeable truth, tells it boldly and has done is both bolder and milder than he who nibbles in a low voice and never ceases nibbling.[1]

The public seldom forgive twice.

Venerate four characters: the sanguine, who has checked volatility and the rage for pleasure; the choleric who has subdued passion and pride; the phlegmatic emerged from indolence; and the melancholy who has dismissed avarice, suspicion and asperity.

Trust not him with your secrets, who, when left alone in your room, turns over your papers.

[1] Blake's marginal comment on this was "Damn such!"

GABRIEL ROMANOVITCH DERZHAVIN
[1743–1816]

O Thou eternal One, whose presence bright
All space doth occupy, all motion guide;
Unchanged through time's all-devastating flight,
Thou only God, there is no God beside.

Ode to God.[1] *Stanza 1*

Thou from primeval nothingness didst call
First chaos, then existence.

Ibid. Stanza 3

JOHANN WOLFGANG VON GOETHE
[1749–1832]

If you inquire what the people are like here, I must answer, "The same as everywhere!"

The Sorrows of Werther.
May 17th

The history of science is science itself; the history of the individual, the individual.

Mineralogy and Geology

Three things are to be looked to in a building: that it stand on the right spot; that it be securely founded; that it be successfully executed.

Elective Affinities.[2] *Book I, Chap. 9*

The sum which two married people owe to one another defies calculation. It is an infinite debt, which can only be discharged through all eternity.

Ibid.

A pretty foot is a great gift of nature.

Ibid. Chap. 11

One is never satisfied with a portrait of a person that one knows.

Ibid. Book II, Chap. 2

[1] Translated by SIR JOHN BOWRING [1792–1872].
[2] Translated by JAMES ANTHONY FROUDE [1818–1894]

The fate of the architect is the strangest of all. How often he expends his whole soul, his whole heart and passion, to produce buildings into which he himself may never enter.

Elective Affinities. Book II, Chap. 3

Let us live in as small a circle as we will, we are either debtors or creditors before we have had time to look round.

Ibid. Chap. 4

Mediocrity has no greater consolation than in the thought that genius is not immortal.

Ibid. Chap. 5

A teacher who can arouse a feeling for one single good action, for one single good poem, accomplishes more than he who fills our memory with rows on rows of natural objects, classified with name and form.

Ibid. Chap. 7

No one feels himself easy in a garden which does not look like the open country.

Ibid. Chap. 8

We lay aside letters never to read them again, and at last we destroy them out of discretion, and so disappears the most beautiful, the most immediate breath of life, irrecoverably for ourselves and for others.

Ibid. Chap. 9

Who never ate his bread in sorrow,
Who never spent the darksome hours
Weeping, and watching for the morrow, —
He knows you not, ye heavenly Powers.

Wilhelm Meister's Apprenticeship.
Book II, Chap. 13

Who longs in solitude to live,
Ah! soon his wish will gain:
Men hope and love, men get and give,
And leave him to his pain.

Ibid. Book III, Chap. 1

Know'st thou the land where the lemon-trees bloom,

Where the gold orange glows in the deep
thicket's gloom,
Where a wind ever soft from the blue
heaven blows,
And the groves are of laurel and myrtle
and rose? [1]
*Wilhelm Meister's Apprenticeship.
Book III, Chap. 1*

One ought, every day at least, to hear
a little song, read a good poem, see a
fine picture, and, if it were possible, to
speak a few reasonable words. [2]
Ibid. Book V, Chap. 1

To know of some one here and there
whom we accord with, who is living on
with us, even in silence, — this makes
our earthly ball a peopled garden.
Ibid. Book VII, Chap. 5

Art is long, life short; [3] judgment difficult, opportunity transient.
Ibid. Chap. 9

The sagacious reader who is capable
of reading between these lines what
does not stand written in them, but is
nevertheless implied, will be able to
form some conception.
*Autobiography. Book XVIII,
Truth and Beauty*

Know'st thou yesterday, its aim and
reason?
Work'st thou well to-day for worthier
things?
Then calmly wait the morrow's hidden
season,
And fear thou not what hap soe'er it
brings.
Zahme Xenien. Book IV [1821]

Without haste! without rest!
Bind the motto to thy breast!
Bear it with thee as a spell;
Storm or sunshine, guard it well.
Haste Not, Rest Not. Stanza 1

To-morrow sees undone, what happens
not to-day;
Still forward press, nor ever tire!
The possible, with steadfast trust,
Resolve should by the forelock grasp;

Then she will ne'er let go her clasp,
And labors on, because she must. [1]
Faust.[2] Prologue for the Theatre

A king there was once reigning,
Who had a goodly flea,
Him loved he without feigning,
As his own son were he!
*Ibid. Mephistopheles' Song
of the Flea*

The Eternal Feminine draws us on. [3]
Ibid. (closing line)

Light, — more light!
Last words

JOHANN HEINRICH VOSS
[1751–1826]

Who does not love wine, women, and
song
Remains a fool his whole life long.
*Attributed to Voss by REDLICH
in Die poetischen Beiträge zum
Waudsbecker Bothen [Ham-
burg, 1871], Page 67. The couplet has also been attributed to
Luther.*

MADAME ROLAND
[1754–1793]

O Liberty! Liberty! how many
crimes are committed in thy name!
*Quoted by MACAULAY in his
Essay on Mirabeau*

---

[1] See Byron, page 355.
[2] See Charles Eliot Norton, page 572.
[3] See Chaucer, page 3.

[1] Lose this day loitering, 'twill be the same
story
To-morrow, and the next more dilatory;
Each indecision brings its own delays,
And days are lost lamenting o'er lost days.
Are you in earnest? Seize this very minute!
Boldness has genius, power, and magic in
it.
Only engage, and then the mind grows
heated.
Begin, and then the work will be com-
pleted.
JOHN ANSTER [1793–1867]: *Faust,
Prologue for the Theatre, Manager's
Speech*
[2] Translated by ANNA SWANWICK [1813–
1899].
[3] Das Ewig-Weibliche zieht uns hinan.

CHARLES MAURICE DE TALLEYRAND-PÉRIGORD
[1754–1838]

Black as the devil,
Hot as hell,
Pure as an angel,
Sweet as love.[1]
>   *Recipe for Coffee*

Beginning of the end.[2]

BERTRAND BARÈRE
[1755–1841]

The tree of liberty only grows when watered by the blood of tyrants.
>   *Speech in the National*
>   *Convention [1792]*

It is only the dead who do not return.
>   *Speech [1794]*

ANTHELME BRILLAT-SAVARIN
[1755–1826]

Tell me what you eat, and I will tell you what you are.[3]
>   *Physiologie du Goût. Aphorism 4*

We become cooks, but a roast cook is born.
>   *Ibid. Aphorism 15*

GEORGES JACQUES DANTON
[1759–1794]

Boldness, again boldness, and ever boldness.[4]
>   *Speech in the Legislative*
>   *Assembly [1792]*

[1] Noir comme le diable,
Chaud comme l'enfer,
Pur comme un ange,
Doux comme l'amour.
This appears as an inscription on many old coffee-pots.

[2] Fournier asserts, on the written authority of Talleyrand's brother, that the only breviary used by the ex-bishop was *L'Improvisateur Français,* a compilation of anecdotes and *bon-mots,* in twenty-one duodecimo volumes. Whenever a good thing was wandering about in search of a parent, he adopted it; amongst others, "C'est le commencement de la fin."

See Shakespeare, page 43.

[3] See Cervantes, page 1040.

[4] De l'audace, encore de l'audace, et toujours de l'audace.

JOHANN CHRISTOPH FRIEDRICH VON SCHILLER
[1759–1805]

There are three lessons I would write,
Three words as with a burning pen,
In tracings of eternal light,
Upon the hearts of men.
>   *Hope, Faith, and Love. Stanza 1*

Thus grave these lessons on thy soul, —
Hope, faith, and love; and thou shalt find
Strength when life's surges rudest roll,
Light when thou else wert blind!
>   *Ibid. Stanza 5*

Against stupidity the very gods
Themselves contend in vain.[1]
>   *The Maid of Orleans. Act III, Sc. 6*

The richest monarch in the Christian world;
The sun in my own dominions never sets.[2]
>   *Don Carlos. Act I, Sc. 6*

When the wine goes in, strange things come out.
>   *The Piccolomini. Act II, Sc. 12*

This feat of Tell, the archer, will be told
While yonder mountains stand upon their base.
By Heaven! the apple's cleft right through the core.
>   *William Tell. Act III, Sc. 3*

JOSEPH ROUGET DE LISLE
[1760–1836]

Ye sons of France, awake to glory!
Hark! hark! what myriads bid you rise!
Your children, wives, and grandsires hoary,
Behold their tears and hear their cries!
>   *The Marseillaise.*[3]

See Spenser, page 25, and Longfellow, page 438.

[1] Against boredom even the gods themselves struggle in vain. — NIETZSCHE: *The Antichrist, 48*

[2] See Scott, page 311, and Bonaparte, page 1061.

[3] Composed in 1792 in the garrison at Strasbourg, and originally called *Chant de guerre de l'armée du Rhin.* First made known in Paris

To arms! to arms! ye brave!
The avenging sword unsheathe!
March on! march on! all hearts re-
solved
On victory or death!
The Marseillaise.

AUGUST FRIEDRICH FERDINAND VON KOTZEBUE
[1761–1819]

There is another and a better world.
The Stranger. Act I, Sc. 1

CHARLES LOUIS ÉTIENNE, CHEVALIER DE PANAT
[1762–1834]

No one is right; no one could forget
anything, nor learn anything.[1]
*Letter to Jacques Mallet du Pan
[January, 1796]*

JOSEPH FOUCHÉ
[1763–1820]

"It is more than a crime; it is a political fault," [2] — words which I record,
because they have been repeated and
attributed to others.
Memoirs

Death is an eternal sleep.
*Inscription placed by his orders
on the gates of the cemeteries
[1794]*

MADAME DE STAËL
[1766–1817]

The sight of such a monument is like
a continuous and stationary music.[3]
Corinne [1807]. Book IV, Chap. 3

To understand all makes us very in-
dulgent.[1]
Corinne [1807]. Book XVIII, Chap. 5

ERNST F. MÜNSTER [2]
[1766–1839]

Absolutism tempered by assassina-
tion.
*Description of the Russian
Constitution*

HENRI BENJAMIN CONSTANT
[1767–1830]

I am not the rose, but I have lived
with her.[3]

NAPOLEON BONAPARTE
[1769–1821]

Soldiers, from the summit of yonder
pyramids, forty centuries look down
upon you.
In Egypt [July 21, 1798]

Go, sir, gallop, and don't forget that
the world was made in six days. You
can ask me for anything you like, except time.
*To one of his aides [1803]. Quoted
in R. M. JOHNSTON: The Corsican*

What is the throne? — a bit of wood
gilded and covered with velvet. I am the
state [4] — I alone am here the representative of the people. Even if I had done
wrong you should not have reproached
me in public — people wash their dirty
linen at home. France has more need of
me than I of France.
To the Senate [1814]

France is invaded; I go to put myself
at the head of my troops, and, with

---

by patriots from Marseilles, it took the name
from their enthusiasm.

[1] They have learned nothing and forgotten
nothing. — Attributed to Talleyrand, describing the Bourbon dynasty.

[2] Commonly quoted, "It is worse than a
crime, — it is a blunder," and attributed to
Talleyrand.

[3] Since it [architecture] is music in space, as
it were a frozen music. . . . If architecture
in general is frozen music. — FRIEDRICH VON
SCHELLING [1775–1854]: *Philosophie der
Kunst, Pp. 576, 593*

[1] See Henrietta A. Huxley, page 563.

[2] Hanoverian envoy at St. Petersburg.

[3] This saying, "Je ne suis pas la rose, mais
j'ai vécu avec elle," is attributed to Constant
by ABRAHAM HAYWARD [1801–1884] in his
Introduction to the *Autobiography and Letters* [1861] of MRS. PIOZZI.

[4] DULAURE, in *History of Paris* [1863],
P. 387, asserts that Louis XIV interrupted a
judge who used the expression, "the king and
the state," by saying, "I am the state."

God's help and their valour, I hope soon to drive the enemy beyond the frontier.

At Paris [January 23, 1814]

The bullet that will kill me is not yet cast.

At Montereau [February 17, 1814]

The Allied Powers having proclaimed that the Emperor Napoleon is the sole obstacle to the re-establishment of peace in Europe, he, faithful to his oath, declares that he is ready to descend from the throne, to quit France, and even to relinquish life, for the good of his country.

Act of Abdication [April 4, 1814]

Unite for the public safety, if you would remain an independent nation.

Proclamation to the French People [June 22, 1815]

Wherever wood can swim, there I am sure to find this flag of England.[1]

At Rochefort [July, 1815]

Whatever shall we do in that remote spot? Well, we will write our Memoirs. Work is the scythe of time.

On board H. M. S. Bellerophon [August, 1815]

I generally had to give in [speaking of his relations with the Empress Josephine].

On St. Helena [May 19, 1816]

My maxim was, *la carrière est ouverte aux talents,* without distinction of birth or fortune.[2]

On St. Helena [March 3, 1817]

No physicking. We are a machine made to live; we are organized for that purpose, and such is our nature; do not counteract the living principle — let it alone — leave it the liberty of self-defence — it will do better than your drugs. Our body is a watch, intended to go for a given time. The watchmaker cannot open it, and must work at random. For once that he relieves or assists it by his crooked instruments, he injures it ten times, and at last destroys it.

To Dr. Antommarchi [October 14, 1820]

1 See Scott, page 311, and Schiller, page 1059.
2 See Thomas Carlyle, page 377.

Our hour is marked, and no one can claim a moment of life beyond what fate has predestined.

To Dr. Arnott [April, 1821]

I am neither an atheist nor a rationalist; I believe in God, and am of the religion of my father. I was born a Catholic, and will fulfil all the duties of that church, and receive the assistance which she administers.

On St. Helena [April 18, 1821]

I could not unbend the bow; and France has been deprived of the liberal institutions I intended to give her.

BOURRIENNE: *Memoirs, Vol. 10, Page 425 [May 3, 1821]*

All was not lost until the moment when all had succeeded.

Ibid., Page 39. On anniversary of Battle of Waterloo

Madame Montholon having inquired what troops he considered the best, "Those which are victorious, Madame," replied the Emperor.

Ibid. Page 399

Tête d'armée (Head of the army).

Last words [May 5, 1821]

MADEMOISELLE BERTIN
[1744–1813]

There is nothing new except what is forgotten.[1]

PIERRE JACQUES ÉTIENNE, COUNT CAMBRONNE
[1770–1842]

The guard dies, but never surrenders.[2]

Inscribed upon the monument erected to him at Nantes

1 Attributed to Mademoiselle Bertin, milliner to Marie Antoinette.
There is nothing new except that which has become antiquated. — Motto of the *Revue Rétrospective*
A New Thinker is only one who does not know what the old thinkers have thought. — FRANK MOORE COLBY [1865–1925].
2 This phrase, attributed to Cambronne, who was made prisoner at Waterloo, was vehemently denied by him. It was invented by Rougemont, a prolific author of *mots*, two days after the battle, in the "Indépendant." — FOURNIER: *L'Esprit dans l'Histoire*

GEORG WILHELM FRIEDRICH HEGEL
[1770–1831]

Peoples and governments never have learned anything from history, or acted on principles deduced from it.
Philosophy of History.[1]
Introduction

Amid the pressure of great events, a general principle gives no help.
Ibid.

To him who looks upon the world rationally, the world in its turn presents a rational aspect. The relation is mutual.
Ibid.

The history of the world is none other than the progress of the consciousness of Freedom.
Ibid.

We may affirm absolutely that nothing great in the world has been accomplished without passion.
Ibid.

It is easier to discover a deficiency in individuals, in states, and in Providence, than to see their real import and value.
Ibid.

Life has a value only when it has something valuable as its object.
Ibid.

Serious occupation is labor that has reference to some want.
Ibid. Part I, Sect. 2, Chap. 1

It is a matter of perfect indifference where a thing originated; the only question is: "Is it true in and for itself?"
Ibid. Part III, Sect. 3, Chap. 2

When liberty is mentioned, we must always be careful to observe whether it is not really the assertion of private interests which is thereby designated.
Ibid. Part IV, Sect. 3, Chap. 2

The Few assume to be the *deputies*, but they are often only the *despoilers* of the Many.
Ibid. Chap. 3

[1] Translated by J. Sibree.

ANDOCHE JUNOT, DUC D'ABRANTES
[1771–1813]

I know nothing about it; I am my own ancestor.[1]
When asked about his ancestry

MARC ANTOINE DÉSAUGIERS
[1772–1827]

When we are dead, it's for a long time.
Song, Le Délire Bacchique

FRANÇOIS HORACE BASTIEN SÉBASTIANI
[1772–1851]

Order reigns in Warsaw.[2]
Announcement of the fall of Warsaw

ÉTIENNE DE GRELLET [3] (DE MABILLIER)
[1773–1855]

I shall pass through this world but once.[4] If, therefore, there be any kindness I can show, or any good thing I can do, let me do it now; let me not defer it

[1] See Plutarch, page 1003.
Curtius Rufus seems to me to be descended from himself [a saying of Tiberius]. — TACITUS: *Annals, Book XI, Chap. 21, 16*
[2] Des lettres que je reçois de Pologne m'annoncent que la tranquillité règne à Varsovie. — DUMAS [1802–1870]: *Mémoires, Second Series, Vol. IV, Chap. 3*
[3] De Grellet was born in Limoges, France, came to America as Stephen Grellet, became a Quaker, and travelled as a missionary in the United States, Canada, and Europe. He died in Burlington, New Jersey. The saying persistently attributed to him is not found in his existing writings.
[4] If I can any way contribute to the Diversion or Improvement of the Country in which I live, I shall leave it, when I am summoned out of it, with the secret Satisfaction of thinking that I have not lived in vain. — JOSEPH ADDISON: *The Spectator, Vol. I, No. 1, March 1, 1711*
See Underwood, page 682, and Foss, page 732.

or neglect it, for I shall not pass this way again.

Attributed

BARON DE LA MOTTE FOUQUÉ
[1777–1843]

Death comes to set thee free;
Oh, meet him cheerily
  As thy true friend,
And all thy fears shall cease,
And in eternal peace
  Thy penance end.

Sintram and His Companions.[1]
Pilgrim Song, Stanza 3

HENRI BEYLE
(DE STENDHAL)
[1783–1842]

One can acquire everything in solitude — except character.

Fragments. I

Prudery is a kind of avarice, the worst of all.

Ibid. V

In matters of sentiment, the public has very crude ideas; and the most shocking fault of women is that they make the public the supreme judge of their lives.

Ibid. IX

A wise woman never yields by appointment. It should always be an unforeseen happiness.

De l'Amour. Chap. 60

The Baron could not produce epigrams; he required at least four sentences of six lines each to be brilliant.

The Red and the Black.[2] *Chap. 34*

I see but one rule: *to be clear.* If I am not clear, all *my world* crumbles to nothing.

Reply to Balzac. Oct. 30, 1840 [3]

Wit lasts no more than two centuries.

Ibid.

[1] Translated by THOMAS TRACY.
[2] Translated by C. K. SCOTT-MONCRIEFF (Modern Library ed.).
[3] In *The Charterhouse of Parma* (Modern Library ed.).

JOHANN LUDWIG UHLAND
[1787–1862]

I always have loved thee, I love thee to-day,
And I swear I will love thee, for ever and aye!

The Landlady's Daughter

Take, O boatman, thrice thy fee, —
Take, I give it willingly;
For, invisible to thee,
Spirits twain have crossed with me.

The Passage

ARTHUR SCHOPENHAUER [1]
[1788–1860]

A certain amount of care or pain or trouble is necessary for every man at all times. A ship without ballast is unstable and will not go straight.

Studies in Pessimism.[2] *On the Sufferings of the World*

Suicide thwarts the attainment of the highest moral aim by the fact that, for a real release from this world of misery, it substitutes one that is merely apparent.

Ibid. On Suicide

Hatred comes from the heart; contempt from the head; and neither feeling is quite within our control.

Ibid. Psychological Observations

If a man sets out to hate all the miserable creatures he meets, he will not have much energy left for anything else; whereas he can despise them, one and all, with the greatest ease.

Ibid.

Every man takes the limits of his own field of vision for the limits of the world.

Ibid.

[1] Schopenhauer was furious and refused to pay his debts to any one who spelled his name with a double "p". — CESARE LOMBROSO: *The Man of Genius, Part I, Chap. 2*
[2] Translated by T. BAILEY SAUNDERS. Modern Library ed.
Schopenhauer wrote at an epoch in which pessimism was beginning to be fashionable, together with mysticism, and fused the whole into one philosophic system. — LOMBROSO: *Ibid., Part III, Chap. 4*

Not to go to the theatre is like making one's toilet without a mirror.

Studies in Pessimism. Psychological Observations

Every parting gives a foretaste of death; every coming together again a foretaste of the resurrection.

Ibid.

There is no absurdity so palpable but that it may be firmly planted in the human head if you only begin to inculcate it before the age of five, by constantly repeating it with an air of great solemnity.

Ibid.

Opinion is like a pendulum and obeys the same law. If it goes past the centre of gravity on one side, it must go a like distance on the other; and it is only after a certain time that it finds the true point at which it can remain at rest.

Ibid.

It is a curious fact that in bad days we can very vividly recall the good time that is now no more; but that in good days we have only a very cold and imperfect memory of the bad.

Ibid.

The fundamental fault of the female character is that it has no sense of justice.

Ibid. On Women

Dissimulation is innate in woman, and almost as much a quality of the stupid as of the clever.

Ibid.

Noise is the most impertinent of all forms of interruption. It is not only an interruption, but also a disruption of thought.

Ibid. On Noise

The most general survey shows us that the two foes of human happiness are pain and boredom.

Essays. Personality, or What a Man Is

A man who has no mental needs, because his intellect is of the narrow and normal amount, is, in the strict sense of the word, what is called a *philistine*.

Ibid.

Fame and honor are twins; and twins, too, like Castor and Pollux, of whom one was mortal and the other was not. Fame is the undying brother of ephemeral honor.

Essays. Fame

Pride is an established conviction of one's own paramount worth in some particular respect; while vanity is the desire of rousing such a conviction in others. Pride works from within; it is the direct appreciation of oneself. Vanity is the desire to arrive at this appreciation indirectly, from without.

Ibid. Pride

Ignorance is degrading only when found in company with riches.

Ibid. On Books and Reading

Intellect is invisible to the man who has none.

Ibid. Our Relation to Others, Sect. 23

There is no more mistaken path to happiness than worldliness, revelry, high life.

Ibid. Our Relation to Ourselves, Sect. 24

To be alone is the fate of all great minds — a fate deplored at times, but still always chosen as the less grievous of two evils.

Ibid.

Rascals are always sociable, and the chief sign that a man has any nobility in his character is the little pleasure he takes in others' company.

Counsels and Maxims. Chap. 2

Do not shorten the morning by getting up late; look upon it as the quintessence of life, as to a certain extent sacred.

Ibid.

Speak without emphasizing your words. Leave other people to discover what it is that you have said; and as their minds are slow, you can make your escape in time.

Ibid. Chap. 3

ALPHONSE M. L. LAMARTINE
[1790–1869]

What is our life but a succession of preludes to that unknown song whose first solemn note is sounded by Death?

Love is the enchanted dawn of every heart, but what mortal is there over whose first joys and happiness does not break some storm, dispelling with its icy breath his fanciful illusions, and shattering his altar? What soul, thus cruelly wounded, does not at times try to dream away the recollection of such storms in the solitude of country life? And yet, man, it seems, is not able to bear the languid rest on Nature's bosom, and when the trumpet sounds the signal of danger, he hastens to join his comrades, no matter what the cause that calls him to arms. He rushes into the thickest of the fight and amid the uproar of the battle regains confidence in himself and his powers.[1]

> *Méditations Poétiques* [*1820*].
> *Second Series, XV*

NARCISSE ACHILLE, COMTE DE SALVANDY
[1795–1856]

We are dancing on a volcano.

> *At a fête given by the Duc d'Orléans to the King of Naples* [*1830*]

HEINRICH HEINE [2]
[1797–1856]

Translations by LOUIS UNTERMEYER

"Oh, 'tis Love that makes us grateful,
Oh, 'tis Love that makes us rich!"
So sings man, and every fateful
Echo bears his amorous speech.

> *O, die Liebe macht uns selig.*
> *Stanza 1*

Toward France there journeyed two grenadiers
  Who had been captured in Russia;
And they hung their heads and their eyes had tears

As they came to the border of Prussia.

> *Nach Frankreich zogen zwei Grenadier'. Stanza 1*

Upon the wings of Song, love,
  I would bear thee far, and go
Where the Ganges ripples along, love —
  There is a place I know.

> *Auf Flügeln des Gesanges.*
> *Stanza 1*

A pine tree stands so lonely
  In the North where the high winds blow,
He sleeps; and the whitest blanket
  Wraps him in ice and snow.

> *Ein Fichtenbaum steht einsam.*
> *Stanza 1*

From grief too great to banish
  Come songs, my lyric minions.[1]

> *Aus meinen grossen Schmerzen.*
> *Stanza 1*

When two who love are parted,
  They talk, as friend to friend,
Clasp hands and weep a little,
  And sigh without an end.

> *Wenn zwei von einander scheiden.*
> *Stanza 1*

I do not know why this confronts me,
  This sadness, this echo of pain;
A curious legend still haunts me,
  Still haunts and obsesses my brain.

> *Ich weiss nicht, was soll es bedeuten (The Lorelei). Stanza 1*

The years keep coming and going,
  Men will arise and depart;
Only one thing is immortal:
  The love that is in my heart.

> *Die Jahre kommen und gehen.*
> *Stanza 1*

Child, you are like a flower,
So sweet and pure and fair.

> *Du bist wie eine Blume. Stanza 1*

---

[1] Heading for the score of Franz Liszt's Symphonic Poem No. 3, *Les Préludes*.

[2] Therefore a secret unrest
Tortured thee, brilliant and bold.
MATTHEW ARNOLD: *Heine's Grave*

[1] Out of my own great woe
  I make my little songs.
        Translated by MRS. BROWNING
  When other men can only curse
  The poet puts his woes in verse.
    CHRISTOPHER MORLEY: Translation
      from the Chinese of NO SHO

He who, for the first time, loves,
Even vainly, is a God.
But the man who loves again,
And still vainly, is a fool.
          Wer zum erstenmale liebt.
                 Stanza 1

Oh what lies there are in kisses!
        In den Küssen, welche Lüge.
                 Stanza 1

Death — it is but the long, cool night;
And Life is but a sultry day.
     Der Tod, das ist die kühle Nacht.
                 Stanza 1

The sea has its pearls,
The heaven its stars, —
But my heart, my heart,
My heart has its love.
        Das Meer hat seine Perlen.
                 Stanza 1

Thalatta! Thalatta!
Hail to thee, oh Sea, ageless and eternal!
    Thalatta! Thalatta! Stanza 1

The deep, blue eyes of Springtime
  Peer from the grass beneath;
They are the tender violets
That I will twine in a wreath.
       Die blauen Frühlingsaugen.
                 Stanza 1

Your eyes' blue depths are lifted,
  With love and friendship stirred.
They smile; and, lost in dreaming,
  I cannot speak a word.
        Mit deinen blauen Augen.
                 Stanza 1

Good-Fortune is a giddy maid,
  Fickle and restless as a fawn;
She smooths your hair; and then the jade
Kisses you quickly, and is gone.
    Das Glück ist eine leichte Dirne.[1]
                 Stanza 1

But Madam Sorrow scorns all this,
  She shows no eagerness for flitting;
But with a long and fervent kiss
  Sits by your bed — and brings her knitting.
               Ibid. Stanza 2

This is America!
This is the new world!

[1] Quoted by GEORGE ELIOT in *Daniel Deronda.* See John Hay, page 639.

Not the present European
Wasted and withering sphere.
    Vitzliputzli. Prelude, Dieses ist
             Amerika! Stanza 1

For Sleep is good, but Death is better
  still —
The best is never to be born at all.
    Gross ist die Ähnlichkeit der
            beiden schönen

If one has no heart, one cannot write
for the masses.
      Letter to Julius Campe
        [March 18, 1840]

Ordinarily he is insane, but he has
lucid moments [1] when he is only stupid.
    Of Savoye, appointed ambassa-
    dor to Frankfurt by Lamartine
    [1848]

To publish even one line of an author
which he himself has not intended for
the public at large — especially letters
which are addressed to private persons
— is to commit a despicable act of felony.
    Quoted by A. C. SWINBURNE *as*
    heading for In Sepulcretis

AUGUST HEINRICH HOFFMANN [2]
[1798–1874]

Pauline now no more was there;
She burnt from pantalette to hair,
But in the place where she had been
A heap of ashes could be seen.
    Pauline and the Matches. Stanza 6

Anything to me is sweeter
Than to see Shock-headed Peter.
               Struwwelpeter

HONORÉ DE BALZAC
[1799–1850]

In the matter of commerce, encouragement does not mean protection. A
nation's true policy is to relieve itself
of paying tribute to other nations, but

[1] See South, page 183.
[2] Dr. Hoffmann, a physician in Frankfurt-am-Main, wrote the famous *Slovenly Peter* verses [1845] to amuse children who had to wait in his office. A free translation was done in 1891 by MARK TWAIN, then living in Berlin, for his daughters.

to do so without the humiliating assistance of custom houses and prohibitory laws. Manufacturing industry depends solely on itself, competition is its life. Protect it, and it goes to sleep; it dies from monopoly as well as from the tariff. The nation that succeeds in making all other nations its vassals will be the one which first proclaims commercial liberty; it will have enough manufacturing power to supply its productions at a cheaper price than those of its rivals.

> *The Country Doctor.*[1] *Chap. 1*

I believe in the incomprehensibility of God.

> *Letter to Madame de Hanska*
> *[1837]*

ALEXANDRE DUMAS THE ELDER
[1802–1870]

All for one, one for all, that is our device.[2]

> *The Three Musketeers. Chap. 9*

There are virtues which become crimes by exaggeration.

> *The Count of Monte Cristo.*
> *Chap. 90*

Great is truth. Fire cannot burn, nor water drown it.

> *Ibid. Chap. 113*

All human wisdom is summed up in two words, — wait and hope.

> *Ibid. Chap. 117*

Nothing succeeds like success.[3]

> *Ange Pitou [1854].*
> *Vol. I, Page 72*

Look for the woman.[4]

> *The Mohicans of Paris. Vol. III,*
> *Chaps. 10 and 11*

VICTOR HUGO
[1802–1885]

The three problems of the age — the degradation of man by poverty, the ruin of woman by starvation, and the dwarfing of childhood by physical and spiritual night.

> *Les Misérables.*[1] *Preface*

Far be it from me to insult the pun! I honour it in proportion to its merits — no more.

> *Ibid. Fantine, Book III, Chap. 7*

Indigestion is charged by God with enforcing morality on the stomach.

> *Ibid.*

Mothers' arms are made of tenderness, and sweet sleep blesses the child who lies therein.

> *Ibid. Book IV, Chap. 1*

The supreme happiness of life is the conviction that we are loved.

> *Ibid. Book V, Chap. 4*

For prying into any human affairs, none are equal to those whom it does not concern.

> *Ibid. Chap. 8*

The malicious have a dark happiness.

> *Ibid. Chap. 9*

Great grief is a divine and terrible radiance which transfigures the wretched.

> *Ibid. Chap. 13*

No human feeling can ever be so appalling as joy.

> *Ibid. Book VIII, Chap. 3*

Death has its own way of embittering victory, and it causes glory to be followed by pestilence. Typhus is the successor of triumph.

> *Ibid. Cosette, Book I, Chap. 2*

Napoleon . . . mighty somnambulist of a vanished dream.

> *Ibid. Chap. 13*

An effluence from the divine afflatus.

> *Ibid. Chap. 15*

Thank heaven, nations are great aside from the dismal chances of the sword.

> *Ibid. Chap. 16*

Waterloo is a battle of the first rank won by a captain of the second.

> *Ibid.*

---

[1] Translated by KATHERINE PRESCOTT WORMELEY.
[2] See Shakespeare, page 106.
[3] Rien ne réussit comme le succès. — French proverb
[4] Cherchez la femme.

[1] Translated by CHARLES E. WILBOUR, Modern Library Giant.

Would you realize what Revolution is, call it Progress; and would you realize what Progress is, call it To-morrow.

> *Les Misérables. Cosette,*
> *Book I, Chap. 17*

What is that to the Infinite?

> *Ibid. Chap. 18*

The doll is one of the most imperious necessities, and at the same time one of the most charming instincts of female childhood.

> *Ibid. Book III, Chap. 8*

Great blunders are often made, like large ropes, of a multitude of fibres.

> *Ibid. Book V, Chap. 10*

Upon the first goblet he read this inscription: Monkey wine; upon the second: lion wine; upon the third: sheep wine; upon the fourth: swine wine. These four inscriptions expressed the four descending degrees of drunkenness: the first, that which enlivens; the second, that which irritates; the third, that which stupefies; finally the last, that which brutalizes.

> *Ibid. Book VI, Chap. 9*

Philosophy should be an energy; it should find its aim and its effect in the amelioration of mankind.

> *Ibid. Book VII, Chap. 6*

A man is not idle because he is absorbed in thought. There is a visible labour and there is an invisible labour.

> *Ibid. Chap. 8*

To be buried in Père Lachaise is like having mahogany furniture.

> *Ibid. Book VIII, Chap. 5*

No one ever keeps a secret so well as a child.

> *Ibid. Chap. 8*

The peculiarity of prudery is to multiply sentinels, in proportion as the fortress is less threatened.[1]

> *Ibid. Marius, Book II, Chap. 8*

Nothing will mix and amalgamate more easily than an old priest and an old soldier. In reality, they are the same

---

[1] That is the refuge of all old coquettes; it is hard for them to be deserted by the gallants, and from such a desertion, in their spite, they take refuge in the trade of a prude. — MOLIÈRE: *Tartuffe*, Act I, Sc. 1

kind of man. One has devoted himself to his country upon earth, the other to his country in heaven; there is no other difference.

> *Les Misérables. Marius,*
> *Book III, Chap. 2*

To err is human.[1]

> *Ibid.*

He declared that man is a magnet, like the needle, and in his room he placed his bed with the head to the south and the foot to the north, so that at night the circulation of the blood should not be interfered with by the grand magnetic current of the globe.

> *Ibid.*

He had the appearance of a caryatid in vacation; he was supporting nothing but his reverie.

> *Ibid. Book IV, Chap. 2*

Peace is happiness digesting.

> *Ibid. Chap. 4*

Life, misfortunes, isolation, abandonment, poverty, are battlefields which have their heroes; obscure heroes, sometimes greater than the illustrious heroes.

> *Ibid. Book V, Chap. 1*

A creditor is worse than a master; for a master owns only your person, a creditor owns your dignity, and can belabour that.

> *Ibid. Chap. 2*

Seeing that Mother Plutarch had a gloomy and thoughtful air, he tapped her on the shoulder and said with a smile: "We have the indigo."

> *Ibid. Chap. 4*

Social prosperity means man happy, the citizen free, the nation great.

> *Ibid. Saint Denis, Book I, Chap. 4*

Nothing is more dangerous than discontinued labour; it is habit lost. A habit easy to abandon, difficult to resume.

> *Ibid. Book II, Chap. 1*

Thought is the labour of the intellect, reverie is its pleasure.

> *Ibid.*

---

[1] See Pope, page 211.

Where the telescope ends, the microscope begins. Which of the two has the grander view?

> *Les Misérables. Saint Denis,*
> *Book III, Chap. 3*

A compliment is something like a kiss through a veil.

> *Ibid. Book VIII, Chap. 1*

Situated in the moon, kingdom of dream, province of illusion, capital Soap-Bubble.

> *Ibid. Chap. 3*

Great perils have this beauty, that they bring to light the fraternity of strangers.

> *Ibid. Book XII, Chap. 4*

Philosophy is the microscope of thought.

> *Ibid. Jean Valjean,*
> *Book II, Chap. 2*

When grace is joined with wrinkles, it is adorable. There is an unspeakable dawn in happy old age.

> *Ibid. Book V, Chap. 2*

Angel is the only word in the language which cannot be worn out. No other word would resist the pitiless use which lovers make of it.

> *Ibid. Chap. 4*

Let us, while waiting for new monuments, preserve the ancient monuments.

> *Note added to the Definitive*
> *Edition of Notre Dame de Paris*
> *[1832]*

The sea never tells what it means to do. There is everything in this abyss, even chicanery. One might almost say that the sea had designs; it advances and retreats, it proposes and retracts, it prepares a squall and then gives up its plan, it promises destruction and does not keep its word. It threatens the North, and strikes the South.

> *Ninety-Three. Part I,*
> *Book II, Chap. 7*

Nothing is more gentle than smoke, nothing more frightful. There is the smoke of peace, and the smoke of villainy. Smoke, the density and colour of smoke, makes all the difference between peace and war, between brotherhood and hatred, between hospitality and the grave, between life and death. Smoke rising through the trees may signify the most charming thing in the world, the hearth; or the most terrible, a conflagration.

> *Ninety-Three. Part I,*
> *Book IV, Chap. 7*

There is a sacred horror about everything grand. It is easy to admire mediocrity and hills; but whatever is too lofty, a genius as well as a mountain, an assembly as well as a masterpiece, seen too near, is appalling. . . . Hence, there is more dismay than admiration.

> *Ibid. Part II, Book III, Chap. 1*

The sublimest song to be heard on earth is the lisping of the human soul on the lips of children.

> *Ibid. Part III, Book III, Chap. 1*

Nothing is so like a soul as a bee. It goes from flower to flower as a soul from star to star, and it gathers honey as a soul gathers light.

> *Ibid. Chap. 3*

Popularity? It is glory's small change.

> *Ruy Blas. Act III, Sc. 5*

Each has his share of a mother's love, and all have it all.

> *Feuilles d'Automne*

To rise at six, to dine at ten,
To sup at six, to sleep at ten,
Makes a man live for ten times ten.

> *Inscription over the door of*
> *Hugo's study*

I represent a party which does not yet exist:
the party of revolution, civilization.
This party will make the twentieth century.
There will issue from it first
the United States of Europe, then
the United States of the World.

> *Prophecy in autograph on the*
> *wall of the room in which Hugo*
> *died, Place des Vosges, Paris*

CHARLES-AUGUSTIN SAINTE-BEUVE
[1804–1869]

Hugo, strong partisan
. . . fought in armor,

And held high his banner in the midst
of the tumult:
He still holds it; and Vigny, more discreet,
As if in his tower of ivory,[1] retreated
before noontime.
> *To M. Villemain. Pensées d'Août,
> Stanza 3 [October, 1837]*

ALEXIS CHARLES HENRI CLÉREL DE TOCQUEVILLE
[1805–1859]

The profession of law is the only aristocratic element which can be amalga-
mated without violence with the natural
elements of democracy, and which can
be advantageously and permanently
combined with them.
> *Democracy in America.
> Vol. I, Chap. 16*

I cannot believe that a republic could
subsist at the present time if the influence of lawyers in public business did
not increase in proportion to the power
of the people.
> *Ibid.*

Connecticut, the little yellow spot
[on the map] that makes the clock-
peddler, the schoolmaster, and the senator. The first, gives you time; the second, tells you what to do with it; and
the third makes your law and your civilization.
> *Address at an American Fourth
> of July celebration in Paris, soon
> after the publication of Democ-
> racy in America*

VON MÜNCH BELLINGHAUSEN
[1806–1871]

Two souls with but a single thought,
Two hearts that beat as one.[2]
> *Ingomar the Barbarian.[3] Act II*

---

[1] See Lindsay, page 858.
[2] Zwei Seelen und ein Gedanke,
Zwei Herzen und ein Schlag.
See Pope, page 219, and Motherwell, page
389.
[3] Translated by MARIA ANNE LOVELL [1803–
1877]. The play was first produced at Drury
Lane Theatre, London, in 1851.

HERMAN NEUMAN
[1806–1875]

Two chambers has the heart,
Wherein dwell Joy and Sorrow;
When Joy awakes in one,
Then slumbers Sorrow in the other.
O Joy, take care!
Speak softly,
Lest you awaken Sorrow.
> *The Heart*

MARSHAL MAURICE DE MacMAHON
[1808–1893]

I am here: I shall remain here.
> *Reply to the Commander-in-
> Chief, from the trenches before
> the Malakoff, in the siege of
> Sebastopol [September, 1855],
> when warned to beware of an ex-
> plosion which might follow the
> retreat of the Russians*

GENERAL PIERRE BOSQUET
[1810–1861]

It is magnificent, but it is not war.
> *Said of the charge of the Light
> Brigade at the battle of Bala-
> klava [October 25, 1854]*

FERDINAND FREILIGRATH
[1810–1876]

O love, while still 'tis yours to love!
O love, while love you still may keep!
The hour will come, the hour will come,
When you shall stand by graves and
weep!
> *Liebestraum*

ALFRED DE MUSSET
[1810–1857]

How glorious it is — and also how
painful — to be an exception.
> *The White Blackbird. I*

Things they don't understand always
cause a sensation among the English.
> *Ibid. VIII*

Never were there so many sleepless
nights as in the time of this man [Na-

poleon]. Never did one see so many anguished mothers gaze from the ramparts of the towns. Never was there such silence when one spoke of death. And yet there was never so much joy, life, warlike music, in all hearts. There was never such pure sunshine as that which dried all this blood. People said that God made it for this man; they called it Austerlitz weather. But he made it himself with his incessant gunfire, and the only clouds were on the morrow of his battles.

> *Confession of a Child of His Century. Chap. 2*

POPE LEO XIII (GIACCHINO PECCI)
[1810–1903]

Every man has by nature the right to possess property as his own.

> *Encyclical Letter on the Condition of Labour [May 15, 1891]*

It is impossible to reduce human society to one level.

> *Ibid.*

It is one thing to have a right to the possession of money, and another to have a right to use money as one pleases.

> *Ibid.*

When a society is perishing, the true advice to give to those who would restore it is to recall it to the principles from which it sprung.

> *Ibid.*

Among the purposes of a society should be to try to arrange for a continuous supply of work at all times and seasons.

> *Ibid.*

THÉOPHILE GAUTIER
[1811–1872]

All things return to dust
  Save beauty fashioned well;
The bust
  Outlasts the citadel.[1]

> *L'Art*

[1] Tout passe. L'art robuste
  Seul a l'éternité;
 Le buste
  Survit à la cité.
See Austin Dobson, page 648.

I am the spectre of the rose
You wore but last night at the ball.

> *The Spectre of the Rose. Stanza 1*

JULIUS KARL REINHOLD STURM
[1816–1896]

Pain's furnace heat within me quivers,
  God's breath upon the flame doth blow,
And all my heart in anguish shivers
  And trembles at the fiery glow,
And yet I whisper — as God will!
And in His hottest fire — hold still.

> *God's Anvil.[1] Stanza 1*

KARL MARX
[1818–1883]

From each according to his abilities, to each according to his needs.

> *The German Ideology[2] [1845–1846]*

Nothing can have value without being an object of utility. If it be useless, the labor contained in it is useless, cannot be reckoned as labor, and cannot therefore create value.

> *Capital.[3] Part II, Chap. 3, Page 33*

The capitalist himself is a practical man, who, it is true, does not always reflect on what he says outside his office, but who always knows what he does inside the latter.

> *Ibid. Chap. 5, Page 43*

Constant labor of one uniform kind destroys the intensity and flow of a man's animal spirits, which find recreation and delight in mere change of activity.

> *Ibid. Chap. 9, Page 74*

[1] Translated by Bishop G. W. Doane.
[2] Translated by Max Eastman.
[3] Abridged edition prepared by Julian Borchardt. Translated by Stephen L. Trask. Modern Library edition.

The intellectual desolation, artificially produced by converting immature human beings into mere machines.

Capital. Part II, Chap. 10, Page 102

Where is the medal without its reverse?

Ibid. Page 137

The battle of competition is fought by cheapening of commodities.

Ibid. Chap. 13, Page 168

The only part of the so-called national wealth that actually enters into the collective possessions of modern peoples is their national debt.

Ibid. Chap. 14, Page 199

Capitalist production begets, with the inexorability of a law of nature, its own negation.

Ibid. Chap. 15, Page 204

When commercial capital occupies a position of unquestioned ascendancy, it everywhere constitutes a system of plunder.

Ibid. Chap. 21, Page 262

The history of all hitherto existing society is the history of class struggles.

Manifesto of the Communist Party [1] *[1848]. I*

Of all the classes that stand face to face with the bourgeoisie to-day the proletariat alone is a really revolutionary class. The other classes decay and finally disappear in the race of modern industry; the proletariat is its special and essential product.[2]

Ibid.

Pauperism develops more rapidly than population and wealth.

Ibid.

In proportion as the antagonism between classes within the nation vanishes, the hostility of one nation to another will come to an end.

Manifesto of the Communist Party [1848]. *II*

The ruling ideas of each age have ever been the ideas of its ruling class.

Ibid.

Christian Socialism is but the holy water with which the priest consecrates the heartburnings of the aristocrat.

Ibid. III

The proletarians have nothing to lose but their chains. They have a world to win. Workers of the world, unite!

Ibid. IV

IVAN SERGEYEVICH TURGENIEV
[1818–1883]

That air of superiority to the rest of the world which usually disappears when once the twenties have been passed.

Fathers and Sons.[1] *Chap. 4*

That awkwardness which overtakes a young man when, just ceased to be a boy, he returns to the spot where hitherto he has ranked as a mere child.

Ibid.

That dim, murky period when regrets come to resemble hopes, and hopes are beginning to resemble regrets.

Ibid. Chap. 7

I agree with no man's opinions. I have some of my own.

Ibid. Chap. 13

The temerity to believe in nothing.

Ibid. Chap. 14

A picture may instantly present what a book could set forth only in a hundred pages.

Ibid. Chap. 16

The sensuous joy of magnanimity.

Ibid. Chap. 17

Whatever a man prays for, he prays for a miracle. Every prayer reduces itself to this: "Great God, grant that twice two be not four."

Prayer

---

[1] Written in collaboration with FRIEDRICH ENGELS. Translated by SAMUEL MOORE.

[2] By bourgeoisie is meant the class of modern capitalists, owners of the means of social production and employers of wage-labor. By proletariat, the class of modern wage-laborers who, having no means of production of their own, are reduced to selling their labor-power in order to live. — FRIEDRICH ENGELS: [1820–1895]: *Footnote to Manifesto of the Communist Party, Part I, Bourgeois and Proletarians*

---

[1] Translated by C. J. HOGARTH.

Don't forget me, but do not call me to mind either, in the midst of daily cares, pleasures and needs. . . . I do not want to disturb your life, I do not want to impede its quiet course.

> *Literary Remains [published in 1930]. When I Shall Be No More*

MAX SCHNECKENBURGER
[1819–1849]

So long as blood shall warm our veins,
While for the sword one hand remains,
One arm to bear a gun, — no more
Shall foot of foeman tread thy shore!
Dear Fatherland, no fear be thine,
Firm stands thy guard along the Rhine.

> *The Watch on the Rhine.*[1]
> *Stanza 4*

GUSTAVE NADAUD
[1820–1893]

I'm growing old, I've sixty years;
  I've labored all my life in vain.
In all that time of hopes and fears,
  I've failed my dearest wish to gain.
I see full well that here below
  Bliss unalloyed there is for none,
My prayer would else fulfilment
  know —
Never have I seen Carcassonne! [2]

> *Carcassonne.*[3] *Stanza 1*

They tell me every day is there
  Not more nor less than Sunday gay;

---

[1] Written in 1840, when France was threatening the left bank of the Rhine. Set to music by Carl Wilhelm [1815–1873] in 1854.

[2] Those towers gold as ripened grain
  Perchance we may not gaze upon,
  And yet, through sunshine, wind and rain,
  We're on our way to Carcassonne.
    BERTON BRALEY: *Carcassonne*
  For the sake
  Of the old man who longed to hie
  Him forth when autumn's work was done,
  I thank the Fates that let him die
  Before he looked on Carcassonne.
    GRACE NOLL CROWELL: *Carcassonne Attained*

[3] Translated by JOHN R. THOMPSON [1823–1873].

In shining robes and garments fair
  The people walk upon their way.
One gazes there on castle walls
  As grand as those of Babylon,
A bishop and two generals!
  What joy to be in Carcassonne!
Ah! might I but see Carcassonne!

> *Carcassonne. Stanza 3*

Thy pardon, Father, I beseech,
  In this my prayer if I offend;
One something sees beyond his reach
  From childhood to his journey's end.
My wife, our little boy Aignan,
  Have travelled even to Narbonne;
My grandchild has seen Perpignan;
  And I — have not seen Carcassonne.

> *Ibid. Stanza 5*

HENRI-FRÉDÉRIC AMIEL
[1821–1881]

Truth is the secret of eloquence and of virtue, the basis of moral authority; it is the highest summit of art and of life.

> *Journal*

Life is the apprenticeship to progressive renunciation, to the steady diminution of our claims, of our hopes, of our powers, of our liberty.

> *Ibid.*

Doing easily what others find difficult is talent; doing what is impossible for talent is genius.

> *Ibid.*

A man without passion is only a latent force, only a possibility, like a stone waiting for the blow from the iron to give forth sparks.

> *Ibid.*

If ignorance and passion are the foes of popular morality, it must be confessed that moral indifference is the malady of the cultivated classes.

> *Ibid.*

Pure truth cannot be assimilated by the crowd; it must be communicated by contagion.

> *Ibid.*

FYODOR DOSTOYEVSKY
[1821–1881]

Man is a pliable animal, a being who gets accustomed to everything!

> *The House of the Dead (Prison Life in Siberia).*[1] *Part I, Chap. 2*

With ready-made opinions one cannot judge of crime. Its philosophy is a little more complicated than people think. It is acknowledged that neither convict prisons, nor the hulks, nor any system of hard labour ever cured a criminal.

> *Ibid.*

Humane treatment may raise up one in whom the divine image has long been obscured. It is with the unfortunate, above all, that humane conduct is necessary.

> *Ibid. Chap. 9*

Tyranny is a habit capable of being developed, and at last becomes a disease. . . . The man and the citizen disappear for ever in the tyrant.

> *Ibid. Part II, Chap. 3*

Consolation is not what you need. Weep and be not consoled, but weep. Only every time that you weep be sure to remember that your little son is one of the angels of God, and rejoices at your tears, and points at them to the Lord God; and a long while yet will you keep that great mother's grief. But it will turn in the end to quiet joy, and your bitter tears will be only tears of tender sorrow that purifies the heart.

> *The Brothers Karamazov.*[2] *Part I, Book II, Chap. 3*

Even those who have renounced Christianity and attack it, in their inmost being still follow the Christian ideal, for hitherto neither their subtlety nor the ardour of their hearts has been able to create a higher ideal of man and of virtue than the ideal given by Christ of old. When it has been attempted, the result has been only grotesque.

> *Ibid. Part II, Book IV, Chap. 1*

---

[1] Everyman edition.
[2] Translated by CONSTANCE GARNETT. Modern Library edition.

Until you have become really, in actual fact, a brother to every one, brotherhood will not come to pass. No sort of scientific teaching, no kind of common interest, will ever teach men to share property and privileges with equal consideration for all. Every one will think his share too small and they will be always envying, complaining and attacking one another.

> *The Brothers Karamazov.* *Part II, Book VI, Chap. 2*

The true security is to be found in social solidarity rather than in isolated individual effort.

> *Ibid.*

Be not forgetful of prayer. Every time you pray, if your prayer is sincere, there will be new feeling and new meaning in it, which will give you fresh courage, and you will understand that prayer is an education.

> *Ibid. Chap. 3*

Love all God's creation,[1] the whole and every grain of sand in it. Love every leaf, every ray of God's light. Love the animals, love the plants, love everything. If you love everything, you will perceive the divine mystery in things. Once you perceive it, you will begin to comprehend it better every day. And you will come at last to love the whole world with an all-embracing love.

> *Ibid.*

Much on earth is hidden from us, but to make up for that we have been given a precious mystic sense of our living bond with the other world, with the higher heavenly world, and the roots of our thoughts and feelings are not here but in other worlds. That is why the philosophers say that we cannot comprehend the reality of things on earth.

> *Ibid.*

Men reject their prophets and slay them, but they love their martyrs and honour those whom they have slain.

> *Ibid.*

---

[1] See *Book of Common Prayer*, page 1128.

ALEXANDRE DUMAS
THE YOUNGER
[1824–1895]

Business? It's quite simple. It's other people's money.

La Question d'Argent [*1857*].
Act II, Sc. 7

GESTA ROMANORUM [1]

We read of a certain Roman emperor who built a magnificent palace. In digging the foundation, the workmen discovered a golden sarcophagus ornamented with three circlets, on which were inscribed, "I have expended; I have given; I have kept; I have possessed; I do possess; I have lost; I am punished. What I formerly expended, I have; what I gave away, I have." [2]

Tale 16

See how the world rewards its votaries.[3]

Tale 36

If the end be well, all is well.[4]

Tale 67

---

[1] A collection of 181 stories, first printed about 1473. The first English version appeared in 1824, translated by the Reverend C. Swan (Bohn Standard Library).

[2] Richard Gough [1735–1809] in *Sepulchral Monuments of Great Britain*, gives this epitaph of Robert Byrkes, which is to be found in Doncaster Church, "new cut" upon his tomb in Roman capitals: —

Howe: Howe: who is heare:
I, Robin of Doncaster, and Margaret my feare.
    That I spent, that I had;
    That I gave, that I have;
    That I left, that I lost.
        A.D. 1579.

The following is the epitaph of Edward Courtenay, Earl of Devonshire, according to Cleaveland's *Genealogical History of the Family of Courtenay, P. 142*, and quoted by Gibbon: *Decline and Fall of the Roman Empire*, Chap. 61: —

    What we gave, we have;
    What we spent, we had;
    What we left, we lost.

[3] Ecce quomodo mundus suis servitoribus reddit mercedem (See how the world its veterans rewards). — Pope: *Moral Essays, Epistle 2, L. 243*

[4] Si finis bonus est, totum bonum erit. — Probably the origin of the proverb, "All's well that ends well."

Whatever you do, do wisely, and think of the consequences.

Tale 103

HENRIK IBSEN
[1828–1906]

A community is like a ship; every one ought to be prepared to take the helm.

An Enemy of the People. Act I

The most crying need in the humbler ranks of life is that they should be allowed some part in the direction of public affairs. That is what will develop their faculties and intelligence and self-respect.

Ibid. Act II

The public doesn't require any new ideas. The public is best served by the good, old-fashioned ideas it already has.

Ibid.

An editor cannot always act as he would prefer. He is often obliged to bow to the wishes of the public in unimportant matters. Politics are the most important thing in life — for a newspaper.

Ibid. Act III

The most dangerous enemy to truth and freedom amongst us is the compact majority.

Ibid. Act IV

You should never wear your best trousers when you go out to fight for freedom and truth.

Ibid. Act V

To crave for happiness in this world is simply to be possessed by a spirit of revolt. What right have we to happiness?

Ghosts. Act I

It is not only what we have inherited from our fathers that exists again in us, but all sorts of old dead ideas and all kinds of old dead beliefs and things of that kind. They are not actually alive in us; but there they are dormant, all the same, and we can never be rid of them. Whenever I take up a newspaper and read it, I fancy I see ghosts creeping between the lines. There must be ghosts all over the world.

Ibid. Act II

There can be no freedom or beauty about a home life that depends on borrowing and debt.

A Doll's House. Act I

A barrister's profession is such an uncertain thing, especially if he won't undertake unsavoury cases.

Ibid.

There are some people one loves best, and others whom one would almost always rather have as companions.

Ibid. Act II

Marriage is a thing you've got to give your whole mind to.

The League of Youth. Act IV

These heroes of finance are like beads on a string — when one slips off, all the rest follow.

Ibid.

He has the luck to be unhampered by either character, or conviction, or social position; so that Liberalism is the easiest thing in the world for him.

Ibid. Act V

Rob the average man of his life-illusion, and you rob him of his happiness at the same stroke.

The Wild Duck. Act V

Look into any man's heart you please, and you will always find, in every one, at least one black spot which he has to keep concealed.

Pillars of Society. Act III

The spirit of truth and the spirit of freedom — they are the pillars of society.

Ibid. Act IV

A lie, turned topsy-turvy, can be prinked and tinselled out, decked in plumage new and fine, till none knows its lean old carcass.

Peer Gynt. Act I

For fortune such as I've enjoyed I have to thank America. My amply-furnished library I owe to Germany's later schools. From France, again, I get my waistcoats, my manners, and my spice of wit, — from England an industrious hand, and keen sense for my own advantage. The Jew has taught me how to wait. Some taste for *dolce far niente* I have received from Italy, — and one time, in a perilous pass, to eke the measure of my days, I had recourse to Swedish steel.

Peer Gynt. Act IV

I hold that man is in the right who is most closely in league with the future.

Letter to Georg Brandes
[January 3, 1882]

COUNT LYOF NIKOLAYE-VITCH TOLSTOI
[1828–1910]

The Frenchman is conceited from supposing himself mentally and physically to be inordinately fascinating both to men and to women. An Englishman is conceited on the ground of being a citizen of the best-constituted state in the world, and also because he as an Englishman always knows what is the correct thing to do, and knows that everything that he, as an Englishman, does do is indisputably the best thing. An Italian is conceited from being excitable and easily forgetting himself and other people. A Russian is conceited precisely because he knows nothing and cares to know nothing, since he does not believe it possible to know anything fully. A conceited German is the worst of them all, and the most hardened of all, and the most repulsive of all; for he imagines that he possesses the truth in a science of his own invention, which is to him absolute truth.

War and Peace.[1] Part IX, Chap. 11

The subject of history is the life of peoples and of humanity. To catch and pin down in words — that is, to describe directly the life, not only of humanity, but even of a single people, appears to be impossible.

Ibid. Epilogue, Part II, Chap. 1

If the will of man were free, that is, if every man could act as he chose, the whole of history would be a tissue of disconnected accidents.

Ibid. Chap. 8

[1] Translated by CONSTANCE GARNETT. Modern Library Giant.

The most powerful weapon of ignorance — the diffusion of printed matter.

> *War and Peace. Epilogue, Part II,*
> *Chap. 8*

Time is infinite movement without one moment of rest.

> *Ibid. Chap. 10*

All happy families resemble one another; every unhappy family is unhappy in its own fashion.

> *Anna Karénina.*[1] *Part I, Chap. 1*

War on the one hand is such a terrible, such an atrocious, thing, that no man, especially no Christian man, has the right to assume the responsibility of beginning it.

> *Ibid. Part VIII, Chap. 15*

The whole trade in the luxuries of life is brought into existence and supported by the requirements of women.

> *The Kreutzer Sonata. Chap. 9*

His face was of that insipidly pleasing kind which women call "not bad-looking."

> *Ibid. Chap. 19*

Error is the force that welds men together; truth is communicated to men only by deeds of truth.

> *My Religion. Chap. 12*

The happiness of men consists in life. And life is in labor.

> *What Is to Be Done? Chap. 38*

The vocation of every man and woman is to serve other people.

> *Ibid. Chap. 40, Note*

The only significance of life consists in helping to establish the kingdom of God; and this can be done only by means of the acknowledgment and profession of the truth by each one of us.

> *The Kingdom of God. Chap. 12*

Art is a human activity having for its purpose the transmission to others of the highest and best feelings to which men have risen.

> *What Is Art? Chap. 8*

The more is given the less the people will work for themselves, and the less

they work the more their poverty will increase.[1]

> *Help for the Starving. Part III*
> *[January, 1892]*

WILHELM BUSCH [2]
[1832–1908]

Youth should heed the older-witted
When they say, don't go too far —
Now their sins are all committed,
Lord, how virtuous they are!

> *Pious Helen (Die fromme*
> *Helene)*

CESARE LOMBROSO
[1836–1909]

Not only is fame (and until recent years even liberty), denied to men of genius during their lives, but even the means of subsistence. After death they receive monuments and rhetoric by way of compensation.

> *The Man of Genius. Preface*

Good sense travels on the well-worn paths; genius, never. And that is why the crowd, not altogether without reason, is so ready to treat great men as lunatics.[3]

> *Ibid.*

A patient one day presented himself to Abernethy; after careful examination the celebrated practitioner said, "You need amusement; go and hear Grimaldi; he will make you laugh, and that will be better for you than any drugs." "My God," exclaimed the invalid, "but I *am* Grimaldi!" [4]

> *Ibid. Part I, Chap. 2*

Klopstock was questioned regarding the meaning of a passage in his poem. He replied, "God and I both knew what it meant once; now God alone knows." [5]

> *Ibid.*

---

[1] Translated by NATHAN HASKELL DOLE [1852–1935].

[1] If you stop supporting that crowd, it will support itself. — SENECA: *Epistle 20, 7*

[2] Famous artist and cartoonist, author of the German classic for children, *Max and Moritz* [1865].

[3] See Seneca, page 991.

[4] See Thackeray, page 484.

[5] Also attributed to Browning, apropos of his *Sordello*.

The appearance of a single great genius is more than equivalent to the birth of a hundred mediocrities.
The Man of Genius. Part II, Chap. 2

The strange insane poet, John Clare, who believed himself a spectator of the Battle of the Nile, and the death of Nelson; and was firmly convinced that he had been present at the death of Charles I.
Ibid. Part III, Chap. 2

"Lawsuit mania" . . . a continual craving to go to law against others, while considering themselves the injured party.
Ibid. Chap. 3

The ignorant man always adores what he cannot understand.
Ibid.

Men in general, but more particularly the ·insane, love to speak of themselves, and on this theme they even become eloquent.
Ibid. Part IV, Chap. 1

HENRI CAZALIS
(JEAN LAHORS)
[1840–1909]

Click, click, click . . . Death is prancing;
Death, at midnight, goes a-dancing,
Tapping on a tomb with talon thin,
Click, click, click, goes the grisly violin.
". . . Equality, Fraternity." [1]
Stanza 1

ANATOLE FRANCE
[1844–1924]

I do not know any reading more easy, more fascinating, more delightful than a catalogue.
The Crime of Sylvestre Bonnard. [2]
The Log, December 24, 1849

All the historical books which contain no lies are extremely tedious.
Ibid.

---

[1] Translated by BERTRAM GALBRAITH. This poem inspired Camille Saint-Saëns' *Danse Macabre*, Opus 40.
[2] Translated by LAFCADIO HEARN. Modern Library edition.

Lovers who love truly do not write down their happiness.
The Crime of Sylvestre Bonnard.
The Log, November 30, 1859

The time God allots to each one of us is like a precious tissue which we embroider as we best know how.
Ibid. The Daughter of Clémentine.
Chap. 2

To know is nothing at all; to imagine is everything.
Ibid. Part II, Chap. 2

The domestic hearth. There only is real happiness.
Ibid. Chap. 3

He flattered himself on being a man without any prejudices; and this pretension itself is a very great prejudice.
Ibid. Chap. 4

Those who have given themselves the most concern about the happiness of peoples have made their neighbours very miserable.
Ibid.

Man is so made that he can only find relaxation from one kind of labor by taking up another.
Ibid.

People who have no weaknesses are terrible; there is no way of taking advantage of them.
Ibid.

The whole art of teaching is only the art of awakening the natural curiosity of young minds for the purpose of satisfying it afterwards.
Ibid.

The faculty of doubting is rare among men. A few choice spirits carry the germs of it in them, but these do not develop without training.
Penguin Island. Book VI, Chap. 2

We have medicines to make women speak; we have none to make them keep silence.
The Man Who Married a Dumb Wife. [1] *Act II, Sc. 4*

They saw Barnaby before the altar of the Blessed Virgin, head downwards, with his feet in the air, and he was juggling six balls of copper and a dozen knives. In honor of the Holy Mother of

---

[1] Translated by CURTIS HIDDEN PAGE.

God he was performing those feats, which aforetime had won him most renown.

Our Lady's Juggler [1]

The good critic is he who narrates the adventures of his soul among masterpieces.

La Vie Littéraire. Preface

We reproach people for talking about themselves; but it is the subject they treat best.

Ibid. Journal des Goncourt

FRIEDRICH WILHELM NIETZSCHE
[1844–1900]

Our destiny exercises its influence over us even when, as yet, we have not learned its nature: it is our future that lays down the law of our to-day.

Human, All Too Human. [2] *7*

Much more happiness is to be found in the world than gloomy eyes discover.

Ibid. 49

One must have a good memory to be able to keep the promises one makes.

Ibid. 59

One will rarely err if extreme actions be ascribed to vanity, ordinary actions to habit, and mean actions to fear.

Ibid. 74

How poor the human mind would be without vanity! It resembles a well stocked and ever renewed ware-emporium that attracts buyers of every class: they can find almost everything, have almost everything, provided they bring with them the right kind of money — admiration.

Ibid.

Every man who has declared that some other man is an ass or a scoundrel, gets angry when the other man conclusively shows that the assertion was erroneous.

Ibid. 90

Every tradition grows ever more venerable — the more remote is its origin, the more confused that origin is. The reverence due to it increases from generation to generation. The tradition finally becomes holy and inspires awe.

Human, All Too Human. 96

I teach you the Superman. Man is something that is to be surpassed.

Thus Spake Zarathustra. [1] *Prologue, Chap. 3*

Man is a rope stretched between the animal and the Superman — a rope over an abyss.

Ibid. Chap. 4

I want to teach men the sense of their existence, which is the Superman, the lightning out of the dark cloud man.

Ibid. Chap. 7

No small art is it to sleep: it is necessary for that purpose to keep awake all day.

Ibid. Part I, Chap. 2

This is hardest of all: to close the open hand out of love, and keep modest as a giver.

Ibid. Part II, Chap. 23

Beggars, however, one should entirely do away with! Verily, it annoyeth one to give unto them, and it annoyeth one not to give unto them. [2]

Ibid. Chap. 25

The sting of conscience teacheth one to sting.

Ibid.

Distrust all in whom the impulse to punish is powerful.

Ibid. Chap. 29

Ah, there are so many things betwixt heaven and earth of which only the poets have dreamed!

Ibid. Chap. 39

Believe me, friend Hollaballoo! The greatest events are not our noisiest, but our stillest hours.

Ibid. Chap. 40

Thoughts that come with doves' footsteps guide the world.

Ibid. Chap. 44

---

[1] Translated by FREDERIC CHAPMAN.
[2] Translated by ALEXANDER HARVEY.

[1] Translated by THOMAS COMMON.
[2] There is surely a Physiognomy, which those experienced and Master Mendicants observe, whereby they instantly discover a merciful aspect, and will single out a face wherein they spy the signatures and marks of Mercy. — SIR THOMAS BROWNE: *Religio Medici* (Everyman ed.), *P. 66*

Winter, a bad guest, sitteth with me at home; blue are my hands with his friendly handshaking.
> *Thus Spake Zarathustra.*
> *Part III, Chap. 50*

Better know nothing than half-know many things.[1]
> *Ibid. Part IV, Chap. 64*

We ought to learn from the kine one thing: ruminating.
> *Ibid. Chap. 68*

Then learnedst thou how much harder it is to give properly than to take properly, and that bestowing well is an art — the last, subtlest master-art of kindness.[2]
> *Ibid.*

If ye would go up high, then use your own legs! Do not get yourselves *carried* aloft; do not seat yourselves on other people's backs and heads!
> *Ibid. Chap. 73, Sect. 10*

From people who merely pray we must become people who bless.
> *Notes on Thus Spake*
> *Zarathustra. 82*

It is certainly not the least charm of a theory that it is refutable.
> *Beyond Good and Evil.*[3] *I, 18*

No one is such a liar as the indignant man.
> *Ibid. II, 26*

Books for the general reader are always ill-smelling books, the odour of paltry people clings to them.
> *Ibid. 29*

It is not the strength but the duration of great sentiments that makes great men.
> *Ibid. IV, 72*

Woman learns how to hate in proportion as she forgets how to charm.
> *Ibid. 84*

[1] See H. W. Shaw, page 518.
[2] Some is for gift sae lang required,
  While that the craver be so tired,
  That ere the gift delivered be,
  The thank is frustrate and expired;
  In Giving sould Discretion be.
    WILLIAM DUNBAR [1460–1530]·
    Discretion in Giving
  In Taking sould Discretion be
    WILLIAM DUNBAR: *Discretion in Taking*
[3] Translated by HELEN ZIMMERN.

Our vanity is most difficult to wound just when our pride has been wounded.
> *Beyond Good and Evil. IV. 111*

Where there is neither love nor hatred in the game, woman's play is mediocre.
> *Ibid. 115*

In revenge and in love woman is more barbarous than man.
> *Ibid. 139*

The thought of suicide is a great consolation:[1] by means of it one gets successfully through many a bad night.
> *Ibid. 157*

There are few pains so grievous as to have seen, divined, or experienced how an exceptional man has missed his way and deteriorated.
> *Ibid. V, 203*

Blessed are the forgetful: for they get the better even of their blunders.
> *Ibid. VII, 217*

Is not life a hundred times too short for us to bore ourselves?
> *Ibid. 227*

One does not know — cannot know — the best that is in one.
> *Ibid. VIII, 249*

The melancholia of everything completed!
> *Ibid. IX, 277*

The "masters" have been done away with; the morality of the vulgar man has triumphed.
> *Genealogy of Morals.*[2] *First Essay,*
> *Aphorism 9*

The broad effects which can be obtained by punishment in man and beast, are the increase of fear, the sharpening of the sense of cunning, the mastery of the desires; so it is that punishment tames man, but does not make him "better."
> *Ibid. Second Essay, Aphorism 15*

A married philosopher belongs to comedy.
> *Ibid. Third Essay, Aphorism 7*

[1] We are in the power of no calamity while death is in our own. — SIR THOMAS BROWNE: *Religio Medici* (Everyman ed.), *P. 50*
[2] Translated by HORACE B. SAMUEL.

Every tiny step forward in the world was formerly made at the cost of mental and physical torture.

Genealogy of Morals. Third Essay,
Aphorism 9

The sick are the greatest danger for the healthy; it is not from the strongest that harm comes to the strong, but from the weakest.

Ibid. Aphorism 14

A strong and well-constituted man digests his experiences (deeds and misdeeds all included) just as he digests his meats, even when he has some tough morsels to swallow.

Ibid. Aphorism 16

Nothing ever succeeds which exuberant spirits have not helped to produce.

The Twilight of the Idols.[1]
Preface

Contentment preserves one even from catching cold. Has a woman who knew that she was well dressed ever caught cold? — No, not even when she had scarcely a rag to her back.

Ibid. Maxims and Missiles, 25

Without music life would be a mistake.

Ibid. 33

He who laughs best to-day, will also laugh last.[2]

Ibid. 43

That which needs to be proved cannot be worth much.

Ibid. The Problem of Socrates, 5

History is nothing more than the belief in the senses, the belief in falsehood.[3]

Ibid. "Reason" in Philosophy, 1

Unconscious gratitude for a good digestion (sometimes called "brotherly love").

Ibid. Morality as the Enemy
of Nature, 3

---

[1] Translated by ANTHONY M. LUDOVICI.
[2] Better the last smile than the first laughter. — JOHN RAY: *Compleat Collection of English Proverbs* [1742]. This is a variant of the familiar saying, "He laughs best who laughs last," known in all languages.
[3] See Matthew Arnold, page 548.

Two great European narcotics, alcohol and Christianity.

The Twilight of the Idols.
Things the Germans Lack, 2

Dancing in all its forms cannot be excluded from the curriculum of all noble education: dancing with the feet, with ideas, with words, and, need I add that one must also be able to dance with the pen?

Ibid. 7

In the architectural structure, man's pride, man's triumph over gravitation, man's will to power, assume a visible form. Architecture is a sort of oratory of power by means of forms.

Ibid. Skirmishes in a War
with the Age, 11

If a man have a strong faith he can indulge in the luxury of scepticism.

Ibid. 12

The sick man is a parasite of society. In certain cases it is indecent to go on living. To continue to vegetate in a state of cowardly dependence upon doctors and special treatments, once the meaning of life, the right to life, has been lost, ought to be regarded with the greatest contempt by society.

Ibid. 36

Liberal institutions straightway cease from being liberal the moment they are soundly established: once this is attained no more grievous and more thorough enemies of freedom exist than liberal institutions.

Ibid. 38

It is my ambition to say in ten sentences what everyone else says in a whole book, — what everyone else does *not* say in a whole book.

Ibid. 51

Love is the state in which man sees things most widely different from what they are. The force of illusion reaches its zenith here, as likewise the sweetening and transfiguring power. When a man is in love he endures more than at other times; he submits to everything.

The Antichrist.[1] *Aphorism 23*

---

[1] Translated by ANTHONY M. LUDOVICI.

Our statesmen — a body of men who are otherwise so unembarrassed, and such thorough anti-Christians in deed — still declare themselves Christians and still flock to communion.[1]

The Antichrist. Aphorism 39

God created woman. And boredom did indeed cease from that moment — but many other things ceased as well! Woman was God's *second* mistake.

Ibid. Aphorism 48

Life always gets harder toward the summit — the cold increases, responsibility increases.

Ibid. Aphorism 57

I call Christianity the one great curse, the one enormous and innermost perversion, the one great instinct of revenge, for which no means are too venomous, too underhand, too underground and too petty, — I call it the one immortal blemish of mankind.

Ibid. Aphorism 62

My doctrine is: Live that thou mayest desire to live again, — that is thy duty, — for in any case thou wilt live again!

Eternal Recurrence.[2] 27

Even a thought, even a possibility, can shatter us and transform us.

Ibid. 30

Let us stamp the impress of eternity upon our lives!

Ibid. 35

Nothing on earth consumes a man more quickly than the passion of resentment.

Ecce Homo [2]

Where one despises, one cannot wage war. Where one commands, where one sees something beneath one, one ought not to wage war.

Ibid.

I believe only in French culture, and regard everything else in Europe which calls itself "culture" as a misunderstanding. I do not even take the German kind into consideration.

Ibid.

Wherever Germany extends her sway, she ruins culture.

Ecce Homo

As an artist, a man has no home in Europe save in Paris.

Ibid.

Simply by being compelled to keep constantly on his guard, a man may grow so weak as to be unable any longer to defend himself.

Ibid.

Pathetic attitudes are not in keeping with greatness.

Ibid.

My time has not yet come either; some are born posthumously.

Ibid.

No one can draw more out of things, books included, than he already knows. A man has no ears for that to which experience has given him no access.

Ibid.

I am not successful at being pompous, the most I can do is to appear embarrassed.

Ibid.

The Germans are like women, you can scarcely ever fathom their depths — they haven't any.[1]

Ibid.

After coming in contact with a religious man, I always feel that I must wash my hands.

Ibid.

All prejudices may be traced back to the intestines. A sedentary life is the real sin against the Holy Ghost.[2]

Ibid.

One must separate from anything that forces one to repeat No again and again.

Ibid. P. 41

---

[1] The reference is to Bismarck, a sincere Christian and forger of the Ems telegram which precipitated the war of 1870.

[2] Translated by ANTHONY M. LUDOVICI.

[1] Man thinks woman profound — why? Because he can never fathom her depths. Woman is not even shallow. — *The Twilight of the Idols, Maxims and Missiles, 27*

[2] Translated by CLIFTON P. FADIMAN. Modern Library edition, P. 27.

HENRYK SIENKIEWICZ
[1846–1916]

The greater philosopher a man is, the more difficult it is for him to answer the foolish questions of common people.
Quo Vadis.[1] *Chap. 19*

A man who leaves memoirs, whether well or badly written, provided they be sincere, renders a service to future psychologists and writers.
Without Dogma.[2] *Page 1*

JORIS KARL HUYSMANS
[1848–1907]

The pleasure of travel, which only exists as a matter of fact in retrospect and seldom in the present, at the instant when it is being experienced.
Against the Grain[3] *[1884].*
Chap. 3

One could revel, for instance, in long explorations while near one's own fireside, stimulating the restive or sluggish mind, if need be, by reading some narrative of travel in distant lands.
Ibid.

Is there a woman, whose form is more dazzling, more splendid than the two locomotives that pass over the Northern Railroad lines?
Ibid.

The diamond has become notoriously common since every tradesman has taken to wearing it on his little finger.
Ibid. Chap. 5

The loveliest tune imaginable becomes vulgar and insupportable as soon as the public begins to hum it and the hurdy-gurdies make it their own.
Ibid. Chap. 9

Perfumes, in fact, rarely come from the flowers whose names they bear . . . with the exception of the inimitable jasmine which it is impossible to counterfeit.
Ibid. Chap. 10

---

[1] Translated by JEREMIAH CURTIN [1838–1906].
[2] Translated by IZA YOUNG.
[3] Translated by JOHN HOWARD.

Art is the only clean thing on earth, except holiness.
Les Foules de Lourdes [1906]

BARONESS BERTHA VON SUTTNER
[1848–1914]

After the verb "To Love," "To Help" is the most beautiful verb in the world!
Epigram

FRIEDRICH A. J. VON BERNHARDI
[1849–1930]

Political morality differs from individual morality, because there is no power above the State.
Quoted as the theme of The Search-lights by ALFRED NOYES

MARSHAL FERDINAND FOCH
[1852–1929]

A guest at a dinner given in honor of Marshal Foch in Denver, Colorado, said that there was nothing but wind in French politeness. Marshal Foch retorted: "Neither is there anything but wind in a pneumatic tire, yet it eases wonderfully the jolts along life's highway."

My center is giving way, my right is pushed back — excellent! I'll attack.
Said at the Battle of the Marne, 1918.[1]

MUTSUHITO, EMPEROR OF JAPAN
[1852–1912]

Be ever careful in your choice of friends,
And let your special love be given to those
Whose strength of character may prove the whip

---

[1] *"Mon centre cède, ma droite recule, situation excellente, j'attaque."* Quoted by B. H. LIDDELL HART, *Reputations Ten Years After* [1928].

That drives you ever to fair Wisdom's
goal.

Wisdom's Goal [1] [*1904*]

ARTHUR RIMBAUD
[1854–1891]

A, black; E, white; I, red; O, blue;
U, green.

Sonnet, Vowels

REMY DE GOURMONT
[1858–1915]

Aesthetic emotion puts man in a state
favourable to the reception of erotic
emotion. Art is the accomplice of love.
Take love away and there is no longer
art.

Decadence [2]

I do not believe it useful to generalize
opinions, to teach admirations. It is for
each man to procure himself the emotion he needs, and the morality which
suits him.

Ibid.

It is because peoples do not know
each other that they hate each other so
little.

Ibid.

There are too few obscure writers in
French. We accustom ourselves like
cowards to love only writing that is
easy and that will soon be elementary.

Ibid.

RABINDRANATH TAGORE
[1861–   ]

Peace, my heart, let the time for parting be sweet.
Let it not be a death but completeness.
Let love melt into memory and pain
into songs.

Peace

When one knows thee, then alien
there is none, then no door is shut. Oh,
grant me my prayer that I may never
lose the touch of the one in the play of
the many.

Gitanjali

Things that I longed for in vain and
things that I got — let them pass. Let
me but truly possess the things I
spurned and overlooked.

Gitanjali

Come out of thyself,
Stand in the open;
Within thy heart wilt thou hear
The response of all the world.

Sheaves. The Invitation

When I bring you coloured toys, my
child, I understand why there is such
a play of colours on clouds, on water,
and why flowers are painted in tints.

*The Crescent Moon. When and
Why*

I do not love him because he is good,
but because he is my little child.

Ibid. The Judge

I alone have a right to blame and
punish, for he only may chastise who
loves.

Ibid.

Years mature into fruit
So that some small seeds of moments
May outlive them.

On Visiting Yale University
[*1932*]

MAURICE MAETERLINCK
[1864–   ]

The future is a world limited by ourselves; in it we discover only what concerns us and, sometimes, by chance,
what interests those whom we love the
most.

Joyzelle. Act I

Men's weaknesses are often necessary
to the purposes of life.

Ibid. Act II

All our knowledge merely helps us to
die a more painful death than the animals that know nothing. A day will
come when science will turn upon its
error and no longer hesitate to shorten
our woes. A day will come when it will
dare and act with certainty; when life,
grown wiser, will depart silently at its
hour, knowing that it has reached its
term.

Our Eternity

---

[1] Translated by ARTHUR LLOYD.
[2] Translated by W. A. BRADLEY.

I have never for one instant seen clearly within myself; how then would you have me judge the deeds of others? [1]
Pelleas and Melisande.
Act I, Sc. 3

Activity and duty are not to be found by the roadside. One must await them on the threshold, ready to bid them enter at the moment of passing, and they pass every day.
Ibid. Act II, Sc. 4

Each young and beautiful being shapes around it events that are themselves young, beautiful, and happy.
Ibid. Act IV, Sc. 2

Old men have need to touch sometimes with their lips the brow of a woman or the cheek of a child, that they may believe again in the freshness of life.
Ibid.

JOSÉ ASUNCIÓN SILVA
[1865–1896]

Verse is a chalice; place within it only
A stainless thought;
From out whose deeps the smouldering radiance sparkles
Like bubbles in a golden vintage caught.
Art.[2] Stanza 1

EDMOND ROSTAND
[1868–1918]

A great nose indicates a great man —
Genial, courteous, intellectual,
Virile, courageous.
Cyrano de Bergerac [3] [1897].
Act I

Lightly I toss my hat away,
Languidly over my arm let fall
The cloak that covers my bright array —

Then out swords, and to work withal!
Cyrano de Bergerac [1897]. Act I.
Ballade of the Duel,[1] Stanza 1

Free fighters, free lovers, free spenders —
The Cadets of Gascoyne — the defenders
Of old homes, old names, and old splendors.[1]
Ibid. Act II

What would you have me do?
Seek for the patronage of some great man,
And like a creeping vine on a tall tree
Crawl upward, where I cannot stand alone?
No, thank you.
Ibid.

There comes one moment, once — and God help those
Who pass that moment by! — when Beauty stands
Looking into the soul with grave, sweet eyes
That sicken at pretty words.
Ibid. Act III

And what is a kiss, when all is done?
A promise given under seal — a vow
Taken before the shrine of memory —
A signature acknowledged — a rosy dot
Over the i of Loving.
Ibid.

In the volume whose sublime
Chapters are headed with proud capitals
You are the titles and you catch the eye.
L'Aiglon[2] [1900]. Act II

How do you know I am a diplomat?
By the skilful way you hide your claws.
Ibid. Act IV

My splendid cradle, Prudhon's masterpiece!
Amidst its gold and mother-o'-pearl I slept,
A babe, whose christening was a coronation.
Ibid. Act VI

---

[1] No man can justly censure or condemn another, because indeed no man truly knows another. . . . Further, no man can judge another, because no man knows himself. — SIR THOMAS BROWNE: *Religio Medici* (Everyman ed.), *P. 72*

[2] Translated from the Spanish by THOMAS WALSH [1875–1928].

[3] Translated by BRIAN HOOKER.

[1] See Edward A. Church, page 671.

[2] Translated by LOUIS N. PARKER.

I fall back dazzled at beholding myself
    all rosy red,
At having, I myself, caused the sun to
    rise.
    Chantecler [*1907*]. *Act II, Sc. 3*
And sounding in advance its victory,
My song jets forth so clear, so proud,
    so peremptory,
That the horizon, seized with a rosy
    trembling,
Obeys me.
                  Ibid.

ANDRÉ PAUL GUILLAUME GIDE
[1869–   ]

What another would have done as
well as you, do not do it. What another
would have said as well as you, do not
say it; written as well, do not write it.
Be faithful to that which exists nowhere but in yourself — and thus make
yourself indispensable.
    Les Nourritures Terrestres. Envoi

A unanimous chorus of praise is not
an assurance of survival; authors who
please everyone at once are quickly exhausted. I would prefer to think that a
hundred years hence people will say we
did not properly understand him [Ana-
tole France].
                Pretexts

NIKOLAI LENIN
[1870–1924]

Political institutions are a superstructure resting on an economic foundation.
    The Three Sources and Three
    Constituent Parts of Marxism [1]
    [*1913*]
Capital, created by the labour of the
worker, oppresses the worker by undermining the small proprietor and creating an army of the unemployed.
                Ibid.
Capital has conquered throughout
the world, but its victory is only an

[1] Translated by MAX EASTMAN.

earnest of the victory of labour over
capital.
    The Three Sources and Three
    Constituent Parts of Marxism
    [*1913*]
People always have been and they always will be stupid victims of deceit
and self-deception in politics, until
they learn behind every kind of moral,
religious, political, social phrase, declaration and promise to seek out the interests of this or that class or classes.
                Ibid.
It is true that liberty is precious —
so precious that it must be rationed.
    Quoted by SIDNEY AND BEA-
    TRICE WEBB *in Soviet Commu-*
    nism: a New Civilization? Page
    1035
Uneven economic and political development is an absolute law of capitalism. Hence, the victory of socialism is
possible, first in a few or even one single
capitalist country taken separately.
    Collected Works. Vol. XVIII,
                Page 272

MARCEL PROUST
[1871–1922]

(*From À la Recherche du temps
perdu, translated* [1] *as Remembrance
of Things Past, Random House edition*)

In his younger days a man dreams of
possessing the heart of the woman whom
he loves; later, the feeling that he possesses the heart of a woman may be
enough to make him fall in love with
her.
        Swann's Way. Page 253
What artists call posterity is the posterity of the work of art.
    Within a Budding Grove. Part I,
                Page 147
The time which we have at our disposal every day is elastic; the passions
that we feel expand it, those that we in-

[1] By C. K. SCOTT MONCRIEFF, except the last
section, *The Past Recaptured,* which was
translated by FREDERICK A. BLOSSOM.

spire contract it; and habit fills up what remains.

Within a Budding Grove. Part I, Page 264

Untruthfulness and dishonesty were with me, as with most people, called into being in so immediate, so contingent a fashion, and in self-defence, by some particular interest, that my mind, fixed on some lofty ideal, allowed my character, in the darkness below, to set about those urgent, sordid tasks, and did not look down to observe them.

The Guermantes Way. Part I, Page 82

Like everybody who is not in love, he imagined that one chose the person whom one loved after endless deliberations and on the strength of various qualities and advantages.

Cities of the Plain. Part I, Page 132

We passionately long that there may be another life in which we shall be similar to what we are here below. But we do not pause to reflect that, even without waiting for that other life, in this life, after a few years we are unfaithful to what we have been, to what we wished to remain immortally.

Ibid. Part II, Page 8

It is often simply from want of the creative spirit that we do not go to the full extent of suffering. And the most terrible reality brings us, with our suffering, the joy of a great discovery, because it merely gives a new and clear form to what we have long been ruminating without suspecting it.

Ibid. Page 363

The almost sacred character of all flesh upon which the sufferings that we have endured on its account have come in time to confer a sort of spiritual grace.

The Captive. Page 2

I thought how markedly . . . these works [Richard Wagner's music dramas] participate in that quality of being — albeit marvellously — always incomplete, which is the peculiarity of all the great works of the nineteenth century, with which the greatest writers of that century have stamped their books, but, watching themselves at work as though they were at once author and critic, have derived from this self-contemplation a novel beauty, exterior and superior to the work itself, imposing upon it retrospectively a unity, a greatness which it does not possess.

The Captive. Page 211

The bonds that unite another person to ourself exist only in our mind. Memory as it grows fainter relaxes them, and notwithstanding the illusion by which we would fain be cheated and with which, out of love, friendship, politeness, deference, duty, we cheat other people, we exist alone. Man is the creature that cannot emerge from himself, that knows his fellows only in himself; when he asserts the contrary, he is lying.

The Sweet Cheat Gone. Page 47

We believe that according to our desire we are able to change the things round about us, we believe this because otherwise we can see no favourable solution. We forget the solution that generally comes to pass and is also favourable: we do not succeed in changing things according to our desire, but gradually our desire changes. The situation that we hoped to change because it was intolerable becomes unimportant. We have not managed to surmount the obstacle, as we were absolutely determined to do, but life has taken us round it, led us past it, and then if we turn round to gaze at the remote past, we can barely catch sight of it, so imperceptible has it become.

Ibid. Page 48

There is not a woman in the world the possession of whom is as precious as that of the truths which she reveals to us by causing us to suffer.

Ibid. Page 111

We are healed of a suffering only by experiencing it to the full.

Ibid. Page 165

Happiness is beneficial for the body but it is grief that develops the powers of the mind.

The Past Recaptured. Page 237

As for happiness, it has hardly more than one useful quality, namely to make unhappiness possible. In our happiness, we should form very sweet bonds, full of confidence and attachment, in order that the sundering of them may cause us that priceless rending of the heart which is called unhappiness.

The Past Recaptured. Page 238

PAUL VALÉRY
[1871–   ]

[Of Anatole France.] A dreamy laziness, a laziness of enormous reading difficult to distinguish from study, a laziness like the repose of a fluid overrich with substance and which in its stillness begets crystals of perfect form.

Discours de Réception, at the French Academy [1927], where he succeeded to the chair of Anatole France

The folly of mistaking a paradox for a discovery, a metaphor for a proof, a torrent of verbiage for a spring of capital truths, and oneself for an oracle, is inborn in us.

Introduction to the Method of Leonardo da Vinci [1]

Collect all the facts that can be collected about the life of Racine and you will never learn from them the art of his verse. All criticism is dominated by the outworn theory that the man is the cause of the work as in the eyes of the law the criminal is the cause of the crime. Far rather are they both the effects.

Ibid.

PAUL RICHARD
[1874–   ]

The vagabond, when rich, is called a tourist.

The Scourge of Christ [1929]. Page 40

When the rich assemble to concern themselves with the business of the poor it is called charity. When the poor

assemble to concern themselves with the business of the rich it is called anarchy.

The Scourge of Christ [1929]. Page 63

Hunting — the least honourable form of war on the weak.

Ibid. Page 142

THOMAS MANN
[1875–   ]

Space, like time, engenders forgetfulness; but it does so by setting us bodily free from our surroundings and giving us back our primitive, unattached state. . . . Time, we say, is Lethe; but change of air is a simi'ar draught, and, if it works less thoroughly, does so more quickly.

The Magic Mountain. [1] *Chap. 1*

A man lives not only his personal life, as an individual, but also, consciously or unconsciously, the life of his epoch and his contemporaries.

Ibid. Chap. 2

It gives me a most peculiar feeling, when somebody is so stupid, and then ill into the bargain. It must be the most melancholy thing in life. . . . One always has the idea of a stupid man as perfectly healthy and ordinary, and of illness as making one refined and clever and unusual.

Ibid. Chap. 4

The solemn, discreet, almost overawed bearing which the young German's respect for authority leads him to assume in the presence of pens, ink, and paper, or anything else which bears to his mind an official stamp.

Ibid.

I have the feeling that once I am at home again I shall need to sleep three weeks on end to get rested from the rest I've had!

Ibid.

The only religious way to think of death is as part and parcel of life; to regard it, with the understanding and

---

[1] Translated by Thomas McGreevy.

[1] Translated by H. T. Lowe-Porter. Modern Library edition.

the emotions, as the inviolable condition of life.

The Magic Mountain. Chap. 5

Time has no divisions to mark its passage, there is never a thunder-storm or blare of trumpets to announce the beginning of a new month or year. Even when a new century begins it is only we mortals who ring bells and fire off pistols.

Ibid.

Order and simplification are the first steps toward the mastery of a subject — the actual enemy is the unknown.

Ibid.

The proud embarrassment of the artist, tasting the enjoyment of looking on his own works with the eyes of strangers.

Ibid.

Human reason needs only to will more strongly than fate, and she *is* fate.

Ibid. Chap. 6

Opinions cannot survive if one has no chance to fight for them.

Ibid.

Chop-fallen funeral processions, with their dignity curtailed by present-day traffic conditions.

Ibid.

One quickly gets readiness in an art where strong desire comes in play.

Ibid.

All interest in disease and death is only another expression of interest in life, as is proven by the humanistic faculty of medicine, that addresses life and its ails always so politely in Latin, and is only a division of the great and pressing concern which, in all sympathy, I now name by its name: the human being, the delicate child of life, man.

Ibid.

What perplexes the world is the disparity between the swiftness of the spirit, and the immense unwieldiness, sluggishness, inertia, permanence of matter.

Ibid.

The invention of printing and the Reformation are and remain the two outstanding services of central Europe to the cause of humanity.

The Magic Mountain. Chap. 6

Speech is civilization itself. The word, even the most contradictory word, preserves contact — it is silence which isolates.

Ibid.

A man's dying is more the survivors' affair than his own.

Ibid.

What we call mourning for our dead is perhaps not so much grief at not being able to call them back as it is grief at not being able to want to do so.

Ibid. Chap. 7

Time cools, time clarifies; no mood can be maintained quite unaltered through the course of hours.

Ibid.

Seven is a good handy figure in its way, picturesque, with a savour of the mythical; one might say that it is more filling to the spirit than a dull academic half-dozen.

Ibid.

RAINER MARIA RILKE
[1875–1926]

Her smile was not meant to be seen by anyone and served its whole purpose in being smiled.

The Journal of My Other Self [1]

He was a poet and hated the approximate.

Ibid.

Is it possible that nothing real or important has yet been seen or known or said? Is it possible that mankind has had thousands of years in which to observe, reflect, and record, and has allowed these millennia to slip past, like a recess interval at school in which one eats one's sandwich and an apple?

Yes, it is possible.

Is it possible that every individual has had to be reminded that he is indeed sprung from all those who have gone before, that he has known this and

[1] Translated [1930] by JOHN LINTON.

ought not to have been persuaded differently by others?

Yes, it is possible.

The Journal of My Other Self

Love consists in this, that two solitudes protect and touch and greet each other.

Letters to a Young Poet [1]

The future enters into us, in order to transform itself in us, long before it happens.

Ibid.

ALEXANDER BISSON
[*Floruit* 1900]

Our life is like some vast lake that is slowly filling with the stream of our years. As the waters creep surely upward the landmarks of the past are one by one submerged. But there shall always be memory to lift its head above the tide until the lake is overflowing.

Madame X [2]

BENITO MUSSOLINI
[1883–   ]

Italians, love bread, heart of the home,
    savor of the repast, joy of health;
Respect bread, sweat of the brow, pride
    of labor, poem of sacrifice;
Honor bread, glory of the fields, fragrance of the earth, feast of life;
Do not waste bread, richness of the
    fatherland, sweetest gift of God,
    most holy reward of human toil.

Proclamation [*April 14–15, 1928*]

Speeches made to the people are essential to the arousing of enthusiasm for a war.

Quoted by EMIL LUDWIG *in Talks
    with Mussolini* [*1932*]

Ludwig. How do you find it possible to put up with the multitude of faces you have to look at here day after day?

Mussolini. I merely see in them what they say to me. I do not let them come into contact with my inmost being. I am no more moved by them than by

this table and these papers. I preserve my loneliness untouched.

*Quoted by Emil Ludwig in Talks
    with Mussolini* [*1932*]

War alone brings up to its highest tension all human energy and puts the stamp of nobility upon the peoples who have the courage to face it.

*Written for The Italian
    Encyclopedia* [1]

Three cheers for war in general!

Speech [1]

Fortunately the Italian people is not yet accustomed to eating several times per day.

Speech [*December, 1930*] [1]

We have buried the putrid corpse of liberty.

Speech [2]

FRANZ KAFKA
[1884–1924]

The true way goes over a rope which is not stretched at any great height but just above the ground. It seems more designed to make people stumble than to be walked upon.

The Great Wall of China. [3]
Reflections

You do not need to leave your room. Remain sitting at your table and listen. Do not even listen, simply wait. Do not even wait, be quite still and solitary. The world will freely offer itself to you to be unmasked, it has no choice, it will roll in ecstasy at your feet.

Ibid.

ADOLF HITLER
[1889–   ]

Then will come a National-Socialist State tribunal; then will November, 1918, be expiated; then heads will roll!

*Spoken in testimony at a trial of
    German army officers, in Leipzig
    [1930]* [4]

[1] Translated [1934] by M. D. HERTER NORTON.
[2] Translated by J. W. McCONAUGHY.
[3] Translated by MR. and MRS. EDWIN MUIR.
[4] Quoted in KONRAD HEIDEN: *Hitler, A Biography* [1936].

[1] Quoted in GEORGE SELDES: *Sawdust Caesar.*
[2] Quoted in MAURICE PARMELEE: *Bolshevism, Fascism and the Liberal-Democratic State.*

BARON EHRENFRIED GUNTHER VON HUENEFELD
[1893–1929]

To-morrow, we shall start on our great journey. After a trying period of expectancy, we have entered upon the stage of certainty. Now the last word lies with the God of weathers and to confide in Him is the duty of every sincere sportsman.

> *Interview, before his transatlantic air flight in the Bremen [April 12–13, 1928]*

Silent I ponder. Ended is the flight,
And He whose hands upheld us in the air,
Whose grace has calmed the snowstorm and the night,
Is now with me and folds my hands in prayer.

> *Song of Thanks in the Lighthouse at Greenly, after the safe landing of the Bremen*

He who has glimpsed the awful face of Death
Can but confess Thy mercy and Thy might;
Who never bowed his heart before Thy cross,
He never saw the unadulterate Light.

> *Ibid.*

MISCELLANEOUS TRANSLATIONS

Arbor viva, tacui; mortua, cano
(When I was part of a living tree, I was
silent; now dead, I sing).

> *Inscription found on an old violin* [1]

A shipwrecked sailor, buried on this
    coast,
    Bids thee take sail —
Full many a gallant ship, when we were
    lost,
    Weathered the gale.[2]

> *Palatine Anthology. VII, 283,*
> *Theodoridas* [3]

Dansons la Carmagnole,
Vive le son du canon!

> *La Carmagnole* [*France, 1792*]

Dead on the field of honour.

> *From the death of Latour d'Au-*
> *vergne at Oberhausen, Bavaria*
> [*June 27, 1800*] *until 1814, his*
> *name was retained on the roll of*
> *his company of grenadiers, as a*
> *mark of honour. At each roll-*
> *call the color-sergeant made this*
> *response.*

Death is never at a loss for occasions.

> *Greek Anthology. Book IX, 488,*
> *Trypho*

Dum tacent, clamant (Though silent,
they cry aloud).

> *Inscription on a monument,*
> *Union Soldiers' Cemetery, Chal-*
> *mette, near New Orleans, Lou-*
> *isiana*

Ea discamus in terris quorum scientia
perseveret in caelis (Let us learn on
earth those things whose knowledge
might continue in heaven).

> *Motto of Saint Paul's School,*
> *Concord, New Hampshire*

Laissez faire, laissez aller (Let it be,
let it go; viz., let nature take its course).

> *Attributed to* BOISGUILBERT
> [*1646–1714*], *also to* GOURNAY,
> *Minister of Commerce at Paris*
> [*1751*], *and to* QUESNAY, *writer*
> *on political economy. Quoted by*
> ADAM SMITH *in The Wealth of*
> *Nations*

Mater ait natae, dic natae, natam
Ut moneat natae, plangere filiolam.
(The mother says to her daughter:
"Tell your daughter that she advise her
    daughter
That her daughter is crying.")

> *A distich, according to Zwingler,*
> *on a lady of the Dalburg family*
> *who saw her descendants to the*
> *sixth generation*

Medicine for the soul.

> *Inscription over the door of the*
> *Library at Thebes. —* DIODORUS
> SICULUS [*second half of first*
> *century*]: *I, 49, 3*

Never believe the impossible,
Never regret the past,
Do not long for the unattainable.

> *Aucassin and Nicolette* [*13th cen-*
> *tury*]. *Le Lai de l'Oiselet*

Nothing is changed in France; there
is only one Frenchman more.

> *According to the Contemporary*
> *Review* [*February, 1854*] *this*
> *sentence formed the opening of*
> *an address written in the name*
> *of the Comte d'Artois by Count*
> *Beugnot, and published in the*
> *Moniteur* [*April 12, 1814*]

Terrible he rode alone,
    With his Yemen sword for aid;

---

[1] Oh all you safe and smooth of heart
    Listen to song from me,
  Whose wooden throat was once a part
    Of the north side of a tree!
        WINIFRED WELLES: *The Violin*

[2] Tomb of a shipwrecked seafarer am I;
    But thou, sail on!
  For homeward safe did other vessels fly,
    Though we were gone.
      ANDREW LANG [*1844–1912*]: *The*
        Sailor's Grave (from the Greek)

[3] Translated by HENRY WELLESLEY [*1791–*
1866].

Ornament it carried none
But the notches on the blade.
> *The Death Feud, an Arab War
> Song, of an age earlier than that
> of Mahomet. Anonymous trans-
> lation from Tait's Magazine
> [July, 1850]*

The world is merely a bridge; ye are
to pass over it, and not to build your
dwellings upon it.
> *Inscription on the Victory
> Gate, Fathepur, India. From
> Agrapha, Unwritten Sayings
> of Jesus*

Thou who passest on this path,
If haply thou dost mark this monu-
ment,
Laugh not, I pray thee, though it is a
dog's grave.
Tears fell for me, and the dust was
heaped above me
By a master's hand.
> *Greek Anthology. Epitaph (of un-
> known authorship)*

Whatever kind of word thou speakest
the like shalt thou hear.
> *Ibid. Book IX, 382
> A Homeric Cento*

When I am dead let fire destroy the
world;
It matters not to me, for I am safe.
> *Ibid. Fragment 430 (of unknown
> authorship)*

Toil does not come to help the idle.
> *Greek Anthology. Fragment 440
> (of unknown authorship)*

Nothing equals the joy of the drinker,
except the joy of the wine in being
drunk.
> *Anonymous. Quoted by* Mau-
> rice des Ombiaux: *Nouveau
> Manuel de l'Amateur de Bour-
> goyne [1921]*

In the U.S.S.R. work is the duty of
every able-bodied citizen, according to
the principle: "He who does not work,
neither shall he eat."

In the U.S.S.R. the principle of socialism is realised: "From each according to his ability, to each according to
his work." [1]
> *Constitution of the Union
> of Soviet Socialist Republics
> [1936]. Article 12*

Citizens of the U.S.S.R. have the
right to work.
> *Ibid. Article 118*

Citizens of the U.S.S.R. have the
right to rest.
> *Ibid. Article 119*

Citizens of the U.S.S.R. have the
right to maintenance in old age.
> *Ibid. Article 120*

Citizens of the U.S.S.R. have the
right to education.
> *Ibid. Article 121*

---

[1] See Karl Marx, page 1071.

THOMAS RUSSELL

The great Jehovah speaks to us
In Genesis and Exodus;
Leviticus and Numbers see,
Followed by Deuteronomy.
Joshua and Judges sway the land,
Ruth gleans a sheaf with trembling hand,
Samuel and numerous Kings appear,
Whose Chronicles we wondering hear;
Ezra and Nehemiah now
Esther, the beauteous mourner, show;
Job speaks in sighs, David in Psalms,
The Proverbs teach to scatter alms.
Ecclesiastes then comes on
And the sweet Song of Solomon.
Isaiah, Jeremiah then,
With Lamentations takes his pen.
Ezekiel, Daniel, Hosea's lyres
Swell Joel, Amos, Obadiah's.
Next Jonah, Micah, Nahum come,
And lofty Habakkuk finds room.
While Zephaniah, Haggai call,
Rapt Zechariah builds his wall,
And Malachi with garments rent,
Concludes the ancient Testament.

*Old Testament. (American Tract
Society, 1852)*

Matthew and Mark, and Luke and John,
The Holy Gospels wrote,
Describing how the Saviour died —
His life — and all He taught;
Acts prove how God the Apostles owned
With signs in every place;
St. Paul, in Romans, teaches us
How man is saved by grace;
The Apostle, in Corinthians,
Instructs, exhorts, reproves;
Galatians shows that faith in Christ

Alone the Father loves.
Ephesians and Philippians tell
What Christians ought to be;
Colossians bids us live to God
And for eternity.
In Thessalonians we are taught
The Lord will come from Heaven;
In Timothy and Titus
A bishop's rule is given.
Philemon marks a Christian's love,
Which only Christians know;
Hebrews reveals the Gospel
Prefigured by the law;
James teaches without holiness
Faith is but vain and dead;
St. Peter points the narrow way
In which the saints are led;
John, in his three Epistles,
On love delights to dwell;
St. Jude gives awful warning
Of judgment, wrath, and hell;
The Revelation prophesies
Of that tremendous day
When Christ, and Christ alone, shall be
The trembling sinner's stay.

*New Testament. (American Tract
Society, 1852)*

These are the twelve Apostles' names:
Peter and Andrew, John and James,
Two pair of brothers who lived by the sea,
When Jesus said to them, "Follow me."
Then James the Less and Jude were called,
   too,
Philip, and also Bartholomew,
Matthew, and Thomas who doubted His word,
Simon, and Judas who sold his Lord.

ANONYMOUS: *The Apostles*

THE KING JAMES BIBLE [1]

OLD TESTAMENT

And God said, Let there be light: and there was light.

Genesis. I, 3

It is not good that the man should be alone.

Ibid. II, 18

Bone of my bones, and flesh of my flesh.

Ibid. 23

They sewed fig-leaves together, and made themselves aprons.

Ibid. III, 7

In the sweat of thy face shalt thou eat bread.

Ibid. 19

For dust thou art, and unto dust shalt thou return.

Ibid.

The mother of all living.

Ibid. 20

Am I my brother's keeper?

Ibid. IV, 9

My punishment is greater than I can bear.

Ibid. 13

And the Lord set a mark upon Cain.

Ibid. 15

Jubal: he was the father of all such as handle the harp and organ.

Ibid. 21

And all the days of Methuselah were nine hundred and sixty years.

Ibid. V, 27

There were giants in the earth in those days.

Ibid. VI, 4

[1] Among all our joys, there was no one that more filled our hearts, than the blessed continuance of the preaching of God's sacred Word among us; which is that inestimable treasure, which excelleth all the riches of the earth; because the fruit thereof extendeth itself, not only to the time spent in this transitory world, but directeth and disposeth men unto that eternal happiness which is above in heaven. — THE TRANSLATORS

And the rain was upon the earth forty days and forty nights.

Genesis. VII, 12

The dove found no rest for the sole of her foot.

Ibid. VIII, 9

In her mouth was an olive leaf.

Ibid. 11

While the earth remaineth, seedtime and harvest, and cold and heat, and summer and winter, and day and night shall not cease.

Ibid. 22

Whoso sheddeth man's blood, by man shall his blood be shed.

Ibid. IX, 6

I do set my bow in the cloud.

Ibid. 13

Nimrod the mighty hunter.

Ibid. X, 9

Babel; because the Lord did there confound the language of all the earth.

Ibid. XI, 9

Let there be no strife, I pray thee, between me and thee.

Ibid. XIII, 8

In a good old age.

Ibid. XV, 15

His [Ishmael's] hand will be against every man, and every man's hand against him.

Ibid. XVI, 12

Old and well stricken in age.

Ibid. XVIII, 11

His [Lot's] wife looked back from behind him, and she became a pillar of salt.[1]

Ibid. XIX, 26

The voice is Jacob's voice, but the hands are the hands of Esau.

Ibid. XXVII, 22

[1] Of all Metamorphoses or transmigrations. I believe only one, that is of Lot's wife. — SIR THOMAS BROWNE: *Religio Medici* (Everyman ed.), *P. 42*

He [Jacob] dreamed, and behold a ladder set up on the earth, and the top of it reached to heaven: and behold the angels of the Lord ascending and descending it.

Genesis. XXVIII, 22

Jacob served seven years for Rachel.

Ibid. XXIX, 20

Mizpah . . . The Lord watch between me and thee, when we are absent one from another.

Ibid. XXXI, 49

I will not let thee go, except thou bless me.

Ibid. XXXII, 26

They stript Joseph out of his coat, his coat of many colours.

Ibid. XXXVII, 23

He left his garment in her hand, and fled.

Ibid. XXXIX, 12

There come seven years of great plenty throughout all the land of Egypt: And there shall arise after them seven years of famine.

Ibid. XLI, 29, 30

Bring down my gray hairs with sorrow to the grave.

Ibid. XLII, 38, and XLIV, 29

His life is bound up in the lad's life.

Ibid. XLIV, 30

Unstable as water, thou shalt not excel.

Ibid. XLIX, 4

I have been a stranger in a strange land.

Exodus. II, 22

Put off thy shoes from off thy feet, for the place whereon thou standest is holy ground.

Ibid. III, 5

A land flowing with milk and honey.[1]

Ibid. 8, and XXXIII, 3

I am slow of speech, and of a slow tongue.

Ibid. IV, 10

Ye shall no more give the people straw to make brick.

Ibid. V, 7

Darkness which may be felt.

Ibid. X, 21

[1] Also in *Jeremiah, XI, 5,* and *XXXIII, 22.*

This day [passover] shall be unto you for a memorial; and ye shall keep it a feast to the Lord throughout your generations.

Exodus. XII, 14

There was not a house where there was not one dead.[1]

Ibid. 30

The Lord went before them by day in a pillar of a cloud, to lead them the way; and by night in a pillar of fire.

Ibid. XIII, 21

They could not drink of the waters of Marah, for they were bitter.

Ibid. XV, 23

When we sat by the fleshpots.

Ibid. XVI, 3

It is manna.

Ibid. 15

Honour thy father and thy mother.[2]

Ibid. XX, 12

Eye for eye, tooth for tooth, hand for hand, foot for foot.[3]

Ibid. XXI, 24

I send an Angel before thee, to keep thee in the way.[4]

Ibid. XXIII, 20

He wrote upon the tables the words of the covenant, the ten commandments.

Ibid. XXXIV, 28

The swine . . . is unclean to you. Of their flesh shall ye not eat.

Leviticus. XI, 7, 8

[1] See John Hay, page 639.
[2] Also in *Apocrypha, Ecclesiasticus, III, 8.*

Have no other gods but me;
Unto no image bow the knee;
Take not the name of God in vain;
Do not the Sabbath day profane;
Honour thy father and thy mother too;
And see that thou no murder do;
From vile adultery keep thou clean;
And steal not, though thy state be mean;
Bear not false witness — shun that blot;
What is thy neighbour's covet not.
   The Decalogue. Found in Parish Register, Lancaster, Nottinghamshire, England, 1689.

[3] Also in *Deuteronomy, XIX, 21.*
[4] I could easily believe that not only whole countries, but particular persons, have their Tutelary and Guardian Angels. — SIR THOMAS BROWNE: *Religio Medici* (Everyman ed.), P. 36

Love thy neighbour as thyself.
Leviticus. XIX, 18

The Lord bless thee, and keep thee: The Lord make his face shine upon thee, and be gracious unto thee: The Lord lift up his countenance upon thee,[1] and give thee peace.
Numbers. VI, 24, 25, 26

The Lord opened the mouth of the ass, and she said unto Balaam, What have I done unto thee, that thou hast smitten me these three times?
Ibid. XXII, 28

Let me die the death of the righteous, and let my last end be like his!
Ibid. XXIII, 10

How goodly are thy tents, O Jacob, and thy tabernacles, O Israel!
Ibid. XXIV, 5

Man doth not live by bread only.[2]
Deuteronomy. VIII, 3

The wife of thy bosom.
Ibid. XIII, 6

The poor shall never cease out of the land.
Ibid. XV, 11

In the morning thou shalt say, Would God it were even! and at even thou shalt say, Would God it were morning! [3]
Ibid. XXVIII, 67

Be strong and of a good courage.[4]
Ibid. XXXI, 6, 7, 23

He kept him as the apple of his eye.[5]
Ibid. XXXII, 10

Jeshurun waxed fat, and kicked.
Ibid. 15

As thy days, so shall thy strength be.
Ibid. XXXIII, 25

Underneath are the everlasting arms.
Ibid. 27

The wall of the city shall fall down flat.
Joshua. VI, 5

His fame was noised throughout all the country.
Ibid. 27

The sun stood still, and the moon stayed.
Joshua. X, 13

I am going the way of all the earth.
Ibid. XXIII, 14

I arose a mother in Israel.
Judges. V, 7

The stars in their courses fought against Sisera.
Ibid. 20

At her feet he bowed, he fell, he lay down: at her feet he bowed, he fell: where he bowed, there he fell down dead.[1]
Ibid. 27

Why tarry the wheels of his chariots?
Ibid. 28

Is not the gleaning of the grapes of Ephraim better than the vintage of Abi-ezer?
Ibid. VIII, 2

There was a swarm of bees and honey in the carcase of the lion.
Ibid. XIV, 8

He smote them hip and thigh.
Ibid. XV, 8

With the jaw of an ass have I slain a thousand men.
Ibid. 16

And Delilah said to Samson, Tell me, I pray thee, wherein thy great strength lieth.
Ibid. XVI, 6

The Philistines be upon thee, Samson.
Ibid. 9

So the dead which he slew at his death were more than they which he slew in his life.
Ibid. 30

From Dan even to Beer-sheba.
Ibid. XX, 1

The people arose as one man.
Ibid. 8

Whither thou goest, I will go; and where thou lodgest, I will lodge: thy people shall be my people, and thy God my God.
Ruth. I, 16

---

[1] Lift thou up the light of thy countenance upon us. — *Psalm IV, 6*
[2] Also in *Matthew, IV, 4.*
[3] See Swinburne, page 632.
[4] Also in *Joshua, I, 6* and *X, 25.*
[5] See Cervantes, page 1040. See page 1103.

[1] Such repetitions [in this verse from the Song of Deborah] I admit to be a beauty of the highest kind. — COLERIDGE: *Biographia Literaria, Chap. 17*

Let me glean and gather after the reapers among the sheaves.

Ruth. II, 7

Go not empty unto thy mother in law.

Ibid. III, 17

The Lord called Samuel; and he answered, Here am I.

1 Samuel. III, 4

Speak, Lord; for thy servant heareth.

Ibid. 9

Quit yourselves like men.

Ibid. IV, 9

The glory is departed from Israel.

Ibid. 21

Is Saul also among the prophets?

Ibid. X, 11

And all the people shouted, and said, God save the king.

Ibid. 24

A man after his own heart.

Ibid. XIII, 14

Now there was no smith found throughout all the land of Israel.

Ibid. 19

So David prevailed over the Philistine with a sling and with a stone.[1]

Ibid. XVII, 50

Saul hath slain his thousands, and David his ten thousands.

*Ibid. XVIII, 7; XXI, 11;
XXIX, 5*

For he loved him as he loved his own soul.

Ibid. XX, 17

David therefore departed thence, and escaped to the cave Adullam.

Ibid. XXII, 1

And every one that was in distress, and every one that was in debt, and every one that was discontented, gathered themselves unto him; and he became a captain over them.

Ibid. 2

Tell it not in Gath, publish it not in the streets of Askelon.

2 Samuel. I, 20

Saul and Jonathan were lovely and pleasant in their lives, and in their death they were not divided.

2 Samuel. I, 23

How are the mighty fallen!

Ibid. 25, 27

Thy love to me was wonderful, passing the love of women.

Ibid. 26

Abner . . . smote him under the fifth rib.

Ibid. II, 23

Know ye not that there is a prince and a great man fallen this day in Israel?

Ibid. III, 38

Tarry at Jericho until your beards be grown.[1]

Ibid. X, 5

Set ye Uriah in the forefront of the hottest battle.

Ibid. XI, 15

Thou art the man.

Ibid. XII, 7

I shall go to him, but he shall not return to me.[2]

Ibid. 23

As water spilt on the ground, which cannot be gathered up again.

Ibid. XIV, 14

Would God I had died for thee, O Absalom, my son, my son!

Ibid. XVIII, 33

They were wont to speak in old time, saying, They shall surely ask counsel at Abel: and so they ended the matter.

Ibid. XX, 18

The Lord is my rock, and my fortress, and my deliverer.

Ibid. XXII, 2

The sweet psalmist of Israel.

Ibid. XXIII, 1

Oh, that one would give me to drink of the water of the well of Beth-lehem, which is by the gate!

Ibid. 15

A wise and an understanding heart.

1 Kings. III, 12

---

[1] A boy with the heart of a king
Fitted the stone to his shepherd sling,
And a giant fell, and a royal race was free.
EDWARD ROWLAND SILL: *Field Notes, VII*

[1] Also in *1 Chronicles, XIX, 5.*
[2] With a change of pronouns, Lord Byron asked to have this line inscribed on the gravestone of his daughter, Allegra. — In a letter to Murray [May 26, 1822].

Many as the sand which is by the sea in multitude.

1 Kings. IV, 20

He [Solomon] spake three thousand proverbs: and his songs were a thousand and five.

Ibid. 32

So that there was neither hammer nor axe nor any tool of iron heard in the house, while it was in building.[1]

Ibid. VI, 7

A proverb and a byword.[2]

Ibid. IX, 7

The half was not told me.

Ibid. X, 7

Once in three years came the navy of Tharshish, bringing gold and silver, ivory, and apes, and peacocks.[3]

Ibid. 22

King Solomon loved many strange women.[4]

Ibid. XI, 1

I have commanded a widow woman there to sustain thee.

Ibid. XVII, 9

An handful of meal in a barrel, and a little oil in a cruse.

Ibid. 12

And the barrel of meal wasted not, neither did the cruse of oil fail.

Ibid. 16

How long halt ye between two opinions?

Ibid. XVIII, 21

There ariseth a little cloud out of the sea, like a man's hand.

Ibid. 44

A still, small voice.

Ibid. XIX, 12

Let not him that girdeth on his harness boast himself as he that putteth it off.

Ibid. XX, 11

Busy here and there.

Ibid. 40

Hast thou found me, O mine enemy?

Ibid. XXI, 20

Is it well with the child?

2 Kings. IV, 26

Death in the pot.

2 Kings. IV, 40

Are not Abana and Pharpar, rivers of Damascus, better than all the waters of Israel?

Ibid. V, 12

Is not the sound of his master's feet behind him?

Ibid. VI, 32

Is thy servant a dog, that he should do this great thing?

Ibid. VIII, 13

Like the driving of Jehu, the son of Nimshi; for he driveth furiously.

Ibid. IX, 20

Jezebel heard of it; and she painted her face, and tired her head, and looked out at a window.

Ibid. 30

A land of corn and wine.

Ibid. XVIII, 32

Set thine house in order.

Ibid. XX, 1

Our days on the earth are as a shadow.[1]

1 Chronicles. XXIX, 15

The man whom the king delighteth to honour.

Esther. VI, 6

One that feared God, and eschewed evil.

Job. I, 1

Satan came also.

Ibid. 6

The Lord gave, and the Lord hath taken away; blessed be the name of the Lord.

Ibid. 21

All that a man hath, will he give for his life.[2]

Ibid. II, 4

There the wicked cease from troubling, and there the weary be at rest.

Ibid. III, 17

Night, when deep sleep falleth on men.

Ibid. IV, 13; XXXIII, 15

---

[1] See Cowper, page 266.
[2] Also in *2 Chronicles, VII, 20*.
[3] See Masefield, page 832.
[4] See Naylor, page 754.

---

[1] Also in *Job, VIII, 9*.
[2] Satan's old saw being apt here — skin for skin,
All a man hath that will he give for life.
ROBERT BROWNING: *The Ring and the Book, Book I*

Man is born unto trouble, as the sparks fly upward.

Job. V, 7

He taketh the wise in their own craftiness.

Ibid. 13

Thou shalt come to thy grave in a full age, like as a shock of corn cometh in in his season.

Ibid. 26

How forcible are right words!

Ibid. VI, 25

My days are swifter than a weaver's shuttle.

Ibid. VII, 6

He shall return no more to his house, neither shall his place know him any more.[1]

Ibid. 10

I would not live alway.

Ibid. 16

The land of darkness and the shadow of death.

Ibid. X, 21

Canst thou by searching find out God?

Ibid. XI, 7

Clearer than the noonday.

Ibid. 17

No doubt but ye are the people.[2]

Ibid. XII, 2

Wisdom shall die with you.

Ibid.

Speak to the earth, and it shall teach thee.

Ibid. 8

Man that is born of a woman is of few days, and full of trouble.

Ibid. XIV, 1

If a man die, shall he live again?

Ibid. 14

Miserable comforters are ye all.

Ibid. XVI, 2

The king of terrors.

Ibid. XVIII, 14

[1] When a few years are come, then I shall go the way whence I shall not return. — *Job, XVI, 22*

The place thereof shall know it no more. — *Psalm CIII, 16*

[2] No doubt but ye are the People — your throne is above the King's.

KIPLING: *The Islanders*

I am escaped with the skin of my teeth.

Job. XIX, 20

Oh that my words were now written! oh that they were printed in a book!

Ibid. 23

Seeing the root of the matter is found in me.

Ibid. 28

Though wickedness be sweet in his mouth, though he hide it under his tongue.

Ibid. XX, 12

The land of the living.

Ibid. XXVIII, 13

The price of wisdom is above rubies.

Ibid. 18

When the ear heard me, then it blessed me; and when the eye saw me, it gave witness to me.

Ibid. XXIX, 11

I caused the widow's heart to sing for joy.

Ibid. 13

I was eyes to the blind, and feet was I to the lame.

Ibid. 15

The house appointed for all living.

Ibid. XXX, 23

Companion to owls.

Ibid. 29

My desire is . . . that mine adversary had written a book.

Ibid. XXXI, 35

Great men are not always wise.

Ibid. XXXII, 9

He multiplieth words without knowledge.

Ibid. XXXV, 16

Fair weather cometh out of the north.

Ibid. XXXVII, 22

Who is this that darkeneth counsel by words without knowledge?

Ibid. XXXVIII, 2

The morning stars sang together, and all the sons of God shouted for joy.

Ibid. 7

Hitherto shalt thou come, but no further; and here shall thy proud waves be stayed.

Ibid. 11

Canst thou bind the sweet influences of Pleiades, or loose the bands of Orion?
Job. XXXVII, 31

Canst thou guide Arcturus with his sons?
Ibid. 32

He smelleth the battle afar off.
Ibid. XXXIX, 25

Hard as a piece of the nether millstone.
Ibid. XLI, 24

He maketh the deep to boil like a pot.
Ibid. 31

I have heard of thee by the hearing of the ear; but now mine eye seeth thee.
Ibid. XLII, 5

His leaf also shall not wither.
Psalms. I, 3

I will both lay me down in peace, and sleep.[1]
Ibid. IV, 8

Out of the mouth of babes and sucklings.
Ibid. VIII, 2

When I consider thy heavens.
Ibid. 3

What is man, that thou art mindful of him.
Ibid. 4

Thou hast made him a little lower than the angels.
Ibid. 5

Flee as a bird to your mountain.
Ibid. XI, 1

The fool hath said in his heart, There is no God.
Ibid. XIV, 1; LIII, 1

He that sweareth to his own hurt, and changeth not.
Ibid. XV, 4

The lines are fallen unto me in pleasant places; [2] yea, I have a goodly heritage.
Ibid. XVI, 6

Keep me as the apple of the eye, hide me under the shadow of thy wings.
Ibid. XVII, 8

The sorrows of death compassed me.
Ibid. XVIII, 4

[1] I will lay me down in peace, and take my rest. — *Book of Common Prayer*
[2] The lot is fallen unto me in a fair ground. — *Ibid.*

He rode upon a cherub, and did fly: yea, he did fly upon the wings of the wind.
Psalms. XVIII, 10

The heavens declare the glory of God; and the firmament showeth his handiwork.
Ibid. XIX, 1

Day unto day uttereth speech, and night unto night showeth knowledge.
Ibid. 2

And there is nothing hid from the heat thereof.
Ibid. 6

More to be desired are they than gold.
Ibid. 10

Sweeter also than honey and the honeycomb.
Ibid.

Cleanse thou me from secret faults.
Ibid. 12

Let the words of my mouth, and the meditation of my heart, be acceptable in thy sight.
Ibid. 14

I may tell all my bones.
Ibid. XXII, 17

He maketh me to lie down in green pastures: he leadeth me beside the still waters.
Ibid. XXIII, 2

The valley of the shadow of death.
Ibid. 4

Thy rod and thy staff they comfort me.
Ibid.

My cup runneth over.
Ibid. 5

Weeping may endure for a night, but joy cometh in the morning.
Ibid. XXX, 5

My times are in thy hand.
Ibid. XXXI, 15

From the strife of tongues.
Ibid. 20

He fashioneth their hearts alike.
Ibid. XXXIII, 15

Keep thy tongue from evil, and thy lips from speaking guile.
Ibid. XXXIV, 13

I have been young, and now am old; yet have I not seen the righteous forsaken, nor his seed begging bread.

Psalms. XXXVII, 25

Spreading [1] himself like a green bay-tree.

Ibid. 35

Mark the perfect man, and behold the upright.

Ibid. 37

While I was musing the fire burned.

Ibid. XXXIX, 3

Lord, make me to know mine end, and the measure of my days, what it is; that I may know how frail I am.

Ibid. 4

Every man at his best state is altogether vanity.

Ibid. 5

He heapeth up riches, and knoweth not who shall gather them.

Ibid. 6

Blessed is he that considereth the poor.

Ibid. XLI, 1

As the hart panteth after the water-brooks.

Ibid. XLII, 1

Deep calleth unto deep.

Ibid. 7

My tongue is the pen of a ready writer.

Ibid. XLV, 1

God is our refuge and strength, a very present help in trouble.

Ibid. XLVI, 1

Beautiful for situation, the joy of the whole earth, is Mount Zion, . . . the city of the great King.

Ibid. XLVIII, 2

Man being in honour abideth not; he is like the beasts that perish.

Ibid. XLIX, 12, 20

The cattle upon a thousand hills.

Ibid. L, 10

Wash me, and I shall be whiter than snow.

Ibid. LI, 7

Create in me a clean heart, O God; and renew a right spirit within me.

Ibid. 10

A broken and a contrite heart.

Psalms. LI, 17

Oh that I had wings like a dove!

Ibid. LV, 6

But it was thou, a man mine equal, my guide, and mine acquaintance.[1]

Ibid. 13

We took sweet counsel together.

Ibid. 14

The words of his mouth were smoother than butter, but war was in his heart.[2]

Ibid. 21

They are like the deaf adder that stoppeth her ear; which will not hearken to the voice of charmers, charming never so wisely.[3]

Ibid. LVIII, 4, 5

Vain is the help of man.

Ibid. LX, 11; CVIII, 12

Lead me to the rock that is higher than I.

Ibid. LXI, 2

Surely men of low degree are vanity, and men of high degree are a lie: to be laid in the balance, they are altogether lighter than vanity.

Ibid. LXII, 9

Thou renderest to every man according to his work.

Ibid. 12

Thou crownest the year with thy goodness.

Ibid. LXV, 11

We went through fire and through water.

Ibid. LXVI, 12

God setteth the solitary in families.

Ibid. LXVIII, 6

He shall come down like rain upon the mown grass.

Ibid. LXXII, 6

His enemies shall lick the dust.

Ibid. 9

---

[1] Flourishing. — *Book of Common Prayer*

[1] But it was even thou, my companion, my guide, and mine own familiar friend. — *Book of Common Prayer*. See note, page 1128.
Mine own familiar friend. — *Psalm XLI, 9*
[2] The words of his mouth were softer than butter, having war in his heart. — *Book of Common Prayer*
[3] Like the deaf adder, that stoppeth her ears; which refuseth to hear the voice of the charmer, charm he never so wisely. — *Ibid.*

As a dream when one awaketh.
Psalms. LXXIII, 20

Promotion cometh neither from the east, nor from the west, nor from the south.
Ibid. LXXV, 6

He putteth down one and setteth up another.
Ibid. 7

They go from strength to strength.
Ibid. LXXXIV, 7

A day in thy courts is better than a thousand. I had rather be a door-keeper in the house of my God, than to dwell in the tents of wickedness.
Ibid. 10

Mercy and truth are met together: righteousness and peace have kissed each other.
Ibid. LXXXV, 10

A thousand years in thy sight are but as yesterday when it is past, and as a watch in the night.
Ibid. XC, 4

We spend our years as a tale that is told.[1]
Ibid. 9

The days of our years are threescore years and ten; and if by reason of strength they be fourscore years, yet is their strength labour and sorrow; for it is soon cut off, and we fly away.[2]
Ibid. 10

So teach us to number our days, that we may apply our hearts unto wisdom.
Ibid. 12

Establish thou the work of our hands upon us; yea, the work of our hands establish thou it.
Ibid. 17

I will say of the Lord, He is my refuge and my fortress: my God; in him will I trust.
Ibid. XCI, 2

Nor for the pestilence that walketh in darkness; nor for the destruction that wasteth at noonday.
Psalms. XCI, 6

He shall give his angels charge over thee, to keep thee in all thy ways.
Ibid. 11

The righteous shall flourish like the palm-tree: he shall grow like a cedar in Lebanon.
Ibid. XCII, 12

The noise of many waters.
Ibid. XCIII, 4

The Lord reigneth; let the earth rejoice.
Ibid. XCVII, 1

As for man, his days are as grass: as a flower of the field, so he flourisheth.
Ibid. CIII, 15

The wind passeth over it, and it is gone; and the place thereof shall know it no more.[1]
Ibid. 16

Wine that maketh glad the heart of man.
Ibid. CIV, 15

Man goeth forth unto his work and to his labour until the evening.
Ibid. 23

They that go down to the sea in ships, that do business in great waters.
Ibid. CVII, 23

At their wits' end.
Ibid. 27

Thy people shall be willing in the day of thy power, in the beauties of holiness from the womb of the morning: thou hast the dew of thy youth.
Ibid. CX, 3

From the rising of the sun unto the going down of the same.
Ibid. CXIII, 3

I said in my haste, All men are liars.
Ibid. CXVI, 11

Precious in the sight of the Lord is the death of his saints.   *Ibid. 15*

---

[1] We bring our years to an end, as it were a tale that is told. — *Book of Common Prayer*

[2] The days of our age are threescore and ten; and though men be so strong that they come to fourscore years, yet is their strength then but labour and sorrow; so soon passeth it away, and we are gone. — *Ibid.*

[1] *Gone with the Wind*, novel by MARGARET MITCHELL [1936]. The title is from *Non Sum Qualis Eram* ("Cynara") by ERNEST DOWSON: —
I have forgot much, Cynara! gone with the wind,
Flung roses, roses riotously with the throng.

The stone which the builders refused is become the head stone of the corner.[1]

Psalms. CXVIII, 22

This is the day which the Lord hath made.

Ibid. 24

I have more understanding than all my teachers: for thy testimonies are my meditations.

Ibid. CXIX, 99

A lamp unto my feet, and a light unto my path.

Ibid. 105

The sun shall not smite thee by day, nor the moon by night.

Ibid. CXXI, 6

Peace be within thy walls, and prosperity within thy palaces.

Ibid. CXXII, 7

They that sow in tears shall reap in joy.

Ibid. CXXVI, 5

Except the Lord build the house, they labour in vain that build it.

Ibid. CXXVII, 1

He giveth his beloved sleep.[2]

Ibid. 2

Happy is the man that hath his quiver full of them.

Ibid. 5

Thy children like olive plants [3] round about thy table.

Ibid. CXXVIII, 3

I will not give sleep to mine eyes, or slumber to mine eyelids.[4]

Ibid. CXXXII, 4

Behold how good and how pleasant it is for brethren to dwell together in unity.

Ibid. CXXXIII, 1

By the rivers of Babylon, there we sat down, yea, we wept, when we remembered Zion.[5]

Ibid. CXXXVII, 1

[1] Also in *Matthew, XXI, 42.*
[2] See Mrs. Browning, page 427.
[3] Like the olive branches. — *Book of Common Prayer*
[4] Also in *Proverbs, VI, 4.*
[5] By the waters of Babylon we sat down and wept, when we remembered thee, O Sion. — *Book of Common Prayer*

We hanged our harps upon the willows.

Psalms. CXXXVII, 2

If I forget thee, O Jerusalem, let my right hand forget her cunning.

Ibid. 5

If I take the wings of the morning, and dwell in the uttermost parts of the sea.

Ibid. CXXXIX, 9

I am fearfully and wonderfully made.

Ibid. 14

That our sons may be as plants grown up in their youth; that our daughters may be as corner stones.

Ibid. CXLIV, 12

Put not your trust in princes.

Ibid. CXLVI, 3

My son, if sinners entice thee, consent thou not.

Proverbs. I, 10

Wisdom crieth without; she uttereth her voice in the streets.

Ibid. 20

Length of days is in her right hand; and in her left hand riches and honour.

Ibid. III, 16

Her ways are ways of pleasantness, and all her paths are peace.

Ibid. 17

Wisdom is the principal thing; therefore get wisdom; and with all thy getting get understanding.

Ibid. IV, 7

The path of the just is as the shining light, that shineth more and more unto the perfect day.

Ibid. 18

Keep thy heart with all diligence; for out of it are the issues of life.

Ibid. 23

Go to the ant, thou sluggard; consider her ways, and be wise.

Ibid. VI, 6

Yet a little sleep, a little slumber, a little folding of the hands to sleep.

Ibid. 10; XXIV, 33

Can a man take fire in his bosom, and his clothes not be burned?

Ibid. VI, 27

As an ox goeth to the slaughter.[1]

Ibid. VII, 22

[1] Also in *Jeremiah, XI, 19.*

Wisdom is better than rubies.
Proverbs. VIII, 11

I love them that love me; and those that seek me early shall find me.
Ibid. 17

Stolen waters are sweet, and bread eaten in secret is pleasant.
Ibid. IX, 17

A wise son maketh a glad father.
Ibid. X, 1

The memory of the just is blessed.
Ibid. 7

In the multitude of counsellors there is safety.
Ibid. XI, 14; XXIV, 6

He that is surety for a stranger shall smart for it.
Ibid. 15

As a jewel of gold in a swine's snout, so is a fair woman which is without discretion.
Ibid. 22

Hope deferred maketh the heart sick.
Ibid. XIII, 12

The way of transgressors is hard.
Ibid. 15

He that spareth his rod hateth his son.
Ibid. 24

Fools make a mock at sin.
Ibid. XIV, 9

The heart knoweth his own bitterness; and a stranger doth not intermeddle with his joy.
Ibid. 10

The prudent man looketh well to his going.
Ibid. 15

The talk of the lips tendeth only to penury.
Ibid. 23

Righteousness exalteth a nation.
Ibid. 34

A soft answer turneth away wrath.
Ibid. XV, 1

A merry heart maketh a cheerful countenance.
Ibid. 13

He that is of a merry heart hath a continual feast.
Ibid. 15

Better is a dinner of herbs where love is, than a stalled ox and hatred therewith.
Proverbs. XV, 17

A word spoken in due season, how good is it!
Ibid. 23

A man's heart deviseth his way; but the Lord directeth his steps.
Ibid. XVI, 9

Pride goeth before destruction, and an haughty spirit before a fall.
Ibid. 18

The hoary head is a crown of glory.
Ibid. 31

He that is slow to anger is better than the mighty; and he that ruleth his spirit than he that taketh a city.
Ibid. 32

A gift is as a precious stone in the eyes of him that hath it.
Ibid. XVII, 8

He that repeateth a matter separateth very friends.
Ibid. 9

A merry heart doeth good like a medicine.
Ibid. 22

Even a fool, when he holdeth his peace, is counted wise.
Ibid. 28

Whoso findeth a wife findeth a good thing.
Ibid. XVIII, 22

A man that hath friends must show himself friendly; and there is a friend that sticketh closer than a brother.
Ibid. 24

Wealth maketh many friends.
Ibid. XIX, 4

He that hath pity upon the poor lendeth unto the Lord.[1]
Ibid. 17

Wine is a mocker, strong drink is raging.
Ibid. XX, 1

Every fool will be meddling.
Ibid. 3

[1] There is more Rhetorick in that one sentence, than in a Library of Sermons. — SIR THOMAS BROWNE: *Religio Medici* (Everyman ed.), P. *87*

The hearing ear and the seeing eye.
Proverbs. XX, 12

It is naught, it is naught, saith the buyer; but when he is gone his way, then he boasteth.
Ibid. 14

Meddle not with him that flattereth with his lips.
Ibid. 19

The beauty of old men is the grey head.
Ibid. 29

It is better to dwell in a corner of the housetop, than with a brawling woman in a wide house.
Ibid. XXI, 9; XXV, 24

A good name is rather to be chosen than great riches.[1]
Ibid. XXII, 1

Train up a child in the way he should go: and when he is old he will not depart from it.
Ibid. 6

The borrower is servant to the lender.
Ibid. 7

Remove not the ancient landmark.
Ibid. 28

Seest thou a man diligent in his business? He shall stand before kings.
Ibid. 29

Put a knife to thy throat, if thou be a man given to appetite.
Ibid. XXIII, 2

Riches certainly make themselves wings.[2]
Ibid. 5

As he thinketh in his heart, so is he.
Ibid. 7

Drowsiness shall clothe a man with rags.
Ibid. 21

Despise not thy mother when she is old.
Ibid. 22

Look not thou upon the wine when it is red, when it giveth his colour in the cup; . . . at the last it biteth like a serpent, and stingeth like an adder.
Ibid. 31, 32

[1] See Cervantes, page 1041.
[2] See Cowper, page 265.

A wise man is strong; yea, a man of knowledge increaseth strength.
Proverbs. XXIV, 5

If thou faint in the day of adversity thy strength is small.
Ibid. 10

A word fitly spoken is like apples of gold in pictures of silver.
Ibid. XXV, 11

Heap coals of fire upon his head.
Ibid. 22

As cold waters to a thirsty soul, so is good news from a far country.
Ibid. 25

Answer a fool according to his folly.
Ibid. XXVI, 5

Seest thou a man wise in his own conceit? There is more hope of a fool than of him.
Ibid. 12

There is a lion in the way; a lion is in the streets.
Ibid. 13

Wiser in his own conceit than seven men that can render a reason.
Ibid. 16

Whoso diggeth a pit shall fall therein.
Ibid. 27

Boast not thyself of to-morrow; for thou knowest not what a day may bring forth.
Ibid. XXVII, 1

Open rebuke is better than secret love.
Ibid. 5

Faithful are the wounds of a friend.
Ibid. 6

Better is a neighbour that is near than a brother far off.
Ibid. 10

A continual dropping in a very rainy day and a contentious woman are alike.
Ibid. 15

Iron sharpeneth iron; so a man sharpeneth the countenance of his friend.
Ibid. 17

The wicked flee when no man pursueth; but the righteous are bold as a lion.
Ibid. XXVIII, 1

He that maketh haste to be rich shall not be innocent.
Ibid. 20

He that giveth unto the poor shall not lack.

Proverbs. XXVIII, 27

Where there is no vision, the people perish.

Ibid. XXIX, 18

The horseleach hath two daughters, crying, Give, give.

Ibid. XXX, 15

The way of an eagle in the air; the way of a serpent upon a rock; the way of a ship in the midst of the sea; and the way of a man with a maid.[1]

Ibid. 19

In her tongue is the law of kindness.

Ibid. XXXI, 26

She looketh well to the ways of her household, and eateth not the bread of idleness.

Ibid. 27

Her children arise up, and call her blessed.

Ibid. 28

Many daughters have done virtuously, but thou excellest them all.

Ibid. 29

Vanity of vanities, . . . all is vanity.

Ecclesiastes. I, 2; XII, 8

One generation passeth away, and another generation cometh.

Ibid. I, 4

The eye is not satisfied with seeing.

Ibid. 8

There is no new thing under the sun.

Ibid. 9

Is there anything whereof it may be said, See, this is new? It hath been already of old time, which was before us.[2]

Ibid. 10

All is vanity and vexation of spirit.

Ibid. 14

He that increaseth knowledge increaseth sorrow.

Ibid. 18

One event happeneth to them all.

Ibid. II, 14

To every thing there is a season, and a time to every purpose under the heaven.

Ecclesiastes. III, 1

A time to keep silence, and a time to speak.

Ibid. 7

A threefold cord is not quickly broken.

Ibid. IV, 12

Let thy words be few.

Ibid. V, 2

Better is it that thou shouldest not vow, than that thou shouldest vow and not pay.

Ibid. 5

The sleep of a labouring man is sweet.

Ibid. 12

A good name is better than precious ointment.

Ibid. VII, 1

It is better to go to the house of mourning than to go to the house of feasting.

Ibid. 2

As the crackling of thorns under a pot, so is the laughter of the fool.

Ibid. 6

In the day of prosperity be joyful, but in the day of adversity consider.

Ibid. 14

Be not righteous overmuch.

Ibid. 16

One man among a thousand have I found; but a woman among all those have I not found.

Ibid. 28

God hath made man upright; but they have sought out many inventions.

Ibid. 29

There is no discharge in that war.[1]

Ibid. VIII, 8

To eat, and to drink, and to be merry.[2]

Ibid. 15

All things come alike to all.

Ibid. IX, 2

A living dog is better than a dead lion.

Ibid. 4

---

[1] There be triple ways to take, of the eagle or the snake,
Or the way of a man with a maid.
KIPLING: *The Long Trail*
[2] See Terence, page 979.

[1] There's no discharge in the war. — KIPLING: *Boots*
[2] Also in *Luke, XII, 19.*

Whatsoever thy hand findeth to do, do it with thy might.
Ecclesiastes. IX, 10

The race is not to the swift, nor the battle to the strong.[1]
Ibid. 11

A bird of the air shall carry the voice, and that which hath wings shall tell the matter.
Ibid. X, 20

Cast thy bread upon the waters: for thou shalt find it after many days.
Ibid. XI, 1

He that observeth the wind shall not sow; and he that regardeth the clouds shall not reap.
Ibid. 4

In the morning sow thy seed, and in the evening withhold not thine hand.
Ibid. 6

Rejoice, O young man, in thy youth.
Ibid. 9

Remember now thy Creator in the days of thy youth.
Ibid. XII, 1

The grinders cease because they are few.
Ibid. 3

He shall rise up at the voice of the bird.
Ibid. 4

The grasshopper shall be a burden, and desire shall fail; because man goeth to his long home, and the mourners go about the streets.
Ibid. 5

Or ever the silver cord be loosed, or the golden bowl be broken, or the pitcher be broken at the fountain, or the wheel broken at the cistern.
Ibid. 6

Then shall the dust return to the earth as it was; and the spirit shall return unto God who gave it.
Ibid. 7

The words of the wise are as goads, and as nails fastened by the masters of assemblies.
Ibid. 11

Of making many books there is no end; and much study is a weariness of the flesh.
Ecclesiastes. XII, 12

Let us hear the conclusion of the whole matter: Fear God, and keep his commandments; for this is the whole duty of man.
Ibid. 13

I am the rose of Sharon, and the lily of the valleys.
The Song of Solomon. II, 1

For, lo! the winter is past, the rain is over and gone; the flowers appear on the earth; the time of the singing of birds is come, and the voice of the turtle is heard in our land.
Ibid. 11, 12

The little foxes, that spoil the vines.
Ibid. 15

Until the day break, and the shadows flee away.
Ibid. 17; IV, 6

Terrible as an army with banners.
Ibid. VI, 4, 10

Thy neck is as a tower of ivory.
Ibid. VII, 4

Like the best wine, . . . that goeth down sweetly, causing the lips of those that are asleep to speak.
Ibid. 9

Set me as a seal upon thine heart.
Ibid. VIII, 6

Love is strong as death; jealousy is cruel as the grave.
Ibid.

Many waters cannot quench love, neither can the floods drown it.
Ibid. 7

The ox knoweth his owner, and the ass his master's crib.
Isaiah. I, 3

The whole head is sick, and the whole heart faint.
Ibid. 5

As a lodge in a garden of cucumbers.[1]
Ibid. 8

Bring no more vain oblations.
Ibid. 13

Come now, and let us reason together.
Ibid. 18

---

[1] See Henry van Dyke, page 710.

[1] See Rossiter Johnson, page 652.

Though your sins be as scarlet, they shall be white as snow.

Isaiah. I, 18

They shall beat their swords into plowshares, and their spears into pruning-hooks; nation shall not lift up sword against nation, neither shall they learn war any more.[1]

Ibid. II, 4

In that day a man shall cast his idols . . . to the moles and to the bats.

Ibid. 20

Grind the faces of the poor.

Ibid. III, 15

Walk with stretched-forth necks and wanton eyes, walking and mincing as they go.

Ibid. 16

In that day seven women shall take hold of one man.

Ibid. IV, 1

Woe unto them that call evil good, and good evil.

Ibid. V, 20

I saw also the Lord sitting upon a throne, high and lifted up, and his train filled the temple.

Ibid. VI, 1

Holy, holy, holy, is the Lord of hosts: the whole earth is full of his glory.

Ibid. 3

Shall call his name Immanuel.

Ibid. VII, 14

A stone of stumbling.

Ibid. VIII, 14

His name shall be called Wonderful, Counsellor, The mighty God, The everlasting Father, The Prince of Peace.

Ibid. IX, 6

The ancient and honourable.

Ibid. 15

The wolf also shall dwell with the lamb, and the leopard shall lie down with the kid.

Ibid. XI, 6

How art thou fallen from heaven, O Lucifer, son of the morning!

Ibid. XIV, 12

Is this the man that made the earth to tremble, that did shake kingdoms?

Ibid. 16

[1] Also in *Joel, III, 10* and *Micah, IV, 3.*

Like the rushing of mighty waters.

Isaiah. XVII, 12

Babylon is fallen, is fallen.

Ibid. XXI, 9

Watchman, what of the night?

Ibid. 11

Let us eat and drink; for to-morrow we shall die.

Ibid. XXII, 13

Fasten him as a nail in a sure place.

Ibid. 23

Whose merchants are princes.

Ibid. XXIII, 8

A feast of fat things.

Ibid. XXV, 6

He will swallow up death in victory; and the Lord God will wipe away tears from off all faces.

Ibid. 8

Hide thyself as it were for a little moment, until the indignation be overpast.

Ibid. XXVI, 20

Leviathan, that crooked serpent . . . the dragon that is in the sea.

Ibid. XXVII, 1

For precept must be upon precept, precept upon precept; line upon line, line upon line; here a little, and there a little.

Ibid. XXVIII, 10, 13

We have made a covenant with death, and with hell are we at agreement.

Ibid. 15

It shall be a vexation only to understand the report.

Ibid. 19

Their strength is to sit still.

Ibid. XXX, 7

Now go, write it before them in a table, and note it in a book.

Ibid. 8

As the shadow of a great rock in a weary land.

Ibid. XXXII, 2

The desert shall rejoice, and blossom as the rose.

Ibid. XXXV, 1

Thou trustest in the staff of this broken reed.

Ibid. XXXVI, 6

Set thine house in order.[1]

>   *Isaiah. XXXVIII, 1*

I shall go softly all my years.[2]

>   *Ibid. 15*

Comfort ye my people.

>   *Ibid. XL, 1*

All flesh is grass.

>   *Ibid. 6*

The nations are as a drop of a bucket.

>   *Ibid. 15*

They that wait upon the Lord shall renew their strength; they shall mount up with wings as eagles; they shall run, and not be weary; and they shall walk, and not faint.

>   *Ibid. 31*

They helped every one his neighbour: and every one said to his brother, Be of good courage.

>   *Ibid. XLI, 6*

A bruised reed shall he not break, and the smoking flax shall he not quench.

>   *Ibid. XLII, 3*

The astrologers, the stargazers, the monthly prognosticators.

>   *Ibid. XLVII, 13*

There is no peace, saith the Lord, unto the wicked.

>   *Ibid. XLVIII, 22*

How beautiful upon the mountains are the feet of him that bringeth good tidings, that publisheth peace.

>   *Ibid. LII, 7*

They shall see eye to eye.

>   *Ibid. 8*

A man of sorrows, and acquainted with grief.

>   *Ibid. LIII, 3*

All we like sheep have gone astray.

>   *Ibid. 6*

He is brought as a lamb to the slaughter.[3]

>   *Ibid. 7*

Ho, everyone that thirsteth, come ye to the waters.

>   *Ibid. LV, 1*

---

[1] Also in *2 Esdras, XIV, 13.*
[2] He hoped now to walk softly all his days
In soberness of spirit.
    ROBERT BROWNING: *The Ring and the Book, II, Half-Rome*
Walk softly — and carry a big stick. —
THEODORE ROOSEVELT
[3] Also in *Jeremiah, LI, 40.*

Let the wicked forsake his way, and the unrighteous man his thoughts.

>   *Isaiah. LV, 7*

A little one shall become a thousand, and a small one a strong nation.

>   *Ibid. LX, 22*

Give unto them beauty for ashes, the oil of joy for mourning, the garment of praise for the spirit of heaviness.

>   *Ibid. LXI, 3*

I have trodden the wine-press alone.

>   *Ibid. LXIII, 3*

We all do fade as a leaf.

>   *Ibid. LXIV, 6*

I am holier than thou.

>   *Ibid. LXV, 5*

Peace, peace; when there is no peace.

>   *Jeremiah. VI, 14; VIII, 11*

Stand ye in the ways, and see, and ask for the old paths, where is the good way, and walk therein.[1]

>   *Ibid. VI, 16*

Amend your ways and your doings.

>   *Ibid. VII, 3; XXVI, 13*

Is there no balm in Gilead?[2] Is there no physician there?

>   *Ibid. VIII, 22*

Oh that I had in the wilderness a lodging-place of wayfaring men!

>   *Ibid. IX, 2*

I will feed them . . . with wormwood, and give them water of gall to drink.

>   *Ibid. 15; XXIII, 15*

Can the Ethiopian change his skin, or the leopard his spots?

>   *Ibid. XIII, 23*

Her sun is gone down while it was yet day.

>   *Ibid. XV, 9*

A man of strife and a man of contention.

>   *Ibid. 10*

Written with a pen of iron, and with the point of a diamond.

>   *Ibid. XVII, 1*

He shall be as a tree planted by the waters, and that spreadeth out her roots by the river.

>   *Ibid. 8*

---

[1] Stare super vias antiquas. — *The Vulgate.*
[2] *Is* there balm in Gilead?
    POE: *The Raven*

He shall be buried with the burial of an ass.

Jeremiah. XXII, 19

Rahel [Rachel] weeping for her children, refused to be comforted.[1]

Ibid. XXXI, 15

The fathers have eaten a sour grape, and the children's teeth are set on edge.[2]

Ibid. 29

With my whole heart and with my whole soul.

Ibid. XXXII, 41

Is it nothing to you, all ye that pass by? behold, and see if there be any sorrow like unto my sorrow.

Lamentations. I, 12

A wheel in the middle of a wheel.

Ezekiel. I, 16; X, 10

I will cause you to pass under the rod.[3]

Ibid. XX, 37

Stood at the parting of the way.

Ibid. XXI, 21

His feet part of iron and part of clay.

Daniel. II, 33

Shadrach, Meshach, and Abed-nego fell down bound into the midst of the burning fiery furnace.[4]

Ibid. III, 23

Nebuchadnezzar . . . was driven from men, and did eat grass as oxen.

Ibid. IV, 33

Belshazzar the king made a great feast to a thousand of his lords.

Ibid. V, 1

Thou art weighed in the balances, and art found wanting.

Ibid. 27

His windows being open in his chamber toward Jerusalem.

Ibid. VI, 10

According to the law of the Medes and Persians.

Ibid. 12

They brought Daniel, and cast him into the den of lions.

Ibid. 16

The Ancient of days.

Daniel. VII, 13

Many shall run to and fro, and knowledge shall be increased.

Ibid. XII, 4

They have sown the wind, and they shall reap the whirlwind.

Hosea. VIII, 7

I have multiplied visions, and used similitudes.

Ibid. XII, 10

Your old men shall dream dreams, your young men shall see visions.

Joel. II, 28

Multitudes in the valley of decision.

Ibid. III, 14

Can two walk together, except they be agreed?

Amos. III, 3

And Jonah was in the belly of the fish three days and three nights.[1]

Jonah. I, 17

They shall sit every man under his vine and under his fig-tree.[2]

Micah. IV, 4

What doth the Lord require of thee, but to do justly, and to love mercy, and to walk humbly with thy God?

Ibid. VI, 8

Write the vision, and make it plain upon tables, that he may run that readeth it.

Habakkuk. II, 2

The Lord is in his holy temple: let all the earth keep silence before him.

Ibid. 20

Your fathers, where are they? And the prophets, do they live forever?

Zechariah. I, 5

Comfortable words.

Ibid. 13

The four winds of the heaven.

Ibid. II, 6

Not by might, nor by power, but by my spirit, saith the Lord of hosts.

Ibid. IV, 6

---

[1] Also in *Matthew, II, 18.*
[2] Also in *Ezekiel, XVIII, 2.*
[3] See Mrs. Dana, page 474.
[4] See Bert Leston Taylor, page 795.

[1] There are in Scripture stories that do exceed the fables of poets. — SIR THOMAS BROWNE: *Religio Medici* (Everyman ed.), P. 25
[2] See *1 Maccabees XIV, 12* on page 1125.

For who hath despised the day of small things? [1]

Zechariah. IV, 10

Prisoners of hope.

Ibid. IX, 12

I was wounded in the house of my friends.[2]

Ibid. XIII, 6

Have we not all one father? hath not one God created us?

Malachi. II, 10

But unto you that fear my name shall the Sun of righteousness arise with healing in his wings.

Ibid. IV, 2

He shall turn the heart of the fathers to the children, and the heart of the children to their fathers.

Ibid. 6

NEW TESTAMENT

Ye are the salt of the earth: but if the salt have lost his savour, wherewith shall it be salted?

Matthew. V, 13

Ye are the light of the world. A city that is set on an hill cannot be hid.

Ibid. 14

Take heed that ye do not your alms before men, to be seen of them.

Ibid. VI, 1

When thou doest alms, let not thy left hand know what thy right hand doeth.

Ibid. 3

They think that they shall be heard for their much speaking.

Ibid. 7

Give us this day our daily bread.

Ibid. 11

Lay up for yourselves treasures in heaven.

Ibid. 20

---

[1] Hereby I learned have, not to despise
What ever thing seemes small in common eyes.
SPENSER: *Visions of the Worlds Vanitie, Sonnet 5*

[2] From the house of friends comes the death stab.
WALT WHITMAN: *Wounded in the House of Friends, St. 1*

Where your treasure is, there will your heart be also.

Matthew. VI, 21

The light of the body is the eye.

Ibid. 22

No man can serve two masters. . . . Ye cannot serve God and Mammon.

Ibid. 24

Take no thought for your life, what ye shall eat, or what ye shall drink.

Ibid. 25

Consider the lilies of the field, how they grow; they toil not, neither do they spin.

Ibid. 28

Take therefore no thought for the morrow; for the morrow shall take thought for the things of itself. Sufficient unto the day is the evil thereof.

Ibid. 34

Neither cast ye your pearls before swine.

Ibid. VII, 6

Ask, and it shall be given you; seek, and ye shall find; knock, and it shall be opened unto you.

Ibid. 7

Every one that asketh receiveth; and he that seeketh findeth.

Ibid. 8

Or what man is there of you, whom if his son ask bread, will he give him a stone?

Ibid. 9

Therefore all things whatsoever ye would that men should do to you, do ye even so to them: for this is the law and the prophets.

Ibid. 12

Wide is the gate, and broad is the way, that leadeth to destruction.

Ibid. 13

Strait is the gate, and narrow is the way.

Ibid. 14

By their fruits ye shall know them.

Ibid. 20

It was founded upon a rock.

Ibid. 25

The foxes have holes, and the birds of the air have nests; but the Son of Man hath not where to lay his head.

Ibid. VIII, 20

The harvest truly is plenteous, but the labourers are few.

Matthew. IX, 37

Be ye therefore wise as serpents, and harmless as doves.

Ibid. X, 16

The very hairs of your head are all numbered.

Ibid. 30

Wisdom is justified of her children.[1]

Ibid. XI, 19

The tree is known by his fruit.

Ibid. XII, 33

Out of the abundance of the heart the mouth speaketh.

Ibid. 34

Pearl of great price.[2]

Ibid. XIII, 46

A prophet is not without honour, save in his own country, and in his own house.[3]

Ibid. 57

Be of good cheer: it is I; be not afraid.

Ibid. XIV, 27

If the blind lead the blind, both shall fall into the ditch.[4]

Ibid. XV, 14

The dogs eat of the crumbs which fall from their masters' table.

Ibid. 27

When it is evening, ye say it will be fair weather: for the sky is red.[5]

Ibid. XVI, 2

The signs of the times.

Ibid. 3

Thou art Peter, and upon this rock I will build my church.

Ibid. 18

I will give unto thee the keys of heaven.

Ibid. 19

[1] Also in *Luke, VII, 35*.
[2] See Hawthorne, page 422.
[3] Prophets have honour all over the Earth, Except in the village where they were born.
KIPLING: *Prophets at Home, St. 1*
See Oxyrhynchus Logia, page 1126.
[4] Quoted by CERVANTES: *Don Quixote, Part II, Book III, Chap. 13*.
[5] Red sky at night, sailors' delight, Red sky at morning, sailors take warning.
Old weather rhyme

Get thee behind me, Satan.[1]

Matthew. XVI, 23

What is a man profited, if he shall gain the whole world, and lose his own soul?[2]

Ibid. 26

It is good for us to be here.

Ibid. XVII, 4

The ninety and nine.

Ibid. XVIII, 12, 13

Where two or three are gathered together in my name, there am I in the midst of them.

Ibid. 20

What therefore God hath joined together, let not man put asunder.

Ibid. XIX, 6

Love thy neighbour as thyself.

Ibid. 19

It is easier for a camel to go through the eye of a needle, than for a rich man to enter into the kingdom of God.

Ibid. 24

Borne the burden and heat of the day.

Ibid. XX, 12

Is it not lawful for me to do what I will with mine own?

Ibid. 15

They made light of it.

Ibid. XXII, 5

For many are called, but few are chosen.

Ibid. 14

Render therefore unto Cæsar the things which are Cæsar's.[3]

Ibid. 21

Whosoever shall exalt himself shall be abased; and he that shall humble himself shall be exalted.

Ibid. XXIII, 12

Woe unto you, . . . for ye pay tithe of mint and anise and cummin.

Ibid. 23

Blind guides, which strain at a gnat, and swallow a camel.

Ibid. 24

[1] Also in *Luke, IV, 8*.
[2] Also in *Mark, VIII, 36*.
[3] Also in *Mark, XII, 17*.

Whited sepulchres, which indeed appear beautiful outward, but are within full of dead men's bones.
Matthew. XXIII, 27

As a hen gathereth her chickens under her wings.
Ibid. 37

Wars and rumours of wars.[1]
Ibid. XXIV, 6

The end is not yet.
Ibid.

Abomination of desolation.[2]
Ibid. 15

False prophets.
Ibid. 24

Wheresoever the carcass is, there will the eagles be gathered together.
Ibid. 28

Heaven and earth shall pass away, but my words shall not pass away.
Ibid. 35

Well done, thou good and faithful servant.
Ibid. XXV, 21

Unto every one that hath shall be given, and he shall have abundance; but from him that hath not shall be taken away even that which he hath.
Ibid. 29

Inasmuch as ye have done it unto one of the least of these my brethren, ye have done it unto me.
Ibid. 40

An alabaster box of very precious ointment.
Ibid. XXVI, 7

Thirty pieces of silver.
Ibid. 15

The spirit indeed is willing, but the flesh is weak.
Ibid. 41

All they that take the sword shall perish with the sword.
Ibid. 52

The potter's field, to bury strangers in.
Ibid. XXVII, 7

Go ye therefore, and teach all nations.
Ibid. XXVIII, 19

[1] Also in *Mark, XIII,* 7.
[2] Also in *Mark, XIII, 14.*

Lo, I am with you alway, even unto the end of the world.
Matthew. XXVIII, 20

The voice of one crying in the wilderness.
Mark. I, 3

The latchet of whose shoes I am not worthy to stoop down and unloose.
Ibid. 7

I came not to call the righteous, but sinners to repentance.
Ibid. II, 17

New wine into old bottles.
Ibid. 22

The Sabbath was made for man, and not man for the Sabbath.
Ibid. 27

If a house be divided against itself, that house cannot stand.
Ibid. III, 25

He that hath ears to hear, let him hear.
Ibid. IV, 9

First the blade, then the ear, after that the full corn in the ear.
Ibid. 28

Peace, be still.
Ibid. 39

My name is Legion.
Ibid. V, 9

Clothed, and in his right mind.[1]
Ibid. 15

My little daughter lieth at the point of death.
Ibid. 23

I see men as trees, walking.
Ibid. VIII, 24

Overthrew the tables of the money-changers.
Ibid. XI, 15

He [Judas] goeth straightway to him, and saith, Master, master; and kissed him.
Ibid. XIV, 45

There was no room for them in the inn.[2]
Luke. II, 7

Glory to God in the highest, and on earth peace, good will toward men.
Ibid. 14

[1] Also in *Luke, VIII, 35.*
[2] See B. Y. Williams, page 904.

Lord, now lettest thou thy servant depart in peace.
Luke. II, 29

A light to lighten the Gentiles.
Ibid. 32

Wist ye not that I must be about my Father's business?
Ibid. 49

His mother kept all these sayings in her heart.
Ibid. 51

The axe is laid unto the root of the trees.
Ibid. III, 9

Physician, heal thyself.
Ibid. IV, 23

Woe unto you, when all men shall speak well of you!
Ibid. VI, 26

Nothing is secret which shall not be made manifest.
Ibid. VIII, 17

No man, having put his hand to the plough, and looking back, is fit for the kingdom of God.
Ibid. IX, 62

Peace be to this house.
Ibid. X, 5

The labourer is worthy of his hire.[1]
Ibid. 7

A certain man went down from Jerusalem to Jericho, and fell among thieves.
Ibid. 30

He passed by on the other side.
Ibid. 31

A certain Samaritan . . . had compassion on him.
Ibid. 33

Go, and do thou likewise.
Ibid. 37

But one thing is needful; and Mary hath chosen that good part which shall not be taken away from her.
Ibid. 42

He that is not with me is against me.
Ibid. XI, 23

[1] Also in *1 Timothy, V, 18.*

Soul, thou hast much goods laid up for many years; take thine ease, eat, drink, and be merry.[1]
Luke. XII, 19

This night thy soul shall be required of thee.
Ibid. 20

Let your loins be girded about, and your lights burning.
Ibid. 35

Which of you, intending to build a tower, sitteth not down first, and counteth the cost, whether he have sufficient to finish it.
Ibid. XIV, 28

Wasted his substance with riotous living.
Ibid. XV, 13

Bring hither the fatted calf.
Ibid. 23

The children of this world are in their generation wiser than the children of light.
Ibid. XVI, 8

He that is faithful in that which is least is faithful also in much; and he that is unjust in the least is unjust also in much.
Ibid. 10

It were better for him that a millstone were hanged about his neck, and he cast into the sea.
Ibid. XVII, 2

Out of thine own mouth will I judge thee.
Ibid. XIX, 22

This do in remembrance of me.[2]
Ibid. XXII, 19

He was a good man, and a just.
Ibid. XXIII, 50

Did not our heart burn within us while he talked with us?
Ibid. XXIV, 32

There was a man sent from God, whose name was John.[3]
John. I, 6

[1] To eat, drink, and be merry, because tomorrow we die.
  G. J. WHYTE-MELVILLE [1821–1878]:
      The Object of a Life
[2] Also in *1 Corinthians, XI, 24.*
[3] Inscription on the tomb of Don John of Austria [1547–1578], in the Escorial, Spain.

The true light, which lighteth every man that cometh into the world.

John. I, 9

Can there any good thing come out of Nazareth?

Ibid. 46

Make not my Father's house an house of merchandise.

Ibid. II, 16

The wind bloweth where it listeth.

Ibid. III, 8

For God so loved the world, that he gave his only begotten Son, that whosoever believeth in him should not perish, but have everlasting life.

Ibid. 16

He was a burning and a shining light.

Ibid. V, 35

Gather up the fragments that remain, that nothing be lost.

Ibid. VI, 12

I am the bread of life.

Ibid. 35

Judge not according to the appearance.

Ibid. VII, 24

He that is without sin among you, let him first cast a stone at her.

Ibid. VIII, 7

Neither do I condemn thee: go, and sin no more.

Ibid. 11

I am the light of the world: he that followeth me shall not walk in darkness, but shall have the light of life.

Ibid. 12

The truth shall make you free.

Ibid. 32

There is no truth in him.

Ibid. 44

The night cometh, when no man can work.

Ibid. IX, 4

I am come that they might have life, and that they might have it more abundantly.

Ibid. X, 10

I am the resurrection and the life.

Ibid. XI, 25

The poor always ye have with you.

Ibid. XII, 8

Walk while ye have the light, lest darkness come upon you.

John. XII, 35

A new commandment I give unto you, That ye love one another.

Ibid. XIII, 24

Let not your heart be troubled.

Ibid. XIV, 1

In my Father's house are many mansions.

Ibid. 2

I will not leave you comfortless.

Ibid. 18

Peace I leave with you.

Ibid. 27

Greater love hath no man than this, that a man lay down his life for his friends.

Ibid. XV, 13

Be of good cheer; I have overcome the world.

Ibid. XVI, 33

Now Barabbas was a robber.

Ibid. XVIII, 40

Thy money perish with thee.

Acts. VIII, 20

It is hard for thee to kick against the pricks.

Ibid. IX, 5

Now there was at Joppa a certain disciple named Tabitha, which by interpretation is called Dorcas: this woman was full of good works and almsdeeds which she did.

Ibid. 36

Come over into Macedonia, and help us.

Ibid. XVI, 9

Lewd fellows of the baser sort.

Ibid. XVII, 5

I found an altar with this inscription, To the Unknown God.[1]

Ibid. 23

Great is Diana of the Ephesians.

Ibid. XIX, 28

---

[1] The inscription did not run "To the unknown God," but "To the Gods of Asia and Africa, to the unknown and foreign Gods." — JEROME: *Commentar. in Epist. ad Titum I. verses 10* and *11*, in FATHER LARGENT: *St. Jerome* [1913], *P. 31*, translated by HESTER DAVENPORT.

It is more blessed to give than to receive.

Acts. XX, 35

Brought up in this city at the feet of Gamaliel.

Ibid. XXII, 3

When I have a convenient season, I will call for thee.

Ibid. XXIV, 25

I appeal unto Caesar.

Ibid. XXV, 11

Much learning doth make thee mad.

Ibid. XXVI, 24

Words of truth and soberness.

Ibid. 25

For this thing was not done in a corner.

Ibid. 26

Almost thou persuadest me to be a Christian.

Ibid. 28

Wherein thou judgest another, thou condemnest thyself.

Romans. II, 1

There is no respect of persons with God.

Ibid. 11

God forbid.

Ibid. III, 31

Who against hope believed in hope.

Ibid. IV, 18

Death hath no more dominion over him.

Ibid. VI, 9

Speak after the manner of men.

Ibid. 19

The wages of sin is death.

Ibid. 23

For the good that I would I do not; but the evil which I would not, that I do.[1]

Ibid. VII, 19

Heirs of God, and joint-heirs with Christ.

Ibid. VIII, 17

For we know that the whole creation groaneth and travaileth in pain together until now.

Ibid. 22

[1] See Euripides, page 967.

All things work together for good to them that love God.

Romans. VIII, 28

If God be for us, who can be against us.

Ibid. 31

Neither death, nor life . . . shall be able to separate us from the love of God.

Ibid. 38, 39

Hath not the potter power over the clay, of the same lump to make one vessel unto honour, and another unto dishonour?

Ibid. IX, 21

Given to hospitality.

Ibid. XII, 13

Be not wise in your own conceits.

Ibid. 16

Recompense to no man evil for evil.

Ibid. 17

If it be possible, as much as lieth in you, live peaceably with all men.

Ibid. 18

Vengeance is mine; I will repay, saith the Lord.

Ibid. 19

If thine enemy hunger, feed him; if he thirst, give him drink: for in so doing thou shalt heap coals of fire on his head.

Ibid. 20

Be not overcome of evil, but overcome evil with good.

Ibid. 21

The powers that be are ordained of God.

Ibid. XIII, 1

Render therefore to all their dues.

Ibid. 7

Owe no man anything, but to love one another.

Ibid. 8

Love is the fulfilling of the law.

Ibid. 10

Let every man be fully persuaded in his own mind.

Ibid. XIV, 5

None of us liveth to himself.

Ibid. 7

Let us therefore follow after the things which make for peace.

Ibid. 19

God hath chosen the foolish things of the world to confound the wise; and God hath chosen the weak things of the world to confound the things which are mighty.

1 Corinthians. I, 27

I have planted, Apollos watered; but God gave the increase.

Ibid. III, 6

Every man's work shall be made manifest.

Ibid. 13

Not to think of men above that which is written.[1]

Ibid. IV, 6

We are made a spectacle unto the world, and to angels, and to men.

Ibid. 9

Absent in body, but present in spirit.

Ibid. V, 3

A little leaven leaveneth the whole lump.[2]

Ibid. 6

The fashion of this world passeth away.

Ibid. VII, 31

I am made all things to all men.

Ibid. IX, 22

Let him that thinketh he standeth take heed lest he fall.

Ibid. X, 12

If a woman have long hair, it is a glory to her.

Ibid. XI, 15

Though I speak with the tongues of men and of angels, and have not charity,[3] I am become as sounding brass, or a tinkling cymbal.

Ibid. XIII, 1

Though I have all faith, so that I could remove mountains, and have not charity, I am nothing.

Ibid. 2

Charity suffereth long and is kind; charity envieth not; charity vaunteth not itself, is not puffed up.

Ibid. 4

We know in part, and we prophesy in part.

1 Corinthians. XIII, 9

When I was a child, I spake as a child. . . . When I became a man, I put away childish things.

Ibid. 11

Now we see through a glass, darkly.

Ibid. 12

And now abideth faith, hope, charity, these three; but the greatest of these is charity.

Ibid. 13

If the trumpet give an uncertain sound.

Ibid. XIV, 8

Let all things be done decently and in order.

Ibid. 40

Evil communications corrupt good manners.[1]

Ibid. XV, 33

One star differeth from another star in glory.

Ibid. 41

The first man is of the earth, earthy.

Ibid. 47

In the twinkling of an eye.[2]

Ibid. 52

O death, where is thy sting? O grave, where is thy victory? [3]

Ibid. 55

Quit you like men, be strong.

Ibid. XVI, 13

Not of the letter, but of the spirit; for the letter killeth, but the spirit giveth life.

2 Corinthians. III, 6

We have such hope, we use great plainness of speech.

Ibid. 12

The things which are seen are temporal; but the things which are not seen are eternal.

Ibid. IV, 18

We walk by faith, not by sight.

Ibid. V, 7

---

[1] Usually misquoted, "To be wise above that which is written."
[2] Also in *Galatians, V, 9*.
[3] In the Revised Version, the word "love" is substituted for "charity" throughout the chapter.

[1] Communion with the bad corrupts good character. — MENANDER: *Thais* (Loeb Classical Library, page 357)
[2] See Shakespeare, page 45.
[3] See William Watson, page 736.

Now is the accepted time.
> *2 Corinthians. VI, 2*

By evil report and good report.
> *Ibid. 8*

As having nothing, and yet possessing all things.
> *Ibid. 10*

God loveth a cheerful giver.
> *Ibid. IX, 7*

Though I be rude in speech.
> *Ibid. XI, 6*

For ye suffer fools gladly, seeing ye yourselves are wise.
> *Ibid. 19*

Forty stripes save one.
> *Ibid. 24*

A thorn in the flesh.
> *Ibid. XII, 7*

Strength is made perfect in weakness.
> *Ibid. 9*

The grace of the Lord Jesus Christ, and the love of God, and the communion of the Holy Ghost, be with you all.
> *Ibid. XIII, 14*

The right hands of fellowship.
> *Galatians. II, 9*

Weak and beggarly elements.
> *Ibid. IV, 9*

It is good to be zealously affected always in a good thing.
> *Ibid. 18*

Ye are fallen from grace.
> *Ibid. V, 4*

Every man shall bear his own burden.
> *Ibid. VI, 5*

Whatsoever a man soweth, that shall he also reap.
> *Ibid. 7*

Let us not be weary in well doing.
> *Ibid. 9*

God forbid that I should glory, save in the cross of our Lord Jesus Christ.
> *Ibid. 14*

Carried about with every wind of doctrine.
> *Ephesians. IV, 14*

Be ye angry, and sin not: let not the sun go down upon your wrath.
> *Ibid. 26*

To live is Christ, and to die is gain.
> *Philippians. I, 21*

Work out your own salvation.
> *Philippians. II, 12*

I press toward the mark for the prize of the high calling of God in Christ Jesus.
> *Ibid. III, 14*

Whose God is their belly, and whose glory is in their shame.
> *Ibid. 19*

The peace of God, which passeth all understanding.
> *Ibid. IV, 7*

Whatsoever things are true, whatsoever things are honest, whatsoever things are just, whatsoever things are pure, whatsoever things are lovely, whatsoever things are of good report; if there be any virtue, and if there be any praise, think on these things.
> *Ibid. 8*

I have learned, in whatsoever state I am, therewith to be content.
> *Ibid. 11*

Touch not; taste not; handle not.
> *Colossians. II, 21*

Set your affections on things above, not on things on the earth.
> *Ibid. III, 2*

Let your speech be alway with grace, seasoned with salt.
> *Ibid. IV, 6*

Luke, the beloved physician.
> *Ibid. 14*

Labour of love.
> *1 Thessalonians. I, 3*

Study to be quiet.
> *Ibid. IV, 11*

Putting on the breastplate of faith and love; and for an helmet, the hope of salvation.
> *Ibid. V, 8*

Prove all things; hold fast that which is good.
> *Ibid. 21*

The law is good, if a man use it lawfully.
> *1 Timothy. I, 8*

Not greedy of filthy lucre.
> *Ibid. III, 3*

Drink no longer water, but use a little wine for thy stomach's sake.
> *Ibid. V, 23*

We brought nothing into this world, and it is certain we can carry nothing out.

1 Timothy. VI, 7

The love of money is the root of all evil.

Ibid. 10

Fight the good fight.

Ibid. 12

Rich in good works.

Ibid. 18

Science falsely so called.

Ibid. 20

A workman that needeth not to be ashamed.

2 Timothy. II, 15

I have fought a good fight, I have finished my course, I have kept the faith.

Ibid. IV, 7

Alexander the coppersmith did me much evil: the Lord reward him according to his works.

Ibid. 14

Unto the pure all things are pure.

Titus. I, 15

Making mention of thee always in my prayers.

Philemon. I, 4

Such as have need of milk, and not of strong meat.

Hebrews. V, 12

Strong meat belongeth to them that are of full age.

Ibid. 14

Faith is the substance of things hoped for, the evidence of things not seen.

Ibid. XI, 1

A cloud of witnesses.

Ibid. XII, 1

The author and finisher of our faith.

Ibid. 2

Whom the Lord loveth he chasteneth.

Ibid. 6

The spirits of just men made perfect.

Ibid. 23

Be not forgetful to entertain strangers, for thereby some have entertained angels unawares.

Ibid. XIII, 2

Yesterday, and to-day, and forever.

Hebrews. XIII, 8

For here we have no continuing city, but we seek one to come.

Ibid. 14

Let patience have her perfect work.

James. I, 4

Blessed is the man that endureth temptation; for when he is tried, he shall receive the crown of life.

Ibid. 12

Every good gift and every perfect gift is from above.

Ibid. 17

No variableness, neither shadow of turning.

Ibid.

Be swift to hear, slow to speak, slow to wrath.

Ibid. 19

Unspotted from the world.

Ibid. 27

Faith without works is dead.

Ibid. II, 26

How great a matter a little fire kindleth!

Ibid. III, 5

The tongue can no man tame; it is an unruly evil.[1]

Ibid. 8

Resist the Devil, and he will flee from you.

Ibid. IV, 7

The effectual fervent prayer of a righteous man availeth much.

Ibid. V, 16

Hope to the end.

1 Peter. I, 13

Fear God. Honour the king.

Ibid. II, 17

Ornament of a meek and quiet spirit.

Ibid. III, 4

Giving honour unto the wife, as unto the weaker vessel.

Ibid. 7

Charity shall cover the multitude of sins.

Ibid. IV, 8

A crown of glory that fadeth not away.

Ibid. V, 4

---

[1] Usually misquoted, "The tongue is an unruly member."

Be sober, be vigilant; because your adversary, the Devil, as a roaring lion, walketh about, seeking whom he may devour.

I Peter. V, 8

And the day star arise in your hearts.

2 Peter. I, 19

The dog is turned to his own vomit again.

Ibid. II, 22

Bowels of compassion.

I John. III, 17

God is love.

Ibid. IV, 8

There is no fear in love; but perfect love casteth out fear.

Ibid. 18

Be thou faithful unto death.

Revelation. II, 10

He shall rule them with a rod of iron.

Ibid. 27

Behold, I stand at the door and knock.

Ibid. III, 20

A pale horse: and his name that sat on him was Death.[1]

Ibid. VI, 8

All nations, and kindreds, and people, and tongues.

Ibid. VII, 9

As the voice of many waters.[2]

Ibid. XIV, 2

They may rest from their labours; and their works do follow them.

Ibid. 13

And he gathered them together into a place called in the Hebrew tongue Armageddon.

Ibid. XVI, 16

Another book was opened, which is the book of life.

Ibid. XX, 12

I saw a new heaven and a new earth.

Ibid. XXI, 1

The holy city, new Jerusalem.

Ibid. 2

I am Alpha and Omega, the beginning and the end, the first and the last.

Ibid. 6

[1] See John Hay, page 639.
[2] The noise of many waters. — *Psalm XCIII, 4*

There shall be no night there.

Revelation. XXII, 5

Without are dogs.[1]

Ibid. 15

THE APOCRYPHA [2]

How exceeding strong is wine! it causeth all men to err who drink it.

1 Esdras. III, 18

Ye must know that women have dominion over you: do ye not labour and toil, and give and bring all to the woman?

Ibid. IV, 22

Great is truth, and mighty above all things.[3]

Ibid. 41

Do right to the widow, judge for the fatherless, give to the poor, defend the orphan, clothe the naked.

2 Esdras. II, 20

What is past I know, but what is for to come I know not.

Ibid. IV, 46

Unto you is paradise opened.

Ibid. VIII, 52

Now therefore keep thy sorrow to thyself, and bear with a good courage that which hath befallen thee.

Ibid. X, 15

I shall light a candle of understanding in thine heart, which shall not be put out.[4]

Ibid. XIV, 25

If thou hast abundance, give alms accordingly: if thou have but a little, be not afraid to give according to that little.

Tobit. IV, 8

God, which dwelleth in heaven, prosper your journey, and the angel of God

[1] See E. A. Church, page 671.
[2] These books form part of the sacred literature of the Alexandrian Jews, and with the exception of *2 Esdras* are found interspersed with the Hebrew Scriptures in the ancient copies of the Septuagint, or Greek Version of the Old Testament. — *The Apocrypha According to the Authorized Version, Preface* (Oxford University Press)
[3] Magna est veritas et praevalet. — *The Vulgate, Book III* (uncanonical)
[4] See Hugh Latimer, page 10.

keep you company. So they [Azarias and Tobias] went forth both, and the young man's dog went with them.

Tobit. V, 16

Honour thy father and thy mother in law, which are now thy parents.

Ibid. X, 12

So they went their way, and the dog went after them.

Ibid. XI, 4

Ye cannot find the depth of the heart of man, neither can ye perceive the things that he thinketh: then how can ye search out God, that hath made all these things, and know his mind, or comprehend his purpose?

Judith. VIII, 14

Put on her garments of gladness.

Ibid. X, 3

Ye shall therefore among your solemn feasts keep it an high day for all feasting.[1]

Esther. XVI, 22

Our time is a very shadow that passeth away.

Wisdom of Solomon. II, 5

Let us crown ourselves with rosebuds before they be withered.

Ibid. 8

The souls of the righteous are in the hand of God, and there shall no torment touch them. In the sight of the unwise they seemed to die: and their departure is taken for misery, and their going from us to be utter destruction: but they are in peace.

Ibid. III, 1–3

They that put their trust in him shall understand the truth.

Ibid. 9

Wisdom is the gray hair unto men, and an unspotted life is old age.

Ibid. IV, 9

When I was born, I drew in the common air, and fell upon the earth, which is of like nature, and the first voice

which I uttered was crying, as all others do.[1]

Wisdom of Solomon. VII, 3

All men have one entrance into life, and the like going out.

Ibid. 6

Who can number the sand of the sea, and the drops of rain, and the days of eternity?

Ecclesiasticus. I, 2

Honour thy father and mother [2] both in word and deed, that a blessing may come upon thee from them.

Ibid. III, 8

If his understanding fail, have patience with him.

Ibid. 13

Observe the opportunity.

Ibid. IV, 20

Let not thine hand be stretched out to receive, and shut when thou shouldest repay.

Ibid. 31

A faithful friend is a strong defence: and he that hath found such an one hath found a treasure.

Ibid. VI, 14

Be not slow to visit the sick.

Ibid. VII, 35

Whatsoever thou takest in hand, remember the end, and thou shalt never do amiss.

Ibid. 36

Rejoice not over thy greatest enemy being dead, but remember that we die all.

Ibid. VIII, 7

Miss not the discourse of the elders.

Ibid. 9

Forsake not an old friend, for the new is not comparable to him. A new friend is as new wine: when it is old, thou shalt drink it with pleasure.

Ibid. IX, 10

In the day of prosperity there is a forgetfulness of affliction: and in the day of affliction there is no more remembrance of prosperity.

Ibid. XI, 25

---

[1] The Feast of Purim, celebrating the deliverance of the Jews from the persecution of Haman through the influence of Esther, Mordecai's queen.

[1] See Pliny the Elder, page 993.
[2] *Exodus*, XX, 12

He that toucheth pitch shall be defiled therewith.
Ecclesiasticus. XIII, 1

He will laugh thee to scorn.
Ibid. 7

A rich man beginning to fall is held up of his friends: but a poor man being down is thrust also away by his friends.
Ibid. 21

The heart of a man changeth his countenance, whether it be for good or evil: and a merry heart maketh a cheerful countenance.
Ibid. 25

Wine and women will make men of understanding to fall away.
Ibid. XIX, 2

Whether it be to friend or foe, talk not of other men's lives.
Ibid. 8

If she go not as thou wouldst have her, cut her off from thy flesh, and give her a bill of divorce, and let her go.
Ibid. XXV, 26

Gladness of the heart is the life of man, and the joyfulness of a man prolongeth his days.
Ibid. XXX, 22

Consider that I laboured not for myself only, but for all them that seek learning.
Ibid. XXXIII, 17

Honour a physician with the honour due unto him.
Ibid. XXXVIII, 1

When the dead is at rest, let his remembrance rest; and be comforted for him, when his spirit is departed from him.
Ibid. 23

Whose talk is of bullocks.[1]
Ibid. 25

Look upon the rainbow, and praise him that made it.
Ibid. XLIII, 11

Let us now praise famous men.[2]
Ibid. XLIV, 1

These were honoured in their generations, and were the glory of their times.
Ecclesiasticus. XLIV, 7

There be of them that have left a name behind them.
Ibid. 8

His word burned like a lamp.
Ibid. XLVIII, 1

A scarecrow in a garden of cucumbers keepeth nothing.
Baruch. VI, 70

Was not Abraham found faithful in temptation, and it was imputed unto him for righteousness?
1 Maccabees. II, 52

With the God of heaven it is all one, to deliver with a great multitude, or a small company: For the victory of battle standeth not in the multitude of an host; but strength cometh from heaven.
Ibid. III, 18, 19

The noble acts which he did, and his greatness, they are not written: for they were very many.
Ibid. IX, 22

Ask and learn.
Ibid. X, 72

Every man sat under his vine and his fig tree.[1]
Ibid. XIV, 12

We have been careful that they that will read may have delight, and that they that are desirous to commit to memory might have ease, and that all into whose hands it comes might have profit.
2 Maccabees. II, 25

It is a foolish thing to make a long prologue, and to be short in the story itself.
Ibid. 32

Leaving his death for an example of a noble courage, and a memorial of virtue, not only unto young men, but unto all his nation.
Ibid. VI, 31

Nicanor lay dead in his harness.
Ibid. XV, 28

---

[1] Quoted by DR. SAMUEL JOHNSON. — BOSWELL's *Life of Dr. Johnson* (Everyman ed.), Vol. II, P. 133
[2] "Let us now praise famous men." — KIPLING: *A School Song*

[1] See *Micah, IV, 4* on page 1113.

If I have done well, and as is fitting,
. . . it is that which I desired; but if
slenderly and meanly, it is that which
I could attain unto.

2 Maccabees. XV, 38

Speech finely framed delighteth the
ears.

Ibid. 39

OXYRHYNCHUS LOGIA
(AGRAPHA) [1]

Wherever there are two, they are not
without God; and wherever there is one
alone, I say I am with him. Raise the
stone, and there thou shalt find me;
cleave the wood, and there am I.[2]

Fifth Logion

A prophet is not acceptable in his
own country,[3] neither doth a physician
work cures upon them that know him.

Sixth Logion

A city built upon the top of a hill and
stablished can neither fall nor be hid.[4]

Seventh Logion

DOUAY BIBLE [5]
[1609]

I am the angel Raphael, one of the
seven, who stand before the Lord.

Tobias. XII, 15

Now Susanna was exceeding delicate,
and beautiful to behold.

Daniel. XIII, 31

[1] In the rubbish heaps of the ancient city
of Oxyrhynchus, near the River Nile, a party
of English explorers, in the winter of 1897,
discovered a fragment of a papyrus book,
written in the second or third century, and
hitherto unknown. This single leaf contained
parts of seven short sentences of Christ, each
introduced by the words, "Jesus says." —
HENRY VAN DYKE: *The Toiling of Felix,
Preface*
[2] See van Dyke, page 709.
Raise thou the stone and find Me there,
Cleave thou the wood and there am I.
SIR WILLIAM WATSON:
The Unknown God
[3] See *Matthew, XIII, 57* on page 1115.
[4] See *Matthew, V, 14* on page 1114.
[5] The English version of the Bible for Roman Catholics was first printed in Douay,
France.

He hath sold the just man for silver,
and the poor man for a pair of shoes.

Amos. II, 6

Houses of ivory shall perish.

Ibid. III, 15

The faces of them all are as the
blackness of a kettle.

Nahum. II, 10

You have sowed much, and brought
in little.

Aggeus. I, 6

He that hath earned wages put them
into a bag with holes.

Ibid.

THE KORAN
Translated [1734] by GEORGE SALE
[1697–1736]

Turn, therefore, thy face towards the
holy temple of Mecca; and wherever ye
be, turn your faces towards that place.

Chap. 2

Wherever ye be, God will bring you
all back at the resurrection.

Ibid.

As for him who voluntarily performeth a good work, verily God is grateful
and knowing.

Ibid.

Your God is one God; there is no
God but He, the most merciful.

Ibid.

O true believers, take your necessary
precautions against your enemies, and
either go forth to war in separate parties, or go forth all together in a body.

Chap. 4

Fight for the religion of God.

Ibid.

O men, respect women who have
borne you.

Ibid.

Wheresoever ye be, death will overtake you, although ye be in lofty towers.

Ibid.

Whosoever flieth from his country
for the sake of God's true religion, shall
find in the earth many forced to do the
same, and plenty of provisions.

Ibid.

God loveth not the speaking ill of any one in public.

Chap. 4

Let not thy hand be tied up to thy neck; neither open it with an unbounded expansion, lest thou become worthy of reprehension, and be reduced to poverty.

Chap. 17

Of his mercy he hath made for you the night and the day, that ye may rest in the one, and may seek to obtain provision for yourself of his abundance, by your industry, in the other.

Chap. 28

If God should punish men according to what they deserve, he would not leave on the back of the earth so much as a beast.

Chap. 35

God obligeth no man to more than he hath given him ability to perform.

Chap. 65

Woe be unto those who pray, and who are negligent at their prayer: who play the hypocrites, and deny necessaries to the needy.

Chap. 107

O unbelievers, I will not worship that which ye worship; nor will ye worship that which I worship. . . . Ye have your religion, and I my religion.

Chap. 109

BOOK OF COMMON PRAYER [1]

We have left undone those things which we ought to have done; and we have done those things which we ought not to have done.

Morning Prayer

The noble army of Martyrs.

Ibid. Te Deum

Make them to be numbered [2] with thy Saints, in glory everlasting.

Ibid.

Whose service is perfect freedom.

Ibid. A Collect for Peace

[1] American Revision [1928].
[2] In the Latin, this word is *munerari* (rewarded), and was mistaken, perhaps, by an early copyist, for *numerari* (numbered).

Afflicted, or distressed, in mind, body, or estate.

Morning Prayer. A Prayer for All Conditions of Men

Grant us grace fearlessly to contend against evil, and to make no peace with oppression; and, that we may reverently use our freedom, help us to employ it in the maintenance of justice among men and nations.

Prayers and Thanksgivings. A Prayer for Social Justice

Deliver us, we beseech thee, in our several callings, from the service of mammon, that we may do the work which thou givest us to do, in truth, in beauty, and in righteousness, with singleness of heart as thy servants, and to the benefit of our fellow men.

Ibid. A Prayer for Every Man in His Work

From envy, hatred, and malice, and all uncharitableness.

The Litany

The world, the flesh, and the devil.

Ibid.

Give to all nations unity, peace, and concord.[1]

Ibid.

The kindly fruits of the earth.

Ibid.

Miserable sinners.[2]

Holy Communion. Exhortation

Read, mark, learn, and inwardly digest.

Collect for the Second Sunday in Advent

Renounce the devil and all his works.

Holy Baptism. Of Children

The pomps and vanity of this wicked world.

Offices of Instruction (Catechism)

[1] The desire for unity, the wish for peace, the longing for concord, deeply implanted in the human heart, have stirred the most powerful emotions of the race, and have been responsible for some of its noblest actions. — SIR WILLIAM OSLER: *Aequanimitas* (2d ed.), *XXI, Unity, Peace and Concord*
[2] The invocation, "Have mercy upon us miserable sinners," was included in the Litany prior to the Revision of 1928. "Miserable offenders" appears in *Morning Prayer, A General Confession.*

To keep my hands from picking and stealing.

Offices of Instruction (Catechism)

To do my duty in that state of life unto which it shall please God to call me.

Ibid.

An outward and visible sign of an inward and spiritual grace.[1]

Ibid.

Let him now speak, or else hereafter for ever hold his peace.

Solemnization of Matrimony

To have and to hold from this day forward, for better for worse, for richer for poorer, in sickness and in health, to love and to cherish, till death us do part.

Ibid.

With this Ring I thee wed.

Ibid.

In the midst of life we are in death.[2]

Burial of the Dead. At the Grave

Earth to earth, ashes to ashes, dust to dust; in sure and certain hope of the Resurrection unto eternal life.

Ibid.

Show thy servant the light of thy countenance.

The Psalter. Psalms, XXXI, 18

But it was even thou, my companion, my guide, and mine own[3] familiar friend.

Ibid. LV, 14

God that maketh men to be of one mind in an house.

Ibid. LXVIII, 6

[1] The Sacrament.
[2] This is derived from a Latin antiphon, said to have been composed by Notker, a monk of St. Gall, in 911, while watching some workmen building a bridge at Martinsbrücke, in peril of their lives. It forms the groundwork of Luther's antiphon *De Morte*.
[3] Through a typographical error, the word "own" was changed to "old" in the first printing of the Revision of 1928.

The iron entered into his soul.

The Psalter. Psalms, CV, 18

God, in whom we live and move and have our being.

Family Prayer. Morning

O Lord, support us all the day long, until the shadows lengthen and the evening comes, and the busy world is hushed, and the fever of life is over, and our work is done. Then in thy mercy grant us a safe lodging, and a holy rest, and peace at the last.[1]

Ibid. At Night

O God of peace, who hast taught us that in returning and rest we shall be saved, in quietness and in confidence shall be our strength; By the might of thy Spirit lift us, we pray thee, to thy presence, where we may be still and know that thou art God.

Ibid. For Quiet Confidence[2]

O Heavenly Father, who hast filled the world with beauty; open, we beseech thee, our eyes to behold thy gracious hand in all thy works; that rejoicing in thy whole creation, we may learn to serve thee with gladness.[3]

Ibid. For Joy in God's Creation[4]

BOOK OF COMMON PRAYER, ENGLISH

Grant that the old Adam in these persons may be so buried, that the new man may be raised up in them.

Holy Baptism. Of Those of Riper Years

With all my worldly goods I thee endow.

Solemnization of Matrimony

[1] By Cardinal Newman.
[2] Added in the Revision of 1928.
[3] See Dostoyevsky, page 1074.
[4] Added in the Revision of 1928.

INDEX

In such indexes, although small pricks
To their subsequent volumes, there is seen
The baby figure of the giant mass
Of things to come at large.
SHAKESPEARE: *Troilus and Cressida, Act I, Sc. 3, Line 343*

INDEX

A.B.C. of reading, 886
A, black E white I red, 1084
A, the letter on the breast of her gown, 422
Aaron's serpent, like, 208
Abana and Pharpar, rivers of Damascus, 1101
Abandon, all hope, 1020
Abandonment poverty are battle-fields, 1068
Abashed the devil stood, 153
Abates, that never falters nor, 438
Abbey, buried in the great, 399
population of the, 787
within the, 562
Abbots, where slumber, 215
Abdallah's dead, 596
Abdiel, so spake the seraph, 153
Abdul the Bulbul Amir, 951
Abel, ask counsel at, 1100
Abhorred in my imagination, 97
Abhorrence, repudiate with indignation and, 419
Abide, and work in our stations, 519
men must needs, what fates impose, 70
our question, others, 545
with me, 365
Abides, peace of thine, that there, 546
God, 654
Abi-ezer, vintage of, 1099
Abilite to lerne sciences, 8
Abilitics as a writer, 235
each according to his, 1071
Ability, from each according to his, 1093
knowing how to conceal, 1044
out of my lean and low, 56
that they never perform, 75
to execute, 258
to make love frivolously, 898
to perform, he hath given him, 1127
Abject and humble, believed to be most, 1048
intercourse, love an, 253
Able, as far as he is, 702
for thine enemy, 52
more performance than they are, 75
to pay for it, I pray God make me, 180
Able-bodid relations, shed ev'ry drop of blud, 606
Ablest navigators, 271
Ablution, how many poor that lack, 760
of pure, round earth's, 385
Abnormal energy, wielded by, 636
Abode, dread, 245
Kubla Khan's, 879
rich man's, 515
where the eternal are, 366

Abode, without suspecting our, 586
Abodes, august, 325
Abominable custom swearing, 268
newspapers are, 278
Abomination of desolation, 1116
Abora, singing of Mount, 316
Aborigines and then upon the, 518, 815
Abou Ben Adhem, 346
Above, affections on things, 1121
all Greek fame, 214
all low delay, 336
all Roman fame, 214
all, this, 91
any Greek or Roman, 173
know the rage that yells, 375
that which is written, 1120
the reach of ordinary men, 297
the smoke and stir, 157
there is a life, 306
thy deep and dreamless sleep, 612
us, starlight of heaven, 502
Abra was ready ere I called, 190
Abraham found faithful in temptation, 1125
god of, 166
Lincoln in the tombs, 854
sat at his tent door, when, 166
Abraham's bosom, sleep in, 72
deaf ear, 892
Abram, O father, 45
Brown is dead and gone, 404
Abreast with Truth, who would keep, 525
Abridgment of all that was pleasant in man, 252
Abroad, before he goes, 242
let the soldier be, 331
the school master is, 331
Absalom my son, would God I had died for thee O, 1100
Abscess on his liver, 811
Absence, a cry of, 903
at his, 823
conquers love, 448
heard of my behavior in her, 183
I dote on his very, 44
makes the heart grow fonder, 388
of mind, your, 324
of occupation is not rest, 263, 501
reopens the springs of love, 506
still increases love, 388
the common cure, 1036
which must needs be endless, 506
Absent child, my, 58
face that fixed you, 428
friend is far away, 587
from Him I roam, 306
from you I have been, 108

Absent in body, but present in spirit, 1120
one from another, when we are, 1098
or dead, let a friend be dear, 393
thee from felicity awhile, 98
Absents, presents endear, 323
Absent-minded beggar, he's an, 782
Absolute, how, the knave is, 97
shall, 76
strong and wise, 780
sway, with, 172
trust, I built, 84
unvarying rigidity, 777
with good men not so, 386
Absolution of a faithful fight, 556
Absolutism tempered by assassination, 1060
Abstain from beans, 1001
Abstinence, easiness to the next, 95
easy as temperance is difficult, 238
Abstracts and brief chronicles, 93
qualities begin, 599
truths are strong meat, 477
Absurd of mankind, creatures most, 214
remark sight of a Dissenter, 314
sacredly, 783
to blame him were, 753
to slight for the hereafter, 484
Absurdity of conduct, 232
so palpable, no, 1064
the privilege of, 132
Abundance he shall have, 1116
if thou hast, 1123
in all, 971
of the heart, out of the, 1115
poorest lived in, 435
Abundant shower of curates, 507
summer redundant blueness, 493
Abundantly, might have life more, 1118
Abuse, bad language or, 622
loudest of its, 1049
rain a tempest of, 971
stumbling on, 78
Abuses and encroachments, 329
they that level at my, 108
Abused, better to be much, 102
or disabused, by himself, 207
too much, 728
Abusing the king's English, 34
Abysm of time, dark, 32
Abysmal dark, or the, 386
Abyss, a rope over an, 1079
everything in this, 1069
Abyssinia, Prince of, 232
Abyssinian maid, it was an, 315
Academe, grove of, 156

Academes that nourish all the world, 41
Academic life, 121
Academical Pharisees, our, 397
Accent of an angel's whisper, 645
  English without an, 905
Accents, copious, 218
  flow with artless ease, 275
  he caught the first, 548
  of old Wabash days, some wild, 676
  that are ours, 30
  yet unknown, 82
Accept a miracle instead of wit, 203
  commotion before stagnation, 543
Acceptable in his own country, not, 1126
  to have been, 985
Acceptation, worthy of all, 188
Accepted time, now is the, 1121
Access, experience has given him no, 1082
Accident, a happy, 117, 254, 1042
  counts for much, 635
  good action found out by, 324
  of sentiment to the literary man, 611
  the purest, by, 645
Accidents by flood and field, 100
  chapter of, 222
  failure and success not, 589
  miracles are propitious, 770
  runs into, 852
  tissue of disconnected, 1076
  will occur in the best, 496
Accommodated, excellent to be, 65
Accommodatin' character, pollertics of an, 606
Accompany old age, that which, 88
Accomplice of love, 1084
Accomplish as you may, you must, 77
Accomplished female friend, 942
Accord, good people all with one, 252
According to the appearance, 1118
Account, beggarly, of empty boxes, 80
  closing your, 1018
  endured on its, 1087
  sent to my, 92
Accoutred as I was I plunged in, 81
Accretion, cold, 651
Accuracy in newspaper account, 803
  that may exclude, 1017
Accurate mind, logic of an, 454
  refined and chaste, 972
Accursed and unfair, thieves, 1022
  deadly magic and, 928
  fear is most, 68
Accurst, not what God blessed, 490
Accusation, tamper not with, 688
Accuse not nature, 154
Accusing spirit, the, 242

Accustomed sight of death, the, 50
  to obsequiousness and flattery, 272
Ace, coldest that ever turned up, 105
  death's, 639
Ache, charm, with air, 40
  penury and imprisonment, 36
  while his heart doth, 172
Achieve a just and lasting peace, 457
  all we, or are, 572
  in time, I shall, 624
  what you cannot as you would, 77
Achieved through liberty, that little, 493
Achievement of any age, total scientific, 543
  to-day's, 629
  turns the bane, 651
Achievements, raise a monument, 1027
Achilles absent was Achilles still, 219
  assumed, what name, 145
  whom we knew, 464
Achilles' tomb, stood upon, 360
  wrath to Greece, 218
Aching, ease one life the, 583
  hands and bleeding feet, with, 546
  members into a chair, 938
  void, left an, 266
Achings and quakings, 453
Achromatic white light of heaven, 432
Acid sect, melt not in an, 443
Acids stain you, 918
Acknowledged worth, for their, 972
Acknowledgment of inferiority, 339
  of the truth, 1077
Acme of romance, 723
A-cold, owl was, 383
  poor Tom's, 99
Acorn falls to die, many an, 681
  heart of the buried, 753
  lofty oak from a small, 292
Acorns on the lea, strewed, 504
  tall oaks from little, 292
Acquaint ourselves with ev'ry zone, 114
  when we were first, 286
Acquaintance among men and nations, mutual, 608
  decrease it upon better, 34
  make a new, 238
  many of mine old, are dead, 65
  people for a visiting, 278
  should auld, be forgot, 286
  that begins with a compliment, 724
Acquaintances, new, 233
Acquire and beget a temperance, 94
Acre, every square, of land and sea, 415
  in Middlesex is better than, 398
  of barren ground, 32
Acres, Cleon hath a million, 503
  few paternal, 216

Acres of diamonds, 665
  over whose, walked, 60
Across the silent stream, 717
Act and know, does both, 169
  and speech, 572
  by what you see them, 100
  done at haphazard, 1010
  each, a course, 200
  from thought, 937
  in the living present, 433
  in the noon, 282
  may show in some fifth, 472
  my wish that failed of, 444
  of common passage, 106
  of fear, distill'd with the, 90
  of God, man think himself an, 506
  of life, dignity in every, 1010
  of order to a peopled kingdom, 1032
  of Parliament, through an, 945
  or passion, no single, 667
  proved all its thought, 487
  that roars so loud, 95
  you reap an, 954
Acts being seven ages, 49
  exemplary, lives in, 28
  five, the just measure of a play, 180
  four first, already passed, 203
  illustrious, high raptures do infuse, 146
  in memory, to keep good, 113
  like a Samaritan, 426
  little nameless, 295
  noble, which he did, 1125
  nobly does well, 201
  of Betsey or any of her, 678
  of government, examination of the, 320
  our, our angels are, 126
  so or so, to say why gals, 527
  the best who thinks most, 506
  those graceful, 154
  unremembered, 295
Acting bravely a silent desperate part, 533
  lies, not in, 209
  of a dreadful thing, 82
  only when off the stage, 252
Action action action, 1005
  and counteraction, 260
  circumstance gives character to, 999
  crowded with glorious, 311
  eases his way of, 1000
  faithful in, 210
  feeling for one single good, 1057
  fine, makes that and the, 135
  for a man of great spirit, chiefest, 128
  good, do by stealth, 324
  great end of life is, 564
  how like an angel in, 92
  I may soar as high in my, 514
  in the tented field, 100
  justice is truth in, 419
  lose the name of, 93
  man's power of, 1048
  materials of, are variable, 1007
  no noble, done, 202
  no stronger than a flower, 107

Action, no worthy, done, 202
of the tiger, imitate in war, 66
pious, we sugar o'er, 93
Puritans gave the world, 479
single lovely, 529
so in each, 199
suit the, to the word, 94
surfeit out of, 76
the glory of, 953
thought is the child of, 420
vice dignified by, 78
Actions, all her words and, 154
extreme, be ascribed to vanity, 1079
fretful foam of vehement, 548
ghost of forgotten, 681
great, no opportunities for, 999
habits increased by correspondent, 1008
mean, to fear, 1079
most brilliant, 395
no other speaker of my living, 74
not always show the man, 209
not our fears make us traitors, 87
ordinary, ascribed to habit, 1079
performance of pleasant, 877
speech the image of, 1013
than hostile, 997
the morality of his, 1055
which work out the good, 1048
words the shadows of, 1001
Actives to passives, fit, 118
Activity and duty, 1085
in mere change of, 1071
Actor, after a well-graced, 60
condemn not the, 36
stops, a moment yet the, 481
the charm of the act, 660
Actors are the usual three, 574
God and nature fill with, 129
jealousies and petulances of, 617
no, without a gallery, 726
these our, were all spirits, 33
Actor's gift, this is the, 649
Actresses excite my amorous propensities, 233
Actual existence, sordid perils of, 723
A-cursing like a very drab, fall, 93
Ad infinitum, so proceed, 190
Adad inundate his field, 958
Adage, like the poor cat in the, 85
Adam and Eve, believe, 810
cup of cold, 190
Cupid, young, 77
gardener, and his wife, 462
saw her prime, 328
so starved me, 490
the goodliest man of men, 152
the offending, 66
the old, 1128
waked so customed, 153
was a gardener, 785
Adam's ale, and drink of, 190
arm, from under, 953
ear left his voice, in, 154
fall, we sinned all, in, 947
feet, taken from, 953

Adam's head, taken from, 953
profession, they hold up, 96
sons born in sin, 124
Adam-zad, no truce with, 779
Adamas de rupe præstantissimus, 145
Add another hue unto the rainbow, 58
to golden numbers, 116
Adder, like the deaf, 1104
stingeth like an, 1108
Addict themselves to sack, 65
Adding fuel to the flame, 157
Addison, days and nights to, 233
Addition, come as an agreeable, 985
Address, wiped with a little, 264
Addressing myself to my cap, 1046
Adds a precious seeing to the eye, 41
Adhem, Abou Ben, 346
Adhere, nor time nor place did, 85
Adieu, drop a tear and bid, 225
for evermore, 288
had not bade, 384
my native shore, 352
she cried, 205
Adjunct, learning is but an, 41
useful, 325
Adjustment, the great, 651
Administered, whate'er is best, 208
Administration, because in the, 969
cannot injure government in four years, 455
genius for, 693
Administrations, most competent, 273
Admirable, how express and, 92
Admiral fame of the, 737
last of all an, 322
of the north, one was, 780
to kill one, 1052
Admirals all they went, 764
Admiralty, price of, 778
Admiration and pity, human affairs deserve, 727
from most fastidious critics, 398
greatest and most worthy of, 120
of virtue, 162
of weak minds, 156
season your, for a while, 90
the right kind of money, 1079
Admirations, to teach, 1084
Admire, for to, for to see, 782
like those who, us, 1044
men of sense approve, fools, 211
where none, 239
Admired, by their domestics, 1030
celerity is never more, 104
Admirers, complaisance for their, 1037
Admiring bog, to an, 584
in the gloomy shade, 145
Admitted to that equal sky, 207
Admonition of the higher instincts, 476
Adolescens moritur, 302
Adonais, soul of, 366

Adonis hath a sweet tooth, my, 24
Adoption tried, their, 90
Adorable, grace joined with wrinkles is, 1069
Adoration, breathless with, 297
Adore the hand that gives the blow, 179
Adored in every clime, 216
Adores and burns, 207
Adorn a tale, point a moral, 230
looks the cottage might, 251
nothing he did not, 231
Adorned in her husband's eye, 295
in naked beauty more, 152
the most when unadorned, 224
whatever he spoke upon, 222
Adorning with so much art, 167
Adornings, or gat ye these, 748
Adornment without embellishment, 980
woman's best, 976
Adorns and cheers our way, 252
Adrift! A little boat adrift, 585
with one, her heart's, 568
Adsum, word used at school, 483
Adulation fawning and flattery, 981
windy, 635
Adullam, cave, 1100
into his political cave of, 478
Adulterate complexion, 115
Adulteries of art, 119
Adultery, gods call, 358
Advance, moral, 572
not to go back is to, 214
spare not nor look behind, 417
Advantage be, find its proper use and of, 706
dressed, nature to, 211
feet nailed for our, 60
forget at times with, 987
in the past, every, 976
itinerant preachers have, 228
keen sense for my own, 1076
of a good light, give the, 413
of a hotel, 720
of them, no way of taking, 1078
to philosophy, 769
Advantages of being an island race, 906
that occur every day, 228
the great have, 1040
various qualities and, 1087
Advantageous to life, 32
Advent of each dangerous day, 825
Adventure and pain, used to, 909
death a beautiful, 534
hopeless his, 624
in experience, life is, 930
is not death the great, 881
lit her stars, 847
of the diver, 484
of to-morrow, 58
retaking up of his, 908
with a song, meet, 825
Adventures of his discontent, 898
of his soul, 1079
relate and embellish his, 1056
Adventurer is within us, the, 908
Adventurers, miscellaneous set of, 739

Adventuring both, oft found both, 44
Adventurous simplicissimus, the, 1045
Adversaries, as, do in law, 52
Adversary had written a book, 1102
  the devil, your, 1123
Adversitee, fortunes sharpe, 4
Adversity, blazes in the dark hour of, 344
  blessing of the New Testament, 109
  bruised with, 37
  day of, 1108, 1109
  education a refuge in, 1015
  good things that belong to, 109
  great men contending with, 124
  hard upon a man, 381
  is not without comforts, 109
  more supportable than great prosperity, 613
  of our best friends, 259
  presses, if, 478
  strength in his, 120
  strokes of, 985
  sweet are the uses of, 48
  tries friends, 990
  what way to endure, 980
Adversity's sweet milk, 79
Advertised by our loving friends, we are, 71
Advertisement, gods had special, 184
  one effective, 921
Advertisements show ideals of a, 802
Advice, and with my, 389
  ask a woman's, 337
  cannot inspire conduct, 1044
  Creator had not taken, 1020
  few profit by, 987
  in a position to give, 772
  nothing given so profusely as, 1044
  of a man in difficulties, 963
  to give, the true, 1071
  worst men often give best, 507
Advices, lengthened sage, 287
Advise another, easy to, 1013
  whom none could, 22
Ae, twa bairns and but, heart, 389
Aegean seas, the dog by the, 674
Aegroto dum anima est, 206
Aeon, an, or two, 779
Aery-light, his sleep was, 153
Aesop's fly, 376
Aesthetic emotion, 1084
Afar and asunder, 621
  from the great sea-deeps, 675
Afeard, soldier and, 88
Affair, consider what precedes in every, 1008
  this world is a strange, 1046
Affairs, debate of commonwealth, 66
  direction of public, 1075
  every man's, 234
  of love, office and, 38
  of men, tide in the, 83
  prying into human, 1067
  quit public, 921
  ridiculous in serious, 1003
  sight of human, 727,

Affairs would be far happier, 1048
Affect little minds, little things, 420
  study what you most, 52
Affected, to be zealously, 1121
Affecting, natural simple, he was, 252
Affection and love for one another, 268
  and recollection, with deep, 423
  but the power we give another, 425
  calls, where, 418
  cannot hold the bent, 54
  equal application to, 661
  hath an unknown bottom, my, 51
  I pine, with blighted, 791
  immortality born of human, 603
  my fond, thou hast seen, 388
  never was wasted, 435
  preferment by letter and, 100
  rests upon vision, 799
  rule the hour, 364
  strong to me-wards, 133
  sustained by its, 942
  talk not of wasted, 435
  the purest, 775
  two sorts of, 716
Affections dark as Erebus, 47
  holiness of the heart's, 385
  mild, of, 217
  on things above, 1121
  which attend human life, 197
Affectionate, compassionate, great individual, 537
Affects to nod, 176
Affinity with the soul of man, such, 476
Affirmation, green towers of, 925
  or denial, whose, 1021
Afflatus, effluence from divine, 1067
Afflicted or distressed, 1127
Affliction, acquainted with, 645
  comforts us in our, 977
  forgetfulness of, 1124
  in the day of, 1124
  is digested, before an, 241
  may smile again, 41
  whether light or grave, 503
Affliction's sons are brothers, 285
Affluence to poverty, 615
Affrayed me out of slepe, 3
Affrighted ostrich, 683
Affront, fear is, 204
  me, a well-bred man will not, 263
  no woman can bear, 1040
Afire with God, every bush, 442
A-fishing, laid aside business and gone, 139
Afraid, and in short I was, 900
  and the just man is, 375
  any more, not be, 901
  be not, it is I, 1115
  in a world I never made, 743
  of whom am I afraid, 584
  that I am not, 845
  to do anything, 226
  to pray, 386
  whistling to keep from being, 179

Afric maps, geographers in, 190
Afric's burning shore, 319
  sunny fountains, 343
Africa and golden joys, 65
African birth, 600
After its life, fleeing to ocean, 501
  looking before and, 96
  the revel was done, 600
  the verb to love, 1083
  times, written to, 162
  us the deluge, 1055
  you with equal grace force, 536
After-life, some letter of that, 1019
Afternoon, custom of the, 91
  multitude call the, 41
  of her best days, 72
  sunshine, time asleep in, 588
  tea, 666
  took long to die, 923
  vacant, 258
Afternoons in Montana, hot, 945
Afterthought, our life is but an, 924
After-times every poet hopes that, 447
Afton, flow gently sweet, 286
Again, come never back, 390
  cut and come, 280
  not look upon his like, 90
  oh to be home, 508
Against me, not with me is, 1117
  sleep, who can wrestle, 478
Agamemnon, brave men before, 358, 984
Agape, cried one, 620
Agate-stone, no bigger than an, 77
Agayns the proces of nature, 8
Age ache penury, 36
  against time and, 27
  and body of the time, 94
  and clime, in every, 206
  and dust, pays us with, 22
  and hunger, 49
  and youth are reconciled, 699
  as if old, were never kindly, 530
  be comfort to my, 48
  become a stonie one, 25
  begins anew, the world's great, 367
  best in four things, 113
  best viaticum of old, 1015
  calmly waits, while old, 954
  cannot wither her, 104
  carries all things, 982
  certain, 357
  come to thy grave in full, 1102
  companions for middle, 110
  crabbed, and youth, 109
  cradle of reposing, 213
  dallies like the old, 55
  dawn in happy old, 1069
  disease or sorrows strike him, when, 519
  disgrace of wickedness added to old, 1003
  draw out his old, 978
  each, is a dream that is dying, 676
  every, has its pleasures, 1049
  every, to souls who live in 't, 430
  excel in pride of life, 546

Age, father of all in every, 216
finds out was dew, 493
folly in all of every, 1050
give me bless'd, 736
golden, exists only in, 400
grow dim with, 195
hardly feel the pressure of, 973
he was not of an, 119
heads of strong old, 895
heritage of old, 420
his wealth a well-spent, 121
I make light of it, 555
I may not drift, in, 649, 983
I summon, 489
immobile hieratic or without art, 723
in a full, come to thy grave, 1102
in a good old, 1097
in a green old, 178, 219
in a virtuous person of either sex, 197
in commendation of, 113
in the summer of her, 179
is as a lusty winter, 48
is dull and mean, the, 442
is full of care, 109
is grown so picked, 97
is in the wit is out, when the, 39
is not all decay, 559
is opportunity, 438
is weary with work and gold, 507
know old, may come after you, 535
know your, 729
labour of an, 161
lends a double charm, 451
made, for talking, 250
master spirits of this, 82
men grow virtuous in their old, 217
monumental pomp of, 302
most blessed memory of mine, 463
most remote from infancy, 1047
most terrible misfortune, 395
naked in mine, to mine enemies, 74
narrative with, 218
new words well suited to the, 180
no longer is a burden, 967
of chivalry is gone, 260
of discord and continual strife, 68
of ease, youth of labor, 250
of giants, ends the, 780
of gold, comes round the, 477
of gold, fetch the, 161
of gold, happier, 649
of miracles, 380
of revolution and reformation, 273
of sophisters, 260
of wisdom the age of foolishness, 497
old and well stricken in, 1097
old, as spectator, 700
old content to sit and watch, 700
old, hand in hand with experience, 185

Age, old, on tiptoe, 770
olives of endless, 108
our fathers', 983
patriot a fool in every, 214
prayer-books are the toys of, 208
proper, for pleasure, 182
pyramids doting with, 147
ripe, 573
ruling ideas of each, 1072
scarce expect one of my, 292
serene and bright, an old, 299
shall not weary them, 804
should accompany old, 88
silvered o'er with, his head was, 206
smack of, in you, 64
small for its, 1012
soul of the, 119
staff of my, 45
still leaves us, 335
strong meat for full, 1122
that darkens, 869
that first was named golden, 25
that is past to the age that is waiting, 363
that which should accompany old, 88
the golden, 32, 984
thinks better of a gilded fool, this, 115
those who compare the, 400
thou art shamed, 81
thou waitedst, wait death, 489
to age succeeds, 462
to cheated age, 780
to come my own, make the, 167
too late, 154
torrent of a downward, 224
tuneless in old, 649
'twixt boy and youth, 307
vastness and, and memories, 459
veracity which increases with old, 1044
what more honourable than, 113
where youth and manhood, if there's an, 685
wherein he lived was dark, 167
will marry, widow of doubtful, 479
will perform promises of youth, 232
with fears and ills is rife, 812
with his stealing steps, 96
without a name, 310
without criticism, 723
woman and her, 724
you live in, 986
you'd scarce expect one of my, 292

Ages, belongs to the, 706
buried in the dust of, 509
ere Homer's lamp appeared, 262
ere the Mantuan swan was heard, 262
famous to all, 162
heir of all the, 464
heirs of all the, 542
hence, how many, 82
his acts being seven, 49

Ages, millions of, to making of man, 581
name curst to all succeeding, 173
of eternity, mighty, 553
of your sires, 546
onward roll, the great, 463
passed away, forms of, 423
past a blank would be, 288
probably pervaded all, 479
rock of, 272
roll forward, 594
stamp and esteem of, 172
the emptiness of, 708
three poets in three, 175
through the, 464
unborn crowd not on my soul, 244
wakens the slumbering, 402
ye unborn, 244
Age's alms, prayers which are old, 28
tooth, poison for the, 57
Aged and poor and slow, for all she's, 715
bosom, confidence in an, 230
ears play truant at his tales, 41
later times are more, 112
men full loth and slow, 309
owl abode, 662
seer alone, laid the, 372
Ageless and eternal sea, 1066
Agencies vary, how widely its, 391
Agency, bestowed by some divine, 975
Agent despised, thus is the poor, 75
good of the, 1048
most precious conservative, 662
powerful, is the right word, 615
trust no, 38
Agents of Congress, I took you for one of the, 283
Agesilaus toying with his children, 1004
Aggravate your choler, 65
Aggravation of self, 635
Aggressive fancy working spells, 650
Agile bookworm eats, 865
A-gley, gang aft, 284
Agnes, the world dear, 1046
Ago, in the olden time long, 459
mighty while, 118
Agonies, dismays doubts and spiritual, 787
exultations, 297
fiercest, have the shortest reign, 373
of all the past, 765
Agony, a great heart's overmastering, 192
all we know of, 363
distrest, though oft to, 303
leave off the, 685
strength in some great, 520
swimmer in his, 359
with words, charm, 40
Agree, agreed that we can't never, 678
not well together, 531

Agree, this world and I shall ne'er, 168
    those who, with us, 1044
    though all things differ, all, 216
Agreeable bountiful constant dutiful, 1037
    person, my idea of an, 421
Agreed, except they be, 1113
    to differ, 321
Agreement about books, 865
    with hell, 1111
Agrees with me, agreeable person, 421
Agricultural population the bravest, 994
Agriculture, I know nothing about, 909
Agriculturist works the farmer, 661
Ahab went to Ascalon, 853
Ahead, then go, 349
A-hunting goes, when tuckt up she, 134
    we daren't go, 573
Ah Sin was his name, 644
Ahkoond is dead, 499, 679
Aid, alliteration's artful, 262
    else small, 967
    friend of pleasure wisdom's, 248
    from a chink in the floor, 817
    from men, need no, 783
    me for to win her, 818
    of ornament, the foreign, 224
    prepare with mutual, 1049
    the truth, cannon-balls may, 504
    then Heaven be thy, 375
    to every poor man, to give, 1049
    win our battles by its, 504
Aids in the ebb-tide or flow, 504
Aïdes' den, imminent to, 652
Ailments and grievances, clod of, 720
Aim and its effect, find its, 1068
    and reason, its, 1058
    attainment of the highest moral, 1063
    better have failed in the high, 492
    mind thine own, 408
    most skilful archer miss his, 180
    of modern societies, 762
    of true philosophy, 646
    our being's end and, 208
    rivalry of, 636
    seems their only, 875
    take glittering, 586
    the star, your, 957
    to serve God's, 575
Aims other than my delight, 651
    unsearchable and secret, 668
Aiming at what's far, 968
Ain countree, in my, 346
Air a chartered libertine, 66
    along the heedless, 541
    and a peculiar grace, an, 199
    around with beauty, 354
    babbling gossip of the, 54
    be shook to, 75
    bird of the, 1110
    birds of the, have nests, 1114
    bites shrewdly, 91

Air, blasted the very, 421
    breasts the keen, 249
    breath of flowers sweeter in the, 111
    burns frore, the parching, 150
    castles in the, 122
    charm ache with, 40
    couriers of the, 85
    cutting the, 1036
    dewy freshness fills the, 322
    do not saw the, 94
    dyes the wide, 701
    eating the, 64
    every flower enjoys the, 295
    fairer than the evening, 32
    faith and philosophy are, 531
    fanes quiver in the, 403
    field of, through the, 267
    fields of, 364, 1051
    freshness fills the silent, 322
    from wild spring, 866
    gather rubies from the, 877
    gave to the common, 954
    gloomy and thoughtful, 1068
    he'd fly through the, 640
    her keel plows, 28
    his happy good-night, 651
    his love was like the liberal, 626
    hurtles in the darkened, 244
    I drew in the common, 1124
    into the murky, 155
    is also man's dominion, 572
    is calm and pleasant, when the, 162
    is chilly in Cremona, 738
    is delicate, the, 85
    is filled that she passes through, 644
    is full of sunlight, 710
    is hush'd, 247
    love free as, 216
    man's life is but, 577
    melted into thin, 33
    meteor to the troubled, 244
    might wash me, 630
    mocking the, with colors, 58
    most excellent canopy, 92
    mounting into the, 238
    my highway is unfeatured, 517
    nipping and an eager, 91
    of delightful studies, 162
    of gloom, ceremonious, 547
    of glory, walking in an, 170
    of great solemnity, 1064
    of night, through the balmy, 460
    of superiority, 1072
    of the New World, 726
    on the haunted, 904
    or fly the, 953
    perfuming, morning, 482
    programs, between, 852
    recommends itself, 85
    round and round as if with, 672
    russet year inhaled the dreamy, 551
    scent the morning, 91
    seen in the, 940
    sewers annoy the, 154
    shut up want, 202
    sightless couriers of the, 85
    silence and the homeless, 629
    slowness of gloried, 920
    so fair that like the, 405

Air, soft somewhat languid, 932
    splitting the, 76
    spread his sweet leaves to the, 77
    summer's noontide, 150
    sweetness in the desert, 245
    sweetness on the desert, 245
    their lungs receive our, 264
    thoughts shut up want, 202
    through the field of, 267
    throw a straw into the, 130
    to Britons dearest, 443
    trifles light as, 102
    vague thunder, in the, 926
    was cooling, 385
    was littered, 699
    wet woolen, of Europe, 932
    when you whistle the, 821
    whose hands upheld us in the, 1091
    wild, world-mothering, 672
    with barbarous dissonance, 158
    with beauty, fills the, 354
    with idle state, mock the, 244
    wool-gray, 932
    world's vaporous vitiate, 652
Airs and madrigals, 163
    ecstatic, 873
    lap me in soft Lydian, 160
    melting, or martial, 266
    of England, martial, 341
    who shall silence all the, 163
Air-drawn dagger, 87
Airly, to take in God, gut to git up, 526
Airship, keeps her course, his, 841
Airy a tread, so, 469
    footsteps of strange things, 421
    nothing, a local habitation, 43
    reveries so, 265
    servitors, nimble and, 162
    tinklings come and go, 618
    tongues that syllable, 157
    voices lead, 382
Aisle, the longest, 927
Aisles of Christian Rome, 408
    on my heart monastic, 408
Aisne-Marne Chavignon St. Mihiel, 866
Ajax, prayer of, was for light, 434
    strives some rock to throw, 211
    the great himself a host, 218
Akond of Swat, who is the, 499
Al his chere, she was, 6
    the night with open yë, 5
Alabama, I've come from, 567
Alabaster arms of death, 646
    as monumental, 103
    box of very precious ointment, 1116
    boxes, do not keep the, 577
    cities gleam, 737
    grandsire cut in, 44
Alacrity in sinking, a kind of, 35
Aladdin's lamp, 361, 528
    tower, window in, 437
Alamo, remember the, 427
Alarms of struggle and flight, 546
    three years of war's, 899
    used to war's, 392
Alas, who cried in goose, 903
Albany to San Diego, towns from, 884

Alcatraz tow'rd Orient skies, past, 643
Alchemy, courtesy is the true, 574
Alcibiades and his dog, 1002
  could adapt himself, 997
Alcides' equal, 991
Alcohol and Christianity, narcotics, 1081
Alcoran, the Talmud and the, 110
Aldeborontiphoscophornio, 189
Aldermanbury to Bunhill Fields, from, 933
Alderman's forefinger, 77
Ale, all-powerful, 258
  and safety, a pot of, 66
  doth bring men to, the bliss good, 20
  drank a pint of English, 827
  drink of Adam's, 190
  God send thee good, 20
  in fear, cakes and, 961
  is the stuff to drink, 743
  no more cakes and, 54
  older than their, 251
  pined for cheerful, 258
  quart of mighty, 6
  size of pots of, 141
  spicy nut-brown, 160
  turn out more, 610
  we drank, 610
Ale-house, an honest, 139
Alembics turn to stranger things, 897
Alexander and Diogenes, 999
  and the Gordium knot, 999
  how great was, 564
  I would be Diogenes if I were not, 1005
  in the Olympic race, 1002
  noble dust of, 97
  Selkirk used, as, 622
  the coppersmith did me much evil, 1122
  wept that he had not conquered a world, 1001
Alexandrine, needless, 211
Alfarata, Indian girl bright, 406
Algebra, tell what hour by, 141
Algiers, soldier lay dying in, 447
Alice! a childish story, 598
  don't you remember sweet, 521
Alien corn, amid the, 383, 390
  realms of night, 764
  there is none, 1084
Aliens into trusting friends, transmutes, 508
Alike are sent, joys and tears, 423
  if you see us naked, 124
  they're needful to the flower, 423
  were they free from fear, 435
Alive and so bold O earth, 367
  as sure as I'm, 1036
  assume we are, 780
  at this day, the bricks are, 69
  bliss to be, 300
  if I shouldn't be, 584
  with a terrible might, 681
All along the pleasant way, 619
  are folded now, 848
  are needed by each one, 408
  are presumed good, 138
  are sleeping on the hill, 806
  around them trembling, 931

All at once and nothing first, 453
  be true that I do think, 184
  but one passed by, 924
  cared not to be at, 149
  cry and no wool, 142
  dies! and not alone, 531
  else had perished, 289
  flesh is grass, 1112
  flesh must die, 892
  for immortality, 535
  for love, 24, 274
  for one, 106
  for one, one for all, 1067
  go to pot, 254
  goes onward and outward, 535
  goned afay mit de lager beer, 559
  good dead men, 710
  good things together come, not, 540
  good to me is lost, 151
  grief and misery, 596
  happy families resemble one another, 1077
  has happened long ago, 531
  have given him over, when, 31
  have it all, 1069
  have not the gift of martyrdom, 174
  have passed away, 364
  having nothing yet hath, 114
  he hath seen forgets, 1021
  he read of any book, 275
  I ask the heaven above, 703
  I better know than, 444
  I can give you, I give, 633
  I fail of win, and, 444
  I had you thought, 887
  I heard it, 816
  I know is what I read, 859
  I meant to say, 850
  I see is mine, but, 568
  in all, manner is, 262
  in all, take him for, 90
  in all to one another, 623
  is best, 157
  is blue, 492
  is done that men can do, 287
  is for the best, 478, 1052
  is illusion till the morning bars, 643
  is lost by a collapse, 661
  is not as it seemeth, 643
  is not gold that glisteneth, 117
  is not Gospell, 15
  is not lost, 148
  is not true, 643
  is ordered well, that, 501
  is vanity, 1109
  is well, 907
  is well and shall be well, 875
  is well, God is and, 444
  is well, if the end be well, 1075
  is well that ends well, 53
  is well, they who assert that, 1052
  is well, to know that, 966
  is well with you, 718
  its all, though, 822
  knowledge is delight, 299
  love except what trade can give, 492
  love, trust a few, 52
  loved art in a seemly way, 686
  men are liars, 1105
  men desire to be immortal, 477

All men have their price, 200
  must come to the self-same bay, 1022
  my days are trances, and, 460
  my nightly dreams, and, 460
  my pretty chickens, 88
  my ways are dewy wet, 572
  of a heap, 279
  of their singing, 757
  of them that seek learning, 1125
  of us fell down, 83
  of us live too much in a circle, 420
  one and, 610
  other time is peace, 132
  our calm is in that balm, 447
  places are distant from heaven alike, 124
  please, 962
  present or accounted for, 550
  quiet along the Potomac, 569
  rosy red, 1086
  seas all ships, 536
  shall die, 65
  she had, purchased with, 422
  she had to say, for, 861
  that a man hath will he give, 1101
  that glisters is not gold, 45
  that glitters is not gold, 174
  that he loves or fears or hates, 306
  that he will know on earth, 841
  that I am to be, I would give, 366
  that I could see, 915
  that I could think of, 702
  that I was I am, 869
  that I would and cannot be, 731
  that is above fulfilment, 799
  that's dusty tame and old, 912
  that is human, 965
  that is left of the Caesars' gold, 841
  that lies on the ocean's floor, 910
  that live must die, 89
  that makes a man, and, 471
  that mankind has done thought gained or been, 381
  that may become a man, 85
  that men held wise, 146
  that once was I, 916
  that once you knew, 879
  that time could wither, 373
  that to heaven and earth relates, 306
  that was beautiful, 771
  that was exquisite and rare, ignoring, 788
  that we cherished, 666
  that we have lost, live as much in, 534
  that we see or seem, 459
  the bright company, 900
  the brothers valiant, 943
  the difference lies, 941
  the fields are lying brown and bare, 552
  the flowers sprang up to see, 619
  the learned and authentic fellows, 53

All the same a hundred years
    hence, 607
    the sisters virtuous, 943
    the translations and editions,
        238
    the trees are brown, and, 523
    the uses of this world, 90
    the voyage of their life, 83
    the world and his wife, 192
    the world in love with night, 79
    the world's a stage, 49
    the world is old lad, when, 523
    the world must see the world,
        559
    the years, hopes of, 612
    these are for you, 917
    these tidal gatherings, 895
    they that take the sword, 1116
    things all day long, on, 470
    things are fleeting, 772
    things are passing, 437
    things can be borne, 596
    things come alike to all, 1109
    things give God glory, 673
    things, he who seeks, 592
    things that are, 45
    things, there's a time for, 37
    things to all men, 1120
    things work and move, 502
    things work together, 1119
    to understand, makes us in-
        dulgent, 1060
    was for best, 486
    was not lost, 1061
    was young, you loved when,
        523
    we ask is to be let alone, 539
    we had of joy, 887
    we have built do we discern,
        546
    we lacked before, learn, 893
    we like sheep have gone astray,
        1112
    we love foregathers, 851
    we would, because we can't do,
        519
    which I took, 749
    who die at sea, 693
    who perceive, belong to, 629
    who turn to it, receives, 1021
    who write, 850
    will be well for us all, 608
    will yet be well, let us hope
        that, 455
    you can hold, 658
    you pitied all you bore, 703
    your danger is in discord,
        436
    your strength is in your union,
        436
    your wish is woman to win,
        481
Allah, the peace of, 952
Allan Percy used to roam with
    me, 447
Allarums, warres and, 25
Allaving Thames, with no, 168
    Tiber, not a drop of, 76
Allegiance to the flag, 718
Allegorical, great literature al-
    ways, 826
    way of expressing it, 496
Allegory, headstrong as an, 278
    life a continual, 385
    on the banks of the Nile, 278
    out, spinning, 893

Alleluia, Alleluia sang the choir,
    653
All-embracing love, 1074
All-enacting Might, 651
All-enclosing freehold of content,
    573
Alleviation, seem to be an, 927
Alley, his soul lives in an, 118
    she lives in our, 189
    titanic of cypress, through an,
        461
Alliance, abroad they purchase
    great, 70
Alliances, entangling, 273
    permanent, 268
Allied powers having proclaimed,
    1061
    to the great truths, 396
Allies, thou hast great, 297
    three grand, 203
Alligator-horses, Kentucky boys
    are, 348
Alliteration's artful aid, 262
Allone, with-outen any com-
    panye, 6
Allotment, corner of God's, 651
Allowance made without equiva-
    lent, 233
    though small your, 481
Allowances for rests and nodding-
    places, 196
Allowed indulgence in such fool-
    ishness, 522
All-powerful ale, 258
    time, 966
    who is, 1043
All-seeing sun ne'er saw her
    match, 77
All's-well, he who breathes, 651
Allured to brighter worlds, 250
Allure thee, if parts, 208
Alluring yet ineluctable problem,
    871
Ally, woman's natural, 968
Alma Mater, to our old, 401
Almanack, look in the, 43
Almighty, difference of purpose
    between, 457
    dollar, the, 119, 343, 656
    eye, could not 'scape the,
        204
    gave the dog to be companion,
        311
    God, first planted a garden,
        111
    God, we make our prayer, 268
    gold, 119, 656
    has His own purposes, 457
    Lord, vicaire of the, 4
Almighty's bow, arrow from the,
    282
    gentlemen, God, 174
    hand, led by the, 168
    orders, 194
Almonds to those who have no
    teeth, 434
Almoner best, is he who keeps
    back nothing, 1016
Almost at odds with morning, 87
Alms accordingly, give, 1123
    before men, 1114
    for oblivion, 75
    prayers which are old age's, 28
    were money put to interest,
        321
    when thou doest, 1114

Alms, who gives himself with
    his, 525
Almsdeeds, good works and, 1118
Almshouse, windows of the, 515
Aloe, how to plant the, 476
    plant, tale of the, 507
Aloe-like hearts, 507
Aloft, cherub that sits up, 274
    his soul has gone, 274
    now he's gone, 274
    on sky and mountain wall, 445
Aloha means I love you, 920
Aloha Oe, so I say, 920
Alone all all alone, 315
    and shut the door, once we are,
        841
    and thou, art there, 403
    at night, flying, 841
    give me to live with love, 406
    how can it be said I am, 42
    I did it. — Boy! 76
    I lie down, 744
    I lingered, on the shore, 418
    in solitude we are least, 353
    in the midst of crowds, 324
    leaving me never, 652
    left too much, 808
    made up of loveliness, 405
    man dwells apart though not,
        540
    man should not be, 1097
    needs must act, 80
    never say that you are, 1007
    never would leave me, 850
    no man can feel himself, 750
    on a wide wide sea, 315
    shut to him who comes, 444
    sing when all, 484
    speaks to the heart, 501
    strongest man most, 487
    than pine in a palace, 545
    than when alone, never less,
        271, 289
    that worn-out word, 425
    thou workest never, 573
    travels fastest who travels, 783
    upon the other side, step, 603
    use sometimes to be, 136
    with his friends, 190
    with his glory, 364
    with my conscience, 681
    with noble thoughts, 27
    with silence, to be, 688
Along the pleasant way, 619
Alonso of Arragon, 113
Aloof with hermit-eye, 316
Aloud before him I may think,
    411
Alp, many a fiery, 150
Alph, the sacred river, 315
Alpha and Omega, 1123
Alphabet, back into the, 660
    man's, 657
    the whole, 1037
Alphonso's hints for the creation,
    1020
Alpine snow, purple lights on,
    442
    summits of great pain, 570
Alps on Alps arise, 210
    there shall be no, 413
Alraschid, golden prime of, 462
Already   the   dandelions   are
    changed, 619
Alsatian mountains, by the blue,
    582

Altama murmurs wild, 251
Altar, before the same, 335
　die, at the, 816
　God's, 165
　kneel not before the same, 657
　lays upon the, 747
　learning's, vanish, 517
　Lord to burn, on thine, 671
　love I bow before thine, 248
　of freedom, costly sacrifice upon, 457
　of the Blessed Virgin, 1078
　of the Lord, on the, 934
　reach the skies, let its, 294
　to publicity, 856
　with this inscription, I found an, 1118
Altars and tombs, bow bare-headed before, 787
　lights of a thousand, 752
　priests, victims, 216
　strike for your, 362
Altar's God, 165
Altar-stairs, world's, 468
Alter? When the hills do, 584
Alteration finds, alters when it, 108
Altered and worn and weak, 484
Alternative, forced to the dreadful, 1020
Although I enter not yet round, 481
Altissima quæque flumina, 21
Alway, I would not live, 387, 1102
Always blind and often tipsy, 406
　find us young, 409
　making them, I am, 449
　right, feels and never reasons is, 412
　to be blest, 207
Am, I am that I, 108
Amalfi in the heat, sits, 438
Amaranth, no fields of, 326
Amaryllis in the shade, 159
Amateur marks down his quarry, 906
Amateurs, a nation of, 686
　ruined by, 897
Amaze, filled the painter with, 511
　me, it doth, 81
　the unlearned, 211
Amazed at life, be not, 556
　the gazing rustics, 251
Amazing how little literature, 237
Amazon, broad mouth of the, 733
Ambassador from Britain's crown, 474
　is an honest man sent to lie abroad, 114
　of loss, love's the, 748
　so gorgeous and so filthy, 400
Ambassadors cabinet-officers and others, 935
Amber, bee enclosed, 995
　flies in, 111
　pipe tipped with, 358
　scent of odorous perfume, 157
　snuff-box, 212
　whose foam is, 166
Amber-dropping hair, 158
Amber-Locks a little child, 699
Ambient ether, slight toss over, 569

Ambition and pride of kings, low, 206
　and thirst of praise, low, 262
　choked with, 68
　distraction, uglification, 598
　fling away, 73
　has no risk, 425
　heart's supreme, 239
　I had, 814
　is no laudable one, 971
　joined, with, 193
　loves to slide not stand, 173
　made of sterner stuff, 83
　of kings, 128
　of man, crueltie and, 22
　or commercial stake makes wars, 874
　to say in ten sentences, 1081
　virtue, wars that make, 102
　which o'erleaps itself, vaulting, 85
　whose lovely, 938
Ambitions lawful, all, 727
　meteorological, 530
Ambition's ladder, lowliness is, 82
Ambitious and envious, usually most, 1048
　finger, from his, 72
　liar, 616
　poverty, 1006
Ambrose and his friends, 1034
　Phillips creator of Namby Pamby, 399
Ambrosia he feeds, on finest, 774
Ambrosial curls, 218
Ambulance comes round, till the, 782
　down in the valley, 640
Ambush of my name, 35
Amelioration of mankind, 1068
Amen I heard me cry, 816
　stuck in my throat, 86
Amend your ways, 1112
Amends, and then make, 935
　by way of, 109
　death by beauty made, 798
　for all these thorns, 834
　for broken hearts, 593
　for everything, 330
　for the toiling and moiling, 486
　for this general defect, 217
Amended, little said is soon, 1036
America! America! God shed his grace, 737
　a rich and populous nation, 637
　at last I was going to, 862
　epocha in history of, 268
　equal to the whole of that commerce, 259
　for me, home again, 710
　for sins, fashionable to blame, 871
　greatest potential force, 762
　half-brother of the world, 506
　has furnished a Washington, 340
　has joined forces with the Allied Powers, 747
　have no meaning, without, 932
　I have to thank, 1076
　I love you, 921
　nervous organization in, 571
　not a good place for genius, 614

America, not a place so happy as, 271
　not endurable for inspired writer, 614
　one hundred per-cent, 866
　privileged to spend her blood, 725
　settles in the mould, 894
　short, don't sell, 944
　singing, I hear, 534
　staring apprehensively, 926
　this is, 1066
　tongue of, 929
　traveling roads all even, 536
　what it is, makes, 836
　you cannot conquer, 230
America's history and biography, 538
American aristocracy, 510
　book, who reads an, 314
　complex fate being, 666
　continent, consider the, 762
　continents not for colonization by European powers, 283
　credo, 863
　empire careens onward, 926
　empire, formers of the, 707
　fear of literature, 885
　flag, haul down the, 390
　I also am an, 340
　I was born an, 342
　I will live and die an, 342
　if I were an, 230
　leader steady of soul, 483
　life powerful solvent, 769
　literature, not constitute, 476
　muse whose strong, 927
　names, fallen in love with, 929
　nation will speak softly, if the, 734
　not a Virginian, but an, 270
　professors like literature, how, 885
　strand, 136
　student familiar with Federalist, 872
　Washington make one proud to be an, 637
Americans and not dwellers in polyglot boarding house, 734
　and trains, 769
　content with newspapers magazines, 755
　detest the pageantry of a king, 393
　educated, first or last go to Europe, 413
　go to Paris when they die, 454, 724
　let us all be, 700
American's creed, 803
Americanism, doctrine of, 701
　of the right sort, 700
Amethyst and rose, edges foamed with, 801
　supposed to keep wearer sober, 713
Amfalula tree, in the, 699
Amiable child, an, 596
　lovely death, 58
　more, than beauty, 196
　weakness, 229, 279
　weaknesses, 270
　words and courtliness, 471
Amicably if they can, 319
Amice gray, in, 156

Amid measureless grossness and slag, 535
the city's jar, mine to feel, 546
Amir, Abdul the Bulbul, 951
Amiss, better to love, 280
nothing comes, 52
once, grows daily wourse, 25
thou shalt never do, 1124
Ammiral, mast of some great, 148
Amo shall be the watchword, 648
Among them but not of them, 353
Amoebas at the start, 815
Amor vincit omnia, 5
Amorous of their strokes, as, 104
be not too wildly, 823
causes, offence springs from, 212
delay, reluctant, 152
of his art, 669
propensities, 233
war, in the, 1022
Amount, certain, of pain or care, 1063
of minor irritation, 853
Amphitrio, into the shape of, 23
Amphitryon, the real, 1046
the true, 179
Ample room and verge enough, 179
Ampler ether, diviner air, 303
Ampliat ætatis spatium, 217
Amuck, to run, 213
Amulet that makes this world a garden, 704
to love is the great, 704
Amused, we are not, 534
Amusement, education a sort of, 974
grows out of work, 532
of the idle, 1054
you need, 1077
Amusements, friend to public, 235
for the mind, 509
Amusing than we thought, more, 673
Amytis made for, 956
Analogy is milk for babes, 477
is often misleading, 614
least misleading thing, 614
Analytic, with a glance, 508
Anarch lets the curtain fall, 216
literary Nihilist, sweet, 893
Anarchy, digest of, 260
no greater fiend than, 964
of drink, wild, 120
Anatomies, make them so many, 123
Anatomy, a mere, 38
arrive, the clear, 934
Ancestor, I am my own, 1062
Ancestors are good kind of folks, 278
derived from, 1051
familiarly pious, 323
forget all about its, 422
glorious, 203
have wisely thrown away, 232
look backward to their, 260
no need of, 311
that come after him, 34
the glory belongs to our, 1001
we owe it to our, 949
wisdom of our, 259

Ancestral tree, 451, 768
trees, 370
voices, 315
Ancestry, men have their intellectual, 529
pride of, 558
without pride of, 260
Anchor, all sail and no, 400
heaves the ship swings free, 406
lost, the holding, 71
might have bought an, 868
of a love is death, 676
of our peace at home, 273
steamer that rode at, 925
up, 579
Anchors, moor with two, 987
of a mother's life, 966
that faith has cast, 624
Anchorage, drawing the soul to its, 644
the long long, 537
unstable, 965
Anchored ships, among the, 873
Anchorite, saintship of an, 352
Ancient and fish-like smell, 32
and holy things fade, 523
and honorable, 1111
and new monuments, 1069
as the sun, hills, 371
authors, praise of, 132
crime, track-mark of an, 965
grudge I bear him, 44
grudges, nurse the, 612
heart-breaking wordless splendorous, 896
heavens are fresh and strong, 299
hollow oak, within an, 662
landmark, remove not the, 1108
law of youth, 811
limits, confines himself within, 422
Mariner called the Old Sailor, 614
modes and former ways, 186
of days, 1113
race by birth, of, 174
riddles, 736
right unnoticed, 780
roots of man's nature, 736
sacred custom, according to, 1050
sacrifice, 780
Saxon phrase, I like that, 434
seat of pedantry, 707
splendors fling, its, 477
tales say true, if, 352
times, these are the, 112
trusty drouthy cronie, 287
Ancients of the earth, we are, 465
Andalusian snare, 331
Anderson my jo John, John, 286
Andrew with the brindled hair, 703
Andromeda provides a starry frame, 795
Ane I'll get better, 291
Anecdotage, man into his, 421
Angel air, with your, 850
appear to each lover, 201
before thee, I will send an, 1098
bosoms know no jealousy, 714

Angel by divine command, 194
came by night, 565
consideration like an, 66
crept through a little, 507
curse his better, 103
Death, his Maker and, 317
down, she drew an, 176
drew one, 488
ended, the, 154
gentle, smile on me, 659
good and bad, 122
guardian, o'er his life, 289
hands to valour given, 382
hold the fleet, 226, 440
I'm no, 482
in action how like an, 92
is man an ape or an, 419
is word which cannot be worn out, 1069
Israfel, none sing so wildly well as the, 460
kneels in woman's form, 405
like the patriarch's, 441
ministering, 97, 308
of Death abroad throughout the land, 478
of God keep you company, 1123
of the backward look, 443
of the darker drink, 1018
of the Lord went out, 356
on the outward side, 37
or earthly paragon, 106
out of heaven, if an, 827
presided at my birth, 282
pure as an, 1059
sings, in his motion like an, 47
standing on the ground, 511
the recording, 242
think him an, 482
those, faces smile, 403
visits few and far between, 327
whiteness, 39
who wrote like an, 243
woman yet think him an, 482
writing in a book of gold, 346
Angels all glorious, 648
alone enjoy such liberty, 168
and ministers of grace, 91, 241
and to men, a spectacle to, 1120
are bright still, 88
are, our acts our, 126
charge over thee, 1105
could no more, 201
entertained, and, 146
face shyned bright, 24
fear to tread, where, 71, 212
fell by that sin, 73
forget-me-nots of the, 435
flutter down, when, 940
from heaven into hell, 3
guard thy bed, holy, 199
he will not play, with other, 842
I am on the side of the, 419
keep their ancient places, 749
laugh too at the good he has done, 452
little lower than the, 1103
may be familiar, 556
may, love as the, 428
must love Ann Hathaway, 274
ne'er like, till passion dies, 116

Angels of God, one of the, 1074
  of God upturned the sod, 372
  of the Lord ascending and de-
    scending, 1098
  plead like, 85
  preventing, 175
  pure in thought as are, 289
  sad as, 327
  said to be the speech of, 378
  sing, which now the, 477
  sung the strain, guardian, 225
  swearing I was right, ten, 458
  to fall, caused the, 110
  tremble while they gaze, 243
  trumpet-tongued, 85
  Tutelary and Guardian, 1098
  unawares, entertained, 220
  weep, make the, 36
  weep, tears such as, 149
  whispering to one another, 460
  white, like two, 669
  wings for, feet for men, 521
  with us unawares, 574
Angel's lips, might tempt, 634
  tear, passage of an, 383
  whisper, accent of an, 645
  wing, dropped from an, 304
  wing, quill from an, 304
  wings, clip an, 383
Angels' ken, far as, 148
  laughter as far as, 721
  visits short and bright, 186
Angela, gotta love for, 813
Angelic songs are swelling, 503
Angelina Johnson comes a-swingin', 820
Angelus, once at the, 648
Anger, April's, is swift, 764
  biting for, 147
  cease from, 493
  forget his, 347
  he that is slow to, 1107
  holy, 351
  hunger and dismay, poetry
    comes with, 912
  impatient and prone to, 318
  is like a full-hot horse, 72
  is one of the sinews of the
    soul, 147
  more in sorrow than, 90
  of heaven, they read in this
    omen, 593
  of his lip, contempt and, 55
  of lovers, 987
  of the gods, 175
  of the guns, monstrous, 918
  rise, if the one's, 968
Angers in unison rising, 937
Angie anything whatever, nor,
  952
Angle, a brother of the, 139
  themselves in every, greet, 169
  would rejoice, I with my,
  140
Angler hath a jolly life, 674
  if he be an honest, 139
  no man is born, 139
  now with God, excellent, 140
  signs of the experienced, 745
  who has no rod, 733
Anglers or very honest men, 140
Angle-worm in halves, he bit an,
  585
Angling, be quiet and go a, 140
  innocent recreation, 140
  like mathematics, 139

Angling, like virtue, 139
  pleasantest, is to see the fish,
    39
  produces gentleness of spirit,
    344
  wagered on your, 104
Angling-rod, a sturdy oak his,
  146
Anglo-Saxon speech, I like the,
  698
Angry, be ye, and sin not, 1121
  creeds oppose, 453
  flood, leap into this, 81
  heaven is not always, 190
  look, when I feigned an, 185
  passions rise, never let such,
    198
  prayers, knelt down with, 816
  reckon the days you have not
    been, 1008
  repeated the four-and-twenty
    letters when, 1003
  roar, contend with, 480
  that you cannot make others
    as you wish, 8
  while I sing, 199
  with my foe, 281
  with my friend, I was, 281
Anguish and the loss, above the,
  875
  another's, 77
  arrows of our, 784
  calmly bear, can every, 459
  hopeless, poured his groan,
    231
  keeps the heavy gate, 723
  of the singer, 661
  of your bereavement, 457
  one minute's, 565
  or in your, 923
  pay, we must an, 584
  rend your heart, 760
  rides swift after pleasure, 551
  shivers, heart in, 1071
  wring the brow, 308
Anguished mothers gaze from the
  ramparts, 1071
Angularity of facts, 411
Animal and Superman, between
  the, 1079
  imperfectly denatured, 787
  is dead and dumb and done,
    823
  kingdom, cannot be found in
    the, 592
  lies, a suffering, 660
  man is a noble, 145
  man is a pliable, 1074
  man is a reasoning, 990
  man is a social, 1049
  man is a two-legged, 1015
  produced by a man an, 930
  self-preservation of an, 1016
  some new kind of, 908
  spiteful envious ungrateful,
    330
Animals end by different rule,
  758
  insolence of enormous, 969
  is justifiable, experiment on,
    449
  love the plants, love, 1074
  souls of, 46
  turn and live with, 535
Animal's vanity, if she flatters,
  786

Animated bust or storied urn,
  244
  only by faith and hope, 233
Anise and cummin, 1115
Ann Ann! Come! quick as you
  can, 823
Arbor, scenes of, 756
  Hathaway, angels must love,
    274
  trips down the street, 908
Ann's suitor, think you are, 720
Anna whom three realms obey,
  212
Annabel Lee, I and my, 459
  McCarty was invited, 667
Annals are blank in history, 379
  bravest spirits in all our, 124
  of the poor, 244
  writ your, true, 76
Anne, across the fields to, 757
  Rutledge, I am, 806
  yes, by St., 54
Annette! Sweetheart good-night,
  702
Annihilate space and time, 216
Annihilating all that's made, 169
Annihilation, man not doomed to
  complete, 449
Anniversaries of uninteresting
  events, 723
  secret, 439
Anniversary festival, great, 268
Announce a life that shall be co-
  pious, 537
  the great individual, I, 537
Announcements, endless, 534
Annoyances, petty repeated, 997
Annual expenditure nineteen nineteen, 496
  income twenty pounds, 496
Annuities, persons living on, 359
  those who are paying your,
    1053
Annuity cheap, buy an, 495
Anointed king, balm from an, 59
  rail on the Lord's, 72
  sovereign of sighs and groans,
    41
Another and a better world, 1060
  entirely, know, 1056
  had said it to him, as if, 110
  horse, give me, 72
  I'm an owl, you're, 508
  if it enrich not the heart of,
    435
  man's ground, built on, 34
  must wait, who travels with,
    514
  rock would crown the work,
    484
  setteth up, 1105
  steals my honours, 982
  story, 241, 785
  to plead before, 998
  wherein thou judgest, 1119
  world, search well, 170
  would have done as well, 1086
  would have said as well, 1086
  yet the same, 215
Another's face commend, 240
  woe, to feel, 216
Answer a fool, 1108
  a wise man with silence, 1001
  dusty, 574
  fynal, 8
  give truthful, 716

Answer in his own words and propositions, 110
is possible, precise, 926
make, I can no other, 55
me in one word, 50
not every question, 989
soft, turneth away wrath, 1107
the better, 39
the silver, 428
to a wise man, silence is an, 1001
to my word, made, 587
ye evening tapers, 451
Answered you last night, yes I, 428
Answering tone, awoke an, 405
too late, or, 924
Answers till a husband cools, never, 209
Ant finds kingdoms, the, 928
for ant doth long, 977
go to the, thou sluggard, 1106
its labor has begun, 345
Ants entombed, 111
Antagonism between classes, 1072
Antagonist is our helper, our, 261
Antecedent thought, 543
Antelope, I'll chase the, 395
swift as an, 406
Anthem of the destinies, 443
Anthems, singing of, 64
Anthology, a well-chosen, 924
Anthosmial divine, sweet apples, 431
Anthracite, glossy cherished, 911
like jet, piled with, 926
Anthropophagi, the, 100
Antic hay, dance the, 32
old father, the law, 60
Anti-Christians in deed, thorough, 1082
Anticipate the past, 278
seldom occurs, what we, 420
Anticipated, satisfaction not lessened by being, 330
Antidote, bane and, 195
some sweet oblivious, 88
turns the bane to, 651
Anti-everythings, lean hungry savage, 453
Antigonus and his ill son, 1000
the son of Helios, 1005
Antioch, walls of, 939
Antique book, to meet an, 584
Persians, 361
Roman than a Dane, 98
song, metre of an, 107
song, old and, 54
towers, ye, 243
world, service of the, 48
Antiquitas sæculi, 112
Antiquities, living men were, 145
Antiquity, crowned of, 889
herbs from all, 664
is accounted by farther distance, 112
ways of hoar, 258
Anti-republican tendencies, 273
Antiseptic baby, 815
Antoninus, reign of, 270
Antony, no man like, 1001
Anvil bear, when you are the, 708
iron did cool on the, 58
is unharmed, 622
lay me on an, 855

Anvil of God's word, 622
of thy wrath, on the, 836
ring the vesper chime, 622
still on life's, 736
wears the hammers out, 622
when it is beaten upon, 708
when you are an, 137
Anvils, how many, 622
Anxiety, inclined to some, 910
strive with the greatest, 1049
Anxious and distrustful, the, 931
convoy in to shore, 839
strife, 326
to have our way, 690
Anybody might have found it, 777
Anyone may be an honourable man, 1046
who comes between them, punishing, 313
Anything astounding, you are not, 893
awful makes me laugh, 325
but gay, a face that's, 481
but history, 200
does for me, 655
for a quiet life, 117
God ever made, 807
green that grew, 783
I can say about New Hampshire, 838
I've done, for, 630
moved to smile at, 82
no one could forget, nor learn, 1060
of human trial, not, 626
owe no man, 1119
sets me sneezing, 314
so beautiful as words, 841
that forces one to repeat No, 1082
that's fit to eat, 955
what is worth in, 142
which I should be afraid to do, 226
you like except time, 1060
Anywhere, it isn't really, 876
Apace, ill weed grows, 28
Apart, are scarce long leagues, 519
forever, two are walking, 540
though not alone, man dwells, 540
Ape, descendant of the, 867
like an angry, 36
or an angel, is man an, 419
played the sedulous, 704
there was an, 569
Apes and ivory from Tarshish, 777
and peacocks, ivory, 832, 1101
of Nikko, 752
Apert, privee and, 7
Aphorisms, interline such of these, 1056
Aplomb stand before presidents or generals with, 539
Apocalyptic commonplace, 889
Apollo garlanded, 892
is an imbecile, 410
Pallas Jove and Mars, 479
physician, I swear by, 971
Apollo's laurel bough, burned is, 32
lute, musical as bright, 41, 158

Apollodorus tied up the bedding, 1000
Apollos watered, 1120
Apology too prompt, 155
Apostle, golden-tongued, 813
Apostles, names of the, 1095
shrank, while, 349
twelve, he taught, 5
would have done as they did, the, 358
Apostolic blows and knocks, 142
Apothecary, ounce of civet good, 99
should never be out of spirits, 278
Appalling as joy, no feeling so, 1067
seen too near, 1069
Apparel, every true man's, 37
fashion wears out more, 39
oft proclaims the man, 91
took fresh, 927
womanliness of woman's, 731
Apparelled in more precious habit, 40
Apparent, one that is merely, 1063
Apparition, a lovely, 299
Apparitions, seen and gone, like, 186
thousand blushing, 39
Appeal from Philip drunk, 969
seldom the same, 930
unto Cæsar, 1119
Appear, beacons of Hope ye, 547
Appearance, in, glad to be at friendship, 183
not according to the, 1118
of a caryatid, 1068
of a certain greatness, 999
of a single great genius, 1078
of things to the mind, 1007
truculent, shy heart within, 709
what a poor, 974
Appearances are deceptive, 962
keep up, 495
Appearest thou, present to my mind, 393
Appendix to nobility, 123
Appetite, a universal wolf, 75
ate umble pie with an, 497
breakfast with what, 73
cloy the hungry edge of, 59
colours were then to me an, 296
comes while eating, 1030
coquetry whets the, 551
for bogus revelation, 862
good digestion wait on, 87
grown by what it fed on, 90
healthy, 599
man given to, 1108
may sicken and so die, 53
quench, check impulse, 1012
still importunate, 1051
that I have, 493
whet the, 599
with cloyless sauce, sharpen his, 104
with that keen, 45
work sharpens his, 1054
Appetites, abandon yourselves to irregular, 188
Appius says in his verses, 981

Applaud thee to the very echo, 88
Applause, attentive to his own, 213
delight the wonder, the, 119
from none but self expect, 544
of a single human being, 237
steered by popular, 1000
their sole, 856
they deserve, deference and, 1056
won their frank, 713
Apple any serpent pushed my way, 490
art thou the topmost, 960
blooms, with, 793
eaten of the, 956
grows so bright and high, 910
of his eye, 1099
of the eye, 1103
on the corner, buy an, 898
orchard smells like wine, 719
pie, ends its days in, 910
pies, abominate dried, 955
reddens, where the, 485
rotten at the heart, 44
trees will never get across, 837
who love the, 626
Apples, anthosmial divine, sweet, 431
behold in the bloom of, 445
have you had, how many, 630
in her skirt, 917
of gold, 1108
of his eyes, 1040
on the Dead Sea's shore, 352
shrivel like old, 123
silver, 790
since Eve ate, 361
small choice in rotten, 52
you steal green, 856
Apple-blossom, and a cheek of, 470
Apple-blossoms fill the air, 904
Apple-boughs down by the mill, 508
Apple-pie and cheese, 698
Appleseed, Johnny, swept on, 858
remember Johnny, 626
story of Johnny, 596
Apple-tree, under the blossoming, 699
when we plant the, 373
with its famous, 578
Apple-trees, drenched and dripping, 915
Apple-wood, that piece of, 621
Appliance, desperate, 96
Appliances and means, 65
Application of a verse of Virgil, happy, 415
of Becky Sharp's remark, 563
to affection, have an equal, 661
Appointed limits, 566
ways, 591
Appointment, never yields by, 1063
not by, 574
on presidential, 935
Appomattox court-house, from near, 578
Appreciate heaven well, to, 678
Appreciated, she must be seen to be, 423
Apprehend some joy, 43

Apprehension, death most in. 36
how like a god in, 92
of a vision, 972
of His displeasure, 329
of the good, 59
Apprenticeship to progressive renunciation, 1073
Approach like the rugged Russian bear, 87
of even or morn, 151
to a false pretence, 599
to good, near, 229
Approbation from Sir Hubert Stanley, 290
if it meet their, 969
of every reader, secure the, 1039
think of their imagined, 448
Appropriate, as difficult to invent as to, 415
conditions, under, 581
Approved good masters, 100
Approximate, and hated the, 1089
April airs were abroad, 758
and over me bright, 882
came to bloom, 703
comes again, grimy, 929
day, a peevish, 348
day, how it is with an, 838
day, uncertain glory of an, 33
evening, all in the, 758
hieth April spieth, 929
is here, now that, 486
is the cruelest month, 899
June and November, 18
laugh thy girlish laughter, 735
of her prime, 107
prepares her green traffic light, 912
proud-pied, 108
rain a fragrance, 665
Rome was founded, in, 706
wears, pinks that, 127
wet by kind, 30
when they laid the martyr's crown, 706
when they woo, 51
with his shoures, 4
Aprils, how many million, 883
April's anger is swift, 764
fledge, a part of, 933
ivory moonlight, 401
lady, if you were, 631
sowing, 485
Aprons of fig-leaves, 1097
with greasy, 105
Apt alliteration's artful aid, 262
and gracious words, 41
to be proud, poor are, 55
Arab tents are rude for thee, 338
Arabs could be swung on an idea, 901
fold their tents like the, 434
obedient servants, 901
of the air, 756
proverb of the, 425
without a creed, 901
Arabesque borders, she stood on the, 432
Arabia, all the perfumes of, 88
breathes from yonder box, 212
Arabian trees, 104
Araby the blest, 151
Arbiter is taste, its sole, 461
of every one's own fortune, 987

Arbitrary stomach, 247
Arbitrator time, old common, 75
Arbitress, moon sits, 149
Arbor viva tacui mortua cano, 1092
Arcades ambo, 360
Arcadia, I too was born in, 1043
Arcadian scenes, 266
Arcady, as I went on to, 619
broken flutes of, 807
I hied me off to, 619
many a flute of, 468
see fair, 715
Arch, comes over the sunlit, 839
experience is an, 635
night's black, 287
night's blue, 267
that fill'st the sky, 328
Arches, I saw the world's, 932
of the years, 748
triumphal, 212
views from eternal, 891
Archaisms of Chaucer's English, 412
Archangel a little damaged, 325
arteries of an, 615
befriended, by an, 897
ruined, 149
Archelaus and the barber, 1002
Archer, little meant, mark the, 309
miss his aim, most skilful, 180
Tell the, 1059
that keen, 588
well-experienced, 106
Archimedes cried I have found it Eureka, 1004
Architect, fate of the, 1057
man is his own, 492
of airy rhyme, 621
of his own fortune, 111, 981
Architects, skilful, have tendency to build high, 532
Architectural structure, in the, 1081
Architecture an art for all men, 570
is a sort of oratory, 1081
is frozen music, 1060
is music in space, 1060
is what you do to it, 535
sculpture painting, 580
surest test of civilization, 387
Archways and the pavement, 500
Arcs, on the earth the broken, 489
Arcturus with his sons, 1103
Arden, now am I in, 48
Ardent longings that I lack, 533
love of glory, most, 197
marigolds, 385
temperature, 686
Ardor, blunt his, 978
compulsive, gives the charge, 95
of their hearts, 1074
radiant with, divine, 547
Ardors from me, it wrenches such, 535
Are, we know what we, 96
Area gates, sprouting despondently at, 900
unlocated spiritual, 787
Areas of rain, snow, hail, and drought, 617
Arena, gladiators' cry in the, 438

Arg'ed the question, the more we, 678
Argos has the curse of fleas, 674
Argosy, a wrecked, 587
Argosies of magic sails, 464
Argue not against Heaven's hand, 162
    though vanquished, 251
Argues with women, the heart, 547
    yourselves unknown, 152
Arguing, owned his skill in, 251
    with Johnson, no, 255
    with you I'm telling, not, 612
Argument and intellects too, 254
    for a week, 61
    force instead of, 950
    has sometimes shaken my reason, 342
    heard great, 1018
    height of this great, 148
    I have found you an, 238
    knock-down, 179
    lack of, 66
    maintain his, 66
    not to stir without great, 96
    sheathed their swords for lack of, 66
    staple of his, 41
    stateliest and most regal, 162
    to thy neighbor's creed, 408
    versed in, 933
    when blood is their, 67
    with an east wind, 530
    wrong, his, 252
Arguments and questions, all kind of, 109
    I have no mockings or, 534
    interminable and inconsistent, 420
    nor waste, where they will be lost, 424
    of deep, 806
    of its opposers, 184
    use wagers, fools for, 142
Argus' eyes, closed forever faithful, 220
Argyments, for the sake of, 853
Aright, always dress, 501
Ariosto of the North, 354
Arise, my maiden Mabel, 394
    my lady sweet, 105
Aristocracy a corporation of the best and bravest, 378
    American, 510
    codfish, 843
    clover to him is, 584
    harmless inoffensive untitled, 453
    is always cruel, 480
Aristocrat, heartburnings of the, 1072
    I am no, 374
Aristocratic element, only, 1070
    flavor to a dead language, 607
Aristotle and his philosophy, 5
Arithmetic cannot number, whose wealth, 129
    different branches of, 598
Arithmetician, skilfulest, 517
Arizona and the Potomac, 932
Ark, hunt it into Noah's, 263
    mouldy rolls of Noah's, 173
    to lay their hand upon the, 264
    walked straight out of the, 312
Arks like foundered galleons, 851

Arkansas, change the name of, 564
    Kansas Iowa, rolling from, 929
Arm and nerve must feel, 309
    fold me with thine, 485
    from under Adam's, 953
    hath bound the restless wave, 566
    he flung against the world, 487
    in love enfolds, one, 931
    is long, but his, 893
    jewelled, 814
    let fall, over my, 1085
    lifted the right, 929
    she leant on her lover's, 465
    short, needs man, 749
    some undone widow sits upon mine, 129
    the obdured breast, 150
    to bear a gun, 1073
    what a waist for an, 545
    what an, what a waist, 545
    which now is free, 447
Armes, by force of, 256
Arms against a sea of troubles, 93
    against a world in, 399
    and idleness, 270
    and the man I sing, 177
    are empty, my, 642
    at the journey's end, two brown, 757
    fall into her, 662
    glorious in, 41
    good laws and good, 1023
    had seven years' pith, 100
    hath goodness, so wide, 1021
    I fill, half sad half proud, 714
    imparadised in one another's, 152
    it, Washington, 414
    land of scholars nurse of, 250
    lord of folded, 41
    might'st seek it in my, 749
    never would lay down my, 230
    of chalk, 864
    of death, the alabaster, 646
    of seeming, 177
    on armour clashing, 153
    others rush to, 982
    prove thou the, 519
    puking in the nurse's, 49
    ridiculous, made, 156
    so he laid down his, 392
    sure-enwinding, of cool-enfolding death, 536
    take your last embrace, 80
    that meet and clasp, 677
    the brilliant limbs, rounded, 763
    the Smiths never had any, 312
    the world in, 58
    to, ye brave, 1060
    trial of everything before, 979
    underneath are the everlasting, 1099
    unstained and free, my, 517
    upbear, and men my giant, 517
    were full of blossom, 850
    ye forge, another bears, 368
Armageddon came, ere, 779
    in the day of, 778
    of the race, 442
    place called, 1123
Armament factories start, when, 930

Arm-chair, old, 512
Armed at points exactly cap-a-pe, 90
    great individual fully, 537
    host, fort nor, 954
    rhinoceros, 87
    so strong in honesty, 83
    thrice is he, 69
    thus am I doubly, 195
    with more than complete steel, 31, 69
    without, he's, 214
Armies clad in iron, 156
    clash by night, where ignorant, 546
    disbanding hired, 379
    ignorant, clash, 546
    join not, pray that our, 64
    not count her, 747
    swore terribly, our, 241
    whole have sunk, where, 150
Armor, against fate, 141
    champion in invincible, 930
    clashing brayed, 153
    Hugo fought in, 1069
    is his honest thought, 114
    knight in glittering, 888
    of a righteous cause, 752
    of Montrose, close around the, 758
    on my eldest son, 901
    on, who puts his, 438
    their dusty, 576
Armor's slave, 491
Armory, all wisdom's, 574
Armourers accomplishing knights, 67
Army again, back to the, 782
    and the Navy, if the, 953
    backbone of the, 782
    grafted him into the, 600
    hum of either, stilly sounds, 67
    of martyrs, the noble, 1127
    of the unemployed, 1086
    of the world's desires, 40
    of unalterable law, 575, 900
    with banners, terrible as an, 1110
Aroma to Louisburg Square, 711
Aromatic pain, die of a rose in, 207
    plants bestow no fragrance while they grow, 252
Around to say farewell, and looks, 481
    us like a cloud, lies, 480
Arrant, thankless, 21
    thief, the moon's an, 81
Arras, slogged up to, 892
Array, bedecked in her snowy, 474
    cloak that covers my bright, 1085
    in trim, 300
    lo! in bright, 423
    mine in bright, 828
    spoiled my best, 217
Arrayed in flames, 66
    in his beauty, king all, 387
Arrays our battalions, field-marshal who, 519
Arrears of pain and darkness, 480
Arrest, death is strict in his, 97
    stiffness and the soul's, 827
Arrival of your audience, speak until the, 329

Arrivals of pleasure, 588
Arrogance pedantry and dogmatism, 849
Arrow and hand and eye were one, 576
flown off with the, 855
for the heart, 361
from a well-experienc'd archer, 106
from the Almighty's bow, 282
haft of the, 962
into the air, I shot an, 434
spoken word sped, 180
that it sends, comes the, 570
Arrows, children living, 879
flew like hail, 897
love's, 50
of desire, 282
of light, swift-winged, 264
of our anguish, 784
of outrageous fortune, 93
of the early frost, slain by, 565
Arrowy Rhone, rushing of the, 353
Ars longa, vita brevis, 3
Arsenal, shook the, 156
Arsenals or forts, no need of, 434
Art, adorning thee with so much, 167
adulteries of, than all the, 119
all loved, in a seemly way, 686
all nature is but, 207
all the gloss of, 251
alone enduring stays, 648
and part, 943
and science international possessions, 740
aspires towards condition of music, 645
atheism in, ridiculous, 556
bestowing well is an, 1080
can wash her guilt away, what, 253
colors life, 605
concealed by, 202
cookery is become an, 123
do whate'er one likes in, 485
ease in writing comes from, 211
elder days of, 436
every enduring work of, 710
every genuine work of, 414
every walk of, 290
failed in literature and, 421
fault of all, 675
first professor of our, 177
France, supreme in no, 545
galleries a refinement for people, 571
gives highest quality to your moments, 646
glib and oily, 98
had invented the, of printing, 379
he tried each, 250
her guilt to cover, the only, 253
imitates nature, 171
in her glorious mind, 889
in rendering itself invisible, 654
in the vaunted works of, 410
includes humor pain and evil, 771
independent of all clap-trap, 611

Art is a human activity, 1077
is a jealous mistress, 413
is but imitation, 991
is it to sleep, no small, 1079
is limitation, 827
is long, less that, 757
is long, life short, 971, 1058
is long though time is short, 433
is long time is fleeting, 433
is man's nature, 506
is quite useless, 723
is the accomplice of love, 1084
is the only clean thing, 1083
is the painting of soul, 767
is too precise, 133
it's pretty but is it, 780
knew 'twas, 595
last and greatest, 214
laughter oft is but an, 386
life without, 533
made it smaller with their, 927
made tongue-tied, 107
may err Nature cannot miss, 176
more matter with less, 92
nature's above, in that respect, 99
nature is but, 207
nature is God's, 506
nearly allied to invention, 278
not dull, 403
not learned by, 128
not strength obtains the prize, 219
number who practice this, 969
of any profundity, 824
of awakening curiosity, 1078
of beginning, 439
of being kind, just the, 718
of cookery, the, 1051
of dancing source of all the arts, 740
of ending greater, 439
of God, nature is the, 144, 202
of medicine in Egypt, 969
of perceiving how not to do it, 497
of poisoning mankind, 1051
of scratch, engraving is the, 533
of supporting beggars, 976
of teaching, the whole, 1078
of telling you nothing, 1046
outraged, 892
pleasure disguised by, 258
poetry a mere mechanic of, 262
posterity of the work of, 1086
power of, 235
preservative of all, 943
safest and surest civilizer, 571
schoolman's subtle, 213
seems antiquated to succeeding generation, 675
shall give such piles of curls, 373
so vast is, 210
summit, 1073
teaching her an, to plague himself, 134
than force, more by, 219
there is no longer, 1084
to blot, 214
to find the mind's construction, 84

Art trained in exercise and, 972
trained in the holy, 453
vaunted works of, 410
war's glorious, 203
we can realize perfection through, 723
we may live without, 592
where strong desire comes in play, 1089
winter the paragon of, 934
with curious, 262
with easy, 218
with the living hues of, 472
Arts and sciences not in a mould, 1029
are one, all, 534
divorced from truth fall mad, 379
fashion's brightest, 251
Greece mother of, 156
hammer out divers, 982
in which the wise excel, 185
letters society, no, 132
lose virtue, all, 895
love greatest of the, 670
no relish of these, 196
of peace, inglorious, 169
of power, 329
remote from common use, 358
taught the wheedling, 205
the academes, 41
the fine, once divorcing themselves, 379
there are three, 974
vulgar, beneath thy care, 242
well fitted in, 41
where life's busy, 403
which I loved, 167
with lenient, 213
Art's long hazard, 808
perfect forms, 441
Artaxerxes' throne, 156
Artery, each petty, 91
Artful part, the most, 1038
Arthritis, your benighted foe, 910
Arthur first in court, when, 256
Article of luxury, do without any, 387
snuffed out by an, 361
stale, 422
Articles, all agree in the essential, 234
legs are staple, 942
Articulate monotony, bleats, 300, 747
stone shall be, 688
Artifice, make themselves by, 1050
Artificer, another lean unwashed, 58
believe any man than an, 147
made my mate, 704
of his own fortune, 377
Artificial manner, men die and kill one another in, 381
Artisans, body's, 823
Artist appeals to us, how the, 726
greatest, has embodied greatest ideas, 531
has always the masters in his eye, 423
has no home save in Paris, 1082
was forgotten, work lived, 717
nature's son and master, 611

Artist, no man is born an, 139
  proud embarrassment of the, 1089
  should paint as he sees, 717
  speaks to our capacity for delight, 726
  who retains his integrity, 871
Artists call posterity, what, 1086
  great, never Puritans, 862
  or pictures, none of the, 538
  tedious, many excellent, 789
  true, are a rare breed, 792
Artistic temperament, 571
Artless in its vanity so fleeting so eternal, 180
  jealousy, 96
Arwes brighte and kene, he bar, 6
Ascalon, a youth of, 855
Ascendancy, position of unquestioned, 1072
Ascent, spiral of its steep, 840
Asclepius by health by panacea, I swear by, 971
  I owe a cock to, 970
Asepsis of clothes is neatness, 696
Ashamed, needeth not to be, 1122
  of being loved, 1044
  the more, a man is, the more respectable, 720
  to be seen with him, because of his red nose, 182
  to buy, we are, 812
  to own he is in the wrong, 217
  with the noble shame, 524
Ashbourn, romantic, 294
Ashen and sober, skies they were, 460
Ashes, a handful of grey, 553
  and the dust, in the, 875
  beauty for, 1112
  follow blaze inevitably, 551
  from truth's sad, 531
  had cigarettes no, 674
  handful of, 832
  in fleeing the, 960
  in your wine, 913
  just to spoil our slide, 699
  laid old Troy in, 185
  lie beneath his own Virginian sky, 445
  man is splendid in, 145
  oaks and maples, 637
  of his fathers, 400
  of yesterday in its hair, 821
  or it prospers, turns, 1018
  out of dead cold, 681
  past is a bucket of, 854
  the colder and deader the, 717
  to ashes, 671
  to ashes, dust to dust, 1128
  to the taste, 352
  urn of his last, 898
  violet made from his, 468
  wonted fires live in our, 245
Ashore with me, didn't come, 655
Ashy the tall skull, 903
Aside, human to step, 285
  last to lay the old, 211
Ask and it shall be given you, 1114
  and learn, 1125
  me no questions, 253
  my wants are few, little I, 451
  no more I, 591

Ask no more of fate, man could, 528
  not, wealth I, 703
  the brave soldier, 335
  to see, I do not, 403
Asked of echo 't other day, I, 511
Askelon and Samarkand, to, 906
  in the streets of, 1100
Asketh, every one that, 1114
Asking eye, explain the, 213
Asleep, hope they have not been, 592
  in lap of legends old, 383
  know they have been, 592
  lips of those that are, 1110
  the very houses seem, 297
  tide as moving seems, 472
  time has fallen, 588
  when he is, 1002
Aspect, meet in her, 356
  more favourable, look with, 56
  of princes, sweet, 73
  presents a rational, 1062
  with grave, he rose, 150
Aspen leaf, right as an, 4
  light quivering, 308
Aspics' tongues, 103
Aspiration, every inmost, 474
  of humanity, 862
  you cannot prove an, 641
Aspired to be, what I, 489
Aspiring youth, 193
Ass, a idiot, the law is a, 494
  burial of an, 1113
  countryman who looked for his, 1041
  egregiously an, 101
  knoweth his master's crib, 1110
  man is an, 1079
  of Balaam, 1099
  Robin thou 'rt an ass, 394
  upon an, 851
  will carry his load, 1042
  write me down an, 40
Asses, bridge of, 977
  mankind are the, 361
  poor human, 700
  to live according to the convenience of, 1002
Assassination, absolutism tempered by, 1060
  could trammel up, if the, 85
Assault, death preparing his, 202
Assay, so hard so sharp, 3
Assayed, thrice he, 149
Assembled souls, 146
Assemblies, masters of, 1110
Assembly as well as a masterpiece, 1069
  of good fellows, 232
  of portable plumbing, 912
  posterity is a most limited, 419
Assent with civil leer, 213
Assertion is erroneous, shows that the, 1079
  of private interests, 1062
Assertions, of his own, 970
Assessor, tax-bill and, 453
Asshen olde is fyr y-reke, 6
Assiduous wait upon her, 285
Assisian, of the loved, 813
Assistance, cause that lacks, 543
  of custom houses and laws, 1067
  which she administers, 1061

Association of literary men, 400
Associations and societies lost, 800
Assume a virtue, if you have it not, 95
Assumes the god, 176
Assumption, gave without, 999
Assurance, before society with glib, 419
  double sure, I'll make, 87
  enough, what man has, 1037
  given by lookes, 26
  most dear, 555
  of a man, give the world, 95
  of survival, 1086
  to the contrary, no, 132
Assured, ignorant of what he's most, 36
Assyrian bull, curled, 469
  came down like the wolf, the, 356
Assyrians, smote in the camp of the, 356
Asterisk of death, fatal, 438
  to do his dirty work, 907
  writer owned an, 907
Asthma and other annoyances, 754
Astolat, come again to, 916
  Elaine the lily maid of, 470
Astray, and they fall, they go, 483
  light that led, 285
  like me, art thou, 548
  like one that had been led, 160
Astrolabie suffisant as for oure orizonte, 8
Astrologers the stargazers, the, 1112
Astronomer knows about th' stars, 797
  undevout is mad, 202
Astronomers, confounding her, 816
  who totter off to bed, 807
Astronomy compels the soul, 974
Asunder, let not man put, 1115
  put this man and woman, 191
Asylum, lunatic, 741
Asylums, padded lunatic, 877
Atavistic features of college life, 731
Athanasian Creed, the, 421
  creeds, weary of mumbling, 609
Atheism in art may become ridiculous, 556
  my, denies gods fashioned by men, 769
  philosophy inclineth to, 110
  the owlet, 316
  true piety, 769
Atheist at twenty-one, 744
  by night half believes a God, 202
  nor a rationalist, neither an, 1061
  novelist realist play your, 471
Atheist's laugh, 285
Athens a fragile kingdom, 903
  immortal influence of, 397
  maid of, ere we part, 351
  sending owls to, 1014
  shall appear great, when, 970
  the eye of Greece, 156

Atlantean shoulders, 150
Atlantic continents or islands, 361
for whales, drag, 616
gem the blue, 756
ocean and Mrs. Partington, 314
the deep immense, 667
Atlas unremoved, 153
Atmosphere of dreams, softness like the, 447
of pomp and glory, 896
thought's, 669
Atom knows its own, each, 669
Atomies, team of little, 77
Atoms, fortuitous concourse of, 187
into ruin hurled, 207
move in the void, 970
or systems, 207
somewhere up in space, 647
Atrocious bow-wow public park manner, 312
crime of being young, 239
Atropos of the future, 974
Attachment, full of confidence and, 1088
Attack is the reaction, 236
would not risk an, 975
Attacks made on Lincoln, 458
Attacked, rather be, than unnoticed, 237
Attain her, in hope to, 24
Attainment of the highest moral aim, 1063
Attains the shore, the fragile skiff, 640
the utmost round, 82
Attar of the ore, recast that, 928
Attempt and not the deed, 86
by fearing to, 35
failed in their, 970
the end, 134
to divert, 236
to extend their system dangerous, 283
Attendance, to dance, 74
Attending ears, 78
strictly to business, 617
Attention like deep harmony, 59
still as night, 150
to others' grief, 223
Attentions, kind, 827
Attentive to his own applause, 213
Attic bird trills her notes, 156
salt, 601
salt, seasoned with, 1047
shape! fair attitude, 383
taste, light and choice of, 162
tragedies, 162
Atticus were he, 213
Attila, my Attila, 575
pensioned slave of, 338
Attire be comely, let thy, 23
her rich, 383
Attired with stars, 161
Attitude, a respectful, 922
O Attic shape! fair, 383
Attitudes, pathetic, 1082
stained-glass, 623
Attitudenize, don't, 238
Attorney's office, pay to go into, 505
Attraction of cities on country people, 739
robs the vast sea, 81

Attractive grace, sweet, 152
Attribute power but his, 617
to awe and majesty, 46
to God himself, 46
Attributes of God, 1048
Attunes the spheres, with one breath, 514
Auber, dank tarn of, 461
Auburn, a mound in sweet, 527
locks, ye golden curls, 451
loveliest village, 250
Aucassin and Nicolete, how far away with, 673
Auction mart, brawlers of the, 722
Audacity, color of, 879
Audience, a sitting, 200
always laughs at, 972
arrival of your, 329
fit, though few, 153
for the sake of a crowded, 971
his look drew, 150
procure me an, 886
sits before us, 326
Audiences about him, collected, 972
there must be great, 539
Aught do touch the utmost thread, if, 115
I loved, change in, 484
if we've promised them, 487
in malice, nor set down, 103
that dignifies humanity, 401
that I could ever read, 42
Augur schœnobates, 174
Augurs, ill name of, 525
turned pale, 593
August, never return in, 926
nor this September, not this, 930
past surprises notes, 493
Augustine to his mother sailed, 568
Auld acquaintance, should, 286
claes, gars, 284
lang syne, 286
Lang Syne, air of, 443
moon in her arm, 255
nature swears, 284
Robin Gray he is kind to me, 277
Aulus Gellius or Macrobius, 1031
Aunt Maggie's cretonne, sat on, 909
Aurora, danced with the, 660
daughter of the dawn, 220
Leighs, no more, 449
shows her face, 225
Auspicious eye, an, 89
Austere, but I rode on, 610
man the most, 651
Austerity, priest of, 656
Austerlitz and Waterloo, 854
weather, 1071
Austrian army awfully arrayed, 950
Aut viam inveniam aut faciam, 510
Authentic watch, 164
Author and critic, at once, 1087
and finisher of our faith, 1122
and statesman, pen of the, 730
choose as a friend, 180
in each son, an, 1050
influence of an, 636

Author, man of rank as an, 237
of liberty, 447
of lies, the devil the, 126
of one of the great histories, 902
owns his stuff, 852
puts between the two covers of his book, 638
richest, that ever grazed, 239
teaches such beauty, where is any, 41
test of an, 554
that's all author, 357
what I like in an, 788
who speaks about his own books, 419
worst thing to do to an, 237
would his brother kill, 167
Authors and instigators of war, 20
are swallowed, many noble, 196
do not make acknowledgment, 992
essayist atheist novelist play your part, 471
everywhere renowned, 713
have established a kind of rule, 196
proof against the mutability of language, 344
shelved round us lie mummied, 565
shipt for foreign shores, 337
to read, 113
useful and entertaining, 196
who please everyone, 1086
Author's intention, consider the, 680
literary reputation, 255
prospects, gloomy as an, 421
soul, comes sincerely from the, 921
Authority, age carries an, 197
and show of truth, 39
art made tongue-tied by, 107
contempt of, 179
drest in a little brief, 36
from others' books, 40
has so great, 981
in discussion adduces, 1022
laws derive their, 949
resist him that is set in, 958
the basis of moral, 1073
Autobiography, British, never good, 738
saves one from memoirs, 521
Autocracy, ocean's deep, 843
Autograph at the beginning, 324
of God, 658
Automaton, mechanized, 368
Automobilus, ran his, 867
Autumn and the leaves were dry, 'twas, 369
dew, bright with, 372
fruit, fell like, 178
hails anew, 681
nodding o'er the plain, 224
poured from out her lavish horn, 441
saw old, in the misty morn, 392
sheaves are dewless, 580
some of us call it, 491
that grew more by reaping, 105
the windy lights of, 673

Autumn trees, sing from, 885
Autumn's hush, still small voice
  in, 431, 442
Autumn-fields, happy, 466
Autumnal face, beauty in one,
  117
  leaves in Vallombrosa, 148
  leaves, thick as, 218
Availeth, say not the struggle
  naught, 519
Avalanche of echoes, 706
Avarice ambition lust, etc., 1049
  and luxury, to gratify, 1051
  dreams of, 237
  envy pride, 1020
  lust and rum, crazed with, 759
  of which old men sicken, 116
  old-gentlemanly vice, 116, 359
  prudery is a kind of, 1063
  seems not so much a vice, 1049
  suspicion and asperity, 1056
Ave materna loving and wise, 579
Avengers of Religion's cause,
  1050
Avenging day, the great, 218
Avenues of ill, seal up the, 409
Aver 't is better than many, 750
Average, cold calculating, 645
  man, in the, 732
Avernus, descent to, 982
Aversion, begin with a little, 277
  to labour, idleness, 1051
Avilion, island-valley of, 463
Avoid shame do not seek glory,
  312
Avon, sweet swan of, 119
  to the Severn runs, 303, 304
A-wait at the gate of the west,
  663
Await no gifts from chance, who,
  546
Awake, my St. John, 206
  my soul, 225
Awakening, a sense of glad, 915
Awareness, rich returns of, 788
Away, and Sheridan twenty miles,
  552
  owes its charm to the far, 426
  pray scourge of war may pass,
  457
Awe and dread of a savage for
  mother-in-law, 713
  and majesty, attribute to, 46
  becomes holy and inspires,
  1079
  of such a thing as I, 81
Aweary of the sun, 88
A-wearyin' fer you, jest, 730
Awful darkness and silence reign,
  when, 498
  goodness is, how, 153
  guide in smoke and flame,
  310
  insane and, passion, 393
  lightning, 429
  Mabel, ain't it, 870
  memory, 321
  moment, face some, 300
  pause, Nature made an, 201
  phantom of the hungry poor,
  619
  volume, within that, 310
Awhile, loved long since and lost,
  403
Awkward hand in a row, 639
  of leg, the, 930

Awkwardness has no forgiveness,
  414
  which overtakes, 1072
Awning scaffolded, 867
Axe laid unto the root of the
  trees, 1117
  Lizzie Borden took an, 957
  many strokes with little, 69
  neither hammer nor, 266
  to grind he has an, 333
  upon the humbled neck, falls
  not the, 50
  woodman's, lies free, 370
Axes, no ponderous, rung, 266,
  342
Axis of the earth, 454
Axle of the universe, great, 566
Aye from thee, dissever, 1022
Ayont the twal, short hour, 284
Azan, he who died at, 596
Azores, lay the gray, 658
Azrael angel of death, 836
Azure brow, no wrinkle on thine,
  355
  deeps, 434
  dome, his hall the, 410
  hue, mountain in its, 327
  main, from out the, 225
  robe of night, the, 382
  skies, into the, 710
  we shall navigate the, 572

B AND C in love with A, 795
  with a Y — Y with an N, 350
Baälim and Peor, 161
Babbie, the most beaut-iful, 634
Babbitt changes his clothes, 884
Babbitt's spectacles, 884
Babble of the brook, careless, 665
Babbled of green fields, 66
Babbling gossip of the air, 54
Babby in a wad of straw, 375
Babe all burning bright, a pretty,
  30
  bent o'er her, 269
  I slept a, 1085
  in a house, a, 477
  pity like a naked new-born, 85
  she lost in infancy, 322
  was sleeping on her breast, the,
  369
Babes alone in the dark, 323
  and sucklings, 1103
  in the wood, 527
  milk for, 477
Babel; because the Lord did
  there confound, 1097
  stir of the great, 265
Babette, I am so old! good-night,
  648
Babies haven't any hair, 910
  we stand on common ground,
  as, 617
Baboon's sister, married the, 954
Baby and the prophylactic pup,
  815
  at my breast, dost not see my,
  105
  dear, where did you come from,
  559
  figure of the giant mass, 75
  he didn't give you that, 678
  shoes tying sashes fitting, 429
  small, only a, 589
  thing that made a woman cry,
  559

Baby thinks, what a, 522
  to bear my, 447
  was sleeping, 389
  who came a month ago, 569
  with my blue-eyed laughing,
  650
Baby's brain is tired, 686
  dimple, 522
  face, folded round a, 682
  feet, a, 634
  hands, 634
  laugh, echoed a, 890
  precious eyes are blinking, 686
  stocking, hang up the, 604
Babylon, by the rivers of, 1106
  by the waters of, 633
  glorious glamorous, 920
  in all its desolation, 941
  is fallen, 600, 1111
Babylon's garden, next, 956
Babylonish dialect, 141
Bacchus ever fair and young, 176
  plumpy, with pink eyne, 104
  that first from grape, 157
Bachelor, acquainted with a, 325
  I would die a, 39
  may risk his 'ide, 782
  of threescore, shall I never see
  a, 38
  widower or a, 346
Bacillus, each microbe and, 860
Back and side go bare, 20
  at my, I always hear, 169
  borne me on his, 97
  carried it on his, 1000
  carries the sky on his, 515
  cast-iron, with a hinge, 582
  cross' upon my rough grey, 758
  die with harness on our, 88
  door robs the house, 137
  haven't a shirt to my, 639
  never a shirt on his, 188
  not to go, 214
  on itself recoils, 154
  over the devil's, 1026, 1052
  scarcely a rag to her, 1081
  shout, our peals of laughter,
  554
  so much upon his, 121
  their opinions by a wager, 357
  those before cried, 400
  through creeks and inlets, far,
  519
  thumping on your, 267
  thumps upon the, 203
  ticklings down the, 929
  to the field, with his, 327
  to their springs like the rain,
  435
  turned his, 494
  unto the ladder turns his, 82
  wallet at his, 75
Backs and covers of books, 494
  and heads, other people's, 1080
  on your sturdy, 458
  raiment to our, 309
  read their stoic, 903
  wallets at our, 992
Backaches in an old stun' wall,
  775
Backbone of the army, 782
Backed like a weasel, 95
  with God and with the seas,
  70
Back-friend a shoulder-clapper,
  38

Background, see fit to keep me in the, 455
Backing of your friends, 61
plague upon such, 61
Backside, breeches upon his, 241
Backward and abysm of time, 32
look, angel of the, 443
look, to take a, 584
turn backward O Time, 595
Backwards, yesterdays look, 202
Bacon, broken bones for, 1042
could as easily have created, 382
great secretary of nature, 140
in peace, beans and, 961
save our, 1026
shined, think how, 208
Bad affright afflict the best, the, 243
and good of every land, 506
as falling, the fear 's as, 105
as we appear, not so, 874
beginning makes a bad ending, 968
better for being a little, 37
digestion inclines to skepticism, 727
dog a mad dog, 912
eminence, to that, 149
for the, all that was theirs dies, 968
himself thought nothing good, 661
in the best, 109, 657
— indifferent — good, 241
indifferent or good, 280
language or abuse, 622
man, this bold, 72
men live to eat and drink, 1004
moral character, bird of, 228
most men were, 1013
news, learning, 521
news, messenger who brings, 964
news, never good to bring, 104
ones bring about worse, 1054
rhyming a disease, 214
she was horrid, 440
the world is grown so, 71
two nations, good and the, 169
weather, no such thing as, 729
what is it makes you, 630
wiser being good than, 489
work follers ye, 527
work, get rid of, 613
world called, 771
Bad-looking, women call not, 1077
Bade each other stand, 620
Badge, nobility's, true, 76
of all our tribe, sufferance is the, 44
of honour is bestowed, 1036
Badness choose in a heap, 959
Badoura is unknown, where, 437
Baedeker to life, 914
Baffled get up and begin again, 487
oft is ever won, 355
still, betrayed and, 628
Baffling foes, beat down, 547
Bag and baggage, 50
empty, to stand upright, 227
full of gold, bought for a, 600
of masks, with a, 927

Bag of tools, each is given a, 680
to hold, give Camacho the, 1040
to hold, given us the, 283
which hangs on our back, 992
with holes, puts them into a, 1126
Bags, creased and flapping, 701
Baggage of life, women are the, 163
Baghdad, death at, 767
Bagman mounts, every, 728
Bagpipes a trying instrument, 745
Bail no demurrer, no, 278
Bailey, unfortunate Miss, 288
Bairns, at scule, sad time twa, 389
twa, and but ae heart, 389
Bait, devour the treacherous, 39
hook without the, 414
the hook well; this fish will bite, 39
this melancholy, 44
Baits, good news, 157
Baited like eagles, 63
with dragon's tale, 146
Baker's dozen, 1026
Balaam's ass, 1099
Balance, in nice, 215
of power, 200, 725
of the old world, 293
Balances, weighed in the, 1113
Bald by nature, 37
eagle representative of our country, 228
followers, time will have, 37
time himself is, 37
Bald-headed, go into it, 526
seaman, that talkative, 881
Baldric, milky, of the skies, 382
Baleen, with huge and dark, 888
Baleful star, beck of a, 756
Bales, costly, 464
of sweet Kentucky hay, 926
unopened to the sun, 202
Ball, a costume charity, 935
fun of the victory, 864
join to get Him back His, 681
of our vision, 576
only wind it into a, 282
roll on thou, 622
the earth, came down to find His, 681
this makes our earthly, 1058
wore last night at the, 1071
Balls of copper, Barnaby juggling, 1078
Ballad, a simple, 759
I met with a, 590
in print, a-life, I love a, 57
is sure to meet you, fragment of a, 589
of Sir Patrick Spence, 316
to his mistress' eyebrow, woful, 49
world was guilty of such a, 41
Ballads from a cart, sung, 177
of Green Erin or Gray Highlands, 361
of the people, 660
of the slums, 887
sing from door to door, 123
twenty, stuck about the wall, 139
ye are better than all the, 437

Ballad-mongers, same metre, 62
Ballast, a ship without, 1063
is old wine, 347
more sail than, 184
to keep the mind steady, 529
Balliol made me, fed me, 809
Ballot to the bullet, appeal from the, 456
Ballots, worthy of their, 934
Ballot-box, 'tis the, 348
Ballyshannon foundered, the, 622
Balm, all our calm is in that, 447
for every pain, and a, 390
from an anointed king, 59
in Gilead, is there no, 1112
night-dew's cooling, 445
of hurt minds, 86
sovereign, 248
sweet hope ethereal, 385
tropic for your, 923
Balms and hieroglyphics, 620
for all our pain, there are, 565
Balmy air of night, through the, 460
pain, full of sweet desolation, 385
sweets, diffuse their, 252
Balsam for mistakes, no, 659
Baltimore, ever go back to, 826
Bamboo-brier, sharp ez a, 689
Ban of labour, bears the, 983
on it lays her, 665
Band, forth we went a gallant, 455
if you haven't got a, 849
in Butte, 910
of brothers, 67
of exiles, 370
preacher in that little, 834
that Marion leads, 372
they march a blustering, 177
worries me to beat the, 870
Bands, cancels all, end of life, 62
of Orion, loose the, 1103
Bandusia's fount, 983
Band-wagon shone, how the grand, 696
Bane and antidote, my, 195
ignorance thy deadliest, 544
morality thou deadly, 284
of all genius virtue freedom, 368
precious, 149
to antidote, turns the, 651
to friendship, no greater, 981
Banff to Painted Post, from, 867
Bang but a whimper, not a, 899
Bangor to the Rocky Range, from, 868
Banish plump Jack, 62
Banished from these works, 179
Banishment, bitter bread of, 59
Banjo on my knee, 567
Banjos rattled and the tambourines, 856
Bank and bush, over, 24
and shoal of time, 85
cathedral like first supernatural, 902
moonlight sleeps upon this, 47
of violets, breathes upon a, 53
whereon wild thyme blows, 42
Banks and braes o' bonny Doon, 287
of Loch Lomond, bonnie, 952

Banks of that lonely river, 396
  of the crystalline waters, 432
  of the Sacramento, on the, 502
  of the Yuba, played on the,
    432
  to see, crowd the, 806
Banker bees are busy, 756
  making the loan, 937
Bankless streams, 882
Bank-note world, this, 363
Banner, blood-red, 343
  earth's green, 576
  Freedom yet thy, 354
  held high his, 1070
  in the sky, to see that, 450
  is unfurled, 502
  of Scotland, 390
  pride carries its, 591
  star-spangled, 332
  the royal, 102
  with the strange device, 434
Banners, army with, 1110
  confusion on thy, 244
  fold up the, 690
  hang out our, 88
  of thy dead, 765
  wave, all thy, 328
Banquet's o'er, when the, 205
  song and dance, 363
  tables, a hundred thousand,
    601
  when love sits down to the,
    610
Banquet-hall deserted, 336
Banqueter on worms, 725
Banqueters sit up in evening
  dress, 601
Banshee, mem'ry comes like a,
  715
Baptis' Baptis' is my name, 733
  pie, eat all de, 733
Baptist bell, clear-toned, 566
Baptized in de Baptis' church,
  733
  in tears, 269
Bar, back of the, 844
  be no moaning of the, 472
  birth's invidious, 468
  is, met where any, 651
  man at the turn-pike, 389
  of heaven, 577
  soon beyond the harbor, 579
  when I have crossed the, 472
Bars, behind the western, 668
  nor iron, a cage, 168
  on their clanged, 748
  till the morning, 643
  to their windows, nor, 435
Barabbas, crucify the Jew, give
  us, 763
  was a robber, 1118
  with wrists unfettered, 686
Barbara Allen, name was, 257
Barbarian, autocrat must be a
  great, 726
  weeping above his dead, 602
Barbaric pearl and gold, 149
  yawp, I sound my, 535
Barbarism, war at best is, 542
Barbarous dissonance, 158
  in beauty, 672
  skill, is but a, 167
Barber, Caesar's, a busy, listening fellow, 1000
  and a collier fight, 229
  imprudently married the, 246

Barber, kept on shaving, and
  the, 508
  the fat colored, 756
Barbers cutting each other's hair,
  878
Barber's shear, never has known
  the, 481
Barber-shop, lights burn low in
  the, 878
Bard here dwelt more fat, 225
  on Chian strand, that blind,
    317
  whom there were none to
    praise, 296
  whose lay resounds, 258
Bards, Eighth Commandment not
  made for, 316
  gather all our Saxon, 397
  of earth, all the, 626
  of long ago, 816
  of passion and of mirth, 384
  of rhyme and metre free, 868
  place 'mid the, 982
  saints heroes if we will, 545
  who sung, Olympian, 409
Bare, and strips it, 675
  and the walls around are, 554
  back and side go, 20
  fields are lying brown and, 552
  gift without the giver is, 525
  imagination of a feast, 59
Barefoot boy with cheek of tan,
  442
  dervishes, like, 410
  him that makes shoes, 15, 122
Barère's Memoirs, never read,
  399
Bargain catch cold, lest the, 105
  in the way of, 62
  never a better, 27
Bargains in books, 674
Barge, clung about the, 948
  drag the slow, 267
  mean to buy a, 899
  she sat in, 104
Barge's prow, watched a, 899
Bark, above below our, 401
  and bite, dogs delight to, 198
  and thong, temple made of, 896
  at me, see they, 99
  attendant sail, 209
  be sailing, shall my, 579
  but not our, 994
  critic peep or cynic, 408
  exiles moored their, 370
  fatal and perfidious, 159
  is on the sea, my, 356
  is wafted, my, 473
  is worse than his bite, 138
  let no dog, 44
  of man could navigate, 393
  of my genius, 1021
  sinks, if my, 517
  that he feels afraid of its, 592
  that held a prince, 371
  that slowly held its way, 424
  watch-dog's honest, 358
Barks, Nicæan, 460
Barkis is willin', 496
Barleycorn, bold John, 287
Barmecide, where is thy feast O,
  649
Barn, grew behind the, 953
  well filled, farm well tilled, 275
Barnaby before the altar, 1078
Barnes, slipped through, 862

Barney Buntline turned his quid,
  274
Baron could not produce epigrams, 1063
Barrage and gas-cloud, above the,
  937
Barrel, handful of meal in a, 1101
  is sprung, 810
  of gold, 686
  of meal wasted not, 1101
Barrel-house kings, 857
Barrel-load, save them by the,
  749
Barren earth, small model of the,
  59
  life and hand, stand with, 689
  peaks of two eternities, 602
  regrets, 592
  't is all, 242
Barricade, at some disputed, 904
Barrie, Sir James, with milk of
  human kindness, 906
Barrier between day and day, 301
  insurmountable, 691
  of loneliness, break through its,
    852
  of senses, no, 861
Barriers, burned away all, 773
  of race and nationality, 711
Barring that natural expression
  of villainy, 616
Barrister's profession, a, 1076
Barter nought but pain, 567
Bartlett of market quotations,
  910
Bartley will have a fine coffin, 817
Barty, Hans Breitmann gife a,
  559
Base born, bravest have been,
  124
  contempts of sect and creed,
    864
  earth, glory fall to the, 59
  fly from its firm, 308
  him that uttered nothing, 462
  ignoble throng, 972
  in man, to keep down the, 471
  men in love have then a no-
    bility, 101
  of the Yankee commonwealth,
    926
  passions, of all, 68
  stand upon their, 1059
  uses we may return, 97
  world and worldlings, 65
Baseless fabric of this vision, 33
Basement, little sick child in the,
  715
Baseness, to write fair, hold it, 97
  we will smite, 806
Baser quality, fruit of, 66
Bashaw, three-tailed, 288
Bashful fifteen, maiden of, 279
  stream, 165
  virgin's sidelong looks, 250
Basic clod, 732
Basil-tree, Isabella did her, 722
Basis, moral authority, 1073
  no broader, for any govern-
    ment, 424
  of all health sinlessness, 548
Basket, eggs in one, 1036
  of fruit, I'll bite this, 362
  piled, you had your, 291
  who was in the, 34
Baskit er kittens, 688

Bass eternal of the sea, the, 609
Bass, the first string, 172
Bassarid of Boston, blatant, 635
Bastard Latin, soft, 357
  to the time, he is but a, 57
Bastards, ancient families, 124
  live like nature's, 158
Bastion fringed with fire, 468
Bastion's mole, 248
Bat, Casey at the, 770
  or any other creature, 592
  tongue of dog, wool of, 87
  weak-eyed, 247
Bats, to the moles and the, 1111
Bate a jot of heart or hope, 162
Bated breath, 45
Batcese, Leetle, 713
Bath in the Styx, 652
  sore labour's, 86
  stirring the water in his, 900
Bathe all the hills in melancholy
    gold, 418
  in fiery floods, 36
Bathing, caught Whigs, 419
  do it while, 984
Batrachian chirrup, gay, 933
Battalions, field-marshal who ar-
    rays our, 519
  heaviest, 1053
  sorrows come in, 96
  through the naked, 738
Batter'd bruised and brown, old
    pipe, 578
  caravanserai, this, 1018
Batteries of China, past the, 746
Battle, after, sleep is best, 609
  and the breeze, 327
  Ben, was a soldier bold, 392
  care for him who shall have
    borne the, 457
  cowards do not count in, 968
  crimson flower of, blooms, 522
  day is past, 402
  division of a, 100
  done ere the last echo, 719
  flags were furled, 464
  for the free, won the, 363
  for the last, of the world, 442
  formost in, 257
  fought the victory won, the,
    305
  freedom's, once begun, 355
  he who is in, slain, 254
  in her face, 814
  in the forefront of the hottest,
    1100
  is lost and won, when the, 84
  life is a, 1010
  lost and battle won, 292
  my child, a, 564
  news of, 500
  noble honorable, 390
  not to the strong, 270
  of competition, 1072
  of life, who fell in the, 533
  of the first rank, 1067
  or business, in, 510
  or the chase, 681
  perilous edge of, 148
  prize o' death in, 527
  raged loudest, 390
  rages loud and long, the, 328
  see the front of, lour, 286
  sees the other's umbered face,
    67
  smelleth the, afar off, 1103

Battle, stay, I made my, 806
  storms dismay, 864
  the bravest, 657
  they joined, 969
  they went forth to, 891
  through defeat, through the,
    535
  was cn once more, telling, 552
  with my peers, delight of, 464
  won, returned from, 432
Battles are transacted by mecha-
    nism, 381
  fight our country's, 953
  fought all his, o'er again, 176
  long ago, 298
  rains fall after great, 998
  sieges attacks campaigns, 1045
  sieges fortunes, 100
  so bravely won, 31
  still are won by justice, 806
  that I have fought his, 172
  win our, by its aid, 504
Battle's sound, no war or, 161
  van, in the, 511
Battle-blood gory, 571
Battle-cry, blood my, 447
  freedom their, 552
  of freedom, 541
Battled for the true and just,
    468
Battlefield, on our last, 401
  rides God's, 891
Battlefields which have their he-
    roes, 1068
Battle-flags unfurled, 397
Battleground fortress tent, away
    from, 816
  world is a, 926
Battle-king's ringlets of light,
    643
Battlements, fate sits on these
    dark, 290
  of eternity, 749
  towers and, 160
Battle-shout, and with, 659
Bauble, pleased with this, 208
Baucis' busy care, 177
Bay, and every stagnant, 761
  bare of, 743
  come to the self-same, 1022
  dead calm rested on the, 405
  of Biscay O, 288
  of Portugal, bottom like, 51
  somebody bet on de, 568
  the moon, be a dog and, 83
Bays burn deep and chafe, 631
  the faded, 896
Bay-tree, like a green, 1104
Bayard, knight like, 442
Bayonet's contrition, 586
Be, and so it might not, 510
  dreamed a dream that could
    not, 558
  ever careful in your choice,
    1083
  favourable to bold beginnings,
    982
  fearful of the night, 661
  gleam on the years that shall,
    426
  good sweet maid, 523
  home again, oh to, 508
  lief not be as live to, 81
  loved by me, to love and, 459
  matters not what you are
    thought to, 980

Be, may bring us there to, 480
  no better than you should, 131
  not afraid, it is I, 1115
  not afraid of life, 663
  not overcome of evil, 1119
  not righteous overmuch, 1109
  not slow to visit the sick, 1124
  now, 'tis not to come, if it, 97
  o'er lesser powers that, 534
  of good cheer, 1118
  of good courage, 1112
  or not to be, to, 93
  patient O be patient, 499
  powers that, 1119
  sure you are right then go
    ahead, 349
  systematically ascetic or he-
    roic, 662
  the great business of life is to,
    641
  we know not what we may, 96
  were it not better not to, 462
  wery careful o' vidders, 494
  ye angry and sin not, 1121
Beach, fishermen that walk upon
    the, 99
  my life is like a stroll upon the,
    513
  pebbles smoothed on rolling,
    572
  shell from the strown, 577
  there came to the, 328
Beacon bright, for a, 807
  of the wise, 75
Beacons, mark as ye go the, 765
  of hope ye appear, 547
  of wise men, logical conse-
    quences, 564
Beacon-tip, topmost, 490
Bead, I kiss each, 765
  on the string of confusions, 837
Beads and prayer-books, 208
  few, are best when we goe a-
    Maying, 134
  in drops of rain, tell their, 433
  of a young Senegambian, 857
  on a string, 1076
  pictures, rosaries, 143
  there are, how many, 406
  they told, their, 394
Beade of amber, flie within a,
    112
Beades, to tell his, 256
Beadle to a humorous sigh, 41
Beadroll, Fames eternall, 25
Beagle bit a kleagle, 824
Beak from out my heart, take
    thy, 460
  upon my face, 647
Beaker, fill every, up my men,
    404
  full of the warm South, 383
Beaker's brim, bubbles that swim
    on the, 431
Be-all and the end-all, 85
Beam, full midday, 163
  of some medicinal star, 923
  unpolluted in his, 112
Beams athwart the sea, 464
  benign, temper with, 522
  display or in clouds hide them,
    168
  from happy human eyes, 703
  full-dazzling, all his, 536
  little candle throws his, 47
  of love, learn to bear the, 281

Beams, spreads his orient, 152
  tricks his, 159
Bean, takes the hair right off
  your, 943
Beans, a certain meal on, 493
  abstain from, 1001
  and bacon, better, 961
  and brown bread, as well as,
  714
  determined to know, 515
  eat no, 122
  there will be no, 853
Bean-rows, nine, 790
Bear a charmed life, 88
  another's misfortunes, 217
  borne and yet must, 367
  can every anguish calmly, 459
  exit, pursued by a, 816
  how easy is a bush supposed a,
  43
  if I were a, 876
  in mind your labor is for future, 417
  it calmly, we, 190
  lick into form as a, 122
  like the Turk, 213
  or lion, sometime like a, 105
  pain to the, 400
  rugged Russian, 87
  that walks like a man, 779
  the burden and the heat, we,
  546
  the palm alone, 81
  those ills we have, 93
  to live or dare to die, 208
  up and steer right onward,
  162
  we 've fought the, before, 562
  with him one night, 228
Bears and lions growl, 198
  in the bush, 565
  lick their cubs, 122, 1029,
  1031
  like the fur of winter, 929
  when first born, 994
Bear-baiting esteemed heathenish, 400
Beard, an old man with a, 499
  and his silence, wrapped in his,
  928
  and hoary hair, 244
  built their nests in my, 499
  caught in student's, 706
  Dutchman's, 55
  he that hath a, 38
  husband with a, 38
  of formal cut, 50
  put aside my, for that never
  committed treason, 10
  singed the Spanish king's, 439
  the lion in his den, 308
  to shave a man's, 1035
  tradition wears a snowy, 442
  was grizzled, 90
Beards be grown, until your,
  1100
  wag all, in hall where, 19
  waveth all, when the, 19
Bearded great and swaggering
  files, 842
  like the pard, 49
  lips, 436
Bearing boughs may live, that, 60
  there was pride in Casey's, 770
Bearings of this observation, 496
Beast, leave so much as a, 1127

Beast, little better than a, 44
  man a, no more, 528
  man is but a, 258
  man this mongrel, 898
  that wants discourse of reason,
  90
  very gentle, 43
  watch the captured, 687
Beasts, brutish, 83
  man's injustice to, 1006
  nature teaches, 76
  pair of very strange, 51
  that perish, like the, 1104
  who have never a friend, 877
  with the kingly eyes, 929
Beat, flow with measured, 685
  John Bull was, at Waterloo,
  406
  the bush, 12, 133
  waves that, our coast, 386
  wild on this world's shore, 447
  your pate, you, 217
Beaten gold my throne, of, 822
  hymn of the wounded the, 533
  with his own rod, 11
Beatific bosom of Penn Yan Bill,
  700
  vision, 149
Beating hammer, back of the,
  873
  of my own heart, 458
  of the storm-waves, 770
Beatitude, eighth, 220
Beaumont lie a little further, 119
  lie a little nearer Spenser, rare,
  119
Beauteous eye of heaven, 58
  flower, may prove a, 78
  idiot speaks, when the, 193
  landscape bright, 942
  looks win love, 52
  thing, if you see a, 553
  thing raises the pure, any, 1023
Beauties hid from common sight,
  557
  lovers admire thy naked, 358
  modestly conceals her, 240
  of Dutchtown, 756
  of holiness, 1105
  of the night, meaner, 114
  of the north, unripened, 194
  see, in small proportions, 120
  we dimly remember, 927
  who followed him, petted by,
  253
Beautifier of complexion or form
  or behavior, no, 413
  rank is a great, 425
Beautiful and best, 809
  and just, 771
  and to be wooed, 68
  as woman's blush, 404
  babbie, the most, 634
  beneath his touch, grow, 327
  birds let me go with you, 845
  dreamer, wake unto me, 568
  early summer weather, 395
  eyes of my cash-box, 1046
  for patriot dream, 737
  for situation, 1104
  in this living, 834
  is love, 834
  is night, how, 322
  loved her for that she was, 506
  most, verb in the world, 1083
  mouth in the world, most, 222

Beautiful necessity, from a, 477
  new cases of curved spine, 430
  nothing happen more, than
  death, 534
  old rhyme, 108
  outward, appear, 1116
  over house-tops, moon, 536
  palace, the, 171
  pale clay, 595
  palms of Allah, 952
  pea-green boat, in a, 498
  Rosalie Lee, was my, 432
  seems right by force, 430
  that war and all its deeds, 536
  the seeds of godlike power, 545
  the, the bright, 665
  things and wept, they said, 931
  upon the mountains, how, 1112
  what a deal of scorn looks, 55
  what could be more, 921
  whole out of commonplace
  things, 683
  wisdom, even in, 960
  within, make thee, 442
Beautifully blue, 322
Beautifying touch, its, 690
Beauty, a hint of the old lost,
  445
  a thing of, 382
  a witty, 576
  about a home life, 1076
  adorned in naked, 152
  an attractive, 1036
  and emotion in sea, 856
  and goodness, connection of,
  571
  and her chivalry, 352
  and mystery of the ships, 436
  and the stars were one, 816
  and truth are worthy to be
  sought, 655
  as could die, as much, 119
  barbarous in, 672
  be with me, 834
  being the best of all, 668
  bereft of, 52
  born of murmuring sound, 297
  but skin deep, 506
  calls and glory shows the way,
  186
  come near your, 68
  courage youth, 832
  crieth in an attic, 614
  crowned, by mourning, 581
  curved is the line of, 444
  dead, black chaos comes again,
  106
  dedicate his, to the sun, 77
  dim, at the heart of things, 754
  divinely superfluous, 895
  double, whenever a swan, 391
  draws us with a single hair,
  125, 212
  dreamed that life was, 508
  drunk with a, 801
  e'er gave, all that, 244
  Elysian, 303
  fades away, slowly thy perfect,
  619
  fashioned well, 1071
  fatal gift of, 354
  fed my common earth, 832
  filling all the land with, 705
  fills the air around with, 354
  flowing curves of, 444
  for ashes, 1112

Beauty, form of manliest, 274
full-blown flower of glorious, 179
furled in the commonplace, 625
garmented in light from her own, 367
great perils have this, 1069
grew, the conscious stone to, 408
has no ebb, 790
hath its source in itself, 1010
hath strange power, 157
hold a plea, shall, 107
home, come with, 834
humbled to the earth, 931
if she unmask her, 90
I'm not a great star, as a, 845
impassioned for its, 429
in a brow of Egypt, 43
in all things, 385
in his life, daily, 103
in the heart, 833
in the, of the lilies, 522
in this plain room, 866
invisible, 849
is a flower, 840
is a joy forever, thing of, 382
is a pledge, 770
is a short-lived tyranny, 1014
is a silent deceit, 1014
is an ivory mischief, 1014
is eternity, 880
is indescribable, 770
is its own excuse, 409, 441
is its own reward, 918
is not immortal, 836
is pleasure, 769
is that Medusa's head, 914
is the best introduction, 1014
is the gift of God, 1014
is truth, truth beauty, 383
isle of, fare thee well, 388
itself doth of itself persuade, 106
king arrayed in his, 387
led captive, 156
left thee but, 628
lies in many eyes, 335
lies, the cynosure, 160
lies unseen, in the rough marble, 445
like the night, walks in, 356
lingers, lines where, 355
lives though lilies die, 881
makes this vault a feasting presence, 80
making beautiful old rhyme, 108
met some young, 1000
more amiable than, 196
must be truth, 385
no, that hath not some strangeness, 111
nor good talk, 786
of a butterfly's wing, 930
of a human face, with the little, 834
of a thousand stars, clad in the, 32
of an aged face, 868
of growing plants, 1049
of old men is the grey head, 1108
of style and harmony, 973
of surpassing, 979

Beauty of the good old cause, 298
of the house is order, 953
of the slender red line, 542
of the world, 169
of things, 895
old age, ill layer-up of, 68
on the shore, left their, 408
or form we are borrowers, to, 480
perception of, a moral test, 515
perils have this, 1069
poetry as rhythmical creation of, 461
possessor of, 483
power of, I remember the, 176
principal, 147
provoketh thieves, 48
pure classic, 930
put on, 811
rings of, 572
rules the roast, 984
scandal the doom of, 986
see naught but vanity in, 522
seems right by force of, 430
seen in one autumnal face, 117
shall be, so long as, 1017
share, unashamed his, 931
she walks in, 356
should harbour a heart, 256
slain, with him is, 106
smiling in her tears, 327
soon grows familiar, 194
stands in the admiration, 156
stands looking, when, 1085
still, such seems your, 108
such, as a woman's eye, 41
that is to be, 757
that underlies, for the possible, 560
the mate for, 425
the splendor of, 953
there is music in the, 145
there's too much, 792
thou art all, 187
though injurious, 157
to die for, 409
to sport with, 337
truly blent, 54
truth and love are one, 668
waking or asleep, 153
wandering, eternal, 790
what so nameless as, 868
which old Greece or Rome, 442
who walks with, 891
why talk of, 921
will decay, 269
winds of March with, 56
with thee in, 555
without grace, 414
without vanity strength without insolence, 351
wrought from within, 645
yet to find, is there, 893
Beauty's chain, hour with, 337
ears, gem that hangs from, 267
ensign is crimson, 80
heavenly ray, 356
perfect round, 682
self rose visible, 869
Beaux, where none are, 239
Beaver hat, on account of his, 498
in Canadian brooks, 451
Becalmed at eve, as ships, 519

Becalmed by the shores of age, 644
Beck, they follow the, 756
Beckoning shadows dire, 157
Beckons me away, a hand which, 205
Becks and wreathed smiles, 160
Become what we are capable of becoming, 704
Becomes him ill, nothing, 41
the throned monarch, 46
Becoming mirth, limit of, 41
Bed, all of man's peril comes of, 610
and board, peace and plenty, 936
and so to, 180, 867
as you lay in your, 941
at Ware, 200
bad luck sits by your, 640
be blest that I lie on, 164
born in, we die in, 1043
bravely thou becomest thy, 105
by night, 251
cottage-chamber, 568
cursed him in, 351
day-star in the ocean, 159
delicious, 391
died quietly in his, 577
dread grave as little as my, 183
dreamless, 446
early to rise, early to, 227
first and worst one is a, 610
from his brimstone, 321
goes to, mellow, 127
gravity out of his, 62
half-hidden in its grassy, 637
hath she for narrow, 823
holy angels guard thy, 199
hue as red as the rosy, 431
I want to go to, 667
if they seldom die in, 683
in the dark, in, 1023
into the coverlet of a, 1000
is narrow, every, 915
is the boon for me, 817
lies in his, 58
little rudely sculptured, 682
little, to rest my head, 382
made his pendent, 85
mighty large, 200
no use in my going to, 389
of ancient mould, 848
of death, faith kneeling by his, 31
of death, smooth the, 213
of honour, 200
of squills how blue, 883
on glory's brightest, 386
on my grave as now my, 145
placed in his room, 1068
should be of ivory, my, 822
sits by your, 1066
sleeping mourn upon thy, 632
sober, will go to, 127
they died in, 610
to-night, I will not go to, 610
up in my, now, 391
we laugh in, we cry in, 1043
welcome to your gory, 286
with the lambe, to, 23
Beds made level, 552
of raging fire, from, 150

Beds of roses, make thee, 31
  to make bloom, 738
Bedazzled with the sun, 52
Beddes heed, lever have at his, 5
Bedding, tied up the, 1000
Bedecked in her snowy array, 474
Bedfellows, strange, 33, 582
Bedford and Exeter, 67
Be-diamonded be-damned, be-decked, 768
Bedlam, mad as, 496
Bednall-greene, blind beggar's daughter of, 257
Bedstead of a crimson rose, 911
Bedtime, would it were, 63
Bedward, dormitive I take to, 145
Bedwarfed the man, o'ergrown the brute, 759
Bee, a vagrant, 728
  bringeth home the, 328
  brisk as a, 233
  buried in his own juice, 112
  busie as a, 23
  busy, has no time for sorrow, 282
  does not concern the, 584
  enclosed in amber, 995
  had stung it newly, 163
  is on the wing, 345
  like the industrious, 910
  love in my bosom like a, 27
  may work like the, 431
  nothing so like a soul as a, 1069
  sparrow and, 570
  the little busy, 199
  weak as a rained-on, 840
  where sucks the, 33
  would choose to dream in, 431
  would know, the curtained, 911
Bees are busy with their gold, 756
  his helmet, a hive for, 28
  honied words like, 898
  human race organized like, 769
  humming of the, 955
  murmuring of innumerable, 466
  rob the Hybla, 84
  store up your honey, 982
  the government of, 1032
Bee-loud glade, alone in the, 790
Beechen tree, spare the, 328
Beef, I am a great eater of, 54
  of England, roast, 229
Beehive's hum, 289
Beelzebub arose early in the morning, 368
Been and may be again, 298
  as things have, they remain, 519
  fall from the days that have, 426
  forgot in the hatred, 459
  here before, I have, 577
  more happy thou hadst, 389
  that the world had never, 559
  what has been has, 177
  who that hath ever, 306
Beer and skittles, 551
  and spirits, throw all the, 695
  bemused in, 212
  chronicle small, 101

Beer, cold small, 226
  come my lad and drink some, 239
  felony to drink small, 69
  idly sipping here my, 605
  knocking off the, 909
  pints and quarts of Ludlow, 743
  poor creature small, 64
  small, that questionable super-fluity, 417
  take you on trust for, 715
Beers, match with destiny for, 778
Beersheba, Dan to, 242, 1099
Beetle balanced bottles, 691
  booms adown the glooms, 696
  brows, 77
  intolerable to a black, 361
  that we tread upon, 36
  three-man, 64
  winds his small horn, 247
Beetle's wing, no thicker than a, 803
Beeves and home-bred kine, 298
  broad as ten thousand, 575
Befall a soul, 587
Befell at forty-odd, 392
Before and after, looking, 96
  dreams no mortal ever dreamed, 460
  fantastic terrors never felt, 460
  her on a shutter, borne, 481
  not lost but gone, 188, 447
  souls gone, 627
  that which has gone, 1011
  the beginning of years, 633
  the better foot, 58
  the bird can fly, break, 471
  the thing we may, 559
  the whole world, 1047
  we've fought the Bear, 562
  you could say Jack Robinson, 540
Beg, Homer himself must, 123
  I give, they, 20
  or borrow or get a man's own, 185
Began best can't end the worst, 490
Begetter, to the onlie, 107
Beggar don't know nor do, 782
  he's an absent-minded, 782
  maid, loved the, 78
  maid shall be my queen, 465
  may crawl at his side, 449
  on horseback, 124, 1041
  slightly alcoholic, 898
  that is dumb may challenge double pity, 21
  with bruised feet, 708
  would enfold himself, 786
Beggars and vagabonds, best of all, 1045
  art of supporting, 976
  at your gate, are there no, 462
  entirely do away with, 1079
  in the streets mimicked, 398
  mounted run their horse to death, 69, 124
  must be no choosers, 131
  should be no choosers, 14
Beggar's daughter, blind, 257
Beggared all description, 104

Beggarly account of empty boxes, 80
  elements, weak and, 1121
  Scotchman, 233
Beggary in the love, 104
Begging bread, nor his seed, 1104
  the question, 944
Begin, finish what I, 444
  way that boys, 481
Beginning and end of political education, 635
  and the end, 1123
  bad, bad ending, 968
  every day is a fresh, 682
  good end good, 14
  hard, 12
  is the most important, 973
  late, choosing and, 154
  mean and end to all things, 506
  never ending, still, 176
  no great love in the, 34
  of a feast, 63
  of a fray, 17
  of a new month or year, 1089
  of his journey, 970
  of Knowledge, love is ever, 378
  of my end, I see the, 43
  of our end, the true, 43
  of years, before the, 633
  who has made a, 985
Beginnings and endings of under-takings, 798
  and new shoots, new, 924
  are, where our, 966
  favourable to bold, 982
  friendships from, 979
  God of Fair, 778
Begone dull care, 170
Begot, by whom, 217
  how nourished how, 45
  in the ventricle of memory, 41
  of nothing but vain fantasy, 77
Begotten of a summer dream, 407
Beguile light of light, 40
  the thing I am, 101
  the time look like the time, 84
Beguiled by one, 103
Begun, between things ended and, 537
  for, wonder what I was, 948
Behaviour, check to loose, 197
  during good, 945
  of silk-sack clouds, 672
  upon his good, 360
  which is intrinsically corrupt, 917
Behind, spare not nor look, 417
  the western bars, 668
Behold a smile of God, 539
  and fear, 129
  hath power to say, 42
  in the bloom of apples, 445
  the upright man, 1104
  we live through all things, 596
Beholds her image in her eyes re-flected, 555
Beholder, lights the heart of the, 933
Beholders, strike awe into the, 191
Beholding myself all rosy red, 1086

Behoof, wassail for new love's, 600
Being, a fallible, 235
  beauty its own excuse for, 409
  each young and beautiful, 1085
  God a necessary, 172
  God-given rights inherent in that, 424
  hath a part of, 353
  holiest end of woman's, 454
  intellectual, 149
  is holiness harmony, 549
  momentary taste of, 1018
  of an accommodatin' character, 606
  one principle of, 1011
  pleasing anxious, 245
  scarcely formed, a lovely, 361
  shot my, through earth, 316
  state of this strange, 247
  who gets accustomed, a, 1074
Beings, peopled it with living, 508
  reasoning, 1010
Being's end and aim, our, 208
Belabored hound, cower like a, 502
Belated peasant, 149
  quip, not even a, 924
Beldame nigh, have a, 977
Belgium's capital had gathered then, 352
Belgrade, by battery besiege, 950
Belial, sons of, 148
Belief, hope is the, 312
  I will to live and die, in this, 1022
  in a beneficent power, 651
  in falsehood, 1081
  in the senses, 1081
  in transmigration of souls, 798
  lightened by the, 922
  my most ethereal, 767
  my sure my very firm, 894
  points of, 335
  ripened into faith, 302
  sad past all, 607
  too great for our, 503
  within the prospect of, 84
Beliefs agonized hopes, tremulous, 798
  all kinds of old dead, 1075
  forsaken, 548
  swallow more, than man can digest, 741
Believe a man repents, will not, 470
  have heard and do in part, 89
  her, though I know she lies, I, 109
  it because it is impossible, 1012
  it or not, 943
  oft repeating they, 190
  some make themselves believe that they, 1028
  what varies every day, who can, 174
  yet they, me who await, 546
Believed, who never doubted never half, 469
Believers, speak long enough he will get, 705
  take your necessary precautions, 1126

Believes his own watch, each, 210
Believing as I do that man, 449
  heart hath gone, 507
  souls, God gives to, 69
Bell and his book, his, 351
  and the sexton tolled the, 392
  as a sullen, 64
  book and candle, 1034
  chimed in the Roman Catholic, 566
  chimed out the Episcopalian, 566
  church-going, 264
  doth toll no passing, 349
  good old Dutch church, 566
  in a cowslip's, I lie, 33
  in rapture rang the Temperance, 566
  invites me, 86
  merry as a marriage, 352
  prompter's hand is on his, 644
  prophet's camel, 881
  rang out the Unitarian, 566
  rang out the Universalist, 566
  Roland spoke, the great, 620
  shouted the Methodistic, 566
  signalling with the, 929
  silence that dreadful, 101
  slow falling to the prompter's, 481
  softly, ring the, 665
  sound as a, 39
  swung to and fro, 705
  tocsin of the soul, the dinner, 360
  tolling from some gray old steeple, 554
  twilight and evening, 472
Bells and fire pistols, ring, 1089
  and Fudges and their historians, respective merits of the, 399
  creed of the, 566
  have knolled to church, 49
  hear the mellow wedding, 460
  I hear, the port is near, 536
  jangled out of tune, 94
  music of those village, 266
  musically wells from the, 459
  of heaven, all the, 634
  of Shandon that sound so grand, 423
  of the Holy City, 443
  of the kirk, 709
  of the past, 644
  pealing at every step, 903
  play uppe O Boston, 540
  rang mad with glee, all the, 600
  ring happy, 469
  ring no, 955
  ring out wild, 469
  sound of all, 323
Belle, where none are beaux 'tis vain to be a, 239
  Aurore, thy wife the, 492
Belligerent discordant States, 341
Bellman, the owl the fatal, 86
  would cry, so the, 599
Bellowing, with troublous, 24
Bellows full of angry wind, 790
  I never will lend, 374
Belly and no bowels, no, 903
  eye is bigger than the, 138
  God send thee good ale, 20

Belly has no ears, 998, 1026
  in its dull quiet way, 961
  man must mind his, 234
  spent under the devil's, 1026
  who does not mind his, 234
  whose God is their, 1121
  with good capon lined, 50
  your back and your feet, 985
Belly-need, beyond his, 777
Bellyful of fighting, 105
Bellywash, slippers and warm, 925
Beloved fill the cup, ah my, 1018
  from pole to pole, 315
  He giveth his, 427
  in life of Abraham Lincoln, 806
  in vain, fields, 243
  of a king, 257
  over all, 779
  sleep, he giveth his, 1106
Below, my thoughts remain, 95
  thy element is, 98
Belshazzar the king made a great feast, 1113
Belshazzar's wall, as on, 807
Belting, lilting at loom and, 936
Bemused in beer, a parson, 212
Ben Adhem's name led, 346
Ben Battle was a soldier bold, 392
Ben Bolt, 521
Ben Johnson and Shakespear gathered humours of men daily, 171
Ben Jonson, rare, 118
Benches, on the platinum, 937
  dark with people, 770
Bend a knotted oak, 193
  low, 619
  low, shall I, 45
  round the, 862
  your eye on vacancy, 95
Bendemeer's stream, roses by, 337
Bends, though she, him she obeys, 436
Beneath soft clouds along the, 418
  far, the tainted foam, 375
  the chestnut-tree, since first, 446
  the crisp and wintry carpet, 668
  the milk-white thorn, 284
  the noise of tempests, far, 480
  the rule of men, 425
  the wild commotion, far down, 480
Benedick the married man, 38
Benediction, memory a, 860
  of nature, is grass, 602
  out of Heaven's, 16
  said, is my, 428
Benedight, sëynt, blesse this hous, 6
Benefaction, a previous, 971
Benefactor was unknown, where the, 323
Benefactors in the newspapers, 321
Beneficence of grass, 602
  private, inadequate, 750
Benefit, he who confers a, 1028
  in making failures early, 563

Benefit of men, use and, 172
  of our fellow men, 1127
  to go over again in imagination, 1023
  with gratitude, receives a, 991
Benefits, desire for greater, 200
  how great, 985
  in refusing, 1049
  of a college education, 413
Benevolence, universal, 253
Benicia boy, now the, 490
Benighted 'eathen, 781
  foe, your, 910
Benign is solitude, 299
Benignant information is his hobby, 815
  spirit, 659
  toils and tender cares, 373
Benison of hot water, 894
  to fall, for a, 134
Benny Havens, oh! drink to her and, 401
Bent, affection cannot hold the, 54
  find out the natural, 974
  him o'er the dead, 355
  just as the twig is, 209
  o'er her babe, 269
  though on pleasure she was, 264
  top of my, 95
  what avails the classic, 780
Benumbs, care's a canker that, 624
Bequeath my soul to God, 113
Bequeathed by bleeding sire, 355
Bequest of wings was but a book, 584
  sun's supreme, 642
Bereavement pain, 596
Bereft of beauty, 52
Berkeley, said there was no matter, 360
Berkshire boulders, ferns by these, 915
  loam, dumb loving of the, 834
Bermoothes, still-vexed, 32
Berries, come to pluck your, 159
  moulded on one stem, two, 43
  where are your, 291
  wholesome, thrive and ripen, 66
Berry, God could have made a better, 140
Berry's cheek is plumper, 584
Berth, death which happened in his, 392
  was of the wombe of morning dew, 24
Berye, as broun as is a, 5
Beryl-rimmed rebecs of ruby, 432
Beryline buckets, the ruby-rimmed, 431
Besançon's alien sky, beneath, 297
Beside a blacksmith's door, 622
  a human door, 298
  the evening sea, I walked, 558
  the springs of Dove, 296
  the still waters, 1103
Bess, image of good queen, 391
Best, a vapor at the, 577
  administered, whate'er is, 208
  and the worst of this is, 633
  are but shadows, 43

Best, as heaven and hell, worst and, 470
  bad in the, 109
  companions, 250
  company when you read, 313
  cosmopolite, that man's the, 471
  days, afternoon of her, 72
  did it for the, 747
  each thing in its place is, 436
  fear not to touch the, 21
  fools be little wise, 118
  friends ever known, 750
  good man, 184
  he should, he could, he would, he did the, 29
  heart the best brain, 602
  his at last who says it, 415, 528
  his circumstance allows, 201
  honest tale speeds, 72
  hope for the, 312
  I loved you, 185
  I scent which pays the, 526
  in kind but in degree, no, 436
  is bad, though the, 743
  is like the worst, 782
  is never to be born, 1066
  is yet to be, the, 489
  it was her, and she was vauntie, 287
  king of good fellows, 68
  laid schemes of mice and men, 284
  liar does smallest amount of lying, 613
  love our own the, 642
  loving and serving highest and, 501
  men moulded out of faults, 37
  men of few words are the, 66
  never manifest their, 609
  never to have been born, 966
  of all possible worlds, 1052
  of all ways, 336
  of dark and bright, all that's, 356
  of friends, a good book the, 478
  of him, these are the, 805
  of luck is always waiting, 679
  of me is diligence, 98
  of me, what's, 984
  of men that e'er wore earth, 115
  of noble work silent part is, 533
  o' noose, git the very, 527
  of now and here, 443
  of our past moments, remember all the, 573
  of possible worlds, 1052
  of this, if there is none he made the, 285
  of thoughts which he hath, 540
  of times the worst of times, 497
  of us, having lost the, 922
  of us, little do or can the, 493
  of wine, king can drink, 504
  old fashions please, 52
  old friends are, 130
  part of valour, discretion the, 131
  past and to come seem, 64

Best portion of a good man's life, 295
  prayeth best who loveth, 315
  profits most who serves, 804
  regulated families, accidents in, 496
  second thoughts are, 179, 465
  state, every man at his, 1104
  stolen sweets are, 194
  that is in one, 1080
  that must be somehow, 594
  the kingdom provides, 799
  the next, 261
  thing one can do when it is raining, 437
  to forget, good to forgive, 492
  to swap horses, not, 457
  to trust that all is, 501
  vindication against slander, 457
  way out is always through, 838
  who does the, 201
  who laughs last, laughs, 812
  who loves his native country, 471
  who serves his country, 219
  will come back to you, 671
  wine is the last, 445
  yield thy poor, 694
  you get is an even break, 868
  yuh ever poured yuh, 927
Best-conditioned and unwearied, 46
Best-humoured man, 184
Best-seller is a gilded tomb, 788
Bestial, what remains is, 101
Bestowed on camps and courts, wealth, 434
Bestowing and so good-night, love's, 607
  honour pudding pence, 406
  most princely in, 74
Bestride the narrow world, 81
Beteem the winds of heaven, 90
Bethlehem, O little town of, 612
  the time they came to, 919
  water of the well of, 1100
Bethumped with words, 57
Betray, Fortune flatters to, 58
  nature never did, 296
  that men, 253
Betrayed and baffled still, 628
Betrothal-ring of song, with a, 910
Betsey and I are out, 678
Betsies Katies and Jennies, 231
Better a bad epitaph, 93
  a little chiding, 35
  be damned, 272
  berry, never made a, 140
  bettered expectation, he hath, 38
  boundless worse, is boundless, 462
  build schoolrooms for the boy, 512
  by their presence, minds made, 520
  day, known a, 306
  day the better deed, 116
  days, friend of my, 363
  days, if ever you have looked on, 49
  days, seen, 357
  days, we have seen, 49, 81

Better elements, to whom the, 405
enemy than friend, weak man a, 518
far to share, 601
fifty years of Europe, 465
foot before, 58
for being a little bad, 37
for worse for, 1128
friend than old dog Tray, a, 567
grace, does it with a, 54
grow wiser and, 172
had they ne'er been born, 310
half, my dear my, 27
hap to worse, from, 30
heresy of doctrine than of heart, 442
his, doth not breathe upon the earth, 71
hopes, the strivings after, 666
horse, grey mare the, 16
I do find myself much, 181
if we better deemed of them, 506
is a dinner of herbs, 1107
is a neighbour that is near, 1108
is a temple made of bark, 896
is half a loaf than no bread, 15
is to bow then breake, 13
it is to dare, 734
it were, for the world, 559
know nothing than half-know, 518
know than all, I, 444
late than never, 14, 188
love given unsought is, 55
made by ill, good are, 289
man than I am Gunga Din, 781
mind their p's and q's, 614
much more the, 37
not to be, were it not, 462
'ole, if you know a, 943
part of human days, 703
part of valour is discretion, 63
reck the rede, may ye, 285
selves, parted from our, 299
so much the, 242
spared a better man, 63
strangers, desire we may be, 50
striving to, 98
than a principality in Utopia, 398
than all the ballads, ye are, 437
than all the heads, good heart, 426
than all to sleep, 817
than false knaves, 40
than he knew, builded, 408
than his dog, something, 464
than his neighbor, 685
than many aver, 750
than nothing, little is, 988
than she should be, no, 1035
than those that are, were, 479
than you dare to think, 440
than you knew, loved you, 596
than you should be, 131
the instruction, 45
the lowly deed were done, 687
the more it made them cry, 253

Better the world with a song, 833
the worse appear the, 149
thou shouldest not vow, 1109
to be able neither to read nor write, 331
to be eaten to death with rust, 64
to be lowly born, 73
to be much abused, 102
to be than not to be, 656
to be vile than vile esteemed, 108
to deal by speech than letter, 111
to dwell in a corner, 1108
to fail in attempting exquisite things, 768
to forget than remember and regret, 404
to give than to take, 13
to have fought and lost, 468
to have loved and lost, 468
to hunt in fields, 175
to know nothing than to know what ain't so, 518
to learn late than never, 46
to live rich, 237
to love amiss, 280, 468
to love in the lowliest cot, 545
to reign in hell, 148
to sink beneath the shock, 355
to travel than to arrive, 704
to want a teacher than desire to learn, 563
to wear out than to rust out, 179
to weep at joy than joy at weeping, 38
world, another and a, 1060
world than this, 48
ye like vice, the more, 797
Betters, mock at your, 913
what is done, what you do, 56
Bettered by the borrower, 162
expectation, 38
Bettering of my mind, 32
Betting is best that way, 270
Betty Haigh, Johnny Sands had married, 941
Zane, the blood of, 521
Between a sleep and a sleep, 634
conflicting vague probabilities, 449
rushes, the one and the other, 425
the cradle and the grave, 223
the cup and lip, many things happen, 124
the election and my hopes, 97
the nightfall and the light, 630
the poles, that wheel, 471
the sundawn and the sun, 630
things ended and things begun, 537
this time and that sweet time, 454
two stooles, 12
Betwixt my lord the king and me, 504
us twain, no passages of love, 470
Bevy of fair women, 155
Beware lest stern heaven hate you, 528, 835
my lord of jealousy, 102

Beware of all enterprises that require new clothes, 514
of desperate steps, 267
of entrance to a quarrel, 90
of had I wist, 11
of hasty connections, 511
of rashness, but with energy, 456
that your Northern laurels do not change, 267
the fury of a patient man, 174
the ides of March, 81
Beweep my outcast state, I all alone, 107
Bewildered lost alone in that dim way, 842
Bewrayed by his manners, 25
Beyond the practice of physicians, 450
the range of sight, I see, 514
the range of sound, I hear, 514
the silent night, 603
Bezonian, under which king, 66
Bias, rules with strongest, 210
Bible by myself, with my, 170
is literature not dogma, 770
knows her true, 263
more and Euclid less, read my, 655
nothin' truer in the, 687
of the race, 525
shows the extent of the English language, 397
studie was but litel on the, 5
tales, tender, 657
text of the, 738
too early familiarity with, 739
Bibles laid open, 136
Bibliomaniac arts, 698
Bibliophiles, Brooklyn has more distinguished, 844
Bickerings to recount, 163
Bid him delay not, 672
me discourse, 106
Bids expectation rise, 252
Bidding, done Thy, 844
thousands speed at his, 162
Bier, murdered Lincoln's, 513
waste sorrows at my, 374
Big Bow-wow strain, 312
for me, I'm just as, 761
manly voice, 50
round tears, 48
with the fate of Rome, 194
with vengeance, 229
Big-endians and small-endians, 191
Bigger than an agate-stone, no, 77
than anything that can happen, 746
than his head, seems no, 99
they come, the, 969
Biggest rascal that walks, 1008
Bigness which you see, 171
Bigotry for objects which please them, 295
Bigwig family, the, 498
Bilbow, the word it was, 222
Bile, sentences that stir my, 747
Bilious, when I am only, 392
Bill, all out of step but, 515
and I was Joe, when you were, 452
as if God wrote the, 409
for a darker ill, larger, 512

Bill, in his little, 444
of divorce, give her a, 1125
patience for his, 225
presented for payment, 381
somebody else pays the, 624
Bills make known she must be dearly let, 135
Billboard lovely as a tree, 934
Billboards fall, unless the, 935
Billion, minus one, 922
Billions, roll in royal, 656
Billows duskier than the gloomy Nile, 647
have rolled, seas where the, 504
never break, where, 187
pilot cannot mitigate the, 1002
swelling and limitless, 317
that never shall break, 609
trusted to thy, 355
wild contend with angry, 480
Bin of wine a spice of wit, 702
sparkling from the, 940
Bind more fast, it doth, 686
safe find safe, 21
up my wounds, 72
up the nation's wounds, to, 457
Binde, fast finde fast, 12
Binds its body in chains, 655
too strictly snaps, vow that, 471
Binding, book in the dingy, 842
nature fast in fate, 216
shoes, Hannah's at the window, 568
steadfast in the broken, 916
Biographer, comes the, 675
first thing done by a, 580
has this problem, 377
Biographical sharpshooter, rifle of some, 638
Biographies, essence of innumerable, 378
geniuses have the shortest, 412
Biography, an heroic poem is a, 377
diminishes in interest, 521
good portrait a kind of, 589
kept posted up for the national breakfast-table, 505
of distinguished individuals, 379
of great men, the history of the world, 380
only, no history, 411
recognized form of sport, 906
should be written by acute enemy, 687
unfair, 906
Biological inequality, 830
Birch most shy and ladylike, 525
tree, that old white, 886
Bird I am, a little, 1051
and rose with rapture, 642
appears a thoughtless thing, 324
aren't we like that wise old, 836
at break of day, 885
butterfly and brook, 595
call, let no, 916
came down the walk, a, 585
can fly, break before the, 471
celestial, 338

Bird each fond endearment tries, 250
first spoke to me, 896
flight of a, 590
hath made his pendent bed, 85
hath perched upon a spray, 735
he starved, he stiffened worm, 576
in the air, better than a, 137
in the hand, 15, 1005, 1037
is on the wing, 1018
let loose, 336
like that stoic, 897
music, time to hear, 930
night with this her solemn, 152
O cuckoo! shall I call thee, 299
of bad moral character, 228
of dawning singeth all night, 89
of the air, 1110
of the solemn strain, 370
of the wilderness, 294
of time has but a little way, 1018
on pinions free joyous, 537
rare, in the land, 1024
rise up at the voice of the, 1110
sang in the apple-tree, 793
sense the, 649
sings the selfsame song, 651
small hot, 699
song of night's sweet, 366
sunward-soaring, 634
sweet-voiced, has flown, 665
that cries La sol me, 912
that fyleth hys own neste, 10, 16
that shun'st the noise, 160
the Attic, 156
thou never wert, 366
to have held the, 793
to others flew, the, 133
to your mountain, flee as a, 1103
waketh and the shadows flee, 480
with the broken pinion, 643
Birds all the year round, 621
and they who wield, 931
and trees and flowers and water-craft, 538
are flying south, 830
are moulting, 691
as choirs of singing, 583
can fly, reason, 751
charm of earliest, 152
confabulate, if, 264
construct your nests, 982
depart the groves decay, 735
eagle suffers little, to sing, 77
feed on sugar and seed, 655
fine feathers make fine, 961
flowers and stones precious things, 741
flying after, holy white, 832
fragmentary conversation going on among, 582
from east to west, of all the, 758
go north again, 763
God's poor, 438
golden troop of, 847
haul in their white-winged, 677

Birds, I see my way as, 484
in cages as with, 1030
in last year's nest, 434, 1042
in their little nests agree, 198
like those of morning, 405
melodious, sing madrigals, 31
morning, were mad with glee, 619
music of the woodland, 625
named without a gun, 409
no, so happy as we, 499
of a feather, 125, 1039
of heaven, 634
of self-same feather, 70
of the air have nests, 1114
other, will sing as gay, 581
out in the meadow, 886
sang, where late the sweet, 108
sing, and no, 385
singing of the, 955
sweet sold in the shops, 816
that eternally flew, 673
that fly with careless ease, 201
that sing and fly, 910
that sing, where will be the, 581
time of the singing of, 1110
too precise or scientific about, 538
whose domestic affairs, 930
will serenade in bush and tree, 646
with chaff, catch old, 1037
without despair to get in, 128
Bird-cage in a garden, 128
Birdie, is it weakness of intellect, 624
Birken'ead drill, be still to the, 782
Birnam wood, 87, 858
Birth, ancient race by, 174
and at his death, at his, 985
and death, lie 'twixt, 822
boasts his, 357
boy of heavenly, 681
came to the place of my, 356
death borders upon our, 121
for honourable, 972
from the moment of, 975
is but a sleep, 301
is death, end of, 597
lucid in that second, 626
months of human, 832
must come to, 843
not broken in from the, 398
nothing but our death begun, 202
of a hundred mediocrities, 1078
of that significant word, 222
or fortune, distinction of, 1061
or one that is coming to, 676
our Saviour's, is celebrated, 89
people own by, 754
rate insolence or inefficiency, 909
rejoice at a, 616
render, to dim enchantments, 447
repeats the story of her, 194
revolts from true, 78
Science frowned not on his, 245
second, 337

Birth, smiled on my, 345
  the secret lords of, 771
  the sunshine is a glorious, 301
  trembling from its, 587
  walked he from his, 777
  was of the wombe, 24
Births, empires' kings' captives', 652
Birth's invidious bar, 468
Birthday blessings, 182
  celebrate the anniversary, of his, 330
Birthless and deathless and changeless, 597
Birthplace, great Homer's, 124
Birthright from of old, 760
Biscay, bay of, 288
Biscuit, dry as the remainder, 49
Bishop and two generals, 1073
  church without a, 393
  Ernulphus, curses of the good, 241
  Hatto hastened away, 320
  hypocrisy of a, 949
Bisier semed than he was, 5
Bisy a man, no-wher so, 5
Bit me, though he had, 99
  of blue amid the grass, 756
  of truth, is a, 939
  with an envious worm, 77
Bits, shattered in myriad, 544
Bitch, son of a mongrel, 98
Bite, bark worse than his, 138
  dogs delight to bark and, 198
  man recovered of the, 254
  of the critical mosquito, 589
  the hand that fed them, 261
Bites, give it the first two, 801
  three, of a cherry, 1026
  shrewdly, the air, 91
Biteth like a serpent, 1108
Biting for anger, eager soul, 147
Bitten by meteorological ambitions, 530
Bitter a thing, how, 630
  across the wild moor, 951
  all we know in love is, 904
  are the tears of a child, 814
  arises something, 352
  as coloquintida, 101
  ballads of the slums, 887
  barren truth, take away the, 533
  bitter is the smart, 343
  bread of banishment, 59
  change, feel the, 150
  cold, 't is, 89
  cross, on the, 60
  dregs of strife, 608
  end, 944
  ere long, 154
  fancy, food of, 51
  for each other, mortals make this earth, 381
  grave or over wise, no one, 790
  hour, it will come the, 596
  is a scornful jest, 230
  it is indeed, 834
  look, some do it with a, 722
  Lord knows it's, 873
  memory, wakes the, 151
  moments given bitter pay, for, 833
  news to hear and bitter tears to shed, 553

Bitter o'er the flowers, some, 352, 981
  past, more welcome is the sweet, 53
  pinch of pain and fear, 780
  tone, oft for our own the, 642
  waters of Marah were, 1098
Bittern booming in the weeds, 399
Bitterns, London an habitation of, 399
Bitterness, knoweth his own, 1107
  of things, from out the, 304
Bivouac of the dead, 541
Bizziness, gang about his, 294
Blabbing and remorseful day, 69
  eastern scout, 157
Black A, 1084
  already with blood, 781
  and midnight hags, 87
  and unknown bards, 816
  as the pit from pole to pole, 692
  beetle, intolerable to a, 361
  brows become some women best, 56
  creeping through the, 857
  customary suits of solemn, 89
  enough to make them frown, 665
  every white will have its, 255
  eyes and lemonade, 334
  flower of civilized society, 421
  for heaven, too, 174
  hung be the heavens with, 68
  I am, but O my soul is white, 281
  in the blue of the sky, 568
  is a pearl in woman's eye, 28
  is not so black, 293
  it stood as night, 150
  lees where lurks, 629
  let the devil wear, 94
  men are pearls, 28
  men of Coromandel, 399
  mountains, among the, 929
  nor yet too light, 451
  or reed, bokes clad in, 5
  or white, whether we played the, 401
  pall of nothing, 914
  spirits and white, 117
  statement of pistons, 938
  to red began to turn, 142
  tragedy lets slip her grim disguise, 620
  white shall not neutralize the, 491
  with tarnished gold, 288
Blackberries, plentiful as, 62
  sit round it and pluck, 431
Blackbird plays but a boxwood flute, 693
  the dearest of all, where is my, 758
  'tis to whistle, 141
Blackest features of the human face, 949
Blackguards both, 360
Black-lettered list, 294
Blackness of a kettle, 1126
  of heart, 657
  there in the sudden, 914
Blacksmith's door, I paused beside, 622

Bladder, blows a man up like a, 62
Bladders, boys that swim on, 73
  of philosophy, swim with, 185
Blade answered, little, 813
  brightest, grows dim with rust, 453
  from the first, 633
  heart-stain away on its, 334
  learn to wield the, 544
  not alone for the, 504
  notches on the, 1093
  of grass a quill, every, 1017
  of grass, best little, 813
  of grass is always a blade of grass, 124
  of grass, when you destroy a, 826
  stands up in a day, 499
  then the ear, first the, 1116
  trenchant, Toledo trusty, 142
Blades, between two, 68
  shall thrust, her million, 937
  to Meg and Molly dear, 604
  two, of grass to grow, 191
Blade-straight, steel-blue and, 704
Blaize, lament for Madam, 252
Blake, shut in cells some, 879
Blame and misrepresentation, by, 997
  dispraise or, 157
  in part to, is she, 128, 221
  neither is most to, 633
  without shame or, 132
Blameless life, white flower of a, 469
  style, test of a, 319
  vestal's lot, 216
Blanch without the owner's crime, 303
Blanche and Sweethearts Tray, 99
Bland as a Jesuit, 692
  childlike and, 644
Blandishments will not fascinate us, 274
Blank, creation's, 246
  eyes know each other not, 685
  misgivings of a creature, 301
  my lord, a, 55
  of Nature's works, 151
  splendor, 666
Blanket and the whitest, 1065
  round you fold, 501
  tied with yellow strings, 279
Blankets, rough male kiss of, 894
Blare of bugles a ruffle of drums, 767
  of the trumpet, 521
  of trumpets, never a, 772
  of trumpets to announce, 1089
Blasphemy in the soldier, 36
Blast, a welding, 686
  a young builder in the budding, 147
  bowed low before the, 547
  chill November's surly, 284
  drives the furious, 194
  from the lungs, 905
  gather on the evening, 568
  he died, of no, 178
  is frantic, though the, 667
  of war blows in our ears, 66
  of wind, but a, 1021

Blast, rushing of the, 372
  shattered in the, 508
  striding the, 85
  that blows, for any, 1021
  that will quickly pass, 1025
  upon his bugle horn, 308
  with contrary, 157
Blasts, many, to shake them, 71
  of wind, hollow, 205
Blasted with excess of light,
  243
Blastments, contagious, 90
Blatant Bassarid of Boston, 635
  mechanical specious electrical
  light, 857
Blaze, ashes inevitably follow,
  551
  burst out into sudden, 159
  laugh out, let the, 484
  of noon, 156
  with your serried columns, 447
Blazed with lights, 81
Blazing galleon the sun, that,
  801
Blazoned roll of heroes, 561
Blazoning pens, quirks of, 101
Bleach of the light of years,
  854
Bleak December, I remember it
  was in, 460
Bled, truest hearts that ever, 386
Bleed, carcasses, at the sight of
  the murderer, 122
  heart for which others, 193
  they have torn me and I,
  353
Bleeding feet, with aching hands
  and, 546
  piece of earth, 82
Blemish of mankind, the one immortal, 1082
Blending of moral courage with
  physical timidity, 651
Bless me this is pleasant, 510
  the day ere the toil, 501
  the hand that gave the blow,
  179
  the hand that gives the, 179
  the man who invented sleep,
  510
  thee Bottom, 43
  thee, hold fast till he, 226
  this house from wicked wight,
  164
  to cheer and, 626
  us please sah, 712
  you with the sunniest weather,
  406
  your haters, love your enemy,
  471
Blessed are the forgetful, 1080
  are the merciful, 25
  are the peacemakers on earth,
  69
  are those that nought expect,
  272
  barrier, 301
  be letters they are the monitors, 551
  candles of the night, 47
  children call her, 1109
  damozel leaned out, 577
  do above, what the, 146
  feet nailed on the bitter cross,
  60
  he alone is, 190

Blessed, he that considereth the
  poor, 1104
  he who expects nothing, 220
  I have been, 355
  is the healthy nature, 377
  it is twice, 46
  Land of Room Enough, 710
  little, with the soft phrase of
  peace, 100
  man, half part of a, 57
  martyr, thou fallest a, 74
  mood, that, 295
  more, to give, 1119
  mutter, 488
  part to heaven, gave his, 74
  plot, this earth, this, 59
  strains are telling, those, 503
  the man who has nothing to
  say, 520
  them unaware, I, 315
  threads of gold, some, 501
  times of old, 507
  to give than to receive, more,
  13
  who ne'er was born, 190
Blessedness, no other, 379
  single, 42
Blesses his stars, 194
  still the generous thought, 441
  us, God does and, 513
Blesseth her with happy hands,
  26
  him that gives, 46
Blessin' we'll need de, 712
Blessing dear, makes a, 163
  health is the second, 140
  I had most need of, 86
  lies, the, 573
  Lord dismiss us with thy, 280
  may come upon thee, that a,
  1124
  more than a common, 323
  national debt a national, 341
  no harm in, 221
  not my doom, my, 710
  of earth is toil, 709
  of tact, 696
  of the house, 953
  of the Old Testament, 109
  on the hearth, 491
  or woe, not a, 638
  out of God's, 16, 1034
  paid thy utmost, 822
  possessing the superior holy,
  972
  steal immortal, from her lips,
  79
  sweet was her, 240
  that money cannot buy, 140
  the Pretender, no harm in, 221
  till it gives its, 441
  which men fly from, death that
  553
Blessings, abundance of, 981
  be upon the head of Cadmus,
  375
  brighten as they take their
  flight, 202
  from whom all, flow, 183
  love disguise, 910
  of dew and shade, 712
  on him that invented sleep,
  1042
  on thee little man, 442
  surrender thee o'er, with, 363
  two of life's greatest, 989

Blessings, wife children and
  friends, 294
  without number, 199
Blest, Araby the, 151
  Hy-Brasail the isle of the, 416
  I have been, 355
  it is twice, 46
  kings may be, 287
  never is, but always to be, 207
  nor it is, 928
  paper-credit, 210
  rest in the land of the, 658
  thought that morning cloud
  was, 375
  where they that love are, 503
  with ease of body and peace of
  mind, 200
  with milk and honey, 518
  with some new joys, 178
Blew cold on my desolate heart,
  418
  great guns, 274
  you hither, what wind, 65
Blight upon the tree, 820
Blind, all the discomforts that
  accompany my being, 183
  always, and often tipsy, 406
  and ignorant in all, 114
  and naked ignorance, 470
  and now I see, once was, 639
  bard, be that, 317
  be to her faults a little, 189
  beggar's daughter, 257
  believe old Homer, 167
  beside, he begged for certain
  and was, 493
  eyes to the, feet to the lame,
  1102
  Fortune though she is, 111
  fury, comes the, 159
  goddess, that, 67
  guides strain at a gnat, 1115
  he that is strucken, 77
  he was, as it is ofte sene, 6
  his soul with clay, 466
  hysterics of the Celt, 469
  in the rain and the cold, 832
  lead the blind, if the, 1115
  love is, 7
  Love must needs be, 317
  man's erring judgment to, 210
  man's stick, 850
  more than, 811
  none so, as will not see, 17,
  188, 192
  speaks in parables to the, 282
  spinner, 591
  suppliant, when the, 373
  'tis we are deaf are dumb are,
  604
  when Milton went, 853
  winged Cupid is painted, 42
Blindly, loved sae, 287
Blindness, bless your, 913
  children of, 736
  is my sight, my, 540
  or I all, 187
  pitied him in his, 880
  sight out of, 663
  we may forgive, 806
Bliss, and gain the coast of, 393
  asks for, 735
  avid of earth's, 736
  bowers of, 205
  brightly glow the hues of, 245
  certainty of waking, 158

Bliss, endure a rival's, 279
  good ale doth bring men to, 20
  he lives in, 285
  health the vital principle of, 225
  how exquisite the, 285
  ignorance is, where, 243
  in possession will not last, 306
  in that dawn to be alive, 300
  it excels all other, 20
  like thine is bought by years, 516
  momentary, 243
  of growth, 953
  of solitude, inward eye the, 299
  perfect, be found, 343
  possession the grave of, 772
  promise of pneumatic, 900
  should have immortall, 24
  source of all my, 251
  sum of earthly, 154
  that earth affords, 20
  the contrary bringeth, 68
  to die for our country, 219
  to press the pillow, 568
  unalloyed, 1073
  virtue makes the, 247
  which centres in the mind, 250
  winged hours of, 327
Blissful and dear, 335
  dreams of long ago, 638
Blister, so much as raised a, 973
Blithe and generous and bold, 686
  as wont, be, 403
  Irish lad, 328
  merry music of harp, 600
  moment, in some, 685
  no lark so, 269
  spirit, hail to thee, 366
Blithesome and cumberless, 294
Block, chip of the old, 145, 261
Blockhead, no man but a, 236
  the bookful, 212
Blonde or brunette, this rhyme applies, 1022
Blondel when his lay, 541
Blood and guile, 316
  and state, glories of our, 141
  and tongue our brothers, 443
  astir, sets the gypsy, 757
  be the price, 778
  beats with his, 466
  brain may devise laws for the, 44
  burns, when the, 91
  calls to heaven for human, 282
  chill, with cold small, 226
  circulation of the, 1068
  clean from my hand, wash this, 86
  cold in clime cold in, 355
  drawn with the lash, 457
  drenched in fraternal, 341
  dried all this, 1071
  endures, so long as the, 778
  enriched our, and ennobled our hearts, 193
  escaped, furious, 903
  falling like red, 931
  fierce as frenzy's fevered, 308
  flesh and, can't bear it, 221
  freeze thy young, 91
  glories of our, 141
  guiltless of his country's, 245

Blood, hand raised to shed his, 207
  hath run in peasant veins, 499
  her pure and eloquent, 118
  hey-day in the, 95
  in him, so much, 88
  in our veins, the, 679
  in torrents pour, 728
  inhabits our frail, 56
  is a rover, 742
  is their argument, when, 67
  is thicker sir than water, 746
  is thicker than water, 310
  is very snow-broth, 35
  is warm within, 44
  moistened with the precious, 681
  my battle-cry, 447
  no sure foundation set on, 58
  of a British man, 99
  of a nation, 1051
  of all the Howards, 208
  of beauty wealth and power, 424
  of Betty Zane, mingles the, 521
  of patriots and tyrants, 273
  of the martyrs, 1012
  of the vine, 668
  of the world, 922
  of tyrants, 1059
  on his sword, 806
  our Saxon, 443
  rebellious liquors in my, 48
  ruddy drop of manly, 410
  sensations sweet felt in the, 295
  shall warm our veins, 1073
  show the father's, 967
  signe to know the gentle, 26
  single drop of my country's, 478
  so cheap, flesh and, 392
  some son of Martha spilled, 781
  spoke in her cheeks, 118
  stepped so far in, 87
  stirs to rouse a lion, 61
  strong as flesh and, 301
  summon up the, 66
  that healest with, 132
  thought to stir the, 954
  to quicken the, 633
  upon the snow, 904
  vengeance desolation, cry aloud for more, 542
  weltering in his, 176
  which stir the, 911
  whoso sheddeth man's, 1097
  with, and with iron, 634
  young, must have its course, 523
Bloods, breed of noble, 81
  richest, on earth, 860
Bloodbeats of song, 633
Blood-fed captains, 857
Bloodless race with feeble voice, 218
  sportsman, 733
  substitute, books a, 704
  triumph, Nature's, 443
Blood-red banner, 343
Bloodshed, fear and, 300
Blood-tinctured heart, 428
Bloody but unbowed, 692
  instructions, we but teach, 85
  Mary, image of, 391
  old sins, 892

Bloody war is made, likes o' that that, 845
  work, then do, 502
Bloom and the passion is past, 792
  comes over the earth, 392
  drives full on thy, 285
  I find some misty purple, 845
  is hung with, 742
  is shed, seize the flower its, 287
  lips he has pressed in their, 450
  of apples, 445
  of young desire, 243
  of youth, in the, 979
  rooting to wondrous, 848
  sight of vernal, 151
  that kill the, 303
  the fire-escapes, 929
  will, another year, 385
Blooms, crimson flower of battle, 522
  next year's, 569
  with statues, the world, 613
Bloomed and died, the lilacs, 437
  lilacs last in the door-yard, 536
  up into love again, 654
Blooming alone, left, 335
  fresh and gay, lovely, 276
  lyre, when 'Omer 'is, 784
Bloomsbury and the British Museum, 932
Blossom then bear fruit, let it, 1007
  and June and rapture pass away, 836
  as the rose, 1111
  bright with autumn dew, 372
  in, last spring, 621
  in the dust, 141
  love's perfect, 556
  of health, from the, 362
  that hangs on the bough, 33
  the, time, 655
  to-morrow, 73
Blossoms, a myriad lovely, 697
  all around me sighing, 375
  borders of the beautiful, 432
  have the mightiest power, 516
  of my sin, cut off in the, 91
  stay, if last year's, 569
  to-morrow, 73
  wet with weeping, 570
Blossom-bald, then, 681
Blossom-burdened bough, 777
Blossomed a few short hours, 446
  the lovely stars, 435
Blossoming, a million buds but stay their, 668
  apple-tree, under a, 699
Blot, art to, 214
  creation's, 246
  in thy scutcheon, 1041
  known what they discreetly, 146
  not one line he could wish to, 239
  on his name, no, 327
  where is the, 493
Blotted it out forever, 242
  paper, that ever, 46
Blow a shepherd's reed, just to, 406
  adore the hand that gives the, 190
  and swallow at the same moment, 978

Blow, bless the hand that gave the, 179
bold I can meet his, 293
buds forgot to, 642
bugle blow, 466
death loves a signal, 202
forbear the bitter, 904
full many a thoughtless, 718
give for blow in the foray, 800
hand that gives the, 190
himself, puff and, 635
in the teeth of a wrong, 833
kindness tempered every, 626
liberty is in every, 286
might be the be-all, 85
on the head, 1015
on whom I please, 49
perhaps may turn his, 293
rain-drop makes some floweret, 504
remember thy swashing, 77
the horrid deed in every eye, 85
the trumpet to arms, 271
thou winter wind, 50
to strike the, 873
what wood a cudgel's of by the, 142
wind! come wrack, 88
winds and crack your cheeks, 98
with a silver, 855
word and a, 79, 179
Blows and buffets of the world, 86
and knocks, apostolic, 142
deal out murderous, 870
guarding his heart from, 905
man up like a bladder, 62
of circumstance, 468
of sound, to heal the, 451
skeptic, 622
Bloweth where it listeth, 1118
Blown through the Conchimarian horns, 432
with restless violence, 36
Blud my able-bodied relations has, shed every drop of, 606
Bludgeonings of chance, 692
Bludso's ghost went up alone, 605
Blue above and blue below, 350
all the time a-feelin', 730
Alsatian mountains, by the, 582
and gold, clad in, 288
and purple hollows, 710
and their hands are, 498
are my hands, 1080
bide by the buff and, 286
bonnets over the border, 588
colour appointed by the Deity, 532
comes to earth, 701
coming into the, 385
dark indigo, 845
darkly deeply beautifully, 322
doubted truth in, 939
een, saw ye the lass wi' the, 388
ethereal sky, 194
eyes blue, kept their, 903
eyes of unholy, 335
faded coat of, 579
for hopes and red for fears, 664
gentle cousin, 385
get those eyes so, 559

Blue heavens above us bent, 462
heaven's height, 701
heaven's own, 372
in eyes as awful as in stockings, 430
in here and there a bird, 839
is but a mist, 838
is the quaker-maid, 806
jays chatter tcha tcha, 912
Juniata, waters of the, 406
meagre hag, 158
my prospects all look, 622
of day, beneath the, 743
of halcyon seas, 760
Presbyterian true, 142
ran the flash across, 493
roses red and violets, 24
rushing of the Rhône, 353
sky bends over all, 315
something borrowed something, 956
speedwell's darling, 469
stars in the green firmament, 433
summer skies are darkly, 418
the fresh the ever free sea, 350
trip slip for an eight cent fare, 583
under the laurel the, 571
were her eyes, 433
Bluebell is the sweetest flower, 516
Blue-bird carries the sky on his back, 515
Blue-birds, ghosts of the, 621
Blue-eyed laughing baby, 650
my, 590
Blue-fringed lids, 316
Blueness abundant, 493
Blue-print devices, are only the, 939
Bluest of things grey, 632
Blue-stocking, sagacious, 399
Bluid is thicker than water, 310
Blunder free us, frae monie a, 285
life is a, 692
notes and names each, 493
worse than a crime, 1060
you find in men this, 275
youth is a, 420
Blunders about a meaning, 213
are often made, 1068
better even of their, 1080
wise, make our, 858
Blunderbuss against religion, 233
Blundering kind of melody, 174
Blunting the fine point of seldom pleasure, 107
Blush, beautiful as woman's, 404
of maiden shame, 372
shame! where is thy, 95
that flies at seventeen, 776
to find it fame, do good and, 214
to give it in, 327
unseen, born to, 245
upon thy breast, that so the, 586
Blushes at the name, 555
bear away those, 39
man that, not quite a brute, 202
Blushed as he gave in the oath, 242
before, we never, 168
the conscious water, 165

Blushed, young men that, 1003
Blushful Hippocrene, 383
Blushing apparitions, 39
honours, bears his, 73
is the colour of virtue, 188, 1015
like the morn, 154
Blustering band, they march a, 177
railer, 247
Blythe blink he had, 345
Boar, saw a crystal, 938
Board, crown the, 941
cursed him at, 351
her father kept a social, 501
we go, still fasting from thy, 649
Boards nailed together, a few crooked, 147
ships are but, 44
still hold the, 648
Boast, almost like a vulgar, 806
can imagination, 224
he lives to build not, 223
independence be our, 294
is poor, the, 504
no more your mighty deeds, 141
not of what thou wouldst have done, 157
not thyself of to-morrow, 1108
of heraldry, 244
our fondest, 386
such is the patriot's, 249
Boasts inhabitants like me, town that, 437
Boasted line, your, 510
Boastful neighs, high and, 67
Boat, adrift, a little, 585
float as easy as a wooden, 940
float in a well-trimmed, 718
going towards my, 187
he's gwine to build a, 712
hundred builds o', 764
in a beautiful pea-green, 498
in an open, 873
in better trim, 348
is on the shore, 356
mysterious happy twilight, 692
oar in every man's, 1040
of life be light, let your, 745
oh here is a, 371
swiftly glides the bonnie, 288
to the place where he sits a, 766
went down, broke the oar and the, 572
will no one guide a little, 585
wrecked on rocky shore, 363
Boats, light, sail swift, 75
messing about in, 742
not steer'd, fortune brings in some, 106
should keep near shore, 227
Boatman, take thrice thy fee, 1063
takes no bribe, 983
Bob, death of old, 731
Bobbed for whale, 146
Bobby, is the London, 815
Bob-o'-link, bob-o'-link, 373
Bobolink for a chorister, 584
Bobtail nag, bet my money on de, 568
tike, 99

Bobtails fu' de rabbits, 820
Bocara's vaunted gold, 275
Boccaccio, with my friend, 843
Bodes me no good, 206
  some strange eruption, 89
Bodies are our gardens, our, 101
  diseases attenuate our, 123
  ghosts of defunct, 142
  high, pile the, 854
  into life, brought dead, 415
  one soul in two, 1015
  princes like to heavenly, 110
  soldiers bore dead, by, 61
  souls and consciences, danger
    to, 1045
  two, with one soul, 219
Bodiless creation, 95
Bodily exercise when compulsory,
  974
  fatigue no such bad succeda-
    neum, 402
Boding tremblers, 251
Bodkin, with a bare, 93
Body, absent in, 1120
  all together in a, 1126
  and soul, damned of, 784
  and spirit are twins, 634
  as well as the, 975
  before the spirit, puts the, 794
  beneficial for the, 1087
  blameless mind and faultless,
    220
  brevity and wit its soul, 316
  by the wall, find thy, 547
  Charlotte having seen his, 481
  cleanness of, 112
  clog of his, 147
  covered thick with hair, 890
  demd damp moist, 494
  distressed in mind, or estate,
    1127
  does no harm to the, 974
  doing necessary work for the,
    961
  drew after it his whole, 948
  enough to cover his mind, not,
    313
  eye is the light of the, 1114
  filled and vacant mind, 67
  five times sensitive, 897
  form doth take, of the soul, 26
  grimly stamped, 845
  in Sussex grass, bury my, 929
  is a watch, 1061
  is my house, this, 805
  is under hatches, 274
  lie lightly upon my burned,
    130
  lies a-mouldering in the grave,
    John Brown's, 612
  little, with a mighty heart, 66
  lodged a mighty mind whose,
    218
  mind, or estate, 1127
  nature is, whose, 207
  nought cared this, 317
  of poetic genius, 318
  of poetry, its, 826
  of the mind, 869
  of the time, very age and, 94
  one of a lean, 147
  pent, here in the, 306
  poison to his mind and peril
    to his, 401
  presence of, 324
  rich, mind that makes, 52

Body, sickness-broken, 147
  so young with so old a head,
    46
  that lived, when the, 783
  the soul was never put into the,
    128
  thought, almost say her, 118
  to be buried obscurely, be-
    queath my, 113
  to that pleasant country's
    earth, his, 60
  took root in my horse's, 1056
  trouble of washing my dead,
    970
  we must part, my, 653
  what this tumultuous, 894
  which my dungeon is, 703
  will go to pieces, 961
  will possibly be old, in, 981
Body's artisans sustain their toil,
  823
  comrade and its guest, 1009
  guest, go soul the, 21
  hunger, because of the, 880
  joy, how the, 869
  power, it's hardly in a, 284
  use, for more than the, 869
  vest aside, casting the, 169
Bog, to an admiring, 584
  Serbonian, 150
Bogs dens and shades of death,
  150
  granddad in the Flemish, 956
  no purple in the, 721
  unapproachable, 996
Bogey, school-room, 756
Bohea, helps to sugar her, 430
Bohemia, rather live in, 676
  where's, 57
Boil at different degrees, we, 414
  her down until she simmers,
    689
  like a pot, maketh the deep,
    1103
  on his ear, 697
Boilers, human beings are like,
  661
Boisterous captain of the sea, 248
Boke and my devocion, farewel
  my, 4
Bokes clad in blak or reed, 5
Boket in a welle, as, 6
Bold, a life that shall be, 537
  and a captain, 622
  and fearless, my eye was, 973
  as a lion, 1108
  bad man, 24, 72
  be bold be not too, 438
  be not too, 25
  Ben Battle was a soldier, 392
  bright rover bad and free, 837
  everywhere be, 25
  I can meet his blow, 293
  John Barleycorn, 287
  man that first eat an oyster,
    192
  relief, stand with, 332
  things in a quiet way, 521
  Turpin vunce on Hounslow
    Heath, 494
  virtue is, 37
  what makes robbers, 70
  who durst be so, 147
  with our songs, 858
Boldest held his breath, 328
  painters cannot trace, 199

Boldness, again boldness, 1059
  is a mask for fear, 994
Bolingbroke was a scoundrel, 233
Bolt of Cupid fell, where the,
  42
  a fooles, is soone shot, 16
Bomb, dash the, 737
  path to the, 641
Bombastes, must meet, 319
Bombastic and truculent appearance, 709
Bond, death breaks every, 1051
  living, with the other world,
    1074
  nominated in the, 47
  of brotherhood, a mystic, 378
  of fate, take a, 87
  of one immortal look, 489
  scatter and unloose it from
    their, 106
  there's never a, 578
  tied by a chance, 514
  't is not in the, 47
  trust man on his oath or, 80
  word good as his, 1041
Bonds, flee new, 853
  form very sweet, 1088
  in your possession, 235
  of ignorance, 473
  of love, in, 120
  that gall, bear the, 631
  that unite, 1087
  were brittle, 631
Bondage led, when Israel was
  from, 168
  out of the land of, 310
  to reproduction marks lower
    animals, 740
Bondman, if any be a, 21
Bondman's key, in a, 45
  two-hundred and fifty years,
    457
Bondsman's chain, links in the,
  686
Bone and Skin, two millers, 221
  as curs mouth a, 262
  bites him to the, 229
  bred in the, 17, 977
  if he flings it a, 592
  of manhood, 259
  of my bones, 1097
  of thy bone, 1033
  rain-washed, 781
  wasted to skin and, 1033
Bones ache with the day's work,
  413
  are coral made, of his, 32
  cursed be he that moves my,
    109
  England keep my, 58
  for bacon, broken, 1042
  from these mother's, 923
  full of dead men's, 1116
  good oft interred with their,
    83
  his honour'd, 161
  I wouldst thou had'st my, 79
  jest breaks no, 237
  leave their valiant, 67
  made no more, 1033
  misery worn him to the, 80
  mutine in a matron's, 95
  of coral, 938
  paste and cover to our, 59
  rattle his, over the stones, 395
  salted it down with our, 782

Bones, sit in my, 313
  sulks in the, 910
  tell all my, I may, 1103
  to lay his weary, among ye, 74
  weave thread with, 54
  whose dice were human, 357
Bonfire, everlasting, 86
  how great a, 912
Bong-tree grows, land where the, 498
Bon mots, not enough, 921
Bons mots, in travail to produce, 1046
Bonnet, foolish little, 653
  I lo'e your very, 770
  is trimming, while the, 625
  under her chin, tying her, 600
Bonnets, blue went over the border, 588
Bonnie bonnie banks of Loch Lomond, 952
  saw ye the lass wi' the, 388
Bonny, brave and, 956
  buds, of all the, 612
  Doon, banks and braes o', 287
  here at home, it's, 836
Bononcini, compared to, 221
Boob may die, one, 853
Booby, mother who'd give her, 206
Boojer is always a Boer, 782
Book, a bad, 921
  about, do not throw this, 809
  adversary had written a, 1102
  all he read of any, 275
  all the world knows me in my, 1030
  and creed, lives alone by, 657
  and heart must never part, 947
  and volume of my brain, 92
  another, was opened, 1123
  barrows in Charing Cross Road, 892
  becomingly, who praises a, 415
  bequest of wings was but a, 584
  but its ghost returneth, 673
  cannot contain actual full-size person, 913
  Carlyle's long-labored, 879
  collect one, 238
  collecting most exhilarating sport, 844
  constitute a, 995
  containing such vile matter, 79
  could set forth, what a, 1072
  dainties bred in a, 41
  does not say in a whole, 1081
  doth share the glory, 77
  entred it into his, 171
  face is as a, 84
  go forth my, 893
  go little, 4, 702
  good kill a man as kill a good, 162
  half a library to make one, 236
  has its fortunes, 646
  he made them a, 499
  he that publishes a, 1039
  his teaching, beyond the, 764
  honestly come by, 530
  I read in an old, 766
  I'll drown my, 33
  in breeches, Macaulay is a, 313

Book in gold clasps, 77
  in sour misfortune's, 80
  in the dingy binding, 842
  is a book, 351
  is closed and prayers are said, 691
  is good which puts me in a working mood, 410
  is like a hat or coat, 571
  is lucky or unlucky, 646
  is not a continent, 913
  is the best of friends, a good, 478
  is the precious life-blood, a, 163
  it's like a, 777
  it was, an excellent, 935
  let my temptation be a, 698
  life is a torn, 594
  lift this little, 916
  like the same, 886
  look not at his picture but his, 119
  loved by those too simple, 398
  make a great, 313
  man better than a, 753
  man knows style of, 826
  many editions of a, 238
  Mohammed's truth in a holy, 458
  most wondrous, bright candle, 393
  no, but has something good, 1009, 1039
  no frigate like a, 585
  no get him a' in a, 886
  no moral or immoral, 723
  nook dedicated to a, 756
  not read, ever new, 330
  note it in a, 1111
  now become your, 756
  O for a, 654
  of Common Prayer, I shall want my, 557
  of fate, heaven hides the, 207
  of female logic, 482
  of gold, writing in a, 346
  of human life, time has torn leaves from the, 439
  of knowledge fair, 151
  of life, the, 955
  of life, which is the, 1123
  of memory, 68
  of nature short of leaves, 391
  of secrecy, nature's infinite, 104
  of songs and sonnets, 34
  of toil is read, 446
  of verses, a, 1018
  on the trail of the, 709
  only read perhaps by me, 297
  or friend, with a religious, 114
  originated in publisher's suggestion, 826
  part of him found in a, 426
  poor copy of a, 773
  published, after my first, 752
  question of the best, 753
  read from a sense of duty, 234, 629
  reads but one, 139
  reading a borrowed, 228
  right good from a, 430
  security in an old, 530
  so fairly bound, 79

Book such as all English people might peruse, 292
  that is not a year old, never read, 414
  that's borrowed is lost, 816
  that's not too new, 845
  the better, liked the, 253
  then shut the, 556
  this is no, camerado, 538
  thou art the, 134
  to meet an antique, 584
  unread a flower unblown, 568
  what everyone says in a whole, 1081
  what is even a wise, 905
  what to put first in a, 1047
  when a nobleman writes a, 237
  which can maintain its value, 825
  who reads an American, 314
  words printed in a, 1102
  worth reading is worth buying, 532
  you hold, the little, 703
Booke, for a jollie goode, 655
Books a bloodless substitute for life, 704
  a university, 381
  about scenery, 542
  agreement about, 865
  all the historical, 1078
  and my food and summer rain, 703
  are a part of man's prerogative, 128
  are a substantial world, 301
  are best, old, 734
  are friends, 711
  are gates, 711
  are keys, 711
  are legacies, 196
  are not companions, worthy, 506
  are paths, 711
  are ranged, antique, 899
  are solitudes, 506
  as schoolboys from their, 78
  assume the care of, 203
  authority from others', 40
  away from art away from, 537
  backs and covers of, 494
  bargains in, 674
  bear him up a while, 185
  best, haven't been written, 872
  by which the printers lost, 147
  cannot always please, 280
  can not learn men from, 420
  comments on, 1031
  cover country in, 673
  creep into the hearts of, 717
  dear human, 798
  deep versed in, 156
  demand for, 500
  do with friends as with, 411
  doth hoard rich, 760
  draw more out of, 1082
  dreams, are each a world, 301
  English in children's, 766
  fate of borrowed, 673
  few friends and many, 168
  finest music from, 691
  for a house full of, 673
  for the general reader, 1080
  forefathers had no other, 69
  friends to borrow my, 807

Books from my room, 374
  from which lectures are taken, 235
  gentleman is not in your, 38
  Gospell, 26
  have grown fewer, her, 804
  have stamped their, 1087
  he comes not in my, 131
  he loves, show me the, 579
  here stand my, 673
  I read and the life I lead, 907
  ill-smelling, 1080
  in a bookcase, 1027
  in her mind the wisest, 168
  in the Charing Cross Road, to hunt, 803
  in the running brooks, 48
  in torrents run, 1050
  inside, no, 715
  invented, 375
  knowing I loved my, 32
  lard their lean, 121
  like proverbs, 172
  like that, no more, 794
  magazines and newspapers in United States, 476
  men do not understand, 886
  men that will make you, 1039
  might spoil its looks, 715
  mortality of, 629
  must be read deliberately, 514
  must follow sciences, 111
  next o'er his, 215
  no other, but the score and tally, 69
  not in your, 38
  nothing so old as his, 691
  obedient to my hand, 759
  of honour razed from the, 107
  of making many, 1110
  of nature, 1033
  of the Old and New Testament, 1095
  old manners old, 253
  old wine old Nankin blue, old, 650
  on the soul, I have written three, 488
  only shut his, 763
  peace of great, 854
  philosophers will put their names to their, 123
  readers and hearers like my, 29
  reading new, 525
  reading valueless, 532
  some are lies, 284
  some, to be tasted, 111
  speaks about his own, 419
  spectacles of, to read nature, 179
  sure companionship of, 673
  sweet serenity of, 438
  tenets turn with, 209
  that never can be mine, 673
  that nourish all the world, 41
  that people give us, 813
  that people talk about, 812
  that were soon forgotten, 788
  the children of the brain, 191
  there is no end, of making, 759, 868
  these trees shall be my, 50
  they read, their, 394
  they will not buy, borrow, 813
  think for me, 324

Books to hold in the hand, 238
  toil o'er, 206
  unread, worthiest, 441
  up and quit your, 295
  upon his head, so many, 290
  we may live without, 592
  we think we ought to read, 812
  we would like to read, 812
  were read, 811
  were woman's looks, my only, 336
  when we are collecting, 892
  which are no books, 324
  which are your very own, 737
  which cannot be reviewed, 641
  wiser grow without, 266
  with homing pigeons, cross my, 813
  world of men not the world of, 625
  you need, Homer all the, 185
Book's profound, 429
Bookbuyer pays for what he must have, 500
Bookcase, I have a, 715
  too many books in a, 1027
Book-club guarded from your modern trick, 429
Bookful blockhead, 212
Bookish theoric, 100
Booklovers have spent, many, 899
Book-making machinery, with proper, 337
Bookmen, you two are, 41
Bookseller who seizes copies, 233
Bookseller's his copy from the, 255
Booksellers' catalogues, 729
Bookshop has a thousand books, 866
Bookstore, nature weak in a, 500
Bookworm, agile, 865
Boomerang to you, it's a, 684
Boomlay boomlay boom, 857
Booms adown the glooms, 696
Boon I beg of fate, 812
Boone the pioneer, 552
Boon's for me, that, 493
Boot, appliances and means to, 65
  heels, bleating to your, 786
  saddle to horse and away, 485
Boots and shoes my greatest trouble, 520
  boots movin' up and down, 782
  displace, dares this pair of, 319
  dying in my, 833
  gentleman looks at his, 721
  hauled on his, and roared, 508
  I died in my, 927
  it at one gate, what, 156
  not to resist both wind and tide, 70
  ran out at the heels of their, 246
  they wear long, 855
Booted and spurred, 169
Bo-peep, played at, 134
Booth died blind, 856
  the other one was, 792
Booze, Georgia booze is mighty fine, 927
Border, let that ay be your, 285
  lies in silent shade, 568

Border nor breed nor birth, 779
  of a wood, 662
Borders of the beautiful blossoms, 432
Borderline, boast such, 954
  miles of, 954
Bore: a person who talks, 662
  but as a, 360
  cleanliness a, 570
  every hero becomes a, at last, 412
  his part, 626
  more contemptible than the, 615
  my point, thus I, 62
  the world, him who, 303
  to the man with a flute, 685
  waking up, 787
  without abuse, 469
Bores and bored, the, 361
  because they were, 525
  through his castle wall, 60
Boreas, blustering railer, 247
Boredom, against, the gods struggle in vain, 1059
  did indeed cease, 1082
  is prolific in church, 213
  pain and, 1064
Born across the sea, Christ was, 522
  and taught, happy is he, 114
  below par, 800
  better ne'er been, 310
  better to be lowly, 73
  blessed who ne'er was, 190
  cry for being, 113
  dat's the charge, I was, 902
  days, in my, 1034
  dreamer, out of my due time, 608
  follow the king else wherefore, 470
  for success, 409
  for the universe, 252
  genius must be, 175
  great, some are, 55
  house where I was, 390
  how happy is he, 114
  in a bower, 388
  in a cellar, 246
  in Arcadia, I too was, 1043
  in bed in bed we die, 1043
  in silent darkness, 30
  in sin, Adam's sons, 124
  knew that before you were, 992
  or taught, happy is he, 114
  poet's made as well as, 119
  that ever I was, 92
  they can't be, 497
  to blush unseen, 245
  to die that were not, 363
  to do, the thing that I was, 30
  to inquire after truth, 1030
  to set it right, 92
  to the manner, 91
  under a rhyming planet, 40
  when I was, 1124
  with the gift of laughter, 840
  would thou hadst ne'er been, 103
Borne, all things can be, 596
  and yet must bear, 367
  before her on a shutter, 481
  his faculties so meek, 85

Borne like thy bubbles, onward, 355
  with him and nourished and clothed him, 228
Borough clock, on time with the, 939
Borrioboola Gha, land of, 475
Borrow its mirth, 718
  live within our means, even if we, 606
  the name of the world, to, 110
  to beg or to, 185
Borrowed plumes, 961
  things, disguising, 1030
  wit, wings of, 133
Borrower, bettered by the, 162
  is servant to the lender, 1108
  nor a lender be, 91
  of the night, 86
Borrowers are ill-spenders, 532
  of books, 323
  we are all wholesale, 480
Borrower-and-not-returner, curses on the, 241
Borrowing and debt, 1076
  dulls the edge, 91
  such kind of, 162
  who goeth a, goeth a sorrowing, 19, 227
Bos'n brained with a marlinspike, 710
Bos'n's pike, fixed by the, 710
Bo'sun tight and a midshipmite, 622
Bosom bears, snow which thy frozen, 127
  captive, 396
  cleanse the stuffed, 88
  heaves and spreads, her, 303
  love in my, 27
  man take fire in his, 1106
  of God, her seat is the, 22
  of his Father and his God, 245
  of Jesus, 817
  of the sea, 69, 121
  of the urgent west, 668
  on thy fair, silver lake, 386
  sleep in Abraham's, 72
  slow growth in an aged, 230
  sweep earth's resonant, 503
  swell, with thy fraught, 103
  the throbbing, 942
  third in your, 78
  thorns that in her, lodge, 92
  warm another's, 1021
  warm cheek and rising, 243
  who charge within the, 584
  wife of thy, 1099
  with a glory in His, 522
  with his hand on his, 256
  wring his, is to die, 254
Bosoms, come home to men's, 109
  of your actresses, 233
Bosom's lord sits lightly, 80
Bosomed deep in vines, 215
  high in tufted trees, 160
Bosom-friend of the maturing sun, 384
Bosom-weight, your stubborn gift, 304
Boston and Concord, there is, 341
  cursed with an army of cranks, 714
  J. Winthrop Wiggins, 686
  knew the most, 410

Boston, New York and Philadelphia, they ask in, 617
  runs to brains, 714
  State-House the hub, 454
  this is good old, 752
Bostonian who leaves Boston, 629
Bostonitis, chronic irritability, 636
Botanize upon his mother's grave, 297
Botany, Latin names all their, 409
Both and either, 1002
  more and less than just, Heaven, 565
  o' dem, no can marry, 813
  of them are thine, 71
  sides, much may be said on, 196, 229
  thanks and use, 35
  true both wise and both delightful, 168
Bothe riche and nigard is, 3
Bother it, 622
Bottle, a large cold, 699
  bauble peppermint nurse, 802
  little for the, 274
  of Burgundy, treat a wretch with a, 188
  of rum, yo-ho-ho and a, 704, 710
  of salvation, 22
  on the chimley-piece, 495
Bottles, a beetle balanced, 691
  narrow-necked, 217
  new wine into old, 1116
Bottom, my affection hath an unknown, 51
  my ventures are not in one, 43
  of the cup, 629
  of the deep, dive into the, 61
  of the economic pyramid, 876
  of the worst, 75
  reasons for remaining at the, 775
  search not his, 167
  see not the, 75
  thou art translated, 43
  tub upon its, 171
Bottoms of my trousers rolled, 900
Bottomless gulf, 338
  ponds will be thought to be, 515
Bough, Apollo's laurel, 32
  blossom that hangs on the, 33
  blossom-burdened, 777
  old forsaken, 450
  reddening on the, 960
  sang upon the, 621
  touch not a single, 328, 404
  underneath the, 1018
Boughs are daily rifled, 391
  bearing, 60
  does glide, soul into the, 169
  hide God, 719
  of love and hate, 790
  of the may, 673
  the shuddering, 668
  under the shade of melancholy, 49
  what soft incense hangs upon, 383
  which shake against the cold, 107

Bought in the market, knowledge is, 519
  now cheaply, 288
Bouillabaisse a noble dish, 481
Boulder's shade, long in the, 806
Bound by strong roots, 619
  heaven not reached at a single, 521
  in shallows and miseries, 83
  in those icy chains, 127
  in to saucy doubts, 87
  short and narrow, 450
Bounds be set, wider shall thy, 761
  breakers of ordered, 757
  dances in his crystal, 158
  increase, her shining, 747
  keep within, 1038
  of earth and sky, in the, 545
  of freakish youth, 265
  of freedom wider yet, 462
  of law and duty, 320
  of modesty, 80
  of place and time, 243
  of possibility, within the, 1037
Boundaries, morality knows nothing of, 581
  which divide life from death, 461
Boundary between God's patience and His wrath, 395
Bounding bug dance a jig, 691
  within limits of its race, 553
Boundless and bare, colossal wreck, 367
  better, boundless worse, is, 462
  contiguity of shade, 264
  deep, drew from out the, 472
  his wealth, 307
  in faith, 479
  ineffable prairie, 590
  seas, 'twixt two, 337
  sky, 372
  universe is life, 618
  universe, that in a, 462
Bounteous fare, had such, 737
  field of wheat, 362
Bounties all may share, 447
  and supreme, shadowy, 673
  of an hour, 201
Bountiful colored my morning rose, 586
Bounty fed, those his former, 176
  he may show to the few, 185
  heaven's, 403
  large was his, 245
  no winter in his, 105
  of earth, fed by the, 417
  receives part of its value, 234
Bouquets while I'm living, 855
Bourgeois artist, the, 871
  tradition of the Victorian, 925
Bourgeoisie, definition of, 1072
  face to face with the, 1072
  in the god-damn, 883
Bourn no traveller returns, 93
Bout, many a winding, 160
Bow before thine altar love, 248
  better to, than break, 13
  cannot always stand bent, 1038
  had flown off, 855
  I hear him draw his, 638
  in the cloud, do set my, 1097
  many strings to your, 15

Bow, moon like to a silver, 42
never to the, 570
none that hath bent his, 958
of burning gold, 282
or cursory salutation, 234
the cord is, as unto the, 436
themselves when he did sing, mountain-tops, 73
thy head in gentle spite, 555
to that whose course is run, 242
too tensely strung, 988
two strings to his, 15
unbend the, 1061
was made in England, 738
you're bucketing, 862
Bowe he bar and arwes brighte and kene, 6
Bows, you are the, 879
Bowed, at her feet he, 1099
by the weight of centuries, 708
Bowels, diseases of the, 969
have molten, 826
of compassion, 1123
of the earth, 121
of the harmless earth, 61
of the land, 72
Bower, born in a, 388
by Bendemeer's stream, 337
flower in heaven's high, 281
led her to the nuptial, 154
of roses, 337
orange flower perfumes the, 310
over me, formed a, 1056
Bowers are bare of bay, 743
of bliss, 205
summer stands, pale in her, 565
Bowery hollows crowned with summer, 463
Bowl brimming over, 599
capacious salad, 703
eternal Sáki from that, 1018
fill high the, 359
golden, be broken, 1110
mingles with my friendly, 213
of brass, a bright, 934
of summer-time, 982
onion atoms lurk within the, 313
put it in a crystal, 846
so free, whither in your, 347
they call the sky, 1019
Bowstring is to the shaft, what the, 888
Bow-wow strain, the big, 312
Bow-wows, gone to the demni-tion, 494
Box, breathes from yonder, 212
brought a light and smallish, 700
twelve good men into a, 331
want with a, 823
where sweets compacted lie, 135
Boxes, alabaster, 577
beggarly account of empty, 80
Boy a dog, give a, 873
and be a farmer's, 950
and youth, 'twixt, 307
barefoot, with cheek of tan, 442
better build schoolrooms for the, 512
called Wolf Wolf, 962
Chatterton the marvelous, 297

Boy fell dead, smiling the, 487
get money, 118
have not a woman's gift, 52
I wouldn't give much for the, 699
in love with the janitor's, 938
just ceased to be a, 1072
lad of mettle a good, 61
little, that died, 580
love is a, by poets styled, 142
no could wait, my leetla, 813
oh would I were a, again, 454
of heavenly birth, 681
— oh, where was he, 370
parlous, 71
playing on the sea-shore, 184
steals from his morning play, 699
stood on the burning deck, 370
than when I was a, 390
that shoots so trim, 255
that was half-past three, 715
the noblest work of God, 571
there a-whistling, unless there's a, 619
when I was a, 809
when I was a beggarly, 528
whose voice shall rise, 896
with a spelling-book, 714
with the heart of a king, 1100
you hear that, laughing, 452
Boys are laid, lightfoot, 743
begin, way that, 481
beware of it prepare for it, 531
bright, mention, when, 907
claret the liquor for, 237
come home, till the, 824
fear, with bugs, 52
flying kites, 677
go wooing in my, 257
got any, the marshal said, 510
grown tall, men are, 953
handsome were the, 936
keep kicking my dawg, 956
learn to spell by reiteration, 430
like little wanton, 73
made of snips and snails, 322
that met him out'n Denver, 698
three merry, are we, 127
throughout eternity, 819
throw stones at frogs, 1006
to learn, what is necessary for, 1014
would gather there, young, 501
Boy's will is the wind's will, 436
Boyhood past in Spain, 629
visions of, 621
Boyhood's years, tears of, 336
Boy-scouts practising again, 896
Bozzy, come to me, my dear, 237
Brach or lym, 99
Bradford, governor of Plymouth, 541
Braes, among thy green, 286
we twa hae run about the, 286
Brag of came and saw and over-came, 105
one went to, 165
Brags, made his, 349
Braggart with my tongue, 88
Brahmin caste, comes of the, 453
sings, hymn the, 410
Braid, blowing the ringlet from the, 465

Braids of lilies, twisted, 158
Brain and heart alike depart, 578
as ear-wax, not so much, 75
book and volume of my, 92
books the children of the, 191
burn from my, 827
children of an idle, 77
coinage of your, 95
dry as the remainder biscuit, 49
feed my, 827
first it warms the, 814
folded in my, 789
has corridors, 585
haunts and obsesses my, 1065
heat-oppressed, 85
him with his lady's fan, 61
in his daft old, 816
inherit your father's cracked, 818
is in a muddle, 792
like madness in the, 315
may devise laws, 44
memory warder of the, 85
mint of phrases in his, 40
more brawn than, 982
of a walk-ecstatic dog, 858
of feathers, 215
paper bullets of the, 39
school-masters puzzle their, 253
shallow draughts intoxicate the, 210
should possess a poet's, 30
tires the, 735
too finely wrought, 262
vex the, with researches, 280
would swim, poor little, 648
written troubles of the, 88
Brains better for living on their own fat, 530
could not move, 290
cudgel thy, no more about it, 96
enough to make a fool of him-self, 704
exudations of a man's, 241
new eras in their, 732
of men, care draws in the, 82
quicker than their, 873
steal away their, 101
unhappy, for drinking, 101
when the, were out, 87
Brain's old ghostly house, within the, 914
Brakemen walk along the roof-tops, 926
Bramble-dew, eyes of gold and, 703
Brambles were always catching, 883
Branch a bird a child a rose, a, 807
cut is the, 32
from the gardens above, 271
Branches, giant, tossed, 370
of arithmetic, 598
of learning, 45
of the pencil-tree, 701
superfluous, 60
Branch-charmed, oaks, 384
Brand in the dark ashes, hides a, 373
of the dog is upon him, 776
Brandy, a hero must drink, 237
and water, sipped, 289

Brandy, nothing extenuate for
  the, 417
Branksome Hall, custom of, 306
Brass, a bright bowl of, 934
  cast in, 956
  events are, 531
  evil manners live in, 74
  like cymbals, polished, 934
  nor stone nor earth, 107
  sounding, 1120
Brass-bound man, robust and,
  784
Brat, Polack's, joylessly torments
  a cat, 841
Bravado, met the Sun's, 861
Brave, a day to fire the, 219
  and bonny and good and gay,
  956
  and strong, remembering you,
  825
  and the great lie there in state,
  540
  days of old, 400
  deserve the lovely, the, 559
  deserves the fair, none but the,
  176
  endeavor to do thy duty, 686
  easy to be, 961
  faith, but that, 507
  forlornly, 428
  fortune helps the, 980
  friends of old all, 470
  heat, life's, 604
  home of the, 332
  how sleep the, 247
  I would be, 880
  man chooses, 525
  man dies, how a, 886
  men and bold, 951
  men before Agamemnon, 358
  of all the earth, 764
  that are no more, 267
  to fight aloud is very, 584
  to satirize the, 927
  toll for the, 267
  went down, the, 690
  who rush to glory, 328
  your storm, 638
Brave-hearted O wise man, O,
  857
Bravely, acting, a desperate part,
  533
  becomest thy bed, 105
  fleshed thy maiden sword, 63
Braver to keep brave thing hid,
  117
Bravery, all her, 157
  never goes out of fashion, 484
  of his grief, 97
Bravest are the tenderest, the,
  565
Braw brass collar, 285
Brawlers of the auction mart,
  722
Brawling judgments unashamed,
  delivers, 470
  woman in a wide house, 1108
Brawn than brain, more, 982
Brawny or rough, no matter how,
  589
Brayed with minstrelsy, 81
Brazen throat of war, 155
Breach endure not yet a, 118
  imminent deadly, 100
  more honoured in the, 91
  once more unto the, 66

Bread, a loaf of, 1018
  and butter, it's my, 937
  and butter of mine, no, 1036
  and butter, quarrel with my,
  192
  and butter, smell of, 357
  and butter, went on cutting,
  481
  and salt, eaten your, 776
  and the barley, 694
  and the gospel is good fare,
  188
  and wine, believe in your, 892
  and wine, dark hands for, 935
  and work for all, there 's, 432
  ask them for, 815
  better is halfe a lofe than no,
  15
  broken it for your daily, 631
  crammed with distressful, 67
  crust of, and liberty, 214
  daily, 850
  die for beauty than live for,
  409
  do not waste, 1090
  ears produce loaves of, 1056
  eaten in secret, 1107
  half-penny worth of, 62
  he dunks his, 923
  he is, 21
  He took the, and brake it, 118
  heart of the home savor of the
  repast, 1090
  home-made miracles of, 887
  Homer begged his, 123
  honor, 1090
  I broke with you, 904
  I like good, 955
  if his son ask, 1114
  in one hand stone the other,
  978
  in sorrow ate his, 439, 1057
  is buttered, which side my, 17
  is the staff of life, 188, 191
  its wondrous, 823
  labour for our, 890
  like eating new, 525
  living corn made, 834
  looked to government for, 261
  man doth not live by only,
  1099
  nor his seed begging, 1104
  of banishment, eating the bitter, 59
  of idleness, 1109
  of life, I am the, 1118
  of life, not daily bread but
  the, 380
  pudding, 795
  Royal slice of, 876
  savor is of other's, 1021
  should be so dear, that, 392
  sir, if you please, a piece of,
  555
  spoiled the, 556
  sweat of the brow, respect,
  1090
  sympathy's sustaining, 595
  that bringeth strength, 682
  they fling to their dogs to-
  night, 559
  upon the waters, cast thy, 1110
  wholesomeness of oaten, 122
  with one fish-ball, don't give,
  555
Breadlines, heard of, 935

Bread-sauce, time-honored, 666
Breadth of heaven betwixt you,
  428
  of my nail, taller by the, 191
Break before the bird, shell must,
  471
  best you get is an even, 868
  better to bow than, 13
  into foam of flowers, 630
  it to our hope, 89
  of day, eyes the, 37
  of day, until the, 660
  of the wave, 362
  on the lips while meeting, 431
  the hearts of kith and kin, 844
  their eggs at the smaller end,
  191
Breakers, the Euxine's dangerous,
  360
  wantoned with thy, 355
Breakfast, contentment that
  comes with, 930
  on a lion's lip, 67
  scheme for her own, 203
  with what appetite you have,
  73
Breakfast-table, neatly arranged
  and well-provisioned, 422
Breakfast-tables garnished by
  newspapers, 798
Breaking flood, murmur of the,
  679
  waves dashed high, 370
  while the tired waves vainly,
  519
Break-o'-day in a boozing ken,
  710
Breast, arm the obdured, 150
  at rest on the quiet earth's,
  523
  baby at my, 105
  bind the motto to thy, 1058
  cross on her white, 212
  earth's half-shielded, 586
  encloseth my poor heart, thy,
  71
  eternal in the human, 207
  fair as thine ideal, 354
  feeble woman's, 303
  forward, marched, 494
  get a hairy, 833
  heart within your, 928
  hold me to your deep, 619
  knock the, 157
  love's ripening, 385
  marble of her snowy, 145
  master-passion in the, 208
  monuments upon my, 374
  no, shall know save mine, 892
  of her gown, 421
  of the old nurse death, 693
  of the waters, 712
  on her white, 212
  reddened all his, 681
  round its, the rolling clouds,
  251
  see the mark on his red, 444
  so peacefully within her, 848
  soft hand and softer, 385
  soothe the savage, 193
  straying to find the, 548
  tamer of the human, 243
  that gives the rose, 575
  the living fires, wake in our,
  451
  thine ideal, 354

Breast, thinking of it on her, 683
  told but to her mutual, 328
  toss him to my, 136
  truth hath a quiet, 59
  two hands upon the, 567
  was in some quiet, 687
  where learning lies, 217
  where roses could not live, 808
  with dauntless, 245
Breasts are orbs of heavenly
  frame, 27
  beat their manly, 761
  must suckle slaves, such, 359
  oppose gallant, 985
  that heave, 763
  the keen air, 249
  within our, this jewel lies, 226
Breast-high amid the corn, 390
Breast-knot gay, scarlet, 573
Breastplate of faith and love,
  1121
  what stronger, 69
Breath, a sweeter woman ne'er
  drew, 540
  able to take his, 490
  all incense, 353
  and die, hold my, 905
  and finer spirit, 295
  attunes the spheres, with one,
  514
  bated, 45
  blew back, when, 585
  boldest held his, the, 328
  by the gate of, 631
  call back the fleeting, 244
  can make them, 250
  divine, by, 473
  down and out of, 63
  eulogy's blandest, 541
  extend a mother's, 213
  Faith hath a fleeting, 761
  for the whole tune before you
  start, 745
  grey from thy, 631
  hot and cold with the same,
  962
  hurricane's sultry, 554
  in labor, draws his, 932
  in our mouth, 780
  is a ware, 742
  is never shaken, whose, 888
  lack of, want of words, 157
  last moment of his, 252
  life of mortal, 436
  life that breathes with human,
  462
  lightly draws its, 295
  little flesh a little, 1009
  most breathes, where, 108
  of decay, 575
  of eternal morning, 583
  of flowers sweeter in the air,
  111
  of God, his life a, 506
  of heaven, 264
  of ice, blooms o'er, 642
  of kindness, 567
  of kings, princes are, 284
  of life, the, 154
  of life, the most immediate,
  1057
  of men, she takes away the,
  429
  of morn, sweet is the, 152
  of the multitude, not the
  musty, 750

Breath of the wind, mist from
  the, 838
  of twilight, when the, 801
  one mighty, 337
  one more unfortunate weary
  of, 392
  places of my, 896
  regular as infant's, 317
  rich perfume of her, 421
  rides on the posting winds, 105
  say beneath my, 938
  shapen by my, 756
  skies were purple and, was
  praise, 395
  smells wooingly, heaven's, 85
  summer's, 659
  summer's ripening, 78
  thou art, a, 36
  to cool your porridge, 1026,
  1039
  to cool his pottage, 1004
  to the latest, 209
  twilight hour of, 796
  we are to utter sweet, 43
  we waste our, 924
  what chisel could cut, 57
  wit is the only, 923
  with tempestuous, 629
  with their short, 729
  with uninforming, 868
  wither at the north-wind's, 370
Breaths, we live in thoughts not,
  506
Breathe not his name, 334
  thoughts that, 244
  were life as though to, 464
Breathed a word, that ever, 516
  the long long night, 473
Breathers of this world, 108
Breathes from yonder box, 212
  must suffer, who, 190
  there the man, 307
  upon a bank of violets, 53
  with human breath, life that,
  462
Breathing, closer is He than, 467
  household laws, 298
  of strength, but as a, 1025
  of the common wind, 297
  rose, friendship is the, 453
  time of day with me, 97
  time, peace only a, 258
  we watched her, 390
  what is it to cease, 880
Breathless with adoration, 297
Bred at Edinborough, 228
  at Oxford or Cambridge was
  not enough, 170
  in a book, dainties that are,
  41
  in the bone, 17, 977
  where is fancy, 45
Breech where honour 's lodged,
  143
Breeches are so queer, 450
  cost but a crown, 101, 256
  Macaulay is like a book in,
  313
  upon his backside, 241
  were blue, coat was red, 321
  women wear the, 122
  wouldn't hurt, 738
Breed a habit, use doth, 34
  artists are a rare, 792
  of men, this happy, 59
  of noble bloods, 81

Breed of their horses and dogs,
  184
  the past again, only, 472
Breeds by a composture, 81
Breeding, another man's want of,
  999
  care in my, 199
  due to gentle, 965
  test of, 720
  to show your, 279
Breeze, as if upon the, 847
  battle and the, 327
  drops in the pool when the,
  516
  every passing, 342
  free as the, 305
  is on the sea, the, 310
  of the morning, 813
  send me a little garden, 905
  summer, waves the bush, 309
  the freshened fragrant, 915
  without a, without a tide, 315
Breezes blow, hot, 445
Breezy hill that skirts the down,
  269
Breffny, little waves of, 820
Brekeke-kesh koash koash, 972
Brent, your bonny brow was,
  286
Brer Fox he lay low, 688
Brethren, all mankind are my,
  271
  born, likenesses in, 967
  great twin, 400
  to dwell together in unity,
  1106
Brevity is the soul of wit, 92
  its body, 316
  of life, 1051
  use of, 995
Brews, as he, 118
Bribe, boatman takes no, 983
  too poor for a, 246
Bric-à-brac, falls heavily among
  the, 900
Brick, straw to make, 1098
Bricks are alive this day, 69
  by chance or fortune, 1005
  sold him gilded, 853
  triumphal arch build of, 796
Brickbats, inability to dodge,
  818
Brick-dust man, the, 229
Bridal chamber, come to the, 362
  of the earth and sky, 135
Bride, foeman's, 306
  hail the, 624
  half of the world a, 735
  I saw the young, 474
  in her rich adornin', 685
  made the world his, 910
  society my glittering, 302
  to a lad gone down, 916
  wife dearer than the, 239
Brides, as the lion woos his, 248
  of Enderby, play up the, 540
Bride-bed to have decked, 97
Bridegroom, fresh as a, 61
  hail the, 624
  is half of the world, 735
Bridge across a hundred years,
  510
  don't cross the, 440
  grave a covered, 440
  habit builds the, 676
  he lives near the, 246

Bridge, Horatius kept the, 400
  in wait, under the, 926
  is a sad song, 934
  of asses, 977
  of blue, 439
  of Sighs, on the, 353
  of time, meet we on the, 543
  that arched the flood, 409
  the world is merely a, 1093
  to the moon, build a, 515
Bridge-head, come up to, 926
Bridle, between spur and, 138
  reins a shake, and gae his, 287
  taxed, 314
Brief as a dragon-fly's repose, 529
  as the lightning, 42
  authority, drest in a little, 36
  candle, out out, 88
  command of Lee, 690
  darkness, 440
  even as bright, 368
  let me be, 91
  life our portion, 518
  terms art of scratch, engraving in, 533
  thanksgiving, 632
  words are well, 644
  year of the rose is, 633
Brier-patch, bred en bawn in a, 689
Brier, as if in the, 629
Briers, working-day world full of, 48
Brig, transom of a merchant, 413
Brigades, give me but two, 552
Bright, a quenchless star forever, 393
  and beautiful English girl, 624
  and yellow gold, 391
  angels are still, 88
  array, in, 423
  as a berry, 842
  as wine, 897
  as young diamonds, 178
  best of dark and, 356
  brokenly, 573
  candle of the Lord, 393
  cloud of tears, through a, 900
  consummate flower, 153
  dark with excessive, 151
  day is done, 105
  days are still and, 418
  her angels face shyned, 24
  honour, pluck, 61
  hour to waste, nor suffer one, 474
  I saw her eye was, 387
  in hue, quaint in form and, 569
  in thy eyes, 579
  is the ring of words, 703
  need to make it, 718
  old age serene and, 299
  or cloudy weather, 612
  or good, not too, 299
  particular star, a, 53
  promise of your early day, 342
  smile haunts me still, 501
  star would I were, 385
  streams play, tripping where the, 568
  suns may scorch, 404
  the pure the beautiful the, 665
  the sunshine as to-day, as, 581
  things come to confusion, 42
  tragic thing, glory is that, 585
  waters meet, where the, 335
Brighten as I draw near, 626

Brighten, blessings, as they take their flight, 202
Brightening to the last, 250
Brightens, how the wit, 211
Brightest and best of the sons, 342
  blade grows dim with rust, 453
  day hath a cloud, 69
  fell, though the, 88
  heaven of invention, 66
  on glory's bed, 386
  wisest, meanest, 208
Bright-eyed fancy, 244
  science watches, 244
Brightly smile and sweetly sing, 365
Brightness break, sudden, 903
  in our breath, 867
  lost her original, 149
  waned, 936
Brignall banks are wild, 309
Brilliance, no conceit of, 928
Brilliant actions brought about from meanest motives, 395
  and warm, 923
  Frenchman, 263
  lamp in that dogged mind, 928
  like chrysophrase glowing, 432
  stream of verbiage, 578
  yet so corrupt, 320
Brillig, 't was, 598
Brim, bubbles that swim on the beaker's, 431
  o'er night's, 485
  pleasure drown the, 53
Brimstone bed, from his, 321
Brine, oh give me the flashing, 502
Bring me no more vain oblations, 1110
  that chance will, us through, 547
  the day, sweet Phosphor, 134
  the rathe primrose, 159
Bringer of that joy, 43
  of unwelcome news, 64
Brings the constant sun, but, 501
Brink, pause upon the, 626
Brisk and giddy-paced times, 54
  as a bee in conversation, 233
  is London's air, 833
Bristol channel, swam across the, 498
Britain at Heaven's command, 225
  boasts, mountains, 575
  where now is, 399
Britain's crown, ambassador from, 474
Britannia needs no bulwarks, 327
  over pale, 194
  rules the waves, 225
Brither, like a vera, 287
British autobiography never frank, 737
  calf is laid mouldering in the grave, 293
  constitution most subtle organism, 450
  eloquence and British indelicacy, 906
  Empire, distribution of, 909

British Isles, the little speck, 452
  man, smell the blood of, 99
  manhood, piece of, 378
  muse, 185
  oak, shadow of the, 260
  public in a fit of morality, 398
  public-school system, 607
  race and empire, 921
  stare, with a stony, 469
British-Americans and Irish-Americans and German-Americans, 700
Briton even in love should be a subject, 304
Britons, air dearest to, 443
  compared with children across the Atlantic, 483
  confidence and self-esteem of, 483
  never shall be slaves, 225
  strolling around among the, 1009
  true, and while we're, 562
Brittle, glass of the years is, 631
Broad acres a patent of nobility, 582
  as ten thousand beeves, 575
  as the blue sky above, 441
  as the kingdoms and empires of old, 504
  based upon her people's will, 462
  blown all his crimes, 95
  brimming water, off a, 873
  earth of ours, in this, 535
  effects which can be obtained, 1080
  for self-complacent British sneer, 513
  hard-beaten road to his house, 416
  is the way, 1114
  mantle of charity, 329
  margin to my life, I love a, 514
  need to make it, 718
  river ebbed and flowed, 437
  way, shun the, 305
Broad-backed hippopotamus, 900
Broadcast doings of the day and night, 539
Broadcloth without, 266
Broader mark, nearer and a, 588
Broad-streeted Richmond, 928
Broadway, the shadows lay along, 431
Broccoli, it's, 932
Brogues, my clouted, 106
Broke the die, nature, 356
Broken and a contrite heart, 1104
  as an egg when, 432
  flutes of Arcady, 807
  friendships, find, 848
  hearts and heads, land of, 828
  in heart, hymn of the, 533
  Jerusalem, 524
  not, in from the birth, 398
  pinion, 643
  reed, this, 113, 1111
  relations, renewal of, 636
  with the storms of state, 74
Broken-hearted for his sins, 719
  half, 351
  languish, 620
  lean above me, 882

Broken-hearted, ne'er been, 287
  you hoped we were both, 633
Brokenly bright, 573
Bromley to the city, daily she
  came from, 911
Bron-rhuddyn, breast-burned, 444
Broncho that would not be
  broken, 856
Bronze and gold and brawn, they
  built with, 282
  and salt and the free grasses,
  929
  and some of, 927
  is the mirror of the form, 964
  Jove changed, to, 984
  out of the eternal, 789
  seems, gold that dull, 597
  that sings, 897
  then iron stamped, with, 984
Bronzed lank man, 857
Brood, idle, be fed, 973
  of folly without father bred,
  160
  we'll leave that's viler, 983
Brook and river meet, where,
  434
  as thou these ashes little, 303
  can see no moon but this, the,
  335
  fast by a, 269
  I could not hear, the, 458
  is deep, where the, 21, 69
  noise like of a hidden, 315
  sparkling with a, 346
  that turns a mill, 289
  the weather, many can, 41
Brooks, are drenched sands, 587
  beaver in Canadian, 451
  books in the running, 48
  in Vallombrosa, 148
  make rivers, 177
  moon looks on many, 335
  of the blond country, sweet-
  tasting, 929
  panteth after the water, 1104
  rodless Walton of the, 733
  shallow, and rivers wide, 160
  sloping into, 346
  too broad for leaping, 743
Brook's motion, 't is the, 501
Brook'd the eternal devil, 81
Brooklyn has more distinguished
  bibliophiles, 844
  moon comes over, 939
Brookside, wandered by the, 458
Broom, new, sweeps clean, 15
Broomstick, witch upon a, 1036
  write finely upon a, 192
Broth, Tammany cooks spoil the,
  935
Brother, a man and a, 941
  am I not a man and a, 941
  and good friend the sun, 881
  author expects a book of yours,
  324
  call my, back to me, 370
  courtly cruel, 478
  do not stumble, courage, 499
  every author would his, kill,
  167
  every one said to his, 1112
  exquisite to relieve a, 285
  far off, better a neighbour near
  than a, 1108
  followed brother, fast has, 305
  from the dust, raised a, 504

Brother, help my ailing, 955
  in dealing with a, 959
  John, buried, 630
  jostle a, 657
  little brown-frocked, 813
  near the throne, no, 167, 213
  of all, equal and kindly, 379
  of death, sleep the, 958
  of the angle, 139
  sleep, death and his, 368
  so like my, 630
  somewhere in the gloom, 664
  souls, my friends and, 471
  stick more close than a, 783
  sticketh closer than a, 1107
  to death, sleep, 30
  to every one, 1074
  to his side, to draw a, 881
  to them that toil, 642
  undying, of ephemeral honor,
  1064
  will follow the plow, 675
Brothers, all the, of my father's
  house, 55
  all valiant, 943
  counterfeit presentment of two,
  95
  forty thousand, 97
  in blood and tongue, 443
  in distress, affliction's sons are,
  285
  in the tavern room, 664
  live together, and as, 436
  men my, 464
  punch with care, punch, 583
  row, the stream runs fast, 334
  seeking the ideal, 801
  sons and kindred slain, 167
  the Romans were like, 400
  to help and save his, 591
  we band of, 67
  were valiant, all the, 943
Brother's father dad, called, 57
  keeper, am I my, 1097
  murder, curse upon a, 95
Brother-devil to despair, 675
Brotherhood, a meaner law than,
  597
  a mystic bond of, 378
  crown good with, 737
  faith in, 954
  of venerable trees, 298
  over food and wine, 381
  that binds the brave, 764
  will not come to pass, 1074
Brother-in-law is haberdasher,
  614
Brotherly affection and love,
  268
Brought fresh from the hyaline,
  432
  low, when false things are,
  650
  nor, too long a day, 390
Broun as is a berye, 5
Brow, a cloud is on thy, 446
  back from your, 639
  child of pure unclouded, 598
  flushing his, 383
  for my dead cold, 681
  furrows on another's, 202
  grace was seated on this, 95
  hallow my unelected, 746
  indifferent godlike, 594
  is wet with honest sweat, 433
  life's evening tinge his, 679

Brow, May-blossom, and a, 470
  no wrinkle on thine azure, 355,
  440
  o'er that, a shadow fling, 365
  of a woman or cheek of a child,
  1085
  of Egypt, beauty in a, 43
  of labor, 753
  pain and anguish wring the,
  308
  pregnant with thought in-
  breathed, 562
  seal of a king on his, 706
  serene, with, 544
  sweat of man's, 959
  the garlands wither on your,
  141
  twitched in their, 490
  upon earth's fevered, 445
  was brent, your bonny, 286
  weariness not on your, 547
Brows, beetle, 77
  black, become some women
  best, 56
  fit them to our, 927
  gathering her, 287
  night-cap decked his, 253
  of him that uttered nothing
  base, 462
  sweat of a man's, 241
  sweat of my, 1033
Brown, and all the trees are, 523
  and bare, fields are lying, 552
  as leather, 737
  bread and the Gospel, 188
  bread, as well as beans and,
  714
  earthly, 701
  for ladies' eyes the only color,
  911
  hand, little, 730
  Missouri Mule, 816
  of the fruitful clay, 523
  study, some, 23
Brown-frocked brother, 813
Brown-handed children, from
  these, 729
Browning, a prose Browning, 526
  and brief for, 326
  is laid to rest, 563
  is riddle redundant, baldness
  abundant, 493
  picked up a fair-coined soul,
  749
  plain, did you once find, 487
Browning's reply to Fitzgerald,
  449
Brownstone will do, a very plain,
  451
Bruce and the spider, 512
  has often led, Scots whom,
  286
Bruise, parmaceti for an inward,
  61
Bruised reed shall he not break,
  1112
  with adversity, 37
Brunette, blonde or, 1022
Brushers of noblemen's clothes,
  113
Brutal savages in an unknown
  island, 418
Brutality, life without art is, 533
Brute, et tu, 82
  love of a, 461
  morose, horned, 543

Brute, not quite a, 202
Brutes, dumb, we call them, 754
  men and men divine, 556
  without women we had been, 185
Brutish, life of man, 132
Brutus and Cassius, meaning, 1001
  Caesar had his, 270
  I am no orator as, 83
  is an honourable man, 83
  there was a, once, 81
Bubble blown by teacher, 695
  burst and now a world, 207
  fire burn and cauldron, 87
  froth and, 601
  honour but an empty, 176
  in the molten mass, 894
  last remark was a, 630
  life is a, 133
  life's troubled, 823
  on the fountain, like the, 308
  pricking our gonfalon, 867
  reputation, seeking the, 49
  whose life is a, 133
  world's a, 112
Bubbles, borne like thy, 355
  do when they burst, just as, 453
  in a golden vintage, 1085
  life is made up of mere, 750
  like us, millions of, 462, 1018
  that swim on the beaker's, as, 431
  the earth hath, 84
  with beaded, 383
Bubbling cry of some strong swimmer, 359
  groan, sinks with, 355
  loud-hissing urn, 265
  venom, flings its, 352
  well-spring, 575
Buccaneer, the last, 401
Buck of the first head, 41
Bucks in a wine-barrel room, 857
Buckbasket, meanings in the, 874
Bucket, as a drop of a, 1112
  just drop your, 732
  of ashes, 854
  the old oaken, the iron-bound, 348
Buckets into empty wells, 265, 313
  the ruby-rimmed beryline, 431
Buckhurst choose, I would, 184
Buckle on it, silver, 770
Buckled sword, that ever, 516
Buckler of the Gaul, 779
Buckram, four rogues in, 62
Bucolical juvenal, 310
Bud bit with an envious worm, 77
  like a, in the frost, 389
  like a worm in the, 55
  nipped i' the, 164
  of love, this, 78
  promise of an incipient, 627
  rose is sweeter in the, 24
  shut and be a, again, 383
  to heaven conveyed, 316
Buds forgot to blow, 642
  of all the bonny, 612
  of roses in your hair, 830
  sleep in the root's white core, 385
  young, sleep in the root's, 385

Buddhas in a private shrine, 1027
Budding Shakespeare drink, sold some, 879
Budge an inch, I'll not, 51
  doctors of the Stoic fur, 158
  significant and, 263
Budget, smelling like a municipal, 910
Buff and the blue, bide by the, 286
  bare to the, 703
  trip slip for a six cent fare, 583
Buffs, drunken private of the, 474
Buffalo, the great old, 929
Buffaloes of the spring, 856
Buffet take the, 781
Buffets and rewards, fortune's, 94
  of the world, blows and, 86
Buffler, he's gone with the, 888
Buffoon, statesman and, 174
Buffoonery of American enterprises, 863
Bug, bounding, went to see a, 691
  crawl out of crack, 929
  in a rug, snug as a, 227
  some little, 860
Bugs and fleas, free from, 972
  fear boys with, 52
  in a basket, three little, 540
  off a sweet-potato vine, 927
Bugbear, no greater, 422
Bugle, blow, 466
  grieves, lonely, 684
  horn, one blast upon his, 308
  sounding, I heard a, 635
Bugles, blow out you, 894
  shake me like a cry of, 757
Build as chance will have it, 401
  as thou wilt, 621
  beneath the stars, who, 202
  not boast, he lives to, 223
  schoolrooms for the boy, better, 512
  the ladder by which, we, 521
  the lofty rhyme, 159
  thee more stately mansions, 452
  when we mean to, 64
Builds a church to God, 210
  it, Wren, 414
Builded better than he knew, 408
Builder also grows, unless the, 688
  blast a young, in the budding, 147
Builders refused, stone which the, 1106
  wrought with greatest care, 436
Buildeth on the vulgar heart, 64
Building, light principal beauty in a, 147
  stole the life o' the, 86
  things to be looked to in, 1057
Buildings apparatus and libraries, you may have, 591
  are books, 570
  to produce, 1057
Built a lordly pleasure-house, 462
  a paper-mill, 69
  all we have, do we discern, 546
  God a church, 263
  in one day, Rome was not, 15

Built in such a logical way, 452
  in the eclipse, 159
  on another man's ground, 34
  their nests in my beard, 499
Bulk, estimated not by its, 1000
Bull, Assyrian, 469
  his iron spouse, a great, 926
  or forge a, 392
  to beguile Io, 23
  supreme, once again the, 816
Bulls and bears, play with the, 910
  in Cymbrian plaine, 24
Bullen's eyes, gospel-light from, 246
Bullet, damn tough, 782
  from the ballot to the, 456
  golden, 109
  that will kill me, 1061
  true as the, 686
Bullets, charming the, 643
  of the brain, paper, 39
Bullocks, how a good yoke of, 65
  whose talk is of, 1125
Bully, like a tall, 210
Bulrush, knot in a, 978
  tripped her, 375
Bulwark of our island, floating, 248
Bulwarks against anti-republican tendencies, 273
  Britannia needs no, 327
  of the state, 660
  round its sacred, 392
Bumble bee, I sat down on a, 939
  if the law supposes that, said Mr., 494
Bumper of claret, 348
  of good liquor, 279
  toast when Peter poured, 348
Bumpity ride a, 823
Bumps along the dusk, 696
Bunbury, invaluable invalid called, 724
Bunch of words, take a little, 829
Bunches, shakes down a few, 712
Buncombe, speaking through reporters to, 379
Bundle of relations, man a, 411
  were put in a, 747
Bung-hole, stopping a, 97
Bunhill Fields, from Aldermanbury to, 933
Bunk below, in his, 655
Bunker-hill, there is Lexington and, 341
Bunny gamboled up, 815
Bunyan the swart convict, 531
  was his name, 779
Buoyant hearts, 698
Burbadge played, when, 649
Burden, age no longer is a, 967
  and heat of the day, 1115
  every man bear his own, 1121
  grasshopper shall be a, 1110
  lay down my, 921
  mad cause and senseless, 922
  of a sigh, 306
  of another, ease the, 955
  of having nothing to do, 1050
  of his song, this the, 269
  of long living, 632
  of our civilization, 866

Burden of our common need, 445
of responsibility, heavy, 921
of the mystery, 295
of the pride of thought, 789
of the world, 708
prosperous fool a grievous, 964
sacred, is this life, 454
superfluous, loads the day, 162
thought about the, 748
to me, leaving the, 583
upon the Lord, 781
we bear the, and the heat, 546
weight of another's, 138
white man's, 780
youth and age equally a, 973
Burdens, heir to the bearing of, 642
that a man can bear, 25
the ease of, 1036
up the hill, all your, 953
Burden-bearer, what careth the, 686
Burdened heart, filled his, 513
Burdensome, nothing harsh or, 1016
Burglaree, vary piracee with a little, 623
Burglary, as ever was committed, flat, 40
Burgundian glass, deepened in the full, 911
Burgundy the winiest wine, 800
Burial, anoint beforehand for their, 578
no, this pretty pair, 258
of an ass, 1113
of Joseph Conrad, 708
of the flame, 671
with such honour, 780
Burial-ground God's acre, 434
Buried in that vast abyss, 347
Burn a Poland winter, will, 36
daylight, 34, 178
it when you've read it, 198
to the socket, hearts, 302
while the lamp holds out to, 199
within us, heart, 1117
words that, 244
Burns, adores and, 207
how it, on the edge, 389
out another's burning, 77
will pay to Robert, 603
Burned is Apollo's laurel bough, 32
on the water, 104
Burning and a shining light, 1118
burns out another's, 77
bush for every day, 873
bush, yon maple wood the, 431, 442
deck, boy stood on the, 370
fiery furnace, midst of the, 1113
haystack, like a, 871
marle, over the, 148
soul, man with his, 832
terms of love, 460
your lights, 1117
Burnished dove, 464
sun, livery of the, 45
Burn-mill meadow, sweets of, 298
Burnt, all the whores were, alive, 189
child craves the flame, 912
child fire dredth, 15

Burnt, half his Troy was, 64
Burs, conversation's, 451
Burst just as bubbles do when they, 453
of bells, hear the, 903
of music, 719
of thunder sound, 370
Burthen of the mystery, 295
ships of this vast, 230
Bury Cæsar, I come to, 83
in oblivion, 133
me on my face, 1015
Bush, both over bank and, 24
and tree, birds will serenade in, 646
beat the, 133
burning, for every day, 873
every common, afire with God, 431, 442
good wine needs no, 51
hawthorn, with seats beneath, 250
if you can't be a tree, be a, 846
nor preface, good wine needs neither, 311
poem hangs on the berry, 650
supposed a bear, how easy is a, 43
the thief doth fear each, 71
waves the, 309
yon maple wood the burning, 431, 442
Bushel, do not sit down on a, 1016
of silver, 686
Bushels of chaff, 44
Busier seemed than he was, 5
Business, a man of, 1016
about my Father's, 1117
and his wife, leaves his, 674
attending strictly to, 617
best, you can go into, 479
better, do mind my, 181
chief, in life, 654
come to men's, 109
could not make dull, 545
crises, 697
despatch is the soul of, 222
dinner lubricates, 275
end of this day's, 84
every man mind his own, 1035
everybody's, is nobody's, 139
fit for the, 188
goes off a man's hands when he stays by it, 182
I have laid aside, 139
in great waters, 1105
is business, 867
is other people's money, 1075
is to be good and happy to-day, 314
man diligent in, 1108
man, the tired, 919
mind your own, 1037
never blush to tell, 219
no, carried on without dissimulation, 222
no feeling of his, 96
nobody's, 139
of life, the great, 641
of one who studies philosophy, 1008
of the citizens, 1054
of the day, be drunk the, 177
of the hour, 670

Business on the jury's done, 677
politics conviviality, when you have exhausted, 538
prayer all his, 201
prosperous man of, 720
putting him in the way of, 1020
quickly, dispatch that, 1022
set aside, his graver, 757
so ends the bloody, 220
some men take to, 209
talents equal to, 1006
talk of nothing but, 1022
tangled, 466
that we love, 104
unembarrassed by cares of, 989
unremitted attention to, 259
will never hold water, this, 194
with an income at its heels, 263
with the grass, 771
won't do any, 849
Businesses, its customs and, 267
Businese, I have partly succeeded in my, 198
Business-like, more, than business men, 838
Buskin, shuffles off the, 452
strait and terse, 648
Buskins shortned, with, 134
Bust, animated, 244
her friendly, uncorseted, 900
outlasts the citadel, 1071
outlasts the throne, 648
Busts between, placed the, 204
but I've three, 715
Bustle, love of, not industry, 990
of man's work-time, in the, 494
so illustrious, 584
Busy, a man, so, 5
about the main chance, 198
and cheerful folk, 875
as a bee, 23
bee, how doth the, 199
career, not quitting the, 501
curious, thirsty fly, 223
hammers, closing rivets up, 67
haunts of men, in the, 370
here and there, 1101
hum of men, 160
listening fellow, a, 1000
straightway he wants to be, 487
we are on Tom Tidler's ground, 512
whisper circling round, 251
with the crowded hour, 409
world an idler to, 265
world and I shall ne'er agree, 168
But me no buts, 946
Butcher, Shakespear's father was a, 171
Butchers, gentle with these, 82
Butcher's bill is due, 622
Butchered to make a Roman holiday, 354
Butler, the ladies remember, 928
Butt end, knocks you down with the, 255
Butt-ends, stick with two, 347
Butter and eggs and a pound of cheese, 590
bread and, of mine, 1036
bread and, smell of, 357

Butter for the royal slice of bread, 876
quarrel with my bread and, 192
she was cutting bread and, 481
to my bread, bit of, 876
words smoother than, 1104
would not melt in her mouth, 14, 192
Buttercup, God wished for a, 693
Buttercups and daffodils do, as, 901
Buttered, which side my bread is, 17
Butterflies no bees, no, 391
Butterfly flitted across the field, 793
I am touching a, 923
I'd be a, 388
upon a wheel, 213
upon the road, 776
Butterfly's wing, beauty of a, 930
Button, did not care a, 1025
little brown, 630
little round at top, 246
sacred bronze, 630
the dearly bought, 630
the highly prized, 630
Buttons be disclosed, 90
gold, 180
I had a soul above, 288
matched our, 625
transitory nature of, 654
Buttoned down before, coat, 404
Button-hole lower, let me take you, 41
Buttress nor coign of vantage, 85
Buy it, they lose it that do, 43
land as cheap as stinking mackerel, 62
whom spoils of office cannot, 522
with you sell with you, 44
Buyer, it is naught saith the, 1108
needs a hundred eyes, 137
Buyers of every class, 1079
Buying or selling of pig, 18
By and by is easily said, 95
day by night, 393
hoke ne by croke, 10
Nebo's lonely mountain, 516
shore at sea, where'er I am, 393
what eternal streams, 460
By-and-by, street of, 693
Bygone measure, move to a, 842
Bygones be bygones, let, 587
Byngo, hys name was littel, 350
By-product more valuable than product, 740
Byrde in hande, better one, 962
Byron, sad as grave and salt as life, 428
words no, 716
Byron's poetry, ethics from, 398
Byword, proverb and a, 1101
Byzantium is not big enough to hold us, 1006
Byzantium's conquering foe, 299, 353

CABBAGE leaf to make an apple pie, 246
pepper his, 989
with a college education, 615

Cabbages and kings, 598
imitating when planting, 649
nobody has ever seen any, 455
Cabin build there, a small, 790
clean, and keep your, 875
empty stand, every, 653
entered Logan's, 249
was, that part of ship where the, 247
Cabined cribbed confined, 87
loop-hole, 157
Cabinet, from his moist, 106
Cabin-walls were gleaming, 562
Cable broke, the holding anchor lost, 71
for a line, 146
scrape the, 505
Cabots talk only to God, 752
Cabriolet, rang for his, 350
Cackle, hungry rooster don't, 688
Cactus spines would tear, 801
Cad and coward, cocoa is a, 828
Cadence of a rugged line, harsh, 175
of consenting feet, 919
sweet in, 266
Cadets of Gascony, 671
of Gascoyne, 1085
Cadmean victory, it was a, 969
Cadmus, blessings upon, 375
gave the letters, 359
Caesar and his fortunes, 1000
and wealthy strangers, 996
bled, where some buried, 1018
dead and turned to clay, 97, 882
feed, doth this our, 81
great, fell, 83
had his Brutus, 270
I appeal unto, 1119
I come to bury, 83
imperious, dead, 97
in every wound of, 83
I've no mind to be a, 1009
made here a kind of conquest, 105
made not here his brag, 105
never here, regions, 263
not that I loved, less, 83
rebellion fraud and, 194
render therefore unto, 1115
stained with blood, 292
treads the deck, 994
upon what meat doth, feed, 81
we who are about to die, 438
with a senate at his heels, 208
without his ambition, Frederick without his tyranny, 599
would relinquish all, 412
yesterday the word of, 83
you carry, and his fortune, 1000
Caesars, those unbred, 903
swords of, 735
Caesar's apartment, carried to, 1000
barber, 1000
hand and Plato's brain, 410
things which are, 1115
wife above suspicion, 999
Café, haunting the little snug, 905
Cage, form is the, 649
gets into the lion's, 952

Cage, I sit and sing, in my, 1051
of laws, make a, 908
nor iron bars a, 168
put me in a, 902
Cages, as with birds in, 1030
of bright-plumaged rhythms, 831
Caged I pine, like an eagle, 502
Cain, old Tubal, 504
the first city made, 168
the Lord set a mark upon, 1097
Cairn, king of Ireland's, 792
Caityf, lyk a restelees, 7
Cake, eat thy, and have it, 136
eat your, and have your cake, 18
is dough, my, 52
not always the fanciest, 923
Cakes and ale in fear, 961
and ale, no more, 54
and friends, 923
Calamities, for the greatest, 995
of life shared among the upper and lower, 187
Calamity, child of, 616
enigmatical sort of, 1012
fortune not satisfied with one, 987
is man's true touchstone, 131
learn from another's, 987
of so long life, 93
Calculation, defies, 1057
past, 625
Caledonia stern and wild, 307
Caledonia's cause, support, 286
Calendar, among the high tides in the, 57
look in the almanack, a, 43
our crowded, 848
striking from the, 1019
Calendars, modern, 723
the basis of culture, 723
Calf, bring hither the fatted, 1117
near three centuries dead, 733
when Shakespear killed a calfe, 171
Calf's-skin on those recreant limbs, 57
Calico cat, the, 699
California, cheer for, 912
go, to, 502
Californian who would talk California, 838
Californians are a race, 800
southerners of the west, 800
Call, a bawd a bawd, 976
a spade a spade, 976
answered to my, 890
back yesterday, 59
clarion, 693
evil good good evil, 1111
for me, and one clear, 472
heard his country's, 782
it by some better name, 337
it holy ground, 370
me early mother dear, 463
me spade, don't, 192
my brother back to me, 370
my own, that I may, 451
no faith false, 604
no man foe, 913
of waters flowing, 755
pity's, 557
spirits from the vasty deep, 62

Call, ten shall heed the, 851
the cattle home, 523
the gods to witness, 80
these delicate creatures ours, 102
thing they, a conscience, 392
things by their right names, 290
to battle, 719
to hail a second, 576
to him, I may not, 672
to-day his own, he who can, 177
you that backing your friends, 61
Called about him everyone, 478
him dead, 591
many are, 1115
the new world into existence, 293
Callers, destitution of morning, 312
Calling, answer that sweet, 850
follow your own, 407
followed their mercenary, 744
shapes, 157
true path of his, 407
Calliope, tout the loud, 912
Calls back the lovely April, 107
Calm, after storm, 188, 923
and serene he drives, 194
and silent night, 478
and tideless sea, 869
and very coldly wise, 882
guest serenely, 248
hats, I like, 907
is in that balm, all our, 447
lights of mild philosophy, 194
me my God and keep me calm, 445
of idle vacancy, 234, 266
of mind, all passion spent, 157
of water which receives and reflects, 636
on the listening ear, 477
patience of the woods, 445
peace is what I seek and, 547
region, in that, 134
rested on the bay, 405
sepulchral spot, 475
so deep, I never felt a, 297
soul of all things make it mine, 546
that must follow all storms, 497
thou mayst smile, 275
through all coming days, 649
to face what's pressing, 984
when sternest, 539
Calme, Sea is as deepe in a, as in a storme, 118
Calmer of unquiet thoughts, 139
Calmly bear, can every anguish, 459
Calmness made, keeps the law in, 300
to remember, 582
Calomel, science and sense in, 951
the remedy is, 951
Calumet, smoke of many a, 681
Calumnious strokes, 90
Calumny, shalt not escape, 93
Calvaries, all must have our, 805
and crucifixions, 609
Calvin, oat-cakes, land of, 312

Calvin, my name was, 746
Calvin's dam, Luther's dike or, 453
Calypso, wake not sad, 570
Camaralzaman is famous, 437
Cambridge, ye fields of, 167
Cambridgeshire of all England, 893
Cambuscan bold, story of, 161
Came, I saw, I conquered, 1003
never, a wink too soon, 390
peeping in at morn, 390
prologue, excuse, 155
saw and overcame, 65, 105
through, out of the sky as I, 559
to the making of man, 633
Camel bell, prophet's, 881
cloud in shape of a, 94
like a, indeed, 94
swallow a, 1115
through the eye of a needle, 60, 1115
thrust his face, 364
to thread the postern, 60
Camel's-bell, tinkling of the, 544
Camel's nose, nor e'en admit the, 364
Camelot, I forgot in, 916
Camerons by, and fifty, 500
Camilla scours the plain, 211
Camlet cloak with gold buttons and a silk suit, 180
Camomill the more it is trodden, 23
Camp that is struck, 618
Camps and courts, wealth bestowed on, 434
Campaspe, Cupid and, 23
Camp-fires dead long ago, 766
in the rain, 847
Camp-ground, tenting on the old, 608
Camping ground, fame's eternal, 541
Can have no lack of good society, 437
it be that this is all, 355
it till this outworn earth, 472
neither when we will enjoy, 547
not feel the sun, 501
not order rain or shine, 504
till we, and do obey, 559
we love but on condition, 492
Canada, mighty voice of, 738
Canadian hills, cold on, 269
Canal in Flanders, by the, 899
Canals and dockyards, 959
by the sour, 936
Canaries, when off the blue, 544
Canary birds feed on sugar, 655
Cana's marriage-feast, as at, 445
wedding feast, 474
Canceled skies, across the, 914
Cancels all bands, end of life, 62
Cancer, I cannot put up with, 754
rot their herring gut, 937
Candid and simple and nothing-withholding, 663
discontent, a kind of, 646
flame ardent temperature, 686
friend, the, 293
where we can, be, 206
Candied tongue, let the, 94
Candle after supper, burne, 171
bright, of the Lord, 393

Candle burns at both ends, 915
farthing, 324
from their torches I light my, 125
his bell and his book, his, 351
hold a, 221
in the sun, 125
light sit spinning, in the, 1027
looking in the daytime with a, 1015
natural, 184
of understanding, light a, 10, 1123
or the mirror, 766
out brief, 88
poor sport not worth the, 138
scarcely fit to hold a, 221
shall never be put out, 101
throws his beams, 47
to my shames, 45
to the sun, 170, 203
two old chairs and half a, 498
white, in a holy place, 868
Candles are all out, 85
are out, when the, 1005
be out all cats be gray, 13, 1041
night's, are burnt out, 79
of the night, 47
Candled dimness smoke and talk, 905
Candle-light, by yellow, 702
colors seen by, 428
marked my love by, 541
Candy is dandy, 935
Cane, conduct of a clouded, 212
Canker and the grief are mine, the, 358
care's a, 624
galls the infants of the spring, 90
in it, I find a, 276
or cark, there's a joy without, 673
Cankers of a calm world, 63
Cannibals, some of us are, 788
that eat each other, 100
Cannikin, why clink the, 487
Cannon his name cannon his voice, 575
to right of them, 467
took off his legs, 392
Cannon's mouth, even in the, 49
Cannon-balls may aid the truth, 504
Cannot come to good, 90
tell how the truth be, 306
Canoe, lies at its moorings the old, 642
light, 396
paddles her white, 334
Canon 'gainst self-slaughter, 90
of the social code, 736
Canon-guarded streams, 831
Canopus, so far away, 794
Canopy, most excellent, the air, 92
of light and blue, 326
of love, 441
the skies, my, 207
under the, 76
which love has spread, 369
Canst not say I did it, 87
thou guide Arcturus, 1103
Cant, clear your mind of, 238
of criticism, 241

Cant of hypocrites, 241
Cants, clear myself of, 378
    which are canted, 241
Cantankerous, you won't be so, 278
Canteen, drunk from the same, 578
Canter that brings you to a standstill, 655
Canterbury bells, te deums of the, 831
    Tales wrote at sixty, the, 438
Canticles and hymns, sings his, 922
Cantilena of the law, 331
Canting world, in this, 241
Cantrips of unicorns, 865
Canvas, crowd your, 472
    drooping, that lay with, 519
    fisted the beating, 726
    flapping on an idle mast, 688
    in, take thy, 267
    is rent, when his, 990
    of his time, the, 572
    that throbs, 609
Canyon, last dark, 738
Cap, addressing myself to my, 1046
    and gown in college life, 731
    by night a stocking all the day, 251, 253
    feather put into his, 241
    ivory, 451
    of youth, riband in the, 96
    velvet, out of a sow's ear, 241
    whiter than driven snow, 242
Caps, feather in their, 1039
Capabilities, betray their, 931
Capability and godlike reason, 96
    certain maximum of, 379
Capable and wide revenge, 103
    of becoming, become what we are, 704
    of nothing but dumb-shows, 94
Capacity for pain, 661
    for stimulating pleasure, 755
    infinite, for taking pains, 379
    of the human mind to resist, 278
    to become happy, 166
    transcendent, of taking trouble, 379
Cap-a-pe, armed at point exactly, 90
Caparisons don't become a young woman, 278
Cape Horn for all, some sort of, 531
    round the, 485
    round the stormy, 224
Capital A, an earnest soul and a, 686
    and labor, 797
    Belgium's, 352
    created by the labour, 1086
    has conquered, 1086
    is the fruit of labor, 456
    ship, a, 655
    solicits the aid of labor, 341
    swimmer, the second mate, 577
    victory of labour over, 1086
    when commercial, 1072
    who was't betrayed the, 185
Capitals, begin with, 599
    headed with proud, 1085
    rise her timeless, 785

Capitalism, absolute law of, 1086
    is doomed, 909
Capitalist country, one single, 1086
    is a practical man, 1071
    production begets, 1072
Capon, lined with good, 50
Caprice and lifelong passion, difference between, 723
    overcome, 1017
Capricious, with love, 676
Captain, a fig for your great, 1037
    be the proud, 693
    becomes his captain's, 104
    bold, 622
    but a choleric word in the, 36
    can, more than his, 104
    Christ, soul unto his, 60
    ill, good attending, 107
    in the army, 664
    jewels in the carconet, 107
    Jinks of the Horse Marines, 664
    lies fallen cold and dead, 536
    my captain our fearful trip, 536
    of all these men of death, 172
    of compliments, 78
    of my soul, I am the, 470
    of the sea, a boisterous, 248
    of the second rank, 1067
    of the wars, 748
    over them, he became a, 1100
    Reece, than that of worthy, 622
    still of thine own fate, 470
    these same ways, your, 875
    Wattle, ever hear of, 274
    with the mighty heart, 708
Captains and conquerors leave, 735
    and the kings depart, 780
    great nature's, 519
    may have grown as quaint, 889
    nod, the blood-fed, 857
    of horse, 141
Captaines couragious, 257
Captain's forequarters, at the, 600
    mind, or troubled the, 655
Captive bosom, within this, 396
    good attending captain ill, 107
    locks love's, 609
    whose words all ears took, 53
Captives free, set all, 697
Captives' births and deaths, 652
Captor, forgive our, 578
Capture of men, for the, 482
Captured beast, as they watch the, 687
Capulets, tomb of the, 261
Car, drive the rapid, 267
    looked after the low-backed, 389
    never wait for an uptown, 414
    rattling o'er the street, 352
    sat in the low-backed, 389
Caravan, innumerable, 371
    put up your, 816
    the phantom, 1019
Caravans of brown, noisy, 756
    of freight, 926
Caravanserai, this batter'd, 1018
Caravels, Columbus's doomburdened, 882
Caraway, a splitting, 977

Carbon de Castel Jaloux, with, 671
Carcass is, wheresoever the, 1116
    of Robinson Crusoe, 246
    none knows its lean old, 1076
    of all that we have, to cover this, 19
Carcasses bleed at the sight of the murderer, 122
Carcassonne, never have I seen, 557, 1073
    we're on our way to, 562
    you have been to, 562
Carconet, jewels in the, 107
Card, cheery old, 892
    clere conscience is a sure, 23
    he's a sure, 179
    reason the, passion the gale, 208
    speak by the, 97
Cards, holding the best of the, 640
    patience and shuffle the, 311, 1040
    played for kisses, 23
    were fairly shuffled, 660
Cardinal rose, the, 351
Care, a certain amount of pain or, 1063
    and disapproves that, 162
    and I was full of, 938
    and pain, if, 662
    and strife, to mingle in its, 474
    and wrong, loads of, 738
    begone dull, 170
    beyond to-day, 243
    buy it with much, 43
    can fashion so the infant heart, 326
    cast away, 1035
    choose with, 923
    compounded with what, 664
    deliberation and public, 150
    delivered to our, 949
    draws in the brains of men, 82
    earliest, latest, 239
    fig for woe and a fig for, 11
    follows, as riches grow, 984
    for naebody, 269, 286
    for nobody, no not I, 269
    for these others have no, 814
    forgot, be every, 364
    from much corroding, 719
    gives without a, 877
    golden, 65
    grown so free from, 916
    his useful, was ever nigh, 231
    I, how chaste she be, 22
    I, how fair she be, 22, 132
    in my breeding, 199
    is an enemy to life, 54
    is like my shadow, 20
    is no cure, 68
    it is their, 781
    keeps his watch, 78
    lift her with, 392
    lightly with tenderest, 628
    live aloof from, 977
    lodges where sleep will never lie, 78
    lost all, 936
    make pale my cheeks with, 132
    merry heart that laughs at, 363
    names that banish, 231
    not, I may although I, 21
    of a brother's name, 690

Care of children, through the, 790
of the sense, 598
on speaking terms with, 754
on the windy side of, 38, 55
or thought, all things without, 556
ravelled sleave of, 86
reach thee with his tender, 562
so wan with, 60
that buy it with much, 43
that life is brief, have little, 757
that the gear engages, 781
the least as feeling her, 22
there's neither cauld nor, 291
things past redress are past, 59
to keep fear to lose, 138
to our coffin adds a nail, 272
we, little we fear, little, 481
weep away the life of, 367
what has he to do with, 446
will kill a cat, 118, 133
with human bosoms human, 601
with judicious, 284
with wine drown, 983
without, a world of, 544
wrinkled, derides, 160
Cares and delicate fears, humble, 297
and joys abound as seasons fleet, 69
are all ended, his, 65
beguiled by sports, 249
clouding, 574
depressed with, 205
dividing his, 289
ever against eating, 160
far from mortal, 345
fret thy soul with, 25
has his little, 324
if nobody, for me, 269
kingdoms are but, 9
lose ourselves and all our, 506
midst of daily, 1073
naebody, for me, 269, 286
of business, unembarrassed by, 989
of gain, unvexed with the, 206
old, 619
on God, cast your, 465
or knows what I am, who, 369
put by your, 757
that fretted me, little, 955
that infest the day, 434
unvexed with all the, of gain, 206
whether it prevail or not, none, 556
whose constant, 248
Care's a canker, 624
an enemy to life, 54
Care-charmer sleep, 30
Cared not to be at all, 149
Career, is not quitting the busy, 501
of his humour, 39
they let nothing hinder, in this, 1045
Careful glance, with, 954
of the main chance, 68
of the type, 468
o' vidders, be wery, 494
that they that will read, 1125

Careful thought for the stranger, 642
ways of duty, 444
Careless babble of the brook, 665
childhood strayed, 243
desolation, 50
ease, 201
eye on men who drown, with, 649
flowing fountains, 583
hand, once my, 848
in deeds, be not, 1011
of my dress, I'm, 509
of sunshine or storm, 602
of the single life, 468
rhyme, some, 640
shoe-string, 133
song now and then, 246
step, with, 811
their merits or faults, 250
tread, walk beneath with, 641
trifle, as 't were a, 84
Carelessness of life and beauty, 834
Caress, answered the, 696
kept so long for one, 766
naught but weakness in fond, 522
wooing the, 358
Caressing, kind her, 240
Cargo of ivory and apes and peacocks, 832
Cargoes of meat drink, our, 950
of my lading, 778
Cargo-boats, but oh, the little, 778
Carian guest, my dear old, 553
Cariboo, off the coast of, 622
Caribous and partridges, in search of, 935
Caricatures, parodies and, 922
Cark, there's a joy without canker or, 673
Carlotta too, I love, 813
Carlyle, scolding from, 452
Carlyle's long-labored book, 879
Carmen travesty on, 902
Carnage bent, the orthodox on, 1050
war and its deeds of, 536
Carnation withered, green, 827
Carnations and my first love, 866
Carnegie in praise of poverty, 714
Johnnie, lais heer, 190
Carol, in a tuneful, 927
or weep, whether we, 449
Carols as he goes 249
varied I hear, 534
Carouse, an eerie faint, 914
Carpenter known by his chips, 192
Carpet, beneath the crisp and wintry, 668
knights, 123, 1027, 1032, 1035
Carriage held but just ourselves, 584
may ride, king in a, 449
Carriages without horses, 940
Carrier of love and sympathy, 608
of news and knowledge, 608
Carry Caesar, you, 1000
gentle peace, right hand, 73
Cart before the horse, 17
creak of a lumbering, 790
sung ballads from a, 177

Carts, passage of, 198
Carthage ought utterly to be destroyed, 998
Cartoons by Goya, 937
to furnish sporting page, 934
Carve to all but just enough, 191
Carved for many a year, names, 450
not a line, we, 364
work and imagery, 247
Carves it, Phidias, 414
out his own fortune, 1033
Carving, conversation is but, 191
Caryatid, appearance of a, 1068
Casca, the envious, 83
Case, and pay the cost, lose their, 456
as plain as a pack-staff, 116
I am in, what a, 51
of anything turning up, 496
of dissension, in a, 968
stands, as the, 116
when a lady is in the, 206
Cases, circumstances alter, 387
in these, we have judgment here, 85
tenures and tricks, 96
won't undertake unsavoury, 1076
Casement, I stood by the open, 552
love-lamps in the, 482
ope at night, 384
slowly grows, 466
Casements, charmed magic, 383
Casey at the bat, 770
Jones orders in his hand, 817
Casey's tabble dote, 698
visage shone, 770
Cash in hand, sweeter than, 986
my last remaining, 909
ready, 1039
take the, 1018
to spare him, yet hae nae, 285
Cash-box, beautiful eyes of my, 1046
Cashiering most kings and senates, 379
Casius, old Mount, 150
Cask, at the beginning of the, 959
Casket with its gifts concealed, 568
Caskets and burial, 423
Cassio, I love thee, 101
Cassius, darest thou, leap in with me, 81
forever and forever farewell, 84
has a lean and hungry look, 81
help me, or I sink, 81
no terrors in your threats, 83
Cast before the Moone, 23
beyond the moon, 12
bread upon the waters, 1110
I have set my life upon a, 72
look on this, 604
of thought, the pale, 93
off his friends, 252
to the ground, 574
your pearls before swine, 1114
Castaway, both, 789
Caste, comes of the Brahmin, 453
of Vere de Vere, 453
Castilian, what best becomes a brave, 388

Casting a dim religious light, 161
Cast-iron back with a hinge, 582
Castle a man's house is his, 21
  called doubting castle, 172
  gray, habitant of, 517
  hath a pleasant seat, 85
  house of every one is his, 21
  in Spain, there's a, 509
  my whinstone house my, is, 382
  tower and town, the strongest, 109
  wall, bores through his, 60
  walls, splendour falls on, 466
Castles in Spain, to build, 138
  in the air, 122, 1040
  in the clouds, 224
  most magnificent of, 1052
Castle's strength will laugh a siege, 88
Castled crag of Drachenfels, 353
  Rhine, dwelleth by the, 433
Castor and Pollux, twins, 1064
Castor-oil, gave it a dose of, 313
Casts out fear, as love, 470
Casual clod, 887
Casualty, road of, 45
Casuists, convocation of, 1035
Cat, bell the, 962
  care killed a, 40
  care will kill a, 118, 133
  drink a college or a, 210
  endow a college or a, 210
  feet, on little, 854
  had Tiberius been a, 546
  hanging of his, 940
  harmless necessary, 46
  if you go outdoors, 917
  in the adage, like the poor, 85
  in the pan, 110
  is averse to fish, what, 243
  languishes loudly, a, 692
  lion look no larger than the, 471
  may looke on a king, 16
  monstrous tail our, has, 189
  nine lives like a, 16, 976
  on your hearthstone, 815
  pains, gave the big, 664
  pensive, gives o'er her frolic, 815
  played, a little, 664
  room to swing a, 497
  so sweet a mistress, no, 748
  that worried the, 543
  the calico, 699
  vice in a, 638
  watches a mouse, as a, 192
  what d'ye think of that my, 390
  when I play with my, 1028
  whose one extravagance, 691
  will mew, 97
  would eate fish, 14
Cats and dogs, rain, 192
  and dogs, raining, 721
  be gray, when all candles bee out, all, 13, 1041
  those who play with, 1035
Cat's ear, breeds in the, 16
  strains, little, 664
Cataclysm, out of their, 922
Catacomb where early Christians pray, 880
Catalogue, go for men in the, 86
  more delightful than a, 1078
  of common things, 383

Catalogue of dogs, 922
  of human woes, 262
  of things necessary, 183
Catalogues, booksellers', 729
  say, seed, 813
Cataract, the sounding, 296
Cataracts, silent, 316
Catastrophe, I'll tickle your, 64
  or exaltation, without, 589
Catastrophes due, to love of pleasure, 532
Catch and conquer, 575
  and hold, 12
  as catch can, game of, 246
  ere she change, 209
  her lovely floating hair, 600
  larks, hoped to, 1025
  old birds with chaff, 1037
  the conscience of the king, 93
  the driving gale, 208
  the manners living, 206
  the transient hour, 231
Catechism, first question in engagement, 793
  so ends my, 63
Categorical, in order, 623
Caterpillars of the commonwealth, 59
  to blame for being, 578
Caters for the sparrow, 48
Cathay, cycle of, 465
  drink the poppies of, 444
Cathedral, inspired mankind made a, 704
  like the first supernatural bank, 902
Cathedrals, luxury liners, 937
Catholic, born a, 1061
  Church understands how to deal with enthusiasts, 399
  man, the, 663
  Roman, bell, 566
Cato, big with the fate of, 194
  give his senate laws, 213
  heroic stoic, 360
  learned Greek at eighty, 438
  on good acts, 113
  statue of, 1006
  the sententious, 360
Cattle are grazing, the, 297
  call the, home, 523
  come back with hogs and, 926
  home, followed the, 658
  thousands of great, 260
  train, goes the, 754
  upon a thousand hills, 1104
  who died as, 918
Caucasus, thinking on the frosty, 59
Caught by glare, maidens, 352
  my heavenly jewel, have I, 27
  Whigs bathing and walked away, 419
Cauld nor care there, neither, 291
Cauldron bubble, fire burn and, 87
Cauliflower nothing but cabbage, 615
Cause above renown, to set the, 764
  avengers of religion's, 1050
  be some first martyr in every, 518
  beauty of the good old, 298
  defile the, 941
  effect defective comes by, 92

Cause, every, produces more than one effect, 580
  evolution is not a, 641
  for order's, 576
  for our, it is just, 332
  goes hard, when the, 174
  hear me for my, 82
  idea of oneself as a, 1048
  is just, our, 332
  jealous though with little, 121
  judge in his own, 988, 1047
  little shall I grace my, 100
  mad, and senseless burden, 922
  magnificent and awful, 265
  may move dissension, 338
  me no causes, 946
  mightier than ever the sword had pleaded, 347
  nothing without, 226
  of all men's misery, 22
  of all things, 1014
  of covetousness, 31
  of disease quarrels sedition, 1051
  of dulness in others, 238
  of mankind, in the, 335
  of policy, turn him to any, 66
  of this defect, 92
  of this effect, 92
  patriots who for a theory risked a, 430
  perseverance in a good, 241
  report me and my, aright, 98
  saved a great, 659
  stands not on eloquence, every, 332
  that lacks assistance, 543
  that wit is in other men, 64
  was this, 217
  whatever be her, 157
Causes, occasions and, 67
  are too much, 405
  cause me no, 946
  conquered by external, 1049
  judges of important, 975
  just, whatever is, is in its, 178
  offence from amorous, 212
Caused the sun to rise, 1086
Caution against the stumbling stone, 879
  must be used, 1049
Caution's lesson scorning, 285
Cautious statistical Christ, 676
Cavalier, my faithful, 638
Cavalry of woe, 584
Cavalrymen, not many dead, 502
Cave Adullam, 1100
  of Adullam, into his political, 478
  vacant interlunar, 156
Caves, dark unfathomed, 245
  lakes, fens, bogs, 150
Cave-man clasps the seer, 892
Cavern choicer than the Mermaid Tavern, 384
  misery's darkest, 231
Caverns, gluts twice ten thousand, 385
  measureless to man, 315
  memory's, pure and deep, 388
Caviare to the general, 93
Cavil on the ninth part of a hair, 62
Caw, what says he, 267
Cease every joy to glimmer, 327

Cease from troubling, the wicked, 1101
  let the long contention, 547
  rude Boreas, 247
  things at worst will, 88
  to be ere one can say, 78
  to die, by dying, 128
  to do and be, 594
  to grieve, cease to be fortune's slaves, 128
  your tears and let it lie, 596
Ceased to be, years sailed by and, 437
Ceaseless clouds, charging like, 536
  devouring of the weak, 580
  strife, death and life in, 447
Ceases to be a virtue, 259
Ceaseth to enlarge itself, 68
Ceasing of exquisite music, 435
  swiftness never, 27
Cedar green with boughs, 708
  in Lebanon, 1105
  to the hyssop, from the, 398
  upright as the, 41
Cedarhurst to San Jose, 867
Cedarwood, sandalwood, 832
C'est un verre qui luit, 250
Celebrations, centenary, 892
Celebrated, Saviour's birth is, 89
Celerity is never more admired, 104
Celestial bird, like that, 338
  fire, spark of, 268
  peace, pattern of, 68
  street, strolling down the, 878
  temper, touch of, 152
  tower, from some, 635
Celestials directed the way, 271
Celibate, still is largely, 911
Cell, becomes a man, a single, 581
  dwell on a rock or in a, 22
  each in his narrow, 244
  in his, he meditates alone, 200
  is free from chimney-tax, 948
  was life's retreat, this narrow, 338
Cells and gibbets for the man, than, 512
  by unresting, 833
  of stone, 848
Cellar, born in a, 246
  damp, lived in a, 528
Cellarer, old Simon the, 647
Celluloid Babylon, glorious, 920
Celt, blind hysterics of the, 469
Cement glue and lime of love, 133
Cemetery, father's plot in the, 829
  gravestones in the, 938
  of Caius Cestius, 750
Censer, thine eye was on the, 451
Censors lurk, carping, 907
Censure from a foe, 219
  is the tax eminent men pay, 191
  mouths of wisest, 101
  of sarcastic tongues, 1017
  or praise, 232
  take each man's, 91
Census among pastors, 860
Cent, not one for tribute, 276
  what he did with every, 839

Cents, minutes to be dollars and, 387
  now I feel like thirty, 791
Centenary celebrations, 892
Centipede was happy, the, 942
Central heart nestles the seed, within its, 535
Centre, faith has, everywhere, 468
  from the thickening, 895
  is giving way, 1083
  of gravity, goes past the, 1064
  of the unfathomed, 386
  where the spinning world, 919
Centuries ago, in the solemn midnight, 479
  ago, restless, 805
  but this, all, 624
  come and go, 921
  down these nineteen, 763
  dusk of misty, 688
  every man has all the, in him, 641
  fall like grains of sand, 445
  forty, look down, 1060
  how shall I lie through, 488
  lasts no more than two, 1063
  may come and pass away, 369
  more gave a thumb, 569
  nor sequent, hit, 409
  of story, through, 443
  passed and his hair, 569
  the weight of, 708
Century begins, when a new, 1089
  dead, for a, 469
  in sight once in a, 524
  make the twentieth, 1069
  of sonnets, 488
  reclaimed for half a, 591
Cerberus, not like, 278
  of, and blackest midnight born, 160
Cerements, the Christ, rises from dead, 609
Ceremonial, in some sad, 755
Ceremonious air of gloom, 547
Ceremony, enforced, 83
  of the air, 867
  that to great ones 'longs, 36
  was devis'd to set a gloss on deeds, 80
Certain air to the countenance, 196
  amount of trouble, 853
  guests of state, 579
  life achiev'd by others' death, no, 58
  one thing, 271
  people call a certain age, 357
  the future is, how, 534
  to all, death is, 65
  unsoundness of mind, 397
Certainties, full of, 885
  hot for, 574
  sweet with, 692
Certainty, and quiet kind, 893
  for an uncertainty, 233
  man's, 785
  needs must spy some, 490
  of waking bliss, 158
  stage of, 1091
  to please, 289
  you have no, 966
Certum est, quia impossibile est, 1012

Cervantes and Will Shakespeare low, laid, 840
  on his galley, 827
  paupered arm of old, 531
  smiled Spain's chivalry away, 361
Cervantes' serious air, 214
Cessation from the pain of thought, 604
Chafed and hunted and much as may be, 144
Chaff and grain together, 567
  catch old birds with, 1037
  hope corn in, 351
  two bushels of, 44
Chaff-threshing churl, 1040
Chafferers, like friendly, 692
Chain about his wits, 960
  beads there are in a, 406
  death broke the vital, 231
  drags a lengthening, 249
  hanging in a golden, 151
  hour with beauty's, 337
  I forged in life, I wear the, 495
  joy so seldom weaves a, 334
  links in the bondsman's, 686
  of all virtues, 121
  slumber's, 336
  tempest scorns a, 402
  time winds the exhausted, 286
  to sport with beauty's, 337
Chains, a race that binds its body in, 655
  and slavery, price of, 270
  at curfew time, 158
  bound in those icy, 127
  crushed with, 764
  I break all, 697
  of chances, 565
  that bind the heart to home, 432
  untwisting all the, 160
Chained in the market-place, 372
Chair, members into a, 938
  no vacant, 677
  one vacant, 435
  sleep in the President's, 954
  there will be one vacant, 502
  vacant, is thine, 439
Chairs and half a candle, two old, 498
  three, in my house, 515
Chalice, our poisoned, 85
  verse is a, 1085
Chaliced flowers, 105
Chalk, arms of, 864
Chalky floor, march the, 907
Challenge double pity, 21
  life that dares send a, 165
Challenged, seen him damned ere I would have, 56
Chamber, come to the bridal, 362
  get you to my lady's, 97
  in the heart's inner, 446
  in the silent halls of death, 371
  in thy, kneeling, 480
  one need not be a, 585
  was peace, the name of the, 172
  whose window opened toward the sun-rising, 172
Chambers, gnats in our, 166
  of the sky, 364
  two, has the heart, 1070
  whisper softness in, 163
Chameleon cannot appear white, 997

Chameleons feed on light and air, 366
Chameleon's life is confusing, 909
Champagne and a chicken, 221
Champak odours pine, 368
Champion Alexander of Clane o' Wind-Holme, 922
  Darwinism had a, 930
  people have always some, 974
  thou fortune's, 57
  waiting in his place, our, 442
Champions fierce, four, 150
  pugilistic encounter between two, 407
Champmedy, my tongue at, 929
Chance, all, direction, 207
  await no gifts from, 546
  bludgeonings of, 692
  born without a, 792
  comes by gift of, 983
  comes from art, not, 211
  control, from, 735
  erring men call, 158
  for safety, our fairest, 972
  for you son, no, 872
  give them a, 512
  have the smallest, 864
  his counselor, 847
  is a sobriquet for providence, 1056
  luck is a, 743
  main, 68, 143, 1035
  now and then be right by, 263
  of Fortune's calms, no, 30
  of future meeting, 324
  or death, nativity, 35
  save by an evil, 791
  set my life on any, 86
  shall not control, 546
  skirts of happy, 468
  strike, should, 853
  that passed, never comes the, 570
  that, will bring us through, 547
  threw it in his way, 984
  to fight for them, 1089
  to show it, if you've not a, 942
  wisdom controlled by, 1030
Chances and mishaps, worldly, 76
  are I go, 601
  change by course, 30
  in trust to fortune's, 404
  like sunbeams pass you by, 591
  most disastrous, 100
  of the sword, dismal, 1067
Chancellor's conscience, 130
  encyclopedic mind, 398
  foot, 130
Chancery, up to heaven's, 242
Change and migration of the soul, 970
  and such a, 353
  be no robbery, 16
  can give no more, 183
  enchanting miracles of, 683
  ever-whirling wheele of, 25
  everything is the result of a, 1010
  fear of, perplexes monarchs, 149
  for progress, mistake, 396
  for worse pray gods, 28
  from day to night, 247
  from rocks to roses, with rapid, 405

Change, heavy, oh the, 159
  I detest all, 484
  in my face, like the, 697
  it brings but, 847
  manifold features of, 767
  nature loves so well to, 1010
  of fierce extremes, 150
  of flesh is here, what a, 129
  of many-coloured life, each, 231
  old love for new, 28
  ringing grooves of, 464
  seasons and their, 152
  strike me and you, 486
  the place but keep the pain, 199
  the stamp of nature, 95
  the universe is, 1010
  was his mistress, 847
  we think we see in life, 838
  with me, perhaps king would, 504
  within us, 441
Changes all your swells, ply all your, 540
  in our face, fortune's, 180
  works through endless, 378
Changed and such a change, 353
  in nothing am I, 99
  mind not to be, 148
  not in kind but in degree, 487
  the dandelions are, 619
Changeful dream, fickle as a, 308
Changeless glimmer of dead gray, 807
  prime, serene in, 375
  through joy or woe, 416
  would fain keep her, 575
Changelings, deformed children, which we call, 122
Changing seasons come and go, 442
Channel, and drum them up the, 765
  bare, lay its secret, 374
  diverted from its natural, 1051
  terrible gale in the, 906
Channels, flows through countless, 570
  for the stream of love, 441
Chanticleer, crow like, 49
  they call him, 758
Chants a doleful hymn, 58
Chaos and cosmos Hegel and Kant, 595
  and old night, 148
  black, comes again, 106
  breeds like, 636
  doth inherit, waste, 841
  is come again, 102
  is restored, empire of, 215
  now, come, 770
  of thought and passion, 207
Chaos-gloom, foot in, 544
Chaos-like together crushed, 216
Chap with wagging tail, 760
Chaps, three roguish, 954
Chapel, Devil builds a, 138, 187
  Devil will have a, 126
  dome, swelling out from, 554
  God's grand greenwood, 626
  of my soul, 816
Chapels had been churches, 44
Chap-fallen, quite, 97
Chaplain of the fleet, 780

Chaplet, rose hath fallen from thy, 309
Chapter of accidents, 222
  to the end of the, 1026
Chapters, whose sublime, 1085
Character any nobility in his, 1064
  bestowed by nature, 975
  bird of bad moral, 228
  elevate, 549
  everything except, 1063
  fault of the female, 1064
  hereditary strokes of, 949
  inward springs and relations of his, 376
  limitations of his own, 641
  man that makes a, 203
  of every man, tell the, 991
  of President Lincoln, 580
  of the Prince of Denmark left out, 311
  of the son, 974
  of the writer, 376
  of woman cannot be altered, 556
  one rag of, 675
  or conviction or social position, 1076
  pollertics of an accommodatin', 606
  propagates his, 950
  say nothing against a, 236
  set at thirty, 662
  simplicity of, 641
  talks away his own, 750
  the almost sacred, 1087
  to set, allowed my, 1087
  unaffected by maxims and sentiments, 662
  wholesome for the, 529
  will appear in spite of himself, 613
  with piety is packed, 830
  you reap a, 954
Characters, high, cries one, 164
  most women have no, 209
  of hell to trace, 244
  venerate four, 1056
Characteristic of the present age, 419
Characteristics, permanent and certain, 231
Charco! Charco! he cries, 572
Charge Chester charge, 308
  compulsive ardour gives the, 95
  God's holiest, 248
  if it be in his, 5
  in peace, a, 177
  is prepared, the, 205
  lay not my transgression to my, 57
  so stern a, 500
  when your daemon is in, 787
  with all thy chivalry, 328
Charges, die to save, 123
  for matter of, 147
Charged with punishments the scroll, 693
Charger, he turned his, 288
Chariest maid is prodigal enough, 90
Charing Cross in London Town, by, 899
Chariot of light, 271

Chariot that bears a human soul, 585
  the flying, 267
  time's winged, 169
Chariots, brazen, raged, 153
  of gold, says Timothy, 823
  why tarry the wheels of his, 1099
Chariot-wheel stands midway, 325
Charioteers, periwigged, 831
Charitable breast, at thy, 898
  intents, wicked or, 91
Charity, all mankind's concern is, 208
  anticipate, 1020
  as frozen as, 322
  be overstrained, 794
  begins at home, 144, 279
  broad mantle of, 329
  Christian pearl of, 443
  covers multitude of sins, 1122
  dependents on, 421
  envieth not, 1120
  faith, hope, 1120
  for all, malice toward none, 457, 806
  give him a little earth for, 74
  gracious, 612
  greatest of these is, 1120
  holding out his hand for, 1020
  nothing if I have not, 1120
  organized, scrimped and iced, 676
  pity gave ere, began, 250
  rarity of Christian, 392
  suffereth long, 1120
  the living need, 605
  to all mankind, 291
  vaunteth not itself, 1120
  will be rewarded, 166
  with the world, 192
Charity's eight degrees, 1020
  golden ladder, 1020
Charlatan, defamed by every, 469
Charles First had his Cromwell, 270
  gentle-hearted, 316
  V and the clocks, 739
Charlie is my darling the young chevalier, 294
Charlotte having seen his body, 481
  lived by a mountain-side, 501
  Werther had a love for, 481
Charm ache with air, 40
  age lends a double, 451
  blest with that, 289
  can soothe her melancholy, what, 253
  fades on nearer approach, 344
  for none, some have, 751
  from the skies, 365
  in melancholy, such a, 289
  indispensable to women, 751
  is a sort of bloom on a woman, 751
  no need of a remoter, 296
  nor witch hath power to, 89
  of a deed, 660
  of a life, 660
  of a love, 660
  of a theory, 1080
  of all the muses, 471
  of earliest birds, 152
  of Mrs. Jones, 788

Charm of poetry and love, 304
  of the act, 660
  one native, 251
  peculiar and indescribable, 645
  people who have, 606
  the grace that time makes strong, 650
  the interval, how shall I, 454
  there is a strange, 1042
  to stay the morning star, 316
  to the far away, owes its, 426
  us orator till the lion, 471
  what is, exactly, 751
Charms and talismans, wearing, 731
  freedom has a thousand, 262
  her modesty concealed, 224
  music hath, 193, 223
  of spring awaken, 573
  proclaimed unto Eve her dainty, 956
  Sabina has a thousand, 193
  solitude where are the, 263
  strike the sight, 212
  to rate her, 274
  were broken if revealed, 507
Charmed life, I bear a, 88
  with the foolish whistling of a name, 168
Charmer, sinner it or saint it, 209
  were t'other dear, away, 205
Charmers, hearken to the voice of, 1104
  wooing the caress like other, 358
Charming, he saw her, 224
  instincts, one of the, 1068
  is divine philosophy, 158
  left his voice so, 154
  little cupboard, 702
  never so wisely, 1104
Charon by the Stygian coast, 858
  has ferried poets, 811
  may forget, 326
Charon's staircase, 656
Charter large as the wind, 49
Chartered libertine, air a, 66
Charybdis your mother, 46
Chase big round tears in piteous, 48
  give her, 736
  now for a madcap galloping, 365
  unhurrying, 748
  wild-goose, 79
Chased with more spirit, 45
Chases the gloom of night, 604
Chasm, displayed a horrid, 200
  if in some desolate, 909
  which nothing can fill up, 261
Chasms and watery depths, 318
Chaste, accurate refined and, 972
  affectionate, great individual, 537
  and unexpressive she, 50
  as ice, be thou, 93
  as morning dew, 202
  as the icicle, 76
  as unsunned snow, 105
  many generous and some, 470
  pronounce it, 623
  to me, if she seem not, 22
  what care I how, she be, 22
Chasteneth whom he loveth, 1122
Chastises whom most he likes, 190

Chastity of honour, 260
  salamander a heroine in, 196
Chat, lingering for a moment's, 926
Chatter of irresponsible frivolity, 420
  silvern, 748
  we are undone of, 650
Chatters of science and logic, he, 406
Chatterton marvellous boy, 297
Chaucer at Woodstock, 438
  Dan, 25
  glossary necessary for, 886
  I will not lodge thee by, 119
  influence of, 412
  learned, 119
  that broad famous poet, 117
  through all the works of, 318
  was alive and hale, 326
  with his clasp of things, 428
Chaucer's speech, rich as, 558
Chaunge be no robbry, 16, 357
Chavender or chub, 140
Chavignon St. Mihiel Meuse-Argonne, 866
Cheap as stinking mackerel, 62
  as wishing, so very, 509
  defence of nations, 260
  fame then was, 178
  good counsel is, 124
  labor, Chinese, 644
  obtain too, 271
  provision, 217
  standing as sitting, 192
Cheapness of literature, 532
Cheat, life 't is all a, 178
  oneself is the first and worst fraud, to, 506
  three Greeks to, a Jew, 559
  three Jews to, an Armenian, 559
Cheated, impossible to be, 411
  pleasure of being, 143
  stockings lean and long, 763
  worth while to be, 788
Cheater time, old bald, 119
Check to loose behaviour, 197
Checked for silence, never tax'd for speech, 53
Checkered dress, 696
Cheek a little red, 209
  by joule, 1031
  changing, sinking heart, 356
  chin knuckle or knee, 522
  drew iron tears down Pluto's, 161
  feed on her damask, 55
  he that loves a rosy, 140
  her lip, language in her, 75
  like the rose is, her, 388
  o'er her warm, 243
  of a child, brow of a woman or, 1085
  of apple-blossom, and a, 470
  of night, hangs upon the, 77
  of tan, barefoot boy with, 442
  of the noble and bold, 479
  tear down virtue's manly, 267
  that I might touch that, 78
  upon her hand, 78
Cheeks, blow winds crack your, 98
  crimson in thy, 80

Cheeks, eloquent blood spoke in her, 118
  famine is in thy, 80
  make pale my, with care, 132
  may fade and hollow, 690
  of sorry grain, 158
  stain my man's, 98
Cheel's full joys, 765
Cheer, be of good, 1118
  but not inebriate, 204, 265
  greet with a, 494
  hearty faith and honest, 574
  make good, play and, 19
  onward with a, 825
  small, and great welcome, 37
  to, and bless, 626
  unite with a, 271
Cheers for the sailors, 664
  for the soldiers, 664
  no worse than, 743
  the tar's labour tobacco, 358
  three, and a tiger, 521
  three, for war, 1090
Cheer'd with ends of verse, 142
Cheerer of his spirits, 139
  at morn he wakes, 249
  clatter of Barrie's cans, 906
  countenance, 1107
  dawn, May-time and the, 299
  godliness in, 298
  hour, God sends a, 162
  on the days they worked, 228
  ways of men, 151
  yesterdays, man of, 303
Cheerfulness a kind of daylight in the mind, 197
  a manly hilarity, 318
  no warmth no, 391
Cheering wine, pour forth the, 404
Cheerly she loves me dearly, 382
Cheese, island of, 1056
  moon made of green, 17, 1025
  muscular, 887
  toasted mostly, dreamed of, 704
Chef-d'oeuvre for the highest, 535
Chelsea, dead as, 944
Cheops' pyramid, hid under, 776
Cheque at a good restaurant, able to pay with, 803
Cheque-books, stubs of the victim's, 580
Chequer-board of nights and days, 1019
Chere, she was al his, 6
Cherish a just and lasting peace, 457
  those hearts that hate thee, 73
  to love and to, 1128
Cherished in slimy waters, 551
  memory of the loved and lost, 457
  secret wish, now obey thy, 537
Cherokee, hears the last cry of the wild, 508
Cherries grow that none may buy, 121
  those, fairly do enclose, 121
Cherry bough could be, white a, 883
  like to a double, 43
  loveliest of trees the, 742

Cherry ripe ripe ripe I cry, 133
  ripe themselves do cry, 121
  three bites of a, 1026
  tree, Washington and the, 941
Cherry-isle, there's the land, 133
Cherry-orchards blow, 692
Cherry-pit, to play with Satan at, 55
Cherub, he rode upon a, 1103
  sweet little, 274
Cherubs earn their wage, 851
  rise, poor black, 936
  will begin, 940
Cherubim, heaven's, 85
Cherubin, rose-lipped, 103
Cherubins, young-eyed, 47
Chest against the foes, his, 248
  of drawers by day, 251
  on a dead man's, 704
Chests of the eight are tightening, 862
Chess-board, world is a, 563
Chester charge on Stanley on, 308
Chestnut is proud and the lilac's pretty, 732
  salute each mouldy, 601
Chestnut-tree, since first beneath the, 446
Chevalier, Charlie is my darling the young, 294
Cheveril consciences, 126
Chew the cud and are silent, 260
Chewed and digested, books to be, 111
Chewing the food of fancy, 51
Chi fa ingiuria non perdona mai, 178
Chian strand on the, 317
Chicago sitteth at the northwest gates, 806
Chicane, over violence or, 925
Chicanery, everything even, 1069
Chickamauga's solitudes, 690
Chicken and champagne, 221
  I'm not a, 451
  in every pot, 588
  once a pretty, 665
  she's no, 192
Chickens, all my pretty, 88
  before they are hatched, reckon not on, 369
  come home to roost, 425
  count their, ere they are hatched, 143, 1042
  count your, 963
  curses are like young, 425
  hen gathereth her, 1116
  quarrelling like people, 852
Chidden still murmurs, 802
Chiding, better a little, 35
Chief a rod, wit's a feather a, 208
  business in life is to pay, 654
  hail to the, 308
  the, octogenarian, 299
  want in life, 414
Chiefs in bloody fights, 218
Chief's pride, vain the, 214
Chief-justice was rich quiet and infamous, 399
Chiel's amang ye takin' notes, 286
Child a home, gives a, 832
  a naked, new-born, 275
  a puppy and a kitten, 812
  a rose, or anything, 807
  a simple, draws its breath, 295

Child a treat, gives a, 832
  again just for tonight, 595
  an amiable, 596
  and she was a child, I was a, 459
  as yet a, nor yet a fool, 213
  because he is my little, 1084
  because I am nobody's, 557
  burnt, craves the flame, 912
  came with her, 951
  counted each His loving, 755
  did cry, how that, 802
  doth reap one precious gain, 299
  dreads the fire, a burnt, 15
  duty's faithful, 393
  fast fold thy, 672
  get with, a mandrake root, 117
  give a little love to a, 532
  great with, 35
  happy Christian, 345
  has its fairy godmother in its soul, 749
  her innocence, a, 175
  hid in the womb of time, 369
  I have seen a curious, 302
  I stand, here a little, 134
  in simplicity, a, 217
  in the basement, little sick, 715
  infirm, fear not then thou, 409
  is a little lonely, 915
  is father to the man, 156, 297
  is it well with the, 1101
  is ready for either world, 313
  keeps a secret so well as a, 1068
  learn sooner than a song, what will a, 214
  like a froward, 172
  like a marvelous old wise, 929
  like a tired, 367
  like the hands of a little, 639
  listens like a three years', 314
  may joy to hear, songs every, 281
  meet nurse for a poetic, 307
  men ne'er spend their fury on a, 71
  misses the unsaid good-night, 838
  name in the heart of a, 859
  never saw a sweeter, 919
  of action thought is the, 420
  of calamity, 616
  of earth and sky, 794
  of hope, wait thou, 477
  of immortal youth, gained a, 558
  of misery, baptized in tears, 269
  of our grandmother Eve, 41
  of pure unclouded brow, 598
  of the boundless prairie, 642
  of the Cyclades, 808
  of thought, experience is the, 420
  of Ver, first-born, 132
  old man is twice a, 92
  on a cloud, saw a, 281
  on the homeless street, 708
  pleased with a rattle, 208
  ranked as a mere, 1072
  Roland to the dark tower came, 309

Child Rowland to the dark tower came, 99
  saving a little, 639
  Shakespeare fancy's, 160
  should always say what's true, 702
  should grow into the man, 439
  spake as a, 1120
  speaking angrily to any, 429
  sports of children satisfy the, 249
  that is born on the Sabbath, 956
  the thoughts of a, 600
  to have a thankless, 98
  to its mother, bringest the, 960
  train up a, 1108
  use of a new-born, 868
  was carried, my third, 1055
  was diseased at birth, 902
  what constitutes a, 1007
  what it is to be a, 749
  when I was a, 1120
  where is my, 356
  wise father knows his own, 45
Child's heart to a child, 800
  kiss, a, 427
  sob in the silence, 428
  strength, credulity is the, 323
Childes pley, it is no, 7
Childhood again, give me my, 595
  careless strayed, 243
  dwarfing of, 1067
  fleeted by, how my, 405
  from, to his journey's end, 1073
  in my days of, 325
  instincts of female, 1068
  manhood and decrepit age, 135
  of eternity, 576
  of the world, 694
  old age but second, 972
  scenes of my, 348
  shows the man, 156
  womanhood and, fleet, 434
Childhood's cheek, tear down, 309
  dreams are twined, 598
  hour, from, 338, 590
Childish days, sweet, 297
  ignorance, it was a, 390
  things, I put away, 1120
  treble, turning again toward, 50
Childishness, second, 50
Childlike and bland, 644
  heaven is of the, 705
Children and fooles cannot lye, 15
  and fools want everything, 183
  and their parents, 723
  ardent for some desperate glory, 918
  are what mothers are, 326
  as gypsies serve stolen, 278
  as living arrows, 879
  breed of their, 184
  bright and agreeable, 1008
  bright faces of, 643
  but for my, 895
  call her blessed, 1109
  clinging to their gown, 665
  comfort of thy, 71
  do, calling out as, 917
  father's sin upon the, 46

Children, fear in, increased with tales, 109
  fear to go in the dark, 109
  followed with endearing wile, 251
  from play, holdeth, 27
  from these brown-handed, 729
  gathering pebbles, 156
  hapless, 586
  have their little language, 564
  I have had five, 1055
  impediments to great enter- prises, 110
  in a house, too many, 1027
  in their laughter, follow after, 839
  inter their parents, in peace, 967
  kind and natural, were all thy, 66
  laugh and play, that made the, 362
  learn to walk, 809
  learne to creepe, 15
  like olive plants, 1106
  like truant, 809
  lips and hearts of little, 482
  lisping soul on the lips of, 1069
  lost, silent above the flowers her, 565
  mother who talks about her, 419
  neighbors', are the worst, 907
  never forgot his, 948
  nine small, 947
  no longer any, 1047
  nor God, neither, 778
  of a larger growth, 177
  of an idle brain, 77
  of blindness, 736
  of light, 1117
  of men! not that your age, 546
  of necessity, 617
  of one family fall out, 198
  of pride, king over, 783
  of the brain, books the, 191
  of the great mother-tongue, 558
  of the wind, 717
  of this world, 1117
  of yesterday, 656
  on wheels, put our, 849
  parents bore their, 721
  Rahel weeping for her, 1113
  should never be lazy and sad, 431
  so dear that I held, 567
  spoke bad English, 766
  sports of, 249
  tale which holdeth, from play, 27
  to their fathers, heart of the, 1114
  toys to the great, leave, 225
  turn the fathers to the, 1114
  way to rear up, 429
  weep when we lie low, 553
  weeping, do ye hear the, 428
  were not used to bearing, 996
  who tumble barefooted, 854
  wisdom justified of her, 1115
  with high spirits, mirth of, 426
  wives and grandsires, 1059
  you will rise, sweet happy, 474
Children's children will have to toil, 689
  griefs, 749

Children's hour, known as the, 434
  teeth set on edge, 1113
  ways and wiles, 634
Chill all its own, 815
  detraction, 651
  no, in wintry age, 263
  November's surly blast, 284
  of its dark-running wave, 652
  penury, 245
  September, full many a, 451
  winds whistle shrill icy and, 481
Chills and fever she died, of, 903
  breathed its killing, 703
  the lap of May, 249
Chillun in de bed, tu'nin' of de, 820
Chilly winds went whistling by, 369
Chimborazo Cotopaxi took me by the hand, 907
Chime, ever peacefully, silver waves, 480
  faintly as tolls the evening, 169, 334
  sun with his planets in, 449
  to guide their, 169
Chimes at midnight, 65
  detected by the poverty of his, 415
  of eternal peace, 443
Chimera, what a, is man, 1047
Chimeras dire, Hydras and, 150
Chimings from the far-off tower, 618
Chimley-piece, leave the bottle on the, 495
Chimney, and heated hot, a little, 52, 436
  in my father's house, 69
  stockings were hung by the, 332
Chimney-corner, men from the, 27
Chimney-sweepers come to dust, 106
Chimney-tax, this cell is free, from, 948
Chimpanzee, behold the, 768
Chin, buries her, 858
  close-buttoned to the, 266
  new-reaped like a stubble-land, 61
  pretty page with dimpled, 481
  some bee had stung, 163
  tying her bonnet under her, 600
  with an upward, 913
  woo with an unhairy, 618
China bowl of ice, 637
  'crost the bay, 782
  dishes, not, but good, 35
  fall, though, 209
  luxury of tea, 323
  plates, them that has, 750
  that's ancient and blue, 673
  to Peru, mankind from, 230, 258
Chinaman, every fourth person born is a, 943
Chinaman's chance, not a, 644
Chinee, the heathen, 644
Chinese cheap labor, 644
  nightingale, 856
  poetry, 762

Chink, importunate, 260
  in the roof, stopping a, 620
Chinks of her body, 147
  that time has made, 146, 289
Chip of the old block, 145, 261
Chips, carpenter is known by his,
  192
  fall where they may, 578
Chirps and twitters, 621
Chirrup, gay batrachian, 933
Chisel keen, the sculptor's, 445
  plough loom and, 950
  trace, ne'er did Grecian, 308
  what fine, could ever cut
  breath, 57
Chivalrous, quixotic sense of the,
  461
Chivalry, age of, is gone, 260
  and state, with their, 507
  beauty and her, 352
  charge with all thy, 328
  Spain's, 361
Chloroform, peaceful departure
  by, 695
Choice, all hev our, 699
  and master spirits, 82
  challenged with a peace-time,
  830
  feast us, light and, 162
  hidden handful, 531
  Hobson's, 126
  in rotten apples, there's small,
  52
  makes our friends, 1056
  of a horse and a wife, 545
  of friends, careful in your,
  1083
  the difficulty in life is the, 709
  the terrible, 491
  word and measured phrase, 297
Choices, passion of their, 888
Choicely good, old-fashioned poetry but, 140
Choir above her head, sang, 653
  invisible, O may I join the, 520
  sorry I disturb the, 692
Choirs, bare ruined, 108
Choked with ambition of the
  meaner sort, 68
Chokin' in my throat, 698
Choler, aggravate your, 65
  consume your own, 379
Choleric who has subdued, 1056
  word in the captain's, 36
Choose a firm cloud, 209
  an author as you choose a
  friend, 180
  my own, if life's a flower I,
  406
  not alone a proper mate, 264
  thine own time, 273
  where to, their place, 156
  which of the two to, 195
  while yet unborn, things we,
  572
Choosers, beggars no, 14, 131
Choosing and beginning late, 154
Chop-fallen funeral processions,
  1089
Chopin, when George Sand met,
  911
Chord, harping on that minor,
  718
  in melancholy, 390
  in unison is touched, 266
  life's common, 492

Chord, lyre of one rich-hearted,
  728
  one mournful, 647
Chords in the most reckless heart,
  461
  most fit, 664
  that vibrate sweetest pleasure,
  287
Chores, celestial, 936
Chorister, bobolink for a, 584
Chortled in his joy, 598
Chorus fortissimo ha, ha, ha, 283
  has a rousing, 810
  landlord's laugh was ready, 287
  of praise, unanimous, 1086
  what a, 326
Chorus-ending from Euripides,
  488
Chorus-note, the fisher's, 288
Chosen and chainless land, 634
  but few are, 1115
  start content with ruin, 834
  the less is to be, 9
Christ a man like us, was, 547
  again should visit earth, if, 578
  ain't a-going to be too hard,
  639
  Child, that frightens the, 898
  everyone in the world is, 841
  Gethsemane, for, 851
  have wrought this miracle,
  would, 541
  He rides the lowly, 851
  himself chose only twelve, 657
  himself was poor, 124
  his pure soul unto his captain, 60
  ideal given by, 1074
  if haloed, 828
  in heaven, the sin forgiven by,
  431
  in the name of a cautious, 676
  Jesus, I served, 758
  on Calvary, torn O, 686
  ring in the, 469
  rises from dead cerements the,
  609
  save us all from a death, 433
  sees white in Judas's heart, 650
  simplicity there is in, 247
  so Judas did to, 60
  stood in the court, 688
  that it were possible, ah, 469
  the plough, O, 832
  to live is, 1121
  took the kindness and forgave
  the theft, 490
  walking on the water, 749
  was born across the sea, 522
  was born, ere, 573
  was crowned in cruel scorn, 586
  was taken from the rood, when,
  681
  was the soul of rapture, 880
  went agin' war an' pillage, 526
  who drives the furrow straight,
  832
  who holds the open gate, 832
Christ's chosen flock, 305
  in a sacred life, 458
Christ-like for sin to grieve, 435
Christendom, last link with, 787
  may be coming to an end, 769
Christening was a coronation,
  1085
Christian bell was heard, 375

Christian charity, rarity of, 392
  child, a happy, 345
  creed, who gave your, 657
  days, in these, 345
  duty, pitied men whose views
  of, 522
  every inch of him, 1034
  faithful man, as I am a, 71
  ground, buried not so far from,
  928
  ground, every vice on, 215
  is God Almighty's gentleman,
  a, 174
  is the highest style of man, a,
  174, 202
  love among the churches, 471
  Mohammedan agnostic monist,
  728
  pearl of charity, the, 443
  perfectly like a, 217
  Protestant or priest, 657
  religion dissipating itself into
  metaphysics, 378
  Science, definition of, 549
  slave, you were a, 693
  socialism is but the holy water,
  1072
  souls, 611
  thou persuadest me to be a,
  1119
  without hypocrisy, 599
  word of a gentleman and a,
  1037
Christians agree in essential articles, 234
  good, good citizens, 339
  have burnt each other, 358
  love one another, how these,
  1012
  of the best edition, 1026
  pray, where early, 880
  still declare themselves, 1082
  want something for nothing,
  721
  were on the earth, 573
  what these, are, 45
Christianity, a local thing called,
  650
  abandoned at thirteen, 744
  alcohol and, 1081
  essential part of, 762
  fault of, 1016
  great deal of, 785
  in the world not a miracle, 415
  open to question, 556
  the one great curse, 1082
  was muscular, his, 421
  who have renounced, 1074
Christmas, a sweeter, 935
  and New Years, best of wishes
  for, 498
  board around the, 653
  books incident upon new year,
  483
  brought his sports again, 305
  but jest 'fore, 699
  comes but once a year, 19, 446
  day may ever come, 653
  desire a rose, at, 40
  home at, 498
  in lands of the fir-tree and
  palm, 612
  is here winds whistle, 481
  is over and business is business,
  867
  merry still, we'll keep our, 308

Christmas morn, blest, 549
  to-night, everywhere every-
    where, 612
  't was the night before, 332
  well, how to keep, 495
  wid dem sheriffs in de sky,
    712
  yet, ne'er saw, 604
Christmas-tide, I love the, 812
Christopher Robin goes hoppity,
    876
Chronic melancholy, 651
Chronicle, his own glass, his own
    trumpet, his own, 75
  of day by day, 33
  of nations, 609
  small beer, 101
Chronicles, look in the, 51
  love to read their, 507
  of the time, 93
Chronicler of time oldest, 681
  such an honest, 74
Chrononhotonthologos, 189
Chrysophrase glowing, brilliant
    like, 432
Chub, chavender or, 140
Chuck 'im out, the brute, 781
Chuckle, make one's fancy, 172
  replied, with a, 870
Church and mart, press too close
    in, 428
  and Sabbath, resolved that,
    924
  and science two powerful sets
    of vested interests, 614
  and state separate, keep, 550
  army, physic law, 267
  beyond the village, 517
  built God a, 263
  by daylight, can see a, 38
  clock at ten, stands the, 893
  duties of that, 1061
  forgotten the inside of a, 62
  I like a, I like a cowl, 408
  I will build my, 1115
  in its place shall rise another,
    647
  keep the Sabbath going to, 584
  mother, hold by the ould, 786
  naught in world or, or state,
    528
  of England best religion, 744
  of Jesus constant will remain,
    605
  plain as way to parish, 49
  seed of the, 1012
  should have a tapering spire,
    789
  the neer to, the further from
    God, 13
  to be of no, is dangerous, 233
  to, with a great show, 182
  where bells have knoll'd to, 49
  where God built a, 1024
  white, above thin trees, 831
  who builds to God a, 210
  without a bishop, 394
Churches and creeds are lost in
    the mists, 569
  bless all the, 456
  chapels had been, 44
  Christian love among the, 471
  grow, lived where, 878
  peace of great, 854
  the scab of, 114
  with spire steeples, 302

Church's strength, emblem of the,
    789
Church-door, wide as a, 79
Church-going bell, 264
Churchman be, would I that
    cowléd, 408
Churchyard mould, 391
  never can see the old, 517
  sod, nest in the, 523
  thing, a palsy-stricken, 383
Churchyards yawn, when, 95
Churl, chaff-threshing, 1040
Churlish, the reply, 51
Chymist, fiddler statesman, 174
Cicero, Demosthenes or, 292
Cigar, a good five-cent, 714
  an end of a, 590
  give me a, 358
  I smoked my last, 544
  is a smoke, a good, 776
  is as great a comfort, 425
  smoke-wreaths of this free,
    605
  smokes a fifty-cent, 867
Cigars, women poets who smoke,
    931
Cigarette and cigar men were
    smitten, 902
  the amulet, 746
Cigarettes no ashes, had, 674
Cigarettum, smoked his, 867
Cimmerian darkness, 327
Cincinnatus of the west, 357
  ploughing in his field, 994
Cinders ashes dust, 383
Cinnamon-bear in spring, brown
    as a, 928
Cipher too, he could write and,
    251
Circle, all of us live too much in
    a, 420
  call fools into a, 48
  enchanted, 576
  grazes confines of space, whose,
    553
  he drew a, 708
  in as small a, 1057
  in water, like a, 68
  in which his claims are rec-
    ognized, 421
  life a self-evolving, 420
  of ideas, think beyond present,
    689
  of the golden year, 464
  spreads, the desert, 322
  swinging round the, 446
  that took him in, 708
  vicious, 607
  which can amuse itself, 645
  within that, none durst walk,
    178
Circles of unimpaired delight, 933
Circled orb, changes in her, 78
Circling faces, from the, 879
Circuit, runs the great, 265
Circuitous and obscure, 735
Circular madness on them shut,
    937
Circulating library, 277
Circulation of the blood, 1068
Circumcised dog, 104
Circumference, fatal, 602
Circumlocution office, 497
Circumnavigator of the soul, 789
Circumspection, pink of courtesy
    and, 253

Circumstance allows, best his,
    201
  breasts the blows of, 468
  lie with, 51
  of glorious war, 102
  pomp and, 102
  shrieking, 783
Circumstances alter cases, 387
  concatenation of, 342
  creature of, 420
  creatures of men, 420
  discordant harmony of, 260
  fortuitous, 310
  make the man, 377
  not to blame, 720
  over which I have no control,
    293
  train of, 271
Circumstantial evidence is very
    strong, 515
  things, 172
Circumvent God, one that would,
    96
Cistern, wheel broken at the,
    1110
Citadel, bust outlasts the, 1071
  towered, 105
Citandum, ane thing they call,
    11
Citations from the poets, avoid,
    971
Cities, alabaster, 737
  attraction of, 739
  crowded, wail its stroke, 363
  fouled by smoke, 814
  glorious, why build these, 688
  hum of human, 353
  lie at the monster's feet, 895
  of old time, 691
  of men and manners, 464
  of the soul, mist-blue, 889
  remote from, lived a swain,
    206
  seven, claimed him, 493
  seven, warred for Homer, 129
  soar along the stormy coast,
    410
  that claimed Homer, 910
  towered, please us, 160
Citizen, a solid, 884
  disappear, man and, 1074
  free nation great, 1068
  of all the land, humblest,
    752
  of the best-constituted state,
    1076
  of the world, 424, 1005, 1016
  of the world, essayist a, 753
  private, without reproach, 599
Citizens, chief business of the,
    1054
  fat and greasy, 48
  good Christians good, 339
  hearts of the, 268
  how to make people respon-
    sible, 722
  of death's grey land, 891
  of New York, 935
  of the middle class, 975
  of the U.S.S.R., 1093
  typical, all born British, 871
City, a populous and smoky,
    367
  adorned by private effort, 532
  and proud seat of Lucifer, 155
  at large, infecting the, 998

City, better than he that taketh a, 1107
built upon the top of a hill, a, 1126
Cain made the first, 168
canals and dockyards make the, 960
extol the absent, 985
great, makes a, 688
great, that with greatest man, 535
in the sea, 289
is not builded in a day, 857
is the teacher, 960
is thy seat, a prostrate, 403
kind to actresses, 859
kind to the poor dull, 732
land, thing raised on, is taxes, 582
lies, unheaven'd the, 701
long in populous, pent, 154
lyric city, 859
much like London, 367
new Jerusalem, the holy, 1123
obedient to his will, 973
of all time and all the world, 422
of carpenters, 859
of dreadful height, 819
of gold, went to the, 798
of New York, 859
of Prague, the beautiful, 625
of sleep, back from the, 784
of the big shoulders, 855
of the great king, 1104
of the soul, Rome the, 354
pent, long in, 383
proud is the, 811
red of the marvellous, 931
rose-red, 500
seemed a speck of light, 705
some calm place, some, 834
that I love be great, may the, 688
that is set on a hill, 1114
that was her destination, 933
the eternal, 231
to be admired by Americans, 637
wanting to a, 970
we have no continuing, 1122
what is the, but the people, 76
when in strange, worship its gods, 126
worn and gray, little, 673
worth visiting, 859
wrought in flame, 859
you will read of, 784
City's disinherited, 750
infamy, worst of the, 806
jar, mine to feel amid the, 546
smoke-stained walls, 571
City-builder, envy not the, 380
Civet, give me an ounce of, 99
in the room, talk with, 263
Civic manhood firm against the crowd, 466
Civil discord, effects from, 195
law, maxims of the, 232
limitation daunts, 575
over violent or over, 174
political and religious rights, 949
sea grew, at her song, 42
so, that nobody thanked him, 236

Civil, too, by half, 278
Civilian, one to a million that any, 623
Civilities of life, the sweet, 176
Civility, I see a wild, 133
Civilization a crust over revolution, 740
and prosperity not synonymous, 739
approaching a long winter, 769
fragments of, 937
itself, speech is, 1089
of to-day, in the, 538
only a wrappage, 381
progresses towards death, 741
the first old, 926
the first permanent, 926
to conquer another one, 762
true test of, 235
value of a Pullman, 635
what a, 980
Civilized life, efflorescence of, 580
man can not live without cooks, 592
world a-wondering and worshipping, 490
Civilizers of man, the two, 419
Clad, go poorly, 620
in blak or reed, bokes, 5
in blue and gold, 288
in russet mantle, 89
venture thinly, 501
Claes, gars auld, 284
Claim higher, Stuart or Nassau, 190
is just, her, 424
stake out your, 936
Claims, answer a thousand, 565
of long descent, 462
vaunt their empty, 700
who make no, 574
Clamor always more or less insane, 377
of the crowded street, 439
peace amidst the, 931
the workshop's, 873
Clamours, Jove's dread, 102
of a venal press, 478
Clamorous pauperism feasteth while honest, 477
Clan, sophist schools and learned, 408
Clans, what time the plaided, 500
Clang of hurrying feet, 500
Clap of thunder in a fair day, 172
Clap-trap, art independent of all, 611
Clare, John, that strange insane poet, 1078
Claret, a bumper of, 348
and sherry theorbo and voice, 164
is the liquor for boys, 237
Clarion, sound sound the, 310
Clash by night, where ignorant armies, 546
Clasp clasping a shred of gold, 289
its dear detaining, 682
ne'er let go her, 1058
of things divine, 428
Clasps, that book in gold, 77
Claspèd hands, new Niobe with, 565

Class and clan, 'gainst, 424
buyers of every, 1079
citizens of the middle, 975
his, is extinguished with him, 412
lies late and snores, 935
nor rank, we consider neither, 970
or classes, this or that, 1086
women of the better, 768
Classes are exasperated, when, 582
decay and disappear, 1072
of intellects, three, 1023
tempt the upper, 730
that stand face to face, 1072
Classic bent, 780
everybody wants to have read, 615
ground, 195
nobody wants to read, 615
produced by coöperation, 771
that the world has lost, 845
Classics as voucher of scholastic respectability, 731
are always modern, the, 426
evidence of wasted time, 731
have a strange charm in a country inn, 413
only primitive literature, 805
science more stimulating than, 914
Classical quotation, 237
Claw, painting a lion from the, 960
Claws, skilful way you hide your, 1085
Clay and wattles made, of, 790
at last but breathing, 223
beautiful pale, 595
blind his soul with, 466
Caesar dead and turned to, 97
cloven, 631
consume this, 671
feet part of iron and part of, 1113
fruitful, 523
has its own, 857
has such red mouths, 803
if, could think, 303
imprisoned in the, 677
inhabits common, 767
kind embrace of, 898
lies still, 742
love not ye hopeless sons of, 446
merely a compost of, 927
mortal made of, 274
of humankind, porcelain, 179
porcelain of human, 179, 360
potter power over the, 1119
querulous and uncivil, 938
reverence the, 449
tenement of, 173
to glorify his, 880
wrought in common, 784
Clay-shuttered doors, 749
Claymore, Scotland's broad, 500
Clean, hath gone from thee, 590
keep, be as fruit, 170
of all my dust, 886
sweet summer sky, grant me a, 905
thing, art the only, 1083

Clean-shirt-day, 233
Clean-winged hearth, 443
Cleanliness a bore, 570
　is a great virtue, 570
　next to godliness, 112, 226
Cleanly, leave sack and live, 63
Cleanness of body, 112
Cleanse the stuffed bosom, 88
　thou me from secret faults,
　1103
Clear and manifest as the nose,
　33, 125
　as a whistle, 221
　call for me, and one, 472
　cold depths, 675
　day that maketh all things,
　643
　deep yet, 167
　fire and a clean hearth, 323
　for life, 214
　from any image of offence,
　55
　his right was, 948
　if I am not, 1063
　in his great office, 85
　the coast was, 31
　to, myself of cants, 378
　unconquerable cry, 654
　without strife, brook's motion,
　501
Clearer than the noonday, 1102
Clearing-house of the world,
　London, 621
Clearness is treason, 811
　of the intuitive powers, 475
　of the sky, 666
Cleave ever to the sunnier side,
　471
Cleaving to the dream, 650
Cleon dwelleth in a palace, 503
　hath a million acres, 503
Cleopatra night drinks all, 664
　nose of, 1047
　wrapped in the coverlet, 1000
Clergyman, duty of a, 312
　who is also a man of business,
　1016
Clergymen, men, women and, 313
Clergymen's households gener-
　ally unhappy, 613
Clerical printless toe, 893
Clerk, every solicitor's, 850
　foredoomed, 212
　me no clerks, 946
　scarce less illustrious, 264
　ther was of Oxenford, 5
Clerks greatest not the wisest, 6,
　16
　have missed the mark, 325
　one can hardly bother the, 928
Clever, he means to be, 426
　let who will be, 523, 868
　man by nature, 290
　men are good, 376
　people were good, 942
　so rude to the good, 942
Click click death is prancing,
　1078
Clicked behind the door, 251
Clients, good counsellors lack no,
　35
Cliff, as some tall, 251
　glittering night-time, 933
　I saw, once on a, 920
　in a coign of, 633
　'round the top of the, 640

Cliffs, pillared, like sentries, 707
Climate, change in moral, 877
　change their, 985
　coal is a portable, 413
　cold, or years, 154
　heaven for, 750
　in the market with a, 838
　Pilgrims fell upon an un-
　genial, 550
Climates councils governments,
　464
Climax of human philosophy,
　803
　some flaming fatal, 891
　verging toward some, 733
Climb, fain would I, 22
　high climb far, 957
　to what they were before, 87
　not at all, 22
　out beyond the limitations of
　his character, 641
Climber-up of knees, 290
Climber-upward turns his face,
　82
Climbing sorrow, down thou, 98
Climbs as rarely falls, who never,
　443
Clime, cold in blood, cold in,
　355
　crusaders from some infernal,
　451
　deeds done in their, 355
　in every, adored, 216
　in every age and, 206
　in some brighter, 273
　in the eastern, 153
　linger in our northern, 308
　our tongue is known in every,
　394
　to clime, from, 840
　to make a happy fireside, 286
Climes beyond the western main,
　250
　cloudless, and starry skies,
　356
　humours turn with, 209
　in all, we pitch our tents, 771
Cling, the greenest mosses, 441
Clink of cups, 771
　of the ice in the pitcher, 698
Clip an angel's wings, 383
　his morning nap, thought to,
　510
Clipper rolled in a great swell,
　833
Clique that styles itself, 426
Cliques, the worst, 721
Cloak be threadbare, though
　your, 690
　camlet, with gold buttons, 180
　dropped your dusty, 652
　martial, around him, 364
　not alone my inky, 89
　take thy old, about thee, 256
　that covers my bright array,
　1085
　when you sleep in your, 545
Cloaked from head to foot, 468
Clock collected in the tower, 743
　condition of being turned into
　a, 564
　in the steeple, 600
　indicates the moment, 535
　is always slow, 845
　like the finger of a, 265
　long hour by Shrewsbury, 63

Clock, my grandfather's, 601
　on time with the borough, 939
　or bell, no slave of, 878
　stands the church, 893
　strikes two, when the, 644
　the varnished, 251
　ticks on, the old, 909
　was in the tower, before a, 681
　worn out with eating time,
　178
Clocks, cannot make two, agree,
　739
　what need of, 801
Clock-peddler the schoolmaster
　the senator, 1070
Clockwork joints of supple gold,
　632
Clod a piece of orange peel, 590
　from which we grow the demi-
　god, 732
　of ailments, feverish selfish
　little, 720
　one with the heavy, 880
　push away the, 648
　to become a kneaded, 36
Clog of his body, 147
Cloistered virtue, fugitive and,
　163
Close against the sky, 390
　and sharp on heart and brain,
　662
　at home, beauty wrought lies,
　442
　but untouching, 903
　have mournful, 809
　music at the, 59
　of day, at, 1027
　of life, at the, 966
　of one sad day, 705
　of the day, at the, 269
　of the envoy, 671
　one stands up, 165
　our souls sit, 177
　the shutters fast, 265
　the wall up with our English
　dead, 66
　up his eyes and draw the cur-
　tain, 69
　we press too, 428
　yet lived she at its, 473
Close-buttoned to the chin, 266
Closed lips hurt no one, 1001
Close-knit strands, 955
Closeness, all dedicated to, 32
　of family ties in Scotland, 751
　of the place, 984
Close-shorn sheep, 138
Closet, do very well in a, 222
　of her mind, in a, 883
Closing of an eye, yet the sweet,
　480
Cloth, cut my coat after my, 13
　to us, meat and drink and,
　1026
Cloths, heavens' embroidered, 790
Clothe a man with rags, 1108
　my naked villany, 71
Clo'es an' good styla an' playnta
　cash, 814
Clothes, brushers of noblemen's,
　113
　came in, since, 498
　cargoes of meat drink and, 950
　distinguished men and clothes,
　629
　fond to shew our, 199

Clothes for myself and wife, 181
  good smell of old, 894
  let us wear theirs and they our,
    124
  liquefaction of her, 134
  nothing to wear but, 729
  old, are not venerable, 380
  on a hickory limb, hang your,
    957
  require new, 514
  through tattered, 99
  thrown on with a pitchfork,
    192
  walked away with their, 419
  wantonness in, 133
  when he put on his, 254
Clothed and in his right mind,
    1116
Clothing resumed its, 889
  the palpable and familiar, 318
  silkworm wore the very, 199
  wolf in sheep's, 962
Clotho of the present, 974
Cloud, a fast-flying, 362
  a silence, out of the, 681
  a wisp of, 795
  and clod, in, 877
  and foam, 588
  ascending seems a soul, 688
  at each wandering, 722
  before the skies, like a, 339
  brightest day hath a, 69
  by day, 1098
  choose a firm, 209
  comes over the sunlit arch,
    839
  do set my bow in the, 1097
  engenders not a storm, every,
    70
  I thought that morning, 375
  in shape of a camel, 94
  inner half of every, 837
  is on thy brow, 446
  is scattered, when the, 368
  lies around us like a, 480
  lightning out of the dark, 1079
  like a man's hand, 1101
  nature is a mutable, 411
  of tears, 664
  of witnesses, 1122
  on a, I saw a child, 281
  or sun, as comes to me or,
    423
  out of the sea, 1101
  riding high, white, 924
  sable, 157
  sits in a foggy, 87
  sky what a scowl of, 493
  so fades a summer, 273
  spot and vein that runs through
    the body, 196
  sun will pierce the thickest,
    490
  that's dragonish, 105
  the flying, 588
  through a fleecy, 160
  when skies are clear expect the,
    509
  will turn to rain, mist and,
    438
  with silver lining, 157
Clouds about, turn my, 837
  across the sky, ceaseless, 536
  and changing skies, 372
  and stars and birds, of, 841
  and the only, 1071

Clouds are blowing, look when
    the, 667
  are marching slow, 710
  as they pass, 771
  blue-massing, 894
  castles in the, 224
  dropping from the, 224
  have dropped their garnered
    fullness, 349
  he that regardeth the, 1110
  heavily in, brings the day,
    194
  hide them, 168
  hooded like friars, 433
  I saw two, at morning, 375
  in eternal shadow lie, 373
  look black the glass is low,
    276
  looks in the, 82
  lovely behavior of silk-sack,
    672
  never king dropped out of the,
    130
  no more through rolling, 351
  of crying witnesses, 170
  of glory, trailing, 301
  of opal and amethyst, 522
  on water, colours on, 1084
  pack away, 129
  peaks most wrapt in, 352
  play i' the plighted, 158
  robe of, throne of rocks, 357
  rolling, are spread, 251
  sees God in, 207
  shining, through dark, 824
  sit in the, and mock us, 64
  so cool and gray, 638
  soft, along the horizon rolled,
    418
  soon dimmed the ether blue,
    382
  spots and, in the sun, 124
  sun breaks through darkest, 52
  suns scorch and dark, lower,
    404
  that gather round the setting
    sun, 302
  thy, dispel all other, 364
  travels in, 170
  which seem pavilions of the
    sun, 425
  will always lour, fear not, 284
  would break, never doubted,
    494
Cloud-born squadrons, I see the,
    586
Cloud-calligraphers, the gulls,
    the, 894
Cloud-capped towers, 33
Clouded eyes miss, my, 669
  sky, from out yon, 418
Clouding cares, 574
Cloudless hours, none but the,
    597
Cloudy collar and a shirt that
    isn't white, 754
  seas, tossed upon, 864
  symbols, 384
Clouted brogues, 106
Cloven clay, clothed in the, 631
Clover, how to live in, 976
  or the snow, in the, 552
  to him is aristocracy, 584
  underneath the, 872
Clover-scented grass, among the,
    955

Clown, meat and drink to me to
    see a, 51
  the stupid and the, 661
Cloy the hungry edge of appetite,
    59
Cloyless sauce, sharpen with, 104
Club, an assembly, 232
Clubs, luncheon, 926
  typical of strife, 266
Clueless we go, 922
Clutch, claw'd me in his, 96
  or with sudden, 924
  the golden keys, 468
  thee, come let me, 85
Coach and six, 945
  calm Johnny who upset the,
    425
  come my, 96
  is forced to cheer, 862
  not too much to keep a, 182
  on the launch, 862
Coach-house, a double, 321
Coachman, prouder with her, 650
Coal and salt, mines for, 363
  cars down from Scranton, 926
  his eyeball, like a, 248
  hissing hot from hell, envy's
    a, 506
  is a portable climate, 413
Coals, all eyes else dead, 57
  blows the, 971
  fallen into the, 960
  far innumerable burning, 874
  of fire on his head, 1108,
    1119
  of fire, with, 889
  to Newcastle, carrying, 984
Coarse, familiar but not, 233
  or fine, all work, 437
Coast, along the stormy, 410
  buried on this, 1092
  from east to western, 954
  of bliss, gain the, 393
  of Cariboo, 622
  of France, and o'er its lee the,
    424
  stern and rock-bound, 370
  to reach the distant, 264
  was clear, the, 31
  waves that beat our, 386
Coasts, in glorious, 707
  with lamps, line the, 914
Coat, after my cloth cut my, 13
  buttoned down before, 404
  he used to wear an old drab,
    404
  herald's, without sleeves, 63
  of many colours, 1098
  riband to stick in his, 485
  thousand kinds o', 764
  was red his breeches were blue,
    321
Coats and all, eat 'em, 952
  and capes, maketh winter, 929
  changed and lost our, 674
  hole in a' your, 286
Coats-of-arms, is worth a hun-
    dred, 462
Cobbler stick to his last, let the,
    994
Cobham, brave, 209
Cobweb bridge, like a, 766
Cobwebs, laws were like, 1013
  peep, spiders from their, 276
Cobweb-covered maimed and set
    at naught, 614

Cock can crow louder in its own
farmyard, 505
early village, 72
of the heath, 288
on his own dunghill, 988
on the crowing of the, 89
only the lion and the, 851
the trumpet of the morn, 89
this is a, 1038
to Asclepius, I owe a, 970
who thought the sun had risen,
520
Cocks that will kill fighting,
1003
together crow, two, 855
Cockatoo, cage not natural to a,
720
Cockle hat and staff, 256
Cockles of my heart, 1039
of the heart, 944
Cockleburs and Democrats, 714
Cockloft is empty, often the, 148,
1026
Cockney initials, notches his,
528
Cockroach, the hellish, 865
Cocksure of anything, wish I
could be as, 332
Cocoa is a cad and coward, 828
Cod by mail, sent the, 775
Code, canon of the social, 736
palace priest or, 597
shrines to no, 363
Codeless myriad of precedent,
465
Codfish aristocracy, 843
Codham Cockridden and Chil-
derditch, 855
Codicil this and codicil that,
453
Coffee, after the, 831
makes the politician wise, 212
strong, make my, 504
Coffee-pot, small grey, 887
Coffin asks us whither, 602
care adds a nail to our, 272
money in his, 330
plain, without a flower, 578
Cofre, litel gold in, 5
Cogibundity of cogitation, 189
Cogitative faculties immersed,
his, 189
Cogs, earth's worn, 956
Cohesion, held in, 833
Cohesive power of public plunder,
339
Cohorts were gleaming, 356
Coign of the cliff, 633
of vantage, 85
Coil, shuffled off this mortal, 93
Coin, hold earth's, 754
is spurious nail it down, 504
is the sinews of war, 1025
of any realm, 847
of brass instead of silver, 504
paid him in his own, 1034 *
pays him in his own, 192
silver and gold not the only,
968
runs to hide itself, 654
small, of great value, 1000
that purchases all things, 1042
Tiberius, the, 648
unsordid as a bond of love,
711
would stretch, far as my, 60

Coins, hours are as a miser's, 620
Coinage, little avails that, 574
of your brain, 95
Coincidence, a strange, 360
Cold accretion called the world,
651
and cruel winter, oh the, 436
and hardship such work, 576
and hungry, alas for the, 475
and naked, 249
and stupid marbles, 657
an' the rain, out of the, 782
and unhonoured, 334
as a cucumber, 131
as paddocks, 134
catch your death of, 501
dead and dumb to all, 626
ear of death, 244
embraces of the tomb, 218
foot and hand, 20
for loving, too, 834
friendship sounds too, 337
from catching, 1081
gray dawn of the morning
after, 359, 791
he was so, 813
healthy dog's nose always is,
815
hearts hate union drear, 685
hunger and thirst, inconveniences of, 1039
if the world seems, 568
in clime cold in blood, 355
in the earth, 516
in the summer of her age, 179
increases responsibility increases, 1082
indifference came, 198
lest the bargain catch, 105
marble leapt to life, 363
marble, sleep in dull, 73
meat on washing day, 182
melt me this, 983
monument slab of marble, 448
neutrality of a judge, 261
night-wind blew, on my desolate, 418
obstruction, to lie in, 36
of cheerless, know the, 823
on Canadian hills, 269
peaks of two eternities, 602
performs the effect of fire, 150
perverted will, 369
poverty famished and gaunt,
873
proves you, 937
shake against the, 107
shelter me from the, 810
so, no fire can warm me, 586
that moderates heat, 1042
the stars are, and cold the
earth, 626
thought and fancy faint with,
544
'tis bitter, 89
to you, is not more, 462
warm the, 219
waters to a thirsty soul, 1108
well dressed ever caught, 1081
wind it blew, 951
words congealed by, 1005
words, of all, 815
world, beg the, 847 ·
world, Curtis, in every office
but thine, 52
wrathful, nipping, 69

Cold-blooded premeditated unpalliated murder, 479
Colder, the heart of friendship,
405
those wild words of doom, 418
Coldest man that ever turned up
ace, 105
Coldly furnish forth, 90
heard, so, 425
sweet so deadly fair, so, 355
think'st I speak too, 336
Coldness dwells within thine
heart, 446
Cold-pausing caution, 285
Coleridge, mortal power of, 305
Colin's eyes, kiss in, 883
Coliseum, when falls the, 354
while stands the, 354
Collapse, all is lost by a, 661
Collar, braw brass, 285
cloudy, 754
creditor's name on his, 560
Collateral security, religion a,
222
Collection of books a university,
381
Collections, mutilators of, 323
of books, in public, 526
Collective possessions of modern
peoples, 1072
Collector should not be too care-
ful, 869
Collectors, eccentricities of, 865
Colledges has much to do with th'
progress, 797
College joke to cure the dumps,
190
life is my, 595
not much between unless a,
839
or a cat, endow a, 210
Colleges, give money to, 453
Collegiate life, map of my, 300
Collie aristocracy, flower of, 735
on my plaid keeps watch, 288
Collied night, lightning in the,
42
Collier and a barber fight, 229
Collision, to avoid foreign, 328
Collop of thy own flesh, 14
Cologne, wash your city of, 317
Colonels full of corn, 746
Colonies are free and independent States, 268
Colonization, American continents not for, 283
Colonquintida, bitter as, 101
Colony times, good old, 954
Color, all but cry with, 916
answer for the, 939
as the curtained bee, 911
as the unborn Juliet felt, 911
as the vineyard speck, 911
comes and goes, 648
every gaudy, 939
horse of that, 54
imbues with a new, 354
in his cheek and courage in his
eye, 571
O heavenly, 701
of audacity, 879
of faith and truth, 523
of romance, 644
of the ground was in him, 708
of the sky, none knew the, 813
of virtue, blushing is the, 188

Color, of what, it please God, 38
    the chameleon cannot assume,
        997
    the glory the gold, the, 832
Colors all our own, 441
    and lustres to recommend
        them, 831
    blent, enough that Raphael's,
        561
    false, last after true be dead,
        115
    have faded, 779
    hues and tinges, all, 866
    idly spread, mocking the air,
        58
    noticed what curious, 909
    of the rainbow, 158
    of the sunset stream, 889
    or crest, carries no, 778
    seen by candle-light, 428
    slit up, 831
    stripped of the, 974
    such a play of, 1084
    that are but skin-deep, 169,
        187
    that never fade, 761
    to the mast, nailed her, 307
    under whose, he had fought
        so long, 60
Color's infamy, redeemed from,
    297
Colorless photography of a
    printed record, 686
Colossal and alone, inscrutable,
    683
    on a more, scale than ever be-
        fore, 679
    wreck boundless and bare, 367
Colossus bestride the world, 81
    of Rhodes, 956
Coloured toys, when I bring,
    1084
Colouring, take a sober, 302
Colt must be taught to feel, 783
    who is wise, 776
Columbia happy land, 294
    Tennessee, the Hudson, 932
Columbines, a host of, 937
    hothouse-nurtured, 904
Columbus discovered numberless
    isles, 523
    dreamed, 870
    found a world, 770
    get over, how did, 519
    sails it, wisdom, 414
    wrote an account of his jour-
        ney, 844
Columbus's doom-burdened cara-
    vels, 882
Column pointing at the skies,
    210
    rising towards heaven, 339
    sunlight on a broken, 899
    throws up a steamy, 265
    where London's, 210
Columns left alone, we are, 501
    serried, 447
Combat deepens, the, 328
    whose wit in the, 334
Combe, cowslips from a Devon,
    778
Combed their beautiful hair, 600
Comber wind-hounded, crash of
    the, 777
Combination and a form, 95
    no comparison no judgment, no,
        261

Combination of circumstances,
    310
    of tenderness and manliness,
        538
Combine, when bad men, 259
Come after you with equal grace,
    535
    again, cut and, 280
    all you rounders, 817
    along follow me, none ever
        said, 519
    and men may go, 465
    and trip it as you go, 160
    as the waves come, 309
    as the winds come, 309
    by their deserts, and they,
        483
    forth into the light, 295
    gentle spring, 224
    hitherto shalt thou, 1102
    home to men's bosoms, 109
    if it be now, 'tis not to, 97
    in our time to, 80
    in the evening or morning, 502
    into the garden, Maud, 469
    jump the life to, 85
    leave to those to, the house
        itself, 537
    like shadows so depart, 87
    live with me and be my love,
        31, 936
    lovely and soothing death, 536
    men may, 465
    my friends to seek a newer
        world, 464
    my lad and drink, 239
    never back again, 390
    now and let us reason together,
        1110
    of things to, 75
    of waiting for some one to, 439
    oh! wherefore, ye forth, 401
    one come all, 308
    out my lord it is a, 472
    over into Macedonia, 1118
    past and to, seem best, 64
    peace and rest at length have,
        392
    perfect days, if ever, 525
    then expressive silence, 224
    they from cottage or come, 448
    thou monarch of the vine, 104
    time, when darkies have to
        part, 567
    to forty year, wait till you, 481
    to good, it cannot, 90
    to me come to me, crying, 432
    to the bridal chamber, 362
    to the sunset tree, 370
    to this, that it should, 90
    to you, whistle and she'll, 131
    unto these yellow sands, 32
    uppe Whitefoot, come uppe
        Lightfoot, 540
    walk abroad with me, 321
    Watson come, 737
    what come may, 84
    what may I have been blessed,
        355
    when it will come, 82
    when sorrows, 96
    when the heart beats, 363
    when you call them, 62
    when you're looked for, 502
    where did you, from baby dear,
        559
    whistle and I'll, 286

Come with me into my country.
    938
    within a pint of wine, 198
    without warning, 502
    you must promise to, 388
Comes a reckoning, 205
    after, that which, 1011
    and goes, 648
    in the sweet o' the year, 56
    not in my books, 131
    not slape that, into my, 389
    of music, by man than, 493
    round the age of gold, 477
    silence like a poultice, 451
    silent flooding in the main,
        519
    take it as it, 624
    then, a mist a weeping rain,
        559
    till the cow, home, 131
    to be denied, 128, 221
    to me or cloud or sun, as, 423
    to pass, never never, 288
    unlooked for if at all, 216
Comedies are ended by a mar-
    riage, 359
Comedy appears unmasked, 620
    married philosopher belongs to,
        1080
    the world is a, 246
Comeliness, success that gives it,
    199
Comely but not costly, 23
    fashion to be glad, 540
    grace, love me not for, 950
    Jack was so, 274
Comet, families are like a, 558
    shake out your locks, 853
Comets amongst the stars, 1054
    meet above, 879
Comfits, sack of tobacco and, 928
Comfort, a good cigar as great a,
    425
    all his friends, 596
    and command, 299
    ask no warmer, 793
    be to my age, 48
    continuall, in a face, 26
    fellowship and social, 430
    for great bereavement, 402
    from above, 280
    in despair, 69
    lend, but never, 942
    lies in not forgetting the past,
        613
    like cold porridge, 32
    of feeling safe with a person,
        567
    of the miserable, 1036
    of thy children left thee, 71
    society is no, 106
    speak, to that grief, 40
    take, 619
    the lust for, 879
    to the unhappy, 990, 1049
    with them, carry their, 520
    ye my people, 1112
Comforts, adversity is not with-
    out, 109
    of life, 985
    of life, many so-called, 514
    of this weary pilgrimage, 237
    our creature, 187
Comfortable feel in any member,
    391
    lies in books, 912
    words, 1113

Comfortable words, large divine and, 469
Comforted, then I pray be, 586
Comforters are ye all, miserable, 1102
Comforting thought, always a, 853
Comfortless, I will not leave you, 1118
Comfortlesse dispaires, 26
Comic, mirthful shows, 71
  perception of the, 415
Coming events cast shadows, 327
  eye will mark our, 358
  far off his, shone, 153
  glory of the, of the Lord, 522
  good time, there's a, 504
  guest, welcome the, 213, 220
  hither, endure even as their, 100
  hour o'erflow with joy, 53
  men go, where do, 717
  on of grateful evening, 152
Comma on thy page of victories, 369
Command, angel by divine, 194
  correspondent to, 32
  much more invitation than, 197
  my heart and me, 165
  of truth, 543
  success, not in mortals to, 194
Commanded good, thy great, 556
  tears, a shower of, 52
Commanders by medalled, 936
Commandeth her husband, she, 147
Commandment, eighth, 316
  new, I give unto you, 1118
Commandments, complained of the ten, 478
  keep his, 1110
  set my ten, 69
  ten, will not budge, 529
  two great, 398
Commandress of the world, 28
Commend, another's face, 240
Commends the ingredients, 85
Commendations, good at sudden, 74
  satiety of, 80
Comment, meek nature's evening, 303
Commentators, plain, give me, 280
  shun each dark passage, 203
Commerce between equals, 253
  combined, with, 950
  heavens fill with, 464
  in the matter of, 1066
  is a kind of spring, 1051
  less convenient, render, 1051
  long prevails, where, 249
  wealth and, 518
  which attracts envy, 259
Commercial liberty, how to procure, 1067
  stake or ambition makes wars, 874
Commercing with the skies, 160
Commit the oldest sins, 65
Commodities by cheapening of, 1072
  tax levied upon, 232
Commodity of good names, 60
Common arbitrator time, 75
  as light is love, 367

Common bush afire with God, every, 431, 442
  daylight sweet, found the, 687
  executioner, 50
  fame, trust to, 416
  friend or foe, death is a, 511
  he nothing, did, 169
  make it too, 64
  men, in the roll of, 62
  mind, education forms, 209
  natures, same with, 204
  of literature, grazed the, 239
  on Thy Earth, naught, 783
  passage, act of, 106
  people of the skies, 114
  prejudice, 235
  problem, the, 488
  property, 481
  sense and plain dealing, 412
  sense, dictate of, 226
  sense, rarely cited, 837
  stock of intellectual enjoyment, 750
  sun the air the skies, 245
  talk of the town, 181
  task, trivial round, 365
  that men are merriest when from home, 66
  thought, to have, 209
  to friends, all things, 980
  to mankind, 965
  use of the sea and air is, 19
  use, remote from, 358
  way, life's, 298
  words turn oracles, 429
Common-looking people, the Lord prefers, 457
Commoner, Bryan the great, 753
Commonplace, apocalyptic, 889
  book which he keeps, 346
  life, a, 682
  of friends, 593
  of nature, 298
  passion, 545
  people dislike tragedy, 834
  stuff of the every-day world, 625
  sun in the commonplace sky, 682
Common-sense, rich in saving, 466
Commonwealth affairs, debate of, 66
  caterpillars of the, 59
  do good service to the, 970
  of thought, great green, 833
  to lie abroad for the, 114
Commotion, far down beneath the wild, 480
  in every place, 365
Commotion's roar, heed the wild, 517
Communicated, good the more, 153
Communication with his constituents, 259
Communications, evil, 1120
Communion, still flock to, 1082
  sweet, quaff in, 153
  that will not grow strange, 676
  with nature's visible forms, 371
  with the bad corrupts, 1120
Communists, high-brow, 871
Communities, individualities may form, 419
Community by the ears, setting the, 343

Community is like a ship, 1075
  of power, 725
  of thought, 636
  the best political, 975
Compact are of imagination, all, 43
  highest, we can make, 413
  majority, 1075
Companion, better, than fear, 478
  even thou my, 1128
  I never found the, 514
  lone man's, 524
  none is like, 19
  on a journey, 987
  so companionable as solitude, 514
  to owls, 1102
  with whom he has shared, 237
Companions, conversation of a few select, 195
  for middle age, 110
  I have had playmates, 325
  in misery, 990, 1049
  innocence and health his best, 250
  keep pace with his, 515
  musing on, gone, 307
  of a disturbed imagination, 949
  of the spring, 276
  rather have as, 1076
  speak their praise, 931
  thou'dst unfold, 103
  true, I think of those, 293
  worthy books are not, 506
Companionable as solitude, so, 514
Companioned years, 835
Companionless, strengthless, 966
Companionship as in marriage, in, 635
  in peace, 76
  in your eyes I read, 690
  of books, 673
  of waxen vines, 904
Company and mirth, stay with, 744
  bright, of heaven, 900
  crowds, without, 271
  fellow who makes no figure in, 239
  from four to ten, 667
  G, I belong to, 612
  good, and good discourse, 140
  great multitude or a small, 1125
  he keeps much, 181
  hell for, 750
  high-lived, 254
  in a journey, good, 139
  is an everlasting pleasure, 977
  is Spartan, 985
  little pleasure in others', 1064
  live always in the best, 313
  man is like the, 968
  no more, I bear you, 1021
  not so much to enjoy, 232
  of ladies, fond of the, 239
  of righteous men, 968
  poverty parts good, 311
  shirt and a half in my, 63
  sicken of men's, 829
  sorry work to lose your, 653
  steal out of your, 39
  tell me thy, 1040
  villainous, the spoil of me, 63
  wait in kindly, 674
  when you are gone, 868

Company with pain and fear in, 300
Companye, allone, with-outen any, 6
Compare great things with small, 151
the age, those who, 400
thee to a summer's day, shall I, 107
with thee in beauty can, 555
Comparisons are odious, 9, 31, 117, 1040
are odorous, 39
make no, 251
of a disturbed imagination, 261
Compass, a narrow, 146
chart and calendar, past, 823
I mind my, and my way, 223
of the notes, through all the, 176
things of smallest, 647
Compassed by the inviolate sea, 462
Compass-flower, this is the, 435
Compassion, bowels of, 1123
courage and, joined, 194
on him, had, 1117
Compassionate fully armed, great individual, 537
turquoise, 118
Compatriots, all men as my, 1030
Compeers, from his, 438
Compelled tu, say nothin' without you're, 527
Compelling thoughts, for those, 738
Compensation, by way of, 1077
for renouncing hope, 729
Competence, health peace and, 208
Competency lives longer, 44
Competition and mutual envy of the living, 132
is fought, battle of, 1072
Complacency and satisfaction which beam, 324
Complain of Betsey, I don't, 678
Complained of the ten commandments, 478
Complaining, from wild and weak, 546
Complaint, the violoncello the heart's, 535
Complaints is many and various, 924
libraries querulous criticisms, 535
Complaisance, reserve a little, 1037
Complaisant, humble and, 199
Complete, carelessly, 684
steel, armed with more than, 31
steel, dead corse again in, 91
Completeness, not a death but, 1084
Complex built for two, 882
fate being American, 666
were not, 815
Complexion, buy adulterate, 115
mislike me not for my, 45
of the sky, men judge by the, 60
of virtue, 188

Complexion, of what, soever, 35
smirch'd, 66
to this, thou must come, 243
whatever may be the sex or, 424
Complexions, coarse, 158
suitors of swarthy, 511
Complicated ill, scene of, 942
thing really becomes, 931
Complies against his will, 144
Compliment, acquaintance that begins with a, 724
is something like a kiss, 1069
returning the, 1040
to the first, 235
Compliments, captain of, 78
only things we can pay, 724
reaching proper ears, 785
Composite things, coming into being of, 970
Composition, regular and orderly, 232
Compositions, read over your, 235
Compost of clay, most merely a, 927
Composture of excrement, 81
Composure of settled distress, 321
Compound for sins, 142
of glory and shame, 570
of villanous smell, 35
Compounded of many simples, 51
Comprehend all vagrom men, 39
is to forgive, to, 563
Comprehends some bringer of joy, 43
Compromise, founded on, 260
Compulsion, a reason on, 62
acquired under, 974
fools by heavenly, 98
Compulsive ardour gives the charge, 95
course, icy current and, 103
Compunctious visitings, 84
Computation backward, 112
Compute, we partly may, 285
Comrade, and cry, 811
body's, 1009
I too grow old old, 895
neither glum nor merry, 757
Comrades and love, evangel-poem of, 534
are, all his other, 847
hastens to join his, 1065
lovers friends, kindred, 557
stand, faiths by which my, 651
twelve patient, 881
warriors Thracians, 502
Comrade-love is as a welding blast, 686
Comradeship, foundation laid in youth, 739
hold him in their high, 900
of an equal birth, 860
that lies beyond a kiss, 835
Concatenation accordingly, 253
of circumstances, 310, 342
Concave, that tore hell's, 148
Conceal his thoughts, speech to, 1052
the mind, talk only to, 203
Concealed beauties of a writer, 196
throughout the war, lay, 624

Concealing, hazard of, 285
Concealment like a worm i' the bud, 55
Concealments, without soft, 725
Conceit, in their high, 408
of brilliance, no, 928
wise in his own, 1108
wiser in his own, 1108
Conceits, wise in your own, 1119
Conceited Frenchmen Englishmen Russians and Germans, 1076
whelp, 458
Conceive nor name thee, 86
the rest, by this, 29
Concentred in a life intense, 353
Conception of a Nashville drizzle, 800
of the joyous prime, 24
Concern, charity all mankind's, 208
given themselves the most, 1078
great and pressing, 1089
Concerns of man, indifferent to the, 979
Concessions of the weak, 259
Conchimarian horns, blown through the, 432
Conciliation of interests, 1044
Concludendum, half gate to, 11
Conclusion, a foregone, 103
lame and impotent, 101
of the whole matter, 1110
Conclusions, sufficient, from insufficient premises, 614
Conclusiveness, supported by, 1017
Concord ice had bubbles, 890
love quarrels oft end in pleasing, 157
of sweet sounds, 47
sweet milk of, 88
to America's credit, 825
town, rang out from, 706
travelled a good deal in, 514
unity peace and, 1127
Concourse of all songs, 601
of atoms, fortuitous, 187
Condemn it as an improbable fiction, 55
the fault, 36
the wrong yet pursue it, 187
worst way to improve world to, 506
you me, 128
Condemns me, every tale, 72
Condemned alike to groan, 243
into everlasting redemption, 40
the wretch, 252
to have an itching palm, 83
Condensed in, 338
Condescend here to sit by me, 634
men of wit will, 191
Condition, can we love but on, 492
content with his, 984
highest, rises in the lowest, 989
not a theory, 419
of a man, alter the, 76
unguarded, 166
wearisome, 27
Conditions and circumstances, under all, 921
life's, 650

Conditions, meeting under certain, 232
  no matter what, 698
  stars govern our, 99
  under appropriate, 581
Condor's quill, give me, 531
Conduct, absurdity of, 232
  advice cannot inspire, 1044
  gives room for talk, 1046
  humane, is necessary, 1074
  of a clouded cane, 212
  on my official, 329
  paradoxes of, 800
  still right, his, 252
Conductor when you receive a fare, 583
Cones under his pines, 837
Confabulate or no, if birds, 264
Confer, minds nothing to, 305
Conference maketh a ready man, 111
Confession, suicide is, 342
Confessions muttered at my ears, 905
Confessional, sewing-circle the Protestant, 571
Confessor minus Latin, 917
Confetti, into streaming, 831
Confided power, the less, 412
Confidence and attachment, full of, 1088
  however gradual the growth of, 419
  in himself, regains, 1065
  in ultimate justice, patient, 455
  of twenty-one, towering in the, 233
  of your fellow citizens, if you once forfeit the, 457
  plant of slow growth, 230
  withdraw the, 972
Confident easy mind, with a, 870
  to-morrows, man of, 303
Confidential with him, could be, 742
Confiding prodigal the blissful oriole, 585
Confine, on the very verge of her, 98
  spirit hies to his, 89
Confines of earth, on the, 290
  of space, whose circle grazes, 553
  on the, of two everlasting, 378
Confined, bound in to doubts and fears, 87
Confirm the tidings as they roll, 194
Confirmation, sacrament of, 1053
Confirmations strong, 102
Confirming cleansing raising making free, 503
Conflagration, most terrible thing, 1069
  of the dust, first, 927
Conflict, dire was the noise of, 153
  heat of, through the, 300
  the rueful, 298
Conflicts, life's stormy, 536
Conflicting faiths, by, 1050
  vague probabilities, between, 449
Conformity is the virtue in most request, 411
Confound all unity on earth, 88

Confused alarms of struggle and flight, 546
  sound, rise from this, 604
Confusion, end my dream's, 856
  made his masterpiece, 86
  on thy banners wait, 244
  so quick bright things come to, 42
  to-morrow's, 629
  worse confounded, 151
Confusions, bead on the string of, 837
Congenial page of tenth-rate poeticule, 635
  to my heart, 251
Congo, saw the, 857
Congratulatory regrets, a series of, 420
Congregate, merchants most do, 44
Congregation, devil has the largest, 187
  of vapours, 92
Congress of Vienna dances, 1055
  President executes the laws of, 638
Conjectures, I am weary of, 195
  obtain, 698
Conjugal fence, 333
Conjure him, in vain did she, 257
Conjuror — he knew everything, 1006
Connecticut, heaven is no larger than, 757
  the little yellow spot, 1070
Connection of beauty and goodness, 571
  of the individual man, 952
Connections, beware of hasty, 511
Conned by rote, 83
Conning tower, sit in a, 785
Connubiality, the wictim of, 494
Conquer a crown, 676
  again and again, fight and, 243
  like Douglas, 248
  love, they that run away, 141
  she is hard to catch and, 575
  truth will, 8
  we must, then, 332
Conquer'd fame of heroes, when I peruse, 535
Conquered fate, await no gifts have, 546
  I sing the hymn of the, 533
Conquering hero comes, see the, 186
  science war its way, 539
  so sharpe the, 3
Conqueror and victor, thou too art a, 380
  came in with the, 51
  every, creates a muse, 146
  lie at the proud foot of a, 58
  or city-burner, pity the, 380
  worm, 459
Conquerors, crier that proclaims the, 1002
Conquest and defeat, results of, 740
  brings self-conceit and intolerance, 740
  Caesar made here, 105
  home did bring, 256

Conquest of the west, 707
  or treaty, by, 974
  the right of, 1054
  which is service, 805
Conquests, their, ask oblivion, 282
  tramplings of three, 145
Conquest's crimson wing, 244
Conrad, burial of, 708
Consanguinity, degrees of, 1035
Conscience, alone with my, 681
  and cowardice, 723
  and upright, O clear, 1021
  bend to our dealings, 529
  coward, 72
  does make cowards, 977
  does make cowards of us all, 93
  fierce thing they call a, 392
  guilty, 977, 989
  hath a thousand tongues, 72
  internal evidence of his, 950
  is a sure card, a clere, 23
  is corrupted with injustice, 31, 69
  laws of, 1027
  less my mind indicts, 823
  makes egotists, 723
  of a good, 43
  of her worth, 154
  of the king, catch the, 93
  policy sits above, 81
  private, for guide, 174
  spiral of his, 881
  still and quiet, 73
  that spark of celestial fire, 268
  the chancellor's, 130
  the courage of, 393
  the disease of an evil, 450
  the guardian, 835
  the sting of, 1079
  thing I cannae bear an' that's my, 681
  tongue confuted by his, 147
  uncreated, of my race, 874
  wakes despair, 151
  we may live without, 592
  with gallantry, 279
Consciences, cheveril, 126
  guilty, make cowards, 977
  historian of fine, 728
Conscient reason, is our, 669
Conscientiously no, 426
Conscious step and hat and all, 755
  stone to beauty, grew, 408
  water blushed, 165
Consciousness human, in relation to the divine, 549
  of freedom, 1062
  of good day's work, 228
  remained, a, 303
Conscripted unvictorious ones, 892
Consecration and the poet's dream, 299
Consent, never with my, 320
  silence gives, 253
  whispering I will ne'er, 358
Consents, my poverty not my will, 80
Consequence, deepest, 84
  enough to have his life and character recorded, 376
  life is not a thing of, 1011
  'tis almost, 584

Consequence, trammel up the, 85
  what you say not of much, 588
Consequences are scarecrows,
  logical, 564
  think of the, 1075
Conservative, be a, 854
  government, 419
Consider the end, 1045
  the lilies of the field, 1114
  too curiously, 97
Consideration has nothing in
  common, 1027
  like an angel, 66
  one, with another, 623
  take the German kind into,
    1082
Considereth the poor, 1104
Consisted of lines like these, 590
Consistency is a hobgoblin, 411
  thou art a jewel, 944
  wuz a part of his plan, 526
Consolation, edifying words of,
  787
  ever comes too soon, 241
  is not what you need, 1074
  no greater, 1057
  priceless, 478
  that character of woman can-
    not be altered, 556
  thought of suicide a great,
    1080
Consoler of the lonely, 608
Consonant they had, surrendered
  every, 661
Consonants and vowels, only, 903
Consorts are the sleepless stars,
  my, 517
Conspicuous becomes more, 999
  by his absence, 1006
  maladies which are less, 969
Conspiracy, by whose, 1001
Constable, in case to justle a, 33
  with lifted hand, 773
Constancy in wind, hope, 351
  of women, infernal, 720
  plain and uncoined, 68
  to purpose, success is, 419
Constant as Penelope, 258
  as the northern star, 82
  as various, 924
  friendship is, save in love, 38
  heart, for a, 950
  is a wondrous excellence, 108
  marigold springs, 924
  most, of all my friends, 597
  only the, know, 416
  service of the antique world, 48
  still, 396
  sun, but brings the, 501
  to me and so kind, 382
  to one thing, never, 38, 256
Constantinople, Russians shall
  not have, 562
Constellation of O'Ryan, 578
  set against the Northern sky,
    nobles, 552
Constellations, happy, 154
Constituents, communication
  with his, 259
Constitution, conditions of our
  mental, 450
  doctor who knows, 520
  has placed it, where the, 320
  is all sail and no anchor, 400
  is openly invaded, 949
  laws and, 949

Constitution, most remarkable
  work of modern times, 450
  one country, one, 340
  proportioned to the human, 204
Construction and creation, differ-
  ence between, 826
  minds, in the face, 84
Consul or president, king or, 686
Consul's open door, 645
Consultation comes in order
  next, 451
Consultations, doctors', 717
Consume their own smoke, chimneys, 379
Consumed the midnight oil, 206
Consumedly, they laughed, 201
Consummate flower, bright, 153
Consummation devoutly to be
  wished, 93
  of life, old age is the, 981
Consumption, birds are in, 128
  brought him down to his grave,
    172
Consumption's ghastly form, 363
Contact with a religious man,
  1082
  with manners is education, 200
  with my inmost being, 1090
Contagion, communicated by,
  1073
  hell itself breathes out, 95
  of the world's slow stain, 366
Contagious blastments, 90
  to the Nile, 375
Contemplation, become wise
  from, 773
  beneath thy, 518
  formed for, 152
  gave a spiritual significance,
    669
  her best nurse, 158
  in leisurely, 824
  mind serene for, 195
  of my travels, 51
  was much more than reading,
    171
Contemplative serene sublime,
  248
Contemporaneous posterity, 227
Contemporaries, disesteem of my,
  788
  homage from, 398
Contemporary spites, 675
Contempt and anger of his lips,
  55
  familiarity breeds, 34, 961
  for the wildest blow, 655
  for their oppressors, 886
  from the head, 1063
  it is not, 376
  of authority, 179
  regarded with greatest, 1081
  tail that wagged, 736
  treat you with, 538
  upon familiarity, 34
Contempts of sect and creed, base,
  864
Contemptible vessel, faintly, 927
Contemptuous of death, 809
Contend with angry roar, 480
Content as the years wear
  through, 631
  elegant sufficiency, 224
  farewell, 102
  freehold of, 573
  good pleasure ease, 208

Content, humble livers in, 73
  I would be well, 63
  land of lost, 743
  live together with any, 997
  majority of men live, 1023
  many a life of sweet, 685
  might be, else they, 729
  my crown is called, 70
  myself with wishing, 239
  o'erlaps them evermore, 517
  of religion, 670
  or joy fame sorrow, 954
  poor and, is rich, 102
  shut up in measureless, 85
  sweet, passing all wisdom, 417
  therewith to be, 1121
  though it go that it came, 868
  thoughts that savour of, 940
  to barter, those, 518
  to follow, 219
  travellers must be, 48
  wants money means and, 50
  wisdom of a just, 595
  with a vegetable love, 623
  with harmless sport, 479
  with small means, live, 473
Contents, lived part of its, 886
Contented, be, 391
  employed men best, 228
  he forgets to fly, 735
  when one is, 1038
  with little, 287
Contentedness, procurer of, 139
Contention, a man of, 1112
  cease, let the long, 547
Contentions, fat, 162
  of the Great Hall, 399
Contentious woman, 1108
Contentment, blessing of the
  house is, 953
  fails and honour sinks, 249
  of the inner man, 930
  preserves one, 1081
  to that toad, preaches, 776
  with the goodness, 971
  within despair, 771
Contest fall, who lets the, 968
  follows, great, 265
  quicker, will end a, 279
Contests allow no excuses, 963
  rise from trivial things, 212
Contiguity of shade, 264
Continent, cannot continually disappoint a, 612
  isolated, 906
  one small spot a, 595
  unshaken as the, 436
  whole boundless, 276
Continents or islands, 361
Continental Congress, the great
  Jehovah and the, 344
Continentals, stood the old, 579
Contingent a fashion, so, 1087
Continual dropping wears, 981,
  1108
  feast, merry heart a, 1107
  noise, sleeps in, 629
  plodders, small have, won, 40
  state of inelegance, 323
Continuing city, here we have no,
  1122
Continuity of nature, 542
Continuous excitement written
  under, 745
  supply of work, 1071
Contortions of the sibyl, 261

Contract, I've filled my, 844
'twixt Hannah God and me, 603
Contract-tablet, alter his, 958
Contractor did Cheops out of several millions, 776
Contradiction an absurd remark, 314
to life, death is in, 709
woman's a, 209
Contrairies, dhrames go by, 389
Contrairy, everythink goes, 496
Contrary blast proclaims most deeds, 157
bringeth bliss, whereas the, 68
dreams are ever, 116
runneth not back to the, 413
runneth not to the, 248
to the king, his crown and dignity, 69
Contrasts and comparisons, happiness a thing of, 608
Contribution, beg a trivial, 760
made a most honourable, 970
make a generous, 949
to the happiness of others, 605
Contrition, a bayonct's, 586
Contrivances to facilitate motion, 232
Contrive, head to, 270
Control feels less the outer world's, 444
neither is quite within our, 1063
not within our, 975
preserved from chance, 735
stops with the shore, his, 354
Controls them and subdues, 300
Controversial polymath, 900
Controversies, for their private, 970
Contumely, proud man's, 93
Convalescence makes illness worth while, 721
Convenience, profit and, 1051
Convenient to great families of doubtful origin, 343
Convent, it was a stately, 423
Convents bosomed deep in vines, 215
Convention of free speech, 558
Conventional signs, merely, 599
Conversation among birds, fragmentary, 582
brisk in, 233
different name for, 241
does not show the minute-hand, his, 239
hinges in French, 242
in his eyes, there lies a, 438
is but carving, 191
lettuce is like, 582
long and dull, 312
more scope of, 128
of the most sincere and searching sort, 411
perfectly delightful, 313
questioning is not the mode of, 236
wants leisure, 835
was by much too strong, 272
when you fall into a man's, 197
Conversation's burs, stick on, 451
Conversationalist, industrious, 921
Converse, an hour's, 587

Converse, formed by thy, 209
spend in pure, 893
with the mighty dead, 224
Conversing with thee I forget all time, 152
Converted because you have silenced, not, 641
Convex mound, seated upon the, 922
Convey the wise it call, 34
Conveyed, bud to heaven, 316
the dismal tidings, 251
Conviction, desire of rousing such a, 1064
faithful to his, 975
heaven of fabulous, 932
more striking, 231
pride is an established, 1064
that we are loved, 1067
Convictions that what was was wrong, 821
Convinced me, unwillingly, 230
Convincing, thought of, 252
Convivial upon tears, grow, 530
Convocation of casuists, 1035
Convolutions of a shell, 302
Convoy, anxious, 839
Convulsions, periodical, 697
Cook and a captain bold, 622
his merit, makes his, 1046
is born, a roast, 1059
oh, I am a, 622
was a good cook, 812
Cooks are gentlemen, 123
can not live without, 592
devil sends, 19, 243
epicurean, 104
go, she went, as, 812
we become, 1059
Cook's tourists, 715
Cookery is an art a noble science, 123
receipts of, 184
the art of, 1051
Cookey's throat was marked, 710
Cook-shops, skulking round among the, 1009
Cool and all unconscious, 425
and gray, 638
iron on anvil did, 58
kindliness of sheets, 894
reflection came with the morning, 198, 310
sequestered vale, 245, 268
sweet day so, 135
to try to keep, 637
waves break, 576
Cools, answers till a husband, 209
Cool-enfolding death, arms of, 536
Cool-headed Saxons with hearts aflame, 553
Coolidge prosperity, 922
Cooling plash of rain, 709
Coolness, dripping with, 348
Coon, I'm a gone, 349
thing's a gone, 527
Coonskin sack, whose wit was a, 927
Cooped, whereunder crawling, 1019
Cop, the one lonesome, 756
Cope, his glossy, 629
of heaven, the starry, 153

Cophetua, king, 78
sware a royal oath, 465
Copies of other men, 233
Copious, a life that shall be, 537
accents, 218
Dryden, 214
Copper, juggling six balls of, 1078
Copper-plated throat, 816
Copy from the bookseller's, 255
leave the world no, 54
nature's, is not eterne, 87
of a book which does not sell, 324
the princeps, 288
then shew your, 1056
Copyists, shortened the labor of, 379
Coquetry, too innocent for, 447
whets the appetite, 551
Coracle I ride, dusky, 801
Corages, nature in hir, 5
Coral bones of, 938
insects multitudinous, 540
lip admires, 140
of his bones are, made, 32
strand, from India's, 343
Corals on, maple puts her, 529
Cord, a threefold, 1109
as unto the bow the, is, 436
cannot hold as love with twined thread, 125
consume the strongest, 309
no force can stretch a, 375
silver, be loosed, 1110
Cordial, a sad man's, 524
and frank, that's, 828
gold in phisik is a, 5
heart, owing to his, 586
old and rare, death a, 664
speech, 410
to the soul, 147
Core, golden to the, 927
hear it in the deep heart's, 791
right through the, 1059
sleep in the root's white, 385
wear him in my heart's, 94
Corinth, lot to gain, 985
one road to, 646
Corinthian lad of mettle, 61
Cormorant, sat like a, 151
Corn, amid the alien, 383
and beans, good, 664
and clothing, no more need we, 651
and wine, a land of, 1101
breast-high amid the, 390
dragging the, 814
flies o'er the unbending, 211
for the rich men only, 76
full, in the ear, then the, 1116
golden, 441
grows a plenty of, 1056
in chaff, hope, 351
is full of kernels, 746
like a field of ripe, 900
like as a shock of, 1102
on his chin, 697
Romans threw in their, 593
sickle in another man's, 989
tasselled, 642
three grains of, 558
two ears of, where one grew, 191
where drowsy poppies nod, 955

Corn, cometh al this newe, 4
  the staffe of life, 188
Corns, toes unplagu'd with, 77
  tread on my, 955
Cornea, speck in, 694
Cornelia, jewels of, 125
Cornfield, dew of the, 668
Corn-fields lie sunny and bright, 613
  rich tint of the, 737
Corner, head stone of the, 1106
  in the streets, round some, 574
  in the thing I love, 102
  of a foreign field, 894
  of a street, lightly turn the, 707
  o' airth, a li'l lew, 765
  of God's allotment, shabby, 651
  of nonsense, 319
  of the breast, hide it in some, 581
  of the house-top, 1108
  sits the wind in that, 39
  stones, that our daughters may be as, 1106
  was not done in a, 1119
Corners of the world, all, 105
  of the world, four, 1032
  of the world, the three, 58
  of their eyes, out of the, 936
  to care for, 738
Cornered in an inch, 689
Cornish men, twenty thousand, 416
Coromandel, black men of, 399
  coast of, 498
Coronation day, kings upon their, 174
  whose christening was a, 1085
Coronets, kind hearts are more than, 462
Corporal Madden to Private McFadden, 774
  oath, take my, 1037
  pain, 669
  sufferance, 36
Corporation of the goose-quill, the press, 483
Corporations have no souls, 21
Corpse of liberty, buried the putrid, 1090
  of public credit, 340
  pain lays not its touch upon a, 964
  that here in fourteen lines, 943
Corpse-gazings, tears black raiment, 573, 978
Correct, easier to be critical than, 419
  errors, I shall try to, 456
  in cypress wood, 919
  thing to do, 1076
Correctly informed, no man who is, 400
Corrector of enormous times, 132
Correggios and their Raphaels, 252
Correspondence and personal intercourse, 475
  closest, 259
Correspondences are like smallclothes, 314
Correspondent habit of feeling, 318
  has decided, 922
  to command, 32

Corridor of years, fair-chambered, 874
Corridors like windy tulip beds, 891
  of light, through, 938
  surpassing material place, 585
Corroded human nature, 641
Corrosive, care is, 68
  dewdrop eats, time's, 564
Corrupt a saint, able to, 60
  good manners, 1120
Corrupted the youth of the realm, 69
Corruption and the worm, 671
  fill our stomachs with, 166
  guilty of, 113
  honest words have suffered, 117
  keep mine honour from, 74
  lends, lighter wings, 210
  may our frame consume, 332
  never has been compulsory, 895
  pass, wilt not let, 725
  strong, 56
  wins not more than honesty, 73
Corrymeela and the blue sky, 840
Corsair's name, he left a, 356
Corse, dead, again in complete steel, 91
  slovenly unhandsome, 61
  to the rampart we hurried, his, 364
Corset, stabbed myself right in the, 756
Cortez, like stout, 384
Cosmic process works, 667
  urge, one with a, 907
Cosmopolite, that man's the best, 471
Cosmopolouse, sort of bloomin', 782
Cost a sigh a tear, 273
  be fed at our, 973
  counteth the, 1117
  give and not count the, 1024
  little less than new, 193
  me much money, 180
  of mental and physical torture, 1081
  tell thee all the, 147
Costs dearest, most valued, 1038
  only the first step which, 1053
Costly, comely but not, 23
  sacrifice on altar of freedom, 457
  thy habit, 23
Costume charity ball, getting up a, 935
Cot beside the hill, 289
  better to love in the lowliest, 545
  except her father's, 501
Cote, after my cloth, cut my, 13
Cotopaxi, Chimborazo, 907
Cotswold lanes, along the, 873
Cottage lamp shines white, 890
  might adorn, looks the, 251
  my lowly thatched, 365
  of gentility, 321
  or come they from hall, 448
  poorest man in his, the, 230
  rung as they sung Dulce dulce domum, 294
  the soul's dark, 146

Cottage was near, knew a, 333
  with double coach-house, 321
Cottages, poor men's, 44
Cottage-chamber bed, 568
Cotton is king, 432
  woven in, sell for silk the, 566
Cotton-spinners all, we are not, 467
Couch, drapery of his, 372
  frowsy, in sorrow steep, 286
Coude songes make, 5
Cough and love cannot be hid, 136
  modest, 721
Coulter and share of the wind, 712
Council, mortal instruments in, 82
  statesmen at her, 462
  two heads in, 466
Councils set on every hill, 681
Counsel and constructive leadership, 877
  and speak comfort, 40
  at a glance, gave him, 620
  by words, darkeneth, 1102
  friendly, cuts off foes, 68
  good is cheap, 124
  hard for women to keep, 82
  in his face yet shone, 150
  is more trustworthy, no, 1022
  keep his own, 1037
  take and sometimes tea, 212
  the best, 478
  three may keepe, 16
  took sweet, together, 1104
  two may keep, 77
  who cannot give good, 124
Counsels, dash maturest, 149
  monie, sweet, 287
Counselor, chance his, 847
Counsellors, good, lack no clients, 35
  if with our present, 972
  multitude of, 1107
Count a man's years until he has nothing else to, 415
  as naught in world or church, 528
  myself in nothing else so happy, I, 59
  our spoons, let us, 234
  that day lost, 950
  their chickens, 143
  them all my friends, I, 471
  this time, I won't, 579
  time by heart-throbs, 506
Counted ere I see thy face, must be, 454
Countenance and profit, 109
  brightened with joy, 302
  cannot lie, that, 26
  certain air to the, 196
  changeth his, 1125
  light of thy, 1128
  maketh a cheerful, 1125
  man sharpeneth the, of his friend, 1108
  merry heart maketh a cheerful, 1107
  more in sorrow than in anger, 90
  never fading serenity of, 195
  of Harlequin without his mask, 484
  of truth, bright, 162

Countenance, place implicit confidence in a man's, 407
that warms and lights, every, 933
the light of thy, 1099
Countenances of a new-married couple, 324
Counteraction, action and, 260
Countercheck quarrelsome, 51
Counterfeit a gloom, 160
presentment, 95
sleep death's, 86
true friends less moved than, 180
Counterfeited glee, with, 251
Counterpane, the pleasant land of, 702
Counterparts in the world of fact, 542
Counters, words are wise men's, 132
Counteth the cost, 1117
Counthry takes what's left, 796
Counties, six, overhung with smoke, 608
Countless channels, flows through, 570
cousins of the Czar, 910
generations pass, 857
ripples laugh, 760
stories spread, 847
thousands mourn, 284
Countree, in my ain, 346
is this mine own, 315
Countries here nor there, 889
in other, 405
newe, seeing, 257
physicians of all the, 450
Country, a slow sort of, 598
absorbs him, 539
afar beyond the stars, 170
and his town estate, his, 867
another, I've heard of, 747
behind officers and government, 550
best, who loves his native, 471
bliss to die for our, 219
but his own, every, 624
churchyard, corner of a, 261
cover a great deal of, 673
dare to love their, 217
desert, near the sea, 57
die nobly for their, 76
die to save our, 195
down, pride that puts the, 256
eagle representative of our, 228
essential service to his, 191
every, needs to be saved from itself, 740
faith and best of all, 763
for our country's good, left our, 281
for the good of his, 1061
for the good of my, 201
gains nothing by war, 740
God forgot, the, 822
God made the, 264, 759
good news from afar, 1108
grows polite, when my, 779
hath Machiavel, every, 1023
he loved his, 550
he sighed, for his, 328
his first best, is at home, 249
his, ruling passion of his life, 701
honestly served my, 329

Country, I love thee still my, 264
I tremble for my, 274
in heaven, his, 1068
is the richest, that, 533
kitchen or house in town, 795
kitchen, remember dot oldt, 661
know something of his own, 242
left for country's good, 201, 281
life in literature, 571
long for the, 985
look like the open, 1057
love of, 494
man dear to all the, 250
my, is the world, 424
my, 'tis of thee, 447
needs, what this, 714
nothing but our, 340
O dear dear, 1017
of air, into my, 938
of fair report, 960
of snow and wheat, 929
one constitution, one, 340
one day in the, 587
one life to lose for my, 195
open, where gathering speed, 938
or seaside a gallery, 563
our, however bounded, 472
our, is the world, 424
our, right or wrong, 262, 472, 580
our whole, 340
resistance in this, 949
save in his own, 1115
seats, not built of, 911
severs me from mine heart's, 796
the undiscover'd, 93
'tis of centuries, my, 921
to be cherished and defended, 472
to die for one's, 930
undone his, 195
upon earth, his, 1068
virtuous and wise every moment, no, 740
wakes, sung ballads at, 177
what, before ever existed, 273
who serves his, best, 219
whosoever flieth from his, 1126
with all her faults she is my, 262
world is my, 271
Country's battles, fight our, 953
cause, his, 219
earth, that pleasant, 60
ends thou aim'st at be thy, 73
fame, raise his, 1027
glory, stood for his, 307
good, my, 76
good, no glory but his, 374
heart, here in the, 763
own heart's-blood, 806
pride, peasantry their, 250
ruin, see my, 940
stead, in their suffering, 973
wishes blessed, 247
Countryman who looked for his ass, 1041
Countrymen fed on oats and base grain, 122
friends Romans, 83
hearts of his, 281

Countrymen, now, all one, 29
of ours lie neglected, 292
Romans, and lovers, 82
unscottified of your, 235
what a fall was there my, 83
Counts his sure gains, 306
County Guy the hour is nigh, 310
Couple, countenances of a new-married, 324
or must die, must, 545
plighted, here they come the, 624
Couple-colored as a brindled cow, 672
Couplet, the fool south-border, 895
Courage, and bear with a good, 1123
and compassion, 194
and gaiety and the quiet mind, 705
and other types, 975
and skill to him that can get it, 172
and submission, bear with, 563
be of good, 1112
brother do not stumble, 499
consists in fear and retreat, 1051
fail, hope or, 567
foes, his, 173
give you fresh, 1074
good of the agent to, 1048
in his eye, 571
in our own, 601
is a virtue, 1051
is better than fear, 625
mounteth with occasion, 57
never to submit, 148
of conscience, 393
of heart or holiness, 810
of New England, the, 393
of the Negro, 480
of unmatchable, 67
screw your, to the sticking-place, 85
shall bring you, 849
species of, 1048
stout will be put out, 22
to face, who have the, 1090
to forget, 582
with his high, 676
without ferocity, 351
Courageous captain of compliments, 78
Courageous, captaines, 257
Couriers of the air, 85
Course, chances change by, 30
each act a, 200
far and brilliant, 362
forgot his, 881
here and there along the, 699
I have finished my, 1122
I must stand the, 99
icy current and compulsive, 103
impede its quiet, 1073
impediments in fancy's, 53
in how to live, 773
in its brief, 953
is steadied, my preudunt, 526
nature's second, 86
of empire, westward the, 30, 203
of human events, in the, 273
of justice, in the, 46

Course of life's few fleeting years, 707
of love, my whole, 100
of man's regeneration, 693
of nature is the art of God, 202
of one revolving moon, 174
of true love, 42
of untold millions of years, 581
planets in their, 289
slays a bad man in its, 966
turned from one's, 997
unbroken, keep your, 760
westward the, of empire, 203
when this my mortal, 878
whose, is run, 242
world's, will not fail, 556
young blood must have its, 523
Courses, like ships they steer their, 142
stars in their, 1099
steer their, 142
Coursed down his innocent nose, 48
Coursers like a page, 585
Court it, the more I, 164
love rules the, 306
of justice, in and out in the, 958
of justice in his breast, 465
sun that shines upon his, 57
when Arthur first in, 256
Courts, a day in thy, 1105
of heaven, high up in the, 842
of hell, roamed the, 685
wealth bestowed on camps and, 434
Courted by all the winds, 157
in your girls again, 257
Courteous, the retort, 51
to a man as to a picture, 413
Courtesies of life, ye small sweet, 242
unwearied spirit in doing, 46
which sweeten life, effect of, 343
Courtesy, always time for, 415
and circumspection, 253
greater man, the greater, 471
grows chill, when, 648
has done its most, sweet, 620
in the heart of, 27
is the true alchemy, 574
it is much less, 810
mirror of all, 72
no joints for courtesy, 75
pink of, 79, 1039
princes of, 765
receive him, with, 503
sense which men call, 508
wins woman as well as valor, 471
Court-house Appomattox, 578
Courtier, heel of the, 97
Courtiers were good, 193
Courtier's scholar's eye, 93
Courtliness and the desire of fame, 471
Courtship love and matrimony, say of, 511
preceded by a long, 196
snaffle of, 776
Courtsied when you have, 32
Cousin of the forest-green, 385
Cousins of the Czar, 910
to the war, given two, 606
Coûte, le premier pas qui, 1053

Cove, there sot an Old, 539
Coves where safety hides, 707
Covenant, be this our, 658
the words of the, 1098
with death, 424
word, whose, 647
Covenants of peace, open, 725
Coventry had already feathered his nest, 181
will surely ride through, 346
Cover is a door, every, 866
my head now, 391
to our bones, which serves as, 59
Covered bridge, 440
way, death but a, 443
Coverlet of a bed, 1000
Covet honour, sin to, 67
those that much, 106
Covetous man ever in want, 985
sordid fellow, 222
Covetousness, cause of, 31
Cow, brindled, 672
comes home, kiss till the, 131
gently waving her hand, 345
I never saw a purple, 792
I wrote the purple, 792
in a pale green mead, 896
very good in the field, 235
Cows are coming home, 618
Coward, a man's an awful, 754
can fight a battle he's sure of winning, 520
conscience, 72
does it with a kiss, 722
flattery to name a, 295
greatest, in the world, 1001
in the fight, 505
scoundrel and a, 233
soul is mine, no, 516
stands aside, while the, 525
that would not dare, 307
Cowards, accustom ourselves like, 1084
conscience does make, 93
die many times, 82
do not count in, 968
guilty consciences make, 977
in reasoning, 377
insult, only, 961
mannish, many other, 48
may fear to die, 22
mock the patriot's fate, 555
plague of all, 61
what can ennoble, 208
Cowards' funerals, 743
Cowardice and conscience, 723
that clings, 827
Cowboy's brief brief story, 822
Cowl, I like a church I like a, 408
Cowlèd churchman, would I that, 408
Cowley said it engagingly, 758
Cowslip loves the lea, 565
Cowslips from a Devon combe, 778
in a hat, bring you, 917
wan, 159
Cowslip's bell, in a, I lie, 33
Coxswain's call, they stop at the, 862
Coy and hard to please, 308
excuse and denial vain, 159
fame will still be, 385

Coy submission, yielded, 152
Coyness, in spite of all their, 1037
lady were no crime, 169
Cozen him whom he salutes, 122
Cozenage, strange, 178
Crabbed age and youth, 109
not harsh and, 158
Crabs, diplomats women and, 640
Crack, bug crawl out of, 929
like that in her head, 679
of doom, stretch out to the, 87
the voice of melody, 451
would hear the mighty, 194
your cheeks, blow winds, 98
Crackers, mottoes inside the, 622
Crackling of thorns, as the, 1109
pile nor cursing creed, 452
Cracks a noble heart, 98
Cradle and the grave, between the, 223, 910
asks us whence, 602
endlessly rocking, 536
may Old Nick rock my, 1034
my splendid, 1085
of American liberty, 342
of every science, 930
of reposing age, 213
of the deep, 350
our, stands in the grave, 121
procreant, 85
the hand that rocks the, 534
Cradles, a-lying in our, 496
we would preserve as sacred things, 617
Cradled into poetry by wrong, 367
Craft, almost touching the, 934
gentle, 945
of will, 109
or custom, no, 808
so long to lerne, 3
the queerest little, 670
to seme flee, it is, 4
Craftiness, wise in their own, 1102
Craftsman jealous of craftsman, 206
toilworn, I honour, 380
Craftsmanship, easier than, 975
Crag of Drachenfels, 353
Crags, upon the, 886
Craggy hills and running streams, 447
Crammed, as they on earth were, 296
with distressful bread, 67
with heaven, earth's, 431
with observation, 49
Cramp rack their limbs, 937
Cranes of Ibycus, 963
Cranks and wanton wiles, 160
in Boston, 714
Crannies, pluck you out of the, 467
Cranny, every, but the right, 267
Crannying wind, save to the, 353
Crape on the door, 665
Cras amet qui nunquam amavit, 201
Crash, fall with heavier, 983
of deafening thunder, 688
of '93, 715
Cravat, in my large white, 729
virtue may flourish in an old, 451

Cravattum, and elegant, 867
Crave for rest, who doth not, 503
  my mind forbids to, 20
  no pelf, I, 80
Craven, down went dauntless, 764
  spoke as he lived, 764
Cravens my weak hand, 106
Craving credulity, 419
  minds are not ever, 280
  to go to law, 1078
Crawl at his side, beggar may, 449
Crawling foam, the cruel, 523
Crazy Horse and Rain-in-the-Face, 707
  understanding, evidence of a, 183
Creak of a lumbering cart, 790
Creaking old mill, 640
Cream and mantle, 44
  skim milk masquerades as, 623
Creamy sea, chin in the, 858
Create a nation, institutions alone, 419
  in me a clean heart, 1104
  wise to learn God-like to, 511
Created, Bacon could as easily have, 382
  equal, all men, 273
  half to rise and half to fall, 207
  in bounds of earth, everything, 545
  suddenly, no great thing, 1007
Creates, or what it can not find, 438
Creating a whole new democratic world, 379
Creation, amid nature's gay, 224
  better, I love, 878
  bodiless, 95
  by right of an earlier, 397
  death and love the double gate, 833
  from every scene of the, 290
  from heat-oppressed brain, 85
  glows, a new, 364
  groaneth and travaileth in pain, 1119
  hints for the, 1020
  lords of the, 285
  love all God's, 1074
  must despise a tailless man, all, 665
  object of the whole, 253
  of beauty and invulnerability, 813
  of beauty, poetry as rhythmical, 461
  of some heart, sweet, 354
  of the world, no tyrant like intemperance, 424
  ploughshare o'er, 202
  rejoicing in thy whole, 1128
  since the world's, 112
  sleeps, 201
  think, makes, 780
  through all, 670
  tire of all, 454
  widened, 326
Creations of the brain, 551
Creation's blank creation's blot, 246
  cry, 780

Creation's dawn beheld, such as, 355
  death behold, 328
  wide domains, 343
Creative spirit, want of the, 1087
Creator drew his spirit, his great, 175
  duty to his, 977
  endowed by their, 273
  glory of the, 112
  remember now thy, 1110
  voice of the great, 501
Creators of odd volumes, 323
Creature, be a far more perfect, 449
  comforts, our, 187
  drink pretty, drink, 298
  every, lives in a state of war, 190
  every, shall be purified, 31
  formed of joy and mirth, 282
  good wine is a good familiar, 102
  heaven-eyed, 305
  in creator meeting, 688
  in whom excelled, 155
  is made so mean, no, 492
  is subject, no living, 132
  literary, 634
  looked upon the, 815
  man is an inconstant, 1001
  misgivings of a, 301
  not too bright or good, 299
  of an hour, fair, 384
  of an hour, the, 1021
  of circumstances, 420
  of the moment, 330
  small beer, 64
  smarts so little as a fool, 213
  stirs to its own impulse, each, 546
  that thou madest, 744
  tired and lone, unmated, 503
  was stirring, not a, 332
  what more felicitie can fall to, 26
  why should every, drink but I, 167
Creatures, desolate, 430
  England breeds valiant, 67
  everywhere, little, 877
  God made all the, 486
  going about their business, 895
  he meets, miserable, 1063
  heaven from all, hides, 207
  kill these weary, 754
  lacking the little, 872
  millions of spiritual, 152
  most absurd of mankind, 214
  of all God's, man alone is poor, 402
  of men, circumstances are the, 420
  of one great law, 619
  of the element, 158
  pent-up, 489
  that creep swim or fly, 1050
  these delicate, 102
  too many, 853
  use living, 997
  you dissect, 209
Creatures' lives, human, 310
Crebillon, romances of, 246
Credit, and it's greatly to his, 623
  any thing light gives life to, 131

Credit, blest paper, 210
  corpse of public, 340
  go, let the, 1018
  goes in science, where, 696
  growth of, requires time, 419
  his own lie, 32
  I have used my, 60
  in ilka town, 311
  in that, there ain't much, 495
  in this world, 1019
  not to thy, 589
  of human nature that it loves more readily, 422
  private, is wealth, 950
Creditor, glory of a, 35
  is worse than a master, 1068
  owns your dignity, 1068
Creditors, either debtors or, 1057
Creditor's name on his collar, 560
Credo then but Amo, not, 648
Credulity, craving, 419
  helps, a little, 475
  is the man's weakness, 323
  most charming characteristic, 694
  ye who listen with, 232
Credulous mother Eve, 154
Credulousness, cursed his, 465
Creed, an Athanasian, 175
  argument to thy neighbor's, 408
  cursing, 452
  is a rod, a, 633
  put your, into your deed, 409
  sapping a solemn, 353
  simple, for word or deed, 686
  suckled in a, outworn, 300
  would stifle me, 848
Creeds agree, ask if our, 335
  and schools in abeyance, 534
  churches and, lost in mists, 569
  grow so thick, 719
  human hopes and human, 660
  iron, 709
  keys of all the, 468
  oppose with Luther's dike, 453
  religion without any, 837
  so many gods so many, 718
  speak not of men's, 354
  than in half the, 469, 506
  that refuse and restrain, 632
  to me are but new names, 657
  weary of mumbling Athanasian, 609
Creek and creaking old mill, 640
Creeks and inlets, back through, 519
  and golden sands beneath the waters, 732
Creep, children learn to, 15
  in one dull line, ten low words, 211
  into his study of imagination, 40
  kind will, 14
  wit that can, 213
Creeping hours of time, 49
  like snail to school, 49
  thing in sober way, 517
  vine, like a, 1085
Creeps in this petty pace, 88
  slowly on, wisdom of mankind, 417
Creetur, I am a lone lorn, 496

Cremona, evening air is chilly in, 738
masters of, 738
Crept into the bosom of the sea, 69
upon our talk, 83
Cressy and Poictiers, shrined with, 518
Crest, below the high hill's, 916
must have passed the, 883
strange to have crossed the, 883
Crests and pedigrees, 671
that front the morning, 755
Crested fortune, 267
Cretan against Cretan, 998
Cretonne, Aunt Maggie's, 909
Crew and captain in the sea, 655
and captain understand, 784
darling of our, 274
dismayed her, 655
he left behind, pities the, 200
laughing, set the, 881
of the captain's gig, 622
went one by one, 576
were much pleased when they found, 599
Crews are laid away to rest, 832
Crib, ass knoweth his master's, 1110
Cribbed confined, 87
Cribs from your field, tampers with rent or lease, 490
Cricket is to cricket dear, 977
my dusky little, 638
on the hearth, 160
Crickets, merry as, 1025
Cried, served him right, 510
Crier of green sauce, 1025
rings his bell, 908
that proclaims the conqueror, 1002
Cries, hear their, 1059
Crime and poverty ever be links, 686
and the much vaunted, 991
blanch without the owner's, 303
called virtue, fortunate, 991
coyness were no, 169
forgive the, 294
it is worse than a, 1060
judge of, 1074
like virtue has degrees, 1050
madden to, 355
more than a, 1060
not failure but low aim is, 528
numbers sanctified the, 268
of being a young man, 239
parent of revolution and, 975
popularity is a, 183
profane swearing sufficient, 180
punishment fit the, 624
that devil's madness, that, 845
the curious, 491
to be nobly born, 128
track-mark of an ancient, 965
want exasperated into, 472
Crimes, all his, broad blown, 95
are not to be measured, 981
as a torment for our, 828
empty pocket's the worst of, 560
may reach the dignity of, 275
never among my, 599
teems with, 950

Crimes, virtues which become, 1067
Criminal, ever cured a, 1074
history is the register of, 270, 1053
in the name of liberty, 1058
is absolved, when the, 988
one virtue and a thousand, 356
Crimp and curdled leaf, 369
Crimson flower of battle blooms, the, 522
in thy lips, 80
life-tide, ebbs the, 568
moon and azure eye, 288
wing, conquest's, 244
Cripples, the six beggared, 937
Crises, business, 697
in American industrial system, 715
of anguish advancing, learn from, 536
real, of lives, 837
Crisis, force the moment to its, 900
of human history, every great, 558
that in a, 922
Crisp and white their flashing old racemes, 843
and wintry carpet, 668
Crisped and sere, leaves they were, 460
Crispian, feast of, 67
rouse him at the name of, 67
Cristemasse, at, merie may ye daunce, 6
Cristes lore and his apostles, 5
Critic, at once author and, 1087
attribute of a good, 529
good, is he who, 1079
leaves at curtain fall, 931
not too inquiring, 921
peep or cynic bark, 408
praise not the, 725
regarded his fault-finding, 508
sir, good day, 508
spot a bad, 886
the youngest, has died, 779
would, well if every, 649
Critick ought to dwell upon excellencies, 196
Critics, admiration from most fastidious, 398
before, there were, 649
before you trust in, 351
between me and my, 685
challenge and defend, 759
Cultured Critics O, 615
gallery, 265
just the same, 615
lie, for, 523
like brushers of clothes, 113
love is the coldest of, 558
men who have failed, 319, 421
our English, 942
praise and blame of, 615
with a poisonous sting, 533
who have stamped out, 430
who will praise me after I am dead, 615
whose verdicts are always so new, 649
you know who the, are, 421
Critic's eye, don't view me with, 292

Critic's satires shall have crumbled, 660
Critical, easier to be, than correct, 419
nothing if not, 101
Criticising elves, 262
Criticism, bad and indifferent, 825
cant of, 241
comes easier, 975
contemporary, 675
definition of, 680
dusty and stony ways of, 675
is the endeavor to find the best, 680
with every wind of, 238
Criticisms, most penetrating of, 922
Critique, killed off by one, 634
Croak, his ill-betiding, 206
Crock two-eared of Sabine make, 983
Crocked crucible, burst like a, 928
Crocodile does not move the lower jaw, 136
tears of the, 29, 125
Croesus hast thou riches, 504
Cromwell, Charles the First had his, 270
damned to fame, 208
guiltless of his country's blood, 245
if thou fall'st, O, 74
said paint me as I am, 508
Cromwell's deed and Shakespeare's fame, 443
Crone, drab as a shawl-hooded, 815
Cronie, trusty drouthy, 287
Cronies of the elements, 771
Crook, by hook or, 15
shepherd's, lays the, 425
the pregnant hinges of the knee, 94
Crooked instruments, by his, 1061
lane, straight down the, 391
roads are roads of genius, 282
straight, strive to set the, 608
street goes past my door, 906
way, they followed his, 733
wiles, by, 964
Crop than corn, nobler, 755
Crops failed, 604
little good watering last year's, 520
the flowery food, 207
Cross, all through life I see a, 560
ensign of His, 875
I bear His, 758
last at his, 349
leads generations on, the, 367
little, to tell my loss, 382
nailed on the bitter, 60
never bowed his heart before Thy, 1091
of gold, crucify mankind upon a, 753
of our Lord, save in the, 1121
Patch Town, 667
she wore a sparkling, 212
that rules the Southern sky, 776
the heavier, 1052
to bear my, 647

Cross, to kiss the, 765
  upon His back, lie easier, 891
  was borne, 375
Crosses are hewn, our, 805
  fret thy soul with, 25
  relics crucifixes, 143
  row on row, 820
Crossed in love, an oyster may be, 279
Crossing a stream, not to swap horses, 457
Crossroads, dirty work at the, 944
Cross-starr'd lovers, a pair of, 77
Crossways, things at home are, 678
  to part familiar feet, no, 596
Cross-word puzzle makers, 882
Crost, sure my love is all, 389
Crotchets in thy head, 34
Crow, gran'ther's rule safer'n 'tis to, 527
  like chanticleer, 49
  might be supposed a, 267
  pluck a, 37
  think thy swan a, 77
  thought sun risen to hear him, 520
Crows and jays to peck, for, 839
  swans seem whiter when by, 1031
  wars of kites or, 163
Crowbar, hammer me into a, 855
  hoe and barrow, 348
  tire of all creation for a, 454
Crowche, to fawne, to, 26
Crowd, a host of golden daffodils, a, 299
  and marvellously fed, 694
  and that is why the, 1077
  and through the, 807
  assimilated by the, 1073
  come up from the, 732
  far from the madding, 245
  finish sentences in a, 550
  gives tongue, when the, 928
  not feel the, 265
  not on my soul, unborn ages, 244
  of common men, 141
  of jollity, I live in the, 232
  stop supporting the, 1077
  the gay and festive, 656
  the velvet imperial, 714
  unless you can muse in a, 428
  we met 't was in a, 388
  you were a good, brothers, 726
Crowds, alone in the midst of, 324
  go forth with, 913
  of people came, 475
  talk with, 783
  without company, 271
Crowded audience, for the sake of a, 971
  hour of glorious life, 310
  public way, 403
  tavern's din, 829
Crowing of the cock, 89
Crown and glory that it asks, 525
  and kingdom is, both, 940
  ask for any, 595
  better than his, 46
  emperor without his, 202
  England's glorious, 371

Crown, every noble, crown of thorns, 378
  fame-wreathed, 659
  galling, 808
  gem of the city's, 687
  has cost a, 572
  head that wears a, 65, 910
  his breeches cost him but a, 101, 256
  immortal, 225
  is in my heart, not on my head, 70
  is of night, 633
  likeness of a kingly, 150
  my, is called content, 70
  not the king's, 36
  of glory, hoary head is a, 1107
  of glory that fadeth not, 1122
  of gold, sunflower with gaudy, 453
  of his head, 351
  of life, receive the, 1122
  of one's reading life, Moby Dick the, 530
  of sorrow, a sorrow's, 464
  of the head, from the, 39, 116, 131
  of the house, 953
  of thorn, 647, 753
  perhaps upon my head, 699
  promise uv the golden, 698
  richer than a, 940
  shall go forth and conquer, 676
  that seldom kings enjoy, 70
  the people snatched my, 620
  the work, another rock would, 484
  though I put on a starry, 557
  to gain, a kingly, 343
  tramp on a daisy's, 877
  upon her lordly, 364
  uv silver hair, 698
  will forever be a, of thorns, 378
  with a hairy gold, 782
Crowns a youth of labour, 250
  all, the end, 75
  and thrones may perish, 605
  be scant, if store of, 120
  of roses fade crowns of thorns endure, 609
  twenty mortal murders on their, 87
Crowned and again discrowned, 798
  and dead, poets, 634
Crowner's quest law, 96
Crowning curl to restless toe, 569
Crow-toe, tufted, 159
Crucible, burst like a cracked, 928
  of her ire, melt in the, 801
Crucified to the world, 247
Crucifixes beads pictures, 143
Crucifixions, Calvaries and, 609
Crucify mankind upon a cross of gold, 753
  the soul of man, diseases, 123
Crude hard-fisted tale, 713
  surfeit reigns, where no, 158
Cruel and blind and cold, 879
  aristocracy is always, 480
  as death, 224
  as the grave, jealousy is, 1110
  crawling foam, the, 523

Cruel death is always near, 947
  only to be kind, 95
  records, 570
  rule, better no rule than, 961
  war is, 542
  war is over, when this, 604
  winter, oh the cold and, 436
Cruelest lies are told in silence, 704
Cruell'st she alive, you are the, 54
Cruelly sweet, 512
  treated, no slaves so, 424
Crueltie and ambition of man, 22
Cruelty of pirates, wonder at the, 529
  to load a falling man, 74
Cruise, depart upon thy endless, 537
  we are all on our last, 704
Crumb, a memorial, 584
Crumbs from the table, 1115
Crumbling, old fetish raiments, 609
  teeth well filled, 473
Crumpetty tree, on the top of the, 498
Crusaders, think they are, 451
Cruse, little oil in a, 1101
Crush of worlds, 195
  the infamous thing, 1053
Crushed egg for ever, be same, 432
  odours, 289
  to earth, truth, 373
Crusoe, poor Robinson, 246
Crust, bore through the tough, 936
  of bread and liberty, 214
  of earth in earth and rust, 564
  share her wretched, 525
  the nightmare, 937
  water and a, 383
  with a piece of, 923
Cry and no wool, 9, 142
  break into a bitter, 694
  bubbling, the, 359
  but little wool, great, 1039
  for being born, 113
  gladiators' in the arena, 438
  goes up on high, 780
  have a good, 391
  havoc and let slip the dogs, 82
  he flings to the wind, this the, 676
  he heard the plaintive, 513
  hounds in glorious, 229
  in bed we, 1043
  is still they come, 88
  Life is all their, 922
  mad wind's panther, 905
  Mum, 35
  my eyes out, I shall, 1036
  no language but a, 468
  no sound no, 927
  not when his father dies, 238
  of a child by the roadway, 790
  of a thousand souls, 847
  of bugles going by, 757
  of the critic, in spite of the, 611
  of the wild Cherokee, 508
  raise a hue and, 1035
  the harsh, of, 930
  to him, I may not, 672
  to Lochow, far, 310

Cry to pierce the gray perhaps, 871
  try with a childish, 761
  war is still the, 352
Crye al-day and crave, 7
  and no wull, moche, 9
Cry-babies of the western world, 898
Crying, come to me come to me, 432
  first voice I uttered was, 1124
  give give, 1109
  made her eyes more bright, 801
  solitary in lonely places, 717
Cryptic mirth laconic and Olympian, 808
Crystal boar, saw a, 938
  bounds, dances in his, 158
  bowl, in a, 846
  clearness through, swam its, 658
  cup, into a, 809
  enraged at the breaking of a, 166
  fount more bright than, 983
  light, on a river of, 699
  river, fair and, 128
  springs would solace me, 140
  what youth deemed, 493
Crystals, an eye like its, 560
Crystalline revelator of the achromatic, 432
  waters, banks of the, 432
Cub, tiger's, 395
Cubic inch of space a miracle, every, 537
Cuccu, lhude sing, 3
Cuckold, despite the, 886
Cuckoo buds of yellow hue, 42
  mocks married men, 42
  shall I call thee bird, 299
Cuckoos still call, 758
Cucumbers, as cold as, 131
  lodge in a garden of, 652, 1110, 1125
  sunbeams out of, 191
Cucumber-tree, wild emerald, 431
Cud, chew the, and are silent, 260
  of bitter fancy, 51
Cudgel know by the blow, 142
  thy brains no more about it, 96
Cue, lightly we follow our, 56, 816
Cuirassiers go, the, 738
Cuirass literature on oatmeal, we, 312
Cultivation, gratitude the fruit of, 239
Culture, education and, 970
  I believe only in French, 1082
  she ruins, 1082
Cultured word, 780
Cummin, mint and anise and, 1115
Cumnor Hall, the walls of, 269
Cunning before, she was never so, 350
  hand, nature's sweet and, 54
  in fence, 55
  little ear-ring caught, 706
  livery of hell, 36
  point of, 110
  right hand forget her, 1106
  seldom gain, the, 951
  sin cover itself, 39

Cunning stagers, old, 142
  strong in, 282
  times, 46
Cunningest pattern, 103
Cup afloat of the lake-lily, 484
  and each bitter, 848
  and the lip, 124
  bring another, 441
  come fill the, 1018
  glory in a shallow, 1019
  I fill this, to one, 405
  I have drained, 441
  into a crystal, 809
  leave a kiss but in the, 119
  life's bitter, 948
  my, runneth over, 1103
  of English mead, 864
  of hot wine, 76
  of kindness yet, we'll take a, 286
  of life, in the, 730
  of still and serious thought, 297
  of strength, 520
  of water, little thing, 386
  offering his, 1018
  runneth over, my, 1103
  that clears to-day, 1018
  there's sky-blue in thy, 391
  to the dead already, 554
  'twixt the lip and the, 425
Cups, clink of, 771
  in their flowing, remembered, 67
  flowing, pass swiftly round, 168
  of love, emptier, 625
  that cheer but not inebriate, 204, 265
Cupboard where the jam-pots grow, 702
Cupid and my Campaspe, 23
  bolt of, fell, 42
  giant-dwarf Dan, 41
  is painted blind, 42
  note which, strikes, 145
  young Adam, 77
Cupid's curse, concludes with, 28
Cupido, up-on his shuldres winges, 6
Cur, fur fly about the ears of the old, 142
  mastiff dog may love a puppy, 472
Curs, common lot of, 449
  mouth a bone, as, 262
  of low degree, 254
Curate thinks you have no soul, 858
Curates, abundant shower of, 507
  long dust, 893
Curb and rein, be sure of your, 402
  that galls, 783
  use the snaffle and the, 933
Curdied by the frost, 76
Curds, quivering, 599
Cure, care is no, 68
  desperate, for desperate disease, 1028
  drugs to work the, 997
  for birth and death, no, 769
  for life's worst ills, 401
  for pain is pain, 998
  is not worth the pain, 998

Cure, kings can cause or, 231
  of love, that common, 1036
  of maladies, attend to the, 969
  on exercise depend for, 175
  prevention as, 924
  the dumps, college joke to, 190
Cures, desperate, applied to desperate ills, 175
Cured, what can't be, 124, 1026
Curfew it must ring to-night, 705
  long years I've rung the, 705
  time, magic chains at, 158
  Time to the next prime, 164
  tolls the knell of parting day, 244
Curiositie after the affairs of others, 166
Curiosity a valuable trait, 828
  awakening natural, 1078
  by way of, 222
  damnable and detestable, 449
  gratify no, 238
  newspapers excite, 324
  of a simian, 828
  one of permanent characteristics, 231
  with what a dreadful, 186
Curious, amazed and, 287
  child, I have seen a, 302
  colors he'd gone, 909
  fancy, 'tis a, 916
  for knowledge and for love, 536
  minds, girls have, 430
  thirsty fly, 223
  time, 112
  volume of forgotten lore, 460
Curiously, consider too, 97
Curl to the rosy point, crowning, 569
Curls as nature never knew, 373
  auburn locks ye golden, 451
  Hyperion's, 95
  shakes his ambrosial, 218
  strokes the, 639
  ye golden, 451
Curled Assyrian bull, 469
  darlings of our nation, 100
  smoke that so gracefully, 333
  up on the floor, 644
Currants, full of, 932
Currency, inflation of the, 930
Current and compulsive course, 103
  beat back the, 640
  glide with the, 223
  go with the, 785
  grand magnetic, 1068
  in which he lives, 670
  noiseless strong obscure and deep, 548
  of the soul, the genial, 245
  unperceived because so fleet, 503
  when it serves, take the, 83
Currents turn awry, 93
Current's flow, drift with the, 865
Curriculum of all noble education, 1081
Currid, short horse soon, 13
Curse all men's, 988
  become all men's, 959
  Christianity the one great, 1082
  concludes with Cupid's, 28
  his better angel, 103

Curse, inherit the primal, 890
  middle age is a, 851
  of marriage, 102
  of service, 't is the, 100
  on all laws, 216
  on his virtues, 195
  primal eldest, 95
  selfishness is the greatest, 450
  terrible, 351
  this her, 918
  traditional, 818
  turn your mind to this little, 314
Curses are like young chickens, 425
  dark, rigged with, 159
  of the good Bishop Ernulphus, 241
  so, all Eve's daughters, 35
Cursed alway, by man is, 431
  be he that moves my bones, 109
  be the verse, 213
  spite, 92
  war and racking tax, 309
Cursing creed, crackling pile nor, 452
  like a very drab, 93
Cursory salutation, 234
Curst and shrewd as Socrates' Xanthippe, 52
  be the gold and silver, 247
  by heaven's decree, 251
  hard reading, easy writing's, 279
Curtain call, there's no, 849
  close up his eyes and draw the, 69
  draw the, 54
  drew Priam's, 63
  drops slow falling, the, 481
  fall, Anarch lets the, 216
  her sleeping world to, 369
  lecture worth sermons, 344
  lectures, 217
  let down the, 1024
  let the thick, fall, 444
  never outward swings, 439
  rustling of each purple, 460
  twilight's, spreading far, 389
Curtains, fringed, of thine eye, 32
  let fall the, 265
  of night, 389
  of the east, 604
  rich lace, 559
Curtain's mystic fold, 644
Curtained bee, such color as the, 911
Curtis, cold world, 52
Curtius revering the oracle, 593
Curve, around the, 717
  for the shore, 882
  in the road, a, 924
  of Regent Circus, 683
  they flow, round the, 926
Curves of beauty, flowing, 444
Curved is the line of beauty, 444
  spine, cases of, 430
Cusha! Cusha! Cusha! calling, 540
Cushion and soft dean invite, 210
  lay your golden, down, 374
Cussedness, had trust in his, 639
Custer, Cody and Carson, 707
  our hero, first in the fight, 643

Custom, a thing of, 87
  always of the afternoon, 91
  ancient sacred, 1050
  followed because it is a custom, 1047
  is second nature, 34
  more honoured in the breach, 91
  nature her, holds, 96
  nothing is stronger than, 986
  of Branksome Hall, 306
  of saying grace at meals, 323
  of swearing, ungodly, 179
  permit, neither nature and public use and, 19
  presses, when, 834
  reconciles us to everything, 259
  shall obliterate, 808
  should corrupt the world, one good, 463
  stale her infinite variety, 104
  tyrant, 1033
  what is done against, 1005
Customs and its businesses, 267
  new, though ridiculous, are followed, 72
  politics and tongue of woman, 557
  rise up from the spirit of this world, 247
Customary employment, forego their, 324
  fate of new truths, 564
  suits of solemn black, 89
Customed hill, missed him on the, 245
Customers, sign brings, 1045
Custom-house opens not on road to Paradise, 421
Cut and come again, 280
  beard of formal, 50
  breath, what fine chisel could, 57
  him out in little stars, 79
  is the branch, 32
  loaf, to steal a shive of a, 77
  most unkindest, of all, 83
  take the short, 1011
Cuts through the meadows of ease, short, 818
Cut-throat dog, 44
Cutting bread and butter, she was, 481
Cutty sark, her, 287
Cyclades, child of the, 808
Cycle impenitently, the whole, 895
  of Cathay, 398, 465
Cycles of heaven, the, 899
Cyclones, whirled in, 660
Cydonian suckets sweet apples, mellow, 431
Cygnet to this pale faint swan, 58
Cymbal, tinkling, 1120
Cymbals crash, the, 864
  kiss, when, 879
  of King David's dancers, 934
Cymbrian plaine, 24
Cynara, faithful to thee, 796
Cynic from study of mankind, 661
  knows the price of everything, 724
  knows value of nothing, 724
  tribe, sneer and jibe of the, 843

Cynic's ban, hurl the, 733
Cynosure of neighbouring eyes, 160
  upon the sea obscure, 1032
Cynthia fair regent of the night, 269
  of this minute, 209
Cypress, an alley titanic of, 461
  and myrtle, land of the, 355
  tree, nor shady, 587
Cypress-trees bear no fruit, 1003
  stars shine through the, 444
Cyprus, of Malmsey and Malvoisie and, 647
Cyrus, palace of, 956
Czar, countless cousins of the, 910
  troops that were led by the, 951

D, NEVER use a big, big, 622
Dab at an index, 254
  at electricity and crime, 828
Dachs-hound Geist, their little friend, 547
Dad, a little song to, 873
  called my brother's father, 57
Daddy heered him bawl, 696
Dadoes, he cut up, 888
Daemon is in charge, when your, 787
Daffadills fair, we weep to see, 133
Daffed the world aside, 63
Daffodils a crowd a host of golden, 299
  are blowing, 831
  before the swallow, 56
  it's raining, 772
  yellow shine of, 867
Daft old brain, in his, 816
  to refuse the Laird o' Cockpen, 291
Dagger, air-drawn, 87
  I see before me, is this a, 85
  in my mouth, my, 106
  of the mind a false creation, 85
  smiles at the drawn, 195
Daggers, I will speak, to her, 95
  though it rain, 125
Dahlias that reign, 714
Daily beauty in his life, 103
  bread, 850
  life, lies before us in, 154
  rations, live upon our, 495
  sight, he who in our, 572
Daintier sense, hath the, 96
Dainties bred in a book, 41
  might hurt their health, 252
  of riches, 589
  on the docks, handle, 936
Daintiest last to make the end most sweet, 59
Dainty charms proclaimed, 956
Daisies go down to the sea, 757
  grow, April shower that makes the, 618
  grow, hear the, 722
  myriads of, 304
  pied, and violets blue, 41
  pied, meadows trim with, 160
  that men callen, in our toun, 4
Daisy dear, above all flowers, 1022
  in the dell, every, 717

Daisy lives and strikes its little root, 369
  never dies, 305
  protects the dewdrop, 305
  starred the sod, 539
  there's a, 96
Daisy's crown, tramp on a, 877
Dakotas under her hull, rolling, 915
Dale, haunted spring and, 161
  or piny mountain, 317
  under the hawthorn in the, 160
Dales and fields hills and valleys, 31
Dalliance, primrose path of, 90
Dallies like the old age, 55
  with the innocence of love, 55
Dam, pretty chickens and their, 88
Damaged, archangel a little, 325
Damascus, rivers of, 1101
Damask cheek, feed on her, 55
Dame, eye hath chose the, 109
  Fortune is a fickle gipsy, 406
  Fortune's golden smile, catch, 285
  hither conducted the, 271
  life in the old, 852
  Margery said, 569
  of honor, when I was, 186
  sulky sullen, 287
Dames, haughty, in jewelled velvets, 531
  it gars me greet, ah gentle, 287
  squire of, 24
Damiata and Mount Casius, 150
Damn, he doesn't give a, 957
  his treacherous flatteries, 522
  I do not give a, 630
  the torpedoes! Go ahead, 402
  tough bullet to chew, 782
  with faint praise, 213
  your precious soul, 1026
Damnable and detestable curiosity, 449
  deceitful woman, 185
  iteration, thou hast, 60
  mouldy a hundred years hence, 165
Damnation, distilled, 290
  of his taking off, 85
  round the land, deal, 216
  within two fingers' breadth of, 1013
Damned, all silent and all, 296
  be him that first cries hold, 89
  better be, 272
  conjecturally, 651
  democrats, the, 360
  ere I'd have challenged him, 56
  first, I will see thee, 293
  seen him, ere I would, 55
  spot, out I say, 88
  the public be, 946
  to everlasting fame, 208
  to fame, 223
Damning those they have no mind to, 142
Damozel, the blessed, 577
Damp and mould, fireflies gleam in the, 841
  fell round, when a, 304
  my intended wing, 154

Damp sheiling, from the, 674
  souls of housemaids, 900
Dampness of that dreadful rain, 815
Damsel lay deploring, a, 205
  of high lineage, a, 470
  with a dulcimer, 315
Damsels of time, 410
Dan Chaucer, well of English undefyled, 25
  Cupid regent of love-rhymes, 41
  to Beersheba, from, 242, 1099
Dana uv the Noo York Sun, 698
Dance and jollity, 157
  and Provençal song, 383
  and wine, banquet song with, 363
  attendance, 74
  mehitable dance, 852
  on with the, 352
  rhythmic tribal, 879
  the Pyrrhic, 359
  their wayward round, 297
  when you do, 56
  who have learned to, 211
Dances, Congress of Vienna but, 1055
  in his crystal bounds, 158
  in the wind, 177
  in what ethereal, 460
  sacred, and in song, 972
  such a way, she, 163
Danced, and then she, 405
  laughed and, 342
Dancers, King David's, 934
  walk, and the, 864
Dancing as an art, 740
  days, past our, 77
  drinking time, a merry, 176
  in all its forms, 1081
  is life itself, 740
  more like wrestling than, 1011
  O Heaven her, 405
  on a volcano, 1065
  with the feet ideas words, 1081
  you would be, if, 743
Dandelions and the daisies, I leave to children, 732
  are changed, 619
  golden kisses over the meadow, 500
Dandin, George, you would have it so, 1046
Dandolo, hour of blind old, 299, 353
Dane, an antique Roman than a, 98
  never get rid of the, 784
Danegeld, paid him the, 784
Danger, be in less, 935
  delay always breeds, 1037
  escape every other, 976
  gleams like sunshine, 967
  in it, there may be, 324
  is in discord, all your, 436
  lurks within, 70
  man who can be out of, 564
  moment of difficulty and, 949
  of popery, never in, 197
  on the deep, 388
  out of this nettle, 61
  pleased with the, 173
  presence of mind in, 1048
  shape of, cannot dismay, 300
  sick are the greatest, 1081

Dangers, fronting all, 553
  loved me for the, 100
  of the seas, 115
  sing the, of the sea, 247
  they may fear, though little, 521
  thou canst make us scorn, what, 287
  to their states, 20
Danger's troubled night, 328
Dangerous Dan McGrew, 844
  delays are, 178
  ends, delays have, 68
  females are most, 853
  if a little knowledge is, 564
  literature the most, of professions, 641
  little learning is, 210
  principles, 950
  questions, 429
  sea, most, 46
  something, in me, 97
  such men are, 81
  thing, thirst is a, 745
  times, say nothing in, 130
  to be of no church, 233
  to our peace and safety, 283
  tongue's magic most, of spells, 426
Daniel, a second, a Daniel Jew, 47
  come to judgment! yea a Daniel, 47
  in the den of lions, 1113
Danish sculptor, from the dead, 621
Dank tarn of Auber, 461
Danny Deever, an' they're hangin', 781
Dansons la Carmagnole, 1092
Dante brought to Beatrice, 680
  of the dread Inferno, 488
  sleeps afar like Scipio, 354
Danube River, upon the, 582
Dappled turf, on the, 298
Darby my own, always the same, 690
Dare and yet I may not, 21
  do all becomes a man, 85
  fain would I but I, not, 21
  not do an ill thing, I, 1001
  not wait upon, I would, 85
  to be true, 135
  to chide her, who shall, 512
  to die, bear to live or, 208
  to love their country, 217
  what man, I dare, 87
  what men, do, 39
  will to do the soul to, 308
Dared, what none hath, thou hast, 22
Dares do more, who, 85
  not put it to the touch, 164
  this pair of boots displace, 319
Darien, silent upon a peak in, 384
Daring half discover, the, 839
  hand he flings, 364
  in full dress, 358
  pilot in extremity, 173
  the loving are the, 565
Darius was of the opinion, 572
Darius's horse, 395
Dark, after that the, 472
  age wherein he lived was, 167
  all that led up is, 563

Dark amid the blaze of noon, 156
and bloody ground, sons of the, 541
and bright, best of, 356
and doubtful, from the, 280
and dreary, some days, 434
and dusty as themselves, 899
and lonely hiding-place, 316
and silent grave, 22
and still we inly glow, 338
and the daylight, between the, 434
as children fear to go in the, 109
as Erebus, affections, 47
as night, thy path be, 499
as one's own heart, 422
as pitch, 171
as sages say, not a dream so, 507
at one stride comes the, 315
backward in the, 32
between us and the, 923
blue depths, 322
but through, no time so, 501
clouds lower, suns may scorch and, 404
cottage, the soul's, 146
deeds of men, 350
dcep emerald that Rossetti wrought, 680
economy of Heaven is, 325
ever-during, surrounds me, 151
every hour of light and, a miracle, 537
eye glances, are where thy, 460
eye in woman, 353
for us i' the, 491
fountain, choke the, 364
go to sleep in the, 323
God's ways seem, 442
heart of mine, so shall this, 432
horse, 420
illumine, what in me is, 148
infinite, 758
irrecoverably, 156
leap into the, 1024
most brightly for the, 911
out of that, 936
pines knew, 847
Plutonian shadows, 568
rigged with curses, 159
shining nowhere but in the, 170
streets, in thy, 612
sun to me is, 156
swearing to keep it, 850
the night is, and I am far, 403
'twill soon be, 408
vistas of the reboantic Norns, 432
was the night, 258
ways that are, 644
we are for the, 105
what lieth, 643
what looks, in the distance, 626
when I face the, 682
with excessive bright, 151
with stormy riot, 910
Dark-blue hunter, night the, 801
Darkeneth counsel by words, 1102
Darker grows the night, as, 252
grows the valley, 575

Darkest clouds, as sun breaks through, 52
day, the, 267
Darkies have to part, time when, 567
Darkling plain, as on a, 546
Darkly blue, summer skies are, 418
deeply beautifully blue, 322
dreaming, 590
see through a glass, 1120
Darkness, a distant voice in the, 437
a knock at the door a voice in the, 437
again and a silence, then, 437
amid later, 396
among the gusty trees, 864
and silence reign, when awful, 498
and the cold, in the, 702
and wandered through the, 746
another of, on the confines, 378
as they slide from, 933
be, and thine my, 823
be over me, 423
born, in silent, 30
Cimmerian, 327
cleaving the, 855
come not in, come not in light, 386
dawn on our, 342
distinguishable as light from, 247
distrust the, 621
door of, 1019
down, never comes, 891
encompass the tomb, 343
falls from the wings of night, 434
feel a way in, 936
gathers over all, when the, 452
God gives light in, 69
goes and bird and rose, 642
house in the, 750
in the school of, 682
instruments of, tell us truths, 84
is half withdrawn, 633
jaws of, devour it, 42
land of, 1102
leaves the world to, 244
let us weep in our, 431
like a dream, following, 674
lost for aye in the, 538
night, and light day, 154
night and storm and, 353
of night and the winter's snow, 282
of the land, ring out the, 469
oh so sore afraid of, 822
out of one, 933
peering, deep into that, 460
pestilence that walketh in, 1105
pray in the, 386
prince of, 99, 164
raven down of, 158
round me falling, 850
shall not walk in, 1118
shares the, 915
snow nor rain nor heat nor, 969
sorrows and, 343
struggling, through, 596
that one day out of, 597

Darkness, they go, into the, 917
through a brief, 440
through, up to God, 468
to the happy morn, yields, 672
universal, buries all, 216
unsearchable, 669
we feel is green, 773
which may be felt, 1098
which permits them to see nothing, 995
who would answer, in the, 939
Dark-running wave, 652
Darksome statesman, 170
Darling, an old man's, 17
and my wife, my, 576
of my heart, she is the, 189
of my manhood, 463
of nature, 1029
of our crew, 274
plains, substantiate with his, 810
sin, his, 316
that mashed Romeo, 755
the dear little dimpled, 604
the Frenchman's, 266
the poet's, 298
Darlings, wealthy curled, 100
Darning ragged hose, passed night away, 557
Dart, death shook his, 155
every look a, 193
feather on the fatal, 145, 351
laughter winged his, 626
like the poisoning of a, 167
shook a dreadful, 150
stricken with a, 145, 964
time shall throw a, at thee, 120
Darts, breaking the bundle of, 1002
to its delight, soul that, 556
wards off the, 453
Darwin, Abraham of scientific men, 543
Darwinian man though well-behaved, 624
Darwinism had a champion in Huxley, 930
Dash between the two, 574
maturest counsels, 149
o'er the surface skims with a, 675
Dashing of waves on the sandy bar, 565
Dateless oblivion and divine repose, 610
Dates of wars and deaths of kings, 621
which made me, 832
Daughter am I in my mother's house, 778
blind beggar's, 257
dear, O, her mother said, 501
is my daughter all her life, 567
left-lonesome, 817
let them all to my, 855
lieth at the point of death, 1116
Light god's eldest, 147
made love to his, 996
O my, 670
of a hundred earls, 462
of Bednall-greene, 257
of earth and water, 366
of earth, never a, 954
of his voice, sole, 155

Daughter of Jove, relentless power, 243
of the dawn, 220
of the voice of God, 299
one fair, and no more, 92
still harping on my, 92
than lovely mother, 983
that was all to him, 784
went to bathe in style, 375
yes my darling, 957
Daughters ever since, her, 490
fairest of her, 152
horseleech hath two, 1109
many, have done virtuously, 1109
may be corner stones, 1106
of earth, words are the, 232
of my father's house, 55
of necessity, 974
of the game, 75
so curses all Eve's, 35
stepmother of ministers', 654
sterile be, 937
words are men's, 204, 232
Daughter's daughter cries, 1092
heart, preaching done a, 464
Daughters' minds, trust not your, 100
Daunce, merie may ye, 6
Dauntless in war, 307
mind ride in triumph over all mischance, 70
Dauphiness at Versailles, 260
David and Josias, 947
Garrick, here lies, 252
his little lad, 719
his ten thousands, 1100
in slaying Goliath, assisted, 1056
not only hating, 173
prevailed over the Philistine, 1100
wrote the Psalms, 755
David's psalms had ne'er been sung, 1052
Davil, sea, dat ole, 902
Davy Crockett, all knew, 686
Daw, no wiser than a, 68
Daws to peck at, 100
Dawg around, quit kicking my, 956
Dawn, breaks brightest into, 967
comes up like thunder, 782
conscious of the secret, 773
creation's, 355
daughter of the, 220
exhortation of the, 953
face of the live new, 633
golden exhalations of the, 318
in the sky, 813
is breaking, grey, 396
is my brother, 810
is overcast, the, 194
light-giving, 960
may-time and the cheerful, 299
no, no dusk no noon, 391
of ampler life, 760
of day, two towers of sail at, 519
of light, 364
of music poetry and art, 411
of the morning after, 791
on our darkness, 342
on the other, 810
parting is with, 771
sacred wine of, 764
salutation of the, 953

Dawn saw his campfires, 847
the eternal, 702
the wind that sighs before the, 604
unspeakable, in happy old age, 1069
watching in the twilight, 918
whitened and the east was clear, 659
with silver-sandaled feet, 723
Dawns, the diamond, 572
Dawn's early, can you see by the, 921
Dawn-encircled sea, 889
Dawning, bird of, 89
is the night for you, 625
of her thigh, 134
tongue and pen aid the, 503
what makes his, glow, 416
Day a happy one to a fellow-creature, 313
a perfect picnic, 691
advantages that occur every, 228
advent of each dangerous, 825
after the fair, 13
afterwards, 583
again, would that it were, 916
alternate night and, 1018
and equal night, equal, 561
and had his, 925
and in my, the sun doth, 514
and night, more sure than, 317
and the light need thee so, 644
and the way we met, 633
another blue, 381
are scarce descried, at dawn of, 519
arriving in, in night to all, 536
as it fell upon a, 120
as one shall see in a summer's, 42
as she lay on that, 288
at night, praise, 136
at the close of the, 269
be drunk the business of the, 177
be she fairer than the, 132
before yesterday, the, 892
better, the better deed, 116
beyond the night across the, 465
big with the fate of Cato, 194
blabbing and remorseful, 69
boils at last, 485
break of, 37
break, until the, 1110
breaks not, it is my heart, 117
breathing time of, with me, 97
bright, is done, 105
brought back my night, 162
brought too long a, 390
burden and heat of the, 1115
by algebra tell what hour of, 141
by day, chronicle of, 33
by day, I shall find how, 405
by the fire at close of, 1027
by water fire or air, that, 577
can prostrate, 965
cap by night a stocking all the, 253
cares that infest the, 434
cast not the, 633
chest of drawers by, 251
clean-shirt, 233
close the drama with the, 203

Day, close the eye of, 161
comes on, 886
cometh night, goeth, 643
compare as, with night, 555
compare thee to a summer's, 107
continual dropping in a rainy, 1108
count that, lost, 950
darkest, the, 267
dawns to which we are awake, only that, 515
deficiencies of the present, 232
denies to gaudy, 356
deserved, what hath this, 57
dies like the dolphin, parting, 354
dog and you've had your, 712
dog will have his, 97
drink oblivion of a, 574
dye before his, 255
entertains the harmless, 114
erased the lesson done, the, 537
ere the dawning of the, 738
even and morn, 154
every dog has his, 1035
every, is a fresh beginning, 682
every, should be passed as if it were our last, 989
eye of, 161, 273
faster and more fast, 484
fills his blue urn with fire, 409
five hours in a, 234
for ever and a, 51
for toil an hour for sport, 410
fretting all the, 889
gather honey all the, 199
gaudy blabbing and remorseful, 69
God's interminable, 504
goes by like a shadow, 567
good-bye sweet, 619
great avenging, 218
great the important, 194
grow milder when 'tis, 967
gwine to run all, 568
has begun, 801
has ever failed me, no, 845
hast thou forgotten this, 396
he that outlives this, 67
heat of the long, and wish, 546
her suffering ended with the, 473
her washing ended with the, 557
hoping for the perfect, 477
how troublesome is, 348
I asked of echo t' other, 511
I dearly love but one, 189
I hate the, 26
I have had the, 580
I stand outside, every, 793
I've lived, this, 984
I've lost a, 201
idle singer of an empty, 608
in a hot, 64
in clouds brings on the, 194
in every scene by, 393
in golden letters should be set, 57
in its hotness, 547
in June, what so rare as a, 525
in melting purple dying, 375
in the country, 587
in the light of fuller, 523
in thy courts, 1105
infinite, excludes the night, 199

Day, into the light of common, 301
is a perpetual morning, 514
is always coming, 763
is at the morn, 485
is aye fair, 291
is dim, only my, 761
is done and darkness falls, 434
is dying in the west, 656
is long, merry as the, 38
is out and the labor done. 430
is over, now the, 605
is past and gone, 370
is too near, 643
jocund, stands tiptoe, 79
joint labourer with the, 89
July's, short as December, 56
kings upon their coronation, 174
knell of parting, 244
known a better, 306
laugh to the summer's, 371
life confined within the space of a, 1004
life is but a, 384
life is but a sultry, 1066
little rain foretells a pleasant, 507
live-long, the, 81
loitering, lose this, 1058
long, on all things all, 470
long, support us all the, 1128
longer than a wonder lasts, a, 70
look to this, 953
lord it but a, 687
luve o' life's young, 389
maddest merriest, 463
made black by morning storms, 325
makes up the commonplace, 682
marked with a white stone, 1039
may bring forth, what a, 1108
merry heart goes all the, 56
more work in a, 345
morning shows the, 156
most splendid, I was thinking the, 537
must follow as the night the, 91
ne'er dawns again, this, 1021
next, never so good, 989
night is mother of the, 441
no proper time of, 391
nor looks to see the breaking, 444
not to me returns, 151
now's the, now's the hour, 286
of adversity, 1108, 1109
of Armageddon, in the day of, 778
of crisis and of ultimate hope, 347
of death, ere the first, 355
of deliverance, 268
of empires, 622
of grief and glory, 759
of judgment, vulgarize the, 417
of nothingness, first dark, 355
of prosperity, in the, 1109, 1124
of small nations, 622
of small things, 26
of spring and spring day, 710

Day of thy power, in the. 1105
of woe the watchful night, 322
old blue flower of, 801
on any particular, 935
on any reckoning, 847
one of the great lost days, 796
open as, and the hearts, 435
our eternal, 893
our little systems have their, 467
painted this perfect, 761
parting, linger and play on its summit, 339
pollutes the, 368
posteriors of this, 41
precincts of the cheerful, 245
promise of your early, 342
rain it raineth every, 56
ran a hundred years to a, 452
right must win the, 503
rival in the light of, 303
Rome was not built in a, 15, 1042
sailed away for a year and a, 498
seated one, at the organ, 564
seek all, ere you find them, 44
seen us walking every, 167
serene, rarely is a, 942
shall be beautiful, 802
shall clasp him, 900
shall not be up, the, 58
shining hills of, 442
short or never so long, 17
sir critic good, 508
smiled up across the tide, 772
so calm so cool, 135
so shuts the eye of, 273
star arise in your hearts, 1123
state and inclination of the, 60
sufficient unto the, 1114
summer's, hath a, 165
sun shall not smite thee by, 1106
sunbeam in a winter's, 223
superfluous burden loads the, 162
sweet Phosphor bring the, 134
take thou in charge this, 400
that comes betwixt a Saturday and Monday, 189
that comes by gift of chance, 983
that is dead, grace of a, 465
that maketh all things clear, 643
that shines, think every, 985
that surely dawning, 954
that unforgettable, 627
the bricks are alive at this, 69
the dying, pause, 848
the, is gone, 385
the most useless, 1056
the order of the, 941
they pass every, 1085
they read no more, that, 346
thou wilt bless the, 501
through the long polar, 552
through the Lord's word named, 3
thunder in a fair frosty, 172
time and hour runs through the roughest, 84
to be lost, every, 238

Day to day, from, 88
to fire the brave, 219
to keep awake all, 1079
to-morrow will be a new, 1040
to-morrow will be another, 732
to night pass life pleasantly, 491
to search for God, took a, 758
too solemn for, 386
toward dying, crawled another, 889
travailes of the painefull, 26
trust some later, 983
turned to his rest, 368
uncertain glory of an April, 33
unto day, uttereth speech, 1103
unto the perfect, 1106
varies every, 174
very rainy, 1108
we pluck, one, 843
wealthy gallant always gains the, 1022
well-spent brings happy sleep, 1023
were here, would God, 632
what thou hast done by, 136
when I must die, 577
when like the rising, 416
when skies are fair, 567
when you shall depart, 930
which the Lord hath made, 1106
who won the success of a, 533
will carry the, 1034
will not cannot last for aye, this bright, 516
will not look the same by, 428
wish for your last, 995
with me to stay, came a, 668
without all hope of, 156
wrong side of thirty if she be a, 192
yield, to night, 68
you do not write, 896
you finished it, 878
you shall seek all, 44
Days, a few prosaic, 585
afternoon of her best, 72
among the dead, 321
among the peaceful harvest, 561
and hours, do with all the, 454
are all alike, 916
are as grass, his, 1105
are done, my fighting, 901
are hastening on, lo the, 477
are in the yellow leaf, 358
are phantom days, 847
are still and bright, 418
are swifter than a shuttle, 1102
are told, 1022
are trances, all my, 460
are young and careless-hearted, 840
as thy, so thy strength, 1099
be as a marriage bed, all thy. 135
begin with trouble here, 947
by dreams, measure, 774
called the feast of Crispian, 67
count on two, 966
dead-letter, 323
dividing lover and lover, 633
dull and hoary, 170
eke out the measure of my, 1076

Days fill so much, winter, 669
find it after many, 1110
flight of future, 150
for all the frittered, 881
forty, and forty nights, 1097
friend of my better, 363
full of sweet, and roses, 135
giants in those, 1097
golden olden glory of the, 973
grow dark, if the, 662
halcyon, 68, 972
hand in hand in the golden, 395
happy mixtures of happy, 357
have been so wondrous free, 201
have crackled, 749
have grown to months, 707
heavenly, one of those, 296
hypocritic, 410
I meet him, greet him the, 673
immelodious, 735
in bad, we can vividly recall, 1064
in good, we have imperfect memory, 1064
in her right hand, length of, 1106
in the week, of all the, 189
in these Christian, 345
joyfulness prolongeth his, 1125
light doth trample on my, 170
light of other, 336
like the good old, no, 453
live laborious, 159
long as twenty, are now, 297
looked on better, 49
loved three whole, 163
may come the days may go, 638
measure of my, 1104
melancholy, are come, 372
men in these degenerate, 218
my, are dull and hoary, 170
o' auld lang syne, 286
of a man are counted, 766
of art, elder, 436
of childhood, in my, 325
of few, and full of trouble, 1102
of his pilgrimage, 499
of indigestion, 860
of joy, to remember, 1020
of labor, through, 952
of langsyne, 390
of long-haired poets, 661
of my distracting grief, 248
of my youth, in the, 718
of necessity, prepare for the, 962
of old, in the brave, 400
of old Rameses, 953
of old, which I heard in, 446
of our years are threescore, 1105
of palmy prosperity, 374
of thy youth, in the, 1110
of yore, sad and happy, 703
of your life, live all the, 192
on evil, though fallen, 153
on the earth are as a shadow, 1101
one of those heavenly, 296
our deeds, our, 572
pain of lonely, 596
past our dancing, 77

Days perfect, if ever come, 525
prepare, for all your, 708
pride of former, 334
red-letter, 323
rye-bread, dull and damp, 476
salad, when I was green, 104
see those halcyon, 972
seen better, 357
shuts up the story of our, 22
some, must be dark and dreary, 434
supported by precedents, 999
sweet childish, 297
tale of her, 954
teach us to number our, 1105
than dreamless nights, idle, 823
that are gone by, 973
that are no more, 466, 973
that have been, from, 426
that keep us still apart, 793
that make us happy, 832
that need borrow, 165
that saw us young, bless the, 522
the ancient of, 1113
the errant, 871
the great of older, 579
the whole forty, 815
thirty, hath November, 18
those were happy, 197
though fall'n on evil, 153
though shortening, 335
through endless summer, 584
to lengthen our, 336
to loose good, 25
town-meeting, 404
trample on my, 170
two carefree, 670
unquiet, he lived in, 445
we have seen better, 49, 81
weaving the web of, 631
were circles, 933
when birds come back, 584
when the ball of our vision, 576
with God he passed the, 201
with toil winding up, 63
who creeps his, 905
world of happy, 71
world was made in six, 1060
Day's autumn, 799
business, end of this, 84
garish eye, 161
life, death of each, 86
long toil is past, 392
march nearer home, 306
occupations, pause in the, 434
sorrow of each, growing, 607
tramp is over, 873
work and his night's work, 630
work, done a good, 228
work was done, soon as your, 600
Daybreak everywhere, it is, 439
Daylight and air, and, 744
can see a church by, 38
finish, must in death your, 492
in the mind, 197
sick, this night is but the, 47
sweet, found the common, 687
that we may rejoice like the lark, 431
we burn, 34, 178

Daysies, swiche as men callen, in our toun, 4
Day-star arise in your hearts, 1123
so sinks the, 159
Daze the world, 402
Dazzle the vision feminine, 401
Dazzling fence of rhetoric, 158
immortality, 366
Dazzlingly in full dress, 358
De mortuis nil nisi bonum, 1013
Deacon, I was junior, 782
swear, enough to make a, 527
Dead a thousand years, 881
and all the rest are, 437
and dumb and done, 823
and gone, he is, 256
and the seas give up their, 375
and turned to clay, 97
are always pop'lar, 796
as a doornail, 66, 495
as Chelsea, 944
as mutton, 497
away, hopeless lays his, 444
being, with him is beauty slain, 106
bivouac of the, 541
close the wall with English, 66
coals, 57
converse with the mighty, 224
could find out, if only the, 594
cup to the, already, 554
day that is, grace of a, 465
days among the, 321
death is to the, 638
deathless hour, 577
democracy of the, 602
disembodied spirits of the, 373
do the meanest thing after he's, 687
don't die, 884
evil become lost and, 536
for a ducat, 95
for we bore our, 845
game sport, 803
has a dear one, 676
have consciousness of our presence, 350
he is not, 366
he is not, but departed, 591
heart's, are never buried, 910
hosts of the mighty, 641
how fares it with the happy, 468
how living are the, 697
if I were, you'd sometimes say, 556
I'm king of the, 448
in look so woe-begone, 63
in the streets, truth never fell, 476
Indians only good ones, 594
is at rest when the, 1125
is it possible, 643
it seems that the, are there, 554
it's for a long time, 1062
knocking when I'm, 855
language impart to a, 607
languages, 358
litigate over me when I'm, 605
living dog better than a, 1109
man cannot bite, 999
Man's Chest, 524

Dead, many of mine old ac-
    quaintance are, 65
marks our English, 778
men, down among the, 941
men grin by the wall, 864
men in the loam, sows, 712
men rise up never, 632
men, who wait for, 15
men's bones, full of, 1116
most deadly when most, 914
mourning for our, 1089
my dearest, when I am, 587
nature seems, 85
no pageant train when I am,
    374
not, but gone before, 188, 289
not to speak evil of the, 1013
nothing to the, 586
now behold him, 756
of midnight, 273
of night, 63
old lion is, 276
on the face of the, 569
on the field of battle, 706
on the field of honour, 1092
only the, who do not return,
    1059
out of reach your, 696
over mounds of the, 576
over the rich, 894
past bury its dead, 433
past clear of all regret, keep
    the, 960
Petra in her hill-tomb, 443
pity tenderness and charity
    when we're, 520
pleasure of not being, 1054
poets in their misery, 297
posture that we give the, 279
profiteering in the, 908
remembered footsteps, 807
rest for the, 605
rest her soul, she's, 97
reverence of the, 132
risen from the, 699
rises from, cerements the
    Christ, 609
say I'm sick, I'm, 212
Sea, one social, 716
Sea's shore, 352
secrets arise, 913
sepulchres of mighty, 386
she is not, 817
sheeted, did squeal, 89
should still be near, desire the,
    468
sleeping but never, 524
some hundred years, 657
the breathers of this world are,
    108
the law hath not been, 36
the noble living and the noble,
    300
the unreplying, 602
the world has no power, over
    the, 1051
there are no, 618
these heroic happy, 921
this earth that bears thee, 63
this man is, 925
those immortal, who live again,
    520
though the house of it seems,
    597
thought it happier to be, 409
to bewail the, 959

Dead together, wish we were,
    631
understand that you are, 896
vast and middle of the night,
    90
volcanoes only, on, 690
wake the, 886
we become the lumber of the
    world, 185
weep not for the silent, 290
when a man is, 330
when but for those our mighty,
    288
when honour dies the man is,
    442
when I am, let fire destroy the
    world, 1093
when I am, no pageant train,
    374
when it is said, word is, 585
when the living might exceed
    the, 145
which he slew at his death,
    1099
who fed the guns, 892
who go, are from the, 683
who hath bent him o'er the,
    355
will not say that he is, 696
will stare and sting, 914
would I were now, 391
you are the, 929
you never shall return, 1018
Dead-letter days, 323
Deadlock, holy, 909
Deadly breach, imminent, 100
    fair so coldly sweet, 355
Dead-sure thing, a, 639
Deadwood and Lost Mule Flat,
    929
Deaf adder, like the, 1104
    are dumb are blind, 'tis we are,
    604
    neither good nor bad to the,
    1049
    none so, that will not hear, 17,
    136, 187
    world does not hear, 706
Deal damnation round the land,
    216
    in giving a great, 1050
    of nothing, infinite, 44
    of sack, intolerable, 62
    of scorn, what a, 55
    of skimble-skamble stuff, 62
    square, 734
Deals, piled-up, 873
Dealing, common sense and plain,
    412
Dealings, he was faultless in his,
    406
    whose hard, 45
Dean, cushion and soft, 210
Deans, dowagers for, 466
    prudes for proctors dowagers
    for, 466
Dear a price, too, 229
    and true industrious friend,
    here is a, 60
    as the light of these sad eyes,
    244
    as the ruddy drops, 82, 244
    beauteous death, 170
    charmer away, 205
    common flower, 525
    creations, so will these, 551

Dear dead women, 486
    five hundred friends, 265
    for his whistle, paid, 227
    for my possessing, too, 108
    glad faces long away, 619
    guest and ghost, 439
    hut our home, 226
    makes the remembrance, 53
    man to all the country, 250
    my, better half, 27
    near and true, 467
    none less, than thine and my
    good Marcius, 76
    old friend to me, 678
    old-fashioned posies, where are
    the, 569
    our very dearest, 642
    pay a great deal too, 56
    sixpence all too, 101
    so, I love him, 155
    son of memory, 161
    the merry cries, 619
    the people coming home, 619
    the spot, matters not how,
    432
    the thanks, 619
    to God, worthy patriots, 162
    to home and memory, 734
    to me as are the ruddy drops,
    82
    to me as life and light, 286
    to them that love her, 747
    to this heart, how, 348
    where did you come from baby,
    559
    wisdom is never, 479
    work good-night, 458
    you will be, how, 895
Dears, the lovely, 284
Dearer than his horse, something,
    464
Dearest enemy, nearest and, 117
    thing he owed, 84
    through every season, 393
Dearly let or let alone, 135
Dearness only gives value, 271
Dearth, but a lack and, 597
    of woman's tears, was, 447
Death a cordial old and rare,
    664
    a delightful journey, 520
    a door that leads to light, 603
    a hideous show, 547
    a necessary end, 82
    a state of rest, 350
    after life, 24
    aims with fouler spite, 134
    all in the valley of, 467
    anchor of a love is, 676
    and Chance and time, triumph-
    ing over, 161
    and failure and fame forever,
    737
    and General Putnam, 816
    and his brother sleep, 368
    and life, bane and antidote, 195
    and life in ceaseless, 447
    and night, hands of the sisters,
    536
    and pain, they fear, 995
    and sleep, twins, 219
    and taxes, 228
    and that vast forever, 523
    and the Roman populace, 438
    and the stars, night sleep, 537
    and the sultan, 767

Death and time bring on the prime, 693
armed with new terror, 331
at midnight goes a-dancing, 1078
at the point of, 80, 1051
be called unhappy, no one till his, 430
be careful of the rest, 793
be good, whether, 632
be not proud, 118
be thou faithful unto, 1123
begun, birth is nothing but, 202
between us, 480
birth and, 985
borders upon our birth, 121
breaks every bond, 1051
broke the vital chain, 231
brother to sleep, 30
but a tavern, 833
but an eternal sleep, 972
but life, and see not, 575
by beauty made amends, 798
by inches, give him, 76
by slanderous tongues, done to, 40
calls ye, 141
came with friendly care, 316
cannot slay, 736
captain of all these men of, 172
chooses his own time, 596
clear, will make, 634
closes a man's reputation, 196
cold not daunte, 257
come lovely and soothing, 536
come to the bridal chamber, 362
comes at last, 592, 792
comes to all, 1027
comes to set thee free, 1063
comes, when, 670
cometh, soon or late, 400
content to have from, 746
continue after, 981
could not stop for, 584
covenant with, 424
creation's, 328
cruel as, 224
cruel, is always near, 947
danger of violent, 132
dear beauteous, 170
defend to the, 1053
delicately takes the best, 793
deprive him of, 738
devise, he did my, 136
devours all lovely things, 915
died there a natural, 838
disregard for, 930
divorce or, 624
doors that lead to, 144
drawing near her, 147
draws near, when, 967
dread of something after, 93
dull cold ear of, 244
early, to favourites, 354
éclat of, 584
eclipsed the gayety of nations, 233
effect of, on the world, 670
eleven thousand persons suffered, 191
eloquent just and mightie, 22
end of a journey, 520
ending in, at last, 608
epitaph after your, 93
ere thou hast slain another, 120

Death, faithful unto, 1123
fatal asterisk of, 438
fell sergeant, 97
final taunt of, 924
first day of, 355
first solemn note is sounded by, 1064
for an example of noble courage, 1125
for thee was glorified, 823
for who is he, 584
forgotten, were, 933
four fingers from, 1013
gallop Pegasus to, 214
gates of glory and of, 789
gave all that we possess, 651
give me liberty or give me, 270
gives a foretaste of, 1064
glimpsed the awful face of, 1091
gone to her, 392
grants us yet a little time, 664
gray, sets me free, 774
grim, 129
guilty of his own, 96
had left it almost fair, 681
had the majority long since, 145
happy people not afraid of, 788
has broached him to, 274
has carved me, when, 892
has choked a great man's voice, 429
has ever truly longed for, 462
has its own way, 1067
has shaken out, 375
hath a thousand doors, 128, 129
hath no more dominion, 1119
hath not touched it at all, 597
hath so many doors, 131
hath ten thousand several doors, 127
he taketh all away, 554
heaven gives to its favourites early, 354
heavy page of, 938
herald after my, 74
his ladder to the skies, 26
his Maker and the angel, 317
how wonderful is, 368
hymn to his own, 58
I would fain die a dry, 32
in battle, prize of, 527
in France, walked with, 904
in itself is nothing, 178
in life, found, 319
in life, oh, 466
in life or after, 970
in love with easeful, 383
in strange contradiction to life, 709
in that sleep of, 93
in the afternoon, 930
in the alabaster arms of, 646
in the hour of, 561
in the midst of life, 1128
in the pot, 1101
in victory, swallow up, 1111
into the world, brought, 148
intrenched, 202
is a common friend or foe, 511
is a great disguiser, 37
is a secret of nature, 1010
is a sleep, 631
is a state of nothingness, 970

Death is a thing which makes men weep, 361
is an eternal sleep, 1060
is at the bottom of the cup, 629
is beautiful, 528
is better, sleep is good but, 1066
is birth, end of, 597
is but an open door, 843
is but one more to-morrow, 579
is but the long cool night, 1066
is certain to all, 65
is life, perhaps, 972
is life's high meed, 385
is love's friend, 690
is master, 678
is most in apprehension, 988
is never at a loss for occasions, 1092
is new, life's old, 493
is no evil, 594
is no foeman, 896
is no punishment, 164
is not the worst evil, 965
is only a beautiful adventure, 534
is only a horizon, 653
is our master, 917
is prancing, 1078
is slumber, 366
is strict in his arrest, 97
is strong, stronger than, 612
is such waste of me, 798
is the ugly fact, 588
is the veil, 367
just and mightie, 22
just, kind umpire of men's miseries, 68
kneeling by his bed of, 31
laid low in, 327
laugh myself to, 33
lays his icy hand, 141
lead him to, 185
let it not be a, 1084
lieth at the point of, 1116
life achieved by others', 58
life is ever lord of, 444
life perfected by, 428
life well used brings happy, 1023
like a friend unseen, 808
long mysterious exodus of, 436
looks gigantically down, 459
love is strong as, 1110
love thee better after, 429
loves a mining shark, 661
loves a shining mark, 134, 202
lurks in every flower, 342
makes equal the high and low, 11
makes his arrest, when, 833
may bring our friend, 587
means, know what, 595
meetest for, 46
men equal in presence of, 986
men fear, 109
most in apprehension, 36
my name is, 659
name is admiral, 764
name that sat on him was, 1123
nativity chance or, 35
no, for such as he, 595
no kind of, 887
no other herald after my, 74
nor change, there is no, 368

Death nor life, neither, 1119
  not, but love, 428
  not divided in, 1100
  nothing happen more beautiful
    than, 534
  nothing our own but, 59
  O amiable lovely, 58
  of a dear friend, the, 43
  of Charles I, 1078
  of cold, catch your, 501
  of each day's life, 86
  of friends, feel for the, 1043
  of his saints, 1105
  of kings, and tell sad stories
    of the, 60
  of one who is young, 887
  of some of her, through the,
    832
  of the flowers, after the, 952
  of the righteous, 1099
  of the saints of the Lord, 1105
  old men's prayers for, 967
  on his pale horse, 155, 639
  on the reef of Norman's Woe,
    433
  or dreamful ease, dark, 463
  or honour or of love's sweet
    smart, of, 911
  outrage worse than, 316
  paleness of, 362
  paradise to what we fear of,
    36
  pause for, 491
  pigeon that has been starved
    to, 458
  plague us to, 1052
  prayers for, 967
  prepare as though for, 907
  provides Anglo-Saxons amuse-
    ment, 919
  quiet us in, so noble, 157
  reads the title clear, 492
  reaper whose name is, 433
  remembered after, 928
  remembered kisses after, 466
  rendezvous with, 904
  rides a camel, 544
  rides on every breeze, 342
  ruling passion strong in, 209
  sail on the sea of, 832
  sallied forth, 840
  seems but a covered way, 443
  sends a radiogram, 854
  sense of, most in apprehension,
    36
  shades of, 150
  shadow of, 1102
  shall be no more, 118
  shook his dart, 155
  should sing, 't is strange that,
    58
  silence deep as, 328
  silent halls of, 371
  simplest of human rights to
    choose, 754
  slavery or, when to choose, 195
  sleep before, 1004
  sleep is a, 145
  slue not him, 26
  smooth the bed of, 213
  sole equality on earth, 506
  sooner or later delicate, 536
  sorrows of, compassed me,
    1103
  speak me fair in, 47
  strikes down the innocent, 495

Death, struck sharp on, 429
  studied in his, 84
  succeeded life so softly, 175
  sure-enwinding arms of cool-
    enfolding, 536
  sweats to, Falstaff, 61
  swerved from, 773
  takes toll of beauty, 832
  that cuts in marble, 916
  that makes life live, 491
  the blessing men fly from, 553
  the discourse of everybody, 182
  the fear of, 988
  the great adventure, 881
  the healer, scorn thou not, 964
  the jaws of, 56, 467
  the lover of life, 692
  the nature of his, 969
  the old nurse, 693
  the punishment for murder,
    479
  the sable smoke, 354
  the serenity of, 602
  the stern sculptor, 595
  the valley of the shadow of,
    1103
  there is no, 435, 618
  there is not room for, 516
  they said that in, 929
  they were not divided, in,
    520
  things that nature wills, 1011
  think not disdainfully of, 1011
  this is the taste of, 958
  thou hast all seasons, 370
  thy sting, O, 736
  till, us do part, 1128
  't is not all of, to die, 306
  to die a more painful, 1084
  to life, from, 31
  to those who mourn, 371
  to us play to you, 167
  to what we fear of, 36
  tragedies finished by a, 359
  triumphant, 155
  true face of, 796
  tryst with, 767
  turn ice in the grasp of, 554
  twitching my ear, 982
  unexpected, the best sort, 1003
  vacancies by, are few, 274
  valiant taste but once of, 82
  vasty hall of, 546
  victory or, resolved on, 1060
  wages of sin is, 1119
  wait, nor be afraid, 489
  way to dusty, 88
  ways and words of, 692
  we must stoop to, 19
  went out to, 867
  what should it know of, 295
  what ugly sights of, 71
  where is thy sting, 1120
  which happened in his berth,
    392
  which he slew at his, 1099
  whispers of heavenly, 537
  who puts, sweet is, 470
  whose portal we call, 436
  will overtake you, 1126
  will seize the doctor, 106
  will soon be past, 396
  with anxious strife, 326
  with rust, eaten to, 64
  world easily reconciles itself
    to his, 422

Death, worse things waiting than,
  631
  worst friend and enemy is but,
    894
Deaths, cowards die many times
    before their, 82
  glorious in thy just defence,
    194
  happen at ebb tide, 713
  I could endure, all, 155
  many, have place in men, 826
  more than one must die, 722
  of kings and dates of wars, 621
  thousand dreadful, 728
  unknown to fame, 219
  ye died I have watched, 776
Death's a debt, 278
  ace, he trumped, 639
  boatman, 983
  brink, Shelley to, 879
  call, why should I fear, 534
  counterfeit, sleep, 86
  dark encounter, for, 508
  door, brought to, 525
  dream kingdom, 899
  familiar tale, 554
  fearful forehead, 658
  iron guard, through, 937
  pale flag, 80
  road we all must go, 983
Death-bed of fame, from the, 327
Death-complete to die, a life-
  complete in, 682
Deathless chains, 432
  deed or word, 879
  fame, to give her features, 561
  lines, for all your, 868
  page, traced on the, 516
Deathly slumber, seal thy sense
  in, 822
Death-wave o'er, sailed long
  since the, 568
Death-winter, so after the, 560
Death-wound of Dundee, 758
Debatable land, 651
Debate of commonwealth affairs,
  66
  Rupert, of, 419, 425
Debauchee of dew, 584
Deborah danced, 901
Debt, a double, to pay, 251
  a national, is a national bless-
    ing, 341
  by no means run in, 136
  death is a, 278
  depends on borrowing and,
    1076
  don't allow us to be in their,
    509
  due in May or in December,
    698
  every one that was in, 1100
  expedient of going into, 715
  if a man owe a, 958
  infinite, 1057
  instalment on his, 991
  not dishonest because in, 627
  produce their, instead of dis-
    charge, 203
  that one man owes, 873
  their national, 1072
  those who are in debt, 482
  to nature is quickly paid, 135
  to you, my, 847
Debts, a quantity of, 811
  are paid, my, 406

Debts, he that dies pays all, 33
　words pay no, 75
Debtor class, the so-called, 627
　earthly, but accounts to fate,
　　833
　is but a shamefaced dog, 560
　to his profession, 109
Debtors or creditors, either, 1057
Decalogue, can hear the, 296
　futile, 736
　the, 1098
Decay, age is not all, 559
　by a gentle, 172
　fondest hopes would not, 590
　found her, 240
　fretted the pigmy body to, 173
　general flavor of mild, 452
　gradations of, 231
　make haste on, 895
　may talk of degeneracy and,
　　400
　moist breath of, 575
　muddy vesture of, 47
　of that colossal wreck, 367
　the great and wise, 640
　upon old, greenest mosses, 441
　wealth accumulates and men,
　　250
Decays, age unconscious of, 178,
　　219
　glimmering and, 170
Decay's effacing fingers, 355
Deceased, he first, 114
　he is indeed, 45
　name of the late, 783
Deceit and self-deception in pol-
　　itics, 1086
　aside, to turn, 710
　health to fond, 774
　hug the dear, 226
　I am not up to small, 644
　in gorgeous palace, 79
　incapable of, 311
　men favour the, 178
　shine deceitful flow, 336
　woman damnable, 185
Deceive, easiest person to, is one's
　　self, 426
　when first we practise to, 308
Deceived, true way to be, 1044
　which cannot be, 949
Deceiver, memory thou fond, 252
　to deceive the, 1045
Deceivers ever, men were, 38, 256
Deceiving, literature the most, of
　　professions, 641
　what is hope but, 592
December and May, when were,
　　620
　debt due in May or in, 698
　in a drear-nighted, 383
　it was in the bleak, 460
　July's day short as, 56
　love you in, 656
　mirth of its, 405
　never dim, 703
　seek roses in, 351
　shortest in, 668
　snow, wallow naked in, 59
　when men wed, 51
Decembers, fifteen wild, have
　　melted into spring, 516
　golden Junes and bleak, 690
Decencies, those thousand, 154
Decency, fits best with, 966
　right meet of, 242

Decency, sea's respect for, 726
　want of, is want of sense, 180
Decent and manly examination,
　　320
　mammalian philosophy, 905
　provision, 235
Decently and in order, 1120
Deceptive, appearances are, 962
Decide, moment to, 524
　when doctors disagree who
　　shall, 210
Decider of dusty and old titles,
　　132
Decimal point, the humble, 830
Decision by majorities is as much,
　　450
　grasp on the bow was, 576
　in the valley of, 1113
Deck, boy stood on the burning,
　　370
　Caesar treads the, 994
　coming o'er, from the cold, 645
　my captain lies, walk the, 536
　our girls for gay delights, to,
　　522
　passengers along the, 933
Decks and scrape the cable, holy-
　　stone the, 505
Decked, thy bride-bed to have,
　　97
　with diamonds and Indian
　　stones, 70
Declamation, air favorable to,
　　726
　roared, 231
Declaration and promise, phrase,
　　1086
　of independence, generalities
　　of, 394
　with the written, 696
Declarations of pretended pa-
　　triots, 200
Declination, letters of, 716
Decline, in our long, 810
　of belief, 651
Declined into the vale of years,
　　102
Decorous, my prose is, 767
Decorum, observances of paltry,
　　311
Decoy, fashion's brightest arts,
　　251
Decree, curst by heaven's, 251
　hot temper leaps over a cold,
　　44
Decrees, a mighty state's, 468
Dedalus, symbolism in name, 874
Dedes, gentil, to do the, 7
Dedicate his beauty to the sun,
　　77
Dedicated to closeness, 32
Dedis, gentil that doth gentil, 7
Dee, across the sands o', 523
　lived on the river, 269
　rises o'er the source of, 277
Deed, attempt and not the, 86
　better day the better, 116
　charm of a, 660
　dieth, every noble, 964
　dignified by doer's, 53
　done, half the, 985
　faintly praises the, 213
　in every eye, blow the, 85
　is in itself a, 471
　is wrought, a noble, 436
　kind of good, to say well, 73

Deed, no evil, 660
　no noise over a good, 1011
　of mercy, each pure and gentle,
　　427
　of mischief, every, 270
　of shame, each, 436
　purpose is equal to the, 201
　put your creed in your, 409
　ruleth over every, 964
　shall blow the horrid, 85
　so shines a good, 47
　tells of a nameless, 290
　this, writ in marble, 130
　trace back the greatest, 578
　whereat valour will weep, 76
　will for the, 192, 194, 1026
Deeds are done in thee, 804
　are done, where glorious, 688
　are men, 138, 204
　be not careless in good, 1011
　be thy prayer to thy God, 499
　better, shall be in water writ,
　　130
　boast no more your mighty,
　　141
　both great and small, 955
　by great thoughts and good,
　　506
　doe die, 25
　done, any of my real, 847
　done in their clime, 355
　excused his devilish, 152
　fruitful of golden, 151
　gloss on faint, 80
　He quickens into, 442
　high, haunt not the fringy
　　edges, 519
　if I did good, 813
　ill, doubled with an evil word,
　　38
　inimitable his, 28
　is known by gentle, 25
　longer than, 964
　matter for virtuous, 28
　means to do ill, make deeds ill
　　done, 58
　not words, 127
　of carnage, war and its, 536
　of honour, 972
　of kindness, little, 553
　of men, looks quite through
　　the, 81
　of men, within this book the
　　pious, 346
　of men, write the pious, 511
　of mercy, teach us to render,
　　47
　of others, have me judge the,
　　1085
　of truth, 1077
　our days our, 572
　relate such brave, 507
　seeds of future, 755
　that are done of Mrs. Jones,
　　715
　the circle growing, 574
　unlucky, relate, 103
　we live in, not years, 506
　with contrary blasts proclaims
　　both, 157
　words are no, 73
　worthy of praise, 981
　years of golden, 471
Deem it not an idle thing,
　　474
Deemed of them, if we better, 506

Deep and dark blue ocean, 354
  and dreamless sleep, 612
  and gloomy wood, 296
  and long lesson, 434
  are dumb, 21
  are the thoughts, 815
  as a well, 't is not so, 79
  as death, silence, 328
  as ever death can be, 638
  as first love, 466
  beauty of the world 'tis but
    skin, 169
  bottom of the, dive into the,
    61
  breast, hold me to your, 619
  but far on the, 609
  calleth unto deep, 1104
  damnation of his taking off, 85
  danger on the, 388
  dear silence, 429
  deep sea, under the, 390
  drink, or taste not, 210
  embosomed in the, 249
  exhaustless, his numbers
    flowed, 393
  fishes that tipple in the, 168
  for his hearers, too, 252
  from out the boundless, 472
  greater hulks draw, 75
  home is on the, 328
  home on the rolling, 502
  immense Atlantic, 667
  in the lowest, a lower, 151
  into new land, 310
  into that darkness peering, 460
  moans round, 464
  of night is crept upon our talk,
    83
  of world-accusing waves, 836
  on his front engraven, 150
  philosophy, search of, 167
  plough the watery, 218
  plow, and straight, 417
  potations pottle, 101
  rocked in the cradle of the, 350
  she goes through the, 588
  sleep falleth on men, 1101
  spirits from the vasty, 62
  thoughts too, for tears, 302
  versed in books, 156
  where the brook is, 69
  wisdom from the central, 524
  yet clear, 167
Deeps, far in yon azure, 434
  from out whose, 1085
Deep-contemplative, fools so, 49
Deeper in my sighs, I'm growing,
    509
  sea, disturbs the Sabbath of
    that, 480
  than all speech, 501
  than ocean, 386
  than the depth of waters, 577
Deepest consequence, 84
  grief and woe, 729
  loathing to the stomach brings,
    43
Deeply beautifully blue, 322
Deep-meadowed happy fair with
    orchard lawns, 463
Deep-mouthed welcome, 358
Deep-seated repugnance, 865
Deep-toned voice of the digger,
    952
Deer, a-chasing the, 286
  be killed, before the, 144

Deer, let the stricken, go weep,
    94, 265
  mice and such small, 99
  poor, thou mak'st a testament,
    48
  stricken, I was a, 265
  to the wholesome wold, 778
Deeth is an ende of every worldly
    sore, 6
  of every man is writen, 6
Dee-vice, it's a, 852
Defamed by every charlatan, 469
Defeat as great, in, 928
  brings prudence and concentra-
    tion, 740
  ill-health is, 378
  is great that can not be helped,
    533
  mankind is sentenced to, 926
  the gloom of, 571
  wounds and sore, 806
  wrested from a sure, 901
Defeats more triumphant than
    victories, 113
Defeated personally, our princi-
    ples never, 424
  valor lies, 581
Defeatures, life's, 445
Defect, amends for this general,
    217
  cause of this, 92
  caused by any natural, 112
  fine by, 209
  noble manners veil, 556
Defective comes by cause, 92
Defence against injury and vio-
    lence, 21
  against lightning, 989
  against reproach, no, 196
  at one gate, to make, 156
  deaths glorious in thy just, 194
  faithful friend is a strong, 1124
  immodest words admit of no,
    180
  in war a weak, 177
  mathematics in their, 937
  millions for, 276
  of nations, cheap, 260
  of our Liberty Tree, 271
  of weak minds, first, 318
  skilful in its own, 591
Defend me from my friends, 293
  the right, God, 69
  what's mine, I will, 129
  your departed friend, 175
Defenders, heat of its, 184
  of old homes, 1085
Defensive, as a moat, 59
Defer, madness to, 201
  not till to-morrow, 193
Deference and applause, refuse
    that, 1056
  duty, friendship politeness,
    1087
Deferential glad to be of use, 900
Deferred, hope, 1107
Defiance, in their eye, 250
Deficiencies of the present day,
    232
Deficiency in individuals, 1062
Defied all portents of impending,
    418
Definite debt, it is a, 1057
Definition of a gentleman, 403
  of bourgeoisie, 1072
  of expert, 761

Definition of proletariat, 1072
  of pure poetry, 709
Definitions are hazardous, 232
  I hate, 420
  of poetry, the, 926
  of prose and poetry, 319
Deformity which beggars mim-
    icked, 398
Defunct bodies, ghosts of, 142
Defy the devil, 55
  the tooth of time, 203
Degeneracy and decay, may talk
    of, 400
Degenerate days, in these, 218
Degenerates from the sire, the
    son, 218
Degradation of man by poverty,
    1067
Degree, curs of low, 254
  difference lies in the, 1050
  each in our, 652
  is preserved, unless, 990
  men of low and high, 1104
  take but, away, 74
Degrees, crime like virtue has,
    1050
  entangled in various, 970
  ill habits gather by unseen, 177
  it grows up by, 131
  of consanguinity, 1035
  scorning the base, 82
  virtue has its, 131
  we boil at different, 414
Deified by our own spirits, 297
Deity, down with ridiculous no-
    tions of, 569
  ever vindictively made, 461
  man's genius is a, 1006
  offended, for, 285
  omnipresent like the, 342
Dejected thing of fortune, the
    most, 99
Delaware, ice on the, 784
Delay, above all low, 336
  always breeds, 1037
  chides his infamous, 201
  excuse in, longer than the tale,
    79
  is ever fatal, 994
  lets you go without, 802
  Mecca saddens at the long, 224
  reluctant amorous, 152
  reproved each dull, 250
  sick with long, 386
  the law's, 93
  wove of my, 807
Delays, after some, 186
  are dangerous, 68, 178
  have dangerous ends, 68
  life admits not of, 236
  unless he recommends, 945
Delectable, sweet and, 59
  mountains, 172
Deliberates, woman that, 195
Deliberation, retreat without,
    1051
  sat on his front, 150
  spent in idle, 235
Deliberations, after endless, 1087
Delicacies, ear for verbal, 862
Delicacy beyond the China lux-
    ury, 323
Delicate and beautiful to behold,
    1126
  child of life, man, 1089
  creatures, call these, 102

Delicate death, sooner or later, 536
 duty of devising schemes, 320
 ears and superfine long nose, 735
 the air is, 85
 thing, you'll hurt the, 924
 weed, like that, 592
Delicately weak, 209
Delicious bed, O bed O bed, 391
 egotist, 893
Delight, afford, 942
 and dole, in equal scale, 89
 and joy, do we meet, 574
 and thy delight, my, 669
 ay in the very temple of, 384
 bring, as summer, 133
 centres of, 27
 circles of unimpaired, 933
 eternal quiet, brief, 759
 even the purest, 561
 faints with its own, 356
 flies, whom, 736
 give back the lost, 619
 go to it with, 104
 he drank, 280
 how they ring out their, 460
 in love, if there's, 193
 in mere change, find, 1071
 in nature, 656
 in others' misfortunes, 259
 in simple things, 783
 into a sacrifice, 135
 is in the pursuit, 217
 lady of my, 701
 land of pure, there is a, 199
 lap me in, 364
 life not life at all without, 556
 lose their dear, 108
 lost in divine, 850
 my ever new, 153
 my private hours, 156
 my solitary sole, 393
 of battle, drunk, 464
 of her husband, 903
 of the race, commonest, 582
 other aims than my, 651
 over-payment of, 322
 paint the meadows with, 42
 plaything gives his youth, 208
 she that was the world's, 618
 she was a phantom of, 299
 slight the to-day's, 484
 some are born to sweet, 282
 soul that darts to its, 556
 stars gave the first, 145
 that shadowy thought can win, 384
 that shatters, 736
 the wonder of our stage, 119
 the world's, 587, 630
 to do the things I ought, 339
 to muse, 773
 to see a wedding, 182
 we all quote by, 415
 with liberty, to enjoy, 26
 with silent, 281
 with sorrow where all was, 567
Delights, all passions all, 316
 hence all you vain, 127
 not me, man, 92
 that witchingly instil, 224
 to deck our girls for gay, 522
 to scorn, 159
 violent, have violent ends, 79
 winter hath his, 121

Delightful human tadpole, shapes of the, 775
 old diarist Pepys, 637
 studies, still air of, 162
 task, 224
 thing is a turnpike road, 360
 ugly as sin almost as, 545
Delilah said to Samson, 1099
Delineation of its varieties, happiest, 323
Delirious riot of religion, 635
Deliver us from the service of mammon, 1127
Deliverance, day of, 268
Delivered upon the mellowing of occasion, 41
Delivers brawling judgments, ignorance, 470
Delivery may secure, 850
 of a sermon, improve their, 228
Dell, every daisy in the, 717
Delmonico's, we sit at, 734
Delphian vales, the, 363
Delphic oracle, sayings of the, 1004
Deluge, after us the, 1055
 pedigree reaching back to the, 483
 showers, the rain a, 288
Delusion a mockery and a snare, a, 331
 and cruel snare, heart-rending, 1042
 of some major purpose, 895
 of youth, 420
 Solon was under a, 974
 to the philanthropist, 611
Delusive train, waiting for that, 551
 vain and hollow, 395
Demagogue, men who can stand before a, 522
Demands strong minds great hearts, time, 522
Demd damp moist body, 494
 horrid grind, 494
Demesne, allowed to man for his, 909
Demigod, clod from which we grow the, 732
Demi-Paradise, this other Eden, 59
Demise, morning after his, 505
Demi-tasses, with your villainous, 730
Demnition bow-wows, gone to the, 494
Democracie, among our fierce, 510
Democracy a charming form of government, 974
 a self-cancelling business, 378
 chiefly to be found in, 975
 egg of, 529
 future of essential, 876
 idea of, 455
 is called a, 970
 is on trial in the world, 679
 natural elements of, 1070
 of the dead, 602
 political, 538
 sail ship of, 537
 world safe for, 725, 769
Democratic party is like a mule, 260
 world, whole new, 379

Democratie, fierce, 156
Democrats, the damned, 360
Democritus would not weep, what, 304
Demon lover, 315
 of despair, unacquainted with the, 754
Demoniac throng, 677
Demonstrate a providence, to, 1007
 an emotion, 641
Demonstrating a careless desolation, 50
Demonstrations of love, 1037
Demosthenes and Phocion, 1000
 and Pythias, 1000
 chance to fall below, 292
 with pebbles in his mouth, 1000
Demure, sober stedfast and, 160
Demurrer, no bail no, 278
Den, Aïdes', 652
 beard the lion in his, 308
Denial vain and coy excuse, 159
 whose affirmation or, 1021
Denied, who comes to be, 128, 221
Denmark, it may be so in? 92
 something is rotten in, 91
Den-O, could reach his, 951
Denoted a foregone conclusion, 103
Density and colour of smoke, 1069
Deny us for our good, 104
Depart, come like shadows, so, 87
 loth to, 189
 the great business of life is to, 641
 upon thy endless cruise, 537
Departing friend, knolling a, 64
Department of utterly contemptible, 768
Departure from the simplicity of Christ, 247
 is taken for misery, 1124
Departures of pleasure, 588
Dependence upon doctors and special treatments, 1081
 upon relief, 876
Dependent on one another, all, 721
Deplore thee, we will not, 343
Deploring, a damsel lay, 205
Deposit, hack through much, 780
 in some sacred, 545
Depravity doctrine and origin of, 654
 of ear, a sweet, 709
 of inanimate things, 654
 of their nature, perverse, 1051
Depressed by poverty, 231
 with cares, 205
Depth, drawn out of this, 895
 far beyond my, 73
 in philosophy, 110
 of grief, make less the, 70
 of some divine despair, 466
 of the heart of man, cannot find the, 1124
 of the soul, gods approve the, 303
 of waters stilled at even, 577

Depths and shoals of honour, 73
 chasms and watery, 318
 dark blue, 322
 of blue, 442
 of the ocean, 290
 pellucid in thy azure, 538
 scarcely ever fathom their, 1082
 sinks into thy, 355
 your eyes' blue, 1066
Deputed sword, nor the, 36
Deputies, assume to be the, 1062
Derangement of epitaphs, 277
Derby dilly with three insides, 294
 domes its meed of woe, 910
Derision, clothed with, 634
 marked for, 1021
 uglification and, 598
Derisive skies twinkle, 895
Dervishes, barefoot, 410
Descendant of the ape, 867
Descending from the train, loveliness, 559
 never ending always, 321
Descent, by a long, 1051
 claims of long, 462
 is from heroic sires, 1050
 no record of her high, 561
 to Avernus, easy is the, 982
 to Hades, 1014
 wealth nor high, 499
Describe the undescribable, 354
Descrie the happy dawning of her thigh, 134
Descried, sail long leagues apart, 519
Description, beggared all, 104
 would make it less, 268
Desert air, sweetness on the, 245
 as I came through the, 610
 blossom as the rose, 1111
 domes across a, 923
 far in the, 933
 from the sown, 1018
 gardens of the, 372
 in the wide, 390
 island, upon a, 622
 isle, hunt for a, 938
 limitless waste of the, 435
 Mr. Micawber, I never will, 496
 of a thousand lines, 214
 of London town, grey miles long, 610
 of the mind, the leafless, 355
 spot, garden makes a, 820
 use every man after his, 93
 were my dwelling-place, 264, 354
 where no life is found, 390
 wildernesses, 157
Deserts, and they come by their, 483
 full of wild beasts, 996
 his, are small, 164
 of vast eternity, 169
 too small, fears his, 164
Desert's awful frame, in the, 528
 dusty face, 1018
Deserted at his utmost need, 176
Desert-wind, whispers of the, 544
Deserve better of mankind, 191
 praises, 679

Deserve the lovely, the brave, 559
 we'll do more we'll, 194
Deserving, honour without, 28
 lost without, 101
Desideratum of a volume, 324
Design, carved me to his stern, 892
 thine of fair, 777
 things difficult to, 232
Designs, getting up new, 617
 of his imagination, 749
Desire, according to our, 1087
 and mystery, the same, 577
 arises from sated, 776
 because of his, 777
 bloom of young, 243
 changes, gradually our, 1087
 comes in play, where strong, 1089
 dream and unaccountable, 806
 drink provokes the, 86
 end of every man's, 632
 fierce, liveth not in, 307
 from what I've tasted of, 839
 heart's, 471
 her for her state's sake, 133
 hour that wakens fond, 1021
 imp of blind, 780
 is a perpetual rack, 123
 is the wish, 312
 kindle soft, 176
 more love, I shall, 48
 my inexpressible, 689
 nearer to the heart's, 1020
 of fame and love of truth, 471
 of knowledge, 669
 of knowledge in excess, 110
 of life prolongs it, 359
 of man, pure and just, 1023
 of power in excess, 110
 of receiving greater benefits, 200
 of the moth for the star, 368
 satisfied of your, 966
 shall fail, 1110
 shining with, 960
 should outlive performance, 65
 spent with, 889
 the soul's sincere, 306
 this fond, 195
 to appear so, as the, 1044
 to be immortal, all men, 477
 to move in harmony, 563
 to purchase, some toy you have, 55
 to quench the fierce, 586
 to take medicine, 694
 vision of fulfill'd, 1019
 which has his, 482
 wonder and a wild, 490
Desires, army of the world's, 40
 mastery of the, 1080
 of our nameless, 771
 of the mind, 112
 sordid hopes and vain, 345
 weaned my heart from low, 1023
 wild and weak, 864
 your hearts, be with you, 48
Desired, no more to be, 1038
Desks, stick close to your, 623
Desk's dead wood, 325
Desolate creatures, how many, 430
 heart, blew cold on my, 418
 no one so utterly, 434

Desolate, none are so, 434
 sands eternal moan, on its, 503
 streams, sitting by, 676
 whisperings around, shores, 385
 wind-swept space, 620
Desolated years, amends for, 593
Desolation, abomination of, 1116
 and dim night, silence and, 459
 build on waste and, 925
 careless, 50
 earth knows no, 575
 enlinked to waste and, 66
 full of sweet, 385
 intellectual, 1072
 o'er my heart's, 507
 the foe's, 332
 your map of, 937
Despair, bawl out their strange, 928
 brooding over putrid eggs of hope, 292
 comfort in, 69
 conscience wakes, 151
 depth of some divine, 466
 doubt is brother-devil to, 675
 fiercer by, 149
 from hope and from, 219
 hopeless love finds comfort in, 279
 hurried question of, 356
 I can endure my own, 189
 lean and swarthy poet of, 881
 master my, 411
 midnights of, 878
 my ending is, 33
 nympholepsy of some fond, 354
 of getting out, 128
 or hope of joy, texts of, 525
 our final hope is flat, 149
 parent of, 385
 seldom comes with first shock of misfortune, 494
 shall I wasting in, 132
 that slumbered, 151
 the message of, 327
 the twin-born of devotion, 632
 the warder is, 723
 the winter's gray, 692
 whence groweth this, 918
 where reason would, 239
 where seraphs might, 352
 wrath and infinite, 151
Despaires, comfortlesse, 26
Despatch is the soul of business, 222
Despatchful looks, 153
Desperadoes, buffler an' the, 888
Desperate appliance, relieved by, 96
 cures must be to desperate ills applied, 175
 disease, desperate cure for, 1028
 diseases grown, 96
 part, acting a silent, 533
 steps, beware of, 267
 the joy, 346
 thing, marriage is a, 130
Despicable enemies, notice of, 961
Despise me, ay do, 269
 not thy mother, 1108
Despised, causes you to be, 1023
 weak and, old man, 98

Despoilers of the many, 1062
Despond, slough of, 171
Despondency and madness, 297.
Desponding, morose or, view, 400
Destination, city that was her, 933
Destined prey, 720
  snare, the, 577
Destinies, anthem of the, 443
  fates and, 45
  prepare, heavy-fisted, 893
  presides over, 895
  we bind our, 425
Destiny a kind of heavenly, 298
  dread heights of, 690
  exercises its influence, our, 1079
  for beers, match with, 778
  great hour of, 891
  hanging and wiving goes by, 45
  has more resources, 716
  in shady leaves of, 165
  in the field of, 441
  is a strange, 651
  is that of Florence, 926
  marriage and hanging go by, 125
  of men, marks the, 395
  one country, one, 340
  rendezvous with, 877
  waiteth alike for them, 963
  wedding is, 12
  you reap a, 954
Destinye, never man's, 255
Destiny's sea, launch us on, 363
Destitution of morning callers, 312
Destroy is murder, one to, 203
Destroyed by thought, 262
  once, never supplied, 250
  so cowardly, 61
Destroyer of the human spirit, 877
Destroying, fighting and still, 176
Destruction, going from us to be, 1124
  it promises, 1069
  lurks within poisonous dose, 226
  means of our own, 962
  pride goeth before, 14
  self-conceit may lead to, 961
  startles at, 195
  that wasteth at noonday, 1105
  to say that for, 839
Destruction's reach, out of, 647
Destructive man, smiling, 186
  woman, damnable deceitful, 185
Desuetude, innocuous, 627
Detached as nurses in a hospital, 912
Detail, frittered away by, 514
Detect, lose it the moment you, 209
Detection, in May escaped, 493
Detective story, not a, 925
Determined mind, soften the, 933
  not to do it, 1048
  to know beans, 515
Detestable curiosity, damnable and, 449
Detestation of the high, 497
Detraction, scared by a, 716
  stirs no sigh, 651
  will not suffer it, 63

Detractions, they that hear their, 39
Development, economic and political, 1086
Deviates into sense, never, 175
Device, banner with the strange, 434
  of movable types, 379
  that is our, 1067
Devices of love, blue-print, 939
Devil a monk was he, 1025
  as a roaring lion, 1123
  at everything, 1036
  author of lies, 126
  black as the, 1059
  brooked the eternal, 81
  builds a chapel, 126, 138, 187
  can cite Scripture, 44
  defy the, 55
  devised forgetfulness, 774
  did grin, the, 316
  dream of the, 351
  dressed, how was the, 321
  drives, when the, 17, 53, 1026, 1037
  drove them, as if the, 1026
  eat with the, 7, 16
  enters the prompter's box, 844
  every man was God or, 174
  for all, 125
  go poor, get thee gone, 241
  God or, every man was, 174
  has the largest congregation, 187
  have all the good tunes, why should the, 274
  he's a very, 55
  his due, give the, 61
  in all his quiver, 361
  in that little jackdaw, 351
  is a gentleman, the, 99, 367
  is asleep, 719
  is gone, a-walking the, 321
  is in, the place the, 144
  laugh to see a biter bit, 559
  let us call thee, 101
  resist the, 1122
  ruled by the, 956
  said then, 316
  sends cooks, 19, 243
  stood abashed, 153
  sugar o'er the, himself, 93
  synonym for the, 397
  speak the truth and shame the, 1040
  splashing and plunging like a, 241
  take the hindmost, 142, 322
  talk of the, 319
  tell truth and shame the, 62, 235, 1026
  to pay, 334
  was ringing his knell, 321
  was sick, 1025
  wear black, let the, 94
  when most I play the, 71
  when thou wast made a, 127
  will have a chapel, 126
  world flesh and the, 1127
  would build a chapel, 1024
Devils, more, than vast hell can hold, 43
Devil's back, got over the, 1026
  leavings, 217
  luck, the, 792
  madness, war that, 845

Devil-and-all to pay, 1037
Devilish deeds, excused his, 152
  sly, tough and, 496
Devious ways, down, 853
Devise wit write pen, 41
Devised at first to set a gloss on faint deeds, 80
Devoid of significance, his claims are, 421
Devon, if the Dons sight, 765
Devonshire lane, in a, 333
  shrimpers, learned from the, 599
Devotee of the gospel of getting on, 720
Devotion, despair the twin-born of, 632
  earnest and entire, 477
  ignorance mother of, 126, 178
  look of, 645
  man capable of, 645
  object of universal, 343
  of a lifetime, 724
  perpetual, 704
  pity love patriotism no concern of art, 611
  solemn acts of, by, 268
  the still prayer of, 336
  they gave the last full measure of, 456
  to organization standardization, 824
  to something afar, 368
  to virtue, 776
Devotion's visage, 93
Devour, seeking whom he may, 1123
  the treacherous bait, 39
  thy heart, do not, 1016
Devouring of the weak by the strong, 580
Devoutly to be wished, 93
Dew, age finds out was, 493
  and glory love and truth, 857
  and shade, blessings of, 712
  anywhere, there's no, 801
  as sunlight drinketh, 462
  bespangling Herbe and Tree, 134
  bright with autumn, 372
  chaste as morning, 175, 202
  cumbers, at mid-day the, 652
  diamonds in their infant, 178
  drenched with, 822
  drop of ink falling like, 359
  dwells a draught of, 730
  exhaled as the morning, 175
  faded like the morning, 327
  fed it with silver, 368
  from the heath-flower, 308
  glistering with, 152
  he brings cool, 444
  her eye dissolved in, 269
  into a sea of, 699
  is full of heavenly love, 696
  mists of silver, 367
  of sleep, timely, 152
  of slumber, honey-heavy, 82
  of the cornfield, 668
  of thy youth, 1105
  of yon high eastern hill, 89
  of youth, morn and liquid, 90
  on his thin robe, 328
  on the mountain, like the, 308
  rained a ghastly, 464

Dew, sage in the silver, 830
  silence of the hours of, 691
  soft falls the, 569
  thaw and resolve itself into a, 89
  the hours of, 691
  upon a thought, like, 359
  walks o'er the, 89
  wombe of morning, 24
Dews, his wrath allay, no twilight, 309
  morn the mother of, 224
  of summer nights, 269
  of the evening, 222
Dew-damp sands, kneel on the, 845
Dewdrop, daisy protects the, 305
  fragile, 384
  from the lion's mane, 75
  gleaming in the, 512
  on the rose, 309
  starlight and, 568
  there 's a woman like a, 487
  time's corrosive, eats, 564
Dewdrops which the sun impearls, 153
Dewey at Manila, 711
  feel discouraged, 660
  was the admiral, 660
  was the morning, 660
  were the regent's eyes, 660
Dewy eve, from noon to, 149
  freshness fills the silent air, 322
  morn to dewy night, from, 608
  wet, 572
Dexterity, avoided with incredible, 871
Dhrains, undernaith the, 819
Dhrames always go by contrairies, 389
  and not slape, for 't is, 389
Diabolical knowledge, 277
Diadem of snow, 357
Diadems and fagots in their hands, 410
Dial from his poke, drew a, 49
  hour by his, 49
  not in figures on a, 506
  takes no note of clouded hours, 330
  to the sun, true as, 143
  usefulness of a, 1016
Dialect, a Babylonish, 141
  and different skill, 109
Dialogue, wooden, 75
Diamond cut diamond, 132
  Dante brought to Beatrice, 680
  dawns are set, 572
  form, of, 266
  great rough, 222
  has become notoriously common, 1083
  in the sky, like a, 345
  is the crystalline revelator, 432
  me no diamonds, 946
  more valuable than a, 1034
  pen with point of a, 1112
Diamonds, acres of, 665
  and Indian stones, decked with, 70
  bright as young, 178
  diamond me no, 946
  sown with, 933
Dian, temple of, 956
Dian's temple, hangs on, 76

Diana, burnt the temple of, 145
  of the Ephesians, great is, 1118
  shows, legs were such, 134
Diana's foresters, 60
Diapason closing full in man, 176
Diarist Pepys, delightful old, 637
Diary, life a, 750
  memory is the, 724
Dice, ought to take the, 967
  were human bones, whose, 357
Dicers' oaths, false as, 95
Dickens Dumas or Walter Scott, can equal, 793
  what the, 34
Dicks, Dick me no, 946
Dictate of common sense, 226
Dictionaries are like watches, 238
  histories, and temporary poems, 232
Dictionary can be called a grammar, than a, 403
  no such literature as a, 694
  words, 319
Didacus Stella, 122
Did it, thou canst not say I, 87
Diddle we take it is dee, 634
Die a bachelor, I would, 39
  a dry death, I would fain, 32
  a little trust that when we, 607
  a more painful death, 1084
  all alone we, 365
  all, 65
  all that live must, 89
  and endow a college, 210
  and go we know not where, 36
  and there an end, 87
  as much beauty as could, 119
  at the top like that tree, 192
  bear to live or dare to, 208
  because a woman's fair, 132
  before I wake, if I, 947
  better, how can man, 400
  but first I have possessed, 355
  but once, a man can, 65
  but once, we can, 195
  by inches, 187
  cowards may fear to, 22
  fall mad if they do not, 379
  for her is serving thee, to, 451
  for love, 53
  for our country 't is a bliss to, 219
  for the truth he ought to, 410
  free men, we will, 274
  freedom or leave to, 552
  greatly think or bravely, 217
  harder lesson how to, 268
  hazard of the, 72
  here in a rage, 191
  I must, 940
  in the last ditch, 940
  in yon rich sky, they, 466
  informs me I shall never, 195
  is a debt we must all discharge, to, 135
  is cast, 396, 1000
  it must couple or must, 545
  it taught me how to, 405
  landing on some silent shore, 187
  leisure as to, 1003
  let us do or, 127
  let us, to make men free, 522
  look about us and to, 206
  lot of man to suffer and to, 220

Die many times, cowards, 82
  men, but sorrow never dies, 682
  names that were not born to, 363
  nature broke the, 356
  nor all of death to, 306
  not born to, 363
  not, those thou think'st thou dost overthrow, 118
  not willingly let it, 162
  O last regret regret can, 469
  of a rose in aromatic pain, 207
  or the world, old men must, 472
  or, unknown, 216
  see London once ere I, 65
  since I needs must, 22
  speak or, 66
  taught me how to, 405
  taught us how to, 205
  teach men to, 205
  that the thing we love must, 492
  the day when I must, 577
  there let me sing and, 359
  these things can never, 666
  thoughts that shall not, 303
  to, is gain, 1121
  to save charges, 123
  to, to sleep no more, 93
  to-morrow we shall, 1111
  to-night, if I should, 729
  unlamented let me, 216
  wandering on as loth to, 304
  we can not, 596
  we must, live we how we can, 70
  when brains were out, 87
  when he shall, 79
  who tell us love can, 322
  with harness on our back, 88
  without or this or that, 210
  without thee I dare not, 365
  young, whom the gods love, 360
Died as one that had been studied, 84
  away in hollow murmurs, 248
  for liberty, 602
  for men, 639
  had no poet and they, 214
  heroes as great have, 219
  if I had thought thou couldst have, 364
  in bed they, 610
  last night, I only, 620
  liked it not and, 114
  of no blast he, 178
  the lilacs bloomed and, 437
  to make men holy, as He, 522
  who, overwhelmed in the strife, 533
Dies a wave along the shore, so, 273
  alas how soon he, 231
  an honest fellow, 127
  and makes no sign, 69
  he that, pays all debts, 33
  hurrah for the next that, 554
  in single blessedness, 42
  nothing, but something mourns, 359

Diet, be sober in your, 221
  benefits a temperate, 985
  directly traceable to, 910
  Doctor, Doctor Quiet, 192
  ill, was the mother, 138
  is the cause love lasts, 163
  prescribed by doctors, 976
Dieth, the noise of tempests, 480
Dieu mésure le froid, 242
Differ, agreed to, 321
  as heaven and earth, men, 470
  though all things, all agree, 216
Diff'ence foller, den de, 682
Difference between a dog and a man, 615
  between construction and creation, 826
  distinction without a, 229
  lies, all the, 941
  lies in the degree, only, 1050
  made all the, 838
  of opinion makes horse races, 616
  of purpose between Almighty, 457
  strange all this, should be, 221
  then where 's the, 504
  to me, but oh the, 296
  wear your rue with a, 96
  whose ox, it makes a, 1024
Different branches of arithmetic, 598
  dish, each scene a, 200
  drummer, hears a, 515
  like but oh how, 300
  name for conversation, 241
  to die is, 535
  way to kill us, 860
Difficile, Latin was no more, 141
Difficult, nothing more, 1023
  to be emphatic, 582
  to design things, 232
  to know one's self, 1012
  to make a man miserable, 456
  to please, she is not, 802
  to stay a moral infection, 497
  world, make it a, 895
Difficulties, a man in, 963
  an even mind in, 399
  and dangers, complicators of the, 606
  cannot be great, 1023
  knowledge under, 331
  show what men are, 1007
Difficulty in life is the choice, 709
  of saying no, 318
  pluck brings us into, nerve takes us out of, 545
Diffused knowledge immortalizes itself, 290
Diffusion of printed matter, 1077
Dig and heap lay stone on stone, we, 546
  the grave and let me die, 703
Digest, divine, to, 753
  mark and inwardly, 1127
  of anarchy, 260
Digested, books to be chewed and, 111
  it comes too late, after it is, 241
Digestion, bred from pure, 153
  gratitude for a good, 1081
  ill, 38
  importance of good, 727

Digestion, question about my, 655
  side of the best, 853
  sour in, 59
  wait on appetite, 87
Digger, deep-toned voice of the, 952
Diggeth a pit, whoso, 1108
Dignified by the doer's deed, 53
  look, with a, 351
  vice sometimes by action, 78
Dignities of earth, 427
  peace above all earthly, 73
Dignity and honour, received with, 999
  conciliate with, 240
  creditor owns your, 1068
  curtailed by traffic conditions, 1089
  in every act, 1010
  in tilling a field, 734
  of crimes, reach the, 275
  of history, 200, 229, 400
  of man, only true, 770
  of truth, 118
  Washingtonian, 619
Digression, there began a lang, 285
Dilemma, two horns of my, 241
Diligence, best of me is, 98
  few things are impossible to, 232
  is the mother of good fortune, 1041
  with the same, 118
Diligent in his business, 1108
Dim and joyless, 338
  and yet so familiar, 766
  beauty at the heart of things, 754
  blue hills of dream, 717
  dominions on the nights, 418
  eclipse, in, 149
  enchantments, render birth to, 447
  halls of night, through the, 418
  hope's star grows, 405
  monument where Tybalt lies, in that, 80
  night, desolation and, 459
  religious light, 161
  the light was, 936
  uncertain sight, 821
  with age, sun shall grow, 195
  with looking for some star, 484
  with rust, brightest blade grows, 453
  world of clouding cares, 574
Dim-discovered, ships, 224
Dimes and dollars! dollars and dimes, 560
Dime's worth of something, 870
Dimensions, hath not a Jew, 45
  sickness enlarges the, 324
Diminished heads, hide their, 151
  rays, hide your, 210
Diminution of our claims, 1073
Dimmed the light of heaven, 709
Dimmer in the eyes, I'm growing, 509
Dimmycratic party ain't on speaking terms, 796
Dimness, candled, smoke and talk, 905
  of sight came over many, 247

Dimness, sight faints into, 356
Dimple, he calls it a, 697
  the baby's, 522
Dimples stick in, 697
Dimpled chin, pretty page with, 481
Dimpling all the way, run, 213
Dim-seen track-mark, 965
Din and riot, hater of, 445
  crowded tavern's, 829
  of its loud life, 443
  of town, all the, 674
  of turmoil hinder, 725
  sick of all the, 593
Dine and dress, let the world go, 406
  has enough when he would, 504
  that jurymen may, 212
  to call, to, 736
Dined, to-day, I have, 313
Dinero, no tengo, 895
Diners-out from whom we guard our spoons, 401
Dingle, far down the dusky, 618
Dingy days, danced along the, 584
Dining, the man that can live without, 592
  thought of, 252
Dinkey-Bird goes singing, 699
Dinner among old soakers, 181
  bell the tocsin of the soul, 360
  good enough, 234
  lubricates business, 275
  much depends on, 361
  nap after, 236
  no gravy and no grub, no, 903
  of herbs, better is a, 1107
  speeches tire me, 601
  talk, 751
  to ask a man to, 234
Dinners, fish, will make a man spring, 164
  the world visits his, 1046
  were precarious things, 323
Dinner-bell's a sound of ruth, 599
Dinner-time fur some folks, twelve o'clock for me, 599
Dinotherium wandered by, a, 664
Diogenes, were I not Alexander, I would be, 1005
  struck the father when the son swore, 125
Dip, she tuk her, 375
Diplomacy begun, what, 644
  is to do and say, 894
Diplomat, know I am a, 1085
  no doubt, some, 728
Diplomats women and crabs, 640
Dipper, long-handled, 661
Dipt in night, 588
Dirce in one boat, 326
Dire revenge these redmen planned, 714
  was the noise of conflict, 153
Direct and honest, to be, 103
  revealings, with its, 698
  the lie, 51
Directs the storm, 194, 215
Direction, all chance, 207
  I cannot leave you my, 406
  in which education starts, 973
  of his dreams, advances in the, 515
  of public affairs, 1075
  that may chance, any, 970

Directions, moving in opposite, 313
Directness, with admirable, 923
Dirge for her, a, 460
  in marriage, 89
  is sung by forms unseen, 247
Dirges, singers chanting, 554
Dirt and dross, mine be the, 832
  delve in nice clean, 761
  faithless leather met the, 203
  loss of wealth is loss of, 11
  of Londontown, 864
  was trumps, if, 325
Dirty fingers soil no gold, 395
  work at the crossroads, 944
Disadvantages of reading books, 542
Disagree, when doctors, 210
Disagreeable man, such a, 623
  more, to say than do, 1000
  truth, speak a, 1056
Disappear, evil tends to, 581
Disappointed, shall not be, 272
  tide, I heard recede, 585
  unaneled, 91
  woman, fury of a, 193
Disappointment and regret, 309
  endears, love's, 493
  follow, lest, 395
  of manhood, 420
  lays one down with a feeling of, 324
  parent of despair, 385
  to ourselves, 507
  trips you up, 865
  we endure, no, 507
Disappointments, familiar with, 455
Disapprobation, gravest moral, 788
  imagined approbation or, 448
Disarray it lays its wing, on, 841
Disaster and ill fortune, 999
  occasions and not causes of, 734
  to ward off, 747
  unmerciful, 460
Disasters have their use, 590
  in his morning face, 251
  middle station had fewest, 187
  weary with, 86
Disastrous chances, 100
  end, borne to, 26
  night, 477
  pledges, 888
  twilight, 149
Disbanding hired armies, 379
Discern, all we have built do we, 546
Discerning, gives genus a better, 253
Discharge in that war, no, 782, 1109
Discharged with greater ease than made, debt. 135
Disciple, he will have no, 393
Disciples devout, 595
Discipline, no, without pain, 741
  of shrews at home, under the, 344
Disciplines of wars, I know the, 66
  to dance most austere of, 741
Disciplined inaction, 290
Discobolus standeth, 614
Disconsolate, a Peri stood, 337

Discontent, adventures of his, 898
  both of, 973
  candid, 646
  discontented with divine, 524
  first step in progress, 724
  nights in pensive, 25
  winter of our, 71
Discontented, everyone that was, 478, 1100
  mourner, many a, 667
  strife, 121
  with the divine discontent, 524
Discord, all your danger is in, 436
  and continual strife, age of, 68
  brayed horrible, 153
  dire effects from civil, 195
  follows, hark what, 75
  harmony not understood, 207
  must investigate, 1000
Discords, straining harsh, 80
Discordant harmony of circumstance, 260
  life, echo from our, 564
  sound, drum's, 261
Discourse, bid me, 106
  good company and good, 140
  kind of excellent dumb, 33
  like a Persian carpet, 996
  of reason, beast that wants, 90
  of the elders, miss not the, 1124
  rather hear thy, than see a play, 125
  rather than not, he will hire hearers, 120
  such large, 96
  sweet and voluble is his, 41
  Sydneian showers of sweet, 165
  your fair, 59
Discourses in our time to come, 80
Discourtesy, holding it as a gross, 931
Discovered, how easily murder is, 77
Discoverers, for the true, 1054
Discovery, joy of a great, 1087
  made a great, 913
  of divine truths, 200
  portals of, 874
  still to be made in literature, 377
Discreetly blot, 146
Discretion is the better part of valour, 63, 131
  destroy them out of, 1057
  in the man, 1006
  of speech, 111
  philosophy is nothing but, 130
  tested, 702
  thou art a jewel, 944
Discrimination, attain, 1017
  is protection, 762
Discuss it freely, as when they, 398
Discussed with buoyant hearts, 698
Discussion, family, to close, 582
  whoever in, 1022
Discussions, part of all political, 775
Disdain, in patient deep, 547
Disease and death, interest in, 1089

Disease, as physician observes the, 118
  bad rhyming, 214
  becomes a, 1074
  called lack of money, 1025
  complicated and chronic, 997
  each season has its own, 342
  father of a, 138
  has to examine, 1000
  Ireland a fatal, 709
  long, 213
  management of one, 969
  new and smart, 821
  of an evil conscience, the, 450
  of not listening, the, 64
  of talking, 120
  of thought, 461
  of which old men sicken, 116
  remedy too strong for the, 966
  remedy worse than the, 110, 987
  shapes of foul, 469
  that minor chord, 718
  this strange, of modern life, 547
  young, 208
Diseases crucify the soul of man, 123
  desperate grown, 96
  enter there, 136
  enumerated among, 1049
  extreme, 971
  new-fangled names to, 973
  number of, is a disgrace, 1051
  occupational, of teachers, 849
  of the bowels, 969
  of the mind, all the, 198
Diseased, minister to a mind, 88
  nature breaks forth, 62
Disembodied spirits, 373
Disesteem of my contemporaries, 788
Disgised, fack can't be no longer, 606
Disgrace, before their loved ones in, 728
  he bears his unforeseen, 199
  the shadow of, 696
  to mankind, 1051
  with fortune, when in, 107
Disgraces, scorned all, 856
Disgraceful, nothing more, 981
Disguise, a flower in, 525
  blessings love, 910
  brooked no, 735
  perseverance in, 731
  the sweet soul, 593
  thyself as thou wilt, 242
Disguises thrown away, 591
  troublesome, 152
Disguiser, death's a great, 37
Disgust to marriage, 235
Disgusted with the task, 948
Dish, each scene a different, 200
  fit for the gods, 82
  for the gods, 105
  if there's a, 908
  upon a golden, 846
  wish I hadn't broke that, 908
Dishes, are these choice, 243
  home-made, that drive, 391
  not China, but very good, 35
  use like old shoes or, 997
  with his wife, washed the, 911
Dishonest because in debt, not, 627

Dishonesty and untruthfulness, 1087
will stare honesty out of countenance, 498
Dishonored star, waste of this, 836
Dishonour, honour rooted in, 470
of God and contempt of authority, 179
sensible of, 970
Dishonourable graves, 81
Disinfected, it wasn't, 815
Disingenuousness of years, penance for the, 400
Disinherited, vast numbers of the city's, 750
Disinheriting countenance, 279
Disinterested and patriotic find their way to control of affairs, 374
commerce, friendship is a, 253
Disinterestedness, all parts even that of, 1043
Disjoined from the only mind, 237
Dislike, hesitate, 213
of interruption, 324
Dislimns, the rack, 105
Dislocated, feel all broke up and, 661
Disloyalty, to doubt would be, 503
Dismal scene I needs must act alone, 80
science, professors of the, 379
svamp, valked by a, 539
swamp, lake of the, 333
tidings, conveyed the, 251
treatise rouse, would at a, 88
universal hiss, 155
Dismay, grief and sorrow and lifelong, 799
than admiration, more, 1069
Dismayed, when the sinner is, 375
Dismiss us with thy blessing, 280
Dismissing the doctor, 288
Disobedience, man's first, 148
the reward of, 153
to nature, 1008
Disorder, every species of domestic, 1051
full of variety and, 974
sweet, in the dress, 133
which is in, 869
Disorders, more common mental, 924
of the eyes, 969
Dispaires, comfortlesse, 26
Disparity between the swiftness of spirit, 1089
Dispatch, let your watchword be, 591
Dispense with trifles, 34
Dispensation of pleasure, diligent, 344
Dispensary of medicine, 924
Disperse to nought, 68
Display of jocularity, every possible, 283
would cause grief, 799
Displeasure, apprehension of His, 329
Dispoged, when I am, 495
Disposal, time we have at, 1086

Disposed to take a morose or desponding, 400
Disposer of other men's stuff, 114
Disposes, man proposes God, 8
Disposition, not their, 985
of an opposite, 973
shake our, 91
to be pleased, 236
to repay them, shows his, 1042
to war, 132
very melancholy, 38
wisdom acquired by, 978
you inherit, 830
Dispraise or blame, 157
other men's, 167
Dispraised no small praise, 156
Disprized love, pangs of, 93
Disputants like true sportsmen, 217
Disputation, seldom fall into, 228
Dispute endeavour and, 1019
engaged in a, 970
my right there is none to, 263
Disputing, itch of, 114
warmer way of, 1036
work without, 1052
Disquantity your train, a little to, 98
Disquietudes, fears and, 985
Disraeli by descent a Jew, 418
possesses qualities of the impenitent thief, 419
Disregard for death, 930
Disrespectfully of the equator, speak, 312
Disruption of thought, 1064
Dissatisfaction with the world, 762
Dissect, creatures you, 209
Dissemble, right to, 283
Dissension between hearts that love, 338
in a case of, 968
Dissent, dissidence of, 259
Dissimulation is innate, 1064
playing the knave and, 181
without some, 222
Dissipation without pleasure, 271
Dissolve, empires, 735
great globe itself shall, 33
Dissolves, all the world, 31
Dissolving score, on thy, 664
Dissonance, air with barbarous, 158
Distance, but keep your, 928
dear enchanter, 327
from a safe, 961
frozen by, 298
have them keep their, 895
hid each shining sail, 605
lends enchantment, 327
looking blue, no, 391
notes by, more sweet, 248
on the other, go a like, 1064
smooth at a, 127
sometimes endears friendship, 388
there's a magic in the, 864
what looks dark in the, 626
Distant and more solemn, more, 899
clime, envy heard in many a, 305
fields, 373
scene, I do not ask to see the, 403

Distant shore, on a stern but, 770
spires, ye, 243
Trojans never injured me, 218
voice in the darkness, and a, 437
Distemper, died of no, 178
Distempers, a forbidden topic, 414
Distil goodness out of evil, 67
Distilled damnation, 290
to jelly with the act of fear, 90
Distinct persons, two, 122
Distinction between vice and virtue, 234
is without, 1021
no, so little, 1051
of birth or fortune, 1061
of the Greeks, 571
without a difference, 229
Distinctions, levels all, 415
of race, morality knows nothing of, 581
Distinctly I remember, ah, 460
Distinguish and divide a hair, 141
Distinguishable as light from darkness, 247
shape had none, 150
Distinguished abilities as a writer, 235
for ignorance, 420
guest the ornament of our town, 497
Distracted in a ditch, 942
Distraction to mankind, 127
uglification and derision, 598
waft me from, 353
Distress and need, pray in your, 880
brothers in, 285
called everyone that was in, 478
composure of settled, 321
every one that was in, 1100
waken my, 375
Distresses, in all your, 478
Distressed in mind body or estate, 1127
Distressful bread, crammed with, 67
Distrest, griefs that harass the, 230
Distributed among the whole species, 197
Distrust all in whom, 1079
broods the dull, 851
one safeguard known to the wise, 277
unsophisticated with, 927
Distrustful, the anxious and, 931
Distrusting asks if this be joy, 251
Disturb it it stings, 592
Disturbed at the passage of carts, 198
its solitude, 687
Disturber, music the beautiful, 938
Disturbs the Sabbath of that deeper sea, 480
Ditch, both fall into the, 1115
die in the last, 940
lay distracted in a, 942
Ditches, at hedges or, 589

Diver, adventure of the, 484
did hang a salt-fish, 104
Divers paces with divers persons, 50
queens who die, 856
relieved by exonerating themselves, 125
Diverse points, blows from, 1021
things they see, 575
Diversion or improvement of the country, 1062
Diversions of life, of all the, 196
Diversity is most universal quality, 144
Diverter of sadness, 139
Divide a hair, distinguish and, 141
lives that part are as ships that, 425
Sunday from the week, 89
Divided against itself, house, 1116
duty, perceive a, 101
excellence, fair, 57
in death, they were not, 1100
we fall, united we stand, 404, 962
Dividend, drawing no, 891
Dividends, incarnation of fat, 364
make them pay you, 910
Dividing, his cares, 289
Divina natura dedit agros, 111
Divine agency, bestowed by some, 975
all save the spirit of man is, 355
an errand all, 445
and comfortable words, large, 469
called human or, 683
delight, lost in, 850
discontent, discontented with, 524
good amiable, 155
hand that made us is, 194
how, a thing, 299
how, woman may be made, 299
human face, 151
I am more, 476
idea, crystalline revelation of the, 432
image long been obscured, 1074
in hookas, tobacco, 358
insanity of noble minds, the, 438
love meets every human need, 549
love something so, 268
love which greybeards call, 71
made service seem, 437
makes drudgery, 135
Milton, the, 302
mystery in things, 1074
O light, we need no fuller, 501
of kings, the right, 215
or holy, aught, 149
philosophy, 158, 468
plain face, 325
power plans evils, when, 175
radiant with ardour, 547
right, government by, 319
she 's lovely she 's, 362
sound, 263
sweet apples anthosmial, 431
think how, he himself is, 534

Divine, to digest is, 493, 753
to forgive, 211
to love, too, 363
to walk unswerving were, 453
unreason, 922
which is, 410
whose toys are, 555
Divinely fair, 463
tall, daughter of the gods, 463
Divineness, participation of, 112
Diviner things, by contemplation of, 546
Diviner's theme, the glad, 173
Divinest hope which none can know of, 406
Divinity doth hedge a king, 96
I understand, all the, 1040
in odd numbers, there is, 35
sacred and inspired, 112
schools join devoutly in credo, 654
sold, for ten cents an ounce is, 870
that shapes our ends, 97
that stirs within us, 195
Division of a battle, 100
of the great and pressing concern, 1089
when we came to, 678
Divisions, time has no, 1089
Divorce or death, till, 624
Divyne wel she sang the service, 5
Dixie land I'll take my stand, in, 505
Dizziness, love is like a, 294
Dizzy way, across that, 849
D.L.W. Jersey Central, 926
Do always, what is right, 564
as you would be done by, 222
good by stealth, 214
good, it is not enough to, 641
if to, were as easy as to know, 44
it with thy might, 1110
justly and to love mercy, to, 1113
lovely things not dream them, 523
not ask for what you will wish, 991
not what we ought, we, 547
nothing left to, 999
or can the best of us, little, 493
or die, let us, 127, 286
so many worlds so much to, 469
some noble work of love to, 474
strange what a man may, 482
the great business of life is to, 641
the right, trust in God and, 499
the thing we must, we must, 559
well and right, 136
what has by man been done, 202
what I will with mine own, 1115
what men dare, 39
what then thou wouldst, 157
with all the days, what shall I, 454
with nothing in the world to, 406

Do ye even so to them, 1114
you know old age may come, 535
Docile as the gentlest thing, 888
Dock the tail of rhyme, 451
Docks, handle dainties on the, 936
Dock-yard fellow, prison-mate and, 604
Dockyards, canals and, 960
Doctor and saint, frequent, 1018
death will seize the, 106
dismissing the, 288
Fell, I do not love thee, 188
for a nauseous draught, fee the, 175
kind old country, 678
of divinity, man his own, 704
old because you never were my, 1004
silent, shook his head, 206
wears three faces, 698
well-trained sensible family, 445
who knows her constitution, 520
Doctors and special treatments, 1081
best in the world, 192
diet prescribed by, 976
differ, when, 544
disagree, when, 210
give what they would take, 452
is all swabs, 704
live lives of self-sacrifice, 445
meet to discuss a case, 451
men must have, 1054
of the Stoic fur, 158
Doctor's nose, slam the door on the, 435
peaceful mission, 698
rules, mocks the, 442
Doctors' consultations, 717
spite, in learned, 364
Doctrine, all the winds of, 163
Christianity the broadest and most humane, 415
from women's eyes, 41
not for the, but the music, 211
of Americanism, 701
of ignoble ease, 734
of the strenuous life, 734
orthodox, prove their, 142
sanctified by truth, 303
than of heart, better heresy of, 442
the Monroe, 734
to-day is, 949
with every wind of, 238
Doctrines of paternalism and state socialism, 830
plain, what makes all, 143
Documents about seekers and makers, 795
Doer and the thing done, 314
Doers, talkers are no good, 71
Does well acts nobly, 201
Doff it for shame, 57
Doffed his hat, when he lightly, 770
Dog, Alcibiades and his, 1002
and I are old, my, 834
and you, my, 842
barked at the ox, 962
biggest, has been a pup, 658

Dog bites a man, not news when a, 677
  by the Aegean seas, 674
  circumcised, 104
  companion of our pleasures and our toils, 311
  difference between a man and a, 615
  faithful, his, 207
  fleas good for a, 687
  give a boy a, 873
  hair of the, 15
  has his day, every, 1035
  he could not keep a, 1017
  his day, every, 523
  holds a well-assured place in men's regard, 730
  how many legs has a, 458
  hunting on my own, 912
  hunts in dreams like a, 464
  I had a little, 890
  I have no, 760
  in the manger, 123
  infidel as a, 235
  is thy servant a, 1101
  is turned to his vomit, 1123
  it was that died, 254
  lapped by a, 424
  let no, bark, 44
  like Tim, wasting a, 875
  living, better than dead lion, 1109
  love me love my, 17
  may love a puppy, a mastiff, 472
  mine enemy's, 99
  misbeliever, cut throat, 44
  most constant, my dear old, 597
  named Rover Towser Sport Spot or Fido, 922
  next-door, the, 925
  of Gettysburg, I was a, 936
  of old, be thy, 766
  old, Tray's ever faithful, 567
  shall bear him company, 207
  sleeps the, 822
  smarts, this, 229
  something better than his, 464
  stands by in prosperity and poverty, 352
  starved at his master's gate, 281
  takes a last look, 220
  teasing silly sheep, 912
  that keeps out of the fight, 610
  that tossed the, 543
  the firmest friend, 352
  the gingham, 699
  therefore to this, 428
  to tear, give your heart to a, 784
  tribute to the memory of a, 352
  walk-ecstatic, 858
  was found, 254
  went after them, the, 1124
  went mad and bit the man, 254
  went with them, young man's, 1124
  what d'ye think of that my, 390
  whose, are you, 216
  wild and lone, 912
  will do for a friend, 920
  will have his day, 97
  wool of bat tongue of, 87

Dog, word to throw at a, 48
  you will die like a, 930
  you're only a, 712
Dogs and bears, and dancing, 816
  and men never meet again, 875
  are faithful, 873
  between two, 68
  conceited quite as you, 458
  delight to bark and bite, 198
  don't bite at front gate, 688
  drinking from the Nile, 992
  eat of the crumbs, 1115
  fighting in the streets, 229
  have had a good long wait, 956
  helping lame, 523
  in the show, catalogue of, 922
  isn't there heaven for, 758
  lie, let sleeping, 497
  lies with the, 137
  little, and all, 99
  little, cause as large griefs, 607
  of war, let slip the, 82
  rain cats and, 192
  there be, as many, 254
  things were going to the, 956
  throw physic to the, 88
  without are, 1123
  would bark, all the, 850
Dog's grave, it is a, 1093
  walking on his hind legs, 234
Dog-angel waits, a little, 842
Dogerel, this may wel be rym, 6
Dogged and grim, if, 873
  as does it, it's, 506
Dogma or want of dogma, danger not in, 614
Dogmatism is puppyism come to full growth, 417
Dog-star and the sisters seven, 900
Doing and saying are two things, 188
  good to good-for-nothing, 430
  or suffering, 148
  what is, 650
  whatever is worth, 222
Doings, amend your ways and your, 1112
  of thy soul, beautiful, 427
Dole, and with the, 682
  by silly fortune's, 931
  delight and, in equal scale, 89
  happy man happy, 12
  of praise, for an instant, 778
Doles that you are now distributing, 976
Doleful dumps, 255
  hymn to his own death, 58
  sound from the tombs, 199
  stories, 384
Doll in the world, prettiest, 523
  one of the most imperious, 1068
  sweet little, 523
Dolls with jeers, treated the, 691
Dollar a line, a, 852
  bill once broken, 518
  farmer covetous of his, 413
  owe no man a, 560
  the almighty, 343, 656
Dollars and cents, minutes to be, 387
  and dimes, 560
  will not be distributed as gifts, 627

Dolly is dead, I tell you my, 679
Dolphin, dies like the, 354
Dolphins play, pleased to see the, 223
Dolphin-chamber, in my, 64
Domain, over the hushed, 478
Domains, creation's wide, 343
Dome and crowd, see beyond the, 814
  fired the Ephesian, 193
  hand that rounded Peter's, 408
  him of the western, 174
  his hall the azure, 410
  life like a, 366
  no gilded, 374
  of many-coloured glass, 366
  of Paul's, on the, 737
  of thought, 352
  orchard for a, 584
  poor or proud the, 432
Domes of Lucknow, silver, 443
  week was seven, 923
Domestic affairs can be observed, 930
  hearth, the, 1078
  malice, 87
  sentiment of mankind, 419
Domestics, few admired by their, 1030
Dominations princedoms, 153
Dominion absolute as I, 504
  for an instant means, 585
  I traversed a, 652
  man's, 572
  no such strange, 369
  over him, no more, 1119
  their true, 911
  ultimate, 851
  wants of his own, 499
Dominions, raven from the dim, 418
  sun never sets in, 1059
Domus sua cuique, 21
Don Alonzo Estabán San Salvador, 559
  fellow is some mighty, 511
  John of Austria is going to the war, 827
  Juan Gomez, I am, 917
  Juan, I am, 881
  Juan is praying, 917
  poor at bed and worse at table, 810
  Quixote de la Mancha, 1034
  Quixote, O great, 878
  that shall never be my friend, 810
Done, all is, that men can do, 287
  decently and in order, 1120
  ere the toil be, 501
  father thy will not mine be, 423
  for, so soon that I am, 948
  heat of long day and wish 't were, 546
  if it were, when 't is, 85
  in a corner, 1119
  in vain, all is, 287
  knowing when to have, 378
  life's work well, 555
  like lightning, 118
  makes ill deeds, 58
  my duty and no more, 229
  quickly, 't were well it were, 85
  reward of a thing well, 412

Done, such things to be so little, 469
the play is, 481
things which we ought to have, 1127
to death by slanderous tongues, 40
to have, 594
we may compute what 's, 285
well, is done soon enough, 1031
what 's, is done, 86
where much is to be, 239
with so much ease, 173
work is, lie shall rot, 556
Donkeys in outstripping, 995
Donne, a new, 922
enjoy with, 898
I suppose was such another, 899
Don't give up afore the ship goes down, 527
shoot colonel, I'll come down, 349
want to fight, we, 562
you ever try to go there, 919
Doom be a noble one, may your, 407
days that wove your, 631
defied all portents of impending, 418
dementia and death, poet of, 793
grisly mask of, 725
had an early, 423
his high, 672
of beauty, scandal the, 986
regardless of their, 243
shall be eternal, 263
takes, the widest land, 429
the crack of, 87
those wild words of, 418
to come, wistful of the, 843
Doom-burdened caravels, Columbus's, 882
Doomed conscripted unvictorious ones, 892
Doomsday shadows fall, till, 712
Doon, ye banks and braes of bonny, 287
Dooney, play on my fiddle in, 791
Door and knock, behold I stand at the, 1123
at mine hostess', 57
at my, the pale horse stands, 639
at some forgotten, 914
bar a single, 722
beside a human, 298
call from his back, 922
clicked behind the, 251
close the, 811
ever-opened, 218
for the moneyless man, no open, 609
going out the, 710
great shining, 787
haunt the rich man's, 267
he watches at the, 410
hole like a, 857
howled about our, 917
is ajar and the barrel is sprung, 810
is shut, then no, 1084
kicked them out the, 954
know the grass beyond the, 577
lamp beside the golden, 694

Door, loved and closed the, 703
marble, 659
met it going out the, 1000
moonlit, 822
my, should be the one, 904
nail in, 66
of darkness through, passed the, 1019
of death is made of gold, 282
of heaven ajar, left the, 507
of his prison, open the, 970
of life, at the, 631
on the doctor's nose, slam the, 435
opens the enchanted, 673
over that same, was writ, 24
pamphlet under every, 933
shut shut the, 212
shut the stable, 14
stand outside your, 793
standing in every, 826
then shuts the, 584
to door, sing ballads from, 123
to her own father's, 951
to which I found no key, 1018
to your friendly, 708
turn in at the open, 873
unlock the, 890
wave and flutter round my, 418
where in I went, same, 1018
wolf from the, 10
Doors and windows, locking the, 629
clay-shuttered, 749
death hath a thousand, 127, 128, 144
death hath so many, 131
death hath ten thousand several, 127
I bar the, 986
men shut their, 80
neither locks to their, 435
nor locks can shield you, 348
of sleep, keys of all the, 810
or turn her out of, 948
quiet shutting of, 874
shut not your, 534
soundless, beat in vain, 444
swing open wide, let your, 742
to be open, O for, 937
to close and ope the, 746
write on your, 438
Doorbells are like a magic game, 323
Doorkeeper in the house of my God, 1105
Doorkeepers that fight, 960
Door-key remember to take the, 482
Doornail, dead as a, 495
Doorstep terror, 787
Doorway, shaded, 552
Door-yard, when lilacs last in the, 536
Dorcas, a woman called, 1118
Dorian mood of flutes, 149
Dorians pray, to whom the, 400
Doric lay, warbling his, 160
Dorg which you've got, 699
Dormant in daylight of prosperity, 343
they are, 1075
Dormitive I take to bedward, 145
Dormouse, my dear little, 876

Dose of castor-oil and then I christened it, 313
Dost thou love life, 227
Dot, rosy, over the i, 1085
though such a, 553
Dotage, old age to, 978
Dotages and plagues of human kind, 123
Dote on his very absence, 44
upon, how fading the joys we, 186
Doting with age, pyramids, 147
Double beauty whenever a swan, 391
cherry, like to a, 43
debt to pay, contrived a, 251
double toil and trouble, 87
erasings, 664
my life's fading space, 168
personality, newspaper-man, 636
pity, challenge, 21
pulses that beat, 429
sure, I'll make assurance, 87
surely you'll grow, 295
swan and shadow, float, 298
thereon, on a lake with her, 391
Double-faced, if not, is double-mouthed, 157
Doubling his pleasures, 289
Doubly armed, thus am I, 195
dead, a dirge for her, 460
dying, 307
feel ourselves alone, 307
Doubt and darkness danger and long tempest of the war, 483
and dismay, with, 872
beyond, all, 452
but ye are the people, no, 1102
dumb-founder, and repay scorn in kind, 490
every, that can retard, 417
faith in honest, 469, 506
I show you, 488
is brother-devil to despair, 675
is slow to clear, 489
light of heaven dimmed with, 709
man that feareth Lord to, 559
mists of, 644
modest, 75
never caught at fault or, 429
never, I love, 92
never stand to, 134
no possible, 624
nor loop to hang a, 103
of my veracity, entertain a, 1056
or shame, knows not, 912
or two of sorts, 811
sunnier side of, 471
that the sun doth move, 92
thou the stars are fire, 92
trieth troth in every, 17
truth to be a liar, 92
uttered ignorance and morbid, 718
where, there truth is, 506
who read to, 310
win the trick, when in, 197
would be disloyalty, to, 503
Doubts and ignorance, through my, 820
are more cruel, 1046
began with the fall, 810

Doubts, bound in to saucy, 87
  from what he sees, 281
  our, are traitors, 35
Doubted, heard Troy, 360
  never half believed, who never, 469, 506
Doubter and the doubt, I am the, 410
Doubteth thee, in that fear, 559
Doubtful, love to run from the dark and, 280
Doubting Castle, called, 172
  dreaming dreams no mortal, 460
  in his abject spirit, 525
  the faculty of, 1078
Dough, my cake is, 52
Douglas, could ye come back, 567
  deals in red herrings, 363
  in his hall, 308
  like, conquer or die, 248
  song of Percy and, 27
  tender and true, 567
Dove, beside the springs of, 296
  burnished, 464
  found no rest, 1097
  gently as any sucking, 42
  go forth my, 881
  instinct for the homing, 711
  more of the serpent than, 31
  shall warm her bosom, 805
  white rose is a dove, 675
  wings like a, oh that I had, 1104
Doves, harmless as, 1115
  moan of, 466
  two, I bring, 896
Doves' footsteps, 1079
Dove-cote, eagle in a, 76
Dowagers for deans, 466
Dower, given you for a priceless, 760
  of bird and of flower, 846
Dowered with the hate of hate, 462
Down and out of breath, 63
  beneath the wild, far, 480
  but up, look not, 489
  by the mill, apple-boughs, 508
  death looks gigantically, 508
  eternity's river, flow in one, 503
  from his perch, gravely got, 508
  he that is, 142, 172
  hill that skirts the, 269
  I grant you I was, 63
  level, 234
  of darkness, the raven, 158
  on your knees and thank heaven, 50
  pillow hard, finds the, 106
  so he laid, his arms, 392
  the base in man, to keep, 471
  the dark vistas of the rebeantic, 432
  the nights and down the days, 748
  the wind, let her, 102
  this story will not go, 229
  thou climbing sorrow, 98
  with ridiculous notions of Deity, 569
Downs, all in the, 205
  unhabitable, 190
Downcast modesty, 224

Downfall, surest road to national, 450
Downward age, torrent of a, 224
  bent, thoughts, 149
  to toil, 663
Downy sleep, death's counterfeit, 86
Doxy, another man's, 223
Dozen, a baker's, 1026
Dr. Livingstone, I presume, 653
Drab, cursing like a very, 93
  is the town, 815
Drabs and vixens, 856
Drachenfels, castled crag of, 353
Draff, still sow eats all the, 14
Drag the Atlantic for whales, 616
  the slow barge, 267
Draggled island, on the, 674
Dragon, before he killed the, 827
  Saint George that swinged the, 57
  that is in the sea, 1111
Dragons by surprise, 857
Dragon's tale, baited with a, 146
Dragon-flies that skim the surface, 732
Dragon-fly? A stranger hither, 730
  beside the stream the, 746
Dragon-fly's repose, brief as a, 529
Dragonish, cloud that is, 105
Dragoon, heavy, 623
Drags at each remove, 249
  its slow length along, 211
Drain, roots are in a, 814
Drained by fevered lips, 386
Drake he was a Devon man, 765
Drakes, ducks and, 29
Drama, grand divine eternal, 508
  has outgrown such toys, the, 430
  means, what this wild, 472
  with the day, close the, 203
Dramatic reminiscence, its most, 538
Dramatist who discovered himself, 812
Drank, and ale we, 610
  delight, 280
Drapery, fancy its, 318
  of his couch, 372
Draught above heat, one, 54
  from a cup of cold pizen, 652
  of a breath, 362
  of bitter dew, dwells a, 730
  nauseous, 175
  of cool refreshment, 386
  of red cow's milk, 140
  slavery a bitter, 242
  starlight's a steadying, 895
Draughts, shallow, 210
Draw men as they ought to be, 252
  the curtain and show the picture, 54
  the curtain close, 69
  the model, 64
  you with a single hair, 177
Drawback, fame has this great, 1049
Drawers, chest of, by day, 251
  of water and hewers of wood, 625
  sewing red flannel, 931
Drawn dagger, smiles at the, 195

Draws him yet she follows, though she, 436
  us with a single hair, beauty, 125, 212
Dread and fear of kings, 46
  heights of destiny, 690
  held in, 360
  mingled love and, 678
  O majesty unspeakable and, 503
  of something after death, 93
  of writers, 766
  stands up for, 966
  temple of thy worth, 783
  whence this secret, 195
Dreadful bell, silence that, 101
  curiosity, 186
  laughter, grief and, 913
  note of preparation, 67
  reckoning, 205
  thing, between the acting of a, 82
  things apt to happen, 852
  thought, thou pleasing, 195
  urs, those, 451
Dreads to the dust returning, who, 554
Dream, a far illusive, 573
  a hideous, 82
  a shadowy lie, was my, 509
  all night without a stir, 384
  an evening thought a morning, 594
  and unaccountable desire, 806
  and wish, beat with, 444
  as we glide through a quiet, 350
  as youthful poets, 160
  awaken'd, who from a, 1021
  awaking, from a troubled, 396
  beautiful for patriot, 737
  beyond the shadow of a, 382
  by day, those who, 461
  come true, making the, 873
  consecration and the poet's, 299
  deeper, one, 592
  delicious, when a, 675
  dim blue hills of, 717
  dreamed a, that could not be, 558
  feeling in his, 1021
  fickle as a changeful, 308
  from deed, 693
  gone like a beautiful, 392
  grandeur is a, 265
  has power to poison sleep, 368
  hath possessed, 891
  heart not able to report my, 43
  her face stirred with her, 360
  holy things fade like a, 523
  I have had a, 43
  I saw as in a, 423
  I took a rampin', 878
  in cleaving to the, 650
  in joy and wake in love, 375
  in reverential, 896
  in the night, a, 789
  iridescent, 601
  is born, when a, 924
  is past, die when the, 428
  is true, know the, 924
  life is an empty, 577
  life is but an empty, 433
  love's young, 335

Dream, man's life is but a, 577
  meditation changed to, 1021
  moon kingdom of, 1069
  new-risen from a, 52
  no more, said dreamer, 558
  none thrives long on happiest, 556
  not Homer nods but we, 210
  of a face, occupy age with the, 490
  of, a sight to, 315
  of a waking man, 1014
  of happiness, 953
  of heaven, she did but, 175
  of home, the, 337
  of life, he hath awakened from the, 366
  of loveliness descending, saw a, 559
  of peace, deep, 346
  of sleeping innocence, 645
  of things that were, 352
  old men's, 173
  one man with a, 676
  one with twilight's, 801
  or dust, 851
  or grave apart, keep a, 428
  our suffering life the, 480
  past the wit of man to say what, 43
  problem flowered from a, 823
  record of a fevered, 685
  scraps of, 757
  short as any, 42
  silently as a, 266
  so climbs my, 889
  somnambulist of a vanished, 1067
  sprite begotten of summer, 407
  still mounts the, 851
  sweet thoughts in a, 368
  that I forget, 632
  that is dying, 676
  the glory and the, 301
  to sleep perchance to, 93
  we thought was lost, every, 557
  when one awaketh, 1105
  when the long trick's over, 832
  which was not all a dream, 356
  with the first, 701
  within a dream, is but a, 459
Dreams, and all my nightly, 460
  and slumbers light, 308
  and visions, distraught with, 439
  are best, 844
  are ever contrary, 116
  awake, from pleasant, 348
  be thine, sweetest, 642
  blissful, of long ago, 638
  blowing loudly in, 967
  books are each a world, 301
  come in, to me, 869
  depart and the vision falls, 521
  direction of his, 515
  dreamer of, 952
  dreamer of, born out of my, 608
  emptied of all my, 882
  feed on, 963
  full of ghastly, 71
  glimpses of forgotten, 462
  ground not upon, 116
  gone to smoke, 766
  green dusk for, 823
  had never known, 696

Dreams, have only my, 790
  help us incarnate, 860
  I have spread my, 790
  I see thee ever in my, 417
  lies down to pleasant, 372
  like a dog he hunts in, 464
  like the atmosphere of, 447
  no mortal ever dreamed before, 460
  not the England of our, 782
  not with, shall a nation be moulded, 634
  of avarice beyond the, 237
  of childhood, 497
  of doing good, 430
  of love and truth, 665
  of men, 726
  of my infinite, 761
  of thee, I arise from, 368
  of those who wake, 995
  old men shall dream, 173
  saddle your, 872
  season of our lonely, 843
  she grows not older, in, 675
  songs she heard in her, 432
  such stuff as, are made on, 33
  that count with men, 952
  that fooled me, 533
  that wave before the half-shut eye, 224
  their own, deceive 'em, 190
  to sell, if there were, 406
  tread on my, 790
  true I talk of, 77
  what, may come, 93
  winged, 256
  yet in my, 423
Dream's confusion, end my, 856
Dream-beguiled, their paths are, 756
Dreamed a dream that could not be, 558
  before, dreams no mortal ever, 460
  that life was beauty, 508
Dreamer awake, where shall the, 618
  beautiful, 568
  dream no more, said, 558
  of dreams, 952
  of dreams born out of my, 608
  who's making the dream, 873
Dreamers of dreams, 676
  of the impossible, 491
Dreamer's wine, drunken with the, 871
Dreamful eyes my spirit lies, with, 552
Dream-house anyway, it's just a, 920
Dreaming darkly of a Dun, 590
  dreams no mortal ever dreamed, 460
  eyes of wonder, 598
  past the size of, 105
  upon Salmon's height, sunshine, 556
Dreamland, the ventures of, 579
  you hail from, 730
Dreamless bed, 446
  rest is mine, when, 681
  sleep, 612
Dream-like trade of blood and guile, 316
Dream-shadows go, where the, 717

Dreamt I dwelt in marble halls, 386
  of in your philosophy, 92
Dreamy air, russet year inhaled the, 551
  eyes, they tell sweet lies, 336
Drear-nighted December, 383
Dreary and cold with a chill, 815
  dumps, these, 77
  never-ending tale, 718
  once upon a midnight, 460
  to be somebody, 584
  winter, oh the long and, 436
Dregs of life, from the, 178
  of strife, bitter, 608
Drenched and dripping apple-trees, 915
  sands, 587
Drenching, because of which, 815
Dress and manners in England, 720
  be plain in, 221
  by yellow candle-light, 702
  changed for sake of leg, 701
  daring in full, 358
  fair undress, best, 224
  felt through this fleshly, 170
  his century wore, in the, 584
  I'm growing careless of my, 509
  let the world go dine and, 406
  little checkered, 696
  music sports and theatres, 1049
  of thoughts, style is the, 222
  sweet disorder in the, 133
  though in another, 438
  to, to call, 736
Dresses for breakfast and dinners and balls, 561
  for winter spring summer and fall, 561
  to dance in and flirt in and talk in, 561
  to sit in and stand in and walk in, 561
Dressed in all his trim, 108
  in good temper when well, 495
Dress-suit city, 859
Drest in little brief authority, 36
  still to be neat still to be, 119
  world you are beautifully, 553
Drew an angel down, she, 176
  breath, a sweeter woman ne'er, 540
  from out the boundless deep, 472
Dried and vanished stream, 480
  apple pies, poorest is, 955
Drift, I will tell you my, 38
  of pinions, 749
  wait and obey, 787
  we know your, 38
Drifting sands, 231
  seed, the, 619
Driftwood tossed on a stormy sea, 437
Drill and plough, spade and mattock, 919
  Birken'ead, 782
  ye tarriers drill, 644
Drink, a little in, but yr. faith-full husband, 198
  and the devil had done, 704
  and to be merry, 1109, 1117
  angel of the darker, 1018
  as friends, 52

Drink, as he brews so shall he, 118
  cannot make the horse, 14
  deep of life's fond illusion, 583
  deep or taste not, 210
  for once dead, 1018
  he has taken to, 809
  I said before and perish, 441
  if he thirst give him, 1119
  it down, 645
  let us eat and, 1111
  mandragora, 104
  meat and, to me, 51, 1026
  no longer water, 1121
  no more than a sponge, 1024
  no sperit, I never, 527
  nor any drop to, 315
  old wine to, 113
  pretty creature drink, 298
  small beer, felony to, 69
  strong, is raging, 1107
  takes the man, 659
  that quenches thirst, 1042
  the best of wine, king can, 504
  the poppies of Cathay, and, 444
  they eat they, 153
  till they nod and wink, 20
  to me only with thine eyes, 119
  to the general joy of the table, 87
  to the lass, 279
  to-day drown all sorrow, 127
  victuals and, 972
  what to read and say and eat and, and, and wear, 398
  what ye shall eat or, 1114
  why should every creature, but I, 167
  wild anarchy of, 120
  with him that wears a hood, 20
  with me and drink as I, 223
  with you eat with you, 44
  ye to her that each loves best, 328
Drinks and gapes for drink again, 167
  banishment of intoxicating, 455
  long time between, 786
Drinker, equals the joy of the, 1093
Drinking a mere pause from thinking, 357
  after they have been, 969
  dancing laughing, 176
  in an inn, 940
  largely sobers us, 210
  not to be blamed, 130
  rule for, 196
  thirsteth still, 587
  unhappy brains for, 101
  when I had a mind to, 810
Drink-shops, among the, 1009
Drip of the suspended oar, 353
Drive a coach and six, 945
  a flock to feed, and just to, 406
  four rogues let, 62
  him away, grief can not, 567
  one from home, dishes that, 391
  whom the devil doth, 17, 53
Driven ice, facing the, 923
Driving of Jehu, like the, 1101
Droghte of Marche, 4

Droll situations, sense to appreciate, 695
Dronkenesse is verray sepulture, 6
Drooped in the western sky, star, 536
Drooping head, repairs his, 159
  that lay with canvas, 519
Drop a tear and bid adieu, 225
  by drop, 978
  greedy for the last, 930
  hinders needle and thread, every, 392
  in every dimpled, 772
  into thy mother's lap, 155
  life and strength in every, 404
  of a bucket, 1112
  of allaying Tiber, 76
  of ink, small, 359
  of manly blood, ruddy, 410
  one other bitter, 626
  raineth, 886
  the line that marks the, 926
  to drink, nor any, 315
Drops, dear as the ruddy, 82, 244
  from off the eaves, 161
  his blue-fringed lids, 316
  like kindred, 264
  of light, these little, 145
  of rain and days of eternity, 1124
  of rain pierce the marble, 23
  of water, little, 553, 764
  play is done the curtain, 481
  that make a lakeful, 867
  that often doe redound, 26
  that sacred pity hath engendered, 49
  the light drip, 353
  to wash a single rose, 707
  what precious, are those, 178
  wiped our eyes of, 49
Dropped a tear upon the word, 242
  from an angel's wing, 304
  from the zenith, 149
  manna, his tongue, 149
  out of the clouds, 130
Droppeth as the gentle rain, 46
Dropping buckets into wells, 265
  continual, in a rainy day, 1108
  continual, wears a stone, 981
  eye, an auspicious and a, 89
Dropt from the skies, 589
Dross, men call treasure Gods call, 528
  of Earth, slough the, 777
  stoops not to show of, 45
Drought or tempest, 677
Drown all sorrow, 127
  my book, 33
  the brim, 53
  the outcry of the heart, 386
  what pain it was to, 71
Drowned honour, pluck up, 61
Drowning ship sank low, 475
  would be happiness and peace, 494
Drowsiness clothe man in rags, 1108
Drowsy ear of night, 352
  head, land of, 224
  man, dull ear of a, 58
  paw, each, 858
  poppies nod, where, 955

Drowsy syrups of the world, 102
  with the harmony, 41
Drudge sold to futurity, 930
Drudgery at the desk, 325
  divine, makes, 135
Drug, humour is a, 624
Drugs are quick, thy, 80
  better than any, 1077
  better than your, 1061
  cause cramp, 918
  to work the cure, 997
Drum as a madman beats upon a, 129
  ecclesiastick, 141
  glittering knife and a jubilant, 925
  made of his, 122
  rumble of a distant, 1018
  spirit-stirring, 102
  throbbed no longer, 464
  to England, take my, 765
  was heard, not a, 364
Drums and fifes, 679
  and tramplings of three conquests, 145
  beat the, 186
  like muffled, are beating funeral marches, 433
  quietly rested under the, 145
Drum's discordant sound, 261
Drum-beat and heart-beat, 571
  the morning, 341
Drumfires, walking into the, 854
Drummer, hears a different, 515
Drunk, all learned all, 266
  appeal from Philip, 969
  debating when, 969
  gloriously, 266
  hasten to be, 177
  ink, he hath not, 41
  is he who prostrate lies, 348
  it is our pleasure to be, 228
  joy of the wine in being, 1093
  let us be, 692
  though he never was, 289
  with a beauty, 801
  with being young, feel, 913
Drunkard, rolling English, 827
Drunkards, notorious, 651
Drunken and magnificent hope, 932
  dog ragged head, 325
  private of the Buffs, 474
  sailor on a mast, 72
Drunkenness, four descending degrees of, 1068
  identical with ruin, 1016
  or any taint of vice, 56
Dry and trodden sand, 659
  as summer dust, hearts, 302
  as the remainder biscuit, 49
  death, I would fain die a, 32
  fields burn, 664
  light, 996
  or lest we should be, 184
  prairies, fires the, 856
  sun dry wind, 19
  volumes of ethics and divinity, 273
Dryad in a tree, 888
Dryden, copious, 214
Drying up a single tear, 360
Du sublime au ridicule, 272
Dubiety, transfixing all, 889
Ducat, dead for a, 95
Ducdame, what's that, 48

Duchesses, Du Maurier's incomparable, 907
Duck or plover, aimed at, 277
Ducks and drakes, 29
Duds of daring, 757
Due, give the devil his, 61
　more is thy, than more than all, 84
　respective thrift, spent with, 556
　season, word in, 1107
　that you may have your, 191
　time, born out of my, 608
Dues of fellowship, simple, 430
　render to all their, 1119
Duke of Norfolk deals in malt, 363
　the, did love me, 128
Dukedom, my library was, 32
Dulce dulce domum, they sung, 294, 365
　et decorum est, 219, 918
Dulcimer, damsel with a, 315
Dull academic half-dozen, a, 1089
　and flowerless weed, 441
　and mean, the age is, 442
　as night, the motions of his spirit are, 47
　beyond all conception, 367
　business could not make, 545
　cold ear of death, 244
　cold marble, sleep in, 73
　commercial liturgies, 806
　ear of a drowsy man, 58
　gentle yet not, 167
　naturally, 234
　Peter was dull very, 367
　pomp the life of kings, 546
　quiet way, in its, 961
　sight to see the year dying, 449
　sleep and a downy bed, 229
　tame shore, on the, 350
　unchanging shore, on this, 502
　wits keep straining, 942
Dullard, George the Third an honest, 713
Dulled with sin, 709
Duller than the fat weed, 91
Dulness call a halt, to, 601
　gentle, ever loves a joke, 215
　in others, cause of, 238
　is in the mind, all, 800
　of the fool is whetstone of the wits, 47
　power to shed anything but, 800
Duluth the word fell upon my ear, 645
Dum tacent clamant, 1092
　vivimus vivamus, 225
Dumb, beggar that is, 21
　creatures we have cherished, 545
　deep heart be no longer, 540
　discourse, kind of excellent, 33
　forgetfulness a prey to, 245
　friend, my dear, 522
　from scandal and from scare, 674
　hearts of the English kind, 834
　kings of modern thought are, 546
　lips are, 463
　modest men are, 288
　name him I am, 917

Dumb, properly walloped is forever, 802
　region of the heart, 663
　the deep are, 21
　the oracles are, 161
Du Maurier's duchesses, 907
Dumb-shows and noise inexplicable, 94
Dumferling toune, king sits in, 316
Dumps, college joke to cure the, 190
　get out of your doleful, 1042
　the mind oppress, doleful, 255
　these dreary, 77
Dumpy woman, I hate a, 358
Dun, dreaming darkly of a, 590
Duncan hath borne his faculties so meek, 85
　hear it not, 86
　is in his grave, 86
Dunce kept at home, 262
　sent to roam, 262
　with wits, 215
Dundee, single hour of that, 298
　death-wound of, 758
Dune, shoulders and slopes of the, 757
Dunedin's streets, that day through high, 500
Dungeon comes a ray, to every, 504
　is so dark, what, 422
　is, which my, 703
　the vapour of a, 102
Dungeon-tomb, sleep calmly in thy, 297
Dunghill, cock on his own, 14
　cover a, 1041
Dunsinane, come to, 87
Dupe of dream, this, 816
　of the heart, 1044
Durable as possible, 228
　make life, 634
Durance vile, in, 286
Duration is always short, their, 271
　of great sentiments, 1080
Dusk a shadow, out of the, 681
　above the roof-tops, 904
　faces with turbants, 156
　he draweth near, at, 638
　of eternity, 571
　of June, 693
　of misty centuries, 688
Dusky hour, midnight brought on the, 153
　little cricket, 638
　night, 619
　pinions, oft I hear thy, 418
　race, she shall rear my, 464
　wine, 809
Dust, a peddler deals in, 711
　all things return to, 1071
　an' smoke an' divilmint, 820
　and dirt, clean of all my, 886
　and heat, not without, 163
　and scum of the earth, 832
　and silence of the upper shelf, 397
　and soot of your complaints, 694
　and strike to, 212
　and the sun, with the, 929
　be light, may the, 897

Dust, blossom in their, 141
　chimney-sweepers come to, 106
　crumbling to the, 427
　destroy their, 364
　down to the vile, 307
　dry as summer, 302
　enemies shall lick the, 1104
　farewell sweet, 897
　first conflagration of the, 927
　glories in the, shall lay, 218
　go toppling to the, 871
　grain of, 887
　heap of, alone remains, 217
　heap, too much litter in a, 1027
　hearts dry as summer, 302
　hopes and fears lie in the, 348
　I raise, what a, 376
　I stand amid the, 748
　is gold, whose, 154
　less than the, 775
　lie still dry, 463
　much learned, 265
　must come to, 106
　mysteries lie beyond thy, 170
　nearer to the, 899
　of ages, from the, 916
　of Alexander, trace the noble, 97
　of death, when the, 429
　of my bosom, from the, 806
　of strife, 604
　of systems and of creeds, 462
　one English tear o'er English, 401
　over the hedges, 926
　pays us with age and, 22
　perishes among the, 373
　pride that licks the, 213
　proud and angry, 743
　provoke the silent, 244
　rain upon the blinding, 498
　redskins bit the, 713
　return, shalt to, 155
　return to the earth, 1110
　returneth to dust, 601
　returning, dreads to the, 554
　shall live, so all now, 892
　sleeps in, 185
　so nigh is grandeur to our, 409
　that drives, as, 692
　that is a little gilt, 75
　the knight's bones are, 316
　they make, terrible, 595
　this earth this grave this, 22
　this quiet, 585
　thou art and shalt to dust return, 155, 1097
　thou art to dust returneth, 433
　to dust ashes to ashes, 1128
　to dust beneath the sod, 560
　to dust in an alien land, 866
　thrown in my eyes, 839
　thy mercy warms, 452
　was heaped above me, 1093
　was once the man, 536
　what would have sunk in, 916
　white, o' the road, 873
　would hear her, 469
　writes in, 113
　wrote them in the, 204
Dusty and old titles, 132
　answer, 574
　cloak, 652
　cobweb-covered maimed, 614
　death, the way to, 88

Dusty spiteful and divided, 810
Dutch, beat the, 950
church bell, good old, 566
fault of the, 293
Dutchman in the garden of Eden, 518
Dutchman's beard, icicle on a, 55
Cap, 524
Duties as a king, 921
back to joyless, 690
new occasions teach new, 525
of that church, 1061
property has its, 420
Duty, a divided, 101
activity and, 1085
and leave the rest, do your, 1043
and my life, my heart, my, 66
but to sing, 736
delicate, 320
demands every faculty, when, 725
do out the, 491
England expects every man to do his, 284
ever, I have done my, 705
faithful below he did his, 274
found that life was, 509
gives from a sense of, 525
has been done, that our, 624
he has seen his, 639
in that state of life, 1128
is a term, plain, 822
I've done my, 229
I've watched my, 677
let us dare to do our, 455
live above the fog in public, 522
men that learned their, 970
not a sin, this is a, 226
obedience into, 1054
of a clergyman, 312
of being happy, 704
of every Irishman, 709
of every sincere sportsman, 1091
of happiness, dwell on the, 605
of humanity, general, 1028
of some, right of all, 319
picket's off, forever, 569
pursues us ever, sense of, 342
service sweat for, 48
so trying, no, 274
some sense of, 466
stern and pressing, 560
straight is the line of, 444
subject's, is the king's, 67
such, as the subject owes, 52
that is thy, 1082
the hard ways of, 445
the path of, 467
to do my, in that state, 1128
to do thy, 686
to avoid religious subjects, 312
to his Creator, 977
to sacrifice his repose, 259
to this body, doing my morning, 907
to worship the sun, 641
trespasses against his, 259
views of Christian, allowed indulgence, 522
walks the careful ways of, 444
we all did our, 1056

Duty wed, those to, 955
whispers low, when, 409
whole, of man, 1110
with pleasant, 572
Duty's faithful child, 393
path, from, 671
Dwarf on a dead giant's shoulders, 592
on a giant's shoulders, 122, 136, 318
Dwarfs and giants tall, all the, 712
Dwarfed and abased below them, 708
Dwarfish whole, a, 316
Dwell like an hermit, 22
together in unity, 1106
Dwelle with sothfastnesse, 4
Dwellers by the sea, 713
Dwellest thou, where, 76
Dwelling, back to his vacant, 649
is light of setting suns, 296
place, man's safe, 370
those that are content with their, 872
Dwellings, soon or late to all our, 443
upon it, not build your, 1093
were open as day, 435
Dwelling-place, the desert were my, 264, 354
Dwells apart though not alone, man, 540
ever in her words, 405
in a poor house, honesty, 51
in that mighty tone, 501
no greatness, in me there, 470
within thine heart, coldness, 446
Dwelt all that's good, 146
among the untrodden ways, 296
Dwindle peak and pine, 84
Dwindles, man only, 249
Dyer's hand, like the, 108
Dying, a man's, 1089
and letting die, 854
and no tomb, no, 843
cease to die by, 128
ember wrought, each separate, 460
experiment so great as, 147
eyes read a mystic meaning, 583
eyes, unto, 466
eyes were closed, 217
fall, it had a, 53
I am dying Egypt, 105
in Algiers, soldier lay, 447
like men, 67
man to dying men, 166
nothing sweet in your, 930
preacher I have been, 948
strife, some, 186
to-morrow will be, 133
we live, living we fret, 492
when she slept we thought her, 390
Dynamite, cook the frozen, 779
Dynamos bridges towers, 936
Dyspepsy, death's door of a mental, 525
is the ruin of most things, 347
Dyspeptic come to feaze, 698

E WHITE I red O blue, 1084
Ea discamus in terris, 1092
Each according to his abilities, from, 1071
can make but once, 584
day is like a year, 722
day will bring its task, 591
for one another, 630
hath back, 719
heart is whispering Home, 392
plays his part and has his day, 844
unto each, 567
was naught to each, 485
Eager fluttering of life's wings, 736
once to win it, 276
Eagerness for flitting, no, 1066
Eagle caged I pine, like an, 502
forgotten, sleep softly, 857
in a dove-cote, 76
in the air, the way of an, 1109
like a young, 334
mewing her mighty youth, 163
of the rock, 897
old age of an, 980
or the snake, ways of the, 778
representative of our country, 228
so the struck, 351
stricken with a dart, 145, 964
suffers little birds to sing, 77
Eagles be gathered together, 1116
dare not perch, 71, 212
having lately bathed, like, 63
mount up with wings as, 1112
never flew, 263
that flew unabashed, 576
Eagle's fate and mine are one, 145
own plumes, feathered with, 962
wings, beneath the, 805
Eagle-eye, lion-heart and, 248
Ear, Abraham's deaf, 892
adder that stoppeth her, 1104
against the earth, 499
and the chin and the nose, pecked on the, 776
and the seeing eye, hearing, 1108
applying shell to his, 302, 325
cap out of a sow's, 241
death twitching my, 982
dull, of a drowsy man, 58
enchant thine, 106
falling at intervals upon the, 266
flattery ne'er lost on poet's, 307
flea in mine, 1025
for each red, a general kiss, 280
give every man thy, 91
hark in thine, 99
he scratched his, 360
heard, eye hath not seen nor, 43
heard me, when the, 1102
hearing, the, 413
I will enchant thine, 106
in at one, 17
in many a secret place, 296
it came o'er my, 53
it heard, one, 4

Ear, jest's prosperity lies in the, 41
jewel in an Ethiop's, 77
lend their, 30
more meant than meets the, 161
nor glance nor smile, lend neither, 364
of death, dull cold, 244
of Eve, close at the, 152
of man hath not seen, 43
of night, the listening, 477
piercing the night's dull, 67
ring sweet in mine, 387
so tough-gristled, 492
thundering in thine inner, 544
to lip from lip to ear, 499
we lack but open eye and, 442
whorled, 672
with a flea in his, 127
word of promise to our, 89
Eare, did heare that tong, was never, 26
went in at tone, and out at the tother, 4
wrong sow by the, 17
Ears, aged, play truant at his tales, 41
as walls have, 470
belly has no, 998, 1026
blast of war blows in our, 66
can hear them, while their, 577
delighteth the, 1126
earth has stopped the, 743
forehead and the little, 808
given two, but only one mouth, 420
hangs from beauty's, 267
he that hath, to hear, 1116
his delicate, 735
in the, of gentle and simple, 545
lend me your, 83
look with thine, 99
music to attending, 78
napkin behind his, 923
noise of waters in mine, 71
of Midas, to have the, 893
of the groundlings, 94
of the old cur, 142
of the world, 633
of which produce loaves, 1056
polite, mentions hell to, 188, 210
she gave me, 297
small pitchers have wide, 16, 52
sounds of music creep in our, 47
that are hushed in death, 541
the woods have, 6, 16
to hear, for, 794
to music, open my, 887
took captive, whose words all, 53
two, of corn where one grew, 191
walls have, 6, 1041
with ravished, 176
wolf by the, 980
woman's, too lightly opened, 963
Earl can last but a few years, 573

Earls, daughter of a hundred, 462
Earldom, insignificancy and an, 222
Earlier time, back upon an, 417
Earliest at his grave, 349
to the ground, drops, 46
Early and sere its end, 586
beautiful, summer weather, 395
bright transient chaste, 202
days of his power, 974
death, heaven gives its favourites, 354
find the peaceful skies, 474
frost, slain by arrows of the, 565
Greece she sung, 247
nothing is too, for thee, 1010
nothing to him falls, 126
rising, worm punished for, 510
root and early doom, 423
seen unknown, too, 77
songster caught, worm by, 510
time, friends in, 247
to bed early to rise, 227
Earn, little to, and many to keep, 523
that I eat, 50
Earnest, between jest and, 1036
I am in, 424
in a world like ours, all must be, 445
life is, 433
soul, with an, 686
stars, 384
Earnestness, thinks with more, 361
Ear-piercing fife, 102
Ear-ring caught in student's beard, 706
Earth, a bit of, 887
a hell, making, 352
a sphere, preserves the, 289
a stage, 129
a stepdame, 1032
affords or grows by kind, 20
alive and so bold, O, 367
all, forgot, 336
all things in heaven and, 22
all unity on, 88
all ye know on, 383
ancients of the, and in the morning of the times, 465
and fell upon the, 1124
and heaven, glories float between, 425
and on, will forever be, 378
and the future, roast him on, 774
and the sky, theirs are the, 846
bards of, 626
be the indifferent, 730
bears no balsam, 659
beauty humbled to the, 931
being so good, would heaven seem best, 487
bleeding piece of, 82
bliss that, affords, 20
blunders along, somehow the poor old, 528
bowels of the, 61, 121
breaks up, when, 486
breathe upon the, 71

Earth, bridal of the, and sky, 135
cannot love and think, 553
confound all unity on, 88
cruel records keeps the, 570
crust of, in earth, 564
daughters of, 232
dust return to the, 1110
embroil the, 1050
exposed he lies on the bare, 176
fall to the base, 59
fed by the bounty of, 417
felt the wound, 155
flowers appear on the, 1110
for sixty year, served the, 919
fragrant the fertile, 152
frame in, 25
from heaven, we hold the, 659
from lowly, to vaulted skies, 521
full of woes, 959
fuming vanities of, 303
gazing forever on the, 773
get away from, 837
giants in the, there were, 1097
girdle round about the, 28, 42
give him a little, for charity, 74
give some special good to the, 78
glance from heaven to, 43
glory passed from the, 301
goes over to the squall, 915
green firmament of the, 433
has got him, 575
has one tale to tell, 619
has stopped the ears, 743
has suffered, on, 668
hath bubbles, 84
healest with blood the, 132
heaven on, 151
heaven tries the, 525
hell on, 720
his hearth the, his hall the azure, 410
his journeys are, beyond the, 911
his sober inn and quiet pilgrimage, 121
holds the rest of him, 805
in an earthy bed, 469
in May like the, 911
in this broad, of ours, 535
insensible, and be, 155
is a mill, 492
is a sepulchre, 970
is a thief, 81
is but a star, 881
is but the frozen echo, 688
is crammed with heaven, 431
is full of his glory, 1111
is hidden, much on, 1074
is not on this, 927
is not the steadfast place, 806
is round and like a ball, 369
is the right place for love, 837
it fell to, 434
it is well, 757
joy of the whole, 1104
kindled, 357
kindly fruits of the, 1127

Earth knows a little God the rest, 609
knows no desolation, 575
lards the lean, 61
lay her in the, 97
less of, than heaven, 308, 405
let me enjoy the, 651
let us learn on, 1092
lie lightly gentle, 130
like an orange was round, 519
loveth the shower, 1012
making, a hell, 352
man marks the, with ruin, 354
man's temporal station, 856
may run red, 602
may sing and earth shall smart, 575
melting heaven with, 447
men differ as heaven and, 470
model of the barren, 59
more than the, 553
more things in heaven and, 92
must borrow its mirth, 718
must have a touch of, 470
my footstool, 207
never a daughter of, 954
nightly to the listening, 194
none on, above her, 289
nor boundless sea, but sad mortality, 107
not gray but rosy, 492
nought so vile that on the, 78
of him, rid the, 807
of majesty, this seat of Mars, 59
of states, dyed with the, 929
of the, earthy, 1120
on the confines of, 290
on this beautiful, 446
on this hapless, 386
on this round, 725
once more may live, upon the, 984
one society alone on, 300
or air, whether in, 89
part of the salt of the, 600
peace good-will, on, 1116
peace shall over all the, 477
peacemakers on, 69
plants suck in the, 167
pleasant country's, 60
poetry of, is never dead, 385
power is passing from the, 301
prepare, for the, 867
proudly wears the Parthenon, 408
rejoice, let the, 1105
revives day breaks, 837
salt of the, ye are the, 1114
scum of the, 860
shall smart, 575
slough the, 777
so much of heaven, so much of, 298
soaks up the rain, the thirsty, 167
sovereign'st thing on, 61
speed the, 854
spot which men call, 157
steer, on does the old, 806
sure and firm-set, 85
take of English, 782
ten metres thick, 891
than heaven, 't is less of, 405
that bears thee dead, 63
that e'er wore, 115

Earth that hides things old, 832
the broken arcs, on the, 489
the reality of things on, 1074
the waters and the sky, peopling the, 1050
they sink to the, 929
this blessed plot, this, 59
this goodly frame the, 92
this grave this dust this, 22
this is the last of, 292
through, sea and air, 316
tickle the, with a hoe, 417
tideless and inert, 687
to earth ashes to ashes, 1128
to every man upon this, 400
to God, raises from, 1023
to lighten, from Paradise, 634
to make, happy, 553
to the sapphire walls, from, 521
to tremble, made the, 1111
truth crushed to, 373
turning, hear, 882
unfolds both heaven and, 42
upon the lap of, 245
walk the, unseen, 152
was nigher heaven, when, 485
way of all the, 1099
ways are sweet on, 963
when it is sick, 132
whereon thy feet do tread, 24
which, can never tame, 404
whole, and stars in sky, 534
whose table, 357
will be stained red from veins, 729
will live by hers, 546
will not see such ships, 834
with her thousand voices, 316
with orient pearl, sowed the, 153
word of the, 633
would not hold it, 747
ye have left your souls on, 384
yours is the, 783
Earths and skies and seas, new, 514
Earth's bitter leaven, 298
bliss, avid of, 736
breast, at rest on the, 523
coin of less account, hold, 754
cold dust and ashes, 765
elements, 570
farthest hills, beyond, 850
fevered brow, 445
firmament, stars in, 433
foundations fled, 744
foundations stand and heaven endures, 744
full rivers, 587
golden time, 984
green banner, 576
green fields and ocean's, o'er, 503
half-shielded breast, 586
last picture is painted, 779
paths are cleared, 840
philosopher, and never, 516
proud masquerade, 774
pure ablution round, human shores, 385
resonant bosom, 503
smoothness rough, 489
undecaying monuments, 423
worn cogs, 956
Earth-and-autumn of the setting sun, 843

Earth-born joy renew, 668
Earthless hour, in an, 920
Earthlier happy is the rose, 42
Earthly bliss, the sum of, 154
debtor, no, 833
dignities, peace above all, 73
flowers, hope's wreaths are made of, 446
godfathers of heaven's lights, 40
hope and heavenly hope, 343
nothing, bounds her, 336
nothing, could surpass her, 358
paragon, 106
power show likest God's, 46
spring, water from some, 586
things, living intensely in, 684
Earthquake, gloom of, 365
Earthquakes, succeeded or preceded by, 617
Earthquake's shock the ocean storm, 363
Earth-worm, like a giant, 926
Earthy grossness, all this, 161
Ear-trumpet, down the horn of her, 896
Ear-wax, not so much brain as, 75
Ease after warre, 24
age of, 250
and home-keeping habits, 997
and plenty, with, 967
and speed in doing a thing, 7
death or dreamful, 463
despise them with greatest, 1063
discharged with greater, than made, 135
doctrine of ignoble, 734
done with so much, 173
flow with artless, 275
fly from tree to tree with careless, 201
for another gives its, 281
for aye to dwell, at, 462
hours of, 289, 308
I was weary and ill at, 564
in Casey's manner, 770
in mine inn, 12, 63
in writing comes from art, 211
is not for any man, 378
live at home at, 115
mob who wrote with, 214
no cheerfulness no healthful, 391
nor peace that heart can know, nor, 248
of body blest, with, 200
of burdens, 1036
on the other, and, 476
or leaves them, 214
rots itself in, on Lethe wharf, 91
sleep and lazy, 1035
tanned reaper in his hour of, 552
that brings long, 24
things which men confess with, 1008
thrall to the gilded, 808
with grace, 225
with the greatest of, 640
would recant vows made in pain, 151
you write with, 279
Eased the putting off, 152

Easeful death, 383
Easier for a camel, 60
  not to speak, 9
  to be played on than a pipe, 94
Easiest person to deceive is one's
  self, 426
Easily as a king, 81
  Bacon could as, created, 382
  things go wrong, how, 559
Easiness to the next abstinence,
  95
  property of, 96
East and west, 389
  arise facing, 802
  bowed low, the, 547
  curtains of the, 604
  golden window of the, 77
  is east, 779
  it is the, and Juliet is the sun,
  78
  like a great chancel, 764
  moon ascending up from, 536
  or blow it west, blow it, 555
  or west, ask me no more if, 140
  remote part of the, 977
  side west side, 761
  to the west blow the trumpet,
  from, 271
  tried to hustle the, 783
  where the gorgeous, 149
  will be found, 519
  wind an impassive-faced tyrant, 726
  wind never blow, may the, 139
Easter won, lent is over and their,
  597
Easter-day, sun upon an, 163
Eastern clime, save in, 500
  kings, guilt of, 167
  skies, sun illumed the, 473
  windows only, not by, 519
Easterners do, as the, 952
Easy as a wooden boat, float as,
  940
  faithful gallant honourable,
  1037
  if to do were as, as to know, 44
  it is missed, 866
  leap, methinks it were an, 61
  live and quiet die, 309
  lives, do not pray for, 613
  to be true, 183
  to call them back, not, 855
  to crawfish and crawl, 844
  to cry when you're beaten, 844
  to despise, it is, 961
  to get up of a cold morning,
  346
  to marry a rich woman, as, 483
  to sit in the sunshine, 718
  writing curst hard reading, 279
Easy-chair, Rabelais', 214
Eat and drink as friends, 52
  and drink, bad men live to,
  1004
  and drink, let us, 1111
  and eat I swear, 67
  drink and be merry, 1109, 1117
  each other, cannibals that, 100
  earn what I, 50
  I cannot, but little meat, 20
  in the evening sleep at night,
  282
  is human, to, 753
  of a king, worm that hath, 96
  or drink, what ye shall, 1114

Eat paper, he hath not, 41
  some hae meat and canna, 287
  the lotus of the Nile, to, 444
  thy cake and have it, 136
  thy heart, 26
  to live, we must, 229
  what to, and drink and wear,
  398
  with a feend, 7
  with the devil, 16
  with you, I will not, 44
  your cake and have your cake,
  18
Eats till he is sick, 577
  time's corrosive dewdrop, 564
Eaten out of house and home, 64
  sour grapes, 1113
  to death with rust, better be,
  64
Eater of beef, I am a great, 54
  'Eathen, pore benighted, 781
Eating, appetite comes with, 1025
  cares, 160
  the air on promise of supply,
  64
  time, worn out with, 178
Eaves, drops from off the, 161
  observed under the, 930
Eb and Flo, you should see them,
  813
Ebb, ne'er feels retiring, 103
  to humble love, ne'er, 103
Ebbed and flowed the tide, 437
Ebbs and flows the muddy Pei-
  Ho, 746
Ebb-tide or flow, aids in the, 504
  deaths happen at, 713
Ebullience, superabundance random, 930
Eccentricities of collectors, 865
Ecclesiastical lyric, 421
Ecclesiastick drum, 141
Echo answers where, 356
  applaud thee to the very, 88
  caught faintly the sound, 290
  dies within our ears, 719
  earth is but the frozen, 688
  everywhere, to find its, 512
  every fateful, 1065
  faint and far replies Hark O!,
  572
  I asked of, t' other day, 511
  is not faint at last, 326
  it seemed the harmonious, 564
  of our wailing cry, 602
  of the sad steps, 303
  of the whole sea's speech, 577
  quoth, plainly matter-o-money,
  511
  to the sense, sound an, 211
  translation is at best an, 407
Echoes, avalanche of, 706
  down the creaking floor, 914
  dying dying dying, 466
  hints and, 443
  how cruelly sweet are the, 512
  of dreamland, 621
  roll from soul to soul, 466
  set the wild, flying, 466
Éclat of death, 584
Eclipse, built in the, 159
  first the rest nowhere, 246
  in dim, 149
  nature's last, 452
  of sorrow and of death, 373
  total, without hope of day, 150

Eclipsed the gayety of nations,
  233
Economic and social forces flow
  with tidal sweep, 641
  foundation, 1086
  issues, obsession by, 866
  M.D.'s, 715
  pyramid, bottom of the, 654,
  876
  royalists, 877
Economics, heedless self-interest
  bad, 877
Economy and good management,
  by, people make a show, 482
  expense essential part of true,
  261
  in things inanimate, 998
  is a distributive virtue, 261
  is the fuel of magnificence, 413
  of heaven, 325
Ecstasies of appreciation, toothy,
  871
  scoff at others', 808
  to those sharp, 897
Ecstasy a growing, 930
  at your feet, will roll in, 1090
  cunning in bodiless creation, 95
  of the modern world, supreme,
  932
  ratio to the, 585
  together to be blown, 773
  waked to, the living lyre, 244
Ecstatic airs and sparkling skies,
  873
  instant, for each, 584
Eddies and tangles, wildest, 629
Edelweiss, who find the, 642
Eden, close to, 824
  Englishman, Yankee Irishman
  Dutchman in garden of, 518
  every pool in, 956
  if woman lost us, 444
  is that old-fashioned house, 585
  keeps, still his, 393
  older place than, 827
  one morn a Peri at the gate of,
  stood disconsolate, 337
  rose, scent of the, 954
  slip, her, 424
  solitary way through, 156
  this other, demi-paradise, 59
  to live in, 667
Edens, lest we lose our, 485
Eden's gate is barred, 890
Edenhall, luck of, 433
Edge, at the sea-down's, 633
  cloy the hungry, of appetite, 59
  finest, made with blunt whetstone, 23
  hardest knife doth lose its, 108
  is sharper than the sword, 105
  near ocean's, as I can go, 513
  of battle, the perilous, 148
  of husbandry, dulls the, 91
  of tempestuous years, 389
  of the grave, on the, 635
  of the steep, 633
  of time, this little, 851
  teeth are set on, 1113
  thin face sharpened to an, 594
  tools, jesting with, 131
  wield thy double, 576
Edges foamed with amethyst, 801
  invite with gilded, 937
  of the fight, fringy, 519
Edication, she had an, 678

Edifices, Niagara of, 479
Edified, whoe'er was, 265
Edinborough, bred at, 228
Edition, Christians of the best, 1026
    if life had a second, 369
Editions of a book, many, 238
    which had variations, 238
Editor cannot always act, 1075
Editors, fourth estate of able, 381
    poll of newspaper, 860
Editorial we, use of the, 430
Edom's plain, 443
Educated Americans all go to Europe, 413
    man in the midst of a boundless arsenal, 376
    Southerner, 616
Education a refuge in adversity, 1015
    and culture, but her, 970
    and practice, poets by, 412
    be a sort of amusement, 974
    beginning and end of political, 635
    benefits of a college, 413
    common to all, making, 529
    contact with manners, 200
    every Englishman's, 551
    felicity of good, 1001
    few are capable of, 729
    forms the common mind, 209
    freemen without, 473
    in the paths of duty, 636
    in this land, there shall be, 752
    is making men, 815
    men of liberal, 1035
    most valuable result of, 563
    must ultimately be limited, 886
    persons without, 330
    prayer is an, 1074
    should be gradual as the moonrise, 545
    soul without, 196
    starts, direction in which, 973
    the ignorant despise, 988
    the instruction of the intellect, 563
    to love her was a liberal, 197
    travel is a part of, 110
    viaticum of old age, 1015
    whole drift of my, 663
Education's sway, neath, 447
Educational relations strongest tie, 712
Educing good from evil, 224
Edward, sons of, 72
Eel of science, 215
    uneasy as an, 661
E'en, the lass wi' the bonnie blue, 388
Effect, aim and, 1068
    an electrical, 686
    cause of this, 92
    defective comes by cause, 92
    does not follow, from whose nature, 1048
    of good wines, 680
    of power and publicity, 635
    produces more than one, 580
Effects and dresses, played with new, 648
    are pernicious, 422
    what dire, 195
    which can be obtained, 1080
Effective strength, 491

Effectual fervent prayer of a righteous man, 1122
Efficiency, goddess of, 910
    of a flawless kind, 726
    to meet the requirements of economic, 731
Efficient, luck is infatuated with the, 514
Effigy about me, bear in, 789
Efflorescence of civilized life, 580
Effluence cannot die, 366
    from divine afflatus, 1067
Effort, does it without, 532
    done by great, 531
    is not lost, smallest, 504
    isolated individual, 1074
    name given to, 892
    of the human soul, 852
    of thinking, 637
    to speak it, 791
    whose constant, 921
Efforts, directs not his, 637
    of race due to love of praise, 532
Egeria! sweet creation, 354
Egg, as innocent as a new-laid, 622
    as one, is like another, 1040
    be the same crushed, for ever, 432
    full of meat, 79
    hard-boiled unbroken, 923
    he that steals an, 138
    of democracy, 529
    when broken, as an, 432
    without salt, 774
Eggs, as if he trod upon, 125
    as like as, 56
    in one basket, all his, 1036
    new-laid roasted rare, 177
    silent when they have hatched their, 147
Egg's way of making another egg, 614
Egotism characteristic of self-taught men, 331
Egotist, delicious, 893
    most eminent in the world, 197
Egotists, conscience makes, 723
Egotistical imagination, gifted with an, 420
Egregiously an ass, 101
Egypt, art of medicine in, 969
    beauty in a brow of, 43
    flesh-pots of, 1035
    I am dying, 105, 568
    Pharos of, 956
    plenty throughout all the land of, 1098
    were laid, in, 956
Egypt's dark sea, o'er, 336
    land, in, 375
    pearl dissolved, 664
    pyramid, the mystery of, 429
Egyptian kings, hieroglyphics of, 620
Eight strong fellows, 862
    times to-day that 's, 389
Eighth Commandment not made for bards, 316
    day of the week, 733
Eileen aroon, when like the rising day, 416
Either may undo thee, so much of, 128

Elaine, is this, 471
    the lily maid of Astolat, 470
Elastic and vigorous thought, 514
    band, garter an, 662
Elated, art thou, 586
Elbow, 'twixt shoulder and, 222
Elbows, horizon never at our, 514
Elbow-room, my soul hath, 58
Eld, palsied, 36
    vastness and age and memories of, 459
Elder days of art, 436
    how much more, 47
    let the woman take an, 54
Elders, the discourse of the, 1124
Eldorado, land of, 861
    that looked like, 460
Elect, heaven does not choose its, 482
    mode of God with his, 556
Elected silence, 672
Election and my hopes, between the, 97
    Day is a holiday, 934
    right of the white, 584
    to public offices, in, 970
Electric power, genius hath, 404
    touch, 412
Electrical display of God the Father, 903
    effect, an, 686
Electricity and crime, 828
Elegance in prose composition, 326
    of female friendship, 232
Elegant but not ostentatious, 233
    simplicity of three per cents, 275
    sufficiency content, 224
Element, creatures of the, 158
    farewell incomparable, 898
    of earth hail, 898
    one God one law one, 469
    thy, is below, 98
    which can be amalgamated, 1070
Elements assemble, there your, 892
    cronies of the, 771
    I tax not you, you, 98
    of democracy, natural, 1070
    of nature, earnest, 895
    out of earth's, 570
    so mixed in him, 84
    to whom the better, 405
    unhurt amidst the war of, 195
    weak and beggarly, 1121
Elemental force is ruthlessly frank, 726
    things, tang of, 708
Elementary, my dear Watson, 737
    writing that will soon be, 1084
Elenore, tread the region, 749
Elephant ate all day, 700
    ate all night, 700
    hath joints, 75
    leans or stands, 136
    learns to dance, 1005
    man's plaything, 1005
    went to see the, 510
    what is bigger than an, 1005
Elephants for want of towns, 190
    indorsed with towers, 156
    never forget, 812, 919
    wild, are caught by tame, 977

Elevate, in thoughts more, 150
Elevation of mankind, hindrances to, 514
Eleven die nobly, 76
hardly more, I was, 938
points in the law, possession is, 193
Eleventh hour, it is the, 635
Elf, joyous, singing sweet songs, 915
Elfland, horns of, 466
Elgin's place, stands in, 474
Eliot, left to an American, T. S., 937
Eliza crossing the river, 480
Elizabeth, my sonne's wife, 540
spacious times of great, 463
Elizabethans, inconsistency of the, 865
Ell, tooke an, 17
Ellen down the lane, old, 828
Elm freshened in the, 659
pears from an, 1041
Elms, immemorial, 466
Elmer's incantation, 885
Elocution flows, 218
wherefore waste our, 624
Elopement would be preferable, 791
Eloquence a hundred times has turned, 425
and indelicacy, British, 906
and poetry, 167
heavenly, 174
mother of arts and, 156
resistless, 156
splendid, 222
stands not on, 332
than speech, silence hath more, 478
Thou hast inspired, 1017
truth is the secret of, 1073
unspoken, 690
woke poetic, 669
Eloquent just and mighty death, 22
Elusiveness of soap, 654
Elves, criticising, 262
fairy, whose midnight revels, 149
whose little eyes, 134
Elysian beauty, 303
life, suburb of the, 436
Elysium have ye known, what, 384
lap it in, 158
Embarrassed gods, greets the, 778
most I do is to appear, 1082
people, 360
Embarrassment of riches, 1053
of the artist, 1089
Embattled armies, 156
farmers stood, here the, 409
hosts on land and sea, 513
soldiery, 964
Ember wrought its ghost, each, 460
Embers, glowing, 160
of the past, 710
Emblem of the Church's strength, 789
of truth, 348
to friends and enemies, 303
to humanity, 497
Emblems of deeds, 355
of untimely graves, 266

Emblems right meet of decency, 242
Embodied greatest number greatest ideas, 531
Embodiment, the law is the true, 623
Embody the law, 623
Embosomed in the deep, 249
Embrace, arms take your last, 80
endure then pity then, 208
for lingering, 824
leaped to ruin's red, 690
me she inclined, 162
thy friends leave all in order, 537
Embraces of the tomb, 218
Embracing to cheer and bless, all, 626
vines, 602
Embroidery, every flower that sad, wears, 159
Embryo novelist, be born anywhere, 913
yesterday in, 1011
Emelye, up rose, 6
Emerald cucumber-tree, wild, 431
dark deep, 680
hue, a little peach of, 698
Isle, men of the, 941
Emergencies, maintain its existence in great, 457
untried, 530
Emergency, whatever the, 622
Emerson advised his fellow-townsmen, 890
first there comes, 526
now the Benicia boy, now, 490
out of Charles Lamb, by, 863
whose rich words, 526
Eminence, that bad, 149
Eminent egotist, most, in the world, 197
man's conversation, 426
tax for being, 191
Emotion, aesthetic, 1084
cannot be touched without, 461
he needs, procure for himself the, 1084
plumb the depths of, 710
reception of erotic, 1084
you can not demonstrate an, 641
Emotions, with understanding and, 1088
Emotional and spiritual intensity, 930
storms, weather in safety, 870
Emperor, in mine own house an, 129
without his crown, 202
Emperors, purple of, 786
ridiculous, pomp of, 414
Emphatic, difficult to be, 582
Empire and 'igh destiny, of, 845
and victory, 367
British race and, 921
lost or won by a single word, 395
my mind to me an, 20
no more than power in trust, 173
of habit is powerful, 987
of land to the French, 376
of the air to Germany, 376
of the sea to the English, 376

Empire, sun never sets on the immense, 311
swayed the rod of, 244
thickening to, 894
thy dread, chaos, 215
westward the course of, 203
westward the star of, 203
Empires daily born, 785
day of, 622
dissolve, 735
expeditions and everything else, 347
two everlasting hostile, 378
whose game was, 357
Empires' kings' captives' births, 652
Employ, if you'll give me, 950
in some unknown Power's, 547
rest from thy loved, 305
teach heaven's, 489
the present well, 217
Employed men best contented, 228
Employers wanting all sorts of servants, 495
Employment, forego their customary, 324
for his idle time, 139
hand of little, 96
may afford, chance, 936
Employments, how various his, 265
public, 190
Emptiness of ages in his face, 708
smiles betray his, 213
stones of, 443
wonder out of, 811
Empty boxes, beggarly account of, 80
bubble, honour but an, 176
chair, toys and his, 580
day, idle singer of an, 608
dream, life is an, 433
heads, tall men have, 113
house like a stray dog, 614
louder but as, quite, 208
music floods the ear, 735
name, fame is but an, 288
often the cockloft is, 148
pocket, an, 560
praise, pudding against, 215
stomach, patriot on an, 714
thanks, words are but, 194
vessel makes greatest sound, 67
when I have made it, 48
windows, smites all the, 594
Empty-vaulted night, 158
Emulation, propensity for, 730
Enamelled eyes, quaint, 159
stones, sweet music with, 33
Enamored architect, 621
Enamoured, hung over her, 153
Enchant thine ear, 106
Enchanted circle of the upper ten, 576
Enchanter Indolence, 300
Enchanting miracles of change, 683
Enchantment, distance lends, 327
fosters it no more, 927
it gave, 954
Enchantments of the Middle Age, 548
render birth to dim, 447

Enchantress of the stormy seas, 418
Encircling gloom, lead kindly Light amid the, 403
Enclosed, safe within its central heart, 535
Encompasseth thy finger, 71
Encounter, death's dark, 508
  free and open, 163
  of our wits, keen, 71
Encounters between two champions, 407
Encourage no vice, 251
Encouragement does not mean protection, 1066
  more than sufficient, 422
Encreasing, youth waneth by, 27
Encroachments, abuses and, 329
Encumbers him with help, 233
Encyclopedic mind, 398
End and aim, our being's, 208
  and beginning are dreams, 597
  and to this, 1022
  assured, some sort of, 490
  at his wit's, 1037
  at my finger's, 13, 125
  at our wittes, 13
  at their wit's, 13, 1105
  attempt the, 134
  be set to them, if an, 804
  be well all is well, 1075
  beginning and the, 1123
  beginning of our, the true, 43
  beginning of the, 1059
  bitter, 944
  born to desastrous, 26
  break eggs at the smaller, 191
  broken only by my life's, 896
  calculate the, 271
  come out all right in the, 495
  crowns all, 75
  death a necessary, 82
  die and there an, 87
  do not forsake me at my, 180
  each particular hair to stand on, 91
  early and sere its, 586
  fortune's, 429
  good beginning, good, 14
  guide original and, 231
  half-won, baulking the, 778
  happiness our being's, 208
  hope to the, 1122
  how dull to make an, 464
  if there's an, 909
  in a golden hour, 664
  in wandering mazes, found no, 150
  is not mere speculative knowledge, 975
  is not yet, the, 1116
  justifies the means, 987
  life's great, 202
  look backward longingly to the, 930
  make me to know mine, 1104
  me no ends, 946
  means unto an, 506
  minutes hasten to their, 107
  most sweet, to make the, 59
  must justify the means, 189
  my last, be like his, 1099
  nearing our journey's, 690
  of a fray, latter, 63
  of a golden string, 282
  of a perfect day, 761

End of a shot, 17
  of an Indian June, 776
  of every man's desire, 632
  of everything, fain would know the, 430
  of government, 393
  of government the happiness of the governed, 401
  of it, there is an, 1038
  of language, nature's, 203
  of life cancels all bands, 62
  of life not knowledge but action, 564
  of my tether, 283
  of reckoning, 37
  of the chapter, 1026
  of the fight, 783
  of the town, never go down to the, 876
  of the world, even unto the, 1116
  of this day's business, 84
  of woman's being, holiest, 454
  of work, look at the, 487
  one must consider the, 1045
  original and, 231
  prophetic of her, 201
  remember Milo's, 180
  remember the, 1124
  served no private, 210
  set gray life and apathetic, 463
  sigh without an, 1065
  swan-like, fading in music, 45
  that shall lightly meet, an, 537
  the finest one in the, 923
  the, is the same, 792
  the sooner to make an, 113
  then, for what, 1052
  this is the silent, 586
  to all an end, an, 789
  to all at length an, 692
  to all things, 506
  to pain, death who puts an, 470
  to quiet age a peaceful, 984
  towards its unpredicted, 926
  try the man, 64
Ends are out of sight, both, 870
  at my fingers', 54
  delays have dangerous, 68
  divinity that shapes our, 97
  end me no, 946
  every man for his own, 125
  human, ultimately answered, 339
  neglecting worldly, 32
  of the earth, come from the, 779
  of verse, cheered with, 142
  of which were twisted, 999
  old odd, of holy writ, 71
  out to the undiscovered, 810
  private, 254
  seldom gain their, 951
  sought his, 649
  this strange eventful history, 50
  thou aimest at, 73
  violent delights have violent, 79
  well, all is well that, 13, 1075
End-all, might be the, 85
  of deep arguments, 806
Ende of every worldly sore, deeth is, 6

Endearing elegance, 232
  wile, children with, 251
Endearment, each fond, 250
Endeavour and dispute, 1019
  brave your storm with firm, 638
  fruit of our long, 659
  glowing mind of all, 889
  no, is in vain, 437
  riven with vain, 298
  to do thy duty, a brave, 686
  vain is my weak, 501
  with impotent, 405
Ended and begun, between things, 537
  his cares are now all, 65
  with the day, her washing, 557
Ending, a good, 12
  always descending, never, 321
  in death at last, 608
  is that our, 575
  life that knows no, 1017
  my, is despair, 33
  on the rustling leaves, 161
  still beginning, never, 176
Endite, songes make and wel, 5
Endless announcements, 534
  cruise, depart upon thy, 537
  day, an, 603
  error, in, 208
  extinction of unhappy hates, 547
  file, single in an, 410
  imitation, 301
  merit, 378
  night, closed his eyes in, 243
  pain, the weariness the, 439
  rue, sold for, 742
  sleep He wills, 563
  surges of the deep, 517
  there is, merit in a man's, 378
  time, with liberty and, 551
  to dispute upon everything disputable, 184
  unfathomable rest, 655
  voyage gone, one on an, 568
En-dor, on the road to, 781
Endow a college or a cat, 210
Endued with sanctity of reason, 154
Endurance, foresight, 299
  made lighter, are by, 983
  of sufferings, 350
  patient, 438
Endure, human hearts, 231
  the like himself, 40
  the toothache patiently, 40
  we first, then pity, 208
Endured, what can't be cured must be, 124, 1026
Endures and waits, labors and, 438
  no tie, love, 176
Enduring as marble, 357
Endymion wrote, letters which, 722
Enemies, a man's worst, 282
  borrowed from his, 481
  both surrounded by, 877
  die loving their, 573
  disposed of foreign, 974
  fallen among, 1003
  fourth for mine, 196
  hast got an hundred, 241
  he has made, love him most for the, 569

Enemies in the face, look his, 181
intimate, 577
naked to mine, 74
no! Can such a grace, 686
no more grievous and thorough, 1081
notice of despicable, 961
of nations, mountains make, 264
of truth, 144
secret history of our, 440
shall lick the dust, 1104
take precautions against your, 1126
their sworn, 20
to flight, put, 122
unhappy lot which finds no, 988
we often give our, 962
wish to make no, 685
you have no, 504
Enemy, able for thine, 52
actual, is unknown, 1089
against such an, 1051
being dead rejoice not over thy, 1124
beyond the frontier, 1061
biography written by acute, 687
dies, no tears are shed when an, 988
down, hewed his, 659
faints not nor faileth, the, 519
goes over to the, 259
good bye to peace, priest for, 423
has no definite name, 794
has risen from his chair, 893
hast thou found me, O mine, 1101
he who has one, 1017
hunger, if thine, 1119
in a single, 1017
in their mouths, 101
is loose on the other side, 675
love your, bless your haters, 471
nearest and dearest, 117
nobody's, 496
of one the enemy of all is, 623
one, is too much, 137
persuaded his, 948
proud of the, 901
to life, care 's an, 54
to mankind, 55
to pomp and noise, 195
to truth, most dangerous, 1075
vision's greatest, 282
we have met the, 348
who has one, 410
you are now my, 227
Enemy's dog, mine, 99
pinions, on an, 962
toils, easier to get into, 962
Energies of our system will decay, the, 687
that can not die, 654
Energy and sleepless vigilance, with, 456
has been spent, much, 925
left, not much, 1063
of thought which keeps thee, 403
of will, who has, 1056
philosophy should be an, 1068

Energy, power wielded by abnormal, 636
release and increase of, 795
to its highest tension all human, 1090
Enfolded passion of the rose, 923
Enforced ceremony, 83
Engaged in opposing wrong, 450
Engagement catechism, 793
Engenders not a storm, every cloud, 70
Engine swerve, feel my, 717
two-handed, 159
wit 's an unruly, 136
Engines, great, move slowly, 112
said, what was it the, 644
smoke from all the, 926
spouting steam like whales, 926
there were two, 926
you mortal, 102
Engineer, while smoking there an, eloquently spat, 926
Enginer hoist with his own petar, 96
England a paradise for women and hell for horses, 125
an industrious hand, from, 1076
and the English, drink to, 787
at her roots, poison, 826
be what she will, 262
best thing between France and, 417
better without beer and spirits, 695
breed again such a King Harry, 31
breeds very valiant creatures, 67
commend me to merry owld, 550
do not grieve, 823
expects every man to do his duty, 284, 320
fallen upon the north of, 507
given, thoughts by, 894
governed by Scotsmen, 906
has no name for prairies, 372
hath need of thee, 298
hedges of, 831
high-road that leads to, 234
his first works in old, 685
interests of individual predominate in, 739
is a cruel place, 523
is a garden, 785
is a pleasant place, 523
is far and honour a name, 765
is the one land, 893
keep my bones, 58
keep untamed, 475
martial airs of, 341
may your doom be a noble one, 407
men of light and leading in, 261
meteor flag of, 328
model to thy inward greatness, 66
my mother, 864
never shall lie at the proud foot of a conqueror, 58
not three good men unhanged in, 61
Oh to be in, 486

England of our dreams, 782
of Queen Victoria, 906
old, on the lee, 345
old, is our home, 394
one day in, 777
paradise of individuality, 769
perfidious, 1048
roast beef of, 229
roast beef of old, 193
rose may bloom for, 642
royal navy of, 248
Scotland's invasion of, 588
slaves cannot breathe in, 264
sporting, 906
St. George he was for, 258
stands sentry, 647
stately homes of, 370, 877
summer in, 197
that is for ever, 894
there shall be in, 69
they that fought for, 826
this flag of, 1061
this realm, this, 59
true to itself, 58
was merry England, 305
was what England seems, 782
what have I done for you, 693
what is left of, 432
where the sacred flame, 765
with a kiss, hid all, 447
with all her faults, 262
with all thy faults, I love thee, 264
wooden walls of, 946
ye gentlemen of, 115
ye mariners of, 327
yet shall stand, 634
England's dead, rest not, 370
glorious crown, 371
glory, 845
lordliest singers, 634
mountain green, walk upon, 282
noblest heritage, names that are, 518
singing soul, 931
slaughter-house, 814
sun was slowly setting, 705
English, abusing the king's, 34
air, sweet as, 466
amused themselves sadly, 331
breach with America, 713
buccaneers, 523
cause a sensation among the, 1070
claim supreme poetic literature, 740
critics, our, 942
dead, close the wall up with our, 66
dress and manners, 720
empire of the sea to the, 376
fam'ly, capital and labor like an, 797
history, heaviest calamity in, 713
in children's books, 766
language only one here, 734
legs, one pair of, 67
literature is a flying fish, 856
mother made her moan, 525
nation, trick of our, 64
nobility, lineage of, 739
oak and holly, 644
orthography, 731
parsonage, an old, 653

English people are snobs, 721
 poor, the, 827
 Scotchmen Jews in Ireland, 709
 spelling, 731
 style, to attain an, 233
 temperament not a national
  trait of, 571
 tongue, our sweet, 881
 undefyled, well of, 25
 unofficial rose, 893
 weather in his heart, 769
 without an accent, 905
Englishman acknowledge he is
  happy, 483
 afraid to feel, 856
 could beat three Frenchmen,
  one, 197
 he is an, 623
 how she wooed an, 257
 in the garden of Eden, 518
 is conceited, 1076
 lives on a island, 906
 Lord Byron was an, 685
 prejudices of a true, 197
 pretended I was an, 884
 rights of an, 949
 says nothing if he has nothing
  to say, 237
 stands firmest in his shoes, 413
 the dying, 314
Englishman's education, every,
  551
 food roast beef, 193
Englishmen in hope and creed,
  443
 of pith, 360
 with such acts, when shall, 31
English-speaking peoples, union
  of, 711
Engraving is the art of scratch,
  533
Engulfing sea, 605
Enigma, sphinx with her, 965
Enigmatical sort of calamity,
  1012
Enjoy, can neither when we will,
  547
 delight with libertie, 26
 her while she's kind, 177
 nought better than to, 489
 or even, without a certain, 397
 there is much to, 605
 we prize not whiles we, 39
 your dear wit, 158
Enjoyed, with more spirit chased
  than, 45
Enjoying, think it worth, 176
Enjoyment of looking on his own
  works, 1089
 of one's self, 195
 of the comforts, 985
 of these things, helps your, 538
 to enjoyment, 236
 variety is the mother of, 420
 youth the only season for, 407
Enjoyments, wonderful seasoning
  of all, 1046
Enlarge itself, never ceaseth to,
  68
Enlarger of the public life, 608
Enlargement, to look out of the
  little world, 554
Enlightenment that buys peace,
  bitter, 895
Enlinked to waste and desolation,
  66

Enliven morality with wit and
  temper wit with morality,
  195
Enmities of twenty generations,
  399
Ennoble sots, what can, 208
Ennobled our hearts and enriched
  our blood, 193
Ennobling dull pomp the life of
  kings, 546
Enormous and innermost perversion, 1082
 animals, insolence of, 969
 times, corrector of, 132
E-nor-mouse, his tail is, 876
Enough for great and small, 394
 his words were simple, 524
 I was thinking this globe, 537
 is equal to a feast, 229
 is good as a feast, 18, 29
 it is not, 804
 one step, for me, 403
 that Raphael's colors blent,
  561
 to have perished once, 982
 to help the feeble up, it is not,
  80
 to make a deacon swear, 527
 to trust that all, know, 501
 't will serve, 79
 verge, for more, 179
 when he would dine, has, 504
 with over-measure, 76
 you know, 610
Enquiry about a woman's pedigree, 1036
Enraged at the breaking of a
  crystall, 166
Enrich not the heart of another,
  if it, 435
Enriches not him and makes me
  poor, 102
Ensample O great, 760
 this noble, 5
Ensanguined hearts, 266
Ense petit placidam, 169
Enshrined but not apart, 697
Ensign, beauty's, is crimson, 80
 fly, let that, 552
 imperial, high advanced, 148
 of His cross, 875
 tear her tattered, down, 450
Enskyed and sainted, a thing, 35
Enslaved illogical elate, 778
 once fully, 534
Enslaved-by-convention, 886
Entanglement, break off from
  that, 972
Entangling alliances, 273
Enter not, although I, 481
Enterprise, heroic, is gone, 260
 life-blood of our, 63
 quixotic is his, 624
Enterprises, impediments to, 110
 lifted to buffoonery, 863
 of great pith and moment, 93
 that require new clothes, 514
Entertain, content to, 63
 strangers, to, 1122
Entertained angels unawares,
  1122
 certain guests of state, 579
Entertaining, all is, 942
Entertainment and wise instruction, 166
 martyrdom involved in, 729

Entertainments, stage a source of
  noble, 196
 without cost of money, 182
Entertains the harmless day, 114
Enthroned in hearts of kings, 46
Enthusiasm for a war, 1090
 nothing achieved without, 412
Enthusiasms, give me the old, 533
Enthusiast who keeps cool, 870
Enthusiasts, how to deal with,
  399
Enthusiastic tone, praises with,
  624
Entice thee, if sinners, 1106
Entire and holiest end of woman's, 454
 and whole and perfect, 747
 complacency and satisfaction,
  324
Entity and quiddity, 142
Entrails spin, from their, 177
Entrance of the Custom-house,
  421
 one, into life, 1124
 to a quarrel, beware of, 90
 too easy, into her heart, 155
 wisdom at one, 151
Entrances, have their exits and,
  49
Entranced, touched his harp and
  nations heard, 393
Entries to the land, 707
Entuned in hir nose, 5
Envelope, return, a mistake, 884
Envious hand, some, 699
 people, disposition of, 1015
 tongues, to silence, 73
 worm, bit with an, 77
Environment, a certain outward,
  379
 whose virtue is, 685
Envoy, lead the way and we'll
  precede, 278
 strike at close of the, 671
Envoys, two punctilious, 1050
Envy and an evil minde, 166
 and calumny and hate and
  pain, 366
 dared not hate, 357
 hatred and malice, 1127
 heard in many a distant clime,
  305
 is a pain of mind, 1006
 no man's happiness, 50
 no torment greater than, 985
 none no not I, 269
 of less happier lands, 59
 of the living, competition and
  mutual, 132
 of the world, 259
 pride avarice, 1020
 provoketh, 669
 shown by collectors, 772
 so little excites, 1051
 strongly rooted in the human
  heart, 278
 the vice of republics, 435
 time transported with, 257
 will merit pursue, 211
Envy's coal hissing hot, 506
Eohippus, said the little, 753
Epaminondas, witty saying of,
  1003
Ephemeral is fame, 1010
Ephesian dome, fired the, 193
Ephesians, Diana of the, 1118

Ephraim, grapes of, 1099
Epic, rather than the, 620
Epics in each pebble, 523
Epic's stately rhyme, 442
Epicure, judicious, 323
  would say, the, 177, 225, 313
Epicurean cooks, 104
Epicurus owne sone, 5
Epicurus' sty, fattest hog in, 985
Epidemical or pernicious, 198
Epigram in two lines, 995
  purrs like an, 724, 853
  what is an, 316
Epigrams, could not produce, 1063
  I write long, 995
Epimenides, the sleep of, 1013
Episcopalian bell, chimed the, 566
  bore, 213
Epitaph, believe a woman or an, 351
  better a bad, 93
  can say as much, 479
  fixed him up an, 661
  no man write my, 329
  not remembered in thy, 63
Epitaphs, derangement of, 277
  let's talk of, 59
Epithet, which belongs to the gentleman, 325
Epithets like pepper, 599
Epitome, all mankind's, 173
Epoch, comfort that bewildered, 787
Epocha in history of America, 268
Epochs in our lives are three, 579
Equal, all men created, 273
  and exact justice, 273
  day and equal night, 561
  grace force fascination, with, 535
  thanks, ta'en with, 94
  that they may be, 975
  to all things, 252
Equals and unequals alike, to, 974
  commerce between, 253
  that they may be superior, 975
Equality amongst all men, 970
  dispensing a sort of, 974
  liberty and, 975
  on earth is death, sole, 506
  we shall not produce, 909
Equanimity, cultivate a measure of, 695
Equator, speak disrespectfully of the, 312
Equilibrists lie here, 903
Equity is a roguish thing, 130
  is according to conscience, 130
Equivalent, made without an, 233
  more than, 1078
Equivocate, I will not, 424
Equivocation will undo us, 97
Era of wonderful nonsense, 922
  there will come another, 683
Eras, new, in their brains, 732
Erant quibus appetentior famæ, 159
Erasings, double, 664
Ercles' vein, this is, 42
Ere I was old, 317
  it herde, oon, 4
  sin could blight, 316

Ere the toil be done, 501
  they have blossomed for a few, 446
Erebus, dark as, his affections are, 47
Erect and strong face to face silent, 429
  by bending, he stands, 602
  unless above himself he can himself, 30
Erected look, with, 174
  spirit, the least, 149
Erection, we rate the cost of, 64
Eremite, nature's patient sleepless, 385
Erie Reading P.R.R., 926
Erin, a poor exile of, 328
Erly and late, bothe, 7
Ermined and minked and Persian-lambed, 768
Ernulphus cursed, was, 241
Eros, mock not, 912
  of his wings, remind not, 735
Err, art may, 176
  in opinion, human to, 1006
  to, is human, 174
Errand all divine, 445
  sleeveless, 13, 75
  upon a Tom Fool's, 241
Errants, sleeveless, 1039
Erring mortal fall, to any, 686
  reason's spite, 207
  rod to check the, 299
  sisters, go in peace, 349
  sister's shame, 355
  spirit hies to his confine, 89
  thought, 628
Erroneous, truth in things, 580
Error, an old and gray-headed, 145
  chokes the windows of the mind, 114
  destroy all, 549
  hosts of, 752
  hurled, in endless, 208
  in narration, 1017
  is a hardy plant, 477
  liable to be perplexed with, 969
  love truth but pardon, 1053
  of opinion may be tolerated, 163, 273
  of the would-be scholar, 426
  redeem the human mind from, 434
  to rectify, 235
  welds men together, 1077
  wounded, writhes with pain, 373
Errors agonies and fears, ere, 618
  are volitional, his, 874
  committed many gross, 1042
  I shall try to correct, 456
  like straws, 177
  seem, stratagems which, 210
  some female, 212
  some truths more harmful than, 564
  where shown to be errors, 456
  yesterday's, 682
Eruption, bodes some strange, 89
Eruptions, breaks forth in strange, 62
Esau, the hands of, 1097
Escape calumny, shalt not, 93
  in time, make your, 1064

Escape me? Never—beloved, 487
  shifts to, thinking. 530
Escapes, hair-breadth, 100
Eschewed evil, 1101
Escurial, my house to me art the, 137
Espousal lay, 669
Essay a loose sally, 232
  impurities of literature in an, 878
  in Atlantic Monthly, 863
  to make a short, 177
Essayist, atheist novelist play your, 471
  typical, 753
Essence, and if the, 669
  glassy, 36
  history is the, of innumerable, 378
  is love, its, 376
  love is God's, 617
  of a thing, look to the, 1011
  of Boston, 711
Essential liberty, 226
  poetry, 318
Essex Junction, who first invented, 551
Establish the kingdom of God, 1077
Estate, fallen from his high, 176
  flies of, and sunneshine, 135
  fourth, of the realm, 397
  hopes of an, 1042
  of man, fleeting is the, 1011
  relief of man's, 112
  that man's, owns him, 1014
  though he hath no, 955
Estates, three in parliament fourth in reporters' gallery, 380
Esteem in which he is held, 970
  they give to get, 249
Esteeming, love whose rich, 108
Estranged faces, 'tis your, 749
Et majores vestros, 291
  tu, Brute!, 82
Etching a mezzotint, 490
Eternal arches, views from, 891
  bass, of the sea, 609
  beadroll, fame's, 25
  city stands, 231
  dance and sing we are, 728
  devil, brooked the, 81
  Father strong to save, 566
  feel and know that we are, 1049
  feminine draws us, 1058
  fitness of things, 229
  friendship, swear an, 292, 1047
  frost, that skirts the, 316
  home, near to their, 146
  hope springs, 207
  house not built with mortal hands, 174
  I rise impalpable, 538
  keeps, whisperings around, 385
  moan, on its desolate sands, 503
  morning, breath of, 583
  new romances, 246
  now does always last, 167
  partnership, 807
  passion eternal pain, 546
  passion of song, 736
  Providence I may assert, 148
  punishment, idea of, 641

Eternal right, through present wrong the, 442
  shadow lie, clouds in, 373
  silent beautiful alone, 500
  smiles emptiness betray, 213
  stars, sky studded with, 536
  streams, by what, 460
  summer gilds them yet, 359
  summer shall not fade, 107
  sunshine settles on its head, 251
  things which are not seen are, 1120
  thought alone is, 593
  truths, wrote down, 684
  verdure, 231
  vigilance, price of liberty, 277
  with, lids apart, 385
  year, heaven's, 175
  years of God are hers, 373
Eternally new, there's a pleasure, 673
Eterne, nature's copy is not, 87
Eternities, past and future, two, 337
  peaks of two, 602
  time between two, 337
Eternity, amid the waste perilous, 867
  and I are one, 628
  are from, 743
  babble of, 851
  childhood of, 576
  deserts of vast, 169
  discharged through all, 1057
  dusk of, 571
  feeling of, 330
  gazing at itself, 880
  hath triumphed over time, 22
  heirs of all, 40
  in an hour, 281
  indicate, what does, 535
  intimates, to man, 195
  is thrust upon, 887
  like a great ring of pure and endless light, 170
  memorial from the soul's, 577
  mighty ages of, 553
  mourns that, 401
  number the days of, 1124
  passing through nature to, 89
  pilgrim of, 366
  plant for, 380
  portions of, great souls are, 524
  put forth the blossom time, 655
  sea of vast, 187
  silence is deep as, 377
  slided, with his best girl to, 755
  speak to age out of, 524
  stamp the impress of, 1082
  star of, the only star, 393
  teacher affects, 636
  tears of, 744
  the horologe of, 434
  their hour is their, 617
  thou pleasing dreadful thought, 195
  time is the image of, 1014
  to the genius of, 432
  uplands of, 850
  use again until, 584
  wander through, 149
  white radiance of, 366
  without injuring, 514

Eternity's river, flow in one down, 503
  sunrise, lives in, 281
Ether, ampler, diviner air, 303
  dissipates to shining, 411
  like a diamond glows, 801
  slight toss over ambient, 569
  the holy, knows what love is, 1012
  through the clear, silently, 383
  what patients say under, 912
Ether's long bankless streams, 882
Ethereal dances, in what, 460
  mildness, come, 224
  minstrel, 304
  mould incapable of stain, 149
  sky, the blue, 194
  spirit full, 338
  warmth, soft, 150
Ethics and divinity, 273
  from Byron's poetry, 398
  or religions, no, 813
Ethiopian change his skin, 1112
Ethiop's ear, jewel in an, 77
Eton, Waterloo won on playing fields of, 293
Euclid alone has looked on beauty bare, 915
  less, read my Bible more and, 655
Eugene Aram walked between, 391
Eulogy, deserving of an, 716
  funeral without a, 578
  or fault-finding, beyond the reach of, 675
Eulogy's blandest breath, 541
Eunuchs guardians of the fair, 203
Euphrasy and rue, 155
Eureka, the cry of Archimedes, 1004
Euripides, chorus, ending from, 488
  plays of, 879
  the human, 967
Europe, better fifty years of, 398, 465
  by conflicting faiths, 1050
  complexity of, 762
  he sauntered, round, 215
  outstanding services of central, 1089
  peace in, 1061
  regard everything else in, 1082
  rings, of which all, 162
  safe, kept, 891
  wool-soft air of, 932
European narcotics, 1081
Europeans for the most part, 932
Euxine, dangerous breakers of the, 360
Evanescence, pathetic, 606
Evanescent as woman's blush, 404
Evangelical things, 172
Evangelists record, all the words the, 671
Evangel-poem of comrades and love, 534
Evangels of the mind, 873
Eve and I, 485
  as ships becalmed at, 519
  ate apples, since, 361

Eve, close at the ear of, 152
  fairest of her daughters, 152
  for Adam's fall, blame, 768
  from noon to dewy, 149
  grandmother, a female, 41
  oh had our simple, 816
  orange band of, 744
  our credulous mother, 154
  son of Adam and, 190
  that unto, 956
  was led astray, when Mistress, 768
  with a berry, 816
Eve's daughters, 35
Even as you and I, 779
  gray-hooded, 157
  mind in difficulties, 399
  star that ushers in the, 108
  such is time, 22
  sweet approach of, 151
  tenor of their way, 245
  to the old, 620
  ushers in the, 108
  would God it were, 632, 1099
Even-balanced soul, whose, 545
Even-handed justice, 85
Evening air, fairer than the, 32
  borrowed in the, 228
  chime, faintly tolls the, 169, 334
  come in the, 502
  dews of the, carefully shun, 222
  exhalation in the, 73
  flowers at shut of, 154
  folded on Tennessee, 798
  grateful, mild, 152
  is spread out, the, 900
  must usher night, 365
  never morning wore to, 468
  not unpeaceful, 325
  now came still, on, 152
  one, with my friend Boccaccio, 843
  sea, I walked beside the, 558
  shades prevail, soon as the, 194
  spent jollily, 228
  star love's harbinger, 155
  star so holy shines, 408
  star, sunset and, 472
  sun shine sweetly, 269
  sunshine, while streams the, 373
  thou that bringest all, 960
  thought a morning dream, 594
  trails her robes of gold, 418
  twilight of the heart, 363
  waits, for which all, 809
  welcome peaceful, 265
  when it is, 1115
Evenings, long dark, 486
Evening's close, at, 245
Even-song, ringeth to, 17
Event, far-off divine, 469
  great, 818
  one, happeneth to all, 1109
  say not small, 485
Events, anniversaries of uninteresting, 723
  are brass, 531
  are writ by history's pen, 405
  begin, we fancy new, 531
  coming, 327
  course of human, 273
  greatest, are not our noisiest, 1079

Events, issue of, 981
  not to lead but follow, 1008
  pressure of great, 1062
  repeat themselves, 999
  river of passing, 1010
  spirits of great, 318
  that are themselves young,
    1085
Eventful history, this strange, 50
  present, the great, 443
Ever and a day, for, 51
  be the same crushed egg, 432
  do nothing but that, 57
  fair and ever young, 176
  hardly, 622
  have the measels, did you, 606
  his time is for, 167
  thus from childhood's hour,
    338
  were lost, 611
Ever-circling years, when with
  the, 477
Ever-during dark surrounds me,
    151
  gates, opened wide her, 154
Everest, watch from, 735
Evergreen tree of diabolical
  knowledge, 277
Evergreens associated with death,
    617
  emblems of immortality, 617
Everich a word, he moot reherce,
    5
Everlasting arms, underneath are
  the, 1099
  bonfire, primrose way to, 86
  fame, damned to, 208
  father the prince of peace, 1111
  fixed his canon, 89
  flint, wear out the, 79
  light, 612
  preordained from, 1012
  redemption, condemned into,
    40
  rest, 396
  two hostile empires, 378
Everlastingness, shoots of, 170
Evermore, one nation, 452
  peaceful stillness reigneth, 480
  thanks, 59
Ever-moving spheres of heaven,
    32
Ever-opened door, 218
Ever-returning spring, yet shall
  mourn with, 536
Every age unheroic, 430
  clime adored, in, 216
  cubic inch of space a miracle,
    537
  day's news, 37
  doubt that can retard, 417
  evil its good, 411
  fool will be meddling, 1107
  hero becomes a bore at last,
    412
  hour of light and dark a mir-
    acle, 537
  inch a king, 99
  look a dart, 193
  man for himself, 18, 1036
  man has all the centuries in
    him, 641
  man is the center of a circle,
    602
  man's work, 1120
  mile is two in winter, 138

Every, of, noble work the silent
  part is best, 533
  one as heaven made him, 1039
  one can master a grief, 39
  one that asketh, 1114
  one that hath, unto, 1116
  one thinks his sack heaviest,
    138
  pain, a balm for, 390
  scene by day by night, 393
  star in place, 821
  sweet has its sour, 411
  sweet its sour, 255
  through, season dearest, 393
  tone is music's own, 405
  volume of poems, 236
  why hath a wherefore, 37, 142
  woe, a hope for, 390
  woe a tear can claim, 355
  woman may be won, 559
  woman should marry and no
    man, 421
Everybody as passed that road,
  at, 539
  says I'm such a disagreeable
    man, 623
  wants a classic to be read, 615
  who is not in love, like, 1087
Everybody's business, 139
  looks discourse is of death, 182
Every-day words, 625
Everyone in the world is Christ,
    841
Everything advantageous to life,
    32
  and anything, sing of, 877
  by starts and nothing long, 174
  comes if man will wait, 414,
    421
  comes to him who waits, 414
  created in bounds of earth, 545
  custom reconciles to, 259
  demonstrating a careless deso-
    lation, 50
  devil at, 1036
  disputable, 184
  either at sixes or sevens, 623
  fain would know end of, 430
  find a tale in, 295
  find and have almost, 1079
  for the security of the future,
    591
  good in, 48
  handsome about him, 40
  happens to everybody, 721
  has been said, 1050
  has got a moral, 598
  has two handles, 1008
  hath two handles, 124
  he read, believed, 791
  he submits to, 1081
  here that they want, 799
  I cannot do, 550
  in earth or sky or sea, 706
  is grim and cold, 626
  is made of one hidden stuff, 411
  is nought, 332
  is right when it is wrong, 1052
  is sweetened by risk, 588
  known is forgotten, 809
  nourishes what is strong, 322
  result of change, 1010
  rustles to him in fear, 967
  sans taste sans, 50
  seemeth green, 52
  that deceives, 973

Everything that pretty is, 105
  that's excellent, 623
  that's old, I love, 113, 253
  there is a season to, 1109
  time tries the troth in, 17
  to imagine is, 1078
  you can say, 925
Everythink goes contrairy with
  me, 496
Everywhere be bold, 25
  his place, 167
  out of the, into the here, 559
  the gods see, 436
  the human soul stands, 378
  the sun shines, 55
Evidence against himself, 996
  boundary of experimental, 543
  circumstantial, 515
  of a crazy understanding, 183
  of his conscience, 950
  of industry a blemish in art,
    611
  of life, growth is the only,
    403
  of things not seen, 1122
  of truth, 329
Evil and good are God's right,
    506
  and good pretty nearly balance,
    556
  and they become, 1054
  around these hearthstones,
    speak no, 691
  be ignorant in foreboding,
    963
  be not overcome of, 1119
  be thou my good, 151
  bent on doing, 988
  but good, what is, 880
  can befall me, no, 911
  communications, 1120
  conscience, the disease of an,
    450
  cut them for, 956
  days, though fallen on, 153
  death is no, 594
  death is not the worst, 965
  deed, no, 660
  feared God and eschewed, 1101
  folly that seeks through, good,
    443
  for himself, man work, 959
  fruit of a bad man, 959
  good and good evil, 1111
  good from seeming, 224
  goodness in things, 67
  guest, it comes an, 960
  habit's earliest wile, 364
  hacking at the branches of, 514
  hastening to merge itself, 536
  if it have mastery over man,
    670
  ignorance is the one only, 1014
  in others, nature of, 973
  in themselves, not only, 970
  infect the soul with, 970
  is null, is nought, the, 489
  is wrought by want of thought,
    390
  its good, every, 411
  keep thy tongue from, 1103
  learned to know, 973
  love of money is the root of all,
    1122
  mainly done with lent money,
    532

Evil manners live in brass, 74
    may nothing, 886
    moral, and of good, 295
    new and untried, 1030
    news rides post, 157
    no, can happen, 970
    not into, wrought, 628
    obscures the show of, 46
    of that purpose, I know the,
        967
    of the dead, speak not, 1013
    oldest and best known, 1030
    out of good find means of, 148
    partial, universal good, 207
    recompense to no man evil for,
        1119
    refrain from, 975
    report and good report, 1121
    root of all, love of money is
        the, 1122
    shared much good and, 237
    shed away, all, 894
    soul of goodness in things, 580
    spiretes fairies wezles bats and
        ferrytes, 164
    submit to the present, 991
    supernatural source of, 726
    tends to disappear, 581
    that men do lives after them,
        83
    thereof, sufficient unto the day
        is the, 1114
    thing that walks by night, 158
    those who plan some, 606
    to contend against, 1127
    to resist him in authority, 958
    tongue an unruly, 1122
    universal good all partial, 207
    vice itself lost half its, 260
    which I would not I do, 1119
    witcheries weave me a spell,
        'gainst, 747
    woman necessarily an, 976
    word, doubled with an, 38
Evils, less grievous of two, 1064
    less of two, 4, 9
    of the night and an unguarded
        condition, 166
    of the sea, 834
    philosophy triumphs over past,
        253
    three great, 1052
    two, monstrous either one, 903
    two weak, 49
    when divine power plans, 175
    which being unarmed brings,
        1023
    which never arrived, 410, 420
Evolution is not a force, 641
    of things, always on the, 733
    some call it, 737
Ewigkeit, afay in de, 559
Ex umbris et imaginibus, 403
Exactness, with, grinds He all,
        435
Exaggerated distorted blurred
        pictures, 542
Exaggeration, crimes by, 1067
    truth that has lost its temper,
        880
Exaltation, crave for mental, 737
    of the defective, 730
    the divine insanity, thine the,
        438
Exalted ideas of fancy, 972
    sat, Satan, 149

Examination of the acts of gov-
        ernment, 320
Examine, the laws of heat, 641
Example from lives of men, 980
    greatest original practical, 537
    is the best precept, 962
    make him an, 35
    more efficacious, 232, 962
    of noble courage, 1125
    profit by terrible, 153
    profit by their, 270
    results of his own, 992
    salutary influence of, 233
    set the, 962
    thy stream my great, 167
    to deter, as an, 949
    you with thievery, 81
Examples, philosophy teaching
        by, 200
Exceedin' accommodatin' charac-
        ter, an, 606
Exceeding fair she was not, 28
    wise, fair-spoken, 74
Exceedingly well read, 62
Excel, 't is useless to, 239
    unstable thou shalt not, 1098
Excels all earthly bliss, 20
    another, one man, 979
    the quirks of blazoning pens,
        101
Excellence, do not know the, 965
    fair divided, 57
    for some special, 970
    gardener grafts the, 491
    is a wondrous, 108
    incredible standards of, 927
    smallest scruple of her, 35
    to maturity, 989
Excellencies than imperfections,
        dwell upon, 196
Excellent dumb discourse, 33
    first is most, 1023
    herb, was an, 783
    in neither, 109
    original, just to an, 217
    thing in woman, 100
    things that are more, 736
    to have a giant's strength, 36
Excelling nature, pattern of, 103
Except the Lord build the house,
        1106
Exception, glorious and painful
        to be an, 1070
    of the jasmine, with the, 1083
    prove the rule, 123
Excess, desire of knowledge in,
        110
    desire of power in, 110
    nothing in, 1013
    of glory obscured, 149
    of it, give me, 53
    of light, blasted with, 243
    of severity, 641
    of stupidity, 234
    of wealth is cause of covetous-
        ness, 31
    surprise by a fine, 385
    there is moderation even in,
        420
    to be blamed, 130
    wasteful and ridiculous, 58
    will be carried to an, 318
Excessive literary production a
        social offence, 520
Exchange, always credited to, 868
    by just, 27

Exchequer of the poor, 59
    rob me the, 63
Excise a hateful tax, 232
Excitable and easily forgetting,
        1076
Excitement, be not hurried by,
        1008
    continuous, written under, 745
Exciting, found it less, 624
Exclusive love, give, 564
Excrement, general, 81
Excrescence superabundance ran-
        dom ebullience, 930
Excuse, beauty is its own, 441
    coy, and denial vain, 159
    every man will plead, 130
    fault worse by the, 58
    for being, beauty is its own,
        409
    for the glass, she'll prove, 279
    I will not, 424
    in her face, came prologue,
        155
    not a single, 780
    that thou dost make in this de-
        lay, 79
    will serve, any, 961
Excuses, contests allow no, 963
    patch'd up your, 104
Excused his devilish deeds, 152
Excusing a fault makes it worse,
        58
Execrable shape, what art thou,
        150
Execute, the villany you teach
        me, 45
Executed, that it be successfully,
        1057
Executes a freeman's will, 348
Executioner, the common, 50
Executors, choose, 59
Exemplary, lives in acts, 28
Exempt from a mixture of mad-
        ness, 173
    from fear, 69
    from public haunt, 48
Exercise and art, trained in, 972
    bodily, 974
    butchered to make a school-
        girl's, 756
    for cure depend on, 175
    the principle of health, 225
    the sad mechanic, 468
Exertion, every form of mental,
        865
Exhalation, like a bright, 73
Exhalations of the dawn, 318
Exhaled and went to heaven, 202
    he was, 175
Exhausted chain, time winds the,
        286
    worlds, 231
Exhaustless deep his numbers
        flowed, 393
Exhibited, I saw what the not-
        day, 537
Exhilaration of success, 719
Exhortation of the dawn, 953
Exile from home, 365
    in the isles of death, from its,
        626
    lingering here, 618
    of Erin, poor, 328
    perpetual, 629
Exiles moored their bark, 370
Exiled son's appeal, hark to, 646

Existence, closing your account, 1018
depends for its, 935
dull routine of, 737
I called the new world into, 293
love is woman's whole, 358
medicine labors to destroy reason for its, 637
might bring into, 974
of me, stop the, 537
of supernatural, 769
realities of your, 953
should be justified, 722
sordid perils of actual, 723
soul secure in her, 195
squander two-thirds of its, 247
struggle for, 448
suck bare, 927
the sense of their, 1079
Exists only in imagination, golden age which, 400
Exit, called to make our, 274
pursued by a bear, 56, 816
ten thousand doors for men to take their, 127
Exits and their entrances, 49
Exodus of death, long mysterious, 436
Expanse, Lake Erie's broad, 605
still fills the wide, 644
Expansion, like gold to thinness beat, 118
open it with unbounded, 1127
Expatiate free o'er all this, 206
Expectancy, heed not our, 574
period of, 1091
Expectant of her, I wait, 481
Expectation, better bettered, 38
fails, oft, 53
makes a blessing dear, 163
rise, bids, 252
short of the wearer's, 498
to bury them, merely in, 147
Expected generally happens, least, 420
Expects nothing, blessed is he who, 220
Expedient as lighting by gas, as much an, 450
free trade is an, 419
of going into debt, 715
to forget sometimes, 987
Expeditious road, 749
Expenditure nineteen nineteen, annual, 496
of human voice, vast, 972
Expense and fatigue of travelling, 1039
employed at less, 242
of the general intellect, 461
of the present, at the, 314
Expenses, money to defray such, 247
Expensive, his wife is, 166
things, women are, 575
Experience and old age, hand in hand, 185
and passion, loneliest places of, 589
be a jewel, 34
has given him no access, 1082
has had the, 921
has shown, 981
hope over, 235
ignorant in spite of, 239

Experience is an arch, 635
is the child of thought, 420
keeps a dear school, 227
lamp of, 270
length of time and frequency of, 239
life is adventure in, 930
made him sage, long, 206
more than sufficiently, 1048
name for mistakes, 724
not personal, 973
of women, had some, 483
old, do attain, 161
our own, 465
parallel of any one man's, 529
remotely comparable, no other, 932
small, grows at home, 52
tells in every soil, 250
the short process guides, 280
the universal mother, 1035
tired of, 693
to make me sad, 51
travel a part of, 110
void of knowledge and, 977
Experiences, digests his, 1081
Experienced angler, signs of the, 745
liar, 616
Experiment, full tide of successful, 273
on animals is justifiable, 449
so great, as dying, 147
social and economic, 830
who makes the, 985
Experiments foolish to make, 776
I love fools', 449
Experimental, youth is wholly, 704
Expert, definition of, 761
designing, the, 937
Explain a thing till all men doubt it, 215
spoil it by trying to, 278
the asking eye, 213
Expletives their feeble aid do join, 211
Explicitness not a necessary virtue, 789
Exploits, relating his own, 1048
Explorations, revel in long, 1083
Explore the thought, 213
Expose thyself to feel, 99
Exposition of sleep, I have an, 43
Express and admirable in form, 92
grant of power, 320
not so much to, as to conceal, 254
Expressed felicitously risks being worse, 291
in fancy, not, 91
of expression that which can not be, 533
thought but ne'er so well, 211
Expression, beyond, 119
brief, pregnant in matter, in, 332
in that happier sphere, find, 540
in the countenance of all Science, 295
of interest, only another, 1089
of this man's face, 538
of villainy, 616
peculiar indescribable, 592

Expression, that which can not be expressed, 533
Expressive silence, come then, 224
Exquisite, joys too, 306
touch is denied me, 312
Exquisitely fine, how, 207
Exudations of a man's brains, 241
Extend a mother's breath, 213
Extent, my offending hath this, 100
of life, long, 967
of our inheritance, learn the, 542
of suffering, full, 1087
of your treasures, 640
Extenuate, as for the brandy nothing, 417
nothing, 103
Exterior and superior to the work, 1087
fair, a recommendation, 987
Extinction of unhappy hates, endless, 547
Extinguisher, frown is no, 510
Extortion, becomes ruthless, 628
Extracted from many objects, 51
Extraordinary spectacle, most, 689
toil, youth the time for, 974
Extravagance, he calls his, generosity, 253
was clothes, 691
Extravagant and erring spirit, 89
Extreme diseases, 971
essential part, 261
perplexed in the, 104
remedies, 96
Extremes, avoid all, 996
by change more fierce, 150
fate of all, 209
from being dominant, prevents, 975
heard so oft in worst, 148
limits of its race utmost, 553
meet, 1056
Extremities of earth and to the latest generations, 376
Extremity, a daring pilot in, 173
in the utmost, 1051
Exuberance of enterprise, 396
Exuberant spirits, 1081
Exultancy its drunken and magnificent hope, 932
Exultations, agonies and loves, 297
Exulting, bells I hear the people all, 536
Eye, a fearful, 30
and ear, we lack but open, 442
and prospect of his soul, 40
apple of his, 1099
apple of the, 1103
bear welcome in your, 84
bend your, on vacancy, 95
black is a pearl in woman's, 28
blow the horrid deed in every, 85
brighter when we come, 358
choose with careful, 914
could not 'scape the Almighty, 204
courtier's soldier's, 93
dares not send his, 165
day's garish, 161

Eye, defiance in their, 250
did see that face, 26
discern with this clear, 514
dissolved in dew, 269
distinguish not by the, 991
don't view me with a critic's, 292
doth level at, 106
explain the asking, 213
fades in his, 194
fire in each, 212
foot were equal with his, 70
for eye tooth for tooth, 1098
fringed curtains of thine, 32
glad me with its soft black, 338
glances, are where thy dark, 460
God caught his, 927
great, of heaven, 24
great task-master's, 161
grows bright, the hollow, 541
half hidden from the, 296
harmony in her bright, 168
harvest of a quiet, 297
hath chose the dame, when as thine, 109
hath not seen, nor ear heard, 43
he casts a sheep's, 1039
hearing ear and seeing, 1108
her cheek, her lip, language in her, 75
hide her shame from every, 254
however blue, doth not weary, 384
I ey'd, when first your, 108
I have a good, 38
in a fine frenzy rolling, 43
in my mind's, 90
in the twinkling of an, 940, 1039
is bigger than the belly, 138
lack-lustre, looking on it with, 49
light of a dark, 353
light of the body is the, 1114
like its crystals a heart like its glow, 560
like Mars to threaten, 95
lion-heart and eagle-, 248
locked up from mortal, 165
look squarely in thine, 760
looked with wistful, 722
looks down with careless, on men who drown, 649
looks farthest into heaven, 442
looks with a threatening, 58
looks yellow to the jaundiced, 211
lovely in her husband's, 295
muse on nature with a poet's, 327
negotiate for itself, 38
not satisfied with seeing, 1109
of a needle, camel through the, 1115
of a yellow star, threading the, 406
of day, 161, 273
of each man, 675
of Greece, Athens the, 156
of heaven, beauteous, 58
of heaven visits, places that the, 59
of man hath not heard, 43
of nature, lived in, 296
of newt and toe of frog, 87

Eye of solitude, that inward, 299
of the intellect, 378
of vulgar light, 334
one auspicious and one dropping, 89
or face, pleasing, 950
peril in thine, 78
postern of a small needle's, 60
power behind the, 413
precious seeing to the, 41
pupil of the human, 334
saw me it gave witness to me, 1102
see with half an, 1040
serene, see with, 299
shall light upon some toy, your, 55
sleep all night with open, 5
smile in her, 389
so inquiring, 326
still-soliciting, 98
such beauty as a woman's, 41
sun cannot be looked at with a steady, 1043
sun with one, vieweth, 68
tear in her, 307
tear stands trembling in her, 220
that inward, 299
the seeing, 1108
they shall destroy his, 958
thoughts are legible in the, 26
thy glorious, shines on me still, 418
to eye, they shall see, 1112
to watch, no, 336
twinkling of an, 45, 1039
unborrowed from the, 296
unforgiving, an, 279
upward glancing of an, 306
was bold and fearless, my, 973
was bright, I saw her, 387
was closed, mine, 1021
was in itself a soul, that, 356
was on the censer, 451
watch in every old man's, 78
wave before the half-shut, 224
welcome in your, your hand, 84
when comes the poet's, 650
which hath the merriest, 68
white wench's black, 78
who sees with equal, 207
will mark our coming, 358
with his glittering, 314
with its little brimming, 369
with threatening, 58
yet the sweet closing of an, 480
you catch the, 1085
Eyes, a smile from her bright, 1045
all, else dead coals, 57
and shame them with thine, 405
apples of his, 1040
are homes of silent prayer, 468
are in his mind, his, 317
are small, 876
are sunlight, 899
are what one is, 798
as stars of twilight fair, 299
baby's precious, 686
beasts with the kingly, 929
beauty lies in many, 335

Eyes, beheld by mortal, 634
beholds her image in her, 555
bend on me thy tender, 426
black, and lemonade, 334
blank, know each other not, 685
bless and astonish my, 913
blinded by our, 894
blue, as the fairy-flax, 433
blue in, 430
book in many, 77
bright in thy, 579
buyer needs a hundred, 137
can see, so long as, 1017
close up his, 69
closed his, in endless night, 243
colored like a water-flower, 632
conversation in his, 438
corners of their, 936
could meet, that ever your, 890
could see, sewing as long as her, 458
cynosure of neighboring, 160
deeper than depth of waters, 577
deeply buried from human, 442
discover, than gloomy, 1079
disenchants the winner's, 309
disorders of the, 969
drink into my, 915
drink to me only with thine, 119
drop out, his, 545
dry one's, 487
dulled their, with sin, 709
dying, read a mystic meaning, 583
faithful Argus', 220
fearless blue, 562
feed deep upon her peerless, 384
fields have, 16
for ladies', brown the only color, 911
for the blind strength for the weak, 602
forgetful, 632
gazed with tearful, 424
get those, so blue, 559
gifts that took all, 409
glow like the sparks of fire, 134
good for sore, 191
gospel-light from Bullen's, 246
had tears, their, 1065
hands were never made to tear each other's, 198
happiness through another man's, 51
happy human, 703
hath not a Jew, 45
have all the brighter shone, 432
have grown dim, 484
I blinded my, 859
I dare not meet, 899
I'm growing dimmer in the, 509
I wait, with longing, 481
I will not give sleep to mine, 1106
in April, men's, 873
in common, 26
innocence closing up his, 31
kindling her undazzled, 163
kiss that mortal's, 715
ladies whose bright, 160

Eyes, laughing lips and roguish. 620
lift my dreaming, 697
light comes from thine, 117
light that lies in woman's, 336
light that visits these sad, 244
like stars start from their spheres, 91
look down like mothers', 574
look from an infant's, 449
look your last, 80
looked in loving, 707
looked love to eyes, 352
love darting, 158
love looks not with the, 42
maidens quiet, 703
make pictures when shut, 317
man may see with no; 99
may be beguiled, wariest, 564
may weep, these wakeful, 325
meet far off, when, 177
men with sore, 995
mine, have seen the glory, 522
mortal, cannot behold, 282
my clouded, 669
night has a thousand, 707
no speculation in those, 87
not a friend to close his, 176
not see, let mine, 54
not withheld from your, 780
not yet created, 108
of gallery critics, 265
of gold and bramble-dew, 703
of men are idly bent, 60
of men, persuade without an orator, 106
of men, sweetly sliding into the, 26
of my cash-box, 1046
of pure women wholesome stars, 470
of sentiment, pluck the, 451
of strangers, with the, 1089
of unholy blue, 335
on the passing world, 230
ope their golden, 105
painted to the, 648
pearls that were his, 32
pictures in our, 117
play the woman with mine, 88
poorly satisfy our, 114
quaint enamelled, 159
rain influence, 160
sans, sans teeth, 50
saw with lifted, 764
severe, 50
shall cry my, out, 1036
she gave me ears she gave me, 297
show his, and grieve his heart, 87
sight for sore, 330
sights of death within mine, 71
so bright so bright, 875
soon will seal these, 396
sought each other's, 382
sought the west afar, 306
soul sitting in thine, 160
sparkle Promethean fire, 41
star-like, 140
still dazzled, 856
strain my, 717
sublime with tears, 428
sunshine to a brave man's, 967
tears gather to the, 466
than a nose, rather have, 791

Eyes, that ever looked with human, 468
that never quail, 760
that remember, 632
that roam, 361
that say you never must, 751
that see them, 412
that shone now dimmed, 336
that stare, better than, 904
that would not look on me, 279
the books, the arts, the academes from women's, 41
the break of day, 37
the glow-worm lend thee, 134
their vigils keep, mine, 1017
there lies a conversation in his, 438
they strike mine, 119
those silent tongues, 1034
those, the greenest of things blue, 632
though not ours shall see, 937
thy dying, were closed, 217
tired eyelids upon tir'd, 463
to behold, open our, 1128
to see, give us the, 757
to see, may I have, 866
to the blind, feet to the lame, 1102
too pure and too honest, 593
toothache or sore, 955
touch her marvelling, 911
unfaltering, 736
unto dying, 466
unveil thine, 960
up to the lion to lift your, 931
visible to the, 905
wanton, 1111
were bright, whilst still my, 1027
were closed, thy dying, 217
were deeper than the depth, 577
were filled with love, your, 521
were fixed above, 891
were made for seeing, 409
where'er I turn my ravished, 195
which fail with wakefulness, 397
whose language is fidelity, 665
whose subdued, 104
wildly fixed, 321
will not give sleep to mine, 1106
wipe my weeping, 199
wiped our, 134
with clearer, 134
with dreamful, my spirit lies, 552
with grave sweet, 1085
with lenient, 560
with light, fill your eager, 854
with purple, 938
women's, from, 41
would that his human, 834
Eyes' blue depths, your, 1066
Eyeball like a coal, 248
Eyebrow, ballad to his mistress', 49
Eyelids close, when my tired, 810
heavy and red, 391
of the morn, opening, 159
slumber to mine, 1106
warm, keeps our, 923
weigh down my, 65

Eyelids winking, are not their, 903
you should kiss my, 626
Eyesight, live giant's, 592
treasure of his, 77
Eyne, Bacchus with pink, 104

Fable, Golden Age is not a, 445
in the Libyan, 964
read my little, 467
Fables in the legends and the Talmud, 110
Fabric of the world to be, 952
of this vision, baseless, 33
rose silently as a dream, 266
the mystic, sprung, 342
Face a world, each, 874
absent, that fixed you, 428
all steeped in smiles, 691
and hand and feet, wash your, 875
and limb, form and feature, 630
and memory out of mind, 854
apparitions start into her, 39
as round as appel, 3
aside, put a tempting, 725
Aurora shows her brightening, 225
autumnal, 117
be by me, may thy, 497
beauty of an aged, 868
below the sun, not a, 596
blackest features of the, 949
bury me on my, 1015
can't I commend another's, 240
child is fair of, 956
climber-upward turns his, 82
continual comfort in a, 26
counted ere I see thy, 454
desert's dusty, 1018
died for, sung of, 773
disasters in his morning, 251
divine, human, 151, 220
divine plain, 325
downward in the sun, 914
excuse in her, 155
familiar with her, 208
finer form or lovelier, 308
fortune's changes in our, 180
garden in her, there is a, 121
give me a look give me a, 119
God grant you find one, 523
God has given you one, 93
gone before your, 596
grows old while the bonnet, 625
half known, like a, 736
he carries or what form, 662
her fair and fickle, 870
hides a shining, 266
hills of manhood a noble, 458
hungering for her, 736
I don't mind it, my, 845
I shall behold your, 600
in his morning, 251
in many a solitary place, 296
in my poor lean lank, 455
in some other, 887
in the sweat of thy, 1097
is as a book, 84
is the worst thing about him, his, 36
is writ with scars, 570
it, fearlessly, 592
labour bears a lovely, 116

Face, length of shambling limb,
his furrowed, 513
less deadly fair, 593
licked me in the, 890
like a benediction, 1034
like a blessing, 1034
like the milky way, 164
look down, if any, 892
look in my, 577
look on her, and you'll forget,
212
magic of a, 141, 451
man had fixed his, as if the,
296
mention with a cheerful, 907
might of one fair, 1023
mind's construction in the, 84
most fair to our vision, 593
muse on the absent, 428
music breathing from her, 356
music of her, 168
never eie did see that, 26
never see your, 881
no odious furrows in my, 280
nor miss my, 403
nose on a man's, 33, 125, 1026,
1034
nose upon his, 263
not seen, the voice not heard,
587
ocean on whose awful, 440
of all the faces, one, 796
of death, the awful, 1091
of death, true, 796
of God shine through, 915
of heaven, fair and open, 383
of heaven so fine, 79
of his desire and shape of his
dream, 727
of nature a study in old gold,
742
of that insipidly pleasing kind,
1077
of the dead, on the, 569
of the live new dawn, 633
of them all are as the blackness, 1126
of this round world, 370
one to himself and another to
the multitude, 422
one would meet in every place,
384
one you loved when all was
young, 523
painted her, and tired her head,
1101
pardoned all except her, 360
praise a poet to his, 657
princely counsel in his, 150
puff it in your, 624
remembered, thy, 773
saw the manners in the, 231
shall wear a mask, 814
sharpened to an edge, his thin,
594
shining morning, 49
shyned bright, her angels, 24
silly hanging, 199
some awful moment, 300
something in a, 199
sorrows of your changing, 790
spit in m , 62
spoil upon my, 68
stirred with her dream, 360
sweetest, in all the world, 665
ten commandments in your, 69

Face that a man might die for,
490
that flies, dearest, 674
that's anything but gay, a, 481
that launched a thousand ships,
31
that makes simplicity a grace,
119
that well might buy, 665
the world with, one to, 488
through her thinking, 911
to face with death, 438
to feel the mist in my, 489
to lose youth for, 490
to the rock, turn your, 889
towards the holy temple, turn
thy, 1126
transmitter of a foolish, 223
truth has such a, 174
umbered, see the other's, 67
visit her, too roughly, 90
was homely, whose weathered,
927
we encounter and lose, 593
we love, to think the, 730
wish I loved it silly, 759
with love capricious, 676
within that passport book, 847
you could not see, but his, 498
you have set your, 930
you wear the thoughts you
bring, 474
your lighted, 335
Faces all along the rails, 925
awful and still their, 933
bid them wash their, 76
blows back in their, 736
driven disenchanted anxious,
889
dusk, with turbans, 156
estranged, 749
folk with friendly, 875
grieved and wistful, 642
I have seen better, 98
in, of men and women I see
God, 535
in the town by day, 896
lifted in single supplication,
933
lifted in the phantasmal light,
933
new, strange with, 529
none alike, 144
of his friends long dead, 766
of old sorrows, 848
of the poor, grind the, 1111
old love look out from old, 560
old men have rosy, 703
on a cigar-box lid, 842
one can put on two several,
181
praise people to their, 390
put up with the multitude of,
1090
sea of upturned, 310, 340
stained and aging, 824
suddenly became as bright,
1050
that he hath not seen, 710
the old familiar, 325
those angel, smile, 403
three, wears a doctor, 698
towards that place, turn your,
1126
turned to the wall, 563
white nameless, 874

Faces would be fain, 709
Facility of octosyllabic verse, 356
Facing fearful odds, 400
Fack can't be no longer disgised,
606
Facks other similar, 853
Fact, but in one, 519
counterparts in world of, 542
has not created, 813
it is a curious, 1064
nobler than any, 444
or fiction life or play, 795
subtract faith and fallacy from,
910
that you're hurt, isn't the, 792
the ugly, 588
to reflect upon, 497
what yesterday was, 949
Facts and figures, 495
and the laws, 203
and told each other, 678
angularity of, 411
are apt to alarm us, 950
are contrary 'z mules, 527
are stubborn things, 248, 1052
don't tell me, 313
exist of his life, some, 493
for poor men's, 28
I never believe, 313
imagination for his, 279
injurious to science, false, 449
not to our taste, 543
nothing so fallacious as, 313
of life, to front the essential,
514
that are, fancies that might be,
493
the years will show, strange
new, 539
will promptly blunt his ardor,
978
Factor, now is its principal, 660
Factories start, when armament,
930
Factory, steps of the paper-box,
939
Faculties, benumbs all his, 233
develop their, 1075
hath borne his, 85
Faculty, infinite in, 92
of beholding at a hint, 727
of doubting, 1078
of entertaining ourselves, 1029
of humanity, characteristic,
669
Fad, place for many a, 811
Fade, as a leaf, we all do, 1112
away, which was first to, 590
gods, 654
made to, and fall away, 446
may flourish or may, 250
nothing of him that doth, 32
thy eternal summer shall not,
107
Faded bays, bring back the, 896
coat of blue, 579
like the morning dew, 327
on the crowing of the cock,
89
prints and massive tomes, 899
tastes, they speak of, 673
things, we fondly cherish, 677
Faded-brown as a cinnamon-bear,
928
Fades a summer cloud, so, 273
in his eye, 194

Fading are the joys we dote upon, 186
  bowers summer stands, in her, 565
  in music, a swan-like end, 45
  never, serenity of countenance, 195
Faery elves whose midnight revels, 149
  lands forlorn, 383
  of the mine, swart, 158
Faggot, fling on any, 751
Fagots and fagots, there are, 1046
  diadems and, 410
Fail, if we should, 85
  no such word as, 425
  not ashamed to, 231
  not for sorrow, 454
  of win, and all I, 444
  sun and breath, 533
  to meet thee, I will not, 134
  we'll not, 85
  world's course will not, 556
Failed of act, my wish that, 444
  sunrise never, 619
  the bright promise, 342
  who strove and who, 533
Faileth, the enemy faints not nor, 519
Failing, every, but their own, 355
  wound, how doth a little, 1021
Failings and faults of individuals, 998
  leaned to virtue's side, 250
Fails, oft expectation, 53
Failure and despair, known, 690
  and fame forever, 737
  and success not accidents, 589
  barks your shin, 865
  cannot quell, 692
  fear not sensible, 758
  not a fiercer hell than the, 382
  not, but low aim is crime, 528
  of years, pays the, 493
  reasons for, 780
Failures, all thought of your, 848
  benefit in making, 563
  of others and merits of thyself, 566
  worst of all, 326
Fain die a dry death, 32
  would I but I dare not, 21
  would I climb yet fear I to fall, 22
Faint and fear to live alone, 365
  and fretful, grown, 632
  and worn, 596
  far murmur of the flood, 679
  heart ne'er won fair lady, 1039
  in the day of adversity, 1108
  so spiritless so, 63
  why should we, 365
Fainter in my laugh, I'm growing, 509
Fainting, help the, 682
Faints not nor faileth, the enemy, 519
Fair adventure of to-morrow, 58
  and crystal river, 128
  and ever young, ever, 176
  and good as she, 120
  and kind and young, still, 675
  and never proud, 101
  and open face of heaven, 383
  and softly goes far, 1034

Fair and unpolluted flesh, 97, 468
  as a star, 296
  as she, 645
  as Spenser's dream, 558
  as the beautiful snow, 560
  as you were, Maggie, 640
  be all thy hopes, 68
  brave deserves the, 176
  budding branch, 271
  chaste and unexpressive she, 50
  daffadills we weep to see, 133
  day after the, 13
  day's wage for fair day's work, 589
  day's-wages for a fair day's-work, 378
  die because a woman's, 132
  discourse hath been as sugar, your, 59
  divided excellence, 57
  eunuchs guardians of the, 203
  exchange not robbery, 357
  face, lift up the same, 560
  fat, and forty, 311
  find out how to make it, 488
  for all that is, 26
  form so, that like the air, 405
  good as she was, 289
  good-night, to each a, 308
  hand that hath made you, 26, 37
  Harvard, thy sons, 363
  humanities of old religion, 317
  if ladies be but young and, 49
  if she was, 840
  in death, speak me, 47
  in life, not to fancy what were, 488
  laughs the morn, 244
  little girl, a, 458
  lov'd the brightest, 239
  maid dwelling, 257
  maid, let each, 226
  maidens are commonly fortunate, 23
  Melrose, would'st view, 306
  mistress moderately, 168
  opportunities, a woman with, 482
  or good alone, nothing is, 408
  or smell so sweet, look so, 569
  round belly with capon lined, 50
  science frowned not, 245
  sepulchre in the grateful stomach, 323
  sex called, 198
  she was not exceeding, 28
  so deadly, 355
  spoken and persuading, 74
  supreme ambition to be, 239
  sweet and, she seems to be, 146
  the rose looks, 107
  to fair he flew, from, 307
  to outward view, she is not, 386
  to visit all the blame, not, 768
  too, to worship, 363
  tresses insnare, 212
  undress best dress, 224
  weather it will be, 1115
  weather out of the north, 1102

Fair, were it fifty times as, 432
  what care I how, she be, 22, 132
  women and brave men, 352
  words never hurt the tongue, 29
  words shall prevail, 783
  words, to give, 13
  young and so, 392
Fair-chambered corridor of years, 874
Faire and fetisly, spak ful, 5
Fairer ladye never was seene, 257
  she never studied to be, 28
  spirit conveyed, 205
  than at first more strong greater, 108
  than my love, 77
  than the day, be she, 132
  than the evening air, 32
Fairest meadow white with snow, 453
  of creation, 155
  of her daughters Eve, 152
  of the learned, 215
Fairfield County, no larger than, 757
Fairies, as well not believe in, 643
  do you believe in, 751
  gave me, one gift the, 673
  have never a penny, 846
  rewards and, 128
Fairies' midwife, 77
Fairy elves, 149
  fair wish thou me well, 747
  fiction drest, by, 244
  forms, their dirge is sung by, 247
  fruits and flowers, 460
  gold is all their gain, 673
  gold, this is, 56
  hands their knell is rung, by, 247
  takes nor witch hath power, 89
  went a-marketing, 846
Fairy-flax, blue as the, 433
Fairy-folk in our southwest, no, 801
Fairy-tale, love-gift of a, 598
Faith a bracing gospel, 704
  a passionate intuition, 302
  and fallacy, we subtract, 910
  and hope, animated by, 233
  and hope, freight of, 459
  and hope, world will disagree in, 208
  and love and gratitude, boundless in, 479
  and morals Milton held, 298
  and no stoicism, there is no, 531
  and philosophy are air, 531
  and ready hands, true, 522
  and trust, for all my, 682
  and unfaith can ne'er be equal, 470
  author and finisher of our, 1122
  be for aye, 650
  before the world confest, 555
  belief ripened into, 302
  beyond the forms of, 471
  can last, no, 867
  deciphered in the skies, 770
  dream that his, is fast, 428

Faith, fanatic, 337
firmer than our fathers knew, 604
full of, that something would turn, 421
grope with little, 887
guardians of the, 900
has centre everywhere, 468
has not lived in vain, 507
hath a fleeting breath, 761
he slept, in that, 732
he trod, by, 856
heart of little, 691
I have kept the, 1122
I wish you 'd take me, 389
if a man have a strong, 1081
if ye break, 821
I'll give no, 563
in any Greek, 967
in brotherhood, 954
in faith established, 634
in God and woman, 587
in honest doubt, 469, 506
in Massachusetts, have, 819
in some nice tenets, 167
in the tale is old, 982
in womankind, 466
is but an idle canvas, 688
is false all faith is true, all, 544
is kneeling by his bed, 31
is like a lily, 587
is lost when honor dies, when, 442
is the substance of things hoped for, 1122
is to have wings, to have, 751
is truer than doubt, 625
made whole in, 1022
man should render reason for his, 312
modes of, for, 167, 208
moves mountains, till, 490
nothing more wonderful than, 695
now abideth, 1120
o'ercomes doubt, 488
of reason, no longer in the, 318
of Tennessee, 828
or creed, who care enough for, 591
perhaps wrong, 167
pity their want of, 1056
plain and simple, 83
simple, more than Norman blood, 462
something of a, 466
staff of, 22
sublime and true, one, 813
talk, 718
that all things are possible to God, 548
that right makes might, 455
that sees the ring of light, 452
that warmed, the holy, 451
this is the country, 763
triumphant over fears, 435
unfaithful kept him, 470
we walk by, not by sight, 1120
wears his, as the fashion of his hat, 38
which hath brought relief, 604
who breaks his, 1033
will trust, love will dream and, 444
with freedom reigns, 612
without good works, 1038

Faith without works is dead, 1122
ye that have, 760
yet not for all his, can see, 408
you call for, 488
Faiths, by conflicting, 1050
by which my comrades, 651
old, loosen and fall, 631
strange, 652
Faith's defender, the, 221
pure shrine, 370
Faithful Argus' eyes, 220
as the turning tide, 824
below he did his duty, 274
cavalier, my, 638
dog bear him company, 207
fight, absolution of a, 556
found among the faithless, 153
friend is the best, 594
friends, 596
Gêlert roam, 294
I would be, so, 567
in action in honour clear, 210
in love and dauntless in war, 307
in that which is least, 1117
is the spirit that remembers, 516
loves shall moralize my song, 24
old dog Tray 's ever, 567
only he, 153
the kneeling, 755
the wounds of a friend, 1108
to his conviction, 975
to that which exists, be, 1086
to thee Cynara, 796
trusty and true, 660
unselfish and patient, 596
unto death, be thou, 1123
Faithfull frends, fallyng out of, 19
Faithfully to serve it, if they be willing, 141
Faithfulness, for want of, 247
Faithless, among the, faithful, 153
Falcon flying, like a, 887
gentle as, 10
glance and lion bearing, 364
red rose is a, 675
towering in her pride, 86
Falcons for swiftness, as, 895
hopes like towering, 189
Falero, lero loo, 132
Fall and swell, its soft, 385
away ere they have blossomed, 446
brook with many a, 289
caused man to, 110
caused the angels to, 110
dig 'em in the, 952
divided we, 404
fain would I climb yet fear to, 22
from the days that have been, 426
hastening to thy, 427
haughty spirit before a, 1107
he that is down needs fear no, 142, 172
hurry to that fatal, 966
it had a dying, 53
laugh at a, 487
leaves at curtain, 931
let the thick curtain, 444

Fall like a bright exhalation, 73
like sweet strains or pensive, 408
no lower, he that 's down can, 142
nodding to its, 994
not far from its, 1054
of a sparrow, 97
of Niagara, 228
of rivers winds and seas, 301
of the snow, marked but the, 119
out and chide and fight, 198
plant them in the, 952
pride will have a, 14
shoots to the, 467
take heed lest he, 1120
they go astray and they, 483
to rise, held we, 494
upon the sea, 667
what a, was there, 83
Falls as I do, 73
as the leaves do, 127
early or too late, 126
like Lucifer, 73
shallow rivers to whose, 31
so low, man never, 477
the dew, 569
upon the ground, leaf, 407
who never climbs as rarely, 443
with the leaf, 127
Fallacious as facts, nothing, 313
Fallen, arise or be forever, 148
Babylon is, 1111
from grace, 1121
from his high estate, 176
how are the mighty, 1100
into the sere the yellow leaf, 88
on evil days, though, 153
so lost, so, 442
Fallest a blessed martyr, 74
Fallible being, 235
Falling at intervals upon the ear, 266
fear 's as bad as, 105
in melody back, 317
man, cruelty to load a, 74
man, press not a, 73
of a tear, the, 306
pillars are, at thy feet, 403
star, came down with a, 507
tears, I can see your, 596
to the prompter's bell, slow, 481
world, secure amidst a, 194
Fallings from us vanishings, 301
Falling-off was there, what a, 91
Fallow as it will, be, 459
for a while, well to lie, 478
Fallyng out of faithfull frends, 19
False facts injurious to progress of science, 449
and fleeting as 't is fair, 343
and hollow, all was, 149
and true, a hair divides the, 1019
as dicers' oaths, 95
colours last after true be dead, 115
distinguish the true from the, 1048
fires, kindles on the coast, 304
forget, the, 653

False, framed to make women, 101
history must be, 200
Jewes, amonge the, 257
prophets, 1116
restrictions on style, 923
things are brought low, 650
to any man, canst not be, 91
views do little harm, 449
volume of his single mind, 661
within, betrayed by what is, 574
words are not only evil, 970
Falsehood and truth grapple, 163
belief in, 1081
can no longer deceive, 949
down, beats some, 851
fear and wrong, challenge, 816
froth of, 635
hath a goodly outside, 44
huge Mississippi of, 337, 548
lingers on, no, 967
meet with a, 655
no, can endure, 152
strife of truth with, 524
to the heart, stabs, 524
wedded to some dear, 337
Falsely luxurious man, 224
Falser than vows made in wine, 51
False-refined weakness, 491
Falstaff sweats to death, 61
Falter not for sin, 454
to, would be sin, 503
When the sun, 584
Faltering feet embraced, 448
Falters, insanity of noble minds that never, 438
Fame, above all Roman, 214
and honor are twins, 1064
and love of truth, desire of, 471
and pelf, cares for naught but, 719
and unspotted, 1036
been raised, by, 31
best of, rival's praise, 337
blush to find it, 214
church to God not to, 210
damned to, 223
damned to everlasting, 208
death-bed of, 327
demands prolonged reverberation, 529
denied to men of genius, 1077
does not record, 879
elates thee, while, 334
family of, 316
fed with, 335
fool to, nor yet a, 213
for a pot of ale, 66
from the field of his, 364
gives immortal, 203
grant an honest, 216
great heir of, 161
has this great drawback, 1049
hath created something of nothing, 147
I care for, only, 588
I slight, nor, 216
I won a noble, 620
if not double-faced is double-mouthed, 157
is a food, 650

Fame is nothing but an empty name, 288
is ephemeral, 1010
is everlasting, its, 982
is good, so will avoid making more speeches, 182
is in the song, 757
is no plant, 159
is not bought and sold, 604
is on Torres Vedras, 765
is the scentless sunflower, 453
is the spur, 159
is the thirst of youth, 353
is the undying brother, 1064
is what some wan writes on ye'er tombstone, 796
lifts it to eternal, 772
lives in, 76
man who never knew taste of, 426
most infamous are fond of, 262
no one shall work for, 779
no sure test of merit, 376
noise of worldly, 1021
nor yet a fool to, 213
nothing can cover his high, 131
of any work of science, 426
of friend or foe, fair, 696
of the admiral falls, 737
on lesser ruins built, 167
over his living head, 366
posthumous, 614
raise his country's, 1027
so false as common, 185
sorrow or sacrifice, 954
surest road to, 432
talks about the where and when, 405
temple of, 950
that comes after life, 1010
that I should chuse, sort of, 292
the breath of power, 728
the pious fool, outlives in, 193
then was cheap, 178
to give her features deathless, 561
too fond of, 1007
too mighty such monopoly of, 124
trust to common, 416
unknown to, 219
unknown to fortune and to, 245
was noised throughout all the country, 1099
well known to, 951
what rage for, 272
will still be coy, 385
Fame's eternal bead-roll, 25
eternal camping ground, 541
illusive light, 572
ladder, ascended, 431
thunders wake, 690
Famed rock, this is, 647
they shall be, 67
Fame-wreathed crown, no, 659
Familiar, angels may be, 556
as his garter, 66
as household words, 67
as the rose in spring, 1011
be thou, but not vulgar, 90
beauty soon grows, 194
but not coarse, 233
clothing the palpable and, 318

Familiar creature, good wine is a, 102
faces, the old, 325
feet, to part, 596
friend, mine own, 1104, 1128
grown, never yet, 736
names, 438
now as heart-beats, 866
with her face, 208
with his hoary locks, 393
word, how fondly each, 405
Familiarity breeds contempt, 34, 961
with Bible, too early, 739
Familiarly talks of roaring lions, 57
Families, accidents occur in best regulated, 496
but two, in the world, 1040
God setteth the solitary in, 1104
like a comet, 558
most ancient, 124
of doubtful origin, 343
Family, children of one, 198, 486
discussion, most effective way to close, 582
father of a, 1009
great and wide-spread, 942
just as in a, 130
may be distinguished, 949
of fame, all the, 316
party tribe or clan, 952
relationship only one aspect of life, 740
should be merged, 422
thread you can't ascend, 510
world like a great, 184
Family-trees that remember, 928
Famine flood and fire, including, 907
is in thy cheeks, 80
philanthropists in time of, 417
seven years of, 1098
they that die by, 187
thirst, bereavement, 596
would depopulate the world, 602
Famous by my pen, 164
by my sword, 164
Camaralzaman is, 437
found myself, 361
high top-hat, 857
orators repair, thence to the, 156
to all ages, 162
victory, it was a, 322
Famoused for fight, 107
Fan, brain him with his lady's, 61
Fanatic faith wedded fast, 337
Fanatiques predict end of the world, 181
Fancied that Deity ever vindictively made in his image, 461
Fancies fugitive, stray thoughts, 492
men's more giddy, 54
that might be, 493
thick-coming, 88
Fancy bred, where is, 45
bright-eyed, 244
busy, 395
by hopeless, feigned, 466
chuckle, make one's, 172

Fancy deemed was only truth
  my, 455
  draws, give a glimpse and, 240
  exalted ideas of, 972
  food of sweet and bitter, 51
  free, keep your, 742
  free, maiden meditation, 42
  free, with, 716
  from a flower-bell, 488
  given, were it to my, 274
  his imperial, 290
  homebound, 401
  in every way, I'll suit my, 920
  its drapery, 318
  like the finger of a clock,
    265
  most excellent, 97
  motives of more, 53
  not expressed in, 91
  of men, please the, 1049
  painted her, all my, 362
  reason virtue, 225
  roam, let the, 384
  styles of active mendicancy,
    645
  'tis a curious, 916
  wavering, 500
  whispers of, 232
  working spells, aggressive, 650
  young man's, 464
Fancy's child, Shakespeare, 160
  course, impediments in. 53
  flight restrain, 776
  meteor ray, misled by, 285
  rays the hills adorning, 285
  strangest child, 893
Fane that stands, marvelous, 541
Fanes, Paestum's ancient, 653
  quiver in the air, 403
Fangs invade the golden stores,
    543
Fanny Kelly's divine plain face,
    325
Fanny's way, pretty, 201
Fantasies, no figures nor no, 82
  thousand, begin to throng, 157
  to me, seem, 651
Fantastic, alike, if too new or old,
    211
  as a woman's mood, 308
  fickle fierce and vain, 308
  summer's heat, 59
  terrors never felt before, 460
  toe, light, 160
  tricks, plays such, 36
  tripped the light, 761
Fantastical, not in fashion is, 125
Fantasy, nor lure thy, 823
  nothing but vain, 77
Fantasy's hot fire, 307
Far amid the melancholy main,
    225
  and brilliant course to run,
    362
  and few are the lands, 498
  and the near unite, 271
  as angels' ken, 148
  as my coin would stretch, so,
    60
  as the solar walk, 207
  away, my soul to-day is, 552
  away, owes its charm to the,
    426
  back through creeks and inlets,
    519
  beneath the tainted foam, 375

Far beyond the village church,
    not, 517
  corner of thy heart, in some,
    582
  cry to Lochow, 310
  down beneath the wild commo-
    tion, 480
  far ahead is all her seamen
    know, 519
  far beneath the noise of tem-
    pests, 480
  far better rest, 498
  far better thing that I do, 498
  far the mountain peak, 697
  from home, and I am, 403
  from mortal cares, 345
  from the lips we love, 335
  from the madding crowd, 245
  he seems so near yet so, 469
  illusive dream, a, 573
  in the stillness a cat, 692
  innumerable burning coals, 874
  less sweet to live, 335
  more than the witnesses said,
    599
  off his coming shone, 153
  on the wild raging sea, 389
  out of reach, the sky, 536
  press not a falling man too, 73
  retreat, withdraw to, 878
  stretched greatness, 22
  till near and, ray on ray, 493
  when seen from, 458
Farce is done, the, 1024
  played by kings and republics,
    1029
Fardels bear, who would, 93
Fare, bounteous, 737
  brown bread and the Gospel is
    good, 188
  thee well and if forever, 356
  thee well isle of beauty, 388
  when you receive a, 583
  ye well brother Watkins, 512
  you well old house, 678
  you 'd not pay any, 954
Fared worse, further and, 16
Farewel my boke and my devo-
    cion, 4
Farewell, a long farewell, 73
  agonize them in, 775
  and looks around to say, 481
  bade the world, 327
  content, 102
  forever and forever, 84
  goes out sighing, 75
  hope fear remorse, 151
  I am called, 577
  I only feel — farewell, 351
  if ever fondest prayer, 351
  in this one cry, 619
  journey to that promised land,
    817
  Leicester Square, 836
  rewards and fairies, 128
  should be but for one night,
    707
  the neighing steed, 102
  the plumed troop, 102
  the tranquil mind, 102
  then O Luck of Edenhall, 433
  to all my greatness, 73
  to earth, final long, 713
  to every fear, I 'll bid, 199
  to hope, bid, 703
  to Lochaber, 204

Farewell, wave their hands for a
    mute, 540
  yet not, 596
Farewells, many, as be stars in
    heaven, 75
  should be sudden, 357
Far-fatiguing trade, 247
Far-flashed to Cape St. Vincent,
    765
Far-heard whisper, 315
Far-hidden heart of the moun-
    tains, 572
Farm, moderate-sized, 959
  of the world, 321
  well-situated well-cultivated,
    374
  well tilled, barn well filled, 275
Farms away, twenty, 871
Farmer covetous of his dollar,
    413
  I have fed like a, 193
  Johnson shouldered his gun,
    755
  understands, every, 282
  works the soil, 661
Farmers are founders of civiliza-
    tion, 340
  embattled, 409
Farmer's boy, and be a, 950
  daughter hath soft brown hair,
    590
  land, on a, 677
  wintry hoard, 441
Farmyard bird, I love that, 758
Far-off divine event, one, 469
  land, plucked in a, 598
  shore, spies a, 70
  things, old unhappy, 298
  touch of greatness, some, 470
Far-seeing places, high, 879
Farther off from heaven, 390
Farthing candle, do not care a,
    324
  candle to the sun, 203
Farthings, Latin word for three,
    41
Fascinate, blandishments will not,
    274
Fascinating, inordinately, 1076
Fascination of a name, 266
  youth full of grace force, 535
Fashion, bravery never goes out
    of, 484
  fantastical that is not in, 125
  fight, the hard, 648
  glass of, 93
  high Roman, 105
  it is a comely, 540
  made of such good, 948
  medicine is all the, 1054
  never go out of, 942
  of his hat, his faith the, 38
  of these times, 48
  of this world passeth away,
    1120
  olden, in a, 914
  out of the world as out of, 193
  so immediate so contingent a,
    1087
  the world's new, 40
  to abuse, the, 624
  wears out more apparel, 39
Fashions, in words as, 211
  intellectual and literary, 829
  old, please me best, 52
Fashion's brightest arts, 251

Fashionable and momentary things, 895
  prattle of the world, 656
  to blame America, 871
  topics, 254
Fashioned so slenderly, 392
  us holler, providence, 526
Fashioneth their hearts alike, 1103
Fast and the world goes by, 718
  as he can, fine and as, 406
  bind fast find, 12
  by a brook, 269
  go out so, 935
  hold, that which is good, 1121
  rising from affluence, 615
  run at least twice as, 598
  spare, 160
  they stumble that run, 78
  till he is well, 577
  too late who goes too, 989
Fasts, surfeits sooner kill than, 163
Fast-anchored isle, 264
Fasten him as a nail, 1111
Fast-flitting meteor, 362
Fast-flying cloud, 362
Fasting for a good man's love, 50
Fat and greasy citizens, 48
  better for living on their own, 530
  black bucks, 857
  contentions, 162
  dividends, incarnation of, 364
  eef she don'ta be, 813
  fair and forty, 311
  feed, the ancient grudge, 44
  I am resolved to grow, 178
  is in the fire, 12
  laugh and be, 127
  men about me that are, 81
  men heading a riot, 343
  more, than bard beseems, 225
  must stand upon his bottom, 171
  of other's works, 121
  of the years, to lap the, 831
  oily man of God, 225
  one of them is, and grows old, 61
  oxen, who drives, 238
  shall be in the fire, 1042
  souls from sleep, keep, 912
  things, feast of, 1111
  waxed, and kicked, 1099
  weed on Lethe wharf, 91
  with the lean, take the, 497
Fatal and perfidious bark, 159
  as it is cowardly, 543
  asterisk of death, 438
  bellman the owl, 86
  circumference, 602
  fall, hurry to that, 966
  gift of beauty, the, 354
  good neighbour is sometimes, 430
  shadows that walk by us, 126
Fate affright your quiet, 725
  and jeers at, 867
  and time and change good-bye, 790
  await no gifts have conquered, 546
  binding nature fast in, 216

Fate by the throat, take, 595
  cannot harm me, 177, 313
  coughed and called it, 808
  cowards mock the patriot's, 555
  cries out, my, 91
  customary, of new truths, 564
  deplored at times, 1064
  determines or indicates his, 514
  did, begin, 631
  eagle's, and mine are one, 145
  fears his, too much, 164
  fixed, freewill foreknowledge, 150
  forbids to heal, ills which, 983
  forced by, 177
  foulness of their, 892
  gave his sad lucidity, 546
  gave me whate'er else denied, 528
  grappling with direst, 536
  had granted to behold his lord, 220
  hanging breathless on thy, 435
  harries us, 924
  has predestined, 1061
  has written a tragedy, 844
  he either fears his, too much, 164
  heart for any, 433
  heart for every, 357
  heaven hides the book of, 207
  hour of, 602
  I am the master of my, 470
  inward, 360
  iron hand of, 778
  is a fiddler life's a dance, 692
  laughs at probabilities, 426
  lord of my unchallenged, 579
  makes our relatives, 1056
  master of his, 470
  master of my, 579
  no armour against, 141
  no one is so accursed by, 434
  of a nation, 437
  of all extremes, 209
  of all great minds, 1064
  of borrowed books, 673
  of empires changed by a bottle of Johannesberg, 279
  of Rome, big with the, 194
  of the architect, 1057
  or caprice may lead his feet, 707
  or the gods may give, what, 775
  proud captain of thine own, 470
  seemed to wind him up, 178
  she is, 1089
  sits on these dark battlements, 290
  stamp of, 218
  take a bond of, 87
  things of the future to, 418
  to-day, whatever be thy, 509
  torrent of his, 230
  true as, 116
  turns on its, 566
  unchallenged, 579
  why should they know their, 243
  wilfully misunderstand me, 837
  will give me life, 777
  will more strongly than, 1089
  wisest man ask no more of, 528

Fate, with a heart for any, 357, 433
  with appointed strength, 870
Fates a jest, owe the, 784
  and destinies, 45
  anger at the, 493
  are not quite obdurate, 528, 835
  impose, what, 70
  men are masters of their, 81
  moulding her mighty, 806
  these are the, 974
Fate's saddest jokes, one of, 528
Fated all to part, 557
  always to disagree, 796
Fateful lightning, He hath loosed the, 522
Father Abraham, we are coming, 475
  Abram, 45
  all the world and one's, 1045
  and I went to camp, 283
  and mother, honour thy, 963
  and ny friend, my, 180
  and thy mother, honour thy, 1098
  antic the law, 60
  be kind to thy, 548
  bred, brood of folly without, 160
  calls me William, 699
  dear father come home with me now, 600
  deigns to touch, if the, 753
  eternal strong to save, 566
  feeds his flocks, 118
  forty-one, gave her, 957
  gave a name, when the, 658
  greatness of name in the, 120
  has written for thee, thy, 437
  have a turnip than his, 238
  hoarding went to hell, 70
  home feet first, brought my, 577
  I like the lad who when his, 510
  I scarcely dare to pray, 591
  in every O my, 474
  in thy gracious keeping, 402
  lies, full fathom five thy, 32
  looked him down, kindly the, 658
  make a gentleman of you, why did not your, 344
  more than schoolmasters, 138
  of a disease, whatsoever was the, 138
  of a family, 1009
  of all in every age, 216
  of lies, nuts to the, 337
  of the man, the child is, 297
  of waters goes unvexed to the sea, 456
  of Waters, the matchless, 929
  on her face, so dwelt the, 471
  religion of my, 1061
  should have had, the praise, 873
  Son and Holy Ghost, 183
  struck when son swore, 125
  thy will not mine be done, 423
  to that thought, wish was, 65
  unto many sons, happy thing to be, 70
  was a gentleman, 344
  was Knott before him, 948

Father William, you are old, 320, 598
wise, knows his own child, 45
wise son maketh a glad, 1107
Fathers, ashes of his, 400
bought for us, 779
came trusting in God, 553
died, die as my, 631
have eaten sour grapes, 1113
inherited from our, 1075
learned to do, the things my, 904
passed to fight, your, 765
sins of the, 46, 968
where are thy, 1113
worshipped stocks, our, 162
Father's blood, show the, 967
business, I must be about my, 1117
fondest care, 326
fortunes and his places, 128
granfer's father's father's name, 811
house, chimney in my, 69
house, daughters of my, 55
house, many mansions in my, 1118
joy mother's pride, 309
printing-office, Spain in my, 629
trade, my, 344
Fathers' age, our, 983
God, our, 445
God to Thee author of liberty, 447
Fathered, so, and so husbanded, 82
Fatherhood, special providence for, 491
Father-in-law, fine thing to be, 288
Fatherland no fear be thine, 1073
the very idea of, 500
to die, for, 983
Fatherless, judge for the, 1123
Fathom five, thy father lies, 32
line could never touch ground, 61
Fathoms many, and down in, 622
Fathomless universe, praised be the, 536
Fatigue give oneself bodily, 402
of judging for themselves, 278
Fattenin' hogs aint in luck, 688
Fattest hog in Epicurus' sty, 249
Fatuity, officialized, 891
Fatuous ineffectual yesterdays, 693
Faubourg St. Germain, portières of, 532
Fauld, when the sheep are in the, 277
Fault at all, who hath no, 470
common to all singers, 984
condemn the, and not the actor, 36
every man has his, 81
excusing of a, makes it worse, 58
eye on thine own, 566
found in a, 138
grows two thereby, 135
I see, hide the, 216
in its flow, never a, 651
is not in our stars, 81

Fault, it has no kind of, 623
just hint a, 213
man's own, 236
of a penetrating wit, 1044
of Christianity, 1016
of the Dutch in matters of commerce, 293
of women, most shocking, 1063
on one side, 1044
only is that he has none, 380
or doubt, never caught at, 429
perhaps it was Lord Byron's, 685
political, 1060
proudly clung to their first, 484
seeming monstrous, 50
talk and find, 1034
the fundamental, 1064
their stars were more in, 189
who hath, he is all, 470
Faults, all his, observed, 83
are locked securely, all his, 883
be blind to her, 189
cleanse thou me from secret, 1103
England with all her, 262
England with all thy, 264
greatest of, 380
if we were without, 1043
lie gently on him, 74
loves him better for his, 253
men moulded out of, 37
of criticism, 680
of fools, wise men avoid the, 998
of individuals, failings and, 998
of man, bear with all the, 121
one loves him better for all his, 253
tells my, 217
thou hast no, 187
to be conscious of no, 380
to scan, careless their, 250
world of vile ill-favoured, 34
Fault-finding critic, regarded his, 508
Faultily faultless, 469
Faultless body, 220
in his dealings, he was, 406
monster, 164
piece to see, thinks a, 164, 210
Faulty we are, why not, 486
Faust, Goethe completed, 438
Faustine, no more, 632
Fauts to tell, ill I like my, 284
Favour, contests for our, 908
in old Virginny, never found, 630
must come to this, 97
nothing is, without whose, 920
of the gods was equal, 969
refused a, 966
smaller injustice as a, 402
we entreat, one, 738
well bestowed, 198
with less offence, asked a, 999
Favours are denied, when, 226
call, nor for her, 216
given, pleased with, 226
hangs on princes', 73
I've felt all her, 240
lively sense of future, 200
sweet and precious, 287
we get, we are certain to pay for the, 509

Favourable, heavens look with aspect more, 56
Favoured land, somewhere in this, 770
Favourite has no friend, 243
sin, his, 321
subject myself, 272
Favourites early death, heaven gives its, 354
Favouritism in public and private life, 727
Fawn at his feet, 592
fickle and restless as a, 1066
Fawne and crouch, 26
Fawning and flattery, adulation, 981
thrift may follow, 94
Fayre and fetisly, spake ful, 5
Fear above, all, 452
act of, 90
among fears, 789
and amazement, 129
and bloodshed, 300
and danger of violent death, continual, 132
and retreat, courage consists in, 1051
and sorrow, pine with, 25
arming me from, 516
as love casts out, 470
at my heart, 315
be thine, no, 1073
bid farewell to every, 199
boys with bugs, 52
cannot be without hope, 1048
cold exhaustion hunger, 754
courage is better than, 625
death, men, 109
doubteth Thee, in that, 559
each bush an officer, 71
exempt from, 69
from hope and, set free, 632
full of, 952
get rid of, 380
God honour the king, 1122
has no need of, 891
I was sick with, 938
in that, doubteth thee, 559
in the night, imagining some, 43
is a rot, 924
is affront, 204
is as bad as falling, the, 105
is increased with tales, 109
is most accurs'd passion, 68
is sharp-sighted, 1035
itself, thing we have to fear is, 876
little care we little we, 481
mask for, 994
may force a man, 12
mean actions be ascribed to, 1079
met without a, 628
no hope could have no, 610
no, in love, 1123
none has merited my, 897
not and be just, 73
not guilt, those who, 262
not to touch the best, 21
o' hell's a hangman's whip, 285
of death has even bygone, 651
of death is more to be dreaded, 988

Fear of divine powers keeps men
  in obedience, 126
  of having to repay, for, 1049
  of kings, 46
  of little men, 573
  of the children's lacking, 894
  of the lack of shelter, food,
    894
  perfect love casteth out, 1123
  rather than by reverence,
    swayed by, 975
  remember that small, 822
  reproach or, 442
  rule by love than, 473
  shame coward, 447
  so hate casts out, 470
  strange and speechless, 699
  strange that men should, 82
  that lurks in most men's eyes,
    894
  that reigns with the tyrant,
    435
  the increase of, 1080
  the lightest heart, 447
  they call courage, 817
  thy nature, yet do I, 84
  to be we know not what, 178
  to die, cowards may, 22
  to fall yet fain would climb, 22
  to him who is in, 967
  to live alone, 365
  to lose, 138
  to the wind, throw, 972
  unaccustomed to, 951
  undraped without a single, 956
Fears and disquietudes, in the
  midst of, 985
  and distastes, 109
  and interest, 237
  and saucy doubts, 87
  blue for hopes and red for,
    664
  do make us traitors, 87
  faith triumphant o'er our, 435
  gamut of human, 824
  his fate too much, 164
  humanity with all its, 435
  humble cares and delicate, 297
  I cannot quite repress, 682
  more, than wars or women
    have, 73
  no. to beat away, 303
  of all the years, 612
  our hopes belied our, 390
  past regrets and future, 1018
  prosperity is not without many,
    109
  shall cease, all thy, 1063
  that I may cease to be, 384
  that make a death, 164
  the foolish, 955
Feared, it is just as I, 499
  the shadows that I, so long,
    540
  to run away, has fought be-
    cause he, 771
Feareth Lord to doubt, man that,
    559
Fearful fire, saved them from
    the, 605
  goodness is never, 37
  joy, snatch a, 243
  odds, facing, 400
  of the night, 661
  summons, upon a, 89
  symmetry, frame thy, 281

Fearful trip is done, my captain
    our, 536
  unbelief, alas the, 380
Fearfully and wonderfully made,
    1106
Fearing, long I stood there won-
    dering, 460
  to attempt, 35
Fearless for unknown shores, 537
  host no slave, 386
Fearlessly face it, 592
Feast and your halls are crowded,
    718
  as you were going to a, 119
  beginning of a, 63
  chief nourisher in life's, 86
  enough is good as a, 18, 29,
    229
  for your scholars and sages,
    590
  imagination of a, 59
  invite your friend to a, 959
  merry, great welcome makes,
    37
  merry heart hath a continual,
    1107
  none better knew the, 348
  O Barmecide, where is thy, 649
  of Crispian, is called the, 67
  of fat things, 1111
  of languages, have been at a,
    41
  of life, bread, 1090
  of love is song, 610
  of nectared sweets, 158
  of Purim, 1124
  of reason and flow of soul,
    213
  or else a, 65
  sat at any good man's, 49
  to a thousand of his lords, 1113
  to the Lord, keep it a, 1098
  who riseth from a, 45
Feasts, among your solemn, 1124
  wedlock compared to public,
    115
Feasteth while honest labor,
    pauperism, 477
Feasting, house of, 1109
  keep it an high day for, 1124
  presence, full of light, 80
Feat, foretells a future, 955
  of Tell the archer, 1059
  sturdiness which does the, 491
  which would make time break,
    489
Feats enlink'd to waste and des-
    olation, 66
  performing those, 1079
Feather, a wit's a, and a chief a
    rod, 208
  and a bit of lace, 653
  birds of a, 70, 125, 1039
  for each wind that blows, I am,
    56
  from an angel's wing, 304
  in hand, a, 137
  in their caps, 1039
  is wafted downward, 434
  never moults a, 494
  of his own, espied a, 145
  on the fatal dart, his own, 351,
    962
  pluck out his flying, 631
  put into his cap, 241
  showed their own white, 826

Feather that adorns the royal
    bird, 950
  to tickle the intellect, 324
Feathers, beat all your, 116
  brain of, 215
  fine, make fine birds, 961
  saffron-tipt, 448
  she plumes her, 158
  two-legged animal without,
    1015
Feather's weight of worth, 638
Feathered foot, youth now flees
    on, 702
  his nest, 181
  my nest, 1025
  well her nest, 181
Feature, abhor that grim, 788
  headed Died, 861
  one, quite distinguished him,
    665
  outward form and, 317
  so scented the grim, 155
Features, as by the blackest, 949
  cut in the sleepy, 927
  deathless fame, to give her, 561
  homely, 158
  of change, manifold, 767
  of men, differences in, 993
February hath twenty-eight, 18
Fed of the dainties, bred in a
    book, 41
  on poetry, as one who, 425
  show lowly taught and highly,
    53
Federal union must be preserved,
    our, 292
Federation of all humanity, 795
  of the world, 464
Fee, another would have his, 808
  set my life at a pin's, 91
  the doctor, than, 175
Fees, contentions and, flowing, 162
  we need a bank, to pay their,
    951
Feeble, if virtue, were, 159
  industry, to quote them argues,
    971
  most forcible, 65
  not enough to help the, 80
  temper, man of such, 81
  wrong because of weakness,
    430
Feed clothe and house the world,
    754
  fat the ancient grudge, 44
  He that doth the ravens, 48
  just to drive a flock to, 406
  on hope, to, 25
  on prayers, 28
Feeds and breeds by a compos-
    ture, 81
  himself his neighbor and me,
    525
Feel another's woe, teach me to,
    216
  but can't define, what I, 268
  it most, those who, 367
  like one who treads alone, 336
  like, what did it, 748
  mine to, amid the city's jar,
    546
  no comfortable, in any mem-
    ber, 391
  no time to, 401
  that I am happier than I know,
    154

Feel the sun, can not, 501
 those who would make us, 262
 to feel what wretches, 99
 which they themselves not, 40
 your honour grip, 285
Feeld hath eyen and the wode hath eres, 6, 470
Feeling, can arouse a, 1057
 deeper than thought, 501
 experience a choked, 931
 hearts touch them but rightly, 289
 hidden founts of, 557
 high mountains are a, 353
 in his dream, impression of the, 1021
 is bad form, 856
 is quick and transient, 488
 is quite within control, 1063
 new, and new meaning, 1074
 of eternity, 330
 of his business, 96
 of sadness and longing, 434
 of vengeance, not one, 941
 petrifies the, 285
 pleasurable and genial, 318
 sensible to, as to sight, 85
 so deem'd not by our, 108
 that he possesses, 1086
 the gratifying, 624
 to the worse, gives greater, 59
 which prompts prayer, 542
Feelings, great, came to them, 458
 run, who lets his, 403
 to mortals given, some, 308
 unemployed, waste of, 355
 way down into your, 698
 wild and vagrant, 589
Feels and never reasons, heroism, 412
 at each thread, 207
 the noblest acts the best, 506
 the wanton stings, 35
Feend, shal ete with a, 7
Feet, a baby's, 634
 a measure, teach his, 631
 are always in the water, 581
 are cold, and my, 924
 are heavy, my, 728
 at her, he bowed, 1099
 bairnies', 807
 bar my constant, 225
 beggar with bruised, 708
 beneath her petticoat, 163
 came on the following, 748
 clang of hurrying, 500
 clouted brogues from off my, 106
 crawl and kiss his, 220
 dancing with the, 1081
 dawn with silver-sandaled, 723
 doe ever tread, thy innocent, 24
 every turf beneath their, 328
 fall in destined snare, 577
 fetter his, in shackles, 147
 friends' departing, 528
 held up his stumbling, 890
 hours with flying, 352
 in his stocking, 927
 in soda water, wash their, 899
 keep thou my, I do not ask, 403
 lamp unto my, 1106

Feet, leaden, 628
 lie close about his, 458
 like snails did creep, 134
 many-twinkling, 243
 may leave but not our hearts, 453
 more would be laid at your, 633
 nailed on the bitter cross, 60
 of Gamaliel, at the, 1119
 of Nemesis, 735
 of the rain, small, 794
 on little cat, 854
 on pink rheumatic, 881
 our unchained, walk freely, 386
 part familiar, 596
 part of iron and part of clay, 1113
 pillars are falling at thy, 403
 rats', 899
 roll in ecstasy at your, 1090
 shall fall in the destined snare, 577
 sound of his master's, 1101
 standing with reluctant, 434
 still under the night, 866
 't will fawn at his, 592
 taken from Adam's, 953
 te thousand silver, 814
 that bringeth good tidings, 1112
 the wind's, shine along the sea, 630
 they rise to their, 777
 through faithless leather, 203
 time's iron, 440
 to the foe, his, 327
 to the lame, eyes to the blind, 1102
 town is at her twinkling, 908
 two pale, crossed in rest, 567
 unstable, with, 857
 was boun' wif twine, 820
 with aching hands and bleeding, 546
 with its silvery, 395
 with their goat, 32
 within a trap, 904
 your, and your raiment all red, 401
 your belly your back and your, 985
Feetur, haint one agreeable, 334, 526
Feigning like froth shall go, 650
Feldes, out of olde, 4
Felicitie, what more, can fall, 26
Felicities, nature's old, 304
 of all man's, 911
Felicity, absent thee from, 98
 and flower of wickedness, 491
 comes, so pure, 1038
 God made man to enjoy, 1008
 human, 228
 is quaffed from a golden cup, 727
 our own, we make, 231
Felix Plater on physicians, 124
Fell by that sin, the angels, 73
 dead in the streets, truth never, 476
 Doctor, I do not love thee, 188
 down, all of us, 83
 feats, all, 66
 great Caesar, 83

Fell in the battle of life, who, 533
 like autumn fruit, 178
 of hair would rouse and stir, 88
 purpose, shake my, 84
 sergeant death, 97
 swoop, at one, 88
 though the brightest, 88
Feller, do unto the other, 687
 sweetes' li'l', 730
 w'en you're beeg, 713
Fellers call me Bill, 699
Fellow and drink with me, sit down good, 626
 at a gift, take the, 965
 covetous sordid, 222
 dies an honest, 127
 do at least that much for a, 898
 down you 'd treat, shoot a, 651
 fault came to match it, 50
 hail, well met, 191
 he seemed a silent, 839
 hook-nosed, of Rome, 65
 in the firmament, 82
 many a good tall, 61
 mortals, naught beside, 485
 no feeling of his business, 96
 of but one idea, 235, 420
 of infinite jest, 97
 of no mark nor likelihood, 62
 of plain and uncoined constancy, 68
 of the selfsame flight, 44
 Officers congratulate me, 182
 raw, and ate the, 585
 that hath had losses, 40
 that hath two gowns, 40
 that will have no sovereign, 21
 touchy testy pleasant, 196
 vindictive and touchy, 1002
 want of it the, 208
 with the best king, 68
Fellows, all the learned and authentic, 53
 are out to row, 862
 best king of good, 68
 chance to be capital, 511
 damned his, 661
 nature hath framed strange, 43
 of the baser sort, 1118
 only in himself, knows his, 1087
 that were good and brave, 744
 we're all good, together, 276
 whom it hurts to think, 743
 without any hurt to his, 1049
Fellow-being yet may fall so low, 696
Fellow-citizens of the United States at large, 268
Fellow-creature, happy day for a, 313
Fellow-creatures, he loved his, 445
 I love my, 623
Fellow-feeling, help others out of, 121
 makes one wondrous kind, 121, 242
Fellow-men, born to marshal, 604
 in bondage, hold their, 291
 one who loves his, 346

Fellow-mortals, propose to show my, 1055
  see, to what thy, 749
Fellow-rover, laughing, 832
Fellowship glows warm, 879
  manhood nor good, 61
  right hands of, 1121
  which warms us, 522
Fellow-sufferers by the shipwreck spared, 300
Fellow-travellers, all but, 774
Felony, despicable act of, 1066
  to drink small beer, 69
Felt along the heart, 295
  as a man, thought as a sage, 269
  before, terrors never, 460
  darkness which may be, 1098
  in the blood, 295
  slippers and warm bellywash, 925
  the halter draw, 277
  with spirit so profound, 298
Female, child of our grandmother Eve, a, 41
  errors fall, if to her share, 212
  friendship, elegance of, 232
  mouth, kisses from a, 357
  murderers get offers of marriage, 720
  of sex it seems, 157
  of the species, 781
  sex, occupied with the, 877
Females of all species, 853
Feminine, eternal, draws us, 1058
  gender of vessels, 859
  the vision, 401
Fen, wild-fire dances on the, 288
Fens and the sedges, the, 888
  bogs dens, 150
Fence, cunning in, 55
  downtrod, her, 963
  impregnable, seas given for, 70
  looms up, last, 807
  of rhetoric, dazzling, 158
  put a strong, 640
  which forbids us to roam, 333
Fences, good, make good neighbors, 837
Fere, darling of his, 977
  the Goodly, 886
Fern and flower, beading, 590
  and stir the, 792
  grasshoppers under a, 260
  of sunset, 920
Ferns by these Berkshire boulders, 915
Ferned grot, 583
Ferny floor, forest's, 822
Ferryman, grim, which poets write of, 71
Fervently do we pray that this, 457
Festival rites, by these, 363
  season, there comes a, 952
Festus, I plunge, 484
Fetch me the handkerchief, 103
Fetid stillness of the swamp, 543
Fetish raiments of the past, old, 609
Fetisly, faire and, spak ful, 5
Fettered hope, set wild the, 868
  poetry, 282
  to an office stool, 622
Fetters breaks, servile, 193
  leaving the, 583

Fetters off, throws its last, 371
  threw aside all, 402
Fettle, in self-admiring, 938
Feud, cherish far-off, 612
Feuds and jealousies and sorrows, 891
  forget all, 401
Fever, after life's fitful, 86
  bringeth, 929
  called living, 460
  famine and war three enemies, 694
  has just left me, 1000
  high, of, 951
  in the mind, 184
  most terrible enemy to mankind, 694
  of life is over, 1128
  or a pimpled nose, 226
  so when a raging, burns, 199
  sweat them, let, 937
  to the questing hound, 834
Fever-fit with paroxysms, 544
Few, address in science the, 426
  and far between, 327
  are capable of education, 729
  are chosen, many called but, 1115
  are grasped by mortal ear, 503
  are the lands, far and, 498
  assume to be the deputies, the, 1062
  but with how splendid stars, 882
  die and none resign, 274
  fit audience though, 153
  friends and many books, both true, 168
  grinders cease because they are, 1110
  immortal names, 363
  is all the world, that, 30
  just four, very, 971
  know their own good, how, 177
  let thine occupations be, 1010
  let thy words be, 1109
  little I ask my wants are, 451
  of the unpleasant'st words, 46
  of us fall very low, 750
  plain rules, a, 302
  real friends, 239
  respect not to the, 969
  safe from many honored by the, 528
  seemed frightened, 576
  shall part where many meet, 328
  sheep quiet fond and, 406
  strong instincts, 302
  that only lend their ear, 30
  the rare, 611
  things impossible to diligence, 232
  thoughts of the, 640
  trust a, 52
  we happy, 67
  who pass above him, 444
  words are, and often funny, 511
Fezziwig, in came Mrs., 495
Fiat justitia ruat cœlum, 136, 145
Fibres, multitude of, 1068
Fibs, I'll tell you no, 253
Fickle and changeful thing, 1037
  and wavering, 611
  as a changeful dream, 308

Fickle, fierce and vain, 308
  gipsy, Dame Fortune is a, 406
  wanderer else will stray, 450
Fickleness of women, 720
Fico for the phrase, 34
Fiction, by fairy, drest, 244
  condemn it as an improbable, 55
  in the form of, 645
  lags after truth, 259
  more truth in, 484
  truth stranger than, 361
  turns the Muses' mangle, 759
  up-to-date, 650
Fictions like to truths, 958
  nautical, caulked with hokum, 871
Fiddle, playing on the, 235
  we know is diddle, 634
  when I play on my, 791
Fiddler, fate's a, 692
  statesman buffoon, 174
Fiddlestring tune-swept, 871
Fidelity, friendship and gossamer, 461
  genius for, 608
  whose language is, 665
Fidget and no reformer, no, 757
Fido, named Rover Towser Sport Spot or, 922
Fie foh and fum, 99
  on possession, 8
Field, accidents by flood and, 100
  and fold, singer of the, 649
  as a flower of the, 1105
  be lost, what though the, 148
  by the gale, ploughed like a, 712
  calmly to the, 371
  corner of a foreign, 894
  cow a good animal in the, 235
  dignity in tilling a, 734
  homely as a plowed, 927
  in the tented, 100
  lilies of the, 1114
  never had they faced in, 500
  of air, through the, 267
  of battle, dead on the, 706
  of destiny, in the, 441
  of his fame, from the, 364
  of honour, dead on the, 1092
  of ripe corn, 900
  or a green tree, sight of a green, 869
  Prussia hurried to the, 280, 307
  red morn betoken'd tempest to the, 106
  six Richmonds in the, 72
  so truth be in the, 163
  squadron in the, 100
  upon a stubborn, 816
  when you walk in a, 877
  where men unknown might win, 432
  with his back to the, 327
Fields above the sea, among the, 955
  and gliding streams, 982
  and skies, watch the same, 632
  and waters shout, 576
  are green and fair her skies, 382
  are lying brown and bare, 552
  babbled of green, 66
  beloved in vain, 243
  better to hunt in, 175

Fields, boundless and beautiful, 372
burn, dry, 664
come flowers, to the, 672
dales and, 31
dwelling in distant, 373
flowering of His, 471
happy autumn, 466
have eies, 16, 470
in those holy, 60
little tyrant of his, 245
o'er earth's green, 503
of air, 364
of air, shut from the, 1051
of amaranth, 326
of Cambridge, ye, 167
of heaven, 364
of yesterday, across the, 874
out of the old, 4
plow with salt your, 756
poetic, encompass me, 195
rude militia, raw in, 177
sanguine, 848
sniffed for their green, 814
with God, out in the, 956
Field-Marshal, there is a great, 519
Fiend, a frightful, 315
hell contains no fouler, 220
no greater, than anarchy, 964
no, in hell can match, 193
thou marble-hearted, 98
with all his comrades fell, 3
Fiends, array'd in flames like to prince of, 66
juggling, 89
Fiend-like to dwell therein, 435
Fient a plack was left, 11
Fier, youk'n hide de, 688
Fierce and vain, fickle, 308
as ten furies, 150
as they paint him, the lion is not so, 137, 147
democracie, 510
democratie, 156
discordant meter, 579
electric fire, 806
for the right, 626
lion is not so, 137
she is, 43
soe'er it flieth, how, 480
that, thing they call, 392
Fiercer by despair, 149
there is not a, hell, 382
Fiery floods, to bathe in, 36
pain, throbs of, 231
rod, reached a, 658
soul working its way, 173
Fife and drum, follow the, 765
ear-piercing, 102
needle-note of a, 925
sound the clarion fill the, 310
squealing of the wry-necked, 45
Fifteen, maiden of bashful, 279
men on a dead man's chest, 704
minutes of hell, 678
Fifth act, may show in some, 472
of November, remember the, 945
stone shall not fail you, 913
year in succession, for the, 922
Fifty above more than fifty below, dread, 839
north and forty west, 784

Fifty, of elder years than, 879
times as fair, were it, 432
Fifty-four forty or fight, 427
Fig a fig, call a, 976
for care and a fig for woe, 11
for him who frets, 772
for your great captain, a, 1037
Figs, in name of the prophet, 332
out of thistles, 471
Figger wants padd'n, yer, 774
Fight, absolution of a faithful, 556
again, those that fly may, 143
and conquer again and again, 243
another day, live to, 143, 254
another such, I were undone, 1002
begins within himself, 488
but when her ladyship is by, 57
cleanly then, 924
coward in the, 505
did Ye smite, in what, 748
dog that keeps out of the, 610
famoused for, 107
fifty-four forty or, 427
for freedom, 1075
for love, as men may do, 42
for such a land, dare to, 307
for the religion of God, 1126
fringy edges of the, 519
good at a, 334
he fought was good, 806
how goes the, 400
I give up the, 484
I have fought a good, 1122
I'll rise and, again, 256
it out on this line, 549
of all, last great, 778
on, merry men, 256
perish in the, 447
rushes into the thickest of the, 1065
the good fight, 1122
the last in, 218
they too have had a, 865
to the last gasp, 48, 68
we don't want to, 562
well hast thou fought the better, 153
ye till I die, 447
Fights and runs away, 143, 254
historical, 623
Fighter, am I no a bonny, 705
fits a dull, 63
twenty years a, 786
Fighters, free lovers, free, 1085
Fightin' tu, you're up to, 527
Fighting, bellyful of, 105
lovely, along the whole line, 604
men, I'd have no, 432
races don't die out, 683
rusty for want of, 142
still destroying and still, 176
Fighting's the game, wherever, 683
Fig-leaves, they sewed, together, 1097
Fig-tree, under his, 1113
Figure and form'll surpass, my, 623
for the time of scorn, 103
in company, makes no, 239
mean and small, 572

Figure, no great, were he not rich, 197
of nobody in sodden khaki, 825
of the giant mass, baby, 75
of the house, 64
that men love, 857
the thing we like, we, 401
Figures as fallacious as facts, 313
facts and, 495
on a dial, 506
thou hast no, 82
Filches from me my good name, 102
File, single in an endless, 410
Files, burial in the, 780
of time, foremost, 464
Filial duty, sense of, 273
Filibuster, high calling of a, 906
Fill a pit as well as better, 63
drank their, 732
every beaker up my men, 404
I, this cup to one, 405
the nights, solemn marches, 522
the seats of justice, 386
them full of refreshment, 435
to-night with hearts as light, 431
Filled me with fantastic terrors, 460
with love, your eyes were, 521
Filler now for cross-word puzzle, 882
Fillet, under her solemn, 410
Filling all the land with beauty, 705
Fillip with a three-man beetle, 64
Fills, he bounds connects, he, 207
the world with terror, power that, 434
Filthy Jersey, nothing there but, 919
lucre, not greedy of, 1121
Fins or pinion, 572
Final goal of ill, 468
hope is flat despair, 149
issue, light of the, 976
long farewell to earth, 713
ruin fiercely drives, 202
Finance, heroes of, 1076
Financial throe volcanic, 733
Finches are merry, 758
Find and not to yield, to, 464
how day by day, I shall, 405
I'll never never, 567
one face, God grant you, 523
or what it can not, creates, 438
seek and ye shall, 1114
the Orient's marvels here, 442
the peaceful skies, or early, 474
Finde, fast binde fast, 12
Findeth, he that seeketh, 1114
Finds the down pillow hard, 106
till all that it foresees it, 438
tongues in trees, 48
too late that men betray, 253
Fine a point, not to put too, 497
and as fast as he can, as, 406
arts once divorcing themselves, 779
by defect, 209
copy of a good book cheap, 773
feathers make fine birds, 961
fellows, some are, 574

Fine frenzy rolling, poet's eye in a, 43
glossy surface, 253
he may be just as, 925
house a master and a task for life, 415
how exquisitely, 207
manners need the support of fine manners in others, 413
passage particularly, 235
prosperity, befall that, 585
puss-gentleman, 263
so exacting so strange so, 767
thing to be father-in-law, 288
too, a point to your wit, 1043
Finely touched, spirits are not, 35
Fineness which a hymn affords, 136
Finer form or lovelier face, 308
than the staple of his argument, 41
Finery, dressed out in all her, 253
Finger and thumb, 'twixt, 61
freed from his ambitious, 72
in every pie, 1035, 1040
more goodness in her little, 192
of a clock, like the, 265
of God has planted, 435
on the place, struck his, 546
pipe for fortune's, 94
pointed to the lips of Julia, 133
points to heaven, whose silent, 302
ring encompasseth thy, 71
slow and moving, 103
thou'lt cut thy, 977
wearing it on his little, 1083
whoso touched his, 948
writes and having writ, 1019
Fingers, decay's effacing, 355
dirty, 395
four, from death, 1013
he licks his, 923
of brass, 804
of the rain, kiss the, 915
on one hand, 534
rude, with forced, 159
scrawled words with careless, 845
tapped the pane, gentle, 794
ten, gripped by, 710
than toes, rather have, 791
through reverent, 785
touched him, God's, 469
wandered idly, and my, 564
weary and worn, with, 391
were made before forks, 192
within two, of death, 1013
Fingers' end, at his, 125
ends, at my, 13, 54
Finis comes, when, 649
Finish the work we are in, strive to, 457
what I begin, 444
Finished by such a she, 57
from the beginning, master's work, 611
my course, I have, 1122
Finitude, man's terror at his own, 770
Finney had a turnip, 953
Finnigin, off ag'in on ag'in gone ag'in, 805
Fire, a chilly man's, 524
alive, keeping the seeds of, 373
and blow, sit at my, 374

Fire and fever, beyond the, 736
and through water, through, 1104
and water, would run through, 34
answers fire, 67
at close of day, by the, 1027
bastion fringed with, 468
beginning of knowledge as, is of light, 378
best of servants but what a master, 378
blaze up in combined, 378
books that you may carry to the, 238
burn and cauldron bubble, 87
burn low, every, 653
burned, while I was musing, 1104
burnt child dreads the, 15
cannot burn nor water drown it, 1067
careful with, 677
clean hearth a clear, 323
coals of, on his head, 1108, 1119
cold performs the effect of, 150
come holy, 671
compact of, 106
day fills his blue urn with, 409
doubt thou the stars are, 92
fantasy's hot, 307
fat is in the, 12
fat shall be in the, 1042
fierce electric, 806
for winter's cold, 894
fretted with golden, 92
fringed with, 468
from beds of raging, 150
from the sun, moon snatches her, 81
frying-pan into the, 16, 1034
glass of liquid, 290
glow like sparks of, 134
hold still, in His hottest, 1071
I built her many a, 843
if I can, excluding the, 1029
in each eye, 212
in his bosom, 1106
in his hand, who can hold a, 59
is dying in the grate, 574
is the test of gold, 991
kneel when you light a, 794
like green, 923
lips still touched with, 938
little, kindleth, 1122
little, quickly trodden out, 70
melt in her own, 95
most tolerable third party, 515
motion of a hidden, 306
my cat, stay by the, 917
never from Hell's, 867
nodding by the, 790
not long life by the, 758
now stir the, 265
O for a muse of, 66
O love O, 462
of life, 326
of spring, 1018
of thine, some, 648
one, burns out another's, 77
other irons in the, 971
outlives the parent spark, 366
pillar of, by night, 1098

Fire, pistol misses, 255
purge off the baser, 149
ruthless, 586
shirt of, martyr in his, 587
sitting by a sea-coal, 64
snatches from the sun, 81
source of motion, 1032
spark of that celestial, 268
sparkle the right Promethean, 41
stood against my, 99
that once was singing gold, 883
that warms cold, 1042
those who favor, 839
three removes as bad as a, 227
to burn together, in perpetual, 773
to the Thames, 246
to warm, to light, 686
touch the sacred, 816
treads upon, 196
turn from any, 776
two irons in the, 129
uneffectual, 'gins to pale his, 92
we cannot kindle when we will the, 546
what, was near, 30
when ready Gridley, 638
with white, laden, 366
without some smoke, no, 16, 23
worshiped, 166
you may sit by my, 374
y-reke in our asshen olde, 6
Fires, a remnant of their, 1050
are dead on hearths and altars, 507
burning, keep the home, 824
kindles false, 304
live their wonted, 245
of passion, to light the, 440
religion veils her sacred, 215
that pass, forest, 827
that scorch, mark of, 444
the tops of the eastern pines, 59
to warm it, kindle, 568
truth lend her noblest, 351
wake in our breast the living, 451
Fire-coals, on the lagging, 879
Fired another Troy, 176
the Ephesian dome, 193
Fire-escapes, maketh bloom the, 929
Fireflies gleam in the damp, 841
Firefly lamp, by a, 334
Fire-hearts sowed our furrows, 428
Firelit homes, clean beds and wives, 891
Firelogs throwing on hearth, freely the, 983
Fireside happiness, 289
howsoe'er defended, no, 435
is a great opiate, 346
king by your own, 1033
near one's own, 1083
to make a happy, 286
Fireworks, somersaults and, 937
Firm endeavor, with, 638
hands to grasp, 803
nerves shall never tremble, 87
of Grin and Barrett, 733
restraint, praise the, 933
thy purpose, 201
to us, seems so, 900

Firmament, fall to earth from, 59
  no fellow in the, 82
  now glowed the, 152
  o'erhanging, 92
  of the earth, 433
  on high, the spacious, 194
  pitiless sapphire, 666
  showeth his handiwork, 1103
  stars in earth's, 433
  the sun in the, 340
Firmer habit than before, 271
Firmness in the right, 291, 457
  of purpose, 1017
Firm-set earth, thou sure and, 85
First, all at once and nothing, 453
  and best, our, 445
  and last of all the songs, 855
  and the last, 1123
  be not the, by whom the new
    are tried, 211
  dark day of nothingness, 355
  day even and morn, 154
  he met her, know how, 481
  he who, shortened the labor,
    379
  he wrought, 5
  human principle, 65
  I had thee, 632
  in banquets but last in fight,
    218
  in everything, one cannot be,
    961
  in the hearts of his country-
    men, 281
  in war first in peace, 281
  invented sleep, bless man who,
    510
  joys of our heart, 390
  last love, my, 463
  magnitude, liar of the, 193
  of the new party, 478
  on the scroll of Fame, 512
  step which costs, 1053
  sweet sleep, 368
  thing he weighed, 345
  thing, let's kill all the lawyers,
    69
  time, does a thing for the, 589
  to breast the swelling tide, 603
  to fade away, 590
  to go, which of us, 603
  to welcome, 352
  true gentleman, 115
  who came away, 358
  wife had given him, 235
First-born's breath, feels her, 362
First-class fightin' man, 781
Firstling of the infant year, 141
Fir-trees dark and high, 390
Fish all is, that cometh to net, 15
  and I was a, 734
  bought a little, 846
  cat would eat, 14
  crier, a Jew, 855
  dinners will make a man
    spring, 164
  flesh nor good red herring,
    1039
  game, swims up stream, 733
  I caught, biggest, 698
  in troubled waters, 188
  Jonah in the belly of the, 1113
  kettle of, 623
  leap like little, 908
  never lost a little, 698
  no, ye're buying, 310

Fish nor flesh, 13
  not with this melancholy bait,
    44
  only the game, 733
  pleasantest angling is to see
    the, 39
  poets are like stinking, 320
  sensible, swims down, 865
  sold for more than an ox, 1003
  spouts music, 922
  still left, plenty of, 733
  that swim or swish, 843
  that talks, 823
  this, will bite, 39
  to fry, other, 1026, 1041
  what cat's averse to, 243
  with the worm, man may, 96
Fishes, all the worse for the, 454
  little, talk like whales, 255,
    649
  live in the sea, how do the, 106
  men lived like, 170
  men first produced in, 1005
  that tipple in the deep, 168
  the two small, 694
Fish-ball, one, 555
Fisher's chorus-note, 288
  life, gallant, 140
Fishermen on the beach, 99
  three, Wynken Blynken and
    Nod, 872
Fishified, how art thou, 79
Fishing, may the east wind never
    blow when he goes a, 139
Fish-like smell, very ancient and,
    32
Fish-shaped Paumanok, 827
Fist instead of a stick, 141
Fit and qualify men to be min-
    isters, 170
  audience though few, 153
  for every change and chance,
    620
  for the gods, a dish, 82
  for treasons stratagems and
    spoils, 47
  historic pride, share her, 952
  instruments, 212
  it with some better time, 57
  punishment, the crime, 624
  's upon me now, the, 131
  survive, only the, 844
  to catch it, 236
  to hold a candle, 221
Fits, 't was sad by, 248
Fitful fever, after life's, 86
Fitness of things, eternal, 229
Fitted him to a T, 238
  in arts, well, 41
Fitter being sane than mad, 490
Fittest place man can die, 511
  survival of the, 448
Fitting of self, rest is the, 501
  season is best, 959
  word He speeds, still the, 441
Five acts the just measure of a
    play, 180
  before the age of, 1064
  hundred friends, 265
  hundred leads to five hundred
    thousand, 636
  reasons we should drink, 184
  small loaves had failed to take,
    541
  thousand a year, on, 482
  you're late, 862

Fives did fit her shoe, 132
Five-cent cigar, a good, 714
Five-star final in the raw, 934
Five-thirty from Paddington, 892
Five-words-long, jewels, 466
Fixed fate free will, 150
  figure for the time, 103
  like a plant, 208
  star, name to every, 40
Flag, carry the, 394
  death's pale, 80
  despairing fondness for, 813
  floats o'er the water, 670
  goes by, as the, 715
  has braved a thousand years,
    327
  has come back to Tennessee,
    569
  here comes the, 664
  is companionship and country
    itself, 481
  is full of stars, 710
  is known in every sea, 394
  is passing by, 767
  nail to the mast her holy, 450
  o' my land, 813
  of all that float, senior, 764
  of breezes free, 715
  of England, sure to find this,
    1061
  of England, the meteor, 328
  of our union forever, 405
  of the free heart's hope, 382
  one land one heart, one, 452
  spare your country's, 443
  stepped out for the, 824
  the embodiment of history, 725
  there is a national, 480
  to haul down the American,
    390
  unfurled, seemed to see our,
    442
  with its stripes untarnished,
    821
  yellow quarantine, 925
Flags, nothing but, 641
  were furled, battle, 464
Flagon, out of an English, 827
Flagstones, hawthorns heave cold,
    905
Flail, with a silver, 888
Flakes were folding it gently, 527
Flame, adding fuel to the, 157
  adore before the, 928
  burnt child craves the, 912
  cannot quench the, 356
  cleanly burial of the, 671
  from virtue flow, pure, 1021
  God's breath upon the, 1071
  if you nurse a, 328
  is out, since the, 882
  like wine, like, 889
  love's devoted, 336
  love's holy, 322
  mingled with, 570
  nor public, nor private, 215
  of freedom, 654
  of the maple tree, 882
  spark of immortal, 890
  strikes out, 725
  swept the land like, 779
  tells in notes of, 309
  that kindled the, 857
  that lit the battle's wreck, 370
  the gold, like, 629
  where is the sea the, cried, 658

Flame, the higher the, 717
vanishes the, 354
vital spark of heavenly, 216
without heat rainbow without
color, 551
words so full of subtile, 129
Flames, like thin, 577
lives in the midst of, 196
through their paly, 67
war arrayed in, 66
Flaming fatal climax, 891
youth, 95
Flanders fields, though poppies
grow in, 821
lost in, 936
no such place as, 698
received our yoke, 146
swore terribly in, 241
Flanged and battering tail, 888
Flannel, piece of scarlet, 498
Flannels of the poor, short and
simple, 911
Flannelled fools, with the, 780
Flare the windy lights of autumn,
673
Flash across, blue ran the, 493
born in the, 736
is still the same, its, 404
of color beneath the sky,
767
of intelligence, 479
of lightning, mirth is like a,
197
of the lightning, 362
of unforeseen remembrance,
807
Flashes in the world of thought,
542
of merriment, 97
of silence, occasional, 313
Flashing and golden car, 891
brine, oh give me the, 502
Flat and unprofitable, 90
as pancakes, 116
burglary as ever was com-
mitted, 40
despair, our final hope is, 149
I drop him, 878
sea sunk, in the, 158
steam-heated, with no ventilation, 801
Flathouse roof, linger on the, 938
Flatter Neptune for his trident,
76
Flattered, being then most, 82
to tears this aged man, 383
whom all the world hath, 22
Flatterers besieged, by, 213
from friends, distinguish, 180
he hates, 82
Flatteries, outlandish, compliments and lies, 156
without winking, damn treacherous, 522
Flattering friends, wooed by, 335
painter, a, 252
tale, hope tells a, 395
unction to your soul, 95
word, with a, 722
Flattery and falsehood, 949
and obsequiousness, 272
be sure the salve of, 699
imitation is the sincerest, 333
is the food of fools, 190
love of, 198
more taken in by, 1049

Flattery never lost on poet's ear,
307
soothe cold ear of death, 244
to name a coward, 295
Flaunting extravagant quean,
279
Flavor of an old pair of sox, 714
of mild decay, general, 452
that aristocratic, 607
Flaw in a donkey's will, 453
it has no kind of, 623
or stain, with no, 924
which is hidden, 995
Flaws! what faults! what, 649
Flax, smoking, 1112
Flea does all the harm he can,
118
has smaller fleas, 190
in his ear, 127, 1025
spring like a, 164
that's a valiant, 67
who had a goodly, 1058
Fleas, Argos has the curse of,
674
free from bugs and, 972
good for a dog, 687
great, have little, 190
little fleas have lesser, 190
riseth with, 137
that on him prey, 190
that tease, 811
Fled Him, I, 748
I waked she, 162
like a passing thought, 285
whose lights are, 336
Fledge of green, April's, 933
Flee fro the prees, 4
when no man pursueth, 1108
Fleece, put on your, 982
was white as snow, 362
Fleeces, heavens are out in, 576
of descending snows, 218
trailed its ravelled, 722
Fleeing to ocean after its life,
501
Flees on feathered foot, 702
Fleet, all in the Downs the, 205
is a glance of the mind, 264
O little, 459
of fishing boats, a, 934
of stars is anchored, 881
so long as we took care of our,
197
that such sweet things should
be, 632
Fleets are useless things, 805
of iron framed, 475
ten thousand, 354
Fleeth the tyme, 7
Fleeting as bubbles, gay and, 431
as 't is fair, 343
guest, please the, 718
is the estate of man, 1011
shibboleths, 652
show, this world is all a, 336
sweeting little soul, 1009
Flesh and blood can't bear it, 221
and blood, merely, 900
and blood, strong as, 301
and the devil, the world the,
1127
character of all, 1087
collop of thy own, 14
come out of the, 977
cut her off from thy, 1125
fair and unpolluted, 97, 468

Flesh fowl or red herring, 606
going the way of all, 128
has dwindled, where, 936
his virgin sword, 220
how art thou fishified, 79
in the soul in the clod, God
in the, 486
is grass, all, 1112
is heir to, the shocks that, 93
is weak, but the, 1116
little breath little, 1009
may suffer, how much the, 596
nor good red herring, 13
of mine, would God this, 630
of my flesh, 1097
of thy flesh, 1033
shall ye not eat, of their, 1098
strange, 166
take off my, 313
that this too solid, would melt,
89
the spirit strives with, 670
the way of all, 128, 493
this wandering, 832
thorn in the, 1121
tinder to your lecheries, 903
weariness of the, 1110
what change of, 129
will not out of the, 17
Fleshe a pound, your owne, 256
Flesh-disguise, arrayed in some
new, 833
Fleshed thy maiden sword, 63
Flesh-pots of Egypt, return to
our, 1035
when we sat by the, 1098
Flexible, important principles
may be, 457
Flexure, necessity not for, 75
Flies, close mouth catches no,
1036
in amber, 111
molasses catches, 700
of estate and sunneshine, 135
on me, there ain't no, 699
preyed on half-starved, 262
summer will have its, 412
the higher pitch, 68
Flight, attained by sudden, 436
brighten as they take their,
202
confused alarms of struggle
and, 546
ended is the, 1091
in his wild aery, 157
into the wordless, thy free, 537
love is conquered only by, 1051
O time in your, 595
of a bird, 590
of a joke, 590
of future days, 150
of years, unmeasured by the,
306
put old cares to, 619
put them all to, 952
selfsame, the selfsame way, 44
the freedom of my soul, 1051
thy certain, 372
time's all-devastating, 1057
Flights, poetic, 332
Flim-flam stories, mere, 1036
Fling away ambition, 73
but a stone the giant dies, 223
it back upon an earlier time,
417
its ancient splendors, 477

Flings it a bone, 592
Flint, everlasting, 79
  the firmest, 26
  weariness can snore upon the,
    106
Flirtation depraves the appetite,
    551
  that significant word, 222
Flirtations with the moon, 933
Flo was fond of Ebenezer, 813
Float along the moonlit floor, 418
  between earth and heaven,
    glories, 425
  double swan and shadow, 298
Floating bulwark of our island,
    248
  hair, 600
Floats above the wrecks of time,
    640
Flock, Christ's chosen, 305
  for every lamb for every, 453
  however watched, no, 435
  just to drive a, to feed, 406
  of geese, charged upon a, 952
  of sheep that leisurely pass by,
    300
  of sheep, to have kept a, 141
  of thoughts, Oh, 907
  pilgrim, 403
  shun the polluted, 897
  tainted wether of the, 46
Flocks in ferny glens are feed-
    ing, 516
  my father feeds his, 248
  of them come, 621
Flogging in schools, 236
Flood and field, accidents by, 100
  bridge that arched the, 409
  far murmur of the breaking,
    679
  gently swelling, 240
  half our sailors swallow'd in
    the, 71
  is behind, 676
  leap into this angry, 81
  not properly born till, 497
  of mortal ills prevailing, 1023
  pass the, 858
  seems motionless as ice, yon,
    298
  taken at the, 83
  the matchless the great, 929
  the melancholy, 71
Floods, bathe in fiery, 36
  great, flown from simple sourc-
    es, 53
  of love and light, 452
  of other being, sweet, 670
  passions are likened best to, 21
  that are deepest, 258
  which are deepest, 864
Flooding in the main, comes si-
    lent, 519
Floor, all that lies on the ocean's,
    910
  curled up on the, 644
  float along the moonlit, 418
  forest's ferny, 822
  from the, can rise alone, 348
  his shadow on the, 410
  I have been given the, 558
  modest front of this small, 165
  nicely sanded, 251
  of heaven is thick inlaid, 47
  reorganized upon the, 900
  scratching at the, 754

Floor, seems to have the, 661
  shadow lies floating on the,
    460
  slimed Hell's worn, 836
  stone from the chancel, 737
  stood ninety years on the, 601
  unswept, leave the, 757
  wrought its ghost upon the,
    460
Floors, along the forest, 757
  footsteps on old, 807
Florence or Venice not Milan, of,
    926
  ungrateful, 354
Florist's triumph, modern, 569
Florus, no mind to be a, 1009
Flounder, squat as a, 1025
Flour, back of the, 731
  of knighthode and of fredom, 6
  of wyfly pacience, 7
  snowy, 731
Floures in the mede, of alle the, 4
  white and rede, 4
Flourish in immortal youth, 195
  princes and lords may, 250
Flourished, whilst bloody treason,
    83
Flourisheth in every soil, it, 477
Flow, aids in the ebb-tide or, 504
  fault in its, 651
  gently sweet Afton, 286
  how well so e'er it, 213
  in one down eternity's river,
    503
  in soft luxurious, 403
  like thee, could I, 167
  of soul, feast of reason and,
    213
Flowed and opened new foun-
    tains, numbers, 393
  the tide, ebbed and, 437
Flower, alike they're needful to
    the, 423
  an army's, 737
  and bee, summer cometh with,
    370
  and fruitage is the world, 411
  between the horses' feet and
    the wheel track, 515
  born to blush unseen, 245
  breaks like a, 833
  bright consummate, 153
  can say it, 849
  canst not stir a, 749
  cherish some, 499
  crimson, of battle blooms, 522
  dear common, 525
  death lurks in every, 342
  every, enjoys the air, 295
  every leaf and every, 153
  every opening, 199
  glistering with dew, 152
  if life 's a, I choose my own,
    406
  in heaven's high bower, 281
  in the crannied wall, 467
  is dry, 309
  is forgotten, as a, 883
  it fell upon a little western, 42
  lightly like a, 469
  look like the innocent, 84
  lovely little, is free, 305
  lowly as a, 774
  man a, he dies, 231
  meanest, that blows, 302
  near the lark's nest, 304

Flower, never loved a tree or, 338
  no stronger than a, 107
  of all his race, 294
  of collie aristocracy, 735
  of glorious beauty, 179
  of olden sanctities, 556
  of our young manhood, 965
  of perfect speech, 735
  of the field, as a, 1105
  of wickedness, 491
  one, no garland, 137
  or wearing-stone or open eye,
    839
  or weed, love is a wild plant,
    797
  pale and sweet, a tiny, 642
  passing all wisdom or its fair-
    est, 417
  pleasure like the midnight,
    334
  proved a beauteous, 78
  safety, pluck this, 61
  that grow'st beside the way,
    525
  that once has blown, 1019
  that opens but at night, 793
  that sad embroidery wears,
    159
  that seemed the very pattern,
    820
  that smiles to-day, 133, 368
  the sculptured, 372
  the splendid, 619
  the summer's, 108
  thou the tree and I the, 623
  tip-tilted like the petal of a,
    470
  to flower, bee goes from, 1069
  unblown a book unread, 568
  up there came a, 574
  will bloom another year, 385
  without perfume, woman with-
    out religion is, 551
  you are like a, 1065
  you might have sent, 642
Flowers, all the sweetest, 24
  and fruits of love, 358
  appear on the earth, 1110
  are at my feet, 383
  are lovely love is flower-like,
    317
  are made of earthly, 446
  are painted in tints, 1084
  are springing, sweet, 336
  bitter o'er the, 352
  by the opening and folding,
    371
  chaliced, 105
  crown old winter's head with,
    165
  death of the, 952
  deck with fragrant, 439
  foam of, 630
  for color, as, 895
  for your table, buy some, 909
  green leaves with golden, 597
  have their sober use, 646
  have their time to wither, 370
  howe'er they bloom, spring's,
    983
  I find the daisy dear, above all,
    1022
  idler than the idlest, 579
  in her hair, 710
  in the garden meat in the hall,
    702

Flowers in the mede, all the, 4
June reared that bunch of, 485
most can raise the, 467
no path of, leads to glory, 1046
nosegay of culled, 1030
o' the forest are a' wede away,
240, 936
of all hue, 152
of Friendship faded, before the,
836
of the town, 936
of the valleys, and the, 889
of Thy heart, 338
of transient fragrance, 231
on the coffin, 578
on the hills, wild, 772
only treads on, 294
promote friendship and social
amity, 646
purple with vernal, 159
say it with, 821
she comes again, with the, 793
showers for the thirsting, 366
shut of evening, 154
silent above the, her children,
565
so beautiful, when to the, 658
so blue and golden, 433
soil's fertility from wholesome,
60
some bitter o'er the, 352
soonest awake to the, 334
sprang up to see, 619
spring to blossom, 444
sweeter in the air, breath of,
111
sweetest, in all the world, 634
that come and go, of all the,
612
that do best perfume the air,
111
that fade, loved, 668
that in the forest grew, 24
that laugh to the summer's day,
371
that skirt the eternal frost, 316
they were radiant with glory,
432
touch a hundred, 916
we are the roadside, 757
were mine, all the, 460
when spring unlocks the, 342
white and red, 4
whose names they bear, 1083
with its all-late, 714
without fragrance, no perfect,
789
Flower-bell, fancy from a, 488
Floweret blow, rain-drop makes
some, 504
can endure the storm, what,
269
of the vale, meanest, 245
Flowerets that shine, 433
Flower-fed buffaloes, 856
Flowery meads, I would be in,
140
meads in May, 132
oratory he despised, 200
Flowing cups pass swiftly round,
168
cups, remembered in, 67
curves of beauty, 444
fees and fat contentions, 162
limb in pleasure drowns, 225
with milk and honey, 1098

Flown from simple sources, floods
have. 53
with insolence and wine, 148
Flows in fit words, sense, 174
Floyd Ireson, for his hard heart,
443
Fluent men, 806
tongue the only thing, 278
Fluid as nature chaste affectionate, 537
Flunked and he never lied, he,
639
Flush as May, 95
in the sunset's, 833
Flushed and magnificent song,
693
Flushes have their laurels, 428
Flushing his brow, 383
Flute, a boxwood, 693
bore to the man with the, 685
high and silver, 922
listen to a, 910
of Arcady, many a, 468
played on a silver, 664
Flutes and drums, spring's first,
887
and soft recorders, 149
broken, 807
of April, hear the, 755
of Greece, 634
to the tune of, 104
Flutter round my door, wave and,
418
Fluttered your Volscians in Corioli, 76
Fluttering about the fruit-trees,
621
Fly, a tiny metal insect-pin, 683
betimes, then, 141
busy curious thirsty, 223
from pleasure, I, 232
is hell, which way I, 151
not yet 't is just the hour, 334
O could I, I'd fly with thee, 276
or I can run, I can, 158
poor harmless, 77
said a spider to a, 394
shell must break before the
bird can, 471
that sips treacle, 205
those that, may fight again,
143
to him, I may not, 672
to others that we know not of,
93
to the desert fly with me, 338
which way shall I, 151
within a bead of amber, 112
would not kill a, 331
Flyeth, how fierce soe'er it, 480
Flyin'-fishes play, where the, 782
Flying chariot, 267
cloud, 588
Dutchman, they who see, 675
feather, 631
hour, wait for love one, 691
trapeze, man on the, 640
Fly-wheel of society, habit the,
662
Foam, far beneath the tainted,
375
house of, 916
is amber, whose, 166
long furrows of, 712
mist and cloud and, 588
o'er the dark sea's, 503

Foam of flowers, 630
of perilous seas, 383
on the river, like the, 308
passes like the, 834
the cruel crawling, 523
too full for sound and, 472
whiter grows the, 668
wiped away the weeds and, 408
Foam-bell more or less of no consequence, 548
Foaming lips of inebriated virtue,
635
Fodder is in the shock, 697
Foe, Byzantium's conquering,
299, 353
censure from a, 219
dare molest, no, 950
grim death my son and, 150
heat not a furnace for your, 72
if, love shall conquer, 815
in strife with many a valiant,
626
is faithful, know that every,
919
learned to treat my, 965
let in the, 156
manly, give me the, 293
meet the insulting, 280
my dearest, 117
never-slumbering, 453
no friend who never made a,
471
overcome but half his, 149
quarrel with the, 820
that comes with fearless eyes,
764
the, they come, 352
to favouritism, 727
to love, unrelenting, 225
to make one worthy man my,
213
to meet the insulting, 80
was it a friend or, 577
where breathes the, 382
with his feet to the, 327
without hate friend without
treachery, 599
Foes, beat down baffling, 547
chief of, 865
comfort friends and, 254
friendly counsel cuts off many,
68
his chest against the, 248
his fellest earthly, 735
judge a man by his, 727
laugh at any but, 214
long inveterate, 174
must have made, 504
proclaim his courage, 173
their friends, make, 425
thrice he routed all his, 176
two, of human happiness, 1064
we were fierce to our, 390
Foe's desolation, 332
Foeman, death is no, 896
foot of, 1073
Foeman's bride, be our, 306
frown, 474
Foemen in the fray, 771
worthy of their steel, 308
Fog and fire, shipwreck and collision, 834
betwixt us and the sun, 719
comes on little cat feet, 854
comes through, 858
in my throat, to feel the, 489

Fog, like a thick midnight, 170
  men who live above the, 522
  or fire by lake or fen, 158
  that may not lift, 926
Foggy cloud, sits in a, 87
Foibles, misery from our, 275
Fold, curtain's mystic, 644
  entered that beautiful, 798
  like the wolf on the, 356
  rose with sweets in every, 453
  within its magic, 630
Folds, blending your, 813
  where it hath lain, 789
Folded arms, lord of, 41
  blooms, o'er, 696
  glory of his wings, 922
  in our infancy, 572
  mates, from their, 756
  orbs would open, 626
  seven, fondly, 642
  wing, 888
Folding of the hands, 1106
Folio, whole volumes in, 41
Folk, advise not wayside, 784
  as poor as they, 792
  dance like a wave, 791
  drinking the gospels in, 891
  I write about, all the, 784
  of all, queerest, 754
  should carry bright, 923
  that depend on us, 872
  to goon on pilgrimages, 5
  who lived in Shakespeare's day, 621
  with friendly faces, 875
Folks ain't got no right, 820
  ancestors good kind of, 278
  at home, far from the old, 567
  expect a street parade, 849
  got taking me for him, 630
  never understand folks they hate, 527
  out in front that I jar, 845
  say our lives is grand, 870
  went to bed, the big, 667
  were growing old, 702
Follies, count o'er their youthful, 309
  may cease with their youth, 239
  teach us not, others', 465
  'tis by our, 659
  that themselves commit, 45
  youthful, 309
Follow as the night the day, 91
  the king else wherefore born, 470
  the vision, 864
  to the last gasp, 48
Followers, to advance her, 28
Following his plough, 297
  take to, where He leads, 609
Follows but for form, 98
  she draws him yet she, 436
Folly, a tale of, 608
  according to his, 1108
  another man's, 785
  as it flies, shoot, 206
  asks the why and wherefore, 406
  brood of, 160
  but vanity, cured of every, 1054
  even in pleasantry, 1017
  fool serviceable according to his, 726

Folly, forts of, 547
  grow romantic, if, 209
  has not fellow, his, 743
  in all of every age, 1050
  ineluctable problem of human, 871
  into sin can glide, 309
  is all they've taught me, 336
  is at full length, 204
  is worth, a good, 791
  mirth can into, glide, 309
  no soul exempt from, 1028
  of others, the irritating, 746
  of the age, some rooted, 1050
  or urbanity, from, 390
  shielding men from the effects of, 581
  shun'st the noise of, 160
  stays and genius goes, 409
  stoops to, 899
  that seeks through evil good, 443
  the slightest, 48
  to be wise, 243
  to tell women truth, 507
  when lovely woman stoops to, 253
Follye of people, 10
Fond affection thou hast, my, 388
  and wayward thoughts, 296
  caress, naught but weakness in, 522
  deceiver, 252
  for what they have not, 106
  imagination, so fair to, 303
  kiss and then we sever, 225
  never prove so, 80
  of quoting Homer, 819
  of uttering platitudes, 623
  recollection presents them to view, 348
  sheep quiet, and few, 406
  to rule alone, man too, 213
  to shew our clothes, 199
  too, for idle scorning, 447
  tyrant, late the, 847
  unalterably and pesteringly, 472
Fonder of my staff, I'm growing, 509
Fondest hope decay, seen my, 338
  hopes would not decay, 590
  our, boast, 386
Fondly do we hope fervently do we, 457
  folded seven, 642
Food and drink, with moderate pleasant, 1049
  and fire for winter's cold, 894
  as it comes, take, 923
  as luscious as locusts, 101
  at noon he bounded out for, 515
  between two kinds of, 1021
  crops the flowery, 207
  for powder, 63
  for unattainable, 890
  give us better, 496
  harmless sport and simple, content with, 479
  his, was glory, 401
  human nature's daily, 299
  hungry man's, 524
  if there 's a, 908
  minds not craving for, 280

Food, nothing to eat but, 729
  of fools, flattery 's the, 190
  of love, if music be the, 53
  of sweet and bitter fancy, 51
  of sweetly uttered knowledge, 27
  one man's, is another's poison, 132
  pined and wanted, 295
  rapture and response of, 887
  rats and mice have been Tom's, 99
  stomach and no, 65
  that appeases hunger, 1042
  that dead men eat, 650
  to furnish him, 700
  was dear, 917
Fool, a ful gret, 3
  all of the people, can not, 457
  almost at times the, 900
  and jester, white hairs ill become a, 66
  and knows not, is a, 706
  and still vainly is a, 1066
  answer a, 1108
  as he was, as much a, 1037
  at forty is a fool indeed, 203
  be merciful to me a, 659
  believed a, 881
  brains enough to make a, of himself, 704
  can noght be stille, 4
  contends that God is not, 583
  describe a, 775
  difference between a wise person and a, 979
  doth think he is wise, the, 51
  dulness of the, 47
  every inch that is not, 174
  every, will be meddling, 1107
  from the next they said, 930
  gudgeon, for this, 44
  hath said there is no God, 362, 1103
  he is a, 966
  his whole life he is a, 481
  hold his tongue, let a, 990
  in every age, 214
  in the forest, I met a, 49
  is counted wise when he holdeth his peace, 1107
  is man, greatest, 1050
  knows himself to be a, 51, 201
  laughter of the, 1109
  lies here, 783
  man at thirty suspects himself a, 201
  may eek a wys man ofte gyde, 4
  me no fools, 947
  me to the top of my bent, they, 95
  more hope of a, 1108
  more knave than, 31, 1037
  motley, 49
  must now and then be right, 263
  no creature smarts so little as a, 213
  old doting, 131, 1001
  old man who will not laugh is a, 769
  one draught makes him a, 54
  only good for, 1045
  outlives in fame the pious, 193

Fool, plague on the, 1050
play the, 326
resolved to live a, 129
said my muse to me, 27
some of the people, 457
south-border couplet, 895
that eats till he is sick, 577
the more, I, 48
there is more hope of a, 1108
there was, a, 779
thinks better of a gilded, 115
though he be a, 181
thought I was just a crazy, 934
to fame, nor yet a, 213
to make me merry, 51
to manage a, 785
what, first invented kissing, 192
when he holdeth his peace, 1107
with judges, 215, 263
you damned old, 875
Fools, a judge amongst, 215, 263
admire, men of sense approve, 211
are my theme, 351
at the wicket, flannelled, 780
best, are a little wise, 118
by heavenly compulsion, 98
call nature what I call God, 491
chronicle small beer and suckle, 101
contest for forms of government, 208
decoyed into our condition, 182
eternally, they are, 886
fool me no, 947
flattery's the food of, 190
for arguments use wagers, 142
gladly, suffer, 1121
gladly, to suffer, 811
greatest, oft most satisfied, 1050
in all tongues are called, 51
in idle wishes, 280
in Paradise, no, 668
into a circle, call, 48
learn only in school of experience, 227
let them use their talents, 54
like you, we thrive on, 216
little wise are the best, 118
make a mock at sin, 1107
measure themselves, greedy, 814
my lord it is a world of, 472
never-failing vice of, 210
of nature, 91
old men know young men are, 28
only good for, 1045
or foes, laugh at any but, 214
paradise of, 79, 151, 280
print it and shame the, 212
profit less by wise men, 998
rush in where angels fear to tread, 71, 212
scarecrows of, beacons of wise men, 564
should be so deep-contemplative, 49
simpleton sages and reasoning, 335
still take for that, 749
supinely stay, 280

Fools that crowd thee so, 168
the privilege of, 1050
the way to dusty death, lighted, 88
these mortals be, what, 43, 990
to be wise among, 995
to fill the world with, 581
to take and break, 703
twenty-seven millions, mostly, 379, 472
unfit to be alive, 754
who came to scoff, 175, 251
who roam, they are, 226
wise men avoided the fault of, 998
with the time, thus we play the, 64
words are the money of, 132
young men think old men, 28
Fool's bolt is soon shot, 16
most artful part is the, 1038
paradise, 607
talke, 25
Fools' experiments, I love, 449
Fooled with hope, 178
Foolery, a little, governs the world, 130
that wise men have, 47
walks about the orb, 55
Fooles and children cannot lie, 15
bolt is soon shot, 16
Foolish and so false, so, 185
fears of what might pass, 955
like you better, 901
little maiden, 653
or though you be wise, be, 846
questions, answer, 1083
ruin the, 995
tears would flow, 583
thing, never says a, 184
thing to make a long prologue, 1125
things to confound the wise, 1120
too, for a tear, 316
whistling of a name, 168
Foolishness allowed indulgence in such, 522
Foot, a pretty, 1057
and hand go cold, 20
before, the better, 58
chancellor's, 130
equal with his eye, wishing his, 70
for foot hand for hand, 1098
has music in 't, 270
in chaos-gloom, 544
in the grave, one, 131, 1001
is on my native heath, my, 310
it's trod, though under, 548
less prompt, 547
more light, step more true, 308
no rest for the sole of her, 1097
nor hand, moving not, 757
of a conqueror, lie at the proud, 58
of foeman tread, 1073
of ground, kingdoms in a, 928
of time, noiseless, 53, 294
on the stair, light, 850
on the table, your, 778
one, in sea and one on shore, 38, 256
one, in the grave, 131
print of a naked, 187

Foot, put forward your best, 58
set his light little, 804
shall slide, no, 957
so light a, 79
sole of our, 116, 131
stranger's, 552
to the north, head to the south, 1068
to the sole of his, 39
unwearied, thy, 371
upon a worm, needlessly sets, 266
with equal, 983
youth now flees on feathered, 702
Football captain, Sir Stafford Cripps, 909
life but a game at, 309
of destiny, 551
Foothold sure, one more, 889
Footman hold my coat, seen the eternal, 900
Footmen whisper have a banana, 937
Footprint in the sod, 758
Footprints on the sands of time, 433
walking in human, 589
when the days are wet, 665
Footstep falls, soft the, 424
gleams, and where thy, 460
never strayed, furthest, 771
Footsteps, airy, 421
come with doves', 1079
he hath turned home, 307
hurrying, 818
in the sea, 266
may roam, though the, 511
of a throne, 22
pressing on of many, 497
remembered, on old floors, 807
stray, lest my, 549
willing, meeting here, 345
Footstool, the earth my, 207
Fop, some proud, 226
the solemn, 263
For to admire and for to see, 782
Forbearance ceases to be a virtue, 259
Forbid, God, 1119
it almighty God, 270
Forbidden tree, fruit of that, 148
Forbids to crave, my mind, 20
Force and road of casualty, 45
and sequence, terms of, 731
because persuasion fails, 491
elemental, 726
enormous, 412
evolution is not a, 641
faith the one great, 695
impostor employs, 950
is mighty, I know some, 888
is no remedy, 478
knowledge more than equivalent to, 232
may reap, what you, 1035
mightiest practical, 678
more by art than, 219
naturally lose their, 949
no, can stretch a cord, 375
of armes, by, 256
of beauty, seems right by, 409, 430
of his own merit makes his way, 72
of illusion, the, 1081

Force of nature, 175
  of temporal power, 46
  of the wind, 753, 962
  of words, by the, 1001
  outside ourselves, beneficent, 738
  patient, 466
  shall have spent its novel, 464
  some mighty, 820
  some plastic, 647
  to shape it, 471
  tyrant, 576
  unite, if their, 219
  who overcomes by, 149
  youth full of grace, fascination, 535
Forces, by united, 1049
  economic and social, 641
  of American civilization, triumph over, 755
  politics a struggle of, 636
Forced by fate, 177
  from their homes, 250
Forcible are right words, 1102
  Feeble, 65
Forcibly if we must, 319
Fordoes me quite, makes me or, 103
Forefathers had no other books, 69
  of the hamlet, 244
  our rude, 590
  think of your, 291
Forefended spheres, music of, 556
Forefinger of all time, 466
  of an alderman, 77
Foregone conclusion, 103
Forehead and the little ears, 808
  cool, keep your, 875
  in the middle of her, 440
  lowers, instantly your, 240
  of the frowning skies, 1032
  of the morning sky, 159, 1032
  on death's fearful, 658
  resting in the, 938
  the godlike, 305
  upon his, 808
Foreheads villanous low, 33
Foreign aid of ornament, 224
  collision, to avoid, 328
  hands, by, 217
  language, value of, 740
  office where everybody is a gentleman, 906
  things, 172
  travel ought to soften prejudices, 571
  troop landed in my country, 230
Foreigners, spell better, 615
  two things which invite, 1051
Foreknowledge absolute, 150
  will and fate, 150
Forelock grasp, should by the, 1058
  time by the, 26
Foremast, drooping at the, 925
Foremost files of time, 464
  man of all this world, 83
  to defend, 352
Forequarters, at the captain's, 600
Foresaw, sees what he, 300
Foreseen, ordained decreed, 777
Foresees, till all that it, it finds, 438

Forespent night of sorrow, 165
Forest by slow stream, 318
  fires, as in, 827
  floors, along the, 757
  flowers o' the, are a' wede away, 240
  king, never became a, 847
  met a fool in the, 49
  primeval, this is the, 435
  wolves in the, 565
Forests are rended, when, 309
  enchanted filled with magic dreams, 831
  let me court the rivers and, 982
  noises that old houses and, hold, 928
  of the night, in the, 281
  sublimity of primeval, 449
  which shake in the wind, 590
Forest's ferny floor, 822
Foresters, Diana's, 60
Forest-green, cousin of the, 385
Forest-nymphs are beading fern and flower, 590
Foretaste of death, 1064
  of the resurrection, 1064
Foretells, happiness their harmony, 460
Foretold by prophet-bards, 477
  that danger lurks within, are, 70
Forever and a day, 51
  and forever farewell, 84
  and on earth will, be, 378
  bright, a quenchless star, 393
  death and that vast, 523
  fallen, arise or be, 148
  fare thee well, 356
  fortune, wilt thou prove, 225
  his time is, 167
  honoured, forever mourned, 219
  known, to be, 167
  now and, 341
  singing as they shine, 194
  still forever, 356
  strange, 568
  take into the vast, 659
  that no life lives, 632
  thou art gone and, 308
  'tis a single word, 590
  yesterday to-day and, 1122
Forever-never never-forever, 434
Fore-warned fore-armed, 1039
Forfeit, all the souls that were, 36
  fair renown, 307
Forfeyture, this shall be the, 256
Forgave the offence, 177
Forges, quit not their, 736
Forget all time with thee, 152
  and forgive, 99
  and forgive that we did you wrong, 860
  and smile, 587
  as to, what human frailty is, 386
  at times with advantage, 987
  can this fond heart, 388
  courage to, 582
  dream that I, 632
  expedient sometimes to, 987
  forgive, 653
  good to forgive, best to, 492
  knew we should both, 633
  lest we, 780

Forget me, go, 365
  never never can, 389
  nor, that sunrise never failed, 619
  old Ireland, I'll not, 432
  six counties overhung with smoke, 608
  taught me at last to, thee, 587
  that I remember, 632
  the human race, that I might, 354
  thee, 395
  thee O Jerusalem, 1106
  thyself to marble, 160
Forgetful, be not, to entertain strangers, 220
  blessed are the, 1080
Forgetfulness anodyne of regret, 774
  mercy of, 794
  not in entire, 301
  of affliction, there is a, 1124
  of slepe, 26
  prey to dumb, 245
  steep my senses in, 65
  sweets of, 269
Forget-me-not, and said, 658
  the blue bell, 385
Forget-me-nots of the angels, 435
Forgets the truly loved never, 335
Forgetting, a sleep and a, 301
  could be willed, if, 575
  if this thou call'st, 395
  more and more, 575
  the world, 216
Forgive, best to forget, good to, 492
  divine to, 211
  forget and, 99
  me not! hate me, 689
  our enemies, 113
  our friends, 113
  the crime, 294
Forgiven by Christ in heaven, the sin, 431
Forgiveness, awkwardness has no, 414
  but to speak, 763
  finds its home, 690
  is better than revenge, 1013
  one step from toleration to, 716
  to the injured, 178
Forgot, and all the rest, 107
  are we so soon, 579
  by the world, 216
  for which he toiled, 107
  in the hatred of a minute, 459
  propos'd as things, 212
  should auld acquaintance be, 286
  thou art not, 448
  what we have been, we have, 531
  when by thy side, 364
Forgotten dreams, glimpses of, 462
  even by God, 484
  lore, curious volume of, 460
  man, 654, 876
  melody, like a, 582
  my kisses, 633
  nothing new except what is, 1061
  the inside of a church, 62

Forgotten, the names of their founders, 147
Fork drive nature out, with a, 924, 985
Forks, fingers made before, 192
Forked mountain, 105
Form, a new and clear, 1087
  all matter is indifferent to, 144
  and colour, and grow to, 533
  and feature face and limb, 630
  and feature, outward, 317
  and follows but for, 98
  and moving, admirable in, 92
  and pressure, show his, 94
  assume a visible, 1081
  cliff that lifts its awful, 251
  combination and a, 95
  divine, the human, 220
  finer, or lovelier face, 308
  from off my door, take thy, 460
  give this well-beloved, 671
  glass of fashion and mould of, 93
  had yet not lost, 149
  he wears, what, 662
  is the cage and sense the bird, 649
  lick it into, 122
  lifeless, 511
  of government, our, 970
  of government, the Republican, 581
  of life and light, 355
  of manliest beauty, 274
  of mingled mist and light, 439
  or formula of peace, all seek some, 726
  so fair that like the air, 405
  spoiled the, 1030
  stuffs vacant garments with his, 58
  was ponderous and his step, 437
  we are borrowers, to use or, 480
  yielding metal flow'd to human, 214
Forms more real than living man, 367
  mould it into heavenly, 452
  no moral need, 441
  of ages passed away, 423
  of ancient poets, 317
  of faith, 471
  of government, fools contest for, 208
  of life and feeling, 934
  of life arise, some, 504
  of things unknown, 43
  or crosses or books, no, 558
  power by means of, 1081
  unseen their dirge is sung, by, 247
  vents in mangled, 49
Formal cut, beard of, 50
Formalism is the hall-mark, 862
Formation of right habits, 542
Formed by thy converse, 209
Former living, talked of my, 681
Formost in battle was Mary Ambree, 257
Formula for complete happiness, 773
Formulas, clear myself of cants and, 378

Forrest, flowres that grew in, 24
Forsake me, do not, 180
  not an old friend, 1124
Forsaken, I feel like one, 573
  not seen the righteous, 1104
  when he is, 390
Forswear thin potations, 65
Forsworn, that so sweetly were, 37
Fort nor armed host, 954
Forts of folly, 547
  no need of arsenals or, 434
Forth we went a gallant band, 455
  wherefore come ye, in triumph, 401
  your rout send, a joyous shout, 401
Fortitude and delicacy all a man has of, 705
  of mind, great, 233
Fortress and my deliverer, my, 1100
  built by nature, 59
  house of every man is his, 21
  is a faithful heart, 747
  is less threatened, 1068
  mighty, is our God, 1023
  my refuge and my, 1105
  of his 'stablisht soul, 735
Fortuitous circumstances, 310
  concourse of atoms, 187
  concurrence, 254
Fortune and to fame unknown, 245
  architect of his own, 111, 981
  as she list, do, 1020
  be bereft, of, 682
  beguiling, 240
  brings in some boats not steer'd, 106
  carves out his own, 1033
  crested, 267
  Dame, is a fickle gipsy, 406
  distinction of birth or, 1061
  doth give too much to many, 29
  down, can cast my, 30
  easy to get a favour from, 987
  fair, deserves not any, 1022
  fill thy sail, if, 267
  flatters, when, 58
  forever, wilt thou prove, 225
  good night, smile once more turn thy wheel, 98
  great commandress, 28
  hath cruelly scratched, 53
  hath divers ways, 28
  here would try, 693
  hostages to, 109
  I care not, 225
  in disgrace with, 107
  insults of, 229
  is a god, 963
  is a great slavery, a great, 991
  is blind, 111
  is like glass, 987
  is like the market, 110
  is on our side, when, 987
  leads on to, 83
  leaves some door open, 1034
  may have a better success, 1033
  may ill, never pry, 886

Fortune, means to men most good, 58
  method of making a, 246
  modern, result of private information, 724
  most dejected thing of, 99
  mould of a man's, 111
  never come with both hands full, will, 65
  not easy to keep a favour from, 987
  not satisfied with one calamity, 987
  out of suits with, 48
  prospereth, whom, 963
  railed on Lady, 49
  sends, gifts that, 664
  slings and arrows of outrageous, 93
  smiles, when, 30, 986
  such as I've enjoyed, 1076
  to prey at, 102
  told, O man thy, 681
  tugged with, 86
  unwilling to mix my, 181
  use you hard an' sharp, 284
  vicissitudes of, 271
  virtues to sustain good, 1043
  waited thousands to, 496
  watcheth o'er our lives, 967
  well-favoured man gift of, 39
  wishes to destroy, whom, 990
  you and, will agree, 508
Fortunes, battles sieges, 100
  cannot tell man's, 966
  carry Caesar and his, 1000
  father's, 128
  hazard of new, 57
  he will vote away, 573
  lest you may mar your, 98
  lie within you, what, 687
  lives and sacred honour, 273
  low, hearts high and, 906
  manners turn with, 209
  my pride fell with my, 48
  of the British race, 921
  parcel of their, 104
  ready to try our, 65
  seekers and makers of great, 795
  to seek their, 52
Fortune's buffets and rewards, 94
  calms, no chance of, 30
  champion, thou, 57
  chances, 404
  changes in our face, 180
  dole, by silly, 931
  end, too straight for, 429
  finger, pipe for, 94
  furious fickle wheel, 67
  ice prefers to virtue's land, 173
  power, not now in, 142
  sharp adversitee, 4
  yoke, 70
Fortunate, at best but, 969
  deserve to be called, 975
  habit, by a, 345
  isle, abode of the blest, 982
  Isles, safely reach the, 435
  they who though once only, 915
Fortunatus, wishing-cap of, 299
Forty centuries look down, 1060
  days and forty nights, 1097
  fat fair and, 178
  feeding like one, 297

Forty, fool at, is a fool indeed, 203
  knows it at, 201
  minutes about the earth, in, 42
  pounds a year, rich at, 250
  stripes save one, 1121
  year, wait till you come to, 481
  years old, 454
Forty-odd befell, at, 392
Forum, in the middle of the, 984
  voice of the, 889
Forward and frolic glee, 308
  as occasion offers, 1012
  nor behind, no longer, 443
  the ages roll, 594
  those behind cried, 400
Fossils in Portland stone, 819
  who are they, 795
Foster-child of silence, 383
Foster-nurse of nature is repose, our, 99
Foster's songs in the world's choir, 711
Fetching him to his own, 639
Fou for weeks thegither, 287
Fought a good fight, 1122
  a long hour, 63
  all his battles o'er again, 176
  and bled in freedom's cause, 294
  the better fight, 153
  we've, the Bear before, 562
Foul and pestilent congregation of vapours, 92
  as Vulcan's stithy, 94
  oyster, pearl in your, 51
  play, 90
  to fair, from, 30
  weather lieth not in a shower, 132
Foulest letters, write fair words in, 65
Foulness of their fate, 892
  rather than because of its own, 975
Found, best gift my latest, 153
  both, adventuring both, 44
  make a note of, when, 496
  myself famous, 361
  no tongue, my songs that, 444
  only on the stage, 360
  pity in his tenderness, 626
  respectable, when was genius, 431
  the companion, I never, 514
Foundation, conquest has no, 1054
  no sure, set on blood, 58
  of comradeship laid in youth, 739
  of morals and legislation, 222
  resting on economic, 1086
  stone of American liberty, 830
Foundations, earth's, 744
  loosen old, 855
  of all states, chief, 1023
Founded, that it be securely, 1057
  upon a rock, 1114
Foundered galleons, 851
Founders of civilization, 340
  the pyramids have forgotten the names of their, 147
Foundling hospital, carried to the, 1055
Found'st me poor at first, and keep'st me so, 252

Fount, God the eternal, 1023
  more bright than crystal, 983
  of joy's delicious springs, 352
Fountain and a shrine, a, 460
  by a forest side, 149
  ere it flows, 364
  heads and pathless groves, 144
  "I have" is a, 676
  like the bubble on the, 308
  of industry, choke the, 340
  of life in every creature, 476
  of sweet tears, a heart the, 297
  of tears, stem the great, 676
  of wit, 352
  overflows for every flock, 453
  pitcher broken at the, 1110
  rise like a, 463
  stealing forth, 645
  stirr'd, like a, 75
  stream and sea, at once, 306
  troubled, is like a, 52
  yet unsealed, 568
Fountains, Afric's sunny, 343
  careless flowing, 583
  in intelligent, 572
  in the human heart, opened new, 393
  large streams from little, 292
  of my hidden life, 411
  of the Nile, show me the, 412
Fountain's murmuring wave, 269
  silvery column, 317
Four be the things, 918
  descending degrees of drunkenness, 1068
  larks and a wren, 499
  little foxes, 904
  rogues in buckram, 62
  seasons, 385
  seasons of the year, 915
  speeches, 550
  square walls, home's not, 418
  walls, I have my own, 382
  winds of the heaven, 1113
  years old, of being only, 911
Four-in-hand, the fiery, 319
Four-legged brain, 858
Fourscore years, numbered more than, 438
  years, wind him up for, 178
Four-square to all the winds, 467
Fourteen hundred years ago, 60
Fourth estate of the realm, 397
  estate, the stupendous, 377
  person born is a Chinaman, every, 943
Foutra for the world, 65
Fowles, smale, maken melodye, 5
Fox and the pack, 807
  cannot reach the grapes, 137
  from his lair, 397
  the tailless, 635
  went out, a, 951
  when he had lost his tail, 122
Fox's skin, patch it with the, 998
Foxes have holes, 1114
  saw their mother go, 904
  that spoil the vines, 1110
Fox-terriers have more original sin, 745
Fraction of a product, 380
Fractions, life made of minute, 318
Fragile dewdrop, a, 384
  kingdom, Athens a, 903
  skiff attains the shore, 640

Fragment of a ballad sure to meet you, 589
  torn out of his heart, 908
Fragments, gather up the, 1118
  of a once glorious union, 341
  of civilization, 937
  of steak, chases, 923
  practice old lovely, 854
Fragmentary blue, make so much of, 839
Fragrance backward, cast no, 578
  ere it gives forth, 592
  from the lilies straying, 375
  of the earth, 1090
  placed beside a rose and caught its, 560
  plants while they grow bestow no, 252
  smells to heaven, 226
  such as never clings, 915
  transient, 231
Fragrant limes, 396
  most, when crushed, 109
  poses, thousand, 31
  still faintly, 828
  the fertile earth, 152
Fraid-cat, en' I wasn't a, 792
Frail a thing is man, so, 947
  and erring men, tales of, 907
  blood, 56
  I am, how, 1104
Frailties from their dread abode, 245
  truce with rosy, 576
Frailty, forget what human, is, 386
  from the organ-pipe of, 58
  of a man, 109
  of the mind, 193
  subsist, human, 1038
  thy name is woman, 90
Frame, a shining, 194
  giant, 372
  of nature, the whole, 194
  of shining golden hair, 665
  orbs of heavenly, 27
  provides a starry, 795
  quit this mortal, 216
  rapture-smitten, 327
  the essence of every picture, 827
  this goodly, the earth, 92
  this universal, 110, 176
  tremble for this lovely, 326
  was dust, nor that his, 584
  whatever stirs this mortal, 316
Framed in prodigality of nature, 71
  strange fellows, nature hath, 43
  to make women false, 101
France and England, best thing between, 417
  autumn in, 197
  beloved of every soul, 779
  by the laws of, 1050
  famed in all great arts, 545
  has been deprived, 1061
  has more need of me, 1060
  her giant limbs uprear'd, 316
  I get my waistcoats, from, 1076
  ill unto the realm of, 1022
  in one easy lesson, 923
  in the light of evening, 424
  is invaded, 1060

France, king of, went up the hill, 950
leave their bones in, 67
managed so well in, 644
march forever from, 930
never go to, 390
nothing is changed in, 1092
of President Thiers, 906
order this matter better in, 242, 644
ready to quit, 1061
St. Dennis was for, 258
they'll swear to that in, 406
threatening, 173
unathletic, 906
unfold, the lily for, 642
ye sons of, 1059
Frank, elemental force is ruthlessly, 726
haughty rash, 425
Franklin's quiet memory, 357
Franklyn's dogge leped over a style, 350
Frantic, the lover all as, 43
though the blast is, 667
Fraternity of strangers, 1069
of the Henpecked, 197, 358
Fratricidal slaughter, no, 686
Fraud, notorious by base, 991
Frauds, first and worst of all, 506
have an interest, 788
Fraught, swell bosom with thy, 103
Fray, beginning of a, 17
foemen in the, 771
latter end of a, 63
lawsuits and the reckless, 984
mingled in the, 504
rode from the bloody, 659
Frayd, more, then hurt, 12
Frayed and soiled and torn, wings so, 633
Freakish young zephyr, palm yourself off as a, 660
youth, 265
Free and whole, keep me, 853
as air, love, 216
as nature first made man, 178
battle for the, 363
but sorrow's purse is, 565
costs me to be, 868
days have been so wondrous, 201
fain have her, 575
fighters lovers spenders, 1085
from fear that reigns, 435
from hope and fear set, 632
from scars, arms unstained and, 517
God wills us, 272
hath made our nation, 451
homestead of the, 442
kind, mate with my, 886
land of the, 332
let us die to make men, 522
my remembrance is very, 55
nature's grace, 225
no one can be, till all are free, 581
show himself too, 933
soil free men free speech Fremont, 945
spirit of mankind, 371
till thou at length art, 452
to think or act, 612

Free trade is not a principle, 419
trade the greatest blessing, 397
truth shall make you, 1118
use of my understanding, 322
we must be, or die, 298
will fixed fate, 150
will, hostile empires Necessity and, 378
will is, strong is the soul, 545
Freed from his ambitious finger, 72
Freedom, all we have of, 779
and peace, 357
bounds of, wider yet, 462
comrades, love, 834
consciousness of, 1062
costly sacrifice on altar of, 457
enemies of, 1081
enemy to truth and, 1075
fail, what avail if, 410
fight for, 1075
from her mountain height, 382
girls display shocking, 691
has a thousand charms, 262
Holland traditional land of, 739
idea of, 477
in my love, if I have, 168
in that, bold, 305
in the souls, flame of, 654
leaning on her spear, 452
new birth of, 456
of Europe, 799
of my soul, 1051
of religion of the press, 273
of the press, 830
or beauty, no, 1076
or leave to die, 552
reverently use our, 1127
ring from mountain-side, let, 447
shouting the battle-cry of, 541
shrieked as Kosciusko fell, 327
so complete, made my, 878
so long as faith reigns with, 612
suggest the wildest, 416
that fills all the space, 663
their battle-cry, 552
thoroughfare for, 600
thou cravest, take back the, 583
thought and truth, it goes with, 397
to speak, 526
to the free, 456
to the slave, 456
to think, 526
to worship God, 370
where wealth and, reign, 249
whose service is perfect, 1127
yet thy banner torn, 354
Freedoms, revolutions do not always establish, 396
Freedom's banner, streaming, 382
battle once begun, 355
cause, fought and bled in, 294
crowning hour, 760
holy light, bright with, 447
soil beneath our feet, 382
Freehold, all-enclosing, 573
Freely, as when they discuss it, 398
Freeman shall stand, when, 332

Freeman with unpurchased hand, 451
Freeman's will, executes a, 348
Freemen, we will die, 274
who rules o'er, 238
without education, 473
Freest of the free, 348
Freeze thy young blood, 91
Freight, caravans of, 926
of faith and hope, 459
of value is thy, 537
yards, the, 926
Freighted hour one moment opportune, one, 626
Freighters, when I rode the, 926
Fremont, free men free speech, 945
French air, there is an old, 607
avoid no hazards, 923
combine the greatest simplicity, 922
culture, I believe only in, 1082
guard fire first, 941
guard private life, 739
have empire of the land, 376
or Turk or Proosian, 623
own supreme prose literature, 740
peasant than Napoleon, rather have been a, 603
politeness, nothing but wind in, 1083
spoken, hear, 592
wiser than they seem, 110
Frenchman I praise the, 263
is conceited, the, 1076
like the old Scotch golfer, 923
must be always talking, a, 237
only one, more, 1092
the brilliant, 263
Frenchman's darling, 266
Frenchmen, three, on one pair of English legs, 67
unhappy lovers should be, 911
Frensh of Paris was to hir unknowe, 5
she spak ful faire and fetisly, 5
Frenzy, poet's eye in a fine, 43
Frenzy's fevered blood, 308
Frequency of experiment, 239
Fresh and crisp and sparkling, 582
and full of faith, he was, 421
as a bridegroom, 61
as when it first arose, 445
as when the first sunrise, 687
from birth, 634
from the hyaline streams, 432
one that you've scowled upon, 422
to start again, 972
while grief is, 236
woods and pastures new, 160
Freshened fragrant breeze, catch the, 915
Fresher I ween, like the rose is but, 388
Freshly ran he on, 178
Freshness fills the air, a dewy, 322
of life, believe again in the, 1085
there lives the dearest, 672
Fret a passage, 147
dying we live, living we, 492

Fret thy soul with crosses, 25
Fretful porpentine, 91
Frets his hour upon the stage, 88
  that, above our peaceful home, 375
Fretted the pygmy body, 173
  with golden fire, 92
Friar of orders gray, 52, 256
Friars, hooded clouds like, 433
Friday, his name should be, 187
  I had that fellow, 655
  the day I saved his life, 187
  with me, took my man, 655
Friday's child is full of woe, 956
Friend, a better, than old dog Tray, 567
  a great field-marshal my, 519
  accomplished female, 942
  after friend departs, 306
  and enemy, worst, 894
  and the plainest, 923
  as you choose a, 180
  be dear, let a, 393
  become your, 789
  best mirror is an old, 137
  countenance of his, 1108
  dear and true industrious, 60
  death how now, 591
  death of a dear, 43
  defend your departed, 175
  equal to a brother, 959
  every man will be thy, 120
  faithful, is a strong defence, 1124
  faithful, is the best, 594
  faithful the wounds of a, 1108
  fav'rite has no, 243
  forsake not an old, 1124
  gained from heaven a, 245
  guide philosopher and, 209
  hast thou a, 19
  house that shelters a, 411
  house to lodge a, 214
  I had a, 524
  I have valued and tried, 335, 657
  if, we greet thee, 815
  in life our absent, 587
  in misery, no, 120
  in my poor dog Tray, 567
  in my retreat, 263
  in need, 978
  in power is a friend lost, 635
  indeed, he that is thy, 120
  indeed to pardon or to bear it, 267
  is a person with whom I may be sincere, 411
  is another I, 1016
  is another self, 977
  is best, what, 19
  is never known, 15
  is one soul in two bodies, 1015
  is to be one, way to have a, 411
  keep thy, 53
  knolling a departing, 64
  life is too short for a, 410
  loan oft loses itself and, 91
  man ever had, deepest rarest, 918
  meet him as thy true, 1063
  men esteem a real, 977
  mine own familiar, 1128
  much too patient, 780

Friend, my dear dumb, 522
  my Father and my, 180
  need be very much his, 267
  new, is as new wine, 1124
  nor a, to know me, 703
  not a, to spare, 410
  nothing so much as a real, 977
  of a man, appear the, 1055
  of all my friends, never a, 712
  of all the world, 786
  of every friendless name, 231
  of man, and be a, 733
  of man desires, 546
  of my better days, 363
  of pleasure wisdom's aid, 248
  of sun and sky, plants the, 715
  of those who have no friend, 697
  of woe, sleep the, 322
  oh, I fear the lightest heart, 447
  one absolutely unselfish, 352
  one, I had, 604
  or foe, was it a, 577
  or foe, whether it be, 1125
  polished female, 394, 942
  praise from a, 219
  received with thumps, 203
  religious book or, 114
  save me from the candid, 293
  should bear friend's infirmities, 83
  sincere, made a, 474
  so good a, 175
  sometimes a, sometimes the engineer, 136
  speak now as with a, 1021
  speaks to a precious, 716
  stands at the door, 567
  stately kindly lordly, 634
  sticketh closer than a brother, 1107
  that loved her, if I had a, 100
  the firmest, 352
  the masterpiece of nature, 411
  thou art not my, 353, 408
  to another friend, 850
  to close his eyes, not a, 176
  to friend, they talk as, 1065
  to her virtues be a, 240
  to human race, 218
  to me, a dear old, 678
  to me he is all fault, 470
  to public amusements, 235
  to truth, statesman yet, 210
  to-day, where is my, 761
  too true to keep a, 429
  treat your, as if he might become an enemy, 988
  unseen unborn unknown, 881
  who deserts you, 962
  who hath not lost a, 306
  who lost no, 210
  who loved his, 948
  who never made a foe, he makes no, 471
  who passeth all the rest, have God thy, 19
  whom fortune prospereth, 963
  whose face will never change, 676
  whose presence, 474
  world is not thy, 80
  worth loving, if you have a, 679

Friend, you never can be old, 108
Friends, a good book the best of, 478
  advanced true, 547
  adversity of our best, 1045
  advertised by our loving, 71
  again with roses, 631
  and brother souls, my, 471
  and foes impartially, 910
  and foes, to comfort, 254
  and many books, 168
  and relatives here below, 605
  and wine, 335
  are born not made, 635
  are exultations agonies, thy, 297
  are sore, if your, 214
  are we, staunch, 619
  as I do with my books, do with my, 411
  at ease alone, two, 822
  at home, make, 996
  begin to compliment about looking young, 343
  best way to make, 935
  better than through mortal, 579
  cakes and, 923
  call you that backing of your, 61
  can go, the nearest, 838
  choice makes our, 1056
  could say, spite of all their, 498
  dear five hundred, 265
  defend me from my, 293
  depart and memory takes them, 388
  distinguish flatterers from, 180
  eat and drink as, 52
  embrace thy, leave all in order, 537
  enter on my list of, 266
  faithful, 120
  fallyng out of faithfull, 19
  farewell, have bid sweet, 1021
  fear to join our, 851
  forsake me like a memory lost, 369
  go with us, our, 851
  good thoughts his only, 121
  had quite such pleasant, 810
  have perished so, 610
  he cast off his, 252
  he loved, his, 735
  he made a thousand, 774
  he who has a thousand, 1017
  held up by his, 1125
  house of my, 1114
  how we should behave to, 1015
  I have had, 610
  I loved, how many, 793
  in early time refused, 247
  is without three good, 50
  I've met many, 388
  joy has its, 922
  laugh at your, 214
  lay down his life for his, 1118
  like summer, 135
  little, may prove great, 961
  loved his, 649
  make foes their, 425
  make pretence, 838
  man that hath, 1107
  many, had me, 774
  many many lady, 755

Friends, my never-failing 321
nature teaches beasts to know
their, 76
never without, 951
of humblest, scorn not one, 304
of my youth a last ad.eu, 544
of my youth where are they,
356
of old all brave, my, 470
of our childhood the place of
our birth, 446
of the unlucky, 967
old, are best, 130, 650
old, are most too home-like,
729
old times old, 253
old, to trust, 113
out of sight we lose, 365
people have for, 754
perform for the sake of our,
980
poor make no new, 432
power in the hands of, 636
princes find few real, 239
proclaim his truth, 173
property of, is common, 1015
prosperity makes, 990
quote one of my, 1031
remembering my good, 59
Romans countrymen, 83
separateth very, 1107
show me his, 579
some honest friends, I have
some, 845
soon be, 965
tell my bestest, 765
thanks to my, 199
that I knew in my Maying,
718
the auldest, 703
the more we love our, 1046
the nearest, 703
the ornament of a house. 414
thou hast grapple to thy soul,
90
thousand, sufficeth not, 1017
three firm, more sure than day,
317
thrust away by his, 1125
to borrow my books, 807
to congratulate their, 174
troops of, 88
true, less moved than counterfeit, 180
we have been, together, 446
we may live without, 592
we need new, 788
we were kind to our, 390
wealth maketh many, 1107
were poor but honest, 53
were pretty few, 665
who come and gape and go, 547
who has a thousand, 410
will be so clever, 952
with himself, to keep, 705
would look upon my quiet face,
680
you and I were long, 227
your choice of, 1083
Friend's departing feet, 528
illness, to hear of, 520
infirmities, bear his, 83
license, with a, 1021
Friendless name, friend of every,
231
Friendliest to sleep, hour, 153

Friendliness, more than common,
669
Friendly and comforting breast,
693
counsel cuts off many foes, 68
critics, my, 886
faces, love the, 848
must show himself, 1107
Friendship an unstable anchorage,
965
and conversation of a few select companions, 195
and gossamer fidelity of man,
461
and took away Love, came for,
336
cold and I was sick, 938
colder, and the heart of, 405
constant save in love, 38
die by negligence, 237
distance sometimes endears,
388
elegance of female, 232
exchange of good offices, 1044
fair, are through thy, 411
gift of, 695
greatest ornament of, 981
in appearance glad to be at,
183
in constant repair, keep his,
233
is a little truer, 822
is a sheltering tree, 317
is disinterested commerce, 253
is love without his wings, 361
is the breathing rose, 453
last long as our love, 612
laughter in, 723
like the holly-tree, 516
lived on terms of, 981
love and liberty, 317
love like, steady, 336
needs emotion to become love,
617
needs parallelism of life, 636
no greater bane to, 981
of the many, 611
of two men, 725
offer a man, 716
precise moment formed, 272
retirement rural quiet, 224
sounds too cold, 337
subsistin' 'tween him an' a
pup, 699
sudden, springs from wine, 206
swear an eternal, 292, 313,
1047
that like love is warm, 336
waned, where good, 794
where there is true, 80
which they owe me, 1028
while wine and, 941
wing of, 494
with all nations, 273
Friendships break and bend, if
my, 919
no more do, 963
round its inner wall, 848
Friendship's laws, 220
name, speak to thee in, 336
Frieth in her own grease, 7, 15
Frieze buttress nor coign of vantage, 85
Frigate like a book, no, 585
Fright, perfect, 358
wake in a, 351

Frightful fiend behind him, 315
idea, the most, 641
Frights the isle, 101
Frigid tranquillity, 232
Fringe, lunatic, 734
upon her gown, like, 1050
Fringes raining, slant sunbeams
through the, 418
Fringed curtains of thine eye, 32
pool, 583
with fire, 468
Fringing the dusty road, 525
Fringy edges of the fight, 519
Frisk away like schoolboys, 285
Frittered days, for all the, 881
Frivolity, chatter of irresponsible,
420
how precious is, 856
Frivolous work of idleness, 290
Frocks and curls, 585
read of summer, 936
Frog, eye of newt toe of, 87
in Calaveras county, 615
my lads, be a, 977
outjump any, 615
plaintive piping, 691
the funniest thing 's a. 953
thus use your, 140
Frogs, boys throw stones at,
1006
Frog-rhetoric of the marsh, 889
Frolic, a metaphysical, 898
and the gentle Lamb, the, 305
now for a, now for a leap, 365
pay dear for their, 1040
Frond on frond opening, 920
Fronds, waves its green, 792
Front, deep on his, 150
me no fronts, 946
of battle lour, see the, 286
of Jove himself, 95
of my offending, 100
of this small floor, 165
smoothed his wrinkled, 71
star of resplendent, 418
Frontier, drive the enemy beyond
the, 1061
neighbor-ground, 954
Frontier-grave is far away, 764
Frore, parching air burns, 150
Frost, a killing frost, 73
curdied by the, 76
death's untimely, 286
flowers that skirt the eternal,
316
is on the punkin, 697
itself as actively doth burn, 95
like a bud in the, 389
said a New Year's gift to the
world, 559
slain by arrows of the early,
565
to-night so clear and dead-still,
714
was near, feels like, 840
Frosts, encroaching, 200
Frosty but kindly, 48
Caucasus, thinking on the, 59
day, thunder in a, 172
night, on such a, 911
prairie brightens, 565
Froth and bubble, 601
feigning shall go like, 650
of falsehood, 635
Frouzy or thin, locks, 373
Frown cannot fear me, 240

Frown, foeman's, 474
  is no extinguisher, 510
  never seen without a, 667
  trembled with fear at your, 521
  with a sudden, 620
  yesterday's sneer and, 523
Frowns, her very, are fairer, 387
Frowning providence, 266
Frozen as charity, as, 322
  at its marvellous source, 305
  by distance, 298
  music, architecture is, 1060
  toes, 809
Frozen-hearted, he who was, 654
Frugal is the chariot, how, 585
  mind, she had a, 264
  of my gold, I'm growing, 510
  pastures, on such, 934
  swain, 248
Fruit, cankers root and, 924
  fell like autumn, 178
  from every tree, 735
  from such a seed, 353
  his firstborn, 898
  is golden to the core, 927
  keep clean bear, 170
  let it blossom then bear, 1007
  of all our long endeavor, 659
  of baser quality, 66
  of cultivation, gratitude a, 239
  of loyal nature, manners the, 471
  of memory, in plucking the, 728
  of sense is rarely found, 211
  of that forbidden tree, 148
  ripest, first falls, 59
  takes all my, 820
  that can fall without shaking, 221
  that mellowed long, 178
  thou drop like ripe, 155
  to me, thy seasons bring, 1010
  tree is known by his, 1115
  unheard-of, 807
  weakest kind of, 46
  well, bear, 546
  which I bore was the sun, 1005
  who gave this, 596
  would spring from such a seed, I should have known what, 353
  years mature into, 1084
Fruits, all pleasant, do grow, 121
  by their, ye shall know them, 1114
  kindly, of the earth, 1127
  no, no flowers no leaves, 391
  of love are gone, 358
  of Rome, spent their, 903
Fruit's rich core, 920
Fruit-tree tops, 78
Fruit-trees, fluttering about the, 621
Fruitage thicken as they once did, 459
Fruitful clay, 523
  mind, 112
  of golden deeds, 151
Fruitfulness, mellow, 384
Fruition, crowned with, 254

Fruitless tears, back to, 690
  wishes, torment themselves with, 1052
Frustrate of his hope, 162
Fry, inches o'er the common, 575
  other fish to, 1041
Frye in his owene grece, 7
Frying-pan into the fire, 16, 1034
  talks in the, 823
Fuddled, too, to observe your orders, 198
Fudge, two fifths sheer, 526
Fuel of magnificence, 413
  to maintain in his fires, 140
  to the flame, adding, 157
  was scarce, 917
Fugitive and cloistered virtue, 163
Fujisan, shade of, 692
Ful wel she song the service divyne, 5
Fulfil the entire and holiest, to, 454
Fulfilling of the law, 1119
Fulfilment, no glad, 626
Fulfilments, gleam, sublime, 626
Full age, thou shalt come to thy grave in a, 1102
  are, of life and light, 540
  experiencing it to the, 1087
  fathom five thy father lies, 32
  for sound and foam, too, 472
  little knowest thou, 25
  man, reading maketh a, 111
  many a flower, 245
  many a gem, 245
  my soul is, of whispered song, 540
  of a number of things, 72
  of briers is this working-day world, 48
  of dead men's bones, 1116
  of faith, he was fresh and, 421
  of good works, 1118
  of good-nature as an egg's full of meat, 79
  of grace force fascination, youth, 535
  of honour and years, 431
  of life, 40
  of marble, 613
  of misery, thou art so, 462
  of quarrels as an egg of meat, 79
  of sound and fury, 88
  of spirit as the month of May, 63
  of strange oaths, 49
  of sweet days and roses, 135
  of sweet indifference, 655
  of valour as of kindness, 67
  of wise saws, 50
  peal of praise, wood-world one, 470
  rivers, 587
  round of truth, morning-star to, 471
  serenely, 313
  tide of successful experiment, 273
  well the busy whisper, 251
  well they laughed, 251
  without o'erflowing, 167
Full-blown rose, like a, 383
Full-dazzling, all his beams, 536

Full-grown souls, nurse of, 524
Full-hot horse, anger like a, 72
Full-orbed glory, in, 322
Fuller day, in the light of, 523
  test, we need no, 501
Fully armed, great individual, 537
Fulmin'd over Greece, 156
Fulness like to the sea, 689
  of death, 631
  of perfection, 57
  of your joy, pray in the, 880
Fumes more precious, 848
  sharp, of necessity, 749
Fun grew fast and furious, 287
  keep it for, 833
  of the victory ball, 864
  roared with the, 639
  to match the sorrow, little, 607
  until a toad in, said, 942
  where I've found it, 782
  wish I thought what jolly, 759
  you think he's all, 452
Function, as to a holy, 261
  best memorial beneficent, 753
  of criticism, 772
  paralyzed in every, 551
Functions of government, 628
Functionaries, public, 320
Fund of good sense, 949
Fundament, the deep verbal, 932
Funeral baked meats, 90
  gloom, no, 573, 978
  gone by, a, 692
  grieve at a, 616
  marches to the grave, 433
  mirth in, dirge in marriage, 89
  misbehaved at a, 325
  no tear shed at their, 129
  note, not a, 364
  processions, chop-fallen, 1089
  rites, my, 340
  with mourning, celebrate my, 978
  without a eulogy, 578
Funerals, cowards', 743
  men that truly grieve at, 180
Funny as I can, to write as, 451
  leedle poy, 661
  things that live, 953
  words are few and often, 511
Fur, doctors of the Stoic, 158
  ever blinked in, 888
  fly, make the, 142
  of winter bears, like the, 929
Furs to touch, 894
Furies, fierce as ten, 150
  harpy-footed, 150
Furious blast, 194
  blood escaped, 903
  fickle wheel, Fortune's, 67
  in luxury, 779
  propaganda, 856
  temperate and, 86
  winter blowing, 903
Furlongs of sea, a thousand, 32
Furnace bright, within the, 795
  heat not a, for your foe, 72
  lover sighing like, 49
  the burning fiery, 1113
Furnaces, worship is your, 826
Furnish all we ought to ask, 365
  forth the marriage tables, 90
Furniture is love, his, 585
  like having mahogany, 1068
  too much, 1026

Furor fit læsa sæpius patientia, 174
Furred gowns, robes and, 99
Furrows in my face, no odious, 280
time's, 202
Furrow's end, at the, 683
Furrowed face, his, 513
Furside is the outside, 817
Further and fared worse, 16
Fury, full of sound and, 88
in your words, 103
like a woman scorned, 193
men ne'er spend their, on a child, 71
of a disappointed woman, 193
of a patient man, beware, the, 174
of heard-of things, 903
of their going, in, 667
with the abhorred shears, 159
withstood the winter's, 200
Fur'z you can look or listen, 527
Fuss, they made, how little, 795
without more, 938
Fust in us unused, 96
Fustian is so sublimely bad, 213
Futile classicism, 731
decalogue of mode, 736
Future, anticipate the, 237
Atropos singing of the, 974
days, flight of, 150
dipt into the, 464
enters into us, 1090
favours, sense of, 200
fits us for the, 506
hours, your labor is for, 417
how certain the, is, 534
I thought of the, 320
in league with the, 1076
in the distance, 543
is a world limited by ourselves, 1084
is only the past again, 716
judged by the past, 270, 1028
lies unrolled, 644
life, as for a, 449
life, determine his, 973
like an unwelcome guest, 692
lot, all my, 395
meet the shadowy, 440
of essential democracy, 876
past acclaims our, 634
prophets of the, 361
provident for the, 985
retrospection to the, 278
security for the, 230
sure, the, 303
that lays down the law, our, 1079
the, His mercy shall clear, 626
there is a, 560
trust no, howe'er pleasant, 433
will be a more perfect, man in, 449
yawning void of the, 1011
Futurists, glad young mad young, 795
Futurity, a drudge sold to, 930
casts, shadows which, 318
to all, 1041
Fyr y-reke, in our asshen olde, 6

G shall not be jellified, 952
Gaarge would bwoast, 550

Gaberdine, Jewish, 44
Gabriel! rang Gabriel! sang, 667
the archangel, 668
Gadding vine, the, 159
Gadire or Javan, bound for, 157
Gaels of Ireland, great, 828
Gaffer Death drags me away, 725
Gage, ere we lift the, 806
Gain and bitter loss, O barren, 765
and gain is gain, joy is, 484
better incur loss than make, 978
every way my, 103
fairy gold is all their, 673
is at least some, 966
is it, what, 686
no, except by loss, 560
nobody's, 1022
not base gains, 959
of a few, 217
of man, the steady, 442
of our best glory, 30
one precious, 299
or lose it all, 164
seem here no painful inch to, 519
so fond, are with, 106
that which serves and seeks for, 98
the coast of bliss, 393
the timely inn, to, 87
the whole world, 1115
to die is, 1121
turns his necessity to, 300
unbribed by, 333
unvexed with all the cares of, 206
Gains, base, the same as losses, 959
counts his sure, 306
for all our losses, there are, 565
Gained from heaven a friend, 245
how little I have, 444
Gait if she be walking, for her, 133
ruffling cut-throat, 842
Gal, swing dat yaller, 689
you loves, f'om de, 820
Gals acts so or so, to say why, 527
and cotton bags, he'd have their, 349
Galaxy that milky way, 154
Gale borne to me on every, 562
bow me to the threatening, 561
catch the driving, 208
down he bears before the, 386
dragging in the, 624
it takes a, 784
more than a propitious, 267
note that swells the, 245
partake the, 209
passion is the, 208
scents the evening, 284
so sinks the, 273
squadrons of the, 586
that blew, no, 655
the lightning and the, 450
wafted by thy gentle, 289
weathered the, 1092
Gales that from ye blow, I feel the, 243
Galen ever cured, more killed than, 137

Galilean, O pale, 631
lake, pilot of the, 159
Galileo with his woes, 354
Gall enough in thy ink, 55
Galls his kibe, 97
the infants of the spring, 90
Gallant band, we went a, 455
fisher's life, 140
gay Lothario, 198
ninetieth, tell aught of the, 539
old soldier of Tippecanoe, 404
spirit, many a, 431
steamer Ocean Queen, 605
tars are our, 242
wealthy, always gains, 1022
Gallantry, conscience with, 279
what men call, 358
Galled jade wince, let the, 94
Galleon, a ghostly, 864
that blazing, 801
Galleons of Greece, all the, 805
sucked down, foundered, 851
Gallery country or seaside a, 563
critics, 265
envenoms the play, 726
in which the reporters sit, 377, 397
Galley, Cervantes on his, 827
to-day I leave the, 777
what the devil did he want in that, 1047
Galleys went, over the sea our, 484
Galligaskins long withstood, 200
Galling crown, bowed with a, 808
to a people, nothing so, 398
Gallons, spilt in white, 814
Gallop of verses, 50
Gallops, time, 50
Gallows-foot and after, to the, 783
Gallows-tree, under the, 127
Galoot, last, is ashore, 639
Gamaliel, feet of, 1119
Gambols, where be your, 97
Game above the prize, to love the, 764
and play the, 765
daughters of the, 75
fighting's the, 683
fish swims up stream, 733
hunt for the gunless, 409
I like the, 660
is afoot, the, 737
is only square, 878
is up, 105
little pleasure of the, 189
lost or won the, 401
love nor hatred in the, 1080
nor covet the, 758
of catch as catch can, 246
of goose royal, 251
of right, lose the, 865
of them all, the best, 844
of three, little, 795
rigour of the, 323
savage tribes pursue their, 279
that must be played, 807
to play the, 893
war is a, 266
was empires, whose, 357
Games, or any sinful, 644
rules the, 895
Game-law, moral, 589
Gamefish swims up stream, 865

Gamesome and gallant, not, 936
Gamester, a wise, 967
Gamut of human fears, 824
Gang a kennin' wrang, 285
  aft a-gley, 284
  is all here, hail hail the, 623
  shoot the holl, 526
Gangs, don't join too many, 839
Ganges ripples, where the, 1065
Ganges' side, by the, 639
Gangway for the Lawd God Jehovah, 908
Gaol, we who lie in, 722
Gap, a huge, 961
  in society, leaves a, 331
Garb half hid, in homely, 573
  jester's motley, 851
Garcia, carry a message to, 745
Garden, a peopled, 1058
  a secret, 875
  and greenhouse too, 265
  ask not for a larger, 665
  bird-cage in a, 128
  bloom, leaves that in the, 1021
  can't forget a, 837
  come into the, Maud, 469
  come into thy, 701
  cultivate our, 1052
  fair, go make thy, 573
  feels himself easy in a, 1057
  for Amytis, Babylon's, 956
  God first planted a, 111
  God once loved a, 875
  God the first, made, 168
  in heaven set, 715
  in her face, 121
  in her looks, 168
  in this delightfull, 24
  is a lovesome thing, 583
  makes a desert spot, 820
  nearer God's heart in a, 918
  no, complete without a toad, 582
  o'ergrow the, 69
  of cucumbers, lodge in a, 1110
  of cucumbers, scarecrow in a, 1125
  of flowers, for a, 673
  of girls, the rosebud, 469
  of life, in my, 714
  of old St. Mark, 597
  of Shut-eye town, 699
  of sleep, 633
  of song, 738
  of the Lord, beauty of the, 445
  over old Marm Hackett's, 508
  rocks trees and herbs in a, 1027
  sea is death's, 712
  small house and large, 168
  so she went into the, 246
  the ghost of a, 633
  through this same, 1020
  was a wild, the, 327
  we turn the cow out of a, 235
  when she walked the, 569
  who loves a, 393
  will contain potatoes and pot-herbs, 476
  within a, 820
Gardens above, 271
  and gardening, liking for, 589
  are not made, such, 785
  in the spring, seeing, 875
  leisure that in trim, 160

Gardens of kings, as well as the, 939
  of the desert, 372
  of the night, 669
  our bodies are our, 101
  with their broad green walks, 424
  worms in our, 166
Garden's end, river at my, 214
Garden-close, I know a little, 608
Garden-pot wherein she laid it by, 384
Garden-side, reign by the, 714
Gardener, baffled, 924
  grafts the excellence, 491
  of God, 864
  the grand old, 462
Gardeners, no ancient gentlemen but, 96
  our wills are, 101
Gardener's work, half a, 785
Garfield sat on the other end, 815
Gargoyle often makes his perch, 768
Garish eye, day's, 161
  sun, worship to the, 79
Garland and singing robes, 162
  green willow is my, 11
  immortal, is to be run for, 163
  of the war is withered, 32
  one flower makes no, 137
  to the sweetest maid, 205
Garlands dead, whose, 336
  of flowers dancing elves, 595
  that fell forgot, 848
  to the day, green, 760
  wither on your brow, 141
  would grace a summer's queen, 309
Garlanded Apollo, and, 892
Garlic, eat no onions nor, 43
  Spanish smell I fancy of, 592
Garment, an outworn, 671
  every new and eagerly expected, 498
  in her hand, left his, 1098
  of praise, 1112
Garments fair, 1073
  nothing changed but in my, 99
  of gladness, 1124
  of the night, trailing, 418, 433
  stuffs out his vacant, 58
Garmented in light, 367
Garner, to guard in thy, 590
Garners be full of fruits, 959
Garnered fullness, dropped their, 349
  lore, no, 659
Garnish, eye of heaven to, 58
Garret aloof, live in a, 620
  born in the, 246
  jewels into a, 113
  living in a, 246
  lonesome, 258
Garrick is a salad, our, 252
Garrulous gossip, mention the, 637
Garrulous to the very last, 538
Gars auld claes, 284
  me greet, it, 287
Garter, definition of, 662
  familiar as his, 66
  mine host of the, 34
Garters fast, tie her, 226

Garters, gold amuse, 208
Gas, as much an expedient as lighting by, 450
  smells awful, 919
Gas-pipe down, we're laying a, 952
Gascony, cadets of, 671
Gascoyne, cadets of, 1085
Gashed with wars, rough with age and, 508
Gasp, fight till the last, 68
  follow to the last, 48
Gasworks and at last the heavy, 938
Gat ne'er my gude grey meir again, 11
Gate, after we pass the, 795
  and near the sacred, 481
  built in Jerusalem's wall, Heaven's, 282
  come in the, 710
  dogs don't bite at front, 688
  Heaven's, is shut, 444
  it matters not how strait the, 693
  lark at heaven's, 105
  latch ter de golden, 689
  levels of the eastern, 643
  love the double, 833
  of breath, by the, 631
  of Eden, Peri at the, 337
  of the west, at the, 860
  of the west, the ponderous, 663
  on the king's, 591
  passing through this, 892
  strait is the, 1114
  swing wide, let your, 890
  there at the beautiful, 608
  to the sea, here is the, 913
  what boots it at one, 156
  wide is the, 1114
Gates, beyond to-morrow's mystic, 568
  her ever-during, 154
  lion on your old stone, 462
  of death, pallid, 851
  of glory and of death, 789
  of gold, three, 716
  of heaven a-gleam with pearl, 746
  of heaven, to the, 298
  of Hercules, 658
  of light, unbarred the, 153
  of Luthany, pass the, 749
  of mercy shut, 245
  she claps her wings at heaven's, 23
  sits alone at the, 842
  these narrow, 716
  to Caesar's apartment, 1000
  to lands of pleasure, 711
Gate-post, twixt you me and the, 492
Gateway, massive, 373
  of my heart, 809
  of the eyes, 801
  shall be free, 686
Gateways of the stars, 748
Gath, tell it not in, 1100
Gather a shell from the strown beach, 577
  them in I gather them, 448
  up the fragments, 1118
  ye rosebuds while ye may, 133
Gathered every vice, 215
Gatherer and disposer, 114

Gatherers could not reach topmost apple, the, 960
Gathering her brows, 287
Gathering is growth and decay, tidal, amid the, 372
Gatherings growth and decay, tidal, 895
Gathers no moss, rolling stone, 14, 988
Gatling is jammed and the colonel dead, 765
Gaudy crown of gold, sunflower with, 453
  neat not, 325
  night, let's have one other, 104
  rich not, 91, 325
  show, augments its, 309
Gaul, buckler of the, 779
  to Greece to, 263
Gaunt, old John of, 58
  siege of the citty of, 257
Gauntlet of all zones, run the, 923
  with a gift in 't, 430
Gauze about her loins, 913
Gave to mis'ry all he had, 245
  what we, we have, 1075
Gawain to gaze upon the Grail, 491
Gay, a face that 's anything but, 481
  and fleeting, to loves as, 431
  and ornate, 157
  be not too, temper thy joy, 586
  delights, to deck our girls for, 522
  from grave to, 177, 209
  gilded scenes, 195
  guiltless pair, 364
  it ain't so very, 845
  laugh of pleasure grows less, 405
  life was, 702
  Lothario, haughty gallant, 198
  'nineties were not really, 847
  rhetoric, dear wit and, 158
  than I, more, 394
  to affront the, 927
  would not if I could be, 289
Gayest wreaths are made, hope's, 446
Gayety of nations, eclipsed the, 233
Gayly the troubadour, 388
Gaze and show of the time, 89
  bent his eager, 511
  hid from public, 404
  secure in his, 938
  thou art gone from my, 392
  with all the town, 374
Gazed, and still they, 251
Gazelle, nursed a dear, 338
  with its silvery feet, 395
Gazing at the gleam, 650
  rustics, amazed the, 251
Gear by every wile, gather, 285
Gee, by gosh by gum, by, 921
Geese are flying, when the, 845
  are swans, all our, 123
  are swans and swans are, 547
  flock of, 952
  sailing high, wild, 737
  tending, 924
  the lazy, 903
  wild, are flighting, 778
  will gabble everywhere, 931

Gehenna, down to, 783
Geist, the dachs-hound, 547
Gêlert roam, where does faithful, 294
Gem carbonaceous, 345
  how many a thing becomes a, 574
  of purest ray serene, 245
  of the city's crown, 687
  of the old rock, 145
  upon her zone, the best, 408
Gems, hard twinkle of cut, 933
  of heaven, 152
  of purest ray serene, 607
  of Samarcand, all the, 275
  or gold, richer than, 443
  rich and rare were the, 334
  the starry girdle of the year, 327
  unmined on earth, 889
General defect, 217
  flavor of mild decay, 452
  good captain lost in an ill, 1030
  invitation, here's a, 502
  maxim, nothing is so useless as a, 397
  merit of a, 966
  office and duties of a, 997
  race, but in the, 449
  't was caviare to the, 93
Generals, I do not envy, 535
  Ireland gives England, 576
  or poets or statesmen, we haven't been, 617
Generalities, glittering, 394
Generality of men, the, 975
Generally happens, least expected, 420
Generation, dissenting opinions of one, 943
  fog that may not lift in this, 926
  from generation to, 1079
  men from a former, 339
  of men, lived with one, 998
  of self-salesmanship, 896
  passeth away, 1109
  to benefit another, 979
  to generation, delivered, 196
  will witness, as the next, 528
Generations, a kindness for many, 710
  countless, 857
  enmities of twenty, 399
  honoured in their, 1125
  pass, how the, 857
  succeeding, may be idle, 689
  the cross leads, on, 367
  to the latest, 376
  too long a series of, 421
Generosity, calls extravagance, 253
  such as is possible, 702
Generous, and some chaste, many, 470
  be just before you're, 279
  contribution in support, 949
  giver, 434
  thought, God blesses the, 441
Genevieve, sweet, 638
Genial current of the soul, 245
  feeling, 318
  morn appears, when, 327
Genius, America not a good place for, 614

Genius and mortal instruments, 82
  appearance of a single great, 1078
  aptitude for patience, 379
  as well as a mountain, 1069
  baffled, 594
  bane of all, 368
  capacity for taking trouble, 379
  consummate sense of proportion, 379
  does what it must, 594
  doing what is impossible for talent, 1073
  finds in our every-day words, 625
  fit, one science only will one, 210
  for administration, 693
  for fidelity to old ones, 608
  found respectable, when was, 431
  goes and folly stays, 409
  hath electric power, 404
  is master of man, 594
  is not immortal, 1057
  leaves books as legacies to mankind, 196
  less good from, 521
  light bark of my, 1021
  makes a bad husband and an ill-provider, 413
  man of, 234
  means the transcendent capacity, 379
  must be born and never can be taught, 175
  nearer to the fool, 896
  never travels well-worn paths, 1077
  no, without some touch of madness, 991
  nursing mother of, 476
  of eternity, to the, 432
  of William Hamilton, 823
  parting, is with sighing sent, 161
  personal history of any, 667
  proof of, 397, 892
  sup late, often does, 892
  that power which dazzles, 731
  the faculty of perceiving, 663
  the substitute for, 262
  three fifths of him, 526
  trust to native, 617
  will thrive without training, 476
  work of, 529
Geniuses have the shortest biographies, 412
Gennesareth but Thames, not of, 749
Genteel and refined obliging and cheerful, 394
  known as the shabby, 954
  thing, the, 253
Gentian, God made a little, 585
Gentil dedes, to do the, 7
  herte, priketh every, 5
  knight, a verray parfit, 5
  man, tak him for the grettest, 7
  that doth gentil dedis, 7
Gentiles, light to lighten the, 1117
Gentility, cottage of, 321

Gentle and low her voice, 100
and merciful and just, 373
and simple, rung in ears of, 545
angel, smile on me the, 659
as falcon or hawk, 10
beast, very, 43
breeding, due to, 965
craft, 945
deeds, to do the, 7
dulness ever loves a joke, 215
earth, lie lightly, 130
figure, saw that, 621
he is, he is kind, 567
his life was, 84
I am meek and, 82
in their manner, 521
knight, a verray parfit, 5
lark weary of rest, 106
lights without name, 164
limbs did she undress, her, 315
murmur of a low fountain, 645
peace, carry, 73
rain from heaven, 46
sex, a woman of her, 405
simple or, from vanity fair, 545
sleep nature's soft nurse, 65
spite, bow thy head in, 555
spring, come, 224
yet not dull, 167
Zitella whither away, 387
Gentle-hearted Charles, my, 316
in print, 325
Gentleman and a Christian, 1037
and scholar, 285
born, I was no, 57
caught Whigs bathing, 419
first true, that ever breathed, 115
Gay, said old, 665
grand old name of, 469
he was a, on whom I built absolute trust, 84
in the parlour, 330
is not in your books, 38
is the first, the right honorable, 478
nature puts forth her, 512
never inflicts pain, 403
nomination of this, 97
prince of darkness is a, 99, 164
since I was a, 115
so stout a, 63
soils the spot, 328
that loves to hear himself, 79
the devil is a, 367
to match the best, 499
where everybody is a, 906
writes well for a, 199
young, is indeed deceased, 45
Gentlemen and ladies and lads and girls, 585
cooks are, 123
farmers, 360
God Almighty's, 174
great-hearted, 485
mob of, 214
no ancient but gardeners, 96
not to forget we are, 259
of the French guard, fire first, 941
of the shade, 60
one of nature's, 499
some pious, 639

Gentlemen, the seamen were not, 400
three, at once, 278
unafraid, 777
we have lost, 651
were not seamen, 400
who reach posterity, 419
who wrote with ease, 214
whom do we dub as, 511
whose hair is gray, 847
Gentleness, knows power of, 491
to all mankind, 837
ways of, 747
yet is that giant very, 478
Gently as any sucking dove, 42
do my spiriting, 32
on him, his faults lie, 74
rapping, as of some one, 460
scan your brother man, 285
time has touched me, 280
touch us, time, 350
upon my heart, 440
Genuine and less guilty wealth, 166
power, possesses, 318
provided the article be, 479
work of art, every, 414
Genus a better discerning, liquor gives, 253
define a thing in terms, 886
Geographers in Afric maps, 190
in their maps, 995
Geographical boundaries, morality knows nothing of, 581
Geography, isle in our, 938
Geometric scale, 141
Geometry, no royal road to, 977
George and the cherry tree, 941
died, when Henry, 684
if his name be, 57
never called a waiter, 867
Sand when she met Chopin, 911
says verily and there is no altering him, 170
that swinged the dragon, 57
the Third an honest dullard, 713
the Third was king, when, 358
Washington commanded sun and moon, 228
Georgia booze is mighty fine, 927
Georgian poets, the, 937
Geranium holds its dew, the wild, 806
Germ of first upgrowth of virtue, 524
of the seed has birth, 499
Germs of empires, 726
of it, carry the, 1078
German, conceited, is worst of all, 1076
foot goes seldom back, 500
gives me a cold, 592
heart is stout and true, 500
lacks jealousy, 739
people whisper when they hear the bell, 554
Germans are like women, 1082
glorious in war, 901
have the empire of the air, 376
Germany extends her sway, wherever, 1082
indication of pre-eminence in, 906
Germany's downfall, 799

Germany's later schools, 1076
Gesture, with too much, 895
Gestures, weapons or fancy, 923
Get a man's own, to, 185
money still get money, 118
out of my house, 1041
place and wealth, 214
that I wear, 50
thee behind me Satan, 1115
thee to a nunnery, 93
those eyes so blue, where did you, 559
understanding, 1106
Gethsemane, for Christ, 851
pass somewhere through, 570
some lonely soul's, 570
Gets him to rest, 67
Getting and spending, 300
on, the gospel of, 720
Gettysburg, dog of, 936
or Waterloo, grown a, 772
Ghastly dreams, 71
phantom moon, 536
Ghent, all who slept in, 620
Ghost am I of winds, 681
dear guest and, 439
faithful barking, 858
give up the, 1035
Hosier's injured, 240
of a garden, the, 633
of forgotten actions, 681
of him, I'll make a, 91
of shores, 658
of what was fair, 825
sometimes comes up them, 656
stubborn, unlaid, 158
talk with some old lover's, 117
upon the floor, wrought its, 460
vex not his, O let him pass, 100
was Lancelot, one poor, 685
Ghosts all over the world, 1075
are your haunting, 642
creeping between lines, 1075
into vanishing, 619
'mid the unfriendly, 842
of defunct bodies, 142
of the robins, 621
only, are dead young mothers, 751
true love is like, 1044
Ghoul-haunted woodland of Weir, 461
Giant arms upbear, and men my, 517
branches tossed, 370
Despair, owner whereof was, 172
dies, fling but a stone the, 223
dies, pang as great as when a, 36
earth-worm, like a, 926
eats the, warrior to a crust, 564
frame, man of, 372
hit into a double, making a, 867
limbs uprear'd, 316
lode, you're still the, 929
mass, baby figure of the, 75
mould, a man of, 572
on the shoulders of a, 122, 136, 318
shadow on the wall, 572
shot that kills, 737
the western, 452
tyrannous to use it like a, 36
very gentleness, yet is that, 478

Giants in the earth, 1097
  tall, dwarfs and, 712
Giant's eyesight, 592
  grasp, else in a, 575
  shoulders, on a dead, 592
  strength, excellent to have a,
    36
  unchained strength, 371
Giant-born prowess, 479
Giant-dwarf Dan Cupid, 41
Gibber, squeal and, 89
Gibbets for the man, than cells
    and, 512
  keep in awe, 203
Gibbon, no Gibbon but, 906
Gibes, where be your, 97
Giddy and unfirm, our fancies are
    more, 54
  and unsure habitation, 64
  fortune's furious fickle wheel,
    67
  he that is, 52
  paced times, 54
Gift, back of the, 609
  every good and perfect, 1122
  fellow at a, 965
  heaven's last, 153
  her priceless, 556
  horse in the mouth, 13, 142,
    1025
  is a portion of thyself, 412
  is as a precious stone, 1107
  nature of a, 704
  no richer, 441
  of beauty, the fatal, 354
  of chance, comes by, 983
  of fortune, well-favoured man
    is a, 39
  of friendship, most essential is
    the, 695
  of God, bread sweetest, 1090
  of God, greatest, 887
  of Heaven, good sense the, 210
  of Heaven, moderation the, 967
  of heavenly peace, 924
  of martyrdom, 174
  of nature, great, 1057
  of poesy, heavenly, 175
  of sleep, great, 693
  of strength, 575
  of taciturnity, 694
  of tears, 633
  or a sum of money, 1020
  or grace, surpassing this for,
    427
  sae lang required, 1080
  small, though the, 106
  spirit in which, is offered, 704
  that no philosophy can lift, 304
  the fairies gave me, 673
  to each to charm, 436
  to know it, they have the, 49
  which God has given, 307
  with a little, 977
  without the giver, 525, 879
  woman's, to rain commanded
    tears, 52
  worth more than the, 1043
Gifts, await no, from chance, 546
  even when bringing, 982
  for his lord's, 441
  hiding rich, 567
  honors offices or places, win
    with, 171
  I get, always like the, 812
  I give, love the, 812

Gifts, if you have, 689
  misspent and resolutions vain,
    601
  more of his grace than, 114
  nor gain, neither, 776
  of a bad man, 967
  of God, debauched the, 871
  of the wise ones, 792
  perforce he has given, two, 632
  rich, wax poor, 93
  seven hundred pounds is good,
    34
  than gold, made us rarer, 894
  that fortune sends, 664
  that took all eyes, 409
  to friends, 967
  to range her little, 918
  to thank Thee for these, 554
  well-timed, 1050
Gifted poet, this the most, 516
  with egotistical imagination,
    420
Gift-horse should not be looked,
    1042
Giftie gie us, 285
Gig, crew of the captain's, 622
Gigantic wilful young Chicago,
    806
Gigantically down, death looks,
    459
Gild refined gold paint the lily, 58
  the vernal morn, 267
Gilded and sticky with a little
    sting, 898
  bricks, sold him, 853
Gilead, balm in, 1112
Gilpin long live he, 264
Gilt, dust that is a little, 75
  o'erdusted, more laud than, 75
Gin or brandy, who worships, 578
Gineral C. is a dreffle smart man,
    526
Ginevra, engraven with the name,
    289
Ginger shall be hot in the mouth,
    54
Gingerbread better than I do,
    likes, 458
Gingerly, took up so, 33
Gingham and calico, bits of, 699
  dog went Bow-wow-wow, 699
Gipsy, Dame Fortune is a fickle,
    406
Girdeth on his harness, 1101
Girdle of the year, starry, 327
  round about the earth, 42
  round about the world, 28
Girl, and when I see a, 917
  beautiful English, 624
  don't cry, little, 696
  goes walking, not a, 873
  is mine, and the, 957
  like a frightened, 723
  never mind the, 792
  of Gath, loved a, 855
  sat under a tree sewing, 458
  the silver, 875
  then spoke I to my, 133
  there was a little, 440
  unschooled unpractised, 46
  with teeth of pearl, 510
Girls, be courted in your, 257
  be more than women wise, 131
  between two, 68
  display shocking freedom, 691
  gayest of all gay, 639

Girls, golden lads and, 106
  have curious minds, 430
  he could please, all, 640
  of swaying, 891
  rosebud garden of, 469
  talk about, what do, 824
  to deck our, for gay delights,
    522
  un-idea'd, 233
  were gay, 936
  who wear glasses, 918
  with golden hair, 808
Girl-graduates, sweet, 466
Girth, maned neck of massy, 931
Give a cup of water, to, 386
  a little love to a child, 532
  a man a boat he can sail, 610
  a man a book he can read, 610
  a man a horse he can ride, 610
  a man a pipe he can smoke, 610
  according to that little, 1123
  all thou canst, 304
  ample room and verge enough,
    244
  an inch he'll take an ell, 17
  and take, one must know how
    to, 740
  back the lost delight, 619
  crowns and pounds and guin-
    eas, 742
  every man thy ear, 91
  give, crying, 1109
  him a little earth for charity,
    74
  him always of the prime, 191
  his little senate laws, 213
  it a slight toss over ambient,
    569
  it an understanding, 90
  me a cigar, 358
  me a look give me a face, 119
  me again my hollow tree, 214
  me another horse, 72
  me back my heart, 351
  me but two brigades, 552
  me health and a day, 414
  me liberty or death, 270
  me my childhood again, 595
  me that man, 94
  me the flashing brine, oh, 502
  me the making of the songs,
    186
  me the ocular proof, 102
  me the splendid silent sun, 536
  me three grains of corn mother,
    558
  me to die, 604
  me to live with love alone, 406
  me what this riband bound, 146
  me your hand, 38, 589
  more blessed to, 1119
  my spirit rest, 619
  no inconsiderable sum, 590
  no quarter, to tyrants I will,
    424
  on till he can give no more,
    173
  plenty of what is given, 557
  sorrow words, 88
  than take, better to, 13
  the devil his due, 61
  the soul fit nourishment, to,
    423
  the world the lie, 22
  thee sixpence, I, 293
  them the roll of the drum, 521

Give, they beg, I, 20
　thy thoughts no tongue, 90
　to all nations unity peace, 1127
　to get esteem, they, 249
　to, her features deathless fame, 561
　us grace and strength, 705
　us men from every rank, 561
　us men time demands, God, 522
　what you have, 440
Given, and kindly stars have, 405
　freely, pay too dear for what's, 56
　in vain, true love tho', 470
　of God, grace is, 519
　that way, something, 127
　them the slip, 188
　to him that hath shall be, 1116
　to hospitality, 1119
　to men of middle age, 56
　to redeem the human mind, 434
　unsought is better, love, 55
　us two ears but only one mouth, 420
　you, ask and it shall be, 1114
Giver, God loveth a cheerful, 1121
　keep modest as a, 1079
　thou hast been a generous, 434
Givers prove unkind, 93
Gives, blesseth him that, 46
　he that lends, 138
　much receives but nothing, 246
　the nod, 218
Giveth his beloved sleep, 427, 563, 1106
Giving, godlike in, 334
　just in taking and in, 565
　thy sum of more, 48
Glacial springs, the, 929
Glad and gay because of you, 825
　confident morning, 485
　did I live, 703
　diviner's theme, 173
　father, wise son maketh a, 1107
　for the country lanes, 719
　fulfilment and no sad denial, no, 626
　I must be, 737
　I'm living, mighty, 849
　me with its soft black eye, 338
　of other men's good, 50
　or sad, to be, 594
　shall make thee, 427
　surprise, our hearts in, 436
　that I live am I, 719
　the heart of man maketh, 1105
　to fall away, 223
　would lay me down, 155
Glade, alone in the bee-loud, 790
　peace of the forest, 712
Gladiators' cry, 438
Gladly wolde he lerne, 5
　would I meet mortality, 155
Gladness, for daily, 967
　for the, 854
　learn to serve thee with, 1128
　of the heart, 1125
　on the paths of men, strew, 732
　overflow of, 373
　put on her garments of, 1124
　some with, 576
　taunt with, 952
　that thy brain must know, 366
　youthful poets begin in, 297

Gladsome, it made me, 872
　light of jurisprudence, 21
　thing in the world, most, 750
Glamor day, 892
　of the goldenrod, 882
　pierced the, 751
Glance analytic, with a, 508
　from heaven to earth, 43
　of the mind, how fleet is a, 264
　their many-twinkling feet, 243
　with careful, 954
Glances, are where thy dark eye, 460
Glancing of an eye, upward, 306
Glare, maidens caught by, 352
　of life, sunburnt by the, 430
Glaring sunshine never knew, 442
Glas, clerer than is, 6
Glasgerion swore a full great othe, 257, 782
Glass, broken, in our dry cellar, 899
　darkly, see through a, 1120
　dome of many-coloured, 366
　doth fall, if this, 433
　drink not the third, 135
　excuse for the, she'll prove, 279
　first for myself, 196
　fourth for mine enemies, 196
　green sea's, 632
　he was indeed the, 64
　I take a, 795
　in the full Burgundian, 911
　is at ninety, 637
　is good and a lass is good, 276
　is low, the, 276
　is not large, my, but I drink out of my own, 51
　it's broken, 807
　mist congealing on the, 554
　not through a, 651
　of fashion and mould of form, 93
　of liquid fire, 290
　of the years, 631
　of water, drank rapidly a, 921
　pride is his own, 75
　shaken out the sands of thy, 375
　she made mouths in a, 98
　that ran, grief with a, 633
　third, for good humour, 196
　thou art thy mother's, 107
　too near that, 625
　turn down an empty, 1020
　wherein the noble youth, 64
Glasses, fill all the, 167
　itself in tempests, 355
　on them, set wet, 807
　Shakespeare and musical, 254
　stand to your, steady, 554
Glassy essence, his, 254
Glaze and the mark of china, 673
Glazen shelves, upon the, 900
Gleam, follow the, 472
　of the far-off sail, 327
　on the years that shall be, 426
　some portion of my early, 573
Gleams, and where thy footstep, 460
　of a remoter world, 366
　of star and depths of blue, 442
Gleamed upon my sight, first she, 299
Gleaming lamps of London, 687
　taper's light, 252

Glean and gather after the reapers, 1100
Gleaning of the grapes of Ephraim, 1099
Glee, birds were mad with, 619
　forward and frolic, 308
　innocent, 548
　its own forgotten, 935
　laughed with counterfeited, 251
　songs of a pleasant, 281
Glen, down the rushy, 573
　lilting wildly up the, 291
Glens, no music in the, 721
Glib and oily art, I want that, 98
Glide through a quiet dream, 350
Glides the bonnie boat, 288
Glimmer of dead gray, 807
　on my mind, to, 327
Glimmering and decays, 170
　square, slowly grows a, 466
　tapers to the sun, 280
　through the dream of things, 352
Glimpse divine, is left, nor, 215
　give but a, 240
　of happiness, 147
　of paradise, same old, 746
Glimpses of forgotten dreams, 462
　of notes, 621
　of the moon, 91
　on my sight, sometimes, 442
　that would make me less forlorn, 300
Glisteneth, all is not gold that, 117
Glistering grief, perked up in, 73
　with dew, 152
Glisters, all that, is not gold, 45
Glitter, for sheer, 930
　how much detestable is expressed in, 461
　of their rifles, 372
Glittering aim, take, 586
　eye, with his, 314
　generalities, 394
　knife and a jubilant drum, 925
　like the morning star, 260
　moments, those, 832
Glitters is not gold, all that, 174
Gloaming light, shuddering in the, 620
Gloat on the glaze and the mark, 673
Globe, all that tread the, 371
　annual visit o'er the, 276
　blown about the, 773
　I was thinking this, enough, 537
　in this distracted, 92
　in this world's, 69
　itself shall dissolve, 33
　magnetic current of the, 1068
　on the teeming, 917
　passport round the, 508
　twirls the spotty, 452
Globes, around me myriads of other, 537
Globed, ere systemed suns were, 650
Gloom, brother somewhere in the, 664
　chase my, away, 289
　counterfeit a, 160
　haunts its ruddy, 809
　is soft and the light is dim, 386

Gloom, lead kindly Light amid the encircling, 403
lit our aimless, 826
no funeral, 573, 978
nor tinge with, 403
of clouds, 197
of defeat, 571
of earthquake, 365
of lonesome garret, 258
of night, chases the, 604
shall melt in, 328
tempted her out of her, 461
through hours of, 546
where life began, primal, 682
Glooms, the beetle booms adown the, 696
Gloomy and peculiar, 362
as an author's prospects, 421
calm of idle vacancy, 234
shadowed tower, 705
Glorie, thyn be the, 6
Gloried air, slowness of, 920
Glories float between earth and heaven, 425
gain new, 219
in the dust shall lay, 218
like glow-worms, 127
of a throne, 424
of our blood and state, 141
of the sunset, 625
were purchased, her, 970
Glorify himself, malign opponent and, 420
what else is damned, 223
Glorious and also how painful, 1070
by my pen, 164
by my sword, 164
city in the sea, 289
cry, hounds join in, 229
eye shines on me still, thy, 418
haven, canst not miss a, 1020
in a pipe, tobacco, 358
in arms, 41
morning, full many a, 107
song of old, that, 477
summer, 71
Tam was, 287
to write, 524
war, circumstance of, 102
works, these are they, 153
Gloriously drunk, 266
Glory, agaze at your, 813
air of, walking in an, 170
all, that can be, 873
all that is of, 350
all things give God, 673
among men dies also, 959
an unremaining, 561
and blue air, vortices of, 430
and peace, he died in, 374
and shame of the universe, 1047
and the dream, 301
another sort of, 1029
be the perfect one, if his, 584
but his country's good, no, 374
country's, 307
desire of, 1007
differeth from another in, 1120
do not seek, 312
excess of, obscured, 149
for all time, 924
from his gray hairs gone, 442
full meridian of my, 73
full-orbed, 322

Glory, glittered with a, 696
go where, waits thee, 334
gown of, 22
guards with solemn round, 541
have drown'd my, 1019
his food was, 401
hoary head is a crown of, 1107
honour praise and, 199
in a great mistake, 939
in a sea of, 73
in one day doth fill the stage, whose, 135
in outstripping donkeys, no, 995
is all moonshine, its, 542
is departed from Israel, 1100
is in their shame, whose, 1121
is like a circle in water, 68
is that bright tragic thing, 585
jest and riddle of the world, 208
leads the way, 186
left him alone with his, 364
like a shooting star, 59
long has made the sages smile, 359
lose all their, when he flies, 338
love of, 197
man the wonder and the, 448
most desirous of honour and, 1049
never sung, a, 445
no need at all of, 1000
no path of flowers lead to, 1046
nothing so expensive as, 312
of a creditor, 35
of a representative, 259
of action, 953
of an April day, the uncertain, 33
of eternal partnership, 807
of far-off mountains, 327
of God, heavens declare the, 1103
of his wings, 922
of man, to the, 789
of the coming of the Lord, 522
of the Creator, 112
of the house, 953
of the Lord is all in all, 561
of the sun will be dimmed, 687
of the universe, 448
of the west, 642
of the winning, 575
of their times, were the, 1125
of this world, vain pomp and, 73
one shame and one, 526
or despair, 395
or the grave, rush to, 328
passed from the earth, 301
path of duty the way to, 467
paths of, lead to the grave, 244
pristine, 396
rainbow's, 368
Rome in the height of her, 341
set the stars of, 382
shall not descend, 960
share the, in many eyes, 77
shows the way, 186
shut with us, too much, 903
slide into, 831
sons of France, awake to, 1059
sudden, is the passion, 132
that belongs, share of, 1023

Glory that was Greece, 460
that we wrestle so valiantly, oh, 458
the quickly faded, 822
the robings of, 571
the shadow and the, 443
the whole earth is full of his, 1111
they talk of England's, 845
this, and this grief, 531
this gain of our best, 30
to be followed by pestilence, 1067
to God in the highest, 1116
to her, it is a, 1120
trailing clouds of, 301
trod the ways of, 73
vain pomp and, 73
visions of, 244
waits ye, this goin' ware, 526
was their dream, 848
who walked in, 297
who works for, 719
with a, in His bosom, 522
Glory's morning-gate, 473
page, rank thee upon, 333
small change, 1069
thrill is o'er, 334
who sleep on, brightest, 386
Gloss of art, than all the, 251
on faint deeds, set a, 80
Glossary necessary to understand Chaucer, 886
Glossy cherished anthracite, 911
cope, his, 629
surface, fine, 253
Gloucester wave, breaks in every, 677
Glove, her torn veil, her, 828
O, that I were a, 78
Gloves not black nor yet too light, 451
too big for white-kid, 927
wear seemly, 451
Glow changeless through joy, 416
flushes up a rosy, 926
of a kindly heart, 676
of brotherhood, 381
sunbeams' golden, 562
through the silver, 865
trembles at the fiery, 1071
waking a, 479
Glowered, amazed and curious, 287
Glowing life of its own times, 710
like chrysophrase, 432
mind of all endeavor, 889
more fervent, 686
Glows in every heart, 202
Glow-worm lend thee her eyes, 134
shows the matin to be near, 92
Glow-worms, glories like, 127
Glozed the tempter, 154
Glum nor merry, a comrade neither, 757
Gluts twice ten thousand, 385
Glutted market, 217
Glutton the idler and the fool, the, 834
Gluttony and drunkenness hunger and thirst, 1045
Glynn, liberal marshes of, 663
Gnat, strain at a, 1115
Gnats in our chambers, 166
Gnawing of a mouse, 916

Go ahead, be sure you are right
  then, 349
and do thou likewise, 1117
and I'll not, 610
and sin no more, 1118
boldly forth my simple lay, 275
bow thy head in gentle spite,
  555
by, the silent stars, 612
call it madness, 289
can't remember how they, 590
dine and dress, let the world,
  406
down to the sea in ships, 1105
forget me, 365
forth to seek, 834
forth under the open sky, 371
his halves, I'll, 1025
in, those without would, 115
into it baldheaded, 526
litel book, 4
little booke, 868
lovely rose, 146, 788, 868
my songs to the lonely, 886
no more a-roving, 357
on forever, but I, 465
out, those within would, 115
poor devil get thee gone, 241
shall I bid her, 256
sir gallop and don't forget,
  1060
soul the body's guest, 21
that the devil drives, 53
think of it in silence and alone,
  424
to grass, 131
to the ant thou sluggard, 1106
to the dreamless bed, 446
we know not where, 36
west young man, 505
when the morning shineth, 480
where glory waits thee, 334
where he will the wise man,
  410
whither thou goest I will, 1099
whom the devil doth drive, 17
with fainting steps they, 251
ye therefore and teach all nations, 1116
Goa where munny is, 467
Goad, with a sharp and ready,
  686
Goads, words of the wise as,
  1110
Goal, do not turn back just at
  the, 988
drives you to fair Wisdom's,
  1084
in sight, keep your, 868
meeting strangely at one sudden, 597
misses oft the, 719
must be thy, 1009
not on the prize, on the, 735
of ill, final, 468
onward to his, 444
passes life's, 966
pilgrimage and, 873
set by the, 309
the grave is not its, 433
the sky your, 957
we still shall gain, 562
when they reach the, 655
ye win, till the, 454
Goals, muddied oafs at the, 780
Goat, thou bringest the, 960

Go-between through Thee their,
  1022
Gobble-uns 'll git you, 696
Goblet, broke is the, and wasted
  the wine, 447
found growing on the wild, 431
inscription on, 1068
parcel-gilt, 64
God a necessary Being, 172
abides, 654
above is great to grant, 485
above or man below, 207
ain't a bed of roses, bein', 908
all things are possible to, 548
allots to each, time, 1078
Almighty first planted a garden, 111
Almighty has hung out a sign,
  342
Almighty's gentlemen, 174
alone knows now, 1077
alone, leaves us, 444
an atheist half believes a, 202
an attribute to, 46
an honest, 603
and all the attributes, 1048
and do the right, trust in, 499
and hold me, be a, 485
and I both knew once, 1077
and Mammon, cannot serve,
  1114
and man decree, let, 743
and nature together shaped,
  642
and nature with actors fill, 129
and right our standard, 954
and the angels, believe in, 639
and the soldier, 698
and woman, faith in, 587
and your native land, 362
announced themselves descended from a, 343
answers sudden on some prayers, 430
arose from His throne, 813
as lightning does the will of,
  348
assumes the, 176
at all, who think not, 156
attribute to, 46
autograph of, 658
backed with, 70
be for us, if, 1119
be praised, 69
be praised, who ne'er cry, 428
be thy guide, 881
be thy shade, 881
be wasting a dog like Tim, 875
be with you, 1021
be with you Balliol men, 809
beginning mean and end, 506
beheld you, as if, 990
beholds, only my wrathful, 931
beside, there is no, 1057
best by remembering, 780
bless no harm in blessing, 221
bless the king, 221
bless the little church around
  the corner, 579
bless the man who first, 510
bless the Prince of Wales, 392
bless the train, 890
bless them all, 693
b'ess us all, 221
bless us every one, 495, 696
bless you, my dear, 238

God blesses still the generous,
  441
blundering back to, 738
bosom of his, 245
bosom of, the seat of the law,
  22
bring us farther from, 899
bring you to a fairer place,
  875
builds a church to, 210
built, a church, 263
but this thing is, 633
by searching find out, 1102
can give no more, even, 840
can't be always everywhere,
  597
can't kill them when they're
  said, 180
caught his eye, by and by, 927
clad the country, 759
comes down in the rain, 763
conceived the world, 508
conscious water saw its, 165
could hardly love and be wise,
  a, 987
created woman, 1082
dear to, and famous to all ages,
  162
declare the glory of, 1103
defend the right, 69, 561, 765
deigns not to overthrow, 886
delights in an odd number,
  389
designed us to live in society,
  1053
did all the work, 757
dishonour of, 179
disposes, man proposes but, 8,
  136
does more for, 657
does not pay Saturdays, 491
does not send strange flowers,
  560
doth not slumber, 832
doorkeeper in the house of my,
  1105
due reverence to, 112
erects a house of prayer, wherever, 187
eternal years of, 373
even vainly is a, 1066
every common bush afire with,
  431
every, did seem to set his seal,
  95
excellent angler now with, 140
favours the heaviest battalions,
  1053
feared, and eschewed evil, 1101
first planted a garden, 111
follows nature up to nature's,
  200
fool hath said there is no, 362
fools call nature what I call,
  491
for dappled things, glory to,
  672
for sleep, thank, 794
for thee, if there is no, 841
for us all, 18
forbid, 1119
forbid that I should glory,
  1121
fortune is a, 963
found stronger than death, no,
  631

God, freedom to worship, 370
from thee we spring, great, 231
from whom all blessings flow, 183
fulfils himself in many ways, 463
further from, 13
gave a loaf to every bird, 585
gave the increase, 1120
gave them love, 840
gave them youth, 840
give each moment to, 225
give me love and care, 955
give such dawns, 858
give thee fruit of thy reading, 1020
give them wisdom, 54
give us men from every rank, 561
give us men time demands, 522
gives light in darkness, 69
gives us daylight, 431
gives us love, 463
gives wind by measure, 138
giveth His beloved sleep, 427, 563, 1106
glory, all things give, 673
go with you, 875
good to Indiana, ain't, 824
grace is given of, 519
grant beneath the desert stars, 881
grant that twice two be not four, 1072
grant to my country and Europe in general, 284
grant you find one face, 523
had I but served my, 74
had set upon his head, 698
had sifted three kingdoms, 436
has a few of us whom he whispers, 489
has given you one face, 93
hath a temple, where, 126
hath joined together, 1115
hath made man upright, 1109
hath made them so, 198
have mercy on the sinner, 903
have mercy on this sot, 940
he kept them, by, 774
he thinks that I am, 597
he walks with, 671
heavens declare the glory of, 1103
help the horse, 877
help those who pass that moment, 1085
help thyself and, will help thee, 137
helps them that help themselves, 227
helps those who help themselves, 170
her fathers', before her, 310
himself, a bit of, 892
himself can't kill them, 677
himself scarce seemed to be, 315
his life a breath of, 506
I believe in, 1061
I saw, 877
I want to be forgotten by, 484
I will find, 666
if, in His wisdom have, 577
if some lesser, 471
if this were enough, 703

God if Thou livest, 918
if You wish for our love, 887
in apprehension how like a, 92
in clouds, sees, 207
in faces of men I see, 535
in him, she for, 152
in His wisdom created them all, 570
in his wisdom, if, 577
in his works and word, 200
in me is, 811
in the star in the stone in the flesh, 486
incomprehensibility of, 1067
is a gallant foe, 886
is an unutterable sigh, 738
is and all is well, 444
is God, since, 503
is grateful and knowing, 1126
is in his heaven, 444, 485
is living working still, 502
is love, 452, 477, 1123
is near, none but, 306
is not, cannot be where, 648
is not willing to do everything, 1023
is on the side, 853
is one God, your, 1126
is our refuge, 1104
is our trust, in, 332
is overhead, 638
is the only mind, 548
just are the ways of, 156
justify the ways of, 148
keep you dearest, 671
keeps an open house, 757
knowing that, 952
label men for, 749
laid down His life, 686
laughs in heaven, 429
lead us past, 858
learned to fear, 407
let us worship, 284
looked down and smiled, 755
loves an idle rainbow, 816
loves, those that, do not live long, 138
loveth a cheerful giver, 1121
loveth not the speaking ill, 1127
made a heart of gold, 844
made a little gent'an, 585
made all the creatures, 486
made and eaten all day long, 488
made him let him pass, 44
made his grave, 372
made it for this man, 1071
made man frail as a bubble, 767
made memory cruel, 774
made the country, 111, 264, 759
make thee beautiful within, 442
make them dream, 693
make us better men, 864
make our blunders wise, 858
makes all things good, 1054
makes such nights all white, 527
man think himself an act of, 506
marble leapt to life a, 363
may be had for the asking, 525
may meet, with, 408
might have bade the earth, 394

God, mighty fortress is our, 1023
moves in a mysterious way, 266
my father and my friend, 180
nature is the art of, 144, 202
necessary to invent, 1052
never changeth, 438
never sends the mouth, 12
no, dare wrong a worm, 409
noblest work of, 208, 284
not worshipped by the herd, 834
O, a sweet good-will, 620
obedience to, 945
obligeth no man, 1127
of Abraham, 166
of battles Lord of might, 845
of fair beginnings, 778
of heaven it is all one, with the, 1125
of love was born, before the, 117
of music dwelleth out of doors, 714
of my idolatry, 78
of nature has placed in our power, 270
of sleep, Morpheus, 3
of storms, give her to the, 450
of the granite and rose, 570
of the stars, 895
of things as they are, 779
on our side, 321
on the side of the heaviest battalions, 271, 1053
on whom each one depends, 597
once loved a garden, 875
one, and no more, 271
one law one element one, 469
one that feared, 1101
one that would circumvent, 96
only, can make a tree, 890
only, he for, 152
only knows, 717
only knows which is which, 634
only who made us rich, 429
or devil, every man was, 174
or something very like Him, 519
others call it, 737
our mind is, 1006
our souls at home with, 523
out of knowledge, 663
passed the days with, 201
planted a garden, 633
plays upon this string first, 172
powers ordained of, 1119
put another in for luck, 763
put your trust in, 329
reason and the will of, 548
reigns and the Government lives, 591
rest ye merry gentlemen, 567
rest you happy gentlemen, 875
rest you merry innocents, 935
round fat oily man of, 225
said I am tired of kings, 409
said what did you do, 813
sanction of the, 218
save the king, 189, 921
save the king, and the people shouted, 1100
save the mark, 61
save the people, 338

God saw light was good, 154
scourge of, 374
security of a, 109
send his hail, unless, 484
send thee good ale enough, 20
sendeth and giveth, 19
sends a cheerful hour, 162
sends meat, 19
sent his singers, 436
servant of, well done, 153
service greater than the, 75
service ranks the same with, 485
setteth the solitary in families, 1104
shall hear your words, 718
shall raise me up, 22
she for, in him, 152
should give me a choice, 796
should punish men, if, 1127
sifted a whole nation, 179
signs and steps of a, 618
silent voice of, 688
sits all the year, where, 827
sleeps in the stone, 486
so loved the world, for, 1118
so near is, to man, 409
speed that surely dawning day, 954
speed the mark, 408
speed the plough, 512
spirit shall return unto, 1110
stern daughter of the voice of, 299
sufficeth, 438
summons him, until, 970
sunflower turns on her, 335
tempers the wind, 242
temple built to, 138
that doomed us, the same, 578
that gave the power divine, 756
that hath made all these things, 1124
the eternal fount of all, 1023
the Father God the Son, 199
the first garden made, 168
the herdsman, 790
the soul, 207
the Spirit three in one, 199
the varied, these are but, 224
the world and love, 617
thou great democratic, 531
thought which keeps thee from thy, 403
thoughts of, 427
through darkness up to, 468
thy God my, 1099
thy friend, who passeth all the rest, 19
to angel His new heaven, 650
to be nearer, 656
to ruin designed, 175
to scan, presume not, 207
to take in, 526
to the unknown, 1118
up to nature's, 209
upon the ocean, is n't, 508
vindicate the ways of, 206
walks in Dublin, if, 875
walks in mine, 583
wash the world, 886
we trust in, 332
we trust, may the, 821
were back, wish that, 767
whate'er we leave to, God does, 513

God, who builds a church to, 210
who gave us life, 273
who gave your very, 657
who is not we see, 634
who is our home, 301
who made boys, 759
who made thee mighty, 761
whom we see not is, 634
whose, is their belly, 1121
will be with His people, 141
will bring you all back, 1126
will help thee, 1045
will not put strange signs, 560
wills but ill the doubter said, 539
wills that it continue, if, 457
wills us free, 272
wish is like a prayer with, 430
wished for a buttercup, 693
wishes to destroy, those whom, 968
wisheth none should wreck, 119
won't and we can't mend it, 519
wove a web of loveliness, 841
wrestled with him, 140
wrote the bill, as if, 409
Gods, a thousand false, 752
alone, to the, 966
approve the depth, 303
are just, the, 100
are old, forget the, 687
are we bards saints, 545
arrive, when half-gods go, 409
before these weapons of the, 969
but me, have no other, 1098
call adultery, 358
call dross, men call treasure, 528
call Lord Houghton Dicky Milnes, 458
daughter of the, 463
dish fit for the, 82
don't allow us to be in their debt, 509
dwells with, above, 75
fade, 654
fast doth diet oft with, 160
for giving, generous, 693
for themselves are monuments enough, 612
fulfill, the, 858
greets the embarrassed, 778
had made thee poetical, 50
had special advertisement to impart, 184
help them, 962
how he will talk, 186
it doth amaze me, 81
kings it makes, 72
labour of the, 212
little tin, 776
love, whom the, 360
of Asia and Africa, to the, 1118
of the copybook maxims, 785
of the market place, 785
of the place, worship the, 126
on the knees of the, 958
once more, 964
one of the immortal, 330
out of their skies, hurled the, 1045
pleased to see great men contend with adversity, 124
provide thee, the good the, 176

Gods returned to earth, 889
right idea of the, 975
see everywhere, 436
sent not corn for rich men only, 76
so many creeds, so many, 718
strive for him, 967
temples of his, 400
the gift of, 26
themselves throw incense, 100
there are no, 975
they knew, reached Him through the, 755
they serve the vintage that they drink, 775
to reverent youth, 984
to witness, call the, 80
unfold so many, 653
utterance of the early, 384
voice of all the, 41
were good to you, 631
whatever, may be, 632
when the favor of the, 969
wish to punish, when the, 724
woman is a dish for the, 105
would destroy, whom the, 175
God's Acre, burial ground, 434
aim, to serve, 575
altar trod, one nearer to, 165
angel undefiled, 474
anvil stands, 706
art, nature is, 506
battlefield, rides, 891
blessing, out of, 16, 1034
breath upon the flame, 1071
critters tempting decent men, 750
earthly power show likest, 46
eldest daughter, light, 147
essence, 617
eternal word, rock of, 305
fingers touched him, 469
first temples, the groves were, 372
goodness and mysterious ways, 922
grand greenwood chapel, 626
great judgment seat, 779
great pictures, 445
great universe, 562
greatness flowed around, 428
Green Inn, rest in, 829
hand drawn, by, 756
hand through a lifetime, 486
hand, we are in, 67
heart, nearer, 918
help and their valour, with, 1061
holiest charge, 248
image, man, 162
instant men call years, 491
interminable day, 504
keeping, in, 626
messenger, employed to write, 346, 511
mill grinds slow, 138, 435
name, produce it in, 380
own chosen weather, 693
own mould, 604
patience, abusing of, 34
patience and His wrath, 395
peculiar light, 1023
plenty, here is, 179
poor, the birds, 438
quiet, taste, 834
residence is next to mine, 585

God's right hand and left, 506
  side, one is a majority on, 479
  skirts, caught at, 487
  sons are things, 232
  thy country's, and truth's, 74
  ways seem dark, 442
  ways to man, justify, 743
  will be done, 272
  works, last and best of all, 155
God damned phrases, 852
Goddamm, sing, 886
Goddess blind, the, 67
  constant and glad, to keep the, 620
  like a thrifty, 35
  night sable, 201
  of efficiency, 910
  of Liberty came, 271
  she moves a, 218
  sing, heavenly, 218
  slipped in three blessings, 294
  write about it and about it, 215
Godfathers of heaven's lights, 40
God-given rights inherent, I see, 424
  trait common sense, 580
Godheads, even old, 851
Godlike forehead, the, 305
  hours, hath not known his, 299
  in giving, 334
  is it all sin to leave, 435
  reason, capability and, 96
  seeds of, power are in us, 545
  to create, wise to learn, 511
Godliness, cheerful, 298
  cleanliness next to, 226
  the crown of the house, 953
God-send a benefit received, 323
Goes against my stomach, 50
  day, by like a shadow, 567
  honest as this world, 92
  out of fashion, bravery never, 484
  to bed sober, 127
  to bed wi' the sun, 56
  to the wall, weakest, 77
Goeth a-borrowing, 19
Goethe at Weimar completed Faust, 438
  has done his pilgrimage, 546
Go-ethe, Shake Mulleary, 715
Goethe's sage mind, 546
Goin' 'ware glory waits ye, this, 526
Going down of the sun, 1105
  down the wind, 181
  guest, speed the, 213
  hence, men must endure their 100
  home, I am, 408
  home like going to render an account, 727
  lingered in my, 873
  looketh well to his, 1107
  no use at all in my, 389
  of time, marketh the, 449
  reading-machine wound up and, 526
  the way of all flesh, 128
  the way of all the earth, 1099
  to keep us and so good-day, 607
  upon the order of your, 87
Gold, a good heart's worth, 64
  a mint of, 292
  a shower of, 381

Gold, age of, 161
  all Bocara's vaunted, 275
  all is not, that doth golden seem, 24
  all is not, that glisteneth, 117
  all that glisters is not, 45, 1041
  all that glitters is not, 174
  almighty, 119
  and amber shore, 744
  and bramble-dew, 703
  and lands, she brought him, 941
  and mother-o'-pearl, amidst its, 1085
  and no such pearl, no such, 624
  and pleasure, youth love, 455
  and purple thoughts, 938
  and silver, curst be the, 247
  and silver light, 790
  and silver, looking for, 512
  and silver not the only coin, 968
  apples of, 1108
  as a jewel of, 1107
  as good as, 495
  ballasted with, 870
  bar of heaven, 577
  barbaric pearl and, 149
  bathe the hills in melancholy, 418
  beauty provoketh thieves sooner than, 48
  better to me than, 655
  black with tarnished, 288
  bow of burning, 282
  bright and yellow, 391
  cemented with, 956
  clad in blue and, 288
  clasps, book in, 77
  comes round the age of, 477
  despise, what female can, 243
  evening trails her robes of, 418
  fairy, 56
  find them lined with, 836
  fire the test of, 991
  fools' gold, we quarry for, 929
  from here to Babylon, 845
  gateways of the stars, 748
  gild refined, paint the lily, 58
  give our, 750
  gives only the worthless, 525
  gleaming in purple and, 356
  gold gold gold, 391
  great gates of, 653
  harmless, 525
  he loved, in special, 5
  I'm growing frugal of my, 510
  in bright, 384
  in cofre, but litel, 5
  in itself so useless a thing, 10
  in ph'sik is a cordial, 5
  in the realms of, 384
  in the world, plenty of, 502
  into a shower of, 23
  is fair, rank is good and, 443
  is the kindest, 960
  left of the Caesars', 841
  less account than fairy, 754
  locks of, 681
  manner not, 976
  missing the, 893
  more to be des'red than, 1103
  narrowing lust of, 469
  no acid test, give your, 844
  once was singing, 883
  or gear, wait for, 628

Gold, patines of bright, 47
  pioneering for, 859
  plating from the chains of matrimony, 801
  poop was beaten, 104
  ring so thin is yet of, 280
  road whose dust is, 154
  ruste, if, 5
  saint-seducing, 77
  soil no, 395
  some blessed threads of, 501
  strive not for, 814
  sunflower with gaudy crown of, 453
  that dull bronze seems, 597
  that shyneth as the, 8
  the goose could give, 962
  thombe of, had a, 5
  three gates of, 716
  thrice their weight in, 288
  to airy thinness, 118
  trodden, 149
  truth purer than the purest, 119
  turning to, 574
  unfolding those portals of, 387
  upon a cross of, 753
  weighs truth with, 215
  whose dust is, 154
  whose gift was, 792
Gold-bright morning gleams, 417
Golden age behind him, 529
  Age is not a fable, 445
  age that first was named, 25
  age, the, 32, 984
  age, their lot has fallen with a, 400
  Age upon the earth, 984
  apples of the sun, 790
  bells, mellow wedding bells, 460
  bowl be broken, 1110
  bullet beats it down, 109
  care, 65
  corn, heap high the, 441
  days, hand in hand in the, 395
  days of good Queen Bess, 186
  deeds, fruitful of, 151
  deeds, years of, 471
  exhalations of the dawn, 318
  goblet found growing, 431
  guess is morning-star, the, 471
  hour, once in a, 574
  journey, we make the, 882
  joy in a silver mirth, 610
  joys, Africa and, 65
  Junes and bleak Decembers, 690
  keys, clutch the, 468
  kisses over the cheeks of the meadow, 500
  lads and girls, 106
  lamps in a green night, 169
  languor, summer's, 692
  letters, should be set in, 57
  locks, his, 27
  mean, 267
  mechanical hammer, 933
  mind stoops not, a, 45
  moments quick to haste, 474
  numbers, add to, 116
  oars, cut with her, 39
  olden glory of the days gone by, 973
  opes the iron shuts amain, the, 159

Golden opinions, I have bought, 85
orb of perfect song, 429
paths, you trod, 837
pen, traced with his, 516
prime of Haroun Alraschid, 462
Rule, act the, 695
rule, guided by this, 623
rule works like gravitation, 679
seem, gray things, 650
seeme, that doth, 24
silence is, 380
sorrow, wear a, 73
story, locks in the, 77
suns and silver rain, 581
time of long ago, 626
troop of birds, 847
window of the east, 77
world, as they did in the, 47
youth is lying, 867
Golden-rod a fairy magical flower, 476
glamour of the, 882
shriveled stalks of, 843
Golden-tongued apostle, 813
Gold-fish in a glass bowl, 812
Goldsmith foolish without a pen, 237
here lies Nolly, 243
wrote better than any man, 236
Goldsmith's jasmine flowers, 716
Golfer, like the old Scotch, 923
Goliath, assisted David in slaying, 1056
tall, like, 564
Gone, and forever, thou art, 308
and past help, what 's, 56
before, not dead but, 289
before, not lost but, 188, 447
before, souls, 627
coon, I'm a, 349
far away, 587
for ever, I am, 56
further and fared worse, 16
now thou art, 159
one on an endless voyage, 568
the day is, 385
to the demnition bow-wows, 494
with the wind, 1105
Gonfalon bubble, pricking our, 867
Gong is sounding, 893
Good action by stealth, do a, 324
all are presumed, 138
all that once was, 887
all things work together for, 1119
always, but the, 966
Americans when they die, 454
and bad angel, 122
and crown thy, 737
and evil, shared much, 237
and great, proclaim him, 194
and ill, share with you its, 443
and ill together, 53
and the bad, two nations, 169
apprehension of the, 59
are always the merry, 791
are better made by ill, 289
are so harsh, 942
as a feast, enough is, 18, 29
as a nod, wink as, 593
as a play, 940

Good as gold, 495
as hurt, produce as much, 271
as I kin be, I'm as, 699
as she was fair, she was, 289
at a fight, 334
at sudden commendations, 74
bad indifferent, can be, 1048
—bad—indifferent, 241, 280
be each man's rule, 463
be out of the world, as, 193
befriend himself by doing, 966
beginning good end, 14
bodes me no, 206
book is the best of friends, 478
books however, 280
but pine, the, 941
by being ungenerous, we get no, 429
by nature, 26
by stealth, do, 214
cannot come to, 90
captive, 107
cheer, play and make, 19
cheer the best of healers, 964
children should never be lazy, 431
clever men are, 376
company and good discourse, 140
company in a journey, 139
conscience, 43
considers his own, 973
critics who have stamped out, 430
cry to a woman, 425
day, sir critic, 508
dealt by the eternal hand, 1021
deed, dying tongueless, 56
deed in a naughty world, 47
deed, kind of, to say well, 73
deeds, by great thoughts and, 506
die first, the, 302, 978
digestion wait on appetite, 87
discerns the good, only the, 429
do you a world of, 1041
every evil its, 411
evil and, are God's right hand, 506
evil be thou my, 151
felawe, he was a, 5
fellow, he's a, 1019
fellow Robin, 164
fellows, assembly of, 232
fellows get together, when, 771
fellows, king of, 5
fellows together, we're all, 276
fellowship in thee, 61
fences make good neighbors, 837
few know their own, 177
folly that seeks through evil, 443
for a million more, 843
for good-for-nothing people, 430
for her, and that was, 678
for our country's, 281
for sore eyes, 191
for us to be here, 1115
fortune, diligence mother of, 1041
fortune, great pieces of, 228
fortune means to men most, 58
fortune will elevate, 999
from seeming evil educing, 224

Good from the heart of a man, 639
glad of other men's, 50
gods! how he will talk, 186
gray head, oh, 467
great and joyous, 367
great man inherits, how seldom a, 317
hand that made you fair made you, 37
hater, he was a, 238
heart is better than all heads, 426
heart's worth gold, a, 64
hold fast that which is, 1121
hold thou the, 468
I do all the, I can, 623
I do love my country's, 76
I know, all the, 916
ill wind blows no man to, 65
ill wind turns none to, 19
ill-gotten is nobody's gain, 1022
in everything, 48
in that I wrought, 783
in the worst of us, so much, 657
intentions, hell paved with, 662
interred with their bones, 83
is as, as infinite, 379
is good from east to east, 657
is mine, your, 778
it is always, 129
it is not enough to do, 641
kill a man as good book, 162
know what were, to do, 44
lectures can do so much, 235
leisure to make, 38
life, who leads a, 276
likely not so, 777
little, watering last year's crops, 520
love him because he is, 1084
love sought is, 55
luck in odd numbers, 35
luck is the gayest, 639
luck shall fling her old shoe, 465
luck would have it, 35
luxury of doing, 187, 249, 280
makes his promise, 185
man prolongs his life, 995
man's feast, sat at a, 49
man's life, best portion of, 295
man's love, thank heaven for a, 50
man's sin, 327
man's smile, 251
means of evil out of, 148
men and true, are you, 39
men like to make the public stare, 359
men must associate, 259
men not so absolute in, 386
men were only better, if, 648
more of moral evil and of, 295
morning, bid me, 273
morning, only a glad, 689
mouth-filling oath, 62
my stomach is not, 20
name better than precious ointment, 1109
name, filches from me my, 102
name in man and woman, 102

Good name is rather to be chosen, 1108
nature more agreeable than wit, 196
near approach to, 229
neighbour is fatal sometimes, 430
never shall be one lost, 489
never, to bring bad news, 104
news baits, 157
news from a far country, 1108
night and joy be wi' you, 291
night, my native land, 352
night, my old Kentucky home, 567
night! no night is good, 580
night, say not, 273
night till it be morrow, 78
night, to each a fair, 308
no glory but his country's, 374
noble to be, 't is, 462
nor aught so, 78
not a politician other habits, 606
not, that man should be alone, 1097
not too bright or, 299
nothing, or bad. 92
notion is lost, by which means many a, 171
of all, greatest, 1049
of his country, 1061
of my country, 201
of themselves, hearkners seldom hear, 188
oft interred with their bones, 83
old age, in a, 1097
old cause, beauty of the, 298
old colony times, 954
old man he will be talking, 39
old rule, the, 298
old-fashioned but choicely, 140
old-gentlemanly vice, 359
old times, 357
old times the grand old times great old times, 495
opinion of the law, 277
or evil side, 524
or evil times, 110
or ill of man, 1007
or ill we choose, things of, 572
or whether bad, depends, whether, 505
orators when they are out, 51
out of infinite pain, 663
overcome evil with, 1119
parent of, 153
part, hath chosen that, 1117
partial evil universal, 207
patriots who for a theory, 430
people all with one accord, 252
people were clever, if all, 942
pleasure ease content, 208
report and evil report, 1121
saw the little that is, 536
see speak hear but the, 752
sense the body of poetic genius, 318
sense the gift of heaven, 210
sense travels, 1077
set terms, 49
smell of old clothes, 894
so much to the, 983
society, no lack of, 437
some said it might do, 171

Good, some special, 78
spirits, any man may be in, 495
statesmen who pulled ruin, 430
stomach excels them all, 184
stomachs that would fall to, 163
sword rust, 317
temper when, in good spirits and, 495
that call evil, 1111
that I can do, 543
that I would I do not, 1119
that is not evil, no, 670
the gods provide thee, 176
the law is, 1121
the more communicated, 153
the second is, 1023
the true the beautiful, the, 599
there dwelt all that's, 146
thing out of Nazareth, 1118
thing too common, 64
thing, too much of a, 51
things come together, not all, 540
things of life come with a mixture, 324
think of any other, 1049
think they 're doing, 661
those that do them, 977
thou doest nobly, 427
thy great commanded, 556
time coming, there's a, 310, 504, 600
'tis and fine, 983
to be believed in once, 497
to be honest and true, 286
to be merry and wise, 11, 29
to be noble we 'll be, 257
to be remembered when outgrown, 497
to be true, too, 188
to be zealously affected, 1121
to forgive best to forget, 492
to know what were, 44
to live and learn, 493
to me is lost, all, 151
to step outside the narrow circle, 421
to the heels the slipper, 452
to whomsoever I do, 960
tortured by its own hunger, 880
train for ill and not for, 743
truly great who are truly, 29
turn when we can, do a, 418
turns you have done him, 976
undone and gifts misspent, 601
universal, all partial evil, 207
very excellent, 51
war or bad peace, 227
we may do here, 473
we naturally know what is, 968
we oft might win, lose the, 35
what has been was, 692
what was, shall be good, 489
when she was, 440
will be the final goal of ill, 468
will is great, 106
will, on earth, 1116
will the mightiest practical force, 678
will toward men, 1116
wind that bloweth no man, 17
wind turns none to, 19
wine — a friend — or being dry, 184

Good wine needs neither bush, 311
wine needs no bush, 51
wine till now, thou hast kept the, 445
wits jump, 1041
woman on five thousand a year, 482
words ne'er be said, 679
work for some, 499
works, full of, 1118
works, rich in, 1122
world to live in, 185
you can, do all the, 226
Goods, all my worldly, 1128
away, bearing eastern, 926
his worldly, 404
man who delivers the, 764
thou hast much, laid up, 1117
were all his worldly, 498
Good-breeding no special connection with wealth or birth, 380
Good-by, and so, 607
brothers! You were a good crowd, 726
dear clouds, 638
for casual, 920
Piccadilly, 836
proud world, 353, 408
sweet day, 619
to peace, priest for enemy, 423
Good-byes, dwelling on, 914
Good-day, keep us going and so, 607
Goodest man you ever saw, 697
Goodfellowship, sham, of democratic public men, 721
Good-for-nothing people, good for, 430
Good-fortune, I myself am, 535
is a giddy maid, 1066
Good-humored stomach, 991
Goodliest man of men, Adam the, 152
Good-looking men more beautiful, made, 998
Goodly are thy tents, 1099
Fere, the, 886
gift of sight, 850
heritage, 1103
outside, falsehood hath a, 44
Good-morrow, and so, 607
I bade to sorrow, 382
to thy sable beak, 288
Good-natured and cheerful, 228
lounging, 300
Goodness and grace, I thank the, 345
crownest the year with thy, 1104
God's, and mysterious ways, 922
greatness and, are not means, 317
how awful is, 153
in her little finger, more, 192
in things evil, there is some, 67
infinite, wide arms hath, 1021
lead him not, if, 136
men not so absolute in, 386
never fearful, 37
of good men, 968
sorry ere 'tis shown, 80
soul of, 580
tainted, arises from, 514

Goodness that comes by nature, 975
  the only investment that never fails, 515
Goodnesse, greatnesse on, loves to slide, 173
Goodness-sake, for, 1036
Good-night a thousand times, 78
  and sweetest dreams, 642
  gives the stern'st, 86
  love's bestowing and so, 607
Good-will, a sweet, 620
Goose could give, gold the, 962
  from off the common, steals the, 659
  girl still, a, 916
  hangs high, 945
  royal game of, 251
Goose-pen, write with a, 55
Goose-quill, corporation of the, 483
Goosegirl ermined is a goosegirl, 931
Gopher Prairie, citizens of, 884
Gorboduc, king, 56
Gordian knot unloose, 66
Gordium knot, unable to untie, 999
Gore O, and this preserved his, 624
  shedding seas of, 360
Gorge rises at it, my, 97
Gorgeous east, 149
  as the sun at midsummer, 63
  palace, deceit in, 79
  palaces the solemn temples, 33
Gorgons hydras and chimæras dire, 150
Gorilla, any man distinguishable from a, 482
Gorry by jingo by gee, by, 921
Gory locks at me, never shake thy, 87
  with the battle-blood, 571
Gospel, all is not, 15
  brown bread and the, 188
  of getting on, 720
  of Jesus Christ divine reality, 342
  of labour, 709
  you do not speak, 15
Gospel-light first dawned, 246
Gossip dost thou soe, 648
  hating ill-natured, 812
  history merely, 724
  most knowing of persons, 990
  of the air, babbling, 54
  to all the, 563
Gossip-ground, held from the general, 839
Got without merit, 101
Goth and Moor and Hercules, 647
  and never may retourne, 3
  and the shameless Hun, 779
Gotham, a flute in, 910
Gotham's three wise men, 347
Gott pulls mit me und I mit him, 684
Gout asthma and seven other maladies, 313
  or stone, without, 172
Govern my passions, may I, 172
  stars above us, 99

Govern the world, syllables, 130
  they that, make least noise, 130
  those that toil, 250
  thou my song, 153
Governed, happiness of the, 401
  only by their will, 129
Government, a conservative, 419
  at Washington still lives, 591
  by divine right, 319
  cannot be seriously injured in four years, 455
  controlled by minorities, 762
  democracy a charming form of, 974
  final end of, 393
  for forms of, 208
  founded on compromise, 260
  functions do not include support of people, 628
  grow oppressive, old forms of, 581
  half slave half free, 455
  in which all people have part, 716
  is a trust, 329
  made for and by the people, 341, 456
  no broader basis for any, 424
  no, ever had provision for its own termination, 455
  no place in the, 974
  obedience to, 268
  of all the people, 477
  of the people by the people for the people, 456, 477, 803
  often decided over a cup of coffee, 279
  our form of, 970
  paternal or meddling, 398
  preservation of the general, 273
  Republican form of, 581
  resting on valuation, 974
  share alike in the, 975
  strong enough to maintain its existence, 457
  the best, 397
  the less, the better, 412
  the principles the truths the history, 500
  under petticoat, 343
  undertaken this, 141
  was laying on their shoulders, 748
  which tells them what to do, 398
  wise, knows how to enforce, 240
  without a king, 394
Governments, councils, 464
  never have learned, 1062
Governors, bear the name of, 1000
Governs land and sea, he, 534
Gowan glitters on the sward, 288
Gowans fine, and pu'd the, 286
Gowd, man's the, for a' that, 287
Gown, ease a heart like a satin, 918
  feel quite lost without my, 557
  in a green, 759
  in her old torn, 807
  like fringe upon her, 1050
  of glory, hope's true gage, 22

Gown, plucked his, 251
  wife who preaches in her, 392
Gowns, fellow that hath two, 40
  furred, hide all, 99
  of silk or suits of grey, 558
Goya, cartoons by, 937
Grab-bag at a fair, 323
Grace, a sort of spiritual, 1087
  and good rhythm depend on simplicity, 973
  angels and ministers of, 91
  at meals, 323
  beauty without, 414
  child is full of, 956
  does it with a better, 54
  ease with, 225
  fallen from, 1121
  force fascination, youth full of, 535
  free nature's, 225
  from which they take their, 458
  grace me no, 947
  half so good a, 36
  has calmed the snow-storm, 1091
  heart which lives in, 1021
  Heaven's good, 513
  hidden, 811
  if possible with, 214
  inward and spiritual, 1128
  is given of God but knowledge, 519
  is joined with wrinkles, 1069
  it is enough that through Thy, 783
  kindness loses its, 1043
  let your speech be with, 1121
  light of His peace and, 821
  melancholy, 303
  melody of every, 168
  mickle is the powerful, 78
  moments of glad, 790
  more of his, than gifts, 114
  my cause, little shall I, 100
  never minde did minde his, 26
  not for comely, 950
  of a day, the tender, 465
  of finer form, 308
  of God, but for the, 18
  of God is in courtesy, 810
  of life, unbought, 260
  of the Lord Jesus Christ, 1121
  of youth, beyond all, 895
  power of, 327
  powerful, that lies in herbs, 78
  prologue is the, 200
  purity of, 356
  swears with so much, 186
  sweet attractive, 26, 152
  that makes simplicity a, 119
  that sweet time of, 454
  that won, 154
  to live, truer, 689
  to win with, 409
  unlooking for such, 600
  was graceless, all the, 966
  was seated on this brow, 95
  we say to God, joy is the, 540
  which boldest painters cannot trace, 199
  with a better, 999
  youthful, 373
Graces, all other, 170, 221
  choice of, 796
  Faith Hope and Charity, 326

Graces, I wish thee all thy mother's, 128
lead these, to the grave, 54
long, 163
not without our, 874
peculiar, shot forth, 153
pride envy malice are his, 326
sacrifice to the, 222
Graced with polished manners, 266
Graceful acts, those, 154
and fair, growing old gracefully, 628
resignation, die with, 330
smoke-wreaths, 605
Graceless zealots fight, 208
Gracious charity remains, 612
how benign is solitude, how, 299
in every kind, 712
is the time, 89
parts remembers me of his, 58
Tam grew, 287
those dews of solace, how, 698
words and apt, 41
Gradation, not by old, 100
Gradations, no pale, 309
of decay, 231
Gradual as scarcely to be perceived, so, 247
may be the growth of confidence, 419
swim, with a, 385
Graduate of Harvard, must be a, 768
Græcia Mæonidam jactet sibi, 176
Grail, gaze upon the, 491
Grain, cheeks of sorry, 158
given to horses, 232
gold as ripened, 1073
have not grown in the field, 958
life in the, of wheat, 753
of dust, 887
of manhood, a, 156
of mustard-seed, 639
of salt, with a, 1041
of sand, weigh against a, 424
of sand, world in a, 281
say which, will grow, 84
Grains of sand, little, 553
of wheat, two, 44
Grainy wood, 894
Grammar and nonsense and learning, 253
controls kings, 1047
has a rule absurd, 872
heedless of, 351
juiceless weeds of, 756
than a dictionary can be called a, 403
Grammar-school, erecting a, 69
Grammaticus, rhetor, 174
Gramophone, puts a record on the, 899
Grampian hills, on the, 248
Granada, there was crying in, 374
Grand a personage as the fastest walker would find, 494
and comfortable, baith, 750
Army button, 630
as those of Babylon, 1073
divine eternal drama, 508
Duke or Duchess, 910
gloomy and peculiar, 362
indifferent godlike brow, 594

Grand leap of the whale, 228
old ballad of Sir Patrick Spence, 316
old gardener and his wife, 462
old harper, wind that, 587
old name of gentleman, 469
Panjandrum himself, 246
shone afar so, 458
that sound so, 423
you look, O Ireland, 685
Grandam, soul of our, 46
Grandchild come oftener to be heir of the first, 120
Grandchildren will be better, hopes her, 346
Granddad in the Flemish bogs, 956
viewing earth's worn cogs, 956
Grandeur is a dream, 265
moon's unclouded, 369
of God, charged with the, 672
of these states their religion, 534
old Scotia's, 284
size is not, 563
steady and bright, 350
that was Rome, 460
to our dust, so nigh is, 409
with a disdainful smile, 244
Grandfather, since the days of the first, 529
we never knew his, 928
Grandfather's clock was too large, 601
house we'll go, to, 404
Grandma couldn't stand it, 638
danced, how she danced, 638
gave her lovers, 569
told me all about it, 638
Grandmother Eve, child of, 41
Grandsire cut in alabaster, 44
phrase, proverbed with a, 77
Grandsires, wives and, 1059
Grandson of your son, 857
Grange, in the moated, 37
Granite against which they make their way, 926
from the deeper, 925
God of the, 570
they have lived on, 926
Gran'pere, your old, 713
Gran'ther's rule was safer 'n 't is, 527
Grant an honest fame, 216
granite dome is over, 596
of power, 320
there is no brilliant, 928
us grace fearlessly to contend, 1127
us this day, 1021
Grape, from out the purple, 157
that can with logic, 1019
Grapes are not ripe, 137
are sour, 961
from thorns and figs from th'stles, 735
have eaten sour, 1113
of Ephraim, 1099
of wrath are stored, where, 522
sour, 1045
whence be the, of the wine-press, 401
wine must taste of its own, 429
Grapevine, keeps pullin' de, 712
swing, on a, 431
Grapple them to thy soul, 90

Grasp, exceed his, 488
in a giant's, 575
it firmly, it stings not, 593
it like a man of mettle, 204
of a friendly hand, 676
of fellowship, keep the, 522
on the bow, 576
the ocean, 199
till the swimmer's, 541
Grass above their graves, 693
all flesh is, 1112
as oxen, did eat, 1113
beyond the door, I know the, 577
blade small, common thing is a, 712
can't make a blade of, 712
go to, 131
green, keeps the, 932
groweth, while the, 14
grows on the weirs, 790
handkerchief of the Lord, 534
his days are as, 1105
I am the, 854
is immortal, 602
is the forgiveness of nature, 602
kissed the lovely, 893
like rain upon the mown, 1104
long dappled, 790
more enchanting than the lily or rose, 602
nibbling inward, 923
no, to make them fairy rings, 801
of the cliff, 633
of yesteryear is dead, 735
peer from the, 1066
people may eat, 381
quick-mown away, is mere, 680
sloping under trees, 867
splendour in the, 301
starred with the flower of blue, 830
stoops not, the, 106
that is made each year, 895
the clover-scented, 955
tides of, 630
together, as once in the, 693
two blades of, 191
under the greenwood tree, 394
universal beneficence of, 602
upon your breast, 553
wind in dry, 899
Grasses, champed the, 822
in the meadows that blossom but to die, 561
salt and the free, 929
Grass-grown headstone, 716
Grasshopper knew, then the, 962
lyrics occur to him, 857
not kill one, 857
shall be a burden, 1110
Grasshoppers rejoice, like, 218
under a fern, 260
Grassy hollow, 575
Grate, she passed about the kitchen, 557
Grateful evening mild, 152
for anything, if you are, 935
for the prize, ever, 294
heart, graven on this, 953
mind by owing owes not, 151
must we be, 986
stomach of an epicure, 323
they are so, 228

Gratiano speaks an infinite deal, 44
Gratification to a taste for the beautiful, 374
Gratified desire, lineaments of, 282
  to answer promptly, 616
Gratifying feeling, the, 624
Gratitude and wonder, with simple, 856
  but a lame sentiment, 702
  for a good digestion, 1081
  fruit of great cultivation, 239
  goes out to ye, 868
  is the sign, 961
  of most men, 200
  of place-expectants, 200
  receives a benefit with, 991
  still small voice of, 244
  two kinds of, 807
Gratulations flow in streams, 189
Grave a covered bridge, 440
  a little little, 60
  a nation's heart, his, 555
  almost to see myself go into my, 183
  an obscure, 60
  and reverend signiors, 100
  aspect he rose, with, 150
  between the cradle and the, 223
  botanize upon his mother's, 297
  bring my tribute to his, 307
  buries empires and cities in a common, 271
  but she is in her, 296
  come to thy, in a full age, 1102
  consumption brought him to his, 172
  could not cheat the, 662
  dark and silent, 22
  descend to the, 168
  digg'st thou this, 952
  dread as little as my bed, 183
  Duncan is in his, 86
  earliest at his, 349
  funeral marches to the, 433
  glory lead but to the, 467
  he bade them lie in the, 204
  honoured in his, 428
  hungry as the, 224
  ignominy sleep with thee in the, 63
  in a common, 271
  in quiet, 24
  in the cold, 390
  is not its goal, 433
  is the place to seek them, 703
  it is a dog's, 1093
  jealousy is cruel as the, 1110
  kingdom for a little, 60
  laid their dearest in the, 406
  lead these graces to the, 54
  Lucy is in her, 296
  mouldering in the, 293
  none on earth shall know his, 575
  now in his colde, 6
  of Mike O'Day, 948
  on my, as now my bed, 145
  on the edge of the, 635
  one foot in the, 131
  one small, 382
  or mellow, humours whether, 196
  our cradle stands in the, 121

Grave, paths of glory lead to the, 244
  pompous in the, 145
  rather follow you to your, 278
  rest in the, 362
  resting-place in a cold, 652
  rush to glory or the, 328
  secret as the, 1042
  sing at Lincoln's, 676
  strewed thy, 97
  study, law's, 21
  sun shine sweetly on my, 269
  there lies a lonely, 516
  thine be the, 823
  this earth, this, 22
  this side the, 326
  thou art gone to the, 343
  thy humble, adorned, 217
  to gay lively to severe, 177, 209
  to lie, in one small, 887
  to light from, pleasant to severe, 177, 1049
  to light, gently steer from, 1049
  to men unknown, 372
  to view, come my, 948
  too cold and damp, 333
  too full the, 744
  under my very little, 382
  unknelled without a, 355
  untimely, 141, 185
  what carry we but a sheet to the, 19
  where English oak and holly, 644
  where is thy victory, 1120
  where Laura lay, 22
  with sorrow to the, 1098
Graves afar, have their, 826
  and weep, stand by, 1070
  are pilgrim shrines, 363
  dishonourable, 81
  emblems of untimely, 266
  give to women's, 596
  grass above their, 693
  let's talk of, 59
  nothing marks their, 937
  of little magazines, 882
  of personal likings, 589
  of your sires, green, 362
  remembers so many, 685
  stood tenantless, 89
  two memoried, 596
Grave-digger or hangman, 417
Gravel gold, streams their, 166
Gravely got down from his perch, 508
Graven imagist, 893
Gravestone meets the sun, this, 854
Gravestones in the cemetery, 938
  milestones are, 482
Graveyard grimness, 573, 978
  stones, plain as, 903
Gravitation, man's triumph over, 1081
  the Golden Rule works like, 679
Gravity and concision of Thucydides, 641
  humour the test of, 377
  out of his bed at midnight. 62
  past the centre of, 1064
  to play at cherry-pit, 55
Gravy, person who disliked, 313

Gray and full of sleep, 790
  and trailing, wings are, 836
  Azores, behind him lay the, 658
  despair, winter's, 692
  flocks, where the, 516
  friar of orders, 256
  hair unto men, wisdom is the, 1124
  hairs with sorrow, 1098
  it is gone and all is, 354
  Marathon, age spares, 352
  mare the better horse, 16
  red spirits and, 117
  spires of Oxford, 875
  the moss grew, 591
  things golden seem, 650
  under the willow the, 571
Grays, dappled, to draw it, 650
Gray-eyed people, all the, 916
Gray-hooded even, 157
Grazed the common of literature, 239
Grazes confines of space, whose circle, 553
Grease, frieth in her owne, 15
  one that gets the, 518
  wharbouts you spill de, 688
Greasy aprons, slaves with, 105
  citizens, you fat and, 48
Great a poet and so good a friend, 175
  a thing as a great love, 808
  acceptable to the, 985
  adjustment is taking place, 651
  adventure, meet the, 825
  an honour to him who confers, 198
  and small, all the peoples, 471
  and wealthy not heaven's elect, 482
  and wise decay, 640
  are slaves, 394
  as a king, 274
  as I am good, 292
  bad man worse, 395
  beautifier, rank is a, 425
  between the little and the, 267
  Caesar fell, 83
  Caesar grown so, 81
  city that with greatest man, 535
  contest follows, 265
  Creator, voice of the, 501
  divide, upward toward the, 878
  eater of beef, 54
  end of life not knowledge, 564
  engines move slowly, 112
  eventful present hides the past, 443
  failure in a, object, 382
  field-marshal, there is a, 519
  fleas have little fleas, 190
  floods have flown from simple sources, 53
  for our belief, too, 503
  friends, little friends may prove, 961
  gates of gold, 653
  God our king, 447
  good and, 194
  good will is, 106
  green commonwealth of thought, 833
  gromboolian plain, over the, 498
  guns, blew, 274

Great Hall, contentions of the, 399
have, advantages the, 1040
hearts, time demands strong minds, 522
history of the land, 436
hoard is little but hearts are, 470
humble and poor become, 729
ill can he rule the, 25
important day, 194
in mouths of wisest censure, 101
individual fluid as nature, 537
interpreter, it is the, 840
inwardly in secret to be, 528
is Diana of the Ephesians, 1118
is the age, 909
is the art of beginning, 439
is truth, 701
is truth and mighty, 1123
know it shall be, 771
labours of the, 961
lord of all things, 207
lords' stories, 288
man dies, when a, 438
man humbled, the, 905
man's memory outlive his life, 94
many a small maketh a, 8, 15
memory does not make, a, 403
men gain doubly, 425
men hallow a whole people, 312
men not always wise, 1102
none unhappy but the, 198
not like Caesar, 292
nothing, achieved without enthusiasm, 412
of older days, 579
ones, ceremony to, 36
ones eat up the little ones, 106
our loss and grievous, 780
pieces of good fortune, 228
protection, shadow of the, 473
right, do a little wrong, to do a, 47
rightly to be, 96
said the greatest of the, 471
sensibility, 234
shade of that which once was, 297
some are born, 55
souls are portions, 524
soul's wealth, a, 587
star early drooped, 536
taskmaster's eye, 161
that he is grown so, 81
there is no small no, 410
thing to pursue, with a, 487
things are made of little things, 490
things of life, all the, 833
things with small compare, 151
those who were truly, 938
though fallen, 352
thoughts and good deeds, by, 506
thoughts great feelings, 458
to be, is to be misunderstood, 411
to grant as mighty to make, 485
to Him no high no low, no, 207
to know well I am not, 470
to them that know, 747

Great, truth is, and shall prevail, 556
truths are portions, 524
twin brethren, 400
valiant pious good and clean, 248
voyage, meditates on his, 200
vulgar and the small, 168
whatever was little seemed, 398
who are truly good are truly, 29
who have passed beyond reach of eulogy, 675
who is what he is, he is, 412
wide beautiful wonderful world, 553
winds let them be, 849
with child, 35
wits allied to madness, 173
wits jump, 241
Greater courtesy, greater man the, 471
feeling to the worse, 59
heights than we can reach, 238
love hath no man, 1118
man the greater courtesy, 471
than it is, deemed, 995
than the king himself, 230
than we know, 305
yes but there's something, 501
Greatest artist has embodied greatest ideas, 531
clerks not the wisest men, 16
comforts, throw away one of the, 237
curse, selfishness is the, 450
efforts of race due to love of praise, 532
happiness of the greatest number, 222
love of life, 272
men and women, great city has, 535
men, the world knows nothing of its, 401
of faults to be conscious of none, 380
of the great, said the, 471
only are, as the, 466
scandal on greatest state, 107
Great-heart away, with, 785
Great-hearted gentlemen, singing this song, 485
Greatly to his credit, 623
Greatness and goodness, 317
and perfection of soul, 689
and stateliness, 999
definition of, 483
eternal substance of his, 131
far stretched, 22
farewell to all my, 73
floated on the Thames, what, 726
God's, flowed around, 428
greatest, is unknown, 609
he could not want, for, 120
heights of, 991
highest point of all my, 73
if honour gives, 274
in me there dwells no, 470
inward, 66
is a-ripening his, 73
is unconscious, 377
noble acts and his, 1125
not in keeping with, 1082

Greatness, nurse into, 974
of God, 663
of his name, 74, 564
of name in the father, 120
passing by, worship, 873
penalty for, 745
proof of, 745
sense of, 736
some achieve, 55
some far-off touch of, 470
thrust upon 'em, some have, 55
which it does not possess, 1087
within the range, 663
Greatnesse on goodnesse loves to slide, 173
Grece, in his owene, 7
Grecian chisel trace, ne'er did, 308
spirit, the old, 502
Venus, the, 240
Greece, Achilles' wrath to, 218
Athens, the eye of, 156
boasts her Homer, 176
but living Greece no more, 355
can show, sage whom, 1050
flutes of, 634
fulmined over, 156
glory that was, 460
in early, she sung, 247
isles of, the, 359
John Naps of, 52
might still be free, 359
most power of any in, 996
or Rome, beauty which old, 442
she sung, in early, 247
Greed, die to, 864
Greedily devour the treacherous bait, 39
Greedy for the last drop, no longer, 930
men whom hope of gain, 622
of filthy lucre, 1121
wish ensued, which his, 1021
Greek, above all, 214
arts, 571
at eighty, Cato learned, 438
come in Latin or in, 146
faith in any, 967
invocation to call fools, 48
isles of the yellow bird's song, 435
or Roman name, above any, 173
puzzles me more than, 767
small Latin and less, 119
thought and life, 571
't is known he could speak, 141
to me, 't was, 82
trying to be, 903
Greeks, highest distinction of the, 571
I fear the, 982
in common, all the, 968
joined Greeks, when, 186
three, to cheat an Armenian, 559
Green, admits no vegetable, 933
and yellow melancholy, 55
bay-tree, like a, 1104
be the turf above thee, 363
but not quite so, 785
carnation withered, 827
content, whose, 517

Green darkness we feel, 773
 dry smooth-shaven, 160
 dusk for dreams, 823
 everything seemeth, 52
 fields and ocean's, o'er earth's, 503
 fire, like, 923
 for a season, laurel is, 631
 from the ferns, sucking the, 915
 gits back in the trees, 697
 God's, inn, 829
 grassy turf, 269
 graves of your sires, 362
 hands are blue, their heads are, 498
 in all the sweetest flowers, 385
 in judgment, when I was, 104
 in youth, 218
 is the colour of faith, 523
 isle in the sea, love, 460
 jealousy's eyes are, 367
 keep his memory, 334
 keep my memory, 496
 lassie that trips on the, 388
 leaves with golden flowers, 597
 mantle, 99
 mantling the sea, 789
 memory be, 89
 night, golden lamps in a, 169
 old age, 178, 219
 one red, making the, 86
 pastures, lie down in, 1103
 quiet place, we have found her a, 931
 sea's glass, greener than the, 632
 swell, 672
 tents, 763
 the memory be, 89
 the orator too, 106
 thought in a green shade, 169
 thy leaf has perished in the, 469
 towers of affirmation, 925
 traffic light, April prepares her, 912
 U, 1084
 wickedly red or malignantly, 857
Greenest, mosses cling, on old decay, 441
 of things blue, 632
Green-eyed monster, 102
Greenhouse too, loves a, 265
Greenland's icy mountains, 343
Greenness pleasure, miscalling, 856
Green-robed senators, 384
Greenwood, long ruled in the, 446
 tree, under the, 48, 394
Greet cheep is holde at litel prys, 7
Greeting, gayer than a, 920
 give us joyous, 545
 to 'change one, 543
Gregory remember thy swashing blow, 77
Grenadier, strode like a, 726
Grenadiers of Austria, 738
 two, journeyed toward France, 1065
 were lunging, 579
Greta woods are green, 309

Gretchen, little Gretchen, 394
Grettest gentilman, tak him for the, 7
Grew a little peach in an orchard, 698
 together like to a double cherry, 43
Grey beginning of years, 633
 fancy's strangest child, 893
 forgotten years, 832
 friar of orders, 52
 head the beauty of old men, 1108
 mare the better horse, 16
 the bluest of things, 632
 to pearl and pearl to gold, 861
Greybeards call word love divine, 71
 hoary, 759
 thank God it is passed, 531
Greyhound mongrel grim, 99
Greyhounds in the slips, 66
Gridley you may fire when ready, 711
Grief, acquainted with, 1112
 and laughter, with, 851
 and misery, 596
 and pain, naught but, 284
 and sorrow and lifelong dismay, 799
 and stay my, 918
 at not being able to want to do so, 1089
 bravery of his, 97
 but aggravates thy losse, 256
 canker and the, are mine, 358, 567
 cannot drive him away, 328, 567
 days of my distracting, 248
 depth of, 70
 do I give you, 913
 every one can master a, 39
 every, that mortals share, 626
 fills the room up of my absent child, 58
 has most of, 660
 hath known, all that, 425
 his heart had never wrung, if, 1052
 holy anger and pious, 351
 I feel, 467
 is a divine and terrible radiance, 1067
 is a matter of relativity, 749
 is bound up with our love, 613
 is fresh, while, 236
 is proud, 57
 its loneliness, 922
 lies onward, my, 107
 makes his owner stoop, 57
 may be joy misunderstood, 429
 no greater, 1020
 not so much, 1089
 of a child, 815
 of a wound, 63
 once, was there, 918
 only time for, 392
 past help should be past, 56
 patience on a monument smiling at, 55
 perked up in a glistering, 73
 plague of sighing and, 62
 reposes. where, 446
 seems quiet and apart, 922
 shall pass away, thy, 586
 should be like joy, 503

Grief, sickening, 269
 silent manliness of, 251
 that develops the powers, 1087
 that does not speak, 88
 that great mother's, 1074
 that is but passion, 546
 this glory and this, 531
 tires and brings a deeper slumber, 607
 to others', 223
 to the physician, for every, 137
 too deep, physic for a, 922
 too great, from, 1065
 torments of, 410
 touched these eyes of mine, 719
 treads upon the heels, 193
 wailings and reproachful, 697
 well ended, 963
 which they themselves not feel, 40
 with a glass that ran, 633
 with proverbs, patch, 40
 you must first feel, 262
Griefs are gone, when all my, 30
 desolate passions, solitary, 798
 griping, 255
 large, little dogs cause, 607
 of kin, 966
 some, are medicinable, 105
 that destroy, 869
 that harass the distrest, 230
 what private, they have, 83
Grief's slow wisdom, 593
Grievance, no, a fit object of redress by mob law, 455
Grievances naturally lose, inferior, 949
 repeat no, 251
Grieve his heart, show his eyes and, 87
 make the judicious, 94
Grieved and wistful, faces, 642
 is to have, 773
 we sighed we, 168
 when rigid for justice sake, 539
Grieving, what is knowledge but, 592
Grievous ill, vexed by no, 966
 pleasure and pain, 631
 wound, 463
Griffith, such an honest chronicler as, 74
Griggsby's station, a-visitin' back to, 697
Grim death, 129, 150
 disguise, 620
 feature, scented the, 155
 repose, hushed in, 244
 sardonic way, they have a, 835
Grimaces called laughter, 132
Grimaldi, but I am, 1077
Grimes is dead, old, 404
Grim-visaged war, 71
Grin and Barrett, firm of, 733
 one universal, 228
 owned with a, 321
 sin to sit and, 450
 so merry, every, 272
 take it with a, 865
 the devil did, 316
Grind, axe to, 333
 one demd horrid, 494
 the faces of the poor, 1111
 the poor, laws, 250
Grinders cease because they are few, 1110

Grindstone, noses to the, 13, 116, 125, 227
Grinning, mock your own, 97
Grip, a middlin' tight, 639
  where ye feel your honour, 285
Grips, I come to, 834
Gripinge grefes, 255
Grisildes, in hope to finde, 7
Grisly mask of doom, 725
  thing, when I face the, 871
  violin, click goes the, 1078
Grist at hand to grind, 521
Gristle, people in the, 259
Grizzled, his beard was, 90
  his hair just, 178
Groan, anguish poured his, 231
  bubbling, sinks with, 355
  condemned alike to, 243
  laugh that brings the, 777
  nor sigh nor, 127
  of a martyr's woe, 282
  the, the knell the pall, 363
Groans, sovereign of sighs and, 41
Grocer's assets swell, 764
  boy, my own my golden, 890
Grog-shop appears, wild-blazing, 389
Groined the aisles of Christian Rome, 408
Gromboolian plain, over the great, 498
Grooves of change, ringing, 464
Groping, glory in your, 913
  hands, laid our, 894
Gross and scope of my opinion, 89
  discourtesy, holding it as, 931
Grossly close it in, doth, 47
Grossness, all this earthy, 161
  and slag, amid measureless, 535
  by losing all its, 260
Grot, ferned, 583
Grotesque irrational, 823
Grotesquely wrong, she was, 666
Grouch, I like a good, 845
Ground, acre of barren, 32
  already broken, 552
  another man's, 34
  as water spilt on the, 1100
  bump the, 575
  call it holy, 370
  cannot dedicate cannot consecrate cannot hallow this, 456
  drops earliest to the, 46
  every vice on Christian, 215
  fathom-line could never touch, 61
  in the hard, 917
  kingdoms in a foot of, 928
  leaf falls upon the, 407
  least willing to quit the, 272
  let us sit upon the, 59
  my taile goe to the, 12
  not so far from Christian, 928
  not upon dreams, 116
  one's own sole, 647
  parts the scarcely broken, 499
  purple all the, 159
  seem to tread on classic, 195
  six foot of, to lie upon, 481
  stand on your own, 506
  stretched on the, 938
  that creep the, 953
  the only, 669

Ground, to own a bit of, 581
  which is my modres gate, 7
  who might well be under, 624
  withering on the, 218
Grounds, whose very charming, 511
Grounded on just and right, 154
Groundlings, ears of the, 94
Groundwork of all happiness is health, 346
Group of willful men, 725
Groups of citizens, does not visit, 912
Grouse worth a sonata, 637
Grove, nightingale's song in the, 269
  of Academe, the olive, 156
  of myrtles, 120
Groves are of laurel and myrtle and rose, 355, 1058
  fountain heads and pathless, 144
  frequenting sacred, 146
  God's first temples, 372
Grow dim with age, the sun, 195
  double, surely you 'll, 295
  learning wiser, 266
  mouldy, world would, 472
  old along with me, 489
  old, always find time to, 203
  to what they seem, 249
  up as soon as you can, 905
  wiser and better, 172
Growed, I 'spect I, 480
Groweth sed and bloweth med, 3
Growing fonder of my staff, I'm, 509
  old, yes I'm, 510
  sorrow of each day's, 607
  sweet golden goblet found, 431
  when ye 're sleeping, 311
Grown by what it fed on, 90
  so great, he is, 81
Grown-up people careful about breaking their word, 742
  people correct on facts lack imagination, 742
Grows dim with rust, brightest blade, 453
  land where the bong-tree, 498
  less gay, laugh of pleasure, 405
  old and is fat, 61
  with his growth, 208
Growth, a thornless, 587
  bless thy secret, 170
  children of a larger, 177
  choke the true, 864
  confidence a plant of slow, 230
  is the only evidence of life, 403
  man seems the only, 249
  of confidence, however gradual the, 419
  of the public mind toward refinement, 500
  on cedars, high, 30
  shadow kills the, 120
  soil for aesthetic, 826
  the bliss of, 953
Grub, of all poor, 955
Grubstreet, near Moorsfield, 232
Grudge and carp, ne'er, 284
  feed fat the ancient, 44
  some who bear a, 977
  the throe, never, 489
Grudges, nurse the ancient, 612

Grumble and rumble and roar, the terrible, 552
Corner in Cross Patch Town, 667
Grundy say, what will Mrs., 290
  tyranny of Mrs., 581
Grunt and sweat, 93
Gruntin', you do de pullin' en I'll do de, 689
Guarantee for being right, slender, 450
Guard along the Rhine, 1073
  constantly on his, 1082
  dies never surrenders, 1061
  gentlemen of the French, 941
  our native seas, 327
  our spoons, from whom we, 401
  through death's iron, 937
  thy bed, holy angels, 199
Guardian angel o'er his life, 289
  angels sung the strain, 225
  on the tower, the, 517
  Tutelary and Angels, 1098
Guardians of the fair, eunuchs, 203
Guardianship of the strong over the weak, 717
Gude nicht and joy be wi' you, 291
  time coming, 310
  to be honest and true, 611
  to be merry and wise, 611
Gudeman who sleeps sound by me, 277
Gudeman's awa', when our, 269
Gudgeon, this fool, 44
Gudgeons, to swallow, 143
Guerdon, the fair, 159
Guermantes Way, The, 1087
Guess is morning-star, the golden, 471
  northern word, 616
  now who holds thee, 428
  woman's more accurate, 785
Guesseth but in part, he, 317
Guest and ghost, dear, 439
  body's comrade and its, 1009
  divine, entertain and honor the, 640
  forget, made each, 620
  give no more to every, 191
  gives her, 737
  is coming, there is a, 890
  it comes an evil, 960
  keen, fits a dull fighter, 63
  like a satisfied, 984
  like an unwelcome, 692
  lingering like an unloved, 368
  love is but a, 114
  my dear old Carian, 553
  my welcome, 258
  of those infinitely privileged ones, 891
  our distinguished, 497
  Perfect, 700
  please the fleeting, 718
  serenely calm, 248
  smiles for the sometime, 642
  soul the body's, 191
  speed the going, 213
  speed the parting, 213, 220
  that graced his board, 348
  tie of host and, 963
  winter a bad, 1080

Guests do go, how fast the, 653
  like hungry, 200
  of state, certain, 579
  should praise it, not the cooks,
    29
  start at one fishball, 555
Guid to be honest and true, 286
  to be merry and wise, 286
Guide and a guard, vouchsafe
    him to me as a, 450
  and mine acquaintance, mine,
    1104
  be Thou our, 957
  from camp to camp, 881
  in smoke and flame, 310
  knowledge should be his, 973
  leaves the private conscience
    for, 174
  my companion my, 1128
  philosopher and friend, 209,
    868
  providence their, 156
  take my stories, for a, 784
  the humble, a star to, 499
  vexes me to choose another,
    516
  was a beautiful wonderful star,
    439
Guides, choose ideals as your,
    580
  the planets in their course, 289
Guilders, a thousand! Come take
    fifty, 487
Guile, lips from speaking, 1103
  words replete with, 155
Guiled shore, 46
Guilt away, wash her, 253
  can look on, 194
  is in that heart, I ask not if,
    336
  of Eastern kings, 167
  secret, is betrayed by silence,
    175
  so full of artless jealousy is,
    96
  those who fear not, 262
  to cover, the only art her, 253
  tomb of affection and, 956
Guiltier than him they try, 35
Guilty consciences, 977
  land, shakes a, 194
  man escape, let no, 549
  man excepts and thins his jury,
    174
  mind, suspicion haunts the, 71
  of corruption, I am, 113
  of his own death, 96
  of such a ballad, 41
  splendour, 265
  thing, started like a, 89
  thing surprised, 301
  wealth, his genuine and less,
    166
Guinea, first, is more difficult,
    1054
  jingling of the, 464
Guineas, I enclose two, 198
Guinea's stamp, rank is but the,
    287
Guinea-pig up by the tail, lift a,
    545
Guinevere, and one was, 685
Guise it wears, whatever the,
    843
Guiseppe da barber, 814
Guitar, touched his, 388

Gulf between, a stately, 866
  first across the, 676
  no line can sound, 401
  profound, 150
  too long the, 735
  yawned as wide, 593
Gulled, if the world will be, 126
Gulls the cloud-calligraphers,
    894
Gum and grin and lariat, worked
    with, 859
  medicinal, 104
Gun, birds named without a, 409
  designing the long-range, 937
  fire your little, 823
  hate of the, 795
  one arm to bear a, 1073
  shouldered his, 755
  sure as a, 179
  that a woman manned, 659
  that is not loaded, 779
Guns, all-shattering, 475
  aren't lawful, 918
  begin to shoot, 781
  begin, when the, 891
  blew great, 497
  but for these vile, 61
  smelt the, 690
  that spoke at Lexington, 771
  though winds blew great, 274
Gunfire, with his incessant, 1071
Gunga Din, better man than I
    am, 781
Gunpowder, glories in, and loves
    parade, 507
  ran out at the heels, 246
  treason and plot, 945
Gust hath blown his fill, the, 161
Gusty thieves, 391
Gutter, idealists walk into the,
    788
Guv'ment choose, on'y wut, 527
Guy, county, the hour is nigh,
    310
  some kind Burbankian, 813
Gwent, that green pap in, 814
Gymnasium, life's, 538
Gymnastics as well as music,
    973
Gypsies serve stolen children, as,
    262, 278
Gypsy blood astir, 757
Gypsy-man built life well, 407
Gyre and gimble in the wabe,
    598
Gyve, stern, 685
Gyves upon his wrist, 391

Habeas Corpus, protection of,
    273
Haberdasher to Mr. Spurgeon,
    614
Haberdashery of success, 787
Habersham, hills of, 663
Habit, apparelled in more pre-
    cious, 40
  builds the bridge, 676
  capable of being developed,
    1074
  costly thy, 23, 91
  easy to abandon, difficult to
    resume, 1068
  except that of, 975
  fills up what remains, 1087
  firmer than before, 271
  honour peereth in meanest, 52

Habit is second nature, 1030
  lost, it is a, 1068
  most precious conservative
    agent, 662
  of being contented, 345
  of feeling in the author, 318
  of reading, how tyrannical is,
    530
  of the soul, here the, 444
  or training, 975
  order breeds, 636
  ordinary actions ascribed to,
    1079
  powerful is the empire of, 987
  the fly-wheel of society, 662
  use doth breed a, in a man, 34
  will encroach, 313
  you reap a, 954
Habits, censuah folks about dey,
    820
  formation of right, 542
  home-keeping, 997
  ill, gather by unseen degrees,
    177
  induced by public practices,
    998
  not a politician other, good,
    606
  of peace and patience, 139
  small, well pursued, 275
Habitable world, look round the,
    177
Habitant of castle gray, 517
Habitation, giddy and unsure, 64
  local, and a name, 43
Habitual, practise what you
    would make, 1008
Hack and Hew were the sons, 757
Hackett's garden, over old Marm,
    508
Hackneyed phrase of vagrant
    worm, 510
  roadster, wind-broken lame,
    728
Had we never loved sae kindly,
    287
Hades, descent to, 1014
  he needs, about all the, 774
  no one goes to, with his wealth,
    960
Hades' shore, back from, 983
Haft of the arrow, 962
Haggard, if I do prove her, 102
  shapes, two, 685
Hags, black and midnight, 87
Haig shall be Haig, 3
Hail Columbia happy land, 294
  fell like the plunging cannon-
    shot, 579
  fellow well met, 191
  hail the gang's all here, 623
  harrow of, 712
  holy light, 151
  or rain or any snow, falls not,
    463
  the rising sun, let others, 242
  to the chief, 308
  to the land whereon, 386
  to thee blithe spirit, 366
  unless God send his, 484
  wedded love, 152
Hail-fellow-well-met, now am I,
    965
Hails you Tom or Jack, 267
Hair, amber-dropping, 158
  and as for my, 791

Hair and finger-tips, through his, 900
and rifles both, were long, 815
Andrew with the br.ndled, 703
as free, robes loosely flowing, 119
babies haven't any, 910
beauty draws us with a single, 177, 212
became curlier, 569
bright over Europe fell her, 448
by her golden, 814
crown uv silver, 698
distinguish and divide a, 141
divides the false and true, 1019
each particular, stand an end, 91
floating, 600
flowers in her, 710
frame of shining golden, 665
from pantalette to, 1066
girl-graduates in their golden, 466
has become very white, 598
her rain-drenched, 882
if a woman have long, 1120
is tumbled, maiden's, 706
just grizzled, 178
less golden about the, 593
long, made good-looking men, 998
loose his beard and hoary, 244
man that coloured his, 1002
most resplendent, 303
my fell of, 88
ninth part of a, 62
no wider than a, 849
odour of her wild, 736
of a woman, one, 125
of Him, never hurt a, 880
of silver or gold, 846
of the same dog, 15
on my head, the very, 966
only a woman's, 192
right off your bean, takes the, 943
ripples of her, 583
sacred, dissever, 212
shall be of what colour it please God, her, 38
she smooths your, 1066
single, casts its shadow, 987
skipper stormed and tore his, 508
smooths her, 899
so there be not too much, 56
streamed like a meteor, 244
strung with his, 41
tangles of Neæra's, 159
that grows bald by nature, 37
that is shining and free, 894
the stars in her, 577
there's no time for a man to recover his, 37
trimmed in silence, 1002
turns gray, toil till his, 714
upon the upper lip, eccentric pattern in, 906
was curly, his, 840
was so charmingly curled, 523
wavelets of soft, 562
whar you fine a bunch er, 688
would rouse and stir, 88
Yoland with the yellow, 592
Hairs, bring down my gray, 1098

Hairs, glory from his gray, 442
of the hapless owner, 654
property of gray, 495
superfluity comes sooner by white, 44
white, become a fool, 66
Hair's-b eadth of time, 1011
Hairbreadth missings, 229
'scapes, 100
Haircut and a shave, lies a, 910
Hairpins, pluck out the, 853
Hairy and silent, like mountains, 929
breast, get a, 833
gold crown on her head, 782
Haiti, graves of soldiers in, 480
Hal, no more of that, 62
the captain's son, when little, 405
Halcyon days, 68, 972
when shall I see those, days, 972
Half a candle, two old chairs and, 498
a life asunder, 598
a proper gardener's work, 785
a world behind, 490
angel and half bird, 490
believed, who never doubted never, 506
broken-hearted, 351
earth, when we are, 574
exceeds the whole, 959, 1013
garden and half house, 466
gate to concludendum, 11
hidden from the eye, 296
his present repute, sink, 526
his Troy was burnt, 64
I hear, don't believe, 813
in love with easeful death, 383
in shade and half in sun, 336
knows everything, 398
my better, 27
of Creation she owns, 782
of it is mine, 690
of music, 773
of ten lines just a, 578
of the world a bridegroom is, 735
part of a blessed man, 57
restaurant and home, 905
slave and half free, 455
so good a grace, 36
so sage as he wrote, truths, 516
the creeds, faith in, 469
the power that fills the world, 434
the wealth bestowed on camps, 434
the world knows not how other half lives, 138, 1025
their remedies, 783
to what I see, 563
too civil by, 278
was more than the whole, 959
was not told me, the, 1101
you may carry, 953
Half-a-crown, help to, 651
Half-brother of the world, 506
Half-dozen, than a dull academic, 1089
Half-gods go, when, 409
Half-hidden in its grassy bed, 637
Half-moon made with a pen, 56
Half-pay for life, 360

Halfpence to tramps and such-like, 512
Halfpenny loaves for a penny, 69
Half-pennyworth cf bread, 62
Half-phrasings, harsh, 664
Half-shirt is two napkins, 63
Half-shut eye, before the, 224
Half-sunlight and half-storm, 879
Half-w tte l sheep, old, 747
Half-world, now o'er the one, 85
Hall, cottage or come they from, 448
Douglas in his, 308
his, the azure dome, 410
merry in, where beards wag all, 19
merry swithe it is in, 19
valleys of, 663
vasty, of Death, 546
Halls are crowded, 718
dwelt in marble, 386
of death, the silent, 371
of learning fair, 447
of Montezuma, 953
of night, d.m, 418
sea-weed in her palace, 363
sweep through her marble, 418, 433
Hallelujahs, as they've sounded, 587
Hallie is no longer with me now, 573
Hall-mark of national culture, 862
of quality, unsaleability, 788
Halloo your name, 54
Hallowed is the time, 89
relics should be hid, 161
thing, poet's mistress is a, 458
Hallucination, universal, 721
Halo, but pray his, 725
of immortality, 291
Halt between two opinions, 1101
learn to, 1001
Halter draw, felt the, 277
in hope one will cut the, 147
threats of a, 274
Halters, talking of, 1036
Halves, I'll go his, 1025
Hame hame to my ain countree, 346
ye maun bide at, 345
Hamlet, as he could have written, 382
at the close of the day, 269
how boring, 883
I am not prince, 900
rude forefathers of the, 244
tragedy of, with the prince of Denmark being left out, 311
Hammer away ye hostile hands, 706
'ammer 'ammer, it's the, 955
beating, 873
golden mechanical, 933
no sound of, 266
nor axe, neither, 266
smith stand with his, 58
strike, when you are the, 708
when you are a, 137
Hammers, anvil wears the, 622
aprons rules and, 105
break, your, 706
closing rivets up, 67
no, fell, 266, 342

Hammersmith on Sunday, 932
Hampden, some village, 245
Hand, adore the, 190
  an easy shoe, an open, 757
  and brain went ever paired, what, 487
  and heart, I give my, 340
  and heart, seeking with, 595
  and mind can use the tools, 928
  and part with laughter, take, 632
  at, its wondrous bread, 823
  be stretched out to receive, 1124
  be tied up to thy neck, thy, 1127
  beckons on every, 826
  bird in the, 15, 1005
  books to hold in the, 238
  brought in her, 271
  but the understanding, not the, 1038
  cheek upon her, 78
  close the open, 1079
  cloud like a man's, 1101
  compelled it, Thy, 783
  cravens my weak, 106
  divine, combine to shut out the, 403
  emprison her soft, 384
  encumbers them with helping, 649
  farther away on either, 915
  feel a vanished, 688
  findeth to do do it, 1110
  foot and, go cold, 20
  for hand foot for foot, 1098
  forget her cunning, 1106
  freeman with unpurchased, 451
  from England an industrious, 1076
  from out whose, 445
  gave her a hero's, 659
  give me your, 38, 589
  glove upon that, 78
  God's right, and left, 506
  good dealt by the eternal, 1021
  handle toward my, 85
  hath made our nation, thy, 451
  hath sown, harvests what his, 657
  heaped above me by a master's, 1093
  heaving up my either, 134
  held in a mighty, 848
  held in the little brown, 730
  her 'prentice, 284
  his red right, 150
  hold a fire in his, 59
  hold in your cold dead, 658
  I argue not against Heaven's, 162
  I kiss my, 672
  imposition of a mightier, 397
  in all thy works, thy gracious, 1128
  in either tight-closed, 567
  in hand, 156
  in hand in the golden, 395
  in the sun, thrust your, 890
  in thine, press thou his, 707
  in thy right, carry gentle peace, 73
  is a stronger one, 311
  is humbled, into dust his, 660

Hand, larger heart the kindlier, 469
  led by the Almighty's, 168
  length of days in her right, 1106
  let not thy left, know, 1114
  let slip, careless, 848
  lick my phantom, 858
  licks the, just raised, 207
  lifted in awe, 203
  lightly in mine, jeweled, 770
  like the dyer's, 108
  little thing in, 962
  man's, is not able to taste, 43
  master lent his, 408
  may no rude, deface it, 297
  may rightly clutch, 782
  misery is at, 1020
  morn with rosy, 153
  mortality's strong, 58
  nature's sweet and cunning, 54
  not able to taste, 43
  of little employment, 96
  of war, 59
  on me, laid not your, 882
  on you, laid his ancient, 841
  one flag one heart one, 452
  one, if it's true, 589
  one, is as good as another, 589
  or fold in its, 589
  other than mine, 473
  paid for, his, 948
  pearly shell in my, 362
  prospered here my, 778
  put in every honest, a whip, 103
  receive it in their, 960
  remains, one, 1073
  riches and honour in her left, 1106
  Satan was now at, 150
  shake you by the, 881
  some envious, 699
  still I got no, 660
  stole forth a, 881
  stretch a, 794
  stretched forth in blessing, 697
  sweet lips soft, 385
  sweet Roman, 55
  sweeten this little, 88
  tender inward of thy, 108
  thank the lavish, 522
  that bore a nation in its hold, 604
  that fed them, bite the, 261
  that gave the blow, 179
  that gives the blow, 190
  that hath made you fair, 37
  that held it, 687
  that is honest and hearty, 305
  that kindles, 356
  that made us is divine, 194
  that made you fair hath made you good, 26
  that ope'd the gate, 686
  that rocks the cradle, 534
  that rounded Peter's dome, 408
  that rules the world, is the, 534
  thunder in his lifted, 173
  time has laid his, gently, 440
  time hath a taming, 403
  to execute, 270
  to give, freer, 689
  to shake the, 928
  to take occasion by the, 462
  touch of a vanished, 465

Hand, unblessed thy, 220
  uncarved, by the, 594
  upon a woman, man that lays his, 295
  upon his head, with my, 428
  upon the ark, to lay their, 264
  upon the ocean's mane, 393
  upon thy mane, 355
  was on the oar, 973
  was resting on a mountain, 877
  wash this blood from my, 86
  waved her lily, 205
  we are in God's, 67
  welcome in your, 84
  white wonder of dear Juliet's, 79
  with my heart in 't, 33
  withhold not thine, 1110
  who sets no, 964
  will miss, my, 736
  will multitudinous seas incarnadine, 86
  with a thankful, 985
  with automatic, 899
  you cannot see, 205
Hands, a baby's, 634
  and then take, 32
  and thighs, horseman's, 928
  and weep, clasp, 1065
  are blue, and their, 498
  are linked, when, 343
  are the hands of Esau, 1097
  as he licks your, 920
  at the piping of all, 375
  blue are my, 1080
  by angel, 382
  by foreign, 217
  clasp him with strong, 900
  death lays his icy, 141
  diadems and fagots in their, 410
  establish the work of our, 1105
  feed out of tribe's, 786
  for bread and wine, dark, 935
  from failing, 820
  from picking and stealing, 1118
  full, fortune with both, 65
  has such small, 921
  hath not a Jew, 45
  his two good honest, 750
  hold much of heat, 903
  hold thou my, 682
  I loved beside the Shalimar, 775
  in prayer, folds my, 1091
  invisible, restore, 891
  it comes, all into whose, 1125
  laid our groping, 894
  little folding of the, 1106
  man's fortune in his own, 111
  many, make light work, 16
  mischief for idle, 199
  mouths without, 177
  must wash my, 1082
  never made to tear each other, 198
  new Niobe with claspèd, 565
  not built with mortal, 174
  not hearts, 103
  not without men's, 520
  of a little child, 639
  of fellowship, the right, 1121
  of memory weave, 638
  of the sisters death and night, 536
  off! Stand back! 954

Hands on high, lift their, 1022
promiscuously applied, 355
puny, 402
rude, have touched it, before, 119
shake, with a king, 363
some with Pilate wash your, 60
that folded are, 671
that might have swayed, 244
their knell is rung, by fairy, 247
then take, 32
to grasp, firm, 803
to valour given, 382
to wuk, sot his, 712
tools were made and born were, 282
true faith and ready, 522
two, upon the breast, 567
upheld us on the air, 1091
washing with invisible soap, 391
watch that wants both, 263
wave their, for a mute farewell, 540
were always too big, whose, 927
were made before knives, 192
with aching, and bleeding feet, 546
what is in their, 965
white as a king's, 686
with his two happy, 26
with those that stay, touch, 653
with your, and your feet, 401
without falling into her, 662
ye hostile, 706
Hands' doings, harms of our own, 965
Hand-clasp and a heart-throb, 746
is a little stronger, 821
Handel, care a farthing candle for, 324
is but a ninny, 221
sings it, wisdom, 414
Handfasted, when we are, 310
Handfasting, this we call, 310
Hand-flung spears, 504
Handful, just take a trifling, 569
of ashes, mine be a, 832
of grey ashes, 553
of meal in a barrel, 1101
of silver, just for a, 485
of stars, 887
of the divine inert, 531
o' things I know, 639
Handicraft of art, rest the, 533
Hand-in-glove, were, 192
Handiwork, showeth his, 1103
you give to God, 708
Handkerchief, fetch me the, 103
of the Lord, 534
Handle not taste not, 1121
one old jug without a, 498
to everything, right and wrong, 1056
toward my hand, 85
Handles, everything hath two, 124, 1008
Hand-organs are playing the tune Shoo fly, 517
Hand-saw, hawk from a, 92
Handshaking, with his friendly, 1080

Handsome at twenty nor strong at thirty, 137
everything about him, 40
house to lodge a friend, 214
hunting man, 823
in three hundred pounds a year, 34
is that handsome does, 7, 253
pigtail wore, 482
slab in the graveyard, 912
strong rich or wise, will never be, 137
than homely, I'd rather be, 686
wee thing, 286
young man on the flying trapeze, 640
Handsomer man than you, 678
Handy-dandy, change places and, 99
Hang a calf's skin, 57
a doubt on, nor loop to, 103
in the air, musicians that shall play, 62
like an icicle, 55
on him, she would, 90
out our banners, 88
sorrow care will kill a cat, 118, 133
the pensive head, 159
themselves in hope one will come and cut the halter, 147
themselves in their own straps, 54
together, we must all, 227
upon his pent-house lid, 84
us every mother's son, 42
Hanging and marriage go by destiny, 125
and wiving go by destiny, 2, 45
his cat on Monday, 940
in a golden chain, 151
was the worst use man could be put to, 114
Hangman's whip, fear o' hell, 285
Hangs a tale, thereby, 34, 1026
his head for shame, 555
on Dian's temple, 76
on prince's favours, 73
upon the cheek of night, 77
Hank of hair, 779
Hannah Cook, doesn't amount to, 944
God and me, contract 'twixt, 603
Hannah's at window binding shoes, 568
Hanner, lost our little, 684
Hannibal had mighty virtues, 122
Hanover, the home of the Indian voice, 752
Hans Breitmann gife a barty, 559
Hap, fear thou not what, 1058
so hard, no, 30
Haphazard, let no act be done at, 1010
Hapless children sent heavenward, 586
Happen more beautiful than death, nothing can, 534
Happened in his berth, death which, 392
once, this could but have, 490

Happens at all, whatever, happens as it should, 1010
least expected generally, 420
Happier in the passion we feel, 367
than I know, feel that I am, 154
things, remembering, 464
Happiest is he who suffers least, 1054
dream, none thrives for long on, 556
Happiness, a lifetime of, 720
a wine of rarest vintage, 788
always be an unforeseen, 1063
and glory, 259
and peace, drowning would be, 494
and powers as a state, 420
and prosperity, 921
attained by true philosophy, 646
best, a woman can boast, 394
consume without producing, 719
depends as nature shows, 262
digesting, peace is, 1068
do not write down their, lovers who love truly, 1078
envy no man's, 50
every one seeking, 795
fireside, 289
first condition of social, 670
foes of human, 1064
formula for complete, 773
gives men, 214
glimpse of, saw a, 147
has hardly more than one, 1088
in the hands of others, trust our, 330
in the married estate, overexpecting, 147
is beneficial, 1087
is like time and space, 608
is speechless, 558
is the only good, 603
is the shadow, 749
is to be found, much more, 1079
lies in superfluities, 454
malicious have a dark, 1067
missings of, 229
mistaken path to, 1064
nineteen six result, 496
no sure, 25
of duty, 605
of life, supreme, 1067
of life, the, 318
of peoples, concern about the, 1078
of the greatest number, 222
opportunity to work out, 333
or misery of life, trifles make the, 589
our being's end and aim, 208
our pastime and our, 301
produced by a good inn, 236
pursuit of, 273
rob him of his, 1076
spectacle of human, 314
sum of human, 734
talk, 718
task of, 703
that makes the heart afraid, 390
the thirst after, 1055

Happiness their harmony foretells, world cf. 460
there only is real, 1078
thought of tender, 300
through another's eyes, 51
to crave for, 1075
too swiftly flies, 243
true, is of a retired nature, 195
was born a twin, 359
we prize, if solid, 226
Happy accident, 117, 254, 1042
and so pore, we ust to be so,
697
are they that hear their detractions, 39
as a lover, 300
as a married man, 235
as America, 271
as kings, 702
as the daisies that dance, 568
as we can, let us be, 237
be, and live within our means,
606
breed of men, 59
call no man, 969
capacity to become, 166
children you will rise, 474
comprehend, and the, 839
constellations, 154
could I be with either, 205
days, a world of, 71
days, those were, 197
earthlier, is the rose distilled,
42
fam'les resemble one another,
1077
few, we band of brothers, 67
field or mossy cavern, 384
goes as lucky goes, 843
he with such a mother, 466
health unto the, 772
highways, 743
hills pleasing shade, 243
how to be, 960
I and wretched he, 504
in nothing else so, 59
inexperience, 494
is he born or taught, 114
is he who heareth, 443
is he who knows them not,
1022
is the blameless vestal's lot,
216
is the house, 411
is the man who hath never
known, 426
land, would not seek the, 503
little, if I could say how much,
38
live completely, 960
make Englishman acknowledge
he is, 483
man that hath his quiver full,
1106
man's without a shirt, 11, 639
mixtures of happy days, 357
never so, as we suppose,
1043
New Year! there's always hope,
837
no one can be, till all are
happy, 581
once been, 647
pair live while ye may, 152
people not afraid, 788
she is not yet so old, 46

Happy soul that all the way,
165
that have called thee so, 322
the heart that sighed, 30
the man and happy he alone,
177
the man whose wish, 216
the mortal, 715
they whose walls, 982
time place and way to be, 603
to think more, thou hadst,
389
visions of my youth, the, 455
walks and shades, 155
Warrior, who is he, 300
was it for that son, 70
ways of doing things, manners
are the, 413
who in his verse, can steer, 177,
1049
world, where all things live,
619
Harangue, nothing in a great,
1046
Harass the distrest, 230
Harbinger, perfume her, 157
spring-time's, 132
the evening star love's, 155
Harbingers to heaven, 147
Harbour bar be moaning, though,
523
bar, soon beyond, 579
even if it is a little, 693
give, in life did, 119
never one in the, 689
of Mahon, in the, 405
safe she lay, in, 772
through the haze, 490
to some unseen, 692
town for thee, what, 806
where lies the final, 531
Hard a keeping oath, sworn too,
40
and inflexible hearts, 166
as a Turk, 950
as I, though none so, 816
doubtful unprosperous and
dangerous times, 374
for an empty sack, 227
for him, it was, 998
harbour a heart that's so, 256
he often fares, 324
heart, sight of death makes, 50
heroic for earth too, 489
is his herte, 3
it is for women to keep counsel,
how, 82
it is to make an Englishman,
how, 483
lessons, 229
long is the way and, 150
nothing so, but search will find
it, 134
service, shrinks when, 403
stiff lines of life, 444
the task I find, 595
things to bear and grin, 557
though, be the task, 557
times come again no more, 567
times were not, and money
scarce, 415
to catch and conquer, 575
to come as, 60
to part when friends are dear,
273
to please everybody, 989

Hard to please, uncertain coy
and, 308
way of transgressors is, 1107
way sweet and delectable, making the, 59
Hard-boiled unbroken egg, 923
Hardens all within, 285
Harder they fall, the, 969
to give properly than to take,
1080
Hardest-timbered oak, 70
Hardihood endurance and courage
of Englishmen, 804
Hardship bred, out of, 934
cold and, 576
Hardy as the Nemean lion's
nerve, 91
plant, error is a, 477
Hare awoke, when the, 962
hold with the, 13
mad as a March, 17, 1041
to run with the, 23
to start a, 61
Hares, little hunted, 816
Hare's foot my preservative, 181
Harebell, hope is like a, 587
Hare-brained chatter of frivolity,
420
Hark from the tombs, 199
hark my soul angelic, 503
hark the lark, 105
Harlequin without his mask, 484
Harm comes to the strong, 1081
flea does all the, 118
in sometimes painting, no, 833
me, fate cannot, 313
nothing do much, 923
that women have done, 747
to my wit, I believe that does,
54
to the body, does no, 974
when you fly from, 966
win us to our, 84
Harms, not only for thy, 749
of our own hands', 965
of the world have come, 609
we beg often our own, 104
Harm's way, get out of, 1035
Harmed by speech, 19
Harmes two the lesse, of, 4
Harmful than errors, some truths
more, 564
Harmless as doves, 1115
day, entertains the, 114
earth, bowels of the, 61
fly, poor, 77
inoffensive untitled aristocracy, 453
necessary cat, 46
pleasure, stock of, 233
sport and simple food, 479
Harmonics far and faint, 492
Harmonies, hear the heavenly,
794
of music, 641
Harmonious bubbling noise, 140
echo, it seemed the, 564
hymn, the whole, 816
madness, such, 367
sound on golden hinges, 154
Harmoniously confused, 216
Harmony between sea and life of
man, 713
composed into a kind of real,
379
for thee O universe, 1010

Harmony foretells, happiness their, 460
heaven drowsy with, the, 41
heavenly, 176
hidden soul of, 160
in her bright eye, 168
in immortal souls, 47
like deep, enforce attention, 59
not understood, 207
of circumstances, 260
of the unive.se, 260
of the world, her voice the, 22
order or proportion, 145
rhythm and, 973
rule of universal, 549
sentimentally disposed to, 323
to create, 1000
to harmony, 176
touches of sweet, 47
Harness, him that girdeth on his. 1101
Nicanor lay dead in his, 1125
on our back, die with. 88
Haroun Alraschid, good, 462
Harp and nations heard, touched his, 393
and of horn, music of, 600
and organ, such as handle the, 1097
Angel Gabriel! give him a, 773
in divers tones, 436
like my own, no, 328
not on that string, 72
of Innisfail, 327
of Tara, 792
of thousand strings, 199
open palm upon his, 440
sings to one clear, 436, 467
through Tara's halls, 334
which I wake, 335
Harps and hearts be strung, let, 397
upon the willows, 1106
Harper, wind that grand old, 587
Harpers, the notes of the, ring, 387
Harping on my daughter, 92
Harp-strings of the mind, 549
Harpy-footed Furies, 150
Harrisburg to Monterey, 867
Harrow of hail, 712
the toad beneath the, 776
up thy soul, 91
Harry the King Bedford, 67
Harsh and wild, their ways seem, 756
as truth, I will be as, 424
face of life, in the, 704
half-phrasings, 664
of cry, the, 930
the words of Mercury are, 42
to the clever, 942
Harshness gives offence, no, 211
Hart, panteth after water brooks, 1104
panteth for the water-brooks, 645
ungalled play, 94
Harvard, fair, 363
must be graduate of, 768
Harvest early, but the, 840
earth laughs with a, 417
golden sheaves after the, 638
grows, there no, 756
of a quiet eye, 297
of barren regrets, 592

Harvest of old age, 981
truly is plenteous, 1115
Harvests, wholesome, 393
Harvest-home, a stubble-land at, 61
Harvest-song and shout, with, 443
Harvest-time of love, 322
Hassan, King, well-beloved, 732
looked around with sudden anger, 511
Haste, golden moments quick to, 474
I am always in, 226
make, the better foot before, 58
maketh waste, 7, 11
married in, 193
mounting in hot, 352
one with moderate, 90
sweaty, 89
to be rich, 1108
to repay an obligation, 1044
to shed the sovereign balm, 248
to wed at leisure, wooed in, 52
without rest! without, 1058
Hasten to be drunk, 177
Hastening ills, piey to, 250
on, lo the days are, 477
to merge itself, evil, 536
towards immortality, good, 536
Hastings Mill, went down by, 873
Hasty marriage seldom proveth well, 70
Hasty-Pudding purest of all food, 280
Hat away, I toss my, 1085
by his cockle, 256
fashion of his, 38
forbade me to put off my, 171
gnaws my, 857
have a good, 451
not the worse for wear, 264
off with your, 715
organ-grinder's, 660
stopping a chink, 620
the ultimum moriens of respectability, 454
three-cornered, the old, 450
throw in his, 941
upon my head, with my, 238
weareth a runcible, 499
Hats, I like calm, 907
off! along the street, 767
shocking bad, 293
Hatched, chickens ere they are, 143, 1042
Hatches, his body's under, 274
Hatchet, I did cut it with my, 941
Hate a dumpy woman, 358
and lust, heats of, 742
and mistrust, 736
cherish those hearts that, 73
definitions, I, 420
him mortally, 217
if hate be perfect, so, 470
immortal, 148
in fee, holds, 851
is a fear, 924
Juno's unrelenting, 177
know enough of, 839
looked the twin of heathen, 471
lost between us, no, 117
more hot, with a, 795
no sport in, 368
of hate scorn of scorn, 462
of the millions, 795

Hate of those below, 353
one another and know it on both sides, 183
out, strong to keep, 887
owe no man, 50
your neighbour, 398
Hates, endless extinction of unhappy, 547
Hated needs, but to be seen, to be, 208
with a hate, 360
Hateful tax, 232
to us, those, 965
Hater, he was a good, 238
of din and riot, 445
Haters, love your enemy bless your, 471
Hating David, not only, 173
no one love but her, 354
Hatred as well as love, 1055
battered by, 881
comes from the heart, 1063
love turned to, 193
neither love nor, 1080
of a minute, forgot in the, 459
of scoundrels, a healthy, 379
public odium and public, 329
Hatreds, die to the little, 864
Hattum, such a stylish, 867
Haud your hands frae inkhorns, 523
Haughtiness, none possess such, 843
of soul, 194
Haughty barbers, to hide the, 878
brought to dust, 905
cry, one, 871
hizzie die, for a, 285
spirit before a fall, 1107
valor, sweet mouth, 418
yearning of the soul, 554
Hauled on his boots and roared, 508
Haunch and the hump is obey, 783
Haunt, exempt from public, 48
Haunts, for love hath lowly, 406
in dale or mountain, 317
of men, the busy, 370
the guilty mind, suspicion, 71
welcome to no editorial, 797
Haunted air, far off on the, 904
houses where men have lived and died, 436
me like a passion, 296
spring and dale, from, 161
town, a, 673
Haunting ghosts, are your, 642
Have a thing is nothing, to, 942
a touch of earth, must, 470
and to hold, 1128
it so, you would, 1046
mercy upon us miserable sinners, 1127
more than thou showest, 98
my own four walls, 382
no mockings or arguments, I, 534
nought venter nought, 15
taste of fame is purgatory, 426
to hold and let go, to, 775
we prize not to the worth what we, 39
you heard of the wonderful, 452

Haven, a glorious, 1020
  down to the, 472
  in sunny Palestine, 832
  under the hill, 764
Havens dumb, is in the, 672
  ports and happy, 59
Have-much and Have-little, 1040
Having nothing yet hath all, 114, 1121
Havoc, cry, and let slip the dogs, 82
Hawk from a hand saw, 92
  's the darling of his fere, 977
  over cypress tree, a white, 798
  the wild, 778
Hawks, between two, 68
Hawk-eyes, cheek of apple-blossom, 470
Hawser's tie no more returning, to, 537
Hawthorn bush with seats, 250
  in the dale, under the, 160
Hawthorns heave cold flagstones, 905
Hay, among the new-mown, 955
  bales of sweet Kentucky, 926
  cry was still more, 700
  goat feet dance the antic, 32
  live on, 957
  make, while the sun shines, 1036
  needle in a bottle of, 132, 1039
  reposing himself in the, 254
  wagon of, 823
  when the sun shineth make, 12
  world a bundle of, 361
Haydn, some Mozart, some cry up, 324
Haystack, like a burning, 871
Haytien, dark, 297
Hazard, art's long, 808
  march to the unseen, 772
  of concealing, 285
  of new fortunes, 57
  runs a very great, 1039
Hazards, French avoid no, 923
Hazardous, definitions are, 232
Haze, and that side of the, 585
  in the mountain-pass, 830
  on the far horizon, 737
He alone is blessed, 190
  and she to bed, bringeth, 929
  as, died to make men holy, 522
  best can paint them, 216
  can't possibly stop, says, 876
  cleansed and anointed, 927
  comes too near, 128, 221
  cometh unto you, 27
  could see naught but vanity, 522
  does not die, 810
  does not write at all, 995
  doesn't get to tell it, if, 661
  doth but sit and wait, 674
  first deceased, 114
  for God only, 152
  governs land and sea, 534
  hath loosed the fateful lightning, 522
  is above everything, 1052
  is gentle he is kind, 567
  is not, 630
  is or was or is to be, 1053
  is trampling out the vintage, 522
  knew what's what, 10

He laughs best who laughs last, 1081
  loves me best that calls me Tom, 129
  may look just the same, 925
  may run that readeth, 1113
  not, that merely says one, 378
  only may chastise who loves, 1084
  passed by on the other side, 1117
  preaches well that lives well, 1040
  profits most who serves best, 804
  quickens into deeds, 442
  rose and was himself again, 903
  sendeth sun he sendeth shower, 423
  shall be as a tree, 1112
  shall give his angels charge, 1105
  speaketh not and yet there, 438
  speeds, still the fitting word, 441
  take to following where, leads, 609
  that doth the ravens feed, 48
  that gets the most tolerable one, 976
  that gives quickly, 1037
  that giveth unto the poor, 1109
  that high growth on cedars did bestow, 30
  that is down, 142, 172
  that is faithful in that, 1117
  that is giddy thinks world turns round, 42
  that is not with me, 1117
  that is proud eats himself, 75
  that is robbed, 102
  that is without sin, 1118
  that lends, gives, 138
  that lives more lives than one, 722
  that runs may read, 266
  that shall humble himself, 1115
  that wants money, means and content, 50
  that with his hand, 1019
  that won't with us comply, 941
  that works and does, 378
  that would live, 960
  that wrestles with us, 261
  to whom you betray another, 1029
  touched his harp and nations, 393
  travels the fastest, 783
  walks among his peers unread, 540
  was fresh and full of faith, 421
  was like a cock who thought, 520
  was rich and she was poor, 510
  was the word that spake it, 118
  who busies himself, 996
  who can call to-day his own, 177
  who died at Azan, 596
  who does not work, 1093
  who for the first time loves, 1066
  who is of a calm and happy nature, 973

He who knows not, 706
  who laughs best to-day, 1081
  who lies to hide one fault makes it two, 135
  who sees takes off his shoes, 431
  who strives, 967
  who would write heroic, 376
  whose hands upheld us, 1091
  wields a mighty scepter, 534
  will swallow up death, 1111
  without whose favour, 920
  would have sinned, 808
  wrote down for men, as, 516
Head a little, turned his, 925
  an inch above general level, 638
  an' brains, moidhered, 820
  and front of my offending, 100
  and saw the wind, turned my, 814
  and the hoof of the law, 783
  and tummy, mainly, 785
  aside, turned her little, 948
  brought in upon a platter, 900
  buck of the first, 41
  coals of fire on his, 1108, 1119
  contempt from the, 1063
  cover my, now, 391
  crotchets in thy, thou hast some, 34
  crown of his, 39, 116, 131
  crown of our, 116
  crown old winter's, 165
  disorders of the, 969
  dissever from the fair, 212
  erect beneath the tragic years, 728
  eternal sunshine settles on its, 251
  every tooth in a man's, 1034
  fame over his living, 366
  gently falling on thy, 199
  gently lay my, 145
  go bow thy, in gentle spite, 555
  good gray, 467
  green grass turf at his, 256
  grown gray in vain, 366
  hairs of your, all numbered, 1115
  hang the, 121
  hang the pensive, 159
  hangs his, for shame, 555
  hapless owner's, 654
  hat upon my, 238
  heart may give a lesson to the, 266
  heaven to the weary, 391
  helmet for a blow on the, 1015
  here rests his, 245
  hit the nail o' the, 1042
  hoary, is a crown of glory, 1107
  how sober, a, 539
  if a thing comes in his, 71
  imperfections on my, 92
  in the lion's mouth, 952
  incessantly stand on your, 320
  inside a wolf's mouth, 961
  into the shop, pops its, 246
  is as full of quarrels, 79
  is bloody but unbowed, 692
  is fancy bred, in heart or, 45
  is sick and the heart faint, 1110

Head is the brightest part, 558
is worth showing to the people, 381
keep a good tongue in your, 33
learned lumber in his, 212
lock upon the shapely, 665
lodgings in a, 142
mouse poked its little, 961
my hand upon his, 428
nail on the, 18, 127, 1042
no roofe to shrowd his, 129
not slape that comes into my, 389
not where to lay his, 1114
not yet completely silvered, 265
of a household twenty years, 786
of his staffe a pen and ink-horne, 171
of my troops, at the, 1060
of the army, 1061
of the table, 1040
of the table, Macdonald sits at the, 414
of things, great, 992
of this great and wide-spread family, 942
of Voltaire, 345
off with his, 72
old men's, are just as bare, 910
on horror's, 103
one small, 251
or hand for self or others, 459
or heart or nerve or vein, of, 951
planted in the human, 1064
precious jewel in his, 48
repairs his drooping, 159
scratched his, 808
seems no bigger than his, 99
silent doctor shook his, 206
silvered o'er by time, 265
slide into a lover's, 296
so many books upon his, 290
so young a body so old a, 46
stroked with a slipper, 979
sweet tooth in his, 24
taken from Adam's, 953
that wears a crown, 65, 910
the very hair on my, 966
the wise the reverend, 199
this man held up his, 925
this old gray, 443
to be let unfurnished, 142
to contrive, 270
to the south and foot to the north, 1068
turn not away that sweet, 388
turns no more his, 315
uneasy lies the, 65
upon his hoary, 446
wagging his wicked, 933
was heavy, poor little, 648
was silvered o'er with age, 206
were less golden, 593
what seemed his, 150
which statuaries loved to copy, 398
with reading, stuff the, 215
Heads are green hands are blue, their, 498
beneath their shoulders, 100
hide their diminished, 151
houseless, 99
hover in their restless, 32

Heads in the world, heart better than, 426
lifted tossing, 891
never raising, 297
never scratching their, 891
of strong old age, 895
of the people, over the, 560
of the same material, 893
on your own, 780
so many wits so many, 12
sometimes so little, 147
tall men had empty, 113
they hung their, 1065
too little for wit, 147
touch heaven, hills whose, 100
two better than one, 13
two in council, 466
will roll, then, 1090
without turning their, 877
wooden, are inherited, 818
Head-dress, lady's, 196
Headings reduced to three, 1049
Headlands of home, 889
Headlines, they read the, 935
Headpiece filled with straw, 899
Headstone every day, come not to the, 553
grass-grown, 716
of the corner, 1106
stood, where a little, 527
Headstones change, milestones into, 529
Headstrong as an allegory, 278
Headwaters, the cold lakes, the, 929
Heal the blows of sound, to, 451
Healer, scorn not death the, 964
Healers, the best of, 964
Healing in his wings, 1114
is a matter of time, 971
of the world, 566
out of doors, 757
that night has shed, 682
Health alone is victory, 378
and a day, give me, 414
and wealth have missed me, 346
back to, 967
best physic to preserve, 111
blossom of, 362
by panacea, I swear by, 971
cut them for, 956
dainties might hurt their, 252
enjoy good, 985
good sense and good, 989
holy, 960
hunt in fields for, 175
is the second blessing, 140
medicine to produce, 1000
my nerves and fibres brace, 225
of the people, 420
peace and competence, 208
poor in, 65
sinlessness and immortality, 548
talk, 718
that mocks the doctor's rules, 442
the groundwork of all happiness, 346
to fond deceit, here's a, 774
to the native-born, 778
unbought, 175
vital principle of bliss, 225
while grace affordeth, 20

Health, wealth and beauty, 165
Healthful ease, no cheerfulness no, 391
Healthy appetite, what you call a, 599
greatest danger for the, 1081
hatred of scoundrels, 379
let all men contrive to be, 378
nature, blessed is the, 377
to care for the, 971
token when women love to sew, 422
wealthy and wise, 227
Heap, dead beneath the, 748
high the farmer's wintry hoard, 441
lay stone on stone, dig and, 546
logs and let the blaze, 484
misfortunes laid in one, 1003
o' good, it does a, 829
o' livin', it takes a, 870
o' sun an' shadder, 870
of ashes could be seen, 1066
of dust alone remains of thee, 217
of stick and stone, 651
struck all of a, 279
Heaps of miser's treasure, 158
of money, 166
of things, what, 971
unsunned, of treasure, 158
Heapeth up riches, 1104
Hear a voice you cannot hear, 1, 205
be silent that you may, 82
be swift to, 1122
beyond the range of sound, 514
by tale or history, 42
he that hath ears to, 1116
heavenly music what is it I, 387
him crow, thought sun risen to, 520
him prate, 575
it not Duncan, 86
listening still they seemed to, 220
me for my cause, 82
me, time will come when you will, 419
none so deaf that will not, 187
port is near the bells I, 536
so are those who, me, 606
the mellow wedding bells, 460
these tell-tale women, 72
thy dusky pinions, oft I, 418
wail in the wind is all I, 517
who so deafe as will not, 17
Heard a wise man say, I, 742
and do in part believe it, 89
for much speaking, 1114
I will be, 424
in days of old, which I, 446
in her dreams, songs she, 432
it said full oft, 109
melodies are sweet, 383
nations, entranced, 393
of the wonderful one-hoss shay, 452
of thee by the hearing of the ear, 1103
round the world, 409
so coldly, 425
the trailing garments, 433

Heard the world around, 161
wail still is, yet its notes, 545
wished she had not, it, 100
Hearer better than the utterer
knows, 748
Hearers, convince his, 970
such as you, to dying, 948
too deep for his, 252
Hearing ear, the, 413
ear the speaking tongue, 413
of the ear, heard of thee by the,
1103
Hearings, younger, quite ravished, 41
Hearkeners seldom hear good of
themselves, 188
Hearse, draw by the gilded, 900
underneath this sable, 119
Heart, a broken and a contrite,
1104
a good, better than heads, 426
a little heaven in each, 190
a loving, is the beginning, 378
a merry, 1107
a rapture, out of the, 681
a widowed woman's, 677
a wise and understanding, 1100
afraid, that makes the, 390
alike conceived and dared, 487
alone in the midst of crowds,
324
alone records my days, 774
alone, speaks to the, 501
almost gay, the poor, 541
and also my poor human, 514
and brain, for the unquiet, 467
and brain, to the near, 738
and hand and eye, vacant, 309
and lip, held his, 444
and my duty, 66
and passion, his whole, 1057
and soul away, his, 743
and the, of friendship colder,
405
and voice oppressed, sink, 518
and voice would fail me, 583
arrow for the, 361
as he thinketh in his, 1108
as sound as a bell, 39
at home, never find thy, 135
at Wounded Knee, bury my,
929
awake to the flowers, 334
ballads, 361
be lonely, seldom can the, 625
be no longer dumb, 540
be troubled, let not your, 1118
beat thick, 818
beating of my own, 458
beats to do some miracle, 683
before the cross, bowed Thy,
1091
believing, 507
bends with love's true instinct,
335
bitten me to the, 971
blew cold on my desolate, 418
blood-tinctured, 428
bread which strengthens man's,
188
breaks because you and I must
part, 117
bring back her, 789
broke, since my, 916
bruised, that knew him well,
836

Heart, build on the human, 484
buildeth on the vulgar, 64
burn within us, 307
bursting with the strain, 598
bury your, 812
but not your, away, 742
by one great, 728
can know, ease the, 248
can push the sea and land, 915
can this fond, forget, 388
cannot break, which the, 511
careful soul and troubled, 781
chains that bind the, 432
close to my, 445
cockles of the, 944, 1039
coldness dwells within thine,
446
command my, and me, 165
congenial to my, 251
console the, 942
create in me a clean, 1104
creep out of the, 666
crown is in my, 70
dark as one's own, 422
darling of my, 189
despair of doing some goodly
thing, 512
distrusting asks, 251
doth ache, while his, 172
dumb region of the, 663
dupe of the, 1044
each, is whispering Home, 392
encloseth my poor, 71
evening twilight of the, 363
every, to heaven aspires, 345
every woman is a rake at, 209
everywhere he feels his, 958
fails thee, if thy, 222
faint and the head is sick, 1110
faint, ne'er won fair lady, 1039
fear and amazement beat upon
my, 129
felt along the, 295
find out her, 594
first joys of our, 390
first set my poor, free, 127
flowers of Thy, 338
flutter and beat of the wild,
787
fool hath said in his, 1103
for a constant, 950
for any fate, 357, 433
for every fate here's a, 357
for every one, 418
for falsehood framed, 279
for his hard, 443
for pain and very shame would
break, 804
for such a kind, 34
fountain of sweet tears, 297
from blows, guarding his, 905
from breaking, stop one, 583
from itself, kept, 628
from low desires, weaned my,
1023
from red, change the, 659
gateway of my, 809
gathered to thy, 701
gently upon my, 440
gets his speeches by, 289
give lesson to the head, 266
give me back my, 351
glows in every, 202
goes wrong, no human, 698
good, is worth gold, 64
graven on this grateful, 953

Heart, griping griefs the, wound,
255
grow fonder, absence makes
the, 388
grown cold a head grown gray,
366
grows weary, darkies how my,
567
had never wrung, his, 1052
hand with my, in 't, 33
happy the, 30
has always assured me, 342
has desired, 780
has hidden treasures, 507
has its love, my, 1066
has learned a lesson, 888
hath builded shrines, 418
hath 'scaped this sorrow, 108
hatred comes from the, 1063
have its say, let the, 715
he seeth with the, 317
here in the country's, 763
heresy of doctrine than heresy
of, 442
his sentient, 839
hope in my, 955
how spacious, 539
hymn of the broken in, 533
I am sick at, 89
I give my hand and, 340
I hold to my, 845
I hope with all my, 878
I said to, 811
if guilt 's in that, 336
if one has no, 1066
in anguish shivers, my, 1071
in conjecture of a neighbour's,
1009
in his hand like a palm branch,
558
in its central, nestles the seed,
535
in my hand, 33
in unison with mankind, 692
incense of the, 226
infant, 326
is a ball of string, 630
is a lonely hunter, 717
is all a-flutter, 938
is at liberty, 1051
is filled with praise, 692
is genuinely Highland, 674
is in a vein, when the, 337
is in a whirl, 792
is in the highlands, my, 286
is laden, with rue, 743
is like a singing bird, 587
is like, we must guess what
the, 594
is met by throbbing heart, 343
is of steel, 804
is on the mountain, my, 760
is open wide to-night, 722
is pure, because my, 465
is right there, but my, 836
is the poet's, 887
is true as steel, 42
is turning home again, my, 508
is warm, my, 916
is wax to be moulded, 357
is where the hills, 760
is wide, no wider than the, 915
is young when, 881
it is an honest, 716
just as high as my, 50
kind and gentle, 254

Heart, kindlier hand the larger, 469
knew of pain, all the, 455
know it all by, 1035
know truth by the, 1047
knoweth his own bitterness, 1107
language of the, 213
languor is not in your, 547
larger was his, 174
less bounding, 547
let in either to the other's, 730
let me wring your, 95
level in her husband's, 54
lightest, heaviest mourning, 447
like a shadow o'er the, 567
like nothing so much as a bowl, 599
little watchman in my, 808
look in thy, 27
look into any man's, 1076
look then into thine, 433
lord of the lion, 248
love that is in my, 1065
lover who unlocks his, 134
loving, I will give to thee, 133
maketh glad the, 1105
man after his own, 1100
man's, deviseth his way, 1107
may bear, how much the, 596
may go whithersoever, 986
may heal or break, 474
may quail, stoutest, 564
melts their thoughtful, 1021
merry, 363
merry, doeth good, 1107
merry, goes all the day, 56
merry, maketh a cheerful countenance, 1107, 1125
mother, within me, 642
moved more than with a trumpet, 27
music in my, I bore, 298
must pass me by, many a, 681
must speak when lips are dumb, 658
my book and, 947
my fond, shall pant for you, 225
my true-love hath my, 27
naked human, 202
nature's, beats strong, 458
ne'er within him burned, 307
never extinguished in the, 1055
new fountains in the human, 393
new opened, I feel my, 73
next our own, 365
not able to report my dream, 43
not thy woman's, 560
notation of the, 927
now cracks a noble, 98
O tiger's, 69
of a child, soft is the, 815
of a dog may never forget, 831
of a maiden is stolen, when the, 335
of a man, 778
of a man changeth, 1125
of a man is depressed, 205
of a man is like that delicate weed, 592
of a true Englishman, 197

Heart of a woman, possesses the, 1086
of another, enrich not the, 435
of childhood, Santa Claus will make glad, 643
of courtesy, seated in the, 27
of heart, in my, 94
of her sons, the strong, 475
of her who bore him, 836
of lead, 215
of little faith, 691
of man depressed with cares, 205
of man, the devil dwells in, 144
of mine, this dark, 432
of my heart, 633
of my mystery, pluck out the, 94
of Shelley, 750
of the beholder, 933
of the fathers, turn the, 1114
of the king or humblest thrall, 713
of the minstrel, 335
of the mountains, 572
of the people! Workingmen, 458
of the woman he loves, 1086
of things, all the rapturous, 735
often healed the, 474
on my, monastic aisles, 408
one hand one flag one, 452
one who thrills your, 679
or head, where is fancy bred in, 45
or hope, nor bate a jot of, 162
out of the abundance of the, 1115
out of the bosom, 742
overcharged, 321
owing to his cordial, 586
pang that rends the, 252
passion or excitement of the, 461
plan my ways and rule my, 403
plays an old tune on the, 512
preaching down a daughter's, 464
priceless rending of the, 1088
prosperity with all my, 921
raise the dead, 868
razors to my wounded, 76
refreshing, the, 735
remembers, playing all my, 690
replete with thankfulness, 68
replies, and the, 266
responds unto his own, 434
rest thou troubled, 396
retain at, 964
reveal, doth the full, 317
riven with vain endeavour, 298
rotten at the, 44
ruddy drops that visit my sad, 82
ruddy drops that warm my, 244
run over, one kindness which makes the, 272
savage indignation no longer tear his, 193
search thine own, 442
secret anniversaries of the, 439
seeth with the, 317
Shakespeare unlocked his, 304, 492

Heart shall be thy garden, my, 701
shall keep the child, 901
shall not dissever, my, 1022
shot full of pain, 854
show his eyes and grieve his, 87
shy in truculent appearance, 709
sick, maketh the, 1107
sigh in the human, 738
silence in the, 922
singeth low in every, 648
sink into the, 218
sinking, changing cheek, 356
sky did never melt into his, 296
some, did break, 468
some far corner of thy, 582
song that nerves a nation's, 471
soothes one humble human, 793
sorrow that purifies the, 1074
spring of love gushed from my, 315
stabs falsehood to the, 524
strike mine eyes not my, 119
strong and diverse, 927
stuff that weighs upon the, 88
subdue the, 983
suffered idleness to eat his, 26 .
sullen, 703
sweet creation of some, 354
sweetly tender, 463
take thy beak from out my, 460
tears rise in the, 466
tenderest, even the, 365
thanked God, 850
that ever beat, happiest, 687
that forgets us, 1046
that gives it love, 828
that has truly loved, 335
that is broken, soothe a, 309
that is soonest awake, 334
that loved her, betray the, 296
that mighty, is lying still, 297
that not yet, 587
that swelling of the, 952
that thou gavest, take back the, 583
that was humble, 333
that's so hard, 256
the cockles of my, 1039
the sesoun priketh every gentil, 5
the sight of death makes hard, whose, 50
the sweeping up the, 584
the waes o' my, 277
they say Ward has no, 289
through that velvet and lace, 594
till the tired, 438
to a dog to tear, 784
to an ancient mould, shape your, 842
to break, when there is no, 895
to captivate my, 193
to conceive, 270, 949
to drown the outcry of the, 386
to eate thy, 26
to fight and lose, 887
to fold, entered into my, 907
to heart mind to mind, 307
to heart up there, 560
to my heart, never a, 718

Heart to resolve, 270
  to thy heart, my, 668
  toil on sad courageously, 509
  tongue nor, cannot conceive, 86
  too easy entrance into her, 155
  too little for our, 503
  touching that wild wild, 911
  turning in unison, 1017
  twa bairns and but ae, 389
  two chambers has the, 1070
  unpack my, with words, 93
  untainted, 69
  until it reached a gentle, 499
  untravelled fondly turns to thee, 249
  upon my sleeve, wear my, 100
  upon 't, break your, 430
  upon the goal, set his, 735
  utmost passion of her, 422
  veracity the, of morality, 563
  want of, 390
  war was in his, 1104
  warm within, 266
  was as great as the world, 415
  was breaking breaking, his, 738
  was kind and soft, 274
  was wax to receive, 357
  watched above the blighted, 544
  way to hit a woman's, 417
  we may live without, 592
  weary, can rest, 548
  weed's plain, 524
  were just frank kindly, every, 1046
  what female, can gold despise, 243
  when the high, 873
  when we meet a mutual, 225
  where your treasure is, 1114
  which lives in grace, 1021
  which most enamour us, 357
  which others bleed for, 193
  whispers the o'erfraught, 88
  whose lines are mottoes of the, 327
  whoso says in his, 1055
  widow's, to sing for joy, 1102
  wilt thou hear, within thy, 1084
  with a manly, 440
  with a mighty, 66
  with all diligence, keep thy, 1106
  with my whole, 1113
  with women the, argues, 547
  with your treasure, 1114
  within and God o'erhead, 433
  within me faints, 823
  within your breast, 928
  would hear her and beat, my, 469
  yet O stricken, 703
Hearts aflame, cool-headed with, 553
  aloe-like, flower once and die, 507
  an open book, he had read in women's. 865
  and heads, broken, 828
  and heads, higher than the, 808
  ardour of their, 1074
  are breaking in Vanity Fair, 690

Hearts are great, hoard is little but, 470
  are hard and sour, 522
  are sair, mony, 952
  are yearning, while your, 824
  as breaks the dumb, 834
  as light, fill to-night with, 431
  believe the truths I tell, 247
  cheerful, now broken, 336
  cherish those, that hate thee, 73
  cherished by all our, upheld by all our hands, 481
  cold, beat hot, 652
  cold, hate the union, 685
  complaisance in their, 1037
  contemptuous of death, 809
  day-star arise in your, 1123
  dissension between, 338
  don't change much, 953
  dry as summer dust, 302
  dust overlying our hard, 498
  endure, of all that human, 231
  ensanguined, 266
  feeling, touch but rightly, 289
  great are always lone, 609
  hands not, 70, 103
  he fashioneth their, alike, 1103
  home-keeping, are happiest, 439
  hot, beat cold, 652
  in glad surprise, our, 436
  in love use their own tongues, 38
  kind, are more than coronets, 462
  lie withered, when true, 335
  light and free, 403
  like doors will ope with ease, 746
  men with splendid, 893
  mystery in human, 955
  of gallant men, 746
  of his countrymen, 281
  of his fellow-citizens, 281
  of kings, enthroned in the, 46
  of men, upon the, 1059
  of oak are our ships, 242
  of the citizens, incline the, 268
  of the owners, open as the, 435
  once so happy and free, 567
  our, are hard and inflexible, 166
  our, our hopes are all with thee, 435
  our, our hopes our prayers, 435
  resolved on victory or death, 1060
  shall breathe the old refrain, 443
  shrined in our, with Cressy, 518
  shutting away of loving, 917
  sing to find our, 881
  steal away your, 83
  still, there are kind, 703
  talk out their, 822
  that break and give no sign, 452
  that love will know, 690
  that once beat high, 334
  that roam, 778
  that the world in vain had tried, 338

Hearts that trust in me, 813
  that weep, waiting, 563
  the truest, that ever, 386
  there are loyal, 671
  there is no union here of, 306
  though stout and brave, 433
  thousand, beat happily, 352
  time demands strong minds great, 522
  to apprehend, 794
  to ease our, 629
  to live in, we leave behind, 328
  too full for utterance, 475
  two, that beat as one, 219
  union of, union of hands, 405
  unto wisdom, apply our, 1105
  upon, men set their, 1018
  were drunk with a beauty, 801
  were high fortunes low, 906
  were not so clever, young, 743
  wiser manfuler happier, 379
Heart's blood, country's own, 806
  core, wear him in my, 94
  dead are never buried, 910
  desire, and may the, 834
  desire, deceived in your, 565
  desire, land of, 790
  desire, nearer to the, 1020
  desire, remould it to the, 471
  desires, be with you, your, 48
  desolation, o'er my, 507
  eternal torture, 889
  hope and home, 382
  inner chamber, in the, 446
  Oh her, adrift with one, 568
  supreme ambition, 239
Heartache, end the, 93
  falls asleep with, 838
  "I had" is a, 676
Heartaches, lock all your, 848
Heart-blood of a queen, 424
Heartbreak, a great deal of, 35
  Mary, helper of, 866
Heart-breaking beauty will remain, 895
Heart-broken husband, 817
Heartburnings of the aristocrat, 1072
Hearth acold, and the, 757
  and stool and all, 869
  and wayside lurking, by, 453
  blessing on the, 491
  clean fire and clean, 323
  cricket on the, 160
  firelogs throwing on, 983
  his, the earth his hall the azure, 410
  most charming thing, 1069
  our old familiar, 364
  the domestic, 1078
  to light his, 373
  two beside the, 466
  vanished from his lonely, 305
  we sat the clean-winged, 443
Hearths and altars fires are dead, on, 507
Hearthfire smoke, sees his, 911
Hearthstone, cat on your, 815
  on any man's, 776
Hearthstones, speak no evil around these, 691
Heart-leaves of lilac, 831
Heartless Godless hell's delight, 759
  owners' hands, in, 618
Heartsome wi' thee, 205

Heart-stain, ne'er carried a, 334
Heart-strings are a lute, 460
  jesses were my dear, 102
  magnetic, 633
  quivering, 553
  rip your very, 777
Heart-talkers, letters are true, 551
Heart-throbs, count time by, 506
Heart-whole, I'll warrant him, 51
Heart-wounded by a subtle spell, 891
Hearty faith and honest cheer, 574
  hand that is honest and, 305
  old man, 320
Heat, cold that moderates, 1042
  fantastic summer's, 59
  for the cold and cold for the hot, 1042
  have neither, nor light, 127
  heraldic in the, 936
  in little storage, 903
  ma'am it was so dreadful, 313
  nor darkness, snow nor rain nor, 969
  not a furnace for your foe, 72
  o' the day, clean of the, 873
  o' the sun, fear no more the, 106
  of blood, in, 871
  of conflict, through the, 300
  of its defenders, 184
  of the day, burden and, 1115
  of the wheel, white, 928
  one, doth drive another, 28
  one draught above, 54
  some human, 853
  sudden, which made my heart to glow, 30
  that flamed, came, 903
  that Promethean, 103
  to examine the laws of, 641
  we bear the burden and the, 546
  within me, pain's furnace, 1071
Heats of hate and lust, 742
Heated hot in a moment, little chimney, 436
Heath, land of brown, 307
  likewise a wind on the, 407
  my foot is on my native, 310
  shy cock of the, 288
Heathen Chinee is peculiar, 644
  hate, looked the twin of, 471
  thousands of miles afar, 475
Heather looks, I know how the, 584
  tumble on, 309
Heath-flower dashed the dew, from the, 308
Heating, warm without, 204
Heat-oppressed brain, 85
Heave and the halt and the hurl, 777
  of the surging world, 735
  of water, one great, 498
Heaves, with oily gradual, 833
Heaven a time ordains, 162
  above us, starlight of, 502
  achromatic white light of, 432
  again for goal, 634
  all places alike distant from, 124
  all the starry host of, 910

Heaven, all the way to, 165
  all things in, and earth, 22
  alone is given away, 525
  and Charing Cross, betwixt, 749
  and earth, men differ as, 470
  and earth, more things in, 92
  and earth shall pass away, 1116
  and earth suspended, 'twixt, 705
  and earth unfolds, 42
  and happy constellations, 154
  and hell, believe in, 728
  and hell, myself am, 1019
  and hell, worst and best as, 470
  and home, points of, 304
  and the earth and all the elements, 9
  around our infancy, 525
  around us, all, 336
  ascribe to, 53
  be thronged, 759
  beauteous eye of, 58
  behaving as if you were in, 721
  breaks the serene of, 322
  breath of, 264
  bright sun of, 74
  cast out of, 633
  commences, his, 250
  deprived of, 1021
  does not choose its elect from great, 482
  drowsy with the harmony, 41
  earth's crammed with, 431
  endures, 744
  even up in, 935
  ever-moving spheres of, 32
  every heart aspires to, 345
  every purpose under the, 1109
  exhaled and went to, 202
  expands, when earth breaks up and, 486
  face of, so fine, 79
  fantastic tricks before high, 36
  farther off from, 390
  feeds the stars, 982
  fell from, 149
  fiercest spirit that fought in, 149
  first-born, offspring of, 151
  floor of, is thick inlaid, 47
  for climate, 750
  for dogs, isn't there, 758
  fragrance smells to, 226
  from all creatures hides, 207
  from, it came, 322
  from yon blue, 462
  gained a friend from, 245
  gates of, to the, 298
  gems of, 152
  gentle rain from, 46
  gives almonds, 434
  gives its favourites early death, 302, 354
  glories float between the earth and, 425
  God's in his, 485
  gold bar of, 577
  good sense the gift of, 210
  got the most of, 391
  grants before the prayer, 175
  great eye of, 24
  had made her such a man, 100
  had sent, herald, 933

Heaven, harbingers to, 147
  has no rage like love to hatred turned, 193
  has not power upon the past, 177
  has willed we die alone, 365
  have ye souls in, too, 384
  he gained from, a friend, 245
  he hath in him, most of, 506
  hell I suffer seems a, 151
  hell or Hoboken, 861
  hills whose heads touch, 100
  his blessed part to, 74
  holds all, 696
  honours reeking up to, 67
  hours before, warned by, 933
  husbandry in, 85
  I'm bound for, 557
  in a poet's secret, 887
  in a rage, puts all, 281
  in a wild flower, 281
  in each heart a little, 190
  in hell's despair, builds a, 281
  in hope to merit, 352
  in plain terms, gone to, 45
  is above all, 73
  is blest with perfect rest, 709
  is love for love is heaven, 306
  is more and less than just, 565
  is no larger than Connecticut, 757
  is not always angry, 190
  is not built, 911
  is not reached at a single bound, 521
  is to be at peace, 770
  is touching earth, 656
  is yours at last, 565
  its stars, the, 1066
  itself would stoop to her, 159
  keep the great professor, 453
  kind not heard in, 1021
  kindred points of, 304
  laid on few curse of poetry, 716
  lay not my transgression to my charge, 57
  leave her to, 92
  led the way to, 205
  less of earth than, 308, 405
  let through, such light as never, 634
  lies about us in our infancy, 301
  light from, 285
  made him, every man is as, 1039
  man alone beneath the, 307
  many farewells as stars in, 75
  marriages are made in, 465
  matches are made in, 125
  may decrease it upon better acquaintance, 34
  moderation the gift of, 967
  my offence is rank it smells to, 95
  no more subtle master under, 471
  not grim but fair of hue, 492
  nothing can cover his fame but, 131
  nothing true but, 336
  O, her dancing, 405
  of all their wish, 893
  of each what each desires, 337
  of fabulous conviction, 932

Heaven of hell, in itself can make
    a, 148
  of invention, the brightest, 66
  of my heart, sing to the, 811
  offspring of, 151
  on earth, 151
  on earth display, 274
  one minute of, 338
  opened wide her ever-during
    gates, 154
  opening bud to, conveyed, 316
  or hell, summons thee to, 86
  permit to, 155
  Persian's, is easily made, 334
  places shall be hell that are
    not, 31
  points out an hereafter, 195
  prepare for His beautiful, 291
  presents in sheets the solid hue,
    839
  reach that purest, 520
  recompense did send, 245
  remedies we ascribe to, 53
  resplendent and fair, 798
  ring the bells of, 816
  seem best, earth being so good,
    would, 487
  sends us good meat, 243
  sent us soda water, 828
  settin' up in, 851
  shall be fulfilled, in, 557
  shall glow, lights of, 401
  shall harbor me, never a, 712
  she did but dream of, 175
  shut thee from, 452
  silent finger points to, 302
  silver bow new-bent in, 42
  so much of earth so much of,
    298
  soul white as, 131
  spectral in, 889
  spires point to, 302
  starry cope of, 153
  starved for, 642
  steep and thorny way to, 90
  sweetened by the airs of, 417
  sword of, 37
  take my soul, 58
  teaching from, 653
  thank, fasting, 50
  that smiles above me, 543
  the gold bar of, 577
  the sin forgiven by Christ in,
    431
  then, be thy aid, 375
  there is a, 820
  things are the sons of, 232
  thunderbolt of, 969
  thy hues were born in, 382
  'tis less of earth than, 405
  to appreciate, well, 678
  to be young was very, 300
  to earth, doth glance from, 43
  to gaudy day denies, which,
    356
  to stoop, so ready is, 749
  to the weary head, 391
  too black for, 174
  tries the earth, 525
  try snow of, 923
  't was whispered in, 't was mut-
    tered in hell, 290
  upon earth, that, 391
  upon the earth, if there's a, 677
  visits, places the eye of, 59
  wanted one immortal song, 173

Heaven was all tranquillity, 338
  was falling, day when, 743
  was not heaven if Phaon was
    not there, 458
  were not heaven if we knew
    what it were, 163
  when earth was nigher, 485
  will protect the working-girl,
    730
  winds of, visit her face, 90
  with all its splendors, 525
  with earth, melting, 447
  without horses, forbid that I
    should go to, 708
  words without thoughts never
    go to, 95
  yet, I'll get you into, 875
Heavens are fresh and strong, an-
    cient, 299
  are out in fleeces, 576
  be penetrable and no lets, if
    the, 124
  declare the glory of God, 1103
  fill with commerce, 464
  fill with shouting, 464
  hear these tell-tale women, 72
  hung be the, with black, 68
  look with aspect more favour-
    able, 56
  should fall, if ever the, 1025
  spangled, a shining frame, 194
  starry, and sense of moral re-
    sponsibility, 542
  that which we call the, 992
  when I consider thy, 1103
Heaven's blue hour-glass, 857
  bounty lends, gifts, 403
  breath smells wooingly, 85
  chancery, flew up to, 242
  cherubim horsed, 85
  decree, curst by, 251
  ebon vault, 369
  eternal year is thine, 175
  gate is shut, 444
  gate, the lark at, 105
  gates, she claps her wings at,
    23
  gates, storming, 918
  glories shine, 516
  good grace, 513
  hand, argue not against, 162
  help is better than early rising,
    1041
  immortal noon, 367
  jeweled crown, 618
  last best gift, 153
  lights, godfathers of, 40
  melodious strains, 477
  own blue, 372
  own light, 306
  pavement, riches of, 149
  protecting power, 395
  scenes, look on, 953
  self, Ann hath a way to be,
    274
  Sovereign saves, 202
  street, 832
  wide pathless way, 160
Heavens' embroidered cloths, 790
Heaven-born band, 294
Heaven-eyed creature, 305
Heaven-gates are not so highly
    arch'd, 128
Heaven-kissing hill, 95
Heavenly blessings, 199
  days that cannot die, 296

Heavenly Father may assuage
    pray the, 457
  forms, mould it into, 452
  gift of poesy, profaned thy,
    175
  harmony, from, 175
  hope is all serene, 343
  host, ye, 183
  jewel, have I caught my, 27
  maid was young, 247
  music, that, 387
Heaven-rescued land, 332
Heaven-taught lyre, 239
Heaven-wander'd princess, to
    lodge this, 867
Heaviest battalions, 1053
  mourning, lightest heart makes,
    447
Heaviness, spirit of, 1112
  that's gone, with a, 33
Heaving up my either hand, 134
Heavy and red, eyelids, 391
  change, but oh the, 159
  dragoon is the residuum, 623
  soft and slow brilliant and
    warm, 923
Heavy-fisted destinies prepare,
    893
Hebrides, in dreams behold the,
    674
  seas colder than the, 881
Hector in the field, better like,
    438
Hecuba to him, what's, 93
Hedge a king, divinity doth, 96
  hide it in a, 285
  leaping over the, 1034
  of thorns, amid a, 857
  yet pull not down your, 137
Hedges and ditches, at, 589
  dust, over the, 926
  of England, 831
  unkempt about those, 893
Hedgehog rolled up, lies like a,
    391
Hedger and ditcher, 345
Hedgerow, see in every, 523
Hedgerows, with the wild, 810
Heed, take, lest he fall, 1120
Heedless of grammar, 351
  unwise to be, 991
Heel of the courtier, 97
  of the north-east trade, 778
  tread upon another's, 96
  trod on by a princely, 590
  with an unused, 783
Heels a stone, at his, 256
  Caesar with a senate at his,
    208
  I am almost out at, 34
  I took to my, 979
  of joy, misery treads on the,
    551
  of pleasure, treads upon the,
    193
  of sleet, 917
  of spring, 984
  of their boots, gunpowder ran
    out the, 246
  slipper good to the, 452
  with an income at its, 263
Heeltap! a heeltap! 348
Hegel and Kant, chaos and cos-
    mos, 595
Height, blue heaven's, 701
  city of dreadful, 819

Height, many on its, 700
  not stretched at any great, 1090
  oaks of towering, 231
  objects in an airy, 189
  of man, measure of the, 993
  of the houses, 1022
  of this great argument, 148
  sunshine dreaming upon Salmon's, 556
Heights by great men reached, 436
  greater than we can reach, 238
  here are the, 735
  look beyond the, 602
  of destiny, 690
  of greatness, 991
  where the far, 865
  yet unconquered, 972
Heimgang, German people whisper, 554
Heir, grandchild come more and oftener to be, 120
  of a mongrel bitch, 98
  of all the ages, 464
  of fame, great, 161
  to, shocks that flesh is, 93
  to the bearing of burdens, 642
  to the first, each second, 100
Heirs of all eternity, make us, 40
  of all the ages, 542
  of God and joint-heirs with Christ, 1119
  of Runnymede, 443
  of the island race, 760
  of to-morrow, 656
Heiresses, first American, 907
Held tu, say nothin' thet you can be, 527
Helen, like another, 176
  thy beauty is to me, 460
Helen's beauty in a brow of Egypt, 43
  lips are drifting dust, 805
Helicon's harmonious springs, 243
Helios, Antigonus the son of, 1005
Hell, agreement with, 424, 1111
  all places shall be, 31
  ascended into, 814
  better to reign in, 148
  broke loose, all, 153
  can hold, more devils than, 43
  characters of, to trace, 244
  contains no fouler fiend, 220
  cunning livery of, 36
  explores His lowest, 650
  fear of, 's a hangman's whip, 285
  for company, 750
  for hoarding went to, 70
  for horses, England, 125
  for women, Italy, 125
  got started, how, 852
  has no fury like a woman scorned, 193
  hath no limits, 31
  horrible light-house of, 389
  hot as, 1059
  I suffer seems a heaven, 151
  ignorance maker of, 736
  in, their souls may dwell, 551
  injured lover's, 153
  into the mouth of, 467

Hell is a city, 367
  is full of good meanings, 137
  is paved with good intentions, 236, 662
  it is in suing long to bide, 25
  itself breathes out contagion, 95
  long is the way out of, 150
  lost in, 915
  making earth a, 352
  milk of concord into, 88
  myself am, 151
  myself am heaven and, 1019
  no, 566
  no fiend in, can match, 193
  of heaven in itself can make a, 148
  of witchcraft, 109
  on earth, 720
  part steered clear of, 677
  procuress to the lords of, 468
  rebellious, 95
  riches grow in, 149
  roamed the courts of, 685
  shall stir for this, all, 67
  should bar the way, 864
  some fifteen minutes of, 678
  souls in trouble here and in, 418
  summons thee to heaven or to, 86
  taste of fame to want is a, 426
  terrible as, 150
  the luckless pots, toss to, 1019
  there is a, 820
  there is not a fiercer, 382
  to ears polite, never mentions, 210
  too white for, 174
  'twas muttered in, 290
  war is, 542
  we make for ourselves, 663
  wedlock forced but a, 68
  where we are is, 31
  which way I fly is, 151
  within him, 151
  within myself, I feel a, 144
  worst and best as heaven and, 470
Hell's broke loose in Georgia, 927
  concave, tore, 148
  despair, builds a heaven in, 281
  fire escape, never from, 867
  worn floor, slimed, 836
Hellespont and the Propontic, 103
  Leander swam the, 453
Hellish cockroach is the chief of foes, 865
Helm, and on the, 473
  Palinurus nodded at the, 215
  pleasure at the, 244
  prepared to take the, 1075
  when the sea is calm, 988
Helmet for blow on head, 1015
  shall make a hive for bees, 28
  that is Mambrino's, 1035
  the hope of salvation, for an, 1121
Help, after verb to love to, most beautiful, 1083
  and ornament, 109
  and support of the woman, 921
  by so much reading, so much, 429
  encumbers him with, 233

Help for the living hope for the dead, 603
  for these things, no, 634
  hindrance and a, 298
  his ready, was ever nigh, 231
  in trouble, a very present, 1104
  it, wicked anyhow I can't, 480
  me Cassius or I sink, 81
  me, who ran to, 345
  me with knowledge, 493
  nobody came to his, 962
  of a surgeon, with the, 43
  of anything on earth, 282
  of man, vain is the, 1104
  others out of a fellow-feeling, 121
  past, should be past grief, 56
  since there's no, let us kiss, 31
  themselves, God helps them that, 227
  thyself and God will help thee, 137, 1045
Helper, of heartbreak, 866
  our antagonist is our, 261
  our, He amid the flood, 1023
Helpless to speak comfort for great bereavement, 402
Helter-skelter hurry-scurry, 321
Hem and Haw were the sons of sin, 757
  lay 'round and Haw looked on, 757
  of my gown, catching the, 883
Hemisphere divided, light from darkness, 154
  of light and darkness, 378
Hemlock cup, the, 851
  for his wage, 853
Hemlocks, the sad, 602
Hemp and steel, that which moulders, 309
Hempen string, sing in a, 127
Hen gathereth her chickens, 1116
  has a right to set, 606
  in the pot, have his, 588
  is an egg's way of making another egg, 614
  two owls and a, 499
Henceforth in me instil, 620
Henceforward betwixt us twain, 470
  therefore be at peace, 436
Henpecked, fraternity of the, 197, 358
  you all, 358
Henry George friend of the race, 684
  Morgan, old bold mate of, 833
  Pimpernell, 52
Her Majesty's councils his words, 573
Heraclean courage and cheerfulness, 702
Heraclitus, they told me you were dead, 553
  would not laugh, what, 304
Herald Mercury, like the, 95
  no other, after my death, 74
  of joy, perfectest, 38
  of the morn, the lark, the, 79
  the owl, night's, 106
  they killed me, 933
Heralds, love's, should be thoughts, 79
Herald's coat without sleeves, 63
Heraldic in the heat, 936

Heraldry, our new, is hands, 103
the boast of, 244
Herb and tree, dew bespangling, 134
to our fathers, excellent, 783
Herbs, better is a dinner of, 1107
bruised, most fragrant are, 1052
from all antiquity, 664
powerful grace that lies in, 78
Herbage strown, strip of, 1018
Hercules and Goth and Moor, 647
do what he may, 97
gates of, 658
he is a second, 996
with strangled serpents, 930
Herd, avoid the reeking, 897
in Mammon's mesh, 759
milky mothers of the, 310
not worshipped by the, 834
singling him out from the, 590
spirit, resistance to the, 824
the lowing, 244
unmotived, 528
Herds, lowing of the, 955
of walruses and whales, 531
Herd-leaders, the buffalo, the, 929
Here a little and there a little, 1111
am I, and he answered, 1100
and there, 'twixt the, 544
he lies, 703
in the body pent, 306
lies a truly honest man, 165
lies our sovereign, 184
nor there, neither, 103, 1039
once through an alley, 461
out of everywhere into the, 559
rests his head, 245
we are, as on a darkling plain, 546
we are, Nantucket's sunk and, 508
we will sit, 47
Hereafter, pathway to the grand, 713
points out an, 195
Hereditary strokes, some, 949
Here's to the housewife, 279
to the maiden, 279
to the widow of fifty, 279
Heresies, new truths begin as, 564
Heresy of doctrine than heart, better, 442
Heretic rebel a thing to flout, 708
Heretofore sin-spotted soul, most, 556
Heritage, come into our, 894
I have a goodly, 1103
names that are England's noblest, 518
of old age, 420
of sorrow and suffering, 453
of woe, lord of himself, that, 356
service is no, 53
sold our loftiest, 806
the sea, our, 345
to grant youth's, 489
to take, 760
Hermit, a sceptred, 362
dwell, shall I like a, 22
man the, sighed, 327
of Prague, the old, 56

Hermit, peculiarity of New England, 683
Hermitage, take that for an, 168
Hermit-eye I scan, with, 316
Herne the hunter, an old keeper, 35
Hero and the man complete, 194
every, becomes a bore at last, 412
he who aspires to be a, 237
is a man of peace, 848
made by murder of millions, 268
may be dragged, a, 1050
most glorious, that ever desolated nations, 343
of the pathetic tale, 364
of this little tale, 755
perish or sparrow fall, 207
see the conquering, 186
stuff that rules the world, 732
the conqueror worm, 459
to his valet, no one is a, 1005
wanders free, 570
Heroes as great have died, 219
battlefields which have their, 1068
for the star-crowned, 772
hail ye, heaven-born band, 294
if we will, Gods are we, 545
lovers, kings, the coming, 644
more than all mad, 657
obscure, greater than illustrious, 1068
of finance, 1076
of old, my peers the, 489
saints and sages face the world alone, 802
these, are dead, 602
walk with laughing, 725
we aren't no thin red, 781
were plenty, 951
Herod, out-herods, 94
Heroic enterprise is gone, 260
for earth too hard, 489
happy dead, these, 921
he who would write, poems, 376
his whole life a, poem, 376
poem a biography, 377
sires, descent is from, 1050
soul in homely garb, 573
stoic Cato, 360
womanhood, type of good, 436
Heroine in chastity, 196
of this tale of woe, 755
Heroism feels and never reasons, 412
persons burning to display, 740
Heron, a strange white, 888
soon, start a, 887
Herostratus lives, 145
Herring, fish flesh nor good red, 13, 1039
flesh fowl or good red, 606
Herrings, Douglas in red, 363
Herte, mouses, nat worth a leek, 7
sesoun priketh every gentil, 5
that loveth nought in May, 3
Herveys, men women and, 313
Hesitancies of Henry James, 766
Hesitate dislike, 213
Hesperus that led the starry host, 152
with the host of heaven, 326

Heterodoxy another man's, 223
Heu! quanto minus est cum reliquis versari, 335
Hevinesse, right sory for your, 4
Hew and hack, somebody to, 142
and Hack were the sons of God, 757
down and fell the hardest-timbered oak, 70
to the line of right, 578
Hewers of wood and drawers of water, 625
Hexameter, in the, 317
Hey-day in the blood, 95
Hic habitat felicitas, 756
jacet, its forlorn, 297
jacet these two narrow words, 22
Hickory limb, clothes on a, 957
Hicks, royal race of, 853
Hid battlements, from the, 749
murder cannot long be, 45
things, 54
Hidden boundary, 395
founts of feeling, 557
room, the, 827
soul of harmony, 160
treasures, heart has, 507
valley pool, 755
Hide, bachelor may risk his, 782
her shame, 254
man within him, 37
myself in thee, let me, 272
the fault I see, to, 216
their diminished heads, 151
those hills of snow, 37, 127
thou wear a lion's, 57
thyself as it were, 1111
virtues in, a world to, 54
wrapped in a woman's, 69
you'll sholy fine de, 688
your diminished rays, 210
Hideous, makes night, 215
making night, 91
town, forget the spreading of the, 609
Hides a shining face, 266
beauties while she, reveals, 240
from himself his state, 230
what they are, 458
Hideth his sharp ribs, labor pining, 477
Hiding-place, dark and lonely, 316
Hied me off to Arcady, 619
Hierophants of inspiration, 318, 369
Hies to his confine, erring spirit, 89
Higgledy-piggledy, 1037
High and haughty yearning of the soul, 554
and low barometer, 617
and low, death makes equal, 11
and low mate ill, 443
and miraculous skies, 913
and palmy state of Rome, 89
as a star, 774
as my heart, 50
be yours to hold it, 820
characters cries one, 164
comradeship, in their, 900
conceit, in their, 408
converse, hold, 224

High courage and unselfish ways, with his, 676
day for all feasting, 1124
deeds, haunt not the fringy edges, 519
deeds in Hungary, 885
descent, no record of her, 561
detestation of the, 497
diddle diddle, 623
erected thoughts, 27
estate, fallen from his, 176
far-seeing places, 879
heaven rejects the lore, 304
hopes, stirred up with, 162
if ye would go up, 1080
imagining, to their, 620
instincts, 301
know it shall be, 771
lineage, a damsel of, 470
mountains are a feeling, 353
mysteries, priestess of night's, 418
never soared as, 643
nor low nor broad nor deep, 786
of night, go in the, 480
on a throne of royal state, 149
pitch this one, 547
price is cruel, 786
so, to bring in sight, 687
spirits jar our quiet mood, children with, 426
that proved too high, 489
the goose hangs, 945
thinking and plain living, 298
thought and amiable words, 471
tides in the calendar, among the, 57
to Him no, no low, 207
we never know how, 585
we seldom rise, 750
wordy pillars, 932
High-blown pride broke under me, 73
High-brow communists, 871
stuff, pull no, 867
Higher levels rise, our hearts to, 436
purposes, life given for, 232
than himself, see nothing, 477
Highest and best, loving and serving, 501
compliment, pays the, 235
felt the spirit of the, 667
form of government, 581
on the tree, the ripest peach is, 696
peppered the, 252
suffer most, 661
summit of art, 1073
thing is truth, 8
High-flyer, no, 181
Highgate Hill, as I came down, 861
Highland, heart is genuinely, 674
home, our rock-bound, 401
host, led the, 500
Mary, my sweet, 286
Mary, spare his, 442
Highlands, in the, 703
my heart's in the, 286
of the mind, 735
Highlanders, pipes of, like the voice of God, 509
High-lived company, 254

Highly fed and lowly taught, 53
Highness' dog at Kew, 216
High-road to England, 234
Highway, down their ancient, 765
is unfeatured air, my, 517
jolts along life's, 1083
Highways, happy, 743
rivers are, 1047
Highwayman came riding, 864
Hilarity, a manly, 318
Hill, a city built upon the top of a, 1126
all are sleeping on the, 806
all your burdens up the, 953
and glen, gone from, 771
and plain, break on, 702
apart, sat on a, 150
a-sitting on a, 839
behind the western, 671
by the wind-beaten, 328
city that is set on an, 1114
cot beside the, 289
flung us on the windy, 893
had climbed the highest, 277
heaven-kissing, 95
hunts on a lonely, 717
is this the, 315
it's the steep, 914
king of France went up the, 950
Maggie, wandered to-day to the, 640
Mahomet and the, 110
of dream, 717
on the 'customed, 245
onward to the eternal, 371
over the, to the poor-house, 678
that skirts the down, 269
tip-toe upon a little, 385
up a steep, 223
valley grove and town, 349
yon high eastern, 89
Hills ancient as the sun, 371
and holds, lingers in the, 810
and valleys dales and fields, 31
are reared, 517
beyond earth's farthest, 850
cattle upon a thousand, 1104
craggy, and running streams, 447
far across the, they went, 465
fling up green garlands, 760
for your lives, to the, 676
from the adoring, 725
from these brown, 516
happy, pleasing shade, 243
hewn on Norwegian, 148
hillmen desire their, 777
immutable as the, 785
in melancholy gold, bathe the, 418
indenting, silent, 744
no lovelier, 823
of Habersham, 663
of Holland, heavenly, 710
of home, 703
of manhood wear a noble face, 458
of peace or pain, 738
of San Francisco bay, 763
of snow, hide those, 37, 127
of the south country, 810
of the stormy north, 370
over the, and far away, 186, 205, 465, 699

Hills peep o'er hills, 210
river and the wooded, 774
rock-ribbed and ancient, 371
shining, 442
strong amid the, 458
that dim and distant rise, 424
that encircles the scanty vale, 318
that fold, great, 873
the, are full of marble, 613
the old green, 737
thy thousand streams thy hundred, 417
to the reverberate, 54
tower waves fall, 895
Vermont O maiden of the, 760
we'll bound, over the, 574
whose heads touch heaven, 100
Hillmen desire their hills, 777
Hillside clear-cut, 924
Hill-tomb, Petra in her, 443
Hill-top, dip down from some, 873
Hill-tops far away, o'er the, 705
Hilt-buried in the dry and trodden sand, 659
Hilted silence, carve thy life to, 688
Hilts, red to your battle, 800
Him, from, that hath not, 1116
no high no low to, 207
of the western dome, 174
that hath, to, 669
walked directly through, 754
who once was kind and dear, 553
who pitieth suffering men, 963
who placed me there, 1051
who rules the thunder, 191
Himalayan dews impearled, with, 735
Himself a host, 218
each man for, 5
from God he could not free, 408
in both, always, 928
Hind mated by the lion, 53
of princes peer, 513
Hinder us in the great march, 163
Hinders needle and thread, 392
Hindmost, devil take, 142, 322
Hindoo died, a, 668
Hindrance and a help, 298
Hindu king, sad-eyed, 618
Hinge, cast-iron back with a, 582
nor loop, 103
Hinges, golden, moving, 154
in French conversation, 242
pregnant, of the knee, 94
turn for me, till the, 373
turns on magic, 866
Hint a fault, just, 213
affords a, 652
never a whispered, 806
of the old lost beauty, a, 445
upon this, I spake, 100
Hints and echoes from the life behind, 443
Hip and thigh, smote them, 1099
have ye him on the, 16
I have thee on the, 47
Orion's belt and sworded, 900
Hippocrene, blushful, 383
Hippopotamus rests on his belly, 900

Hire, labourer worthy his, 1117
  those that cry for, 180
Hirelin' shepa'd, 719
Hireling, given to a state, 233
Hirelings subsist on less, 618
His faith might be wrong, 167
  Majesty has 'em, see that, 909
  requiring taught, truth at, 442
  terrible swift sword, 522
  time is forever, 167
  truth is marching on, 522
Hiss, a dismal universal, 155
Historian must have some con-
    ception, 856
  of fine consciences, 728
  of my country's woes, 220
  poet naturalist and, 231
  shackles of a, 147
  take him into favor, did not
    some, 343
Historian's ignorance of women,
    636
  style, depending on the, 359
Historical fights, 623
Histories charm, 337
  dictionaries and temporary
    poems, 232
  lie, 337
  make men wise, 111
History a whiz, 599
  anything but, 200
  biggest in, 872
  could not be written, 236
  dignity of, 200, 229, 400
  embraces small part of reality,
    548
  ever hear by tale or, 42
  every great crisis of human,
    558
  falsehood called, 337, 548
  hath triumphed over time, 22
  he has invented, 1053
  human, history of ideas, 795
  in all men's lives, 65
  is a fable, 337
  is bunk, 337
  is falsehood, 548
  is merely gossip, 724
  is nothing more than belief,
    1081
  is philosophy teaching by ex-
    amples, 200
  is the essence of innumerable,
    biographies, 378
  land without memories is with-
    out, 609
  make the boy interested in nat-
    ural, 803
  must be false, 200
  never learned anything from,
    1062
  no, only biography, 411
  of a hundred years, 652
  of a soldier's wound, 241
  of any absolute genius, 667
  of class struggles, 1072
  of disconnected accidents, 1076
  of hitherto existing society,
    1072
  of science, 1057
  of the individual, 1057
  of the world, 1062
  of world but biography, 380
  outwrought, 652
  picture of human crimes, 1053
  rattling good, 650

History register of crimes, 270
  repeats itself, 998
  secret, 440
  shall stand in the great, 436
  speak, Who are life's victors,
    533
  strange eventful, 50
  study of, 636
  tale which men call, 373
  the belief in the senses, in false-
    hood, 548
  the soul's, 938
  the subject of, 1076
  their sum, 565
  through the whole, 1042
  truth of anything by, 997
  what is her, 55
  when at our, 889
  while we read, we make, 558
  with all her volumes, 354
  would be a history of accidents,
    1076
History's page, names inscribed
    in, 518
  pen, events are writ by, 405
  purchased page, 353
Hit, a very palpable, 97
  lucky, 199
  the nail on the head, 127
  without striking back, I never
    like being, 621
Hitch your wagon to a star, 414
Hitherto shalt thou come, 1102
Hits the mark, 106
Hive for bees, his helmet a, 28
  for the honey-bee, 790
Hiving wisdom, 353
Hizzie die, for a haughty, 285
Hoar antiquity, ways of, 258
Hoard, farmer's wintry, 441
  is little but our hearts, our,
    470
  of maxims preaching, 464
Hoarding went to hell, for his, 70
Hoarse rough verse, 211
  with tempestuous breath, 629
Hoarseness of his note, 267
Hoarse-throated brutalized re-
    frain, 763
Hoary head is a crown of glory,
    1107
  head, upon his, 446
  my days but dull and, 170
Hob, nob is his word, 55
Hobbies, all on their, 595
Hobby and rides, straddles a, 695
  information is his, 815
  young man get a, 772
Hobbyhorse, rides his, 241
Hobgoblin, consistency is a, 411
Hobson's choice, 126
Hocus pocus nickname for jug-
    glery, 628
Hoe, tickle the earth with a, 417
Hog and dog begun, was in the,
    544
  butcher for the world, 855
  in Epicurus' sty, fattest, 249
Hogs and cattle, come back with,
    926
  eat acorns, greater ease than,
    141
  fattenin', aint in luck, 683
Hoist with his own petar, 96
Hoke ne by croke, 10
Hold a candle, 45

Hold a fire in his hand, 59
  an hour's converse, 588
  enough, cries, 89
  fast that which is good, 1121
  high converse, 224
  his peace hereafter, forever,
    1128
  it takes a, 698
  makes nice of no vile, 58
  me to your deep breast, 619
  on the mind, obtains no, 974
  scepter of rule is spade I, 448
  the fleet angel, 226, 440
  the fort I am coming, 542
  the mirror up to nature, 94
  their noses to grinstone, 13
  thou the good, 468
  to have and to, 1128
  with the hare, 13
  with the hound, 23
Holder-on, quiet equable dead-
    ly, 928
Holding, life is but a little, 575
Holds fast the golden mean, 267
  some joy of silence, 407
Hole, Caesar might stop a, 97
  estopped a, 882
  gnawed a little, 711
  if you know a better, 943
  in a' your coats, 286
  in my shirt, eats a, 857
  like a poisoned rat in a, 191
  mouse of one poor, 7, 139
  oon, for to sterte to, 7
  square peg in round, 314
  where his tail came through,
    321
  without room, gloomy old, 756
Holes, foxes have, 1114
  triangular and square, 314
Holiday, to make a Roman, 354
Holidays, all the year were play-
    ing, 61
  holiest of all, 439
Holiday-rejoicing spirit, 325
Holier laws, of purer science, 523
  than thou, I am, 1112
Holiest end of woman's being,
    454
  thing alive, 316
Holiness, courage of heart or, 810
  harmony immortality, 549
  in the beauties of, 1105
  of the heart's affections, 385
  only clean thing except, 1083
Holla your name, 54
Hollaballoo, believe me friend,
    1079
Hollaing and singing of anthems,
    64
Holland lies, where, 249
  the heavenly hills of, 710
  traditional land of freedom,
    739
Holler, Providence fashioned us,
    526
Hollow, all was false and, 149
  blasts of wind, 205
  compliments and lies, 156
  eye grows bright, 541
  lands and hilly lands, 790
  men, we are the, 899
  murmurs died away, in, 248
  oak our palace is, 345
  phrase, 806
  sea-shell, 679

Hollow, some deep green, 812
  the grassy, 575
  vale, in that, 134
  welcomes recanting goodness, 80
  winds begin to blow, 276
Hollows, bowery, 463
  radiance fills their, 849
  with blue and purple, 710
Hollow-eyed, sharp-looking, 38
Holly is dark when rose-briar blooms, 516
  wreaths, the genial, 935
Holly-tree, friendship like the, 516
Hollywood, fabulous Hollywood, 920
Holy and enchanted, 315
  angels guard thy bed, 199
  anger and pious grief, 351
  as He died to make men, 522
  as severe, 37
  book, Mohammed's truth in a, 458
  Church, when this our, 647
  City, bells of the, 443
  day comes to-morrow, 291
  deadlock, 909
  divine good amiable or sweet, 155
  faith that warmed, the, 451
  fields, in those, 60
  Ghost, sin against, 641, 1082
  ground, call it, 370
  ground, where sorrow is, 723
  health, unless one have, 960
  holy holy is the Lord of Hosts, 1111
  more profound, more, 76
  one of those who think thee, 935
  reward of human toil, 1090
  seal, it sets a, 690
  sea-sick people look, 614
  thing, like some, 337
  time is quiet as a nun, the, 297
  'tis and true, so, 953
  towers of the silences, 914
  white birds flying after, 832
  writ, old odd ends stolen out of, 71
  writ, proofs of, 102
Homage, all things do her, 22
  bring, to him your, 706
  from contemporaries, 398
  of the low, 497
  vice pays to virtue, 1044
  worthless pomp of, 374
Home a week, been away from, 677
  again, as coming, 642
  again, oh to be, 508
  amusing or attractive, 884
  anchor of our peace at, 273
  and fare, partner of my, 522
  and friends once more, we think of seeing, 541
  and I am far from, 403
  art gone and ta'en thy wages, 106
  at ease, live at, 115
  at evening's close, hie him, 245
  beauty wrought lies close at, 442

Home, best country ever is at, 249
  charity begins at, 144. 279
  come, to supper, 60
  day's march nearer, 306
  decked with the comforts of, 333
  deep imaged in his soul, 220
  do they miss me at, 555
  draw near their eternal, 140
  dream of, 337
  each heart is whispering, 392
  exile from, 365
  for ever, I came, 325
  from the sea, 703
  God who is our, 301
  going far from, 916
  has right here at, 824
  have yet the gift of, 890
  headlands of, 889
  Heimgang! always going, 554
  hills of, 703
  his footsteps he hath turned, 307
  home at last, 392
  homely features to keep, 158
  how to value, 425
  I'm going, 408
  I was leaving, 702
  in a better place at, 48
  in the ambush of my name strike, 35
  in the dark, want to go, 801
  is bright with a calm delight, 610
  is home though never so homely, 365
  is on the deep, 328
  is the place where, 838
  is the safest refuge to every one, 21
  is the sailor, home from the sea, 703
  is where affection calls, 418
  keep his only son at, 248
  keep it staying, 584
  kiss till the cow comes, 131
  life not natural, 720
  love of, 494
  make friends at, 996
  makes her loved at, 284
  man goeth to his long, 1110
  men merriest when from, 66
  more delightful than, 981
  my old Kentucky, good night, 567
  no place like, 365
  not wept so well at, 743
  of fairest mould, 844
  of lost causes, 548
  of love, this is my, 108
  of the bean and the cod, 752
  of the brave, 332
  old England is our, 394
  on stone at, 970
  on the rolling deep, 502
  our rest, this is our, 672
  our souls at, with God, 523
  out of house and, 64
  points of heaven and, 304
  revered abroad and loved at, 284
  rise and go, 640
  sitteth with me at, 1080
  snail is at, 117

Home, stored for thee at, 749
  sweet home had stirred, 557
  sweet, sweet, 294
  that dear hut our, 226
  that drive one from, 391
  that frets above our peaceful, 375
  that our feet may leave, 453
  the nineties provided, 849
  the wise man is at, 410
  there's nobody at, 217
  they dream of, 824
  to dinner, dear Prue I can't come, 198
  to her own father's door, 951
  to make it, 870
  to men's bosoms, 109
  to rest, lead one, 742
  to roost, chickens come, 425
  to-day nearer, 557
  true nature of, 532
  turns again, 472
  tyrants safely govern, 70
  unquiet at, 183
  we first knew, 446
  when you knock is never at, 263
  where small experience grows, 52
  where we love is, 453
Homes, and filled their, 899
  clean beds and wives, firelit, 891
  for spiders, engine shops, 825
  forced from their, 250
  from quiet, 810
  give us better, 496
  homeless near a thousand, 295
  of England, the stately, 370
  of silent prayer, eyes are, 468
  old names old, 1085
  their loved, 332
Home's heart, I'm, 814
  not merely four square walls, 418
Homebound fancy, 401
Home-bred kine, beeves and, 298
Home-brought stuff, 757
Home-keeping hearts are happiest, 439
  youth, 33
Homeless and sobbing, 588
  near a thousand homes, 295
  tempest-tossed to me, 694
Homely as a plowed field, 927
  features to keep home, 158
  garb, 573
  wits, home-keeping youth have, 33
Home-made dishes, 391
  miracles of bread, 887
Homer all the books you need, 185
  all the world knows, 493
  and Whitman roared in the pines, 806
  blind, believe old, 167
  cities that claimed, 910
  Greece boasts her, 176
  hath been observed to nod, 180
  himself must beg, 123
  his sight, 719
  living begged his bread, 124
  living had no roofe to shroud his head, 129
  nods, nor is it, 210

Homer, our poets steal from, 121
seven cities warred for, 129
sometimes nods, 984
those incomparable poets, 819
Homer's birth, seven cities claim,
129
lamp appeared, ere, 262
place of birth, 493
rule the best, 213
verse, met him first in, 674
works your study, 210
Homesick unto death, 868
Homestead of the free, 442
Home-truth seem more true,
513
Homeward, and draw me, 798
Honest and true, 286
as any man living, 39
as this world goes, 92
business never blush, 219
enough so it be large enough,
533
exceeding poor man, 45
friends are few, 845
God, 603
heart it is an, 716
if, I love it the same, 589
if, why sure that's enough, 589
labor, pauperism feasteth
while, 477
labour bears a lovely face, 116
love of a nine-year-old, 775
man is aboon his might, 287
man is the noblest work of
God, 126, 208, 284
man looked, 616
man, other than an, 64
men, a few, are better than
numbers, 141
my friends were poor but, 53
prejudices, 197
rude effective strength, 491
tale speeds best, 72
things, tired of, 916
though it be, 104
to be direct and, 103
to steal, too, 954
whatsoever things are, 1121
wives may be merry, yet, 35
Honester, old man and no, 39
Honesty and love doth mince this
matter, 101
armed so strong in, 83
corruption wins not more than,
73
dwells like a miser, 51
is his fault, 81
is praised and starves, 1006
is the best policy, 1041
neither manhood nor, 61
no legacy so rich as, 53
no, nor manhood in thee, 61
out of countenance, stare,
498
rare as a man, 927
spring and root of, 1001
Honey and the honeycomb, 1103
as a soul gathers light, gathers,
1069
bees store up your, 982
flowing with milk and, 1098
from the poisoned lips, 889
gather, all the day, 199
in the carcase of the lion, 1099
is sweeter than cash, 986
of Hymettus, 601

Honey or the gall, 774
still for tea, 893
the pedigree of, 584
with milk and, 1017
words sweet as, 218
Honey-dew, hath fed on, 316
Honeyed dew, 958
showers, 159
Honey-heavy dew of slumber, 82
Honey-lands of milk and wine,
657
Honeyless, leave them, 84
Honi soit qui mal y pense, 35,
258
Honied words like bees, 898
Honour a physician, 1125
and a quantity of debts, 811
and clean mirth, 777
and glory forever more, 657
and glory, most desirous of,
1049
and greatness of his name, 74
and my life, all is lost save,
1024
and the reward, claims the,
985
and truth and manhood, 843
and years, full of, 431
as in war, 76
bed of, 200
bestowing, pudding pence, 406
bread glory of the fields, 1090
brother of ephemeral, 1064
but an empty bubble, 176
chastity of, 260
dead on the field of, 1092
depends on the opinion, 1049
depths and shoals of, 73
dies, when faith is lost when,
442
faithful and clear in, 210
France love thy wife, 492
from corruption keep, 74
from me, take, 59
gives greatness, if, 274
grip, where feel your, 285
has come back, 894
hath no skill in surgery, 63
his memory and loved the man,
120
hurt that, feels, 464
in a sure success, no, 901
is a mere scutcheon, 63
is at the stake, 96
is dearer to me, 1037
is lodged, place where, 143
is lost, what is left when, 987
is the subject of my story, 81
jealous in, 49
let no one pay me, 978
like your sabre bright, keep,
447
love and, with my soul, 66
love obedience troops of
friends, 88
loved I not, more, 168
man being in, abideth not,
1104
manly deeds of, 972
meaning and import, of great,
1056
men who have, 522
mine, is my life, 58
mine shall be the post of, 206
new made, doth forget men's
names, 57

Honour, nice points of, 680
no longer live with, 759
not to be crowned, 620
of more weight than an oath,
1013
of religion, 179
one vessel unto, 1119
our fortunes and our sacred,
273
peereth in meanest habit, 52
perfect truth, in perfect, 837
perfect ways of, 74
pluck up drowned, 61
post of, is a private station,
195, 206
praise and glory given, 199
pricks me on, 63
prophet not without, 1115
public, is security, 950
razed from the books of, 107
rest, in peace and, 76
rooted in dishonour, 470
set to a leg, 63
she knew what was, 154
sin to covet, if it be a, 67
sinks where commerce long prevails, 249
that part more hurts, 143
the king, fear God, 1122
the louder he talked of his, 401
their property nor their, 1023
thy father and thy mother,
963, 1098, 1124
thy father and thy mother in
law, 1124
thy name and thy praises endure, thy, 982
to die with, 759
to him who confers as to him
who receives, 198
to its high, 890
to pluck bright, 61
truth and loyalty, map of, 69
turns with frown defiant, 452
unto the wife, giving, 1122
use me in, 758
virtue sense, 242
what is in that word, 63
with dignity and, 999
without deserving, 28
would thee do, that, 66
Honours and draw their, reeking
to heaven, 67
another steals my, 982
bears his blushing, 73
earn some, 595
especially promoted to city,
343
more substantial, 257
of illustrious men, 981
rais'd and swell'd with, 972
three, wi' a' the, 393
to the world, he gave his, 74
Honour's voice, can, 244
Honourable, ancient and, 1111
contribution, a most, 970
gentleman caught Whigs, 419
gentleman is the first, right,
478
men, all, 83
professions of law and physic,
328
quixotic sense of the, 461
retreat, 50
to tell lies is not, 966
wife, true and, 82

Honoured bones, Shakespeare's, 161
by strangers, 217
by the few, safe from many, 528
how loved how, 217
in his grave, 428
in the breach, 91
Hood, a page of, 452
drink with him that wears a, 20
Hooded clouds like friars, 433
mantle, under thy, 562
Hoodwinked, judgment, 266
Hoof-marks going in, 962
Hoofs of a swinish multitude, 260
Hook, bait well the, 39
baited with a dragon's tale, 146
or by crook, by, 1038
or crook, 15, 24
salt-fish on his, 104
without the bait, 414
Hooks forsake their lawful eyes, 654
Hookas, divine in, 358
Hooker at fortified Lookout, 552
Hook-nosed fellow of Rome, 65
Hooping, out of all, 50
Hoops of steel, grapple them with, 90
three-hooped pot shall have ten, 69
Hoop's bewitching round, 240
Hooting at the glorious sun, 316
Hope abandon who enter here, 1020
against hope, 306, 608, 1119
and be happy, 478
and call it, 711
and care, in the midst of, 985
and creed, O Englishmen in, 443
animated by faith and, 233
as giving it a, 119
bade the world farewell, 327
bate a jot of heart or, 162
be weak, though, 386
beacons of, ye appear, 547
beyond the shadow of a dream, 382
break it to our, 89
but not another's, 189
compensation for renouncing, 729
constancy in wind, 351
critics who stamped out poets', 430
deferred, 1107
despair brooding over the putrid eggs of, 292
drunken and magnificent, 932
earthly, how bright soe'er, 343
earthly, still fluctuates, 343
ethereal balm, 385
faith and love, 1059
farewell, fear remorse, 151
fettered, 868
final, is flat despair, 149
flag of the free heart's, 382
fondly do we, 457
fooled with, 178
for poetry, a, 937

Hope for the dead, help for the living, 603
from, and fear set free, 632
frustrate of his, 162
hath happy place with me, 517
heavenly, is all serene, 343
her to attain, 24
I laugh for, 517
I live on, 668
in sure and certain, 1128
in the world, equal, 455
is a better companion, 478
is all serene, 343
is ever livelier, 669
is like a harebell, 587
is the belief, 312
is there no, the sick man said, 206
less quick to spring, 547
light of, leave the, 327
like the gleaming taper, 252
lined himself with, 64
loyal, 612
mayflower of our, 550
men set their hearts upon, 1018
my fondest, 338
my, is in thee, 20
my life's best, 309
never comes that comes to all, 148
never to, again, 73
no, could have no fear, 610
no other medicine but only, 36
none e'er loved without, 239
nor bate a jot of heart or, 162
nursing unconquerable, 547
o'ercome the steeps in, 570
of a fool, more, 1108
of day, without all, 156
of getting the straw, 962
of happy inexperience, 494
of my spirit, the, 337
of the resurrection, 1128
one only, my heart can cheer, 392
or courage fail, nor let, 567
or fear, I look in, 443
owes its charm, memory no less than, 426
past cure past help past, 80
phantoms of, 232
pleasure, yet all, 178
prevail, let not, 395
prisoners of, 1114
repose in trembling, 245
sees a star, 602
shadow of a, 847
some blessed, 651
some sweet, lies, 442
springs eternal, 207
still relies on, 252
strength is felt from, 219
tells a flattering tale, 395
that divinest, 406
that hath been crossed, every, 557
that stings, 736
the wretch relies on, 252
there's a, for every woe, 390
thou thy hope and pray thy prayer, 473
to attain her, 24
to feed on, 25
to have mercy, 25

Hope to make the day go through, 757
to meet again, the, 392
to meet when life is past, 373
to merit heaven, 352
to see London, 65
to the end, 1122
to write well hereafter, 162
told a flattering tale, 395
triumph of, 235
true, is swift, 72
wait thou child of, 477
we give up, 952
we have such, 1120
what is, but deceiving, 592
whence this pleasing, 195
where reason would despair love can, 239
while there's life there's, 206, 1038
whispered, when every tale, 455
without fear, nor, 1048
world will disagree in faith and, 208
Hopes and ashen flowers, agonized, 798
and fears and interest, 237
and fears lie in the dust, 348
and this of all my, 586
are beginning to resemble regrets, 1072
are water, 897
avail, little can all our, 668
belied our fears, 390
bright, yet to find me, 543
exactly to fulfil, 556
fair be all thy, 68
high faint, 507
high up and spirits down, 578
laid waste, 425
like towering falcons, 189
man's nobler, 736
may be frail but fond, 761
of all the years, 612
of an estate, 1042
of future years, 435
of honest men, 503
of living, high, 162
only reaps from the, 592
resigned, all, 888
sordid, and vain desires, 345
stirred up with high, 162
tender leaves of, 73
that after-times, every poet, 447
that can not die, 654
unsubstantial, 965
vanity of human, 231
wither, high, 507
Hope's dear delusive spell, 406
gayest wreaths are made, 446
star to man grows dim, 405
Hoped we were both broken-hearted, 633
Hopeful hearts, 638
Hopeless and grim, 879
anguish, 231
fancy feigned, by, 466
his adventure, 624
lays his dead away, 444
love finds comfort in despair, 279
rubbish, write such, 300
sons of clay, love not ye, 446
wrestler, 575

Hoping more, they have but less, 106
Hopkins, Mark, a true teacher, 591
sat on one end of a log, 815
Horace whom I hated so, 354
Horas non numero nisi serenas, 330
Horatio, I knew him, 97
in my mind's eye, 90
more things in heaven and earth, 92
thrift, thrift, 90
to what base uses we may return, 97
Horatius kept the bridge, 400
Horde, one polished, 361
Horizon, along the far, 710
clouds along the, rolled, 418
death is only a, 653
for a successor, explore the, 412
for the majority, 318
haze on the far, 737
I saw her just above the, 260
is limit of our sight, 653
is never at our elbows, 514
the, obeys me, 1086
upon the dull, 445
wear so wide a grin, 775
Horizons, lord of the far, 757
Horizontal line, 375
Horn, barter that, 790
from out her lavish, 441
huntsman winds his, 229
is there a, 905
Moorish, 375
of her ear-trumpet, 896
of the hunter, 396
one blast upon his bugle, 308
small but sullen, 247
sound of his, 397
the lusty horn, 51
Triton blow his wreathed, 300
tunes were frozen in the, 1056
Horns and motors, sound of, 899
appear, devil and his, 319
blown through the conchimarian, 432
her two little, 350
not defeated by the, 857
of elfland, 466
of my dilemma, 241
they blew their, also, 229
with great ragg'd, 35
Horner, his name was, 667
Horologe of eternity, 434
Horrible discord, brayed, 153
light-house of hell, 389
shadow hence, 87
Horrid grind, one demd, 494
tale, 373
Horror of falling into naught, 195
of outer darkness, 601
sacred, about everything grand, 1069
secret dread and inward, 195
Horrors accumulate on horror's head, 103
supped full with, 88
Horse, a pale, 639, 1123
and a wife, choice of a, 545
and the driver too, 877
anger is like a full-hot, 72
back, sits on his, 57

Horse, call me, 62
captains of, 141
cart before the, 17
Darius's, 395
dark, 420
Death on his pale, 155
give me another, 72
good corn, I give my, 664
grey mare the better, 16
he can ride a boat he can sail, give a man a, 610
he used to ride, 580
I am going to be a, 753
in the silence champed, 822
keep fussing the, 928
knows the way to carry the sleigh, 404
lies about his wooden, 881
little dearer than his, 464
looke a given, in the mouth, 13
lost for want of a shoe, 137, 227
made fat by the king's eye, 1001
Marines, Captain Jinks of the, 664
misused upon the road, 282
move a, 263
my kingdom for a, 72
of that colour, 54
philosophy is a good, 253
races, difference of opinion makes, 616
ride a free, to death, 1042
short, soon curried, 13
sick as a, 242
spontaneous product of the, 491
spur not an unbroken, 310
starveth, while grasse groweth, 14
talk of his, 44
than to saddle a, 1035
that which is now a, 105
the taxed, 314
to the water, 14
to which I tied my, 1055
too big to keep changing the saddle, 927
where's the bloody, 933
working for a dead, 1042
would my, had the speed of your tongue, 38
Horses against a son, a thousand, 817
and cars and yachts and planes, 899
are the jewels, such, 928
between two, 68
carriages without, 940
England is hell for, 125
heaven without, 708
in England, 232
in Virginia, bred such, 928
Italy a paradise for, 125
not best to swap, 457
oats food for, 122
of the sun, 53
of the sun, who drives the, 53, 687
that were remembered after death, 928
Horse's neighing, sweetness in his, 395
shoe, if you pick up a, 679
Horseback, beggar on, 124

Horseback, set beggar on, 1041
the man on, 945
Horsed, heaven's cherubim, 85
Horsehair, steep, 491
Horseleach hath two daughters, 1109
Horseman's hands, jewels of the, 928
Horse-meat, fitter juments, 122
Horsemill, perpetual rack or, 123
Horse-sense in an atmosphere, 896
Horse-shoe upside down, nailed the, 508
Hortensius, his friend, 360
Hos ego versiculos feci, 982
Hose a world too wide, 50
in darning ragged, 557
Hosier's injured ghost, 240
Hospitable entertainment and wise instruction, 166
thoughts intent, 153
Hospital, carried to the foundling, 1055
grey quiet old, 692
social comfort in a, 430
Hospitals, old men are walking, 180
Hospitality and the grave, 1069
given to, 1119
glory of the house, 953
I like his, 828
Host, a fearless, no slave, 386
and guest, tie of, 963
encircled by a, 955
fort nor armed, 954
himself a, 218
himself is not the, 620
mingling with the vulgar, 220
of columbines and pathics, 937
of friends, you'll have a, 986
of golden daffodils, 299
of heaven, came with the, 326
of mariners perpetual sleep, 517
of the Garter, 34
reckeners without their, 13
that led the starry, 152
universal, up sent a shout, 148
ye heavenly, 183
Hosts behind, fling to the, 765
embattled, 513
kindest of all, 960
of error, 752
of the mighty dead, 641
that march, 397
Hostage, he who knows a, 824
Hostages to fortune, 109
Hostelry of Never, stands the, 693
Hostess, dares to wrong his, 737
ideal, 802
of the sky, the moon, 728
Hostess' door, at mine, 57
without his, 23
Hostile actions, than, 997
empires, two everlasting, 378
hands, ye, 706
Hostility against all established institutions, 340
disarm all, 440
of one nation to another, 1072
reckless of world's, 811
Hot afternoons have been in Montana, 945
and bothered, 786

Hot and cold with the same breath, 962
and rebellious liquors, 48
breezes blow, while these, 445
cold moist and dry, 150, 1032
day, armies join not in a, 64
for certainties, 574
for reason, much too, 637
hammer your iron when it is, 987
haste, mounting in, 352
heat not a furnace so, 72
in a moment, little chimney, 436
in the mouth, 54
little pot soon, 52
not so, 56
temper leaps o'er a cold decree, 44
that they hurt, so, 932
time in the old town, 767
water is to remain upon it, 144
with the bloodbeats of song, 633
Hotel, advantage of a, 720
Hothouse-nurtured columbines, 904
Hound, belabored, 502
fever to the questing, 834
holde with the, 23
if he is a, 956
old, wags his shaggy tail, 574
or spaniel, 99
run with the, 13
slain his gallant, 294
Hounds all join in glorious cry, 229
cry of his, 397
get out the, 577
of spring, 633
Hounslow Heath, Bold Turpin vunce on, 494
Hour and sweet, one far fierce, 828
at the fit, 984
await the inevitable, 244
before the dawn, 849
before the worshipped sun peered forth, 77
bounties of an, 201
busied with the crowded, 409
by his dial, 49
by Shrewsbury clock, 63
catch the transient, 231
crowded, 310
dead deathless, 577
dedicated to afternoon tea, 666
divine, that coming, 954
ever thus from childhood's, 338, 590
every, brings palpable access of knowledge, 299
every, of light and dark a miracle, 537
every, takes away part, 236
every, the apotheosis, 870
fair creature of an, 384
finds end in a golden, 664
for a dark, 86
for a minute, for an, 736
for one short, 469
Freedom's crowning, 760
friendliest to sleep, 153
has set, sailing, 847
he knows the very, 373

Hour, I also had my, 828
I have had my, 177
if we do but watch the, 357
if you work by the, 582
improve each shining, 199
in that most lovely, 833
insects of the, 260
is marked, our, 1061
it is the eleventh, 635
kind affection rule the, 364
lives its little, 372
Lord through this, 957
make the coming, o'erflow, 53
matched us with his, 894
morning, to sadden, 453
nothing can bring back the, 301
now's the day and now's the, 286
O my soul, this is thy, 537
of blind old Dandolo, one, 299, 353
of breath, 832
of destiny, great, 891
of ease, tanned reaper in his, 552
of fate, 602
of glorious life, one crowded, 310
of her nativity, 522
of ill, darkest, 967
of life crowded to the full, 311
of night, the cheerless, 369
of that Dundee, single, 298
of the dawn, 804
of youthful joy, for one, 452
offspring of an idle, 640
one little, 588
one self-approving, 208
one short, spent in Thy presence, 441
once in a golden, 574
or two, lighting a little, 1018
pensioner on the bounties of an, 201
rose that lives its little, 372
serve the future, 305
some wilder darker, 817
something in the parting, 557
steals into a musing, 675
strikes, appointed, 774
take our mortal momentary, 895
talk always by the, 582
that brought the scent, 954
that is, seize the, 983
that summer, 737
that wakens fond desire, 1021
the business of the, 670
the creature of an, 1021
time and the, 84
to hour we ripe and ripe, 49
to open for the world a purer, 517
to put away childish things, 889
to sit up till the, 667
to waste, nor suffer one bright, 474
told the twilight, 705
torturing, 243
troublesome insects of the, 260
upon the stage, frets his, 88
waste not your, 1019

Hour, whatever prosperous, 985
when earth's foundations, 744
when God sends a cheerful, 162
wherein a man might be happy, 139
which shall not be expected, 985
while in an earthless, 920
will come, the, 1070
with beauty's chain, 337
you use your power, from this, 754
Hours and minutes, reckon, 387
are as a miser's coins, 620
are scourges, 582
are suns, where the, 938
as they floated away, 370
better three, too soon, 34
blossomed for a few short, 446
count only the sunny, 330
delight my private, 156
do with all the days and, 454
five, in a day, 234
I once enjoyed, peaceful, 266
I spent with thee dear heart, 765
in love with, 879
in the shrinking, 714
lazy leaden-stepping, 161
lost two golden, 387
lover of lost, 579
lovers of idle, 757
mournful midnight, 439
music of the languid, 674
none but cloudless, 597
not till the, of light return, 546
of bliss, winged, 327
of dew, 691
of ease, to, 289
of ease, woman in our, 308
of gloom, 546
of time, creeping, 49
on angel wings, 286
our stillest, 1079
quiet, 63
reposing, 71
seven, to law, 275
six, in sleep, 21
so fast the lone, 473
some wee short, 284
sport away the, 445
steal a few, from the night, 336
strike, hear the slow, 916
unaltered through a course of, 1089
unheeded flew the, 294
waked by the circling, 153
were all serene, if, 330
with flying feet, 352
your labor is for future, 417
Hour's converse, 587
talk withal, never spent an, 41
Hour-glass, Heaven's blue, 857
Houris, lying with, 246
Hourly victory, thy, 736
Hous, lady of the, 7
House, a man builds a fine, 415
and home, out of, 64
appointed for all living, 1102
at ease, I sit in mine, 757
at night, 750
babe in a, 477
back door robs the, 137
be divided against itself, 1116
be small, if your, 890

House, beauty of the, 953
  bless this, 164
  brain's old ghostly, 914
  brawling woman in a wide,
    1108
  by the side of the road, 218,
    733
  chimney in my father's, 69
  dark, and long sleep, 397
  daughter in my mother's, 778
  daughters of my father's, 55
  empty, like a stray dog, 614
  except the Lord build the, 1106
  fare you well, old, 678
  full of books, for a, 673
  get out of my, 1041
  half garden and half, 466
  he who loves an old, 828
  I am in the, 746
  in mine own, I am an emperor,
    129
  in order, set thine, 1101
  in Thanks-giving Street, 667
  in the way in the, 475
  is of glass, whose, 137
  is to be let for life, 134
  is turned upside down, this, 61
  lady of the, 7
  leave to those to come the, it-
    self, 537
  like a miser in a poor, 51
  little pleasure in the, 269
  man's, his castle, 21
  mansions in my Father's, 1118
  may dwell, who in this
    splendid, 511
  May is building her, 793
  moat defensive to a, 59
  my whinstone my castle, 382
  nae luck about the, 269
  new, no sense of have-beens,
    651
  no, is good for anything with-
    out a master, 412
  no, like God's out-of-doors,
    704
  not built with mortal hands,
    eternal, 174
  not made with hands, 486, 678
  of dreams untold, 759
  of dust, mind the, 742
  of every one is his castle, 21
  of feasting, 1109
  of flesh, in the, 742
  of friends, from the, 1114
  of logs, granddad in his, 956
  of mourning, better go to the,
    1109
  of my friends, 1114
  of my God, 1105
  of my own, a, 869
  of prayer, wherever God erects
    a, 187
  of the interpreter, 171
  on another man's ground, 34
  one mind in an, 1128
  one need not be a, 585
  open, in the evening, 827
  or home, at whose, 640
  ornament of a, 414
  paths to the, I seek to make,
    537
  peace be to this, 1117
  prop of my, 47
  reject him, fired that the, 212

House, return no more to his,
    1102
  rich honesty dwells in a poor,
    51
  says stay, the little, 836
  set thine, in order, 1112
  she hath, a, 948
  small and large garden, 168
  snail carrying his own, 117
  stand together, that our, 778
  talking of halters in the, 1036
  that doth sustain my, 47
  that has echoed, 890
  that I'll have, this, 920
  that Jack built, 543
  that looks to east, 672
  that shelters a friend, 411
  though small art to me the
    Escurial, 137
  to grandfather's, 404
  to have a little, 869
  to such a, 948
  too many children in a, 1027
  tragic, 614
  treasure, land slipped from my
    hold, 604
  we dwell in every day, 585
  we inhabit together, 487
  we two kept, 652
  when I have a, 920
  when we see the figure of the,
    64
  where a great man, 565
  where I was born, 390
  where none hath ever died,
    639
  where there was not one dead,
    not a, 1098
  whose rooms lack, 568
  with a deep thatch, 810
  with lawns, 702
  with love for timber, 916
  with nobody in it, 614
  within so small a, 823
  you mislike, 872
  you take my, when you take
    the prop, 47
Houses, all, wherein men have
    lived, 436
  and forests hold, noises that
    old, 928
  are communicative, 869
  finely roofed, not, 959
  in it, build, 568
  mended, old, 193
  of ivory shall perish, 1126
  or for kine, for, 628
  out of doors, turns, 964
  plague o' both your, 79
  seem asleep, the very, 297
  thick and sewers annoy, 154
  which humbly crowd, 938
  wide as the height of the,
    1022
Housed where it gets possession,
    38
House-fly goes tasting, 926
Household, head of a, 786
  still, the, 870
  ways of her, 1109
  words, familiar as, 67
  worth in his own, 964
Households, clergymen's, 613
Housekeeper chambermaid laun-
    dress, 446

Housekeeping, when you break
    up, 640
Houseless heads, 99
  shadow evermore, 618
  wild, here in the, 435
Housemaids, damp souls of, 900
Housemaid's knee to heart dis-
    ease, 821
Housetop, corner of the, 1108
Housetops and the sky, between
    the, 910
  moon beautiful over the, 536
  over the, over the street, 560
Housewife that's thrifty, 279
Housewife's happiest season, 552
Hovels of the poor, 983
Hover, about the spot ofttimes I,
    481
How and where and who, 784
  are the mighty fallen, 1100
  blest is he, 250
  he will talk, 186
  I pities them, 275
  it talked, Lord, 131
  little I have gained, 444
  not to do it, 497
  pleasant it is to have money,
    519
  shall I charm the interval, 454
  sweet the truth, 503
  the world wags, 49
  they ring out their delight, 460
  vast the unattained, 444
Howards, blood of all the, 208
Howdy howdy won't you step,
    820
Howe'er it be it seems to me, 462
Howells, tribute to, 628
Howling of the wolf, 29
Howls along the sky, 248
Hub of the solar system, 454
  the king pin the main spring,
    Logan is the, 601
Huckleberry Finn, book called,
    930
Huddle up their work, 265
Huddled masses, 694
Hudibras cried up to be an ex-
    ample of wit, 181
Hue and cry, raise a, 1035
  as red as the rosy bed, 431
  cuckoo-buds of yellow, 42
  flowers of all, 152
  harried every, 939
  locks of an unlovely, 373
  of resolution, the native, 93
  sinuous shells of pearly, 302,
    325
  unto the rainbow, add another,
    58
Hues, like nature's, 224
  masts against the western, 576
  of art, with the living, 472
  of bliss, 245
  that seem ever to vary, 590
  were born in heaven, thy, 382
Hug the dear deceit, we, 226
Huge cloudy symbols, 384
  piles of stone, 688
  way off from the Kingdome of
    God, 166
Hugeness of depriving deep,
    mute, 920
Hugged by the old, 391
  the offender, 177

Hugo Huxley Darwin too, 713
  strong partisan, 858, 1069
Hugs it to the last, 337
Hulk, here lies a sheer, 274
Hulks, convict prisons nor the,
  1074
  greater, draw deep, 75
  nor the, 1074
Hull, vast black cliff of her, 933
Hulls of stone, 937
Hum, beehive's, 289
  no voice or hideous, 161
  of either army sounds, 67
  of human cities torture, 353
  of men, the busy, 160
  of mighty workings, 383
Human affairs deserve admiration
  and pity, 727
  all that is, a day can prostrate,
  965
  all that is, must retrograde, 271
  as to forget what, frailty is,
  386
  being, wherever there is a, 424
  beings are like boilers, 661
  beings, noble and happy, 533
  bliss to human woe, 1043
  body is sacred, 535
  breath, life that breathes with,
  462
  creatures' lives, 391
  ends are ultimately answered,
  339
  events, course of, 273
  everywhere the, soul, 378
  face divine, 151, 220
  features, differences in, 993
  felicity, 228
  form divine, 220, 282
  hands predatory, 741
  heart a human hand, 601
  heart, and also my poor, 514
  heart, naked, 202
  heart, new fountains in the,
  393
  hearts endure, all that, 231
  hopes and human creeds, 660
  kind, of all tyrannies on, 174
  kind, plagues and dotages of,
  123
  kindness, milk of, 84
  mind from error, redeem the,
  434
  mind in ruins, 941
  mortals, 42
  natur' to surrender, not in, 387
  nature, corroded, 641
  nature shows marks of divine
  origin, 333
  nature, the highest type of,
  581
  nature will not change, 457
  nature will not flourish in
  worn-out soil, 421
  nature, you must alter, 753
  nature's daily food, 299
  offspring, true source of, 152
  or divine, called, 683
  race, forget the, 354
  race from China to Peru, 230
  race organized like bees, 769
  race, selfishness is the greatest curse of, 450
  race, survival of the, 846
  round earth's, shores, 385

Human soul take wing, to see
  the, 356
  spark is left, nor, 215
  thought is the process, 339
  to eat is, to digest divine, 493,
  753
  to err in opinion, 1006
  to err is, 174, 211, 1068
  to step aside is, 285
  which is, which divine, 410
  wish I loved the, 759
  woe, each struggle lessens, 504
Humane men I will plead, with,
  424
Humanistic faculty of medicine,
  1089
Humanities of old religion, 317
Humanity, aught that dignifies,
  401
  be the predominant feature in
  the British fleet, 284
  characteristic faculty of, 669
  emblem to, 497
  has three enemies, 694
  imitated abominably, 94
  needs pity and mercy, 728
  of a veined, 428
  packed with poor, 180
  so packed with poor, 650
  still sad music of, 296
  there is but one race, 709
  wearisome condition of, 27
  with all its fears, 435
Humanity's poor sum and story,
  350
Humankind, lord of, 179
  lords of, 250
  porcelain clay of, 179
Humble, star to guide, 499
  and a contrite heart, 780
  and how complaisant, how, 199
  and poor become great, 729
  be it ever so, 365
  but umble, not only, 496
  cares and delicate fears, 297
  heart that was, 333
  hymn of the low and, 533
  livers in content, 73
  one of us that's, 719
  pride were not also, 493
  tranquil spirit, 115
  voyagers are we, 350
  way, kept the, 687
  wisdom is, 266
Humbled neck, upon the, 50
Humbleness, whispering, 45
Humbug lied, the dear old, 721
Humiliation, pride and, 436
Humility and modest stillness,
  66
  is a virtue all preach, 130
  like the virtue of, 139
  love's highway of, 840
  pride that apes, 316, 321
  proud in, 123
  that low sweet root, 338
  week of passionate, 666
Humming of the bees, 955
Humour, career of his, 39
  is a drug, 624
  of it, there's the, 34
  own up to a lack of, 775
  sense of, balance of all the
  faculties, 459
  spoils romance, 724

Humour springs not more from
  the head, 376
  the only test of gravity and
  gravity of humour, 377
  third for good, 196
  void of wit and, 246
  was ever woman in this, won,
  71
  which gains force by unusualness, 835
  will not be comprehended, 877
Humours, in all thy, 196
  of men, gathered, 171
  turn with climes, 209
Humorist, desires to be a, 877
  is like a man firing at a target,
  750
Humorous ladyship, 57
  sadness, wraps me in, 51
  sigh, very beadle to a, 41
Hump, without an absolute, 482
Hun and Roman and vandal, 625
  Goth and the shameless, 779
Hundred, covered with a, 943
  isles, throned on her, 353
  little things, a, 967
  thousand men were led by one
  calf, 733
  while one might tell a, 90
  years are gone, when a, 446
  years from now, 774
  years hence, damnable mouldy
  a, 165
  years to a day, ran a, 452
  years to come, a, 581
Hundreds talk for one who
  thinks, 531
Hundred-fold, catch and produce
  its, 476
Hundredth part of its members,
  270
Hung be the heavens with black,
  68
  over her enamoured, 153
Hungarian wight, 34
Hungary, do high deeds in, 885
Hunger, a man might die of, 1021
  and by contriving, 880
  and war and weather, 737
  food that appeases, 1042
  for unattainable food, 890
  haunted, 937
  if thine enemy, feed him, 1119
  is our work well done, because
  of, 880
  is the teacher of arts, 171
  man be done with, 967
  no sauce like, 1039
  presseth behind him, 686
  thirst and pain, 754
  two weak evils, age and, 49
Hunger's savage tooth, 599
Hungering wings of His, 920
Hungry, a poet should always be,
  930
  and he gave him not meat, 249
  and squalid population, 563
  as the grave, 224
  guests, like, 200
  judges, 212
  lean-faced villain, 38
  look, a lean and, 81
  plight, in a, 951
  poor, the, 619
  rooster don't cackle, 688

Hungry, savage anti-everythings, lean, 453
  sheep look up and are not fed, 159
  sinner, the, 361
Hunt in fields for health unbought, 175
  it in the dark, 263
Hunted and chafed as much as may be, 144
Hunter have you at last, 929
  heart is a lonely, 717
  home from the hill, 703
  horn of the, 396
  Indian, 364
  Nimrod the mighty, 1097
  tongues are cut by the, 929
Hunters of Kentucky, 815
  who hunt for gunless game, 409
Hunter-state of man, 323
Hunting amusement of English gentlemen, 239
  labour of savages of North America, 239
  morning, proclaim a, 229
Hunts in dreams, like a dog, 464
Huntsman the fox and the pack, 807
  his pack, as a, 252
  winds his horn, 229
Huntsmen, three jovial, 229
Hurdy-gurdies make it their own, 1083
Hurdy-gurdy, violin is not a, 593
Hurdy-gurdy's whine, to a, 929
Hurl and the crash of the comber, 777
Hurly-burly's done, when the, 84
Hurrah for the next that dies, 554
Hurricane, night came on a, 274
  win' can blow lak, 712
Hurricane's sultry breath, 554
Hurry, in haste but never in a, 226
  invariably in a, 914
  the noise and the fray, leave all the, 673
Hurrying shapes, two, 620
  world, parted by the, 299
Hurry-scurry helter-skelter, 321
Hurt, as much good as, 271
  cannot be much, 79
  do a mortal little, 761
  he that sweareth to his own, 1103
  more frayd than, 12
  past all surgery, 101
  stays in the heart, 763
  that honour feels, 464
  to his fellows, 1049
  with a thousand tongues, 802
Hurts, you have cured some of your, 410
Hurting and harming, 1045
Hurtles in the darkened air, 244
Husband and wife and lever, 574
  bad, and an ill-provider, 413
  cools, ne'er answers till a, 209
  crying over a, 785
  drink before his wife, 322
  for her, was far, 389

Husband frae the wife despises, advices the, 287
  grief-stricken son, heart-broken, 817
  has no place in the government, 974
  her aunts an infant of three, 903
  in drink but yr faithfull, 198
  light wife doth make a heavy, 47
  lover may be lost in the, 239
  shape a, 482
  she commandeth her, 147
  such duty woman oweth to her, 52
  truant, should return, 358
  with a beard, 38
Husbands look behind and wish, 908
Husband's eye, lovely in her, 295
  heart, level in her, 54
  name find her, 853
Husbanded and so fathered, 82
Husbandman, life of the, 417
Husbandry, dulls the edge of, 91
  in heaven there's, 85
Hush, moaning and sighing and saying, 833
  my dear lie still, 199
  still small voice in autumn's, 442
Hushaby street, lady from, 699
Hushed be every thought, 304
  in grim repose, 244
  in the alabaster arms of death, 646
Hushing of the corn, 955
Husking, laws of, 280
Husks, fresh life withers and bursts, 559
Huswife's wool, tease the, 158
Hut beyond the blue haze, 751
  he made him a, 246
  love in a, 383
  of stone, I only wish a, 451
  of the peasant, 713
  that dear, our home, 226
Huxley, in Darwinism had a champion, 930
Huzzas, loud, 208
Hwang, in the reign of the emperor, 673
Hyacinth, the garden wears every, 468
Hyacinths to feed thy soul, 682
Hyaline, buckets star-gemmed lily-shaped, 431
  streams, fresh from the, 432
Hybla bees, words rob the, 84
Hy-Brasail the isle of the blest, 416
Hydras and Chimæras dire, 150
Hyena, voice of the, 29
Hygiene is rather a virtue, 1054
  the only useful part, 1054
Hymettus, honey of, 601
Hymn affords, fineness which a, 136
  dat good ole, 733
  I sing the, of the conquered, 533
  o' the low and humble, 533
  of the wounded the beaten, 533
  sober as a, 692

Hymn the Brahmin sings, 410
  the whole harmonious, 816
  to his own death, 45, 58
Hymns are sung, what, 887
  sings his canticles and, 922
Hyperion to a satyr, 90
Hyperion's curls, 95
Hypocrisy, an organized, 419
  is a homage, 1044
Hypocrite falls into sin, 1016
Hypocrites, cant of, 241
  in our sleep, 331
  who play the, 1127
Hypocritic days, the, 410
Hyrcan tiger, 87
Hyssop, from the cedar to the, 398
Hysterica passio, down, 98
Hysterics of the Celt, 469

I ALMOST know you are kissing to deceive, 540
  alone have a right to blame, 1084
  always have loved thee, 1063
  am able to say a few words, 921
  am being woman hard beset, 897
  am bigger than anything, 746
  am come that they might have life, 1118
  am here, he answered, 565
  am here: I shall remain here, 1070
  am holier than thou, 1112
  am I and you are you, while, 487
  am no orator, 83
  am not one, 933
  am not the thing you kiss, 596
  am not worthy to unloose the latchet, 1116
  am praying God on high, 869
  am Sir Oracle, 44
  am the angel Raphael, 1126
  am the bread of life, 1118
  am the light of the world, 1118
  am the resurrection and the life, 1118
  am the rose of Sharon, 1110
  am the state, 1060
  am true, know, 888
  am that I am, 108
  am with you alway, 1116
  ask to know, 843
  assume you shall assume, what, 534
  benefit myself in aiding, 965
  called the New World into existence, 293
  came I saw I conquered, 1003
  came not to call the righteous, 1116
  can be pushed, 801
  can cheerfully take it now, 535
  can take it if they can, 877
  cannot see nor breathe nor stir, 832
  cannot stand alone, where, 1085
  can't tell a lie, pa, 941
  can't think why, 623
  celebrate myself and sing myself, 534
  come in the little things, 840

I disapprove of what you say, 1053
do not know why this, 1065
do not understand, 1031
don't think, said Alice, 598
drink to one, 953
flatter you, 888
generally had to give in, 1061
ha' lived an' I ha' worked, 777
have been here before, 577
have forgot much Cynara, 1105
have found it impossible, 921
have loved many, 843
have never wanted to withhold, 921
have nothing, I owe much, 1024
have overcome the world, 1118
is an unfortunate intruder, 938
is surrounded, central, 938
knew him when, 815
know not I ask not, 336
know what I like, 867
laboured not for myself only, 1125
laugh'd till I cried, 972
lie here, here let me lie, 875
like the game and want to play, 660
love it I love it, 512
love them that love me, 1107
loved him and honoured him, 890
loved thee Atthis once, 960
my lords embody the law, 623
my religion, and, 1127
myself am heav'n and hell, 1019
myself caused the sun to rise, 1086
myself have done no less, 781
never like being hit, 621
often stop to wonder, 935
on my path belated, 565
once utter the, 640
pause I examine, 1031
planted in him, the great, 938
put myself forward, neither will, 888
red O blue U green, 1084
remember I remember, 390
rise again, quietly, 925
rose again but, 939
said I didn't know, 616
saw a new heaven and a new earth, 1123
saw the Lord sitting upon a throne, 1111
say Come Jack with me, 941
say I am with him, 1126
say it that should not, 131
set facing mother, 884
shall be telling this, 838
shall cause it not, 652
shall go softly all my years, 1112
shall go to him, 1100
shall have more to say, 808
shall not be there, 929
shall not smile beloved, 920
shall not wholly die, 984
shouldn't much care if it froze or snew, 876
sleep or no, whether, 896

I stand at the door and knock, 1123
still should long for more, 292
swear by Apollo physician, 971
swear I will love thee, 1063
think that I shall never see, 934
turned down one little street, 882
vow to thee my country, 747
wad do, as, 948
want to understand others, 907
wants to go somewhere, 934
was about to multiply, 925
was being human born alone, 897
who am dead, 881
who died I do not chide, 553
will be the gladdest thing, 916
will blow you out, said the wind to the moon, 559
will feed them with wormwood, 1112
will lay me down in peace, 1103
will look at you grimly, 888
will love thee forever, 1063
will not doubt nor scoff, 781
will not hang myself to-day, 827
will not leave you comfortless, 1118
will not let thee go, 1098
will not worship that which ye worship, 1127
will say no more, 582
wish he were here, 555
wish I'd said that, 612
with mournful tread walk the deck, 536
wonder why we either of us came, 730
would bear thee far, 1065
would change with him, 867
would I were alive again, 915
wouldn't eat I wouldn't sleep, 839
I'd sit and sit a thousand years, 839
I'll attack, excellent, 1083
tak' the low road, 952
I'm done gone Massa step on me, 557
for drinking honestly, 833
not goin' back on him, 639
I's all those other, 938
Iago, the pity of it, 103
Iago's soliloquy, 319
Iambics, what little, 806
Ibsen spent, years with, 843
Ibycus, cranes of, 963
Ice and snow, wraps him in, 1065
be thou chaste as, 93
blooms o'er breath of, 642
china bowl of, 637
facing the driven, 923
fortune's, to virtue's land, 173
gave way and fled, 552
in June, seek, 351
in skating over thin, our safety, 412
in the grasp of death, 554
is also great, 839
motionless as, 298
on the Delaware, 784
one night's, 137
some say in, 839

Ice, starve in, 150
thick-ribbed, 36
to smooth the, 58
Iceberg or two at control, 652
Iceland, no snakes in, 237
to Molokai, drifting from, 920
Ich singe wie der vogel singt, 468
Icicle, chaste as the, 76
on a Dutchman's beard, hang like an, 55
Icily regular splendidly null, 469
Iconoclast, what if some unshamed, 609
Icy and chill, winds whistle shrill, 481
current and compulsive course, whose, 103
hands, death lays his, 141
Idea, don't trust that conventional, 498
gained, for every, 689
he had only one, 235, 420
isn't responsible, 854
must have an adequate, 1048
of an agreeable person, my, 421
of eternal punishment, 641
of her life shall sweetly creep, 40
of immortality, 603
of oneself as a cause, 1048
one sole, 964
possess but one, 235
shock your first, 754
teach the young, 224
Ideas, all sorts of old dead, 1075
and opinions have normal rate of growth, 614
are common property, 990
good old-fashioned, 1075
greatest number of greatest, 531
history of, 795
of each age, ruling, 1072
of fancy exalted, 972
of its ruling class, 1072
public doesn't require, 1075
public has very crude, 1063
who sung divine, 409
with words, with, 1081
Ideal, follow the Christian, 1074
given by Christ, 1074
his brothers seeking the, 801
mind fixed on some lofty, 1087
of man and of virtue, 1074
polity, the, 974
Ideals are like stars, 580
of a nation, 802
three personal, 695
true to certain, 694
Idealists walk into the gutter, 788
Idealizing, whatever that may mean, 475
Identity, tormenting everlasting, 330
Ides of March, beware the, 81
Idiot, beauteous, 193
name given to effort, 892
tale told by an, 88
the law is a ass a, 494
who praises, 624
you ignominious, 753
Idle and false imposition, reputation is an, 101

Idle and unemployed, amusement of the, 1054
  as a painted ship, 315
  biologically speaking, is, 917
  brain, children of an, 77
  brood be fed, 973
  days mutinous and quarrelsome, 228
  deliberation, 235
  for manners are not, 471
  hands to do, mischief for, 199
  heedless pace, 600
  is, he who most, 660
  man cannot enjoy rest, 605
  man has so much to do, 639
  rainbow, 816
  ripples that come and go, 865
  scorning, too fond for, 447
  show, seems but, 436
  singer of an empty day, 608
  thing, not an, 474
  thou art not, 525
  thunder in his lifted hand, 173
  toil does not come to help the, 1093
  vacancy, 234
  waste of thought, 332
  whom the world calls, 265
  wild and young, 342
  wind, pass by me as the, 83
  wishes, stay in, 280
  with impunity, 344
Idleness an appendix to nobility, 123
  and lack of occupation, 995
  arms and, 270
  bread of, 1109
  frivolous work of polished, 290
  sorrow a friend and a foe, 918
  sterile with, 101
  't is love in, 406
  to eat his heart away, 26
Idler, busy world an, 265
  is a watch, 263
Idly, and my fingers wandered, 564
  spoken, word so, 425
Idol, a superannuated, 196
  in New York harbor called Liberty, 722
  of my youth, 463
  thou the, I the throng, 623
Idols I have loved so long, 1019
  lost obscenes, old, 826
  to the moles and bats, 1111
Idolatry, god of my, 78
  mad, 75
  on this side, 120
Idyll, will rank as an, 623
If any speak, 83
  I should die to-night, 729
  is the only peacemaker, 51
  it be now 't is not to come, 97
  much virtue in, 51
  she be not so to me, 132
  there be or ever were, 105
  we do meet again, 84
  we should fail, 85
Ignis aurum probat, 131
  fatuus of the mind, 185
Ignoble ease, doctrine of, 734
  selves we knew, 864
  things, sands, 129
  throng, base, 972
Ignominious idiot, 753

Ignominy of popular applause, 707
  sleep with thee, 63
Ignorance and morbid doubt, uttered, 718
  blind and naked, 470
  bonds of, 473
  consists in, 965
  distinguished for, 420
  in education, 636
  is bliss, 't is folly to be wise, 243
  is degrading, 1064
  is the only slavery, 603
  is thy fiercest foe, 544
  it was a childish, 390
  knew nothing but the fact of his, 1014
  let, talk as it will, 1046
  like a fire, 566
  man sedate in, 230
  most powerful weapon of, 1077
  mother of devotion, 126, 178
  never settles a question, 419
  no allowance for, 563
  of the law excuses no man, 130
  of wealth, best riches, 250
  one only evil, 1014
  only is maker of hell, 736
  plays the chief part among men, 1013
  wage eternal war, with, 544
  would die war would cease, 588
Ignorant armies clash by night, where, 546
  despise education, the, 988
  in foreboding evil, 963
  in spite of experience, 239
  man adores, 1078
  of music, 660
  of ourselves, 104
  of what he 's most assured, 36
  who had a capacity for knowledge, 380
Ignorantly read, blockhead, 212
Iliad and Odyssey, 317
  the Shanameh or the Nibelungenlied, the, 527
Iliction returns, follows th', 796
Ilion is consumed with lust, 805
Ilium, topless towers of, 31
Ill and not for good, train for, 743
  at ease, I was weary and, 564
  better made by, 289
  blows the wind that profits nobody, 65
  can he rule the great, 25
  cure all, 410
  darkest hour of, 967
  deeds done, makes, 58
  deeds doubled with an evil word, 38
  diet was the mother, 138
  digestion, unquiet meals make, 38
  does not dawn, what human, 927
  fares the land, 250
  final goal of, 468
  fit instruments of, 212
  for ill, 620
  fortune never pry, 886
  go by, bid all, 977
  good and, together, 53

Ill habits gather by unseen degrees, 177
  know I am, 883
  luck would have it, as, 35
  news goes quick, 1004
  no grievous, 966
  nor has he lived, 985
  nothing becomes him, 41
  of any one in public, speaking, 1127
  of digestion, 310
  panacea for every conceivable, 624
  pleasure, one of the great being, 614
  prest with, 263
  report while you live, 93
  scene of complicated, 942
  seal up the avenues of, 409
  success, nothing more aggravates, 229
  suffer no, 995
  talking of halters, 'tis, 1036
  the good are better made by, 289
  they reckon, 410
  things of good or, we choose, 572
  thoughts die, where, 956
  to maidenhead, bringeth, 929
  to quit an inn, 737
  weede growth fast, 14
  who would wish, 1022
  wind blows no man to good, 65
  wind turns none to good, 19
  winde that bloweth no man to good, 17
Ills, at the long string of, 294
  bear those, we have, 93
  betide, resigned when, 226
  cure for life's worst, 401
  desperate cures applied to desperate, 175
  flood of mortal, 1023
  he can't prevent, 223
  marvelling sweetly on her, 903
  most of our, 967
  of life, victorious o'er a' the, 287
  of men, in the, 965
  the scholar's life assail, what, 230
  to come, no sense of, 243
  to hastening, a prey, 250
  what mighty, done by woman, 185
  which fate forbids, 983
Ill-favoured faults, 34
  thing but mine own, 51
Ill-gotten good is nobody's gain, 1022
Ill-health is defeat, 378
Illinois, and winds of, 676
Illiterate him from your memory, 277
Ill-looking men more terrible, 998
Ill-luck, as, would have it, 1033
  if by, 1054
  people fond of, 417
  seldom comes alone, 1035
Ill-natured gossip, anything in the way of, 812
Illnesses, not of their, 1047
Ill-seeming thick, 52

Ill-spenders, borrowers are nearly always, 532
Ill-timed release, ask for no, 671
truth, 659
Illumed the eastern skies, 473
the eastern skies, sun in state, 557
Illuminated manuscripts, look like, 507
Illumine, what in me is dark, 148
Illusion, all is, 643
by which we would be cheated, 1087
given, for man's, 336
in everything, 618
life's fond, 583
loom weaving, 856
province of, 1069
reaches its zenith, 1081
that times that were are better, 479
victuals and drink an, 972
Illusive dream, 573
light, 572
Illusory from the true, 910
Illustrious acts high raptures do infuse, 146
bustle so, 584
predecessors, 230, 259
spark, the parson, 264
Ils sont si transparents qu'ils laissent voir votre âme, 593
Image, cherished thine, 587
divine, obscured, 1074
in her eyes reflected, beholds her, 555
let them applaud the, 928
made in his, a mannikin, 461
never may depart, 953
of an apprehended object, transfigured, 799
of bloody Mary, 391
of eternity, time is the, 1014
of good Queen Bess, 391
of her, flashed with the, 903
of offence, clear from any, 55
that blossoms, wronging your, 790
Images and precious thoughts, 303
Pygmalion's, 37
receives and reflects, 636
Imagery, carved work and, 247
Imaginary world of lovers, 732
Imagination, abhorred in my, 97
all compact, are of, 43
as a pint-pot, as much, 367
as good as many voyages and cheaper, 558
boast, can, 224
bodies forth the forms of things, 43
cold and barren, 259
comparisons of a disturbed, 261
fame of any work of, 426
gifted with an egotistical, 420
golden age which exists only in, 400
indebted to his, for his facts, 279
into his study of, 40
lacking in grown-up people, 742
like the wings of an ostrich, 397

Imagination of a feast, bare, 59
pours, all that, 305
so fair to fond, 303
solitude needful to the, 529
such tricks hath strong, 43
supreme master of art, 727
that minister of ministers, 728
the soul of poetic genius, 318
to sweeten my, 99
trace the noble dust, 97
travelling is to regulate. 238
truth of, 385
Imaginations are as foul, 94
Imaginative literature, whole range of, 480
stimulus, need for, 646
Imagine why or whence, you can't, 406
Imagined approbation or disapprobation, 448
Imagining fear in the night, 43
to their high, 620
Imagist, O graven, 893
Imbecile, Apollo is an, 410
Imbecility, nor is he convinced of his, 239
Imitate the action of the tiger, 66
Imitated humanity abominably, 94
Imitates nature, art, 171
Imitation, arises from the, 232
is the sincerest flattery, 333
men often applaud an, 963
of nature, all art is but, 991
vocation were endless, 301
Imitator a poor kind of creature, 611
will have no, 1055
Immanuel, shall call his name, 1111
Immaterial wind, into an, 933
Immature human beings, converting, 1072
Immediate jewel of their souls, 102
Immelodious days, crown'st our, 735
Immemorial elms, 466
plan, achieve my, 840
year, of my most, 461
Immense and lonely land, 932
and silent moon, 536
at twelve I felt, 791
Atlantic, 667
ocean, consider time as an, 196
Imminent deadly breach, 100
Immoderate sleep, 239
Immodest words, 180
Immodesty, an excellent, 933
Immoral thought, not one, 239
Immortal, all men desire to be, 477
as they quote, 203
blemish, one, 1082
blessing from her lips, 79
crown, 225
dead who live again, those, 520
fame gives, 203
garland is to be run for, 163
genius is not, 1057
gods I crave no pelf, 80
happened to be born, 1054
hate and courage, 148
longings in me, 105
man meant to be, 421

Immortal names, one of the few. 363
noon, heaven's, 367
part of myself, have lost the, 101
reign, where saints, 199
sea, sight of that, 301
song, wanted one, 173
soul is passing, an, 349
soul of man is, 974
souls, such harmony is in, 47
spirit in the skies, 332
that the soul was, 1014
verse, married to, 160, 303
with a kiss, make me, 31
youth, flourishing in an, 195
youth to mortal maids, 326
Immortals await great men who die, 751
Immortality, all all for, 535
cities have promised themselves, 398
endow with personal, 803
good hastening towards, 536
he ne'er is crowned with, 382
idea of, 603
longing after, 195
mortal shall assume its, 328
nurslings of, 367
of the human soul, 449
ourselves and, 584
quaff, and joy, 153
robed in dazzling, 366
scale the steeps of, 837
think there is nothing but, 537
Immortality's portal, 590
Immovable, infixed to pine, 150
Immutable as the hills, 785
Imp of blind desire, 780
Impalpable out of the land and bottomless sea, 538
Imparadised in one another's arms, 152
Impartial laws were given, by whom, 205
Impassioned expression, 295
for its beauty and salt of truth, 429
onset of life and passion, 531
Impatient and prone to anger, 318
but I am, 812
had we not been, 796
with over-praise, 529
years, outlive the, 780
Impeachment, own the soft, 278
Impearls on every leaf, 153
Impediment, marched on without, 72
Impediments, admit, 108
in fancy's course, 53
to great enterprises, 110
to the marriage of true minds, 108
Impending doom, defied all portents of, 418
Imperceptible, so, has it become, 1087
water, 391
Imperfect gloomy scene, in this, 942
offices of prayer, 302
urn, of his last ashes, 898
work, nature abhors, 665

Imperfections, excellencies than, 196
on my head, 92
pass my, by, 292
Imperial Caesar dead, 882
ensign high advanced, 148
fancy, his, 290
towers of Troy, 212
votaress passed on, 42
Imperious Cæsar dead, 97
mouth whose haughty, sweet, 418
necessities, doll one of the, 1068
pride, 591
Imperishable, immortal and, 974
peace, 744
stone against, 923
Impersonation of force and murder, Napoleon, 603
Impertinence and lack of taste to bare private love, 608
in joy or grief, 566
lesson in grammar an, 554
of childhood, 530
Impervious and immune, 933
Impetuous and near, 679
down, rolls, 223
Impetus of the morning, 786
Impiety may be banished from these works, 179
of the pious, 580
Impious men bear sway, 195
war, 66
Import and value, see their real, 1062
honour meaning and, 1056
points of gravest, 644
Importance of good digestion, 727
of serious, 974
of the world justifies, 786
of well-instructed men, 448
to me, of no, 1027
Important causes, judges of, 975
day, the great the, 194
to himself, 234
what he says is least, 641
Imports the nomination, what, 97
Importunate, rashly, 392
tormenting everlasting identity, 330
Importune, too proud to, 246
Impose, what fates, 70
Imposes an oath, he that, 142
Imposition, an idle and false, 101
of a mightier hand, 397
Impossibility, metaphysical, 376
not to be happy in United States, 863
of changing, 797
Impossible, because it is, 1012
dreamers of the, 491
few things, to diligence, 232
for a man to be cheated, 411
not, though hard to master, 1011
nothing is, 12
remedies, propose, 962
she, that not, 165
solution, 624
specialize in the wholly, 872
that is not physically, 279
to be soiled, truth is, 162
to please all the world, 1045
what 's, can't be, 288

Impostor employs force, 950
Impostors treat those two, 783
Impotence and insignificance, man's, 570
Impotent conclusion, 101
endeavor, 405
thing, a vain and, 959
Impoverished by payment of taxes, 974
Impregnable, fence, 70
Impress of eternity, stamp the, 1082
Impressed on the mind, 273
Impression of the feeling, still retains, 1021
Impressions, courting new, 646
freshness of first, 542
unweaving of false, 520
Impressive, if you'd be, 599
Imprisoned in the viewless winds, 36
soul, rapture the, 274
Imprisonment, penury and, 36
Improbable fiction, condemn it as, 55
Impromptu and full of unexpectedness, 800
Impropriety soul of wit, 835
Improve each moment, 231
each shining hour, 199
the world, worst way to, 506
Improvement makes straight roads, 282
of his originality, 324
Impulse from a vernal wood, one, 295
of indiscretion, that strange, 727
quench appetite check, 1012
still our fate controls, 879
to a wordless prayer, 665
to its own, 546
to punish is powerful, 1079
Impulses of recklessness and despair, 494
primitive, 461
Impunity, idle with, 344
ravage with, 484
Impurities of literature, 878
In God is our trust, 332
his owene grece I made him frye, 7
pace ut sapiens, 268
Inability to remember, 325
Inaccessible tower of the past, 529
vine of song, 635
Inaction disciplined, 290
Inactivity, masterly, 290
Inanimate things, total depravity of, 654
Inattention, patient, 575
Inaudible foot of time, 53
Incalculable up-and-down of time, 664
Incapable of a tune, 323
of deceit, 311
of relishing wit, 246
of stain, 149
Incarnadine, multitudinous seas, 86
Incarnate I told you so, seemed the, 437
Incarnation of fat dividends, 364
Incarnations in every age, 785
Incense, breath all, 353

Incense, gods themselves throw, 100
hangs upon the boughs, 383
of the heart, 226
Incense-breathing morn, 353
Incensed, odours most fragrant when, 109
so that I am reckless, 86
Incense-smoke, strong thick stupefying, 488
Incessant gunfire, with his, 1071
Incessantly, stand on your head, 598
wash this soiled world, 536
Inch, every, a king, 99
every cubic, of space a miracle, 537
every, that is not fool, 174
gave an, you tooke an ell, 17
I'll not budge an, 51
I will not retreat a single, 424
of earth's old mire, 806
of him, Christian every, 1034
of joy, one, 1024
of land, I do not own an, 568
of land, own one, 725
of rigging, without an, 670
thick, let her paint an, 97
to gain, seem here no painful, 519
would not budge an, 1041
Inches, death by, 76
die by, 187
drops below twenty, 926
o'er the common fry, 575
Inchcape bell, with the, 321
Inch-long eager ardent feathered, 823
Inch-rule of taste, 635
Incident that actually occurred, 780
Incidis in Scyllam, 46
Incipient somnolence, with, 686
Inclination, a treacherous, 285
gets the better of judgment, 967
leads him, 234
leads, read as, 234
of the day, state and, 60
thereto of many days together, 132
to hear you, whether he has an, 197
to make or meddle with it, no, 330
Inclined, lest I be, 620
to embrace me she, 162
to sing, never, 984
Incognito, pleasantest condition of life is in, 758
Incoherence, well of soft, 893
Income at its heels, 263
on the same amount of, 973
tears, her, 134
twenty pounds, annual, 496
Income-tax gout umbrella for three, 599
pay the, 430
when there is an, 973
Incommunicable, pressure from the, 347
Incomparable oil Macassar, 358
Incompatibles, these two sorts are, 908
Incomplete, quality of being, 1087

Incompleteness, greatness flowed around our, 428
Incomprehensibility of God, 1067
Incongruity of character, from, 997
Incongruous with intelligence, 543
Inconsiderable sum, 590
Inconsistencies in principle, 650
of opinion, 341
Inconsistency of Elizabethans, 865
Inconsistent man, 202
series of arguments to malign, 420
Inconsolable, they would be, 1051
Inconstant moon, 78
Inconveniences, modern, 616
of cold hunger and thirst, 1039
Incorrectness, exclude, 1017
Increase, God gave the, 1120
of appetite grew by what it fed on, 90
of fear, the, 1080
to her truth, time brings, 240
Incredible standards, known, 927
Incredulous, the world is so, 974
Ind, wealth of Ormus and of, 149
Indebted and discharged at once, 151
to his memory, 279
Indecency, as a public, 1040
Indecent to go on living, 1081
Indecision brings its own delays, 1058
nothing habitual but, 662
Indecorous womanhood in sculpture, 422
Indemnity for the past, 230
Independence be our boast, let, 294
great step towards, 991
let me share, thy spirit, 248
now and forever, 340
secure the, through which, 376
when they planted, 586
Independent, glorious privilege of being, 285
Indescribable charm, 645
expression, 592
Indestructible, love is, 322
states, union of, 445
Index, dab at an, 254
of a mind, the marble, 299
thunders in the, 95
Index-learning, 215
India's coral strand, 343
Indian girl, wild roved an, 406
hunter pursued, 364
like the base, 104
lo the poor, 207
Ocean's bed, through the, 679
of falcon glance and lion bearing, 364
only in this, 842
steep, on the, 157
summer comes at last, 561
summer of life, 637
Indians, only good, were dead, 594
out of the land, 714
Indictment against an whole people, 259
Indies, come you from the, 539
wealth of the, 237
Indifference bring, 248

Indifference, cold, 198
full of sweet, 655
is the tragedy of love, 835
matter of perfect, 1062
moral, 1073
to the concerns of man, 979
Indifferent — good — bad, 241
Indifferently, we have reformed that, 94
Indigested piece, irregular, 232
Indigestion, in these days of, 860
is charged by God, 1067
is that inward fate, 360
Indignant man, such a liar as the, 1080
Indignation and abhorrence, repudiate with, 419
be overpast, until the, 1111
I survey with, 242
savage, 193
Indigo, we have the, 1068
Indiscreet, wanting to be, 925
Indiscretion, a lover without, 651
strange impulse of, 727
Indispensable, make yourself, 1086
so-called comforts not, 514
toiling for the spiritually, 380
Indisposition to what is good, 996
Indistinct as water in water, 105
Individual, every, has had to be reminded, 1089
I announce the great, 537
injustice to an, 950
man, connection of the, 952
of sufficient consequence, 376
one single, you, 537
the history of the, 1057
Individuals, biography of distinguished, 379
discover a deficiency in, 1062
have capacity for better things, 729
have no virtues, if, 950
Individual's rights in England and France, 739
Individualism, rugged, 830
Individualities may form communities, 419
Individuality the salt of common life, 710
Individually but nationally, not only, 991
Indolence, emerged from, 1056
Indolent, common fate of the, 277
the voluptuous and the, 1051
vacuity of thought, 266
Indoor complaints libraries criticisms, done with, 535
Indostan, six men of, 510
Indulgence, I beg your, 320
in such foolishness, allowed, 522
Indurated veins distorted joints, 430
Indus to the Pole, 216
Industrial system gets the jimjams, 715
Industries, innocent, 860
wrecked the, 697
Industrious and grave, 190
and kind, 394

Industrious conversationalist, 921
friend, dear and true, 60
liar, 616
Industry and all the virtues, 922
argues feeble, 971
choke the fountain of, 340
in art a necessity, 611
life without, 533
love of bustle is not, 990
obtain provision by your, 1127
of exclusive predominance, 866
only, not his, 259
race of modern, 1072
Inebriate, cheer but not, 204, 265
of air am I, 584
Inebriated virtue, foaming lips of, 635
with exuberance of verbosity, 420
Ineffable, life, 629
Inelegance, continual state of, 323
Inequality, biological, 830
Inert facts, in the form of, 636
handful of the divine, 531
tideless and, 687
Inertia permanence of matter, 1089
Inevitable, arguing with the, 530
hour, await the, 244
Inexhaustible self-inexhausting Possible, existed in the, 627
Inexorability of a law, 1072
Inexorable, jailer so, 422
Inexperience, hope of happy, 494
Inexplicable dumb-shows, 94
Inexpressible as sweet, 718
desire, give me my, 689
Infallible proceeding, my, 590
resource, 360
test, 319
Infamous are fond of fame, 262
delay, chides his, 201
rich quiet and, 399
thing, crush the, 1053
Infamy, who prefer any load of, 314
worst of the city's, 806
Infancy, age most remote from, 1047
folded in our, 572
heaven around our, 525
heaven lies about us in, 301
old age is most remote from, 112
the babe she lost in, 322
we played in, 446
Infant crying for the light, 468
crying in the night, 468
heart, fashion the, 326
lived and died and lived again, 450
mewling and puking, 49
ripe for his birth, 581
sighed out its little breath, 746
those who have lost an, 346
year, firstling of the, 141
Infants, canker galls the, 90
unbaptized, 651
Infant's breath, regular as, 317
eyes, outlook from an, 449
Infantry class, train him up well in the, 600
moved out the matchless, 690
Infatuated with the efficient, 414

Infected, all seems, 211
Infection, fortress against, 59
  moral and physical, 497
Inferior grievances naturally lose,
  949
  multiplication of the, 580
  while he is with them, 235
Inferiors, advantages great have
    over their, 1040
  is to live with your, 483
  revolt, 975
Inferiority, acknowledgment of,
  339
Infernal, have the most, 809
  newspapers are, 278
Infidel as a dog is an infidel, 235
  now, I have you on the hip, 47
Infidels adore, Jews kiss and, 212
  sextillions of, 535
Infinite dark, leap to the, 758
  day excludes the night, 199
  deal of nothing, speaks an, 44
  dreams, friend of my, 761
  faculties of man, 380
  in faculty, 92
  is as good as, 379
  jest, fellow of, 97
  love, 631
  meadows of heaven, 435
  men believe in the, 515
  pain, good out of, 663
  plan, parts of an, 627
  riches in a little room, 31
  sea, time's, 594
  the cause of all things, 1014
  variety, nor custom stale her,
    104
  what is that to the, 1068
  wrath and despair, 151
Infinite-stepped, ladder, 544
Infinitesimal fraction, 380
Infinitesimals of pleasurable and
    genial feeling, 318
Infinitude of silence beyond, 542
Infinity in the palm of your hand,
  281
Infirm of purpose, 86
  weak and despised old man, 98
Infirmities, bear his friend's, 83
  of age, 324
Infirmity of noble mind, 159
Infixed and frozen round, 150
Inflation of the currency, 930
Inflexible, hearts are hard and,
  166
Influence and power, 235
  bad, 300
  bequeath some, 810
  destiny exercises its, 1079
  have so little, 969
  may fall, our, 666
  of an author, 623
  of example, salutary, 233
  of lawyers, 1070
  of wealth, under the, 973
  shed their selectest, 154
  stops, where his, 636
  unawed by, 333
  whose bright eyes rain, 160
  widest helpful, 533
Influences of Pleiades, sweet,
  1103
  servile to the skyey, 36
Informal is what women say,
  912
Information and belief, on, 911

Information, benignant, 815
  know where we can find, 236
  only ask for, 496
Informed, no man who is correct-
    ly, 400
Infortune, worst kind of, 4
Infusion of milk and sugar, 323
Ingenious assembly of portable
    plumbing, 912
  contrivances, 232
  kind loyal mild noble, 1037
Inglorious arts of peace, 169
  Milton, some mute, 245
Ingloriously, we do, 163
Ingrate thought, 888
Ingratitude in a man, I hate more,
  56
  of men, 236
  thou marble-hearted fiend, 98
  unkind as man's, 50
Ingredients, commends the, 85
Ingress into the world, man's, 276
Inhabit this bleak world, 336
Inhabitants, like me, town that
    boasts, 437
Inhabits our frail blood, 56
Inhaled the dreamy air, russet
    year, 551
Inherent beauties, shows none of
    its, 196
Inherit, all which it, shall dis-
    solve, 33
Inheritance, enter into their, 817
  extent of our, 542
  is held in store, 496
  to be destroyed, their dearest,
    949
  with him, divided an, 1056
Inhuman, ev'y thin' thet 's done,
  526
Inhumanity to man, man's, 284
Inimies make life worth living,
  796
Inimitable his deeds, 28
  jasmine, exception of the, 1083
Iniquity, know about, 785
  laurel of approved, 808
  of oblivion, 145
  that grey, 62
Initials, notches his cockney, 528
Injured, forgiveness to the, 178
  ghost, Hosier's, 240
  hate whom they have, 991
  lover's hell, jealousy, 153
  peevish look, 879
Injuries, forgive and forget, 1037
Injurious, beauty though, 157
  to the freshness of first impres-
    sions, 542
Injury, adding insult to, 992
  and harm, protect her from,
    953
  elephants never forget an, 812
  ever done him an, 997
  means of doing him an, 1055
  or of the greatest, 970
  passes over without, 969
  to the meaning, without, 319
Injustice, corrupted with, 69
  is the surest road, national,
    450
  jealousy is, 204
  mankind censure, 973
  nothing so finely felt by chil-
    dren as, 498
  of our fellows, 1046

Injustice, rigorous, is rigorous
    law, 980
  threatened with a great, 402
  to an individual, 950
  to beasts, man's, 1006
Ink, gall enough in thy, 55
  he hath not drunk, 41
  in formal, 128
  shelter of his, 725
  small drop of, 359
  take a little bit of, 829
  that never saw pen and, 56
  the ocean fill, with, 1017
Inkdrop scent the world, 814
Inkhorns, haud your hands frae,
  523
Inkstand, Vesuvius' crater for,
  531
Inky cloak, not alone my, 89
Inland far we be, though, 301
  island, 633
Inlets making, through creeks
    and, 519
Inmate of the skies, some, 220
Inn, charm in a country, 413
  die drinking in an, 940
  earth his sober, 121
  happiness produced by a good,
    236
  ill to quit an, 737
  Miranda, remember an, 810
  no room for them in the, 1116
  of earth, wayside, 771
  rest in God's green, 829
  take mine ease in mine, 12, 63
  to gain the timely, 87
  warmest welcome at an, 242
  was full, the, 904
Inns of molten blue, 584
Inn-door, up to the old, 864
Inner flow of things, 524
  half of every cloud, 837
  vision quick to find, 557
Innisfail, harp of, 327
Innisfree, go to, 790
Innocence and health, 250
  closing up his eyes, 31
  dream of sleeping, 645
  endures, while, 935
  her, a child, 175
  mirth and, 357
  of love, dallies with the, 55
  of our neighbors, 515
  our fearful, 298
  recovered, 515
  silence of pure, 56
  was never known, timid, 1050
Innocency, no, in modern paint-
    ing, 709
Innocent and young, 495
  as a new-laid egg, 622
  as June, 586
  curly-browed, they sink, 929
  flower, look like the, 84
  for coquetry, too, 447
  glee, joined in their, 548
  grieves not at ills, 223
  lamb, skin of an, 69
  minds, 168
  nose, coursed down his, 48
  one, condemn an, 1053
  shall not be, 1108
  shames, a thousand, 39
  sincere officious, 231
  sleep, 86
  thoughts like rose leaves, 360

Innocent within is armed without, 214
Innocents, rest you merry, 935
Innocuous desuetude, 627
Innumerable as the stars, 153
  bees, murmuring of, 466
  burning coals, 874
  caravan, join the, 371
  essence of biographies, 378
  race of men, 154
Inquirer, modest not presumptuous, 200
Inquiring, eye so, 326
Inquisitive, man should be, 775
Insane and awful passion, 393
  men eloquent, 1078
  more or less, loud clamor, 377
  ordinarily he is, 1066
  root, 84
Insanity is often the logic, 454
  of noble minds, the divine, 438
  power to charm down, 413
Insatiable and unhappy, the, 788
Inscribed in history's page, names, 518
Inscription, altar with this, 1118
  on stone, by the, 970
  upon my tomb, no, 329
Inscriptions, four, expressed the degrees, 1068
  lapidary, 236
Inscrutable colossal and alone, 683
  invisible, 33
Insect scraping about, small, 629
Insects and humans, both, 853
  multitudinous, coral, 540
  of the hour, 260
Insect's wing, tenderness with which we take up an, 331
Insensible, honour is, 63
  of the brevity of life, 1051
Insensibility, it argues an, 324
  stark, 233
Inseparable, one and, 341
Inside, in your little, 624
  of a church, forgotten the, 62
Insight, in hours of, 546
Insignificancy and an earldom, 222
Insignificant, passes over the weak and, 960
Insinuated nose, miss the, 736
Insipid to a vulgar taste, 788
Insolence and wine, flown with, 148
  of enormous animals, 969
  of office, 93
  or inefficiency, 909
  strength without, 351
Inspector of snow-storms, self-appointed, 514
Inspiration beyond efficiency, 726
  contortions without the, 261
  glows, in iron, 292
  lack for an, 854
  like a low, 653
  no more, than in a plate of muffins, 720
  sources of joyous, 476
  unapprehended, 318, 369
  without the, 261
Inspiring John Barleycorn, 287
Instalment, repays the first, 991
Instances, wilderness of single, 465

Instances, wise saws and modern, 50
Instant a mystery, the, 883
  before me at this, 98
  for each ecstatic, 584
  never for one, 1085
  we rose both at an, 63
  when it is being experienced, 1083
Instants, soul's superior, 585
Instant's truce, never an, 515
Instil a wanton sweetness, 224
  in me, 620
Instinct, generous, in boys, 571
  of passing around, 538
  of revenge, one great, 1082
  of the homing dove, 711
  of the soul, indulging every, 489
  political, 722
  truth was felt by, 490
  with love's true, 335
Instincts, a few strong, 302
  feelings came to them like, 458
  high, 301
  of female childhood, 1068
  plant himself indomitably on his, 414
  satisfied in its double, 636
  unawares, like, 458
  uncivilized Eastern, 785
Instinctive taste, an, 318
Institution is the lengthened shadow, 411
  life's a pleasant, 624
  strains until it breaks, 720
Institutions alone create a nation, 419
  cease from being liberal the moment, 1081
  I sought to destroy, 535
  in England, 720
  liberal, I intended, 1061
  neither for nor against, 535
  political, a superstructure, 1086
Instruct my sorrows to be proud, 57
Instruction, better the, 45
  by others, 975
  in the laws of nature, 563
  wise, 166
Instructions, we but teach bloody, 85
Instrument, a more potent, 973
  God's most awful, 303
  of executive will, 320
  of trade and commerce, 608
  stringed, 996
  to know if the moon shine, 143
  trouble to invent an, 933
  with a certain range, musical, 542
Instruments, his crooked, 1061
  mastery over musical, 742
  mortal, 82
  of darkness tell us truths, 84
  of ill, 212
  to plague us, 100
Insubstantial pageant faded, 33
Insult like a slight bow, 234
  look that threatened, 260
  to injury, added, 992
Insults of fortune, 229
  unavenged, 302
Insulting foe, to meet the, 280

Insupportable, the unreasonable, 1007
Insured, they were heavily, 622
Insurmountable barrier a myth, 691
Insurrection, nature of an, 82
Integrity, clothed with, 1046
  health soundness to the full, 895
  of nature, in all the, 1055
Intellect but memory, uses not, 1022
  education the instruction of, 563
  eye of the, 378
  feather to tickle the, 324
  is improperly exposed, 313
  is invisible, 1064
  is of the narrow and normal, 1064
  or will, 612
  subtlety of, 641
  the march of, 259, 321
  thought the labour of the, 1068
  truth or satisfaction of, 461
  weakness of, 624
  will and, 1048
  will find pure pleasure, 669
Intellects, argument and, 254
  three classes of, 1023
Intellectual ancestry, 529
  anti-Darwin, 867
  being, would lose this, 149
  desolation, 1072
  enjoyment, common stock of, 750
  lords of ladies, 358
  nature abhors a vacuum, 235
  passion drives out sensuality, 1022
  preserved her, 429
  product judged, 645
  splendor, no, 543
  thing, a tear is an, 282
  thing, no great, 531
  virile courageous, 1085
Intelligence and reflection and judgment, 981
  and self respect, develop their, 1075
  capable of grasping whole truth, 643
  controlling, 1011
  enables man to get along without education, 818
  flash of, 479
  incongruous with, 543
  madness the loftiest, 461
  takes, form which, 872
  to our, 358
Intelligent fountains, 572
  obligation to be, 856
Intelligible forms of ancient poets, 317
  the less, 1049
Intemperance, to know her an, 586
  world has no tyrant like, 424
Intense, concentred in a life, 353
  reply of hers, 358
  verse fame and beauty are, 385
Intensity and flow, destroys the, 1071
  emotional and spiritual, 930
Intent on all the wondrous plan, 286

Intent, on hospitable thoughts, 153
  pious passion, grave, 736
  quite so single in, 927
  spur to prick the sides of my, 85
  to do mischief, 122
  truth told with bad, 282
  working out a pure, 303
Intents wicked or charitable, be thy, 91
Intention of communicating truth, 318
  to read it, 235
Intentions are honourable, your, 1055
  hell paved with good, 137, 236
  hell paved with mere good, 662
  in spite of your good, 629
  of men, bad, 981
Interchange of courtesies which sweeten life, 343
Intercourse between tyrants and slaves, 253
  lived in social, 235
  speed the soft, 216
Interdependence absolute, 777
Interest, at small, 235
  by some particular, 1087
  equal to the proudest, 949
  exceed in, 323
  first condition of, 646
  for that year, shall not pay, 958
  in all parts of the universe, 207
  in disease and death, 1089
  in planting a tree, 589
  in things that are fine, 858
  in your movements, 785
  no kind of common, 1074
  of man, justice the great, 340
  paid by those who borrow trouble, 946
  proof a man gives of his, 786
  speaks all sorts of tongues, 1043
  unborrowed from the eye, 296
  was high and security small, 593
  with profound, 921
Interests, assertion of private, 1062
  conciliation of, 1044
  most concerned in my own, 979
  of our fellow-citizens, 273
  of this or that class, 1086
  prefer their, to his own, 259
Interested in others, when, 986
Interesting but tough, statement was, 615
Interim is like a phantasma, 82
  when the gloom is soft, 386
Interior, whose sources are, 585
Interludes in the electrical display, 903
Interlunar cave, her vacant, 156
Interminable series of arguments to malign, 420
Intermission, sans, 49
Internal evidence, confides in the, 950
Interposition, spiritual, 738
Interpretation, interpreter of life not need, 641
Interpretations, necessary to interpret, 1031

Interpreter hardest to be understood, 278
  it is the great, 840
  my fond, 873
  of life, 641
  the house of the, 171
Interred with their bones, the good is oft, 83
Interrupted by experiment of dying, 147
Interruption, dislike of, 324
  of all forms of, 1064
Interstellar spaces, meditate on, 794
Interval, lucid, 183
  that lowers, charm the, 454
Intervals, falling at, 266
  lucid, 1038
Intestines, traced back to the, 1082
Intimate and free, 771
  enemies, 577
Intimates are predestined, 635
  eternity to man, 195
Intolerable deal of sack, 62
  in Almighty God, 361
Intoxicating drinks, banishment of, 455
Intrepid sparrows Arabs of the air, 756
Intricate meaning and pith, 590
Introduced, they had not been, 622
Introduction of a new order of things, 1023
  to any literary work, 254
Intruder, an unfortunate, 938
Intrusive, sorrow's held, 401
Intuition, passionate, 302
Inurned weep a people, 399
Invaded hearers, encompass'd and drown'd, 649
Invasion of the rights of others, 396
Invent, as difficult to appropriate as to, 415
  God, necessary to, 1052
  young men fitter to, 111
Invented history, 1053
  sleep, God bless the man who first, 510
  sleep, this same, 1042
  the art of printing, 379
  work, who first, 325
Invention, art allied to, 171
  art so nearly allied to, 278
  brightest heaven of, 66
  every matter that relates to, 480
  is unfruitful, 259
  means another multi-millionaire, 618
  mother of, 654
  necessity the mother of, 171, 200
  of printing and the Reformation, 1089
  science of his own, 1076
  use of this new, 868
Inventions, sought out many, 1109
Inventor blundered, its, 943
  return to plague the, 85
Inventor's wife, I'm an, 733
Inverted bowl, 1019
  year, ruler of the, 224, 265

Investigate things, men ought to, 1013
Investigation, experiment for real, 449
  guided by principles, 1012
Investment, goodness the only, 515
Inveterate dislike of interruption, 324
  foes saluted, 174
Invidious bar, birth's, 468
Invigorated and reimpressed, 233
Invincible as they, none, 263
  locks, shaking her, 163
Inviolable shade, clutching the, 547
Inviolate sea, compassed by the, 462
Invisible and mute, 872
  beauty, 849
  coat of Jack the Giant-Killer, 299
  inscrutable, 33
  intangible unknowable world, 749
  oh may I join the choir, 520
  soap, 391
  spirit of wine, 101
  through the, 1019
  wounds, 50
Invitation of her host, 700
  than command, more, 197
  to the people of the world, 502
Invite my soul, I loafe and, 534
  with gilded edges, 937
Invites you by his looks, 263
Invocation, Greek, to call fools, 48
Invoked, though oft, 155
Involuntary homage, 497
Involvements and feelings and characters, 312
Inward and spiritual grace, 1128
  bruise, parmaceti for, 61
  eye the bliss of solitude, 299
  judge obey more strictly, 547
  light, men of, 143
  places of the soul, 973
  quality, do draw the, 104
  self-disparagement, 302
Inwardly digest, 1127
  in secret to be great, 528
Io, a bull to beguile, 23
Iona, ruins of, 233
Ipsa quidem virtus, 139
Ipse dixit, 1016
Ire, condensed in, 338
Ireland a fatal disease, 709
  all is changed in, 792
  but I'll not forget old, 432
  ever ye ride in, 828
  first named Emerald Isle, 941
  free, I'd have, 954
  gives England her soldiers, 576
  isn't it grand you look, 685
  may honor the shamrock, 642
  no more, it's, 779
  romantic, is dead and gone, 791
  taught me love, 746
  the right road to, 934
Iridescent dream, 601
Iris, livelier, 464
  that shall find thee out, 69
Iris' woof, spun out of, 157
Irish are the cry-babies, 898
  came in the spring, wild, 925

Irish eyes and London cries and streams of Wales, 746
lad, no blithe, 328
Shilelah, 347
shore, round about upon the, 287
where there are, 778
Irishman in the garden of Eden, 518
is lined with copper, 616
plain duty of every, 709
Irishmen in Ireland, 709
Irksome word and task, it is an, 481
Iron and part of clay, part of, 1113
armies clad in, 156
bands, harness me down with your, 402
bars a cage, 168
creeds, 709
did on the anvil cool, 58
entered into his soul, 1128
from rare springs, drink, 923
front of, 521
hand of fate, 778
in the water, 940
inspiration glows, 292
is hot, strike when the, 12
is hot, striking while the, 1042
lilies, 793
nor any tool of, 1101
sharpeneth iron, 1108
shuts the golden opes, 159
sleet, before the, 431
sleet of arrowy shower, 244
some are of, 927
spouse, his, 926
stamped the age, with, 984
tears down Pluto's cheek, 161
tongue of midnight, 43
when it is hot, hammer your, 987
winter, 576
with a rod of, 1123
with blood and with, 634
written with a pen of, 1112
Irons, everywhere he is in, 1054
in the fire, other, 971
in the fire, two, 129
Iron-armed soldier, 404
Ironies, jokes malices, 766
Irradiancy of love, full, 889
Irradiating word, 588
Irrationally held truths more harmful, 564
Irrecoverably dark, 156
Irregular indigested piece, 232
Irreparable ravages of time, 1050
Irresponsible frivolity, harebrained chatter of, 420
Irritability, Bostonitis a certain chronic, 636
Irritating folly of others, bearing the, 746
Irritation, amount of minor, 853
Irving, Halleck and Dana uncontaminated, 766
Is and all is well, God, 444
but hadn't ought to be, 442
the was the might have been, the, 579
Isabella did her basil-tree, keep green as, 722
Iscariot, mother of, 817

Island, as an inland, 633
bulwark of our, 248
cast on to an, 958
in the silent sea, 874
of cheese, 1056
of England, that, 67
of ruins towers cloisters grey, 396
of Saints, 396
on the draggled, 674
tight little, 305
Islands lift their fronded palms, 444
of august surprise, 858
of the blest, 780, 832
when the, and the lands, 375
Island-valley of Avilion, 463
Isle a sickle moon a ship, an, 882
fast-anchored, 264
fortunate, 982
green, in the sea, 460
hunt for a desert, 938
in far-off seas, 485
it frights the, 101
men of the Emerald, 941
of Beauty fare thee well, 388
of rest, 874
this sceptred, 59
where the nations throng, 860
Isles Columbus discovered, 523
extreme, from, 848
of death, exile in the, 626
of Greece, the, 359
ships that sailed for sunny, 423
that o'erlace the sea, 488
the old Greek, 435
throned on her hundred, 353
we shall touch the happy, 464
Islington, village less than, 168
Isolated individual effort, 1074
Isolation abandonment poverty, 1068
Israel, I arose a mother in, 1099
Jephthah judge of, 92, 255
of the Lord beloved, when, 310
sweet psalmist of, 1100
was from bondage led, when, 168
Israfel, as the angel, 460
Issue, expects the, 303
in the light of the final, 976
of events, measured by the, 981
Issues good or bad, 300
of life, out of it are the, 1106
touched but to fine, 35
Isthmus, this narrow, 337
I-tiddly-iddly-i-ti-iddly-ay, 911
It is here, but only, 928
it's just, 786
might do good, some said, 171
might have been, 442
must be so, 195
were all one, 53
why doth, so and so, 650
would never do with us, 801
Italia O Italia, 354
Italian lake, my blue, 899
people is not yet accustomed, 1090
Itali-an, or perhaps, 623
Italians have voices like peacocks, 592
love bread heart of the home, 1090
Italy a hell for women, 125

Italy a paradise for horses, 125
I have received from, 1076
jewelled all, 889
lieth thine, 570
my Italy, 486
spring in, 197
Itch of disputing, 114
poor, of your opinion, 75
Itching palm, 83
Iteration, thou hast damnable, 60
Ithaca full of moths, did but fill, 76
oars of, 570
Ither weel, we luvit ilk, 389
Ithuriel with his spear, 152
Ithuriel's spear, like, 889
Itinerant preachers, 228
Ivan Petruski Skavar, name of, 951
Ivan's bivouac, 543
Ivory apes and peacocks, 832, 1101
cap and stopper too, 451
Gate, come through the, 674
gate, comes up to the, 570
houses of, 1126
in his tower of, 858, 1070
moonlight, 401
my bed should be of, 822
neck a tower of, 1110
towers dwell upon, 893
Ivory-towers, let us forget our, 858
Ivrything worth havin' goes to th' city, 796
Ivy from a sacred tree, 758
to the wall, clings the, 427
Ivy-branch over the wine, 51, 990

JABBER of a waterside saloon, 925
Jack, banish plump, 62
built, house that, 543
life of poor, 274
loved his friend, 274
mansion reared by daedal, 543
Robinson, before you could say, 540
spanking, 274
Jackass, cudgel his own, 654
Jackdaw, devil in that little, 351
Jackson picked from the pebbles, Andrew, 531
Jacksonian vulgarity, the, 619
Jacob dreamed and behold a ladder, 1098
served seven years for Rachel, 1098
Jacob's ladder, talk to him of, 417
ladder, traffic of, 749
voice, the voice is, 1097
Jade, arrant, on a journey, 253
kisses you quickly, 1066
let the galled, wince, 94
Jail, in a ship is being in a, 234
jail afore us everywhere, 496
patron and the, 230
the world's thy, 117
Jailer so inexorable, 422
Jam to-morrow and jam yesterday but never jam to-day, 598
James I, James II and the Old Pretender, 906

James James Morrison Morrison, 876

Jam-pots grow, where the, 702

Jane, and simply, 903
  Shore with sorrowe sing, 257

Jangled out of tune, 94

Janitor's boy, I'm in love with the, 938

Janus, two-headed, 43

Japan, loved you once in old, 692

Jar, mine to feel amid the city's, 546
  through all will run, the paining, 441

Jars, fretted to dulcet, 748

Jargon of the schools, 189, 263

Jarring sects confute, 1019

Jasmine is impossible to counterfeit, 1083

Jasper cup, like jewels in a, 728
  wall, seek to cross the, 671

Jaundice of the soul, jealousy the, 174

Jaundiced eye, all yellow to the, 211

Jaunt must be put off, our, 277

Javan or Gadire, bound to, 157

Javelin, never handled oar or, 973

Jaw-breaking woodnotes wild, 893

Jaws of darkness to devour it up, 42
  of death, 56, 467, 1032
  ponderous and marble, 91, 615

Jay-bird don't rob his own nes', 688

Je ne vous aime pas, 188

Jealous be, men will sometimes, 121
  in honour, 49
  mistress, art is a, 413
  mistress, law is, 477
  one not easily, 103
  they're apt to be, 511

Jealousies and petulances of actors, 617
  and sorrows, feuds, 891

Jealousy, beware my lord of, 102
  full of artless, 96
  is cruel as the grave, 1110
  is injustice, 204
  of the French, 739
  the injured lover's hell, 153
  the jaundice of the soul, 174

Jealousy's eyes are green, 367

Jean, farewell to my, 204
  Jacques Rousseau, ask, 264

Jeanie with the light brown hair, 568

Jedgment, I'd run my chance with Jim at, 639

Jefferson Davis, first message, 539
  galled by, 928
  trumpet word of, 771

Jeffersonian simplicity, the, 619

Jehovah has triumphed, 336
  Jove or Lord, 216

Jehu, like the driving of, 1101

Jelly, distill'd almost to, 90

Jenkin Grout, Sir, epitaph of, 948

Jennies, Betsies Katies and, 231

Jenny kissed me, 346

Jephthah was judge of Israel, 92, 255

Jericho, may go to, 334
  tarry at, 1100

Jersey meadows, 372
  on a drizzly night, 919

Jerusalem, if I forget thee, O, 1106
  lunatic asylum in, 741
  meet with joy in sweet, 71
  the golden, 518, 1017
  the holy city new, 1123
  till we have built, 283
  to Jericho, man went down from, 1117
  windows open toward, 1113

Jerusalem's wall, gate built in, 282

Jes' to show you're up to fightin' tu, 527

Jeshurun waxed fat, 1099

Jessamine, pale, 159

Jesse James was a two-gun man, 888

Jesses were my dear heart-strings, 102

Jest and earnest, between, 1036
  and riddle of the world, 208
  and youthful jollity, 160
  be laughable, Nestor swear the, 43
  bitter is a scornful, 230
  breaks no bones, 237
  fellow of infinite, 97
  given to, 539
  I am a merry, 673
  it would be a good, forever, 61
  life is a, 206
  man's life is but a, 577
  may yet be said, 828
  owe the fates a, 784
  put his whole wit in a, 129
  unseen inscrutable, 33
  while laughing at some, 781

Jests at scars that never felt a wound, 78
  indebted to his memory for, 279
  life and death are equally, 461

Jest's prosperity lies in the ear, 41

Jester, fool and, 66

Jester's motley garb, 851

Jesting dancing drinking, 'tis, 743
  some sly way of, 197
  with edge tools, 131

Jesu Crist and sëynt Benedight, blesse this hous, 6

Jesuit, bland as a, 692

Jesus and the dead dog, 566
  came to Birmingham, when, 880
  Christ our Saviour was born on Christmas, 567
  resting in the bosom of, 817
  wast Thou shy once, little, 748

Jet, anthracite like, 926
  of memory, a, 888
  pansy freaked with, 159

Jetty to the milking shed, rise and follow, 540

Jew and prostitute, ruled by, 759
  fish crier, I knew a, 855
  has taught me how to wait, 1076

Jew, hath not a, eyes, 45
  I am proud to be a, 418, 797
  I thank thee, 47
  that Shakespeare drew, 221
  wandring, 257
  your hated, 657

Jews, among the false, 257
  and Gentiles most are wont, 604
  chosen people of God, 419
  give value, 721
  might kiss, cross which, 212
  three, to cheat a Greek, 559

Jewel carved, precious, 672
  consistency thou art a, 944
  discretion thou art a, 944
  experience be a, 34
  have I caught my heavenly, 27
  immense and brilliant, 932
  in an Ethiop's ear, 77
  in his head, wears a precious, 48
  lies within our breast, this, 226
  of gold in a swine's snout, 1107
  of the just, 170
  of their souls, 102
  or plate, weight of, 792

Jewels, Cornelia's, 125
  five-words-long, 466
  in a jasper cup, like, 728
  in the carconet, 107
  into a garret, Nature never put her, 113
  of the mine, bright, 370
  of the horseman's hands, 928

Jewelled arm, 814
  mass of millinery, 469
  unicorns, while, 900

Jeweller's trays of spangle-glitter, 683

Jewish gaberdine, 44
  race older than savages, 797

Jezebel heard of it, 1101

Jibe of the cynic tribe, 843

Jig upon a rug, dance a, 691

Jill-o'er-the-ground purple blue, 806

Jim, I'd run my chance with, 639
  was a keerless man in his talk, 639
  well good-by, 696

Jingling of the guinea, 464

Jingo, by the living, 283
  if we do we've got the ships by, 562

Joan, Darby and, 345
  your old wife, 690

Job, as to a pitiful, 261
  back of the, 873
  do things by the, 582
  for this Panama gang, 872
  on the top of the earth, 782
  you find, scared of the, 870

Job's curses, breathed, 660

Joblillies, Picninnies and the Garyulies, 246

Jock be aye sticking in a tree, 311

Jocularities, who seeks for, 624

Jocularity from an affettuoso smile to a piano titter, 283

Jocund day stands tiptoe, 79

Joe Millers are a pest, 673
  voices calling Old Black, 567

Joe, when you were Bill and I was, 452
who rode so straight, 577
Joh, Mayor on oaten bread, 122
John and Peter and Robert and Paul, 570
Barleycorn, bold, 287
Barleycorn got up again, 284
Bird a laborer, 919
Bradford, but for the grace of God, there goes, 18
Brown's body lies a-mouldering, 612
Bull, a typical, 706
Bull greatest of all, 361
Bull was beat at Waterloo, 406
Grumlie swore, 345
Harvard from Stratford town, 834
Knott, here lies, 948
Lee is dead that good old man, 404
man whose name was, 1117
Naps of Greece, 52
of Gaunt, old, 58
P. Robinson he, 526
Peel at the break of day, 396
Peel with his coat so gay, 396
Peel's view-hallo would waken the dead, 397
print it, some said, 171
Smith, that homeliest name, 561
Tompkins a hedger and ditcher, 345
why don't you speak for yourself, 436
Johnny Appleseed swept on, 858
Sands had married Betty Haigh, 941
who upset the coach, 425
Johnson knew and well, 649
put you in mind of, 261
there is no arguing with, 255
Johnson's conversation was too strong, 272
Join the choir invisible, oh may I, 520
Joined together, God hath, 1115
Joint labourer with the day, 89
of mutton, 65
time is out of, 92
Joints, indurated veins distorted, 430
of supple gold, 632
the elephant hath, 75
Joint-heirs with Christ, 1119
Joke, college, to cure the dumps, 190
flight of a, 590
for the ages, 590
gentle dulness ever loves a, 215
good, cannot be criticized, 826
into a Scotch understanding, 246
many a, had he, 251
peace on earth is a, 850
that's possible, every, 624
Jokes at which the mob laughs, 827
begin with the usual, 972
ever funny, were, 913
family, 913
for every ten, 241

Jokes, one of fate's saddest, 528
wooden-shoes are standing, 195
Jollity, I live in the crowd of, 232
jest and youthful, 160
tipsy dance and, 157
Jolly and comfortable bourgeois tradition, 925
miller, there was a, 269
old pedagogue, 605
Jolts along life's highway, 1083
Joly whistle wel y-wet, 6
Jonah, Noah an', 851
prays and sings, 922
was in the belly of the fish, 1113
Jonathan, Saul and, 1100
Jones, deeds that are done of Mrs., 715
Jonson, rare Ben, 118
Jonson's learned sock, 160
Jordan's holy harvest vales, 657
wave, on this side, 516
Joses the brother of Jesus, 880
Jostle, come up from the, 732
Jostling in the street, not done by, 282
Jot of heart, nor bate a, 162
Journalists most old-fashioned, 775
Journey, agreeable companion on a, 987
arrant jade on a, 253
direct the traveller's, 435
ends, here they say the, 765
God prosper your, 1123
good company in a, 139
is done, when, 887
is done, when the, 873
is over, when the, 742
of life, toilsome, 558
on Sundays, to begin a, 192
one of the pleasantest things is going a, 329
prepare for a, 907
to Samarkand, 882
to the sea, begins its, 637
to-morrow we start on our great, 1091
took his farewell, 817
women too personal for a, 861
Journeys are, beyond the earth his, 911
end in lovers' meeting, 54
Journey's end, nearing our, 690
Journeymen, nature's, 94
Journey-work of the stars, 535
Jove bestows, ask me no more where, 140
changed earth's golden time, 984
daughter of, 243
for his power to thunder, 76
intended, what omen, 184
laughs at lovers' perjuries, 78, 176
like a painted, 173
strikes the Titans down, 484
the front of, himself, 95
thou regent of the skies, 269
young Phidias brought his awful, 408
Jove's dread clamours, 102
own eagle sundered, from, 292
Joy, a secret thing, make my, 814

Joy, a sober, 983
added to the sum of human, 602
again, take up my, 551
and freedom are, that's where, 926
and love triumphing, 151
and not pain, scatter, 413
and sorrow, wherein dwell, 1070
and temperance and repose, 435
and woe, changeless through, 416
apprehend some, 43
asks if this be, 251
awakes in one, when, 1070
be the reality, your, 480
be unconfined, let, 352
be wi' you a', 291
behind, and my, 107
better to weep at, 38
beyond all dignities of earth, 427
cease every, 327
cometh in the morning, 1103
desperate the, 346
dream in, and wake in love, 375
eet ees too late, 813
enter thy master's, 305
for life and, and for objects, 536
forever, thing of beauty is a, 382
has its friends, 922
how pure the, 288
in man in leaf in star, 736
in sailing outward, 642
in the gifts, 403
incredible beauty of, 895
is gain, every, 484
is the grace we say to God, 540
is wisdom, 790
its exultancy, its sense of, 932
kisses the, as it flies, 281
life warlike music, never so much, 1071
livelier and more abiding, 669
loses its beauteous summer glow, 540
Marcellus exil'd feels, and more true, 208
may be a miser, 565
misunderstood, grief may be, 429
mother's pride father's, 309
no feeling so appalling as, 1067
now lives in me, 869
o'erflow with, 53
of a great discovery, 1087
of all the earth, 587
of health, savor of the repast, 1090
of hearts, never know the, 628
of his death, none hath, 631
of life, light sane, 779
of life, unto all the, 693
of silence, holds some, 407
of the drinker, nothing equals the, 1093
of the rose, this is the, 841
of the whole earth, 1104
of the whole table, 87

Joy of the wine in being drunk, 1093
of the working, 779
of youthful sports, 355
oil of, for mourning, 1112
one inch of, 1024
or grief conflicting, 566
pain for promised, 284
partakes of our, 977
present, therein I find, 20
quaff immortality and, 153
quick mint of, 346
remember days of, 1020
reminded us of an original, 809
renew, earth-born, 668
renews the life of, 386
riding is a, 487
scrip of, immortal diet, 22
shall be yours in the morning, 742
shall reap in, 1106
shipmate joy, 537
shouted for, 1102
sleeping lords of, 896
smiles of, the tears of woe, 336
snatch a fearful, 243
so seldom weaves a chain, 334
so great, no, 30
some bringer of that, 43
sweeten present, 393
take care speak softly, 1070
temper thy, 586
the perfectest herald of, 38
there is no, in Mudville, 770
there 's no, 960
to death, hunt a, 814
to forgive and joy to be forgiven, 617
turn in the end to quiet, 1074
turns at the touch of, 248
which warriors feel, the stern, 308
who are capable of, 788
widow's heart to sing for, 1102
within us, 887
without canker or cark, 673
would win, all who, 359
you may impart, 679
youthful, 452
Joys, Africa and golden, 65
all we have our youth our, 22
and prosperity only, learned from, 536
and tears alike are sent, 423
are not the property, 985
are withered like the grass, 406
as winged dreams, 256
be as the month of May, all thy, 135
blest with some new, 178
but lasting, 942
cares and, 69
confess his, 220
fairest, give most unrest, 382
flow from our own selves, 226
in youth, many are our, 299
I 've had, half the, 850
life's sweetest, 665
mingle your, 1054
must be used and spent, 826
no one believes in, 850
of our heart, first, 390
of sense, all the, 208
of the open road, 757
past, remembrance of, 312

Joys, profanation of our, 118
remembered, are never past, 306
society's chief, 263
such present, 20
summer hath his, 121
that both afford, 941
that came down shower-like, 317
that faded like morning dew, 327
that we 've tasted, 447
the most prized, 666
three parts pain, be our, 489
to rob us of our, 257
too exquisite to last, 306
vain deluding, 160
we dote upon, fading are the, 186
we made our, of what toys, 536
with age diminish, do your, 492
Joy's delicious springs, 352
fleeting sigh, 406
rebirth, for, 889
Joyance in its stead, bringeth, 929
Joy-bells ring in heaven's street, 832
Joyful in the day of prosperity, be, 1109
let the poet be, 517
nations join, 218
school days, my, 325
Joyfully meet its translation, 538
Joyfulness of a man prolongeth his days, 1125
Joyless duties, back to, 690
if not shared, 338
stupor, 247
Joyous beautiful and free, 367
greeting when we pass the golden gate, 545
prime, 24
shout, send forth a, 401
time will not be staid, 26
we too launch out, 537
Jubal he was the father of all such, 1097
Jubilee throng, thy sons to thy, 363
Jubilo, year ob, 600
Judas did to Christ, so, 60
goeth straightway to him, 1116
has given them the slip, 188, 1038
Judas's heart, Christ sees white in, 650
Judea stretches far, wild, 477
Judee, down in, 526
Judge amongst fools, 215, 263
an upright learned, 47
and jury, himself the, 465
enforcing obsolete law, 937
for himself, man, 449
in heaven, sits there no, 547
in his own cause, 988, 1047
neutrality of an impartial, 261
not by appearance, 1118
of all things, 1047
of Israel, Jephthah was, 92, 255
of the highest matters, 974
of the man, mind is the, 991
of their lives, supreme, 1063
of truth, sole, 208

Judge should not be young, 973
sober as a, 229
strictest, 779
that no king can corrupt, 73
then, of my regret, 388
though I am no, of such matters, 406
you as you are, 36
Judges alike of the facts and laws, 203
all ranged a terrible show, 205
fool with, 215
hungry, soon the sentence sign, 212
of important causes, 975
of property, common, 232
self-appointed, 612
Judge's robe, the, 36
Judgment, a Daniel come to, 47
and a taste accurate, 972
book, leaves of the, 565
but his, 259
day, it is, 896
day, waiting the, 571
defend against your, 175
enough for me, 681
falls upon a man, we say, 130
fled to brutish beasts, 83
green in, when I was, 104
he which is the top of, 36
hoodwinked, surrender, 266
inclination gets the better of, 967
intelligence and reflection and, 981
man's erring, 210
no one complains of his, 1044
of any man or thing, right, 376
on my official conduct, 329
on the few, force their, 426
reserve thy, 91
shallow spirit of, 68
skill and, 242
suspension of, 1016
thunders, 708
vulgarize the day of, 417
we still have, here, 85
young in limbs old in, 45
Judgments as our watches, 164, 210
ignorance delivers brawling, 470
men's, are a parcel of their fortunes, 104
of the English law, 818
of the Lord are true, 457
Judgment-signal's spread, when the, 375
Judicious care, with, 284
epicure, 323
grieve, make the, 94
readers, a few, 985
Judy O'Grady, the colonel's lady an', 782
Jug, gits loose from de, 688
of wine a loaf of bread, 1018
without a handle, one old, 498
Juggling fiends no more believed, 89
Juice, bee buried in its own, 112
nectarian, 386
of the snail, 923
the old familiar, 1019
Juiceless weeds of grammar, 756
Julep in the ever-brimming glass, 768

Julep is built, 791
  this cordial, 158
Julia goes in silks, 134
  lips of, 133
Juliet felt, the unborn, 911
  is the sun, 78
  Juliet, I'm, 755
Juliet's hand, white wonder of, 79
Julius fell, ere the mightiest, 89
  live first with, 856
  ye towers of, 244
July, second day of, 268
  warmth of its, 405
July's day short as December, 56
Jumblies live, lands where the, 498
Juments than men, fitter, 122
Jumna, on the banks of the distant, 541
Jump both sea and land, nimble thought can, 107
  or trot, hear a, 652
  the life to come, 85
Junction invented Essex, 551
Junctions, as she should, changed at, 700
June, as innocent as, 586
  beside the dusk of, 693
  do you recall that night in, 582
  end of an Indian, 776
  is past, when, 140
  knee-deep in, 696
  leafy month of, 315
  longest day is in, 668
  reared that bunch of flowers, 485
  rose newly sprung in, 287
  seek ice in, 351
  slower sweet, 603
  suns and skies and clouds of, 591
  what so rare as a day in, 525
Jungle, cutting through the, 857
  laws of the, 783
  pack in the, 783
Juniata, waters of the blue, 406
Junior deacon in my mother-lodge, 586, 782
Juniper juice, and, 851
Junks along the lazy river, 746
Juno's unrelenting hate, 177
Jupiter a bull to beguile Io, 23
  in the shape of Amphitrio, 23
Jupiter's statue by Phidias, 956
Juries, trial by, 273
Jurisprudence, gladsome light of, 21
Jury passing on the prisoner's life, 35
  thins his, 174
Jurymen may dine, 212
Jus' man do not waller, 682
Just, actions of the, 141
  and lasting peace, cherish a, 457
  and mightie death, 22
  and perfect purpose, 661
  and resolute, man, 536
  and right, grounded on, 154
  and the, man is afraid, 375
  are the ways of God, 156
  as bubbles do when, 453
  as I feared, it is, 499
  as the twig is bent, 209

Just, battled for the true the, 468
  be, and fear not, 73
  before you 're generous, 279
  coldly sublime intolerably, 667
  frank kindly, every heart were, 1046
  he was a good man and a, 1117
  hearing him called the, 997
  heaven more and less than, 565
  hint a fault, 213
  jewel of the, 170
  knows and knows no more, 263
  less than sage, 333
  memory of the, is blessed, 1107
  men, as the light for, 967
  men, spirits of, 1122
  or wise, not very, 328
  path of the, 1106
  prosperous to be, 525
  remembrance of the, 141, 185
  the gods are, 100
  the same as on the land, 508
  then with a wink and a sly, 508
  through a woman, 687
  to blow a shepherd's reed, 406
  to drive a flock to feed, 406
  whatever is is in its causes, 178
Justice a tendency to temperance, 975
  among men and nations, 1127
  and injustice, sense of, 1053
  as uncompromising as, 424
  be thy plea, 46
  Bennet was first that called us Quakers, 171
  course of, 46
  even-handed, 85
  fill the seats of, 386
  has no sense of, 1064
  in fair round belly, 50
  in the court of, 958
  in the land, law and, 958
  is a machine, 797
  is forever in a passion, 482
  is the only worship, 603
  judge or vicar, 279
  loftier tower by, 964
  love of, 1044
  maintenance of, 1127
  mercy seasons, 46
  moderation and good faith, 1051
  of my quarrel, 31
  of the people, confidence in, 455
  poetic, with lifted scale, 215
  prayer for social, 1127
  rails upon yon thief, 99
  revenge a kind of wild, 109
  shall be done, 503
  sleeps, waiting, 525
  sufficient measure of social, 795
  the great interest of man, 340
  to all men, equal and exact, 273
  to be patient is a branch of, 1010
  virtue of the soul, 1015
  was done, 651
  which the, which the thief, 99
  with mercy I shall temper, 155
  wrong rules waiting, sleeps, 525
Justifiable for real investigation, 449

Justifiable inconsistencies, 341
  to men, 156
Justification in every line, 726
Justified of her children, 1115
Justify the means, the end must, 189
  the ways of God to men, 148
Justinian's Pandects, 490
Justle a constable, to, 33
Justling time, in such a, 63
Jutty frieze buttress, no, 85
Juvenal, most bucolical, 310
Juventus mundi, 112

Kaiser auf der Vaterland, der, 684
  und Gott on high, 684
Kansas, grow small in, 952
  with her woes and glory, 660
Karaman, O Karaman, 417
Kate Ketcham on a winter's night, 557
  Vane, eyes were filled with love, 521
Kathleen mavourneen, 396
Katies Jennies and Betsies, 231
Keats, sick heart of, 669
Keel, on even, 964
  plows air, her, 28
  she steadies with upright, 315
  upon the shore, 954
Keels of my command, 778
Keen and quivering ratio, 585
  archer sorrow, 588
  dog a wild dog and lone, 912
  encounter of our wits, 71
  for lawsuits, 984
  intellects too sharp for common service, 343
  sense of my own advantage, 1076
  smell, 577
  with memories, 866
Keep a stiff upper lip, 557
  a-goin', 730
  and pass and turn again, 410
  clean bear fruit, 170
  down the base in man, to, 471
  little to earn and many to, 523
  me through the coming day, 845
  moving, push on, 290
  no bad company, 251
  o' the windy side of the law, 55
  step to the music of the Union, 394
  the faculty of effort alive, 662
  the word of promise to our ear, 89
  thou my feet I do not ask, 403
  thy heart with all diligence, 1106
  thy shop and thy shop will keep thee, 29
  to, us going and so good-day, 607
  up appearances, 495
  who can, they should, 298
  your powder dry, 329
Keeper, am I my brother's, 1097
  here in Windsor forest, a, 35
Keeping, in thy gracious, 402
  the past in God's, 626
  time time time, 459
Keeps thee from thy God, thought which, 403

Keep'st the ports of slumber open, 65
Keer of yourse'f, take, 696
Keerless man in his talk, 639
Kelly and Burke and Shea, 683
Kellys, wherever there's, 683
Kelmscott Press books, 730
Kelt I count them, Slav Teuton, 471
Ken, break-o'-day in a boozing, 710
    far as angels', 148
    much has lain outside our, 652
    years beyond our, 438
Kendal green, knaves in, 62
Kennebec the Rappahannock the Delaware, 932
Kennel, couched in his, 822
Kennin' wrang, gang a, 285
Kentuckian rocks, carved so deep in the, 552
Kentucky boys are alligator-horses, 348
    home good night, my old, 567
    in spite of old, 349
    moonlight in, 675
    politics in, 675
Kepe wel thy tonge, 8
Kept on shaving, and the barber, 508
    the faith, I have, 1122
Kerke, the narre, 25
Kettle black, pot calls the, 1041
    blackness of a, 1126
    of fish, here 's a pretty, 623
Kew, his highness' dog at, 216
Key, departed with my, 715
    find the, 564
    found no, 1018
    I have the, 746
    I wish I were a little, 609
    in a bondman's, 45
    life's, 53
    sealed with a golden, 610
    Shakespeare unlocked his heart with, this, 304, 492
    shall forever hold the, 686
    since you gave me the, 913
    that opens the enchanted door, 673
    to your heart, gave me the, 676
Keys belonging to the locks, 700
    break one of a thousand, 441
    clutch the golden, 468
    of all the creeds, 468
    of all the doors, 810
    of heaven, I will give unto you the, 1115
    over the noisy, 564
    to wisdom's treasure, 711
    two massy, he bore, 159
    we Thy, 443
Keystane o' night's black arch, 287
Kibe, galls his, 97
Kick against the pricks, 1118
    in that part more hurts honour, 143
    me down stairs, why did you, 283
    that scarce would move a horse, 263
    their owners over, 277
Kicked until they can feel, 142
    waxed fat and, 1099

Kickshaws, little tiny, 65
Kid has gone to the colors, 824
    lie down with the, 1111
    oh you, 890
    we have loved and cuddled, 824
Kidney, man of my, 35
    of one vast, 922
Kilkinny, skies of ould, 820
Kill a man as a good book, 162
    a wife with kindness, 52
    if you could, time, 514
    princes privileged to, 268
    the bloom before its time, 303
    time, how to, 1026
    too apt before to, 167
    whom lust of office does not, 522
Killed off by one critique, 634
    sire, I'm, 487
Killing chills, breathed its, 703
Kills the thing he loves, 722
Kilmeny was born, blest be the day, 294
Kilmer tongue in his cheek, 898
Kin and kith, one's own, 935
    little more than, 89
    the griefs of, 966
    the whole world, 75
Kind and gentle heart, 254
    and little fair, little, 916
    and natural, children, 66
    as kings upon their coronation day, 174
    attentions, thank him for his, 827
    be to her virtues very, 189
    best in this, 43
    but in degree, not in, 487
    cruel only to be, 95
    discovered to be, 897
    embrace of clay, 898
    enjoy her while she 's, 177
    having to repay them in, 1049
    he is gentle he is, 567
    hearts are more than coronets, 462
    her caressing, 240
    is it, 716
    just the art of being, 718
    kiss before we part, one, 225
    makes one wondrous, 242
    more than kin and less than, 89
    no best in, 436
    of alacrity in sinking, 35
    of easiness, lend a, 95
    of excellent dumb discourse, 33
    of good deed to say well, 73
    of heaven to be deluded by him, 186
    of heavenly destiny, 298
    of semi-Solomon, 398
    of ways, newest, 65
    old country doctor, 678
    other places of this, 1049
    porcelain clay of human, 179
    stop to be, 872
    that loves or serves its, 779
    the larger, 807
    till now, never found it, 919
    to her virtues, 189
    to my remains, 175
    will creep where it may not go, 14
    will not ask you to be, 916
    yet there is plenty of the, 462

Kind, yet was he, 251
Kinds of weather, puffed thee in all, 578
Kinder than is necessary, be, 751
Kindest man, the, 46
Kindle soft desire, 176
Kindled by the master's spell, 289
    earth, from the no less, 357
Kindles false fires, 304
    wantonness in clothes, 133
Kindlier hand, the larger heart, 469
Kindliness of sheets, cool, 894
Kindling her undazzled eyes, 163
Kindly, frosty but, 48
    fruits of the earth, 1127
    had we never loved sae, 287
    light, lead, 403
    lordly friend, 634
    stars have given, and, 405
    wanderer loved and known, 596
Kindness as large and plain, 927
    for many generations, 710
    from the unkind, learned, 880
    greater than, 1054
    I can show, any, 1062
    in another's trouble, 601
    in women, not their beauteous looks, 52
    kill a wife with, 52
    law of, 1109
    little deeds of, 553
    loses its grace, 1043
    master-art of, 1080
    milk of human, 84
    nameless acts of, 295
    not quite free from ridicule, 456
    save in the way of, 295
    shown, pass it on, 647
    tempered every blow, 626
    the very road into his, 76
    to his majesty, 363
    who does a, 209
Kindnesses, able to do great, 1041
    do me some mischief for these, 1002
    he has received, proclaims, 1042
    in a series of, 272
    she doeth little, 524
Kindred, a medley of, 1035
    comrades lovers friends, 557
    only should behold, 966
    points of heaven, 304
    soul, pros and cons of a, 803
    to the great God, claims, 456
Kine, beeves and home-bred, 298
King, acts like a, 1055
    all arrayed in his beauty, 387
    and slave, life the mirror of, 671
    and the pope together, 610
    and you are queen, while I am, 560
    Arthur had three sons, 954
    balm from an anointed, 59
    beloved of a, 257
    betwixt my lord the, and me, 504
    by your own fireside, 1033
    came not, 591
    can corrupt, a judge that no, 73

King can drink the best of, 504
cat may looke on a, 16
Charles, and who'll do him, 485
Charles's Head, 496, 752
city of the great, 1104
conscience of the, 93
contrary to the, 69
Cophetua loved, 78
cotton is, 432
David wrote the psalms, 755
David's dancers, cymbals of, 934
delighteth to honour, man whom the, 1101
duties as a, 921
else wherefore born, follow the, 470
equals the shepherd with the, 1042
every inch a, 99
farewell, 60
fellow with the best, 68
first who was, 1053
God bless the, 221
God save our gracious, 189
God save the, 189, 921, 1100
Gorboduc, niece of, 56
great as a, 274
grew vain, the, 176
Harry, England breed again such a, 31
Hassan well beloved, 732
he is rightful, 706
here lies our sovereign, 184
himself, greater than the, 230
I fought my, 1045
if I were, 759
in a carriage may ride, 449
in Babylon, I was a, 693
is a thing men have made for their own sakes, 130
James called for his old shoes, 130
Lear, by reading, 273
live one's own sole, 647
lived under the, 954
long live our noble, 189
long live the, 264
lustre that surrounds a, 1030
may not see her, 747
never dropped out of the clouds, 130
never smiled again, this, 577
not only hating David but the, 173
now we all have a new, 921
of Boyville, 804
of England cannot enter, 230
of France went up the hill, 950
of good fellows, 5, 68
of hearts the only one, 855
of Ireland's cairn, 792
of men, precedent is, 634
of pain, I were, 631
of realms of endless joy, 890
of shreds and patches, 95
of snow, mockery, 60
of song, 562
of terrors, 1102
of the dead, I'm, 448
of the night is the bold brown owl, 350
of the sea, 859
or consul or president, 686
or humblest thrall, 713

King over all the children, 783
pageantry of a, 949
Pandion he is dead, 120
Pharaoh's daughter, 375
reigns but does not govern, 1031
ruin seize thee ruthless, 244
shake hands with a, 363
show 'em who is, 853
sits in Dumferling, 316
Solomon drew merchantmen, 777
Solomon wrote the proverbs, 755
son of Heaven's eternal, 161
speak to you as, 921
state without, or nobles, 393
Stephen was a worthy peer, 101, 256
such divinity doth hedge a, 96
there was once, a, 1058
they were all looking for a, 559
to the Execushioner, 853
to whom the power, 814
under which, Bezonian, 66
wants me out of his eyesight, 611
was a' for our rightfu', 287
when George the Third was, 358
who pretender is and who, 221
who would wish to be thy, 308
will be well, 639
worm that hath eat of a, 96
would change with me, perhaps, 504
Kings, all the rivers of the, 927
ambition of, 128
and parliaments, heavier hand than, 227
and republics, farce of, 1029
and walk with, 783
are like stars, 367
are not born, 721
are sepulchred, 562
as happy as, 702
cabbages and, 598
can cause or cure, 231
cashiering most, 379
change my state with, 107
death lays his icy hands on, 141
dread and fear of, 46
dull pomp the life of, 546
enjoy, crown that seldom, 70
enthroned in the hearts of, 46
for such a tomb would die, 161
good, are mourned for after life, 129
guilt of Eastern, 167
he shall stand before, 1108
I am tired of, 409
invest knights and barons, 123
it makes gods, 72
leave a dubious legend of their reign, 735
may be blest, 287
may love treason, 116
meaner creatures, 72
must show their might, 432
of earth, saddest among, 808
of England, I know the, 623
of modern thought are dumb, 546
one of nature's little, 114
pride of, the, 206

Kings, princes are the breath of, 284
reigned in green palaces, 146
right divine of, 215
ruined sides of, 129
saddest of all, 798
setter up and plucker down of, 70
ships and towns and roaring, 903
showers on her, barbaric pearl, 149
stories of the death of, 60
the gardens of, 939
this royal throne of, 59
three, came riding, 439
to fight, were only, 433
twilight of the, 763
upon their coronation day, 174
will be tyrants from policy, 260
would not play at, 266
war's a game which, 266
King's crown, not the, 36
English, abusing the, 34
every subject's duty is the, 67
eye, horse made fat by the, 1001
fair daughter, each a, 914
gate, on the, 591
head, no, 850
highway, rides along the, 241
motto, keep the, 718
name a tower of strength, 72
own daughter, like a, 840
son, came the, 659
Kingdom by the foam, 903
by the sea, 459
coming, mus' be now the, 600
for a horse, 72
found in the animal, 592
good mind possesses a, 20, 991
I possess, a little, 594
in death's dream, 899
is best fortified, 1051
like to a little, 82
my large, for a little grave, 60
my mind to me a, is, 20
none can take, 764
of dream, 1069
of God, is fit for the, 1117
of heaven is of the childlike, 705
of his soul, 522
of perpetual night, unto the, 71
palace and a, 522
snug little, 482
Kingdoms are but cares, 9
God had sifted three, 436
man that did shake, 1111
the ant finds, 928
Kingly crown, likeness of a, 150
line in Europe, the longest, 311
Kingsley, Charles, answer to Mrs. Browning, 524
Kinship to their sisters, 934
with the deathless dead, 764
with the stars, 574
Kirk, bells of the, 709
is this the, 315
the narre, from God more farre, 25
the near to, from God more far, 25
Kiss a baby's feet, to, 634

Kiss but in the cup, leave a, 119
  coming to you, a, 898
  drew my soul with one long,
    31, 462
  flamed upon the, 903
  had won, many a glowing, 390
  he gains, a general, 280
  I am not the thing you, 596
  immortal with a, 31
  in Colin's eyes, 883
  lies beyond a, 835
  me and be quiet, 221
  me sweet-and-twenty, 54
  me though you make believe,
    540
  of blankets, rough male, 894
  of the sun, 918
  one kind, before we part, 225
  set on thy sighing lips, 427
  she with traitorous, 349
  snatched hasty, 224
  the coward does it with a, 722
  the place to make it well, 345
  through a veil, 1069
  till the cow comes home, 131
  to every sedge, giving a gentle,
    33
  too long, a sigh too much or a,
    559
  was lost in jest, 883
  what is a, 133, 1085
  which Jews might, 212
  with a long and fervent, 1066
  without a moustache, 774
  you take is better than you
    give, 75
Kisses bring again, my, 37
  dear as remembered, 466
  from a female mouth, 357
  if you have forgotten my, 633
  keep not your, 681
  of a summer night, 875
  on your mouth, 830
  play'd at cards for, 23
  smacking, 937
  tears and smiles, 299
  thinking their own, sin, 79
  touch her marvelling eyes, 911
  what lies there are in, 1066
Kissed her on the spot, up and,
    427
  lips that I have, 97
  me before, that you 've, 389
Kissing, what fool first invented,
    192
Kit Carson, General Custer and
    Colonel Cody, 707
Kitchen bred, in the, 246
  country or house in town, 795
  floor, easy to turn on the, 912
  grate, she passed about the,
    557
  ruled the rost in the, 129
  to de big woods, 820
Kite-borne threads, 676
Kites or crows, wars of, 163
Kith and kin, break the hearts of,
    844
Kitten, I had rather be a, 62
  my love she is a, 630
  playing with dead leaves, 516
Kittens, ez soshubble ez a baskit
    er, 688
  maketh baby, maketh, 929
  were rude and grabbed their
    food, 691

Kittery to Calais, from, 707
Kivvers down, when they turn't
    the, 696
Kleagle of the Ku Klux Klan,
    824
Klingle klangle klingle, 618
Knack of tying sashes fitting
    baby-shoes, 429
Knave and dissimulation, with-
    out playing the, 181
  coined an epithet for a, 397
  how absolute the, is, 97
  men crown the, 659
  more, than fool, 31, 1037
  presume to sneer and laugh,
    293
  rascally yea-forsooth, 64
  thank God you are rid of a, 39
  the fool the brute, the, 511
Knavery, best defence against
    knave, 1001
Knaves, he called them untaught,
    61
  in Kendal green, 62
  little better than false, 40
Kneaded clod, to become a, 36
Knee, bend the reverent, 910
  his head on his, 256
  I will not bend the, 447
  pregnant hinges of the, 94
  under each bending, 858
Knees and then upon the abori-
    gines, fell upon their, 518
  done upon his, 785
  down on your, 50
  man-at-arms must serve on his,
    28
  of the gods, on the, 958
  on parent, 275
  rustling to her, 383
  they fell upon their, 815
  woo her with too slavish, 385
Knee-deep in June, 696
Kneeling take aim, 417
Knell, devil below was ringing
    his, 321
  is rung by fairy hands, 247
  of parting day, 244
  overpowering, 360
  sighed at the sound of a, 264
  sound like a rising, 352
  that summons thee to heaven,
    86
  the pall the bier, the, 363
Knells in that word alone, 425
Knew, all declared how much he,
    251
  her loveliness I never, 386
  himself to sing, 159
  more, no man spoke less and,
    1004
  that before you were born, 992
  that one small head could carry
    all he, 251
  thee but to love thee, 363
  we should both forget, 633
  what 's what, 10, 142
Knife and fork, picks up a, 923
  hardest, ill-used doth lose his
    edge, 108
  like a glittering, 925
  to thy throat, put a, 1108
  use thy sharp, 864
  war even to the, 352
  war to the, 657
Knife-grinder, weary, 293

Knight, a prince can make a
    belted, 287
  in glittering armor, 888
  lean and foolish, 827
  like Bayard, O for a, 442
  like the young Lochinvar, 307
  of rueful countenance, 1034
  of the woeful figure, 1034
  parfit gentil, a verray, 5
  pricking on the plaine, 24
Knights, accomplishing the, 67
  barons kings can invest, 123
  carpet, 123, 1027, 1032
Knight's bones are dust, 316
Knighthode and of fredom flour,
    6
Knightly pennon furled, 878
  years were gone, 693
Knitters in the sun, spinsters and,
    54
Knitting, and brings her, 640,
    1066
Knives and scissors to grind, 293
  balls of copper and a dozen,
    1078
  hands made before, 192
  mishaps are like, 530
Knock and it shall be opened,
    1114
  as you please, 217
  at the door, exceed in interest
    a, 323
  it never is at home, 263
  the breast, nothing to, 157
  whom should I, 52
Knocks, apostolic blows and, 142
  open locks whoever, 87
Knock-down argument, 179
Knocker, tie up the, 212
Knocking when I 'm dead, and
    the, 855
Knokke with my staf, 7
Knolled to church, bells have, 49
Knolling a departing friend, 64
Knot, in a bulrush, 978
  nuptial, 624
  of roots, man is a, 411
  unable to untie the Gordium,
    999
  unloose the Gordian, 66
Knott, and still is, 948
  christened Knott begot, 948
  died Knott, lived, 948
Knotted and combined locks. 91
  oak, to bend a, 193
Knottiness of strings, 654
Know, a subject ourselves, 236
  a thing is nothing, to, 942
  a trick worth two of that, 61
  again, would that I could, 455
  all except myself, 1022
  all words are faint, 275
  all ye need to, 383
  but can't express, 268
  does both act and, 169
  enough to trust, we, 501
  enough you, 610
  happier than I, 154
  her was to love her, 289
  him any more, shall, 1102
  how first he met her, 481
  how frail I am, 1104
  it is not safe to, 147
  me, not to, 152
  me, when it came to, 338
  mine end, make me to, 1104

Know much and think for nothing, 121
my place, as they should do theirs, 55
myself, not if I, 323
never prophesy onless ye, 527
not I ask not, 336
not well the subtle ways, 410
not what is to come, 692
not what, to be we, 178
not what we may be, 96
not what 's resisted, 285
old age may come after you, 535
one's self, difficult to, 1012
one's self, to, 6
only the constant, 416
or dream or fear all we, 363
other people, more practical to say, 976
reason but from what we, 207
than all, I better, 444
that I love thee, 336
that thou art God, 1128
the sweet Roman hand, 55
the table round, I, 470
the very road into his kindness, 76
thee not, who, 275
their own good, how few, 177
then thyself, 207
thought so once now I, 206
thyself, 1041
thyself and nothing too much, 1004
thyself is not well said, 976
unless others, you know it, 942
we believe what we least, 1028
we loved in vain, 351
well I am not great, 470
what I mean to do, 486
what lays before us, little we, 495
what Virgil sings, you, 472
what we are, 96
what were good to do, 44
what you don't, 313
whatever there is to, 577
where to find information, 236
where'er I go, yet I, 301
ye the land of cypress and myrtle, 355
Knowe, wys is he that can himselven, 6
Knowest, speak less than thou, 98
Knoweth of such an one, none, 630
Knowing, greater than their, 783
he that is most, 166
mastered what was not worth, 526
of persons, most, 990
when to have done, 378
Knowledge, a great deal of, 234
ample page of, 244
and experience, void of, 977
and timber, 454
book of, 151
by suffering entereth, 428
comes but wisdom lingers, 464
comes only from study, 773
curious and for love, for, 536
diffused, immortalizes itself, 290
dwells, in me all human, 305
end of life not, but action, 564

Knowledge, ever the beginning of, 378
evergreen tree of, 277
grow from more to more, let, 467
hath won God out of, 663
he that increaseth, 1109
help me with, 493
helps us to die a more painful death, 1084
hid from public gaze, 404
if a little, is dangerous, 564
in excess, desire of, 110
increaseth strength, 1108
is bought in the market, 519
is but sorrow's spy, 147
is more than equivalent to force, 111
is of two kinds, 236
is power, 111
is proud, 266
is sympathy, 736
is the great sun in the firmament, 340
is the one only good, 1014
light of, 654
lost in information, 899
manners must adorn, 222
may starve while law grows fat, 453
more than equivalent to force, 232
multiplieth words without, 1102
never learned of schools, 442
night unto night showeth, 1103
not mere speculative, 975
of hard things, 926
of human nature, 635
of human nature, most thorough, 323
of what a rare rare world it is, 732
of you, love and, 48
out-topping, 545
palpable access of, 299
shall be increased, 1113
should be his guide, 973
sovereign, of duty done, 427
sweet food of sweetly uttered, 27
too high the price for, 205
under difficulties, 331
what is, but grieving, 592
which is acquired, 974
will more scope of conversation impart, 128
Known, best thoughts which he hath, 540
no more than other men, 171
the barber's shear, never has, 481
to be forever, 167
too late, 77
Knows and knows no more, 263
man who, he knows, 706
not how to know, 544
not till he tries, 989
Knuckle or knee, cheek chin, 522
Knuckle-end of England, 312
Kopje is always a kopje, 782
Koran, passed away the, 375
Kosciusko fell, shrieked as, 327
Kotal, unhappy land ill-fated spot, 679
Krysis is onto us, that a, 606

Kubla Khan, 315
Khan's abode, 879
Kye's come hame, 277

L. & N., D.L. AND W., Erie, 926
La carrière est ouverte aux talents, 377, 1061
donna è mobile, 472
Label, bear the glorious, 846
Labored nothings, 211
Laborin' man an' woman, 526
Laborious days, to live, 159
Labors and endures and waits, but, 438
Labour and intent study, 162
and sorrow, their strength is, 1105
and the wounds are vain, the, 519
and time wasted, 689
and to wait, learn to, 433
aversion to, 1051
bears a lovely face, 116
capital solicits the aid of, 341
cheers the tar's, 358
Chinese cheap, 644
constant, uniform kind, 1071
contained in it is useless, 1071
disgraces no man, 550
done, day 's out and, 430
even in the meanest sorts of, 378
for his pains, 74, 1033
for my travail, I have had my, 74
good week's, 117
he who first shortened the, 379
in his vocation, 60
is done, 567
is for future hours, your, 417
is independent and proud, 341
is noble and holy, 499
is past, hands upon the breast and, 567
is prior to and independent of, 456
is to pray, to, 499
lent to do a mighty, 575
life is in, 1077
mountain in, 984, 992
nothing more dangerous than discontinued, 1068
of an age in piled stones, 161
of love, 1121
of the gods, 212
of the worker, 1086
pauperism feasteth while honest, 477
preserves us, 1052
process of acquiring property, 662
relaxation from one kind of, 1078
restores vigor to, 1051
system of hard, 1074
that has reference, 1062
the brow of, 753
this is the gospel of, 709
through days of, 952
to write, as much of a, 921
visible and invisible, 1068
we delight in physics pain, 86
what to speak, 112
why should life all, be, 463
wisdom gives poignancy, by, 1051

Labour without end, 983
wrought as wavering fancy planned, 500
youth of, with age of ease, 250
Labours and peregrinations, 112
long and sometimes anxious, 942
of the great, 961
the line too, 211
they may rest from their, 1123
who from their, rest, 555
Labour's bath, sore, 86
Labourer free, sett'st the weary, 328
I am a true, 50
is worthy of his hire, 1117
swearing 'a sufficient crime to dismiss any, 180
Labourers are few, 1115
Labourer's task is o'er, 402
Labouring incessant, 224
man, sleep of a, 1109
mountain scarce brings forth a mouse, 180
seas, no less than, 816
surges of the world, 748
Labyrinthine ways of my own mind, 748
Lac St. Pierre, drown on, 713
Lace, folds of marble, 682
Laces and ivory and gold, 848
Lacedaemonians and the enemy, 1003
Lachesis singing of the past, 974
Lack and dearth, but a, 597
but open eye and ear, 442
I have they, 20
in all abundance, 971
of argument, 66
of decent clothing, 422
of energy distinguishes dependents, 421
of faith, except for, 1021
of good society, no, 437
of humor, own up to a, 775
of listeners are not said, for, 540
of many a thing, 107
of something within, 651
of wit, plentiful, 92
of woman's nursing, there was, 447
Lacked and lost we rack the value, 39
Lackest, mind not what thou, 1011
Lack-lustre eye, looking on it with, 49
Lacqueys make, little laws that, 736
Lad and all the sport is stale, 523
both brave and good, 405
I used to be, 874
just back from play, little, 874
lightfoot, 743
of mettle a good boy, 61
so brave and true, my, 579
that day his five small loaves, 541
that's born to be king, 752
was ever a rover, 866
when all the world is old, 523
who when his father, I like the, 510

Lads are far away, though your, 824
of the village are banished, 936
underground, lays, 743
Ladder by which we rise, build the, 521
charity's golden, 1020
from earth to heaven, 781
infinite-stepped, life is a, 544
Jacob's, 417
of human thought, highest rung of, 741
of our vices, 436
only in dreams is a, 521
rounds of life's long, 493
set up on earth, 1098
to the skies, 26
who ascended Fame's, 431
young ambition's, 82
Laddie, my laddie, 770
Laden life, 604
Ladies, a lion among, 43
be but young and fair, 49
fond of the company of, 239
good night sweet, 96
have too-long memories, 928
hop light, 689
intellectual, lords of, 358
not the good fortune to be, 617
of St. James's, 648
over offended, 198
read, why, 674
remember Butler, 928
sigh no more, 256
what would ye, 881
when they write letters, 347
whose eyes rain influence, 160
Ladies' love, unfit for, 176
Lady cheer up, 967
Diana, the poet reciting to, 937
Disdain are you yet living, 38
doth protest too much, 94
faint heart ne'er won fair, 1039
fair, 779
Fortune, railed on, 49
from over the Rhine, 510
garmented in light, 367
he's dead and gone, 256
help wanted, 394
here comes the, 79
here lies a most beautiful, 822
in a villa, dwelt a, 478
is in the case, when a, 206
Jane was tall and slim, 350
Luck, insulted you as, 923
married to the Moor, 301
Moon where are you roving, 459
of beauty and high degree, 903
of my delight, 701
of pain, our, 632
of the hous, 7
old, and a boy, 715
or the tiger, 610
protests too much, 94
sat, and on its deck a, 424
sweet arise, 105
that's known as Lou, 844
to remove the toll, 346
weep no more, 256
who lent his, to his friend, 360
Willy, leave the, 792
with a Lamp, 436
would remind you, 952
you are the cruell'st she alive, 54

Ladye, a fairer, 257
Lady's fan, brain him with his, 61
head-dress, nothing so variable as, 196
Ladyship, humorous, 57
Lady-smocks all silver white, 41
Lafayette we are here, 747
Lag-end of my life, entertain the, 63
Lager beer, all goned afay mit de, 559
beer and hops, 451
give an Irishman, 616
Lagging fire-coals, on the, 879
Lagoon, across the still, 889
Lags the veteran, superfluous, 230
Laid me down with a will, 703
on with a trowel, 47
Lair, rouse the lion from his, 311
Laissez faire laissez aller, 1092
Laity our love, tell the, 118
Lake brims her cup, blue, 760
Erie's broad expanse, 605
I know a, 576
is overflowing, until the, 1090
life is like some vast, 1090
of the Dismal Swamp, 333
or moorish fen, 158
pilot of the Galilean, 159
silver, on thy fair bosom, 386
Superior put half a drop into, 454
swan on still St. Mary's, 298
swan swims on a, 391
the blue-eyed Walden, 517
thou in thy, dost see, 555
where drooped the willow, 405
Lakes, the headwaters the cold, 929
Lamb, and read Charles, 793
at home a lion in the chase, 294
for miles, propelled a, 691
God tempers the wind to the shorn, 242
of God on England's pleasant pastures seen, 282
of God, thought on the, 758
one dead, is there, 435
skin of an innocent, 69
snow-white, 505
that belonged, 962
the frolic and the gentle, 305
to the slaughter, as a, 1112
Una with her milk-white, 301
was sure to go, the, 362
when the lion fawns upon the, 70
who made thee, little, 281
wolf dwell with the, 1111
Lamb's great discovery, 803
Lamb-devouring kind, of the, 691
Lame and blind, heal the, 886
and impotent conclusion, 101
dogs over stiles, helping, 523
feet was I to the, 1102
man, live with a, 1001
messenger, 137
to march, too, 834
Lament for Madam Blaize, 252
Lamentable difficulty of saying no, 318
thing, is not this a, 69
Lamentation, hear my unblest, 508
Lamorna Cove, our great, 814
Lamp, a lady with a, 436

Lamp, arguments smelt of the, 1000
  beside the golden door, 694
  burn low and dim, 867
  ere Homer's, appeared, 262
  hold thy lighted, 647
  holds out to burn, 199
  I had Aladdin's, 528
  is shattered, when the, 368
  of a ship's berth, 825
  of experience, 270
  of human hope, 834
  of life, hand over the, 981
  of truth, held the, 687
  shall burn unquenchably, 263
  shines white and clear, 890
  smell of the, 134
  there is no brilliant, 928
  ungirt loin and the unlit, 488
  unto my feet, 1106
  word burned like a, 1125
Lamps are white, 717
  in a green night, golden, 169
  in sepulchral urns, 263
  of London, O gleaming, 687
  shone o'er fair women, 352
Lancaster, time-honoured, 58
Lance in rest, lay his, 648
  may fail, stoutest, 564
  white plume and a green, 925
Lances, leveled, 586
Lancelot, one poor ghost was, 685
Land, a thousand miles from, 350
  and no, beside, 57
  and sea, he governs, 534
  as cheap as stinking mackerel, 62
  as on the sea, on the, 953
  as various as your, 927
  be bright with freedom's holy light, 447
  beyond the sea, 438
  beyond, there was a, 834
  bowels of the, 72
  chosen and chainless, 634
  citizens of death's grey, 891
  cleaner greener, 782
  darkness of the, 469
  deal damnation round the, 216
  deep into new, 310
  fight for such a, 307
  flowing with milk, 1098
  forlorn, makes the, 346
  French have the empire of the, 376
  from out of foreign, 168
  give an acre of bare, 32
  great rock in a weary, 1111
  hail to the, whereon, 386
  has appeared, a shadowy, 416
  hour later I saw, 934
  I do not own an inch of, 568
  I have loved my, 804
  I went into a golden, 907
  ill fares the, 250
  immense and lonely, 932
  in a blatant, 469
  in No-man's, 620
  in the stranger's, 714
  in this part of the, 952
  in which he lives, 1055
  into the silent, 587
  is man's safe dwelling place, 370
  just the same as on the, 508
  knowest thou the, 355

Land, law and justice in the, 958
  light that never was on sea or, 299
  lost and ancient, 746
  madden round the, 212
  my native, good night, 352
  my own my native, 307
  never cease out of the, 1099
  occupy de, 600
  ocean leans against the, 249
  o'er all the pleasant, 370
  of all I love fade, 544
  of beginning again, 879
  of bondage, out of the, 310
  of broken heads, 828
  of broken hearts, 828
  of brown heath, 307
  of Calvin and oat-cakes, 312
  of corn and wine, 1101
  of counterpane, 702
  of darkness, 1102
  of darkness called Borrioboola Gha, 475
  of drowsy head it was, 224
  of Eldorado, 861
  of faery, 789
  of freedom, 630
  of heart's desire, 790
  of hope and glory, 761
  of liberty, sweet, 447
  of Moab, a vale in the, 516
  of no name, 758
  of nowadays we never discover, 809
  of our birth, 783
  of our home, 511
  of pure delight, 199
  of room enough, blessed, 710
  of sand and ruin and gold, 631
  of scholars nurse of arms, 250
  of shadows, in that, 842
  of the cypress and myrtle, 355
  of the free, 332
  of the heart is the land of the west, 405
  of the island kingdom, 752
  of the leal, in the, 291
  of the living, 1102
  of the mountain, 307
  of the pilgrims, 921
  of the pilgrims' pride, 447
  of the spirits, 294
  of Thought, and returned to the, 294
  one heart one hand, one, 452
  or cherry-isle, there's the, 133
  or water, travel by, 192
  plucked in a far-off, 598
  proud lords on the, 390
  rare bird in the, 1024
  rent with civil feuds, 341
  return to my native, 921
  robbed each other's, 674
  say fish, no more, 893
  seek the happy, 503
  sees across a weary, 827
  shakes the turret of the, 451
  shaven, 576
  speed and post o'er, 162
  stranger in a strange, 1098
  sunshine to the sunless, 305
  that bears a well-known name, 512

Land, the only thing that can't fly away, 506
  there her kindred, there her, 593
  they love their, 363
  think of some strange, 911
  this delightful, 152
  through the, let the sound flee, 271
  to-day, our glorious, 447
  to which the ship would go, 519
  to which yon ship must go, 300
  violet of his native, 468
  wakes in a foreign, 932
  walk precariously through waste, 937
  we dream about, 492
  where all the men are stones, 541
  where lies the, 300
  where my fathers died, 447
  where newspapers were dumb, 674
  where sorrow is unknown, 264
  where the bong-tree grows, 498
  where the lemon-trees bloom, 355
  where the years increased, 681
  wisest in this whole wide, 658
  without memories is land without history, 609
  without ruins is land without memories, 609
  woman is a foreign, 556
Lands and gold, empowered with, 879
  as they shall see or not see, 337
  brought him gold and, 941
  but in all, 970
  forlorn, in faery, 383
  hollow and hilly, 790
  less happier, 59
  lord of himself though not of, 114
  profoundly shaded, 796
  roamed o'er many, 388
  that in fondest memory, 396
  travel in distant, 1083
  unvisited, so many, 441
  when the islands and the, 375
  where the Jumblies live, 498
  wrought in Thy many, 844
Land-flower broken from the stem, 756
Landing on some silent shore, 187
Landlady and Tam grew gracious, the, 287
Ländler-tune, we listened to the, 582
Landlord ever raise her rent, 948
  really, every tramp's a, 937
Landlord's laugh, the, 287
Landmark, ancient, 1108
Landmarks of the past, 1090
Land-rats and water-rats, 44
Landscape bright, a beauteous, 942
  is the grandest, 675
  love is like a, 127
  whose wide border, 568
Landsknechte, mercenary foot soldiers, 1045
Landsmen all, 622
  all, list ye, 247

Landsmen build upon, we, 806
Land-thieves and water-thieves, 44
Lane highway or open street, meet in, 441
it's a long, 487
marriage is much like a Devonshire, 333
of beams athwart the sea, 464
straight down the crooked, 391
Lanes, along the Cotswold, 873
glad for the country, 719
laughter and loving in the, 936
Langsyne, could not match, 393
in the days of, 390
Language adorned with veracity, 1017
an art and refuge, 700
as in our native, 156
children have their little, 564
conveyed in best chosen, 323
flavor to a dead, 607
gone before we can frame it in, 593
gradually varies, 344
in every, 921
in her eye her cheek her lip, 75
in such lovely, 883
in words of the same, 319
is fidelity, whose, 665
is plain, my, 644
is too worn, 728
life is a foreign, 912
loosed a shaft of, 808
most astonishing creation, 866
music is the universal, 440
nature speaks a various, 371
nature's end of, 203
no, but a cry, 468
no, like the Irish, 818
Oh that those lips had, 267
of all the earth, confound the, 1097
of my own country, 405
of the devil is sarcasm, 379
of the heart, 213
of the message, comprehend the, 610
of the nation, don't confound the, 292
one, held his heart and lip, 444
or abuse, bad, 622
patriot's soldier's and gentleman's, 1056
perspicuity of, 1017
profane, for, 698
quaint and olden, 433
reduced to seven words, 880
trouble to learn a, 236
under the tropic is our, spoke, 146
use in measured, 467
Languages, especially the dead, 358
have been at a feast of, 41
of all the, 840
the first among, 1053
Languishes loudly, a cat, 692
Languor is not in your heart, 547
smile, make, 213
summer's golden, 692
Lank and brown, thou art, 315
Lap, drop into thy mother's, 155
in my mother's, 155
it in Elysium, 158
me in delight, 364

Lap me in soft Lydian airs, 160
of earth, his head upon the, 245
of legends old, asleep in, 383
of May, chills the, 249
of Thetis, sun in the, 142
of time, 369
upon the valley's, 707
Lapidary inscriptions, 236
Lapland night, lovely as a, 299
Lapped by a dog, 424
Lapse of murmuring streams, 154
of thrice a thousand years, 621
of time, 18
Larch has hung his tassels, 370
Lards the lean earth as he walks, 61
Large a world we stray, how, 840
as life, 599
divine and comfortable words, 469
style, whose, 68
was his bounty, 245
was his wealth, 174
youth, lusty loving, 535
Large-brained woman, 427
Large-hearted man, 427
Larger than the cat, lion look no, 471
than the sky, soul of man is, 386
Lark, as sings the, 430
at heaven's gate sings, 105
fresh as a, 300
in the noon sky, 758
is up to greet the sun, 345
lo here the gentle, 106
mounting at break of day, 269
no, so blithe as he, 269
now leaves his wat'ry nest, 146
rejoice like the, 431
rise with the, 23
sings like a, 1040
the herald of the morn, the, 79
twitters, a late, 693
you need not fly, 811
Larks and a wren, four, 499
to catch, 1025
Lark's is a clarion call, the, 693
Larkes, when the skie falth we shall have, 12
Lasca used to ride, 711
Lash, blood drawn with the, 457
that falls, 783
the rascals naked, 103
the shallows that line the beach, 675
the sounding shore, 211
Lashes, teary round the, 527
Lass, drink to the, 279
is good and a glass is good, 276
more bright than May-day morn, 280
penniless, wi' a lang pedigree, 291
wi' the bonnie, saw ye the, 388
Lasses lilting before dawn, 936
then she made the, 284
Lassie, she 's the loveliest, 388
Lassitude, yield now to, 851
Last and best of all God's works, 155
at his cross, 349
at long, 921
battle of the world, for the, 442
best gift, heaven's, 153

Last, best wine is the, 445
best work the human mind, 286
comes at the, 60
dark canyon, shoots the, 738
ditch, die in the, 940
embrace, take your, 80
every hero becomes a bore at, 412
eyes look your, 80
first and the, 1123
galoot 's ashore, till the, 639
gasp, fight till the, 68
home home at, 392
hour of my life, 226
in fight first in banquets, 218
is best, he that comes, 122
kind word to Christ, 490
legs, on his, 116
long sleep, 275
love thyself, 73
night, yes I answered you, 428
not least in love, 82
of all the Romans fare thee well, 84
of earth, this is the, 292
of human mould, 328
of life for which the first was made, 489
out a night in Russia, 36
pleased to the, 207
reader reads no more, 451
remaining cash, spend my, 909
remark was a bubble, 630
returns the first, after, 490
rose of summer, 335
scene of all, 50
sex to the, 177
still loveliest, 354
syllable of recorded time, 88
taste of sweets is sweetest, 59
the daintiest, 59
thing to grow old, wrath the, 960
to lay the old aside, 211
was like the first, 915
whoever had thee, 632
words Narcissa spoke, 209
words of Marmion, 308
year's blossoms stay, if, 569
year's crops, little good watering, 520
Lasting peace among ourselves, 457
power, 640
rest, to their, 58
Latakia, about some, 630
Latch, en fin' no, 689
Latchet of whose shoes, 1116
Late and long observation, from, 973
better, than never, 14, 188, 990
born too, 710
choosing and beginning, 154
everything comes too, 625
into the night, so, 357
known too, 77
lark singing, some, 693
line of crimson sun, 845
love that comes too, 53
soon or, shall navigate, 572
though lingered the snow, 642
to trouble, 'tis somewhat, 601
too, I stayed, 294
too, who goes too fast, 989

Lated traveller, now spurs the, 87
Latent force, a man without passion, 1073
Later than you think, 845
  times are more aged, 112
  to each sooner or, delicate death, 536
Lath, thin as a, 497
Latin, addresses politely in, 1089
  and Greek, speaks, 141
  beauty of, 861
  has incalculable advantage, 802
  meanings fixed by authority, 802
  minus beads, minus, 917
  names, all their botany is, 409
  or in Greek, must come in, 146
  small, and less Greek, 119
  soft bastard, 357
  was no more difficile, 141
Latitude and opulence of a writer, 415
  for a seine, parallels of, 616
  is rather uncertain, 625
  of Oxenforde, 8
  sixty miles in, 600
Latter, carry off the, 348
  end of a fray, 17, 63
Lattices, lean from their, 643
Latyn, wolde he speke no word but, 5
Laud more than gilt o'erdusted, 75
L'audace encore de l'audace, 25
Laudanum, whipping and abuse like, 480
Lauded in song, many once, 1011
Laugh a siege to scorn, 88
  an atheist's, 285
  and be fat, 127
  and be merry, 833
  and be proud to belong, 833
  and be well, 223
  and the world laughs with you, 718
  answered with a, 953
  at any mortal thing, 360
  at everything make haste to, 360
  explode a huge, 766
  for hope, I, 517
  for the time is brief, 833
  gladden with a wholesome, 453
  I'm growing fainter in my, 509
  in bed we, 1043
  it is to, 716
  make the unskilful, 94
  not any more, 634
  not granted man to, 993
  of pleasure grows less gay, 405
  of the vacant mind, 250
  of war, the red, 864
  proper to the man to, 1024
  sans intermission, 49
  that I may not weep, 360
  that win, they, 103
  the children, 452
  thence had he the, 575
  to death, 33
  to make the weeper, 109
  to scorn, 51
  upon their lips, with a, 807
  was ready chorus, the landlord's, 287
  where we must, 206

Laugh, who but must, 213
  will then be mine, 984
  with a tear in the middle, 751
  world's dread, 224
  yourself into stitches, 55
Laughable, swear the jest be, 43
Laughed and danced, 342
  and said his say, when he's, 481
  and talked in the chamber there, 600
  as we laboured, how we, 625
  consumedly, 201
  full well they, 251
  his word to scorn, 263
Laugher weep, to make the, 109
Laughing, always leave them, 849
  Ann trips down the street, 908
  fellow-rover, 832
  fellowship, 879
  giant, laughs louder than, 452
  heroes walk with, 725
  in your sleeve, 277
  lips and roguish eyes, 620
  quaffing and unthinking, 176
  soil, paint the, 342
  you hear that boy, 452
Laughing-stock, make myself anybody's, 1039
Laughs at lovers' perjury, 78, 176
  at probabilities, fate, 426
  fair, the morn, 244
  Jove, 78, 176
  louder than the giant, 452
  with a harvest, earth, 417
Laughter, a little more, 691
  and ability and sighing, 585
  and loving in the lanes, 936
  and memories and few regrets, 811
  and the love of friends, 810
  filled my heart with, 668
  fleers and jeers, thing for, 510
  for a month, 61
  for all time, 428
  from a cloud, 759
  gift of, 840
  gits ye, fit of, 684
  holding both his sides, 160
  in friendship, 723
  indulged to excess, 973
  is my shield, 816
  it issues not in, 376
  laugh thy girlish, 735
  mirth and, 359
  no one ever died of, 819
  of a fool, 1109
  of a girl that's dead, 773
  of children, 854
  of the years, 335
  of time, troubled, 869
  oft is but an art, 386
  part with, 632
  running, 748
  shakes the skies, 218
  shout back our peals of, 554
  shows, when her lovely, 121
  stood up at his side, 888
  their hearty, 713
  they shook, with, 499
  those grimaces called, 132
  winged his polished dart, 626
Launch into the sea of vast eternity, 187
Launch'd a thousand ships, 31

Launching, committed at her, 505
  desire of those who speed your, 834
Laura lay, grave where, 22
  wore when Petrarch cut it, 680
Laurel above and wrinkle below, 594
  and myrtle, groves are of, 1058
  bough, Apollo's, 32
  greener from the brows, 462
  is green for a season, 631
  is not mine, 760
  love or crown, sans, 851
  of approved iniquity, 808
  outlives not May, 631
  trees are clipped, 743
  under the, the blue, 571
  wreaths entwine, 644
  wreaths, pile, 890
Laurels all are cut, 743
  grew, while his, 972
  of eternal verdure, 231
  the Flushes have their, 428
Laureled ox, at the heels of the, 635
Laurie, all sang Annie, 565
Lavender in the windows, 139
Laverock's in the sky, 288
  note sweet and lang, 291
Lavish hand, thank the, 522
  horn, from out her, 441
  waste of worth, 597
Law a sort of hocus-pocus science, 628
  accumulate and constitute, 949
  and justice, I established, 958
  and order known as man's, 823
  and physic, professions of, 328
  and the prophets, 1114
  and your civilization, third makes your, 1070
  army of unalterable, 575, 900
  as adversaries do in, 52
  but is this, 96
  call in, 490
  crowner's quest, 96
  demands entire devotion, 477
  eleven points in the, 193
  enforcing obsolete, 937
  evolution is a, 641
  fulfilling of the, 1119
  good opinion of the, 277
  grows fat, knowledge may starve while, 453
  has no power, 975
  hath not been dead, the, 36
  he who has mastered any, 414
  ignorance of the, 130
  in calmness made, keeps the, 300
  in point of, 970
  is a ass a idiot, the, 494
  is a jealous mistress, 477
  is good, the, 1121
  is nothing else but reason, 21
  is perfection of reason, 21
  is the true embodiment, 623
  it has honored us, the, 341
  last result of human wisdom, 238
  lawless science of our, 465
  locks up both man and woman, 659
  love has never known a, 443
  maxims of the civil, 232
  measure for, 130

Law, murder by the, 203
  must have the credit of the conduct, 387
  nature's kindly, 208
  necessity has no, 1026
  not to be heard in war, 998
  obeys the same, 1064
  of capitalism, 1086
  of culture, the great, 376
  of kindness, 1109
  of our to-day, 1079
  of the jungle, this is the, 844
  of the Medes and Persians, 1113
  of the Yukon, the, 844
  of youth, ancient, 361, 811
  offends no, 28
  old father antic the, 60
  one God one element one, 469
  one principle of Being and one, 1011
  or in love, in, 510
  ought to weed out revenge, 109
  possession eleven points in the, 193
  preserves the earth a sphere, 289
  public opinion is in advance of, 797
  reason is the life of the, 21
  rich men rule the, 250
  rigorous, is rigorous injustice, 980
  runs true O little son, 361, 811
  seat of, is the bosom of God, 22
  seven hours to, 275
  strongest tenure of the, 977
  supposes that, if the, 494
  than brotherhood, a meaner, 597
  the craving to go to, 1078
  the, is good, 1121
  the profession of, 1070
  the ultimate angels', 489
  these nice sharp quillets of the, 68
  thine own soul's, 473
  truly kept the, 163
  unchanging, of God, 477
  underneath the, 780
  we have a measure for, 130
  wedded love mysterious, 152
  what plea so tainted in, 46
  which moulds a tear, 289
  who to himself is, 28
  will go, who to, 225
  windy side of the, 38, 55
  world's, is not thy friend, 80
  written and unwritten, 1014
Laws, abounds with, 950
  and constitution of his country, 949
  and learning die, 518
  are with us, the, 321
  ascribed to Triptolemus, 963
  better none than too many, 1030
  breathing household, 298
  curse on all, 216
  derive their authority, 949
  end tyranny begins, 230
  facts and the, judges of the, 203
  for the blood, 44

Laws for themselves, 743
  give us kinder, 496
  gives his little senate, 213
  good, and good arms, 1023
  good, lead to the making of better, 1054
  grind the poor, 250
  have been written down, 975
  he ever keeps so well, no, 280
  I care not who makes its, 186
  impartial, 205
  imperfect and unjust, whose, 661
  keeps his self-made, 544
  like cobwebs, 1013
  love knoweth no, 23
  nature's, lay hid in night, 214
  obedient to their, 961
  of Congress, execute the, 638
  of conscience, 1027
  of France, by the, 1050
  of God the laws of man, 743
  of heat, to examine the, 641
  of husking, 280
  of nature, 273
  of nature the rules of the game, 563
  of purer science holier, 523
  of servitude began, 178
  of the jungle, 783
  of their own nature, things have, 827
  of time and space, 553
  or kings can cause or cure, 231
  ourselves have made, 466
  precept of her peaceful, 1050
  repeal of bad, 549
  stands on, 332
  that bound with, 820
  that lacqueys make, 736
  the fewer, 412
  there cannot be good, 1023
  to execute the, 627
  true friendship's, 220
  with sweeter manners purer, 469
Law's delay, the, 93
  grave study, 21
Lawful for me to do what I will with mine own, 1115
Lawn, rivulets hurrying through the, 466
  with rosy lustre, 220
Lawns, fair with orchard, 463
Lawrence more incredible than Prester John, 902
Lawsuit mania, 1078
Lawsuits and the reckless fray, 984
Lawyer, every quarrel to the, 137
  the skull of a, 96
  without literature a mechanic, 309
Lawyers are met, the, 205
  Cantilena of, 331
  in public business, influence of, 1070
  I've watched the, 677
  let's kill all the, 69
  take what they would give, when, 452
  university men and men of all sorts, 228
  whose profession it is to disguise matters, 10

Laxity of their mothers, 691
Lay dying in Algiers, 447
  espousal, 669
  go forth my simple, 275
  her in the earth, 97
  him low, 552
  his Doric, 160
  his weary bones among ye, 74
  like a warrior, 364
  low, Brer Fox he, 688
  me down to sleep, now I, 947
  no wagers, 251
  not that flattering unction, 95
  on Macduff, 89
  on that day, as she, 288
  pierced the strong tower, 541
  resounds, 258
  set some value on his votive 447
  stone on stone, dig and heap, 546
  thou thy soul, 533
  'tis a melancholy, 673
  with canvas drooping, that, 519
  your golden cushion down, 374
Lays before us, little we know what, 495
  constructing tribal, 780
Layer-up of beauty, that ill, 68
Lazy and sad, children should never be, 431
  fokes's stummucks, 688
  geese like a snow cloud, 903
  junks, westward still you see, 746
  leaden-stepping hours, 161
Le Chevalier sans peur et sans reproche, 442
  véritable Amphitryon, 179
Lea, across the green, 758
  standing on this pleasant, 300
  the sun has left the, 310
  winds slowly o'er the, 244
Leas no larks no rooks, no, 707
Lead, heart of, 215
  in the introduction, take the, 1023
  kindly Light, 403
  't were a pleasant life to, 406
  thou me on, 403
Leads me on forever, 573
  take to following where He, 609
Lead-colored lips, life into, 928
Leaden feet, move with, 628
Leader of his own generation, 675
  of men, to be, 738
  of the herd, 816
  people may require a, 974
Leaders have spoken, till the, 783
Leader's indomitable soul, the American, 483
Leadership, calm counsel and constructive, 877
Leadeth me beside the still waters, 1103
Leading, men of light and, 261
Leaf, all do fade as a, 1112
  and I were like the, 631
  crimp and curdled, 369
  falls with the, 127
  from the thin green, 633
  impearls on every, and flower, 153
  is for hope, one, 763

Leaf is lost, not a beam or, 353
last, upon the tree, 450
let fall no burning, 916
love every, 1074
my days are in the yellow, 358
of grass is no less, 535
or a shaken, 849
perished in the green, 469
right as an aspen, 4
sere the yellow, 88
shall not wither, his, 1103
sorrow and scarlet, 531
that falls, there's not a, 407
turn over a new, 116, 117, 1039
upon the stream, vain as the, 308
upon the tree, the last, 450
Leafless all the winter, 482
desert of the mind, 355
there by my door, 629
trees, sober realm of, 551
Leafy month of June, 315
League, a symbol, that, 908
with the future, in, 1076
Leagues apart descried, scarce long, 519
beyond those leagues, 577
from hence, a thousand, 62
of peace, 218
Leal, to the land o' the, 291
we were dear we were, 718
Lean and foolish knight, 827
and hungry look, 81
and low ability, 56
and slippered pantaloon, 50
and swarthy poet, 881
books, lard their, 121
dog a keen dog a wild dog, a, 912
earth, lards the, 61
hungry men continually worry-ing society, 343
hungry savage anti-every-things, 453
makes you, 943
unwashed artificer, 58
upon the thought that chance, 547
Leander swam the Hellespont, 453
Leaned to virtue's side, 250
Lean-faced villain, hungry, 38
Leanness of his purse, the, 68
Leans upon his hoe, 708
Leap, an easy, 61
into the dark, 1024
into this angry flood, 81
look before you, 11, 143
of the torrent, breezy, 543
of the Whale, 228
to light, 572
to pluck bright honour, 61
Leape, look ere ye, 11
Leaps the live thunder, 353
Leapt to life a god, 363
Learn and inwardly digest, 1127
ask and, 1125
craft so long to, 3
gladly would he, 5
late than never, better, 46
live and, 1041
men from books, we can not, 420
not so old but she may, 46

Learn of the little nautilus, 208
to labour and to wait, 433
to live and live to learn, 566
to read slow, 170
what is necessary for boys to, 1014
while you're young, 605
wise to, God-like to create, 511
Learned about women from 'er, 782
and all drunk, 266
and authentic fellows, 53
and conned by rote, 83
and fair and good as she, 120
Chaucer, 119
doctors' spite, 364
dust, much, 265
have said, in spite of all the, 279
here I'm; this I understand, 429
length, words of, 251
lumber in his head, 212
much by art, not, 128
of the fair, 215
say what they can, 199
smile, make the, 211
sock, Jonson's, 160
to dance, who have, 211
upright judge, 47
Learning, all that seek, 1125
and infused opinions, 111
become mad out of too much, 126
branches of, 45
breast where, lies, 217
cast into the mire, 260
dote on scraps of, 203
find time to be, 1009
grace nor gear, 780
has its value, 1046
hath gained most by those books which printers have lost, 147
I desire, that's a' the, 284
is but an adjunct to ourself, 41
is it a time to be, 1014
laws and, die, 518
little, is a dangerous thing, 210
love he bore to, 251
love of, 469
much, doth make thee mad, 1119
no man wiser for his, 130
no royal road to, 977
progeny of, 277
somewhat good, 1009
study of, 162
to misquote, just enough, 351
university should be place of, 420
unto which we come, 802
weight of, 469
whence is thy, 206
wiser grow without books, 266
with grammar and nonsense and, 253
Learning's altar vanish from the plain, 517
Lease of beauty, forty years', 483
Least alone in solitude, 353
although the last not, 82, 98
and vilest things, 115
considerable man, the, 949

Least expected generally happens, what we, 420
of all that goes, 883
of these, done it unto the, 1116
said soonest mended, 497
word, done for the, 630
Leather, brown as, 737
feet through faithless, 203
light of years held in, 854
on shoe of, 1034
or prunella, 208
Spanish or neat's, 142
there's nothing like, 955
trod upon neat's, 81
Leathern wing, 247
Leave all in order, embrace thy friends, 537
all meaner things, 206
but never takes his, 510
her to heaven, 92
it unpicked, 65
live by no man's, 780
not a rack behind, 33
often took, 189
thee, must I thus, 155
to coin new words, 180
to die, freedom or, 552
to God God does, whate'er we, 513
to those to come the house it-self, 537
us alone! 954
what with his toil he won, 173
Leaves all point to the north, 435
bordered with autumn, 890
by hundreds came, 637
cover them with, 258
depart, when, 934
do fall, falls as the, 127
do hang, when yellow, 107
ending on the rustling, 161
getteth short of, 391
harping in the, 922
have their time to fall, 370
long, cover me, 630
no man has aught of what he, 97
of destiny, in shady, 165
of hopes, puts forth the tender, 73
of life keep falling, 1018
of stone nor paper, 525
of the judgment book, 565
of the willow are bright, 897
on the tree, green, 345
on trees, like, 218
quick as a kitten playing with dead, 516
shatter your, 159
showed the white of their, 620
spread his sweet, to the air, 77
swept away like, 496
that in the garden bloom, 1021
they were crisped and sere, 460
thick as autumnal, 148, 218
were calling me, 793
were dry and rustled, 369
where, might cover me, 630
which remain are few, 440
whisp'ring overhede, 654
will be rust, along the, 926
words are like, 180, 211
Leaven, a little, leaveneth the whole lump, 1120
earth's bitter, 298

Leaven, had song for its, 633
  lowly lives, 612
Leaving, nothing in his life be-
  came him like the, it, 84
  on craggy hills and running
    streams, 447
Leavings, devil's, 217
Leave-takings are but wasted
  sadness, 746
Lebanon, like a cedar in, 1105
Lecheries, tinder to your, 903
Lecture, any subject for a, 829
  wish to hold a, 971
Lectures can do so much good,
  235
  I do not give, 535
  in her night-dress, 392
  made a restless night, 217
Led by my hand, 215
Leda, a swan to enjoy, 23
Ledge, trod by rocky, 758
Lee, at the brief command of,
  690
  waters of the river, 423
Leek, by this, 67
  nat worth a, 7
Leer, assent with civil, 213
Lees, black, where lurks, 629
  the mere, is left, 86
Left an aching void, 266
  blooming alone, 335
  free the human will, 216
  God's right hand and, 506
  hand know, let not thy, 1114
  thunder on the, 184
  to be finished by such as she,
    57
  undone those things, 1127
  what we, we lost, 1075
  ye have, your souls on earth,
    384
Leg, can honour set to a, 63
  caper and shake a, 852
  goes after which, which, 942
  the awkward of, 930
  the best part of the figure, 701
Legs, a cannon-ball took off his,
  392
  are legs for necessity, 75
  are staple articles, 942
  are uncontrolled, 785
  biggest rascal on two, 1008
  brushed against his, 936
  lost on him, 293
  of time, break the, 451
  on his last, 116
  three Frenchmen on one pair
    of English, 67
  use your own, 1080
  walk under his huge, 81
  were such Diana shows, 134
Legacies that a genius leaves to
  mankind, 196
Legacy, no, so rich as honesty, 53
  thoughts of a good, 1042
Legalizer, time a great, 862
Legend, dubious, 735
  quaint Saxon, 653
  still haunts me, curious, 1065
Legends old, lap of, 383
  told, to hear their, 507
Legion lay dying in Algiers, soldier of, 447
  my name is, 1116
  that never was 'listed, 778
Legions thunder past, let the, 547

Legislators of the world, 369
Legislature, public opinion is
  stronger than, 582
Legree and Uncle Tom, 480
Lehigh Valley B. and O., 926
Leisure for love or hope, no, 392
  forbid I should be at, 1002
  he hath no, 138
  I have no superfluous, 36
  is the repose of passions, 330
  of the crew, beguiled the, 622
  one with true toil, true, 501
  repent at, 193
  retired, 160
  to be sick, 63
  to contrive, 258
  to die, so much, 1003
  to grow wise, 547
  to make good, 38
  wooed in haste to wed at, 52
Leman doeth, tell me how thy,
  255
Lemon, in the squeezing of a,
  253
  twelve miles from a, 313
Lemonade, black eyes and, 334
  of a watery grade, 578
Lemon-peel, shred of, 889
Lemon-trees bloom, where the,
  1057
Lend a hand, 550
  me a heart replete with thank-
    fulness, 68
  me your ears, 83
  or to spend or to give in, 185
  you something out of my lean
    and low ability, 56
Lender, borrower is servant to
  the, 1108
  nor borrower be, 91
Lendeth unto the Lord, 1107
Lends, he that, 138
Length, 900 feet of, 933
  drags its slow, 211
  folly's at full, 204
  of days O Lord, for, 813
  of shambling limb, his fur-
    rowed face, 513
  of time and frequency of ex-
    perience, 239
  peace and rest at, 392
  words of learned, 251
Lengthened sage advices, 287
  shadow of one man, 411
Lengthening chain, 249
  shadows, the, 173
Lenient eyes, with, 560
Lenity, too much, 70
Lens of even, 442
Lent is over and Easter won, 597
Leonidas and three hundred, always, 558
Leopard change his spots, 1112
  lie down with the kid, 1111
Leprechauns, red flannel drawers
  for, 931
Lerne, gladly wolde he, 5
Lesbia with her sparrow, 915
Less alone, I was never, 271
  alone than when alone, never,
    289
  and what worlds away, the lit-
    tle, 486
  description would make it, 268
  expense, employed at, 242
  happier lands, 59

Less he spoke the more he heard,
  836
  heaven more and, than just,
    565
  hoping more, they have but,
    106
  mighty than Thou art, wert,
    503
  of earth in them than heaven,
    308
  of earth than heaven, 't is, 405
  of two evils, 9
  or more, nicely calculated, 304
  people will work for them-
    selves, 1077
  rather than be, 149
  spend, 237
  than a span, 112
  than archangel ruined, 149
  than hope, memory no, 426
  than kind, more than kin, 89
  than prison fare, 618
  than the journey-work of the
    stars, 535
  what we do than what we
    think, 506
Lesse, of harmes two, the, 4
Lessened by another's anguish,
  77
Lessening up the skies, 574
Lessens human woe, each struggle, 504
Lesser powers that be, o'er, 534
Lesson, Caution's, scorning, 285
  first to be learned, 564
  had a jolly good, 780
  in grammar seems an imperti-
    nence, 554
  in the world, most difficult,
    544
  its grandest, 658
  last, that he learns, 564
  learnt his, 796
  many a, deep and long, 434
  nature let me learn, 545
  odd quaint, 752
  of St. Christopher, 591
  still harder, 268
  take to our hearts a, 569
  that I can never teach, 888
  this, seems to carry, 264
  time has taught us a, 996
  to the head, heart give a, 266
  we speak a, 748
Lessons and tasks are all ended,
  662
  I would write, three, 1059
  learned great, 538
  lie, beyond and on his, 657
  of paternalism, 628
  of the violet, 657
  on my soul, grave these, 1059
  represented as so hard, 229
  that I teach, 306
  time teaches many, 963
  undone and play forgot, 595
Lest we forget, 780
Let a fool be made serviceable,
  726
  a man be glad, 631
  all the earth keep silence before
    him, 1113
  bygones be bygones, 587
  de blessin' stay wid us, 712
  dearly, or let alone, 135
  down the curtain, 1024

Let each man think himself, 506
each try by great thoughts, 506
early education be a sort, 974
for life or years, 134
God and man decree, 743
head to be, unfurnished, 142
her alone, she will court you, 119
her down the wind, 102
him first cast a stone, 175, 1118
him not boast, 438
him now speak, 1128
him show himself what he is, 39
him that thinketh, 1120
in the foe, 156
it be, let it be, so, 889
it rain, 437
knowledge grow, 467
me alone, song of, 539
me go where'er I will, 408
me hide myself in thee, 272
me live out my years, 871
me not defer it, 1062
me see, the difference, 504
me tell the world, 36
men tremble to win the hand of woman, 422
my voice ring out, 610
nature take its course, 1092
Newton be, God said, 214
no guilty man escape, 549
no maid nor matron grieve, 373
no saucy knave sneer and laugh, 293
no such man be trusted, 47
not the heavens hear, 72
not thine hand be stretched out, 1124
not your heart be troubled, 1118
nothing disturb thee, 437
or let alone, must be dearly, 135
others hail the rising sun, 242
sleeping dogs lie, 497
the end try the man, 64
the far and the near all unite, 271
the guiltless throw the stone, 175
the learned say what they can, 199
the long contention cease, 547
the man who woos to win, 618
the spiritual grow through the common, 473
the thick curtain fall, 444
the toast pass, 279
the words of my mouth, 1103
the world go dine and dress, 406
the world sink, 136
the world slide, 11, 51, 131
the world slip, 52
them clash, 285
them go over us all I say, 914
them loiter in pleasure or, 448
them say, 22
there be light, 1097
there be no strife, 1097
there be truth between us, 413
this be your motto, 510
those love now, 201

Let thy words be few, 1109
to-morrow take care of to-morrow, 418
us all to meditation, 69
us be happy and live within, 606
us be merry, 133
us call thee devil, 101
us crown ourselves with rose-buds, 133
us die like men, 447
us die to make men free, 522
us do or die, 127, 286
us drink and be merry, 164
us eat and drink, 1111
us forget we ever loved, 730
us have peace, 549
us hope that all will yet be well, 455
us kiss and part, 31
us love our occupations, 495
us not be weary in well doing, 1121
us now praise famous men, 783, 1125
us sit upon the ground, 59
us talk of graves of worms, 59
us therefore follow after, 1119
us to providence trust, 519
us work without disputing, 1052
us worship God he says, 284
who can be clever, 523
your boat of life be light, 745
your loins be girded, 1117
your neighbour carve, 191
Lethe the river of oblivion, 150
wharf, fat weed on, 91
Lethean, drunken from things, 631
Lets in new light through chinks, 146
me, I'll make a ghost of him that, 91
Letter, better speech than, 111
declining Pulitzer prize, 885
going to him, happy, 585
if she have written a, 776
of that after-life, some, 1019
pleasant to get a, 621
pleasanter to be able to decipher a, 621
preferment goes by, 100
short, an insult, 234
singular and perpetual charm in your, 621
the, killeth, 1120
you did not write, 642
your, will last a lifetime, 621
Letters addressed to private persons, 1066
again became as racy, 925
are monitors and comforters, 551
Cadmus gave, the, 359
come to a War Department, 928
fair words in foulest, 65
I have read your glorious, 402
listening, writing, 928
man of, 398
man of the world among men of, 398
of declination, 716
of the sky, large gold, 657
republic of, 229, 241

Letters, safe, best way to make, 483
search the fading, 916
should be set in golden, 57
spelling of, 1041
that we ought to burn, 844
watch and wallet, lost his, 645
we lay aside, 1057
which Endymion wrote, 722
Letter-writing, uncertain process of, 520
Letting I dare not, 85
Lettuce is like conversation, 582
Leve moder, leet me in, 7
Levee, played for his lordship's, 648
Level and lone at morning, sands are, 618
at, his eye doth, 106
in the balances of love, 617
lines of woodwork, 759
met upon the, 782
musket-flashes, 604
of its great men, 713
reduce society to one, 1071
so sways she, 54
we meet upon the, 586
Levels, hearts to higher, rise, 436
of the eastern gate, 643
Leveled lances of the rain, 586
Levellers wish to level down, 234
Lever have at his beddes heed, 5
of all scientific advance, 449
of all things, mind is the, 339
Leviathan that crooked serpent, 1111
where the vast, sleeps, 675
Levity, say the right thing with, 719
with strength, unite, 232
Levy, malice domestic foreign, 87
Lewd fellows of the baser sort, 1118
Lexicography, lost in, 232
Lexicon of youth, in the, 425
Lexington and Bunker Hill, there is, 341
guns that spoke at, 771
Leyser, this wol be doon at, 7
Liar, best, 613
doubt truth to be a, 92
lest the loud, 888
no one is such a, 1080
of the first magnitude, 193
old time is a, 452
or a madman, either a, 1055
quite picturesque, 616
will not be believed, 962
Liars, all men are, 1105
cities that claimed Homer were, 910
ought to have good memories, 169, 995, 1027
Libel on architecture, buildings a, 570
Liberal air, his love was like the, 626
education, of good natural parts and of a, 1035
education, to love her was a, 197
institutions, 1081
marshes of Glynn, 663
offices of life, 466
year, once more the, 443

Liberalism is the easiest thing, 1076
Liberality consists less in giving, 1050
Liberate me, implore that thou, 20
Liberator for her teacher for us, 595
Liberties, he takes the strangest, 510
  people never give up, 261
Libertine, puffed and reckless, 90
  the air a chartered, 66
Liberty a loosened spirit brings, 584
  an idol in New York harbor, 722
  and endless time, 551
  and equality, 975
  and glory of his country, 339
  and property and no stamps, 950
  and union now and forever, 341
  angels alone enjoy such, 168
  author of, 447
  binds in chains and calls them, 655
  burst in its ray, 512
  cradle of American, 342
  crimes in the name of, 1058
  crust of bread and, 214
  definition of the word, 456
  enjoy delight with, 26
  essential, 226
  eternal vigilance is the price of, 277
  exists in wholesome restraint, 340
  God gave us, at the same time, 273
  Hall is an American heart, 253
  Hall, this is, 253
  I must have withal, 49
  inspire our souls, 194
  is in every blow, 286
  is mentioned, when, 1062
  is precious, true that, 1086
  is to be subserved, 537
  least, because they are most observed, 173
  mountain nymph sweet, 160
  my heart's at, 1051
  my spirit felt thee, 316
  of a poet, take away the, 147
  of self-defence, 1061
  of the press, 949
  of thought, 1053
  only to those who love it, 341
  or death, give me, 270
  packed his load, 686
  price of, 277
  resumes its, 534
  set his mind at, 237
  statue of, inscription, 694
  sweet land of, 447
  that little achieved through, 493
  the putrid corpse of, 1090
  the soul of a journey, 330
  they died for, 602
  to pray, for simple, 591
  treacherous phantom which men call, 532
  Tree, in defence of our, 271
  tree of, 1059
  Tree, plant she named, 271

Liberty, university should be place of, 420
  voices of, 921
  what things are done in thy name, 381
  when they cry, 161
Librarian, matrimony no fit diversion for, 865
Libraries grow, 697
  of heaven, 551
  proud, 534
  provided us many well-furnished, 125
Library being always open, 998
  better to collect a, 697
  books from mine own, 32
  circulating, 277
  here in my, 713
  Lucullus' furnishing a, 998
  money invested in a, 465
  my amply-furnished, 1076
  others have a, 313
  public, 238
  such be the, 756
  to myself, have the, 322
  turn over half a, 236
  was dukedom large enough, 32
  whereon I look, the book the, 134
  which is your paradise, 1023
Libyan fable, in a, 964
License, blossom suddenly into extreme, 1050
  they mean, 161
  thing called poetical, 1042
  with a friend's, 1021
Lick absurd pomp, 94
  the dust, enemies shall, 1104
Licker talks mighty loud, 688
Licks the dust, pride that, 213
  the hand just raised, 207
Lid and laugh, sit on the, 848
  hang upon his pent-house, 84
Lids, drops his blue-fringed, 316
  lift their heavy, 556
  with eternal, apart, 385
Lie as it was of yore, is a, 843
  asks no questions isn't told a, 253
  children and fools cannot, 15
  direct, the, 51
  fallow for a while, well to, 478
  give the world the, 22
  how still we see thee, 612
  I can't tell a, 941
  in your throat, you, 64
  is the handle which fits them all, 454
  isn't told a, 784
  it's a, 957
  its work done the, shall rot, 556
  lightly, gentle earth, 130
  like a bill on nature's reality, 381
  men who will not, 522
  nothing can need a, 135
  of the blackest can clear, 776
  shelved round us, mummied authors, 565
  spit in my face if I tell a, 62
  still and slumber, 199
  that saves their pride, 725
  to credit his own, 32
  to tell a, 234
  turned topsy-turvy, 1076

Lie was dead and damned, the, 487
  was my dream a shadowy, 509
  whatever the guise, 843
  which is all a, 467
  which is half a truth, 467
  with a purpose th' mos' profitable, 796
  with circumstance, 51
  with me, who loves to, 48
Lies a conversation in his eyes, yet there, 438
  a lonely grave, there, 516
  about his wooden horse, 881
  and truths and pain, the, 893
  around us like a cloud, 480
  books which contain no, 1078
  close at home, sung painted, 442
  comfortable, in books, 912
  devil author of, 126
  down to pleasant dreams, 372
  for himself, tell many, 234
  in his bed, 58
  in woman's eyes, light that, 336
  is not honourable, to tell, 966
  like a hedgehog, 391
  nothing but shams and, 1036
  or tell me, 955
  outlandish flatteries, 156
  rather live on, 507
  some books are, 284
  there are in kisses, 1066
  told in silence, 704
  under the walls of Paradise, 552
  what is gained by telling, 1014
  with the dogs, he that, 137
  you can invent, beats all the, 282
Lied, he never, 639
Lief not be as live to be in awe, 81
Liege of all loiterers, 41
Life a breath of God, his, 506
  a by-product, 846
  a discipline to the artist, 741
  a dream and delusion, is, 618
  a galling load, 285
  a great interpreter of, 641
  a harbor through the haze, 490
  a hundred times too short, 1080
  a long disease, 213
  a man's real, 726
  a medicine for, 963
  a richer, 573
  a sweet submissive, 691
  a tale of wasted, 608
  a thousand doors to let out, 129
  a weary pilgrimage, 135
  above, there is a, 306
  add what we can to, 694
  admits not of delays, 236
  again, out of ashes, 681
  age is ripening of fresh, 559
  all dark and bitter be, 601
  all labour be, why should, 463
  all other passions fly, with, 322
  all the diversions of, 196
  always gets harder, 1082
  an affair of being rather frightened than hurt, 613

Life an eagle poised, 881
an' love an' youth, who ventured, 527
anchors of a mother's, 966
and death are equally jests, 461
and death like friendly chafferers, 692
and death upon one tether, 914
and feeling, kills all, 934
and I are old, 626
and its ails, addresses, 1089
and its few years, 719
and joy and objects, for, 536
and ladies, you were wrong, 887
and liberty, God gave us, 273
and light be thine, 484
and light, form of, 355
and spend its, 901
and strength in every drop, 404
and universe show spontaneity, 569
angler hath a jolly, 674
announce a, that shall be copious, 537
anything for a quiet, 117
are full of, and light, 540
art colors, 605
as for a future, 449
as I have seen it in his, 90
as, is to the living, 638
as large as, 599
as the light, live out thy, 633
as the wind is, so is mortal, 597
as though to breathe were, 464
at a pin's fee, do not set my, 91
at all, lives no, 960
at hazard, nation's, 551
at least it will not be, 632
at the close of, 966
at the door of, 631
at the end, praise, 136
atom of infinite space, 544
ay soon upon the stage of, 474
baggage of, 163
bane and antidote, death and, 195
be just with, 809
be that which men call death, 968
beauty about a home, 1076
becomes a spasm, when, 599
behind, hints and echoes from the, 443
believe in the freshness of, 1085
beyond life, 163
beyond the grave, if there be, 834
bread is the staff of, 188, 191
breathe strong, 928
brief, is here our portion, 1017
brought dead bodies into, 415
but a game at football, 309
but a succession of preludes, 1064
but not his love, lived out his, 597
by the waters of, we sat, 395
calamities of, 187
calamity of so long, 93
calling me as crystal-clear, 850
can little more supply, 206

Life, cannot tell what other men think of this, 81
careless of the single, 468
care's an enemy to, 54
charm of a, 660
charmed, I bear, 88
Christ's in a sacred, 458
claim a moment of, 1061
clear for, 214
comes before literature, 613
commands, eternal, 595
commands, for, 922
condemned to part with, 252
confined to the space of a day, 1004
consist in sleeping and eating, does not, 972
consists in mutual service, 754
consummation of, 981
content with his, 984
could navigate the sea of, 393
crowded hour of glorious, 310
crown of, receive the, 1122
cut short just as triumph came, 513
daily beauty in his, 103
dawn of ampler, 760
dear to me as light and, 286
death after, 24
death and all that is of glory, 350
death and, bane and antidote, 195
death and, in ceaseless, 447
death hath so many doors to let out, 131
death in the midst of, 1128
death of each day's, 86
deep enough, dig my, 848
delicate child of, 1089
denied, what, 738
describe directly the, 1076
desire of, 359
determine his future, 973
dignity in every act of, 1010
din of its loud, 443
distasteful, have you found your, 492
disturb your, 1073
divine, through right of, 445
doctrine of the strenuous, 734
does smack sweet, my, 492
dost thou love, 227
dry, wrung, 631
dull pomp the, of kings, 546
durable, 634
easy, take, 790
echo from our discordant, 564
elysian, suburb of the, 436
emits a fragrance, if, 515
end of, not knowledge but action, 564
even to relinquish, 1061
every lovely organ of her, 40
everything advantageous to, 32
except by death, no, 560
exempt from public haunt, 48
father, what is, 564
fed by the bounty of earth, 417
feeds it, ever, 736
first part of their, 1050
fleeing to ocean after its, 501
for her love's sake fail, 631
for the living, 605
for which they stand, not the, 610

Life, fountains of my hidden, 411
from death to, 31
from the dregs of, 178
fury slits the thin-spun, 159
gave thee, 281
give for his, all he hath, 1101
given for higher purposes, 232
glare of, 430
God who gave us, 273
goes on forever, 916
good man's, best portion of, 295
great thing to start, 737
great things of, 833
grew cold, saw her as, 631
growth is the only evidence of, 403
had a second edition, if, 369
hand over the lamp of, 981
happiness consists in, 1077
harsh face of, 704
has a value, 1062
has enough of love, when my, 836
has passed but roughly, 267
has taken us round it, 1087
hath man no second, 547
have everlasting, 1118
have, more abundantly, 1118
he only is advancing in, 532
he passes from, 362
highest summit of, 1073
his, I'm sure was in the right, 167
his, is a watch, 634
honour is dearer than my, 1037
hour of glorious, 310
how good is man's, 486
how pleasant in thy morning, 285
how short this, how long withal, 544
I am the resurrection and the, 1118
I have, will keep the little, 559
I long to meet, another, 548
idea of her, shall sweetly creep, 40
in death, may find, 319
in every limb, feels its, 295
in short measures, 120
in so long tendance spend, 26
in that state of, 1128
in the conditions of its, 926
in the eyes, look, 882
in the interior, 533
in the midst of, 1128
in the old dame yet, 852
in the saddle, a short, 758
Indian summer of, 637
inflicts its worst, 596
insensible of the brevity of, 1051
intense, concentrated in a, 353
interesting, make your, 495
into each, some rain, 434
is a battle, 1010
is a blunder and a shame, 692
is a bubble, whose, 133
is a copycat, 898
is a dance, fate's a fiddler, 692
is a disease, 721
is a dream, 789

Life is a foreign language, 912
  is a good thing, 887
  is a jest and all things show it, 206
  is a ladder infinite-stepped, 544
  is a lie and love's a cheat, 774
  is a loom, 856
  is a mystery, 638
  is a narrow vale, 602
  is a progress, 236
  is a short summer, 231
  is a shuttle, 35
  is a torn book, 594
  is a very funny proposition, 849
  is a watch or a vision, 634
  is a wave, 542
  is adventure in experience, 930
  is all a cheat, 178
  is already a treason and a stratagem, 379
  is an empty dream, 577
  is at an end, 256
  is bound up in the lad's life, 1098
  is brief, 718
  is but a day, 384
  is but a day at most, 284
  is but a jest, 577
  is but a little holding, 575
  is but a means unto an end, 506
  is but a span, our, 947
  is but a sultry day, 1066
  is but a walking shadow, 88
  is but a wraith, 887
  is but an afterthought, 924
  is but an empty dream, 433
  is but like a child when all is done, 172
  is but the pebble, 574
  is closed our life begins, our, 537
  is death, 972
  is eternal, love immortal, 653
  is ever lord of death, 444
  is frittered away by detail, 514
  is gliding downward, 738
  is good be it stubbornly long, 895
  is he, to dead men, 21
  is in labor, 1077
  is in the loom, 656
  is in the right, whose, 208
  is just one damned thing after another, 843
  is like a stroll upon the beach, 513
  is like some vast lake, 1090
  is love, all that, 306
  is lovelier, rest of, 887
  is made up of marble and mud, 422
  is made up of mere bubbles, 750
  is made of, the stuff, 277
  is many days, 875
  is mine, my, 441
  is more amusing, 673
  is more terrible than death, 965
  is more than fruit or grain, 820
  is mostly froth and bubble, 577, 601
  is my college, 595
  is never the same again, 559
  is not a dream so dark, 507

Life is not long, 235
  is not too long, 405
  is of a mingled yarn, 53
  is old, death's new, 493
  is one demd horrid grind, 494
  is ordained to bear, 459
  is over, do not wait till, 872
  is over life was gay, 702
  is perhaps the only riddle, 624
  is real life is earnest, 433
  is rounded with a sleep, 33
  is short a fleeting vapor, 689
  is short and art is long, 433
  is short, since, 718
  is so short, 473
  is sweet, 528
  is the apprenticeship to renunciation, 1073
  is the art of drawing sufficient conclusions, 614
  is the game, 807
  is the mirror, 671
  is the rose's hope, 384
  is the same sweet life, 763
  is the thing, 788
  is their madness, 922
  is too short to waste, 408
  is very short and uncertain, 238
  is very sweet, 407
  is what our thoughts make it, 1010
  is worth living, 663
  is worth the living, 894
  isn't all beer and skittles, 551
  it lights my, 573
  joy empire and victory, 367
  knocks, when, 833
  lag-end of my, 63
  larger, 563
  last hour of my, 226
  lay down his, for his friends, 1118
  lead an academic, 121
  leaves of, 1018
  lies before us in daily, 154
  like a dome, 366
  like following, 209
  little needed to make a happy, 1011
  live thou thy, 668
  living one's, over again, 228
  loathed worldly, 36
  long, a fool his whole, 481
  long extent of, 967
  loosened, 223
  love but as a part of, 581
  love of, increased with years, 272
  luxuries of, 454
  made up of minute fractions, 318
  make his whole, a heroic poem, 376
  man's, is but a jest, 577
  many-coloured, 231
  map of busy, 265
  marble softened into, 214
  may be prolong'd, 106
  may long be borne, 371
  may you live all the days of your, 192
  means, never know what, 491
  might e'en be too sunshiny, 590
  mine honour is my, 58
  misfortunes isolation, 1068

Life, more profound than mine own, 76
  moving to one measure, 850
  moving-delicate and full of, 40
  multiple in seed and cell, new, 936
  my joy my, 1033
  my sole rule of, 378
  my way of, 88, 376
  near the bone is sweetest, 515
  never was begun, real, 847
  next at hand, out of, 629
  no certain, 58
  no man loves, 967
  no more, know the, 1018
  nor love thy, nor hate, 155
  not a thing of consequence, 1011
  not death for which we pant, 462
  not life at all without delight, 556
  not numbered by years, 1033
  not take his own, 970
  not the whole of, to live, 306
  nothing half so sweet in, 335
  nothing in his, became him, 84
  nothing in human, 969
  of a man a poem of its sort, 377
  of a man faithfully recorded, 377
  of a man, nobody can write the, 235
  of a seafaring man, 871
  of any worth is a continual allegory, 385
  of battle good, 764
  of care, weep away the, 367
  of earth that you shall see, 539
  of every man a diary, 750
  of joy, renews the, 386
  of life, the very, 953
  of man a self-evolving circle, 420
  of man brutish and short, 132
  of man but a point of time, 1001
  of man less than a span, 112
  of mortal breath, 436
  of peoples and of humanity, 1076
  of poor Jack, watch for the, 274
  of sweet content, many a, 685
  of the building, stole thence the, 86
  of the husbandman, 417
  of the law, reason is the, 21
  of the soul, 1053
  oh death in, 466
  on any chance, set my, 86
  on the ocean of, we pass, 437
  on the ocean wave, 502
  once in a, 808
  only changes with age, 700
  or after death, in, 970
  or death or birth, 638
  our chief want in, 414
  out of it are the issues of, 1106
  outlive his, half a year, 94
  over, live the same, 601
  parallelism of, 636
  pass into another, 576
  passing on the prisoner's, 35

Life, passionately long for another, 1087
perfected by death, 428
perhaps death is, 972
permanent national, 876
poor as it is, love your, 515
presiding angel o'er his, 289
prosperous be thy, 68
protracted is protracted woe, 230
pulse of, stood still, 201
pursue, not for nothing that we, 178
questioned me the story of my, 100
retrace his, 796
rides through hell to save his country's, 542
ring in the nobler modes of, 469
rules men's, 963
sacred burden is this, 454
sad as grave and salt as, 428
save honour and my, 1024
sedentary, is the real sin, 1082
see you owe your, to any but, 278
seemed formed of sunny years, 454
seems a jest, 577
sequestered vale of, 245, 268
set gray, 463
set upon a cast, 72
sharing its, 942
short art is long, 1058
shortens not his own, 96
show in your, 1050
significance of, 1077
so dear or peace so sweet, 270
so precious, is, 620
so softly death succeeded, 175
some good things in, 594
sooth 't were a pleasant, 406
spirit giveth, 1120
spun out, were, 393
staff of my, 1036
steadily and saw it whole, saw, 545
struck sharp on death, 429
struggling for, 233
sunset of, 327
sure there is another, 753
surrender of, 339
sweat under a weary, 93
sweet civilities of, 176
sweetest near the bone, 515
take no thought for your, 1114
tedious as a twice-told tale, 58
thanks for mere, 538
that all night long, 922
that breathes with human, no, 462
that dares send a challenge, 165
that had song for its leaven, 633
that, is long, 202
that knows no ending, 1017
that man liveth, 1009
that startled them, deny the, 931
the breath of, 154
the happiest, 965
the meaning of life, the right to, 1081

Life, the tearless, 1017
there is one, 843
there's hope, while there's, 1038
they could not lose, 1054
they've dealt with, 895
this house to be let for, 134
this if, a poor, 814
this strange disease of modern, 547
this was their whole, 1045
this, we live and see, 638
thou art a galling load, 285
thou art good, 757
time of, is short, 63
't is all a cheat, 178
't is of thee they fable, 649
to be still the unguessed mystery, 444
to be, tissue of the, 441
to come, we'd jump the, 85
to lead a tranquil, 1010
to live not the whole of, 306
to lose for my country, one, 195
to simplify my way of, 376
tolerable, only way to render, 1052
too long, think, 1051
too precious to be spent, 520
too short for reading inferior books, 532
took a man's, with him, 378
trade in the luxuries of, 1077
treads on life, 428
tree of, the middle tree, 151
trifles make the sum of, 497
true pleasure of, 483
unbought grace of, 260
unspotted, is old age, 1124
unsupportable, which renders, 1051
unworthy of my principles, 479
urban, 739
vanities of, forego, 309
variety's the spice of, 265
veil those who live call, 367
victorious o'er all the ills of, 287
voyage of their, 83
walking in daily, 670
was an inspiration, whose, 860
was beauty, dreamed that, 508
was duty, found that, 508
was full of misfortunes, 685
was gentle, 84
was in the right, I am sure, 167
was like a London fog, 390
was like the movies are, wish, 908
was worth, much as my, 241
waste not the remnant of thy, 1010
wave of, kept heaving, 390
we have lost in living, 899
web of our, is of mingled yarn, 53
welcome O, 874
well or ill, live your, 975
well used brings happy death, 1023
were in 't, stir as, 88
we've been long together, 272
what am I, 833
what is the prime of, 973

Life, what more I asked of, 746
wheels of weary, 179
when sin, of that new, 503
while there's, there's hope, 206, 981
white flower of a blameless, 469
who fell in the battle of, 533
will depart silently at its hour, 1084
will have given me, 883
wine of, is drawn, 86
with love forever, 686
within doors, 422
without art is brutality, 533
without him live no, 155
without industry is guilt, 533
without the sweetness of love, 578
without waiting for that other, 1087
worth living, is, 617
would be a mistake, 1081
would come gladly back, 626
would have paid, 847
you take my, 47
Life's a flower I choose my own, 406
a little thing, 491
a pain and but a span, 115
a pleasant institution, 624
a pudding full of plums, 624
anvil, still on, 736
best hope, my, 309
bitter cup, 948
blessings, two greatest of, 989
brave heat, 604
bright promise, 373
business being the terrible choice, 491
busy arts combine, 403
common chord, 492
common way, 298
compound, 570
conditions, 650
dark road through, 364
defeatures, whate'er his, 445
dim unsounded sea, 350
dull round, travelled, 242
evening tinge his brow, ere, 679
fading space, 168
farthest reach, at, 714
feast, chief nourisher in, 86
fine loyalties, 648
fitful fever, 86
fond illusion, 583
great end which answers, 202
gymnasium, not of good only, but of all, 538
hard school, in, 444
high meed, 385
highway, eases the jolts along, 1083
history, 570
ignorant wings, 736
journey gaily start, on, 624
key, thine own, 53
long ladder, climb the rounds of, 493
long night is ended, 597
many fears, calmed, 692
meaning, and read, 597
moving-pictures, well-wrought plays, 223
poor play is o'er, 208
prose turned to poetry, 595

Life's race well run, 555
  retreat, 338
  rough sea, 28
  sea, o'er, 401
  small things, 529
  star, our, 301
  storm, when in, 405
  stormy conflicts, no more for
    him, 536
  stress and its strains, 851
  sunset, stand in, 643
  supreme temptation, 834
  surges rudest roll, 1059
  sweet morning yield to noon,
    555
  sweetest joys are hidden, 665
  swift river, my, 665
  terminal swift towards, 717
  troubled bubble broken, 823
  troubles come never too late,
    418
  uncertain voyage, 81
  unequal lot, to balance, 544
  vast ocean we sail on, 208
  victory won, 556
  water turned to wine, 474
  wine, 823
  work well done, 555
  worst ills, ill cure for, 401
  year begins, 335
  young day, luve of, 389
Life-blood of a master-spirit, 163
  of our enterprise, 63
  seemed to sip, 315
  stain its soil, 771
Lifeboat, tale of a, 658
Life-complete in death-complete
    to die, 682
Life-illusion, rob man of his,
    1076
Lifeless form dissolves again to
    dust, where the, 511
  old beliefs, 1075
Lifelike portrait drew, well that,
    649
Life-long martyrdom, she knew
    the, 439
  romance, beginning of a, 724
  struggle ended, 671
Life-melody, missing that part of
    the, 532
Life-saver, vague generality a,
    791
Life-tide, ebbs the crimson, 568
Lifetime of happiness, a, 720
  through a, 486
  wakes men once a, 556
Life-to-be shall ever crave, 544
Liffy's tide, laughter in the
    smelly, 721
Lift a thought in prayer, 319
  her with care, 392
  it bear it solemnly, 454
  of mine, if any, 955
  slight gives the greatest, 116
Lifted high and white, 587
  shield, 453
Light a cause, how, 338
  a door that leads to, 603
  a foot so, 79
  a little warmth a little, 607
  a spring of, 387
  advantage of a good, 413
  and air, feed on, 366
  and calm thoughts, 317
  and choice of Attic taste, 162

Light and fleeting, thoughts were,
    744
  and leading, men of, 261
  and life and pleasure and pain,
    601
  and life, dear to me as, 286
  and smallish box, 700
  are full of life and, 540
  as air, trifles, 102
  as fire is of, 378
  as if they feared the, 163
  as soon as he rises, 228
  asking toward the, 802
  beautiful with, 802
  between the nightfall and the,
    630
  blasted with excess of, 243
  boats sail swift, 75
  brings an added, 557
  burning and a shining, 1118
  by her own radiant, 158
  can thus deceive, 326
  canoe, come with me in my,
    396
  chariot of, 271
  children of, 1117
  come in when daylight comes,
    519
  common as, is love, 367
  dear as the, 244
  dies before thy uncreating
    word, 215
  dim religious, 161
  divine we need no, O, 501
  drips through the shutters, 904
  dry, 996
  dust contradiction, 314
  enough for wot I've got to do,
    494
  every hour of, and dark a
    miracle, 537
  every ray of God's, 1074
  fades the, 643
  fading, dims the sight, 643
  fantastic toe, 160
  far back through creation, 670
  feasting presence full of, 80
  fervid earnest, 555
  fill to-night with hearts as, 431
  foot, hear a, 850
  for after times, 321
  for just men, 967
  forever shine, let thy pure,
    731
  form of life and, 355
  from darkness divided, 154
  from grave to, 177, 1049
  from heaven, 285
  from which they take, 458
  gains make heavy purses, 29
  gentles and the wind is soft,
    833
  gives life to, any thing, 131
  gleaming taper's, 252
  God's eldest daughter, 147
  God's peculiar, 1023
  goes out forever, before my,
    796
  gold and silver, 790
  green traffic, 912
  hail holy, 151
  hate the day it lendeth, 26
  have neither heat nor, 127
  he leaves behind him, 438
  hemisphere of, and another,
    378

Light, here's the happiest, 867
  hide your golden, 434
  high in the heavens, 760
  his shining sword of, 756
  his sleep was aery, 153
  in darkness, God gives, 69
  in darkness wait the coming,
    509
  in fame's illusive, 572
  in heaven's own, 306
  in liquid, 431
  in shadow and shadow in light,
    568
  in the dust lies dead, 368
  is as the shining, 1106
  is low in the west, 844
  is low, when my, 468
  it gives a lovely, 915
  itself is not so fleet, 628
  lady garmented in, 367
  lead kindly, 403
  leap to, 572
  let there be, 1097
  lets in new, 146
  like a shaft of, 463
  like the, silently wrapping all,
    535
  live by thy, 546
  lives, remember while the, 632
  may kindle, humblest, 643
  mellowed to that tender, 356
  men of inward, 143
  mingled mist and, 439
  more, 434
  more light, 1058
  most lightless, 749
  o' love, hold a winking, 776
  of a dark eye in woman, 353
  of a whole life, 707
  of common day, 301
  of day, prayed to behold the,
    373
  of day, rival in the, 303
  of fuller day, in the, 523
  of heaven, men have dimmed,
    709
  of heaven restore, 434
  of hope, leave the, 327
  of it, they made, 1115
  of jurisprudence, gladsome, 21
  of knowledge in their eyes, 654
  of life, shall have the, 1118
  of light beguile, 40
  of lost time, 933
  of love, 356
  of love, purple, 243
  of morn, golden, 390
  of other days, 336
  of setting suns, 296
  of step and heart was she, 822
  of the ages, 579
  of the body is the eye, 1114
  of the final issue, 976
  of the land and the sea, 671
  of the moon, by the, 345, 693
  of the morning gild it, 339
  of the world, I am the, 1118
  of the world — remember that
    fear, 822
  of the world, ye are the, 1114
  of things, come forth into the,
    295
  of thy countenance, 1128
  of what you may do, 691
  out of hell leads up to, 150
  out of the, 631

Light painful, find the, 995
    perfect pursuit of sweetness and, 548
    possessed with inward, 317
    presence full of, 80
    pure and endless, 170
    put out the, 103
    quivering aspen, 308
    relume, that thy, 103
    remnant of uneasy, 298
    restore, thy former, 103
    return, not till the hours of, 546
    ringlets of, 643
    rule of streaming, 158
    scorns the eye of vulgar, 334
    seeking light, 40
    she fled in, away, 285
    shine manifestly forth, 1021
    shines, where no, 1020
    shineth the everlasting, 612
    shows sufficient of his, 491
    shuddering in the gloaming, 620
    silver, on tower and tree, 277
    so dark there wasn't, 760
    sounds possessed with inward, 317
    specious electrical, 857
    spreading roots of, 932
    stand in thy own, 1039
    stand in your own, 16
    streakings of the morning, 382
    succeeds the keen and frosty night, 372
    such a candle, 10
    such a dawn of, 364
    such, as never heaven let through, 634
    summer-shine of lengthened, 561
    sunny, for sullen gloom, 392
    sunset seams with lines of, 417
    sweetness and, 191
    swift-winged arrows of, 264
    takes away the, 699
    tan cow in a pale green mead, 896
    that guides, 477
    that hath no name, 445
    that leads toward perfection, 691
    that led astray, 285
    that lies in woman's eyes, 336
    that loses, 633
    that never was on sea, 299
    that shines comes from thine eyes, 117
    that visits these sad eyes, 244
    the day and darkness the night, 154
    the one true, 1019
    the sun doth pale his, 514
    the true, which lighteth, 1118
    the unadulterate, 1091
    the world rolls into, 439
    those little drops of, 145
    through chinks, lets in new, 146
    through corridors of, 938
    through failing, 850
    through love to, 672
    through yonder window, 78
    to counterfeit a gloom, 160
    to give him, 951
    to guide rod to check, 299

Light to lighten the Gentiles, 1117
    tracings of eternal, 1059
    truth and noonday, 509
    truth will come to, 45
    twinkling out with silvery, 301
    two ways of spreading, 766
    unbarred the gates of, 153
    university should be place of, 420
    unreflected, 401
    unto my path, 1106
    unveiled her peerless, 152
    walk while ye have the, 1118
    was born, thy, 549
    was first, 3
    we almost had, 659
    we seek it ere it come to, 267
    when into shadow, a, 714
    when thou wert blind, 1059
    which beats upon a throne, 469
    which once he wore, 442
    which opens into, 443
    wild crackling intermitting, 888
    will repay the wrongs of night, 134
    with a newer, 807
    with all her, 385
    withdrawn, the, 442
    word part us now, shall a, 446
    worship its, 512
    you are, as, 889
    you move, in, 889
Lights and net-work rails, 926
    are fled whose garlands dead, 336
    are on the sleepy uplands waning, warm, 418
    around the shore, 577
    burn blue, the night comes down, 639
    burn low in the barber-shop, 878
    burned row by row, 933
    earthly godfathers of heaven's, 40
    every room blazed with, 81
    let your, be burning, 1117
    my life, it, 573
    of a thousand altars, 752
    of autumn flare, 673
    of heaven, 401
    of His peace and grace, 821
    of London Town, 687
    of mild philosophy, 194
    of the world, 262
    over mounds of the dead, 576
    purple, 442
    shifting fancies and celestial, 430
    that do mislead the morn, 37
    truth may bear all, 377
    turn up the, 801
    without a name, 164
Lighted lamp, hold thy, 647
Lighten earth from Paradise, 634
Lightens, ere one can say it, 78
Lighter passions long have passed, 953
Lightest heart makes sometimes, 447
Lightfoot lad, 743
Light-giving dawn, 960
Lighthouse of hell, horrible, 389

Lighting by gas, an expedient as, 450
Lightly and joyfully meet its translation, 538
    draws its breath, 295
    from fair to fair he flew, 307
    like a flower, 469
    turns to thoughts of love, 464
    was her slender nose, 470
Lightnin' out of sight, went like, 919
Lightning and the gale, 450
    as quick as, 143
    calming the, 357
    defence against, 989
    does the will of God, as, 348
    done like, 118
    fateful, of His terrible swift sword, 522
    flash of the, 362
    from heaven, he snatched the, 226
    in the collied night, brief as the, 42
    in the dead of night, 888
    makes awful, 429
    or in rain, in thunder, 84
    out of the dark cloud, 1079
    reached a fiery rod, 658
    scratch my head with, 616
    that breaks through a gloom of clouds, 197
    that mocks the night, 368
    too like the, 78
    vanish like, 402
Lightnings of his song, veiling the, 366
Lightning-flash of sympathy, 736
Lightning-spark of thought, 378
Light-o'-love, watching his luck was his, 844
Like a bud in the frost, 389
    a church I like a cowl, I, 408
    a cloud, lies around us, 480
    a cock who thought the sun, 520
    a new Niobe with claspèd, 565
    a poultice comes, silence, 451
    a prayer with God, wish is, 430
    a well-conducted person, 481
    all good women, 678
    an eagle caged I pine, 502
    as eggs, 56
    as one pease to another, 23
    but oh how different, 300
    clouds which seem pavilions, 425
    endure the, himself, 40
    following life, 209
    not look upon his, again, 90
    of each thing in season, 40
    one who treads alone, 336
    shalt thou hear, the, 1093
    some tanned reaper, 552
    the air 't is less of earth, that, 405
    the lad who when, I, 510
    the light silently wrapping all, 535
    the petal of a flower, tip-tilted, 470
    the sweet golden goblet, 431
    those of morning birds, 405
    to a little kingdom, 82
    will to like, 12

Liked it not and died, 114
Likelihood, fellow of no, 62
Likeness not a lion, in, 897
　of a kingly crown, 150
　of the earthly pilgrimage of a
　　man, 377
　that I knew, old, 567
Likenesses in brethren born, 967
Likes, a woman may marry whom
　she, 482
Likewise, go and do thou, 1117
Liking for gardens and garden-
　ing, 589
　old for thee, 589
Lilac and larkspur and an elm
　above, 828
　heart-leaves of, 831
　in me, 831
　is pretty and the chestnut's
　　proud, 732
　out of my head, made the,
　　887
　thought of the, 887
　under the soil, roots of, 831
Lilacs bloomed and died, the, 437
　last in the door-yard bloomed,
　　536
　out of dead land, breeding,
　　899
　this year's, 569
Lilac-time, go down to Kew in,
　864
Lilies and with laurel, with, 917
　in her hand, three, 577
　in the beauty of the, 522
　of the field, consider the, 1114
　of the Strand, iron, 793
　twisted braids of, 158
Lily, a most unspotted, 74
　Adair, bleeds for my, 432
　and the rose, between the,
　　814
　faith is like a, 587
　flamed, where one scarlet, 758
　for France unfold, 642
　grow before rude hands have
　　touched it, 119
　hand, waved her, 205
　how sweet the, grows, 342
　it trembles to a, 648
　of the valleys, 1110
　to paint the, 58
　white, bow thy head thou, 555
Lily-shaped, beryline buckets
　star-gemmed, 431
Lima, traveller from, 399
Limb, feels its life in every, 295
　flowing, in pleasure drowns,
　　225
　of Satan, 616
　pain has exhausted every, 561
　sound wind and, 1040
　where is your mannish, 701
Limbs and brighter brain, with
　sturdier, 833
　and hearts and brains of liv-
　　ing men, 932
　are of iron, 804
　at rest on the quiet earth's,
　　our, 523
　cramps rack their, 937
　decent, composed, 217
　her gentle, did she undress,
　　315
　mangled, 262
　on those recreant, 57

Limbs, on your light, 897
　run to all his, 958
　uprear'd in wrath, her giant,
　　316
　will quiver after the soul is
　　gone, 238
　young in, 45
Lime of love, 133
Limes their boughs unite, 396
Limehouse to Blackwall, 780
Limit, as though it had a, 638
　of becoming mirth, 41
　of human felicity, 697
　of the world, quiet, 464
　to the giant's strength, 371
Limits but the sky, no, 1034
　hell hath no, 31
　its own appointed, 566
　of his own field of vision, 1063
　of its race utmost extremes,
　　553
　of the world, for the, 1063
　stony, cannot hold love out, 78
　within ancient, 422
Limitation, civil, 575
Limitations of his own character,
　641
Limited assembly, posterity is a
　most, 419
Limitless billows, swelling and,
　317
　waste of the desert, 435
Limns on water, 113
Limousine, one perfect, 919
Limping pilgrim leaning on his
　staff, 453
Lincoln at home with the hum-
　blest, 415
　beloved of Abraham, 806
　character of, 419
　his education and manners,
　　580
　six feet one, 927
　was, how large a mould, 604
Lincoln's bier, wreath on mur-
　dered, 513
　brow, martyr's crown on, 706
　grave, stand and sing by, 676
Lindbergh flies alone, 841
Lindbergh's flight to Paris, 934
Line, a-swingin' down de, 820
　about a fancied, 1050
　along the whole, 604
　by us unseen, 395
　cancel half a, 1019
　creep in one dull, 211
　dare to draw a, 657
　draw the mystic, 410
　drawn ringing hard, 834
　fight it out on this, 549
　for the lea, 882
　harsh cadence of a rugged, 175
　he never blotted out a, 120
　in the very first, 252
　lives along the, 207
　longest kingly, 311
　Marlowe's mighty, 119
　may end in a loop of twine,
　　510
　move on a rigorous, 547
　not one, to blot, 239
　of light, 531
　or two, in a, 20
　parts, the, 893
　stretch out to the crack of
　　doom, 87

Line, there is scarcely a, 925
　thin red, 541, 542
　to publish even one, 1066
　too labours, the, 211
　upon line, 1111
　washing on the, 938
　we carved not a, 364
　which marks the drop, 926
　which shall be absolutely
　　straight, 375
　within a measured, 1050
　write a living, 119
Lines accords, soul unto the, 136
　desert of a thousand, 214
　each, sentences of six, 1063
　for all your deathless, 868
　ghosts creeping between the,
　　1075
　in Lucretius, not eight finer,
　　178
　in pleasant places, 1103
　is wrapped, in fourteen, 943
　let a lord once own the, 211
　made I, these, 982
　mottoes of the heart, 327
　of life, hard stiff, 444
　of rain like glittering spears,
　　586
　reading between the, 1058
　see two dull, 203
　where beauty lingers, 355
　where go the poet's, 451
Lineage, a damsel of high, 470
　proud old, 881
　prouder, no one has, 521
Lineaments, of gospel-books, 26
　of gratified desire, 282
Lined himself with hope, 64
Linen, at home, wash their dirty,
　1060
　dirty, to wash, 1052
　old, wash whitest, 128
　you're wearing out, not, 310,
　　391
Liner she's a lady, 778
Liners laden with souls, 937
Linger and loiter as you go, 603
　do not live but, 123
Lingered alone on the shore, I,
　418
　the snow, 642
Lingering look behind, 245
　winter, chills the lap of May,
　　249
Lingers, lines where beauty, 355
Lingo, unless you know the, 242,
　390
Lining, silver, on the night, 157
　there's a silver, 824
　to show the, 837
L'injure se grave en métal, 74
Link, silver, silken tie, 307
　with Christendom, last, 787
Links in the bondsman's chain,
　686
　pain to break its, 334
Linked sweetness, 160
　with one virtue, 356
Linnet sings wildly, and a, 758
Linnets, pipe but as the, 468
Lintel low enough, 710
　pass the low, 840
Lion, a raging roaring, 691
　among ladies, 43
　and the cock, only the, 851
　as a roaring, 1123

Lion at Lucerne, 621
  better than a dead, 1109
  blood more stirs to rouse a, 61
  bold as a, 1108
  breakfast on the lip of a, 67
  but a pard, not a, 897
  fawns upon the lamb, when the, 70
  from his lair, rouse the, 311
  heart and eagle eye, 248
  honey in the carcase of the, 1099
  hungry, give a grievous roar, 319
  in his den, beard the, 308
  in the chase, 294
  in the way, there is a, 1108
  is dead, now that the old, 276
  is in the streets, 1108
  is not so fierce as they paint him, 137, 147
  lift your eyes up to the, 931
  like a bear or, 105
  look no larger, till the, 471
  mated by the hind, 53
  on your old stone gates, 462
  painting a, 960
  righteous are bold as a, 1108
  sheep swine monkey wine, 1068
  woos his brides, as the, 248
Lions, Daniel in the den of, 1113
  growl and fight, 198
  rushed like, 921
  talks familiarly of, 57
Lion's cage, gets into the, 952
  hide, thou wear a, 57
  mane, dew-drop from the, 75
  mouth, head in the, 952
  nerve, the Nemean, 91
  skin will not reach, 998
Lion-like March, 629
Lip and the cup, 'twixt the, 425
  between the cup and the, 124
  contempt and anger of his, 55
  coral of his, admires, 140
  is curved with pain, never a, 644
  keep a stiff upper, 557
  language in her, 75
  meets lip at the lastward, 776
  miraculous, at, 823
  nectar on a, 279
  of a lion, eat breakfast on the, 67
  perjured, 504
  quivered on their, 490
  reproof on her, 307, 389
  save whitening, 452
  vermeil-tinctured, 158
Lips and eyes, leave your, 887
  and part with tears, touch, 632
  and take her hands, kiss her, 790
  apply its polisht, 325
  are dumb in a little while, 463
  are laughing but eyes are wet, 690
  are now forbid to speak, 388
  are sealed, thy, 776
  beauty's ensign crimson in thy, 80
  but half regretful, 632
  can move or a man is alive, 776
  closed, hurt no one, 1001
  control, why do her, 875

Lips, divine persuasion flows from his, 219
  drop gentle words, 958
  fevered, 386
  flattereth with his, 1108
  foaming, of inebriated virtue, 635
  from speaking guile, 1103
  had language, oh that those, 267
  half-way to her, 816
  Helen's, 805
  here hung those, 97
  I tighten my, 845
  immortal blessing from her, 79
  in poverty to the very, 103
  let no dog bark when I ope my, 44
  life into lead-colored, 928
  listen at its, 577
  long silent, on, 690
  might tempt an angel's, 634
  mouldered the, 903
  name of God upon his, 1055
  of Julia, 133
  of life, poisoned, 889
  of poets crowned, 634
  of the unreplying dead, 602
  of those that are asleep, 1110
  of truth, 337
  of woe, still inclining to, 539
  once sanctified by hers, 449
  only sing when they cannot kiss, 610
  poisoned chalice to our, 85
  prophetic, 633
  say God be pitiful, 428
  set on thy sighing, 427
  smacked his, 954
  smile on her, 307
  smily round the, 527
  soul through my, 462
  steal blessing from her, 79
  still touched with fire, 938
  suck forth my soul, her, 31
  sweet voice sweet, 385
  take those, away, 37
  talk of the, 1107
  that are for others, 466
  that he has prest, 450
  that I have kissed, 97
  that love thy name, 765
  that nothing answer, 671
  that touch liquor, 791
  that touch, or, 904
  that were forsworn, 37
  to it, let me put my, 495
  to quaff, forth to your, 1018
  to speak, causing the, 1110
  to touch the sacred fire, 816
  touch sometimes with their, 1085
  touched not, 384
  truth from his, prevailed, 250
  we are near, make love to the, 335
  we love, far from the, 335
  were four red roses on a stalk, 72
  were less red, 593
  were red and one was thin, 163
  were so near, her, 685
  while meeting, and break on the, 431
  whispering with white, 352
  wine-cup to my, 940

Lips would keep from slips, 716
Liquefaction of her clothes, 134
Liquescent and nebulous lustre, 461
Liquid dew of youth, 90
  fire, glass of, 290
  in which the bitter, 927
  lapse of murmuring streams, 154
  light, sparkling and bright in, 431
  notes, 161
Liquor, bumper of good, 279
  gives genus a better discerning, 253
  is quicker, 935
  lips that touch, 791
  livelier, than the muse, 743
  love or fights, with, 743
  never brewed, I taste a, 584
  swims enough good, 629
Liquors, hot and rebellious, 48
Lisette, my pretty, 690
Lisped in numbers, 213
Lisping of the human soul, 1069
Lissom clerical printless toe, 893
List, black lettered, 294
  I would make a, 793
  I'm on your, 284
  I've got a little, 624
  of friends, enter on my, 266
  ye landsmen all to me, 247
Lists of dates and facts, 832
Listen at its lips, 577
  fur 'z you can look or, 527
  my children and you shall hear, 437
  where thou art sitting, 158
  with credulity, ye who, 232
Listeners are not said, for lack of, 540
Listening ear of night, 477
  earth, nightly to the, 194
  for the voices, I am, 446
  love, 602
  mood, in, 308
  shadowless like silence, 392
  still they seemed to hear, 220
  the disease of not, 64
Listens like a three years' child, 314
Listeth, wind bloweth where it, 1118
Listlessness, that weary, 1051
Litany, lovers', 776
Litel gold in cofre, 5
  on the bible, his studie was, 5
Literal translation can be just, no, 217
Literary creature, 634
  men are a perpetual priesthood, 376
  men paid by the quantity they do not write, 377
  men, parole of, 237
  product of America, typical, 863
  reputation, no luck in, 411
  reputation to be alive, 255
  scenes, among our, 882
  world is made up of little confederacies, 344
Literature a fairy land viewed at a distance, 344
  all modern American, 930
  always allegorical, great, 826

Literature, amazing how little, 237
American, 476
American fear of, 885
as a trade, never pursue, 318
as with law or empire, it is with, 461
belong to sacred, 924
charms of country life in, 571
cheapness of, 532
complete statement which is, 878
consoles sorrow, 397
critical spirit in, 772
dominates over all the arts, 538
failed in, and art, 421
furthest reach of, 898
good, must affect the reader, 744
grazed the common of, 239
greatest source of refined pleasure, 563
his profession, 318
is an art, 768
is my Utopia, 861
keep up with current, 791
life comes before, 613
never was much given to, 804
of England and America, 872
of modern Europe, 740
of the music-hall, 919
on a little oatmeal, 312
out of life, 629
read the oldest works, 426
students' choice in, 872
success of, depends on, 768
the many, address in, 426
the most seductive of professions, 641
whole purport of, 927
whole range of imaginative, 480
without charm, no fine, 789
Lithe and long as the serpent train, 431
Litigious terms, 162
Litter in a dust heap, 1027
Little, a, warmth a little light, 607
a, work a little play, 607
added to a little, 1005
advantages that occur every day, 227
and the great, between the, 267
at a time, 191
avails that coinage, 574
Bateese, 713
Billee drowned in a surge of love, 606
birds that fly with careless ease, 201
black-eyed rebel, 677
boats should keep near shore, 227
body with a mighty heart, 66
book I never wrote, 845
Boy Blue kissed them and put them there, 699
boy that died, 580
boys made of, such are, 322
Broom Gardens, live in, 864
brown hand, held in the, 730
but our hearts, our hoard is, 470

Little, but 'tis all I have, 307
but to the purpose, said, 360
by little does the trick, 962
care we little we fear, 481
chimney and heated hot, 52, 436
church around the corner, 579
contented with, 287
deeds of kindness, 553
do or can the best of us, 493
do we know wot lays afore us, 495
done, so much to do, so, 712
drops of water, 553
earth for charity, 74
employment, hand of, 96
enough endures, 761
faith, O heart of, 691
faithful barking ghost, 858
finger, more goodness in her, 192
fire kindleth, 1122
fire is quickly trodden out, 70
fishes talk like whales, 255
folding of the hands, 1106
foolery that wise men have, 47
for our heart, too, 503
for the bottle, 274
foxes that spoil the vines, 1110
friend of all the world, 786
friend of man, here lies, 382
fun to match the sorrow, 607
girl with a little curl, 440
gold in cofre, 5
good watering last year's crops, 520
grave, my kingdom for a, 60
Gretchen, little Gretchen, 394
hands were never made to tear each other's eyes, 198
happy if I could say how much, 38
hate each other so, 1084
have, and seek no more, 20
here a, and there a little, 1111
his study on the bible was, 5
I ask my wants are few, 451
I have gained, how, 444, 469
I need so, 605
if a, knowledge is dangerous, 564
if thou have but a, 1123
in drink, a, 198
in his purse, much upon his back, 121
in one's own pocket, 1039
is achieved through that, 493
is better than nothing, 988
Jesus, wast Thou shy once, 748
jingles, little rhymes, 189
kingdom, like to a, 82
knowest thou that hast not tride, 25
lay up little upon a, 959
learning dangerous, 210
less anxious, 690
light, a little warmth a, 607
longer, wait a, 504
lore of loving, 649
love me, love me long, 16, 31, 133
loved me ever so, 631
lower than the angels, 1103
man, there was a, 334
man wants but, 202, 254
men, for fear of, 573

Little minds, little things affect, 420
moment what one knows in youth, 636
more care, 690
more than a little is too much, 62
more than kin, 89
moulted feathers saffron-tipt, 448
needed to make a happy life, 1011
Nell, had writ of, 644
of this vicissitude, 197
one become a thousand, 1112
one come to my knee, 565
one-horse town, 615
ones gather around me, 662
or nothing between them, 975
our fathers, wonderful, 783
play, a little work a, 607
pot and soon hot, 52
round button at top, 246
safer to know too, 613
said is soon amended, 133
said is soonest mended, 1036
saw the, that is good, 536
severs me from mine heart's country, 796
shall I grace my cause, 100
sick child in the basement, 715
sleep a little slumber, 1106
soul let us try, 334
talk too much and think too, 173
tasks make large return, 566
thing to do, seeks a, 487
things affect little minds, 420
things, don't despise the, 578
this side of the snow, 585
those who have too, 877
though, 950
though she be but, 43
tin gods on wheels, 776
to disquantity your train, 98
to earn and many to keep, 523
to fear or hope, 232
too wise never live long, 116
town of Bethlehem, 612
trust that when we die, 607
we fear, little care we, 481
we know about the age, 986
we need, how, 751
we see in nature that is ours, 300
whatever was, 398
window where the sun, 390
wise the best of fools, 118
worth a sigh, 601
wrong, to do a, 47
you give is great, 557
Littlenesses, a thousand peering, 469
Liturgies, dull commercial, 806
Live a fool the rest of his life, 129
above the fog, men who, 522
again in minds made better, 520
all that, must die, 89
all the days of your life, 192
alone, why should we fear to, 365
alway, I would not, 387, 1102
among men, 990

Live and die, though to itself it only, 108
and learn, 493, 1041
and let live, 632
and move and have our being, we, 1128
and see, this life we, 638
at home at ease, 115
but linger, do not, 123
by bread only, man doth not, 1099
by one man's will, 22
cleanly, leave sack and, 63
dare to die bear to, 208
good men eat to, 1004
good world to, in, 185
hair that is shining, 894
I still, 342
in an alley, I, 118
in brass, men's evil manners, 74
in deeds not years, 506
in hearts we leave behind, 328
in peace, adieu, 216
in pleasure when I live to thee, 225
in snuff, rather than, 22
in teaching me the way to, 405
innocently, God is here, 1054
it matters not how long you, 989
lands where the Jumblies, 498
leave to, 780
living we fret dying we, 492
long, those that God loves do not, 138
means to, 32
means whereby I, 47
more virtue than doth, 119
not in myself, I, 353
not three good men unhanged, 61
on hope, 668
or die sink or swim, 340
past years again, none would, 178
peaceably with all men, 1119
pure speak true right wrong, 470
so may'st thou, 155
so that when the mighty caravan, 371
so wise so young never, long, 72
taught us how to, 205
teach him how to, 268, 1027
teach men to, 205
that thou mayst desire to live, 1082
things in their pride, 857
through all things, 596
thus let me, 216
till I were married, 39
till to-morrow, 267
to be in awe of such a thing, 81
to be the show and gaze, 89
to eat, bad men, 1004
to fight another day, 143, 254
to, is Christ, 1121
to please must please to live, 231
together, and as brothers, 436
too much in a circle, all of us, 420
true as I, 116
unblemished let me, 216

Live undaunted, 985
unnumbered years, names that shall, 518
unseen unknown, let me, 216
upon the vapour of a dungeon, 102
we, but a world has passed away, 628
we how we can, die we must, 70
we must eat to, 229
we never live but hope to, 1047
well what thou liv'st, 155
while ye may happy pair, 152
while you live, 225
with love alone, give me to, 406
with me and be my love, 31
with the gods, 1011
with thee and be thy love, 21
with them less sweet, 335
with your inferiors, is to, 483
within our means if we borrow, 606
without him, tried to, 114
without poetry, 592
without thee I cannot, 365
Lives along the line, 207
and dies in single blessedness, 42
and sacred honour, 273
are but our marches to the grave, 433
are padded, 891
are strange dark interludes, 903
as he ought to do, 127
buying men's, 310
contentedly, 267
desire the rest of their, 785
devote to love and truth, 522
do not pray for easy, 613
fortunes and, vote away, 573
history in all men's, 65
how a man, 235
how the other half, 138
impress of eternity upon our, 1082
in acts exemplary, our, 28
in fame that died in virtue's cause, 76
in sleep, our, 527
in the midst of flames without hurt, 196
join, oft a scar if two, 486
led merry merry, 754
longer, competency, 44
may last but never, 246
most who thinks most, 506
must direct our, 1049
nine, like a cat, 16
of great men all remind us, 28, 433, 844
of most women and men, 594
of obscure persons, 761
of others happier, make the, 694
pleasant in their, 1100
sublime, make our, 28, 433
supreme judge of their, 1063
talk not of other men's, 1125
that no life, forever, 632
the sweetest, 955
to build not boast, he, 223
to leaven lowly, 612

Lives, two, that once part are as ships, 425, 437
watcheth o'er our, 967
with sweetness, fill their, 577
working for our, 496
would grow together, 631
ye led were mine, 776
Lived in abundance, the poorest, 435
in the eye of nature, 296
in the tide of times, 82
in vain, 318
she at its close, yet, 557
the yonghy-bonghy-bo, 498
to-day, I have, 177
unknown, she, 296
with no other thought, maiden, 459
Livelier iris, 464
plaything, some, 208
Livelihood, earn an honest, 1020
slave for, 867
Live-long day, 81
day, tell your name the, 584
Lively and lasting sense, 273
sense of future favours, 200
to severe, grave to gay, 177, 209
Liver, abscess on his, 811
flow through one small, 360
on his sleeve, 933
Livers in content, with humble, 73
Livery of hell, the cunning, 36
shadowed, of the burnished sun, 45
twilight gray in her sober, 152
Living all there is in, 655
and my uttermost power, my, 66
and we the, 963
art of, 1011
bond with the other world, 1074
dead man, 38
dog better than dead lion, 1109
fires, wake in our breast the, 451
from too much love of, 632
high hopes of, 162
house appointed for all, 1102
hues of art, with the, 472
land of the, 1102
life for the, 605
line, who casts to write a, must sweat, 119
makes up the sum of, 565
might exceed the dead, the, 145
mother of all, 1097
name, leave a, 128
nature not dull art, 403
need charity, 605
one's life over again, 228
only cannot be forgiven, 520
plain, and high thinking, 298
poems, for ye are, 437
proof to all the world, 954
sanity and perfection of, 549
seed, 575
soul, in all that makes a, 424
talked of my former, 681
the fever called, 460
there is hope for the, 206
to one's self, 330
toil for a, 589

Living, wasted his substance with riotous, 1117
  waters, lie by, 725
  we fret dying we live, 492
  who must stay behind, 683
  will it not live with the, 63
  with thee nor without thee, no, 196
  working still, God is, 502
  works hard for a, 956
Living-room, too much furniture in one's, 1026
Lizette, hear the word of old, 817
Lizzie Borden took an axe, 957
Llewellyn's heir, to save, 294
Lloyd's, too new for the British, 670
Lo all things can be borne, 596
  as the wind is, 597
  the poor Indian, 207
Load a falling man, a cruelty to, 74
  again, wake and take your, 765
  ass will carry his, 1042
  life thou art a galling, 285
  of infamy, any, 314
  of sorrow, wring under the, 40
  to bear, heaviest, 625
  travels without a, 757
  would sink a navy, a, 73
Loads of care and wrong, 738
  of learned lumber, 212
Loaf back of the, 731
  half a, is better than no bread, 15
  of bread, a, 1018
  of bread, leads to a, 733
  of bread, like giving a, 716
  to every bird, God gave a, 585
  to steal a shive of a cut, 77
Loafe and invite my soul, I, 534
Loafing around the throne, 639
Loam, Berkshire, 834
  sows dead men in the, 712
Loan for the war, making the, 937
  oft loses both itself and friend, 91
Loath to lay out money on a rope, 123
Loathe the taste of sweetness, 62
Loathed melancholy, hence, 160
  worldly life, 36
Loathing, deepest, to the stomach brings, 43
  undisguised, with a, 815
Loaves, five small, 541
  half-penny, 69
  of bread, ears produce, 1056
  there be but left two, 682
Lobster boil'd, like a, 142
Local habitation and a name, 43
  thing called Christianity, 650
Loce Ang-El-Ess, all about, 952
Loch Lomond, bonnie bonnie banks of, 952
Lochaber back, bring, 361
  farewell to, 204
Lochaber's snows, through wild, 500
Lochinvar, young, never a knight like, 307
Lock, cryin' at the, 475
  last night I changed the, 676
  of Whistler, white, 826
  upon the shapely head, 665

Locks, familiar with his hoary, 393
  had they to their doors, 435
  in the golden story, 77
  invincible, 163
  knotted and combined, 91
  left you are gray, the few, 320
  loose were her jetty, 406
  may lose their brown, 690
  never shake thy gory, 87
  nor doors nor, 348
  of an unlovely hue, 373
  of gold to-day, 681
  pluck up drowned honour by the, 61
  shake out your, 853
  time his golden, 27
  were like the raven, 286
  whoever knocks open, 87
  with their whitening, 983
  without any, 823
  ye auburn, 451
Locked lettered collar, 285
  up from mortal eye, 165
  up in steel, naked though, 69
Locksmith, epitaph of, 948
Locomotives, more splendid than the two, 1083
  sing, ranged where, 856
Locusts, luscious as, 101
Lode we quarry, the giant, 929
Lodge in a garden of cucumbers, 652, 1110
  oh for a, 264
  porter of my father's, 584
  thee by Chaucer, 119
  to prick and sting her, 92
  where thou lodgest I will, 1099
Lodger for the night, 771
Lodges, where care, 78
Lodging, grant us a safe, 1128
  sleep in your cloak there's no, 545
Lodgings free from bugs, 972
  in a head unfurnished, 142
Lodging-place of wayfaring men, 264
Lodore, this way the water comes down at, 321
Loftier race, a, 654
Loftiness of thought, 175
Lofty and sour, 74
  name, 620
  rhyme, build the, 159
  scene, this our, 82
Log, not a, but its memories has got, 677
  sat on one end of a, 815
  tough wedge for a tough, 989
  you roll my, 991
Logs, granddad in his house of, 956
Logan is the head center the hub the king pin, 601
Logan's cabin, ever entered, 249
Logic absolute, with, 1019
  and history only external guides, 680
  and rhetoric, 111
  down to fishing, from, 509
  of science and, he chatters, 406
Logical consequences are scarecrows, 564
  way, built in such a, 452
Loin, the ungirt, 488

Loins be girded, let your, 1117
Loiter in pleasure or toilfully, 448
Loiterers and malcontents, 41
Loke who that is most vertuous, 7
London air, brisk 's the, 833
  ale is right ale, 833
  bridge, arch of, 398
  Bridge, his frequent way, 621
  finest thing in, 815
  fog, 390
  fossils in Wren's buildings in, 819
  gave me breath, 746
  gleaming lamps of, 687
  habitation of bitterns, 399
  has all that life can afford, 236
  hell a city much like, 367
  is a man's town, 709
  lane and street, in every, 793
  like a land of old, 861
  monster, 168
  neighbourhood, things to be guarded against in a, 402
  on an early autumn afternoon, 799
  our delight, 793
  see, once ere I die, 65
  sights are rare, 833
  small and white and clean, 609
  streets, sighing through, 683
  swallowed up in, 751
  the clearing-house of the world, 621
  town, desert of, 610
  town has blurred it, 701
  town, heart of, 952
  town, passed over, 565
  town, rather than pace up and down, 478
  Town's a fine town, 833
  whistled up to, 241
London's column pointing, 210
  lasting shame, 244
Lone and high, 771
  and level sands, 367
  He stands, where, 697
  hours fly so fast, 473
  lorn creetur, 496
  our path be, 406
  o'er the world I wander, 579
  unmated creature tired and, 503
  woman, a poor, 64
Loneliness, around thee in thy, 427
  grief its, 922
  is danger, in, 913
  is ended, 794
  mete out my, 683
  sense of utter, 955
  sick of, 375
  untouched, preserve my, 1090
  without me, to prove his, 598
Lonely and poor of old, 894
  and unsatisfied, 886
  art thou, 794
  bugle grieves, 684
  fire, I sit beside my, 582
  forest way, 562
  grave he sleeps, in his, 579
  grave, there lies a, 516
  is thenceforth, 556
  men, there's too much beauty for, 792
  mountain, by Nebo's, 516

Lonely now Mary, I am very, 432
  our path be, 406
  paths, 588
  places, crying solitary in, 717
  sea and the sky, 832
  season, this is the, 843
  so, it was, 315
  soul's Gethsemane, 570
  the way is, 681
  want retired to die, 231
  waste of Edom's plain, 443
  we shall be, how, 858
Lonesome garret, 258
  October, night in the, 461
  place against the sky, 708
  place, it's in a, 817
  road, like one on a, 315
  streets, 565
Long, a fool his whole life, 481
  after it was heard no more, 298
  ago, in the olden time, 459
  ago, the golden time of, 626
  and dreary winter, oh the, 436
  and loath at going, were, 903
  and silent street, down the, 723
  as ever you can, 226
  be it stubbornly, 895
  be the day never so, 17
  boots hard boots, they wear, 855
  bright tresses, 600
  brought too, a day, 390
  choosing beginning late, 154
  contention cease, let the, 547
  courtship, preceded by a, 196
  dark evenings come, 486
  day closes, 446
  day's, toil is past, 392
  disease my life, 213
  drawn out, linked sweetness, 160
  dull and old, 288
  enough for living well, 981
  for a mornin's mornin', 715
  for perishing meat, 166
  furrows of foam, 712
  has it waved on high, 450
  has lain, that which, 647
  heat of the, day and wish, 546
  heave of the surging world, 735
  home, man goeth to his, 1110
  I stood there wondering, 460
  in city pent, 383
  in one place, 639
  in populous city pent, 154
  is the way and hard, 150
  it sha'n't be, 222
  lane that knows no turnings, 487
  lank and brown, 315
  leagues apart descried, scarce, 519
  life is not too, 405
  live our noble king, 189
  live the king, 264
  living, burden of, 632
  long ago, 388
  long anchorage we leave, 537
  long shift is over, 844
  long thoughts, thoughts of youth are, 436
  long way to Tipperary, 836
  long wintry nights, through, 499

Long, love me little love me, 16, 31, 133
  loved long woo'd and lately won, 309
  may it be ere the sun of thy glory, 407
  may it wave, 332
  may our land be bright, 447
  merry as the day is, 38
  mysterious exodus of death, 436
  narrow shallow, so, 823
  night away, passed long, 557
  none thrives, upon happiest dreams, 556
  on all things all day, 470
  path, down the, 851
  pull and a strong pull, 497
  rest or death, give us, 463
  road that knows no turning, 965
  short and the, of it, 34
  sigh too much or a kiss too, 559
  since, which I have loved, 403
  small showers last, 59
  so, as we love we serve, 705
  string of ills, 294
  that life is, 202
  the shadows that I feared so, 540
  time ago, 405
  to long in solemn sort, 317
  to spend shortness basely were too, 63
  too long America, 536
  trips from, to short, 317
  tumult of the land and sea, 848
  vacation, long for a, 854
  way, in the, 372
  we live, but how, not how, 506
  yet too short, 120
  you wish to stay, how, 802
Longed for death, has ever truly, 462
Longer disgised, fack can't be no, 606
  wait a little, 504
Longest kingly line, 311
Longevity, increase, 549
  waste of, 247
Longfellow a gentleman, 766
Long-forgotten music, 644
Long-haired poets, 661
Long-handled dipper, und dot, 661
Longing after immortality, 195
  eyes I wait, with, 481
  feeling of sadness and, 434
  leans and beckons, 529
  lingering look behind, 245
  more than all, 836
  more, wavering, 54
  of my soul, the upward, 820
  that lies dormant, 607
  to be mated, has such, 545
  to be seen, no, 933
Longings after something lost, 665
  give me the ardent, 533
  immortal, 105
Longitude for a seine, meridians of, 616
  likewise is vague, 625
  tho' sorely scanty, in, 287
Longitudes, time in two, 641

Long-lasht eyes abased, her, 326
Long-levelled rule, 158
Long-lost multitude of ships, 552
Longmans' shop, it's still in, 296
Long-range gun, designing the, 937
'Longside of some pious gentlemen, 639
Long-tailed words, 292
Look a gift horse in the mouth, 13, 142
  amaist as weel's the new, 284
  and a voice, only a, 437
  angel of the backward, 443
  before and after, we, 366
  before you ere you leap, 143, 1039
  behind, spare not nor, 417
  beneath the surface, 1011
  beyond the heights, 602
  brighter when we come, 358
  caressing, with, 697
  deep in mine, 960
  drew audience, his, 150
  ere thou leap, 11, 143
  feigned an angry, 185
  forward not back, 550
  gave it a second, 935
  give me a, give me a face, 119
  here upon this picture, 95
  in my face, 577
  in the chronicles, 51
  in your eyes, 868
  into happiness through another man's eyes, 51
  into the seeds of time, 84
  into thy heart, 27, 433
  lean and hungry, 81
  like the innocent flower, 84
  longing lingering, 245
  men met with erected, 174
  no larger than the cat, 471
  no way but downwards, 172
  not mournfully into the past, 440
  not thou down but up, 489
  not thou upon the wine, 1108
  older, all thoughts, things, 405
  on her face and you'll forget, 212
  on it lift it bear it, 454
  one immortal, 489
  one quick wordless, 647
  or listen, fur'z you can, 527
  out and not in, 550
  out upon the stars my love, 405
  proudly to heaven, 327
  round the habitable world, 177
  so dull so dead in, 63
  starved for a, 108
  takes a last, 220
  that threatened insult, 260
  the same by day, will not, 428
  through a milstone, 24
  to have, I must not, 88
  to take a backward, 584
  to the essence of a thing, 1011
  to thy mouth; diseases enter there, 136
  up and not down 550
  upon his like again, 90
  upon the rainbow, 1125
  when clouds are blowing, 667
  with a bitter, 722
  with a dignified, 351
  with injured peevish, 879

Look with thine ears, 99
  without a backward, 930
  would begin it, 736
  your last, 80
Looks a queen, she, 218
  around to say farewell, and, 481
  clear your, 295
  commercing with the skies, 160
  fairest garden in her, 168
  full assurance given by, 26
  gigantically down, death, 459
  in the clouds, 82
  invites you by his, 263
  meagre were his, 80
  more elder than thy, 47
  of love, sidelong, 250
  only books were woman's, 336
  pallid Virtue's sidelong, 912
  praising God with sweetest, 390
  profound, statesmen with, 251
  puts on his pretty, 58
  quite through the deeds of men, 81
  somehow from her, 427
  that will part from us, 406
  the cottage might adorn, 251
  through nature, 209
  Up! up! my friend and clear your, 295
  were fond and words were few, 345
  with despatchful, 153
Looked after the low-backed car, 389
  honest, 616
  no sooner, but loved, 51
  on better days, if ever you have, 49
  sighed and, 176
  the twin of heathen hate, 471
  unutterable things, 224
Looking before and after, 96
  ill prevail, 163
  well can't move her, 163
Lookout, fortified, 552
Loom and belting, lilting at, 936
  and chisel, plough, 950
Looming bastion, 468
Looms again, look to your, 656
  weave no more silks ye Lyons, 522
Loony now, who's, 762
Loop, no, nor hinge, 103
Looped and windowed raggedness, 99
Loophole, cabined, 157
Loopholes barred, 320
  of retreat, 265
Loose, all hell broke, 153
  good dayes, 25
  his beard, 244
  sally of the mind, 232
  way of talking, 293
  were her jetty locks, 406
Loosed string, lest the, 226
  the fateful lightning, He hath, 522
Loosely-sandalled verse, 648
Loosened spirit, 584
Lopsided man runs fastest, 775
Loquacity, poetry checks, 412
Lord, am an attendant, 900
  among wits, 215
  are true, judgments of the, 457

Lord, as Thy temple's portals close, 450
  be thankit, let the, 287
  beloved, when Israel of the, 310
  bless thee and keep thee, the, 1099
  Byron was an Englishman, 685
  called Samuel, 1100
  Christ's heart, 410
  directeth his steps, 1107
  dismiss us with thy blessing, 280
  for the erring thought, 628
  for the wicked will, 628
  gave and hath taken away, 1101
  glory of the coming of the, 522
  God, were I, 948
  God will wipe away tears, 1111
  handkerchief of the, 534
  he knew his, 220
  help 'em how I pities them, 275
  himself forgot, 441
  how it talked, 131
  in a tuneful carol, worshiped the, 927
  in mariage, 8
  in May, if I were, 631
  is beautiful to the, 934
  is in his holy temple, the, 1113
  is my rock, 1100
  it is a world of fools, my, 472
  keep my memory green, 496
  lays it on Martha's sons, 781
  lendeth unto the, 1107
  lift up his countenance upon thee, 1099
  Lobcock and Count Asthma, dine with, 937
  make his face shine upon thee, 1099
  man that feareth, to doubt, 559
  my bosom's, 80
  my, I meet, 793
  of all things great, 207
  of death, life is ever, 444
  of folded arms, 41
  of Glory, how they served the, 199
  of himself that heritage of woe, 356
  of himself though not of lands, 114
  of humankind, 179
  of Love came down, 709
  of my unchallenged fate, 579
  of Tartary, if I were, 822
  of the far horizons, 757
  of the lion-heart, 248
  of the pots and pipkins, 918
  of the sun, not, 907
  of the Wessex coast, 780
  of thy presence no land beside, 57
  once own the happy lines, let a, 211
  oppressed with pride and poverty, 184
  precious in the sight of the, 1105
  reward him according to his works, 1122
  set a mark upon Cain, 1097
  St. Albans on tall men, 113
  Stafford mines for coal, 363

Lord than God, a lower, 597
  that lends me life, 68
  till his, is crucified, 525
  Tomnoddy got up one day, 350
  Tomnoddy is thirty-four, 573
  too great, Thou wert O, 503
  transformed to devils, them all, the, 3
  vicaire of th' almyghty, 4
  we thank Thee, 794
  went before them, 1098
  what a change within us, 441
  who ordainest for mankind, 373
  whom the, loveth he chasteneth, 1122
  wondrous book bright candle of the, 393
  you know what Virgil sings, my, 472
Lords may flourish or may fade, 250
  of an empire wide, 558
  of birth, the secret, 771
  of hell, procuress to the, 468
  of humankind, 250
  of ladies intellectual, 358
  of the creation, 285
  or kings of the earth, true, 532
  to a thousand of his, 1113
  women who love their, 248
Lord's anointed, rail on the, 72
  anointed temple, broke ope the, 86
  gifts, for his, 441
Lords' stories, great, 288
Lordly cedar, as when a, 708
  friend, 634
  pleasure-house, 462
Lordship rang for his cabriolet, 350
Lordship's levee, 648
Lordships' pleasures, on their, 74
Lore and the pride of man, 408
  Cristes, and his apostles, 5
  curious volume of forgotten, 460
  lacking in, 776
  mystical, 327
  of loving, little, 649
  of nicely calculated less or more, 304
  Thanksgiving, 935
  this is the, 439
  we leave you, 652
  who follow not her, 156
Lorn, creetur, I am a lone, 496
  with-outen remedye, 8
Los Angeles, 952
Lose his own soul, 1115
  it that do buy it with much care, 43
  its own, love can never, 444
  no man can, what he never had, 140
  nothing having, nothing can he, 70
  of no account what you can, 987
  the good we oft might win, 35
  the power to love, 502
  the power to will, work or, 502
  who never wins can rarely, 443
  your way, cannot, 76
Loser's woe, to enhance the, 309

Loses faith in God and woman, 587
Losing office, hath but a, 64
  profit by, 104
  rendered sager, by, 357
Loss, and is it all, 881
  is no loss if unknown, 987
  lament their triumph and his, 444
  most patient man in, 105
  nor gain nor change, 682
  of life and of heaven, 1045
  of sight of thee I most complain, 156
  of the sun, 222
  of time most grieves, 1021
  of wealth is loss of dirt, 11
  pleasure without, 21
  though he promise to his, 185
  thy so sore, 749
  to make of every, 647
  voice of woe for a lover's, 517
Losse, grief but aggravates thy, 256
Losses are restor'd and sorrows end, 107
  fellow that hath had, 40
  have ye met, sad, 507
  there are gains for all our, 565
Lost a day, I've, 201
  a hundred years a day, 733
  all good to me is, 151
  all is not, 148
  and ancient land, 746
  and dead, evil become, 536
  and won, when the battle's, 84
  and worn, sooner, 54
  associations and societies, 800
  battle won and battle, 292
  being lacked and, 39
  but gone before, not, 447
  count that day, 202, 950
  delight, give back the, 619
  for aye in the darkness, soon to be, 538
  forever, what I forego is, 305
  in lexicography, 232
  in mists, churches, creeds, 569
  in the sweets, 205
  in wandering mazes, 150
  loved long since and, awhile, 403
  my reputation, 101
  no hate, 117
  no love, 118
  not, but gone before, 188, 447
  ones, counting all our, 963
  praising what is, 53
  reputation, comes not again, 324
  silent above the flowers her children, 565
  smallest effort is not, 504
  than ever were, 611
  the immortal part of myself, 101
  think that day, 202, 950
  to sight to memory dear, 392
  war and deeds of carnage be, 536
  was Solomon's purple show, 805
  waste arguments where they will be, 424
  what though the field be, 148
  whatsoever thing is, 267

Lost, when faith is, when honor dies, 442
  when I was saved, just, 585
  with much protesting, dignity of truth, 118
  without deserving, 101
  woman that deliberates is, 195
Lot, balance life's unequal, 544
  be content with your, 961
  blameless vestal's, 216
  compare the age in which their, 400
  God wot, as by, 255
  in thy young, 391
  matters not what be thy, 549
  not every man's, 985
  of all of us, the, 1054
  of man but once to die, 135
  of man to suffer and to die, 220
  our high imperial, 780
  scot and, 118
  strange was his, 685
  this is our, 780
  to find no enemies, unhappy, 988
  with all my future, 395
Lot's wife, metamorphosis of, 1097
Loth and slow, aged men, 309
  to depart, and often took leave, 189
  to depart, O so, 538
  to die, wandering on as, 304
Lothario, gay, 198
Lotus, of the Nile, to eat the, 444
  tied, bring me a, 639
Loud and quick, it's, 698
  had spoken, not as the, 652
  hissing urn, 265
  laugh of the vacant mind, 250
  not so, as those that cry for hire, 180
  roared the dreadful thunder, 288
  the torrent's roar, 258
  through the width of the land, 843
  with shallow waterfalls, 438
  yet was never, 101
Louder but as empty quite, 208
Loudly, a cat languishes, 692
Louis of the awful cheek, 703
Louisburg Square, lends its aroma to, 711
Louisiana, retired upon, in good order, 616
Lounsbury, will of Charles, 732
Lousy, poor and very, 228
Love a bright particular star, that I should, 53
  a perceptual anæsthesia, 862
  a puppy cur, mastiff may, 472
  a simple ballad of, 759
  a well of, 387
  a wild plant, 797
  absence conquers, 448
  absence still increases, 388
  after the verb to, 1083
  all for, 24
  all hearts in, 38
  all that life is, 306
  all the world in, with night, 79
  all, trust a few, 52
  alone can pore, 664
  alone, give me to live with, 406

Love among the churches, Christian, 471
  an abject intercourse, 253
  and a cough cannot be hid, 136
  and all his pleasures are but toys, 121
  and be loved by me, than to, 459
  and be my, 936
  and beauty and delight, for, 368
  and care and strength, 955
  and constancy, those marriages abound with, 196
  and desire and hate, 795
  and devotion that never shall die, 813
  and faith, compel such, 692
  and fame, I dreamt of, 746
  and fame, poets' food is, 366
  and friendship stirred, with, 1066
  and goodness, not enough of, 520
  and gratitude of united America, 374
  and hers, my, 1036
  and I had the wit, 708
  and idleness, sing for, 885
  and knowledge of you, 48
  and laughter's there, when, 905
  and let love, 632
  and life eternal youth, 857
  and light and calm thoughts, 317
  and light, floods of, 452
  and power untold, with, 501
  and putting steam on, making, 661
  and roses, youth gave, 335
  and the commonplace things, 939
  and thought and joy, 297
  and to cherish, 1128
  and toil in the years to be, 783
  and truth, the dreams of, 665
  and war the same thing, 1040
  and wisdom dwell, where, 501
  are blest, where they that, 503
  art the accomplice of, 1084
  as a debt, 698
  at first sight, 785
  away, and putting, 584
  away, take, 1084
  be now no passages of, 470
  be younger than thyself, let thy, 54
  beauteous looks not win my, 52
  beauty truth and, 668
  begins to sicken, when, 83
  better to, in the lowliest cot, 545
  between predilection and, 651
  beyond, a better, 596
  bow before thine altar, 248
  bread, Italians, 1090
  breastplate of faith and, 1121
  Briton even in, 304
  burning terms of, 460
  business that we, 104
  but as a part of life, 581
  but her forever, 287
  but love in vain, 167

Love but on condition, can we, 492
but one day, I dearly, 189
but only her, 354
by candle-light, I marked my, 541
by reason of respect or natural, 726
came laughing by, 809
can die, they sin who tell us, 322
can hear the rustling of a wing, 602
can hold with twined thread, 125
can hope where reason despairs, 239
can never fail to warm, 1021
can never lose its own, 444
can never more grow old, 690
can scarce deserve the name, 355
can tell and love alone, 669
canopy of, 441
canst thou not wait for, 691
change old, for new, 28
close the open hand out of, 1079
comes back, 649
comes to all, 713
comforteth like sunshine after rain, 106
common as light is, 367
conquers all, 982
consists in this, 1090
content with a vegetable, 623
could never change, thought, 669
could teach a monarch, 246
could you and I with Him conspire, 1019
course of true, 42
curiosity freckles and doubt, 918
dallies with the innocence of, 55
deep as first, 466
deeper than speech our, 778
demonstrations of, 1037
deplored or sorrow knew, 626
despised and of disgraces, 824
die for, 53
dream in joy and wake in, 375
each in my, alike, 76
each time we, we turn, 588
earth's the right place for, 837
endures no tie, 176
ennobles all, where, 955
evangel-poem of comrades and, 534
fairer than my, 77
false or true, 790
fans it ever life feeds, 736
fasting for a good man's, 50
first, 724
flowers and fruits of, 358
fools' experiments, I, 449
for Charlotte, Werther had a, 481
for ever wilt thou, and she be fair, 383
for me shall last, one whose, 953
for mirth, for, 843
for the woman you love, 716
for them is great my, 1021

Love for things afar, 964
free as air, 216
freedom comrades, 834
friendship constant save in, 38
friendship politeness deference, 1087
friendship that like, is warm, 336
from whom the world begun, 669
full of heavenly, 696
gather the rose of, 133
gilds the scene, 278
give exclusive, 564
God from necessity is, 477
God gives us, 463
God is, 1123
God, the world and, 617
God thou art, 452
goes here, a great, 977
goes toward love, 78
gold and pleasure, youth, 455
greater, hath no man, 1118
greater than his power, 617
greatest of the arts, 670
greatest pain it is to, 167
grown faint and fretful, 632
grows bitter with treason, 631
hail wedded, 152
half angel and half bird, O lyric, 490
harvest-time of, 322
has crossed an ocean, my, 869
has gone and left me, 916
has never known a law, 443
has overflowing streams, 441
hath lowly haunts, for, 406
hath no physic, 922
hatred as well as, 1055
he bore to learning, 251
he may live without, 592
he purloined away, my, 640
he spake of, 303
he was all for, 274
her, to know her was to, 289
her, to see her was to, 287
her was a liberal education, to, 197
him ere he seem worthy, 297
his furniture is, 585
his, was like the liberal air, 626
how should I know your true, 256
how vast a memory has, 216
hunt down, 631
I cannot show the, 766
I fear to, thee Sweet, 748
I, my fellow-creatures, 623
I stroll, a while with, 889
if I have freedom in my, 168
if love be perfect, as, 470
if there's delight in, 193
in a hut, 383
in, and hold, 887
in idleness, 't is, 406
in my bosom like a bee, 27
in my degree, I must have, 601
in revenge and in, 1080
in search of a word, 664
in the beginning, no great, 34
in the open hand, 917
in, to let, 384
in yours Nora Creina, 335
infinite, 631
is a boy by poets styled, 142
is a flame, 833

Love is a frailty of the mind, 193
is a kiss, 711
is a mood, 718
is a proud and gentle thing, 896
is a sickness, 30
is a spirit compact of fire, 106
is blind, 7, 45, 317
is blind, believe her, 883
is but a girdle of the love, 474
is conquered, 1051
is doomed to mourn, 395
is enough, though the world be a-waning, 609
is ever the beginning, 378
is flower-like, 317
is full of showers, 30
is God's essence, 617
is grown to ripeness, when, 463
is heaven and heaven is love, 306
is indestructible, 322
is justified of love, 429
is left alone, and, 463
is like a dizziness, 294
is like a landscape, 127
is like a red red rose, my, 287
is like a rose, 587
is like the meazles, 518
is like the wild rose-briar, 516
is merchandiz'd, that, 108
is more richer than my tongue, 98
is nature's second sun, 28
is noght old, 7
is not love which alters, 108
is o'er a water, 869
is over, 789
is something so divine, 268
is strong as death, 1110
is sweet for a day, 631
is sweet given or returned, 367
is that orbit of the soul, 553
is the ambassador of loss, 748
is the coldest of critics, 558
is the enchanted dawn, 1065
is the fulfilling of the law, 1119
is the gift God has given, 307
is the jewel that wins the world, 840
is the lord and slave of all, 559
is the mellow glow of autumn, 700
is the only priest, 603
is the part and love is the whole, 559
is the robe and love is the pall, 559
is the state in which, 1081
is the sweetest thing on earth, 686
it would conceal, 317
kisses the lips of death, 603
knoweth no lawes, 23
labour of, 1121
last not least in, 82
lasts because of spare diet, 163
laws which, has made, 216
lay thy phobias to rest, 882
least that let men know, 33
let those, now, 201
let your special, 1083
level in the balances of, 617
levels all, 425
lies for ever yesterday to-day, 587

Love life, dost thou, 227
light and calm thoughts, 317
light of, 356
like a bird, 735
like friendship steady, 336
like the light silently wrapping, 535
live with me and be my, 31
live with thee and be thy, 21
lodged in woman's breast is but a guest, 114
look out upon the stars my, 405
looks not with the eyes, 42
lose the power to, 502
lost between us, no, 117, 253
lost, no, 118
lost sir, no, 1040
machine, 632
made trouble, 767
made visible, work is, 879
maid with few to, 296
man can stand much in the cause of, 742
many waters cannot quench, 1110
may lift his head, 696
me, all that, 459
me little love me long, 16, 31, 133
me love my dog, 17
medicines to make me, 61
melt into memory, let, 1084
men have died but not for, 51
might enter in, 722
mightier far is, 303
mighty pain to, it is, 167
ministers of, 316
music be the food of, 53
must die, that the thing we, 492
must have wings, 808
must kiss, 715
must needs be blind, 317
my country's good, I do, 76
my first last, 463
my heart has its, 1066
my life has enough of, 836
my, returns no more again, 673
my whole course of, 100
never doubt I, 92
never ebb to humble, 103
never quite forgets his first, 628
never seek to tell thy, 282
no, but vanity, 346
no fear in, 1123
no, like mother-love, 595
nor hatred, neither, 1080
nor says nor thinks, 618
not death but, 428
not love not ye hopeless, 446
not man the less I, 354
not the wind, many, 41
now who never loved before, 201
O beautiful is, 834
O fire O, 462
O human! 460
of a brute, unselfish and self-sacrificing, 461
of a devoted woman, impertinence to tell, 608
of a nine-year-old, 775
of a woman you respect, 716

Love of all that is and ever was, 606
of books the golden key, 673
of bustle, 990
of country has its rise in love of home, 494
of every land, entwining, 906
of flattery, 198
of glory is most ardent, 197
of God above, the, 1017
of God and communion of the Holy Ghost, 1121
of good Allah, 953
of home, in, 494
of justice, 1044
of learning, 438
of life increased with years, 272
of life's young day, 389
of living, from too much, 632
of man and woman, 686
of money the root of all evil, 1122
of my life, the, 714
of nature, in the, 371
of praise, efforts of race due to, 532
of praise howe'er concealed by art, 202
of the dearest friends grow small, 561
of the old for the old, 745
of the turtle, 355
of the young for the young, 745
of truth and all that, 471
of virtue, and the, 1055
of war for itself, the, 393
of women, passing the, 1100
office and affairs of, 38
once possessed, to regain, 157
once, was there, 918
one another, 1119
one another, that ye, 1118
only they conquer, 141
or bid me, 133
or have a lost, 930
overcomes all obstacles, 5
oyster may be crossed in, 279
pains of, be sweeter far, 178
pangs of dispriz'd, 93
pardon in the degree that we, 1044
part us from his, 473
paths to woman's, 131
perdition catch my soul but I do, 102
perfect, casteth out fear, 1123
perfect, casts out prudery, 617
permanent, interwreath, 810
pity melts the mind to, 176
play a dominant part, 774
pleasure of, is in loving, 367
poet without, 376
power and effect of, 125
prove variable, 78
purple light of, 243
quietly falling in, 592
remember'd, for thy sweet, 107
renewal of, 979
renuyng is of, 19
requires of me all, 804
rhymes, regent of, 41
right to dissemble your, 283
ruin'd, built anew grows fairer, 108
rules the court the camp, 306

Love, say of courtship, and matrimony, 511
seals of, but sealed in vain, 37
seeketh not itself to please, 281
seemed, so sweet, 669
seldom haunts the breast, 217
sends his early ray, 416
service of my, 747
shall be love till death, 761
shall lose, who wins his, 675
share of a mother's, 1069
she is a kitten, 630
she never told her, 55
should mend and sew no more, 912
shows itself, by excusing nothing, 1046
shut in, a world of, 544
sidelong looks of, 250
silence in, bewrays more woe, 21
silent tongues of, 1034
sits long, 610
soft eyes looked, 352
something to, God lends us, 463
sometimes called brotherly, 1081
sought is good, 55
speak low if you speak, 38
speaks, when, 41
spring of, 33, 315
still retains some deathless chains, 432
stony limits cannot hold, 78
straitened him, of an old, 470
sublimes my, 1023
such, as spirits feel, 303
such I believe my, 1023
sure my, is all crost, 389
swears she is made of truth, 109
sweet are the words of, 618
sweet as, 1059
sweet love, and for, 536
takes my voice away, 718
tale of wayward, 685
taught him shame, 176
ten thousand fathoms deep, 760
than fear, rule by, 473
thank Heaven for a good man's, 50
that asketh love again, 567
that asks no questions, 747
that can be reckon'd, beggary in, 104
that circles home, 403
that comes too late, 53
that common cure of, 1036
that giveth in full store, 567
that is in my heart, 1065
that makes undaunted, 747
that makes us grateful, 1065
that makes us rich, 1065
that never falters, 747
that pays the price, 747
that should help you to live, 633
that so desires, 575
that stands the test, 747
that the winged seraphs, 459
that they sing that they, 146
that took an early root, 423
that was more than love, we loved with a, 459

Love that was sleeping, 937
  that we knew of yore, old old, 649
  that's wise, 808
  the game beyond the prize, 764
  the more, now, 201
  the offender, 216
  the pest of, 382
  the sure sweet cement glue and lime of, 133
  thee, but I do, 102
  thee dear so much, 168
  thee Doctor Fell, I do not, 188
  thee, how do I, 429
  thee, I but know that I, 336
  thee, none knew thee but to, 363
  thee still, with all thy faults I, 264
  their lords, women who, 248
  their lovers, women, 1044
  they conquer, that run away, 141
  they who inspire, 367
  this bud of, 78
  this is my home of, 108
  tho' given in vain, true, 470
  thoughts of, 464
  three more, am like to, 163
  thy life nor hate, nor, 155
  thy neighbour as thyself, 1099, 1115
  thyself last, 73
  to do, some noble work of, 474
  to hatred turned, like, 193
  to have known, 630
  to light, through, 672
  to lips we are near make, 335
  to me was wonderful, 1100
  to reward the love, creates, 486
  to see all things and not my, 26
  to woman is life or death, 718
  too divine to, 363
  too young for puppy, 824
  took away, 336
  triumph in redeeming, 280
  true, is never blind, 557
  trust thou thy, 533
  truth of truths is, 507
  tunes the shepherd's reed, 306
  unfit for ladies', 176
  united, bonds of, 120
  unkynde, 257
  unrelenting foe to, 225
  unreturned has its rainbow, 750
  unto others is cast, as, 714
  vows of the first lover, 660
  wakes men once a lifetime, 556
  was consummated, by, 644
  was false, when, 938
  was loveliest, 619
  was the pearl of his oyster, 632
  was young, here we came when, 757
  waters cannot quench, 1110
  we cannot fight for, 42
  well to be off with the old, 611
  were begun, 736
  were what the rose is, 631
  were young, if all the world and, 21
  what we choose, make, 833

Love what we give, 506
  when I, thee not chaos is come, 102
  when silence speaks for, 617
  when we love them, not to, 1035
  whence descended wisdom and, 572
  which greybeards call divine, 71
  while still 'tis yours, O, 1070
  wholesome stars of, 470
  wholly could escape, 1017
  whom none can, 246
  whose eyelids dropped, 959
  will creep in service, 14
  will do no wrong, 556
  will dream and faith will trust, 444
  will find out the way, 258, 864
  will not grieve for thy, 632
  wish for our, 887
  with all their quantity of, 97
  with an all-embracing, 1074
  with as much, as his friends, 181
  with night, all the world in, 79
  with the innocence of, 55
  with their own graces, in, 390
  without his wings, 361
  woman I, 921
  woman's whole existence, 358
  worthy of your, 297
  would be merely you, 893
  would have the lily win, 814
  would prove so hard, 669
  wroth with one we, 315
  years of, have been forgot, 459
  you happy wayfarer, 873
  you still may keep, 1070
  young, may go to Jericho, 334
  your enemy bless your haters, 471
  your eyes were filled with, 521
  your life, poor as it is, 515
  your neighbour's wife, 398
Loves and lures, the, 631
  as gay and fleeting, to, 431
  endure, weeps that no, 632
  faithfull, 24
  his native country best, who, 471
  kills the thing he, 722
  me best that calls me Tom, 129
  me must, for who, 470
  more readily than it hates, 422
  never think she, him, 883
  not wine woman and song, 481
  oblique, 169
  of many a mood, 633
  to hear himself talk, 79
  to revel in a summer, sound, 459
  where are the, 841
Love's altar-stone, Mizpah, 658
  arrows make, invisible wounds, 50
  best habit is a soothing tongue, 109
  captive in, locks, 609
  devoted flame, 336
  disappointment endears, 493
  fire still burns, 690
  harbinger the evening star, 155

Love's heralds should be thoughts, 79
  highway of humility, 840
  holy flame, 322
  land, walked in, 796
  of, bestowing and so good-night, 607
  old drink of Yule, 600
  old songs, 600
  perfect blossom, 556
  picture or letter under the pillow, 617
  repaid with scorn, 269
  ripening breast, 385
  ritornella, 387
  sake only, except for, 429
  shock, withstand, 851
  sweet smart, 911
  tender human touch, 682
  true instinct, 335
  wound, purple with, 42
  young dream, 335
Loved and known, shall I miss the, 568
  and lost, better to have, 468
  and near she lies, 911
  and still loves, 289
  arts which I, 167
  ashamed of being, 1044
  at first sight, 28, 31
  at home, revered abroad, 284
  but one, sighed to many, 352
  by me, to love and be, 459
  Caesar less, not that I, 83
  dear, lad, 285
  gold in special, 5
  heart that has truly, 335
  her that she did pity them, 100
  him for himself alone, 279
  him not, sour to them that, 74
  him, use him as though you, 140
  how honoured, how, 217
  I never, a tree or flower, 590
  I not honour more, 168
  I saw and, 28, 271
  in vain, I know we, 351
  lad convenience snug a treacherous inclination, 285
  let those who always, 201
  like to be told I am, 521
  long since, which I have, 484
  me for the dangers, 100
  me still the same, dreamt that you, 386
  needs only to be seen, to be, 174
  no sooner, but they sighed, 51
  none without hope e'er, 239
  not wisely but too well, 103
  one all together, and the, 493
  passing well, 92
  Rome more, but that I, 83
  sae blindly, had we never, 287
  sae kindly, had we never, 287
  so long and sees no more, 289
  the great sea, 350
  the stars too fondly, 661
  the world, I have not, 353
  three whole days together, I have, 163
  to plead lament and sue, 307
  when all was young, you, 523
  which I have, long since, 403
  who never, before, 201
Love-darting eyes, 158

Love-gift of a fairy-tale, 598
Love-in-idleness, maidens call it, 42
Love-lamps in the casement, 482
Lovelier face, finer form or, 308
  things have mercy, 355
Loveliest lassie, she's the, 388
  last still, 354
  of lovely things, 372
  of trees the cherry, 742
  the, ever was seen, 388
  village of the plain, 250
  when love was, 619
Love-light lies — and lies, 336
Loveliness, dream of, descending, 559
  fashioned forth its, 651
  I never knew her, 386
  increases, its, 382
  is enough, 655
  keeps house, 774
  lay down in her, 315
  made up of, alone, 405
  majesty of, 356
  needs not ornament, 224
  which once he made more love-ly, 366
  yet not without such, 837
Lovely and pleasant in their lives, 1100
  and soothing death, come, 536
  apparition sent, 299
  as a Lapland night, 299
  as you are, 924
  blooming fresh and gay, 276
  fair, who art so, 103
  female shapes complicators, 606
  fighting along the whole line, 604
  floating hair, 600
  I say the world is, 655
  in her husband's eye, 295
  in sun and shadow, 712
  in thy youthful grace, 373
  in your strength, 353
  is the rose, 301
  more, than Pandora, 152
  O amiable, death, 58
  organ of her life, every, 40
  pictures still shall bloom, 662
  pupils fear to chill, 226
  river, a, 810
  she's, she's divine, 362
  Thais sits beside thee, 176
  the brave deserve the, 559
  thing, fold each, 445
  thou art, 886
  thought to mark the hours, 370
  whatsoever things are, 1121
  when decked with the comforts of home, 333
  woman stoops to folly, 253
  you were not, 905
Love-match a failure, 802
Love-quarrels oft in pleasing con-cord end, 157
Lover all as frantic, 43
  all mankind love a, 411
  and find a foe, scratch a, 918
  and the poet, the lunatic, 43
  and the young of soul, 839
  beauty grows familiar to, 194
  been so great a, 894
  disturbs an absent, 1034
  e'er do as I did, 755

Lover, give repentance to her, 254
  happy as a, 300
  having been your, 789
  I am a, 841
  in the husband lost, 239
  lieth, everywhere a, 929
  like an island shore, no, 824
  loose or hold me fast, 632
  of all beauty, 445
  of life, 692
  of lost hours, no dearer, 579
  of poetry can spare Chaucer, no, 412
  of pompous title, no, 20
  of the Lord shall trust in Him, 561
  or nightingale, for, 711
  receive him as thy, 898
  required in every good, 1037
  rooted stays, the, 411
  sighing like furnace, 49
  still an angel appear to each, 201
  sulk no more, 937
  their millionth millionth, 914
  to listening maid, 372
  wailing for her demon, 315
  who unlocks his heart, 134
  why so pale and wan, 163
  without indiscretion, 651
  woman loves her, 359
Lovers, a pair of star-cross'd, 77
  alas for, 759
  anger of, renews the strength of love, 19
  are commonly industrious, 1036
  are losers, tell me if, 854
  between true, 933
  cannot see their pretty follies, 45
  eloped in the dark, 673
  find their peace at last, 881
  happy, and make two, 216
  imaginary world of, 732
  like sunset and sunrise, 613
  love the western star, 306
  meeting, journeys end in, 54
  never tired of each other, 1044
  of idle hours, 757
  of virtue, all that are, 140
  old, are soundest, 128
  quarrels of, 979
  Romans countrymen and, 82
  swear more performance than they are able, 75
  whispering, 250
  who love truly, 1078
  women love their, 1044
Lover's hell, injured, 153
  ghost, some old, 117
  loss, voice of woe for a, 517
  pride, blithesomely with, 757
  star, the, 798
Lovers' litany, hear the, 776
  meeting, of, 744
  perjuries, Jove laughs at, 78
  perjury, Jove but laughs at, 176
  songs turned to holy psalms, 28
  thoughts, a pansy for, 28
  tongues by night, 78
Love-rhymes, regent of, 41
Lovesick, the winds were, 104

Lovesome thing, 583
Loving and laughing and free, 866
  and lovely of yore, 452
  and serving, 't is, 501
  are the daring, the, 565
  dot over the i of, 1085
  heart to thee, I will give a, 133
  hearts divide, 675
  hearts, shutting away of, 917
  lady moon whom are you, 459
  little lore of, 649
  never call it, 428
  to my mother, so, 90
  youth large lusty, 535
Low ambition and the pride, 206
  and humble, hymn of the, 533
  and pensive sound, 369
  and trembling tone, in, 658
  bend, 619
  death makes equal high and, 11
  degree, curs of, 254
  foreheads villanous, 33
  in his seemed musical and, 524
  it is not that I deem them, 590
  lay him low lay him, 552
  lintel of the human heart, 840
  lone song, hear but their, 500
  man never falls so, 477
  my work is done, lay me, 601
  nothing useless is or, 436
  raise and support, what is, 148
  so, that none could miss, 687
  speak, if you speak love, 38
  to Him no high no, 207
  to whisper, 625
  too, they build, 202
  uplift the trodden, 575
  voice calling fancy, 484
  when my light is, 468
Low-backed, looked after the, car, 389
  she sat in the, car, 389
Low-breathed or loudest, shrill or deep, 503
Lowells talk only to Cabots, 752
Lower, bright suns scorch and dark clouds, 404
  can fall no, 142
Lowers between this time and that, 454
  the morning, 194
Lowest and most dejected thing of fortune, 99
  deep a lower, in the, 151
  ranks, work up from the, 519
Low-hung clouds, 349
Lowing herd winds slowly, 244
  of the herds, 955
Lowland and range fair meadow, 831
Lowliest cot, better to love in the, 545
Lowliness ambition's ladder, 82
Lowly born, better to be, 73
  earth to vaulted skies, from, 521
  haunts, for love hath, 406
  lives, 612
  taught, highly fed and, 53
Lown, called the tailor, 101
Loyal and neutral in a moment, 86
  be to loyal friends, 910

Loyal hope survives, 612
  nature and of noble mind, 471
  to your highest, 895
Loyalties, impossible, 548
  life's fine, 648
Loyalty, follow with truth and, 48
  map of honour truth and, 69
Lubricates business, dinner, 275
Lucas crushed with chains, 764
Lucent and large signories, 920
Lucerne, lion at, 621
Lucid in that second birth, 626
  interval, 183
  intervals, 1038
  moments, he has, 1066
Lucidity of soul, sad, 546
Lucifer, city and proud seat of, 155
Lucius, fast asleep, 82
Luck about the house, nae, 269
  and chance, sense of, 731
  bad, soberly comes, 640
  best of, 679
  God put another in for, 763
  grumble at his, 967
  in literary reputation, no, 411
  in odd numbers, 35, 389
  insulted you as lady, 923
  is a chance, 743
  is infatuated with the efficient, 414
  it was to land upon almost the only rock, 403
  of Edenhall, 433
  old shoe for, 13
  shallow men believe in, 414
  the determining factor, 836
  till with good, 966
  to be away, in, 674
  to be unhampered, 1076
  true, consists not in, 640
  watching his, 844
  would have as good, 1033
  would have it, as good, 35
Luckiest he who knows when, 640
Luckless pots he marr'd, 1019
Lucknow, silver domes of, 443
Lucky hit, but a, 199
  who gets the most tolerable one is, 976
Lucre, not greedy of filthy, 1121
Lucrece swears he did her wrong, 107
Lucullus dines with Lucullus, 998
Lucy ceased to be, when, 296
  should be dead, if, 296
Ludlow fair, I have been to, 743
Lug, let me whisper i' your, 285
Lugger, once aboard the, 957
Luke the beloved physician, 1121
Lumber, learned, in his head, 212
  of the world, 185
Luminous self-possession of ships, 938
Lump of clay beside a rose, 560
Luna, lux of, 951
Lunatic asylum in the suburbs of Jerusalem, 741
  asylum place where optimism flourishes, 740
  fringe in reform movements, 734
  lover and the poet, 43
Lunatics, treat great men as, 1077

Luncheon clubs are unsatisfactory, 926
Lungs, arbitrary stomach as well as, 247
  began to crow, 49
  blast from the, 905
  receive our air, 264
Lurch, a wink and a sly normal, 508
Lure more strong, a, 685
  of green things, 755
  time stoops to no man's, 632
Luscious as locusts, 101
Lust for comfort, 879
  not serving shame or, 650
  of gold, the narrowing, 469
  of office does not kill, 522
Lusts or wine, not in toys or, 167
Lustre amid the stars, like the, 586
  doubtful, of a jewel, 10
  liquescent and nebulous, 461
  ne'er could any, see, 279
  purpled with rosy, 220
  shine with such, 266, 267
Lusty days of long ago, 452
  loving, youth large, 535
  winter, 48
  young, kill the, 879
Lute, heart-strings are a, 460
  little rift within the, 470
  musical as Apollo's, 41, 158
  Orpheus with his, 73
  this time-worn, 337
Lutes were strung, 482
Luthany, pass the gates of, 749
Luther preaches it, wisdom, 414
  sang, sing as Martin, 481
Luther's dike or Calvin's dam, 453
Luve is like a red red rose, my, 287
  is like the melodie, 287
  of life's young day, 389
Luvit ilk ither weel, we, 389
Lux of Luna, lit by, 951
Luxuries, afford the most unnecessary, 802
  most of the, positive hindrances, 514
  of life, give us the, 454
  of life, trade in the, 1077
Luxurious man falsely, 224
Luxury and indolence, parent of, 973
  blesses his stars and thinks it, 194
  curst by heaven, 251
  do without any article of, 387
  furious in, 779
  in self-dispraise, there is a, 302
  morality a private and costly, 636
  of doing good, 187, 249, 280
  of scepticism, 1081
  of woe, I'll taste the, 333
  to be, it was a, 316
  to gratify avarice and, 1051
Lyciscus' beauty rules, 984
Lydian airs, lap me in soft, 160
  measures, softly sweet in, 176
  notes of Andrew Carnegie, 714
Lyf so short, the, 971
Lyfe so short the craft so long, 3, 433

Lying brown and bare, fields are, 552
  let me have no, 57
  vainness, babbling drunkenness, 56
  with houris, 246
  world is given to, 63
Lyke as one pease is to another, 23
Lym, spaniel brach or, 99
Lynn, set out from, 391
Lyons looms, weave no more silks ye, 522
Lyre, beauty of the minstrel's, 816
  forgot, long years my, 649
  forgot, my, 983
  had been discovered, 528
  heaven-taught, 239
  like half a silver, 920
  of gold, 693
  smote 'is blooming, 784
  the living, 244
Lyric, I would be the, 620
  lord of England's lordliest singers, 634
  love, 490
  splendid ecclesiastical, 421
Lyrical grave or satirical musical miracle, 805
Lytton Bulwer, Sir Bulwer Lytton or, 400

Ma'am Allison learned, 569
Mab, Queen, hath been with you, 77
Mabel, ain't it awful, 870
Macassar, incomparable oil, 358
Macaulay is a book in breeches, 313
  is cocksure of everything, 332
  out of literature, 313
Macbeth does murder sleep, 86
  shall never vanquished be, 87
Macdonald sits, wherever, is the head of the table, 414
Macduff, lay on, 89
Macedon, fulmined over Greece to, 156
  there is a river in, 67
Macedonia and help us, come into, 1118
MacGregor, my name is, 310
  where sits, 414
Machiavel, every country hath its, 1023
  had ne'er a trick, 143
  says virtue and riches, 124
Machine called man, 496
  made to live, 1061
  pulse of the, 299
  unpassioned beauty of a great, 894
Machines, human beings into mere, 1072
  for making more machines, 826
  slaves instead of masters, 740
  that equity demands, 618
Machinery of the state, 331
  proper book-making, 337
Mackerel by moonlight, 320
  cheap as stinking, 62
Macrobius, quote Aulus Gellius or, 1031
Mad as a March hare, 17, 1041

Mad, break out and go, 850
cause and senseless burden, 922
fust gits, 's 'most ollers wrong, 527
heroes dare, 657
idolatry, 75
if I am Sophocles I am not, 967
it is fitter being sane than, 490
it was, how sad bad and, 489
merry music that set us a-dancing, 600
much learning doth make thee, 1119
on one point, more or less, 785
out of too much learning, 126
pleasure in being, 179
prose run, 213
quite certain to fall, 379
saint run, 214
they first make, 175
't is true he is, 92
undevout astronomer is, 202
we are, 991
whom fortune makes, 990
wind's panther cry, 905
with drinking, 728
with glee, morning birds were, 619
world mad as Bedlam, 496
Madam Bad Luck soberly comes, 640
Blaize, lament for, 252
Madcap galloping chase, 365
me no madam, 947
Sorrow scorns all this, 1066
Madden it, made a mannikin to, 461
round the land, 212
to crime, now, 355
Maddest merriest day, 463
Madding crowd, far from the, 245
Made a foe, makes no friend who never, 471
annihilating all that's, 169
better by their presence, minds, 520
fearfully and wonderfully, I am, 1106
glorious summer, 71
his eldest son slave, 591
light of it, 1115
me, don't think nobody never, 480
no more bones, 1033
our nation free, thy hand hath, 451
to fade and fall away, 446
Madman beats upon a drum, as a, 129
either a liar or a, 1055
lived, if he like a, 1043
Madmen know, none but, 179
seize the story, 889
Madness caused by thinking, 728
count with men for, 952
despondency and, 297
from my lips would flow, 367
genius has a touch of, 991
go you may call it, 289
great wits allied to, 173
in the brain, work like, 315
is or is not the loftiest intelligence, 461
less infernal, 728
lies, that way, 98

Madness, life is their, 922
melancholy, of poetry, 261
method in, 92
midsummer, this is very, 55
moon-struck, 155
of maintaining, 1052
of many for gain of a few, 217
on them shut, circular, 937
species of, 1049
still he did retain that fine, 30
strike with no, 924
to defer, 201
to live like a wretch and die rich, 123
Madonnas, Rafael of the dear, 488
Madrigals, hope to hear some, 936
melodious birds sing, 31
that whisper softness, 163
Maenad of Massachusetts, rampant, 635
Magazine filled with all the weapons and engines, 376
of matter, out of the general, 144
with a paid circulation, to a, 931
Magazines, graves of little, 882
into the big, 811
of myth, 851
that died to make verse free, 882
Magdalena's grace, 478
Magic casements, 383
comes, still the, 842
flood me, with their, 801
fold, within its, 630
hinges, turns on, 866
in the distance, 864
it is a deadly, 928
matter, trifling handful of, 569
numbers and persuasive sound, 193
of a cheerful face, 451
of a face, 141
of a name, 327
of the sea, 436
of the tongue most dangerous spell, 426
potent over sun and star, 303
preservation in the pages of books, 381
shadow-shapes, row of, 1019
Shakespeare's, 178
turn this bronze, shall, 897
wand, the, 746
words or phrases, 917
Magical tie there's a, 511
Magister artis, 171
Magistracy is a great trust, 188
Magistrate of his country's good, 374
Magna Charta will have no sovereign, 21
est veritas et praevalet, 1123
Magnanimity of thought, 201
sensuous joy of, 1072
Magnet and the steel, you are the, 936
as true as a, 435
man is a, 1068
Magnetic heartstrings, 633
Magnificence comes after, 324
fuel of, 413
of the dead, 905

Magnificent and awful cause, 265
but it is not war, 1070
spectacle of human happiness, 314
three-tailed Bashaw, 288
Magnify, the high heart, 873
Magnifying-glass, beneath a, 725
Magnitude, liar of the first, 193
Magnolia trees, gossip in, 905
Magnolia-blossoms star the twilight, 443
Magyars are a very old race, 418
Mahogany furniture, like having, 1068
tree, shelter about the, 481
Mahomet and the mountain, 110
moon of, 367
to Moses, passed from, 405
Mahometans, pleasures of the, 246
Mahone, sweet Belle, 579
Mahoun, some calling on, 374
Maid, be good sweet, 523
dwelling in Scarlet towne, 257
Good-Fortune is a giddy, 1066
here lies our little, 822
is for him who can know her, 751
it was an Abyssinian, 315
lover to listening, 372
maiden passion for a, 471
meek as is a, 5
nor matron grieve, 373
of all work, a, 437
of Athens ere we part, 351
of the mill, remember the, 582
snatched from the sidelong, 224
snivelling servant, 879
sphere-descended, 248
sweetest garland to the sweetest, 205
the chariest, 90
to the heart of a, 778
was young, Music heavenly, 247
when King Cophetua loved the beggar, 78
who fears to be disgraced, 226
who modestly conceals, 240
whom there were none to praise, 296
widow nor wife, neither, 37
Maids are May when they are maids, 51
in clinging gowns of golden, 914
in modesty, say No, 33
mortal, 326
must be wives and mothers, 454
of thirteen talk of puppy dogs, 57
that weave thread with bones, 54
weeping at home, 432
were old, her, 358
who love the moon, 334
Maide, wydowe or wyffe, 10
Maiden, a foolish little, 653
a neater sweeter, 782
deny thee, if a, 776
in her flower, 462
lived with no other thought, 459
meditation fancy-free, 42

Maiden of bashful fifteen, 279
　only, love one, 471
　passion for a maid, the, 471
　presence, scanter of your, 91
　rose-lipt, 743
　shame, blush of, 372
　sings, the village, 249
　sword, bravely fleshed thy, 63
　was delighted, 667
　will steal after her heart, the,
　　335
　with white fire laden, 366
　young and fair, dwelt a, 582
　young heart of a, 335
Maidens, as many, be, 386
　call it love-in-idleness, 42
　caught by glare, like moths,
　　352
　fair are commonly fortunate,
　　23
　in the little town, 653
　quiet eyes, young fair, 703
　smiles of other, 387
　withering on the stalk, 42,
　　301
Maiden's hair is tumbled, 706
Maiden-fair wine-scented and po-
　etic soul, 703
Maidenhead, bringeth ill to, 929
Maid-servant the sailor and the
　schoolboy, 347
Mail, need of triple, 886
Mails from the north east south
　west, 347
Maimed mind, 147
　the halt and the blind, the, 832
Main, beyond the western, 250
　Camilla skims along the, 211
　chance, 23, 68, 143, 198
　comes silent flooding in the,
　　519
　far amid the melancholy, 225
　from out the azure, 225
　mixed with the, 663
　Street bordered with autumn
　　leaves, 890
　three hundred to the, 600
　unravelled from the, 406
Mainbrace of the mind, 893
Maine, compares with, 707
　here's to the, 683
Mainly right, wise world is, 470
Mainspring of his own volition,
　715
Maintain his argument, he will,
　66
　no ill opinions, 251
Maintenance of justice, 1127
Mair they talk I'm kend the bet-
　ter, 285
Majestic equable sedate, 503
　silence, 342
　though in ruin, 150
　world, get the start of the, 81
Majesty, attribute to awe and, 46
　in rayless, 201
　insult dying, 961
　next in, 175
　obsequious, approved, 154
　of loveliness, 356
　rising in clouded, 152
　this earth of, 59
　unspeakable and dread, O, 503
　will rise in, 524
Majesty's free and loyal subjects,
　His, 950

Major and minor poets, 931
Majors we can make every year,
　123
Majorities have been wrong, 580
　is as much, decision by, 450
Majority, long since death had
　the, 145
　of its inhabitants, 318
　of men live content, 1023
　of one, constitutes a, 514
　one on God's side is a, 479
　stirred by ignoble motives, 802
　the compact, 1075
Make a deacon swear, enough to,
　527
　a note of, when found, 496
　a sky, why you should n't, 569
　history, while we read we, 558
　languor smile, 213
　let us die to, men free, 522
　man did not, and can not mar,
　　546
　me a child again, 595
　me to know mine end, 1104
　men holy, as He died to, 522
　my throne on a, and I, 448
　paths to the house I seek to,
　　537
　the angels weep, 36
　yourself necessary to some-
　　body, 414
Make-believe, no time for, 933
　seen through the, 816
Maker and the angel death, his,
　317
Makes a man, and all that, 471
　his promise good, 185
　me or fordoes me, 103
　my gain, every way, 103
　no friend who never, he, 471
　on its desolate sands, 503
　sech nights all white and still,
　　527
　some floweret blow, rain-drop,
　　504
　that and the action fine, 135
　up the sum of living, 565
　us or it mars us, 103
　what, his dawning glow, 416
Maketh haste to be rich, 1108
Making beautiful old rhyme, 108
　many books there is no end,
　　1110
　night hideous, 91
　of man, the, 633
　pies, and went to, 557
　the green one red, 86
　them, I am always, 449
　through creeks and inlets, 519
Maladies, asthma and seven
　other, 313
　people are liable to in cold
　　weather, 402
　which are less conspicuous, 969
Malady, medicine worse than the,
　127
　of not marking, 64
Malaria's countless treasons, 811
Malbrook s'en va t'en guerre mi-
　ronton, 483
Malcontents, loiterers and, 41
　thou art the Mars of, 34
Male and female tissue, 903
　more deadly than the, 781
　never yet walked, 880
　sadly susceptible, 755

Malefactors of great wealth, 734
Male-lands, loved all the more by
　earth's, 486
Malice, bearing no, 291
　domestic foreign levy, 87
　envy hatred and, 1127
　hold out against, 1046
　in his mind, he had no, 404
　nor set down aught in, 103
　of the storm, 199
　toward none, charity for all,
　　806
　towards none, 457
Malicious have a dark happiness,
　1067
Malign an opponent, arguments
　to, 420
Malignant its inventor, 943
Malignity, motiveless, 319
Malindy sings, when, 820
Mallecho, this is miching, 94
Malmsey and Malvoisie, 647
Malt does more than Milton, 743
　Duke of Norfolk deals in, 363
　stored in many a plethoric
　　sack, 543
Mambrino's helmet, 1035
Mammon, from the service of,
　1127
　is like fire, 378
　least erected spirit, 149
　wins his way, 352
　ye cannot serve God and, 1114
Mammy heered him holler, 696
Man a flower he dies, 231
　a fool at forty, 203
　a great bad, 395
　a hundred years of age, 166
　a merrier, 41
　a plain blunt, 83
　a reasonable creature, 162
　a, sat on a rock, 664
　a single cell becomes a, 581
　a tailless, 665
　a thinking being, 344
　a two-legged animal, 1015
　after his desert, use every, 93
　after his own heart, 1100
　after sleep, like a strong, 163
　aid to every poor, 1049
　all that a, hath, 1101
　all that may become a, 85
　all that was pleasant in, 252
　alone is poor, 402
　already in no mean Paradise,
　　641
　alter the condition of a, 76
　always adores, ignorant, 1078
　always better than a book, 753
　among men, 706
　an animal and a piece of scar-
　　let serge, 930
　an ape or an angel, is, 419
　an honest, is aboon his might,
　　287
　an honest, like the true reli-
　　gion, 950
　an inconstant creature, 1001
　and a Positivist, 569
　and all that makes a, 471
　and beast, punishment in, 1080
　and brother, am I not a, 941
　and fold me, be a, 485
　and his Maker, between, 354
　and nature scorn the shocking
　　hat, 451

Man and of virtue, ideal of, 1074
  and the citizen disappear, 1074
  and the just, is afraid, 375
  and wife for a year and a day, 310
  and wife to live together, 997
  and woman enter paradise together, 617
  and woman together, I marry this, 191
  any military, in the world, 66
  apparel oft proclaims the, 91
  appeal to any white, 249
  appoints and God disappoints, 1042
  architect of his fortune, 111
  arms and the, I sing, 177
  arose, whence, 898
  as a dying, to dying men, 166
  as good kill a, as kill a good book, 162
  as happy as any in the world, 181
  as he is humour the, 980
  as the indignant, 1080
  asleep sight to make angels weep, 801
  assurance of a, 95
  at a station, 499
  at all times, necessary for, 1063
  at arms must now serve on his knees, 28
  at his best state, 1104
  at his birth, 993
  at his worst is the real, 750
  at the point of death, a, 1051
  at the turn-pike bar, 389
  at the wheel, 655
  at thirty, suspects himself a fool, 201
  attend, joys the, 942
  back to health, sick, 967
  bad, never for good service, 261
  bad, war never slays, 966
  be done with hunger, 967
  be drunk for ever, could, 743
  be fully persuaded, let every, 1119
  be insensible, can any, 1051
  be vertuous withal, if a, 8
  be wise, though a, 965
  bear his own burden, 1121
  bear with all the faults of, 121
  before thy mother, 132
  before your mother, 132, 267
  begins to see that the leaves, 440
  being in honour, 1104
  being too proud to fight, 724
  believes he shall ever die, no young, 330
  below, God above or, 207
  bend other faces, around the, 326
  Benedick the married, 38
  best good, 184
  best-humoured, 252
  better spared a better, 63
  between man and, 111
  beware the fury of a patient, 174
  bewrayed by his manners, 25
  bites a dog, when a, 677
  blush, make, 357

Man, bold bad, 24, 72
  brave, chooses, 525
  brave, draws his sword, 219
  breathes there the, 307
  brick-dust, 229
  broken with the storms of state, 74
  Brutus is an honourable, 83
  builds no structure, 660
  built up again to a whole, 144
  by, is cursed alway, 431
  by man was never seen, 501
  by the name of Skavar, 951
  by which the bark of, could navigate, 393
  called, machine, 496
  came to the making of, 633
  can be a patriot, no, 714
  can be absolutely true to himself, no, 476
  can be idle, happy age when a, 344
  can boast that he has trod, 374
  can die but once, 65
  can play the pipes, 774
  can work, when no, 1118
  cannot be as he would be, 980
  cannot be happy alone, 667
  cannot emerge from himself, 1087
  cannot live without playing the knave, 181
  cannot lose the past nor future, 1009
  canst not be false to any, 91
  capable of devotion, 645
  capitalist is a practical, 1071
  caverns measureless to, 315
  certain of immortality, 727
  cheated only by himself, 411
  child is father of the, 297
  child should grow into the, 439
  childhood shows the, 156
  Christian faithful, 71
  city the teacher of the, 960
  civilizers of, 419
  clever at envying a, 959
  clever, by nature, 290
  close-buttoned to the chin, 266
  clothe a, with rags, 1108
  coldest that ever turned up ace, 105
  complete, hero and the, 194
  conceited, is satisfied, 818
  conference maketh a ready, 111
  consists of body mind and imagination, 835
  consumes a, more quickly, 1082
  contact with a religious, 1082
  could act as he chose, 1076
  could ask no more of Fate, 528
  could call me a fussy, 876
  could ease a heart, 918
  could moult, if, 691
  covetous, ever in want, 985
  crime of being a young, 239
  crueltie and ambition of, 22
  cruelty to load a falling, 74
  dare do all that may become a, 85
  Darwinian, 624
  dead, cannot bite, 999
  debtor to his profession, 109
  deep infinite faculties of, 380
  delights not me, 92

Man depressed with cares, 205
  der shturdy oak, 661
  destroy the eye of another, 958
  destructive, smiling, 186
  devil in the heart of, 144
  diapason closing full in, 176
  die better, how can, 400
  die shall he live again, if a, 1102
  dies, how a, 235
  dies on a tree, 886
  dies, when a, 959
  dies, when a great, 438
  dies, when an old, 935
  diligent in business, 1108
  diseases crucify the soul of, 123
  distracted melancholic, 128
  do but die, what can an old, 390
  does, 't is not what, 486
  dog went mad and bit the, 254
  doth not live by bread only, 1099
  dreams of possessing, 1086
  drest in a little brief authority, 36
  dull ear of a drowsy, 58
  dwells apart though not alone, 540
  dying, to dying men, 166
  ear of, hath not seen, 43
  eloquent, that old, 161
  England expects every, 284
  enough for a tear, 715
  escape, though a, 976
  ever become a rich, 810
  ever saw, nor no, 52
  every, a scribe by trade, 1017
  every, according to his work, 1104
  every, after his desert, 93
  every, architect of his, 981
  every, can tame a shrew, 125
  every, desires to live long, 191
  every, has his fault, 81
  every, has his price, 425
  every, hath a good and bad angel, 122
  every, hath sins enough and trouble enough, 166
  every, is the builder of a temple, 515
  every, is wanted, 412
  every, sat under his, 1125
  every, who has declared, 1079
  every woman should marry and no, 421
  exceeding poor, 45
  exceptional, has missed his way, 1080
  excepts and thins his jury, the guilty, 174
  expatiate o'er this scene of, 206
  eye of, hath not heard, 43
  false man smiling, 186
  falsely luxurious, 224
  far better, know the, 579
  fashion wears out more apparel than the, 39
  fear may force a, 12
  fell into his anecdotage, 421
  finds what he travels for at home, 709
  first in hearts of his countrymen, 281

Man, first, is of the earth earthy, 1120

first years of, 232

fittest place for, to die, 511

flattered to tears this aged, 383

for himself, every, 18, 125, 1036

for his demesne, allowed to, 909

foremost, of all this world, 83

foretells the courses of the stars, 373

fortunes of a, 966

frailty of a, 109

free as nature first made, 178

Friday with me, I took, 187

from Porlock, 879

fury of a patient, 174

gains largely if he has intellectual taste or skill, 413

gazing on the stars, 588

genial courteous intellectual, 1085

gentle plain just and resolute, 536

gently scan your brother, 285

give back the singing, 836

give every, thy ear, 91

go to worship sinful, 728

God or devil, every, 174

goeth forth unto his work, 1105

goeth to his long home, 1110

good easy, when he thinks, 73

good great, 317

good name in, and woman, 102

good old, 39, 48, 404

good or ill of, 1007

good, prolongs his life, 217

goodliest, of men, 152

got to have something to cuss, 852

greater love hath no, 1118

greatest fool is, 1050

had a little soul, 334

had fixed his face, as if the, 296

half part of a blessed, 57

hand against every, 1097

handsome hunting, 823

handsomer, than you, 678

hanging the worst use of, 114

happy as a married, 235

happy, call no, 969

happy citizen free nation great, 1068

happy, confines himself, 422

happy dole, happy, 12

happy is the, 972

happy, 's without a shirt, 11

happy the, 177

happy the innocent, 223

happy, thenceforth is he, 322

has an axe to grind, 333

has assurance enough, what, 1037

has by nature the right, every, 1071

has no ears, 1082

has no home in Europe, 1082

has no morrow, 966

has shop to mind, 492

has usually some sly way of jesting, every rich, 197

Man hath over-greet a wit, 8

have a strong faith, if a, 1081

he felt as a, 269

he's a good, 1034

he that hath no beard is less than a, 38

he was a good and just, 1117

healthy wealthy and wise, 227

hearty old, 320

heaven had made her such a, 100

held up his head, this, 925

her wit was more than, 175

here lies a truly honest, 165

highest style of, 202

his own doctor of divinity, 704

honest as any, living, 39

honest is the only perfect, 126

honest, the noblest work, 208

how poor a thing is, 30

I am the inferior of any, 602

I didn't like, never met a, 859

I know myself a, 115

I know not, the, 994

I love not, the less, 354

I loved in Rome, 916

I marry, that I love the, 860

I might have been, 874

I pray for no, 80

I saw the almighty, 877

I see the steady gain of, 442

I would be, what a, 955

idle, cannot enjoy rest, 605

idle, has so much to do, 639

ignorance of the law excuses no, 130

ignorant without knowledge of the Greeks, 571

imagines he cannot do, 1048

impossible to be cheated, 411

in a state favourable, 1084

in all the integrity, 1055

in all the world's new fashion, 40

in armor is armor's slave, 491

in arms would wish to be, that every, 300

in difficulties, 963

in ignorance sedate, 230

in prosperitee, 4

in the bush with God, 408

in the distant future will, 449

in the making of, 669

in the mind of, 296

in the mire, 80

in the unsearchable darkness, 669

in wit a, 217

indulges himself in murder, if once a, 347

ingratitude in a, 56

inherits honor or wealth, a good great, 317

intimates eternity to, 195

is a bundle of relations, 411

is a knot of roots, 411

is a magnet, 1068

is a mere insect, 643

is a military animal, 507

is a noble animal, 145

is a pliable animal, 1074

is a prisoner, 970

is a reasoning animal, 990

is a rope stretched, 1079

is a social animal, 1049

is a torch, 856

Man is able to master, what, 676

is accommodated, 65

is an ass or a scoundrel, 1079

is as great, poor, 955

is as heaven made him, 1039

is as old as he's feeling, 570

is as true as steel, 79

is born free, 1054

is born unto trouble, 1102

is busy, when a, 487

is but a beast, 258

is but a mind, 662

is by no means poor, 985

is content to know he is loved, 533

is curled, in the average, 732

is dead, once a, 963

is dead, this, 925

is dead, when honor dies the, 442

is found, the race of, 218

is great and strong and wise, 887

is his own architect, 492

is his own star, 126

is immortal sage or fool, 758

is in love, when a, 1081

is in the right, 1076

is little to be envied, that, 233

is man and master of his fate, 470

is mighty, they say that, 534

is never alone, 1007

is not idle, 1068

is not mad, provided a, 1054

is preferred, each, 970

is small potatoes, 786

is so in the way, 475

is so made, 1078

is the gowd for a' that, 287

is the richest, 533

is the richest whose pleasures are cheapest, 515

is thy most awful instrument, 303

is vile, and only, 343

is worth something, 488

it is for each, to procure, 1084

judged by friends and foes, 727

judgment falls upon a, 130

justice the great interest of, 340

kindest, best-conditioned, 46

knotty and tough, the lank, 927

knows what comes after, no, 851

laborin', an' laborin' woman, 526

large-hearted, 427

laugh if such a, there be, 213

lay asleep, a great, 565

lay down his life for his friends, 1118

learns how to value at sixty, 425

let him pass for a, 44

let no guilty, escape, 549

let no such, be trusted, 47

let not, put asunder, 1115

let the end try the, 64

life of a, a poem, 377

life of a, faithfully recorded, 377

life of, a point of time, 1001

life of, less than a span, 112

Man, life of, solitary, 132
like a phonograph, 720
like to a little kingdom, 82
little friend of, 382
little round fat oily, 225
little worse than a, 44
living dead, 38
look sad, near to make a, 43
looked honest enough, 616
lore and pride of, 408
lot of, but once to die, 135
love is a mood to, 718
loves life, no, 967
made the town, 264, 759
made wine to drown trouble, 768
makes friends without half trying, 822
makes his own circumstances, 377
maketh glad the heart of, 1105
man's inhumanity to, 284
many million ages to making of, 581
mark the perfect, 1104
marks the earth with ruin, 354
married, will wait, 782
marry any sort of white, 479
master of his time, 86
may be in good spirits, any, 495
may be sinner or saint, 639
may become proud, vain, 1048
may choose, no, 808
may do, strange what a, 482
may fish with the worm, 96
may grow so weak, 1082
may last but never lives, that, 246
may redeem the past, 711
may see how this world goes, 99
may take money from his wife, 680
may understand what the common talk is, 181
may use without any hurt, 1049
may work from sun to sun, 205
meaning in saying he is a good, 44
meant to be immortal, 421
measure of the height of, 993
meddles with them, 1054
meets his Waterloo, every, 479
melancholic distracted, 128
memory of, runneth not, 248
merit that which he obtains, 317
might be happy all his life, 139
might die of hunger, 1021
might honor and woman trust, 443
might know the end, that, 84
mildest mannered, 359
mind the standard of the, 199
mine equal, it was thou a, 1104
misery acquaints a, 33
mistakes of a good, 950
moneyless, no open door for the, 609
more sinned against, 98
most married, I ever saw, 606
mounts through all the spires, 409
must bear a nation's stain, 763

Man must have patience with his wife, 225
must judge for himself, 449
must mind his belly, 234
must not accept money from a woman, 680
must not swallow beliefs, 741
must play a part, every, 44
must take the fat, 497
my foe, to make one worthy, 213
my son, you'll be a, 783
nameless amid a crowd, 504
nation needed a, 642
naturally persuades himself, 239
nature formed but one such, 356
nature made thee to temper, 185
needs in gardening, what a, 582
needs, what every, 837
never falls so low that, 477
never is but always to be blest, 207
never quite forgets, 628
never was so wise a, before, 437
no, but a blockhead, 236
no, can be living for ever, 817
no, can feel himself alone, 750
no, can justly censure another, 1085
no, can lose what he never had, 140
no, can put you in mind of Johnson, 261
no, can serve two masters, 1114
no, can wear two faces, 422
no Christian, 1077
no creature so blind as, 592
no, deserved less at her hands, 550
no, ever asked a favour, 999
no, ever felt the halter draw, 277
no, ever repented that he rose sober, 166
no evil can happen to a good, 970
no good, grew rich at once, 990
no, happy without a hobby, 695
no, has aught of what he leaves, 97
no, hath walked along our roads, 326
no, having put his hand to the plough, 1117
no, is born an angler, 139
no, is born an artist, 139
no, is wanted much, 412
no, knows what then, 808
no, lives without jostling, 377
no, loseth other life than that which he liveth, 1009
no, loth to sit for portrait, 818
no, of elder years, 879
no right to be a public, 495
no, ruleth safely, 9
no, who is correctly informed, 400
no, wicked at once, 1006
no wiser for his learning, 130
no, would be old, 191

Man, noncommissioned, 782
not a money-chest, 425
not a, who hath not known godlike hours, 299
not able to bear languid rest, 1065
not always, actions show the, 209
not good to be alone, 1097
not made for the Sabbath, 1116
not passion's slave, 94
not so good a Christian, 705
not so great a coward as he thinks, 705
not the best, 456
not the creature of circumstances, 420
nothing more fun than a, 919
nothing so becomes a, 66
nowhere so bisy a, 5
obliged to be thrifty, 908
obtains that which he merits, if a, 317
of action forced into state of thought, 797
of business clergyman also, a, 1016
of cheerful yesterdays, 303
of contention, 1112
of every age and clime, 681
of genius has been seldom ruined, 234
of genius makes no mistakes, 874
of genius pays in affliction, 818
of genius sees the world, how a, 741
of giant frame, 372
of giant mould, 572
of God, round fat oily, 225
of God's own mould, 604
of great estate, hard to find a, 180
of great spirit, chiefest action for a, 128
of his time, no, 1001
of knowledge increaseth strength, 1108
of letters amongst men of the world, 398
of letters has sensitive skin, 589
of men, the goodliest, 152
of mettle, 1040
of mettle, grasp it like a, 204
of morals, why, 167
of most distinguished abilities, 235
of my kidney, 35
of my town, 576
of rank as an author, 237
of renown, I'm a, 954
of sense, tailor is a, 451
of sorrows and acquainted with grief, 1112
of sovereign parts, 41
of strife, 1112
of such a feeble temper, 81
of the future what shall be, 539
of the world amongst men of letters, 215, 398
of toil and care, 578
of unbounded stomach, 74
of worth in his own household, 964
of worth, preferred the, 996

Man of worth, so acts your, 978
office which the false, does easy, 86
old age in this universal, 112
old, and no honester than I, 39
old, broken with storms of state, 74
old, in whom there is something, 981
old, is twice a child, 92
old, may learn many things, 974
old, to have had so much blood, 88
on his oath or bond, 80
on horseback, 945
on the flying trapeze, 640
on the planet, every, 676
one, among a thousand, 1109
one, excel another, 979
one, is appointed to buy the meat, 130
one, with a dream, 676
one worthy, my foe, 213
only knows nothing, 993
ought to be dull sometimes, 196
ought to be inquisitive, 775
overtakes a young, 1072
owe a debt, if a, 958
owes not any, 433
parchment undo a, 69
part of a wise, 1049
partly is and wholly hopes to be, 489
pass unquestioned and bold, 653
past the wit of, 43
patient in loss, 105
patronage of some great, 1085
pays the public, the tax a, 191
peace of thine, did not make, 546
people arose as one, 1099
perceives, soon as a, 985
perils doe enfold the righteous, 24
picked out of ten thousand, 92
plain, is the basic clod, 732
plants a tree for posterity, 589
plays many parts, in his time, 49
poet still more a, 376
poor, being down is thrust, 1125
poorest, in his cottage, 230
prays for, whatever a, 1072
'prentice han' she tried on, 284
present work of present, 316
press not a falling, 73
profited, what is a, 1115
proper, as one shall see, 42
proper judge of the, 991
proper study of, 803
proposes God disposes, 8, 136
proud man, 36
prudent, looketh well, 1107
pure young, 623
reading maketh a full, 111
ready money makes the, 199
recovered of the bite, 254
reduced to want, 199
remote from, 201
repents, will not believe a, 470
rich, beginning to fall, 1125
rides his hobbyhorse, 241

Man, right, in the right place, 513
right judgment of, 376
rights of, 260
rob the average, 1076
robust and brass-bound, 784
rousing herself like a strong, 163
ruins of the noblest, 82
Sabbath was made for, 1116
sadder and a wiser, 315
said to the universe, 813
same kind of, 1068
say go to your, 941
says of the affairs of the state, 1054
says what he knows, 1055
secret thoughts of a, 132
see me more, no, 73
seems the only growth, 249
sees things most widely different, 1081
sensible well-bred, 263
sent from God whose name was John, 1117
sets out to hate, if a, 1063
seven women hold of one, 1111
shall be surpassed, 1079
shall bear his own burden, 1121
shall cast his idols, 1111
shall these paper bullets awe a, 39
shall walk transparent, 337
sharpeneth the countenance, 1108
she had was kind and clean, 919
she knows her, 177
she matches, for a' that, 424
shirt of a happy, 11, 639
should always consider, 197
should be upright, 1010
should choose, 914
should earn his bread, 835
should know something of his own country, 242
should live in a garret, 620
should never be ashamed, 217
should not be alone, 1097
should render a reason for his faith, 312
should surely keep, 965
should wait, 970
sick, is a parasite, 1081
sleep of a labouring, 1109
sleeps, an old, 926
slumbers of the virtuous, 195
smell the blood of a British, 99
snarl and be an angry, 933
so faint so spiritless, 63
so frail a thing is, 947
so much one, can do, 169
so sings, 1065
so unto the, is woman, 436
so various, 173
social friendly honest, 284
soul of, is larger than the sky, 386
soul of, like rolling world, 588
sour-complexioned, 139
soweth that he reaps, 1121
state of, like to a little kingdom, 82
stood up in Panama, 839

Man, strong and well-constituted, 1081
strong, in his wrath, 428
strong, when is, 487
strongest, stands most alone, 487
struggling for life, 233
study of mankind is, 207
such a disagreeable, 623
such affinity with the soul of, 476
such master such, 19
suffers or woman may soothe, wherever, 593
sure he's a talented, 406
suspects himself a fool at thirty, 201
take him for all in all, 90
takes a drink, 659
takes the limits, every, 1063
teach you more of, 295
telle a tale after a, 5
terribly glad to be selling fish, 855
tested, metal of a, 530
than cells and gibbets for the, 512
than comes of music, by, 493
thankless inconsistent, 202
that blushes, 202
that died for men, 639
that endureth temptation, 1122
that feareth Lord to doubt, 559
that first eat an oyster, 192
that fortune's buffets and rewards, 94
that hails you Tom or Jack, 267
that hangs on princes' favours, 73
that has a taste of musick, a, 196
that hath a tongue, 34
that hath friends, 1107
that hath his quiver full, 1106
that hath no music in himself, 47
that I love and honour, 66
that is born of woman, 1102
that is not passion's slave, 94
that lays his hand upon a woman, 295
that low, 487
that made the earth to tremble, 1111
that makes a character, 203
that meddles with cold iron, 24
that mourns, vile, 207
that old, eloquent, 161
that thou art mindful of him, what is, 1103
that was hanged, 1036
that was in th' evening made, 145
that's stubbed his toe, 829
the catholic, 663
the country turns out, 414
the dark cloud, 1079
the delicate child of life, 1089
the first, found that to his cost, 687
the forgotten, 654, 876
the greater courtesy, greater, 471

Man the hermit sighed, 327
the kindest, the best conditioned, 46
the least considerable, 949
the making of, 633
the most austere, 651
the noblest work of, 603
the raggedy, 697
the tragedy, 459
the whole soul of a, 378
the wonder and glory of the universe, 448
there was a little, 334
think himself an act of God, 506
thinks woman profound, 1082
this, and that man fixt, 735
this high, 487
this is the state of, 73
this mongrel beast, this, 898
this was a, say to all the world, 84
thou art the, 1100
thou shalt never die, 350
thoughtless inconsistent, 202
to all the country dear, 250
to fall, caused, 110
to good, ill wind which blows no, 17, 65
to hold against the world, 708
to keep down the base in, 471
to labour in his vocation, 60
to match the mountains, 708
to mend God's work, 175
to remind the, 976
to the last, 65
to whom all Naples is known, 1046
to whom old men hearkened, 1003
to you refused, if a, 966
too fond to rule alone, 213
trubbled with melankolly, 518
turn over half a library, 236
unclubable, 234
under his fig-tree, 1113
unfit to hold office, 997
upon this earth, to every, 400
upright, God hath made, 1109
use doth breed a habit in a, 34
use it lawfully, if a, 1121
used to vicissitudes, 232
useless while he has a friend, no, 705
vain is the help of, 1104
vindicate ways of God to, 206
virtue and riches seldom settle one, 124
vulgar, has triumphed, 1080
wants but little, 202, 254
warning for thoughtless, 302
was a pinhead, 791
was not born with a silver spoon, 1042
weak and despised old, 98
well-bred, will not affront me, 263
well-favoured, to be a, 39
went down from Jerusalem, 1117
went down to Panama, 839
were never made for, 924
what a piece of work is a, 92
what can old, do but die, 390
what, dare I dare, 87
what has been done by, 202

Man, what is good in, 722
what keeps pullin' de grapevine, 712
what manner of, 54
when I became a, 1120
when I get to be a, 809
where he dies for, 511
where lives the, 309
which lighteth every, 1118
who acts the least, 218
who can be out of danger, 564
who can blow hot and cold, 962
who can call, 922
who can keep the whiteness of his soul, 588
who can say he has lived happy, 984
who cannot laugh, 379
who comes up from the crowd, 732
who could make so vile a pun, 186
who craves more, 990
who delivers the goods, 764
who does a thing for the first time, 589
who does himself no wrong, 1023
who during the war, 921
who first invented sleep, 510, 1042
who first invented the art of supporting beggars, 976
who found himself out, 751
who goes alone, 514
who goes with all the shows, 952
who had many friends, 774
who has a city, 973
who has been able to learn, 994
who has had the experience, 921
who has, let the, 877
who has never looked on Niagara, 399
who has no gift of speech, 738
who has no mental needs, 1064
who has none, to the, 1064
who has not yet grown old, 1006
who has nothing to say, 520
who has power and skill, 204
who has too little, 990
who hath never known fame, 426
who idly sits and thinks, 755
who is always achieving, 663
who is completely wise, 1000
who is high up thinks he has done it all, 751
who is not too young, 1006
who knew more and spoke less, 1004
who knows and knows, 706
who knows it all, 669
who leaves memoirs, 1083
who lets himself be bored, 615
who lets the contest fall, 968
who lives for self alone, 657
who looked with wistful eye, 722
who loves again, 1066
who makes the experiment, 985

Man who much receives, 246
who never in his life, 911
who never works, 855
who opens the door, 914
who owes nothing to the land, 1055
who plants cabbages, 649
who plays on the violin, 685
who run, here sleeps the, 698
who seeks one thing, 592
who smokes, 426
who tells his wife all he knows, 147
who tells the truth is disagreeable, 418
who touches this touches a, 538
who turnips cries, 238
who wants a shirt, 252
who was altogether void, 977
whole duty of, 1110
whole, must be greater, 426
whom Fortune hath cruelly scratched, 53
whom the king delighteth to honour, 1101
who's had almost every tooth out, 482
whose acquisitions stick, 663
whose blood is very snow-broth, 35
whose blood is warm within, 44
whose name was Johnny Sands, 941
whose wish and care, 216
whoso would be a, 411
wicked all at once, no, 1006
will do the foolishest thing, 687
will feel all broke up, 661
will go down into the pit, 687
will lord it over his fellow, 729
will pay more, the just, 973
will supply thy want, no, 120
will wait, everything comes if, 421
wills us slaves, 272
wise in his own conceit, 1108
wise, knows himself to be a fool, 51
wise, should have so little influence, 969
wit and wisdom born with a, 130
with a beard, an old, 499
with a dungfork, 673
with a maid, way of a, 1109
with a terrible name, 322
with his burning soul, 832
with his heart in his hand, 478
with soul so dead, 307
with spondulix, woes of the, 714
with thy might, be, 633
within him hide, what may, 37
within this learned, 32
without a tear, 328
without any prejudices, 1078
without feeling, I never see that, 538
without one scar, 997
without passion, 1073
without religion, 551
without riches, 996

Man without self-pity, rare as a, 927
woman is the lesser, 464
woman more barbarous than, 1080
woman younger than a, 430
worth makes the, 208
would die when the brains were out, 87
would do, what, 486
writing maketh an exact, 111
written out of reputation, 187
yields up his trust, 348
you'll walk like a, 753
young, in Boston town, 451
young, in whom there is something, 981
young, married is man marr'd, 53
young, pension never enriched, 137
Man's affairs, however little, 234
aims, above, 595
alphabet, 657
animal spirits, flow of a, 1071
apparel, every true, 37
beard, to shave a, 1035
bedevilment and God's, 743
best things are nearest him, 458
blood, whoso sheddeth, 1097
books, 657
brains, exudations of a, 241
brows, sweat of a, 241
capacity to despise himself, 770
censure, take each, 91
certainty, 785
cheeks, stain my, 98
contumely, the proud, 93
conversation, an eminent, 426
creative hand, 500
days have been a mixture, 804
derling, old, 17
desire, end of every, 632
destinye to dye before his day, 255
distinctive mark, 489
dominion, 572
dying, a, 1089
erring judgment, 210
estate, relief of, 112
every wise, son, 54
eye, watch in every old, 78
eyes, to a brave, 967
face, nose on a, 33, 125
feast, sat at any good, 49
felicities, of all, 911
first disobedience, 148
foot, rung to hold a, 563
fortune, mould of a, 111
friendships invalidated by marriage, 614
genius is a deity, 1006
good qualities, see a, 376
ground, built on another, 34
hand against him, every, 1097
hand, cloud like a, 1101
hand is not able to taste, 43
heart deviseth his way, 1107
heart, which strengthens, 188
honest will, 513
house his castle, 21
illusion given, for, 336
imperial race, 212
ingratitude, unkind as, 50

Man's ingress to the world, 276
inhumanity to man, 284
injustice to beasts, 1006
leg the best, 701
life, he took a, 378
life, how good is, 486
life is but a jest, 577
love, a good, 50
love is a thing apart, 358
memory, a great, 94
merit in a, knowing, 378
might, to be wise and love exceeds, 75
mind, interested in, 709
mortality, watch o'er, 302
naked foot, print of a, 187
nature, art is, 506
nature runs to revenge, 109
noble memories, 736
nobler hopes, 736
own littleness, 380
own, to get a, 185
perdition to be safe, 410
peril comes of bed, all of, 610
poison, what's one, 132
power of action, 1048
power to live long, in no, 990
prerogative, books a part of, 128
pride, man's triumph man's will, 1081
profit nor pleasure, opposeth no, 132
progress through the world, 276
reach should exceed his grasp, 488
real possession, 588
reputation, good or bad, 196
road marked by graves of personal likings, 589
safe dwelling place, 370
smile, to share the good, 251
spirit stirred, 777
temporal station, 856
the best cosmopolite, that, 471
thinking too highly, 1048
tongue not able to conceive, 43
training begins early, 564
true remedies, 1054
true touchstone, 131
truest monument, 658
ultimate good work, 613
unconquerable mind, 297
virtue nor sufficiency, 40
want of breeding, 999
weakness, credulity is the, 323
wickedness, a method in, 131
will, to live by one, 22
work a portrait of himself, 613
work come to, what a, 486
work is born with him, 524
work made manifest, 1120
work-time, 494
worst enemies those of his own house and family, 282
yesterday never like his morrow, 368
Mandalay, on the road to, 782
Mandamus binds us all, his, 278
Mandarin, a great yellow, 828
Mandragora, give me to drink, 104
not poppy nor, 102

Mandrake root, get with child a, 117
Mane, dew drop from the lion's, 75
hand upon the ocean's, 393
hand upon thy, 355
of snows, tossing his, 629
Manes, long streaming, 934
Maned neck of massy girth, his, 931
Manger, dog in the, 123
when it approached the, 962
Mangle, turn the muses', 759
Mangled forms, vents in, 49
limbs and dying groans, 262
youth lies dead, my, 748
Manhattan transfer, 925
Manhood, a grain of, 156
bone of, 259
civic, 466
darling of my, 463
disappointment of, 420
flower of our young, 965
is a struggle, 420
mother of, 994
moulded to, by thee, 363
nor good fellowship in thee, 61
of Rome, 593
sounder piece of British, 378
wear a noble face, hills of, 458
Mania, lawsuit, 1078
Maniac, who is yonder poor, 321
world, 588
Manifest but this, no, 670
destiny, science of, 518
made, 1117, 1120
Manifestation of an unfriendly disposition towards the United States, 283
Manifesto, first plain powerful, 938
Manifold stories, 589
Manila Bay, down in, 660
Mankind a future life must have, 544
agree, let, 176
all the better for, 454
amelioration of, 1068
are my brethren, 271
are my subjects all all, 448
are the asses, 361
art of poisoning, 1051
be for all, 647
brightest meanest of, 208
by perverse depravity, 1051
cause of, 335
censure injustice, 973
common to, 965
creeps slowly on, wisdom of, 417
crucify, upon a cross of gold, 753
deserve better of, 191
diseases unbidden haunt, 959
distraction meant to, 127
enemy to, 55
example the school of, 261
free spirit of, 371
from China to Peru, 230
has had thousands of years, 1089
hindrances to elevation of, 514
in charity to all, 291
is dead, when, 826
is sentenced to defeat, 926

Mankind looks forth, 954
love a lover, all, 411
mischiefs that afflict, 1051
misfortunes of, 270
nationality is, 795
never so happily inspired, 704
nor sift, 410
ordainest for, 373
proper study of, is man, 207
read the chapters of, 763
respect to the opinions of, 273
surpasses or subdues, 353
things are in the saddle and ride, 409
think their little set, 275
to all, 620
to hate, 353
to live in, 857
upper and lower part of, 187
what was meant for, 252
wine pernicious to, 219
woman that seduces all, 205
worth destroying, 360
would be less bored, 760
Mankind's concern, charity, 208
epitome, not one but all, 173
interest in famous writers, 588
Manliest beauty, form of, 274
Manlike is it to fall into sin, 435
Manliness, native western form of, 538
of grief, silent, 251
Manly blood, ruddy drop of, 410
deeds of honour, 972
foe, give me the, 293
sentiment, nurse of, 260
to be simple modest true, 528
voice, his big, 50
Manna, his tongue dropped, 149
it is, 1098
this day our daily, 1021
where none is, seeks, 170
Manne, anye, may blameless kiss, 768
Manner, artificial, 381
bold things in a quiet, 521
born, to the, 91
disposed of in the same, 1055
equal with high or low, 539
in a very painful, 684
in good Queen Bess's golden days, 186
in which it is bestowed, 234
is all in all, 262
most eloquent or acute, 1048
not gold, 976
of doubt, no, 624
of giving, the, 1043
of man, what, 54
of men, after the, 1119
same for all human souls, 721
urbanity of, 828
was the foe, what, 748
Manners and carriage, 776
and my spice of wit, my, 1076
are always under examination, 413
are awarding or denying you prizes, 413
are not idle, for, 471
are the happy ways, 413
catch the, living as they rise, 206
climates councils governments, 464

Manners, corrupt good, 1120
different, worse than different souls, 797
gentle of affections mild, of, 175, 217
graced with polished, 266
had not that repose, her, 462
in the face, saw the, 231
man bewrayed by his, 25
men with beautiful, 886
men's evil, live in brass, 74
must adorn knowledge, 222
need the support of manners, 413
noble, veil defect, 556
purer laws, with sweeter, 469
turn with fortunes, 209
Mannikin merely to madden it, made a, 461
Mannish cowards, 48
Man-o'-war is 'er 'usband, 778
Man-preacher against vanity of raiment, 691
Mansion reared by daedal Jack, 543
Mansions, build thee more stately, 452
in my Father's house, 1118
in the skies, 199
Manslaughter and isolated murders, 991
Mantelpiece, commanding of the, 622
Mantle, hooded, 562
like a standing pond, 44
morn in russet, 89
o'er the dark her silver, threw, 152
of charity, 329
of the standing pool, 99
that covers all human thoughts, 1042
Mantling blood, 226
Mantuan swan, ages ere the, 262
Manuals, and read their, 576
Manufacturing industry depends on itself, 1067
Manure, natural, 273
Manured with industry, 101
Manus haec inimica tyrannis, 169
Manuscript, rolls his, 797
youth's sweet-scented, 1019
zigzag, 265
Manuscripts, collected many choice, 998
illuminated, 507
Many a mood and many a kind, 633
a poem is marred, 439
a slip 'twixt cup and lip, 124
a smale maken a grate, 8
and mighty are they, 783
are called but few chosen, 1115
despoilers of the, 1062
eyes that look on it, 575
forced to do the same, 1126
generous and some chaste, 470
maidens be, as, 386
mellow Cydonian suckets, 431
of mine old acquaintance, 65
safe from, honored by the few, 528
small make a great, 8, 15
to keep, little to earn and, 523
we were not, 431

Many-coloured glass, dome of, 366
life, 231
Many-headed monster, 129, 214, 308
multitude, 27
Many-splendoured thing, 749
Many-twinkling feet, 243
Map me no maps, 947
of busy life, 265
of desolation, fold your, 937
of honour truth and loyalty, see the, 69
of my collegiate life, 300
over the universe in a, 1039
representing the sea, 599
they could all understand, 599
Maps, as geographers crowd their, 995
geographers in Afric, 190
map me no, 947
of the world, on the, 657
Maple and oak and pine, 712
puts her corals on in May, 529
tree, flame of the, 882
wood the burning bush, yon, 431, 442
Maples, scarlet of the, 757
Mar, man did not make and can not, 546
what's well, oft we, 98
your fortunes, lest you, 98
Marah, drink of the waters of, 1098
Marathon looks on the sea, 359
mountains look on, 359
plain of, 233
to Waterloo, from, 623
Marble and mud, life is made of, 422
changes to, 595
cold, monument slab of, 448
deed writ in, 130
door admits no fruit, 659
enduring as, 357
forget thyself to, 160
front, Treasury's, 604
halls, I dreamt that I dwelt in, 386
halls, sweep through her, 418, 433
index of a mind, 299
jaws, ponderous and, 91
leapt to life a god, 363
made you out of, 982
many a braver, 165
minds, men have, 107
nor gilded monuments, 107
of her snowy breast, 145
or bronze, lodge in, 612
poets that lasting, seek, 146
quilt of, 682
shows none of its inherent beauties, 196
sleep in dull cold, 73
soft rain perce the hard, 23
softened into life, 214
some write their wrongs in, 204
the hills are full of, 613
to retain, 357, 1043
wastes, more the, 1023
with his name, mark the, 210
Marbles cold and stupid, 657
mossy, rest, 450

Marbles, mournful, 444
Marbled steep, Sunium's, 359
Marblehead, by the women of, 443
Marble-hearted fiend, ingratitude, 98
Marcellus exiled feels, 208
  our young, sleeps, 646
March, beware the ides of, 81
  droghte of, 4
  hare, mad as a, 17
  hinder us in the great, 163
  ides of, are come, 1000
  is o'er the mountain waves, 328
  lion-like, cometh in, 629
  nearer home, day's, 306
  of intellect, 259, 321
  of the human mind, is slow, 259
  on march on, 1060
  stormy, has come, 372
  walk softly, 904
  winds of, with beauty, 56
Marches fill the nights, and solemn, 522
  funeral, to the grave, 433
Marched on without impediment, 72
Marching on, His truth is, 522
Marcia towers above her sex, 195
Marciful Providence fashioned us, 526
Marden, roared to, Nantucket's sunk, 508
Mare Bess bestrode, 494
  grey, the better horse, 16
  my old gray, 512
Margaret be our foeman's bride, 306
Marge, whose, the wistful waves, 874
Margent of the world, across the, 748
Margery Grey the young wife, 562
Margin a certain free, 538
  meadow of, 279
  to my life, broad, 514
  vanishes over the, 472
Margins of her book, 595
Mariana, this dejected, 37
Marie, dare not tell sweet, 717
Maries, the queen had four, 953
Marigold springs, the constant, 924
  that goes to bed wi' the sun, 56
Marigolds, ye ardent, 385
Mariner, O young, 472
Mariners of England, ye, 327
  travelers, 851
Marines, tell that to the, 311
  that will do for the, 358
  United States, 953
Marion leads, band that, 372
Marivaux, romances of, 246
Mark Antony, who lost, the world, 185
  death loves a shining, 134, 202
  fellow of no, nor likelihood, 62
  God save the, 61
  God speed the, 408
  Haley drives along the street, 572

Mark, hits the, 106
  Hopkins and I, 591
  Hopkins sat on one end of a log, 815
  I press toward the, 1121
  measures not men my, 253
  miss the, 277
  now how a plain tale, 62
  of rank in nature, 661
  of virtue, 46
  on his red breast, see the, 444
  push beyond her, 468
  slander loves a shining, 571
  the archer little meant, 307
  the marble with his name, 210
  the perfect man, 1104
  to such, set a, 1056
  Twain, one book by, 930
  upon Cain, the Lord set a, 1097
  well experienced archer hits the, 106
  wisest clerks have missed the, 325
Marks and scars I carry with me, 172
  death aims at fairer, 134
  of angels' feet, 523
  of divine origin in human nature, 333
  of God in the heavens and the earth, 333
Marked him for her own, 245
  him for his own, 140
  of many, the, 652
Marked-down quarry, 720
Market, considering the, 838
  fortune is like the, 110
  glutted, makes provision cheap, 217
  knowledge is bought in the, 519
  quotations, Bartlett of, 910
  with a climate, in the, 838
Market-place, chained in the, 372
  of war, 806
Marketh the going of time, 449
Marking, malady of not, 64
Marle, over the burning, 148
Marley was as dead as a doornail, 495
Marlinspike, brained with a, 710
Marlowe's mighty line, 119
Marm Hackett's garden, over old, 508
Marmalade, this bit of, 927
Marmion, last words of, 308
Maro sings, scenes that, 266
Maroons and schooners and buried treasure, 842
Marred, young man married is, 53
Marriage, an excellent, 505
  an open question, 412
  and hanging go by destiny, 125
  and the stars, 797
  arrives a reaction, after, 785
  bell, merry as a, 352
  comedies ended by a, 359
  community of two, 662
  curse of, 102
  day, all thy days as a, 135
  definition of, 848
  disgust to, 235

Marriage, female murderers get offers of, 720
  give your whole mind to, 1076
  hasty, seldom proveth well, 70
  in companionship as in, 635
  invalidated by, 614
  is a desperate thing, 130
  is a noose, 1040
  is an evil, 976
  is, in heaven no, 903
  is much like a Devonshire lane, 333
  made, rich hues have, 668
  mirth in funeral and with dirge in, 89
  of true minds, 108
  offers of, to female murderers, 720
  resembles a pair of shears, 313
  tables, furnish forth the, 90
  terrible thorn-bit of, 776
  ye know a lot about, 797
Marriages abound most with love and constancy, 196
  are made in heaven, 465
Marriage-feast, as at Cana's, 445
Married and lived happily ever after, 773
  estate, happiness in the, 147
  he is dreadfully, 606
  in haste, 52, 193
  live till I were, 39
  man, Benedick the, 38
  man, happy as, 235
  man must sink or swim, 782
  most, man I ever saw, 606
  philosopher, a, 1080
  to immortal verse, 160
Marrow and nerve of human powers, 458
  Yankees have the, 348
Marrow-nerve, nimble of the, 576
Marry a rich woman, as easy to, 483
  ancient people, 147
  every woman should, 421
  proper time to, 264
  whether it was better to, 1014
  whom she likes, a woman, 482
  widow of doubtful age will, 479
Mars, eye like, to threaten, 95
  of malcontents, 34
  potent planet, 586
  this seat of, 59
  us, it makes us or it, 103
Marsh beneath the moon, 888
  or bog, in woodland, 953
Marshes how candid and simple, ye, 663
  old, dig deep in, 847
  range of the, 663
Marshal's truncheon, 36
Marsh-grass, roots as the, 663
Marsh-hen flies, as the, 663
  secretly builds, as the, 663
Mart, thronged the daily, 504
Martial airs of England, 341
  cloak around him, 364
  outside, swashing and, 48
Martin Elginbrodde, here lie I, 948
  Luther sang, sing as, 481
Martini, chilled, like Ithuriel's spear, 889
Martyr, fallest a blessed, 74

Martyr, like a pale, 587
  to suffer and fall, some first, 518
Martyrs, blood of the, 1012
  noble army of, 1127
  or Nero, 533
  or reformers, what makes men, 574
  they love their, 1074
Martyr's crown on Lincoln's brow, 706
  woe, 282
Martyrdom involved in entertainment, 729
  of John Rogers, 947
  she knew the life-long, 439
  the gift of, 174
Marvel how men toil and fare, 673
  match me such, 500
  of great renown, 699
  of her face, 774
Marvels here, to find the Orient's, 442
Marvelling eyes, touch her, 911
Marvellous boy, Chatterton the, 297
  fane, 541
  mercies and infinite love, 631
  old wise child, like a, 929
  things appear, 993
Mary A, portrait of, 751
  Ambree was formost in battle, 257
  and her Son, to shut out, 904
  Carmichael and me, 953
  go and call the cattle home, 523
  had a little lamb, 362
  hath chosen that good part, 1117
  helper of heartbreak, 866
  image of Bloody, 391
  my sweet Highland, 286
  my, to be lovely still, 263
  Seaton and Mary Beaton, 953
  she came, young, 951
  weep no more for me, 277
Marys and Anns and Elizas, 452
Mary-buds, winking, 105
Mask for fear, boldness a, 994
  Harlequin without his, 484
  he shows as he removes the, 481
  of care, wear a, 814
Masks outrageous and austere, 897
  with a bag of, 927
Masked words abroad, there are, 532
Masquerade, earth's proud, 774
Masquerades as cream, skim milk, 623
Mass, a shapeless, 680
  blessed mutter of the, 488
  bubble in the molten, 894
  enormous, a, 218
  of humanity, obscure, 422
  of matter lost, in the, 220
  of millinery, 469
  of things to come, 75
  resisting, 648
  swells forward in a, 498
Masses, cannot write for the, 1066
  huddled, 694

Massa ob de sheepfol', 719
Massachusetts, have faith in, 819
  the home of the sacred cod, 752
  there she is, behold her, 341
  wears it, 364
  with her Plymouth rock, 660
Massive gateway, 373
  sandal, have heard her, 915
Mast be now blown over-board, 71
  bends the gallant, 345
  clinging to a, 622
  colors to the, 307
  cut away the, 508
  flapping on an idle, 688
  like a drunken sailor on a, 72
  nail to the, her holy flag, 450
  of some great ammiral, 148
Masts against the western hues, 576
  crack, 28
  sail crowded fit to break, 834
Master a grief, every one can, 39
  always the, 1054
  behold thy, 1053
  both of science and of art, 678
  for life, 321
  had writ of Little Nell, 644
  I would not be a, 455
  I've filled my contract, 844
  in the sky, 811
  is coming, the, 640
  master and kissed him, and saith, 1116
  melody, feels the, 871
  mine lo I remember, 766
  of all good workmen, 779
  of all men, 414
  of his fate, 470
  of his time, every man be, 86
  of men was Goodly Fere, 886
  of my fate, I am the, 470, 579
  of the mainspring, 715
  of the Thames, 780
  owns only your person, 1068
  salute his, 220
  so hard a, 669
  speaker is the tear, 840
  spirit of the earth, 879
  spirits of this age, 82
  such, such man, 19
  the eternal, found, 231
  the great, 436
  the passive, 408
  thy, missed it, 73
  Traveller and his, 928
  under heaven, no more subtle, 471
  we Thy keys, Thou the, 443
  went clean forspent, 664
  who crown'st, 735
  will choose to stay, 640
  without a, 412
Masters, frightfulest of all, 378
  have been done away with, 1080
  have wrought, 848
  I have to tell a tale, 608
  in his eye, 423
  little better than false knaves, 40
  lords and rulers in all lands, 708
  no man can serve two, 1114

Masters, noble and approv'd good, 100
  of assemblies, 1110
  of Cremona, 738
  of the subtle schools, 900
  of the things they write, few are, 130
  of their fates, men are, 81
  spread yourselves, 42
  two, with a single blow, 840
  we cannot all be, 100
Master's hand, string may jar in the best, 180
  joy, enter thy, 305
  spell, kindled by, 289
  touch, beauty needs the, 445
Master-art of kindness, last subtlest, 1080
Mastered whatever was not worth knowing, 526
Master-key, comes with a, 854
Masterly inactivity, 290
Master-passion in the breast, one, 208
Masterpiece, assembly as well as a, 1069
  designed, nature her great, 286
  made his, 86
  nature's chief, 185
  of nature, a friend is the, 411
  Prudhon's, 1085
  should appear as flower to painter, 611
Masterpieces, acclaimed as, 788
  among, 1079
  are intended, for which, 927
  of the world belong to me, 913
Master-spirit embalmed, 163
Master-stroke is nature's part, the, 410
Mastery of a subject, 1089
  of the desires, 1080
  over musical instruments, 742
  strive here for, 150
Mast-fringed port, each estuary, 761
Mast-heads ever bowing, 914
Mastiff dog may love a puppy, a, 472
  greyhound, 99
Mastiffs are of unmatchable courage, 67
Match, ne'er saw her, 77
  the sorrow, little fun to, 607
  took care to strike a, 761
Matches are made in heaven, 125
Matchless bard, 258
Mate, choose not alone a proper, 264
  each may choose another, 310
  for beauty, the, 425
  great artificer made my, 704
  I'll call him, 878
  of Henry Morgan, old bold, 833
  of the Nancy brig, 622
  of the wind and sea, 886
  replies O blow me eyes, 843
  talked, listen when his, 880
  the second, 577
  was fixed, the, 710
Mates, from their folded, 756
Mated by the lion, the hind, 53
  has such longing to be, 545
Mater ait natae, 1092

Materia medica could be sunk, whole, 454
Material comes before the work, 613
  heads of the same, 893
  nature, of, 235
  place, corridors surpassing, 585
  wrought in common crude, 629
Materials of action, 1007
  youth gets together his building, 515
Mathematical motion, 128
Mathematician capable of reasoning, 974
  on highest rung of ladder, 741
Mathematics, angling like, 139
  in the region of absolute necessity, 821
  makes men subtile, 111
  possess supreme beauty, 821
  show the poor by, 937
Matilda though a pleasant child, 339
Matin, glow-worm shows, 92
Matrimony, begin with aversion in, 277
  no fit diversion for librarian, 865
  say of courtship love and, 511
Matron's bones, mutine in a, 95
Matt Minikin won't set fire, 246
Matter, a little fire kindleth, 1122
  all, is indifferent to form, 144
  Berkeley said there was no, 360
  book containing such vile, 79
  can never die, 753
  conclusion of the whole, 1110
  for a May morning, 55
  for scorning, no, 493
  for virtuous deeds, 28
  half know a, 990
  he that repeateth a, 1107
  in bright gold, 384
  it is no, 82
  lost in the mass of, 220
  love doth mince this, 101
  magazine of, 144
  mince the, 101
  more, with less art, 92
  no, what he said, 360
  of perfect indifference, 1062
  of time and opportunity, 971
  of wonder, 247
  permanence of, 1089
  quite, spoil the, 599
  root of the, found in me, 1102
  so they ended the, 1100
  success in the smallest, 1012
  thought immersed in, 393
  to a T, manage this, 241
  trifling handful of magic, 569
  what is, never mind, 360
  where the lifeless form, what, 511
  will make a Star-chamber, 34
  wreck of, the, 195
Matters, I am no judge of such, 406
  in practical, 975
  in unimportant, 1075
  judge of the highest, 974
  men may read strange, 84
  not how a man dies, it, 235
  of importance, decides, 984

Matters of the highest moment, 969
  serious, must be seen to, 701
  that perplex it, 795
  they used to pride, 936
  were or were not true, 936
  you mince, 1033
Matter-o'-money, quoth Echo plainly, 511
Matthew and Waldo, guardians of the faith, 900
  Prior, here lies, 189
Maturest counsels, dash, 149
Maturity, credit requires time to arrive at, 419
  excellence to, 989
  is the gate of Paradise, 558
Maud, come into the garden, 469
Maudlin poetess, a, 212
Maunder and mumble, let her, 378
Mauritius issue, came the first, 842
Mausoleum, Westminster Abbey is a, 892
Mausolos' tomb of affection, 956
Maxim I would teach, 591
  in the schools, an old, 190
  nothing is so useless as a general, 397
  scoundrel, 225
  this great, be my virtue's guide, 221
  true and wise graved upon his signet ring, 620
  universally known, 229
  was la carrière est ouverte, 1061
  who follows this, 981
Maxims, gods of the copybook, 785
  little hoard of, 464
  of the civil law, 232
May, all the months were, 687
  although I care not, 21
  and June then dead December, 856
  as flush as, 95
  before the thing we, 559
  breathing of the, 864
  bring us there to be, 480
  call my own, that I, 451
  fair fresshe, wel-come be thou, 5
  flowery meads in, 132
  full of spirit as the month of, 63
  he that will not when he, 11
  I be there to see, 264
  I join the choir invisible, oh, 520
  I were lord in, 631
  in the merry month of, 120
  in the middle of, 838
  is building her house, 793
  is full of flowers, 30
  it was the month of, 619
  joys be as the month of, 135
  love I gave in, 656
  maids are, when they are maids, 51
  morning, more matter for a, 55
  never was month of love, 30
  not, I dare and yet I, 21
  prosperous morn in, 735
  Queen o' the, 463

May there be no moaning, 472
  winter chills the lap of, 249
  with alle thy floures and thy grene, 5
  wol have no slogardye, 5
May's new-fangled mirth, 40
  warm slow yellow moonlit summer nights, 485
May-bells clash and chime, 649
May-blossom and a brow, 470
Mayd, not-browne, 257
Mayde he canne, kiss what, 768
  meke as is a, 5
May-flower in her face, 864
  of our hope, 550
Maying, friends that I knew in my, 718
  oh that we two were, 523
  when we goe, 134
May-morn, till that, 492
May-time and cheerful dawn, 299
Maze, mighty, not without a plan, 206
Mazes, in wandering, lost, 150
Mazy progress, 243
Me and Mamie Rorke, 761
  as comes to, or cloud or sun, 423
  but not for, 646
  could determine which is, 719
  make mention, of, 1020
  pinguem et nitidum, 249
  the same as, 784
Mead and hill, water fresh from, 733
  by the streams and o'er the, 281
  flowers in the, 4
  in a pale green, 896
Meads, flowery, I would be in, 140
  in May, flowery, 132
Meadow flower-girt hill, 831
  mist, out in the, 886
  of margin, 279
  seek thee in vain by the, 392
  sweets of Burn-mill, 298
  wealth of the fruitful, 712
  white with snow, fairest, 453
Meadows brown and sere, 372
  deep, 893
  do paint the, with delight, 42
  fresh and green, 372
  gloomerin', 719
  of heaven, 435
  trim with daisies pied, 160
Meadow-flower its bloom unfold, 305
Meagre were his looks, 80
Meal in a barrel, handful of, 1101
  in, cook a, 850
  kindle for their evening, 912
  on beans, a certain, 493
  something more than a common blessing, 323
Meals, hunted for their, 622
  make no long, 251
  o' you, to mak' their, 523
  saint by getting, 918
  unquiet, 38
Meal-drift, wilder wilful-wavier, 672
Mean and cold, hated all that's, 912
  and self-conscious, so, 883
  and small, 572

Mean between ostentation and rusticity, 218
made so, 492
observances of paltry decorum, 311
the golden, 267, 990
the proper, 1053
things put on beauty, 811
yes an' say no, mebby to, 527
Means and content, he that wants, 50
and leisure, increased, 419
appliances and, 65
end must justify the, 189
every, shall be present to sate, 625
get wealth by any, 118
if we borrow, within our, 606
most good, when fortune, 58
no matter by what, 118
not, but ends, 317
of doing him an injury, 1055
of evil out of good, 148
of our own destruction, 962
of preserving peace, 268
of subsistence, even the, 1077
one certain, 940
quite beyond my, 664
the end justifies the, 987
to be of note, youth that, 105
to do ill deeds, 58
to live, save, 32
too venomous too underhand, no, 1082
unto an end, life 's but a, 506
up to our, 488
what this wild drama, 472
whereby I live, 47
which the God of nature has placed, 270
you can, by all the, 226
Meander, as streams, 440
Meaner beauties of the night, 114
creatures kings, 72
Meanest flower that blows, 302
floweret of the vale, 245
habit, honour peereth in, 52
of mankind, wisest brightest, 208
of us all, for the, 905
Meaning, a little aside from common, 709
blunders round about a, 213
mystic, 583
of life the right to life, 1081
permeate, let its, 718
seems to be, the, 953
to our life, gives a, 788
without injury to the, 319
Meanings and wishings, good, 137
Meanness and viciousness, 973
avarice or pride, unstained by, 479
Meant, more, than meets the ear, 161
Measels, did you ever have the, 606
Measles fade at last, 910
Measure for law, we have a, 130
God gives wind by, 138
its narrow, 744
move to a bygone, 842
not the work, 430
of a man's height, 993
of a play, five acts the just, 180
of my days, eke out the, 1076

Measure of my days what it is, 1104
often have I sighed to, 297
take thine own, 136
teach his feet a, 631
that it spans, knows the, 677
there is no, 804
three with a new song's, 676
tread a stately, 770
undertaken, every, 969
Measures bind the power of pain, 549
life in short, may perfect be, 120
Lydian, softly sweet in, 176
not men, 253, 259
Measured beat serene and slow, 685
by my soul, 199
phrase and choice word, 297
Measureless content, shut up in, 85
grossness and slag, amid, 535
to man, caverns, 315
Measurement is found, in his, 575
Meat, after, comes mustard, 1035
and cannot eat, some have, 287
and drink, nor easy, 780
and drink to me, 51
as an egg is full of, 79
benison fall on our, 134
drink and cloaths, cargoes of, 950
eaten without mirth or music, 310
for little guests, mighty, 750
God sendeth both mouth and, 12, 19
he gave him not, 249
heaven sends us good, 243
I cannot eat but little, 20
I have no stomach for such, 650
I like good, 955
in the hall, 702
is too good for any but anglers, 140
it feeds on, mock the, 102
long for perishing, 166
one appointed to buy the, 130
or drink, is another's, 132
out-did the, 134
sit down and taste my, 135
so dressed and sauced and seasoned, 606
strong, for age, 1122
truths are strong, 477
upon what, doth Caesar feed, 81
Meats, as he digests his, 1081
funeral baked, 90
Meazles, love is like, 518
Mebbe, yes an' no an', 687
Mebby to mean yes an' say no, 527
Mecca saddens at the delay, 224
Meccas of the mind, 363
Mechanic art, made poetry a mere, 262
lawyer without literature, a, 309
operation, 143
pacings to and fro, 463
slaves, 105
Mechanician, visible sage, 517
Mechanized automaton, 368

Mechanizes it, Watt, 414
Medal without its reverse, 1072
Meddle not with him that flattereth, 1108
Meddlesome tongues, 474
Meddling, every fool will be, 1107
paternal or, government, 398
Mede, alle the floures in the, 4
Medes and Persians, law of the, 1113
Medical men entered into agreement, 402
Medici, Miniver loved the, 808
Medicinable, some griefs are, 105
Medicinal gum, 104
star, beam of some, 923
Medicine as it came, took his, 882
by, life may be prolong'd, 106
complete dispensary of, 924
desire to take, 694
doeth good like a, 1107
for case like mine, 538
for life, find a, 963
for the soul, 1092
Hat, plumed war-bonnet of, 929
humanistic faculty of, 1089
is all the fashion, 1054
labors to destroy the reason for its existence, 637
miserable have no other, 36
only useful part of, 1054
the art of, 969
thee to that sweet sleep, 102
to live by, 1054
to produce health, 1000
worse than the malady, 127
Medicines at the outset, use, 990
to make me love, 61
to make women speak, 1078
Medicos marvelling sweetly, 903
Mcdio de fonte leporum, 352
Mediocrities, birth of a hundred, 1078
Mediocrity and hills, easy to admire, 1069
gratified with, 291
has no greater consolation, 1057
of middle life, 530
safeguard of, 413
Meditate by night, 210
the thankless muse, 159
Meditation changed to dream, 1021
let us all to, 69
maiden, fancy-free, 42
of my heart, and the, 1103
Méditations Poétiques, 1065
Meditations, thy testimonies are my, 1106
Meditative spleen, 302
Medley of kindred, 1035
Medusa's head, beauty is that, 914
Meed, life's high, 385
of some melodious tear, 159
sweat for duty not for, 48
Meek and gentle, I am, 82
and quiet spirit, 1122
as is a mayde, 5
borne his faculties so, 85
nature's evening comment, 303
patient humble spirit, 115
than fierce, safer being, 490

Meek, the terrible, the fierce agonizing, 817
Meek-eyed morn, 224
Meekness and modesty, with, 972
Meet again, if we do, 84
  it is I set it down, 92
  me by moonlight alone, 388
  mortality, how gladly would I, 155
  neath the sounding rafter, 554
  no more, 588
  nurse for a poetic child, 307
  parted to, nevermore, 418
  thee like a pleasant thought, 298
  when shall we three, 84, 951
  with joy in sweet Jerusalem, 71
  you and them, 627
Meetest for death, 46
Meeting and the spot, bless the, 364
  break on the lips while, 431
  is a summary, that silent, 933
  journeys end in lovers, 54
  of gentle lights, 164
Meetings of men's lives, 933
Meets the ear, more than, 161
Meinherr from Almany, let some, 874
Meinself — und Gott, 684
Meir, my gude grey, 11
Meke as is a mayde, 5
Melancholia of everything, 1080
Melancholic distracted man, 128
Melancholy as a battle won, 292
  bait, fish not with this, 44
  boughs, under the shade of, 49
  but my soul is, 673
  chord in, 390
  chronic, 651
  days are come, 372
  disposition, he is of a very, 38
  flood, I passed the, 71
  gold, bathe the hills in, 418
  grace, elysian beauty, 303
  green and yellow, 55
  main, amid the, 225
  marked him for her own, 245
  men are most witty, 124
  moping, and moon-struck madness, 155
  most musical most, 160
  music good to the, 1048
  naught so sweet as, 121, 127
  never give way to, 313
  O sweetest melancholy, 144
  of Cerberus and blackest midnight born, 160
  of mine own, it is a, 51
  quaint sincere, 573
  slow, remote unfriended, 249
  there's such a charm in, 289
  to purge, 57
  train, forced from their homes a, 250
  veil'd, has her sovran, 384
  waste, ocean's gray and, 371
  what charm can soothe her, 253
  who has dismissed, 1056
Melankolly, I never knu a man trubbled with, 518
Melchior and Gaspar and Baltasar, 439
Melchizedek, Ucalegon, 807
Mellow and yellow and rounded, 764

Mellow Cydonian suckets sweet apples, 431
  goes to bed, 127
  rich and ripe, 358
  too, for me, 221
  wedding bells, hear the, 460
  whether grave or, 196
Mellowed long, fruit that, 178
  to that tender light, 356
Mellowing of occasion, 41
  year, before the, 159
Mellows the spirit, 573
Melodie, my luve's like the, 287
Melodies, heard, are sweet, 383
  thousand, unheard before, 289
Melodious birds sing madrigals, 31
  strains, heaven's, 477
  tear, meed of some, 159
Melodist of the mind, 691
Melody, and something more than, 405
  blundering kind of, 174
  crack the voice of, 451
  fall like strains of, 586
  falling in, back, 317
  feels the Master, 871
  forgotten, 582
  fowles maken, 5
  is best expressed, 533
  of Chaucer's verse, 412
  of every grace, 168
  of song, enchanted by, 677
  sonnet is a wave of, 600
  the clearest, 922
  to the voice, 984
Melrose by pale moonlight, 306
Melt and dispel ye spectre-doubts, 327
  in her mouth, butter would not, 14, 192
  in her own fire, 95
  into sorrow, 355
  not in an acid sect, 443
  thaw and resolve itself into a dew, 89
  too solid flesh would, 89
Melted in his own grease, 7
  into air into thin air, 33
Melting airs or martial, 266
  heaven with earth, 447
  mood, unused to the, 104
Melts the mind to love, pity, 176
Melville a deplorable Bohemian, 766
  in Whitman and, 925
Member, comfortable feel in any, 391
  joint or limb, 150
  no, needs so many muscles, 1022
  of the rabble, 922
  tongue an unruly, 1122
Members, fling down its aching, 938
  in arms and idleness, 270
Memnonium was in all its glory, 332
Memoirs, man who leaves, 1083
  saves man or woman from, 521
  we will write our, 1061
Memoir-writers for governing persons, 381
Memorable epocha, 268
  on account of some single word, 588

Memorandum of it, if you don't make a, 598
Memorial, best, for the common man, 753
  crumb, 584
  from the soul's eternity, 577
  of virtue, 1125
  this day shall be unto you a, 1098
Memories and sighs, a night of, 325
  brave with faint, 848
  ladies have too-long, 928
  liars ought to have good, 169
  man's noble, 736
  no pyramids set off his, 131
  of eld, vastness and age and, 459
  of those they left, 866
  precious ever-lingering, 538
  that bless and burn, 765
  wane, 507
  without ruins is without, 609
Memory, a jet of, 888
  a very cold and imperfect, 1064
  all that reflective, stores, 305
  and desire, mixing, 899
  and name of Washington, 374
  as it grows fainter, 1087
  at the expense of his, 1052
  be dead, till, 953
  be green, 89
  before the shrine of, 1085
  begot in the ventricle of, 41
  blushes at the sneer, 452
  book of, 68
  ceases to be, only when, 406
  climbs to heaven, 357
  clings, 677
  comes like a banshee, 715
  dear, lost to sight to, 392
  dear son of, 161
  dear, thoughts to, 309
  desirous to commit to, 1125
  does not make, a great, 403
  everyone complains of his, 1044
  fond, brings the light, 336
  for a politician, 641
  great man's, 94
  green in our souls, 334
  green, keep my, 496
  green, tears will keep thy, 722
  has love, how vast a, 216
  has painted, 761
  he shall have a noble, 76
  he who fills our, 1057
  holds a seat, while, 92
  how sweet their, 266
  I bequeath to foreign nations and next age, 114
  if there be, 540
  illiterate him from your, 277
  indebted to his, for his jests, 279
  is bitter to me, 813
  is fairly spoilt on me, 840
  is so bad, my, 1036
  is sweet to me, 438
  is the diary, 724
  left his awful, 321
  lends her light no more, 309
  let love melt into, 1084
  lets slip, epic, 620
  liar should have a good, 995
  lost, like a, 369

Memory, made such a sinner of his, 32
man's real possession, 588
morning-star of, 355
no less than hope owes its charm, 426
of a wrong, 415
of all he stole, pleasing, 215
of Boatswain a dog, 352
of earth's bitter leaven, 298
of her name, nor, 561
of man runneth not back, 413
of mine age, most blessed, 463
of scene or incident echoed and reduplicated, 423
of the just is blessed, 1107
of the movements they made, 933
of their absent conquering earls, 531
of their worth, 373
of those who lie below, 495
one must have a good, 1079
place in thy, dearest, 416
plays an old tune, 512
plays lurid tricks with our, 727
pluck from, a rooted sorrow, 88
retained in the, 1049
runneth not to the contrary, 248
shall be ours, 439
silent shore of, 303
still is dear, the, 960
strengthens as you lay burdens upon it, 347
surrendered sword of, 848
table of my, 92
takes them to her caverns, 388
that which I gave thee, 590
things to hold in, 793
thou fond deceiver, 252
throng into my, 157
to convict of plagiarism, a, 238
to keep good acts in, 113
to lift its head above the tide, 1090
unexampled voice of awful, 301
uses not intellect but, 1022
vibrates in the, music, 367
wakes the bitter, 151
warder of the brain, 85
watches o'er the sad review, 327
Memory's mystic band, 598
room, 662
Men, a few honest, 141
a man that died for, 639
able to use opportunity, 960
about me that are fat, 81
above that which is written, 1120
above the common herd, 702
above the reach of ordinary, 297
admire virtue who follow not her lore, 156
adversity is the test of strong, 131
after the manner of, 1119
afraid of the sea, 818
aged, full loth and slow, 309
all, are created equal, 273
all, are liars, 1105
all earth, God gives all, 779
all good dead, 710

Men, all, have one entrance into life, 1124
all, know the law, 130
all things to all, 1120
and boys as thick as hasty pudding, 283
and mountains meet, when, 282
and things we love, near the, 834
and toward God, toward, 922
and women creeping through the red, 931
and women forget they have been children, 558
and women inaccessible, 775
and women merely players, 49
apt to tell secrets, 222
are April when they woo, 51
are at the point of death, when, 80
are but children of a larger growth, 177
are fit for, which ordinary, 98
are free in homeland, 883
are free to think and act, 612
are merriest when from home, 66
are moulded out of faults, 37
are my teachers, 207
are naturally apt to be swayed, 975
are never so likely to settle, 398
are not flattered by being, 457
are on this account, 1048
are only boys grown tall, 953
are polished, 572
are so completely corrupted, 995
are the mountains Britain boasts, 575
are the universe, 728
are too cowardly, 995
are unwise, 881
are used as they use others, 977
are we and must grieve, 297
are you good, and true, 39
as He died to make, holy, 522
as he wrote down for, 516
as need, help such, 783
as trees walking, I see, 1116
at most differ as heaven, 470
at sea, desire in, 1021
at the top, 775
bad intentions of, 981
bad, live to eat and drink, 1004
ballooning high, mighty, 575
base, in love have a nobility, 101
become the better for being a little bad, 37
being once lost, 997
believe in the infinite, while, 515
below and saints above, 306
beneath the rule of, 425
best of, sometimes forget, 101
best of, that e'er wore earth, 115
betray, finds too late that, 253
black, are pearls, 28
bossing eight hundred, 785
both good and wise, 545
brave and bold, 951
busy haunts of, 370

Men, busy hum of, 160
by losing rendered sager, 357
by whom impartial laws were given, 205
call gallantry, what, 358
call treasure the gods call dross, 528
callen daysies in our toun, 4
can counsel and speak comfort, 40
can not learn, from books, 420
cannot devise some scheme, 894
capable of every wickedness, 726
cause that wit is in other, 64
chatter and love and hate, 547
cheerful ways of, 151
chortle, real estate, 912
cigarette and cigar, 902
circumstances the creatures of, 420
claret for boys port for, 237
clever, are good, 376
command women, 996
company of righteous, 968
comprehend all vagrom, 39
condemned alike to groan, 243
contending with adversity, 124
could still be holy, if, 914
cradled into poetry, 367
creep not walk, 442
crowd of common, 141
crown the knave, 659
cuckoo mocks married, 42
daily do, not knowing what they do, 39
dare do what men may do, 39
dared to die loving their enemies, 573
decay, wealth accumulates and, 250
December when they wed, 51
deeds are, 138, 204
deep, natural philosophy makes, 111
desire to be immortal, all, 477
die but sorrow never dies, 682
die fast enough, 1051
die, long before, 903
die of their remedies, 1047
disgrace labor, 550
distinguished, and clothes, 629
do aland, live as, 106
do not care, 990
do not think of sons and daughters, 430
do not your alms before, 1114
doubt, till all, 215
down among the dead, 941
draw, as they ought to be, 252
dying like, 67
dying man to dying, 166
eddy about, 547
employed best contented, 228
equal in presence of death, 986
equal in the democracy of the dead, 602
erring, call chance, 158
ever will have leave to coin new words, 180
everlastingly, remain with all, 970
evil that, do, 83
eyes of, are idly bent, 60

Men favour the deceit, 178
  fear death, 109
  feel an honorable bigotry, 295
  few, admired by their domestics, 1030
  few, masters of things they write or speak, 130
  few, own own property, 603
  fifteen, on a dead man's chest, 704
  fighting, 432
  fill every beaker up my, 404
  fill up their pockets, 935
  find me the, 591
  find that they can prepare, 1049
  first produced in fishes, 1005
  fly from death, 553
  follow me, if ye are, 502
  foolery of wise, 47
  for not many, 963
  for the use and benefit of, 172
  from a former generation, 339
  from every rank, give us, 561
  from particular vice, to save, 582
  from the chimney-corner, 27
  gallant tars are our, 242
  gather and squander, 547
  get opinions as boys learn to spell, 430
  go armed to seek, 914
  go at set of day, 766
  go by, where the race of, 733
  go, where'er, 706
  God give us, time demands, 522
  godly honest, to be captains of horse, 141
  good, eat and drink to live, 1004
  good, what makes, 975
  good will toward, 1116
  goodliest man of, 152
  govern nothing with more difficulty, 1048
  gratitude of most, 200
  great city has greatest, and good women, 535
  great, gain doubly, 425
  great, hallow a whole people, 312
  great, not always wise, 1102
  great, not great scholars, 454
  greatest clerks not the wisest, 16
  greatest, oftest wrecked, 156
  gregarious animals, 663
  grind in the mill, 414
  grow virtuous in their old age, 217
  grown, understand it, 1038
  hang out their signs, 342
  happy breed of, 59
  hate thee have no care, and if, 473
  have always done, wondering, 816
  have bags of money, good, 933
  have consecrated it, brave, 456
  have died not for love, 51
  have dulled their eyes, 709
  have laughed at me, 893
  have lost their reason, 83
  have marble minds, 107
  have rosy faces, 703
Men have their intellectual ancestry, 529
  have their price, all, 200
  have tried to understand, 927
  heard thunder on the left, 184
  heights by great, reached, 436
  hemmed in with the spears, 831
  histories make, wise, 111
  honest, esteem and value, 977
  honours of illustrious, 981
  hopes of living to be brave, 162
  hunte faste, 4
  I want to teach, 1079
  I've studied, from my, 574
  ignorance plays the chief part among, 1013
  ill at ease, 422
  impatient with over-praise of others, 529
  impious, bear sway, 195
  in a world of men, 778
  in argument with, 157
  in exile, 963
  in faces of, I see God, 535
  in great place, are servants, 110
  in impotence, old, 879
  in independent position and of honest purpose, 532
  in obedience, supreme powers keep, 126
  in the brains of, 82
  in the catalogue ye go for, 86
  in the ills of, 965
  in the mouths of, 108
  in these degenerate days, 218
  incomprehensible wavering and misty, 727
  innumerable race of, out of one man, 154
  inordinately like to do, 936
  insane, eloquent about themselves, 1078
  into an error, surprising honest, 1055
  it ain't my princerples nor, 526
  judge by the complexion of the sky, 60
  judge, by their success, 1044
  justifiable to, 156
  justify the ways of God to, 148
  kind-hearted business, 935
  know love, most, 581
  know, old, 935
  know so little of men, 802
  know their love, let, 33
  known by their cigars, 797
  learn that poetry is, 912
  let us die like, 447
  let us die to make, free, 522
  let us now praise famous, 783, 1125
  light for just, 967
  like satyrs grazing, 32
  like to make the public stare, 359
  literary, a perpetual priesthood, 376
  little group of willful, 725
  live peaceably with all, 1119
  lived and toiled with, 777
  lived like fishes, 170
  lives of great, all remind us, 433
Men, lodging-place of wayfaring, 1112
  logical consequences beacons of, 564
  looks through the deeds of, 81
  loven newfangelnesse, 8
  macerate for advertising, 934
  made, and not made them well, 94
  make use of the first part, 1050
  makes all, one, 378
  man of letters among, 215
  marry again when, 723
  masters of their fates, 81
  may be read, 209
  may come and men may go, 465
  may err was never yet denied, 174
  may read strange matters, 84
  measures not, 253, 259
  melancholy, are the most witty, 124
  met each other with erected look, 174
  might be better if we, 506
  might know remorse, 774
  miscall delight, 366
  mispronounce it, 912
  modest, are dumb, 288
  more careful of the breed of horses and dogs, 184
  more or less impatient, 318
  most infamous, 262
  most, were bad, 1013
  most wretched, 367
  moulded out of faults, best, 37
  move under a canopy of love, 441
  must be taught, 212
  must die or the world, old, 472
  must endure their going hence, 100
  must have doctors, 1054
  must needs abide, what fates impose, 70
  must see love before death, 729
  must work, 523
  my giant arms upbear, and, 517
  nation of gallant, 260
  ne'er spend their fury on a child, 71
  nobleness that lies in other, 524
  nor wrong these holy, 352
  not so old, 936
  not superior by accidents of race or color, 602
  obsequious and conciliating abroad, 344
  of death, captain of all these, 172
  of few words are the best, 66
  of genius do not excel because they labor, 331
  of genius, fame denied to, 1077
  of high degree and low degree, 1104
  of honour and of cavaliers, 260
  of inward light, 143
  of letters, best thoughts of, 588
  of light and leading, 261, 561
  of little showing, 783

Men of loyal breeding, 561
  of middle age, marigolds given to, 56
  of most renowned virtue, 163
  of perverse opinion, 965
  of place and consequence, 806
  of sense approve, 211
  of sense, to laugh at, 1050
  of the Emerald Isle, 941
  of the present day, 346
  of the same religion, sensible, 421
  of these degenerate days, 218
  of thought and men of action, 503
  of thought and reading, 561
  of understanding to fall away, make, 1125
  of weak nerves, 926
  of wit will condescend, 191
  often applaud imitation, 963
  old are walking hospitals, 180
  old, have need to touch, 1085
  old, know young men fools, 28
  old, shall dream dreams, 1113
  ordinary, are fit for, 98
  other, our lands will till, 581
  ought not to investigate things, 1013
  over seventy, 724
  owe most of their greatness, 727
  patient with over-praise of themselves, 529
  pell-mell of, 519
  persist in doing so, how, 767
  pitieth suffering, 963
  please the fancy of, 1049
  poet still more a man than are, 376
  poets or sages, what makes, 574
  possess a poison for serpents, 993
  power makes slaves of, 368
  prevailin' weakness of, 606
  prize the thing ungain'd, 74
  proper and tall, 738
  proper, as ever trod, 81
  propose, why don't the. 388
  proud, small things make base, 69
  purchased by valiant, 970
  put an enemy in their mouths, 101
  quit yourselves like, 1100
  quotation the parole of literary, 237
  read it with joy, reasonable, 415
  read poetry, why, 680
  reject their prophets, 1074
  reside in old, 981
  rich, rule the law, 250
  rise on stepping stones, 436, 467
  rise, where great men, 688
  risk their luck, 723
  roll of common, 62
  ruined by their propensities, 261
  sailors are but, 44
  say nothing in dangerous times, wise, 130
  say, of what, 967
  say the winter, 917

Men, schemes o' mice and, 284
  science that, lere, 4
  seems vilest of, 964
  seldom make passes, 918
  self-made, 453
  self-taught, 331
  shall be seen in the air, 940
  shall walk under water, 940
  shallow, believe in luck, 414
  she takes the breath of, away, 429
  should be judged, 775
  should be what they seem, 102
  should fear, strange that, 82
  showed their own white feather, 826
  shut doors against a setting sun, 80
  sicken of avarice, old, 116
  sin without intending it, 1010
  sit down to nourishment called supper, 40
  sleek-headed, 81
  smile no more, 205
  so are they all honourable, 83
  so many minds, as many, 12, 980
  Socrates the wisest of, 156
  some, have only one book in them, 313
  some to business take, 209
  some to pleasure take, 209
  speak after the manner of, 1119
  speak with the tongues of, 1120
  spirits of just, made perfect, 1122
  stand amazed, 889
  stand face to face, 779
  steered by popular applause, 1000
  strength of twenty, 80
  strive, all, 487
  successful, cause, 1006
  such, are dangerous, 81
  such names and, 52
  superiority of educated, 1015
  suspect your tale, 206
  talk only to conceal the mind, 203
  tall, had empty heads, 113
  tall, sun-crowned, 522
  ten, went along, 924
  that be lothe to departe, 189
  that can have communion, 381
  that can render a reason, 1108
  that conquer and slay, 772
  that God made mad, 828
  that learned their duty, 970
  that makes great, 1080
  that perished to make us, 628
  that put quarrels purposely on others, 55
  that stood for office, 972
  that stumble at the threshold, 70
  that truly grieve at funerals, 180
  that were boys, 810
  that were sensible of dishonour, 970
  that which flees from, 930
  the world's great, 454
  think all men mortal, 201
  think, what you and other, 81

Men, this blunder find in, 275
  thought it a region of sunshine, 416
  thought of less value than gold, 10
  thoughts of, are widened, 464
  thoughts of, do decay, 25
  three good, unhanged, 61
  three sorts of wise, 976
  thwart thee, if, take no heed, 473
  tide in the affairs of, 83
  to be leader of, 738
  to be of one mind in an house, 1128
  to err, it causeth, 1123
  to famous, 970
  to follow far-fatiguing trade, persuade, 247
  to foolish, 964
  to hear him, hire, 120
  to live, teach, 205
  to match my mountains, 732
  to match my plains, 732
  to remember, I want, 774
  to share, teach, 1074
  to take their exit, doors for, 127
  tongues of dying, 59
  toppling lift of the young, 914
  treacherous phantom, call liberty, 532
  trunks of, 46
  truths which are not for all, 1053
  turn and see the stars, 674
  twelve good, into a box, 331
  twelve honest, have decided, 203
  two, of all mankind, 807
  two stern-faced, 391
  under steadfast, 475
  unknown might win themselves a name, 432
  unlearned, of books, 203
  upon the paths of, 438
  usually more stung, 997
  wait their good and truth, 410
  want woman's first love, 724
  we are, my liege, 86
  we are the hollow, 899
  we petty, walk under his legs, 81
  weep, death makes, 361
  well-fed long-haired, 1000
  were all transported, 954
  were deceivers ever, 38, 256
  were listening, as if, 990
  were living before Agamemnon, 358
  were men, trod when, 490
  we've got the, 562
  what if, take to following, 609
  what scanted in hair, given in wit, 37
  when bad, combine, 259
  when, speak well of you, 1117
  which never were, 52
  which ordinary, are fit for, 98
  whilst they are awake, 1002
  who are occasions and not causes of disaster, 734
  who are richer, 936
  who borrow and men who lend, 323
  who brag and bluster, 761

Men who can hear the Decalogue, 296
who can stand before, 522
who clung to their first fault, 484
who died, poor, 823
who do the work, 780
who drown, 649
who go on losing, 807
who grasp the standard, 561
who have failed in literature, 421
who have honour, 522
who have this life in them, 532
who keep on playing, 807
who know much, 1055
who lend and men who borrow, 323
who live by sharping and robbing, 228
who perhaps down wells, 879
who possess opinions and a will, 522
who prefer any load of infamy, 314
who strike for home and altar, 561
who understand, shire of, 893
who will not lie, 522
whom men condemn, 657
whom men pronounce divine, 657
whom the lust of office, 522
whom the spoils of office, 522
whose heads do grow beneath their shoulders, 100
whose views of Christian duty, 522
whose visages do cream and mantle, 44
will arise and depart, 1065
will sometimes jealous be, 121
will stand saddening, 632
wise, refraine to medle, 10
wiser become, 146
wisest of all mortal, 114
with beautiful manners, 886
with empires in their purpose, 732
with good, not so absolute, 386
with humane, I will plead, 424
with mothers and wives, 391
with reasonable, I will reason, 424
with sisters dear, 391
with sore eyes, like, 995
with splendid hearts, 893
with the muck-rake, 734
women and Herveys, 313
won eight victories, 969
world knows nothing of its greatest, 401
world was worthy of such, 428
worth a thousand, 308
would sooner face, 728
you took them for, not the, 39
young, fitter to invent, 111
young, regard their elders as senile, 635
young, shall see visions, 1113
young, think old men fools, 28
Men's believing, pass all, 885
bones, full of dead, 1116
business and bosoms, 109
charitable speeches, 114
company, sicken of, 829

Men's cottages princes' palaces, 44
counters, words are, 132
creeds, 354
daughters, words are, 204, 232
dream, the old, 173
evil manners live in brass, 74
eyes in April, 873
eyes, sparkled in, 490
facts, precedents for poor, 28
judgments are a parcel, 104
labours and peregrinations, port of all, 112
lives are chains, 565
lives deaths toils and teens, 651
lives, history in all, 65
lives, music of, 60
lives, ye are buying, 310
minds, can lead, 649
miseries, kind umpire of, 68
misery, became the cause of all, 22
names, that syllable, 157
noses when they lie asleep, athwart, 77
nurses, wives are old, 110
office to speak patience, 40
prayers for death, old, 967
private lives, into, 998
souls, times that try, 271
stuff, disposer of other, 114
thoughts according to their inclinations, 111
vision, the young, 173
weaknesses are often necessary, 1084
wives are young, mistresses, 110
Mencken and Nathan's American credo, 863
Nathan and God, these three, 872
Mend God's work, man to, 175
it or be rid on 't, 86
lacks time to, 401
your speech a little, 98
Mendacity, tempted into, 472
Mended, little said is soonest, 133
never can be, but must ever, 432
old houses, 193
Mender of bad soles, 81
Mendicancy, fancy styles of active, 645
Mending, in need of, 575
put their detractions to, 39
Menial's hire, worked for a, 847
Mens aequa in arduis, 399
regnum bona possidet, 20
Mental constitution, conditions of our, 450
dyspepsy, of a, 525
exaltation, 737
exertion, escape the need for, 278
fight, I will not cease from, 283
Mention her, no we never, 388
of thee always in my prayers, making, 1122
Mentioned as having suffered, 995
better be damned than not, 272

Mentions hell to ears polite, never, 210
Mercator's north poles and equators, 599
Mercenary calling, 744
Merchant, over-polite, 333
who for silk would sell, 566
Merchants are princes, whose, 1111
where, most do congregate, 44
Mercies, marvellous, 631
Merciful as constant, 924
no God but he the most, 1126
proud and strong, 765
to a broken reed, be, 113
Merciless in toil, 779
stepmother, 993
Mercury can rise, Venus sets ere, 217
like the herald, 95
the words of, are harsh, 42
Mercy and truth are met, 1105
asked, mercy I found, 21
can but confess Thy, 1091
charity and love, shapes of, 495
courage kindness mirth, for, 804
deed of, 427
do justly and to love, 1113
ever hope to have, 25
his, shall clear, 626
I to others show, 25, 216
is above this sceptred sway, 46
is nobility's true badge, 76
is not strained, 46
la belle dame sans, 383
nothing becomes them as, 36
o' my soul, ha'e, 948
of a rude stream, 73
of forgetfulness, 794
of the puddles, at the, 588
on this sot, 940
render the deeds of, 47
seasons justice, 46
shown, lovelier things have, 355
shut the gates of, 245
signatures and marks of, 1079
temper justice with, 155
unto others, 25, 216
upon us miserable sinners, 1127
we do pray for, 46
wound with, 672
Mere anatomy, a, 38
white truth in simple, 470
Meredith is only a prose Browning, 526
Merge itself and become lost, evil, 536
Meridian of my glory, 73
third hour after, 799
Meridians for a seine, 616
Merit, as if her, lessened yours, 240
endless, in a man's knowing, 378
envy will pursue, 211
force of his own, 72
got without, 101
heaven by making earth a hell, 352
makes his cook his, 1046
name vain without the, 219
next in, 415
of a general, 966
raised, by, 149

Merit, sense of your great, 267
spurns that patient, takes, 93
unassisted advances slowly,
231
wins the soul, 212
Merits, careless their, 250
dumb on their own, 288
handsomely allowed, 237
honour it in proportion of its,
1067
of thyself, look not on, 566
to disclose, no farther his, 245
told the utmost of their, 931
Mermaid Tavern, choicer than
the, 384
things done at the, 129
Meroë Nilotic isle, 156
Merrier man, a, 41
more the, 17
Merriest, men are, when from
home, 66
Merrily shall I live now, 33
Merriment, flashes of, 97
Merry, all their wars are, 828
and glad, all things are, 431
and wise, 11, 29, 286, 611
as a marriage-bell, 352
as the day is long, 38
boys are we, three, 127
dance joke and rejoice, be, 164
dancing drinking time, 176
eat drink and be, 1109
England, they called thee, 305
feast, great welcome makes a,
37
fool to make me, 51
have they been, at point of
death, 80
heart goes all the day, 56
heart hath a continual feast,
1107
heart that laughs at care, 363
I am not, 101
in hall where beards wag all,
19
jest, I am a, 673
let's be, 133
love the fiddle, 791
men, fight on, 256
monarch scandalous and poor,
184
month of May, 120
roundelay, 28
swithe it is in halle, 19
was he, 190
when I hear sweet music, 47
Merryman and Doctor Quiet, 192
Mesa grass, dreamed of the, 830
Meself and me wealth between,
715
Mess of 'em, cleanin' up de whole,
908
Message of comfort "Easy all,"
862
for the age, 787
from the skies, many a, 286
he may have a, 797
of despair, 327
sweet, give to him a, 664
to Garcia, carry a, 745
to me, came in the twilight,
653
writ, whose hand the, 445
Messenger chanced to drown, 572
employed to write within this
book, 511

Messenger, God's, sent down, 503
I am God's, 346
lame, 137
no rest for a, 727
of friendship, 608
of sure and swift relief, 697
who brings bad news, 964
Messengers, Persian, 969
take these two, 746
words for, 881
Messmates hear a brother sailor,
247
Met face to face, 620
hail fellow well, 191
her, know how first he, 481
if we had never, 389
in thee to-night, are, 612
night that first we, 388
no sooner, but they looked, 51
part of all that I have, 464
the day and the way we, 633
't was in a crowd, we, 388
Metal flowed to human form, 214
insect-pin a fly, 683
O hearts of, 760
of a man tested, 530
pure as finest gold, 760
rang true, 527
shout of golden, 938
sonorous, 148
Metals, all the earthy, 929
Metallic pens disclose the poet's
numbers, 292
Metamorphosis, in a state of,
1012
Metaphor and dream, verbiage,
578
betrayed into no, 331
Metaphysic wit, high as, 142
Metaphysical frolic, 898
Meteor flag of England, 328
like a fast-flitting, 362
ray, fancy's, 285
streamed like a, 244
streaming to the wind, 148
Meteors are not needed, 895
Meter, rang a fierce discordant,
579
Method in madness, 92
in man's wickedness, 131
of making a fortune, 246
of mounting, 238
of pleasing, surest, 222
resort to any, 858
Methodist Church sends more
soldiers to the field, 456
Methodistic bell, shouted the, 566
Methought I heard a voice, 86
Methuselah, all the days of, 1097
Metre ballad-mongers, 62
of an antique song, 107
Metres, mouse-traps of, 831
Metropolis of flowers, in their
bright, 756
Mettle, a lad of, a good boy, 61
a man of, 1040
grasp it like a man of, 204
of your pasture, 66
puts us on our, 1046
Mew, be a kitten and cry, 62
the cat will, 97
Me-wards, affection's strong to,
133
Mewing her mighty youth, 163
Mewling and puking, 49
Mezzotint, an etching, 490

Micawber, I never will desert
Mr., 496
Mice and rats and such small
deer, 99
best-laid schemes o', 284
desert a falling house, 993
feet like little, 163
fishermen appear like, 99
Miching mallecho, this is, 94
Mickle is the powerful grace, 78
Microbe and bacillus, each, 860
Microbes, foolish thoughts swarm
like, 671
Microcosm of a public school,
420
Microscope begins, 1069
of thought, 1069
Microscopes cease to be of use,
543
Midas me no Midas, 947
the ears of, 893
the woes of, 1021
touched, one of the ones, 585
Midday beam, at the full, 163
Middle age, companions for, 110
age, enchantments of, 548
age is a curse, 851
age on his bold visage, 308
class is large, 975
class morality, 721
life, a thousand years of, 812
mind, beware the, 898
of March back in the, 839
of the night, vast and, 90
of the woods lived, in the,
498
station had fewest disasters,
187
tree, tree of life the, 151
Middle-aged have all their five
senses, only, 905
man builds a woodshed, 515
Middle-class, last enchantment
of the, 906
Middlesex, an acre in, is better
than, 398
Middlin' tight grip, 639
Midland furze afire, 778
Midnight, at still, 35
born, of Cerberus and blackest, 160
brought on the dusky hour,
153
clear, it came upon the, 477
dead of, the noon of thought,
273
drink no water, at, 801
flower, pleasure like the, 334
gravity out of bed at, 62
hags, secret black and, 87
heard the chimes at, 65
hours, mournful, 439
in the solemn, centuries ago,
479
iron tongue of, 43
murder many a foul and, 244
oil consumed, 206
on the seas, in the, 501
on the stroke of, 801
once upon a, dreary, 460
one hour's sleep before, 138
over the, came stealing the
morn, 600
pity the, 898
revels by a forest side, 149
shout and revelry, 157

Midnight, spend my time till, 931
  stars of, shall be dear, 296
  strikes and hastens, 744
  train is slow, 890
  we galloped, into the, 485
  with streamers flying, 240
Midnights, bring back those, 832
  of despair, through, 878
Midriff from its moorings, tear
  the, 863
Midshipmite, a bo'sun tight and
  a, 622
Midst of life we are in death,
  1128
  of them, there am I in the,
  1115
Midsummer, as the sun at, 63
  golden sun of, 394
  madness, this is very, 55
Midwife, she is the fairies', 77
Mien carries more invitation, 197
  monster of so frightful, 208
  such a face and such a, 174
Might, alive with a terrible, 681
  all-enacting, 651
  be better if we better, men, 506
  do it with thy, 1110
  faith that right makes, 455
  have been, it, 442
  honest man 's aboon his, 287
  if kings must show their, 432
  nor by power, not by, 1113
  not be, and so it, 510
  of one fair face, the, 1023
  of the gods, 968
  of thy spirit, by the, 1128
  protect us by thy, 447
  Thy mercy and Thy, 1091
  try with all my, 339
  would not when he, 257
Might-have-been, my name is,
  577
Might-have-beens, these poor,
  693
Mightier far is love, 303
Mightiest in the mightiest, 46
  Julius fell, 89
  practical force in the universe,
  678
Mightily, strive, 52
  won, 663
Mighty ale a large quart, of, 6
  all the proud and, 223
  and dreadful death, 118
  crack, hear the, 194
  crowd, spread a, 694
  dead, converse with the, 224
  death, eloquent just and, 22
  deeds, boast no more your, 141
  fallen, how are the, 1100
  fortress is our God, 1023
  have no theory, 893
  heart is lying still, 297
  heart, little body with a, 66
  ills, what, 185
  large bed, bed of honour a, 200
  line, Marlowe's, 119
  maze but not without a plan,
  206
  men ballooning high, 575
  minds of old, 321
  name of Rome, 401
  orb of song, 302
  pain to love, it is, 167
  race, 373
  scepter, he wields a, 534

Mighty sepulchres of, dead, 386
  shrine of the, 355
  state's decrees, mould a, 468
  than Thou art, wert less, 503
  they say that man is, 534
  thought in a mighty mind, 675
  tone, dwells in that, 501
  voice of Canada, 738
  while ago, 118
  wicked anyhow, I's, 480
  withered, how are the, 756
  workings, hum of, 383
  youth, mewing her, 163
Mignonette, pitcher of, 715
  the Frenchman's darling, 266
Migration of the soul, 970
Mike O'Day, grave of, 948
Mild decay, general flavor of, 452
  philosophy, calm lights of, 194
Mildest mannered man, 359
Mildew mould and stain, 725
Mildness, ethereal, 224
Mile, by a hundred thousand, 678
  with Sorrow, walked a, 861
Miles away, and Sheridan
  twenty, 552
  long, grey, 610
  they came three thousand, 525
  three thousand, 954
  to go before I sleep, 839
  to go that night, 951
  twelve, from a lemon, 313
Milestones are gravestones, 482
  into headstones change, 529
Military animal, man is a, 507
  man, any, 66
Militia, the rude, 177
Milk, adversity's sweet, 79
  and honey blest, with, 1017
  and honey, flowing with, 1098
  and water, happy mixtures of,
  357
  draught of red cow's, 140
  from many a rocky teat, 814
  likely to be watered, 614
  of concord, sweet, 88
  of human kindness, 84
  of human kindness, with the,
  906
  of Paradise, drunk the, 316
  skim, masquerades as cream,
  623
  such as have need of, 1122
  trout in the, 515
  white doe with dust is dark
  and dim, 296
Milkie mothers, for the, want
  complaine, 24
Milkmaids, no singing, 707
Milk-white, before, now purple,
  42
  lamb, Una with her, 301
  thorn, beneath the, 284
Milky baldric of the skies, 382
  mothers of the herd, 310
  way i' the sky, 164
  way of souls, 874
  way, solar walk or, 207
Mill a-going, keep the, 521
  back of the flour the, 731
  brook that turns a, 289
  cannot grind with water that is
  past, 137, 666
  earth is a, 492
  God's, grinds slow but sure,
  138

Mill, I wandered by the, 458
  in the selfsame, 675
  more water glideth by the, 77
  much water goeth by the, 17
  of a truism, 414
  that makes th' wather run, 797
  the creaking old, 269
  under the apple-boughs, down
  by the, 508
  waters under a ruined, 868
  were it but a, 649
Mills are to turn, 664
  of God grind slowly, 435
Millennia to slip past, allowed
  these, 1089
Miller knoweth not of, much water, 17
  sees not all the water, 125
  there was a jolly, 269
Millers thin, bone and skin two,
  221
Miller's golden thumb, 5
Milliard-headed throng, 544
Milliner, perfumed like a, 61
Millinery, mass of, 469
Million acres, Cleon hath a, 503
  buds but stay their blossoming,
  668
  it's one to a, 623
  million men are sped, 844
  million spermatozoa, 922
  misses a unit, aiming at a,
  488
  of ages have gone, 581
  pleased not the, 93
  stars are in the sky, 844
  than the second, 1054
  you made, not the, 676
Millions boast, who dost thy, 168
  for defence, 276
  in it, there's, 617
  in tears, leaves, 431
  leave your many, 656
  of bubbles like us, 1018
  of spiritual creatures, 152
  of surprises, 136
  of years, untold, 581
  saddled and bridled, 169
  think, perhaps makes, 359
  toil unblessed, 735
  twenty-seven, mostly fools, 379
  who've choked you down, 795
  with millions agree, 271
  yet to be, thanks of, 363
Millstone hanged about his neck.
  1117
  hard as the nether, 1103
  look through a, 24
  see into a, 1040
Milnes, the gods call Dicky, 458
  will visit you in disgrace, 458
Milo's end, remember, 180
Milstone, seene far in a, 14
Milton, faith and morals of, 298
  malt does more than, 743
  round the path of, 304
  shouldst be living, 298
  some mute inglorious, 245
  that mighty orb of song, 302
  the divine, 302
  the sightless, 303
  to give a, birth, 262
Milton's faith and Wordsworth's
  trust, 634
  immemorial theme, 558
Mimic sky, 701

Mimsy were the borogoves, 598
Mince this matter, 101, 1033
Mincemeat of the very smallest
  talk, 430
Mincing, walking and, 1111
Mind, absence of, 324
  all with a joyful, 765
  alone, companion none is like
    unto, 19
  amusements for the, 509
  and feeling, go with pure, 480
  and soul and senses, fill my,
    888
  appearances to the, 1007
  as the, is pitched, 266
  at liberty, 237
  at peace, from a, 986
  away, even the, 982
  bear in, your labor is, 417
  bettering of my, 32
  blameless, a, 220
  bliss centres in the, 250
  blotted from his, 204
  body or estate, 1127
  breathing from her face, 356
  calm of, all passion spent, 157
  cheerfulness a daylight in the,
    197
  clothed and in his right, 1116
  conscious of rectitude, 986
  content, a, 940
  couldn't copy my, 777
  dagger of the, 85
  damning those they have no, to,
    142
  dauntless, 70
  desires of the, 112
  destroys their, 175
  develops the powers of the,
    1087
  did minde his grace, never, 26
  diseased, minister to a, 88
  diseases of the, 198
  education forms the common,
    209
  encyclopedic, 398
  envy and an evil, 166
  envy is a pain of, 1006
  equal to any undertaking, 496
  error chokes the windows of
    the, 114
  evangels of the, 873
  even, in difficulties, 399
  exist only in our, 1087
  farewell the tranquil, 102
  fixed on some lofty ideal, 1087
  fleet is a glance of the, 264
  for it was happy, 595
  forbids to crave, 20
  from care, house the, 809
  from moods of, 461
  gentle, is knowne, 25
  gentlest of man's, 779
  glimmer on my, to, 327
  glowing, 889
  God is the only, 548
  golden, stoops not to show of
    dross, 45
  good, possesses a kingdom, 20
  grand prerogative of, 344
  grateful, by owing owes not,
    151
  great fortitude of, 233
  great, knows the power of gen-
    tleness, 491
  grows old, for the, 975

Mind grows torpid, 236
  had grown Suspicion's sanctu-
    ary, 353
  has seldom had an equal, his,
    930
  hath a maimed, 147
  her opinionated, 790
  his, a thought his life, 506
  his Euclid, 576
  his eyes are in his, 317
  ignis fatuus of the, 185
  in a mighty, 675
  in ruins, the human, 941
  in the victor's, 194
  ingratiate deeply with the, 223
  is bent, when to ill thy, 220
  is divided, my, 964
  is free to go, 814
  is gay, my, 673
  is God, our, 1006
  is its own place, 148
  is like a catacomb, 880
  is pitched, as the, 266
  is so engrossed, 1049
  is the judge of the man, 991
  is the lever of all things, 339
  lamp in that dogged, 928
  large and fruitful, 112
  last infirmity of noble, 159
  laugh that spoke the vacant,
    250
  leafless desert of the, 355
  lets go, my, 621
  looke cleane through the, 24
  loose sally of the, 232
  love looks with the, 42
  love's a frailty of the, 193
  loyal nature and of noble, 471
  mainbrace of the, 893
  man is but a, 662
  man's unconquerable, 297
  marble index of a, 299
  march of the human, 259
  Meccas of the, 363
  men to be of one, 1128
  might satisfy his, 511
  misguide the, 210
  mostly in your, 919
  mould the secret, 633
  narrowed his, 252
  never be an old man in, 981
  no hold on the, 974
  noble, o'erthrown, 93
  nobler in the, to suffer, 93
  not acquainted with his, 994
  not body enough to cover his,
    313
  not to be changed, 148
  not what thou lackest, 1011
  o'erwrought, 650
  of a son or daughter, 273
  of cant, clear your, 238, 241
  of man, in the, 296
  of man like musical instrument,
    542
  of man, wine shows the, 960
  one, in an house, 1128
  oppressed with dumps, 255
  oppression of the, 184
  out of sight out of, 9, 27, 519
  overtaxed, an accurate, 454
  passion is a fever in the, 184
  pen is the tongue of the, 1040
  permit the, to look, 30
  persecutes the, 174
  persuaded in his own, 1119

Mind, philosophy inclineth man's,
    110
  pity melts the, to love, 176
  plumb the Oriental, 776
  poison to his, and peril to his
    body, 401
  professional military, is inferi-
    or, 795
  pulse in the eternal, 894
  quiet, is richer, 940
  quite vacant, 263
  raise and erect the, 112
  redeem the human, from error,
    434
  rehearse, this truth within thy,
    462
  reign of, 337
  require a new social, 637
  riddle of a woman's, 1037
  sad thoughts to the, 295
  seize upon the, 507
  serene for contemplation, 195,
    206
  shall heal the tortured, 373
  she had a frugal, 264
  soften the determined, 933
  soon grows through them, 271
  spectres of the, 443
  standard of the man, 199
  steady, ballast to keep the, 529
  strength both of body and,
    1048
  suspicion haunts the guilty, 71
  talk only to conceal the, 203
  that has the same hopes, 237
  that makes the body rich, 52
  that purrs, 898
  that very fiery particle, 361
  the last best work the human,
    286
  the philosophic, 301
  the restive or sluggish, 1083
  thou present to my, appearest,
    393
  time out of, 1033
  'tis peace of, 977
  to be a Florus, no, 1009
  to change thy, 1011
  to, give your whole, 1076
  to glimmer on my, 327
  to laugh, have a, 985
  to me a kingdom is, 20
  to me an empire is, 20
  to mind heart to heart, 307
  to see if this boat will float, 371
  to such a pitch, worked her,
    942
  to this little curse, 314
  touch my country's, 834
  treasures he found in his, 791
  unmoved, show a, 983
  untutored, sees God in clouds,
    207
  unwritten record of the, 970
  vacant, and body filled, 67
  vacant, is a mind distressed,
    263
  vigorous, 231
  waiting harp-strings of the, 549
  weakness of the human, 1048
  well-ordered, 1010
  well-stored, 692
  were weight, if, 303
  what I am pleased to call my,
    794
  what I am taught, 339

Mind, what is, 360
 what you are pleased to call, 402
 whose body lodged a mighty, 218
 wisest books in her, 168
 with a confident easy, 870
 with its own eyes, 814
 with women heart argues not, 547
 without a certain unsoundness of, 397
 would be, poor the human, 1079
 your little, 910
Minds, activity unfamiliar to people's, 670
 admiration of weak, 156
 all, are little, 643
 are not ever craving, 280
 are slow, as their, 1064
 are turned, their, 838
 as many men, so many, 12
 balm of hurt, 86
 curiosity of young, 1078
 divine insanity of noble, 438
 elevate even petty, 999
 fate of all great, 1064
 govern lesser restless, 506
 happiest and best, 369
 innocent and quiet, 168
 led captive, 156
 little things affect little, 420
 made better by their presence, 520
 marriage of true, 108
 men have marble, 107
 of old, the mighty, 321
 of some of our statesmen, 334
 powers which impress our, 295
 recriminate, weak, 318
 speech to communicate their, 183
 strongest, world hears least, 302
 that have nothing to confer, 305
 time demands strong, great hearts, 522
 true dull, preferred, 343
 trust not your daughters', 100
 women have waxen, 107
 world must have great, 506
Mind's construction in the face, 84
 eye Horatio, in my, 90
 own fire, 869
Minden's plain, on, 269
Mind-events, in, 937
Mindful what it cost, ever, 294
Mindfulness, some, 965
Mine and thine, two fatal words, 1034
 be a cot beside the hill, 289
 be the breezy hill, 269
 bright jewels of the, 370
 but all I see is, 568
 by the royal seal, 584
 ease in mine inn, take, 63
 equal mine guide and mine acquaintance, 1104
 eye seeth thee, 1103
 eyes have seen the glory, 522
 fairy of the, 158
 Father thy will not, be done, 423

Mine, it was, 596
 of cleverness and wit, 713
 own, do what I will with, 1115
 soul of all things make it, 546
 the matchless, 929
 thou still art, 576
 were of trouble, 744
 what is yours is, 37
Mines for coal and salt, 363
Mingle in its care and strife, to, 474
 mingle mingle, 117
Mingled love and dread, 678
 mist and light, 439
 yarn, 53
Mining-claims, snakeskin-titles of, 929
Mining stock, better returns than, 465
Minions, nature's, 808
 of the moon, 60
 power and its, 329
 songs my lyric, 1065
Minister came to tea, 818
 of God, 779
 of ministers, 728
 of praise at large, 248
 one fair spirit for my, 354
 so sore, no, 213
 thou flaming, 103
 to a mind diseased, 88
 to himself, patient must, 88
Ministers, fit and qualify men to be, 170
 of grace defend us, 91, 241
 of love, all are but, 316
Ministers' daughters, 654
Ministering angel, 97, 308
Miniver Cheevy, born too late, 808
 loved the Medici, 808
Minnows, Triton of the, 76
Minor and major poets, 931
 chord, harping on that, 718
 key, sings in, 912
 of Thy loftier strain, 443
 pants for twenty-one, the, 214
Minority achieved all that is noble in history, 512
 have stood in the van, 512
 what is a, 512
Minstrel is breaking, heart of the, 335
 lead, Mercy this, 298
 pilgrim of the sky, 304
 raptures swell, no, 307
 wandering, 95
Minstrel's lyre, 816
Minstrelsy, brayed with, 81
Mint and anise, tithe of, 1115
 is in the liquor, 768
 of gold, were each wish a, 292
 of joy, 346
 of phrases in his brain, 40
Minute, better too soon than a, too late, 34
 crowd whole thing in a, 689
 Cynthia of this, 209
 drops from the eaves, 161
 forgot in the hatred of a, 459
 of heaven, one, 338
 once for a, 897
 speak more in a, 79
 that ye sling it, 684
Minutes are whereof our life is made, 540

Minutes, few, every day for inner life, 572
 few, utterly alone, 907
 hasten to their end, 107
 in forty, 42
 make the ages, 553
 set with sixty diamond, 387
 we reckon hours and, 387
Minute's space, the unbounded shut in one small, 647
 success, a, 493
Minute-hand, his conversation shows not the, 239
Miracle and mystery, 672
 believes in the, 932
 beside the lake, 541
 every hour of light and dark a, 537
 grave or satirical musical, 805
 he prays for a, 1072
 instead of wit, 203
 r'ar back and pass a, 908
Miracles, age of, 380
 are past, 53
 are propitious accidents, 770
 for home-made, 887
 miracle me no, 947
 of precocity, 993
 of the Church, 842
 one of God's, 870
Mirage that lured me, 533
Mirage-mists their shining land, 651
Miranda, remember an inn, 810
Mire and fen, sunk in the, 771
 cheat men into, 833
 in the, 620
 inch of earth's old, 806
 learning will be cast into the, 260
 water never left man in the, 80
Mironton, mironton mirontaine, 483
Mirror always nigh, keep a, 760
 best, is an old friend, 137
 break, what if the, 618
 every pool was a, 956
 honest wife's truest, 295
 in that just, 202
 of all courtesy, 72
 of king and slave, 671
 of the soul, speech, is a, 990
 strains to kiss, 882
 thou glorious, 355
 toilet without a, 1064
 truth is the shattered, 544
 up to nature, holds the, 94, 898
Mirrors of the gigantic shadows, 318, 369
 showing stained and aging faces, 824
Mirth and fun grew fast and furious, 287
 and innocence, 357
 and laughter, it is no time for, 359
 and tears, they are by with, 783
 bards of passion and of, 384
 can into folly glide, how, 309
 company and, 744
 far from all resort of, 160
 golden joy in a silver, 610
 he is all, 39
 honour and clean, 777

Mirth in funeral dirge in marriage, 89
is a relaxation from gravity, 331
is like a flash of lightning, 197
laconic and olympian, 808
limit of becoming, 41
May's new-fangled, 40
must borrow its, 718
my spirit enough of, 836
of children with high spirits, 426
of its December, 405
of others only saddens, times when, 426
or music, meat eaten without, 310
song of the birds for, 918
songs of sadness and, 436
string attuned to, 390
that after no repenting draws, 162
that has no bitter, 783
that is but feigning, 546
there's small sincerity of, 386
vexed with, 352
with a shout of, 854
Mirth's boat, 348
Mirthful comic shows, 71
Misanthropos, I am, and hate mankind, 81
Misapplied, virtue turns vice being, 78
Misbegotten knaves, 62
Misbeliever, you call me, 44
Mischance, broke to every known, 779
triumph over all, 70
Mischief, are a, 960
beauty is an ivory, 1014
for idle hands, 199
in every deed of, 270
it means, 94
mortals bend their will to, 212
neglect may breed, 227
place which has done man, 992
Satan finds some, 199
smile with an intent to do, 122
the very virtuous do, tell the, 483
to this nation, public wonder and, 182
Mischiefs, the most dreadful, 1051
Mischievous thing spoken unawares, 1003
Misdeeds, mankind's most terrible, 917
Miser, honesty dwells like a, 51
I was never a, 897
joy may be a, 565
little more than a, 869
Misers of time, 330
Miser's coins, the hours are as a, 620
treasure, unsunned heaps of, 158
Miserable comforters are ye all, 1102
have no other medicine, 36
made their neighbours very, 1078
monster whom I had created, 389
most, is he who enjoys least, 1054

Miserable night, I have passed a, 71
only comfort of the, 1036
sinners, 1127
to be weak is, 148
Miserere Psalm, say very leisurely the, 144
Miseries, in shallows and in, 83
or credulities of mankind, 727
umpire of men's, 68
we call a ship, 787
Misery acquaints a man with strange bedfellows, 33
are from, some to, 282
art thou in, 586
became cause of all men's, 22
child of, baptized in tears, 269
cold to distant, 270
companions in, 990, 1049
finds himself loses his, 546
had worn him to the bones, 80
half our, from our foibles, 275
happy time in, 440
having no relief, one, 347
he gave to, all he had, 245
is at hand, 1020
no friend in, 120
poets in their, dead, 297
power naught but, brings, 388
thou art so full of, 462
treads on heels of joy, 551
twenty ought and six result, 496
vow an eternal, together, 185
Misery's darkest cavern, 231
hand bestows, 262
Misfortune, age the most terrible, 395
delight in another's, 988
made the throne her seat, 198
punished by, 969
remembrance of my former, 1036
Misfortunes, bear another's, 217
delight in others', 259
hardest to bear, 530
laid in one heap, 1003
life was full of, 685
occasioned by man, 993
of mankind, 197, 270
of others, to endure the, 1043
Misfortune's book, writ in sour, 80
Misgivings, blank, 301
Mishaps are like knives, 530
fell into, 954
sad stories of my own, 37
will entail the same, 661
wisdom from another's, 989
worldly chances and, 76
Misled by fancy's meteor ray, 285
Mislike me not for my complexion, 45
Mismanaged nation, for a, 930
Misprint, poet can survive everything but, 723
Misquote, enough learning to, 351
Miss Annabel McCarty was invited, 667
Austen had a talent, 312
Emily, what can, want with a box, 823
McFlimsey of Madison Square, 561

Miss, nature cannot, 176
T. eats, whatever, 823
Missed it lost it forever, we, 490
or wanted, lest it be, 228
who never would be, 624
Missings of happiness, 229
Mission, the doctor's peaceful, 698
Mississippi, at last it is, 929
it's your, 616
of falsehood, 337, 548
ran into, 927
Mississippi's winding stream, from, 475
Missouri, I am from, 714
mule has a copper-plated throat, 816
rolls down to the sea, 504
Missouri's plain, on green, 518
Misspending a man's time a kind of self-homicide, 183
Mist and a weeping rain, follows a, 559
and cloud and foam, 588
and cloud will turn to rain, 438
and the blowing of winds, 891
and there a mist, here a, 583
cold and heavy, 391
has wrapped hill valley grove and town, 349
in my face, to feel the, 489
is dispelled when a woman appears, 205
is rising to the eyes, 643
obscures, no, 322
of light from which they, 458
of shadowy things, 811
of tears, in the, 748
on the glass, 554
pale in a saffron, 904
resembles rain, as, 434
Mists and mellow fruitfulness, 384
churches and creeds lost in, 569
lie low on hill and bay, 580
of doubt prevail, 644
of silver dew, 367
that roll and rise, 916
Mist-blue cities of the soul, 889
Mistake, a great, 217
all which thy child's, 749
glory in a great, 939
life would be a, 1081
never overlooks a, 563
of my life, 616
there is no, 293
woman God's second, 1082
Mistakes, do not even make, 854
experience name for, 724
no balsam for, 659
of a good man, 950
Mistletoe, beneath the holye, 768
Mistress, change was his, 847
in my own house, 778
is a hallowed thing, poet's, 458
jealous, 413, 477
moderately fair, a, 168
of herself, 209
simplicity most deceitful, 637
so sweet a cat, no, 748
such, such Nan, 19
unlocks his heart unto his, 134
Mistresses, wives are young men's, 110
Mistress' eyebrow, 49

Mistrust, hate and, 736
Misty mountain-tops, 79
    old Autumn in the, morn, 392
    purple bloom, I find some, 845
Misunderstanding,   everything
    else a, 1082
Misunderstood, joy, 429
    to be great is to be, 411
Misused wine, poison of, 157
Mite of unfitness, adding his, 528
Mither instead of mother, 723
Mithridates, half, 399
    he died old, 743
Mitten, to see me get the, 604
Mixture of all that constitutes,
    804
    of sorrow, some, 1038
    things come with a, 324
    well, stir the, 454
Mixtures of more happy days,
    357
Mizaru Kikazaru and Iwazaru,
    752
Mizpah, sign upon love's altar-
    stone, 658
    the Lord watch between me
    and thee, 1098
Moab, in the land of, 372, 516
Moab's rocks, 372
Moan, a sigh a sob, a, 597
    English mother made her, 525
    for rest, 597
    of doves, 466
    of thunder, 366
    on its desolate sands eternal,
    503
    paid with, 748
Moaning and groaning and bend-
    ing the knee, 20
    and the harbor bar is, 523
    of the bar, be no, 472
Moat defensive to a house, 59
Moat-by-the-Castle, Nettlecombe
    Hants, 864
Moated grange, at the, 37
Mob is varied and inconstant,
    1049
    laughs at jokes, 827
    law, 455
    of gentlemen, 214
    opinion of the, 1049
    'twas in a, 388
Mobs, herding in turbulent, 343
Mock at sin, fools make a, 1107
    sit in the clouds and, 64
    the air with idle state, 244
    the meat it feeds on, 102
    Turtle replied, 598
    your own grinning, 97
Mocked himself, smiles as if he,
    81
    sense is, 115
Mocker of all degrees, 808
    wine is a, 1107
Mockeries, whole dark pile of
    human, 337
Mockery and a snare, 331
    and contradiction, world a,
    769
    hence unreal, 87
    king of snow, 60
    of monumental stone, 366
Mocking pencil, with, 513
    sneer or the sharp cry, 192
    the air with colours idly
    spread, 58

Mockings or arguments, I have
    no, 534
Mocking-bird is singing, 573
    music of a lovesick, 820
Mocking-bird's throat the musi-
    cal shuttle, 536
Mocking-master mock'd not, 114
Mocks married men, the cuckoo,
    42
Mode, effective, of saying things,
    548
    futile decalogue of, 736
    of God with his elect, 556
Modes, ancient, and former ways,
    186
    of faith, 167, 208
    of life, ring in the nobler, 469
Model of the barren earth, 59
    then draw the, 64
    to thy inward greatness, 66
Moderate, be moderate, be, 75
    haste, one with, 90
    pleasant food, 1049
Moderation and good faith, jus-
    tice, 1051
    even in excess, there is, 420
    is best, 996
    is the silken string, 121
    observe, 959
    the gift of heaven, 967
Moderator of passions, 139
Modern American literature, all,
    930
    classics are always, 426
    inconveniences, 616
    instances, wise saws and, 50
    life, this strange disease of,
    547
    painting, no innocency in, 709
    trick, 429
Modest as a giver, keep, 1079
    cough of a minor poet, 721
    doubt, 75
    men are dumb, 288
    pride and coy submission, 152
    stillness and humility, 66
    the quip, 51
    to be simple, manly true, 528
    woman dressed in all her fin-
    ery, 253
Modesty, bounds of, 80
    clemency etc. are species, 1048
    downcast, concealed, 224
    is a virtue not often found,
    1040
    of nature, o'erstep not the, 94
    pure and vestal, 79
    with meekness and, 972
Modification, bad plan that ad-
    mits no, 988
Modres gate, 7
Mogul and mugwump, 601
Moist breath of decay, 575
Mohammed's truth lay in a holy,
    458
Molasses catches flies, 700
Mold of pain, in the strong, 928
Mole, bastion's, 248
    live like the velvet, 897
Moles and to the bats, 1111
Mole-hill and mare's nest, 650
    mountain of, 329
Molly Pitcher, bright name of,
    659
    was true to his, 274
Molokai's lord of love, 705

Molten blue, inns of, 584
    bowels, 826
Mome raths outgrabe, 598
Moment, as it were for a little,
    1111
    clock indicates the, 535
    deem of no, 975
    deep, the, 773
    did cease from that, 1082
    every, is supreme, 870
    face some awful, 300
    give to God each, 225
    glitters for a, 197
    has gone by for hoping, 913
    improve each, as it flies, 231
    in some blithe, 685
    it is possessed, the, 1051
    least happiest, present, 494
    little chimney heated hot in
    a, 436
    little, what one knows, 636
    loyal and neutral in a, 86
    matters of the highest, 969
    of difficulty, there is a, 949
    of life, claim a, 1061
    of my greatness, 900
    of passing, enter at the, 1085
    of rest, without one, 1077
    of sweet peril, 593
    on moment there rushes, 425
    opportune, one, 626
    pith and, enterprises of, 93
    psychologic, 723
    then in a, presto pass, 406
    there comes one, 1085
    they are soundly established,
    1081
    to decide, 524
    when all had succeeded, 1061
    when all would go smooth, 594
    work of a, 1033
    yet the actor stops, a, 481
Moments, all the best of our past,
    573
    fall, one by one, 564
    given, for bitter, 833
    happiest and best, 369
    in man's mortal years, 647
    make the year, 203
    may outlive them, 1084
    of glad grace, 790
    of surplus power, 872
    quick to haste, the golden, 474
    that a spirit lends, 832
    when he is only stupid, 1066
Moment's monument, 577
    ornament, to be a, 299
    time a little space, 596
Momentary bliss, bestow a, 243
    things we need not see, 895
Momentous to himself, 736
Monarch, does not misbecome a,
    246
    hears assumes the god, 176
    in his throne, any, 1033
    is night, 888
    love could teach a, 246
    morsel for a, 104
    of all I survey, 263
    of mountains, 357
    of the vine, 104
    scandalous and poor, 184
    the throned, 46
Monarchs, change perplexes, 149
    must give place, 512
    ought to put to death, 20

Monarchs seldom sigh in vain, 307
Monarchies, mightiest, 150
Monarchy is a merchantman, 581
Monastic aisles fall like sweet strains, 408
Monday, betwixt Saturday and, 189
hanging his cat on, 940
Monday's child is fair of face, 956
Money, and do spend less, 181
as one pleases, use, 1071
bags of, 933
business is other people's, 1075
can still be made without, 930
cannot buy, blessing that, 140
comes withal, 52
from women, 680
goes as well as my song, my, 610
good provision of, 1025
he loved, 1037
heaps of, 166
how goes the, 510
how pleasant it is to have, 519
I do not mind his, 828
I write for, 685
I'll bet my, 568
if you have, 1022
in thy purse, put, 101
in trust, but put your, 454
invested in a library, 465
is beautiful as roses, 412
is the seed of money, 1054
it is just the same, with, 977
make, is to coin it, 236
means and content, that wants, 50
money money, O, 935
much, as 't will bring, 142
my new play yields, 933
no one shall work for, 779
not scarce, times not hard and, 415
of fools, words the, 132
or toil, built without, 509
painful to keep as well as get, 182
people who despise, 751
perish with thee, thy, 1118
possessed by their, 123
possession of, 1071
put not your trust in, 454
put to interest in the other world, 321
rather serve with their, 1054
ready, Aladdin's lamp, 361
ready, makes the man, 199
right kind of, 1079
spent, never ask of, 839
still get, boy, 118
store her, 1016
the love of, root of all evil, 1122
time is, 227
to a starving man at sea, 1035
to colleges, give, 453
to defray such expenses, 247
to go over the world, 413
to your neighbours, lending, 235
too, we've got the, 562
unless you've got, 685
waste of public, 641

Money which represents the prose of life, 412
who works for, 719
without, George, 258
wrote except for, 236
you would sell, for, 964
Money-changer near the temple, 898
Money-changers, overthrew the tables of the, 1116
Money-chest, man not a, 425
Moneyless man, no open door for the, 609
Money-maker, not a mere, 973
Money-making, is but, 998
Money-match a mistake, 802
Mongoose where were you, 768
Mongrel best in man or dog, 721
bitch, son and heir of a, 98
mastiff, 99
puppy whelp and hound, 254
Monie a blunder free us, 285
Monitions, time's, 650
Monk distraught with dreams and visions, 439
the devil a, would be, 1025
Monks of old, I envy those, 394
Monkey climbing on a yellow stick, 684
married the Baboon's sister, 954
shaved, is only a, 624
wine lion wine sheep wine, 1068
Monkeys, men were developed from, 448
sensibly refrain from speech, 742
two great stems of, 448
wilderness of, 45
Monmouth, river at, 67
Monna Lisa, beauty of, 645
Monomania, cleanliness a, 570
Monongahela, the Colorado the Rio Grande, 932
Monopoly of fame, 124
Monotonous, nothing so, as the sea, 529
Monotony, bleats articulate, 300, 747
Monroe Doctrine will go far, 734
Monster, faultless, 164
green-eyed, it is the, 102
London, 168
makes one a, 685
many-headed, 129, 214, 308
of so frightful mien, 174, 208
whom I had created, 389
Monster's feet, lie at the, 895
Monstrous anger of the guns, 918
every fault seeming, 50
little voice, 42
tail our cat has got, 189
Mont Blanc is the monarch, 357
Montaigne, author of the celebrated essays, 197
Montana, hot afternoons in, 945
Monterey, been with us at, 431
Montezuma, from the halls of, 953
Month between them, 710
follow month with woe, 365
in town, 587
it was the, of May, 619
laughter for a, 61
march stout once a, 177

Month, more than he will stand to in a, 79
next, I'm going to move, 898
of greatest joy, 181
of June, leafy, 315
of love, May never was, 30
of May, in the merry, 120
this is the, and this the happy morn, 161
Months go to the shaping of an infant, nine, 581
of human birth, 832
to lagging years, 707
were May, all the, 687
Montparnasse, rest quiet in, 929
Montreal lumber room, stowed away in a, 614
O God! O, 614
Montrose, around the armor of, 758
to battle with, 500
Monument a people free, his, 555
build their, 364
dim, where Tybalt lies, 80
dost mark this, 1093
enduring, 366
far beyond any, 970
has reared his, 573
man's truest, 658
my gentle verse your, 108
patience on a, 55
slab of marble cold, 448
sonnet is a moment's, 577
which shall endure, 1027
would be a new Europe, 799
ye who pass this, 961
Monuments and rhetoric, 1077
for themselves are, 612
mountains earth's undecaying, 423
of princes, 107
of wit survive monuments of power, 110
to his memory, 330
to your great dead, 722
upon my breast, 374
while waiting for new, 1069
Monumental alabaster, smooth as, 103
pomp of age, 302
stone, 366
Moo-cow-moo, held me up to the, 792
Mood, answered your every, 784
can be maintained, no, 1089
Dorian, of flutes, 149
fantastic as a woman's, 308
in a working, 410
in any shape in any, 356
in his high singing, 890
in listening, she stood, 308
jar on our own quiet, 426
let your reckless, 878
sweet, when pleasant thoughts, 295
that blessed, 295
unused to the melting, 104
Moods all passions, to share all, 649
Moo-hoon, ro-holl on silver, 616
Moon a chill and friendless thing, 761
and I could keep this up, 868
ascending up from the east, 536
auld in hir arme, 255

Moon, be a dog and bay the, 83
begged of the, 951
beneath a waning, 315
beneath the visiting, 105
by night, nor the, 1106
by yonder blessed, 78
cast before the, 23
cast beyond the, 12
close by the, 151
comes over Brooklyn, 939
course of one revolving, 174
drops down, 671
fair and friendly, 372
frail veiled, 889
from out the sea, rake the, 347
glimpses of the, 91
had climbed the highest hill, 277
honour from the pale-faced, 61
hung on the silver, 447
in full-orbed glory, 322
inconstant, 78
into salt tears resolves the, 81
is a silver pinhead, 389
is an arrant thief, 81
is my sister, 810
lifting her silver rim, 385
like a flower, 281
like to a silver bow, 42
looks on many brooks, 335
love to sit and bay the, 912
lucent as a rounded, 528
made of green cheese, 17
maids who love the, 334
minions of the, 60
more interested in the earth, 709
mortals call the, 366
night-flower sees but one, 335
no sun — no, 391
nor stars do shine, 823
of Mahomet, 367
on the one hand, 810
our flirtations with the, 933
pale ports o' the, 748
rising in clouded majesty, 152
roll on silver, 616
shall rise, when the, 114
shine at full or no, 143
shone bright, O the, 899
sigh for the, 608
silent as the, 156
silent night with this fair, 152
silver apples of the, 790
sits arbitress, 149
situated in the, 1069
so round and yellow, 589
swear not by the, 78
sweet regent of the sky, 269
takes up the wondrous tale, 194
that looks for us again, 1020
that monthly changes, 78
the hostess of the sky, 728
the innocent, 748
the sweet surprise of heaven, 601
thou climb'st the skies, 27
unmask her beauty to the, 90
walks the night, 822
wandering, behold the, 160
was a ghostly galleon, 864
was balanced on the sea, 920
went up the sky, the moving, 315

Moon, whom mortals call the 366
will wax the moon will wane, 438
with a rag of gauze, 913
with lifted wing, 798
yestreen I saw the new, 255
Moons lie mirrored, 816
my old and new, 672
wasted, some nine, 100
waxed and waned the lilacs, 437
Moon's unclouded grandeur, 369
Moonbeams on a river, 573
quiver, 582
Moon-calf, 33
Moonlight and feeling, music, 368
April's ivory, 401
come to thee by, 864
glutinous a syrup as, 933
in Kentucky, 675
is divine, 938
lulled by the, 568
meet me by, alone, 388
not of the, 472
of a perfect peace, 717
over the purple moor, 864
sleeps upon this bank, 47
tale told by, 388
visit Melrose by, 306
Moonlit door, knocking on the, 822
floor, float along the, 418
sails, 673
Moonrise, gradual as the, 545
Moonshine, find out, 43
its glory is all, 542
Moon-struck madness, 155
Moon-touched mountains, climb the, 688
Moor, bitter across the wild, 951
I never saw a, 584
lady married to the, 301
moonlight over the purple, 864
Moore, Tom, a health to thee, 356
Moorings, lies at its, 642
Moorish fen, lake or, 158
horn, 375
Moorsfield, London, street near, 232
Moping melancholy, 155
Moral advance, 572
and immoral, significance of, strictly limited, 741
authority, the basis of, 1073
climate of America, 877
culture, highest possible stage in, 448
enterprise does not depend upon numbers, 424
everything's got a, 598
evil and of good, 295
game-law were passed, time a, 589
habits, 998
indifference, 1073
infection difficult to stay, 497
nature, with a higher, 580
need, no, 441
no man's sufficiency to be so, 40
no one can be, till all are, 581
obligation, 856
point a, or adorn a tale, 230

Moral religious political social phrase, 1086
sensible and well-bred man, 263
settling the, 635
test, perception of beauty a, 515
things, 172
topsy-versy, turneth, 929
Morals manners scenery of all such lands, 337
simply blind obedience, 741
which Milton held, 298
why man of, 167
Morality a private and costly luxury, 636
and politics, treat apart, 641
but as his best garment, 880
has become democratic, 572
knows nothing of boundaries, 581
middle class, 721
needs emotion, 617
no, where there is no free agency, 387
of his actions, 1055
of the vulgar man, 1080
on the stomach, enforcing, 1067
periodical fits of, 398
pernicious to general, 422
political differs from individual, 1083
religion and, 233
sexless orgies of, 635
thou deadly bane, 284
unawares expires, 215
veracity the heart of, 563
which suits him, 1084
with wit, enliven, 195
Moralize my song, 24
Mordre wol out, 6
More an antique Roman than a Dane, 98
and how much it is, a little, 486
and less than just, heaven, 565
angels could no, 201
blessed to give, 1119
cantie wi', 287
eloquence, silence hath, 478
frayd then hurt, 12
giving thy sum of, 48
have been wrecked, 611
he saw the less he spoke, 836
honoured in the breach than the observance, 91
I do not know nor need, 657
in man than breath of his body, 449
in sorrow than in anger, 90
is given, the, 1077
is meant than meets the ear, 161
is thy due than more than all, 84
it made them cry, the better the, 253
knave than fool, 31
know less and understand, 877
matter for a May morning, 55
matter with less art, 92
no man see me, 73
nor less, neither, 598
of giving and less of buying, 822

More of singing and less of sighing, 822
of the serpent than dove, 31
please sir I want some, 494
said dreamer dream no, 558
she yaf awey, the more she hadde, 3
sinned against than sinning, 98
still should long for, 292
than a crime, it is, 1060
than a little, 62
than all can pay, 84
than he wants, how much he has, 197
than is necessary, never say, 277
than kin less than kind, 89
than melody, and something, 405
the merrier, 17
the, we arg'ed the question, 678
things in heaven and earth, 92
when sin shall be no, 503
who dares do, 85
would be laid at your feet, 633
Morgan, old bold mate of Henry, 604
the buccaneer, sailed with, 604
Morn, a red, 106
a thousand roses, each, 1018
and cold indifference came, 198
and liquid dew of youth, 90
and with the, those angel faces, 403
begins her rosy progress, 155
blushing like the, 154
breaks, when the, 582
came peeping in at, 390
came stealing the, 600
cheerful at, he wakes, 249
day's at the, 485
fair laughs the, 244
first day even and, 154
furthers a man on his road, 959
genial, appears, 327
golden light of, 390
her rosy steps, 153
herald of the, 79
in russet mantle clad, 89
is up again, 353
lights that do mislead the, 37
like a lobster boiled, the, 142
meek-eyed, appears, 224
night ushers in the, 229
no, no noon no dawn, 391
not waking til she sings, 23
of toil nor night of waking, 308
old Autumn in the misty, 392
on the Indian steep, 157
one, I missed him, 245
opening eyelids of the, 159
prophesied the, 681
salutation to the, 72
set a-sparkle, 493
suns that gild the vernal, 267
sweet approach of even or, 151
sweet is the breath of, 152
the east has crimsoned, 590
this the happy, 161
till night, he sung from, 269
to noon he fell, from, 149

Morn, tresses like the, 158
trumpet of the, 89
waked by the circling hours, 153
who in the, 1021
with rosy hand, 153
Morns are meeker than they were, 584
greeteth a million, 891
in the music of the, 432
Morn's sun may bring, next, 983
Morning, a perpetual, 514
after, cold gray dawn of the, 359, 791
again, never glad confident, 485
air, scent the, 91
as this that drowning, a, 494
at odds with, 87
best of the sons of the, 342
between four and six in the, 930
bid me good, 273
birds, like those of, 405
birds were mad with glee, 619
clock wound up every, 564
come in the, 502
cool reflection came with the, 310
dew, as the sun the, 175
dew, chaste as, 202
dew, faded like the, 327
dew, womb of, 24
do not shorten the, 1064
drum-beat, 341
earliest light of the, 339
evening noon and night, 487
face, disasters in his, 251
face, schoolboy with his shining, 49
fair came forth, 156
found myself famous one, 361
full many a glorious, 107
haze in the mountain-pass, 830
hour to sadden, 453
I thought that, cloud, 375
in the, thou shalt hear, 199
life how pleasant in thy, 285
like the spirit of a youth, 105
lowers, the dawn is overcast the, 194
make me over in the, 757
more matter for a May, 55
nap, thought to clip his, 510
never, wore to evening, 468
night and, Hannah's at window, 568
no this, sir I say, 428
noon and evening cry, 415
o' May, like a, 840
of a mighty day, 347
of the times, in the, 465
of the world, in the, 485
our share of, 583
prime, taste the, 692
purple, 480
reflection came with the, 198
returned in the, 228
rose, bountiful colored my, 586
rose-streak of, 493
rouse at, 743
saw them masters, 738
saw two clouds at, 375
Senlin says, it is, 904
shineth, go when the, 480
shows the day, as, 156

Morning, simply another, 903
sky, forehead of the, 159
sky, shall not see the, 650
somewhere, 't is always, 417
sow thy seed in the, 1110
stars of, dewdrops, 153
stars sang together, 1102
throws a thousand pearly drops, 707
time you wake up next, 935
up, cuts your, 430
wait for the, 643
we will remember, in the, 804
what if some, 659
when you rise in the, 535
wings of the, 342
would God it were, 632, 1099
Mornings face to face, meet our, 810
Morning's glory, spread the, 689
Morning-gate, through glory's, 473
Morning-star, glittering like the, 260
of memory, 355
to the full round of truth, 471
Mornin's mornin', long for a, 715
Moron, I wish I were a, 957
see the happy, 957
Morose, disposed to take a, view, 400
Morpheus, the god of sleep, 3
Morrow, desire of the night for the, 368
did a new, 867
free of thought, 651
good night till it be, 78
knoweth God, the, 677
makes it hope, 566
man has no, 966
no part of their good, 165
of his battles, clouds on the, 1071
take no thought for the, 1114
watching for the, 1057
windy night a rainy, 108
Morrows, thought-worn eves and, 651
Morrow's hidden season, 1058
Morsel for a monarch, 104
sweetest, of the night, 65
under his tongue, 187
Morsels, tough, to swallow, 1081
Mortal and is mine, the wound is, 922
breathes but one, 917
cares, far from, 345
coil, shuffled off this, 93
course, this my, 878
engines, O you, 102
ever dared to dream before, dreams no, 460
eyes cannot behold, 282
frame, quit this, 216
frame, stirs this, 316
free and independent, 715
hands, not built with, 174
known, meanest, 657
ills prevailing, flood of, 1023
instruments, 82
life, as the wind is, so is, 597
made of clay, 274
men think all men, 201
momentary hour, 895
murders, twenty, 87
one was and one was not, 1064

Mortal resting-place so fair, no, 354
  say, of no, 966
  shall assume immortality, 328
  shame of nature, paint the, 472
  spirit of, be proud, 362
  splendor, suddenly a, 895
  taste brought death, 148
  thing, laugh at any, 360
  to any erring, 686
  to the skies, he raised a, 176
  what you desire is not, 986
Mortals, barrenest of all, 378
  be, what fools these, 990
  bend their will to mischief, 212
  call the moon, 366
  crave, whatever, 405
  for of, 965
  given, some feelings to, 308
  happiest of, 1052
  human, 42
  share, every grief that, 626
  to command success, not in, 194
  we all are, and as mortals err, 283
  what fools these, 43
  who ring bells, 1089
Mortality behold and fear, 129
  gladly would I meet, 155
  is too weak to bear them, 186
  kept watch o'er man's, 302
  o'ersways their power, 107
  of books, 629
  thoughts of, 147
  to frail, 113
  weighs heavily on me, 385
Mortality's strong hand, 58
Mortgage beats 'em all, 677
Moses and de profets, 733
  from Mahomet to, 405
  the servant of the Lord died in the land of Moab, 372
Moslem mosque and pagan shrine, 443
  palace, read of the, 541
Mosquito, bite of the critical, 589
  critics, 533
Mosquitoes, fat-gorged, 1009
  we must feed, 412
Moss for a pillow, 823
  grew gray, 591
  rolling stone gathers no, 14
  starved bank of, 492
Mosses cling, on old decay green-est, 441
Moss-covered bucket that hung in the well, 348
Moss-grown walls, who storms the, 851
Mossy cavern, 384
  marbles rest, the, 450
  stone, violet by a, 296
Most beautiful verb in the world, 1083
  dangerous of all spells, 426
  forcible feeble, 65
  gifted poet, this the, 516
  he serves me, 219
  mutable, woman is various and, 472
  of all that comes, 883
  of Heaven he hath in him, 506

Most of the rest did give more, 181
  of them never occur, 750
  unkindest cut of all, 83
  who is it that says, 108
  wondrous book bright candle, 393
  you need me, when, 814
Motes that people sunbeams, 160
Moth, desire of the, for the star, 368
  ne'er spoiled my best array, 217
  vestments of the May, 939
Moths, fill Ithaca full of, 76
  maidens like, 352
Mother an aching heart, caused their, 691
  and lover of men, the sea, 631
  April, make me over, 757
  back to the great sweet, 631
  bore me in the southern wild, 281
  bought it for the sink, 917
  calls me Willie, 699
  child to its, 960
  complaining, hears his, 974
  don't like her daughter to re-semble her, 278
  Eve our credulous, 154
  forty whacks, gave her, 957
  gives him birth, another, 833
  had the money, 884
  happy he with such a, 466
  heart within me, 642
  honour thy father and, 963
  Hubbard, mock sermon on, 678
  ill diet was the, 138
  in Israel, I arose a, 1099
  in place of God to child, 683
  in whose eyes I see, 731
  is a mother still, 316
  is more let and hindered, 872
  is the name for God, 482, 683
  kept all these sayings in her heart, His, 1117
  like son, like, 692
  lovelier still than lovely, 983
  man before thy, 132
  man before your, 132, 267
  may I go out to swim, 957
  meets on high her babe, 322
  mighty, turns in tears, 690
  my, says I must not pass, 625
  never is afraid, 429
  none so devotional as that of, 460
  o' mine, 784
  of a mighty race, 373
  of all living, 1097
  of arts and eloquence, 156
  of devotion, ignorance the, 126, 178
  of dews, morn appears, 224
  of enjoyment, variety is the, 420
  of God, in honour of the holy, 1078
  of good fortune, 1041
  of invention, 654
  of invention, necessity the, 171, 200
  of Iscariot, 817
  of manhood, 994
  of sciences, universal, 1035

Mother of so sweet a son, 817
  of the careful soul, 781
  of the day, night is, 441
  of the free, 761
  ran away, his, 638
  set facing the front, 884
  she's somebody's, 715
  so loving to my, 90
  stand by as for your, 550
  state to thee I kneel, 646
  tells me happy dreams, 699
  the holiest thing alive, 316
  this is my, 665
  time only comforter for the loss of a, 402
  to her daughter says, 1092
  to the child, ties that bind the, 373
  took great care of his, 876
  virgin, wedded maid and, 161
  wandered with her child, 369
  was a superior soul, 883
  was weeping, its, 389
  when she is old, despise not thy, 1108
  who call her, 575
  who has lost an infant, every, 558
  who loves his, 521
  who ran to help me? my, 345
  who talks of her children, 419
  who'd give her booby, 206
  wit, nature by her, 25
Mothers, and so invented, 597
  and wives, men with, 391
  are, children are what, 326
  braver than they, 772
  ever fret, wonder that, 665
  maids must be wives and, 454
  milky, 24, 310
  of men, fought by the, 657
  only ghosts are dead young, 751
  relative laxity of their, 691
  so many anguished, 1071
Mother's ample breast, common, 479
  are not alone our, 443
  bones, from these, 923
  breath, extend a, 213
  eyes like, 574
  face and voice, 683
  graces, thy, 128
  grave, botanize upon his, 297
  house, daughter am I in my, 778
  lap, 155
  life, anchors of a, 966
  life made me a man, 832
  pride a father's joy, 309
  son, hang every, 42
  son, know he was his, 919
  tears, could not bear a, 982
  thanks, shall have a, 539
Mothers' arms are made of ten-derness, 1067
Motherhood woman's great work, 670
Mother-in-law, go not empty unto thy, 1100
  untutored savage contemplates his, 713
Mother-land, sent her from the, 864
Mother-lodge, in my, 782
Mother-love, no love like, 595

Mother-tongue, children of the great, 558
Motion and a spirit, 296
  and rest which we call life, 197
  between the acting and first, 82
  clear without strife, brook's, 501
  guide, all, 1057
  in his, like an angel sings, 47
  its life and imagination the soul, 318
  mathematical, 128
  money sets the world in, 989
  of a hidden fire, 306
  of but an ebb and flow, 869
  or a tear, 474
  scoured with perpetual, 64
  so gradual, 247
  this sensible warm, 36
  to facilitate, 232
  two stars keep not their, 63
Motions of his spirit dull as night, 47
  of the sense, 35
Motionless as ice, 298
  torrents silent cataracts, 316
Motive guide original and end, 231
Motives of more fancy, 53
  meanest, 395
Motive-hunting of a motiveless malignity, 319
Motley fool, 49
  garb, jester's, 851
  rout, 267
  to the view, made myself, 108
Motley's the only wear, 49
Motor-car rich man has his, 867
Motto of a Latin make, 756
  of Warren Hastings, 399
  rely on yourself, 510
  to thy breast, bind the, 1058
  writ so fair, the tender, 776
Mottoes inside the crackers, 622
  of the heart, 327
Mouf, heish yo', 820
Mould, a man of giant, 572
  covered it with, 384
  ethereal, 149
  God's own, 604
  grew out of the, 783
  how large a, 604
  last of human, 328
  mouthful of, 832
  nature lost the perfect, 356
  nature's happiest, 243
  of a man's fortune, 111
  of form, glass of fashion, 93
  of its vulgarity, 894
  of vaster powers, 670
  shape your heart to an ancient, 842
  splashing the wintry, 790
  verge of the churchyard, 391
Moulded on one stem, two lovely berries, 43
  out of faults, best men are, 37
  scarcely formed or, 361
  shall a nation be, 634
Moulder piecemeal on the rock, 355
Moulding Sheridan, 356
Mouldy chestnut, salute each, 601

Mouldy, damnable, 165
  rolls of Noah's ark, 173
  the world would grow, 472
Mound in sweet Auburn, 527
  upon the convex, 922
Mounded years, 748
Mount Abora, singing of, 316
  Casius old, 150
  to its summit round by round, 521
  Zion city of the great king, 1104
Mountain, a genius as well as a, 1069
  and lake, splendor of, 590
  brought forth a mouse, 961, 984, 999
  by Nebo's lonely, 516
  flee as a bird to your, 1103
  haunt dale or piny, 317
  if I never see a, 325
  in its azure hue, robes the, 327
  land of the, 307
  like the dew on the, 308
  nymph sweet liberty, 160
  of a mole-hill, 329
  or sea, path o'er, 406
  pendent rock a forked, 105
  scarce brings forth a mouse, 180
  see one, see all, 124
  sheep are sweeter, 348
  small sands the, 203
  up in the airy, 573
  wall, aloft on sky and, 445
  was in labor, 961, 992
  waves, march is o'er the, 328
  wilderness field and farm, 816
Mountains, above the tops of the highest, 238
  among our ancient, 392
  among the black, 929
  and a wood, three long, 915
  and the sea, man to match the, 708
  are earth's undecaying monuments, 423
  bind him to his native, 249
  Britain boasts are men, 575
  build their monument, 364
  Delectable, 172
  differ in their, 838
  divide you and no end of seas, 674
  faith moves, 490
  faith to remove, 1120
  far-hidden heart of the, 572
  for mass and quiet, 895
  Greenland's icy, 343
  high, are a feeling, 353
  how beautiful upon the, 1112
  in her past, 895
  in the side of the, 961
  interposed make enemies, 264
  let me go, into the, 735
  look on Marathon, 359
  men to match my, 732
Mont Blanc is the monarch of, 357
  moon-touched, 688
  needed less than, 895
  of foam, 857
  one of the, 304
  rolling, sea was, 274
  shall bend, 306
  sink to the earth like, 929

Mountains stand, while yonder, 1059
  stood aside, 839
  that can't be cut through, 872
  there are left the, 895
  to slit the sliding, 839
  while on the, 982
  wide seas and the, 847
  will be in labour, 984
  woods or steepy, 31
Mountain's rim, 485
Mountain-height, freedom from her, 382
  winds swept the, 369
Mountain-piling, they set about their, 484
Mountain-side, from every, 447
  sheer precipitous, 621
  wild wind blows on the, 516
Mountain-stream shall turn, 374
Mountain-tops, and jocund day stands tiptoe on the, 79
  that freeze, 73
Mounted and finished and polished down, 451
Mounteth with occasion, courage, 57
Mounting in hot haste, 352
  up to God, 577
Mourn, countless thousands, 284
  her, all the world shall, 74
  lacks time to, 401
  love is doomed to, 395
  the unalterable days, 409
  who thinks must, 190
Mourned and yet shall mourn, I, 536
  by strangers, 217
  her soldier slain, 269
  honoured and forever, 219
Mourner, many a discontented, 667
Mo'ners up higher, fetch de, 689
Mourners go about the streets, 1110
  remorseful, 596
Mourner's tears, dried one, 593
Mournful about it, nothing, 651
  close, day have, 809
  marbles, across the, 444
  midnight hours, 439
  numbers, tell me not in, 433
  truth, this, 231
Mourning beauty crowned, by, 581
  celebrate my funeral with, 978
  for our dead, 1089
  house of, 1109
  lightest heart makes heaviest, 447
  oil of joy for, 1112
Mourns, nothing dies but something, 359
  vile man that, 207
Mouse, ardent feathered, 823
  as a cat would watch a, 192
  is miracle enough, 535
  killing a, on Sunday, 940
  like the gnawing of a, 916
  mountain brought forth a, 961, 984, 999
  mountain scarce brings forth a, 180
  need to bee a wylie, 16
  never entrusts his life, 7
  not even a, 332

Mouse of the scrolls, 886
  poked its little head, 961
  stirring, not a, 89, 332
  the prowling, 865
  with one poor hole, 139, 978
Mouse-gray mustang, ride on a,
  711
Mouses herte nat worth a leek, 7
Mousetrap, if you build a better,
  416
Mouse-traps of metres, 831
Mousie chuckled to himself, 711
Mousing owl hawked at, 86
Moustache, da bigga da blacka,
  814
  kiss without a, 774
  only one that hasn't a, 855
Mouth a rein, find his, 631
  an thou 'lt, I'll rant, 97
  and the meat, God sendeth, 12,
    19
  ate, what his, 948
  butter would not melt in her,
    14, 192
  close, catches no flies, 1036
  even in the cannon's, 49
  familiar in his, 67
  gift-horse not looked in the,
    1042
  ginger shall be hot i' the, 54
  given two ears but only one,
    420
  he remembered, 903
  head in the lion's, 952
  inside a wolf's, 961
  is too full to express, 441
  is what one becomes, 798
  let the words of my, 1103
  like kisses from a female, 357
  look a gift horse in the, 13,
    142
  look to thy, 136
  most beautiful, in the world,
    222
  mustard in a child's, 272
  O sad kissed, 630
  of babes and sucklings, 1103
  of hell, into the, 467
  of one just dead, 849
  of. the Amazon, 733
  out of thine own, 1117
  purple-stained, 383
  tells it with his tiresome, 669
  that says I rather wish, 751
  to water, made his, 142
  unctuous, 465
  utters, which your, 964
  was an olive leaf, in her, 1097
  wear not my dagger in my,
    106
  which hath the deeper, 68
  whose haughty valor, sweet,
    418
  wickedness sweet in his, 1102
  with a red, 625
  with open, swallowing a
    tailor's news, 58
Mouths, enemy in their, 101
  fill their, 806
  in a glass, made, 98
  not descended from Odin, 592
  of men, in the, 108
  of nations, 1027
  of wisest censure, 101
  to kiss, such red, 803
  what in other, was rough, 524

Mouths without hands, 177
Mouth-filling oath, 62
Mouthful of mould, 832
Movable types, device of, 379
Move, all things work and, 502
  easiest, those, 211
  on a rigorous line, 547
Moved, a woman, 52
  it, so sweetly to the west, 375
  to smile at anything, 82
  with concord of sweet sounds,
    47
Movement misrepresented, every
  new, 670
  new, a stampede, 775
  time is infinite, 1077
Movements, exceeds in the number of its, 1022
  slow and vital, 932
  they made, memory of the, 933
  were graceful, his, 640
Movers and shakers of the
  world, 676
Moves a goddess, 218
  as I move, 573
  in a mysterious way, God, 266
Moveth all together, if it moves
  at all, 297
Movie show, two seats for an
  elegant, 907
Movie-star, wish I was a, 908
Moving accidents, 100
  push on keep, 290
  seems asleep, tide as, 472
  within the family circle, 943
Moving-delicate and full of life,
  40
Moving-pictures well-wrought
  plays, 223
Mown grass, like rain upon the,
  1104
Mr. Dick and his illness, 496
Mr. Lear, pleasant to know, 499
Mr. Micawber, never will desert,
  496
Mrs. Browning's death, 449
Mrs. Lofty keeps a carriage, 650
Much an expedient as lighting,
  450
  as my life was worth, 241
  credit in that, there ain't, 495
  goods laid up, 1117
  he reads, 81
  he thinks too, 81
  I owe, I have nothing, 1024
  I want which most would have,
    20
  is there waits you, 652
  may be made of a Scotchman,
    235
  may be said on both sides, 196,
    229
  more than little, is by much
    too, 62
  more to that which had too,
    48
  of a muchness, 190
  of earth so much of heaven,
    298
  one man can do, 169
  sigh too, or a kiss too long, 559
  so, said and so well said, 550
  so, to do so little done, 469
  some have too, 20
  something too, of this, 94
  that I found, 856

Much that I freed, 856
  that I sought, 856
  that well may be thought, 955
  the better, 214
  to say, 617
  too, of a good thing, 51, 1033
  you get is small, 557
Muchness, much of a, 190
Muck of sweat, all of a, 254
Muckle, twice as, as a' that, 284
Muck-rake in his hand, 172
  men with the, 734
Mud and scum of things, 409
  belly in the, 900
  marble and, 422
  sun reflecting upon the, 112
Muddied oafs, 780
Muddy, ill-seeming thick, 52
  Pei-Ho, ebbs and flows, the,
    746
  sparrow, mean and small, 910
  vesture of decay, his, 47
Mudsills of society, 432
Mudville nine, for the, 770
  there is no joy in, 770
Muezzin's call for prayer, 755
Muffins, no more inspiration than
  in a plate of, 720
Muffled and dumb like barefoot
  dervishes, 410
  drums are beating, 433
  oar, I wait the, 444
  roar, 770
Mufflers, where we wear, 492
Mugwump is a person educated
  beyond his intellect, 601
  mainspring mogul and, 601
Mulberry-trees, amid her, 438
Muldoon. He's a solid man, 679
Mule, Democratic party is like a,
  260
  kicked by a, 791
  reason with a, 712
Mules, facts are contrary 'z, 527
Mulligan Guard, as we marched
  in the, 679
Mulligrubs, died merely of the,
  1042
Multiplication of the inferior, 580
Multiplicity in uniformity, 769
  unity to, 637
Multiplied visions, 1113
  wave, drops on the, 601
Multiplieth words, he, 1102
Multiply, I was about to, 925
Multitude admire you, make, 985
  but to the, 969
  call the afternoon, 41
  for addressing a, 1001
  great, or a small company,
    1125
  is always in the wrong, 180
  many-headed, 27
  of an host, 1125
  of counsellors, 1107
  of faces, put up with the, 1090
  of fibres, 1068
  of projects, 988
  of ships, 552
  of sins, charity shall cover the,
    1122
  swinish, hoofs of a, 260
  that shrunk to hear his name,
    372
  underlings of the, 1000
  with the ignorant, 426

Multitudes in the valley of decision, 1113
  of hours pilfered, 300
  to mirth, 713
  who dwell, vast, 688
Multitudinous are, as, 910
  seas incarnadine, 86
Mum, cry, 35
  is the word, 1041
  it is a secret, 236
Mumble, a sort of, 550
  let her maunder and, 378
  of the wind, 905
Mumbles Head, that happened
  off, 658
Mumbling Athanasian creeds,
  weary of, 609
Mumbo-Jumbo is dead, 858
Mumbojumbos, popinjays or
  soot-smeared, 376
Mummer's part, woman the, 844
Mummied authors, shelved round
  us lie, 565
Mundus, scattered o'er this, 951
Munich, over Paris and Rouen,
  over, 932
  wave, all thy banners, 328
Municipal budget, smelling like
  a, 910
Munificent Ptolemies, bountiful
  Maecenates, 124
Munny, doant thou marry for,
  467
Murder, a brother's, 95
  and spoil which men call history, 373
  by the law, 203
  cannot be long hid, 45
  charge me with, 599
  ez fer war I call it, 526
  is discovered, how easily, 77
  many a foul and midnight, 244
  one, made a villain, 268
  one to destroy is, 203
  sacrilegious, hath broke ope,
  86
  shrieks out, 128
  sleep, Macbeth does, 86
  thousands takes a specious
  name, to, 203
  to robbing to drinking to Sabbath-breaking, 347
  will out, 6
Murders, manslaughter and isolated, 991
  twenty mortal, 87
Murderer, carcasses bleed at the
  sight of the, 122
Murillo said whose work is this,
  511
Murky air, into the, 155
Murmur of a low fountain, 645
  of the breaking flood, 679
  the shallow, 21
Murmurs as the ocean murmurs,
  325
  died away in hollow, 248
  hear our mutual, 359
  to their woe, 251
Murmuring of innumerable bees,
  466
  of many voices, 497
  streams, lapse of, 154
Murmurings were heard within,
  302
Muscle trained, keep thy, 529

Muscles as the tongue, needs so
  many, 1022
  strain'd, toil and sweat, 223
Muscular cheese, 887
  his Christianity was, 421
  training of a philosopher, 1007
Muse and her song, 977
  every conqueror creates a, 146
  his chaste, 239
  His praise, expressive silence,
  224
  meditate the thankless, 159
  of fire, O for a, 66
  on nature with a poet's eye,
  327
  said look in thy heart, 27
  Sappho the tenth, 960
  transports of a British, 185
  what I mean by the, 475
  whose strong and diverse heart,
  927
  worst-humoured, 252
  worst-natured, 184
Muses are nine, 960
  charm of all the, 471
  recorded by the, 25
  sacrifice to the, 222
  spirit back the, 807
  to their ancient rule, 896
  wore, that once the, 743
Mushrumps leave to grow, gave
  lowly, 30
Music, a sky-born, 408
  and an eerie faint carouse, 914
  and moonlight, 368
  and the flying cloud, 588
  and women, give way to, 182
  architecture is frozen, 1060
  at the close, setting sun and, 59
  be the food of love, 53
  breathing from her face, 168,
  356
  by man than comes of, 493
  ceasing of exquisite, 435
  cried for madder, 796
  die in, 45
  down an unlistening street,
  719
  dwells lingering, where, 304
  fading in, a swan-like end, 45
  fall like harmonies of, 641
  floods the ear, 735
  from a thousand stops, one,
  684
  from the grey forgotten years,
  832
  from the soul of things, 687
  from their voice and song, 659
  hath charms, 223
  hath charms to soothe the
  savage breast, 193
  heavenly maid was young, 247
  here that softer falls, 463
  highest of fine arts, 581
  his very foot has, 270
  how sour sweet, is, 60
  I heard with you, 904
  I'm ignorant of, 660
  in its roar, 354
  in my heart I bore, 298
  in that land, heard, 881
  in the beauty, there is, 145
  in their home, 697
  in 't, foot has, 270
  in them, die with all their, 451
  influence of, 772

Music is a psychical storm, 772
  is good to the melancholy,
  1048
  is like a voice, 484
  is love, 664
  is not immortal, 864
  is the thing I love most, 182
  is the universal language, 440
  is well said to be the speech,
  378
  is what awakes from you, 535
  let him step to the, 515
  lies unheard, in the still air,
  445
  like a little river's, no, 704
  like continuous and stationary, 1060
  like softest, 78
  like the warbling of, 111
  long-forgotten, 644
  man that hath no, in himself,
  47
  ministers to human welfare,
  581
  mute, will make the, 470
  my rampart, 916
  neither secular nor religious,
  821
  never heard such, 606
  never merry when I hear sweet,
  47
  never prize the, 665
  nighest bordering upon heaven,
  323
  night shall be filled with, 434
  no, in a rest, 532
  no truer truth than comes by,
  493
  not for the doctrine but the,
  211
  odorous, 693
  of a lovesick mockin'-bird, 820
  of forefended spheres, 556
  of her face, 145, 168
  of humanity, still sad, 296
  of men's lives, so is it in, the,
  60
  of the flutes, pure, 634
  of the languid hours, 674
  of the morns, in the, 432
  of the sea, rose to the, 317
  of the spheres, 55, 145
  of the Union, keep step to the,
  394
  of the woodland birds, 625
  of their names, mighty, 932
  of those village bells, 266
  passed away, though all their,
  626
  Psalmist's, 427
  puts upon them, colours, 974
  rang the gay, 600
  slumbers in the shell, 289
  some to church repair for, 211
  soul of, shed, 334
  sounds of, creep in our ears,
  47
  sphere-descended maid, 248
  sports and theatres, 1049
  tells no truths, 506
  that brings sweet sleep, 463
  that can deepest reach, 410
  that gentlier on the spirit lies,
  463
  that heavenly, 387
  that I care to hear, 672

Music that set us a-dancing, 600
  that you made below, 728
  the beautiful disturber, 938
  the sea-maid's, to hear, 42
  the wine of love is, 610
  theirs be the, 832
  this shall be for, 703
  time to hear bird, 930
  to attending ears, softest, 78
  to create harmony, 1000
  vibrations of deathless, 806
  we may live without, 592
  when soft voices die, 367
  wherever there is harmony,
    there is, 145
  will not be complete, 619
  with her silver sound, 255
  with its voluptuous swell, 352
  with, or with poem, 156
  with the enamelled stones, 33
  without, life would be, 1081
Music's golden speech, in holy,
    503
  golden tongue, 383
  own, every tone is, 405
  soothing sound, 942
Musical and low, in his seemed,
    524
  as bright Apollo's lute, 41,
    158
  glasses, Shakespeare and the,
    254
  most, most melancholy, 160
  silence, 587
  training a more potent instru-
    ment, 973
Musically wells, tintinnabulation
    that so, 459
Musician usually touches bass
    string first, 172
  who tries to rival painter, 821
Musicians know, we, 489
  that shall play to you, 62
Music-makers, we are the, 676
Musing hour, steals into a, 675
  on companions gone, 307
  there an hour alone, 359
  while, the fire burned, 1104
Musk, swirls of, 696
Musket moulds in his hands, 699
Muskets aimed at duck, 277
Musket-flashes, level, 604
Musk-rose and woodbine, 159
Must be counted ere I see thy
    face, 454
  be now no passages of, 470
  couple or must die, it, 545
  do the thing we must, 559
  genius does what it, 594
  have a touch of earth, 470
  I thus leave thee, 155
  not what we would but what
    we, 565
  why must we bear this yoke of,
    543
  youth replies I can, 409
Mustang, ride on a mouse-gray,
    711
Mustard, after meat comes, 1035
  in a young child's mouth, 272
Mutable nature, fix her, 1037
  rank-scented many, the, 1037
  woman is various and most,
    472
Mutability, naught endure but,
    368

Mutability of language, proof
    against the, 344
Mutantur nos et mutamur, 209
Mute, are not soon, 326
  farewell, wave their hands for
    a, 540
  had thought, as the, 652
  hugeness, from the, 920
  I shall be, 650
  inglorious Milton, 245
  is she not pure, if she be, 533
  make the music, 470
  nature mourns, 307
  sink among the naked, 575
  unchanged hoarse, 153
  witness, from this, 604
Mutilators of collections, 323
Mutine in a matron's bones, 95
Mutinous and quarrelsome, 228
Mutiny, stones to rise and, 83
Mutter of the mass, 488
Muttered in hell, 't was, 290
Mutton and Brussels sprouts,
    into, 932
  dead as, 497
  joint of, 65
  scrags, our scanty, 177
Muttons, to return to our, 1024
Mutual heart, when we meet a,
    225
Muzzle thrust out, with his, 815
My better half, 27
  country 't is of thee, 447
  ever-new delight, 153
  idea of an agreeable person,
    421
  life is like a stroll upon the
    beach, 513
  lord the king and me, betwixt,
    504
  opinion is and so and so, 1014
  own, thou art, my darling, 576
  own to-day, whether I come to,
    535
  sole rule of life, almost, 378
  whinstone house my castle is,
    382
Mynheer Vandunck, 289
Myriad lovely blossoms, 697
  moving water, by the, 914
  of precedent, codeless, 465
  scattered stars, a, 566
Myriads bid you rise, what, 1059
  infatuated and besotted, 123
  of daisies, 304
  of other globes, around me,
    537
  of rivulets hurrying, 466
  who before us pass'd, 1019
Myriad-minded Shakespeare, 318
Myrrh, whose was the gift of,
    792
Myrtle, groves of laurel and,
    1058
  land of the cypress and, 355
Myrtles, grove of, 120, 1058
Myself am hell, 151
  clear, of cants, 378
  enabled to remain true to, 376
  favourite subject, 272
  I live not in, 353
  never less alone by, 271
  not if I know, 323
  seen clearly within, 1085
  speaking alone for, 914
  such a thing as I, 81

Myself unwitting where their
    master, 833
  when I give I give, 535
  when young, 1018
Mysteries lie beyond thy dust,
    170
  of machine called man, 496
  priestess of night's high, 418
Mysterious exodus of death, the
    long, 436
  happy twilight boat, 692
  independent variable, 563
  union with its native sea, 302
  voice, the same, 635
  way, God moves in a, 266
Mystery and the dark way, 931
  around her sculptured, 443
  burthen of the, 295
  desire and, 577
  divine, in things, 1074
  heart of my, 94
  hid under Egypt's pyramid,
    429
  in human hearts, 955
  life is a, 638
  must be instressed, 673
  new names for, 657
  of beauty, 789
  of mysteries, 310
  of that magic tool, 348
  of the ships, 436
  profound secret and, 497
  profound, some, 820
  sea's works wrapped in, 726
  she acquires, 938
  this the miracle and, 672
  unguessed, 444
Mystic bond of brotherhood, 378
  fabric sprung, the, 266, 342
  line, draw if thou canst, the,
    410
  meaning, 583
  sees the ineffable, 835
  the improbable the rose, the,
    923
  too full of God, 789
Mystical lore, 327
Myth, call an outworn, 872
  of weak men, 691
Myths, the same old, 648

N. AND W. the Great Northern,
    926
Naebody cares for me, 269, 286
Nag, bobtail, 568
Naiad of the strand, 308
  or a grace, 308
Nail, breadth of my, 191
  fasten him as a, 1111
  in door, 66
  not a, but touches a tender
    spot, 678
  on the head, hit the, 18, 127,
    1025, 1042
  shoe lost for want of a, 137,
    227
  to our coffin, care adds a, 272
  to the mast her holy flag, 450
  tooth and, 1032
Nails, come near your beauty
    with my, 68
  fastened by the masters,
    1110
  on Monday, cut your, 956
Nailed on the bitter cross, 60

Naked, alike if you see us, 124
and he clothed him not, 249
and outcast, with the, 282
as she was born, 346
came I into the world, 1036
clothe the, 1123
every day he clad, 254
human heart, 202
I saw thee, 859
ignorance, blind and, 470
in December snow, 59
mute, 575
new-born babe, 85
new-born child, 275
soul of Tomlinson, 781
though locked up in steel, 31, 69
to lash the rascals, 103
to mine enemies, 74
truth, the, 41
villany, clothe my, 71
woods, wailing winds, 372
wretches, poor, 98
Nakedness, not in utter, 301
white truth in simple, 470
Nam et ipsa scientia, 111
Namby Pamby, 400
Namby-Pamby's little rhymes, 189
Name a person leaves behind, 359
acclaim thy glorious, 921
Achilles assumed, 145
Ah Sin was his, 644
an established, 461
and form, classified with, 1057
and memory, 114
another and prouder, 596
at which the world grew pale, 230
be George, if his, 57
behind them, left a, 1125
beyond the sky, but waft thy. 351
breathe not his, 334
call it by some better, 337
cannon his, 575
cannot conceive nor, 86
current but not appropriate, 290
different, writing but a, 241
fascination of a, 266
filches from me my good, 102
foolish whistling of a, 168
for which my soul had panted, 645
forget my own, 1036
friend, of every friendless, 231
good, better than precious ointment, 1109
good, better than riches, 1041, 1108
good, in man and woman, 102
good, is like precious ointment, 110
grand old, of gentleman, 469
greatness of his, 74, 564
Greek or Roman, 173
happy people won for thee that, 305
her, is never heard, 388
holla your, to the reverberate hills, 54
I know his note, I know his, 629
if I have forgotten your, 633

Name in print, pleasant to see one's, 351
in the ambush of my, 35
in the heart of a child, 859
is Admiral Death, 764
is carved in the Kentuckian rocks, 552
is death, my, 659
is great in mouths, 101
is Legion, my, 1116
is MacGregor, my, 310
is Norval, my, 248
is not Lost Angie Lees, 952
is on your waters, 364
is taboo, yet the, 883
is the human heart, 844
is woman, frailty thy, 90
is worthy of the, of poet, 378
is writ in water, 761
king's, is a tower of strength, 72
lights without, 164
link deathless to his, 756
live in a, 857
living, 128
local habitation and a, 43
love can scarce deserve the, 355
magic of a, 327
make for its owner a, 589
man with a terrible, 322
mark the marble with his, will never, 210
may be recorded, that my, 20
may not stink, 958
murder takes a specious, 203
no blot on his, 327
no one can speak, 322
no parties, I, 131
nor memory of her, 561
not knowing each the other's, 300
of action, lose the, 93
of Crispian, rouse at the, 67
of God upon his lips, 1055
of perseverance, 241
of the great Jehovah and the Continental Congress, in the, 344
of the late deceased, 783
of the Prophet figs, 332
of the slough was Despond, 171
of the world, borrow the, 110
pessimism is only the, 926
ravished with the whistling of a, 208
remember your grandfather's, 928
rose by any other, 78
Shakespeare's use of his, 874
shall be called wonderful, His, 1111
shall be redeemed from color's infamy, 297
shifts its, 1021
should be Friday, his, 187
shrunk to hear his, 372
speak to thee in friendship's, 336
that lives in song, 815
that love waxed weary, 632
that never felt the sun, warms some poor, 585
the world grew pale at, 230
— the year — the day, 362

Name, their race their nation clan, their, 612
thence, they had their, 158
thou didst write thy, 594
though late redeem thy, 223
Thy, O Jesus be forever blest, 555
to all succeeding ages curst, 173
to be known by, no, 101
to every fixed star, that give a, 40
to every nook, 714
to orb your, 888
to posterity, transmit his, 343
to tell your, 584
trod down my lofty, 620
vain without the merit, 219
was a kind of ducdame, 48
was Horner, his, 667
was Johnny Sands, man whose, 941
was littel Byngo, 350
was nought, the place was all, 686
was writ in water, 29, 386, 722
we will not ask her, 328
what the dickens his, is, 34
what 's in a, 78, 875
which no one can spell, 322
worth an age without a, 310
will insure a good price, 255
Names, a few of their princely, 932
against whose familiar, 438
athwart the dusk, 688
call things by their right, 290
called him soft, 383
commodity of good, 60
fallen in love with American, 929
familiar as household words, 67
for my disease, no, 868
great proud glittering, 932
greatest, in his wild aery flight, 157
he loved to hear, 450
hyphenated, phalanx of, 935
inscribed in history's page 518
mighty music of their, 932
new-made honour doth forget men's, 57
of Gray Dukes and Oscar Baer, 878
of our fearless race, 364
of railroad presidents, 906
of the Apostles, 1095
of their founders, forgotten the, 147
old splendours, old, 1085
on earth are dark, 366
one of the few immortal, 363
respected in former ages, 292
Scotland boasts a thousand, 603
strange and new-fangled, 973
syllable men's, 157
that are England's noblest heritage, 518
that banish care, 231
that never get fat, 929
that shall live unnumbered years, 518

Names, the old strange, 866
  twenty more such, 52
  unpopular, and impossible loy-
  - alties, 548
  unremembered, 700
  we know your, 929
  which never were, 52
  win ourselves good, 28
Named thee but to praise, 363
Nameless as beauty, what so, 868
  deed, tells of a, 290
  man amid a crowd, 504
  pathos in the air, 581
  saints, 566
  unremembered acts, 295
Nan, such mistress such, 19
Nancy brig, mate of the, 622
Nantahala, the French Broad the
  Chattahoochee, 932
Nantucket Light, never watch
  for, 929
Nantucket's sunk and here we
  are, 508
Nantucketer out of sight of land,
  531
Nap after dinner, 236
  definition of a, 721
  hare awoke from his, 962
  thought to clip his morning,
  510
Naps, afternoon, 788
  old John, of Greece, 52
Napkin behind his ears, ties his,
  923
  while we wait for the, 625
Napkins tacked together, two, 63
Naples is known, man to whom
  all, 1046
Napoleon and his letters, 413
  impersonation of force and
  murder, 603
  is the sole obstacle, 1061
  mighty somnambulist, 1067
  without his selfishness, 599
Napoleon's presence in the field,
  293
Napping, while I nodded nearly,
  460
Narcissa's last words, 209
Narcotics numbing pain, 468
  two great European, 1081
Narration, error in, 1017
Narrative of travel, reading
  some, 1083
  over-voluminous, 641
  with age, 218
Narrow and normal amount,
  1064
  and opaque, walls too, 903
  as the neck of a vinegar-cruet,
  239
  cell, this, 338
  compass, 146
  human wit so, 210
  isthmus, this, 337
  measure, its, 744
  our span, 418
  thraldom, first in, 1050
  two, words hic jacet, 22
  world, he doth bestride the, 81
Narrowed his mind, 252
Narrowing lust of gold, 469
Narrow-souled people and narrow-necked bottles, 217
Nashville drizzle, conception of a,
  800

Natal day celebrate this, 522
  star that ruleth, 964
Natchez, to beat de steamah, 712
Nation and its flag, 500
  confound the language of the,
  292
  curled darlings of our, 100
  evermore, one, 452
  free, hath made our, 451
  God sifted a whole, 179
  great, keeps a, 736
  hand that bore a, 604
  he hates our sacred, 44
  how enormously rich and populous a, 637
  institutions alone can create a,
  419
  language of the, 292
  made and preserved us a, 332,
  404
  making of the songs of a, 186
  needed a man, 642
  ne'er would thrive, 189
  noble and puissant, 163
  not lift sword against, 1111
  nun hath no, 593
  of amateurs, 686
  of gallant men, 260
  of men of honour, 260
  of shop-keepers, 240
  panacea for a mismanaged,
  930
  remain an independent, 1061
  righteousness exalteth a, 1107
  shall a, be moulded, 634
  small one a strong, 1112
  state city, no, 534
  strong, father a, 860
  sympathy of a, 419
  territory does not make a, 563
  that succeeds in making nations vassals, 1067
  that's dead and gone, 652
  the blood of a, 1051
  the fate of a, 437
  there was a famous, 748
  trick of our English, 64
  unto all his, 1125
  void of wit and humour, 246
  we trust as a, 821
Nations, among ourselves and
  with all, 457
  are destroyed or flourish, 282
  are great aside from, 1067
  as a drop of a bucket, 1112
  but two, in all, 169
  cheap defence of, 260
  cry to thee, 889
  day of small, 622
  eclipsed the gayety of, 233
  enrich unknowing, 30
  fierce contending, 195
  friendship with all, 273
  give to all, 1127
  greatness of his name make
  new, 74
  heard entranced, touched harp
  and, 393
  join in leagues of peace, 218
  kindreds and tongues, 1123
  maintain their armaments,
  how, 762
  most advanced, 414
  mountains make enemies of,
  264
  Niobe of, 354

Nations, not kings lords but, 338
  of the earth, all the, 954
  teach all, 1116
  tend to stupidity and baseness, 729
  to belong to other, 623
  Wall Street's mingled, 604
  yet unborn, 1027
Nation's art-products and scientific activities, 740
  flag a symbol of the nation,
  500
  freighthandler, 855
  heart, his grave a, 555
  heart, song that nerves a, 471
  life at hazard, 551
  praise, filled with a, 649
  slumbers, interrupted a, 935
  stain, bear a, 763
  true policy, 1066
  trust, a, 373
  Valhalla, 696
  welfare speeding, 561
  wounds, to bind up the, 457
Nations' airy navies grappling,
  464
National debt a national blessing, 341
  downfall, surest road to, 450
  honor is national property, 283
  injustice is the surest road, 450
  prowess and glory, 396
Nationalism, gain of, from war
  and bloodshed, 908
Nationality, true, is mankind,
  795
National-Socialist State tribunal,
  1090
Native and to the manner born,
  91
  charm, one, 251
  country best, who loves his,
  471
  heath, my foot is on my, 310
  hue of resolution, 93
  land good night, my, 352
  of America, Turky original,
  228
  personality endows a man, 538
  seas, guard our, 327
  shore, adieu my, 352
  shore, fast by their, 267
  to them, more than is, 101
  wood-notes wild, 160
Native-born, health to the, 778
Nativity chance or death, 35
  hour of her, 522
Natur', not in human, to surrender, 387
Natural bent, find out the, 974
  candle, extinguishes the, 184
  children kind and, 66
  defect, not caused by any, 112
  expression of villainy, 616
  history better than games, 803
  I do it more, 54
  in him to please, 173
  manure, 273
  more than, 92
  nothing prevents our being,
  1044
  on the stage he was, 252
  selection, 448
  sorrow loss or pain, 298
  twice as, 599
Naturalist and historian, 231

Naturalists observe a flea, so, 190
Naturally as pigs squeak, 141
Naturam expelles furca, 924
Nature, a great gift of, 1057
  abhors a vacuum, 1048
  abhors imperfect work, 665
  accuse not, 154
  and books belong to eyes that see them, 412
  and nature's God, 200, 273
  and nature's laws, 214
  and of noble mind, loyal, 471
  and the open, influence in, 671
  art imitates, 171
  art is man's, 506
  bald by, 37
  be your teacher, let, 295
  blessed is the healthy, 377
  book of, 1033
  book of, short of leaves, 391
  broke the die, 356
  broke the mould, 356
  built many stories high, 148
  by her mother wit, 25
  cannot miss, 176
  careless-handed, 736
  character bestowed by, 975
  clever man by, 290
  commonplace of, 298
  compunctious visitings of, 84
  continuity of, 542
  could no further go, the force of, 175
  course of, is the art of God, 202
  credit to human, 422
  custom is almost, 1003
  darling of, 1029
  deals with us, 439
  death is a secret of, 1010
  debt to, 's quickly paid, 135
  diseased, breaks forth, 62
  disobedience to, 1008
  earnest elements of, 895
  everything contains all the powers of, 411
  fast in fate, binding, 216
  first made man, free as, 178
  fits all her children, 526
  fitted by, to bear, 1011
  fix her mutable, 1037
  fluid as, chaste affectionate, 537
  fools of, 91
  for 't is their, too, 198
  formed but one such man, 356
  forms and softens us within, 180
  forms us for ourselves not for others, 1029
  foster-nurse of, 99
  framed strange fellows, 43
  friend a masterpiece of, 411
  from her seat sighing, 155
  from whose, some effect, 1048
  goodness that comes by, 975
  great secretary of, 140
  habit is second, 1030
  had but little clay, 348
  has given us two ears, 420
  has presented us, 1029
  he is great who is what he is from, 412
  held by some to be, 975
  her custom holds, 96

Nature, her great masterpiece designed, 286
  hides the fact well, 588
  his, is too noble, 76
  hold the mirror up to, 94
  holds communion with, 371
  how unjust to, 202
  human, will not change, 457
  I do fear thy, 84
  I loved, 326
  I'll walk where my own, 516
  imitation of, 991
  in hir corages, 5
  in spite of, and their stars, 142
  in the love of, 371
  in you stands on the very verge, 98
  includes men and their ways, 563
  integrity of, 1055
  intellectual, 235
  is a mutable cloud, 411
  is above art in that respect, 99
  is all aglow, when, 952
  is but art unknown, 207
  is God's art, 506
  is subdued to what it works in, 108
  is the art of God, 144, 202
  is thought immersed in matter, 393
  is too noble for the world, 76
  learned its, 1079
  lengths unknown, to carry, 262
  liberty taken with, 637
  little we see in, that is ours, 300
  lived in the eye of, 296
  looks through, 209
  lost the perfect mould, 356
  loves so well to change, 1010
  made a pause, 201
  made her, fairer than, 28
  made thee to temper man, 185
  might stand up, 84
  modesty of, o'erstep not the, 94
  mortal, did tremble, 301
  mourns her worshipper, 307
  muse on, with a poet's eye, 327
  must obey necessity, 84, 1013
  never did betray, 296
  never lends her excellence, 35
  never put her jewels into a garret, 113
  noble and incapable of deceit, 311
  nor public use and custom permit, 19
  not dull art, 403
  not man the less but, more, 354
  of a calm and happy, 973
  of an insurrection, 82
  of evil in others, 973
  of his death, know the, 969
  of material, 235
  of war, 132
  of women, 1035
  one touch of, 75
  out, drive, 924
  paint the mortal shame of, 472
  paints the best part of a picture, 410
  passing through, to eternity, 89
  pattern of excelling, 103

Nature, permit, to take her own way, 1031
  prodigality of, 71
  prompting of, 993
  puts forth her gentleman, 512
  remains, 538
  removes a great man, when, 412
  repugnant to their, 1049
  rich with the spoils of, 144
  roots of man's, 736
  rose above man's aims, 595
  rough paths of peevish, 190
  secret aims of, 668
  seems dead o'er one half-world, 85
  shows, happiness depends as, 262
  sings her exquisite song to artist alone, 611
  sink in years, 195
  so mild and benign, 203
  so weak, where is human, 500
  some things are of that, 172
  speaks a various language, 371
  speaks in symbols and in signs, 442
  spectacles of books to read, 179
  state of war by, 190
  still to poets kind, 933
  strong propensity of, 162
  such is our, 1061
  sullenness against, 162
  swears the lovely dears, 284
  take its course, let, 1092
  teaches beasts, 76
  that is the seal, 1021
  the vicar of the Lord, 4
  this fortress built by, 59
  't is their, too, 198
  to advantage dressed, 211
  to write and read comes by, 39
  under tribute, laid all, 290
  unjust to, and himself, 202
  use can almost change the stamp of, 95
  voice of, cries, 245
  wants of, are supplied, 1051
  war was the state of, 258
  weaknesses of human, 270
  wears one universal grin, 228
  what I call God and fools call, 491
  what is done against, 1005
  what, wishes should be said, 626
  who can paint like, 224
  whole frame of, 194
  whose body, is, 207
  will out, 963
  wills, death a thing that, 1011
  with a fork, drive out, 985
  you must alter human, 753
Natures, nobility in their, 101
  same with common, 204
Nature's bastards not her sons, 158
  bloodless triumph, 443
  chief masterpiece, 185
  choice, was it, 685
  cockloft is empty, 148
  constant benediction, 602
  copy is not eterne, 87

Nature's daily food, for human, 299
  debt almost escaped my recollection, 406
  end of language is declined, 203
  evening comment, 303
  gentlemen, one of, 499
  God, through nature up to, 200, 209
  grace, rob me of free, 225
  happiest mould, 243
  heart beats strong, 458
  infinite book of secrecy, 104
  journeymen, 94
  kindly law, 208
  last eclipse, 452
  laws lay hid in night, 214
  little kings, one of, 114
  minions, 808
  own nobleman, 478
  own sweet cunning hand, 54
  part, the master-stroke is, 410
  patient sleepless Eremite, 385
  plan, 439
  plan, 'tis he fulfils great, 284
  'prentice han', 284
  purpose, that was, 669
  real king, 814
  second course, 86
  second sun, love is, 28
  soft nurse, gentle sleep, 65
  son and master, 611
  sternest painter, 351
  sweet restorer balmy sleep, 201
  teachings, list to, 371
  universal throne, 358
  walks, eye, 206
  works, universal blank of, 151
Nature-faker, 734
Naught a trifle, think, 203
  availeth, say not the struggle, 519
  better than to enjoy, 489
  but misery brings, 388
  but the nightingale's song, 269
  but vanity in beauty, see, 522
  but weakness in fond caress, 522
  can me bereave, 225
  else worth the having, 885
  for tomorrow's passer-by, 553
  horror of falling into, 195
  in the waters below, 652
  in this life sweet, 127, 144
  in world or church or state, 528
  may endure but mutability, 368
  my sighs avail, 395
  paramour is a thing of, 43
  projects come to, 491
  saith the buyer it is, 1108
  so sweet as melancholy, 121
  venture naught have, 19
  woman's nay doth stand for, 109
Naughty night to swim in, 99
  world, good deed in a, 47
Nautilus, learn of the little, 208
Navarre, helmet of, 400
Navee, rulers of the Queen's, 623
Navies are forgotten, when, 805
  are stranded, when, 309
  grappling in the central blue, 464

Navigate, bark of man could, 393
  the azure, 572
  the most, nations that, 414
Navigation, truce to, 623
Navigators, winds and waves on the side of the ablest, 271
Navy, load would sink a, 73
  of England, royal, 248
  of Tharshish, bringing gold and silver, 832, 1101
  rode triumphant, 240
Nay he shall have, 11
  turn not away that sweet head, 388
  woman's, doth stand for naught, 109
Nazareth, good thing out of, 1118
Ne supra crepidam, 994
Neæra's hair, tangles of, 159
Near and far ray on ray, till, 493
  and yet so far, so, 469
  approach to good, 229
  as, the ocean's edge as I, 513
  he comes too, 128, 221
  he seems so, 469
  I still am, 403
  is God to man, so, 409
  port is, the bells I hear, 536
  the sacred gate, and, 481
  to be thought so, will go, 40
  to heaven by sea as by land, 508
  to us and dear, those who are most, 600
Nearer and a broader mark, 588
  home to-day, 557
  my God to Thee, 423
Nearest and dearest enemy, 117
Nearing the solution of some theme, 733
Nearness, grant me a sense of his, 450
Neat not gaudy, 325
  repast light and choice, 162
  still to be, still to be drest, 119
Neat's leather, ever trod on, 81
  leather, shoe of, 142
Neatness the asepsis of clothes, 696
Nebo's lonely mountain, by, 516
Nebuchadnezzar did eat grass as oxen, 1113
Nebula by name, 795
Nebulae, each in its own, 874
Nebulous star we call the sun, 466
Necessaries to the needy, deny, 1127
Necessary being, God a, 172
  end, death a, 82
  harmless cat, 46
  never say more than is, 277
  to invent God, 1052
  to somebody, make yourself, 414
  work, doing, 961
Necessitatem in virtutem, 4
Necessite, maketh vertue of, 4
Necessities, most imperious, 1068
  of life, toil for the bare, 689
Necessity, beautiful, 477
  can set me helpless, 805
  children of, 617
  daughters of, 974
  days of, 962

Necessity engendered and justified by science, 543
  has no law, 1026
  hostile empires, and free will, 378
  knows no law, 988
  legs for, 75
  made a virtue of, 1037
  nature must obey, 84
  never refuses anything, 988
  none sorer than, 965
  proper parent of an art, 171, 278
  stern, 654
  the gods cannot strive against, 1013
  the mother of invention, 171, 200
  the tyrant's plea, 152
  three eldest children of, 617
  to make virtue of, 4, 34, 125
  turns to glorious gain, 300
  villains by, 98
  we give the praise of virtue to, 995
Necessity's sharp pinch, 98
Neck and cease, break his, 877
  do not fall on the, 778
  for an ax, measure his, 853
  is as a tower of ivory, thy, 1110
  millstone hanged about his, 1117
  of massy girth, his, 931
  or nothing, 360
  upon the humbled, 50
  yield not thy, 70
Necks, and arching, 934
  walk with stretched-forth, 1111
Necklaces of tan, 763
Necktie, left my, 743
Neckties wild, I want my, 907
Nectar on a lip, 279
Nectarean juice, 386
Nectared sweets, feast of, 158
Neebor's part, a man may tak a, 285
Need at all of glory, no, 1000
  at his hardest, 898
  burden of our common, 445
  deserted at his utmost, 176
  ever but in times of, 177
  friend in, 978
  friend indeed will help thee in thy, 120
  has he of clocks, what, 801
  in their common, 781
  love meets every human, 549
  many things I do not, 1014
  no fuller test, we, 501
  of a remoter charm, 296
  of a world of men, 485
  of arsenals and forts, no, 434
  of blessing, I had most, 86
  of me, France has more, 1060
  of milk not strong meat, 1122
  of prayer, ye have no, 364
  of the sky, I have, 771
  of valour, no, 999
  satisfies no normal, 943
  the most crying, 1075
  to be ashamed, she had, 956
  to cry, little, 919
  to doff his pride, 777
  to fly from, 353

Need to make an enquiry, no, 1036
train to stand the test of, 663
Needs and woes, for its, 649
go that the devil drives, 17, 53
man who has no mental, 1064
my soul's or body's, 917
no record of her descent there, 561
of the age, 787
of the least of you, 879
only to be seen, 174
root in human, 660
to each according to his, 1071
Needed by each one, all are, 408
Needful, is it, 716
one thing is, 1117
to flower, alike they're, 423
Needle and thread, hinders, 392
and thread, plying her, 391
eye of a, go through the, 1115
howsoe'er it swerve, 661
in a bottle of hay, 132, 1039
in my hand, 699
magnet like the, 1068
points faithfully, the, 337
true, like the, 248
Needle's eye, postern of a, 60
Needless alexandrine, 211
Needle-note, like a silver, 925
Needy hollow-eyed sharp-looking, 38
stomachs of the, 1016
Neer to the church, 13
Negation, begets its own, 1072
Negatives, make much of, 538
Neglect may breed mischief, 227
perpetual, 704
such sweet, 119
wise and salutary, 259
Neglected opportunity, 180
Neglecting worldly ends, 32
Negligé, display contributory, 768
Negligence and indisposition, 996
and silence, 237
Negligences, his noble, 190
Negligent at their prayer, who are, 1127
more admir'd than by the, 104
Negotiate for itself, every eye, 38
Negro, courage of the, 480
minstrel singing the answer, every, 516
Neighbour, a good, 430
breaks your fence, when a, 490
carve for you, let your, 191
desirous of being a good, 876
do good to our, 976
hate your, 398
helping every feeble, 601
love thy, as thyself, 1099, 1115
love your, yet pull not down your hedge, 137
pines upon its, 517
policy of the good, 876
says, looks not to what his, 1010
that he might rob a, 399
that is near, better is a, 1108
they helped every one his, 1112
to wrangle with a, 1028
well, to love my, 657
Neighbours, cause their, 1006
first to attack their, 1046
go, where would my, 820

Neighbors, good fences make good, 837
innocence of our, 515
lending money to your, 235
reasonable, 415
some new, 402
the clatter they make abroad, 182
very miserable, made their, 1078
Neighbor's birth, thought on my, 878
creed, argument to thy, 408
grandfather, what is it to me if my, 166
heart, in conjecture of a, 1009
wife, love your, 398
Neighbors' children are the worst, 907
Neighboured by fruit of baser quality, 66
Neighbor-ground, frontier, 954
Neighbourhood, a London, 402
Neighbouring eyes, cynosure of, 160
states are convinced, 1051
Neighbourly, keep up our spirits and be, 495
Neighing, his horse's, 395
steed, farewell the, 102
Neighs, high and boastful, 67
Nein, civilly answered, 510
Neither heat nor light, 127
here nor there, 103
is most to blame, 633
rhyme nor reason, 37, 50
starve nor stuff, 191
Nelson, death of, 1078
on board the Victory, 623
waiting his turn, 764
Nelson's hand, Shakespeare's voice and, 634
Nemean lion's nerve, 91
Nemesis, the feet of, 735
Neptune obey, which, 258
would not flatter, 76
you shall never sink this ship, 1029
Neptune's ocean, all great, 86
Nerve brings us out of difficulty, 545
marrow and, 458
O iron, 467
or vein, or, 951
strength of, 303
stretch every, 225
the Nemean lion's, 91
the visual, 155
Nerves a nation's heart, song that, 471
and finer fibres brace, 225
are scant, whereof our, 462
at angry tension, 895
men of weak, 926
new-string, shattered, 248
Oh, the, 496
sensitive, 609
shall never tremble, 87
throbbing jumping, 473
Nerve-wracked, go also to the, 886
Nervous matter, 636
Nes', jay-bird don't rob his own, 688
Nessus, as of poisonous, shirts, 378

Nessus, shirt of, is upon me, 105
Nest, byrd that fyleth his owne, 10, 16
crosswise in his, 681
feathered his, 181
I will build me a, 663
no birds in last year's, 434
of robins in her hair, 890
the phoenix builds her spicy, 140
this delicious, 224
watery, 146
Nests, birds in their little, agree, 198
birds of the air have, 1114
birds of this year in the, of the last, 1042
construct your, 982
in my beard, built their, 499
Nestles the seed perfection, 535
Nestor swear, though, 43
Net, all is fish that cometh to, 15
fain would fling the, 575
Nets to catch the wind, 128
Nether millstone, hard as, 1103
Nettle danger, out of this, 61
tender-handed stroke a, 204
the world is a, 592
Nettles grow, lets the, 651
Nettlecombe, Hants, 864
Neutral, loyal and, in a moment, 86
Neutrality of an impartial judge, 261
Never asked for the toll, 389
better late than, 14
can be mended, egg, 432
can fall from the days, ah, 426
climbs as rarely falls, who, 443
come, back again, 390
comes to pass, 288
constant to one thing, 38
earth's philosopher, and, 516
ending still beginning, 176
flunked and he never lied, 639
found the companion, I, 514
give up, 478
go to sea, 623
goes out of fashion, bravery, 484
has known the barber's shear, 481
I'll, never find, 567
knew, her loveliness I, 386
less alone, 271, 289
life is, the same again, 559
loved sae blindly, had we, 287
mention her, no we, 388
merry when I hear sweet music, 47
met or never parted, had we, 287
never can forget, 389
read any book that is not a year old, 414
say nothin' without you're compelled, 527
says a foolish thing, 184
takes his leave, but, 510
that dead men rise up, 632
the time and the place, 493
the twain shall meet, 779
to hope again, 73
use a big big D, 622
was a better bargain driven, 27

Never was seen nor never shall be, 121
was so wise a man, there, 437
what, 622
will desert Mr. Micawber, 496
wins can rarely lose, who, 443
would be missed, 624
would lay down my arms, 230
yet fair woman but made mouths, 98
yet was a springtime, 642
you mind, 622
Never-ending flight of days, 150
Never-failing friends, 321
vice of fools, pride the, 210
Nevermore be officer of mine, 101
parted to meet, 418
quoth the raven, 460
shall be lifted, 460
would come again, 439
New acquaintance, make a, 238
and smart disease, 821
before one is on with the, 611
broom sweeps clean, 15
clothes rich and, 199
cost little less than, 193
creation, a, 364
Deal, accounts of, 830
departure, 338
earths and skies and seas, 514
England, happy in, 768
England hermit, 683
England, how we love, 700
England, I sing, 517
England is a finished place, 926
England lights her fire in every prairie, 517
England shore, 370
England, the courage of, 393
England there she stands, 926
England weather, variety about the, 617
England, whence he came, in, 596
England's own, still, 866
England's shore, 475
Englanders love pie, as, 853
fangled theories, repudiate those, 419
fashion, the world's, 40
fountains in the human heart, opened, 393
Hampshire, in the mountains of, 342
Hampshire mountains curl up in a coil, 838
hat to church, 347
Haven the home of the truth and the light, 752
heaven and a new earth, 1123
house has no sense, 651
in connection with our country, 616
is but the old come true, the, 591
is not comparable, for the, 1124
is not valuable, what is, 341
it is ever, 855
life when sin, of that, 503
look amaist as weel's the, 284
Niobe with claspèd hands, 565
off with the old before on with the, 611
or old, ale enough whether, 20

New or old, alike fantastic if too, 211
over-use of the word, 616
party who has retired, first of, 478
see this is, it may be said, 1109
something old, something, 956
Testament, blessing of the, 109
Testament, books of the, 1095
thing came, a, 849
thing under the sun, no, 1109
things succeed, 134
thoughts new fancies, 670
what is valuable is not, 341
whole, democratic world, 379
wind blew, a, 849
wine into old bottles, 1116
World into existence, called the, 293
Year that for you waits, 568
Year waited for with welcomes presents and rejoicings, 495
Year's gift to the world, 559
yielding place to, 463
York, citizens of, 935
York, city of, 859
York City, sick of, 819
York thy name's delirium, 759
Zealand, traveller from, 398
News and knowledge, carrier of, 608
bringer of unwelcome, 64
brought me bitter, 553
comes by cable led, 679
cut them for, 956
evil, rides post, 157
from a far country, 1108
good, baits, 157
if a man bites a dog, 677
in the case of, 1053
is old enough, this, 37
messenger who brings bad, 964
much older than their ale, 251
never good to bring bad, 104
of battle, 500
on the Rialto, what, 44
our morning noon and evening cry, 415
suspense in, is torture, 157
swallowing a tailor's, 58
the magical word, 347
to impart good, 966
when I was told the, 925
wouldst I had thy, 79
New-bathed in light of Paradise, 671
New-bent in heaven, silver bow, 42
New-born babe, pity like a, 85
child, a naked, 275
child, what's the use of a, 868
Newcomers all, 860
Newest kind of ways, 65
works, in science read the, 426
Newfangelnesse, of propre kinde, 8
New-fangled mirth, May's, 40
New-fashioned, deem our lives, 670
New-fledged offspring, 250
New-laid egg, as innocent as a, 622
eggs roasted rare, 177
New-lighted, herald Mercury, 95
New-made grave to-day, there is a, 891

New-made honour doth forget men's names, 57
New-married couple, 324
New-mown hay, among the, 955
Newness is worn off, uncomfortable until, 571
New-risen from a dream, 52
Newsboys cry the worst, 806
New-spangled ore, 159
Newspaper at the breakfast-table, 415
guy, he's a, 653
most important thing for a, 1075
never to look into a, 278
poet's a commonplace, 811
read nothing but a, 720
take up a, 1075
Newspapers are villainous, 278
ceaselessly querulous, 862
excite curiosity, 324
were dumb, 674
Newspaper-death, amounts to, 636
Newspaper-man a double personality, 636
Newt, eye of, and toe of frog, 87
Newton a new Donne, another, 922
be, God said let, 214
where stood the statue of, 299
Next doth ride abroad, 264
good an understanding wife, 128
Next-door dog, but the, 925
neighbours lived as strangers, 300
Niagara, Fall of, 228
of edifices, 479
stuns with thundering sound, 250
Nibbling, never ceases, 1056
Nicæan barks of yore, like those, 460
Nicanor lay dead in his harness, 1125
Nice as woman, sleep is as, 164
of no vile hold to stay him up, 58
sharp quillets of the law, 68
too, for a statesman, 252
Nicely sanded floor, 251
Niceties, no time for me to mind, 1041
Nicht-goun, in his, 475
Nick Machiavel had ne'er a trick, 143, 397, 1034
of time, 164
our old, 143
rock my cradle, 1034
stopped them in the, 1038
Van Stann, what seemed like, 511
Nickname for jugglery, hocus-pocus, 628
Nicodemus the slave, 600
Niggardly rich man, 1014
Nigger Jim is stolen, stop where, 930
Nigh is grandeur to our dust, 409
Night, a cap by, 251, 253
acquainted with the, 838
across the day beyond the, 465

Night, all this lonely, 671
an atheist half believes a God by, 202
and day, alternate, 1018
and day brother both sweet things, 407
and death, out of, 760
and morning Hannah's at the window, 568
and storm and darkness, 353
and the curtains drawn, 870
and the day, made for you the, 1127
and the firelit dark, 870
antique song heard last, 54
arriving in day in, to all, 536
as darker grows the, 252
attention still as, 150
azure robe of the, 382
bear with him one, 228
bed by, chest of drawers by day, 251
before Christmas, 't was the, 332
behind me in the, 850
beyond the silent, 603
black it stood as, 150
blossom in the winter, 814
borrower of the, 86
breathed the long long, 473
breathing through the, 390
bring stars, how doth the, 672
brooding through the, 924
by day by, 393
calm and silent, 478
came on a hurricane, 274
candles of the, 47
change from day to, 247
chaos and old, 148
cheek of, hangs upon the, 77
climbing, and the, 915
closed his eyes in endless, 243
comes down the lights burn blue, 639
cometh when no man can work, 1118
compare as day with, 555
course with tempests through the, 934
danger's troubled, 328
darkens the streets, 148
day brought back my, 162
day of woe the watchful, 322
deep of, is crept upon our talk, 83
desolation and dim, 459
drawing nigh, falls the, 643
drooped in western sky at, 536
drowsy ear of, 352
empty-vaulted, 158
fair regent of the, 269
falling in disastrous, 477
flower that opens but at, 793
follows the day, 91
for the morrow, desire of the, 368
from old to new, only a, 591
go one and all, into the, 692
golden lamps in a green, 169
good, and joy be wi' you, 291
good night good, 78
greatest part of the, 228
gwine to run all, 568
hands of the sisters death and, 536
has a thousand eyes, 707

Night he should dream of the devil, 351
heard the trailing garments of the, 418
hideous, makes, 215
hideous, making, 91
hoary winter, 30
how beautiful is, 322
how you'll reach tomorrow, 754
I never seen a, 760
imagining some fear in the, 43
in its silence, 547
in June, recall that, 582
in love with, 79
in Russia, this will last out a, 36
in the dead of, 63
in the first sweet sleep of, 368
in the lonesome October, 461
infant crying in the, 468
infinite day excludes the, 199
innumerable as the stars of, 153
is beginning to lower, 434
is but the daylight sick, 47
is drawing nigh, 605
is mother of the day, the, 441
is near at hand, 580
is the dawning, 625
is the safe time, 967
is too young, 643
it is not, 42
joint labourer with the day, 89
keen and frosty, 372
king of the, 350
kingdom of perpetual, 71
life's long, 597
light will repay the wrongs of, 134
lightning in the collied, 42
lightning in the dead of, 888
listening ear of, 477
lone splendour hung aloft the, 385
long, all, 922
lovely as a Lapland, 299
lovers' tongues by, 78
loves to revel in a summer, 459
made a restless, 217
many a dreadful, 224
many a watchful, 65
meaner beauties of the, 114
meditate by, 210
mid the cheerless hours of, 369
miles to go that, 951
morning, sorrow makes, 71
most holy, 810
motions of his spirit are dull as, 47
my native land good, 352
my old Kentucky home good, 567
mysterious, 326
nature's laws lay hid in, 214
naughty, to swim in, 99
no, can hide us from each other's sight, 134
no evil thing walks by, 158
no, is good for me, 580
nor the moon by, 1106
O dusky, 619
of cloudless climes, 356
of death, 602

Night of memories and of sighs, 325
of sorrow, a fore-spent, 165
of the year, darkest, 625
of waking, morn of toil, 308
oft in the stilly, 336
one other gaudy, 104
or day, either by, 901
out of the, 855
passed a miserable, 71
passed long long, away, 557
physical and spiritual, 1067
pillar of fire by, 1098
pilot 't is a fearful, 388
pitch-black, 565
praise day at, 136
regent of the, 269
rides down the sky, 229
sable goddess, 201
say not good, 273
seal thy sense, let no, 822
shaded in the solemn, 555
shall be filled with music, 434
shall fold him, 900
ships that pass in the, 437
silver lining on the, 157
singeth all, 89, 315
skirts of the dead, 633
sleep death and the stars, 537
so full of ghastly dreams, 71
so late into the, 357
so wild but brings, no, 501
soft stillness and the, 47
son of the sable, 30
soon comes the, 401
sound of revelry by, 352
starless unknown, 850
stars break up the, 566
stars in empty, 306
steal a few hours from the, 336
stronger, one, 592
such, ne'er had been nor e'er shall be, 401
sum up at, what thou hast done by day, 136
sung from morn till, 269
sweeps along the plain, 348
sweetest morsel of the, 65
swiftly goes the, 886
that covers me, 692
that first we met, 388
that makes me or fordoes me, 103
that slepen al the, 5
that wins, 633
the dark-blue hunter, 801
the, is dark and I am far, 403
the long cool, 1066
there shall be no, 1123
this frosty, 924
through many a bad, 1080
through the balmy air of, 460
through the dim halls of, 418
thy path be dark as, 499
till it be morrow, 78
time of innocent industries, 860
to bloom for sons of, 334
to dawn from dawn to night, 888
to each a fair good, 308
toiling upward in the, 436
too sweet for, 386
unto night showeth knowledge, 1103
upon its throne, 505

Night, upon the cheek of, 77
  urge the morrow, 365
  vast and middle of the, 90
  very different from the day, 247
  vigil at my heart, 896
  vindication of, 860
  waits all, one, 983
  was riding that, 437
  was senescent, as the, 461
  was thick and hazy, 655
  watch in the, 1105
  watches of the, 673
  watchman what of the, 1111
  we banish sorrow, with, 129
  we parted by, 396
  weaker beauties of the, 166
  what is the, 87
  when she came home, 850
  when the wind, one, 951
  where ignorant armies clash by, 546
  will not last the, 915
  windless, 833
  windy, a rainy morrow, 108
  wings of, 434
  witching time of, 95
  with her train, 693
  with me, come into the, 903
  with this her solemn bird, then silent, 152
  with thy black mantle, 1032
  womb of uncreated, 149
  world in love with, 79
  would not spend another such, 71
  yes I answered you last, 428
  yield day to, 68
Nights, all white and still, sech, 527
  and days, chequer-board of, 1019
  and solemn marches fill the, 522
  are longest in Russia, when, 36
  are wholesome, 89
  as there are days, as many, 915
  delights as short as are the, 127
  dews of summer, 269
  forty days and forty, 1097
  idle days than dreamless, 823
  lay down of, 743
  May's yellow moonlit summer, 485
  of rest, 952
  profit of their shining, 40
  shorten tedious, 121
  starred and stately, 531
  such as sleep o', 81
  through long long wintry, 499
  to waste long, in pensive discontent, 25
  with sleep, winding up, 67
  with sleepless sorrow, 596
Night's black arch, 287
  black mantle, 1032
  blue arch adorn, 267
  brim, o'er, 485
  candles are burnt out, 79
  dull ear, piercing the, 67
  herald, the owl, 106
  high mysteries, priestess of, 418
  Plutonian shore, 418, 568
  repose, earned a, 434

Night's work, his day's work and his, 630
Night-cap decked his brow, 253
  wave had its, 701
Night-dew's cooling balm, 445
Night-dress, lectures in her, 392
Nightfall and the light, between the, 630
Night-flower sees but one moon, 335
Nightingale as amorous, 669
  dies for shame if another bird sings, 123
  has a lyre of gold, 693
  in the sycamore, 702
  lover or, 711
  man who imitated the, 999
  roar an 't were any, 42
  said the Chinese, 856
  that never dies, the new year's, 554
  to act the part of a, 1007
Nightingales live on, thy, 554
  thy pleasant voices, thy, 554
  which sing only in the spring, 147
Nightingale's song in the grove, 269
Nightly dreams, all my, 460
  pitch my moving tent, 306
  to the listening earth, 194
Nightmare and the goblin, 164
  crust, throw off the, 937
  Life-in-death, 315
Night-time I shall not forget, 632
Night-wind blew cold on my desolate, 418
  sigh, hear the, 650
Nihilist, literary, 893
Nile, allegory on the banks of the, 278
  dogs drinking from the, 992
  outvenoms all the worms of, 105
  show me the fountain of the, 412
  to eat the lotus of the, 444
  where is my serpent of old, 104
Nilotic isle, 156
Nimble and airy servitors, 162
  and full of subtle flame, 129
  of the marrow-nerve, 576
  thought can jump both sea and land, 107
Nimbly and sweetly recommends itself, 85
Nimrod the mighty hunter, 1097
Nine days' wonder, 4, 15
  hundred and sixty years, 1097
  lives like a cat, 16, 976
  moons wasted, 100
  tailors make a man, 380
  tailors of Tooley Street, 578
Nineteenth century, great works of the, 1087
Nineties were not really gay, 847
Ninetieth, aught of the gallant, 539
Ninety and nine, the, 1115
  in the shade, worse than, 795
  when the glass is at, 637
Ninety-eight, to speak of, 555
Nineveh and Tyre, one with, 780
Ninny, Handel's but a, 221

Ninth part of a hair, I 'll cavil on, 62
Niobe, like, all tears, 90
  of nations, 354
  with clasped hands, new, 565
Nipped i' the bud, 164
Nipping and an eager air, 91
Nipple in a cloud, its dark, 814
Nips his root, 73
Nirvana or the heavenly courts, in, 826
  strive to reach thee, 664
Nis nat gold, as that I have herd, 8
Nisi suadeat intervallis, 945
Nix shallow et non profundus, 951
No better than you should be, 131
  day without a line, 994
  great and no small, there is, 207
  herb like tobacco, 524
  high-flyer, 181
  love lost between us, 117
  matter where it's going, 916
  mebby to mean yes an' say, 527
  more of that Hal, 62
  name whose echo is not faint, 326
  one is injured save by himself, 1023
  one stops to listen, if, 661
  place to sit down, 166
  sooner looked but they loved, 51
  sooner met but they looked, 51
  sooner sighed but asked the reason, 51
  tengo dinero, God damn it to hell, 895
Noah an' Jonah an' Cap'n John Smith, 851
  but one poor, 922
  often said to his wife, 827
  tuk de Herald, 712
Noah's ark, hunt it into, 263
  ark, mouldy rolls of, 173
Nob, hob, is his word, 55
Nobilitas sola est atque unica virtus, 257
Nobility, base men in love have a, 101
  betwixt the wind and his, 61
  broad acres a patent of, 582
  good of others to, 1048
  idleness is an appendix to, 123
  in his character, 1064
  my, begins with me, 1003
  of ascent and descent, 619
  our old, 518
  species of, 1048
  stamp of, 1090
  true, is exempt from fear, 69
Nobility's true badge, mercy is, 76
Noble, all work is, 378
  and approved good masters, 100
  and happy human beings, greatest number of, 533
  and incapable of deceit, 311
  and most sovereign reason, 94
  and useful entertainments, 196
  and well-beloved souls, 627

Noble and wise of the land. 730
army of martyrs, 1127
be, 524
bloods, the breed of, 81
deed, every, 964
deed is wrought, where'er a, 436
every, crown is and, 378
face, hills of manhood a, 458
fame, 620
in a death so, 157
in reason, 92
living and the noble dead, 300
manners veil defect, 556
memory, he shall have a, 76
mind, loyal nature and of, 471
mind o'erthrown, 93
minds, divine insanity of, 438
my longing to be, 862
negligences, teach his, 190
of every, work silent part is best, 533
race and brave, 364
shame, ashamed with the, 524
thought, whene'er is spoken a, 436
thoughts, never alone with, 27
through and through, 671
to be good, 'tis only, 29, 462
to be, we'll be good, 257
too, for the world, 76
trustworthy consistent, not one is, 795
type of good heroic womanhood, 436
work of love to do, some, 474
youth did dress themselves, 64
Nobles and heralds, 189
by the right of an earlier creation, 397
Nobleman, equal to the proudest, 949
friendly and frank, 478
writes a book, when a, 237
Noblemen, towns and, are made, 931
Nobleness has taught, me too, 411
in other men, 524
of another person, 841
walks in our ways, 894
Nobler in the mind to suffer, whether 'tis, 93
modes of life, ring in the, 469
than any fact my wish, 444
yet in his own worth, 174
Noblest acts the best, feels the, 506
heritage, names that are England's, 518
Roman of them all, 84
things, sweetness and light the two, 191
work of God, an honest man, 208, 284
work of man, 603
Nobly born is now a crime, 128
born must nobly meet his fate, 968
die, for their country, 76
planned, perfect woman, 299
Nobody at home, there's, 217
came to his help, 962
can write the life of a man, 235
ever could do, things, 872
gave it a second, 935

Nobody gets old and godly and grave, 789
has ever expected me to be, 455
I care for, 269
I'm, who are you, 584
never made me, 480
not even the rain, 921
the figure of, 825
there is, 261
wants to read a classic, 615
was ever meant to remember, 839
writes for humanity, 802
Nobody's business, 139
child, because I am, 557
enemy but his own, 496
Nocturne deserves another, one good, 911
Nod, affects to, 176
an esteemed person's, 1000
Homer observ'd to, 180, 984
ready with every, to tumble, 72
shakes his curls and gives the, 218
the shepherd goes, old, 822
wink as good as a, 593
Wynken Blynken and, 699, 872
Nods and becks, 160
Homer sometimes, 984
nor is it Homer, 210
Nodded at the helm, Palinurus, 215
nearly napping, while I, 460
Noddin', nid nid, 291
Nodosities of the oak, 261
Noise and rout, out from, 829
dire was the, of conflict, 153
enemy to pomp and, 195
enough, were not, 910
from good toast, 803
harmonious bubbling, 140
is the most impertinent, 1064
just like the sea, 910
like of a hidden brook, 315
no, over a good deed, 1011
nor make a, 404
of falling blows, 622
of folly, shun'st the, 160
of it would put his enemies to flight, 122
of many waters, 1105, 1123
of tempests dieth, the, 480
of these, bear forever, 838
of tongues and deeds, 462
of waters in mine ears, 71
of worldly fame, 1021
people who make no, 1046
sleeps in continual, 629
so close to our dwelling-place, 838
splitting the air with, 76
they make in pouring out, 217
they that govern make least, 130
tranquillity, after, 609
Noises, popular, 166
the small dim, 928
Noiseless around me myriads of other globes, 537
current strong obscure and deep, 548
fabric sprung, 342
falls the foot of time, 294

Noiseless foot of time, inaudible and, 53
tenor of their way, 245
Noisome weeds, the, 60
Noisy caravans of brown, 756
keys, over the, 564
when he is too, 561
world hears least, 302
Noli me tangere, 18
Noll for shortness called, 243
No-man's land, 620
Nomen alias quære, 114
Nominated in the bond, 47
Nomination of this gentleman, 97
to office, 261
No-more, I am also called, 577
Non amo te, Sabidi, 188
Non-combatant, no fury like, 800
Non-conformist, whoso would be a man must be a, 411
None are equal to those not concerned, 1067
are quite so single, 927
beside us wrought, 965
but himself his parallel, 221
but the brave deserves the fair, 176
can tell when 'twas finished, 502
ever loved but at first sight, 28
has begun to think how divine, 534
have yet come home, 566
knew thee but to love thee, 289
more taken in by flattery, 1049
of these finally satisfy, 538
of these so lonely, there's, 894
of us liveth to himself, 1119
old or young has ever died, 639
on earth above her, 289
other can pain me, 692
other can please me, 692
padre none; I slew them all, 686
resign, few die and, 274
saw it begin, 502
shall part us, 623
so blind that will not see, 188, 192
so deaf that will not hear, 17, 187
so poor to do him reverence, 83
thrives for long upon, 556
to mend and none to mar, 634
to praise, maid with, 296
unhappy but the great, 198
who dares do more is, 85
without hope e'er loved, 239
will sweat but for promotion, 48
you will please, 962
Nongtongpaw again, what, 511
Non-payment, turn her out for, 948
Nonsense and learning, 253
and sense, through, 174
era of wonderful, 922
now and then, a little, 246
the corner of, 319
vast quantity of, 498
Noodles have chicken and cream, 655
Nook, fastened a name to every, 714
for me, an obscure, 484

Nook of God's creation a little
  fruitfuller, make some, 379
  seat in some poetic, 346
  unknown, in some, 648
Nooke, and a shadie, 654
Nooks to lie and read in, 346
Noon, blaze of, 156
  heaven's immortal, 367
  morning yield to, 555
  no sun no moon no, 391
  of thought, 273
  quick dried, 493
  sailing athwart the, 316
  to dewy eve, from, 149
Noons and nights, 672
Noon's broad fervid earnest light,
  555
Noonday, clearer than the, 1102
  light, truth and, 509
  no at, 494
  that wasteth at, 1105
Noontide air, summer's, 150
  hour, shadow for the, 373
  night, sorrow makes, 71
Noontime, retreated before,
  1070
Noose, get the very best o',
  527
  marriage is a, 1040
Nooses give, 918
Nor can I, 504
Nor'-east to sou'-west winds,
  617
Normal lurch, a wink and a sly,
  508
  need, satisfies no, 943
Norman blood, 462
Normans a miscellaneous set of
  adventurers, 739
Norman's Woe, on the reef of, 433
Norns, dark vistas of the reboantic, 432
North and strikes the South,
  threatens the, 1069
  and the south and, 375
  and west they lie, 929
  Ariosto of the, 354
  fair weather out of the, 1102
  far north are the sources, 929
  forth in triumph from the, 401
  hills of the stormy, 370
  no east no west no, 329
  Ocean girds it round, 673
  unripened beauties of the, 194
  where the high winds blow,
  1065
  wind ceases, 576
Northern laurels, 267
  Railroad, locomotives on the,
  1083
  Sea, on this side the, 954
  thought is slow, 488
  word guess imported from
  England, 616
North-wind's breath, 370
Norval, my name is, 248
Norwegian hills, hewn on, 148
Nor'-wester is blowing, a strong,
  275
Nose, a pouncet-box he gave his,
  61
  ashamed of his red, 182
  doctor's, 435
  down his innocent, 48
  entuned in hir, 5
  frozen was his honest, 815

Nose, great, indicates a great
  man, 1085
  he wrapped his, 498
  his own, would not assert his,
  263
  into other men's porridge, 1036
  is as red as a pink, 320
  is cold he meekly cried, 364
  I've only one, 702
  jolly red nose, 135
  may ravage a rose, any, 484
  miss the insinuated, 736
  of a healthy dog, 815
  of Cleopatra, 1047
  on a man's face, 33, 125, 1034
  paying through the, 945
  pimpled or a fatal fever, 226
  salt-lick of his, 926
  sharp as a pen, 66
  spectacles on, and pouch on
  side, 50
  superfine long, 735
  that says why don't you, 751
  that's his precious, 391
  tip-tilted, her slender, 470
  to the grindstone, 227
  wipe a bloody, 206
Noses, athwart men's, 77
  to the grindstone, 13, 116, 125
Nosegay of culled flowers, 1030
Nostril, that ever offended, 35
  upturned his, 155
Not a drum was heard, 364
  at all surprising, it's, 510
  dead but gone before, 289
  if I know myself at all, 323
  in the vein, I am, 72
  in toys we spent them, 167
  lost but gone before, 188
  of an age but for all time, 119
  that I loved Cæsar less, 83
  to know me, 152
  to speak it profanely, 94
  too much, rule of, 155
  with me is against me, he that
  is, 1117
Notation of the heart, 927
Not-browne mayd, 257
Notches on the blade, 1093
Not-day exhibited, till I saw
  what the, 537
Note, bid for each poor blotted,
  722
  deserving, 133
  first solemn, 1064
  hits an upper, 816
  it in a book, 1111
  of every bell, every, 667
  of him take no, 39
  of preparation, give dreadful,
  67
  of that immortal song, 684
  of, when found make a, 496
  take note take, O world, 103
  that means to be of, 105
  that swells the gale, 245
  which Cupid strikes, 145
  who takes, 1020
  you in my book of memory, 68
  youth that means to be of, 105
Notes, all the compass of the, 176
  and clear, whose large, 735
  between the grace, 822
  by distance made more sweet,
  248
  chiel's amang ye takin', 286

Notes, disjointed series of stac-
  cato, 906
  like the catch of a song, 621
  never scare, yet its, 545
  of Andrew Carnegie, Lydian,
  714
  of flame, 309
  of gladness, strung to, 327
  of the harpers ring, the, 387
  of woe, the deepest, 287
  on the next war, 930
  on theology lecture, 885
  thick-warbled, 156
  thy liquid, 161
  to notes respond, remotest,
  503
  with many a winding bout, 160
  you cain't sta't no, 820
Notebook, bring novelist your,
  658
  set in a, 83
Note-booke in his pocket, carried always a, 171
Notebooks, laugh at my, 893
Nothin' thet you can be held tu,
  say, 527
  without you're compelled, say,
  527
Nothing, a thing cannot go back
  to, 1010
  affright thee, 437
  all come to, 165
  artistic out of mere art, 826
  as good since, 930
  astonishes men so much, 412
  at all, black pall of, 914
  at all, to know is, 1078
  away, when he dieth, 960
  becomes him ill, 41
  before and nothing behind, 317
  begins and nothing ends, 748
  behind me, leave, 859
  better know, 1080
  blessed is he who expects, 220
  but flags, 641
  but his reverie, supporting,
  1068
  but his violin, 628
  but I never seed, 639
  but immortality, think there
  is, 537
  but talk of his horse, 44
  but that, might ever do, 57
  but vain fantasy, begot of, 77
  but well and fair, 157
  but what hath been said before,
  979
  can be more disgraceful, 981
  can be more impossible, 1039
  can be well done hastily, 988
  can bring back the hour, 301
  can bring you peace, 411
  can come out of nothing, 1010
  can cover his high fame, 131
  can freeze, 452
  can happen more beautiful
  than death, 534
  can have value, 1071
  can need a lie, 135
  can shake or slay, 813
  can touch him further, 87
  can we call our own but death,
  59
  cares to know, 1076
  certain but death and taxes,
  228

Nothing collapses, 535
comes amiss so money comes, 52
comes to pass without cause, 226
comes to thee new or strange, 463
common did or mean, 169
condition of doing, 1009
created something of, 147
death in itself is, 178
dies but something mourns, 359
do much harm, 923
earthly could surpass her, 358
either good or bad, 92
equals the joy of the drinker, 1093
ever succeeds, 1081
evil cross this door, 886
except a battle lost, 292
extenuate, 103, 417
first, all at once and, 453
for himself, keeps back, 1016
for mere vengeance, do, 591
for reward, 24
for thee is too early, 1010
full of sound and fury signifying, 88
gives to airy, 43
God can send, 913
good counsel costs them, 124
good, thought, 661
great in the world, 1062
habitual but indecision, 662
half so sweet in life, 335
happens unless first a dream, 854
harsh or burdensome, 1016
having, nothing can he lose, 70
having, yet hath all, 114
hid from the heat thereof, 1103
human can equal, 969
I have caused or done, 854
I have everything yet have, 979
I owe much, I have, 1024
I want nothing and I possess, 979
if not critical, 101
in, am I changed but in my garments, 99
in excess, 1013
in front but the master, 807
in his life became him, 84
in human life, 969
in my hand, turn to, 458
in particular, did, 623
in poverty borne so ill, 230
in the world but what he knew, 665
in the world is single, 368
in the world to do, with, 406
infinite deal of, speaks an, 44
interesting wholly loses vitality, 645
into this world, we brought, 1122
is changed in France, 1092
is fair or good alone, 408
is good, to do, 519
is had for nothing, world when, 519
is here for tears, 157
is impossible, 12

Nothing is law that is not reason, 21
is little, 234
is lost, one on whom, 667
is lost that's wrought with tears, 728
is more confident, 995
is more dangerous, 1068
is more troublesome, 637
is so galling to a people, 398
is so hard but search will find it out, 134
is so useless as a general maxim, 397
is to pay, 311
is there to come, 167
is too late, 438
is unnatural, 279
is wanting, 438
knew when to say, 723
left remarkable beneath the visiting moon, 105
like being used to a thing, 278
like leather, there's, 955
little is better than, 988
long, everything by starts and, 174
more aggravates ill success, 229
more can I do, 660
more difficult, there is, 1023
more fun than a man, 919
more gentle than smoke, 1069
more of me, ask, 633
more tiresome than a superannuated pedagogue, 636
more to see, 796
my own but the thread, 114
new except what is forgotten, 1061
now can make us twain, 576
of him that doth fade, 32
of nothing comes, 572
on earth consumes, 1082
on earth that will stay, 666
on God's earth, 652
out of senseless, 461
paint costs, 414
profits more than self-esteem, 154
real or important has yet been seen, 1089
says, when nothing to say, 237
scoured to, 64
signification of word, 482
so active is, 749
so becomes a man as modest stillness, 66
so difficult but it may be found out, 980
so expensive as glory, 312
so finely perceived as injustice, 498
so precious as time, 1026
so tragic as death of young one, 887
so well known, 711
speaks, yet says, 78
starve with, 44
succeeds like success, 945, 1067
than to know, 991
thank you for, 1034
that he did not adorn, 231
that is can pause or stay, 438
that is evil except, 670

Nothing that's worth lying awake, 817
the world knows, of its greatest men, 401
'tis not for, we life pursue, 178
'tis something, 102
to do but trade with them, 271
to do but work, 729
to do with all these, 938
to fear from them, 974
to have a thing is, 942
to have, yet think we have enow, 121
to him falls early, 126
to look backward to, 838
to look forward to, 838
to this, but, 241
to wail or knock the breast, 157
to write about, 1008
to you, is it, 1113
true but heaven, 336
useless is or low, 436
very beautiful and nothing very gay, 895
we desire, so much as what we ought not to have, 988
whatever to wear, 561
who cares for, 626
will come of nothing, 98
will help, 923
will mix and amalgamate, 1068
will sustain you more potently, 695
wise for saying, 44
wise men say, in dangerous times, 130
world crumbles to, 1063
worth a tear, 601
worth the doing, 677
worth the wear of winning, 810
worthy in the past departs, 378
would give, 966
wouldst thou be, 854
yet thou hast seen, 1036
zealous for, 237
Nothings, such laboured, 211
Nothingness, day of, 355
death is a state of, 970
pass into, 382
towers and ships are, 965
Nothing-withholding and free, 663
Nothynge that more dyspleaseth God, 9
Notice of their opinions, state takes no, 141
Notion, blunder and foolish, 285
good, is lost, 171
Notions fudge, we call old, 529
of Deity, down with ridiculous, 569
spite all modern, 780
Notionable dictes of antique Rome, 184
Notoriety may be achieved in a narrow sphere, 529
Notorious by base fraud, 991
rather be, 995
Nought but a lovely sighing of the wind, 385
but that he nought did know, 114
disperse to, 68
except for love's sake only, 429

Nought expect, blessed are those that, 272
is everything, 332
n'assayeth, nought n'acheveth, 4
shall make us rue, 58
so vile that on the earth, 78
that He has made, 473
time's enormous, 823
to do with a man, 962
to have, is to have all things, 556
venter, nought have, 15
Nouns, whose verbs and, do more agree, 645
Nourish all the world, 41
Nourished in the womb of Pia Mater, 41
Nourisher in life's feast, 86
Nourishment called supper, 40
I get, the little, 897
to give the soul fit, 423
Novel beauty, derived a, 1087
last fashionable, 399
only a, 323
Novels, three-volume, those signs-manual, 1050
Novelist, advice to unborn, 913
first duty of a, 580
psychological, 797
realist rhymester play your, 471
Novelties, full of untold, 563
November glooms are barren, 693
hold in the month of, 541
no leaves no birds, 391
remember the fifth of, 945
thirty days hath, 18
November's surly blast, 284
Novice she could say, what to a, 511
Now and forever, 341
came still evening on, 152
eternal, does always last, 167
everlasting, 167
I know it, thought so once, 206
I lay me down to sleep, 947
if it be, 't is not to come, 97
is the accepted time, 1121
or never, 241
's the day, now's the hour, 286
the, is its principal factor, 660
Nowadays, land of, 809
Nowhere else than where I am, 904
to come but back, 729
to go but out, 729
Nox most opportuna, 951
was lit by lux, 951
Noyance or unrest, 224
Nozzle agin the bank, 639
Nude, to keep one from going, 729
Nuffin' in de pot, w'en dey's, 820
Nuisance, in reality a universal, 1048
one to the other, a, 1048
Null, splendidly, 469
the evil is, 489
Nulla dies sine linea, 994
Nullos his mallem ludos spectasse, 940
Nullum magnum ingenium, 173
quod tetigit non ornavit, 231
Number, blessings without, 199

Number, happiness of the greatest, 222
largest, of excellent works, 1053
of diseases, the, 1051
of things, the world is full of, 702
our days, teach us to, 1105
than your light, more by, 114
Numbers, a few honest men are better than, 141
add to golden, 116
are but few, 807
good luck in odd, 35
lisped in, 213
luck in odd, there is, 389
magic, and persuasive sound, 193
round, are false, 238
sanctified the crime, 268
stream in smoother, 211
success does not depend upon, 424
tell me not in mournful, 433
there is divinity in odd, 35
warmly pure, 247
wise wordes taught in, 25
wrong but similar, 935
Numbered with Thy Saints, 1127
Numerous as the concourse of all songs, 601
train below, 185
Nun hath no nation, 593
holy time is quiet as a, 297
Nunc scripsi totum, 957
Nunnery, get thee to a, 93, 615
Nunquam se minus otiosum, 289
Nuptial bower, led her to the, 154
knot, 624
ring and a small seal, 289
Nurse a flame, if you, 328
asleep, sucks the, 105
contemplation, her best, 158
for a poetic child, 307
nature's soft, 65
of arms and land of scholars, 250
of full-grown souls is solitude, 524
of manly sentiment, 260
of our souls, 363
rocked me to patience, 382
Nurses in a hospital, detached as, 912
wives are old men's, 912
Nurse's arms, puking in the, 49
Nursed a dear gazelle, 338
Nurseries of heaven, 748
Nursery rhyme, first made the, 924
Nursing her wrath, 287
there was lack of woman's, 447
Nursling of the sky, 366
Nurslings of immortality, 367
Nuts and things happen, we're all poor, 902
are getting brown, 584
to crack, 434
to the father of lies, 337
Nut-brown ale, the spicy, 160
Nutmeg-graters, rough as, 204
Nutrition, to draw, 208
Nutty and so knowing, so, 361
Ny as ever he can, 5
Nymph, haste thee, 160

Nymph in thy orisons, 93
indifference bring, 248
mountain, sweet liberty, 160
Naiad or a Grace, 308
Nymphs blush, not he, 575
Nympha pudica Deum vidit, 165
Nympholepsy of fond despair, 354
O ME no O's, 947
Oafs at the goals, 780
Oak and ash and thorn, 782
becomes the greenest, 814
bend a knotted, 193
brave old, the, 446
for angling rod a sturdy, 146
from a small acorn grows, 292
hardest-timbered, 70
hearts of, are our ships, 242
hollow, our palace is, 345
in the forest, 381
little strokes fell great, 227
many strokes overthrow the tallest, 23
nodosities of the, 261
raven on yon left-hand, 206
shadow of the British, 260
walk round about an, 35
within an ancient hollow, 662
Oaks, branch-charmed, 384
fell great, 227
from little acorns, tall, 292
of towering height, 231
Oake and ashe and thorne, 257
Oak-tree and the cedar-tree without a flower, 394
Oar, drip of the suspended, 353
in every man's boat, 1040
my hand was on the, 973
put in her, 1039
soft moves the dipping, 288
spread the thin, 208
steady plies the, 954
sweating at the, 881
take awhile his, 777
wait the muffled, 444
we broke the, 572
when for me the silent, 568
who never handled, 973
Oars alone can ne'er prevail, 264
cut with her golden, 39
keep time and voices tune, 288, 334
of Ithaca, 570
over the courtyard, 894
ply back again, 475
trouble dangerous seas with, 982
were silver, the, 104
with falling, 169
Oat-cakes and sulphur, the land of, 312
Oaten bread, wholesomeness of, 122
Oates walking to his death, 804
Oath, a full great, 257
and song, all day long with, 829
corporal, 1037
faithful to his, 1061
good mouth-filling, 62
he never made, to break an, 142
he that imposes an, 142
not the, makes us believe, 964

Oath, royal, 465
  spirit flew up with the, 242
  sworn too hard-a-keeping, 40
  the physician's, 971
  trust no man on his, 80
Oaths, false as dicers', 95
  soldier full of strange, 49
Oatmeal, literature on a little, 312
Oats and base grain, fed on, 122
  definition of, meant to vex, 233
  food for horses, 122
  for people in Scotland, 232
  given to horses in England, 232
  when to sow wild, 793
Obadias David Josias, 947
Obdurate and blind, believed me, 897
  fates are not quite, 528, 835
Obdured breast, arm the, 150
Obedience bane of all genius, 368
  into duty, 1054
  is best, 764
  morals simply, 741
  power to command, 975
  supreme powers keep men in, 126
  to God, 260, 945
  to government, 268
  to the voice of God, 445
Obedient to their laws, 961
Obelisk, strong and upright like an, 726
Obey the important call, 266
  the voice at eve, 410
  thy cherished secret wish, now, 537
  till we can and do, 559
  whom three realms, 212
Obeys him, though she bends him she, 436
Obits improving reading, 861
Obituary in Boston Transcript, 768
Object all sublime, 624
  be our country, let our, 340
  black ceremonial, 787
  failure in a great, 382
  has he not also another, 974
  in possession, 254
  of the whole creation, 253
  of utility, without being an, 1071
  passion or the excitement of the heart, 461
  something valuable its, 1062
  truth or the satisfaction, 461
Objects and knowledge curious, for, 536
  extracted from many, 51
  in an airy height, 189
  of all thought, 296
  of sense, significance to, 669
  rows on rows of natural, 1057
  sees in all, eye of intellect, 378
  tries for great, 998
Oblations, bring no more vain, 1110
Obligation, a sense of, 813
  haste to pay an, 1044
  to be intelligent, 856
  to posterity, 277
Obliging and cheerful, 394
  so, ne'er obliged, 213

Oblique loves greet themselves in every angle, 169
Obliteration, between us and utter, 772
Oblivion, after life is, 1010
  alms for, 75
  ask, 853
  consign other works to, 324
  dateless, 610
  gently replacing in, 585
  iniquity of, 145
  largely lit, blue, 888
  Lethe the river of, 150
  of a day, 574
  second childishness and mere, 50
  shimmering all around us, 850
  six months', 636
  tooth of time and razure of, 37
Oblivion's silence seal, or in, 305
Oblivious antidote, some sweet, 88
Obnoxious thought, to expel an, 670
Obscene in life, 739
  only great men dare be, 739
Obscure and illustrious heroes, 1068
  circuitous and, 735
  grave, a little little, 60
  he died, and though, 910
  mass of humanity, merged into the, 422
  momentous souls, 879
  not necessarily, 319
  palpable, 150
  writers in France, 1084
Obscures the show of evil, 46
Obscurity, gradually shaded into, 558
  of his person, 970
  often brings safety, 962
  only defence against reproach, 196
  the least of outward evils, 377
Obsequious majesty, 154
Obsequiousness and flattery, 272
Observance, breach than the, 91
  with this special, 94
Observances of paltry decorum, 311
Observation, bearings of this, 496
  is the best physic, 111
  of the nature of evil, 973
  smack of, 57
  strange places crammed with, 49
  that each by, 511
  things worth their, 196
  with extensive view, 230
  without punishment or, 949
Observations which we make, 209
Observe the opportunity, 1124
Observed, they are most, 173
Observer, he is a great, 81
  of ought and must, a calm, 757
Observers, observed of all, 94
Observer's sake, partial for the, 209
Obsession by economic issues, 866
Obstacle, managed to surmount the, 1087
  Napoleon is the sole, 1061

Obstacles, love overcomes all, 5
  ride over all, 497
  we combat, 636
Obstinacy in a bad one, 241
Obstinate questionings of sense, 301
Obstruction, to lie in cold, 36
Obstructionists, fossils, scoffers, 795
Obtainable, no truer truth, 493
Obtained, but when once, 387
Occasion, courage mounteth with, 57
  for every social, 921
  for the vigilant, 966
  learn to make, 621
  mellowing of, 41
  of such estrangement, 997
  requires, silent when, 1001
  to know one another, 34
  when to take, by the hand, 462
  who would do ill never wants, 137
Occasions and causes, 67
  death is never at a loss for, 1092
  new, teach new duties, 525
Occident, in the yet unformed, 30
Occupation, absence of, 263
  idleness and lack of, 995
  is labor, serious, 1062
  's gone, Othello's, 102
  with your earnest, 1054
Occupations, in mean, 996
  let thy, be few, 1010
  love our, 495
Occur in the best regulated families, 496
  the most of them never, 750
  things that did n't, 733
Occurs, liberty be subserved whatever, 537
  what we anticipate seldom, 420
Ocean, abandon the, 328
  after its life, fleeing to, 501
  bars, beyond the, 710
  bed, daystar in the, 159
  bidd'st the mighty, 566
  current is the whole ocean, thinks the, 670
  deeper than, 386
  depths of the, 290
  dry, drain the, 1017
  each wavelet on the, tost, 504
  echoes of the, rang, 446
  fill, with ink the, 1017
  girdled with the sky, 322
  grasp the, with my span, 199
  great Neptune's, 86
  I have loved thee, 355
  in a moving ring, 761
  in which many noble authors are swallowed, 196
  is forever asking questions, 808
  is not God upon the, 508
  is this the mighty, 326
  is turned up and rent, 712
  leans against the land, 249
  like a man's, 677
  like the round, 322
  murmurs as the, 302, 325

Ocean no longer beckons me, 836
　nothing but sky and, 317
　o'er which no breezes, 869
　of crime, one on the, 521
　of life we pass, so on the, 437
　of truth all undiscovered, 184
　on a western beach, like, 674
　on life's vast, 208
　on whose awful face, 355, 440
　Queen, gallant steamer, 605
　raging o'er the upper, 480
　roll on thou dark blue, 354
　sepulchre and pall, 349
　sunless retreats of the, 336
　that hollows the rocks, 416
　the round, 296
　they've sailed o'er, 513
　title to the, 19
　to adventure into the, 147
　unfathomed caves of, 245
　upon a painted, 315
　wave, life on the, 502
　wherein the whale, 888
Ocean's bosom ever borne, 459
　deep autocracy, 843
　dreamless peace, drink the,
　　805
　edge as I can go, as near the,
　　513
　mane, hand upon the, 393
　melancholy waste, 371
　paths charted, 840
　wave-beat shore, and, 503
Ocean-furrows, breasts the, 570
O'clock, it's ten, 49, 475
　what's, 61
Octave is a world, each, 503
October, dies in, 127
　gave a party, 637
　in New England, 882
　night in the lonesome, 461
　something in, 757
October's bright blue weather,
　591
Octogenarian chief, the, 299, 353
　poet, enjoy the, 788
Octosyllabic verse, the, 356
Ocular proof, give me, 102
Odd number, God delights in an,
　389
　numbers, divinity in, 35
　numbers, luck in, 35, 389
　numbers most effectual, 994
　numbers, the god delights in,
　　994
　volumes, creators of, 323
Odds, facing fearful, 400
　how am I to face the, 743
　life must one swear, 189
　what is the, 494
　with morning, night almost at,
　　87
Ode, I intended an, 649
　to the moon, sweet, 815
Odin, mouths not descended from,
　592
Odious, comparisons are, 9, 31,
　117
　in woollen, 209
Odium and public hatred, 329
　of success, 707
Odour, fairer for that, 107
　of her wild hair, 736
　of its sanctity, 828
　of paltry people, 1080
　so bad, no, 514

Odour, stealing and giving, 53
Odours, Champak, 368
　crushed are sweeter, 289
　of ointments more durable than
　　those of flowers, 110
　Sabean, 151
　virtue is like precious, 109
　when sweet violets sicken, 368
Odourous, comparisons are, 39
　music, listened to his, 693
Odyssey, surge and thunder of
　the, 674
　the Iliad and the, 317
Oedipus, Sophocles wrote his
　grand, 438
O'er folded blooms, 696
　the hill-tops far away, 705
O'er-dusted, than gilt, 75
O'erflowing full, without, 167
O'erfraught heart, whispers the,
　88
O'erhanging firmament, 92
O'erstep not the modesty of na-
　ture, 94
O'erthrown, noble mind is here,
　93
O'erwrought, a mind, 650
Off ag'in on ag'in gone ag'in
　Finnigin, 805
　with his head, 72
Offence, almost gives, 1043
　detest the, 177, 216
　forgave the, 177
　from amorous causes springs,
　　212
　image of, done to any man, 55
　is rank, my, 95
　no harshness gives, 211
　returning after, 157
　to learning and to taste, 332
　with less, 999
Offended, for him have I, 83
Offender, hugged the, 177
　love the, 177, 216
　never pardons the, 137
Offenders, of social, 624
Offending Adam, whipped the, 66
　front of my, 100
　soul alive, most, 67
Offer yourselves to the sea, 663
Offering pure of love, 549
　too little and asking too much,
　　293
Office and affairs of love, 38
　and so to bed, up to the, 867
　but thine, cold in every, 52
　circumlocution, 497
　clear in his great, 85
　due participation of, 274
　for life, hold, 975
　hath but a losing, 64
　he'll hold, 573
　insolence of, 93
　men that stood for, 972
　never ask refuse or resign, 228
　nomination to, 261
　of a wall or as a moat, 59
　of government not to confer
　　happiness, 333
　of more trust, 'tis an, 1035
　of the President not so difficult,
　　638
　return to the, 198
　tender, long engage me, 213
　to speak patience, 't is all
　　men's, 40

Office was to fit actives to pas-
　sives, 118
　what he says outside his, 1071
　which the false man does easy,
　　86
　whom lust of, does not kill,
　　522
　whom spoils of, cannot buy,
　　522
Offices and duties of a general,
　997
　as public trusts, 339
　election to public, 970
　friendship an exchange of good,
　　1044
　liberal, 466
　of friendship which they owe,
　　1028
　of prayer and praise, 302
　or places, people I cannot win
　　with, 171
Office-pens skewered with, 497
Officer and the office, 314
　fear each bush an, 71
　of mine, never more be, 101
　of the people, 320
　public, without vices, 599
Officers and government, country
　behind, 550
　but not scholars, 123
　nosed among the, 936
　public, servants and agents,
　　627
Officious innocent sincere, 231
　prudent quiet rich secret, 1037
Offspring, new-fledged, 250
　of an idle hour, 640
　of heaven first-born, 151
　of the gentilman Jafeth, 115
　time's noblest, 203
　true source of human, 152
Oft expectation fails, 53
　in the stilly night, 336
　is but an art, laughter, 386
　repeating they believe 'em, 190
Often, always blind and, tipsy,
　406
　been so, it has, 476
　funny, words are few and, 511
Ofttimes I hover, about the spot,
　481
Ohio Missouri and Mississippi
　rivers, along the, 538
　Wisconsin Illinois, rolling
　　from, 929
Ohio's deeper boom was there,
　676
Oil, business furnishes, 263
　everything is soothed by, 992
　incomparable Macassar, 358
　little, in a cruse, 1101
　midnight, consumed the, 206
　neither did the cruse of, fail,
　　1101
　of joy for mourning, 1112
　unprofitably burns, our, 263
Oily art, that glib and, 98
　man of God, round fat, 225
Ointment, box of very precious,
　1116
　like a precious, 110
　precious, better than, 1109
　prize at three hundred, 136
　smeared with political, 935
Ointments more durable, odours
　of, 110

Ol' Man River, 456
Old age a good and pleasant time, 700
age a regret, 420
Age and Experience, hand in hand, 185
age but second childhood, 972
age, dallies like the, 55
age, harvest of, 981
age, honored, 981
age in this universal man, 112
age is by nature, 981
age is consummation, 981
age, lingers on into, 967
age live under the shadow of death, 613
age may come after you, know, 535
age serene and bright, 299
age, that ill layer-up of beauty, 68
age, torpid in, 236
age, which should accompany, 88
ale enough whether new or, 20
alike fantastic if too new or, 211
all brave, my friends of, 470
always find time to grow, 203
and antique song, 54
and fat, grows, 61
and gray and full of sleep, 790
and gray-headed error, 145
and lofty walls, 423
and weak and near to death, 766
and young, 610
and young we are on our last cruise, 704
are tenacious, 330
as I am for ladies' love unfit, 176
as time, 500
authors to read, 113
Autumn in the misty morn, 392
Black Joe, 567
blessed times of, 507
bokes, out of olde, 4
bold mate of Henry Morgan, 604, 833
camp-ground, tenting on the, 608
cares, 619
chairs and half a candle, two, 498
Cove, sat an, 539
Decay the greenest, ever upon, 441
died years ago very, 600
dog Tray's ever faithful, 567
ere I was, 317
even to the, 620
ever grow to be, 810
familiar Juice, the, 1019
fashions please me best, 52
father antic the law, 60
fetish raiments of the past, 609
feldes, out of olde, 4
Floyd Ireson, 443
folks at home, far from the, 567
forms of government, 581
forsaken bough where I cling, 450

Old friend you never can be, 108
friends are best, 113, 130
friends old times, 253
friends to trust, 113
Glory, I name thee, 407
Glory, who gave you the name, 408
godheads sink, even, 851
Greece or Rome, beauty which, 442
grow lovely growing, 848
growing, in drawing nothing up, 265
growing, gracefully, 628
hands to young, 653
have been young and now am, 1104
he grew, and trod the path to hell, 802
he will make us, 883
head, young body with so, 46
homes names and splendors, 1085
hugged by the, 391
I grow, 900
I love everything that 's, 253
I was thrice as, 485
in the brave days of, 400
Ireland, I'll not forget, 432
Ironsides at anchor lay, 405
jug without a handle, one, 498
Kentucky home good night, my, 567
like him that's growing, 967
linen wash whitest, 113, 128
lion is dead, now that the, 276
love for new, 28
love shall look out, 560
love straitened him, of an, 470
love that we knew, 649
lovers are soundest, 128
man, a good, 39
man at a station, there was an, 499
man died, when the, 601
man do, what can an, 390
man eloquent, 161
man is twice a child, 92
man to have so much blood, 88
man, weak and despised, 98
man with a beard, an, 499
man's darling, 17
manners old books old wine, 113, 253
Marm Hackett's garden, over, 508
men are walking hospitals, 180
men fools, young men think, 28
men in love, 842
men must die or the world, 472
men shall dream dreams, 1113
men with beautiful manners, 886
men's dream, 173
mighty minds of, 321
monks of, those, 394
never to be, 966
Nick, 143
Nick, gave his name to our, 397
no man would be, 191
nobility, leave us still our, 518
nor young, she was not, 357

Old, not so, but she may learn, 46
odd ends stolen out of holy writ, 71
old old old lady, 715
old sea comes murmuring, 552
pair of sox, 714
pippins toothsomest, 113, 128
plain men have rosy faces, 703
poll, just rubbed his, 389
Queen of the waters, styled the, 407
roads winding, 443
shall not grow, 804
she is not, 737
soldiers are surest, 128
soldiers more accostable than old sailors, 423
some day before I'm, 784
something new, something, 956
songs, I cannot sing the, 583, 590
soul takes the roads again, 833
sweetheart of mine, 696
Testament, blessing of the, 109
Testament, books of the, 1095
that glorious song of, 477
the public is an, woman, 378
the text is, 106
the thought and oft exprest, 415, 528
they think he is growing, 343
time, cities of, 691
time to be, 410
to care, you shall be too, 868
too old for roving, 834
Tubal Cain, 504
when all the world is, lad, 523
when I am, 555
when you are, 1027
which I heard in days of, 446
who remain shall grow, 823
wine to drink, 113
wine wholesomest, is not, 113, 128
with service, weary and, 73
with wandering, 790
wood burns brightest, 128
wood to burn, 113
world and the new, 513
yes I'm growing, 510
yes yes I am, 652
you are, Father William, 320
Olden sanctities, flower of, 556
time long ago, this was in the, 459
Older and wiser people, 913
days, the great of, 579
place than Eden, 827
thoughts and things look, 405
Older-witted, youth should heed the, 1077
Oldest colours have faded, 779
in literature read the, 426
sins the newest kind of ways, 65
Old-fashioned house, Eden is that, 585
Old-gentlemanly vice, 359
'Ole, if you know a better, 943
O'Leary in the grave, with, 791
Oligarchy, definition of, 974
Olive branches twine, 392
oiled by an, 889

Olives of endless age, peace proclaims, 108
Olive-leaf he brings, 155
in her mouth was an, 1097
Olive-plants, children like, 1106
Oliver, Rowland for an, 946
Olympian bards who sung, 409
mirth, 808
Olympic games, conqueror in the, 1002
race, Alexander in the, 1002
Omar should you chance, 664
Omega, Alpha and, 1123
Omen, asks no, 219
Jove intended, to study what, 184
read in this, 593
'Omer smote 'is blooming lyre, 784
Omnia mutantur, 209
Omnipotence and the Infinite, 901
in fighting, 901
Omnipotent, rise in arms against the, 153
Omnipresent, like the Deity is, 342
and up amid the hills, 458
On dit que dans ses amours, 252
his last legs, 116
Stanley on, 308
the wild emerald cucumber-tree, 431
this hapless earth, 386
with the dance, 352
ye brave, 328
Once a year, Christmas comes but, 19
and nothing first, all at, 453
have a priest for enemy, 423
I thought so, now I know it, 206
man can die but, 65
more, telling battle was on, 552
more unto the breach, 66
my soul possest, 619
to every man and nation, 524
upon a midnight dreary, 460
went to pieces all at, 453
One all poets have outgrown, 911
all together, and the loved, 493
alone, wherever there is, 1126
and all, 610
and inseparable, 341
and the other a sea, between the, 425
and the same thing, 1048
another, they stand too near, 120
as in Thy sight, 567
at his right hand, one at his left, 757
beyond all others vile, 747
both grow in, 58
breath attunes the spheres, with, 514
bright hour to waste, nor suffer, 474
broods all day, 896
brotherhood makes all men, 378
by one in the moonlight, 904
by one the phantoms go, 807

One by one you mark them twinkling, 301
can know nothing of giving, 740
can put on two several faces, 181
clear call for me, and, 472
coming, do you see any, 946
commands, where, 1082
country one constitution, 340
day in the country, 587
day, that shall we know, 577
despises one cannot wage war, where, 1082
does not know, 1080
down eternity's river, flow in, 503
draught above heat makes him a fool, 54
enemy too much, 137
fair daughter and no more, 92
fair spirit, with, 354
fell swoop, 88
fishball, and gently whispers, 555
flag one land one heart, 452
foot in sea and one on shore, 38
for all, or all for one, 106
for solitude two for friendship, 515
forty feeding like, 297
friend is much two are many, 636
full peal of praise, is, 470
God grant you find, face, 523
God one law one element, 469
good custom, lest, 463
good old man more than many sermons, 558
great law, 619
has a broken wing, 896
he loved in secret and apart, 722
heart, if I can stop, 583
her heart's adrift with, 568
hundred per-cent American, 866
I fill this cup to, 405
if by land and two if by sea, 437
in life and death, 623
in red cravat, give the, 584
is all right, when, 698
is alone and dies more alone, 838
is for love, you know, 763
is never entirely without the instinct, 538
kind kiss before we part, 225
led astray, like, 160
less travelled by, 838
little hour, 588
little word, how long a time lies in, 59
long buried, 730
made for this soul, 553
man among a thousand, 1109
man can do, so much, 169
man's poison, 132
man's will, to live by, 22
man's wit, 946
may go first and one remain, 576
mind in an house, 1128
more unfortunate, 392

One mouth, two ears only, 420
must learn by doing, 966
nation evermore, 452
near one is too far, 486
night last spring, ever sence, 639
night's ice, trust not, 137
O thou eternal, 1057
of a thousand keys, 441
of God's miracles, 870
of the many, 234
of the ones that Midas touched, 585
of the two best states, 838
old jug without a handle, 498
on God's side is a majority, 479
only but still I am one, 550
other gaudy night, let's have, 104
rich-hearted chord, lyre of, 728
scene no more than three should speak in, 180
science only, 210
seated, day at the organ, 564
should walk with me, rather, 870
step enough for me, 403
still strong man in a blatant land, 469
sweetly solemn thought, 557
that feared God, 1101
that flatters is no friend, 120
that got away, the, 919
that has another sense, 196
that hath, unto every, 1116
that loved not wisely, 103
that stands upon a promontory, 70
that was a woman, 97
that would be thinned, 933
that would circumvent God, 96
that would peep and botanize, 297
thet fust gits mad 's 'most, 527
thing, the man who seeks, 592
thought of thee, 216
thought, one grace, one wonder, 32
to give, it annoyeth, 1079
truth is clear, 207
two and the third in your bosom, 78
voice of sympathy and shame, 513
was me, but the, 922
went to brag, 165
what are his qualifications, 573
which uses, another which makes, 974
who bears beneath, 924
who fed on poetry, as, 425
who goes is happier, 557
who loves his neighbor, 719
who prospers, to fear for, 966
who threatens, 1019
who walked with starry feet, 840
will rarely err, 1079
with empty music, 735
with heaven and the stars, 575
with nature, 366

One with Nineveh and Tyre, 780
with true toil, true leisure, 501
woman and none but she, 631
Ones, great many smaller, 645
the saddest, 851
One's inmost thoughts in another, 717
own self, care for, 971
own self, easiest to deceive, 426
own sole ground, 647
sphere, fitting of self to, 501
One-and-twenty, but I was, 742
One-book man, he was a, 313
One-horse town, this poor little, 615
One-hoss shay, wonderful, 452
One-night stand, try some, 870
Oneself, to love, 724
Onion atoms lurk within the bowl, 313
flourish there, 703
will do well, 52
Onions in the stew, 906
nor garlic, eat no, 43
Onlie begetter, to the, 107
Only a baby small, 589
a little while now, 627.
a look and a voice, 437
a signal shown, 437
Onset, impassioned, 531
just girt me for the, 585
word of, 298
Onward impulses owed to men ill at ease, 422
steer right, 162
upward till the goal ye win, 454
Onwards unswerving, 't is, 501
Ootah's explanation, 719
Opal and amethyst, clouds of, 522
Ope, murder hath broke, 86
my lips, when I, 44
the sacred source, 243
Open as day and the hearts, 435
covenants of peace, 725
eye and ear, we lack but, 442
house to an, 827
locks whoever knocks, 87
our eyes to behold, 1128
rebuke is better, 1108
stand in the, 1084
time and let him pass, 758
yë, slepen al the night with open, 5
Opened new fountains in the human heart, 393
Opening bud to heaven conveyed, 316
eyelids of the morn, 159
flower, every, 199
paradise to him are, 245
Openings, spots of sunny, 346
Open-wood-fire, what is more cheerful than an, 621
Opera guyed, 902
Operas that Verdi wrote, 594
Operation, by mere mechanic, 143
it requires a surgical, 246, 312
Ophelia, ope not thy ponderous and marble jaws, 615

Opiate, fireside is a great, 346
Opiates for the conscience, 917
Opinion and advice, ignoring the, 545
corrupted by, 995
error of, 273
from the surface of, 972
having too good an, 1029
high respect, 259
human to err in, 1006
inconsistencies of, 341
is like a pendulum, 1064
keep, my old, 279
men of perverse, 965
my deliberate, 319
of his own, still, 144
of the law, with good, 277
of the mob, 1049
of the public, 972
of the strongest, 1045
public, 499
sacrifices it to your, 259
scope of my, 89
soon estranged, 369
the poor itch of your, 75
this fool gudgeon, this, 44
trammels of public, 330
ultimately governs the world, 724
was clearly of the, 572
with Pythagoras, 46
Opinions and a will, men who possess, 522
back with wager, 357
cannot survive, 1089
dissenting, of one generation, 943
force of, 1028
halt between two, 1101
I agree with no man's, 1072
I have bought golden, 85
maintain no ill, 251
men get, 430
never two, alike, 144
notice of their, 141
of mankind, 273
public buys its, 614
ready-made, 1074
reverse many of your, 974
stiff in, always in the wrong, 173
testing new, 646
turned by men's, 997
useful to generalize, 1084
winnowed, 97
Op'ning day, it is our, 288
Opponent, arguments to malign an, 420
unenlightened, of the children of light, 548
Opportoonity, ain't it the land of, 925
Opportunists, political and economic, 930
Opportunities, a woman with fair, 482
Opportunity, able to use their, 960
age is, 438
also a matter of, 971
neglected, 180
observe the, 1124
of getting to know, 921
of saying, occurred an, 748
to work out happiness, 333
watch your, 1013

Opposed, that the, may beware, 90
Opposers, arguments of its, 184
Opposing end them, by, 93
wrong, engaged in, 450
Opposite directions, moving in, 313
shore will be, and I on the, 437
Opposites we might succeed, with, 972
Opposition may become sweet, 520
Oppressed, will not submit to be, 949
with two weak evils, age and hunger, 49
Oppression of the mind, 184
make no peace with, 1127
rumour of, 264
Oppression's passion, 937
Oppressor's wrong, 93
Oppugnancy, in mere, 75
Optics sharp it needs, 277
turn their, in upon 't, 143
Optimism and pessimism both needed, 740
flourishes in the lunatic asylum, 740
is the madness, 1052
Opuscules denominated Christmas books, 483
Oracle, I am Sir, 44
of oracles, the, 305
pronounced Socrates wisest, 156
said, 593
Oracles are dumb, 161
common words turn, 429
Oracular tongue, use of my, 277
Orange band of eve, 744
bright, like golden lamps, 169
flower perfumes the bower, 310
glows in the deep thicket's gloom, 355
glows, where the gold, 1058
peel an end of a cigar, 590
Oration, made a promiscuous, 499
Orations, objections against, 1004
Orator bite us, lest an, 972
I am no, 83
persuade the eyes of men without an, 106
shame's, 38
till the lion, charm us, 471
too green, the text is old. the, 106
Orators, loud-bawling, 1003
repair, the famous, 156
very good, when they are out, 51
Oratory, architecture is a sort of, 1081
flowery, he despised, 200
Phocion's, 1000
Orb, drop some golden, 429
foolery does walk about this, 55
monthly changes in her circled, 78
of living light, 294
of one particular tear, 109
of song, that mighty, 302
there is not the smallest, 47
this wretched, 588

Orbs in town, deem all other, 911
 of heavenly frame, 27
 of royal blue, 660
 would open at thy breath, 626
Orbaneja the painter, 1038
Orbed maiden with white fire,
 366
Orbit and sum of Shakespeare's
 wit, 326, 409
 of the restless soul, love the,
 553
Orchard for a dome, 584
 keep cold young, 839
 or the fields, I would get into
 the, 170
 sleeping within my, 91
Orchestra, poets', 684
 whirls me wider, 535
Orchestral silences, grand, 430
 strand, conducting the, 773, 799
Ordained of God, 1119
Ordains, heav'n a time, 162
Order and simplification, 1089
 beauty of the house is, 953
 breeds habit, 636
 categorical, 623
 changeth, the old, 463
 decently and in, 1120
 embrace thy friends leave all
 in, 537
 gave each thing view, 72
 his mistress', to perform, 215
 in variety we see, 216
 introduction of a new, 1023
 is a lovely thing, 841
 of the day, the, 941
 of your going, stand not upon
 the, 87
 path to, 641
 rain or shine, can not, 504
 reigns in Warsaw, 1062
 set thine house in, 1112
 this better in France, 242
 to haud the wretch in, 285
Orders, Almighty's, to perform,
 194
 both under secret, 801
 grey, friar of, 52, 256
 too fuddled to observe your,
 198
Order's cause, for, 576
Ordered formal passionate, 930
 well, that all is, 501
Orderly and regular composition,
 232
 sergeant — Robert Burton, 635
Ordinances, external, 233
 profane no divine, 251
Ordinary men are fit for, 98
 men, reach of, 297
Ordine retrogrado, 112
Ordure of the sty, 889
Ore, in darkness to good, 936
 new-spangled, 159
 that attar of the, 928
Organ of her life, every lovely, 40
 seated one day at the, 564
 surges, when they hear the, 554
 swell, a full, 937
Organs dimensions senses, 45
 players of lofty pipe, 854
Organ-grinder's hat, 660
Organically incapable of a tune,
 323
Organism, British constitution
 most subtle, 450

Organized charity scrimped and
 iced, 676
 hypocrisy, 419
Organ-pipe of frailty, 58
Orgies of morality, sexless, 635
Orient beams, spreads his, 152
 pearl, a double row, 121
 pearl, sowed the earth with,
 153, 1032
 pearls at random strung, 275
 pearls, puddly thoughts to,
 1032
Orient's marvels here, to find the,
 442
Oriental mind, never plumb the,
 776
 quest for righteousness is, 696
Oriflamme, the helmet of Navarre, 400
Orifice, the quaint, 903
Origin, the more confused that,
 1079
 the more remote its, 1079
Original, a thought is often, 453
 and end, 231
 brightness, lost her, 149
 excellent, 217
 he would have the, 238
 just to an excellent, 217
 practical example, contributes
 the, 537
 proclaim, their great, 194
 purely, 804
 right of the people, 949
Originals, reading books in the,
 414
 Shakespeare more original than
 his, 415
Originality, solitude of his own,
 362
 to the great improvement of
 his, 324
Originator and quoter, 415
Oriole, the blissful, 585
Orion and Andromeda, beyond,
 667
 ignorantly and falsely spelled,
 578
 loose the bands of, 1103
 plunges prone, 744
Orion's belt and sworded hip,
 900
Orisons, nymph in thy, 93
 patter out their hasty, 918
Ormus and of Ind, wealth of,
 149
Ornament, foreign aid of, 224
 greatest defence and, 248
 is but the guiled shore, 46
 it carried none, 1093
 of a house, 414
 of a meek and quiet spirit,
 1122
 of friendship, greatest, 981
 of her sex, 494, 1037
 of our town, 497
 only for, 518
 sent to be a moment's, 299
 to his profession, 109
 to society, 325
Ornamental cloud spot and vein,
 every, 196
Ornate and gay, 157
Orphan, for his widow and his,
 457
 or destitute lady, 394

Orphans, peace and freedom of
 being, 720
Orphans' moans and widows'
 tears, 262
 tears, wronged, 129
Orphan-boy to read, 463
Orphan-girl to sew, 463
Orpheus, bid the soul of, sing,
 161
 with his lute, 73
Orthodox on carnage bent, 1050
 prove their doctrine, 142
Orthodoxy is my doxy, 223
O'Ryan, constellation of, 578
Oscar you will (say that), 612
Osity and ation, words in, 292
Osler quotes Trollope on chloroform, 695
Oslerize, a byword, 695
Ossa on the top of Pelion, 1025
 upon Olympus, 986
Ostentation and rusticity, 218
 more, than real utility, 230
Ostentatious, elegant but not,
 233
 show, shuns all, 802
Ostrich dare not dust her wings,
 683
 resembled the wings of an, his
 imagination, 397
Oswego spreads her swamps,
 250
Othello's occupation's gone, 102
Other, between the one and the,
 a sea, 425
 birds and other men, 581
 men think of this life, 81
 side, sounded on the, 172
 than an honest man, if you say
 I am, 64
 things to drink, 827
 useless each without the, 436
Others apart sat on a hill, 150
 are handsomer, 845
 know you know it, unless, 942
 our streets will fill, 581
 service to, 943
 shall right the wrong, 444
 shall sing the song, 444
 times when mirth of, only saddens, 426
Others' uses, corner for, 102
Ought, we do not what we, 547
Ould Church mother of them all,
 786
 shebeen, Shanahan's, 715
Ounce of civet, give me an, 99
 of poison in one pocket, 399
Our academical Pharisees, 397
 acts our angels are, 126
 champion waiting in his, 442
 flag unfurled, seemed to see,
 442
 glories float between earth and,
 425
 hearts in glad surprise, 436
 old gentleman, 346
Oursels, to see, as others see,
 285
Ourselves, always meeting, 875
 and immortality, 584
 and not our words, 626
 and with all nations, among,
 457
 are great, 873
 however we do praise, 54

Ourselves, in them and in, our safety lies, 70
the fault is in, 81
to bore, 1080
Out at heels, I am almost, 34
brief candle, 88
damned spot, 88
good orators when they are, 51
it does not put him, 510
mordre wol, 6
of breath, down and, 63
of house and home, 64
of my due time, born, 608
of my lean and low ability, 56
of olde bokes, 4
of olde feldes, 4
of sight out of mind, 9, 27, 519
of suits with fortune, 48
of the everywhere into the here, 559
of the frying-pan, 16
of the night that covers me, 692
of the sky as I came through, 559
of thine own mouth, 1117
the boundless deep, from, 472
to sea, when I put, 472
upon the stars, look, 405
Outcast state, beweep my, 107
with the naked and, 282
Outcome, much outcry little, 961
Outcry, little outcome, much, 961
of the heart, to drown the, 386
Outdid the frolic wine, 134
the meat, 134
Outer world's control, the soul feels less the, 444
Out-herods Herod, 94
Outlandish lingo, 283
Outlined in fame's illusive light, 572
Outlines of forms previously studied, 1023
Outlive his life half a year, memory, 94
so many years, 65
this powerful rhyme, shall, 107
Outlives in fame, 193
this day and comes safe home, 67
Outlook wasn't brilliant, 770
Out-of-doors, no house like God's, 704
Out-paramoured the Turk, 99
Outrage from lifeless things, 654
on the spirit of justice, 711
worse than death, 316
Outrageous and austere, masks, 897
fortune, arrows of, 93
Outrageously virtuous, 198
Outram coveting right, 764
Outshone the wealth of Ormus, 149
Outside of that part of the ship, 247
show is a poor substitute, 961
swashing and a martial, 48
what a goodly, falsehood hath, 44
Outskirts of the crowd, in the, 497

Outstanding, two, services of central Europe, 1089
Out-topping knowledge, 545
Outvenoms all the worms of the Nile, 105
Out-vociferize even sound itself, 189
Outward and visible sign, 1128
appear beautiful, 1116
form and feature, 317
part, for any, 950
parts, mark of virtue on his, 46
pity, showing an, 60
side, angel on the, 37
things, do draw the inward quality, 104
view, she is not fair to, 386
walls, banners on the, 88
Outward-parting throng, behind the, 450
Outworn garment, 671
myth, 872
Ovation, named it, 997
Over all the earth, peace shall, 477
all the sky, 536
old Marm Hackett's garden, 508
the great gromboolian plain, 498
the hill to the poor-house, 678
the hills and far away, 205
the noisy keys, 564
the roofs of the world, 535
the sea, roving, 459
violent or over civil, 174
Overcame, I came saw and, 65
Overcharged heart, 321
Overcoat, get off your, 893
Over-coloured and over-voluminous narrative, 641
Overcome but half his foe, 149
evil with good, 1119
Overcomes by force, 149
Overfed overdressed and underbred, 759
Overflow, dar's gwine to be a, 712
of gladness, 373
Over-flowing full, without, 167
Overgrow the garden, suffer them and they'll, 69
Overhead, I believe that God is, 638
Overloaded undermanned, meant to founder, 777
Over-measure, enough with, 76
Overmuch, be not righteous, 1109
Over-payment of delight, 322
Over-poetical for poetry, 484
Overpowering knell, 360
Oversoul well in the van, 595
Overthrow of militarism, 799
purposed, 108
wrought their, 748
Overwhelmed in the strife, who died, 533
Overwhelming, let it be, 839
Overwork, men killed by, 786
Ovis a sheep, from the Latin, 997
Owe, if I can't pay, I can, 11
much I have nothing, 1024
no man anything, 1119
no man hate, 50

Owed, dearest thing he, 84
Owes its charm to the far away, 426
Owing owes not, a grateful mind by, 151
Owl abode, aged, 662
and the pussy-cat, the, 498
bold brown, 350
for all his feathers, 383
hawked at by a mousing, 86
I'm an, you're another, 508
in the whole island, no, 237
night's herald, the, 106
sat on an oak, 836
that shrieked, it was the, 86
very gravely got down, the, 508
Owls and a hen, two, 499
companion to, 1102
to Athens, sending, 1014
Owlet atheism, the, 316
Own and only love, 519
do what I will with mine, 1115
every subject's soul is his, 67
God marked him for his, 140
how to hold your, 721
I do not, an inch of land, 568
I have my, four walls, 382
no superior, soul walk free and, 537
rob us of our, 954
sweet will, beyond its, 443
that I may call my, 451
the soft impeachment, 278
would not assert his nose his, 263
Owned with a grin, 321
Owner a name, make for its, 589
grief makes his, stoop, 57
in fee of this handsome estate, 509
of the sphere, 410
ox knoweth his, 1110
whereof was Giant Despair, 172
Owners, down went the, 622
kick their, 277
open as the hearts of the, 435
Owner's tongue doth publish, 108
Ox, at the heels of the laureled, 635
dog barked at the, 962
fish sold for more than an, 1003
goeth to the slaughter, 1106
he that steals an egg will steal an, 138
is gored, whose, 1024
knoweth his owner, 1110
than a stalled, 1107
Oxen bear the yoke, 982
like great black, 790
who drives fat, 238
Oxenford, clerk ther was of, 5
Oxford Book of English Verse, 813
gray spires of, 875
or Cambridge was not enough, 170
spoke to me at, 896
Street, stony-hearted stepmother, 347
Oxyrhynchus, ancient city of, 1126
Oyster crossed in love, 279
man that first eat an, 192

Oyster, pearl in your foul, 51
  secret and solitary as an, 495
  sick, at low tide, 595
  solitary as an, 495
  the world's mine, 34
  'twas a fat, 216
Oysters, season for, 798
Ozymandias king of kings, 878

P's AND Q's, better mind their, 614
Pablo of San Diego, 565
Pace, are traveling all the same, 449
  creeps in this petty, 88
  follow on His, 888
  heavy plummet's, 161
  idle heedless, 600
  she varies, 806
  silent, 219
  thoughts with violent, 103
  unperturbed, 748
  with the sun, keeps, 514
Paces, time travels in divers, 50
Pacience, flour of wyfly, 7
  is an heigh vertu, 8
  t'assaille his wyves, 7
Pacific sign an olive-leaf, 155
  stared at the, 384
  to the great, 858
Pacings, the long mechanic, 463
Pack, as a huntsman his, 252
  beneath my, 891
  clouds away and welcome day, 129
  meets pack, when, 783
  when it begins to rain, will, 98
Package, in this bright little, 870
Packed with poor humanity, 180
Packet of assorted miseries, 787
  the only certain, 780
Pack-horse on the down, 609
Pack-staff, plain as a, 116
Padded lunatic asylums, 877
  petrified and pleasant, 891
Paddington, five-thirty from, 892
Paddle or fins or pinion, 572
Paddocks, cold as, 134
Paddy had not a shirt to his back, 309
Paestum's ancient fanes, 653
Pagan, fought like a, 813
  suckled in a creed, 300
Paganini, tours de force of the great, 630
Paganism to Christianity, prefer, 744
Page, ample for a want ad, 934
  beautiful quarto, 279
  history hath but one, 354
  history's purchased, 353
  I didn't write, tell him the, 585
  names inscribed in history's, 518
  never printed in a, 801
  of gold, wrought on a, 842
  of knowledge, ample, 244
  of prancing poetry, 585
  of some tenth-rate poeticule, 635
  of victories, 369
  pictures for the, atone, 215
  prescribed, all but the, 207
  quite fair is saved, 594
  rank thee upon glory's, 333

Page, refine her sterling, 1050
  traced on the deathless, 516
  what one sweet, 556
  when ended is the, 833
  with bended knee, no, 447
  with dimpled chin, ho pretty, 481
  you're reading done, get the, 777
Pages and pages of colours, 831
  in only a hundred, 1072
  line as good as, 925
  of her battle years, 690
  turn the tattered, 916
Pageant, insubstantial, 33
  of man, old proud, 833
  ranks the yearly, 833
  train when I am dead, no, 374
Pageantry of a king, 949
Paid dear for his whistle, 227
  well that is well satisfied, 47
Pail, boiled in a, 932
Pain, a balm for every, 390
  akin to, 434
  all the heart then knew of, 455
  and affright, 888
  and anguish wring the brow, 308
  and boredom, 1064
  and evil, proportion of, 563
  and falsehood grow, 531
  and fear, who have known, 690
  avoid this, 473
  barter nought but, 567
  be our joys three parts, 489
  bind the power of, 549
  born in other's, 748
  can be, whose only, 773
  capacity for, 661
  change the place and keep the, 199
  clings cruelly to us, 382
  cure is not worth the, 998
  death who puts an end to, 470
  die of a rose in aromatic, 207
  dull narcotics numbing, 468
  engendereth corporal, 669
  error wounded writhes with, 373
  eternal passion eternal, 546
  famine thirst bereavement, 596
  for any kind of, 911
  for my lost, 918
  for promised joy, 284
  gentleman never inflicts, 403
  glad life's arrears of, 489
  good out of infinite, 663
  greatest, it is to love, 167
  groaneth and travaileth in, 1119
  has exhausted every limb, 561
  in company with, 300
  into songs, 1084
  is felt in every member, 1038
  is, where no, 652
  it is that pain to miss, 167
  it was to drown, 71
  kicked me to my, 936
  labour we delight in physics, 86
  laughter is fraught with some, 366
  lessened by another's anguish, 77

Pain, life's a, 115
  mighty, to love it is, 167
  naught but grief and, 284
  no fiery throbbing, 231
  no throbs of fiery, 231
  of finite hearts that yearn, 486
  of lonely days, 596
  of mind, envy is a, 1006
  of thought, cessation from the, 604
  of thought, spun from, 804
  or ache if any, 596
  or care, a certain amount of, 1063
  or cool one, 583
  out of my, 901
  perhaps in, 929
  pleasure out of, 827
  pleasures banish, 199
  she cures me of my, 193
  shews the signature of, 933
  short, well borne, 24
  short-lived, 307
  sigh yet feel no, 337
  slow moving o'er his, 717
  some natural sorrow loss or, 298
  stranger yet to, 243
  strong mold of, 928
  sudden cry of, 877
  supported her in, 948
  sweet desolation — balmy, 385
  sweet is pleasure after, 176
  tender for another's, 243
  tenseness of humiliating, 939
  that has been and may be, 298
  the weariness the endless, 439
  there are balms for all our, 565
  this echo of, 1065
  this is my last worst, 895
  though full of, 149
  to break its links so soon, 334
  to end, bring my, 918
  to the bear, 400
  too much rest becomes a, 220
  too soon we part with, 437
  turns with ceaseless, 249
  vows made in, 151
  when, grows sharp, 272
  whines out his, 802
  with a sudden clamorous, 924
Pains and drugs, gives him, 997
  and take no, 985
  are past, their sorrows o'er, 290
  died in bitter, 591
  few, so grievous, 1080
  for all the, 703
  he takes about things, 996
  it took, regret the, 292
  labour for his, 74
  of love be sweeter far, 178
  of prose, 649
  pleasure in poetic, 179
  stings you for your, 204
  to get, care to keep, 138
  we have for our, 625
  which only poets know, 265
  world of sighs for my, 100
Pain's furnace heat within, 1071
  resistless power, 522
Pained surprise, with, 912
Painful and long search, 185
  inch to gain, seem here no, 519

Painful manner, in a very, 684
  thought, 318
  to keep money, 182
  vigils keep, pensive poets, 215
  warrior famoused for fight, 107
Paint all off, sucked the, 684
  an inch thick, 97
  and powder, make them with, 1051
  chisel then or write, 648
  costs nothing, 414
  does he? He fain would write, 488
  like nature, who can, 224
  lion not so fierce as they, 137
  me as I am said Cromwell, 508
  no words can, 275
  pomade and eau de rose, 510
  success is a rare, 163
  the laughing soil, 342
  the lily gild refined gold, 58
  the meadows with delight, 42
  the mortal shame of nature, 472
  them, he best can, 216
Painted blind, winged Cupid, 42
  Jove, like a, 173
  lion is not so fierce as, 147
  ocean, upon a, 315
  she's all my fancy, her, 362
  ship, idle as a, 315
  to the eyes, 648
  wrought lies close at home, the beauty, 442
Painter admitted behind the scenes, 589
  flattering, a, 252
  great, dips his pencil, 365
  gymnastic teacher, 1006
  is hinted and hidden, 609
  nature's sternest, 351
  no, has the colorin', 697
  with amaze, filled the, 511
Painters, boldest, 199
Painting, colored it that was, 508
  do, what good can, 833
  is silent poetry, 1006
  music and poetry, 580
  poetry as speaking, 1006
Paintings, I have heard of your, 93
Paints wisdom, Raphael, 414
Pair, gay guiltless, 364
  of star-cross'd lovers, 77
  of very strange beasts, 51
  that once was white, 451
  this pretty, 258
Pairing is as good as another, one, 651
Pakenham he made his brags, 349
Palace alone, than pine in a, 545
  and a prison, 353
  be thine own, 117
  beautiful, the, 171
  built upon the sand, 915
  deceit in gorgeous, 79
  hollow oak our, 345
  I gave my son a, 522
  of Cyrus, 956
  of his body, 522
  of no mortal architect's art, 253
  of rest, 602
  of the soul, 146, 352
  priest or code, take from, 597

Palaces, gorgeous, 33
  in kingdom come, 832
  in such green, 146
  marble of her, 289
  'mid pleasures and, 365
  of the greatest kings, 166
  princes', cottages had been, 44
  prosperity within thy, 1106
  seen how the proudest, 969
Palates, such refined and delicate, 934
Pale and hungry-looking, 1001
  and white and cold as snow, 596
  anguish keeps the heavy gate, 723
  Britannia passed, o'er, 194
  cast of thought, 93
  faint swan, cygnet to this, 58
  feet crossed in rest, 567
  Galilean, 631
  gradations, no, 309
  haggard uncertain shuddering me, 767
  hands I loved, 775
  his light, the sun doth, 514
  his uneffectual fire, 'gins to, 92
  horse, 1123
  horse of death, 155
  Horse stands, 639
  in a saffron mist, 904
  in her fading bowers summer, 565
  jessamine, crow-toe and, 159
  martyr in shirt of fire, 587
  my cheeks make, 132
  passion loves, places which, 144
  patient volunteers, 772
  ports o' the moon, 748
  procession, this, 874
  realms of shade, 371
  unripened beauties, 194
Paleface I defy, the, 447
Pale-faced moon, 61
Paleness of death, 362
Paleozoic time, 734
Palestine, happy peaceful, 657
  haven in sunny, 832
Palestines, Delphian vales the, 363
Palinurus nodded at the helm, 215
Pall, in sceptred, 161
Palladium of all the civil, 949
Pallas Jove and Mars, 479
  perched upon a bust of, 460
Pallid gates, pass the, 851
  vestal, once a, 939
  Virtue's sidelong looks, 912
Palls upon the sense, 194
Palm, bear the, alone, 81
  branch, heart in his hand like a, 558
  itching, 83
  like some tall, 266, 342
  of my hands, oozing out at the, 278
  of your hand, infinity in the, 281
  open upon his harp, 440
Palms before my feet, 828
  his islands lift their fronded, 444
  of Allah, beautiful, 952

Palms of your hands, 753
  toil-worn by nails, 686
Palmer kings with pontiffs, 396
Palmer's weed, votarist in, 157
Palmetto and the pine, planted the, 586
Palm-tree and vine, lands of the, 612
  flourish like the, 1105
Palmy prosperity, 374
  state of Rome, 89
Palmyra, the same that saw, 939
Palos, sailest from, 459
Palpable access of knowledge, 299
  and familiar, 318
  hit, 97
  obscure, the, 150
  that thou hast never loved, 618
Palsied eld, 36
Palsy-stricken, poor weak, churchyard thing, 383
Palter in a double sense, 89
Paltry compensations and commendations, 461
  people, odour of, 1080
Paly flames, through their, 67
Pamphlet under every door, 933
Pan is dead, the great, 428
  leap out of the frying, 16
Pan's pipe was thine Theocritus, 649
Panacea, a mighty, 630
  old wine is a true, 624
  the first, 930
Panaceas, tobacco beyond all, 125
Panama Canal, Bryce's opinion of, 637
  gang, job for this, 872
  with its poverty, 388
Pancakes, flat as, 116
Pandects, Justinian's, 490
Pandemonium, city and proud seat of Lucifer, 155
Panders will, reason, 95
Pandion is dead, king, 120
Pandora, more lovely than, 152
Pane, gentle fingers tapped the, 794
Panegyric, practitioner in, 278
Pang as great as when a giant dies, 36
  learn nor account the, 489
  of all the partings, 748
  preceding death, 252
  that rends the heart, 252
  without one, 223
Pangs and fears, 73
  of dispriz'd love, 93
  the wretched find, 355
  which it hath witnessed, 303
Panic, never yet was any, 733
  of the times, 908
Panics have their uses, 271
Panks of de Rhine, coom to de, 559
Panoplies of red, in, 586
Panorama of human existence, 863
Pansies for thoughts, 28
Pansy for lovers' thoughts, 28
  freaked with jet, 159
  purple, brings thoughts, 612

Pant for you, till we meet shall, 225
Pants begin to go, when his, 754
  for twenty-one, 214
Pantalette to hair, she burnt from, 1066
Pantaloon, lean and slippered, 50
Panted, my soul had, 645
Panteth, as the hart, 1104
Panther caged within my breast, 892
Panting syllable, chase a, 263
  time toiled after him in vain, 231
Pap in Gwent, that green, 814
Paps are centres of delight, 27
Paper and print, except as to, 238
  best 'nd brightest, Noo York Sun, 698
  bullets of the brain, 39
  credit, blest, 210
  fill the whole blamed, 689
  he hath not eat, 41
  leaves nor leaves of stone, 525
  that ever blotted, 46
  they take a, 935
  tiny, tightly rolled, 630
Papers don't purtend to print, 527
  everything he read in the Sunday, 791
  in each hand, 212
  speak from your folded, 451
  turns over your, 1056
  what I read in the, 859
Paper-box factory, steps of the, 939
Paper-mill, thou hast built a, 69
Parables to the blind, 282
Parade and uniforms so grand, 849
  glories in gunpowder and loves, 507
Parading round and round, 261
Paradisal nature, Eve's, 490
Paradise, and walked in, 473
  as in that lost, 931
  awoke the lark in, 687
  custom-house does not open on road to, 421
  drunk the milk of, 316
  enow, wilderness were, 1018
  fool's, 79, 280, 607
  for horses, Italy a, 125
  for women, England a, 125
  heavenly, that place, 121
  how grows our store in, 365
  how has she cheapened, 556
  itself were dim and joyless, 338
  lead again to, 871
  library which is your, 1023
  lived it in, 954
  man and woman enter, 617
  maturity the gate of, 558
  must I thus leave thee, 155
  new-bathed in light of, 671
  no fools in, 668
  O Paradise, O, 503
  of fools, 151
  opened unto you is, 1123
  spirit lies under walls of, 552
  the soldiers' earthly, 1045
  thought would destroy their, 243
  to him are opening, 245

Paradise to lighten earth from, 634
  to what we fear of death, 36
Paradisiacal pleasures, 246
Paradoxes of conduct, 800
Paragon, an earthly, 106
  of art, winter the, 934
  of her gentle sex the seeming, 405
Paragraph to make one laugh, 578
Paragraphs, to be made into, 934
Parallax, no, to speak of, 794
Parallel, admits no, 221
  none but himself his, 221
  startling, of man's real experience, 529
  though infinite can never meet, 169
Parallels, for a seine, 616
  of cloth, 701
Paralyzed in every function, 551
Paramount lord of the soil, 509
Paramour is a thing of naught, 43
Paranoia, madness on them shut or, 937
Paraphrase can make amends, 217
Parasite of society, 1081
Parcel of their fortunes, 104
  of vain strivings, 514
Parcel-gilt goblet, 64
Parch or swell, or, 951
Parched way, world's wide, 450
Parchment should undo a man, that, 69
  world of, 1017
Pard, bearded like the, 49
Pards below, tell my, 878
Pard-like spirit, 366
Pardon, first begs, 50
  father I beseech, thy, 1073
  I don' ax no, 630
  in the degree that we love, 1044
  kiss of the sun for, 918
  no word like, 60
  or to bear it, 267
  quick to crave our, 875
  remorseful, 53
  thee, we may not, 37
  they ne'er, 178
Pardonable to speak dishonourably, 966
Pardoned all except her face, 360
Pardons, the offender never, 137
Parent from the sky, keep one, 213
  knees a new-born child, on, 275
  of an art so nearly allied to invention, 171
  of despair, 385
  of good, 153
  of invention, necessity the, 278
  of luxury and indolence, 973
  of revolution and crime, 975
  the people's, 220
  thou wert our, 363
  too experienced a, 912
  when our first, 326
Parents bore children, 721
  do not know what they do, 323
  foreigners to their sons and daughters, 558
  think calmly of coming years, 646

Parents, which are now thy, 1124
  would not have been cursed, 768
Parentage of antecedent thought, 543
Paresis, that story had, 953
Parfit gentil knight, a verray, 5
Paris, before he gets to, 242
  counts an author, 1050
  for French of, 5
  good Americans when they die go to, 454
  is a woman's town, 710
  like a perfumed, 438
  Lindbergh's flight to, 934
  no home save in, 1082
  peep-shows, 863
  to Japan, from, 1050
  town, speech out of, 1022
Parish church, plain as way to, 49
  me no parishes, 947
  priest of austerity, 656
Parishes, parish me no, 946
Park where the peach-blossoms blew, 673
Parks and palaces, 703
Parliament, a, speaking through reporters, 379
  of Man the Federation of the world, 464
  of the present, in the, 529
  through an act of, 945
Parlour, gentleman in the, 330
  is it a party in a, 296
  will you walk into my, 394
Parlous boy, 71
Parmaceti for an inward bruise, 61
Parnassus and flush, 807
  has its flowers, 231
Parochial, to be, 554
Parodies and caricatures, 922
Parole of literary men, 237
Paroxysms to mark its opening and close, 544
Parrots have crackers, 655
Parsimony is not economy, 261
  requires no providence no sagacity, 261
Parsnips, proverbial, 887
Parson bemused in beer, 212
  lost his senses, if, 816
  owned his skill, in arguing the, 251
  there goes the, 264
Parsonage, English, 653
Part, a kick in that, 143
  acting a silent desperate, 533
  allowed some, 1075
  art and, 943
  authors essayist play your, 471
  believe it, I do in, 89
  choosest not the better, 770
  each minute and unseen, 436
  escaped him, no, 241
  every man must play a, 44
  for any outward, 950
  for my own, 29, 82
  hard to, when friends are dear, 273
  has not been given, blessed, 811
  hath chosen that good, 1117
  he bore his, 626

Part I come, to a, 1020
  immortal, of myself, 101
  in freedom's crowning hour, 760
  is done, our, 931
  is to uplift, thy, 575
  less than the tenth, of one, 75
  master-stroke is nature's, 410
  nature hath done her, 154
  of a hair, ninth, 62
  of a wise man, 1049
  of all that I have met, 353, 464
  of April's fledge, 933
  of being, hath a, 353
  of noble work silent, is best, 533
  of sight, became a, 355
  of the countless dead, 691
  of the land, in this, 952
  of the things, 236
  of the time kept heaven in view, 677
  of valour, the better, 63
  of wisdom, 266
  so he plays his, 50
  take my own, 407
  taken thus the peaceful, 984
  that makes the illness worth while, 721
  then we twa did, 389
  time when darkies have to, 567
  to heaven gave his blessed, 74
  two lives that once, are as ships, 425
  us now, shall a light word, 446
  we die in, 223
  we know in, 1120
  we sadly in this troublous world, 71
  which he means to be clever, 426
  whole greater than a, 426
  words of doom ye must, 418
  wretched, render the other, 1050
Parts, all his gracious, 58
  allure thee, if, 208
  applaud or stickle at, 325
  backs and covers best, 494
  man of sovereign, 41
  mark of virtue in outward, 46
  of an infinite plan, 627
  of good natural, 1035
  of one stupendous whole, all are but, 207
  one man plays many, 49
Partake the gale, 209
Parted, double cherry seeming, 43
  I remember the way we, 633
  never met or never, 287
  when we two, 351
  where we, in sorrow, 418
Parthenon, as though it were the, 831
  Earth proudly wears the, 408
Partial evil universal good, 207
  for the observer's sake, 209
Participation of divineness, 112
  of office, 274
Particle, that very fiery, 361
Particular hair, each, 91
  star, a bright, 53
  tear, orb of one, 109
Parties, I name no, 131
  in a republic, if, 320

Parties the rich and the poor, opposite, 975
Parting day dies like the dolphin, 354
  day, knell of, 244
  day linger and play, 339
  gives a foretaste, 1064
  guest, speed the, 220
  is such sweet sorrow, 78
  is with dawn, 771
  of the way, 1113
  was well made, 84
Partings gone and yet to be, 748
Partington, Dame, 314
Partisan, strong, 1069
  when engaged, 970
Partition, union in, 43
Partitions, what thin, 173, 207
Partly may compute, we, 285
Partner, most gracious, 770
  of my home, 522
Partners at the whist-club said, 406
  in their woes, 1036
Partnership, glory of eternal, 807
Partridges, in search of caribou and, 935
Party, Annabel McCarty was invited to a, 667
  come to the aid of the, 854
  dressed in white, went to a, 557
  fire most tolerable third, 515
  gave up to, 252
  I represent a, 1069
  in a parlour, is it a, 296
  is the madness of many, 217
  October gave a, 637
  of revolution civilization, 1069
  stick the less, the other, 110
  themselves the injured, 1078
  unshackled by, 305
  who has, first of new, 478
Parvis e glandibus quercus, 292
Paso del Mar, rode down to the, 565
Pass and turn again, I keep and, 410
  away, even this shall, 509
  by me as the idle wind, 83
  'e doesn't want no, 845
  for a man, let him, 44
  he carries a, 653
  heluva, 654
  in a perilous, 1076
  in the night, ships that, 437
  into nothingness, 382
  it so came to, 255
  let him, 100
  my imperfections by, 292
  never never comes to, 288
  on the ocean of life we, 437
  presto, your joys are withered, 406
  this way again, will not, 732
Passage, act of common, 106
  as a race of men, 834
  at night, in the, 929
  each dark, shun, 203
  in so considerable a, 1042
  of a song, sweetest, 701
  of an angel's tear, 383
  particularly fine, 235
  to descend and climb, hard the, 1021

Passage, to fret a, 147
  to mark its, 1089
  to riches, shortest, 950
  with you, dispute the, 538
Passages cut out of newspapers, 346
  of love, now no, 470
Passed about the kitchen grate, she, 557
  long long night away, 557
Passenger pukes in, sea the, 360
Passengers by reason of their clinging, 622
  silent row of, 933
Passenjare, punch in the presence of the, 583
Passer-by, naught for to-morrow's, 553
Passers-by are rare, 878
Passeth all understanding, 1121
  show, that which, 89
Passing all wisdom or its fairest flower, 417
  phase, underlies the, 560
  rich with forty pounds, 250
  salute to this world, 738
  scene, what is this, 348
  speak each other in, 437
  strange, 't was, 100
  sweet is solitude, 263
  the love of women, 1100
  thought, like a, 285
  through nature to eternity, 89
  tribute of a sigh, 245
  well, daughter which he loved, 92
Passing-bell, some cost a, 406
Passing-bells for these who died, 918
Passion, accomplished without, 1062
  and blood and tears, from, 804
  and pride, subdued, 1056
  bards of, and of mirth, 384
  chaos of thought and, 207
  commonplace, 545
  dies, till our, 116
  driven by, 285
  expends his whole heart and, 1057
  for a maid, the maiden, 471
  haunted me like a, 296
  intellectual, 1022
  is a fever in the mind, 184
  is the gale, 208
  lifelong, and caprice, 723
  most violent insane delusive and transient, 720
  of resentment, 1082
  of tears, depart in a, 493
  of the rose, 923
  of their choices, 888
  one, doth expel another, 28
  only I discern infinite, 486
  oppression's, 937
  or the excitement of heart, 461
  pale, 144
  put me into a towering, 97
  red rose whispers of, 675
  ruling, 209, 210
  sets the spindrift flying, 834
  slept, 231
  so strongly rooted, 278
  spent, all, 157

Passion spent its novel force, 464
  still makes, whose, 823
  sudden glory is the, 132
  that insane and awful, 393
  that lasted not, 848
  that left the ground, 489
  to light the fires of, 440
  to tatters, tear a, 94
  vows with so much, 186
  we feel, happier in the, 367
  what is, but pining, 592
  whirlwind of, 94
  woman in her first, 359
  women love in their first, 1044
Passions, aching hours, desolate, 798
  all, all delights, 316
  are likened best to floods, 21
  catching all, 109
  fly with life, all other, 322
  may I govern my, 172
  never let such angry, rise, 198
  noblest, to inspire, 239
  of all base, 68
  repose of, 330
  rise and swell, 820
  rule, wherein old, 755
  should be held in reverence, 461
  spin the plot, 574
  that we feel, 1086
  to be relished, 1027
  when lighter, 953
Passion's slave, man not, 94
  sway, undisturbed by, 685
Passionate after rings and seals, 166
  increasing disregard for death, 930
  intuition, 302
  simple sensuous and, 162
Passion-flower, he who gives a, 849
Passion-flowers, leave the sultry, 849
Passion-waves lulled to rest, 363
Passive master lent his hand, 408
Passives, fit actives to, 118
Passiveness, in a wise, 295
Passport book, within that, 847
  round the globe, 508
Past acclaims our future, 634
  again, only breed the, 472
  all surgery, 101
  and I, the, 652
  and to come seems best, 64
  anticipate the, 278
  at least is secure, 341
  bells of the, 644
  clear of all regret, 960
  comes not back again, 440
  conclude the future by the, 1028
  day's long toil is, 392
  enjoy, and even the, 217
  extolling the, 314
  forgive the, 796
  gaze at the remote, 1087
  grieve for the, 320
  grieve not for what is, 256
  hallowed quiets of the, 528
  heaven has not power upon the, 177
  help should be past grief, 56
  hope past cure past help, 80

Past I know, what is, 1123
  indemnity for the, 230
  is a bucket of ashes, 854
  is also stored in thee, 537
  is future, all the, 895
  is heavy and hindereth, 664
  is only the present, 872
  is stone, 680
  leave thy low-vaulted, 452
  let the dead, bury its dead, 433
  long and glorious, 748
  man may redeem the, 711
  man who is correctly informed as to the, 400
  miracles are, 53
  neither the, nor the future, 1009
  never plan the future by the, 261
  nothing to come and nothing, 167
  old fetish raiments of the, 609
  our dancing days, 77
  parcels of the dreadful, 463
  present future I reveal, 305
  retrace the, 237
  same rehearsal of the, 354
  singing of the, 974
  the bitter, more welcome the sweet, 53
  the bounds of freakish youth, 265
  the, in God's keeping, 626
  the, like a funeral gone by, 692
  the size of dreaming, 105
  the wit of man, 43
  unsighed for, 303
  upon its throne, died to keep the, 525
  voice of the, 380
  we are to-morrow's, 872
  what calls back the, 441
  woman may not redeem the, 711
  world is weary of the, 367
Paste and cover to our bones, 59
Pastime and delight, universal, 440
  and our happiness, 301
Pastoral visiting, notes on, 884
Pastors, as some ungracious, 90
  census among, 860
Pasture, mettle of your, 66
Pastures above the smooth green, 710
  and fresh woods, 160
  fairer greener, 824
  lie down in green, 1103
  on such frugal, 934
  pipe me to, 672
Patch grief with proverbs, 40
Patch'd up your excuses, 104
Patches, king of shreds and, 95
Patchwork used by the blind, 716
Pate, you beat your, 217
Patent of nobility, broad acres a, 582
Paternal acres, a few, 216
  or meddling government, 398
Paternalism and state socialism, doctrines of, 830
  lessons of, 628
Path, at the end of our, 461
  be dark as night, though thy, 499

Path be hewn out of the rock, 305
  belated, I on my, 565
  crosses every, 395
  err from the right, 965
  from duty's, 671
  he is a, 21
  is wholly rough, no, 718
  light unto my, 1106
  more fair or flat, 781
  motive guide original and end, 231
  no, of flowers leads to glory, 1046
  o'er mountain or sea, 406
  of dalliance treads, 90
  of duty was to glory, 467
  of Milton, round the, 304
  of sorrow and that alone, 264
  of the just, 1106
  smooth that leadeth on to danger, 106
  swerve often from your, 872
  that I must wend, I trace the, 683
  that leads to a loaf of bread, 733
  that leads to a suit of clothes, 733
  the world advances along its, 336
  thou who passeth on this, 1093
  through life, hew your, 699
  to happiness, mistaken, 1064
  to hell, trod the, 802
  to order, 641
  to the bomb, 641
  untrod, 568
  we tread, side of every, 266
  where beauty wends, 851
Paths are dream-beguiled, 756
  are hard to tread, 733
  are peace, all her, 747, 1106
  ask for the old, 1112
  his bruised feet trod, 738
  in the world diverged so wide, 485
  of glory lead to the grave, 244
  of men, strew gladness on the, 732
  of men, upon the, 438
  of peevish nature, 190
  of youth, golden, 837
  on lonely, 588
  pacing up and down the, 875
  that have been or shall be, 570
  that upward lead, 711
  that wind and wind, so many, 718
  to the house I seek to make, 537
  to woman's love, 131
  travels on well-worn, 1077
  walk down garden, 831
Pathetic attitudes not in keeping, 1082
  evanescence of things, 606
  spondees, laments in, 714
Pathics, columbines and, 937
Pathless realms of space, 622
  was the dreary wild, 369
  way, heaven's wide, 160
  woods, pleasure in the, 354
Pathos and jest of him, 805
  spring with that nameless, 581
  that is the true, 286

Pathway to the grand hereafter, 713
Patience, abusing of God's, 34
bow, must to, 225
by your gracious, 100
cousin and shuffle the cards, 311, 406
flour of wyfly, 7
gentlemen and shuffle, 406
habits of peace and, 139
have her perfect work, let, 1122
He stands waiting, with, 435
is a remedy, 978
make us bear with, 1046
may compass anything, 1025
men's office to speak, 40
on a monument, sat like, 55
poor are they that have not, 102
possess your soul with, 175
rocked me to, 382
stubborn, 150
thou rose-lipped cherubin, 103
with him, have, 1124
with the calm, 445
you tread upon my, 61
Patient confidence in ultimate justice, 455
deep disdain, 547
endurance, 350, 438
etherized upon a table, 900
force to change them, 466
humble spirit, 115
inattention, 575
man, fury of a, 174
man in loss, 105
merit of the unworthy takes, 93
must minister to himself, 88
O be, 499
our playwright may be, 472
remedy for every trouble, 978
restores the strength of the, 976
search and vigil long, 357
stars, the, 643
the good of his, 973
the moderate use, allows his, 997
to be, is a branch of justice, 1010
to perform, 220
when favours are denied, 226
when saddest, calm when sternest, 539
with over-praise, 529
Patients, in all his, 692
may complain, 951
recover their health, 971
say under ether, what, 912
when the doctor's, 451
Patiently to endure the toothache, 40
Patines of bright gold, 47
Patria an illusion and a curse, 729
Patriarch, the venerable, 268
to the command of God, 543
Patriarch's angel, 226, 441
Patrick Spence, ballad of, 316
Patriot is a fool, 214
on an empty stomach, 714
peer and king, names of, 603
truth, 333

Patriots all, true, 280
and tyrants, blood of, 273
so to be, 259
who for a theory risked, 430
worthy, dear to God, 162
Patriot's boast, such is the, 249
fate, cowards mock the, 555
soldier's and gentleman's language, 1056
Patriotic, disinterested and, 374
Patriotism and protection, 338
is the last refuge of a scoundrel, 236
whose, would not gain force on the plain of Marathon, 233
Patron and the jail, 230
one who looks with unconcern, 233
what is a, 649
who looks down, 649
Patrons that have provided us libraries, 125
Patronage of capital, 341
of some great man, 1085
sway, 573
Patter of the soft rain, 568
Patterings of an April shower, 618
Pattern called a war, 831
is sold, 625
of all patience, I will be a, 98
of all propriety, 820
of celestial peace, a, 68
of excelling nature, 103
to imitate, not as a, 949
willow, 439
Patterns for, what are, 831
Paul, by the apostle, 72
rob Peter and pay, 14, 122, 1025
Pauline now no more was there, 1066
Paumanok, far out of fish-shaped, 827
Paunch, fat, never breeds fine thoughts, 1016
Pauper, he's only a, 395
Paupers, came here to see the, 687
Pauperism develops more rapidly, 1072
feasteth while honest labor, 477
Pause, an awful, 201
and look back, 416
for a reply, I, 83
in the day's occupations, 434
must give us, 93
nature made a, 201
or stay, nothing that is can, 438
upon the brink, one little, 626
Pauses speak the overflow of gladness, 373
Paved, hell is, with good intentions, 137, 236, 662
Pavement, riches of heaven's, 149
stars, dust is gold and, 154
Pavilions of the sun, clouds seem, 425
Paw is doubled, each drowsy, 858
Paws of silver, 822
Pay, a double debt to, 251
given to a state hireling, 233
haven of, 582

Pay him in his own coin, 192
if I can't, why I can owe, 11
more due than more than all can, 84
sleep in cloak no lodging to, 545
Paying through the nose, 945
Paynter's, to the, and sat, 181
Pays all debts, he that dies, 33
the best, I scent which, 526
us but with age and dust, 22
Peace, a charge in, 177
a thought, what, 909
above all earthly dignities, 73
all her paths are, 747, 1106
all should be at, 432
amidst the clamor, hold their, 931
among ourselves, just and lasting, 457
anchor of our, 273
and competence, health, 208
and darkness, we now to, 744
and give thee, 1099
and good will, promoter of, 608
and grace, light of His, 821
and honour rest, in, 76
and in eternal, 1063
and pain, that, 738
and plenty bed and board, 936
and quiet, calm, 160
and rest at length have come, 392
and rest can never dwell, 148
and villainy, smoke of, 1069
and war brotherhood and hatred, 1069
and war, in, 68
around, throw sweet, 942
as a breathing time, 258
assert her power, 364
at last, spoke of, 856
be still, 1116
be with you, 1055
be within thy walls, 1106
beans and bacon in, 961
being a form of, 918
beyond these voices there is, 471
brooded o'er the hushed domain, 478
can pierce your, 913
cankers of a long, 63
carry gentle, 73
chimes of eternal, 443
deep dream of, 346
depart, lest, 986
drowning would be happiness and, 494
ef you want, 527
first in war first in, 281
fool when he holdeth his, 1107
forever hold his, 1128
gift of heavenly, 924
grant us thy, 671
great war and petty, 795
habits of patience and, 139
hath her victories, 162
henceforward, therefore be at, 436
hero is a man of, 848
hold companionship in, 76
I have won a solemn, 562
I leave with you, 1118
imperishable, 744

Peace in themselves, 856
  in thy right hand, 73
  inglorious arts of, 169
  is happiness digesting, 1068
  is poor reading, 650
  is thine whate'er betide, 549
  is what I seek and calm, 547
  its ten thousand slays, 268
  lay me down in, to sleep, 350
  leagues of, 218
  let us have, 549
  live in, adieu, 216
  lovers find their, 881
  makes desolation which they
    call, 1007
  makes solitude and calls it,
    356
  means of preserving, 268
  moonlight of a perfect, 717
  my preservation of, 20
  never a good war or bad, 227
  never hold his, 120
  no, unto the wicked, 1112
  nor ease of heart, 248
  nothing can bring you, 411
  ocean's dreamless, 805
  of Allah, may the, 952, 953
  of evening in your quiet ways,
    871
  of God, 1121
  of great books, 854
  of great churches, 854
  of lovelier valleys, 823
  of mind, blest with, 200
  of mind, dearer than all, 365
  of mind, 'tis, 977
  of mind, to insure, 791
  of the done, 605
  of the forest glade, 712
  of the great release, 693
  of thine, there abides a, 546
  on earth good will toward
    men, 1116
  on earth is a joke, 850
  on dim Plutonian shore, 658
  only as a breathing time, 258
  open covenants of, 725
  pattern of celestial, 68
  prepare for war in, 985, 989
  priest for enemy good bye to,
    423
  proclaims olives of endless age,
    108
  righteousness and, 1105
  save what pertains to, 971
  shall over all the earth, 477
  sleep in, 76
  slept in, 74
  so sweet, life so dear or, 270
  soft phrase of, 100
  some form or formula of, 726
  spirit entering into living, 532
  star of, return, 328
  that publisheth, 1112
  the name of the chamber was,
    172
  the re-establishment of, 1061
  things that make for, 1119
  thinks of war in time of, 125
  thousand years of, 469
  to be found in the world, 333
  to be taken, no, 890
  to kiss with, 842
  universal, lie across the land,
    463
  unjust, before a just war, 227

Peace, uproar the universal, 88
  veriest school of, 583
  victory which is, 805
  what we need in war, provide
    in, 989
  when all at, 822
  when there is no peace, 1112
  with oppression, make no, 1127
  within my breast, 823
  yet for thy, 533
  your valor won, enjoyed the,
    294
Peaceably if we can, 319
  with all men, live, 1119
Peaceful end, to quiet age a, 984
  evening, welcome, 265
  hours I once enjoyed, 266
  or no more, or, 931
  skies, or early find the, 474
  stillness reigneth evermore,
    480
Peacefully, silver waves chime
    ever, 480
Peacemaker, If is the only, 51
Peacemakers, blessed are the, 69
Peach in an orchard grew, 698
  the ripest, is highest, 696
Peach-blossoms blew, in a park
    where the, 673
Peacocks apes and ivory, 777,
    832, 1101
  voices like, 592
Pea-green boat, in a beautiful,
    498
Peak and pine, dwindle, 84
  comes off a frozen, 839
  far the mountain, 697
  in Darien, upon a, 384
  is fame's, sturdiest, 700
  to peak, far along from, 353
Peaks are gilt and rose, highest,
    801
  of dazzling snow, 710
  of two eternities, 602
  wrapped in clouds, 352
Peal for years, wildest, 816
  of praise, wood-world one, 470
  which rings out the old year,
    323
Peals of laughter, shout back our,
    554
Pearl an emerald stone a golden
    clasp, 289
  and gold, barbaric, 149
  as being of great price, 422
  chain of all virtues, 121
  double row of orient, 121
  Egypt's, 664
  for carnal swine, too rich a,
    142
  he rises with his, 484
  in a woman's eye, 28
  in your foul oyster, 51
  many a fair, laid up, 121
  named the infant, 422
  no radiant, 267
  no such, 624
  of charity, the Christian, 443
  of great price, 1115
  of his oyster, 632
  quarelets of, 133
  seas, the, 744
  sowed the earth with orient,
    153
  tankards scooped in, 584
  threw a, away, 104

Pearls and vermin, dropping, 400
  are not equal in whiteness, 566
  at random strung, orient, 275
  before swine, 1114
  did grow, asked how, 133
  I can not buy, 899
  of thought, 528
  puddly thoughts to orient,
    1032
  that were his eyes, 32
  the sea has its, 1066
  who would search for, 177
Pearly light of summer twilight,
    670
  shell that murmurs, 672
  shell was in my hand, 362
Pears from an elm, 1041
  go to a pear-tree for, 989
Peasant, French, and worn wood-
    en-shoes, 603
  hut of the, 713
  some belated, 149
  toe of the, 97
  veins, 499
Peasants plow with salt your
    fields, 756
Peasantry, country's pride, 250
Pease, like as one, is to another,
    23, 1026
Pebble, epics in each, 523
  sunk, life is but the, 574
Pebbles, children gathering, 156
  on the rolling beach, 572
Pebbly spring, stream or, 318
Peccavi (I have Sind), 339
Peck at, for daws to, 100
  of salt, 1034
  of troubles, 1034
Peculiar and indescribable charm,
    645
  grace, 199
  graces, shot forth, 153
  grand gloomy and, 362
  kind of fear, 817
Peculiarity of all the great works,
    1087
  of prudery, 1068
Pedagogue, superannuated, 636
  the jolly old, 605
Pedal, poverty is the soft, 862
Pedantry, ancient seat of, 707
Pedants much affect, learned, 141
Pedestal these words, on the,
    878
Pedestaled in triumph, 491
Pedigree, enquiry about a wom-
    an's, 1036
  lass wi' a lang, 291
  match the best of any, 499
  of honey, 584
  reaching back to the deluge,
    483
Peep and botanize upon his
    mother's grave, 297
  or cynic bark, critic, 408
  to what it would, 96
Peeps, talkative Samuel as, 637
Peeping in at morn, came, 390
Peer, King Stephen was a worthy,
    101, 256
  of England, many a, 743
  rhyming, a, 212
  you'll rarely find his, 499
Peers, a couple of rotten, 510
  my, the heroes of old, 489
  sunk beneath my, 618

Peers, walks among his, unread, 540
will take his place, in the, 573
Peering, deep into that darkness, 460
littlenesses, 469
too far, refrain from, 964
Peerless eyes, feed deep upon her, 384
fearless an army's flower, 737
Peevish April day, 348
Peewee bird alone is sad, 912
bird, there is a, 912
Pegasee, the hors that hadde winges, 7
Pegasus, never gallop, 214
Pei-Ho by the Gulf of Pechili, 746
Pejorist, not a pessimist but a, 744
Pelf, I crave no, 80
no meaner, 514
Pelicans went over, four, 894
Pelion, from Ossa hurled, 986
on the top of Ossa, 1025
Pell-mell of men, 519
Pellucid in thy azure depths, 538
Pelops' line, Thebes or, 161
Pelt, to dry her royal, 375
Pelting of this pitiless storm, 98
Pembroke's mother Sidney's sister, 119
Pen and ink, never saw, 56
and ink-horne in the head of his staffe, 171
as with a burning, 1059
aside, lay my, 685
becomes a torpedo, 233
bring dramatist your, 658
dance with the, 1081
devise wit write, 41
do things with a, 785
famous by my, 164
glorious by my, 164
half-moon made with a, 56
history's, 405
in hand, foolish without, 237
in trust, held his, 650
is mightier, 787
is preferable to the sword, 1038
is the tongue of the mind, 1040
learn to ply the, 544
mightier than the sword, 425
nose sharp as a, 66
of a ready writer, 1104
of iron, written with a, 1112
of the author and statesman, 730
poet's, turns them to shapes, 43
such virtue has my, 108
through every other word, run your, 313
traced with his golden, 516
was shaped, 304
worse than the sword, 123
Pens a stanza, who, 212
in a stand, too many, 1027
quirks of blazoning, 101
scholars', carry farther, 1038
Penalty for greatness, 745
Penance end, thy, 1063
in their strange, 588
Pence, bestowing honour pudding, 406

Pence, for thirty, 136
or pounds might purchase, 850
take care of the, 222
Pencil and confute my pen, lame my, 513
wayward, 595
with mocking, 513
Pencil-tree, branches of the, 701
Pendent bed and procreant cradle, 85
rock a towered citadel, 105
world, 36, 151
Pendulum, opinion is like, 1064
Penelope, constant as, 258
out there somewhere, my sweet, 830
Penelophon O king quoth she, 255
Penetrable stuff, made of, 95
to a shower of gold, most things are, 381
Pen-holders, thin as a pair of, 774
Penitence, vague kind of, 495
Penn Yan Bill, beatific bosom of, 700
Penn's town New York and Baltimore, 410
Pennant universal subtly waving, 536
Penned it down, so I, 171
Penniless lass, a, 291
Pennon, his knightly, 878
Penny for your thoughts, 16, 191
plain and twopence coloured, 705
saved is a penny got, 229
seven halfpenny loaves for a, 69
the worse, one, 351
wise pound foolish, 122
worser than hee, 257
Penobscot, the Wabash the Chesapeake, 932
Penrod was a state of being, 809
Pension — an allowance, 233
never enriched, 137
Pensions, civil, and family gratuities, 338
Pensioned sailor lies, the, 199
slave of Attila, 338
Pensioner on the bounties of an hour, 201
Pensive beauty, like, 327
discontent, waste nights in, 25
gaze, do probe my heart with, 760
poets painful vigils keep, 215
smiles, like sweet strains or, 408
through a happy place, 303
Pent, here in the body, 306
long in populous city, 154
Pentameter, in the, 317
Pent-house lid, hang upon his, 84
Pent-up love of my heart, all the, 685
Utica, 276
Penurious woman, his wife was a, 171
Penury and imprisonment, 36
houses that confess intellectual, 869
repressed their noble rage, 245
People, all of the time, can not fool all of the, 457

People, all power springs from the, 420
all sorts of, 85
all the time, fool some of the, 457
all with one accord, 252
always stupid victims of deceit, 1086
and beasts, 877
any streetful of, 854
are good enough for me, 781
are good, the, 276
are hard to suit, 685
are like here, what, 1057
arose as one man, 1099
become wise in their own eyes, 247
behold you, let the, 813
bells I hear, all exulting, 536
by the people for the, 456
can't die along the coast, 497
careful when suspected, 422
common-looking, 457
confidence in justice of the, 455
did by this stone intend, 546
did older and wiser, 913
doubt that ye are the, 780
eternally seeking, are, 618
explore the horizon, 412
first original right of the, 949
fond of ill-luck, 417
foolish questions of common, 1083
for practical, 895
for talking, we reproach, 1079
free, his monument a, 555
go from earth to paradise, 849
God save the, 338
God will be with His, 141
good for good-for-nothing, 430
governed by grave magistrates, 393
government of the, 456
hallow a whole, 312
happy, not afraid, 788
have always some champion, 974
have hesitated, 924
here among my, 656
home to bed, carries, 890
I pity who know not the city, 625
in grief their own way, 475
in Scotland, oats for, 232
in the gristle, 259
in their wisdom, if the good, 455
indictment against an whole, 259
inurned, weep a, 399
judge men by success, 1044
last, I should choose, 278
made for the, by the, 341
make a great show with little means, 482
may eat grass, 381
may require a leader, 974
may sit them down and rest, 916
narrow-souled, 217
never give up their liberties, 261
nod our heads, we common, 764
not a book-reading, 755
nothing is so galling to a, 398

People of his best, gave the, 465
of nearly every country, 921
of the skies, common, 114
of Vermont, 819
often grudge others, 962
old, applaud it, 1038
one loves best, 1076
our sovereign the, 341
owe, sum which married, 1057
pacing restless up and down, 551
people marry, 754
people work with best, 754
perish where there is no vision, 1109
pity me, when, 868
pleurisy of, 132
poor, putting on style, 685
read a song who will not read a sermon, 405
representative of the, 1060
risen, there is a, 171
say behind your back what, 711
say of us, what, 788
serviceable to God and His, 141
snatched my crown, 620
some of the time, all the, 457
songs of a, 186
speak unreservedly, if, 613
stumble, designed to make, 1090
the sunbeams, motes that, 160
they that marry ancient, 147
think, more complicated than, 1074
think they're thinking, 854
thy people shall be my, 1099
to discover, leave other, 1064
to the goal, to pint the, 526
to us, has gathered, 839
troops of solemn, 924
two kinds of, 718
walking through, and, 920
wash their dirty linen, 1060
we cheat other, 1087
were clever, if all good, 942
what is the city but the, 76
when wilt Thou save the, 338
who are very resourceful, 935
who bless, become, 1080
who do things, 842
who eat peppermint, 624
who have charm, 606
who have no weaknesses, 1078
who keep shops, 875
who know little, 1055
who lift and people who lean, 718
who make no noise, 1046
who make no roads, 805
who merely pray, 1080
who truly deserve, 975
who understand, 786
who will not believe anything, 1031
who would have been poets, 319
whom we most despise, 498
whose annals are blank, 379
will say we did not understand, 1086
will talk and find fault, 1034
wish him and you his, 921

People with all their rights in their hands, 424
you can, to all the, 226
Peoples and governments never have learned, 1062
and of humanity, life of, 1076
crime of slaughtering whole, 991
disappear, 735
do not know each other, because, 1084
great and small, all the, 471
happiness of, 1078
People's backs and heads, other, 1080
government, 341
little frauds, 788
prayer, 173
right maintain, 333
will, based upon her, 462
Peopled garden, a, 1058
the world must be, 39
Peor and Baälim, 161
Pepper, epithets like, 599
his cabbage, 989
Peppercorn, I am a, 62
Peppered the highest, who, 252
two of them, I have, 61
Peppermint nurse, bottle bauble, 802
people who eat, 624
Pepys his journal, know as, 650
Journal of, 180
pleased to see his wife's company, 181
pronunciation of, 637
Pepys' advice to his family, 181
Perceptible not in progress but in result, 545
Perception and attempt, time-lag between, 795
end, till our, 492
of beauty a moral test, 515
of the comic, 415
Perceptions are made finer, our, 842
Perceptual anaesthesia, love a, 862
Perch, gravely got down from his, 508
on a cathedral or a church, 768
where eagles dare not, 71
Perches which his faltering feet embraced, 448
Perchance to dream, to sleep, 93
Perched and sat, 460
upon a bust of Pallas, 460
Percipience, awful, 889
Percy and Douglas, song of, 27
Perdition catch my soul, 102
Père Lachaise, to be buried in, 1068
Peregrinations, labours and, 112
Peremptory tone, with a, 263
Perennial pleasures, 393
Perfect as love if love be, 470
day, end of a, 761
day, from darkness to the, 672
day, unto the, 1106
days, then if ever come, 525
fright, 358
liberty to do just as one pleases, 330
love casteth out fear, 1123
love casts out prudery, 617
man, mark the, 1104

Perfect picnic day, 'tis a, 691
poem the crystalline revelation, 432
pursuit of, pursuit of light, 548
rounded symmetrical complete swindle, 616
so hate if hate be, 470
they are, how else, 486
understanding may extinguish pleasure, 745
ways of honour, 74
woman nobly planned, 299
Perfectest herald of joy, 38
Perfection, fulness of, 57
happen, I saw, 920
nestles the seed, 535
of reason, 21
of ten, vowing more than the, 75
perishes, what's come to, 486
pink of, 253
praise and true, 47
pursuit of an unattainable, 788
realize our, 723
songs spring thought, 493
Perfections, his sweete, 26
Perfectly free moral happy, 581
Perfidious bark, that fatal, 159
England, 1048
Perform, an ability that they never, 75
patient to, 220
Performance, lovers swear more, than they are able, 75
maketh best return, silent, 1020
of pleasant actions, 877
takes away the, 86
viewing them as a literary, 538
which is without precedent, 1055
Perfume doth remain, 789
for vapour cold, 392
of her breath, 421
on the violet, to throw a, 58
puss-gentleman that's all, 263
scent of odorous, 157
the air, what flowers and plants best, 111
with a subtle sad, 644
Perfumes of Arabia, 88
rarely come from flowers, 1083
take pleasure with, 1049
that are richest, 666
Perfumed like a milliner, 61
Paris, like a, 438
Perhaps no person can be a poet, 397
the king would change, 504
to pierce the gray, 871
turn out a sermon, 285
turn out a sang, 285
Peri at the gate of Eden, 337
Peril, all of man's, 610
every hour, 342
in thine eye, 78
moment of sweet, 593
on the sea, those in, 566
poison to his mind and, to his body, 401
ships that are in, 1022
Perils do environ, what, 24
doe enfold, how many, 24

Perils have this beauty, great, 1069
of actual existence, sordid, 723
past, spoke of, 856
which beset them, 1049
Perilous and beautiful, lie, 903
edge of battle, 148
nothing more, 1023
pass, in a, 1076
stuff which weighs upon the heart, 88
sweet, 593
way from a tree's summit, 384
Period of about twenty years, 973
of expectancy, after a, 1091
of life, the short, 981
of spending and speculation, 922
that dim murky, 1072
Periods of time, 150
Periodical fits of morality, 398
Perish, no seed shall, 654
where there is no vision, the people, 1109
with him the folly that seeks, 443
Perished, friends have, 610
in his pride, 297
years that, to make us men, 628
Perishing republic, shine, 895
Periwigged charioteers, 831
Periwig-pated fellow, 94
Perjured lip, dashed no cup from, 504
Perjuria ridet amantium Jupiter, 78
Perjuries, Jove laughs at lovers', 78
Perjury and strife murder and spoil, 373
lovers', 176
Perked up in a glistering grief, 73
Permanence, things have a terrible, 901
Permanent alliances, 268
and certain characteristics, 231
fame, doubt the, 426
grandeur of these states religion, 534
Permit to heaven, 155
Pernicious than the love of flattery, more, 198
to general morality, 422
to mankind, wine, 219
weed, 263
Perpetual devotion to business, 704
exile, condemned to, 629
motion, scoured with, 64
neglect sustained by, 704
night, kingdom of, 71
priesthood, literary men a, 376
serenity, 197
source, stage might be a, 196
Perpetually, tends to disappear, 581
Perplex and dash maturest counsels, 149
Perplexed in the extreme, 104
with error, 969
Perplexes monarchs, 149

Persecution, christened it, 520
in a good cause, 241
Persephone take her head upon your knee, 915
Perseverance better than violence, 999
flowing, from, 521
in disguise, 731
Persia reigned a king, once in, 620
Persian and Arab and Greek and Hun, 625
carpet, discourse like a, 996
give, to the noble, 441
Gulf the Red Sea and the Mediterranean, 679
gulfs, pearls of thought in, 528
messengers, 969
Persians and Xerxes, 533
are accustomed to deliberate, 969
law of the Medes and, 1113
taught three useful things, 361
Persian's heaven is easily made, 334
Person, a really busy, 711
adorning, with care his sweet, 368
always the same, 787
as he is, such a, 976
desires to be a humorist, 877
dies, when a, 833
forth to sell, set thy, 109
freedom of, 273
has to be scaled to fit a book, 913
I'm a very umble, 496
in the first, 955
knows a story, when a, 661
like a well-conducted, 481
master owns only your, 1068
my idea of an agreeable, 421
no sich a, 495
oblong square triangular, 314
of most respectable connections, 614
one knows, portrait of a, 1057
one loved, chose the, 1087
perhaps no, can be a poet, 397
risk saving a guilty, 1053
to deceive is one's self, easiest, 426
who agrees with me, is a, 421
who can't pay, 497
who collects objects, 691
who disliked gravy, looking for a, 313
who has died, I know a, 890
Persons, all, share alike, 975
burning to display heroism, 740
divers paces with divers, 50
great, are able to do great, 1041
grown old in active business, caution, 324
letters addressed to private, 1066
more lives of obscure, 761
no respect of, place nor, 54
of good sense, 228, 1044
of such mark, 292
than with their, 1054
there is no respect of, with God, 1119

Persons, two distinct, 122
who constantly clamor, 340
without education, 330
Personage, as grand a, 494
less imposing, 331
this goodly, 302
Personal experience, not, 973
identity, lose our, 330
Personalities decomposing in print, 878
to greater, 853
Personality, most characteristic artistic moral, 538
Personally defeated our principles never, 424
Perspicuity of language, 1017
Perspicuous work, 319
Persuade the eyes of men, 106
Persuaded in his own mind, 1119
whom none could advise thou hast, 22
Persuades when speaking fails, silence, 56
Persuading, fair-spoken and, 74
Persuasion fails, because, 491
flows from his lips, 219
of whatever state or, 273
ripened into faith, 302
shine all silver, 960
Persuasive sound, 193
Perturbed spirit, rest, 92
Peru, from China to, 230, 258
with its riches, 388
Peruvian mine, shares in some, 465
Perverse opinion, men of, 965
Perverseness one of the primitive impulses, 461
Perversion, one enormous and innermost, 1082
Pessimism and optimism both needed, 740
is only the name, 926
refuge from, 572
Pest, Joe Millers are a, 673
of love, 382
Pesteringly fond, inalterably and, 472
Pestilence, breeds, 281
glory followed by, 1067
like a desolating, 368
seals that close the, 363
that walketh in darkness, 1105
Pestilences dire, of all the, 907
Pestilent congregation of vapours, 92
Petal of a flower, tip-tilted like the, 470
Petals fade away, 801
float away, its, 912
from blown roses, 463
Petar, hoist with his own, 96
Peter denyed his Lord, 947
feared full twenty times, 296
I'll call him, 57
poured and passed it round, 348
rob, and pay Paul, 14, 122, 1025
spoke, the thought that, 671
thou art, 1115
Turf, 52
Peter's dome, that rounded, 408
Peterkin, quoth little, 322
Petition me no petitions, 947

Petra in her hill-tomb sleeps, 443
Petrarch cut it sparkling out of
    thought, 680
Petrified truth, this is, 615
Petrifies the feeling, 285
Petticoat government, under, 343
    her feet beneath her, 163
    swift-descending, 763
    tempestuous, 133
Pettiest form of his kind, 675
Pettifogger and quack, 329
Petty done the undone vast, con-
    trast the, 487
    pace, creeps in this, 88
Pewter and no pub, no, 903
Phalanx, in perfect, 149
    of hyphenated names, 935
    the Pyrrhic, 359
Phantasies, seas of, 664
Phantasma, like a, 82
Phantom blade, her, 888
    hand, leap to lick my, 858
    moon, ghastly, 536
    of delight, she was a, 299
    the awful, 619
    treacherous, men call liberty,
        532
    tribes pursue, 681
Phantoms go, one by one, 807
    of hope, 232
Phaon was not there, if, 458
Pharisees, our academical, 397
Pharos of Egypt, 956
Phase, passing, of the meanest
    thing, 560
Phials hermetically sealed, 191
Phidias carves it, wisdom, 414
    his awful Jove young, 408
    statue by, 956
Philadelphia, in, Who were his
    parents? 617
    most pecksniffian of cities, 863
    off to, 784
    probably leads the world, 863
Philanthropists in time of famine,
    417
Philanthropy only virtue suffi-
    ciently appreciated, 514
Philatelic fame, a year of, 842
Philip, appeal from, drunk, 969
    receiving news of success,
        1002
    when arbitrator, 1002
Philippi, I will see thee at, 84
Philistine in the strict sense,
    1064
    originally meant unenlightened
        opponent, 548
    slay the, 913
Philistines be upon the, 1099
    opponent of the children of
        light, 548
Philobiblos knows, be assured
    that, 865
Philologists who chase a panting
    syllable, 263
Philosopher a man is, the great-
    er, 1083
    a man up in a balloon, 595
    a trifling handful O, 569
    and friend, 209
    and never earth's, 516
    can scorn, scarce the firm, 224
    equal and kindly brother, 379
    great memory does not make
        a, 403

Philosopher, he was a, 5
    married, belongs to comedy,
        1080
    muscular training of a, 1007
    never yet that could endure
        the toothache, 40
    thinks like a, 1055
Philosophers exchange their
    wares for money, 646
    have judged, as wise, 143
    have sought, all that, 305
    say, why the, 1074
    sayings of, 142
    sit in their sylvan hall, 595
    will put their names to their
        books, 123
Philosopher's scales, produced
    the, 345
Philosophic mind, the, 301
Philosophical argument, 342
Philosophie, Aristotle and his, 5
Philosophy a little more compli-
    cated, 1074
    advantage to, 769
    adversity's sweet milk, 79
    and wine are alike, 646
    bladders of, 185
    bringeth men's minds about to
        religion, 110
    climax of human, 803
    conformable to truth, 669
    could find it out, if, 92
    decent mammalian, 905
    depth in, 110
    dreamt of in your, 92
    for fear divine, 468
    hast any, in thee shepherd, 50
    how charming is divine, 158
    I ask not proud, 328
    inclineth to atheism, 110
    is a good horse in the stable,
        253
    is nothing but discretion, 130
    is the microscope, 1069
    lights of mild, 194
    makes men deep, 111
    may determine, 235
    of one who studies, 1008
    search of deep, 167
    should be an energy, 1068
    teaching by examples, 200
    that no, can lift, 304
    triumphs over past evils, 253
    what he gained from, 1015
    what matters in, 741
    will clip an angel's wings, 383
Phlegmatic emerged, 1056
Phobias to rest, lay, 882
Phocaeans won, the, 969
Phocion and Demosthenes, 1000
    saying of, 1003
Phocion's oratory, 1000
Phoebe are you come so soon,
    291
Phœbus 'gins arise, 105
Phœbus' wain, wheels of, 157
Phœnicians or whoever invented
    books, 375
Phœnix builds her spicy nest,
    140
    risen, no flaming, 889
Phonograph, man is like a, 720
Phosphor, sweet, bring the day,
    134
Photographer would be king of
    artists, 611

Photography of a printed record,
    colorless, 686
Phrase, a fico for the, 34
    behind every kind of, 1086
    choice word and measured, 297
    every, is a string of gems,
        607
    of his espousal lay, 669
    of peace, the soft, 100
    of vagrant worm, hackneyed,
        510
    one translucent, 647
    proverbed with a grandsire, 77
    quaint and stilted, 596
    suitable vesture of, 972
    that ancient Saxon, 434
    that with the public took, 275
    wings of a, 788
    with hollow, 806
    with pompous, 332
Phrases, find the secret, 873
    I detest, 747
    mint of, in his brain, 40
    similar goddamned, 852
Phyllida, but Phyllida my, 648
Physic, gold in, is a cordial, 5
    love hath no, 922
    minus robe, minus, 917
    pomp, take, 99
    throw, to the dogs, 88
    to preserve health, 111
    wisdom beyond the rules of,
        111
Physics pain, labour we delight
    in, 86
Physical and metaphysical im-
    possibility, 376
    arguments and opinions, 1031
Physically impossible, 279
Physician and man of letters,
    450
    chief, out of London, 313
    confessor nor lawyer, deceive
        not, 137
    considers his own good, no,
        973
    every grief to the, 137
    goodness of the, 971
    he bawls for a, 698
    heal thyself, 1117
    honour a, 1125
    I observe the, 118
    is also a ruler, the true, 973
    is confined to study, one, 969
    is there no, there, 1112
    like a skilful, 997
    Luke the beloved, 1121
    makes his rounds, the great,
        757
    minus physic, 917
    of the iron age, 546
    or my lawyer is, my, 1027
    presumed to call himself a, 977
    regular-bred, 278
    the flower of civilization, 702
    who can do no good, 808
    work cures, neither does a,
        1126
Physicians, best of all, 698
    beyond the practice of all, 450
    catch diseases to cure them,
        124
    of the highest rank, 951
Physician's oath, the, 971
Physick substitute of exercise or
    temperance, 196

Physicking, no, 1061
Physiognomy, nothing so easy nor so useful as, 407
Physiological experiment on animals, 449
Pia mater, womb of, 41
Pianist, please do not shoot the, 724
Pianoforte lapdog parrot, 402
Piano's tune, a new, 776
Piccadilly Daisy, when the, 655
Pick a pocket, not scruple to, 186
no quarrels, 251
Pickaxe shovel spade, 348
Picked, age is grown so, 97
out of ten thousand, 92
Picket's off duty forever, 569
Pickett leading grandly down, 690
Pickett's Virginians were passing, 737
Picking and stealing, 1128
Pickle, in such a, 33
put you in this, 1033
Pickwickian sense, in a, 494
Picninnies, Joblillies and the Garyulies, 246
Pictur' that no painter, 697
Picture, a dark and gloomy, 804
and fell across the, 665
as a whole requires distance, 543
but his book, look not at his, 119
I fear, will not be like me, 181
is not wrought by hands alone, 533
look here upon this, 95
may instantly present, 1072
nature paints the best part of a, 410
painted well, a little, 672
placed the busts between, 204
see a fine, 1058
show you the, 54
to say of a, in praise, 611
to see her is a, 586
who looks at an American, 314
Pictures and verse and statues, 610
eyes make, 317
for the page atone, 215
God's great, 445
hung and gilded, 418
in Afric maps, savage, 190
in our eyes, 117
lovely, shall bloom, 662
merely mental, 937
of silver, 1108
often exaggerated distorted blurred, 542
people who understand, 786
well-wrought plays, 223
Pictured truth that Shakespeare drew, 626
urn, fancy from her, 244
Picturesque liar, 616
with a savour, 1089
Picturs of his birth-place prof'tible cherishing, 606
Pie, a finger in every, 1035, 1040
cabbage leaf to make an apple, 246
ends its days in apple, 910
I ate umble, 497
in the sky, you'll get, 957

Pie, New Englanders love, 853
no man's, is freed from his finger, 72
the rich pumpkin, 441
Pies, abominate dried apple, 955
and went to making, 557
Piece, faultless, to see, 164, 210
judge of the whole, 1033
of British manhood, sounder, 378
of earth, thou bleeding, 82
of foreign sky, my, 899
of work is a man, what a, 92
Pieces, all at once, it went to, 453
body will go to, 961
of eight, 842
of mathematical motion, 128
Piecemeal on the rock, 355
Pier, leave upon the, 642
Piers, knocking at the vacant, 552
Piercing the night's dull ear, 67
Pierian spring, taste not the, 210
Piety is packed, character with, 830
nor wit shall lure it, 1019
Pig in a poke, buying or selling of, 18
Pigs have wings, 598
squeak, naturally as, 141
Pig's tail can never make a good shaft, 138
Pigeon, boiling the shadow of a, 458
Pigeons, cross with homing, 813
in the grass, 836
Pigtail, wore a handsome, 482
Pike-staff, plain as a, 221, 1052
Pilate, court of, 688
or Christ, 533
slaves of, 686
took water and washed his hands, 60
Pile, crackling, 452
of human mockeries, 337
old, 427
Pilgrim flock, I mused upon the, 403
limping, 453
of the sky, 304
of eternity, 366
shrines, such graves are, 363
soul in you, 790
steps in amice gray, 156
steps of spring, 668
they laid the, 172
way, finding upon my, 873
Pilgrims and strangers, 553
crossed the sea, 442
foundation of greatness of, 550
if Plymouth rock had landed on the, 403
land of the, 921
landed, the, 815
Pilgrim's Progress interesting but tough, 615
Progress, that wonderful book, 398
withered wreath, 598
Pilgrimage and goal, 873
days of his, 499
earth his quiet, 121
Goethe has done his, 546
I'll take my, 22

Pilgrimage it goes, and the, 939
overtaketh in his, 33
savage enough, 883
succeed me in my, 172
tavern on our, 833
this weary, 237
to Paradise, her long, 822
weary, life a, 135
with songs beguile your, 881
Pilgrimages, folk to goon on, 5
Pilgrimes, passing to and fro, we ben, 6
Pilgrim-manned the Mayflower in a dream, 839
Pill of turpentine every morning, 181
Pills political, quacks with, 794
Pillar of fire by night, 1098
of salt, 1097
of state, seemed a, 150
Pillars are falling at thy feet, 403
do not fall, the, 778
high wordy, 932
last tottering, 452
of society, 1076
that hold all upright, 932
Pillared cliffs like sentries, 707
where they run, 688
Pillow, bliss to press the, 568
hard, finds the down, 106
moss for a, 823
of stone, 521
Pilot, after you, 764
can sail, a great, 990
cannot mitigate the billows, 1002
I hope to meet my, 472
in extremity, a daring, 173
lifts it, as a, 929
of the Galilean lake, 159
of the state, 964
our, lives still, 71
that weathered the storm, 294
'tis a fearful night, 388
Pilots of the purple twilight, 464
touching head to head, 644
Pimpernell and twenty more, 52
Pin, bores with a little, 60
tiny metal insect, 683
to be chosen between them, not a, 339
what the world may say, I care not a, 610
Pins, by not swallowing, 799
it with a star, 389
Pin's fee, do not set my life at a, 91
Pinch, a lean-faced villain, 38
bitter, 780
deserts you at a, 962
necessity's sharp, 98
Pinches, put up with the, 928
where the shoe, 997
Pine, dwindle peak and, 84
for thee, then most I, 426
forests mighty, 590
I live they lack I have they, 20
if you can't be a, 846
immovable infixed, 150
it is the lofty, 969, 983
like an eagle caged I, 502
planted the palmetto and the, 586
spray of Western, 644

Pine, than, in a palace alone, 545
  to equal which the tallest, 148
  tree stands so lonely, 1065
  where the rugged, 642
  with fear and sorrow, 25
Pines, eat the cones under his, 837
  knew his whistle, 847
  silent sea of, 316
  smile upon its neighbor, 517
  star the twilight of the, 443
  stretched beneath the, 408
  the solemn, 602
  thunder-harp of, 587
  tops of the eastern, 59
Pine-apple of politeness, 277
Pined and wanted food, 295
  in thought, 55
Pine-roots to last, 766
Pinhead in many respects, 791
Pining hideth his sharp ribs, labor, 477
  what is passion but, 592
Pinion, bird with the broken, 643
  on shining, 851
  with paddle or fin or, 572
Pinions, drift of, 749
  oft I hear thy dusky, 418
  on an enemy's, 962
  shadow of thy, float along, 418
  silver, 385
Pinioned sentiment, each, 1050
Pink and the pansy, 159
  and white are everywhere, its, 550
  as any shell, 890
  eyne, Bacchus with, 104
  of courtesy and circumspection, 253
  of courtesy, the very, 79, 1039
  of perfection, 253
  rheumatic feet, 881
  sea-shells, 634
  sunbonnet, I can see the, 696
  trip slip for a five cent fare, 583
Pinks that grow, the, 127
Pinned with a single star, 389
Pin-pricks, killed by, 589
Pint of English ale, drank a, 827
Pints and quarts of Ludlow beer, 743
Pint-pot, as much imagination as a, 367
Piny mountain, 317
Pioneer, Boone the, 552
  in my boots like a, 927
Pioneers! O pioneers, 535
Pioneering for gold, 859
  for spinach, 859
Pious action we do sugar o'er, 93
  deeds of men, 346, 511
  gentlemen, some, 639
  good and clean, 248
  impiety of the, 580
  not the less a man though, 1046
  ones of Plymouth, 517
  passion, grave intent, 736
  seem when only bilious, 392
  thoughts, she sent, 147
Pipe but as the linnets sing, 468
  easier to be played on than a, 94
  for fortune's finger, 94

Pipe, glorious in a, 358
  he can smoke a book he can read, give a man a, 610
  light my, 793
  now battered bruised and brown, old, 578
  of briar my open fire, my, 845
  over a, 693
  tipped with amber, 358
  to smoke in cold weather, 276
Pipes and whistles in his sound, 50
  any man can play the, 774
  of the Highlanders, 509
  than poetry, brisker, 743
Piping, at the, of all hands, 375
Pippins, old, toothsomest, 128
Piracee with a little burglaree, vary, 623
Pirate, a sea robber, 233
Pirates, cruelty of, 529
Pistol let off in the ear, 324
  misses fire, if his, 255
  what wind blew you hither, 65
Pistols, ring bells and fire, 1089
Pistons, black statement of, 938
Pit, black as the, 692
  down to the, 847
  man will go down into the, 687
  monster of the, 214
  they 'll fill a, as well as better, 63
  what we should call the, 656
  whoso diggeth a, 1108
Pitch, dark as, 171
  he that toucheth, 1125
  my moving tent, nightly, 306
  of the word, 858
  out of tune above the, 1025
  they that touch, 39
  which flies the higher, 68
  worked her mind to such a, 942
Pitch-black night, in the, 565
Pitched, as the mind is, 266
Pitcher broken at the fountain, 1110
  clink of the ice in the, 698
  costly, I'll burst in three, 362
  of mignonette, 715
  of singing, fetch in a, 910
  that wouldn't spill, 453
Pitchers have ears, 16, 52
Pitchfork, clothes thrown on with a, 192
Piteous chase, 48
  thing, it will be a, 887
Pith and moment, enterprises of, 93
  Englishmen of, 360
  intricate meaning and, 590
  seven years', these arms had, 100
Pitied men whose views of Christian, 522
  who do not complain are never, 322
Pitiful, lips say God be, 428
  sound to hear, 699
  strife, pity us all in our, 657
  't was wondrous pitiful, 100
Pitiless sapphire firmament, 666
  storm, pelting of this, 98
  use which lovers make of it, 1069

Pity and mercy, man needs, 728
  challenge double, 21
  drops of sacred, 49
  for conceited people, 520
  gave ere charity began, 250
  hath engendered, sacred, 49
  in his tenderness, found, 626
  is the feeling, 874
  is the straightest path to love, 131
  like a new-born babe, 85
  melts the mind to love, 176
  no, could change the heart, 659
  of it Iago the pity of it, 103
  of others' woe, seek love in, 282
  on her, have, 804
  showing an outward, 60
  tenderness and charity, 520
  that it was great, so it was, 61
  then embrace, endure then, 208
  though not pardon thee, we may, 37
  'tis 'tis true, 92
  unites the mind with the sufferer, 874
  upon the poor, he that hath, 1107
Pity's call, listen to, 557
Pity-pat, his heart kep' goin', 527
Pity-Zekle, but hern went, 527
Pixes and rosaries, 143
Pizen a cup of cold, 652
Place, all other things give, 206
  and enough, 649
  and time, bounds of, 243
  and wealth, get, 214
  appointed, the lowly, 994
  as a nail in a sure, 1111
  as from their high, 999
  at home in a better, 48
  at its accustomed, 824
  begins to forgive a, 497
  beneath, 46
  convenient handy sort of, 760
  did then adhere, nor time nor, 85
  dignified by the doer's deed, 53
  distressed and forsaken, 182
  each in its accustomed, 681
  ear in many a secret, 296
  everywhere his, 167
  fittest, where man can die, 511
  for everything, 706
  for many a fad, 811
  for the boys to play, 811
  from lowest, 53
  get wealth and, 214
  has changed, wonder if the old, 898
  I know my, 55
  in a certain, 451
  in heaven or earth, not a, 638
  in many a solitary, 296
  in the unchanging, 810
  in the world, 47
  in thy memory dearest, 416
  it's in a lonesome, 817
  keep the pain but change the, 199
  kiss the, to make it well, 345
  know him any more, 1102

Place, leaves a lonesome, 708
  may be better supplied, 48
  men are servants in great, 110
  'mid the bards, 982
  mind is its own, 148
  more beautiful for dead poets, 675
  more delightful, no, 981
  never claim its true, 938
  never the time and the, 493
  no, affords a more striking conviction, 231
  no, like home, 365
  no respect of, 54
  nor trusted to one, 43
  O give me a, 738
  of light, university should be, 420
  of my birth, came to the, 356
  of peace, home is the, 532
  of rest, where to choose their, 156
  of thine, that there abides a, 546
  on earth hath he, what, 604
  or time, not to be changed by, 148
  our champion waiting in his, 442
  pensive though a happy, 303
  plant another in its, 1054
  pride of, 86
  right man in the right, 513
  some wonderful, 879
  stands upon a slippery, 58
  sunshine in the shady, 24
  takes her unassuming, 774
  that has known him, 1102
  that is better than this, 955
  thereof shall know it no more, 1102
  to be happy is here, 603
  to place, from, 257
  to sit down, here is no, 166
  towering in her pride of, 86
  travels in a distant, 911
  was all, the name was nought, 686
  wharbouts you spill de grease, 688
  where honour's lodged, 143
  where loveliness, 774
  where men can pray, 827
  where she had been, in the, 1066
  where thou standest is holy, 1098
  where time had ceased, 681
  wherein to sleep, quiet, 931
  which 't is not good manners to mention, 188
  world was an enchanted, 811
  worship the gods of the, 126
Places all alike distant from heaven, 124
  fill up their proper, 221
  keep their ancient, 749
  lines in pleasant, 1103
  of my breath, 896
  other graces follow in proper, 170
  shall be hell, all, 31
  strange, crammed, 49
  stretches forth from shadowed, 935
  that look on plains, 879

Places the eye of heaven visits, 59
  those in the highest, 173
  to wade, point out the, 718
  you can, in all the, 226
Place-expectants, gratitude of, 200
Placid and self-contained, 535
Plagiarè, among authors, 162
Plagiarism, memory to convict of, 239
Plague, avoid as you would the, 1016
  every one has his particular, 1001
  my wife is my particular, 1001
  o' both your houses, 79
  of all cowards, 61
  of sighing and grief, 62
  proved a terrible, 941
  the inventor, return to, 85
  us, instruments to, 100
Plagues and common dotages, 123
  of heaven, 293
  that haunt the rich, 267
Plaid, collie on my, 288
Plaided clans came down, what time the, 500
Plaidie, I lo' your very, 770
Plain, a darkling, 546
  and clear, 143
  and flat, 526
  and simple faith, 83
  and to the purpose, 38
  and uncoined constancy, 68
  as a pack-staff, 116
  as a pike-staff, 221, 1052
  as a prairie wind, 927
  as the beak, 647
  as way to parish church, 49
  blunt man, 83
  brownstone will do, a very, 451
  Camilla scours the, 211
  coffin, I would rather have a, 578
  here as on a darkling, 546
  in dress, be, 221
  knight pricking on the, 24
  living and high thinking, 298
  lonely waste of Edom's, 443
  loveliest village of the, 250
  night sweeps along the, 348
  nodding o'er the yellow, 224
  of Marathon, 233
  over the, 395
  over the great gromboolian, 498
  stood out in the open, 846
  stretched upon the, 351
  tale shall put you down, 62
  to be seen on the sand, 187
Plains behind, leave the, 735
  die on the, 929
  half-sunlight and half-storm, 879
  men to match my, 732
  of faraway, 738
  of windy Troy, 464
  ravaged, 262
  silver-mantled, 477
  tolerant, 663
  with his darling, 810

Plainness of speech, use great, 1120
Plaintive cry of that poor soldier, 513
  piping frog, 691
  strings, 798
Plan, achieve my immemorial, 840
  build up no, 913
  nature's, 439
  not without a, 206
  of attack, 892
  parts of an infinite, 627
  that admits no modification, 988
  that they should take, 298
  the simple, sufficeth them, 298
  to forget it, pretty good, 799
  to make a man, surest, 506
Plans and projects, all human, 491
Plancus' day, in, 984
Plane tree's kind to the poor dull city, 732
Planet, born under a rhyming, 40
  on a swiftly tilting, 904
  ranges, some other, 847
  ship like a small, 726
  skin-diseases of the, 925
  some ill, reigns, 56
  swims into his ken, when a new, 384
Planets, as easily have created the, 382
  engulf the, 770
  guides the, 289
  in chime, sun with his, 449
  in their turn, all the, 194
  not more numerous than the, 419
  plunge and die, a million, 844
  then no, strike, 89
Plank of driftwood, 437
Planks, two floating, 437
Planned, perfect woman nobly, 299
Plant, error is a hardy, 477
  fame is no, 159
  fixed like a, 208
  in a garden grew, 368
  look at this delicate, 435
  love a wild, 797
  of slow growth, confidence is a, 230
  she named Liberty Tree, 271
  that grows on mortal soil, 159
  whose virtues have not been discovered, 415
Plants, aromatic, 252
  beauty of growing, 1049
  children like olive, 1106
  dried and fresh flowers, 475
  suck in the earth, 167
  that our sons may be as, 1106
Planted a garden, God Almighty, 111
  Apollos watered, I have, 1120
  of the tree I, 353
Planting, wheat for this, 436
Plaster saints, 781
Plastic force, moulded by some, 647
Plates and cups clean-gleaming, 894

Platinum benches, on the, 937
Platitude, effect of good, 724
  stroke a, 853
Platitudes, fond of uttering, 623
Plato old, prayer of, 442
  taught of the rule of, 162
  thou reasonest well, 195
Plato's brain, Caesar's hand and,
  410
  retirement, 156
Platonic mind, preoccupied by a,
  897
Platonick, been purely, 1036
Plausibility, one grain of, 476
Play, a little work a little, 607
  and make good cheer, 19
  artful part in a, 1038
  at cherry-pit, 55
  better at a, 334
  foul, 90
  good as a, 940
  hart ungalled, 94
  holdeth children from, 27
  in the plighted clouds, 158
  is done, the, 481
  is mediocre, woman's, 1080
  is ready to start, 844
  is the thing, 93
  is the tragedy Man, 459
  just as of a, 981
  life's poor, is o'er, 208
  me no plays, 947
  of colours on clouds, 1084
  of the many, in the, 1084
  on give me excess of it, 53
  out the play, 62
  pleased not the million, 93
  pleasure when I, not, 21
  rather hear a discourse than
    see a, 125
  run, they will not let my,
    186
  scarcely saw the, 931
  the devil, seem a saint and, 71
  the fools with the time, 64
  the just measure of a, 180
  the swan and die in music, 45
  the woman with mine eyes, 88
  to you is death to us, 167
  up! and play the game, 765
  uppe play uppe O Boston bells,
    540
  what is a good, 825
  whatever a body is not obliged
    to do, 615
  who goes to an American, 314
  with similes, 298
  wouldst have me sing and, 337
  yields, money my new, 933
  your part, authors essayist,
    471
Plays his part, so he, 50
  many parts, one man, 49
  of Euripides, 879
  play me no, 947
  such fantastic tricks, 36
  to others' grief attention raise,
    223
  with happy endings, 794
  writing of, 721
Playbill of Hamlet, 311
Played and sung, as once I, 337
  at bo-peep, 134
  familiar with his hoary locks,
    393
  in fancy we, 446

Played on the banks of the Yuba,
  432
  upon a stage, if this were, 55
Player, life's a poor, 88
  shuffles off the buskin, 452
  with railroads, 855
Players, attitude of professional,
  897
  honor Shakespeare, 120
  men and women merely, 49
  of lofty pipe organs, 854
  though the most be, 120
  upon plaintive strings, 798
Playful breeze, when the, 516
  when I'm, 616
Playing holidays, if all the year
    were, 61
Playmate always true and faith-
    ful, 873
  sweet, I'll give thee for a, 395
  time's but our, 555
Playmates have answered his call,
  362
  I have had, 325
Plaything, elephant man's, 1005
  some livelier, 208
Playthings, takes away our, 439
Playwright may show in some
    fifth act, our, 472
Playwrights mouth, the, 759
Plea, necessity the tyrant's, 152
  shall beauty hold a, 107
  so tainted, in law what, 46
  though justice be thy, 46
Plead lament and sue, 307
  like angels, his virtues will, 85
  with humane men I will, 424
Pleasant and cloudy weather, 272
  bless me this is, 510
  bread eaten in secret is, 1107
  country's earth, 60
  duty, 572
  fellow, touchy testy, 196
  for brethren to dwell together,
    1106
  fruits do grow, wherein, 121
  how, it is to have money, 519
  in man, all that was, 252
  in their lives, 1100
  institution, 624
  is Saturday night, 291
  is thy morning, life how, 285
  land of counterpane, 702
  life to lead, 't were a, 406
  memory of their worth, 373
  nothing half so, 642
  places, lines in, 1103
  thought, we meet thee like a,
    298
  thoughts bring sad thoughts,
    295
  time with my mind, 595
  to know Mr. Lear, 499
  to see one's name in print, 351
  to severe, grave to light, 177,
    1049
  to think on, 164
  vices, our, 100
  way, all along the, 619
Pleasantest angling is to see the
    fish, 39
Pleasantness, ways of, 1106
Pleasantry, folly even in, 1017
Please, books cannot always, 280
  certainty to, 289
  everybody, hard to, 989

Please, live to, must please to
    live, 231
  natural in him to, 173
  studious to, 231
  surest to, 252
  uncertain coy and hard to, 308
Pleased, I would do what I, 1038
  not the million, 93
  the ear is, 266
  they please are, 249
  to the last, 207
  with a rattle, 208
  with the danger, 173
  with this bauble, 208
Pleases all the world, he, 1050
Pleasing anxious being, 245
  dreadful thought, 195
  dreams and slumbers light,
    308
  hope, whence this, 195
  memory of all he stole, 215
  punishment that women bear,
    37
  shade, ah happy hills, 243
  ware is half sold, 136
Pleasure, a mile with, 861
  a precious mouldering, 584
  after pain, sweet is, 176
  all hope, 178
  and pain, grievous, 631
  and pain, light and life, 601
  arrivals and departures of, 588
  at the helm, 244
  blossom with, 487
  by myself a lonely, 297
  can be had, 236
  chords that vibrate sweetest,
    287
  company is an everlasting, 977
  costs, a single, 707
  dissipation without, 271
  drink it with, 1124
  drown the brim, 53
  drowns in, 225
  ease content, 208
  eternally new, a, 673
  fine point of seldom, 107
  friend of, 248
  full of, void of strife, 140
  give a shock of, 386
  has ceased to please, 232
  have their moments of, 417
  he takes in others' company,
    1064
  howe'er disguised by art, 258
  I fly from, 232
  I have left, only, 1053
  if a woman gave him, 948
  in being popular, 476
  in poetic pains, 179, 265
  in the pathless woods, 354
  in trim gardens, takes his,
    160
  is oft a visitant, 382
  laugh of, grows less gay, 405
  like the midnight flower, 334
  little, in the house, 269
  live in, when I live to thee,
    225
  loiter in, or toilfully spin, 448
  lost, the just, 108
  love sweeter than all other, 178
  never is at home, 384
  no, is comparable, 109
  no profit grows where is no, 52
  not take so much, 1043

Pleasure of being cheated, 143
  of cutting pictures out, 809
  of life is to, true, 483
  of love is in loving, 367
  of not being dead, 1054
  of the game, the little, 189
  of the time, spoils the, 87
  of travel, 1083
  of your company, 325
  out of pain, 827
  poignancy to, 1051
  praise all his, 201
  pride is therefore, 1048
  read for, I, 773
  reason's whole, 208
  reverie is its, 1068
  riches fame and, 1049
  rides swift after, 551
  self-complacency is, 1048
  she was bent, though on, 264
  sight the purest physical, 312
  so received be vain, 966
  stock of harmless, 233
  sure in being mad, 179
  sweet the, 176
  take, some men to, 209
  they can enjoy, the only, 1054
  thy most pointed, 703
  to be drunk, it is our, 228
  to deceive the deceiver, 1045
  to hear sermons, he that takes,
    130
  to the spectators, 400
  treads upon the heels of, 193
  trip up to the pole, 652
  unseasoned by variety, 988
  was the chief good, 1016
  well-spring of, 477
  what were, 669
  when I live to thee I live in,
    225
  when I play not, 21
  with perfumes, take, 1049
  without loss, 21
  work thou for, 719
  you are viewing, if with, 872
  youth and, 352
  youth love gold and, 455
Pleasures and palaces, 365
  are all alike, 130
  are cheapest, richest man
    whose, 515
  are like poppies, 287
  banish pain, 199
  calm, 224
  catastrophes due to love of,
    532
  doubling his, 289
  every age has its, 1049
  he joyed of life's, 791
  hovered nigh, 224
  lie thickest where no, 407
  like waves, 576
  needs, cares, 1073
  of heroic poesy, 147
  of the Mahometans, 246
  of the present day, 225
  of the spheres, 338
  of weary people, 645
  of youth, preferable to all the,
    198
  of youth, than all the, 981
  pretty, might me move, 21
  prove, we will all the, 31,
    936
  soothed his soul to, 176

Pleasure-dome, stately, 315
Pleasure-house, lordly, wherein
  at ease, 462
Plebeian vocation, by some, 510
Pledge is still the same, 888
  never signed no, 527
  of a nation, 652
  of allegiance, 718
  of conformity, 770
  of her love, 271
  our sacred honour, 273
  with mine, and I will, 119
Pleiades, sweet influences of,
  1103
Pleiads, the rainy, 744
Plenteous, harvest truly is, 1115
Plentiful as blackberries, 62
  lack of wit, 92
Plenty comes and goes, 604
  here is God's, 179
  of gold, there's, 502
  of other irons, 971
  of the kind, yet is there, 462
  reveled in the, 768
  seven years of great, 1098
  shall get a, 481
  with ease and, 967
Plenty's horn, mouth of, 790
Pleurisy of people, 132
Pliant instrument, 320
Plight, went out in a hungry,
  951
Plighted clouds, play in the,
  158
Plinths are laid at midnight, 785
Plodders, continual, 40
Plodding wins the race, 962
Plods his weary way, 244
Ploffskin Pluffskin Pelican jee,
  499
Plot, gunpowder treason and,
  945
  in the cemetery, father and a,
  829
  is next to thine, he whose, 573
  me no plots, 947
  of dust, one little moving, 771
  of Fixed Period, 695
  passions spin the, 574
  this blessed, this earth, 59
  we first survey the, 64
  women guide the, 278
Plots, plot me no, 947
Plough deep while sluggards
  sleep, 227
  following his, 297
  for what avail the, 410
  God speed the, 512
  having put his hand to the,
  1117
  laid by at the furrow's end, 683
  loom and chisel, 950
  the sea, those who, 989
  the watery deep, 218
Ploughs and workshops, we leave
  our, 475
Ploughman homeward plods, 244
Ploughshare o'er creation, 202
  put not your, too deep, 310
  stern Ruin's, 285
  unwilling, 304
Plover, muskets aimed at, 277
Plow, brother will follow the, 675
  deep and straight with all your
  powers, 417
  I maun mind the, 345

Plowmen, ye rigid, bear in mind,
  417
Plowshare, fashioned first, 504
Plowshares, swords into, 1111
Pluck a crow together, we'll, 37
  blackberries, sit round it and,
  431
  bright honour from the moon,
  61
  from memory a rooted sorrow,
  88
  of Lord Nelson, 623
  out the heart of my mystery,
  94
  takes us into a difficulty, 545
  this flower safety, 61
  up drowned honour, 61
  your berries, I come to, 159
Plucked his gown, 251
Plucker down of kings, setter up
  and, 70
Plucky, woodsmen stout and,
  815
Plumage dark and sleek, 288
  new and fine, decked in, 1076
  the brightest, 930
Plumbers and their ways, 582
Plumbing, ingenious assembly of
  portable, 912
Plume a eu d'avantage sur
  l'épée, 123
  and a green lance, 925
  of amber snuff-box, 212
  proudly as a, 826
  to fledge the shaft, 334
Plumes, borrowed, 961
  eagle's own, 962
  her feathers, she, 158
Plumed knight, 583
  troop, farewell, 102
Plummet, deeper than ever, 33
Plummet's pace, speed is but the
  heavy, 161
Plump Jack, banish, 62
  why I'm so, 276
Plumpskin Ploshkin Pelican jill,
  499
Plumpy Bacchus, 104
Plums, life's a pudding full of,
  624
Plunder, constitutes a system of,
  1072
  power of public, 339
Plunge, Festus I, 484
Plunged along the shore, waves
  that, 558
  in, accoutred as I was, I, 81
Plutarch, no such person as,
  1002
Plutarch's men, one of, 528
Pluto knocks at hovels, 983
Pluto's cheek, drew tears down,
  161
Plutonian shore, 418, 658
  shadows, 568
Plymouth, governor of, 541
  pious ones of, 517
  rock, Massachusetts with her,
  660
  sand, rock among the, 403
Po, or wandering, 249
Pobble who has no toes, 498
Pocket, empty, the worst of
  crimes, 560
  in a shroud, no, 656
  little in one's own, 1039

Pocket, not scruple to pick a, 186
the very sling in my, 1056
Pockets, Babbitt's, 884
with cartridges, fill their, 935
Pocket-book, contents of a, 346
Pocket-knife, that magic tool, 348
Poe with his raven, 526
Poe's poetry, in all of, 925
Poem ever known, greatest, 911
goes about the world, 415
hangs on the berry bush, 650
himself to be a true, 162
his whole life a heroic, 376
into the air, shot a, 868
is a proof of genius, a great, 397
is the reader illuminated, 825
life of a man a, of its sort, 377
lovely as a tree, 890
marred by a superfluous verse, 439
not necessarily obscure, 319
of earth, I am the, 538
of sacrifice, pride of labor, 1090
one single good, 1057
perfect, the crystalline revelation, 432
read a good, 1058
recalled by its rhythm, 415
round and perfect as a star, 587
should not mean but be, 914
to which we return, 318
which we have read, not the, 318
Whitman's, 924
with music or with, 156
works and does some, 378
Poems are made by fools, 890
every volume of, 236
for ye are living, 437
no man reads, 995
produced, more, 838
seldom consist of poetry alone, 744
temporary, 232
to pages, commit your, 982
would write heroic, 376
Poesy, heavenly gift of, 175
heroic, pleasures of, 147
some participation of divineness, 112
Poet be, joyful let the, 517
binds by passion and knowledge, 295
can survive everything but a misprint, 723
cannot die, the, 465
classical, 716
dies, when the, 307
does his best, 707
doth remain, 735
gathers fruit, 735
has grudge against poet, 959
he was a, 1089
hopes that after-times, every, 447
I was young, I was a, 881
is a chameleon, 749
is a commonplace fellow, 811
is made as well as born, 119
is worthy of the name of, 378
lies beneath this sod, 319

Poet, lunatic, lover, and the, 43
modest cough of a minor, 721
more confident than a bad, 995
must have love, 765
naturalist and historian, 231
nothing keeps a, 890
of doom dementia and death, 793
Oh for a, 807
or a friend to find, a, 410
or other literary creature, 634
perhaps no person can be a, 397
pleasantest sort of, 890
pointed where a flower, 539
published a book, 935
puts his woes in verse, 1065
reciting to Lady Diana, 937
retired in his tower of ivory, 858
should always be hungry, 930
should avoid religion, 556
sighed I am not fit, 812
sings and guards his grave, 609
sings, this is truth the, 464
so great a, 175
soaring, 162
speak to men with power, 376
still more a man than men, 376
survives the statesman the warrior or the monarch, 423
swarthy, of despair, 881
take away the liberty of a, 147
talk by, dull, 616
tell a major from a minor, 931
that strange insane, 1078
the tadpole, 635
they had no, and they died, 214, 282, 853
this the most gifted, 516
twirls them in his mind, 649
was ever, so trusted before, 235
who is a, 492
who's old and wise, 890
whose works so content us, 243
will follow the rainbow still, 675
with the coward's tongue, 737
without love, 376
young, screams forever, 890
Poets, and I believed the, 524
and romancers corrupt, 771
and their song, 620
are all who love, 507
are like stinking fish, 320
are sultans, 167
are the hierophants of inspiration, 318, 369
are the unacknowledged legislators, 369
avoid citations from the, 971
beautiful place prepared for dead, 675
by education and practice, 412
by nature we love, 412
by their sufferings grow, 144
despise money, 751
dream, as youthful, 160
ever fail in reading, 428

Poets, few, were so mated, 749
forms of ancient, 317
have dreamed, only the, 1079
histories make, witty, 111
in their misery dead, 297
in three distant ages born, 175
in youth begin in gladness, 297
know better than others, 597
lived and died, for this the, 882
long-haired, 661
lose half the praise, 146
of the proud old lineage, 881
only can read them, 514
or sages, what makes men, 574
pensive, painful vigils keep, 215
reading their own works, 931
sing, all that, 425
sing, besides the autumn, 585
so it happens with, 437
sometimes have to seem business-like, 838
steal from Homer, 121
styled, love is a boy by, 142
that, lasting marble seek, 146
the Georgian, 937
the tales of the, 974
things the first, had, 30
thrill the swampy reach, 933
to have great, there must be great audiences, 539
two classes of, 412
virtue not often among, 1040
we, in our youth, 297
who feel great truths, 507
who give it a name, 868
who have sold a sonnet, 931
who read are major, 931
write of that grim ferryman, 71
Poet's brain, should possess a, 30
darling, the, 298
dream, consecration and the, 299
ear, flattery lost on, 307
eye in a fine frenzy rolling, 43
eye, muse with a, 327
lines, where go the, 451
majority, constitutes a, 931
mistress is a hallowed, 458
pen plundered from wing of bird, 292
pen turns them to shapes, 43
secret heaven, 887
triumph, this is the, 672
Poets' food is love and fame, 366
forms of beauty, 531
hope, critics who stamped out, 430
orchestra, 684
Poetess, maudlin, 212
Poetic child, meet nurse for a, 307
fields encompass me, 195
flights belong to prose, 332
justice with lifted scale, 215
nature, safe arrival of the, 667
nook, seat in some, 346
pains, pleasure in, 179, 265
prose, warbler of, 266
Poetics, never indulge in, 978
Poetical, gods had made thee, 50
Poeticule, some tenth-rate, 635
Poetry, a hope for, 937
and prose invite to utterance, 869

Poetry, attainable in, 461
 beautiful impressive mode of
  saying things, 548
 began each day with a passage,
  723
 best words in best order, 319
 brisker pipes than, 743
 call Whitman's poems, 924
 changes every hundred years,
  896
 checks loquacity, 412
 Chinese, 762
 comes fine spun, 986
 comes with anger hunger and
  dismay, 912
 curse of, 716
 definition of, 645, 926
 eschewed, why has our, 887
 exists in hearts of all men,
  380
 fettered fetters the human race,
  282
 from physical causes, 744
 gives pleasure by its form,
  645
 I saw sweet, 822
 in all of Poe's, 925
 innate untold, 911
 is difficult to read, all, 491
 is founded on hearts, 826
 is in the pity, 937
 is not just the skill, 912
 is speaking painting, 1006
 is what Milton saw, 853
 like a page of prancing, 585
 means, what his, 811
 melancholy madness of, 261
 men are cradled into, 367
 mere mechanic art, 262
 most wavering of flames, 667
 never again a popular art, 919
 not a purpose but a passion,
  461
 of earth is never dead, 385
 of ethics from Byron's, 398
 of speech, the, 354
 of the commonplace, 695
 of words as rhythmical creation, 461
 old-fashioned, 140
 or even enjoy, without, 397
 painting and music are destroyed or flourish, 282
 pictures and statues, find more
  in, 423
 power to recognize, 695
 prophecy and religion is to see
  clearly, 531
 prose run mad not, 213
 purest, 716
 record of happiest and best
  moments, 369
 refreshment of your inner life,
  572
 religious, relished by undevout,
  744
 should surprise by a fine excess, 385
 simple passionate and sensuous, 162
 teaches the enormous force of
  few words, 412
 tender charm of, 304
 that was, 508
 the breath and finer spirit of
  knowledge, 295

Poetry, the hand that wrings, 687
 the only ways I know it, 586
 their universal pastime and
  delight, 440
 thoughts over-poetical for, 484
 United States import print and
  read more, 539
 we may live without, 592
 who writes, 889
 why men read, 680
 wit eloquence and, 167
 written while out of health,
  745
 you speak as one who fed on,
  425
Poetry's immortality will pass,
  826
Poictiers, shrined with Cressy
  and, 518
Poignancy to pleasure, gives,
  1051
Poincarés and Ludendorffs, 907
Point a moral or adorn a tale,
  230
 at which it can remain, 1064
 don't put too fine a, 1043
 fine, of seldom pleasure, 107
 his slow unmoving finger at,
  103
 it blows from, shifting the,
  1021
 not to put too fine a, 497
 of a diamond, 1112
 of all my greatness, 73
 of death, at the, 80
 of his appointed sourse, 25
 of view of age and people, 645
 swim to yonder, 81
 thus I bore my, 62
 we know not where, 395
 where carping censors lurk,
  907
Points, arm'd at, exactly cap-
  a-pe, 90
 blows from diverse, 1021
 in the law, eleven, 193
 of gravest import, 644
 of heaven, kindred, 304
 of honour, nice fine, 680
 on trifling, 332
 out an hereafter, 195
 the meeting, 212
 true to the kindred, 304
Pointed pleasure, Lord thy most,
  703
Poise, keep an equal, 685
Poised and bland, nobly, 770
Poison and I suicided, I took
  cold, 755
 bathe before I drink the, 970
 for serpents, 993
 for the age's tooth, 57
 I could drink, know some, 916
 of misused wine, 157
 of sure sleep, 920
 one grain of plausibility is,
  476
 one man's, another's meat, 132
 ounce of, in one pocket, 399
 power is, 636
 steel nor, can touch him, 87
 to his mind and peril to his
  body, 401
 when he's strong, 828
Poisoned chalice, 85
 rat in a hole, like a, 191

Poisoning of a dart, 167
Poisonous dose, 226
 Nessus shirts, 378
Poison-weeds, the vilest deeds
  like, 722
Poke, drew a dial from his, 49
 pig in a, buying or selling of
  a, 18
Poky dull and dry, 812
Polack's brat, a, 841
Poland winter, will burn a, 36
Polar day, through the long, 552
Polaris, southward from, 795
Pole, behold each, 114
 from Indus to the, 216
 hear the latest, 900
 pleasure trip to the, 652
 to Cape Columbia, from the,
  719
 to pole, beloved from, 315
 to pole, truth from, 194
 were I so tall to reach the, 199
Poles, that wheel between the,
  471
Policeman Day, go back with,
  784
 with uplifted hand, 799
Policeman's lot is not a happy
  one, 623
Policemen stand and purr, 908
Policy, exercised over men becomes, 998
 hand to the best, 964
 honesty is the best, 1041
 is to relieve itself, nation's,
  1066
 kings will be tyrants from, 260
 of the good neighbor, 876
 sits above conscience, 81
 stratagems and, 1040
 turn him to any cause of, 66
Polish her until she glimmers,
  689
Polished dart, laughter winged
  his, 626
 female friend, 394, 942
 idleness, 290
 manners, 266
 razor, satire is like a, 221
 through act and speech, 572
Polisher, skill of the, 196
Polite, never mentions hell to
  ears, 210
Politeness, pine-apple of, 277
Politic cautious but a bit obtuse,
  900
Political and economic opportunists, 930
 and individual morality, 1083
 bands, dissolve the, 273
 campaigns, 768
 cave of Adullam, into his, 478
 community, the best, 975
 democracy training-school, 538
 education, 635
 fault, it is a, 1060
 instinct in America, 722
 institutions a superstructure,
  1086
 ointment, smeared with, 935
 subjects purely, 312
Politician, coffee makes the, wise,
  212
 not a, other habits good, 606
 proper memory for a, 641
 that would circumvent God, 96

Politicians, calculated by the ablest, 270
in and out of office, 798
one rule for, 798
whole race of, 191
Politician's pen, stroke of a, 604
Politics a struggle of forces, 636
absorbs, when, 794
and morality, treat apart, 641
conscience with, 279
deceit and self-deception in, 1086
makes strange bedfellows, 582
practical, 636
the damnedest in Kentucky, 675
the most important thing, 1075
the purification of, 601
to puns, slipped from, 405
Polity, the ideal, 974
Poll, just rubbed his old, 389
of newspaper editors, 860
talked like poor, 243
Pollertics like my religion, my, 606
Polluted flock, shun the, 897
Pollutes whate'er it touches, power, 368
Pollutions, sun passeth through, 112
Polygamy may well be held in dread, 360
Polysyllabic words, 319
Pomegranate from Browning, some, 427
Pomp, all his, without his force, 261
and circumstance, 102
and glory of this world, 73
and parade, 268
and pride, keep out, 710
blot out vain, 1012
candied tongue lick absurd, 94
dull, the life of kings, 546
give lettered, 442
of age, monumental, 302
of emperors ridiculous, 414
of power, 244
of writ, 591
of yesterday, all our, 780
rule, reign, what is, 70
sepulchred in such, 161
take physic, 99
to flight, puts all the, 216
worthless, of homage, 374
Pomps and vanity, 1127
Pompous in the grave, 145
not successful at being, 1082
phrase, 332
two-legged dogs, 458
Pond, mantle like a standing, 44
Ponds will be thought bottom-less, 515
Pondered weak and weary, while I, 460
Ponderous and marble jaws, 91
axes rung, no, 342
form was, and his step, 437
gate of the west, 663
stone recoils, 223
woe, though a, 190
Poniard behind his back, with a sharp, 726
Ponies, wretched blind pit, 816
Pons asinorum, 977

Ponsonby Perks fought, 701
Pontic sea, like to the, 103
Pontiffs with palmer kings, 396
Pony over the nose, hit a, 785
Poodles, as for the, 655
Pool, fringed, 583
from the hidden valley, 755
in Eden, every, 956
mantle of the standing, 99
Pool-green valleys, 848
Poop was beaten gold, 104
Poor a thing is man, how, 30
about your lands, any, 462
always ye have with you, 1118
and content is rich enough, 102
and often very lousy, 228
and rascally people, 181
and unhappy brains for drink-ing, 101
annals of the, 244
apt to be proud, 55
are all, rich and, 967
be our purse, though, 418
but honest, my friends were, 53
care of the, 1049
child, sometimes say, 556
Christ himself was, 124
complain, wherefore do the, 321
considereth the, 1104
creature small beer, 64
ever, makes them, 814
exchequer of the, 59
flannels of the, 911
folks as I, for such, 523
garments, 52
give the rest to the, 1024
give to the, 1123
God only can make us, 429
grind the faces of the, 1111
he is so, 1017
he lived among the throng, 910
he that considereth the, 1104
he that giveth unto the, 1109
he that hath pity upon the, 1107
he was, and she was rich, 510
hovels of the, 983
human asses, 700
human heart, and also my, 514
humanity, so packed with, 650
I rich they, 20
in health, such are the, 65
indeed, makes me, 102
infirm weak and despised, 98
knew no more that he was, 584
laws grind the, 250
lean lank face, in my, 455
little one-horse town, 615
lone woman, 64
love their country and be, who dare to, 217
make no new friends, 432
man has grudge against poor man, 959
man is deprived of it, 974
man laughs loudest of all, 452
man who craves more is, 990
men's cottages, princes' pal-aces, 44
must be wisely visited, 472
naked wretches, 98
of England an iron army, 827
old astronomers, 807

Poor or proud the dome. 432
pensioner, 201
people putting on style, 685
prophets apostles all, 124
proud Byron, sad as grave, 428
relieved the, 218
rich gifts wax, 93
richest was, and the poorest, 435
scandalous and, 184
shall never cease out of the land, 1099
splendid wings, 633
that found'st me, 252
that have not patience, 102
that lack ablution, 760
the human mind would be, how, 1079
the hungry, 619
though much they have, 20
to do him reverence, 83
Tom, heaven be thy aid, 375
Tom's a-cold, 99
too, for a bribe, 246
wants that pinch the, 267
weak palsy-stricken, 383
when I am, 311
who are capable of joy, 788
who show the, 937
woman, marry rich woman as, 483
Poorest lived in abundance, 435
man in his cottage, 435
Poor-house, over the hill to the, 678
thrilling glorious hours even in a, 515
Pop goes the weasel, 510
Pope hast thou dominion, 504
wants me out of his see, 611
Popery, never in danger of, 197
Popinjays or soot-smeared mum-bojumbos, 376
Poplar is gentle and tall, 732
pale, edged with, 161
Poplars showed the white of their leaves, 620
Poplar-trees, creep slowly past the, 899
Popp'd in between election and my hopes, 97
Poppies blow in Flanders fields, 820
grow in Flanders fields, though, 821
nod, where drowsy, 955
of Cathay, and drink the, 444
pleasures are like, 287
Poppy, blindly scattereth her, 145
nor mandragora, 102
Populace considered, whom the, 678
Roman, 438
Popular, aim to be, 319
applause, ignominy of, 707
noises, 166
Popularity is a crime, 183
It is glory's small change, 1069
Population, agricultural, bravest, 994
and wealth, than, 1072
hungry and squalid, 563
of world, 853
Populous city pent, long in, 154
Porcelain clay of humankind, 179

Porcelain of human clay, 360
Pore benighted 'eathen, 781
Pores of the ocean and shores, 366
Porlock, man from, 879
Porpentine, upon the fretful, 91
Porpoise, fat as a, 192
Porridge, breath to cool your, 1026, 1039
  nose into other men's, 1036
  receives comfort like cold, 32
Port after stormie seas, 24
  and hawser's tie no more returning, to, 537
  as meke as is a mayde, his, 5
  each estuary, each mast-fringed, 761
  for men, 237
  is near the bells I hear, 536
  o' heaven, I'll quit the, 765
  of all men's labours, 112
  pride in their, 250
  she knew, as if her, 806
  there came to, 670
Ports and happy havens, 59
  of slumber, keeps open, 65
  of the moon, 748
Portable climate, coal is a, 413
Portal, immortality's, 590
  opens to receive me, 290
  the outermost, 632
  we call death, whose, 436
Portals are alternate night and day, 1018
  close behind the outward-parting throng, 450
  of gold, unfolding those, 387
Portents of impending doom, 418
Porter and skittles, 551
  of my father's lodge, 584
Portholes, there were faces in the, 925
Portion, brief life is here our, 518, 1017
  he wales a, 284
  in this life, my, 162
  in us, no, 795
  of my early gleam, 573
  of that around me, I become, 353
  of the loveliness, 366
  of thyself the only gift, 525
  that best, of a good man's life, 295
  this is our, 966
Portions and parcels of the dreadful past, 463
  of eternity, 524
  of the soul of man, 524
Portius, thy steady temper, 194
Portly presence of potentates, 832
Porto-Bello lying, as near, 240
  off to capture, 604
Portrait a kind of biography, 589
  lifelike, 649
  man sitting for a, 818
  of Mary A., 751
  painting more than the model's face, 611
  satisfied with a, 1057
Portraits lumbering in the dark, 292
Portugal, like bay of, 51
Poseidon laughed, 784
Posies, buy my English, 778

Posies, dear old-fashioned, 569
  none of all my, 784
  thousand fragrant, 31
Position of unquestioned ascendancy, 1072
Positions and order, shapes and sizes, 970
Positive truth, this I set down as, 482
Positivist, he was man and a, 569
Positivists, truth be sought with, the, 570
Possess a poet's brain, 30
  but one idea, he seems to, 235
  opinions and a will, men who, 522
  your soul with patience, 175
Possessed by their money, 123
  first I have, 355
  with inward light, 317
Possessing all things, 316
  too dear for my, 108
Possession always cheapens, 629
  bliss in, 306
  bonds in your, 235
  fie on, 8
  housed where it gets, 38
  is eleven points, 193, 977
  man's best, 968
  object in, 254
  of the valuable by the valiant, 533
  of whom is as precious, 1087
  preoccupation with, 821
  the grave of bliss, 772
  was the strongest, 977
  would not show, virtue that, 39
Possessions, enters into the, 1072
  give of your, 879
Possest, that once my soul, 619
Possibilities, pounds and, 34
Possibility, a man without passion, 1073
  bounds of, 1037
  can shatter us, even a, 1082
Possible and proper, things, 1011
  self-inexhausting, 627
  that so short a time, 76
  with steadfast trust, the, 1058
  worlds, best of all, 1052
  yes it is, 1090
Possum or a coona, catch a, 951
Post, answered by return of, 700
  evil news rides, 157
  near the winning, 962
  o'er land and ocean, 162
  of honour is a private station, 195, 206
  of the plot may make light, 578
Postage stamps, pasted a sheet of, 775
Posteriors of this day, 41
Posterity can hardly trace, 398
  contemporaneous, 227
  do something for us, 197
  done for us, what has, 277
  gentlemen who reach, 419
  intimately known to, 398
  is a most limited assembly, 419
  look forward to, 260
  obligation to, 277
  of the work of art, 1086
  of those yet unborn, 196
  owe it to our, 949

Posterity shall sway, thy, 263
  think of your, 291
  to imitate, 949
  we are a kind of, 227
  what artists call, 1086
  what, will say, 227
  will give a man a fair hearing, 614
Postern of a needle's eye, 60
Posthumous fame, 614
Posting winds, rides on the, 105
Post-mortem kindness, 578
Post-office, inscription on New York, 969
Postponed me twa year, 11
Postscripts let out the real objects, 347
Posture that we give the dead, 279
Posy, I pluck a, 492
Pot, boil like a, 1103
  calls the kettle black, 1041
  chicken in every, 427
  death in the, 1101
  every thirst to the, 137
  have his hen in the, 588
  little, soon hot, 52, 436
  of ale and safety, 66
  or pan, left a, 850
  thorns under a, 1109
  three-hooped, 69
  with a cot in a park, 673
  you may all go to, 254
Pots and pipkins, lord of the, 918
  of ale, size of, 141
  the luckless, 1019
Potations, forswear thin, 65
  pottle-deep, 101
Potato, bake him like a sweet, 853
Potatoes, don't forget the, 551
  small and few in a hill, 786
  small, we all are, 582
  they grow small, 952
Potency, promise and, 543
Potent grave and reverend signiors, 100
  over sun and star, 303
  planet Mars, of the, 586
Potentates, portly presence of, 832
Potentiality of growing rich, 237
Potion, refused to drink the, 948
Potomac, all quiet along the, 569
Potomac's jewelled stream, 848
Pottage, breath to cool his, 1004
Potter is jealous of potter, 206
  power over the clay, 1119
Potter's field, to bury strangers in, 1116
Pottle-deep, potations, 101
Pouch, little silver in his, 426
  on side, 50
  with hoarded seed was packed, 596
Poultice comes, silence like a, 451
Pouncet-box 'twixt his finger, 61
Pound foolish penny wise, 122
  had I a golden, 912
  of your owne fleshe, 256
Pounds, annual income twenty, 496
  does the baby weigh, how many, 569
  rich with forty, 250

Pounds, seven hundred, and possibilities, 34
take care of themselves, 222
three hundred, a year, 34
two hundred, a year, 143
Pour forth the cheering wine, 404
of that terrible, 815
Pouter tumbler and fantail are
from, 448
Poverty, and be reduced to, 1127
by preventing, 1020
degradation of man by, 1067
depressed, worth by, 231
famished and gaunt, 873
from affluence to, 615
I pay thy, not thy will, 80
in praise of, 714
is no sin, 138
is the parent, 975
is the soft pedal, 862
iz step-mother ov genius, 518
most deadly and prevalent of
diseases, 902
not my will consents, 80
of his chimes, 415
of meanness and viciousness,
973
or of wealth, influence of, 973
parts good company, 311
pride and, 184
put back through, 970
rustic life and, 327
state of ambitious, 1006
steeped me in, 103
the mother of manhood, 994
will increase, their, 1077
Powder, food for, 63
is running low, when your, 765
keep your, dry, 329
Powdered with stars, 154
Power, a witty beauty is a, 576
above the state, no, 1083
alas naught but misery, 388
alone he dares disown, 648
and beauty and delight, 934
and beauty of the minstrel's
lyre, 816
and effect of love, 125
and energy, 259
and goodness, wisdom, 362
and influence, 235
and its minions, 329
and pelf, 307
and publicity, effect of, 635
balance of, 200
beauty hath strange, 157
behind the eye, 413
behind the throne, 230
belief in a beneficent, 651
blossoms have the mightiest,
516
but his attribute, 617
cohesive, of public plunder,
339
community of, 725
daughter of Jove relentless,
243
day of thy, 1105
divine, an easy thing O, 554
divine that saved his song, 756
dotted over the surface of the
whole globe, 311
early days of his, 974
earthly, show likest God's, 46
fame is the breath of, 728
force of temporal, 46

Power, friend in, 635
genius hath electric, 404
gentle peace assert her, 364
great, make me always think,
564
greater than the people, 339
greatest not exempted from
her, 22
he wields the, 706
heaven upon the past has not,
177
human, which could evade, 357
I scorn the, 402
I trust the, 820
in a spoken word, 727
in excess, desire of, 110
in men to be silent, 1048
in the air, 709
in the hands of friends, 636
in trust, an empire is no more
than, 173
individualize infinite, 549
is a trust, all, 420
is passing from the earth, 301
is poison, 636
knowledge is, 111
lay down the wreck of, 374
like a desolating pestilence,
368
love greater than his, 617
man's will to, 1081
manufacturing, 1067
monuments of, 110
mortality o'ersways their, 107
most serious of facts, 636
must fail and pride must fall,
561
my uttermost, 66
not now in fortune's, 142
o' faith in gert to-morrows,
765
objects wholly out of their
own, 318
o'er true virginity, 158
of art, 235
of beauty I remember, the, 176
of every man, 1049
of gentleness, 491
of grace, 327
of no calamity, in the, 1080
of public plunder, cohesive,
339
of taking delight, 800
of the law, enfeebles the, 975
of the people, 1070
of the press, 532
oratory of, 1081
pain's resistless, 522
passing mine, 491
peculiar, 337
placed in our, 270
pomp of, 244
possesses genuine, 318
rather than use, 53
rob the soul of, 864
seeds of godlike, are in us,
545
shadow of some unseen, 365
should take who have the, they,
298
so by Thy, 957
sun returned to, 937
sweetening and transfiguring,
1081
talent in a man's, 529
that dazzles mortal eyes, 731

Power that fills the world with
terror, 434
that hath made and preserved
us a nation, 332
the giftie gie us, wad some, 285
the less confided, 412
the rich have, 974
they take who have the, 298
to acquire that sense, 1053
to be guided not extinguished,
542
to charm insanity, 413
to charm, nor witch hath, 89
to command obedience, 975
to drink or rise, without, 348
to grow, 809
to keep frae being sour, 284
to know all things, 114
to live and act and serve, 305
to love, lose the, 502
to outsoar, 634
to poison sleep, 368
to prove, I've tried its, 448
to recognize true poetry, 695
to say behold, 42
to thunder, flatter Jove for his,
76
to will, work or lose the, 502
to wound, her very shoe has,
240
tragic effects of, 636
tyrant, 396
united world has no, 1051
untold, with love and, 501
upon the past, heaven has not,
177
was given, to whom the, 814
we give another to torment us,
425
we rise how full of, 441
whence has come thy lasting,
640
which erring men call chance,
158
who have the most, 173
within no man's, 990
Powers, the Allied, having proclaimed, 1061
fear of divine and supreme,
126
grief that develops the, 1087
mould of vaster, 670
ne'er be equal, 470
of combination, parsimony requires no, 261
of darkness, I saw the, 760
of the mind, greatest, are displayed, 323
plow deep and straight with all
your, 417
reasonably full exertion of
their, 422
sphere of human, 236
struggle of discordant, 260
superior to man, 713
supreme, keep men in obedience, 126
that be, 1119
that be, o'er lesser, 534
that will work for thee, 297
thou hast left behind, 297
we lay waste our, 300
which impress our minds, 295
wise, deny us for our good, 104
Power's employ, in some unknown, 547

Powerful agent is the right word, 615
  as truth, nothing so, 342
  grace that lies in herbs, 78
Practical force, the mightiest, 678
  people, for, 895
  politics ignore facts, 636
Practice is everything, 1013
  is the best instructor, 988
  made good, 747
  of all physicians, beyond the, 450
  success in, 650
Practices, induced by public, 998
  long train of these, 230
Practise in little things, 1007
  to deceive, 308
  what we preach, 788
  what you preach, 591
Practising so different from preaching, 509
Practitioner in panegyric, 278
Prague, beautiful city of, 625
  old hermit of, 56
Prairie Bell, in the smoke of the, 605
  boundless ineffable, 590
  child of the boundless, 642
  died on the, 856
  flowers lie low, 856
  frosty, 565
  I have loved the, 854
  mother, I, 854
  we cross the, 442
Prairies, gardens of the desert, 372
  like seas, 504
  of our wide waste land, 856
Prairie's midst, she lights her fires in every, 517
Prairie-lawyer, master of us all, 857
Praise, all his pleasure, 201
  and favor, render, 428
  and true perfection, 47
  at large, minister of, 248
  beat high for, 334
  best of fame, a rival's, 337
  blame love kisses, 299
  censure or, 232
  come to bury Caesar not to, 83
  companions speak their, 931
  damn with faint, 213
  dispraised no small, 156
  efforts of race due to love of, 532
  Father Son and Holy Ghost, 183
  filled with a nation's, 649
  for the sure-enwinding arms, 536
  from a friend, 219
  from Sir Hubert Stanley, 290
  garment of, 1112
  God from whom all blessings flow, 183
  God sang Theocrite, 487
  Him all creatures here below, 183
  how he receives, 991
  I 'll sing thee a song in thy, 286
  if there be any, 1121

Praise, love of, howe'er concealed, 202
  more than this rich, 108
  none named thee but to, 363
  O save this, 756
  of a picture, 611
  of ancient authors, 132
  of poverty, in, 714
  of those about to marry, 1015
  of those who sleep in earth, 373
  only to be praised, we, 1044
  ourselves, however we do, 54
  owes its value to scarcity, 232
  poets lose half the, 146
  pudding against empty, 215
  rest a little from, 631
  silence muse His, 224
  skies were purple and breath was, 395
  slays its victim, 593
  sound of woman's, 401
  splendor of love's, 894
  that father should have had, 873
  that I can raise, all the, 135
  the Frenchman, I, 263
  thirst of, 262
  unanimous chorus of, 1086
  whom there were none to, 296
  wood-world one full peal of, 470
  would be unmeaning flattery, 351
Praises faintly when he must, 213
  not the last of, 985
  of your deeds, singing the, 981
  said, what, 887
  shall be sung, his, 1027
  sound of one's, 1005
  wait deserved, 679
  which remorseful mourners give, 596
Praised be the fathomless universe, 536
Praising God with sweetest looks, 390
  man when he is dead, 959
  most dispraises, 213
  the rose that all are, 388
  what is lost makes the remembrance dear, 53
Prate, hear him, 575
  of my whereabout, stones, 85
Praties they are small, 952
Prattle, fashionable, 656
  to be tedious, thinking his, 60
Pray, doth late and early, 114
  for no man but myself, I, 80
  for peace and grace and spiritual food, 551
  for powers equal to your tasks, 613
  for wisdom, 582
  I scarcely dare to, 591
  remained to, 251
  that our armies join not, 64
  that this mighty scourge, 457
  the Lord my soul to keep, 947
  two went to, 165
  we do, for mercy, 46
  with you drink with you nor, 44
  work not can not, 501
Prayer all his business, 201
  at least, this, 858

Prayer at the moment of greatest suffering, 476
  be not forgetful of, 1074
  be this a, 512
  breathe to God a, 517
  do not aid me, if, 1021
  doth teach us all, 47
  effectual fervent, 1122
  erects a house of, 187
  every, reduces itself, 1072
  folds my hands in, 1091
  for all who lie beneath, 782
  for him, breathes a, 405
  for others' weal, fondest, 351
  four hours spend in, 21
  grant me my, 1084
  have steeped their souls in, 459
  heaven sometimes grants before the, 175
  homes of silent, 468
  I have no words to say, 896
  I make this, 935
  imperfect offices of, 302
  is an education, 1074
  is sincere, if your, 1074
  is the burden of a, 306
  is the soul's sincere desire, 306
  more things are wrought by, 463
  muezzin's call for, 755
  need of, 364
  of Ajax was for light, 434
  of devotion, the still, 336
  of Plato, 442
  of thanks, our, 854
  people's, the, 173
  pray thy, 473
  shrine where a sin is a, 632
  some daily good to do, my, 549
  that reforms the sinner, 548
  that Thou wilt keep the United States, 268
  the Easterners do, pray the, 952
  the heartier, 1052
  the impulse to a worldless, 665
  to Raphael, proper for us travellers, 490
  way he makes his, 878
  when we breathe our evening, 502
  which my mouth, 441
  who are negligent at their, 1127
  will somewhat vary, 860
  wish is like a, with God, 430
Prayers, feed on, 28
  for death, old men's, 967
  God answers sudden on some, 430
  in absence breathed, 395
  knelt down with angry, 816
  losing of our, 104
  making mention of thee in my, 1122
  of the church, 192
  which are old age's alms, 28
  without words, 607
  would make me whole, 784
Prayer-books are the toys of age, 208
Prayeth best who loveth best, 315
  well who loveth well, 315
Praying and sighing through London streets, 683
  be brief in, 134

Preach a whole year, if I, 276
  humility is a virtue all, 130
Preached as never to preach
  again, 166
Preacher I have been, a dying,
  948
  in that little band, 834
  still I am, 948
Preachers, itinerant, 228
  jangle, the, 759
Preaches it, Luther, 414
  wife who, in her gown, 392
Preaching a by-word for long and
  dull conversation, 312
  a woman, 234
  practising so different from,
  509
Precarious things, dinners were,
  323
Precautions, take your necessary,
  1126
Precede, lead the way we'll, 278
Precedence among women, no,
  974
Precedent, codeless myriad of,
  465
  embalms a principle, 419
  for poor men's facts, 28
  hereafter become a, 999
  is a king of men, 634
  one, creates another, 949
  performance without, 1055
  well-established, 733
Precedents are entitled to great
  weight, 329
  day supported by, 999
Precedes, consider what, 1008
Precept, example more efficacious,
  232
  example the best, 962
  forgot each, 1050
  upon precept, 1111
Precepts of the Gospel, 188
Precincts few extol, silver, 889
  of the cheerful day, 245
Precious as the truths she reveals, 1087
  bane, deserve the, 149
  ever-lingering memories, 538
  friend, speaks to a, 716
  gain that he forgets himself,
  299
  in the sight of the Lord, 1105
  jewel carved, 672
  jewel in his head, wears a, 48
  life is, so, 620
  life-blood of a master-spirit,
  163
  mouldering pleasure, 584
  mystic sense, given a, 1074
  nose, that's his, 391
  odours, virtue is like, 109
  ointment, better than, 1109
  ointment, like a, 110
  one half so, 1019
  seeing to the eye, it adds a, 41
  so, that it must be rationed,
  1086
  soul, damn your, 1026
  stone, a gift is as a, 1107
  stone, this, 59
  thing that was, 629
  things in the world of nature,
  741
  tissue, like a, 1078
  treasure of his eyesight, 77

Precious, truth is, 142
  unto one, but is, 596
  what to Rome is most, 593
  words, ate and drank the, 584
Preciousness of the laws and liberties, 500
Precise and pedantic their step,
  637
  art is too, 133
  in promise-keeping, 35
  moment friendship formed, 272
Precocity, miracle of, 993
  price for, 476
Predatory human hands, 741
Predecessors, illustrious, 230, 259
Predestined, intimates are, 635
  of the will, 840
Predilection and love, land between, 651
Predominant feature in the British fleet, 284
Pre-eminence in Germany, indication of, 906
Prees, greet, at market, 7
Preface to make it welcome, 311
Preferable to all the pleasures of
  youth, 198
Preference the newest, in science
  read by, 426
Preferment goes by letter, 100
  passage to riches and, 950
Pregnant hinges of the knee, 94
  in matter in expression brief,
  332
Prejudice, common, 235
  I ran against a, 754
  pretension is a great, 1078
Prejudices, all, may be traced,
  1082
  man without any, 1078
  which cleave to the heart, 197
Prelate Dr. Donne, that worthy,
  878
  religion without a, 394
Prelates, princes and, 831
Preludes, succession of, 1064
  transmit the, 900
Premier pas qui coûte, 1053
'Prentice han' she tried on man,
  284
Preoccupation with possession,
  821
Preordained from everlasting,
  1012
Preparation, dreadful note of, 67
  I make, 508
Prepare to shed tears, 83
Prepared, fatal to those who are,
  994
Preparedness he implores, 848
Preposition is a word, 872
Prerogative, books part of man's,
  128
  of mind, the grand, 344
Presage of his future years, 269
  uninitiate by many a, 610
Presbyterian true blue, 142
Prescription to be taken for life,
  final, 498
Presence bright, whose, 1057
  depart her, 257
  either human or divine, 683
  equal to forty thousand men,
  293
  full of light, 80
  haunts this room, his, 439

Presence, how we come into this,
  684
  in minds made better by their,
  520
  in the house, 474
  lift us to thy, 1128
  lord of thy, and no land beside, 57
  maiden, scanter of your, 91
  makes itself felt, 684
  my, doth trouble ye, 68
  of a benignant Spirit, 659
  of body, 324
  of mind, 979
  of mind in danger, 1048
  of the love it would conceal,
  317
  of the passenjare, 583
  sense of a personal, 683
  spent in Thy, 441
  to depart her, 257
  whose, civilizes ours, 263
  whose wings darken, 670
  with that translucid, 897
Present, Clotho, singing of the,
  974
  desponding view of the, 400
  help in trouble, 1104
  in spirit, absent in body, 1120
  is all thou hast, the, 441
  is eternity, 684
  is mere grass, 680
  joys therein I find, 20
  live in the, 684
  moment least happiest, 494
  of theirs with the hopeful past,
  487
  only, 'tis not the, 537
  or accounted for, 550
  past at the expense of the, 314
  seldom in the, 1083
  sober twilight of the, 644
  the great eventful, 443
  things seem worst, 64
  thou, to my mind, 393
  time travel that of old, 128
  we have never conquered, 883
  well, employ the, 217
  wisely improve the, 440
  work of present man, 316
  wrong the eternal right,
  through, 442
Presents a silver lining, 812
  and rejoicings, 495
  endear absents, 323
  goes for bets, it goes for, 510
  if it were not for, 791
  to posterity, 196
Presentation copy, 324
Presentment, counterfeit, 95
Preservation, except for its own,
  1051
  magic, 381
  of peace, my, 20
  of the wild and vagrant, 589
Preservative, a hare's foot my,
  181
  of all arts, 943
Preserves us a nation, made and,
  404
President, duties of, 638
  ever expected me to be, 455
  holds the rein, 686
  if you are, 853
  Lincoln, you are underrating,
  580

President now Jenny Lind now Emerson, I'm, 490
of the immortals, 651
rather be right than, 329
Presidents, effect of power on, 636
President's chair, sleep in, 951
Press, clamors of a venal, 478
down upon the brow of labor, 753
freedom of the, 273
is too much with us, 650
king over all is the, 783
liberty of the, 949
not a falling man too far, 73
shall vigorously aid, 661
the fourth estate, the, 483
the people's right maintain, 333
voice of the, 479
what is the, 305
where ye see my white plume, 400
with vigour on, 225
Press's freedom, believe in the gret, 526
Pressed clover leaves, stains of, 854
Pressure from the Incommunicable, 347
his form and, 94
of age, 973
of great events, 1062
of taxation, 314
when you get on too much, 661
Prest with ill, 263
Presto pass your joys are withered, 406
Presume not God to scan, 207
Presumptuous folly, 644
Pretence, approach to a false, 599
Pretender, God bless the, 221
Pretension itself is a great prejudice, 1078
Pretty chickens, all my, 88
creature drink, 298
everything that, is, 105
Fanny's way, 201
feet like snails, 134
how-de-do, 624
it's, but is it Art, 780
kettle of fish, 623
looks, puts on his, 58
mottoes. I write the, 622
page with dimpled chin, 481
Sally, there's none like, 189
state of things, 624
the moon looks tonight, how, 350
to walk with, 164
words that make no sense, 429
Preudunt course is steadied, my, 526
Prevail, oars alone can ne'er, 264
or not, none cares whether it, 556
truth is great and shall, 556
Prevailin' weakness of public men, 606
Prevailing sadness, 327
Prevalence of suicide, 741
Prevaricate, thou dost, 142
Prevention, used as much for, 924
Prey at fortune, 102
expects his evening, 244

Prey, fleas that on him, 190
or become a prey, 941
the destined, 720
to dumb forgetfulness, a, 245
to every bird, 578
to hastening ills, a, 250
unresisting, 349
where eagles dare not perch, wrens make, 71, 212
Priam's curtain, drew down, 63
powers and self shall fall, 218
Price, all men have their, 200
at such a, 976
buy at too dear a, 229
every man has his, 425
for knowledge, too high the, 205
for precocity, 476
is cruel high, 786
love that pays the, 747
name will insure a good, 255
of admiralty, 778
of chains and slavery, 270
of liberty, 277
of wisdom is above rubies, 1102
pearl of great, 422, 1115
sell at low, 235
set her own, 556
to five, gave the, 754
we pay, great, 574
will fall, if you stay a little, 110
Priceless gift, given for nought her, 556
rending of the heart, 1088
Prick the sides of my intent, 85
Pricks, kick against the, 1118
me on, honour, 63
Pricking of my thumbs, 87
on the plaine, 24
Prickles, tormenting himself with his, 391
Prickly star, pity the, 898
Pride alone, stands in his, 446
and haughtiness of soul, 194
and humiliation, 436
and poverty, oppressed with, 184
avarice envy, 1020
carries its banner to the last, 591
coy submission modest, 152
crueltie and ambition of man, 22
envy malice are his graces, 326
father's joy mother's, 309
fell with my fortunes, 48
goeth before, 14, 29
goeth before destruction, 1107
has been wounded, 1080
her fit historic, 952
high-blown, broke under me, 73
humble out of, 1029
I thought with, 890
idleness and, 227
imperious, 591
in Casey's bearing, 770
in reasoning, 209
in their port, 250
is an established conviction, 1064
is his own glass, 75
is suffering, her, 747
is therefore pleasure, 1048

Pride, man's, 1081
must fall and power must fail, 561
need to doff his, 777
nursing at home in lonely, 531
of ancestry increases in ratio ot distance, 558
of ancestry, without, 260
of birth, the queerest one is, 510
of former days, 334
of Greece and Rome, 408
of kings, 206
of labor poem of sacrifice, 1090
of place, towering in her, 86
of the father, 889
of thought, 789
peasantry their country's, 250
plastered high with, 824
pomp and circumstance, 102
rank pride, 't is, 194
soldier's, 487
spite of, 207
that apes humility, 316, 321
that licks the dust, 213
that must be yours, solemn, 457
that perished in his, 297
that putts this countrye downe, 256
the vice of fools, 210
they are England's, 778
to relieve the wretched, 250
truths opposed to human, 396
vain was the chief's the sage's, 214, 282
were not also, as if true, 493
when puffed up, 965
who strut in, 700
will have a fall, 14
withered in their, 484
works from within, 1064
works of mortal, 212
Priest and the Quaker and all who died, 558
consecrates the heartburnings, 1072
for enemy good bye to peace, 423
hearing the holy, 26
I would not go to hear the, 170
of the most authentic creed, 602
old, and an old soldier, 1068
Priests altars victims, 216
by the imposition of a mightier hand, 397
in the temple of Solomon, 418
is queer people, 306
tapers temples, 216
Priestess of night's high mysteries, 418
Priesthood, literary men a perpetual, 376
Priestlike, moving waters at their, task, 385
Priestly tract and sentimental stage, 881
vestments, 731
Prigs, manufacture, 707
Primal curse, inherit the, 890
eldest curse, 95
gloom, back to the, 682
Prime, Adam saw her, 328

Prime, April of her, 107
conception of the joyous, 24
give him always of the, 191
golden, of Haroun Alraschid,
462
of body and soul, 375
of life, what is the, 973
of the day, confident, 735
so swell so nutty, so, 361
taste the morning, 692
to the next, 164
voice obeyed at, 410
wisdom, 154
Primer, school master with his,
331
Primeval forests, before even the
grand, 627
forests could boast the promise
of a bud, 627
this is the forest, 435
Primitive music and medicine and
literature, 805
Primrose, bring the rathe, 159
by a river's brim, 296
first-born child of Ver, 132
path of dalliance treads, 90
peeps beneath the thorn, 251
sweet as the, 251
way, go the, 86
way, we have come the, 702
yellow, was to him, 296
Prince, advise the, 900
and a great man fallen this
day, 1100
duty subject owes, 52
make a belted knight, 287
must be a lion, 998
of darkness, 99, 164
of fiends, like to the, 66
of peace, the everlasting father,
the, 1111
of Wales, better known as the,
921
of Wales, God bless the, 392
or prelate, there is no, 911
or rich person hath not, 166
war the only study of a, 258
Princes and lords may flourish,
250
and nobles to patronize literature, 476
and prelates, 831
are the breath of kings, 284
find few real friends, 239
gilded monuments of, 107
like to heavenly bodies, 110
of courtesy, 765
prefers the service of, 977
privileged to kill, 268
put not your trust in, 1106
that sweet aspect of, 73
Prince's court, search in every,
499
Princes' bastards, 124
favours, hangs on, 73
palaces, 128
service of, 977
Princedoms virtues powers, 153
Princely in bestowing, 74
in both valour and kindness,
67
Princeps copy in blue and gold,
288
Princerples, I don't believe in,
526
nor men, it ain't by, 526

Princess, heaven-wander'd, 867
him that beds a, 933
inscribe beneath my name, 882
Principal beauty in a building,
147
duty a parent owed a child,
505
thing, wisdom is the, 1106
Principality in Utopia, better
than a, 398
Principle, clear legal, 331
counteract the living, 1061
first human, 65
free trade is not a, 419
general, gives no help, 1062
inconsistencies in, 650
is old but true as fate, 116
of beauty, 385, 826
of bliss, the vital, 225
of socialism, 1093
on a religious, 247
precedent embalms a, 419
rebels from, 260
Principles, affects to renounce
his, 950
controlled by right, 572
deduced from it, 1062
from which it sprung, 1071
ideas called settled, 571
may be flexible, 457
never defeated, our, 424
of eternal justice, 477
of nature, 1012
of resistance, 259
oftener changed, their, 203
search men's, 1010
that gave birth and happiness
and peace, 725
the most dangerous, 950
to which I am recreant, 479
turn with times, 209
we might our, swaller, 526
Print, all that I own is a, 490
before plain press, 507
decomposing in the eternity of,
878
I love a ballad in, 57
if you see it in, 883
it and shame the fools, 212
it, some said John, 171
of a man's naked foot on the
shore, 187
to see one's name in, 351
transforms old, 265
unless it is in, 1031
Printed in a book, words, 1102
matter, diffusion of, 1077
record, the colorless photography of, 686
Printer instead of laundress, sent
to, 906
Printers have lost, books by
which, 147
Printing, had invented the art of,
379
invention of, 1089
to be used, caused, 69
Printing-office, father's, 629
Printing-press born of mother
earth, 804
halo of immortality encircled,
291
I am the, 805
song of the, 804
Prior, here lies Matthew, 189
Prism and silent face, 299

Prison, bursts its, 889
door of his, 970
from this, my hard, 20
palace and a, 353
self is the only, 710
stone walls do not a, make, 168
the black flower of society, 421
walls cannot control, 1051
Prisons, masters have wrought in,
848
neither convict, 1074
Prison-air, bloom well in, 722
Prison'd soul, take the, 158
Prisoner at the bar, himself the,
465
man is a, 970
no weak-eyed, 878
takes the reason, 84
to be, well pleased a, 1051
Prisoners call the sky, 722
of hope, 1114
Prisoner's life, passing on the, 35
Prison-mate and dock-yard fellow, 604
Pristine glory, 396
Prithee why so pale, 163
Privacy, an obscure nook, a, 484
I got, for all the, 812
let there be an end, a, 484
of storm, 408
Private, a drunken, 474
and costly luxury, 636
beneficence inadequate, 750
conscience for the guide, 174
credit is wealth, 950
end, who served no, 210
ends, to gain some, 254
griefs they have, 83
information source of modern
fortune, 724
property, 638
station, post of honour is a,
195
thinking, above the fog in
public duty and in, 522
under Fairfax, 779
Privee and apert, 7
Privilege of absurdity, the, 132
of being independent, 285
of fools, the, 1050
of putting him to death, 314
of the heroes of yore, 343
sight highest bodily, 312
will occupy a lesser place, 877
Privileges of the government, 455
share property and, 1074
Privileged ones, infinitely, 891
to kill, princes were, 268
Prize, art not strength obtains
the, 219
be a ribbon or throne, 510
ever grateful for the, 294
judge the, 160
light, too light winning make
the, 32
not to the worth whiles we enjoy, 39
o' death in battle, 527
of the high calling of God,
1121
of verse, 438
strips of all its worth the, 309
the thing ungained, men, 74
the vanquished gain, 437
to love the game above the,
764

Prize to some proud fop should fall, 226
  valor's second, 995
  we sought is won, the, 536
Prizes, prize me no, 946
Probabilities, between conflicting vague, 449
  fate laughs at, 426
Probability, keep in view, 206
  only a, 376
Probable nor'-east to sou'-west winds, 617
Probe my heart with pensive gaze, 760
Problem flowered from a dream, 823
  of the head into moral question, 775
  the common, 488
Problems, three, of the age, 1067
Proceed ad infinitum, 190
Proceeding, my infallible, 590
Proceedings interested him no more, 645
Proces of nature, it is agayns, 8
Process, cosmic, 667
  evolution is a, 641
  human thought is the, 339
  of sex, 739
  of the suns, 464
  which serves, 490
Procession goes by, when a, 1041
  out of stellar spaces, 874
  stay with the, 791
Proclaims the man, apparel oft, 91
Procrastination art of keeping up, 852
  is the thief of time, 201
Procreant cradle, 85
Proctors, prudes for, 466
Procurer of contentedness, 139
Procuress to the lords of hell, 468
Prodigal, chariest maid is, 90
  confiding, 585
  of life, 330
  the soul lends the tongue vows, 91
Prodigality of nature, framed in, 71
Prodigious ruin, one, 218
Produce, carry away the, 958
  its hundredfold, catch and, 476
Product, its special and essential, 1072
  of the horse, 491
Production, capitalist, 1072
  excessive literary, 520
Profanation of our joys, 'twere, 118
Profane, hence ye, 168
  no divine ordinances, 251
  swearing sufficient crime to dismiss any laborer, 180
  things, 172
  to pity him were, 753
Profanely, not to speak it, 94
Profession, a barrister's, 1076
  Adam's, 96
  debtor to his, 109
  of law, 1070
  of the truth, 1077

Profession, ornament to his, 109
Professions, the most dangerous of, 641
  two oldest, in the world, 897
Professional military mind inferior, 795
Professor can never better distinguish himself, 1054
  Heaven keep the great, 453
  of our art, 177
  of the art of puffing, 278
Professors, respectable, of the dismal science, 379
Proffered treaty, I scorn your, 447
Profferer construe Ay, 33
Proficient poison, when the, 920
Profit and convenience, 1051
  and title I resign, 206
  countenance and, 109
  no, where is no pleasure, 52
  nor pleasure, opposeth no man's, 132
  of their shining nights, 40
  so find we, 104
  without, 60
Profits, calculating, 429
Profited, what is a man, 1115
Profiteering in the dead, 908
Prof'tible cherishin', 606
Profitless others and stale and flat, 794
Profligate of happiness, 811
Profound as the grave, 636
  makes it more, 688
  than mine own life, more, 76
Profoundest of slumbers, 247
Profusion of days, bestow such a, 247
  of water light and air, 602
Progeny of learning, 277
Prognosticators, the monthly, 1112
Programme has been gone through, 674
Programs, between air, 852
Progress and poverty, in writing, 684
  based on desire to live beyond income, 614
  calls each fresh link, 655
  discontent first step in, 724
  do to swell a, 900
  from want to want, 236
  is at stand, 674
  is, realize what, 1068
  long-continued slow, 449
  man's distinctive mark alone, 489
  morn begins her rosy, 155
  much more general than retrogression, 448
  of the consciousness, 1062
  summer's royal, 833
  their mazy, 243
  war involves in its, 271
Progressive renunciation, 1073
Prohibition, against self-slaughter there is a, 105
  root of all our woe, 155
  tree of, 154
Project failed, or any, 732
Projects, multitude of, 988
  tossed eager, 767
  young men fitter for new, 111
Proletariat, definition of, 1072

Proletariat is a really revolutionary class, 1072
  is its special product, 1072
Prologue, excuse came, 155
  foolish to make a long, 1125
  is the grace, 200
Promethean fire, 41
  heat, where is that, 103
  word, 634
Prometheus back, nor brings, 983
Promiscuous oration, 499
Promiscuously applied hands, 355
Promise and potency of terrestrial life, 543
  dwells, 955
  given under seal, 1085
  keep the word of, 89
  let us keep our, 487
  life's bright, 373
  most given when least said, 29
  never, more than you can perform, 988
  not a bound, skyline is a, 834
  of my years, where is the, 618
  of pneumatic bliss, 900
  of supply, eating the air on, 64
  of your early day, 342
  that if we but wait, 625
  to come for I said, 388
  to his loss, though he, 185
  to seek out the interests, 1086
  who broke no, 210
Promises of youth, 232
  oft fails where most it, 53
  one makes, keep the, 1079
  to keep, but I have, 839
  to make positive, 912
  to pay, keep or break our, 348
Promised land other side of wilderness, 741
  on a time, 26
Promise-keeping, precise in, 35
Promontory, earth seems a sterile, 92
  see one, see all, 124
  stands upon a, 70
  with trees upon 't, 105
Promoter of mutual acquaintance, 608
Promotion cometh neither from the east nor west, 1105
  none will sweat but for, 48
Prompters, how many, 326
Prompter's bell, slow falling to the, 481
  hand is on his bell, 644
Prompting of nature, 993
Prompts the eternal sigh, which, 208
Pronounce, foreigners spell better than they, 615
  it Vinchy, 615
Pronouncing on his bad, before, 376
Pronouns, wise in the use of his, 640
Proof, give me ocular, 102
  of a poet, the, 539
  of genius, a great poem is, 397
  of greatness, 745
  of love and power, 539
  of man's own littleness, 380
  of the pudding, 1037

Proof of thus and so, 696
  putting off the, 839
  the first, 786
  'tis a common, 82
  to all the world, 954
Proofs, how I would correct the, 369
  of holy writ, 102
Proosian, a French or Turk or, 623
Prop, staff of my age my very, 45
  that doth sustain my house, 47
  to save it from sneers, 510
Propaganda and advertising, devotion to, 824
  furious, 856
Propagate and rot, 208
Propagation, pictures all our, 117
Propensities, excite my amorous, 233
  ruined by natural, 261
Propensity for emulation, 730
  of nature, 162
  to forego, 662
  to get ourselves noticed, 663
Proper age of my life for pleasure, 182
  man as one shall see, 42
  mean, the, 1053
  men and tall, 738
  men as ever trod, 81
  stations, know our, 495
  study of man is himself, 803
  study of mankind is man, 207
  time of day, no, 391
  time to marry, 264
  to fill up its empty spaces, 196
  use of and of advantage be, 706
  use of those means, 270
Property, a man's own, 241
  a valuation of, 974
  and no stamps, liberty and, 950
  and privileges, share, 1074
  best ideas common, 990
  common, 481
  has its duties, 420
  nor their honour, their, 1023
  of easiness, 96
  of gray hairs, natural, 495
  of the highest value, 283
  of the rich alone, 985
  owns men, 603
  private, 638
  public, 274
  right to possess, 1071
  thieves respect, 827
Prophesy in part, we, 1120
  never, onless ye know, 527
Prophet, I am no, 900
  in the name of the, 332
  is not acceptable, a, 1126
  not without honour, 1115
  of the soul, I love a, 408
  sons of the, 951
Prophets and apostles all poor, 124
  and the poets, the, 889
  do they live forever, 1113
  don't pan out on the, 639
  false, 1116
  have honour, 1115
  is Saul also among the, 1100
  men reject their, 1074
  of the future, 361

Prophets old or young, 928
  shudder, while the, 928
  the law and the, 1114
  were twice stoned, 912
Prophet's camel bell, 881
  vision, thine was the, 438
  word, sounds like a, 363
Prophet-bards foretold, by, 477
Prophetic lips, 633
  of her end, 201
  soul, O my, 91
  strain, something like, 161
Propitiation or conciliation of powers, 713
Propitious gale, 267
  succor, 1017
Propontic and the Hellespont, 103
Proportion kept, no, 60
  of pain and evil, 563
  preserving the sweetness of, 119
  strangeness in the, 111
  to the power, increase in, 1070
Proportions, in small, we just beauties see, 120
Proposals for distribution of British Empire, 909
Propose, why don't the men, 388
Proposes, man, but God disposes, 8
Proposition, life's a funny, 849
Propositions, own words and, 110
Proprietor, undermining the small, 1086
Propriety, frights the isle from her, 101
  of speech, 112
  pattern of all, 820
Proprium humani ingenii, 178
Pros and cons of a kindred soul, 803
Pro's and con's, from, 1036
Prose and poetry, definition of, 319
  best of Melville's, 925
  composition, elegance in, 326
  is decorous, 767
  is grand verse, whose, 526
  life's turned to poetry, 595
  more attainable in, 461
  no 't is not even, 526
  or rhyme, unattempted in, 148
  pains of, 649
  recited in simple, 974
  run mad, not poetry but, 213
  verse will seem, 185
  warbler of poetic, 266
  what others say in, 214
  words in best order, 319
Prospect, a great thing in, 962
  of belief, within the, 84
  of his soul, into the eye and, 40
  pleases, though every, 343
  Scotchman's noblest, 234
  some have looked on a fair, 296
Prospects all look blue, 622
  brightening, 250
  gilded scenes and shining, 195
  gloomy as an author's, 421
  has few pleasanter, 422
  in view are more pleasing, 254
  see new, 736

Prosper, treason doth never, 29
Prospering, we shall march, 485
Prosperitee, a man to have ben in, 4
Prosperity, a jest's, lies in the ear, 41
  all sorts of, 1052
  and civilization are far from being synonymous, 739
  and trade, can hope, 661
  befall that fine, 585
  both bring temporary, 930
  education an ornament in, 1015
  has turned away, 870
  in the day of, 1109, 1124
  is not without many fears, 109
  keeps people honest, 482
  makes friends, 990
  man that hath been in, 4
  no more remembrance of, 1124
  not favorable to display of public virtue, 374
  not without fears and distastes, 109
  social, means man happy, 1068
  the blessing of the Old Testament, 109
  things which belong to, 109
  times of unexampled, 343
  vulgar, 237
  within thy palaces, 1106
Prosperous be thy life in peace and war, 68
  morn in May, 735
  they are still too, 930
  to be just, 525
Prosperum ac felix scelus, 29
Prostitute, puff away the, 177
  ruled by, 759
Prostrate city is thy seat, a, 403
Prostrations, my proper, 785
Protecting power, 395
Protection and patriotism are reciprocal, 338
  does not mean, 1066
  great, 473
  of habeas corpus, 273
  of the incompetent, 762
  Thy holy, 268
Protector, appears as a, 974
Protest only a bubble, 894
  too much, the lady doth, 94
Protestant to be, I will live thy, 133
Protestantism of the Protestant religion, 259
Protestants or Papists believe in the essential articles, 234
Proteus rising from the sea, 300
Protracted life is woe, 230
Proud and angry dust, 743
  and gentle thing, love is a, 896
  and mighty have, all the, 223
  and yet a wretched thing, 115
  apt the poor are to be, 55
  cirque of Ivan's bivouac, 543
  eyer fair and never, 101
  foot of a conqueror, 58
  fop, prize to some, 226
  for a wit, too, 252
  for tears, too, 760
  God keep me from being, 180
  grief is, 57
  his name, though, 307

Proud in humility, 123
in that they are not proud, 123
instruct my sorrows to be, 57
is she not sweet, if she be, 533
is the city, 811
knowledge is, 266
labour is independent and, 341
lords on the land and kings on the sea, 390
man, but man, 36
man reduced to want, 199
man's contumely, 93
me no prouds, 80, 947
on his own dunghill, 14
one that's, 719
pageant of man, 833
philosophy, I ask not, 328
Poll, the Pirate's Bride, 713
purses shall be, 52
science never taught to stray, 207
seat of Lucifer, 155
setter up of kings, 70
shall be, all the, 217
small things make base men, 69
soul ne'er pays but to the proud, 61
spirit of mortal be, 362
to beg, too, 954
to fight, too, 724
to importune, too, 246
tops of the eastern pines, 59
tower in the town, from a, 459
waves be stayed, 1102
we are, how, 199
who wish to be the first, 1049
world, good bye, 408
Prouds, proud me no, 80, 947
Prouder than rustling in silk, 105
Proud-pied April, 108
Proudest nobleman, equal to, 949
Prove, all the pleasures, 31
all things, 1121
an aspiration, 641
their doctrine orthodox, 142
Proved, true before, was, 143
Provençal song and dance, 383
Proverb and a by-word, 1101
most sensible, ever invented, 607
not wiser if mended, 611
old and of excellent wit, 440
Proverbs, and songs of Solomon, 1101
books like, 172
King Solomon wrote the, 755
patch grief with, 40
unaware of, 912
Proverbed with a grandsire phrase, 77
Proverbial parsnips, 887
Providence, behind a frowning, 266
bestows upon you, 985
fashioned us holler, 526
foreknowledge, will and fate, 150
I may assert eternal, 148
in the fall of a sparrow, 97
of the inferior man, 602
on side of last reserve, 1053
rubs which, sends, 253
seldom vouchsafes more than sufficient encouragement, 422

Providence should bestow such a profusion of days, 247
sobriquet for, 1056
their guide, 156
to demonstrate a, 1007
trust, let us to, 519
ways of God are full of, 1009
wisely has mingled, 478
Providently caters for the sparrow, 48
Province hath its own, every, 437
of illusion, 1069
Provision cheap, 217
for its own termination, 455
for the poor, 235
for yourself of his abundance, 1127
of money beforehand, 1025
Provisions, and plenty of, 1126
Provoke, 'twould a saint, 209
Provokes desire, 86
Provoketh thieves, beauty, 48
Prow, watched a barge's, 899
youth on the, 244
Prowess and glory, national, 396
giant-born, 479
Prowling mouse abhors light, 865
Prude, inclined to be a, 956
trade of a, 1068
Prudes for proctors dowagers for deans, with, 466
Prudence, directed by, 1051
Prudent in their own sight, 247
man looketh well, 1107
pause, then did the, 184
purpose to resolve, 201
Prudery is a kind of avarice, 1063
peculiarity of, 1068
perfect love casts out, 617
Prudhon's masterpiece, 1085
Prunella, leather or, 208
Prunes and prism, 497
are wholesome sweet and cheap, 764
longing for stewed, 35
Pruning-hooks, spears into, 1111
Prussia, came to the border of, 1065
hurried to the field, when, 280, 307
Prys, holde at litel, 7
Psalm, Miserere, 144
Psalms, David's, had ne'er been sung, 1052
King David wrote the, 755
of David, I've sung the, 692
songs be turned to holy, 28
Psalmist of Israel, the sweet, 1100
Psalmist's music deep, 427
Psyche, thus I pacified, 461
with, my soul, 461
Psychologic moment, 723
Psychological moment, 723
novelist can't see an inch, 797
reason, 667
Psychologists and writers, future, 1083
Psycho-pathologist, the unspeakable, 835
Ptolemies, Maecenates, heroical patrons, 124
Ptolemy, as far back as, 519
Pub as a valuable institution, 909

Public amusements, friend to, 235
be damned, 946
begins to hum it, 1083
buys its opinions, 614
calm, peace what I seek and, 547
credit, dead corpse of, 340
decide upon every man's title, 411
doesn't require new ideas, 1075
duty, above the fog in, 522
employments, 190
extempore speech, better in, 550
feasts, wedlock compared to, 115
flame nor private, 215
for sculptor painter, 422
for which masterpieces are intended, 927
functionaries within bounds, 320
gaze, hid from, 404
greatest of cowards, 330
has very crude ideas, 1063
haunt, exempt from, 48
honour is security, 950
intended for the, 1066
is best served, 1075
library, than a, 231
life a situation of power and energy, 259
like a frog, 584
man, no right to be a, 495
men, prevailin' weakness of, 606
must and will be served, 184
must cherish nobler plants, 476
odium and public hatred, 329
of service to the, 950
office is a public trust, 188, 481
offices, keep out of, 1001
opinion, doesn't he care for, 499
opinion is in advance of law, 797
opinion of the, 972
opinion stronger than legislature, 582
opinion variable, 563
plunder, power of, 339
property, 274
rout, where meet a, 115
school, microcosm of a, 420
scorn, sound of, 155
seldom forgive twice, 1056
service ceases, as soon as, 1054
stare, make the, 359
stock, misfortunes cast into a, 197
stock of harmless pleasure, 233
tax eminent men pay to, 191
the, is an old woman, 378
the supreme judge, make the, 1063
to speak in, on the stage, 292
trust, when a man assumes a, 188, 274
trusts, 188
uncritical buying, 921
way, in the crowded, 403
ways, whene'er I walk the, 760

Public weal, 1029
  wonder and mischief to this nation, 182
  would ever stop to read, what, 527
Publick library, present it to a, 238
  made themselves, 234
Public-school system, British, 607
Publish it not in the streets, 1100
  yourselves to the sky, 663
Publishers suggest books, 826
Pudding against empty praise, 215
  bestowing honour, pence, 406
  full of plums, life's a, 624
  proof of the, 1037
Puddings should be full of currants, 932
Puddle is shallow, where the, 865
Puddles, at the mercy of the, 588
Puff and blow himself, 635
  the prostitute away, 177
Puffed and reckless libertine, 90
Puffing, professor of the art of, 278
Pugilistic encounters, 407
Puissant nation, noble and, 163
Pukes in, sea the passenger, 360
Puking in the nurse's arms, 49
Pukka peerless sportsmen, 807
Pulitzer prize, letter declining, 885
Pull, a long strong and altogether, 497
Pulled ruin on the state, statesmen who, 430
Puller down of kings, 70
Pullman cars, ten years on de, 902
  civilization, 635
Pulpit drum ecclesiastick, 141
  press and song, 652
Pulse, by its strong, 728
  in the eternal mind, 894
  let me feel your, 38
  of life stood still, 201
  of the machine, 299
Pulses give, ecstasies the, 897
  temperate, 685
  that beat double, 429
Pulteney's toad-eater, 246
Pumpkin pie, like the rich, 441
Pumpkins blow, early, 498
  grew upon a tree, if, 821
Pun, insult the, 1067
  is a pistol, 324
  who could make so vile a, 186
Puns, from politics to, 405
Punch in the presence of the passenjare, 583
  some sipping, 296
Punch-bowl's brink, 659
Punctilious envoys, two, 1050
  in observance of conventionalities, 614
Punished for the offence they give, 505
  sir for early rising, worm, 510
Punishment, because of the, 975
  death is no, 164
  fit the crime, 624
  for murder, death the, 479
  greater than I can bear, 1097
  idea of eternal, 641

Punishment in man and beast, 1080
  pass by without, 949
  sent heavenward for, 586
  tames man, 1080
  that women bear, 37
Punkin, frost is on the, 697
Puny hands, power of your, 402
Pup, biggest dog has been a, 658
  prophylactic, 815
  the little lost, 815
Pupil, by encouraging a clever, 1054
  of the human eye, 334
Puppets best and worse are we, 485
Puppy cur, mastiff dog may love a, 472
  whelp and hound, 254
Puppy-dogs and monkeys, carrying, 996
  as maids talk of, 57
Puppyism come to full growth, 417
Purchase great alliance abroad, 70
Purchaser will pay the worth of everything, 990
Pure and eloquent blood, 118
  and gentle deed of mercy, 427
  and just desire of man, 1023
  and sad, 771
  and vestal modesty, 79
  and will survive, save what is, 934
  as snow chaste as ice, 93
  by being purely shone upon, 337
  delight, land of, 199
  flame, let its, 1021
  I would be, 880
  in thought as angels are, 289
  intellect will find, 669
  kept thy truth so, 162
  my heart is, 465
  offering of love, 549
  speak true right wrong, live, 470
  the real Simon, 190
  the, the beautiful the bright, 665
  too, and too honest, 593
  unto the pure all things are, 1122
  white diamond Dante brought, 680
  women, eyes of, 470
  young man, particularly, 623
Purer laws, with sweeter manners, 469
  science holier laws, of, 523
  than the purest gold, 119
Purest of all food, Hasty-Pudding, 280
  physical pleasure, sight, 312
  poetry, 716
Purgatory, taste of fame to have it is a, 426
Purge and leave sack, 63
  melancholy, to, 57
  off the baser fire, 149
Purged with euphrasy, 155
Purification of politics, 601
Purified, every creature shall be, 31

Puritanism laid the egg of democracy, 529
Puritans for ancestors, select, 768
  gave the world action, 479
  hated bear-baiting, 400
Purity of grace, the, 356
  out of a stain, 663
  to reverent youth grant, 984
Purple all the ground, 159
  and gold, gleaming in, 356
  as their wines, abbots, 215
  cow, never saw a, 792
  curtain, rustling of each, 460
  eyes and snout of golden, 938
  light of love, 243
  lights on Alpine snow, 442
  monkey, 684
  morning breaketh, 480
  of emperors, 786
  testament of bleeding war, 60
  the sails, 104
  when skies were, 395
  with love's wound, 42
Purpled o'er the lawn, 220
Purple-robed and pauper-clad, 759
Purple-stained mouth, 383
Purport of literature, the whole, 927
Purpose aloft, speeding my, 888
  and opinion, their, 652
  and served its whole, 1089
  between Almighty, difference of, 457
  cite Scripture for his, 44
  comprehend his, 1124
  constancy to, 419
  delusion of some major, 895
  empires in their, 732
  firm, is equal to the deed, 201
  grant us the, 873
  grips with half her, 834
  I know the evil of that I, 967
  infirm of, 86
  is not a slave to, 930
  just and perfect, 661
  listens to good, 1020
  little but to the, 360
  man used for a, 720
  my, is a horse of that colour, 54
  necessary for that, 1079
  of satisfying it, for the, 1078
  one increasing, runs, 464
  organized for that, 1061
  prudent, 201
  runs, her gentle, 690
  serves a certain, 636
  shake my fell, 84
  speak and, not, 98
  that may overcome caprice, 1017
  time to every, 1109
Purposes, Almighty has his own, 457
  of a society, among the, 1071
  of life, 1084
Purposed overthrow, 108
Purr to sleep with thunder, 616
Purse, costly as thy, can buy, 91
  hide it in a, 1016
  is free, but sorrow's, 565
  or pocket, touches the, 490
  put money in thy, 101

Purse, so little in his, 121
the leanness of his, 68
though poor be our, 418
though skinny be your, 813
velvet, of a sow's ear, 272
who steals my, steals trash, 102
Purses, light gains make heavy, 29
shall be proud, 52
Pursue phantoms of hope, 231
the triumph, 209
then be it yours while you, 474
Pursued, it is you who are the, 720
Pursuing, still achieving still, 433
Pursuit, delight is in the, 217
farewell the long, 898
of an unattainable perfection, 788
of happiness, 273
of knowledge, 331
of the perfect, of light, 548
of this and that, vain, 1019
Push on keep moving, 290
us from our stools, 87
Puss-gentleman, a fine, 263
Pussy-cat, the owl and the, 498
Put a tongue in every wound, 83
back to-morrow, 25
him out, it does not, 510
money in thy, 101
not your trust in money, 454
not your trust in princes, 1106
old cares to flight, 619
out the light, 103
out to sea, when I, 472
too fine a point, don't, 1043
too fine a point, not to, 497
up with a great deal, 979
you down, a plain tale shall, 62
your money in trust, but, 454
your trust in God, 329
Putrid corpse of liberty, we have buried the, 1090
eggs of hope, 292
Puts an end to pain, death who, 470
on his pretty looks, 58
Putteth down one, he, 1105
Putting off, eased the, 152
Putty brass and paint, 782
Puzzle to the botanist, 611
Puzzles the will, 93
Pygmalion's images, 37
Pygmy-body, fretted the, 173
Pyramid, bottom of the economic, 654, 876
mystery hid under Egypt's, 429
star-ypointing, 161
Pyramids doting with age, 147
first, the, 956
set off his memories, no, 131
summit of yonder, 1060
Pyrenees, in the high, 811
Pyrrhic dance, you have the, 359
phalanx, where is the, 359
Pyrrhus on victory, 113
Pythagoras, opinion of, 46, 122
Pytheas and Demosthenes, 1000

Quack and pettifogger, 329
Quacks with pills political, 794
Quadrangular spots, 266

Quadruped larger than a cat, 374
Quaff immortality and joy, 153
Quaffing laughing drinking, 176
Quaint and crazed, grown as, 889
and curious volume, many a, 460
and curious, war is, 651
and gray, a sun-dial, 597
and stilted phrase, 596
great figure, make him the, 857
in form and bright in hue, 569
old Quaker town, 551
Saxon legend, 653
wit made home-truth seem more true, 513
Quake, right as an aspen leaf, 4
Quaker, and priest and, 558
town, in the quaint old, 551
Quakers, because I bid them tremble at the word of the Lord, 171
Quaking, achings and, 453
Quaking-asp to glow, 766
Qualifications, what are his, 573
Qualities, abstract, begin with capitals, 599
and advantages, various, 1087
and their true, 78
as would wear well, 253
have very little merit, 830
hid all her better, 339
see a man's good, 376
Quality, each for its, 895
fruit of baser, 66
hardly more than one useful, 1088
no, but poor and rascally people, 181
of a thing, regarded as the, 769
of mercy is not strained, 46
of the stupid, 1064
of thought they think, 776
rather than quantity, 991
taste of your, 92
things outward do draw the inward, 104
things that have a common, 1012
true-fixed and resting, 82
your tragic, 895
Qualms, with many many, 755
Quandary, editor in a, 884
Quangle Wangle sat, 498
Quantitative dispassionate force and sequence, 731
Quantity of love, with all their, 97
of nonsense talked about bad men, 498
Quantum o' the sin, 285
Quareiets of pearl, 133
Quarles saved by beauties not his own, 215
Quarrel, during each successive, 748
entrance to a, 90
in a straw, 96
is a very pretty, 278
just, he that hath his, 69
justice of my, 31
short, cut the fiercest, 406
sudden and quick in, 49
take up our, 820
them who make the, 432
to the lawyer, for every, 137

Quarrel with my bread and butter, 192
with the shirt, no, 738
Quarrels of lovers, 979
on others, men that put, 55
pick no, 251
sedition idleness, 1051
thy head is as full of, 79
who in, interpose, 206
would not last long, 1044
Quarreled and told each other facts, 678
Quarrelling, when chickens quit, 852
Quarrelsome, countercheck, 51
mutinous and, 228
Quarry it shall find, 888
never found, the, 834
sagacious of his, 155
the marked-down, 720
Quarry-slave, like the, 371
Quart of mighty ale, 6
of Sabine, crack a, 868
Quarter, I always drop a, 660
of what I see, 813
to tyrants I will give no, 424
Quartz, rugged as the, 686
Que scais-je, 1031
Quean, extravagant, 279
Queen apparent, 152
Bess, image of good, 391
Bess ruled England's state, 760
Bess's golden days, 186
Elizabeth and the tailors, 380
Elizabeth, no scandal about, 279
gliding like a, 938
had four Maries, 953
hail their, fair regent, 269
heart-blood of a, 424
Mab hath been with you, 77
Mary's saying, 486
o' the May, I'm to be, 463
of France, Oh! if I were, 432
of land and sea, Rome, 478
of pleasure, if you were, 631
of secrecy, 385
our, our rose our star, 405
Prosperity, from whom our, 870
rose of the rosebud garden, 469
shall be as drunk as we, 229
she looks a, 218
show the night-flowers their, 388
this beggar maid shall be my, 465
upon a card, insipid as the, 465
would grace a summer's, 309
Queens, in the hands of, 856
who die with Antony, 856
Queen's delight, for their, 736
navee, 623
Queenly boat, toll for the, 363
Queer, all the world is, 306
kindly though, 874
sometimes very, 754
suburban streets, little, 911
that I should see them, 919
thou art a little, 306
Quem Di diligunt adolescens moritur, 302
Quench, rivers cannot, 70
Quenchless star forever bright, 393

Quern, buy her a little, 912
Querulous and bellicose, news-
    papers, 862
    and uncivil clay, 938
    criticisms, 535
    serenity, 322
Quest divine, on thy, 459
    drives him in relentless, 892
    for knowledge Occidental, 696
    for righteousness, 696
    what thy, 668
    wherefore is a hopeless, 736
Questing hound, fever to the, 834
Question about my digestion,
    never a, 655
    at Faubourg St. Germain, 532
    begging the, 944
    deep, arguments and, 109
    ignorance never settles a, 419
    is like starting a stone, 704
    is this: is man an ape, 419
    marriage an open, 412
    never so likely to settle a, 398
    no, settled until settled right,
    718
    not but live and labor, 601
    not every, deserves an answer,
    989
    now placed before society, 419
    of despair, the hurried, 356
    of loving them enough, 914
    of the best book, 753
    oftentimes a, 860
    rights of the, 970
    that is the, 93
    two sides to every, 1016
Questions, ask me no, 253
    asking dangerous, 429
    briefly and to the point, an-
    swered, 742
    feel strongly about putting,
    704
    foolish, of common people,
    1083
    heads for, 891
    of taste feeling and inherit-
    ance, 635
    them that asks no, 784
    vex the thought, endless, 544
Questionable shape, in such a, 91
    superfluity small beer, that,
    417
Questioning is not the mode of
    conversation, 236
Questionings of sense, 301
Qui ante diem periit, 764
    desiderat pacem, 268
    fuit peut revenir aussi, 143
    nullum fere scribendi genus,
    231
    procul hinc, 764
Quibblin' is all through, 677
Quick and easy death, 754
    bright things come to confu-
    sion, 42
    in quarrel, sudden and, 49
    mint of joy, 346
    of the universe is incarnate
    carnal self, 883
    successive train in, 450
    thy drugs are, 80
    to haste, the golden moments,
    474
Quickens into deeds, He, 442
Quickly, well it were done, 85
Quickness, with too much, 209

Quid, Barney Buntline turned his,
    274
    velit et possit, 260
Quiddities, where be his, 96
Quiddity and entity, 142
Quiet along the Potomac, 569
    and meaningless, are, 899
    and peace, calm, 160
    and they are, 849
    as a nun, the holy time is, 297
    as a plough, 683
    be, and go a-angling, 140
    breast, truth hath a, 59
    brief delight eternal, 759
    conscience, a still and, 73
    die, easy live and, 309
    Doctor Diet Doctor, and Doc-
    tor Merryman, 192
    dream, glide through a, 350
    dust was gentlemen and la-
    dies, 585
    earth's breast, at rest in the,
    523
    equable deadly holder-on, 928
    fate affright your, 725
    fond and few, sheep, 406
    freed from that, 834
    hours, entertain with, 63
    in Montparnasse, rest, 929
    integrity health soundness, 895
    kiss me and be, 221
    light, 372
    mind is richer, 940
    mood, jar in our own, 426
    pilgrimage, 121
    rich, and infamous, 399
    rural and retirement, 224
    self-control, 438
    study to be, 1121
    then, in the awful, 816
    us in a death so noble, 157
Quiets of the past, hallowed, 528
Quietly contentedly silly, 323
Quietness and in confidence, in,
    1128
Quietus make with a bare bodkin,
    93
Quill, every blade of grass a,
    1017
    from an angel's wing, 304
Quills, stops of various, 160
    upon the porpentine, 91
Quillets of the law, nice sharp,
    68
    where be his, 96
Quilt of marble, 682
Quinquireme of Nineveh, 832
Quintessence of life, 1064
Quintilian stare and gasp, made,
    161
Quip modest, 51
    not even a belated, 924
Quips and cranks, 160
    and sentences, 39
Quire of bad verses, 399
Quiring to young-eyed cheru-
    bins, 47
Quirks of blazoning pens, 101
Quit oh quit this mortal frame,
    216
    you like men be strong, 1120
    your books, up my friend and,
    295
    yourselves like men, 1100
Quite the other way, 702
Quitting, rest is not, 501

Quiver, after the soul is gone the
    limbs will, 238
    fanes, in the air, 403
    full, man that hath his, 1106
    starlight in heaven above us
    shall, 502
    the moonbeams, 582
Quiver's choice, devil in his, 361
Quivering curds, 599
    heart-strings prove it, 553
Quixotic is his enterprise, 624
    sense of the honorable, a, 461
Quos Deus vult perdere, 175
    læserunt et oderunt, 178
Quotation, classical, 237
    or chance word, 709
    should come unsought, 869
Quotations a blessing to the pub-
    lic, 758
    from the great filial reverence,
    758
    throng for trade and last, 604
    wrapped himself in, 786
Quote, by delight we all, 415
    grow immortal as they, 203
    to, argues feeble industry, 971
Quoted to be, only fame, 588
Quoter next to the originator, the,
    415
Quoth echo plainly matter-o'-
    money, 511

RA, the great god, 882
Rabbit in the snare, 877
    say scat, ole Miss, 689
    say scoot, ole man, 689
    thoughts of a, 415
Rabbits, bobtails fu' de, 820
Rabbit-flight, deep colon, 927
Rabble, a member of the, 922
    no longer saw a, 801
    run to strip him, 594
    sadly pedestrian, 937
Rabelais, quart d'heure de, 205
Rabelais' easy chair, 214
Race, a loftier, 654
    ancient by birth, 174
    armageddon of the, 442
    best, hasn't been run, 872
    boast a generous, 223
    but in the general, 449
    descended from great cats, 828
    distinctions, of, 581
    efforts of, due to love of
    praise, 532
    figures of a rough-hewn, 784
    forget the human, 354
    heavenly, demands thy zeal,
    225
    heirs of the island, 760
    here lived and loved another,
    364
    is not to the swift, 270
    is run, when his, 649
    is to the strongest, 775
    is won, the, 567
    life's, well run, 555
    limits of its, utmost extremes,
    553
    man's imperial, 212
    may be an accident, 829
    mother of a mighty, 373
    never betted on a, 479
    noble and brave, 364
    not to the swift the, 710
    of man like leaves, 218

Race of men innumerable, 154
of men on earth, 964
of men that don't fit in, 844
of mine, but for this, 935
of modern industry, 1072
of politicians, 191
or section, family party, 952
plodding wins the, 962
rear my dusky, 464
runs twice his, 168
selfishness greatest curse of
the human, 450
slinks out of the, 163
stars of human, 262
swiftness in the forward, 371
that binds its body in chains,
a, 655
that can't stay still, 844
the slaughters of the, 650
there is but one, — humanity,
709
win the, 497
wish I loved the human, 759
worn quite out, 360
younger, succeeds every year,
180
Races, fighting, 683
two distinct, 323.
Racemes, their flashing old, 843
Racer and hack may be traced,
448
Rachel, Jacob served seven years
for, 1098
weeping for her children, 1113
Rachel-Jane, far away the, 857
Rack behind, leave not a, 33
desire is a perpetual, 123
dislimns, 105
glowing through the gray, 871
of this tough world, 100
spread open on the, 616
the value, being lost we, 39
Racket rip, let the, 792
Racy as the jabber, 925
Radiance, divine and terrible,
1067
fills their hollows, 849
of eternity, 366
of the morning, glad, 669
sparkles, a smouldering, 1085
Radiant light, by her own, 158
marginal sand-beach, 663
pearl, no, 267
waters, where such, 730
wings at rest, 338
with ardour divine, 547
with glory, 432
Radiator is absolutely cold, the,
868
Radiators lose their temperature,
911
Radio, around the world by, 815
but had no, 910
Radiogram, death sends a, 854
Rafael made a century of sonnets, 488
of the dear Madonnas, 488
Raft, his fragile, 784
that Homer made for Helen,
850
Rafts, sailors hastily making,
850
thoughts like small lost, 850
Rafter, we meet neath the sounding, 554
Rafters of the home, 708

Rafters, wrenching the, 708
Rag and a bone, to a, 779
of character, one, 675
tied to an upright stick, 147
to her back, scarcely a, 1081
Rags are royal raiment, 942
clothe a man with, 1108
virtue though in, 177
Rag-bag of the world, 757
Rage for fame, 272
for pleasure, the, 1056
heaven has no, 193
is all on one side, 368
nor know the, that yells, 375
not die here in a, 191
of the vulture, 355
penury repressed their noble,
245
strong without, 167
swell the soul to, 176
was vain and to sulk would
nothing gain, 282
Rages, furious winter's, 106
Ragged and weary and swarthy,
753
hose, in darning, 557
regimentals, in their 579
uncomely and old and gray,
807
Raggedness, windowed, 99
Raggedy man he works for pa,
697
Raging fever burns, so when a,
199
o'er the upper ocean, 375, 480
roaring lion, 691
Rail down ribs down, 915
on the Lord's anointed, 72
pleasant riding on the, 510
tough as a hickory, 927
Rails, all along the, 925
lights and net-work, 926
o'er strange, 717
of it crack, 807
Railed on Lady Fortune, 49
Railer, Boreas blustering, 247
Railroad bridge, de, 934
presidents more significant,
906
Railroads, on the, 954
Rail-splitter a true-born king of
men, 513
Raiment, black, graveyard grimness, 573, 978
rags are royal, 942
to our backs, scarcely, 309
vanity of, 691
your feet and your, all red,
401
Raiments of the past, old fetish,
609
Rain a deluge showers, the, 288
a shower of commanded tears,
52
always got its share of, 846
and ruin of roses, 633
as the mist resembles the,
434
at once, sunshine and, 99
back to their springs like the,
435
best to let it, 437
cats and dogs, 192
comes in slanting lines, 587
cooling plash of, 709
daggers, 125

Rain, dull roots with spring, 899
fell on the roof, 929
follows mist and weeping, 559
gentle, from heaven, 46
goes, when the, 814
golden suns and silver, 581
I shall not feel the, 587
in thunder lightning or in, 84
in winter when the dismal, 587
influence, bright eyes, 160
into each life some, must fall,
434
is over and gone, 1110
is pouring, hark how the, 565
it raineth every day, 56
leveled lances of the, 586
like glittering spears, 586
maketh silvers in the, 929
may enter king cannot, 230
mist and cloud will turn to,
438
not even the, 921
of autumn, 824
or shine, can not order, 504
overhead, soft, 568
pack when it begins to, 98
pierces the hard marble, 23
presages the coming of, 815
slash of the, 753
some, must fall, 434
sunshine after, 106
sunshine follows the, 523
sweetest, makes not fresh, 127
that makes things new, 832
thirsty earth soaks up the, 167
to me, not raining, 772
to mist and cloud again, 438
umbrellas in the, 923
unravelled from the tumbling
main, 406
upon the blinding dust, 498
upon the mown grass, 1104
useful trouble of the, 470
voice of the, 538
with a silver flail, 888
Rains fall after great battles,
998
Rainbow, another hue unto the,
58
colours of the, 158
comes and goes, 301
flame of a, 825
hues of song, 794
look upon the, 1125
love unreturned has its, 750
loves an idle, 816
once in heaven, awful, 383
poet will follow the, 675
see how that lovely, 814
span of fifty years, 664
without color a flower without perfume, 551
Rainbows in the rain, wonderful,
609
span it, smile till, 568
Rainbow's glory is shed, 368
Rainbow-crust, rich in, 848
Rain-drenched hair, shakes out
her, 882
Rain-drop makes some floweret,
each, 504
Raineth every day, rain it, 56
Rainfall, the average annual,
926
Rain-in-the-Face, Short Wolf
and Crazy Horse, 707

Raining, it is not, rain to me, 772
daffodils, it's, 772
when it is, 437
Rain-storms, self-appointed inspector of, 514
Rain-washed bone, 781
Rainy day, in a very, 1108
morrow, windy night a, 108
Pleiads wester, 744
Raise me up, God shall, 22
what is low in me, 148
Raised a mortal to the skies, 176
backstayed into, 834
level by the passing, 552
woman is at heart a, 209
Rakes, and a scholar among, 400
Rally round the flag boys, 541
Ralpho thou dost prevaricate, 142
Rambling in thought, 1011
Rameses, in the days of old, 953
Rampant Maenad of Massachusetts, 635
Rampart, my, and my only one, 916
no, will hold out, 1046
Ramparts, anguished mothers gaze from the, 1071
Rampin' dream in tow, took a, 878
Ramrod, swallowed a, 1007
Ramshackled sidewalks, the, 756
Ran a hundred years to a day, 452
grief with a glass that, 633
to help me when I fell, 345
Rancor, tell them with no, 868
this man met, 808
will out, 68
Randolph thy wreath has lost a rose, 309
Random, many a shaft at, sent, 309
many a word at, spoken, 309
pearls at, strung, 275
words at, flung, 275
Range beckons vainly, old, 822
of hills, the first, 318
of sight, I see beyond the, 514
of sound, I hear beyond the, 514
of the marshes, greatness within the, 663
seen at close, 930
with humble livers, 73
Ranges, look behind the, 777
loomin' high and cold and still, 831
of comfortless years, 824
Ranged like him that travels, if I have, 108
Ranger should go, went like a, 831
Rank and wealth his strength and health, 610
give us men from every, 561
is a great beautifier, 425
is but the guinea's stamp, 287
is good and gold is fair, 443
mark of, 661
my offence is, 95
no king can give, 512
physicians of the highest, 951
pride and haughtiness, 194
Ranks are thinned, 917
of life, in the humbler, 1075

Ranks of the shah, in the, 951
thinning of our, 652
whence come great captains, 519
Rankest compound of villanous smell, 25
Rank-scented many, the mutable, 76
Ransom, accept thy, 476
Rant and swear, 177
as well as thou, 97
Raphael, I am the angel, 1126
paints wisdom, 414
prayer to, 490
Raphaels Correggios and stuff, 252
Raphael's colors blent, enough that, 561
Rapid exhaustless deep his numbers, 393
of life shoots to the fall, 467
Rapids are near, the, 334
Rapping, as of some one gently, 460
Rapt one of the godlike forehead, the, 305
ship run on her side, 28
Rapture ahead, heaving for, 576
and response of food, 887
greet the day, with, 642
ineffable, 700
is over by eight, 930
of life ineffable, 629
of pursuing, 437
on the lonely shore, 354
the first fine careless, 486
then a pain, 681
to the dreary void, 355
Raptures, high, do infuse, 146
surgeons spend, 430
swell, for him no minstrel, 307
that yourselves infuse, 186
Rapture's roadway, lead on, 775
Rapture-smitten frame, 327
Rapturous heart of things, 735
wings, 888
Rare and curious pieces, 128
as a day in June, what is so, 525
Ben Jonson, 118
difficult as they are, 1049
new-laid eggs, roasted, 177
paint, success is a, 163
rich and, the gems she wore, 334
treasure-galleon, 576
volumes richly bound, 713
Rarely falls, who never climbs as, 443
lose, who never wins can, 443
rarely comest thou, 368
Rareness, a strain of, 106
Rarity of Christian charity, 392
Rascal, biggest, on two legs, 1008
hath not given me medicines, 61
strove to pass, whenever a, 504
Rascals are always sociable, 1064
in the coach and worth on foot, 525
to lash the, naked, 103
Rascally thief, cursed that, 351

Rascally yea-forsooth knave, 64
Rash paraphrase can make amends, 217
splenitive and, 97
Rashly importunate, 392
Rashness, beware of, but with energy, 456
Rasselas, history of, 232
Rat, I smell a, 116, 142, 1037
in a hole, like a poisoned, 191
that ate the malt, 543
Rats and such small deer, 99
in a ship, 859
instinctively have quit it, the, 32
leave a sinking ship, 993
Rat's felonious fangs, 543
Rats' feet over broken glass, 899
Rate o' speed, an' every, 777
the cost of the erection, 64
Rathe primrose, bring the, 159
Rather be a dog and bay the moon, 83
lie in the woollen, 38
than be less, 149
Ratio, in keen and quivering, 585
Rations, daily, 495
have not your own, 786
Rationalist, atheist nor a, 1061
Rattle his bones over the stones, 395
pleased with a, 208
the thundering, 833
Rattlesnake, fight a, 801
Rattling crags among, 353
good history, 650
Ravage with impunity a rose, 484
Ravages of time, irreparable, 1050
Ravaged plains and burning towns, 262
Ravelled fleeces by, trailed its, 722
sleave of care, 86
Raven down of darkness, 158
from the dim dominions, 418
nevermore, quoth the, 460
on yon left hand, 206, 978
ringlets, 600
was croaking, 206, 978
Ravens feed, he that doth the, 48
Ravished ears, with, 176
eyes, turn my, 195
with the whistling of a name, 208
younger hearings are, 41
Raw in fields, 177
material of opinion, 724
Ray, beauty's heavenly, 356
fancy's meteor, 285
hope emits a brighter, 252
liberty burst in its, 512
love sends his early, 416
of good hope may fall, 641
on ray split the shroud, 493
serene, gem of purest, 245
Rays, hide your diminished, 210
young fancy's, 285
Rayless majesty, 201
Rayn, this is an huge, 4
Raypublican party will keep ye broke, 796
Raze out the written troubles of the brain, 88

Razed from the books of honour, 107
Razor blades, like rusty, 785
  satire like a polished, 221
Razors pain you, 918
  words are, 76
Razure of oblivion, 37
Reach and power, beyond the, 1049
  beyond our, 647
  from the remoter, 738
  I deny your "out of," 696
  man's, should exceed his grasp, 488
  of every man, within the, 990
  of ordinary men, above, 297
  out of destruction's, 647
  sky far out of, 536
  that beyond their, 1052
  the small, the great cannot, 25
  thrill the swampy, 933
Reaches of our souls, beyond the, 91
Reached at a single bound, heaven not, 521
Reaction after marriage, 785
  attack is the, 236
  produces a violent, 973
  to it, watching his, 931
Reactions, unpredictable, 787
Read and write comes by nature, 39
  as inclination leads, 234
  as much as other men, 171
  aught that I could ever, 42
  blockhead ignorantly, 212
  books, from a sense of duty, 629
  exceedingly well, 62
  five hours in a day, 234
  he that runs may, 266
  Homer once, 185
  in science, by preference the newest, 426
  mark and inwardly digest, 1127
  my little fable, 467
  my title clear, 199
  never, book not a year old, 414
  old authors to, 113
  slow, learn to, 170
  the perfect ways of honour, 74
  to doubt or read to scorn, 310
  what do you, 92
  what is, twice, 233
  what to, say and eat, 398
  while we, history we make history, 558
Reader, books for general, 1080
  delights the, 1050
  illuminated is the poem, 825
  most severe, makes allowances, 196
  reads no more, when the last, 451
  the approbation of every, 1039
Readers, a few judicious, 985
  and hearers like my books, the, 29
  are deaf, most, 869
  five hundred, 636
  of the Boston Evening Transcript, 900
  of the hour, partial and noisy, 411

Readers sleep, to give their, 215
Readeth, he may run that, 1113
Readiness in an art, quickly gets, 1089
  is all, 97
  to change, 975
  to stray far, in men, 728
Reading, A.B.C. of, 886
  any, more easy, 1078
  as was never read, 215
  at random, 925
  between these lines, 1058
  coal cars, Pere Marquette, 926
  contemplation more than, 171
  easy writing's curst hard, 279
  effects of, 829
  employ themselves by, 1051
  fruit of thy, 1020
  he that I am, has most force, 1029
  I prefer, 788
  is an oppression of the mind, 184
  maketh a full man, 111
  stuff the head with, 215
  to retain, not, 925
  what they never wrote, 265
Reading-machine always wound up, 526
Reading-rooms about it free, 998
Reads as a task, 234
Ready booted and spurred, 169
  ere I called her name, 190
  money is Aladdin's lamp, 361
  money makes the man, 199
  rough but, 496
  that he may be, 496
  to scold and blame, 690
  to try our fortunes, 65
  we always are, 242
  with every nod to tumble, 72
  writer, pen of a, 1104
Real estate men chortle, 912
  ones right ones straight ones and true, 807
  permanent grandeur of these states, 534
  Simon Pure, 190
Realist rhymester play your part, 471
Realities are melting from me, 497
  face, 725
  of your existence, 953
Reality, against the essential, 895
  of things on earth, 1074
  our only touch with, 830
  the most terrible, 1087
  your joy be the, 480
Realize our perfection, 723
Realm, fourth estate of the, 397
  his sober, of leafless trees, 551
  is diminished, 785
  of France, wish ill unto the, 1022
  of silence, 521
  of the circling sea, 764
  one, we have never conquered, 883
  riding o'er the azure, 244
  that mysterious, 371
  this earth this, 59
  youth of the, 69
Realms, alien, 764

Realms below, nor yet of the, 907
  obey, whom three, 212
  of gold, I have travelled in, 384
  of marvel, what new, 539
  of shade, the pale, 371
  of space, pathless, 622
  to see, whatever, 249
  where sin's forgiven, 789
Reap, as you sow ye are like to, 143
  our sowing and so good-bye, 607
  the whirlwind, 1113
Reaped, his chin new, 61
  the thorns which I have, 353
Reaper in his hour of ease, tanned, 552
  whose name is death, 433
Reapers among the sheaves 1100
  white-winged, 170
Reaper's work is done, 370
Reaping, grew the more by, 105
Reaps from the hopes, 592
Rear my dusky race, she shall, 464
  the tender thought, 224
Rearward of a conquered woe, 108
Reason, a psychological, 667
  a woman's, 33
  according to soundest, say and do everything, 1011
  and conscience of thousands into a mould, 739
  and knowledge, against, 932
  and the will of God, 548
  approved my pleaded, 154
  asked one another the, 51
  but from what we know, 207
  capability and godlike, 96
  common law is nothing but, 21
  die for no good, 930
  discourse of, 90
  endued with sanctity of, 154
  feast of, and flow of soul, 213
  fifty times to one does err, 185
  firm the temperate will, 299
  for its existence, destroy the, 637
  for my rhyme, 26
  for so many senseless scholars, 184
  for the faith in me, 342
  gave it him, 984
  has moons, 816
  how noble in, 92
  ignis fatuus of the mind, 185
  I'll not listen to, 475
  in the faith of, 318
  is left free to combat it, 163, 273
  is our conscient, 669
  is the life of the law, 21
  is what someone else has to say, 475
  itself, kills, 163
  law is the perfection of, 21
  lies between spur and bridle, 138
  men have lost their, 83
  men that can render a, 1108
  most sovereign, 94
  my pleaded, 154

Reason needs only to will, 1089
neither rhyme nor, 37, 50
no sooner knew the, 51
not altogether without, 1077
nothing is law that is not, 21
of his fancies, 162
of strength, if by, 1105
of the case, consider the, 21
on compulsion, 62
panders will, 95
perfection of, 21
prisoner, takes the, 84
regulates all things, 1007
ruling passion conquers, 210
strong and replication prompt, 109
than that the twain, no more, 472
the card passion is the gale, 208
theirs not to, why, 467
think not for such a, 922
to apprehend, 234
too hot for, 637
under control, keep, 1012
virtue naught can me bereave, 225
war with rhyme, 120
what is the, of this thusness, 606
why I cannot tell, 188
why I clasp them, 553
with reasonable men I will, 424
worse appear the better, 149, 1014
would despair, where, 239
Reasons are among the many, 811
as two grains of wheat, 44
for remaining at bottom, 775
forty million, 780
heroism feels and never, 412
plentiful as blackberries, 62
we should drink, 184
who wisely, 209
why we smile and sigh, 365
Reason's spite, in erring, 207
whole pleasure, 208
Reasonable men I will reason, with, 424
number of fleas good, 687
the wrong way seems the more, 709
Reasoned high of providence, 150
Reasonest well, Plato thou, 195
Reasoning beings, 1010
fools, 335
mathematician capable of, 974
pride in, 209
prose, 332
Rebecs of ruby, beryl-rimmed, 432
Rebel, good old, 630
thought the little black-eyed, 677
Rebellion, century and a half without a, 273
notwithstanding his, 228
to tyrants, 260, 945
Rebellious hell, 95
liquors in my blood, 48
Reboantic Norns, dark vistas of the, 432
Rebuff, then welcome each, 489

Rebuke, open, is better, 1108
Recall that night in June, do you, 582
Recanting goodness sorry ere 'tis shown, 80
Receipts of cookery are swelled to a volume, 184
Receive, more blessed to give than to, 1119
thy sight, the Saviour said, 373
Receives, who much, 246
Reception of erotic emotion, 1084
one meets with from women of a family, 347
Recess interval at school like a, 1089
Rechabite poor Will must live, 190
Reciprocal, protection and patriotism are, 338
Recitative I'd bring for thee, 537
Reck the rede, 285
Reckless libertine, 90
mood, let your, 878
of the world's hostility, 811
what I do to spite the world, 86
Recklessness, frank barbarous, 726
Reckon he never knowed how, 639
hours and minutes, we, 387
Southern word, 616
Reckoned, beggary in the love that can be, 104
Reckoners without their host, 13
Reckoneth without his hostesse, 23
Reckoning, I have revised thy, 511
made, no, 92
pay my, 737
so comes the dreadful, 205
to the end of, 37
trim, 63
Recks not his own rede, 90
Recluse would not have been stigmatized, 828
Recoils on itself, revenge, 154
Recollection and abundance of blessings, 981
debt almost escaped my, 406
fond, 348
of that life, 228
that can never never pass, 768
Recommendation, a silent, 987
Recommends itself, sweetly, 85
Recompense, an honest, 427
heaven sent a, 245
service beyond all, 1043
tardy, 596
toil without, 595
Reconciliation, temple of silence and, 399
Reconstructed, I won't be, 630
Reconstructionist, spring a true, 581
Record of a fevered dream, 685
of her high descent, no, 561
of the mind, unwritten, 970
on the gramophone, puts a, 899
tells, the shining, 955
weep to, 327

Records, cruel, 570
of valour decay, till the, 512
that defy the tooth of time, 203
trivial fond, 92
Recorded time, last syllable of, 88
Recorders, flutes and soft, 149
Recording angel dropped a tear, the, 242
Recourse, embarrassed people have, 360
to Swedish steel, 1076
Recover, he might, with the help of a surgeon, 43
Recovered innocence, through our own, 515
Recovery when overthrown, augment your chance of, 542
Recreant limbs, a calf's-skin on, 57
Recreation, angling innocent, 140
of delight, which find, 1071
without some lawful, 1038
Red and they're rare, they're, 842
and white beauty truly blent, 54
as a rose is she, 314
as ruin, listed, 939
black to, began to turn, 142
breast, mark on his, 444
cheek a little, 209
cow's milk, draught of. 140
flannel drawers for leprechauns, 931
for valor blue for justice, 481
gleameth a dusky, 586
gods call for you, 779
her lips were, 163
Hoss Mountain, think of, 698
I, 1084
it never dies, 648
laugh of war, 864
lips were less, 593
making the green one, 86
men scalped each other, 399
morn ever betoken'd wrack, 106
mouth to whisper low, 625
outside the arteries of an archangel, no, 615
red grass a thousand miles, 841
red rose, my luve's like a, 287
right hand, 150
rose is a falcon, 675
rose whispers of passion, 675
roses, and violets blew, 24
Sea place in your life, 763
sky at night sailors' delight, 1115
slayer thinks he slays, if the, 410
slender, line, 542
spirits and gray, 117
star sheds its ray, 288
tape, bound with, 497
their, it never dies, 648
thin, line, 541, 542
to your battle hilts, 800
waves of wretchedness, 389
with other wars, 602

Red with the wreck of a square, 765
  with wrong to white as wool, 659
  your feet and your raiment all, 401
Rede and dryve the nyght away, 3
  better reck the, 285
  floures white and, 4
  recks not his own, 90
  that other folk canst, 4
  you tent it, 286
Redeem the human mind, given to, 434
  thy name, though late, 223
Redeeming love, triumph in, 280
Redemption, everlasting, 40
  from above did bring, 161
Redmen planned, a dire revenge these, 714
Redress by mob law, 455
  things past, are now past care, 59
Redskins, seven, bit the dust, 713
Reduced, assist the, 1020
Redundant blueness abundant, summer, 493
  riddle, 493
Reed, bokes clad in blak or, 5
  broken, 1111
  bruised, shall he not break, 1112
  just to blow a shepherd's, 406
  man is but a thinking, 1047
  the little, 962
  to what a, 475
Reeds at Runnymede, 784
  to blow upon, 849
Reedy stream, along the, 385
Reef may be safely let out, 963
Reeking herd, avoid the, 897
  up to heaven, 67
Reeling and writhing, 598
  from the delirious riot of religion, 635
Re-establishment of peace, to the, 1061
Reference to some want, has, 1062
Refined gold, to gild, 58
Refinement may be found at home, 283
  on the principles of resistance, 259
Refining, still went on, 252
Reflected, beholds her image in her eyes, 555
Reflection, cool, with the morning, 198, 310
  remembrance and, 207
  steals light from past, 717
  strange old woman, 717
Reflections on the greatness of the British nation, 197
Reflective memory stores, all that, 305
Reform, every, will be carried to excess, 318
  it altogether, 94
Reformation, age of, 273
  of religion, the, 20
  printing and the, 1089
Reformed that, we have, 94
Reformer, no fidget and no, 757

Reformers and lawmakers, lost, 800
Refrain, breathe the old, 443
  daily hear the sweet, 533
  from eating as well as breathing, 247
  from setting yourself up, 974
  hoarse-throated brutalized, 763
  to-night, 95
Refreshment, draught of cool, 386
  from his thumb, 664
  mid the dust of strife, 604
  of your inner life, 572
  shall fill them full of, 435
Refuge and my fortress, 1105
  and strength, God is our, 1104
  both are the, 930
  from confession, suicide but, 342
  from home, hotel a, 720
  from pessimism, 572
  of a scoundrel, last, 236
  of all old coquettes, 1068
  to every one, home is the, 21
Refusal to consider the author's intention, 680
Refuse of your teeming shore, 694
Refutable charm of a theory that it is, 1080
Refute a sneer, who can, 274
Regal solitude a sick bed, 324
  wealth can add, 985
Regard, things without all remedy should be without, 86
Regarded his fault-finding critic, 508
Regardless of their doom, 243
Regent Circus I espy, at curve of, 683
  of love-rhymes, 41
  of the night, fair, 269
  of the sky, moon sweet, 269
Regeneration, man's, 693
  she smells, 575
Regiment blind with the dust, 765
  from behind, led his, 624
Reg'ment didn't need to send, 782
Regimental in her fittings, 786
Regimentals, ragged, 579
Region Elenore, tread the, 749
  now, what, 1009
  of day, 271
  of sunshine and rest, 416
  of the dead, 850
  of thick-ribbed ice, 36
  where no night can hide us, 134
Regions Caesar never knew, 263
Register a lie hath told, 522
  of the crimes follies and misfortunes, history a, 270
Regret can die, O last regret, 469
  I do not purchase, 976
  many a fond, 401
  old age is a, 420
  one asked of, 792
  past clear of all, 960
  then judge of my, 388
  wild with all, 466
Regrets, a harvest of barren, 592
  and future fears, past, 1018

Regrets come to resemble hopes. 1072
  series of congratulatory, 420
  the natural property of gray hairs, 495
Regular as infant's breath, 317
  icily, splendidly null, 469
Regular-bred physician, 278
Regulated families, accidents in best, 496
Regulations, under the proper. 196
Rehearsal, go smoothly at, 492
  of the past, 354
Rehearsals, improve sermon by, 228
Rehearse, our being shall, 108
  this truth within thy mind, 462
Reherce, as ny as ever he can, 5
Reign, dubious legend of their. 735
  have the shortest, 373
  in hell, better to, 148
  labours of my, 942
  of Chaos and old Night, 148
  of mind, 337
  undisturbed their ancient, 479
  what is pomp, rule, 70
  when awful darkness and silence, 498
Reigns of terror, risk of, 581
  some ill planet, 56
  with the tyrant, fear that, 435
Reigneth evermore, peaceful stillness, 480
  the Lord, 1105
Rein, find his mouth, a, 631
  hardly need the, 928
  he draws no, 676
  I loose the, 1021
  too much, 33
Reinforcement of forty thousand men, 293
Reiteration, spell by, 430
Reivers and robbers, right thrifty, 1045
Rejoice in thy youth, 1110
  let the earth, 1105
  not over thy greatest enemy, 1124
  the desert shall, 1111
Rejoicing with heaven and earth, 162
Rejoinder repartee, 650
Relation, find the ennobling, 771
  is mutual, 1062
  plagued some worthy, 510
Relations, educational, 712
  man is a bundle of, 411
  were much troubled at me, 170
  with a good joke, our, 826
Relationship of an author to his works, 727
Relative, strong-willed, 422
Relatives, fate makes our, 1056
Relaxation from one kind of labour, 1078
Release, ensured, 744
  ill-timed, 671
  peace of the great, 693
  real, from this world, 1063
  signal of his, 443
Relentless power, 243
  quest, 892

Relics, cold and unhonoured, 334
  crucifixes beads, 143
  deposit for, 545
  hallowed, 161
Relief a narcotic, 877
  continued dependence, 876
  for this, much thanks, 89
  in sight, with no, 795, 868
  of another's care, 282
  of man's estate, 112
  sure and swift, 697
  'tis a poor, we gain, 199
  to any laden life, 604
  work brings its own, 660
Relieve a brother, exquisite to, 285
  the wretched, to, 230
Relieved by exonerating themselves, many, 125
Religion a collateral security, 222
  a definite set of doctrines, 762
  and science not antagonistic, 741
  beats me, 891
  blunderbuss against, 233
  blushing veils her fires, 215
  breathing household laws, 298
  definition of, 713
  delirious riot of, 635
  distant rewards of, 233
  don't go much on, 639
  freedom of, 273
  from any man, take my, 855
  grandeur of these states their, 534
  haven't whipped, 831
  his, an anxious wish, 376
  humanities of old, 317
  if there were no, 500
  in our northern colonies, 259
  inner unity and continuity with the world, 670
  is made, stuff of which, 670
  is what one is most interested in, 751
  John Bullism in, 706
  liberty and law, 333
  like the true, 950
  my, is to do good, 424
  my physician, of what, 1027
  my pollertics like my, 606
  of God, fight for the, 1126
  of late ages, Christian, 378
  of my father, of the, 1061
  of peace, 762
  of war, 762
  one, is as true as another, 126
  philosophy bringeth about to, 110
  pledged to, 333
  poet should avoid, as a subject, 556
  powerless to bestow tranquillity, 415
  reach a man through his own, 721
  rum and true, 359
  sensible men are all of the same, 421
  stands on tiptoe, 136
  superstition constructive, 543
  supported by private contributions, 550
  that sets men to rebel, 457

Religion, the honour of, 179
  the real motive force, 721
  the reformation of, 20
  their ancestral, 926
  to do good is my, 271
  unbeliever and, 403
  which alone rejoices, 604
  who defends his, 813
  whose dark, 653
  without a prelate, 394
  without any creeds, 837
  writers against, 258
  ye have your, 1127
Religions grow by natural laws, 645
  modified by life, 645
Religion's cause, avengers of, 1050
  sake, earth and stars for, 534
  sake, for true, 879
Religious book or friend, with a, 114
  complexion of modern world, 742
  feeling a verity, 543
  light, dim, 161
  people deeply suspicious, 785
  poetry relished by undevout, 744
  principle, on a, 247
  quarrels of seventeenth century, 866
  subjects distorted into political, 312
Relish him more in the soldier, 101
  of the saltness of time, 64
  of those arts, no, 196
Reluctant amorous delay, 152
Remain, as things have been they, 519
Remainder biscuit, dry as the, 49
  viands, 75
Remained to pray, 251
Remains, all that, of thee, 355
  an Englishman, 623
  be kind to my, 175
Remark, last, was a bubble, 630
  was shrewd, his, 263
Remarkable, nothing left, 105
Remedied, things that are not to be, 68
Remedies cured you dead, 783
  for extreme diseases, 971
  man's true, 1054
  men die of their, 1047
  oft in ourselves do lie, 53
  propose impossible, 962
  refusing, all, 30
Remedy for every sorrow, 987
  for every trouble, 978
  force is no, 478
  found out the, 36
  is calomel, 951
  sought the, 51
  things without all, 86
  to all diseases, tobacco, 125
  too strong, 966
  worse than the disease, 110
Remedye, lorn with-outen, 8
  the follye of people, they cannot, 10
Remember and be sad, 587
  and regret, better to forget than, 404

Remember, calmness to, 582
  can't, how they go, 590
  days of joy, 1020
  forget that I, 632
  I remember I, 390, 405
  it is as easy to marry, 483
  it was in the bleak, I, 460
  Johnny Appleseed, 626
  me when I am gone away, 587
  Milo's end, 180
  now thy Creator, 1110
  sweet Alice, don't you, 521
  the Alamo, 427
  the poor creature, I do, 64
  the power of beauty I, 176
  the way we parted, 633
  thee, far less sweet than to, 335
  thee yea, 92
  thy swashing blow, 77
  when times were not hard, 415
Remembered, be all my sins, 93
  in flowing cups, 67
  in thy epitaph, 63
  joys are never past, 306
  kisses after death, 466
  knolling a departing friend, 64
  sorrows, sweeten present joy, 393
Remembering happier things, 464
Remembers me of his gracious parts, 58
Remembrance and reflection, 207
  dear, makes the, 53
  is very free, my, 55
  no word to designate, 312
  of me, this do in, 1117
  of my former misfortune, 1036
  of past happiness, 464
  of the just shall flourish, 185
  of them, longer, 981
  of things past, 107
  rest, let his, 1125
  rise, bids, 252
  rosemary that's for, 96
  unforeseen, 807
  writ in, 59
Remembrances, burden our, 33
Remembren whan it passed is, 4
Reminiscence, most dramatic, 538
Remnant, leaving a, 625
  of decay, from each sad, 504
  of our Spartan dead, 359
  of their fires, 1050
  of uneasy light, 298
Remnants of remnants, deal in, 193
  of the good old time, 308
Remorse, farewell, 151
  men might know, 774
Remorseful day, 69
  mourners, 596
  pardon, 53
  winds, 588
Remote and tempting, equally, 1021
  from all the wrangling world, 271
  from cities lived a swain, 206
  from common use, 358
  from man with God, 201
  unfriended melancholy slow, 249
Remoter world, gleams of a, 366

Remove, drags at each, 249
  not the ancient landmark,
    1108
Removes the mask, he shows as
  he, 481
  three, as bad as a fire, 227
Remuneration Latin word for
  three farthings, 41
Render birth to dim enchantments, 447
  ill for ill, to, 620
  therefore unto Cæsar, 1115
  to all their dues, 1119
Rendezvous and pledge, my, 711
  I shall not fail that, 904
  with death, 904
  with destiny, 877
  with life, I have a, 904
Renew a right spirit within me,
    1104
Renewal of broken relations,
    636
  of life, watch the, 581
  of love, 979, 987
Renewing of love, 19
Renounce the devil, 1127
Renown, filled with, 649
  forfeit fair, 307
  highest of, 661
  left increased, 763
  only title to, 893
  purchased, 344
  runs a road of high, 899
  some for, 203
  to set the cause above, 764
  without a ripple of, 530
  won him most, 1079
Renowned Spenser, 119
  victories no less, 162
Rent is sorrow, her, 134
  landlord ever raise her, 948
  the envious Casca made, 83
Renunciation, progressive, 1073
Repair, friendship in constant,
    233
Reparation for our rights, 230
  pay for, 948
Repast and calm repose, 245
  what neat, shall feast us,
    162
Repay, to-morrow will, 178
Repeal of bad laws, 549
Repeat no grievances, 251
Repeateth a matter, he that,
    1107
Repeating, oft, they believe 'em,
    190
Repeats his words, 58
Repent at leisure, 52, 193
  speak what they will, 121
Repentance, call sinners to, 1116
  for the ill we have done, 1044
  to her lover, and give, 254
  winter-garment of, 1018
Repenting, after no, 162
Repents, will not believe a man,
    470
Replication, prompt, 109
Reply, churlish, 51
  conceives the apt, 924
  I pause for a, 83
  theirs not to make, 467
Report, country of fair, 960
  divine, knew from, 326
  evil and good, 1121
  me and my cause aright, 98

Report retort rejoinder repartee,
    650
  things of good, 1121
  thy words, how he may, 157
  vexation only to understand
    the, 1111
Reports of my death exaggerated, 616
Reporters, speaking through, to
  Buncombe, 379
Reporters' gallery fourth estate,
    397
Repose, dateless oblivion and divine, 610
  earned a night's, 434
  expects the issue in, 303
  foster-nurse of nature is, 99
  hushed in grim, 244
  in trembling hope, 245
  is insupportable, 636
  manners had not that, 462
  of passions, 330
  sacrifice his, 259
  shut my spirit in, 450
  spread out in its ample, 594
  statue-like, 473
  sweet repast and calm, 245
  wakes from short, 249
  what sweet, 396
Reprehend anything, if I, 277
Reprehension, become worthy of,
    1127
Representative, bald eagle, 228
  of the people, 1060
  your, owes you, 259
Representatives of the people,
  immediate, 320
Reproach, much like a, 976
  no defence against, 196
  of being, 108
  or fear, without, 442
  unconscious of, 425
Reproachful words, galled by,
    997
Reprobate the football of destiny, 551
Reprobation, fall to, 103
Reproduction, bondage to, 740
Reproof, brooding on such, 924
  on her lip, 307, 389
  valiant, 51
Reproved each dull delay, 250
Reptile that appears to relish it
  so little, 247
Republic, bloom forever O, 806
  could subsist at the present
    time, 1070
  is a dream, 854
  is a raft, 581
  of letters, 229, 241, 344
  of the grave, 602
  parties in a, 320
  proud, hath not stooped, 806
  shield of the great, 642
  shine perishing, 895
Republics, envy the vice of, 435
Republican form of government
  the highest, 581
Repudiate with indignation and
  abhorrence, 419
Repugnance to every form of
  mental exertion, 865
Reputation dies at every word,
    212
  for being clever and artistic,
    812

Reputation, good or bad, 196
  I have lost my, 101
  is an idle and false imposition,
    101
  is not carefully preserved,
    1049
  lost comes not again, 324
  makes immediate, 426
  men survive their own, 1029
  more than money, 987
  no luck in literary, 411
  reputation reputation, 101
  seeking the bubble, 49
  sold my, 1019
  sugar her bohea with your,
    430
  to be alive, 255
  to retain his, 1049
  written out of, 187
Repute, sink half his present,
    526
Reputed wise, 44
Request, conformity virtue in
  most, 411
  to fair, 1020
Requirements of women, 1077
Rescue by her side, 772
Researches deep, 280
Resentment, passion of, 1082
Reserve, hold the deadlier, 576
  thy judgment, 91
Residence, a forted, 37
  God's, 585
Residue, starve upon the, 910
Residuum, heavy dragoon is the,
    623
Resign, few die and none, 274
  nor when we will, 547
Resignation, die with graceful,
    330
  gently slopes the way, 250
  vacancies by, none, 274
Resigned when ills betide, 226
Resist the devil, 1122
Resistance of a kitten, 812
  of power, 350
  principles of, 259
  spirit of, 949
  wrong that needs, 543
Resisted, know not what 's, 285
Resistless eloquence, 156
Resolute and great, be, 529
Resolution, native hue of, 93
  never tell your, beforehand,
    130
  only take the, 346
  to fire it off himself, 233
  to make the day a happy one,
    313
Resolutions and protests of Irish,
    898
  he can keep his, 239
Resolve, heart to, 270
  itself into a dew, 89
  should by the forelock, 1058
  silence is the best, 1044
  to be thyself, 546
  wise to, 220
Resolved to live a fool, 129
  to ruin or to rule, 173
Resolves the moon into salt
  tears, 81
Resort of mirth, all, 160
Resource, infallible, 360
Resources, has not exhausted its,
    909

Resourceful at being remorseful, 935
Respect all such as sing when all alone, 484
  bread, sweat of the brow, 1090
  is what we owe, 506
  more tender, more holy, more profound, 76
  nature 's above art in that, 99
  of persons, no, 1119
  of place or persons, no, 54
  opinion high, 259
  takes away from it, 981
  that makes calamity of so long life, 93
  that title of, 61
  to the opinions of mankind, 273
  upon the world, too much, 43
Respectability, ultimum moriens of, 454
Respectable bird, turky more, 228
  professors of the dismal, 379
  the more things a man is ashamed of the more, he is, 720
  when was genius found, 431
Resplendent hair, most, 303
  star of, front, 418
Responding to the cheers, 770
Response of all the world, 1084
Responsible citizens, how to make people, 722
Responsibilities of being American, 666
Responsibility, heavy burden of, 921
  increases, 1082
  is like a string, 870
  of beginning war, 1077
Rest a stone, my, 423
  and be thankful, 946
  and peace at the last, 1128
  and that is true, 501
  are dead, and all the, 437
  better than I have ever known, 498
  can never dwell where, 148
  can never find, 597
  detachedly takes, 881
  dove found no, 1097
  dreamless, 681
  endless unfathomable, 655
  fancies that keep her from her, 88
  for the dead, 605
  forgot for which he toil'd, 107
  gets him to, 67
  give my spirit, 619
  good man gone to, 657
  her soul she is dead, 97
  in everlasting, 396
  in one thing excel the, 669
  in the grave, 362
  is but the handicraft of art, 533
  is just cheating, 930
  is not quitting, 501
  is rust, too much, 311
  is silence, the, 98
  is the fitting of self, 501
  life's victory won now cometh, 556
  like a warrior taking his, 364

Rest, master I've earned it, 844
  may reason and welcome, 489
  more frequent than the, 908
  nights of, 952
  no music in a, 532
  nowhere, the, 246
  or death dark death, 463
  palace of, 602
  peace and, at length have come, 392
  perturbed spirit, 92
  profound as the grave, 636
  repose in, 76
  sit round it and pluck; the, 431
  so may he, 74
  speedeth all to their, 643
  strange peace and, 659
  strengthens and supports the, 436
  talk about the, 657
  taste of, 588
  the gift of Gods, 26
  there the weary be at, 1101
  to heaven, leave the, 1043
  to their lasting, 58
  toil and not seek for, 1024
  too much, itself becomes a pain, 220
  veneration but no, 110
  well to come for deeper, 444
  when I slumber there, 517
  whistle for the, 1035
  who doth not crave for, 503
  who find their, 479
  who sink to, 247
  with our limbs at, 523
  without one moment of, 1077
  without haste without, 1058
Rests and nodding-places, 196
Rested under the drums, 145
Restful and agreeable, darkness is, 995
Resting place, laid it in its, 680
  quality, true-fixed and, 82
Resting-place in the cold grave, 652
  so fair, no mortal, 354
Restive or sluggish mind, stimulating the, 1083
Restless, bless Thee Lord that we are, 568
  crew he left behind, 200
  feet still, 866
  heads, 32
  night, lectures made a, 217
  plagued impatient things, 806
  soul, love orbit of the, 553
  stone, rolling, 67
  violence, blown with, 36
  violent hands and casual tongue, 806
  years make men, 490
Restlessness, round our, His rest, 428
Restoration of world trade, 909
Restorer, nature's sweet, 201
Restraint, liberty is wholesome, 340
  praise the firm, 933
Restreyne thy tonge, 8
Restriction on the multiplication of the inferior, 580
Restrictions and conventions, ascend above, 618
  on style or stance, 923

Resty sloth, 106
Result happiness, nineteen six, 496
  has been only grotesque, 1074
  misery, twenty ought and six, 496
Results, simplicity with the best, 922
Resumption, the way to, 446
Resurrection, all back at the, 1126
  and the life, I am the, 1118
  foretaste of the, 1064
  grounds, book barrows are, 892
  hope of the, 1128
  is rare, 636
Retailer of phrases, 193
Retard, every doubt that can, 417
Reticence as regards anything we deeply love, 600
  of soul peculiar to English, 871
Retired into his political cave, 478
  leisure, 160
  nature an enemy to pomp and noise, 195
Retirement, only true, 330
  Plato's, 156
  rural quiet, 224
  short, urges sweet return, 154
Retiring ebb, ne'er feels, 103
Retort courteous, 51
Retreat a single inch, I will not, 424
  according to the rules of war, 617
  among the angels, far, 878
  fear and, 1051
  friend in my, 263
  life's, 338
  loopholes of, 265
  make an honourable, 50
  without deliberation, 1051
Retreats of the ocean, sunless, 336
Retrograde, all that is human must, 271
Retrogression, progress more general than, 448
Retrospect, only exists in, 1083
Retrospection to the future, 278
Retrospections, long, and ironic thoughts, 788
Return, bid time, 59
  he shall not make any, 958
  little tasks make large, 566
  maketh best, 1020
  no more to his house, 1102
  not till the hours of light, 546
  retirement urges sweet, 154
  thou art gone and never must, 159
  to Lochaber no more, 205
  to our wethers, 1024
  to the unconscious vast, 765
  vilest sinner may, 199
Returning and rest, in, 1128
  as tedious as go o'er, 87
  back to their springs, its waters, 435
  port and hawser's tie no more, 537
  who dreads to the dust, 554

Reuben I have long been thinking, 954
Reveal no secrets, 251
Revel in a summer night, loves to, 459
was done, 600
Revels, midnight, 149
now are ended, 33
the winds their, keep, 502
Revelation measured by capacity, 805
of the Divine Idea, crystalline, 432
Revelator of the achromatic white light, 432
Revelry by night, sound of, 352
high life, worldliness, 1064
midnight shout and, 157
Revenge, a dire, 714
and in love, in, 1080
at first though sweet, 154
back on itself recoils, 154
capable and wide, 103
forgiveness better than, 1013
if not victory, 149
is a kind of wild justice, 109
is stamped upon my spear, 447
nation too great for, 591
one great instinct of, 1082
ready, has her, 1046
study of, 148
sweet is, to women, 358
will most horribly, 67
Revenges, time brings in his, 56
Revenons à nos moutons, 1024
Revenue, devising schemes of, 320
streams of, 340
Reverberate hills, holla your name to the, 54
Reverberation, fame demands prolonged, 529
Revered abroad, 284
Reverence, by fear than by, 975
due to it, 1079
for the laws, 466
is lent to well-established precedent, 733
none so poor to do him, 83
of the dead, 132
to God, a due, 112
Reverend head, the wise the, 199
signiors, grave and, 100
vice that grey iniquity, 62
Reverends of every order, 800
Reverent fingers, through, 785
knee, bend the, 910
silence, in, 349
Reverential dream, in, 896
Reverie is its pleasure, 1068
supporting nothing but his, 1068
Reveries so airy, 265
Reverse cannot befall, 585
do the very, 337
medal without its, 1072
Reversion in the sky, 217
Review, can't write can surely, 526
editorial we in a, 430
Reviewers a stupid and malignant race, 319
people who have failed, 319

Revisit'st glimpses of the moon, 91
Revolt, possessed by the, 1075
Revolts from true birth, 78
Revolution, age of, 273
and crime, parent of, 975
civilization, party of, 1069
is, realize what, 1068
opportunities for display, 422
volcano of, 740
Revolutions are not made they come, 479
break out, 975
do not always establish freedom, 396
never go backward, 480
state of mind which creates, 975
Revolves the sad vicissitudes, 249
Revolving moon, of one, 174
Reward, claims the honour and the, 985
enough for you, 961
is in the doing, 437
labour and not ask for, 1024
nothing for, 24
of a thing well done, 412
of disobedience, 153
of virtue is virtue, only, 411
this will be a full, 942
virtue is her own, 139
virtue to itself a, 139
wert not thine own, 760
Rewards and fairies, farewell, 128
fortune's buffets and, 94
not in, but in strength, 573
of religion, the distant, 233
Rewarder, who will now be my, 172
Rhamses knows, she knows what, 429
Rhapsody, three lines is, 995
of words, 95
Rhetoric, could not ope his mouth for, 141
dazzling fence of, 158
logic and, 111
ornate, 162
receive monuments and, 1077
wit and gay, 158
Rhetorically yes, 426
Rhetorician inebriated with exuberance, 420
Rhetorician's rules teach nothing, 141
Rheumatics, down with, 978
Rheumatism, I cotch the, 630
Rhine, guard along the, 1073
panks of de, 559
the castled, 433
the lady from over the, 510
wash the river, 317
wide and winding, 353
without delay, crossed the, 320
Rhinoceros, armed, 87
Rhode Island was the name, 372
Rhodes, colossus of, 956
scholarships, 711
Rhododendron, glory of, 372
Rhodopè, no voices O, 326
Rhone, rushing of the arrowy, 353
Rhyme applies, this, 1022
beautiful old, 108

Rhyme, build the lofty, 159
chained in, 1050
courage with a way-worn, 849
dock the tail of, 451
epic's stately, 442
far too warm for, 637
first made the nursery, 924
forget they the, 736
in many a mused, 383
is the commonplace passion this, 545
nor reason, 27, 37, 50
now I close my, 685
of all the threads of, 756
one for, one for sense, 142
outlive this powerful, 107
reason for my, 26
reason war with, 120
restoring the ancient, 900
ripple of laughing, 650
shall be forgotten, this simple 369
some careless, 640
that fails, it is the, 707
the measure of the latitude. 415
the rudder is of verses, 142
those that write in, 142
time in a sort of runic, 459
too warm for, 637
trouble drives me into, 909
unattempted in prose or, 148
Rhymes, I had store of, 321
love to sing their ancient, 507
Namby Pamby's little, 189
so rare to love, 673
that suggest wildest freedom. 416
Rhymed or unrhymed poem, 377
Rhymester play your part, realist, 471
Rhyming peer, 212
planet, born under a, 40
Rhythm and harmony find their way, 973
depend on simplicity, grace and, 973
poem recalled by its, 415
Rhythms, cages of brightplumaged, 831
Rhythmic tribal dance, 879
Rhythmical creation of beauty. poetry the, 461
Rialto, what news on the, 44
Riant roundelay, warbles a, 714
Ribbed and edged with steel, 873
Riband bound, but what this. 146
in the cap of youth, 96
to stick in his coat, 485
Ribbed sea-sand, 315
Ribber column, he read de, 712
Ribbon and a feather and a bit of lace, 653
of moonlight, 864
Ribs, labor pining hideth his sharp, 477
Rice, best not stir the, 1041
same old, 746
Rich a shrine, so, 809
alone, property of the, 985
and high, pleasant for them that's, 523
and new, 199
and poor are all as one, 967
and proud men, there are. 550

Rich and rare were the gems, 334
  and strange, into something,
  32
  are possessed by their money,
  the, 123
  as Chaucer's speech, 558
  as honesty, no legacy so, 53
  at forty nor wise at fifty, 137
  at once, no good man, 990
  attire, her, 383
  better to live than die, 237
  beyond the dreams of avarice,
  237
  brilliant like chrysoprase, 432
  eat with the, 788
  enough to give us all a farm,
  502
  ever by chance grow, 855
  gifts wax poor, 93
  God who made us, 429
  have power, 974
  he that maketh haste to be,
  1108
  in good works, 1122
  in saving common sense, 466
  jewel in an Ethiop's ear, like
  a, 77
  lace curtains, 559
  live like a wretch and die, 123
  man has sly way of jesting,
  197
  man to enter the kingdom,
  1115
  men only, corn for, 76
  men rule the law, 250
  mind that makes body, 52
  not gaudy, 91, 325
  perfume of her breath, 421
  person, prince or, 166
  plagues that haunt the, 267
  poor and content is, 102
  quiet and infamous, 399
  she was, and he was poor, 510
  soils often to be weeded, 112
  the treasure, 176
  they poor, I, 20
  to the one who was, 996
  wish I was, 883
  with forty pounds a year, 250
  with little store, 20
  with the spoils of nature, 144
  with the spoils of time, 244
  woman, as easy to marry a,
  483
  year, snow year, 137
Riches a valuable thing, 191
  all the dainties of, 589
  and honour in her left hand,
  1106
  and preferment, passage to,
  950
  are ready snares, 9
  best, 250
  fame and pleasure, 1049
  found in company with, 1064
  from every scene of creation,
  290
  good name better than, 1041,
  1108
  grow cares follow, as, 984
  have wings, 265
  he heapeth up, 1104
  I care for, 967
  infinite, in a little room, 31
  make themselves wings, 265
  of heaven's pavement, 149

Riches of the world, 869
  that grow in hell, 149
  that with mine can vie, 504
  the embarrassment of, 1053
  virtue and, seldom settle on
  one man, 124
  without a man, 996
Richard answered it, 541
  conqueror, came in with, 51
  Richard O my king, 1055
  struck terror to the soul of, 72
Richelieu learned that Wallenstein was dead, 594
Richer for poorer, 1128
  life, a, 573
  love, than my tongue, 98
  than all his tribe, 104
Richest author that ever grazed,
  239
  was poor and the poorest, 435
Richmond, broad-streeted, 928
  Hill there lives a lass, on, 280
Richmonds in the field, six, 72
Richness of the fatherland, 1090
Rid on 't, mend it or be, 86
Riddle, monstrous hard, 647
  of a woman's mind, 1037
  of the world, 208
  that we shrink from giving up,
  only, 624
Riddles mar, still the ancient,
  736
Ride abroad, next doth, 264
  in a wagon of hay for me,
  823
  king in a carriage may, 449
  mankind, things, 409
  on, rough-shod if need be,
  496
  to crowche to wait to, 26
Rider, he the bold, 643
  lost, for want of horse, 137,
  227
  that breaks youth, the, 138
Riders in a race, 655
Rides in the whirlwind, 194, 215
  on the posting winds, 105
  post, evil news, 157
  upon the storm, 266
Ridge of life, 186
Ridges, on its, 318
Ridgepole up, held the, 708
Ridicule often decides matters,
  984
  reaches his vitals, 742
  seared by, 881
  the test of truth, 377
  truth the test of, 280
  without malice, endured a
  great deal of, 456
Ridiculous affairs, serious in,
  1003
  at times almost, 900
  atheism in art may become,
  556
  don't make me, 325
  down with, notions of Deity,
  569
  excess, wasteful and, 58
  in serious matters, 1003
  no spectacle so, 398
  sublime to the, 272
  though customs be never so,
  72
Riding is a joy, 487
  o'er the azure realm, 244

Riding on the rail, pleasant,
  510
Rifle and pack, with, 892
  leans on his gleaming, 552
Rifles, glitter of their, 372
Rifles' rapid rattle, stuttering,
  918
Rift through which sublime fulfilments, 626
  within the lute, 470
Rifts between, grope in, 579
Rigdom Funnidos, 189
Rigged with curses dark, 159
Rigging, without an inch of, 670
Right, always do what is, 564
  as a ribstone pippin, 811
  as a trivet, 350
  as God gives us to see the, 291,
  457
  as yourself to the road, as
  much, 676
  be always sure you're, 349
  be sure you're, then go ahead,
  686
  before command, coveting,
  764
  born to set it, 92
  by chance, a fool now and
  then, 263
  by divine, 319
  by force of beauty, seems, 430
  come out all, 495
  cried served him, 510
  divine of kings, 215
  dwelling much on, 1050
  enjoyed in its own high, 930
  every single one is, 780
  fierce for the, 626
  firmness in the, 457
  following him that sets thee,
  1011
  God defend the, 69, 561
  good from a book, 430
  hand and left, God's, 506
  hand forget her cunning, 1106
  hand, his red, 150
  hands of fellowship, 1121
  have we to happiness, what,
  1075
  hew to the line of, 578
  his conduct still, 252
  his life I 'm sure was in the,
  167
  honorable gentleman is the
  first, 478
  I see the, and I approve it too,
  187, 986
  idea of the gods, 975
  if he did thus or thus, 413
  in every cranny but the, 267
  in the use of them, 242
  is chiefly with the strong, 1050
  is pushed back, 1083
  is right since God is God, 503
  little tight little island, 305
  lose his, 225
  makes might, faith that, 455
  man in the right place, 274,
  513
  mind, clothed and in his, 1116
  more, than his neighbors, 514
  more'n ef we's doin', 712
  names, call things by their,
  290
  never reasons and is always,
  412

Right, no one is, 1060
  of all, duty of some, 319
  of coining words, 346
  of conquest, 1054
  of life divine, 445
  of the strongest, 1054
  of the white election, by the, 584
  of way, died maintaining his, 948
  on, I only speak, 83
  onward steer, 162
  or truth were at stake, earnest if, 540
  or wrong, our country, 262
  over old Marm Hackett's garden, 508
  prisoner who has no, 970
  rather be, than president, 329
  serves us jolly well, 780
  shall disestablish wrong, 651
  side, but works for the, 569
  side, follow the, 1029
  slender guarantee for being, 450
  sorry for your heaviness, I am, 4
  speech there's no, 1022
  swear to guard your native, 294
  that man is in the, 1076
  that which they will is, 635
  the day must win, 503
  the wrong, others shall, 444
  there is none to dispute my, 263
  through present wrong the eternal, 442
  to assume the responsibility, 1077
  to be kept right, when, 580
  to blame and punish, 1084
  to dissemble your love, 283
  to do a great, 47
  to education, 1093
  to govern is an express grant, 320
  to maintenance in old age, 1093
  to possess property, 1071
  to pray is, 386
  to relate and embellish, a, 1056
  to say it, your, 1053
  to set, sun has a, 606
  to strike, no, 819
  to use money, 1071
  to work, to rest, 1093
  transforms strength into, 1054
  tried so hard to do the, 628
  trust in God and do the, 499
  unnoticed as the breath, 780
  until it is settled, 718
  was clear, his, 948
  was right, 280
  way, one must do good in the, 641
  were worsted, though, 494
  whatever it is, 207
  whose life is in the, 208
  wise world is mainly, 470
  words, how forcible are, 1102
  wrong follow the king, 470
Rights, equal power to maintain their, 424
Rights, never exceed your, 1054
  of an Englishman, 949
  of individual in England and France, 739
  of man, called the, 260
  of men, bugle forth the, 771
  of the question, 970
  preserve entire those, 949
  property has its duties as well as, 420
  reparation for our, 230
  to social, 424
  unalienable, 273
Righteous altogether, judgments of the Lord, 457
  are bold as a lion, 1108
  cause, armor of a, 752
  die the death of the, 1099
  forsaken, not seen the, 1104
  God, I leave the, 728
  man, prayer of a, 1122
  not, but sinners to repentance, 1116
  overmuch, be not, 1109
  perfect grace, not to the, 710
  perils doe enfold the, 24
  shall flourish, 1105
  souls of the, 1124
Righteousness and peace, 1105
  exalteth a nation, 1107
  imputed unto him for, 1125
  sun of, 1114
Rightful king, and he is, 706
  voice to say, 626
Rightly settle a question, 398
  to be great, 96
Rigid earth revives, 837
  for justice sake, 539
  plowmen bear in mind, 417
Rigidity, absolute unvarying, 777
Rigorous law, 980
  line, move on a, 547
Rigour of the game, 323
  of the statute, 35
Rill, by cool Siloam's shady, 342
  nor yet beside the, 245
Rills, thousand, 243
Rim, lifting her silver, 385
  mountain's, 485
  of shadow is the line of light, 531
  of the far-flung sky, 870
  over the shining, 858
  the sun's, dips, 315
Rims so pale, 369
Ring as to an oak, adds a, 527
  encompasseth thy finger, how my, 71
  get gallantly within the, 941
  going round as in a, 123
  happy bells, 469
  in the Christ that is to be, 469
  in the nobler modes, 469
  in the thousand years of peace, 469
  in the valiant man, 469
  of galloping feet, 676
  of pure and endless light, 170
  on her wand she bore, a, 334
  out old shapes of foul disease, 469
  out the darkness of the land, 469
  out the narrowing lust of gold, 469
Ring out the old ring in the new, 469
  out the thousand wars of old, 469
  out their delight, how they, 460
  out wild bells, 469
  so thin so pale is yet of gold, 280
  sweet, notes of the harpers, 387
  to evensong, 17
  with this, I thee wed, 1128
Rings and seals, passionate after, 166
  make them fairy, 801
  of beauty, 572
  of which all Europe, 162
  on the rakoon's tale, 518
Ringing clear, a good song, 771
  grooves of change, 464
  plains of windy Troy, 464
Ringlet, blowing the, 465
Ringlets, her raven, 600
  of light, 643
Rio Grande, down by the, 711
  love to roll to, 784
Riot, change these for endless, 759
  dark with stormy, 910
  of religion, delirious, 635
  thrown forever in a, 938
Ripe age gives tone to violins, 573
  and good one, a scholar and a, 74
  and ripe, hour to hour we, 49
  cherry, I cry, 133
  rich tint of the cornfields, 737
  shelter to grow, 547
Ripened fruit is golden, 927
  into faith, persuasion, 302
Ripeness, love grown to, 463
Ripening breath, summer's, 78
  his greatness is a, 73
  swelling of fresh life, age is, 559
Ripest fruit first falls, 59
  peach is highest, 696
Ripple of laughing rhyme, 650
  of renown, sank without, 530
Ripples break, round his breast, 386
  of her hair, 583
  where the countless, 760
  with the idle, 865
Rise again, but now they, 87
  build ladder by which we, 521
  by sin, some, 35
  from out the sea, thus did Venus, 555
  in arms against the Omnipotent, 153
  in glad surprise to higher levels, 436
  let it, till it meet the sun, 339
  sweet happy children you will, 474
  to no little surprise, 351
  to the top of the tree, 622
  up never, dead men, 632
  up Xarifa, 374
  with the lark, 23
Risen to hear him crow, thought sun had, 520
Rises from dead cerements the Christ, 609

Rising all at once, their, 150
day, when like the, 416
early, heaven's help better
than, 1041
from affluence, 615
in clouded majesty, 152
in his, seemed a pillar of state,
150
never assisted the sun in his,
514
of the sun, from the, 1105
tempests shakes a guilty land,
with, 194
to a man's work, 1011
worm punished for early, 510
Risk, ambition has no, 425
everything is sweetened by,
588
of spoiling its bloom, 728
worth that brings no, 960
Risks, filled with noble, 311
Risked a cause, patriots for a
theory, 430
Rites, by these festival, 363
thou shouldst have seen, my funeral, 340
Ritornella, love's, 387
Ritter Hugo von Schwillensanf-
tenstein, 559
Rituals and faith excel, in, 566
Rival cities soar, what care
though, 410
in the light of day, 303
to dispose, intrigued a, 479
Rival's bliss, never can endure a
279
praise, 337
Rivalry of aim, 636
River, across the, 811
Alph the sacred, 315
all alone, 810
and the wooded hills, 774
and through the wood, over
the, 404
at Monmouth, 67
at my garden's end, 214
banks of that lonely, 396
by the door, 702
dark brown is the, 702
Dee, lived on the, 269
fair and crystal, 128
flow in one down eternity's,
503
glideth at his own sweet will,
297
how long the, 660
in Macedon, there is a, 67
in the broad, ebbed and flowed,
437
known yet unknown, 929
let us cross the, 928
like the foam on the, 308
like the snow falls in the,
287
moonbeams on a, 573
no sound save the rush of the,
569
of death has brimmed, 765
of his thoughts, 434
of oblivion, Lethe, 150
of passing events, 1010
of time, on the, 933
of unfailing source rapid, vast,
393
parts the silent, 568
see one, see all, 124

River, shining on the weeds of
the, 854
silent, 434
sources of the great, 929
still the rolling, 929
the weariest, 632
they say isn't crossable, 872
upon a golden, 522
whose course we trace, to each
bright, 364
will reach the sea, 660
Rivers and forests, let me court,
982
are damp, 918
are highways, 1047
as with people, with, 710
better than oceans, like, 808
by shallow, 31
cannot quench, 70
disappear in deserts, 378
flow, her hills arise, 382
greatest, not the most agreeable, 710
of Babylon, by the, 1106
of Damascus, 1101
of the kings, 927
run into the sea, 982
run to seas, 177
water that you touch in, 1022
wide and shallow brooks, 160
River's brim, primrose by a, 296
music, 704
River-brink, find you by the,
1018
Riverside on the slow hill-slant,
596
Rivets up, hammers closing, 67
Rivulet of text, a neat, 279
Rivulets dance, where, 297
myriads of, 466
Road, a curve in the, 924
along a rough a weary, 285
along the 'ard 'igh, 955
broad hard-beaten, 416
by me, the western, 840
death's, 983
fast by the, 218
fringing the dusty, 525
grows strange as life runs on,
529
house by the side of the, 218,
733
I travel the open, 535
in Spain, 827
into his kindness, the very, 76
is clear before you, 779
is once built, when a, 705
it is a rough, 991
joys of the open, 757
let me stand by the, 636
like one on a lonesome, 315
long, knows no turning, 965
may lie, wherever my, 577
morn furthers a man on his,
959
no expeditious, 749
no royal, to geometry, 977
no street, no, 391
not built to last, 705
of casualty, 45
of evening, softly along the,
822
of Gratitude in Samoa, 705
of high renown, 899
of it, smooth the, 242
of the bairnies' feet, 807

Road one treads to labour, 742
rolling English, 827
says go, the little, 836
sends him on his heavenly, 362
take the high, 952
takes no private, 208
taxed horse on a taxed, 314
tell us of the, 1019
that leads to Corinth, 646
the, below me, 703
through life's dark, 364
thy feet have trod the, 784
to En-dor, 781
to fame and fortune, 700
to fame, the surest. 432
to hell paved with good intentions, 662
to hell wants mending, 506
to Ireland, the right, 934
to Mandalay, 782
to national downfall, surest,
450
to Paradise, old, 866
to tread, a higher, 596
to virtue, no ready, 144
together to its end, fare the,
835
was a ribbon, 864
went along that, 924
whose dust is gold, 154
wind up-hill, does the, 587
Roads all even and peaceful,
536
between the thunder, 809
improvement makes straight,
282
of genius are crooked, 282
of hell, tread the, 875
their fathers had built, 937
two, diverged in a wood, 838
winding as old roads will, 443
Roadside flowers, we are the, 757
found by the, 1085
Roadway calls no more, 836
lead on rapture's, 775
Roam, absent from Him I, 306
soar but never, 304
some love to, 503
they are fools who, 226
when far o'er sea we, 337
where'er I, whatever realms to
see, 249
Roamed o'er many lands, 388
with my soul, I, 461
Roaming, in the first of my, 718
in thought over the universe,
536
Roar and rains go by, 886
billows wild contend with angry, 480
gently as any sucking dove
42
grumble and, telling the battle
was on, 552
music in its, 354
of conflict, in the, 602
set the table on a, 97
the spray and the tempest's,
502
there went up a muffled, 770
you as 't were any nightingale
42
Roaring crown, rush against the,
690
is ended, when the, 800
lion, as a, 1123

Roaring lions, talks as familiarly of, 57
kings, and the, 903
street, 806
Roast and the smacking kisses, 937
beef of old England, 193, 229
beef the Englishman's food, 193
ruled the, 343
rules the, 9, 984
Roasted rare, new-laid eggs, 177
Rob a neighbour, that he might, 399
me the exchequer, 63
Peter and pay Paul, 14, 122
the Hybla bees, 84
us of our joys, 257
Robbed, he that is, 102
the, that smiles, 101
Robber, Barabbas was a, 1118
particularly a bookseller, 233
Robbers bold, what makes, 70
safe time for, 967
Robbery, fair exchange not, 357
Robbie Burns, send a man like, 777
Robbing, sharping and, 228
Robbry, chaunge be no, 16
Robe, dew on his thin, 328
he is a, 21
of clouds, throne of rocks in a, 357
of night, azure, 382
of purest white, wings of gold and, 511
the judge's, 36
Robes and furred gowns hide all, 99
garland and singing, 162
loosely flowing hair as free, 119
of gold, evening trails her, 418
riche or fithele, 5
shining, 1073
ye weave another wears, 368
Robert and Paul, John and Peter, 570
of Lincoln is telling his name, 373
Robin found and wove it cross-wise, 681
good fellow, 164
is here in a coat of brown, 573
jolly Robin, 255
legend of the, 444
or help one fainting, 583
Redbreast did cover them, 258
Redbreast in a cage, 281
thou'rt an ass, 394
thou wert there upon the day, 586
wears his silver vest, 586, 647
Robins come, when the, 584
ghosts of the, 621
the babes in the wood, as did the, 527
Robin's breast gleameth, 586
lost in play, 883
Robings of glory, 571
Robinson Crusoe, poor, 246
Robs me of that which not en-riches him, 102
the vast sea, the sun, 81
Robust and brass-bound man, 784

Robust spirit grew, 584
Robustious periwig-pated fellow, 94
Robyn jolly Robyn, 255
Rock, a man sat on a, 664
among the Plymouth sand, 403
as if by magic grown, 500
as the shadow of a great, 1111
down, roll a, 831
dwell on a, or in a cell, 22
famed, 647
founded upon a, 1114
gem of the old, 145
I will build my church, upon this, 1115
Island Pere Marquette, 926
meeting rock, 904
moulder piecemeal on the, 355
my fortress and my deliverer, my, 1100
of Ages cleft for me, 272
of God's eternal word, 305
of the national resources, 340
of time, 889
pendent, a towered citadel, 105
reclined, all on a, 205
safe upon the solid, 915
shall fly from its firm base, this, 308
shoal and other evils, 834
stood on, to bob for whale, 146
tall, the mountain, 296
that is higher than I, 1104
the cradle of reposing age, 213
upon the eternal, 231
wish I were a little, 839
would crown the work, an-other, 484
Rocks are gray and shore is steep, 642
caves lakes fens bogs, 150
hollow, water dropping will wear hard, 23
Moab's, 372
music hath charms to soften, 193
ocean that hollows the, 416
that are steepest, 258
the cradle, the hand that, 534
throne of, robe of clouds, 357
to roses, change from, 405
trees and herbs in a garden, 1027
walled round with, 633
whereon greatest men have oftest wrecked, 156
Rock-a-By Lady from Hushaby street, 699
Rock-bound coast, stern and, 370
Highland home, 401
Rocked in the cradle of the deep, 350
Rocket, rose like a, 271
Rocking on a stormy surge, 964
Rock-ribbed hills, 371
Rocky ledge, trod by, 758
Rod, a creed is a, 633
and thy staff, thy, 1103
angler who has no, 733
beaten with his own, 11
he that spareth his, 1107

Rod, lightning reached a fiery, 658
must heal the sin, 659
of criticism, 789
of divination, 789
of empire might have swayed, 244
of iron, rule with a, 1123
pass under the, 474, 1113
spare the, 9, 142, 169
to check the erring, 299
wit's a feather and a chief a, 208
Rode, the six hundred, 467
Roderick, where was, then, 308
Rodin wrought, 789
Rodless Walton of the brooks, 733
Roger in, won't let, 712
is my dog, 572
Rogue, inch that is not fool is, 174
the Roman was a, 867
Rogues in buckram, 62
were dead, when the, 372
Rogue's Island once, 372
Roguish chaps, three, 954
thing, equity is a, 130
Roland for an Oliver, 946
the great bell, 620
Role, play a superior, 883
Roll darkling down, 230
forward, the ages, 594
of common men, 62
on dark blue ocean, 354
on thou ball, 622
Virginia's blazoned, 561
Rolls it under his tongue, 187
of Noah's ark, 173
Rolled up the wrong way, hedge-hog, 391
Rolling beach, 572
deep, home on the, 502
English drunkard, 827
in fine frenzy, 43
restless stone, stands upon 67
stone gathers no moss, 14, 988
world, 588
year is full of Thee, the, 224
Roman came, before the, 827
Catholic bell, 566
conquers, wherever the, 991
fame, above all, 214
fashion, after the high, 105
hand, we do know the sweet, 55
holiday, to make a, 354
more an antique, than a Dane, 98
name, above any Greek or, 173
noblest, of them all, 84
populace, death and the, 438
senate long debate, can a, 195
streets, gibber in the, 89
than such a, 83
thought hath struck him, a, 104
was a rogue, 867
Romans call it stoicism, the, 194
countrymen and lovers, 82
last of all the, fare thee well, 84
pray to Tiber, 400
threw in their corn, 593
were like brothers, the, 400
Roman's life a Roman's arms, a, 400

Romance brought up the nine-
fifteen, 781
color of, 644
dragged in a, 1050
is always young, 442
last, 724
sense of humour spoils, 724
symbols of a high, 384
the thing we call, 751
Romances of Marivaux, 246
Romanism and rebellion, 494
Romantic Ashbourn, down thy
hill, 294
if folly grow, 209
Ireland's dead, 791
plays inferior to tragedies,
794
Romany in June, to, 843
Rome, aisles of Christian, 408
and I, world knows only, 119
and Sion, stray to, 396
beauty old Greece or, 442
big with the fate of, 194
but that I loved, more, 83
can Virgil claim, 176
city of the world, 422
do as they do at, 1042
eternal devil to keep state in,
81
grandeur that was, 460
growing up to might, 478
hath most precious, that
which, 593
hook-nosed fellow of, 65
I do fast on Saturday at, 1016
I gave to, 711
in the height of her glory, 341
in, there opened a gulf, 593
is most precious, what to, 593
man I loved in, 916
mighty name of, 401
move the stones of, 83
not built in one day, 15, 1042
notionable dictes of antique,
184
palmy state of, 89
pride of Greece and, 408
queen of land and sea, 478
shall fall when falls the Coliseum, 354
spent their fruits of, 903
taller town than, 827
than second in, 999
thou hast lost the breed of
noble bloods, 81
time will doubt of, 360
to Iceland, from, 1050
trumpet of a child of, 634
was founded in April, 706
when at, do as they see done,
126
you long for the country, at,
985
Romeo, Romeo, I'm, 755
wherefore art thou, 78
Ronsard sung, thus, 1027
Rood, died without a, 481
has not a star, there's no, 408
Roof, arched, 161
beneath his neighbor's, 924
fretted with golden fire, 92
linger on the flathouse, 938
no gilded dome swells from the
lowly, 374
of mine, beneath this, 439
rain fell on the, 929

Roof, they reach the, 673
to shroud his head, 124, 129
Roofs and men, done with, 758
of the world, yawp over, 535
rowl above the blessed, 819
Roof-garden superimposed, 791
Roof-tops, brakemen walk along
the, 926
on your sliding, 926
Room after room I hunt the
house through, 487
and secondly of my, 322
and verge enough, ample, 179,
244
as your company, 322
be poor indeed, though the,
610
beauty in this plain, 866
blazed with lights, 81
civet in the, 263
finest music from books in the,
691
for all creation, 502
for another rose, 697
for beauty, always, 697
for death, not, 516
for it, room, 656
for only English language in
America, 734
for Shakespeare, 119
for six scotches more, 105
for talk, conduct gives, 1046
for the impurities, no, 878
for them in the inn, no, 904,
1116
for two, and hardly, 540
for wit, heads so little no, 147
I grant him a white man's, 878
I only seek, 738
in a large and lofty, 725
in a man's house, hidden, 827
infinite riches in a little, 31
left alone in your, 1056
no need to leave your, 1090
no wit for so much, 147
paces about her, 899
reading, often sat in my, 228
regulate my, 239
the whispering crowded, 547
there was no, 904
to be quiet in, 887
to hold the memory of a
wrong, no, 415
to room, move from, 843
to swing a cat, 497
to this still, 444
up of my absent child, grief
fills the, 58
walls of memory's, 662
where we shall find a cleanly,
139
who sweeps a, 135
whose every nook, 756
Rooms, glimmering, 793
lack the heart's divine perfumes, 568
Roosian, he might have been a,
623
Roost, as chickens come home to,
425
Rooster crow, watch the, 761
hungry, don't cackle, 688
Root and all in my hand, I hold
you, 467
and flourish, it will take, 548
and fruit alike, cankers, 924

Root, axe is laid unto the, 1117
from which a tyrant springs,
974
humility that low sweet, 338
in human needs, 660
in my horse's body, 1056
insane, 84
love that took an early, 423
mandrake, 117
nips his, and then he falls, 73
of all evil, love of money is
the, 1122
of all our woe, 155
of the matter is in me, 1102
strikes its little, 369
striking at the, 514
to crowning petal, 701
tree of deepest, 272
Roots, bound by strong, 619
by so many, 663
by the river, spreadeth out her,
1112
of light, spreading, 932
of man's nature, 736
of our thoughts and feelings,
1074
of roses are kept alive, 540
polished by digging, 938
springs from hidden, 924
with spring rain, dull, 899
Root's white core, 385
Rooted in the human heart, 278
sorrow from the memory, 88
Rope enough, you shall never
want, 1026
loath to lay out money on a,
123
over an abyss, 1079
stretched, man is a, 1079
the true way goes over a, 1090
what use for the, 541
Rosalie Lee, was my beautiful,
432
Rosaries and pixes, 143
Rosary, my rosary, 765
Rose above the mould, 392
among roots, 703
any nose may ravage a, 484
at Christmas, desire a, 40
Aylmer, 325
bedstead of a crimson, 911
blossom as the, 1111
by any other name, 78
color of a, 939
dewdrop on the, 309
enfolded passion of the, 923
English unofficial, 893
fairer for sweet odour, 107
for a ribbon a wreath, for a,
866
for every perfect, 809
friendship is the breathing,
453
get one perfect, 919
go lovely, 146, 788, 868
granite and, 570
happy is the, distilled, 42
has but a summer reign, 305
hath fallen from thy chaplet,
309
I am not the, 1060
in aromatic pain, 207
in spring, familiar as the,
1011
in the deeps of my heart, 790
is a rose is a rose, 836

Rose is faded, when this our, 796
is fairest when 't is budding, 24
is, her cheek like the, 388
is out of town, 584
it tried to be a, 585
it wavers to a, 648
je ne suis pas la, 1060
last, of summer, 335
like a full-blown, 383
like a rocket, 271
love is like a, 587
love thou the, yet leave it, 593
lovely is the, 301
lump of clay placed beside a, 560
may bloom for England, 642
mighty lak' a, 730
my luve 's like a red red, 287
of evening drops, 912
of love, gather, 133
of Sharon, I am the, 1110
of yesterday, 1018
of youth, he wears the, 104
one, for beauty attracted me, 276
one sad ungathered, 451
our queen our, our star, 405
plot, 583
red as a, is she, 314
robed in dazzling immortality, 366
room for another, 697
scent of the Eden, 954
should shut and be a bud, 383
so red, never blows the, 1018
spectre of the, 1071
sweeter in the bud, 24
that all are praising, 388
that He planted, 709
that lives its little hour, 372, 868
the colour of love and youth, 523
the mystic the improbable the. 923
the year I met with, 604
this is the joy of the, 841
thought like a full-blown, 383
tiger sniffs the, 892
to him that loved the, 748
to wash a single, 707
tree full in bearing, 276
trembled a sense of the, 629
under the, 145
upon my balcony, 482
vanish with the, 1019
when baby smelt the, 702
when June is past the fading, 140
whispers of passion, red, 675
white, breathes of love, 675
with all its thorns, 587
with leaves yet folded, 361
with thorns, 976
without a thorn, 280
without the thorn, 134, 151
wreath has lost a, 309
Roses, a few late, 665
a rain and ruin of, 633
a thousand, 1018
and lilies and violets, 388
and white lilies, 121
are kept alive in snow, 540

Roses at my head, plant thou no, 587
bein' Gawd ain't a bed of, 908
bower of, by Bendemeer's stream, 337
expect to gather, 977
four red, on a stalk, 72
friends again with, 631
full of dew, 696
full of sweet days and, 135
gather her blue, 784
in December seek, 351
make thee beds of, 31
money is beautiful as, 412
must die with the year, 666
ne'er a thorn, 674
never expect to gather, 977
petals from blown, 463
Pyrgo and Lapwater, 855
red and roses white, 784
red and violets blew, 24
roses, strew on her, 546
scent of the, 336
she wore a wreath of, 388
sweet, ain't the, 730
underneath the snow, 638
virgins soft as the, 355
Rose's hope while yet unblown, 384
need, know a, 837
scent is bitterness, 748
Roseate splendors, with, 669
Rose-briar, love is like the wild, 516
Rosebud garden of girls, 469
set with thorns, 466
Rosebuds blow, earlier shall the, 553
filled with snow, 121
gather ye while ye may, 133
let us crown ourselves with, 1124
Rose-land, over the red, 633
Rose-leaves die of grieving, 885
scattered, like, 360
stirred with the air, 360
Rose-lipp'd cherubin, 103
Rose-lipt maiden, 743
Rosemary and rue, there's, 56
for remembrance, 96
Rose-moles all in stipple, 672
Rose-petal down the Grand Canon, 853
Rose-red city half as old as time, 443, 500
Rose-streak of morning, 493
Rosewater on a toad, pour, 417
Rossetti wrought from his own soul, 680
Rost, rule the, 9, 13, 129
Rosy progress, morn begins her, 155
steps, morn her, 153
trembling, 1086
wreath, sent thee late a, 119
Rot and rot, from hour to hour we, 49
propagate and, 208
that cankers root, 924
to lie in cold obstruction and to, 36
work done the lie shall, 556
Rote, learned and conned by, 83
perced to the, 4
sarcastikul, this is, 606
Rots itself in ease, 91

Rotten apples, small choice in, 52
at the heart, a goodly apple, 44
in Denmark, something is, 91
mackerel by moonlight, 320
Rouge Bouquet, wood they call the, 891
Rough and thorny way, 595
and unshod, 592
as nutmeg-graters, 204
but gentle uncouth but gracious, 539
cold weather, there must be, 540
dog a tough dog, 912
male kiss of blankets, 894
road of life, 657
rude sea, all the water in the, 59
sir but ready, 496
way leads to rest, 730
what in other mouths was, 524
with age and gashed with wars, 508
Rough-hew them how we will, 97
Rough-hewn race, 784
Rough island story, 467
Roughly, life has passed, 267
Rough-shod if need be, 496
Round, a perfect, 489
about the spot, yet, 481
and round we run, 503
and yellow, moon so, 589
as appel, 3
at the top, from the, 431
attains the upmost, 82
beauty's perfect, 682
by round, mount to its summit, 521
dance their wayward, 297
earth, of this, 725
fat oily man of God, 225
glory guards with solemn, 541
hoop's bewitching, 240
I know the table, 470
keeps up a continual, 1009
life's dull, 242
moon, ascending silvery, 536
my door, wave and flutter, 418
numbers are false, 238
of starry folds, 385
of truth, the full, 471
shelved, us lie mummied authors, 565
the age of gold, comes, 477
the slight waist, 355
the square, all, 391
the world serenely, undulate, 536
trivial, the common task, 365
unvarnished tale, 100
walked, and regarded his critic, 508
Rounds, great physician makes his, 757
of life's long ladder, 493
Roundabout, lead men's minds the, 649
this great, 267
what's lost upon the, 842
Rounded and permanent national life, 876
with a sleep, life is, 33
Roundelay in praise of poverty, 714

Roundelay, my merry merry, 28
Round-heads and wooden-shoes, 195
Rouse a lion, the blood stirs to, 61
    and stir as life were in 't, 88
    the lion from his lair, 311
Roused woman, something about a, 494
Rousing chorus, has a, 810
Rousseau, ask Jean Jacques, 264
    odd fantastic ass, 767
Rout, breaks up in, 964
    on rout, ruin upon ruin, 151
    was it on a day, of, 748
    we feel our, 652
    where meet a public, 115
    wherefore doth your, send forth, 401
    world with its motley, 267
Routed all his foes, thrice he, 176
Routine of existence, 737
Routine-work large part of life, 646
Rover bad and free, bold bright, 837
    could hear one dreadful sound, 321
    lad was ever a, 866
    whither away fair, 668
Roving, go no more a, 357
    Lady Moon where are you, 459
Row, awkward hand in a, 639
    brothers row, 334
    fellows are out to, 862
    no other than a moving, 1019
    one way and look another, 122
    set 'em in a, 829
Rows on rows of natural objects, 1057
Rowers, like, who advance backward, 122, 1029
Rowland for an Oliver, 946
    to the dark tower came, 99
Royal office to execute laws, 261
    race of hicks, 853
    raiment, rags are, 942
    road to fame, 700
    road to geometry, no, 977
    sport, 54
    throne of kings, this, 59
    train believe me, a, 74
    wage, paid his subjects with a, 894
Royalists, economic, 877
Royalty of virtue, the, 619
Ruat cœlum fiat voluntas tua, 136, 145
Rub, let the world, 1035
    there's the, 93
Rubs which providence sends, 253
Rubbing the poor itch of your opinion, 75
Rubbish heaps of the ancient city, in the, 1126
    of his own monument, 343
    write such hopeless, 300
Rubente dextera, 150
Rubicon, Caesar and the, 1000
    I had passed the, 340
Rubies from the air, gather, 877
    grew, where the, 133
    price of wisdom is above, 1102
    wisdom is better than, 1107

Ruby, beryl-rimmed rebecs of, 432
Ruby Shakespeare hewed, 680
Ruby-rimmed beryline buckets, from the, 431
Rudder is of verses, rhyme the, 142
    or needle, without, 401
    true, steer my, 1029
Ruddy drop of manly blood, 410
    drops, dear as the, 82, 244
    ripe tomata, 637
Rude am I in my speech, 100
    by day and lewd by night, 759
    do not think me, 851
    figures of a rough-hewn race, 784
    forefathers deemed it two, 590
    forefathers of the hamlet, 244
    hand deface it, may no, 297
    in speech, though I be, 1121
    militia swarms, 177
    multitude call the afternoon, 41
    sea grew civil at her song, 42
    storm how fierce soe'er, no, 480
    stream, mercy of a, 73
    the clever so, 942
Rudeliche, speke he never so, 5
Rue and euphrasy, 155
    my heart, with, 743
    nought shall make us, 58
    rosemary and, 56
    sold for endless, 742
    with a difference, wear your, 96
Rueful conflict, the heart riven the, 298
Ruffian, that father, 62
Ruffle of drums, 767
Ruffles on his shirt, no, 404
    sending them, 188, 252
Ruffling cut-throat gait, 842
Rug, snug as a bug in a, 227
Rugged individualism, 830
    line, harsh cadence of a, 175
    pine, where the, 642
    Russian bear, 87
    way, follow all the, 549
Ruin and confusion hurled, in, 194
    behold this, 338
    both bring permanent, 930
    content with, 834
    drunkenness identical with, 1016
    entails tremendous, 966
    final, fiercely drives, 202
    has designed, whom God to, 175
    hath taught me to ruminate, 107
    listed red as, 939
    loaded full o', 677
    majestic though in, 150
    man marks the earth with, 354
    of the state, predicts the, 281
    of worlds, the, 891
    on the state, statesmen pulled, 430
    one prodigious, swallow all, 218
    or to rule the state, 173
    see my country's, 940
    seize thee ruthless king, 244

Ruin, systems into, hurled, 207
    upon ruin rout on rout, 151
Ruins, fame on lesser, built, 167
    human mind in, 941
    of home, o'er the, 507
    of Iona, 233
    of St. Paul's, 398
    of the noblest man, 82
    undistinguished heap of, 398
Ruin's ploughshare, stern, 285
    red embrace, leaped to, 690
Ruined but by himself, 234
    by natural propensities, 261
    sides of kings, 129
Ruing, causes sharp, 965
Ruin-trace, can print no, 355, 440
Rule absurd, grammar has a, 872
    all be done by the, 104
    alone, too fond to, 213
    animals end by different, 758
    authors have established a kind of, 196
    better no, 961
    Britannia, 225
    but one, 1063
    for drinking, 196
    gran'ther's, was safer, 527
    guided by this golden, 623
    Homer's, the best, 213
    I leave this, 349
    little sway, a little, 223
    long-levelled, 158
    muses to their ancient, 896
    my sole, of life, 378
    no, without exception, 123
    nor rhyme, neither, 869
    of life, new, 751
    of men entirely great, beneath the, 425
    of not too much, 155
    of Plato, 162
    of thumb, shared all by the, 704
    one, for politicians, 798
    over others, how shall I, 1025
    reign, what is pomp, 70
    scepter of, is the spade, 448
    sufficeth them, good old, 298
    that was against the, 362
    the good old, 298
    the great, ill can he, 25
    the law, rich men, 250
    the rest, 13, 129
    the state, to ruin or to, 173
    the varied year, to, 224
    them with a rod of iron, 1123
Rules, a book of, 680
    a few plain, 302
    and hammers, 105
    and regulations, ignore the, 791
    and tools, study of the, 922
    it would seem, the same, 661
    let those five make all the, 754
    may be ignored by writer, 741
    mocks the doctor's, 442
    never shows she, 209
    o'er freemen, who, 238
    of the game laws of nature, 563
    the roast, 9, 984
    the twelve good, 251
    the waves, Britannia, 225

Rules the world, is the hand that, 534
Ruled, he that is willingly, 9
Ruler having a human body, 973
  of heart and brain and soul, 559
  of the inverted year, 224, 265
Rulers of state, 729
  of the Queen's navee, 623
Ruleth all the roste, 9
  his spirit, he that, 1107
Ruling passion, 209, 210
Rum alone's the tipple, 833
  and true religion, 359
  cattle to deal with, 687
  Island, 524
  Romanism and rebellion, 494
  yo-ho-ho and a bottle of, 704, 710
Rumble grumble and roar, terrible, 552
  of a distant drum, 1018
Rumbling universe, rearrange the, 693
Ruminate, as thou dost, 102
  ruin hath taught me to, 107
Ruminating, learn from kine, 1080
  long been, 1087
Rumination wraps me, my often, 51
Rumour of oppression, 264
  tamper not with idle, 688
Rumours of wars, 1116
Run amuck, too discreet to, 213
  away, he feared to, 771
  away, they conquer love that, 141
  back, time will, 161
  but through its woof there, 501
  down, and all the wheels, 523
  he may, that readeth it, 1113
  I can, or I can fly, 158
  life's race well, 555
  once more, I'll have a, 577
  red with other wars, 602
  seems short to-night, 717
  to and fro, many shall, 1113
  to waite to ride to, 26
  with the hare, 23
  with the hound, 13
Runs away, he that fights and, 143
  away, he who fights and, 254
  may read, he that, 266, 467
  the great circuit, 265
  the world away, 94
Runcible hat, weareth a, 499
Runes and legends of a thousand years, 911
  of rapture half forgotten, 755
Rung in the ears, vanitas vanitatum, 545
  of a ladder, 563
Rungs, hides its, 544
Runic, something too, 592
  rhyme, time in a sort of, 459
Runner, a naked, 789
  overtaken by a swifter, 888
Runners, the swift, 981
Runneth not to the contrary, 248
  over, my cup, 1103
Running brooks, books in the, 48
  laughter, 748
  sprightly, 178

Running streams, on craggy hills and, 447
  you can do, it takes all the, 598
Runnymede, heirs of, 443
  what say the reeds at, 784
Rupert Brooke's war sonnets, 907
  of debate, 419, 425
Rural quiet, retirement, 224
Rush of faces in the town, 896
  of the river, no sound save, 569
  to glory or the grave, 328
Rushed to meet the insulting foe, 280
Rushes between the one and the other, 425
Rushing of mighty waters, like the, 1111
  of the arrowy Rhone, 353
  of the blast, the, 372
Ruskin and Morris spokesmen of the hand-wrought, 730
Russet mantle clad, morn in, 89
  year inhaled the dreamy air, 551
Russia, last out a night in, 36
  who had been captured in, 1065
Russian bear, the rugged, 87
  is conceited, 1076
  is nothing but sneezing, 592
Russians shall not have Constantinople, 562
Rust along the leaves, 926
  better to be eaten to death with, 64
  brightest blade grows dim with, 453
  in rust, of earth in earth and, 564
  less than, 735
  less than the, 775
  too much rest is, 311
  unburnished, to, 464
Ruste, if gold, 5
Rustic life and poverty, 327
Rustics, amazed the gazing, 251
Rusticity, ostentation and, 218
Rusting in a pool of tears, 749
Rustling in unpaid-for silk, 105
  of each purple curtain, 460
  of the trees, 955
Rusty and dusty of hat and shoe, 737
  for want of fighting, 142
Ruth, dinner-bell's a sound of, 599
  gleaning the fields of childhood, 558
  when sick for home, 383
Ruthless breezes borne, by, 605
  fire, bred in them by, 586
  king, ruin seize thee, 244
Rydal Lake, way that lead to, 296
Rye or out to Severn, to, 827
Rye-bread days, 476
Rym dogerel, this may wel be, 6

SABAOTH and port, 112
Sabbath appear'd, smiled when a, 264
  bill to frame a, 392
  I do not love the, 924

Sabbath, of that deeper sea, disturbs the, 480
  was made for man, 1116
Sabean odours, 151
Sabina has a thousand charms, 193
Sabine make, crock of, 983
Sable beak and glossy plumage, 288
  cloud with silver lining, 157
  goddess, night, 201
  hearse, underneath this, 119
  night, son of the, 30
  shore, who shrinks from the, 554
  silvered, his beard a, 90
Sables, suit of, 94
Sabler tints of woe, 245
Sabra in the forest with St. George, 299
Sabrina fair, listen, 158
Sack, addict themselves to, 65
  empty, hard to stand upright, 227
  heaviest, every one thinks his, 138
  intolerable deal of, 62
  many a plethoric, 543
  of dry tall tales, 927
  of tobacco, with his, 928
  purge and leave, 63
Sackcloth for banner, 913
Sacrament of confirmation, 1053
Sacramento, on the banks of the, 502
Sacred and inspired divinity, 112
  bronze button, 630
  bulwarks, 392
  burden is this life, 454
  deposit, 545
  gate, and near the, 481
  honour, pledge our, 273
  horror, there is a, 1069
  if anything is, 535
  literature, belong to, 924
  nation, he hates our, 44
  page engrossed on the, 686
  pity, drops of, 49
  songs and dances, 972
  to a certain extent, 1064
  water, defile its, 686
  wine of dawn, 764
Sacrifice, costly, on altar of freedom, 457
  fame sorrow or, 954
  makes undaunted the final, 747
  never forgive him for the, 835
  to God, 217
  to the graces, 222
  to the muses, 222
  turn delight into a, 135
  unpitied, an, 259
Sacrifices, such, my Cordelia, 100
Sacrilegious murder, 86
Sad and bad and mad it was, 489
  and happy days of yore, 703
  as angels, 242, 327
  by fits, 't was, 248
  day, at the close of one, 705
  enough without your woe, 718
  experience to make me, 51
  heart, ruddy drops that visit my, 82
  heart tires in a mile-a, 56

Sad hemlocks, 602
  is our life, 503
  is our youth, 503
  kissed mouth, 630
  life cut short, 513
  music of humanity, 296
  near to make a man look, 43
  news bad news, 679
  offence to learning and to
    taste, 332
  old earth, 718
  or singing weather, 631
  past all belief, 607
  remember and be, 587
  say I'm weary say I'm, 346
  soul, 619
  stories of my own mishaps, 37
  stories of the death of kings,
    60
  tale's best for winter, 56
  things stay and glad things
    fly, 632
  thoughts and sunny weather,
    531
  time, sweet time, 389
  uncertain rustling, the silken,
    460
  vicissitude of things, 242, 249
  votarist in palmer's weed, 157
  words of tongue or pen, 442
Saddens us, times when mirth,
    426
Sadder and a wiser man, 315
  even than I, they are, 606
Saddest of year, days the, 372
  thing that befalls a soul, 587
  when I sing, 389
Saddle, a short life in the, 758
  cloth is fringed, my, 917
  fits, as long as the, 928
  things are in the, 409
  to horse and away, boot, 485
  to keep changing the, 927
  your dreams, 872
Saddled and bridled, 169
Sad-eyed Hindu king, 618
Sadness and longing, feeling of,
    434
  diminishes or hinders, 1048
  diverter of, 139
  is a wall, 880
  leave-takings wasted, 746
  out of our, 773
  prevailing, 327
  this echo of pain, this, 1065
  wraps me in a most humorous,
    51
Safe again, hold me, 489
  and smooth of heart, 920
  and sound your trust is, 204
  bind safe find, 19
  comfort of feeling, 567
  for perpetuity, 891
  from the censure, 1017
  from the many honored by the
    few, 528
  in my sylvan home, 408
  on shore the pensioned sailor,
    199
  perdition to be, 410
  silent and, 676
  time for robbers, 967
  to be honest is not, 103
  to-day, may you go, 850
  upon the solid rock, 915
  within the heart, 698

Safe within its heart nestles the
    seed, 535
Safeguard of mediocrity, 413
Safer being meek than fierce, 490
  gran'ther's rule was, 527
  to know too little than too
    much, 613
Safety, ensure your, 976
  fairest chance for, 972
  first, 740
  garnered up in, 725
  in multitude of counsellors,
    1107
  is our speed, over thin ice, 412
  lies in them and in ourselves,
    70
  little temporary, 226
  obscurity often brings, 962
  out again in, 961
  pluck this flower, 61
  pot of ale and, 66
  strike against public, 819
  to teach thee, 57
  unite for public, 1061
Sagacious blue-stocking, 399
  of his quarry from so far, 155
Sagacity, in vast infant, 888
  whereby we may attain, 1017
Sage advices, lengthened, 287
  a-shinin' in the sun, 831
  by saint by savage and by,
    216
  experience, 280
  he stood, 150
  he thought as a, 269
  in the silver dew, 830
  just less than, 333
  long experience made him, 206
  there lived a, 482
  thinks like a, 426
  truths electrify the, 327
  truths half so, as he wrote,
    516
  when they find a, 853
  whom Greece can show, every,
    1050
Sages and reasoning fools, 335
  have died to learn, what, 626
  have seen in thy face, 263
  in all times assert, 11
  smile, made the, 359
  teach more than all the, can,
    295
Sage's pride, vain the, 214
Sage-brush to kindle with, 766
Sager, by losing rendered, 357
Said before, nothing that has not
    been, 979
  for lack of listeners are not,
    540
  his say, when he's laughed
    and, 481
  it, as well as if I had, 192
  little, is soonest mended, 133
  not what we, but what we are,
    626
  on both sides, much may be,
    196, 229
  on the whole so well, 550
  only dreamer dream no more,
    558
  than done, no sooner, 978
  that ever were sung or, 437
  the greatest of the great, 471
  when this is, 610
Sail, bark attendant, 209

Sail, bids thee take, 1092
  breath of heaven swell the,
    264
  clears the top, 963
  far-off, 327
  he bade set, 631
  if fortune fill thy, 267
  is as a noiseless wing, this, 353
  learn of the little nautilus to,
    208
  lifts the, 1021
  of Sir John was blown, 552
  on life's ocean diversely we,
    208
  on O ship of state, 435
  on O union strong and great,
    435
  scarce a, from England, 337
  set every threadbare, 450
  swan spreads his snowy, 386
  than ballast, more, 184
  the sea, as now we, 572
  thy best ship of democracy,
    537
  to take in, 410
  to the west, 519
  two towers of, at dawn, 519
  what avail the plough or, 410
  white and rustling, 345
Sails, and unbent, 833
  argosies of magic, 464
  crowding, thy white, 668
  filled and streamers waving,
    157
  filled with a lusty wind, 28
  it, Columbus, 414
  purple the, 104
  swell full. To sea to sea, 406
  the moonlit, 673
  we see on the ocean, 689
Sailed away for a year and a
    day, 498
  by and ceased to be, years, 437
  for sunny isles, 423
  off in a wooden shoe, 699
  with me before, you never, 292
Sailing hour, ere, 847
  like a stately ship, 157
  on obscene wings, 316
  the Vesuvian Bay, far away,
    552
Sailor, a shipwrecked, 1092
  and passenger, little and great,
    576
  home is the, 703
  looked upon San Salvador, 858
  messmates hear a brother, 247
  on a mast a drunken, 72
  pensioned, lies safe on shore,
    199
  thy endless cruise, old, 537
  would not watch the star, 1052
Sailors are but men, 44
  cheers for the, 664
  hastily making rafts, 850
  jealous for our vessels, 826
  o'er all brave, 536
  soldiers more accostable than
    old, 423
  swallow'd in the flood, 71
  to some unseen harbour, 692
  with bearded lips, 436
  won't believe it, 311
Sailor's trust, warranting the,
    661
  wife the sailor's star, 690

Sailyards tremble, the, 28
Saint an object almost of suspicion, 645
Anne, yes by, 54
Anthony of Padua, 789
as any medieval, 889
Augustine well hast thou said, 436
crowned him, 573
eagerly frequent doctor and, 1018
George and the dragon, 57
he weren't no, 639
in heaven unshod, 688
it, sinner it or, 209
it would provoke a, 209
John, awake my, 206
John mingle with my friendly bowl, 213
Lawrence the Susquehanna the Tombigbee, 932
Mary's lake, swan on still, 298
my late espoused, 22
Nicholas would soon be there, 332
no time to be a, 918
Paul nothing leave, 138
Paul's, ruins of, 398
Peter give not, so much, 138
run mad worst of madmen, 214
savage and by sage, by, 216
seem a, when I play the devil, 71
sustain'd it but the woman died, 217
threadbare, 115
to corrupt a, 60
who findest what is lost, 789
Saints above, men below and, 306
again and made new, 828
all hail ye, 566
bards, heroes if we will, 545
death of his, 1105
for all the, 555
go hurrying to the Virgin, 917
his soul is with the, 317
immortal reign, where, 199
in glory everlasting, numbered with the, 1127
in its nameless, 566
who taught, 205
who wash their hands too clean, 913
will aid if men will call, 315
Sainted, a thing enskyed and, 35
Saint-seducing gold, 77
Saintship of an anchorite, 352
Sair, mony hearts are, 952
Sairey little do we know, oh, 495
Sake, earth and stars for religion's, 534
for my own love's, 486
for quietness', 130
no man do for your, 630
of being supported, for the, 446
of God's true religion, for the, 1126
of our friends, 980
weeping for your, 915
worn for virtue's, 942
Sakes, for their own, 130
Saki from that bowl, has poured, 462, 1018

Salaam aliakum, peace be with you, 1055
Salad days, my, 104
Salads, time of, 242
Salamander, a kind of heroine in chastity, 196
like a freezing, 933
Salary, before spending draw your, 791
Salesmanship, scholarly in regard to, 884
Salisbury and Gloucester, 67
Sally of the mind, a loose, 232
there's none like pretty, 189
Salmons in both, there is, 67
Salmon's height, sunrise dreaming upon, 556
Saloon, jabber of a waterside, 925
Salt and the free grasses, tongue of, 929
have lost his savour, 1114
inhospitable sea, 856
of common life is individuality, 710
of our youth, we have some, 34
of the earth, 600
of the earth, ye are the, 1114
of truth, 429
peck of, 1034
pillar of, 1097
season with, 1121
seasoned with Attic, 1047
seaweed clings to the marble, 289
the savor, how, 1021
thing of watery, 833
upon the tails of sparrows, 191
with a grain of, 1041
Salt-fish on his hook, 104
Salt-lick of his nose, 926
Saltness, oil vinegar sugar and, 252
of time, 64
Saltpeter, villainous, 61, 579
Salutary influence of example, 233
neglect wise and, 259
Salutation, cursory, 234
of the dawn, 953
the common Turkish, 1055
to the morn, 72
Salute to this world, a passing, 758
Salvation, bottle of, 22
for an helmet the hope of, 1121
is free, we tell, 566
march, who to, 924
none of us should see, 46
stand, can, 667
tools of working our, 143
work out your own, 1121
Salve of flattery soaps all you do, 699
Samarcand, all the gems of, 275
here to drowsy, 830
Samaritan, a certain, 1117
acts like a, 426
without the oil and twopence, 313
Samarkand, golden journey to, 882
Same again, life is never the, 559
all the, a hundred years hence, 607

Same always and never the, 411
another and the, 215
as everywhere the, 1057
as on the land, just the, 508
by day, will not look the, 428
dear things lift up the same fair faces, 560
except as to paper and print, 238
its flash is still the, 404
though changed, the, 305
to your old wife Joan, 690
to-day and for ever, the, 478
will it not be then the, 401
Samian wine, 359
Samoa, road of Gratitude in, 705
Samphire, one that gathers, 99
Sample, by a small, 1033
Sampler, ply the, 158
Sanat sanctificat et ditat, 227
Sancho Panza said and so say I, 510
Sanctified the crime, numbers, 268
Sanctimonious theory, veneered with, 465
Sanction of the god, 218
Sanctities, flower of olden, 556
Sanctity, odour of its, 828
of reason, endued with, 154
Sanctuary, suspicion's, 353
Sanctum, supercilious, my, 392
Sand an' ginger when alive, 781
against a grain of, 424
and ruin and gold, land of, 631
and the wild uproar, 408
centuries fall like grains of, 445
dry and trodden, 659
golden is the, 702
he plows the, 898
in it, every grain of, 1074
leaves or driving, 218
little grains of, 553
of the desert, 765
of the sea, who can number the, 1124
on the silver, 576
pass like, 857
plain to be seen on the, 187
roll down their golden, 343
trampled and beaten as the, 436
which is by the sea, 1101
wrote upon the, 362
Sands are flowing, one by one, 564
come unto these yellow, 32
death has shaken out the, 375
drenchèd, 587
drifting, 231
eternal moan, on its desolate, 503
ignoble things, 129
lone and level, 367
o' Dee, across the, 523
of time, footprints on the, 433
small, the mountain make, 203
splendors fall on Syrian, 442
syllable men's names on, 157
that are lamplit at eve, 618
that lie so meek and still, 887
to say, on the dew-damp, 845
Sandal, massive, set on stone, 915
shoon, by his, 256

Sandals for my feet, winged, 807
Sand-dune-hundredfold, 971
Sand-dunes, like the, 1011
Sandalwood cedarwood and sweet white wine, 832
Sanded floor, the nicely, 251
Sandpile we run our fingers in, 855
Sandpiper and I, the little, 619
Sandwich and apple, one eats one's, 1089
Sane 't is fitter being, than mad, 490
San Francisco bay, hills of, 763
Sang, it may turn out a, 285
of love and not of fame, 565
sing as Martin Luther, 481
Sanguine fields, from her own, 848
who has checked, 1056
Sanguine-souled, meet sunrise, 652
Sanity and perfection of living, 549
Sans intermission, 49
taste sans everything, 50
teeth sans eyes, 50
Santa Claus lives forever, 643
not believe in, 643
things in the dark besides, 830
Santa Cruz to Valley Forge, 867
Sap begins to stir, 757
stirred not at whisper, 642
Sapphire Laura wore, 680
violet glow and silver gleam, 801
walls, 521
Sapphires, glowed with living, 152
Sapphire-blaze the living throne, 243
Sappho from Lesbos, 960
loved and sung, where, 359
tenth Muse, 960
Sapping a solemn creed, 353
Saraband, dance a merry, 830
Sarcasm the language of the devil, 379
Sarcastikul, this is rote, 606
Sardonic smile, 426
Sark, her cutty, 287
Sassafras, fill me with, 851
thou art the stuff for me, 323
wood boiled down, 323
Sat and combed their beautiful hair, 600
by the waters of life we, 395
in the low-backed car, 389
like a cormorant, 151
Satan and his imps, 907
came also, 1101
exalted sat, 149
finds some mischief, 199
get thee behind me, 1115
limb of, 616
play at cherry-pit with, 55
was now at hand, 150
wiser than of yore, 210
Satan's old saw, 1101
Satanic school, the, 322
Satchel, schoolboy with his, 49
Sathan that ever waiteth, 6
Satiety of commendations, 80
Satire be my song, 351
ever moral, but, 1050

Satire, for pointed, 184
is my weapon, 213
like a polished razor, 221
or sense, 213
true, 774
Satires, the critic's, 660
Satirical musical miracle, 805
Satisfaction, a present, 971
as the time requires, 112
is spent with, 197
not lessened by being anticipated, 330
of knowing we are avenged, 505
of the tongue, windy, 220
Satisfied, I would be, 659
that is well paid, he is, 47
Satisfy the soul, what will, 537
Saturday and Monday, betwixt a, 291
night, how pleasant is, 291
not always fall on, 491
Saturday's child has far to go, 956
Saturn keeps the years, 808
Satyr, Hyperion to a, 90
man either a stoic or, 716
Satyrs grazing on the lawn, like, 32
Sauce in the world like hunger, no, 1039
sharpen with cloyless, 104
Saucy doubts and fears, 87
Saul among the prophets, 1100
and Jonathan were lovely, 1100
hath slain his thousands, 1100
Sauntered Europe round, 215
Sausage friend and mash, it's, 909
Savage anti-everythings, lean hungry, 453
breast, soothe the, 193
enough pilgrimage, 883
fight them be, 753
indignation tear his heart, 193
place, 315
saint and sage, by, 216
tribes pursue their game, 279
wild in woods the noble, ran, 178
woman, take some, 464
young man who has not wept is a, 769
Savages, brutal, 418
hunting in the swamps, 418
of New York kindle, 912
Save in his own country, 1115
it be some far-off touch, 470
me from the candid friend, 293
means to live, 32
the squadron, honor France, 492
thou a soul, 444
Saving a little child, 639
Savior for a friend, with the, 660
of 'is country, 781
Saviour was sold for thirty pence, 136, 257
Saviour's birth is celebrated, 89
Savour and seeming, all the winter long, 56
how salt the, 1021
of the mythical, 1089
salt have lost his, 1114

Saw and loved, 271
and overcame, 65
her eye was bright, then I, 387
no sound of hammer or of, 266
old Autumn in the misty morn, 392
the air too much, do not, 94
the little that is good, 536
what the not-day exhibited, 537
who, to wish her stay, 154
ye the lass wi' the, 388
Sawe, an old sayd, 25
Saws, full of wise, 50
Saxon bards, 397
blood has flowed, our, 443
legend, 653
phrase, ancient, 434
Saxons cool-headed with hearts aflame, 553
Saxpence under my thumb, 311
Say farewell, and looks around to, 481
I had a thing to, 57
I, Sancho Panza said and so, 510
I'm sick, I'm dead, 212
it that should not, though I, 131
it with flowers, 821
more than this rich praise, 108
neither it is a deadly magic, 928
no, mebby to mean yes an', 527
no this morning sir I, 428
not the struggle naught availeth, 519
nothin' without you're compelled tu, 527
spite of all their friends could, 498
than do, more disagreeable to, 1000
that man is mighty, they, 534
thou lov'st her well, 109
to yourself what you would be, 1008
what say they? Let them, 22
what to a novice she could, 511
what to, and eat and drink, 398
when he's laughed and said his, 481
why gals acts so or so, to, 527
Says a foolish thing, never, 184
nor thinks, 618
not he that merely, one, 378
Saying, wise and old, 438
witty, proves nothing, 1052
Sayings in her heart, kept all these, 1117
of philosophers, 142
such odd, 45
Scab of churches, 114
Scabs, make yourselves, 75
Scabbard, keep the sword within the, 176
of the night, 756
sword glued to my, 129
sword within its, sleeps, 848
Scabbards, swords leaped from their, 260

Scaffold high, on the, 511
  truth forever on the, 525
Scale, geometric, 141
  Justice with lifted, 215
  of war and peace, 425
  on a grand and speculative, 533
  turns the, 975
  weighing in equal, 89
Scales, philosopher's, 345
Scallop-shell of quiet, 22
Scalps of Indians I have slain, 917
Scampering of their steeds, 372
Scan, or their faults to, 250
  presume not God to, 207
  your brother man, 285
Scandal about Queen Elizabeth, no, 279
  and from scare, from, 674
  and the cry, 465
  has ever been the doom, 986
  waits on greatest state, 107
Scandalous and poor, 184
Scant, our nerves are, 462
Scanted men in hair, what he hath, 37
Scanty vale of human life, 318
Scanter of your maiden presence, 91
'Scapes, hair-breadth, 100
Scar, if two lives join there is oft a, 486
  man without one, 997
  mark us with a, 808
Scars, arms unstained and free from, 517
  jests at, that never felt a wound, 78
  marks and, 172
  of woe, writ with, 570
  won ye so great, 748
Scarce expect one of my age, 292
  long leagues apart descried, are, 519
  times were not hard and money, 415
Scarcity, owes its value to, 232
Scare, wail is heard yet its notes never, 545
Scarecrow in a garden of cucumbers, 1125
Scarecrows of fools beacons of wise men, 564
Scared out of his seven senses, 310
Scarfs garters gold, 208
Scarlet breast-knot gay, 573
  creeper loves the elm, 565
  flannel, in a piece of, 498
  leaf, sorrow and, 531
  line was slender, 541
  of the maples, 757
  sins were, 811
  though your sins be as, 1111
  towne, in, 257
Scatter and unloose it, they, 106
Scattered to the wind, thou wert, 462
Scene as false and fleeting as 'tis fair, 343
  be acted o'er, this lofty, 82
  below, to watch the, 640

Scene, care one whit for, 649
  each, a different dish, 200
  ever dear, one, 746
  I do not ask to see the distant, 403
  in every, by day by night, 393
  in this imperfect gloomy, 942
  last, of all, 50
  love gilds the, 278
  my dismal, 80
  not one fair, 388
  o'er this changing, 343
  of living corn made bread, 834
  of man, o'er all this, 206
  on which they gazed, 296
  or incident, memory of previous, 423
  or two, start a, 900
  passing, 348
  that memorable, 169
  tread again the, 306
  was all changed, the, 697
  was changed, the, 424
Scenes, among our literary, 882
  behind your, 233
  gay gilded, 195
  like these, from, 284
  look on heaven's, 953
  of my childhood, 348
Scenery and fresh air, too much, 801
Scent of odorous perfume, 157
  of the Eden rose, 954
  of the roses, 336
  survives their close, 748
  the fair annoys, whose, 263
  the morning air, methinks I, 91
  which pays the best, I, 526
Scents flinging, their fresh, 889
  sweet unmemoried, 668
Scented the grim feature, 155
Scentless sunflower, fame is the, 453
Sceptic could inquire for, 142
Scepticism, luxury of, 1081
Sceptre, beside the, 425
  he wields a mighty, 534
  leaden, stretches forth her, 201
  of rule is the spade, 448
  shows the force of temporal power, 46
  signed with a golden, 610
Sceptred hermit, a, 362
  isle, this, 59
  pall, tragedy in, 161
  sway, mercy is above this, 46
Scheldt or wandering Po, 249
Scheme for her own breakfast, 203
  of life to banish fear, 894
  of the weal and woe, his, 489
  of things, grasp this sorry, 1020
Schemes o' mice, best laid, 284
  of revenue, 320
Schiller has the material sublime, 319
Scholar, a, among rakes, 400
  and a gentleman, 285
  error of the would-be, 426
  more in the soldier than in the, 101
  ripe and good one, 74
Scholars, base born, the greatest, 124
  great men, not great, 454

Scholars, he was a rake among, 400
  officers but not, 123
  so many senseless, 184
  the land of, 250
Scholar's life assail, the, 230
  soldier's eye, 93
School, creeping unwillingly to, 49
  days, in my joyful, 325
  experience keeps a dear, 227
  for the day dismissed, 662
  Germany's later, 1076
  he that travelleth goeth to, 110
  in life's hard, 444
  microcosm of a public, 420
  never at her, 229
  nor creed, question, 657
  of darkness, in the, 682
  of mankind, example is the, 261
  of peace, 583
  of Stratford, 5
  of the Lord's service, 1016
  tell tales out of, 13
  the Satanic, 322
  to see a lamb in, 362
  when you got expelled from, 729
  with heavy looks towards, 78
Schools, flogging in great, 236
  jargon of the, 189, 263
  knowledge never learned of, 442
  masters of the subtle, 900
  old maxim in the, 190
Schoolboy cries, It snows, 362
  hath at his fingers' ends, 125
  were you ne'er, 951
  whining, 49
  whips his taxed top, 314
  with his satchel, 49
Schoolboys, frisk away like, 285
  from their books, as, 78
Schooldays, in my, 44, 325
School-girl's exercise, butchered to make, 756
Schoolman's subtle art, 213
Schoolmaster is abroad, 331
  the senator the clock-peddler, 1070
School-masters puzzle their brain, 253
School-room bogey, shrunk to a, 756
Schoolrooms for the boy, better build, 512
Schooners and the merry crews, 832
Science and his only art, 770
  and of art, master of, 678
  and religion not antagonistic, 741
  and sense in calomel, 951
  bright-eyed, 244
  carries us into speculation, 704
  Christian, defined, 549
  conquering, 539
  cookery a noble, 123
  countenance of all, 295
  cradle of every, 930
  discovered genius wrought, 305
  eel of, by the tail, 215

Science fair, frowned not, on his birth, 245
falsely so-called, 1122
gave law the air of a, 340
good sense though no, 210
in, address the few, 426
in, read by preference the newest, 426
new, that men lere, 4
nosing in the grass, 822
of, and logic he chatters, 406
of his own invention, 1076
of manifest destiny, 518
of our law, the lawless, 465
of purer holier laws, 523
one, will one genius fit, 210
professors of the dismal, 379
proud, never taught to stray, 207
star-eyed, 327
stimulating to imagination, 914
the dismal, 379
the history of, 1057
waves of, beat in vain, 543
where credit goes in, 696
will turn upon its error, 1084
Sciences, all the abstruse, 358
books must follow, 111
touching nombres and proporciouns, 8
Scientific advance, lever of all, 449
Scintillate, scintillate globule vivific, 345
Scilurus on his death-bed, 1002
Scipio buried by the upbraiding shore, 354
Scissors, two halves of a pair of, 495
Scoff, fools who came to, 251
Scoffers, these obstructionists, these, 795
Scolding from Carlyle, 452
Scole of Stratford, 5
Scone in Glasgow, give you a, 815
Scope of conversation, more, 128
of my opinion, 89
to its utmost, 823
Scorch, bright suns may, 404
Score and tally, no books but the, 69
dissolving, 664
muster many a, 291
Scorn all burning hot, said I in, 753
delights, 159
for the time of, 103
hiss sound of public, 155
in spite of, 149
laid in, 824
laugh a siege to, 88
laugh thee to, 1125
laughed His word to, 263
not the sonnet, 304
of scorn the hate of hate, 462
read to doubt or read to, 310
silence perfect expression of, 721
tender love's repaid with, 269
they, the strand, 513
to change my state with kings, 107
to laugh to, 51
under her solemn fillet, 410

Scorn, what a deal of, looks beautiful, 55
Scorns of time, whips and, 93
Scorned, no fury like a woman, 193
slighted, disappointed woman, 193
Scorner's seat, sit in the, 733
Scornful jest, most bitter is a, 230
Scorning the base degrees, 82
too fond for idle, 447
Scorpion died of the bite, 254
on a stone, 936
Scot and lot, 118
Scots, a few industrious, 29
wha hae wi' Wallace bled, 286
wham Bruce has aften led, 286
Scotch mist, umbrella no avail against, 530
nation void of wit, 246
understanding, 246
Scotched the snake, 86
Scotches more, room for six, 105
Scotchman, left to a beggarly, 233
much may be made of a, 235
Scotchman's noblest prospect, 234
Scotchmen Jews English in Ireland, 709
Scotia's grandeur springs, 284
Scotland, banner of, 390
before ye, I'll be in, 952
boasts a thousand names, 603
drink a cup to, 393
family ties in, 751
has invaded England, 588
her thistle bold, 642
oats for people in, 232
stands, where it did, 88
universities of, 752
Scotland's broad claymore, 500
dales and Scotland's vales, 393
strand, fair, 287
Scotsmen, island governed by, 906
Scott's message to the public, 804
Scoundrel, an ass or a, 1079
and a coward, 233
last refuge of a, 236
maxim, 225
Scoundrels, a healthy hatred of, 379
offscouring of, 381
Scoured with perpetual motion, 64
Scourge of God, him that was the, 374
of war, pray this mighty, 457
whose iron, 243
Scourged to his dungeon, 371
Scours the plain, Camilla, 211
Scout, the blabbing Eastern, 157
Scowl of cloud sky, what a, 493
Scramble for pelf, struggle for power or, 510
Scranton, coal cars down from, 926
Scrap of beauty's cloth, 828
of sunset with a voice, dower a, 685
Scraps of dream and duds of daring, 757
of learning, dote on, 203

Scraps, stolen the, 41
Scratch, engraving is the art of, 533
my head with lightning, 616
Scratched, fortune hath cruelly, 53
Scratching at the floor, 754
Scrawl, I read the, 686
Screaming stallions, his, 841
Screw your courage to the sticking place, 85
Scribe by trade, every man, 1017
Scripture, the devil can cite, 44
Scroll, charged with punishments the, 693
fill as it may, 550
nor would the, 1017
of fame, first on the, 512
upon the starry, 561
Scrolls, no mouse of the, 886
Scrub by the side of the rill, best little, 846
in the valley, 846
Scrubby thing, lived and died a, 847
Scrumptious, this is, 599
Scruple, I felt a, 247
of her excellence, 35
Scrutiny of the underside, furtive, 869
Scule, sad time two bairns at, 389
Sculptor, death the stern, 595
on sculptor starved, 594
Sculpture, formed it that was, 508
indecorous womanhood in, 422
Sculptured mystery, around her, 443
Scum of the earth, 832, 860
of the world, 1040
take off the, 623
Scurvy, some right, 574
Scutcheon, blot in thy, 1041
honour a mere, 63
Scuttled ship, mildest manner'd man that ever, 359
Scylla your father, 46
Scyllam, incidis in, 46
Scythe and home he run, he swung his, 345
in the rain and the sun, 755
of time mows down, whatever thing the, 155
of time, work is the, 1061
S'death I 'll print it, 212
Sea a seducer, 859
ageless and eternal, 1066
alone on a wide wide, 315
and land, jump both, 107
and the rains and the sun, 663
as a moral teacher, 570
as now we sail the, 572
as stars look on the, 426
at London, the, 824
bass eternal of the, 609
beheld and fled, the great, 168
beside the silent, 444
beside the western, 912
best thing between England and France, 417
between the one and the other, a, 425
bluffed the eternal, 777
boisterous captain of the, 248
breast the stiller, 850

Sea, by the deep, where none intrude, 354
ceased to be the, 787
chin in the, 858
Christ was born across the,
522
cloud out of the, 1101
cold green mantling, 789
comes murmuring with its
foamy lips, 552
compassed by the inviolate,
462
could navigate the, of life, 393
dat ole davil, 902
dawn-encircled, 889
desire in men at, 1021
desired the, 777
disturbs the Sabbath of that
deeper, 480
down to a sunless, 315
dwellers by the, 713
far on the wild-raging, 389
far-heard whisper o'er the. 315
far-off murmuring, 672
fearful fire and engulfing. 605
fields above the, 955
Floy what it is that it keeps
on saying, the, 496
footsteps in the, 266
fountain stream and, 306
friends who plough the, 623
gently o'er a perfumed, 460
give a thousand furlongs of,
32
go down to the, in ships, 1105
grew civil at her song, 42
had designs, 1069
has its pearls, 1066
he governs land and, 534
his deeds inimitable like the,
28
how the fishes live in the, 106
I never saw the, 584
I walked beside the evening,
558
I'm on the, 350
in a beautiful pea-green, went
to, 498
in a sieve, they went to, 498
in the bosom of the, 69, 121
in the flat, sunk, 158
in the rough rude, 59
into that silent, 315
is a thief, 81
is as deepe in calme as in
storme, 118
is boiling hot, 598
is calm and the sky is blue,
396
is calm, when the, 988
is death's garden, 712
is in the broad the narrow
streets, 289
isles that o'erlace the, 488
lane of beams athwart the, 464
life's dim unsounded, 350
light that never was on, 299
like to the Pontick, 103
lost at, 611
loved the great, more and
more, 350
loved the open, 886
magic of the, 436
Marathon looks on the, 359
materia medica at bottom of,
454

Sea, money to a starving man at,
1035
most dangerous, 46
mother and lover of men, 631
music of the, 317
my bark is on the, 356
never changes, 726
never go to, 623
never tells, 1069
nor earth nor boundless, 107
nothing so monotonous as the,
529
of a sudden came the, 485
of death, beyond the, 587
of dew, 699
of glory, summers in a, 73
of pines, silent, 316
of time to rise, 496
of troubles, arms against a, 93
of upturned faces, 310, 340
of vast eternity, 187
on life's rough, 28
one foot in, and one on shore
38, 256
one if by land and two if by,
437
one is of the, 304
or fire in earth or air, in, 89
or land, thing of, 156
our flag is known in every,
394
our heritage the, 345
owl and pussy-cat went to, 498
precious stone set in the silver,
59
profound and wide, sang of
the misty, 446
Proteus rising from the, 300
realm of the circling, 764
rising nor sky clouding, 668
roaring, 350
robber, any robber, 233
robs the vast, 81
roving over the, 459
run beyond the, 985
running all over the, 726
ships that went to, 566
ships upon the, 587
ships went to, and ships came,
437
sight of that immortal, 301
sing the dangers of the, 247
sings of its home in the, 446
siren who sung under the, 335
stand along the, 810
strongly masculine, 859
swelling of the voiceful, 317
that drinking thirsteth still,
587
that shuts still as it opes, the,
28
the blue the fresh the ever
free, the, 350
the breeze is on the, 310
the passenger pukes in, 360
the wind's feet shine along the,
630
they who plough the, 989
thing I hate the most is the.
599
this side the northern, 954
those in peril on the, 566
thus did Venus rise from out
the, 555
tideless dolorous midland, 631
time's infinite, 594

Sea to shining sea, from, 737
under the deep deep, 390
union with its native, 302
unmated creature tired, the,
503
uttermost parts of the, 342.
1106
was moaning and sighing, 833
was mountains rolling, 274
was roaring, 't was when the.
205
wave o' the, I wish you a, 56
we have fed our, 778
we hear the, 679
what thing of, or land, 156
when I put out to, 472
when she goes over the, 812
where is the, 658
where'er I am by shore at, 393
whether in, or fire, 89
wind of the western, 466
yonder the stormy, 672
Seas again, down to the, 832
and the, give up their dead.
375
are scooped in vain, 517
around, new skies and, 514
blue of halcyon, 760
borne to me o'er the, 697
colder than the Hebrides, 881
dangers of the, 115
enchantress of the stormy, 418
foam of perilous, 383
from the dry lands, like, 526
given for fence impregnable,
70
guard our native, 327
incarnadine, 86
labouring, 816
nor scour the, 410
of dreams, 664
of gore, shedding, 360
of phantasies, 664
of solitudes and vacancies, 664
of talk, huge, 829
of thought, strange, 299
port after stormie, 24
rivers run to, 177
roll to waft me, 207
sail o'er silent, 437
sail through uncharted, 757
Severn to the narrow, 303
shall be thy fate, on what. 771
swept by great, 619
the pearl, 744
trouble the dangerous, 982
two boundless, 337
unsuspected isle in the far,
485
upon cloudy, 864
Sea's red vintage, 664
speech, 577
Sea-born treasures home. I
fetched my, 408
Sea-breakers, wandering by lone,
676
Sea-change, suffer a, 32
Sea-coal fire, by a, 64
Sea-deep and dark indigo blue.
845
Sea-deeps, afar from the great.
675
Sea-down's edge, at the, 633
Sea-faring stuff from far, 757
Sea-fowl and the shark, dies the.
401

Sea-fugue writ from east to west, 664
Sea-gulls cry above them lightly, 904
Seal, a promise given under, 1085
 engraven with the name Ginevra, 289
 mine by the royal, 584
 of a king on his brow, 706
 on all the past, 690
 sealed with the, 671
 seem to set his, 95
 to mortal wax, 1021
 upon thy heart, as a, 1110
Seals of love but sealed in vain, 37
 rings and, 166
 that close the pestilence, 362
Sealed their letters with their thumbs, 313
Sea-like pathless limitless waste, 435
Sea-line, where the, meets the sky, 864
Sealing-wax, of shoes and ships and, 598
Seam, sewing her long white, 541
Sea-maid's music, to hear the, 42
Seaman, betoken'd wrack to the, 106
Sea-mark in the tides of time, 634
Sea-marshes of Glynn, 663
Seamen have a custom, 191
 learnt, but, 776
 said it blew great guns, 497
 the gentlemen were not, 400
 three what men ye be, 347
Search men's principles, 1010
 no, hath found, 401
 not his bottom, 167
 not worth the, 44
 nothing's so hard but, will find it, 134
 of deep philosophy, 167
 patient, and vigil long, 357
 so painful and so long, after a, 185
 vain my weary, 250
Searcher obedient to the command of truth, 543
Searches to the bottom, 75
Sea-rover, seventh son of the old, 914
Sea-sand, brown as the ribbed, 315
Sea-shell of the sea, as a, 446
 the hollow, 679
Sea-shore, boy playing on the, 184
Sea-sick people looking holy, 614
Seaside stroll a walk through a gallery, 563
Season, comes a festival, 952
 each, has its own disease, 342
 each thing that grows in, 40
 ever 'gainst that, 89
 for enjoyment, youth the only, 407
 from that time unto this, 26
 housewife's happiest, 552
 no, such delight can bring, 133

Season of Christmas spend, 687
 of light the season of darkness, 497
 of love and laughter, a little, 601
 of mists and mellow fruitfulness, 384
 of our lonely dreams, 843
 of snows and sins, 633
 shock of corn in his, 1102
 the silent, thro', 406
 things seasoned by, 47
 this is the lonely, 843
 through every, dearest, 393
 to every thing there is a, 37, 1109
 wait the morrow's hidden, 1058
 when I have convenient, 1119
 when ordinarily kind-hearted, 935
 when to come and go, 214
 word spoken in due, 1107
 your admiration for a while, 90
Seasons and reposing hours, sorrow breaks, 71
 and their change, 152
 change, 735
 changing, come and go, 442
 death thou hast all, 370
 fill the measure of the year, 385
 fleet, cares and joys abound as, 69
 in the commercial world, 343
 in the mind of man, 385
 justice, when mercy, 46
 rainy, 811
 return with the year, 151
 roll as the swift, 452
 such as this, defend you from, 99
 vernal, of the year, 162
 who knew the, 462
Seasoned timber never gives, 135
 with a gracious voice, 46
 with salt, 1121
Seasoning of all enjoyments, 1046
Seat, a prostrate city is thy, 403
 his favourite, be woman's feeble breast, 303
 in some poetic nook, 346
 is shaken, his, 917
 is the bosom of God, her, 22
 misfortune made the throne her, 198
 nature from her, 155
 of Mars, this, 59
 of sensation is pit of stomach, 745
 of the Campbells, the original, 310
 scorner's, 733
 this castle hath a pleasant, 85
 thought's mysterious, 338
 while memory holds a, 92
Seats beneath the shade, 250
 built of country, 911
 fill the, of justice, 386
 for an elegant movie show, 907
Seated one day at the organ, 564
Sea-thieves, swaggering files of, 842

Sea-water, by the soft, 914
Seaweed clings to her palaces, 289
 is in her palace halls, 363
Sech nights all white and still, 527
Second birth, as from a, 337
 call, to hail a, 576
 childishness and mere oblivion, 50
 Daniel, a, 47
 draught mads him, 54
 each, stood heir to the first, 100
 in Rome, 999
 mate, a capital swimmer, 577
 nature, custom is, 34, 1003
 thoughts are best, 179
 thoughts, to their own, 187
Second-hand, quote, 426
 three busts all, 715
Secrecy, nature's infinite book of, 104
Secret and mystery to every other, 497
 and self-contained and solitary, 495
 anniversaries of the heart, 439
 as the grave, 1042
 black and midnight hags, 87
 bread eaten in, 1107
 caves of earth, 476
 dread and inward horror, 195
 guilt by silence is betrayed, 175
 hid under Cheops' pyramid, 776
 history of our enemies, 440
 in silence and tears, in, 587
 inwardly in, to be great, 528
 is revealed, 776
 is safe, 492
 it betrays, keeps the, 437
 kept in silence sealed, in, 507
 knows my, 717
 lords of birth, 771
 mind, mould the, 633
 monstrous in the general eye, 422
 mum it is a, 236
 no, can be told, 610
 no one ever keeps a, 1068
 of a uniform, 902
 of nature, death is a, 1010
 of success is constancy, 419
 of the sun, 669
 of your looks, the, 451
 phrases of the soul, 873
 sympathy, it is the, 307
 the universal, 728
 thoughts of a man, 132
 trusted to a woman, 998
 way, shows her the, 134
 window, 827
 wish, now obey thy cherished, 537
Secrets, entrust women with their, 977
 I have no, 848
 men and women apt to tell, 222
 of a weed's plain heart, 524
 of the nether world, 1009
 one of thy, 562
 reveal no, 251
 that everybody guesses, 720

Secrets, trust him not with, 1056
Secretary of nature, 140
Sect and creed, contempts of, 864
  melt not in an acid, 443
  slave to no, 200, 208
Sects, all other, I can win, 171
  confute, jarring, 1019
  vicissitudes of, and religions, 111
Section, first American, 926
Secure amidst a falling world, 194
  from worldly chances and mis-haps, 76
  the past at least is, 341
  unless energy fails, 345
Security for the future, 230
  have we, how little, 330
  is to be found, 1074
  of a god, 109
  of the future, 591
  public honour is, 950
  small, interest high and, 593
  to virtue, 222
Sedentary life, a, 1082
Sedge, giving a kiss to every, 33
Sedition sitting in a tree, 912
Seduces all mankind, woman, 205
Seductive, literature the most, of professions, 641
Sedulous ape to Hazlitt Lamb Wordsworth, 704
See a hand you cannot see, 205
  a world to, 23
  a world we do not, 480
  all things, light to, 26
  and be seen, 7, 986
  and eek for to be seye, 7
  be seen, 217
  beyond the range of sight, 514
  but all I, is mine, 568
  her was to love her, to, 287
  I do not ask to, 403
  is this a dagger which I, 85
  may I be there to, 264
  naught but vanity in beauty, 522
  none so blind as those that will not, 188, 192
  not for all his faith can, 408
  nothing higher than himself, 477
  or seem, all that we, 459
  oursels as others see us, 285
  pope wants me out of his, 611
  sad sights, to, 107
  soft unfolding, and, 387
  the conquering hero comes, 186
  the flowers sprang up to, 619
  the right and approve it, 187
  the shadow of thy pinions, 418
  thee again, then I shall, 84
  thee at Philippi, 84
  thee damned first, I will, 293
  thee still, I have thee not yet, 85
  thou in thy lake dost, thyself, 555
  through a glass darkly, now we, 1120
  thy face, ere I, 454
  what I can't, I never believe, 647

See what I see, to have seen what I have seen, 94
  what is not to be seen, 277
  where the wild-blazing Grog-shop, 389
  your face, not night when I do, 42
Seed, all living, 575
  and cell, life multiple in, 936
  beneath the sod, plants, 648
  begging bread, nor his, 1104
  catalogues say, all the, 813
  fruit from such a, 353
  germ of the, 499
  grows and spreads and sows itself anew, 377
  however broadcast will catch, 476
  I cast to earth a, 574
  in the morning sow thy, 1110
  of commonwealths, 726
  of half the states, 929
  of money, 1054
  of the church, 1012
  of Treasure Island, 524
  perfection, nestles the, 535
  sows himself for, 898
  the drifting, 619
  this supercilious, 820
  when you have planted, 837
  which the soul hath sown, 654
  ye sow another reaps, 368
Seeds, but for finer, 665
  of April's sowing, 485
  of fire alive, 373
  of godlike power are in us, 545
  of last year's spring, 569
  of moments, some small, 1084
  of time, look into the, 84
  wrapped up among the balms, 620
Seedtime and harvest cold and heat, 1097
Seegar, smoke a mild, 794
Seeing and the hearing ear, 1108
  eyes were made for, if, 409
  not by our feeling but by others', 108
  not satisfied with, 1109
  precious, to the eye, 41
  the root of the matter, 1102
Seek and ye shall find, 1114
  it ere it come to light, 267
  peace is what I, and calm, 547
  the happy land, would not, 503
  thee in vain by the meadow, 392
  their fortunes further, to, 52
  to find and not to yield, to, 464
  to make, paths to the house I, 537
Seeker may find the thought, the, 873
Seeking light doth light of light beguile, 40
  the bubble reputation, 49
  whom he may devour, 1123
Seeks one thing, the man who, 592
  through evil good, folly that, 443
Seem a saint when I play the devil, 71

Seem here no painful inch to gain, 519
  is but a dream, all we see or, 459
  men should be what they, 102
  pavilions of the sun, clouds which, 425
  they grow to what they, 249
  things are not what they, 433
  things are seldom what they, 623
Seemed musical and low, in his, 524
  the harmonious echo, it, 564
  the incarnate I told you so, 437
  to see our flag unfurled, 442
Seeming and savour all the win-ter long, 56
  evil still educing good, 224
  of her gentle sex the, paragon, 405
  otherwise, 101
Seemly way, in a, 686
Seems asleep, tide as moving, 472
  madam I know not seems, 89
  no bigger than his head, 99
  right by force of beauty, 430
  that the dead are there, it, 554
Seen and known, much have I, 464
  as the world the world hath, 559
  better days, we have, 49
  by candle-light, colors, 428
  evidence of things not, 1122
  from far, when, 458
  his body, Charlotte having, 481
  mine eyes have, the glory, 522
  my fond affection thou hast, 388
  needs only to be, 174
  never was, nor never shall be, 121
  sweetest that ever was, 388
  'tis the loveliest ever was, 388
  to be appreciated, must be, 423
  too early, unknown, 77
  what I have seen, 94
Seer, aged, 372
  clasps the, 892
Sees God in clouds, 207
  or dreams he sees, 149
  takes off his shoes, he who, 431
  what he foresaw, 300
  with equal eye, who, 207
Seething surge of love, 606
Seine, meridians and parallels for a, 616
Sekret ceases to be a sekret if once confided, 518
Seld-shaven odd-eyed stuttering, 325
Seldom he smiles, 81
  occurs, what we anticipate, 420
  what they seem, things are, 623
Select companions, a few, 195
Selection from a piece that's known as Saul, 845
  natural, 448

Self, as it were another, 977
care for one's own, 971
easiest to deceive one's own, 426
enjoyment of one's, 195
in you, truest, 888
incarnate carnal, 883
is the only prison, 710
must still retreat, 853
Oh sweeter, 548
through my, 664
to its sphere, fitting of, 501
true to thine own, 91
Self-admiring fettle, in, 938
Self-appointed inspector of snow-storms, 514
judges, brood of, 612
Self-approving hour, one, 208
Self-cancelling business, 378
Self-complacency is pleasure, 1048
Self-complacent British sneer, 513
Self-conceit may lead to destruction, 961
of youth, 530
Self-confident, only the stern, 931
Self-consuming die, 686
fires, wastes in, 193
Self-contained and solitary as an oyster, 495
Self-contemplation, derived from this, 1087
Self-control, quiet, 438
Self-defence, love lightly now in, 775
Self-denial is indulgence, 662
Self-disparagement, inward, 302
Self-dispraise, luxury in, 302
Self-distrust, he inspires, 393
Self-effacement in a generation, 896
Self-esteem, nothing profits more than, 154
Self-evident truths, 273
Selfish, very old are the most, 483
Selfishness is the greatest curse, 450
Self-forgetting seeking only emptier cups, 625
Self-homicide, misspending a man's time, 183
Self-interest bad economics, 877
Self-knowledge self-control, 462
Self-love not so vile a sin, 66
Self-made laws, makes and keeps his, 544
men, 453
Self-mettle tires him, 72
Self-neglecting and self-love, 66
Self-pity, man without, 927
Self-place, circumscribed in one, 31
Self-possession of ships, 938
Self-preservation in animals, 1016
Self-reproach, feel no, 296
Self-respect, never lose thy, 1010
Self-reverence self-knowledge, 462
Self-same feather, birds of, 70
flight the selfsame way, 44
men shall meet, never, 544

Self-same song, sings the, 651
sun that shines upon his court, 57
Self-slaughter, canon 'gainst, 90, 105
Self-taught men, egotism characteristic of, 331
Sell America short, don't, 944
with you buy with you, 44
Seller needs not one eye, 137
Selves, from our own, our joys must flow, 226
stepping-stones of their dead, 436, 467
Semblance, wait for me a little, 1008
Semely, ful, in hir nose, 5
Semed bisier than he was, 5
Semi-circle, but in a, 56
Semicircles, sun drew, 923
Semi-Solomon, a kind of 398
Sempronius, we 'll do more, 194
Senate at his heels, Caesar with a, 208
give his little, laws, 213
long debate, can a Roman, 195
Senates, cashiering most kings and, 379
Senate's admiration for itself, 635
Senator seldom proclaims his inferiority, 635
Senators, green-robed, those, 384
Send back the song, whole world, 477
Sendeth sun he sendeth shower, he, 423
Seneca, high speech of, 109
Senegambian queen, young, 857
Senescent, as the night was, 461
Senile, regard their elders as, 635
Senior-junior giant-dwarf, 41
Sensation among the English, 1070
be lost to all, 247
if that is not, 599
Sensations felt in the blood, 295
Sense aches at thee, the, 103
all the joys of, 208
and nonsense, through, 174
and outward things, 301
deviates into, 175
dictate of common, 226
enough to come in out of the rain, not, 10
flows in fit words, 174
from thought divide, 207
fund of good, 949
given a precious mystic, 1074
good health and good, 989
good, the gift of heaven, 210
honour virtue, 242
is mock'd in every thing, 115
joys of, lie in three words, 208
live within the, 368
men of, approve, 211
much fruit of, 211
no substitute for, 899
obstinate questionings of, 301
of being well-dressed, 415
of death is most in apprehension, 36
of duty, some, 466
of filial duty, 273
of future favours, gratitude, 200

Sense of glad awakening, 915
of greatness, 736
of humour is the just balance, 459
of ills to come, no, 243
of justice and injustice, 1053
of justice, it has no, 1064
of moral responsibility, 542
of obligation, a, 813
of shame, lost to all, 219
of the common life, 670
of the have-beens, 651
of the honorable, a quixotic, 461
of the rose, 629
of the uselessness, 786
of the value of time, keener, 330
of their existence, the, 1079
of uneasiness, left a, 1056
of utter loneliness, 955
of your great merit, 267
one for rhyme, one for, 142
one that has another, 196
or want of, 599
palls upon the, 194
palter in a double, 89
persons of good, 228, 1044
pretty words that make no, 429
refine her sterling page, 1050
satire or, 213
served by every, 427
sound an echo to the, 211
stings and motions of the, 35
sublime of something, 296
take care of the, 598
that the world is mad, 840
the bird, 649
the daintier, 96
the pains the fears, 164
to appreciate droll situations, 695
want of decency is want of, 180
which men call courtesy, that fine, 508
whose weighty, 174
women have a positive moral, 635
Senses, belief in the, 1081
deep through all his, 764
first deprives of their, 968
have all their five, 905
illusion of the, 972
seven, out of his, 310
steep my, in forgetfulness, 65
unto our gentle, 85
youth's lively, 850
Senseless stone, 887
wounds, all, 888
Sensibility, great, 234
wanting, 266
Sensible and well-bred man, 263
failure, fear not, 758
men are of the same religion, 234
men never tell, 421
sane and mild, 907
to feeling as to sight, 85
warm motion, 36
Sensitive and timid natures, 637
brave sanguine, 895
nerves of receiving, 609
plant, a, 368
Sensuality, drives out, 1022

Sensuous joy of magnanimity, 1072
simple and passionate, 162
Sent, joys and tears alike are, 423
Sentence, he mouths a, 262
hungry judges sign the, 212
mortality my, 155
my, is for open war, 149
of dismissal, 324
stand with bold relief, 332
uttered, for every, 565
with, mustn't end a, 872
Sentences, ambition to say in ten, 1081
are memorable, 588
quips and, 39
required at least four, 1063
that stir my bile, 747
Sententious, Cato the, 360
Sentient beings are doomed, 449
heart, never wore his, 839
Sentiment, appeals to the domestic, 419
deepest and highest, 725
each pinioned, 1050
he has such faith in, no, 279
my living and dying, 340
no snivelling, 933
nurse of manly, 260
pluck the eyes of, 451
value of a, 797
Sentiments, duration of great, 1080
grandest of all human, 347
in matters of, 1063
them's my, 482, 678
Sentimentalist, barrenest of all mortals, 378
Sentimentally disposed to harmony, 323
Sentinels, fixed, 67
multiply, 1068
of song, 609
Sentries stand, cliffs like, 707
Sentry, England stands, 647
in the silent night, 845
Separate dying ember wrought, each, 460
star, each in his, 779
us from the love of God, able to, 1119
Separateth very friends, 1107
Separation, not through union but through, 806
prepare for a, 319
September, full many a chill, 451
thirty days hath, 18
Sepulchral urns, in old, 263
Sepulchre and pall of thousands, 349
earth is a, 970
in the grateful stomach, 323
no man knows that, 372
soldier's, shall be a, 328
Sepulchres, the, of mighty dead, 386
whited, 1116
Sepulchred in such pomp, 161
Sepulture of mannes wit and his discrecioun, 6
Sequent centuries, 326, 409
Sequestered nooks, 438
vale, 245, 268
Seraph, as the rapt, that adores, 207

Seraph never was sweeter, 823
so spake the, Abdiel, 153
Seraphs might despair, where, 352
winged, 459
Serbonian bog, 150
Sere, leaves were crisped and, 460
the yellow leaf, 88
Serene and bright, old age, 299
and calm, 194
and low, measured beat, 685
at least, 451
gem of purest ray, 245
if hours were all, 330
in changeless prime, 385
of heaven, breaks the, 322
Serenely arriving in the day, death, 536
full the epicure would say, 313
Serenity of books, 438
of countenance, never fading, 195
of death, 602
steady and perpetual, 197
usual querulous, 322
Serfs dig deep, bidding his, 847
Serge, a piece of scarlet, 930
beneath your old blue, 847
when it sees my old blue, 907
Sergeant at Belleau Woods, 854
death, this fell, 97
Series of congratulatory regrets, 420
Serious as a city's careless drainage, 825
importance, no thing of, 974
in ridiculous matters, 1003
thought, still and, 297
Seriphus, if I had been of, 996
Sermon, delivery of a, 228
implies absence of anything agreeable and inviting, 312
on Mother Hubbard, 678
on the Mount not a mere human production, 342
perhaps turn out a, 285
rather see a, 870
two-hour, 475
who flies a, 135
who will not read a, 135, 405
Sermons and soda-water, 359
in stones, 48
one good old man more than many, 558
pleasure to hear, 130
Serpent, biteth like a, 1108
first, seen the, 768
Leviathan, that crooked, 1111
like Aaron's, 208
more of the, than dove, 31
of old Nile, 104
sting thee twice, 46
tempted me, the, 490
that hisses, strike at a, 716
trail of the, 338
train, lithe and long as the, 431
under the innocent flower, 84
upon a rock, way of a, 1109
Serpents, be ye wise as, 1115
poison for, 993
Serpent's tongue, 737
tooth, sharper than a, 98
Serried columns, blaze with your, 447

Servant a dog, is thy, 1101
depart in peace, lettest thou thy, 1117
girls, being said by the, 817
heareth, for thy, 1100
if I accustom a, 234
in love, 8
not judge any public, 734
of God, 710
of God well done, 153, 305
of God's holiest charge, 248
of the eternal must, 875
of the scattered family, 668
sleeping, leave we now Thy, 402
this is Thy, 785
thou good and faithful, 1116
to the lender, 1108
who made service, 437
with this clause, 135
Servants and agents of the people, 627
as good as themselves, 1040
fire the best of, 378
men in great place are thrice, 110
of fame and of business, 110
of the sovereign or state, 110
robbed, what his, 948
sons and, 1022
that spilled water, 441
wanting all sorts of employers, 495
Servant's title, 441
Serve for table-talk, 46
God and mammon, ye cannot, 1114
in heaven, than, 148
other people, to, 1077
they, who stand and wait, 162
'tis enough, 'twill, 79
Served him right, cried, 510
my God, had I but, 74
Serves me most who serves his country best, 219
Serveth not another's will, 114
Servi peregrini, 264
Service, ability for good, 261
all, ranks the same, 485
beyond all recompense, 1043
broken with, 998
conquest which is, 805
curse her, 777
divyne she song, 5
done the state some, 103
greater than the god, 75
is no heritage, 53
is perfect freedom, whose, 1127
life consists of mutual, 754
must be done, 403
of God and the honour of religion, 179
of my love, 747
of princes, prefers the, 977
of the antique world, 48
pressed into, 838
public, 1054
school of the Lord's, 1016
seem divine, 437
simply given, simple, 781
small, is true service, 304
still, strong for, 265
sweat for duty not for meed, 48
these are of the greatest, 970

Service, 'tis the curse of, 100
  to future psychologists, 1083
  to His Majesty, of, 921
  to others highest of distinc-
    tions, 943
  to the commonwealth, 970
  to the public, 950
  to the state, renders a, 191
  unforeseen, 339
  weary and old with, 73
  which thou renderest, 427
  yeoman's, it did me, 97
Services, compensated for his,
    320
  for nothing, give your, 971
  in return for her, 394
  intend to measure, 965
  two outstanding, 1089
Serviceable to God and His peo-
    ple, 141
Servile to skyey influences, 36
Serving thee, to die for her is,
    451
  'tis loving and, 501
Serving-men, six honest, 784
Servitors, nimble and airy, 162
Servitude, base laws of, 178
Sesoun priketh every gentil
    herte, 5
Sesquipedalianism natural to
    Americans, 758
Sessions of sweet silent thought,
    107
Set about their mountain-piling,
    484
  down as a positive truth, 482
  down aught in malice, 103
  mankind their little, 275
  me as a seal upon thy heart,
    1110
  my life at a pin's fee, 91
  my life on any chance, 86
  my ten commandments in your
    face, 69
  sail and away, 579
  some value on his votive lay,
    447
  sun has a right to, 606
  terms, in good, 49
  the cause above renown, 764
  the crooked straight, why
    strive to, 608
  thine house in order, 1101,
    1112
Setter up of kings, 70
Setters from Kerry and Cork and
    Kildare, 842
Setteth up another, 1105
Setting, I haste now to my, 73
  in his western skies, 173
  sun and music at the close, 59
  sun, men shut doors against a,
    80
Settle a question, men never so
    likely to, 398
Settled right, until it is, 718
Settlers put up beam and rafter,
    596
Settles, ignorance never, a ques-
    tion, 419
Seven ages, his acts being, 49
  all at six and, 15
  answered only, 630
  cities claimed him, 493
  cities that claimed Homer, 910
  cities warred for Homer, 129

Seven halfpenny loaves, 69
  hours to law, 275
  hundred pounds and possibili-
    ties, 34
  hundred years and fifty-three,
    478
  is a good handy figure, 1089
  long year, Tom's food for, 99
  men that can render a reason,
    1108
  more redskins bit the dust,
    713
  o'clock is not too late, 930
  one of, who stand before the
    Lord, 1126
  or eight large tears, 691
  senses, scared out of his, 310,
    1036
  stars and the solar year, 410
  that fondly folded, 642
  the stars in her hair were, 577
  wealthy towns, 123, 129
  women hold of one man, 1111
  years, keep a thing, 311
  years of famine, 1098
  years of great plenty, 1098
  years' pith, these arms had,
    100
Seventeen, blush that flies at, 776
  he was, 866
Seventh, and on the, 505
  son of the old sea-rover, 914
Seventies, should have been done
    in the, 791
Seventy, men over, 724
  years is the time of a man, 537
  years young, 454
Several faces, 181
Severe, grave to gay from lively
    to, 177
  holy as, 37
  in aught, if, 251
  pleasant to, 177, 1049
  with eyes, 50
Severed from the heart, 223
Severity, excess of, 641
  in a better manner than, 984
Severn, Avon to the, runs, 303
  to the narrow seas, 303, 304
Sevilla, near the city of, 478
Sewers annoy the air, 154
Sewing at once a double thread,
    392
Sewing-circle the Protestant con-
    fessional, 571
Sex, a woman of her gentle, 405
  and his soul, about his, 890
  and started, 815
  by change of, 424
  female of, it seems, 157
  is ever kind to a soldier, the,
    220
  Marcia towers above her, 195
  occupied with the female, 877
  omnipresent process of, 739
  or complexion, whatever may
    be the, 424
  ornament of her, 1037
  she's the ornament of her, 494
  spirits can either, assume or
    both, 148
  stronger than my, 82
  the fair, 198, 1039
  to the last, 177
  which is therefore called fair,
    198

Sex whose presence civilizes ours,
    263
Sexes, the French say there are
    three, 313
Sex's earliest latest care, 239
Sexless orgies of morality, 635
Sexton, and the, tolled the bell,
    392
  they went and told the, 392
  to willow, 823
Shabby corner of God's allot-
    ment, 651
  genteel, known as the, 954
  slowly-turning shelf, 901
Shackles fall in our country, 264
  ne'er again shall bind, 447
  of a historian, 147
  of an old love, the, 470
Shad, first run of, 925
Shadders, both shores', 527
Shade, admiring in the gloomy,
    145
  ah pleasing, 243
  Amaryllis in the, 159
  boundless contiguity of, 264
  clutching the inviolable, 547
  comes back with rustling,
    904
  from well to well, 881
  gentlemen of the, 60
  green thought in a green, 169
  half in sun half in, 336
  he is old and she a, 326
  how small the, 793
  I am a, 648
  if I have, 689
  in sunshine and in, 446
  let it sleep in the, 334
  more welcome, 205
  ninety in the, 795
  no shine no butterflies, no, 391
  of Fujisan, 692
  of melancholy boughs, 49
  of that which once was great,
    297
  pale realms of, 371
  seats beneath the, 250
  sitting in a pleasant, 120
  sitting in the, 785
  so softening into shade, 224
  soft and luminous, 922
  talk to the man in the, 718
  thought in a green, 169
  through sun and, 465
  unperceived, 224
  variable as the, 308
Shades are about us, 633
  are drawn with care, 878
  are stretching, evening, 652
  happy walks and, 155
  of death, bogs dens and, 150
  slept in their, 146
  soon as the evening, prevail,
    194
  who land, toll of all the, 858
Shaded doorway still, there is
    the, 552
Shadow and sun, 793
  and the glory, the, 443
  both way falls, 156
  cloaked from head to foot,
    468
  days on the earth are as a,
    1101
  dims her way, nor, 336
  fell over his heart, 460

Shadow, float double swan and, 298
for the noontide hour, 373
grasping at the, 961
hence horrible, 87
I have a little, 702
in light and light in shadow, 568
in the street, my, 522
in the sun, care is like my, 20
is heavy the whole day through, 642
it still flies you, follow a, 119
kills the growth, 120
lies floating on the floor, 460
life is but a walking, 88
like a, o'er the heart, 567
man's life is but a, 577
may never be less, that thy, 441
of a great rock, as the, 1111
of a hope, 847
of a tree, from the, 666
of death, darkness and the, 1102
of death like the sword of Damocles, 613
of disgrace, 696
of doubt, no probable possible, 624
of one man, lengthened, 411
of our night, 366
of our travelling earth, 447
of some unseen Power, 365
of the British oak, 260
of the Great Protection, 473
of the night comes on, 914
of things past, 749
of thy pinions float along, 418
of thy wings, under the, 1103
of turning, neither, 1122
on the floor, behold his, 410
on the wall, a giant, 572
proves the substance true, 211
rim of, 531
seemed, that, 150
selves, our, 666
single hair casts its, 987
soul from out that, 460
stand henceforward in thy, 429
swift as a, 42
that passeth away, 1124
then a spark, 681
there truth is 't is her, 506
walks before, 668
was on your floor, 708
Shadows and symbols, from, 403
beckoning dire, 157
best in this kind are but, 43
come like, so depart, 87
coming events cast their, 318
flee away, the, 1110
fold thee, 619
gather, the, 851
I shall not see the, 587
lay along Broadway, 431
lengthen and evening comes, until the, 1128
lengthening, 173
linger longer, evening, 669
melted into mist, 522
mirrors of gigantic, 318, 369
move over the slopes, 982
not substantial things, 141
of actions, words the, 1001

Shadows of coming events, 327
of night, out of the, 439
of the clouds, 602
of the evening, 606
of the things to be, 557
our fatal, 126
our years are like the, 561
overhead, weave their, 765
Plutonian, gather on the evening blast, 568
soft and gray, 669
that I feared so long, the, 540
that walk by us, 126
the, departed, 654
to-night have struck more terror, 72
we are what shadows we pursue, 260
which I now dismiss, 497
wishes lengthen like our, 173, 202
Shadowed livery of the sun, 45
Shadowing folds of marble lace, 682
Shadowless like silence listening, 392
Shadow-shapes, row of magic, 1019
Shadowy bounties and supreme, 673
land, a, 416
lens of even, 442
lie, was my dream a, 509
Shadrach Meshach and Abednego, 1113
Shadwell never deviates into sense, 175
Shady cypress tree, nor, 587
leaves of destiny, 165
place, sunshine in the, 24
Shaft at random sent, 309
lent his plume to fledge the, 334
none that hath turned his, 958
of beauty towering, 715
of language, loosed a, 808
of light across the land, 463
pig's tail can never make a good, 138
that made him die, 145
that quivered in his heart, 351
when I had lost one, 44
winged the, 351
Shafts, thy fatal, 248
Shaggy science nosing in the grass, 822
Shah, in the ranks of the, 951
Shake, Mulleary and Go-ethe, 715
my fell purpose, 84
of his poor little head, 624
our disposition, 91
the saintship of an anchorite, 352
the spheres, seems to, 176
thy gory locks at me, never, 87
Shaken, so, as we are, 60
when taken, to be, 288
withered and, 390
Shaker of o'er-rank states, 132
Shakers of the world, 676
Shakes his ambrosial curls, 218
Shakespeare and musical glasses, 254
another Newton, chanced to be, 922

Shakespeare at his side, 303
died, in April, 706
drew, pictured truth that, 626
drew, this is the Jew that, 221
exercised his father's trade, 171
explained, 905
fancy's child, sweetest, 160
had the largest and most comprehensive soul, 179
hewed from his heart's core, 680
his father was a butcher, 171
is not our poet, 326
more original than his originals, 415
my, rise, 119
myriad-minded, 318
never blotted out a line, 120
on whose forehead climb, 428
passes by, 650
rose, then, 364
said, this is what, 933
shall live no more, 737
the wonder of our stage, 119
to make room for, 119
tongue that, spake, 298
unlocked his heart, 304, 492
was not accounted great, 760
what needs my, 161
when I read, 883
writes it, wisdom, 414
wrote, no words, 716
Shakespeare's day, folk who lived in, 621
fame and Cromwell's deed, 443
hand, shaken, 834
heart, reddest vein of, 911
magic, 178
name in plays, 874
strain, 410
voice and Nelson's hand, 634
wit, orbit and sum of, 409
Shaking, fruit that falls without, 221
Shale, the rock he sat upon was, 665
Shalimar, beside the, 775
Shall a light word part us, 446
call his name Immanuel, 1111
find how day by day, 405
foretells, simply, 955
I wasting in despair, 132
in the second and third, 955
mark you his absolute, 76
not when he wolda, 257
set some value on his, 447
Shallow brooks and rivers wide, 160
cup, in a, 1019
draughts intoxicate the brain, 210
in himself, versed in books, 156
men believe in luck, 414
murmur, the deep are dumb, 21
rivers, 31
spirit of judgment, 68
streams run dimpling, 213
waterfalls, 438
Shallows, bound in, 83
that line the beach, 675
Shallow-rooted, weeds are, 69
Shambling limb, length of, 513
Shame and woe, barbed with, 499

Shame, ashamed with the noble, 524
avoid, 312
blush of maiden, 372
cometh after, 14
coward fear, 447
dies for, 123
doff it for, 57
each deed of, 436
erring sister's, 355
fear not guilt yet start at, 262
for him to live, 965
hide her, from every eye, 254
is the apprehension, 972
life is a, 692
London's lasting, 244
lost to all sense of, 219
love taught him, 176
of nature, paint the mortal, 472
one glory an' one, 526
or blame, without, 132
or lust, not serving, 650
say what it will, 96
scourged with the thing called, 779
the devil, tell truth and, 62
the fools, print it and, 212
them with thine eyes, and, 405
those who start at, 262
where is thy blush, 95
who hangs his head for, 555
whose glory is in their, 1121
will follow after, 29
with love at strife, 176
Shames, hold a candle to my, 45
Shame's orator, thy tongue thy own, 38
Shamed, age thou art, 81
be he who thinks evil of it, 35
Shamefaced dog, debtor is but a, 560
Shammin' when 'e's dead, 781
Shamrock from your hat, take the, 548
Ireland may honor the, 642
Shams and lies, nothing but, 1036
Shanahan's ould shebeen, 715
Shanàmeh or the Nibelungenlied, the, 527
Shandon Bells, I often think of those, 423
Shank, too wide for his shrunk, 50
Shannon, green banks of, 328
Shap, gontradict dot, 661
Shape, bears lick their young into, 122, 994, 1029, 1031
color form verse tone, 534
execrable, what art thou, 150
had none distinguishable, 150
if it might be called, 150
in any, in any mood, 356
no bigger than an agate-stone, in, 77
of a camel, cloud almost in, 94
of danger can dismay, 300
pressed out of, 838
said the second, 620
such a questionable, 91
take any, but that, 87
the strong and awful spirit, 841
virtue in her, 153
ye've no, 774
Shapes, all worldly, 328

Shapes and sizes and positions, symmetry of, 970
are quaint and beautiful, their, 831
calling, 157
complicators, lovely female, 606
of foul disease, 469
of mercy charity and love, 495
our ends, divinity that, 97
the busy thoughts outnumber, 366
the poet's pen turns them to, 43
two haggard, 685
two hurrying, 620
when thy arriving tolls, what, 806
Shapeless ways, spent in, 881
Share, every grief that mortals, 626
of a mother's love, 1069
of night, our, 583
of the wind, coulter and, 712
they are already possessed of, 197
too small, think his, 1074
Shares in some Peruvian mine, 465
Shark, dies the sea-fowl and the, 401
loves a mining, 661
Sharp and so bright, so, 350
as a pen, his nose was, 66
be the weather, 309
cry, mocking sneer or the, 192
fumes of necessity, etched by the, 749
is the grief, 815
it pierced and stung, 659
keen intellects too, 343
knife, use thy, 864
misery had worn him, 80
pinch, necessity's, 98
ribs, labor pining hideth his, 477
ruing, causes, 965
some day will find a sharper, 559
the conquering, 3
Sharps, unpleasing, 80
Sharpen with cloyless sauce, 104
Sharpeneth the countenance, 1108
Sharpening of the sense of cunning, 1080
Sharper than a serpent's tooth, 98
than the sword, whose edge is, 105
Sharping and robbing, men who live by, 228
Sharp-looking wretch, 38
Sharpshooter, unerring rifle of biographical, 638
Sharp-sighted, fear is, 1035
Shatter the vase if you will, 336
your leaves, fingers rude, 159
Shattered nerves new-string, 248
torch, a, 848
Shattering walls are thin, 886
Shaven land, 576
Shaving, and the barber kept on, 508
Shaw on Lawrence, 902

Shawl, plain worn, 857
Shawl-hooded crone, 815
Shay, the wonderful one-hoss, 452
She a fair divided excellence, 57
be not for me, for if, 132
drew an angel down, 176
fair chaste and unexpressive, 50
for God in him, 152
gave me eyes, 297
gave me of the tree, 155
go not as thou wouldst, if, 1125
has been there before, 776
have spoken a word, 776
have written a letter, 776
in part to blame is, 128
is a woman, 77
is all my fancy painted her, 362
is fierce, though she be but little, 43
is lovely she's divine, 362
is not fair to outward, 386
is pretty to walk with, 164
knew the life-long martyrdom, 439
knows her man, 177
lived unknown, 296
loves him wholly, 883
makes him think, 911
never told her love, 55
played on the banks of the Yuba, 432
sways level in her husband's heart, 54
that had no need of me, 915
that not impossible, 165
that was ever fair, 101
that was the world's delight, 618, 630
was one of those rarely gifted beings, 607
was rich, he was poor and, 510
were grave or gay, whether, 931
who had died two days before, 845
will, if she will, 204
with one breath attunes, 514
you are the cruell'st, alive, 54
Sheaf, blown to the, 633
of splendid songs, 910
Shear, never has known the barber's, 481
swine all cry and no wool, 142
Shears, Fury with th' abhorred, 159
resembles a pair of, 313
Sheath, one sword keeps another in, 138
sword back in the, 827
Sheathed their swords, 66
Sheaves, a thousand golden, 808
autumn, 580
golden, 638
She-bear, a great, 246
Shebeen, Shanahan's ould, 715
Shed no tear — O shed, 385
Sheddeth man's blood, whoso 1097
Sheelah was nigh, 328
Sheep and silkworm wore the very clothing, 199

Sheep are in the fauld, 277
  close shorn, 138
  flock of, that leisurely pass by, 300
  have gone astray, like, 1112
  how to feed Thy, 549
  hungry, look up and are not fed, 159
  is dey all come in, 719
  kept a flock of, 141
  lamb that belonged to the, 962
  mountain, 348
  old half-witted, 300, 304, 747
  put on your fleece, 982
  quiet fond and few, 406
  shepherdess of, 701
  swine monkey lion wine, 1068
  thou bringest the, 960
  to his, he yaf, 5
  with their lambs, 758
  would not sail again with, 814
Sheep's black nose, stroke, 814
  eye, he casts a, 1039
Sheepfol' bin, guards de, 719
Sheep-herding, rest is mere, 886
Sheep-men, eight ragged, 814
Sheer hulk, 274
  necessity, 278
  precipitous mountain-side, 621
Sheet, forever float that standard, 382
  of postage stamps, 775
  to the grave, what carry we then but a, 19
Sheets, cool kindliness of, 894
Sheeted dead did squeal, 89
Sheiling, from the damp, 674
Shekels of silver wherewith to pay, 715
Shelf, dust and silence of the upper, 397
  of dreams, 901
  put upon a, 831
  wreck on a strange, 119
Shell, convolutions of a, 302
  disdained a soul had gained, 528
  endures, only the, 892
  ever sings of its home, 446
  far from the sea, I found a, 302
  from the strown beach, 577
  hath speech, my, 446
  leaving thine outgrown, 452
  music slumbers in the, 289
  must break before the bird, 471
  pearly, 672
  smooth-lipped, 302
  take ye each a, 216
Shells of pearly hue, sinuous, 302, 325
  remember the lost sea, 901
Shelley, did you once see, 487
  in a public lavatory, read, 907
  lyric lord, 634
  sing to, such a song, 625
  to death's brink, 879
Shelter about the mahogany tree, 481
  all who ask for, 890
  from injury, 532
  from the summer shower, 373
  lack of, 894
  of his ink, 725
  smiting for, 748
  to grow ripe, 547

Shelved round us lie mummied authors, 565
Shelves as dark and dusty, 899
  lacking on your well-filled, 534
  they're stored, on his, 760
  upon the glazen, 900
Shepa'd, call to de hirelin', 719
Shepherd fear, with their, 907
  hast any philosophy in thee, 50
  of the forest came, 279
  star that bids the, fold, 157
  tells his tale, 160
  with the king, equals the, 1042
Shepherd's crook beside the sceptre, 425
  reed, just to blow a, 406
  reed, love tunes the, 306
  tongue, truth in every, 21
Shepherdess of sheep, 701
Sheridan, in moulding, 356
  twenty miles away, and, 552
Sheriffs in de sky, 712
Sherlock Holmes, to, she is always the woman, 737
Sherry is dull, 234
  pale, too rosy-strong, 530
Shews of things, 112
Shibboleth, the lovely name of, 938
Shibboleths, fleeting, 652
Shield, but left the, 280, 307
  for the defenseless, 602
  laughter is my, 816
  of the great republic, 642
  soul like an ample, 179
  Spartan, 371
  sullen, 891
  wards off the darts, 453
Shields, blazoned, 933
Shielding men from the effects of folly, 581
Shift for myself, 10
  from side to side, 199
  is over, the long long, 844
  onion will do for such a, 52
  thus times do, 134
Shifted his trumpet, he, 252
Shifting fancies and celestial lights, 430
Shilelah, the Irish, 347
Shillings down, fifty thousand, 814
  make ducks and drakes with, 29
  rather than forty, 34
Shilling's praise, splendid, 258
Shiloh's woods, 690
Shin, failure barks your, 865
Shins are as thin as pen-holders, 774
  till I break my, 48
Shine along the sea, the wind's feet, 630
  bright afar off, 127
  can not order rain or, 504
  of every slanting silver line, 915
  singing as they, 194
  with such a lustre, 266
Shines always there, the sun, 432
  everywhere, the sun, 55
  make hay while the sun, 12
  on me still from out yon, 418
  so, a good deed, 47

Shineth as the gold, 8
  the everlasting light, 612
Shingles, played upon the, 568
Shining and sweet and true, 844
  hills of day, 442
  hour, improve each, 199
  land, their, 651
  light, as the, 1106
  light, burning and a, 1118
  mark, 571
  morning face, schoolboy with, 49
  nights, profit of their, 40
  nowhere but in the dark, 170
  of the stars, I found Him in the, 471
  palace, come and see my, 915
  pinion, on, 851
  rim, nestles over the, 858
  robes, 1073
  through them, 593
Shinto temple and shrine, 752
Ship an isle a sickle moon, a, 882
  and a star to steer her by, 832
  ashore, to put their, 784
  being in a, is being in a jail, 234
  committed to her element, 505
  community is like a, 1075
  drowning, 475
  flies, away the good, 345
  for an ocean trip, 655
  full many a gallant, 1092
  glowed like an immense, 932
  goes down, afore the, 527
  goes wop, 784
  has weathered every wrack, 536
  his rapt, 28
  idle as a painted, 315
  in the midst of the sea, way of the, 1109
  is anchor'd safe and sound, 536
  is clear at last she leaps, 537
  is fitted, this new, 787
  is troubled with rats, if the, 859
  lonely and swift like a small planet, 726
  me somewheres east of Suez, 782
  miseries we call a, 787
  no, contained a better crew, 622
  of all, no, 839
  of Democracy, 537
  of souls, vast outbound, 806
  of state, 964
  of state, sail on O, 435
  of the Union, common cause to save the, 455
  of truth, build a, 832
  perished, then the, 958
  sailing like a stately, 157
  sinking of the, 826
  stately, is seen no more, 640
  swings free, the anchor heaves, the, 406
  that ever scuttled, 359
  that part of the, where the cabin was, 247
  that's westward bound, 710
  whither O splendid, 668
  will sail, up the bay my, 567
  without ballast, 1063
Ships and steamboat man, 825

Ships are alive, 932
　are but boards, 44
　are coaffins, 825
　as those, see such, 834
　beauty and mystery of the,
　　436
　becalmed at eve, as, 519
　came home from sea, and,
　　437
　constructed these great, 932
　dim-discovered, 224
　go down to the sea in, 1105
　hearts of oak are our, 242
　I have seen old, 881
　I saw long, 914
　launched a thousand, 31
　like, they steer their courses,
　　142
　long-lost multitude of, 552
　long time together, 678
　number of the enemy's, 997
　of love, here come the, 857
　of vast and unwieldy burthen,
　　230
　on ocean, self-possession of,
　　938
　rafts upon doomed, 850
　sail on the sea, 370
　see silver, 857
　that are in peril, 1022
　that divide, lives that part
　　are as, 425, 437
　that have gone down at sea,
　　338
　that pass in the night, 425,
　　437
　that sailed for sunny isles,
　　423
　that went to sea, 566
　thinking of these, 834
　towers and, 965
　upon the sea, 587
　warn the, 914
　we've got the, 562
　went forth to sea, my, 605
　went to sea and ships came,
　　437
　what you say of our, 826
Ship's great side, waiting at the,
　　933
　way upon the sea, 778
Shipmate, joy, 537
Shipmates die, to see your, 873
　then, shall all the happy, 806
Shipment's worthlessness, of this
　　poor, 845
Shipwreck and collision, may,
　　834
　deserve, 1051
　spared, 300
　terrible storm and, 658
Shipwrecked before I got aboard,
　　991
　kindles false fires, 304
Shire of men who understand,
　　893
Shires where the girls are fonder,
　　744
Shirt, a maxima cum laude, 867
　and a half in all my company,
　　63
　clean, day, 233
　doesn't wear a, 898
　from off her back, 898
　happy man's without a, 11
　no quarrel with the, 738

Shirt, no ruffles on, 404
　of a happy man, 639
　of fire, martyr in his, 587
　of Nessus is upon me, 105
　oftener changed their princi-
　　ples than, 203
　on his back never a, 188
　ruffles when wanting a, 188,
　　252
　shroud as well as, 392
　tail of an old bleached, 932
　that isn't white, 754
　to his back, not a, 309
　to my back, haven't a, 639
Shirts, as of poisonous Nessus,
　　378
　I take but two, 64
　I've got no, to wear, 622
Shirt-cuffs, Mr. Pound's, 906
Shive of a cut loaf, to steal a, 77
Shivering desolate out in the cold,
　　907
　on the ridge of life, 186
Shoal of time, bank and, 85
Shoals of honour, depths and, 73
Shock, cushion the, 781
　fodder's in the, 697
　it was a, 912
　of corn, like as a, 1102
　of pleasure, give a, 386
　sink beneath the, 355
　surge's angry, 231
　them, we shall, 58
　withstand love's, 851
Shocks that flesh is heir to, 93
Shocking bad hats, 293
　fault of women, 1063
Shoe, an open hand an easy,
　　757
　be Spanish or neat's leather,
　　142
　cannot put the same, on every
　　foot, 989
　good luck shall fling her old,
　　465
　has power to wound, 240
　horse lost for want of a, 137,
　　227
　let not a shoemaker judge
　　above his, 994
　lost for want of a nail, 137,
　　227
　of leather, trod on, 1034
　pick up a horse's, 679
　pinches me, my own, 997,
　　1037
　the fives did fit her, 132
　tramp can't eat a silver, 898
　wrings, where the, 137
Shoes, a new pair of, 956
　a surgeon to old, 81
　and ships and sealing-wax, 598
　come back with little white,
　　917
　Englishmen stand firmest in
　　their, 413
　from off thy feet, put off thy,
　　1098
　Hannah's at the window bind-
　　ing, 568
　he who sees takes off his, 431
　him that makes, go barefoot,
　　15, 122
　I felt wings upon my, 925
　like old, 997
　of King James, 130

Shoes, poor man for a pair of.
　　1126
　soles right offen yore, 927
　the latchet of whose, 1116
　walk in velvet, 897
Shoemaker should give no opin-
　　ion beyond shoes, 994
Shoemaker's wife, who is worse
　　shod than the, 15, 122
Shoe-string, careless, 133
Shoke, made dis leedle, 661
Shone, far off his coming, 153
　like a meteor, 148
　she, 654
Shoo fly don't bodder me, 517,
　　612
Shooe for lucke, old, 13
Shook a dreadful dart, 150
　hands and went to 't, 222
　his dart, death, 155
　the arsenal, 156
　to air, like a dew-drop, 75
Shoon, in her silver, 822
　sandal, 256
Shoot folly as it flies, 206
　if you must, 443
　straight, 361, 811
　young idea how to, 224
Shoots and briars, wandering,
　　864
　new beginnings and new, 924
　of everlastingness, 170
　through air and light, 336
Shooting star, glory like a, 59
Shooting-stars attend thee, 134
Shop can never know, the, 875
　coming right home from the.
　　600
　keep thy, 29
　pops its head into the, 246
　to mind, man has, 492
Shops of Stupidity Street, 816
Shop-keepers, nation of, 240
Shore, Afric's burning, 319
　against the distant, 258
　and ocean's wave-beat, 503
　at the rim, unknown, 870
　back from Hades', 983
　beat wild on this world's,
　　447
　control stops with the, 354
　dull tame, 350
　echoed along the, 319
　fades o'er the waters blue.
　　352
　far-off, where he would tread,
　　70
　fast by their native, 267
　few companions on the, 513
　gathering pebbles on the, 156
　gold and amber, 744
　gone to the, 567
　hear from the misty troubled,
　　644
　I lingered alone on the, 418
　I stand upon the, 568
　is steep, rocks are gray and,
　　642
　keel upon the, 954
　landing on some silent, 187
　left their beauty on the, 408
　lights around the, 577
　little boats should keep near,
　　227
　my boat is on the, 356
　my native, adieu, 352

Shore, never was on the dull
    tame, 350
  no search hath found, 401
  odours from the spicy, 151
  of memory, silent, 303
  of the Lollipop sea, 699
  on a stern but distant, 770
  on the night's Plutonian, 418
  on the opposite, 437
  on this dull unchanging, 502
  one foot in sea and one on, 38,
    256
  ornament is but the guiled, 46
  passed to the farther, 781
  pebbled, 107
  rapture on the lonely, 354
  sable, 554
  safe on, 199
  Scipio buried by the upbraid-
    ing, 354
  ships that never came to, 423
  slant to the, 882
  so dies a wave along the, 273
  so long you stay on, 713
  such is the aspect of this, 355
  surges lash the sounding, 211
  the fragile skiff attains the,
    640
  the lights around the, 577
  there comes up the, 766
  to his own native, 460
  to love, set a, 773
  tread thy, 1073
  Troy's doom-crimson, 881
  ulterior, 811
  unhappy folks on, 275
  unknown and silent, 325
  upon the farther, 402
  waves that plunged along the,
    558
  where'er I am by, at sea, 393
  who shrinks from sable, 554
  wrecked on, 611
  wrecked on rocky, 363
  writing them aloud along the,
    808
  your teeming, 694
Shores, fearless for unknown,
    537
  ghost of, 658
  of death, along the, 746
  of Tripoli, 953
  on sands and, 157
  round earth's human, 385
  shipt for foreign, 337
  to what strange, 30
  undreamed, unpathed waters,
    57
  whisperings around desolate,
    385
Shores' shadders kind of mix
    and mingle, 527
Shoreless seas, only, 658
Short and far between, 186
  and long is, 1034
  and narrow bound from morn
    to eventide, 450
  and simple annals of the poor,
    244
  and simple flannels of the
    poor, 911
  and long of it, this is the, 34
  and uncertain, life is, 238
  as any dream, 42
  as are the nights, 127
  as one, appear as, 223

Short be the day, or never so
    long, 17
  comes so far, 838
  cut, always take the, 1011
  don't sell America, 944
  horse soon curried, 13
  letter an insult, 234
  life is too, 408, 410
  of the wearer's expectation,
    498
  on this sad Saturday, for be-
    ing, 715
  potential stir, 584
  retirement urges sweet return,
    154
  shrill shriek, 247
  sleep, one, 118
  stopped, never to go again,
    601
  sudden storms are, 59
  time of life is, 63
  views, take, 312
Shortened, who first, the labor,
    379
Short-haired poet, 661
Short-lived pain, 307
Shortness basely, to spend that,
    63
Shot, beginning of a fray and
    end of a, 17
  fool's bolt is soon, 16
  forth peculiar graces, 153
  heard round the world, 409
  so trim, he that, 77
  that kills Wordsworth, 737
  whose sound rang out, 706
Should auld acquaintance, 286
  keep who can, they, 298
  not say it, say it that, 131
  take who have, they, 298
Shoulder and elbow, 'twixt, 222
  better faces than stands on
    any, 98
  her bosom her face, show us
    her, 594
  perhaps to touch his, 929
  to the wheel, 124, 962
Shoulders ache, my, 891
  and slopes of the dune, 757
  Atlantean, 150
  dwarf on a giant's, 122, 136,
    318
  head and, 1030
  heads grow beneath their, 100
  sight of his, 862
  stick out like two bowlders,
    774
  were His throne, my, 828
  white as snow, 510
Shoulder-clapper, a back-friend,
    a, 38
Shoulder-high we bring you
    home, 743
Shout about my ears, 828
  and revelry, midnight, 157
  and the ring of galloping feet,
    676
  back our peals of laughter,
    554
  is a rattling of chains, 883
  pursued him with one, 170
  ringing through parlor and
    hall, 362
  that tore hell's concave, 148
  your rout send forth a joyous,
    401

Shouts and plaudits of the
    throng, 439
  golden, 576
Shouted for joy, 1102
Shovel and tongs, 389
Show and gaze o' the time, 89
  at Madison Square Garden,
    922
  death a hideous, 547
  great, with little means, 482
  himself what he is, let him,
    39
  his eyes and grieve his heart,
    87
  I would, the night-flowers,
    388
  idle, 436
  in some fifth act, may, 472
  is a poor substitute, outside,
    961
  it, if you've not a chance to,
    942
  judges all ranged a terrible,
    205
  makes a great, 47
  mercie unto others, 25, 216
  never ain't had no, 639
  of dross, 45
  of evil, obscures the, 46
  of truth, authority and, 39
  slaves to their gilded, 394
  spontaneity, life and universe,
    569
  that within which passeth, 89
  the most of Heaven, to, 506
  'tis all a great, 502
  us how divine a thing, 299
  world is all a fleeting, 336
  you 're up to fightin' tu, 527
Shows as he removes the mask,
    he, 481
  comment on the, 303
  goes with all the, 952
  mirthful comic, 71
Showed him the gentleman, 285
Shower, earth loveth the, 1012
  from the south, 668
  he sendeth sun he sendeth,
    423
  of commanded tears, 52
  of curates, 507
  of rain, foul weather lieth not
    in a, 132
  ran white wine, 929
  shelter from the summer, 373
  sleet of arrowy, 244
  the tranquil sun, after the, 638
Showers, April with his, 4
  for the thirsting flowers, 366
  frae my ee, 277
  fragrant after, soft, 152
  love is full of, 30
  small, last long, 59
  suck the honied, 159
  Sydneian, of sweet discourse,
    165
  the sweetest, 256
Shower-like, joys that came, 317
Showest, have more than thou,
    98
Shpeer und helmet, rode out mit,
    559
Shred of lemon-peel, 889
Shreds and patches, king of, 95
Shrew, every man can tame a,
    but he that hath her, 125

Shrew, united to a, 668
Shrews, under the discipline of, 344
Shrewd and over-thrifty, 879
  as Socrates' Xanthippe, 52
Shrewdly, the air bites, 91
Shrewsbury clock, hour by, 63
Shriek, a solitary, 359
  of outraged art, 892
  short shrill, 247
  with a fearful, 665
Shrieked, it was the owl that, 86
Shrieking circumstance, thrones on, 783
Shrill and high newsboys cry, 806
  Christmas is here winds whistle, 481
  trump, 102
  winds whistle free, 503
Shrimpers, Devonshire, 599
Shrine, a vacant, 871
  before the inmost, 765
  faith's pure, 370
  melancholy has her sovran, 384
  Moslem mosque and pagan, 443
  of memory, before, the, 1085
  of the mighty, 355
  once covered acres, 882
  so rich a, 809
  too many Buddhas in a private, 1027
  where a sin is a prayer, 632
  where patriots kneel, 439
  worshiper at nature's, 382
Shrines, such graves are pilgrim, 363
  the heart hath builded, 418
  to no code, 363
Shrined in our hearts with Cressy, 518
Shrinks from the sable shore, who, 554
  the soul, why, 195
Shriveled stalks of goldenrod, 843
Shroud and rigging ran in sport, 405
  as well as shirt, 392
  no pocket in a, 656
  of thoughts, 353
  ray on ray split the, 493
Shrouded day retreats, 668
Shrunk shank, too wide for his, 50
Shudder, regard the world without a, 637
Shuddering boughs, 668
  fall, with, 575
  in the gloaming light, 620
Shuffle the cards, patience and, 311, 1040
Shuffled off this mortal coil, 93
Shuffle-Shoon and Amber-Locks, 699
  is old and gray, 699
Shufflers who slacken their pace, 492
Shut, of evening flowers, 154
  shut the door, 212
  the gates of mercy, 245
  the stable door, 14
  the windows of the sky, 225

Shut up in measureless content, 85
Shuts up the story of our days, 22
Shutter and knock upon her, 917
  borne before her on a, 481
Shutters, close the, 265
  light drips through the, 904
Shuttle, life is a, 35
  mocking-bird's throat the musical, 536
  swifter than a weaver's, 1102
Shuttles, fly the great, 656
  of using his wit, 141
Shy cock of the heath, 288
Shyneth as the gold, 8
Si bene commemini causae sunt quinque bibendi, 184
Sibilants and dentals, omitting, 550
Sibyl, contortions of the, 261
Sic transit, and then, 486
  vos non vobis, 982
Sicilian tyrants never invented greater torment, 985
Sick and blue, you're beaten, 920
  and tired and faint and worn, 596
  are the greatest danger, 1081
  as a horse, 242
  at heart, I am, 89
  be not slow to visit the, 1124
  bed regal solitude, 324
  but when he 's, 698
  enter to help the, 971
  healest the earth when it is, 132
  heart of Keats, 669
  leisure to be, 63
  made him deathly, 684
  maketh the heart, 1107
  man back to health, 967
  not so, as troubled, 88
  of all the din, 593
  of its business, 299
  of lugging, 492
  oyster at low tide, 595
  say I'm, I'm dead, 212
  superintend the, 971
  that eats till he is, 577
  that surfeit with too much, 44
  this night is but the daylight, 47
  whole head is, 1110
  with long delay, 386
Sicken and decay, love begins to, 83
  the appetite may, 53
Sickening grief doth prey, 269
  thought itself, 669
Sickle in another's corn, 989
  keen, death with his, 433
Sicklied o'er with the pale cast of thought, 93
Sickly flame, love is a, 193
  smile, he smiled a kind of, 644
Sickness and in health, in, 1128
  doth infect the life-blood, 63
  enlarges dimensions of man's self, 324
  love is a, 30
  nor pain of body, 873
  out of this sleepy, 936
Sickness-broken body, 147
Side, angel on the outward, 37

Side, back and, go bare, 20
  beggar may crawl at his, 449
  brought to my, 671
  by side for the way was one, 558
  by side, with canvas drooping, 519
  by the Ganges', 639
  down the glowing, 355
  Europe rings from side to, 162
  ever strong upon the stronger, 57
  feel it instantly on every, 115
  forgot when by thy, 364
  God on our, 321
  has his pleasant, 767
  he works on the wrong, 569
  heard the other, 968
  let me warm it by thy, 364
  on this, Jordan's wave, 516
  passed by on the other, 1117
  south and southwest, 141
  stand by your, 783
  stand thou on that, 667
  the sun's upon, 336
  to side, shift from, 199
  truth stood on one, 476
  where my sympathies lie, 904
Sides, equal for both, 969
  laughter holding both his, 160
  much may be said on both, 196, 229
  of kings, ruined, 129
  spur to prick the, of my intent, 85
  unfed, 99
  we see both, 808
  with laughing, split his, 1037
Side-hills of success, 775
Sidelong looks of love, 250
  maid, hasty from the, 224
Sidewalks of New York, 761
Sidmouth, great storm at, 314
Sidney thirsting, 764
  warbler of poetic prose, 266
Sidney's sister Pembroke's mother, 119
Siege to scorn, laugh a, 88
  of the city of Gaunt, 257
Sieges attacks campaigns, 1045
  fortunes, battles, 100
Sieve, can't see through a, 1038
  they went to sea in a, 498
  water in a witch's, 897
Sifted a whole nation, God, 179
  three kingdoms, God had, 436
Sigh a sob a storm a, 597
  at leaving, last, 668
  beadle to a humorous, 41
  from Indus to the Pole, 216
  God is an unutterable, 738
  is the sword of an angel king, 282
  listening to a whisper or a, 927
  no more ladies, 38, 256
  of the weary, 567
  passing tribute of a, 245
  perhaps 't will cost a, 273
  prayer is the burden of a, 306
  sadder than a, 920
  some a light, 406
  the lack of many a thing, 107
  the same desire, 577
  to think he still has found, 242
  to those who love me, 356

Sigh too much or a kiss too long, 559
  which prompts the eternal, 208
  with a smile, part with a, 796
  yet feel no pain, to, 337
Sighs a-plenty, 'tis paid with, 742
  and prayers, 596
  avail, naught my, 395
  before the dawn, 604
  give we to them, 384
  haunted with a million, 937
  I'm growing deeper in my, 509
  in Venice on the bridge of, 353
  night of memories of, 325
  sovereign of, 41
  to find them in the wood, 372
  world of, for my pains, 100
Sighed and looked, 176, 224
  at the sound of a knell, 264
  for his country he, 328
  no sooner, but asked the reason, 51
  no sooner loved but they, 51
  till woman smiled, man, 327
  to many, loved but one, 352
  to measure, often have I, 297
  to think I read a book, 297
  we wept we, 168
Sighing, a plague of, 62
  farewell goes out, 75
  like furnace, the lover, 49
  nought but a lovely, of the wind, 385
  sound, the, 577
  through all her works, nature, 155
  under a sicamore tree, 255
Sight, a dull, 449
  be acceptable in thy, 1103
  became a part of, 355
  because it is not yet in, 279
  charms strike the, 212
  complain most of loss of, 156
  dimness of, came over many, 247
  elude the, 301
  faints into dimness, 356
  for sore eyes, 191, 330
  gleamed upon my, 299
  goodly gift of, 850
  he could not want, 167
  hidden away out of, 631
  hide us from each other's, 134
  hideous, a naked human heart, 202
  highest bodily privilege, 312
  I see beyond the range of, 514
  I would receive my, 669
  in his dim uncertain, 821
  is the saddest, 890
  keen discriminating, 293
  limit of our, 653
  lose friends out of, 365
  lost to, to memory dear, 392
  loved not at first, 28, 31
  my blindness is my, 540
  of a Dissenter, the, 314
  of a white church, 831
  of death makes heart hard, 50
  of human ties, at, 216
  of it, barely catch, 1087
  of it, fear not the, 555
  of means to do ill deeds, 58
  of salt water unbounded, 777

Sight of such a monument, 1060
  of that immortal sea, 301
  of the unwise, in the, 1124
  of vernal bloom, 151
  of you is good for sore eyes, 191
  or sound, spotted, 897
  or thought be formed, whatever can to, 155
  out of blindness, 663
  out of, out of mind, 9, 27
  pass slowly out of, 552
  receive thy, 373
  sensible to feeling as to, 85
  so many a glorious, 441
  spare my aching, 244
  sucked up out of, 430
  swim before my, 216
  thousand years in thy, 1105
  'tis a shameful, 198
  to dream of not to tell, 315
  to thee is sightless, 749
  tracks go out of, 927
  walk by faith not by, 1120
  we lose friends out of, 365
  yet sometimes glimpses on my, 442
Sights and sounds, troublous, 796
  as youthful poets dream, 160
  I would see, what, 955
  moves more than to hear them told, to see sad, 107
  of death, what ugly, 71
  of ghastly dreams and ugly, 71
  the saddest of, 815
Sightless couriers of the air, 85
  heaven a shaven land, a, 576
  Milton with his hair, 303
Sigismund the emperor, 123
Sign brings customers, 1045
  carve thou this, 658
  chief, that a man has nobility, 1064
  dies and makes no, 69
  for him to retire, 421
  give me a, 539
  God Almighty has hung out a, 342
  hearts that break and give no, 452
  of noble souls, 961
  of old age, 314
  outward and visible, 1128
  pacific, 155
  to know the gentle blood, 26
  without a, 219
Signs and steps of a god, 618
  by which one heart, 437
  indicative of their respective trades, 342
  merely conventional, 599
  nature speaks in symbols and in, 442
  of the times, 1115
  of woe, gave, 155
  strange, in heavenly places, 560
  which come before events, 318
Signal flame, sky-high a, 937
  of his release, 443
  shown and a distant voice, only a, 437
Signals and the signs, 437

Signature acknowledged, 1085
  of pain, 933
  of some great master on verse of young poet, 741
Signatures and marks of mercy, 1079
Signet sage, pressed its, 308
Significance devoid of, 421
  gave a spiritual, 669
  of life, 1077
  whatever the, 491
Significant and budge, 263
Signifying nothing, 88
Signiors, most potent grave and reverend, 100
Signories, lucent and large, 920
Silence, a time to keep, 1109
  all the airs and madrigals, 163
  also, in, 960
  and alone, in, 424
  and apart, in, 439
  and desolation and dim night, 459
  and slow time, 383
  and tears, in secret in, 587
  and tears, parted in, 351
  and the homeless air, 629
  and the wakeful stars, 588
  and their still faces, 933
  back of the sound broods the, 609
  before him, let all the earth keep, 1113
  burning, thunder and, 926
  check'd for, 53
  child's sob in the, 428
  clings around me, 798
  conspiracy of, 869
  deep as death, 328
  deep dear, 429
  elected, 672
  envious tongues, 73
  expressive, 224
  flashes of, 313
  float upon the wings of, 158
  foster-child of, 383
  from the talkative, 880
  give me but, 794
  gives consent, 253
  hath more eloquence, well-timed, 478
  have trimmed in, 1002
  hilted, 688
  hour friendliest to sleep and, 153
  implies settled distress, 321
  implying sound, 489
  in love bewrays more woe, 21
  in the far-off, 688
  in the starry sky, 302
  in thy life, a, 594
  infinitude of, 542
  is an answer to a wise man, 1001
  is deep as eternity, 377
  is golden speech is silvern, 380
  is no certain token, 625
  is of eternity, 380
  is so near, because the, 737
  is the best resolve, 1044
  is the perfectest herald of joy, 38
  like a poultice comes, 451
  listening to, 392
  living on even in, 1058
  majestic, 342

Silence more musical than any song, 587
negligence and, 237
never betrays you, 676
never dies, 688
never regretted, 990
none to make them keep, 1078
nothing lives 'twixt it and, 347
of pure innocence, 56
of the ancient world, wander in the, 729
of the receding world, 583
of the upper shelf, 397
or of sound, joy of, 407
parted in, 396
perfect expression of scorn, 721
reign, when awful darkness and, 498
secret guilt betrayed by, 175
sealed, in secret kept, 507
sounds no worse, 743
speaking, 306
speaks for love, 617
speech better than, 973
stand shadowless like, 392
suppressed in, 964
temple of, 399
that dreadful bell, 101
that is in the starry sky, 302
the cruelest lies are told in, 704
the rest is, 98
the wizard, 691
then a lark, 681
then darkness again and a, 437
there is a, 390
thunders of white, 428
to work in, 706
tongueless, 603
true sorrow makes a, 922
wakened by, 629
were fitter, 796
when one spoke of death, 1071
where hath been no sound, 390
where he cannot convince, 950
where no sound may be, 390
whereso'er I go, 350
which isolates, it is, 1089
will fall like dews, 897
wrapped in his beard and his, 928
Silences, grand orchestral, 430
holy towers of the, 914
success is in the, 757
three, there are, 439
we keep, what, 600
Silenced, you have not converted because you have, 641
Silent above the flowers her children, 565
acting a, desperate part, 533
all, and all damned, 296
and all damned to die, 933
and from the world apart, 582
and safe, 676
as the moon, 156
as the trees, can be, 802
as to his works, 237
cataracts, motionless torrents, 316
court of justice, 465
dark o'ershadowing tomb, 672
dead their pains are past, 290
end, this is the, 586

Silent evening skies, under the, 658
face to face, 429
finger, point with, 318
finger points to heaven, 302, 318
flooding in the main, comes, 519
gazing pondering the themes, 537
grave, dark and, 22
halls of death, 371
I ponder, 1091
if I would be loved, 880
land, the, 587
manliness of grief, 251
moon, immense and, 536
not gamesome and gallant, 936
note which Cupid strikes, 145
oar parts the silent river, 568
pace, matchless swiftness but, 219
part is best, of noble work, 533
performance maketh best return, 1020
prayer, homes of, 468
river, thou hast taught me, 434
sea, beside the, 444
sea, into that, 315
sea of pines, 316
season thro', the, 406
shade 'neath silent skies, 568
shore, landing on some, 187
shore of memory, 303
shore, that unknown and, 325
so we stand, 922
spectator, 330
speech, speak with a, 580
stars go by, the, 612
stream, across the, 717
sun, give me the splendid, 536
tents of green, 439
that you may hear, 82
though, they cry aloud, 1092
thought, sessions of sweet, 107
thought, stores of, 295
upon a peak in Darien, 384
voice of God, 688
when occasion requires, 1001
when they have hatched their eggs, 147
when to be, 990
why art thou, 396
worshiper, wiser the, 612
Silently as a dream, 266
steal away, 434
wrapping all, light, 535
Silhouette sublime, a, 572
Silk and fur, fondle of, 792
on his tongue, 426
rustling in unpaid-for, 105
soft as, remains, 204
stockings and white bosoms, 233
suit which cost me much money, 180
umbrella, with a, 857
Silks my Julia goes, in, 134
need not be new, 848
ye Lyons looms, weave no more, 522
Silken sad uncertain rustling, 460
snare, 600

Silken tie, the silver link the, 307
Silkworm, sheep and, 199
Sill, crossed the, 552
Silly and as wise as bad and as good, as, 457
hanging face, 199
quietly and contentedly, 323
sooth, it is, 54
Siloam's shady rill, 342
Silver and gold are not the only coin, 968
answer rang, 428
apples of the moon, 790
blow, with a, 855
bow, moon like to a, 42
chain of evening rain, 406
cord be loosed, 1110
dollars, however plenty, 627
domes of Lucknow, round the, 443
flute, played on a, 664
fruit-tree tops, tips with, 78
girl she came to me, 875
glow, call through the, 865
golden locks to, turned, 27
in his pouch, little, 426
just for a handful of, 485
light on tower and tree, 277
lining on the night, 157
link the silken tie, 307
mantle threw, o'er the dark, 152
needle-note of a fife, 925
on its wings, with, 888
persuasion shine all, 960
pictures of, 1108
pinions, wave thy, 385
plate, polished up the, 911
rings, try not how your, 844
sea, stone set in the, 59
ships, 857
sold the just man for, 1126
spliced and linked together, with, 578
stars when the day is done, 638
the oars were, 104
thirty pieces of, 1116
tips with, 78
to the povre freres, 5
vest, 647
waves chime ever peacefully, 480
wedding, their, 812
Silvered by time completely, 265
his beard was sable, 90
o'er with age, 206
the walls of Cumnor Hall, 269
Silver-footed ironies veiled jokes, 766
Silver-gray, to-morrow, 681
Silver-mantled plains, 477
Silvern, speech is, 380
Silvers in the rain, maketh, 929
Silver-sandaled feet, 723
Silver-sweet sound lovers' tongues, 78
Silver-white lady-smocks, 41
Silvery round moon beautiful over the house-tops, 536
wings says Elaine, 823
Simiadae then branched off, 448
Simians believe knowledge is power, 829
fairy story of, 829

Similar facks, other, 853
  goddamned phrases, 852
  to what we are, 1087
Simile that solitary shines, 214
  wisdom in the, 495
Similes, I sit and play with, 298
Similitudes, used, 1113
Simon Pure, real, 190
  Stone he spied a boat, 371
  the cellarer, 647
Simonides bore off the prize, 438
Simple child, a, 295
  creed for word or deed, 686
  daisy starred the sod, 539
  dues of fellowship and social
    comfort, 430
  either, or gentle from vanity
    fair, 545
  faith, plain and, 83
  gratitude and wonder, 856
  in ears of gentle and, 545
  maiden in her flower, 462
  maxim universally known, 229
  merry tender knack, 429
  modest manly true, to be, 528
  nakedness, white truth in, 470
  no vice so, 46
  silver welcome, 896
  sources, from, 53
  wiles, transient sorrows, 299
  words enough, his words were,
    524
Simples, compounded of many,
  51
Simpleness and gentleness and
  honour, 777
Simpleton sages and reasoning
  fools, 335
Simplicity a child, in, 175, 217
  a grace that makes, 119
  a great, 854
  be imposed upon, don't let
    your, 277
  can no longer be misled, 949
  depend on, 973
  greatest, with best results, 922
  he lived in noble, 374
  in his, sublime, 466
  Jeffersonian, 619
  lost is our old, 950
  most deceitful mistress, 637
  of character, 641
  of the three per cents, 275, 421
  simple truth miscalled, 107
  the mean between ostentation
    and rusticity, 218
  there is in Christ, 247
  to sing, teaching, 841
Simplification, order and, 1089
Simplify, simplify, 514
  to, my way of life, 376
Simulated stature face and
  speech, 430
Simulation of the painted scene,
  430
Sin, a duty not a, 226
  against the Holy Ghost, 641,
    1082
  among you, he that is with-
    out, 1118
  and blot, so much of, 657
  and the saving lies, 780
  angels fell by that, 73
  born of a little, 917
  could blight, ere, 316
  cunning, can cover itself, 39

Sin deprived of heaven, for no,
  1021
  dulled their eyes with, 709
  except stupidity, no, 723
  falter not for, 454
  folly can glide into, 309
  fools make a mock at, 1107
  for me to sit and grin, 450
  forgiven by Christ in heaven,
    the, 431
  fox-terriers have more orig-
    inal, 745
  has cast away, 681
  has many tools, 454
  hate the, but love the sinner,
    552
  his darling, 316
  his favourite, is pride, 316,
    321
  hold it half a, 467
  hypocrite falls into, 1016
  impute, 488
  in the blossoms of my, 91
  is a prayer, 632
  is ez sharp ez a bamboo-brier,
    689
  is forgiven, realms where, 789
  is not so prejudicial, private,
    1040
  laughed at original, 810
  man-like is it to fall into, 435
  men, without intending it,
    1010
  no, for a man to labour, 60
  not, be ye angry and, 1121
  not only as a, 360
  of self-neglecting, 66
  poverty is no, 138
  quantum o' the, I waive the,
    285
  rod must heal the, 659
  sad as angels for the good
    man's, 242, 327
  self-love is not so vile a, 66
  shall be no more, when, 503
  some rise by, 35
  suffered for all, 668
  take me from my, 940
  the angels fell, by which, 814
  they do by two and two, 781
  they, who tell us love can die,
    322
  think it little, 566
  thinking their own kisses, 79
  to covet honour, if it be a, 67
  to falter would be, 503
  to gladden this vale, 453
  unconsciousness of, 828
  wages of, is death, 1119
  world's as ugly ay as, 545
Sins are all committed, 217, 1077
  be as scarlet, though your,
    1111
  compound for, 142
  enough, every man hath, 166
  multitude of, 1122
  no, to be forgiven, 364
  of the fathers, 46, 968
  oldest, the newest kind of
    ways, 65
  only speak, murder shrieks
    out, 128
  remembered in thy orisons, 93
  that are common heritage, 871
  that tarnish, 767
  washed white, 892

Sins were scarlet, 811
  wilt Thou judge me, not by
    my, 844
Sinais climb and know it not, 525
Sinament and ginger, 135
Since first beneath the chestnut,
  446
  the creation of the world no
    tyrant, 424
  when was genius found, 431
  which I have loved long, 403
Sincere sagacious melancholy
    quaint, 573
  to be quite, 893
Sincerest laughter, our, 366
Sincerity of mirth, there's small,
    386
  wrought in a sad, 408
Sinew nerve and brain, in, 823
Sinews of the soul, anger one of
    the, 147
  of virtue, 140
  of war, coin is the, 1025
  stiffen the, 66
Sing again with your dear voice,
    368
  alas for those that never, 451
  and die, let me, 359
  and play, wouldst have me,
    337
  and that they love, 146
  as Martin Luther sang, 481
  because I must, I do but, 468
  bird on green Missouri's plain,
    518
  eagle suffers little birds to, 77
  for joy, widow's heart to, 1102
  he knew himself to, 159
  heavenly goddess, 218
  I am saddest when I, 606
  I can't, as a singist, 606
  I'm saddest when I, 389
  in a hempen string, 127
  strange that death should, 58
  sweetly, and brightly smile,
    365
  the hymn of the conquered, I,
    533
  the old songs, 590
  the song, others shall, 444
  them, I pray you, 982
  though I shall never hear thee,
    365
  which now the angels, 477
Singe yourself, so hot that it, 72
Singed the Spanish king's beard,
    439
Singer, anguish of the, 661
  comes the song, to the, 672
  dries one tear, 793
  idle, of an empty day, 608
  in France of old, 631
  long after the death of the, 539
  of the field and fold, 649
  passes, though the, 575
  thou the, I the song, 623
  wait, do not let the, 679
  where is the, 735
Singers chanting dirges, 554
  fault common to all, 984
  God sent his, 436
  love the sweetest, 930
  with vocal voices, 189
Singeth a quiet tune, 315
  all night long, 89
Singing as they shine, 194

Singing bird, my heart is like a, 587
birds sweet sold, 816
is sweet but be sure of this, 610
man, 836
milkmaids, no, 707
of anthems, 64
of birds is come, time of the, 1110
of Mount Abora, 316
of the birds, 955
robes, garland and, 162
seamen, 864
ships, 857
sick of, 631
singers with vocal voices, 189
when I felt inclined to, 810
whisper, a, 873
with happier, 596
Singist I am not a success, as a, 606
Single blessedness, dies in, 42
bound, heaven not reached at a, 521
cell becomes a man, 581
hour of that Dundee, 298
in intent, 927
life, careless of the, 468
man plant himself on his instincts, 414
men in barricks, 781
nothing in the world is, 368
song and carelessly complete, 684
talent well employed, 231
track, facing on the, 644
volume brought to land, 300
word, 't is a, 590
Singleness of heart, with, 1127
Sings from the organ-pipe of frailty, 58
I held it truth with him who, 467
it, Handel, 414
like an angel, 47
the lark at heaven's gate, 105
you know what Virgil, 472
Singular, in the, 952
Singularity, trick of, 55
Sink a navy, a load would, 73
beneath the shock, 355
bought it for the, 917
hangs py der, 661
let the world, 136
or swim live or die, 340
pour them down the, 827
unrespective, 75
Sinking, a kind of alacrity in, 35
in thy last long sleep, 275
Sinks the day-star, so, 159
Sinned against than sinning, more, 98
all in Adam's fall, 947
Sinner, art thyself a, 228
hate the sin but love the, 552
it or saint it, 209
of his memory, made such a, 32
or saint, man may be, 639
prayer that reforms, the, 548
the hungry, 361
too weak to be a, 80
vilest, may return, 199
when the, is dismayed, 375

Sinner who must write, mercy on the, 903
Sinners, how many po', 689
if, entice thee, 1106
lift their hands, all, 1022
miserable, 1127
Sinning, more sinn'd against than, 98
Sin-spotted soul, most heretofore, 556
Sinuous shells of pearly hue, 302, 325
speech of schools, 891
Sir Amice Pawlet on haste, 113
Bulwer, Lytton, I met, 400
critic good day, 508
Henry Wotton on critics, 113
Jenkin Grout, here lies, 948
John, the sail of, 552
Oracle, I am, 44
which serves and seeks for gain, 98
Sire of fame, toil is the, 968
son degenerates from the, 218
to son, bequeathed by, 355
Sires, descent is from heroic, 1050
green graves of your, 362
holy faith that warmed our, 451
strong speech of our, 771
Sires' not so good, than their, 983
Siren, song of the, 29
waits thee, 326
Sirens sang, what song the, 145
Sirrahs, sirrah me no, 947
Sisera, stars fought against, 1099
Sister and golden brother, silver, 889
Anne do you see any one, 946
calls me Will, 699
in, shut my little, 866
married the baboon's, 954
shall be a ministering angel, 97
to a sister, never praise, 785
was not gratified, 812
woman, still gentler, 285
Sisters, all the, virtuous, 943
and his cousins and his aunts, 622
dear, men with, 391
death and night, hands of the, 536
of the sea, 934
seven, dog-star and the, 900
three and such branches of learning, 45
two, by the goal are set, 309
under their skins, 782
wayward, depart in peace, 349
weird, the, 87
Sister's, erring, shame, 355
Sisyphus by fate doomed, 983
who bears the ban, 983
with toil and sweat, 223
Sit attentive to his own applause, 213
beside my lonely fire, 582
closer friends, 664
down and taste my meat, 135
down now but the time will come, 419
here we will, 47
in my bones, 313

Sit in the clouds and mock us, 64
round it and pluck, the rest, 431
still, their strength is to, 1111
studious let me, 224
thee down sorrow, 41
upon the ground, let us, 59
where I will, let me, 1040
you may, by my fire, 374
Sits as one new-risen from a dream, 52
in a foggy cloud, 87
on his horse back, 57
the wind in that corner, 39
upon mine arm, 129
Sitting audience looks like hungry guests, 200
Bull, the Short Wolf, Crazy Horse, 707
cheap as standing, 192
in a pleasant shade, 120
in my dolphin-chamber, 64
Situation, beautiful for, 1104
becomes unimportant, 1087
is remote, 271
of power and energy, 259
Situations, droll, 695
Six and seven, at, 15
beggared cripples, 937
days shalt thou labor, 505
feet one in his stocking feet, 927
get on to it, 862
honest serving-men, 784
hours in sleep, 21
hundred pounds a year, 214
men of Indostan, 510
months' oblivion, 636
of the seven cities, which, 910
Richmonds in the field, 72
scotches more, room for, 105
to dine at ten, to rise at, 1069
to sleep at ten, to sup at, 1069
Sixes and sevens, 15
or sevens, either at, 623
Sixpence all too dear, 101
I give thee, 293
thing that costs, 235
Sixteen were called Thompson, 360
Sixty miles in latitude, 600
Sixty-first minute, 733
Size, he could not suffer, such in, 933
is not grandeur, 563
no virtue goes with, 409
of dreaming, past the, 105
of pots of ale, 141
Skating on the Tiber, 868
over thin ice our safety, in, 412
Skeleton clothed with life, 340
if you know of a, 799
lo a, 289
Skeptic blows have beat upon, 622
Skepticism of a skeptical age, 643
Skewered through with office-pens, 497
Skie falth, have Larkes when, 12
Skies and seas around, new, 514
are a trifle bluer, 822
are blue and fields are green, as long as, 365

Skies as couple-colored, 672
  as I came through, out of the, 559
  be just as blue, other, 625
  beneath the, 955
  bird let loose in eastern, 336
  blows to flame the misty, 801
  books and my food, 703
  cloudless climes and starry, 356
  commercing with the, 160
  common people of the, 114
  death his ladder to, 26
  double-darken gloomy, 528
  from lowly earth to vaulted, 521
  from the blissful, 463
  glorify the, 669
  have many, 759
  hurled the gods out of their, 1045
  illumed the eastern, 473
  immortal spirit in the, 332
  into the azure, 710
  laughter shakes the, 218
  let its altar reach the, 294
  milky baldric of the, 382
  my canopy the, 207
  of ould Kilkinny, 820
  or early find the peaceful, 474
  pointing at the, 210
  raised a mortal to the, 176
  setting in his western, 173
  shine in other, 445
  some inmate of the, 220
  stars are in the quiet, 426
  steelyards of the, 725
  summer, are darkly blue, 418
  sun illumed the eastern, 557
  they change their, 778
  they were ashen and sober, 460
  to mansions in the, 199
  twinkle against our wrongs, 895
  upon you frown, 508
  watcher of the, 384
  when, were purple, 395
  wide laughed the, 889
Skiff does with current glide, 223
  fragile, attains the shore, 640
Skilful in its own defence, 591
Skill, all wisdom art and, 951
  and judgment thrown away, 242
  courage and, 172
  in arguing, 251
  in curing, 977
  in surgery, honour hath no, 63
  is but a barbarous, 167
  of a coin in hiding, 654
  of the polisher fetches out the colours, 196
  of words long dead, 912
  simple truth, his utmost, 114
  strengthens our nerves and sharpens our, 261
  'tis God gives, 520
  to do more, 882
Skim milk masquerades as cream, 623
Skimble-skamble stuff, a deal of, 62
Skin and bone, two millers, 221
  and bone, wasted to, 1033
  arm impregnably the, 409

Skin, come off with a whole, 1035
  deep, beauty but, 506
  drum made of his, 122
  Ethiopian change his, 1112
  lion's, will not reach, 998
  of an innocent lamb, 69
  of my teeth, 1102
  of the man of letters sensitive, 589
  of your cheek will tan, 753
  played, beneath the cool, 869
  scar to show on his, 997
  the wolf was wearing, 962
Skins and all, eat 'em, 952
Skin-deep, colours that are, 169, 187
  't is but, 169
Skin-diseases of the planet, 925
Skinside is the inside, 817
Skipper, hire out as a, 851
  stormed and tore his hair, 508
  with a groan, says the, 843
Skirmish of wit between them, 38
Skirt the eternal frost, 316
Skirts, caught at God's, 487
  no one ever lifted my, 1005
  of happy chance, 468
  of the dead night, 633
Skittles, beer and, 551
Skull, ashy the tall, 903
  of a lawyer, 96
  once of ethereal spirit full, 338
Sky above, the whole wide, 927
  admitted to that equal, 207
  and sea and land and earth's foundations, 744
  and sea but not our bark, 994
  and the ocean, nothing behind but the, 317
  banner in the, 450
  beneath what, 771
  bends over all, the blue, 315
  black in the blue of the, 568
  blue, and living air, 296
  blue ethereal, 194
  bridal of the earth and, 135
  bright reversion in the, 217
  chambers of the, 364
  changes when they are wives, the, 51
  clean sweet summer, 905
  clear-cut against the, 924
  clearness of the, 666
  climb the upper, 340
  close against the, 390
  complexion of the, 60
  could not enfold it, 747
  dusky night rides down the, 229
  extends around it all, 369
  far out of reach, the, 536
  flushing round a summer, 224
  forehead of the morning, 159
  girdled with the, 322
  gloomy as an author's prospects, 421
  go forth under the open, 371
  howls along the, 248
  I have need of the, 771
  in the bounds of earth and, 545
  infinite tender, 737
  inverted bowl they call the, 1019

Sky is blue the land is glad, 912
  is changed and such change, 353
  is filled with stars, 438
  is like a woman's love, 677
  is red, for the, 1115
  is the limit, 1034
  keep one parent from the, 213
  look bravely up into the, 693
  lose itself in the, 489
  milky way i' the, 164
  muse on the misty, 867
  my lad, shoulder the, 743
  no limits but the, 1034
  red, at night, sailors' delight, 1115
  regent of the, 269
  reversed and evil-starred, 897
  rim of the far-flung, 870
  shining in the, 589
  shines from out yon clouded, 418
  shines in the, 960
  silence in the starry, 302
  smile into the sullen, 923
  soft blue, did never melt, 296
  soul of man is larger than the, 386
  stared into the, 816
  stars in the, for religion's sake, 534
  steeples point to the, 318
  stepped to the, 431
  storm that howls along the, 248
  sunshine aye shall light the, 503
  tears of the, 222
  the moving moon went up the, 315
  they die in yon rich, 466
  through the boundless, 372
  to sky, stretched from, 1017
  triumphal arch that fill'st the, 328
  wait thy name beyond the, 351
  Washington is in the upper, 340
  were to fall, if the, 980
  what a scowl of cloud, 493
  whatever, is above me, 357
  why you should n't make a, 569
  windows of the, 225
  witchery of the soft blue, 296
  woods against a stormy, 370
  your goal the, 957
Sky-blue in thy cup, 391
Sky-born music, I hear a, 408
Skye, over the sea to, 752
Skyey influences, servile to the, 36
Skylark singing sweet and clear, 847
Skyline is a promise, 834
Sky-robes, these my, 157
Slab in the graveyard, handsome, 912
  of marble cold, monument, 448
Slackness, to brace our, 936
Slag, amid measureless grossness and, 535
Slain by arrows of the early frost, 565
  care little, 963
  he can never do that's, 143

Slain, he who is in battle, 254
  I could consent to be, 979
  in your country's wars, 76
  of the war, swear by the, 891
  think he is slain, if the, 410
  thrice he slew the, 176
  with him is beauty, 106
Slander, and would bring, 794
  like death loves a shining
    mark, 571
  lives upon succession, 38
  sharper than sword, 105
  truth best vindication against,
    457
Slanderous tongues, done to
  death by, 40
Slant sunbeams through fringes
  raining, 418
Slanted radiance, 849
Slape, 't is dhrames and not, 389
Slapped and rapped complain,
  802
Slash of the rain, 753
Slattern, a wandering, 820
Slatting, thundering rattle of,
  833
Slaughter, as a lamb to the, 1112
  as an ox goeth to the, 1106
  no fratricidal, 686
  to a throne, wade through, 245
  to the roaring, 921
Slaughters a thousand waiting,
  56
  of the race, 650
Slaughter-house, sailing to England's, 814
Slav Teuton Kelt I count them,
  471
Slave, armor's, 491
  as I would not be a, 455
  frees her, again, 193
  I am your, 858
  in his father's stead, 591
  king and, 671
  no, is here, 386
  of whistle clock or bell, 878
  of words, 379
  passion's, man that is not, 94
  pensioned, 338
  sleepy features of a, 927
  stone walls do not make a, 168
  subject not a, 304
  to no sect, 200, 208
  to purpose, not a, 930
  to thousands, has been, 102
  trade, that execrable sum of all
    villanies, 226
  You, Señor, said the trembling,
    511
  you were a Christian, 693
Slaves, Britons never shall be,
  225
  cannot breathe in England,
    264
  cease to be fortune's, 128
  five-and-thirty black, 736
  freeing the, 456
  man wills us, 272
  must suckle, 359
  of Pilate, 686
  so cruelly treated, no, 424
  to their gilded show, 394
  tyrants and, 253
  what can ennoble sots or, 208
  who dare not be in the right,
    524

Slaves, who fear to speak for the
  fallen, 524
  whose servitude is made sweet,
    799
  with greasy aprons, 105
Slavery thou art a bitter draught,
  242
  fortune is a great, 991
  ignorance the only, 603
  is but half abolished, 473
  or death, which to choose, 195
  price of chains and, 270
  remitted, hundred years of,
    689
Slavish knees, 385
Slayer, if the red, think he slays,
  410
Sleave of care, ravelled, 86
Sleek-headed men, 81
Sleep a dream a story, a, 561
  a wink, I cannot, 213
  after toil, 24
  and a forgetting, 301
  and a quiet, 832
  and be glad, 631
  and death, twins, 219
  and lazy ease, 1035
  between a sleep and a, 634
  bless man who first invented,
    510
  blesses the child, 1067
  blessings on him who invented,
    1042
  brings happy, 1023
  calls us from, 348
  care-charmer, 30
  dark house and long, 397
  days with toil nights with, 67
  death and his brother, 368
  death but an eternal, 972
  death is an eternal, 1060
  death's counterfeit, 86
  death's twin-brother, 468
  deep and dreamless, 612
  drowne in forgetfulnesse of, 26
  end the heartache, by a, 93
  exposition of, I have an, 43
  falleth on men, when deep,
    1101
  folding of the hands to, 1106
  from night to morn, only a,
    591
  full of rest from head to feet,
    463
  God giveth his beloved, 563
  great gift of, 693
  He giveth his beloved, 427,
    1106
  heavily on me like unwilling,
    385
  holy spirit blessed soul, 463
  hour friendliest to, 153
  how, the brave, 247
  hypocrites in our, 331
  I lay me down in peace to, 350
  if an endless, 563
  in Abraham's bosom, 72
  in dull cold marble, 73
  in peace, 76
  in thy last long, 275
  in your cloak there's no lodg-
    ing, 545
  is a death, 145
  is as nice as woman, 164
  is best after battle, 609
  is best, know that, 759

Sleep is good but death is better,
  1066
  it is a gentle thing, 315
  life is rounded with a, 33
  like unwilling, 385
  Macbeth does murder, 86
  medicine thee to that sweet,
    102
  miles to go before I, 839
  music that brings sweet, 463
  nature's soft nurse, 65
  nature's sweet restorer balmy,
    201
  neither night nor day, 84
  no more, I heard a voice cry,
    86
  no more, to die to, 93
  no small art to, 1079
  not dream not, 516
  nothing is gone save his, 683
  now I lay me down to, 795,
    947
  O gentle sleep, 65
  of a labouring man, 1109
  of death, in that, 93
  of nights, such as, 81
  one hour's, before midnight,
    138
  out of his, to sterte, 5
  passed in, 361
  passed it in my, 685
  past, one short, 118
  perchance to dream, to, 93
  sinking in thy last long, 275
  six hours in, 21
  sleepless to give their readers,
    215
  some must watch while some
    must, 94
  soul's nurse, 279
  strong man after, 163
  sweetly tender heart, 463
  that giv'st what life denies,
    673
  that is among the lonely hills,
    302
  that knits up the ravelled
    sleave of care, 86
  that knows not breaking, 308
  the friend of woe, 322
  the innocent, 86
  the universal vanquisher, 965
  they, in the land they made
    free, 602
  through darkness falls, 813
  till the end true soul, 463
  timely dew of, 152
  to mine eyes, I will not give,
    1106
  unseasonable and immoderate,
    239
  was aery light, his, 153
  whether we wake or we, 449
  while sluggards, 227
  who can wrestle against, 478
  who, on glory's brightest bed,
    386
  will never lie where care
    lodges, 78
  will sometimes surprise, 984
  winding up nights with, 67
  without a wink of, 1034
  yet a little, 1106
  young buds, in the root's, 385
Sleeper, rule not to waken a, 713
  wakes on his pillow, 521

Sleeping but never dead, 524
  growing when ye 're, 311
  in thy "Come O Lord," 474
  innocence, 645
  lords of joy, 896
  when she died, we thought
    her, 390
  within my orchard, 91
Sleeping-car, struggle with a, 635
Sleepless Eremite, nature's pa-
    tient, 385
  nights, so many, 1070
  soul that perished, 297
  stars, my consorts are the,
    517
  to give their readers sleep, 215
  yet do lie, 301
Sleeps creation, 201
  ill, who knows not that he, 987
  in dust, flourish when he, 185
  the pride of former days, 334
  till tired he, 208
  upon this bank, the moonlight,
    47
  well, after life's fitful fever,
    he, 86
Sleepy features of a slave, 927
  uplands waning, lights are on
    the, 418
Sleepy-town express, take the,
    824
Sleet of arrowy shower, 244
  stood before the iron, 431
Sleeve, heart upon my, 100
  laughing in her, 1046
  laughing in your, 277
  wear his liver on his, 933
Sleeves, herald's coat without, 63
Sleeveless errand, a, 13, 75
Sleigh, way to carry the, 404
Slender debt to nature, the, 135
  nose tip-tilted, her, 470
  silver thread, 637
Slenderly fashioned, so, 392
Slepen al the night with open
    yë, 5
Slept and dreamed, 508
  dying when she, 390
  one wink, 106
Sleveless errand, 13
Slew the slain, thrice he, 176
Slice of bread, the royal, 876
Slide, ashes just to spoil our, 699
  let the world, 11, 51, 131
  not stand, loves to, 173
Slides, don't hurry the, 862
Sliding mountains, to slit the,
    839
  roof-tops, riding on your, 926
Slight bow or cursory salutation,
    234
  nor fame I, 216
  not strength, 116
  not what is near, 968
  toss over ambient ether, 569
Slightest folly love did make thee
    run into, 48
Slime on water-plants, 551
  slimier, 893
Sling and with a stone, with a,
    1100
  in my pocket, 1056
Slings and arrows of fortune, 93
Slinks out of the race, 163
Slip, give them the, 1038
  if I, Thou dost not fall, 519

Slip, Judas had given them the,
    188
  let the world, 52
  many a, 425
  may come to all, de, 682
  of a lad to guide, 862
  the dogs of war, let, 82
Slips, greyhounds in the, 66
Slipped from my hold, 604
Slipper, good to the heels the
    well-worn, 452
  head stroked with a, 979
Slippers, composed of felt, 925
  of snow, little white, 917
  same old, 746
Slippered pantaloon, lean and,
    50
Slippery place, stands upon a, 58
  words are, 637
Slithy toves, 598
Slits the thin-spun life, 159
Slogan cry, had pealed the, 500
Slogans both exciting and com-
    forting, 917
  popularity of, 427
Slogardye a-night, May wol have
    no, 5
Slop over, prevailin' weakness to,
    606
  staineth, 886
Slope laughs with its white and
    red, 550
  through darkness, 468
  upward and downward, 703
Slopes, over the, of the dune,
    757
  shadows move over the, 982
Sloping into brooks, 346
  to the southern side, 528
Sloth and the cowardice, 827
  resty, 106
Slough was Despond, 171
Slovenly unhandsome corse, 61
Slow and moving finger, 103
  and silent stream, 150
  falling to the prompter's, 481
  form ponderous and step was,
    437
  go a little, 829
  hours strike, hear the, 916
  learn to read, 170
  of speech and of slow tongue,
    1098
  of study, 42
  rises worth, 231
  selection, rather a, 845
  Spondee stalks, in solemn sort,
    317
  sweet piece of music, 832
  to anger, he that is, 1107
  to smite and swift to spare,
    373
  to speak, 1122
  too swift arrives as tardy as
    too, 79
  tranquilities, 920
  'twill be very, 474
  unfriended melancholy, 249
  years sailed by and ceased, 437
Slowly and sadly we laid him,
    364
  silence all, ever widening, 470
Slowness, opening in a rare, 920
Slug-a-bed, get up sweet, 134
Sluggard, go to the ant thou,
    1106

Sluggard, 't is the voice of the,
    199
Sluggards sleep, while, 227
Sluggishness inertia permanence
    of matter, 1089
Slumber, a little, 1106
  again, too soon I must, 199
  awaits to house the mind, 809
  death is, 366
  grief brings a deeper, 607
  honey-heavy dew of, 82
  lie still and, 199
  ports of, 65
  seven hours to soothing, 275
  still repel you, 867
  to mine eyclids, 1106
Slumbers, in the profoundest of,
    247
  in the shell, 289
  interrupted a nation's, 935
  light, dreams and, 308
  of the virtuous man, 195
Slumber's chain has bound me,
    336
Slumbering ages, wakens the,
    402
  world, o'er a, 201
Slums, bitter ballads of the, 887
Slush, buried beneath the, 804
Sly normal lurch, wink and a,
    508
  Stephen, 52
  tough and devilish, 496
  way of jesting, 197
Smack and tang of elemental
    things, 708
  of age, 64
  of observation, 57
  sweet, my life does, 492
Smacked of noyance, 224
Smale, manye, maken a greet, 8
Small, all the peoples great and,
    471
  beer, felony to drink, 69
  beer, ostensibly drinking, 937
  beer, poor creature, 64
  beer that questionable super-
    fluity, 417
  beer, to chronicle, 101
  but how dear to us, 589
  but sullen horn, 247
  cannot reach the, 25
  choice in rotten apples, 52
  compare great things with, to,
    151
  deer, rats and such, 99
  experience grows, home where,
    52
  few pleased me, a, 971
  gain is gain however, 484
  great vulgar and the, 168
  habits well pursued, 275
  have continual plodders won,
    40
  her waist exceeding, 132
  his deserts are, 164
  house and large garden, 168
  in common eyes, 26
  interest, 235
  Latin and less Greek, 119
  many, make a great, 8
  moon lightens more, 668
  nations, day of, 622
  no low no great no, 207
  number of those who judge for
    themselves, 278

Small of all that human hearts endure, 231
one a strong nation, 1112
potatoes, we all are, what, 582
praties they are, 952
rare volume, 288
sands the mountain, 203
seems a figure mean and, 572
service is true service, 304
showers last long, 59
sincerity of mirth, there's, 386
so trifling or so mean, so, 339
sweet courtesies of life, 242
there is no great no, 410
things, day of, 1114
things make base men proud, 69
vices do appear, 99
voice in autumn's, the still, 442
voice spake unto me, still, 462
yet they grind exceeding, 435
Small-clothes before the invention of suspenders, 314
Small-endians and big-endians, 191
Smallest effort is not lost, 504
worm will turn, 70
Small-knowing soul, 40
Smart for it, 1107
of all the girls that are so, 189
of them that bid farewell, 343
Smarts so little as a fool, 213
this dog, 229
Smell a rat, 116, 142
ancient and fish-like, 32
as sweet, a rose by any other name would, 78
of bread and butter, 357
of him, liked the, 936
of piled-up deals, 873
of the lamp, 134
rankest compound of villanous, 35
stale, came from the tubby steamer, 925
sweet and blossom in their dust, 141
the blood of a British man, 99
the sweet keen, 577
Smelleth the battle afar off, 1103
Smells to heaven, 95, 226
wooingly, heaven's breath, 85
Smelly Liffy's tide, in the, 721
Smelt of the lamp, 1000
Smile again, affliction may, 41
an early-Gothic, 768
and be a villain, 92
and sigh, reasons why we, 365
at anything, could be moved to, 82
better the last, 1081
brightly, and sweetly sing, 365
calm thou mayst, 275
cannot cheer me, 240
clasp us with a, 574
dwells a little longer, 822
escaped my, 897
falls heavily, my, 900
followed perhaps by a, 264
forget and, 587
from her bright eyes, 1045
good warm, sunny, 422
greets you with a, 952

Smile haunts me still, her bright, 501
he smiled a kind of sickly, 644
hear with a disdainful, 244
if we do meet again, we shall, 84
in her eye, 307, 389
is sweet, his wise rare, 692
is the sweetest, her, 388
lit up the grim old face, 686
look backwards with a, 202
make languor, 213
make the learned, 211
no more, men, 205
of Christian charity, 770
on her lips, 307
one vast substantial, 495
sympathetic tear, the social, 246
tear followed perhaps by a, 264
that was childlike, 644
that won't come off, 813
those angel faces, 403
though I shall not be near thee, 365
to share the good man's, 251
to those who hate, 356
too wicked for a, 316
vain tribute of a, 307
was not meant to be seen, 1089
we would aspire to, 73
wept with delight at your, 521
when you call me that, 756
with an intent to do mischief, 122
Smiles all other maids' surpass, 280
and tears, her, 99
at the drawn dagger, 195
becks and wreathed, 160
for the sometime guest, 642
full of, 974
his emptiness betray, 213
in such a sort, 81
kissed into, 644
kisses tears and, 299
live upon remembered, 793
of joy the tears of woe, 336
of other maidens, 387
on glory's bloody face, 690
seldom he, 81
still, which lie far deeper, 376
sweet strains or pensive, 408
the robbed that, steals something from the thief, 101
the tears of boyhood, the, 336
to those who love you, 335
to-day to-morrow will be dying, 133
welcome ever, 75
Smiled a kind of sickly smile, 644
all around thee, 275
hermit sighed till woman, 327
on me, until she, 386
she, and the shadows departed, 654
when a sabbath appeared, 264
Smiling and the weeping, beyond the, 445
at grief, patience on a monument, 55
babby in a wad of straw, 375
damned villain, 92
destructive man, 186

Smiling in her tears, pensive beauty, 327
of fortune, 240
with a never-fading serenity, 195
Smirched complexion, with his, 66
Smite once, stands ready to, 159
Smith found, there was no, 1100
his name was, 664
hyphenated with, 935
nineteen were called, 360
stand with his hammer, 58
would have rejoiced Sydney, 590
Smiths never had any arms, the, 312
Smoke, a good cigar is a, 776
against the sky, 911
and flame, awful guide in, 310
and stir of this dim spot, 157
burn your own, 379
cities fouled by, 814
consume your own, 380, 694
from all the engines, 926
full of fancies, 766
gone up in, 749
is only smoke to me, 766
no fire without some, 16, 23
nothing more frightful than, 1069
of many a calumet, 681
of peace and of villainy, 1069
rising through trees, 1069
sable, 354
suffering man ought to consume his own, 381
that so gracefully curled, 333
w'at you gwine do wid de, 688
worth its weight in, 916
Smokes, the man who, 426
Smoke-wreaths of this free cigar, 605
Smoking flax, 1112
Smooth and sleek with ease, 997
as monumental alabaster, 103
at a distance rough at hand, 127
course of true love never did run, 42
do ye make the road of it, 242
runs the water, 69
stream in smoother numbers, 211
the bed of death, 213
the ice, 58
Smoother than butter, 1104
Smoothing the raven-down, 158
Smooth-lipped shell, 302
Smoothly done, my task is, 158
Smoothness, temperance that may give, 94
Smooth-shaven green, 160
Smooth-shod if that will do, 496
Smote him thus, 104
him under the fifth rib, 1100
'is blooming lyre, 784
them hip and thigh, 1099
Smouldering radiance sparkles, 1085
Snaffle and the curb, they use the, 933
of courtship, 776
Snail, carrying his own house, 117
creeping like, 49

Snail, juice of the, 923
Snails, feet like, 134
Snake, like a wounded, 211
  produced a, 491
  scotched the, not killed it, 86
  should pass the apples round, 956
  unwary may tread on a, 590
Snakes in Iceland, no, 237
Snakeskin-titles of mining-claims, 929
Snap av a finger, care a, 786
Snapper-up of unconsidered trifles, 56
Snaps itself, vow that binds too strictly, 471
Snare Andalusian, 331
  fall in the destined, 577
  mockery and a, 331
  rabbit in the, 877
  the destined, 577
  the silken, 600
Snares, riches are ready, 9
  traps gins and pitfalls for the capture of men, 482
Snatch a fearful joy, 243
Snatched my crown, 620
Sneaking off, my valour is, 278
Sneer and jibe, through the, 843
  shame me from my, 513
  teach the rest to, 213
  who can refute a, 274
  with solemn, 353
  yesterday's frown and, 523
Sneezing, Russian is nothing but, 592
Snips and snails and puppy dog tails, 322
Snivelling servant maid, 879
Snobs, English people are, 721
Snore, teach the rest to, 213
  upon the flint, 106
Snorting steam and piston stroke, 609
Snout clear down to the tail, 775
  jewel in a swine's, 1107
  of golden metal, 938
Snow, a-campin' in the, 630
  a ghastlier whiteness every year, 459
  a little this side of the, 585
  Alpine, 442
  and wheat, country of, 929
  appearing above the, 1055
  buried in, 952
  chaste as ice as pure as, 93
  chaste as unsunned, 105
  diadem of, 357
  fairest meadow white with, 453
  fall of the, 119
  falls in the river a moment white, 287
  from purest, 76
  had melted, beautiful, 804
  hide those hills of, 37, 127
  I shall be whiter than, 1104
  in May's new-fangled mirth, 40
  in the clover or the, 552
  is on the grass again, 560
  it can do no wrong, beautiful, 560
  late though lingered the, 642
  lies on dead volcanoes only, 690

Snow lies thick on Valley Forge, 784
  mockery king of, 60
  nor rain nor heat nor darkness, 969
  of heaven, try, 923
  on the green grass, 903
  or rain, step softly under, 827
  peaks of dazzling, 710
  peaks wrapt clouds and, 352
  rosebuds filled with, 121
  roses underneath the, 638
  shall be their winding sheet, 328
  shoulders white as, 510
  stood shivering in the, 30
  the beautiful snow, O the, 560
  the emerald leaves, after the, 638
  the falling, 849
  they shall be white as, 1111
  under the, 722
  upon the desert's dusty face, 1018
  walk in the, 897
  wallow naked in December, 59
  white and drifted, 404
  whiter than the driven, 242
  wraps him in ice and, 1065
  year, rich year, 137
  you must walk in the, 917
Snows and sins, season of, 633
  mane of, 629
  of yester year, where are the, 434
  of yesterday, where are the, 759
  soft as fleeces of descending, 218
  through the drifting, 369
  were falling on our oaks, 843
Snow-broth, whose blood is, 35
Snow-flakes, as still as, 348
  fall thickest, where the, 452
  on the wave, 553
Snow-peaks stand solemn and white, 612
Snow-storm and the night, calmed the, 1091
Snow-storms, self-appointed inspector of, 514
Snow-white lamb left alone, 505
Snowy beard, tradition wears a, 442
  summits old in story, 466
Snuff, only took, 252
  rather than live in, 22
Snuff-box, amber, 212
  no right to sneeze, 882
Snuffed out by an article, 361
Snug as a bug in a rug, 227
  little island, 305
  little kingdom, 482
So and so and ever so, 650
  and so and my opinion is, 1014
  can I, 62, 504
  dies a wave along the shore, 273
  have I, 504
  is good very good, 51
  it is but so, 51
  it might not be, and, 510
  much to do, 469, 712
  near and yet so far, 469
  on the ocean of life we pass, 437

So or so, to say why gals acts. 527
  so is good, very excellent good, 51
  soon that I am done for, 948
  to bed, 180, 867
  unto the man is woman, 436
  wise so young never live long, 72
Soakers, dinner among the old. 181
Soaks up the rain, the thirsty earth, 167
Soap, elusiveness of, 654
  in the suds and in the, 660
  invisible, 391
  what no, 246
Soap-bubble, capital, 1069
Soapsuds and the starch, 924
Soar but never roam, 304
  through rolling clouds to, 351
Soaring head, with, 983
Sob a storm a strife, 597
  child's, in the silence, 428
Sobbing through the deeps she goes, 588
Sober, appeal to Philip, 969
  as a hymn, 692
  as a judge, 229
  be vigilant, be, 1123
  certainty of waking bliss, 158
  goes to bed, 127
  healthful and with his wits about him, 166
  in your diet, be, 221
  inn, earth his, 121
  livery twilight gray in her, 152
  realm of leafless trees, the, 551
  skies they were ashen and, 460
  stedfast and demure, 160
  twilight of the present, 644
  whatever they discuss when, 969
  will to bed go, 127
Soberness, truth and, 1119
Sobers us again, drinking largely, 210
Sobriquet for Providence, 1056
So-called debtor class, 627
Sociable, no comfort to one not, 106
Social and economic experiment, 830
  and family relationship, 740
  board, father kept a, 501
  comfort in a hospital, 430
  Dead Sea, one, 716
  friend I love thee well, 364
  happiness and prosperity, 670
  intercourse, lived in, 235
  philosophical spine-character. 538
  position, conviction or, 1076
  rights 'gainst class and clan, 424
  smile the sympathetic tear, 246
  solidarity, 1074
  soporific, serve as, 213
  system could not subsist, 1053
  tact how to acquire, 724
Socialism, principle of, 1093
  victory of, 1086
Societies, modern, aim at equality, 762

Society among unequals, 154
  as is quiet wise and good, 368
  black flower of civilized, 421
  death leaves a gap in, 331
  designed us to live in, 1053
  in shipwreck, 987
  incumbent on, 1049
  is commonly too cheap, 515
  is no comfort to one not so-
    ciable, 106
  is one polished horde, 361
  is perishing, when a, 1071
  mudsills of, 432
  my glittering bride, 302
  no lack of good, 437
  offenders, 624
  one, alone on earth, 300
  ornament to, 325
  pillars of, 1076
  purposes of a, 1071
  question placed before, with
    glib assurance, 419
  sick man is a parasite of, 1081
  solitude sometimes is best, 154
  soul selects her own, 584
  spread over the whole earth,
    295
  the vanilla of, 313
  three chairs for, 515
  to one level, impossible to re-
    duce, 1071
  waits unformed, 537
  we owe ourselves partly to,
    1029
  where none intrudes, 354
  with contempt by, 1081
  wholesome for the character,
    529
Society's chief joys, 263
Sock, Jonson's learned, 160
Socket, burn to the, 302
Socrates or Plato, sweet as, 853
  the hemlock for, 851
  was persuaded to go to a fair,
    1014
  wisest of men, 156
Socrates' Xanthippe, 52
Sod above, green, 702
  and the dew, under the, 571
  as snow-flakes fall upon, 348
  cast it on the, 548
  in the churchyard, 523
  no stone marks the, 579
  sprung from the, 794
  treads our native, 811
Soda-water the day after, ser-
    mons and, 359
Sofa soft, woman was the, 576
  wheel round the, 265
Soft and luminous shade, 922
  answer turneth away wrath,
    1107
  as fleeces of descending snows,
    218
  as silk remains, 204
  as the underside of soap, 868
  bastard Latin, 357
  brown hair, 590
  clouds along the horizon, 418
  droppes of rain, 23
  eyes looked love, 352
  falls the dew, 569
  gray mist, 349
  her voice was ever, 100
  impeachment, own the, 278
  is the heart, 815

Soft is the strain when zephyr
    blows, 211
  Kentucky strain, 676
  light tone and low, 499
  meek patient, 115
  moves the dipping oar, 288
  nurse, nature's, 65
  stillness and the night, 47
  sweet accent of an angel's
    whisper, 645
  the music of those village
    bells, 266
  the zephyr blows, 244
  unfolding, and see, 387
  voices die, when, 367
Soften to us our enemies, 705
Softening into shade, 224
Softer, music that, falls, 463
Softest music to attending ears,
    78
Softly, I shall go, 1112
  speak, and carry a big stick,
    734
  sweet in Lydian measures, 176
Softness and harmony unparal-
    leled, 330
  like the atmosphere of dreams,
    447
  madrigals that whisper, 163
  she and sweet attractive grace,
    for, 152
  untouched by, 834
Soil, flowerless, 733
  good to be born on, a, 530
  grows on mortal, 159
  hath smutched it, before the,
    119
  it flourisheth in every, 477
  may best deserve, that, 872
  nor yet within the common,
    374
  of an unknown country, 804
  paramount lord of the, 509
  planted in the same worn-out,
    421
  son of the virgin, 642
  there must be rich moral, 826
  they struck deep, 586
  thorn-curst, 709
  thus leave thee native, 155
  to paint the laughing, 342
  where first they trod, 370
Soils, rich, to be weeded, 112
Soil's fertility, suck the, 60
Soiled by any outward touch,
    162
  with all ignoble use, 469
  world, incessantly wash this,
    536
Sojourn shall be long, 742
Solace, whence comes, 650
  where find that, 156
Solar system, hub of the, 454
  walk or milky way, 207
Soldier among sovereigns, 215,
    311
  and afeard, 88
  and sailor too, 782
  be abroad, let the, 331
  blasphemy in the, 36
  bold, Ben Battle was a, 392
  brave enough to tell, 542
  brave, when falls the, 609
  first who was king a fortu-
    nate, 1053
  flat blasphemy in the, 36

Soldier full of strange oaths, 49
  I ask the brave, 335
  lay in prison, doomed to die,
    513
  marches by, a, 571
  mourned her, slain, 269
  no, in that gallant band, 624
  of the Legion lay dying,
    447
  old, and an old priest, 1068
  relish him more in the, 101
  rest! thy warfare o'er, 308
  successful, 311
  the iron-armed the true-
    hearted, 404
  the sailor the shepherd, the,
    702
  the sex is ever kind to a, 220
  thou more than, 333
  would himself have been a, 61
Soldiers are citizens, 891
  are dreamers, 891
  are sworn to action, 891
  bore dead bodies by, 61
  cheers for the, 664
  from the summit, 1060
  Ireland gives England, 576
  of King George, poor dead,
    784
  of the Thirty Years' War,
    1045
  old, more accostable, 423
  old, sweetheart are surest, 128
  sovereign among, 311
  sterner, the world saw never,
    737
  substance of ten thousand, 72
  to the field more nurses to the
    hospitals, more, 456
  were brave and courtiers were
    good, 193
  with him, carrying, 1001.
Soldier's and gentleman's lan-
    guage, 1056
  pride touched to the quick,
    487
  scholar's eye, 93
  sepulchre, shall be a, 328
  training and his Euclid mind,
    576
  wound, history of a, 241
Soldiery, embattled, 964
Sole almost my, rule of life,
    378
  daughter of his voice, 155
  delight, my solitary, 393
  idea, one, 964
  judge of truth, 208
  of her foot, no rest for the,
    1097
  of his foot, from the crown of
    his head to the, 39, 116, 351
  of our foot, from the crown of
    our head to the, 116
  of the foot, from the crown of
    the head to the, 131
Soles, mender of bad, 81
  right offen yore shoes, 927
Solemn and touching is the peal,
    323
  black, suits of, 89
  councils, from, 681
  creed, sapping, a, 353
  fillet, under her, 410
  fop, the, 263
  marches fill the nights, 522

Solemn midnight, in the, 479
  outlook from an infant's eyes,
    449
  pines, 602
  sanctimonious face, no, 392
  sneer, with, 353
  strain, bird of the, 370
  temples, 33
  too, for day, 386
  way, in such a, 451
Solemnity, air of great, 1064
Solicitor's clerk, every, 850
Solid citizen, a, 884
  flesh would melt, too, 89
  happiness we prize, 226
  man, Muldoon, 679
  pudding against empty praise,
    215
Solidarity, social, 1074
Solidity or exactness of beauty,
  7
Solitary as an oyster, 495
  in families, setteth the, 1104
  in lonely places, crying, 717
  life of man is, 132
  my, sole delight, 393
  place, in many a, 296
  precedent not conclusive, 329
  shriek, a, 359
  way, never have a, 955
  when young, 704
Solitude, acquire everything in,
  1063
  he makes a, and calls it peace,
    356
  how gracious how benign is,
    299
  how passing sweet is, 263
  I love tranquil, 368
  in seeing you, 868
  intrude on that, 576
  Islington will grow a, 168
  least alone in, 353
  may give, thoughts and voices,
    128
  midst of a vast, 398
  needful to the imagination,
    529
  nurse of full-grown souls,
    524
  of country life, 1065
  of his own originality, 362
  one chair for, 515
  regal, 324
  shrinks from the dismaying,
    399
  so companionable a compan-
    ion as, 514
  sometimes is best society, 154
  sweet retired, 158
  terror to infancy, 663
  that inward eye which is the
    bliss of, 299
  the safeguard of mediocrity,
    413
  where are the charms, 263
  which they call peace, 356
Solitudes, books are not companions — they are, 506
  two, protect and touch, 1090
Solitudinem faciunt, 356
Solo game, in a, 844
Solomon drew merchantmen, 777
  loved many strange women,
    1101
  priests in the temple of, 418

Solomon spake three thousand
  proverbs, 1101
  wine cups of, 934
  wrote the Proverbs, 755
Solomon's purple show, 805
Solon was under a delusion, 974
Solution of some theme he could
  not solve, 733
  see no favourable, 1087
  that generally comes to pass,
    1087
  waste on impossible, 624
Solvency a matter of temperament, 788
Solvent, American life a powerful, 769
Solway Firth to Skye, from, 780
Sombre face the storm defies, 572
  ship sweeps silently, 643
Some are born great, 55
  are born posthumously, 1082
  are fine fellows, 574
  are jolly, 911
  asked how pearls did grow,
    133
  asked where rubies grew, 133
  blessed threads of gold, 501
  books are drenchèd sands, 587
  books to be tasted, 111
  chaste, many generous and,
    470
  cost a passing-bell, 406
  days must be dark, 434
  do it with a bitter look, 722
  far-off touch of greatness, 470
  fifth act what this, in, 472
  floweret blow, each rain-drop
    makes, 504
  have too much, 20
  keep the Sabbath, 584
  love to roam, 503
  must watch some must sleep,
    94
  noble work of love to do, 474
  of them go plaintively, 911
  of us will smart for it, 40
  of you will travel, 943
  one dash it from them, 965
  one gently rapping, as of, 460
  one here and there, know, 1058
  one or nobody knows, 499
  one terrible gets elected, 934
  one to come who nevermore,
    439
  pray to marry, 860
  rain must fall, 434
  rise by sin, 35
  said John print it, 171
  sprite begotten of summer, 407
  sudden thought, some careless
    rhyme, 640
  there are who tell, 1019
  to church repair, 211
  undone widow, 129
  vast river of unfailing source,
    393
  weep because they part, 620
  what if, unshamed iconoclast,
    609
  who bear a grudge, 977
  with gladness and few with
    fear, 576
  with Pilate, wash your hands,
    60
  write their wrongs in marble,
    204

Somebody, dreary to be, 584
  else pays the bill, 624
  said it couldn't be done, 870
  to hew and hack, 142
  who shall make us do what we
    can, 414
Somebody's mother, boys, 715
Someone miles and years away,
  608
  worse off than yourself, 961
Somer, welcom, with thy sonne
  soft, 4
Somersaults and fireworks, with
  the, 937
Something a boy should never
  see, 938
  about a roused woman, 494
  after death, dread of, 93
  attempted something done,
    434
  away in her old torn gown,
    807
  better than his dog, 464
  between a hindrance and help,
    298
  borrowed something blue, 956
  dangerous in me, 97
  depressing comes, 877
  for nothing, should not ex-
    pect, 711
  for posterity, 197
  from our hands have power,
    305
  gained for every thing missed,
    411
  given that way, 127
  good be said, 696
  good may be found, 236
  greater, yes but there's, 501
  I'll lend you, 56
  in a face, 199
  in her gizzard, waiting oppor-
    tunity to bring up, 182
  in him we cannot abide, 130
  in October, there is, 757
  in the doings of man, 539
  in the parting hour, 557
  in the wind, there is, 37
  in this more than natural,
    there is, 92
  in us never dies, 286
  is rotten in Denmark, 91
  known only to God, 870
  lost behind the ranges, 777
  lost, longings after, 665
  more than melody, and, 405
  more to do than feel, 325
  mourns, 359
  nothing, 't is, 102, 359
  of nothing, created, 147
  poet creates outside his per-
    sonality, 709
  provoke a conscious, 461
  rich and strange, 32
  sings, alway, 409
  still alive in the body before
    us, 350
  still I can do, 550
  sure silent slow and large, 899
  tells me, there's, 45
  to cuss about, 852
  to love He lends us, 463
  too much of this, 94
  very like Him, God or, 519
  wicked this way comes, 87
  would turn up, faith that, 421

Something you somehow haven't to deserve, 838
Sometimes counsel take, 212
  for years and years together, 406
  glimpses on my sight, 442
Somewhere else instead, it's, 876
  in desolate wind-swept space, 620
  in this favored land, 770
  you wait for me, 830
Somnambulist of a vanished dream, 1067
Somnolence, blinking with incipient, 686
Son, a wise, maketh a glad father, 1107
  an author in each, 1050
  and foe, grim death my, 150
  and heir of a mongrel bitch, 98
  ask bread, if his, 978
  at home, keep his only, 248
  by God I have a, 911
  degenerates from the sire, 218
  every mother's, 42
  every wise man's, 54
  father overwhelms the, 120
  go cheerily, let my, 850
  God the Father God the, 199
  happy was it for that, 70
  hateth his, 1107
  He gave his only begotten, 1118
  is my son, 567
  is one of the angels, 1074
  Joe who rode so straight, 577
  left-lonesome daughter, grief-stricken, 817
  like mother like, 692
  of Adam and Eve, 190
  of God goes forth to war, 343
  of heaven's eternal king, 161
  of his own works, 1033
  of memory, dear, 161
  of mine did I hurt you, 836
  of sable night, 30
  of the virgin soil, 642
  swore, Diogenes struck the father when the, 125
  the character of the, 974
  two-legged thing a, 173
  was killed while laughing, 781
  were he, as his own, 1058
  who wept a, 371
Sons acclaim thy glorious name, 921
  affliction's, are brothers in distress, 285
  and daughters, 430
  and servants, 1022
  Arcturus with his, 1103
  are the anchors, 966
  father unto many, 70
  few, are like their father, 983
  God's, are things, 204, 232
  had I a dozen, 76
  if I had a thousand, 65
  King Arthur had three, 954
  lamenting all her fallen, 690
  may be as plants grown, 1106
  no two of earth's degenerate, 218
  of Belial, flown with insolence, 148
  of clay, ye hopeless, 446

Sons of Edward sleep in Abraham's bosom, 72
  of France awake to glory, 1059
  of God, Hack and Hew were the, 757
  of God shouted for joy, 1102
  of God yield up their breath, 560
  of heaven, things are the, 232
  of Martha favour their mother, 781
  of Mary seldom bother, 781
  of night, bloom for, 334
  of sin, Hem and Haw were the, 757
  of the dark and bloody ground, 541
  of the morning, 342
  of the prophet, 951
  tell your, 760
  the goodliest man since born his, 152
Sonata, grouse worth a, 637
Sone, Epicurus owne, 5
Song, a new unhallowed, 710
  a shell a moth, a, 828
  a tiny broken, 756
  always one last, 887
  and died, sang one, 684
  and jest and rhyme, welcome, 664
  as Shelley sang to you, 625
  betrothal-ring of, 910
  burden of his, 269
  can ever attain full purport, no great, 539
  can't keep back a, 692
  careless, with a little nonsense, 246
  certain of my, 814
  clothed from head to foot in, 938
  eternal passion of, 736
  flushed and magnificent, 693
  for our banner, 404
  for singing, the fine, 703
  for song, singing, 326
  for those that bore them, 772
  full lasting is the, 575
  golden orb of perfect, 429
  hear a little, 1058
  I can give thee but a, 434
  I have no words to sing, 896
  I know, really the best, 911
  in de air, bridge's a sad, 934
  in the garden of, 738
  in thy praise, I 'll sing, 286
  inaccessible vine of, 635
  into the air, breathed a, 815
  is but a solace for a day, 711
  is more lasting, 869
  it may turn out a, 285
  jets forth so clear, 1086
  leads to another, one, 850
  learn sooner than a, 214
  let satire be my, 351
  loves not wine woman and, 481
  low lone, 500
  many once lauded in, 1011
  many read a, who will not read a sermon, 135
  metre of an antique, 107
  mighty orb of, 302
  moralize my, 24

Song, my soul is full of whispered, 540
  needless Alexandrine ends the, 211
  no sorrow in thy, 276
  note of that immortal, 684
  nothing but my, 628
  o' steam, sing the, 777
  of beauty rare, 815
  of certain wing, thy, 697
  of every bird, low sweet, 729
  of home and friends, 608
  of loneliness and grief, 607
  of night's sweet bird, 366
  of old, that glorious, 477
  of Percy and Douglas, 27
  of sorrow, the saddest, 518
  of the birds, 918
  of the siren, 29
  of those who answer not, 648
  old and antique, 54
  one immortal, 173
  others shall sing the, 444
  passes not away, 735
  people read a, 405
  preludes to that unknown, 1064
  pulpit press and, 652
  rainbow hues of, 794
  remembered by a, 588
  sea grew civil at her, 42
  senseless burden of their, 922
  sentinels of, 609
  silence more musical than any, 587
  sing thou thy, 473
  snare it in a, 849
  so mystical and calm, 885
  sold my reputation for a, 1019
  still govern thou my, 153
  swallow flights of, 468
  swear to the truth of a, 189
  sweet archaic, 881
  that nerves a nation's heart, 471
  that should spur you, 633
  that thrills you, hear a, 679
  the sigh of the weary, 567
  the sirens sang, 145, 799
  till I end my, 932
  to be heard, sublimest, 1069
  to cheer our weary hearts, 608
  to Dad, a little, 873
  to hear, the rare, 703
  to the oak, 446
  to the singer comes the, 672
  tremble with, 737
  unlike my subject shall be my, 222
  veiling lightnings of his, 366
  was ever sung, forget that any, 879
  we loved, she whose, 897
  what they teach in, 367
  whole world send back the, 477
  without love, no true, 765
  woven a little, 901
  wrote one, 488
  yet cast out of man, 633
  you can't forget, 821
Songes make and wel endyte, 5
Songs and ballads, Scotch, 588
  and dances, sacred, 972
  and sonnets, book of, 34
  are best, old, 734

Songs are swelling, angelic, 503
  be fashioned, 832
  be turned to holy psalms, 28
  beguile your pilgrimage, 881
  cannot sing the old, 583
  endure, have your, 484
  every child may joy to hear, 281
  from far away, old, old, 690
  greater than all my, 910
  half written, 738
  I sang long years ago, 583
  my lyric minions, come, 1065
  of a nation, 186
  of a people, 186
  of pleasant glee, 281
  of Apollo, 42
  of modern speech, 674
  of one who strove, 807
  of sadness and mirth, 436
  pain into, 1084
  she heard in her dreams, 432
  sheaf of splendid, 910
  sing no sad, 587
  spring thought perfection, 493
  Stephen Foster's, 711
  sweetest, are of saddest thought, 366
  that found no tongue, my, 444
  that must be sung, 890
  that never shall float into speech, 609
  to sing, sweeter, 452
  we sung, 610
  well sung our, 880
  were a thousand and five, 1101
  are sad, all their, 828
  without words are best, 607
  you'll sing my, 1027
Song-crowned immortal, 850
Songsmiths, yet do the, 736
Songster, worm by early, caught, 510
Songsters, envy of the lesser, 669
Sonne, up roos the, 6
Sonne's wife Elizabeth, than my, 540
Sonnet is a moment's monument, 577
  is a wave of melody, 600
  is composed of fourteen lines, 931
  it turned to a, 649
  scorn not the, 304, 943
  scribbled off a, 812
  than St. Paul's, rather have built a, 588
  what is a, 672
Sonnets, book of songs, and, 34
  Rafael made a century of, 488
  ten passably effective, 921
Sonorous metal blowing martial sounds, 148
Soon, born too, 710
  never came a wink too, 390
  or late shall navigate, 572
  that I am done for, so, 948
  upon the stage of life, 474
Sooner lost and worn, 54
  or later delicate death, to each, 536
  to make an end, the, 113
Soonest mended, little said is, 133

Soot falls down, 276
Sooth 't were a pleasant life, 406
Soothe a heart that 's broken, 309
  and smile, I began to, 282
  the savage breast, 193
Soothed his soul to pleasures, 176
  with the sound, 176
Soothing death, come lovely and, 536
  idea, cherish the, 624
  slumber, 275
Sophist schools and learned clan, 408
Sophisters, age of, 260
Sophisticated rhetorician inebriated with exuberance, 420
Sophocles, not mad if I am, 967
  poetic eloquence in, 669
  wrote his grand Oedipus, 438
Sophonisba, O, 225
Soporific, serve as social, 213
Soracte's crest is white, 868
Sorceries more excellent, 927
Sordid hopes and vain desires, 345
  perils of actual existence, 723
Sore labour's bath, 86
  store is no, 12, 1041
  worldly, deeth is an ende of, 6
Sorrow, a little fun to match the, 607
  alleviates the, 1042
  and death, eclipse of, 373
  and death they have often brought, 628
  and scarlet leaf sad thoughts, 531
  and suffering in each man's life, 440
  anticipate, 418
  ate his bread in, 439
  break its chain, 371
  breaks seasons and reposing hours, 71
  but more closely tied, 338
  calls no time that 's gone, 127
  comes with years, 428
  cut them for, 956
  down thou climbing, 98
  drown all, 127
  ever held a crocus back, no, 837
  fade, ere sin could blight or, 316
  fail not for, 454
  for the dead, 344
  from which we refuse to be divorced, 344
  give, words, 88
  hang, care will kill a cat, 118, 133
  hath scaped this, 108
  her rent is, 134
  I bade good morrow to, 382
  I had a little, 917
  in the other, slumbers, 1070
  in thy song, thou hast no, 276
  increaseth, 1109
  is hard to bear, 489
  is held intrusive, 401
  is in vain, thy, 256
  is mine but no more dread, 706
  is unknown, where, 264

Sorrow, it is to go with, 834
  labour and, is their strength, 1105
  last, should, 256
  lest you awaken, 1070
  like unto my sorrow, any, 1113
  literature consoles, 397
  Madam, scorns all this, 1066
  makes a silence, true, 922
  makes night morning and noontide night, 71
  melt into, 355
  misfortune and suffering, 746
  more in, than in anger, 90
  nae, there John, 291
  never comes too late, 243
  never dies, 682
  night of, from a fore-spent, 165
  not mine but man's, 744
  now melt into, 355
  out of my, 821
  parting is such sweet, 78
  path of, and that alone, 264
  patience a remedy for, 978, 987
  pine with feare and, 25
  resembles, only as the mist resembles the rain, 434
  rooted from the memory, 88
  short-lived care, brief, 1017
  show an unfelt, 86
  sickness and a troubled mind be stranger, 135
  sing away, 1035
  sing, with, 257
  sit thee down, 41
  some mixture of, 1038
  some natural loss or pain, 298
  sphere of our, from the, 368
  steep, my couch in, 286
  than joy, ever more, 1054
  that could compare, known, 544
  that keen archer, 588
  that purifies the heart, 1074
  there is no greater, 440
  time assuages, 979
  to lift this, 668
  to the grave, 1098
  to thyself, keep thy, 1123
  under the load of, wring, 40
  walked a mile with, 861
  we parted in, to meet nevermore, 418
  wear a golden, 73
  where there is, is holy ground, 723
  which is never spoken, 625
  wild, with sleepless, 596
  with night we banish, 129
  with, where all was delight, 567
Sorrows, a man of, 1112
  and darkness encompass the tomb, 343
  at my bier, waste their, 374
  bury thy, 574
  come not single spies, 96
  crowd, how many, 309
  end, losses are restor'd and, 107
  flow, as thy, 333
  I will instruct my, 57
  may be a man of, 754

Sorrows, more abiding than our, 669
  of death compassed me, 1103
  of your changing face, 790
  remembered, 393
  simple wiles transient, 299
  to be proud, I will instruct my, 57
  which do not belong to them, 197
Sorrow's crown of sorrow, 440, 464
  purse is free, but, 565
  spy, knowledge is but, 147
Sorrowing, he that goes a borrowing goes a, 19, 227
Sorrow-soothing sweets, 258
Sorry scheme of things, 471, 1020
  work to lose your company, 653
Sort, ambition of the meaner, 68
  of bloomin' cosmopolouse, 782
  of runic rhyme, time, 459
  smiles in such a, 81
Sorts, men of all, 228
  of carved work, sundry, 247
  of people, all, 85
  of prosperity, I wish you all, 1052
  of things and weather, 408
Sory, I am right, 4
Soshubble ez a baskit er kittens, 688
Sot, have mercy on this, 940
Sots, what can ennoble, 208
Sought, lack of many things I, 107
  love, is good, 55
  prize we, is won, 536
  the world, I never have, 237
  with positivists, truth be, 570
Soul a thousand tears, 707
  abhors less than truth, 508
  above buttons, 288
  above the soul of each, 601
  among masterpieces, adventures of his, 1079
  and body to lasting rest, 58
  and scars our, 694
  and soul, link together, 438
  angelic, hark hark my, 503
  another lonely soul, for one lone, 597
  as good-natured a, 1034
  as in a, remembering my good friends, 59
  aspiring pants, the, 440
  astronomy compels the, 974
  awake my, 225
  away, he gives his, 672
  be built up again to a whole man, 144
  beautiful doings of thy, 427
  befall a, 587
  biting for anger, eager, 147
  blind his, with clay, 466
  bruised with adversity, 37
  calm, of all things make mine, 546
  can split the sky in two, 915
  change and migration of the, 970
  circumnavigator of the, 789
  cloud and conceal, 671
  coins his very, 719

Soul, cold waters to a thirsty, 1108
  conquered for itself, each, 492
  cordial to the, 147
  crowd not on my, 244
  darkness o'er the parting, 327
  deceived and half divined, 897
  deep imaged in his, 220
  did pine, for which my, 460
  dinner-bell the tocsin of the, 360
  does in this world, greatest thing the, 531
  does not bring, if your own, 620
  enchanted by melody, 677
  ever bind the, 710
  every, on board went down, 576
  everywhere the human, 378
  expends his whole, 1057
  eye and prospect of his, 40
  feast of reason and flow of, 213
  feed some hungry, 595
  fiery, working out its way, 173
  for my unconquerable, 692
  for these things lives, 736
  forth, invite your, 1018
  fortress of his 'stablisht, 735
  forward draw my, 594
  free from this my hard prison, set my, 20
  freed his, the nearest way, 231
  fresh from birth, 634
  fret thy, with crosses, 25
  from death, it saved a, 504
  from out that shadow, 460
  genial current of the, 245
  go stumbling through my, 820
  goes from star to star, 1069
  goes marching on, his, 612
  grapple them to thy, 90
  grasp my, 853
  grave these lessons on my, 1059
  green England's singing, 931
  happy, that all the way, 165
  harrow up thy, 91
  has gone aloft, his, 274
  has not learned to read, 657
  has power to clothe itself, 753
  hath elbow-room, 58
  hath power to know all things, 114
  hath sown, seed which the, 654
  haughtiness of, 194
  he had a little, 334
  her lips suck forth my, 31
  his father's, to cross, 212
  human, take wing, 356
  I am the captain of my, 693
  I build my, 462
  I have them in my, 485
  I love a prophet of the, 408
  I loafe and invite my, 534
  I roamed with my, 461
  I sent my, 1019
  if stout within, 409
  if you would keep your, 897
  immortality of the human, 449
  in sleep, visit the, 366
  in the shining eyes of him, 875
  in tune, sets the, 172

Soul in you, loved the pilgrim, 790
  indeed is far away, 449
  indulging every instinct of the, 489
  into the boughs does glide, 169
  into the eye and prospect of his, 40
  inward places of the, 973
  iron entered into his, 1128
  is all but out of me, 916
  is dark with stormy riot, 910
  is dead that slumbers, 433
  is forme and doth the bodie make, 26
  is full of whispered song, my, 540
  is gone, limbs will quiver after the, 238
  is high, no higher than the, 915
  is his own, even subject's, 67
  is melancholy, 673
  is passing, 349
  is sailing, 664
  is the captain and master, 693
  is the captain and ruler, 470
  is wanting there, 355
  is with the saints, 317
  it fortifies my, 519
  it is this that oppresses my, 599
  it offends me to the, 94
  jealousy the jaundice of the, 174
  justice is a virtue of the, 1015
  keep your distance and your, 928
  life of the, 1053
  lends the tongue vows, 91
  like an ample shield, 179
  like seasoned timber, 135
  listened intensely, his very, 302
  little, scarce fledged for earth, 634
  lives in an alley, his, 118
  loafe and invite my, 534
  longed to go, shore where my, 567
  locking into the, 1085
  lose his own, 1115
  love orbit of the restless, 553
  loved him as he loved his own, 1100
  makes a living, 424
  may pierce, such as the, 160
  may sail on the sea of death, 832
  measured by my, 199
  medicine for the, 1092
  merit wins the, 212
  most heretofore sin-spotted, 556
  most offending, alive, 67
  must mount on wings of deeds, 626
  my, had panted, 645
  my heart and my duty, my, 66
  my own, not dare to call my, 430
  my, today is far away, 552
  no coward, 516
  not from his own, 973
  now to want them feels sorry, 432

Soul, O my prophetic, 91
O strong-winged, 633
of a friend we've made. 761
of a journey, 330
of a sleeper away, 713
of Adonais, 366
of business, despatch is the, 222
of cypress with Psyche my, 461
of goodness in things evil, 67, 580
of harmony, the hidden, 160
of man, diseases crucify the, 123
of man is immortal, 974
of man is larger than, 386
of man is like the rolling world, 588
of man, portions of the, 524
of man, such affinity with the, 476
of music shed, 334
of music slumbers in the shell, 289
of Orpheus sing, 161
of our grandam, 46
of Richard, 72
of the age, 119
of the capacious salad bowl, 703
of the fact, 660
of the sculptor is bidden, 609
of the sparrow and bee, 570
of the whole past time, 380
of this world, time is the, 1006
of truth, 580
of wit, brevity is the, 92
old, takes the roads again, 833
on the lips of children, 1069
one, in two bodies, 1015
only the naked, 889
palace of the, 146, 352
perdition catch my, 102
possest, once my, 619
proud, ne'er pays, 61
rapt, sitting in thine eyes, 160
returned to me, by and by my, 1019
returns again to earth, 833
sad, 619
sad lucidity of, 546
sail leagues, 577
save thou a, 444
saved his. by hard work, 591
saw a glimpse of happiness, 147
secure in her existence, 195
selects her own society, 584
seriously yearns, my fond, 920
Shakespeare had the largest and most comprehensive, 179
shall be required, this night thy, 1117
shall see, 736
she's dead, rest her, 97
shining through them, 593
sighing under a sicamore tree, 255
sincere, 210, 245
sincerely from the author's, 921
sinews of the, 147
sits hushed and calm, 473

Soul, sleep holy spirit blessed, 463
small-knowing, 40
so dead, man with, 307
so warm and true, 333
soothed his, to pleasures. 176
speech is a mirror of the, 990
stands shivering on the ridge of life, 186
startled heaven of my, 853
stature of my, 574
still flies above, 888
stream which overflowed the, 303
studies each commonplace, 682
sweet and virtuous, 135
sweetest, that ever looked with human eyes, 468
sweeting fleeting little, 1009
swell the, to rage, 176
take the prisoned, 158
takes nothing with her, 970
that can be honest, 126
that eye was in itself a, 356
that feeds on books alone, 657
that's feelin' blue, 684
that o'er him planned, 408
that passed on high, 688
that perished in his pride, 297
that rises with us, 301
the body's guest, go, 21
the flight the freedom of my, 1051
the whiteness of his, 588
the whole, of a man, 378
the wild of, 930
thou hast much goods laid up, 1117
three books on the, 488
through my lips, 462
through time and space, send my, 881
to dare the will to do, the, 308
to give the, fit nourishment, 423
to God, bequeath my, 113
to its anchorage, 644
to keep, pray the Lord my, 947
to sleep, layes the, 24
to soul, intercourse from, 216
to stray, never taught his, 207
to tears, move the, 911
to the air, flung my, 887
to-day is far away, my, 552
tumult of the, 303
two bodies with one, 219
unacquainted still with our own, 114
unborn ages crowd not on my, 244
unction to your, 95
unlettered small-knowing, 40
unto his captain Christ. gave his, 60
unto the lines accords, 136
walk slowly, let thy, 688
wan numb naked, 1009
was immortal, that the, 1014
was like a star, thy, 298
was never put into the body, 128
what will satisfy the, 537
white as heaven, 131
whose even-balanced. 545

Soul, why shrinks the, 195
will is free strong is the, 545
windows of my, 443
wit its, 316
with crosses and cares to fret thy, 25
with evil, infect the, 970
with my whole, 1113
with patience, possess your, 175
withdrawn from us, dwells a, 875
without education like marble in a quarry, 196
would love her, 875
yearning of the, sting no more. 554
you would sell your, 964
Souls, adorn and beautify, 646
apart, presses on the, 834
are like the sparrows, 677
are restless plagued impatient, 806
assembled, 146
at home with God, and our, 523
at last, possess our, 796
beyond the reaches of our, 91
corporations have no, 21
flow in one down eternity's. 503
great, are portions of eternity 524
great obscure momentous, 879
have ye, in heaven too, 384
his memory green in our, 334
immediate jewel of their, 102
in prayer, steeped their, 459
in trouble here and in hell, 418
inward into, 427
laden with, 937
liberty inspire our, 194
little lonely, 755
milky way of, 874
mounting up to God, 577
my friends and brother, 471
noble and well-beloved, 627
of all that men held wise, 146
of animals infuse themselves. 46
of Christian, 611
of poets dead and gone, 384
of sin, lets it fall on the, 444
of the English, fatted, 779
of the righteous, 1124
of thought, thoughts that are the, 459
perplexed and distressed, 671
powerless, 1049
revive our, 474
rise as, 574
should not be, 767
sign of noble, 961
sit close and silently, our, 177
stand up, when our two, 429
such harmony is in immortal, 47
sympathy with sounds in, 266
that are pure and true, 671
that Azrael brings, 836
that cringe and plot, 525
that were forfeit once, 36
through unbegotten, 667
times that tried men's, 271. 453
to souls can never teach, 501

Souls, two, which are one, 118
two, with a single thought, 219
unfree, go west, 883
we loved, to see the, 469
what men are pleased to call
their, 544
whose sudden visitations daze
the world, 402
ye have left your, on earth,
384
you may grind their, 675
Soul's dark cottage, 30, 146
eternal sleep, points out the,
279
good, two things for the, 835
history, remembered the, 938
invincible surmise, trust the,
770
law, thine own, 473
or body's needs, 917
sincere desire, prayer is the,
306
superior instants, 585
wealth, 587
Soul-animating strains, 304
Souldiers, they mustred their, 257
Soul-forward headlong into a
book, plunge, 429
Soul-house built of mud, 871
Soul-sides, the meanest boasts
two, 488
Sound an echo to the sense, 211
and foam, too full for, 472
and fury, full of, 88
as a bell, heart as, 39
as if with the Inchcape bell,
321
as of some joyous elf, 915
born of murmuring, 297
divine, kill a, 263
empty vessel makes greatest,
67
hark from the tombs a doleful,
199
harmonious, 154
however rude the, 249
I hear beyond the range of, 514
joy of silence or of, 407
like the sweet, 53
loves to revel in a summer,
459
made of all human speech,
601
music with her silver, 255
music's soothing, 942
my barbaric yawp, I, 535
Niagara stuns with thundering, 250
no cry, no, 927
no, save rush of the river, 569
no war or battle's, 161, 409
not a fourth, but a star, 289
of a knell, sighed at the, 264
of a voice that is still, 465
of clashing wars, no, 478
of friends' departing feet, 528
of hammer or of saw, 266
of his master's feet behind
him, 1101
of horns and motors, 899
of my name, hearest the, 416
of one's praises, 1005
of public scorn, 155
of rain and bees murmuring,
301
of revelry by night, 352

Sound of the church-going bell,
264
of thunder heard remote, 150
of voices, confused, 604
of woman's praise, 401
out-vociferize even, itself, 189
persuasive, 193
pipes and whistles in his, 50
pitiful to hear, 699
shall end in silence, 688
silence implying, 489
silence where hath been no, 390
silver-sweet, 78
so fine, 347
soothed with the, 176
strikes like a rising knell.
deep, 352
sweet is every, 466
that breaks the silence, 688
the clarion fill the fife, 310
the loud timbrel, 336
the trumpet beat the drums,
186
therefore thou sleep'st so, 82
to heal the blows of, 451
trumpet give an uncertain,
1120
was heard, no, 565
what a torrent of, 649
what stop she please, 94
whistles in his, 50
with low and pensive, 369
words of thundering, 251
Sounds, all sweet, 634
all urban and all rural, 323
are dulled, all other, 619
as a sullen bell, 64
blowing martial, 148
concord of sweet, 47
of music creep in our ears, 47
of the rude world, 568
out of three, 489
possessed with inward light.
317
sympathy with, 266
will take care of themselves,
598
Sounded all the depths of honour, 73
Sounder piece of British manhood, 378
Sounding brass, 1120
cataract haunted me, 296
rafter, we meet neath the, 554
Soundless doors in vain, beat
the, 444
Soup gets cold while we wait,
625
or broth or brew, Bouillabaisse
a, 481
thin as homœopathic, 458
Soup-tureen, falls into the, 784
Sour, every sweet has its, 255,
411
grapes, 1045
grapes, have eaten, 1113
hearts are hard and, 522
in digestion, things sweet
prove, 59
lofty and, 74
misfortune's book, 80
sweet music is, how, 60
the grapes are, 961
Source of all my bliss, 251
of human offspring, 152
of sympathetic tears, 243

Source of terror to infancy, 663
point of his appointed, 25
springs rise not above their.
572
that keeps it filled, 575
vast river of unfailing, 393
Sources are interior, 585
from simple, 53
of the great river, 929
Sour-complexioned man, 139
Soured the milk of human kindness, 84
South, alas! for the, 804
and southwest side, 141
and the, and North shall,
375
beaker full of the warm, 383
cheering on her sons, 690
fought in honor for the, 676
head of bed to, 1068
in Dixie, away down, 505
no North no East no West, no,
329
Street, as I came down to, 914
threatens North and strikes
the, 1069
was in the glory, 768
winds blow so softly, 625
Southerly wind and cloudy sky.
229
Southern, warm, wind, 702
wild, mother bore me in the,
281
willows, 267
Southerner has no use for r, 616
Southerners say reckon, 616
South-west awakes, the warm,
576
Southwind sweet and low, 642
Sovereign among soldiers, 215,
311
balm, 248
heaven's, 202
knowledge of duty done, 427
lord the king, here lies our,
184
Magna Charta will have no
21
of sighs and groans, 41
or state, servants of, 110
parts, a man of, 41
reason, noble and most, 94
spirit will accept thy ransom.
476
Sovereigns, soldier among, 311
Sovereignest thing on earth, 61
Soviet constitution, extracts
from, 1093
Sovran seats, 668
veil'd melancholy has her
shrine, 384
Sow, he that observeth the wind
shall not, 1110
thy seed in the morning, 1110
wrong, by the ear, 17, 1034
ye are like to reap, as you.
143
Sowe eats all the draffe, still, 14
Sow's ear, velvet cap out of a
241
ear, velvet purse of a, 272
Soweth here with toil and care
322
whatsoever a man, 1121
Sowing and so good-bye, reap
our, 607

Sowing and the reaping, beyond the, 445
  seeds of April's, 485
Sown, divides the desert from the, 1018
  the wind, 1113
Sox, subtle flavor of an old pair of, 714
Space a moment's time, a little, 596
  and time, annihilate but, 216
  and time, behind, 893
  and time the universes, in, 538
  as history, cover, 710
  atom of infinite, 544
  desolate wind-swept, 620
  doth occupy, all, 1057
  double life's fading, 168
  every cubic inch of, a miracle, 537
  laws of time and, 553
  on earth a little, 281
  open window's, 364
  pathless realms of, 622
  sink in, 851
  'twixt the marsh and the skies, 663
  was thought's mysterious seat, 338
  where nobody is, more, 836
  whose circle grazes confines of, 553
Spaces, fill up its empty, 196
  in your togetherness, 879
  meditate on interstellar, 794
  procession out of stellar, 874
  wide, heavenly, 820
Spacious firmament on high, 194
  times, the, 463
Spade a spade, call a, 976, 1002
  and mattock, drill and plough, 919
  I hold, scepter of rule is the, 448
  if you don't call me a, 192
  who wield the, 931
Spades emblems of untimely graves, 266
Spain, a castle in, 509
  and England for a mighty prey, through, 840
  boyhood past in, 629
  castles in, 138
  I'm sorry for, 683
  singed the beard of the king of, 439
  winter in, 197
Spain's chivalry, 361
Spak Frensh ful faire, 5
Spake as a child when I was a child, 1120
  the seraph Abdiel, 153
  unto me, still small voice, 462
  upon this hint I, 100
Span, gaze for a, 631
  grasp the ocean with my, 199
  in length a, 133
  length of a, 833
  less than a, 112
  my life is but a, 115
  narrow our, 418
  new, spick and, 116, 1042
  of our brief, 441
  ye spread and, 663
Spangled heavens, 194

Spangle-glitter, trays of, 683
Spaniards seem wiser than they are, 110
  two, to come a Yankee o'er, 559
Spaniel, hound or, 99
Spaniels sleep and spiders from cobwebs peep, 276
Spanish dominions, the sun never sets on, 312
  fleet thou canst not see, 279
  Johnny you, 841
  lady, hear a, 257
  monk, 439
  or neat's leather, 142
  sailors with bearded lips, 436
  smell of garlic, 592
  waters, you are ringing, 832
Spanking Jack was so comely, 274
Spar, cling to the last, 789
Spare diet is the cause love lasts, 163
  Fast, 160
  my aching sight, 244
  not nor look behind, 417
  that tree, woodman, 404
  the beechen tree, 328
  the rod, 9, 142, 169
  to us our friends, 705
  your country's flag, 443
Spared a better man, better, 63
Spareth his rod, he that, 1107
Spark divine, not without a, 475
  illustrious, 264
  nor human, is left, 215
  of beauty's heavenly ray, 356
  of celestial fire, 268
  of heavenly fire in every woman's heart, 343
  of heavenly flame, vital, 216
  of immortal flame, 890
  of nature's fire, 284
  outlives the parent, 366
Sparks fly upward, as the, 1102
  from the anvil, like, 758
  of fire, eyes like, 134
  three fatal, 1020
Sparkle at the top, 629
Sparkled was exhal'd, she, 202
Sparkling and bright, 431
  cross she wore, a, 212
  from the bin, 940
  with a brook, 346
Sparrow, caters for the, 48
  fall or hero perish, 207
  muddy, mean and small, 910
  providence in the fall of a, 97
Sparrows, intrepid, 756
  our souls are like the, 677
  salt upon the tails of, 191
Sparta dead, is, 502
Spartan dead, remnant of our, 359
  shield, 371
  the company is, 985
Spartans, go tell the, 961
  who fell at Thermopylae's tryst, 533
Spasm, where life becomes a, 599
Spats, I don't wear, 907
Speak after the manner of men, 1119
  and purpose not, 98
  as one who fed on poetry, you, 425

Speak, be slow to, 1122
  by the card, 97
  comfort to that grief, 40
  daggers to her, 95
  each other in passing, 437
  for yourself, why don't you 436
  from your folded papers, 451
  gently, 473
  grief that does not, 88
  if any, for him have I offended, 83
  in a monstrous little voice, 42
  in good order, 111
  in public on the stage, 292
  it profanely, not to, 94
  labour what to, 112
  less than thou knowest, 98
  let him now, 1128
  lips are now forbid to, 388
  long enough he will get believers, 705
  low if you speak love, 38
  me fair in death, 47
  more in a minute, 79
  more words than we should, 9
  name which no one can, 322
  not what we mean, 36
  of me as I am, 103
  one another, we pass and, 437
  or die, 66
  patience, all men's office to, 40
  right on, I only, 83
  sins only, 128
  tears that, 168
  to me as to thy thinkings, 102
  to the earth, 1102
  to thee in friendship's name 336
  too coldly, thou think'st I, 336
  true right wrong, live pure, 470
  up Ike an' 'spress yo'se'f, 820
  well of no man living, he can, 1004
  what straight they will repent, 121
  when I think I must, 50
  with the tongues of men, 1120
  without emphasizing, 1064
Speaker, no other, of my living actions, 74
Speakest wiser than thou art ware, 48
Speaketh not and yet there lies, he, 438
Speaking fails, persuades when, 56
  heard for their much, 1114
  terms with itsilf, 796
  thought him still, 154
  tongue, the, 413
Speaks an infinite deal of nothing, 44
  in symbols, nature, 442
  she, yet she says nothing, 78
  the truth stabs falsehood, who, 524
  to the heart alone, that, 501
Spear a hundredweight, 564
  benignant, holds the, 725
  freedom, leaning on her, 452
  is song, 816
  Ithuriel with his, 152
  like Ithuriel's, 889

Spear, put up his, 878
  revenge is stamped upon my,
    447
  snatched the, 280, 307
  to equal the tallest pine, 148
  took the, 280
  with its shattered, 898
Spears, hemmed in with the, 831
  into pruning-hooks, 1111
  lost in a storm of, 789
  rain like glittering, 586
  the hand-flung, 504
Special advertisement to impart,
    184
  loved gold in, 5
  providence, 97
  providence for fatherhood, 491
Species, distributed among the
    whole, 197
  every, of domestic disorder,
    1051
  female of the, 781
  human, composed of two dis-
    tinct races, 323
  not too shy to be seen, 930
  of madness, nothing but, 1049
Specious electrical light, 857
Speck in cornea, 694
  vineyard, 911
  within vast star-space, 889
Spectacle, most extraordinary,
    689
  of human happiness, 314
  so ridiculous, no, 398
  to conjure with, a, 954
  unto the world, we are made a,
    1120
Spectacles, grandest of all
    earthly, 347
  in nature, one of the finest,
    228
  of books, he needed not the,
    179
  on nose and pouch on side, 50
Spectator of Battle of the Nile,
    1078
Spectators, pleasure to the, 400
  some must be, 120
Spectre not within the door, 618
  of the rose, I am the, 1071
Spectres of the mind, 443
Spectre-bark, off shot the, 315
Spectre-doubts, dispel, ye, 527
Speculation in those eyes, 87
  ingenious, 1023
  watches the, 495
  zones of, 704
Speech abroad, there is a, 110
  and thoughts, apprehend both,
    492
  be alway with grace, let your,
    1121
  bears his amorous, 1065
  better than silence, 973
  cordial, 410
  day unto day uttereth, 1103
  deeper than, 778
  desire thought, 439
  discretion of, 111
  echo of the whole sea's, 577
  finely framed, 1126
  flower of perfect, 735
  free men, free, 945
  free, Frémont, 427
  given men to communicate
    their minds, 183

Speech, grease our, 934
  harmed by, 19
  I will speak thy, 485
  is a mirror of the soul, 990
  is civilization itself, 1089
  is of time, 380
  is reported in the newspaper,
    492
  is shallow as time, 377
  is silvern silence is golden, 380
  is spun from pain, 804
  is truth, 307
  men polished by act and, 572
  mend your, a little, 98
  monkeys sensibly refrain from,
    742
  most I lose my, 649
  never made a, 709
  no gift of, 738
  of England has no name, for
    which the, 372
  of our sires, strong, 771
  of the world, speak with, 640
  often regretted my, 990
  on him no, 326
  out of Paris town, no right,
    1022
  plainness of, 1120
  poetry of, 354
  propriety of, 112
  public extempore, 550
  result of, 716
  returns to dying lips, native,
    714
  rude am I in my, 100
  rude in, though I be, 1121
  said to be the, of angels, 378
  seasoned with salt, 1121
  silence hath more eloquence
    than, 478
  silent, 306
  sinuous, of schools, 891
  than letter, better to deal by,
    111
  the Anglo-Saxon, 698
  the best they ever heard, 182
  the image of actions, 1013
  the whole sea's, 577
  they called but would not
    come, 490
  thought deeper than, 501
  thought wed itself with, 468
  to conceal thoughts, 183, 1052
  trembles a rarer, 822
  true use of, 254
  was like to tapestry, 996
  what is the use of, 796
  when thought is, 307
  word for word twice over,
    made this fine, 921
Speeches, after-dinner, 825
  compared to cypress trees
    1003
  four, 550
  his wonderful, 883
  made to the people, 1090
  that you do mislike, 68
  which have produced an elec-
    trical effect, 686
Speechless, happiness is, 558
  pride, 700
Speed, be wise with, 203
  bonnie boat, 752
  deliberate, majestic instancy,
    748
  of your tongue, 38

Speed on lonely paths, away they,
    588
  over thin ice safety is our, 412
  permitted to obstruct their,
    969
  the going guest, 213
  the parting guest, 220
  the soft intercourse, 216
  thousands at his bidding, 162
  to-day put back to-morrow, 25
  whose, is but the heavy plum-
    met's pace, 161
Speeds, still the fitting word He,
    441
Speedwell blue, go to make one
    722
Speedwell's darling blue, 469
Speke he never so rudeliche, 5
Spell, as a, 1058
  better than they pronounce
    615
  heart-wounded by a subtle, 891
  hope's dear delusive, 406
  it Vinci, 615
  kindled by the master's, 289
  soon fades the, 401
  who lies beneath your, 775
Spells, aggressive fancy working
    650
  magic of tongue most danger-
    ous of, 426
  of art, enchaunt me with your,
    798
Spelling of the English language,
    731
Spelling-book, boy with a, 714
Spence, Sir Patrick, ballad of,
    316
Spend another such a night, 71
  less, whatever you have, 237
  or to lend or to give in, 185
  to give to want to, 26
Spender thinks it went, where
    the, 839
Spenders, free lovers free, 1085
Spending, getting and, 300
Spenser, lie a little nearer, 119
  lodge thee by Chaucer, or, 119
Spenser's dream, fair as, 558
Spent dayes that might be better
    25
  them not in toys, 167
  under the devil's belly, 1026
  what we, we had, 1075
Sperit, never drink no, 527
Spermatozoa, a million million,
    922
Spet upon my Jewish gaberdine,
    44
Sphere, European wasted and
    withering, 1066
  fitting of self to one's, 501
  know thee in the, 373
  of human powers, 236
  of our sorrow, from the, 368
  of time, beyond the, 375
  owner of the, 410
  she just began to move in, 260
  talk about a woman's, 638
  to make up a year and a, 408
  travel the splendid, 903
  two stars in one, 63
Spheres, forefended, 556
  music of the, 55, 145, 728
  of heaven, ever-moving, 32
  or suns, even as great, 506

Spheres, pleasures of the, 338
  seems to shake the, 176
  stars shot madly from their, 42
  start from their, 91
  who borrow from the sun, 910
  with one breath attunes the, 514
Sphere-descended maid, 248
Sphinx, initials on the, 528
  with her enigma, 965
Sphinx-like into space, stare, 907
Spice of danger, or a, 683
  of life, variety is the, 265
  of wit, 702
Spick and span new, 116, 1042
Spicy nest, the phoenix builds her, 140
  nut-brown ale, 160
  shore of Araby the blest, 151
Spider a ghost, 599
  Bruce and the, 512
  much like a subtle, 115
  to the fly, said the, 394
Spiders and flies in the palaces, 166
  flies or ants in amber, 111
  from cobwebs peep, 276
  half-starved, 262
  homes for, 825
Spider's touch how exquisitely fine, 207
Spider-like we feel the tenderest touch, 177
Spies a far-off shore, 70
  sorrows come not single, 96
  thee waving here, she who, 555
Spight of his teeth, 10
Spigot wield, wilt thou the, 34
Spills itself in fearing to be spilt, 96
Spin, loiter in pleasure or toilfully, 448
  toil not neither do they, 1114
Spinach, I say it's, 932
  pioneering for, 859
Spindrift flying, sets the, 834
Spine, as if sunlight stroked the, 929
  is feelin' proud, 684
  new cases of curved, 430
Spines would tear their filmy wings, 801
Spine-character of the states, 538
Spinner, blind, 591
Spinster, knows more than a, 100
  for a wife, wed a woolly, 691
Spinsters and knitters in the sun, 54
Spiracle, spouts blithely from his, 888
Spiral of his conscience, 881
  of its steep ascent, 840
Spirals, windy, before a storm, 894
Spire, should have a tapering, 789
Spires of form, 409
  of Oxford, I saw the, 875
  whose silent finger, 302
  ye antique towers ye distant, 243
Spirit broad awake, stab my, 703
  but by my, 1113
  calms, nought so much the, 359

Spirit chased, are with more, 45
  clear, doth raise, 159
  close by, walks a, 880
  clothed from head to foot, 938
  comes at will, her, 501
  compact of fire, love is a, 106
  Creator drew his, 175
  doth dwell in heaven, 460
  dull as night, 47
  enough of mirth, my, 836
  extravagant and erring, 89
  fairer, or more welcome shade, 205
  filling to the, 1089
  for my minister one fair, 354
  free and warm deserts it, when the, 511
  full of, as the month of May, 63
  given on earth, 460
  giveth life the letter killeth, 1120
  God the Son God the, 199
  grew robust, 584
  haughty, before a fall, 1107
  haunted by a demoniac throng, 677
  he that ruleth his, 1107
  hies to his confine, 89
  his great Creator drew his, 175
  holiday-rejoicing, 325
  humble tranquil, 115
  in which the gift is rich, 792
  indeed is willing, 1116
  independence, thy, 248
  is departed, when his, 1125
  is entering into living peace, 532
  lack all life, needs, 492
  liberty a loosened, 584
  lies, with dreamful eyes my, 552
  many a gallant, 431
  meek and quiet, 1122
  meet and mingle, in one, 368
  mellows, the, 573
  motions of his, are dull as night, 47
  no, can walk abroad, 89
  not of the letter but the, 1120
  of a youth, morning like the, 105
  of all childhood, 862
  of delight, rarely comest thou, 368
  of heaviness, 1112
  of judgment, some shallow, 68
  of man is divine, all save the, 355
  of man suffer annihilation, will the, 753
  of mankind, free, 371
  of mortal be proud, 362
  of resistance, 949
  of revolt, 1075
  of subordination, 268
  of the Highest, felt the, 667
  of truth and of freedom, 1076
  of wine, O thou invisible, 101
  of wine sang, 693
  of youth in everything, 108
  or more welcome shade, 205
  pard-like, 366
  present in, 1120

Spirit rest, give my, 619
  rest perturbed, 92
  say to the, 747
  shall cease to be never, 597
  shall return unto God, 1110
  sits in a foggy cloud, 87
  so profound, he felt with, 298
  standing near, benignant, 659
  straight in the strength of thy, 633
  strives with flesh, 670
  strongest and fiercest, 149
  subtle, has my path attended, 897
  swiftness of the, 1089
  that answered your every mood, 784
  that could be moved to smile, 82
  that dost render birth, 447
  that loved thee, wounded the, 587
  the accusing, 242
  the least erected, 149
  the strong and awful, 841
  to bathe in fiery floods, 36
  truly noble and resolved, 999
  unwearied, best conditioned and, 46
  uprisen, soars upward, my, 20
  vanity and vexation of, 1109
  was born, never the, 597
  will atrophy, sporting, 869
  with one fair, 354
  with spirit can meet, 467
Spirits, a few choice, 1078
  any man may be in good, 495
  are not finely touched, 35
  black and white, 117
  brave, there are, 671
  can either sex assume, 148
  choice and master, 82
  clad in veils, 501
  deified by our own, 297
  did not make us, their own, 981
  flow of a man's animal, 1071
  from the vasty deep, 62
  have not helped, exuberant, 1081
  keep up, 495
  more vast than earth or sea or sky, 612
  never out of, 278
  of great events, 318
  of just men made perfect, 1122
  of power and beauty, 934
  of the dead, 373
  of the wise sit in the clouds, 64
  our actors were all, 33
  stories from the land of, 317
  tread, dear immortal, 618
  twain have crossed with me, 1063
Spirit's yearning cry, 666
Spiriting gently, do my, 32
Spiritless, so faint so, 63
Spirit-stirring drum, 102
Spiritual, a life that shall be, 537
  area, unlocated, 787
  creatures, millions of, 152
  force greater, 416
  grace, confer a sort of, 1087
  grace, inward and, 1128

Spiritual interposition, 738
  unbidden and unconscious, 473
  wild oats, all sow, 614
Spit brown my son, 833
  in my face, 62
  orators when out will, 51
Spite, bow thy head in gentle,
    555
  death aims with fouler, 134
  in erring reason's, 207
  in learned doctors', 364
  O cursed, 92
  of all their friends could say,
    498
  of criticising elves, 262
  of his teeth, 10
  of nature and their stars,
    142
  of scorn, thrice in, 149
  the world, reckless what I do
    to, 86
  wretched yet inevitable, 441
Spites, contemporary, 675
Spiteful and divided, dusty, 810
Spittoon all newly polished. 934
  on the altar, a clean, 934
Spleen about thee, mirth and,
    196
  meditative, 302
Splendid, a star, 493
  cradle, my, 1085
  flower, the, 619
  I was thinking the day most,
    537
  in ashes, 145
  shilling's praise, 258
  silence, 798
  silent sun, give me the, 536
  was its station, 748
Splendidly null, 469
Splendor all its own, with a, 696
  blank, 666
  dazzles in vain, 365
  falls on castle walls, 466
  guilty, 265
  in the grass, 301
  not in lone, hung aloft, 385
  of beauty, 953
  of love's praise, 894
  of mountain and lake, 590
  of their dying, 867
Splendors fall on Syrian sands,
    what, 442
  fling, its ancient, 477
  now clouded, 447
  old names old, 1085
  with roseate, 669
Splenitive and rash, 97
Split the ears of groundlings, 94
  the shroud, ray on ray, 493
Splitting the air with noise, 76
Spoil of gems, like a, 889
  of me, villanous company the,
    63
  the child, spare the rod, 9, 142,
    169
  upon my face, can do no more,
    68
  will not share the, 961
Spoils, is fit for stratagems and,
    47
  of nature, rich with the, 144
  of office cannot buy, whom,
    522
  of time, rich with the, 244
  of war the wealth of seas, 370

Spoils, the pleasure of the time,
    87
  to the victors belong the, 349
Spoilers of symmetry of shelves,
    323
Spoke less, knew more and, 1004
Spoken a noble thought, where'er
    is, 436
  word be again unsaid, 570
  word the sped arrow, 180
Spokesman spake out strong, 652
Spondee stalks, slow, 317
Spondees, laments in pathetic,
    714
Spondulix, man with, 714
Sponge, drink no more than a,
    1024
Spontaneity, life and universe
    show, 569
Spontaneous product of the
    horse, 491
Spoon, a ful long, that shal ete
    with a feend, 7
  by the gret horn, 526
  embellished by a notable, 869
  in his mouth, silver, 1042
  must have a long, 16
Spoons, count our, 234
  from whom we guard our, 401
Sport an hour with beauty's
    chain, 337
  book collecting most exhilarat-
    ing, 844
  day for toil and hour for, 410
  in hate, no, 368
  is stale lad, and all the, 523
  is there, never know what, 814
  not worth the candle, 138
  of bear-baiting gave offence,
    400
  of every wind, 204
  royal, 54
  that wrinkled care derides, 160
  to have the enginer, 96
  with Amaryllis in the shade,
    159
  with Tess, ended his, 651
  would be as tedious as to
    work, 61
Sports, my joy of youthful, 355
  of children, 249
Sporting man's sense of luck and
    chance, 731
Sportsman, bloodless, 733
  duty of every sincere, 1091
Sportsmen, pukka peerless, 807
  true disputants like, 217
Sporus feel, can, 213
Spot, at least one black, 1076
  calm sepulchral, 475
  do in that remote, 1061
  he stands upon, soils the, 328
  kissed her on the, 427
  leave this barren, 328
  long buried in a distant, 730
  no holier, 581
  of earth, 303
  of ground, no, like Eldorado,
    460
  ordains for each one, 779
  out damned, 88
  plant on his peculiar, 208
  she hath, the loveliest, 570
  stand on the right, 1057
  stir of this dim, 157
  the little yellow, 1070

Spot where he has ranked as a
    child, 1072
  which men call earth, 157
  yet round about the, 481
Spots in the sun, 124
  leopard change his, 1112
  of sunny openings, 346
  quadrangular, 266
Spouse, his iron, 926
Spoyle the childe, 169
Sprang out so noiseless around
    me, 537
  up to see, the flowers, 619
Spray, across the dashing, 864
  and flutter that we loved, 448
  and the tempest's roar, the,
    502
  of western pine, 644
  of yew, never a, 546
  the bird clung to, 487
  wet with Channel, 778
Spread and span like the cath-
    olic man, 663
  by little and little, 247
  his sweet leaves, 77
  the thin oar, 208
  the truth from pole to pole,
    194
  with colours idly, 58
  yourselves, masters, 42
Spreading, by broad, 68
  himself, 1104
  roots of light, 932
Spreads his light wings, 216
  his orient beams, 152
Spreeng ees com', da, 813
Sprightly running, 178
Sprigs took root, 1056
Spring and root of honesty, 1001
  and with a, 941
  be far behind, can, 366
  came on forever, 856
  canker galls the infants of the,
    90
  cinnamon-bear in, 928
  come gentle, 224
  comes back, when, 904
  comes slowly up this way, 315,
    758
  commerce is a kind of, 1051
  companions of the, 276
  different kinds of weather in,
    617
  evening's twilight, long, 926
  first day of, and first spring
    day, 710
  from haunted, 161
  full of sweet days, 135
  had come, 925
  has less of brightness, 459
  hounds of, 633
  I firmly believe, each, 813
  in blossom last, 621
  in England now, 777
  in the, a livelier iris, 464
  in the fire of, 1018
  is a true reconstructionist, 581
  is gone, 665
  is with us once again, 581
  more remarkable for biting
    east winds, 613
  my twentieth, 452
  of hope the winter of despair,
    497
  of light, a, 387
  of love, 33, 315

Spring of virtues, 28
  of woes unnumbered, 218
  Pierian, taste not the, 210
  pilgrim steps of, 668
  pining for the, 482
  rides no horses down the hill, 916
  shall be forever, 824
  shall mourn with ever-returning, 536
  should vanish, ah that, 1019
  slow stream or pebbly, 318
  some earthly, 586
  supplies another race, the, 219
  the winter of the, 441
  the year's at the, 485
  through death's iron guard, 937
  to have lived light in the, 547
  treads on heels of, 984
  trips north, when, 904
  unlocks the flowers, 342
  was dancing green, 875
  was late that year, 840
  what shall be done with, 812
  when God gives us, 445
  wild Irish came in the, 925
  winds blow, 560
  with that nameless pathos, 581
Springs, back to their, like the rain, 435
  crystal, should solace me, 140
  drink iron from rare, 923
  Helicon's harmonious, 243
  joy's delicious, 352
  no bitter, 783
  of Dove, beside the, 296
  of peace, at the wilding, 757
  rise not above their source, 572
  steeds to water at those, 105
  the glacial, 929
Spring's first flutes and drums, 887
  flowers must fade, 983
Springes to catch woodcocks, 91
Springfield, Massachusetts, in, 923
Spring-fret comes o'er you, 779
Springtime, deep blue eyes of, 1066
  never yet was a, 642
Spring-time's harbinger, 132
Sprite begotten of summer, some, 407
Sprouting, ever seen any cabbages, 455
Spur and bridle, between, 138
  fame is the, 159
  to prick the sides of my intent, 85
  unto strife, 964
Spurious, the coin is, 504
Spurned but spurned in vain, 27
  by the young, 391
Spurns that patient merit takes, 93
Spurs the lated traveller, 87
Spy, knowledge is sorrow's, 147
Squadron in the field, 100
  save the, 492
Squadrons, I see the cloud-born, 586
Squall, it prepares a, 1069
  of time, 915
Squander time, do not, 227

Square, all round the, 391
  deal, 734
  everything upon the, 1039
  faithful thronged the, 755
  grows a glimmering, 466
  hole, has got into the, 314
  I have not kept my, 104
  parted on the, 782
  peg in a round hole, 314
  root of minus one, 823
  we part upon the, 586
  world is runne quite out of, 25
Squat in his hole, 635
  like a toad, 152
Squeal and gibber, 89
  as naturally as pigs, 141
Squealing of the wry-necked fife, 45
Squeezing of a lemon, in the, 253
Squills, a bed of, 883
  and the bright blue, 831
Squire and his relations, bless the, 495
  I need no, 447
  of dames, 24
Squirrel sits, the, 887
  with his tail curved, 920
Squir'ls de bushtails, giv' de, 820
St. Agnes' Eve, bitter chill it was, 383
  Andrews by the northern sea, 673
  Bavon's tower, in old, 620
  Christopher, lesson of, 591
  Dennis was for France, 258
  Francis and St. Benedight, 164
  George for England, 258
  George he was for England, 258, 827
  George, Sabra in the forest with, 299
  James's, ladies of, 648
  Louis, price of, 616
  Mark, garden of old, 597
  Paul's, passing near, 814
  Paul's, ruins of, 398
  Peter slept, one night as old, 507
  Ursula's day, discovered on, 523
Stab, for a treacherous, 726
  my spirit, 703
Stabbed with a white wench's black eye, 78
Stability, to achieve, 926
Stable door, shut the, 14
  good horse in the, 253
Stabs falsehood to the heart, 524
Staff and comfort, been my, 692
  and load, lay down, 873
  cockle hat and, 256
  I'm growing fonder of my, 509
  leaning on his, 453
  of faith to walk upon, 22
  of life, 188, 191
  of my age my very prop, 45
  of my life, 1036
  of this broken reed, 1111
  on which my years should lean, 340
  thy rod and thy, 1103
Stage a perpetual source of noble entertainments, 196
  after a well-graced actor leaves the, 60

Stage, all the world's a, 49
  amuse his riper, 208
  as poets do, walk the, 889
  directions from Shakespeare, 905
  found only on the, 360
  frets his hour upon the, 88
  God and nature fill the, 129
  if this were played upon a, 55
  is not as once it was, 792
  natural on the, 252
  of certainty, entered upon the, 1091
  of life, ay soon upon the, 474
  speak in public on the, 292
  successes, early, 648
  the earth is a, 129
  the wonder of our, 119
  the world but as a, 1033
  the world's a, 117
  then to the well-trod, 160
  veteran on the, 230
  where every man must play a part, 44
Stages, beyond all mummed on any, 652
  in our latter, 272
  where'er his, may have been, 242
Stagers, old cunning, 142
Stagirite, that stout, 325
Stagnation, commotion before, 543
Stain, dyed with an ancient, 804
  incapable of, 149
  like a wound, felt a, 260
  my man's cheeks, 98
  of sin, keep me my God from, 645
  purity out of a, 663
  with no flaw or, 924
  world's slow, 366
Stains of pressed clover leaves, 854
Stained web that whitens, 337
Stained-glass attitudes, 623
Stainless, the flag they rendered, 602
  thought, only a, 1085
Stair, a crystal, 849
  as he comes up the, 270
  I'll build a, 821
  or path or plot, on the, 652
  up steep and weary, 598
Stairs, descend and climb by other's, 1021
  kissing on the, 929
  up four pair of, 482
  why did you kick me down, 283
Staircase, Charon's, 656
Stairway to the sky, 688
Stake, I am tied to the, 99
  out your claim, 936
  to eat a, 198
  when honour's at the, 96
Stakes were thrones, 357
Stalactite meets stalagmite, 688
Stalagmite meets stalactite, 688
Stale article, if you dip it in a smile, 422
  flat and, 713
  flat and unprofitable, 90
  lad, and all the sport is, 523
  nor custom, 104
  tale is more than, 718

Stalk a silhouette sublime, 572
four red roses on a, 72
left it on its, 409
of the tasselled corn, 642
withering on the, 42, 301
Stalks of goldenrod, shriveled, 843
Stalled ox and hatred, 1107
Stallions maned with whistling wind, 841
Stamford fair, bullocks at, 65
Stamp and esteem of ages, 172
is a tiny flimsy thing, 803
of fate, 218
of nature, use can almost change the, 95
of nobility upon the peoples, 1090
quick delivery, 775
rank is but the guinea's, 287
Stamps, property and no, 950
Stamped out poet's hope, critics who, 430
Stampede, new movement a, 775
Stand a tip-toe, 67
and wait, they serve who, 162
bade each other, 620
before a demagogue, men who can, 522
before kings, 1108
by to crash, 913
close around, 326
face to face friend, 960
how if a' will not, 39
in your own light, 16
like greyhounds in the slips, 66
not upon the order of your going, 87
on your head, 598
shadowless like silence, 392
the hazard of the die, 72
time to, and stare, 492, 814
to doubt, never, 134
to your glasses steady, 554
too many pens in a, 1027
try some one-night, 870
united we, 404
upon his bottom, 171
ye in the ways, 1112
Standard, God and right our, 954
of morals, uplift the, 549
of the man, 199
of their fathers, 561
sheet, forever float that, 382
unfurled her, to the air, 382
Standards of excellence, incredible, 927
still being richer men, 814
Standeth, thinketh he, 1120
Standing, as cheap sitting as, 192
in the community, 711
jokes, wooden-shoes are, 195
member in good, 922
on this pleasant lea, 300
pond, mantle like a, 44
pool, green mantle of the, 99
upon the vantage ground of truth, 109
with reluctant feet, 434
Standpoint of a succeeding age is desirable, 543
Stands as never it stood, wind, 19

Stands, as the case, 116
not within the prospect of belief, 84
on tiptoe, religion, 136
pale in her bowers summer, 565
Scotland where it did, 88
the church clock, 893
tiptoe, jocund day, 79
upon a slippery place, 58
Stanhope's pencil writ, lines with, 203
Stanley, approbation from Sir Hubert, 290
charge Chester charge on, 308
Stanza has been sung in vain, 793
who pens a, 212
Staple articles, legs are, 942
of his argument, 41
Star, a bright particular, 53
a quenchless, forever bright, 393
and there a star, here a, 583
as I watched a, 596
beck of a baleful, 756
bright, would I were, 385
came down with a falling, 507
camps to-night upon a, 847
catch a falling, 117
constant as the northern, 82
danced and I was born, 38
desire of the moth for the, 368
dropped like a falling, 149
early drooped in the western sky, 536
emigrated to another, 591
every, in place, 821
evening, love's harbinger, 155
fair as a, 296
follow but thy, 1020
following a fallen, 826
for every state, 472
for which all evening waits, 809
gather me a, 849
give a name to every fixed, 40
gleams of, and depths of blue, 442
glittering like the morning, 260
guide was a beautiful wonderful, 439
hitch your wagon to a, 414
hope's, to man grows dim, 405
I feel like a morning, 612
in bigness as a, 151
in place, every, 821
in someone's sky, 647
in the west that shall never go down, 512
in waters red, not the, 773
is not extinguished, 445
it is the natal, 964
lamp of human hope become a, 834
leadeth all, 643
looks down at me, 652
lovers love the western, 306
man is his own, 126
many a young new, 759
not a fourth sound, but a, 489
of empire, westward the, 203
of Eternity the only star, 393
of its worship, as still to the, 337
of peace return, 328

Star of resplendent front thy glorious, 418
of smallest magnitude, 151
one, differeth from another in glory, 1120
or two beside, a, 315
our life's, 301
our queen our rose our, 405
pinned with a single, 389
pins it with a, 389
pity the prickly, 898
pursue, nor any, 913
round and perfect as a, 587
sailor would not watch the, 1052
seems nothing, each separate, 566
so holy shines, evening, 408
some medicinal, 923
splendid a, 493
state for every, 472
strives to touch a, 25
sunset and evening, 472
than a fading, 899
that bids the shepherd, 157
that bringeth home the bee, 328
that has no parallax, 794
that haunts, 809
that once had shone, 881
that ushers in the even, 108
there's no rood has not a, 408
threading the eye of a yellow, 406
thy soul was like a, 298
to guide the humble, a, 499
to stay the morning, 316
troubling of a, 749
twinkle twinkle little, 345
wearies every, 424
which breaks on him, 484
wind each ticking, 851
your aim the, 957
Stars above us govern our conditions, 99
across the sky in, 901
afar beyond the, 170
agree, when good, 522
an endless number, count of, 867
and all eyes else dead coals, 57
and candles out, put all, 702
and kindly, have given, 405
and pavement, 154
and space above, 850
and wave beyond the, 825
are in the quiet skies, 426
are old, till the, 565
are shining bright, 368
are shining there, 370
are strewn, million, 669
are twinkling there, 590
at heaven's border, 869
attired with, 161
beauty of a thousand, 32
beneath the desert, 881
blesses his, 194
blossomed the lovely, 435
blue, 433
branch-charmed by the earnest, 384
climb the darkening blue, 728
comets amongst the, 1054
courses of the, 373
cut him out in little, 79
doubt thou the, are fire, 92

Stars, fault is not in our, 81
flag is full of, 710
fling us a handful of, 887
fought against Sisera, 1099
from wrong, thou dost preserve, 299
gave the first delight, 145
gem the sky, 643
go down to rise, 618
gold gateways of the, 748
half quencht in mists, 367
have influence upon me, 207
have lit the welkin dome, 382
have their time to set, 370
heaven feeds the, 982
heaven's vault studded with,
  369
her eyes as, 299
hide their diminished heads,
  151
hide your diminished rays, 210
how like the, 874
ideals are like, 580
in empty night, sink those, 306
in heaven, as be, 75
in heavenly spaces wide, 820
in her hair were seven, 577
in spite of nature and their,
  142
in the purple dusk, 904
in the right places, 914
in the sky for religion's sake,
  534
in the universe, number of,
  846
in their calm, 547
in their circling, 737
in their courses, 1099
innumerable as the, 153
invisible by day, 438
journey-work of the, 535
kings are like 367
kinship with the, 574
kiss my hand to the, 672
lean from their lattices, 643
like measles fade at last, 910
look for the, 301
look on the sea, as, 426
look out upon the, 405
loved the, too fondly, 661
morning, sang together, 1102
my consorts are the sleepless,
  517
of glory there, set the, 382
of heaven, strike the, 983
of human race, 262
of love, wholesome, 470
of midnight shall be dear, 296
of morning, 153
of the summer night, 434
over the heavens blown, 896
powdered with, 154
rise and vanish, 318
rush out, the, 315
seen in the galaxy, 154
shall fade away, 195
shine through the cypress-
  trees, 444
shining of the, 471
shot madly from their spheres,
  42
sky studded with eternal, 536
start from their spheres, 91
steal to their sovran seats, 668
teetered a little nearer the,
  431

Stars, thank your, 1037
that come in sight, 524
that come once in a century,
  524
that round her burn, 194
that sweep and turn and fly,
  776
the heaven its, 1066
the silent, go by, 612
the wakeful, 588
two, keep not their motion in
  one sphere, 63
untriangulated, 807
unutterably bright, 369
were more in fault than they,
  189
were paling, 659
which night's blue arch adorn,
  267
who build beneath the, 202
will shine, the little, 30
Star-captains glow, young, 881
Starch, the soapsuds and the, 924
Star-chamber matter of it, 34
Star-crowned heroes, 772
Star-dials pointed to morn, 461
Stare, grave and tranquil, 933
  stony British, 469
  time to stand and, 814
Starers, stupid, 208
Star-eyed science, 327
Stargazers, the monthly prognosticators, 1112
Star-gemmed, ruby-rimmed beryline buckets, 431
Stark insensibility, 233
Starless unknown night, 850
Starlight and dewdrop, 568
  is a steadying draught, 895
  lovely-asunder, 672
  not of the, 472
  of heaven above us, 502
  Winchelsea, 873
Star-like eyes, 140
Starred silence and the homeless
  air, 629
Starry cope of heaven, 153
  crown, though I put on a, 557
  folds, 385
  Galileo with his woes, 354
  girdle of the year, 327
  heavens fill me with awe, 542
  host of heaven, to all the, 910
  host, that led the, 152
  skies and cloudless climes, 356
  sky, silence in the, 302
  sky, under the wide and, 703
  stranger, entertain this, 165
  train, heaven's, 152
  tree eternity, 655
  wings I do forsake, my, 840
Star-space, within vast, 889
Star-spangled banner, 332
Start a hare, to, 61
  a thrill a rattle, a, 854
  of the majestic world, 81
  straining upon the, 66
Starts everything by, and nothing
  long, 174
  't was wild by, 248
Started like a guilty thing, 89
Starting tear, dry the, 622
Startled heaven of my soul, 853
Startles at destruction, 195
  of water, 833
Startling genius, he had a, 733

Starvation, ruin of woman by,
  1067
Starve, catch cold and, 105
  in ice, 150
  nor stuff, 191
  with nothing, 44
Starved bank of moss, 492
  for a look, 108
  for heaven, 642
Starving dog made prosperous
  will not bite, 615
  or depressed, when, 908
  tramp can't eat a silver shoe,
  898
Star-ypointing pyramid, 161
State, affairs of the, 1054
  almost perfect, 853
  and church separate, keep, 550
  and inclination of the day, 60
  beweep my outcast, 107
  brave and great lie there in,
  540
  broken with the storms of, 74
  bulwarks of the, 660
  certain guests of, 579
  compares with Maine, what
  other, 707
  favourable, puts man in a,
  1084
  for every star, 472
  grow mighty rulers of, 729
  he hails from, 578
  hides from himself his, 230
  high and palmy, of Rome, 89
  high on a throne of royal, 149
  hireling, 233
  House, Boston, 454
  I am the, 1060
  in Rome, devil to keep his, 81
  in sober, 268
  is devoid of stay, 9
  is not far from its fall, 1054
  is not well armed, where the,
  1023
  man at his best, 1104
  matters, touch no, 252
  may be given up for lost, 1054
  mock the air with idle, 244
  naught in world or church or,
  528
  no, can maintain members in
  arms, 270
  no power above the, 1083
  of ambitious poverty, 1006
  of cowardly dependence, 1081
  of life, duty in that, 1128
  of life, no, 225
  of man like a little kingdom,
  82
  of man, this is the, 73
  of mind can recur and be identical, no, 663
  of mind composed of felt slippers, 925
  of nature, war was the, 258
  of nothingness, 970
  of things, here's a pretty, 624
  of this strange being, 247
  of war by nature, 190
  pillar of, seemed a, 150
  pilot of the, 964
  Queen Bess ruled England's,
  760
  ruin or rule the, 173
  sail on O ship of, 435
  scandal waits on greatest, 107

State, scorn to change my, 107
so blessed in climate, 838
some service, I have done the, 103
some strange eruption to our, 89
star for every, 472
statesmen who pulled ruin on the, 430
that raises corn and cotton and cockleburs, 714
the, in choosing men to serve it, 141
the ship of, 964
upright in the, 964
when fair thy, 983
when the sun in all its, 557
where Venice sate in, 353
who mutually injure the, 969
without a king, 394
without king or nobles, 393
States and in providence, deficiency in, 1062
are convinced, neighbouring, 1051
are likely to be well administered, 975
chief foundations of all, 1023
could exist, no, 981
dangers to their, 20
dissevered discordant, 341
free and independent, 268
free from moral obligation, 319
grandeur of these, their religion, 534
in seven, 888
indestructible, 445
move slowly, 112
of all the, but three, 660
saved without the sword, 425
seed of half the, 929
shaker of o'er-rank, 132
she ruins, 964
unborn, scene be acted o'er in, 82
with others' ruin built, 30
State's decrees, mould a mighty, 468
Stateliest and most regal argument, 162
Stately convent, it was a, 423
gulf between, 866
homes of England, 370
kindly lordly friend, 634
mansions, build thee more, 452
pleasure-dome, 315
ship is seen no more, 640
Statement, complete, which is literature, 878
solemn inevitable appalling, 787
was interesting but tough, the, 615
Statesman and buffoon, 174
and the saint, 661
hung with weights and woe, 170
throws his shoulders back, 764
too nice for a, 252
warrior or monarch survived by the poet, 423
yet friend to truth, 210
Statesmanship, highest, 445
Statesmen at her council met, 462

Statesmen declare themselves Christians, 1082
minds of some of our, 334
talked, where village, 251
these our present, 972
to give an account of themselves, 1006
who pulled ruin on the state, 430
wise, foresee changes, 641
Station, an old man at a, 499
can disgrace, no, 512
in a private, 921
like the herald Mercury, 95
post of honour is a private, 195, 206
she leaves the, 938
splendid was its, 748
take another, 623
your unique and moping, 937
Stations, abide and work in our, 519
proper, 495
Stationary, over those who are, 228
Statists hold it baseness to write fair, 97
Statistics influenced by circumstance, 741
variable and uncertain, 741
Statuaries, loved to copy, 398
Statue by his touch grew into youth, 340
by Phidias, Jupiter's, 956
grows, more the, 1023
in the public square, 862
of Cato, 1006
of Newton stood, where, 299
that breathes, 609
Statues and pictures and verse may be grand, 610
the world blooms with, 613
Statue-like repose, 473
Stature grows, her, 303
is she of, what, 50
made him great, not his, 564
of my soul, 574
tall, her, 358
toys of simulated, 430
undepressed in size, 302
Statures touch the skies our, 585
Statute, the rigour of the, 35
Staunch friends are we, 619
Stay at home my heart, 439
I ask not to, 387
in which she made so long a, 449
nor ever will be at a, 174
nothing that is can pause or, 438
staff and the, 188
weary by a longer, 898
who saw to wish her, 154
why should I, 681
Stayed, too late I, 294
Stead, in their suffering country's, 973
Steadfast as the scene, 296
Steadied, my preudunt course is, 526
Steadies with upright keel, she, 315
Steadily hastening towards immortality, 536
Steady and perpetual serenity, 197

Steady boys steady, 242
candle-flame and feel the, 488
gain of man, I see the, 442
self-esteem and confidence of Britons, 483
temper, thy, 194
Steak and gravy, fragments of, 923
Steal a few hours from the night, 336
a shive of a cut loaf, 77
away give little warning, 273
away their brains, 101
away your hearts, 83
"Convey" the wise it call, 34
foh a fico for the phrase, 34
from the world, 216
immortal blessing from her lips, 79
my thunder, 186
out of your company, 39
to their sovran seats, 668
young children, witches, 122
Stealer of this book, 241
Stealin' for de big, 902
for de little, 902
Stealing and giving odour, 53
forth in the midst of roses, 645
hands from picking and, 1128
will continue stealing, 529
Steals an egg will steal an ox, he that, 138
from the thief, 101
my purse steals trash, who, 102
Stealth, do good by, 214
treasure without, 21
Steam, know where you are with, 871
like whale, spouting, 926
on, putting, 661
song of, 402
to affection and to, 661
to sing the song o', 777
unconquered, 267
Steamboat man on ships, 825
Steam-engine in trousers, 313
Steam-engines are very human, 871
Steamer that rode at anchor, 925
Stedfast and demure, sober, 160
of thought, 10
would I were, as thou art, 385
Steed, farewell the neighing, 102
mounts the warrior's, 306
threatens steed, 67
Steeds, scampering of their, 372
to water at those springs, 105
Steel, and pour its, 928
as with triple, 150
could the labour of the gods destroy, 212
foemen worthy of their, 308
grapple with hoops of, 90
heart is true as, 42
in complete, 91
is wrought, 873
made was the bright, 504
magnet and the, 936
more than complete, 31
my man is as true as, 79
no workman's, 342
nor poison can touch him further, 87
of spirit, 888

Steel Potomac's jewelled stream, 848
  recourse to Swedish, 1076
  ribbed and edged with, 873
  sting of the rowelled, 783
  supple as, 737
  though locked up in, 69
Steel-true and blade-straight, 704
Steelyards of the skies, 725
Steep and thorny way, 90
  and weary stair, daily up, 598
  guards them from the, 701
  hill, up a, 223
  my senses in forgetfulness, 65
  no towers along the, 327
  o'er the hillside, 549
  on Sunium's marbled, 359
  on the Indian, 157
Steeps God set for thee, 570
  of immortality, scale the, 837
Steeped me in poverty, 103
  their souls in prayer, 459
Steeple, climbed up a high church, 656
  cried out from the, 656
  some gray old, 554
  weathercock of the church, 1055
  weathercock on a, 33
Steeples point to the sky, 318
Steepy mountains, 31
Steer clear of permanent alliances, 268
  from grave to gay, 177
  from grave to light, 177
  right onward, 162
Stein, a notable family called, 836
  on the table, with a, 771
Stem, cut the weak, 864
  land-flower broken from the, 756
  leave it on its, 593
  moulded on one, 43
Stenches, two-and-seventy, 317
Step above the sublime, 271
  all out of, but Bill, 515
  and summit, highest, 1020
  aside is human, to, 285
  brings with careless, 811
  conscious, hat and all, 755
  every, is an end, 682
  first, which costs, 1053
  forward, every tiny, 1081
  I see not a, before me, 626
  more slow, each, 603
  more true, foot more light, 308
  one, enough for me, 403
  precise and pedantic their, 637
  so active, 326
  to the music of the Union, 394
  towards independence, 991
  was slow, and his, 437
Steps, age with his stealing, 96
  and tongues resound, where stranger, 541
  aright, lead my, 372
  beware of desperate, 267
  echo of the sad, 303
  hear not my, 85
  intrude, and no, 576
  Lord directeth his, 1107
  morn her rosy, advancing, 153
  of the paper-box factory, 939
  of the ploughman, heavy, 790
  our truest, 453

Steps, pilgrim, in amice gray, 156
  that may make us good, 975
  thy, I follow with bosom bare, 248
  to support uneasy, 148
  were higher that they took, 174
  with fainting, they go, 251
  with how sad, 27
  with wandering, and slow, 156
Stephen Sly, 52
  was a worthy peer, 101, 256
Stephen's Green, lead through, 875
Stepmother, merciless, 993
  of genius, poverty the, 518
  of ministers' daughters, 654
Steppe in other men and catch the burdes, 12
Stepped so far in blood, 87
  to the sky, 431
Stepping o'er the bounds, 80
Stepping-stone or a stumbling-block, 680
Stepping-stones, men may rise on, 436, 467
Sterile promontory, earth seems a, 92
  with idleness, 101
Sterilized, it wasn't, 815
Sterling page, refine her, 1050
  worth, of, 465
Stern and pressing duty, 560
  and rock-bound coast, 370
  but distant shore, 770
  design, to his, 892
  friend to genius, 413
  gyve, joined by a, 685
  necessity, 654
  ruin's ploughshare, 285
  self-confident, only the, 931
Sterner stuff, made of, 83
Stern-faced men, two, 391
Stern'st good-night, which gives the, 86
Sterte, out of his slepe to, 5
  to, but oon hole for to, 7
Stethoscope nice and new, 451
Stew, fretted and kept in a, 474
  is smokin' hot, 820
  onions in the, 906
Steward falls into the soup-tureen, 784
Stick and stone, heap of, 651
  beat with fist instead of a, 141
  blind man's, 850
  climbing on a yellow, 684
  close to your desks, 623
  fell like the, 271
  more close than a brother, 783
  on conversation's burrs, 451
  or a stone this old cove throwed, 539
  serge draped over a, 930
  standing upright, a, 147
  with two butt-ends, 347
Sticking-place, screw your courage to the, 85
Stiff and old, the wrist grows, 544
  in opinions, 173
  upper lip, keep a, 557
Stiffen the sinews, 66
Stiffening of the vertebrae, young men need, 745

Stiffness and the soul's arrest, 827
Stile, before you come to the, 1034
Stiles, helping lame dogs over, 523
Still achieving still pursuing, 433
  an angel appear, 201
  and bright, the days are, 418
  and quiet conscience, 73
  and serious thought, 297
  and solitary, be quite, 1090
  as night, attention, 150
  beginning never ending, 176
  beneath the waves, 667
  destroying fighting still, 176
  from out yon clouded sky, 418
  God is living working, 502
  govern thou my song, 153
  harping on my daughter, 92
  morning brightened, 659
  prayer of devotion, 336
  room, to this, 444
  sad music of humanity, 296
  sech nights all white and, 527
  seeds of godlike power are in us, 545
  small voice, 244, 1101
  small voice in autumn's, 442
  small voice spake unto me, 462
  small voice thundering, 544
  small voice, with, 305
  soliciting eye, 98
  sowe eats up all the draffe, 14
  still with Thee, 480
  the fitting word He speeds, 441
  the same, its flash is, 404
  the wonder grew, 251
  their strength is to sit, 1111
  to be neat still to be drest, 119
  waters, beside the, 1103
  we see thee lie, how, 612
  when you are an anvil hold, 137
  where we may be, 1128
Stille, a fool can noght be, 4
Stilled at even, 577
Stillness and the night, 47
  drowned, in sweet blue, 688
  modest, and humility, 66
  reigneth evermore, peaceful, 480
Still-vexed Bermoothes, 32
Stilly night, oft in the, 336
  sounds, the hum of either army, 67
Stimulus, imaginative, need for, 646
Sting, death where is thy, 1120
  no more, yearning of soul, 554
  of conscience, 1079
  of poverty of love despised, 824
  of the rowelled steel, 783
  poisonous, 533
  that bids not sit nor stand, 489
  thee twice, have a serpent, 46
  there O death, thy, 736
Stings and motions of the sense, 35
  disturb it, it, 592
  never feels the wanton, 35
  you for your pains, 204
Stinger, 't is a, 117
Stingeth like an adder, 1108
Stingy with your blooming, 853

Stinking altar, one, 856
　fish, 320
Stinks, rotten mackerel shines
　and, 320
　well defined, 317
Stippled, rose-moles all in, 672
Stir, all hell for this shall, 67
　as life were in 't, 88
　by secret, 834
　of echoes down the creaking
　　floor, 914
　of the great Babel, 265
　of this dim spot, smoke and,
　　157
　that short potential, 584
　the fire with a sword, 1016
　things that make the greatest,
　　733
　without great argument, 96
Stirs of discontented strife, 121
　to rouse a lion, blood, 61
Stirred at the whisper, the sap,
　642
　our hearts in youth, 665
Stirring, not a creature was, 332
　not a mouse, 89
Stirrup and the ground, 21
Stitch stitch stitch, 391
Stitches, laugh yourself into, 55
Stithy, as foul as Vulcan's, 94
Stock, cast into a publick, 197
　of enjoyment, common, 750
　of harmless pleasure, 233
　Virginia with her noble, 660
　with a new, 921
Stocks and stones, worshipped,
　162
Stocking all the day, 251, 253
　blue, 399
　hang up the baby's, 604
　up, yawns and draws a, 900
Stockings and the tree, the, 935
　blue in eyes as awful as in,
　　430
　hung by the chimney, 332
　lean and long, 763
　with blue silk, 864
Stocking's crowded toe, 711
Stoic backs, read their, 903
　fur, doctors of the, 158
　of the woods, 328
　or satyr, 716
Stoics, after the manner of the,
　109
Stoicism and no philosophy no,
　531
　the Romans call it, 194
Stolen forth of holy writ, 71
　not wanting what is, 102
　sweets are best, 194
　waters are sweet, 1107
　when the steed is, 14
Stomach, a good-humored, 991
　and no food, she either gives,
　　65
　and takes away the, 65
　as well as lungs, arbitrary, 247
　deepest loathing to the, 43
　enforcing morality on the,
　　1067
　for such meat, no, 650
　good, excels them all, 184
　goes against my, 50
　mutinied against the, 997
　my, is not good, 20
　of unbounded, 74

Stomach, patriot on an empty,
　714
　the seat of this sensation, 745
　underneath, his little, 890
Stomachs, good, that would fall
　to, 163
　of the needy, 1016
Stomach's sake, wine for thy,
　1121
Stone, a gift is as a precious,
　1107
　against imperishable, 923
　and thou shalt find me, raise
　　the, 709
　at her, let him first cast a,
　　175, 1118
　at his heels, 256
　carve not upon a, 596
　caution against the stumbling,
　　879
　cold as any, 66
　continual dropping wears away
　　a, 981
　fling but a, the giant dies, 223
　from the chancel floor, 737
　give him a, 978
　goes starting others, 705
　huge piles of, 688
　I only wish a hut of, 451
　if any have a, 897
　in one hand bread in the other,
　　978
　inscription on, 970
　let the guiltless person throw
　　the, 175
　look about under every, 972
　many a rich, laid up, 121
　mark with a white, 1039
　marks the sod, no, 579
　mockery of monumental, 366
　my rest a, 423
　of stumbling, a, 1111
　of the corner, head, 1106
　of walls, 959
　on stone, dig and heap lay,
　　546
　out of your shoe, shake a, 670
　people did by this, 546
　pillow of, 521
　ponderous, 223
　raise the, 709, 1126
　raise ye the, 781
　rolling, gathers no moss, 14,
　　988
　rolling, restless, 67
　scorpion on a, 936
　senseless, 887
　set in the silver sea, 59
　shall be articulate, 688
　sling your fifth, 913
　squeezing from a, 897
　strength, lend me the, 895
　survive in wistful, 648
　tell where I lie, not a, 216
　the past is, 680
　their hulls of, 937
　this precious, 59
　to beauty grew, the, 408
　turn but a, 749
　two things stand like, 601
　underneath this, doth lie, 119,
　　948
　unturned, leave no, 968
　violet by a mossy, 296
　virtue is like a rich, 111
　waiting for the blow, 1073

Stone walls do not a prison
　make, 168
　we raised not a, 364
　which the builders refused,
　　1106
　without gout or, 172
Stones and poets, from, 749
　are men and men are stones,
　　541
　existence from the broken, 927
　labour of an age in piled, 161
　music with the enamelled, 33
　of emptiness remain, 443
　of it are laid in scorn, 824
　of Rome to rise, 83
　of worth, like, 107
　plain as graveyard, 903
　prate of my whereabout, 85
　rattle his bones over the, 395
　sermons in, 48
　stocks and, worshipped, 162
　towns of, 810
　whose house is of glass must
　　not throw, 137
Stone's throw, within a, 1036
Stone-wall Jackson, 552
　Jackson wrapped in his beard,
　　928
Stony limits cannot hold love
　out, 78
Stony-hearted stepmother, 347
Stood against my fire, 99
　against the world, 83
　among them but not of them,
　　353
　and gazed, 316
　fixed to hear, 154
　in Venice on the bridge of
　　sighs, 353
　there wondering fearing, 460
　upon Achilles' tomb, 360
Stooks rise around, 672
　she stood amid the, 390
Stool, fettered to an office, 622
Stools, between two, 12
　push us from our, 87
　trying to sit on two, 12
Stoop, grief makes his owner, 57
　to Death we must, 19
Stoops not, the grass, 106
　to folly, lovely woman, 253
Stop a hole, might, 97
　to sound what, she please, 94
Stops, a moment yet the actor,
　481
　and strings, 684
　music from a thousand, 684
　of various quills, 160
Stopping a bunghole, 97
Store, how grows in Paradise our,
　365
　is no sore, 12, 1041
　of crowns, 120
　rich with little, 20
　to increase his, 248
　you saved a little, 481
Stores as silent thought can
　bring, 295
　enrich with our, 30
　in John's pavilion laid, 543
　of Attic salt, 601
　richer than gems or gold, 443
Stored, where grapes of wrath
　are, 522
Storied urn, can, 244
　windows richly dight, 161

Stories come true, dead, 913
  do we see, too many doleful, 384
  for a guide, take my, 784
  from the land of spirits, 317
  great lords', 288
  mere flim-flam, 1036
  nature built many, 148
  of the death of kings, 60
  only two or three human, 841
  sad, of my own mishaps, 37
  tall men are like houses of four, 113
  there are countless, 847
Storm a strife, a, 597
  after a, comes a calm, 188
  after storm, 387
  and after storm calm, try, 923
  and darkness, night and, 353
  as deepe in calme as in, 118
  cable that ne'er broke in, 146
  called life must hush, 497
  cloud, gaze on the, 583
  dark the night and wild the, 258
  descends, when the, 986
  directs the, 194, 215
  dispelling his fanciful illusions, 1065
  endure the, 269
  euchred God Almighty's, 777
  every cloud engenders not a, 70
  great music a psychical, 772
  had passed, when the, 962
  head to the, 778
  how fierce soe'er, no rude, 480
  ice of an old, 923
  is oftener tossed, by the, 983
  leave thee in the, 98
  like gathering, 287
  malice of the, 199
  midway leaves the, 251
  of spears, lost in a, 789
  of war was gone, when, 294
  of words, I 'll raise a, 971
  or sunshine guard it, 1058
  pelting of this pitiless, 98
  pilot that weathered the, 294
  rides upon the, 266
  sublime and terrible, 314
  that howls along the sky, 248
  tumultuous privacy of, 408
  upon the mountain, 505
  when in life's, 405
  when waves were rough, 338
  whose might can reach, 675
  will break in a little time, 183
Storms, black by morning, 325
  calm that must follow all, 497
  come, asked to be where no, 672
  emotional, weather, 870
  give her to the god of, 450
  he sought the, 173
  may enter, the king cannot, 230
  of state, broken with the, 74
  sudden, are short, 59
Stormed and tore his hair, skipper, 508
Stormie seas, port after, 24
Storm-troubled sphere, in the world's, 516
Storm-waves on a stern but distant shore, 770

Stormwind, outracing the, 758
Stormy cape, round the, 224
  husky brawling, 855
  March has come, 372
  North, hills of the, 370
  parent, 679
  sea, to be tossed on the, 437
  seas, enchantress of the, 418
  surge, rocking on a, 964
  waters threw, 300
  winds do blow, 115, 328
Story, Alice a childish, 598
  being done, my, 100
  found in the Jews' Books, 165
  had paresis, 953
  honour is the subject of my, 81
  I have none to tell, 293
  itself, be short in the, 1125
  locks in the golden, 77
  of Cambuscan bold, 161
  of her birth, repeats the, 194
  of Johnny Appleseed, 596
  of my life, questioned me the, 100
  of our days, shuts up the, 22
  of Sussex told, 810
  rough island, 467
  some pretty, tell, 345
  standing in every door, 826
  teach him how to tell my, 100
  that 's another, 241, 785
  the cowboy's brief brief, 822
  through centuries of, 443
  well-nigh told, like a, 555
  when a person knows a, 661
  will not go down, this, 229
Story-book, read it in the, 453
  thy Father has written for thee, 437
Story-books, for all the, 703
Story-dressers do as much, 122
Stout Cortez with eagle eyes, 384
  courage will be put out, 22
  not alive so, a gentleman, 63
  once a month, 177
  watchword, 478
  within, well the soul if, 409
Stradivari's violins, Antonio, 520
Straggler into loving arms, 290
Straggling road in Spain, 827
Straight down the crooked lane, 391
  from absolution of faithful fight, 556
  in the strength, grow, 633
  is the line of duty, 444
  out of the ark, 312
  plow deep and, with all, 417
  strive to set the crooked, 608
  was the path of gold, 485
  we walked too, 429
Straight-jacket or a swamp-elm club, 714
Strain, along the reedy stream a half-heard, 385
  at a gnat, 1115
  Christ's heart and Shakespeare's, 410
  low sad and sweet, 549
  of rareness, a, 106
  of the doing, 605
  soft is the, 211
  soft Kentucky, 676
  solemn, 370
  something like prophetic, 161

Strain, strive and hold cheap the, 489
  subdued subduing, 568
  sweetness of the, 661
  that, again it had a dying fall, 53
  that, once more, 252
  the big Bow-wow, 312
  the minor of Thy loftier, 443
  the simplest can touch it, 337
Strains are telling, those blessed, 503
  fall like sweet, or pensive, 408
  heaven's melodious, 477
  little cat's, 664
  of melody, fall like, 586
  soul-animating, 304
  to home and memory dear, 734
  who delight in her, 335
Strained from that fair use, 78
  quality of mercy is not, 46
Straining harsh discords, 80
  upon the start, 66
Strait and terse, the buskin, 648
  is the gate, 1114
  the gate, it matters not how, 693
Straits, in financial, 971
Straitened him, an old love, 470
Strand, American, 136
  conducting the orchestral, 773, 799
  disturbs the, 576
  fair Scotland's, 287
  I walked along the, 238
  India's coral, 343
  iron lilies of the, 793
  on the Chian, 317
  the guardian Naiad of the, 308
  walked the ocean, 362
  wandering on a foreign, 307
Strands, close-knit, 955
Strange all this difference, 221
  and drear the sound, 626
  and new-fangled names, 973
  and speechless fear, 699
  as truth, nothing so, 342
  bedfellows, 33
  but true, 't is, 361
  coincidence, a, 360
  cozenage, 178
  disease of modern life, this, 547
  dominion, 369
  eruption, this bodes some, 89
  eruptions, breaks forth in, 62
  eventful history, that ends this, 50
  fellows, nature hath framed, 43
  flesh, no love for anything but, 166
  forever, shore of the, 568
  land, stranger in a, 1098
  matters, men may read, 84
  men of old, 653
  oaths, soldier full of, 49
  peace and rest, 659
  penance, 588
  something rich and, 32
  that death should sing, 58
  that desire should outlive performance, 65
  that men should fear, 82

Strange the world, 736
  things, footsteps of, 421
  to see, 431
  to think by the way, 577
  truth is always, 361
  'twas passing strange, 100
  was his lot, 685
  what a man may do, 482
Strangeness in the proportion, 111
Stranger and afraid, I a, 743
  careful thought for the, 642
  entertain this starry, 165
  from the wiles of the, 935
  if, such no longer, 815
  in a strange land, 1098
  in financial straits, 971
  kith or kin, 722
  never love a, 913
  pause and look, 916
  preached, a, 475
  surety for a, 1107
  than fiction, truth is, 361
  to thee, a troubled mind be, 135
  would come, what, 850
  would do well, 242
  yet to pain, 243
Strangers as 'tis offered up by, 645
  he barks at, 674
  honoured, by, 217
  I desire we may be better, 50
  in, potter's field to bury, 1116
  mourned, by, 217
  not knowing each the other's name, 300
  pilgrims and, 553
  the fraternity of, 1069
  to entertain, 220
  waiting to entertain, 166
  with the eyes of, 1089
Stranger's foot has crossed, 552
  yoke, assumed the, 903
Strangest liberties, he takes the, 510
Strangled serpents, Hercules was with, 930
Straps, hang themselves in their own, 54
Stratagem, nor take tea without a, 203
Stratagems and policy are allowable, 1040
  and spoils, is fit for, 47
  which errors seem, oft are, 210
Stratford atte bowe, scole of, 5
  upon Avon in the county of Warwick, 171
Straw, did not care one, 979
  for a bedding, 810
  hope of getting the, 962
  nor do they care a, 1035
  quarrel in a, 96
  stumbles at a, 25
  tickled with a, 208
  to make brick, 1098
  to see which way the wind is, 130
Straws, errors like, 177
  that blow, as, 692
Strawberries, great, 113
  melts on the vine, 696
  what Dr. Boteler said of, 140
Strawberry wives, like the, 113

Stray thoughts fancies fugitive, 492
Streakings of the morning light, 382
Stream, a slow and silent, 150
  along the reedy, 385
  as the leaf upon the, 308
  at eve, by living, 225
  bashful, 165
  central, 548
  cut the silver, 39
  dried and vanished, 480
  in smoother numbers flows, 211
  left to the mercy of a rude, 73
  let us glide a-down thy, 350
  make channels for the, of love, 441
  Mississippi's winding, 475
  no striving against the, 1038
  not to swap horses crossing a, 457
  of love that circles home, 403
  of our years, filling with the, 1090
  of time, 289
  of verbiage metaphor and dream, 578
  Potomac's jewelled, 848
  runneth smoothest, where, 24
  runs fast, the, 334
  shallow and light, 547
  summer eves by haunted, 160
  that brawls, 438
  thy, my great example, 167
  time is but a, 514
  which overflowed the soul, 303
  which runs with rapid change, 405
Streams and woods belong, 409
  are running, while its, 738
  ascend, 306
  bright, 568
  by what eternal, 460
  canon-guarded, 831
  ether's long bankless, 882
  feed by the, 281
  fresh from the hyaline, 432
  from little fountains, large, 292
  gold-sanded, 597
  in the valleys, 982
  liquid lapse of murmuring, 154
  love has overflowing, 441
  meander, as, 440
  no resemblance with those, 166
  of music, swift, 670
  of revenue gushed forth, 340
  on craggy hills running, 447
  our gratulations flow in, 189
  passions are likened to floods and, 21
  run dimpling all the way, 213
  that glide, 527
  their gravel gold, 166
  thy thousand, 417
  upon the, 912
Streamed like a meteor, 244
Streamers flying at midnight, 240
  waving, 157
Streaming time, through, 459
  to the wind, like a meteor, 148
Street, as I walk the, 679
  be as wide, let the, 1022
  begins to masquerade, 650
  but he shakes the, 676

Street car rattling over the stony, 352
  child on the homeless, 708
  clamor of the crowded, 439
  cryes all about, 654
  down an unlistening, 719
  down the long and silent, 723
  gallivanted down the, 925
  goes past, a crooked, 906
  half garden and half house, 466
  is hung for miles, 806
  live in a trading, 198
  my shadow in the, 522
  of by-and-by, 693
  ringing down the, 500
  threading the, 600
  turn the corner of a, 707
  wanders up and down the, 394
Streets, along its lonesome, 565
  are guarded, 953
  are packed, 785
  dogs fighting in the, 229
  gibber in the Roman, 89
  in thy dark, 612
  little queer suburban, 911
  mourners go about the, 1110
  of air, bright, 889
  of Askelon, 1100
  of life, corner in the, 574
  truth never fell dead in the, 476
  utters her voice in the, 1106
  were rife with people, 551
  when night darkens the, 148
Strength, a breathing of, 1025
  and thou shalt find, 1059
  be, as thy days so shall thy, 1099
  be sapped, though its, 943
  both of body and mind, 1048
  but art obtains the prize, not, 116
  but the duration, not the, 1080
  collected its, 743
  cometh from heaven, 1125
  enough to do the work, 787
  exact quality matters, 727
  excellent to have giant's, 36
  for others, spent his, 591
  for the weak shield for defenceless, 602
  giant's unchained, 371
  gift of, 575
  grant us the, 873
  honest rude effective, 491
  if by reason of, 1105
  in every drop, there's life and, 404
  into right, transforms, 1054
  is as the strength of ten, 465
  is felt from hope, 219
  is in your union, your, 436
  is to sit still, their, 1111
  is yours, my, 778
  its ancient and natural, 248
  king's name a tower of, 72
  knowledge increaseth, 1108
  labour and sorrow is their, 1105
  lieth, wherein thy great, 1099
  lovely in your, 353
  magnifies the idea of, 894
  my sword is, 816
  nor hold thy, in vain, 570
  not, but art, 210

Strength of character may prove
the whip, 1083
of might of power, of, 789
of nerve and sinew, 303
of the past, 895
of the patient, restores the,
976
of thy spirit, 633
of twenty men, 80
of various qualities, 1087
our castle's, will laugh a siege
to scorn, 88
our refuge and, 1104
perfect in weakness, 1121
prayed that God would give
him, 120
relied, on what have you for,
855
renewed, thy, 371
revealing, thine old, 546
shall renew their, 1112
slight not, 116
spend your, 862
to finish well our task, 671
to force the moment, 900
to help, 955
to perfect what it dreamed of,
525
to strength, pass from, 837
to strength, they go from,
1105
to strive, 573
to the thought, adds, 204
tower of, 72, 467
truth ever has most, 967
unguessed unproved, leave
their, 931
union gives, 962
unite levity with, 232
wears away, as my, 172
wisdom overmatch for, 992
yet stayed to, 834
Strengthens our nerves, 261
with his strength, 208
Strengthless companionless, 966
Strenuous life, doctrine of the,
734
Strephon's kiss was lost in jest,
883
Stress of the wildest weather,
642
terrestrial, 651
Stretch every nerve, 225
him out longer, 100
out to the crack of doom,
87
Stretched metre of an antique
song, 107
upon the plain, 351
Stretched-forth necks, 1111
Strew gladness on the paths of
men, 732
Strewed thy grave, 97
Stricken deer go weep, let the,
94, 265
in age, well, 1097
in life's brave heat, 604
Strictest union, live in, 259
Strictly snaps itself, vow that
binds too, 471
Stride, comes the dark at one,
315
Striding the blast, 85
Strife, a sob a storm, a, 597
and confusion, through, 583
bitter dregs of, 608

Strife, brook's motion clear
without, 501
clubs typical of, 266
death and life in ceaseless,
447
discord and continual, 68
dust of, 604
full many a, 225
full of pleasure, void of, 140
in our pitiful, 657
in, with many a valiant foe,
626
let there be no, 1097
madding crowd's ignoble, 245
man of, 1112
none was worth my, 326
of tongues, 1103
of truth with falsehood, 524
shut out, a world of, 544
spur unto, 964
stirs of discontented, 121
to heal, no, 303
to mingle in its care and,
474
who died overwhelmed in the,
533
with anxious, 326
with the palm, 547
world at, 760
Strike an awe into the beholders,
191
afraid to, 213
but hear, 996
for your altars, 362
home in the ambush, 35
mine eyes but not my heart,
119
shook but delayed to, 155
the tent! 565
then no planets, 89
Thou the master, 443
when the iron is hot, 12
you on such a morning, 494
your fill, when you are a hammer, 137
Strikes the Titans down, Jove,
484
Striking conviction, 231
String after string is severed
from the heart, 223
and tying it with, 866
attuned to mirth, 390
bead on the, of confusions, 837
beads on a, 1076
catch one or two on a, 909
few can touch the magic, 451
harp not on that, 72
harp so on the same, 1037
heart's a ball of, 630
hempen, under a gallows-tree,
127
lest the loosed, 226
may jar in the best master's
hand, 180
moderation is the silken, 121
of pearls, as a, 765
the first, 172
untune that, 74
warbled to the, 161
Strings, bruised albeit at the,
687
harp of thousand, 199
knottiness of, 654
many, to your bow, 15
players upon plaintive, 798
trembling, 364

Strings, two, to his bow, 15
were on the banjo, 768
Stripes, forty, save one, 1121
untarnished, with its, 821
Strip lads and to it, 309
of herbage, 1018
Stripling Will, has, 757
Strive here for mastery, 150
in strength to, 573
mightily, 52
to seek to find and not to yield,
to, 464
to set crooked straight, 608
Strives to touch a star, 25
Striving against the stream, no,
1038
and struggling the worst way,
720
to better oft we mar, 98
Strivings after better hopes, 666
parcel of vain, 514
Stroke a nettle, 204
at the same, 1076
feel the friendly, 187
for a gull, 882
kept, to the tune of flutes, 104
of a politician's pen, 604
of all, bitterest, 973
Strokes, as amorous of their, 104
calumnious, 90
fell great oaks, little, 227
many, though with a little axe
69
of adversity, 985
of character, hereditary, 949
overthrow tallest oaks, many,
23
Stroll upon the beach, my life
like a, 513
Strong alone, not to the, 270
already, what is, 322
and content I travel, 535
and rugged as the quartz, 686
and upright like an obelisk,
726
and well-constituted man,
1081
as a bull moose, 734
as death, love is, 1110
as flesh and blood, 301
as proofs of holy writ, 102
as your hand can make, 848
battle is not to the, 1110
bird, as a, 537
command, when the, 764
constant pleasant wise, 248
convictions, he had, 821
corruption inhabits our frail
blood, 56
devouring of the weak by the,
580
drink is raging, 1107
fence 'round the top, 640
for a person, 272
for service still, 265
for the disease, too, 966
for the man who named it, 830
hand, mortality's, 58
hands to weak, 653
his will was, 948
I would be, 880
in beauty's passion, 794
in cunning, 282
in death, ruling passion, 209
in honesty, I am armed so, 83
is the lion, 248

Strong man free, set some, 777
man in his wrath, 428
men, not two, 218
minds great hearts, time demands, 522
nor'wester's blowing, 275
numbers pure and sweetly, 247
poison when he's, 828
quit you like men be, 1120
right is chiefly with the, 1050
roots, bound by, 619
shall thrive, only the, 844
the fight, not to the, 710
thick stupefying incense-smoke, 488
to consume small troubles, 503
to keep hate out, 887
to run the race, 340
upon the stronger side, 57
will is free, is the soul, 545
wise man is, 1108
without rage, 167
ye are wondrous, 353
Strong-backed and neat-bound, 324
Strong-box, build for yourself a, 848
Stronger by weakness, 146
than my sex, 82
thought 's a weapon, 504
to yield to the, 995
Strongest, opinion of the, 1045
is never strong enough, 1054
minds, 302
wander farthest, 661
Strongly it bears us along, 317
Strong-willed relative a bugbear, 422
Strong-winged soul, O, 633
Strove and who failed, who, 533
Strown beach, 577
Struck eagle, so the, 351
Strucken blind, he that 's, 77
Structure, architectural, 1081
no, outlives a book, 660
Struggle and flight, alarms of, 546
ended, lifelong, 671
for existence, 448
for power or scramble for pelf, 510
for room and food, 448
in a contemptible, 259
lessens human woe, each, 504
manhood is a, 420
naught availeth, say not, 519
not the prize, in the, 458
o'er, 346
of discordant powers, 260
of forces, politics a, 636
with a sleeping-car, 635
Struggles, history of class, 1072
Struggling for life, man, 233
Strumming, wild joy of, 742
Strung, pearls at random, 275
with his hair, Apollo's lute, 41
Struts and frets his hour, 88
Stuart or Nassau, 190
race, noblest of the, 424
Stubble land at harvest home, 61
Stubborn gift, 304
patience, 150
things, facts are, 248, 1052
unlaid ghost, 158
Stubs of the victim's cheque-books, 580

Studded with stars, 369
with the eternal stars, sky, 536
Student of our sweet English tongue, 881
pale, turns no, 215
Studibus, wore a diamond, 867
Studie was but litel on the bible, his, 5
Studied in his death, 84
men close, 574
never to be fairer, 28
Studies, still air of delightful, 162
Studious let me sit, 224
to please, 231
Study, all in all his, 66
and delight, Homer's works your, 210
and management of one disease, 969
in law's grave, 21
in old gold, nature a, 742
is a weariness of flesh, 1110
labour and intent, 162
of a prince, war the only, 258
of history useful, 636
of imagination, creep into his, 40
of learning, enflamed with the, 162
of mankind is man, 207
of revenge immortal hate, 148
of the rules and tools, 922
slow of, 42
some brown, 23
to be quiet, 1121
what you most affect, 52
Stuff as dreams are made on, 33
disposer of other men's, 114
everything made of one hidden, 411
from far sea-faring, 757
it 's the worst darn, 943
life is made of, 227
made of penetrable, 95
not made of rarer, 803
perilous, which weighs upon the heart, 88
should be made of sterner, 83
skimble-skamble, 62
that it is made of, 887
the head with reading, 215
they sell, so precious as the, 1019
without that, 910
wrapping your, 866
youth 's a, 54
Stuffed bosom, cleanse the, 88
his critic who thought he was, 508
men, we are the, 899
Stuffs out his vacant garments, 58
Stumble at the threshold, men that, 70
courage brother do not, 499
that run fast, they, 78
Stumbles at a straw, 25
Stumbling, a stone of, 1111
in disastrous night, 477
on abuse, 78
Stumbling-block or a stepping-stone, 680
Stummucks, lazy fokes's, 688
Stump of a little tree, taken to be a, 1055

Stuns, Niagara, 250
Stupendous fourth estate, 377
whole, one, 207
Stupid and the clown they remain, 661
crime, end that, 845
people control, when, 852
starers, 208
Stupidity, an excess of, 234
and baseness, nations tend to, 729
god of our gods, 889
not be guilty of, 1030
only sin, 723
Street, shops of, 816
the gods contend against, 1059
Stupor, in a joyless, 247
Sturdier limbs and brighter brain, 833
Sturdiness, decry plain, 491
Sturdy and stanch he stands, 699
Sturgeon belongs to the king, 909
Stuttering rifles' rapid rattle, 918
Sty, fattest hog in Epicurus', 249
ordure of the, 889
Stygian coast, Charon by the, 858
set, 326
Style agrees not with leanness of his purse, 68
amid ecclesiastic, 768
and harmony and grace, 973
and my sentiments are my own, my, 804
bewrays us, our, 122
blameless, 319
give vigor to your, 314
historian's, 359
is but the faintly contemptible vessel, 927
is the dress of thoughts, 222
leave off, 685
of man, Christian is the highest, 174
of the day of judgment, 704
or stance, restrictions on, 923
putting on, 685
read him for, 649
refines, how the, 211
supported by conclusiveness, 1017
to attain an English, 233
went in pretty, 927
your own delightful, 402
Styles, know all fancy, 645
Style 's the man, the, 453
the woman, anyhow, 453
Styx, bath in the, 652
through one small liver flow, 360
Subdue, disease that must, 208
what will not time, 200
Subdued, by time, 200
subduing strain, 568
to what it works in, 108
Subdues mankind, surpasses or, 353
Subduing tongue, tip of his, 109
Subject for song, in want of a, 333
human body as a, 973
man only, 132
myself favourite, 272
not a slave, 304
of all verse, 119

Subject of history the, 1076
of my story, honour is the, 81
such duty as the, owes, 52
they treat best, 1079
to every doubt that can retard, 417
unlike my, shall be my song, 222
we know a, 236
Subjects and paid his, 894
free and loyal, 950
mankind are my, 448
of lives rarely alive, 906
purely political, preach on, 312
wise, were their, 266
Subject's duty is the king's, 67
soul is his own, 67
Subjection, implied, 152
Sublime and the ridiculous, 271
as Milton's immemorial theme, 558
chapters are headed, 1085
contemplative serene, 248
dashed to pieces, the, 319
fulfilments gleam, 626
hope cheers ever the faithful heart, 597
in his simplicity, 466
intolerably just, coldly, 667
make our lives, 433
object all, 624
Schiller has the material, 319
tobacco, 358
Sublimely bad, fustian is, 213
Sublimity of primeval forests, 449
Submerged, landmarks one by one, 1090
Submission, yielded with coy, 152
Subordination and obedience to government, 268
Subscribers, ten and twenty pound, 321
Subsequent proceedings, 645
Subserved whatever occurs, liberty be, 537
Subsistence, even the means of, 1077
obtaining mere, 689
Substance, like a living, 932
lose the, 961
might be called, 150
of his greatness, 131
of ten thousand soldiers, 72
of things hoped for, 1122
there, spent their, 899
true, proves the, 211
wasted his, 1117
Substantial honours, in more, 257
smile, one vast, 495
world, books are a, 301
Substitute, books a bloodless, 704
for inner worth, 961
for sense, no, 899
for talent, no, 922
of exercise or temperance, 196
Sub-Subs, give up, 530
Subtle and indirect expression, 538
flavor of an old pair of sox, 714

Subtle, master under heaven, no more, 471
sad perfume, 644
spell, 891
spider, much like a, 115
thief of youth, 161
ways I keep and pass, 410
Subtle-sweet, more, 596
Subtlety nor the ardour of their hearts, 1074
of intellect, 641
Suburb of the life elysian, 436
Suburban streets, little queer, 911
Succedaneum, no such bad, 402
Success, a minute's, 493
among us render his bettering impossible, 497
as a singist I am not a, 606
but was, 890
depends on three things, 641
gives action its comeliness, 199
haberdashery of, 787
has come too late, 533
he has achieved, 860
how to know, 515
ill, 229
in life means, 904
in practice, 650
in reserve for you, 1033
in smallest matter, 1012
is a rare paint, 163
is counted sweetest, 583
is in the silences, 757
is secure, 345
is your religion, 751
its own reward, 707
men judged by their, 1044
more uncertain in its, 1023
not in mortals to command, 194
nothing succeeds like, 945, 1067
odium of, 707
of a day, 533
of any great moral enterprise, 424
secret of, is constancy, 419
seemed born for, 409
the inevitable result, 513
things ill got had ever bad, 70
unexpected in common hours, 515
with his surcease, 85
Successful at being pompous, not, 1082
experiment, full tide of, 273
soldier, 311
teacher, the, 695
whether the appeal is, 331
Succession, fifth year in, 922
slander lives upon, 38
Successive rise and fall, 219
title long and dark, 173
Successors gone before him, 34
Succor, propitious, 1017
Succory flower is blue, 719
Such a logical way, built in, 452
a questionable shape, 91
a tide as moving, but, 472
apt and gracious words, 41
as sleep o' nights, 81
as words could never utter, 481
has, longing to be mated, 545

Such master such man, 19
mistress such Nan, 19
songs as she heard in dreams, 432
things to be, 469
Suck forth my soul, 31
Suckets, many mellow Cydonian, 431
Suckin' a li'l sleepin', a li'l, 765
Sucking dove, gently as any, 42
Suckle fools and chronicle small beer, 64, 101
Suckled in a creed outworn, 300
Suckling in that mighty land, 932
Sucklings, babes and, 1103
Sucks the nurse asleep, 105
where the bee, 33
Sudden a thought came, 383
and quick in quarrel, 49
clamorous pain, with a, 924
commendations, good at, 74
cry of pain, 877
farewells should be, 357
frown, 620
glory is the passion, 132
if a thing comes in his head, he's, 71
kind, the, 807
storms are short, 59
thought, some, 640
thought strikes me, 292
Suddenly there came a tapping, 460
Suds and in the soap, in the, 660
Suffer a sea change, 32
all alike, 104
fools gladly, 1121
hell l, seems a heaven, 151
lot of man to, 220
nobler in the mind, 93
one bright hour to waste, nor, 474
the sea and the rains, 663
them and they'll o'ergrow the garden, 69
who breathes must, 190
Sufferance, corporal, 36
is the badge of all our tribe, 44
Suffered him these hundred years, 166
you to impose on him, 281
Sufferer, best of men was a, 115
comfort every, 606
pity for the human, 874
says his say, each, 489
Suffering country's stead, 973
ended with the day, her, 473
full extent of, 1087
healed of a, 1087
knowledge entereth by, 428
makes men petty and vindictive, 835
they learn in, 367
to be weak is miserable doing or, 148
undergo severe, 995
yours the, 439
Sufferings of right, 609
poets grow by their, 144
that we have endured, 1087
to each his, 243
Suffice, let this, 29
Sufficiency, an elegant, 224
to be so moral, no man's, 40

Sufficient crime, profane swearing is, 180
  understand me that he is, 44
  unto the day, 1114
Sugar and spice and all things
  nice, 322
  mingled with the sand, 764
  o'er the devil himself, 93
  oil vinegar and saltness, 252
  your fair discourse hath been
  as, 59
Sugar-plum tree, ever heard of
  the, 699
Suicide acts as judge jury and
  executioner, 852
  is a person, 852
  is confession, 342
  no refuge from confession but,
  342
  prevalence of, 741
  proof of insanity, 892
  test of civilization, 741
  the thought of, 1080
  those who commit, 1049
  thwarts the attainment, 1063
Suicides, notorious drunkards,
  651
Suing long to bide, hell it is in,
  25
Suit lightly won, 307
  of ancient black, 857
  of clothes, leads to a, 733
  of sables, 94
  the action to the word, 94
  thrown off this old, 575
  wear a courtly, 511
Suits of grey or gowns of silk,
  558
  of solemn black, 89
  of woe, trappings and the,
  89
  out of, with fortune, 48
  rogues in buckram, 62
Suitable vesture of phrase, 972
Suitors of swarthy complexions,
  511
Sullen dame, our sulky, 287
  heart, knocked on my, 703
  horn, 247
  shields, above the, 891
  sky, smile into the, 923
Sullenness against nature, 162
Sulphur, land of oat-cakes and,
  312
Sultans, poets are, 167
Sultry breath, hurricane's, 554
  passion-flowers, 849
Sum and story, humanity's poor,
  350
  gold in a princely, 750
  make up my, 97
  no inconsiderable, 590
  of a lasting lore, 918
  of all villanies, 226
  of earthly bliss, 154
  of human achievement, 694
  of human happiness, 734
  of human joy, added to the,
  602
  of human things, 275
  of living, makes up the, 565
  of more, giving thy, 48
  of Shakespeare's wit, 409
  swindling with a petty, 533
  total of Thanksgiving lore,
  935

Sum which two married people
  owe, 1057
Sumer is icumen in, 3
Summary of all the meetings,
  933
Summer afternoon, most beautiful words, 766
  and winter, and day and
  night, 1097
  beautiful early, weather, 395
  bird-cage, 128
  cannot last, 665
  comes with flower and bee,
  370
  criticizes, 493
  days come oftest in Kentucky,
  675
  do with this strange, 812
  dream, sprite begotten of, 407
  dust, dry as, 302
  ends now, 672
  eternal, gilds them yet, 359
  evening ripened, 920
  eves by haunted stream, 160
  flowers quicken autumn fruitage thicken, 459
  friends, like, 135
  hath his joys, 121
  in England autumn in France,
  197
  in, quite the other way, 702
  in, whole flocks come, 621
  in your eyes, 871
  labor there all, 738
  last rose of, 335
  laughed, and all the, 585
  life's a short, 231
  made glorious, 71
  night, sound loves to revel in
  a, 459
  nights, dews of, 269
  of her age, in the, 179
  one swallow maketh not, 16
  one swallow never makes a,
  1034
  pale in her bowers, stands, 565
  redundant blueness abundant,
  493
  reign, rose has but a, 305
  sang in me, 915
  skies are darkly blue, 418
  succeeds barren winter, after,
  69
  sweet as, 74
  thy eternal, shall not fade, 107
  to your heart, but, 915
  treads on heels of spring,
  984
  will have its flies, 412
Summers in a sea of glory, 73
  raw inclement, 191
  three-score, appear short as
  one, 223
Summer's day, as one shall see
  in a, 42
  day, compare thee to a, 107
  day, hath a, 165
  flower is to the summer sweet,
  108
  golden languor, 692
  heat, fantastic, 59
  noontide air, 150
  queen, would grace a, 309
  ripening breath, 78
  rose, vernal bloom or, 151
  royal progress, 833

Summer's warmth is in them
  still, 690
  wonder-land, 864
Summer-shine of lengthened
  light, 561
Summer-tide, often in the, 757
Summer-time, in a bowl of
  982
Summit, from the eastern, 277
  harder toward the, 1082
  linger and play on its, 339
  of art, 1073
  of yonder pyramids, 1060
  round by round, mount to its,
  521
  tree's, 384
Summits of great pain, Alpine,
  570
  snowy, 466
Summon up remembrance, 107
  up the blood, 66
Summons, each must go at his,
  511
  thee to heaven or to hell, 86
  upon a fearful, 89
  when thy, comes, 371
Summum nec metuas diem, 155
Sumner's mind, 636
Sumptuous dress, without ruffling
  her, 594
  variety, 617
Sumter far and wide, 706
Sun, a blind spinner in the, 591
  a duty to worship, 641
  a little rain, a little, 348
  all except their, is set, 359
  all-seeing, ne'er saw her match,
  77
  and moon and stars keep pace,
  891
  and moon, commanded to
  stand still, 228
  and moon should doubt, if the,
  281
  and rain, used to, 828
  and shade, through, 465
  and sky and air and light, for,
  846
  and the Father's will, 731
  and the seed, the dust and the,
  929
  as comes to me or cloud or,
  423
  as the, drew the morning dew,
  175
  aweary of the, 'gin to be, 88
  bales unopened to the, 202
  be in eclipse, 807
  bedazzled in the, 52
  before the worshipped, 77
  behold for the last time the,
  341
  between the sundawn and the,
  630
  bewitched, like a, 764
  breaks through darkest clouds,
  as the, 52
  brother and good friend the,
  881
  but brings the constant, 501
  can not be looked at with a
  steady eye, 1043
  can not feel the, 501
  candle in the, 125
  candle to the, 170, 203
  climbs slow, in front the, 519

Sun, clouds around the setting, 302
clouds which seem pavilions of the, 425
comes out as well, 908
common, the air the skies, 245
dawdle in the, 833
declines, our wishes lengthen as our, 202
dedicate his beauty to the, 77
dewdrop from the, 305
die we with the, 575
doth pale his light, the, 514
doubt the, doth move, 92
drew semicircles, 923
dropp'd from the zenith, 149
dry, dry wind, 19
excludes you, not till the, 537
exterminate everyone under the, 937
faces the setting, 759
follow the, 923
from the rising to the going down of the, 1105
fruit I bore was the, 1005
give me the splendid silent, 536
gives light soon as he rises, 228
goes round, take all the rest the, 146
going down of the, at the, 804
golden apples of the, 790
gone down, the, 423
gorgeous as the midsummer, 63
greater are none beneath the, 782
grow dim with age, 195
grows cold, till the, 565, 1027
had risen to hear him crow, thought, 520
had tired the, 553
half in, half in shade, 336
has a right to set, 606
has gone in, 788
has left the lea, the, 310
he sendeth, he sendeth shower, 423
heat o' the, 106
hides not his visage, 57
hills ancient as the, 371
himself must die, 328
his beams display, 168
hooting at the glorious, 316
horses of the, 53, 687
how great the, 793
impearls on every leaf, 153
in all his state, 473
in his coming, meet the, 339
in my dominions never sets, 1059
in the firmament, knowledge is the, 340
in the lap of Thetis, 142
into the warm, 16, 1034
is a thief, 81
is born on its ridges, 318
is but a morning star, 515
is coming down, 576
is gone down while it was yet day, her, 1112
is out and the wind is still, 838

Sun is setting low, 926
Juliet is the, 78
laughed in the, 893
let others hail the rising, 242
lighted nor warmed by the, 747
little window where the, 390
livery of the burnished, 45
looked over the mountain's rim, 485
loss of the, 222
love is nature's second, 28
low descending, 202
magic potent over, 303
marigold goes to bed with, 56
maturing, 384
may bring, next morn's, 983
melts in the sea, 643
moon and stars all sweet things, 407
moon and stars, we might have been, 882
more worshipped the rising, 999
moves always west, 742
mus'n't set on yo' sorrer, 689
nebulous star we call the, 466
never assisted the, in rising, 514
never sets in Spanish dominions, 312
never sets on the empire of Charles V, 311
no new thing under the, 1109
no, no moon no morn, 391
not a face below the, 596
not polluted, 1016
of heaven shall shine, 74
of life has crossed the line, 561
of life is low, my, 795
of righteousness, 1114
of York, 71
once beneath the, 954
passes through dirty places, 112
pay no worship to the garish, 79
pleasant the, 152
question if his glory, when the, 584
reflecting upon the mud, 112
rested on the moor, 920
returned to power, 937
rises bright in France, 345
secret of the, 669
self-same, that shines upon his court, 57
sets on despair, 565
sets to rise again, my, 492
setting, and music at the close, 59
shall greet them, 67
shall not smite thee by day, 1106
shine sweetly on my grave, 269
shines always there, and the, 432
shines everywhere, the, 55
shines, make hay while the, 12, 1036
shineth upon the dunghill, 112
shut doors against a setting, 80
snatches from the, 81
somewhere beneath the, 553

Sun, spinsters and knitters in the, 54
spots and clouds in the, 124
stand still, we cannot make our, 169
stood still and the moon stayed, 1099
surer, one, 592
sweetheart of the, 390
tapers to the, 280
that side the, is upon, 336
the glory of the, 687
the, is a-wait, 663
the tranquil, 638
tinged with the rising, 375
to have enjoyed the, 547
to me is dark, 156
to-morrow's, may never rise, 193
true as the dial to the, 143
unkindly hot, 820
unpolluted, 112
up before the, 424
up rose Emelye and up rose the, 6
upon an Easter-day, 163
viewteh all the world, 68
walk about the orb like the, 55
warm summer, 702
was warm but the wind was chill, 838
web that whitens in the, 337
when the, in all its state, 557
which passeth through pollutions, 112
who lights the morning, 362
wide open to the, 443
will pierce the thickest cloud, 490
with a golden ball, 888
with his planets in chime, 449
with the setting, 149
yet cast out of heaven, 633
Suns and showers, beyond these, 735
and skies and clouds of June, 591
bright, may scorch, 404
golden helmeted, 531
have been, where summer, 933
light of setting, 296
process of the, 464
systemed, 650
that gild the vernal morn, 267
think of all the, 722
to light me rise, 207
where the hours are, 938
will shine, other, 625
Sun's a thief, 81
beams, faster than the, 79
bravado, I met the, 861
rim dips, the, 315
supreme bequest, 642
Sunbeam in a winter's day, 223
soiled by outward touch, 162
Sunbeams, motes that people the, 160
out of cucumbers, 191
pass you by, chances like, 591
play and the women weep, 763
through the fringes raining, 418
Sunbeams' golden glow, gleaming in the, 562
Sunbonnet, pink, 696

Sunburnt by the glare of life, a
    little, 430
    mirth, song and, 383
Sunburst break, saw the dazzling,
    690
Sun-crowned, tall men, 522
Sundawn and the sun, between
    the, 630
Sunday clothes, put on his, 368
    cut your nails on, 956
    from the week divide, 89
    gay, 1073
    killing of a mouse on, 940
Sundays, begin a journey on, 192
Sunday's best, in his, 321
Sunday-school superintendent
    touring peep-shows, 863
Sun-dial quaint and gray, 330,
    597
Sundown, verge of the, 757
Sundry contemplation of my
    travels, 51
Sunflower, fame is the scentless,
    453
    turns on her god, 335
Sung ballads from a cart, 177
    from morn till night, 269
    or said, that ever were, 437
    painted wrought, 442
    songs we, 610
    sweeter than any, my songs,
    444
    under the sea, 335
Sunium's marbled steep, 359
Sunk and here we are, Nantuck-
    et's, 508
Sunless land, sunshine to the, 305
    pleasures of weary people, 645
    retreats of the ocean, 336
    sea, down to a, 315
Sunlight, air is full of, 710
    drinketh dew, as, 462
    not of the moonlight, not of
    the, 472
    on a broken column, 899
    stroked the spine, as if, 929
    strong, somewhere in the, 793
Sunne shineth, make hay when
    the, 12
Sunneshine, flies of estate and,
    135
Sunniest weather, bless you with
    the, 406
Sunny and a little sad, a little,
    637
    fountains, Afric's, 343
    hour, in a, 338
    openings, spots of, 346
    weather, sad thoughts and, 531
    years, life formed of, 454
Sunrise awoke the lark, 687
    falling like red blood, 931
    I face the, 904
    never failed, 619
    sees a new year born, 591
    we who met, 652
Sun-rising, window opened to-
    wards the, 172
Sunset, a little south the, 832
    and evening star, 472
    of life, 't is the, 327
    seams with lines of light, 417
    stand in life's, 643
    tree, come to the, 370
Sunsets have their birth, 814
Sunset's changing hue, 728

Sunset's flush, in the, 833
Sunset-touch just when we are
    safest, 488
Sunshine, after rain, love com-
    forteth like, 106
    and in shade, in, 446
    and laughter, exulted in, 798
    and rain at once, 99
    and rest, region of, 416
    aye shall light the sky, 503
    danger gleams like, 967
    dreaming upon Salmon's
    height, 556
    easy to sit in the, 718
    every hour, hope not, 284
    follows the rain, 523
    glaring, 442
    guard it, storm or, 1058
    hits ye, a bit of, 684
    if all the skies were, 709
    in one eternal, 374
    in the shadie place, 24
    is a glorious birth, the, 301
    joy and life to us, 845
    just think you need some, 678
    of the world's new spring, 337
    on quiet wood and lea, 373
    settles on its head, eternal, 251
    sick of endless, 777
    time asleep in afternoon, 588
    to the lives of others, bring,
    750
    to the sunless land, 305
    which dried all this blood,
    1071
Sun-starts on a stream, as, 749
Sunthin' thet ain't jes' like either
    single, 527
Sun-treader life and light be
    thine, 484
Sunward-soaring bird, power to
    outsoar, 634
Superabundance of life, 330
    random ebullience, 930
Superannuated idol, 196
    pedagogue, 636
Supercilious, my sanctum, 392
    seed, this, 820
Superfluities, happiness lies in,
    454
    make or trade in, 247
Superfluity comes sooner by
    white hairs, 44
    that questionable, small beer,
    417
Superfluous branches, we lop
    away, 60
    lags the veteran, 230
    leisure, 36
    the, a very necessary thing,
    1053
    verse, 439
    weapons, without, 923
Superior holy blessing, possess-
    ing, 972
    man the providence of the infe-
    rior, 602
    soul, mother was a, 883
    soul walk free and own no,
    537
    that they may be, 975
    were manifestly, 975
    who have the best heart the
    best brain, 602
Superiors kindred and friends, we
    face our, 727

Superiority of educated men,
    1015
    of Senate members, 635
    to the rest of the world,
    1072
Superlatives, pestiferous, 771
Superman, between the animal
    and, 1079
    the lightning, 1079
Supernatural, existence of, 769
Superstition defined as construc-
    tive religion, 543
Superstitions, new truths end as,
    564
Superstructure resting on eco-
    nomic foundation, 1086
Supinely stay, fools, 280
Supped full with horrors, 88
Supper, come home with me to,
    60
    I want my, 667
    nourishment called, 40
    proper time for, 1015
    what say you to such a, 221,
    361
Suppers, more have been killed
    by, 137
Suppertime milk toast would do,
    by, 515
Supple as steel, 737
Suppliant, blind, 373
Supplication, lifted in single, 933
Supplied, may be better, 48
Supply, last and best, 210
    on promise of, 64
Support him after, but to, 80
    of the state governments, 273
    of the woman I love, 921
    us all the day long, 1128
    what is low, raise and, 148
Supposes that, if the law, 494
Supreme Coort follows th' ilic-
    tion returns, 796
    hour in woman's life, 717
    worth, it boasts its, 492
Surcease, success with his, 85
Sure and certain hope, 1128
    and firm-set earth, 85
    and slow, reclaimed it, 591
    as a gun, 179
    belief, this is my, 894
    card, he's a, 179
    foundation, no, 58
    he's a talented man, 406
    make assurance doubly, 87
    nor can be true, it is not, 519
    of power and influence, 235
    of, what a man has he is, 1041
    possessing, for thy, 441
Sure-enwinding arms of cool-
    enfolding death, 536
Surely you'll grow double, 295
Surest method of pleasing, 222
    road to national downfall, 450
Surety for a stranger, 1107
Surface, fine glossy, 253
    flow, straws upon the, 177
    flower above the, 575
    look beneath the, 1011
    of opinion, reflected from the,
    972
    stream, below the, 547
Surfeit of the sweetest things, 43
    out of action, 76
    reigns, no crude, 158
    with too much, 44

Surfeits sooner kill than fasts, 163
Surfeiting the appetite may sicken, 53
Surge and thunder of the Odyssey, 674
of cheers, never a, 772
rocking on a stormy, 964
she rides the, 363
whose liquid, resolves, 81
Surges, beneath the endless, 517
labouring, 748
lash the sounding shore, 211
rudest roll, life's, 1059
sing, what the, 501
Surge's angry shock, 231
Surgeon to old shoes, 81
with the help of a, 43
Surgeons spend raptures, 430
Surgeon's hand, waiting his turn for the, 764
Surgery, honour no skill in, 63
hurt past all, 101
Surging of the sea, like the, 568
sea outweighs, the, 410
Surmise, soul's invincible, 770
Surpasses or subdues, 353
Surpassed, man shall be, 1079
Surpassing beauty, 979
Surprise, disturbs me with, 736
flash of a mighty, 736
our hearts in glad, 436
rise to no little, 351
with pained, 912
Surprises, millions of, 136
Surprising, it's not at all, 510
Surrender it voluntarily, not to, 387
of life, 339
unconditional, 549
Surrendered sword of memory, 848
Surrenders, dies but never, 1061
Survey, monarch of all I, 263
the most general, 1064
the plot, we first, 64
Survival, assurance of, 1086
of children through the, 646
of human race, 846
of the fittest, 448, 580
Survive or perish, live or die, 340
Survivors' affair, more the, 1089
Susanna! O don't you cry, 567
was exceedingly delicate, 1126
Suspect teaches them, 45
Suspended oar, drip of the, 353
Suspenders, before the invention of, 314
inclination to twist, 654
Suspense in news is torture, 157
Suspicion and asperity, dismissed, 1056
Caesar's wife above, 999
haunts the guilty mind, 71
Suspicion's sanctuary, 353
Suspicious, religious people deeply, 785
Susquehanna's utmost springs, 279
Sussex grass, bury my body in, 929
songs be sung, 810
Sustaining bread, sympathy's, 595
Susurrus, blue tide's low, 570
Swabs, doctors is all, 704

Swaggering files of sea-thieves, 842
Swain, frugal, 248
remote from cities lived a, 206
Swains commend her, all our, 34
no nightingales, no, 707
ruined, 262
Swaller, we might, our principles, 526
Swallow a camel, 1115
give it the, 812
one, maketh not summer, 16
one, never makes a summer, 1034
swift as the wing of a, 362
that come before the, 56
Swallow's wings, flies with, 72
Swallowed a ramrod, 1007
some books to be, 111
Swallow-flights of song, 468
Swam before my sight, 216
Swamp, fetid stillness of the, 543
lake of the Dismal, 333
Swamps of toil, 733
Oswego spreads her, 250
Swampy bed, from out this, 848
Swan a crow, make thee think thy, 77
and shadow, float double, 298
cygnet to the pale faint, 58
double beauty whenever a, 391
jalous, ayens his deth that singeth, 4
Jupiter in the form of a, 23
Mantuan, ages ere the, 262
of Avon, sweet, 119
on still St. Mary's lake, 298, 391
shook slowly free, 922
spreads his snowy sail, the, 386
to act the part of a, 1007
Swans are geese, all our, 123
asleep, sail like, 881
geese are, and swans are geese, 547
seem whiter when by crows, 1031
Swan-like end fading in music, 45
let me sing and die, 45, 359
Swank, do not like his, 828
Swannanoa, Indian River the Niagara, 932
Swap horses, not best to, 457
Sward, the gowan glitters on the, 288
Swarm, not good for the bee not the, 1011
of bees and honey, 1099
Swashing and martial outside, 48
blow, remember thy, 77
Swat, it borders upon, 679
what's the news from, 679
Sway, above this sceptred, 46
extends her, 1082
impious men bear, 195
little rule a little, 223
of magic potent, 303
prevailed with double, 250
required with gentle, 152
sweeping whirlwind's, 244
undisturbed by passion's, 685
with absolute, 172
Sways she level in her husband's heart, 54

Swear an eternal friendship, 292, 1047
by yonder blessed moon, I, 78
enough to make a deacon, 527
I eat and eat, I, 67
I think there is nothing but immortality, 537
not by the moon, 78
to me upon a parcel-gilt goblet, 64
to that in France, they'll, 406
to the truth of a song, 189
when you rant and, 177
Sweareth to his own hurt, 1103
Swearing is too frequently heard, 179
Swears with so much grace, 186
Sweat but for promotion, 48
for duty not for meed, 48
muck of, 254
of a man's brows, 241
of my brows, 1033
of thy face, in the, 1097
to write a living line, 119
under a weary life, 93
wet with honest, 433
Sweats to death, Falstaff, 61
Sweaty haste, 89
Swedish and Danish have something too Runic, 592
Sweeney shifts from ham to ham, 900
to Mrs. Porter, bring, 899
Sweep for the main, 882
on you fat and greasy citizens, 48
through her marble halls, 433
Sweeping round from place to place, 617
up the heart, the, 584
waves, 371
whirlwind's sway, 244
Sweeps a room, who, 135
clean, new broom, 15
Sweet Afton, flow gently, 286
Alice whose hair was so brown, 521
and bitter fancy, food of, 51
and cunning hand, nature's own, 54
and dear, what is so, 735
and fair she seems to be, 146
and fair, so wondrous, 146
and fitting to die, 930
and for love, love, 536
and gracious even in common speech, 508
and grow old, time to be, 633
and low wind of the western sea, 466
and musical as Apollo's lute, 41
and of their nature vacant, 683
and pure and fair, so, 1065
and twenty, kiss me, 54
and virtuous soul, 135
and voluble is his discourse, 41
and white, sunshine not so, 556
apples anthosmial divine, 431
approach of even, 151
are the thoughts, 940
are the uses of adversity, 48
are the words of love, 618
as English air could make her, 466

Sweet as melancholy, 121
  as Socrates or Plato, 853
  as summer, 74
  as the primrose, 251
  as year by year we lose, 365
  attractive grace, 152
  attractive kinde of grace, 26
  Auburn loveliest village, 250
  Basil, her tears kept ever wet, 384
  Belle Mahone, 579
  bells jangled out of tune, 94
  bitter past more welcome is the, 53
  but then how it was, 489
  childish days, 297
  civilities of life, 176
  closing of an eye, yet the, 480
  content passing all wisdom, 417
  counsel together, we took, 1104
  cruelly, are the echoes, 512
  dashed with a little, 349
  day so cool so calm, 135
  days and roses, 135
  discourse, Sydneian showers of, 165
  disorder in the dress, 133
  doing-nothing, 1009
  every, its sour, 255, 411
  flowers are springing, 336
  food of knowledge, 27
  full of, desolation — balmy pain, 385
  girl graduates, 466
  golden goblet growing, 431
  good-will, 620
  happy children you will rise, 474
  head, turn not away that, 388
  heard melodies are, 383
  I fear to love you, 748
  imperious mouth whose haughty, 418
  in cadence, upon the ear, 266
  in communion, 153
  in faith to muse, 365
  in his mouth, wickedness, 1102
  indifference, 655
  inexpressible as, 718
  influences of Pleiades, 1103
  is a grief, 963
  is death, and, 470
  is every sound, 466
  is half so, 335
  is pleasure after pain, 176
  is revenge to women, 358
  is solitude, how passing, 263
  is the breath of morn, 152
  is true love tho' given, 470
  it is to us, how, 638
  it must be, 671
  keen smell sighing sound, 577
  land of liberty, 447
  little cherub sits up aloft, 274
  lovely fair and smellest so, 103
  Marie, 717
  mercy is nobility's true badge, 76
  milk of concord, 88
  mood, in that, 295
  morsel under his tongue, 187
  naught in this life, 144
  notes of the harpers ring, 387
  nothing half so, in life, 335

Sweet o' the year, 56, 574
  oblivious antidote, 88
  on earth, ways are, 963
  perfections caught, 26
  peril, 593
  Phosphor bring the day, 134
  poison for the age's tooth, 57
  poison of misused wine, 157
  potato, bake him like a, 853
  psalmist of Israel, 1100
  rather have my, 885
  reluctant amorous delay, 152
  repast and calm repose, 245
  revenge at first though, 154
  Roman hand, we do know the, 55
  rose would smell as, 78
  serenity of books, 438
  she is coming my own my, 469
  silent thought, sessions of, 107
  simplicity of the three per cents, 421
  sleep of a labouring man is, 1109
  so coldly, so deadly fair, 355
  so lovely fair and smell'st so, 103
  softly, in Lydian measures, 176
  solitude is, 263
  sorrow, parting is such, 78
  soul shining through them, 593
  sound, o'er my ear like the, 53
  spring full of sweet days, 135
  stolen waters are, 1107
  strains or pensive smiles, 408
  swan of Avon, 119
  sweet sweet, 857
  sweets to the, 97
  tears, fountain of, 297
  the dream of home, 337
  the lily grows, how, 342
  the memory is to me, 438
  the moonlight sleeps, how, 47
  the truth those blessed, how, 503
  their memory still, 266
  Themmes runne softly, 26
  things should be fleet, that such, 632
  time of grace, and that, 454
  time sad time, 389
  to hear the strains, 734
  to hear the watch-dog's bark, 358
  to live with them is far less, 335
  to make the end most, 59
  to taste, things, 59
  to unbend, 'tis, 984
  tooth in his head, 24
  understanding, for thy more, 41
  upon the ear in cadence, 266
  voices, your most, 76
  will, at his own, 297
Sweets, and all its, are gone, 385
  compacted lie, where, 135
  diffuse their balmy, 252
  feast of nectared, 158
  fly lost in the, 205
  grown common lose their delight, 108
  in every fold, rose with, 453
  last taste of, is sweetest last, 59
  of Burn-mill meadow, 298

Sweets of forgetfulness, 269
  of summer, locked from, 866
  sorrow-soothing, 258
  stolen, are best, 194
  to the sweet, 97
  wilderness of, 153
Sweeten my imagination, 99
  present joy, 393
  this little hand, 88
Sweetened by risk, 588
Sweetening and transfiguring power, 1081
Sweeter his thoughts, 618
  manners purer laws, with, 469
  pains of love be, 178
  rose in the bud is, 24
  than any sung my songs, 444
  than honey, 1103
  thy voice, 466
  unsung melodies are, 383
  woman ne'er drew breath, a, 540
Sweetest and the best, 339
  flowers in all the world, 634
  flowres in the forrest, 24
  garland to the sweetest maid, 205
  her smile is the, 388
  li'l feller everybody knows, 730
  morsel of the night, 65
  of all, 618
  Shakespeare fancy's child, 160
  thing on earth, 686
  thing that ever grew, 298
Sweet-fed will flit away, 823
Sweetheart, good-night, 702
  lift to my Western, 864
  light of land and sea, 671
  of mine, that old, 696
  of the sun, 390
  to-morrow, see, 956
  Tray Blanch and, 99
Sweetly to the West, moved so, 375
  played in tune, 287
  sing, brightly smile, 365
  uttered knowledge, 27
  were forsworn, 37
Sweetness and light, 191
  and light, perfect pursuit of, 548
  bringeth fever, bringeth, 929
  fill with, 577
  in the desert air, 245
  instil a wanton, 224
  linked, long drawn out, 160
  loathe the taste of, 62
  of proportion, preserving the, 119
  of the strain, 661
  on the desert air, 245
Sweet-potato vine, bugs off a, 927
Sweet-scented herbs, like flowers and, 515
Sweet-tasting brooks, by the little, 929
Sweet-voiced bird, 665
Swell, and with its mighty, 385
  bosom with thy fraught, 103
  music with its voluptuous, 352
  the soul to rage, 176
  with oily gradual heaves, 833
Swelling and limitless billows, 317

Swelling, angelic songs are, 503
of fresh life within, age, 559
of the heart, 952
of the voiceful sea, 317
Swells from the vale, cliff that, 251
the gale, note that, 245
Swept by great seas, 619
with confused alarms, 546
Swering, false, is yet more re-prevable, 7
gret, is a thing abhominable, 7
Swift and free she carries me. 717
as a shadow, 42
as an antelope, 406
as the wing of a swallow, 362
is less than to be wise, 219
light boats sail, 75
race is not to the, 1110
sharp pain, strike with a, 920
sword, lightning of His ter-rible, 522
the race, not to the, 710
time too, 27
to hear, be, 1122
to spare and slow to smite, 373
too, arrives as tardy as too slow, 79
true hope is, 72
with wings, 855
Swifter than a weaver's shuttle. 1102
Swiftly glides the bonnie boat, 288
Swiftness, curb his, 371
never ceasing, O, 27
of matchless, 219
Swift-winged arrows of light, 264
Swim before my sight, temples, 216
gradual, 385
in, naughty night to, 99
on the beaker's brim, bubbles that, 431
sink or, live or die, 340
to yonder point, 81
Swimmer, a capital, 577
in his agony, 359
like waves to the, 576
Swimmers, the waders and, 930
Swimmer's grasp, till the, 541
Swimmin'-hole, the old, 696
Swims, whenever a swan, 391
Swindles, without a compeer among, 616
Swindling, what looks like, 533
Swine is unclean to you, 1098
pearls before, 1114
shear, all cry and no wool, 142
too rich a pearl for carnal, 142
Swine's snout, jewel in a, 1107
Swing of the sea, out of the, 672
on a grapevine, 431
ports gush, 833
Swinged the dragon, 57
Swinging round the circle, 446
Swings, we pulls up on the, 842
Swinish multitude, 260
Swirls of musk, 696
Switches lock, care that the, 781
Swoop, at one fell, 88
Sword against nation, 1111
and pen, certain of, 778
and the flame, with the, 782
back in the sheath, 827
blood drawn with the, 457

Sword, by her, lay her, 888
character by the, 950
cut it asunder with his, 999
dismal chances of the, 1067
edge sharper than the, 105
famous by my, 164
flesh his virgin, 220
fleshed thy maiden, 63
gird on thy, 668
glorious by my, 164
glued to my scabbard, 129
good, rust, 317
I with, will open, 34
in hand, with, 500
is strength, my, 816
like a surrendered, 848
lightning of his terrible swift, 522
never stained thy, 775
of an angel king, 282
of common sense, 576
of heaven, the, 37
of light, his shining, 756
of power, 373
one, keeps another in sheath, 138
or tongue or pen, done by, 864
pen is preferable to the, 1038
pen mightier than the, 425
rust the sharpest, 309
saw the broken, 659
shall perish with the, 1116
sleep in my hand, 283
stir the fire with a, 1016
take away the, 425
that ever buckled, 516
the avenging, unsheathe, 1060
the brave man draws, 219
the brave man with a, 722
the chisel and palette, the, 730
the deputed, 36
to him that shall succeed me, my, 172
while for the, 1073
within its scabbard, 848
within the scabbard keep, 176
worse than the, 123
Swords and to work, then out, 1085
into ploughshares, 1111
leaped from their scabbards, 260
of Caesars, 735
sheathed their, for lack of ar-gument, 66
twenty of their, 78
Sworn to weed and pluck away, 59
twelve, 35
Sycamore tree, under a, 255
Sydneian showers of sweet dis-course, 165
Syene Meroë Nilotic isle, 156
Syllabes jar with time, 120
Syllable, chase a panting, 263
men's names, 157
No, could not pronounce that, 1001
of recorded time, to the last, 88
Syllables govern the world, 130
Sylvan hall, 595
home, when I am safe in my, 408
Sylvia, who is, 34

Symbol and a sign, as a, 586
wrong, interpreting the sim-plest, 893
Symbols and in signs, nature speaks in, 442
of a high romance, 384
Symmetry, frame thy fearful, 281
of shelves, 323
of their shapes and sizes, 970
Sympathetic tear, the, 246
tears, sacred source of, 243
Sympathies, killing the victim's, 635
Sympathy and shame, one voice of, 513
charity kindness, 736
cold to distant misery, 270
lightning-flash of, 736
of a nation, 419
the silver link the secret, 307
with other men, tie of, 415
with sounds, in souls, 266
Sympathy's sustaining bread, 595
Symphony of living, 473
Symptoms as her own, recognized the, 821
they find, appropriate all, 124
Synonym for the devil, 397
Syntax, I only said the, 585
Syracusans, eight victories over the, 969
Syrian sands, 442
Syrup, so glutinous a, 933
Syrups, drowsy, of the world, 102
System, apparatus of the, 331
hub of the solar, 454
of hard labour, 1074
of plunder, 1072
social, could not subsist, 1053
survived unshaken, if our, 909
the energies of our, 687
Systems and of creeds, dust of, 462
into ruin hurled, 207
our little, 467
Systemed suns, 650

T, fitted him to a, 238
manage this matter to a, 241
performed to a, 1025
Tabaco, no tengo, no tengo papel, 895
Tabernacles of Israel, 1099
Tabitha, disciple named, 1118
Table, adorn the proudest, 846
and listen, remain at your, 1090
and these papers, moved by this, 1090
at the round, 64
behave mannerly at, 702
best of the cards at the, 640
crumbs which fall from the, 1115
earth, whose, 357
general joy of the whole, 87
head of the, 1040
Mountain, I reside at, 644
of my memory, 92
on a roar, set the, 97
pounded on the, 857
rose from the, sober, 166
Round, I know the, 470
write it before them in a, 1111
Tables brown and bare, 905

Tables, he wrote upon the, 1098
  make it plain upon, 266
  my, meet it is, 92
  near a thousand, pined, 295
  of the money-changers, 1116
  the marriage, 90
Tablecloths, no one thinks of, 905
Table-talk, serve for, 46, 1028
Taboo, inhibit thy, 882
Tackle trim, sails filled, 157
Tact blessing to a woman, 696
  possessing the most social, 724
  tried, 702
  unaccompanied by, 830
Tadpole poet, 635
  shapes of the human, 775
  when you were a, 734
Tail a leg, if you call a, 458
  as sharp and narrow, 855
  came through, hole where his, 321
  eel of science by the, 215
  flanged and battering, 888
  fox when he lost his, 122
  go to the ground, 12
  gradually shades into obscurity, 558
  hangs loose, 858
  he had a, 665
  his distinguished, 735
  his ears his eyes, 220
  is enormouse, 876
  little chap with wagging, 760
  monstrous, our cat has, 189
  of rhyme, dock the, 451
  pig's, never a good shaft, 138
  that wagged contempt, 736
  tied in the, 932
  tucked in, with his, 815
  wags his shaggy, 574
Tails of sparrows, salt upon the, 191
  smoking free, white, 934
Tailless fox, 635
  man, a, 665
Tailor is a man of sense, 451
  lown, he called the, 101
  my Balfour, 629
Tailors, nine, make a man, 380
  Tooley Street, 578
Tailor's news, swallowing a, 58
Taine, and all is entertaining, enter, 942
Taint of vice, 56
Tainted, in law what plea so, 46
  wether of the flock, 46
Take a seat said the cow, 345
  a wyf with-oute avysement, 7
  all the rest, 146
  any shape but that, 87
  away the sword, 425
  better to give than to, 13
  care of the pence, 222
  care of the sense, 598
  comfort, 619
  each man's censure, 91
  heed lest he fall, 1120
  her up tenderly, 392
  him for all in all, 90
  I give it willingly, 1063
  I wish you 'd, me, 389
  it as it comes, 624
  just, a trifling handful, 569
  mine ease in mine inn, 63
  no note of him, 39

Take note take note O world, 103
  O boatman thrice thy fee, 1063
  O take those lips away, 37
  physic pomp, 99
  some savage woman, 464
  some to pleasure, 209
  the current when it serves, 83
  the good the gods provide thee, 176
  the prison'd soul, 158
  the whole range of imaginative literature, 480
  their grace, from which they, 458
  time enough, 221
  to following where He leads, 609
  who have the power, they should, 298
  ye each a shell, 216
  you a button-hole lower, 41
Taken at the flood, 83
  that which he hath, shall be, 1116
  to be well shaken, when, 288
Takin' notes, a chiel's amang ye, 286
Taking and in giving, just in, 565
  having and giving, worth the, 894
  trouble, capacity for, 379
  what a, was he in, 34
Taking-off, deep damnation of his, 85
Takes his leave, but never, 510
  off his shoes, he who sees, 431
  the strangest liberties, he, 510
Tale, a plain, shall put you down, 62
  an honest, speeds best, 72
  and rhyme float with us, 734
  as 't was said to me, 306
  baited with a dragon's, 146
  crude hard-fisted, 713
  every, condemns me, 72
  every shepherd tells his, 160
  every tongue brings in a several, 72
  faith in the, 982
  goes that Herne the hunter, an old, 35
  has got little in it, 689
  hope tells a flattering, 395
  hope told a flattering, 395
  hope whispered, when every, 455
  in everything, find a, 295
  moon takes up the wondrous, 194
  must be told by moonlight, 388
  of a lifeboat, 658
  of a tub, some, 1025
  of an ancient wrong, 612
  of folly, a, 608
  of her days is done, 954
  of more prevailing sadness, 327
  of mortal maladies, 718
  of my whole course of love, 100
  of perjury and strife, 373
  of Troy divine, 161
  of wayward love, 685
  of woe, to tell, 608
  or history, ever hear by, 42
  point a moral or adorn a, 230

Tale, round unvarnished, 100
  sad, is best for winter, 56
  scarce believe the, 562
  telle his, untrewe, 5
  tempted to reveal a, 716
  that I relate, 264
  that is told, as a, 1105
  that's easy told, 851
  thereby hangs a, 34, 49, 1026, 1042
  thou dost excuse, longer than the, 79
  to tell, just one, 851
  to tell, thy humble, 544
  told by an idiot, 88
  told by moonlight alone, 388
  told by one who had it of his father, 616
  twice-told, tedious as a, 58, 220
  unfold, I could a, 91
  untrue, lest men suspect your, 206
  was undoubtedly true, 673
  which holdeth children, 27
  whoso shal telle a, 5
  you may tell the, 716
Tales, aged ears play truant at his, 41
  be told, my, 832
  fear in children increased with, 109
  if ancient, say true, 352
  of frail and erring men, 907
  of the poets, 974
  out of school, 13
  sack of dry tall, 927
  tell and gather, 217
  that to me were so dear, 388
Tale-bearers bad as tale-makers, 279
Talent does what it can, 594
  doing easily what others find difficult, 1073
  for making new friends, 608
  his single, well employed, 231
  no substitute for, 922
  to each a certain inward, 379
  tomb of a mediocre, 788
Talents, Dryden possessed of splendid, 397
  in a man's power, 529
  let them use their, 54
Talented man, sure he's a, 406
Talk among people, great, 181
  and never think, 120
  from getting overwise, 839
  gives room for, 1046
  how he will, 186
  is of bullocks, whose, 1125
  loves to hear himself, 79
  mincemeat of the very smallest, 430
  night is crept upon our, 83
  not of wasted affection, 435
  of dreams, true I, 77
  of graves of worms, 59
  of his horse, nothing but, 44
  of many things, to, 598
  of nothing but high life, 254
  of the lips, 1107
  of the town, 181
  of wills, choose executors and, 59
  one thing think another, 988
  only to conceal the mind, 203

Talk, small, dies in agonies, 367
  spent an hour's, withal, 41
  then you shouldn't, said the Hatter, 598
  'tis no time to, 70
  to beare, fooles, 25
  too much, think too little and, 173
  was like a stream, 405
  who never think, they always, 173, 189
  with, witty to, 164
  with you walk with you, 44
Talkative bald-headed seaman, 881
  old age by nature rather, 981
  Samuel as Peeps, 637
Talked like poor Poll, 243
  Lord how it, 131
  of me, I believe they, 201
Talker, he is a, 968
  he is a wonderful, 1046
Talkers are no good doers, 71
  are usually great, 1055
Talking age, for, 250
  disease of, 120
  Frenchman always, 237
  good old man, he will be, 39
Talks mighty loud, 688
  of roaring lions, 57
Tall ancestral trees, 370
  daughter of the gods divinely, 463
  fellow, many a good, 61
  if she was, 840
  men had empty heads, 113
  men sun-crowned, 522
  oaks from little acorns grow, 292
  ship, all I ask is a, 832
  stone temple, 896
  to reach the pole, so, 199
Taller, sorry you are, 901
  than any of his court, 191
Tally, score and, no books but, 69
Talmud and Alcoran, 110
Talon thin, with, 1078
Tam o' Shanter dog, 691
Tam was glorious, 287
Tambourines jing-jing-jingled, 856
Tame lover, 134
  the heyday in the blood is, 95
  the tongue no man can, 1122
  though I seem, 18
  which earth can never, 404
  which thou canst not, 135
Tamed and shabby tigers, 816
Tamer of the human breast, 243
Taming hand, time hath a, 403
Tammany cooks spoil the broth, 935
Tammie glow'red amazed, 287
Tangible whole, blend in one, 767
Tangle, to-morrow's, 1018
Tangles of Neæra's hair, 159
Tangled business of the world, 466
  web we weave, 308
Tankards scooped in pearl, 584
Tanned reaper in his hour of ease, 552
Tant pis and tant mieux, 242
Tape, bound with red, 497
Taper lights, a thousand, 643

Tapers, answer ye evening, 451
  swim before my sight, 216
  to the sun, glimmering, 280
Taper's light, hope like the, 252
Taper-light, to seek the eye of heaven, 58
Tapestry, speech like to, 996
  weavers, 569
  with a piece of, 1041
Tapping of a blind man's stick, 850
  suddenly there came a, 460
Taproots of New England trees, 927
Tar water is of a nature so mild, 203
  wine that tasted of, 811
Tars, gallant, are our men, 242
Tar's labour, cheers the, 358
Tara lieth low, 792
Tara's halls, harp through, 334
Tardy as too slow, too swift as, 79
  recompense, 596
  though somewhat, 1020
Tare-and-agers girls, which av yez owns the child, 375
Tariffs, trade a matter of, 739
Tarn of Auber, dank, 461
Tarnish that goes at a touch, 838
Tarnished gold, black with, 288
Tarred and feathered and carried in a cart, 443
Tarry at Jericho, 1100
Tarshish unto Tyre, from, 777
Tarsus, ship of, 157
Tartary, talked it out in, 889
Task accomplished, my, 693
  and though hard be the, 557
  before civilization, greatest, 740
  by God assigned, 543
  common, trivial round, 365
  delightful, 224
  disgusted with the, 948
  each day will bring its, 591
  finish well our, 671
  is smoothly done, now my, 158
  it is an irksome word and, 481
  labourer's, 402
  moving waters at their priest-like, 385
  no, too steep for human wit, 983
  of governing it well, 595
  of happiness, 703
  of life and art, 771
  reads as a, 234
  remaining before us, dedicated to the great, 456
  that comes your way, 870
  the holiest, 445
  to Englishmen becomes romance, 727
  to mankind given, not a, 638
  trained by a, 872
  undertaken in adventurous spirit, 727
  whose sore, 89
  worldly, 106
Tasks are done, 682
  bends itself to loving, 525
  equal to your powers, 613
  in hours of insight, 546
  little, make large return, 566
  urgent sordid, 1087

Tasks, years have hardier, 927
Task-master's eye, in my great, 161
Tasselled corn, stalk of the, 642
Tassels, the larch has hung his, 370
Taste accurate refined and chaste, 972
  ashes to the, 352
  choice of Attic, 162
  feeling and inheritance, questions of, 635
  for dolce far niente, 1076
  for popular tunes, 821
  has reigned, except where pure, 680
  inch-rule of, 635
  insipid to a vulgar, 788
  its sole arbiter is, 461
  last, of sweets is sweetest last, 59
  man's hand is not able to, 43
  never, who always drink, 189
  not handle not, 1121
  of death but once, the valiant, 82
  of death, this is the, 958
  of fame, man who never knew 426
  of musick painting or architecture, 196
  of rest, 588
  of sweetness, loathe the, 62
  of your quality, give us a, 92
  sans, sans everything, 50
  the whole of it, let me, 489
  their valour, to, 55
  when you married me, you had no, 279
  whose mortal, brought death, 148
  wild vicissitudes of, 231
  with a little more, 1052
Tastes, speak of faded, 673
Tasted, some books to be, 111
Tattered and torn and hanging in rags, flags, 641
  clothes, through, 99
  ensign down, tear her, 450
Tatters, tear a passion to, 94
Taught, being, return to plague, 85
  following what we are, 1007
  genius never can be, 175
  happy is he born or, 114
  her dazzling fence, 158
  highly fed and lowly, 53
  him shame, love, 176
  it, me how to die, 405
  me at last to forget thee, 587
  me, folly's all they, 336
  me to love working and reading, 199
  men must be, 212
  mind what I am, 339
  saints who, 205
  the wheedling arts, we first were, 205
  the world to see, 167
  to stray, science never, 207
  too much quickness ever to be, 209
  truth at His requiring, 442
  us how to die, 205
  us how to live, 205
Taughte, afterward he, 5

Taughte and first he folwed it himselve, 5
Taunt of death, final, 924
  with gladness, take the, 952
  ye with my latest breath, 447
Tavern, I am come to a, 198
  I'll keep a little, 916
  on our pilgrimage, 833
  one flash of it within the, 1019
  opened a, instead of a home, 802
  or inn, a good, 236
  room, brothers in the, 664
  tidy, to keep the, 655
Tax, cursed war and racking, 309
  for being eminent, 191
  levied on commodities, 232
  not you you elements, 98
Taxes, certain to increase, 271
  death and, 228, 314
  generally raised on city land, 582
  impoverished by payment of, 974
  nothing truer than, 496
Taxation, pressure of, 314
  unnecessary, becomes extortion, 628
  would be lightened, 588
Tax-bill and assessor, 453
Taxed for speech, 53
  horse and bridle, 314
  top, whips his, 314
Taxpayer incapable of a grand passion, 774
Te deums of the Canterbury bells, 831
Tea and cakes and ices, after, 900
  boiled down to a kind of, 323
  glad I was not born before, 314
  hour dedicated to afternoon, 666
  is like the east, 828
  minister came to, 818
  some sipping, 296
  sometimes take, 212
  thank God for, 313
  what would the world do without, 313
  without a stratagem, take her, 203
Teas where small talk dies in agonies, 367
Teach bloody instructions, 85
  gladly would he learn and, 5
  high thought, but to, 471
  him how to live, 268
  him how to tell my story, 100
  in song, what they, 367
  me only teach Love, 485
  me to feel another's woe, 216
  me to live, 183
  men to die, 1027
  men to live, 1027
  souls to souls can never, 501
  the rest to sneer, 213
  the young idea how to shoot, 224
  thee all things, time shall, 477
  thee safety, ladyship is by to, 57
  us good Lord to serve Thee, 1024

Teach us to number our days, 1105
Teacher affects eternity, 636
  better to want a, 563
  defends his pupils, 393
  for us a liberator for her, 595
  let nature be your, 295
  of the man, 960
  sea as a moral, 570
  successful, 695
  who can arouse, 1057
  whom she learned to love, 595
Teachers, men are my, 207
  more understanding than my, 1106
  nine tenths of our university, 871
Teacher's doctrine sanctified, 303
Teaching by examples, philosophy, 200
  in, me the way to live, 405
  no sort of scientific, 1074
  the whole art of, 1078
  was quite untrue, 783
Teachings, list to nature's, 371
Team of little atomies, 77
Teapot, tempest in a, 1012
Tear a passion to tatters, 94
  bedims the eye, never a, 644
  cost a sigh a, 273
  down childhood's cheek, 309
  drop a, 168
  drop a, and bid adieu, 225
  drying up a single, 360
  each others' eyes, 198
  every woe can claim a, 355
  falling of a, 306
  followed perhaps by a smile, 264
  gave to misery all he had a, 245
  her tattered ensign down, 450
  in her eye, 307
  is an intellectual thing, 282
  law which moulds a, 289
  little, all I crave, 382
  man without a, 328
  master speaker is the, 840
  may be forgotten, 763
  meed of some melodious, 159
  nothing worth a, 601
  on his eyelids, 664
  one particular, 109
  passage of an angel's, 383
  perhaps 't will cost a sigh a, 273
  recording angel dropped a, 242
  shed no, 129, 385
  shed one English, 401
  stain it with hypocritic, 374
  stands trembling in her eye, 220
  sympathetic, the, 246
  that flows for others' woes, 267
  that we shed, 334
  the groan the knell, the, 363
  to memory given, 291
  wiped with a little address, 264
Tears, alike are sent, joys and, 423
  all her sorrow all her, 322
  all in vain, 595
  and kiss again with, 466
  and laughters, 428

Tears, and smiles, kisses 299
  are even their, 634
  are in the falling rain, 793
  are shed, 682
  back to fruitless, 690
  beauty smiling in her, 327
  behold their, hear their cries, 1059
  big round, in piteous chase, 48
  blotted all over with, 482
  bored to, 781
  bring me your, 335
  child of misery baptized in, 269
  cloud of, 664
  costs the soul a thousand, 707
  could not bear a mother's, 982
  crocodile, 29, 125
  declined into the vale of, 102
  dimmed them too, 382
  dip their wings in, 468
  down Pluto's cheek, 161
  dried one mourner's, 593
  drop fast as the Arabian trees, 104
  droppings of warm, 967
  far fewer far softer, 553
  fell for me, 1093
  flattered to, 383
  foolish, would flow, 583
  for all souls in trouble, 418
  for lovers, too many, 384
  for me, keep your, 335
  for the men, 664
  fountain of, 676
  fountain of sweet, 297
  from some divine despair, 466
  from off all faces, wipe away, 1111
  he slipped, on its slow, 836
  hence these, 979
  her income, 134
  her smiles and, 99
  idle tears, 466
  if you have, prepare to shed them now, 83
  in a passion of, 493
  in secret in silence and, 587
  in the mist of, 748
  kept ever wet, 384
  leaves millions in, 431
  like Niobe all, 90
  must stop for every drop, 392
  need never be ashamed of our, 498
  nor all your, wash out a word, 1019
  nothing is here for, 157
  now am full of, 790
  of a child, 814
  of boyhood's years, 336
  of eternity, 744
  of tender sorrow, 1074
  of the mother, 889
  of the sky for loss of the sun, 222
  of woe, smiles of joy, 336
  part with, 632
  parted in silence and, 351
  pay me honor with, 978
  rejoices at your, 1074
  resolves the moon into salt, 81
  seven or eight large, 691
  shall drown the wind, 85
  she stood in, 383
  shower of commanded, 52

Tears, so weary of toil and of, 595
source of sympathetic, 243
sprang to their meeting eyes, 658
such as angels weep, 149
that bring no healing, 546
that speak, 168
that's wrought with, 728
their eyes had, 1065
there was dearth of woman's, 447
they that sow in, 1106
thoughts too deep for, 302
through a bright cloud of, 900
time with a gift of, 633
too proud for, 760
undimmed by human, 737
vale of, beyond this, 306
we waste, 779
weep thy girlish, 735
wept away in transient, 455
were given, all my, 475
world's a vale of, 568
wronged orphans', 129
Tearful willows, 602
Tearing, give me but a, 828
Teat, milk from many a rocky, 814
Teche, and gladly, 5
Technique! the very word, 892
Techstone, war's red, 527
Tedious as a twice-told tale, 58, 220
as go o'er, returning as, 87
as to work, to sport as, 61
books without lies extremely, 1078
flat and stale, dinner speeches are, 601
nights, shorten, 121
pomp of writ, 591
thinking his prattle to be, 60
waste of time, what honour that but, 156
years, twenty, 220
Teeming globe, on the, 917
wonder of his words, 847
Teeth are set on edge, the children's, 1113
clean, keep their, 76
crumbling, 473
in spite of my, 10
of time, give lettered pomp to, 442
sans eyes sans taste sans, 50
skin of my, escaped with the, 1102
spight of his, 10
take care of the, 969
those who have no, 434
whiteness of his, 566
Teetot'lers seem to die, 909
Tegumai alone, comes, 784
Telephone, some one invented the, 935
Telescope ends, where the, 1069
Tell a hundred, might, 90
a tale of woe, 608
all he sees or hears, 181
all my bones, I may, 1103
and gather tales, 217
him I lingered alone on the shore, 418
how the truth may be, I cannot, 306

Tell it not in Gath, 1100
it to forget, 575
me not in mournful numbers, 433
me the tales, 388
me what you eat, 1059
the archer, this feat of, 1059
the mischief the virtuous do, 483
the world, I'll, 36
them I came, 822
when or how I can not, 577
your resolution beforehand, never, 130
Telle his tale untrewe, 5
Telling not arguing, 612
that goes with the giving, 660
the battle was on once more, 552
those blessed strains are, 503
Tells no truths, music, 506
Tell-tale women, hear these, 72
Temerity to believe in nothing, 1072
undertaken with, 969
Temper, enforce with, 240
hot, leaps over cold decree, 44
justice with mercy, 155
man of such a feeble, 81
of chums, the, 776
of her own, 678
thy steady, 194
touch of celestial, 152
when he's well dressed, in good, 495
which bears the better, 68
Temperance, a tendency to, 975
and industry, 1054
bell, rapture rang the, 566
more difficult than abstinence, 238
sobriety presence of mind, 1048
substitute of exercise or, 196
teaches him to control it, 1054
that may give it smoothness, 94
Temperament and not income, 788
artistic, 571
of Americans, 571
Temperate and furious in a moment, 86
diet, benefits a, 985
pulses flow, whose, 685
will, the reason firm the, 299
Temperature, radiators lose their, 911
Tempered every blow, 626
Tempers the wind, God, 242
Tempest and from sun. shaded from, 796
description of a, 1012
in a teapot, 1012
itself lags behind, 264
of abuse, rain a very, 971
scorns a chain, 402
the, raves, 667
they that defy the, 1051
to the field, 106
weather, better the, 678
Tempests dieth, the noise of, 480
glasses itself in, 355
loved to course with, 934
roar, billows never break nor, 187

Tempests, with rising, 194
Tempest's roar, the spray and the, 502
Tempest-tossed, the homeless, 694
Tempestuous petticoat, 133
Temple, better than in the, lost, 1019
built to God, 138
called his body, builder of a, 515
hangs on Dian's, 76
his train filled the, 1111
Holy, of Mecca, 1126
in that dread, 783
in the very, of delight, 384
let each new, 452
Lord's anointed, 86
made of bark and thong, 896
of Dian in Ephesus, 956
of Diana, burnt the, 145
of fame, 950
of silence and reconciliation, 399
of Solomon, priests in the, 418
once complete, of a, 501
that may stand too long, 896
the Lord is in his holy, 1113
where God hath a, 126
within my earthly, 719
Temples bare, my, 316
dedicated to God, 339
groves were God's first, 372
like gold nails in, 526
of his gods, 400
solemn, the great globe itself, 33
swim before my sight, 216
to the market-place, 896
Temple-walls to shut thee in, 709
Temporal power, shows the force of, 46
things which are seen are, 1120
Temporary safety, to obtain a little, 226
Tempt the pilgrim steps of spring, 668
Temptation, Abraham found faithful in, 1125
be a book, let my, 698
comes in fine gay colors, 187
greater is he who is above, 393
life's supreme, 834
little claim to virtue without, 387
many a dangerous, 169
resist everything but, 724
that endureth, 1122
to yield is the way to get rid of, 723
why comes, 491
ye're aiblins nae, 285
Temptations, in spite of all, 623
into account, take, 685
Tempter, so glozed the, 154
Tempting, equally remote and, 1021
Ten and twenty pound subscribers, 321
cents an ounce, 870
commandments, complained of the, 478
commandments, covenant. the. 1098
commandments, my, 69

Ten commandments, nearly as strong as the, 582
days' wonder at the least, 70
hours to the world allot, 275
low words in one dull line, 211
men went along, 924
passably effective sonnets, 921
shall heed the call, 851
shillings and no more, I did give, 181
thousand a year, virtuous on, 563
thousand celestials, 271
thousand several doors, death hath, 127
thousand soldiers, 72
thousand strong to the end, 850
times faster glide than the sun's beams, 79
times more comfort, 29
times ten, live for, 1069
to one, 'tis, 1036
winters more, ran he on, 178
years' war, cause of a long, 185
Tens o' thousands thou hast slain, 284
Tenacious of life, 330
Tenant be, who would not, 948
ne'er shall pay, 948
Tenantless, graves stood, 89
save to the wind, 353
Tend, to thee we, 231
Tendance spend, in so long, 26
Tendency to fill up, nothing has a, 261
Tender and true, Douglas, 9, 567
babes alone in the dark, 323
Bible tales, taught you, 657
for another's pain, 243
inward of thy hand, 108
of our friends, 197
pauses speak, 373
respect more, 76
spot, 678
word forgotten, 642
Tenderest, the bravest are the, 565
touch, we feel the, 177
Tender-handed stroke a nettle, 204
Tenderly, take her up, 392
Tenderness for which I long, 681
found pity in his, 626
mothers' arms are made of, 1067
purest heartiest, 538
takes up the meanest subjects with, 331
Tendrils strong, with, 301
Tends to disappear, evil, 581
Tenement of clay, 173, 753
Teneriff or Atlas unremoved, 153
Tenets, his faith in some nice, 167
turn with books, 209
Tennessee, evening folded on, 798
flag's come back to, 569
Tenor of his way, 268
of their way, noiseless, 245
of whose way, even, 685
Tenseness of humiliating pain, 939
Tension, nerves at angry, 895

Tension of a man, try the, 651
war brings to its highest, 1090
Tent, made a white-walled, 922
battleground fortress, 816
nightly pitch my moving, 306
of blue, upon that little, 722
strike the, 565
that is gathered and gone, 618
that searches to the bottom, 75
the little green, 439
thrust out of his, 166
Tents, Arab, 338
armourers from the, 67
fold their, like the Arabs, 434
how goodly are thy, 1099
in all climes pitch our, 771
of green, silent, 439
of wickedness, 1105
strike its white, 371
the little green, 439, 763
their silent, are spread, 541
within whose magic, 668
Tented field, action in the, 100
Tenth transmitter of a foolish face, 223
Tenth-rate poeticule, 635
Tenting on the old camp-ground, 608
Tenui musam meditamur avena, 312
Tenure of the law, strongest, 977
Terbaccy, eatin' their, 851
Terence O'Reilly, I'm, 954
Term that is harsh, 822
Terms, good set, 49
in plain, 45
in uncompromising, 748
litigious, 162
of friendship, lived on, 981
of its own genus, 886
Termagant, o'er-doing, 94
Terminal, swift towards life's, 717
Terrace walk and half a rood of land, 214
Terrene form a terrene use, body but a, 826
Terrestrial life, 543
stress, feel of old, 651
Terrible as an army with banners, 1110
as hell fierce as ten furies, 150
atrocious thing, war a, 1077
do something, 935
example, profit by, 153
grumble rumble and roar, 552
he rode alone, 1092
hour, it is the, 804
lightning of His, swift sword, 522
man with a terrible name, 322
meek, the, 817
plague, she proved a, 941
pour, 815
storm and shipwreck, 658
Territories will never be usurped, 1051
Territory does not make a nation, 563
vast, and its, 748
Terror, death armed with a new, 331
doubt and division, shelter from, 532
fills the world with, 434

Terror in your threats, there is no, 83
risk of reigns of, 581
shadows have struck more, 72
shows, all ways of dying, 824
tongued-tied through some, 964
touches me when, 923
Terrors clad, come not in, 349
king of, 1102
never felt before, fantastic, 460
Tess, ended his sport with, 651
Test, love that stands the, 747
of a blameless style, 319
of an author, 554
of breeding, 720
of brine, stand the, 834
of civilization, 235, 414
of merit, 376
of our progress, 877
of ridicule, truth the, 280
of truth, ridicule the, 377
we need no fuller, 501
Testament as worldlings, a, 48
blessing of the old, 109
of bleeding war, open the purple, 60
of Grunnius Corocotta Porcellus, 125
Testimonies are my meditations, 1106
Testy pleasant fellow, 196
Testyment, no furder than my, 526
Tetchy and wayward, 72
Tête d'armée, 1061
Tether, at the end of my, 283
life and death upon one, 914
stronger than life our, 778
Teuton Kelt I count them, Slav, 471
Texas, lie buried there in, 711
Text is old, 106
neat rivulet of, 279
one unquestioned, 452
variations in the, 238
Texts of despair of hope of joy or moan, 525
Texture of every enduring work of art, 710
of men's souls, know the, 797
Thais sits beside thee, lovely, 176
Thalatta! Thalatta! hail to thee, 1066
Thaliarchus, it is cold O, 868
Thames afire, bids you set the, 780
and all the rivers, 927
fire to the, 246
flow gently, sweet, 932
most loved of ocean's sons, 166
runne softly, sweete, 26
the noblest river in Europe, 197
the tiny, 637
with no allaying, 168
Thamus uttered with a loud voice, 428
Thane, your face my, 84
Thank God for life, 610
God for work, 524
God you are rid of a knave, 39

Thank heaven fasting, 50
  me no thankings, 80
  thee Jew for teaching word, 47
  with brief thanksgiving, 632
  you and if you please, 746
  you for your voices, 76
Thanks and thanks, no answer
    but, 55
  and use, both, 35
  do you get, what, 909
  embarrassing, 702
  evermore, 59
  for health the midday sun the
    impalpable air, 538
  for life and loves and lures,
    631
  for this relief much, 89
  in old age, 538
  my special, 545
  of millions yet to be, 363
  taken with equal, 94
  the exchequer of the poor, 59
  to my friends, 199
  to thee, Most High, 777
  words are but empty, 194
Thanked, when I'm not, at all,
    229
Thankful for, what you're being,
    935
  hand, receive it with a, 985
  rest and be, 946
Thankfulness, replete with, 68
Thankings, thank me no, 947
Thankless arrant, 21
  child, to have a, 98
  inconsistent man, 202
  muse, meditate the, 159
Thanksgiving day, for all of this,
    619
  like ambassadors, 935
  lore, sum total of, 935
  our, accept, 628
  Street, house in, 667
  to the vine, 404
  unto the Lord, 541
  we thank with brief, 632
Thar and then, 639
Tharshish, the navy of, 1101
That and a' that, 284
  ever buckled sword, 516
  ever I was born, 92
  fierce thing they call, 392
  has been and may be, 298
  I may call my own, 451
  in a boundless universe, 462
  it should come to this, 90
  questionable superfluity small
    beer, 417
  that is, 56
  the world had never been, 559
  we two were Maying, oh, 523
  which I desired, it is, 1126
  which needs to be proved,
    1081
  which we wish, believe, 1043
That's another story, 241
Thatch, deep, 810
Thatched cottage, my lowly, 365
Thaw and resolve itself into a
    dew, 89
Theatre, as in a, 60
  expands, how wide the, 326
  is the house of life, 844
  not to go to the, 1064
  universe serves for a, 1029
  wide and universal, 49

Theatre, world's a, the earth a
    stage, 129
Theatres and other places, 1049
Theban, this same learned, 99
Thebes or Pelops' line, present-
    ing, 161
Thebes's streets, walked about in,
    332
Thee fully forth emerging, 537
  I think of, 393
  there's no living with, 196
  to die for her is serving, 451
Theft, took the kindness and for-
    gave the, 490
Theirs but to do and die, 467
  not to make reply, 467
  not to reason why, 467
Them by others mastered, 963
  that has gits, 687
  that help themselves, help, 962
  that men call free, 963
Theme, choose a mighty, 531
  example as it is my, 167
  fools are my, 351
  glad diviner's, 173
  I scarce can name, 475
  of the touching ballad, 364
  they become eloquent, on this,
    1078
  what is their, 824
Themmes, sweete, 26
Themselves and that is all, they
    find, 706
Theocrite, sang, 487
Theocritus! Pan's pipe was thine,
    649
Theologians, surrounded by dead,
    930
Theology lecture, notes on, 885
Theorbo and voice, 164
Theoric, bookish, 100
Theories in face of opposition,
    support his, 837
  repudiate these new fangled,
    419
Theory, condition not a, 419
  of technique, no, 893
  of the universe, 537
  risked a cause, patriots for a,
    430
  sanctimonious, 465
There are times when the mirth,
    426
  is no death, 435
  is not a fiercer hell, 382
  lies a lonely grave, 516
  neither here nor, 103
Thereby hangs a tale, 34, 49,
    1026, 1042
Therefore be at peace hence-
    forward, 436
Thereon, with her double, 391
Thermopylae, crisis of history a
    pass of, 558
  sires at old, 502
  to make a new, 359
These are thy glorious works,
    153
  are weighty secrets, 682
  only are reputed wise, 44
  things can never die, 666
Thespis professor of our art, 177
Thetis, sun in the lap of, 142
They are good they are bad, 733
  are weak they are strong, 733
  can take it, I can, if, 877

They conquer love that run away,
    141
  goes up and down or else goes
    round, 842
  knew that they had died, 881
  labour in vain that build it,
    1106
  say there's bread and work,
    432
  shall grow not old, 804
  shall run and not be weary,
    1112
  shall see eye to eye, 1112
  shall walk and not faint, 1112
  that are desirous to commit to
    memory, 1125
  that put their trust in him,
    1124
  that sow in tears, 1106
  that stand high, 71
  that wait upon the Lord, 1112
  went and told the sexton, 392
  were they are they yet shall
    be, 306
  who have steeped their souls,
    459
  who mutually injure the state,
    969
  wither, 909
Thick and hazy, night was, 655
  and thin, through, 6, 24, 174,
    241, 1033
  and wide, between us, 824
  as autumnal leaves, 218
  creeds grow so, 719
  curtain fall, let the, 444
  lay them on too, 599
  midnight fog, 170
  muddy ill-seeming, 52
  with lily and red rose, 608
Thick-coming fancies, 88
Thicker, blood is, than water,
    310, 746
  than water in one rill, 443
Thickest, pleasures lie, 407
Thicket rang, all the, 468
Thick-ribbed ice, region of, 36
Thick-warbled notes, 156
Thief, apparel fits your, 37
  doth fear each bush an officer,
    71
  each thing's a, 81
  earth's a, 81
  if you do take a, 39
  in the sworn twelve, 35
  moon's an arrant, 81
  of time, procrastination is the,
    201
  of youth, 161
  one turned out a, 657
  rascally, 351
  steals something from the, 101
  sun's a, the sea's a, 81
  that said the last kind word,
    490
  to catch a thief, 1001
  turns thief-catcher, 319
  which the justice which the, 99
  yond justice rails upon yon,
    99
Thievery, I'll example you with,
    81
Thieves, and fell among, 1117
  beauty provoketh, 48
  moth or rust, molested by, 593
  respect property, 827

Thieves, rifled by the gusty, 391
  these traitorous, 1022
Thigh, happy dawning of her,
  134
  smote them hip and, 1099
Thighs, horseman's hands and,
  928
Thikke and thenne, thurgh, 6
Thin a veil, so, 670
  air, melted into, 33
  as a lath, 497
  as homoeopathic soup, 458
  flames, like, 577
  green leaf to the gold, 633
  ice, in skating over, 412
  it makes you, 943
  partitions, 173, 207
  potations, forswear, 65
  red line, 541, 781
  spun life, slits the, 159
  through thick and, 6, 24, 174,
    241, 1033
Thine and mine, two punctilious,
  1050
  enemy hunger, if, 1119
  for a day, 579
  the exaltation the divine, 438
  was the prophet's vision, 438
Thing abhominable, gret swering
  is, 7
  acting of a dreadful, 82
  any good, out of Nazareth,
    1118
  as odd as can be, 823
  as steadfast as the scene, 296
  became a trumpet, the, 304
  before the, we may, 559
  better than I have ever done,
    498
  but one, is needful, 1117
  came, a new, 849
  dearest, he owed, 84
  don't mind the, 883
  each, his turn does hold, 134
  each, in its place is best, 436
  each, is a thief, 81
  enskyed and sainted, 35
  excellent, in woman, 100
  explain a, till all men doubt,
    215
  fearful, to see, 356
  finds good in every, 48
  finished, the one, 528
  for every, missed something
    else is gained, 411
  for laughter fleers and jeers,
    510
  give if she would have a, 569
  give me one perfect, 881
  give you any goodlier, 759
  good, I can do, 1062
  have said a foolish, 1052
  he understood, he praised the,
    649
  highest, is truth, 8
  hiss the real, 963
  holiest, alive, 316
  how bitter a, it is, 51
  how poor a, is man, 30
  I am, I do beguile the, 101
  I should be nor the thing I
    could be, 285
  I was born to do, this is the,
    30
  if they have a good, 64
  ill-favoured, but mine own, 51

Thing immoral, deemed he was
  a, 938
  in awe of such a, 81
  in hand, a little, 962
  in prospect, a great, 962
  is a gone coon, 527
  is immortal, only one, 1065
  is of serious importance, no,
    974
  is over, if the, 866
  is right, that the, 964
  is sweet, one, 835
  it's a very terrible, 866
  laugh at any mortal, 360
  life's a little, 491
  like of each, 40
  lion among ladies is a dreadful,
    43
  little, a cup of water, 386
  little learning is a dangerous,
    210
  look to the essence of a, 1011
  miss the many-splendoured,
    749
  more intelligible a, 1049
  more, now put in one, 711
  most like living over again,
    228
  nastiest, in the nicest way, 894
  never says a foolish, 184
  no evil, that walks by night,
    158
  no great, created suddenly,
    1007
  no man may explain, 674
  no new, under the sun, 1109
  not the least, 1034
  nothing like being used to a,
    278
  of beauty is a joy forever, 382
  of custom, 87
  of fortune, most dejected, 99
  of naught, paramour is a, 43
  of sea or land, 156
  of shreds and patches, 95
  of watery salt, 833
  on earth, not a, 185
  one and the same, 1048
  one damned, after another, 843
  only, that sighs, 912
  order gave each, view, 72
  originated, where a, 1062
  palsy-stricken churchyard, 383
  play's the, 93
  poet's mistress hallowed, 458
  possessed by man, most pre-
    cious, 1055
  proud and yet wretched, 115
  reminding yourself of a, 912
  seemes small in common eyes,
    what ever, 26, 1114
  show us how divine a, 299
  sigh the lack of many a, 107
  singing the same sad, 500
  so frail a, is man, 947
  sovereign'st, on earth, 61
  started like a guilty, 89
  such an uncertain, 1076
  sweetest, that ever grew, 298
  that costs sixpence, 235
  that fierce, they call, 392
  that I was born to do, 30
  that's quite another, 221
  that is seyd, is seyd, 8
  that life can give, 909
  that numbs the heart, 894

Thing that pleased him once, any,
  965
  that was precious, 629
  that you want, 873
  the, as he sees it, 779
  the first damn, 761
  the genteel, 253
  the scythe of time mows down,
    155
  the sweet day yields, each
    lovely, 445
  they call citandum, 11
  thou lovest, carve the, 719
  to every, there is a reason, 37
  to have a, is nothing, 942
  to have a right, one, 1071
  to know a, is nothing, 942
  to laugh to scorn, is not a, 51
  to love, have not found my,
    841
  to master all, one, 886
  to one, constant never, 38, 256
  to say, find the right, 719
  to say, I had a, 57
  to say, when you've got a, 689
  too much of a good, 51, 1033
  tremble like a guilty, 301
  true that any beauteous, 1023
  truth is the highest, 8
  two-legged, a son, 173
  under the common, 811
  undisputed, thou say'st an, 451
  was not done in a corner, this,
    1119
  we like, we figure the, 401
  we love must die, that the,
    492
  we may nat lightly have, 7
  we must do the, we must, 559
  well done, reward of a, 412
  when two do the same, 988
  which that shyneth, 8
  which we cast to the ground,
    574
  winsome wee, 286
  would please us best, one, 655
  you'll hurt the delicate, 924
  you've gut tu du, 527
Things, a hundred little, 967
  above, affections on, 1121
  afar, love for, 964
  ain't so bad, 831
  all, are now as they were, 1012
  all, are the same, 1012
  all day long, on all, 470
  all other, give place, 206
  all poor foolish, 790
  all, that are, 45
  all thinking, 296
  all thoughts and, look older,
    405
  all, to all men, 1120
  all, work together for good,
    1119
  ancient and holy, 523
  and as, have been they remain,
    519
  are as difficult as they are rare,
    excellent, 1049
  are as they are, why, 669
  are honest, whatsoever, 1121
  are in common among friends,
    all, 1015
  are in the saddle, 409
  are just, whatsoever, 1121
  are lovely, whatsoever, 1121

Things are managed so well in France, 644
are merry and glad, when all, 431
are moulded by some plastic, 647
are not what they seem, 433, 992
are of good report, whatsoever, 1121
are passing, all, 437
are pure, whatsoever, 1121
are seldom what they seem, 623
are taken from us, all, 463
are the sons of heaven, 232
are true, whatsoever, 1121
are wrought by prayer, more, 463
as are worth their observation, 196
as we wish them to be, 962
at home are crossways, 678
at night, an' seein', 699
at worst will cease, 88
bare to the buff, 703
behind, left no little, 700
beneath the sun, 835
better to know useless, 991
between, ended and begun, 537
betwixt heaven and earth, so many, 1079
both great and small, all, 669
bright, come to confusion, 42
by a law divine, 368
by contemplation of diviner, 546
by season seasoned are, 47
by their right names, call, 290
bygone are the only things, 680
can be, how such, 915
can come, before such, 753
cannot always go your way, 694
capable of higher, 856
cloy, the best of, 219
come out, strange, 1059
compare great, with small, 151
comprehend the reality of, 1074
conceived by ingenious speculation, 1023
created, these are all, 9
day of small, 1114
differ all agree, though all, 216
do not say, 415
done at the Mermaid, 129
done decently and in order, 1120
draw more out of, 1082
else about her drawn, 299
else melt, all, 966
equal to all, for all things unfit, 252
erroneous, 580
essential or circumstantial, 172
evil, 67, 580
evil, there is some goodness in, 67
facts are stubborn, 248, 1052
fairest have fleetest end, 748
feast of fat, 1111
five, observe, 716
for which we live, beauteous, 553
foreign or at home, 172

Things, former, grow old, 134
frequently happen which you do not hope, 978
friendship is constant in all other, 38
from out the bitterness of, 304
glad and sad, 632
go at sixes and sevens, 1037
God's sons are, 232
great, are done when men and mountains meet, 282
great, are made of little things, 490
great head of, 992
great lord of all, 207
greatest vicissitude of, 111
half-know many, 1080
have a terrible permanence, 901
have bitten me to the heart, 971
have come to a heluva pass, 654
have laws of their own nature, 827
have not spoken of these, 798
he has discarded, 985
he might have sold, 802
heavenly or things earthly, 172
hid, wherefore are these, 54
holy profane clean obscene, 132
hoped for, substance of, 1122
how easily, go wrong, 559
I am wiser to know, 918
I do not need, many, 1014
I learned from her, 861
I miss, thank Thee for the, 555
I ought, to do the, 339
I thought were dead things, 681
I'd been better without, 918
I've done and known, 850
ignoble, 129
ill got had ever bad success, 70
in the dark besides Santa Claus, 830
in the mud and scum of, 409
inanimate, economy in, 998
into the light of, 295
just to sit and fancy, 844
learned on earth, 486
leave all meaner, 206
left behind him, 453
left undone those, 1127
Lethean, 631
little, affect little minds, 420
little go lessening, 490
living in earthly, 684
long past, more than, 59
looked unutterable, 224
loose type of, 298
love and the commonplace, 939
loveliest of lovely, 372
lovely, like that is always, 919
lovely, look thy last on all, 822
made entirely by the human hand, 842
man's best, are nearest him, 458
men ought not to investigate, 1013
mighty contests rise from trivial, 212
more, in heaven and earth, Horatio, 92

Things more pleasing to the eye, few, 374
move the under-jaw, most, 130
necessary, catalogue of, 183
needed for happy work, 531
not made for words, 1013
not seen, evidence of, 1122
of good or ill we choose, 572
of life come with a mixture, 324
of little or no, 996
of smallest compass, 647
of that kind, 1075
of the future to fate, leave, 418
of the world in store, 826
other, ceased as well, 1082
outward do draw the inward quality, 104
past redress are now past care, 59
past, remembrance of, 107
pick up, way, 930
possessing all, 316
present seem worst, 64
prove all, 1121
rarely go smoothly at rehearsal, 492
remembering happier, 464
return to dust, all, 1071
rolls through all, 296
round about us, change the, 1087
sacred or profane things past or to come, 172
sad vicissitude of, 242, 249
seem fairer when we look back, 529
sense and outward, 301
shall be added, these, 719
shews of, 112
silenced here, some, 540
silently gone out of mind, 295
sleep lying, most, 136
smack and tang of elemental, 708
small, make base men proud, 69
sorry scheme of, 471
soul of all, make it mine, 546
surfeit of the sweetest, 43
sweet to taste, prove sour in digestion, 59
sum of human, 275
taught three useful, 361, 811
that almost happen, 421
that are and have been, 1005
that are, do not care for the, 711
that are made to fade, 446
that are might be otherwise, 936
that are more excellent, 736
that are not to be remedied, 68
that began, twilight of, 633
that belong to adversity, 109
that cannot fail, 625
that chiefly excite us, two, 1036
that have a common quality, 1012
that have caught my eye, 920
that haven't been done, 870
that he thinketh, perceive the, 1124
that I got, 1084
that I longed for in vain, 1084

Things that I spurned and overlooked, 1084
  that live, funny, 953
  that mar or bless, 734
  that nature wills, 1011
  that ne'er were nor are, 164
  that pay, these are the, 599
  that please us, 236
  that soon are old, 561
  that stand, these are the, 843
  that trouble us, forget the, 601
  that we seek, find all the, 733
  that were, dream of, 352
  that wouldn't divide, 678
  there be, all the loveliest, 916
  these, shall be, 654
  they don't understand, 1070
  they said beautiful, 931
  they understand, 838
  they wanted yesterday, 528,
    835
  they write or speak, masters of,
    130
  think on these, 1121
  this sorry scheme of, 1020
  those who want fewest, 1014
  though all, differ all agree, 216
  three silent, 849
  through the dream of, 352
  time for all, 37
  time ordains for other, 162
  time shall teach thee all, 477
  to aim at, two, 788
  to aught save happy living,
    915
  to be guarded against, 402
  to be, lies and dreams of the,
    699
  to be remembered by, 914
  to bear, of all hard, 557
  to come, giant mass of, 75
  to do two, at once, 986
  to have nought is to have all,
    556
  to hold in memory, lovely, 793
  to tell, many, 661
  to write well in laudable, 162
  too fur, carryin', 678
  translunary, 30
  trophies and dead, 128
  turn to stranger, strange
    things, 897
  two, I can do very well, 254
  unattempted, 148
  uncomely and broken, 790
  unfit for all, 252
  unhappy far-off, 298
  unknown, forms of, 43
  unknown proposed, 212
  unsaid, wishing, 796
  unseen, what mean the, 682
  upon earth, of all best, 594
  very much as 'ow I've always
    found, 842
  violently destroyed, 295
  virtuous, from lowest place
    when, 53
  we have seen and known and
    heard, 668
  we need not see nor speak of,
    895
  we ought to have done, 1127
  we see are shadows, 557
  were going to the dogs, 956
  which are Caesar's, 1115
  which are esteemed, 1049

Things which are not seen are
    eternal, 1120
  which are seen are temporal,
    1120
  which belong to prosperity,
    109
  which for our own sake, 980
  which invite foreigners, 1051
  which make for peace, 1119
  which men confess with ease,
    1008
  why and wherefore in all, 67
  without all remedy, 86
  words are, 359
  work and move, all, 502
  work for worthier, 1058
  worn out and old, 790
  ye lef' behind, 870
  you read about, 891
Think and act, free to, 612
  always, what is true, 564
  before thou speakest, 1037
  comedy to those that, 246
  him an angel, a woman yet,
    482
  him so because I think him so,
    33
  himself an act of God, man,
    506
  how Bacon shined, 208
  how divine he himself is, 534
  how many never, 345
  I don't, said Alice, 598
  I, of thee, 393
  I must speak, when I, 50
  if the red slayer, he slays, 410
  in the morning, 282
  makes millions, 359
  may sigh to, 242
  naught a trifle, 203
  nobody never made me, don't,
    480
  not disdainfully of death, 1011
  of your forefathers, 291
  of your posterity, 291
  on, pleasant to, 164
  on thee, while I, 107
  on these things, 1121
  talk and never, 120
  that day lost, 202
  there is nothing but immortal-
    ity, I, 537
  they talk who never, 189
  those that, must govern, 250
  those who greatly, 217
  thy swan a crow, 77
  to, more happy thou, 389
  to-morrow will repay, 178
  too little and talk too much,
    173
  what you and other men, 81
  within thyself, 1020
Thinker, a new, 775
  new, does not know, 1061
Thinkers, greatest, have been am-
    ateurs, 741
  no better or happier, 773
Thinketh in his heart, as he, 1108
  let him that, he standeth take
    heed, 1120
Thinking, above the fog in pri-
    vate, 522
  being, man a, 344
  comparable to paper money,
    740
  face, through her, 911

Thinking few, how few think
    justly of the, 345
  few or none harmed by, 19
  is a kind of poetry, 740
  is an idle waste of thought, 332
  makes it so, 92
  nothing more troublesome than
    effort of, 278, 637
  of the days that are no more,
    466
  on fantastic summer's heat, 59
  on the frosty Caucasus, 59
  pause from, 357
  plain living and high, 298
  reed, man is but a, 1047
  the day most splendid, I was,
    537
  their own kisses sin, 79
  things, impels all, 296
  this globe enough, I was, 537
  weary of, 618
  with too much, 209
  worlds of fine, 347
Thinkings, speak to me as to thy,
    102
Thinks like a sage, 426
  says nor, 618
  too much, he, 81
  what ne'er was, 211
  who, must mourn, 190
Thinne, my wit is, 7
Thinness beat, gold to airy, 118
Thin-spun life, slits the, 159
Third draught drowns him, 54
  hour after the meridian, 799
  is away, when the, 77
  of life is passed in sleep, and
    yet a, 361
  which imitates, 974
Thirst after happiness, 1055
  bereavement pain, 596
  dying of, 716
  for more and more, 984
  if he, give him drink, 1119
  is a dangerous thing, 745
  of praise, 262
  of youth, 353
  to the pot, for every, 137
  where a man can raise a, 782
Thirsteth, ho everyone that, 1112
  still, drinking, 587
Thirsty earth soaks up the rain,
    167
  fly, busy curious, 223
  live, bids the, 682
  soul, cold waters to a, 1108
  think, let the, 659
Thirteen, maids of, 57
  or so, when I was, 907
Thirty days hath September, 18
  in a man's, and, 973
  man a fool at, 201
  on the wrong side of, 192
  pence, for, 136, 257
  pieces Judas sold himself, for,
    136
  pieces of silver, 1116
Thirty-second day of the thir-
    teenth month, 733
This above all, 91
  all this was in the olden time,
    459
  be the verse, 703
  is a cock, 1038
  is petrified truth, 615
  is the thing, 30

This or that to me, what is, 889
  shall pass away, even, 620
  that it should come to, 90
  the most gifted poet, 516
  too, shall pass away, 509, 718
  was a man, say to all the world, 84
  was the truest warrior, 516
  will pass away, 509
Thistle bold, Scotland her, 642
Thistles, figs from, 735
  figs out of, 471
Thombe of gold, he hadde a, 5
Thompson, sixteen were called, 360
Thorn, and bore away one bleeding, 586
  beneath the milk-white, 284
  crown of, 647
  in the flesh, 1121
  kissed beside the, 669
  oak and ash and, 782
  or rose, if you strike a, 730
  primrose peeps beneath the, 251
  rose without a, 280
  rose without the, 134, 152
  that guards the rose, 551
  this crown of, 753
  upon the ground, one, 681
  with every rose, 730
  withering on the virgin, 42
Thorns, amid a hedge of, 857
  bear a thousand, 809
  forever be a crown of, 378
  grapes from, 735
  he that plants, 977
  of life, fall upon the, 366
  pricked by the, 976
  rosebud set with little wilful, 466
  that in her bosom lodge, 92
  the rose with all its, 587
  through which we walk, 834
  touched by the, 334
  under a pot, crackling of, 1109
  which I have reaped, the, 353
Thorn-bit of marriage, terrible, 776
Thorn-curst soil, 709
Thornless growth, 587
Thorny way, steep and, 90
Thoroughbreds the fleetest in Kentucky, 675
Thoroughfare for freedom, 600
  no, 809
Thorwaldsen carved his lion, 621
Those angel faces smile, 403
  hateful to us, 965
  immortal dead who live again, 520
  that leave their valiant bones, 67
  that seek me early, 1107
  that talk and never think, 120
  that think must govern, 250
  that vexed, 971
  that whine, 887
  which he pursues, 985
  which he relinquished, resume, 985
  who bring sunshine, 750
  who have loved forget, can, 370
  who have wealth, 388
  who know thee not, 275

Those who live toil lowly die, 870
  who look backward longingly, 930
  who love me, I live for, 543
  who love us well, 955
  who reject you and brace themselves against you, 538
  who toil bravely, 729
  who wait for gold or gear, 628
  who walk with Him, 955
  who whipped you, let, 865
  who will never return, 807
  whom God wishes to destroy, 175, 968
  whom they have slain, honour, 1074
  whom we mistrusted, 972
  whom we obey and those whom we love, 727
Thou ailest here and here, 546
  alone art there, and, 403
  and I are parted, when, 840
  art all beauty, 187
  art gone from my gaze, 392
  art gone to the grave, 343
  art so full of misery, 462
  art the man, 1100
  art the whole wide world, 672
  art to me a delicious torment, 411
  art, wert less mighty than, 503
  beside me singing, 1018
  canst not say I did it, 87
  crownest the year with thy goodness, 1104
  hast left behind powers, 297
  keep, my feet I do not ask, 403
  lead, me on, 403
  more happy, hadst been, 389
  my fond affection, hast seen, 388
  present to my mind appearest, 393
  the tree and I the flower, 623
  wert O Lord too great, 503
  wert scattered to the wind, 462
Though I am no judge of such matters, 406
  I say it that should not, 131
  lost to sight, 392
  thy path be dark as night, 499
Thought, absorbed in, 1068
  adds strength to the, 204
  again, plunged in, 547
  all objects of all, 296
  all things without care or, 556
  almost say her body, 118
  alone is eternal, 593
  always a comforting, 853
  an intolerable, that he, 449
  and amiable words, high, 471
  and craft and deed, 777
  and fancy faint with cold, 544
  and joy, love and, 297
  and passion, chaos of, 207
  armour is his honest, 114
  as a sage, 269
  be formed, whatever can to sight or, 155
  be not rambling in, 1011
  but ne'er so well expressed, 211
  came like a full-blown rose, 383
  can mend, another, 29
  can think, what, 29
  careful, 642

Thought, confine the swelling, 1050
  consolation in the, 1057
  could wed itself, ere, 468
  darted, as soon as a, 171
  destroyed by, 262
  disruption of, 1064
  divide, sense from, 207
  dome of, the, 352
  eies and eares and ev'ry, 26
  elastic and vigorous, 514
  even a possibility, a, 1082
  even with a, 105
  evil is wrought by want of, 390
  exhausting, 353
  experience is the child of, 420
  explore the, 213
  feeling deeper than all, 501
  flashes in the world of, 542
  for the morrow, take no, 1114
  for your life, take no, 1114
  God blesses still the generous, 441
  grows old and worn with usage, 588
  hath struck him, a Roman, 104
  her dying when she slept, 390
  him still speaking, 154
  his mind a, his life, 506
  human, is the process, 339
  hushed be every, 304
  I shun the, 701
  I, that morning cloud, 375
  I waste no, 878
  I'd think of thee, America, 537
  immersed in matter, 393
  in a green shade, green, 169
  in prayer for S.T.C., 319
  in the head, with the, 594
  is a weapon stronger, 504
  is added will, unless to, 410
  is deeper than all speech, 501
  is often original, a, 453
  is speech, when, 307
  is the child of action, 420
  is the labour of the intellect, 1068
  is the property of him who can entertain it, 412
  is tired of wandering, 401
  is viscous, 637
  it is a cheering, 853
  kings of modern, 546
  lean upon the, that chance, 547
  leapt out, 468
  liberty of, 1053
  lightning-spark of, 378
  like a passing, 285
  like a pleasant, 298
  like dew upon a, 359
  like this can give, 909
  loftiness of, 175
  lovely, 370
  magnanimity of, 201
  maiden lived with no other, 459
  microscope of, 1069
  midnight is the noon of, 273
  mighty, in a mighty mind, 675
  nimble, 107
  no noble human, can come to naught, 509
  Northern, is slow and durable 488
  not one immoral, 239
  obnoxious, 670

Thought of convincing, 252
  of dining, 252
  of her own, not a, 726
  of some one miles and years away, 608
  of suicide, 1080
  of tender happiness, 300
  of thee, hold a, 580
  of thee, one, 216
  of you remaining, 789
  of your failures, 848
  old the, and oft exprest, 528
  one, one grace, one wonder, 32
  one sweetly solemn, 557
  one wandering, 368
  only a stainless, 1085
  our ingrate, 888
  pain of, 604
  painful to any man, 318
  pale cast of, 93
  parentage of antecedent, 543
  pearls of, 528
  pined in, 55
  pleasing dreadful, 195
  plunged into a sea of words, 878
  practice by taking, 982
  pure in, as angels are, 289
  recur to some things, if, 540
  roaming in, over the universe, 536
  satisfied, no, 689
  sessions of sweet silent, 107
  shadowy, 384
  should quickly follow, act from, 937
  sickening, 669
  so, go near to be, 40
  so once but now I know it, I, 206
  some sudden, 640
  soul of the thing is the, 660
  sow a, 954
  spontaneous, 414
  still and serious, 297
  strange seas of, 299
  such stores as silent, 295
  sudden, strikes me, 292
  takes one's breath away, 554
  that baffles you, 972
  that he sung while he whistled, 492
  that most thrills, 593
  that would delight thy love, 618
  the erring, 628
  the travell long, 26
  think thy, 485
  thinking an idle waste of, 332
  those that tell of saddest, 366
  thou couldst have died, if I had, 364
  thy wish was father to that, 65
  'tis the immortal, 823
  to have common, 209
  to rear the tender, 224
  to stir the blood, 954
  two souls with a single, 219, 1070
  vacuity of, 266
  vain or shallow, 408
  vein of tender, 337
  very energy of, which keeps, 403

Thought, what oft was, 211
  whene'er is spoken a noble, 436
  whistled for want of, 176
  who would have, 88
  whose armour is his honest, 114
  will strike with a swift, 920
  withdraws to poetry, 492
  would destroy their paradise, 243
Thoughts, a penny for your, 191
  all, all passions, 316
  all, and things look older, 405
  all man's, will perish, 687
  among my fairest, 701
  and acts, all my, 832
  and actions, less conscious, 613
  and feelings dwell, 594
  and feelings, the roots of our, 1074
  and kind, loving, 700
  and voices our solitude may give, 128
  are legible in the eie, 26
  are seeds of future deeds, 755
  as harbingers, most pious, 147
  as still as the waters, 868
  as thunders, 633
  beyond the reaches of our souls, 91
  by England given, 894
  by great, and good deeds, 506
  calmer of unquiet, 139
  employ speech to conceal, 183, 1052
  even so my bloody, 103
  fond and wayward, 296
  for those compelling, 738
  give thy worst of, 102
  grave thoughts, great, 503
  great feelings, great, 458
  high erected, 27
  his only friends, 121
  ill, die, 956
  images and precious, 303
  in a shroud of, 353
  in another, one's inmost, 717
  in our head, 780
  ironic, and retrospections, 788
  lasting to the end, 503
  lead men's, 789
  life is what our, make it, 1010
  like rose leaves scattered, 360
  like small lost rafts, 850
  looks and, were downward, 149
  love light and calm, 317
  love's heralds should be, 79
  mantle that covers human, 1042
  may be over-poetical, 484
  men's, according to inclination, 111
  more elevate, 150
  never alone with noble, 27
  never breeds fine, 1016
  no tongue, give thy, 90
  nor measure words, weigh, 567
  of a child, 600, 815
  of a good legacy, 1042
  of a turtle, 415
  of God, of all the, 427
  of love, turns to, 464
  of men are widened, 464
  of men do decay, 25
  of mortality, 147
  of others, 744

Thoughts of the few, 640
  of the sweetest saddest things, 612
  of those who wake and live, 366
  of youth are long long, 436
  on hospitable, intent, 153
  our most secret, 977
  pansies for, there is, 96
  pleasant, bring sad thoughts, 295
  ran a wool-gathering, 1041
  regular as infant's breath, 317
  remain below, my, 95
  riot of gold and purple, 938
  river of his, 434
  rule the world, 416
  run over all things, 132
  sad, and sunny weather, 531
  second, are the best, 179, 465
  second, are wiser, 968
  serve your best, as gypsies do children, 278
  shall fly, around the world, 940
  shut up want air, 202
  soars to 'igher things, 629
  style is the dress of, 222
  sweeter his, 618
  teaches them suspect the, 45
  that are the souls of thought, 459
  that breathe, 168, 244
  that come with doves' foot-steps, 1079
  that ennoble, 590
  that glow, hearts that kindle, 554
  that mould the age, 524
  that savour of content, 940
  that shall glad high souls, 524
  that shall not die, 303
  that wander through eternity, 149
  the hopes the dreams, the, 507
  these, inspire my youthful mind, 292
  to distant countries roam, 283
  to rest, tired, 823
  to their own second, 187
  too deep for tears, 302
  unexpressed, 677
  unexpressed sometimes fall back dead, 180
  unrighteous man his, 1112
  upon second, 1040
  we ought to control our, 448
  when shaving, 745
  which he had known, best 540
  which mould our lives, less conscious, 613
  which prompt to speak, 492
  who can mistake great, 507
  winged, 395
  with noble, 27
  words without, 95
Thought's atmosphere, in, 669
  mysterious seat, 338
Thoughtful vaulting, on, 932
Thoughtless blow, full many a, 718
  man, warning for, 302
  thankless man, 202
  thing, bird appears a, 324

Thought-worn eves and morrows, 651
Thousand a year Gaffer Green, 955
blushing apparitions, 39
crimes, one virtue and a, 356
decencies, those, 154
dreadful deaths, a, 728
friends suffice thee not, 1017
girls, as if a, 808
hacking at the branches of evil, 514
hearts beat happily, 352
hills, cattle upon a, 1104
homes, near a, 295
idly watch Him pass, 851
in an hour, 395
in twelve, 60
innocent shames, 39
leagues from hence, a, 62
leagues like a thousand years, 227
little one shall become a, 1112
melodies unheard before, 289
miles from land, 350
natural shocks, end the, 93
one man among a, 1109
picked out of ten, 92
soldiers, substance of ten, 72
sons, if I had a, 65
stars, beauty of a, 32
strings, harp of a, 199
take in a few, 921
thousand voices, 888
times good-night, a, 78
tongues, conscience hath a, 72
tongues to allure him, 257
virtuous on ten, a year, 563
voices, earth with her, 316
waiting, slaughters a, 56
wars of old, 469
we love a, 795
would he had blotted out a, 120
years in thy sight, 1105
years of peace, 469
Thousands at His bidding speed, 162
countless, mourn, 284
die without or this, 210
has been slave to, 102
of undone widows, 116
of years, rung in the ears of simple for, 545
peace slays its ten, 268
think for one who can see, 531
to murder, 203
war slays its, 268
Thousandth man will stand, 783
Thracians, comrades warriors, 502
Thrains, roarin' o' the, 819
Thraldom, in narrow, 1050
Thrall, humblest, 713
to the gilded ease, 808
to the least and vilest things, 115
Thread, feels at each, 207
from a house, 639
hinders needle and, 392
love holds with twined, 125
of his verbosity, the, 41
pluck one, 441
plying her needle and, 391

Thread, sewing at once a double, 392
shall hang to thread, while, 552
slender silver, 637
strands of an unbroken, 955
that ties them, 1030
the length of a span, 833
touch the utmost, 115
weave their, with bones, 54
your family, 510
Threads, cast kite-borne, 676
of gold, some blessed, 501
of rhyme, of all the, 756
will run appointed ways, 591
Threadbare sail, set every, 450
saint in wisdom's school, 115
Threat or else a promise, 955
Threats, no terror in your, 83
of a halter, 274
Threaten and command, an eye to, 95
Threatened with a great injustice, 402
Threatening eye, looks with a, 58
gale, 561
shadows melted, 522
Three arts concerned with all things, 974
cannot take part in a conversation, 411
corners of the world, 58
estates in parliament, 380
fatal sparks, 1020
fifths of him genius, 526
firm friends, more sure than day, 317
friends are hardly possible, 636
gates of gold, 716
gentlemen at once, 278
good friends, 50
good men unhanged in England, 61
hundred and three-score, 567
hundred grant but three, of the, 359
hundred grateful voices, 605
hundred, ointment prize at, 136
hundred pounds a year, 34
hundred thousand more, 475
jovial huntsmen, 229
kingdoms, had sifted, 179
kings came riding, 439
lilies in her hand, 577
little bugs in a basket, 540
long mountains and a wood, 915
may keep counsel, 16
meet again, when shall we, 84, 951
merry boys are we, 127
misbegotten knaves, 62
per cents, simplicity of the, 275, 421
poets in three distant ages, 175
removes bad as a fire, 227
should speak, no more than, 180
silences there are, 439
sons of yore, 954
species of creatures, 640
stories high long dull and old, 288

Three sweet graces, around the child, 326
that enjoy a holiday, 347
things are to be looked to, 1057
things needed for happy work, 531
things never come again, 570
though he was only, 876
thousand miles of borderline, 954
times I came, 708
times three, 348
treasures love light and thoughts, 317
useful things, 361
which of the, 776
with these, 1049
words, joys of sense lie in, 208
years' child, listens like a, 314
Three-cornered hat, the old, 450
Threefold cord, 1109
fourfold tomb, 119
Three-hooped pot, 69
Three-man beetle, 64
Threescore, bachelor of, 38
summers, when they're gone, 223
years and ten, 742, 1105
Three-tailed Bashaw, 288
Three-toed tree-toad, 815
Threshold, await them on the, 1085
high enough, 710
of the new world, 146
stumble at the, 70
whining at the, 754
Thrice he assayed, 149
he routed all his foes, 176
he slew the slain, 176
is he armed, 31, 69
their weight in gold, 288
Thrift may follow fawning, 94
spent with due respective, 556
thrift Horatio, 90
Thrill, glory's, is o'er, 334
the deepest notes of woe, 287
Thrilled me filled me with fantastic, 460
Thrive and ripen, berries, 66
Thrives for long upon, none, 556
Throat, Amen stuck in my, 86
copper-plated, 816
gold beneath his, 629
of war, brazen, 155
put a knife to thy, 1108
scuttled ship or cut a, 359
to feel the fog in my, 489
wooden, was once a part, 920
you lie in your, 64
Throats, cut each other's, 674
engines whose rude, 102
welling, through our, 937
Throb of giving's sweet, 918
Throbs of fiery pain, 231
Throbbing jumping nerves, 473
Throe, never grudge the, 489
volcanic, financial, 733
Throes of bitter pain, 820
Throne, and I make my, 448
any monarch in his, 1033
descend from the, 1061
footsteps of a, 22

Throne, glories of a, 424
  high and lifted up, Lord sitting
    upon a, 1111
  is above the king's, your, 1102
  light which beats upon a, 469
  like a burnished, 104
  loafing around the, 639
  my bosom's lord sits lightly in
    his, 80
  nature's universal, 358
  night from her ebon, 201
  no brother near the, 167, 213
  of beaten gold my, 822
  of kings, this royal, 59
  of rocks in a robe of clouds,
    357
  of royal state, high on a, 149
  sapphire-blaze the living, 243
  shake hands with a king upon
    his, 363
  shape the whisper of the, 468
  something behind the, 230
  through slaughter to a, 245
  to keep the past upon its, 525
  up to the, 783
  what is a, 1060
  wrong forever on the, 525
Thrones and crowns but men, not,
    338
  are rocking, 763
  dominations princedoms, 153
  of tyranny and pride, 706
  whose stakes were, 357
Throned monarch, 46
  on her hundred isles, 353
Throng, base ignoble, 972
  go crowned with blue, 701
  haunted by a demoniac, 677
  into my memory, 157
  milliard-headed, 544
  shouts and plaudits of the, 439
  thoughts as thunders in, 633
Throstle awakes and the morn
    breaks, 582
Through an alley titanic of cy-
    press, 461
  creeks and inlets making, 519
  every season dearest, 393
  love to light, 672
  out of the skies as I came, 559
  the balmy air of night, 460
  the dim halls of night, 418
Throw physic to the dogs, 88
  within a stone's, 1036
Thrummed, I was ne'er so, 115
Thrush sings each song twice, 486
Thrust out of his tent, 166
  that staggers, some, 924
Thucydides, gravity and conci-
    sion of, 641
Thumb, miller's golden, 5
  print is different, every, 859
  rule of, 704
  saxpence under my, 311
  sought refreshment from his,
    664
  to his wrist, 569
  United States under my, 954
Thumbs, pricking of my, 87
  sealed their letters with their,
    313
Thumping on your back, 267
Thumps upon the back, 203
Thunder and the sun, the, 809
  crash of deafening, 688
  glow glory in, 672

Thunder, heard remote, 150
  Him who rules the, 191
  in a fair frosty day, 172
  in his lifted hand, 173
  in the air, vague, 926
  Jove's power to, 76
  leaps the live, 353
  lightning or in rain, in, 84
  loud roared the dreadful, 288
  of those hungering wings, 920
  on the left, 184
  purr to sleep with, 616
  shall not hurt you, 864
  steal my, 186
Thunders, heard fame's, 690
  in the index, 95
  in throng, 633
  of white silence, 428
  the judgment, 708
Thunderbolt of heaven, 969
Thunderbolts of snow, hurl their,
    934
Thunder-harp of pines, 587
Thundering rattle of slatting,
    833
  sound, 250, 251
Thunder-storm against the wind,
    354
  there is never a, 1089
Thurgh thikke and thurgh
    thenne, 6
Thurghfare full of wo, this world
    nis but, 6
Thursday come, week is gone,
    138
  I do not love you, 916
Thursday's child works hard,
    956
Thus let me live unseen un-
    known, 216
  why is this, 606
Thusness, the reason for this,
    606
Thy will not mine be done, father,
    423
Thyme, whereon wild, blows, 42
Thynge, doe ye nexte, 653
Thyself, come out of, 1084
Tiber father Tiber, 400, 932
  not a drop of allaying, 76
Tiberius been a cat, had, 546
  might have sat, so, 546
Ticking star, each, 851
Tickle the earth with a hoe, 417
  your catastrophe, 64
Tickled with a straw, 208
Ticklings down the back, 929
Tide and wind stay no man, 12
  as it moves each day, 865
  as moving seems asleep, 472
  at the turning o' the, 713
  boots not to resist both wind
    and, 70
  brought in upon the, 766
  ebbed and flowed the, 437
  going out with the, 497
  in the affairs of men, 83
  in the smelly Liffy's, 721
  in the sunset, 873
  is pretty nigh out, 497
  lift its head above the, 1090
  lift the eternal, 839
  of being flows, 570
  of successful experiment, 273
  of the years, 595
  of times, lived in the, 82

Tide, pulled against the, 223
  recede the disappointed, 585
  smiled up across the, 772
  swim upon the selfsame, 801
  tarrieth for no man, 12
  this frosty, 742
  turning of the, 66
  twilight, 431
  without a breeze without a,
    315
  writes her will upon the, 761
Tides, among the high, 57
  have for long ages, 707
  in their flowing, 736
  of grass, 630
  of love, talk of, 813
  of men, drew those, 901
  of time, sea-mark in the, 634
Tide's low susurrus, 570
Tideless and inert, 687
  dolorous midland sea, 631
Tidings as they roll, confirm the,
    194
  dismal, when he frowned, 251
  seeks no, 792
  that bringeth good, 1112
Tie, give me a wild, 907
  in whose, a wild civility, 133
  love endures no, 176
  my tie, and, 904
  of host and guest, 963
  of sympathy, 415
  silver link the silken, 307
  that links my soul with thee,
    560
  that will swear and rip and
    tear, 907
  there's a magical, 511
  up the knocker, 212
Ties, human, that bind me, 543
  of mother and son, 773
  pleasantest of all, 963
  sight of human, 216
  that bind, thank thee for the,
    373
Tied to the stake, I am, 99
  up together, twain have been,
    472
Tiger, Hyrcan, 87
  in war imitate the action of
    the, 66
  sniffs the rose, 892
  the lady or the, 610
  three cheers and a, 521
  tiger burning bright, 281
Tigers, tamed and shabby, 816
Tiger's cub I'll bind, 395
Tight little island, 305
Tight-closed hand, in either, 567
Tillage, other arts follow, 340
Tilt at all I meet, 213
  work at any, 777
Tilts, ride in the, 800
Timber into a wood, carrying,
    984
  knowledge and, 454
  like seasoned, 135
  wedged in that, 180
Timber-patches, a-clarin', 712
Timbrel, sound the loud, 336
Time a great legalizer, 862
  above the wrecks of, 640
  age and body of the, 94
  all in good, 1041
  all other, is peace, 132
  already of old, 1109

Time ambles withal, 50
an endless song, 790
and age, his youth 'gainst, 27
and all the world, all, 422
and eternity meet, 690
and race more prosaic, 524
and sense have known, the world that, 444
and sin and fate's control, 375
and space, through, 263
and stars below, 850
and the hour runs, 84
and the place, never the, 493
and the River, of, 932
and trouble, serves a world of, 490
annihilate but space and, 216
anything except, 1060
as an immense ocean, consider, 196
assuages sorrow, 979
back upon an earlier, 417
backward and abysm of, 32
bank and shoal of, 85
bastard to the, 57
be heavy on your hands, if, 462
be ruled by, 997
began since, 718
between drinks, long, 786
between this, and that sweet, 454
born out of my due, 608
bounds of place and, 243
break the legs of, 451
breathing, of day with me, 97
brief chronicles of the, 93
bring back those midnights, 832
brings increase to her truth, 240
brings not death, 847
by stars, reckon, 774
by, subdued, 200
by the forelock, take, 26
cannot age it, 736
carelessly, fleet the, 47
chained to, 366
chinks that, has made, 146, 289
choose some happier, 926
choose thine own, 273
colors history, 892
coming, there's a good, 310, 504
common arbitrator, 75
cools time clarifies, 1089
count, by heart-throbs, 506
creeping hours of, 49
curious, requires, 112
damsels of, 410
dead for a long, 1062
death chooses his own, 596
demands strong minds, the, 522
do not squander, 227
driveth onward, 463
enough for that, there's, 57
enough, take, 170, 221
enough to sleep, there'll be, 742
even such is, 22
every man be master of his, 86
fool all people some of the, 457
fool some people all of the, 457

Time, footprints on the sands of, 433
for a man to recover his hair, there's no, 37
for all good men, now is the, 854
for all things, 37, 1041
for courtesy, always, 415
for extraordinary toil, 974
for grief only, 392
for laughter, little, 701
for living, little, 693
for make-believe, no, 933
for mirth and laughter, no, 791
for parting be sweet, let the, 1084
for payment comes, 833
for robbers, night is the safe, 967
for sorrow, bee has no, 282
for supper, the proper, 1015
for things that matter, 864
forefinger of all, 466
foremost files of, 464
frozen round periods of, 150
gallops withal, 50
gives to her mind, 240
goes by turns, 30
golden, of long ago, 626
good, that is no more, 1064
got his wrinkles, 664
had been, as if the moving, 296
has come, the, 598
has come when the darkies, 567
has fallen asleep, 588
has its way with you, 857
has laid his hand gently, 440
has no divisions, 1089
has not yet come, my, 1082
has taught us a lesson, 996
has touched me gently, 280
hath a taming hand, 403
hath to silver turned, his silver locks, 27
he that lacks, 401
healing is a matter of, 971
held in store for us by, 496
hid in the womb of, 369
himself can prove you no truer, 467
himself is bald, 37
his good time, some, 484
his, is forever, 167
history hath triumphed over, 22
how a man should kill, 1026
how long a, lies in one little word, 59
how small a part of, they share, 146
I count my, 672
I marke the, 648
I won't count this, 579
in God's good, 491
in misery, happy, 440
in store, we have, 486
in your distant, 849
irreparable ravages of, 1050
is a kind friend, 883
is a liar, we're twenty to-night, 452

Time is a peddler, 711
is a river of passing events, 1010
is a sandpile, 855
is all to-day, 305
is broke, when, 60
is but a stream I go a-fishing in, 514
is but our playmate, 555
is elastic, 1086
is fleeting, art is long and, 433
is infinite movement, 1077
is money, 227, 387, 432
is out of joint, 92
is quiet as a nun, the holy, 297
is still a-flying, 133
is the image of eternity, 1014
is the only comforter, 402
is the soul of this world, 1006
it is, telling me what, 808
it may be some, 921
itself grows beautifully dim, 891
kill, as if you could, 514
kill the bloom before its, 303
lapse of, 18
last syllable of recorded, 88
leaves have their, to fall, 370
lettered pomp to teeth of, 442
lift up all who live in their, 312
like the old time, no, 453
look into the seeds of, 84
look like the, 84
long ago, was in the olden, 459
lose breath, till, 718
loss of, 1021
lost in idle company, less, 181
makes ancient good uncouth, 525
makes strong, the grace that, 650
makes these decay, 141
marketh the going of, 449
may cease, and midnight never come, 32
melt with all-powerful, 966
men have died from time to, 51
merry dancing drinking, 176
most valuable thing to spend, 1015
nick of, 164, 1038
nine tenths leisure, 689
no respect of, 54
noiseless falls the foot of, 294
noiseless foot of, 53
nor place adhere, 85
nor space nor deep nor high, nor, 535
nor talents waste, 332
not all people all of the, 457
not of an age but for all, 119
nothing so precious as, 1026
now is the accepted, 1121
of day, no proper, 391
of grace, that sweet, 454
of life is short, 63
of Man, the, 891
of night, witching, 95
of peace, in, 986
of salads, 242
of scorn, figure for the, 103
of the singing of birds, 1110

Time of trouble, 853
  old bald cheater, 119
  oldest chronicler of, 681
  on the way, long long, 600
  only after a certain, 1064
  only given by, 975
  ordains, mild Heaven a, 162
  our, is a very shadow, 1124
  our oars keep, 334
  out of mind, 1033
  Paleozoic, 734
  panting, toiled after him, 231
  peace only as a breathing, 258
  play the fools with, 64
  point of, life of man but a,
    1001
  present, so with, 1022
  present travel that of old, 128
  procrastination the thief of,
    201
  profusely squandered, 242
  promised on a, 26
  quaffing and unthinking, 176
  redeem the, 900
  relish of the saltness of, 64
  remnants of the good old, 308
  return, bid, 59
  rich with the spoils of, 244
  robs us of our joys, 257
  save only one, glad if, 756
  seemed but the vassal, 579
  sense of the value of, 330
  serves we are going, 652
  shall teach thee all things, 477
  shall throw a dart at thee, 120
  show and gaze of the, 89
  silence and slow, 383
  silvered o'er by, 265
  so dark but through its woof,
    no, 501
  so gracious is the, 89
  so hallowed is the, 89
  so short a, 76
  soul of the whole past, 380
  speech is of, 380
  speech is shallow as, 377
  spoils the pleasure of the, 87
  stanchless flows, 922
  stand still withal, 50
  stays, we go, 648
  steady plies the oar, 954
  still as he flies, 240
  stoops to no man's lure, 632
  stream of, 289
  subdue, what will not, 200
  such a justling, 63
  supreme to every life, 626
  sweet, sad time, 389
  syllabes jar with, 120
  teaches many lessons, 963
  tears and laughter for all, 428
  tedious waste of, 156
  tell her that wastes her, 146
  that aged nurse, 382
  that no man knows, 734
  that takes in trust, 22
  that you weep, every, 1074
  the blossom, 655
  the dark whale, 888
  the first gives you, 1070
  the incalculable up-and-down
    of, 664
  the moving, 296
  the rider that breaks youth,
    138
  the scythe of, 155

Time the subtle thief of youth,
    161
  the wisest counsellor, 997
  through streaming, 459
  till midnight, spend my, 931
  time time, keeping, 459
  to arrive at maturity, credit
    requires, 419
  to be happy is now, 603
  to be learning, is it a, 1014
  to be sad, never has, 639
  to be sweet and grow old, 633
  to beguile, 84
  to come, sweet discourses in
    our, 80
  to enjoy a European trip, 791
  to every purpose under heaven,
    37, 1109
  to grow old, we may always
    find, 203
  to hear bird music, 930
  to keep silence, 1109
  to kiss and cling, little, 701
  to lick it into form, 122
  to look around, before we have,
    1057
  to marry, choose a proper, 264
  to mourn, lacks, 401
  to read the libraries of heaven,
    551
  to remember time for a sigh,
    727
  to sing, little, 701
  to speak, 1109
  to sport away the hours, no,
    445
  to stand and stare, 492, 814
  to talk, 'tis no, 70
  to think of men, no, 551
  to turn on the old trail, 778
  too swift, O, 27
  tooth of, 37, 203
  touch us gently, 350
  transported, with envy, 257
  travels in divers paces, 50
  tries the troth in everything,
    17
  trieth troth in every doubt, 17
  trots withal, 50
  turn backward O, 595
  was now or never, 241
  we know not when, 395
  what a, 980
  what to do with their, 1054
  when for the first, 911
  when jests are few, 781
  when one is sick to death, 838
  which was before us, 1109
  which we have at disposal,
    1086
  whips and scorns of, 93
  whirligig of, brings in his re-
    venges, 56
  wil not be staid, 26
  will change and even reverse,
    974
  will come when you will hear
    me, 419, 424
  will consume the strongest
    cord, 309
  will do to help our grief, what,
    613
  will doubt of Rome, 360
  will explain it all, 968
  will have bald followers, 37
  will run back, 161

Time will rust the sharpest
    sword, 309
  will teach thee, 434
  winds the exhausted chain, 286
  wise through, 218
  witching, of night, 95
  with a gift of tears, 633
  with falling oars they kept the,
    169
  with reckless hand, not till,
    439
  with thee conversing I forget
    all, 152
  without injuring eternity, kill,
    514
  work is the scythe of, 1061
  worn out with eating, 178
  wrestle so valiantly with, 458
  writes no wrinkle, 355, 440
  you old gipsy man, 816
  you really live, only, 905
  you will at another, 1029
Times and the Saturday Review,
    622
  and ways they least expect,
    556
  are hard, when, 983
  are in his hand, our, 489
  are in thy hand, my, 1103
  behind the, 793
  brisk and giddy-paced, 54
  corrector of enormous, 132
  cowards die many, 82
  cunning, 46
  derision to all future, 1021
  do change and move, 25
  do shift, thus, 134
  fashion of these, 48
  good old grand old great old,
    495
  good or evil, 110
  hard, come again no more, 567
  I do not tell you, 867
  I've seen, the, 850
  in good old colony, 954
  in the morning of the, 465
  later, more aged, 112
  light for after, 321
  lived in the tide of, 82
  of disaster and ill fortune, 999
  of great Elizabeth, 463
  of need, ever but in, 177
  of unexampled prosperity, 343
  principles turn with, 209
  signs of the, 1115
  simplicity of, 950
  that I meet thee, 672
  that tried men's souls, 453
  that try men's souls, 271
  that were, illusion that, 479
  those golden, 266
  unprosperous and dangerous,
    374
  we know not of, 631
  were not hard and money
    scarce, 415
  when old are good, 357
  when only a dog will do, 920
  when the mirth of others sad-
    dens, 426
  when the world is ancient, 112
  wherein we now live, 112
  wise men say nothing in dan-
    gerous, 130
  without number, 832

Times you can, at all the, 226
Time's all-devastating flight, 1057
  corrosive dewdrop eats, 564
  dark events, no more, 536
  delight hath she, 823
  enormous nought, 823
  furrows on another's brow, 202
  infinite sea, 594
  iron feet can print, 355, 440
  monitions, 650
  noblest offspring is the last, 203
  slow torments free, 837
  to-morrows, 891
  winged chariot, 169
Time-bells tolled, her, 833
Time-honored bread-sauce, 666
  Lancaster, 58
Time-lag in England, 795
Timeless capitals, 785
Timely dew of sleep, 152
  inn, to gain the, 87
Time-worn lute, 337
Timid and the bold, the, 511
Timidity, moral courage with physical, 651
Timothy learnt sin to fly, 947
Tin, treasuring the, 893
  tunes like smitten, 785
Tinged by the rising sun, 375
Tinker out of Bedford, 779
  to Evers to Chance, 867
Tinkling cymbal, 1120
  of the camel's-bell, 544
Tinklings, airy, 618
Tint for the sky, 882
  of skin, judged not by, 775
  released upon the air, 879
Tints of woe, sabler, 245
  painted in, 1084
  that glorify, changing, 669
Tintinnabulation that so musically wells, 459
Tiny bill and wing, 586
  broken song, 756
  flimsy thing, stamp is a, 803
  flower, pale and sweet, 642
  inch-long eager ardent, 823
  Tim said God bless us every one, 495
Tip for you here's a, 813
  of his subduing tongue, 109
Tips with silver, 78
Tippecanoe, gallant old soldier of, 404
Tipperary, long long way to, 836
Tipple in the deep, fishes that, 168
  is aboard, 810
  rum alone's the, 833
Tipsy always blind and often, 406
  dance and jollity, 157
Tip-tilted like the petal of a flower, 470
Tiptoe, jocund day stands, 79
  religion stands on, 136
  upon a little hill, 385
  when this day is named stand, 67
Tire, nothing but wind in pneumatic, 1083
  of all creation, 454
Tired and faint and worn, 596

Tired and lone, unmated creature, 503
  and sick of war, 542
  at close of day, 690
  business man can feel happy, 919
  eyelids upon tir'd eyes, 463
  he sleeps, till, 208
  heart, 438
  my heart and I, we're, 429
  nature's sweet restorer, 201
  of its pleasures, 299
  of hearing him called the just, 997
  voices, is like, 905
  waves vainly breaking, while the, 519
  we are so, 655
  yet strong, 701
  your poor, give me your, 694
  youths and maids, 785
Tires in a mile-a, 56
Tiresome mouth, tells it with his, 669
Tissue, like a precious, 1078
  of the life to be, 441
Titan, one, at a time, 808
Titans down, Jove strikes the, 484
Titanic, through an alley, of cypress, 461
Tithe of gold, own full, 511
  of mint and anise, 1115
Title and profit I resign, 195, 206
  by this, alone, 596
  clear, death reads the, 492
  gained no, lost no friend, 210
  long and dark, successive, 173
  of this brood, show me the, 612
  to renown, only, 893
  true servant's, 441
  when I can read my, clear, 199
Titles, decider of dusty and old, 132
  high though his, 307
  power and pelf, 307
  you are the, 1085
Titwillow titwillow, 256
To all to each a fair good night, 308
  be or not to be, 93
  do easy as to know what to do, 44
  err is human, 1068
  live is to function, 655
  travel better than to arrive, 704
Toad beneath the harrow, 776
  I had rather be a, 102
  in fun, until a, 942
  rose-water on a, 417
  squat like a, 152
  ugly and venomous, 48
  without which no garden is complete, 582
Toad-eater, Pulteney's, 246
Toast, noise from good, 803
  pass, let the, 279
  this almost square of, 927
  works down to babies, when the, 617
Tobacco and comfits, sack of, 928
  anything for thy sake, 325

Tobacco, divine, rare, superexcellent, 125
  is a dirty weed, 943
  is divine, 358
  no herb like, 524
  sovereign remedy to all diseases, 125
  sublime, 358
Tocsin of the soul, 360
To-day and for ever, the same, 478
  be good and happy, 314
  be wise, 305
  he has got through, 966
  his own, who can call, 177
  I have lived, 177
  in, already walks to-morrow, 318
  isn't any other day, 598
  just for, 645
  may bring, whate'er, 793
  may win to-morrow, lose, 1033
  my soul, is far away, 552
  never before, 490
  never do, 553
  nor care beyond, 243
  of past regrets, clears, 1018
  our youth we can have but, 203
  pleasure to be drunk, 228
  speed, to be put back to-morrow, 25
  that's eight times, 389
  the road all runners come, 743
  to-morrow be, 438
  well-lived, but, 953
  what happens not, 1058
  what have we done, 750
  work'st thou well, 1058
Today's achievement, 629
  delight, 484
  Most Indispensables, 776
Toe, light fantastic, 160
  lissom clerical printless, 893
  man that's stubbed his, 829
  of frog, eye of newt, 87
  of the peasant, 97
  rosy point of the restless, 569
  stocking's crowded, 711
Toes, the pobble who has no, 498
  unplagu'd with corns, 77
  walk on frozen, 809
Together, and as brothers live, 436
  and the loved one all, 493
  by the waters of Life we sat, 395
  we have been friends, 446
  we shall be again, 627
Togs, granddad in his old skin, 956
Toil and care, man of, 578
  and fare, 673
  and of tears, weary of, 595
  and sweat and muscles straining, 223
  and trouble, 87
  and trouble, war his, 176
  and trouble, why all this, 295
  be done, ere the, 501
  day's long, is past, 392
  does not come to help the idle, 1093
  envy want and jail, 230
  for waste of scheme and, 553

Toil, govern those that, 250
  he won, what with his, 173
  horny hands of, 524
  hunger nakedness, 388
  is lost, or all the, 264
  is over, my, 808
  is the sire of fame, 968
  isn't worth the, 776
  may be, however bitter, 813
  merciless in, 779
  morn of, nor night of waking, 308
  most holy reward of human, 1090
  not neither do they spin, 1114
  o'er books, 206
  of breath, with, 319
  of dropping buckets into wells, 265
  on sad heart courageously, 509
  sleepe after, 24
  terribly, know that he can, 412
  the blessing of earth, 709
  those that think govern those that, 250
  time for extraordinary, 974
  true leisure one with true, 501
  uselessness of your, 786
  verse sweetens, 249
  waste their, for a smile, 307
  whip of, 725
  winding up days with, 67
  winds through the swamps of, 733
  with servile, 374
  without recompense, 595
  years of unrequited, 457
Toils and teens, 651
  and tender cares, 373
  despair to reach, what others', 190
  enemy's, 962
Toiled after him in vain, panting Time, 231
  forgot for which he, 107
Toilet is not complete, 738
  without a mirror, 1064
Toilfully spin, loiter in pleasure or, 448
Toiling and moiling, amends for the, 486
  upward in the night, 436
Toilsome journey of life, 558
Toilworn craftsman, 380
Token, no certain, 625
  sewing a healthy, 422
Tokens of remembrance, need not send, 413
Told by an idiot, 88
  her love, she never, 55
  they went and, the sexton, 392
  you so, the incarnate I, 437
Toledo trusty, blade, 142
Tolerant plains, 663
Toleration from the intolerant, 880
  to forgiveness, one step from, 716
Toll for the brave, 267
  never asked for the, 389
  of all the shades, take, 858
  Roland toll, 620
  that makes the land forlorn, 346
  without oppress of, 585

Tolled, and the sexton, the bell, 392
Tom beaten by Legree, 480
  Bowling, a sheer hulk lies poor, 274
  Bowling, darling of our crew, 274
  Fool's errand, upon a, 241
  Heaven be thy aid Poor, 375
  keep the boy, 924
  Lincoln's wife to-day, 792
  loves me best that calls me, 129
  or Jack, hails you, 267
  's a-cold, poor, 99
  Tiddler's ground, busy we are, 512
Tom's food seven long year, 99
Tomata, ruddy ripe, 637
Tomb before me, in the, 340
  cold embraces of the, 218
  darkness encompass the, 343
  for its, 384
  is shadowless, dark o'ershadowing, 672
  kings for such a, 161
  more than royal, 111
  nature cries from the, 245
  no inscription on my, 329
  of a mediocre talent, 788
  of affection and guilt, 956
  of him who would have made glad the world, 423
  of the Capulets, 261
  shall 'scape the, 984
  stood upon Achilles', 360
  surviving the voiceless, 848
  tapping on a, 1078
  threefold fourfold, 119
  with no pickaxe to force it, 756
Tombs, hark from the, 199
  in the Abbey, 788
  in the cool, 854
  many fair, 540
Tombstone, cannot read his, 872
  fame what some wan writes on ye'er, 796
  white, is a, 783
Tomes, faded prints and massive, 899
Tomlinson, naked soul of, 781
Tommy this an' Tommy that, 781
To-morrow and dead yesterday, 1019
  and its needs, Lord for, 645
  and to-morrow, 88
  be to-day, 438
  boast not thyself of, 1108
  call it, 1068
  comes down the starry track, 837
  death is but one more, 579
  defer not till, 193
  do thy worst, 177
  fair adventure of, 58
  I may be myself, 1018
  in to-day already walks, 318
  is falser than the former day, 178
  is only a vision, 953
  let my sun, 168
  lose to-day may win, they who, 1033

To-morrow morning, if I stand here until, 558
  never leave that till, 227
  put off till, 553, 791
  sees undone, 1058
  sing, way to make, 793
  speed to-day to be put back, 25
  take care of to-morrow, 418
  the darkest day live till, 267
  to fresh woods, 160
  we know nothing of, 314
  we shall die, 1111
  whoever says, 648
  will be a new day, 1040
  will be another day, 732
  will be dying, 133
  will be the happiest time, 463
  will climb, and every, 821
  will repay, think, 178
To-morrows, confident, 303
To-morrow's confusion, 629
  mystic gates, beyond, 568
  sun may never rise, 193
  tangle, 1018
Tone, awoke an answering, 405
  bitter, 642
  dwells in that mighty, 501
  is music's own, her every, 405
  low and trembling, 658
  of thought, probing the, 858
  ripe age gives, 573
  soft light and low, 499
  with a peremptory, 263
  your wants low enough, 538
Tones, harp in divers, 436, 467
  in its hollow, 363
  like rusty razor blades, 785
  of all great nature's, 503
  that will haunt us, 406
Tong, never eare did heare that, 26
Tonge, restreyne and kepe wel thy, 8
Tongs, shovel and, 389
Tongue, a soothing, 109
  an unruly member, 1122
  at Champmedy, bury my, 929
  at will, yet never loud, 101
  bear welcome in your, 84
  blabs, when my, 54
  braggart with my, 88
  brings a several tale, every, 72
  can no man tame, 1122
  confuted by his conscience, 147
  dropped manna, 149
  fair words never hurt the, 29
  fluent, 278
  from evil, keep thy, 1103
  give thy thoughts no, 90
  give understanding but no, 90
  good, in your head, 33
  hide it under his, 1102
  in every wound of Caesar, 83
  is an unruly evil, 1122
  is known in every clime, our, 394
  is loosed most, 649
  is the only edge tool, 344
  is the pen of a ready writer, 1104
  law of kindness in her, 1109
  let a fool hold his, 990
  let the candied, 94
  man that hath a, 34
  man's, not able to conceive, 43

Tongue, more silk on his, 426
  most dangerous spell, magic of, 426
  muscles in the, 1022
  music's golden, 383
  my love's more richer than my, 98
  my songs that found no, 444
  never eare did heare that, 26
  nor heart cannot conceive nor name thee, 86
  nor speak with double, 409
  not she denied him with unholy, 349
  of bronze and salt, great, 929
  of dog, wool of bat and, 87
  of him that makes a jest, 41
  of midnight hath told twelve, 43
  of the mind, pen is the, 1040
  Oh singing, 929
  our own good Saxon, 397
  our sweet English, 881
  outvenoms all the worms of Nile, 105
  repented that he held his, 990
  restless violent hands and casual, 806
  restreyne and kepe wel thy, 8
  sad words of, 442
  slow of speech and of slow, 1098
  so sharp, with that, 773
  so sweet a, 911
  so varied in discourse, 326
  soul lends the, vows, 91
  sounds as a sullen bell, 64
  such a, glad I have not, 98
  sweet morsel under his, 187
  that Shakespeare spake, 298
  the owner's, doth publish everywhere, 108
  the servile fetters breaks, 193
  the speaking, 413
  thy, thy own shame's orator, 38
  tip of his subduing, 109
  to conceive nor heart to report, 43
  to persuade, 270
  to wound us, no, 336
  treasure of our, 30
  truth in every shepherd's, 21
  unholy, 349
  use of my oracular, 277
  when the crowd gives, 928
  win a woman with his, 34
  windy satisfaction of the, 220
  with fire upon their, 889
  woman with the serpent's, 737
  would my horse had the speed of your, 38
Tongues, airy, 157
  and deeds, noise of, 462
  are cut by the hunter, 929
  as walls, woods have, 470
  aspic's, for 't is of, 103
  called fools in all, 51
  censure of sarcastic, 1017
  conscience hath a thousand several, 72
  evil days and evil, 153
  hearts in love use their own, 38
  in trees books in the running brooks, 48

Tongues, interest speaks all sorts of, 1043
  lovers', by night, 78
  meddlesome, 474
  nations kindreds and, 1123
  of dying men, 59
  of love, silent, 1034
  of men, speak with the, 1120
  shall rehearse, 108
  silence envious, 73
  slanderous, done to death by, 40
  strife of, 1103
  that syllable men's names, 157
  to allure him, thousand, 257
  with more difficulty than their, 1048
  woods have, 6
Tongueless, one good deed dying, 56
  silence of the dreamless dust, 603
Tongue-tied, but remains, 964
  by authority, 107
Tonics and beauty-creams, 901
To-night, are met in thee, 612
  then fill, with hearts as light, 431
Too black for heaven, 174
  civil by half, 278
  fond for idle scorning, 447
  full for sound and foam, 472
  great for our belief, 503
  innocent for coquetry, too fond, 447
  late I stayed, 294
  little for our heart, 503
  low they build, 202
  much rein, 33
  much thinking, 209
  pure in aught to disguise, 593
Took up so gingerly, 33
Tool, magic, 348
  maker stacker of wheat, 855
  no doubt an easy, 900
  of iron, nor any, 266
  scourge the, 659
  that grows keener with constant use, 344
Tools, always work and, 524
  dynamos bridges towers, 936
  given a bag of, 680
  no jesting with edge, 131
  nothing but to name his, 141
  of civilized table warfare, 922
  of working our salvation, 143
  sin has many, 454
  they get, can use the, 928
  to him that can handle them, 377
  were made and born were hands, 282
Too-late, I am called, 577
Tooley Street tailors, 578
Toonerville trolley, 852
Tooth and nail, 1032
  every, in a man's head, 1034
  for tooth, eye for eye, 1098
  hunger's savage, 599
  is out, the, 473
  never shows a, 898
  of time, 37, 203
  poison for the age's, 57
  sharper than a serpent's, 98
Toothache, endure the, 40
  or sore eyes, give me, 955

Toothpicks, supply of, 417
Tooth-point, where each, 776
Toothy ecstasies, 871
Top, die at the, 192
  little round button at, 246
  o' the mornin', 685
  of it reached to heaven, 1098
  of judgment, 36
  of my bent, fool me to the, 95
  of my head were taken off, feel as if the, 586
  of the tree, 622
  of the wave, 963
  recoils, near the, 223
  shakes not its, 1021
  whips his taxed, 314
Tops, fruit-tree, 78
  of the eastern pines, 59
  of the highest mountains, 238
Top-hat and plain worn shawl, 857
Topic peremptorily forbidden, 414
Topics, fashionable, 254
  keep to the old, 752
Topless towers of Ilium, 31
Topmost apple, 960
  beacon-tip, from, 490
Topples round the west, 468
Toppling lift of the young men, 914
Topsy-turvy, from my, 574
Torch, a bright, 384
  held in a mighty hand, 848
  in flame, like a, 765
  man is a, 856
  we throw the, 820
  when once wasted, 447
Torches, light my candle from their, 125
Tore his hair, skipper stormed and, 508
Torment and with tears, dark with, 516
  for our crimes, 828
  greater than envy, 985
  thou art to me a delicious, 411
  touch them, shall no, 1124
Torments, from time's slow, free, 837
  of grief you endured, 410, 420, 733
Torn me and I bleed, they have, 353
Torpedo, pen becomes a, 233
Torpedoes, damn the, 402
Torpid, mind grows, 236
Torrent and whirlwind's roar, 249
  breezy leap of the, 543
  is heard, naught but the, 269
  of a downward age, 224
  of a woman's will, 204
  of darkness, 864
  of his fate, 230
  of sound, 649
  roar, should like the, 211
  so the loud, 249
  tempest and whirlwind of passion, 94
Torrents, motionless, 316
Torrent's roar, 258
Torrid tracts, through, 251
Tortoise has an arbitrary stomach, 247
  near the winning post, 962

Torture, hum of human cities is, 353
  mental and physical, 1081
  one poor word, 175
  out of the heart's eternal, 889
  suspense in news is, 157
Tortured mind, 373
Torturing hour, 243
Toss him to my breast, 136
  slight, over ambient ether, 569
Total depravity of inanimate things, 654
  neglect and oblivion, consign to, 324
Tots sang ring-a-rosie, 761
Touch, beautiful beneath his, 327
  dares not put it to the, 164
  electric, 412
  exquisite, is denied me, 312
  its beautifying, 690
  lose the common, 783
  love's tender human, 682
  my heart, I, 953
  no earthly power can stay, 595
  no state matters, 251
  not taste not, 1121
  of a vanished hand, for the, 465, 688
  of celestial temper, 152
  of earth, must have a, 470
  of fate, hurry at the, 833
  of greatness, some far-off, 470
  of joy or woe, 248
  of nature, one, makes the whole world kin, 75
  of the hand, at a, 838
  of the one, lose the, 1084
  put it to the, 164
  soiled by any outward, 162
  that's scarcely felt, 221
  the best, fear not to, 21
  them but rightly, 289
  truth needs no other, 119
  us gently Time, 350
  we feel the tenderest, 177
  wound with a, 221
  your kiss, your, 870
Touches of sweet harmony, 47
Touched his harp and nations heard, 393
  nothing that he did not adorn, 231
  spirits are not finely, 35
  the highest point, I have, 73
Touchstone, man's true, 131
Touchy testy pleasant fellow, 196
Tough as a hickory rail, 927
  is J. B., 496
  morsels to swallow, 1081
  wedge for a tough log, 989
  world, rack of this, 100
Tough-gristled, ear so, 492
Tough-hearted widow, that frisky, 756
Toujours gai, her word is, 852
Toun, callen daysies in our, 4
Toung to give faire words, 13
Tourist, know the worthy, 645
Tourists, we are Cook's, 715
Tours de force of the great Paganini, 630
Tous les hommes sont fous, 472
Tousle-haired, all, 907
Toves, the slithy, 598
Tower, Aladdin's, 437
  and tree, light on, 277

Tower, be as a, 1021
  came, Child Rowland to the dark, 99
  collected in the, 743
  from some celestial, 635
  from that gloomy shadowed, 705
  from yonder ivy-mantled, 868
  guardian on the, 517
  I like a, 789
  in old St. Bavon's, 620
  in the town, from a proud, 459
  inaccessible, 529
  intending to build a, 1117
  is fallen, 375
  mounteth a loftier, 964
  of ivory, 858
  of ivory, as if in his, 1070
  of strength, king's name is a, 72
  of strength, that, 467
  reached his, 320
  that is left, 668
  town and castle, 109
Towers above her sex, Marcia, 195
  along the steep, 327
  although ye be in lofty, 1126
  and at the tyrant's, 983
  and battlements, 160
  and castles, sure enough the, 919
  and ships, 965
  are grey, 562
  distant spires ye antique, 243
  dwell upon ivory, 893
  elephants indorsed with, 156
  fall with heavier crash, 983
  gold as ripened grain, 1073
  it would be in, 914
  looked its stately, 562
  of affirmation, 925
  of Ilium, burnt the topless, 31
  of Julius, ye, 244
  of sail at dawn, two, 519
  the cloud-capped, 33
  whispering from her, 548
  ye antique, 243
Towered citadel, 105
  cities please us then, 160
Towering falcons, hopes like, 189
  in her pride of place, 86
  in the confidence of twenty-one, 233
  passion, put me into a, 97
Town, a haunted, 673
  all around the, 761
  and in that, 254
  axis of the earth in every, 454
  beyond the, 938
  callen daysies in our, 4
  came out to see, while all the, 600
  cannot complete her soul, 857
  common talk of the, 181
  credit in ilka, 311
  every time I come to, 956
  gaze with all the, 374
  hideous, 609
  hot time in the old, 767
  is at her twinkling feet, 908
  is lighter than vanity, 172
  like a place distressed and for-saken, 182
  London is a man's, 709
  man made the, 264, 759

Town, never go down to the end of the, 876
  no, can hope prosperity, 661
  of Bethlehem, O little, 612
  proud tower in the, 459
  taller, than Rome, 827
  that boasts inhabitants, a, 437
  the messenger lost we lost the, 572
  this poor little one-horse, 615
  unto the nearest, 585
  worth a month in, 587
Towns and noblemen are made, 931
  burning, and ruined swains, 262
  elephants for want of, 190
  from Albany to San Diego, 884
  of stones, hundred little, 810
  where the pots hold more, 744
Town-meeting days, 404
Townsman of a stiller town, 743
Towser, mastiff sent Pepys by a surgeon, 181
  Sport Spot or Fido, 922
Toy you have desire to purchase, some, 55
Toyle, sleepe after, 24
Toys are divine, 555
  bring you coloured, 1084
  I shall see his, 580
  of age, beads and prayer-books, 208
  of stimulated stature, 430
  pleasures are but, 121
  thou rememberest of what, 556
  to the great children, 225
  we spent them not in, 167
Toy dog, the little, is covered with dust, 699
Toy soldier, the little, is red with rust, 699
Trace, leave no lasting, 870
  of kinship, 764
Traces lead 'em, and in the, 526
  on winter's, 633
Traced with his golden pen, 516
Tracings of eternal light, 1059
Track, around the ancient, 575
  pursue, each other's, 178
  single, 644
  with a golden, 857
Tracks go out of sight, 927
Trackless seas, launch out on, 537
Track-mark of an ancient crime, 965
Tract, curst by priestly, 881
  one untrodden, 612
Tracts, leaves no, 28
  through torrid, 251
Tractors and your travelling-cranes, 936
Trade a matter of tariffs, 739
  and last quotations, throng for, 604
  Aquarius, how is your, 924
  can give, except what, 492
  extension of, 739
  follow far-fatiguing, 247
  heel of the north-east, 778
  in the luxuries of life, 1077
  is to rectify error, 235
  literature as a, 318
  of blood and guile, 316
  of lying, 1027
  of using words, 705

Trade, teaching him a, 1020
  thou learned, love the little, 1010
  two of a, 574
  two of a, can never agree, 206
Trades, ugliest of, 417
Tradesman has taken to wearing it, 1083
  must have patience, 225
Tradesmen, lying becomes none but, 57
Trading street, they that live in a, 198
Tradition, desert, for a spontaneous thought, 414
  finally becomes holy, 1079
  grows more venerable, 1079
  of the Victorian age, 925
  wears a snowy beard, 442
Trafalgar, burns from, 765
Traffic conditions, curtailed by, 1089
  of Jacob's ladder, 749
  road collects, 705
Tragedie, go litel myn, 4
Tragedies are finished by a death, 359
  Attic, 162
  generally sincere, 794
  two in the world, 724
Tragedy, black, 620
  comedy through my pages, 652
  gorgeous, 161
  makes vulgar the, 794
  of a world at strife, 760
  of Hamlet with the prince left out, 311
  of love, 835
  of man, 751
  of the age, 802
  to die ignorant, 380
  to those who feel, 246
Tragic effects of power, 636
  life God wot, in, 574
  quality, your, 895
  years, the, 728
Trail ahead, the long dim, 878
  go from the, 783
  held true, 778
  of the serpent, 338
  pull out on the long, 778
  runs to the westward, your, 697
  that is always new, 778
  time to turn on the old, 778
  vagrant beauty's, 828
  whistle up the, 847
Trails await me, far, 831
  her robes of gold, evening, 418
Trail-breaker, still the, 929
Trailing clouds of glory, 301
  garments of the night, heard the, 418, 433
Train, a melancholy, 250
  a royal, believe me, 74
  below, starve the numerous, 185
  caught the, 700
  delusive, 551
  fear and bloodshed miserable, 300
  filled the temple, 1111
  I wouldn't take, 916
  is slow and old, 890
  it was, what a dear old, 892
  little to disquantity your, 98

Train, loveliness descending from the, 559
  of stars, 693
  of thy amber-dropping hair, 158
  of unforeseen and unsupposed circumstances, 271
  serpent, 431
  starry, heaven her, 152
  trotted near the, 936
  up a child, 1108
  when I am dead no pageant, 374
  who follows in His, 343
Trains beyond the Missouri, 841
  pass, ever' time de, 934
Train-attendant, nor for a, 285
Training, do not develop without, 1078
Training-school for making first-class men, 538
Traitor, love treason but hate the, 116
  on the hip, you've hit no, 504
  or true, 792
  well, loves His, 650
Traitors, fears do make us, 87
  our doubts are, 35
Traitorous kiss, 349
  thieves, these, 1022
Trammel up the consequence, 85
Trammels of the world, 330
Tramp is a landlord, every, 937
  the long day's, 873
Trample an empire down, can, 676
  on my days, 170
Trampled and beaten were they, 436
Trampling out the vintage, He is, 522
Tramplings of three conquests, 145
Trances, all my days are, 460
Tranquil mind, farewell the, 102
Tranquilities, slow, 920
Tranquillity after noise, 609
  dismiss it with frigid, 232
  heaven was all, 338
  of mind, 1016
  thou better name, 316
  which religion is powerless to bestow, 415
Transatlantic commentator, 399
Transcendent capacity, genius is the, 379
Transcribed, what is, 233
Transfigures you and me, that, 522
Transforms old print, 265
Transgression, lay not my, to my charge, 57
Transgressors, way of, 1107
Transient chaste, early bright, 202
  fragrance, flowers of, 231
  hour, catch the, 231
  meteors, 344
  sorrows simple wiles, 299
Transition, what seems so is, 435
Translated, thou art, 43
Translation can be just, no literal, this, 217
  is at best an echo, 407
  is no translation, 818
  just as well in a, 236

Translation, lightly and joyfully meet its, 538
Translations and editions, all the, 238
Translucent wave, glassy cool, 158
Translucid presence, with that, 897
Translunary things, 30
Transmigration of souls, belief in, 798
Transmission of the highest feelings, 1077
Transmitted effluence, 366
Transmitter of a foolish face, 223
Transmutes, subdues, 300
Transom of a merchant brig, 413
Transparent like some holy thing, 337
Transport myself with a wish, 197
Transports of a British muse, 185
Transportation in the United States, 906
Trap for pleasure, no, 588
Trapeze, young man on the flying, 640
Trappings and suits of woe, 89
Trash, who steals my purse steals, 102
Travail, labour for my, 74
Travailes of the painefull day, 26
Travaille, myn be the, 6
Travel, foreign, 571
  is a part of education, 110
  narrative of, 1083
  on life's common way, 298
  the pleasure of, 1083
  thought the, long, 25
Travels, contemplation of my, 51
  he, the fastest, 783
  in divers paces, time, 50
Travelled a good deal in Concord, I have, 514
  in realms of gold, 384
  life's dull round, 242
Traveller and his master, 928
  from Lima, 399
  from New Zealand, 398
  from the Zuyder Zee, 399
  has a right, 1056
  hereafter some, 398
  now spurs the lated, 87
  returns, from whose bourn no, 93
  that goes afoot is swiftest, 514
  through a dusty road, 504
Travellers have come to be taken, 933
  must be content, 48
  proper for us, 490
  two, Roger and I, 572
Traveller's journey, to direct, 435
Travelling all same pace, 449
  bad on new or old road, 377
  earth, shadow of our, 447
  expense and fatigue of, 1039
  is to regulate imagination, 238
  on the beaten road, 376
Travelling-cranes, tractors and your, 936
Traverse may the poorest take, this, 585
Tray Blanch and Sweetheart, 99
  my poor dog, 328, 567

Tray's ever faithful, old dog, 567
Treacherous flatteries without winking, damn, 522
phantom men call liberty, 532
Treacle, fly that sips, 205
Tread again the scene, who would, 306
ever so airy a, 469
grapes of the wine-press which ye, 401
in air, seem to, 219
lightly she is near, 722
my days, 591
on another year, 626
on classic ground, 195
softly bow the head, 349
the globe, all that, 371
the land whereon we, 386
upon another's heel, one woe, 96
upon my patience, 61
walk with careless, 641
where angels fear to, 212
Treads alone some banquet-hall, 336
so light the grass stoops not, 106
Treason and plot, gunpowder, 945
bitter with, 631
can but peep, 96
corporations cannot commit, 21
doth never prosper, 29
flourished over us, bloody, 83
has done his worst, 87
if this be, make the most of it, 270
none dare call it, 29
to his country, 233
Treasons, malaria's countless, 811
stratagems and spoils, 47, 379
Treasure, a witty woman is a, 576
hath found a, 1124
is never molested, where, 593
is, where your, 1114
of his eyesight, 77
of our tongue, 30
rich the, 176
schooners and buried, 842
unsunned heaps of miser's, 158
what a, hadst thou, 92
what men call, Gods call dross, 528
without stealth, 21
your choicest, 809
Treasures, extent of your, 640
hath he not always, 317
heart has hidden, 507
in heaven, 1114
love light and calm thoughts, 317
sea-born, fetched my, 408
that were mine, 890
up a wrong, him who, 357
yet richest the, 791
Treasure-galleon, like some rare, 576
Treasure-thoughts friendships and hopes, 363
Treasury's marble front, 604

Treaties, meanest of, signed at Versailles, 799
Treatise on geometry, saved by chance a, 300
rouse at a dismal, 88
Treatment, humane, 1074
most kind, 394
one sort of, may serve for all, 402
to help the sick, 971
Treaty, proffered, 447
Treble, turning again toward childish, 50
Tree, a poem lovely as a, 890
at all, I'll never see a, 935
aye sticking in a, 311
billboard lovely as a, 934
come to the sunset, 370
die at the top like that, 192
dies, if a, 1054
falls, soon as the great, 594
for one that makes a, 681
friendship is a sheltering, 317
from the shadow of a, 666
fruit of that forbidden, 148
give me again my hollow, 214
hale green, 446
he that planteth a, 710
I planted, thorns of the, 353
in a kind old, 812
interest in planting a, 589
is inclined, as twig is bent the, 209
is known by his fruit, 1115
ivy from a sacred, 758
last leaf upon the, 450
light on tower and, 277
like a green bay, 1104
lopped, may grow again, 997
lovely as a pulpwood, 934
near his fav'rite, 245
'neath yon crimson, 372
north side of a, 920
of deepest root is found, 272
of liberty, 1059
of liberty must be refreshed, 273
of life, apples from the, 856
of life, shake the, 807
of life, the middle tree, 151
of prohibition, root of all our woe, 155
on my ancestral, 451
or flower, never loved a, 338
plant a, 712
planted by the waters, 1112
planted for posterity, 589
she gave me of the, 155
shelter about the mahogany, 481
sits on the ancestral, 768
spare the beechen, 328
sprouted up and grew into a, 504
stands so lonely, pine, 1065
stump of a little, 1055
that falls before the saw, 934
that may in summer wear, 890
that never had to fight, 846
the starry, 655
they'd knock on a, 747
to the top of the, 622
too happy happy, 383
tossed by the autumn wind, 924
'twas on a, 664

Tree, under a sycamore, 255
under the greenwood, 48, 394
vine on a tall, 1085
who plants a, 715
whose girth will prove its age, 934
whose roots are in a drain, 814
with fruit unharvested, 568
with grace toward heaven rising, 934
woodman spare that, 328, 404
Zaccheus he did climb the, 947
Trees and fields tell me nothing, 207
and men and grass, 531
are brown, and all the, 523
birch most ladylike of, 525
bosomed high in tufted, 160
brotherhood of venerable, 298
darkness among the gusty, 864
drop tears as Arabian, 104
fall and perish, loftiest, 969
grow and hills tower, 895
has most insincere line, 898
hewn from different, 805
I wonder about the, 838
If and Invictus annoying verse, 898
in a city square, 831
in their blooming, 736
just hid with, 346
like leaves on, 218
on either hand, 702
promontory with, 105
seem more resigned, 841
shade of the, 928
shall be my books, 50
sober realm of leafless, 551
tall ancestral, 370
taproots of New England, 927
that grow, of all the, 782
that would march, 858
the rustling of the, 955
to benefit another generation, 979
tongues in, 48
unto the root of the, 1117
used to living with people, 928
walking, I see men as, 1116
walking with the, 848
when lopped and cut, 997
Tree's summit, from a, 384
Tree-toad is a chef-d'oeuvre, 535
the three-toed, 815
Tree-tops, over the whispering, 759
Trelawney die, and shall, 416
Tremble for my country, I, 274
like a guilty thing, 301
my firm nerves shall never, 87
while they gaze, angels, 243
Trembler in the world's storm-troubled, 516
Tremblers, boding, 251
Trembles, to a lily, 648
too, turning, 248
Trembling, a rosy, 1086
from its birth, 587
strings, across the, 364
Tremendous object, most, 253
ruin, entails, 966
Tremor of heartstrings magnetic, 633
Tremulous beliefs, 798
Trenchant blade, 142
Trencherman, a very valiant, 38

Trespassers, downtrod by many, 963
Trespasses, forgive us all our, 877
Tresses fair, ensnare, 212
    flowing, in wavy, 406
    gray, withered cheek and, 306
    like the morn, 158
    one by one, 600
    whitening lip and fading, 452
Trevi's edge, tossed my coin from, 711
Trial, anything of human, 626
    by juries, 273
    on, in the world, 679
Triangular holes and persons, 314
Tribal lays, constructing, 780
Tribe, hopeless sallow, 530
    increase, may his, 346
    is the badge of all our, 44
    or clan, family party, 952
    richer than all his, 104
    that highly respectable, 954
    were God Almighty's gentle-men, 174
Tribes, formed of two mighty, 361
    phantom, 681
    that slumber in its bosom, 371
Tribe's hands, feed out of, 786
Tribunal, then will come a Na-tional-Socialist State, 1090
Tribute, laid all nature under, 290
    not one cent for, 276
    of a sigh, the passing, 245
    of a smile, vain, 307
    of its love and tears, 603
    or betrayal, 887
    to his grave, 307
    to other nations, paying, 1066
    to the memory of Boatswain, 352
Tributes he pays, one of the, 914
Trick and wile, turning many a, 282
    does the, 962
    is over, long, 832
    of our English nation, 64
    of shaking dangerous ques-tions, 429
    of singularity, 55
    one ugly, 339
    tried the same, 962
    when in doubt win the, 197
    wins the, 649
    worth two of that, I know a, 61
Tricks, his tenures and, 96
    in plain and simple faith, 83
    plays such fantastic, 36
    such, hath strong imagination, 43
    that are vain, 644
Tricking and stopping sleepy and proud, 903
Trident, flatter Neptune for his, 76
Tried each art, 250
    little knowest thou that hast not, 25
    to blame that has been, 221
    to live without him, 114
    without consent been only, 128
Tries, knows not till he, 989

Trifle, as 't were a careless, 84
    at her time of life, no, 520
    for my love, this utter, 683
    think naught a, 203
Trifles, all these things are, 572
    are trifles, 701
    dispense with, 34
    light as air, 102
    make happiness or misery, 589
    make the sum of human things, 275
    make the sum of life, 497
    snapper-up of unconsidered, 56
    which no poet sings, 578
    win us with honest, 84
Trifling handful, just take a, 569
    points, on, 332
Trim array, puts forth in, 300
    dressed in all his, 108
    gardens, in, 160
    gilded vessel in gallant, 244
    he that shot so, 77
    meadows, 160
    reckoning, 63
    that shoots so, 255
Trimmed off when once plucked, 551
Trinity, some calling on the, 374
Trio, consider friends this, 795
Trip I did not take, 899
    is done, my captain our fear-ful, 536
    it as you go, 160
    time to enjoy a European, 791
Triple mail, need of, 886
    ways to take, there be, 1109
Tripoli, shores of, 953
Trips on the green, lassie that, 388
Triptolemus, laws ascribed to, 963
Trissotin, half, 399
Triton blow his wreathed horn, 300
    of the minnows, hear you this, 76
Triumph advances, chief in, 308
    and defeat are in ourselves, 439
    and disaster, meet with, 783
    came, just as, 513
    in redeeming love, 280
    lament their, 444
    modern florist's, 569
    nature's bloodless, 443
    of hope, 235
    of spirit over gross material forces, 755
    over all mischance, 70
    over gravitation, man's, 1081
    pedestaled in, 491
    pursue the, 209
    that last, 735
    this is the poet's, 672
    typhus the successor of, 1067
    wherefore come ye forth in, 401
Triumphs of might are transient, 609
    of our own good Saxon tongue, 397
Triumphal arch, 328
    arch to yer conquering hero, 796
    arches, hew to ground, 212

Triumphant death, 155
    faith, o'er our fears, 435
    in this faith, 805
    navy rode, 240
Triumphed, Jehovah has, 336
    over time, 22
Triumphing over death and chance and time, 161
Trivet, right as a, 350
Trivial contribution, beg a, 760
    dwelling upon the, 893
    fond records, 92
    people should muse and thun-der, 883
    personalities decomposing, 878
    round the common task, 365
    theme, 578
    things, contests rise from, 212
Trochee trips from long to short, 317
Trod down my lofty name, 620
    proper men as ever, 81
    upon eggs, as if he, 125
Trodden low, 575
    out, little fire is quickly, 70
    the wine-press alone, 1112
Trojans, the distant, 218
Trolley that meets all the trains, 852
    the Toonerville, 852
Trollope has written more first-class novels, 505
    plot related by Osler, 695
Troop, farewell the plumed, 102
    of birds, a golden, 847
Troops, at the head of my, 1060
    considered the best, what, 1061
    of error, charged the, 144
    of friends, love obedience, 88
    of solemn people, 924
    that were led, 951
Trope, out there flew a, 141
Trophies and dead things, 128
    need not raise, 167
    pass away, 640
    unto the enemies of truth, 144
Tropic for your balm, try, 923
    love, 879
    under the, 146
Tropics, pass both, 114
    zones and meridian lines, 599
Troth, not break my, 40
    time tries the, in everything, 17
Trots, time, 50
Troubadour, gayly the, 388
Trouble came, ready when, 744
    capacity of taking, 379
    certain amount of, 853
    concerns the sky and sea, 994
    double toil and, 87
    drives me into rhyme, 909
    enough, in his own mind, 166
    enough of its own, 718
    happens to other people, 853
    is a ton, 792
    is a trouble, a, 870
    is sure, 743
    is what you make it, 792
    it is not our, 853
    it is there, 952
    kindness in another's, 601
    man is born unto, 1102
    mine were of, 744
    of few days and full of, 1102
    of liking them, 323

Trouble of the rain, useful, 470
  of washing my dead body, 970
  our days begin with, 947
  pain or care or, 1063
  present help in, 1104
  pressed, pretty hard by, 730
  remedy for every, 978
  soon smooth away, 894
  to herward, 776
  to invent an instrument, 933
  to learn a language, 236
  those who borrow, 946
  war his toil and, 176
  why all this toil and, 295
  wine to drown, 768
  ye, my presence doth, 68
Troubles, a peck of, 1034
  a whole lot of, 750
  against a sea of, 93
  come never too late, 418
  of our proud, 743
  of the brain, the written, 88
  of the little boy, 699
  there, put all your, 848
  we 've a whole lot of, 750
Troubled air, meteor to the, 244
  eyes, poetry turn, 822
  laughter of time, 869
  let not your heart be, 1118
  like a fountain, 52, 75
  waters, fish in, 188
  with thick-coming fancies, 88
Troublesome disguises, 152
  is day, how, 348
  nothing is more, 637
  women are, 163
Troublest me, thou, 72
Troubling, wicked cease from,
  1101
Troublous sights and sounds,
  796
  world, 71
Trousers badly need a patch behind, 754
  best, to fight for freedom, 1075
  steam-engine in, 313
Trout a crystal stair, build the,
  849
  big, would not ever escape,
  674
  in the milk, 515
  stipple upon, 672
  swim down Great Ormond
  Street, 904
Trouts bite best on Sabbath, 750
Trouthe is the hyeste thing, 8
Trovatore, best to my taste is
  the, 594
Trowel, laid on with a, 47
Troy divine, tale of, 161
  fired another, 176
  half his, was burnt, 64
  heard, doubted, 360
  imperial towers of, 212
  laid in ashes, 185
  windy, 464
Troy's doom-crimson shore, 881
  proud glories, 218
Truant, aged ears play, at his
  tales, 41
  children, like, 809
  husband should return, 358
Truce between virtue and vice,
  515
  to navigation, 623
  with Adam-zad, 779

Truce with rosy frailties, 576
Truck stood, on the main, 405
Trudged along unknowing, 176
Trudgin' my weary way, 678
True, all is not, 643
  always think what is, 564
  Amphitryon, 179
  and honourable wife, 82
  and lovely, dream is, 924
  and tender and brave and just,
  443
  are you good men and, 39
  as another, one religion is as,
  126
  as fate, 116
  as I live, 116
  as steel, 42, 79
  as the dial to the sun, 143
  as the needle to the pole, 143
  as turnips is, 496
  battled for the, 468
  beginning of our end, 43
  blue, Presbyterian, 142
  canst thou be, 793
  dare to be, 135
  dull minds generally preferred,
  343
  easy to be, 183
  enabled me to remain, 376
  eyes too pure and too honest,
  593
  faith and ready hands, 522
  friends less moved than counterfeit, 180
  from the false, distinguish the,
  1048
  good to be honest and, 286
  happiness is of retired nature,
  195
  hearts lie withered, 335
  hope is swift, 72
  I would be, 880
  if all be, 184
  if England to itself rest, 58
  in and for itself, is it, 1062
  industrious friend, dear and,
  60
  it is ever, 855
  it 's, I 've got no shirts to
  wear, 622
  joy in life, 720
  leisure one with true toil, 501
  like the needle, 248
  love, course of, never did run
  smooth, 42
  love is like ghosts, 1044
  love tho' given in vain, 470
  man's apparel, every, 37
  nobility is exempt from fear,
  69
  nothing, but heaven, 336
  of most we leave behind, 519
  original native of America, 228
  patriots all, 280
  perfection, praise and, 47
  pleasure of life, 483
  pride were not also, as if,
  493
  religion, like the, 950
  rest, and that is, 501
  retirement, 330
  right wrong, live pure speak,
  470
  science and study of man is
  man, 207
  servant's title, 441

True, so much is, 916
  sportsmen, disputants like, 217
  strange but, 361
  tender and, Douglas, 9
  test of civilization, 235, 414
  that any beauteous thing, 1023
  that liberty is precious, 1086
  that love will do no wrong,
  not, 556
  then we are sure they are, 57
  'tis pity and pity 'tis 'tis true,
  92
  to be simple modest manly, 528
  to certain ideals, 694
  to one another, let us be, 546
  to one party, 526
  to plan, if we are, 585
  to the kindred points of heaven,
  304
  to thine own self be, 91
  to true occasion, 467
  toil, true leisure one with, 501
  too good to be, 188
  unless she's, 628
  use of speech, 254
  valiant wise, 1037
  views, as fast as they appear,
  456
  way to be deceived, 1044
  we loved too, 429
  whatsoever things are, 1121
  which Appius says, 981
  while we 're Britons, 562
  while yet there is time, 847
  wit, the well of, 576
  worship of the infinitely, 604
True-fixed and resting quality,
  82
True-love hath my heart, my, 27
Truer truth obtainable, is no,
  493
Truest, the, hearts that ever, 386
  warrior, this was the, 516
Truism, men grind in the mill of
  a, 414
Truly longed for death, has ever,
  462
  loved never forgets, 335
Trump, come with, 832
  shrill, 102
  we hear, it is the, 896
Trumps, if dirt was, 325
Trumpet give an uncertain sound,
  1120
  hear the rattling, 508
  his own chronicle, his own, 75
  moved more than with a, 27
  of a child, 634
  of the morn, the cock, 89
  shifted his, 252
  sound no, 955
  sound the, beat the drums, 186
  sounds, ever and anon, 749
  the thing became a, 304
  to arms, blow the, 271
Trumpets, blare of, 1089
  silver snarling, 383
  sounded for him, all the, 172
Trumpet-tongued, angels, 85
Truncheon, the marshal's, 36
Trundle-tail, tike or, 99
Trunk, hide it in your, 847
Trunks of men, 46
Trust a few, 52
  a little, that when we die, 607
  a nation's, 373

Trust, all power is a, 420
  but put your money in, 454
  for beer, take you on, 715
  government is a, 329
  in all things high, 466
  in God, 312
  in God and do the right, 499
  in God is our, 332
  in God, put your, 329
  in him, they that put, 1124
  in his cussedness, 639
  in money, put not your, 454
  in princes, put not your, 1106
  in vinegar, put not your, 700
  let us to Providence, 519
  magistracy is a great, 261
  man on his oath, 80
  never threw in, 404
  no agent, 38
  no future howe'er pleasant, 433
  not your daughters' minds, 100
  office of more, 1035
  on whom I built absolute, 84
  power in, 173
  public office is a public, 188, 481
  sailor's, 661
  somehow good will be, 468
  soothed by an unfaltering, 372
  takes in, our youth, 22
  that all is best, to, 501
  that it procures, greater, 1000
  voter exercises a public, 627
  we are unfit for any, 559
  with steadfast, 1058
  yields up his, 348
Trusts, offices as public, 188, 339
Trusted, let no such man be, 47
  was ever poet so, 235
Trustees, officers of government are, 188
Trustful birds have built their nests, 668
Trusting everybody universal benevolence, 253
Trustworthy as you trust it, 347
Trusty drouthy cronie, 287
  dusky vivid true, 703
Truth, acknowledgment of, 1077
  alone with, 789
  and falsehood grapple, let, 1028
  and freedom, the spirit of, 1076
  and love approve, 427
  and loyalty, follow with, 48
  and loyalty, map of honour, 69
  and manhood, honor and, 843
  and noonday light to thee, 509
  and shame the devil, speak the, 62, 1026, 1040
  and soberness, words of, 1119
  appear to lie, 688
  as opposeth no man's profit nor pleasure, 132
  at His requiring taught, 442
  at least, this, 807
  authority and show of, 39
  be in the field, so, 163
  beauty and, are worthy to be sought, 655
  beauty righteousness, in, 1127
  between us forevermore, 413
  bitter barren, 533
  born to inquire after, 1030

Truth, bright countenance of, 162
  but O the, 575
  called to speak a disagreeable, 1056
  cannon-balls may aid the, 504
  cannot be assimilated, 1073
  crushed to earth shall rise again, 373
  desire of fame and love of, 471
  dignity of, 118
  divorcing themselves from, 379
  doubt, to be a liar, 92
  enemies of, 144
  entails tremendous ruin, 966
  even when he speaks the, 962
  ever has most strength, 967
  fancy deemed was only, 455
  fiction lags after, 259
  first to face the, 779
  folly to tell women, 507
  forever on the scaffold, 525
  found, in all but one, 60
  from his lips prevailed, 250
  from pole to pole, spread the, 194
  from symbols into the, 403
  from the people, 847
  great and mighty, 1123
  great is, 701, 1067
  great ocean of, 184
  has such a face, 174
  hath a quiet breast, 59
  he ought to die for, 410
  held the lamp of, 687
  her glorious precepts draw, 333
  His, is marching on, 522
  hold hard by, 491
  I felt this, 736
  I must speak the, 1037
  I will be harsh as, 424
  imagines he possesses, 1076
  impossible to be soiled, 162
  in action, justice is, 419
  in blue, doubted, 939
  in every shepherd's tongue, 21
  in man's imagination, 727
  in simple nakedness, white, 470
  in the ranks of, 550
  in the strife of, 524
  in unison with the, 1017
  in wine there is, 994
  increase to her, 240
  intention of communicating, 318
  is a bit of, 939
  is always strange, 361
  is beauty beauty is truth, 383
  is communicated to men, 1077
  is generally best vindication, 457
  is great and shall prevail, 556
  is precious and divine, 142
  is so though I perish, 519
  is still the light, 477
  is the highest thing, 8
  is the secret of eloquence, 1073
  is the shattered mirror, 544
  is the trial of itself, 119
  is truth, 37
  itself decays, 531
  keep in sight, this, 676
  laugh by speaking the, 835

Truth lay in a holy book, Mohammed's, 458
  lend her noblest fires, 351
  lie which is half a, 467
  love swears she is made of, 109
  man never harmed by, 1011
  may be, tell how the, 306
  may bear all lights, 377
  may sometimes be improbable, 361
  men wait their good and, 410
  mercy and, are met together, 1105
  miscalled simplicity, 107
  most dangerous enemy to, 1075
  mournful, 231
  must be sought with positivists, 570
  my soul abhors, less than, 508
  never an unflattering, 725
  never hurts the teller, 492
  never yet fell dead, 476
  not to be spoken at all times, 1031
  nothing but the, 1037
  nothing so powerful as, 342
  nothing so strange as, 342
  obtainable, is no truer, 493
  ocean of, all undiscovered, 184
  of a song, swear to the, 189
  of all but, 832
  of heaven, this, 669
  of history, 997
  of imagination, 385
  of the thing, know the, 137
  of truths is love, 507
  on the scaffold, 525
  one, is clear, 207
  or the satisfaction of intellect, 461
  out of Tusitala, 827
  pardon error but love, 1053
  patriot, 333
  philosophy conformable to, 669
  precedents evidence of, 329
  proclaim, his friends his, 173
  put to the worse, 163
  quenched the open, 308
  rather than love money fame, 515
  ride shoot straight and speak, 361, 811
  ridicule the test of, 377
  sanctified by, 303
  seeming, 46
  severe by fairy fiction drest, 244
  shall be thy warrant, 21
  shall ever come uppermost, 503
  shall make you free, 1118
  shall understand the, 1124
  simple, his utmost skill, 114
  so absolutely good is, 492
  so pure of old, kept thy, 162
  sole judge of, 208
  something that is not, 566
  soul of, 580
  speak as much as I dare, 1029
  speech is, 307
  statesman yet friend to, 210
  stood on one side, 476
  stranger than fiction, 361
  strife of, with falsehood, 524
  suffers more by heat of its defenders, 184

Truth, tell the, 235
  that has lasted a million years, 843
  that has lost its temper, 880
  the brilliant Frenchman never knew, 263
  the naked, 41
  the nursing mother of genius, 476
  the poet sings, this is, 440, 464
  the soul of the fact, 660
  the test of ridicule, 280
  the well of true wit is, 576
  there is no, in him, 1118
  this I set down as positive, 482
  this is petrified, 615
  those blessed, how sweet the, 503
  throughout the world, 303
  time brings increase to her, 240
  time trieth truth, 17
  time will teach thee soon the, 434
  to side with, is noble, 525
  to tell you the, 1036
  to the full round of, 471
  told with bad intent, 282
  took to telling the, 812
  urge him with, 220
  vantage ground of, 109
  was buried deep below, 114
  was felt by instinct, 490
  way to, 835
  we know, by the heart, 1047
  we might have kept, 659
  well known to most, 267
  were he to tell the, 808
  where doubt there, is, 506
  who has forgotten, 794
  who speaks, stabs falsehood, 524
  will come to light, 45
  will conquer, in the end, 8
  will sometimes lend her noblest fires, 351
  with gold she weighs, 215
  with him who sings, 436
  with the weapon of, 930
  within thy mind rehearse, this, 462
Truths, abstract, 477
  being in and out of favour, 838
  discovery of divine, 200
  electrify the sage, whose, 327
  fictions like to, 958
  great, are portions of the soul, 524
  half so sage as he wrote, 516
  I tell, believe the, 247
  instruments of darkness tell us, 84
  irrationally held, more harmful, 564
  more cruel than the worst of, 1046
  music tells no, 506
  must be sought, 570
  new, begin as heresies, 564
  opposed to human pride, 396
  that wake to perish never, 301
  to be self-evident, 273
  which are not for all men, 1053
  which she reveals to us, 1087
  who feel great, 507
Truth's sad ashes, from, 531

Truth's, thy country's thy God's and, 74
Truthful James, my name is, 644
Try by great thoughts and deeds, 506
  first then call in God, 968
  men's souls, times that, 271
  our fortunes, ready to, 65
  the fair adventure of tomorrow, 58
  the man, let the end, 64
  tropic for your balm, 923
Tryst so faithful, no, 824
Tub, tale of a, 1025
  to the whale, fling a, 191
  upon its bottom, every, 171
Tubal fashioned the hand-flung spears, 504
Tubby steamer, came from the, 925
Tubes are twisted and dried, 779
Tucson and Deadwood and Lost Mule Flat, 929
Tuesday's child is full of grace, 956
Tufted crow-toe, 159
  trees, bosomed high in, 160
Tug of war, then was the, 186
Tugged with fortune, 86
Tugging, don't advance for their, 492
Tulip beds, like windy, 891
Tumble, another, 391
  on heather, worse things than a, 309
  ready with every nod to, 72
Tumbling main, 406
Tumor that ends by killing, 635
Tumours of a troubled mind, 963
Tumult and the shouting dies, 780
  from the long, 848
  hard ye may be in the, 800
  in the city, 551
  in the midst of, 1070
  of the soul, 303
  stilled the rising, 770
Tumultuous body now denies, 894
  privacy of storm, 408
Tune, bells jangled out of, 94
  imaginable, the loveliest, 1083
  incapable of a, 323
  intends to put all in, 172
  is more lasting, 869
  memory plays an old, 512
  of flutes, 104
  our voices keep, 334
  out of, above the pitch, 1025
  should keep so long in, 199
  singeth a quiet, 315
  the drummers play, 845
  the happiest, 922
  to hear her is a, 586
Tunes, devil have all the good, 274
  like smitten tin, 785
  loathe sweet, 631
  taste for popular, 821
  that bring the laugh, 777
  that make you choke, 777
  that mean so much, 777
  were frozen, 1056
  wherein old passions rule, 755
Tuneful are and dear, that, 758

Tuneless in old age, 649
Tune-swept fiddlestring, 871
Turbants, white silken, 156
Turbid dream of life is waning, 396
Turbulence eludes the eye, 298
Turf, at his head a green grass, 256
  beneath their feet, 328
  green be the, above thee, 363
  green grassy, 269
  of fresh earth, smell to a, 147
  oft on the dappled, 298
  Peter, 52
  soft lies the, 479
  that the Puritans trod, 752
Turk and Brahmin monk and Jew, 755
  bear like the, 213
  or Proosian, 623
  out-paramoured the, 99
  the unspeakable, 382
  work as hard as a, 950
Turks becoming somewhat sad, 661
  fought with, 701
Turk's galley, on board a, 1047
Turkish salutation, the common, 1055
Turkman's rest, cheers the, 358
Turky more respectable bird, 228
Turmoil, din of, 725
Turn again, I keep and pass and, 410
  and fight another day, 143
  backward O Time, 595
  do a good, 418
  each thing his, does hold, 134
  it over once more, 402
  nay, not away that sweet head, 388
  one good, asketh another, 15
  over a new leaf, 116, 117
  the smallest worm will, 70
  to rain, mist and cloud will, 438
  turn my wheel, 439
  up, faith that something would, 421
  your hand to anything, 1036
Turns again home, 472
  and turns to say, 638
  at the touch of joy, 248
  good, you have done him, 976
  thought of all by, 301
  time goes by, 30
  with ceaseless pain, 249
Turner of the wheel, 650
Turning o' the tide, 66
  points of lives, 837
  road knows no, 965
  trembles too, 248
Turnings, lane that knows no, 487
Turnip did no harm, 953
  Mr. Finney had a, 953
Turnips, man who, cries, 238
  true as, 496
Turn-pike, man at the, bar, 389
  road is a delightful thing, 360
Turpentine, pill of, every morning, 181
Turpin, bold, 494
Turquoise tells wearer is not well, 118
Turret of the land, the vote that shakes the, 451

Turtle doves is singing sweet, 853
love of the, 355
thoughts of a, 415
voice of the, is heard, 1110
Tusitala, truth out of, 827
Tut tut child, 598
Tutelary and Guardian Angels, 1098
Twa bairns and but ae heart, 389
bairns at scule, 389
did part, 't was then we, 389
Twain have been tied up together, 472
have met like the ships, we, 587
henceforward, betwixt us, 470
never the, shall meet, 779
nothing now can make us, 576
together be, we, 1022
Twal, short hour ayont the, 284
Tweedledum and Tweedledee, 221
Twelve against the gods, 908
Christ himself chose only, 657
Cristes lore and his apostles, 5
good men into a box, 331
good rules, the, 251
honest men have decided, 203
hours longer, 592
in, found truth in all but one, 60
in the sworn, 35
miles from a lemon, 313
thousand, in, found none, 60
times dearer, love thee, 592
tongue of midnight hath told, 43
years, only, 866
Twelvemonth's length again, to run the, 286
Twenties have been passed, when the, 1072
Twentieth century, party will make the, 1069
spring, my, 452
Twenty bokes clad in blak, 5
days are now, long as, 297
kiss me sweet and, 54
men, the strength of, 80
miles away, and Sheridan, 552
more such names, 52
mortal murders, 87
of their swords, 78
pound a year, cannot live on, 136
pounds, annual income, 496
tedious years, 220
will not come again, 742
years on a woman's life, 973
years united, 668
Twenty-fifth hour, on the, 733
Twenty-five years of married life, 812
years of one's life, 407
Twenty-nine, she had a long, 751
Twenty-one, brave days when I was, 482
in the confidence of, 233
the minor pants for, 214
Twice as fast as that, run at least, 598
read, what is, 233
Twice-told tale, life is tedious as a, 58, 220
Twig is bent, just as the, 209
Twilight a timid fawn, 801

Twilight and evening bell, 472
darkened, and the, 929
deep'ning into night, 670
dews, no, 309
dim with rose, 822
disastrous, 149
fades away, as evening, 438
fair, as stars of, 299
gray in sober livery, 152
hour of breath, 796
interim, 386
lets her curtain down, 389
long spring evening's, 926
near, and, 916
of the heart, an evening, 363
of the kings, 763
of the pines, 443
of things that began, 633
repairing, when at, 328
spirit that dost render, 447
than live in the gray, 734
tide, 431
Twilights, her dusky hair like, 299
Twilight's curtain, 389
dream, one with, 801
Twilight-land, in, 620
Twin brethren, great, 400
happiness was born a, 359
of heathen hate, looked the, 471
Twins, body and spirit are, 634
fame and honor are, 1064
of winged race, 219
Twin-born of devotion, despair the, 632
Twin-brother, sleep death's, 468
Twine, loop of stronger, 510
Twinkle in her eye, 677
of cut gems, 933
twinkle little star, 345
Twinkling of an eye, 45, 940, 1039, 1120
Twirl, with a twist and a, 431
Twisted and dried, 779
Twitch quick as lightning, 143
Twitching my ear, Death, 982
Twitters, chirps and, 621
'Twixt two boundless seas, 337
Twm Barlum that green pap, 814
Two and two continue to make four, 611
are many three hardly possible, 636
are walking apart forever, 540
be away, if, 16
brief words, 309
carefree days, 670
clouds at morning, I saw, 375
discourse, where, 968
ears but only one mouth, given, 420
eternities, past and future, 337
good honest hands, 750
gray eyes, was taught me out of, 916
great European narcotics, 1081
halves of a pair of scissors, 495
handles, everything hath, 1008
hands upon the breast, 567
heads better than one, 13
heads in council, 466
hearts in one, 1032
hearts that beat as one, 1070
hit it off, seldom or never the, 942

Two hurrying shapes, 620
irons in the fire, 129
lay sleeping, O that we, 523
little words, in, 941
lives that once part are as ships, 425
lovely berries on one stem, 43
may keep counsel, 77
may talk and one may hear, 411
narrow words hic jacet, 22
of a trade, 206, 574
of that, trick worth, 61
of the great hinges, 242
oh that we, were Maying, 523
old chairs and half a candle, 498
or three are gathered together, where, 1115
owls and a hen, 499
pale feet crossed in rest, 567
rogues in buckram suits, 62
shall be born the wide world apart, 597
sides to every question, 1016
sorts of affection, 716
souls with single thought, 1070
Spaniards to come a Yankee o'er, 559
strings to his bow, 15
things stand like stone, 601
things to believe of any man, 809
to the world, 567
towers of sail at dawn, 519
voices are there, 304
walk together, can, 1113
went to pray, 165
wherever there are, 1126
who love are parted, when, 1065
who made love to his daughter, 996
whose welcome will not fail, 842
Two-and-seventy jarring sects, 1019
stenches, 317
Two-gun man, 888
Two-handed engine, 159
Two-headed Janus, 43
Two-legged animal, man is a, 1015
dogs, pompous, 458
thing a son, 173
Twopence coloured, penny plain and, 705
Two-penny damn, I care not one, 293
Two-thirds of all the time, 909
Tybalt lies, dim monument where, 80
Tying her bonnet under her chin, 600
Tyme goth and never may retourne, 3
it nil no man abyde, 7
that may not sojourne, 3
Type, careful of the, 468
noble, 436
of all her race, 474
of human nature, the highest, 581
of the wise who soar, 304
of things, loose, 298
Types apart, easy to tell the, 931

Types, device of movable, 379
  innumerable, 627
  of character, other, 975
  reproduction of formal, 723
Typhus the successor of triumph, 1067
Typical of strife, clubs, 266
Tyrannical habit of reading, 530
Tyrannies on human kind, of all, 174
Tyrannous to use it like a giant, 36
Tyranny and pride, thrones of, 706
  begins, where law ends, 230
  is a habit, 1074
  of Mrs. Grundy, 581
Tyrant, disappear forever in the, 1074
  east wind an impassive faced, 726
  fear that reigns with the, 435
  force, evermore shall, 576
  has disposed of foreign enemies, 974
  if you are a, 853
  like intemperance, world has no, 424
  of his fields, 245
  power, wrongs or, 396
  springs, root from which a, 974
  who misrules our land, 847
  will serve a, 961
Tyrants and slaves, 253
  from policy, kings will be, 260
  never invented, Sicilian, 985
  rebellion to, 260, 945
  safely govern home, how can, 70
  to, I will give no quarter, 424
  watered by the blood of, 1059
Tyrant's plea, necessity the 152
  towers, and at the, 983
Tyre, village which men call, 881
Tyro cried, a noble theme, 812

U GREEN, I red O blue, 1084
U.P. Railway, working for the, 644
U.S.S.R., in the, 1093
Ubi saeva indignatio ulterius cor lacerare nequit, 192
Ubiquitous press, 483
Ucalegon, Melchizedek, 807
Ugliest of trades, 417
Uglification and derision, 598
Ugliness, success hides all the, 163
Ugly and venomous, the toad 48
  ay as sin, the world 's as, 545
  fact, 588
  houses stand, 915
  sights, so full of, 71
  trick, one, 339
Ulterior shore, to the, 811
Ultimate angels' law, 489
  dominion, shall have, 851
  one, to an, 923
Ultimum moriens of respectability, 454
Ulysses' absence, yarn she spun in, 76
Umbered face, sees the other's, 67
Umbrella and the handle of a broom, 857

Umbrella for three, 599
  of no avail against a Scotch mist, 530
Umbrellas, carry bright, 923
Umpire of men's miseries, 68
Una with her milk-white lamb, 301
Unabashed, eagles that flew, 576
Unable any longer to defend himself, 1082
  as of old to jest, 1009
Unaccompanied by tact, 830
Unaccustomed to fear, 951
Unacknowledged legislators, 369
Unacquainted still with our own soul, 114
  with the A.B.C., 300
Unadorned, adorned the most, when, 224
Unadulterate light, never saw the, 1091
Unalienable rights, 273
Unalloyed, bliss, 1073
Unalterable days, the, 409
Unalterably and pesteringly fond, 472
Unaltered, ought not always to remain, 975
Unaneled, disappointed, 91
Unanimous chorus of praise, 1086
Unappeasable hunger, like, 890
Unapprehended inspiration, 369
Unashamed, delivers brawling judgments, 470
  his beauty share, 931
Unasked they never desist, 984
Unassuming commonplace, 298
Unattained, how vast the, 444
Unattempted yet in prose, 148
Unavenged, insults, 302
Unaware, I blessed them, 315
Unawares, like instincts, 458
Unawed by influence, 333
Unbaptized infants notorious drunkards, 651
Unbegotten souls, through, 667
Unbelief, alas the fearful, 380
  is, in yourself, 380
  there is no, 648
Unbeliever and religion, 403
Unbidden, I knock, 602
Unblemished let me live, 216
Unblest lamentation, hear my, 508
Unborn ages, ye, 244
  in states, 82
  things we choose while yet, 572
Unborrowed from the eye, 296
Unbought grace of life, 260
  health, hunt in fields for, 175
Unbounded courage, 194
  expansion, open it with, 1127
  stomach, man of an, 74
  we hold the, 647
Unbred Caesars, how meek those, 903
Unbribed by gain, 333
Unbroken horse, spur not an, 310
  thread, 955
Uncertain age, 357
  comes and goes, the world, 411
  coy and hard to please, 308
  glory of an April day, 33
  rustling of each purple, 460
  the visible for the, 1012

Uncertain, voyage, life's, 81
Uncertainty, certainty for an, 233
  cloaca of, 1047
Unchained, our, feet walk freely, 386
  strength, the giant's, 371
Unchallenged fate, lord of my, 579
Unchangeable, of the unchanging the, 823
Unchanged through time's flight, 1057
Unchanging law of God, 477
  principles of human nature, 344
  shore, on this dull, 502
Uncharitableness, all, 1127
Uncivilized Eastern instincts, 785
Uncle Fenner's family, besides us and my, 181
  Sam is rich enough, 502
  uncle me no, 947
Unclubable man, a very, 234
Uncoffined and unknown, 219
Uncoined constancy, plain and, 68
Uncompromising as justice, 424
  terms, in, 748
Uncompromisingness of dogma, 614
Unconcern, with restrained, 938
Unconditional surrender, 549
Unconfined, let joy be, 352
Unconquerable cry, 654
  hope, nursing the, 547
  mind, 297
  soul, my, 692
  will and study of revenge, 148
Unconquered, heights yet, 972
Unconscious gratitude, 1081
  greatness is, 377
  of decays, age, 178, 219
  of reproach, 425
Unconsciousness of sin, 828
  utter, 970
Unconsidered trifles, snapper-up of, 56
Uncorseted, her friendly bust, 900
Uncouth but gracious, 539
  makes ancient good, 525
Uncovered stand and sing by Lincoln's grave, 676
Uncreated night, 149
Uncreating word, before thy, 215
Uncritical buying public, 921
Unction, flattering, 95
Unctuous mouth which lured him, 465
Undazzled eyes, 163
Undefyled, well of English, 25
Undepressed in size, 302
Under the apple-boughs, home again, 508
  the rose, 145
Underground, put me, 577
  too petty, too, 1082
Under-jaw, most things move the, 136
Underlings of the multitude, 1000
  we are, 81
Underneath this sable hearse, 119
  this stone doth lie, 119
Understand a fury in your words, 103

Understand, believe what they least, 1030
Understanding and emotions, 1088
appeals to the, 950
dupe of the heart, 1044
fail, if his, 1124
for thy more sweet, 41
give it an, but no tongue, 90
has forsook me, my, 1041
joke into a Scotch, 246, 312
light a candle of, 10, 1123
more, than all my teachers, 1106
not obliged to find you an, 238
of a man, 1038
passeth all, 1121
perfect, may extinguish pleasure, 745
spiritual, 548
to direct, 270
with all thy getting get, 1106
with the hills, 849
Understood, harmony not, 207
interpreter hardest to be, 278
Undertaking, equal to any, 496
Undertone, in a sort of, 660
Undervalue me, if she, 22
Undescribable, describe the, 354
Undevout astronomer is mad, 202
Undiscovered country, 93
universe, the, 728
Undisputed thing, 451
Undisturbed by passion's sway, 685
Undoctored incident, 780
Undone, another victory we are, 113
day's work and night's work are, 630
his country, they 've, 195
in another fight I were, 1002
to want to be, 26
widow, some, 129
widows, thousands of, 116
wrongdoer that has left something, 1012
Undreamed shores, 57
Undress, fair, best dress, 224
her gentle limbs did she, 315
Undulate round the world serenely, 536
Uneasiness, left a sense of, 1056
Uneasy as an eel, 661
industrious to make themselves, 1036
lies the head, 65
light, remnant of, 298
Uneffectual fire, 'gins to pale his, 92
Unelected infant, an, 746
Unemployed, army of the, 1086
Unemployment, heard of, 935
problem, solved the, 898
Unenlightened opponent, 548
Unentreated way, in its own, 629
Unequals, among, 154
to equals and, 974
Unerring wisdom never dwelt, 1050
Uneven economic and political development, 1086
Unexampled prosperity, 343
voice of awful memory, 301
Unexercised, virtue, 163

Unexpected always happens, the, 978
death the best, 1003
Unexpressed thoughts sometimes fall back dead, 180
uttered or, 306
Unexpressive she, fair chaste and, 50
Unextinguished laughter, 218
Unfailing source rapid exhaustless, river of, 393
Unfaith in aught is want of faith, 470
Unfaithful to what we have been, 1087
Unfaltering trust, 372
Unfathomed caves of ocean, 245
center, of the, 386
Unfeathered two-legged thing, 173
Unfeatured air, my highway is, 517
Unfed sides, 99
Unfeeling for his own, 243
Unfelt sorrow, to show an, 86
Unfinished window in Aladdin's tower, 437
Unfirm, more giddy and, 54
Unfit, for all things, 252
for ladies' love, 176
we are, for any trust, 559
Unfitness, mite of, 528
Unfold, I could a tale, 91
Unfolds both heaven and earth, 42
Unfolding, soft, those portals, 387
Unforgettable day, that, 627
Unforgiving eye, 279
Unformed occident, 30
society waits, 537
Unforeseen and unsupposed, 271
disgrace, he bears his, 199
happiness, 1063
service, 339
Unforewarned, come, 373
Unformidable even pitiable, 651
Unfortunate above all, with the, 1074
by a calamity, 1012
Miss Bailey, 288
one more, 392
Unfree souls go west, 883
Unfriended melancholy slow, 249
Unfriendly disposition towards the United States, 283
ghosts, 'mid the, 842
to society's chief joys, 263
Unfruitful, invention is, 259
Unfurled, seemed to see our flag, 442
Unfurnished, head to be let, 142
Ungained, men prize the thing, 74
Ungainliness magnifies the idea of strength, 894
Ungalled play, the hart, 94
Ungemmed unhidden, wishing not to hurt, 917
Ungenerous, no good by being, 429
Ungenial climate, [Pilgrims] fell upon an, 550
Ungodly custom of swearing, 179
Ungracious pastors, 90

Ungrateful, man who is, 1044
Unguessed mystery, 444
unproved, their strength, 931
Unguents, gleaming with, 960
Unhabitable downs, 190
Unhabitual way, perceiving in an, 663
Unhairy chin, 618
Unhand me gentlemen, 91
Unhandsome corse, a slovenly, 61
Unhanged, not three good men, 61
Unhappiness possible, make, 1088
Unhappy, be called, 430
being, not a more, 196
comfort to the, 1049
family is unhappy in its own way, 1077
far-off things, 298
folks on shore, 275
hates, endless extinction of, 547
how much more, he might be, 197
lovers should be Frenchmen, 911
never so, as we suppose, 1043
none but the great, 198
those who think themselves most, 197
Unharmed upon the eternal rock, 231
Unheard beyond the ocean tide, 525
by the world, 336
Unheeded flew the hours, 294
Unheroic dead, remember the, 892
every age most, 430
Unholy blue, eyes of, 335
pleasure, 809
Unhonoured and unsung, 219, 307
by his fellows, 802
his relics are laid, 334
Unhoodwinked wave, 784
Unhouseled, disappointed, 91
Unhurrying chase, still with, 748
Unicorns, cantrips of, 865
come down to the sea, 904
draw by the gilded hearse, 900
Un-idea'd girls, 233
Uniform death's livery, 902
secret of, 902
Uniformity of life, 350
sense of multiplicity in, 769
Unimpaired delight, circles of, 933
Unimportant, busy with the, 773
Uninforming breath, with, 868
Uninitiate by many a presage, none, 610
Unintelligible world, this, 295
Uninterred, he lies, 219
Union, all your strength is in your, 436
are joined, where in, 950
drear, hate the, 685
flag of our, 405
fragments of a once glorious, 341
gives strength, 962
here of hearts, there is no, 306
in partition, 43
indestructible, 445
is too big a horse, 927

Union Jack, his trav'ling rug's a, 845
  liberty and, now and forever, 341
  music of the, keep step to the, 394
  must be preserved, our Federal, 292
  my paramount object is to save the, 456
  of English-speaking peoples, 711
  of hearts union of hands, 405
  of lakes union of lands, 404
  of states none can sever, 404
  our Federal, 292
  sail on O, strong and great, 435
  strictest, 259
  with his native sea, 302
Unique and moping station, 937
Unison, some chord in, 266
  with the truth, in, 1017
Unitarian bell, rang out the, 566
United States and join the family, join the, 839
  States, books magazines and newspapers in, 476
  States bounded, 472
  States import print and read more poetry, 539
  States in Thy protection, 268
  States Marines, guarded by, 953
  States of America, I believe in the, 803
  States of Europe, 1069
  States of Europe Asia and the world, 857
  States of the World, 1069
  States, population of, 853
  States themselves the greatest poem, 539
  States under my thumb, 954
  voice of all His Majesty's subjects, 950
  we stand, 404, 962
Units pitiable in its, 651
Unity, a greatness, imposing upon it a, 1087
  on earth, confound all, 88
  peace and concord, 1127
  to dwell together in, 1106
  to multiplicity, 637
Universal benevolence, 253
  blank, 151
  darkness buries all, 216
  good, partial evil, 207
  grin, nature wears one, 228
  hallucination, 721
  pastime and delight, 440
  peace, uproar the, 88
  quality is diversity, most, 144
  theatre, wide and, 49
  vanquisher, 965
  wolf, appetite, a, 75
Universalist bell, rang out the, 566
Universe, all parts of the, I have an interest in, 207
  better ordering of the, 1020
  born for the, 252
  forsakes thee, 1055
  glory and shame of the, 1047
  God's great, 562
  great axle of the, 566
  harmony of the, 260

Universe in a map, journey over the, 1039
  is change, 1010
  is melting into radiation, 846
  is stirred, 728
  life and, show spontaneity, 569
  loves to create, 1012
  made up of all that is, one, 1011
  praised be the fathomless, 536
  roaming in thought over the, 536
  that in a boundless, 462
  the rumbling, 693
  the undiscovered, 728
  vast, scenes for a theatre, 1029
  whole theory of the, 537
  wonder and glory of the, 448
Universes, in space and time, 538
Universities of Scotland, 752
University, if I were founding a, 805
  men and men of all sorts, 228
  of Göttingen, studied with me at the, 293
  of these days, 381
  should be a place of light, 420
  teachers, our, 871
Unjust in the least, he that is, 1117
  less, and the, 973
  peace before a just war, 227
  to nature and himself, 202
Unkempt about those hedges, 893
Unkind as man's ingratitude, 50
  when givers prove, 93
Unkindest cut of all, the most, 83
Unkindness, I tax not you with, 98
Unknelled uncoffined, 219, 355
Un-know, knows not also how to, 544
Unknowing what he sought, 176
Unknown, accents yet, 82
  and be, 995
  and silent shore, 325
  argues yourselves, 152
  bottom, my affection hath, 51
  forms of things, 43
  god, to the, 1118
  lands, to carry me to, 639
  Power's employ, in some, 547
  she lived, 296
  shore, dreamed of an, 870
  thus let me live, unseen, 216
  to fortune and to fame, 245
  too early seen, 77
  when we come home, 114
Unlamented let me die, 216
Unlearn not what you have learned, 1015
Unlearned, amaze the, 211
  he knew no schoolman's art, 213
  men of books, 203
Unless above himself he can erect himself, 30
Unlessoned girl unschooled, 46
Unlettered small-knowing soul, 40
Unlimited soon become, 1054
Unlined brow, 562
Unlistening street, 719
Unlooked for, she comes, 216
Unloose it from the bond, 106

Unloved guest, 368
Unlovely hue frouzy or thin, 373
Unlucky deeds relate, 103
  friends of the, 967
Unmanly, nay, let them be, 72
Unmannerly untaught knaves, 61
Unmask her beauty to moon, 90
Unmasked, but when, 620
  offer itself to be, 1090
Unmated creature tired, the sea, 503
Unmeaning and abominable custom, 268
Unmeasured by flight of years, 306
Unmerciful disaster, 460
Unmotived herd, 528
Unmoved, can sit, 931
Unnatural, nothing is, 279
Unnecessary to collect many editions, 238
Unnoticed, has passed, 985
  rather be attacked than, 237
  to be, most fiendish punishment, 663
Unnumbered woes, 218
  years, that shall live for, 518
Unpack my heart with words, 93
Unpacking books, happiness of, 729
Unpaid-for silk, rustling in, 105
Unparalleled, softness and harmony, 330
Unpassioned beauty of a great machine, 894
Unpathed waters undreamed shores, 57
Unperceived, current, 503
  shade softening in shade, 224
  the stars steal, 668
Unperturbèd pace, 748
Unpicked, hence and leave it, 65
Unpierced the cloudy walls remain, 444
Unpitied sacrifice, 259
  unrespited, unreprieved, 150
Unplagued with corns, toes, 77
Unpleasant body, moist, 494
Unpleasantest words, 46
Unpleasantness, arising from, 997
Unpleasing sharps, 80
Unpolite to refuse, 1056
Unpolluted flesh, fair and, 97
Unpractised unschooled, 46
Unpredictable reactions, 787
Unpredicted end, toward its, 926
Unpremeditated verse, 154
Unprintable offscouring of scoundrels, 381
Unprofitable, stale flat and, 90
Unprofitably burns, our oil, 263
Unpurchased hand, with, 451
Unquestioned and bold, 653
  text, one, 452
Unquiet at home, 183
  meals, 38
Unread, that what I lose, 551
  vision, redeem the, 900
  walks among his peers, 540
Unreal mockery hence, 87
Unrealized, so many visions, 441
Unreason, divine, 922
Unreasonable, the insupportable is, 1007

Unredressed, wrongs, 302
Unreflected light, 401
Unregenerate, know more about
   iniquity than the, 785
Unrelenting foe to love, 225
   hate, Juno's, 177
Unremaining glory, an, 561
Unremembered acts, 295
   and afar, 596
   names, 700
   shall perish, 427
Unremembering way, went her,
   748
Unremitted attention, 259
Unreplying dead, 602
Unreserved communication, 259
Unresisting prey, 349
Unrespited unpitied unreprieved,
   150
Unresponsive soul, no, 557
Unrest and sorrow, charms afar,
   746
   give most, 382
   in a sweet, 385
   or noyance, 224
   tortured thee, a secret, 1065
   which men miscall delight, 366
Unresting sea, life's, 452
Unrighteous man his thoughts,
   1112
Unripened beauties, 194
Unruly engine, wit's an, 136
   evil, tongue is an, 1122
   member, 1122
Unsaid, meant to say remains,
   850
   unheard, 570
   unheard, word be again, 180
Unsaleability hallmark of quality, 788
Unsatisfied, keep me still, 887
Unsavoury cases, won't undertake, 1076
Unscaled unpierced the cloudy
   walls, 444
Unschooled unpractised, 46
Unscottified of your countrymen,
   235
Unsearchable and secret aims,
   668
   dispose of highest wisdom, 157
Unseasonable and immoderate
   sleep, 239
   unfitting, many things, 966
Unseen and dumb, 170
   born to blush, 245
   hazard, 772
   in the seen, 794
   made her, 931
   to display, 403
   to leave, 441
   walk the earth, 152
   with a cheer, greet the, 494
Unselfed love, 548
Unselfish and patient like yours,
   596
   spirits, let all, 596
Unsettle you, don't let that,
   622
Unshackled by party, 305
Unshaken as the continent, 436
Unshamed iconoclast, what if
   some, 609
Unshod saint, 688
Unshorn fields, 372
Unsighed for past, 303

Unskilful laugh, make the, 94
Unsophisticated with distrust,
   927
Unsought be won, 154
   is better, love given, 55
Unsoundness, without a certain,
   of mind, 397
Unspeakable and dread, O majesty, 503
   dawn in happy old age, 1069
   the, Turk, 382
Unspoilt untitled, 811
Unspoken, what to leave 112
Unspotted from the world, 1122
   life is old age, 1124
   lily, a most, 74
Unstable anchorage, 965
   as water, 1098
   ship without ballast is, 1063
Unstained and free from scars,
   arms, 517
   by meanness avarice, 479
Unsubstantial hopes, 965
   things, 665
Unsuccess, bear up beneath
   their, 487
Unsuccesses to success, 651
Unsuccessful or successful war,
   264
Unsung, unwept unhonoured, 219,
   307
Unsunned heaps of treasure, 158
   snow, chaste as, 105
Unsure habitation, giddy and, 64
Unsuspected, isle in far-off seas,
   485
Unswerving, 't is onwards, 501
Untainted blithe, in beauty's passion, 794
   heart, 69
Untangled, moans to be, 923
Untaught knaves, he called them,
   61
Unthinking idle wild, 342
   time, quaffing and, 176
Unthought-like thoughts that are
   souls, 459
Until she smiled on me, 386
   the day break and the shadows
   flee, 1110
Untimely frost, death's, 286
   grave, 141, 185
   graves, emblems of, 266
Untitled aristocracy, 453
Unto dying eyes, 466
   the pure all things are pure,
   1122
Untold millions of years, 581
   with love and power, 501
Untranslatableness without in-
   jury, 319
Untravelled, my heart, 249
Untrewe, telle his tale, 5
Untriangulated stars, dream of,
   807
Untrodden tract for intellect or
   will, 612
   ways, among the, 296
Untruthfulness and dishonesty,
   1087
Untune that string, 74
Unturned, leave no stone, 968
Untutored mind, 207
Untwisting all the chains, 160
Unused, fust in us, 96
   to the melting mood, 104

Unutterable sigh in the human
   heart, 738
   things, looked, 224
Unutterably bright stars, 369
Unvarnished tale, a round, 100
Unveiled her peerless light, 152
Unvexed to the sea, 456
   with cares of gain, 206
Unwashed artificer, another lean,
   58
Unwearied spirit, 46
Unwelcome guest, like an, 692
   news, bringer of, 64
Unwept unhonoured and unsung,
   219, 307
Unwieldiness sluggishness inertia
   of matter, 1089
Unwieldy burthen, 230
Unwilling alone we embark, 668
   heavily on me like, sleep, 385
   ploughshare, 304
   to mix my fortune with him going down the wind, 181
Unwillingly to school, creeping,
   49
Unwitting of the day, 604
Unwomanly rags, woman in, 391
Unworth, for his own, 661
Unworthiness of the world, 878
Unworthy, patient merit of the,
   93
Unwritten and written law, 1014
   record of the mind, 970
Unwrung, our withers are, 94
Up anchor, 579
   and doing, let us be, 433
   faith that something would
   turn, 421
   game is, 105
   in my bed now, 391
   my friend and quit your books,
   295
   roos the sonne, 6
   rose Emelye, 6
   to the throne, 783
Up-and-down of time, 664
Upbear, and men my giant arms,
   517
Upbraiding shore, buried by the,
   354
Upgrowth of virtue, germ of
   first, 524
Up-hill all the way, wind, 587
Uplands, lights on the sleepy,
   waning, 418
   of eternity, 850
Uplifting get underneath, in, 791
   stuff, the, 852
Upmost round, attains the, 82
Upon this hint I spake, 100
Upper and lower part of mankind, 187
   classes, you may tempt, 730
   lip, keep a stiff, 557
   ocean, raging o'er the, 480
   shelf, silence of the, 397
   ten, circle of the, 576
Upper-crust, they are all, 387
Uppercut, watch for an, 893
Upright as the cedar, 41
   God hath made man, 1109
   judge, a learned judge, 47
   keel, she steadies with, 315
   man, behold the, 1104
Uproar, sand and wild, 408
   the universal peace, 88

Uprouse ye then, my merry men, 288
Ups and downs of this world, 625
Upside down, this house is turned, 61
Upstairs and downstairs, 475
Upturned faces, sea of, 310, 340
Upward and downward slope, 703
Urania govern thou my song, 153
Uranus flies, wider than, 535
Urban and all rural sounds, 323
life saps strength, 739
Urbanity, folly or, 390
of manner, 828
Urge him with truth, 220
no healths, 251
Urgent sordid tasks, above those, 1087
Urges sweet return, retirement, 154
Uriah in the forefront of the hottest battle, 1100
Urn, bubbling and loud-hissing, 265
can storied, 244
day fills his blue, 409
fancy's pictured, 244
for your sovereign's, 374
of his last ashes, 898
Urns, lamps in old sepulchral, 263
Urs, those dreadful, 451
Use, a terrene form a terrene, 826
almost can change the stamp of nature, 95
both thanks and, 35
can serve no, 238
doth breed a habit in a man, 34
for it, sure to find a, 311
from want of, 236
him as though you loved him, 140
if I'm still any, 851
more magnificent, 998
of a new-born child, 868
of brevity, what is the, 995
of everything he wants, 985
of him, what can be the, 702
of my understanding, 322
of speech, the true, 254
of such things, moderate, 997
of the editorial we, 430
of the sea and air is common to all, 19
of them, right in the, 242
or beauty or form, relates to, 480
remote from common, 358
soiled with all ignoble, 469
sometimes to be alone, 136
strained from that fair, 78
them kindly they rebel, 204
there's no, in my going to bed, 389
which lovers make, pitiless, 1069
worst, a man could be put to, 114
Uses, corner for others', 102
of a liberal education, 563
of adversity, sweet are the, 48
of this world, 90
to what base, we may return, 97

Used them so, and yet he, 524
to a thing, 278
to war's alarms, 392
Useful and entertaining authors, 196
be, where thou livest, 136
despise what is most, 961
more than a little, 926
trouble of the rain, 470
Usefulness ends, at that point their, 320
is over, when, 754
Useless away, slip, 381
each without the other, 436
if it goes as if it stands, 263
labor contained in it is, 1071
nothing is so, as a general maxim, 397
third is, 1023
to excel where none admire, 239
Uselessness of men above sixty, 695
of your toil, 786
Ushers in the even, full star that, 108
Usual querulous serenity, 322
Utica, no pent-up, 276
Utility in ships, 230
without being an object of, 1071
Utmost extremes, limits of its race, 553
need, deserted at his, 176
of their merits, 931
passion of her heart, 422
Utopia, better than a principality in, 398
Utopians wonder, 10
Utter inability to remember, 325
such as words could never, 481
sweet breath, 43
Utterance, daunts his, 575
is base, every, 889
of the early gods, 384
with hearts too full for, 475
Uttered and unuttered part of a man's life, 377
knowledge, 27
or unexpressed, 306
Utterer, hearer better than the, 748
Uttermost parts of the sea, 342
power, my, 66

VACANCIES by death are few, 274
by resignation none, 274
seas of solitudes and, 664
Vacancy, bend your eye on, 95
idle, 234
Vacant afternoon, 258
are the days I spend, 683
chair is thine, 439
chair, one, 435, 502
chair, there is no, 677
garments, stuffs out his, 58
heart and eye and hand, 309
interlunar cave, 156
mind a mind distressed, 263
mind and body filled, 67
mind quite, 263
mind, that spoke the, 250
piers, knocking at the, 552
Vacation, long for a long, 854
Vacuity of thought, 266

Vacuum, nature abhors a, 235, 1048
Vagabond began to sketch, 665
Vagabonds, best of all beggars and, 1045
Vagabond's house, 920
Vagrant beauty's trail, 828
bee, a, 728
but rates a, 942
oft in quod, 779
worm, hackneyed phrase of, 510
Vagrom men, comprehend all, 39
Vague generality a life-saver, 791
longing, waking up some, 607
penitence which holidays awaken, 495
probabilities, between conflicting, 449
thunder and silence burning, 926
Vagueness — perhaps ignorance credulity — helps, 538
should not be invoked, 926
Vain and impotent thing, 959
as the leaf upon the stream, 308
call it not, 307
deluding joys, 160
fantasy, nothing but, 77
I only know we loved in, 351
I shall not live in, 583
is my weak endeavor, 501
is the help of man, 1104
mightiest fleets, 475
my weary search, 250
oblations, 1110
pomp and glory of this world, 73
repinings go, let your, 638
seals of love but sealed in, 37
splendour dazzles in, 365
the ambition of kings, 128
the labor and the wounds are, 519
the weakest, not, 219
time toiled after him in, 231
to have lived in, 318
to love in, 167
to rise in arms, against the Omnipotent, 153
true love tho' given in, 470
was the chief's pride, 214
wishes in him were prevented, 345
Vainly breaking, while the tired waves, 519
Vainness, babbling drunkenness, 56
Vale in the land of Moab, in a, 516
meanest floweret of the, 245
meet thee in that hollow, 134
of life, sequestered, 245, 268
of sorrows, gladden this, 453
of tears, beyond this, 306
of years, declined into the, 102
scanty, 318
where bright waters meet, 335
Vales below, leave the, 735
Jordan's holy harvest, 657
our lovely, 392
the Delphian, 363
Valet, no one is a hero to his, 1005

Valet-de-chambre, my, is not aware, 1005
Valhalla, the nation's, 696
Valiant, all the brothers were, 943
and cunning in fence, 55
but not too venturous, 23
foe, in strife with many a, 626
man and free, 469
men, purchased by, 970
pious good and clean, 248
possession by the, 533
taste death but once, 82
the reproof, 51
trencher-man, a very, 38
Valiantly with time, wrestle so, 458
Valley, ambulance down in the, 640
blow softly down the, 792
darker grows the, 575
Forge, snow lies thick on, 784
of death, all in the, 467
of decision, 1113
of the shadow of death, 1103
sheep are fatter, 348
so sweet, 334
that God forgot, 830
Valleys and rocks never heard, 264
delight me, streams in the, 982
hills and, dales and fields, 31
of Hall, 663
of spray to-day, 857
pausing in pool-green, 848
peace of lovelier, 823
vast and still, 831
wild, piping down the, 281
Valley's lap, upon the, 707
Vallombrosa, brooks in, 148
Valour decay, records of, 512
discretion the best part of, 131
formed, for contemplation and, 152
given, angel hands to, 382
God's help and their, 1061
imperious mouth whose haughty, 418
in feasting as in fighting, 123
is certainly going, my, 278
is oozing out, my, 278
is sneaking off, my, 278
lies, defeated, 581
no need of, 999
the better part of, 63
to dare, the truest, 965
to taste their, 55
will weep, whereat, 76
wins woman as well as, 471
Valor's second prize, 995
Valuable result of education, 563
thing, riches a, 191
what he thought he could not do is, 236
what is, is not new, 341
Valuation of Europe, superstitious, 666
of property, a, 974
Value, as of no, 1051
being lost we rack the, 39
cannot create, 1071
dearness gives everything its, 271
estimate their own, 853
learning has its, 1046

Value, life has a, 1062
no, 845
of a Pullman civilization, 635
of a sentiment, 797
of learning a foreign language, 740
of time, 330
on his votive lay, some, 447
owes its, 232
part of its, 234
small coin of great, 1000
than all the pleasures, more, 981
their real import and, 1062
to them, of no, 1054
Valueless books, waste no life in, 532
Van, in the battle's, 511
shaped him to lead in the, 642
Van Amburgh is the man, 952
Vandunck, Mynheer, 289
Vanguard camps, where our, 574
Vanilla of society, 313
Vanish like lightning, 402
Vanished hand, touch of a, 465
Vanishing ghosts, 619
Vanishings blank misgivings, 301
Vanitas Vanitatum, 482
vanitatum has rung in, 545
Vanities of earth, fuming, 303
of life forego, 309
Vanity, all is, 1109
all others are but, 322
and vexation of spirit, 1109
be ascribed to, 1079
beauty without, 351
cause of virtue, 717
cured of every folly but, 1054
eaten up with, 390
Fair, everybody in, 482
Fair, hearts breaking in, 690
Fair, it beareth the name of, 172
Fair, simple or gentle from, 545
flatters the animal's, 786
human mind without, 1079
in beauty, see naught but, 522
in years, 62
is most difficult to wound, 1080
is the desire of rousing, 1064
is the desire to arrive, 1064
lighter than, 172, 1104
man is altogether, 1104
men of low degree are, 1104
of having been trusted, 222
of human hopes, 231
of more benefit than modesty, 837
of the world, 1049
of this wicked world, 1127
of vanities, 1109
plays tricks with memory, 727
sets love a task like that, 346
so artless in its, 180, 650
their voyaging is, 673
wounded, limps off the field, 591
Vanquished, e'en though, 251
gain, prize the, 437
Macbeth shall never be, 87
Vanquisher, the universal, 965
Vantage best have took, 36
coign of, 85
Vantage-ground of truth, 109
Vapor, a fleeting, 689

Vapor at the best, 577
of a dungeon, 102
on the summer air, 568
sometime like a bear, 105
streaks the dawn, 565
Vapours, congregation of, 92
rise shadows lengthening as, 173
Vaporous sapphire, 801
vitiate air, 652
Variable as the shade, 308
lest thy love prove, 78
public opinion, 563
thing, not so, in nature, 196
Variableness no, neither shadow, 1122
Variations in the text, 238
Varied God, are but the, 224
year, to rule the, 224
Variety and disorder, full of, 974
is the mother of enjoyment, 420
is the spice of life, 265
nor custom stale her infinite, 104
order in, 216
pleasure unseasoned by, 988
sumptuous, 617
Various, a man so, 173
and most mutable, woman is, 472
as your land, you are as, 927
gift to each, 436
his employments, 265
is the scene, how, 909
so be, 924
stuff the various Man, she formed of, 286
Varium et mutabile, 472
Vase from its blue, 912
you may shatter the, 336
Vassal at my feet, a willing, 522
of my will, seemed but the, 579
Vassals and serfs at my side, 386
bend the reverent knee, 910
Vast a memory has love, 216
and middle of the night, 90
and unwieldy burthen, 230
expenditure of human voice, 972
expense, maintained at, 177
forever, take into the, 659
infant sagacity, 888
is art, so, 210
return to the unconscious, 765
river of unfailing source, 393
soul, to the, 408
that is evil hastening to merge, 536
the unattained, how, 444, 469
the undone, 487
wings, with, 914
Vastness and age and memories, 459
Vasty deep, spirits from the, 62
hall of death, 546
Vault, heaven's ebon, 369
makes this, a feasting presence, 80
mere lees is left this, 86
resound, making the hollow, 922
Vaulted skies, from lowly earth to, 521
Vaulting ambition, 85

Vaulting interlocked secure, 932
Vaunted works of art, 410
Vaward of our youth, 64
Vegetable green, admits no, 933
  love which would not suit me, 623
Vehemence of youth, fiery, 308
Vehement, a life that shall be, 537
Vehicle, no, but a wheelbarrow, 374
  stickle about the, when flying for life, 381
Vehicles can serve no use, 238
Veil, a kiss through a, 1069
  into eternity, beyond the, 606
  no mortal ever took up my, 1005
  playeth behind the, 886
  so thin a, 670
  through which I might not see, 1018
  which those who live call life, 367
Veils her sacred fires, 215
  pass, from the circling faces, 879
  spirits clad in, 501
Veil'd melancholy has her sovran, 384
Vein, I am not in the, 72
  it checks no, 224
  of poetry, 380
  of Shakespeare's heart, 911
  of tender thought, 337
  this is Ercles', 42
  when the heart is in a, 337
Veins are cold, when the, 804
  indurated, 430
  in the rich, 936
  in your body were dry, 320
  peasant, 499
Velasquez, why drag in, 612
Velocity, travel with a, 969
Velvet cap out of a sow's ear, 241
  gilded and covered with, 1060
  imperial crowd, 714
  purse of a sow's ear, 272
  shoes, walk in, 897
Veneered with sanctimonious theory, 465
Venerable men from a former generation, 339
  old clothes are not, 380
  trees, brotherhood of, 298
Veneration but no rest, 110
Vengeance, do nothing for mere, 591
  is mine I will repay, 1119
  not one feeling of, 941
Veni vidi vici, 65, 1003
Venice broke, when, 889
  I stood in, 353
  in the armoury of, 125
  more than any man in all, 44
  sate in state, where, 353
  woke, when, 889
Venom, bubbling, 352
  himself, all, 254
Venomous, toad ugly and, 48
Ventered life an' love an' youth, 527
Ventricle of memory, begot in the, 41
Ventriloquist, wish I were a, 787

Vents in mangled forms, 49
Venture, all is, 651
  nought, nought have, 15, 19
  o'er, his, 858
Ventures in one bottom, 43
  of dreamland, 579
  or lose our, 83
Venturous, not too, 23
Venus rise from out the sea, thus did, 555
  rose red out of wine, 632
  sets ere Mercury can rise, 217
  the Grecian, 240
Ver, primrose first-born child of, 132
Veracity, a doubt of my, 1056
  does not consist in saying, 318
  increases with old age, 1044
  is the heart of morality, 563
  language adorned with, 1017
Verb and pronoun out, and left the, 585
  most beautiful, in world, 1083
  to love, to help is most beautiful, after, 1083
Verbs and nouns do more agree, 645
Verbal delicacies, an ear for, 862
Verbiage metaphor and dream, 578
Verbosity, inebriated with exuberance of, 420
  thread of his, 41
Verdi, in praising, 593
Verdict, one wise man's, 488
  true, and give my, 677
Verdure, laurels of eternal, 231
Vere de Vere, caste of, 462
Verge enough, ample room and, 179, 244
  enough for more, 179
  of her confine, 98
  of the churchyard mould, 391
  of the sundown, over the, 757
Verging toward some climax, 733
Veriest school of peace, 583
Verily, I use the word, 170
Verities and realities, lie all the, 953
Verity, religious feeling is as much a, 543
Vermeil-tinctured lip, 158
Vermont comes in, that's where, 822
  hikes his way back to, 799
  indomitable people of, 819
  is the other, 838
  mountains stretch exceeding straight, 838
  O maiden of the hills, 760
  serve almost as well about, 838
  Yankee, a, 896
Vermonter in heaven abides, not a, 799
  was there, not a, 798
Vernal bloom or summer's rose, 151
  morn, suns that gild the, 267
  seasons of the year, 162
  wood, one impulse from a, 295
Versailles, dauphiness at, 260
  treaty signed at, 799
Verse badly, write, 1046
  cheered with ends of, 142
  cursed be the, 213

Verse fame and beauty are intense, 385
  free, died to make, 882
  happy who in his, 177, 1049
  herself inspires, decorate the, 351
  hoarse rough, 211
  is a chalice, 1085
  is sad, they say my, 744
  loosely-sandalled, 648
  marred by a superfluous, 439
  married to immortal, 160, 303
  may find him, a, 135
  may find who a sermon flies, 135
  my gentle, 108
  octosyllabic, 356
  of every young poet, 741
  of mine may linger, one, 660
  one, for sense, 142
  one, for the other's sake, 142
  or two, to write a, 135
  publishing a volume of, 853
  restoring with a new, 900
  sweetens toil, 249
  tears the curtain, 767
  that gives immortal youth, 326
  the subject of all, 119
  the, you grave for me, 703
  to God is dear, homely, 793
  tone shape color form, 534
  unpremeditated, 154
  who says in, 214
  whose prose is grand, 526
  will seem prose, 185
  write me a, 854
Verses, a book of, 1018
  false gallop of, 50
  no one will ever get at my, 538
  quire of bad, 399
  rhyme the rudder is of, 142
  wonderful, 779
Versed in books, deep, 156
Version of their lives, ideal, 788
Vertu, pacience is a heigh, 8
  the firste, 8
Vertue of necessitee, 4
Vertue's ferme land, 173
Vertuous alway, who that is most, 7
Very energy of thought, 403
  like a whale, 95
  thing I should not know, 625
Vesper chime, heard the anvil ring the, 622
Vessel, empty, makes greatest sound, 67
  in which the bitter liquid, 927
  launch your, and crowd your canvas, 472
  made, with his hand the, 1019
  one, unto honour, 1119
  suppose that this here, 843
  the gilded, goes, 244
  wife the weaker, 1122
Vessels, feminine gender of, 859
  large may venture more, 227
  run to all his limbs, its, 958
  westward sped, 552
Vest begins, that's where the, 822
  nor pants, he has neither, 614
  Robin wears his silver, 647
  the body's, 169
Vestal modesty, pure and, 79
  once a pallid, 939
Vestal's lot, blameless, 216

Vestige of land, least, 599
Vestments of the May moth, 939
    priestly, 731
Vesture of decay, this muddy, 47
    of phrase, suitable, 972
Vesuvian Bay, far away sailing the, 552
Vesuvius' crater for an inkstand, 531
Veteran, superfluous lags the, 230
Vex not his ghost, 100
    the brain, researches, 280
Vexation of spirit, 1109
    only to understand the report, 1111
Vexed with waiting while his wife dressed, 182
Vexing the dull ear of a drowsy man, 58
Viands he preferred, 698
    the remainder, 75
Viaticum of old age, 1015
Vibrates in the memory, music, 367
Vibrations of deathless music, 806
    to deaden its, 440
Vicaire of th' almyghty lorde, 4
Vice, amusements prevent, 235
    and want, weariness, 1052
    by action dignified, 78
    creature of heejus mien, 797
    distinction between virtue and, 234
    encourage no, 252
    gathered every, 215
    good old-gentlemanly, 359
    in a cat, 638
    in a man, one big, 645
    is a monster, 174, 208
    is sold, almost every, 119
    itself lost half its evil, 260
    of fools, never-failing, 210
    of old age, a common, 980
    of republics, envy the, 435
    pays to virtue, the homage, 1044
    prevails, when, 195, 206
    save men from any particular, 582
    so simple, there is no, 46
    some tincture of, in the best virtue, 1029
    taint of, 56
    that reverend, 62
    truce between virtue and, 515
    virtue itself turns, 78
Vices disguised, virtues are, 1043
    Hannibal had many, 122
    ladder of our, 436
    may be of use, 950
    our pleasant, 100
    small, do appear, 99
    wallets for our, 992
    without man's vices, 351
Vicious circle, 607
Viciousness, meanness and, 973
Vicissitude of motion and rest, 197
Vicissitudes in all things, 979
    man used to, 232
    of fortune, 271
    of human existence, 459
    of sects and religions, 111
    of taste, wild, 231

Vicissitudes of things, the sad, 242, 249
Victim, marks its, 329
    must be found, 624
    of fat-gorged mosquitoes, 1009
    of the Scythian hoar-frosts, 1009
Victims, fearing they may be the, 973
    of deceit and self-deception, 1086
    play, the little, 243
    priests altars, 216
Victim's sympathies, killing the, 635
Victor, a great, 928
    exult, shall, 327
    is he who can go it alone, 510
    ship, from fearful trip the, 536
Victors, to the, belong the spoils, 349
    they whom the world calls, 533
    who are life's, 533
Victoria the faery, dubbed, 865
Victorian age, speak scornfully of, 752
    age, tradition of the, 925
Victories, after a thousand, 107
    go forward and give us, 456
    of mighty generals, 535
    peace hath her, 162
    over the Syracusans, 969
    worse than defeat, 520
Victorious, he rides, 917
    o'er a' the ills o' life, 287
    those which are, 1061
Victory, a Cadmean, 969
    a great and glorious, 284
    and peace, blessed with, 332
    best kind of, 1042
    for their all, their, 518
    grave where is thy, 1120
    health alone is, 378
    how to gain a, 997
    if not, is yet revenge, 149
    is only an earnest, 1086
    of battle standeth not, 1125
    of labour over capital, 1086
    of socialism, 1086
    or death, resolved on, 1060
    or Westminster Abbey, 283
    own way of embittering, 1067
    remembered by a song than by, 588
    rise in open, 302
    thy hourly, 736
    'twas a famous, 322
    undone by another, 113
    which is peace, 805
    won, life's 556
Victorys wanne, great, 256
Victuals and drink an illusion, 972
    holler Uncle, make their, 923
Vidders, be wery careful o', 494
Vidder's one equal to five-and-twenty, 494
Vienna, congress of, dances, 1055
View, he did not bring to, 404
    imagine so absurd a, 590
    keep probability in, 206
    kept ever in his, 972
    me with a critic's eye, 292
    morose or desponding, 400
    motley to the, 108
    no earthly, 391

View, not fair to outward, 386
    order gave each thing, 72
    ourselves with clearer eyes, 134
    quite cut off the, 754
    which has grander, 1069
    widened in man's, 326
    with extensive, 230
Views and patients, seen old, 678
    as fast as they appear true, 456
    false, do little harm, 449
    meets the public, 495
    new, as fast as true views, 456
    of Christian duty, men whose, 522
    of themselves, interested, 200
    take short, 312
Viewless voiceless turner of the wheel, 650
    winds, imprisoned in, 36
Vigil long, patient search and, 357
    night, 896
Vigils, between two, 892
    keep, eyes their, 1017
    keep, poets painful, 215
Vigilance, eternal, 277
    go forward and give victories, 456
    secure a sufficient degree of, 320
    yet above you, 867
Vigilant, be sober be, 1123
    occasion for the, 966
    the active the brave, 270
Vigny more discreet, retreated, 858, 1070
Vigor is found in the man. 1006
    it will give your style, what, 314
    press with, on, 225
    to labor, restores, 1051
Vigorous mind, characteristics of a, 231
Vile, better to be, than vile esteem'd, 108
    durance, 286
    guns, but for these, 61
    hold to stay him up, 58
    ill-favoured faults, 34
    man that mourns, 207
    matter, book containing such, 79
    nought so, that on the earth doth live, 78
    only man is, 343
    squealing of the fife, 45
    to pigeonhole, think it, 803
Vilest deeds like poison-weeds, 722
    sinner may return, 199
Villa, dwelt a lady in a, 478
Village bells, music of those, 266
    cock, early, 72
    Hampden, some, 245
    less than Islington, 168
    maiden sings, 249
    of his birth, 771
    of Yule, I loved in the, 643
    sleeps, the, 771
    sweet Auburn loveliest, 250
    the lads of the, 936
    there was no, 501
    which men still call Tyre, 881
Villagers all, this frosty tide, 742

Villagers came to help, 962
  thought boy deceiving, 962
Villain, branded a, 881
  condemns me for a, 72
  hath done thee wrong, some,
    98
  hungry lean-faced, 38
  need be, no, 574
  one murder made a, 268
  smile and be a, 92
  smiling damned, 92
  still pursued her, 686
Villains by necessity, 98
Villainous demi-tasses, 730
  saltpeter, 579
Villanies, sum of all, 226
Villanous company, 63
  low, foreheads, 33
  saltpetre, 61
  smell, rankest compound of,
    35
Villany, clothe my naked, 71
  natural expression of, 616
  you teach me I will execute,
    45
Villon among the birds, 837
  our sad bad glad mad brother's
    name, 489
Vinchy, pronounce it, 615
Vinci, spell it, 615
Vindicate the ways of God, 206
Vindication against slander, best,
    457
  of night, 860
Vindictively made in His image,
    461
Vine and fig tree, sat under his,
    1125
  blood of the, 668
  bugs off a sweet-potato, 927
  drank at every, 915
  of song, inaccessible, 635
  on a tall tree, creeping, 1085
  thanksgiving to the, 404
  the gadding, 159
  the viol the violet the, 459
  thou monarch of the, 104
  under his, and fig-tree, 1113
Vines, bless with fruit the, 384
  bosomed deep in, 215
  companionship of waxen, 904
  foxes that spoil the, 1110
  the embracing, 602
Vinegar, oil, sugar and saltness
    agree, 252
  put not your trust in, 700
Vinegar-cruet, neck of a, 239
Vineyard speck, such color as the,
    911
Vintage, bubbles in a golden,
    1085
  He is trampling out the, 522
  of a famous, 576
  of Abi-ezer, 1099
  sea's red, 664
  wine of rarest, 788
Vintners buy, wonder often what
    the, 1019
  that put water, 1022
Viol the violet and the vine, the,
    459
Violation of fundamental princi-
    ples, 628
Violence, blown with restless,
    36
  or chicane, over, 925

Violence, perseverance more pre-
    vailing than, 999
Violent and gross, 563
  delights have violent ends, 79
  over civil or over, 174
  reaction, produces a, 973
Violently if they must, 319
Violet and the vine, the viol the,
    459
  by a mossy stone, 296
  glowing, 159
  here and there a, 269
  is here, the, 560
  lessons of the, 657
  loves a sunny bank, 565
  of his native land, 468
  queen of secrecy, 385
  throw a perfume on the, 58
Violets blew, roses red and, 24
  blue, daisies pied and, 41
  breathes upon a bank of, 53
  I would give you some, 96
  in the sward, 445
  it's raining, 772
  of the undercliff, 778
  plucked, 127, 256
  roses lilies and, 388
  sicken, when sweet, 368
  slight the, 665
  spring from her fair flesh, 97,
    468
  they are the tender, 1066
  were born, 493
Violin a bore to the flute, 685
  click goes the grisly, 1078
  is not a hurdy-gurdy, 593
  nothing but his, 628
Violins, ripe age gives tone to,
    573
  without Antonio, 520
Violoncello the heart's complaint,
    535
Virgil, I am, 1021
  Rome can claim, 176
  sings, you know what, 472
Virgin clean, O, 1022
  Garda first of those numberless
    isles, 523
  me no virgins, 947
  mother of, wedded maid and,
    161
  sword, flesh his, 220
  thorn, withering on the, 42,
    301
Virgins are soft as the roses, 355
  virgin me no, 947
Virgin's head, instruction gave
    before that, 511
  sidelong looks, bashful, 250
Virginia, bred such horses in, 928
  he is not from, 928
  with her noble stock, 660
  your little friends are wrong,
    643
Virginia's blazoned roll, 561
Virginian, I am not a, 270
  sky, his own, 445
Virginity, just a little more, 897
  power o'er true, 158
Virginny, favor in old, 630
Virile and odious fiction, 871
  courageous intellectual, 1085
Virility, to prove their, 937
Virtue, according to his, 970
  admiration of, 162
  all that are lovers of, 140

Virtue and riches seldom settle on
    one man, 124
  and the love of, 1055
  as wax to flaming youth, 95
  assume a, if you have it not,
    95
  blushing is the colour of, 188
  blushing is the complexion of,
    188
  collateral security to, 222
  could see to do what virtue
    would, 158
  courage is a, 1051
  courage wit in all men, 199
  crime called, 991
  distinction between vice and,
    234
  feeble were, if, 159
  first upgrowth of all, 524
  flow, flame from, 1021
  foaming lips of inebriated, 635
  for which all, now is sold, 119
  forbearance ceases to be a, 259
  fugitive and cloistered, 163
  has difficulties to wrestle with,
    1028
  has its degrees, 131
  highest proof of, 400
  homage vice pays to, 1044
  humility is a, 130
  in her shape how lovely, and
    saw, 153
  in man can't be vice in a cat,
    638
  in most request, 411
  in the open, 757
  is bold goodness never tearful,
    37
  is environment, 685
  is its own reward, 139
  is like a rich stone, 111
  is like precious odours, 109
  is the performance, 877
  itself 'scapes not, 90
  itself turns vice, 78
  keep your, 783
  lies in the struggle, 458
  linked with one, 356
  lovers of, all that are, 140
  may flourish in an old cravat,
    451
  men admire, 156
  men of most renowned, 163
  more, than doth live, 119
  most in request is conformity,
    411
  much, in If, 51
  no, can digest, 32
  no, goes with size, 409
  no man's, nor sufficiency, 40
  no road or ready way to, 144
  not enough to know about, 975
  not often found among poets,
    1040
  now is sold, 119
  of a sacrament, 1016
  of humility, 139
  of necessity, made a, 1037
  of necessity, to make a, 4, 34,
    125, 1026
  of the soul, justice a, 1015
  of vested power, through, 541
  only reward of, is virtue, 411
  passes current over the world,
    968
  redeem us from, 632

Virtue requires a rough and stormy passage, 1028
  royalty of, 619
  sense, honour, 242
  some fall by, 35
  some healing, 441
  some mark of, 46
  than a science, rather a, 1054
  that possession would not show, 39
  the first, if thou wilt lere, 8
  then we find the, 39
  though in rags, 177
  thousand crimes and one, 356
  tincture of vice in the best, 1029
  to be serviceable must be alloyed, 613
  truth is the secret of, 1073
  vanity is cause of, 717
  wars that make ambition, 102
  where men have it, 183
Virtues, all heavenly, shoot, 338
  average of all the, 645
  be to her, very kind, 189
  but vices disguised, 1043
  curse on his, 195
  display of eminent, 422
  friend to her, 240
  Hannibal had mighty, 122
  he might lack, 767
  if individuals have no, 950
  industry and all the, 922
  is it a world to hide, in, 54
  not yet discovered, 415
  nothing could surpass her in, 358
  of man without his vices, 351
  of patience and long-suffering, 344
  pearl chain of all, 121
  powers, dominations, 153
  shall be testified, their, 970
  spring of, 28
  to sustain good fortune, 1043
  we write in water, 74
  which become crimes, 1067
  which the idle never know, 524
  will plead like angels, 85
  world to hide, 54
  would be well-nigh useless, 1046
Virtue's cause, died in, 76
  guide, this maxim be my, 221
  land, 173
  manly cheek, 267
  sake, worn for, 942
  side, his failings leaned to, 250
  sidelong looks, 912
Virtuous all the sisters, 943
  because thou art, 54
  deeds, matter for, 28
  do, tell the mischief the, 483
  if a man be, withal, 8
  in their old age, 217
  man, slumbers of the, 195
  Marcia towers above her sex, 195
  outrageously, 198
  person of either sex, 197
  soul, only a sweet and, 135
  they are, Lord how, 1077
  things, from lowest place, 53
  who that is most, 7
Virtuously, many daughters have done, 1109

Virulence of the national appetite, 862
Visage as you find it, show my, 508
  devotion's, 93
  hides not his, 57
  lean body and, 147
  on his bold, 308
Visages do cream and mantle, 44
Viscous, thought is, 637
Visible for the uncertain, 1012
  sage mechanician, 517
  world beautiful and interesting, 656
Vision, a more delightful, 260
  apprehension of a, 972
  baseless fabric of this, 33
  beatific, enjoyed in, 149
  between a sleep and a sleep, 634
  but by faith, no, 560
  celebrate, clear, 873
  dies, all the, 1022
  feminine, dazzles the, 401
  four walls cannot limit my, 805
  his life is a, 634
  his own field of, 1063
  I took it for a faery, 158
  in the higher dream, 900
  is machines, 826
  never dazzle the feminine, 401
  of blue wings, 665
  of Christ that thou didst see, 282
  of fulfilled desire, 1019
  of hope, 953
  of it slip, smallest, 807
  of the mind supplements, 543
  of the worker in the work, 794
  of the world, saw the, 464
  on the inward, 770
  quick to find the beauties, 557
  rose, poet, 669
  sensible to feeling, 85
  thine was the prophet's, 438
  to-morrow is only a, 953
  where there is no, 1109
  within him, never a, 880
  write the, make it plain, 266
  ye that follow the, 864
  young men's, 173
Visions bright, so many, 441
  I have multiplied, 1113
  I no longer see, 766
  of boyhood, 621
  of glory, 244
  of my youth, happy, 455
  young men shall see, 173
Vision's greatest enemy, 282
Visionless officialized fatuity, 891
Visit broke the wizard song, 879
  her face too roughly, 90
  my sad heart, 82
  o'er the globe, our annual, 276
  so unexpected a, 254
Visits like those of angels, 186, 327
  went abroad and paid, 233
Visitant, pleasure oft a, 382
Visitations daze the world, 402
  of power to heart and brain, 411
Visiting acquaintance, 278
  moon, beneath the, 105

Visiting, notes on pastoral, 884
Visitings, compunctious, 84
Vistas, dark, of the reboantic norns, 432
  undreamed-of, 831
Visual nerve, 155
Vital spark of heavenly flame, 216
Vitality, hold strange, 621
  nothing interesting loses, 645
  of a work of art, 755
Vitamines, richest in, 846
Vittles said the dear old saint, my, 855
Vivid true, trusty dusky, 703
Vixens, snap like, 898
Vixere fortes ante Agamemnona multi, 358
Vizier, each devoted, 618
Vocal voices, singers with, 189
Vocation of men is to serve others, 1077
  plebeian, 510
  'tis my, 60
  to labour in his, 60
  were endless imitation, 301
Vociferation, in sweet, 189
Vociferous, vocal voices most, 189
Voice above their beat, 748
  ascending high, my, 199
  at eve, obey, 410
  away, love takes my, 718
  big manly, 50
  bird shall carry the, 1110
  but a wandering, 299
  came o'er the waters, 732
  cannon his, 575
  choked a great man's, 429
  cry sleep no more, I heard a, 86
  each a mighty, 304
  first, which I uttered was crying, 1124
  from I knew not where, 651
  give few thy, 91
  gives melody to the, 984
  I have heard thy, 922
  I sing with mortal, 153
  if mine were a solitary, 478
  in all her music, his, 366
  in autumn's hush, still small, 431, 442
  in every wind, 243
  in hollow murmurs, 290
  in the darkness, a distant, 437
  in the streets, uttereth her, 1106
  in the shrinking hours, 714
  is Jacob's voice, 1097
  is still for war, my, 195
  Kentucky strain was in his, 676
  like a prophet's word, 363
  like the north wind, 855
  lives on the breeze, 501
  lost with singing of anthems, 64
  love's familiar, 367
  methought I heard a, 86
  monstrous little, 42
  more safe I sing with mortal, 153
  music is like a low, 484
  nibbles in a low, 1056
  no, disturbs the strand, 576

Voice of all our times, the loveliest, 922
of all the gods, 41
of awful memory, 301
of Canada, mighty, 738
of children gone before, 644
of God, daughter of the, 299
of God, obedience to the, 445
of gratitude, still small, 244
of her God, 'twas the, 474
of love, notes of the, 822
of man, carries the, 375
of many waters, as the, 1123
of my heart, 396
of nature cries, 245
of one crying in the wilderness, 1116
of sea and mountains, 304
of the bird, rise up at the, 1110
of the birds, than the, 869
of the charmer, 1104
of the forum, 889
of the great Creator, 501
of the hyena, 29
of the past, audible, 380
of the press, 479
of the sluggard, 199
of the turtle is heard, 1110
of woe for a lover's loss, 517
one would hear so very oft, 384
only a look and a, 437
or hideous hum, 161
pleasing on their ear, his, 220
ring out, 610
rise like a fountain, 463
seasoned with a gracious, 46
sing with mortal, 153
so charming left his, 154
so soft and kind, your little, 910
sole daughter of his, 155
sounds like a prophet's, 363
spake unto me, still small, 462
still small, 1101
sweet, sweet lips, 385
sweeter thy, 466
that is still, sound of a, 465
that never dieth, 964
that rang through Shiloh's woods, 690
that wakens the slumbering ages, 402
the harmony of the world, 22
the same mysterious, 635
the united, 950
thundering in thine inner ear, 544
vast expenditure of human, 972
was ever soft gentle and low, 100
was heard, 277
watch-dog's, 250
with still small, 305
without reply, 410
years will never drown, 706
you cannot hear, I hear a, 205
Voices, airy, 382
ancestral, 315
are in the wind's singing, 899
beyond these, 471
calling, gentle, 567
earth with her thousand, 316
I am listening for the, 446
keep tune and oars keep time, 288, 334

Voices lead, where airy, 382
most vociferous, 189
murmuring of many, 497
music when soft, die, 367
of duty, downward the, 663
of liberty, the, 921
of the wandering wind, 597
our dried, 899
still are thy pleasant, 554
thank you for your, 76
that have sinned, 905
there are no, O Rhodope, 326
thousand thousand, 888
three hundred grateful, 605
with kindly, 798
your most sweet, 76
Voiceful sea, swelling of the, 317
Voiceless in a sudden night, 897
lips of the unreplying dead, 602
tomb, 848
turner of the wheel, 650
Void, atoms move in the, 970
left an aching, 266
long stood, 135
Ostade went out into the, 871
rapture to the dreary, 355
yawning, of the future, 1011
Volatile, ain't I, 496
Volatility and the rage for pleasure, 1056
Volcanic political instinct, 722
Volcano, dancing on a, 1065
Volition, mainspring of his own, 715
Volscians in Corioli, I fluttered your, 76
Voltaire, head of, 345
Voluble is his discourse, sweet and, 41
Volume, false, 661
made to love, a little, 847
of forgotten lore, curious, 460
of my brain, book and, 92
of poems, in every, 236
saved by chance, 300
small rare, 288
sweet and good and true, many a, 760
swelled to a, 184
whose sublime chapters, 1085
within that awful, 310
Volumes from mine own library, 32
happiness of unpacking, 729
history with all her, 354
in folio, I am for whole, 41
of ethics and divinity, 273
richly bound, 713
through ten long, 1050
Voluminous writer, 196
Voluntarily, not to surrender it, 387
Volunteers, pale patient, 772
Voluptuous and the indolent, 1051
swell, music with its, 352
Voluptuously surfeit out of action, 76
Voman vas der glinging vine, 661
Vomit, dog is turned to his, 1123
Vools gwoes prating, 550
Vortices of glory and blue air, 430

Votaress, imperial, passed on, 42
Votaries credulous, renders its, 1055
how the world rewards its, 1075
Votarist, like a sad, 157
Vote away, fortunes and lives, 573
hand and heart to this, 340
that shakes the turrets of the land, 451
Voter exercises a public trust, 627
Votive lay, set some value on his, 447
Vouchsafe him to me as a guide and guard, 450
Vow and not pay, 1109
better thou shouldst not, 1109
me no vows, 947
taken before the shrine, 1085
that binds too strictly snaps, 471
there I made a, 899
Vows, a woman's, 967
made in pain, recant, 151
made in wine, falser than, 51
our, are heard betimes, 175
soul lends the tongue, 91
vow me no, 947
with so much passion, 186
Vowels, open, tire the ear, 211
Voyage closed and done, 536
dry as the biscuit after a, 49
I have made a, 522
I was born to make, 809
life's uncertain, 81
of their life, 83
one on an endless, gone, 568
to America, 932
to the world unknown, 200
Voyages, imagination as good and cheaper than, 558
Voyager, lands the, 402
Voyagers, humble, 350
Voyaging, their, is vanity, 673
through strange seas, 299
Vulcan's stithy, foul as, 94
Vulgar and insupportable, becomes, 1083
arts beneath thy care, 242
deaths unknown to fame, 219
Discobolus is, 614
familiar but by no means, 90
heart, buildeth on the, 64
of manner overfed, 759
prosperity, 237
the great, and the small, 168
Vulgarity, mould of its, 894
the Jacksonian, 619
Vulgarize the day of judgment, 417
Vulture, rage of the, 355

Wad some power, oh, 285
Wade through slaughter, 245
Waders and swimmers, for them the, 930
Waes o' my heart, 277
Waft me from distraction, 353
thy name beyond the sky, 351
Wafted by thy gentle gale, 289
Wag all, in hall where beards, 19
let the world, 12
of a dog's tail, 920
Wage, cherubs earn their, 851

Wage, fair, for fair day's work, 589
for which they draw the, 780
hemlock for his, 853
I asked of life, 847
one ought not to, war, 1082
with a royal, 894
Wages, a fair day's, 378
and took their, 744
he that hath earned, 1126
home art gone and ta'en thy, 106
I ask not for, 738
of sin is death, 1119
taken, my, 693
taxes debts, it goes for, 510
world looks for, 491
Wager, opinions backed by a, 357
Wagers, fools use arguments for, 142
lay no, 251
Wagner's music dramas, 1087
Wagon, hitch your, to a star, 414
Wagon-seat, high upon his, 572
Wags, see how the world, 49
Waifs of wisdom and of folly, 609
Wail in the wind is all I hear, 517
nothing to, 157
of the remorseful winds, 588
still is heard yet its notes, 545
with old woes, new, 107
Wailing cry, 602
winds and naked woods, 372
Wain, wheels of Phœbus', 157
Waist exceeding small, her, 132
for an arm, what a, 545
lover's arm round her, 465
round the slight, 355
Waistcoats my manners and my
spice of wit, 1076
Wait a little longer, 504
and hope, 1067
for the day, 643
I witness and, 534
thou child of hope, 477
till you come to forty year, 481
upon I would, 85
who only stand and, 162
with longing eyes I, 481
Waiter roars it through the hall, 555
Waiting and watching for me, 608
for some one to come, 439
in his place, our champion, 442
while his wife dressed, 182
Waits, but labors and endures
and, 438
unformed, society, 537
Wake and call me early, 463
and sleep, still did, 109
and weep, here must I, 286
dream in joy and, in love, 375
dreams of those who, 995
if I should die before I, 947
in our breast the living, 451
or we sleep, whether we, 449
to perish never, 301
Wakes, at country, 177
the bitter memory, 151
the morning, 106
Waked by the circling hours, 153
me too soon, you have, 199

Waked, she fled, I, 162
with smale foules, 3
Wakeful stars, 588
Wakefulness, fail with, 397
Wakens the slumbering ages, 402
Wakin' a sudden weepin', a sudden, 765
Waking and the sleeping, beyond the, 445
bliss, certainty of, 158
man, dream of a, 1014
morn of toil nor night of, 308
Walden blue-eyed lake, 517
Wales England wed, so I was bred, 746
Walk about, foolery does, 55
and wot not what they are, 40
beneath it steadfastly, 454
by faith not by sight, 1120
free and own no superior, soul, 537
humbly with thy God, 1113
in fear and dread, 315
into my parlour, 394
milky way or solar, 207
none durst, but he, 178
of art, every, 290
on wings, seem to, 219
our unchained feet, freely, 386
softly and carry a big stick, 1112
the earth unseen, 152
the public ways, 760
under his huge legs, 81
where only saints have been, 913
while ye have the light, 1118
with, pretty to, 164
with stretched-forth necks, 1111
with you talk with you, 44
Walks among his peers unread,
he, 540
and shades, these happy, 155
broad green, 424
eye nature's, 206
happy, and shades, 155
in beauty like the night, 356
o'er the dew, 89
to-morrow, already, 318
up and down with me, 58
Walked away with their clothes, 419
beside the evening sea, I, 558
in glory, him who, 297
in paradise, 473
in Thebes's streets, 332
round and regarded his critic, 508
straight out of the ark, 312
Walker filiburst, 906
mechanically a pirate, 906
Walking and mincing as they go, 1111
apart forever, two are, 540
every day, seen us, 167
in an air of glory, 170
shadow, life 's but a, 88
Walking-stick, purpose of a, 731
the best automobile, 861
Wall and the fire, between the, 783
between two gardens, 880
bores through his castle, 60
braver he that leaps the, 604

Wall, clings to the, 427
close the, up with our English
dead, 66
cross the jasper, 671
die driven against the, 758
flower in the crannied, 467
giant shadow on the, 572
have built a, 824
in the office of a, 59
led her forth to the, 804
mounts the, 966
of the city shall fall flat, 1099
scaled the city, 738
Street's mingled nations, 604
that doesn't love a, 837
the, is strong, 722
twenty ballads stuck about
the, 139
weakest goes to the, 77, 1038
whitewashed, 251
wit is the only, 923
you can scale the, 557
Walls already rise, whose, 982
are thin, shattering, 886
around are bare, and the, 554
banners on the outward, 88
ever widening, 647
from their thick, 848
have ears, 6, 1041
have ears, woods have tongues
as, 470
I have my own four, 382
limit my vision, nor can four, 805
of Antioch, 939
of eld, 851
of England, wooden, 946
of memory's room, 662
of Paradise, spirit lies under, 552
old and lofty, 423
peace be within thy, 1106
prison, cannot control, 1051
pry loose old, 855
remain, the cloudy, 444
still within these, 813
stone, do not a prison make. 168
too narrow and opaque, 903
well-builded, stones of, 959
within wide circling, 688
wooden, of England, 946
worn thin, 30
Wallace bled, Scots wha hae wi'. 286
Wallenstein was dead, 594
Waller's Magdalena, 478
Wallets for our vices, 992
Walloping window-blind, 655
Wallow naked in December snow, 59
Walnuts and the wine, 462
Walton, a rodless, 733
Wan her cheeks are and what
heavy tears, 620
numb naked soul, 1009
with care, so, 60
Wand, bright gold ring on her, 334
he walked with, 148
magic, that can conjure up, 746
Wander through eternity, 149
when you, you wander indeed, 112
Wandered by the brook-side, 458

Wandered east I 've wandered
  west, 389
  idly, and my fingers, 564
Wanderer, fickle, else will stray,
  450
  kindly, 596
  though like the, 423
  weary wayworn, 460
Wandering by lone sea-breakers,
  676
  cloud that trailed, 722
  flesh, long before this, 832
  I love, 887
  mazes lost, in, 150
  moon riding near, 160
  on a foreign strand, 307
  on as loth to die, 304
  shoots and briars, 864
  steps and slow, 156
  voice, but a, 299
  wind, 597
Wandring Jew, so doth this, 257
Wane, moon will wax the moon
  will, 438
Waned, moons waxed and, the lilacs, 437
Waning, lights on the sleepy uplands, 418
  moon, beneath a, 315
Want, covetous man ever in,
  985
  exasperated into crime, 472
  had ceased to weep, 565
  has burnt out, 625
  has reference to some, 1062
  it is a hell, taste of fame to,
  426
  lonely, retired to die, 231
  no man will supply thy, 120
  not waste not, 591
  of a horse the rider was lost,
  137, 227
  of a nail the shoe was lost,
  137, 227
  of a shoe the horse was lost,
  227
  of decency is want of sense,
  180
  of faith, I pity their, 1056
  of faithfulness, 247
  of heart, as well as, 390
  of me, for, 556
  of skill or want of care, 280
  of thought, evil wrought by,
  390
  of thought, whistled for, 176
  of towns, elephants for, 190
  of use, from, 236
  of words or lack of breath, 157
  peace, if you, 527
  proud man reduced to, 199
  though much I, that most
  would have, 20
  to be a fly, I do not, 753
  to be undonne, to, 26
  to want, 236
  we don't, to fight, 562
  weariness vice and, 1052
Wants and tastes down low
  enough, tone your, 538
  are few, little I ask my, 451
  are many, 291
  are many, where, 757
  but little, man, 202, 254
  money means and content, 50
  of his own dominion, 499

Wants of nature are supplied,
  1051
  that pinch the poor, 267
  their daily, 974
Wanted a good word, never, 252
  a lady help, 394
  one immortal song, 173
Wanting, art found, 1113
  is what summer redundant,
  493
  not, what is stolen, 102
Wanton boys that swim on bladders, 73
  eyes, stretched-forth necks
  and, 1111
  stings and motions of the
  sense, 35
  sweetness, witchingly instil a,
  224
  wiles, quips and cranks and,
  160
Wantoned with thy breakers, 355
Wantonness in clothes, 133
War a terrible atrocious thing,
  1077
  alone bring to its highest tension, 1090
  always ready for, 1051
  always stirring up, 974
  and all its deeds of carnage,
  536
  and Peace, 1076
  and peace, scale of, 425
  and racking tax, 309
  and wine throve together, 576
  arousing enthusiasm for a,
  1090
  art statesmanship, be it, 728
  at best is barbarism, 542
  begun without good provision,
  1025
  blast of, blows in our ears, 66
  brazen throat of, 155
  breeds war again, 728
  but in modern, 930
  but what of, 991
  by nature in a state of, 190
  by the slain of the, 891
  cause of a long ten years', 185
  Christ went agin, an' pillage,
  526
  circumstance of glorious, 102
  coin is the sinews of, 1025
  consisteth in the known disposition thereto, 132
  country gains nothing by, 740
  cruel, is over, 604
  delays are dangerous in, 178
  Department, letters come to a,
  928
  drum throbbed, 464
  ease after, 24
  enters but where wealth allures, 174
  even to the knife, 352
  extension of preceding war,
  874
  ez fer, I call it murder, 526
  first in, first in peace, 281
  France and the last blind, 930
  garland of the, 32
  grim-visaged, 71
  hand of, infection and the, 59
  hath no fury like a non-combatant, 800
  he kept us out of, 427

War he sung his toil and trouble,
  176
  impious, array'd in flames, 66
  in general, three cheers for,
  1090
  in separate parties, go forth
  to, 1126
  in the amorous, 1022
  in time of peace thinks of, 125
  involves in its progress, 271
  is a game, 266
  is cruel, 542
  is glorious art, 203
  is hell, 542
  is quaint and curious, 651
  is still the cry, 352
  its thousands slays, 268
  John of Austria is going to,
  827
  law spoke too softly for, 998
  leap out, lurking, 728
  let slip the dogs of, 82
  loan for the, 937
  loves to prey, 967
  magnificent but not, 1070
  makes rattling good history,
  650
  my sentence is for open, 149
  my voice is still for, 195
  neither learn, any more, 1111
  never slays a bad man, 966
  never was a good, 227
  no discharge in that, 782,
  1109
  not inevitable, 762
  of commerce, 874
  of elements, amidst the, 195
  on the men, make, 928
  one cannot wage, 1082
  or battle's sound, 161, 409
  peace and, 68
  peace no less renowned than,
  162
  pray this mighty scourge of,
  457
  protracted, unjust, 532
  provide in peace what we need
  in, 989
  should come, if a, 778
  slogans, 799
  Son of God goes forth to, 343
  spoils of, 370
  storm of, was gone, 294
  superfluous to point out that
  this is, 431
  surest way to prevent, 320
  talk by men interesting, 616
  testament of bleeding, 60
  the authors and instigators of,
  20
  the great, and the petty peace,
  795
  the love of, for itself, 393
  the real, will never get in the
  books, 538
  the red laugh of, 864
  the same thing, love and, 1040
  the second is, 930
  the state of nature, 258
  the study of a prince, 258
  there'd be an end of, 433
  this is, 431
  to be prepared for, 268
  to end war, 799
  trooping from the, 759
  tug of, then was the, 186

War, unjust peace before a just, 227
  unsuccessful or successful, 264
  voices prophesying, 315
  was in his heart, 1104
  weak defence in, 177
  what we need in, 989
  will have its fascinations, 723
  with him, to be at, 981
  with honour as in, 76
  with the words of fate, at, 570
Wars and allarums, 25
  and rumours of wars, 1116
  and ships and towns, the, 903
  are merry, all their, 828
  are over and I am home, 899
  big, that make ambition virtue, 102
  disciplines of, 66
  more pangs and fears than, 73
  no sound of clashing, 478
  of kites or crows, 163
  run red with other, 602
  slain in your country's, 76
  thousand, of old, 469
  to be fought, 890
  to kill, new, 879
  we wage, the, 806
  who does i' the, 104
War's alarms, used to, 392
  glorious art, 203
  red techstone, 527
Warble his native wood-notes, 160
Warbled to the string, 161
Warbler of poetic prose, 266
Warblers roam, where idle, 336
War-bonnet of Medicine Hat, plumed, 929
Ward has no heart they say, 289
  thou knowest my old, 62
Wards, terrible crowded, 928
Warder of the brain, 85
  the, is despair, 723
Ware, great bed at, 200
  pleasing, is half sold, 136
Wares are so much harder to get rid of, 838
Ware-emporium, resembles a, 1079
Warfare, civilized table, 922
  o'er, thy, 308
Waring, what's become of, 478
Warld, it's a weary, and nobody bides in't, 750
Warm for rhyme, far too, 637
  from her wearing, 828
  heart within, 266
  lights are on the sleepy uplands, 418
  without heating, 204
Warmed by the sun, 698
  our sires, holy faith that, 451
Warmest welcome at an inn, 242
Warmth, a little light, a little, 607
  I give and light, 814
  no cheerfulness no healthful, 391
  of feeling turn ice, 554
  of its July, 405
  soft ethereal, 150
Warn comfort and command, 299
Warning, at th' expected, 285
  be, let this to you a, 948
  come without, 502

Warning for a thoughtless man, 302
  give little, 273
  take from others, 979
  to you, that should be, 426
Warp, weave the, 244
Warrant him heart-whole, 51
  truth shall be thy, 21
Warre, ease after, 24
Warren Hastings' motto, 399
Warres and allarums, 25
  and faithful loves, 24
Warrior bold, looking at some, 432
  famoused for fight, 107
  happy, 300
  intrepid and unselfish, 374
  taking his rest, like a, 364
  this was the truest, 516
  to a crust, eats the giant, 564
Warriors their dusty armour doffed, 576
Warsaw, order reigns in, 1062
Warwick and Talbot, 67
Wary, must be watchful, 388
Wash, dirty linen, 1052, 1060
  dresse be brief in praying, 134
  her guilt away, 253
  incessantly softly, soiled world, 536
  me and I shall be whiter, 1104
  me, where air might, 630
  saw God, the world, 886
Washing day, cold meat on, 182
  dry, we won't get the, 867
  ended with the day, her, 557
  his hands with invisible soap, 391
  on the line, like the, 938
Washington a finer and more beautiful city, 637
  America has furnished a, 340
  and the cherry tree, 941
  arms it, wisdom, 414
  bequeathed the name of, 357
  had thanks and nought beside, 357
  is a watchword, 357
  is in the clear upper sky, 340
  name of, shall shed an eternal glory, 374
  never slopt over, G., 606
  rode up, 659
  whose every battleground is holy, 357
  without his reward, 599
Washingtonian dignity, the, 619
Wassail for new love's behoof, 600
Wassail-bowl old arm-chair, 446
Waste and desolation, 66
  and desolation, built on, 925
  arguments where they will be lost, 424
  chaos doth inherit, 841
  haste maketh, 7, 11
  its sweetness on the desert air, 245
  lonely, 443
  long nights, 25
  nor suffer one bright hour to, 474
  not the remnant of thy life, 1010
  not want not, 591
  ocean's melancholy, 371

Waste of feelings unemployed, 355
  of hopes laid, 425
  of longevity, 247
  of public money, 641
  of scheme and toil, 553
  of this dishonored star, 836
  of thought, thinking is idle, 332
  of time, call it, 821
  of time, tedious, 156
  our elocution, 624
  perilous eternity, 867
  sheer delightful, 930
  wail my dear times', 107
  wilful, brings woeful want, 339
Wasted, affection never was, 435
  affection, talk not of, 435
  and withering sphere, 1066
  half my day, 591
  life, a tale of, 608
  some nine moons, 100
Wasteful and ridiculous excess, 58
  and unremorseful as tigers, 908
  woman, ah, 556
Wastes and withers there, 722
  in self-consuming fires, 193
Wasteth at noonday, 1105
Wasting in despair, 132
Watch a mouse, as a cat would, 192
  an idler is a, 263
  authentic, is shown, 164
  call the rest of the, 39
  care keeps his, 78
  each believes his own, 210
  Him pass, a thousand idly, 851
  his life is a, 634
  in every old man's eye, 78
  in the night, 1105
  no eye to, no tongue to wound, 336
  o'er man's mortality, 302
  or a vision, 634
  our body is a, 1061
  sleeps upon his, 259
  some must, while some sleep, 94
  that wants both hands, 263
  the hour, do but, 357
  was worn, e'er a, 681
  whispers of each other's, 67
  with more advised, 44
  your opportunity, 1013
Watches, and in its, 424
  dictionaries are like, 238
  judgments as our, 210
  keep time in two longitudes, 641
  of the night, the, 673
Watch-dog's honest bark, 358
  voice that bayed, 250
Watched her breathing, 390
  the moonbeams quiver, 582
Watcher of the skies, 384
  whose eyes have grown dim, 484
Watchful and wary, must be, 388
  night, the, 65, 322
Watching with eternal lids apart, 385
Watchmaker cannot open it, 1061

Watchman in my heart, little, 808
what of the night, 1111
Watchword, amo shall be the, 648
be dispatch, let your, 591
recall the, 404
stout, 478
Water and a crust, 383
and land upon the face, 370
and wine, drunk your, 776
benison of hot, 894
between our lodges, 697
blood thicker than, 310, 746
blushes into wine, 165
brooks, hart panteth after, 1104
brooks, the hart panteth for the, 645
burn'd on the, 104
but limns on, 113
by the myriad moving, 914
calm of, 636
can but freeze, 882
Christ walking on the, 749
conscious, saw its God, 165
continually dropping, 1001
cup of, a little thing, 386
deeds writ in, 130
deepest in smoothest stream, 24
defile its sacred, 686
don't go near the, 957
drank rapidly a glass of, 921
drink no longer, 1121
dropping will wear hard rocks hollow, 23
drops, women's weapons, 98
drowned them, I think the, 655
earth hath bubbles as the, 84
fresh from mead and hill, 733
from hither and thither, 909
from some earthly spring, 586
froze, the, 882
glass of brandy and, 290
glory is like a circle in, 68
goes, care where the, 827
goes dead, all, 801
holy with which the priest, 1072
horse to the, 14
hot, is to remain upon it, 144
imperceptible, 391
in a sieve, singing, 897
in a witch's sieve, 897
in his bath stirring the, 900
in our wine, put, 1022
in the rough rude sea, 59
in water, indistinct as, 105
into wine, change, 474
iron in the, 940
is a thing of beauty, 512
life is as, 948
like one great heave of, 498
made his mouth to, 142
men shall walk under, 940
milk and, 357
miller sees not all the, 125
moaned like beeves, 833
more, glideth by the mill, 77
much, goeth by the mill, 17
name writ in, 29, 386, 722
ne'er left man in the mire, 80
never miss the, 591
of gall to drink, give them, 1112

Water of that cup, 441
off a broad brimming, 873
or fire or air, by, 577
pure that bids, 682
rats and land rats, 44
servants that spilled, 441
sipped brandy and, 289
slimier slime, wetter, 893
smooth runs the, 21, 69
so runnes the, out, 948
spilt on the ground, 1100
steep horsehair certain weeks in, 491
that doun renneth ay, 3
that is past, grind with, 137, 666
that you touch in rivers, 1022
they've left for me, 362
thicker than, 310, 443, 746
thieves and land thieves, 44
this business will never hold, 194
travel by land or, 192
unbounded, salt, 777
unstable as, 1098
virtues we write in, 74
water everywhere, 315
we went through fire and through, 1104
went by, instead of land, 998
you fetch them, 909
Waters, as the voice of many, 1123
below look dark and deep, 642
beside the still, 1103
blue, fades o'er the, 352
cannot quench love, 1110
cast thy bread upon the, 1110
cold, to a thirsty soul, 1108
come ye to the, 1112
creep surely upward, as the, 1090
crystalline, 432
do business in great, 1105
dreadful noise of, in mine ears, 71
drowned in its, 640
England styled the queen of the, 407
fish in troubled, 188
flowing, the call of, 755
lie by living, 725
like the rushing of mighty, 1111
meet, where the bright, 335
name is on your, 364
noise of many, 1105
of Babylon, by the, 633
of Life we sat together, by the, 395
of Marah, drink of the, 1098
of the blue Juniata, 406
of the river Lee, 423
rave, where the scattered, 502
returning back to their springs, 435
rising world of, 151
round you curled, 553
Spanish, 832
stilled at even, 577
stolen, are sweet, 1107
swell, ye rising, 566
take heed of still, the quick pass, 21
that glass the clouds, 771

Waters, the moving, at their priestlike, 385
under a ruined mill, 868
undreamed shores, unpathed, 57
where such radiant, 730
where the bright, meet, 335
wide as the, be, 304
words writ in, 29
Waterfalls, loud with shallow, 438
Water-flower, colored like a, 632
Watering last year's crops, little good, 520
Watering-pot and pruning-knife, reward the, 476
Waterloo, every man his, 479
from Marathon to, 623
is a battle, 1067
John Bull was beat at, 406
won on playing fields of Eton, 293
Watermen look astern while they row, 1005
row one way and look another, 122
Water-plants, the slime on, 551
Waterside saloon, jabber of a, 925
Water-wagon is the place for me, 791
Watery deep, plough the, 218
nest, lark now leaves his, 146
Watkins, fare ye well, brother, 512
Watt mechanizes it, wisdom, 414
Wattle, did you ever hear of Capt., 274
Wave, all sunk beneath the, 267
and flutter round my door, 418
break of the, 362
bound the restless, 566
chill of its dark-running, 652
clears the top of the, 963
cool translucent, 158
for the next wave, as the, 914
fountain's murmuring, 269
had its nightcap, 701
life is a, 542
life on the ocean, 502
long may it, 332
Munich all thy banners, 328
must be, what a, 584
o' the sea, I wish you a, 56
of all her waves, 778
of life kept heaving, 390
of religious emotion, 606
of the sea, by a, 958
of the sea, folk dance like a, 791
on the multiplied, 601
on this side Jordan's, 516
shall test, you the, 784
so dies a, along the shore, 273
succeeds a wave, 134
their hands for a mute farewell, 540
to wash him from the world, 818
winning, deserving note, 133
write upon the, 967
Waves and mountains meet, 438
break, where the cool, 576
breaking on the farther shore, 583

Waves, Britannia rules the, 225
  chime ever peacefully, silver,
    480
  come as the, come, 309
  dashed high, the breaking, 370
  dashing of, 565
  freely as the, that beat, 386
  lap listlessly, 874
  make towards the pebbled
    shore, as, 107
  may not foam nor wild wind
    sweep, 370
  nothing save the, and I, 359
  o'er the mountain, 328
  of Breffny, 820
  of science beat in vain, 543
  proud, be stayed, 1102
  red, of wretchedness, 389
  rolled on, sweeping, 371 .
  seem ever singing the same sad
    thing, 500
  settled placidly, 630
  sleep in restless, 693
  that plunged along the shore,
    558
  that run like little lambs, 814
  to sleep had gone, 405
  vainly breaking, while the
    tired, 519
  went high, when the, 173
  were rough, storm when, 338
  what are the wild, saying, 500
  whist, the wild, 32
Wave-beat shore, and ocean's,
    503
Waved her lily hand, 205
Wavelet on the ocean tost, each,
    504
Wavelets of soft hair, 562
Wavering, more longing, 54
  wedge, a, 845
Wavers to a rose, 648
Waving here, she who spies thee,
    555
Wax, moon will, the moon will
    wane, 438
  my heart is, to be moulded,
    357
  seal to mortal, 1021
  to flaming youth, virtue be as,
    95
  to receive marble to retain,
    357
Waxed and waned the lilacs,
    moons, 437
  at the farther end, 510
Waxen minds, women have, 107
Way, a grim sardonic, 528
  a little to one, 925
  across that dizzy, 849
  adorns and cheers our, 252
  again, I shall not pass this,
    1063
  all along the pleasant, 619
  all the rugged, 549
  along life's weary, 774
  and that it wastes, this, 1022
  Ann hath a, 274
  as birds I see my, 484
  aught will ever stand in their,
    1045
  back to life and living people,
    838
  best, of doing everything, 413
  built in such a logical, 452
  cannot lose your, 76

Way, come the primrose, 702
  exceptional man has missed
    his, 1080
  face is like the milky, 164
  freed his soul the nearest, 231
  get out of harm's, 1035
  glory leads the, 186
  glory shows the, 186
  God moves in a mysterious,
    266
  Great White, 945
  heaven's wide pathless, 160
  home, the next, 135
  home, the shortest, 135
  homeward plods his weary,
    244
  how she may tyrannize, the
    secret, 134
  I am going a long, 463
  I live because he has passed
    my, 691
  I shall not pass again this, 682
  I shall not pass along, 881
  in its dull quiet, 961
  in such a, 1049
  in such a solemn, 451
  is all so very plain, 827
  kept the humble, 687
  let the wicked forsake his,
    1112
  lies open to eternal day, 597
  life's common, 298
  lion in the, there is a, 1108
  London Bridge his frequent,
    621
  lonely forest, 562
  long is the, and hard, 150
  longest, round, 135
  madness lies that, 98
  man's heart deviseth his, 1107
  merit makes his, 72
  mind my compass and my, 223
  mystery and the dark, 931
  narrow, is the, 1114
  never have a solitary, 955
  no, but through, 763
  no t' other side the, 391
  noiseless tenor of their, 245
  none trod before, 789
  of a man with a maid, 778
  of all flesh, 128, 493
  of all the earth, 1099
  of an eagle in the air, 1109
  of bargain, in the, 62
  of God, stands in the, 847
  of granting men, 835
  of kindness, save in the, 295
  of life, my, 88
  of managing this complicated
    world, 909
  of stealing on us, your sudden,
    842
  of transgressors, 1107
  or make it, I'll find a, 510
  out, best, is always through,
    838
  out of his wrack, 73
  parting of the, 1113
  permit nature to take her,
    1031
  pretty Fanny's, 201
  primrose, to everlasting bon-
    fire, 86
  rough, leads to rest, 730
  she dances such a, 163
  she hath a, 274

Way, skilful, you hide your
    claws, 1085
  smooth the rough and thorny,
    595
  so they went their, 1124
  solar walk or milky, 207
  something given that, 127
  sordid, he wends, 364
  speediest, by the, 966
  spell them the proper, 714
  steep and thorny, to heaven,
    90
  sweet and delectable, making
    the hard, 59
  swept proudly on her, 605
  take the old, 490
  tenor of his, 268
  that boys begin, this is the,
    481
  that I must tread alone, 372
  that leads from darkness, 672
  that milky, which nightly, 154
  that they played together, 715
  the excellent old, 790
  the money goes, that's the, 510
  the wind doth blow, whichever,
    555
  the worst, to improve the
    world, 506
  they fight or love or sin, 775
  through all their shining, 642
  through Eden took their, 156
  through mony a weary, 389
  to avoid it, surest, 1051
  to be deceived, 1044
  to be happy, 603
  to browbeat this world, but
    one, 490
  to dusty death, 88
  to flutter, but a little, 1018
  to have a friend is to be one,
    411
  to heaven, 90, 165
  to heaven led the, 205
  to hit a woman's heart, 417
  to live, in teaching me the, 405
  to look for a thing, 644
  to make sure, 235
  to parish church, plain as, 49
  to prevent war, surest, 320
  to rear up children, 429
  to simplify my, of life, 376
  to spread a work, 235
  too easily explored, 305
  travel on life's common, 298
  trudgin' my weary, 678
  unentreated, 629
  upheaves its little, 499
  upheld you on your, 855
  we may lose the, 827
  we parted, the way we met,
    633
  we will precede, lead the, 278
  went her unremembering, 748
  whence I shall not return, go
    the, 1102
  where is the good, 1112
  which, I fly is hell, 151
  which, shall I fly, 151
  which, the wind is, 130
  which, they walk, 85
  wide is the gate broad the,
    1114
  wisdom finds a, 280
  working out its, 173
  world's wide parched, 450

Ways, a hundred different, 920
amend your, 1112
among the untrodden, 296
and means, 222
and wiles, children's, 634
appointed, 591
are dewy wet, 572
are sweet on earth, 963
are ways of gentleness, 747
cheerful, of men, 151
down devious, 853
fortune hath divers, 28
halting not in your, 778
high courage and unselfish, 676
let me count the, 429
mysterious, 922
newer, are ours, 670
newest kind of, 65
of death, 692
of duty, trod the hard, 445
of duty, walks the careful, 444
of dying, knows all, 824
of glory, trod the, 73
of God, by the, 856
of God, just are the, 156
of God to man, vindicate the, 206
of God to men, justify the, 148
of her household, 1109
of hoar antiquity, 258
of honour, the perfect, 74
of pleasantness, 1106
of spreading light, two, 766
of the gods full of providence, 1009
of the tapestry weavers, 569
seem harsh and wild, 756
shadow falls both, 156
shall plan my, 403
stand ye in the, 1112
sweet accustomed, 887
that are dark, 644
the many thousand, 437
there are nine and sixty, 780
they know not well the subtle, 410
they least expect, 556
to keep thee in all thy, 1105
to lengthen our days, 336
torture ten thousand, 175
walked in our common, 706
wandered all our, 22
with men, in His, 471
you can, in all the, 226
Wayfarer desire moves and wakes, 755
love, you happy, 873
Wayfaring men, 264, 1112
Wayside folk, advise not, 784
inn, in this old, 771
Wayward and tetchy, 72
pencil drew, 595
sisters depart in peace, 349
Way-worn rhyme, 849
We are born to wander, 908
are men my liege, 86
are ne'er like angels, 116
are not amused, 534
are the music-makers, 676
are waiting for you there, 732
beg Thee freely to bestow, 1017
cannot know, 807
dare not think too long, 843

We dying, long for, 938
lack but open eye and ear, 442
live not as we wish to, 976
may live without poetry, 592
must do the thing we must, 559
never mention her, 388
praise Thee O God, 1017
're laying a gas-pipe down, 952
seemed to see our flag, 442
the workers all demand, 845
took off rather suddenly, 934
us and ours, when you're talking, 784
who have sailed together, 678
will be free! 954
will be under it, 914
will lie down and weep, 931
would often be sorry, 962
Weak and as strong as silly and as wise, as, 457
and beggarly elements, 1121
and despised old man, 98
and insignificant, the, 969
and weary, while I pondered, 460
as a rained-on bee, 840
by those who are too, 892
ceaseless devouring of the, 580
concessions of the, 259
fine by defect and delicately, 209
hand, cravens my, 106
in courage is strong in cunning, 282
man better enemy than friend, 518
men, persuade, 247
minds, first defence of, is to recriminate, 318
minds led captive, 156
shall perish, surely the, 844
stem hard back, cut the, 864
the flesh is, 1116
to be a sinner, too, 80
to be, is miserable, 148
we are not, 270
we kneel how, 441
women went astray, if, 189
words are all too, 373
Weaker beauties of the night, 166
than it found us, leaves us, 184
vessel, as unto the, 1122
Weakest goes to the wall, 77, 1038
kind of fruit, 46
not vain the, 219
Weak-eyed bat, 247
prisoner of wall and street, 878
Weak-fish stay, 865
Weakness, amiable, 229, 270
cannot run from a, 704
false-refined, 491
feeble wrong because of, 430
fills me with disgust, 713
in fond caress, naught but, 522
is not in your word, 547
of intellect, 624
of the human mind, 1048
prevailin', of public men, 606
strength perfect in, 1121
stronger by, 146
Weaknesses, amiable, 279

Weaknesses and meannesses, our worst, 498
men's, 1084
people who have no, 1078
Weal and woe, scheme of the, 489
how false its how true its woes, 544
prayer for others', 351
the public, 1029
Wealth, a great soul's, 587
a well-spent age, 121
accumulates, where, 250
allures, but where, 174
and commerce, 518
and freedom reign, 249
and poverty merely mental, 937
bestowed on camps and courts, 434
boundless his, 307
brings, love remember'd, 107
but life, no, 533
by any means get, 214
can add nothing greater, 985
consume without producing, 719
cut them for, 956
e'er gave, all that, 244
excess of, is cause of covetousness, 31
genuine and less guilty, 166
get place and, 214
he boasts not, 499
I ask not, 703
ignorance of, his best riches, 250
large was his, 174
lies hid, 476
loss of, is loss of dirt, 11
maketh many friends, 1107
malefactors of great, 734
meself an' me, 715
nor wit, not too much, 128
of earth's gold-sanded streams, 597
of living, from a, 880
of mankind, 676
of Ormus and of Ind, 149
of our times, increasing, 500
of seas the spoils of war, 370
of the fruitful meadow, 712
of the Indies, 237
of the richest bloods, 860
or of glory, of, 859
part of the so-called national, 1072
piled up by the bondsman's, 457
private credit is, 950
small aid is, 967
takes away liberty, 769
than population and, 1072
the parent of luxury, 973
the possession of the valuable, 533
those that have, 388
took a flight, 604
whose, arithmetic cannot number, 129
ye find another keeps, 368
Wealthy and wise, healthy, 227
curled darlings, 100
gallant always gains the day, 1022
obliged the, 218

Weans in their bed, are the, 475
Weapon never carried a, 786
  of ignorance, most powerful, 1077
  of truth, 930
  satire 's my, 213
  still as snowflakes, 348
  stronger, thought 's a, 504
  that slays, no, 593
Weapons of the gods, 969
  without superfluous, 923
  women's, water-drops, 98
Wear a golden sorrow, 73
  a lion's hide, 57
  a noble face, hills of manhood, 458
  get that I, 50
  in continuance, 26
  motley's the only, 49
  not much the worse for, 264
  not my dagger in my mouth, I, 106
  out than to rust out, better to, 179
  what to eat and drink and, 398
Wearer knows where shoe wrings, 137
Wearer's expectation, the, 498
Weariest river, the, 632
  worldly life, 36
Wearin' awa' to the land of the leal, 291
  the white flower, 469
Wearing, worse for the, 15
Weariness can snore, 106
  may toss him, 136
  not on your brow, 547
  of the flesh, 1110
  the endless pain, the, 439
  vice and want, 1052
Wearisome condition, 27
Wears a hood, drink with him that, 20
  a snowy beard, tradition, 442
  she to him, so, 54
Weary, a song the sigh of the, 567
  and old with service, 73
  and worn cold and forlorn, 551
  and worn, with fingers, 391
  are wearing, 652
  be at rest, there the, 1101
  bones, come to lay his, 74
  creatures sore and worn, 754
  heart can rest, 548
  how my heart grows, 567
  hymn of, and broken in heart, 533
  I was, and ill at ease, 564
  in well doing, let us not be, 1121
  knife-grinder, 293
  land, across a, 827
  land, rock in a, 1111
  lay me low, I am, 601
  leagues two loving hearts divide, 675
  love waxed, 632
  of breath, one more unfortunate, 392
  of conjectures, I am, 195
  of mumbling Athanasian creeds, 609
  of the chill companionship, 904
  of the commonplace, 601

Weary of toil and tears, 595
  or too dull, too, 893
  pilgrimage, 237
  pondered weak and, 460
  say I'm sad say I'm, 346
  stale flat and unprofitable, 90
  warld, it's a, 750
  warld to rest are gone, 277
  way, trudgin' my, 678
  wayworn wanderer, 460
  with disasters, 86
Weasel, it is like a, 95
  pop goes the, 510
Weasel-head, the snout the jowl, 856
Weather a literary speciality, 617
  beautiful early summer, 395
  bless you with the sunniest, 406
  carries English, 769
  crops potatoes pumpkins, 451
  eyes blue to any, 903
  fair, out of the north, 1102
  foul, lieth not in a shower, 132
  God's own chosen, 693
  had cleared, when the, 655
  if it prove fair, 163
  in all kinds of, 578
  in sad or singing, 631
  in stormy, 191
  is always doing something, 617
  many can brook the, 41
  October's bright blue, 591
  one hundred and thirty-six kinds of, 617
  sad thoughts and sunny, 531
  safe from worldly, 796
  sorts of things and, 408
  stress of the wildest, 642
  they called it Austerlitz, 1071
  through pleasant and cloudy, 272
  'tis always fair, 771
  trying to get behind the, 726
  unchangeable, if Providence had made, 312
  variety about the New England, 617
  watched the, 837
  will be dry, unless it rains, 764
  will be fair for the sky is red, 1115
  wind or, nought cared for, 317
  without, little we fear, 481
Weathers, lies with the god of, 1091
Weathercock of the church steeple, 1055
  on a steeple, 33
Weathered every wrack, ship has, 536
  face was homely, whose, 927
  the storm, 294
Weave no more silks ye Lyons looms, 522
  the warp, 244
Weavers, ways of the tapestry, 569
Weaver's shuttle, swifter than a, 1102
Weaving the web of days, 631
Web from their own entrails spin, 177
  in middle of her, 115
  like the stained, 337
  of days, 631

Web of loveliness, God wove a, 841
  of our life is of mingled yarn, 53
  tangled, we weave, 308
  that whitens in the sun, 337
  unbroken, 652
  ye mar, the, 441
Webster a steam-engine, 313
  has the words, 829
Wed at leisure, wooed in haste, 52
  December when they, 51
  itself with speech, thought, 468
  with this ring I thee, 1128
Wedded love, hail, 152
  maid and virgin mother, 161
Wedding bells at end of novels, 773
  bells, hear the mellow, 460
  delight in a, 182
  feast, Cana's, 474
  is destiny, 12
  vow, well-kept, 445
Wedding-gown, as she chose her, 253
Weder for to slepen inne, 4
Wedge, for a tough log a tough, 989
  on the high bright blue, 845
Wedged in that timber, 80
Wedlock compared to public feasts, 115
  forced, what is, 68
Wedlock-treachery, not, 157
Wednesday, he that died o', 63, 604
  if I loved you, 428, 916
  in Wheeson week, 64
Wednesday's child is loving, 956
Wee short hour, some, 284
  thing, handsome, 286
  thing, lo'esome, 286
  wife of mine, sweet, 286
  Willie Winkie, 475
Weed, and found itself a, 820
  and pluck away, 59
  dull and flowerless, 441
  ill, groweth fast, 14
  ill, grows apace, 28
  in palmer's, 157
  is but an unloved flower, 525
  like that delicate, 592
  no more than a flower, 525
  on Lethe wharf, 91
  pernicious, 263
  the people said a, 574
  tobacco is a dirty, 943
  what is a, 415
  who art so lovely fair, 103
Weeds are shallow-rooted, 69
  do grow apace, 14
  juiceless, 756
  noisome, 60
  of the river, 854
  outworn, winter, 367
  pass like, 338
  sleep beneath these, 806
  wiped away the, 408
Weed's plain heart, 524
Weeded, rich soils often to be, 112
Week, a dozen times a, 763
  argument for a, 61
  divide the Sunday from the, 89
  is gone, Thursday come and the, 138

Week, of all the days that's in
    the, 189
    of passionate humility, 666
    the whole of the, 956
    was seven domes, 923
Weeks thegither, fou for, 287
Week's labour, good, 117
Weel, we luvit ilk ither, 389
Weep a people inurned, 399
    and be not consoled, 1074
    and you weep alone, 718
    away the life of care, 367
    here must I wake and, 286
    him dead and mourn, 916
    in our darkness, let us, 431
    laugh that I may not, 360
    let the stricken deer go, 94
    make the laugher, 109
    might not, for thee, 364
    no more lady, 256
    no more nor sigh, 127
    no more — O weep, 385
    not for him, 431
    not for me, 403
    not, weep not, 817
    such tricks as make angels, 36
    tears such as angels, 149
    to, is to make less the depth of
        grief, 70
    to record, 327
    whether we carol or, 449
    while all around thee, 275
    who would not, 213
    women must, 523
    words that, 168
    yet scarce know why, 337
Weeper laugh, make the, 109
Weeping and laughter, not long
    the, 795
    at the feet and head, 596
    eyes, wipe my, 199
    for the morrow, 1057
    joy at, 38
    may endure for a night, 1103
    rain, follows a mist and, 559
    thou sat'st, 275
    upon his bed has sate, 439
Weigh my eyelids down, 65
Weighed in the balances, 1113
Weighing delight and dole, in
    equal scale, 89
Weighs heavily on me, mortality,
    385
    upon the heart, 88
Weight, entitled to great, 329
    have great, 259
    heavy and the weary, 295
    I bear, estimate the, 811
    if clay could think and mind
        were, 303
    in gold, thrice their, 288
    in wildcats, whip his, 698
    of another's burden, 138
    of centuries, 708
    of jewel or plate, 792
    of learning, 469
    of mightiest monarchies, 150
    of seventy years, 302
    the enormous, 218
Weights and woe, hung with, 170
Weighty secrets, 682
    sense flows in fit words, 174
Weir, ghoul-haunted woodland
    of, 461
Weirs, grass grows on the, 790
Weird sisters, 87

Welcome as to himself, as, 1029
    at an inn, warmest, 242
    beneath this roof, 439
    day, pack clouds away, 129
    deep-mouthed, 358
    ever smiles, 75
    friend, when it comes say,
        165
    guest, always my, 258
    in your eye your hand, 84
    on wings, silver, 896
    peaceful evening in, 265
    shade, more, 205
    small cheer and great, 37
    the coming guest, 213, 220
    the sweet, more, 53
    to all men, 132
    whimper of, 783
    wit makes its own, 415
Welcomes presents and rejoic-
    ings, 495
    recanting goodness, hollow, 80
Welding blast of candid flame,
    686
Welds, men together, error, 1077
Welfare a greater place, 877
    music ministers to human, 581
    speeding the nation's, 561
Welkin dome, lit the, 382
    splits apart, 816
Well, agree not, together, 531
    all is, 566
    all is well that endes, 13
    and did it, 623
    descended, desirable to be,
        1001
    do, 566
    done is done soon enough,
        1031
    done, life's work, 555
    done said written as, 1086
    done thou good and faithful
        servant, 1116
    dressed, in good temper when,
        495
    drink from the, 566
    enough for every day, 919
    God is and all is, 444
    good deed to say, 73
    here, if we do, 276
    if I have done, 1126
    if the end be well all is, 1075
    it rose from the, 348
    life's race, run, 555
    live, what thou livest, 155
    not so deep as a, 79
    not wisely but too, 103
    of Beth-lehem, which is by
        the gate, 1100
    of English undefyled, 25
    of love, a, 387
    of soft incoherence, 893
    of St. Keyne, 321
    of true wit, 576
    oft we mar what's, 98
    ordered mind, 1010
    paid that is well satisfied, 47
    read, exceedingly, 62
    runs dry, till the, 591
    said again, 73
    shaken, when taken to be, 288
    still forever fare thee, 356
    stocked and ever renewed,
        1079
    stricken in age, 1097
    sure to live, 276

Well that all is ordered, 501
    that ends well, all's, 53, 1075
    that I am placed so, 878
    they know not, the subtle,
        410
    to be off with the old love,
        611
    to know that all is, 966
    to lie fallow for a while, 478
    'twill all be, 1019
    with him, if it be, 761
    worth doing, 222
Wells, buckets into empty, 265,
    313
    from the bells, musically, 459
    on earth, 634
Well-attired woodbine, 159
Well-being of his fellow men,
    921
Well-beloved, souls, noble and,
    627
Well-born boys, necessary for,
    1014
Well-bred man, sensible and,
    263
    whisper close the scene, 265
Well-chosen anthology, a, 924
Well-conducted person, like a,
    481
Well-defended, walked so, 897
Well-established precedent, 733
Well-experienced archer, 106
Well-favoured man, to be a, 39
Well-fed long-haired men, 1000
Well-fill'd shelves, lacking on
    all your, 534
Well-graced actor, after a, 60
Well-instructed carry on all high
    intellectual work, 448
Well-kept wedding vow, you and
    your, 445
Well-known name, 512
Well-provisioned   breakfast-
    table, 422
Well-situated   well-cultivated
    farm, 374
Well-spring bubbling, 575
    of pleasure, 477
Well-stored mind, hunger for a,
    692
Well-timed silence hath more
    eloquence, 478
Well-trod stage, then to the, 160
Well-wisher what you might say
    a, 812
Well-worn paths, good sense
    travels on the, 1077
Weltering in his blood, 176
    water moaned, 833
Wench, sheep's eye at the, 1039
Wench's black eye, white, 78
Went a gallant band, we, 455
    an' took, 784
    on cutting bread and butter,
        481
    to making pies, and, 557
    to pieces all at once, it, 453
    to sea in a beautiful pea-green
        boat, 498
    to sea in a sieve, they, 498
Weping and preyeres, in stede
    of, 5
Wept away in transient tears,
    455
    out their eyes, 948
    we grieved we sighed we, 168

Wept with delight at smile, 521
Were, illusion that times that, 497
Werke wel and hastily, 7
Werk wel thy-self, 4
Werkman, ther nis no, 7
Werling, young man's, 17
Werther had a love for Charlotte, 481
West begins, out where the, 822, 925
  begins where the average rainfall, 926
  blue eyes sought the, 306
  bosom of the urgent, 668
  go, 505
  history of conquest of, 707
  is San Francisco, 800
  land of the, is the land of the heart, 405
  moved so sweetly to the, 375
  no South no North no East, no, 329
  of these out of seas, 881
  the old time, the old, 841
  to make the, 442
  To the West! to the, 504
  topples round the dreary, 468
  turn your face to the great, 479
  wind, autocratic sway of, 726
  wind blow, I have heard the, 717
  you have reached the, 926
  young man, go, 505
Western bars, behind the, 668
  dome, him of the, 174
  flower, a little, 42
  sea, beside the, 912
  sky in the night, drooped in, 536
  star, lovers love the, 306
Westinghouse, breathing by, 926
Westminster Abbey a mausoleum, 892
  Abbey or victory, 283
  Abbey the nation's Valhalla, 696
  glorious glooms at, 540
  we thrive at, 216
Westward, brightens to the, 565
  look the land is bright, 519
  stepping, 298
  the course of empire, 203
  the star of empire, 203
Westward-going stars, and saw the, 552
Westward-ho, then, 55
West-wind purr contented, 527
Wet by the dew, 698
  dewy, 572
  guess what I should perform in the, 1036
  sheet and flowing sea, 345
Wether, tainted, of the flock, 46
Wethers, return to our, 1024
Whacks, gave her mother forty, 957
Whale, and there was, 888
  bobbed for, 146
  in the cold and green, 888
  like a wounded, 873
  ship my Yale college, 531
  swims minnow-small, 888
  throw a tub to the, 191
  time the dark, 888

Whale, very like a, 95
Whales, little fishes talk like, 255, 649
  spouting steam like, 926
Wharf, fat weed on Lethe, 91
Wharves in sailor town, 873
What a fall was there, 83
  a falling-off was there, 91
  a man thinks of himself, 514
  a monstrous tail our cat has, 189
  a piece of work is a man, 92
  a taking was he in, 34
  a waist for an arm, 545
  a world of happiness, 460
  and where they be, 469
  and why and when, 784
  are the wild waves saying, 500
  asketh man to have, 6
  boots it at one gate, 156
  can an old man do but die, 390
  can ennoble sots, 208
  care I for whom she be, 132
  care I how chaste she be, 22
  care I how fair she be, 22
  dire effects from civil discord, 195
  do I know, 1031
  do you read my lord, 92
  doth the Lord require of thee, 1113
  God hath joined together, 1115
  has been has been, 177
  has posterity done for us, 277
  he knew what's, 10, 142
  I gona do, 813
  I know what's, 1036
  I never knew, 893
  I tell you is so, 535
  if men take to following, 609
  if some unshamed iconoclast, 609
  in other mouths was rough, 524
  is a man profited, 1115
  is and what must be, 151
  is her history, 55
  is knowledge but grieving, 592
  is the night, 87
  is to come I know not, 1123
  is virtue courage wit, 199
  is worth in anything, 142
  is yours is mine, 37, 978
  it can not find creates, or, 438
  makes all doctrines plain, 143
  makes his dawning glow, 416
  man dare I dare, 87
  may man within him hide, 37
  men call treasure, 528
  men daily do not knowing, 39
  men dare do what men may do, 39
  mighty contests rise, 212
  more felicitie can fall, 26
  ne'er was nor is, 211
  never? 622
  news on the Rialto, 44
  none hath dared thou hast done, 22
  oft was thought, 211
  say they, let them say, 22
  seest thou else, 32
  shall I do with all the days, 454

What so rare as a day in June, 525
  sought they thus afar, 370
  strange shores, 30
  summer redundant, wanting is, 493
  the devil did he want in that galley, 1047
  the dickens, 34
  they'd never told, 893
  thou liv'st live well, 155
  though the field be lost, 148
  to recall, 773
  was good shall be good, 489
  was shall live as before, 489
  we anticipate seldom occurs, 420
  we gave we have, 1075
  we have but what we use, not, 734
  we have we prize not, 39
  we least expected happens, 420
  we left we lost, 1075
  we ought not we do, 547
  we see but what we choose, not, 734
  we spent we had, 1075
  we would but what we must, not, 565
  will Mrs. Grundy say, 290
  would you have me do, 1085
  you do betters what is done, 56
  you have done, changing, 797
Whate'er we leave to God God docs, 513
Whatever gods may be, 632
  is best administered, 208
  is is in its causes just, 178
  is is right, 178, 207
  is worth doing at all, 222
  may befall, 576
  there is to know, 577
  was great seemed to him little, 398
  was or is or will be, 1005
  wasn't must be right, 821
What's done is done, 86
  done we may compute, 285
  given freely, 56
  gone and what's past help, 56
  Hecuba to him, 93
  impossible can't be, 288
  in a name, 78
  o'clock, 61
  one man's poison, 132
  that, and say, 729
Whatsoever a man soweth, 1121
  one hath well said, 964
  state I am, in, 1121
  thing is lost, 267
  things are honest, 1121
  things are just, 1121
  things are lovely, 1121
  things are of good report, 1121
  things are pure, 1121
  things are true, 1121
  thou takest in hand, 1124
  thy hand findeth to do, 1110
  ye would that men should do, 1114
Wheat and the shower, 731
  as two grains of, 44

Wheat, bounteous field of, 362
country of snow and, 929
for this planting, 436
life in the grain of, 753
Wheedling arts, the, 205
Wheel, as she turns the giddy, 249
between the poles, that, 471
broken at the cistern, 1110
butterfly upon a, 213
dust beneath thy chariot, 775
fortune turn thy, 98
giddy Fortune's furious fickle, 67
in the middle of a wheel, 1113
noisy, was still, 458
shoulder to the, 124, 962
that squeaks the loudest, 518
the sofa round, 265
the world is a, 421
turn turn my, 439
viewless voiceless turner of the, 650
Wheele of Change, 25
Wheels, little tin gods on, 776
of brazen chariots, 153
of daily life, 717
of his chariots, why tarry the, 1099
of Phœbus' wain, 157
of weary life stood still, 179
run down, and all the, 523
Wheelbarrow, no vehicle but a, 374
Wheeson week, Wednesday in, 64
Wheeze, laugh at his own, 882
Whelp and hound and curs of low degree, 254
conceited, 458
When all its work is done the lie, 556
all the world is old lad, 523
another rock would crown, 484
awful darkness and silence, 498
faith is lost when honor dies, 442
found make a note of, 496
he would he shall have nay, 11
he's laughed and said his say, 481
I ope my lips, 44
I put out to sea, 472
I was one-and-twenty, 742
in doubt win the trick, 197
Israel of the Lord, 310
Israel was from bondage led, 168
like the rising day, 416
lilacs last in the door-yard, 536
love speaks, 41
lovely woman stoops to folly, 253
moment on moment, 425
peace shall over all the earth, 477
probing a bottomless, 747
shall we three meet again, 84, 951
taken to be well shaken, 288
that which drew from out, 472
the age is in the wit is out, 39

When the sea was roaring, 't was, 205
the sun in all its state, 557
we two parted, 351
we will resign, nor, 547
winds are raging o'er, 480
you and I were young, 453, 640
you sleep in your cloak, 545
Whence and what art thou, 150
and whither give no rest, 736
and whither when how, 544
be the grapes of the wine-press, 401
is thy learning, 206
Whene'er a noble deed is wrought, 436
is spoken a noble thought, 436
Where did I come from, 647
doubt there truth is, 506
dwellest thou, 76
go, he will the wise man, 410
go the poet's lines, 451
go we know not, 36
I am, I would be nowhere else than, 904
I would ever be, I am, 350
ignorance is bliss, 243
is my child, an echo answers, 356
is the blot, 493
law ends tyranny begins, 230
lives the man that has not tried, 309
love and wisdom dwell, 501
Macgregor sits, 414, 1040
my Julia's lips do smile, 133
none admire, useless to excel, 239
nothing is had for nothing, world, 519
searching an infinite, 747
the bee sucks there suck I, 33
the shoe pinches, 997
they that love are blest, 503
thou lodgest I will lodge, 1099
was Roderick then, 308
your treasure is, 1114
Whereabout, prate of my, 85
Where'er I am by shore at sea, 393
I roam, 249
Wherefore and the whence, thinking on the, 686
are these things hid, 54
art thou Romeo, 78
doth your rout send forth, 401
for every why a, 37, 142
in all things, why and, 67
is a hopeless quest, 736
of men, what is the, 747
oh, come ye forth in triumph, 401
Wheresoever whensoever, 274
Wherever I will, let me sit, 1040
Macdonald sits, 414
Wherewith to spend, 120
Whether in sea or fire, 89
pigs have wings, 598
we wake or we sleep, 449
Whets appetite, coquetry, 551
Whetstone of the wits, 47
the blunt, 23

Which I have loved long since, 403
is which, knows not, 42
leg goes after which, 942
Whigs bathing and walked away, caught, 419
While, a little, 634
after a little, 647
ago, mighty, 118
ere I go hence, this little, 775
I nodded nearly napping, 460
I pondered weak and weary, 460
I was musing, 1104
stands the Coliseum, 354
the tired waves vainly break-ing, 519
there is life there's hope, 206
well to lie fallow for a, 478
we're Britons true, 562
you pursue, then be it yours, 474
Whim, after this life's, 561
bites, as the, 324
her ladyship's, 648
Whimper, not a bang but a, 899
of welcome, 783
to snarl and, 635
Whimpy, little Whimpy cried, 638
Whining school-boy, 49
Whimsical fellows, included among the, 751
Whine of the amateur, 611
to a hurdy-gurdy's, 929
Whining at the threshold, 754
Whinstone, my, house my castle is, 382
Whip, a hangman's, 285
awaits shirkers, 492
in every honest hand a, 103
of toil no more, 725
pray you spare the, 758
ride with an idle, 783
that drives you ever, 1083
Whips and scorns of time, 93
Whipped for o'erdoing terma-gant, 94
the offending Adam, 66
Whipping and abuse like lauda-num, 480
who should 'scape, 93
Whirligig of time, 56
Whirlwind, fell in, 708
of passion, 94
reap the, 1113
rides in the, 194, 215
scatter in its breeze, 337
Whirlwind's rings, in the, 770
roar, 249
sway, sweeping, 244
Whiskey, couldn't afford good, 715
polishes the copper, 616
yer's yer good old, 645
Whiskies, to the extent of two, 800
Whisper, accent of an angel's, 645
came to me, 777
full well the busy, 251
goes, a singing, 873
of the southwind, 642
of the throne, shape the, 468
of the wind, 801

Whisper on the tumult thrown, 504
 or a sigh, listening to a, 927
 softness in chambers, 163
 well-bred, close the scene, 265
 with far-heard, 315
 woke the air, 499
Whispers low, when duty, 409
 of each other's watch, 67
 of fancy, 232
 of heavenly death, 537
 of the desert-wind, 544
 the o'er-fraught heart, 88
Whispered hint, never a, 806
 in heaven, 't was, 290
 song, my soul is full of, 540
 then, every tale hope, 455
 yes or no, 638
Whispering crowded room, 547
 each heart is, Home, 392
 humbleness, 45
 I will ne'er consent, 358
 lovers made, for, 250
 wind, bayed the, 250
 with white lips, 352
Whisperings around desolate shores, 385
Whist, the wild waves, 32
Whist-club, his partners at the, 406
Whistle and I'll come to ye, my lad, 286
 and she will come to you, 131
 and sing, still he'd, 274
 clear as a, 221
 free, the shrill winds, 503
 her off and let her down, 102
 knew his, 847
 of my call, softest, 671
 paid dear for his, 227
 shrill, Christmas is here winds, 481
 them back, when he pleased, 252
 wel y-wet, 6
Whistled for want of thought, 176
 up to London, 241
Whistler, white lock of, 826
Whistler's ideas about art, borrowing, 724
Whistles in his sound, pipes and, 50
Whistling aloud to bear his courage up, 179
 of a name, 168, 208
 to keep from being afraid, 179
Whit, matter then a, 774
White a cherry bough, how, 883
 a moment, then melts, 287
 and drifted snow, 404
 and still, sech nights all, 527
 as a rain-washed bone, 781
 as heaven, a soul as, 131
 as snow, they shall be, 1111
 as the sails at sea, 689
 bosoms, silk stockings and, 233
 bow thy head thou lily, 555
 candle in a holy place, 868
 canoe, she paddles her, 334
 dust o' the road, 873
 E, 1084
 election, 584
 flesh, no, 903
 flower of a blameless life, 469

White, for hell, too, 174
 hairs become a fool and jester, how ill, 66
 in black in green, in, 940
 is for purity red for valor, 481
 it stays for ever, 648
 magnolia-blossoms, 443
 man, appeal to any, 249
 man, marry any sort of, 479
 man's burden, 780
 man's room on earth, 878
 nameless faces, 874
 or a black stone, 1039
 pair that once was, 451
 plates and cups, 894
 plume and a green lance. 925
 pure celestial, 382
 radiance of eternity, 366
 rose breathes of love, 675
 she keeps them, 701
 shall not neutralize the black, 491
 so very white, nor, 293
 sunshine not so sweet and, 556
 their, it stays for ever, 648
 truth in simple nakedness, 470
 wench's black eye, 78
 went to a party dressed in, 557
 will have its black, 255
 wings lessening up the skies, 574
 with snow, fairest meadow, 453
 wonder of Juliet's hand, 79
Whited sepulchres, 1116
White-hall, by water to, 948
White-hot, before the white heat, 928
Whiteness, angel, 39
 of his soul, 588
Whitens in the sun, web that, 337
Whiter grows the foam, 668
 than driven snow, 242
White-walled tent, made a, 922
Whitewashed wall, 251
White-winged birds, 677
 reapers, 170
Whither thou goest I will go, 1099
Whitman a poet who disdained to be just a poet, 849
 and Melville, in, 925
 with his sack of tobacco, 928
Whitman's poems poetry, call, 924
Whittier thou art not old, 522
Whiz, history a, 599
Who are a little wise the best fools be, 110
 are you, 620
 can be against us, 1119
 can be wise amazed temperate, 86
 can hold a fire in his hand, 59
 can wrestle against sleep, 478
 cannot live on twenty pound a year, 136
 dares do more is none, 85
 does not befriend himself, 966
 doth not crave for rest, 503

Who dreads to the dust returning, 554
 goeth a borrowing, goeth a sorrowing, 19
 has many wishes, 1056
 has not found the heaven below, 585
 hath no fault at all, 470
 knows but on their sleep may rise, 634
 is all-powerful should fear, 1043
 is living on with us, 1058
 is so deafe or so blinde, 17
 is Sylvia, 34
 knows most, 1021
 knows the thoughts of a child, 600
 lined himself with hope, 64
 loves not wine woman and song, 481
 loves to lie with me, 48
 never climbs as rarely falls, 443
 never doubted never half believed, 506
 never wins can rarely lose, 443
 nevermore would come again, 439
 of us being what he is, 808
 or why or which or what, 499
 ran to help me when I fell, 345
 says it what he says how he says it, 641
 should 'scape whipping, 93
 shrinks from the sable shore, 554
 sleep on glory's brightest, 386
 so deaf as he that will not hear, 136
 stands and cheers, 636
 that hath ever been, 306
 think not God at all, 156
 think too little, 173
 thinks must mourn, 190
 will not readily comply, 942
 wooed in haste, 52
 would fardels bear, 93
 would not seek the happy, 503
 would not weep, 213
Whoever tries for great objects, 998
Whole, animate the, 313
 be greater than a part, 426
 cannot grasp at a, 325
 duty of man, 1110
 half was more than the, 1013
 head is sick, 1110
 heart is faint, 1110
 in a flash made, 856
 in faith, made, 1022
 in one tangible, 767
 life long, a fool his, 481
 makes His beautiful, 683
 new democratic world, 379
 of it, let me taste the, 489
 of life to live, 't is not the, 306
 of truth and knowledge, 643
 one beautiful and perfect, 597
 one stupendous, 207
 range of imaginative literature, 480
 scroll contain the, 1017

Whole sea's speech, 577
  sought to see the, 735
  volumes in folios, 41
  wide world, 671
  wood-world is one full peal, 470
  world, if he shall gain the, 1115
  world kin, makes the, 75
  world send back the song, and the, 477
Wholesale borrowers, we are all, 480
Wholesome berries thrive and ripen, 66
  example in these days, 641
  harvests, 393
  laugh, gladden with a, 453
  restraint, liberty is, 340
  stars of love, 470
  the nights are, 89
Wholesomest, old wine is, 128
Wholly consisted of lines like these, 590
Whom should I knock, 52
Whomsoever I do good, to, 960
Whore and thief, tarnish, 767
Whores were burnt alive, 189
Whoring, full of other folks', 883
Whorled ear, beat upon my, 672
Who's loony now, 762
Whose dog are you, 216
  words are few and often funny, 511
Who-so shal telle a tale, 5
Whoso belongs only to his own age, 376
  sheddeth man's blood, 1097
  would be a man, 411
Whosoever believeth in him, 1118
  shall exalt himself, 1115
Whum we stwops at, 550
Why a wherefore, every, 37, 142
  and I can't think, 623
  and wherefore in all things, 67
  is plain as way to parish church, 49
  or whence, you can't imagine, 406
  or wherefore, without knowing, 1037
  the sea is boiling hot, 598
Wicked are wicked no doubt, 483
  be so bad, would the, 648
  cease from troubling, 1101
  flee when no man pursueth, 1108
  forsake his way, 1112
  I's mighty, 480
  must have done something, 1015
  no man all at once, 1006
  no peace unto the, 1112
  or charitable, be thy intents, 91
  something, this way comes, 87
  too, for a smile, 316
  war regarded as, has fascinations, 723
  wight, 164
  will, 628

Wicked world, vanity of this, 1127
  worldliness, more of, 505
Wickedly red or malignantly green, 857
Wickedness, disgrace of, added to old age, 1003
  felicity and flower of, 491
  men capable of every, 726
  methods in man's, 131
  one man's, 959, 988
  sweet in his mouth, 1102
  tents of, dwell in the, 1105
Wicket, flannelled fools at, 780
  wait outside my, 638
Wickliffe's dust shall spread abroad, 304
Wictim of connubiality, the, 494
Wide, a world too, 50
  and starry sky, 703
  and universal theatre, 49
  as a church door, not so, 79
  as Shakespeare's soul, 558
  as the height of the houses, 1022
  as the waters be, 304
  beautiful wonderful world, 553
  enough for thee and me, 241
  impossible stars, all the, 896
  is the gate, 1114
  sea, alone on a, 315
  seas and the mountains, 847
  wide world, 671
Widening, ever, slowly silence all, 470
Wide-waving wings, 267
Widow and his orphan, for his, 457
  at Windsor, 782
  do right to the, 1123
  I took to the hop, e'en the gay, 756
  nor wife, neither, 37
  of doubtful age will marry, 479
  of fifty, here's to the, 279
  some undone, 129
  that gay college, 756
  that tough-hearted, that frisky old, 756
  to one safe home, 916
  woman, I have commanded a, 1101
Widows, thousands of undone, 116
Widow's heart to sing, 1102
  prayer, have a, 539
Widows' tears and orphans' moans, 262
Widowed woman's heart, 677
Widower or a bachelor, 346
Wielded at will, 156
Wields a mighty scepter, he, 534
Wife, all the world and his, 192
  an understanding, 128
  and children hostages to fortune, 109
  and children impediments to great enterprises, 109
  at all, give me no, 275
  but woos your, 490
  Caesar's, free from suspicion, 999
  children and friends, three blessings, 294
  could do in three, 345

Wife dearer than the bride, 239
  edited his works, 889
  expect from a friend's, 325
  first, had given him, 235
  giving honour unto the, 1122
  I chose my, 253
  I'm an inventor's, 733
  in the west country, not a, 321
  is expensive, whether his, 166
  light, doth make heavy husband, 47
  like fringe, follows his, 1050
  love thy, honor France, 492
  love your neighbour's, 398
  make a splendid, 801
  man who tells his, all he knows, 147
  mirror of an honest, 295
  mother nurse seamstress cook, 446
  my particular plague is my, 1001
  neither maid widow nor, 37
  not so much as suspected, 999
  of mine, sweet wee, 286
  of thy bosom, 1099
  or cowl, take, 1034
  outlives a, 237
  patience with his, 225
  poor wretch, my, 181
  smiles and lets it go, 751
  sympathetic, 968
  till he gets him a, 567
  than my sonne's, Elizabeth, 540
  the sailor's star, the sailor's, 690
  the shoemaker's, 15
  the weaker vessel, 1122
  to be, do my best a gude, 277
  to have and to lose a, 237
  true and honourable, 82
  was a penurious woman, his, 171
  w'at good eesa, 813
  well willed, 275
  what would you with my, 1041
  who calls her, 575
  who preaches in her gown, 392
  whoso findeth a, 1107
  will hinder me of a little pleasure, 182
  with kindness, kill a, 52
  with nine small children, 947
Wife's brother, stand reddy to sacrifiss my, 606
Wight, bless this house from wicked, 164
  blesse this hous from every wikked, 6
  borne to desastrous end, 26
  if ever such, were, 101
  O base Hungarian, 34
Wild and dream-like trade, 316
  and lonely spot, in a, 501
  and weak desires, 864
  but brings, no night so, 501
  by starts 't was, 248
  commotion, far down beneath the, 480
  contend with angry, billows, 480
  crackling intermitting light, 888
  drama means, what this, 472

Wild emerald cucumber-tree, 431
gazelle, 395
geese are flighting, 778
geese sailing high, 737
hawk to the wind-swept sky, 778
houseless, 435
in woods, when, 178
New England shore, 370
oats, how to sow, 793
oats, sow spiritual, 614
of soul, 930
on this world's shore, beat, 447
passion could not make, 545
passion-waves lulled to rest, 363
religion, 837
roved an Indian girl, 406
spring air, 866
the garden was a, 327
the storm, 258
thing sorry for itself, 883
thyme blows, bank whereon the, 42
to hold, though I seem tame, 18
vicissitudes of taste, 231
waves saying, what are the, 500
wild heart and thinking hand, 911
wind blows, where the, 516
wind sweep, waves may not foam nor, 370
with all regret, 466
words of doom, but colder those, 418
Wild-blazing grog-shop appears, 389
Wildcats, whip his weight in, 698
Wilder willful-wavier meal-drift, has, 672
Wildered eyes, 574
Wilderness, choice grain into this, 179
field and farm, 816
forth to the, 834
had they been in the, 478
if the world is a, 568
lodge in some vast, 264
of flowers, sleep beneath, 602
of human flesh, 759
of monkeys, 45
of single instances, 465
of sweets, 153
one crying in the, 1116
singing in the, 1018
to seek a barren, 591
were paradise enow, 1018
Wildernesses, desert, 157
Wild-fire dances on the fen, 288
Wild-goose chase, 79, 1035
Wilding springs of peace, at the, 757
Wildings, grafts the excellence on, 491
Wild-raging, far on the, sea, 389
Wild-wood track, through the, 447
Wile, children with endearing, 251
habit's earliest, 364
that is justified by honor, 285

Wiles, cranks and wanton, 160
of the stranger, 935
or by crooked, 964
transient sorrows simple, 299
Wilfrid Owen, killed on the Sambre, 937
Wilful waste brings woeful want, 339
Will a threat, in, 955
across the sky, wrote my, 901
and fate fix'd fate, 150
and intellect are one, 1048
based upon her people's, 462
be done, God's, 272
be done, Thy, 443
be there a, 280
beyond its own sweet, 443
boy's will is the wind's, 436
can neither when we, enjoy, 547
city obedient to his, 973
complies against his, 144
craft of, 109
ends by settling the moral, 635
executes a freeman's, 348
Father thy, not mine be done, 423
flaw in a donkey's, 453
for if she, she will, 204
for intellect or, 612
for the deed, 192, 194, 1026
for the wicked, 628
foretells a future feat, 955
generally but little, 1056
glideth at his own sweet, 297
go where he, the wise man, 410
gods are we heroes if we, 545
good or evil, save in the, 1008
good or ill lies in the, 1007
governed by their, 129
grant us the, 873
had tongue at, 101
Honeycomb, 198
I laid me down with a, 703
I should have my, 1038
instrument of executive, 320
is a solemn matter, a, 732
is bent with energy, 1056
is free strong is the soul, 545
knowing that we do thy, 1024
left free the human, 216
men who possess opinions and a, 522
much against my, 917
my poverty but not my, 80
nor when we, resign, 547
not when he may, 11
of Charles Lounsbury, 732
of man were free, 1076
of their own, by no, 570
one man's, to live by, 22
or won't, a woman, 204
pay thy poverty not thy, 80
predestined of the, 840
puzzles the, 93
reason firm the temperate, 299
reason panders, 95
serveth not another's, 114
take away our free, 1023
the sun and the Father's, 731
the thoughtful-eyed, 757
the vassal of my, 579
to do the soul to dare, 308
to like, 12

Will to mischief, 212
to refrain, 882
tool that did his, 659
torrent of a woman's, 204
unconquerable, 148
upon the tide, writes her, 761
was strong, his, 948
when you, they won't, 979
wielded at, 156
woman's cold perverted, 369
work or lose the power to, 502
ye no come back again, 291
Wills are gardeners, our, 101
talk of, 59
to burn out human, 833
Willful men, little group of, 725
William cook, tell, 65
the Conqueror a son of the people, 739
you are old Father, 320
Willie had a purple monkey, 684
Winkie, wee, 475
Willing hart, 12
the spirit indeed is, 1116
to wound, 213
Willingness is great, where, 1023
Willingnesses, dwell alone with our, 663
Willow, all a green, 11
lake where drooped the, 405
leaves of the, 897
pattern, that we knew in childhood, 439
titwillow, 256
under the, the gray, 571
underneath the abject, 937
willow willow, oh, 255
Willows, harps upon the, 1106
Southern, 267
the tearful, 602
Willowy brook, 289
Wilson, pedestal of, 908
Wilson's adventure was the world's, 908
Win a woman with his tongue, 34
all your wish is woman to, 481
and all I fail of, 444
our battles by its aid, 504
the good we oft might, 35
the trick, when in doubt, 197
they laugh that, 103
us to our harm, 84
us with honest trifles, 84
with grace to, 409
Win' can blow lak hurricane, 712
Wince, let the galled jade, 94
Winchelsea, lie easy at, 929
on starlight, 873
Wind, a wail in, is all I hear, 517
along the sage, 801
among the anchored ships, 873
and clouds now here now there, 369
and cloudy sky, southerly, 229
and his nobility, betwixt the, 61
and limb, come back sound, 1040
and sky were always fair, if, 1052
and tide, 12
argument against an east, 530
bayed the whispering, 250
bellows full of angry, 790
blew a new, 849

Wind blew you hither, what, 65
blow, come wrack, 88
blow thou winter, 50
blow upon me so wild, why does the, 557
bloweth where it listeth, 1118
blowing, feel the salt, 873
blows loudly, nor ever, 463
breathing of the common, 297
but a blast of, 1021
carries their like away, 1022
children of the, 717
comes off a frozen peak, 839
crannying, save to the, 353
doth blow whichever way the, 555
doth ramm, how the, 886
down stream is blowing, 674
dry sun dry, 19
feel the free shrill, 674
float high in the, 390
fly upon the wings of the, 1103
force of the, 962
go Yooooo, heard the, 699
God gives, by measure, 138
God tempers the, 242
going down the, 181
has blown them, 759
he that observeth the, 1110
hears God in the, 207
him up for fourscore years, 178
hollow blasts of, 205
hope constancy in, 351
ill blows the, which profits nobody, 65
ill, turns none to good, 19
ill, which blows no man good, 17, 65
in a pneumatic tire, 1083
in dry grass, 899
in French politeness, 1083
in the woods a-roaring, 565
into an immaterial, 933
is always north-north-east, 809
is chill, 307
is in the tree, 910
is, see which way the, 130
it blew cold, 951
large a charter as the, 49
let her down the, 102
love not the, 41
lovely sighing of the, 385
maned with whistling, 841
may follow and snow beside, 742
may the east, never blow when he goes a-fishing, 139
nets to catch the, 128
of criticism, 238
of doctrine, 238, 1121
of the western sea, 466
on the heath, likewise the, 407
or weather, nought cared for, 317
pass by me as the idle, 83
passeth over it, 1105
plain as a prairie, 927
sails filled with lusty, 28
singing through, the old, 841
sits the, in that corner, 39
something in the, 37
sprang up from sleep, 365
stands as never it stood, 19

Wind, streaming to the, 148
sway in the, 900
tears shall drown the, 85
that blows, feather for each, 56
that blows that wind is best, 555
that carries rain, 814
that follows fast, 345
that grand old harper, 587
that sighs before the dawn, 604
the wandering, 597
they have sown the, 1113
tho' thou wert scattered to the, 462
throw fear to the, 972
thunder-storm against the, 354
to keep the, away, 97
to shake the world, a, 936
to the moon said I will blow you out, 559
tossed by the autumn, 924
upon the wings of the, 1103
voice in every, 243
warm southern, 702
warm western, 702
was a torrent, 864
when she dances in the, 177
with a wolf's head, 917
words are easy like the, 120
Winds and rains so wild, 540
and waves on the side of the ablest navigators, 271
are breathing low, 368
are chill and drear, summer, 669
are fair always, 966
are free, all the, 667
are raging o'er the upper ocean, 375, 480
at play, among the, 955
begin to blow, 276
blew great guns, though, 274
blow, crack your cheeks, 98
blow, where the high, 1065
come, come as the, 309
courted by all the, 157
fed it with silver dew, 368
four, of the heaven, 1113
four-square to all the, 467
happy, upon her played, 465
imprisoned in the viewless, 36
in their hands, 989
let them be, great, 849
loud, when they call, 297
naked woods and wailing, 372
nor'-east to sou'-west, 617
of doctrine were let loose, 163
of heaven visit her face, 90
of March with beauty, take the, 56
of springtime, 777
of winter cry, 673
on earth, 634
resign, to the, 1018
rides on the posting, 105
somewhere safe to sea, 632
stormy, do blow, 115, 328
swept the mountain-height, 369
that die, 681
the remorseful, 588
their revels keep, 502

Winds they shift and veer, 735
thy wide gray skies, thy, 916
went whistling, 369
were love-sick, 104
whistle free, the shrill, 503
whistle shrill, Christmas is here, 481
you are going to tempt, 496
Wind's and the rain's way, out of the, 869
feet shine along the sea, 630
panther cry, 905
soft song, calls me in the, 793
will, a boy's will is the, 436
Wind-beaten hill, 328
Winding bout, with many a, 160
old roads, 443
Rhine, wide and, 353
up days with toil, 67
Winding-sheet of Edward's race, 244
snow shall be their, 328
Windless night, through the, 833
Window, below my, 754
binding shoes, Hannah's at the, 568
light through yonder, 78
little, where the sun, 390
of the east, the golden, 77
opened toward sun-rising, 172
opening, like a big, 872
secret, 827
tired her head and looked out at a, 1101
tirlin' at the, cryin' at the lock, 475
under this, 191
unfinished, 437
Windows and doors and loop-holes barred, 320
being open toward Jerusalem, 1113
eastern, 519
lavender in the, 139
nor bars to their, 435
of mine eyes, 1032
of my soul, 443
of the almshouse, reflected from the, 515
of the mind, 114
of the sky, 225
of the soul, 1032
pry about these, 886
smites all the empty, with sinking light, 594
storied, richly dight, 161
to light my own, 848
Window's space, through the open, 364
Window-blind, the walloping, 655
Windowed raggedness, 99
Windowless palace of rest, 602
Windsor forest, doth walk in, 35
widow at, 782
Wind-swept space, 620
Windy adulation, 635
lights of autumn flare, 673
night a rainy morrow, 108
side of care, the, 38, 55
side of the law, keep on the, 38, 55
Wine, a cup of hot, 76
a jug of, 1018
and friendship, while, 941
and I'll not look for, 119

Wine and wealth and mirth, sing of the, 831
and women dotages of human kind, 123
and women, let us have, 359
and women make men of understanding, 1125
at lip life's, 823
ballast is old, 347
best, is the last, 445
broke is the goblet and wasted the, 447
central essential and typical, 800
come within a pint of, 198
comrades pour the, 771
cups of Solomon, 934
doesn't get into the, 827
drown care, with, 983
falser than vows made in, 51
flown with insolence and, 148
for stronger, 796
for thy stomach's sake, 1121
goes in, when the, 1059
good, needs no bush, 51, 311, 990
how exceeding strong is, 1123
I pour, the dusky, 809
in a keg, fizz like, 852
in being drunk, joy of the, 1093
in toys in lusts or, 167
invisible spirit of, 101
is a good familiar creature, 102
is a mocker, 1107
is a traitor, 711
is a true panacea, 624
is the mirror of the heart, 964
ivy-branch over the, 51
king can drink best of, 504
like the best, 1110
look not thou upon the, 1108
monkey lion sheep swine, 1068
must taste of its own grapes, 429
needs neither bush nor preface, 311
new, into old bottles, 1116
no, so wonderful as thirst, 915
of another, drink the, 1015
of life is drawn, 86
of love is music, 610
old books old, 253
old, to drink, 113
old, wholesomest, 128
one that hath, 960
orchard smells like, 719
our goblets gleam in, 431
outdid the frolic, 134
pernicious to mankind, 219
pour forth the cheering, 404
proceed from, 1051
ripe age gives tone to, 573
Samian, 359
send round the, 335
since my leaving drinking of, 181
spilled the, 556
sudden friendship springs from, 206
sweet poison of misused, 157
that maketh glad the heart, 1105
that tasted of tar, 811
that was spilt, 848

Wine, the shower ran white, 929
there is truth, in, 960, 994
Venus rose red out of, 632
walnuts and the, 462
war and, 576
warms us more than, 522
water in our, 1022
when warm with, 969
will never warm, 530
with four years a-glowing, 983
woman and song, loves not, 481
women and, 1058
Wines, purple as their, 215
when good, 680
Wine-colored amethyst, 713
Wine-cup to my lips, hold the, 940
Wine-press alone, trodden the, 1112
whence be the grapes of the, 401
Wine-red, the gold the crimson the pied, 714
Wine-scented and poetic soul, 703
Wing, as a noiseless, 353
beauty of a butterfly's, 930
bird is on the, 1018
conquest's crimson, 244
damp my intended, 154
dropped from an angel's, 304
flits by on leathern, 247
fur or folded, 888
hear the beating of his, 478
human soul take, 356
is closely bound, though my, 1051
ne'er stoops to earth her, 336
of bird, pen plundered from, 292
of friendship never moults a feather, 494
quill from an angel's, 304
start a, 749
were set off by itself, 526
Wings across the canceled skies, 914
affrighted ostrich dare not dust her, 683
are gray and trailing, 836
at heaven's gate she claps her, 23
beneath those folded, 836
bless Him who gave them, 677
chickens under her, 1116
clip an angel's, 383
damn poor us because we have not, 578
flies with swallow's, 72
fold him in soft, 900
folded glory of his, 922
for angels feet for men, 521
friendship is love without, 361
golden hours on angel, 286
healing in his, 1114
I am the, 410
idly lounging in the, 644
in tears, dip their, 468
it were not amiss to make, 124
lends corruption lighter, that, 210
lessening up the skies, 574
life's ignorant, 736

Wings like a dove, oh that I had, 1104
love without his, 361
may chance take, 578
my starry, 840
of a phrase and a flower, 788
of an ostrich, 397
of borrowed wit, 133
of deeds, on, 626
of gold and robe of purest white, 511
of night, falls from the, 434
of silence, float upon the, 158
of song, love, upon the, 1065
of the future, 895
of the morning, 1106
of the wind, fly upon the, 1103
on wide-waving, 267
one black the other white, 157
poor splendid, 633
radiant when at rest, 338
rapturous, 888
remind not Eros of his, 735
riches have, 265
riches make themselves, 1108
sailing on obscene, 316
seem to walk on, 219
shadow of thy, 1103
shakes his dewy, 146
so frayed and soiled and torn, 633
spreads his light, 216
that which hath, 1110
the swift with, 855
upon my shoes, I felt, 925
vision of blue, 665
with the thought of, 806
wondrous, 652
Wing'd the shaft, 351
Winged Cupid is painted blind, 42
dreams, 256
his polished dart, laughter, 626
hours of bliss, 327
life destroy, doth the, 281
race, twins of, 219
sandals for my feet, 807
thoughts that flit to thee, 395
Winges for to flee, the hors that hadde, 7
hadde he two, up-on his shuldres, 6
Wink and a sly normal lurch, with a, 508
as good as a nod to the wise, 593
I have not slept one, 106
of an eye, 362
of sleep, without a, 1034
sleep a, 213
too soon, never came a, 390
Winkie, wee Willie, 475
Winking, damn treacherous flatteries without, 522
Mary-buds, 105
Winners go by, cheer as the, 636
Winner's eyes, disenchants the, 309
Winning, glory of the, 575
I am not worth the, 436
there's nothing worth the wear of, 810
too light, 32
wave, 133

Winning, world worth thy, 176
Winnowed opinions, 97
Wins not more than honesty, 73
  who never, can rarely lose, 443
  woman as well as valor, courtesy, 471
Winsome wee thing, 286
Winstanley lieth low, 540
Winter a bad guest, 1080
  blowing, in the wood the furious, 903
  cloud, like a, 565
  cold of cheerless, 824
  comes, if, 366
  comes to rule, 224
  every mile is two in, 138
  every year hath its, 763
  fearful thing in, 508
  fire upon the hearth, 843
  hath his delights, 121
  held her firm, 576
  I get up at night in, 702
  in his bounty, no, 105
  in Spain spring in Italy, 197
  in thy year, no, 276
  is icummen in, 886
  is past, for lo the, 1110
  lies too long in country towns, 841
  lingering chills the lap of May, 249
  long, all the, 56
  my age is as a lusty, 48
  night, blossom in the, 814
  of despair, spring of hope the, 497
  of our discontent, 71
  of the Spring, the, 441
  oh the long and dreary, 436
  ruler of the inverted year, 224, 265
  sad tale's best for, 56
  succeeds barren, 69
  the paragon of art, 934
  through, see the, 812
  was bad that year, 917
  weeds outworn, her, 367
  when the dismal rain in, 587
  wind, blow blow thou, 50
  winds set the yellow wood sighing, 449
Winters more, ran he on ten, 178
Winter's day, sunbeam in a. 223
  frost and chill, never, 690
  fury. withstood the, 200
  gray despair, 692
  head, crown old, 165
  rages, nor furious, 106
  rains and ruins, 633
  snow, many a, 446
  traces, 633
Winter-garment of repentance, 1018
Winter-quarters the soldiers' earthly paradise, 1045
Winter-time, doth walk all the, 35
Wintres weders overshake, 4
Wintry age to feel no chill, 263
  nights, through long long, 499
  world, in this, 337
Wipe a bloody nose, 206
  my weeping eyes, 199
Wiped away the weeds, 408
  our eyes of drops, 49

Wiped with a little address, 264
Wisdom, a larger, 579
  all men's, 946
  and guidance, pray for, 551
  and love, whence descended, 572
  and of folly, waifs of, 609
  and wit are born with a man, 130
  and wit are little seen, 204
  apply our hearts unto, 1105
  art and skill, combine all, 951
  at one entrance, 151
  beyond the rules of physic, 111
  can calculate the end, no human, 271
  can you find, what, 1054
  Columbus sails it, 414
  crieth without, 1106
  dwell, where love and, 501
  finds a way, 280
  from another's mishap, 989
  from the central deep, 524
  gives poignancy, 1051
  God give them, 54
  grief's slow, 593
  Handel sings it, 414
  if God in His, have, 577
  is better than rubies, 1107
  is humble, 266
  is justified of her children, 1115
  is never dear, 479
  is summed up, all human, 1067
  is the gray hair unto men, 1124
  is the principal thing, 1106
  is the result of human, 238
  lessons of, 229
  lingers, knowledge comes but, 464
  Luther preaches it, 414
  married to immortal verse, 303
  more than wealth more than, 363
  name men give to, 926
  never comes when it is gold, 574
  never dwelt below, 1050
  never grieves, 922
  never lies, 220
  no joy in beautiful, 960
  not acquired by years, 978
  of a just content, 595
  of mankind creeps slowly, 417
  of many and the wit of one, 946
  of our ancestors, 259, 495
  overmatch for strength, 992
  passing all, or its fairest flower, 417
  Phidias carves it, 414
  point of, to be silent, 1001
  power and goodness meet, 362
  pray for, 582
  Raphael paints, 414
  seems the part of, 266
  Shakespeare writes it, 414
  shall die with you, 1102
  teaches, their, 465
  that will never die, 612
  the prime, 154
  therefore get, 1106
  they leave, the, 676

Wisdom, thou hast taught me, 922
  to be only wise, not, 770
  to believe the heart, 770
  to love to live to take what fate, 775
  unsearchable dispose of highest, 157
  Washington arms it, 414
  Watt mechanizes it, 414
  we have lost in knowledge, 899
  will not enter, there, 401
  will repudiate thee, 669
  with each studious year, 353
  world is governed with little, 130
  Wren builds it, 414
Wisdom's aid, friend of pleasure, 248
  armory, 574
  goal, drives you to fair, 1084
  part, this is, 226
  school, 115
  self oft seeks solitude, 158
  treasure, keys to, 711
Wise, a man before, never was so, 437
  above that which is written, 1120
  all that men held, 146
  amazed temperate and furious, 86
  among fools, 215
  among fools, to appear, 995
  among women, 632
  and good, 161
  and just, be both, 820
  and love, for to be, 75
  and masterly inactivity, 290
  and salutary neglect, 259
  and the lovely, the, 917
  and understanding heart, 1100
  and virtuous, man completely, 1000
  are never without friends, 951
  as a serpent, 791
  as serpents, 1115
  be not worldly, 134
  beacon of the, 75
  by nature, 128
  coffee which makes the politician, 212
  consider her ways and be, 1106
  "convey" the, it call, 34
  defer not to be, 193
  do never live long, so, 72
  enough to keep his own counsel, 1037
  exceeding, fair spoken, 74
  excel, arts in which the, 185
  fair-spoken and persuading, 74
  father knows his own child, 45
  folly to be, 243
  fool doth think he is, 51
  foolish so am I, 733
  for cure on exercise depend, 175
  from contemplation, become, 773
  gamester, a, 967
  girls be more than women, 131
  good to be merry and, 11, 29, 286
  government knows how to enforce, 240

Wise, great men are not always, 1102
he bids fair to grow, 989
healthy wealthy and, 227
histories make men, 111
I count him, 736
I'm growing, 510
immediately, 893
immoderately, 873
in his own conceit, 1108
in show, 162
in the use of his pronouns, 640
in their own craftiness, 1102
in their own eyes, people become, 247
in your own conceits, 1119
is not, 237
learning to be, 230
little, the best fools be, 118
little too, 116
make us happy make us, 832
man is at home, the, 410
man is strong, 1108
man, silence an answer to a, 1001
man, to discover a, 1016
man's son, every, 54
man's verdict, 488
men as far back as Ptolemy, 519
men avoid the faults of fools, 998
men, foolery of, 47
men, logical consequences beacons of, 564
men out of the east, three, 439
men profit more by fools, 998
men say nothing in dangerous times, 130
men's counters, words are, 132
old owl, a, 836
one died, like a, 1043
passiveness in a, 295
person and a fool, difference between, 979
pound foolish penny, 122
powers deny us for our good, 104
rare smile is sweet, 692
saws and modern instances, 50
seeing ye yourselves are, 1121
so young never live long. so, 72
some few ways, 895
son maketh a glad father, 1107
spirits of the, sit in the clouds, 64
strong constant pleasant, 248
strong is the soul and, 545
swift is less than to be, 219
teach a monarch to be, 246
the great and, decay, 640
the light, not to the, 710
the reverend head, 199
these only are reputed, 44
though a man be, 965
through time, 218
to be a poet, not, 657
to learn God-like to create, 511
to resolve patient to perform, 220
to-day be, 201, 305
type of the, 304
who has grown, 895

Wise, who lets the contest fall is, 968
with speed be, 203
words of the, 1110
world of ours is mainly right, and this, 470
years that make us, 522
Wiseacres vow, the, 812
Wisely, charming never so, 1104
one that loved not, 103
whatever you do do, 1075
who reasons, 209
worldly, be, 134
Wiser and better grow, 172
being good than bad, 490
for his learning, no man is, 130
in his own conceit, 1108
in their generation, 1117
second thoughts are ever, 968
sorry you are, 901
than a daw, no, 68
than of yore, 210
than the children of light, 1117
than thou art ware, 48
to-day than yesterday, 217
Wisest brightest meanest of mankind, 208
censure, mouths of, 101
man could ask no more, 528
men not the greatest clerkes, 6, 16
men, relished by the, 246
of all mortal men, 114
of men, Socrates the, 156
to entrap the, 46
Wish a hut of stone, I only, 451
a mint of gold, were each, 292
and care, man whose, 216
desire is the, 312
faith I, you'd take me, 389
granting our, 528
her stay, who saw to, 154
his religion an anxious, 376
I were a moron, 957
is like a prayer with God, 430
is woman to win, all your, 481
more faint, a, 685
now obey thy cherished secret, 537
that failed of act, my, 444
to scatter joy and not pain, 413
transport myself with a, 197
was father to that thought, 65
which his greedy, 1021
Wishes, all their country's, 247
asking our, 875
fixed, 318
for many things, renounce the, 1056
for that beyond their reach, 1052
has few diverging, 1056
in idle, fools supinely stay, 280
lengthen like our shadows, 173, 202
never learned to stray, their sober, 245
of the public, bow to the, 1075
ought to have great weight, 259

Wishes, soon as granted fly, whose, 307
vain, were prevented, 345
were gratified, if our, 962
who has many, 1056
Wished devoutly to be, 93
she had not heard it, 100
Wished-for prize should fall, 226
Wishing, content myself with, 239
his foot were equal with his eye, 70
so very cheap as, 509
Wishing-cap of Fortunatus, 299
Wisp of fog betwixt us, 719
Wist, beware of had I, 11
Wistful ones, do you think of me, 652
stone, survive in, 648
waves, the, 874
Wistfulness abroad, publish their, 798
Wit, a man in, 217
admire her for her, 133
among lords, 215
and gay rhetoric, 158
and wisdom are little seen, 204
and wisdom born with a man, 130
brevity is the soul of, 92
brightens, how the, 211
cause that, is in other men, 64
delectable form of, 872
derive from widows, 116
devise, 41
eloquence and poetry, 167
enjoy your dear, 158
fault of a penetrating, 1044
for so much room there is no, 147
given in, what scanted in hair, 37
good nature more agreeable than, 196
harm to my, 54
hast so much, 196
her, was more than man, 175
high as metaphysic, 142
impropriety is the soul of, 835
in a jest, whole, 129
in all men, 199
in the combat, whose, 334
in the fountain of, 981
in the very first line, 252
invites you, his, 263
is a feather, 208
is an unruly engine, 136
is out when age is in, 39
is the only breath, 923
is the only wall, 923
lasts no more, 1063
learning and sense, 165
makes its own welcome, 415
men of, will condescend, 191
mine of cleverness and, 713
miracle instead of, 203
monuments of, 110
much, but shy of using it, 141
my, is thinne, 7
nature dressed is true, 211
ne'er be ware of mine own, 48
no room for, heads so little, 147
not too much, 128

Wit of man conceives, all the, 305
  of man, past the, to say, 43
  of one, wisdom of many and the, 946
  one man's, all men's wisdom, 946
  or the works of desire, 783
  orbit sum of Shakespeare's, 326
  piety nor, shall lure it back, 1019
  plentiful lack of, 92
  put his whole, in a jest, had meant to, 129
  retained all the, 345
  shines at the expense of his memory, 1052
  skirmish of, there's a, 38
  so narrow human, 210
  spice of, 702
  staggers his unready, 924
  sum of Shakespeare's, 409
  that can creep, 213
  the Scotch are void of, 246
  the well of true, 576
  to distinguish, want, 183
  to mortify a, 214
  too fine a point to your, 1043
  too proud for a, 252
  too steep for human, 983
  was a coonskin sack, 927
  will come, and fancy, 217
  will shine, 175
  wings of borrowed, 133
  with dunces, 215
  with morality, temper, 195
Wits about him, with his, 166
  as a chain about his, 960
  be fresh, so shall your, 972
  dunce with, 215
  encounter of our, 71
  from wool-gathering, summoned your, 116
  good, jump, 1041
  great, jump, 241
  home-keeping youth have homely, 33
  in the keeping of their, 905
  keep straining, their dull, 942
  new-fangled, should find out, 124
  run the wild-goose chase, 79
  so many heads so many, 12
  to madness near allied, 173
  whetstone of the, 47
  write pen devise, 41
Wit's end, at his, 1037
  end, at their, 13, 1105
Witch, a little, that looks like me, 625
  as swift as a, 1036
  hath power to charm, 89
Witches steal young children, 122
Witchcraft, hell of, 109
  this only is the, I have used, 101
Witcheries, 'gainst, 747
Witchery of soft blue sky, 296
Witching time of night, 95
Wither her, age cannot, 104
  high hopes, 507
  his leaf also shall not, 1103
Withers are unwrung, our, 94
  wastes and, 722

Wither'd be, it could not there, 119
Withered and shaken, 390
  cheek and tresses gray, 306
  in their pride, 484
  when true hearts lie, 335
  your joys are, like the grass, 406
Withering and sere, leaves were, 460
  on the ground, 218
  on the stalk, maidens, 301
  on the virgin thorn, 42, 301
Within a dream, is but a dream, 459
  I have that, which passeth show, 89
  is good and fair, 317
  that awful volume lies, 310
  that 's innocent, 214
  the sober realm of leafless trees, 551
  they that are, would fain go out, 115
Without, they that are, would fain go in, 115
Witless way, on all my, 867
Witness and wait, I, 534
  call the gods to, 80
  mute, 604
  that I have fought his battles, 172
  to any creed, 781
  weak, of thy name, 161
Witnesses, cloud of, 1122
  clouds of crying, 170
  ever had said, more than the, 599
Wittes end, at our, 13
Witticism, to fail in a, 326
Witty in myself, I am not only, 64
  it shall be not long, 222
  saying proves nothing, 1052
  to talk with, 164
  woman is a treasure, 576
  words though ne'er so, 21
Wives and children dear, 475
  and mothers, maids must be, 454
  are young men's mistresses, 110
  clean beds and, 891
  many many, 755
  may be merry, yet honest, 35
  men with mothers and, 391
  sky changes when they are, 51
  strawberry, 113
  vexed their, 899
Wiving and hanging go by destiny, 45
Wizard islands, to, 858
  silence, 691
  song, broke the, 879
Wode hath eres, 6
Woe, a voice of, for a lover's loss, 517
  Altama murmurs to their, 251
  and sorrow, 596
  be to those who pray, 1127
  being not unacquainted with, 121
  changeless through joy and, 416

Woe, child is full of, 956
  day of, the watchful night, 322
  deepest notes of, 287
  doth tread upon another's heel, 96
  each struggle lessens human, 504
  enhance the loser's, 309
  every, a tear can claim, 355
  faints at every, 403
  fig for care fig for, 11
  fill the world with, 940
  gave signs of, 155
  groan of a martyr's, 282
  heritage of, 356
  is me to have seen what I have, 94
  its meed of, 910
  life protracted is protracted, 230
  luxury of, 333
  out of my own great, 1065
  ponderous, though a, 190
  rearward of a conquered, 108
  root of all our, 155
  sabler tints of, 245
  silence in love bewrays more, 21
  sleep the friend of, 322
  smiles of joy the tears of, 336
  source of my bliss and, 251
  succeeds a woe, 134
  teach me to feel another's, 216
  the cavalry of, 584
  there 's a hope for every, 390
  to him who reads but one book, 139
  to tell a tale of, 608
  touch of joy or, 248
  trappings and suits of, 89
Woes and glory, Kansas with her, 660
  catalogue of human, 262
  from a thousand, 396
  historian of my country's, 220
  how true its, 544
  love is a sickness full of, 30
  new wail with old, 107
  of man with spondulix, 714
  of Midas, 1021
  of thirty millions, 513
  partners in their, 1036
  shall serve for sweet discourses, 80
  starry Galileo with his, 354
  tear that flows for others', 267
  unnumbered, 218
Woe-begone, so dead in look so, 63
Woeful want, wilful waste brings, 339
Wold, deer to the wholesome, 778
Wolds, forgotten in the western, 810
Wolf actually came, 962
  appetite, a universal, 75
  dwell with the lamb, 1111
  from the door, 10
  has slain his gallant hound, 294
  howling of the, 29
  in sheep's clothing, 962

Wolf is at the door, 754
  on the fold, like the, 356
  was wearing, skin the, 962
Wolf's head, wind with a, 917
  mouth, head inside a, 961
Wolsey, that once trod the ways
  of glory, 73
Wolves in the forest, 565
Woman a contradiction at best,
  209
  a, of her gentle sex, 405
  a sweeter, ne'er drew breath,
  540
  a witty, 576
  a woman's heart, turn to a,
  800
  Ah wasteful, 556
  always has her revenge, 1046
  always in the background of
  man's mind, 725
  among all those, not found a,
  1109
  and may be wooed, she's a, 77
  and song, loves not wine, 481
  as easy to marry a rich, 483
  as nice as, 164
  as old as she looks, 570
  as you are, 924
  asleep better to be that way,
  801
  avenged on a, 662
  believe a, or an epitaph, 351
  born, seen the loveliest, 790
  brawling, in a wide house,
  1108
  bring all to the, 1123
  by an archangel befriended,
  897
  by starvation, ruin of, 1067
  can bear, affront no, 1040
  can forgive a man for harm,
  835
  can manage a clever man, 785
  clever, to manage a fool, 785
  comfort of a good cry to a,
  425
  coming out of her stockings,
  662
  contentious, 1108
  could be a good, 482
  could play the, with mine
  eyes, 88
  cry, baby thing that made a,
  559
  dare, what will not gentle, 322
  desolating the country, 662
  destructive damnable deceitful, 185
  died, the saint sustained it the,
  217
  doubts the instrument is
  broke, 533
  dressed out in all her finery,
  253
  ever goes by the worse, 157
  every, may be won, 559
  every, should marry and no
  man, 421
  excellent thing in, 100
  excite us to love a, 1036
  for courtesy wins, 471
  for thy more sweet understanding, 41
  forgets how to charm, 1080
  frailty thy name is, 90
  fury of a disappointed, 193

Woman gave him pleasure, if a,
  948
  God created, 1082
  good name in man and, 102
  good-natured, 325
  half human half divine is,
  522
  hath nine lives like a cat, 16
  have long hair, if a, 1120
  hell contains no fouler fiend
  than, 220
  how divine a thing, may be
  made, 299
  I am a, 672
  I hate a dumpy, 358
  in God and, 587
  in her first passion, 359
  in our hours of ease, 308
  in this humour won, 71
  in this humour wooed, 71
  in unwomanly rags, 391
  is a dish for the gods, 105
  is a foreign land, 556
  is always younger than a man
  at equal years, 430
  is at heart a rake, 209
  is fair, die because a, 132
  is more barbarous, 1080
  is necessarily an evil, 976
  is not even shallow, 1082
  is only a woman, 776
  is the lesser man, 464
  is various and most mutable,
  472
  is woman's natural ally, 968
  joins herself to man, 593
  laborin' man and laborin', 526
  laid old Troy in ashes, 185
  lays his hand upon a, 295
  learns how to hate, 1080
  left too much alone, 808
  light of a dark eye in, 353
  like a dewdrop, 487
  look for the, 1067
  lost Mark Antony the world,
  185
  lost us Eden, if, 444
  lovely woman, O, 185
  loves her lover, 359
  man delights not me no nor,
  92
  man that is born of, 1102
  may be, ken what a, 294
  mist is dispelled by, 205
  more interested in man's mind,
  709
  moved is like a fountain troubled, 52
  nature made thee to temper
  man, 185
  never can be man, 424
  never show a, 786
  never yet fair, 98
  never yields by appointment,
  wise, 1063
  newly made, 37
  no, is an absolute fool, 727
  no, should be accurate about
  age, 724
  not permitted to kill a, 662
  O woman perfect, 127
  of her unborn child, certain
  as a, 814
  once embraced, 651
  one, and none but she, 631
  one hair of a, 125

Woman, one that was a, 97
  oweth to her husband, 52
  perfect, nobly planned, 299
  poor lone, 64
  possesses the heart of a, 1086
  preaching, 234
  says what will please, 1055
  scorned, no fury like a, 193
  she is a, 68, 77
  she is always the, 737
  she was taken, 953
  should be good for everything
  at home, 968
  should be seen, 965
  smiled, till, 327
  so unto the man is, 436
  something about a roused,
  494
  still be a, to you, 201
  still gentler sister, 285
  stoops to folly, when lovely,
  253, 899
  such duty, oweth to her husband, 52
  supper with such a, 221, 361
  take an elder, let the, 54
  take some savage, 464
  tempted me, 792
  that deliberates is lost, 195
  that seduces all mankind, 205
  the creature of an hour, 1021
  the mummer's part, 844
  the one reward of virtue, 725
  the public is an old, 378
  there is not a, 1087
  therefore may be won, 77
  therefore may be wooed, 77
  therefore to be won, 68
  this the need of, 918
  thou large-brain'd, 427
  to win, all your wish is, 481
  tremble to win the hand of,
  422
  trust and man might honor,
  443
  trusted a secret to a, 998
  wailing for her demon lover,
  315
  walked in a northern town,
  807
  was God's second mistake,
  1082
  was made a devil, 127
  was not taken, the, 953
  was the sofa soft, 576
  well to be off with the, 720
  what mighty ills done by, 185
  who did not care, 779
  who did not know, 779
  who knew she was well
  dressed, 1081
  whose form is more dazzling,
  1083
  widow, 1101
  will or won't depend on't, 204
  with a slop-pail, 673
  with fair opportunities, a, 482
  with the serpent's tongue,
  737
  without religion is flame without heat, 551
  worked a, 660
  would be more charming, 662
  would run through fire and
  water, a, 34
  yet think him an angel, 482

Woman you gave to eat, 708
Woman's advice, ask a, 337
  being, holiest end of, 454
  best adornment, 976
  blush, beautiful as, 404
  body is the woman, 662
  breast his favourite seat, 303
  cold perverted will, 369
  ears too lightly opened, 963
  eye, black is a pearl in a, 28
  eye, such beauty as a, 41
  eyes, light that lies in, 336
  form, angel kneels in, 405
  gift to rain commanded tears, 52
  great and incomparable work, 670
  guess, 785
  hair, only a, 192
  head, would that this, 593
  heart that spoke, not thy, 560
  heart, the way to hit a, 417
  hide, wrapped in a, 69
  looks, only books were, 336
  love, paths to a, 131
  love, sky is like a, 677
  mind, riddle of a, 1037
  mood, fantastic as a, 308
  nay stands for naught, 109
  nursing, lack of, 447
  part, a, 564
  play is mediocre, 1080
  praise, sweeter sound of, 401
  reason, no other but a, 33
  sphere, talk about a, 638
  tears, there was dearth of, 447
  town, Paris is a, 710
  vows, a, 967
  whole existence, love is, 358
  will, torrent of a, 204
  work is never done, 205
Woman-country wooed not wed, 486
Womanhood and childhood, 434
  good heroic, 436
  in sculpture, indecorous, 422
Womankind, faith in, 466
Womanliness of woman's apparel, 731
Womb of morning dew, 24
  of pia mater, in the, 41
  of the morning, 1105
  of uncreated night, 149
  there in the, 936
  where I began, 832
Women all raiment, 911
  an' I learned about, 82
  and birds able to see, 877
  and brave men, 352
  and children first, 475
  and elephants, 812, 919
  and men, lives of most, 594
  and music, give way to, 182
  and not give the, 970
  and song, wine, 1058
  apt to tell secrets, 222
  are such expensive things, 575
  are the baggage of life, 163
  are wiser than men, 877
  bevy of fair, 155
  black brows become some, 56
  call not bad-looking, 1077
  comes natural to, 527
  command us, 996
  dear dead, 486
  displeasing to, 1037

Women, dissimulation innate in, 1064
  do for men, what, 658
  England is a paradise for, 125
  eyes of pure, 470
  extra, in every scene, 897
  fair as she, 645
  fickleness of, 720
  find few real friends, 239
  framed to make, false, 101
  Germans are like, 1082
  great city has greatest men and, 535
  guide the plot, 278
  have positive moral sense, 635
  have dominion over you, 1123
  have done, all the harm that, 747
  have no characters, 209
  have waxen minds, 107
  hear these tell-tale, 72
  in faces of, I see God, 535
  in their first passion, 1044
  Italy is a hell for, 125
  kindness in, 52
  know the way to rear up children, 429
  lamps shone o'er fair, 352
  like not only to conquer, 482
  love the lie, 725
  love to buy adulterate complexion, 115
  love to sew, when, 422
  marry again, when, 723
  men and, merely players, 49
  miss the best in life, 725
  must weep, 523
  nurse that babe to sleep, 561
  of Marblehead, by the, 443
  of the better class, 768
  of the present day too forward, 346
  old, should not be perfumed, 997
  ought to understand this, 930
  pardoned all except her face, 360
  pass the time, how, 801
  passing the love of, 1100
  pleasing punishment of, 37
  poets who smoke cigars, 931
  requirements of, 1077
  's rum cattle, 687
  say they are going to be informal, 912
  seven, take hold of one man, 1111
  should like the birds, 930
  show a front of iron, 521
  Solomon loved many strange, 1101
  speak, medicines to make, 1078
  strive to be constant, 258
  sweet is revenge to, 358
  that remember in the night, 773
  that's the nature of, 1035
  the mothers of all mischief, 561
  to keep counsel, hard it is for, 82
  too personal, 861
  try their luck, 723
  upset everything, 721
  vidders and ordinary, 494

Women wear the breeches, 122
  went astray, if weak, 189
  were by nature, if, 1050
  were created forgiveness but to speak, 763
  when Achilles hid himself among, 145
  who have borne you, respect, 1126
  wine and, 123, 359
  wise among, 632
  wise, girls be more than, 131
  wish to be who love their lords, 248
  with, the heart argues, 547
  with their children, 475
  with their secrets, entrust, 977
  won't, when you will, 979
  words are, deeds are men, 138, 204
  worst and best as heaven, 470
Women's eyes, from, 41
  hearts an open book, 865
  weapons water-drops, 98
Won a noble fame, 620
  every woman may be, 559
  grace that, 154
  life's victory, 556
  not unsought be, 154
  prize we sought is, 536
  she is a woman therefore to be, 68
  the man who hath mightily, 663
  though baffled oft is ever, 355
  was ever woman in this humour, 71
Wonder and a wild desire, 490
  and desire, I know the, 776
  April's, is worth it all, 764
  came the teeming, 847
  dreaming eyes of, 598
  grew, still the, 251
  is basis of worship, 379
  lasted nine daies, 4, 15
  lasts, day longer than a, 70
  matter of, 247
  nine days', 4, 15
  of all the lands, 541
  of Juliet's hand, white, 79
  of our stage, the, 119
  of the world, win that, 1045
  one, one thought, one grace, 32
  out of emptiness, 811
  struck with, 883
  ten days', 70
  that would be, all the, 464
  this year of publick, 182
  to me, is a pure, 519
  what I was begun for, 948
  word becomes a, 471
  world's splendor and, 673
Wonders of the western world, 818
  rare your eyes shall know, 539
  seven, of ancient world, 956
  that I yet have heard, 82
  to perform, his, 266
Wonderful counsellor the mighty God, 1111
  is death, how, 368
  little our fathers knew, 783
  most wonderful, 50
  one-hoss shay, 452
  place, wish there were some, 879

Wonderful rainbows in the rain, 609
speeches, snoring his, 883
the way, 672
thy love to me was, 1100
waters round you curled, 553
yet again, 50
Wonderfully and fearfully made, 1106
Wondering fearing, long I stood there, 460
men, 816
Wonderland, far from our, 857
in summer's, 864
Wondrous excellence, 108
kind, fellow-feeling makes one, 242
most, book bright candle, 393
pitiful, 't was, 100
strong yet lovely in your strength, 353
sweet and fair, so, 146
wealth to view, 559
wings, taken your, 652
Won't, if she, she won't, 204
Wonted fires, e'en in our ashes, 6, 245
Woo her, and that would, 100
her as the lion wooes his brides, 248
men are April when they, 51
were not made to, 42
Wood and there am I, cleave the, 709
can swim, wherever, 1061
carrying timber into a, 984
cleave the, 1126
deep and gloomy, 296
drudgery at the desk's dead, 325
gilded and covered, 1060
heap on more, 307
into a dark and lonely, 814
land set to plant a, 214
of yew wood, of true, 738
old, burns brightest, 128
one impulse from a vernal, 295
or cleave the, 781
set the yellow, sighing, 449
sighs to find them in the, 372
sorts of carved, 247
that skirts the road, 517
till Birnam, do come, 87
to burn, old, 113
two roads diverged in a, 838
we knock against, 747
what, a cudgel 's by the blow, 142
wondrously cut in, 752
yon maple, the burning bush, 442
Woods against a stormy sky, 370
and pastures new, fresh, 160
are full of them, 946
are lovely dark and deep, 839
calm patience of the, 445
Greta, are green, 309
have eares, 16
have tongues, 6, 470
He came, out of the, 664
her wilds her waters, 358
I went to the, 514
I will get me away to the, 771
if we walk in the, 412

Woods in the gay summer time, green, 484
in the middle of the, 498
no more, we'll to the, 743
or steepy mountains, 31
pleasure in the pathless, 354
prowling around the, 935
senators of mighty, 384
stoic of the, 328
that bring the sunset near, 672
this autumn day, thy, 916
to the sleeping, singeth, 315
untamed through, 758
wailing winds and naked, 372
walking in the high, 810
when wild in, 178
with music ring, 345
Woodbine, well-attired, 159
Woodcocks, springs to catch, 91
Wooden dialogue, 75
horse, lies about his, 881
legs not inherited, 818
shoe, sailed off in a, 699
shoes, round-heads and, 195
throat, whose, 920
walls of England, 946
Woodland bower, peeps from a, 676
marsh or bog, 953
of Weir, 461
Woodlands, leafless, 777
Woodman spare that tree, 328, 404
spare the beechen tree, 328
Woodman's axe lies free, 370
Woodnotes, jaw-breaking, 893
wild, native, 160
Wood-rose, loved the, 409
Woodside, glad to have lived under my, 141
Woodsmen stout and plucky, 815
Woodwork, level lines of, 759
Wood-world is one full peal of praise, 470
Wooed, beautiful therefore to be, 68
in haste, 193
in haste to wed at leisure, 52
we should be, 42
woman in this humour, 71
woman therefore may be, 77
would be, not unsought be won, 154
Woof, spun out of Iris', 157
there run, but through its, 501
weave the warp weave the, 244
Wooing, if I am not worth the, 436
in my boys, I'll go, 257
o't, ha ha the, 285
the caress, 358
Wooingly, heaven's breath smells, 85
Wool, all cry and no, 9, 142
great cry but little, 1039
moche crye and no, 9
of bat and tongue of dog, 87
tease the huswife's, 158
Wool-gathering, gone a, 1041
thoughts ran a, 1041
wits from, 116
Wool-gray air is all around, 932

Woollen, odious in, 209
rather lie in the, 38
Woolly spinster for a wife, 691
Wool-soft air of Europe, 932
Word, accoutred as I was upon the, 81
Alone, knells in that, 425
Alone, that worn out, 425
am true, to my pledged, 904
and a blow, 79, 179
and measured phrase, 297
and take back their word, give their, 742
and task, it is an irksome, 481
and what the cultured, 780
answer me in one, 50
answer not a, 924
as fail, no such, 425
as good as his bond, 1041
as we part, 668
at random spoken, 309
awoke an answering tone, 405
be again unsaid unheard, 180
benign, whose gracious, 474
burned like a lamp, 1125
choleric, in the captain, 36
deals destruction, 727
deathless deed or, 879
did make it, what that, 118
done for the least, 630
doubled with an evil, 38
down, hand his, 656
dropped a tear upon the, 242
dwell upon a, 471
everich, he moot reherce, 5
fitly spoken, 1108
flirtation that significant, 222
flowering in a lonely, 471
for teaching me that, 47
for three farthings, 41
go by the, 928
God in his works and, 200
has sometimes lost an empire, a single, 395
having but the, 834
He speeds, still the fitting, 441
He was the, that spake it, 118
honour, what is that, 63
I cannot speak a, 1066
in kindness spoken, 474
is a comprehensive, 1056
is dead when it is said, 585
is like a shriek, 892
is toujours gai, 852
it was bilbow, the, 222
knowed he would keep his, 639
last kind, 490
launch a heedless, 728
let no harsh, 473
lies with the god of weathers, 1091
light dies before thy uncreating, 215
like pardon, no, 60
liveth the, 964
love which greybeards call divine, 71
means just what I choose it to mean, 598
more than just an easy, 920
mum's the, 1041
must be spoken, 791
never break thy, 1010
never shall thy spoken, 570
never wanted a good, 252
no, but Latyn, 5

Word, no man relies on, 184
o' comfort, say a, 829
of a gentleman and a Christian, 1037
of Caesar might have stood, 83
of hope and love unstudied from the heart, 504
of Jefferson, trumpet, 771
of mine, one, 756
of old Lizette, 817
of onset gave, 298
of promise to our ear, 89
of the earth, the, 633
once familiar, 388
one little, 59
our orators let fall, 971
pleasant, to speak, 474
preserves contact, 1089
reputation dies at every, 212
right, a powerful agent, 615
said she, ne'er a, 861
shall a light, part us, 446
single irradiating, 588
so brief. 849
so idly spoken, 425
spoken in due season, 1107
spoken, power in, 727
suit the action to the, 94
sweeps down the ages, 568
tears wash out a, 1019
that ever breathed a, 516
that I kept my, 822
that is overbearing, 964
that one warm, 659
that shall echo forevermore, 437
that the blood, never a, 806
that was bad, not spoke a, 291
that you say, do not agree with a, 1053
that you've often heard, 883
thou speakest, whatever kind of, 1093
through every other, 313
till I can get the, 801
to designate remembrance, no, 312
to say, at last have a, 928
to scorn, laughed His, 263
to the action, suit the, 94
to throw at a dog, 48
torture one poor, 175
voice like a prophet's, 363
was still fie foh and fum, 99
wash out a, of it, 1019.
we had not sense to say, 659
we have no dearer, 694
weakness is not in your, 547
what was the, 590
whose lightest, 91
with this learned Theban, 99
Words, a few small, 809
a storm of, 971
all ears took captive, whose, 53
and actions, from all her, 154
and courtliness, amiable, 471
and deeds, fail I alone in, 487
answer in his own, 110
anything as beautiful as, 841
apt and gracious, delivers in, 41
are all too weak, 373
are but empty thanks, 194
are easy like the wind, 120

Words are faint, all, 275
are few and often funny, 511
are like leaves, 180, 211
are little jars, my, 831
are men's daughters, 204, 232
are no deeds, 73
are razors, 76
are said to me, 888
are slippery, 637
are the daughters of earth, 232
are the physicians of a mind diseased, 963
are things, 359
are wanting to commend, 175
are wise men's counters, 132
are women deeds are men, 138, 204
as in fashions, in, 211
as with a burning pen, three, 1059
at night, read out my, 881
at random flung, 275
be few, let thy, 1109
be not confused in, 1011
bethumped with, 57
brief, are well, 644
bright is the ring of, 703
by the force of, 1001
careful with, 677
charm agony with, 40
comfortable, 469, 1113
congealed by cold, 1005
could never utter, such as, 481
darkeneth counsel by, 1102
deceiving, in, 161
deeds not, 127
drank the precious, 584
dwells ever in her, 405
Emerson whose rich, 526
enormous force of few, 412
fair, never hurt the tongue, 29
false, are not only evil, 970
familiar as household, 67
finde, new, 5
flows in fit, 174
fly up, my, 95
for messengers, send my, 881
for the lips, very good, 497
forcible are right, 1102
galled by reproachful, 997
give sorrow, 88
good, are worth much and cost little, 137
good, ne'er be said of a friend, 679
have suffered corruption, 117
have vanished, 933
he multiplieth, 1102
he scorns, mouthing of, 891
his, replete with guile, 155
how you use proud, 855
I do not know the, 583
I understand a fury in your, 103
illusion wind, 359
immodest, admit of no defence, 180
in their best order, 319
in two little, 941
incarnadine the world, 773
joys of sense lie in three, 208
large divine and comfortable. 469
like airy servitors, 162
long dead, skill of, 912
long-tailed, in osity, 292

Words make friends one with another, 800
masked, 532
Masonic, 586
men of few, are the best men, 66
most wonderful are, 800
move slow, the, 211
multitude of, 1013
Narcissa's last, 209
no Byron penned, 716
no, can paint, 275
no Shakespeare wrote, 716
no virtue can digest into, 32
of all sad, of tongue or pen, 442
of blame, 696
of consecration, 628
of Death, 692
of doom, colder those wild, 418
of learned length, 251
of love, sweet are the, 618
of love then spoken, 336
of Marmion, the last, 308
of Mercury are harsh, 42
of mine, if any, 445
of my own, say a few, 921
of the wise as goads, 1110
of tongue or pen, cold, 815
of truth and soberness, 1119
once spoke can never be recalled, 180, 985
or smiles, sweeter than their, 634
pay no debts, 75
pin down in, 1076
plunged into a sea of, 878
polysyllabic or dictionary, 319
repeats his, 58
report thy, how he may, 157
rhapsody of, 95
right of coining, 346
saying in other, 217
seem flat and stale, 713
shall not pass away, but my, 1116
she thought they said, 653
sicken at pretty, 1085
sing out your, 873
slave of, 379
smelt of the lamp, 1000
smoother than butter, 1104
speak a few reasonable, 1058
speak approving cheering, 577
sublimely beautiful, 586
summed up in two, 1067
sweet as honey, 218
taught in numbers, 25
ten low, in one dull line, 211
that are weighty, 867
that burn, 168, 244
that have been so nimble, 129
that make no sense, 429
that weep and tears that speak, 168
the money of fools, 132
the shadows of actions, 1001
the unpleasantest, 46
these two brief, 309
they rob the Hybla bees, but for your, 84
things not made for, 1013
those two fatal, 1034
though ne'er so witty, 21

Words to convey truth and arouse emotion, 705
to give fair, 13
to put in, 467
to say, I have only a few, 558
to them, wut's, 527
two narrow, Hic jacet, 22
trust not a man's, 407
turn oracles, common, 429
unpack my heart with, 93
want of, or lack of breath, 157
we waited long, 659
weighty sense flows in fit, 174
well suited to the age, 180
were few, looks were fond, 345
were now written, that my, 1102
were simple words enough, his, 524
when men meet, 1027
when we desire to confine our, 145
when you're flying, 677
wing on, 652
without emphasizing your, 1064
without knowledge, 1102
without thoughts, 95
words words, 92
worst of thoughts the worst of, 102
writ in waters, 29, 386
write her fair, 65
Word-coining genius, 878
Wordless prayer, the impulse to a, 665
splendorous things, 896
Wordsworth walking the old green hills, 737
Wordsworth's healing power, 546
trust and Milton's faith, 634
Wore a wreath of roses, 388
Work, a fair day's, 378
a little, a little play, 607
a man is doing, 872
about writing, the only, 866
all day without sugar in your tay, 644
all must, 459
alone will efface the footsteps of work, 611
amusement grows out of, 532
and be wise, stand to your, 778
and called it good, looked upon your, 878
and folded it right, smoothed her, 458
and move, all things, 502
and pray live on hay, 957
and thou wilt bless, 501
and tools, there is always, 524
and your play, what you were like in your, 621
another rock would crown the, 484
at all times and seasons, supply, 1071
bad, follers ye, 527
be perspicuous, if a, 319
begun, no, 491
best, done between twenty-five and forty, 695
better go on with your, 851
blessed is he who has found his, 379
bones ache with the day's, 413

Work born with him, man's, 524
brings its own relief, 660
but just begun, 591
can best be done, 710
continueth, for their, 783
dirty, at the crossroads, 944
distinguish himself in his, 1054
done, I see the, 941
every man according to his, 1104
for a god, 379
for a man, if you, 745
for all, say there's bread and, 432
for man to mend, 175
for some good, 499
for the body, necessary, 961
for the work's sake, 719
for the world's, 567
go to your, 778
grows weary, when dull, 474
hard gives rest to body and peace to mind, 605
his day's work and his night's, 630
huddle up their, 265
if fifty men did all the, 754
in a day, do more, 345
in our stations, abide and, 519
instant he sets himself to, 379
is alone noble, 378
is as seed sown, 377
is done, my, 141
is done, the reaper's, 370
is love made visible, 879
is the duty of every able-bodied citizen, 1093
is the least of my idees, 697
is the scythe of time, 1061
is what a body is obliged to do, 615
it is stern, 890
let patience have her perfect, 1122
life's, well done, 555
like the industrious bee, 910
lives while artist is forgotten, 717
made manifest, 1120
man goeth forth unto his, 1105
man's, a portrait of himself, 613
many hands make light, 16
material comes before the, 613
measure not the, 430
men must, 523
most important part of the, 973
motherhood woman's great, 670
nature's noblest, 284
night cometh when no man can, 1118
noblest, she classes O, 284
not, they that, 501
nothing to do but, 729
of a moment, 1033
of God, the noblest, 208
of Henry James, 906
of life at last, 688
of love to do, some noble, 474
of man's creative hand, 500
of master suggests no effort, 611
of my hands, by the, 844
of our hands, 1105

Work of our head and hand, 779
of polished idleness, 290
of six, doing the, 446
one, transcendently surpassed, 324
or lose the power to will, 502
out your own salvation, 1121
rejoicing in his, 835
rising to a man's, 1011
sharpens his appetite, 1054
silent part is best of every noble, 533
such as few ever had laid on head, 513
tackle your, 870
thank God for, 524
thankless, 785
that aspires to art, 726
that it was made to do, 760
that we may rest from our, 291
that's nearest, do the, 523
the master-word, 694
the open sesame, 694
the true philosopher's stone, 694
this is my, 710
to do, enough, 787
to each according to his, 1093
to sport as tedious as to, 61
together for good, 1119
toil and moil at their, 1045
voluntarily performeth a good, 1126
way to spread a, 235
we are in, strive to finish the, 457
well, act the Golden Rule, 695
what a piece of, is a man, 92
what valid, 728
when all its, is done the lie, 556
which thou givest us to do, 1127
who first invented, 325
why fret you at your, 706
workman known by the, 1045
Works are wrapped in mystery, 726
do follow them, their, 1123
done least rapidly, 486
embodied in, greatest ideas, 531
faith without, 1122
fat of others', 121
follows God in his, 200
full of good, 1118
great, of the nineteenth century, 1087
he that, and does, 378
in science read the newest, 426
in, subdued to what it, 108
intended for the service of God, 179
is dead, without good, 1038
largest number of excellent, 1053
last and best of all God's, 155
many wonderful, 701
nature sighing through all her, 155
of art, in the vaunted, 410
of mortal pride, 212
of the great poets never read by mankind, 514
rich in good, 1122
silent as to his, 237

Works, son of his own, 1033
these are thy glorious, 153
universal, blank of nature's, 151
ye mighty, look on my, 878
Work-a-day world, in the, 649
Worker, created by the labour of the, 1086
oppresses the, 1086
Workers of the world unite, 1072
Working and reading, love, 199
mood, puts me in a, 410
our salvation, tools of, 143
out a pure intent, 303
out its way, fiery soul, 173
spells, 650
still, God is living, 502
Workings, hum of mighty, 383
Working-day world, full of briers, 48
Working-girl, heaven will protect the, 730
Workingmen! Heart of the people, 458
Workman known by the work, 1045
not to be ashamed, 1122
true, were it so bad O, 706
Workmanship common test of merit, 571
superfluity of, 247
Workmen and their work, 973
to displace, competing, 618
Workshop's clamor, back of the, 873
World a better thing, 647
a, has passed away, 628
a maniac, 588
a perpetual caricature, 769
abounds with laws, 950
accidents fill the, 940
ah, happy, 619
all corners of the, 105
all the beauty of the, 169
all the countries in the, 450
all the, must see the world, 559
all the uses of this, 90
all's right with the, 485
along its path advances, 336
always morning somewhere in the, 417
an idler too, busy, 265
and his wife, all the, 192
and its dread laugh, 224
and love, 617
and search the sea, go search the, 624
and shout to all the, 925
and the wrong it does, this, 486
and under the world, over the, 778
and worldlings base, 65
and youth behind, left the, 837
another and a better, 1060
apart, throbbed from all the, 499
appears like a great family, 184
arise, new-bathed, 671
around, spins the heavy, 743
as good be out of the, 193
as the, the world hath seen, 559
at will, roam the, 844
bade the, farewell, 327
balance of the old, 293

World, banish all the, 62
bank-note, 363
barbaric yawp over roofs of, 535
be nobler, O, 804
become the lumber of the, 185
been formed, has this, 1052
before the whole, 1047
began, since the, 77, 432
belongs to the enthusiast, 870
bestride the narrow, 81
better than all heads in the, 426
better, than this, 48
bite my thumb at the, 590
blood of the, 922
blows and buffets of the, 86
books a substantial, 301
borrow the name of the, 110
breathers of this, 108
breathes out contagion to this, 95
brought death into the, 148
browbeat this, 490
busy, is hushed, 1128
but a larger stage, 721
but as a stage, 1033
but not the same, a, 937
but once, through this, 682, 1062
called the new, into existence, 293
calls idle, whom the, 265
can never fill, void the, 266
cankers of a calm, 63
cannot live at high level, 713
cast not out song from the, 633
cast out of the, and despised, 22
children of this, 1117
citizen of the, 424, 1005, 1016
clothe the, 754
cold, in every office but thine, 52
come to love the whole, 1074
commandress of the, 28
credit in this, 1019
crucified to the, 247
crumbles to nothing, 1063
daffed the, aside, 63
dark and wide, 767
deaf, does not hear, 706
death undulate round the, 536
destruction of our, 449
dissolves, when all the, 31
doth but two nations bear, 169
dreams books are each a, 301
drowsy syrups of the, 102
ears of the, 633
ends, the way the, 899
ends, the whole, 870
endures, while the, 631
enough and time, 169
envy of the, 259
equal hope in the, 455
ere the, be past, 250
except the one within, conquer any, 595
falls when Rome falls, 354
far from ours, some, 368
fashion of this, passeth away, 1120
firmament ringing the, 666
flesh and the devil, 1127
flowers, a new, 936
for the last battle of the, 442

World for you, roam the, 803
foremost man of all this, 83
forgetting by the world forgot, 216
four corners of the, 1032
fresh and full of novelties, 563
gain the whole, 1115
girdle round about the, 28
give the, the lie, 22
go dine and dress, let the, 406
go through this, 474
God conceived the, 508
goes, honest as this, 92
goes round, 565
goes round forever, 405
goes up the world goes down, 523
goes with no eyes, 99
good-bye proud, 408
good deed in a naughty, 47
great as the, 415
great wide beautiful wonderful, 553
grew pale, name at which the, 230
guide the, 1079
had ceased to turn, 845 *
half of the, knoweth not how the other half liveth, 1025
half the, 138
half-brother of the, America, 506
harmoniously confused, 216
harmony of the, 22
has but one song, 855
has grown grey, 631
has joked incessantly, 624
has made him free, 686
has made it sweet, 864
has no power, over the dead, the, 1051
has no tyrant like intemperance, 424
has nothing to bestow, 226
hath flattered all the, 22
hath just one tale, 851
he gained the, 658
he gave his honours to the, 74
He looked about the, 877
He looked upon the, 877
he pleases all the, 1050
healing of the, 566
heave of the surging, 735
hero stuff that rules the, 732
him who bore the, 303
his bride, made the, 910
history of the, 1062
hold your own in the, 721
holds hate in fee, 851
house the, 754
how little wisdom governs the, 130
how this, goes with no eyes, 99
I cannot hold thee, 916
I have not loved the, 353
I hold the, but as the world, 44
I never have sought the, 237
I saw God wash the, 886
I'll tell the, 36
if there's another, 285
imaginary, of lovers, 732
impossible to please all the, 1045
in a grain of sand, 281
in arms, against a, 399
in arms, come the, 58

World in as good condition as ever it was, 182
in charity with the, 192
in its turn presents, 1062
in love with night, 79
in one common, 1002
in that new, 465
in the face, looks the, 433
in the golden, 47
in the, I fill a place, 47
in the morning of the, 485
in this canting, 241
in this wintry, 337
in which children have their existence, 498
incessantly wash this soiled, 536
inhabit this bleak, alone, 336
intangible, O, 749
invisible, O, 749
is a battleground, 926
is a bubble, 112
is a bundle of hay, 361
is a chess-board, 563
is a comedy, 246
is a difficult world, 685
is a nettle, 592
is a stage, all the, 49, 117, 1031
is a strange affair, 1046
is a theatre the earth a stage, 49, 129
is a tragedy to those who feel, 246
is a vale of tears, 568
is a wheel, the, 421
is a wilderness, if the, 568
is all a fleeting show, this, 336
is all right, I say, 844
is all wrong, and the, 920
is ancient, when the, 112
is better off, 718
is charged with grandeur, 672
is cold to all, 469
is everything to us, 684
is full of roses, 696
is given to lying, how this, 63
is good and the people are good, 276
is grown so bad, 71
is his who has money, 413
is, know how the, 891
is large when leagues divide, 675
is mad, sense that the, 840
is merely a bridge, the, 1093
is mine oyster, 34
is my country, 271
is nodding, whole, 994
is not so bad a world, 505
is not sweet in the end, 631
is not thy friend, 80
is old lad, when all the, 523
is queer, all the, 306
is runne quite out of square, 25
is sad enough, 718
is so incredulous, 974
is the hand that rules the, 534
is too much with us, 300
is very odd we see, 519
is weary of the past, 367
is wide enough to hold both, 241
is wide, thanks be to God, 916

World is young to-day, 687
it has so modest grown, 657
it were better for the, 559
jest and riddle of the, 208
knows me in my book, 1030
knows nothing of its greatest men, 401
knows only two, 119
lasts, while the, 942
let any man show the, 592
light of the, ye are the, 1114
lights of the, 262
limited by ourselves, 1084
limits of the, 1063
literature in the, 237
little foolery governs the, 130
little friend of all the, 786
look down upon the, 999
look round the habitable, 177
looks for wages, 491
looks small and very dear, 827
macadamize the, 506
made new, every morn, 682
made safe for democracy, 725
make it a difficult, 895
man of letters amongst men of the, 398
man of the, among men of letters, 398
man to hold against the, here was a, 708
man's ingress into the, 276
may give her content, 954
may sound no trumpet, 955
most beautiful verb in, 1083
must be peopled, 39
must follow you, 754
must have great minds, 506
my country is the, 424
naked came I into the, 1036
naked through the, 103
natural and political, 260
naught in, or church or state, 528
needs, is all this sad, 718
no copy, leave the, 54
not in need of new thoughts, 588
not the way to improve the, 720
not too late to seek a newer, 464
nothing to the other, 970
nourish all the, 41
now a bubble burst and now a, 207
O brave new, 33
O carping, 685
O world, thus is the poor agent despised, 75
of care without, a, 544
of clouding cares, 574
of divine delight, 822
of fire and dew, 790
of fools, my lord it is a, 472
of good, do you a, 1041
of happiness their harmony, 460
of happy days, to buy a, 71
of his own, in a, 1002
of light and speech, 521
of love, 647
of love shut in, 544
of memory, 647

World of men not the world of books, 625
of misery, release from this, 1063
of music in one word, 647
of our present consciousness, 663
of ours, and this wise, 470
of parchment made, were the, 1017
of pleurisy of people, curest the, 132
of sighs, for my pains a, 100
of sorrow, 647
of sorrow and pain, 294
of strife, be a, 686
of strife shut out, 544
of thought, 647
of time and trouble, a, 490
of vile ill-favoured faults, 34
of waters, the rising, 151
of wrath and strife, 693
out of bed, get the, 832
out of fashion out of the, 193
over, ever the wide, 778
owes its onward impulses, 422
part sadly in this troublous, 71
peace to be found in the, 333
pendent hanging in a golden chain, 151
pomp and glory of this, 73
prevailed and its dread laugh, 224
proclaim, to all the sensual, 310
Puritans gave action to the, 479
quiet limit of the, 464
rack of this tough, 100
rationally, looks upon the, 1062
ready for either, 313
rebuked by the, 786
reckless what I do to spite the, 86
recommended to the, 927
response of all the, 1084
retire from the, 984
rewards its votaries, 1075
rise up from the spirit of this, 247
rolls into light, 439
round about the pendent, 36
rub, let the, 1035
ruled by best thoughts, 588
's ugly as sin, the, 545
safe for democracy, 769
scum of the, 1040
search well another, 170
secrets of the nether, 1009
secure amidst a falling, 194
seems cold, if the, 568
seems to smile upon me, 181
seen like shadows on water, 618
send back the song, whole, 477
service of the antique, 48
seven wonders of the ancient, 956
shall mourn her, all the, 74
she followed him, through all the, 465
shot heard round the, 409
should listen then, the, 367
sink, let the, 136

World sleeps on its axis, 919
slide, let the, 11, 51, 131
slip, let the, 52
slumbering, o'er a, 201
smooth its way through the, 222
snug farm of the, 321
so beautiful made this, 773
so runs the, away, 94
so wags the, 310
somewhere there waiteth in this, 597
soul of this, 1006
sounds of the rude, 568
speech of the, 640
spin forever, let the great, 464
stand up and say to all the, 84
stands out on either side, 915
start of the majestic, 81
steal from the, 216
stood against the, 83
supreme ecstasy of the modern, 932
sweetest flowers in all the, 634
syllables govern the, 130
tell the, 484
ten hours to the, 275
that few is all the, 30
that nourish all the, 41
that sensitive and timid natures, 637
that the, had never been, 559
that time and sense have known, 444
that we're a-livin' in, 730
the best you have, give to the, 671
the, blooms with statues, 613
the burden of the, 708
the flesh and the devil, 1127
the higher heavenly, 1074
the, is full of a number of things, 702
the, is lovely, 655
the, laughs with you, 718
the lie, give the, 22
the race the soul, the, 538
the rolling, 588
the vanity of the, 1049
the whole, kin, 75
the whole wide, 671
there is not in the wide, 334
thinks Go, 912
this bloomin', 777
this busy, 168
this great roundabout, 267
this is the new, 1066
this little, 59
this, nis but a thurghfare, 6
this unintelligible, 295
this would be, good, 954
thou art the whole wide, 672
thou choosest not the better part O, 770
three corners of the, 58
tired of wandering o'er the, 401
to another, from this, 970, 974
to be, fabric of the, 952
to curtain her sleeping, 369
to darkness, leaves the, 244
to do, with nothing in the, 406
to give the, assurance, 95
to hear, beg the cold, 847
to hide virtues in, 54

World to live in, very good, 185
to open for the, 517
to overcome the, 789
to peep at such a, 265
to rouse and rule the, 397
to see, a, 23
to see, taught the, 167
to the pleasant, 1020
to you bequeaths, 935
too beautiful this year, 916
too glad and free, 423
too much respect upon the, 43
too noble for the, 76
too wide for his shrunk shank, 50
trade, restoration of, 909
turn thine eyes on passing, 230
turns round, giddy thinks the, 52
truth throughout the, 303
two nations bear, the, 169
uncertain comes and goes, 411
unheard by the, 336
unknowable, 749
unknown, voyage to the, 200
unspotted from the, 1122
unworthiness of the, 878
upon the rack of this tough, 100
uses of this, all the, 90
vanity of this wicked, 1127
virtue passes current over the, 968
visitations daze the, 402
visits his dinners, 1046
wag, let the, 12
wags, how the, 49
War, unprecedented upheaval of, 909
was all before them, 156
was all forgot, 346
was always yours, 914
was an enchanted place, 811
was born, 755
was guilty of a ballad, 41
was heard the, around, 161
was made in six days, 1060
was not to seek me, 237
was on thy page, 369
was sad till woman smiled, 327
was worthy of such men, 428
wax colder, all the, 675
we come from a, 927
we do not see, a, 480
were just, if all the, 999
were young, if all the, 21
what I may appear to the, 184
what is all the, 867
what is this, 6
what perplexes the, 1089
what's to be next in the, 914
when all the, dissolves, 31
where is any author in the, 41
where nothing is had for nothing, 519
whereon rests sure the, 932
who feed the, 754
who lost Mark Antony the, 185
who rebukes the, 786
who would inhabit this bleak, alone, 336
who would succeed in the, 640
whole new democratic, 379
wide enough for thee and me, 241

World will be gulled, if the, 126
will come round to him, 414
will disagree in faith and hope, 208
will end in fire, 839
will judge largely of mother, 692
will never starve for wonders, 826
will not believe a man, 470
will offer itself to you, 1090
will sail on, 678
will there be another, 603
will wake anew, 674
wind to shake the, 936
with all its motley rout, 267
with beauty, who has filled the, 1128
with terror, fills the, 434
wonderfully drest, 553
working-day, full of briers, 48
works for to-day, 689
worship of the, but no repose, 367
worst, that ever was known, 185
worst way to improve the, 506
worth th' winning, 176
would be nicer than ever, 942
would grow mouldy, or the, 472
would teach the, 851
you are all the, 42
Worlds, allured to brighter, 250
best of all possible, 1052
both, at once they view, 146
exhausted, imagined new, 231
face is from other, 773
in the yet unformed occident, 30
not realized, in, 301
of fine thinking lie buried, 347
of pain, costs, 832
so many, so much to do, 469
stretch beyond the actually seen, 670
wandering between two, 546
within the hollow of our hand, 647
whose course is equable, 303
wreck of matter and crush of, 195
World's altar-stairs, 468
arches, I saw the, 932
course will not fail, 556
creation, most ancient since the, 112
delight, lovely rose the, 587
delight, what is this, 368
desires, huge army of the, 40
dread laugh, 224
end, to the, 37
far end, journeys to the, 694
globe, wheresoe'er thou art in this, 69
great age begins anew, 367
great light, 687
great men, the, 454
greatest thinkers amateurs, 741
law, nor the, 80
new fashion planted, 40
noble emblem, 825
she that was the, delight, 618, 630
shore, beat wild on this, 447

World's slow stain, 366
  splendor and wonder, 673
  thy jail, 117
  vaporous vitiate air, 652
  way, out of the, 631
  way'll be overthrown, 832
  wide parched way, back to the, 450
  work sake, for the, 567
World-accusing waves, 836
World-forsakers, world-losers and, 676
Worldliness, more of wicked, 505
  revelry high life, 1064
Worldlings do, testament as, 48
  world and, 65
World-losers and world-forsakers, 676
Worldly chances and mishaps, secure from, 76
  ends, thus neglecting, 32
  goods, his, 404
  goods, were all his, 498
  goods, with all my, 1128
  hope, the, 1018
  life, the weariest, 36
  task hast done, thou thy, 106
  wise, be not, 134
World-mothering air, 672
Worm, bit with an envious, 77
  by early songster caught, vagrant, 510
  he stiffened, 576
  i' the bud, concealment like a, 55
  I want to be a, 753
  in your little inside, 624
  man cannot make a, 1028
  needlessly sets foot upon a, 266
  no god dare wrong a, 409
  or beetle, 677
  striving to be man, the, 409
  that hath eat of a king, 96
  the conqueror, 459
  the canker and the grief, 358
  the smallest, will turn, 70
  was punished sir, the, 510
  when trod upon will turn, 1038
Worms and epitaphs, let 's talk of, 59
  banqueter on, 725
  devils at, 1024
  entertains the most exclusive, 919
  have eaten men, 51
  in our gardens, 166
  of Nile, outvenoms all the, 105
Wormwood, feed them with, 1112
  why taste the, 764
Worn and gray, a little city, 673
  and shabby, suddenly all, 929
  and weak and full of tears, 484
  oars, sculled their, 894
  out with eating time, 178
  sick and tired and faint and, 596
  the ring so, 280
Worn-out tale, have done with a, 612
  word Alone, 425
Worried and fretted and kept in a stew, 474
Worry the interest paid, 946
Worse, for better for, 1128
  for the excuse, 58

Worse for the wearing, 15
  for wear, not much the, 264
  further and fared, 16
  greater feeling to the, 59
  is boundless better boundless, 462
  make the, appear the better reason, 149, 1014
  oft cures the, to fear the worst, 75
  pray God they change for, 28
  present things seem, 64
  than a crime, it is, 1060
  than a man, little, 44
  than being talked about, 723
  that which makes man no, 1010
  things waiting than death, 631
  truth put to the, 163
Worser ills to face, there are, 771
Worship deep and wild, 395
  God he says, 284
  is your furnaces, your, 826
  no other, abides, 595
  of the infinitely true, 604
  of the world, they have the, 367
  stated calls to, 233
  still to the star of its, 337
  the gods of the place, 126
  the sun, a duty to, 641
  to the garish sun, pay no, 79
  too divine to love too fair to, 363
  wonder the basis of, 379
Worshiped fire only, 166
  stocks and stones, 162
  sun, hour before the, 77
  the rising than the setting sun, 999
Worshiper at nature's shrine, 382
  nature mourns her, 307
  wiser the silent, 612
Worst and best are both inclined, 898
  and best as heaven and hell, 470
  bottom of the, 75
  comes to the worst, 116, 1035
  he kept his best he gave, his, 465
  is still behind, 1041
  is that which persecutes the mind, 174
  is yet to come, 465
  of madmen a saint run mad, 214
  of thoughts the worst of words, 102
  of woes, it is the, 1020
  part of man's conversation, 426
  pursue, 187
  the best and the, 633
  thing about him, 36
  thing to do to an author, 237
  things present seem, 64
  this is the, 99
  to fear the, oft cures the worse, 75
  to-morrow do thy, 177
  treason has done his, 87
  way to improve the world, the, 506
  what began best can't end, that, 490

Worst world that ever was known, 185
Worst-humored muse, 252
Worst-natured muse, 184
Worth a month in town, 587
  a thousand men, 308
  and pains, with all his, 317
  boasts its supreme, 492
  by its intrinsic, 1000
  by poverty depressed, 231
  conscience of her, 154
  doing well, 222
  dread temple of Thy, 783
  feather's weight of, 638
  going to see, 237
  in anything, what is, 142, 990
  in his own household, 964
  is eulogy's blandest breath, what, 541
  judge of her own, 779
  lavish waste of, 597
  makes the man, 208
  man is, as he esteems himself, 1025
  mastered what was not, knowing, 526
  much and cost little, good words are, 137
  nobler yet in his own, 174
  everything is, 990
  of him, never knew the, 807
  of sterling, 465
  on foot and rascals in the coach, 525
  one's own paramount, 1064
  opinion of our own, 1029
  our while to live, 909
  remembering, this is, 785
  seeing, 237
  slow rises, 231
  stones of, like, 107
  strips of all its, 309
  substitute for inner, 961
  the candle, not, 138
  the search, not, 44
  the wear of winning, nothing, 810
  thy winning, 176
  the wooing, if I am not, 436
  that brings no risk, 960
  their acknowledged, 972
  two of that, I know a trick, 61
  what we have we prize not to the, 39
  what you saved, you're, 676
  whate'er his, howe'er divine, 578
  while, is it, 657
Worthies did, braver thing than all the, 117
Worthless pomp of homage, 374
Worthy of all acceptation, 188
  of reprehension, become, 1127
  of the name of poet, 378
  of their steel, 308
  of your love, 297
  to be read more than once, 985
  to be sought, 655
Wot, a lovesome thing, God, 583
  as by lot God, 255
  not what they are, 40
Would and we would not, 37
  God it were even, 632, 1099
  God it were morning, 632, 1099
  God the day were dead, 632

Would God the day were here, 632
  he shall have nay, when he, 11
  I, fain, but I dare not, 21
  I that cowlèd churchman be, 408
  I were a boy again, 454
  I were dead now, 391
  it were bedtime, 63
  letting I dare not wait upon I, 85
  not if I could be gay, 289
  not live alway, I, 387
  not what we, but what we must, 565
  not when he might, 257
  that I could know again, 455
  that we were young again, 521
  write and can't write, 526
  you know how first, 481
Would-be scholar, 426
Wouldn't you like to know, 510
Wound each weakness, read each, 546
  earth felt the, 155
  felt a stain like a, 260
  grew a pearl, 714
  grief of a, take away the, 63
  heal me of my grievous, 463
  her very shoe has power to, 240
  history of a soldier's, 241
  is mortal and is mine, 922
  mine was a secret, 714
  purple with love's, 42
  that never felt a, 78
  to-day, send me a, 892
  tongue in every, of Caesar, 83
  up and going, reading-machine, 526
  up every morning, clock, 564
  us, no tongue to, 336
  willing to, 213
  with a touch, 221
Wounds and sore defeat, 806
  are in front, 985
  are vain, the labor and the, 519
  bind up my, 72
  bind up the nation's, 457
  fight and not heed the, 1024
  he licked my, 897
  invisible that love's arrows make, 50
  of a friend, faithful are the, 1108
  senseless, 888
  which smarted and bled, 682
Wounded, hymn of the, the beaten, 533
  Knee, bury my heart at, 929
  in the house of my friends, 1114
  snake, like a, 211
  sore bestead, 659
  the spirit that loved thee, 587
  vanity knows when it is hurt, 591
  whale a-sounding, like a, 873
  you're, 487
Wove your doom, days that, 631
Wrack, blow wind come, 88
  ship has weathered every, 536
  to the seaman, 106
  way out of his, 73

Wraith, life is but a, 887
Wrappage through which savage nature can burst, 381
Wrapped in a woman's hide, 69
Wrapping all, light silently, 535
Wrastling for this worlde, 4
Wrath, Achilles', 218
  allay, no twilight dews his, 309
  be slow to, 1122
  can send, good Heaven thy, 293
  destroy, in after, 1019
  did end, I told my wrath my, 281
  did grow, 281
  God's patience and His, 395
  infinite, and infinite despair, 151
  nursing her, 287
  on the anvil of Thy, 836
  soft answer turneth away, 1107
  strong man in his, 428
  sun go down upon your, 1121
  the last thing to grow old, 960
  where grapes of, are stored, 522
Wrathful God beholds, only my, 931
  nipping cold, winter with, 69
Wreath a rank a throne a grave, a, 405
  a rosy, 119
  across my hair, for a, 866
  has lost a rose, thy, 309
  is still as green and red, 446
  of roses, she wore a, 388
  on murdered Lincoln's bier, 513
  pilgrim's withered, 598
  presaging life, 475
  twine in a, 1066
Wreaths are made of earthly, hope's, 446
  genial holly, 935
  upon his grave, 890
Wreathed horn, Triton with his, 300
  smiles, becks and, 160
Wreck, colossal, 367
  I rise, out of the, 493
  of matter, 195
  of power, lay down the, 374
  on a strange shelf, 119
  on error's shore, stand a, 618
  on raging seas, saved from, 815
Wrecks of time, 640
Wrecked argosy, like a, 587
  greatest men oftest, 156
  on shore, 611
Wren builds it, wisdom, 414
  four larks and a, 499
  mighty fleet of, 819
Wrens make prey, 71, 212
Wrestle against sleep, who can, 478
  oh glory that we, 458
  with, virtue has difficulties to, 1028
Wrestled with him, 140
Wrestler, a hopeless, 575
Wrestles with us, he that, 261
Wrestling, more like, than dancing, 1011
Wretch concentred all in self, 307
  condemned with life to part, 252

Wretch, excellent, 102
  hollow-eyed sharp-looking, 38
  I beheld the, 389
  in order, to haud the, 285
  my wife poor, 181
  on hope relies, the, 252
  to live like a, 123
Wretches feel, feel what, 99
  hang that jurymen may dine, 212
  hired, 232
  poor naked, 98
  such as I, weary road to, 285
Wretched blind pit ponies, 816
  he, if happy I and, 504
  made many, 976
  orb, 588
  refuse of your teeming shore, 694
  soul bruised with adversity, 37
  souls of those who lived, 1020
  taste to be gratified with mediocrity, 291
  thing, a man, 115
  to relieve the, was his pride, 250
  transfigures the, 1067
  unidea'd girls, 233
  yet inevitable spite, 441
Wretchedness, red waves of, 389
Wring his bosom, 254
  under the load of sorrow, those that, 40
  your heart, let me, 95
Wrinkle below, laurel above and, 594
  time writes no, 355, 440
Wrinkles, grace is joined with, 1069
  time got his, 664
  won't flatter, 360
Wrinkled care derides, 160
  front of war, 71
  with age and drenched with dew, 822
Wrist grows stiff and old, 544
Writ in remembrance, 59
  in sour misfortune's book, 80
  in water, deeds, 130
  in water, whose name was, 386
  in waters, words, 29
  proofs of holy, 102
  stolen forth of holy, 71
  your annals true, 76
Write a verse or two, 135
  about it goddess, 215
  and cipher too, 251
  and read comes by nature, to, 39
  as funny as I can, 451
  does he, he fain would paint, 488
  fair, hold it baseness to, 97
  finely upon a broomstick, 192
  force them to, 142
  he who would, heroic, 376
  in rhyme, those that, 142
  in water, their virtues we, 74
  it before them in a table, 1111
  look in thy heart and, 27
  me as one who loves, 346
  me down an ass, 40
  nothing to, about, 1008
  pen, devise wit, 41
  the evangel-poem of comrades, 534

Write the vision and make it
plain, 1113
well hereafter, hope to, 162
with a goose pen, 55
with ease, you, 279
Writen, in the sterres, clerer than
is glas, 6
Writer, abilities as a, 235
character of the, 376
may put aside conventional
rules, 741
nodding-places in a voluminous, 196
one, excels at a plan, 254
owned an asterisk, 907
pen of a ready, 1104
who can set down with accuracy, 898
Writers against religion, 258
cannot them digest, 29
future psychologists and, 1083
in France, too few obscure,
1084
mankind's interest in, 588
of his own generation, 675
of small histories, 232
of that century have stamped,
1087
Writes it, Shakespeare, 414
the moving finger, 1019
Writhing, reeling and, 598
Writing, better to read a man's
own, 520
comes from that, American,
930
easy, is curst hard reading, 279
is but a different name, 241
maketh an exact man, 111
putting it down in, 228
scarcely any style of, 231
that is easy, 1084
that will soon be elementary,
1084
true ease in, 211
well, nature's masterpiece is,
185
Writings, in every man's, 376
of authors fade away, 344
on the sand, 553
recite their, 984
the great ancients', 507
Written a book, that mine adversary had, 1102
above that which is, 1120
as he could have, Hamlet, 382
out of reputation by himself,
187
that my words were now, 1102
to after times, 162
troubles of the brain, 88
with a pen of iron, 1112
Wrong, a grievous, 620
all his life he has been in the,
185
always in the, 173
as if he'd been, 948
beautiful snow it can do no,
560
because of weakness, feeble,
430
condemn the, 986
cradled into poetry by, 367
do a little, 47
dwelling much on, 1050
eben ef we 's doin', 712
engaged in opposing, 450

Wrong, falsehood fear and, 816
follow the king, right, 470
forever on the throne, 525
fust gits mad's most ollers,
527
he can't be, whose life is right,
167, 208
him who treasures up a, 357
his argument, 252
how easily things go, 559
in Kentucky, 675
in some nice tenets might be,
167
in the teeth of a, 833
it does, world and the, 486
love will do no, 556
Lucrece swears he did her,
107
majorities have been, 580
multitude is always in the,
180
no room for memory of a, 415
none, 52
nothing marred to do you, 790
of unshapely things, 790
only one idea and that was,
235, 420
oppressor's, 93
others shall right the, 444
own he has been in the, 217
pursue, and yet the, 986
pursue yet condemn the, 187
right shall disestablish, 651
shall fall on it, 688
she was grotesquely, 666
side evermore, on the, 569
side of thirty, 192
some villain hath done me, 98
sow by the ear, 17, 1034
sure way of coming out, 528
tale of an ancient, 612
tell me what's, 883
that needs resistance, 543
that which they reject is, 635
they do me, 793
they may gang a kennin', 285
they ne'er pardon who have
done the, 178
through present, the eternal
right, 442
to be put right, when, 580
too great to be told, 790
way seems the more reasonable, 709
when we're a-going, 496
would triumph never dreamed,
494
Wrongs are borne, what, 804
his friend wrongs himself more,
he that, 465
in marble, some write their,
204
of night, 134
or tyrant power, 396
our rights our power, against
our, 895
unredressed, 302
Wrongdoer has left something
undone, 1012
Wronged orphans' tears, 129
Wrote down for men, as he, 516
like an angel, 243
reading what they never, 265
them in the dust, 204
with ease, gentlemen who, 214
Wroth with one we love, 315

Wrought and afterwards he
taught, 5
brain too finely, 262
by want of thought, 390
in a sad sincerity, 408
in common clay, 784
its ghost upon the floor, 460
lies close at home, beauty,
442
not into evil, 628
whene'er a noble deed is, 436
Wry-necked fife, squealing of the,
45
Wum, w 'en he fine, a, 688
Wut 's words to them, 527
Wyf, to take, with-oute avysement, 7
Wyfly pacience, this flour of, 7
Wyn, he wel dronken had the, 5
Wynken Blynken and Nod, 699,
872
Wys is he, 6

XANADU, Kubla Khan in, 315
Xanthippe, shrewd as Socrates',
52
Xarifa, rise up, 374
Xerxes did die and so must I,
947
Ximena speak and tell us, 441

YACHTS and planes, cars and,
899
Yale college and Harvard, a
whale ship, 531
Yaller gal, swing dat, 689
Yankee boy, before he's sent to
school, 348
commonwealth, base of the,
926
doodle do, 283
in King Ballyhoo's court, 896
in the garden of Eden, 518
is a dab, 828
nation, this glorious, 502
two Spaniards to come a, 559
Yankees have the marrow, 348
killed a chance of, 630
Yard be narrow, if your, 890
Yards unknown at night, 717
Yarn, all the, she spun in Ulysses' absence, 76
from a laughing fellow-rover,
832
is of a mingled, 53
Yawcob Strauss, mine leedle, 661
Yawn, when churchyards, 95
Yawning make another yawn, 123
Yawp, I sound my barbaric, 535
Ye are better than all the ballads,
437
distant spires, 243
gentlemen of England, 115
gods it doth amaze me, 81
have done it unto me, 1116
mariners of England, 327
Ye'll tak' the high road, 952
Yea-forsooth knave, 64
Year, a thousand a, 955
a, whose days are long, 722
across many a, 849
ain't been the very best, 730
and a day, sailed away for a,
498
and a sphere, to make up a,
408

Year by year we lose friends, 365
  Christmas comes but once a, 19
  days saddest of the, 372
  dying a dull sight, 449
  each day is like a, 722
  each, to ancient friendships, 527
  find at last our twentieth, 810
  for seven long, Tom's food, 99
  happiest of the glad new, 463
  hath its winter every, 763
  heaven's eternal, is thine, 175
  I tread on another, 626
  if I had five thousand a, 482
  if I preach a whole, 276
  infant, 141
  is at the spring, 485
  less of brightness, every, 459
  liberal, 443
  life's, 335
  measure of the, 385
  mellowing, 159
  memory outlive life half a, 94
  moments make the, 203
  no winter in thy, 276
  ob Jubilo, 600
  of my most immemorial, 461
  of philatelic fame, 842
  of the rose is brief, 633
  old, never read book that is not, 414
  restore the ruined, 891
  rich with forty pounds a, 250
  rolling, is full of Thee, 224
  russet, inhaled the dreamy air, 551
  seasons return with the, 151
  seven stars and the solar, 410
  some wither every, 180
  starry girdle of the, 327
  sweet o' the, 56
  that for you waits, 568
  the, I met with Rose, 604
  three hundred pounds a, 34
  to do in, you have this, 930
  vernal seasons of the, 162
  virtuous on ten thousand a, 563
  wait till you come to forty, 481
  wake year to sorrow, 365
  was in its yellowing time, 742
  were playing holidays, 61
  where are the snows of last, 1022
  will bloom another, 385
  winter comes to rule the varied, 224
  winter ruler of the inverted, 224, 265
  wisdom with each studious, 353
Years ago, a million, 734
  and years together, 406
  are few, because the, 737
  are like the shadows, 561
  ay, down the, 851
  begin in early, 973
  beyond our ken, 438
  brooding on the, 621
  companioned, 835
  creep slowly by Lorena, 560
  dark with torment and with tears, 516
  days of our, 1105
  declined into the vale of, 102

Years, desolated, 593
  disingenuousness of, 400
  drift long, 983
  drip slowly, long long, 746
  dust of the mounded, 748
  edge of tempestuous, 389
  eternal, of God are hers, 373
  far back into other, 423
  fate seemed to wind him up for fourscore, 178
  flag has braved a thousand, 327
  flight of, unmeasured by the, 306
  fourscore, 438
  fourteen hundred, ago, 60
  from now, a hundred, 774
  full of honor and, 431
  go by, as the, 974
  go by in single file, 897
  go on and heads get gray, as, 653
  have hardier tasks, 927
  have passed, your thousand, 565
  have swept by thee softly, 628
  history of a hundred, 652
  hopes of all the, 612
  I do not think seventy, 537
  if by reason of strength they be fourscore, 1105
  if we should live a thousand, 305
  in the grey beginning of, 633
  instant men call, 491
  it is eighteen, 929
  it may be for, 396
  keep a thing seven, 311
  keep coming and going, 1065
  lamenting all her battle, 690
  lapse of thrice a thousand, 621
  let me live out my, 871
  life seemed formed of sunny, 454
  life's few fleeting, 707
  like great black oxen, 790
  long ranges of comfortless, 824
  love of life increased with, 272
  make men restless, 490
  mature into fruit, 1084
  months to lagging, 707
  music from the grey forgotten, 832
  nature sink in, 195
  new, ruin and rend, 631
  nine hundred and sixty, 1097
  none would live past, again, 178
  not for twenty, but eternity, 603
  O tide of the, 595
  of change and suffering, after such, 516
  of Europe, better fifty, 465
  of gold, forget the, 687
  of golden deeds, 471
  of love have been forgot, 459
  of man, the first, 232
  of mean observances, 311
  of peace, thousand, 469
  of rainy seasons, 811
  outlive so many, 65
  outlive the impatient, 780
  outweighs, whole, 208
  pays the failure of, 493
  rainbow span of fifty, 664

Years return, the golden, 367
  rung in ears for thousands of, 545
  rush by, 520
  sad presage of his future, 269
  sees beyond the, 737
  shall make us other men, 544
  should lean, staff on which, 340
  slow, sailed by and ceased, 437
  sorrow comes with, 428
  tears of boyhood's, 336
  than each will tell, longer, 685
  that are to be, 738
  that bring the philosophic mind, 301
  that make us wise, 522
  that perished to make us men, 628
  that shall be, gleam on the, 426
  that shall live for unnumbered, 518
  that were ere I drew breath, 621
  the knightly, 693
  these hundred ninety and eight, 228
  thousand, in thy sight, 1105
  thousand leagues like a thousand, 227
  three thousand, ago, 332
  threescore, and ten, 1105
  through endless, 338
  through the empty, 690
  to a day, ran a hundred, 452
  to be let for life or, 134
  to come, do so much in the, 750
  to evolve man, taken God, 740
  together through the everlasting, 773
  told our increasing, 691
  twenty tedious, 220
  untold millions of, 581
  vanity in, 62
  walk, the new, 900
  we do not count a man's, 415
  we live in deeds not, 506
  we see, beyond the, 952
  we spend our, as a tale, 1105
  we waste, 779
  we will not speak of, 452
  weight of seventy, 302
  whatever comes with, 632
  when eighty, were past, 438
  when with the ever-circling, 477
  will ever stop the existence, nor that, 537
  wisdom not acquired by, 978
  with all the hopes of future, 435
  with Ibsen spent, better than, 843
  with their whitening locks, 983
  woman's always younger than a man at equal, a, 430
  would give half his, 431
  would prove them true, hoped the, 767
  yesterday's sev'n thousand, 1018
  young, seventy, 454

Year's at the spring, 485
  crops, little good watering last, 520
Years' pith, seven, 100
Yearnin' feel a sort of, 698
Yearning cry, the spirit's, 666
  for something permanent enduring, 842
  of the soul can sting no more, 554
Yell for yell, gave back, 726
Yellow candle-light, 702
  leaf, my days are in the, 358
  leaf, sere the, 88
  leaves, or none or few do hang, 107
  mandarin, a great, 828
  melancholy, green and, 55
  primrose was to him, 296
  quarantine flag, 925
  rims so pale, 369
  sands, come unto these, 32
  shine of daffodils, 867
  shores of creeks and golden sands, 732
  to the jaundiced eye, 211
Yells, know the rage that, above, 375
Yemen sword, with his, 1092
Yeoman's service, it did me, 97
Yes an' no an' mebbe, 687
  an' say no, mebby to mean, 527
  rhyme with, 952
Yesterday and to-day, 1122
  and to-morrow without worry, 670
  in embryo, man, 1011
  is but a dream, 953
  know'st thou, 1058
  O call back, bid time return, 59
  our pomp of, 780
  rose of, 1018
  sweet sleep thou owedst, 102
  the word of Caesar, 83
  unborn to-morrow and dead, 1019
  when it is past, but as, 1105
Yesterdays, cheerful, 303
  fatuous ineffectual, 693
  have lighted fools, 88
  look backwards with a smile, 202
  my morrows noons, my, 672
Yesterday's errors let yesterday cover, 682
  sev'n thousand years, 1018
  sneer and frown, 523
  wounds, 682
Yestreen, I saw the moon late, 255
  the Queen had four Maries, 953
Yew, never a spray of, 546
Yield day to night, 68
  not thy neck to fortune's yoke, 70
Yielded, by her, by him received, 152
  with coy submission, 152
Yielding marble of her snowy breast, 145
Yo-ho-ho and a bottle of rum, 704, 710
Yoke, Flanders hath received our, 146

Yoke, fortune's, 70
  of bullocks at Stamford fair, 65
  oxen bear the, 982
  the stranger's, 903
  to resent the, 461
  why must we bear this, 543
Yoland with the yellow hair, 592
Yonder ivy-mantled tower, from, 868
Yonghy-Bonghy-Bo, lived the, 498
Yorick, alas poor, I knew him, 97
York, this sun of, 71
You alone are you, 108
  and I were young, when, 640
  are afraid, 931
  are all the world, 42
  bequeath to yours, may, 935
  blest it and called it, 844
  can fool some of the people, 457
  have got to show me, 714
  may go when you will, 916
  may take it away, 901
  must come no more, 929
  must follow me, quickly, 948
  never, mind, 622
  saw him, face to face, 929
  say go to your man, 941
  suddenly cried and turned away, 893
  that I might love, 843
  that intend to write, 985
  that mean to fight, 765
  twenty times, utter the, 640
  went up another, 882
  will only injure yourself, 961
  without me I without you, 858
  yourself write nothing, 995
You's and I's, but actual, 912
You-all means a race or section, 952
Young Adam Cupid, 77
  again and sound, 577
  again, would you be, 291
  and beautiful being, each, 1085
  and fair, ladies, 49
  and so fair, 392
  and yare the fond and fair, 759
  and zealous, 1037
  are happy never, 736
  are prodigal of life, 330
  as the fairies are, 846
  as you are young, when he was, 482
  ask much of life, 835
  at whatever age, die, 930
  beautiful and happy, 1085
  body with so old a head, 46
  buds sleep in the root's white core, 385
  climber-up of knees, 290
  disease, the, 208
  ever fair and ever, 176
  face you loved when all was, 523
  I have been, and now am old, 1104
  I want to be, 851
  idea how to shoot, teach the, 224
  idle wild and, 342

Young, if all the world and love were, 21
  if he be caught, 235
  if ladies be but, and fair, 49
  in limbs, in judgment old, 45
  in that she died so, 460
  Lochinvar is come out of the west, 307
  love may go to Jericho, 334
  man believes he shall ever die, no, 330
  man married is man that's marr'd, 53
  man's fancy lightly turns, 464
  man's heart within, she tied, 600
  man's werling, 17
  manhood, flower of our, 965
  men apt to tell secrets, 222
  men are fools, old men know, 28
  men can sing, 879
  men leap like little fish, 908
  men need stiffening of the vertebrae, 745
  men think old men fools, 28
  men's vision, the, 173
  music heavenly maid was, 247
  my son, you are, 974
  next to the very, 483
  Obadias David Josias, 947
  old and, 610
  prey upon the, 967
  romance is always, 442
  seventy years, 454
  she is not, 737
  so wise so, never live long, 72
  spurned by the, 391
  though I am, I scorn to flit, 133
  till forty, look, 178
  Timothy learnt sin to fly, 947
  to be, was very heaven, 300
  we too were, 767
  when we are, 789
  when you and I were, 453, 640
  which always find us, 409
  whom the gods love die, 360
  women of the present day, 346
  would that we were, again, 521
Younger hearings are quite ravished, 41
  race succeeds every year, 180
  than thyself, let thy love be, 54
  we shall ne'er be, 52
Youngest critic has died, 779
Young-eyed cherubins, 47
Youngsters read it, 1038
Youngun born without a chance, 792
Your hands your feet and your raiment, 401
Yours, beloved may it be, 892
  what 's mine is, 37, 978
Yourself as he instead of I, think of, 805
  give of, 879
  go by, watch, 805
  if you mean to know, 1056
  in me, cannot slay, 888
  someone worse off than, 961
Youth against time and age, 27
  age 'twixt boy and, 307
  an over-praised season, 613
  ancient law of, 361, 811

Youth and age are equally a burden, 973
  and caught our, 894
  and I lived in 't together, 317
  and manhood keep an equal
    poise, 685
  and pleasure meet, 352
  as lord of my fate, 579
  begin in gladness in our, 297
  bounds of freakish, 265
  could not last, 320
  crabbed age and, 109
  cry Wel-awaye, 257
  deemed crystal, what, 493
  delight, gives his, 208
  delusion of, 420
  dew of thy, 1105
  did dress themselves, 64
  eagle mewing her mighty, 163
  fame is thirst of, 353
  fantastic panic-stricken, 787
  fiery vehemence of, 308
  flourish in immortal, 195
  flower of, 979
  follies may cease with their,
    239
  for life we both regret, for, 673
  friends of my, where are they,
    356
  full of grace force fascination,
    535
  gained a child of immortal,
    558
  gave love and roses, 335
  gets together his building ma-
    terials, 515
  glass wherein the noble, 64
  grant purity, to reverent, 984
  had been a habit, 785
  happy visions of my, 455
  home-keeping, 33
  idol of my, 463
  immortal, to mortal maids, 326
  in Babylon, there was a, 851
  in my, 48
  in my hot, 358
  in the bloom of, 979
  in the days of my, 320
  in the lexicon of, 425
  is a blunder, 420
  is a silly vapid state, 812
  is alive, 767
  is full of pleasure, 109
  is lying, underground their
    golden, 867
  is more than a, 38
  is the time, 974
  is wholly experimental, 704
  itself, no less than, 438
  large lusty loving, 535
  love gold and pleasure, 455
  many are our joys in, 299
  morn and liquid dew of, 90

Youth, morning like the spirit
    of, 105
  multiply their, 522
  my mangled, 748
  now flees on feathered foot,
    702
  now green in, 218
  of Ascalon, there was a, 855
  of labour with an age of ease,
    250
  of pleasure wasteful, was your,
    492
  of the realm, corrupted the, 69
  of the year, dauntless, 735
  on the prow, 244
  only a moment of romance and
    glamour, 727
  only season for enjoyment. 407
  our joys our, 22
  our, we can have but to-day,
    203
  plaything gives his, delight,
    208
  promises of, 232
  rebellious liquors in my, 48
  rejoice in thy, 1110
  remember thy Creator in, 1110
  replies I can, 409
  riband in the cap of, 96
  sheltered me in, 404
  should heed the older-witted,
    1077
  some salt of our, 34
  spirit of, in everything, 108
  taken in exchange my, 883
  that fired the Ephesian dome,
    193
  that means to be of note, 105
  that would flow to waste, 848
  thoughts of, are long long, 436
  time that takes in trust our, 22
  time the subtle thief of, 161
  to fame unknown, 245
  to serve her, calls, 550
  to whom was given, 298
  twenty years a, 786
  vaward of our, 64
  virtue be as wax to flaming, 95
  waneth by encreasing, 27
  we poets in our, 297
  wears the rose of, upon him,
    104
  what he steals from her, 240
  where are the friends of my,
    356
  who took up in his, 975
  whom the gods favour dies in,
    978
  whoso neglects learning in his,
    968
Youth's a stuff will not endure, 54
  for an hour, 840

Youth's heritage, to grant, 489
  lively senses, all, 850
  sweet-scented manuscript, 1019
  sweet spring grows brown, 628
Youthful follies o'er, count their,
    309
  grace, 373
  hose well saved, 50
  jollity, jest and, 160
  joy, hour of, 452
  poets dream, such sights as,
    160
  sports, my joy of, 355
  than old, I'd rather be, 686
Y-reke, asshen olde is fyr, 6
Yuba, played on banks of, 432
Yukon, the law of the, 844
Yule, love's old drink of, 600
  village of, 643
Y-wet, joly whistle wel, 6

Zaccheus he did climb the tree,
    947
Zeal, heavenly race demands thy,
    225
  served God with half the, 74
Zealand, traveller from New,
    398
Zealots fight, let graceless, 167,
    208
Zealous for nothing, 237
Zealously affected, good to be,
    1121
Zenith, dropped from the, 149
  illusion reaches its, 1081
Zephyr gently blows, when the,
    211
  not a freakish young, 660
  soft the, blows, 244
Zephyrs with my ringlets playing,
    375
Zero, net result of, 378
Zest, tell with such high, 918
  to what you write, 599
Zeus, impossible to escape the
    will of, 959
  pitieth, 963
Zigzag manuscript, 265
Zion the city of the great king,
    1104
  we wept when we remembered,
    1106
Ziska, the great captain, 122
Zitella, gentle, 387
Zogbaum draws with a pencil,
    785
Zone, acquaint ourselves with
    ev'ry, 114
  as a circling, 154
  best gem upon her, 408
  to zone, from, 372
Zones, gauntlet of all, 923
Zuyder Zee, traveller on the, 398